Table of atomic masses listed alphabetically

Scaled to relative atomic mass $^{12}C = 12$ exactly. A number in parentheses is the atomic mass number of the isotope of longest known half-life.

Element	Symbol	Atomic number	Atomic mass	Element	Symbol	Atomic number	Atomic mass
Actinium	Ac	89	227.0278	Molybdenum	Mo	42	95.94
Aluminum	Al	13	26.98154	Neodymium	Nd	60	144.24
Americium	Am	95	(243)	Neon	Ne	10	20.179
Antimony	Sb	51	121.75	Neptunium	Np	93	237.0482
Argon	Ar	18	39.948	Nickel	Ni	28	58.69
Arsenic	As	33	74.9216	Niobium	Nb	41	92.9064
Astatine	At	85	(210)	Nitrogen	N	7	14.0067
Barium	Ba	56	137.33	Nobelium	No	102	(259)
Berkelium	Bk	97	(247)	Osmium	Os	76	190.2
Beryllium	Be	4	9.01218	Oxygen	O	8	15.9994
Bismuth	Bi	83	208.9804	Palladium	Pd	46	106.42
Boron	B	5	10.81	Phosphorus	P	15	30.97376
Bromine	Br	35	79.904	Platinum	Pt	78	195.09
Cadmium	Cd	48	112.41	Plutonium	Pu	94	(244)
Calcium	Ca	20	40.08	Polonium	Po	84	(209)
Californium	Cf	98	(251)	Potassium	K	19	39.0983
Carbon	C	6	12.011	Praseodymium	Pr	59	140.9077
Cerium	Ce	58	140.12	Promethium	Pm	61	(145)
Cesium	Cs	55	132.9054	Protactinium	Pa	91	231.0359
Chlorine	Cl	17	35.453	Radium	Ra	88	226.0254
Chromium	Cr	24	51.996	Radon	Rn	86	(222)
Cobalt	Co	27	58.9332	Rhenium	Re	75	186.207
Copper	Cu	29	63.546	Rhodium	Rh	45	102.9055
Curium	Cm	96	(247)	Rubidium	Rb	37	85.4678
Dysprosium	Dy	66	162.50	Ruthenium	Ru	44	101.07
Einsteinium	Es	99	(252)	Samarium	Sm	62	150.36
Erbium	Er	68	167.26	Scandium	Sc	21	44.9559
Europium	Eu	63	151.96	Selenium	Se	34	78.96
Fermium	Fm	100	(257)	Silicon	Si	14	28.0855
Fluorine	F	9	18.998403	Silver	Ag	47	107.868
Francium	Fr	87	(223)	Sodium	Na	11	22.98977
Gadolinium	Gd	64	157.25	Strontium	Sr	38	87.62
Gallium	Ga	31	69.72	Sulfur	S	16	32.06
Germanium	Ge	32	72.59	Tantalum	Ta	73	108.979
Gold	Au	79	196.9665	Technetium	Tc	43	(98)
Hafnium	Hf	72	178.49	Tellurium	Te	52	127.60
Helium	He	2	4.00260	Terbium	Tb	65	158.9254
Holmium	Ho	67	164.9304	Thallium	Tl	81	204.383
Hydrogen	H	1	1.0079	Thorium	Th	90	232.0381
Indium	In	49	114.82	Thulium	Tm	69	168.9342
Iodine	I	53	126.9045	Tin	Sn	50	118.69
Iridium	Ir	77	192.22	Titanium	Ti	22	47.88
Iron	Fe	26	55.847	Tungsten	W	74	183.85
Krypton	Kr	36	83.80	Unnilhexium	Unh	106	(263)
Lanthanum	La	57	138.9055	Unnilpentium	Unp	105	(262)
Lawrencium	Lr	103	(260)	Unnilquadium	Unq	104	(261)
Lead	Pb	82	207.2	Uranium	U	92	238.0289
Lithium	Li	3	6.941	Vanadium	V	23	50.9415
Lutetium	Lu	71	174.967	Xenon	Xe	54	131.29
Magnesium	Mg	12	24.305	Ytterbium	Yb	70	173.04
Manganese	Mn	25	54.9380	Yttrium	Y	39	88.9059
Mendelevium	Md	101	(258)	Zinc	Zn	30	65.38
Mercury	Hg	80	200.59	Zirconium	Zr	40	91.22

Chemistry with Inorganic Qualitative Analysis
Second Edition

SECOND EDITION

CHEMISTRY

With Inorganic Qualitative Analysis

Therald Moeller
Arizona State University

John C. Bailar, Jr.
University of Illinois

Jacob Kleinberg
University of Kansas

Cyrus O. Guss
University of Nevada at Reno

Mary E. Castellion
Stamford, Connecticut

Clyde Metz
College of Charleston

Academic Press

(Harcourt Brace Jovanovich, Publishers)
Orlando   San Diego   San Francisco   New York   London   Toronto
Montreal   Sydney   Tokyo   São Paulo

Academic Press, Inc.
Orlando, Florida 32887

United Kingdom Edition published by
Academic Press, Inc. (London) Ltd.
24/28 Oval Road, London NW1 7 DX

ISBN: 0-12-503360-5
Library of Congress Catalog Card Number: 83-73687

Printed in the United States of America

CONTENTS

ASIDES

PREFACE

The second edition of *Chemistry with Inorganic Qualitative Analysis* is dedicated to meeting the needs of students and teachers as they exist in the 1980s. In addition, we have maintained our commitment to the philosophy that was our guide in the first edition: Both descriptive chemistry and the principles of chemistry are necessary to the study of the subject, and these topics should be covered with scientific honesty and in the clearest language possible. Each and every aspect of this second edition results from reevaluation of the content of the first edition in terms of our ever-present goals of clarity and scientific honesty. Many individuals who taught from the first edition have helped in this process.

For the students, our major new goal is to provide greater assistance in learning how to solve *both* qualitative and quantitative problems. A second goal is to provide more guidelines for understanding the facts and concepts that are of central importance, especially with respect to descriptive chemistry. For the teachers, our major new goal is to provide a more meaningful approach to the teaching of descriptive chemistry. The outcome of our determined effort to meet these goals has been extensive rewriting, some major reorganization, a new emphasis on chemical reactions, expanded coverage of certain topics, and the introduction of a number of new pedagogical aids.

To assist the students in problem solving, we begin in Chapter 2 with a thorough introduction to significant figures, units, and the dimensional method, and we introduce a method for *thinking* through the solution of a problem (see p. 29)—a method that reappears whenever new types of problems are introduced (see p. 80). We want students to use this book actively, not passively. All worked Examples include not only mathematics, but verbal explanations. Most Examples are followed by similar Exercises that include only answers; by working these Exercises the students can immediately learn whether they have understood the Examples. The application of thoughtful problem solving to the descriptive aspects of chemistry, as opposed to the mathematical aspects, has been sorely neglected in general chemistry textbooks. We have endeavored to provide some Examples that remedy this omission.

Occasionally we have issued warnings about common errors in problem solving (see p. 133). Summary paragraphs, which pull together interrelated concepts, appear immediately after the concepts have been introduced (see p. 99). This is another attempt to keep students reading in an active, rather than a passive, mode. New terms are printed in boldface type where they are first defined, and margin definitions highlight essential terms and relationships. In addition, a substantive summary appears at the end of each chapter, and special tables summarize important aspects of descriptive chemistry.

In revising the sequence of descriptive chemistry topics, we have drawn upon the many years of practical experience that we share in teaching both undergraduate and graduate students and also upon our communications with those of our students who have become teachers. As students, we each began by learning simple facts about simple chemical reactions. Experience has shown that this approach works well and we have chosen to emphasize such learning techniques. It is all too easy for a student, while reading a chemistry textbook, to skim over the chemical equations, which may look like collections of not-very-meaningful symbols. We encourage the students to "read" chemical equations and think about chemical reactions by asking them to recognize simple reaction patterns and to distinguish between redox and nonredox reactions. Such thinking can open the door to curiosity about why reactions occur as they do and to interest in other properties of the substances involved. In addition, familiarity with some simple chemical reactions is an excellent foundation for the topics of kinetics, equilibrium, and electrochemistry.

The introduction of descriptive chemistry by means of chemical reactions begins in Chapter 6, with simple reaction patterns. Chapter 14, on the chemistry of water, provides a logical framework for definitions of chemical equilibrium, electrolytes, and acids and bases. Similarly, Chapter 16, on hydrogen and oxygen, provides a natural place for the introduction of oxidation and reduction. Most of Chapter 17 is devoted to extending the students' abilities to recognize types of chemical reactions and to predict possible products. The remaining descriptive chapters are organized on the basis of the periodic table (Chapter 25–31). Each chapter includes a section devoted to reactions of the elements and compounds under consideration. The relationship between the principles and descriptive aspects of chemistry is demonstrated by the inclusion of Examples in all of the descriptive chapters.

Metals and metallurgy are now covered in a separate chapter. The material on pollution and the environment, which seemed so new just a few years ago, is now incorporated where appropriate, rather than being treated in separate chapters. An introduction to polymer chemistry has been added and the treatment of biochemistry has been expanded.

A number of significant changes have also been made in the presentation of the principles of chemistry. The pace of the early chapters has been slowed a bit by providing expanded and more patient explanations. By the end of Chapter 7, students with diverse backgrounds should be on an equal footing. Chemical bonding is treated in three chapters—the types of bonding are introduced in Chapter 9; Chapter 11 is devoted to the properties of molecules, including an expanded treatment VSEPR (valence shell electron pair repulsion); and molecular orbital theory alone is discussed in Chapter 24. Thermochemistry is presented in Chapter 7, and the remainder of thermodynamics is deferred until Chapter 22, which has been extensively rewritten to provide greater understanding of the *meaning* of entropy and free energy. Chapter 18, on kinetics, has also been completely rewritten. It now *begins* with a description of what happens at the molecular level in an effort to overcome the frequent confusion between the kinetics of elementary reactions and the kinetics of overall reactions. The equilibrium chapters (based on those in the first edition of *Chemistry with Inorganic Qualititative Analysis*) have been expanded. Chapter 23, on electrochemistry, now includes the relationship between electromotive force and free energy.

Chapter 34 is a review of the principles of equilibrium as they are utilized in the qualitative-analysis scheme. Chapter 35 discusses the chemistry of the scheme for the analysis of eleven anions and twenty-two cations. Flow charts are presented, the procedures are outlined in terms of the chemistry involved, and equations are written for all of the important reactions. (Laboratory directions are given in the separate publication, *Chemistry: Inorganic Qualitative Analysis in the Laboratory*, by Clyde Metz and Mary E. Castellion).

At the end of each chapter is an extensive set of questions and problems; these are organized by topic and include several simple problems for each topic, as well as more difficult problems denoted by asterisks. Each descriptive chapter includes some questions concerning simple chemical reactions and also, under the heading "Review of Principles," problems that apply previously learned principles to the chemistry discussed in the chapter. Roughly one-half of the problems and approximately one-third of the questions are answered in the book. [Complete solutions to the answered questions and problems are given in the *Student Solutions Manual*, by John Williams and Clyde Metz, and all solutions and answers are collected in the *Instructor's Manual*, by Clyde Metz and John Williams. In addition, a review of skills, further examples (including some worked by the problem-solving method), practice texts, and a complete glossary are contained in the *Study Guide*, by Clyde Metz.]

In response to many requests, we have included greatly expanded data tables in the Appendix. However, we continue to give all necessary data in the statement of each Example or problem.

Our commitment to clarity, to expanded treatments of problem solving and chemical reactions, and to frequent summaries has lengthened each chapter. We could have shortened the book by giving up the Asides, the Tools of Chemistry essays, or the Thoughts on Chemistry, but users of the first edition of this book clearly found these sections desirable. We could have omitted polymer chemistry, but many teachers wish to add this topic, as well as other industrial chemistry topics. We could have eliminated biochemistry, but that would be unfair to students who will not take another chemistry course or who have a strong interest in biochemistry. We take comfort in the knowledge that most teachers will choose to present those descriptive chapters that they consider most important and that they most enjoy teaching.

The following consultants and reviewers, approximately half of whom have read the entire manuscript, have made significant contributions to the development of this second edition. We are grateful for the enthusiasm and high degree of involvement that they have each displayed:

John L. Bordley, University of the South; Roy D. Catton, Jr., University of New Mexico; Sheldon H. Cohen, Washburn University; Fredrick H. Dahlquist, University of Oregon; Marion C. Day, Louisiana State University; Arnold Drucker, University of Connecticut–Stamford; Wayne Dunbar, Winona State University; Gordon J. Ewing, New Mexico State University; Steven L. Fedder, Arizona State University; Mark Freeman, Dorr–Oliver, Incorporated; Helmi S. Habib, Central Washington University; K. Robert Huffman, American Cyanamid Company; Wilbert Hutton, Iowa State University; James A. Ibers, Northwestern University; Ronald Johnson, Emory University; Edwin Lane, William Jewell College; Vincent Magnuson, University of Minnesota–Duluth; Frank Millich, University of Missouri–Kansas City; David Moseley, Jr., Washington State University; Julian Roberts, University of the Redlands; Rolly Rue, South Dakota State University; Allan L. Smith, Drexel University; Walter Thomas, American Cyanamid Company; Eugene R. Weiner, University of Denver; and Philip K. Welty, Wartburg College.

The dedication of this book is our way of acknowledging the contributions of the many individuals whose names have not been mentioned. Finally, for his eternal vigilance in the interest of clarity, our thanks to Dan Schiller.

Therald Moeller
John C. Bailar, Jr.
Jacob Kleinberg
Cyrus O. Guss
Mary E. Castellion
Clyde Metz

To everyone who helped.

CHAPTER 1

The Nature of Chemistry

(We open this book with a letter to a friend from John C. Bailar, Jr., who has been a member of the chemistry department faculty at the University of Illinois for 56 years.)

Dear Chris:

This letter is an answer to your questions about just what chemistry is and what chemists do. I'm glad that you asked, for many people have a distorted, or at least superficial, view of what the subject is all about. Whether I can give you a clear picture of it in a letter like this, I am not sure, but I shall try.

You know, of course, that chemistry is one of the **physical sciences,** along with physics, geology, and astronomy. Closely related, but in a somewhat different category, are the **biological sciences,** such as botany, physiology, ecology, and genetics. There is no sharp distinction between the two groups of sciences, or between those in either group, for they overlap each other. Often it is difficult to decide whether a specific topic belongs in one area or another. Many important subjects fall within the boundaries of several different disciplines. [Definitions of terms given in boldface type are listed at the end of this letter.]

All of the sciences overlap extensively with chemistry; they depend upon it and, in large measure, are based upon it. By that I mean that chemistry is really a part of all of the natural sciences, and a person cannot go very far in any science without some knowledge of chemistry. It would be possible to be a chemist without much knowledge of astronomy or physiology, but certainly, one could not make great progress in astronomy or physiology without some understanding of chemistry. A knowledge of chemistry is essential in other scientific fields as well. Agriculturists, engineers, and medical doctors use chemical concepts constantly.

Chemistry is concerned with the composition of **matter** and the changes in composition which matter undergoes — in brief, chemistry is the science of matter. Physics is concerned chiefly with energy and with the interactions of matter and energy, including energy in such forms as heat, light, sound, electricity, mechanical energy, and nuclear energy. All changes in the composition of matter either release or absorb energy and for this reason the relationship between chemistry and physics is a most intimate one.

We think of any change in which the composition of matter changes as a **chemical change.** For example, if you pour vinegar on baking soda in a glass vessel, you will see bubbles of gas escaping and the liquid will become warm as energy is released. When the bubbling stops, you can evaporate the liquid by boiling it, until finally only a white powder remains. But this white powder is not the original baking soda. It is a new substance with new characteristics. For example, it won't give off bubbles if you pour vinegar on it. This new material is different in composition from either of the materials which you originally mixed together. A chemical change has taken place.

By contrast, a **physical change** does not involve a change in the composition of matter. The melting of ice or the stretching of a rubber band are physical changes. It is often impossible to say whether a particular change is chemical or physical. Happily, it is not usually necessary to make a clear distinction between the two.

You must not assume that in your first course in chemistry you'll learn about the chemistry of the digestion of food or how a mixture of cement and water sets and hardens. These are complex processes, and before one can understand them one must first learn the chemistry of simpler substances. In learning to play the piano, a student does not start with Rachmaninoff's *Prelude in C# Minor*. A music student must first learn to play scales, and then simple pieces. It is only after months or years of practice that an individual can play the music of the masters. So it is with chemistry. You must first learn the fundamental principles and something about simple substances such as water and oxygen. A good understanding of the behavior of such substances will then allow you to understand the chemical behavior of more complex materials.

The science of chemistry is so broad that no one can be expert in all of its aspects. It is necessary to study the different branches of chemistry separately, and, if you become a chemist, to specialize in one or two branches of the subject.

Until about 150 years ago, it was believed that inanimate matter and living matter were of entirely different natures and had different origins. The inanimate matter was referred to as "inorganic" (meaning "without life") and the living matter and material derived from living matter were called "organic." However, in 1828, a German chemist named Friedrich Wöhler heated a material which was known to be inorganic and obtained a substance which all chemists recognized to be a product formed in life processes. So the distinction between "inorganic" and "organic" broke down. We still use these terms, but they now have different meanings from those they had in the early days. All living matter contains carbon chemically combined with hydrogen, so the chemistry of chemical compounds of carbon and hydrogen, whatever their origin, is called **organic chemistry.** Substances that do not contain carbon combined with hydrogen are "inorganic," and their chemistry is called **inorganic chemistry.** Carbon is very versatile in its behavior and is a key substance in a great many compounds, including most of the compounds essential to life.

There are other branches of chemistry, too. *Analytical chemistry* is concerned with the detection or identification of what substances are present in a material (**qualitative analysis**) and how much of each is present (**quantitative analysis**). *Physical chemistry* is the application of the methods and theories of physics to the study of chemical changes and the properties of matter. Physical chemistry really forms the foundation for all of the other branches of the subject. *Biochemistry,* as the name implies, is concerned with the chemistry of the processes that take place in living things.

Inorganic, organic, analytical, physical chemistry, and biochemistry are the main branches of chemistry, but it is possible to combine portions of them, or to elaborate on them in many ways. For example, *bioinorganic chemistry* deals with the function of the metals that are present in living matter and that are essential to life. *Pharmaceutical chemistry* is concerned with drugs: their manufacture, their composition, and their effects upon the body. *Clinical chemistry* is concerned chiefly with the analysis of blood, urine, and other biological materials. *Polymer chemistry* deals with the formation and behavior of such substances as rayon, nylon, and rubber. (Some people would include inorganic polymers such as glass and quartz.) *Environmental chemistry,* of course, deals with the composition of the atmosphere and the purity of water supplies—essentially, with the chemistry of our surroundings. *Agricultural chemistry* is concerned with fertilizers, pesticides, plant growth, the nutrition of farm animals, and every other chemical topic that is involved in farming.

One more topic should be mentioned. This is *chemical engineering,* which is concerned with the applications of chemistry on a large scale. Chemical engineers design and operate chemical factories; they deal with the economics of making chemicals on a commercial scale. They are also concerned with such processes as distilling, grinding, and drying materials in large amounts—even the study of the friction of liquids and gases flowing through pipes.

Before you can undertake the study of any of these broad fields of chemistry, you will need to take a course, usually called "General Chemistry," which is the basis for more specialized study. You will quickly learn that general chemistry consists of two interrelated parts: **descriptive chemistry** and **principles of chemistry.**

Descriptive chemistry generally deals with the "What . . .?" questions: What does that substance look like? What happens when it is heated? What happens when an electric current flows through it? What occurs when it is mixed with another specific substance? Chemistry is an experimental science and chemists work with a great many substances. It is important that they know the nature of these substances: their solubility in water or other liquids, their flammability, their toxicity, whether they undergo chemical changes in damp air, and many other characteristics. Sometimes the availability and cost of a substance are also important. The descriptive part of the general chemistry course is concerned chiefly with the behavior of some of the simpler inorganic substances, but often includes brief discussions of organic and biochemical materials as well.

The *principles* part of the course is concerned with theories of chemical behavior. That is, it attempts to answer the "Why . . .?" questions: Why won't a substance dissolve in water? Why did an explosion take place when a mixture was heated? Why was a particular substance and not a different one formed in a chemical change? Why does a chemical change speed up dramatically if a tiny amount of something else is added?

The study of chemical principles is of great practical as well as intellectual interest. We can, for example, calculate how much heat is given off when a particular fuel burns, and determine how to speed up or slow down its combustion. When we know why certain substances behave as they do we can often modify their behavior to achieve desirable or useful results.

Chemistry is an experimental science. By this statement, I do not mean that chemists do not have theories about changes in chemical composition—under what conditions they will or will not take place, how they take place, and what the products will be. There are always theories. But **theory** must always be subject to experiment. If one's theory is not in accordance with carefully executed experiments, then the theory, not the experiment, must be wrong. The theory must then be abandoned or modified. In this regard, chemistry is quite different from the social sciences, such as sociology and economics. People who work in those fields may have theories about the causes of inflation or unemployment or marital unhappiness, and they may carry out experiments to test their theories. But these experiments can never be repeated and checked under the same conditions, for in the act of doing the experiment the conditions have been irretrievably changed. This is true to some extent also in the biological sciences. A pharmacologist may test the effect of a given drug on a mouse and draw some conclusions from what happens to the mouse. But he cannot repeat the experiment with that same mouse, for he cannot be sure that the health of the mouse has not been changed by the first administration of the drug. He can do the experiment with another mouse, but he cannot be sure that the second mouse will respond exactly as the first one did. Chemists are more fortunate; under the same conditions, pure chemicals will always react with each other in exactly the same way. The trick is to be sure that the chemicals are pure and that the conditions of the experiment are exactly the same.

But, you will ask, "Just what do chemists do?" That is a difficult question to answer, for chemists do many different things. About half of the chemists in the United States work in laboratories. Some of them are "quality control" chemists. By a variety of laboratory techniques (some simple and some complex), they analyze or otherwise test materials which are to be used or the products of a chemical factory (be it a drug factory, a food factory, or a steel mill) to ensure that these products are uniform and pure. Some chemists do laboratory research, hoping to discover new chemicals or new uses for known chemicals, or to improve methods of making useful chemicals. Some seek to unearth new principles of chemical behavior, and their activities may range from laboratory work to using only pure mathematics. None of this, of course, is hit-and-miss experimentation. A chemist is always guided by a background of both chemical theory and practical experience, and the broader these are the more successful the chemist will be.

But what about those who do not work in laboratories? Are they still chemists? Indeed they are, though they may combine their chemical activity with some other professional work. Some spend their time looking for new uses and markets for substances that the research chemists have discovered; some are teachers (or divide their time between teaching and research); some become writers of scientific articles for newspapers and magazines.

You may be wondering whether you should study chemistry at all. I hope that you will do so, for as I indicated earlier, a knowledge of chemistry is useful, no matter what profession you follow. If you decide to become a mechanical engineer, you'll need to know something about fuels and alloys and corrosion; if a civil engineer, you must have a knowledge of cement, plaster, steel, and other building materials; if an electrical engineer, you'll need a knowledge of how a battery produces electrical energy, and the changes that take place in it when it is recharged, as well as a knowledge of transistors and lasers. Should you become a medical doctor, you'll be dealing with the most complex chemical plant of all — the human body — and the multitude of chemicals in it. My own son, John, studied chemistry for three years as an undergraduate, but after one year in medical school, he returned to his undergraduate college to take a summer course in physical chemistry, for he had discovered that he needed that extra chemical knowledge in his medical studies.

If you decide to go into agriculture, you'll need to know about fertilizers and pesticides, as well as animal nutrition. Even if you enter some profession that seems to have no connection with chemistry, such as law, you'll find a knowledge of chemistry very useful. Lawyers frequently have to deal with patents that concern chemical inventions. Some members of the U. S. Congress have had extensive chemical training, which gives them a great advantage in discussions of environmental pollution, nuclear energy, the regulations of the Food and Drug Administration, and in other legislation that concerns scientific matters.

The chemical profession is so broad that persons of many different interests and temperaments find satisfaction in it. A person who studies chemistry for very long develops habits of thinking logically and clearly. Once he has accomplished that, he can do almost any sort of work.

I hope that you will enjoy your study of chemistry. I have found it to be a fascinating subject, because of its history, the beauty of its logic, and its multitude of applications.

Sincerely,

John C. Bailar Jr.

SIGNIFICANT TERMS

physical sciences	study of natural laws and processes other than those peculiar to living matter
biological sciences	study of living matter
chemistry	the branch of science that deals with matter, with the changes that matter can undergo, and with the laws that describe these changes
matter	everything that has mass and occupies space
chemical change	a change in the composition of matter
physical change	a change in which the composition of the matter involved is unaltered
organic chemistry	the chemistry of compounds of carbon with hydrogen and of their derivatives
inorganic chemistry	the chemistry of all of the elements and their compounds, with the exception of compounds of carbon with hydrogen and of their derivatives
qualitative analysis	the identification of substances, often in a mixture
quantitative analysis	the determination of the amounts of substances in a mixture
descriptive chemistry	description of the elements and their compounds, their physical states, and how they behave
principles of chemistry	explanations of chemical facts, for example, by theories and mathematics
theory	unifying principle or group of principles that explains a body of facts or phenomena

CHAPTER 2

Units, Measurements, and Numbers

Numbers are either exciting or dull. It depends upon how you look at them. Each year after an election the newspapers print columns of numbers tabulating the votes by geographic area. Have you ever read these numbers, or did they look like pretty dreary stuff to you? The winner of the election no doubt finds them quite thrilling. And politicians who need to analyze voting patterns and predict trends must read these numbers with great interest.

Sometimes in science, magnificent success or dismal failure hinges on the results of a few measurements. If you pursue a career in science, you might some day find yourself present at the moment of high drama when years of work are validated by the appearance of the hoped-for numbers on an instrument panel or chart. But it is not only the professional scientist who must pay attention to numbers. Anyone who studies chemistry soon finds that he or she must frequently deal with numbers, measurements, and calculations. To do so requires skills that must be learned.

Some of us have to struggle to overcome a built-in fear of numbers and arithmetic. Have you ever been seized by a helpless feeling when confronted with the need to change the proportions in a recipe or find the number of miles that your car is traveling per gallon of gasoline? The problem–solving approach discussed at the end of this chapter is designed to help everyone who uses this book. If you suspect that you have an inherent uneasiness with numbers, give this section some extra time. It will pay off not only in chemistry, but in many practical, everyday problems.

CHEMISTRY AS A QUANTITATIVE SCIENCE

Every object in the world around you can be described in terms of chemistry. Many events that you can see occurring in nature involve chemical changes: the changing color of the leaves in the fall, the transformation of a pond into a swamp, the rusting of iron. Curiosity about what can be observed in the world has led to the study of chemistry (see A Historical Aside: The Origins of Chemistry).

Let's describe what is seen in one specific chemical change. Two substances are involved. One is a black powdery solid. The other is a colorless liquid that causes irritation if spilled on the skin. If some of the black solid is placed in a container and the liquid slowly added, things happen. The black solid begins to dissolve. The solution that is formed is not black, but very pale green. At the same time, a gas begins to bubble out of the solution. And the air is filled with a terrible smell, like that of rotten eggs.

What a multitude of questions can be asked here. What are these substances? Why did the black solid dissolve? What was formed in its place? *How much* of the liquid does it take to dissolve all of the black solid? *How much* of the gas can be produced? *How long* did the change take? Will events speed up if we heat the mixture? If so, by *how much per degree of temperature?*

Notice how many of the questions are *quantitative* ones. Observation and measurement both play vital roles in answering the questions of chemistry. A chemical change is not completely understood until it is understood quantitatively — in terms of measurements and numbers. Our understanding of chemistry is tested by making measurements. If a prediction is made based on what we think we understand, and if the prediction is shown to be correct by obtaining the predicted numbers in a quantitative test, we have greater confidence in our understanding.

In studying chemistry you will be presented with facts accumulated during hundreds of years of observation and measurement. You will also learn how the principles of chemistry are used to explain what has been observed. To test your understanding of chemical principles, you will solve problems, frequently problems that utilize the results of measurements of physical properties. Therefore, right from the beginning in studying chemistry, it is best to be prepared to solve problems — that is the goal of this chapter.

This chapter may be frustrating to some of you. Here you are ready to study chemistry and your first encounter is with topics that appear very nonchemical, more like the beginning of a mathematics course. We assure you that mastering the subject matter of this chapter is going to make everything that follows easier. Numbers and units of measurement begin to appear in Chapter 3 where we talk about the properties of very small particles of matter. All of the subjects in this chapter are applied in one way or another throughout the rest of this book. Everyone practicing or studying chemistry in any way must at times use significant figures, very large and very small numbers, units of measure, and must solve problems — the topics of the following sections.

NUMBERS IN PHYSICAL QUANTITIES

2.1 MEASUREMENT AND SIGNIFICANT FIGURES

The result of measuring a physical property is expressed by a numerical value together with a unit of measurement, for example

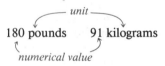

Here and in Sections 2.2 – 2.5 we concentrate on the numerical part of such physical quantities — on how many digits should be included and on the use of scientific notation. In later sections, we discuss the units.

If you count the pencils on your desk, there is no uncertainty in the number that results. You may have, say, 5 pencils, *exactly.* Also, there is no uncertainty in the number of inches in one foot. By definition, 12 inches = 1 foot. These are **exact numbers** — numbers with no uncertainty; they arise by directly counting whole items or by definition.

Exact numbers: no uncertainty (from counting, or by definition)

Numbers that result from *measurements* are never exact. There is always some degree of uncertainty due to experimental errors: limitations of the measuring instrument, variations in how each individual makes measurements, or other conditions of the experiment. For example, with a finely constructed, sensitive balance, it is possible to read the mass of a sample as 3.1267 grams (Figure 2.1). A simple balance might only allow the mass of the same sample to be read as 3.13 grams — such a balance cannot detect differences in mass beyond hundredths of a gram.

In both of these measurements there is a degree of uncertainty in the final digit — the 7 in 3.1267 and the 3 in 3.13. The preceding digits are definitely known, but the final digits are near the limits of what the balances can detect. Physical quantities are reported to the first digit that is uncertain. The **significant figures** in a number include all of the digits that are known with certainty, plus the first digit to the right that has an uncertain value.

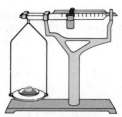

Single-pan balance

Top-loading balance

Automatic single-pan balance

Figure 2.1
Three Different Balances The single–pan balance can weigh to ±0.01 g. The top–loading type of balance can usually weigh to either ±0.01 g or ±0.001 g. The automatic single-pan balance, also known as an "analytical balance," usually weighs to ±0.0001 g, although some are available that weigh to ±0.00001 g.

As an illustration of how many significant figures should be reported in the result of a measurement, consider the following results of weighing a piece of candy as done by the members of a class (g is the abbreviation for grams).

23.1 g	23.3 g	23.0 g	23.3 g	23.2 g	23.2 g
23.3 g	23.4 g	23.2 g	23.1 g	23.3 g	23.2 g

As you can see, there is some uncertainty in the measurements. This uncertainty is in the third figure from the left—the tenths of a gram place. The average of the masses measured by the twelve students is 23.2 g. (The average is the sum of the 12 values divided by 12.) There is no doubt that the piece of candy weighs 23 g plus something more, but here is where the uncertainty is. To reflect the uncertainty in the measurement, we could report the mass as 23.2 ± 0.2 g, which includes all of the class data. (The highest value is 23.4 g and the lowest is 23.0 g.)

However, data are often given without any indication of the amount of uncertainty. For the candy the mass would be reported as 23.2 g. It is the responsibility of an individual reporting the results of experiments to include only the number of digits that are significant. In using experimentally measured data reported by others, we assume that the uncertainty lies in the last significant digit to the right and that it is ± 1. The decimal place of the digit does not matter. For example, the uncertainty in 3285 lies in the 5, and in 0.042, in the 2.

uncertainty of ±1   *uncertainty of ±0.001*

3285   0.042

Errors in measurement can be classified in two broad ways, as random errors or as systematic errors. Random errors result from uncontrolled variables in an experiment. For example, different people read instruments in different ways. The error in the candy-weighing experiment was a random error of this type. The error at the limits of what an instrument can detect is also a random error. Repetition of random errors gives results that randomly fluctuate about the true value. Random errors affect **precision**—the reproducibility of the results of a measurement (Figure 2.2).

Systematic errors can be assigned to definite causes. The measuring instrument may be defective. Or an experiment may be poorly designed and have a built-in error. Repetition of systematic errors gives results that are consistently too high or too low to roughly the same extent. Systematic errors affect **accuracy**—the closeness to the true result of a measurement or an experiment (see Figure 2.2).

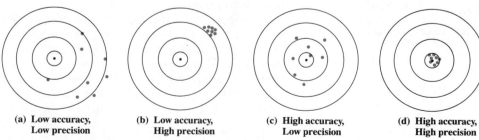

(a) Low accuracy, Low precision   **(b) Low accuracy, High precision**   **(c) High accuracy, Low precision**   **(d) High accuracy, High precision**

Figure 2.2

Accuracy and Precision *Accuracy* refers to the closeness of measured results to the true value. Low accuracy is generally the result of *systematic errors* (e.g., an improperly adjusted rifle sight in this example). *Precision* refers to the reproducibility or consistency of experimental measurements. Low precision is generally the result of *random errors* (e.g., an unsteady hand or gusty winds in this example).

2.2 FINDING THE NUMBER OF
SIGNIFICANT FIGURES

When physical quantities are used in arithmetic, it is important that the number of significant figures in the result represent the uncertainty in the original measurements. First, it is necessary to recognize how many significant figures are included in the physical quantities being used. The last digit to the right is assumed to be uncertain. *The number of significant figures is found by counting from left to right, beginning with the first nonzero digit and ending with the digit that has the uncertain value.* Each of the following numbers has three significant figures.

| *123* | *123* | *1 23* | *123* | *12 3* |
| 454 | 0.296 | 7.31 | 0.00846 | 10.7 |

Zeros that are at the end of a number and *follow* a decimal point are significant. For example, the final zero in 1.520 shows that this number has four significant figures and an uncertainty of ± 0.001. (By contrast, 1.52 would have only three significant figures and an uncertainty of ± 0.01.) Zeros at the end of a number given *without* a decimal point present a problem because they are ambiguous. The terminal zero in the number 1520 may or may not be significant. We have no good way to tell unless more information is given. The uncertainty might be ± 10 or ± 1. In general, we recommend that such terminal zeros be assumed to be *not* significant. The ambiguity is removed if a decimal point is given; then all the zeros preceding the decimal point *are* significant.

123	*1234*
1520	1520.
three significant figures	*four significant figures*

(A still better way of dealing with such cases is presented in Section 2.4, where we discuss scientific notation.)

**Random errors:
reduce precision
Systematic errors:
reduce accuracy**

How to count nonzero digits and zeros in determining the number of significant digits in a number is summarized in the following rules:

1. All nonzero digits are significant.
2. To count significant digits, begin with the first nonzero digit in the number as read from left to right. This means that zeros that *precede* the first nonzero digit are not significant.

| *12* | *1* | *1* |
| 0.096 | 0.000003 | 0.8 |

3. Zeros are significant when they appear
   (a) in the *middle* of a number:

| *1234* | *12 345* |
| 1003 | 70,204 |

   (b) at the *end* of any number that includes a decimal point:

| *1234* | *12* | *12 3456* |
| 0.6900 | 50. | 50.0000 |

4. Zeros at the end of a number given without a decimal point are ambiguous; we choose to assume that they are not significant. Adding a decimal point indicates their significance, according to rule 3b.

| *12* | *1234* |
| 3600 | 3600. |

EXAMPLE 2.1
Counting Significant Figures

How many significant figures are in the numbers (a) 57, (b) 82.9, (c) 340, (d) 700., (e) 10.000, (f) 0.000002, (g) 0.0402, and (h) 0.04020?

(a) Beginning with the 5 and counting gives two significant figures.

$\overset{1\,2}{57}$

(b) Beginning to count with the 8 gives three significant figures.

$\overset{1\,2\,3}{82.9}$

(c) The final zero, because there is no decimal point, is assumed not to be significant (see rule 4, above).

$\overset{1\,2}{340}$

(d) The placement of the decimal point indicates that the final two zeros are significant (rule 4).

$\overset{1\,2\,3}{700.}$

(e) All zeros here are significant (rule 3b).

$\overset{1\,2\,3\,4\,5}{10.000}$

(f) None of the zeros here are significant (rule 2).

$\overset{\qquad\quad 1}{0.000002}$

(g) The zeros at the left are not significant, but the zero in the middle is (rules 2 and 3a)

$\overset{\quad\; 1\,2\,3}{0.0402}$

(h) Here, the zero at the end is significant as well as the zero in the middle (rule 3).

$\overset{\quad\; 1\,2\,3\,4}{0.04020}$

Exercise How many significant figures are in the numbers (a) 234.7, (b) 0.0300, (c) 630, and (d) 1036? *Answer* (a) 4, (b) 3, (c) 2, (d) 4

2.3 ARITHMETIC USING SIGNIFICANT FIGURES

When physical quantities are used in arithmetic, the number of digits that are significant must be maintained. It is poor practice, for example, to divide 3.7 g by exactly 8 and give more than two significant figures in the answer. The uncertainty of the original measurement, which had only two significant figures, has not changed.

too many significant figures ⟶ 3.7 g/8 = 0.4625 g

two significant figures ⟶ 3.7 g/8 = 0.46 g *two significant figures*

Paying attention to the correct number of digits in the result of a calculation is especially important in these days of electronic calculators. With the push of a button, 7.8 divided by 7 is seen to be 1.114285714. *Do not assume that all of the numbers in your digital display are significant.* Limit the number of digits in your answer as explained in the following sections.

a. Addition and subtraction Adding the numbers 23.2 + 6.052 + 139.4 gives 168.652 as an answer. However, this is not the correct answer. The old adage about a chain being only as strong as its weakest link applies here. The answer cannot be more certain than the least certain of these numbers. The greatest uncertainty lies in 23.2 and 139.4, both of which are uncertain to ±0.1. Therefore, the answer should be rounded to 168.7, which also has an uncertainty of ±0.1.

To maintain the correct number of significant figures in addition or subtraction, *round the answer to the place (before or after the decimal point) with the greatest uncertainty.* An easy way to apply this rule is to draw a vertical line after the digit of the greatest uncertainty in the numbers being added or subtracted, and round the *answer* to the same place, as shown.

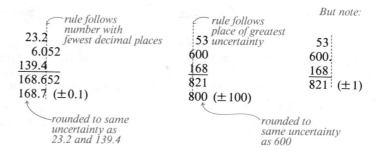

In this book we use the following rule for rounding off an answer: If the numbers following the desired place are between 000 and 499 drop these numbers and do nothing to the number in the desired place; if the numbers following are between 500 and 999 drop these numbers and increase the number in the desired place by one. For example, to round 6.713, and 6.785, and 6.75 to the one-tenths place:

drop these digits	*drop these digits and add 1 to preceding place*	*drop this digit and add 1 to preceding place*
6.713 becomes 6.7	6.785 becomes 6.8	6.75 becomes 6.8

EXAMPLE 2.2
Significant Figures—
Addition/Subtraction

Perform the following additions or subtractions and express the answers to the proper number of significant figures.

(a)   14
   − 0.072

(b) 0.0097
   0.0563

(c) 0.296
   4.41
   8.9273

(d) 1500
    21

(a)   14
   − 0.072
   13.928
   14

(b) 0.0097
   0.0563
   0.0660
   0.0660

(c) 0.296
   4.41
   8.9273
   13.6333
   13.63

(d) 1500
    21
   1521
   1500

In (a), the numbers to the right of the vertical line are greater than 500, so they are dropped and 1 is added. In (b), each number has four decimal places and the answer need not be rounded off. In (c), the numbers to the right of the vertical line are less than 499, so they are dropped and no other change is necessary. In (d), the answer is rounded to the same number of significant digits as the number with the greatest uncertainty.

Exercise Perform the following additions or subtractions and express the answers to the proper number of significant figures: (a) $(16.3) - (10.02)$, (b) $(1462) + (0.036)$, (c) $(6000.) - (32)$, (d) $(0.0327) - (0.0147)$ *Answer* (a) 6.3, (b) 1462, (c) 5968, (d) 0.0180

---

b. Multiplication and division Multiplying the two numbers $(23.2)(0.1257)$ gives 2.91624 as an answer. Here again, this is not the correct answer, because of the difference in the uncertainty of the numbers. To maintain the correct number of significant figures in multiplication and division, *round the answer to the same* *number of significant figures as in the number with the fewest significant figures.* For the problem above, the answer should have three significant figures.

$$\overset{12\ 3}{(23.2)}\overset{1234}{(0.1257)} = [2.91624] = \overset{1\ 23}{2.92}$$

An exact number (a number that has no uncertainty; Section 2.1) does not limit the number of significant figures in the result of a multiplication or division problem. For example, if we are going to perform an experiment exactly six times and need 6.35 g of a substance each time, the total amount needed is 38.1 g.

$$\underset{\substack{exact \\ number}}{exact\ (6)} \times \overset{1\ 23}{(6.35\ g)} = \overset{12\ 3}{38.1\ g} \quad \substack{need\ not\ be\ rounded \\ off\ to\ one\ significant\ figure}$$

EXAMPLE 2.3
Significant Figures —
Multiplication/Division

Perform the following multiplications or divisions and express the answers to the proper number of significant figures. In (b), assume that the factor 100 is exact.

(a) $\dfrac{26.9}{2.69}$ (b) (0.0729)(100)   (c) (13.65)²   (d) $\dfrac{14.89}{0.0003}$

In (a), a zero must be added to the calculated answer to obtain the correct number of significant figures. In (b), the exact factor of 100 does not limit the number of significant figures in the answer. In (d), despite all of the decimal places in the factors, the answer should carry only one significant figure. [Many students at first have trouble accepting this big a difference between the calculated answer and the properly significant answer.]

(a) $\dfrac{\overset{12\ 3}{26.9}}{\underset{1\ 23}{2.69}} = [10] = \overset{12\ 3}{10.0}$

(c) $\overset{12\ 34}{(13.65)^2} = [186.3225] = \overset{123\ 4}{186.3}$

(b) $\overset{123}{(0.0729)}\overset{exact\ number}{(100)} = \overset{1\ 23}{7.29}$

(d) $\dfrac{\overset{12\ 34}{14.89}}{\underset{1}{0.0003}} = [49,633] = \overset{1}{50,000}$

Exercise Perform the following multiplications or divisions and express the answers to the proper number of significant figures: (a) (16.3)/(10.02), (b) (1462)(0.036), (c) (6000.)(32), (d) (0.0327)/(0.0147) *Answer* (a) 1.63, (b) 53, (c) 190,000, (d) 2.22

The question arises of how to determine the number of significant figures in the answer to a problem that includes both multiplication or division, and addition or subtraction. We recommend the following procedure: (1) Solve the problem using all numbers as given. (2) Inspect the problem to determine which factor limits the number of significant digits in the answer. To do this first carry out the addition or subtraction and express the answer to the correct number of digits. Then compare this number of digits with the number in the multiplication or division portion of the expression that has the smallest number of significant figures. Whichever of these two numbers has the smallest number of significant figures is the one that limits the significance of the answer. Finally, (3) round the answer appropriately.

The above sounds rather complicated, but as shown in Example 2.4, the procedure is quite straightforward.

EXAMPLE 2.4
Significant Figures

Perform the following calculation and express the answer to the proper number of significant figures.

$$x = \frac{(95{,}316)}{(2.303)(1.987)}\left(\frac{1}{298} - \frac{1}{308}\right)$$

Solving the expression with a calculator gives

$$x = \frac{(95{,}316)}{(2.303)(1.987)}\left(\frac{1}{298} - \frac{1}{308}\right) = [2.269378954]$$

The next step is to carry out the subtraction. This can also be done in one step on a calculator, or it can be done by finding $\frac{1}{298}$ and $\frac{1}{308}$ and subtracting.

$$\frac{1}{298} = 0.00336 \qquad\qquad \frac{1}{308} = 0.00325$$

$$0.00336 - 0.00325 = 0.00011$$

The answer has two significant digits. Comparison with the rest of the expression above shows that the result of this subtraction is the factor that limits the number of digits in the value of x. Rounding the answer to two significant digits gives $x = 2.3$.

Exercise Perform the following calculation and express the answer to the proper number of significant figures.

$$x = \frac{(44.008)}{(0.0820568)(273.15)(1.976757)} - \frac{1}{1.3}$$

Answer $x = 0.22$

2.4 SCIENTIFIC NOTATION
(EXPONENTIAL NOTATION)

In chemistry we often use very large and very small numbers, and we must be able to represent such numbers in some convenient fashion. Scientific notation (also called exponential notation) is the answer. In standard scientific notation the *significant figures* of a number are retained in a factor between 1 and 10 and the location of the decimal point is indicated by a power of 10.

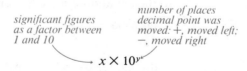

For example, the numbers 0.0063 and 900,000,000 are expressed in scientific notation as follows:

factor — two significant figures   *factor — one significant figure*

$$6.3 \times 10^{-3} \qquad\qquad 9 \times 10^{8}$$

exponent   *exponent*

To change a number greater than unity to scientific notation, we move the decimal point to the left until we reach a number that is between 1 and 10. The power of 10 is equal to the number of digits that the decimal point was moved. For example, to rewrite 2,000,000 in scientific notation the decimal point is moved left six places, giving 10 to the sixth power.

$$2{,}000{,}000 \text{ becomes } 2 \times 10^{6}$$

654 321

Table 2.1
Some Large and Small Physical Quantities

Masses	
Sun	2.0×10^{30} kg
Earth	6.0×10^{24} kg
Person	5.9×10^{1} kg
Basketball	6.0×10^{-1} kg
Virus	2.3×10^{-13} kg
Electron	9.1×10^{-31} kg

Lengths	
Radius of our galaxy	5×10^{20} m
Radius of sun	7.0×10^{8} m
Radius of earth	6.4×10^{6} m
Height of Mt. Everest	8.9×10^{3} m
Person	1.8×10^{0} m
Virus	1.7×10^{-8} m

In rewriting 120, the decimal point is moved two places.

$$120 \text{ becomes } 1.2 \times 10^2$$

To change a number less than unity to scientific notation, the decimal point is moved to the right in the number until a number that is between 1 and 10 is reached. The power of 10 is equal to the number of digits that the decimal point was moved and a minus sign appears in the exponent. For example, we would rewrite 0.0006 and 0.0263 as follows:

$$0.0006 \text{ becomes } 6 \times 10^{-4} \qquad 0.0263 \text{ becomes } 2.63 \times 10^{-2}$$

Usually a number is not written in scientific notation unless it is easier to use than the original number. For example, the numbers 1.32, 0.9624, and 42 are simpler in their original form, and we would probably not use scientific notation for them.

Note that the problem of the significance of the zeros at the end of a number such as 200 can be solved with scientific notation. The number can be written to clearly show one, or two, or three significant digits.

$$2 \times 10^2 \qquad 2.0 \times 10^2 \qquad 2.00 \times 10^2$$

Table 2.1 gives some examples of large and small physical quantities expressed in scientific notation.

EXAMPLE 2.5
Scientific Notation

Express the following numbers in standard scientific notation.

(a) 6100   (c) 10.2   (e) 0.000870
(b) 4,921,000   (d) 0.392   (f) 6.3

In each case the decimal point is moved to the right or left — counting the number of moves — until a number is reached that is between one and ten. The power of ten equals the number of places the decimal point was moved; it is positive for a move to the left and negative for a move to the right.

(a) $6100 = 6.1 \times 10^3$ (d) $0.392 = 3.92 \times 10^{-1}$

(b) $4{,}921{,}000 = 4.921 \times 10^6$ (e) $0.000870 = 8.70 \times 10^{-4}$

(c) $10.2 = 1.02 \times 10^1$ (f) $6.3 = 6.3 \times 10^0$ (note that $10^0 = 1$)

There is no advantage in using scientific notation to express the numbers in parts (c), (d), or (f). [Note that zeros that are not significant are dropped.]

Exercise Express the following numbers in standard scientific notation: (a) 0.0203, (b) 5,260,000, (c) 0.0010   *Answer* (a) 2.03×10^{-2}, (b) 5.26×10^6, (c) 1.0×10^{-3}

EXAMPLE 2.6
Scientific Notation

Write out in full the following numbers.

(a) 4.33×10^4 (c) 6.1234×10^2 (e) 1.348×10^{-3} (g) 3.9×10^{-1}
(b) 9.1×10^2 (d) 9.10×10^2 (f) 2.0×10^{-2}

For positive powers of 10, the decimal point in the factor is moved to the right the number of places equal to the power of 10.

(a) $4.33 \times 10^4 = 43,300$
  1 234

(c) $6.1234 \times 10^2 = 612.34$
  12

(b) $9.1 \times 10^2 = 910$ — *no decimal point shows two figures are significant*
  12

(d) $9.10 \times 10^2 = 910.$ — *decimal point shows three figures are significant*
  1 2

For negative powers of 10, the decimal point in the factor is similarly moved to the left.

(e) $1.348 \times 10^{-3} = 0.001348$
  321

(g) $3.9 \times 10^{-1} = 0.39$
  1

(f) $2.0 \times 10^{-2} = 0.020$
  21

Exercise Write out in full the following numbers: (a) 6.3×10^{-6}, (b) 1.01×10^4, (c) 3.0×10^{-2} *Answer* (a) 0.0000063, (b) 10,100, (c) 0.030

2.5 ARITHMETIC USING SCIENTIFIC NOTATION

In doing arithmetic with numbers expressed in scientific notation, the rules governing significant figures are applied to the factor exactly as for any numbers. To do addition or subtraction with pencil and paper, the numbers must all have the same exponent, even if this produces some numbers with factors not between 1 and 10. For example, to add 99 to 1.23×10^3 the 99 must be expressed with the third power of 10, as 0.099×10^3.

$$\begin{array}{r} 0.099 \times 10^3 \\ 1.23 \times 10^3 \\ \hline 1.329 \times 10^3 \\ 1.33 \times 10^3 \end{array}$$

The power of 10 in the answer is then the same as that in the numbers added or subtracted. Today, of course, most of us need only enter the numbers as originally given into our calculators to do addition or subtraction involving numbers in scientific notation.

To multiply and divide numbers in scientific notation with pencil and paper, multiply and divide the factors, obeying the rules of significant figures. Then find the power of 10 for the answer by *adding* powers of 10 for multiplication and *subtracting* them for division. If necessary, rewrite the answer using a factor between 1 and 10.

equal to 23 + 3

$$(6.022 \times 10^{23})(4.2 \times 10^3) = 25 \times 10^{26} = 2.5 \times 10^{27}$$

restated with factor between 1 and 10

equal to 10 − 6

$$\frac{99 \times 10^{10}}{5.1 \times 10^6} = 19 \times 10^4 = 1.9 \times 10^5$$

equal to (−2) − (−1)

$$\frac{4.3 \times 10^{-2}}{2.01 \times 10^{-1}} = 2.1 \times 10^{-1} = 0.21$$

For multiplication and division, calculators give the answer directly. Where necessary it should be restated with the correct number of significant figures and a factor between 1 and 10.

Table 2.2
Rules for Arithmetic

Significant figures
Addition and subtraction: add or subtract; round the answer to the place (before or after the decimal point) with the greatest uncertainty in the numbers being added or subtracted.
Multiplication and division: multiply or divide; round the answer to the same number of significant figures as in the number with the fewest significant figures.

Scientific notation
Addition and subtraction: Write all numbers in the same power of 10; add or subtract factors; answer has same power of 10.
Multiplication and division: Multiply or divide factors; get power of 10 by adding (multiplication) or subtracting (division) powers of 10.

EXAMPLE 2.7
Scientific Notation—Arithmetic

Perform the following calculations and express the answers in standard scientific notation.

(a) $(6.38 \times 10^4) + (5.2 \times 10^5)$

(b) $(4.77 \times 10^{-4}) - (2.66 \times 10^{-3})$

(c) $(5.3 \times 10^8)(9.62 \times 10^{-4})$

(d) $\dfrac{7.11 \times 10^{-3}}{4.26 \times 10^4}$

(e) $\dfrac{(6.7 \times 10^{-5})(1.2 \times 10^{10})^2}{(8.1 \times 10^{-3})^{11}(2.5 \times 10^2)}$

Each calculation is performed, the answer is expressed to the proper number of significant figures, and the answer is then rewritten with a factor between one and ten.

(a) $\begin{array}{r} 0.638 \times 10^5 \\ \underline{5.2 \times 10^5} \\ 5.838 \times 10^5 \\ 5.8 \times 10^5 \end{array}$
(b) $\begin{array}{r} 0.477 \times 10^{-3} \\ \underline{-2.66 \times 10^{-3}} \\ -2.183 \times 10^{-3} \\ -2.18 \times 10^{-3} \end{array}$

(c) $(5.3 \times 10^8)(9.62 \times 10^{-4}) = 51 \times 10^4 = 5.1 \times 10^5$

(d) $\dfrac{7.11 \times 10^{-3}}{4.26 \times 10^4} = 1.67 \times 10^{-7}$
(e) $\dfrac{(6.7 \times 10^{-5})(1.2 \times 10^{10})}{(8.1 \times 10^{-3})^{11}(2.5 \times 10^2)} = 3.9 \times 10^{36}$

Exercise Perform the following calculations and express the answers in standard scientific notation: (a) $(3.62 \times 10^{-3}) + (2.68 \times 10^{-4})$, (b) $(3.14 \times 10^{-4})(5.1 \times 10^{-5})$, (c) $(4.58 \times 10^4)/(5.44 \times 10^{-14})$, (d) $(7.39 \times 10^5) + (7.39 \times 10^{-5})$
Answer (a) 3.89×10^{-3}, (b) 1.6×10^{-8}, (c) 8.42×10^{17}, (d) 7.39×10^5

In summary, to use numbers correctly in physical quantities, you must know how to express a numerical value to the correct number of significant figures (Section 2.2) and how to use scientific notation (Section 2.4) for very large and very small numbers. You must also know how to do arithmetic with numbers expressed correctly in significant figures and in scientific notation. The rules for arithmetic are summarized in Table 2.2.

A HISTORICAL ASIDE

The Origins of Chemistry

Chemistry is a very old science. The first person who saw a tree burn after it was struck by lightning was observing a chemical change. People learned many centuries ago to cook food and to make pottery vessels by strongly heating clay which they had molded into appropriate shapes.

Modern chemistry grew out of ancient technology, such as the smelting of ores, as well as out of medicine and alchemy. In addition, observations of the world around them led those who were philosophically minded to speculate about the nature of matter. Unfortunately, much of this speculation was far from the mark and actually retarded the progress of science. For example, some philosophers of the sixth century before Christ believed that water was the basis of all substances; others thought air was the primordial substance.

Plato (427–347 B.C.) postulated that there were four elements — earth, air, fire, and water, and perhaps a fifth — an ether which was in some way associated with the material of the heavens. Aristotle (384–322 B.C.) also thought that all matter was composed of these elements, a belief that persisted in science until the end of the eighteenth century.

Alchemy grew out of both technology and philosophical speculation. At first alchemy was concerned with the conversion of base metals into gold, and several experiments were cited to support the belief that this was possible. For example, when impure gold is strongly heated, especially in a molten salt, the impurities are burned away, leaving pure gold. The resulting change in color and other properties was interpreted to mean that the original metal had changed into gold.

Physicians of early times tested all sorts of materials for their medicinal value, not on mice and guinea pigs, as is done today, but on their human patients. Herbs and vegetable extracts were used, as well as inorganic salts and minerals. Some valuable drugs were discovered in this way, and also some deadly poisons! Many physicians practiced alchemy on the side, and eventually alchemy came to include a search for the "elixir of life," a substance that would ensure perpetual youth and health. There were many opportunities for "get rich quick" schemes, and some alchemists took advantage of these. On that account, we often think of the alchemists as quacks and charlatans. Doubtless many of them were, but others were earnest seekers after truth.

The Greek philosophers drew some sound conclusions about the nature of matter (see A Historical Aside: The Concept of the Atom, Chapter 3), and many alchemists correctly recorded the physical and chemical properties of many substances. However, their scientific progress was limited. The philosophers did few experiments, and although the alchemists did many, none involved accurate measurements.

Most areas of science are not considered fully explored until they become quantitative, that is, until accurate measurements are made. To learn about the composition of matter and about changes in the composition of matter, experiments must be performed, most often on weighed amounts of material under carefully controlled conditions. After the changes are complete, the products formed must be weighed before conclusions can be drawn about what has happened. By the middle of the eighteenth century the need for quantitative experiments had been recognized, and progress was aided by the availability of finely made, accurate balances constructed to meet the need. A study of the chemistry of carbon dioxide done by Joseph Black in 1754 has been called "the first example we possess of a clear, reasoned series of chemical researches where nothing was taken on trust, but everything was made the subject of careful, quantitative measurement."

UNITS OF MEASUREMENT

Having looked at how numbers are treated in physical quantities, we now turn our attention to the units.

2.6 SYSTEMS OF MEASUREMENT

If you ask an Englishman his weight, he might reply, "14 stone." An American might say, "180 pounds," and a Canadian might say "91 kilograms," in answer to the same question. These answers leave you in the dark about who is the heaviest person unless you are familiar with three different systems of measurement and the relationships among them.

Easy comparison of measurements made by different people, in different laboratories, or in different countries, is only possible when measurements of the same quantities are expressed in the same units. If our Englishman had used the unit kilograms instead of stones, he would have replied "89 kilograms." Our American, using the same system of measurement, would have replied that he weighs 82 kilograms. Without any effort, we can now see that the Canadian is the heavyweight of the group at 91 kilograms, and the American is the lightweight at 82 kilograms.

The *metric system* was devised by the French National Academy of Sciences in 1793 to replace the profusion of units handed down from medieval times. Since then, various international bodies have been defining and redefining units of measurement and attempting to gain widespread uniformity in their use. For many years people in most European countries and scientists everywhere have used the metric system. The United States, until 1975, officially stayed with a weights and measures system based upon the English system of inches and feet, ounces and pounds, pints and quarts, and so on. The Metric Conversion Act of 1975 committed this country to a policy of voluntary conversion to the metric system by 1985. Although the metric system is finding acceptance, the changeover from the English system is proceeding very slowly because of conversion costs and general public resistance to change.

In 1960, the International Bureau of Weights and Measures adopted the International System of Units, known as the "SI system" (for Système International). The SI system is a revision and extension of the metric system; it provides base units for each type of measurement. Scientists and engineers throughout the world in all disciplines are now being urged to use *only* the SI system of units. However, the scientific community is as resistant to change as the general public. Also, some specific objections to certain SI units have been raised. It will undoubtedly be a long time before the conversion to the SI system is complete. At the present time, everyone working in science must be familiar with both the older metric system of measurement and with many aspects of the SI system.

2.7 THE SI SYSTEM OF MEASUREMENT

In this and the next section we concentrate on defining the units in physical quantities. In later sections of this chapter we discuss how physical quantities are treated in problem solving.

The SI system specifies the units to be used in various types of measurements. Seven base physical quantities have been chosen and their units defined. All other physical quantities are derived from the seven base quantities, and the units for all physical quantities are derived from the base units.

For example, volume is a derived physical quantity that measures space. To find the volume of a box, the lengths of its three sides are multiplied together. Length is a base physical quantity in the SI system, and the base unit of length is the *meter.* With the length of the sides in meters, the volume of a box has units of meters cubed, or cubic meters.

$$(\text{meters})(\text{meters})(\text{meters}) = (\text{meters})^3 \text{ or cubic meters}$$

Cubic meters is the derived unit for volume in the SI system.

The seven base physical quantities are given in Table 2.3, together with the base units and their abbreviations. One of the base quantities, luminous intensity, is rarely encountered in chemistry. In parentheses after the name of the physical quantity in Table 2.3 is given the abbreviation for that quantity. To express, for example, the

Table 2.3
SI Base Physical Quantities and Units The candela is not commonly encountered in chemistry.

Quantity (symbol)	Name of Unit	Abbreviation
Length (l)	meter (or metre)	m
Mass (m)	kilogram	kg
Time (t)	second	s
Electric current (I)	ampere	A
Temperature (T)	kelvin	K
Luminous intensity (I_v)	candela	cd
Amount of substance (n)	mole	mol

Table 2.4
SI Derived Physical Quantities and Units

Quantity (Symbol)	Name of Unit (Symbol)	Derived Unit
Area (A)	square meter	m^2
Volume (V)	cubic meter	m^3
Density (ρ)	kilogram per cubic meter	kg/m^3
Velocity (u)	meter per second	m/s
Pressure (P)	pascal (Pa)	$kg/(m\ s^2)$
Energy (E)	joule (J)	$(kg\ m^2)/s^2$
Frequency (ν)	hertz (Hz)	$1/s$
Quantity of electricity (Q)	coulomb (C)	A s
Electromotive force (E)	volt (V)	$(kg\ m^2)/A\ s^3$
Force	newton (N)	$kg\ m/s^2$

length of a 2 meter long piece of pipe, the unit and quantity abbreviations would be used as follows:

$$\text{physical quantity abbreviation (in italics)} \rightarrow l = 2 \text{ m} \leftarrow \text{unit abbreviation}$$

Table 2.4 lists several derived quantities that are used in chemistry. (A list of additional derived units is given in Appendix II.) Many derived units require several base units. Such derived units are simplified by assigning a single unit to represent the physical quantity. We do not, for example, have to recall each time we use it that pressure is given in "kilograms per meter per second squared," $kg/(m\ s^2)$. The SI approved unit for pressure is the *pascal,* abbreviated Pa. By definition, 1 Pa = 1 $kg/(m\ s^2)$.

Often the SI unit for a physical quantity is inconvenient because it leads to a numerical value that is very large or very small. To solve this problem, multiples and fractions of the base or derived units are indicated by using the prefixes given in Table 2.5. For example, one type of virus is about 0.00000001 m long. The meter is too big a unit for the length of viruses, and it is more convenient to talk about viruses in units of nanometers. One nanometer is equal to 0.000000001 m, and the virus is about 10 nm long. (Note that the prefix, "nano" in nanometer, is written in front of the unit name without a hyphen and that the prefix abbreviation, "n" in nm, is similarly written in front of the unit abbreviation.)

Table 2.5
Prefixes for Multiples and Fractions of SI Units The symbol for the prefix "micro" is the Greek letter mu, μ.

Decimal Location	Prefix	Prefix Symbol
$1{,}000{,}000{,}000{,}000 = 10^{12}$	tera	T
$1{,}000{,}000{,}000 = 10^9$	giga	G
$1{,}000{,}000 = 10^6$	mega	M
$1{,}000 = 10^3$	kilo	k
$100 = 10^2$	hecto	h
$10 = 10^1$	deka	da
$0.1 = 10^{-1}$	deci	d
$0.01 = 10^{-2}$	centi	c
$0.001 = 10^{-3}$	milli	m
$0.000\ 001 = 10^{-6}$	micro	μ
$0.000\ 000\ 001 = 10^{-9}$	nano	n
$0.000\ 000\ 000\ 001 = 10^{-12}$	pico	p
$0.000\ 000\ 000\ 000\ 001 = 10^{-15}$	femto	f
$0.000\ 000\ 000\ 000\ 000\ 001 = 10^{-18}$	atto	a

Table 2.6

Equivalence between Units The equivalences marked by * are exact (see Section 2.1). Appendix II gives additional conversion factors and also some of these factors to a greater number of significant figures. Abbreviations used here that have not yet been introduced are Å, angstrom; L, liter; eV, electron volt; atm, atmosphere; psi, pounds per square inch; mmHg, millimeters of mercury.

Length

1 km = 0.621 mile	1 mile = 1.6093 km
1 m = 3.281 ft	1 ft = 0.3048 m
1 cm = 0.3937 inch	1 inch = 2.54 cm*
1 nm = 10 Å* = 1 mμ*	

Volume

1 L = 1 dm³* = 10^{-3} m³*	
1 cm³ = 1 mL*	
1 L = 1.0567 qt	1 qt = 0.94635 L
	1 gal = 3.785 L

Mass

1 kg = 2.205 lb	1 lb = 0.45359 kg
1 g = 0.0353 oz	1 oz = 28.350 g
1 metric ton = 10^3 kg*	

Energy

1 J = 1 (kg m²)/s²*	
1 J = 0.239 cal	1 cal = 4.184 J*
1 erg = 10^{-7} J*	1 eV = 1.6022×10^{-19} J
1 L atm = 101.325 J*	

Force

1 dyne = 1 g cm/s²*	
1 N = 1 kg m/s²*	
1 N = 10^5 dyne*	1 dyne = 10^{-5} N*
1 N = 0.225 pound (force)	1 pound (force) = 4.45 N

Pressure

1 Pa = 1 N/m²* = 1 kg/(m s²)*	
	1 bar = 10^5 Pa*
	1 psi = 6894.76 Pa
	1 atm = 101,325 Pa*
	1 Torr = 1 mmHg = 133.32 Pa
	1 atm = 760 Torr*

In the section that follows we discuss individually many of the units for physical quantities important to chemistry. To give you a feeling for the magnitude of the SI units, Table 2.6 compares some of these units to those with which you may be more familiar. We suggest that you refer back to this table as you read the following sections.

2.8 UNITS OF MEASUREMENT IN CHEMISTRY

a. Length   In both the older metric and the newer SI systems, the *meter* (m) is the base unit of length. All base units must be defined in terms of something that does not vary and can be used as a reference. Originally the meter was defined as exactly one ten-millionth of the distance from the equator to the North Pole and reference was made to a metal bar of that length kept carefully, by international agreement, in Paris. The new definition of a meter in terms of a particular type of radiation is more precise, and the physical quantity of reference is less subject to variation than a metal bar (all substances vary slightly in size with variations in temperature). The definitions of all of the SI base units are given in Appendix II.

Chemists often have to talk about very small lengths and, as described above, these are conveniently expressed in nanometers (1 nm = 10^{-9} m). An older unit that is still commonly used to express very small distances is the angstrom, abbreviated Å (1 Å = 10^{-10} m = 0.1 nm).

b. Volume   Because of the relationship of length to volume, as illustrated above, the SI unit for volume is the cubic meter (m³). (The SI unit for area is the square meter, m².) However, the milliliter (mL) and the liter (L) are the standard units of volume for liquids in most chemical laboratory work. One milliliter is exactly equal to one cubic centimeter (cm³), and one liter exactly equals 1000 milliliters or 1000

Table 2.7
Densities of Some Common Substances Approximate values for ordinary room temperature and pressure.

Substance	Density (g/cm³)
Ammonia, dilute solution (4%)	0.96
Balsa wood	0.1
Bone	1.9
Chalk	2.4
Chloroform	1.5
Cork	0.24
Corn oil	0.91
Creosote	1.1
Diamond	3.3
Limestone	2.7
Maple wood	0.69
Mercury	13.5
Water	0.99
Whiskey	0.92

$$\text{Density} = \text{mass/volume}$$

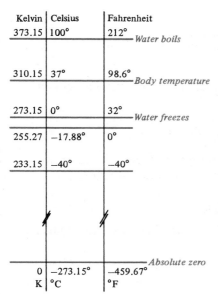

Kelvin	Celsius	Fahrenheit	
373.15	100°	212°	— Water boils
310.15	37°	98.6°	— Body temperature
273.15	0°	32°	— Water freezes
255.27	−17.88°	0°	
233.15	−40°	−40°	
0	−273.15°	−459.67°	— Absolute zero
K	°C	°F	

Figure 2.3
Comparison of Temperature Measured in Kelvin Units and on the Celsius and Fahrenheit Scales

cubic centimeters. The SI system recommends replacing the liter with the cubic decimeter (dm³), but in this book we have chosen to use milliliters and liters. The cubic decimeter has not yet been widely accepted. [From 1901 to 1964, a liter was defined as the volume of 1 kilogram of water at 4 °C. During this period a milliliter was very slightly larger than a cubic centimeter. In 1964, the liter was redefined as exactly equal in volume to 1000 cubic centimeters, thereby eliminating some confusion.]

c. Mass and weight The distinction between mass and weight should be clear to anyone who has seen pictures of the astronauts bounding over the surface of the moon. The gravity of the moon is smaller than that of the earth, and so the weight of the astronauts there was less. Their bodies, however, were unchanged and had the same mass as on earth. **Mass** is a physical property that represents the quantity of matter in a body. **Weight** is the force a body exerts because of the pull of gravity on the mass of that body.

Both the SI and metric systems rely on the gram, and the multiples and fractions of the gram, as the units for mass. The kilogram is the base unit for mass in the SI system. Strictly speaking, weight should be expressed in units of force (Section 2.8 g). In practice, however, the distinction between weight and mass is often ignored. Expressions such as "Weigh out 30 grams of this material," or "How many grams does that sample weigh?" are often used.

d. Density Mass and volume are physical quantities that by themselves disclose nothing about the identity of the substance measured. But, when they are combined, they yield one of the distinctive properties of different substances (Table 2.7). The **density** is the mass per unit volume of a substance. The SI unit for density utilizes the base units of kilograms and meters, and is kilograms per cubic meter (kg/m³). The most common unit for density is grams per cubic centimeter (g/cm³), which is equivalent to grams per milliliter (g/mL). For example, the density of aluminum metal might be given as 2.7×10^3 kg/m³ or 2.7 g/cm³, the density of water as about 1 g/mL, and the density of oxygen gas (at room temperature and pressure) as 1.3 g/L. Note that the volume of a substance varies with temperature (and pressure if it is a gas). In careful work, therefore, the temperature (and pressure) at which a density was measured must be stated.

e. Temperature You should be familiar with three temperature scales: the SI scale, measured in kelvin units; the Celsius scale, measured in degrees Celsius (°C); and the Fahrenheit scale, measured in degrees Fahrenheit (°F). The Fahrenheit scale has been in common use in the United States. The kelvin is the SI unit for temperature. However, most scientific measurements are still reported in Celsius degrees, which are gradually being introduced to common use in the United States.

On the Celsius scale water freezes at 0 °C and boils at 100 °C (at 1 atm pressure). Anders Celsius described a thermometer using such a scale in 1742. The same scale has also been called the centigrade scale. Fortunately, both are represented by °C.

On the Fahrenheit scale water freezes at 32 °F and boils at 212 °F (at 1 atm). Thus there are 100 degrees between these two points on the Celsius scale and 180 degrees between them on the Fahrenheit scale. This makes the Fahrenheit degree equal to 100/180 or 5/9 of a Celsius degree.

The temperatures on the two scales are equal at −40°C (Figure 2.3). This allows for an easy-to-remember way of converting between temperatures on the two scales. Let's start with a Fahrenheit temperature. Adding 40° to a Fahrenheit temperature gives the number of Fahrenheit degrees between −40 °C and that temperature. For example, for 25 °F

25 °F + 40 F degrees = 65 Fahrenheit degrees between −40 °F and 25 °F

To convert 25 °F to temperature on the Celsius scale, it is then only necessary to multiply 65 Fahrenheit degrees by the factor that relates Fahrenheit and Celsius degrees. Then subtract 40 Celsius degrees to get the numerical value of the temperature on the Celsius scale.

$$(65 \text{ F degrees})\left(\frac{5 \text{ C degrees}}{9 \text{ F degrees}}\right) - 40 \text{ C degrees} = -4 \text{ °C}$$

Similarly, to convert from a known temperature on the Celsius scale to temperature on the Fahrenheit scale, 40 ° is added. Then the result is multiplied by the factor that relates Celsius and Fahrenheit degrees, and 40 Fahrenheit degrees subtracted. The conversion of 25 °C to the Fahrenheit temperature is done in one step as follows:

$$(25 \text{ °C} + 40 \text{ C degrees})\left(\frac{9 \text{ F degrees}}{5 \text{ C degrees}}\right) - 40 \text{ F degrees} = 77 \text{ °F}$$

The general expressions for interconversion of Celsius and Fahrenheit temperatures, $T(°C)$ and $T(°F)$, are

$$T(°C) = [T(°F) + 40 \text{ F degrees}]\left(\frac{5 \text{ C degrees}}{9 \text{ F degrees}}\right) - 40 \text{ C degrees} \qquad (2.1)$$

$$T(°F) = [T(°C) + 40 \text{ C degrees}]\left(\frac{9 \text{ F degrees}}{5 \text{ C degrees}}\right) - 40 \text{ F degrees} \qquad (2.2)$$

In the SI system the kelvin (K) is the unit for temperature and it is used without a degree sign. One kelvin is the same size as one degree Celsius. On the Kelvin temperature scale absolute zero, which is the lowest possible temperature, is equal to 0 kelvin, or 0 K. The freezing point of water is 273.15 K and the boiling point of water is 373.15 K. (The physical explanation for the relationship of these two temperature scales is discussed in Section 5.5.) A Celsius temperature can be converted to a Kelvin temperature by adding 273.15.

$$T(K) = T(°C) + 273.15 \qquad (2.3)$$

$$°C = [(°F + 40)\tfrac{5}{9}] - 40$$
$$°F = [(°C + 40)\tfrac{9}{5}] - 40$$
$$K = °C + 273$$

EXAMPLE 2.8
Temperature Conversion

(a) Convert 72 °F to both Celsius and Kelvin temperatures. (b) Convert 64 K to both Celsius and Fahrenheit temperatures.

First use Equation (2.1) to find the Celsius temperature from the Fahrenheit temperature that is given, $T(°F) = 72$ °F.

$$T(°C) = (72 \text{ °F} + 40 \text{ F degrees})\left(\frac{5 \text{ C degrees}}{9 \text{ F degrees}}\right) - 40 \text{ C degrees} = 22 \text{ °C}$$

Then use Equation (2.3) to find the Kelvin temperature from the Celsius temperature. (Note that 273 may be used, because it has enough significant figures.)

$$T(K) = T(°C) + 273$$
$$= 22 + 273 = 295 \text{ K}$$

(b) First the Celsius temperature must be found from the Kelvin temperature that is given.

$$64 \text{ K} = T(°C) + 273$$
$$T(°C) = -209 \text{ °C}$$

Now the Fahrenheit temperature can be found by using Equation (2.2).

$$T(°F) = (-209 \text{ °C} + 40 \text{ C degrees})\left(\frac{9 \text{ F degrees}}{5 \text{ C degrees}}\right) - 40 \text{ F} = -344 \text{ °F}$$

Exercise Convert $-15\,°F$ to both Celsius and Kelvin temperatures. *Answer* $-26\,°C$, 247 K

f. Heat and energy In the SI system the unit for energy of all types is the joule (J; pronounced "jool"), a derived unit defined as $1\text{ J} = 1\text{ (kg m}^2)/s^2$, where m is the abbreviation for meter and s that for second. The joule is being adopted more rapidly than some SI units. At the present time both joules and kilojoules, as well as the older, metric units of calories and kilocalories, are seen often. The calorie is now defined in terms of the joule (1 cal = 4.184 J, exactly). The calorie and the joule are rather small units for the heat exchanged in many chemical processes. Most frequently, the kilocalorie or the kilojoule is used for these purposes.

$$1\text{ kilocalorie (kcal)} = 4.184\text{ kilojoules (kJ)}$$

The "calories" counted by dieters are really kilocalories.

g. Force and pressure If you push or pull an object, you are exerting a force on the object. In chemistry we often deal with forces that are interactions between two bodies. The state of motion of the bodies may be changed, or the shape or size of the bodies altered, when the interaction occurs. The SI unit of force is the newton, N $[1\text{ N} = 1\text{ (kg m)}/s^2]$.

Pressure = force/area

Pressure is a force exerted per unit area. The SI unit of pressure is the pascal $[1\text{ Pa} = 1\text{ N/m}^2 = 1\text{ kg}/(m\ s^2)]$. Other, more commonly used, units for pressure are atmospheres (atm), bars (bar), pounds per square inch (psi), torr (Torr), and millimeters of mercury (mmHg). The relationships among these units are given in Table 2.6. (Pressure is discussed further in Tools of Chemistry: Pressure Units and Pressure Measurement, Chapter 5.)

THE DIMENSIONAL METHOD AND PROBLEM SOLVING

2.9 THE DIMENSIONAL METHOD

The unit should *always* accompany the numerical value of a measurement in writing about the measurement, talking about it, or using it in any kind of calculation. In a numerical problem, units are included in setting up the calculation and are treated exactly as numbers would be. Such treatment of units as numbers is the basis for what is called the dimensional method of calculation.

Because only numbers with the same units can be added or subtracted, units do not change in these operations.

$$9.0\text{ V} + 3.29\text{ V} = 12.3\text{ V}$$
$$635\text{ nm} - 91\text{ nm} = 544\text{ nm}$$

In multiplication the answer has as its units the product of the units multiplied.

read "liter atmospheres"

$$(6\text{ L})(0.3\text{ atm}) = 2\text{ L atm}$$
$$(29.0\text{ cm})^2 = 841\text{ cm}^2$$

In division the units may appear in the answer or they may cancel out.

read "centimeters per second"

$$\frac{3.0\text{ cm}}{2.0\text{ s}} = 1.5\text{ cm/s}$$

units cancelled; a dimensionless quantity

$$\frac{203\text{ kcal}}{69\text{ kcal}} = 2.9$$

(Often a unit that would appear in the denominator of an expression is instead written with a negative exponent. For example, for "centimeters per second," cm s^{-1} would be written instead of cm/s.)

Units are cancelled exactly as numbers (or algebraic variables) would be in calculating the answer to a problem. For example, suppose you wanted to know how many liters of gasoline you needed to travel 650 km each day for 10 days in a car that requires 21 L of gasoline for each 160 km. The correct solution to the problem looks like this:

$$\left(\frac{650\ \text{km}}{1\ \text{day}}\right)(10\ \text{days})\left(\frac{21\ \text{L}}{160\ \text{km}}\right) = 850\ \text{L}$$

The dimensional method of calculation is powerful and useful for several reasons. It is an excellent guide in deciding how to solve some problems. And it makes many errors instantly recognizable. A correct setup usually leads to an answer in the desired units, as is shown by the answer in liters just above. A wrong setup usually leads to an answer in the wrong units. A good question to ask yourself before solving a dimensional problem is, What must the units be in the final answer?

EXAMPLE 2.9
Dimensional Method

How many boxes of candy bars are needed so that 15 people can have 2 candy bars each? There are 6 candy bars in each box.

The solution to the problem, set up dimensionally to give the answer in the unit "boxes," is

$$(15\ \text{persons}) \times \left(\frac{2\ \text{bars}}{1\ \text{person}}\right) \times \left(\frac{1\ \text{box}}{6\ \text{bars}}\right) = 5\ \text{boxes}$$

Five boxes of candy bars are needed. [Note how the units cancel, leaving only the desired unit.]
   Suppose someone quickly figured the answer as $(15)(2)(6) = 180$ and ran out to buy several cases of candy. Including the units in the incorrect setup

$$(15\ \text{persons})\left(\frac{2\ \text{bars}}{1\ \text{person}}\right)\left(\frac{6\ \text{bars}}{1\ \text{box}}\right) = 180\ \frac{\text{bars}^2}{\text{box}}$$

would have revealed the error by giving the answer in meaningless units.

Exercise A newspaper contains 26 sheets of newsprint. An art project calls for 4 sheets of newsprint for each 3 students working together. Will three newspapers provide enough sheets for a class of 18 students? *Answer* Yes, one newspaper will provide enough sheets with 2 sheets left over.

The conversion of units, discussed in the next section, provides further illustration of how the dimensional method is used.

2.10 CONVERSION FACTORS

The conversion of a physical quantity in one unit to the same quantity expressed in another unit is a common necessity in solving problems in chemistry. To carry out such a transformation, conversion factors based on the relationship between the two units are used. The conversion factors are derived from equalities (see Table 2.6) such as

$$1\ \text{cal} = 4.184\ \text{J}$$

Each such equality yields two conversion factors

$$1 \text{ cal} = 4.184 \text{ J} \qquad\qquad\qquad 1 \text{ cal} = 4.184 \text{ J}$$

or

$$\frac{1 \text{ cal}}{1 \text{ cal}} = \frac{4.184 \text{ J}}{1 \text{ cal}} \qquad\qquad \frac{1 \text{ cal}}{4.184 \text{ J}} = \frac{4.184 \text{ J}}{4.184 \text{ J}}$$

$$1 = \frac{4.184 \text{ J}}{1 \text{ cal}} \xleftarrow{\quad} \begin{array}{c} \textit{two conversion} \\ \textit{factors;} \\ \textit{reciprocals} \end{array} \xrightarrow{\quad} \frac{1 \text{ cal}}{4.184 \text{ J}} = 1$$

These conversion factors allow us to change joules to calories and vice versa.

As you can see, these conversion factors are reciprocals of each other and are both equal to 1. The conversion factor on the left is read "4.184 joules per calorie" and tells us how many joules of heat there are for one single calorie of heat. Once we know this, we can easily find how many joules are equivalent to any number of calories simply by multiplying. Similarly, once we know how many calories are equivalent to one joule, we can find the number of calories equivalent to any number of joules. The conversion factor on the right—"one calorie per 4.184 joules"—gives this information.

The two conversions allowed by the conversion factor just derived are from calories to joules, and from joules to calories.

$$\text{Calories} \underset{\times\left(\frac{1\ cal}{4.184\ J}\right)}{\overset{\times\left(\frac{4.184\ J}{1\ cal}\right)}{\rightleftharpoons}} \text{Joules} \qquad\qquad (2.4)$$

For example, given 30.0 cal and needing to express this quantity of heat in joules

$$30.0 \text{ cal} \times \frac{4.184 \text{ J}}{1 \text{ cal}} = 126 \text{ J} \qquad\qquad (2.5)$$

or given 30.0 J and needing to express this quantity of heat in calories

$$30.0 \text{ J} \times \frac{1 \text{ cal}}{4.184 \text{ J}} = 7.17 \text{ cal} \qquad\qquad (2.6)$$

How do you choose which conversion factor to use? It's easy—*choose the conversion factor that eliminates the unit that you do not want.* The cancellation of units by the dimensional method is shown in Equations (2.5) and (2.6). In each case the unit to be eliminated is in the denominator (on the *bottom*) in the conversion factor. Of course, it is possible that the reverse might occur and the unit to be eliminated would have to be in the numerator in the conversion factor.

EXAMPLE 2.10
Unit Conversion

Convert 8160 Å to (a) nanometers and (b) meters.

(a) Table 2.6 shows that 1 nm = 10 Å, giving the conversion factors

$$\frac{1 \text{ nm}}{10 \text{ Å}} \qquad \frac{10 \text{ Å}}{1 \text{ nm}}$$

Choosing the conversion factor that eliminates Å,

$$(8160 \text{ Å})\left(\frac{1 \text{ nm}}{10 \text{ Å}}\right) = 816 \text{ nm}$$

shows that 8160 Å = 816 nm.

(b) The unit equivalence (Table 2.6) and the possible conversion factors are

$$1 \text{ nm} = 1 \times 10^{-9} \text{ m} \qquad \frac{1 \text{ nm}}{1 \times 10^{-9} \text{ m}} \qquad \frac{1 \times 10^{-9} \text{ m}}{1 \text{ nm}}$$

The conversion is accomplished as follows:

$$(816 \text{ nm})\left(\frac{1 \times 10^{-9} \text{ m}}{1 \text{ nm}}\right) = 816 \times 10^{-9} \text{ m} = 8.16 \times 10^{-7} \text{ m}$$

Unit conversion shows that 8160 Å = 8.16×10^{-7} m.

Exercise Convert 265 μL to (a) liters and (b) milliliters. *Answer* (a) 2.65×10^{-4} L, (b) 0.265 mL

EXAMPLE 2.11
Unit Conversion

In planning to cook for a party while on vacation in France, the Jones family made a shopping list that included 2 qt of milk, 3 gal of wine, 6.5 oz of cheese, and 2.5 lb of beef. Convert this into a shopping list for liters of milk and wine, grams of cheese, and kilograms of beef. (See Table 2.6.) How far in miles is it to the store, which is 19 km away?

Choosing in each case (Table 2.6) a conversion factor that eliminates the unwanted unit, and limiting the conversion factors to two significant figures gives

$$(2 \text{ qt milk})\left(\frac{0.95 \text{ L}}{1 \text{ qt}}\right) = 2 \text{ L milk} \qquad (3 \text{ gal wine})\left(\frac{3.79 \text{ L}}{1 \text{ gal}}\right) = 10 \text{ L wine}$$

$$(6.5 \text{ oz cheese})\left(\frac{28 \text{ g}}{1 \text{ oz}}\right) = 180 \text{ g cheese} \qquad (2.5 \text{ lb beef})\left(\frac{0.45 \text{ kg}}{1 \text{ lb}}\right) = 1.1 \text{ kg beef}$$

$$(19 \text{ km})\left(\frac{0.62 \text{ mi}}{\text{km}}\right) = 12 \text{ mi}$$

The Joneses will travel 12 miles to purchase 2 L of milk, 10 L of wine, 180 g of cheese, and 1.1 kg of beef.

Exercise A package weighs 362 g. What is the mass expressed in ounces? *Answer* 12.8 oz

---

The number of significant figures in a conversion factor depends on whether or not the number is an exact number. Note that in part (a) of Example 2.10, the factor 10 Å did not limit the answer to two digits. This is because there are *exactly* 10 Å in exactly 1 nm. An exact conversion factor can be treated as having as many significant figures as are needed. The multiples and fractions of units indicated by the prefixes of Table 2.5 are exact numbers; for example, 1 dL is exactly equal to 0.1 L.

When supplying conversion factors or values of physical constants in a calculation, always make sure that the values you have supplied contain enough significant figures so that the uncertainty in the answer is the same as the uncertainty in the original number. You do not want to decrease the number of significant figures just by choosing a conversion factor with too few significant figures. In addition and subtraction, this means giving the constant as many decimal places as the number in the problem with the fewest decimal places. In multiplication and division, this means giving the constant or conversion factor the same number of significant figures as the other factor.

Confirm for yourself that the following examples illustrate this point.

express conversion factor to two significant figures

$$\text{(1.2 eV)} \left(\frac{1.6 \times 10^{-19} \text{ J}}{1 \text{ eV}} \right) = 1.9 \times 10^{-19} \text{ J}$$

two significant figures

two significant figures

$$\text{(99.94 eV)} \left(\frac{1.602 \times 10^{-19} \text{ J}}{1 \text{ eV}} \right) = 1.601 \times 10^{-17} \text{ J}$$

four significant figures

express conversion factor to four significant figures

four significant figures

Once you understand the use of the dimensional method, many steps in a unit conversion or any other problem can be combined in a single expression, as shown in the following example.

EXAMPLE 2.12
Conversion Factors

How many seconds are there in one day?

The conversion factors needed must come from the following equalities:

$$1 \text{ day} = 24 \text{ h} \qquad 1 \text{ h} = 60 \text{ min} \qquad 1 \text{ min} = 60 \text{ s}$$

We start with days and convert to hours:

$$\text{(1 day)} \left(\frac{24 \text{ h}}{1 \text{ day}} \right) = 24 \text{ h}$$

Next, we convert hours to minutes:

$$\text{(24 h)} \left(\frac{60 \text{ min}}{1 \text{ h}} \right) = 1440 \text{ min}$$

and then we convert to seconds:

$$\text{(1440 min)} \left(\frac{60 \text{ s}}{1 \text{ min}} \right) = 86,400 \text{ s}$$

The individual steps in such a unit conversion can be strung together and the final answer calculated all at once as follows:

$$\text{(1 day)} \times \left(\frac{24 \text{ h}}{1 \text{ day}} \right) \times \left(\frac{60 \text{ min}}{1 \text{ h}} \right) \times \left(\frac{60 \text{ s}}{1 \text{ min}} \right) = 86,400 \text{ s}$$

Exercise How many seconds are there in one hour? *Answer* 3600 s

---

The conversion factors that we have used so far all convert between different units for the same physical property: distance in miles or kilometers, heat in kilocalories or kilojoules, and so on. The dimensional method is also effective in the use of factors that allow conversion between related but different physical properties. For example, density—the mass per unit volume—is a conversion factor that allows us to convert from volume to mass or mass to volume, for example,

$$\begin{array}{ccc} \text{Mass} & = \text{(density)} & \text{(volume)} \\ grams & \dfrac{grams}{cubic\ centimeter} & cubic\ centimeters \end{array}$$

Such conversion factors are ratios between two different physical quantities.

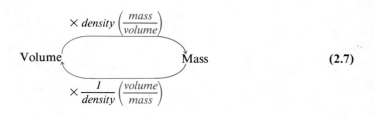

$$\text{Volume} \xrightarrow{\times \, density \left(\frac{mass}{volume}\right)} \text{Mass} \qquad\qquad (2.7)$$

$$\times \frac{1}{density}\left(\frac{volume}{mass}\right)$$

EXAMPLE 2.13
Conversion Factors

What is the mass in grams of a 9.00 cm³ piece of lead? The density of lead is 11.3 g/cm³.

The solution to the problem is set up using the dimensional method.

$$\text{Mass} = (9.00 \text{ cm}^3)\left(\frac{11.3 \text{ g}}{1 \text{ cm}^3}\right) = 102. \text{ g}$$

The piece of lead has a mass of 102. g.

Exercise   What is the volume in cubic centimeters of a 6.35 g piece of lead? *Answer* 0.562 cm³

The ratios needed to solve a problem can be derived from the problem itself, as well as from a defined quantity like density. Two simple problems of this type are given in Examples 2.14 and 2.15. Many chemical problems are of this type.

EXAMPLE 2.14
Conversion Factors

A 250. cm³ volume of a liquid weighs 312 g. What volume of the liquid will weigh 4.5 g?

The information given provides a ratio of mass to volume for this liquid, which can be used in a dimensional calculation as follows:

$$\left(\frac{250. \text{ cm}^3}{312 \text{ g}}\right)(4.5 \text{ g}) = 3.6 \text{ cm}^3$$

A 3.6 cm³ sample of the liquid will weigh 4.5 g.

Exercise   A 100. mL sample of an oil weighs 86.2 g. What is the mass of 16.3 mL of the oil?   *Answer* 14.1 g

---

EXAMPLE 2.15
Conversion Factors

A chemical plant can produce 5.4 kg of a substance each day at a cost of $1300 per kilogram. What will it cost to run the plant for 5 days?

The conversion factors for this problem are derived from the data given: the mass produced per day and the cost per unit mass.

$$\text{Total cost} = \left(\frac{5.4 \text{ kg}}{1 \text{ day}}\right)\left(\frac{\$1300}{1 \text{ kg}}\right)(5 \text{ days}) = \$35,000$$

The total cost for the five days is $35,000.

Exercise   Starting with $8300, how many days can the chemical plant described above operate until the funds are depleted?   *Answer* 1.2 days

EXAMPLE 2.16
Conversion Factors

What is the mass of the snow (in tons) on a 150 ft × 45 ft flat roof after a 6.0 inch snowfall? Assume that 11 inches of snow are equivalent to 1.0 inch of water. Density of water = 1.0 g/cm³; 1 lb = 454 g; 1 T = 2000 lb.

The volume of water equivalent to the volume of snow on the roof is

$$(6.0 \text{ inches snow})\left(\frac{1.0 \text{ inch water}}{11 \text{ inches snow}}\right)(150 \text{ ft})(45 \text{ ft})\left(\frac{12 \text{ inches}}{1 \text{ ft}}\right)^2\left(\frac{2.54 \text{ cm}}{1 \text{ inch}}\right)^3$$

$$= 8.7 \times 10^6 \text{ cm}^3 \text{ water}$$

The mass of this volume of water, which corresponds to the mass of the snow, is found by using the density

$$(8.7 \times 10^6 \text{ cm}^3)\left(\frac{1.0 \text{ g}}{1 \text{ cm}^3}\right)\left(\frac{1 \text{ lb}}{454 \text{ g}}\right)\left(\frac{1 \text{ T}}{2000 \text{ lb}}\right) = 9.6 \text{ T}$$

The roof holds 9.6 T of snow.

Exercise Astronomical distances are often measured in units of light years (the distance that light travels in a year). What is the number of meters in a light year? The speed of light is 3.00×10^8 m/s. *Answer* 9.46×10^{15} m

2.11 A PROBLEM-SOLVING METHOD

Some general steps can be applied to the solution of many problems in chemistry, problems for which the answer is a physical quantity. In following through problem solving by these steps you can ask yourself some general questions while thinking about each step. The questions might vary with the nature of the problem.

a. Study the problem and be sure you understand it To understand a problem, you must know what facts are given—the known information about the system. Read the problem carefully to determine what "knowns" are included. This information might be a single physical quantity or it might be several quantities. In some cases these quantities will be related to each other and can be combined into conversion factors or ratios. Read the problem carefully again to be sure you know what the question is. What is the "unknown" that must be determined from the known information? The unknown might be a single physical quantity or several.

b. Decide how to solve the problem With the known and the unknown clearly in mind, the next step is to figure out what connects them. What have you learned that applies to the physical quantities and the kind of system under consideration? A simple conversion factor or ratio might be all that is needed. A standard mathematical expression might have to be solved for the unknown.

In deciding how to solve the problem, analyze the units of the known and the units desired in the unknown. It may be necessary to find the unknown physical quantity in one unit and then convert it to another unit before the problem is solved. Or it might be necessary to convert the known into other units before it can be used in the appropriate equation. If solving the problem requires conversion factors or equations not in the statement of the problem, be sure you get them right. Check back in the book or some other source if your memory is hazy.

c. Set up the problem and solve it At this step the dimensional method is of primary importance. With practice, many problems can be set up as single expressions to be solved. Check the setup by checking the unit cancellation. Will the answer be in the desired units? In doing the arithmetic the rules for significant figures and scientific notation must be kept in mind.

d. Check the result Solving a problem *is not finished* until you check the result. Do this in two ways. First, check both the numerical part of the answer and the units in terms of the rules. Is the answer OK with respect to significant figures, decimal places, scientific notation, and units? Second, *think* about the answer. Is the magnitude reasonable, or is the answer much larger or smaller than is realistically possible? In some cases, the kind of physical or chemical change under consideration will allow the prediction of whether the answer should be larger or smaller than a known value of the same quantity.

To illustrate the steps and some of the questions that you can ask yourself at each step, we apply the method to the following simple unit conversion problem.

Particles of one type of virus have an average diameter of 98 Å. What is the average diameter in nanometers?

1. Study the problem and be sure you understand it.
   (a) What is unknown?
       The average particle diameter in nanometers.
   (b) What is known?
       The average particle diameter in angstroms.
2. Decide how to solve the problem.
   (a) What is the connection between the known and the unknown?
       The conversion factor for changing angstroms to nanometers.
   (b) What is necessary to make the connection?
       The conversion factor to be found from the prior knowledge that 10 Å = 1 nm.
3. Set up the problem and solve it.

$$\text{Average diameter} = (98\,\text{Å})\left(\frac{1\,\text{nm}}{10\,\text{Å}}\right) = 9.8\ \text{nm}$$

(Remember to choose the conversion factor that cancels the unit to be eliminated.)

4. Check the result.
   (a) Are significant figures and the location of the decimal point correct?
       Yes. The 98 Å limits the answer to two significant figures. (The 10 is exact.)
   (b) Did the answer come out in the correct units?
       Yes.
   (c) Is the answer reasonable?
       Yes, the answer is reasonable, for a nanometer is larger than an angstrom.

We are not suggesting that you write out the solution to any problem as we have just illustrated. (Although it might be helpful to do it if you are stuck.) These steps and questions are simply a guide to a logical approach to thinking about a problem. But it will work in many types of problems in chemistry. If you practice the method consciously for a while, it will become a habit.

Here is a slightly more complicated problem:

A small airplane traveled 128 km in 48 min. What is the speed of the airplane in kilometers per hour?

1. Study the problem and be sure you understand it.
   (a) What is unknown?
       The speed of the plane in kilometers per hour.
   (b) What is known?
       The distance traveled = 128 km; the time to travel that distance = 48 min.

2. Decide how to solve the problem.
   (a) What is the connection between the known and the unknown?
       Speed is a ratio, distance/time.
   (b) What is necessary to make the connection?
       First, the calculation of speed in km/min. Second, a conversion factor
       based on the prior knowledge that 60 min = 1 h.
3. Set up and solve the problem.
   The solution can be set up in two steps:

$$\frac{128 \text{ km}}{48 \text{ min}} = 2.7 \frac{\text{km}}{\text{min}} \qquad \left(2.7 \frac{\text{km}}{\text{min}}\right)\left(\frac{60 \text{ min}}{1 \text{ h}}\right) = 160 \text{ km/h}$$

   or in one step:

$$\left(\frac{128 \text{ km}}{48 \text{ min}}\right)\left(\frac{60 \text{ min}}{1 \text{ h}}\right) = 160 \text{ km/h}$$

4. Check the result.
   (a) Are significant figures used correctly?
       Yes.
   (b) Did the answer come out in the correct units?
       Yes.
   (c) Is the answer reasonable?
       Yes, this is a reasonable speed for a small airplane. (When SI units are
       more widely used we will know that a highway speed limit for a car
       might be about 80 km/h. It is reasonable that a small plane travels
       somewhat faster than a car.)

Occasionally, as we introduce various types of problems, we will present one or
two solutions according to the plan given here. The crucial point is knowing what the
connection is between the known and the unknown. Often chemistry problems can
be characterized by how the connection is made.

*In summary, a physical quantity consists of a number and a unit. At present,
the SI system of units is recommended for use in all scientific work, although
other units are still encountered. Units should always be included in reporting
the results of physical measurements and in working problems using such data.
The dimensional method, in which units are treated like numbers, is a valuable
aid in problem solving. To solve problems in chemistry, identify the known and
the unknown information, then decide how they can be connected.*

SUMMARY   **2.1** MEASUREMENT AND SIGNIFICANT FIGURES   Exact numbers—numbers with no uncertainty—result from counting whole objects or from definitions. All measurements
of physical quantities, however, have some degree of uncertainty. The results of
measurements are reported so as to include only significant figures—all the digits
that are known with certainty, plus the first uncertain digit, which is assumed to have
an uncertainty of ±1.

2.2 FINDING THE NUMBER OF SIGNIFICANT FIGURES   The number of significant figures is
found by counting from left to right, beginning with the first nonzero digit and
ending with the digit that has the uncertain value. All nonzero digits in a number are
significant. Zeros between nonzero digits are significant. Zeros at the end of a
number which includes a decimal point are also significant. Zeros at the end of a
number without a decimal point are ambiguous and are regarded as not significant in
this book. Zeros at the beginning of a number are never significant.

2.3 ARITHMETIC USING SIGNIFICANT FIGURES   In arithmetic involving the results of measurements, the number of digits in the answer must be limited to the correct number of significant figures. In addition or subtraction, round the answer to the place (before or after the decimal point) with the greatest uncertainty. In multiplication or division, round the answer to the same number of significant figures as in the number with the fewest significant figures.

2.4 SCIENTIFIC NOTATION (EXPONENTIAL NOTATION)   In scientific notation, the significant figures of a number appear as a factor between 1 and 10, and the location of the decimal point is indicated by a power of 10. A positive power of 10 indicates that the original number is greater than 1 and gives the number of places the decimal point was moved to the left. A negative power of 10 indicates that the original number was less than 1 and gives the number of places the decimal point was moved to the right.

2.5 ARITHMETIC USING SCIENTIFIC NOTATION   To add or subtract numbers expressed in scientific notation with pencil and paper, the numbers must all be given with the same exponent. In multiplication and division, multiply and divide the factors (obeying the rules for significant figures), and find the power of 10 by adding powers of 10 for multiplication and subtracting powers of 10 for division.

2.6 SYSTEMS OF MEASUREMENT   **2.7** THE SI SYSTEM OF MEASUREMENT   **2.8** UNITS OF MEASUREMENT IN CHEMISTRY   Comparision of measurements is only possible when measurements of the same quantity are expressed in the same units. Scientific measurements are expressed either in metric units or in the units of the newer Système International (SI units). Prefixes and suffixes are used to simplify expression of very large or very small quantities.

2.9 THE DIMENSIONAL METHOD   The numerical value of a measurement should always be expressed together with the correct unit. In a problem, units are multiplied, divided, and cancelled exactly as numbers would be. If the problem is correctly set up and worked, it should produce an answer in the correct units.

2.10 CONVERSION FACTORS   The conversion of a physical quantity from one unit to another is done with conversion factors derived from the numerical relationship between the two units. Choosing the correct conversion factor allows the cancellation of the unwanted units. Conversion factors or physical constants should include a sufficient number of significant figures so as not to affect the uncertainty of the answer. (If a conversion factor is an exact number it can be treated as having as many significant figures as needed.)

SIGNIFICANT TERMS

exact numbers
significant figures
precision
accuracy
mass
weight
density
pressure

2.11 A PROBLEM-SOLVING METHOD   To solve a problem, first make sure that you understand exactly what is known and what is unknown. Then try to figure out how the knowns and unknowns in the problem are connected. Pay special attention to units and conversions. In setting up the problem and solving it, check to see if the answer emerges in the correct units. Make sure to obey the rules for the correct number of significant figures in the answer. Finally, see if the answer seems reasonable.

THOUGHTS ON CHEMISTRY
How to Solve It

HOW TO SOLVE IT, by G. Polya

It would be a mistake to think that solving problems is a purely "intellectual affair"; determination and emotions play an important role. Lukewarm determination and sleepy consent to do a little something may be enough for a routine problem in the classroom. But, to solve a serious scientific problem, will power is needed that can outlast years of toil and bitter disappointments.

Determination fluctuates with hope and hopelessness, with satisfaction and disappointment. It is easy to keep on going when we think that the solution is just around the corner; but it is hard to persevere when we do not see any way out of the difficulty. We are elated when our forecast comes true. We are depressed when the way we have followed with some confidence is suddenly blocked, and our determination wavers.

"Il n'est point besoin espérer pour entreprendre ni réussir pour persévérer." "You can undertake without hope and persevere without success." Thus may speak an inflexible will, or honor and duty, or a noble-man with a noble cause. This sort of determination, however, would not do for the scientist, who should have some hope to start with, and some success to go on. In scientific work, it is necessary to apportion wisely determination to outlook. You do not take up a problem, unless it has some interest; you settle down to work seriously if the problem seems in-structive; you throw in your whole personality if there is a great promise. If your purpose is set, you stick to it, but you do not make it unnecessarily difficult for yourself. You do not despise little successes, on the contrary, you seek them: If you cannot solve the proposed problem try to solve first some related problem. . . .

Incomplete understanding of the problem, owing to lack of concen-tration, is perhaps the most widespread deficiency in solving problems. With respect to devising a plan and obtaining a general idea of the solution two opposite faults are frequent. Some students rush into calcu-lations and constructions without any plan or general idea; others wait clumsily for some idea to come and cannot do anything that would accelerate its coming. In carrying out the plan, the most frequent fault is carelessness, lack of patience in checking each step. Failure to check the result at all is very frequent; the student is glad to get an answer, throws down his pencil, and is not shocked by the most unlikely results.

How To Solve It: A New Aspect of Mathematical Method. Copyright 1945 by Princeton University Press; © 1957 by G. Polya, reprinted by permission of Princeton University Press. Pp. 93–95.

QUESTIONS

Numbers in Physical Quantities

2.1 What are the two major classifications of errors that can be made in measurements? Which classification affects the preci-sion of the measurement? Which affects the accuracy?

2.2 How can we express the uncertainty in a number? If the uncertainty is not expressed for a given number, what do we normally assume?

2.3 How would you determine the number of significant figures in a given number?

2.4 When is a zero considered to be a significant digit and when is it not?

2.5 State the rules for determining the number of significant figures in the answer for calculations involving (a) addition or subtraction and (b) multiplication or division.

2.6 What is an exact number? How do we apply the rules of significant figures to calculations involving exact numbers?

2.7 To how many significant figures should conversion factors, physical constants, or other numbers (such as π) be expressed in a calculation?

2.8 State the rule for adding or subtracting numbers expressed in scientific notation. What is the rule for multiplication or divi-sion?

Units of Measurement

2.9 List the seven base physical quantities as specified by the SI system. How are all other physical quantities treated in this system?

2.10 How can we express multiples or fractions of a given base or derived unit?

2.11 Which of the following units are used to express (a) mass, (b) energy, (c) length, (d) volume, and (e) temperature: (i) erg, (ii) cm, (iii) cm³, (iv) K, (v) Å, (vi) J, (vii) km, (viii) mL, (ix) g, (x) °C, (xi) nm, (xii) L, (xiii) cal, (xiv) m, (xv) dm³, (xvi) kg, and (xvii) mg?

2.12 Which of the following units are correct for the property that is being measured: (a) the area of a football field in m², (b) the volume of an apple juice bottle in L³, (c) the density of wood in kg/m³, (d) the length of an eraser in mL, (e) the radius of a basketball in kg, (f) the length of time of a TV commercial in Ms, and (g) the height of an evergreen tree in cm³?

The Dimensional Method and Problem Solving

2.13 How are the units of a physical quantity treated in a numerical calculation?

2.14 What is a conversion factor? How are these factors derived?

Answers to Selected Questions

2.2 The number and the uncertainty are reported in the form (number ± uncertainty); The right-most digit contains an uncertainty of ±1.

2.7 At least to the same number of significant figures as the other factors in multiplication or division, and at least to the same decimal place as the other factors in addition or subtraction

2.12 (a), (c), (f)

PROBLEMS

Significant Figures

2.1 Express the uncertainty for each of the following numbers, assuming the uncertainty in the last significant figure is ±1: (a) 273; (b) 0.5649; (c) 470; (d) 12.529; (e) 6000; (f) 0.0006; (g) 12.00; (h) 1,300,020; (i) 6.9×10^6.

2.2 Express the uncertainty for each of the following numbers, assuming the uncertainty in the last significant figure is ±1: (a) 1432; (b) 632.2; (c) 710; (d) 0.92; (e) 500; (f) 0.09; (g) 8.0; (h) 3.14159; (i) 4.26×10^{-19}. *Answer* (a) ±1, (b) ±0.1, (c) ±10, (d) ±0.01, (e) ±100, (f) ±0.01, (g) ±0.1, (h) ±0.00001, (i) 1×10^{-21}

2.3 How many significant figures are in each of the numbers in Problem 2.1?

2.4 How many significant figures are in each of the numbers in Problem 2.2? *Answer* (a) 4, (b) 4, (c) 2, (d) 2, (e) 1, (f) 1, (g) 2, (h) 6, (i) 3

2.5 Perform the following calculations and express the answers in the proper number of significant figures.

(a) $\begin{array}{r} 423.1 \\ 0.256 \\ \underline{100} \end{array}$
(b) $\begin{array}{r} 52.987 \\ 9.3545 \\ \underline{6.12} \end{array}$
(c) $\begin{array}{r} 14.3920 \\ \underline{-4.4} \end{array}$
(d) (5183)(2.2)

(e) $\dfrac{14.000}{6.1}$
(f) $(6.11)(\pi)$
(g) (14.3)(60)
(h) $\dfrac{1020}{1.2}$

(i) $\dfrac{(3.2)(454)}{(8.6214)}$
(j) $(4/3)\pi(2.16)^3$

(k) $(6.0 + 9.57 + 0.61)(1.113)$

(l) $(2.93)(14.7) + (1203)(0.0296) + (9.38)(5.2)$

2.6 Perform the following calculations and express the answers in the proper number of significant figures.

(a) $\begin{array}{r} 1900 \\ \underline{-6.25} \end{array}$
(b) $\begin{array}{r} 963.2 \\ 1.46 \\ \underline{10.5} \end{array}$
(c) $\begin{array}{r} 16.3256 \\ \underline{-49.3} \end{array}$

(d) $(1492)(6.3) =$
(e) $\dfrac{0.25}{137} =$
(f) $\dfrac{(9.4)(16)}{(9.354)} =$

(g) $\pi(8.2)^2$
(h) $(6.35 + 2.9 + 163)(7.5 + 6.3) =$

Answer (a) 1900, (b) 975.2, (c) −33.0, (d) 9400, (e) 0.0018, (f) 16, (g) 210, (h) 2380

2.7* A group of students reported the following measurements for the diameter of a quarter: 2.50 cm, 2.42 cm, 2.43 cm, 2.40 cm, and 2.41 cm. (a) Calculate the class average for the diameter and (b) express the uncertainty in the measurement.

To check the accuracy of the result, the "% error" was calculated.

$$\% \text{ error} = \frac{(\text{experimental value}) - (\text{true value})}{(\text{true value})} \times 100\%$$

Using the true diameter as 2.44 cm, (c) calculate the % error of the class average. (d) Do you think that there was a systematic error in the data?

Scientific Notation

2.8 Express the following numbers in standard scientific notation: (a) 6500; (b) 0.0041; (c) 0.003050; (d) 810.; (e) 0.0000003; (f) 9,352,000; (g) 42×10^3; (h) 9 kJ; (i)14.9 cm.

2.9 Express the following numbers in standard scientific notation: (a) 0.0516; (b) 1420; (c) 1260.; (d) 0.0002; (e) 0.010; (f) 6,925,300; (g) 0.28×10^{-5}; (h) 5 Mg; (i) 0.1 ps. *Answer* (a) 5.16×10^{-2}, (b) 1.42×10^3, (c) 1.260×10^3, (d) 2×10^{-4}, (e) 1.0×10^{-2}, (f) 6.9253×10^6, (g) 2.8×10^{-6}, (h) 5×10^6g , (i) 1×10^{-13} s

2.10 Express the following numbers using ordinary notation (for example, $5.2 \times 10^{-2} = 0.052$): (a) 5.26×10^3, (b) 4.10×10^{-6}, (c) 5×10^5, (d) 0.3×10^4, (e) 16.2×10^{-3}, (f) 9.346×10^3.

2.11 Express the following numbers using ordinary notation: (a) 6.90×10^{-4}, (b) 1.426×10^5, (c) 4×10^{-3}, (d) 52.3×10^3, (e) 3.200×10^3, (f) 0.2×10^{-2}. *Answer* (a) 0.000690; (b) 142,600; (c) 0.004; (d) 52,300; (e) 3200.; (f) 0.002

2.12 Perform the following calculations and express the answer in standard scientific notation:

(a) $(6.057 \times 10^3) + (9.35)$
(b) $(2.35 \times 10^{-14}) - (7.1 \times 10^{-15})$

(c) $\dfrac{4.51 \times 10^{-3}}{8.78 \times 10^4}$
(d) $\dfrac{(1812)(1492)}{1979}$

(e) $\dfrac{(7.33 \times 10^{-3}) + (4.29 \times 10^1)}{(5.88 \times 10^{-3}) + (4.29 \times 10^1)}$
(f) (5 km)(14.6)

2.13 Perform the following calculations and express the answer in standard scientific notation:

(a) $(4.3 \times 10^3) + (5.2 \times 10^2) + (6.1 \times 10^1)$
(b) $\dfrac{1.4 \times 10^5}{1.1 \times 10^5}$

(c) $(2.5 \times 10^6)(0.75)$
(d) $\dfrac{(52.6 \times 10^3)(3.86 \times 10^{-4})}{(4 \times 10^4) + (5 \times 10^5)}$

(e) $(10.3 \text{ cm}^2)(0.3)^2$

Answer (a) 4.9×10^3, (b) 1.3×10^0, (c) 1.9×10^6, (d) 4×10^{-5}, (e) 9×10^{-5} m^2

Temperature Conversion

2.14 Convert the following temperatures which are commonplace in our daily lives to the Celsius scale: (a) normal body temperature, 98.6 °F; (b) the temperature on a cold, wintry day, −10. °F; (c) the temperature on a warm fall day, 78 °F; (d) the running temperature of a modern auto engine, 250 °F, and (e) the melting point of ice, 32.00 °F.

2.15 Convert the temperatures given in Problem 2.14 to kelvin units. *Answer* (a) 310.15 K, (b) 250. K, (c) 298.8 K, (d) 390 K, (e) 273.15 K

2.16 Convert each of the following boiling point temperatures to values on the Celsius scale: (a) water, 373.15 K; (b) nitric oxide, 121.4 K; (c) sulfur, 717.8 K; (d) iron, 3020 K; and (e) sulfuric acid, 611 K.

2.17 Convert the temperatures given in Problem 2.16 to values on the Fahrenheit scale. *Answer* (a) 212.00 °F, (b) −241.2 °F, (c) 832.5 °F, (d) 4980 °F, (e) 640. °F

2.18 Confirm the values given in Figure 2.3 for the absolute zero shown on the Fahrenheit and Celsius scales by calculating the corresponding value on each scale from absolute zero on the Kelvin temperature scale.

2.19* At what temperature will a Fahrenheit thermometer give (a) the same reading as a Celsius thermometer, (b) a reading that is twice that on the Celsius thermometer, and (c) a reading that is numerically the same but opposite in sign from the Celsius scale? *Answer* (a) −40 °C = −40 °F, (b) 160 °C = 320 °F, (c) −11.4 °C = 11.4 °F

Dimensional Method

2.20 A roll of quarters obtained at a bank has a value of $10.00. How many quarters are in the roll?

2.21 Each molecule of sucrose (ordinary sugar) contains 12 carbon atoms. How many carbon atoms are present in 5×10^{21} molecules? *Answer* (a) 6×10^{22} carbon atoms

2.22 A chemical plant releases 5.0 tons of gas into the atmosphere each day. The gas contains 5% by mass of sulfur dioxide (i.e., for every 100 parts of gas, 5 parts are sulfur dioxide). What mass of sulfur dioxide is released in a period of one week? *Answer* 2 T sulfur dioxide

2.23 A certain chemical process required 75 gallons of pure water each day. The available water contained 11 parts per million by mass of salt (i.e., for every 1,000,000 parts of water, 11 parts are salt). What mass of salt must be removed each day? A gallon of water weighs 3.78 kg.

2.24* A molecule of palmitic acid has a volume of 110 Å³. When a drop of the acid is placed on water, the molecules spread out on the surface of the water producing a layer that is one molecule thick. The height of the molecule is 4.6 Å in this layer. Calculate the cross sectional area of the molecule. What area in m² will 6.022×10^{23} molecules occupy? The area of 1 Å² is equivalent to 10^{-20} m². *Answer* 24 Å²/molecule, 1.4×10^{5} m²

Unit Conversions

2.25 Make each of the following conversions: (a) 10.3 Å to nm, (b) 635 cal to J, (c) 14.6 L to dm³, (d) 14.6 kg to g, (e) 14.6 atm to Pa, (f) 1.2 eV to J, (g) 735.2 Torr to atm, (h) 21.65 mL to cm³.

2.26 Determine which quantity is larger: (a) 1.0 mg or 1.0 cg, (b) 325 kcal or 95 J, (c) 50 nm or 0.5 m, (d) 0.8 nm or 8 Å, (e) 75 Pa or 747 Torr, (f) 5 L or 3.2 m³. *Answer* (a) 1 cg, (b) 325 kcal, (c) 0.5 m, (d) same, (e) 747 Torr, (f) 3.2 m³

2.27 A very important constant that we encounter in this book is known as the ideal gas constant. It is numerically equal to 8.314 J/K mol. Express the value of this constant in (a) erg/K mol, (b) cal/K mol, (c) L atm/K mol.

2.28 Vinegar has a density of 1.0056 g/cm³. What is the mass of one liter of vinegar?

2.29 The mass of one hundred cubic centimeters of uranium metal is 1.897 kg. What is the density of uranium expressed in kg/m³ and g/cm³? *Answer* 1.897×10^{4} kg/m³; 18.97 g/cm³

2.30 A small crystal of sucrose (table sugar) had a mass of 2.236 mg. The dimensions of the box-like crystal were $1.11 \times 1.09 \times 1.12$ mm. What is the density of sucrose expressed in g/cm³?

2.31* The radius of a hydrogen atom is about 0.58 Å and the distance between the sun and the earth is about 1.5×10^{8} km. Find the ratio of the radius of the hydrogen atom to the sun−earth distance so that the units cancel. *Answer* 3.9×10^{-22}

2.32* The radius of a neutron is approximately 1.5×10^{-15} m. Find the density of a neutron if its mass is 1.675×10^{-24} g.

2.33* A container has a mass of 68.31 g empty and 93.34 g filled with water. Calculate the volume of the container using a density of 1.0000 g/cm³ for water. The container when filled with an unknown liquid had a mass of 88.42 g. Calculate the density of the unknown liquid.

2.34* The mass of an empty container is 66.734 g. The mass of the container filled with water is 91.786 g. (a) Calculate the volume of the container using a density of 1.0000 g/cm³ for water.

A piece of metal was added to the empty container and the combined mass was 87.807 g. (b) Calculate the mass of the metal. The container with the metal was filled with water and the mass of the entire system was 105.408 g. (c) What mass of water was added? (d) What volume of water was added? (e) What is the volume of the metal? (f) Calculate the density of the metal. *Answer* (a) 25.052 cm³, (b) 21.073 g, (c) 17.601 g, (d) 17.601 cm³, (e) 7.451 cm³, (f) 2.828 g/cm³

CHAPTER 3

Chemistry: The Science of Matter

The history of science is highlighted by periods of extraordinary progress. In such periods scientists who are giants in their fields appear on the scene and tackle monumental problems. These individuals and the outstanding work that they do generate excitement, and spur their colleagues and students on to triumphs of their own.

Joseph John Thomson, known as "J.J.," was one such man. When he was only 28 years old (in 1884), his talents were so apparent that he was appointed Cavendish Professor of Experimental Physics and became director of the Cavendish Laboratory at Cambridge University in England. "The Cavendish" became the focal point for the study of matter and the then-mysterious atom. One young man is said to have backed off from working with Thomson, remarking "I thought he was too young to be my professor of physics." This was a mistake. Thomson identified the electron, and seven of his students won Nobel prizes for work related to atomic structure.

After more than 30 years Thomson turned over the Cavendish Laboratory to Ernest Rutherford, who had been his student and who had already won fame for his work on radioactivity. A friend is reported to have said of Rutherford, "He can arouse enthusiasm in anything short of a cow or a cabinet minister." Rutherford went on to give the world the first realistic explanation of what is inside an atom.

ATOMS AND ELEMENTS

We have called chemistry the science of matter. The usual scientific definition of *matter* is "anything that has mass and occupies space." Just what is matter? How many kinds of matter are there? What is matter made of?

3.1 ELEMENTS

Early observations showed that some matter is composed of other kinds of matter. Splitting a rock open frequently reveals the colors and textures of many substances within it. By 1500 B.C. the Hittites knew that if certain rocks were heated, a useful metal (iron) separated from them. More than 3000 years later, the recognition that air is not "pure," but can be separated into several different substances, marked a milestone in the growth of chemistry.

Those who experimented with matter also recognized that some substances, such as iron, could *not* be broken down into other substances. From ancient to medieval times, philosophers had used the word *element* to refer to the simple substances of which all matter was thought to be made (see A Historical Aside: The Origins of Chemistry, Chapter 2). Eventually, substances that cannot be broken down into other kinds of matter came to be called "elements."

Elements known since ancient times are listed in Table 3.1. By the 1770s, oxygen, nitrogen, and hydrogen had also been identified as elements. One by one other elements were discovered, sometimes only after long and tedious experiments.

Today more than one hundred substances are recognized as elements. Some, such as gold and sulfur, can be found in the crust of the earth in their uncombined, elemental forms. Other elements, such as chlorine and uranium, must be obtained by separating them from substances in which they are combined with other elements. And with the advent of our understanding of nuclear chemistry has come a string of man-made elements—elements not found naturally on earth.

Table 3.1
Elements Known in Antiquity

Antimony
Carbon
Copper
Gold
Iron
Lead
Mercury
Silver
Sulfur
Tin

The Names of the Elements

The names of the elements provide a fascinating glimpse into the history of chemistry. Gold, silver, and the other elements listed in Table 3.3 have been known since ancient times, and their names reflect what the Romans observed about them. Gold was called *aurum,* meaning "shining dawn"; mercury was *hydrargyrum,* meaning "liquid silver"; and lead was *plumbum,* which means "heavy." Copper had the name *cuprum,* derived from the name of the island we know as Cyprus, which was the ancient source for most copper.

In the eighteenth century, chemists were intrigued with studies of the atmosphere, and the gases they discovered were given names based on what was then known of their chemistry. "Hydrogen" is from the Greek words meaning water-former, and "nitrogen" and "oxygen" are from the Greek words meaning soda-former and acid-former, respectively. Chlorine, which is a greenish yellow gas, and iodine, which has a violet vapor, are named from the Greek words for their colors. "Bromine" comes from the Greek for stench. Helium was named for *helios,* the sun, because the first evidence for the existence of helium was found in a study of radiation from the sun.

The names of many metals, other than those known since antiquity, end in *ium.* "Aluminium" was the name first given to the metal called "aluminum" in the United States. It is still called "aluminium" in England and many other parts of the world. We are blessed with the four tongue-twisters terbium, erbium, ytterbium, and yttrium because these metals were all isolated from ores found in Ytterby, Sweden.

When faced with the challenge of naming new elements, chemists have turned to the heavens for plutonium, uranium, and cerium (for Ceres, an asteroid discovered at about the same time as the element). They have looked to mythology for thorium (Thor, the Scandinavian god of war), and promethium (Prometheus, the bringer of fire), and for two elements that were tantalizingly difficult to separate, tantalum and niobium (Tantalus and his daughter, Niobe).

Names of some elements honor the places where the elements were discovered: californium, berkelium, europium, americium, francium, germanium. In recent years a series of man-made elements have been named in honor of famous scientists: einsteinium (Albert Einstein), fermium (Enrico Fermi), mendelevium (Dimitri Mendeleev), nobelium (Alfred Nobel), and lawrencium (Ernest Lawrence).

The honor of naming an element has traditionally gone to its discoverer. The prestige associated with discovering an element is reflected in an argument that has lasted for more than 10 years over who should name elements 104 and 105. In the 1960s both American and Russian teams of scientists claimed discovery of elements 104 and 105. The Russians suggested the name khurchatovium (after a Russian scientist) for element 104 and the Americans suggested rutherfordium (Ernest Rutherford).

The International Union of Pure and Applied Chemistry (IUPAC) has been given the responsibility for making rules for naming elements and other chemical substances. In 1978 the conflict over naming element 104, and also the need for establishing the "discoverers" of this and other elements, was partially resolved. It was recommended that, at least for now, elements above 103 be named by a system based on numerical root words. Element 104 becomes unnilquadium ("un" for 1; "nil" for 0, "quad" for 4, plus the "ium" ending). Element 105 becomes unnilpentium, 106 becomes unnilhexium, and the system can cope with elements all the way up to atomic number 999, which will be ennennennium if and when it is discovered. These elements would become the first to have three-letter symbols (104, Unq; 105, Unp; 106, Unh, and so on). The IUPAC commission was careful to make clear that they have not suggested abandoning the old system. They state that the systematic nomenclature "does not deny the right of 'discoverers' of new elements to suggest other names to the Commission after their discovery has been established beyond all doubt in the general scientific community." (The authors of this text favor eventual use of distinctive names rather than the systematic names.)

3.2 SYMBOLS FOR THE ELEMENTS

In talking and writing about chemistry, we come upon a recurring problem: How do we clearly communicate with each other about elements and the more complex substances derived from them? So many kinds of chemicals are now known that the problem can only be solved by a systematic approach. The language of chemistry is really *two* languages. One is based on the names of the elements and more complex chemical substances, the other is based upon symbols for the elements.

Table 3.2 gives the names and symbols for some of the more familiar elements. Thirteen elements have as their symbols the first letter of their modern names or older names. All other elements have two-letter symbols (three-letter symbols have been proposed for elements 104 and those after it; see An Aside: The Names of the Elements).

Single-letter symbols are always capital letters. Other symbols are written with the first letter capitalized and the second small.

The symbols for most of the elements are based on the modern names of the elements, for example,

Ac	Al	Am	Ar	As	At
actinium	*aluminum*	*americium*	*argon*	*arsenic*	*astatine*

Some of the elements have symbols that do not appear to be related to their names. Most of these elements are the ones known since ancient times and their symbols are derived from their Latin names, for example,

Cu	Pb	Fe
copper	*lead*	*iron*
(*Latin* cuprum)	(*Latin* plumbum)	(*Latin* ferrum)

All elements with symbols not based on their modern names are listed in Table 3.3.

The names of the known elements are given in alphabetical order inside the front cover of this book. Opposite the alphabetical list of the elements is a periodic table, which organizes the elements into groups based upon similarities in their chemical behavior and properties. (The format of the periodic table is explained in Chapter 8.)

Table 3.2
Symbols for Some of the Elements

Aluminum	Al
Arsenic	As
Bromine	Br
Calcium	Ca
Carbon	C
Chlorine	Cl
Chromium	Cr
Hydrogen	H
Nitrogen	N
Oxygen	O
Phosphorus	P
Platinum	Pt
Silicon	Si
Sulfur	S
Uranium	U
Zinc	Zn

3.3 ATOMS

Early philosophers wondered whether matter that could be seen was composed of smaller bits of matter. Perhaps the rock, or the iron derived from it, were both "made of" something else—something so tiny that it couldn't be seen. The name *atom* was suggested by the Greeks for such small particles. (A Historical Aside later in this chapter traces the growth of the concept of atoms.)

Table 3.3
Elements with Symbols Not Based on Their Modern Names All of these elements except tungsten (discovered in 1783) and potassium and sodium (both discovered in 1807) have been known since antiquity. All of the symbols are based on Latin names except for W, for tungsten, which derives from the name of an ore, wolfram.

Modern Name	Symbol	Derivation of Symbol
Antimony	Sb	*stibium*
Copper	Cu	*cuprum*
Gold	Au	*aurum*
Iron	Fe	*ferrum*
Lead	Pb	*plumbum*
Mercury	Hg	*hydrargyrum*
Potassium	K	*kalium*
Silver	Ag	*argentum*
Sodium	Na	*natrium*
Tin	Sn	*stannum*
Tungsten	W	*wolfram*

All matter is now understood to be composed of atoms. The description of matter in a scientific manner—what chemistry is all about—began with an understanding of atoms. The period from 1879 to 1932 was an exciting time, as chemists and physicists found out more and more about atoms. Many surprises were part of the story, the first being that atoms themselves have "structure"—atoms contain smaller particles within themselves.

Our modern picture of atomic structure, known as the nuclear model, is based upon a series of classic experiments designed to "see the unseeable and know the unknowable." Atoms are *very* small. Their diameters are on the order of 1×10^{-10} m, or, in the units we use more often, 0.1 nm (nanometer). It has been estimated that 3.8×10^{13} (thirty-eight trillion) atoms of iron can "dance" on the head of a pin.

As knowledge from experiments accumulated, theoretical explanations of the behavior and structure of atoms were developed. Modern atomic theory views an atom as having a dense, central core (a nucleus) containing positively charged particles (protons) and neutral particles (neutrons). Negatively charged particles (electrons) are scattered in a relatively very large space around the nucleus. Nuclei have diameters on the order of 1×10^{-6} nm, one hundred thousand times smaller than atoms. If an atom were expanded to the size of one of our largest football stadiums, the nucleus would be about the size of a marble at the center. The electrons (no more than ninety of them in the most common atoms) would have the entire space above the field in which to fly about.

ATOMIC STRUCTURE: FIVE CLASSIC EXPERIMENTS

In the following sections we describe the series of classic experiments that led to our modern theory of atomic structure.

3.4 CATHODE RAYS: THE ELECTRON

a. Electricity and matter By the end of the nineteenth century it was becoming apparent that electricity had an intimate relationship with matter. It was known that many solids conduct electricity and that when electricity passes through a liquid or a solution, chemical changes often occur. Experiments on the passage of electricity through gases opened the door to an understanding of what is within an atom.

An electrical potential of 10,000 volts between electrodes in the open air will barely cause a spark to jump a gap of a few millimeters. (An **electrode** is a conductor through which electrical current enters or leaves a conducting medium; see Tools of Chemistry: Electricity and Magnetism.) If the electrodes are sealed into a **gas-discharge tube**—a glass tube that can be evacuated—the result is different. As the gas is gradually pumped out a glow appears in the tube, and when the pressure gets down to 1–20 Torr, current flows between the two electrodes. Different gases in the tube give different colors to the glow.

When more gas is pumped out of the tube, so that the pressure is reduced to 10^{-2} Torr and lower, the glow fades out. However, current continues to flow from the negative electrode, and where the current falls on the glass wall at the other end of the tube, a greenish fluorescence is produced (Figure 3.1). (A **fluorescent** substance emits radiation when it is exposed to light or some other form of energy, but stops emitting when the energy no longer falls upon it.)

William Crookes, an English editor, inventor, and scientist studied the behavior of many gases in gas-discharge tubes. He confirmed the important discovery, made earlier by Julius Plücker in Bonn, that the fluorescent spot can be moved by a magnet. Crookes concluded, in 1879, that rays of particles were flowing from the negative electrode, or *cathode,* in a gas-discharge tube. He called them "cathode rays." Cathode rays are the same, Crookes found, no matter what material is used for

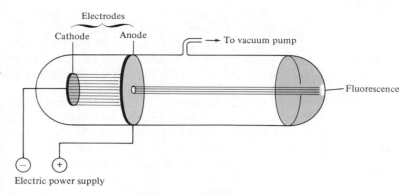

Figure 3.1
A Gas-Discharge Tube Showing Cathode Rays The nature of cathode rays was studied by varying the gases in the tube and placing various targets within the tube. (Source: Reproduced by permission of the publisher from O'Connor et al., *Chemistry: Experiments and Principles,* © 1968, Lexington, Massachusetts: D.C. Heath.)

the negative electrode or what gas is used in the tube.

The *cathode ray tube,* or the Crookes tube, as it was called, is the ancestor of neon signs, fluorescent lights, and television tubes. What we call "neon" signs are cathode ray tubes that may contain neon (which gives a red glow), or other gases that produce other colors. Fluorescent light bulbs are produced by coating the inside walls of long cathode ray tubes with material that emits visible light when struck by cathode rays. A similar coating is placed on the inside of a television tube; a rapidly moving cathode ray continuously sweeps across the coated surface and the television picture is created by varying the intensity of the ray.

b. Discovery of the electron George Johnstone Stoney, a physicist, proposed in 1881 that electricity is carried by individual, negatively charged particles. This was not a completely new idea. Benjamin Franklin had suggested it in about 1750. However, in Stoney's time electricity was thought of by many as a fluid. Stoney named the proposed particle the "electron" (from the Greek for amber, a material known to acquire an electric charge when rubbed with silk).

For many years J. J. Thomson studied cathode rays at the Cavendish Laboratory, pondering the meaning of the properties they exhibited in his own experiments and those of others. (These properties are listed in Table 3.4.) Thomson found that cathode rays are deflected by both electric and magnetic fields. By 1897 Thomson was convinced that cathode rays are streams of negatively charged particles of extremely small mass, much smaller than the mass of atoms. These particles, he reasoned, must be Stoney's electrons. Since cathode rays are the same for any gas or any electrode material, Thomson was sure that electrons must be present in all matter.

Thomson was able to prove experimentally that cathode rays are streams of particles. Obviously, if the rays consist of particles with mass and charge, it should be possible to measure these properties. Thomson could not determine the mass or charge separately. However, by an ingenious method of balancing the forces of electric and magnetic fields, he was able to measure the ratio of the charge of an electron (e) to its mass (m) (Figure 3.2). He found that the value of e/m was constant for different gases and different electrode materials, further evidence that electrons are present in all neutral atoms. The modern value for e/m is 1.76×10^8 C/g (where the units are coulombs per gram).

The charge on the electron was determined experimentally in 1909 by Robert A. Millikan at the University of Chicago. Tiny oil droplets, some of which were charged by friction while passing through an atomizer, were released between two horizontal plates on which the charge could be turned on and off (Figure 3.3). The rate of fall of the droplets under the influence of gravity alone, and then their rate of rise and fall

Table 3.4
Properties of Cathode Rays

1. Travel in straight lines from the cathode to the anode
2. Cast shadows when metal objects are placed in their path
3. Produce fluorescence where they strike the glass walls of the tube
4. Heat thin metal foils to incandescence
5. Cause ionization of gas molecules
6. "Expose" photographic films or plates
7. Produce highly penetrating radiation (x-rays) when directed against a target
8. Impart a negative charge to such a target
9. Undergo deflection parallel to an applied electrostatic field (away from the negative electrode) and perpendicular to an applied magnetic field

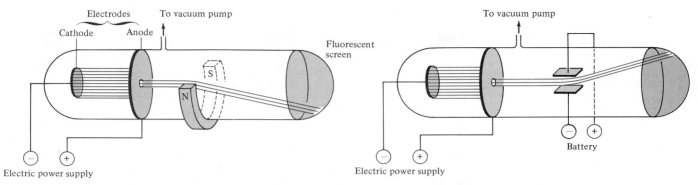

(a) **Deflection of cathode ray by magnetic field**

(b) **Deflection of cathode ray by electric field**

Figure 3.2
Determination of e/m of the Electron The magnetic and electric fields deflect the cathode ray in opposite directions. By varying these two opposing forces until they balance (an often-used principle in the design of experiments), Thomson was able to calculate from the field strengths, the e/m value of the electron. (Source: Reproduced by permission of the publisher from O'Connor et al., *Chemistry: Experiments and Principles,* © 1968, Lexington, Massachusetts: D.C. Heath.)

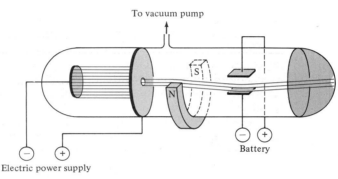

(c) **Balanced deflection of cathode ray by electric and magnetic fields**

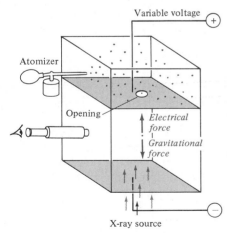

Figure 3.3
Millikan Oil Drop Experiment The velocity of the rise and fall of charged oil drops between the + and − plates is observed through the microscope. Both the charge on the drops and the electric field can be varied. Here again (see Figure 3.2) an experiment makes use of the balancing of opposing forces.

when the electric field was on, were closely observed. Sometimes the rate changed abruptly, showing that the droplet had captured a charged particle from the air.

In some experiments x-rays were passed through the air to assure the formation of charged particles. After many measurements on droplets with different charges, Millikan found that the charge, whether positive or negative, was always a whole-number multiple of the same value, 1.60×10^{-19} C (where the unit is a coulomb). This, therefore, is the charge of the smallest charged particle present during the experiment, the electron. All of the charged particles were formed by the gain or loss by atoms in the air (alone or in combined forms) of one, or two, or more electrons. In relative terms, we express the charges on atoms in terms of the charge on an electron. That is, we refer to a particle with a charge of -1.60×10^{-9} C as having a charge of -1, a particle with a charge of -3.20×10^{-19} C as having a charge of -2, and so on, doing the same for particles with positive charges ($+1$, $+2$, and so on).

Once the charge of an electron was known from Millikan's experiments, the mass could be calculated from the value of e/m. Using the modern value of e/m and solving for the mass gives

$$\frac{e}{m} = 1.76 \times 10^8 \text{ C/g}$$

$$\frac{1.60 \times 10^{-19} \text{ C}}{m} = 1.76 \times 10^8 \text{ C/g}$$

$$m = \frac{1.60 \times 10^{-19} \text{ C}}{1.76 \times 10^8 \text{ C/g}} = 9.09 \times 10^{-28} \text{ g}$$

An electron has a mass of about 9×10^{-28} g, which is $\frac{1}{1837}$ of the mass of a hydrogen atom.

Table 3.5
Fundamental Particles of Importance to Chemistry Electrons and protons are both stable outside of an atom. Neutrons eventually decompose spontaneously.

Particle	Symbol	Mass*†	Charge	
			In Coulombs	Relative
Electron	e^-	9.109534×10^{-28} g (0.0005485802 u)	-1.602×10^{-19}	-1
Proton	p^+	$1.6726485 \times 10^{-24}$ g (1.0072764 u)	$+1.602 \times 10^{-19}$	$+1$
Neutron	n	$1.6749543 \times 10^{-24}$ g (1.0086650 u)	0	0

* Strictly speaking, we should use the term *rest mass.* Physicists have shown that moving particles have greater mass than particles that are "resting." The distinction has little bearing here, and throughout this book we use "mass" to refer to the rest mass of particles.

† The "u" is the abbreviation for "atomic mass unit," which is defined in Section 3.10.

The electron was the first fundamental, subatomic particle to be discovered. A **subatomic particle** is a particle smaller than the smallest atom. A **fundamental particle** is one that is present in all matter. The **electron** is a fundamental, subatomic, negatively charged particle, and **cathode rays,** as Thomson thought, are streams of electrons flowing from the cathode toward the anode in a gas-discharge tube. Modern values for the properties of the electron and other fundamental particles are given in Table 3.5.

The proof of the existence of a particle so much smaller than the smallest known atom unleashed a host of questions that had to be answered. What other particles might be present within an atom? What holds these particles together? What is the arrangement of the particles within an atom?

3.5 CANAL RAYS: THE PROTON

Atoms are electrically neutral. Therefore, the identification of positive charges to balance the negative charge of the electrons was essential. Also, since electrons have such small mass, something else had to be found to account for the much greater mass of atoms.

The first observations of charged particles other than cathode rays were also made in gas-discharge tubes. In 1886, Eugen Goldstein discovered that rays with a positive charge were flowing in the opposite direction from the cathode rays in such tubes. These were named *canal rays,* because they pass through "canals"—openings cut into the cathode.

In 1898, Wilhelm Wien, a German physicist, succeeded in measuring e/m for canal rays by a method similar to that used by Thomson for the electron. The work of Wien and others showed that canal ray particles are much heavier than electrons, and that, unlike cathode ray particles, they vary in mass according to the gas present in the tube. Canal rays have positive charges that are small-whole-number multiples of $+1.60 \times 10^{-19}$ C (a charge equal but opposite to that on the electron). The properties of canal rays are summarized in Table 3.6.

After the discovery of the canal rays, it was possible to explain completely what happens in a gas-discharge tube (Figure 3.4). Electrons released from the cathode collide with atoms of whatever gas is present in the tube, knocking out of each of these atoms one or more additional electrons. These collisions leave behind positively charged particles called *ions,* formed by the loss of electrons from the atoms of the gas. The loss of one electron gives an ion of $+1$ charge, the loss of two electrons gives an ion of $+2$ charge, and so on. Ions can be formed from any atoms by the loss or gain of electrons and can have positive or negative charges. We indicate an ion by writing its unit charge as a superscript after the symbol for the neutral species from

Table 3.6
Properties of Canal Rays These rays are so named because they pass through a hole, or "canal," in the cathode.

1. Travel in straight lines toward the cathode
2. Produce fluorescence when they strike the walls of the tube
3. Are deflected in the opposite direction from cathode rays by both electric and magnetic fields
4. Are deflected less than cathode rays by fields of equal strength
5. Expose photographic plates
6. Differ for different gases in the tube

Figure 3.4
Cathode Rays and Canal Rays Electrons from the atoms of the cathode material are accelerated toward the anode, forming cathode rays. These electrons collide with gaseous atoms, knocking off other electrons and leaving positively charged ions, a process that causes a glow. The positive ions are attracted to the cathode, forming canal rays. As the pressure becomes lower the electrons encounter fewer and fewer atoms, and eventually the glow disappears. However, the electron beam continues to flow from the cathode.

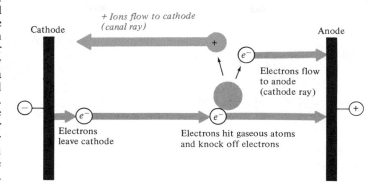

which the ion was formed. For example, a hydrogen ion is H$^+$ and a neon ion is Ne$^+$.

In the gas-discharge tube most of the positive ions collide with the cathode, but a few pass through the holes ("canals") in the cathode. They can be observed as luminous rays and also can be detected as they impinge on a fluorescent material on the inside of the tube (Figure 3.5). The lightest and simplest canal ray particles are formed when a gas-discharge tube contains hydrogen. These hydrogen ions have a positive charge equal to the negative charge of the electron [$1 \times (1.60 \times 10^{-19})$] C.

The hydrogen ion, later named the proton by Ernest Rutherford, was the most likely candidate for the positively charged particle needed to balance the charge of the electron. Rutherford eventually showed that the proton, like the electron, is present in all matter. The **proton** is a fundamental subatomic particle with a positive charge equal in magnitude to the negative charge of the electron (see Table 3.5).

3.6 α-PARTICLE SCATTERING: THE NUCLEUS

a. Radioactivity and α-particles During the years that Rutherford was studying atomic structure, he was also studying radioactive elements—elements that spontaneously break down because they are unstable. (Chapter 12 is devoted to radioactivity and nuclear chemistry.) One result of this work was Rutherford's identification of α-particles ("alpha-particles"), which are given off by some radioactive elements. An **α-particle** is a helium ion with a charge of +2, He^{2+}. α-Particles are also formed in gas-discharge tubes that contain helium. α-Particles have a positive charge of 3.20×10^{-19} C, twice the charge of a proton, and have a mass four times that of a proton.

Although the α-particle is not fundamental to the model of atomic structure, it was used in some pioneering experiments. α-Particles are emitted from radioactive elements with very high speed. For example, they come from radium atoms traveling

Figure 3.5
Canal Rays Positive ions are produced in the gas-discharge tube when electrons from the cathode strike atoms. The positive ions move toward the cathode, forming the "canal ray." Some ions pass through the canals and cause fluorescence on the wall of the tube.

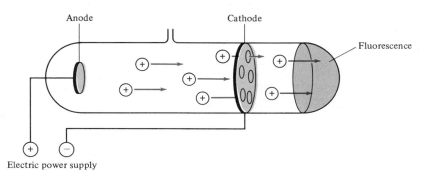

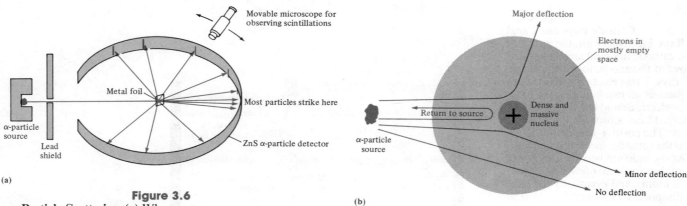

(a)

(b)

Figure 3.6

α-Particle Scattering (a) Where an α-particle strikes the zinc sulfide screen, a flash of light (a "scintillation") can be observed through the microscope. Most α-particles pass through the metal foil undeflected. Some are deflected through varying angles, and a few are deflected back toward the source. (b) This diagram shows how α-particles are scattered by a single atom with a dense positive nucleus.

at 1.5×10^7 m/s—fully five percent of the speed of light—which gives them very high energy. Rutherford and others recognized the value of such particles. Because of their high energy, they could be fired like bullets at atoms and, from what happened when the particles collided, information about the structure of atoms could be obtained.

One result of Rutherford's experiments was the production of H^+ ions—protons—from the bombardment of nitrogen and other elements, which showed that protons are present in atoms other than hydrogen atoms. But the most important result came from the fate of the α-particles themselves in the bombardment of thin foils of metals, as is discussed in the next section.

b. α-Particle scattering and the nuclear atom   The third of the classic experiments on atomic structure was carried out in 1911 in Rutherford's laboratory by his colleagues Hans Geiger and Ernest Marsden. At the time, the prevailing picture of an atom was that proposed by J. J. Thomson after his determination of e/m for the electron. Thomson suggested that an atom is a sphere of positive charge in which electrons are embedded like raisins in a plum pudding. Since the electrons are so light, the mass of this atom would have to be accounted for by the positively charged part of it. The electrons would be distributed at maximum distances from each other because of the repulsion of their negative charges. This model was tested by the experiment of Geiger and Marsden.

A narrow beam of α-particles from a radioactive source was aimed at a thin foil of a metal such as gold, platinum, or copper (Figure 3.6). Here is an account given by Rutherford, beginning with his suggestion to Geiger that Marsden try the experiment:

> "Why not let him see if any alpha particles can be scattered through a large angle?" I may tell you in confidence that I did not believe that they would be since we knew that the alpha particle was a very fast massive particle, with a great deal of energy, and you could show that if the scattering was due to the accumulated effect of a number of small scatterings the chance of an alpha particle's being scattered backwards was very small. Then I remember two or three days later Geiger coming to me in great excitement and saying, "We have been able to get some of the alpha particles coming backwards. . . ." It was quite the most incredible event that has ever happened to me in my life. It was almost as incredible as if you fired a 15-inch shell at a piece of tissue paper and it came back and hit you. (E. Rutherford, in *Background to Modern Science*, J. Needham and W. Pagel, eds. (London: Cambridge University Press, 1938), p. 68.)

If the mass and positive charge were uniformly distributed throughout each atom in the metal foil, as suggested by the Thomson model, there would be no concentration of charge or mass large enough to deflect the α-particles. Faced with this disagreement between fact and theory, Rutherford did what a good scientist must do. He abandoned the old theory and devised a better one. He proposed that each atom has a dense central core, which he called the nucleus. The **nucleus** is a central region, very small by comparison with the total size of an atom, in which virtually all of the mass and positive charge of the atom are concentrated. In this model the electrons were thought of as circling about the nucleus much as planets circle around the sun.

In α-particle bombardment of a foil of such nuclear atoms, the majority of the α-particles would encounter only empty space and pass through undeflected (see Figure 3.6b). Only those coming close to a positively charged nucleus would be deflected by the great forces of repulsion between like charges. And only those few that come very close to the nucleus and experience maximum repulsion would be returned in the direction from which they came.

The nucleus, according to Rutherford, contained closely packed protons. The positive charge of the protons had to be balanced by the negative charge on the electrons outside the nucleus. However, this model was not completely satisfactory because the mass of protons and electrons equal in number to the nuclear charge did not account for the observed atomic masses. For example, a nucleus of two protons —to balance the charge of its two electrons—could not explain the helium atom, which has a mass *four* times that of a proton. For a while, it was thought that the nucleus contained enough additional protons to account for an atom's mass, plus enough electrons inside the nucleus to maintain electrical neutrality. After Chadwick's discovery of the neutron in 1932, a more satisfactory model of the nucleus emerged.

3.7 20 YEARS LATER: THE NEUTRON

Rutherford pursued his studies on radioactivity, the nucleus, and the use of α-particles in bombardment experiments. In 1920 he proposed that the nucleus might contain an uncharged particle with a mass close to that of the hydrogen atom. The search for this "neutron" lasted another 12 years. James Chadwick of Rutherford's laboratory in Cambridge saw the answer in some α-particle experiments reported by other workers. They had produced a "highly penetrating" radiation from beryllium (Figure 3.7). This radiation knocked protons out of paraffin with great force.

Chadwick felt that the "highly penetrating radiation" must be a beam of uncharged particles, each with the mass expected for a neutron. Chadwick performed his own experiments and in 1932 was able to prove conclusively the existence of the neutron. The **neutron** is a fundamental, subatomic particle that has a mass almost the same as the mass of the proton and has no charge (see Table 3.5).

With the discovery of the neutron, it could be assumed that all of the electrons in an atom are outside the nucleus. The nucleus contains *protons equal in number to the*

α-particle source   α-particles   Beryllium   Highly penetrating radiation   Paraffin   High velocity protons

Experimental Discovery of the Neutron Such experiments were first performed by Irene and Frederic Joliot-Curie in Paris, who interpreted the "highly penetrating" radiation as an x-ray. Chadwick recognized that, based on what was known of energy and momentum, only a neutral particle with mass close to that of the proton could knock protons out of paraffin.

Figure 3.7

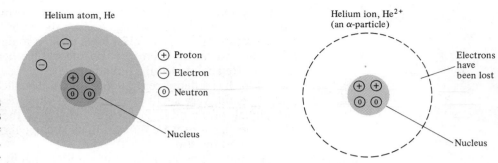

Figure 3.8
The Helium Atom and +2 Ion This is a schematic picture of the location of the electrons, protons, and neutrons in helium.

electrons, plus enough neutrons to account for the total mass of the atom. For example, the helium atom contains two electrons, and in its nucleus, two protons and two neutrons that account for its mass (Figure 3.8).

3.8 X-RAY SPECTRA: ATOMIC NUMBER

Henry G. J. Moseley, a young Englishman, in 1913 performed a series of experiments crucial to the understanding of atomic numbers and the atomic nucleus. It had been found that when the electrons from the cathode in a gas-discharge tube hit a metal target, the metal emits x-rays (Figure 3.9). When the spectra from these x-rays were photographed, series of lines that varied with the metal could be seen. (A **spectrum**—the plural is spectra—is an array of radiation or particles spread out according to the increasing or decreasing magnitude of some physical property. In the case of x-ray spectra, this property is wavelength [see Tools of Chemistry: Electromagnetic Radiation and Spectra, in Chapter 8, and Section 8.5]).

Moseley set out to photograph the x-ray spectra of as many elements as possible. In the remarkably short time of six months, Moseley examined the x-ray spectra of 38 elements from aluminum to gold. Several series of lines appear in the spectrum of each element. Moseley found that, with one or two exceptions, as the relative atomic mass of the target increased, the position of any specific line in a specific series moved by regular intervals toward shorter wavelengths (Figure 3.10). There was a simple mathematical relationship between the position of these lines and a property of the target elements. Here, in his own words, are his conclusions:

1. Every element from aluminum to gold is characterized by an integer N which determines its x-ray spectrum. Every detail in the spectrum of an element can therefore be predicted from the spectra of its neighbors (in the periodic table).

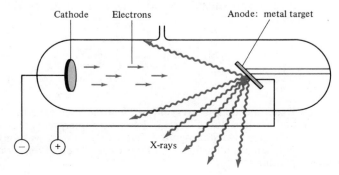

Figure 3.9
An x-ray tube.

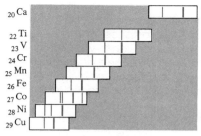

Figure 3.10
Atomic X-Ray Spectra A sketch of
the relative positions of emission
lines in some of Moseley's spectra.
The element scandium, not
available to Moseley, is missing
between titanium and calcium. (For
a discussion of wavelength and
radiation, see Tools of Chemistry:
Electromagnetic Radiation and
Spectra, in Chapter 8.)

2. This integer N, the atomic number of the element, is identified with the number of positive units of electricity contained in the atomic nucleus. (H. J. G. Moseley, in *The World of the Atom*, H. A. Boorse and L. Motz, eds. (New York: Basic Books, 1966), p. 68.)

The **atomic number** of an element, now symbolized by Z, is equal to the number of protons in the nucleus of each atom of that element. Inside the front cover of this book, in the table that lists the elements alphabetically, is a column labeled "atomic number." Look at the periodic table opposite the alphabetical table and you can see that the atomic numbers correspond to the order in which the elements appear in the periodic table. The periodic table was devised before the significance of this arrangement was fully understood. (The history of the periodic table is discussed in the Historical Aside in Chapter 8.)

Rutherford's concept of the nucleus is now universally accepted. Rutherford did not know the whole story of what was inside the nucleus. We still do not know it. Nor did Rutherford have a clear understanding of the location and behavior of electrons in atoms. But he was right in picturing an atom as mostly empty space occupied by electrons moving around a very small, dense central core. The modern picture of the arrangement of electrons in atoms is presented in Chapter 8, and the great significance of this arrangement for chemistry is explained there.

**Atomic number (Z)
= no. of protons in nucleus**

In summary, Dalton's original picture of atoms as hard and indivisible evolved into the nuclear model of the atom used today (Figure 3.11) as a result of a number of classic experiments. First, the electron, a very light, negatively charged particle, was identified in cathode rays by J. J. Thomson, who measured its charge-to-mass ratio. The Millikan oil drop experiment gave a value for the charge on the electron, allowing determination of its mass also. The study of the canal rays in gas-discharge tubes proved the existence of a second fundamental particle, the proton, which is a positively charged particle (an H^+ ion) with much greater mass than the electron.

An experiment by Geiger and Marsden on α-particle scattering led Rutherford to propose that the mass of an atom is concentrated in a small, dense central nucleus, with electrons moving outside the nucleus in mostly empty space. The basic model of the nuclear atom was completed in 1932 with the discovery of the neutron by Chadwick. Neutrons and protons together in the nucleus account for the mass of each atom. The significance of the number of protons in the nucleus, called the atomic number, became clear when Moseley found in x-ray studies that atoms of each element have different and characteristic numbers of protons.

Figure 3.11
Older Models of the Atom
Dalton's atomic theory is discussed
in the Historical Aside on the next
page.

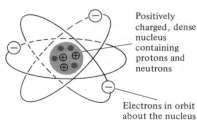

Dalton atom
(hard and
indivisible)

Thomson atom
(the plum pudding atom)

Electrons

Sphere of positive charge

Rutherford atom
(the planetary atom)

Positively
charged, dense
nucleus
containing
protons and
neutrons

Electrons in orbit
about the nucleus

A HISTORICAL ASIDE

The Concept of the Atom

If you divide a drop of water into smaller drops, and one of those into still smaller drops, and so on, will you ultimately reach a point where the drop cannot be further subdivided, even in imagination, without destroying the substance of the water itself? The ancient Greek philosophers debated this question, and were sharply divided on it. Plato and Aristotle argued that all matter is composed of earth, air, fire, and water. Others chose mercury, salt, and sulfur as the basis of all matter. Still others argued in favor of the divisibility of matter into ultimate small particles that retain the properties of the original matter.

Democritus of Abdera, in about 400 B.C., came remarkably close to the modern theory of matter — the atomic theory. He argued that all matter is composed of tiny, homogeneous particles that are hard and impenetrable, differ in size and shape, can come together in different combinations, and are constantly in motion. Democritus named the particles "atoms," from the Greek word meaning "indivisible." Several hundred years later, Lucretius in Rome said it this way: ". . . all nature as it is in itself consists of two things — for there are atoms and there is the void."

For almost 1600 years after Lucretius the concept of the atom dropped from view, and Aristotle's four elements remained dominant in philosophy and science. In the seventeenth century, a revival of interest in atoms coincided with the growing recognition that facts and experimentation are a better basis for science than philosophical speculation. Robert Boyle (1627–1691), although not a firm believer in the existence of atoms, was instrumental in discrediting belief in the Aristotelian elements. In his famous book *The Skeptical Chymist,* Boyle presented strong arguments in favor of experimentally determined facts and against the vague philosophical and alchemical concepts that were then popular.

The remarkable way in which atomic theory can explain the behavior of matter gradually came to be fully appreciated as chemistry became a quantitative science. Let's look at one example of the kind of evidence that led John Dalton (1766–1844) to formulate his atomic theory.

Many compounds containing only carbon and hydrogen are known. One of the simplest of these contains 85.7% carbon and 14.3% hydrogen (by mass). Another common one contains 75.0% carbon and 25.0% hydrogen.

As they stand, these figures are of little interest. But if we calculate from them how much hydrogen is combined with one gram of carbon in each case, we find that in the first compound it is 0.167 g and in the second, 0.333 g. The second of these numbers is almost exactly twice the first ($\frac{0.167}{0.333}$ is approximately equal to $\frac{1}{2}$). Your first reaction to this may be, "An interesting coincidence." But there are hundreds of other cases like it. The amounts of one element that combine with a given amount of another element are small whole-number multiples of each other. From other carbon–hydrogen compounds it can be found that the amount of hydrogen combined with a given amount of carbon is always 1 or 2 or 3 or 4 . . . times a specific amount of hydrogen. So we must conclude that this is not a coincidence. How, then, shall we explain it? The most logical explanation is that the elements exist in the form of extremely small, discrete units — atoms — and that these combine in simple ratios. In other words, one atom of A will combine with one atom of B, or with two atoms of B, or with three atoms of B, and so on.

Dalton was an extraordinary man. His parents were poor, so he had little formal schooling and had to educate himself. He did this so well that he became a school teacher when he was 12 years old. He kept detailed records of the weather for 57 years, and his study of weather led him to study gases in general.

Dalton's atomic theory (see margin), first published in 1808, was based on his observation of the behavior of gases. The importance and usefulness of Dalton's atomic theory are not diminished by the modern knowledge that some of the statements are not correct under all circumstances.

Dalton's Atomic Theory

1. All matter consists of tiny particles. Dalton, like the Greeks, called these particles atoms.
2. Atoms of one element can neither be subdivided nor changed into atoms of any other element.
3. Atoms can neither be created nor destroyed.
4. All atoms of the same element are identical in mass, size, and other properties.
5. Atoms of one element differ in mass and other properties from atoms of other elements.
6. Chemical combination is the union of atoms of different elements; the atoms combine in simple, whole-number ratios to each other.

TOOLS OF CHEMISTRY

Electricity and Magnetism

The study of electricity and magnetism is one of the major areas of physics. By observing the behavior of matter under the influence of electricity or magnetism, much has been learned about the properties of matter. For the purpose of studying chemistry, therefore, it helps to understand in a general way some of the concepts and terms related to electricity and magnetism.

What is commonly thought of as "electricity" is the flow of electrons through a wire. The essential property of electrons is their charge—electrons are negatively charged. Positively charged objects are attracted to negatively charged objects, and objects of the same charge repel each other. Protons are positively charged, and the attraction between electrons and protons holds the particles together in atoms. The charges on electrons and protons, and the attraction and repulsion of charged objects are not *proven* or *explained* by theory. These are fundamental properties that are accepted because they are observed to exist.

The force of electrical attraction or repulsion between charged particles is called the **Coulomb force.** The Coulomb force between two particles is a function of the magnitudes of the charges on the particles and the distance between them.

$$\text{Coulomb force} = k\,\frac{q_1 q_2}{r^2} \qquad (3.1)$$

charge on particles 1 and 2
proportionality constant
distance between particles 1 and 2

We can manipulate charge and measure its effect. The SI unit of charge is the coulomb, abbreviated C.

Matter is ordinarily neutral, that is, it has no net charge: A neutral bit of matter contains equal numbers of electrons and protons evenly distributed throughout. If something happens to separate the protons and electrons from each other, or to redistribute them in an unequal fashion, the presence of charge is observed. For example, charge can be redistributed in a storm cloud on a summer day. Electrons collect at the bottom of the cloud, which thus acquires a negative charge. Eventually, charge balance is restored in a very dramatic way—a bolt of lightning strikes the ground or another cloud. (In a lightning bolt, electrons move in one direction and positive ions in the other.)

Variations in the force of attraction between charged particles and in the distribution of negatively charged electrons among positively charged atoms strongly influence the properties of matter. In later chapters, we find frequent occasion to refer to the Coulomb force and the relationship given in Equation (3.1).

The region around one charged particle or bit of matter in which another charged particle will be attracted (if the charges are opposite) or repelled (if the charges are alike) is an *electric field.* A charged particle in an electric field has *electrical potential energy,* as does the water in a reservoir. The water flows from the reservoir because it has gravitational potential energy and it flows from an area of higher potential energy to one of lower potential energy. Similarly, a charged particle in an electric field moves from an area of higher electrical potential energy to one of lower electrical potential energy. We speak of charged particles in an electric field as moving in response to a *potential difference*.

There is a potential difference between the cathode and anode in a gas-discharge tube (see Figures 3.1 and 3.2) and between the parallel plates in the Millikan experiment (see Figure 3.3). In a diagram of an electrical apparatus or circuit, you can recognize by the location of the + and − the presence of a potential difference that will cause charged particles to flow. The *volt* is the unit of electrical potential difference. To "put a voltage across" something means to apply a potential difference.

The movement of charged particles constitutes an electric current. The metal from which wires are made, and all other substances through which current can flow, are called *conductors*. Substances that do not conduct electricity are called *insulators*. To be conductive, a substance must contain charge carriers—charged particles that are free to move through the material. For example, in a gas-discharge tube (see Figure 3.4), electrons and positive ions flow through a gas.

The ability of different substances to allow charge carriers to move varies widely. The *electrical conductivity* of a substance is a measurable quantity used to compare the ability of different substances to carry current, or the ability of the same substance to carry current under different conditions (for example, at different temperatures). In later chapters, we discuss how the chemical constitution of a substance influences its electrical conductivity.

To close this section, a few words must be said about magnetism. For a long time electricity and magnetism were thought to be different phenomena, and we still frequently talk about them as though they are different. In actuality, electricity and magnetism are two aspects of the same phenomenon. A wire through which an electric current is moving is surrounded by a magnetic field. Whenever charged particles are in motion, a magnetic field is created and, conversely, where a magnetic field is detected, charged particles are in motion nearby. (The magnetic properties of materials derive from the motion of electrons within the atoms of the substance.) A charged particle that is moving in a magnetic field experiences a force. This explains the deflection of cathode rays in a gas-discharge tube when a magnetic field is applied (see Figure 3.2) and the deflection of ions in a mass spectrometer (see Tools of Chemistry: Mass Spectrometer).

NUCLEAR ARITHMETIC

3.9 ATOMIC NUMBER, ISOTOPES, AND MASS NUMBERS

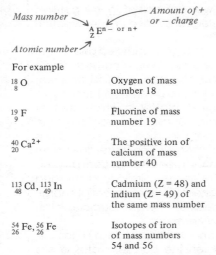

Mass number

Amount of + or − charge

$^{A}_{Z}E^{n-\ or\ n+}$

Atomic number

For example

$^{18}_{8}O$	Oxygen of mass number 18
$^{19}_{9}F$	Fluorine of mass number 19
$^{40}_{20}Ca^{2+}$	The positive ion of calcium of mass number 40
$^{113}_{48}Cd, ^{113}_{49}In$	Cadmium (Z = 48) and indium (Z = 49) of the same mass number
$^{54}_{26}Fe, ^{56}_{26}Fe$	Isotopes of iron of mass numbers 54 and 56

Figure 3.12
Notation for an Atom or Ion of Element E Only the subscripts or superscripts needed for the purpose at hand are used. Often the atomic number is not included. (This is the notation as agreed upon today. Some older publications place the mass number at the right, e.g., O^{18}.)

The atomic number—the number of protons in the nucleus—determines the identity of an atom. Every atom with an atomic number of 8 is an oxygen atom and every oxygen atom contains 8 protons in its nucleus. Atoms with atomic numbers of 9 or 7 are atoms of fluorine or nitrogen, and contain 9 or 7 protons, respectively. Because of the necessity for charge balance in all matter, the atomic number also equals the number of electrons normally present in every atom of the same element. So far, then, we see that atoms of the same element each contain the same number of protons and electrons.

The number of neutrons, however, can vary for atoms of the same element. For example, oxygen as it occurs naturally in the atmosphere and elsewhere includes atoms that contain 8, 9, or 10 neutrons.

The **mass number** is the sum of the number of neutrons and the number of protons in a nucleus. Where A is the mass number, Z is the atomic number, and N is the **neutron number**—the number of neutrons in an atom—

$$\underset{number}{mass}\ A = \underset{neutron\ number\ (=\ no.\ of\ neutrons)}{\overset{atomic\ number\ (=\ no.\ of\ protons)}{Z + N}} \qquad (3.2)$$

The number of neutrons is the difference between the mass number and the atomic number ($N = A - Z$).

In the symbolism used for atoms and ions, the left superscript position is reserved for the mass number and the left subscript position for the atomic number (Figure 3.12). For the naturally occurring oxygen atoms the symbols and their meaning are as follows:

| Symbol | Name | Mass Number | = | Atomic Number | + | Neutron Number |
		A		Z		N
$^{16}_{8}O$	oxygen–16	16	=	8	+	8
$^{17}_{8}O$	oxygen–17	17	=	8	+	9
$^{18}_{8}O$	oxygen–18	18	=	8	+	10

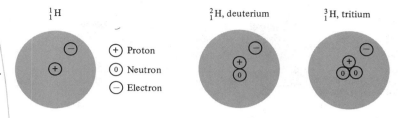

Figure 3.13
The Isotopes of Hydrogen This is a schematic picture of the number of electrons, protons, and neutrons in the hydrogen isotopes.

Mass number (A)
= atomic no. (Z)
+ neutron number (N)
= (protons + neutrons)

Isotopes:
same atomic number,
different mass number

These are atoms of different **isotopes** — forms of the same element with different mass numbers. In other words, isotopes have the same number of protons but different numbers of neutrons. (Note that the formation of ions by loss or gain of electrons does not change the identity of an element or its isotopes.)

Natural hydrogen is almost entirely a mixture of isotopes of mass numbers 1 and 2, $_1^1H$ and $_1^2H$. Each hydrogen atom contains a single proton and a single electron. The nucleus of the heavier hydrogen isotope contains in addition a single neutron. A third and much scarcer isotope of hydrogen has a mass number of 3 (Figure 3.13) and contains two neutrons. Hydrogen-2 is commonly known as **deuterium** or "heavy hydrogen," and hydrogen-3 is known as **tritium**. Most elements, although not all, occur in nature as mixtures of isotopes (see Tools of Chemistry: Mass Spectrometer). For a specific element the composition of the naturally occurring mixture of isotopes is very nearly the same everywhere (on this planet).

EXAMPLE 3.1
Nuclear Arithmetic

What are the compositions of the nuclei of $_{17}^{35}Cl$ and $_{17}^{35}Cl^-$?

The atomic number, Z, of chlorine (found from the table inside the front cover) is 17; thus the nucleus contains 17 protons.

The mass number, A, of this isotope is 35; thus the total number of protons and neutrons in the nucleus is 35.

The neutron number, N, is the difference between the mass number and the atomic number.

$$N = A - Z = 35 - 17 = 18$$

The nucleus of $_{17}^{35}Cl$ consists of 17 protons and 18 neutrons. The electrical charge on an ion is the result of the gain or loss of electrons, which takes place outside the nucleus. Therefore, the nuclear composition of $_{17}^{35}Cl^-$ is the same as that of $_{17}^{35}Cl$.

Exercise What is the composition of the nucleus of $_{11}^{23}Na$? Will this composition be any different from that of the nucleus of $_{11}^{23}Na^+$? *Answer* 11 protons, 12 neutrons; no

---

3.10 ATOMIC MASS

Today we have sophisticated techniques for determining the masses of atoms with great accuracy. We know that one atom of bismuth, one of the heaviest of the elements, has a mass of 3.470256×10^{-22} g, and that one atom of hydrogen ($_1^1H$), the lightest element, has a mass of 1.673559×10^{-24} g. The **actual mass of an atom** is the value of its mass in mass units, such as grams.

There was a time, however, when knowing the actual mass of an atom, or even knowing whether an atom of one element was heavier than an atom of another element, seemed an insurmountable problem. Early chemists had to establish a relative atomic mass scale by assigning a mass to an atom of one kind and then determining all other atomic masses relative to that one. The process is like deciding

Figure 3.14
Length Measured Relative to Royal Feet

A 1.25 foot snake
(King's foot standard)

A 1.66 foot snake
(Queen's foot standard)

1 King's foot   1 Queen's foot

that the king's foot has a length of one "foot." Anything equal in length to five king's feet is then 5 "feet" long, and so on. If the queen's foot is chosen as the relative length scale standard, then all objects in the kingdom have a different measured length (Figure 3.14). (For more on the subject of the masses of atoms, see A Historical Aside: Relative Atomic Masses, in Chapter 4.)

We still use a relative mass scale for atoms, rather than a scale of conventional mass units such as grams. It is much easier to think of an atom of bismuth as about 209 times heavier than a hydrogen atom, than to deal with numbers with more than 20 zeros after the decimal point. By international agreement, the standard for atomic masses is now the isotope of carbon of mass number 12, $^{12}_{6}C$, which is *assigned* an atomic mass of *exactly* 12 units. An **atomic mass unit,** u, is defined as $\frac{1}{12}$ of the mass of one carbon-12 atom. One atomic mass unit is equal to $1.6605655 \times 10^{-24}$ g, often rounded off to 1.6606×10^{-24} g (Figure 3.15).

On this relative atomic mass scale, the mass of any atom is *close* to the whole number that is its mass number. This is so because on this scale the masses of protons and neutrons are each close to 1 (see Table 3.5). For example, for the three naturally occurring isotopes of neon of mass numbers 20, 21, and 22 the relative atomic masses are

$$^{20}_{10}Ne \; 19.992 \; u \qquad ^{21}_{10}Ne \; 20.994 \; u \qquad ^{22}_{10}Ne \; 21.991 \; u$$

The masses of isotopes deviate slightly from whole numbers for several reasons. First, the neutron and proton masses are not *exactly* equal to 1 (see Table 3.5). Second, the isotopic mass includes the masses of electrons, which make a tiny contribution to mass. And third, a relatively small amount of mass is converted into the energy that holds the particles together (known as the binding energy; Section 12.2).

Except in specialized applications, chemists are not concerned with individual isotopic masses (or individual isotopes). What is important is the *average* atomic mass of the naturally occurring mixture of the isotopes of any element. This mass is based on a weighted average found by multiplying the isotopic mass by the fraction of atoms having that mass. For example, for carbon, which is 98.89% $^{12}_{6}C$ and 1.11% $^{13}_{6}C$ (see Table 3.7)

$$\text{Average atomic mass} = (0.9889)(12.0000 \; u) + (0.0111)(13.003 \; u)$$
$$= 12.011 \; u$$

The atomic masses given in the periodic table and the other tables inside the covers of this book and elsewhere are the average, relative atomic masses. **Atomic mass** is defined as the average mass of the atoms of the naturally occurring element relative to $\frac{1}{12}$ of the mass of an atom of $^{12}_{6}C$. The terms "average atomic mass" or "relative atomic mass" are usually shortened to just "atomic mass." When we speak of the atomic mass of, say, bromine, we mean 79.904 u (see Table 3.7)—if we have a bottle of bromine, this is the average relative atomic mass of the bromine atoms it contains. (Note that "atomic weight" is often used instead of "atomic mass.") Table 3.7 gives some additional examples of the relationships discussed in this section and the preceding section.

Atomic mass unit (u)
= 1/12 the mass of
1 atom of ^{12}C
= 1.6606×10^{-24} g

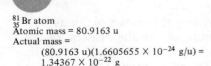

$^{12}_{6}C$ atom
Atomic mass = 12.0000 u
Actual mass =
  $(12.0000 \; u)(1.6605655 \times 10^{-24} \; g/u) =$
  1.99268×10^{-23} g

$^{81}_{35}Br$ atom
Atomic mass = 80.9163 u
Actual mass =
  $(80.9163 \; u)(1.6605655 \times 10^{-24} \; g/u) =$
  1.34367×10^{-22} g

Figure 3.15
Atomic Mass Relationships The relative atomic masses and the actual masses are in the same ratio to each other:
(12.000 u)/(80.9163 u) =
$(1.99268 \times 10^{-23} \; g)/(1.34367 \times 10^{-22} \; g) = 0.148301.$

Table 3.7
Isotopes and Masses The atomic mass of each element, which is the weighted average of the isotope atomic masses, is given in color in the last column. The percentages of the isotopes in naturally occurring mixtures are given in parentheses in the first column. The actual mass in grams of one atom of an isotope can be found by multiplying the atomic mass by 1.66057×10^{-24} g/u.

Element and Isotopes (%)	Protons	Neutrons	Atomic Mass, or Isotope Atomic Mass (u)
Carbon (Z = 6)			12.011
^{12}C (98.89)	6	6	12.000*
^{13}C (1.11)	6	7	13.003
Magnesium (Z = 12)			24.305
^{24}Mg (78.99)	12	12	23.985
^{25}Mg (10.00)	12	13	24.986
^{26}Mg (11.01)	12	14	25.983
Calcium (Z = 20)			40.08
^{40}Ca (96.941)	20	20	39.963
^{42}Ca (0.647)	20	22	41.959
^{43}Ca (0.135)	20	23	42.959
^{44}Ca (2.086)	20	24	43.955
^{46}Ca (0.004)	20	26	45.954
^{48}Ca (0.187)	20	28	47.952
Bromine (Z = 35)			79.904
^{79}Br (50.69)	35	44	78.918
^{81}Br (49.31)	35	46	80.916
Uranium (Z = 92)			238.0289
^{234}U (0.005)	92	142	234.041
^{235}U (0.720)	92	143	235.044
^{238}U (99.275)	92	146	238.051

* By definition

EXAMPLE 3.2
Actual Atomic Mass

The most abundant isotope of uranium is $^{238}_{92}$U, which has an atomic mass of 238.051 u. What is the actual mass of an atom of $^{238}_{92}$U?

To find the actual mass of an atom, we simply convert from atomic mass units to units of mass (g, kg, etc.). Using our knowledge that $1\ u = 1.6605655 \times 10^{-24}$ g,

$$(238.051\ u)(1.6605655 \times 10^{-24}\ g/u) = 3.95299 \times 10^{-22}\ g$$

The actual mass of an atom of $^{238}_{92}$U is 3.95299×10^{-22} g.

Exercise What is the actual mass of an atom of $^{20}_{10}$Ne which has an atomic mass of 19.992 u? *Answer* 3.3198×10^{-23} g

EXAMPLE 3.3
Average Atomic Mass

Naturally occurring iron contains 5.82% $^{54}_{26}$Fe, 91.66% $^{56}_{26}$Fe, 2.19% $^{57}_{26}$Fe, and 0.33% $^{58}_{26}$Fe. The respective atomic masses are 53.940 u, 55.935 u, 56.935 u, and 57.933 u. Calculate the average atomic mass of iron.

To find the weighted average, multiply the mass of each isotope by the fraction of that isotope present and add the results.

$$\begin{aligned} \text{Average atomic mass} &= (0.0582)(53.940\ u) + (0.9166)(55.935\ u) \\ &\quad + (0.0219)(56.935\ u) + (0.0033)(57.933\ u) \\ &= 3.14\ u + 51.27\ u + 1.25\ u + 0.19\ u \\ &= 55.85\ u \end{aligned}$$

The average atomic mass of iron is 55.85 u. (You can check this value in the tables inside the front cover.)

Exercise Naturally occurring neon gas contains 90.92% $^{20}_{10}$Ne, 0.257% $^{21}_{10}$Ne, and 8.82% $^{22}_{10}$Ne. The respective atomic masses are 19.992 u, 20.994 u, and 21.991 u. Calculate the average atomic mass of neon. *Answer* 20.17 u

In summary, the identity of an atom is determined by the number of protons in the nucleus, which is given by the atomic number. Isotopes are forms of the same element with different numbers of neutrons. The mass number of an isotope equals the number of protons plus the number of neutrons. The relative atomic mass scale is based upon carbon-12, which is assigned an atomic mass of exactly 12 u. "Atomic mass" refers to the average mass of the naturally occurring mixture of isotopes of an element.

KINDS OF MATTER

3.11 PURE SUBSTANCES AND MIXTURES

Color, melting point, boiling point, density, and hardness are among the properties of matter. These are **physical properties**—they can be measured or observed without changing the composition and identity of a substance. By contrast, any process in which the *identity* and composition of at least one substance is changed is a **chemical reaction. Chemical properties** can only be observed in chemical reactions, which result in changes in the identity of substances.

Every kind of matter can be classified as a pure substance or a mixture. We identify pure substances by examining their properties. A **pure substance** is a form of matter that has the same physical and chemical properties, no matter what its source. For instance, pure water is colorless and odorless, boils at 100 °C and freezes at 0 °C at atmospheric pressure, weighs 1 gram per milliliter at 4 °C, and does not burn. It has these properties whether it is distilled from sea water or from melted snow, or prepared in a chemical reaction by the union of hydrogen and oxygen. And it is these characteristic properties that enable us to distinguish water from other substances.

Pure substances are either elements or chemical compounds. The modern definition of an **element** is as a substance that contains only atoms of the same atomic number. An **atom** is defined as the smallest particle of an element that can participate in a chemical reaction.

> **Element: a substance containing only atoms of the same atomic number**

A **chemical compound** is a substance of definite, fixed composition in which atoms of two or more elements are chemically combined. For example, under the right conditions, the elements hydrogen and oxygen combine to give water. The properties of water are very different from those of hydrogen and oxygen. Water is a chemical compound in which there are always two hydrogen atoms for every oxygen atom. Thus, the mass ratio of hydrogen to oxygen in water is 1 to 8, *always.*

> **Solution = solute dissolved in solvent**

A **mixture** is composed of two or more substances that retain their separate identities. The substances in a mixture can be present in *any* proportions, and the

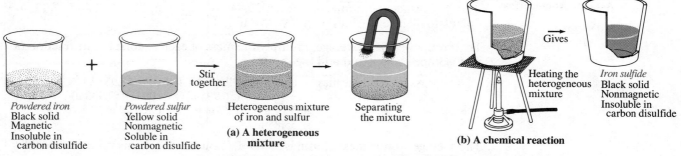

Powdered iron
Black solid
Magnetic
Insoluble in
  carbon disulfide

Powdered sulfur
Yellow solid
Nonmagnetic
Soluble in
  carbon disulfide

Stir together

Heterogeneous mixture of iron and sulfur
(a) A heterogeneous mixture

Separating the mixture

Heating the heterogeneous mixture

Gives

Iron sulfide
Black solid
Nonmagnetic
Insoluble in
carbon disulfide

(b) A chemical reaction

Figure 3.16

Iron Plus Sulfur: A Mixture or a Chemical Compound If iron and sulfur powders are thoroughly mixed but not heated, a mixture results. The iron can be completely removed from the sulfur by a magnet. Conversely, the sulfur can be complete removed from the iron by dissolving it in carbon disulfide, a liquid in which iron is not soluble. Powdered iron and powdered sulfur when heated together give a chemical compound, iron sulfide.

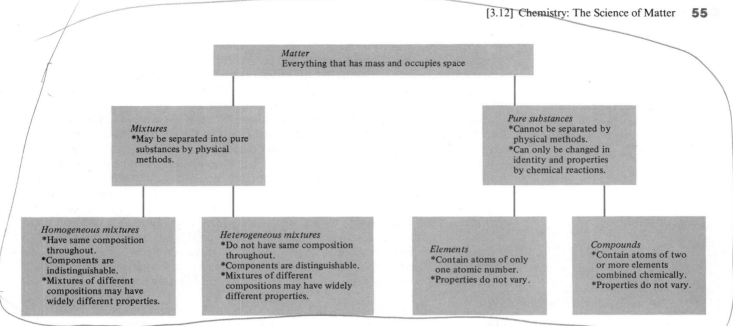

Figure 3.17
The Classification of Matter

components can be retrieved intact from the mixture without a chemical change. A **heterogeneous mixture** is a mixture in which the individual components of the mixture remain physically separate and can be seen as separate components, although in some cases a microscope is needed. Concrete and granite are heterogeneous mixtures. Powdered iron and powdered sulfur, no matter how well stirred, form a heterogeneous mixture. They can be separated by using a magnet to attract the powdered iron (Figure 3.16).

By contrast, when iron and sulfur are heated together, a chemical reaction occurs and iron sulfide, a chemical compound, is formed. The properties of iron sulfide (see Figure 3.16b) are clearly different from those of iron and sulfur.

The substances in a **homogeneous mixture** are thoroughly intermingled, and the composition and appearance of the mixture are uniform throughout. Air is a homogeneous mixture of gases, and motor oil is a homogeneous mixture of liquid petroleum derivatives. Homogeneous mixtures also can be separated by physical means.

We commonly think of solutions as homogeneous mixtures of something with water. Strictly speaking, any homogeneous mixture of two or more substances is a **solution.** A solution of any substance in water is an **aqueous solution.**

Solutions are spoken of as having two components: the solvent and the solute (or solutes). If a handful of salt is dissolved in a bucket of water, the salt is the solute and the water is the solvent. The **solvent** is the component of a solution usually present in the larger amount. The solvent is the medium in which the **solute** — the component of a solution usually present in the smaller amount — has dissolved. However, the terms "solvent" and "solute," while convenient, are often imprecise and do not have a fixed scientific meaning. The process of one substance dissolving in another is called **dissolution.**

The general classification of matter is summarized in Figure 3.17.

3.12 STATES OF MATTER   There are three **states of matter:** the gaseous state, the liquid state, and the solid state. At ordinary temperatures and pressures the pure substances oxygen, nitrogen, hydrogen, carbon dioxide, chlorine, ammonia, and methane (the major component of natural gas) are all gases. The pure substances water, ethyl alcohol, and mercury are liquids at ordinary temperatures and pressures. And solids, of course, are everywhere we look. The majority of the pure substances are solids. Some common pure substances that are solids at ordinary temperatures and pressures include most metals, such as iron, copper, and gold; carbon, as either diamond or graphite; sodium chloride (common salt); and sucrose (common sugar).

Some substances can exist in all three states. Water is known in the solid state as ice, in the liquid state (at room temperature), and in the gaseous state as steam or water vapor. We refer to interconversions between the solid, liquid, and gaseous states as **changes of state.** Many metals, which are usually solid, can be melted, and if heated to even higher temperatures, can become gaseous. Some substances, however, cannot exist in the gaseous state; others cannot exist in the liquid state; and some cannot exist in either the gaseous or the liquid state. For example, calcium carbonate, a solid, cannot be melted or vaporized, for upon heating it decomposes into calcium oxide, a different solid chemical compound, and carbon dioxide, a gas. Upon gentle heating, sugar melts to the liquid state. However, upon heating to higher temperatures sugar does not become gaseous, but instead decomposes into a variety of products that contain carbon. However, all gases and liquids can be condensed to the solid state.

The term **phase** refers to a homogeneous part of a system in contact with but separate from other parts of the system. A glass of iced tea — we might think of the iced tea as the system — has a solid phase (ice, a pure substance) and a liquid phase (tea, a solution), for example. The iced tea includes substances in the solid and the liquid states. A bottle of oil and vinegar contains only substances in the liquid state, but it also has two phases, because the oil phase and the vinegar phase remain in contact with each other but do not mix. It is also possible to have a completely solid substance in which several phases that are different crystalline forms are in contact with each other.

States of matter: solid, liquid, gas

TOOLS OF CHEMISTRY

Mass Spectrometer

Measurements with mass spectrometers are the main source of our highly accurate information about the occurrence of isotopes. The modern mass spectrometer, in which positive ions are produced in the gaseous state, is a direct descendant of the gas-discharge tube in which Goldstein studied canal rays.

A spectrum, as we have said, is an array of radiation or particles spread out according to a continuously changing property. To produce a mass spectrum, a beam of positive ions is spread out according to the mass-to-charge ratio of the ions. Under vacuum, positive ions (most of them of +1 charge) are produced either by bombardment of a gas by an electron beam or by the ionization of a solid by an electric spark. The positive ion beam is lined up ("collimated") by a slit system and accelerated by an electrical field of variable strength. The ions then pass through a magnetic field of variable strength that is perpendicular to their path. This force deflects the ions into curved paths. How far the path of an ion is curved depends upon its mass-to-charge ratio. Ions with the smallest mass are deflected the most.

Figure A

Mass Spectrograph The electron beam ionizes molecules of the gas, which are given a high velocity by the ion accelerators. As the ions pass through the magnetic field, they are deflected from their straight path, the lighter ones being deflected the most. In the instrument shown, the arrival of ions of different *e/m* is recorded on a photographic plate. In a mass spectrometer they are recorded on a graph or chart.

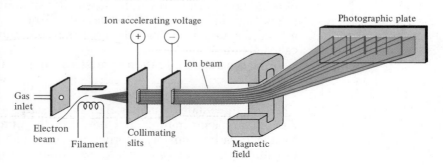

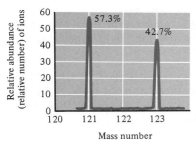

Figure B
Mass Spectrum of Antimony The peak heights show the abundances of antimony 121 and antimony 123 in the naturally occurring mixture.

In a mass spectrograph (Figure A) the spectrum is recorded in a photograph. The locations of the lines show the relative masses of the ions and the intensities of the lines show the relative numbers, or abundances, of ions of each mass.

In a mass spectrometer, the flow of ions is controlled by controlling the electric and magnetic fields so that ions of the same mass and charge arrive at a detector at the same time and are recorded as peaks on a graph. The positions of the peaks give the mass numbers of the ions present. The relative heights of the peaks give the relative abundances of ions of each mass number. Mass spectrometers are very sensitive and can separate ions that differ only slightly in mass. With the aid of a computer coupled to a mass spectrometer, mass spectra are provided directly as printouts of the masses and abundances of the ions present.

Figure B is a simple mass spectrum showing the relative abundances of the two naturally occurring isotopes of antimony. Mass spectra have many uses in addition to the determination of isotopic masses and abundances. The masses of chemical compounds and information about their structures can be found. Also chemical compounds can be identified by their "fingerprints," which are the distinctive patterns of ions formed when compounds break down in the spectrometer. Figure C is such a mass spectrum—only ethyl bromide would give exactly this pattern of peaks.

Figure C
The Mass Spectrum of Ethyl Bromide, C_2H_5Br (mol mass 108.96 u) The principal ions formed in the mass spectrometer by ethyl bromide are $[C_2H_5Br]^+$, symbolized M^+; $[CH_2Br]^+$; Br^-; $[C_2H_5]^+$; and $[C_2H_3]^+$. The natural isotopic distribution of the bromine isotopes, ^{79}Br (50.69%) and ^{81}Br (49.31%), is reflected in the pairs of peaks for each of the bromine-containing ions. (From K. Biemann, *Mass Spectrometry*, New York: McGraw Hill, 1962, p. 127.)

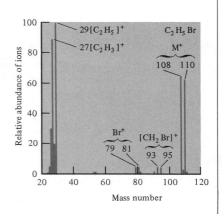

SUMMARY

3.1 ELEMENTS **3.2** SYMBOLS FOR THE ELEMENTS Substances which cannot be broken down chemically into simpler substances have historically been known as elements. Chemical elements are symbolized by one- or two-letter abbreviations derived from their modern names, or in some cases from their old Latin names.

3.3 ATOMS All matter is composed of tiny particles called atoms, which are themselves composed of smaller particles. An atom has a dense central core, or nucleus, containing positively charged protons and uncharged neutrons. Much lighter, negatively charged electrons occupy a relatively large space around the nucleus.

3.4 CATHODE RAYS: THE ELECTRON When an electrical potential is applied across the two electrodes of a gas-discharge tube, the gas within the tube begins to glow, and if the pressure is low enough cathode rays flow from the negative to the positive electrode. These are now known to be streams of the fundamental, subatomic particles called electrons. The electron is assigned a relative charge of -1.

TOOLS OF CHEMISTRY: ELECTRICITY AND MAGNETISM Like electrical charges repel each other, and opposite charges (+ and −) attract each other. The electrical force that acts between charged particles is the Coulomb force. Charged bodies create an electric field within which other charged bodies are attracted or repelled by a difference in potential, commonly measured in volts. An electric current is a flow of electrons or ions. Substances through which current can flow are conductors; substances that do not conduct electricity are insulators. Any electric current creates a magnetic field and a charged particle moving in a magnetic field experiences a force.

3.5 CANAL RAYS: THE PROTON When electrons flow in a gas-discharge tube they leave behind positively charged ions, which can themselves flow from the positive to the negative electrode in the form of canal rays. The positively charged ions of hydrogen are fundamental, subatomic particles called protons. Protons have the same charge as electrons but with a positive sign (a relative charge of $+1$).

3.6 α-PARTICLE SCATTERING: THE NUCLEUS α-Particles are the nuclei of helium atoms. Some radioactive elements break down spontaneously and emit α-particles at high speeds. When such particles strike a metal foil, some of them are deflected back toward their source. Rutherford concluded from this that the target atoms have a dense, central *nucleus* in which most of their mass and their positive charge are concentrated.

3.7 20 YEARS LATER: THE NEUTRON Atomic nuclei contain protons, but protons do not account for all of their mass. Chadwick discovered the neutron, a subatomic particle found in the nuclei of all atoms except ordinary hydrogen. The mass of the neutron is similar to that of the proton, but the neutron has no electrical charge.

3.8 X-RAY SPECTRA: ATOMIC NUMBER From studies of the x-ray spectra of different elements, Moseley found that the wavelengths produced by each element could be related to a single number corresponding to the number of units of positive charge in its nucleus. This atomic number, Z, is equal to the number of protons in the nucleus.

3.9 ATOMIC NUMBER, ISOTOPES, AND MASS NUMBERS The *mass number* of an element (A) is equal to the number of neutrons (N) and protons (Z) in the nuclei of its atoms ($A = Z + N$). Some elements exist in different forms called isotopes, the atoms of which contain different numbers of neutrons and thus have different mass numbers.

3.10 ATOMIC MASS The *actual mass* of an atom is its mass in grams. The *atomic mass unit* (u), a unit of relative atomic mass, is defined as $\frac{1}{12}$ the mass of an atom of $^{12}_{6}C$, or 1.6606×10^{-24} g. The masses of isotopes are usually given in atomic mass units. The *atomic mass* of an element is the average mass (in u) of the atoms in the naturally occurring mixture of isotopes.

3.11 PURE SUBSTANCES AND MIXTURES Physical properties are those that can be measured or observed without changing the identity or composition of a substance. Chemical properties can only be observed in chemical reactions, in which the identity of at least one substance is changed. A pure substance always has the same physical and chemical properties and is either an element or a compound. An element is a substance that contains only atoms of the same atomic number. (An atom can be defined as the smallest particle of an element that can participate in a chemical reaction.) A chemical compound is a substance in which atoms of two or more elements are combined in a definite ratio. A mixture contains two or more substances that retain their identities. Any homogeneous mixture of two or more substances is a solution. The solute—the component present in the smaller amount—is said to be dissolved in the solvent. In an aqueous solution the solvent is water.

3.12 STATES OF MATTER There are three common states of matter: gaseous, liquid, and solid. Transitions between these are known as changes of state. Not all substances can exist in all three states.

TOOLS OF CHEMISTRY: MASS SPECTROMETER In a mass spectrometer, a beam of positive ions is spread out according to the mass-to-charge ratio of the ions. Mass spectra are used to determine isotopic masses and abundances, molecular masses and structures, and to identify known chemical compounds.

SIGNIFICANT TERMS

electrode
gas-discharge tube
fluorescent
subatomic particle
fundamental particle
electron
cathode rays
Coulomb force
proton
α-particle
nucleus
neutron
spectrum
atomic number
mass number
neutron number
isotopes
deuterium
tritium
actual mass of an atom
atomic mass unit
atomic mass
physical properties
chemical reaction
chemical properties
pure substance
element
atom
chemical compound
mixture
heterogeneous mixture
homogeneous mixture
solution
aqueous solution
solvent
solute
dissolution
states of matter
changes of state
phase

THOUGHTS ON CHEMISTRY

Use and Value of a Theory

COLLEGE CHEMISTRY (in 1901),
by Ira Remsen

The relation of a theory to facts is very simple, but is frequently misunderstood. The relation may be conveniently illustrated by the case under consideration. By a careful investigation of a number of chemical compounds it was shown that in each of them the same elements always occur in the same proportion. This led to the belief that this is true of every chemical compound, and after further investigation which, as far as it went, showed the surmise to be correct, the law of definite proportions (in a pure compound, two or more elements are combined in definite proportions by weight; Au. note) was proposed. This law is simply a statement of what has been found true in all cases examined. It involves no speculation. It is a statement of fact. It may be said that the statement or law must be open to some doubt for the reason that all possible cases have not been examined, and it may not hold true for some of these unexamined cases. The reply to this is that it has been found true in a very large number of cases and in all cases which have been investigated. It is true for the present state of our knowledge, and that is all we can demand of any law. Again, further investigation led to the discovery of the law of multiple proportions (If two elements combine in more than one ratio, the amounts of one element that combine with a given amount of the other are in some simple ratio to each other, 1:2, 1:3, and so on; Au. note), which is also a statement of what has been found true in all cases investigated. It, like the law of definite proportions and in the same sense, is a statement of fact. But having gone thus far, we now ask, what is the explanation of these laws? We know the facts—what is the explanation? By experiment we cannot go beyond these facts, but it is possible to imagine a cause and then proceed to see whether the imagined cause is sufficient to account for the facts. This is what Dalton did. He imagined that matter is made up of atoms of definite weights, and that chemical combination takes place in simple ways between these atoms. This imagined cause is the atomic theory. It is not a statement of anything found by investigation. It is not a statement of an established fact. It may or may not be literally true, but at all events it is the best guess that has ever been made as to the cause of the fundamental laws of chemical action, and it furnishes a very convenient means of interpreting the facts of chemistry. Since the atomic theory was first proposed it has been accepted by nearly all chemists. It has been of great value in suggesting methods of work, and has contributed largely to the advance of chemistry. Any theory which is in accordance with the facts and leads to the discovery of new facts is of value, whether it should eventually prove to be true or false. At the same time a false theory may do much harm, as it may lead men to misinterpret the facts which they observe, and thus retard progress.

Ira Remsen, College Chemistry (New York: Henry Holt & Co, 1901) pp. 99, 100.

QUESTIONS

Atoms and Elements

3.1 Name the element which corresponds to each of the following symbols: (a) Be, (b) B, (c) V, (d) As, (e) Ba.

3.2 Write the symbol for each of the following elements: (a) xenon, (b) nickel, (c) magnesium, (d) cobalt, (e) silicon.

3.3 Select the symbols which are not derived from the modern names of the respective elements: (a) Ac, (b) Cs, (c) Cu, (d) Au, (e) Fe, (f) Mn, (g) Th.

3.4 Write the names of all of the elements which have one-letter symbols.

3.5* Name the element which corresponds to each of the following symbols: (a) Al, (b) At, (c) Ca, (d) Cl, (e) Ir, (f) Re. Look up the origins of the names in a suitable reference such as the *Handbook of Chemistry and Physics* (The Chemical Rubber Co.).

Atomic Structure: Five Classic Experiments

3.6 Prepare a sketch of a gas-discharge tube showing the production of cathode rays.

3.7 Are the cathode rays produced in a gas-discharge tube different for different gases in the tube? What conclusion can be drawn from this fact?

3.8 Describe the experiment in which the charge-to-mass ratio of an electron was determined. Once the charge on an electron was determined, the mass could be calculated. What did the value of the mass prove?

3.9 Prepare a sketch of a gas-discharge tube showing the production of canal rays.

3.10 Are the canal rays produced in a gas-discharge tube different for different gases in the tube? What conclusion can be drawn from this fact?

3.11 Explain how cathode rays and canal rays are produced from atoms in a gas-discharge tube.

3.12 Is an α-particle a subatomic particle? What is the relationship of an α-particle to a helium atom?

3.13 What was the major conclusion drawn from the results of the α-particle scattering experiments?

3.14 Describe the experiment in which the neutron was discovered. How does this subatomic particle fit into Rutherford's concept of a nucleus?

3.15 What property of each element did Moseley use to assign atomic numbers to the elements?

3.16 List and briefly discuss the points of the atomic theory as formulated by John Dalton.

Nuclear Arithmetic

3.17 What information about the nucleus is given by the (a) atomic number, (b) neutron number, and (c) mass number?

PROBLEMS

Nuclear Arithmetic

3.1 How many protons are present in each atom of (a) ^{100}Rh, (b) ^{146}Nd, (c) ^{79}Br, (d) ^{7}Li, and (e) ^{159}Tb?

3.2 How many neutrons are present in each atom listed in Problem 3.1? *Answer* (a) 55, (b) 86, (c) 44, (d) 4, (e) 94

3.3 Calculate the mass number for each of the following isotopes: (a) 74 protons and 106 neutrons, (b) 92 protons and 144 neutrons, (c) 38 protons and 46 neutrons. Write the complete symbol for each isotope.

3.18 What is an isotope? What are the special names given to the isotopes of hydrogen?

3.19 How do we write the symbol for an atom of an element if we wish to specify a particular isotope of that element?

3.20 What does the symbol ^{41}Ca represent?

3.21 Write the symbol for the isotope of iron that has 30 neutrons in the nucleus.

3.22 What instrument is used to determine the relative masses of the isotopes of an element? Will this instrument also indicate the relative abundance of each isotope?

3.23 What is the definition of an atomic mass unit?

3.24 Define "actual mass of an atom." What is the relationship between this term and the relative atomic mass?

Kinds of Matter

3.25 What do we mean by a "pure substance"? Is an element a pure substance? Is a chemical compound a pure substance?

3.26 What is the smallest particle of an element that can participate in a chemical reaction?

3.27 What is a chemical compound? What type of process will separate the elements making up a chemical compound?

3.28 A chemical change has taken place if the identity and composition of at least one substance has been changed by the process. Choose from the following list of processes those that are chemical changes: (a) a nail is magnetized, (b) grape juice is fermented, (c) gasoline is burned, (d) meat is cut, (e) meat is cooked, (f) a cake is baked, (g) a leaf changes color in the autumn, (h) concrete becomes hard, and (i) a balloon is inflated.

3.29 Name the three states of matter. Do all substances exist in all of these states?

Answers to Selected Questions

3.3 (c), (d), (e)

3.15 x-ray spectrum

3.21 ^{56}Fe

3.28 (b), (c), (e), (f), (g), (h)

3.4 Complete the following table for the atoms or ions as illustrated for $^{41}_{20}$Ca^{2+}:

Symbol	Z	N	A	Number of Electrons	Electrical Charge
$^{41}_{20}$Ca^{2+}	20	21	41	18	+2
$^{190}_{78}$Pt					
$^{223}_{87}$Fr					
$^{139}_{53}$I^{-}					
$^{3}_{2}$He^{2+}					

3.5 Complete the following table for the atoms or ions as illustrated for $^{13}_{6}C$:

Symbol	Z	N	A	Number of Electrons	Electrical Charge
$^{13}_{6}C$	6	7	13	6	0
	14	15			0
S		18		18	
			56	24	+2
Au			188	76	

Answer $^{29}_{14}Si$, 29, 14; $^{34}_{16}S^{2-}$, 16, 34, -2; $^{56}_{26}Fe^{2+}$, 26, 30; $^{188}_{79}Au^{3+}$, 79, 109, $+3$

3.6* Choose from the following list the symbols that represent (a) groups of isotopes of the same element, (b) atoms with the same number of neutrons, and (c) atoms with the same mass number (4 different sets): (i) ^{12}N, (ii) ^{13}B, (iii) ^{13}N, (iv) ^{14}C, (v) ^{14}N, (vi) ^{15}N, (vii) ^{16}N, (viii) ^{16}O, (ix) ^{17}N, (x) ^{17}F, and (xi) ^{18}Ne.

Actual Mass

3.7 Calculate the actual mass of an atom for each of the following isotopes: (a) ^{78}Kr, (b) ^{80}Kr, and (c) ^{82}Kr. The respective atomic masses are 77.9204 u, 79.9164 u, and 81.9135 u.

3.8 Calculate the actual mass of an atom of (a) ^{6}Li and (b) ^{7}Li. The respective atomic masses are 6.01512 u and 7.01600 u. *Answer* (a) 9.98850×10^{-24} g, (b) 1.16505×10^{-23} g

3.9 Calculate the atomic mass of (a) ^{151}Eu and (b) ^{153}Eu. The respective actual masses are 2.506119×10^{-22} g and 2.539352×10^{-22} g.

3.10 Calculate the atomic mass of (a) ^{231}Np and (b) ^{233}Np. The respective actual masses are 3.836542×10^{-22} g and 3.869792×10^{-22} g. *Answer* (a) 231.0383 u, (b) 233.0406 u

3.11 Calculate the actual mass of an atom for each of the following: (a) ^{56}Mn, 55.93904 u; (b) ^{56}Fe, 55.9349 u; and (c) ^{56}Co, 55.94002 u. Why is there a difference in the masses even though the mass number is 56 in all three cases?

Average Atomic Mass

3.12 Calculate the average atomic mass for lithium using the following data for the percent of natural abundance and mass of each isotope: 7.5% of ^{6}Li (6.01512 u) and 92.5% of ^{7}Li (7.01600 u).

3.13 Calculate the average atomic mass for magnesium using the following data for the percent of natural abundance and mass of each isotope: 78.99% of ^{24}Mg (23.98504 u), 10.00% of ^{25}Mg (24.98584 u), and 11.01% of ^{26}Mg (25.98259 u).

3.14 Calculate the average atomic mass for strontium using the following data for the percent of natural abundance and mass of each isotope: 0.05% of ^{84}Sr (83.9134 u), 9.9% of ^{86}Sr (85.9094 u), 7.0% of ^{87}Sr (86.9089 u), and 82.6% of ^{88}Sr (87.9056 u) *Answer* 87.6 u

3.15 Only two isotopes of copper are present in naturally occurring copper: ^{63}Cu (62.9298 u) and ^{65}Cu (64.9278 u). Calculate the percent composition of naturally occurring copper using the average atomic mass as 63.546 u.

3.16 The average atomic mass of chlorine is 35.453 u. There are only two isotopes in naturally occurring chlorine: ^{35}Cl (34.96885 u) and ^{37}Cl (36.96712 u). Calculate the percent composition of naturally occurring chlorine. *Answer* 75.77% ^{35}Cl and 24.23% ^{37}Cl

3.17* In a suitable reference such as the Table of Isotopes in the *Handbook of Chemistry and Physics* (The Chemical Rubber Co.), look up the following information for selenium: (a) the total number of known isotopes, (b) the average atomic mass, and (c) the percentage of natural abundance and mass of each of the stable isotopes. (d) Calculate the average atomic mass of selenium.

Additional Problems

3.18 The approximate radius of a neutron is 1.5×10^{-15} m and the mass is 1.675×10^{-27} kg. Calculate the density of a neutron. $V = (4/3)\pi r^3$ for a sphere. *Answer* 1.2×10^{17} kg/m^3 = 1.2×10^{14} g/cm^3

3.19 The approximate radius of a hydrogen atom is 0.058 nm and of a proton is 1.5×10^{-15} m. Assuming both the hydrogen atom and the proton to be spherical, calculate the fraction of the space in an atom of hydrogen that is occupied by the nucleus. $V = (4/3)\pi r^3$ for a sphere.

3.20* Consider the earth to be the proton and the moon to be the electron in a hydrogen atom. The radius of a hydrogen atom is 0.058 nm and the approximate radius of the proton is 1.5×10^{-15} m. (a) If the average radius of the earth is 6371 km, what should the distance between the earth and moon be so that it is in the same proportion as the radius of the hydrogen atom to a proton? (b) The actual value of the average earth–moon distance is 3.8×10^{8} m. How visible would the moon be from the earth if it were at this new distance?

3.21 The following data are measurements of the charges on oil droplets using an apparatus similar to that used by Millikan:

11.215×10^{-19} C	14.423×10^{-19} C
12.811×10^{-19} C	24.037×10^{-19} C
14.419×10^{-19} C	9.621×10^{-19} C
12.815×10^{-19} C	16.012×10^{-19} C

Each of these charges should be some integral multiple of a fundamental charge. (a) Calculate the fundamental charge.

The value of e/m for an electron is 1.76×10^{8} C/g. Using your value of the charge calculated above, (b) calculate the mass of an electron. *Answer* (a) 1.602×10^{-19} C, (b) 9.10×10^{-28} g

CHAPTER 4

Atoms, Molecules, and Ions

Almost every introduction to chemistry at some point uses the mental image of taking matter apart down to smaller and smaller bits. A chemical show that traveled the country was called "Taking Things Apart and Putting Them Together." We seem to seek a sense of order in discovering the building blocks of our universe.

Physicists for years have been taking matter apart down to smaller and smaller pieces. They have an array of particles with delightful names — hadrons, leptons, baryons, and quarks — that have the properties of "strangeness" and "charm." The proliferation of particles in physics is fascinating, if bewildering. Lately, a few theoretical scientists have themselves become frustrated with the diversity of the bits of matter needed by physics to explain the nature of matter and energy. These individuals are also disturbed by the need to call on different theories to explain large-scale and small-scale interactions of matter and energy. Once more a search for greater order is under way — a search for a single subatomic building block that may be present everywhere, in all of matter and in all of space. Only time will tell the outcome of this search.

For the purposes of chemistry, atoms, molecules, and ions are the bits of matter with which we are most often concerned. Many of the chemical and physical properties of the substances that chemists deal with are explained by how these bits of matter are assembled. In chemistry we deal with quantities of substances that we can see and weigh, and we also deal with atoms, molecules, and ions that we cannot directly see or weigh. The most important thing for you to learn from this chapter is how we relate seeable, weighable amounts of chemical compounds to the masses of individual atoms and molecules that cannot be seen or weighed directly.

ATOMS AND IONS IN COMBINATION

4.1 MOLECULAR AND IONIC COMPOUNDS

So far in this book we have briefly mentioned ions and have examined atoms in detail. In this chapter we begin to examine how these species combine. All pure substances, whether they are elements or compounds (Section 3.11), are made of atoms or ions combined in various ways.

a. Molecular compounds When two or more atoms combine chemically they form a molecule. A **molecule** is the smallest particle of a pure substance that has the composition and properties of that substance and is capable of independent existence. Suppose we had a pile of crystalline sulfur. If we could divide the pile enough times, we would eventually wind up with individual sulfur molecules, each containing eight sulfur atoms. We write the formula of this molecule as S_8; the subscript 8 shows that eight sulfur atoms are chemically combined. (How to write chemical formulas is discussed in the next section.) The S_8 molecule is a **polyatomic molecule** — a molecule containing more than two atoms. Any further division of the S_8 molecules would give a substance with different properties from those of ordinary sulfur.

Gaseous oxygen usually exists as a **diatomic molecule** — a molecule made of two atoms. The elements hydrogen, nitrogen, fluorine, chlorine, bromine, iodine, and astatine, like oxygen, occur naturally as diatomic molecules (Table 4.1). A few elements — helium, neon, argon, krypton, xenon, and radon — ordinarily exist as single atoms. (We might think of these as *monatomic* molecules.) Elements other

Table 4.1
Chemical Formulas for Molecules of Elements The subscript gives the number of atoms in a molecule of the element. Other elements exist in large aggregates of atoms not thought of as molecules.

Monatomic Molecules		Diatomic Molecules		Polyatomic Molecules	
He	Helium	H_2	Hydrogen	P_4	Phosphorus
Ne	Neon	O_2	Oxygen	As_4	Arsenic
Ar	Argon	N_2	Nitrogen	Sb_4	Antimony
Kr	Krypton	F_2	Fluorine	S_8	Sulfur
Xe	Xenon	Cl_2	Chlorine	Se_8	Selenium
Rn	Radon	Br_2	Bromine		
		I_2	Iodine		
		At_2	Astatine		

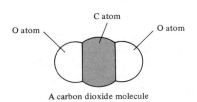

A carbon dioxide molecule

A block of dry ice

Figure 4.1
Carbon Dioxide, a Molecular Compound Dry ice is frozen carbon dioxide.

than those listed in Table 4.1 usually are made up of large aggregates of atoms, and these aggregates are *not* thought of as "molecules."

When one atom of element A combines with one atom of element B, they form a molecule of a compound, written AB, or A—B. Molecules may contain from two atoms to thousands of atoms. There are giant molecules such as that of chlorophyll *a*, a natural compound that traps solar energy in green plants. One chlorophyll *a* molecule is made of 137 atoms of the elements carbon, hydrogen, nitrogen, oxygen, and magnesium. And there are **polymers**—very large molecules formed by linking together smaller molecules. Polymer molecules may contain many thousands of atoms.

The line drawn between A and B, A—B, represents a chemical bond. Until we give a more formal definition later (Chapter 9), simply think of the chemical bond as the force that holds the atoms together.

We speak of chemical compounds composed of molecules as "molecular compounds." Water is a molecular compound. Each water molecule is formed from two hydrogen atoms and one oxygen atom to give H_2O (a triatomic molecule). Carbon dioxide is also a molecular compound. Each carbon dioxide molecule is formed from two oxygen atoms and one carbon atom. A block of *dry ice,* which is solid carbon dioxide, contains *only* carbon dioxide molecules CO_2 (also a triatomic molecule; Figure 4.1).

b. Ionic compounds We first encountered ions as they were formed from gaseous atoms in gas-discharge tubes (Section 3.5). **Ions** are positively or negatively charged atoms or groups of atoms, each formed by the loss or gain of one or more electrons. Positively charged ions are called **cations,** and negatively charged ions are called **anions.** For example, a sodium cation, represented by Na^+, is formed from a sodium atom by the loss of one electron and thus has a single positive charge. A barium cation, Ba^{2+}, is formed from a barium atom by the loss of two electrons and therefore has twice the positive charge of a sodium ion. A chlorine atom gains one electron to form Cl^-, the chloride anion, and an oxygen atom gains two electrons to form the negatively charged oxide anion, O^{2-}.

The existence of ions in the gas phase is very brief. Ions occur most commonly in solid ionic compounds or in the aqueous solutions of such compounds. Table 4.2 lists some of the common cations and anions formed by single atoms of elements (*monatomic* ions). The types of ions formed is a characteristic property of each element. Some elements form no stable ions, some form only one, and some form ions of two different charges (see Table 4.2).

We call a chemical compound composed of ions an "ionic compound." Positive and negative ions combine in ionic compounds in sufficient numbers so that electrical neutrality is maintained—the total positive charge equals the total negative charge. This means, for example, that in an ionic compound there is one Na^+ ion

Table 4.2
Some Monatomic Ions

H^+	Bi^{3+}
Li^+	Cr^{2+}, Cr^{3+}
Na^+	Co^{2+}, Co^{3+}
K^+	Mn^{2+}, Mn^{3+}
Cu^+, Cu^{2+}	Sn^{2+}
Ag^+	Pb^{2+}
Mg^{2+}	F^-
Ca^{2+}	Cl^-
Ba^{2+}	Br^-
Zn^{2+}	I^-
Cd^{2+}	O^{2-}
Hg^{2+*}	S^{2-}
Fe^{2+}, Fe^{3+}	N^{3-}
Al^{3+}	P^{3-}

* Mercury (Hg) also forms an unusual diatomic ion, Hg_2^{2+}.

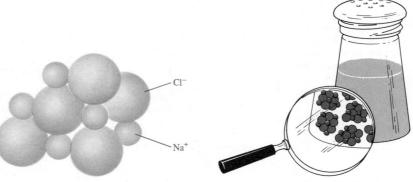

Figure 4.2
Sodium Chloride, an Ionic Compound

A portion of a crystal of NaCl

A salt shaker filled with NaCl crystals

for every one Cl^- ion, or one Ba^{2+} ion for every two Cl^- ions. The resulting ionic compounds are sodium chloride (NaCl) and barium chloride ($BaCl_2$). Most ionic compounds are crystalline solids like sodium chloride, which is table salt. A solid ionic compound is a collection of ions held together by the mutual attraction of positive and negative charges. Independent molecules of NaCl and other ionic compounds do not ordinarily exist. A salt shaker holding pure table salt contains *only* crystals in each of which sodium and chloride ions are combined in a 1-to-1 ratio (Figure 4.2).

+ ions are cations
– ions are anions

In summary, a few elements (e.g., He, Ne, and Ar) are monatomic—their atoms exist independently. A few other elements form diatomic or polyatomic molecules (e.g., O_2, Cl_2, or S_8). In combination, atoms of different elements form molecules that range from simple to very large and complex. The types of ions formed is a characteristic property of each element. Ions combine in ratios that maintain charge neutrality, but truly ionic compounds do not contain any individual molecules. Pure substances are elements or are chemical compounds composed of molecules and ions combined in various ways. (It would be very useful for you to memorize the chemical formulas for the molecules of elements, Table 4.1, and the common monatomic ions, Table 4.2.)

4.2 FORMULAS FOR CHEMICAL COMPOUNDS

Chemical compounds are symbolized by chemical formulas. A **chemical formula** gives the symbols for the elements combined, with subscripts indicating how many atoms of each element are included. As mentioned above, one atom of carbon combined with two atoms of oxygen gives carbon dioxide, which has the formula CO_2. The chemical formula of a molecular compound can be used to represent one molecule of the compound ("a CO_2 molecule") or many molecules of the compound ("25 g of CO_2"). The chemical formulas of a few simple compounds are given in Table 4.3. The correct chemical formula of a compound can be found only by experiment.

As explained in the preceding section, ionic compounds do not consist of separate molecules; they consist of very large numbers of ions mutually attracted to each other. Formulas for these substances represent only the *ratios* in which the ions are combined. For example, the formula $BaCl_2$ indicates that in this substance, barium and chloride ions are present in the ratio 1 : 2. The term **formula unit** refers to the simplest unit indicated by the formula of a nonmolecular compound. For $BaCl_2$, one formula unit is one barium ion plus two chloride ions. From observations of the properties of this ionic compound, it is known that $BaCl_2$ molecules are not present—but we cannot tell this from the formula.

Table 4.3
Chemical Formulas for Some Simple Compounds

Water	H_2O
Carbon monoxide	CO
Carbon dioxide	CO_2
Sulfur dioxide	SO_2
Silver sulfide	Ag_2S
Potassium chloride	KCl
Ammonia	NH_3
Methane	CH_4

Table 4.4
Polyatomic Ions These are some of the more common polyatomic ions.

NH_4^+	Ammonium ion
CN^-	Cyanide ion
CO_3^{2-}	Carbonate ion
ClO_3^-	Chlorate ion
ClO_4^-	Perchlorate ion
CrO_4^{2-}	Chromate ion
$Cr_2O_7^{2-}$	Dichromate ion
MnO_4^-	Permanganate ion
NO_2^-	Nitrite ion
NO_3^-	Nitrate ion
O_2^{2-}	Peroxide ion
OH^-	Hydroxide ion
PO_4^{3-}	Phosphate ion
SO_3^{2-}	Sulfite ion
SO_4^{2-}	Sulfate ion
CH_3COO^-	Acetate ion

Chemical formulas are used to represent ions as well as neutral compounds. For example, one sulfur atom and four oxygen atoms form an ion with a charge of -2, the sulfate ion, SO_4^{2-}. Ions that incorporate more than one atom are called **polyatomic ions**. Table 4.4 lists the formulas and names of some of the common polyatomic ions, most of which are anions, that is, they are negatively charged. (Memorizing these names and formulas will be *very* helpful.)

Like the monatomic anions, polyatomic anions also combine with cations to give ionic compounds in which electrical neutrality is maintained. Here are the formulas of some of the many compounds that are formed between the cations of Table 4.2 and the polyatomic anions of Table 4.4.

read "N-A-oh-H"
Na^+OH^-
1 Na⁺ plus 1 OH⁻

read "C-U-two-S-oh-four"
$Cu^+_2SO_4^{2-}$
2 Cu⁺ plus 1 SO₄²⁻

read "M-G-N-oh-three-taken twice"
$Mg^{2+}(NO_3^-)_2$
parentheses to avoid confusion about what is taken twice

Note that when a formula includes more than one polyatomic ion, parentheses are placed around the formula of that ion.

Remember that the total positive charge must equal the total negative charge. Determining how many ions of each charge must combine is obvious when the charges are equal or when one is two or three times the other. For example, Ca^{2+} plus F^-, Ca^{2+} plus SO_4^{2-}, and Na^+ and PO_4^{3-} obviously give $Ca^{2+}(F^-)_2$, $Ca^{2+}SO_4^{2-}$, and $(Na^+)_3PO_4^{3-}$. In other cases, a number of positive ions equal to the charge on the negative ion and a number of negative ions equal to the charge on the positive ion often gives a correct formula. For example, Al^{3+} plus SO_4^{2-} gives $(Al^{3+})_2(SO_4^{2-})_3$ and Sn^{2+} plus PO_4^{3-} gives $(Sn^{2+})_3(PO_4^{3-})_2$. To check for charge balance, multiply the subscript times the charge on each ion:

total + charge of
$2 \times (+3) = +6$
$(Al^{3+})_2(SO_4^{2-})_3$
total − charge of
$3 \times (-2) = -6$

total + charge of
$3 \times (+2) = +6$
$(Sn^{2+})_3(PO_4^{3-})_2$
total − charge of
$2 \times (-3) = -6$

The charges of ions are not ordinarily included in formulas. The formulas for the compounds described above would normally be written as follows:

$NaOH$ Cu_2SO_4 $Mg(NO_3)_2$ $Al_2(SO_4)_3$ $Sn_3(PO_4)_2$

EXAMPLE 4.1
Chemical Formulas

The compound $Cr_3(SO_4)_2$ is used in manufacturing metal alloys, dyes, and inks. What elements make up this compound? What is the ratio of the atoms of the different elements in this compound?

The formula tells us that this compound is composed of three elements—chromium, sulfur, and oxygen. There are three chromium atoms. The two sulfate groups contain two sulfur atoms. Multiplying the two subscripts gives the number of oxygen atoms, $2 \times 4 = 8$. There are eight oxygen atoms. Any amount of this compound will contain chromium, sulfur, and oxygen atoms in the ratio 3 Cr : 2 S : 8 O.

Exercise Malachite, $Cu_2(CO_3)(OH)_2$, is a common copper mineral. Name the elements in this mineral and give the ratio of the atoms of the different elements. *Answer* Copper, carbon, oxygen, hydrogen; $2\,Cu:1\,C:5\,O:2\,H$

EXAMPLE 4.2
Formulas for Ionic Compounds

Write the formulas for the 12 compounds that might form between the cations Na^+, Zn^{2+}, Al^{3+}, and Th^{4+}, and the anions Cl^-, CO_3^{2-}, and PO_4^{3-}.

The total positive charge in each case must be equal to the total negative charge. For example, for Zn^{2+} with Cl^-

$$\text{total positive charge} = (1)(+2) = +2 \quad Zn^{2+}$$
$$\text{total negative charge} = (2)(-1) = -2 \quad Cl^-, Cl^- \quad \Big\} \quad ZnCl_2$$

The formulas for simple ionic compounds are easily checked by remembering that the subscript on the positive ion times the charge on the positive ion must equal the subscript on the negative ion times the charge on the negative ion.

	Cl^-	CO_3^{2-}	PO_4^{3-}
Na^+	NaCl	Na_2CO_3	Na_3PO_4
Zn^{2+}	$ZnCl_2$	$ZnCO_3$	$Zn_3(PO_4)_2$
Al^{3+}	$AlCl_3$	$Al_2(CO_3)_3$	$AlPO_4$
Th^{4+}	$ThCl_4$	$Th(CO_3)_2$	$Th_3(PO_4)_4$

Note that, except for $ZnCO_3$, $Th(CO_3)_2$, and $AlPO_4$, the number of positive ions equals the charge on the negative ions and vice versa.

Exercise Write the formulas for the six compounds that can form between the cations NH_4^+, Ca^{2+}, and Fe^{3+}, and the anions NO_3^- and SO_4^{2-}. *Answer* NH_4NO_3, $(NH_4)_2SO_4$, $Ca(NO_3)_2$, $CaSO_4$, $Fe(NO_3)_3$, $Fe_2(SO_4)_3$

Sometimes, for molecules or polyatomic ions, we write "structural" formulas in which the symbols for the elements are arranged on the page so that they give information about how the atoms are connected together. For example, instead of SO_4^{2-} and NH_3 we can write

$$\left[\begin{array}{c} O \\ | \\ O-S-O \\ | \\ O \end{array}\right]^{2-} \quad \text{and} \quad \begin{array}{c} H \quad\quad H \\ \diagdown N \diagup \\ | \\ H \end{array}$$

Ethyl alcohol contains two C atoms, six H atoms, and one O atom. Instead of C_2H_6O, the formula is frequently written as either C_2H_5OH (which shows that the C_2H_5 forms a "group" of atoms and so does the OH) or as CH_3CH_2OH (which shows that an OH group is attached to a CH_2 group, which is attached to a CH_3 group). A further expansion of the formula for ethyl alcohol is

$$\begin{array}{c} H \quad H \\ | \quad | \\ H-C-C-O-H \\ | \quad | \\ H \quad H \end{array}$$

Obviously, we are going to encounter many more formulas. Here we just want to mention one additional common practice that applies to compounds in which

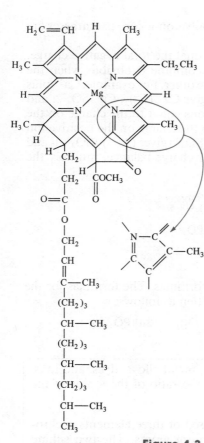

Figure 4.3
The Structure of Chlorophyll *a*, $C_{55}H_{72}MgN_4O_5$ Carbon atoms occur at each unlabeled corner in the rings, as shown in the insert.

carbon atoms form rings. Often just the ring, and not the symbols for the atoms, is used. For example, a five-carbon-atom ring compound is C_5H_{10} and is written as

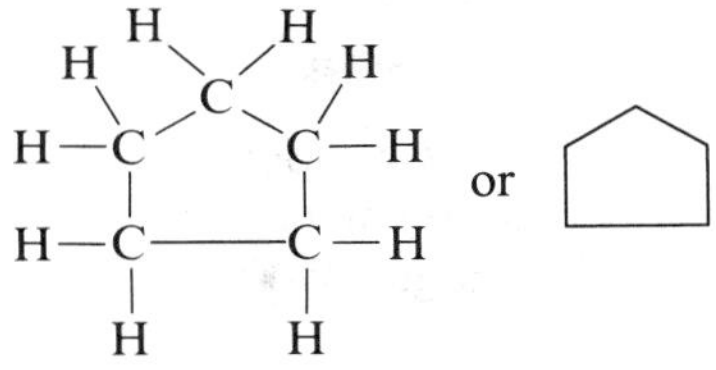

When a double line appears in such a ring, it indicates a carbon-to-carbon double bond.

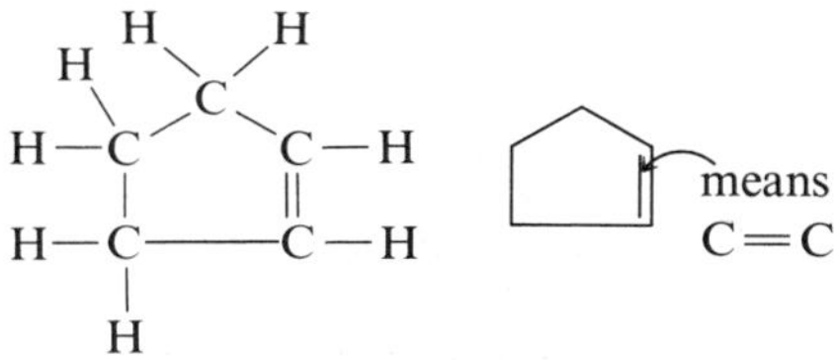

(Double bonds are discussed in Section 9.12.) The structural formula for chlorophyll *a*, shown in Figure 4.3, includes such rings. A carbon atom and whatever hydrogen atoms are attached to it are assumed to be present at each corner.

4.3 NAMING CHEMICAL COMPOUNDS

Ideally, every chemical compound should have a unique name. For simple ionic compounds and relatively small molecules, this requirement is not difficult to fulfill. But when large molecules have to be named, or when there are several molecules that differ only slightly, the situation becomes complicated. **Chemical nomenclature** is the collective term for the rules and regulations that govern naming chemical compounds. The nomenclature of some simple types of compounds is discussed in the following sections.

a. Simple cations Simple cations are formed by the removal of one or more electrons from an atom. The Stock system of nomenclature is recommended for naming simple cations. (The International Union of Pure and Applied Chemistry, IUPAC, sets standards for nomenclature.) In the Stock system, the name of a cation consists of (1) the name of the element, (2) the charge on the ion given inside parentheses as a Roman numeral, and (3) the word "ion." For example,

Cr^{2+}	chromium(II) ion	Fe^{2+}	iron(II) ion
Cr^{3+}	chromium(III) ion	Fe^{3+}	iron(III) ion

For elements that form only one cation (see Table 4.2), the Roman numeral is omitted. Also, the 1 is not written in the superscript for ions of $+1$ (or -1) charge, for example,

H^+ hydrogen ion Na^+ sodium ion

EXAMPLE 4.3
Chemical Nomenclature —
Simple Cations

(a) Name the simple cations K^+ and Cr^{2+}. (b) Write the symbols for tin(IV) ion and nickel(II) ion.

(a) K is the symbol for potassium and, as shown in Table 4.2, potassium commonly forms only one ion, so K^+ is named the potassium ion. Cr is the symbol for chromium, the Roman numeral for a $+2$ charge is II, so Cr^{2+} is called the chromium(II) ion.

(b) The symbols for tin and nickel are Sn and Ni. These ions are written Sn^{4+} and Ni^{2+}.

Exercise (a) Name the simple cations Cr^{3+} and Sc^{3+}. (b) Write the symbols for the cesium ion and the lead ion. *Answer* (a) chromium(III) ion, scandium(III) ion; (b) Cs^+, Pb^{2+}

An older system of naming cations uses word endings instead of numerals. The cation with the lower charge has the suffix "ous" and the cation with the higher charge has the suffix "ic" following the stem of the name of the element.

	Older System	Stock System
Mn^{2+}	**Manganous ion**	**Manganese(II) ion**
Mn^{3+}	**Manganic ion**	**Manganese(III) ion**
Cu^+	**Cuprous ion**	**Copper(I) ion**
Cu^{2+}	**Cupric ion**	**Copper(II) ion**

Frequently, the ancient name of the metal is used as the root in this system, as, for example, in cuprous and cupric, which are based on "cuprum." Although you may encounter this older system for naming cations, the Stock system is now preferred and its use is encouraged.

b. Simple anions Simple anions are formed by the addition of one or more electrons to an atom. Such anions are named by writing (1) the name of the element modified by (2) the ending "ide," followed by (3) the word "ion." Most elements form only one anion and it is not necessary to include the charge in the name. Some examples of simple anions are

Cl^-	chloride ion	O^{2-}	oxide ion	N^{3-}	nitride ion
	(from chlorine)		*(from oxygen)*		*(from nitrogen)*

A few ions have unique names, such as

$$N_3^- \text{ azide ion} \qquad O_2^{2-} \text{ peroxide ion}$$

EXAMPLE 4.4
Chemical Nomenclature —
Simple Anions

(a) Name the anions Te^{2-} and P^{3-}. (b) Write the symbols for the astatide anion, which has a charge of -1, and the sulfide ion, which has a charge of -2.

(a) Te is the symbol for tellurium. Dropping the "ium" and modifying the name with the ending "ide" gives the name "telluride ion" for Te^{2-}. P is the symbol for phosphorus, and P^{3-} is therefore the phosphide ion.
(b) The name "astatide" is derived from the element "astatine," which has the symbol At, so the astatide ion is written At^-. The sulfide ion is derived from the element sulfur and it is written S^{2-}.

Exercise (a) Name the anions F^- and O^{2-}. (b) Write the symbols for the iodide ion, which has a charge of -1, and the nitride ion, which has a charge of -3. *Answer* (a) fluoride ion, oxide ion; (b) I^-, N^{3-}

---

c. Ionic compounds A **binary compound** is a compound that contains atoms or ions of only two elements. A binary compound formed by two ions is named by giving the cation name first, followed by the anion name. The word "ion" does not appear in the name of the compound. For example, these are a few of the many compounds formed between the cations and anions of Table 4.2:

CuCl	copper(I) chloride	Na_3P	sodium phosphide

$CuCl_2$	copper(II) chloride	NaN_3	sodium azide
NaF	sodium fluoride	FeO	iron(II) oxide
Al_2O_3	aluminum oxide	Fe_2O_3	iron(III) oxide

With the older system of naming cations by word endings, names such as the following were used:

CuCl	cuprous chloride	MnF_2	manganous fluoride
$CuCl_2$	cupric chloride	MnF_3	manganic fluoride

Compounds of polyatomic ions are also named by giving the cation name followed by the anion name. For example,

Cu_2SO_4	copper(I) sulfate	$Al_2(SO_4)_3$	aluminum sulfate
$Mg(NO_3)_2$	magnesium nitrate	$ZnCO_3$	zinc carbonate

EXAMPLE 4.5
Chemical Nomenclature — Ionic Compounds

(a) Write the formulas for the following compounds: (i) iron(III) bromide, (ii) calcium phosphide, (iii) calcium permanganate. (b) Name the following compounds: (iv) CaI_2, (v) FeO, (vi) $(NH_4)_2SO_4$, (vii) $K_2Cr_2O_7$.

(a) There are two steps to writing the formulas: (1) Identify the symbols for the ions and the charges of the ions (check Tables 4.2 and 4.4) and (2) combine the ions into a formula based on electrical neutrality (see Example 4.2).
   (i) Fe^{3+} and Br^- give $FeBr_3$
   (ii) Ca^{2+} and P^{3-} give Ca_3P_2
   (iii) Ca^{2+} and MnO_4^- give $Ca(MnO_4)_2$
(b) (iv) Calcium forms *only* an ion with a $+2$ charge (see Table 4.2) and CaI_2 is therefore named calcium iodide.
   (v)   The iron in FeO obviously has a $+2$ charge, since oxygen has a -2 charge. The compound is named iron(II) oxide. (Iron also forms Fe^{3+}.)
   (vi) $(NH_4)_2SO_4$ is simply named ammonium sulfate.
   (vii) Potassium forms only one ion and $K_2Cr_2O_7$ is therefore named potassium dichromate.

Exercise (a) Write the formulas for potassium nitride and strontium carbonate. (b) Name the compounds that have the formulas $Na(CH_3COO)$ and $NiCl_2$
Answer (a) K_3N, $SrCO_3$; (b) sodium acetate, nickel(II) chloride

d. Acids and bases At this point you should become familiar with the names of the common acids and bases. Acids and bases are chemical compounds that are often used in the laboratory and they are mentioned in many of the following chapters. The common acids, some of which are listed in Table 4.5, all contain hydrogen and when dissolved in water give solutions that contain hydrogen ions (H^+) and anions. The common bases all contain OH^- ions and dissolve to give these ions plus cations. The two most common bases are sodium hydroxide, NaOH, and potassium hydroxide, KOH.

The anions formed when the common acids are dissolved in water include many of the simple anions and the polyatomic anions listed in Tables 4.2 and 4.4. In addition, in some cases anions that contain hydrogen are also formed. For example, H_2SO_4 can yield both SO_4^{2-} (sulfate ion) and HSO_4^-. Anions that include hydrogen are named by using either the word "hydrogen" or, in some cases, the prefix "bi" as follows:

HSO_4^-	hydrogen sulfate ion *or* bisulfate ion
HCO_3^-	hydrogen carbonate ion *or* bicarbonate ion

Acid		Anion	
Hydrochloric acid	HCl (*aq*)	Chloride ion	Cl^-
Carbonic acid	H_2CO_3 (*aq*)	Carbonate ion	CO_3^{2-}
		Hydrogen carbonate ion	HCO_3^-
Nitric acid	HNO_3	Nitrate ion	NO_3^-
Nitrous acid	HNO_2 (*aq*)	Nitrite ion	NO_2^-
Perchloric acid	$HClO_4$	Perchlorate ion	ClO_4^-
Phosphoric acid	H_3PO_4	Phosphate ion	PO_4^{3-}
		Hydrogen phosphate ion	HPO_4^{2-}
		Dihydrogen phosphate ion	$H_2PO_4^-$
Phosphorous acid	H_3PO_3	Hydrogen phosphite ion	HPO_3^{2-}
Sulfuric acid	H_2SO_4	Sulfate ion	SO_4^{2-}
		Hydrogen sulfate ion	HSO_4^-
Sulfurous acid	H_2SO_3 (*aq*)	Sulfite ion	SO_3^{2-}
		Hydrogen sulfite ion	HSO_3^-

Ionic compounds formed between cations (except H^+) and the anions of acids are called **salts.** For example, KCl, Na_2SO_4, $Mg_3(PO_4)_2$, and $NaHSO_4$ are all referred to as salts. (In addition, a few types of ionic compounds containing anions for which there are no acids, such as the nitride or phosphide anions, are also thought of as salts.)

Table 4.6
Multiplying Prefixes

Number Indicated	Prefix
1	mono
2	di
3	tri
4	tetra
5	penta
6	hexa
7	hepta
8	octa
9	nona
10	deca

e. Binary molecular compounds The classical system for naming binary molecular compounds is based on the prefixes listed in Table 4.6. The appropriate prefix is placed before the name of the first element in the compound. For example, for N_2O_3 the first part of the name is *di*nitrogen, showing that there are two nitrogen atoms. The second part of the name consists of the appropriate prefix before the name of the second element, which has been modified by adding "ide." For N_2O_3 this would be *tri*oxide, showing that there are three oxygen atoms. Thus, the complete name of N_2O_3 is dinitrogen trioxide.

The prefix "mono" for one atom of an element in a compound is usually omitted, except where there is more than one compound formed between the two elements.

Following are some additional examples of the names of binary molecular compounds:

N_2O	dinitrogen monoxide	ICl	iodine monochloride	SO_2	sulfur dioxide
N_2O_5	dinitrogen pentoxide	ICl_3	iodine trichloride	SO_3	sulfur trioxide

EXAMPLE 4.6
Chemical Nomenclature—Binary Molecular Compounds

(a) Write the formulas for phosphorus triiodide and oxygen difluoride. (b) Write names for BrF_3, S_2O_7, and S_2Br_2.

(a) The formula of each compound consists of the symbols for the elements in the compound, each with a subscript corresponding to the prefix. Phosphorus triiodide is PI_3. Oxygen difluoride is OF_2.

(b) The name of each of these compounds consists of (1) the name of the first element given in the formula modified with a prefix identifying the number of atoms of this element present in the molecule and (2) the name of the second element modified with both a similar prefix and the ending "ide." BrF_3 is named bromine trifluoride because the prefix "mono" is usually not used. S_2O_7 is named disulfur heptoxide. S_2Br_2 is named disulfur dibromide.

Exercise (a) Write the formulas for dialuminum hexachloride and iodine tri-fluoride. (b) Write names for IF_7 and P_4O_{10}. *Answer* (a) Al_2Cl_6, IF_3; (b) iodine heptafluoride, tetraphosphorus decaoxide

4.4 CHEMICAL EQUATIONS

Substances that undergo chemical reactions may be composed of atoms, molecules, or ions. They may be in the gaseous, liquid, or solid states, or in solution. The substances that are changed in a reaction are called the **reactants.** The substances that are produced in a chemical reaction are called the **products.**

Chemical equations are the sentences of the symbolic language of chemistry. A **chemical equation** represents with symbols and formulas the total chemical change that occurs in a chemical reaction. The chemical reaction between the elements phosphorus and chlorine to form the binary compound phosphorus trichloride is represented by the following balanced equation:

$$P_4 + 6Cl_2 \longrightarrow 4PCl_3 \qquad \qquad \textbf{(4.1)}$$
a balanced equation

The arrow means "yields," and so Equation (4.1) can be read as

$$P_4 \quad + \quad 6Cl_2 \quad \longrightarrow \quad 4PCl_3$$
Phosphorus plus chlorine   yields   phosphorus trichloride

or as

$$P_4 \quad + \quad 6Cl_2 \quad \longrightarrow \quad 4PCl_3$$
One P_4 plus   six Cl_2 yields   four molecules
molecule   molecules   of PCl_3

It would be incorrect to write

$$P_4 + Cl_2 \longrightarrow PCl_3$$
an incorrect equation—
not balanced

because this equation is not balanced, that is, the numbers of atoms of phosphorus and chlorine on the two sides of the arrow are different. When the coefficients "6" for Cl_2 and "4" for PCl_3 are added, Equation (4.1) shows 4 P atoms and 12 Cl atoms on each side of the arrow. All chemical equations must be balanced—the number of atoms of each kind must be the same in the products and in the reactants. There is a reason for this—it is what we call the law of conservation of mass, or matter: In ordinary chemical reactions it can be assumed that matter is neither created nor destroyed. This law means that all of the atoms that we start with in an ordinary chemical reaction, however their arrangements or combinations are changed, must still be present when the reaction is finished. (How to balance chemical equations is discussed in Section 6.2.)

The general scheme for writing any chemical equation is

$$\text{reactant}_1 + \text{reactant}_2 + \text{reactant}_3 + \cdots \longrightarrow$$
$$\text{product}_1 + \text{product}_2 + \text{product}_3 + \cdots \quad \textbf{(4.2)}$$

There may be only one reactant or only one product, or there may be several substances as both products and reactants.

Information about the physical state of the reactants and products or about some of the conditions under which a reaction occurs is often added to chemical equations. The states of the substances involved are indicated by placing after the formulas the symbols g for gas, l for liquid, and s for solid, in parentheses (Table 4.7). These designations refer to the states of the pure substances *under the conditions of the*

Table 4.7
Symbols for the States of Reactants and Products

(s)	Solid
(l)	Liquid
(g)	Gas
(aq)	Aqueous solution

reaction. The symbol (*aq*) is used for substances in aqueous solution. For example,

$$3Ca(s) \quad + \quad N_2(g) \quad \longrightarrow \quad Ca_3N_2(s) \qquad \textbf{(4.3)}$$
Solid calcium plus gaseous nitrogen yields solid calcium nitride

$$HCl(aq) \quad + \quad NaOH(aq) \quad \longrightarrow \quad NaCl(aq) \quad + \quad H_2O(l) \textbf{ (4.4)}$$
An aqueous solution of hydrogen chloride plus *an aqueous solution of sodium hydroxide* yields *an aqueous solution of sodium chloride* plus *liquid water*

The capital Greek letter delta, Δ, is often placed over the arrow to indicate that heat has been found necessary to make a reaction take place, for example,

$$CaCO_3(s) \quad \xrightarrow{\Delta} \quad CaO(s) \quad + \quad CO_2(g) \qquad \textbf{(4.5)}$$
Solid calcium carbonate *when heated yields* *solid calcium oxide* plus *gaseous carbon dioxide*

The exact temperature required, as well as the pressure, might be written over the arrow instead, as in the following equation for the industrial preparation of methyl alcohol. (This type of information is derived from experiments. It is not information that you would ever be expected to predict.)

$$CO(g) \quad + \quad 2H_2(g) \quad \xrightarrow{350\,°C,\ 200-300\ atm} \quad CH_3OH(g) \qquad \textbf{(4.6)}$$
Gaseous carbon monoxide plus *gaseous hydrogen* *when heated to 350 °C at pressure of 200 to 300 atm yield* *gaseous methyl alcohol*

This reaction occurs more easily, as do many reactions, in the presence of a **catalyst** — a substance that increases the rate of a reaction, but can be recovered chemically unchanged after the reaction is finished. For reaction (4.6) the catalyst is a mixture of zinc and chromium oxides, and this information can also be placed over the arrow.

$$CO(g) + 2H_2(g) \xrightarrow[\mathrm{ZnO-Cr_2O_3}]{350\,°C,\ 200-300\ atm} CH_3OH(g) \qquad \textbf{(4.7)}$$

Equations are sometimes used to represent the dissolution of a substance in water or another solvent. The presence of solvent can be indicated by writing its formula or name over the arrow.

$$CH_3OH(l) \quad \xrightarrow{H_2O} \quad CH_3OH(aq)$$
methyl alcohol *methyl alcohol in aqueous solution*

The ions in ionic compounds separate from each other in aqueous solutions. In a solution of sodium chloride in water, for example, the presence of separated positive and negative ions is indicated as follows:

$$NaCl(s) \quad \xrightarrow{H_2O} \quad Na^+(aq) \quad + \quad Cl^-(aq) \qquad \textbf{(4.8)}$$
solid sodium chloride *sodium ion in aqueous solution* *chloride ion in aqueous solution*

The **dissociation of an ionic compound** is the transformation of a neutral ionic compound into positive and negative ions, usually by dissolution in water. The term **ionization** is reserved for the formation of ions from a molecular compound or from atoms. For example, ionization occurs when hydrogen chloride, a gas, is dissolved in water to give hydrogen ions and chloride ions.

$$HCl(g) \quad \xrightarrow{H_2O} \quad H^+(aq) + Cl^-(aq) \qquad \textbf{(4.9)}$$
hydrogen chloride *hydrochloric acid*

The solution of hydrogen chloride in water is hydrochloric acid.

EXAMPLE 4.7
Interpreting Chemical Equations

Write a sentence describing in words the chemical reaction represented by the following chemical equation:

$$N_2(g) + 3H_2(g) \xrightarrow[\text{FeO}]{400\ °C,\ 250\ atm} 2NH_3(g)$$

The required description is produced simply by reading the chemical equation from left to right: Gaseous nitrogen reacts with gaseous hydrogen at 400 °C and 250 atm pressure in the presence of FeO as a catalyst to produce gaseous ammonia.

Exercise Write a sentence describing in words the chemical reaction represented by the following chemical equation:

$$(NH_4)_2Cr_2O_7(s) \xrightarrow{\Delta} N_2(g) + Cr_2O_3(s) + 4H_2O(g)$$

Answer Solid ammonium dichromate, when heated, reacts to yield gaseous nitrogen, solid chromium(III) oxide, and steam.

ATOMIC, MOLECULAR, AND MOLAR MASS RELATIONSHIPS

Quantities of substances are dealt with on two levels in chemistry. At times we are concerned with, for example, an individual molecule, or what happens when a few molecules interact with each other. This is sometimes referred to as the *microscopic level*. At other times, we are concerned with the *macroscopic* level — with substances that can be seen and weighed, for example, 30 g of sulfuric acid in a laboratory or a tankcar full of sulfuric acid in an industrial plant.

In Section 4.5 we explain how to find the masses of chemical compounds on the atomic mass scale. The rest of this chapter is devoted to the relationships between the masses of atoms, molecules, and ions (the "micro" level) and the amounts of substances that can be seen and weighed (the "macro" level).

4.5 MOLECULAR MASS

The **molecular mass** (or molecular weight) of a chemical compound is the sum of the atomic masses, in atomic mass units, of the total number of atoms in the formula of the compound. To calculate molecular masses, we must know the correct formula of the compound and the atomic mass of each element in the compound. We use "molecular mass" for all types of chemical compounds or ions, whether molecules are actually present or not. In the case of an ionic compound, the term refers to the sum of the atomic masses in one *formula unit*.

EXAMPLE 4.8
Molecular Mass

Calculate the molecular masses of (a) N_2O_5 and (b) SO_4^{2-}.

Find the molecular mass of each substance by adding the atomic masses of the elements in the substance. The values of the atomic masses are taken from the tables inside the front or back covers of this book. For most calculations, we need only consider the atomic and molecular masses to the nearest 0.01 u (u represents atomic mass units; Section 3.10).

(a) N_2O_5 contains two N atoms and five O atoms, thus

	number of atoms	atomic mass (u/atom)	mass (u)
N	2	× 14.01	= 28.02
O	5	× 16.00	= 80.00
molecular mass of N_2O_5			= 108.02 u

(b) SO_4^{2-} contains on S atom and four O atoms, thus

	number of atoms	atomic mass (u/atom)	mass (u)
S	1	× 32.06	= 32.06
O	4	× 16.00	= 64.00
molecular mass of SO_4^{2-}			= 96.06 u

Note that the mass contribution of the additional two electrons on the ion is not considered in this calculation. These electrons would only contribute an additional 0.001 u, which is negligible. Likewise, the masses of electrons lost in forming a cation are not subtracted from the molecular mass.

Exercise Calculate the molecular mass of KBH_4. *Answer* 53.95 u

4.6 AVOGADRO'S NUMBER, THE MOLE, AND MOLAR MASS

How do we relate visible, weighable masses of matter to the number and masses of the individual atoms and molecules that are present? How much of a reactant must be weighed out to produce a given amount of a product? The chemical equation shows the relative numbers of atoms or molecules needed. But we cannot see or count individual atoms or molecules to get the correct number.

Three quantities are at the heart of the matter in the relationship between weighable masses on the one hand, and the number and masses of the atoms and molecules present, on the other. We define these quantities here so that you can see how they are related to each other. We discuss each of them separately in the following sections. The three quantities are Avogadro's number, the mole, and the molar mass.

> **Avogadro's number** is the number of atoms in exactly 12 g of carbon-12.
>
> The **mole** is a number of anything equal to Avogadro's number.
>
> The **molar mass** of a substance is the mass in grams of one mole of that substance.

You will see that the mole provides the connection between the microscopic and the macroscopic levels in chemistry.

a. Avogadro's number Our discussion of Avogadro's number is based on a simple assumption: If you understand how this number is arrived at, you will find the relationship between masses at the micro and macro levels much easier to understand.

In chemistry the amounts of substances are most commonly measured in grams or milligrams or kilograms. We would like to know how many atoms or molecules are present when we weigh out 0.2 g of X, or 500 g of Y. This is important, because chemical formulas and chemical equations show how atoms combine, not in terms of their masses, but in terms of their relative *numbers.* The formula SO_2, for example, does *not* tell us what *mass* of sulfur will combine completely with a given mass of oxygen; it tells us only that there are two oxygen atoms for every sulfur atom in this compound. But when we weigh out a few grams of sulfur, we are weighing out trillions upon trillions of atoms which are both too small to see and too numerous to count.

What we need is a simple way to *connect* macroscopic masses of various substances, measured in grams or similar units, with relative numbers of atoms or molecules. There is such a way, and it is made possible by the atomic mass scale (Chapter 3). To understand the connection, let us consider an analogy. Suppose that we have some tennis balls and some basketballs. All of the tennis balls weigh the same. All of the basketballs weigh the same. Suppose further that each basketball is $8\frac{1}{4}$ times as heavy as each tennis ball. We can thus say that on a *relative mass scale,* each tennis ball weighs 1, and each basketball 8.25. Now, can we determine when we have equal numbers of tennis balls and basketballs *just by weighing*?

Of course we can. As long as a sample of basketballs weighs 8.25 times as much as a sample of tennis balls, the two samples will contain equal numbers of balls. Say, for example, that we have 100 lb of tennis balls and we want to measure out an equal number of basketballs. All we need do is to take 825 lb of basketballs. The important point is that *we don't have to count the balls.* As long as the *relative* masses are maintained, we *know* that the numbers *must* be equal. Moreover, *the unit of mass chosen doesn't matter.* We can weigh out the basketballs and tennis balls in units of grams, or pounds, or tons. In *any* mass unit, 1 "unit" of tennis balls will contain exactly the same number of balls as 8.25 "units" of basketballs.

Now consider an actual chemical situation. We know that

$$\text{atomic mass of O} = 16.00 \text{ u} \qquad \text{atomic mass of S} = 32.06 \text{ u}$$

How can we use this knowledge? To start with, we can see that a sulfur atom weighs about twice as much as an oxygen atom, so if we take 1 g of each substance, we will have roughly one sulfur atom for every two oxygen atoms. If we take 1 g of oxygen and 2 g of sulfur—or 16 g of oxygen and 32 g of sulfur—then we will have *roughly* the same number of atoms of each element.

Now, suppose that we want to weigh out *exactly* the same number of atoms of each element. Can we achieve this? Yes, if we take *exactly* 15.9994 g of oxygen and *exactly* 32.06 g of sulfur. Just as we saw for the basketballs and tennis balls, once a relative mass scale is established, the relative numbers of individual items can be determined from the masses, regardless of what units of mass are used. Thus, as long as the same mass ratio is maintained, the number of atoms must be equal.

But we can go further. By exactly the same reasoning, 1.0079 g of hydrogen or 238.03 g of uranium must contain *this same number of atoms.* Why? Because these are also masses in grams numerically equal to the relative atomic masses of the respective elements (see the tables inside the front cover). In fact, we can generalize this result: For *any* element, a mass in grams numerically equal to its atomic mass (in u) contains this same number of atoms. This number is *Avogadro's number.*

Recall that on the atomic mass scale, one atom of carbon-12 is assigned a mass of 12 u, and all other atomic masses are measured relative to this value. This is the chemist's "micro" unit. We have chosen the gram as our "macro" unit. Avogadro's number is defined as the number of atoms in exactly 12 g of carbon-12. It is therefore also the number of atoms in a sample of *any* element having a mass in grams numerically equal to its atomic mass. This number is the connecting link between our macro and micro scales of mass. It is also the connecting link between macroscopic masses and specific numbers of atoms.

Note that the same relationship can be extended from atoms to molecules. For a molecular substance of molecular mass *y, y* grams will contain a number of *molecules* equal to Avogadro's number. For example, the molecular mass of sulfur dioxide, SO_2, is

$$
\begin{array}{lll}
\text{S} & 1 \times 32.06 \text{ u} = & 32.06 \text{ u} \\
\text{O} & 2 \times 16.00 \text{ u} = & \underline{32.00 \text{ u}} \\
\multicolumn{2}{l}{\text{molecular mass of } SO_2 =} & 64.06 \text{ u}
\end{array}
$$

Avogadro's number
$= 6.022 \times 10^{23}$

Therefore 64.06 g of SO_2 contains Avogadro's number of molecules.

Avogadro's number has been determined by many methods and with great accuracy. The most up-to-date value is 6.022045×10^{23}. In most calculations in this book, it will be sufficient to use 6.022×10^{23}. (To grasp the magnitude of this number, consider that 6×10^{23} baseballs would cover the entire surface of the earth to a depth of 97 km, or that a digital electronic timer that can register 10 million counts per second would take almost 2 billion years to count Avogadro's number of seconds.)

EXAMPLE 4.9
Avogadro's Number

How many ozone molecules and how many oxygen atoms are present in 48.00 g of ozone, O_3?

The molecular mass of ozone is (3 atoms) (16.00 u/atom), or 48.00 u. Therefore, in 48.00 g of O_3 there will be a number of molecules equal to Avogadro's number. Each molecule contains three O atoms, so the number of O atoms is

$$(6.022 \times 10^{23} \text{ molecules})\left(\frac{3 \text{ O atoms}}{1 \text{ molecule}}\right) = 1.807 \times 10^{24} \text{ O atoms}$$

The 48.00 g sample of ozone contains 6.022×10^{23} molecules of O_3 and 1.807×10^{24} atoms of O.

Exercise How many formula units are present in 238.1 g of K_2MoO_4? How many potassium ions are present? How many MoO_4^{2-} ions are present? How many atoms are present? *Answer* 6.022×10^{23} formula units, 1.204×10^{24} K^+ ions, 6.022×10^{23} MoO_4^{2-} ions, 4.215×10^{24} atoms

b. The mole Because Avogadro's number connects macroscopic masses with numbers of atoms, it enables us to define an extremely convenient unit for dealing quantitatively with what takes place in chemical reactions. This unit is the *mole:* a number of anything equal to Avogadro's number. The mole is a counting unit, like a dozen. You can use the dozen to count anything: a dozen atoms, a dozen eggs, or a dozen butterflies. Similarly, the mole is a definite number of "entities" of any kind whatsoever—ions, or atoms, or molecules. We could also refer to a mole of eggs or a mole of butterflies. One mole is Avogadro's number of *anything*.

What are the advantages of the mole? First, it represents a very large number of atoms, molecules, or ions. When we weigh out 6 g of carbon, for example, we do not have to write that we have "about 3×10^{23} atoms"; we can simply refer to "one-half mole." More important, the way in which Avogadro's number is defined makes it extremely simple, arithmetically, to convert from number of atoms or molecules or ions (in moles) to mass in grams, and vice versa. (The usefulness of the mole will become clearer in Chapter 6, which deals with chemical calculations.)

The mole is one of the seven SI base units. As defined formally, one mole of a substance contains the same number of "elementary entities" as there are atoms in 12 g of carbon-12 (Figure 4.4). The SI definition notes that the "elementary entities," which may be "atoms, ions, electrons, other particles, or groups of such particles," must be specified.

The mole gives us an equality

$$6.022 \times 10^{23} \text{ entities} = 1 \text{ mol}$$

from which we can derive conversion factors, as usual (Section 2.10).

$$\frac{6.022 \times 10^{23} \text{ entities}}{1 \text{ mol}} \quad \text{and} \quad \frac{1 \text{ mol}}{6.022 \times 10^{23} \text{ entities}}$$

Avogadro's number provides the conversion factor between the number of entities on the micro scale and the number of moles, the unit in which we count entities on the macro scale. For example, when the entities are molecules

$$\text{No. of moles} \xrightarrow[\times \left(\frac{1}{Avogadro's\ number}\right)]{\times (Avogadro's\ number)} \text{No. of molecules} \qquad \textbf{(4.10)}$$

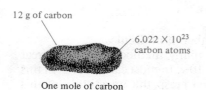

One mole of carbon

Figure 4.4
The mole The word "mole" comes from the Latin *moles,* meaning a mass or a pile of something.

or, stated as equations

$$(\text{No. of moles})\left(\frac{6.022 \times 10^{23} \text{ molecules}}{1 \text{ mol}}\right) = \text{no. of molecules} \qquad \textbf{(4.11)}$$

and

$$(\text{No. of molecules})\left(\frac{1 \text{ mol}}{6.022 \times 10^{23} \text{ molecules}}\right) = \text{no. of moles} \qquad \textbf{(4.12)}$$

Number of molecules = number of moles × Avogadro's number

Once we know the number of moles of a substance, it is always possible to find the number of "entities," such as atoms or molecules, as shown in Equation (4.11). (The usefulness of the mole in dealing with chemical reactions is discussed in Chapter 6.)

It is interesting to note that the first calculation of Avogadro's number was based on the use of the mole as the connection between the micro and macro scales. The value of the charge carried by one mole of electrons had been determined experimentally. Once Millikan found the charge on a single electron in his famous oil drop experiment (Section 3.4b), a simple calculation like the following one (done here with modern values) gave Avogadro's number. (C is the abbreviation for coulombs.)

$$\text{Avogadro's number} = \frac{\text{charge/mole of electrons}}{\text{charge/one electron}}$$

$$= \frac{9.6485 \times 10^{4} \text{ C/mol e}^-}{1.6022 \times 10^{-19} \text{ C/e}^-}$$

$$= 6.0220 \times 10^{23} \text{ electrons/mol}$$

EXAMPLE 4.10
Avogadro's Number and Moles

How many moles of copper are present in a sample containing 1.2×10^{22} copper atoms?

This problem, which is like the molecules → moles conversion, is carried out as follows (see Equation 4.12):

$$(1.2 \times 10^{22} \text{ atoms Cu})\left(\frac{1 \text{ mol Cu}}{6.022 \times 10^{23} \text{ atoms Cu}}\right) = 0.020 \text{ mol Cu}$$

There is 0.020 mol of copper atoms in a sample containing 1.2×10^{22} copper atoms.

Exercise How many moles of CsBr are present in a sample containing 7.8×10^{24} formula units of CsBr? *Answer* 13 mol

---

EXAMPLE 4.11
Avogadro's Number and Moles

A 1 L flask of air contains 0.040 mol of N_2. How many molecules of nitrogen are present?

This problem is a mole → molecules conversion. The number of molecules is given by

$$(0.040 \text{ mol N}_2)\left(\frac{6.022 \times 10^{23} \text{ molecules N}_2}{1 \text{ mol N}_2}\right) = 2.4 \times 10^{22} \text{ molecules N}_2$$

The flask contains 2.4×10^{22} molecules of N_2.

Exercise How many formula units are present in 1.3×10^{-3} mol of $CaCl_2$? How many Cl^- ions are present? *Answer* 7.8×10^{20} formula units, 1.6×10^{21} Cl^- ions

---

c. Molar mass The molar mass of a substance is the mass in grams of one mole of that substance. Here is where the quantities that we have been talking about — relative atomic mass, Avogadro's number, and the mole — come together beautifully.

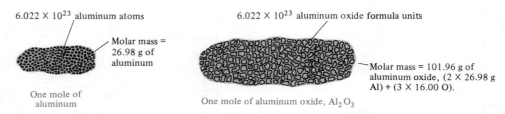

6.022 × 10²³ aluminum atoms

Molar mass = 26.98 g of aluminum

6.022 × 10²³ aluminum oxide formula units

Molar mass = 101.96 g of aluminum oxide, (2 × 26.98 g Al) + (3 × 16.00 O).

One mole of aluminum

One mole of aluminum oxide, Al_2O_3

Figure 4.5
Molar Masses

Molar mass = mass in g of 1 mol; numerically = to molecular mass in u

Mass = number of moles × molar mass

Let's consider a substance made of atoms, for example, pure aluminum. One aluminum atom weighs 26.98 u (or 4.480×10^{-23} g). One mole of aluminum atoms (an Avogadro's number of atoms) weighs 26.98 g ($6.022 \times 10^{23} \times 4.480 \times 10^{-23}$ g). For an atomic substance the molar mass is the mass in grams numerically equal to the atomic mass in atomic mass units. For a compound, the molar mass is the mass in grams numerically equal to the molecular mass in atomic mass units (Figure 4.5). To find the molar mass of a compound, we add the molar masses of all of the atoms present in the chemical formula of that compound. (In an older terminology that you may encounter in other books, the molar masses of atomic, molecular, and ionic substances are called the gram atomic weight, gram molecular weight, and gram formula weight, respectively.)

Table 4.8 gives the molar masses of a variety of chemical "entities." Think for a moment about how the molar masses are related to the atomic masses of the elements involved.

From Table 4.8 it should be clear why it is necessary to specify what "entity" is referred to when the number of moles is used. For example, one mole of oxygen *molecules* contains two moles of oxygen *atoms*. One mole of $NaNO_3$ contains one mole of Na^+ ions and one mole of NO_3^- ions, or a total of two moles of ions.

Molar mass has the units of grams per mole, for example, the molar mass of aluminum is 26.98 g/mol. Molar mass therefore provides the conversion factor between the mass in grams and the number of moles of a substance.

Table 4.8
Molar Masses of Some Different Chemical "Entities"

	Molar Mass (g/mol)
Atoms	
O atoms	16.00
Fe atoms	55.85
S atoms	32.06
N atoms	14.01
Molecules	
O_2	32.00
H_2O	18.02
SO_2	64.06
Ions	
Na^+	22.99
Fe^{3+}	55.85
NO_3^-	62.01
Ionic compounds	
$Na^+NO_3^-$	85.00
$Fe^{3+}(NO_3^-)_3$	241.88

$$\text{Mass} \xrightarrow[\times (molar\ mass)]{\times \left(\frac{1}{molar\ mass}\right)} \text{No. of moles} \qquad \textbf{(4.13)}$$

grams

Stated as equations, the conversion factors are used as follows:

$$(\text{Mass})\left(\frac{1}{\text{molar mass}}\right) = \text{no. of moles} \qquad \textbf{(4.14)}$$

grams $\quad \frac{moles}{grams} \quad$ moles

$$(\text{No. of moles})(\text{molar mass}) = \text{mass} \qquad \textbf{(4.15)}$$

moles $\quad \frac{grams}{mole} \quad$ grams

EXAMPLE 4.12
Molar Mass

What is the molar mass of chlorophyll *a*, $C_{55}H_{72}MgN_4O_5$?

The molar mass is the mass in grams of one mole of a compound. It is found from the molar masses of the atoms present in the compound.

	moles of atoms		molar mass of atoms (g/mol)		mass (g)
C	55	×	12.01	=	660.55
H	72	×	1.01	=	72.72
Mg	1	×	24.31	=	24.31
N	4	×	14.01	=	56.04
O	5	×	16.00	=	80.00

$$\text{molar mass of } C_{55}H_{72}MgN_4O_5 = 893.62 \text{ g}$$

Thus the molar mass of chlorophyll *a* is 893.62 g.

Exercise What is the molar mass of benzoic acid, C_6H_5COOH?
Answer 122.13 g

EXAMPLE 4.13
Molar Mass and Moles

What is the mass of the nitrogen in the flask described in Example 4.11, which contained 0.040 mol of N_2?

The molar mass of N_2 is 28.02 g. This problem is a moles → mass conversion.

$$(0.040 \text{ mol } N_2)\left(\frac{28.02 \text{ g } N_2}{1 \text{ mol } N_2}\right) = 1.1 \text{ g } N_2$$

The nitrogen in the flask has a mass of 1.1 g.

Exercise What is the mass of 1×10^{-10} mol of HCl? *Answer* 4×10^{-9} g HCl

---

EXAMPLE 4.14
Molar Mass and Moles

How many moles of PCl_5 are present in 5.6 g of PCl_5?

The molar mass of PCl_5 is 208.22 g. (We assume that by now you know how to find molar mass. For a reminder, if you need it, look back at Example 4.12). This problem is a mass → moles conversion.

$$(5.6 \text{ g } PCl_5)\left(\frac{1 \text{ mol } PCl_5}{208.22 \text{ g } PCl_5}\right) = 0.027 \text{ mol } PCl_5$$

The 5.6 g sample of PCl_5 contains 0.027 mol of PCl_5.

Exercise How many moles are present in 34 kg of sucrose, $C_{12}H_{22}O_{11}$?
Answer 99 mol $C_{12}H_{22}O_{11}$.

In summary, the three quantities Avogadro's number, the mole, and molar mass provide the means for relating masses of substances on the microscopic level to masses of substances on the macroscopic level. We can proceed, for example, from number of molecules (or atoms) to grams or from grams to number of molecules (or atoms)

$$\times \left(\frac{1}{Avogadro's\ number}\right) \qquad \times (molar\ mass)$$

No. of molecules (or atoms) → No. of moles → Mass *grams*

$$\times \left(\frac{1}{molar\ mass}\right)$$

$$\times (Avogadro's\ number)$$

(4.16)

As you can see, the mole provides the connection. Knowing the amount of a substance in moles, we can find the mass in grams or the number of "entities."

Relationships such as those in Equation (4.16) can be used separately and in combination to solve a wide variety of problems. As an illustration of how you might think about solving such problems, the following example is worked by the problem-solving method introduced in Section 2.12.

EXAMPLE 4.15
Molar Mass, Avogadro's Number, and Moles

What mass of zirconium contains the same number of atoms as 16 g of calcium?

1. Study the problem and be sure you understand it.
   (a) What is unknown?
       The mass of zirconium containing the same number of atoms as 16 g of calcium.
   (b) What is known?
       The sample size — 16 g of calcium. Also the molar masses of calcium and zirconium (from the tables).
2. Decide how to solve the problem.
   (a) What is the connection between the known and the unknown?
       The mole provides the connection between mass in grams and numbers of atoms. *Equal molar amounts* of calcium and zirconium contain equal numbers of atoms.
   (b) What is necessary to make the connection?
       It is necessary to do a mass → moles conversion and then a moles → mass conversion. First, from the known mass of calcium, find the number of moles of calcium

$$16 \text{ g Ca} \xrightarrow{\times \left(\frac{1}{\text{molar mass}}\right)} \text{no. of moles of Ca}$$

Then, taking an equal number of moles of zirconium, (because this amount contains an equal number of atoms), find the equivalent mass of zirconium, which is the unknown.

$$(\text{No. of moles Ca})\left(\frac{1 \text{ mol Zr}}{1 \text{ mol Ca}}\right) = \text{no. of moles Zr}$$

$$\text{No. of moles Zr} \xrightarrow{\times (\text{molar mass Zr})} \text{mass Zr (grams)}$$

3. Set up the problem and solve it.
   First, find the number of moles of calcium in 16 g of calcium.

$$(16 \text{ g Ca})\left(\frac{1 \text{ mol Ca}}{40.08 \text{ g Ca}}\right) = 0.40 \text{ mol Ca}$$

Then, find the number of grams of zirconium that represents the same number of moles:

$$(0.40 \text{ mol Ca})\left(\frac{1 \text{ mol Zr}}{1 \text{ mol Ca}}\right)\left(\frac{91.22 \text{ g Zr}}{1 \text{ mol Zr}}\right) = 36 \text{ g Zr}$$

Or, in a single setup:

$$(16 \text{ g Ca})\left(\frac{1 \text{ mol Ca}}{40.08 \text{ g Ca}}\right)\left(\frac{1 \text{ mol Zr}}{1 \text{ mol Ca}}\right)\left(\frac{91.22 \text{ g Zr}}{1 \text{ mol Zr}}\right) = 36 \text{ g Zr}$$

The answer is that 36 g of zirconium contains the same number of atoms as 16 g of calcium.

4. Check the result.
   (a) Are significant figures used correctly?
       Yes, the answer can have only two significant figures.
   (b) Did the answer come out in the correct units?
       Yes.
   (c) Is the answer reasonable?
       Yes. The molar mass of zirconium (91.22 g/mol) is slightly more than two times the molar mass of calcium (40.08 g). Therefore, it is reasonable that 36 g of zirconium contains the same number of atoms as 16 g of calcium, because 36 g is roughly two times 16 g.

Following are some further examples of problems that require the use of Avogadro's number, moles, and molar masses.

EXAMPLE 4.16
Molar Mass and Moles

Which contains the greater number of moles: 3.5 g of carbon dioxide, CO_2, or 3.5 g of sodium chloride, NaCl?

To answer this question, the conversion required is mass $\rightarrow$ moles. The molar masses are 44.01 g for CO_2 and 58.44 g for NaCl. The number of moles of the substances are

$$(3.5 \text{ g } CO_2)\left(\frac{1 \text{ mol } CO_2}{44.01 \text{ g } CO_2}\right) = 0.080 \text{ mol } CO_2$$

$$(3.5 \text{ g NaCl})\left(\frac{1 \text{ mol NaCl}}{58.44 \text{ g NaCl}}\right) = 0.060 \text{ mol NaCl}$$

The number of moles of CO_2 is larger than the number of moles of NaCl.

Exercise Which contains the larger number of moles: 2.1 g of iron(II) oxide, FeO, or 2.9 g of iron(III) oxide, Fe_2O_3? *Answer* 2.1 g FeO

EXAMPLE 4.17
Molar Mass, Avogadro's Number, and Moles

The nutritional recommended daily allowance (rda) of iron is 18 mg for an adult. How many atoms of iron is this?

We must first convert mass to moles, and then moles to number of atoms, or mass $\rightarrow$ moles $\rightarrow$ atoms. Note that in molar calculations we must convert all masses to *grams*. This problem can also be solved in one step:

$$(18 \text{ mg Fe})\left(\frac{1 \text{ g}}{1000 \text{ mg}}\right)\left(\frac{1 \text{ mol Fe}}{55.85 \text{ g Fe}}\right)\left(\frac{6.022 \times 10^{23} \text{ Fe atoms}}{1 \text{ mol Fe}}\right) = 1.9 \times 10^{20} \text{ Fe atoms}$$

The rda of iron for an adult contains 1.9×10^{20} atoms of iron.

Exercise How many atoms of carbon are present in 14.6 g of $CaCO_3$? *Answer* 8.78×10^{22} C atoms.

4.7 MOLARITY: MOLAR MASS IN SOLUTIONS

The mole and molar mass are used to express the amounts of *pure* substances. Frequently, chemical reactions are performed in aqueous solutions. Such solutions are mixtures and can contain widely varying proportions of dissolved substances and water. To know the amount of a substance present in a given amount of solution, we must have a way of expressing the **concentration** of the solution, which is a quantitative statement of the amount of solute in a given amount of solvent or solution.

The concentration of aqueous solutions is often most conveniently given as moles per liter of solution, which is called the **molarity** of the solution:

$$\text{Molarity} = \frac{\text{moles of solute}}{\text{volume of solution in liters}} \qquad (4.17)$$

A one-molar solution, written 1 M, of a substance contains 1 mol of the substance dissolved in enough water to give exactly 1 L of solution. For example, 1 L of a 1 M NaCl solution contains 58.5 g of dissolved sodium chloride. And 1 L of a 0.1 M NaCl solution contains 5.85 g of dissolved sodium chloride.

The concentration of any solution in moles per liter is found by dividing the number of moles of solute by the number of liters of solution. For example, to find the molarity of 2.92 L of a solution that contains 43.6 g of NaCl we proceed as follows:

$$\text{Molarity} = \frac{\text{no. of moles of solute}}{\text{volume of solution in liters}}$$

$$= \frac{(43.6 \text{ g NaCl}) \left(\dfrac{1 \text{ mol NaCl}}{58.5 \text{ g NaCl}} \right)}{2.92 \text{ L}} = 0.255 \text{ mol/L}$$

or, set up more simply,

$$(43.6 \text{ g NaCl}) \left(\frac{1 \text{ mol}}{58.5 \text{ g NaCl}} \right) \left(\frac{1}{2.92 \text{ L}} \right) = 0.255 \text{ mol/L}$$

This is a 0.255 M NaCl solution.

Molarity, the number of moles per liter, provides the connection between the molar amount of a substance in solution and the volume of the solution.

$$\text{Volume of solution} \underset{\times \left(\frac{1}{molarity} \right)}{\overset{\times (molarity)}{\rightleftarrows}} \text{Moles of solute} \qquad (4.18)$$

or, stated as equations

$$(\text{Volume of solution})(\text{molarity}) = \text{moles of solute} \qquad (4.19)$$

$$\underset{liters}{} \quad \underset{\frac{moles}{liter}}{} \quad \underset{moles}{}$$

$$(\text{Moles of solute}) \left(\frac{1}{\text{molarity}} \right) = \text{volume of solution} \qquad (4.20)$$

$$\underset{moles}{} \cdot \underset{\frac{liters}{mole}}{} \quad \underset{liters}{}$$

EXAMPLE 4.18
Molarity

What is the concentration of a solution which contains 4.03 g of NaOH dissolved in sufficient water to give 500.0 mL of solution?

The number of moles of NaOH is

$$(4.03 \text{ g NaOH}) \left(\frac{1 \text{ mol NaOH}}{40.00 \text{ g NaOH}} \right) = 0.101 \text{ mol NaOH}$$

The molarity of the solution is found by dividing the number of moles by the volume of the solution in liters.

$$\frac{(0.101 \text{ mol NaOH})}{(500.0 \text{ mL})(1 \text{ L}/1000 \text{ mL})} = 0.202 \text{ mol NaOH/L}$$

The solution is 0.202 M in NaOH.

Molarity

$$= \frac{\text{moles of solute}}{\text{volume of solution (L)}}$$

Exercise A solution contains 9.68 g of $Ca(NO_3)_2$ dissolved in 250.0 mL of solution. What is the molarity of this solution? *Answer* 0.236 M

EXAMPLE 4.19
Molarity and Moles

A student transferred 25.00 mL of a 0.0839 M solution of hydrochloric acid solution from a stockroom container into a flask. How many moles of HCl were transferred?

This is a volume of solution → moles of solute problem. The conversion involves multiplying by the concentration of the solution:

$$(25.00 \text{ mL})\left(\frac{1 \text{ L}}{1000 \text{ mL}}\right)\left(\frac{0.0839 \text{ mol HCl}}{1 \text{ L}}\right) = 0.00210 \text{ mol HCl}$$

The student transferred 0.00210 mol, or 2.10 mmol, of HCl.

Exercise How many moles of NaOH are in 10.5 mL of a 6.0 M solution of NaOH? *Answer* 0.063 mol NaOH

EXAMPLE 4.20
Molarity and Moles

An experiment called for the addition of 1.50 mol of NaOH in the form of a dilute solution. The only sodium hydroxide solution that could be found in the laboratory was a 2 L container marked "0.1035 M NaOH." What volume of this solution would be required for the 1.50 mol of NaOH? If the 2 L container was full, would this be enough?

We need to make the following conversion, moles → volume of solution, and the key to this conversion is multiplying by the reciprocal of the molarity:

$$(1.50 \text{ mol NaOH})\left(\frac{1 \text{ L}}{0.1035 \text{ mol NaOH}}\right) = 14.5 \text{ L}$$

We would need to have 14.5 L of this dilute solution. No, there could not be enough in the 2 L container.

Exercise What volume of 6.0 M HCl is needed to obtain 3.0 mmol of HCl? *Answer* 0.50 mL

4.8 COMPOSITION OF A CHEMICAL COMPOUND

The composition of a chemical compound can be stated in terms of atoms, moles, atomic mass units, or grams (Table 4.9). All of this information is known once the correct chemical formula of a compound is known (see A Historical Aside: Relative Atomic Masses).

Table 4.9
Information from a Chemical Formula The information given here is derived from the formula of ethyl alcohol, C_2H_5OH.

46.07 g of ethyl alcohol contains	1 mol of ethyl alcohol contains
24.02 g of carbon	2 mol of carbon atoms
16.00 g of oxygen	(1.204×10^{24} carbon atoms)
6.05 g of hydrogen	1 mol of oxygen atoms
	(6.022×10^{23} oxygen atoms)
Ethyl alcohol is	6 mol of hydrogen atoms
52.14% carbon	(3.613×10^{24} hydrogen atoms)
34.73% oxygen	
13.13% hydrogen	1 molecule of ethyl alcohol contains
46.07 u of ethyl alcohol contains	
24.02 u of carbon	2 carbon atoms
16.00 u of oxygen	1 oxygen atom
6.05 u of hydrogen	6 hydrogen atoms

Another way to express the composition of a chemical compound is as **percentage composition**—the percentage by mass of each element present. To find the percentage composition of a compound from its known chemical formula, we calculate the percentage by mass of each element present in one mole of the compound.

EXAMPLE 4.21
Percentage Composition

What is the percentage composition of sulfur dichloride, SCl_2?

The molar mass of sulfur dichloride, SCl_2, is 102.96 g and one mole of SCl_2 contains one mole, or 32.06 g, of sulfur and two moles, or 70.90 g, of chlorine. The percentage composition is found as follows:

$$\% \text{ S} = \frac{32.06 \text{ g S}}{102.96 \text{ g SCl}_2} (100\%) = 31.14\% \quad \% \text{ Cl} = \frac{70.90 \text{ g Cl}}{102.96 \text{ g SCl}_2} (100\%) = 68.86\%$$

Sulfur dichloride contains 31.14% sulfur and 68.86% chlorine.

The percentage composition is the same, no matter what the size of a sample of the compound. Sulfur dichloride is 31.14% S and 68.86% Cl, whether we have one mole, 1 mg, 1000 kg, or 1000 tons of it.

Exercise What is the percentage composition of DDT, $(ClC_6H_4)_2CHCCl_3$? *Answer* 47.42% C, 2.56% H, 50.01% Cl

---

As shown in the next example, experiments with weighed quantities of reactants and products can be used to determine percentage composition. In this way the composition of a compound can be found without knowing its chemical formula. The percentage composition is found from the experimentally determined mass of each element in a sample of known mass.

EXAMPLE 4.22
Percentage Composition—
Experimental Data

A 3.91 g sample of potassium metal when burned in oxygen formed a compound weighing 7.11 g and containing only potassium and oxygen. What is the percentage composition of this compound?

The percentage composition is the percent by mass of each element in the compound. Thus

$$\% \text{ K} = \frac{(3.91 \text{ g K})}{(7.11 \text{ g compound})} (100\%) = 55.0\%$$

$$7.11 \text{ g compound} - 3.91 \text{ g K} = 3.20 \text{ g O}$$

$$\% \text{ O} = \frac{(3.20 \text{ g O})}{(7.11 \text{ g compound})} (100\%) = 45.0\%$$

The compound contains 55.0% by mass of K and 45.0% by mass of O.

Exercise A 13.73 g sample of a compound of phosphorus and chlorine contained 3.10 g P. What is the percentage of this compound? *Answer* 22.6% by mass of P, 77.42% by mass of Cl

A HISTORICAL ASIDE

Relative Atomic Masses: Gay-Lussac, Avogadro, and Cannizzaro

For someone living today, it is almost impossible to imagine how hard it was for the early chemists to understand the nature of matter. Many of us, even if we know no other chemistry, know that water is "H-2-oh" and unquestioningly accept the fact that all little bits of water contain two H's and one O combined in some way. Even this simple basic assumption—that in a pure substance the elements are combined in fixed proportions—was first arrived at with great difficulty.

In the second half of the eighteenth century, the French chemist Claude Louis Berthollet (1748–1822) believed that he had experimental evidence to prove that the percentages by weight of the elements in the same chemical compound could vary. Berthollet and another French chemist, Louis Joseph Proust (1754–1826), argued for years on this point. Proust was apparently the more exacting experimentalist, for he was careful to use pure chemical compounds (some of Berthollet's materials were mixtures). Proust's results proved that <u>in pure compounds the elements are always combined in the same definite proportions by weight</u>. This is known as the *law of definite proportions,* or definite composition, and it was eventually accepted as a true statement.

From our modern perspective we can easily see that the existence of atoms explains this law. Atoms of different elements have different weights; they combine in a specific way in each pure substance and, therefore, the percentage by weight of each of the elements in the same substance does not vary. Earlier we discussed the need for a relative atomic mass scale and the problem of choosing a standard mass (Section 3.10). A further problem existed because, for a long time, chemists were uncertain of *what* they were weighing. Dalton, working with his own idea that nature followed the greatest simplicity, thought water was HO—one hydrogen atom and one oxygen atom combined. Using the lightest element, hydrogen, as a relative atomic mass standard of mass 1, this gave a mass of 8 for oxygen and of 9 for water.

$$H + O \longrightarrow HO$$
$$1 \quad\ 8 \qquad 9$$

These relative masses agreed with Dalton's limited experimental data, to be sure, but are wrong because the formulas for water, hydrogen, and oxygen are wrong.

A valid relative atomic mass scale could not be developed until the distinctions among "atoms," "molecules," and "elements" were sorted out. This occurred as the direct result of the efforts of three men: Joseph Gay-Lussac, (1778–1850), a Frenchman who made some new observations about the combining volumes of gases; Amadeo Avogadro (1776–1856), an Italian physicist who brilliantly grasped the meaning of Gay-Lussac's results; and Stanislao Cannizzaro (1826–1910), a Sicilian who led chemists to a very belated recognition of the value of Avogadro's insights.

Gay-Lussac became interested in the chemical reactions of gases and in the volumes of the reactants and products. He observed a remarkably simple relationship: When gases react with each other, their volumes (if measured at the same temperature and pressure) are in the ratio of small, whole numbers, and if the products are gases, their volumes are in small, whole-number ratios to the volumes of the reactants. This is called the *law of combining volumes* (Section 5.8). For example,

Hydrogen + oxygen ⟶ steam
2 volumes   1 volume   2 volumes

Hydrogen + chlorine ⟶ hydrogen chloride
1 volume   1 volume   2 volumes

These simple ratios reflect the existence of atoms and molecules. However, explanation of these ratios in terms of atomic theory was a problem that neither Gay-Lussac nor Dalton could solve. Dalton considered the obvious possibility that equal volumes of gases might contain equal numbers of reacting particles (at the same temperature and pressure), but rejected it because he had no answer for questions such as this: If water is HO, shouldn't the formation of two volumes of steam require two volumes of oxygen as well as two volumes of hydrogen?

Avogadro resolved the dilemma by first simply stating that at the same temperature and pressure, equal volumes of gases contain equal number of molecules (now known as Avogadro's law, Section 5.8). He then clarified the matter by concluding that not only do atoms of *different* elements combine, but that atoms of the *same* element can also combine to form molecules.

Let us see what chemical conclusions we can draw from Gay-Lussac's discovery, and Avogadro's law and his understanding of molecules. Consider the reaction of hydrogen with chlorine. If Avogadro's law is correct, the number of molecules of hydrogen chloride gas formed is twice the number of hydrogen molecules consumed. But every molecule of hydrogen chloride must contain at least one atom of hydrogen, so each molecule of the original hydrogen must have broken in two. We should, therefore, write the formula of hydrogen as H_2, H_4, H_6, or some other multiple. Many experiments have been performed with gaseous hydrogen and no case has yet been found in which the volume of the gaseous product is more than twice the volume of the hydrogen consumed. We assume, therefore, that the hydrogen molecule consists of two atoms and we write the formula H_2. By exactly the same reasoning, we deduce the formula Cl_2 for chlorine.

$$H_2 \quad + \quad Cl_2 \quad \longrightarrow \quad 2HCl$$
1 volume   *1 volume*   *2 volumes*

The reaction between hydrogen and oxygen to form steam, by the same reasoning, tells us that the molecule of oxygen consists of two atoms, O_2. It also tells us that the formula of water in the form of steam is H_2O.

$$2H_2 \quad + \quad O_2 \quad \longrightarrow \quad 2H_2O$$
2 volumes   *1 volume*   *2 volumes*

Avogadro's law provided a means of measuring atomic and molecular masses. If equal volumes of gases contain equal numbers of molecules, then by comparing the masses of equal volumes of gases (at the same temperature and pressure), the masses of the individual molecules can be compared. For example, suppose the hydrogen atom has been chosen as the relative mass standard and assigned an atomic mass of one. Measurements would show that (at the same temperature and pressure) a given volume of oxygen is 16 times heavier than an equal volume of hydrogen and that a given volume of steam is nine times heavier than an equal volume of hydrogen. By using the correct molecular formulas, we find molecular masses of 2 for hydrogen, 32 for oxygen, and 18 for water.

$$2H_2 \quad + \quad O_2 \quad \longrightarrow \quad 2H_2O$$
mol. mass 2   *mol. mass 32*   *mol. mass 18*

Obviously, the atomic mass of oxygen is 16 on this scale. Eventually, methods like this were used to develop the first accurate tables of relative atomic masses.

Sadly for the progress of chemistry, however, it took 50 years before the significance of Avogadro's law came to the attention of the scientific community. A Congress was called in 1860 in Karlsruhe, Germany, for the purpose of resolving the confusion among the many different "atomic" and "molecular" mass scales and systems of naming chemical compounds then in use. At this congress, Cannizzaro made a vigorous speech stressing the importance of Avogadro's work. Cannizzaro's reception was not enthusiastic, but the seeds had been sown. As a direct result of Cannizzaro's speech and his distribution of a paper at the congress, the validity of Avogadro's law eventually came to be accepted. One chemist, after reading Cannizzaro's paper, wrote, "The scales seemed to fall from my eyes. Doubts disappeared and a feeling of quiet certainty took their place."

4.9 SIMPLEST AND EMPIRICAL FORMULAS

Determining the correct formula of a chemical compound newly prepared in the laboratory or newly discovered in nature is an essential part of its identification. The first step in the study of such a compound is frequently the experimental determination of the elements present and the percentage composition of the compound. This information is used to find the simplest, or empirical, formula of the compound.

The **simplest formula** of a compound gives the simplest whole-number ratio of atoms in the compound. It represents the chemical composition of the compound in terms of the smallest possible number of atoms of each element present. For example, the simplest formula of diborane, a compound of boron and hydrogen, is BH_3. The simplest formula of ammonia is NH_3. The actual formula of a chemical compound is either the same as the simplest formula or is, as we describe further in Section 4.10, a multiple of the simplest formula. The actual formula of diborane is B_2H_6, which has twice the molar mass of BH_3, but, of course, the same percentage composition.

For an ionic compound, the simplest formula is the only one that is needed. Recall our examples of ionic compounds, NaCl and $BaCl_2$. These are simplest formulas that show the smallest whole-number ratios of the ions present.

An experimentally determined simplest formula is usually called an **empirical formula,** implying that the correct formula is not yet known. (An **empirical relationship** is a relationship based solely on experimental facts or derived without the use of any theory or explanation of the facts.)

In determining an empirical formula, the number of moles of atoms of each element present is calculated from data found experimentally. Suppose a 0.666 g sample of a compound was found by experiment to contain 0.255 g of C, 0.0651 g of H, and 0.346 g of O. We can convert these masses to moles by dividing by the molar masses of C, H, and O. This gives the following (where n indicates the number of moles; e.g., n_C = number of moles of carbon):

$$n_C = (0.255 \text{ g C})\left(\frac{1 \text{ mol C}}{12.01 \text{ g}}\right) = 0.0212 \text{ mol C}$$

$$n_H = (0.0651 \text{ g H})\left(\frac{1 \text{ mol H}}{1.008 \text{ g}}\right) = 0.0646 \text{ mol H}$$

$$n_O = (0.346 \text{ g O})\left(\frac{1 \text{ mol O}}{16.00 \text{ g O}}\right) = 0.0216 \text{ mol O}$$

Because for a given compound atom ratios and mole ratios are the same, we could write an empirical formula of $C_{0.0212}H_{0.0645}O_{0.0216}$. However, this is unrealistic, because whole atoms combine, not fractions of atoms. To proceed to a more reasonable empirical formula, the simplest ratio of moles is found by dividing the number of moles of each element by the number of moles of the element present in the smallest amount (in this case, 0.0212 mol):

$$\frac{n_C}{n_C} = 1.00 \qquad \frac{n_H}{n_C} = 3.04 \qquad \frac{n_O}{n_C} = 1.02$$

Knowing that experimental data usually incorporate some errors, we can safely conclude that the empirical formula of this compound is CH_3O.

EXAMPLE 4.23
Empirical Formula

An oxide contains 0.52 g of phosphorus and 0.67 g of oxygen. What is the empirical formula of this oxide?

The molar masses of atomic P and O are 30.97 g and 16.00 g, respectively. The number of moles of P and O are

$$(0.52 \text{ g P})\left(\frac{1 \text{ mol P}}{30.97 \text{ g P}}\right) = 0.017 \text{ mol P}$$

$$(0.67 \text{ g O})\left(\frac{1 \text{ mol O}}{16.00 \text{ g O}}\right) = 0.042 \text{ mol O}$$

Dividing the number of moles of each element by the number of moles of the element present in the smaller amount gives

$$\frac{n_O}{n_P} = \frac{0.042 \text{ mol}}{0.017 \text{ mol}} = 2.5 \qquad \frac{n_P}{n_P} = \frac{0.017 \text{ mol}}{0.017 \text{ mol}} = 1.0$$

Thus for every mole of P atoms, there are 2.5 moles of O atoms in the compound. This means that there are 2.5 atoms of O for each P atom in the compound. The empirical formula could be written as $PO_{2.5}$. However, fractional numbers of atoms are usually avoided in formulas. The relative numbers are doubled, and the empirical formula becomes P_2O_5.

Exercise   What is the empirical formula of the compound that contains 3.10 g of P and 10.64 g of Cl?   *Answer* PCl_3

The steps in determining an empirical formula are always the same. For this reason, they can be organized into a table. Example 4.24 illustrates the use of a table and also the determination of an empirical formula from percentage composition. If the experimentally determined composition of a compound is obtained as the mass percentage of each element present, it is convenient to take 100 g of the compound as the basis for calculation. Each mass percentage is then taken as the mass in grams of an element. (This is a convenient way to deal with percentages in any dimensional calculation.)

EXAMPLE 4.24
Empirical Formula

The mineral cryolite contains 33% by mass of Na, 13% by mass of Al, and 54% by mass of F. Determine the empirical formula of the compound.

Choose exactly 100 g of cryolite as a basis to solve the problem. The 100 g of cryolite contains 33 g of Na, 13 g of Al, and 54 g of F. The entries in a table summarizing the calculations are as follows:

	Na	Al	F
No. of moles	$\frac{33 \text{ g}}{22.99 \text{ g/mol}} = 1.4 \text{ mol}$	$\frac{13 \text{ g}}{26.98 \text{ g/mol}} = 0.48 \text{ mol}$	$\frac{54 \text{ g}}{19.00 \text{ g/mol}} = 2.8 \text{ mol}$
Mole ratio, n/n_{Al}	$\frac{1.4}{0.48} = 2.9$	$\frac{0.48}{0.48} = 1.0$	$\frac{2.8}{0.48} = 5.8$
Relative no. of atoms	3	1	6

The empirical formula of cryolite is Na_3AlF_6.

Exercise   Sodium thiosulfate contains 29.1% by mass of Na, 40.6% by mass of S, and 30.4% by mass of O. Determine the empirical formula for this compound. *Answer* $Na_2S_2O_3$

4.10 MOLECULAR FORMULAS

For molecular compounds, it is important to know how many atoms are present in each molecule. The **molecular formula** of a compound represents the actual number of atoms of each element that are combined in each molecule. To find the molecular formula from the empirical formula, we must determine the molecular or molar mass of the compound in question. This mass will be equal or nearly equal to some multiple of the mass calculated from the empirical formula. For example, for diborane, which has an empirical formula of BH_3, the molar mass is two times the empirical formula mass and therefore the molecular formula of the compound is B_2H_6.

A molar mass determined experimentally for the compound we described back in Section 4.9, the compound that had an empirical formula of CH_3O, might be 61.43 g. The molar mass based on the empirical formula is 31.04 g [which is 12.01 g + (3 × 1.01 g) + 16.00 g]. Dividing the true molar mass by the empirical formula molar mass

$$\frac{61.43 \text{ g/mol}}{31.04 \text{ g/mol}} = 1.979$$

shows that the empirical formula should be doubled. The molecular formula of the compound is $C_2H_6O_2$. (When we began this example, the compound we had in mind was ethylene glycol, which is used in antifreeze. Its structural formula is $HOCH_2CH_2OH$, but more experiments would be necessary to uncover this information.)

EXAMPLE 4.25
Molecular Formula

The empirical formula for a substance was determined to be CH. The approximate molar mass of the substance was experimentally found to be 79 g. What is the molecular formula of this molecular compound? What is the exact molar mass?

The molar mass of the compound based on its empirical formula is 12.01 g + 1.01 g = 13.02 g. Dividing the true molar mass by the empirical formula molar mass

$$\frac{79 \text{ g/mol}}{13.02 \text{ g/mol}} = 6.1$$

shows that the empirical formula should be multiplied by six to obtain the molecular formula, C_6H_6.

The exact molar mass is

$$(13.02 \text{ g/mol})(6) = 78.12 \text{ g/mol}$$

The molecular formula of the compound is C_6H_6 and its exact molar mass is 78.12 g.

Exercise The empirical formula of enneaborane was determined to be B_3H_5. The approximate molar mass of the compound is 115 g. What is the molecular formula of this compound? *Answer* B_9H_{15}

In summary, the identification of a chemical compound frequently begins with the experimental determination of the masses of the elements present in a sample of known weight, or the percentage composition. The simplest, or empirical, formula is found from such data. In order to determine the molecular formula of a compound—the actual number of atoms in each molecule—both the empirical formula and the molar mass must be known. Table 4.9 summarizes the kinds of information about a chemical compound that are conveyed by its molecular formula.

SUMMARY

4.1 MOLECULAR AND IONIC COMPOUNDS When two or more atoms combine chemically they form a molecule. The naturally occurring forms of some elements are diatomic molecules (molecules consisting of two atoms) or polyatomic molecules (which contain more than two atoms). We refer to the compounds composed of molecules as molecular compounds. When an atom gains one or more electrons it acquires a negative charge and is known as an anion; when an atom loses one or more electrons it acquires a positive charge and is known as a cation. An ionic compound consists of positive and negative ions held together by electrical attraction. The chemical formula of an ionic compound gives the ratio of ions, but individual molecules are not ordinarily present.

4.2 FORMULAS FOR CHEMICAL COMPOUNDS A chemical formula gives the symbols for the elements in a compound with subscripts indicating the number of atoms of each element present. For a molecular compound, the formula represents the number of atoms in one molecule. For an ionic compound, the formula gives the ratio of ions present in the simplest unit, or one formula unit. A structural formula is essentially a diagram showing how the atoms in a compound or ion are linked to each other by chemical bonds.

4.3 NAMING CHEMICAL COMPOUNDS The rules that govern the naming of chemical compounds are known collectively as chemical nomenclature. In the Stock system, the name of a cation consists of the name of the element, the charge on the ion as a Roman numeral in parentheses, and the word "ion." The name of a monatomic anion (e.g., Cl^-) consists of the name of the element with the ending "ide," followed by the word "ion." A binary compound is one containing atoms or ions of only two elements. Salts are ionic compounds formed between cations and the anions of acids. For binary molecular compounds, prefixes (Table 4.6) are used to indicate the number of atoms of each element present.

4.4 CHEMICAL EQUATIONS The substances that undergo changes in a chemical reaction are called the reactants, and the new substances formed are the products. The chemical change that takes place is represented with symbols and formulas in a chemical equation. All chemical equations must be balanced—the correct coefficients must be used for each species so that all the atoms of each element in the reactants can be accounted for in the products. Information about the states of reactants and products may be provided by symbols after the formulas: (g) for gas, (l) for liquid, (s) for solid, and (aq) for substances in aqueous solution. The transformation of a neutral ionic compound into positive and negative ions, usually by dissolution in water, is called dissociation. The formation of ions from a molecular compound is known as ionization.

4.5 MOLECULAR MASS The molecular mass of a chemical compound is the sum of the atomic masses, in atomic mass units, of all the atoms in the formula of the compound.

4.6 AVOGADRO'S NUMBER, THE MOLE, AND MOLAR MASS Avogadro's number is the number of atoms in exactly 12 g of carbon-12; it is equal to 6.022×10^{23}. A mole is a number of anything equal to Avogadro's number. The mole is the unit that provides the connection between masses on the microscopic level (measured in atomic mass units) and masses on the macroscopic level (measured in grams). The molar mass of a substance is the mass in grams of one mole of that substance.

4.7 MOLARITY: MOLAR MASS IN SOLUTIONS The concentration of a substance in solution is a quantitative statement of the amount of solute in a given amount of solvent or solution. Concentrations are often given in moles per liter of solution, or molarity.

4.8 COMPOSITION OF A CHEMICAL COMPOUND **4.9** SIMPLEST AND EMPIRICAL FORMULAS **4.10** MOLECULAR FORMULAS The percentage (by mass) of each element present in a chemical compound is its percentage composition. The simplest formula of a compound gives the simplest whole-number ratio of the atoms it contains. An experimentally determined simplest formula is called an empirical formula; it can be determined from the percentage composition and the molar masses of the elements present. The molecular formula of a compound represents the actual number of atoms of each element present in a molecule. To find the molecular formula of a compound it is necessary to know both its empirical formula and its molecular or molar mass, which is usually some multiple of the mass calculated from the empirical formula.

THOUGHTS ON CHEMISTRY

On the Nature of the Universe

DE RERUM NATURA, by Lucretius
(55 B.C.)

Material objects are of two kinds, atoms and compounds of atoms. The atoms themselves cannot be swamped by any force, for they are preserved indefinitely by their absolute solidity. . . . The atoms must be made of imperishable stuff into which everything can be resolved in the end, so that there may be a stock of matter for building the world anew. The atoms, therefore, are absolutely solid and unalloyed. In no other way could they have survived throughout infinite time to keep the world in being.

Furthermore, if nature had set no limit to the breaking of things, the particles of matter in the course of ages would have been ground so small that nothing could be generated from them so as to attain in the fullness of time to the summit of its growth. For we see that anything can be more speedily disintegrated than put together again. Hence, what the long day of time, the bygone eternity, has already shaken and loosened to fragments could never in the residue of time be reconstructed. As it is, there is evidently a limit set to breaking, since we see that everything is renewed and each according to its kind has a fixed period in which to grow to its prime.

Here is a further argument. Granted that the particles of matter are absolutely solid, we can still explain the composition and behaviour of soft things — air, water, earth, fire — by their intermixture with empty space. On the other hand, supposing the atoms to be soft, we cannot account for the origin of hard flint and iron. For there would be no foundation for nature to build on. Therefore there must be bodies strong in their unalloyed solidity by whose closer clustering things can be knit together and display unyielding toughness.

If we suppose that there is no limit set to the breaking of matter, we must still admit that material objects consist of particles which throughout eternity have resisted the forces of destruction. To say that these are breakable does not square with the fact that they have survived throughout eternity under a perpetual bombardment of innumerable blows.

by Titus Lucretius Carus (c. 94 B.C. – c. 55 B.C.) *De Rerum Natura.* Quoted from Lucretius, *On the Nature of the Universe,* translated by Ronald Latham (London: Penguin Books, 1951), pp. 41–43.

QUESTIONS

Molecular and Ionic Compounds

4.1 Classify each of the following substances as (i) monatomic, (ii) diatomic, or (iii) polyatomic: (a) CO, (b) CO_2, (c) Ne, (d) Cl_2, (e) PCl_5, and (f) N_2O_4.

4.2 Classify each of the following ions as (i) a cation or (ii) an anion: (a) Sn^{2+}, (b) P^{3-}, (c) Cu^{2+}, (d) I^-, (e) K^+, and (f) Fe^{2+}.

4.3 Classify each of the following species as (i) atomic, (ii) molecular, or (iii) ionic: (a) SO_4^{2-}, (b) S_8, (c) Na^+Cl^-, (d) CO_2, (e) NH_4^+, and (f) Fe.

4.4 Classify each of the following species as (i) atomic, (ii) molecular, or (iii) ionic: (a) Cl, (b) Cl_2, (c) Fe^{3+}, (d) Pt, and (e) Ca^{2+} (CO_3^{2-}).

Formulas for Chemical Compounds

4.5 Name the elements present in the following compounds: (a) Ce_2O_3, (b) $Pb(N_3)_2$, (c) $NiSO_4$, (d) K_2Se, and (e) $Th(CO_3)_2$. In what atomic ratios are these elements present in each compound?

4.6 Repeat Question 4.5 for (a) AuCN, (b) $KC_{18}H_{35}O_2$, (c) S_4N_4, (d) $ZnBr_2$, and (e) OF_2.

4.7 Repeat Question 4.5 for

(a)
```
    H  H
    |  |
H — C — C — O — H
    |  |
    H  H
```

(b)
```
    H        H
    |        |
H — C — O — C — H
    |        |
    H        H
```

(c) $O=C=O$

(d)
$$\left[\begin{array}{c} H \\ | \\ H - N - H \\ | \\ H \end{array} \right]^{+} Cl^{-}$$

4.8 What is the difference between (a) 2H and H_2; (b) C_2H_2 and C_6H_6; (c) Hg_2Cl_2 and $HgCl_2$; and (d) O, O^{2-}, O_2, O_2^{2-} and O_3?

4.9 Write the formula for the ionic compound formed between (a) Ca^{2+} and ClO_3^-, (b) Al^{3+} and SO_4^{2-}, (c) Au^{3+} and Br^-, (d) NH_4^+ and CN^-, and (e) K^+ and PO_4^{3-}.

4.10 Write the formula for the ionic compound formed between (a) Na^+ and $Cr_2O_7^{2-}$, (b) Ca^{2+} and MnO_4^-, (c) NH_4^+ and SO_4^{2-}, and (d) Zn^{2+} and N^{3-}.

4.11 Write the formula for the ionic compound formed between (a) Cu^{2+} and SO_4^{2-}, (b) Ba^{2+} and O_2^{2-}, (c) K^+ and CrO_4^{2-}, (d) Cs^+ and OH^-, and (e) La^{3+} and CO_3^{2-}.

4.12* Some chemical formulas are more complex than those discussed in this chapter. For example, the formula for the mineral known as gypsum is usually written as $CaSO_4 \cdot 2H_2O$. This formula tells us that in addition to the one calcium cation and one sulfate anion, there are two molecules of water present. Thus gypsum contains 1 atom of Ca, 1 atom of S, 6 atoms of O (4 from the sulfate ion and 2 from the water molecules), and 4 atoms of H. Two obvious advantages of writing the formula as $CaSO_4 \cdot 2H_2O$ instead of $CaSO_6H_4$ are that we can recognize the simpler ions and molecules that make up the mineral as well as having some information about the arrangement of the atoms, ions, and molecules in the structure of gypsum. Name the elements present and state in what atomic ratios these elements make up the following substances: (a) alum, $K_2Al_2(SO_4)_4 \cdot 24H_2O$; (b) borax, $Na_2B_4O_7 \cdot 10H_2O$; (c) calamine, $2ZnO \cdot SiO_2 \cdot H_2O$; and (d) washing soda, $Na_2CO_3 \cdot 10H_2O$.

Naming Chemical Compounds

4.13 State the rules for naming (a) simple cations, (b) simple anions, (c) binary ionic compounds, (d) binary molecular compounds, and (e) salts containing polyatomic ions.

4.14 Name the following simple cations: (a) Li^+, (b) Cd^{2+}, (c) Fe^{2+}, (d) Mn^{2+}, and (e) Al^{3+}. Use the Stock system of nomenclature.

4.15 Name the following simple cations: (a) Au^+, (b) Au^{3+}, (c) Ba^{2+}, (d) Sn^{2+}, and (e) Ag^+. Use the Stock system of nomenclature.

4.16 Write the formula for each of the following simple cations: (a) sodium ion, (b) zinc ion, (c) silver ion, (d) mercury(II) ion, and (e) iron(III) ion.

4.17 Write the formula for each of the following simple cations: (a) lithium ion, (b) bismuth(III) ion, (c) iron(II) ion, (d) chromium(III) ion, (e) potassium ion.

4.18 Name the following simple anions: (a) N^{3-}, (b) O^{2-}, (c) Se^{2-}, (d) F^-, and (e) Br^-.

4.19 Write the formula for each of the following simple anions: (a) phosphide ion, (b) sulfide ion, (c) telluride ion, (d) chloride ion, and (e) iodide ion.

4.20 Name the following binary compounds: (a) Li_2S, (b) SnO_2, (c) RbI, (d) Li_2O, and (e) UO_2.

4.21 Name the following binary compounds: (a) NaI, (b) Hg_2S, (c) Li_3N, (d) $MnCl_2$, and (e) $ZrBr_4$.

4.22 Name the following binary compounds: (a) $AlCl_3$, (b) CuF_2, (c) FeO, (d) Ba_3N_2, and (e) NaF.

4.23 Write the formula for each of the following binary compounds: (a) sodium fluoride, (b) zinc oxide, (c) barium peroxide, (d) magnesium bromide, and (e) hydrogen iodide.

4.24 Write the formula for each of the following binary compounds: (a) sodium azide, (b) calcium phosphide, (c) iron(II) oxide, and (d) silver fluoride.

4.25 Write the formula for each of the following binary compounds: (a) copper (I) chloride, (b) potassium azide, (c) manganese(IV) oxide, and (d) iron(III) oxide.

4.26 Name the following salts of polyatomic ions: (a) $(NH_4)_2SO_4$, (b) $K_2Cr_2O_7$, (c) $Fe(ClO_4)_2$, (d) $CaCO_3$, and (e) $NaNO_2$.

4.27 Name the following salts of polyatomic ions: (a) NH_4CN, (b) $Al(NO_3)_3$, (c) $Ca_3(PO_4)_2$, (d) Li_2CO_3, and (e) BaO_2.

4.28 Name the following salts of polyatomic ions: (a) K_2CrO_4, (b) Na_2SO_3, (c) $FeCO_3$, (d) $Fe_2(SO_4)_3$.

4.29 Write the formula for each of the following salts of polyatomic ions: (a) potassium sulfite, (b) calcium permanganate, (c) barium phosphate, (d) copper(I) sulfate, and (e) ammonium acetate.

4.30 Write the formula for each of the following salts of polyatomic ions: (a) iron(II) perchlorate, (b) potassium nitrite, (c) sodium peroxide, (d) ammonium dichromate, and (e) sodium carbonate.

4.31 Write the formula for each of the following salts of polyatomic ions: (a) silver nitrate, (b) uranium(IV) sulfate, (c) aluminum acetate, and (d) manganese(II) phosphate.

4.32 What is the name of the acid with the formula H_2CO_3? Write the formulas of the two anions derived from it and name these ions.

4.33 What is the name of the acid with the formula H_3PO_3? What is the name of the HPO_3^{2-} ion?

4.34 Name the following binary molecular compounds: (a) CO, (b) CO_2, (c) SF_6, (d) $SiCl_4$, and (e) IF.

4.35 Name the following binary molecular compounds: (a) AsF_3, (b) Br_2O, (c) BrO_2, (d) CSe_2, and (e) Cl_2O_7.

4.36 Write the formula for each of the following compounds: (a) diboron trioxide, (b) silicon dioxide, (c) phosphorus trichloride, (d) sulfur tetrachloride, and (e) bromine trifluoride.

4.37 Write the formula for each of the following compounds: (a) iodine monobromide, (b) dinitrogen pentasulfide, (c) phosphorus triiodide, (d) silicon monosulfide, and (e) tetrasulfur dinitride.

Chemical Equations

4.38 The chemical equation describing the decomposition of dinitrogen monoxide is

$$2N_2O(g) \xrightarrow{\Delta} 2N_2(g) + O_2(g)$$

(a) What is the reactant? (b) What are the products? (c) What are the physical states of the substances involved in the reaction? (d) What does the "Δ" represent?

4.39 The chemical equation describing the reaction of aluminum with iodine is

$$2Al(s) + 3I_2(\text{in } CS_2) \xrightarrow{45\,°C} 2AlI_3(s)$$

(a) What are the reactants? (b) What is the product? (c) What are the special conditions of the experiment?

4.40 For each of the following chemical equations, write a word sentence that describes the chemical reaction

(a) $SiI_4(s) + 2H_2O(l) \xrightarrow{H_2O} SiO_2(s) + 4HI(aq)$
(b) $2H_3AsO_3(aq) + 3H_2S(g) \longrightarrow As_2S_3(s) + 6H_2O(l)$

4.41 Write a chemical equation representing the reaction of aqueous sodium chloride with liquid water to produce aqueous sodium hypochlorite and gaseous hydrogen. This reaction takes place only if electrical energy is supplied from an outside source, so write "electrolysis" above the reaction arrow to indicate this condition. Balance the equation.

4.42 Write a chemical equation representing each of the following reactions: (a) solid aluminum sulfide reacts with liquid water to give solid aluminum hydroxide and gaseous hydrogen sulfide, (b) solid barium peroxide reacts with aqueous sulfuric acid to give aqueous hydrogen peroxide and solid barium sulfate, (c) liquid phosphorus tribromide reacts with liquid water in the presence of excess water to produce aqueous phosphorous acid

and aqueous hydrogen bromide, and (d) gaseous ozone reacts with gaseous nitrogen monoxide to produce gaseous nitrogen dioxide and gaseous oxygen. Balance each equation (if you can).

Atomic, Molecular, and Molar Mass Relationships

4.43 How do we calculate the molecular mass of a chemical compound? What are the units that are used to express molecular mass?

4.44 What is the numerical value of Avogadro's number? What is the relationship of Avogadro's number to the mole?

4.45 What is the relationship between the molecular mass and the molar mass of a substance?

4.46 Why must we express the concentration of a solution? What is the commonly used unit for expressing concentration which involves the number of moles of solute and the volume of the solution?

4.47 How do we calculate the volume of solution which contains a given number of moles of solute? How do we find the number of moles of solute in a given volume of solution?

4.48 What is the relationship between the empirical formula of a compound and its molecular formula? What information about the compound is usually used to find this relationship?

Answers to Selected Questions

4.1 (a) ii, (b) iii, (c) i, (d) ii, (e) iii, (f) iii

4.2 (a) i, (b) ii, (c) i, (d) ii, (e) i, (f) i

4.4 (a) i, (b) ii, (c) iii, (d) i, (e) iii

4.6 (a) gold, carbon, and nitrogen, 1 atom of Au to 1 atom of C to 1 atom of N; (b) potassium, carbon, hydrogen, and oxygen, 1 atom of K to 18 atoms of C to 35 atoms of H to 2 atoms of O; (c) sulfur and nitrogen, 4 atoms of S to 4 atoms of N; (d) zinc and bromine, 1 atom of Zn to 2 atoms of Br; (e) oxygen and fluorine, 1 atom of O to 2 atoms of F

4.10 (a) $Na_2Cr_2O_7$, (b) $Ca(MnO_4)_2$, (c) $(NH_4)_2SO_4$, (d) Zn_3N_2

4.15 (a) gold(I) ion, (b) gold(III) ion, (c) barium ion, (d) tin(II) ion, (e) silver ion

4.17 (a) Li^+, (b) Bi^{3+}, (c) Fe^{2+}, (d) Cr^{3+}, (e) K^+

4.22 (a) aluminim chloride, (b) copper(II) fluoride, (c) iron(II) oxide, (d) barium nitride, (e) sodium fluoride

4.25 (a) CuCl, (b) KN_3, (c) MnO_2, (d) Fe_2O_3

4.28 (a) potassium chromate, (b) sodium sulfite, (c) iron(II) carbonate, (d) iron(III) sulfate

4.31 (a) $AgNO_3$, (b) $U(SO_4)_2$, (c) $Al(CH_3COO)_3$, (d) $Mn_3(PO_4)_2$

4.35 (a) arsenic trifluoride, (b) dibromine monoxide, (c) monobromine dioxide, (d) carbon diselenide, (e) dichlorine heptoxide

4.37 (a) IBr, (b) N_2S_5, (c) PI_3, (d) SiS, (e) S_4N_2

4.39 (a) Al and I_2, (b) AlI_3, (c) 45 °C, I_2 dissolved in CS_2.

4.40 (a) solid silicon tetraiodide reacts with liquid water in the presence of excess water to produce solid silicon dioxide and an aqueous solution of hydrogen iodide. (b) Aqueous arsenous acid

reacts with gaseous hydrogen sulfide to give solid arsenic(III) sulfide and liquid water.

4.41 $NaCl(aq) + H_2O(l) \xrightarrow{\text{electrolysis}} NaClO(aq) + H_2(g)$.

PROBLEMS

Molecular and Molar Mass

4.1 Calculate the molecular mass for each of the following: (a) Cl_2, (b) Fe, (c) Fe^{3+}, (d) $C_{12}H_{22}O_{11}$, (e) $KClO_3$, (f) $CoWO_4$, and (g) $Pt_2(CO)_3Cl_4$.

4.2 Calculate the molecular mass for each of the following: (a) H_2SO_4, (b) $Ca(OH)_2$, (c) $Ca_3(PO_4)_2$, and (d) $(NH_4)_2SO_4$. *Answer* (a) 98.08 u, (b) 74.10 u, (c) 310.18 u, (d) 132.16 u

4.3 Calculate the molar mass for each of the following: (a) NO_2, (b) $Ba(OH)_2$, (c) XeF_6, (d) Mn^{2+}, (e) $H_2PO_4^-$, (f) N_2, (g) $KAuI_4$, (h) $C_6H_5N_3O_4$, and (i) $Cu(IO_3)_2$.

4.4 Calculate the molar mass for each of the following: (a) H_3PO_4, (b) $(NH_4)_3AsO_4$, (c) $UO_2(SO_4)$, and (d) $HgBr_2$. *Answer* (a) 98.00 g/mol, (b) 193.07 g/mol, (c) 366.09 g/mol, (d) 360.39 g/mol

Avogadro's Number and Moles

4.5 What mass of benzene, C_6H_6, will contain a number of C_6H_6 molecules equal to Avogadro's number? *Answer* 78.12 g

4.6 What mass of $CaCl_2$ will contain a number of Ca^{2+} ions equal to Avogadro's number? What mass of $CaCl_2$ will contain a number of Cl^- ions equal to Avogadro's number? *Answer* 110.98 g, 55.49 g

4.7 How many hydrogen peroxide molecules are present in 34.02 g of H_2O_2? How many hydrogen atoms are present? How many oxygen atoms are present? What is the total number of atoms present?

4.8 How many formula units are present in 222.99 g of AuCN? How many gold(I) ions are present? How many cyanide ions are present? How many atoms are present? *Answer* 6.0220×10^{23} formula units, 6.0220×10^{23} Au^+, 6.0220×10^{23} CN^-, 1.8066×10^{24} atoms

4.9 Calculate the number of moles of each substance present in each of the following: (a) 9.5×10^{21} atoms of Cs, (b) 4.7×10^{27} molecules of CO_2, and (c) 1.63×10^{23} formula units of $BaCl_2$. *Answer* (a) 1.6×10^{-2} mol, (b) 7.8×10^3 mol, (c) 0.271 mol

4.10 Calculate the number of moles of each substance present in each of the following: (a) 5.5×10^{16} atoms of Fe, (b) 1.5×10^{24} atoms of Tc, (c) 3.92×10^{18} molecules of CH_4, (d) 4.61×10^{25} molecules of O_3, and (e) 4.6×10^{25} formula units of $Fe(NO_3)_3$.

4.11 You are given a sample containing 0.37 mol of a substance. (a) How many atoms are present if the sample is uranium metal, U? (b) How many molecules are present if the sample is acetylene, C_2H_2? (c) How many formula units are present if the sample is silver chloride, AgCl? *Answer* (a) 2.2×10^{23} atoms, (b) 2.2×10^{23} molecules, (c) 2.2×10^{23} formula units

4.12* What mass of $Al_2(SO_4)_3$ will contain a number of Al^{3+} ions equal to Avogadro's number? What mass of $Al_2(SO_4)_3$ will contain a total number of ions equal to Avogadro's number? What mass of $Al_2(SO_4)_3$ will contain a total number of atoms equal to Avogadro's number?

Molar Mass and Moles

4.13 What mass corresponds to (a) 5.3 mol of C, (b) 0.1273 mol of N_2O_5, and (c) 1.3 μmol of $AmBr_3$? *Answer* (a) 64 g, (b) 13.75 g, (c) 6.3×10^{-4} g

4.14 What mass corresponds to (a) 0.50 mol of phenol, C_6H_5OH; (b) 1.01 mol of quartz, SiO_2; (c) 3 mol of quicksilver, Hg; (d) 0.42 mol of saccharin, $C_6H_4(CO)(SO_2)NH$; and (e) 0.25 mol of saltpeter, KNO_3?

4.15 Calculate the number of moles present in each of the following samples: (a) 7.9 mg of Tc, (b) 16.8 g of NH_3, and (c) 3.25 kg of NH_4Br. *Answer* (a) 8.0×10^{-5} mol, (b) 0.986 mol, (c) 33.2 mol

4.16 Calculate the number of moles present in each of the following samples: (a) 10.03 g of calcium carbonate, $CaCO_3$; (b) 14 g of iron, Fe; (c) 24.5 g of formaldehyde, H_2CO; and (d) 33.5 g of acetic acid, CH_3COOH.

4.17* A chemist needed 14.6 g of $CuSO_4$ to perform a chemical reaction. (a) How many moles of $CuSO_4$ is this? The only source of $CuSO_4$ in the laboratory was a bottle containing $CuSO_4 \cdot 5H_2O$. (b) How many moles of $CuSO_4 \cdot 5H_2O$ will give the desired amount of $CuSO_4$? (c) What mass of $CuSO_4 \cdot 5H_2O$ contains 14.6 g of $CuSO_4$? *Answer* (a) 0.0915 mol, (b) 0.0915 mol, (c) 22.8 g

Molarity and Moles

4.18 Solutions containing (a) 10.0 g of Na_2SO_4, (b) 56 g of $CaCl_2$, and (c) 42.6 g of $Al(NO_3)_3$, dissolved in sufficient water to make a total volume of 1.00 liter of solution were prepared. What are the concentrations expressed in molarity that should be written on the respective bottles?

4.19 What is the molarity of chloride ion in a solution prepared by dissolving 16.7 g of $CaCl_2$ in sufficient water to obtain 400. mL of solution? Note that 2 mol of Cl^- are released when 1 mol of $CaCl_2$ dissolves in water. *Answer* 0.753 M

4.20* What is the molarity of a solution containing 100.00 g of $Ba(OH)_2 \cdot 8H_2O$ dissolved in enough water to make exactly 1 L of solution?

4.21 What mass of solid sodium hydroxide is needed to prepare 250.0 mL of a 0.100 M NaOH solution?

4.22 What masses of solutes are needed to prepare 250 mL of

1.0 M solutions of each of the following: (a) KCl, (b) NiCl$_2$, and (c) FeSO$_4 \cdot$7H$_2$O?

4.23* How many moles of acid are present in 108 mL of 0.62 M solution? If we add enough water to make 0.300 L of acid solution, how many moles of acid will it now contain? What is the molarity of the final solution? *Answer* 0.067 mol, 0.067 mol, 0.22 M

Percentage Composition

4.24 A 3.56 g sample of iron powder was heated in gaseous chlorine and 10.39 g of a dark substance presumed to be an iron chloride was formed. What is the percentage composition of this compound? *Answer* 34.3% Fe, 65.7% Cl

4.25 A white compound was analyzed and found to contain 0.0944 g of Ca, 0.0283 g of C, and 0.1133 g of O. What is the percentage composition of this compound?

4.26 Calculate the percentage composition of (a) KClO, (b) KClO$_2$, (c) KClO$_3$, and (d) KClO$_4$. *Answer* (a) 43.18% K, 39.15% Cl, 17.67% O; (b) 36.70% K, 33.27% Cl, 30.03% O; (c) 31.91% K, 28.93% Cl, 39.17% O; (d) 28.22% K, 25.59% Cl, 46.19% O

4.27 Calculate the percentage composition of (a) acetone, CH$_3$COCH$_3$; (b) corundum, Al$_2$O$_3$; (c) aspirin, CH$_3$COOC$_6$H$_4$COOH; (d) beryl, Be$_3$Al$_2$(SiO$_3$)$_6$; (e) carborundum, SiC; and (F) LSD, C$_{20}$H$_{25}$N$_3$O.

4.28 What mass of oxygen is contained in 5.5 g of KClO$_3$? *Answer* 2.2 g

4.29 What mass of silver is contained in (a) 0.263 g of AgF, (b) 5.92 g of AgCl, (c) 136.9 g of AgBr, and (d) 1.6 μg of AgI?

4.30 Compare the percentage of iron in (a) FeO, (b) Fe$_2$O$_3$, and (c) Fe$_3$O$_4$. (d) Assuming that the cost of shipping 1.00 lb of each oxide is the same, which oxide would be the most economical to ship in terms of maximum amount of iron delivered? *Answer* (a) 77.73%, (b) 69.94%, (c) 72.36%, (d) FeO

4.31* What mass of water is contained in 15.8 g of CuSO$_4 \cdot$5H$_2$O? *Answer* 5.70 g

4.32* One type of artificial diamond (commonly called YAG, for yttrium aluminum garnet) can be represented by the formula Y$_3$Al$_5$O$_{12}$. (a) Calculate the percentage composition of this compound. (b) What is the mass of yttrium present in a 2.0 carat YAG? (1 carat = 200 mg).

Empirical and Molecular Formulas

4.33 The hormone epinephrine is released in the human body during stress and increases the body's metabolic rate. Like many biochemical compounds, epinephrine is composed of carbon, hydrogen, oxygen, and nitrogen. The percentage composition of the hormone is 56.8% C, 6.56% H, 28.4% O, and 8.28% N. Determine the empirical formula. *Answer* C$_8$H$_{11}$O$_3$N

4.34 Determine the empirical formula for (a) copper(II) tartrate, which contains 30.03% Cu, 22.70% C, 1.91% H, and 45.37% O,

and (b) nitrosyl fluoroborate, which contains 11.99% N, 13.70% O, 9.25% B, and 65.06% F.

4.35 A compound containing 52.2% C, 13.0% H, and 34.8% O has an observed molar mass of 91.6 g. Determine (a) the empirical formula, (b) the molecular formula, and (c) the exact molar mass of the compound. *Answer* (a) C$_2$H$_6$O, (b) C$_4$H$_{12}$O$_2$, (c) 92.16 g/mol

4.36 A compound containing 12.3% N, 3.5% H, 28.0% S, and 56.1% O has an observed molar mass of 228 g. Determine (a) the empirical formula, (b) the molecular formula, and (c) the exact molar mass.

4.37* Find the empirical formula of each of the following minerals: (a) talc (used for talcum powder, ceramics, and laundry tubs), which contains 19.23% Mg, 29.62% Si, 42.18% O, and 8.97% OH; and (b) borax (used for softening water and washing clothes), which contains 12.1% Na, 11.3% B, 29.4% O, and 47.3% H$_2$O. Note that the percentages of OH in (a) and H$_2$O in (b) are given separately from the percentages of O. This is the manner in which geological analyses are stated. *Answer* (a) Mg$_3$Si$_4$O$_{10}$(OH)$_2$, (b) Na$_2$B$_4$O$_7 \cdot$10H$_2$O

4.38* A highly purified sample of carbon tetrabromide, CBr$_4$, contains 96.379% bromine and 3.621% carbon by mass. Using the atomic mass of carbon as 12.011 u, find the exact atomic mass of bromine.

4.39* Calculate the atomic mass of a metal that forms an oxide having the empirical formula M$_2$O$_3$ and contains 68.4% of the metal by mass. Identify the metal. *Answer* 51.8 u, Cr

4.40* A sample of compound weighing 2.00 g gave 4.86 g of CO$_2$ and 2.03 g of H$_2$O upon combustion in oxygen. The compound is known to contain only C, H, and O. What is its empirical formula?

4.41* A 1.000 g sample of an alcohol was burned in oxygen and produced 1.913 g of CO$_2$ and 1.174 g of H$_2$O. The alcohol contained only C, H, and O. What is the empirical formula of the alcohol? *Answer* C$_2$H$_6$O

Additional Problems

4.42 Carbon tetrachloride, CCl$_4$, was formerly used as a dry cleaning fluid. What are the (a) molecular mass and (b) molar mass of this substance? (c) Calculate the mass of one molecule of CCl$_4$. How many (d) moles and (e) molecules of CCl$_4$ are present in 17.93 g of the compound? How many (f) carbon atoms and (g) chlorine atoms are present in the 17.93 g sample? *Answer* (a) 153.81 u, (b) 153.81 g/mol, (c) 2.5541 × 10^{-22} g/molecule, (d) 0.1166 mol, (e) 7.022 × 10^{22} molecules, (f) 7.022 × 10^{22} atoms of C, (g) 2.809 × 10^{23} atoms of Cl

4.43 Test tubes containing 1.00 g samples of (a) lime, CaO; (b) slaked lime, Ca(OH)$_2$; (c) magnesium, Mg; (d) nitroglycerine, C$_3$H$_5$(NO$_3$)$_3$; and (e) water, H$_2$O, are placed in front of you. Which contains the largest number of moles? Which contains the largest number of atoms? *Answer* Water contains the largest number of both moles and atoms.

CHAPTER 5

The Gaseous State

The word "gas" was created in 1662 to describe a specific form of matter. Johann van Helmont, a Belgian physician, derived the word from the Greek word "chaos," which referred to the "great abyss" from which the earth was formed. (Some have suggested that he chose "chaos" because his equipment kept exploding when he tried to make gases.)

Progress in the understanding of gases provides a superb example of how science works. Observations led to quantitative experiments. Laws (the "gas laws") were formulated to summarize the results of the experiments. Ultimately, a theory was developed — the kinetic–molecular theory — that explained the related observations, facts, and laws. (Sometimes in science, of course, it goes the other way. A theory can come first, and then gradually be accepted as more and more experiments support its predictions.)

During the latter part of the eighteenth and the early part of the nineteenth century, chemistry advanced rapidly, largely through the study of gases. At first glance this may appear strange, for to most of us gases seem rather nebulous. Most common gases are invisible and we cannot hold a gas in our hands.

Yet the properties of gases are exactly what made the study of gases so fruitful. Gases, although they differ as widely as solids and liquids in their chemical properties, have many physical properties in common. Eventually, it became clear that these properties all depend upon one thing — the behavior of molecules flying through space. This realization led to the kinetic–molecular theory (the theory of moving molecules), which was completely in harmony with the atomic theory. Both in terms of a model of moving particles, which can be visualized, and in terms of mathematics, the kinetic–molecular theory explained what had already been observed about gas behavior and predicted much of what has since been observed. This theory is still providing new information about the gaseous state.

THE NATURE OF GASES

5.1 GENERAL PROPERTIES OF GASES

Most familiar gases are colorless and odorless — the oxygen and nitrogen of the atmosphere, the bubbles of carbon dioxide that rise in a glass of soda pop, or the hydrogen or helium gas that is used to fill balloons. A few gases are colored; for example, nitrogen dioxide (NO_2) is red-brown, and iodine vapor has a beautiful violet color. And anything that we can smell can exist in the gaseous state, because our sense of smell reacts only to gases.

The names and formulas of some compounds that are gases are given in Table 5.1. Eleven of the elements are also gases (H_2, N_2, O_2, F_2, Cl_2, He, Ne, Ar, Kr, Xe, Rn). The word "gas" is used to refer to a substance that at ordinary temperatures and pressures is present in the gaseous state only. The word "vapor" is reserved for a gas that has evaporated from a material that is usually solid or liquid at ordinary temperatures. The term **volatile** is applied to a substance that forms a vapor very readily. For example, ether is a volatile liquid.

CO	Carbon monoxide	Odorless, poisonous
CO_2	Carbon dioxide	Odorless, nonpoisonous
NH_3	Ammonia	Pungent odor, poisonous
PH_3	Phosphine	Terrible odor, very poisonous
CH_4	Methane	Odorless, flammable
C_2H_2	Acetylene	Mild odor, flammable
HCl	Hydrogen chloride	Choking odor, harmful and poisonous
SO_2	Sulfur dioxide	Suffocating odor, irritating to eyes, poisonous
NO_2	Nitrogen dioxide	Red-brown, irritating odor, very poisonous
H_2S	Hydrogen sulfide	Rotten egg odor, very poisonous

Table 5.1
Gases This is a list of some compounds that are gases at ordinary temperatures and pressures. Pranksters often ask for a harmless gas with a very bad odor, but there is no such thing—all evil-smelling gases are poisonous. Some odorless gases, such as CO, are also poisonous, of course.

Gases have many easily observable physical properties (Table 5.2). They fill whatever space is available, but can be compressed into a smaller volume by applying pressure. They are affected by temperature, for a given quantity of gas can expand and contract, or exert different pressures, depending on the temperature. It is obvious from the force of the wind on a stormy day that gases can flow readily from place to place and that they have mass. However, gases are not very dense—a vessel filled with air floats on the surface of a pond because the air is less dense than the water. (The densities of some common gases are listed in Table 5.3.)

Because of their interrelated effects, temperature, pressure, and volume must always be specified when gases are discussed. (See Tools of Chemistry: Pressure Units and Pressure Measurement; also Sections 2.8 b, e, and g.) The quantitative relationships among the temperature, pressure, and volume of a gas are expressed in the gas laws, which were first explored in the eighteenth and nineteenth centuries (see A Historical Aside: Pneumatic Chemistry). The *kinetic–molecular theory* is a mathematical model that was eventually developed to explain the physical behavior of gases. The model is successful in explaining the gas laws, and it applies to many other aspects of gas behavior as well as to some of the properties of liquids and solids. We have chosen to discuss the kinetic–molecular theory first, so that in subsequent sections it will become apparent how each of the gas laws is explained by the theory.

Table 5.2
Observable Properties of Gases

Fill whatever space is available and take shape of container
Infinitely expandable
Very compressible
Flow rapidly
Expand and contract with changes in temperature
Exert greater pressure when temperature rises
Low density

5.2 KINETIC–MOLECULAR THEORY OF GASES

The essential concept of the kinetic–molecular theory is that molecules are always in motion. The molecules in a gas are continuously and freely moving about, colliding with each other and whatever surfaces are nearby (Figure 5.1). (Molecules in the solid and liquid states are also in motion, but in these states the motion is much more limited than in the gaseous state; Section 13.1.)

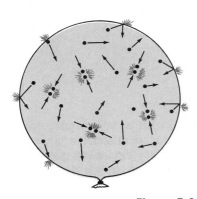

Figure 5.1
Molecular Motion in a Gas Gas molecules are far apart, constantly moving in random straight lines, and colliding with each other and the walls of the container. The pressure on the container walls is the sum of the force of the individual impacts.

Table 5.3 **Densities of Some Gases** The values given are the densities at 0 °C and atmospheric pressure at sea level.

	Density (g/L)
Gas	
Hydrogen (H_2)	**0.090**
Helium (He)	**0.179**
Nitrogen (N_2)	**1.256**
Carbon monoxide (CO)	**1.256**
Air	**1.297**
Oxygen (O_2)	**1.429**
Argon (Ar)	**1.783**
Carbon dioxide (CO_2)	**1.965**
Chlorine (Cl_2)	**3.165**
Sulfur hexafluoride (SF_6)	**6.602 (20 °C)**
For comparison	
Water	**1000 (4 °C)**
Ethyl alcohol	**790**

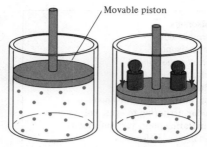

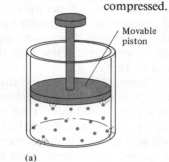

Figure 5.2
Compression of a Gas Gas molecules are far apart relative to their size and gases are easily compressed.

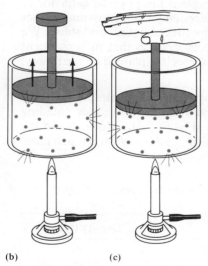

(a)

(b)   (c)

Figure 5.3
Effect on a Gas of Increasing Temperature (a) Gas in a cylinder with a movable piston. (b) With increasing temperature the molecules move faster, hit the piston with greater force, and push it up while the pressure remains the same. (c) When the piston cannot move, as the molecules move faster they hit the piston with greater force and more often, and the pressure increases.

The five statements given below summarize the kinetic–molecular theory of gases. Keep in mind that these statements form the basis for a mathematical model. As is often the case, to develop such a model some simplifying assumptions must be made. In theory, molecules with all of these properties would exactly fulfill the quantitative predictions of the gas laws, which you will be learning in later sections of this chapter. A gas that perfectly obeys the gas laws is called an **ideal gas.** Under many conditions, real gases behave very much like ideal gases. In the discussions and examples in the following sections of this chapter, we deal mostly with ideal gas behavior.

1. Gases are made up of molecules that are relatively far apart; in comparison with their size, the spaces between them are large. A substance in the gaseous state occupies a much larger volume than the same amount of that substance in the liquid or solid state. For example, when liquid water at 100°C and 1 atm pressure changes to steam at the same temperature and pressure, the volume of the steam is about 1700 times greater than the volume of the same amount of water. The same number of water molecules have simply spread out over a much larger space. Gases can be compressed easily because the distances between neighboring molecules decrease when pressure is applied (Figure 5.2). In an *ideal* gas, the molecules are considered to be so small relative to the spaces between them that they occupy virtually no volume.

2. The molecules of a gas are in constant motion, and their collisions with surfaces cause gas pressure. Molecules in the gaseous state are constantly moving at random in straight lines. The molecules change direction only when they collide with each other or with the walls of their container. The gas pressure is the result of impacts with the walls. In an inflated balloon, it is the impact of multitudes of gas molecules with the inside of the balloon that keeps it stretched out and prevents it from collapsing (see Figure 5.1). The pressure does not vary with each blow because the number of gas molecules is very large, the molecules move rapidly, and the impacts are so frequent that they cannot be detected individually. (A molecule of a gas at 25°C and 1 atm undergoes roughly 1×10^9 collisions per second.) Although the spaces between gas molecules are great, gases fill any container by constantly moving about through its entire volume. (Think of how quickly the smell of frying onions fills a house.)

3. The average speed and average kinetic energy of gas molecules are directly proportional to the temperature. The energy of a moving body—kinetic energy, E_k—is a function of the body's mass, m, and its velocity, u. As the velocity of a body increases, its kinetic energy increases.

$$\underset{\substack{kinetic \\ energy}}{\longrightarrow} E_k = \frac{1}{2} m u^2 \overset{mass}{\underset{velocity}{\longleftarrow}} \qquad (5.1)$$

According to kinetic-molecular theory, the kinetic energy of an atom or molecule in a gas, and therefore also its velocity, is a function of temperature. As the temperature increases, the average of the kinetic energy of all of the molecules in a sample of gas increases, and as the temperature falls, the average kinetic energy decreases. We can therefore say that average kinetic energy and temperature are directly proportional to each other. (See the next section for a discussion of proportionality.) Also, the velocities of the individual molecules, and therefore the average speed of all of the molecules in a sample of gas, must also increase and decrease with temperature in a proportional relationship.

As the molecules of a gas confined in a vessel move faster and faster, they collide with the walls more often and with more force. If the walls are fixed, the pressure on the walls increases. If the walls are flexible, they are pushed back and the volume increases instead (Figure 5.3). With lower temperatures and the resulting lower

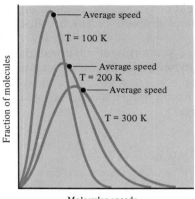

Figure 5.4
**Distribution of Molecular
Speeds** Both the average speed and
the range of speeds increases with
increasing temperature. At any
given temperature, very few
molecules have the highest or the
lowest speeds.

molecular velocities, the opposite effects occur—pressure decreases and volume decreases.

Note that not all the molecules in a gas sample are flying about at the same speed (Figure 5.4). Some go much faster than others. Collisions between molecules continually cause exchanges in energy, slowing down some molecules and speeding up others. It is the *average* speed of all the molecules in a gas that increases as the temperature is raised.

4. At the same temperature, the molecules of every gas have the same average kinetic energy. If $E_k = \frac{1}{2} mu^2$ has the same average value for every gas at a given temperature, then molecules with larger mass must, on the average, move more slowly at that temperature than molecules with smaller mass. In short, the larger the m, the smaller the u. As a consequence, a gas with a lower molar mass released into a container will spread throughout the container more quickly than will a gas with a higher molar mass.

5. Collisions of gas molecules with each other or with the walls of a container are perfectly elastic. When ideal gas molecules collide with each other or with the walls of a container, they bounce off with no loss in energy—they undergo frictionless, or perfectly elastic, collisions. Energy may be exchanged between colliding molecules, but the *total* energy of the molecules that have collided is the same after the collision as it was before. Ideal gas molecules are assumed to exert no forces of attraction or repulsion on each other. If the gas molecules attracted each other, their collisions would not be perfectly elastic.

In summary, gases have in common many easily observable physical properties. The kinetic–molecular theory explains these properties by assuming that gas molecules are constantly in motion in random straight-line paths. Gas pressure is the result of the collisions of gas molecules with the walls of a container. In an ideal gas, the gas molecules occupy a negligible volume, collisions are perfectly elastic, and the molecules exert no forces of attraction or repulsion on each other. The average kinetic energy of gas molecules increases with the temperature, causing increases in pressure or volume. (Average kinetic energy and average speed are both proportional to temperature.) A mathematical model based on these assumptions is successful at explaining gas behavior.

VOLUME, PRESSURE, AND TEMPERATURE RELATIONSHIPS

The pressure, volume, and temperature of a sample of gas are all properties that can be measured, and the value of each is dependent on the values of the other two. The mathematical relationships that express the variations in these properties are referred to as the "gas laws." The gas laws are introduced in Sections 5.4–5.6, 5.8, and 5.10. In the next section, the mathematical concepts of variable quantities and proportionality, which are utilized in the gas laws and numerous other relationships in chemistry, are reviewed.

5.3 VARIABLES AND PROPORTIONALITY

Measurable properties of a system that can change are called **variables.** The pressure, volume, temperature, and the amount of a gas are all variables. To investigate the effects of changes in one variable on changes in a related variable, other quantities must be held constant. If this were not done, it would not be possible to identify which of several variable quantities is related to the changes observed. The study of the gas laws illustrates this experimental approach. Sections 5.4–5.6 discuss the effects of changing variables on a *fixed* amount of gas. Boyle's law experiments deal with changes in volume and pressure, while temperature and the amount of gas are held constant. Charles' law experiments deal with changes in temperature and

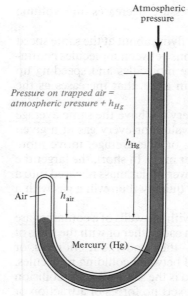

Atmospheric pressure

Pressure on trapped air = atmospheric pressure + h_{Hg}

h_{Hg}

Air — h_{air}

Mercury (Hg)

Figure 5.5
Boyle's Apparatus for Measuring Volume Changes with Changing Pressure The height, h_{air}, is proportional to the volume of the trapped gas. The total pressure on the trapped gas is the atmospheric pressure plus the pressure of the mercury column, which is varied by adding mercury to the open side of the J tube. Boyle said that the particles of air behaved like coiled springs.

volume while pressure and the amount of gas are held constant. The relationship between temperature and pressure while volume and amount of gas are held constant can be studied similarly.

Each of the gas laws is based upon one or more proportional relationships. Proportional quantities are related to each other mathematically by multiplication by a constant.

In a *direct proportion* one variable is equal to a constant times a second variable. A **constant** has a numerical value that does not change.

a direct proportion

variable

$$a = kb \qquad \text{or} \qquad \frac{a}{b} = k \qquad \textbf{(5.2)}$$

variable *constant*

If the value of a doubles, the value of b doubles, so that their ratio a/b remains the same and is equal to k. If a is tripled in value, then b also triples in value, and so on. Whatever changes in a and b occur, a/b is equal to the same constant.

In an *inverse proportion* one quantity is equal to a constant times the *reciprocal* of the other quantity (the reciprocal of b is $1/b$).

an inverse proportion

$$a = k \times \frac{1}{b} \qquad \text{or} \qquad ab = k \qquad \textbf{(5.3)}$$

variable *variable*

constant

Here if the value of variable a doubles, the value of b is halved, so that their product remains constant and equal to k. If the value of a triples, then b is decreased to one-third of its original value, and so on. Whatever changes in a and b occur, $a \times b$ is equal to the same constant.

5.4 VOLUME VERSUS PRESSURE: BOYLE'S LAW

Boyle's law applies to volume and pressure changes when the temperature and amount of a gas are constant. The volume of the gas decreases when the pressure exerted on the gas increases, and vice versa. For example, the helium in a balloon vendor's tank is under high pressure. The pressure within the balloons that the vendor fills is much lower. Therefore, the total volume of all of the balloons that the vendor can fill from the tank will be much greater than that of the tank itself.

The apparatus used by Boyle in his experiments is shown in Figure 5.5. He observed that if the pressure on a gas is doubled while the temperature remains unchanged, the gas volume decreases to one-half the original volume; if the pressure is tripled, the gas volume decreases to one-third the original volume; and so on. These are changes characteristic of an inversely proportional relationship.

Boyle's law is stated as follows: <u>At constant temperature, the volume of a given mass of gas is inversely proportional to the pressure upon the gas.</u> Stated mathematically, Boyle's law is

Boyle's law: At constant T, V is inversely proportional to P.

At constant temperature and mass of gas:

an inverse proportion

volume of the gas

$$V = \text{constant} \times \frac{1}{P} \qquad \text{or} \qquad PV = \text{constant} \qquad \textbf{(5.4)}$$

pressure of the gas

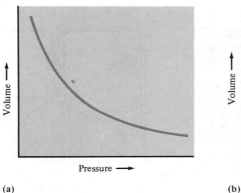
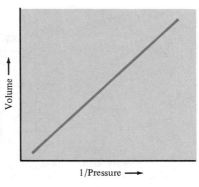

(a)   (b)

Figure 5.6
Boyle's law In (a) volume is plotted versus pressure for a gas at constant temperature. If volume is plotted versus the reciprocal of the pressure (1/P) as in (b), a straight line is obtained. Plots like these are always obtained when the two plotted quantities are inversely proportional to each other.

These relationships hold for any given quantity of gas at a fixed temperature, whether the gas is a pure substance or a mixture. Volume is plotted versus pressure in Figure 5.6, showing the types of curves always obtained for inversely proportional quantities.

According to kinetic–molecular theory, when gas volume decreases, the space between gas molecules becomes smaller (Figure 5.7). With less space to move around in, but no change in the speed with which they are moving (constant temperature), the gas molecules are bound to collide with the walls more often, leading to higher pressure.

For a given amount of the same gas, at constant temperature, we can write $PV = k$, where k is a constant. For the product of P and V to remain equal to the same constant, when P or V changes, then the other quantity must change also. Let's say P_1 is the initial pressure and P_2 is the new pressure. Mathematically,

$$P_1V_1 = k \qquad P_2V_2 = k$$

and therefore P_1V_1 and P_2V_2 must equal each other.

$$P_1V_1 = P_2V_2 \tag{5.5}$$

To find the new pressure, Equation (5.5) can be solved for P_2.

$$P_2 = \frac{P_1V_1}{V_2} \tag{5.6}$$

An application of Boyle's law is shown in Figure 5.8.

The factor V_1/V_2 in Equation (5.6) can be thought of as a correction factor: Multiplying the original pressure, P_1, by this correction factor gives the new pressure.

Figure 5.7
Effect of Volume Change on an Equal Number of Gas Molecules at Constant Temperature For equal amounts of the same gas at the same temperature, the molecules moving at the same speed collide with the walls twice as often at one-half the volume, and so on.

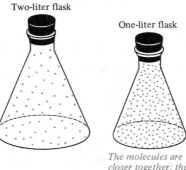

Two-liter flask

One-liter flask

The molecules are closer together; the density is doubled.

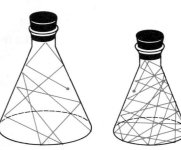

The average molecule hits the wall twice as often. The total number of impacts with the wall is doubled and the pressure is doubled.

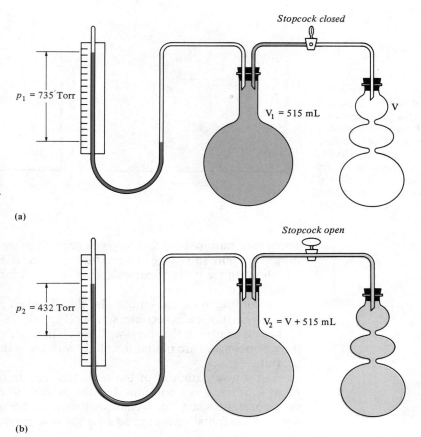

Stopcock closed

$p_1 = 735$ Torr

$V_1 = 515$ mL

V

(a)

Stopcock open

$p_2 = 432$ Torr

$V_2 = V + 515$ mL

(b)

Figure 5.8
Volume Determination Boyle's law can be used to find the volume of an irregularly shaped container by (1) evacuating the container, (2) connecting to it a container holding a gas of known volume (V_1) at a known pressure (P_1), as shown in (a), (3) allowing the gas to fill both containers as shown in (b), (4) measuring the final pressure of the combined system (P_2), and (5) using Boyle's law to calculate the unknown volume (V_2). In the experiment illustrated, the flask on the left held 515 mL of air at 735 Torr. After the stopcock was opened, the pressure was 432 Torr. Solving Equation (5.5) with $V_2 = V + 515$ mL gave 361 mL as the volume of the flask on the right.

Use of this reasoning either to solve a problem or to provide a common-sense check of the answer to a problem is illustrated in the next example.

EXAMPLE 5.1
$P–V–T–n$ Relationships:
V and P

A sample of an ideal gas at 0.93 atm and 25 °C occupied a volume of 17.3 L. This gas was transferred to a 3.7 L container without a temperature change. What was the pressure of the gas under the new conditions?

Because the process involved a fixed mass of gas and was done at a constant temperature, the Boyle's law relationship, $P_1V_1 = P_2V_2$, can be used to find the final pressure. The original conditions of the gas were

$$P_1 = 0.93 \text{ atm} \qquad V_1 = 17.3 \text{ L}$$

and the final conditions are

$$P_2 = ? \qquad V_2 = 3.7 \text{ L}$$

Using Equation (5.5), solving for P_2, and substituting the above values gives

$$P_2 = (P_1)\left(\frac{V_1}{V_2}\right) = (0.93 \text{ atm})\left(\frac{17.3 \text{ L}}{3.7 \text{ L}}\right) = 4.3 \text{ atm}$$

The new pressure is 4.3 atm.

Without using Equation (5.5), this problem can be solved by thinking through what must happen to the original pressure. Because the volume has decreased, the pressure must increase. Therefore, the correction factor for P_1 based on the known volumes must be greater than one, that is, it must be (17.3 L/3.7 L). As a common-sense check on the answer obtained above, we can see that the new pressure found is greater than the original pressure, and this is reasonable, for the volume decreased.

Exercise What will be the volume occupied by an ideal gas at 75 kPa after it has expanded from 10.0 L and 145 kPa at constant temperature? *Answer* 19 L

TOOLS OF CHEMISTRY

Pressure Units and Pressure Measurement

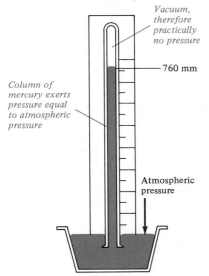

Figure A
Mercury Barometer The height of the column of mercury in millimeters is read as the atmospheric pressure. The space above the mercury is not a complete vacuum, for a little mercury evaporates into it. But at ordinary temperatures this vapor pressure is so small that it can be disregarded.

Vacuum, therefore practically no pressure

760 mm

Column of mercury exerts pressure equal to atmospheric pressure

Atmospheric pressure

---

1 atm = 760 Torr

Pressure is defined as force per unit area. The atmosphere exerts pressure on the surface of the earth and on all sides of all objects on the earth's surface. The first **barometer**—an instrument that measures atmospheric pressure—was made in about 1643 by Evangelista Torricelli, who worked with Galileo.

Torricelli filled a tube with mercury and inverted it in a dish of mercury. He found that whatever the length or diameter of the tube, the mercury always fell in the tube to the same height above the mercury level in the dish, about 760 mm (Figure A). At this height, the weight of the mercury is balanced by the constant pressure exerted by the atmosphere on the surface of the mercury in the dish. Pressure is still sometimes expressed in millimeters of mercury (e.g., a pressure of 20 mmHg).

The height of the liquid column in the barometer depends on the density of the liquid, as well as on the atmospheric pressure. Since it is very dense, mercury is best for barometers, because the column is of a convenient height. The atmosphere supports a column of water about 34 ft high, not too useful for barometers.

The average pressure of the atmosphere at sea level is 760 mmHg. High pressures are frequently expressed in units of atmospheres: 1 atmosphere (atm) = 760 mmHg. For example, a pressure of 25 atm means a pressure equal to 25 × 760 mmHg.

The unit "mmHg" has caused some distress because it makes pressure look like a function of length, which it is not. To avoid this problem, the Torr (for Torricelli) was defined as a unit of pressure: 1 Torr = 1 mmHg and 760 Torr = 1 atm.

Atmospheric pressure is today often measured with an aneroid barometer. An aneroid barometer depends upon the flexibility of the wall of an evacuated box. As atmospheric pressure varies, the wall of the box moves in and out. A mechanical linkage connects the wall to a dial calibrated in pressure units (Figure B). The simple gauges used on gas tanks and for measuring tire pressure operate on the same principle as the aneroid barometer.

A **manometer** is an instrument used to measure gas pressure in closed systems. A manometer that compares the unknown pressure with atmospheric pressure (or with a vacuum) is shown in Figure C.

Uniformity in the choice of units for the measurement of gas pressures seems particularly far off. Each branch of science and engineering has its own preferences. Engineers, in particular, frequently express pressure in units with the dimensions of force per unit area, such as pounds per square inch or dynes per square

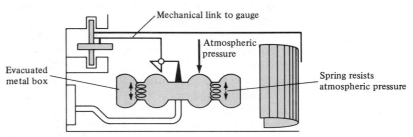

Mechanical link to gauge

Atmospheric pressure

Evacuated metal box

Spring resists atmospheric pressure

Figure B
An Aneroid Barometer One wall of the evacuated metal box is flexible and moves in and out with changes in pressure.

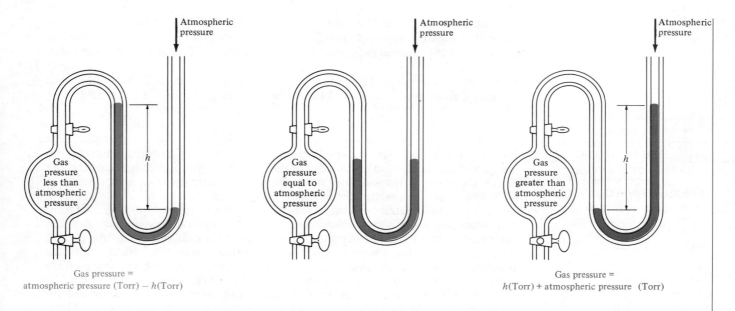

Gas pressure =
atmospheric pressure (Torr) − h(Torr)

Gas pressure =
h(Torr) + atmospheric pressure (Torr)

Figure C
Open-Tube Manometer The difference in the height of the mercury columns in the two arms of the tube is measured in mm Hg, and atmospheric pressure is read from a standard barometer. The unknown pressure in the flask or whatever gas system is attached to the manometer is then calculated as shown. In a closed-tube manometer, the vertical tube is sealed and evacuated.

centimeter. A distinction is sometimes made between "absolute pressure" and "gauge pressure." When, for example, the pressure in a tire is given as 30 lb/sq. inch, or 30 psi, it means that the pressure is 30 psi *greater* than atmospheric pressure. This is sometimes indicated by writing 30 psig, where the "g" stands for "gauge pressure"—pressure greater than that of the atmosphere. Absolute pressure *includes* the atmospheric pressure, and for this tire would be 44.7 psia. In chemistry we usually deal with absolute pressures.

The SI unit for pressure is the pascal. Pressure is force per unit area, and the pascal is related to the SI unit of force, the newton, as follows:

$$1 \text{ newton (N)} = 1 \text{ kg m/s}^2 \qquad 1 \text{ pascal (Pa)} = 1 \text{ newton/m}^2 = 1 \text{ kg/s}^2 \text{ m}$$

The units for pressure are summarized in the following table:

Pressure Units

1 mmHg = 1 Torr (exactly)	1 atm = 760 Torr
1 Pa = 1 kg/m s^2 (exactly)	= 14.7 psi
= 7.50 × 10^{-3} Torr	= 101,325 Pa
	= 1.01325 bar

5.5 VOLUME VERSUS TEMPERATURE: CHARLES' LAW

Charles' law applies to volume and temperature changes when the pressure and amount of a gas are constant. As a gas is heated, it expands, and as it is cooled, it contracts. Have you ever left a balloon or a rubber raft in the bright sunlight and seen it burst? As the temperature rises the balloon or the raft expands. Eventually its maximum volume is reached, and as the temperature increases still further the increasing pressure within causes it to burst.

The increase or decrease in gas volume has been found by experiment to be the *same* for each Celsius degree of temperature change over a large range of temperatures. The volume change is close to $\frac{1}{273}$ of the volume which that quantity of the gas would have at 0 °C. Suppose we start with 273 mL of oxygen at 0 °C and increase the temperature by 1 °C. The volume will increase to 274 mL. At 100 °C this gas sample would have a volume of 373 mL and an increase of the temperature by one more Celsius degree would still increase the volume by 1 mL—to 374 mL.

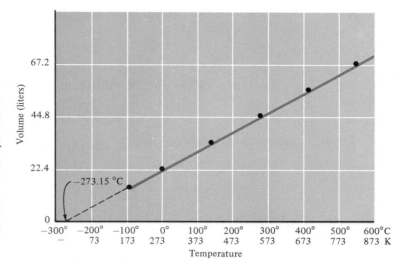

Figure 5.9
Charles' Law Volume is plotted versus temperature at constant pressure. This graph shows the variation in the volume of 1 mol of an ideal gas with changing temperature. The equivalent temperatures on the Celsius and Kelvin scales are shown. Note that when the Kelvin temperature doubles (2 × 273 K) the volume occupied by 1 mol doubles (from 22.4 L to 44.8 L).

Plotting the volume versus the temperature for any quantity of a gas at constant pressure gives a straight line, showing that volume and temperature have a directly proportional relationship. Such a plot for an ideal gas is drawn in Figure 5.9. The dashed portion of the plot illustrates a "logical" conclusion from the observations: When an ideal gas is cooled to −273.15 °C, it should disappear entirely. We know from experiment that this does not happen. Instead, Charles' law becomes a less and less accurate description of gas behavior as the temperature decreases. In other words, at lower temperatures the gas becomes less like an ideal gas. The velocities of the molecules decrease, spaces between them become smaller, and the real forces of attraction that do exist between molecules take effect. Before −273.15 °C is reached, the gas molecules get close enough together for the forces of attraction between them to overcome the energy of their random motion; as a result, the gas liquefies or solidifies.

When extended, a plot of volume versus temperature for any ideal gas will reach zero volume at the same temperature. This temperature is **absolute zero,** −273.15 °C, the lowest possible temperature. According to kinetic–molecular theory, temperature drops as energy is removed. At absolute zero no further energy can be removed and this means that no lower temperature is possible. Absolute zero has been approached to within a few thousandths of a degree in the laboratory, but never attained.

About 100 years after Charles' law was formulated, the British physicist Lord Kelvin realized how useful it would be to define an **absolute temperature scale**—a scale that takes absolute zero as its zero point. The **Kelvin temperature scale** (see Section 2.8e and Figure 2.3) is the absolute temperature scale based on the Celsius scale; 0 K is equal to −273.15 °C. (There are other absolute temperature scales; the only requirement is that on an absolute scale the zero point is absolute zero.) Kelvin's scale allows **Charles' law** to be stated as follows: At constant pressure, the volume of a given mass of gas is directly proportional to the absolute temperature. Mathematically, Charles' law takes the following forms:

Charles' law: At constant P, V is directly proportional to T.

At constant pressure and for a given mass of gas:

temperature of the gas in kelvins

$$V = \text{constant} \times T \quad \text{or} \quad \frac{V}{T} = \text{constant} \qquad (5.7)$$

a direct proportion

By the same reasoning as used for Boyle's law, we can say that since $V_1/T_1 = k$ and $V_2/T_2 = k$, then

$$\frac{V_1}{T_1} = \frac{V_2}{T_2} \tag{5.8}$$

To find a new temperature or volume, therefore, we set

$$V_2 = \frac{T_2 V_1}{T_1} \qquad T_2 = \frac{T_1 V_2}{V_1}$$

The correction factors here are T_2/T_1 or V_2/V_1.

EXAMPLE 5.2
P–V–T–n **Relationships:**
V and *T*

A cylinder with a movable piston (see Figure 5.3) is filled at 24 °C with a gas that occupies 36.2 cm³. If the maximum capacity of the cylinder is 65.2 cm³, what is the highest temperature to which the cylinder can be heated at constant pressure without having the piston come out?

The initial and final conditions of the gas are

$$V_1 = 36.2 \text{ cm}^3 \qquad T_1 = 24° + 273 = 297 \text{ K}$$
$$V_2 = 65.2 \text{ cm}^3 \qquad T_2 = ?$$

(Note that temperature must always be given on the Kelvin scale in gas law problems.) Solving Charles' law, Equation (5.8), for T_2 and substituting the known values gives

$$T_2 = (T_1)\left(\frac{V_2}{V_1}\right) = (297 \text{ K})\left(\frac{65.2 \text{ cm}^3}{36.2 \text{ cm}^3}\right) = 535 \text{ K}$$

The highest temperature to which the gas in the cylinder can be heated is 535 K, or 262 °C. (Let's apply the common-sense check of the solution to make sure that we have not made an error. The volume of the gas increases in this problem. Charles' law tell us that for this to occur, the temperature must have increased. Mathematically, V_2/V_1, the correction factor that must be applied to the temperature, is greater than 1. Thus the answer of 535 K seems reasonable.)

Exercise The temperature of a 35.2-L sample of a gas was changed from 25 °C to 75 °C while keeping the pressure constant. What is the new volume? *Answer* 41.1 L

5.6 *P, V,* AND *T* CHANGES
IN A FIXED MASS OF GAS

The relationships among pressure, volume, and temperature expressed in Boyle's law and Charles' law (Equations 5.5 and 5.8) can be combined mathematically.

For a fixed mass of gas:
$$\frac{P_1 V_1}{T_1} = \frac{P_2 V_2}{T_2} \tag{5.9}$$

Combined gas law: For a fixed amount of gas,

$$\frac{P_1 V_1}{T_1} = \frac{P_2 V_2}{T_2}$$

This equation can be used to solve any problems involving changes in the variables *P, V,* and *T* for a given mass of a gas. Knowing any five of the quantities in Equation (5.9), the sixth can be calculated. When one variable remains unchanged ($P_1 = P_2$, or $V_1 = V_2$, or $T_1 = T_2$), that variable can be cancelled from both sides of the equation (Table 5.4).

To determine the value of one quantity in Equation (5.9), first solve the equation for that quantity. For example, suppose you know the initial conditions P_1, V_1, and

Table 5.4
***P, V, T*, Changes in a Fixed Mass of Gas** The subscript 1 indicates the initial conditions and the subscript 2 the new conditions.

At constant P, $\dfrac{V_1}{T_1} = \dfrac{V_2}{T_2}$

At constant V, $\dfrac{P_1}{T_1} = \dfrac{P_2}{T_2}$

At constant T, $P_1 V_1 = P_2 V_2$

T_1 and the final conditions P_2 and T_2, and you wish to calculate V_2. First determine that

$$V_2 = \left(\frac{P_1}{P_2}\right)\left(\frac{T_2}{T_1}\right)(V_1)$$

Here, the initial volume is multiplied by *two* correction factors to give the new volume.

The first of the following examples is solved by our method for *thinking* through a problem to a logical solution (Section 2.11).

EXAMPLE 5.3
***P–V–T–n* Relationships:**
P* and *T

A sample of gas confined in a 2.0 L container at 930 Torr and 25 °C was heated to 45 °C. What was the final pressure?

1. Study the problem and be sure that you understand it.
   (a) What is known?
       The initial and final conditions for a gas that has been heated at constant volume:

       $P_1 = 930$ Torr $T_1 = 25\,°C$ $V_1 = 2.0$ L
       $T_2 = 45\,°C$ $V_2 = 2.0$ L

   (b) What is unknown?
       The final pressure, P_2.
2. Decide how to solve the problem.
   (a) What is the connection between the known and the unknown?
       This is a gas law problem for a fixed mass of gas. As for all problems of this type, the connection can be made by using

       $$\frac{P_1 V_1}{T_1} = \frac{P_2 V_2}{T_2}$$

       (Alternatively, the correction factors that must be applied to the initial pressure can be employed.)
   (b) What is necessary to make the connection?
       First, recognizing that $V_1 = V_2$, cancel these terms from the equation. Then solve for the unknown, P_2.

       $$\frac{P_1}{T_1} = \frac{P_2}{T_2} \qquad P_2 = \frac{P_1 T_2}{T_1}$$

       This is the same expression that we would obtain by utilizing the other approach — adjusting the initial pressure (P_1) by a correction factor (T_2/T_1) based on the temperature change. Before the problem can be solved, the temperature, which is given in Celsius degrees, must be converted to temperature on the Kelvin scale for use in a gas law calculation.

       $T_1 = 25° + 273 = 298$ K
       $T_2 = 45° + 273 = 318$ K

3. Set up the problem and solve it.

   $$P_2 = (930 \text{ Torr})\left(\frac{318 \text{ K}}{298 \text{ K}}\right) = 990 \text{ Torr}$$

4. Check the result.
    (a) Are significant figures used correctly?
        Yes; the limit is two significant figures.
    (b) Did the answer come out in the correct units?
        Yes; the temperature units in the correction factor cancel.
    (c) Is the answer reasonable?
        An increase in temperature should cause an increase in pressure at constant volume, and the correction factor should be larger than 1, which it is (318 K/298 K). The final pressure is greater than the initial pressure, and the answer is reasonable.

EXAMPLE 5.4
P–V–T–n **Relationships:**
P, V, and T

A sample of hydrogen occupied a volume of 4.00 L at 760. Torr and 31 °C. What volume would the gas occupy at 205 °C and 382 Torr?

All three variables change for this gas sample. The initial and final conditions are

$P_1 = 760.$ Torr $T_1 = 31° + 273 = 304$ K $V_1 = 4.00$ L
$P_2 = 382$ Torr $T_2 = 205° + 273 = 478$ K $V_2 = ?$

Solving Equation (5.9) for V_2 and substituting into it the above values gives

$$V_2 = (V_1)\left(\frac{P_1}{P_2}\right)\left(\frac{T_2}{T_1}\right)$$

$$= (4.00 \text{ L})\left(\frac{760. \text{ Torr}}{382 \text{ Torr}}\right)\left(\frac{478 \text{ K}}{304 \text{ K}}\right) = 12.5 \text{ L}$$

The volume of the gas under the new conditions is 12.5 L. (Even in this more complicated problem, we can apply the common-sense check of the answer. The factor P_1/P_2 should be larger than 1 because the pressure on the hydrogen gas has decreased, which means the volume must increase. Also, the factor T_2/T_1 should be larger than 1 because an increase in the temperature on the gas means the volume must increase. The factors of 760 Torr/380 Torr and 478 K/304 K, both larger than 1, do seem reasonable.)

Exercise An ideal gas that initially had a volume of 175 L at 15 atm and 298 K was compressed to 75 L at 5.0 atm. What was the new temperature of this gas?
Answer 43 K

5.7 STANDARD TEMPERATURE
AND PRESSURE (STP)

Because the volume of a gas changes with both pressure and temperature, stating only the volume of a gas is not sufficient to indicate the quantity of gas present. The temperature and pressure at which the volume was measured must also be given. For example, 4 L of hydrogen at 760 Torr and 30 °C is about three times as much hydrogen as 4 L of hydrogen at 380 Torr and 200 °C.

To simplify comparisons among quantities of gases, scientists have agreed always to state gas volume at a specified temperature and pressure. The **standard temperature and pressure** (abbreviated STP) universally used for this purpose are 0 °C (273 K) and 760 Torr.

STP = 0 °C (273 K),
760 Torr (1 atm)

The volume of a gas is often reported as, for example, 25 L (STP). When the pressure and temperature are not given with a gas volume, you can assume that the conditions are STP. Measurements of gas volumes need not, of course, always be made at STP conditions. But the volume measured under any conditions of temperature and pressure may be converted to the value at STP by the combined expression of Boyle's and Charles' laws.

EXAMPLE 5.5
$P-V-T-n$ **Relationships:**
P, V, **and** T

What is the volume at STP of a sample of gas that occupies 16.5 L at 352 °C and 0.275 atm?

This problem is solved in the same way as Example 5.4. The initial and final conditions are

$$P_1 = 0.275 \text{ atm} \qquad V_1 = 16.5 \text{ L} \qquad T_1 = 352° + 273 = 625 \text{ K}$$

$$P_{\text{STP}} = 1.000 \text{ atm} \qquad V_{\text{STP}} = ? \qquad T_{\text{STP}} = 0° + 273 = 273 \text{ K}$$

$$V_{\text{STP}} = V_1 \left(\frac{P_1}{P_{\text{STP}}} \right) \left(\frac{T_{\text{STP}}}{T_1} \right) = (16.5 \text{ L}) \left(\frac{0.275 \text{ atm}}{1.000 \text{ atm}} \right) \left(\frac{273 \text{ K}}{625 \text{ K}} \right) = 1.98 \text{ L}$$

The volume of the gas at STP will be 1.98 L.

Exercise What will be the volume at STP of a sample of gas that occupies 35.2 mL at 27 °C and 742 Torr? *Answer* 31.3 mL

In summary, for a fixed amount of gas, Boyle's law expresses the relationship of volume to pressure at constant temperature, V = k × (1/P), and Charles' law expresses the relationship of volume to temperature at constant pressure, V = kT. In all calculations dealing with gas laws, temperature is expressed on an absolute temperature scale, usually the Kelvin scale. The combined gas law, Equation (5.9), combines the relationships of pressure, temperature, and volume for a fixed amount of gas. At constant temperature or constant pressure, the combined gas law reduces to Boyle's law or Charles' law, respectively. Gas volumes are reported at STP, standard temperature and pressure, which are 0 °C and 760 Torr.

A HISTORICAL ASIDE

Pneumatic Chemistry

A chapter on gases in a chemistry textbook is overrun with laws named for scientists of the past. A chronology of the study and discovery of gases is given in the table on the next page. What was learned from gases contributed to an understanding of the elements and atomic theory, and to the beginnings of physical chemistry.

The first gas law, which relates changes in pressure to changes in volume, is named for Robert Boyle (English chemist and physicist, 1627–1691). Boyle recognized the critical importance of experimentation to science. As scientists do today, he published accounts of his experiments in great enough detail to allow their repetition by others. Boyle's own experimental data on the relationship between pressure and volume of gases (Section 5.4) are available to this day in his book, *New Experiments Physicomechanical Touching on the Spring of Air and Its Effect.*

In contrast to Boyle, who is a major figure in the history of science, Jacques-Alexandre-César Charles (French physicist, 1746–1823) published nothing of significance. Charles apparently observed that several different gases expanded in the same way when heated and told Joseph Gay-Lussac about it. In his day, Charles was best known for his design of a hydrogen-filled balloon for manned flight. Joseph Gay-Lussac (French chemist and physicist, 1778–1850) was an all-around chemist who made contributions to industrial, organic, and analytical chemistry (see A Historical Aside: Relative Atomic Masses, Chapter 4). Balloon flight also played a role in Gay-Lussac's life, and he held an altitude record that stood for 50 years.

By chance Guillaume Amontons (1663–1705), a man more deserving of a named law than Charles, has been largely overlooked. In 1701, Amontons published experiments on the third of the mathematical relationships for a given amount of gas, the relationship of temperature to pressure. Although it is not customary, a few refer to this as Amontons's law. Amontons was also first to define

Boyle's law (V–P)	1662		1620	**Pilgrims land at Plymouth**
			1672	**Marquette and Joliet explore the Mississippi**
Daniel Bernoulli relates pressure to molecular motion	1738		~1715	**"Age of Reason" begins**
Henry Cavendish discovers hydrogen	1766		1760	**George III begins 60-year reign in England**
			1769	**James Watt invents steam engine; industrial revolution begins in England**
Daniel Rutherford discovers nitrogen	1772			
Joseph Priestley discovers oxygen	1774			
			1776	**U.S. Declaration of Independence**
Charles' law (P–T)	1787		1789	**French revolution**
Dalton's law (partial pressures)	1801			
			1804	**Napoleon I becomes Emperor in France**
Gay-Lussac's law (combining volumes)	1808			
Graham's law of diffusion	1830			
			1837	**Queen Victoria begins 54-year reign in England**
Graham's law of effusion	1846		1860	**Abraham Lincoln elected U.S. President**
J. Clerk Maxwell and Ludwig Boltzmann, mathematics of kinetic theory	1860, 1868			
Noble gases discovered	1894–1898		1885	**Louis Pasteur, first vaccine**
			1904	**Theodore Roosevelt elected U.S. President**

absolute zero as the temperature at which the volume of a gas would decrease to zero (Section 5.5).

Almost 200 years elapsed between Boyle's careful experiments on gas pressure and volume, and the development of the kinetic–molecular theory.

MASS, MOLECULAR, AND MOLAR RELATIONSHIPS

5.8 GAY-LUSSAC'S LAW OF COMBINING VOLUMES AND AVOGADRO'S LAW

In a reaction among gases, the relative gas volumes are the same as the coefficients of the gaseous compounds in the balanced equation (Figure 5.10). For example, 1 volume of chlorine and 3 volumes of fluorine react to give 2 volumes of chlorine trifluoride.

$$Cl_2(g) \; + \; 3F_2(g) \longrightarrow 2ClF_3(g)$$
$$\textit{1 volume} \quad \textit{3 volumes} \quad \textit{2 volumes}$$

"Volume" is used here in the general sense of relative volume in any units. It could, for example, be 1 L of Cl_2, 3 L of F_2, and 2 L of ClF_3 or 0.01 mL of Cl_2, 0.03 mL of F_2, and 0.02 mL of ClF_3.

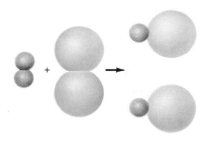

$$H_2 \qquad + Cl_2 \qquad \longrightarrow \quad 2HCl$$
1 molecule + 1 molecule ⟶ 2 molecules
1 volume + 1 volume ⟶ 2 volumes

Figure 5.10
Reaction of Hydrogen with Chlorine

Avogadro's law: Equal volumes of gases, measured at the same T and P, contain equal numbers of molecules.

The relationships among volumes of reacting gases were first observed by Gay-Lussac and then interpreted by Avogadro in the early 1800s. The work of Gay-Lussac and Avogadro was crucial to the understanding of atoms and molecules (see A Historical Aside: Relative Atomic Masses, in Chapter 4). **Gay-Lussac's law of combining volumes** may be stated as follows: When gases react or gaseous products are formed, the ratios of the volumes of the gases involved, measured at the same temperature and pressure, are small whole numbers.

Avogadro was able to give the reason for Gay-Lussac's law. What is now known as **Avogadro's law** can be stated as follows: Equal volumes of gases, measured under the same conditions of temperature and pressure, contain equal numbers of molecules. This law holds for all gases, whether they are elements, or compounds, or the vapors from liquids and solids.

A mole has been defined as an Avogadro's number of molecules, or atoms, or anything else (Section 4.6b). Therefore, equal volumes of gases at the same temperature and pressure, because they contain equal numbers of molecules, must also contain equal numbers of moles of gases. Some chemists at first found it difficult to accept the fact that a mole of a gas with a high molar mass does not, under identical conditions of temperature and pressure, occupy a larger volume than a mole of a gas with a lower molar mass. In terms of the kinetic–molecular theory, however, it makes good sense. A gas is mostly empty space occupied by molecules moving around with an average energy that varies only with the temperature. At any given temperature a mole of gas A and a mole of gas B both contain the same number of particles and the average kinetic energy of the molecules in both samples of gas is the same. Therefore if the pressure is the same, the two gases should occupy the same volume.

Since the number of moles is directly proportional to the volume, Avogadro's law may be stated mathematically as follows:

At constant temperature and pressure:

$$V = \text{constant} \times n \qquad \text{or} \qquad \frac{V_1}{n_1} = \frac{V_2}{n_2} \qquad\qquad (5.10)$$

number of moles of gas

where n_1 and n_2 represent the number of moles of the same gas in different volumes, or the number of moles of different gases in different volumes, both at the same temperature and pressure.

EXAMPLE 5.6
$P-V-T-n$ Relationships:
Gay-Lussac's Law

The chemical reaction in laboratory alcohol burners is

$$CH_3CH_2OH(l) \;+ 3O_2(g) \rightarrow 2CO_2(g) + 3H_2O(g)$$
ethyl alcohol

What volume of CO_2 (at the same pressure and temperature) is produced if 6.0 L of O_2 reacts?

The coefficients in the chemical equation indicate the relative volumes of gaseous reactants and products. For every 3 volumes of O_2 that react, 2 volumes of CO_2 are produced. A factor for "conversion" of oxygen volume to CO_2 volume can be derived from this information:

$$(6.0 \text{ L } O_2)\left(\frac{2 \text{ volumes } CO_2}{3 \text{ volumes } O_2}\right) = 4.0 \text{ L } CO_2$$

The amount of CO_2 produced will be 4.0 L. (Note that we cannot use Gay-Lussac's law to discuss the volume of the original alcohol, because it is a liquid and not a gas.)

Exercise   Bromine trifluoride can be prepared by the direct combination of the elements:

$$Br_2(g) + 3F_2(g) \xrightarrow{\Delta} 2BrF_3(g)$$

What volumes of Br_2 and of F_2 measured at the same temperature and pressure are needed to prepare 50. mL of BrF_3?   *Answer* 25 mL Br_2, 75 mL F_2

EXAMPLE 5.7
P – V – T – n Relationships:
Avogadro's Law

Incandescent light bulbs contain inert gases, such as argon, so that the filament will last longer. The approximate volume of a 100-watt bulb is 130 cm³, and the bulb contains 3×10^{-3} mol of argon. How many moles of argon would be inside a 150-watt bulb under the same pressure and temperature conditions if the volume of the larger wattage bulb is 185 cm³?

For the 100-watt bulb

$$n_1 = 3 \times 10^{-3} \text{ mol} \qquad V_1 = 130 \text{ cm}^3$$

and for the 150-watt bulb

$$n_2 = ? \qquad V_2 = 185 \text{ cm}^2$$

Solving the mathematical statement of Avogadro's (Equation 5.10) law for n_2 and substituting the above values gives

$$n_2 = (n_1)\left(\frac{V_2}{V_1}\right) = (3 \times 10^{-3} \text{ mol})\left(\frac{185 \text{ cm}^3}{130 \text{ cm}^3}\right) = 4 \times 10^{-3} \text{ mol}$$

There will be 4×10^{-3} mol of argon in the 150-watt bulb. (Again we can check our answer by the common-sense method. Because the 150-watt bulb has a larger volume, according to Avogadro's law, there should be a larger quantity of gas in it—our answer of 4×10^{-3} mol seems reasonable.)

Exercise   A flask contains 0.116 mol of nitrogen at a given temperature and pressure. Under the same temperature and pressure conditions, a 6.25 ft³ flask contains 1.522 mol of nitrogen. What is the volume of the first flask?   *Answer* 0.476 ft³

5.9 MOLAR VOLUME

According to Avogadro's law, one mole of any gas should occupy the same volume as one mole of any other gas when the volumes are measured at the same conditions of temperature and pressure. **Standard molar volume** is defined as the volume occupied by one mole of a substance at standard temperature and pressure (STP).

Molar volume of a gas
= 22.4 L (at STP)

On the basis of many measurements, it has been found that at standard temperature and pressure the molar volume averages 22.4 L (Figure 5.11) for gases

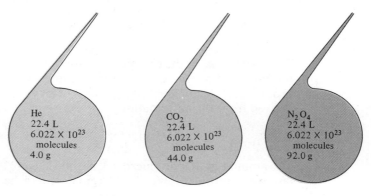

He
22.4 L
6.022×10^{23}
molecules
4.0 g

CO_2
22.4 L
6.022×10^{23}
molecules
44.0 g

N_2O_4
22.4 L
6.022×10^{23}
molecules
92.0 g

Figure 5.11
Avogadro's Law and Molar Volume

that are reasonably close to "ideal." Molar volume has the units of liters per mole. The molar volume gives the factor 22.4 L/mol, which allows conversion between the number of moles of a gas and its volume at STP.

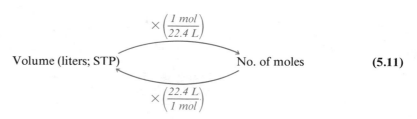

$$\text{Volume (liters; STP)} \quad\rightleftharpoons\quad \text{No. of moles} \qquad (5.11)$$

The molar mass of a substance, as we have seen, is the mass in grams of one mole of that substance. If one mole of gas at STP always occupies 22.4 L, then the molar mass of any gas is simply the mass in grams of 22.4 L of that gas at STP. This is easy to find if we know the density of the gas at STP.

$$\text{(Gas density)(molar volume)} = \text{molar mass} \qquad (5.12)$$

$$\frac{grams}{liter} \qquad\qquad \frac{liters}{mole} \qquad \frac{grams}{mole}$$

(For discussion of density, see Section 2.8d.)

The molar volume of 22.4 L/mol is a useful conversion factor, but remember that it applies *only* to gases *at standard temperature and pressure*. The factor of 22.4 L/mol *cannot* be used for gases at other than standard temperature and pressure *or* for solids or liquids.

Examples 5.8 and 5.9 illustrate the use of molar volume and Example 5.10 shows how to think through solving a problem that requires several steps and brings together concepts presented earlier.

EXAMPLE 5.8
***P–V–T–n* Relationships:**
Molar Volume

What volume would be occupied at STP by 3.25 mol of an ideal gas?

The volume can be found by simply multiplying the number of moles of gas by the molar volume of an ideal gas at STP (22.4 L/mol), giving

$$(3.25 \text{ mol})\left(\frac{22.4 \text{ L}}{1 \text{ mol}}\right) = 72.8 \text{ L}$$

The gas would have a volume of 72.8 L.

Exercise What volume at STP would be occupied by 0.0036 mol of an ideal gas?
Answer 81 mL

EXAMPLE 5.9
***P–V–T–n* Relationships:**
Molar Volume

The limit of sensitivity for the analysis for carbon monoxide, CO, in air is 1 ppb (ppb = parts per billion) by volume. What is the smallest number of CO molecules that can be detected in 10 L of air at STP?

A limit of 1 ppb by volume means that in every 1 L of air one-billionth, or 1×10^{-9} L, of CO could be detected. For 10 L of air (STP), the amount of detectable CO is

$$(10 \text{ L air})\left(\frac{1 \times 10^{-9} \text{ L CO}}{1 \text{ L air}}\right) = 1 \times 10^{-8} \text{ L CO}$$

The molar volume allows us to calculate how many moles of CO are present in this volume, and Avogadro's number enables us to convert the number of moles to the actual number of molecules:

$$(1 \times 10^{-8} \text{ L CO})\left(\frac{1 \text{ mol CO}}{22.4 \text{ L CO}}\right)\left(\frac{6.022 \times 10^{23} \text{ molecules CO}}{1 \text{ mol CO}}\right) = 3 \times 10^{14} \text{ molecules CO}.$$

The smallest number of CO molecules that can be detected is 3×10^{14} molecules.

Exercise How many moles of Cl_2 are present in a 26.5-mL sample measured at STP? *Answer* 1.18 mmol

---

EXAMPLE 5.10
P-V-T-n **Relationships:**
Molar Volume

A pure gas containing 92.3% carbon and 7.7% hydrogen has a density of 1.16 g/L at STP. What is the molecular formula of the gas?

1. Study the problem and be sure that you understand it.
   (a) What is known?
       The percentage composition of a gas and its density at STP.
   (b) What is unknown?
       The molecular formula of the gas—the number of carbon and hydrogen atoms combined in each molecule.
2. Decide how to solve the problem.
   (a) What is the connection between the known and the unknown?
       Making the connection in this problem is going to require several steps. First, we must ask what is directly needed to find the unknown. To find the molecular formula requires knowing the simplest formula and the molar mass (Section 4.10)—both also unknown. Then examine the known data: How do they apply? The percentage composition data can be used to find the simplest formula—the molar masses of carbon and hydrogen provide the connection. This leaves the molar mass of the gas in question unknown. It can be found from the gas density—here the standard molar volume provides the connection. Then, knowing the simplest formula and the molar mass of the compound, it will be possible to determine the molecular formula.
   (b) What is necessary to make the connection?
       There are three steps to solving this problem. (i) Find the simplest formula. To do this, take 100 g of the compound as a basis for calculation and find the number of moles of carbon and hydrogen represented by 92.3 g of carbon and 7.7 g of hydrogen. The simplest formula is then found by determining the ratio of carbon to hydrogen atoms (Section 4.9). (ii) Find the molar mass by multiplying the density by the molar volume. (iii) Decide upon the molecular formula based on the simplest formula and molar mass.
3. Set up the problem and solve it.
   (a) Find the simplest formula.

$$(92.3 \text{ g C})\left(\frac{1 \text{ mol C}}{12.0 \text{ g}}\right) = 7.69 \text{ mol C}$$

$$(7.7 \text{ g H})\left(\frac{1 \text{ mol H}}{1.0 \text{ g H}}\right) = 7.7 \text{ mol H}$$

It is apparent that the C to H ratio is 1 to 1 and the simplest formula is CH.

(b) Find the molar mass.

$$\left(1.16\,\frac{g}{L}\right)\left(\frac{22.4\,L}{mol}\right) = 26.0\ g/mol$$

(c) Find the molecular formula.
The molar mass based on the simplest formula of CH is 13.0 g/mol (12.0 g for C plus 1.0 g for H). The molar mass of the compound in question is twice this value and so the molecular formula is clearly C_2H_2. [The compound is acetylene.]

4. Check the results.
(a) Are the calculations correct?
Yes. Significant figures have been used correctly, and the molar mass units are correct.
(b) Is the answer reasonable?
This is difficult to judge here. Your later studies will show that it is reasonable for a gaseous compound of carbon and hydrogen to have a low molar mass.

5.10 IDEAL GAS LAW

Boyle's law, Charles' law, and Avogadro's law establish relationships for gases among four variables — the volume, the pressure, the temperature, and the amount of gas, which we express in moles, n.

$$V = \text{constant} \times \frac{1}{P},\ \text{at fixed } T \text{ and } n$$

$$V = \text{constant} \times T,\ \text{at fixed } P \text{ and } n$$

$$V = \text{constant} \times n,\ \text{at fixed } P \text{ and } T$$

These proportionalities combine to give a single relationship

$$V = \text{constant} \times \frac{1}{P} \times T \times n \qquad \text{or} \qquad PV = \text{constant} \times T \times n$$

Ideal gas law: $PV = nRT$

The constant is represented by the symbol R and, written in its usual form, we have the **ideal gas law**

$$PV = nRT \tag{5.13}$$

$R = 0.0821$ L atm/K mol

Based as it is on the individual gas laws, which assume ideal behavior of gases, this equation summarizes the behavior of ideal gas. The constant R, called the ideal gas constant, or universal gas constant, is the same for all gases under conditions where their behavior is close to ideal.

The value and units for R depend upon the units of P, V, and T. The value of R can be calculated from molar volume and the standard temperature and pressure. In conventional units, using the most accurate value for the molar volume of an ideal gas, 22.41383 L,

Table 5.5
Ideal Gas Constant Values

$$R = \frac{PV}{nT} = \frac{(1\ atm)(22.41383\ L)}{(1\ mol)(273.15\ K)} = 0.082057\ L\ atm/K\ mol$$

0.0821 L atm/K mol
62.36 L Torr/K mol
8.314×10^3 L Pa/K mol
8.314 m³ Pa/K mol
1.987 cal/K mol
8.314 J/K mol

Usually, this value of R is rounded off to 0.0821 L atm/K mol.

As Table 5.5 shows, pressure and volume can be expressed in many different units, and for each combination of units R has a different numerical value. In working problems with the ideal gas law, it is *essential* that the units of P, V, and T and the units of the gas constant be in agreement. (It is convenient to memorize one value for the gas constant, and convert the pressure and volume to the appropriate units.)

We have followed the historical approach, in which observations led to the gas laws, which were then combined to give the ideal gas law. These relationships based on observation can be verified directly and independently from the kinetic-molecular theory. It can be shown that PV, the pressure times the volume of a gas, is a function solely of the number of molecules, their mass, and their velocity. By combining this relationship with the proportionalities between kinetic energy and temperature, and between the number of molecules and the number of moles, it is possible to arrive at $PV = nRT$.

The following examples show some of the many types of problems that can be solved by using the ideal gas law. Knowing three of the four quantities P, V, n, and T, the ideal gas law can be used to find the fourth.

EXAMPLE 5.11
P-V-T-n **Relationships:**
Ideal Gas Law

What pressure would be necessary to confine 1.38 mol of an ideal gas at 375 °C in a volume of 5.2 L?

The known information is as follows:

$$V = 5.2 \text{ L} \qquad n = 1.38 \text{ mol} \qquad T = 375° + 273 = 648 \text{ K}$$

The pressure can be determined using the ideal gas law, $PV = nRT$.

$$P = \frac{nRT}{V} = \frac{(1.38 \text{ mol})(0.0821 \text{ L atm/K mol})(648 \text{ K})}{(5.2 \text{ L})} = 14 \text{ atm}$$

The pressure is 14 atm.

Exercise A 1.3 mol sample of an ideal gas occupies 74 L at 45 atm. What is the temperature of this gas? *Answer* 3.1×10^4 K

EXAMPLE 5.12
P-V-T-n **Relationships:**
Ideal Gas Law

The statement was made in Section 5.7 that 4.0 L of hydrogen at 760 Torr and 30. °C (sample 1) contains about three times as much hydrogen as does 4.0 L of hydrogen at 380 Torr and 200. °C (sample 2). Prove this statement by using the ideal gas law and comparing the number of moles of each gas.

For sample 1:

$$P = (760 \text{ Torr})(1 \text{ atm}/760 \text{ Torr}) = 1.0 \text{ atm} \qquad V = 4.0 \text{ L}$$
$$T = 30.° + 273 = 303 \text{ K} \qquad\qquad\qquad n = ?$$

which, upon substituting into the ideal gas law, gives

$$n = \frac{PV}{RT} = \frac{(1.0 \text{ atm})(4.0 \text{ L})}{(0.0821 \text{ L atm/K mol})(303 \text{ K})} = 0.16 \text{ mol}$$

For sample 2:

$$P = (380 \text{ Torr})(1 \text{ atm}/760 \text{ Torr}) = 0.50 \text{ atm} \qquad V = 4.0 \text{ L}$$
$$T = 200.° + 273 = 473 \text{ K} \qquad\qquad\qquad n = ?$$

which gives

$$n = \frac{(0.50 \text{ atm})(4.0 \text{ L})}{(0.0821 \text{ L atm/K mol})(473 \text{ K})} = 0.052 \text{ mol}$$

The ratio of the number of moles in sample 1 to the number of moles in sample 2 is

$$\frac{(0.16 \text{ mol})}{(0.052 \text{ mol})} = 3.1$$

Sample 1 contains a little over three times as much hydrogen as sample 2.

Exercise Choose the sample which contains the larger number of moles of gas: (a) 529 L measured at −12 °C and 0.255 atm or (b) 32.6 mL measured at 37 °C and 37.6 atm. *Answer* (a)

5.11 MASS AND DENSITY

Molar mass, gas density, and sample mass can all be determined for gases from P, V, T data and the ideal gas law. The number of moles, n, equals the mass divided by the molar mass, M.

$$\text{No. of moles} = \frac{\text{mass}}{\text{molar mass}} \qquad \text{or} \qquad n = \frac{m}{M}$$

$$moles \qquad \frac{grams}{grams/mole}$$

Substitution of this relationship into the ideal gas equation gives a form convenient for use in problems where masses are unknown.

$$PV = \frac{m}{M} RT \tag{5.14}$$

Equation (5.14) is the basis for a method of molar mass determination (the Dumas method, Figure 5.12). In this method, an empty glass bulb with a known volume is weighed. A few grams of a volatile sample are placed in the bulb. The sample is heated until it is completely vaporized and no excess vapor escapes from the thin neck of the bulb. The bulb is then cooled and weighed. The molar mass is determined from $M = mRT/PV$; $m =$ the mass of the bulb plus the cooled vapor minus the mass of the empty bulb; $T =$ the temperature of the bath; $P =$ the atmospheric pressure, read from a barometer; $V =$ the volume of the flask.

It is also sometimes useful to introduce density into the ideal gas law. Density (d) is mass per unit volume (m/V) and can be used to convert volume into mass (see Equation 2.7):

$$d = \frac{m}{V} \qquad \text{or} \qquad m = dV$$

Substituting $m = dV$ into Equation (5.14), cancelling V from both sides, and rearranging gives a relationship which allows calculation of the density of a gas at a given pressure and temperature if its molar mass is known.

$$PV = \frac{dV}{M} RT \qquad d = \frac{PM}{RT} \tag{5.15}$$

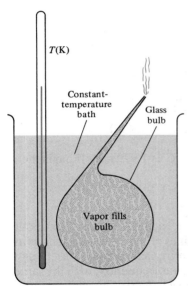

Figure 5.12
Molar Mass Determination (the Dumas Method)

Labels in figure: $T(K)$; Constant-temperature bath; Glass bulb; Vapor fills bulb

---

EXAMPLE 5.13
Molar Mass of Ideal Gases

A liquid was known to be either methyl alcohol, CH_3OH, or ethyl alcohol, CH_3CH_2OH. The Dumas method for determining molar masses (see Figure 5.12) was used to obtain an approximate molar mass, and this value was used to identify the alcohol. The gaseous alcohol at 98 °C and 740 Torr had a mass of 0.276 g in a Dumas bulb of volume equal to 270 mL. Which alcohol was present?

For the alcohol,

$$P = (740 \text{ Torr})\left(\frac{1 \text{ atm}}{760 \text{ atm}}\right) = 0.97 \text{ atm} \qquad T = 98° + 273 = 371 \text{ K}$$

$$V = (270 \text{ mL})\left(\frac{1 \text{ L}}{1000 \text{ mL}}\right) = 0.27 \text{ L} \qquad m = 0.276 \text{ g}$$

Solving Equation (5.14) for the molar mass and substituting the above values, we get

$$M = \frac{mRT}{PV} = \frac{(0.276 \text{ g})(0.0821 \text{ L atm/K mol})(371 \text{ K})}{(0.97 \text{ atm})(0.27 \text{ L})} = 32 \text{ g/mol}$$

The molar mass of the unknown alcohol is 32 g/mol, which agrees with the value calculated from atomic masses for the formula of methyl alcohol.

Exercise An ideal gas had a mass of 0.0218 g and occupied a volume of 1.111 L at 0 °C and 0.0100 atm. What is the molar mass of this gas? *Answer* 44.0 g/mol

---

EXAMPLE 5.14
Density of Ideal Gases

What is the density of acetone vapor, CH_3COCH_3 at 95 °C and 650 Torr?

For the gas:

$$P = (650 \text{ Torr})(1 \text{ atm/760 Torr}) = 0.86 \text{ atm} \qquad M = 58 \text{ g/mol}$$
$$T = 95° + 273 = 368 \text{ K}$$

The density of the gas can be calculated using Equation (5.15).

$$d = \frac{PM}{RT} = \frac{(0.86 \text{ atm})(58 \text{ g/mol})}{(0.0821 \text{ L atm/K mol})(368 \text{ K})} = 1.7 \text{ g/L}$$

The density of acetone vapor under the given conditions is 1.7 g/L.

Exercise The density of ozone at 1.013 atm and 26.5 °C is 1.979 g/L. What is the molar mass of this gas? *Answer* 48.04 g/mol

---

5.12 PRESSURE IN GAS MIXTURES: DALTON'S LAW

In a mixture of gases that do not interact with each other, each molecule moves about independently just as it would in the absence of molecules of other kinds. Each gas in a mixture distributes itself uniformly throughout the entire space available as though no other gas were present. The molecules strike the walls as frequently, with the same energy, and therefore with the same pressure, as they do when no other gas is present.

Among the studies which led John Dalton to the atomic theory were experiments on gas pressures in mixtures. He summarized his conclusions in 1803 in what is known as **Dalton's law of partial pressures:** In a mixture of gases, the total pressure exerted is the sum of the pressures that each gas would exert if it were present alone under the same conditions.

Dalton's law:
$$P_{\text{total}} = p_1 + p_2 + p_3 + \cdots$$

If several different gases (1, 2, 3, . . .) are placed in the same container they form a homogeneous mixture. The pressure of a single gas in a mixture is called its **partial pressure.** We use the small letters p_1, p_2, p_3, . . . , to represent partial pressures. The total pressure of a gas mixture is given by

partial pressures of gas$_1$, gas$_2$, gas$_3$, . . .

$$P_{\text{total}} = p_1 + p_2 + p_3 + \cdots \tag{5.16}$$

Consider a volume of air under a pressure of 1000 Torr. Approximately one-fifth of the molecules are oxygen molecules and approximately four-fifths are nitrogen molecules. The approximate partial pressures are, therefore, 200 Torr for oxygen and 800 Torr for nitrogen.

The fraction of molecules of each gas present in a mixture is given by the **mole fraction, X**—the number of moles of a component in a mixture divided by the total number of moles of all components in the mixture.

$$X_1 = \frac{n_1}{n_1 + n_2 + \cdots} \qquad (5.17)$$

mole fraction of component 1

Because each gas in a mixture exerts the same pressure that it would exert by itself, the mole fraction of a gas is also the fraction of the total pressure exerted by that gas.

$$p_1 = X_1 P_{total} \qquad \text{or} \qquad X_1 = \frac{p_1}{P_{total}} \qquad (5.18)$$

partial pressure of component 1

For example, in a mixture of 3.0 mol of N_2 and 1.5 mol of He, the total number of moles of gas is 4.5 mol. The mole fractions of the two gases present are

$$X_{N_2} = \frac{3.0 \text{ mol } N_2}{3.0 \text{ mol } N_2 + 1.5 \text{ mol He}} = \frac{3.0 \text{ mol}}{4.5 \text{ mol}} = 0.67$$

$$X_{He} = \frac{1.5 \text{ mol He}}{3.0 \text{ mol } N_2 + 1.5 \text{ mol He}} = \frac{1.5 \text{ mol}}{4.5 \text{ mol}} = 0.33$$

If this N_2–He mixture has a total pressure of 0.40 atm, the partial pressures of the two gases are

$$p_{N_2} = X_{N_2} P_{total} = (0.67)(0.40 \text{ atm}) = 0.27 \text{ atm}$$
$$p_{He} = X_{He} P_{total} = (0.33)(0.40 \text{ atm}) = 0.13 \text{ atm}$$

EXAMPLE 5.15
Dalton's Law

A 6.2 L sample of N_2 at 738 Torr is mixed with a 15.2 L sample of O_2 at 325 Torr. The gaseous mixture is placed in a 12.0 L container. What is the pressure of the system?

For each gas we apply Boyle's law independently.

For N_2:

$$P_1 = 738 \text{ Torr} \qquad V_1 = 6.2 \text{ L}$$
$$P_2 = ? \qquad V_2 = 12.0 \text{ L}$$
$$P_2 = (P_1)\left(\frac{V_1}{V_2}\right) = (738 \text{ Torr})\left(\frac{6.2 \text{ L}}{12.0 \text{ L}}\right) = 380 \text{ Torr}$$

For O_2:

$$P_1 = 325 \text{ Torr} \qquad V_1 = 15.2 \text{ L}$$
$$P_2 = ? \qquad V_2 = 12.0 \text{ L}$$
$$P_2 = (325 \text{ Torr})\left(\frac{15.2 \text{ L}}{12.0 \text{ L}}\right) = 412 \text{ Torr}$$

According to Dalton's law of partial pressure,

$$P_{total} = p_{O_2} + p_{N_2} = 412 \text{ Torr} + 380 \text{ Torr} = 790 \text{ Torr}$$

The pressure of the mixture is 790 Torr.

Exercise The total pressure of a mixture of water vapor and helium is 0.893 atm. The partial pressure of water is 27.3 Torr at this temperature. What is the partial pressure of helium? *Answer* 0.857 atm

EXAMPLE 5.16
Dalton's Law

What is the composition (in mole fractions) of the gaseous mixture described in Example 5.15?

The partial pressure of N_2 is 380 Torr, and of O_2 is 412 Torr, giving a total pressure of 790 Torr. The mole fraction of each component in the mixture can be found using Equation (5.18).

$$X_{N_2} = \frac{p_{N_2}}{P_{total}} = \frac{380 \text{ Torr}}{790 \text{ Torr}} = 0.48 \qquad X_{O_2} = \frac{p_{O_2}}{P_{total}} = \frac{412 \text{ Torr}}{790 \text{ Torr}} = 0.52$$

The gaseous mixture has the composition $X_{N_2} = 0.48$ and $X_{O_2} = 0.52$.

Exercise   What are the mole fractions of each gas in a mixture that contains 0.267 atm of He, 0.369 atm of Ar, and 0.394 atm of Xe?   *Answer* $X_{He} = 0.259$, $X_{Ar} = 0.358$, $X_{Xe} = 0.383$

In the experiment shown in Figure 5.13, hydrogen is pumped into a cylinder containing nitrogen until the gas volume is doubled, while the pressure remains the same. The total pressure is then doubled and the volume occupied by the gas mixture returned to what the volume was at the beginning of the experiment. Thus, the nitrogen occupies its original volume and exerts its original pressure, completely independent of the hydrogen that also occupies the cylinder. Because gas particles are so far apart that they interact very little with each other, the old adage that two things cannot occupy the same space at the same time does not seem to apply to gases.

In a closed container partly filled with water, the air over the liquid soon becomes mixed with water vapor. Eventually, the air holds all of the water vapor that it can, and some of the water vapor condenses. For example, in a terrarium (Figure 5.14), water is constantly evaporating from the surface of the plants and soil, and in an equal but opposite change, water is condensing on the walls and lid and running back into the soil. In the terrarium, as in any other closed vessel containing water or any other liquid, the processes of evaporation and condensation eventually reach a state of **dynamic equilibrium**—a state of balance between exactly opposite changes occurring at the same rate.

$$H_2O(l) \rightleftharpoons H_2O(g)$$

Vapor pressure is the pressure exerted by the vapor over a liquid (or solid) once evaporation and condensation have reached equilibrium. The total pressure over a liquid is the sum of the pressure of any gas present plus the vapor pressure of the liquid at the existing temperature.

Figure 5.13
Dalton's Law of Partial Pressures (a) A cylinder with a movable piston contains 500 mL of nitrogen at a pressure 760 Torr. (b) Hydrogen is introduced. The piston rises in the cylinder until the volume is 1000 mL, when the addition of hydrogen is stopped. Each gas now exerts half of the total pressure, or 380 Torr. (c) The piston is next forced down until the volume in the cylinder is again 500 mL. This doubles the total pressure and doubles the pressure of each of the two gases.

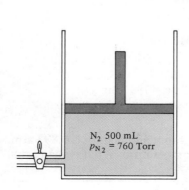

(a)

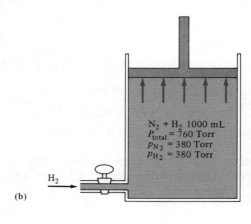

$N_2 + H_2$ 1000 mL
$P_{total} = 760$ Torr
$p_{N_2} = 380$ Torr
$p_{H_2} = 380$ Torr

H_2

(b)

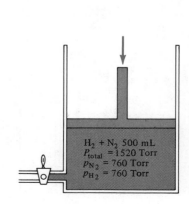

$H_2 + N_2$ 500 mL
$P_{total} = 1520$ Torr
$p_{N_2} = 760$ Torr
$p_{H_2} = 760$ Torr

(c)

N_2 500 mL
$p_{N_2} = 760$ Torr

Frequently a gas is collected in the laboratory over some liquid in which it is not very soluble (Figure 5.15). The procedure is always basically the same: The vessel in which the gas is to be confined is filled with the liquid and inverted in a container of the same liquid. The gas is led through a tube from the apparatus in which it is generated, under the liquid, and to the mouth of the vessel, where it bubbles up into the vessel through the liquid. Once the gas is collected, the bottle is moved up or down until the liquid levels inside and outside the bottle are the same. At this point the gas inside the bottle is at atmospheric pressure.

A gas collected over water is "wet" — it contains water vapor. For a gas collected at atmospheric pressure, the total gas pressure is the sum of the pressure of the water vapor and the pressure of the gas collected, and equals the atmospheric pressure.

$$P_{atm} = p_{H_2O} + p_{gas} \tag{5.19}$$

**Figure 5.14
Dynamic Equilibrium in a
Terrarium** Liquid water and water
vapor are in equilibrium.

The volume of the gas collected is measured at atmospheric pressure (see Figure 5.14). The value of P_{atm} is found by reading a barometer. The value of P_{H_2O} is read from a table of water vapor pressures at various temperatures (Appendix IV). With this information, the partial pressure of the gas collected and the amount of gas collected can be found as shown in Example 5.17.

**EXAMPLE 5.17
Dalton's Law**

Potassium chlorate ($KClO_3$) was heated to give oxygen.

$$2KClO_3(s) \xrightarrow[\text{MnO}_2]{\Delta} 2KCl(s) + 3O_2(g)$$

A volume of 550 mL of gas was collected over water at 21 °C and an atmospheric pressure of 743 Torr. The vapor pressure of water at 21 °C is 19 Torr. How many moles of oxygen were collected?

The pressure of oxygen is the total pressure less the partial pressure of the water vapor. Thus

$$P = (743 \text{ Torr} - 19 \text{ Torr})(1 \text{ atm}/760 \text{ Torr}) = 0.953 \text{ atm}$$
$$V = (550 \text{ mL})\left(\frac{1 \text{ L}}{1000 \text{ mL}}\right) = 0.55 \text{ L}$$
$$T = 21° + 273 = 294 \text{ K}$$

Substituting these values into the ideal gas law gives us

$$n = \frac{PV}{RT} = \frac{(0.953 \text{ atm})(0.55 \text{ L})}{(0.0821 \text{ L atm/K mol})(294 \text{ K})} = 0.022 \text{ mol}$$

The amount of oxygen collected was 0.022 mol (about 0.70 g).

**Figure 5.15
Collecting a Gas over a
Liquid** Atmospheric pressure on the surface in the dish keeps the bottle full (a) until the liquid in it is displaced by the gas (b). When all of the gas is collected its pressure may be smaller (b) or greater (c) than that of the atmosphere. By raising or lowering the bottle, the liquid levels are made equal (d). In this way, the gas is brought to atmospheric pressure (which can be read from a barometer). The gas volume is determined by marking the level of the liquid in the bottle, setting the bottle upright, and measuring the volume of water required to fill the bottle to the mark.

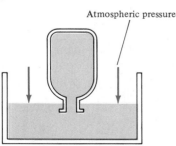
(a)

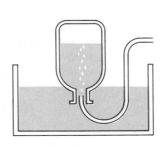
(b)

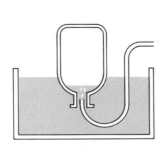
(c)

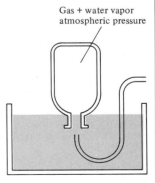
Gas + water vapor
atmospheric pressure
(d)

Atmospheric pressure

Exercise   A volume of 45.2 mL of "wet" hydrogen gas was collected by the displacement of water at 759.3 Torr and 23.8 °C. The vapor pressure of water at this temperature is 22.1 Torr. What mass of "dry" hydrogen gas was collected? *Answer* 0.00364 g H_2

In summary, under the same conditions of temperature and pressure, equal volumes of gases contain equal numbers of molecules (Avogadro's law). As a result, in chemical reactions, the relative volumes of gaseous reactants and products are given by the coefficients in the balanced chemical equation. The ideal gas law summarizes, for any ideal gas, the relationships among pressure, volume, temperature, and amount of gas. Knowing any three of these variables allows calculation of the fourth. Mass, density, and molar mass relationships can also be found by introducing these quantities into the ideal gas law. The sum of the pressures that individual gases would exert if they were present alone under the same conditions is the total pressure of a gaseous mixture (Dalton's law).

BEHAVIOR OF GAS MOLECULES

5.13 EFFUSION AND DIFFUSION: GRAHAM'S LAWS

Effusion is the escape of molecules in the gaseous state one by one, without collisions, through a hole of molecular dimensions (Figure 5.16). Effusion is of interest for three reasons: (1) it is a simple demonstration of the validity of kinetic–molecular theory; (2) it provides a method for determining molecular masses; and (3) it provides a practical method for the separation of gases.

In 1846 Graham found experimentally that the rate of effusion was dependent upon the density of a gas. **Graham's law of effusion** may be stated as follows: The rates of effusion of two gases at the same pressure and temperature are inversely proportional to the square roots of their densities.

$$\frac{\text{rate}_1}{\text{rate}_2} = \frac{\sqrt{d_2}}{\sqrt{d_1}} \tag{5.20}$$

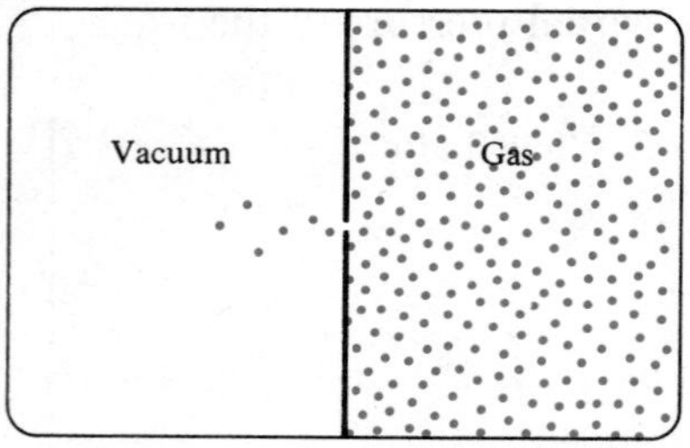

By using Equation (5.15), in which density was introduced into the ideal gas equation, we can relate density to molar mass (M) for two gases at the same temperature and pressure as follows:

$$\frac{d_1}{d_2} = \frac{PM_1/RT}{PM_2/RT} = \frac{M_1}{M_2} \tag{5.21}$$

Figure 5.16
Effusion

Combining this relationship with Graham's law gives

$$\frac{\text{rate}_1}{\text{rate}_2} = \frac{\sqrt{d_2}}{\sqrt{d_1}} = \frac{\sqrt{M_2}}{\sqrt{M_1}} \tag{5.22}$$

The determination of molar mass from an effusion experiment by using Equation (5.22) is illustrated in the following example.

EXAMPLE 5.18
Graham's Law

It is more convenient to measure the time for a gas sample to effuse than to measure its actual rate of effusion. The rate is defined as the number of molecules moving through a molecular-sized hole per unit time. Therefore, rate is inversely proportional to time, giving for the effusion of equal numbers of molecules

$$\frac{\text{rate}_1}{\text{rate}_2} = \frac{\text{time}_2}{\text{time}_1} = \frac{\sqrt{M_2}}{\sqrt{M_1}}$$

Find the molar mass of a gas that takes 33.5 s to effuse from a porous container. An identical number of moles of CO_2 takes 25.0 s.

Solving the above equation for the molar mass of the unknown gas and substituting the respective times and $M = 44.0$ g/mol for CO_2 gives

$$M_2 = M_{CO_2}\left(\frac{time_2}{time_{CO_2}}\right)^2 = \left(44.0 \frac{g}{mol}\right)\left(\frac{33.5 \text{ s}}{25.0 \text{ s}}\right)^2 = 79.0 \text{ g/mol}$$

The molar mass of the unknown gas is 79.0 g.

Exercise   A sample of methane, molar mass $= 16.04$ g, required 23.2 s to effuse from a container. What time was required for a sample of ethane, molar mass $= 30.07$ g?   *Answer* 31.8 s

Graham's law can be derived directly from kinetic–molecular theory. Without going through the mathematics to prove this, we can see qualitatively that Graham's law does provide support for the assumptions of kinetic–molecular theory. According to the theory, at the same temperature gases of different masses have the same average kinetic energy, and therefore gases of higher molar mass must have slower average speeds than gases of lower molar mass. A heavier gas should collide with the hole in an effusion experiment less often and have a slower rate of effusion. Suppose gas 1 is a heavier gas and gas 2 is a lighter gas. From Equation (5.22) you can see that the larger is M_1, the molar mass of the heavier gas, the smaller must be its rate of effusion, rate 1.

When two gases of different masses are confined (at constant temperature and pressure) in two halves of a container divided by a porous membrane, the lighter gas effuses through the membrane faster than the heavier one. As a result, a pressure difference is built up between the two chambers.

Passage of a mixture through a membrane can be used to separate gases of different masses. Separation of forms of uranium of slightly different masses in this manner played an important role in the dramatic effort by the United States to develop an atomic bomb during World War II (see Section 12.15; also An Aside: The Atomic Bomb, in Chapter 12). Naturally occurring uranium contains only 0.72% of uranium-235 in a mixture with uranium-238. This is not a high enough percentage of uranium-235 for use of the uranium in a nuclear fission bomb. The uranium is converted to a mixture of the gaseous hexafluorides, $^{235}UF_6$ and $^{238}UF_6$. By successive passage of the mixture through a series of porous membranes from higher pressure to lower pressure in what is called a uranium enrichment process, the percentage of uranium-235 can eventually be raised to a useful level. This method of uranium enrichment is commonly referred to as the "gaseous diffusion" separation of uranium isotopes. However, diffusion, as it is usually discussed, is a somewhat different physical process.

Diffusion is a more complicated phenomenon that, like effusion, is based on molecular motion. **Diffusion** is the mixing of molecules of different gases by random motion and collisions until the mixture becomes homogeneous (Figure 5.17). Graham also investigated diffusion, and in 1831 stated what is now known as **Graham's law of diffusion:** The rates of diffusion of two gases are inversely proportional to the square roots of their densities (or their molecular masses). The mathematical expression of this law is exactly the same as that of the law of effusion, as given in Equation 5.22.

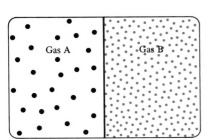

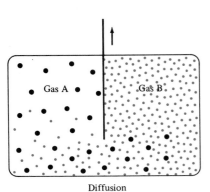

Diffusion

Figure 5.17
Diffusion

$$\frac{rate_1}{rate_2} = \frac{\sqrt{d_2}}{\sqrt{d_1}} \frac{\sqrt{(\text{molecular mass})_2}}{\sqrt{(\text{molecular mass})_1}} = \frac{\sqrt{M_2}}{\sqrt{M_1}} \tag{5.23}$$

5.14 DEVIATIONS FROM THE GAS LAWS

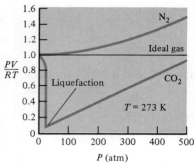

Figure 5.18

Deviations from Ideality for One Mole of Gas with Increasing Pressure For an ideal gas $PV/RT = 1$. For CO_2, attraction between molecules decreases volume as pressure increases. Because nitrogen molecules have low forces of attraction, PV/RT is greater than that of an ideal gas.

Table 5.6
Van der Waals Constants

Gas	a (L² atm/mol²)	b (L/mol)
H_2	0.2444	0.02661
He	0.03412	0.02370
O_2	1.360	0.03183
CO_2	3.592	0.04267
H_2O	5.464	0.03049

Deviations from ideal gas behavior are small for gases that do not liquefy easily, such as oxygen, hydrogen, and nitrogen, but are fairly large for more readily condensable gases, such as carbon dioxide and ammonia. The deviations become greater for all gases as conditions at which a gas will liquefy (low temperature and/or high pressure) are approached.

Real gases differ from ideal gases because some of the assumptions that are made in describing ideal gas behavior are not entirely correct. First, it is assumed that the molecules in a gas exert no forces on each other. This is not quite true. There are some forces of attraction that can act between all molecules. As the pressure is increased and the molecules come closer together, real gas molecules experience these forces. Therefore as the pressure is increased, the volume of the gas tends to decrease more than would be predicted for an ideal gas. This effect influences the nonideal behavior of molecules with strong forces of attraction, such as CO_2 molecules (Figure 5.18). Lowering the temperature causes a similar effect.

Moreover, in deriving the gas laws it is assumed that changes in temperature and pressure affect the entire volume occupied by a gaseous material. This is also not quite correct. The *spaces* between the molecules change with temperatures, but the molecules themselves do not expand or contract. The volume occupied by molecules is so small a fraction of the total that the error introduced by this assumption can be disregarded in most work. However, at high pressures or low temperatures, this error becomes significant. As the pressure is increased or the temperature decreased, the fraction of the total volume not occupied by molecules becomes smaller. As a result, the volume decreases less than the gas laws predict. Nitrogen has low forces of attraction and this effect predominates (see Figure 5.18).

These two sources of error tend to offset each other, but in very exact work, the gas law equation must be corrected to eliminate the inaccuracies. One of several more exact ways of expressing the gas law is the van der Waals equation,

$$\left(P + \frac{an^2}{V^2}\right)(V - nb) = nRT \tag{5.24}$$

in which a is a constant that takes into account the molecular attractions and b is a constant related to the volume actually occupied by the molecules of the substance. The corrections represented by a and b are different for different gases. Therefore, standard tables must be consulted to find the values of a and b needed for various gases. Values of a and b for some common gases are given in Table 5.6.

EXAMPLE 5.19
Real Gases

Using the van der Waals equation, calculate the pressure for a 3.25 mol sample of xenon contained in a volume of 1.000 L at 75 °C; $a = 4.194$ L² atm/mol² and $b = 0.05105$ L/mol for Xe. Compare this result to that predicted by the ideal gas law.

The pressure for the real gas is

$$P = \frac{nRT}{(V - nb)} - \frac{an^2}{V^2}$$

$$= \frac{(3.25 \text{ mol})(0.0821 \text{ L atm/K mol})(348 \text{ K})}{(1.000 \text{ L}) - [(3.25 \text{ mol})(0.05105 \text{ L/mol})]} - \frac{(4.194 \text{ L}^2 \text{ atm/mol}^2)(3.25 \text{ mol})^2}{(1.00 \text{ L})^2}$$

$$= 67 \text{ atm}$$

The ideal gas law would predict

$$P = \frac{nRT}{V} = \frac{(3.25 \text{ mol})(0.0821 \text{ L atm/K mol})(348 \text{ K})}{(1.000 \text{ L})} = 92.9 \text{ atm}$$

The pressure of the gas is 67 atm. The ideal gas law predicts a value of 92.9 atm, which is about 39% too high.

Exercise A 1.75 L container holds 32.5 mol of Xe at 75 °C. Calculate the pressure of the gas (a) assuming ideality and (b) using the van der Waals equation. For Xe, $a = 4.194$ L² atm/mol² and $b = 0.05105$ L/mol. *Answer* (a) 531 atm, (b) 9000 atm

SUMMARY

SIGNIFICANT TERMS

volatile
ideal gas
variables
constant
Boyle's law
barometer
manometer
absolute zero
absolute temperature scale
Kelvin temperature scale
Charles' law
standard temperature and pressure (STP)
Gay-Lussac's law of combining volumes
Avogadro's law
standard molar volume
ideal gas law
Dalton's law of partial pressures
partial pressure
mole fraction
dynamic equilibrium
vapor pressure
effusion
Graham's law of effusion
diffusion
Graham's law of diffusion

5.1 GENERAL PROPERTIES OF GASES Gases fill whatever space is available to them, but are highly compressible. The pressure of a gas and the space that it occupies vary with temperature. Gases have low densities and flow easily.

5.2 KINETIC-MOLECULAR THEORY OF GASES Molecules of gas are very small in comparison to the spaces that separate them. Gas molecules are in constant random motion, and gas pressure is the result of impacts with the walls. The average kinetic energy of gas molecules is directly proportional to the absolute temperature of the gas. At any given temperature, the molecules of every gas have the same average kinetic energy, molecules of lower mass moving with greater speeds. Collisions with each other and with the walls of the container are perfectly elastic — they involve no loss of energy. A gas having all these properties is known as an ideal gas. The behavior of real gases resembles that of an ideal gas under many conditions.

5.3 VARIABLES AND PROPORTIONALITY A variable quantity is one that can change, for example, the pressure, volume, temperature, and amount of a gas. A constant has a fixed value that cannot change. A and B are directly proportional if $A = kB$, and inversely proportional if $A = k(1/B)$, where k is a constant.

5.4 VOLUME VERSUS PRESSURE: BOYLE'S LAW According to Boyle's law, at constant temperature the volume of a given mass of gas is inversely proportional to the pressure upon the gas. For a given mass of gas at constant temperature, $P_1V_1 = P_2V_2$, where the subscripts 1 and 2 designate initial and final conditions.

TOOLS OF CHEMISTRY: PRESSURE UNITS AND PRESSURE MEASUREMENT Pressure is force per unit area. A device that measures the pressure exerted by the atmosphere is called a barometer. In a mercury barometer, atmospheric pressure supports a column of mercury in an evacuated tube. Pressure can be expressed in many different units. Normal atmospheric pressure at sea level is 760 Torr = 1 atm = 1.013 bar.

5.5 VOLUME VERSUS TEMPERATURE: CHARLES' LAW According to Charles' law, at constant pressure the volume of a given mass of gas is directly proportional to the absolute temperature. For a given mass of gas at constant pressure, $V_1/T_1 = V_2/T_2$, where T is the absolute temperature, measured in kelvins (K) on the absolute or Kelvin temperature scale, which has a zero point of -273.15 °C. This is absolute zero, the lowest possible temperature, at which no more kinetic energy can be removed from the molecules of a gas and its volume would in theory fall to zero.

5.6 P, V, AND T CHANGES IN A FIXED MASS OF GAS Boyle's law and Charles' law can be combined into a single expression: for a fixed mass of gas, $P_1V_1/T_1 = P_2V_2/T_2$.

5.7 STANDARD TEMPERATURE AND PRESSURE (STP) Gas volumes are generally given at standard temperature and pressure, STP: 0 °C (273 K) and 760 Torr.

5.8 GAY-LUSSAC'S LAW OF COMBINING VOLUMES AND AVOGADRO'S LAW Gay-Lussac observed that when gases react or gaseous products are formed, the ratios of the volumes of the gases involved, measured at the same temperature and pressure, are small whole numbers. The explanation for this law was provided by Avogadro, who recognized that equal volumes of gases, measured at the same temperature and pressure, contain equal numbers of molecules.

5.9 MOLAR VOLUME   Standard molar volume is the volume of one mole of a substance at STP. For any ideal gas, it is equal to 22.4 L. The density of an ideal gas at STP can be found from its molar mass, or vice versa, by using molar volume.

5.10 IDEAL GAS LAW   **5.11** MASS AND DENSITY   The ideal gas law is $PV = nRT$, where n is the number of moles of gas and R is the ideal gas constant, the value of which depends on the units used for P, V, and T. If m is the mass of gas and M its molar mass, $PV = (m/M)RT$. The density, d, of a gas is given by $d = PM/RT$.

5.12 PRESSURE IN GAS MIXTURES: DALTON'S LAW   In a mixture of gases that do not react, the molecules of each gas move about independently and distribute themselves uniformly throughout the available space as if no other gas were present. Each therefore exerts the same pressure as it would if it were present alone. This is known as Dalton's law of partial pressures. The pressure of a single gas in a mixture is called its partial pressure.

5.13 EFFUSION AND DIFFUSION: GRAHAM'S LAWS   Effusion is the escape of gas molecules, one by one, through a hole of molecular dimensions. Diffusion is the mixing of different gases by random molecular motions and collisions. According to Graham's laws of effusion and diffusion, at the same temperature and pressure, the rates of both processes are inversely proportional to the square roots of the densities (and therefore to the square roots of the molecular masses) of the gases.

5.14 DEVIATIONS FROM THE GAS LAWS   Molecules of all real gases occupy a finite volume and interact with each other to some extent. These factors cause some deviations from the ideal gas law. The van der Waals equation, which introduces corrections that take into account the volumes and interactions of gas molecules, describes more accurately the behavior of real gases.

THOUGHTS ON CHEMISTRY

Scientific Method

ZEN AND THE ART OF MOTORCYCLE MAINTENANCE, by Robert Pirsig

When I think of formal scientific method an image sometimes comes to mind of an enormous juggernaut, a huge bulldozer — slow, tedious, lumbering, laborious, but invincible. It takes twice as long, five times as long, maybe a dozen times as long as informal mechanic's techniques, but you know in the end you're going to get it. There's no fault isolation problem in motorcycle maintenance that can stand up to it. When you've hit a really tough one, tried everything, racked your brain and nothing works, and you know that this time Nature has really decided to be difficult, you say, "Okay, Nature, that's the end of the nice guy," and you crank up the formal scientific method.

For this you keep a lab notebook. Everything gets written down, formally, so that you know at all times where you are, where you've been, where you're going and where you want to get. In scientific work and electronics technology this is necessary because otherwise the problems get so complex you get lost in them and confused and forget what you know and what you don't know and have to give up. In cycle maintenance things are not that involved, but when confusion starts it's a good idea to hold it down by making everything formal and exact. Sometimes just the act of writing down the problems straightens out your head as to what they really are. . . .

The real purpose of scientific method is to make sure Nature hasn't misled you into thinking you know something you don't actually know.

There's not a mechanic or scientist or technician alive who hasn't suffered from that one so much that he's not instinctively on guard. That's the main reason why so much scientific and mechanical information sounds so dull and so cautious. If you get careless or go romanticizing scientific information, giving it a flourish here and there, Nature will soon make a complete fool out of you. It does it often enough anyway even when you don't give it opportunities. One must be extremely careful and rigidly logical when dealing with Nature: one logical slip and an entire scientific edifice comes tumbling down. One false deduction about the machine and you can get hung up indefinitely.

Robert Pirsig, *Zen and the Art of Motorcycle Maintenance* (New York: William Morrow & Co., 1975), p. 100.

QUESTIONS

The Nature of Gases

5.1 List the five statements that summarize the kinetic-molecular theory for an ideal gas. Explain how these might not be valid for a liquid or solid.

5.2 What causes the pressure on the walls of a container holding a gas?

5.3 If two different gases have the same average kinetic energy at the same temperature, how do the average speeds of the molecules differ?

5.4 Explain, in terms of the kinetic-molecular theory, the direct relationship between the pressure and the temperature of a gas in a fixed volume.

Volume, Pressure, and Temperature Relationships

5.5 In sentence and equation forms, state (a) Boyle's law and (b) Charles' law.

5.6 Classify the relationship between the variables (a) P and V, (b) V and T, (c) P and T, (d) V and n as either (i) directly or (ii) inversely proportional.

5.7* Prepare sketches of plots of (a) P vs. V, (b) P vs. $1/V$, (c) V vs. T, and (d) P vs. T for an ideal gas.

Mass, Molecular, and Molar Relationships

5.8 State Gay-Lussac's law of combining volumes. What is the relationship between the "volumes of gases" and the coefficients used to balance the chemical equation?

5.9 State Avogadro's law. How does this explain that any ideal gas will have the same molar volume at STP?

5.10 State Dalton's law of partial pressures. What is the relationship between the partial pressures and the composition of a mixture?

5.11 State the ideal gas law in mathematical form. Identify the variables to which the number of moles is directly proportional.

Behavior of Gas Molecules

5.12 What is the relationship between the rate of effusion of a gas and its density? What is the relationship between the rate of effusion and the molar mass of the gas?

5.13 What two properties of real gas molecules cause deviations from ideal gas behavior?

Additional Questions

5.14 What types of experiments could be used to prove that molecular chlorine is diatomic?

5.15 A local disc jockey commented one morning: "The present temperature is 21 degrees and the outlook for today is for a high of 42 degrees, just twice as hot." Comment on his statement.

5.16* About 20 years ago it was discovered that the "inert" gases are not really inert after all. In particular, xenon reacts with fluorine under various conditions to form a series of compounds.

Colorless crystals of XeF_4 can be prepared by heating a 1 to 5 mixture by volume of Xe to F_2 in a nickel can at 400 °C and 6 atm pressure for a few hours and cooling. The equation for the reaction is

$$Xe(g) + 2F_2(g) \longrightarrow XeF_4(s)$$

After the reaction the nickel container contains gaseous F_2 and a little XeF_4 vapor above the crystals of XeF_4.

According to Gay-Lussac's law of combining volumes, (a) what volume of F_2 would react for every milliliter of Xe that reacts? (b) Which law allows us to deduce that the partial pressure of Xe is 1 atm and the partial pressure of F_2 is 5 atm in the original reaction mixture? Predict what will happen to the gases in the nickel container after the reaction if (c) the pressure is increased at constant temperature (use Boyle's law) and (d) the temperature is increased at constant pressure (use Charles' law). (e) Using Graham's law, predict the increasing order for the rate of effusion of the gases Xe, F_2, and XeF_4. (f) Basing your argument on actual volumes of molecules, which of the three gases — Xe, F_2 or XeF_4 — would you predict would deviate most from ideal gas behavior at high pressures?

Answers to Selected Questions

5.6 (a) ii, (b) i, (c). i, (d) i

5.11 $PV = nRT$, P and V

5.16 (a) 2 mL, (b) Dalton's law, (c) volume decreases, (d) volume increases, (e) $XeF_4 < Xe < F_2$, (f) XeF_4

PROBLEMS

P-V-T-n Relationships: V and P

5.1 What pressure is needed to confine an ideal gas at 75 L after it has expanded from 25 L and 1.00 atm at constant temperature? *Answer* 0.33 atm

5.2 A flask of unknown volume was filled with air to a pressure of 3.6 atm. This flask was then attached to an evacuated flask of known volume and the air was allowed to expand into the flask. The final pressure of the air (in both flasks) was 2.7 atm and the volume of the second flask was 4.9 L. Calculate the volume of the first flask. *Answer* 10 L   14L

5.3 A 0.532 L flask containing helium at 836 Torr was connected to a vacuum system of unknown volume. The helium was allowed to expand into the vacuum system and the final pressure of the system and flask was 262 Torr. Calculate the volume of the vacuum system.

5.4* Demonstrate that the following data for the experimental apparatus depicted in Figure 5.5 are consistent with Boyle's law:

$P_{atm} = 745$ Torr

h_{Hg} in cm	1.0	2.0	3.0	4.0	5.0
h_{air} in cm	25.00	24.68	24.34	24.05	23.75

Answer $(P)(h_{air}) = 18,900$ cm Torr, h_{air} is directly proportional to V, $PV =$ constant

5.5* Trapped air is used as a ballast in water storage tanks so that large quantities of water can be drawn from the tank at fairly uniform pressure. In a typical system used in a home, water is pumped into the storage tank until a pressure of 60. psig is reached. As water is withdrawn for use, the pressure drops. When a pressure of 30. psig is reached, the tank is refilled until a pressure of 60. psig is restored. If the volume of trapped air at 60. psig is about 15 gal, what volume of water is delivered before the pump turns on for refilling?

P-V-T-n Relationships: V and T

5.6 What will be the new volume after 1.000 L of an ideal gas is heated from 0.0 °C to 1.0 °C under constant pressure? *Answer* 1.004 L

5.7 What will be the final temperature after 10.0 L of an ideal gas at 950 K is reduced to a volume of 1.0 L under constant pressure?

5.8* Calculate the volume of an ideal gas at dry ice (−78.5 °C), liquid N_2 (−195.8 °C), and liquid He (−268.9 °C) temperatures if it occupies 10.00 L at 25.0 °C. Assume constant pressure. Plot your results and extrapolate to zero volume. At what temperature is zero volume reached?

P-V-T-n Relationship: P and T

5.9 An ideal gas occupies a certain volume at 600. Torr and 27 °C. If the pressure is reduced to 500. Torr, what will the temperature have to be to keep the volume constant? *Answer* 250. K

5.10 A steel cylinder of fixed volume has an attached pressure gauge which reads 298 Torr at 25 °C. At what temperature should it register 1000. Torr? Could you use this sort of device as a thermometer? Why?

5.11 What will be the final pressure of an ideal gas that is heated from 0 °C and 1.00 atm to 135 °C in a fixed volume? *Answer* 1.49 atm

5.12 A basketball was inflated to 8 psig in a garage at 20. °C. While playing basketball on a driveway at a temperature of −5 °C, the ball seemed "flat." Calculate the pressure of the air in the cold ball assuming the atmospheric pressure to be 14.4 psi. *Answer* 6 psig

P-V-T-n Relationships: P, V, and T

5.13 What is the volume of an ideal gas at −14 °C and 367 Torr if it occupied 3.65 L at 25 °C and 745 Torr?

5.14 What is the volume of an ideal gas at 1246 K and 5.30 atm if it occupied 16.3 L at 273 K and 0.937 atm? *Answer* 13.2 L

5.15 What pressure is necessary to contain an ideal gas at a volume of 37.5 ft³ and 78 °F if it originally occupied 375 ft³ at 135 psi and 85 °F? *Answer* 1340 psi

5.16 What is the pressure of an ideal gas which is confined to 15.9 L at 63 °C if it occupied 22.4 L at 25 °C and 757 Torr?

5.17 What is the temperature of 83 L of an ideal gas at 425 Torr if it occupied a volume of 75 L at 763 Torr and 15.0 K? *Answer* 9.2 K

5.18 What temperature would be necessary to double the volume of an ideal gas initially at STP if the pressure decreased by 25%? *Answer* 410 K

P-V-T-n Relationships: Gay-Lussac's Law

5.19 What volume of chlorine under the same temperature and pressure conditions will react with 2 L of each of the following gases: H_2, C_2H_4, CO, and C_2H_2? The equations are

(a) $H_2(g) + Cl_2(g) \longrightarrow 2HCl(g)$
(b) $C_2H_4(g) + Cl_2(g) \longrightarrow C_2H_4Cl_2(g)$
(c) $CO(g) + Cl_2(g) \longrightarrow COCl_2(g)$
(d) $C_2H_2(g) + 2Cl_2(g) \longrightarrow C_2H_2Cl_4(g)$
Answer (a) 2 L, (b) 2 L, (c) 2 L, (d) 4 L

5.20 Which reaction requires the smallest volume of gaseous oxygen for the reaction of 1 volume of the other gas?

(a) $CH_4(g) + 2O_2(g) \longrightarrow CO_2(g) + 2H_2O(l)$
(b) $2CH_3OH(g) + 3O_2(g) \longrightarrow 2CO_2(g) + 4H_2O(l)$
(c) $2C_2H_2(g) + 5O_2(g) \longrightarrow 4CO_2(g) + 2H_2O(l)$
(d) $CH_3CH_2OH(g) + 3O_2(g) \longrightarrow 2CO_2(g) + 3H_2O(l)$

5.21 One liter of sulfur vapor at 500 °C and 1 atm is burned in pure molecular oxygen to give 8 L of sulfur dioxide gas, SO_2, measured at the same temperature and pressure. How many atoms are there in a molecule of sulfur in the gaseous state? *Answer* 8

5.22 One liter of PCl_3 in the gaseous state at 200 °C and 1 atm reacts with an equal volume of molecular chlorine gas measured under the same temperature and pressure conditions. The product, also a gas, occupies 1 L when measured under the same conditions. What is the formula of this gas?

P-V-T-n Relationships: Avogadro's Law

5.23 A "one-liter" beaker (actual volume = 1.08 L) contains 0.0411 mol of air under a given set of temperature and pressure conditions. How many moles of air are in a "two-liter" beaker (actual volume = 2.23 L) under these same temperature and pressure conditions?

5.24 A 503 mL flask contains 0.0179 mol of an ideal gas under a given set of temperature and pressure conditions. Another flask contains 0.0256 mol of the gas under the same temperature and pressure conditions. What is the volume of the second flask? *Answer* 719 mL

P-V-T-n Relationships: Molar Volume

5.25 What is the volume occupied by 2.25 mol of an ideal gas at STP?

5.26 How many moles of an ideal gas are present in a cubic meter at STP? *Answer* 44.6 mol

5.27 How many molecules of an ideal gas are present in a 1.00 L flask at STP?

5.28 What is the density of gaseous fluorine, F_2, at STP?

5.29 The density of an ideal gas at STP is 6.13 g/L. What is the molar mass of the gas? *Answer* 137 g/mol

P-V-T-n Relationships: Ideal Gas Law

5.30 For an ideal gas, calculate the number of moles in 1.00 L at 25 °C and 1.00 atm. *Answer* 0.0409 mol

5.31 A sample of an ideal gas is confined in a 3.0 L container at a pressure of 2280 Torr and a temperature of 27 °C. How many moles of gas are there?

5.32 For an ideal gas, calculate the pressure needed to contain 5.29 mol at 45 °C in a volume of 3.45 L. *Answer* 40.0 atm

5.33 A 10.0-mol sample of oxygen is confined in a vessel with a capacity of 8.0 L. If the temperature is 0 °C, what is the pressure?

5.34 A 6.00-mol sample of helium is confined in a 4.5 L vessel. What is the temperature if the pressure is 3.0 atm?

5.35 What is the volume occupied by 1.00 mol of an ideal gas at −75 °C and 12.5 atm? *Answer* 1.30 L

5.36 How many gaseous molecules are in a one-liter container if the pressure is 1.6×10^{-9} Torr and the temperature is 1475 K? *Answer* 1.0×10^{10} molecules

5.37* A barge containing 640 tons of liquid chlorine was involved in an accident on the Ohio River. What volume would this amount of chlorine occupy if it were all converted to a gas at 740 Torr and 15 °C? Assume that the chlorine is confined to a width of 0.5 mile and an average depth of 50 ft. How long would this chlorine "bubble" be?

Molar Mass of Ideal Gas

5.38 An ideal gas has a molar mass of 95 g. What volume will 5.0 g of the gas occupy at 25 °C and 776 Torr? *Answer* 1.3 L

5.39 What is the molar mass of an ideal gas if 0.52 g of the gas occupies 610 mL at 385 Torr and 45 °C?

5.40 The Dumas method was used to determine the molar mass of a liquid. The vapor occupied a 103 mL volume at 99 °C and 721 Torr. The condensed vapor had a mass of 0.800 g. Calculate the molar mass of the liquid. *Answer* 250. g/mol

5.41* A highly volatile liquid was allowed to vaporize completely into a 250 mL flask immersed in boiling water. From the following data, calculate the molar mass of the liquid: mass of empty flask = 65.347 g; mass of flask filled with water at room temperature = 327.4 g; mass of flask and condensed liquid = 65.739 g; atmospheric pressure = 743.3 Torr; temperature of boiling water = 99.8 °C; and density of water at room temperature = 0.997 g/mL.

5.42 Cyanogen is 46.2% carbon and 53.8% nitrogen by mass. At a temperature of 25 °C and a pressure of 750 Torr, 1.00 g of cyanogen occupies 0.476 L. Determine the empirical formula and the molecular formula of cyanogen. *Answer* CN, $(CN)_2$

Density of Ideal Gases

5.43 What is the density of an ideal gas at 25 °C and 10.0 atm if the molar mass is 18 g? *Answer* 7.4 g/L

5.44 A laboratory technician forgot what the color coding on some commercial cylinders of gas meant, but remembered that each of two specific tanks contained one of the following gases: He, Ne, Ar, or Kr. Density measurements at STP were made on samples of the gases from these cylinders and were found to be 0.178 g/L and 0.900 g/L. Which of these gases was present in each tank?

Dalton's Law

5.45 A sample of molecular oxygen of mass 24.0 g is confined in a vessel at 0 °C and 1000. Torr. If 6.00 g of molecular hydrogen is now pumped into the vessel at constant temperature, what will be the final pressure in the vessel (assuming only simple mixing)? *Answer* P = 6.52 atm

5.46 A gaseous mixture contains 4.18 g of chloroform, $CHCl_3$, and 1.95 g of ethane, C_2H_6. What pressure is exerted by the mixture inside a 50.0 mL metal bomb at 375 °C? What pressure is contributed by the $CHCl_3$?

5.47 A cyclopropane-oxygen mixture can be used as an anesthetic. If the partial pressures of cyclopropane and oxygen are 150 Torr and 550 Torr, respectively, what is the ratio of the number of moles of cyclopropane to the number of moles of oxygen in this mixture? *Answer* 0.27

5.48 A 5.00 L flask containing He at 5.00 atm was connected to a 4.00 L flask containing N_2 at 4.00 atm. Using Boyle's law for each gas, (a) find the partial pressures of the gases after they are allowed to mix, and, using Dalton's law, (b) find the total pressure of the mixture. (c) What is the mole fraction of the helium?

5.49 A sample of hydrogen was collected over water at 25 °C. The vapor pressure of water at this temperature is 23.8 Torr. A dehydrating agent (something that absorbs water) was added to remove the water. If the original volume of wet hydrogen was 33.3 L and the original pressure of the wet hydrogen was 738 Torr, what volume would the dry hydrogen occupy at 743 Torr? *Answer* 32.0 L

Graham's Law

5.50 A sample of unknown gas flows through the wall of a porous cup in 39.9 min. An equal volume of molecular hydrogen, measured at the same temperature and pressure, flows through in 9.75 min. What is the molar mass of the unknown gas? *Answer* 33.8 g/mol

5.51 What would be the relative rates of effusion of gaseous H_2, HD, and D_2? (D is a chemical symbol used to represent deuterium, an isotope of hydrogen that has an atomic mass of 2.0140 u as compared to that of 1.007825 u for H.)

Real Gases

5.52 A sample of gas has a molar volume of 10.3 L at a pressure of 745 Torr and a temperature of −138 °C. Is the gas acting ideally?

5.53 The van der Waals constants for carbon tetrachloride, CCl_4, are $a = 20.39$ L^2 atm/mol^2 and $b = 0.1383$ L/mol. Find the pressure of a sample of CCl_4 if one mole occupies 30.0 L at 77 °C (just slightly above the boiling point). Assume CCl_4 to obey the (a) ideal gas law and (b) van der Waals gas law.

5.54 Repeat the calculations of Problem 5.53 using a 3.25 mol gas sample confined to 6.25 L at 115 °C. *Answer* 16.6 atm, 12.3 atm

5.55* Values of molar mass calculated using the ideal gas law are good only to the extent that the gas behaves as an ideal gas. However, all real gases approach ideal gas behavior at very low pressures, so a common technique for obtaining very accurate molar masses is to measure the density of a gas at various low pressures, calculate d/P from the data, plot d/P against P, extrapolate the curve to $P = 0$ to find the intercept, and calculate the molar mass, M, using $M = $ (intercept)RT where $R = 0.0820568$ L atm/K mol. Find the molar mass for SO_2 from the following data at 0 °C:

P in atm	0.1	0.01	0.001	0.0001
(d/P) in g/L atm	2.864974	2.858800	2.858183	2.858121

Assume that the temperature and pressure values are exact. *Answer* 64.0612 g/mol

Additional Problems

5.56 The radius of a typical molecule of gas is 0.2 nm. (a) Find the volume of a molecule assuming it to be spherical. ($V = \frac{4}{3}\pi r^3$ for a sphere.) (b) Calculate the volume actually occupied by a mole of these molecules. (c) If a mole of this gas is at STP, find the fraction of the volume of the gas actually occupied by the molecules. (d) Comment on your answer to (c) in view of the first statement summarizing the kinetic-molecular theory of an ideal gas.

5.57* The average speed of oxygen molecules at 25 °C is 4.44×10^2 m/s. What is the average speed of nitrogen molecules at this temperature?

5.58* The density of dry air at STP is 1.2929 g/L, and that of molecular nitrogen is 1.25055 g/L. (a) Find the average molar mass of air from these data. The mole fractions of the major components of air are 0.7808 for N_2, 0.2095 for O_2, 0.0093 for Ar, and 0.0003 for CO_2. (b) Calculate the average molar mass of air and (c) compare your answers from (a) and (b). (d) Why can't Graham's law be used to find the average molar mass of air?

What is the density of (e) dry air at 745 Torr and 25 °C and of (f) wet air at 745 Torr and 25 °C if it contains water vapor at a partial pressure of 13 Torr? (g) Explain why the answer to (f) should be less than the answer to (e).

(h) What is the partial pressure of CO_2 in a room containing dry air at 1.00 atm? (i) What mass of CO_2 will be present at 25 °C in a closet 1.5 m by 3.4 m by 3.0 m if the air pressure is 1.00 atm?

(j) What is the predicted pressure of a molar sample of air at −150 °C in a 1.00 L container assuming ideal gas behavior? (k) Repeat the calculation of (j) assuming air to obey the van der Waals gas law with $a = 1.38$ L^2 atm/mol^2 and $b = 0.037$ L/mol. (l) What is the percentage difference between your answers to (j) and (k)?

Answer (a) 28.962 g/mol, (b) 28.96 g/mol, (c) the same, (d) air is a mixture, (e) 1.16 g/L, (f) 1.15 g/L, (g) H_2O is less dense than the air it replaces, (h) 0.0003 atm, (i) 9 g, (j) 9.9 atm, (k) 8.9 atm, (l) 11%

CHAPTER 6

Atoms, Molecules, and Ions in Action: Chemical Reactions and Stoichiometry

The curious word "stoichiometry" was coined in 1792 by a German engineer who worked in the mines in Silesia. Jeremias B. Richter wondered "how far chemistry is part of applied mathematics." In his search for mathematical relationships in chemistry he measured the amounts of various compounds that combined with each other. Such studies of "equivalents" or "combining weights" were pursued in different ways by many scientists at the time.

Richter titled his book "Foundations of Stoichiometry," explaining the title as follows: "As the mathematical portion of chemistry deals in a great measure with bodies which are either elements or substances incapable of being decomposed and as it teaches also their relative magnitudes, I have been able to find no more fitting name for this scientific discipline than the word stoichiometry, from (the two Greek words meaning) 'something which cannot be divided,' and 'to find out relative magnitudes'."

Richter did a poor job of interpreting his experiments, apparently because of his determination to make the results fit the type of mathematical relationships that he was looking for. Also, his writing style was difficult to understand and did not encourage examination of his results. Eventually, a German chemist, Ernst Fischer, rearranged and clarified the results of Richter's experiments. The work of Fischer and Richter helped to inspire Dalton's concepts of the atom and of relative atomic weights.

CHEMICAL CHANGE: EQUATIONS AND TYPES OF REACTIONS

6.1 CONSERVATION OF MASS AND ENERGY

When chemical changes take place, both matter and energy are redistributed. A guiding principle in studying chemical change is our understanding that the total amounts of matter and energy in the universe are constant.

The *law of conservation of mass* (Section 4.4) tells us that in ordinary chemical reactions matter is neither created nor destroyed. Every chemical change also involves a change in energy. Chemical reactions and all other changes that release or utilize energy are governed by the *law of conservation of energy:* The energy of the universe is constant, or, in other words, energy cannot be created or destroyed. In the next chapter, we discuss the release and absorption of energy as heat in ordinary chemical reactions. Here we are concerned with the consequences of the law of conservation of mass in chemistry.

At the micro level, the law of conservation of mass means that no matter how the atoms of the reactants are rearranged to give the products of a chemical reaction, none of the atoms can disappear, nor can any new atoms appear. Atoms are neither created nor destroyed in ordinary chemical reactions. At the macro level, this means that the total mass of the substances that react must be equal to the total mass of the products.

Consider the following balanced chemical equation:

$$2BaO_2(s) \xrightarrow{\Delta} 2BaO(s) + O_2(g) \qquad \textbf{(6.1)}$$

barium peroxide   *barium oxide*   *oxygen*

Balanced chemical equation:
mass on left = mass on right

$$\frac{\text{charge}}{\text{on left}} = \frac{\text{charge}}{\text{on right}}$$

For each element:
atoms on left = atoms on right

It is *balanced* because there are two barium atoms and four oxygen atoms on each side of the arrow. Without the coefficients of 2 for BaO_2 and 2 for BaO, this equation would not be balanced. The equation would be in violation of the law of conservation of mass, for it would show three oxygen atoms being formed from two oxygen atoms.

Because we know from Equation (6.1) that two formula units of barium peroxide decompose to give two formula units of barium oxide and one molecule of oxygen, we also have the following information:

$$2BaO_2(s) \xrightarrow{\Delta} 2BaO(s) + O_2(g)$$
$$\quad 2\ mol \qquad\qquad 2\ mol \qquad 1\ mol$$

As we have seen, the molar mass is the equivalent in grams of the masses of the individual atoms, ions, or molecules in atomic mass units (Section 4.6). Using the molar masses of the compounds we find that 338.6 g of barium peroxide will decompose to give 306.6 g of barium oxide and 32.0 g of oxygen.

$$2BaO_2(s) \xrightarrow{\Delta} 2BaO(s) + O_2(g)$$
$$(2\ mol)(169.3\ g/mol) = \quad (2\ mol)(153.3\ g/mol) = \quad (1\ mol)(32.0\ g/mol) =$$
$$338.6\ g \qquad\qquad 306.6\ g \qquad\qquad 32.0\ g$$

In accordance with the law of conservation of mass, the mass of the product equals the mass of the reactants:

$$306.6\ g + 32.0\ g = 338.6\ g$$

6.2 BALANCING CHEMICAL EQUATIONS

The objective of this section is to describe how to balance simple chemical equations — how to find the correct coefficients so that for each element, the same number of atoms are present in the products as in the reactants. For the simple reactions discussed here, inspection of the formulas of the reactants and products can give enough information to allow balancing of the equations. Not all chemical equations can be balanced by inspection, and more elaborate methods are sometimes necessary. Balancing more complex equations is discussed in later chapters (Sections 17.8 and 23.2).

Once the reactants and products in a chemical reaction are known, the first step in writing the equation is to write the correct formulas on the appropriate sides of the arrow. Suppose we have found that when aluminum sulfide is mixed with water, the products are aluminum hydroxide and hydrogen sulfide gas. Starting with the formulas, we write

$$Al_2S_3(s) + H_2O(l) \xrightarrow{\text{not balanced}} Al(OH)_3(s) + H_2S(g) \qquad\qquad \textbf{(6.2)}$$
$$\quad aluminum \quad water \qquad\qquad\quad aluminum \quad hydrogen$$
$$\quad sulfide \qquad\qquad\qquad\qquad\quad hydroxide \quad sulfide$$

To balance an equation, it is often easiest to begin with atoms that appear in only one formula on each side of the equation. In Equation (6.2) there are three such atoms, Al, S, and O. It is also often best to begin with the most complicated formula, which in this case is Al_2S_3.

Starting with Al, inspect the formula of the reactant in which it appears, aluminum sulfide, Al_2S_3. The subscript shows that two Al atoms are present, and so there must also be two Al atoms on the right in the equation. To increase the number of Al atoms on the right from one in aluminum hydroxide, $Al(OH)_3$, to two, the *coefficient* 2 must be added.

$$Al_2S_3 + H_2O \xrightarrow{\text{not balanced}} 2Al(OH)_3 + H_2S \qquad\qquad \textbf{(6.3)}$$

We *cannot* write $Al_2(OH)_3$ because this would be a different chemical compound (if it existed, which it doesn't).

In the same manner, inspection shows that there must be three S atoms on the right.

$$Al_2S_3 + H_2O \xrightarrow{\text{not balanced}} 2Al(OH)_3 + 3H_2S \qquad (6.4)$$

Going on to oxygen, there are now six oxygen atoms on the right (2×3, the coefficient times the subscript), so six are needed on the left.

$$Al_2S_3(s) + 6H_2O(l) \longrightarrow 2Al(OH)_3(s) + 3H_2S(g) \qquad (6.5)$$

Now it is necessary to check the number of hydrogen atoms to see if they balance. On the left there are $6 \times 2 = 12$ hydrogen atoms and on the right there are $2 \times 3 = 6$ plus $3 \times 2 = 6$ hydrogen atoms, also giving a total of 12 hydrogen atoms. Equation (6.5) is balanced.

It is important to emphasize that the formulas for the reactants and products in a chemical reaction must represent the species that have been shown, by experience, to take part in the reaction. Any change in the correct chemical formulas of these species makes the equation *wrong,* even if it is balanced. Balancing an equation must never be achieved by changing the chemical formula of a reactant or a product. Do not make the common error of changing subscripts to balance an equation.

Some chemical equations can be balanced by using fractional coefficients, for example

$$Fe(s) + \tfrac{1}{2}O_2(g) \longrightarrow FeO(s)$$
$$\textit{iron(II) oxide}$$

Except in special circumstances, it is customary to use whole numbers as coefficients. This equation would normally be written

$$2Fe(s) + O_2(g) \longrightarrow 2FeO(s)$$

EXAMPLE 6.1
Balancing Chemical Equations

An important step in the treatment of municipal water supplies and sewage is the reaction between $Al_2(SO_4)_3$ and $Ca(OH)_2$, which are added as solids to the water and then dissolve:

$$Al_2(SO_4)_3(aq) + Ca(OH)_2(aq) \xrightarrow{\text{not balanced}} CaSO_4(s) + Al(OH)_3(s)$$

Balance this equation.

First balance the two Al atoms on the left by placing the coefficient 2 in front of $Al(OH)_3$.

$$Al_2(SO_4)_3 + Ca(OH)_2 \xrightarrow{\text{not balanced}} CaSO_4 + 2Al(OH)_3$$

Recognizing that there are $2 \times 3 = 6$ hydroxide ions on the products side, and only two on the reactants side, write a 3 in front of $Ca(OH)_2$.

$$Al_2(SO_4)_3 + 3Ca(OH)_2 \xrightarrow{\text{not balanced}} CaSO_4 + 2Al(OH)_3$$

The balancing is completed by placing a 3 before the formula for $CaSO_4$, which equalizes both the number of Ca atoms and the number of sulfate ions on both sides of the equation:

$$Al_2(SO_4)_3(s) + 3Ca(OH)_2(s) \longrightarrow 3CaSO_4(s) + 2Al(OH)_3(s)$$

Let's make a quick check.

No. aluminum atoms	2 on left	2 on right
No. sulfate ions	3 on left	3 on right
No. calcium atoms	3 on left	3 on right
No. hydroxide ions	$3 \times 2 = 6$ on left	$2 \times 3 = 6$ on right

The equation is balanced. [Note that polyatomic ions can be counted as units in balancing equations.]

Exercise Solid phosphorus pentabromide, PBr_5, reacts with water to form phosphoric acid, H_3PO_4, and hydrobromic acid, HBr. Write the chemical equation for this reaction. *Answer* $PBr_5(s) + 4H_2O(l) \rightarrow H_3PO_4(aq) + 5HBr(aq)$

EXAMPLE 6.2
Balancing Chemical Equations

Some cigarette lighters use butane, C_4H_{10}, as fuel. When butane burns, it reacts with oxygen from the air to produce water and carbon dioxide. Write a balanced chemical equation for this reaction.

The first step in writing the correct equation is to identify the reactants and products. These were given in the statement of the problem: C_4H_{10} and O_2 are the reactants and H_2O and CO_2 are the products. Next set up the equation with the reactants on the left and the products on the right:

$$C_4H_{10}(g) + O_2(g) \xrightarrow{\text{not} \atop \text{balanced}} CO_2(g) + H_2O(g)$$

All that remains is to find the coefficients needed to balance the equation. Beginning with the most complicated formula, C_4H_{10} on the left, add coefficients so that there are also four C atoms and ten H atoms on the right.

$$C_4H_{10} + O_2 \xrightarrow{\text{not} \atop \text{balanced}} 4CO_2 + 5H_2O$$

Note that the coefficient times the subscript shows that there are ten H atoms on the right. Now there are thirteen O atoms on the right and two O atoms on the left. We can balance the number of oxygens by using $\frac{13}{2}$ (or $6\frac{1}{2}$) in front of the O_2, obtaining

$$C_4H_{10} + \tfrac{13}{2}O_2 \longrightarrow 4CO_2 + 5H_2O$$

Ordinarily we do not use fractional coefficients, so we clear the fractions by multiplying all coefficients by 2, obtaining

$$2C_4H_{10}(g) + 13O_2(g) \longrightarrow 8CO_2(g) + 10H_2O(g)$$

Let's make a quick check.

No. carbon atoms	$2 \times 4 = 8$ on left	$8 \times 1 = 8$ on right
No. hydrogen atoms	$2 \times 10 = 20$ on left	$10 \times 2 = 20$ on right
No. oxygen atoms	$13 \times 2 = 26$ on left	$(8 \times 2) + (10 \times 1) = 26$ on right

The equation is balanced.

Exercise When the mineral chalcocite, Cu_2S, is heated in oxygen, the products are copper(I) oxide, Cu_2O, and sulfur dioxide, SO_2. Write the chemical equation for this reaction. *Answer* $2Cu_2S(s) + 3O_2(g) \rightarrow 2Cu_2O(s) + 2SO_2(g)$

6.3 SOME TYPES OF CHEMICAL REACTIONS

Chemical reactions can be categorized in many ways. An important objective in any study of chemical reactions is to recognize similarities in reactions among many different kinds of atoms, molecules, and ions. As a beginning in our study of chemical reactions, we introduce four simple, general types of reactions in the following sections. Knowing the possible types of reactions may, in some cases, help to predict the products. A surprising number of reactions fit into these four reaction categories: combination, decomposition, displacement, and partner exchange. In later chapters further examples of these types of reactions are discussed. However, you must not expect all chemical reactions to be easily categorized.

After we have studied the properties of atoms, molecules, and ions more extensively, we return to these categories of reactions and use them to expand our understanding of chemical reactions in general (Chapter 17). At this point, we suggest that you practice "reading" the chemical equations in the following sections. Think about what the equations mean in terms of the conservation of mass and note the physical states of the reactants and products. The equations given here can be written with confidence because they represent reactions that have been carried out many times with the same results. Never forget that writing a balanced equation does not mean that the reaction described will occur as indicated. Only experiment can prove that an equation is correct.

a. Combination reactions   In **combination reactions,** two reactants combine to give a single product (Figure 6.1). Using those old favorite reactants A and B (which may be atoms, ions, or molecules), a combination reaction may be described as

$$A + B \longrightarrow AB \qquad\qquad (6.6)$$

Many elements undergo combination reactions, for example,

$$2Li(s) + Cl_2(g) \longrightarrow \quad 2LiCl(s) \qquad\qquad (6.7)$$
lithium chloride

$$2Al(s) + 3S(s) \longrightarrow Al_2S_3(s) \qquad\qquad (6.8)$$
aluminum
sulfide

Compounds also take part in combination reactions. Whenever bottles of ammonia and hydrochloric acid stand near each other on the shelf, the fumes escaping from the bottles combine.

$$NH_3(g) + HCl(g) \longrightarrow NH_4Cl(s) \qquad\qquad (6.9)$$
ammonia   hydrogen   ammonium
chloride   chloride

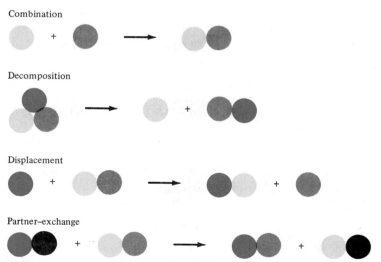

Figure 6.1
Four General Types of Chemical Reactions

Table 6.1
Some Examples of Chemical Reactions

Combination

$$C(s) + O_2(g) \longrightarrow CO_2(g)$$
carbon dioxide

Occurs when coal is burned in an excess of air; large amounts of heat released

$$2C(s) + O_2(g) \longrightarrow 2CO(g)$$
carbon monoxide

CO, a poisonous gas, is formed when coal is burned in a limited amount of air

$$N_2(g) + 3H_2(g) \longrightarrow 2NH_3(g)$$
ammonia

Major industrial preparation of NH_3, which is used as a fertilizer and source of nitric acid, HNO_3

$$S(s) + O_2(g) \longrightarrow SO_2(g)$$
sulfur dioxide

Important reaction in the industrial production of H_2SO_4; reaction also occurs when coal and other fossil fuels are burned; SO_2 is an atmospheric pollutant

$$CaO(s) + H_2O(l) \longrightarrow Ca(OH)_2(s)$$
calcium oxide (lime)   *calcium hydroxide (slaked lime)*

Preparation of "slaked lime," used in mortar and plaster

Decomposition

$$NH_4NO_3(s) \xrightarrow{\Delta} N_2O(g) + 2H_2O(g)$$
ammonium nitrate   *dinitrogen monoxide*

N_2O is "laughing gas," the first synthetic anesthetic discovered

$$CaCO_3(s) \xrightarrow{\Delta} CaO(s) + CO_2(g)$$
calcium carbonate (limestone)   *calcium oxide (lime)*

Source of lime, which is used in the manufacture of mortar and plaster (see above)

$$2Al_2O_3(s) \xrightarrow{\text{electric current}} 4Al(l) + 3O_2(g)$$
aluminum oxide

A major step in the production of aluminum

$$SiI_4(g) \xrightarrow{\Delta} Si(s) + 2I_2(g)$$
silicon (IV) iodide   *silicon*

Reaction by which ultrapure silicon is obtained for the electronics industry

Displacement

$$Fe(s) + H_2SO_4(aq) \longrightarrow H_2(g) + FeSO_4(aq)$$
iron (II) sulfate

First preparation of hydrogen, in 1671

$$Na(g) + KCl(l) \xrightarrow{\Delta} K(g) + NaCl(l)$$

Industrial preparation of potassium

Partner–Exchange

$$BaCl_2(aq) + H_2SO_4(aq) \longrightarrow BaSO_4(s) + 2HCl(aq)$$
barium chloride   *barium sulfate*

Used in analysis for sulfur

$$AgNO_3(aq) + NaCl(aq) \longrightarrow AgCl(s) + NaNO_3(aq)$$
silver nitrate   *silver chloride*

Used in analysis for chloride ion and to make AgCl for photography

The result is a fine frosting of ammonium chloride on everything nearby. Additional examples of combination and the other types of reactions discussed below are given in Table 6.1.

b. Decomposition reactions

In a **decomposition reaction** a single compound breaks down to give two or more other substances. Decomposition is essentially the reverse of combination.

$$AB \longrightarrow A + B \tag{6.10}$$

Metals above H_2 in the activity series displace H_2 from acid.

Energy, most often in the form of heat, usually must be provided to cause a compound to decompose. For example, oxygen was discovered (in 1774) as the product of the thermal decomposition (decomposition caused by heating) of mercury(II) oxide:

$$2HgO(s) \xrightarrow{\Delta} 2Hg(l) + O_2(g) \tag{6.11}$$
$$\textit{mercury(II)}$$
$$\textit{oxide}$$

Compounds that contain three or more elements can decompose to give several different products.

$$2NaHCO_3(s) \xrightarrow{\Delta} Na_2CO_3(s) + H_2O(g) + CO_2(g) \tag{6.12}$$
$$\textit{sodium hydrogen carbonate} \qquad \textit{sodium carbonate}$$

$$2Pb(NO_3)_2(s) \xrightarrow{\Delta} 2PbO(s) + 4NO_2(g) + O_2(g) \tag{6.13}$$
$$\textit{lead(II) nitrate} \qquad \textit{lead(II)} \quad \textit{nitrogen}$$
$$\textit{oxide} \quad \textit{dioxide}$$

c. Displacement reactions; activity series of metals

A reaction in which the atoms or ions of one substance take the place of other atoms or ions in a compound is called a **displacement reaction.**

$$A + BC \longrightarrow AC + B$$

The element hydrogen was first prepared (in 1671) by the displacement of the hydrogen from sulfuric acid by iron.

$$Fe(s) + H_2SO_4(aq) \longrightarrow H_2(g) + FeSO_4(aq) \tag{6.14}$$
$$\textit{sulfuric} \qquad \textit{iron(II) sulfate}$$
$$\textit{acid}$$

A number of metals can displace hydrogen from acids. Such metals are thought of as more "active" than hydrogen. Table 6.2 lists the more common metals in an activity series. Along the left side of the table is summarized the activity of the metals in displacing hydrogen from water and acids. All of the metals above hydrogen, which is included in the series for reference, displace hydrogen from acids.

The reactions with acids of the most active metals—those at the top of the table—can be quite violent. These active metals displace hydrogen from cold water to produce metal hydroxides. The lithium, potassium, and sodium hydroxides are quite soluble and remain in solution, for example,

$$2Li(s) + 2H_2O(l) \longrightarrow H_2(g) + 2LiOH(aq) \tag{6.15a}$$
$$\textit{lithium hydroxide}$$
$$\textit{(in aqueous solution)}$$

The somewhat less active metals displace hydrogen at the temperature of steam and yield metal oxides (which are all solid compounds).

$$Mg(s) + H_2O(g) \xrightarrow{\Delta} H_2(g) + MgO(s) \tag{6.15b}$$
$$\textit{(steam)} \qquad \textit{magnesium oxide}$$

Table 6.2
Activity Series of Metals The most reactive metals are at the top. They form ions readily. The activity of the metals decreases down the series.

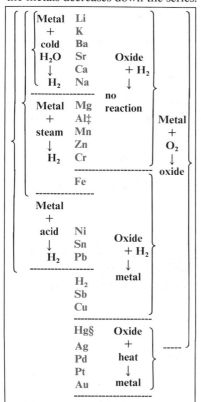

‡ Pure aluminum forms a protective oxide coating in air. When cleaned of this oxide, aluminum will react with water.

§ Mercury adds O_2 to give HgO, and HgO undergoes thermal decomposition.

The still less active metals like nickel, tin, and lead displace hydrogen only from acids and yield solutions of the salts formed between the metal cation and the anion of the acid.

$$Sn(s) + 2HBr(aq) \longrightarrow H_2(g) + SnBr_2(aq) \qquad \text{(6.15c)}$$

hydrobromic   tin(II)
acid   bromide

(Tables 4.2 and 4.4 give the charges of the common ions and can be consulted to determine the formulas of the products of the reactions discussed here and in the next section.)

EXAMPLE 6.3
Activity Series of Metals

Will reactions occur between (a) manganese and hydrochloric acid or (b) platinum and hydrochloric acid? What will be the products of the reactions? Write the balanced equations.

(a) Manganese is above hydrogen in the activity series and should react to displace hydrogen from an acid. The products of the reaction with hydrochloric acid will be hydrogen and the salt formed between the manganese and the chloride ions. The charges of the manganese and chloride ions are, respectively, $+2$ and -1, and the product is $MnCl_2$.

$$Mn(s) + 2HCl(aq) \longrightarrow MnCl_2(aq) + H_2(g)$$

hydrochloric   manganese(II)
acid   chloride

(b) Platinum is one of the least active metals. Since it is below hydrogen in the activity series, it will not react with hydrochloric acid.

$$Pt(s) + HCl(aq) \not\longrightarrow \text{(no reaction)}$$

Exercise Will magnesium react with hydrochloric acid? What are the products of the reaction? Write the equation. *Answer* yes, H_2 and Mg^{2+}, $Mg(s) + 2HCl(aq) \rightarrow MgCl_2(aq) + H_2(g)$

The far right of Table 6.2 shows that all but the least active metals combine with oxygen to give metal oxides, for example,

$$4Al(s) + 3O_2(g) \longrightarrow 2Al_2O_3(s) \qquad \text{(6.16)}$$

aluminum oxide

The activity series also shows the relative ease with which oxides will react to give free metals. The more active the metal, the less easily will the oxide yield the metal. Hydrogen displaces metals of intermediate activity from their oxides, for example,

$$H_2(g) + NiO(s) \xrightarrow{\Delta} H_2O(g) + Ni(s) \qquad \text{(6.17)}$$

nickel(II)
oxide

but does not react with oxides of the most active metals. Heating is sufficient to decompose oxides of the least active metals.

Metal displaces ions of metals below it in the activity series.

Displacement reactions between metals and metal ions also occur in aqueous solutions. A free metal displaces a metal below it in the series. For example, zinc metal displaces copper from a solution of any water-soluble, ionic copper compound such as copper(II) chloride to give a solution of zinc chloride and free copper.

$$Zn(s) + CuCl_2(aq) \longrightarrow ZnCl_2(aq) + Cu(s) \qquad \text{(6.18)}$$

copper(II) chloride   zinc
chloride

In summary, an activity series of metals (Table 6.2) allows the prediction of the results of four types of chemical reactions: (1) displacement of hydrogen from water and acids by metals (e.g., Equations 6.14, 6.15a, b, c), (2) combination of metals with oxygen to give oxides (e.g., Equation 6.16), (3) formation of free metal from oxide by displacement by hydrogen (e.g., Equation 6.17) or heating, (4) displacement of metal ions from solution by more active free metals (e.g., Equation 6.18).

EXAMPLE 6.4
Activity Series of Metals

Compare the activity of strontium, an active metal, and lead, a moderately active metal, by writing chemical equations for the information summarized in Table 6.2. (Strontium forms only Sr^{2+} ions and in these reactions lead will form Pb^{2+} ions.)

Strontium, near the top of the activity series, will displace hydrogen from cold water, from steam, or from acids such as hydrochloric acid. Strontium will form an oxide by direct combination with oxygen, and hydrogen cannot displace strontium from this oxide.

$$Sr(s) + 2H_2O(l) \longrightarrow Sr(OH)_2(aq) + H_2(g)$$
$$Sr(s) + H_2O(g) \xrightarrow{\Delta} SrO(s) + H_2(g)$$
$$Sr(s) + 2HCl(aq) \longrightarrow SrCl_2(aq) + H_2(g)$$
$$2Sr(s) + O_2(g) \longrightarrow 2SrO(s)$$
$$H_2(g) + SrO(s) \xrightarrow{\quad\not\longrightarrow\quad} \text{(no reaction)}$$

Lead displaces hydrogen from acids, but not from water or steam. Lead forms an oxide by direct combination with oxygen, and hydrogen is able to displace lead from this oxide.

$$Pb(s) + H_2O(l \text{ or } g) \not\longrightarrow \text{no reaction}$$
$$Pb(s) + 2HCl(aq) \longrightarrow PbCl_2(aq) + H_2(g)$$
$$2Pb(s) + O_2(g) \longrightarrow 2PbO(s)$$
$$H_2(g) + PbO(s) \xrightarrow{\Delta} Pb(s) + H_2O(g)$$

Exercise   Nickel is a moderately active metal. Write chemical equations describing the chemical behavior of this metal as summarized in Table 6.2.   *Answer* $Ni(s) + H_2O(g \text{ or } l) \not\longrightarrow$ no reaction, $Ni(s) + 2HCl(aq) \rightarrow NiCl_2(aq) + H_2(g)$, $NiO(s) + H_2(g) \rightarrow Ni(s) + H_2O(g)$, $2Ni(s) + O_2(g) \rightarrow 2NiO(s)$

EXAMPLE 6.5
Activity Series of Metals

Use the activity series given in Table 6.2 to predict whether or not reactions will occur between the following substances.

$$Fe(s) + CuCl_2(aq) \longrightarrow$$
$$Mg(s) + NaCl(aq) \longrightarrow$$

Complete the equations if reactions occur.

Iron is more active than copper. Therefore, it will displace copper ions from a solution of copper(II) chloride to give free copper.

$$Fe(s) + CuCl_2(aq) \longrightarrow FeCl_2(aq) + Cu(s)$$

Magnesium is a less active metal than sodium, and therefore it cannot displace sodium from the solution.

$$Mg(s) + NaCl(aq) \not\longrightarrow \text{(no reaction)}$$

Exercise Use the activity series given in Table 6.2 to predict whether or not the following reactions will occur. (a) $2Al(s) + 3Cu^{2+} \rightarrow 2Al^{3+} + 3Cu(s)$; (b) $Mg(s) + 2Na^{+} \rightarrow Mg^{2+} + 2Na(s)$; (c) $4Au(s) + O_2(g) \rightarrow 2Au_2O(s)$. *Answer* (a) yes, (b) no, (c) no

d. Partner-exchange reactions

In **partner-exchange reactions** two compounds interact as follows:

$$AC + BD \longrightarrow AD + BC \tag{6.19}$$

where A, B, C, and D may be atoms, monatomic ions, or polyatomic ions. Many different names have been given to this type of reaction—double decomposition, double displacement, and, often, metathesis—you may see these terms in other books. We feel that "partner exchange" is more descriptive of what takes place in reactions that correspond to the pattern of Equation (6.19).

One step in the production of magnesium metal from seawater is a partner-exchange reaction between magnesium, which is present in seawater mainly as dissolved magnesium chloride or magnesium sulfate, and calcium hydroxide.

$$\underset{\substack{magnesium \\ chloride}}{MgCl_2(aq)} + \underset{\substack{calcium \\ hydroxide}}{Ca(OH)_2(s)} \longrightarrow \underset{\substack{magnesium \\ hydroxide}}{Mg(OH)_2(s)} + \underset{\substack{calcium \\ chloride}}{CaCl_2(aq)} \tag{6.20}$$

In many cases partner exchange takes place between two ionic compounds that are both dissolved in water to yield one product that is a solid, for example.

$$\underset{\substack{barium \\ chloride}}{BaCl_2(aq)} + \underset{\substack{potassium \\ chromate}}{K_2CrO_4(aq)} \longrightarrow \underset{\substack{barium \\ chromate}}{BaCrO_4(s)} + \underset{\substack{potassium \\ chloride}}{2KCl(aq)} \tag{6.21}$$

A solid that forms during a reaction in solution is called a **precipitate.** The formation of a solid when a reaction takes place in solution is called **precipitation.** In the next section, we introduce solubility rules that can be used to predict the products of partner-exchange reactions in which precipitates are formed.

EXAMPLE 6.6
Classification of Reactions

Classify each of the following chemical reactions as combination, displacement, decomposition, or partner exchange.

$$HNO_3(aq) + NH_3(aq) \longrightarrow NH_4NO_3(aq) \tag{a}$$

$$NH_4Cl(s) \overset{\Delta}{\longrightarrow} NH_3(g) + HCl(g) \tag{b}$$

$$ZrCl_4(s) + 2Mg(s) \overset{\Delta}{\longrightarrow} Zr(s) + 2MgCl_2(s) \tag{c}$$

$$CaCl_2(aq) + 2AgNO_3(aq) \longrightarrow 2AgCl(s) + Ca(NO_3)_2(aq) \tag{d}$$

$$Fe_3O_4(s) + 4H_2(g) \overset{\Delta}{\longrightarrow} 3Fe(s) + 4H_2O(g) \tag{e}$$

In reaction (a) two compounds combine to form a single compound. This is a combination reaction.

In decomposition reactions, a single compound decomposes to give other substances. This is the case for reaction (b).

In reaction (c), the Mg atoms replace the Zr atoms in $ZrCl_4$ and in reaction (e), the H atoms replace the Fe atoms in Fe_3O_4. These are displacement reactions.

Reaction (d) fits the pattern of Equation (6.19) and is therefore a partner-exchange reaction.

Exercise Classify each of the following chemical reactions as combination, displacement, decomposition, or partner exchange: (a) $ZnCO_3(s) \overset{\Delta}{\longrightarrow}$

$ZnO(s) + CO_2(g)$. (b) $P_4O_6(s) + 6H_2O(l) \rightarrow 4H_3PO_3(aq)$. (c) $Al_2(SO_4)_3(aq) + 3Ca(OH)_2(aq) \rightarrow 2Al(OH)_3(s) + 3CaSO_4(aq)$. *Answer* (a) decomposition, (b) combination, (c) partner exchange

6.4 NET IONIC EQUATIONS; PRECIPITATION REACTIONS

In the reaction between barium chloride and potassium chromate (Equation 6.21), three of the four chemical compounds involved are soluble and are dissociated into ions in aqueous solution (Section 4.4). Writing out separately all of the ions in solution in Equation (6.21) gives

$$Ba^{2+}(aq) + 2Cl^-(aq) + 2K^+(aq) + CrO_4^{2-}(aq)$$
$$\longrightarrow BaCrO_4(s) + 2K^+(aq) + 2Cl^-(aq) \quad \textbf{(6.22)}$$

Inspection of this equation shows that two of the species present—the K^+ and Cl^- ions—actually undergo no chemical change. We call these **spectator ions**—ions that are present during a reaction in aqueous solution, but are unchanged in the reaction.

Equal numbers of spectator ions that appear on both sides of an equation can be cancelled. Doing so for Equation (6.22) leaves

$$Ba^{2+}(aq) + CrO_4^{2-}(aq) \longrightarrow BaCrO_4(s) \quad \textbf{(6.23)}$$

Equation (6.23) is a **net ionic equation**—an equation that shows only the species involved in a chemical change and excludes spectator ions. Equation (6.23) tells us that barium chromate can precipitate whenever barium and chromate ions are brought together in solution. The barium and chromate ions can be from any source. They need not be only from the compounds we started with in Equation (6.22).

A net ionic equation can be written for any reaction that has ions in solution among the reactants and products. For the displacement of copper ion by zinc [Equation (6.18)],

$$Zn(s) + Cu^{2+}(aq) + 2Cl^-(aq) \longrightarrow Zn^{2+}(aq) + 2Cl^-(aq) + Cu(s)$$
$$Zn(s) + Cu^{2+}(aq) \longrightarrow Zn^{2+}(aq) + Cu(s) \quad \textbf{(6.24)}$$

In writing net ionic equations, only ions in solution are written as ions. As is done in Equation (6.23), complete formulas are given for reactants or products that are insoluble solids, even if they are ionic compounds. Also, complete formulas are written for gases, for water, or for other molecular compounds. The equations for the reaction between solid manganese sulfide and hydrochloric acid are written as follows:

$$MnS(s) + 2HCl(aq) \longrightarrow MnCl_2(aq) + H_2S(g) \quad \textbf{(6.25)}$$
$$MnS(s) + 2H^+(aq) \longrightarrow Mn^{2+}(aq) + H_2S(g) \quad \textbf{(6.26)}$$

Note that although one product is a gas rather than a precipitate, this reaction fits the pattern for partner exchange.

In net ionic equations, the sum of the charges on the left and those on the right must balance. Electrical charge, like mass, must be conserved. Keep in mind in summing the charges, that you are taking an algebraic sum of positive and negative numbers. For Equation (6.23), for example, the charge on the left is zero (+2 plus $-2 = 0$), as is the charge for the compound on the right. As long as charge balance is maintained, the total charge on each side of an ionic equation can have any value. In the following equation the charge on each side is +17.

$$MnO_4^-(aq) + 5Fe^{2+}(aq) + 8H^+(aq) \longrightarrow 5Fe^{3+}(aq) + Mn^{2+}(aq) + 4H_2O(l) \quad \textbf{(6.27)}$$
$$(-1) \quad + \quad 5(+2) \quad + \quad 8(+1) \quad = +17 \quad 5(+3) \quad + \quad (+2) \quad = \quad +17$$

The occurrence of precipitation can often be predicted on the basis of generalizations, or rules, about the solubilities of ionic compounds. Table 6.3 summarizes some solubility rules for common compounds of the types listed. For example,

Table 6.3
Solubility Rules for Common Types of Ionic Compounds These generalities apply to solutions in water at room temperature (20–25 °C). *Soluble* indicates approximately one or more moles of solute per liter of solution; *moderately soluble* (mod. sol.), $0.01 - 0.1$ mol/L; and *slightly soluble*, less than 0.01 mol/L). (*Nothing* is completely insoluble.)

Generally Soluble
All Na^+, K^+, and NH_4^+ compounds
All Cl^-, Br^-, and I^- compounds
Except **those of Ag^+, Pb^{2+}, Hg_2^{2+}, insol.**
$PbCl_2$ sol. in hot water
$HgBr_2$, mod. sol.
I^- with heavier metals, insol.
All SO_4^{2-} compounds
Except **those of Sr^{2+}, Ba^{2+}, Pb^{2+}, insol.**
$CaSO_4$, Ag_2SO_4, mod. sol.
All NO_3^- and NO_2^- compounds
Except **$AgNO_2$, mod. sol.**
All ClO_3^-, ClO_4^-, MnO_4^- compounds
Except **$KClO_4$, mod. sol.**
All CH_3COO^- compounds
Except **$AgCH_3COO$, mod. sol.**

Generally Insoluble
All S^{2-} compounds
Except **those of NH_4^+, Li^+, Na^+, K^+, sol.**
All O^{2-}, OH^- compounds
Except **those of Li^+, Na^+, K^+, sol.**
BaO, $Ba(OH)_2$, CaO, $Ca(OH)_2$, SrO, $Sr(OH)_2$, mod. sol.
All CO_3^{2-}, PO_4^{3-}, CN^-, SO_3^{2-} compounds
Except **those of NH_4^+, Li^+, Na^+, K^+**

consider what might happen when solutions of the soluble salts potassium carbonate (K_2CO_3) and calcium chloride ($CaCl_2$) are mixed. The following ions are present in the solution:

$$2K^+(aq) + CO_3^{2-}(aq) + Ca^{2+}(aq) + 2Cl^-(aq)$$

Possible precipitates — if the compounds are insoluble — would be potassium chloride, KCl, or calcium carbonate, $CaCO_3$. Table 6.3 shows that chlorides are generally soluble, and KCl is not one of the exceptions. Carbonates are generally insoluble, and $CaCO_3$ is not an exception to this rule. Therefore, we can predict that $CaCO_3$ would precipitate when solutions of potassium carbonate and calcium chloride are mixed. The complete equation, the equation showing all of the ions, and the net ionic equations are given below. In these equations and throughout the remainder of this book, we usually omit the designation (aq) after ions. You may always assume that ions are in aqueous solution unless it is explicitly stated that they are not.

$$K_2CO_3(aq) + CaCl_2(aq) \longrightarrow 2KCl(aq) + CaCO_3(s) \qquad \textbf{(6.28)}$$
$$2K^+ + CO_3^{2-} + Ca^{2+} + 2Cl^- \longrightarrow 2K^+ + 2Cl^- + CaCO_3(s) \qquad \textbf{(6.29)}$$
$$Ca^{2+} + CO_3^{2-} \longrightarrow CaCO_3(s) \qquad \textbf{(6.30)}$$

EXAMPLE 6.7
Net Ionic Equations

Based on the solubility rules given in Table 6.3, how would you write the formulas for (a) Na_2S, (b) AgBr, (c) $NH_4(CH_3COO)$, and (d) $Fe(OH)_3$ in the net ionic equations for reactions in aqueous solution?

(a) Na_2S is soluble in water and should be written as $2Na^+(aq) + S^{2-}(aq)$, or $2Na^+ + S^{2-}$.
(b) AgBr is insoluble in water. Thus the formula should be written as AgBr(s).
(c) $NH_4(CH_3COO)$ is soluble in water and should be written as $NH_4^+(aq) + CH_3COO^-(aq)$, or $NH_4^+ + CH_3COO^-$.
(d) $Fe(OH)_3$ is an insoluble hydroxide and the formula should be $Fe(OH)_3(s)$.

Exercise   Based on the solubility rules given in Table 6.3, write the formulas for (a) KNO_2, (b) $BaCO_3$, and (c) Hg_2I_2 that would be used in the equations for reactions in aqueous solution.   *Answer* (a) $K^+ + NO_2^-$, (b) $BaCO_3(s)$, (c) $Hg_2I_2(s)$

EXAMPLE 6.8
Net Ionic Equations

Chlorine gas can be prepared in the laboratory by the reaction of manganese dioxide with hydrochloric acid (an acid which is completely ionized in aqueous solution):

$$MnO_2(s) + 4HCl(aq) \longrightarrow MnCl_2(aq) + 2H_2O(l) + Cl_2(g)$$

Write the net ionic equation for this reaction.

Before we can write the net ionic equation, we must identify which species exist as ions and which ones do not. We know that HCl is completely ionized in aqueous solution. Thus the formula for HCl(aq) should be written as $H^+(aq) + Cl^-(aq)$. Table 6.3 tells us that $MnCl_2$ is soluble in water and therefore the formula should be written as $Mn^{2+}(aq) + 2Cl^-(aq)$. We must write the formula for manganese dioxide as $MnO_2(s)$ because it is a solid, water as $H_2O(l)$, and chlorine as $Cl_2(g)$ because it is a gas.
The original equation, rewritten using the ionic form for the HCl and $MnCl_2$, is

$$MnO_2(s) + 4H^+ + 4Cl^- \longrightarrow Mn^{2+} + 2Cl^- + 2H_2O(l) + Cl_2(g)$$

Two chloride ions are spectator ions and can be cancelled from each side, giving the net ionic equation

$$MnO_2(s) + 4H^+ + 2Cl^- \longrightarrow Mn^{2+} + 2H_2O(l) + Cl_2(g)$$

A check shows that there are equal numbers of Mn atoms (1), O atoms (2), H atoms (4), and Cl atoms (2) on each side of the equation. Likewise, a check shows that the algebraic sum of the charges, $(0) + (4)(+1) + 2(-1) = (+2) + (0) + (0) = +2$, is the same on each side of the equation.

Exercise One industrial method for preparing sodium hydroxide is to allow sodium carbonate to react with calcium hydroxide.

$$Na_2CO_3(aq) + Ca(OH)_2(aq) \longrightarrow 2NaOH(aq) + CaCO_3(s)$$

Write the net ionic equation for this reaction. *Answer* $Ca^{2+} + CO_3^{2-} \rightarrow CaCO_3(s)$

EXAMPLE 6.9
Net Ionic Equations

Using the solubility rules in Table 6.3, determine whether or not precipitation reactions will occur when aqueous solutions of the following compounds are combined. If the reactions occur, write complete and net ionic equations.

$$\text{(a)} \quad ZnI_2(aq) + PbNO_3(aq) \longrightarrow$$
$$\text{(b)} \quad MgBr_2(aq) + Na_2SO_4(aq) \longrightarrow$$

(a) Of the two possible products, zinc nitrate is soluble and lead iodide is insoluble and would precipitate.

$$ZnI_2(aq) + Pb(NO_3)_2(aq) \longrightarrow Zn(NO_3)_2(aq) + PbI_2(s)$$
$$Pb^{2+} + 2I^- \longrightarrow PbI_2(s)$$

(b) The two possible products, magnesium sulfate and sodium bromide, are both soluble salts. Therefore, no reaction will occur and the ions will all remain in solution.

$$MgBr_2(aq) + Na_2SO_4(aq) \not\longrightarrow \text{(no reaction)}$$

Exercise Predict whether or not the following reactions will occur, and if they do occur, write the complete and net ionic equations: (a) $Zn(NO_3)_2(aq) +$ $NaOH(aq) \rightarrow$, (b) $KCl(aq) + NaNO_3(aq) \rightarrow$. *Answer* (a) $Zn(NO_3)_2(aq) + 2NaOH(aq) \rightarrow Zn(OH)_2(s) + 2NaNO_3(aq)$, $Zn^{2+} + 2OH^- \rightarrow Zn(OH)_2(s)$; (b) no reaction

---

STOICHIOMETRY

We have titled this chapter "Atoms, Molecules, and Ions in Action." When these chemical species go into "action" we have chemical reactions—processes of chemical change. The calculation of the quantitative relationships in chemical changes is called **stoichiometry.**

6.5 INFORMATION FROM CHEMICAL EQUATIONS

A balanced chemical equation gives the formulas for the reactants and products. We have already learned how much information can be derived from a chemical formula—information about atomic, molar, and mass relationships (look back at Table 4.9). Stoichiometry uses all of this information and adds to it what chemical equations tell about the ratios of the atoms, molecules, and ions and their masses. When the reactants and products are gases the chemical equation also yields information about the ratios of the volumes of the gases involved (from the law of combining volumes, Section 5.8).

Let's look at the equation for the combination of oxygen with sulfur dioxide to give sulfur trioxide.

$$2SO_2(g) + O_2(g) \xrightarrow{\text{catalyst}} 2SO_3(g) \tag{6.31}$$

Table 6.4
Information from a Chemical Equation This reaction between sulfur dioxide and oxygen accounts for the presence of sulfur trioxide in the air as a pollutant and is a step in the sequence that leads to formation of sulfuric acid in the atmosphere.

Molecular masses =	$2SO_2(g)$	+	$O_2(g)$	$\longrightarrow$	$2SO_3(g)$
	sulfur dioxide 64 u		*oxygen* 32 u		*sulfur trioxide* 80. u
	Each		can react with		to yield
	2 molecules of SO_2		1 molecule of O_2		2 molecules of SO_3
	2 moles of SO_2		1 mole of O_2		2 moles of SO_3
	2 volumes of SO_2‡		1 volume of O_2‡		2 volumes of SO_3‡
	128 u of SO_2§		32 u of O_2		160. u of SO_3
	128 g of SO_2		32 g of O_2		160. g of SO_3
	44.8 L (STP) of SO_2		22.4 L (STP) of O_2		44.8 L (STP) of SO_3

‡ Volumes all measured at same T and P.

§ u is the abbreviation for atomic mass units (Section 3.10).

The coefficients immediately tell us that for every two SO_2 molecules that react, one O_2 molecule is required and two molecules of SO_3 form. Also, the coefficients indicate that every 2 mol of SO_2 requires 1 mol of O_2 and yields 2 mol of SO_3. Because the reactants and the product are gases, the ratios of moles and the ratios of gas volumes (at constant temperature and pressure) are the same. By using our prior knowledge of molar masses, the masses of the reactants and products can also be found (as done in Section 6.1 for Equation 6.1). Table 6.4 summarizes the information derived from Equation (6.31).

The mass ratios found from the molar masses and the coefficients always hold for *any* unit of mass because atomic and molar masses are relative numbers. (Recall our discussion of the masses of tennis balls and basketballs. Take a moment to look back at Section 4.6a if you don't remember, for this is a very important concept.) To prove that the mass ratios apply to any unit, we can take the relative mass ratios given in Table 6.4 in, say, pounds instead of grams, convert the mass in pounds to moles, and demonstrate that the mole ratio is unchanged.

$$2SO_2(g) \qquad + \qquad O_2(g) \qquad \longrightarrow \qquad 2SO_3(g)$$

$$\frac{(128\ lb\ SO_2)(454\ g/1\ lb)}{(64.06\ g\ SO_2/1\ mol\ SO_2)} \qquad \frac{(32\ lb\ O_2)(454\ g/1\ lb)}{(32.00\ g\ O_2/1\ mol\ O_2)} \qquad \frac{(160.\ lb\ SO_3)(454\ g/1\ lb)}{(80.06\ g\ SO_3)(1\ mol\ SO_3)}$$

$$= 907\ mol\ SO_2 \qquad\qquad = 454\ mol\ O_2 \qquad\qquad = 907\ mol\ SO_3$$

mole ratio   2   1   2

6.6 USING MOLE RATIOS

In order to carry out a chemical reaction, many questions must be answered about the mass or volume relationships among the reactants and products. How much of each reactant has to be weighed out and allowed to react in order to produce the desired amount of product? If only a few grams of one reactant are available, how much of the other reactant will be needed? How much product can be prepared from a given amount of starting materials? Will any amount of the reactants be left unchanged? These are all questions about stoichiometry.

To answer such questions, it is necessary to know the balanced chemical equation for the reaction. If the equation is not known, finding it becomes the first step in solving the problem.

The known and unknown facts in stoichiometry problems are different kinds of information about the quantities of reactants and products. In *every* stoichiometry problem, the mole ratios in the balanced chemical equation provide the connection between the known and the unknown information. No matter how complex the problem is, the step that allows its solution will be the use of mole ratios to connect the known and unknown facts.

As an example of how mole ratios are used, suppose you want to produce 0.30 mol of SO_3 by the reaction of Table 6.4. You must find out how many moles of SO_2 and O_2 will be needed. The balanced chemical equation provides the connection between 0.30 mol of SO_3 and the unknown amounts of reactants in the form of mole ratios, which yield the conversion factors needed.

$$2 SO_2(g) + O_2(g) \longrightarrow 2SO_3(g)$$

Two moles of SO_2 are required for the formation of every 2 mol of SO_3, and 1 mol of O_2 is needed for every 2 mol of SO_3, giving the mole ratios

$$\frac{2 \text{ mol } SO_2}{2 \text{ mol } SO_3} \quad \text{and} \quad \frac{1 \text{ mol } O_2}{2 \text{ mol } SO_3}$$

To solve the problem, the amount of SO_3 is converted to the amounts of SO_2 and O_2 needed by using the mole ratios:

$$(0.30 \text{ mol } SO_3)\left(\frac{2 \text{ mol } SO_2}{2 \text{ mol } SO_3}\right) = 0.30 \text{ mol } SO_2$$

$$(0.30 \text{ mol } SO_3)\left(\frac{1 \text{ mol } O_2}{2 \text{ mol } SO_3}\right) = 0.15 \text{ mol } O_2$$

The amounts of reactants required to produce 0.30 mol of SO_3 are 0.30 mol of SO_2 and 0.15 mol of O_2. (Note that mole ratios are exact conversion factors and do not limit the number of significant figures.)

EXAMPLE 6.10
Mole Ratios

Calcium carbide is produced by the reaction of calcium oxide with carbon at high temperatures:

$$CaO(s) + 3C(s) \xrightarrow{\Delta} CaC_2(s) + CO(g)$$

What are the mole ratios that give (a) the amount of CaC_2 produced by each mole of CaO that reacts, (b) the amount of C required by each mole of CaO that reacts, and (c) the amount of CaC_2 produced by each mole of C that reacts?

(a) From the balanced chemical equation we find that 1 mol of CaC_2 is produced by each mol of CaO that reacts, giving the mole ratio

$$\frac{1 \text{ mol } CaC_2}{1 \text{ mol } CaO}$$

(b) Similarly, 3 mol of C is needed for each mole of CaO that reacts.

$$\frac{3 \text{ mol C}}{1 \text{ mol } CaO}$$

(c) And 1 mol of CaC_2 is produced by every 3 mol of C that reacts.

$$\frac{1 \text{ mol } CaC_2}{3 \text{ mol C}}$$

Exercise A beautiful yellow suspension of solid As_2S_3 in water may be prepared according to the following equation:

$$2H_3AsO_3(aq) + 3H_2S(g) \longrightarrow As_2S_3(s) + 6H_2O(l)$$

What are the mole ratios of (a) H_3AsO_3 to H_2S, (b) As_2S_3 to H_3AsO_3, and (c) As_2S_3 to H_2S? *Answer* (a) 2 mol H_3AsO_3/3 mol H_2S, (b) 1 mol As_2S_3/2 mol H_3AsO_3, (c) 1 mol As_2S_3/3 mol H_2S

EXAMPLE 6.11
Mole Ratios

A reaction for producing elemental phosphorus is described by the chemical equation

$$2Ca_3(PO_4)_2(s) + 6SiO_2(s) + 10C(s) \xrightarrow{\Delta} 6CaSiO_3(l) + 10CO(g) + P_4(g)$$

How many moles of each reactant would be required to produce 2.6 mol of P_4?

To solve this problem, the number of moles of P_4 to be produced is "converted" to the number of moles of each reactant by using the mole ratios of each reactant to P_4.

$$(2.6 \text{ mol } P_4)\left(\frac{2 \text{ mol } Ca_3(PO_4)_2}{1 \text{ mol } P_4}\right) = 5.2 \text{ mol } Ca_3(PO_4)_2$$

$$(2.6 \text{ mol } P_4)\left(\frac{6 \text{ mol } SiO_2}{1 \text{ mol } P_4}\right) = 16 \text{ mol } SiO_2$$

$$(2.6 \text{ mol } P_4)\left(\frac{10 \text{ mol } C}{1 \text{ mol } P_4}\right) = 26 \text{ mol } C$$

The production of 2.6 mol of P_4 will require 5.2 mol of $Ca_3(PO_4)_2$, 16 mol of SiO_2, and 26 mol of C.

Exercise Plaster of Paris is produced by heating gypsum.

$$2CaSO_4 \cdot 2H_2O \xrightarrow{\Delta} (CaSO_4)_2 \cdot H_2O + 3H_2O(g)$$

gypsum   *plaster of Paris*

For every 0.25 mol of gypsum that reacts, how many moles of (a) plaster of Paris and (b) water are produced? *Answer* (a) 0.13 mol $(CaSO_4)_2 \cdot H_2O$, (b) 0.38 mol H_2O

A HISTORICAL ASIDE

Priestley, Lavoisier, and Phlogiston

As we have pointed out, early in the history of science many theories were based more on philosophy and speculation than on facts. Once a theory has been generally accepted it is hard to dislodge. The phlogiston theory is the outstanding example of a faulty theory in chemistry that was not readily given up by those who believed in it. Phlogiston theory dominated chemistry for almost 100 years.

The phlogiston theory resulted from efforts to understand fire—the combustion of substances in air. The phenomenon of fire has always been a source of amazement and wonder. Some races had gods and goddesses of fire; others worshipped fire itself. Plato thought that fire was an element. Robert Boyle (1627–1691), who contributed greatly to making chemistry an experimental science, believed that fire could be weighed on a balance.

Johann J. Becher (1635–1682) was a strange man, possibly a charlatan, or perhaps a man who believed that he had the power to solve any problem. With equal confidence he tackled the alchemists' dream of turning ordinary substances into gold, the building of a perpetual motion machine, and the composition of a universal language. In 1669, he decided that a burning substance was releasing something—which he called phlogiston—in the form of the flame. Furthermore, he explained that the calcination of a metal—the heating of a metal in air to give a powdery, nonmetallic substance—was also the release of phlogiston.

Combustible substance $\xrightarrow{\text{burning}}$ ashes + phlogiston

Metal $\xrightarrow{\text{heat}}$ metal ash (calx) + phlogiston

It was known that air was necessary for combustion and calcination. Becher explained that the essential role of air was to absorb the phlogiston as it was released. Air which was exhausted by combustion and in which nothing would burn was said to be ''phlogisticated.'' Such air could absorb no more phlogiston. In some ways phlogiston theory made sense and its followers adapted it to explain many chemical phenomena. It was, in fact, the exact opposite of the correct idea. In combustion and calcination, substances do not release phlogiston to the air. They combine with oxygen that is present *in* the air.

Many prominent chemists of the time were firm believers in the phlogiston theory. Although the theory was wrong, the result of their belief was not entirely negative, for many good experiments were conducted in the interests of investigating the behavior of phlogiston. However, phlogistonists had to struggle to explain why metal calxes were heavier than the metals from which they were formed. Becher resorted to proposing that under some circumstances phlogiston had a negative mass.

The discovery of oxygen, for which Carl W. Scheele (1742–1786), a Swedish apothecary, and Joseph Priestley share the credit, ultimately killed phlogiston theory. Joseph Priestley (1753–1804) was an English clergyman, a multitalented man who developed unorthodox religious and political ideas, with a heavy emphasis on individualism—ideas for which he was forced to flee England to the United States at the time of the French Revolution. While in England, Priestley had been elected to the Royal Society on the basis of his experiments on electricity, and had investigated ''airs,'' or gases.

On August 1, 1774, Priestley heated the red powder we know as mercury(II) oxide and obtained a colorless gas in which substances burned more vigorously than in air. He assumed that the gas was air which had lost all of its phlogiston and was therefore more ready to absorb phlogiston than ordinary air.

Antoine Lavoisier (1743–1794), a brilliant Frenchman whose accomplishments were as diverse as Priestley's, quickly grasped the significance of ''dephlogisticated air.'' In 1776 Lavoisier named ''dephlogisticated air'' oxygen and identified it as a component of air that combines with substances as they burn. He explained that oxygen is the gas released when calxes, which he called oxides, are heated to give metals. This explanation made sense of the fact that calxes are heavier than the metals from which they are formed. Ironically, Priestley never accepted Lavoisier's explanation of combustion and calcination. He remained a staunch defender of the phlogiston theory long after most other chemists had abandoned it.

Lavoisier led the way in disproving phlogiston theory, and also in reforming chemical nomenclature and putting chemistry into language that could be clearly understood. He improved French gunpowder, served in the government assembly, helped to develop the metric system, and ran a farm. On May 7, 1794, Lavoisier was sent to the guillotine by the leaders of the French Revolution because of his connections with the old Royalist government. On that day one of Lavoisier's scientific colleagues said, ''It took but a moment to cut off that head; perhaps a hundred years will be required to produce another like it.''

6.7 SOLVING STOICHIOMETRY PROBLEMS

Many stoichiometry problems, no matter what kind of information is known and what kind of information is unknown, can be solved by using the following four steps:

1. Write the balanced chemical equation.
2. Convert the known information to moles.
3. Use mole ratios from the balanced chemical equation to find the unknown in terms of moles.
4. Convert from moles to the unknown quantity that is desired.

We have already studied everything that is necessary to solve a great many types of stoichiometry problems. Often, balanced equations are known. When only the identities of the reactants and products are known for a simple reaction, the equation can be balanced as discussed earlier in this chapter (see Section 6.2).

Three possible types of known or unknown information about reactants and products are (a) masses, (b) pressure–volume–temperature data for gases, and (c) molarity for reactants or products in aqueous solution. The methods for converting each of these types of information to moles (Step 2) have already been presented.

(a) *Given* mass
   Convert to moles
   By using the molar mass (Section 4.6)

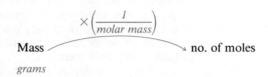

$$\text{Mass} \quad\xrightarrow{\;\times\left(\dfrac{1}{molar\ mass}\right)\;}\quad \text{no. of moles}$$

grams

If masses are given in units other than grams, conversion to grams must be done first.

(b) *Given* for a gas, pressure–volume–temperature data
   Convert to moles
   By using the ideal gas law, $PV = nRT$ (Section 5.10)

$$\frac{PV}{RT} = n$$

(c) *Given* molarity and solution volume
   Convert to moles
   By using the following relationship (Section 4.7)

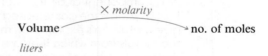

$$\text{Volume} \quad\xrightarrow{\;\times\ molarity\;}\quad \text{no. of moles}$$

liters

We cannot emphasize too strongly that the *essential* step in every stoichiometry problem (Step 3) is the use of a mole ratio to connect the known and unknown quantities. (Finding mole ratios was discussed in the preceding section.)

Step 4, converting moles to the unknown quantity, is often the reverse of one of the conversions (a), (b), or (c) above.

The following two examples represent a simple type of stoichiometry problem in which the known and unknown are both masses of reactants and /or products. How you might think through applying our four-step method for solving stoichiometry problems is illustrated in Example 6.12.

EXAMPLE 6.12
Stoichiometry

How many grams of cobalt(II) chloride and of hydrogen fluoride are needed to prepare 10.0 g of cobalt(II) fluoride by the following reaction?

$$CoCl_2(s) + 2HF(g) \longrightarrow CoF_2(s) + 2HCl(g)$$

1. Study the problem and be sure you understand it.
   (a) What is unknown?
       The masses of the reactants $CoCl_2$ and HF needed.
   (b) What is known?
       The chemical equation and the mass of the product, 10.0 g of CoF_2.
2. Decide how to solve the problem.
   To analyze how to solve a stoichiometry problem, think through what is

necessary to follow the four steps outlined at the beginning of this section.
Step 1. Write the balanced chemical equation. The equation is given in the problem.
Step 2. Convert the known quantity to moles. The known information is the mass of a product, so conversion to moles will be a mass to moles conversion:

$$\times \left(\frac{1}{molar\ mass\ CoF_2} \right)$$

Mass CoF_2 ⟶ no. of moles CoF_2

grams

Step 3. Use mole ratio to find the unknown in terms of moles. Here is the essential step in any stoichiometry problem — making the connection between the known and the unknown by using mole ratios. The necessary connections here are

$\times$ *(mole ratio)*

No. of moles CoF_2 ⟶ no. of moles $CoCl_2$

$\times$ *(mole ratio)*

No. of moles CoF_2 ⟶ no. of moles HF

From the chemical equation, the mole ratios needed are found to be

$$\frac{1\ mol\ CoCl_2}{1\ mol\ CoF_2} \quad and \quad \frac{2\ mol\ HF}{1\ mol\ CoF_2}$$

Step 4. Convert from moles to the desired quantity. The unknowns here are both masses in grams, and this step is essentially the reverse of Step 2.

$\times$ *(molar mass)*

No. of moles $CoCl_2$ ⟶ mass $CoCl_2$

$\times$ *(molar mass)*

No. of moles HF ⟶ mass HF

3. Set up the problem and solve it.
Steps 2, 3, and 4 can be done separately, as follows:
Step 2.

$$(10.0\ g\ CoF_2)\left(\frac{1\ mol\ CoF_2}{96.9\ g\ CoF_2} \right) = 0.103\ mol\ CoF_2$$

Step 3.

$$(0.103\ mol\ CoF_2)\left(\frac{1\ mol\ CoCl_2}{1\ mol\ CoF_2} \right) = 0.103\ mol\ CoCl_2$$

$$(0.103\ mol\ CoF_2)\left(\frac{2\ mol\ HF}{1\ mol\ CoF_2} \right) = 0.206\ mol\ HF$$

Step 4.

$$(0.103\ mol\ CoCl_2)\left(\frac{129.8\ g\ CoCl_2}{1\ mol\ CoCl_2} \right) = 13.4\ g\ CoCl_2$$

$$(0.206\ mol\ HF)\left(\frac{20.0\ g\ HF}{1\ mol\ HF} \right) = 4.12\ g\ HF$$

or, a single expression can be set up for each reactant:

$$(10.0 \text{ g CoF}_2)\overbrace{\left(\frac{1 \text{ mol CoF}_2}{96.9 \text{ g CoF}_2}\right)}^{Step\ 2}\overbrace{\left(\frac{1 \text{ mol CoCl}_2}{1 \text{ mol CoF}_2}\right)}^{Step\ 3}\overbrace{\left(\frac{129.8 \text{ g CoCl}_2}{1 \text{ mol CoCl}_2}\right)}^{Step\ 4} = 13.4 \text{ g CoCl}_2$$

$$(10.0 \text{ g CoF}_2)\overbrace{\left(\frac{1 \text{ mol CoF}_2}{96.9 \text{ g CoF}_2}\right)}^{Step\ 2}\overbrace{\left(\frac{2 \text{ mol HF}}{1 \text{ mol CoF}_2}\right)}^{Step\ 3}\overbrace{\left(\frac{20.0 \text{ g HF}}{1 \text{ mol HF}}\right)}^{Step\ 4} = 4.13 \text{ g HF}$$

To prepare 10.0 g of cobalt(II) fluoride, 13.4 g of cobalt(II) chloride and 4.13 g of hydrogen fluoride will be needed. [The difference in the final digits of the answers from the stepwise and single-step calculations for HF are within the expected ± 1 error. The differences arise because in the stepwise calculations rounding off is done at each step, while in the single-step calculation, it is done once.]

4. Check the result.
   (a) Are significant figures used correctly?
       Yes. In each calculation the three significant figures in the numbers of moles allow three significant figures in the answer. (The numbers of moles in the mole ratios are exact.)
   (b) Is the answer reasonable?
       Yes. By comparing the molar masses of $CoCl_2$ and HF with that of CoF_2 and taking into account the mole ratios, the answers are reasonable— 13.4 g of $CoCl_2$ yields 10.0 g of CoF_2 (their molar masses are roughly equal and the mole ratio is 1 to 1); 4.12 g of HF yields 10.0 g of CoF_2 (the molar mass of HF is one-fifth that of CoF_2, but twice the molar amount is needed.)

EXAMPLE 6.13
Stoichiometry

One of the components of gasoline is isooctane, C_8H_{18}. What mass of oxygen is consumed in the combustion of 1.00 g of isooctane? The balanced equation is

$$2C_8H_{18}(l) + 25O_2(g) \longrightarrow 16CO_2(g) + 18H_2O(g)$$
$$\text{isooctane} \qquad \text{oxygen} \qquad \text{carbon dioxide} \qquad \text{water}$$

Step 1. Write the balanced chemical equation. The equation is given above.
Step 2. Convert the known quantity to moles.

$$(1.00 \text{ g } C_8H_{18})\left(\frac{1 \text{ mol } C_8H_{18}}{114.26 \text{ g } C_8H_{18}}\right) = 0.00875 \text{ mol } C_8H_{18}$$

Step 3. Use mole ratios to find the unknown in terms of moles. The chemical equation states that 25 mol of O_2 react with 2 mol of C_8H_{18}. The amount of O_2 that reacts is

$$(0.00875 \text{ mol } C_8H_{18})\left(\frac{25 \text{ mol } O_2}{2 \text{ mol } C_8H_{18}}\right) = 0.109 \text{ mol } O_2$$

Step 4. Convert from moles to the desired quantity.

$$(0.109 \text{ mol } O_2)\left(\frac{32.00 \text{ g } O_2}{1 \text{ mol } O_2}\right) = 3.49 \text{ g } O_2$$

The 1.00 g of isooctane requires 3.49 g of O_2.

Steps 2–4 may be combined into a single calculation.

$$(1.00 \text{ g C}_8\text{H}_{18})\overbrace{\left(\frac{1 \text{ mol C}_8\text{H}_{18}}{114.26 \text{ g C}_8\text{H}_{18}}\right)}^{Step\ 2}\overbrace{\left(\frac{25 \text{ mol O}_2}{2 \text{ mol C}_8\text{H}_{18}}\right)}^{Step\ 3}\overbrace{\left(\frac{32.00 \text{ g O}_2}{1 \text{ mol O}_2}\right)}^{Step\ 4} = 3.50 \text{ g O}_2$$

The problem-solving method has *not* changed.

Exercise Hydrogen chloride can be prepared by the reaction of sodium chloride with warm concentrated sulfuric acid.

$$NaCl(s) + H_2SO_4(conc) \xrightarrow{\Delta} HCl(g) + NaHSO_4(aq)$$

What mass of HCl can be obtained if 120 g NaCl react with excess H_2SO_4?
Answer 77 g HCl

6.8 REACTIONS INVOLVING GASES

Information is sometimes needed in stoichiometry problems about the amounts of volumes of gaseous reactants or products. The ideal gas law, molar volume, and the relationships among mass, density, and molar mass (Sections 5.8–5.12) are used in solving such problems.

EXAMPLE 6.14
Stoichiometry—Gases

Metallic tungsten is obtained by displacement of tungsten from tungsten(VI) oxide by hydrogen at high temperatures. What volume of H_2 (measured at 0.975 atm and 25 °C) is required to react quantitatively with 46.4 g of WO_3?

Step 1. Write the balanced chemical equation. The displacement reaction is

$$3H_2(g) + WO_3(s) \xrightarrow{\Delta} 3H_2O(g) + W(s)$$

Steps 2 and 3. Convert the known quantities to moles and use mole ratios to find the unknown in terms of moles. The mole ratio must connect H_2, about which information is needed, to WO_3, about which information is known.

$$(46.4 \text{ g WO}_3)\overbrace{\left(\frac{1 \text{ mol WO}_3}{231.85 \text{ g WO}_3}\right)}^{Step\ 2}\overbrace{\left(\frac{3 \text{ mol H}_2}{1 \text{ mol WO}_3}\right)}^{Step\ 3} = 0.600 \text{ mol H}_2$$

Step 4. Convert from moles to the desired quantity.

$$V = \frac{nRT}{P} = \frac{(0.600 \text{ mol})(0.0821 \text{ L atm/K mol})(298 \text{ K})}{(0.975 \text{ atm})}$$
$$= 15.1 \text{ L}$$

The volume of H_2 needed is 15.1 L.

Exercise Hydrazine, H_2NNH_2, is used as a rocket fuel.

$$H_2NNH_2(l) + O_2(g) \longrightarrow N_2(g) + 2H_2O(g)$$

What volume of N_2 will be produced at 850 °C and 0.23 atm for each 15.0 g of hydrazine that reacts? What volume of steam will be produced? *Answer* 190 L N_2, 380 L H_2O

6.9 REACTIONS IN AQUEOUS SOLUTION

When chemical reactions are carried out in aqueous solution, the amounts of reactants and products are best dealt with as concentrations in moles per liter. The amounts are found from the volumes of the solutions and the known molarities, as illustrated in the following examples.

EXAMPLE 6.15
Stoichiometry—Solutions

How many milliliters of 0.10 M barium chloride must be added to 25 mL of 0.23 M solution of sodium sulfate to completely precipitate barium sulfate?

Step 1. Write the balanced chemical equation. This is a partner-exchange reaction.

$$BaCl_2(aq) + Na_2SO_4(aq) \longrightarrow BaSO_4(s) + 2NaCl(aq)$$

Step 2. Convert the known quantity to moles.

$$(25 \text{ mL})\left(\frac{1 \text{ L}}{1000 \text{ mL}}\right)\left(\frac{0.23 \text{ mol Na}_2\text{SO}_4}{1 \text{ L}}\right) = 5.8 \times 10^{-3} \text{ mol Na}_2\text{SO}_4$$

Step 3. Use mole ratio to find the unknown in terms of moles.

$$(5.8 \times 10^{-3} \text{ mol Na}_2\text{SO}_4)\left(\frac{1 \text{ mol BaCl}_2}{1 \text{ mol Na}_2\text{SO}_4}\right) = 5.8 \times 10^{-3} \text{ mol BaCl}_2$$

Step 4. Convert from moles to the desired quantity.

$$(5.8 \times 10^{-3} \text{ mol BaCl}_2)\left(\frac{1 \text{ L}}{0.10 \text{ mol BaCl}_2}\right)\left(\frac{1000 \text{ mL}}{1 \text{ L}}\right) = 58 \text{ mL}$$

To completely precipitate the barium sulfate will require 58 mL of 0.10 M $BaCl_2$.

Exercise   What volume of 0.103 M HCl will react with 25.00 mL of 0.112 M NaOH?

$$HCl(aq) + NaOH(aq) \longrightarrow H_2O(l) + NaCl(aq)$$

Answer 27.2 mL

EXAMPLE 6.16
Stoichiometry—Solutions

The concentration of iodine dissolved in aqueous potassium iodide was determined by allowing the solution to react with 25.00 mL of 0.0397 M arsenous acid, H_3AsO_3.

$$H_3AsO_3(aq) + I_2(aq, KI) + H_2O(l) \longrightarrow H_3AsO_4(aq) + 2H^+ + 2I^-$$

Find the concentration of the solution if 19.9 mL of the iodine solution was used. [The KI does not participate in the reaction.]

Step 1. Write the balanced chemical equation. The equation is given above.
Steps 2 and 3. Convert known quantities to moles and use mole ratios to find the unknown in terms of moles.

$$(25.00 \text{ mL})\underbrace{\left(\frac{1 \text{ L}}{1000 \text{ mL}}\right)}_{\text{Step 2}}\underbrace{\left(\frac{0.0397 \text{ mol H}_3\text{AsO}_3}{1 \text{ L}}\right)}_{}\underbrace{\left(\frac{1 \text{ mol I}_2}{1 \text{ mol H}_3\text{AsO}_3}\right)}_{\text{Step 3}} = 9.93 \times 10^{-4} \text{ mol I}_2$$

Step 4. Convert from moles to the desired quantity.

$$\left(\frac{9.93 \times 10^{-4} \text{ mol I}_2}{19.9 \text{ mL}}\right)\left(\frac{1000 \text{ mL}}{1 \text{ L}}\right) = 0.0499 \text{ mol/L}$$

The concentration of I_2 in the solution is 0.0499 M.

Exercise A 0.863 g sample of impure potassium acid phthalate, $KHC_8H_4O_4$, was dissolved in water and allowed to react with a dilute solution of sodium hydroxide.

$$KHC_8H_4O_4(aq) + NaOH(aq) \longrightarrow NaKC_8H_4O_4(aq) + H_2O(l)$$

What is the purity of the sample if 22.7 mL of 0.106 M NaOH was used? *Answer* 57.0 mass % $KHC_8H_4O_4$

6.10 LIMITING REACTANTS

Sometimes only a limited amount of one of the reactants needed for a chemical reaction is available. Or perhaps it is easier to carry out a reaction by adding an excess of one of the reactants. The maximum amount of product that can be formed is determined by the amount of the reactant that is used up first. The situation is not unlike trying to put together new bicycles in a toy store. Suppose that each bicycle requires six nuts, six bolts, and six washers. If one shipment of parts includes 60 washers, 60 nuts, but only 59 bolts (as is so often the case), then bolts become the limiting factor. Only nine bicycles can be assembled.

We refer to the exact amount of a substance required according to a balanced chemical equation as the **stoichiometric amount.** For example, in the combination of sodium with chlorine

$$2Na(s) + Cl_2(g) \longrightarrow 2NaCl(s)$$

1 mol of Na will react with 0.5 mol of Cl_2 to produce 1 mol of NaCl. These are the stoichiometric amounts required for the reaction of 1 mol of sodium according to the balanced chemical equation.

When more than the stoichiometric amount of one reactant is present, some of it will be left over. If 1 mol of Na is mixed with 2 mol of Cl_2, then 1.5 mol of the chlorine will be left over and the same amount of sodium chloride as before—1 mol—will be produced. In this case, sodium is the **limiting reactant**—the reactant that determines the amount of product that can be formed. Even if 100 mol of chlorine is available, 1 mol of sodium will limit the reaction to the formation of 1 mol of sodium chloride.

In a limiting reactant problem information is known about two of the reactants and it is necessary to determine which is the one that is limiting. First, the number of moles of both reactants is found. Then, the stoichiometric amount of one reactant (A) *required* by the other reactant (B) is calculated. If more of reactant A is required than is available, then A is the limiting reactant. If less of reactant A is required than is available, then B is the limiting reactant.

EXAMPLE 6.17
Stoichiometry—Limiting Reactant

What volume of hydrogen will be produced at 0.861 atm and 22 °C from the displacement reaction of 6.0 g of zinc with 25 mL of 6.0 M by hydrochloric acid?

Step 1. Write the balanced chemical equation.

$$Zn(s) + 2HCl(aq) \longrightarrow ZnCl_2(aq) + H_2(g)$$

Step 2. Convert the known quantities to moles.

$$(6.0 \text{ g Zn})\left(\frac{1 \text{ mol Zn}}{65.38 \text{ g Zn}}\right) = 0.092 \text{ mol Zn}$$

$$(25 \text{ mL})\left(\frac{1 \text{ L}}{1000 \text{ mL}}\right)\left(\frac{6.0 \text{ mol HCl}}{1 \text{ L}}\right) = 0.15 \text{ mol HCl}$$

Step 3. Use mole ratios to find the unknown in terms of moles. For all of the Zn to react, the number of moles of HCl must be

$$(0.092 \text{ mol Zn})\left(\frac{2 \text{ mol HCl}}{1 \text{ mol Zn}}\right) = 0.18 \text{ mol HCl}$$

The amount of HCl available, 0.15 mol, is less than the required amount. There-fore, the HCl is the limiting reactant. (If we had checked to see if we had enough Zn to react with all of the HCl, we would have found that the amount available is greater than the required amount.) The amount of H_2 formed is determined by the amount of HCl,

$$(0.15 \text{ mol HCl})\left(\frac{1 \text{ mol } H_2}{2 \text{ mol HCl}}\right) = 0.075 \text{ mol } H_2$$

Step 4. Convert from moles to the desired quantity. The volume of the gaseous H_2 is found by using the ideal gas law.

$$V = \frac{nRT}{P} = \frac{(0.075 \text{ mol})(0.0821 \text{ L atm/K mol})(295 \text{ K})}{(0.861 \text{ atm})} = 2.1 \text{ L}$$

The volume of hydrogen produced will be 2.1 L.

Exercise A 1.6 L sample of H_2 measured at 15 °C and 0.987 atm was mixed with a 1.0 L sample of O_2 measured at 25 °C and 1.028 atm. An electrical spark ignited this mixture to produce water. Calculate the mass of water produced. *Answer* 1.2 g H_2O

6.11 YIELDS   The maximum amount of a product that can, *according to the balanced chemical equation,* be obtained from known amounts of reactants is called the **theoretical yield.** It is the stoichiometric amount of the product. For many reasons, the amount of a product actually obtained is often less than the theoretical amount. Perhaps some product was lost or spilled in handling, or perhaps not all of the reactant was converted to product. Also, sometimes undesired side reactions occur and use up some of the reactant or product.

The actual yield in a reaction is the weighed mass or measured volume of product formed. The extent to which product has been formed is given as the **percent yield:**

$$\% \text{ yield} = \left(\frac{\text{quantity of product obtained}}{\text{theoretical yield}}\right)(100\%) \tag{6.32}$$

EXAMPLE 6.18
Stoichiometry—Percent Yield

The final step in the industrial production of aspirin (acetylsalicylic acid) is the reaction of salicylic acid with acetic anhydride:

$$\text{HOC}_6\text{H}_4\text{COOH}(s) + (\text{CH}_3\text{CO})_2\text{O}(l) \longrightarrow \text{CH}_3\text{COOC}_6\text{H}_4\text{COOH}(s) + \text{CH}_3\text{COOH}(l)$$

| salicylic acid | acetic anhydride | acetylsalicylic acid (aspirin) | acetic acid |

To test a new method of handling the materials, a chemist ran the reaction on a laboratory scale with 25.0 g of salicylic acid and excess acetic anhydride (over 20 g). The actual yield was 24.3 g of aspirin. What was the percent yield?

We first calculate the theoretical yield, which is the stoichiometric amount of the product. Setting up the dimensional calculation in one expression gives

$$\underbrace{(25.0 \text{ g sal. acid})}\underbrace{\left(\frac{1 \text{ mol sal. acid}}{138.13 \text{ g sal. acid}}\right)}_{Step\ 2}\underbrace{\left(\frac{1 \text{ mol aspirin}}{1 \text{ mol sal. acid}}\right)}_{Step\ 3}\underbrace{\left(\frac{180.17 \text{ g aspirin}}{1 \text{ mol aspirin}}\right)}_{Step\ 4}$$

$$= 32.6 \text{ g aspirin}$$

The percent yield is given by

$$\% \text{ yield} = \frac{\text{actual yield}}{\text{theoretical yield}} \times (100\%) = \left(\frac{24.3 \text{ g}}{32.6 \text{ g}}\right)(100\%) = 74.5\%$$

The percent yield in this reaction was 74.5%.

Exercise The equation for the decomposition of $NH_4Cl(s)$ to $NH_3(g)$ and $HCl(g)$ is

$$NH_4Cl(s) \xrightarrow{\Delta} NH_3(g) + HCl(g)$$

What is the theoretical yield of NH_3 for 1.00 g NH_4Cl? If the percent yield is 78%, what is the actual yield? *Answer* 0.318 g NH_3, 0.25 g NH_3

6.12 STOICHIOMETRY IN INDUSTRIAL CHEMISTRY

Stoichiometry is important. Everyone who works with chemistry in any field is likely to encounter stoichiometry problems at one time or another. In this section we have collected a number of examples that illustrate various practical stoichiometry problems that might be encountered in industrial chemistry.

EXAMPLE 6.19
Stoichiometry — Industrial Chemistry

Each day an electric power plant burns 4000 T of coal which contains 1.2% S by mass. During the combustion process, the sulfur is quantitatively converted to sulfur dioxide. Calculate the mass (in grams) of sulfur dioxide produced each day by the plant. (1 T = 9.07×10^5 g.)

Step 1. Write the balanced chemical equation.

$$S(s) + O_2(g) \longrightarrow SO_2(g)$$

Step 2. Convert the known quantity to moles. The mass of S that reacts each day is

$$(4000 \text{ T coal})\left(\frac{1.2 \text{ T S}}{100.0 \text{ T coal}}\right) = 50 \text{ T S} \qquad \text{or} \qquad (50 \text{ T S})(9.07 \times 10^5 \text{ g/T}) = 5 \times 10^7 \text{ g S}$$

The number of moles of sulfur that react each day is

$$(5 \times 10^7 \text{ g S})\left(\frac{1 \text{ mol S}}{32.06 \text{ g S}}\right) = 2 \times 10^6 \text{ mol S}$$

Steps 3 and 4. Use mole ratios to find the unknown in terms of moles and convert to desired quantity.

$$(2 \times 10^6 \text{ mol S})\overbrace{\left(\frac{1 \text{ mol SO}_2}{1 \text{ mol S}}\right)}^{Step\ 3}\overbrace{\left(\frac{64.06 \text{ g SO}_2}{1 \text{ mol SO}_2}\right)}^{Step\ 4} = 1 \times 10^8 \text{ g SO}_2$$

The power plant will generate 1×10^8 g (about 100 T) of SO_2 each day.

Exercise Limestone, $CaCO_3$, is heated to produce unslaked lime (or quicklime), CaO, and carbon dioxide.

$$CaCO_3(s) \xrightarrow{\Delta} CaO(s) + CO_2(g)$$

What masses (in grams) of CaO and CO_2 are produced from the decomposition of 2.25 T of impure limestone? Assume the limestone is 45% pure. *Answer* 5.2×10^5 g CaO, 4.0×10^5 g CO_2

EXAMPLE 6.20
Stoichiometry — Industrial Chemistry

The sulfur dioxide released by the power plant described in Example 6.23 is removed from the stack gases (the gases that go up the chimney) by passing these gases through a series of scrubbers containing powdered limestone, $CaCO_3(s)$. The following reaction takes place in 100% yield:

$$SO_2(g) + CaCO_3(s) \longrightarrow CaSO_3(s) + CO_2(g)$$

What mass (in grams) of limestone is needed to remove the daily effluent of SO_2 from this plant?

In Example 6.19 we found that the power plant releases 2×10^6 mol of SO_2 each day. Using the mole ratio of SO_2 to $CaCO_3$ we find the mass of $CaCO_3$ needed in one step:

$$(2 \times 10^6 \text{ mol SO}_2)\overbrace{\left(\frac{1 \text{ mol CaCO}_3}{1 \text{ mol SO}_2}\right)}^{Step\ 3}\overbrace{\left(\frac{100.09 \text{ g CaCO}_3}{1 \text{ mol CaCO}_3}\right)}^{Step\ 4} = 2 \times 10^8 \text{ g CaCO}_3$$

The power plant requires 2×10^8 g (about 200 T) of limestone each day.

Exercise   Slaked lime, $Ca(OH)_2$, is produced from CaO by the reaction

$$CaO(s) + H_2O(l) \longrightarrow Ca(OH)_2(aq)$$

What mass (in grams) of slaked lime will be produced from the CaO produced from the 2.25 T of impure limestone described in the exercise following Example 6.19?
Answer 6.8×10^5 g $Ca(OH)_2$

EXAMPLE 6.21
Stoichiometry — Industrial Chemistry

A by-product of an industrial process was a mixture of sodium sulfate, Na_2SO_4, and sodium bicarbonate, $NaHCO_3$. To determine the composition of the mixture, a sample weighing 8.00 g was heated until constant mass was achieved, indicating that the heat-induced reaction was complete. Under these conditions the sodium bicarbonate undergoes the following decomposition reaction:

$$2NaHCO_3(s) \longrightarrow Na_2CO_3(s) + CO_2(g) + H_2O(g)$$
$$\underset{\substack{sodium \\ bicarbonate}}{} \qquad \underset{\substack{sodium \\ carbonate}}{} \quad \underset{\substack{carbon \\ dioxide}}{} \quad \underset{water}{}$$

and the sodium sulfate is unchanged. The mass of the sample after heating was 6.02 g. What was the mass percent of $NaHCO_3$ in the original by-product?

Before we can find the mass of $NaHCO_3$ in the sample before heating, we must determine either the mass of CO_2 or the mass of H_2O that was present in the mixture of gases released during the decomposition process. The molar ratio of CO_2 to H_2O in the mixture of gaseous products is (1 mol CO_2/1 mol H_2O). This means that for each 44.02 g of CO_2, there will be 18.02 g H_2O produced. The mass percent of CO_2 in the gaseous products is

$$\left(\frac{44.02 \text{ g CO}_2}{44.02 \text{ g CO}_2 + 18.02 \text{ g H}_2\text{O}}\right) \times (100\%) = 70.95\%$$

The mass of the gaseous mixture released by the decomposition process was

$$8.00 \text{ g} - 6.02 \text{ g} = 1.98 \text{ g}$$

The mass of CO_2 in 1.98 g of gaseous products was

$$(1.98 \text{ g mixture})\left(\frac{70.95 \text{ g } CO_2}{100.0 \text{ g mixture}}\right) = 1.40 \text{ g } CO_2$$

Using the mole ratio of $NaHCO_3$ to CO_2, we find the mass of $NaHCO_3$ originally present:

$$\overset{\textit{Step 2}}{(1.40 \text{ g } CO_2)\left(\frac{1 \text{ mol } CO_2}{44.02 \text{ g } CO_2}\right)}\overset{\textit{Step 3}}{\left(\frac{2 \text{ mol } NaHCO_3}{1 \text{ mol } CO_2}\right)}\overset{\textit{Step 4}}{\left(\frac{84.01 \text{ g } NaHCO_3}{1 \text{ mol } NaHCO_3}\right)} = 5.34 \text{ g } NaHCO_3$$

The mass of $NaHCO_3$ in 8.00 g of the original mixture was 5.34 g, which corresponds to

$$\left(\frac{5.34 \text{ g}}{8.00 \text{ g}}\right) \times (100\%) = 66.8\%$$

The by-product contained 66.8% $NaHCO_3$.

Exercise A Cu_2O-CuO mixture was analyzed by heating a sample of the mixture with gaseous hydrogen to produce copper metal and water.

$$Cu_2O(s) + H_2(g) \xrightarrow{\Delta} 2Cu(s) + H_2O(g)$$

$$CuO(s) + H_2(g) \xrightarrow{\Delta} Cu(s) + H_2O(g)$$

A 1.351 g sample of the mixture gave 1.152 g of copper metal. What is the composition of this mixture? *Answer* 61 mass % Cu_2O, 39 mass % CuO

EXAMPLE 6.22
Stoichiometry — Industrial Chemistry

The production of potassium permanganate requires two steps. The first reaction involves converting manganese dioxide (a naturally occurring mineral known as pyrolusite) to potassium manganate

$$2MnO_2(s) + 4KOH(aq) + O_2(g) \longrightarrow 2K_2MnO_4(aq) + 2H_2O(l) \qquad \textbf{(a)}$$
$$\underset{\substack{\textit{manganese} \\ \textit{dioxide}}}{} \quad \underset{\substack{\textit{potassium} \\ \textit{hydroxide}}}{} \quad \underset{\textit{oxygen}}{} \quad \underset{\substack{\textit{potassium} \\ \textit{manganate}}}{} \quad \underset{\textit{water}}{}$$

and the second reaction involves changing potassium manganate to potassium permanganate

$$2K_2MnO_4(aq) + Cl_2(g) \longrightarrow 2KMnO_4(aq) + 2KCl(aq) \qquad \textbf{(b)}$$
$$\underset{\substack{\textit{potassium} \\ \textit{permanganate}}}{}$$

What mass, in tons, of $KMnO_4$ will be produced from 1.0 T of MnO_2 (9.07×10^5 g = 1 T)?

This problem illustrates the common situation in which two or more consecutive reactions are involved in a process. The equations for the individual steps can be added together and the mole ratios from the overall equation used to make the connection between the known and unknown information about the original reactants and the final products. The amounts of the intermediate products need not be calculated, nor taken into account, *so long as they cancel out of the overall equation.*

Adding Equations (a) and (b) as they are given allows cancellation of the intermediate, potassium manganate.

$$2MnO_2(s) + 4KOH(aq) + O_2(g) \longrightarrow 2K_2MnO_4(aq) + 2H_2O(l)$$
$$\underline{2K_2MnO_4(aq) + Cl_2(g) \longrightarrow 2KMnO_4(aq) + 2KCl(aq)}$$
$$2MnO_2(s) + 4KOH(aq) + O_2(g) + Cl_2(g) \longrightarrow 2KMnO_4(aq) + 2KCl(aq) + 2H_2O(l)$$

$$\overbrace{(1.0 \text{ T MnO}_2) \left(\frac{9.07 \times 10^5 \text{ g}}{1 \text{ T}} \right)}^{\textit{Step 2. Convert to moles.}} \left(\frac{1 \text{ mol MnO}_2}{86.94 \text{ g MnO}_2} \right) \overbrace{\left(\frac{2 \text{ mol KMnO}_4}{2 \text{ mol MnO}_2} \right)}^{\textit{Step 3. Use mole ratios.}}$$

$$\underbrace{\times \left(\frac{158.04 \text{ g KMnO}_4}{1 \text{ mol KMnO}_4} \right) \left(\frac{1 \text{ T}}{9.07 \times 10^5 \text{ g}} \right) = 1.8 \text{ T KMnO}_4}_{\textit{Step 4. Convert to desired quantity.}}$$

Note that in this calculation the conversion factor between grams and tons is used twice and drops out of the calculation. For this reason, chemical engineers commonly define such terms as "lb-mol" (1 lb-mol = 454 mol) and "T-mol" (1 T-mol = 9.07×10^5 mol) and use these factors to simplify the calculations. One pound-mole of any substance has a mass *in pounds* numerically equal to the molar mass of that substance. When this unit is used in place of moles it allows the masses of reactants and products to be expressed in pounds, without the need for conversion to grams. Similarly, one ton-mole of any substance has a mass *in tons* numerically equal to the molar mass of that substance. When this unit is used in place of moles it allows all masses to be given in tons. For example, the above calculation would be

$$(1.0 \text{ T MnO}_2) \left(\frac{1 \text{ T-mol MnO}_2}{86.95 \text{ T MnO}_2} \right) \left(\frac{2 \text{ T-mol KMnO}_4}{2 \text{ T-mol MnO}_2} \right) \times$$

$$\left(\frac{158.04 \text{ T KMnO}_4}{1 \text{ T-mol KMnO}_4} \right) = 1.8 \text{ T KMnO}_4$$

Reactions (a) and (b) will yield a maximum of 1.8 T of potassium permanganate for each ton of manganese dioxide.

Exercise Antimony can be prepared from its sulfide ore by the following two-step process:

$$2Sb_2S_3(s) + 9O_2(g) \xrightarrow{\Delta} Sb_4O_6(s) + 6SO_2(g)$$

$$Sb_4O_6(s) + 6C(s) \xrightarrow{\Delta} 4Sb(l) + 6CO(g)$$

What mass of elemental antimony will be produced from 1.00 kg of an ore that contains 23.2 mass % Sb_2S_3? *Answer* 166 g Sb

---

EXAMPLE 6.23
Stoichiometry—Industrial
Chemistry

Sodium tripolyphosphate, $Na_5P_3O_{10}$, is used in detergents. The main source of this compound (and other phosphorus compounds) is "phosphate rock," an ore consisting mainly of calcium phosphate, $Ca_3(PO_4)_2$, and silica, SiO_2. Calculate the mass of $Na_5P_3O_{10}$ that can be produced from the complete conversion of phosphorus obtained from processing 60. T of the ore which contains 45% $Ca_3(PO_4)_2$.

Step 1. Write the balanced chemical equation. Not enough information is given to write the complete equation(s). However, we are given the fact that all of the phosphorus from the $Ca_3(PO_4)_2$ will end up in $Na_5P_3O_{10}$. We can write a partial equation which is balanced as far as the atoms of P are concerned:

$$3Ca_3(PO_4)_2 + \cdots \longrightarrow 2Na_5P_3O_{10} + \cdots$$

As long as all of the reactant is converted to only one product, as is the case here, a partial equation such as this provides the necessary mole ratio.

The mass of calcium phosphate present in the ore is

$$(60. \text{ T ore})\left(\frac{45 \text{ T Ca}_3(\text{PO}_4)_2}{100. \text{ T ore}}\right) = 27 \text{ T Ca}_3(\text{PO}_4)_2$$

As illustrated in Example 6.26, ton-moles can be used directly. This problem can be solved in a single dimensional calculation using the mole ratio found in Step 1.

$$\overset{Step\ 2}{(27 \text{ T Ca}_3(\text{PO}_4)_2)}\left(\frac{1 \text{ T-mol Ca}_3(\text{PO}_4)_2}{310.18 \text{ T Ca}_3(\text{PO}_4)_2}\right)\overset{Step\ 3}{\left(\frac{2 \text{ T-mol Na}_5\text{P}_3\text{O}_{10}}{3 \text{ T-mol Ca}_3(\text{PO}_4)_2}\right)}$$

$$\overset{Step\ 4}{\left(\frac{367.86 \text{ T Na}_5\text{P}_3\text{O}_{10}}{1 \text{ T-mol Na}_5\text{P}_3\text{O}_{10}}\right)} = 21 \text{ T Na}_5\text{P}_3\text{O}_{10}$$

Twenty-one tons of sodium tripolyphosphate can be produced from 60. T of phosphate rock.

Exercise Lead is one of the four "workhorse metals" of our modern civilization. The steps in its preparation from the sulfide ore are: (a) roasting to form the oxide and (b) reduction in a blast furnace with coke and scrap iron to give the metal. What mass of lead would be produced from 1.00 kg of an ore which contains 15.2 mass % PbS? (Assume the efficiency of the overall process to be 72%.) *Answer* 95 g Pb

SUMMARY

6.1 CONSERVATION OF MASS AND ENERGY Two conservation laws apply to all chemical reactions: Energy can neither be created nor destroyed, and matter can neither be created nor destroyed. Thus the atoms taking part in a chemical reaction may be rearranged, but all the atoms present in the reactants must also be present in the products, and the total mass of the reactants must equal the total mass of the products.

6.2 BALANCING CHEMICAL EQUATIONS A chemical equation must be balanced. That is, it must be written with the correct coefficients for each species participating so that for each element, the number of atoms in the reactants is the same as the number in the products.

6.3 SOME TYPES OF CHEMICAL REACTIONS In a combination reaction, two reactants combine to give a single product. In a decomposition reaction, a single compound breaks down to give two or more other substances. In a displacement reaction, atoms or ions of one substance replace other atoms or ions in a compound. Metals can be arranged in an activity series based on their ability to displace hydrogen from water or acids and their ability to displace each other in soluble ionic compounds. Partner-exchange reactions have the general form $AC + BD \longrightarrow AD + BC$. Often such reactions occur between ionic compounds in solution when one product is an insoluble solid, known as a precipitate.

6.4 NET IONIC EQUATIONS: PRECIPITATION REACTIONS Ions that are present during a reaction in aqueous solution but undergo no chemical change are called spectator ions. A net ionic equation shows only the species involved in a chemical change, excluding spectator ions. In such an equation charge must always be conserved; the sum of the charges on the left must equal the sum of the charges on the right. Whether a precipitate will form can be predicted from data on the solubility of different types of compounds, summarized in Table 6.3.

6.5 INFORMATION FROM CHEMICAL EQUATIONS **6.6** USING MOLE RATIOS Stoichiometry is the calculation of quantitative relationships in chemical changes. All stoichiometric calculations must begin with the balanced chemical equation. The coefficients of the equation give the mole ratios of the various species. From these ratios, stoichiometry can give us information about the mass ratios of products and reactants, as well as volume ratios of any gases involved in the reaction.

6.7 SOLVING STOICHIOMETRY PROBLEMS **6.8** REACTIONS INVOLVING GASES **6.9** REACTIONS IN AQUEOUS SOLUTION In all stoichiometric problems, the mole ratios from the balanced chemical equation provide the connection between the known and unknown quantities, whether these be masses, pressure-volume-temperature data for gases, or molarities for substances in solution. To solve a stoichiometry problem, first write the balanced chemical equation, convert the known information to moles, use mole ratios to find the unknown in terms of moles, and convert the answer from moles to the desired quantity.

6.10 LIMITING REACTANTS The exact amount of a substance required by a balanced chemical equation is the stoichiometric amount. When reactants are present in non-stoichiometric amounts, the one that determines the amount of product that can be formed is called the limiting reactant. At the completion of the reaction, some of the other reactant(s) will be left over.

6.11 YIELDS The theoretical yield of a reaction is the maximum amount of a product that can be formed according to the balanced chemical equation. The actual yield may be less for various reasons. The percent yield represents the ratio of the actual yield to the theoretical yield expressed as a percentage.

6.12 STOICHIOMETRY IN INDUSTRIAL CHEMISTRY Calculations can be simplified by using such units as pound-moles or ton-moles instead of moles, in order to find masses in pounds, or tons, and so on, instead of in grams. For processes that include consecutive reactions, stoichiometric calculations can be based on overall equations and intermediate products can be disregarded *if* the intermediates cancel out of the equations. Also, *partial* equations can be used *if* the equations are balanced for the element or elements in question.

SIGNIFICANT TERMS

combination reaction
decomposition reaction
displacement reaction
partner-exchange reaction
precipitate
precipitation
spectator ions
net ionic equation
stoichiometry
stoichiometric amount
limiting reactant
theoretical yield
percent yield

THOUGHTS ON CHEMISTRY

On the Constitution of Bodies

A NEW SYSTEM OF CHEMICAL PHILOSOPHY, by John Dalton

Chemical analysis and synthesis go no farther than to the separation of particles one from another, and to their reunion. No new creation or destruction of matter is within the reach of chemical agency. We might as well attempt to introduce a new planet into the solar system, or to annihilate one already in existence, as to create or destroy a particle of hydrogen. All the changes we can produce, consist in separating particles that are in a state of cohesion or combination, and joining those that were previously at a distance.

In all chemical investigations, it has justly been considered an important object to ascertain the relative weights of the simples which constitute a compound. But unfortunately the enquiry has terminated here; whereas from the relative weights in the mass, the relative weights of the ultimate particles or atoms of the bodies might have been inferred, from which their number and weight in various other compounds would appear, in order to assist and to guide future investigations, and to correct their results. Now it is one great object of this work, to shew the importance and advantage of ascertaining the relative weights of the ultimate particles, both of simple and compound bodies, the number of simple elementary particles which constitute one compound particle, and the number of less compound particles which enter into the formation of one more compound particle.

John Dalton, *A New System of Chemical Philosophy*, 1808 (Quoted from *A Treasury of Scientific Prose*, H. M. Jones and I. B. Cohen, eds., New York: Little, Brown & Co., 1963) pp. 135–136.

QUESTIONS

Chemical Change: Equations and Types of Reactions

6.1 What does a balanced chemical equation represent?

6.2 A student wrote the following equation to describe the decomposition of hydrogen peroxide, H_2O_2, into oxygen and water:

$$H_4O_4 \longrightarrow 2H_2O + O_2$$

What is wrong with this equation?

6.3 Balance each of the following chemical equations:
(a) $Cl_2O_7(g) + H_2O(l) \longrightarrow HClO_4(aq)$
(b) $Br_2(l) + H_2O(l) \longrightarrow HBr(aq) + HBrO(aq)$
(c) $Ca_3(PO_4)_2(s) + H_2SO_4(aq) \longrightarrow CaSO_4(s) + H_3PO_4(aq)$
(d) potassium reacts with water to give aqueous potassium hydroxide and gaseous hydrogen
(e) solid magnesium carbonate decomposes to form solid magnesium oxide and gaseous carbon dioxide

6.4 Balance each of the following chemical equations:
(a) $Fe_3O_4(s) + H_2(g) \longrightarrow Fe(s) + H_2O(l)$
(b) $KClO_3(s) \longrightarrow KCl(s) + O_2(g)$
(c) steam and hot carbon react to form gaseous hydrogen and gaseous carbon monoxide.

6.5 What are the names of the four types of reactions discussed in this chapter? Give a suitable definition for each type.

6.6 Classify each of the chemical reactions in Question 6.3 as a (i) combination reaction, (ii) decomposition reaction, (iii) displacement reaction, or (iv) partner-exchange reaction.

6.7 Repeat Question 6.6 for the chemical reactions given in Question 6.4.

6.8 Repeat Question 6.6 for the following reactions:
(a) $NH_4HSO_4 \longrightarrow NH_3 + H_2SO_4$ _decomposition_
(b) $2NaI + Br_2 \longrightarrow 2NaBr + I_2$ _displacement_
(c) $Zn(NO_3)_2 + Na_2S \longrightarrow ZnS + 2NaNO_3$ _Part. exchange_
(d) $4Fe + 3O_2 \longrightarrow 2Fe_2O_3$ _combination_
(e) $2HAuCl_4 \longrightarrow 2Au + 3Cl_2 + 2HCl$ _decomposition_
(f) $Xe + 2F_2 \longrightarrow XeF_4$ _combination_

6.9 Use the activity series to predict whether or not the following reactions will occur:
(a) $Fe(s) + Mg^{2+} \longrightarrow Mg(s) + Fe^{2+}$ _N.R._
(b) $Ni(s) + Cu^{2+} \longrightarrow Ni^{2+} + Cu(s)$ _yes_
(c) $Cu(s) + 2H^+ \longrightarrow Cu^{2+} + H_2(g)$ _N.R._
(d) $Mg(s) + H_2O(g) \longrightarrow MgO(s) + H_2(g)$ _yes_

6.10 Repeat Question 6.9 for
(a) $Sn(s) + Ba^{2+} \longrightarrow Sn^{2+} + Ba(s)$ _N.R._
(b) $Al_2O_3(s) + 3H_2(g) \xrightarrow{\Delta} 2Al(s) + 3H_2O(g)$ _N.R._
(c) $Ca(s) + 2H^+ \longrightarrow Ca^{2+} + H_2(g)$ _yes_
(d) $Cu(s) + Pb^{2+} \longrightarrow Cu^{2+} + Pb(s)$ _N.R._

6.11* Use the following chemical reactions to prepare an activity series for the hypothetical elements A, D, E, G, and R.

(a) $2R + 3D^{2+} \longrightarrow 2R^{3+} + 3D$
(b) $E^+ + A \longrightarrow A^+ + E$
(c) $R + G^+ \nrightarrow$ no reaction
(d) $D + A^+ \nrightarrow$ no reaction
(e) $R + 3A^+ \longrightarrow R^{3+} + 3A$
(f) $D + 2E^+ \longrightarrow D^{2+} + 2E$

6.12 Based on the solubility rules given in Table 6.3, how would you write the formulas for the following substances in a net ionic equation: (a) $PbSO_4$, (b) $Na(CH_3COO)$, (c) $(NH_4)_2CO_3$, (d) MnS, and (e) $BaCl_2$?

6.13 Repeat Question 6.12 for (a) $(NH_4)_2SO_4$, (b) $NaBr$, (c) $Ba(CN)_2$, (d) $Mg(OH)_2$, and (e) Li_2CO_3.

6.14 Using the solubility rules given in Table 6.3, determine whether or not the following will react when aqueous solutions of the compounds are mixed:
(a) $Hg(NO_3)_2(aq) + Na_2S(aq) \longrightarrow$
(b) $Al(NO_3)_3(aq) + LiOH(aq) \longrightarrow$
(c) $Li_2SO_3(aq) + NaCl(aq) \longrightarrow$
(d) $Fe(OH)_3(s) + KNO_3(aq) \longrightarrow$

Write net ionic equations for those reactions that occur.

6.15 Repeat Question 6.14 for
(a) $Al(OH)_3(s) + NaNO_3(aq) \longrightarrow$
(b) $NaBr(aq) + NH_4I(aq) \longrightarrow$
(c) $AgNO_3(aq) + HCl(aq) \longrightarrow$
(d) $CaCl_2(aq) + Na_2CO_3(aq) \longrightarrow$

Stoichiometry

6.16 List the four steps that are used to solve stoichiometry problems.

6.17 How does a chemical equation provide the connection between the known and unknown facts in a stoichiometry problem?

6.18* Consider the hypothetical equation describing photosynthesis:

$$CO_2(g) + H_2O(l) \xrightarrow[\text{chlorophyll}]{\text{light}} C_6H_{12}O_6(aq) + O_2(g)$$

(unbalanced)

(a) Identify the (i) reactants, (ii) products, and (iii) catalyst. (b) What else is needed for the reaction to occur? (c) Balance the equation. (d) What is the mole ratio of (i) O_2 to CO_2, (ii) $C_6H_{12}O_6$ to O_2, and (iii) CO_2 to H_2O? (e) Does the reaction obey the law of conservation of mass? (f) If the reaction were carried out in a closed container, would there be a pressure change?

Answers to Selected Questions

6.4 (a) $Fe_3O_4(s) + 4H_2(g) \rightarrow 3Fe(s) + 4H_2O(l)$; (b) $2KClO_3(s) \rightarrow 2KCl(s) + 3O_2(g)$; (c) $H_2O(g) + C(s) \xrightarrow{\Delta} H_2(g) + CO(g)$

6.7 (a) iii, (b) ii, (c) iii   **6.10** (a) no, (b) no, (c) yes, (d) no

6.11 $G > R > A > D > E$

6.13 (a) $2NH_4^+ + SO_4^{2-}$; (b) $Na^+ + Br^-$; (c) $Ba(CN)_2$; (d) $Mg(OH)_2$; (e) $2Li^+ + CO_3^{2-}$

6.15 (a) no reaction; (b) no reaction; (c) $Ag^+ + Cl^- \rightarrow AgCl(s)$; (d) $Ca^{2+} + CO_3^{2-} \rightarrow CaCO_3(s)$

PROBLEMS

Interpreting Chemical Equations

6.1 Give an interpretation for the following equation

$$C_7H_{16}(l) + 11O_2(g) \longrightarrow 7CO_2(g) + 8H_2O(g)$$

in terms of (a) moles, (b) molecules, (c) volumes of gases, and (d) mass. *Answer* (a) 1 mol C_7H_{16} reacts with 11 mol O_2 to give 7 mol CO_2 and 8 mol H_2O; (b) 1 molecule of C_7H_{16} reacts with 11 molecules of O_2 to give 7 molecules of CO_2 and 8 molecules of H_2O; (c) for every 11 volumes of O_2, 7 volumes CO_2 and 8 volumes of H_2O vapor are produced at the same temperature and pressure; (d) 100.23 g C_7H_{16} react with 352.00 g O_2 to give 308.07 g CO_2 and 144.16 g H_2O.

6.2 Interpret the following equation

$$SO_2(g) + Br_2(g) + 2H_2O(g) \xrightarrow{\Delta} 2HBr(g) + H_2SO_4(aq)$$

in terms of (a) moles, (b) molecules, (c) volumes of gases, and (d) mass.

6.3* Nitrous oxide, N_2O, undergoes decomposition when heated to give N_2 and O_2.

$$2N_2O(g) \xrightarrow{\Delta} 2N_2(g) + O_2(g)$$

What is the molar composition of the gaseous mixture produced? Compare this composition to that of air and predict whether the mixture will support combustion or not. *Answer* 1 mol O_2 to 2 mol N_2; The mixture is slightly richer in O_2 than air, and so will support combustion.

Mole Ratios

6.4 The equation which describes the commercial "roasting" of zinc sulfide is

$$2ZnS(s) + 3O_2(g) \xrightarrow{\Delta} 2ZnO(s) + 2SO_2(g)$$

What is the mole ratio of (a) O_2 to ZnS, (b) ZnO to ZnS, and (c) SO_2 to ZnS? *Answer* (a) 3 mol O_2/2 mol ZnS, (b) 2 mol ZnO/2 mol ZnS = 1 mol ZnO/1 mol ZnS, (c) 2 mol SO_2/2 mol ZnS = 1 mol SO_2/1 mol ZnS

6.5 The reaction between dilute nitric acid and copper is given by the equation:

$$3Cu(s) + 8HNO_3(aq) \longrightarrow$$
$$3Cu(NO_3)_2(aq) + 2NO(g) + 4H_2O(l)$$

What is the mole ratio of (a) HNO_3 to Cu, (b) NO to Cu, and (c) $Cu(NO_3)_2$ to Cu?

6.6 How many moles of oxygen can be obtained by the decomposition of one mole of reactant in each of the following reactions?

(a) $2KClO_3(s) \longrightarrow 2KCl(s) + 3O_2(g)$ $\frac{3}{2}$ mole O_2
(b) $2H_2O_2(aq) \longrightarrow 2H_2O(l) + O_2(g)$ $\frac{1}{2}$ mole O_2
(c) $2HgO(s) \longrightarrow 2Hg(l) + O_2(g)$ "
(d) $2NaNO_3(s) \longrightarrow 2NaNO_2(s) + O_2(g)$ "

Answer (a) 1.5 mol O_2, (b) 0.5 mol O_2, (c) 0.5 mol O_2, (d) 0.5 mol O_2

6.7 Consider the reaction

$$NH_3(g) + O_2(g) \xrightarrow{\text{not balanced}} NO(g) + H_2O(l)$$

For every 1.50 mol of NH_3, (a) how many moles of O_2 are required, (b) how many moles of NO are produced, and (c) how many moles of H_2O are produced?

Stoichiometry

6.8 Calculate the mass of sodium required to produce 80.0 g of sodium hydroxide by direct reaction with water

$$2Na(s) + 2H_2O(l) \longrightarrow 2NaOH(aq) + H_2(g)$$

(Although this reaction is performed frequently, it is rather dangerous because the hydrogen can form an explosive mixture with the oxygen in the air and bits of molten sodium metal may fly off and start a fire.) *Answer* 46.0 g Na

6.9 Find the mass of chlorine that will combine with 1.38 g of hydrogen to form hydrogen chloride

$$H_2(g) + Cl_2(g) \longrightarrow 2HCl(g)$$

6.10 What mass of solid AgCl will precipitate from a solution containing 1.50 g of $CaCl_2$ if an excess amount of $AgNO_3$ is added?

$$CaCl_2(aq) + 2AgNO_3(aq) \longrightarrow 2AgCl(s) + Ca(NO_3)_2(aq)$$

Answer 3.87 g AgCl

6.11 A sample of magnetic iron oxide, Fe_3O_4, reacted completely with hydrogen at red heat. The water vapor formed by the reaction

$$Fe_3O_4(s) + 4H_2(g) \xrightarrow{\Delta} 3Fe(s) + 4H_2O(g)$$

was condensed and found to weigh 7.5 g. Calculate the mass of Fe_3O_4 that reacted.

6.12 An impure sample of $CuSO_4$ weighing 5.52 g was dissolved in water and allowed to react with excess zinc.

$$CuSO_4(aq) + Zn(s) \longrightarrow ZnSO_4(aq) + Cu(s)$$

What is the percent $CuSO_4$ in the sample if 1.49 g of Cu was produced? *Answer* 67.6%

Stoichiometry—Gases

6.13 What volume of carbon dioxide, measured at STP, can be obtained by the reaction of 50.0 g of $CaCO_3$ with excess hydrochloric acid?

$$CaCO_3(s) + 2HCl(aq) \longrightarrow CaCl_2(aq) + CO_2(g) + H_2O(l)$$

What would be the volume of CO_2 had it been measured at 25 °C and 0.975 atm? *Answer* 11.2 L, 12.5 L

6.14 Aqueous ammonium nitrite decomposes upon heating to form water and nitrogen. What volume of N_2, at STP, will be released by the decomposition of 80.0 g of NH_4NO_2?

$$NH_4NO_2(aq) \xrightarrow{\Delta} N_2(g) + 2H_2O(g)$$

6.15 What volume of hydrogen fluoride at 743 Torr and 24 °C will be released by the reaction of 47.2 g of xenon difluoride with a stoichiometric amount of water? The unbalanced equation is

$$XeF_2(s) + H_2O(l) \longrightarrow Xe(g) + O_2(g) + HF(g)$$

What volumes of oxygen and xenon will be released under these conditions? *Answer* 13.9 L HF, 3.48 L O_2, 6.95 L Xe

6.16 Many woodsmen use small propane stoves to cook meals.

How many liters of air (assumed to be 20.% O_2 by volume) will be required to burn 10.0 L of propane, C_3H_8? Assume all gas volumes are measured at the same temperature and pressure. The equation is

$$C_3H_8(g) + 5O_2(g) \longrightarrow 3CO_2(g) + 4H_2O(g)$$

Answer 250 L air

6.17* A common laboratory preparation of oxygen is

$$2KClO_3(s) \xrightarrow[\Delta]{MnO_2} 2KCl(s) + 3O_2(g)$$

If you were designing an experiment to generate four bottles (each containing 250 mL) of O_2 at 25 °C and 723 Torr and allowing for 50% waste, what mass of potassium chlorate would be required? As a laboratory instructor, how would you explain to your students the symbol Δ and MnO_2 written near the arrow?

6.18* A sheet of iron was galvanized (plated with zinc) on both sides to protect it from rust. The thickness of the zinc coating was determined by allowing hydrochloric acid to react with the zinc and collecting the resulting hydrogen. (Note: The acid solution contained an "inhibitor" ($SbCl_3$) which prevented the iron from reacting.)

$$Zn(s) + 2HCl(aq) \longrightarrow ZnCl_2(aq) + H_2(g)$$

Determine the thickness of the zinc plate from the following data: sample size = 1.50 cm × 2.00 cm; volume of dry hydrogen = 30.0 mL; temperature = 25 °C; pressure = 747 Torr; and density of zinc = 7.11 g/cm³. *Answer* 0.00185 cm each side

Stoichiometry — Solutions

6.19 What volume of 0.50 M HBr is required to react with 0.75 mol of $Ca(OH)_2$?

$$2HBr(aq) + Ca(OH)_2(aq) \longrightarrow CaBr_2(aq) + 2H_2O(l)$$

6.20 What volume of 0.324 M HNO_3 solution is required to completely react with 22.0 mL of 0.0612 M $Ba(OH)_2$?

$$Ba(OH)_2(aq) + 2HNO_3(aq) \longrightarrow Ba(NO_3)_2(aq) + 2H_2O(l)$$

Answer 8.31 mL

6.21 What is the concentration of an HCl solution if 23.65 mL neutralizes 25.00 mL of a 0.1037 M solution of NaOH?

$$HCl(aq) + NaOH(aq) \longrightarrow NaCl(aq) + H_2O(l)$$

6.22 An excess of $AgNO_3$ reacts with 100.0 mL of an $AlCl_3$ solution to give 0.275 g of AgCl. What is the molarity of the $AlCl_3$ solution?

$$AlCl_3(aq) + 3AgNO_3(aq) \longrightarrow 3AgCl(s) + Al(NO_3)_3(aq)$$

Answer 0.00640 M

6.23 An impure sample of solid Na_2CO_3 was allowed to react with 0.1026 M HCl.

$$Na_2CO_3(s) + 2HCl(aq) \longrightarrow 2NaCl(aq) + CO_2(g) + H_2O(l)$$

A 0.1247 g sample of sodium carbonate required 14.78 mL of HCl. What is the purity of the sodium carbonate?

6.24 Calculate the theoretical yield of AgCl formed from the reaction of 5.23 g $ZnCl_2$ with 35.0 mL of 0.325 M $AgNO_3$.

$$ZnCl_2(aq) + 2AgNO_3(aq) \longrightarrow Zn(NO_3)_2(aq) + 2AgCl(s)$$

Answer 1.63 g AgCl

Stoichiometry — Limiting Reactant

6.25 What is the maximum mass of sodium chloride that can be formed by the reaction of 5.00 g of sodium with 7.10 g of chlorine? Which substance is the limiting reactant? Which substance is in excess?

$$2Na(s) + Cl_2(g) \longrightarrow 2NaCl(s)$$

Answer 11.7 g NaCl, Cl_2, Na

6.26 What mass of $BaSO_4$ will be produced by the reaction of 33.2 g of Na_2SO_4 with 43.5 g of $Ba(NO_3)_2$?

$$Ba(NO_3)_2(aq) + Na_2SO_4(aq) \longrightarrow BaSO_4(s) + 2NaNO_3(aq)$$

6.27* Consider the reaction for making DDT:

$$CCl_3CHO + 2C_6H_5Cl \longrightarrow \underset{DDT}{(ClC_6H_4)_2CHCCl_3} + H_2O$$

If 100.0 g of CCl_3CHO is treated with 100.0 g of C_6H_5Cl, (a) what mass of DDT would be formed and (b) what amount of water would be formed? What would happen if the amount of CCl_3CHO was doubled?

6.28* Consider the following reaction:

$$HNO_3(aq) + Cu(s) \longrightarrow Cu(NO_3)_2(aq) + NO_2(g) + H_2O(l)$$

(a) Balance the equation. A piece of Cu metal 3.31 cm × 1.84 cm × 1.00 cm reacts with 157 mL of 1.35 M nitric acid solution. The density of copper is 8.92 g/cm³. (b) Find the number of moles of each reactant. (c) What volume of NO_2 at 1.01 atm and 297 K will be formed? (d) Describe what would happen if the amount of Cu were doubled.

Stoichiometry — Percent Yield

6.29 The percent yield for the reaction

$$PCl_3(g) + Cl_2(g) \longrightarrow PCl_5(g)$$

is 85%. What mass of PCl_5 would be expected from the reaction of 38.5 g of PCl_3 with excess chlorine? *Answer* 50. g PCl_5

6.30 The percent yield for the following reaction carried out in carbon tetrachloride solution

$$Br_2(CCl_4) + Cl_2(CCl_4) \longrightarrow 2BrCl(CCl_4)$$

is 57%. (a) What amount of BrCl would be formed from the reaction of 0.0100 mol Br_2 with 0.0100 mol Cl_2? (b) What amount of Br_2 is left unchanged?

6.31 A student prepared copper by the following displacement reaction

$$Zn(s) + Cu^{2+} \longrightarrow Cu(s) + Zn^{2+}$$

The student started with 1.00 g Zn and turned in a 1.26 g sample of Cu. What was the percent yield of the reaction? Comment on your answer.

6.32 For the reaction

$$cis\text{-}[Pt(NH_3)(H_2O)Cl_2] \xrightarrow{H_2O} trans\text{-}[Pt(NH_3)(H_2O)Cl_2]$$

the yield of trans-$[Pt(NH_3)(H_2O)Cl_2]$ was 1.36 g when starting with 14.2 g of cis-[Pt(NH$_3$)(H$_2$O)Cl$_2$]. What was the percent yield of the reaction? *Answer* 9.58%

6.33* Hydrogen reacts with some of the more active metals to form crystalline ionic hydrides. For example, Li forms LiH

$$2Li(s) + H_2(g) \longrightarrow 2LiH(s)$$

(a) What mass of LiH would be produced by allowing 10.0 g of Li to react with 10.0 L of H$_2$ (measured at STP)? (b) If the actual yield was 6.7 g of LiH, what is the percent yield?

Stoichiometry — Industrial Chemistry

6.34 Zirconium is obtained industrially using the Kroll process

$$ZrCl_4(s) + 2Mg(s) \longrightarrow Zr(s) + 2MgCl_2(s)$$

Calculate the mass of Zr obtainable for each ton of Mg consumed.

6.35 What mass of potassium chlorate would be required to supply the proper amount of oxygen needed to burn 35.0 g of methane, CH$_4$?

$$2KClO_3(s) \longrightarrow 2KCl(s) + 3O_2(g)$$
$$CH_4(g) + 2O_2(g) \longrightarrow CO_2(g) + 2H_2O(g)$$

Answer 357 g KClO$_3$

6.36 Hydrogen, obtained by the electrical decomposition of water, was combined with chlorine to produce 51.0 g of hydrogen chloride. Calculate the mass of water decomposed.

$$2H_2O(l) \longrightarrow 2H_2(g) + O_2(g)$$
$$H_2(g) + Cl_2(g) \longrightarrow 2HCl(g)$$

6.37 Two moles of acetone react to give diacetone alcohol (an industrial solvent). This compound, however, can lose water giving mesityl oxide.

$$2CH_3COCH_3 \xrightarrow[\text{71\% yield}]{Ba(OH)_2} HOC(CH_3)_2CH_2COCH_3 \xrightarrow[\text{65\% yield}]{I^-}$$
$$(CH_3)_2CCHCOCH_3$$

What would be the theoretical yield of mesityl oxide from one mole of acetone? What is the actual yield?

6.38* What mass of H$_2$SO$_4$ can be produced in the process given below if 1.00 kg of FeS$_2$ is used? The unbalanced equations for the process are

$$FeS_2(s) + O_2(g) \longrightarrow Fe_2O_3(s) + SO_2(g)$$
$$SO_2(g) + O_2(g) \longrightarrow SO_3(g)$$
$$SO_3(g) + H_2SO_4(l) \longrightarrow H_2S_2O_7(l)$$
$$H_2S_2O_7(l) + H_2O(l) \longrightarrow H_2SO_4(aq)$$

6.39* The chief ore of zinc is the sulfide, ZnS. The ore is concentrated by flotation and then heated in air, which converts the ZnS to a mixture of ZnO and ZnSO$_4$.

$$2ZnS(s) + 3O_2(g) \longrightarrow 2ZnO(s) + 2SO_2(g)$$
$$ZnS(s) + 2O_2(g) \xrightarrow{H_2O} ZnSO_4(aq)$$

The mixture is then treated with dilute H$_2$SO$_4$, which converts the ZnO to ZnSO$_4$,

$$ZnO(s) + H_2SO_4(aq) \longrightarrow ZnSO_4(aq) + H_2O(l)$$

to produce an aqueous solution containing only ZnSO$_4$. An electrical current is passed through the solution to produce the metal.

$$2ZnSO_4(aq) + 2H_2O(l) \longrightarrow 2Zn(s) + 2H_2SO_4(aq) + O_2(g)$$

What mass of Zn will be obtained from an ore containing 100. kg of ZnS? Assume the flotation process to be 91% efficient, the electrolysis step to be 98% efficient, and the other steps to be 100.% efficient.

Additional Problems

6.40* Ethylene can be produced from ethyl alcohol as follows:

$$CH_3CH_2OH(g) \xrightarrow[210\,°C]{H_3PO_4} CH_2{=}CH_2(g) + H_2O(g)$$

ethyl alcohol   *ethylene*

(a) What amount of ethyl alcohol is needed to produce 0.1 mol of ethylene? (b) Would 4 L or 2 mL of steam be produced when 0.1 mol of ethyl alcohol reacts? (c) How many molecules of water are produced for each mole of ethylene? (d) How many molecules of hydrogen are involved in this reaction for each mole of ethylene? (e) How many atoms of hydrogen are involved in this reaction for each mole of ethylene? (f) What is the catalyst? *Answer* (a) 0.1 mol alcohol, (b) 4 L, (c) 6.022 × 10^{23} molecules of H$_2$O, (d) none, (e) 3.613 × 10^{24} atoms of H, (f) H$_3$PO$_4$

6.41 Fluorescein is an orange-red powder which dissolves in alkaline solution to produce a strong green fluorescence. (The alkaline solution looks like yellow-green from the reflected light, but is reddish-orange by transmitted light.) Fluorescein is produced by heating a mixture of phthalic anhydride and resorcinol

$$C_6H_4(CO)_2O + 2C_6H_4(OH)_2 \xrightarrow[\substack{190-200\,°C \\ 10\,hr}]{\substack{anhydrous \\ ZnCl_2}} C_{20}H_{12}O_5 + X$$

phthalic anhydride   *resorcinol*   *fluorescein*

(a) Identify the missing product, X, in the above equation and (b) write the complete balanced equation. (c) How many molecules of resorcinol are needed to react with 1 mol of phthalic anhydride? (d) What conditions are indicated for the reaction? (e) Show that the equation is an example of the law of conservation of mass.

6.42 Bromine may be prepared in the laboratory by treating NaBr with a mixture of MnO$_2$ and H$_2$SO$_4$

$$NaBr(s) + H_2SO_4(aq) \longrightarrow HBr(aq) + NaHSO_4(aq)$$
$$2HBr(aq) + MnO_2(s) + H_2SO_4(aq) \longrightarrow$$
$$Br_2(l) + MnSO_4(aq) + 2H_2O(l)$$

What mass of bromine can be produced from the reaction of 100.0 g of NaBr with excess H$_2$SO$_4$ and MnO$_2$? *Answer* 77.66 g Br$_2$

6.43* A standard qualitative analysis scheme for the separation and identification of Ba^{2+}, Sr^{2+}, and Ca^{2+} ions in solution is

$$[Ba^{2+}, Sr^{2+}, Ca^{2+}](NO_3)_2(aq) + K_2CrO_4(aq)$$
     mixture

$$\xrightarrow{CH_3COOH,\ NH_4(CH_3COO)} BaCrO_4(s) +$$
$$[Sr^{2+}, Ca^{2+}](NO_3)_2(aq) + 2KNO_3(aq)$$
     mixture

$$[Sr^{2+}, Ca^{2+}](NO_3)_2(aq) + K_2CrO_4(aq) \xrightarrow{OH^-}$$
$$SrCrO_4(s) + Ca(NO_3)_2(aq) + 2KNO_3(aq)$$

$$Ca(NO_3)_2(aq) + K_2C_2O_4(aq) \longrightarrow CaC_2O_4(s) + 2KNO_3(aq)$$

What is the composition of a mixture of these ions if 1.00 g of each of the precipitates was collected? Assume each precipitate to be completely insoluble.

CHAPTER 7

Thermochemistry

What is heat? What is temperature? Answering these questions ought to be easy. Everyone knows what heat and temperature are. Heat is what makes water boil. Temperature is what you read from a thermometer. And yet, when we try to go beyond our intuitive understanding of heat and temperature, answering the questions becomes harder. We have to use imagination and mathematics to picture and explain events that we can observe only indirectly.

Kinetic-molecular theory tells us that as a substance is heated, the molecules have more energy and move around faster. If heat is associated with the random motion of the particles of which a substance is composed, then a larger mass of something ought to contain more heat than a smaller mass of the same substance at the same temperature. Also, at the same temperature, equal masses of different substances should contain different amounts of heat. Can we tell from looking at a large block of metal and a small one, or from looking at blocks of two different metals, which ones "contain" more heat? No. Can we measure the amount of heat in these samples? Not really.

But we can measure the amount of heat transferred between two objects at different temperatures. If a hot block of metal is placed in contact with a cold block of metal, the hot one will cool down and the cold one will warm up until they both reach the same temperature. This demonstrates a law about the behavior of heat: Heat always flows naturally from a hot body to a colder body. In fact, this law leads to a definition of temperature: If heat can flow from one body to another, they are at different temperatures; if no heat flows between two bodies, they are at the same temperature. Although we cannot measure the amount of heat within a single body, we can measure temperature changes and calculate from them the amounts of heat involved in those changes.

If we burn a block of wood, we can measure the amount of heat given off in the reaction of the wood with oxygen. In fact, we can measure the heat given off in any chemical reaction.

Being able to find the amount of heat associated with chemical reactions is of great practical importance. Our industrial society is powered to a great extent by the heat derived from chemical reactions. The major portion of the cost of many industrial processes is the cost of the heat that they require. Also, the dynamics of our environment must be examined in light of the heat which accompanies the chemical and physical changes that occur in the atmosphere and the oceans.

ENERGY

7.1 ENERGY IN CHEMICAL REACTIONS

Exactly what is it that happens in chemical reactions? So far, we have learned that reactants, chemical species with their own distinctive compositions and properties, are transformed into products, other chemical species with different compositions and properties. In the course of the reactions mass is neither lost nor gained.

The balanced chemical equation for the reaction of sulfuric acid with calcium carbonate is

$$CaCO_3(s) + H_2SO_4(aq) \longrightarrow CO_2(g) + H_2O(l) + CaSO_4(s) \tag{7.1}$$

Careful observation of this reaction as it occurs would reveal that something else is involved in addition to the transformation of reactants into products. When the sulfuric acid is poured on the calcium carbonate, the mixture gets hot.

The thermal decomposition of sodium hydrogen carbonate gives similar products

$$2NaHCO_3(s) \xrightarrow{\Delta} CO_2(g) + H_2O(g) + Na_2CO_3(s) \tag{7.2}$$

Sodium hydrogen carbonate ("bicarbonate of soda") sits unchanged in a box on the kitchen or bathroom shelf without decomposing. But when the compound is heated, the reaction takes place.

Why is heat involved in these chemical reactions? Heat is, we know, a form of energy. Is it possible that changes in energy accompany chemical reactions? "Yes, always," is the answer. Experience has shown that energy changes accompany all chemical reactions.

Chemical compounds are held together by the forces that we refer to as chemical bonds. When new substances are produced by a chemical reaction, existing chemical bonds are broken and new ones are formed. In general, breaking chemical bonds requires energy and making new ones releases energy. Whether a specific reaction requires energy or releases energy depends upon the final balance between the energy used to break old bonds and the energy released as new ones are formed. Despite the similarity of the products in reactions (7.1) and (7.2), the overall result in one case is the release of energy as heat, while in the other case, the reaction does not take place *unless* the substance is heated. Careful investigation of chemical reactions has shown that for the same amounts of reactants under identical conditions, the same amount of energy is always involved.

7.2 THERMODYNAMICS

Thermodynamics is the study of energy transformations. The question that immediately arises is, What is energy? This is a hard question to answer because we cannot see energy or directly measure it. But we *accept* the existence of energy because we can see and measure the effects of energy changes. When energy is available, things happen.

Kinetic energy (see Section 5.2) is energy of motion, and depends upon both the mass and the velocity of the moving object. A train roaring down the tracks has kinetic energy, as do the molecules of a gas. An object has *potential energy* by virtue of its position with respect to a force acting on it that could cause it to move. A boulder poised at the top of a cliff, for example, has potential energy with respect to the Earth's gravity. An electron in an atom has potential energy with respect to the force of electrical attraction of the nucleus.

In the study of thermodynamics, it is convenient to discuss a process in terms of a system and its interaction with the surroundings. The system and the surroundings are defined according to what is being studied. A **system** is the portion of the universe under study. A system can be simple or complex—the boulder on the cliff, the contents of a test tube, or an entire train with its engine and all of its cars. A system in chemistry is usually the substances undergoing a physical or chemical change. In the decomposition of sodium hydrogen carbonate, the sample of the compound would be defined as the system.

The **surroundings** is everything in the universe that is not part of the system. The flask in which the sodium hydrogen carbonate was heated, the hot plate on which it was heated, and everything else in the universe would be the surroundings. In this case we can say that heat was added to the system from the rest of the universe and caused a change in the system.

Most commonly, chemical systems exchange energy with their surroundings in the form of heat—thermal energy. **Thermochemistry,** which is the study of the

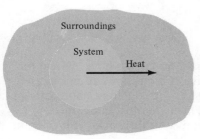

Figure 7.1
Exothermic Processes

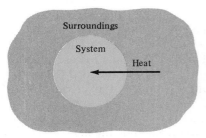

Figure 7.2
Endothermic Processes

thermal energy changes that accompany chemical and physical changes, is the principal subject of this chapter.

Heat is the energy transferred between objects or systems at different temperatures. Note that energy is a property of a system or a substance, but heat is not. Heat, which is detected by temperature changes (Section 7.12), is something happening — it is energy in transit between objects or systems that are at different temperatures and are in contact with each other.

Any process that releases heat from the system to the surroundings is referred to as **exothermic** (Figure 7.1). When an exothermic chemical reaction occurs, the temperature of the reacting substances increases and heat is transferred to the surroundings. The reaction of calcium carbonate with sulfuric acid (Equation 7.1) is exothermic. Any process in which the system absorbs heat from the surroundings is **endothermic** (Figure 7.2). For an endothermic chemical reaction to occur, the necessary amount of heat must be available from surroundings that are at a higher temperature than the reacting substances. The decomposition of sodium hydrogen carbonate (Equation 7.2) is endothermic.

7.3 INTERNAL ENERGY

All of the energy contained within a chemical system is **internal energy.** It is the internal energy of a substance that participates in thermal energy exchange with the surroundings. A chemical system might also have gravitational potential energy (a beaker might be poised on the lab bench) or it might have kinetic energy (a tankcar full of chlorine might be speeding along as part of a freight train), but these types of energy on a macro scale are usually not of interest in the study of chemistry.

Internal energy is the sum of all of the energy of all of the atoms, molecules, or ions within a system. For example, if the system is an ideal gas (Section 5.2), there is a large contribution to the internal energy from the kinetic energy of the molecules moving about randomly. Additional energy is contributed by the molecules rotating in space and the atoms in the molecules moving with respect to each other (Figure 7.3).

An *increase* in the internal energy of a chemical system has three possible results:

1. The temperature can increase. The increased internal energy of a system when the temperature rises is demonstrated visibly by the expansion of an ideal gas at constant pressure (see Figure 5.3).
2. A phase change — melting or vaporization — can occur (Section 13.2). For example, consider the molecules in a liquid. All molecules are influenced by forces known collectively as **intermolecular forces** — the forces of attraction

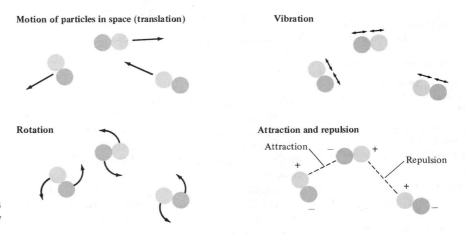

Figure 7.3
Contributions to Internal Energy

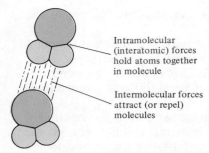

Figure 7.4
Intermolecular and Intramolecular Forces When the forces acting between atoms—the interatomic forces—are strong enough to hold atoms together, we say that a chemical bond has been formed.

and repulsion between individual molecules (Figure 7.4; discussed in Sections 11.10–11.12). By contrast, forces that act between atoms in the same molecule are known as **intramolecular forces.** The molecules in a liquid are attracted to each other and held together by the intermolecular forces. When the liquid boils and changes into a gas, it is because the heat added to keep the liquid boiling is giving the molecules sufficient energy to overcome the intermolecular forces.

3. A chemical reaction can occur. When the increase in internal energy of a system is sufficient to cause chemical bonds to break, allowing new ones to form, a chemical reaction takes place. A chemical reaction that results from the absorption by the system of energy from the surroundings is an endothermic reaction.

A *decrease* in the internal energy of a system can result in either a decrease in temperature or different phase changes, for example, freezing or condensation. While a decrease in internal energy rarely initiates a chemical reaction, frequently the outcome of an exothermic chemical reaction (one in which the system releases thermal energy) is that the system has a lower internal energy than it had before the reaction.

The total internal energy, E, of a system cannot be determined. However, changes in internal energy

$$\underset{\substack{\text{change in} \\ \text{energy}}}{\nearrow} \Delta E = E_{\text{final}} - E_{\text{initial}}$$

can be both measured and calculated. The **internal energy change** of a system, ΔE, is the amount of energy exchanged with the surroundings during a chemical or physical change of the system.

The symbol Δ is used to represent a change in a variable that is a property of a system. For most variables, it is customary to find the change by subtracting the *initial* value from the *final* value.

7.4 ENERGY, HEAT, AND WORK

The **first law of thermodynamics** is called the law of conservation of energy. It is often stated as follows: The energy of the universe is constant. (Other ways of stating the first law are given in Table 7.1.) The first law is accepted because no observation contrary to it has ever been made. The energy changes in any system and in its surroundings are always observed to offset each other so that the total energy of the universe remains constant.

In the interaction between a system and its surroundings, the entire energy change must be accounted for by heat, q, and/or work, w.

$$\Delta E = \overset{\overset{\text{heat}}{\downarrow}}{q} + w \longleftarrow \text{work} \tag{7.3}$$

This equation is a mathematical statement of the first law.

We choose to set up and use Equation (7.3) so that ΔE is negative when a system loses energy and positive when a system gains energy. To do this, heat that has been added to the system and work that has been done *on* a system—both of which can increase the internal energy of the system—are given positive values. Heat lost by a system or work done *by* a system on the surroundings—both of which can decrease the internal energy of the system—are given negative values (Figure 7.5). [Until the mid-1970s, a sign convention for work opposite to that just described was used. It results in Equation 7.3 taking the form $\Delta E = q - w$. Always check the author's definitions when reading about heat and work in other books and publications.]

Table 7.1
Statements of the First Law of Thermodynamics

> The energy of the universe is constant.
>
> Energy can be converted from one form to another, but cannot be destroyed.
>
> The change in energy of a system equals the heat exchanged by the system plus the work done on or by the system.
>
> $\Delta E = q + w$
>
> You can't get something for nothing.
>
> There is no such thing as a free lunch.

1 cal = 4.184 J

The SI unit for heat and for energy in any form is the joule (Section 2.8f).

1 calorie (cal) = 4.184 joules (J), exactly

The magnitude of energy changes in chemical reactions makes it frequently convenient to use the kilojoule (1 kJ = 1000 J). Work, because of the way it is calculated, is expressed in various units, but these can all be converted to joules (see Appendix II).

Work is performed when a force moves an object over a distance. Obviously, since all energy transfer other than heat is defined as work, there are many different kinds of work. Only pressure–volume, or expansion, work is of significance in chemical systems (other than those of electrochemistry; Chapter 23). And pressure–volume work is of significance only when gases are present.

We have already encountered pressure–volume work in the expansion of a gas that pushes back a piston (see Figure 5.3). Similarly, in a system open to the atmosphere, an expanding gas does work by pushing back the atmosphere. For a gas *expanding* against a constant external pressure

$$\text{work} \quad w = -\underbrace{P\Delta V}_{\text{work done by system}} \quad \overset{\text{constant pressure}}{} \quad \overset{\text{final volume minus initial volume}}{} \tag{7.4}$$

This equation also represents the work done when the *amount* of gas in a system open to the atmosphere changes due to a chemical reaction in which gaseous substances are consumed or produced. If the volume of a system does not change ($\Delta V = 0$), no work is done. (The pressure within the system may increase or decrease, but nothing moves and therefore no work is done.) From the first law (Equation 7.3), it can be seen that at constant volume, with $w = 0$, the change in internal energy of a system is equal to the heat exchanged with the surroundings.

$$\Delta E = q_V \tag{7.5}$$

This is a useful relationship—heat can be measured and this equation shows that the value of ΔE can be found by measuring q_V.

Chemicals are commonly handled in the laboratory and industrial plants at constant external pressure, most often atmospheric pressure. Therefore, we are often interested in q_P—the heat at constant external pressure—rather than q_V. For a system at constant external pressure, which can exchange energy with the surroundings only as heat or work,

$$\Delta E = q + w$$
$$\Delta E = q_P - P\,\Delta V \tag{7.6}$$

or

$$E_2 - E_1 = q_P - (PV_2 - PV_1) \tag{7.6a}$$

Rearranging gives

$$q_P = (E_2 + PV_2) - (E_1 + PV_1) \tag{7.6b}$$

Because of the interest in q_P and our ability to measure it, $E + PV$ is defined as a quantity called *enthalpy, H* (from the Greek *enthalpo*, warming up). **Enthalpy** is a thermodynamic property of a system defined so that a change in enthalpy is equal to the amount of heat exchanged with the surroundings in processes that occur at constant external pressure.

$$\text{enthalpy} \longrightarrow H = E + PV \tag{7.7}$$

$$\text{enthalpy} \longrightarrow \Delta H = \Delta E + \Delta(PV) \tag{7.8}$$
$$\text{change}$$

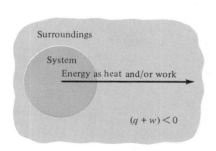

(a) Energy of system decreases, $\Delta E < 0$

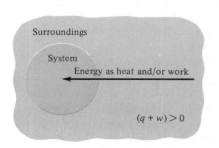

(b) Energy of system increases, $\Delta E > 0$

Figure 7.5
Energy Flow, Heat, and Work

At constant external pressure

$$\Delta H = \Delta E + P\,\Delta V \tag{7.9}$$

and, from Equation (7.6b)

$$\Delta H = H_2 - H_1 = (E_2 + PV_2) - (E_1 + PV_1)$$
$$\Delta H = q_P \tag{7.10}$$

The value of ΔH can be both calculated theoretically and measured. (The measurement of ΔH is discussed in Section 7.13.) Both ΔE and $\Delta(PV)$ have units of energy, and therefore ΔH also is expressed in energy units, usually joules or kilojoules.

For many processes, particularly those involving solids and liquids, $\Delta(PV)$ in Equation (7.8) is quite small and the change in enthalpy is close in value to the change in internal energy. In such cases, $\Delta(PV)$ is usually neglected. Frequently, even in reactions involving gases, the contribution of $\Delta(PV)$ to ΔH is relatively small.

EXAMPLE 7.1
Energy, Heat, and Work

In a single process, a system does 125 J of work on its surroundings while 75 J of heat is added to the system. What is the internal energy change for the system?

A system loses energy when it performs work on its surroundings, therefore, $w = -125$ J. The energy of the system is increased by the flow of heat into the system, so q is given a positive value, $q = 75$ J. To find ΔE

$$\Delta E = q + w = 75\ \text{J} + (-125\ \text{J}) = -50.\ \text{J}$$

The change in internal energy is $-50.$ J. The system has lost energy.

Exercise The internal energy of a system increased by 323 kJ while the system performed 111 kJ of work on its surroundings. How much heat was transferred between the system and its surroundings during this process? In which direction did the heat flow? *Answer* system absorbed 434 kJ of heat

---

EXAMPLE 7.2
Energy, Heat, and Work

For each of the following chemical and physical changes at constant pressure, is work done by the system (the substances undergoing the change) on the surroundings, or by the surroundings on the system, or is the amount of work negligible?
(a) $Sn(s) + 2F_2(g) \longrightarrow SnF_4(s)$
(b) $AgNO_3(aq) + NaCl(aq) \longrightarrow AgCl(s) + NaNO_3(aq)$
(c) $C(s) + O_2(g) \longrightarrow CO_2(g)$
(d) $SiI_4(g) \xrightarrow{\Delta} Si(s) + 2I_2(g)$

(a) There are 2 mol of gaseous reactant and no gaseous product. The volume of the system decreases and, therefore, work is done *on* the system by the surroundings (w is positive).
(b) No gaseous reactants or products are involved and therefore the work is negligible.
(c) With one mole of gaseous reactant and one mole of gaseous product, $\Delta V = 0$ and the amount of work is negligible.
(d) One mole of gaseous reactant yields two moles of gaseous product. Therefore, the volume increases as work is done by the system (w is negative).

Exercise In which of the following chemical and physical changes is work being done by the system (the substances undergoing the change) on the surroundings: (a) $I_2(g) \rightarrow I_2(s)$, (b) $CaCO_3(s) \xrightarrow{\Delta} CaO(s) + CO_2(g)$, (c) $H_2(g) + Cl_2(g) \rightarrow 2HCl(g)$, and (d) $H_2O(l) \rightarrow H_2O(s)$? *Answer* (b)

EXAMPLE 7.3
Energy, Heat, and Work

For the thermal decomposition of potassium chlorate at constant external pressure

$$2KClO_3(s) \xrightarrow[\text{MnO}_2]{\Delta} 2KCl(s) + 3O_2(g)$$

discuss the relationships among ΔE, ΔH, q_P, and w.

A thermal decomposition is an endothermic reaction. Therefore, ΔH and q_P both have positive values. With no gaseous reactants and 3 mol of gaseous products, $P \Delta V$ is positive, the system does work on the surroundings, and the work done is given by $w = -P \Delta V$. The internal energy change for this reaction, which involves pressure–volume work, is $\Delta E = q_P - P \Delta V$, or $\Delta E = \Delta H - P \Delta V$. The value of ΔE will be positive unless the amount of work done by the system is so great that $P \Delta V$ is larger than ΔH (which is unlikely).

Exercise   The combustion of benzoic acid

$$C_6H_5COOH(s) + \tfrac{15}{2}O_2(g) \longrightarrow 7CO_2(g) + 3H_2O(l)$$

was carried out under constant volume conditions. Discuss the relationships among ΔE, ΔH, q_V, and w.   *Answer* $w = 0$, $\Delta E = q_V < 0$, $\Delta H < 0$

Exothermic: releases heat
Endothermic: requires heat

In summary, to examine energy changes in thermodynamics, we define a system and its surroundings. Heat is energy in transit between objects or systems at different temperatures, or between a system and its surroundings. Exothermic processes release heat to the surroundings and endothermic processes absorb heat from the surroundings. In either case, the total amount of heat gained and lost is equal to zero, a consequence of the first law of thermodynamics (the law of conservation of energy).

In chemistry, we deal mainly with substances and their internal energy—the total energy of all the atoms, molecules, or ions within the substances. Changes in internal energy (ΔE) are exhibited as temperature changes, phase changes, or chemical reactions. At constant volume, ΔE equals the heat exchanged with the surroundings ($\Delta E = q_V$). The thermodynamic quantity enthalpy, H, is defined as $H = E + PV$. At constant external pressure, $\Delta H = \Delta E + P \Delta V$, and ΔH equals the heat exchanged with the surroundings ($\Delta H = q_P$). For many processes, especially those involving solids and liquids, $P \Delta V$ is small and ΔH is approximately equal to ΔE.

HEATS OF REACTION AND OTHER ENTHALPY CHANGES

7.5 HEATS OF REACTION

Enthalpy change, ΔH = heat of reaction at constant pressure

In studying thermodynamics, a chemical reaction is considered complete when no further changes in composition take place and the substances have returned to their original temperature, usually room temperature. The total amount of heat released or absorbed between the beginning of a reaction and the return of the substances present to the original temperature is referred to as the **heat of reaction.** When the reaction occurs at constant pressure, the heat of reaction is equal to the enthalpy change. Thus, ΔH is correctly referred to as either the enthalpy change or the heat of reaction. The value of ΔH depends on the specific reaction that has taken place, the amounts of the substances involved, and the temperature. Enthalpy changes, therefore, must be expressed as the quantity of heat per quantity of the substance or substances in question, and the temperature must be specified.

The value of ΔH is usually given as the heat released or absorbed in the reaction of the molar amounts of reactants that appear in a balanced equation. A **thermo-**

Heat is evolved
Products have lower energy than reactants

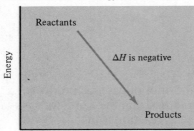

(a) **Exothermic reaction**

Heat is absorbed
Products have higher energy than reactants

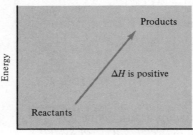

(b) **Endothermic reaction**

Figure 7.6
Energy of Reactants and Products in Exothermic and Endothermic Reactions

chemical equation includes ΔH for the balanced equation as written. For example, the following thermochemical equation

$$2HgO(s) \xrightarrow{\Delta} 2Hg(l) + O_2(g) \qquad \Delta H_{298} = 181.67 \text{ kJ} \qquad \textbf{(7.11)}$$

tells us that 181.67 kJ of thermal energy must be *added* (because ΔH is positive) to convert 2 mol of solid mercury(II) oxide to 2 mol of liquid mercury and 1 mol of gaseous oxygen. (The meaning of the specified temperature is discussed in the next section.) The equation

$$K_2O(s) + CO_2(g) \longrightarrow K_2CO_3(s) \qquad \Delta H_{298} = -391.1 \text{ kJ} \qquad \textbf{(7.12)}$$

tells us that when one mole of solid potassium oxide reacts with one mole of gaseous carbon dioxide to produce one mole of solid potassium carbonate, 391.1 kJ of energy is *released* as heat.

Another way to express heats for chemical changes is as the heat involved in a particular reaction for *one mole* of a compound, the heat per mole. For example, Equation (7.11) represents a decomposition reaction and, as written, gives ΔH for the decomposition of 2 mol of HgO. The heat of decomposition could be given *per mole of HgO,* which is one-half the value given, or 90.84 kJ/mol. To write thermochemical equations for ΔH values given per mole of a reactant, the equation must be balanced so that just one mole of the compound under consideration appears in the equation. This sometimes requires fractional coefficients for other reactants or products. The thermochemical equation for the decomposition of one mole of HgO(s) is

$$HgO(s) \xrightarrow{\Delta} Hg(l) + \tfrac{1}{2}O_2(g) \qquad \Delta H_{298} = 90.84 \text{ kJ} \qquad \textbf{(7.13)}$$

Because ΔH in a thermochemical equation always refers to the molar amounts in the equation *as written,* it is not necessary to write 90.84 kJ/mol in Equation (7.13).

It might be helpful to think of the heat exchanged in a reaction as one of the reactants or products. In an exothermic reaction such as the combustion of carbon disulfide

$$CS_2(l) + 3O_2(g) \longrightarrow CO_2(g) + 2SO_2(g) + 1075 \text{ kJ} \qquad \textbf{(7.14)}$$

energy has been released and therefore, the total internal energy of the products is less than that of the reactant (Figure 7.6a). For an endothermic reaction such as the thermal decomposition of mercury(II) oxide

$$2HgO(s) + 181.67 \text{ kJ} \longrightarrow 2Hg(l) + O_2(g)$$

energy has been added to the system and therefore the total internal energy of the products is greater than that of the reactants (Figure 7.6b).

If the amounts of reactants change, the amount of heat changes too. For the reaction of three times as much carbon disulfide via Equation (7.14), $\Delta H = 3 \times (-1075 \text{ kJ}) = -3225 \text{ kJ}$.

$$3CS_2(g) + 9O_2(g) \longrightarrow 3CO_2(g) + 6SO_2(g) + 3225 \text{ kJ}$$

A HISTORICAL ASIDE

Heat and Caloric Theory

Several eminent early students of nature, such as Francis Bacon and Robert Boyle, thought that heat might be the result of the motion of "corpuscles" of matter. These ideas were forerunners of the kinetic–molecular theory. However, in the eighteenth century, an alternative view was popular. Heat was thought to be the result of the presence in all matter of a fluid substance called "caloric." When heat flowed from a hotter body to a cooler one, caloric was thought to be flowing from one to the other.

Attempts to show the loss or gain of mass when heat flowed were never successful. The definitive word on the subject was written by one of the most

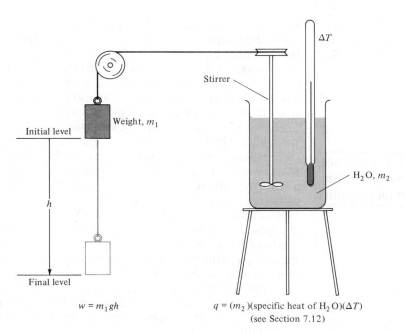

$$w = m_1 gh$$

$$q = (m_2)(\text{specific heat of } H_2O)(\Delta T)$$
(see Section 7.12)

Figure A
Apparatus for Determining the
Mechanical Equivalent of Heat

fascinating characters in the history of science, Count Rumford (1753–1814). In his "Inquiry Concerning the Weight Ascribed to Heat" he reported meticulous experiments on the weight of water at various temperatures and in various states. He ended his paper with the statement, "I think we may safely conclude that all attempts to discover any effect of heat upon the apparent weights of bodies will be fruitless."

Rumford, who was born Benjamin Thompson in Woburn, Massachusetts, was a man of many parts—a politician, a military man, and a scientist. He was also an unscrupulous scoundrel. He managed to be a spy for both the British and the French, in each instance to his financial advantage. More than once, Rumford married for money.

At 60 Rumford married Madame Lavoisier, the wealthy lady widowed when Antoine went under the guillotine. Their marriage did not last long. Rumford described the final six months of his marriage as ". . . a purgatory sufficiently painful to do away with the sins of a thousand years."

While Rumford was supervising the boring of cannon barrels at an arsenal at Munich, he observed that a great amount of heat was generated in the process. He pursued this observation with experiments showing that work and heat were related. Rumford immersed the cannon-boring equipment in water and found, much to his delight, that after $2\frac{1}{2}$ hours of work by the borer, the water had absorbed enough heat to come to a boil (see Thoughts on Chemistry at the end of this chapter). His calculations showed that mechanical work is an inexhaustible source of heat. The result argued strongly against the existence of caloric, for an inexhaustible supply of a physical substance is not to be expected.

In the 1840s James Joule, an English brewer, quantitatively measured the mechanical equivalent of heat. Joule measured the temperature rise in water heated by stirring with a paddle wheel. In essence, his apparatus was as shown in Figure A. The mass of the weight times the gravitational constant times the distance the weight drops gives the mechanical work. The amount of heat generated in the water by this amount of work was calculated from the mass of water and ΔT, as discussed in Section 7.12. Joule is honored in the modern system of units by the name of the standard unit of energy, the joule.

7.6 STANDARD STATE AND STANDARD ENTHALPY CHANGES

In order to make meaningful comparisons among heats of reactions, it is necessary to know the temperature at which ΔH was measured and the physical state of each of the reactants and products. Chemists have agreed to report heats of reaction for reactions carried out with reactants in what is called the standard state. The **standard state** of any substance is the physical state in which it is most stable at 1 atm pressure and a specified temperature. The usual specified temperature is 298 K (25 °C, roughly room temperature). For substances that are solid at this temperature and pressure, and can also have several different crystalline forms, it is necessary to specify for which form the heat of reaction is given.

Standard state of a substance: most stable state at 1 atm, specified temperature

---

Standard enthalpy changes are enthalpy changes expressed for chemical reactions or other transformations of substances in their standard states. The symbol for a standard enthalpy change is $\Delta H°$, and the specified temperature is often given as a subscript, $\Delta H°_{298}$. We have chosen to omit specifying the temperature if it is 298 K. Unless otherwise stated, all $\Delta H°$ values in this book are given for 298 K. When changes in internal energy are reported for substances in their standard states, the symbol $\Delta E°$ is used. (It is important to note that the standard state of a substance is a specific physical state and is in no way related to the "standard conditions" of temperature and pressure, STP, used most often in discussing gases.)

Many chemical reactions, of course, do not actually take place at 298 K, but require higher or lower temperatures. The standard enthalpy changes at 298 K reported for such reactions are calculated from ΔH values measured at other temperatures.

EXAMPLE 7.4
Standard States

What would be the standard states at 25 °C of the following substances?

Ca	GeCl$_4$	GeH$_4$	CH$_3$(CH$_2$)$_6$CH$_3$
Calcium	Germanium tetrachloride	Germanium hydride	Octane
m.p. 839 °C	m.p. −49.5 °C	m.p. −165 °C	m.p. −56.8 °C
b.p. 1484 °C	b.p. 84 °C	b.p. −88.5 °C	b.p. 125.7 °C

By examining the melting and boiling points, we find that in their standard states at 25 °C calcium is a solid (m.p. > 25 °C), germanium tetrachloride and octane are liquids (m.p. < 25 °C, b.p. > 25 °C), and germanium hydride is a gas (b.p. < 25 °C).

Exercise What would be the standard states of the substances listed above at 100 °C? *Answer* $Ca(s)$, $GeCl_4(g)$, $GeH_4(g)$, $CH_3(CH_2)_6CH_3(l)$

7.7 HEATS OF FORMATION

One of the simplest chemical reactions is the formation of a compound from its elements, a combination reaction. The **standard enthalpy of formation** of a compound, $\Delta H_f°$, is the heat of formation of one mole of the compound in its standard state by combination of the elements in their standard states at a specified temperature. The thermochemical equation for the formation of water at 298 K by combination of hydrogen and oxygen is

$$H_2(g) + \tfrac{1}{2}O_2(g) \longrightarrow H_2O(l) \qquad \Delta H_f° = -285.83 \text{ kJ}$$

Hydrogen and oxygen are gases, and water is a liquid at this temperature and therefore the standard enthalpy of formation of water is given for the reaction with the substances in these states.

Some standard heats of formation are given in Table 7.2. (A more comprehensive table is given in Appendix IV.) To write the chemical equations for the combination reactions to which these heats of formation apply, the reactants must be

Table 7.2
Standard Heats of Formation at 298 K The values of ΔH_f° are for the formation of one mole of the given compound in its standard state by combination of the elements in their standard states at 298 K. A compound that is a gas or a liquid at 25 °C and 1 atm has that form as its standard state. For solids that can have several different crystalline states, it is necessary to specify for which form the value of ΔH_f° is given.

Substance	ΔH_f° (kJ/mol)	Substance	ΔH_f° (kJ/mol)
Standard state			
of all elements	0.00	$Ca(OH)_2(aq)$	−1002.82
C(graphite)	0.00	$HCl(g)$	−92.31
C(diamond)	1.90	$PCl_3(l)$	−319.7
P(s, red)	−17.6	$PCl_5(s)$	−443.5
P(s, black)	−39.3	$AgCl(s)$	−127.07
P(s, white)	0.00	$NaCl(s)$	−411.00
		$KCl(s)$	−435.87
$H_2O(l)$	−285.83	$HF(g)$	−271.1
$SO_2(g)$	−296.83	$HBr(g)$	−36.40
$SO_3(g)$	−395.72	$HI(g)$	26.48
$NO(g)$	90.25	$H_2S(g)$	−20.63
$NO_2(g)$	33.18	$NH_3(g)$	−46.11
$CO(g)$	−110.53	$CS_2(l)$	89.70
$CO_2(g)$	−393.51	$CH_4(g)$	−74.81
$PbO(s,\ yellow)$	−217.32	$C_2H_2(g)$	226.73
$PbO(s,\ red)$	−218.99	$CF_4(g)$	−925
$PbO_2(s)$	−277.4	$H_2SO_4(l)$	−813.99
$Al_2O_3(\alpha\text{-solid})$	−1675.7	$HNO_3(l)$	−174.10
$Ag_2O(s)$	−31.05	$PbSO_4(s)$	−919.94
$Fe_2O_3(s)$	−824.2	$CaCO_3(calcite)$	−1206.87
$Fe_3O_4(s)$	−1118.4	$CaCO_3(aragonite)$	−1207.04
$CaO(s)$	−635.5	$CaSO_3 \cdot 2H_2O$	−1762.3
$CaC_2(s)$	−62.8	$CaSO_4 \cdot 2H_2O$	−2021.12
$Ca(OH)_2(s)$	−986.6	$(CaSO_4)_2 \cdot H_2O$	−3150.30

elements in their standard states at 298 K and the product must be *one mole* of the substance in its standard state. For example,

$$3Fe(s) + 2O_2(g) \longrightarrow Fe_3O_4(s) \qquad \Delta H_f^\circ = -1118.4 \text{ kJ}$$
$$\tfrac{1}{2}H_2(g) + \tfrac{1}{2}I_2(s) \longrightarrow HI(g) \qquad \Delta H_f^\circ = +26.48 \text{ kJ}$$
$$Pb(s) + \tfrac{1}{8}S_8(s) + 2O_2(g) \longrightarrow PbSO_4(s) \qquad \Delta H_f^\circ = -919.94 \text{ kJ}$$

By convention, the standard enthalpy of formation of an element in its standard state is taken to be zero.

EXAMPLE 7.5
Heats of Reaction

Using the data given in Table 7.2, write the thermochemical equations for the formation of (a) $PbO(s,\ yellow)$ and (b) $PCl_3(l)$.

(a) The equation must give the elements in their standard states at 298 K as reactants and one mole of $PbO(s,\ yellow)$ in its standard state as the only product. Oxygen in its standard state is $O_2(g)$ and lead is a solid.

$$Pb(s) + O_2(g) \xrightarrow{\text{(unbalanced)}} PbO(s,\ yellow)$$

We must balance the equation by putting a coefficient of $\tfrac{1}{2}$ before the O_2 term

$$Pb(s) + \tfrac{1}{2}O_2(g) \longrightarrow PbO(s,\ yellow)$$

The heat of formation of $PbO(s,\ yellow)$ is given as −217.32 kJ/mol in Table 7.2, so the complete equation is

$$Pb(s) + \tfrac{1}{2}O_2(g) \longrightarrow PbO(s,\ yellow) \qquad \Delta H_f^\circ = -217.32 \text{ kJ}$$

(b) We know that chlorine, Cl_2, is gaseous in its standard state and that phosphorus is a solid. The table shows that there are three forms of elemental phosphorus, and the $\Delta H°$ value of zero for white phosphorus shows that this is considered the standard state. The complete equation is

$$P(s, \text{white}) + \tfrac{3}{2}Cl_2(g) \longrightarrow PCl_3(l) \qquad \Delta H_f° = -319.7 \text{ kJ}$$

Exercise Use the data given in Table 7.2 to write the thermochemical equations for the formation of (a) iron(III) oxide, Fe_2O_3, and (b) calcite, $CaCO_3$. *Answer* (a) $2Fe(s) + \tfrac{3}{2}O_2(g) \rightarrow Fe_2O_3(s) \qquad \Delta H° = -824.2 \text{ kJ}$; (b) $Ca(s) + C(\text{graphite}) + \tfrac{3}{2}O_2(g) \rightarrow CaCO_3(\text{calcite}) \qquad \Delta H° = -1206.87 \text{ kJ}$

7.8 HEATS OF COMBUSTION

Many chemical compounds, particularly organic compounds containing carbon and hydrogen, react exothermically with oxygen. **Combustion** is a general term for any chemical change in which heat and light are given off. Usually "combustion" refers to combination with oxygen. The **standard enthalpy of combustion, $\Delta H_c°$,** is the heat for the reaction of one mole of a substance in its standard state with oxygen at 25 °C. Obviously combustion of most substances does not take place at 25 °C. As for any enthalpy values reported for 25 °C, the value is equal to the total amount of heat released or absorbed once the products have returned to 25 °C; there can be wide variations in temperature during the process.

$$\text{Reactants (25 °C)} \xrightarrow{\text{combustion}} \text{products (high T)} \longrightarrow \text{products (25 °C)}$$

Some standard enthalpies of combustion, often referred to as heats of combustion, are given in Table 7.3. [Many reference sources list heats of combustion as positive rather than negative. Because heat is generated, it is preferable to give negative values for $\Delta H_c°$.]

When compounds containing only carbon and hydrogen burn completely, they produce only carbon dioxide and water. The thermochemical equation for the combustion of a compound containing carbon and hydrogen (oxygen may also be present in the compound) must show the reaction of the compound with sufficient oxygen to convert all of the carbon and hydrogen present to carbon dioxide and

Table 7.3
Heats of Combustion Values at 298 K except those marked(*) at 293 K.

Substance	$\Delta H_c°$ (kJ/mol)	Substance	$\Delta H_c°$ (kJ/mol)
Carbon, C(graphite)	-394	Formaldehyde, $CH_2O(g)$	-571
Hydrogen, $H_2(g)$	-286	Formic acid, $HCOOH(l)$	-255
Acetic acid, $CH_3COOH(l)$	-875	n-Heptane, $C_7H_{16}(l)$	$-4811*$
Acetone, $CH_3COCH_3(l)$	$-1790.$	n-Hexane, $C_6H_{14}(l)$	-4163
Acetylene, $C_2H_2(g)$	$-1300.$	Methane, $CH_4(g)$	$-890.$
Benzene, $C_6H_6(l)$	-3268	Methyl alcohol, $CH_3OH(l)$	-727
Benzoic acid, $C_6H_5COOH(s)$	-3227	Naphthalene, $C_{10}H_8(s)$	-5154
Diethyl ether,		Nicotine, $C_{10}H_{14}N_2(l)$	$-5974*$
$\quad(CH_3CH_2)_2O(l)$	-2751	n-Octane, $C_8H_{18}(l)$	$-5451*$
Dimethyl ether,		n-Pentane, $C_5H_{12}(g)$	-3536
$\quad(CH_3)_2O(g)$	$-1454*$	n-Pentane, $C_5H_{12}(l)$	-3509
Ethane, $C_2H_6(g)$	$-1560.$	Propane, $C_3H_8(g)$	$-2220.$
Ethyl alcohol,		Sucrose, $C_{12}H_{22}O_{11}(s)$	-5641
$\quad CH_3CH_2OH(l)$	-1367	Toluene, $C_6H_5CH_3(l)$	$-3909*$
Ethylene, $C_2H_4(g)$	-1411		

water. Thermochemical equations for combustion of some of the substances listed in Table 7.3 are as follows:

$$CH_4(g) + 2O_2(g) \longrightarrow CO_2(g) + 2H_2O(l) \qquad \Delta H_c^\circ = -890.\ kJ$$
methane

$$C_6H_6(l) + \tfrac{15}{2}O_2(g) \longrightarrow 6CO_2(g) + 3H_2O(l) \qquad \Delta H_c^\circ = -3268\ kJ$$
benzene

$$CH_3CH_2OH(l) + 3O_2(g) \longrightarrow 2CO_2(g) + 3H_2O(l) \qquad \Delta H_c^\circ = -1367\ kJ$$
ethyl alcohol

7.9 FINDING ENTHALPY CHANGES

The enthalpy changes for many chemical reactions have been measured and are recorded in standard tables of thermochemical data. To find a desired heat of reaction, these tables may be consulted. If necessary, the desired value is calculated from other values available in the tables. Heats of formation and heats of combustion like those given in Tables 7.2 and 7.3 (and Appendix IV) are two of the types of data given in standard thermochemical tables. In finding enthalpy changes, it is necessary to recognize what types of tabulated data will provide the necessary known information. In the following sections we discuss methods for finding the desired data from known data.

So far, we have mentioned heats of formation and heats of combustion. The heats associated with many other types of chemical and physical changes are introduced in later chapters. Table 7.4 lists these and some other commonly encountered quantities. All of these changes involve thermal energy and are carried out at constant pressure. Their "heats" are all changes in enthalpy and can be used as described in the following sections. What is explained in these sections applies not just to heats of reaction, but to enthalpy changes of any type.

a. Reversing reactions Suppose we want to know the standard enthalpy change for the decomposition of one mole of silver oxide, Ag_2O.

$$Ag_2O(s) \xrightarrow{\Delta} 2Ag(s) + \tfrac{1}{2}O_2(g) \qquad \Delta H^\circ = ?$$

This thermal decomposition of silver oxide is the reverse of the formation of silver

Table 7.4
Types of Enthalpy Changes

Heat of formation, ΔH_f° (Section 7.7)
elements $\longrightarrow$ 1 mol substance
Heat of combustion, ΔH_c° (Section 7.8)
1 mol substance + $nO_2(g) \longrightarrow$ combustion products
Heat of change of state   (Section 7.11 and Figure 7.9)
1 mol substance in state A $\longrightarrow$ 1 mol substance in state B
Heat of neutralization, $\Delta H_{neutralization}^\circ$ (per 1 mol of acid or base)
acid + base $\longrightarrow$ salt(aq) + $H_2O(l)$
Heat of solution, ΔH_{soln}° (Section 15.5)
1 mol solute $\xrightarrow{n\ solvent}$ 1 mol solute (in n mol solvent)
Heat of dilution, ΔH_{dil}°
1 mol solute (in n mol solvent) $\xrightarrow{m\ solvent}$ 1 mol solute (in $n + m$ mol solvent)
Bond dissociation energy   (Section 9.18)
$X_2(g) \longrightarrow 2X(g)$
Ionization energy   (Section 10.4)
$X(g) \longrightarrow X^+(g) + e^-$
Electron affinity   (Section 10.6)
$X(g) + e^- \longrightarrow X^-(g)$

oxide from the elements in their standard states, and the ΔH_f° for this reaction appears in Table 7.2.

$$2Ag(s) + \tfrac{1}{2}O_2(g) \longrightarrow Ag_2O(s) \qquad \Delta H_f^\circ = -31.05 \text{ kJ}$$

The decomposition of Ag_2O, the reverse of this reaction, is endothermic and requires 31.05 kJ/mol.

$$Ag_2O(s) \longrightarrow 2Ag(s) + \tfrac{1}{2}O_2(g) \qquad \Delta H^\circ = 31.05 \text{ kJ}$$

Reversing a reaction changes the sign of its ΔH.

The energy required to decompose a compound to its constituent elements equals the energy released in forming the compound from the elements. In general, $\underline{\Delta H \text{ for a}}$ $\underline{\text{reaction in one direction is equal in magnitude to } \Delta H \text{ for the reaction in the reverse}}$ $\underline{\text{direction, but opposite in sign.}}$ This is a consequence of the first law of thermodynamics.

b. Changing quantities Suppose we are interested in the standard enthalpy change for the decomposition of 2 mol of Ag_2O. To find the value of ΔH° for this reaction, the heat of reaction for one mole must be multiplied by 2, as are the coefficients for the reactants and products.

$$2[Ag_2O(s) \longrightarrow 2Ag(s) + \tfrac{1}{2}O_2(g)] \qquad \Delta H^\circ = (2)(31.05 \text{ kJ})$$
$$2Ag_2O(s) \longrightarrow 4Ag(s) + O_2(g) \qquad \Delta H^\circ = 62.10 \text{ kJ}$$

This illustrates the second important principle of thermochemistry: For a given chemical reaction or change of state, $\underline{\Delta H \text{ is directly proportional to the quantities of}}$ $\underline{\text{reactants or products.}}$

To find the heat of reaction for any amount of a substance, known in mass units, the mass is first converted to moles as in any stoichiometry problem. Then the enthalpy change is multiplied by the number of moles of the substance.

EXAMPLE 7.6
Heats of Reaction

What is the thermochemical equation for burning acetylene, $C_2H_2(g)$, in oxygen? What is the heat of reaction for burning 65 g of acetylene in oxygen (at 298 K)?

Burning in oxygen is combustion, so a table of the heats of combustion should be consulted; ΔH_c° for acetylene appears in Table 7.3. Acetylene contains only carbon and hydrogen, and therefore must burn to give CO_2 and H_2O

$$C_2H_2(g) + \tfrac{5}{2}O_2(g) \longrightarrow 2CO_2(g) + H_2O(l) \qquad \Delta H_c^\circ = -1300. \text{ kJ}$$

The heat of combustion is given per mole of reactant. Therefore, to find the heat of combustion for 65 g of acetylene, the value of ΔH_c° is multiplied by the number of moles of acetylene. Doing the calculation in one step gives

$$(65 \text{ g C}_2\text{H}_2)\left(\frac{1 \text{ mol C}_2\text{H}_2}{26.04 \text{ g C}_2\text{H}_2}\right)\left(\frac{-1300. \text{ kJ}}{1 \text{ mol C}_2\text{H}_2}\right) = -3200 \text{ kJ}$$

The heat of reaction for burning 65 g of acetylene is -3200 kJ (at 298 K). [This is a highly exothermic reaction which is used in welding.]

Exercise Use the data in Table 7.3 to write the thermochemical equation for the complete combustion of benzoic acid, $C_6H_5COOH(s)$, in oxygen. What is the heat of reaction for the combustion of 1.00 g of benzoic acid? *Answer* $C_6H_5COOH(s) + \tfrac{15}{2}O_2(g) \rightarrow 7CO_2(g) + 3H_2O(l) \qquad \Delta H^\circ = -3227$ kJ; heat of reaction is -26.4 kJ/g

---

EXAMPLE 7.7
Heats of Reaction

Aluminum displaces chromium from chromium(III) oxide.

$$2Al(s) + Cr_2O_3(s) \longrightarrow Al_2O_3(s) + 2Cr(s) \qquad \Delta H^\circ = -536 \text{ kJ}$$

How much heat will be released in the reaction (under standard state conditions at 298 K) of 10.0 g of aluminum with 25.0 g of Cr_2O_3?

1. Study the problem and be sure you understand it.
   (a) What is unknown?
       The heat released in the reaction of known amounts of Al and Cr_2O_3 according to the equation given.
   (b) What is known?
       The thermochemical equation for the reaction under consideration and the masses of the two reactants.
2. Decide how to solve the problem.
   (a) What is the connection between the known and the unknown?
       Several steps will be necessary to make the connection. We can analyze the problem beginning with the unknown and working backwards. To find the unknown heat, the number of moles of reactant that are completely consumed must be known. Because masses of both reactants are given, it will first be necessary to determine which is the limiting reactant. To find the limiting reactant, the known masses must be converted to moles and mole ratios then used to determine which reactant is limiting.
   (b) What is necessary to make the connection?
       (i)   Convert masses of Al and Cr_2O_3 to moles.
       (ii) Check amount of one reactant, say Cr_2O_3, required by the other, Al, to see which is limiting.
       (iii) Use molar amount of limiting reactant to find how much heat will be released.
3. Set up and solve the problem.
   (i)

$$(10.0 \text{ g Al})\left(\frac{1 \text{ mol Al}}{26.98 \text{ g Al}}\right) = 0.371 \text{ mol Al}$$

$$(25.0 \text{ g Cr}_2\text{O}_3)\left(\frac{1 \text{ mol Cr}_2\text{O}_3}{151.99 \text{ g Cr}_2\text{O}_3}\right) = 0.164 \text{ mol Cr}_2\text{O}_3$$

   (ii)

$$(0.371 \text{ mol Al})\left(\frac{1 \text{ mol Cr}_2\text{O}_3}{2 \text{ mol Al}}\right) = 0.186 \text{ mol Cr}_2\text{O}_3$$

   More Cr_2O_3 is required than is available. Therefore, Cr_2O_3 is the limiting reactant.
   (iii) The value of $\Delta H°$ is the amount of heat for the reaction as written and can be expressed, for this reaction, as either -536 kJ/1 mol Cr_2O_3 or -536 kJ/2 mol Al. Since Cr_2O_3 is the limiting reactant, it is used to find the amount of heat released.

$$(0.164 \text{ mol Cr}_2\text{O}_3)\left(\frac{-536 \text{ kJ}}{1 \text{ mol Cr}_2\text{O}_3}\right) = -87.9 \text{ kJ}$$

4. Check the result.
   The answer is reasonable. The units came out correctly, significant digits are used correctly (limited to three throughout by 10.0 g and 25.0 g), and the magnitude of the answer is reasonable (25.0 g of Cr_2O_3 is roughly 0.2 mol and 87.9 kJ is roughly two-tenths of the value of $\Delta H°$).

c. Hess's Law: Combining ΔH values **Hess's law,** discovered experimentally in 1840, is the third important principle of thermochemistry: The enthalpy change of a chemical reaction is the same whether the reaction takes place in one step or several steps. In other words, the heat absorbed or evolved in going from the initial state to the final state is the same no matter by what route the reaction takes place (Figure 7.7).

Hess's Law: ΔH for a reaction is independent of the number of steps.

Hess's law and the other thermochemical principles are all consequences of the law of conservation of energy. It is impossible to reverse a reaction and get more heat out than was put in, or to go from the same reactants to the same products by different intermediate steps and get more heat out by one route than by another.

The very useful result of Hess's law is that thermochemical equations can be dealt with algebraically to find enthalpy changes that are not known or are difficult to measure. The desired ΔH value is calculated from a sequence of thermochemical equations that can be combined algebraically to give the desired equation. *It doesn't matter whether the sequence of reactions will actually take place or exists only on paper.*

A method for using known enthalpies to calculate unknown enthalpies can be summed up in five general steps. In all Hess's law problems, the unknown is the enthalpy change of a particular chemical reaction; the knowns are thermochemical equations for changes involving the substances in the process in question; and the connection between the unknown and the knowns is an algebraic manipulation of the known thermochemical equations. The objective is to write the known thermochemical equations in such a way that they will add up to the desired equation. This can be accomplished by following the steps outlined below and used to solve the following problem: Given the enthalpy changes for the following two reactions:

$$\tfrac{1}{2}N_2(g) + \tfrac{1}{2}O_2(g) \longrightarrow NO(g) \qquad \Delta H° = 90.25 \text{ kJ} \qquad \textbf{(7.15)}$$
$$2NO_2(g) \longrightarrow 2NO(g) + O_2(g) \qquad \Delta H° = 114.14 \text{ kJ} \qquad \textbf{(7.16)}$$

find the standard enthalpy of formation of NO_2.

1. Write the desired thermochemical equation.
   The equation for the formation of NO_2 from the elements in their standard states is

   $$\tfrac{1}{2}N_2(g) + O_2(g) \longrightarrow NO_2(g) \qquad \textbf{(7.17)}$$

2. If necessary, reverse some of the known thermochemical equations so that the major reactants and products of the desired reaction are on the reactants and products sides.
   Comparison of Equations (7.15) and (7.16) with Equation (7.17) shows that the reactants are on the desired side in Equation (7.15), but Equation (7.16) must be reversed so that the product NO_2 will be on the appropriate side.

   $$2NO(g) + O_2(g) \longrightarrow 2NO_2(g) \qquad \Delta H° = -114.14 \text{ kJ} \qquad \textbf{(7.16a)}$$

3. If necessary, multiply the known equations by appropriate coefficients so that the major reactants and products have the same coefficients as they do in the desired equation.
   Because NO_2 has the coefficient of 1 in the desired reaction, Equation (7.16a) must be multiplied by $\tfrac{1}{2}$.

   $$\tfrac{1}{2}[2NO(g) + O_2(g) \longrightarrow 2NO_2(g)] \qquad \Delta H° = \tfrac{1}{2}(-114.14 \text{ kJ})$$
   $$NO(g) + \tfrac{1}{2}O_2(g) \longrightarrow NO_2(g) \qquad \Delta H° = -57.07 \text{ kJ} \qquad \textbf{(7.16b)}$$

   Nitrogen, N_2, has the same coefficient in both Equations (7.15) and (7.17), so no further change is necessary.

4. If unwanted reactants or products appear in the equations after Step 3, further equations must be included so that the unwanted species will cancel out when all of the equations are added to give the desired equation. This is accomplished by having the unwanted species, with the same coefficients, on opposite sides of the equations. In this case, the only

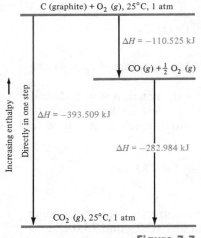

C (graphite) + O_2 (g), 25°C, 1 atm

$\Delta H = -110.525$ kJ

CO (g) + $\tfrac{1}{2} O_2$ (g)

$\Delta H = -393.509$ kJ

$\Delta H = -282.984$ kJ

CO_2 (g), 25°C, 1 atm

Increasing enthalpy →
Directly in one step

Figure 7.7
Hess's Law The total amount of heat released in the combustion of graphite is the same whether the reaction takes place in one step $(C + O_2 \rightarrow CO_2)$ or in two steps $(C + \tfrac{1}{2}O_2 \rightarrow CO,$ $CO + \tfrac{1}{2}O_2 \rightarrow CO_2)$.

unwanted species is NO and it already appears on opposite sides of Equations (7.15) and (7.16b) with the same coefficient (see Example 7.8, where this step must be followed).

5. Add the known equations and the values of $\Delta H°$ as they appear after Steps 2, 3, and 4.

$$
\begin{array}{ll}
\frac{1}{2}N_2(g) + \frac{1}{2}O_2(g) \longrightarrow \cancel{NO(g)} & \Delta H° = 90.25 \text{ kJ} \\
\cancel{NO(g)} + \frac{1}{2}O_2(g) \longrightarrow NO_2(g) & \Delta H° = -57.07 \text{ kJ} \\
\hline
\frac{1}{2}N_2(g) + O_2(g) \longrightarrow NO_2(g) & \Delta H° = 33.18 \text{ kJ}
\end{array}
$$

The standard heat of formation of NO_2 is 33.18 kJ/mol.

EXAMPLE 7.8
Heats of Reaction

Combine the following thermochemical equations

$$
\begin{array}{ll}
N_2O_4(g) \longrightarrow 2NO_2(g) & \Delta H° = 57.20 \text{ kJ} \\
2NO(g) + O_2(g) \longrightarrow 2NO_2(g) & \Delta H° = -114.14 \text{ kJ}
\end{array}
$$

to find the heat of reaction for

$$2NO(g) + O_2(g) \longrightarrow N_2O_4(g)$$

The equation for the desired reaction was given in the statement of the problem (Step 1). The first known equation gives $N_2O_4(g)$ as a reactant and so it must be reversed (Step 2). The coefficients are all as they should be (Steps 3 and 4), so the resulting two equations can be added (Step 5).

$$
\begin{array}{ll}
2\cancel{NO_2(g)} \longrightarrow N_2O_4(g) & \Delta H° = -57.20 \text{ kJ} \\
2NO(g) + O_2(g) \longrightarrow 2\cancel{NO_2(g)} & \Delta H° = -114.14 \text{ kJ} \\
\hline
2NO(g) + O_2(g) \longrightarrow N_2O_4(g) & \Delta H° = -171.34 \text{ kJ}
\end{array}
$$

The desired heat of reaction is -171.34 kJ.

Exercise Use the data given in Table 7.2 to find the heat of reaction for

$$P(s, \text{red}) + \tfrac{5}{2}Cl_2(g) \longrightarrow PCl_5(s)$$

Answer $\Delta H° = -425.9$ kJ

EXAMPLE 7.9
Heats of Reaction

Use the following thermochemical equations:

$$
\begin{array}{ll}
Ca(s) + 2C(\text{graphite}) \longrightarrow CaC_2(s) & \Delta H° = -62.8 \text{ kJ} \\
Ca(s) + \frac{1}{2}O_2(g) \longrightarrow CaO(s) & \Delta H° = -635.5 \text{ kJ} \\
CaO(s) + H_2O(l) \xrightarrow{\text{H}_2\text{O}} Ca(OH)_2(aq) & \Delta H° = -653.1 \text{ kJ} \\
C_2H_2(g) + \frac{5}{2}O_2(g) \longrightarrow 2CO_2(g) + H_2O(l) & \Delta H° = -1300. \text{ kJ} \\
C(\text{graphite}) + O_2(g) \longrightarrow CO_2(g) & \Delta H° = -393.51 \text{ kJ}
\end{array}
$$

to find $\Delta H°$ for

$$CaC_2(s) + 2H_2O(l) \xrightarrow{\text{H}_2\text{O}} Ca(OH)_2(aq) + C_2H_2(g)$$

The complete equation for the desired reaction is given in the statement of the problem (Step 1). The first, third, and fourth known equations include the major reactants and products, and the first and fourth equations must be reversed, giving the following three equations that include the main reactants and products (Step 2).

$$
\begin{array}{ll}
CaC_2(s) \longrightarrow Ca(s) + 2C(\text{graphite}) & \Delta H° = 62.8 \text{ kJ} \\
CaO(s) + H_2O(l) \xrightarrow{\text{H}_2\text{O}} Ca(OH)_2(aq) & \Delta H° = -653.1 \text{ kJ} \\
2CO_2(g) + H_2O(l) \longrightarrow C_2H_2(g) + \frac{5}{2}O_2(g) & \Delta H° = 1300. \text{ kJ}
\end{array}
$$

No changes in coefficients are needed (Step 3).

We have $CaO(s)$ and $2CO_2(g)$ as unwanted reactants and $Ca(s)$, $2C(graphite)$, and $\frac{5}{2}O_2(g)$ as unwanted products. These can be eliminated by using the second and fifth equations (Step 4). The objective now is to have formulas on the *opposite* sides from their positions in the first three equations. By including the second equation as it is and the fifth equation multiplied by 2 to allow the elimination of $2CO_2$, the desired equation is obtained.

$$CaC_2(s) \longrightarrow \cancel{Ca(s)} + \cancel{2C(graphite)} \qquad \Delta H° = 62.8 \text{ kJ}$$
$$\cancel{CaO(s)} + H_2O(l) \xrightarrow{H_2O} Ca(OH)_2(aq) \qquad \Delta H° = -653.1 \text{ kJ}$$
$$\cancel{2CO_2(g)} + H_2O(l) \longrightarrow C_2H_2(g) + \cancel{\tfrac{5}{2}O_2(g)} \qquad \Delta H° = 1300. \text{ kJ}$$
$$\cancel{Ca(s)} + \cancel{\tfrac{1}{2}O_2(g)} \longrightarrow \cancel{CaO(s)} \qquad \Delta H° = -635.5 \text{ kJ}$$
$$\cancel{2C(graphite)} + \cancel{2O_2(g)} \longrightarrow \cancel{2CO_2(g)} \qquad \Delta H° = -787.02 \text{ kJ}$$
$$CaC_2(s) + 2H_2O(l) \xrightarrow{H_2O} Ca(OH)_2(aq) + C_2H_2(g) \qquad \Delta H° = -713 \text{ kJ}$$

The $\Delta H° = -713$ kJ for the reaction of $CaC_2(s)$ with water.

Exercise The following thermochemical equations can be written for the oxides of iron:

$$Fe(s) + \tfrac{1}{2}O_2(g) \longrightarrow FeO(s) \qquad \Delta H° = -272.0 \text{ kJ}$$
$$3Fe(s) + 2O_2(g) \longrightarrow Fe_3O_4(s) \qquad \Delta H° = -1118.4 \text{ kJ}$$

Find $\Delta H°$ for $4FeO(s) \rightarrow Fe(s) + Fe_3O_4(s)$. *Answer* $\Delta H° = -30.4$ kJ

7.10 HEATS OF REACTION FROM STANDARD HEATS OF FORMATION

When standard enthalpies of formation are known for all of the reactants and products in a desired thermochemical equation, the heat of reaction can be found by a more simple method than that of the preceding section. Subtraction of the sum of the $\Delta H_f°$ values of all of the *reactants* from the sum of the $\Delta H_f°$ values of all of the *products* gives the $\Delta H°$ value for a desired reaction.

$$\Delta H° = (\text{sum of } \Delta H_f° \text{ products}) - (\text{sum of } \Delta H_f° \text{ reactants}) \qquad \textbf{(7.18)}$$

In using Equation (7.18) keep in mind that for elements in their standard states, $\Delta H_f° = 0$.

To find $\Delta H°$ for the reaction

$$2A + B \longrightarrow 3C + 2D \qquad \Delta H° = ?$$

$\Delta H_f°$ values would be combined according to Equation (7.18) as follows:

$$\Delta H° = [(3 \text{ mol})\Delta H_f° (C) + (2 \text{ mol})\Delta H_f° (D)] - [(2 \text{ mol})\Delta H_f° (A) + (1 \text{ mol})\Delta H_f° (B)]$$

$\Delta H° = \Delta H_f°$ of products $- \Delta H_f°$ of reactants

Note that each value must be multiplied by the number of moles that appear in the desired reaction.

EXAMPLE 7.10
Heats of Reaction

Find the heat of reaction for

$$CH_4(g) + 4F_2(g) \longrightarrow CF_4(g) + 4HF(g)$$

using the heat of formation data given in Table 7.2.

The heats of formation of all of the reactants and products are known. Therefore,

$$\Delta H° = [(1\ mol)\Delta H_f°\ (CF_4) + (4\ mol)\Delta H_f°\ (HF)] - [(1\ mol)\Delta H_f°\ (CH_4) + (4\ mol)\Delta H_f°\ (F_2)]$$
$$= [(1\ mol)(-925\ kJ/mol) + (4\ mol)(-271.1\ kJ/mol)]$$
$$\quad - [(1\ mol)(-74.81\ kJ/mol) + (4\ mol)(0)]$$
$$= -1935\ kJ$$

The heat of reaction is -1935 kJ.

Exercise Use the heat of formation data given in Table 7.2 to find the heat of reaction for $2Fe_3O_4(s) + \frac{1}{2}O_2(g) \rightarrow 3Fe_2O_3(s)$. *Answer* $\Delta H° = -235.8$ kJ

7.11 HEATS OF CHANGES OF STATE

A change in the internal energy of a substance or a mixture of substances can cause a change in temperature or a change of state, or both, rather than a chemical reaction. Suppose we begin with one mole of ice at -25 °C and carefully measure the temperature of the system as heat is added at a constant rate until the temperature reaches 125 °C. We would find that the ice gradually increases in temperature until the temperature reaches 0 °C (Figure 7.8). The temperature then remains constant, even as more heat is added, until all of the ice has melted into liquid water. All of the added thermal energy has gone into melting the ice.

Once the ice is melted and only liquid water is present, the system again increases in temperature, this time until the boiling point of water is reached (100 °C at 1 atm pressure). Again, the temperature remains constant as more heat is added, this time until the liquid water has completely vaporized into steam. All of the thermal energy has gone into breaking up clusters of water molecules held together by the intermolecular forces. After the vaporization is complete, the steam can again increase in temperature.

A dramatic demonstration of the constant-temperature, liquid-to-steam portion of the heating curve for water (Figure 7.8) is the boiling of an egg in a paper bag full of water (Figure 7.9). The paper will not reach its kindling point until all of the water has evaporated, because until that point is reached the temperature of the bag and its contents cannot exceed 100 °C.

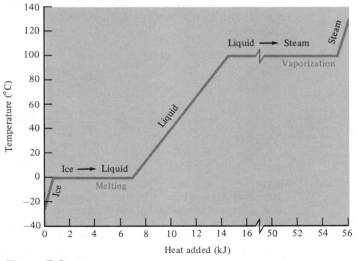

Figure 7.8
Heating Curve from -25 °C to 125 °C for One Mole of Water Note that more heat is required for vaporization than for melting.

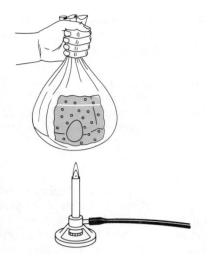

Figure 7.9
Boiling Water, a Phase Transition at Constant Temperature Until all of the water has evaporated, the temperature cannot exceed 100 °C and the bag will not burn.

One of the many practical applications of the heat transferred in phase changes is in steam-heated buildings. Water is converted to steam in a boiler and the steam is piped around the building. Then the steam is allowed to condense in radiators in the rooms to be heated and the heat of vaporization is released. In this way the two transitions — from water to steam, and from steam to water — transfer heat from the furnace to all of the rooms.

The transformation of a solid to a liquid and a liquid to a gas are examples of changes of state. The enthalpy for a change of state is the amount of heat absorbed or released in the process (at constant pressure) of completing the transformation from one state to the other, without any change in the temperature. The enthalpies for changes of state (Figure 7.10) are usually referred to as heats of vaporization, heats of fusion, and so on. These quantities are nothing more nor less than enthalpies of physical changes. They change sign for reverse processes (e.g., ΔH for condensation is equal in magnitude but of the opposite sign as ΔH for vaporization), are directly proportional to the amount of material involved, and can be used in Hess's law calculations. Some examples of enthalpy changes for phase transitions are given in Table 7.5. (Substances that have melted and then resolidified are sometimes referred to as "fused." This causes some confusion — note that "fusion" means melting, not solidification.)

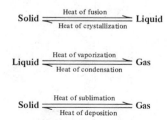

Figure 7.10
Changes of State Enthalpy values for changes of state are usually given in kilojoules per mole of substance changed at constant temperature. The heat added to raise the substance to the temperature at which vaporization, for example, begins is not included. Sometimes values for changes of state are given in joules per gram. Usually the enthalpies of fusion, vaporization, and sublimation are tabulated in handbooks of chemistry. For a further discussion of changes of state, see Section 13.2.

**Table 7.5
Enthalpy Changes for Changes of
State**

Substance	Transformation	T (K)	ΔH (kJ/mol)
Br$_2$	fusion	265.9	10.54
CO	solid II $\longrightarrow$ solid I	61.52	0.632
	fusion	68.09	0.837
	vaporization	81.65	6.042
CO$_2$	sublimation	194.67	25.23
CH$_3$OH (methyl alcohol)	solid II $\longrightarrow$ solid I	157.4	0.644
	fusion	175.25	3.17
	vaporization	337.9	35.27
CH$_3$CH$_2$OH (ethyl alcohol)	fusion	158.6	5.02
	vaporization	351.7	38.58
(CH$_3$)$_2$O (dimethyl ether)	fusion	131.65	4.94
	vaporization	248.33	21.51
Cl$_2$	fusion	172.15	6.41
	vaporization	239.09	20.41
HF	fusion	190.08	4.58
	vaporization	293.1	7.5
H$_2$	fusion	13.95	0.117
	vaporization	20.38	0.904
H$_2$O	fusion	273.15	6.01
	vaporization	373.15	40.66
H$_2$O$_2$ (hydrogen peroxide)	fusion	271.2	10.54
Pb	fusion	600.6	5.10
	vaporization	2023	179.9
Hg	fusion	234.28	2.33
	vaporization	629.72	58.12
O$_2$	fusion	54.39	0.444
	vaporization	90.18	6.82
Na	fusion	371	2.64
NaCl	fusion	1081	28.5
	vaporization	1738	170.7

MEASURING HEAT

7.12 HEAT CAPACITY

When a hotter object is placed in contact with a cooler object, energy in the form of heat flows between them until they reach the same temperature. Heat flow is detected by changes in temperature. The symbol ΔT represents a change in temperature. The value of ΔT is taken as the difference between the final and the initial temperatures of a substance or a system.

$$\underset{\substack{change \\ in}}{\xrightarrow{\hspace{1cm}}} \overset{temperature}{\Delta T} = T_{final} - T_{initial} \tag{7.19}$$

Temperature is most often reported in Celsius degrees, °C. In thermodynamics, as in the gas law calculations (Chapter 5), temperature should be expressed in an absolute temperature unit, commonly the kelvin. However, because the Celsius degree and the kelvin are the same size, ΔT has the same value in Celsius degrees as it does in kelvins. Simply write the value of ΔT in kelvins, where these are needed. For example, for a temperature increase from 23 °C to 47 °C

$$\Delta T = T_{final} - T_{initial} = 47 \text{ °C} - 23 \text{ °C} = 24 \text{ °C, or 24 K} \tag{7.20}$$

For a temperature decrease from 100. °C to 35 °C

$$\Delta T_{final} - T_{initial} = 35 \text{ °C} - 100. \text{ °C} = -65 \text{ °C, or } -65 \text{ K} \tag{7.21}$$

Table 7.6
Molar Heat Capacity Data at
Constant Pressure for Selected
Substances at 298 K

Substance	Molar Heat Capacity (J/K mol)	Substance	Molar Heat Capacity (J/K mol)
Ag(s)	25.35	FeO(s)	48.12
Al(s)	24.35	HCl(g)	29.12
Ar(g)	20.79	HF(g)	29.13
Au(s)	25.42	H₂(g)	28.82
Br₂(l)	75.69	H₂O(l)	75.29
C(graphite)	8.53	H₂O(g)	33.58
C(diamond)	6.11	H₂O₂(l)	89.1
CO(g)	29.12	H₂SO₄(l)	138.91
CO₂(g)	37.11	I₂(s)	54.44
CH₃CH₂OH(l)	111.46	N₂(g)	29.13
CH₃COOH(l)	124.30	NH₃(g)	35.06
Cl₂(g)	33.91	NO(g)	29.84
Cu(s)	24.44	NO₂(g)	37.20
F₂(g)	31.30	O₂(g)	29.36
Fe(s)	25.10	Pb(s)	26.44

Note: The values given here are heat capacities under constant pressure, as for a substance at atmospheric pressure. Values of heat capacity when the volume is constant and the pressure can vary are slightly different for solids and liquids and appreciably different for gases.

As you can see in Equations (7.20) and (7.21), when temperature increases, ΔT is positive; when temperature decreases, ΔT is negative.

The magnitude of the heat flow that accompanies an increase in temperature is dependent upon the mass and the identity of the substance involved. To determine the amount of heat associated with a known ΔT for a given substance, it is necessary to know the **heat capacity** of that substance — the amount of heat required to raise the temperature of a given amount of a substance by one kelvin. The units that we use for heat capacity are

$$\frac{(\text{joules})}{(\text{kelvins})(\text{moles, or mass unit})}$$

Heat capacities are usually tabulated in one of two ways: (1) as **molar heat capacity,** the amount of heat required to raise the temperature of one *mole* of substance by one kelvin (J/K mol), or (2) as what is known as **specific heat,** the amount of heat required to raise the temperature of one *gram* of a substance by one kelvin (J/K g). Some molar heat capacity values are given in Table 7.6. (Additional values are given in Appendix IV.)

Molar heat capacity and specific heat provide the connections between heat, q, and the amount of substance and the change in temperature.

$$\text{Heat } (q) = (\text{no. of moles})(\text{molar heat capacity})(\Delta T) \qquad \textbf{(7.22)}$$

$$\text{joules} \qquad \text{moles} \qquad \frac{\text{joules}}{\text{kelvin mole}} \qquad \text{kelvins}$$

$$\text{Heat } (q) = (\text{mass})(\text{specific heat})(\Delta T) \qquad \textbf{(7.23)}$$

$$\text{joules} \qquad \text{grams} \qquad \frac{\text{joules}}{\text{kelvin gram}} \qquad \text{kelvins}$$

Specific heat: heat needed to raise temperature of 1 g of a substance by 1 K

EXAMPLE 7.11
Heat Flow – Specific Heat

How much is needed to raise the temperature of 21 g of aluminum from 25 °C to 161 °C (no phase changes occur)? The specific heat of aluminum is 0.902 J/K g.

The amount of heat needed is found from the known mass of aluminum, the change in temperature and the specific heat.

$$\Delta T = 161 \ °C - 25 \ °C = 136 \ °C, \text{ or } 136 \ K$$

$$q = (\text{mass})(\text{specific heat})(\Delta T)$$

$$= (21 \ g)\left(\frac{0.902 \ J}{K \ g}\right)(136 \ K)$$

$$= 2600 \ J$$

A total of 2600 J of heat must be added to the aluminum. Note that the temperature increased, and q is positive.

Exercise Exactly 100 J of heat was absorbed by 55.85 g of iron and the resulting temperature change was 3.98 °C. Calculate the specific heat of iron. *Answer* 0.450 J/K g

7.13 CALORIMETRY

A **calorimeter** is a device used for measuring the heat absorbed or released during a thermochemical process. Many different types of calorimeters have been designed for different purposes (see Tools of Chemistry: Calorimeters). In all of them, simple or very complex, the objective is to measure ΔT for the calorimeter, to calculate from it the amount of heat that has been exchanged between the calorimeter and its contents, and thus to determine the heat of a reaction or change of state. To do this requires knowing the heat capacity of the calorimeter itself (how much heat is required to raise the temperature of the entire calorimeter by one kelvin and also, in some cases, the heat capacity of the contents of the calorimeter.

The heat capacity of a calorimeter is determined experimentally by one of several standard methods. For example, a known amount of heat is introduced into the calorimeter with an electric heater and the temperature rise measured. Or a known amount of heat is introduced by means of a heated metal of known specific heat (see Example 7.12). A reaction for which the heat of reaction is known can also be used. The heat capacity of the calorimeter is found from the relationship

$$q_{known} = (\text{calorimeter heat capacity})(\Delta T) \tag{7.24}$$

$$\underset{joules}{} \quad \underset{\frac{joules}{kelvin}}{} \quad \underset{kelvins}{}$$

Examples 7.12–7.14 illustrate calculations necessary in calorimetry. The heat flow in a constant-volume calorimeter is equal to the internal energy change ($\Delta E = q_V$; Section 7.4) and the heat flow in a constant-pressure calorimeter is equal to the enthalpy change ($\Delta H = q_P$; Section 7.4).

TOOLS OF CHEMISTRY

Calorimeters

One of the most common types of calorimeters is a bomb calorimeter (Figure A). The reaction takes place in a "bomb," a chamber strong enough to withstand high temperatures and pressures. The heat flow measured in a bomb calorimeter is equal to ΔE because the reaction is carried out at constant volume ($\Delta E = q_V$).

Heats of combustion and the caloric values of foods are frequently measured in bomb calorimeters. The substance to be burned is weighed and placed in the reaction chamber, which is then sealed and filled with oxygen under pressure in order to assure complete combustion. The reaction chamber is placed in the water bath. The reaction is then initiated by a small, electrically heated wire in the calorimeter. The stirrer keeps the water in motion so that heat evolved by the reaction is evenly distributed and the temperature is uniform. The temperature of the water, once it has become constant, is accurately measured.

The total heat produced by an exothermic reaction is equal to the heat

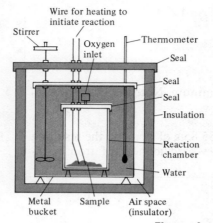

Figure A
Bomb Calorimeter Volume is constant and ΔE is measured.

absorbed by the water plus the heat absorbed by all of the parts of the calorimeter within the insulated chamber. The heat evolved is calculated from the recorded temperature increase by using the known specific heat of water and the heat capacity of the calorimeter, which is determined experimentally (Section 7.13). (In highly accurate work, the heat capacity of the products of the reaction must also be taken into account.)

A calorimeter for use with processes that take place in solution is shown in Figure B. The pressure in this apparatus is constant and is equal to atmospheric pressure. Therefore, the heat flow in such a solution calorimeter is equal to ΔH ($\Delta H = q_P$). The sealed glass ampoule holds a substance that will react with the solution or dissolve in it. A Dewar flask, which is like the silvery lining of a thermos bottle, but much larger, insulates the solution. After the calorimeter is tightly sealed and the temperature recorded, the ampoule is broken to initiate the process to be studied. As in a bomb calorimeter, the temperature change is recorded. The heat is calculated from the heat capacity of the calorimeter and, in this case, also the heat capacity of the solution, for a significant amount of the heat evolved will raise the temperature of the substances present.

A simple, constant-pressure calorimeter can be made from a Styrofoam coffee cup (Figure C). Styrofoam is a good insulator and prevents heat exchange with the surroundings. The calorimeter has four parts—the coffee cup holding a solution, a lid, preferably of an insulating substance such as Styrofoam or cardboard, a thermometer, and a rod for stirring.

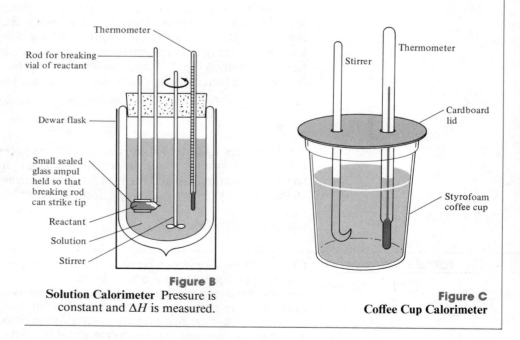

Figure B
Solution Calorimeter Pressure is constant and ΔH is measured.

Figure C
Coffee Cup Calorimeter

EXAMPLE 7.12
Calorimetry

In order to determine the heat capacity of a solution calorimeter, 75.3 g of copper at 370.5 K was placed into 100.3 g of water in the calorimeter. The initial temperature of the water was 294.4 K. The final temperature of the system was 298.8 K. What is the heat capacity of the calorimeter? For Cu, specific heat = 0.385 J/K g and for H_2O, specific heat = 4.184 J/K g.

The copper loses energy and decreases in temperature and the water and the calorimeter gain energy and increase in temperature.

$$\Delta T_{Cu} = 298.8 \text{ K} - 370.5 \text{ K} = -71.7 \text{ K}$$
$$\Delta T_{H_2O} = 298.8 \text{ K} - 294.4 \text{ K} = 4.4 \text{ K}$$

The amount of heat lost by the copper was

$$q_{lost, \, Cu} = (\text{mass})(\text{specific heat})(\Delta T) = (75.3 \text{ g})(0.385 \text{ J/K g})(-71.7 \text{ K}) = -2080 \text{ J}$$

The heat lost was transferred to the water and the calorimeter.

$$q_{gained, \, H_2O} = (100.3 \text{ g})(4.184 \text{ J/K g})(4.4 \text{ K}) = 1800 \text{ J}$$
$$q_{gained, \, calorimeter} = (\text{calorimeter heat capacity})(4.4 \text{ K})$$

From the first law, we know that the sum of the heat lost and the heat gained must be zero. The heat capacity of the calorimeter can therefore be calculated as follows:

$$q_{lost, \, Cu} + q_{gained, \, H_2O} + q_{gained, \, calorimeter} = 0$$
$$-2080 \text{ J} + 1800 \text{ J} + (\text{calorimeter heat capacity})(4.4 \text{ K}) = 0$$
$$\text{calorimeter heat capacity} = \frac{(2080 \text{ J} - 1800 \text{ J})}{4.4 \text{ K}} = 60 \text{ J/K}$$

The heat capacity of the calorimeter is 60 J/K.

Exercise A calorimeter was calibrated by mixing together dilute solutions of HCl and NaOH. The amount of heat released by the reaction was 5583.5 J. The 200.7 g of solution that resulted from the reaction had a specific heat of 3.97 J/K g. A temperature increase of 6.5 °C was observed for the calorimeter and the contents. Calculate the heat capacity of the calorimeter. *Answer* 60 J/K

EXAMPLE 7.13
Calorimetry

The calorimeter described in Example 7.12 was used to find the heat flow associated with the dissolution of 24 g of NaCl in 176 g of water. The observed ΔT was -1.6 K. The calorimeter heat capacity is 60 J/K. The specific heat of the resulting NaCl solution is 3.64 J/K g. (This value is found from a standard table of specific heats.) What is the heat flow for this process?

The total heat flow in this experiment is accounted for as follows:

$$q_{dissoln} + q_{calorimeter} + q_{NaCl \, soln} = 0$$

The negative ΔT shows that the dissolution process is endothermic; the solution and the calorimeter lose energy during the dissolution.

$$q_{lost, \, NaCl \, soln} = (\text{mass})(\text{sp ht})(\Delta T) = (176 \text{ g} + 24 \text{ g})(3.64 \text{ J/K g})(-1.6 \text{ K}) = -1200 \text{ J}$$
$$q_{lost, \, calorimeter} = (\text{calorimeter heat capacity})(\Delta T) = (60 \text{ J/K})(-1.6 \text{ K}) = -100 \text{ J}$$

Solving the first law expression above gives the heat absorbed in dissolving 24 g of NaCl

$$q_{dissoln} - 100 \text{ J} - 1200 \text{ J} = 0$$
$$q_{dissoln} = 1300 \text{ J}$$

The heat of solution for dissolving 24 g of NaCl in 176 g of water is 1300 J.

Exercise The heat capacity of a calorimeter is 7.3 J/K. This calorimeter was used to measure the heat of reaction for mixing 100. mL of 0.0100 M Ag^+ with 100. mL of 0.0100 M Cl^-. The observed temperature change was 0.077 K for the 200. g of solution (specific heat = 4.35 J/K g) and calorimeter. What is the heat of reaction for $Ag^+ + Cl^- \rightarrow AgCl(s)$? *Answer* $\Delta H° = -68$ kJ

EXAMPLE 7.14
Calorimetry

A bomb calorimeter was used to measure the heat evolved in the combustion of naphthalene, $C_{10}H_8$, in oxygen (at 298 K). The reaction of a 0.640 g sample of naphthalene raised the temperature of the calorimeter and its contents by 2.54 K. The calorimeter was of a type that has a relatively large heat capacity. The heat gain of such a calorimeter is so much larger than the heat gain of its contents that the amount of heat gained by the contents of the calorimeter can be neglected. Calculate the heat involved in the combustion of one mole of naphthalene ($\Delta E = q_V$). The heat capacity of the calorimeter is 10.13 kJ/K.

In this experiment the total heat flow, neglecting the heat absorbed by the contents of the calorimeter, is

$$q_{rxn} + q_{calorimeter} = 0$$

The heat gained by the calorimeter is

$$q_{calorimeter} = (\text{calorimeter heat cap})(\Delta T) = (10.13 \text{ kJ/K})(2.54 \text{ K}) = 25.7 \text{ kJ}$$

giving for the combustion of the sample

$$q_{rxn} + 25.7 \text{ kJ} = 0$$
$$q_{rxn} = -25.7 \text{ kJ}$$

The amount of naphthalene that reacted was

$$(0.640 \text{ g } C_{10}H_8)\left(\frac{1 \text{ mol } C_{10}H_8}{128.17 \text{ g } C_{10}H_8}\right) = 0.00499 \text{ mol}$$

giving the heat of reaction on a molar basis as

$$\frac{-25.7 \text{ kJ}}{0.00499 \text{ mol}} = -5150 \text{ kJ/mol}$$

The value of -5150 kJ/mol, because it was measured in a constant volume calorimeter, is the internal energy change (ΔE) for the combustion of naphthalene.

Exercise The same bomb calorimeter was used to measure the heat of combustion of urea, $(NH_2)_2CO(s)$. The temperature increase of the calorimeter and contents was 1.05 K for the combustion of 1.013 g of urea. Calculate the molar heat of combustion of urea. *Answer* $\Delta E = -628$ kJ/mol

[The data of the experiment described in Example 7.14 can be used to demonstrate the relationship between the internal energy change and the heat of a reaction involving gases. The reaction was

$$C_{10}H_8(s) + 12O_2(g) \longrightarrow 10CO_2(g) + 4H_2O(l) \qquad \Delta E = -5150 \text{ kJ}$$

Recall that the heat of reaction, ΔH, is defined as $\Delta H = \Delta E + \Delta(PV)$. Using the ideal gas equation for a change from state 1 to state 2 shows that we can replace $\Delta(PV)$ by $\Delta(RTn)$:

$$P_1V_1 = n_1RT_1 \qquad P_2V_2 = n_2RT_2$$
$$P_2V_2 - P_1V_1 = n_2RT_2 - n_1RT_1$$
$$\Delta(PV) = \Delta(nRT)$$

At constant temperature

$$\Delta(PV) = RT(\Delta n_g) \quad \overset{\frown}{} \quad \begin{array}{l}\text{change in}\\ \text{no. of moles of gas}\end{array}$$

The reaction of Example 7.14 was carried out at 298 K and the change in the number of moles of gas is 10 mol − 12 mol = −2 mol. The value of ΔH is found as follows:

$$\Delta H = \Delta E + RT(\Delta n_g)$$
$$= -5150 \text{ kJ} + (8.314 \times 10^{-3} \text{ kJ/K mol})(298 \text{ K})(-2 \text{ mol})$$
$$= -5150 \text{ kJ} + (-4.96 \text{ kJ}) = -5160 \text{ kJ}$$

The difference between ΔE and ΔH in this reaction is about 0.2% of the value of ΔE. You can see that in reactions involving only solids and liquids the difference would be negligible.]

In summary, processes of importance in chemistry are usually carried out at constant pressure. The heats of such processes are expressed as changes in enthalpy, ΔH. Exothermic reactions have negative ΔH values; endothermic reactions have positive ΔH values. Thermochemical equations include ΔH for the reaction as written. Standard enthalpy changes, $\Delta H°$, apply to reactants and products in their standard states—the states most stable at 1 atm and a specified temperature (most often 298 K). Standard heats of formation are enthalpy changes for the formation of compounds from the elements in their standard states.

Thermochemical equations can be dealt with algebraically to find unknown heats of reaction from known heats of reaction. When the direction of a reaction is reversed, the sign of ΔH must be reversed. When a chemical equation is multiplied or divided by a factor, the value of ΔH changes by the same factor. The heats of changes of state and many other processes are the enthalpy changes for these processes and may be dealt with as described for heats of reaction.

The amount of heat evolved or absorbed in a chemical process can be found from the change in temperature and the heat capacity of the substance or system that has changed temperature. The enthalpy change is found by carefully measuring the change of temperature in a calorimeter, for which the heat capacity has been determined experimentally.

SUMMARY

7.1 ENERGY IN CHEMICAL REACTIONS All chemical reactions are accompanied by energy changes. In general, breaking chemical bonds requires energy and the formation of chemical bonds releases energy.

7.2 THERMODYNAMICS In thermodynamics—the study of energy transformations—we define the area of study as the system and consider the rest of the universe to be the surroundings. Heat is the energy transferred between objects that differ in temperature; it represents the random kinetic energy (energy of motion) of atoms and molecules. Any process that releases heat from a system to its surroundings is exothermic; any process in which a system absorbs heat from its surroundings is endothermic.

7.3 INTERNAL ENERGY All of the energy contained by a chemical system is classified as internal energy. An increase in internal energy can have three consequences: It can raise the temperature, it can cause a phase change, or (if it is sufficient to break chemical bonds, allowing new ones to form) it can produce a chemical reaction. The internal energy change of a system is symbolized by ΔE.

7.4 ENERGY, HEAT, AND WORK The first law of thermodynamics, known as the law of conservation of energy, states that the energy of the universe is constant. Thus any energy lost by a system must be transferred to its surroundings, and vice versa. The entire energy change must be accounted for by heat and/or work. Mathematically, $\Delta E = q + w$. Work is performed when a force moves an object over a distance. For a gas expanding against constant pressure, the work, w, is equal to $-P\Delta V$. At constant volume, the flow of heat in a chemical change is equal to the change in internal energy: $\Delta E = q_V$. Enthalpy, H, is a thermodynamic property of a system defined by the formula $H = E + PV$. The change in enthalpy in a process at constant pressure is equal to the amount of heat exchanged with the surroundings: $\Delta H = q_P$. H has units of energy.

7.5 HEATS OF REACTION Many chemical reactions are carried out at constant pressure (usually atmospheric). Under these conditions, the heat of reaction — the amount of heat released or absorbed from the start of the process to the time when the system has returned to its original temperature — is equal to the enthalpy change, ΔH. A thermochemical equation is one that includes ΔH for the balanced equation as written. For exothermic processes, ΔH is negative; for endothermic processes, ΔH is positive.

7.6 STANDARD STATE AND STANDARD ENTHALPY CHANGES **7.7** HEATS OF FORMATION **7.8** HEATS OF COMBUSTION The standard state of any substance is the physical state in which it is most stable at 1 atm and a specified temperature (usually 298 K). Enthalpy changes for chemical reactions of substances in their standard states are known as standard enthalpy changes ($\Delta H°$). The standard enthalpy of formation of a compound, $\Delta H_f°$, is the heat of formation of one mole by combination of its elements in their standard states at a specified temperature. The standard enthalpy of combustion, $\Delta H_c°$, is the heat for the reaction of one mole of a substance in its standard state with oxygen.

7.9 FINDING ENTHALPY CHANGES **7.10** HEATS OF REACTION FROM STANDARD HEATS OF FORMATION The enthalpy change, ΔH, for a reaction is equal in magnitude to ΔH for the reverse reaction but opposite in sign. If the quantities of reactants and products in a reaction are changed, ΔH for that reaction changes proportionately. For any chemical reaction, ΔH has the same value whether the reaction takes place in one step or in several steps. This means that thermochemical equations can be manipulated and combined algebraically to find unknown enthalpy changes from known ones.

7.11 HEATS OF CHANGES OF STATE The enthalpy for a change of state (see Figure 7.10) is the amount of heat absorbed or released at constant pressure and without any change in temperature, for example, in melting or freezing, evaporation or condensation.

7.12 HEAT CAPACITY The heat capacity of a substance is the amount of heat needed to raise the temperature of a given amount of the substance by 1 K. The amount of the substance may be 1 mol (molar heat capacity, C_p) or 1 g (specific heat).

7.13 CALORIMETRY A calorimeter is used for measuring the heat flow during a thermochemical process. The heat of the process is found from the change in temperature of the calorimeter and its contents, ΔT, and the heat capacity of the calorimeter (which must be experimentally determined).

TOOLS OF CHEMISTRY: CALORIMETERS Heats of combustion are measured in bomb calorimeters. The reaction chamber is sealed, and since the reaction is carried out at constant volume, the heat flow measured is equal to ΔE. This is found by adding the heat absorbed by the water bath surrounding the reaction chamber to the heat absorbed by all parts of the calorimeter itself. For reactions that take place in solution, heat flow is measured in a calorimeter at atmospheric pressure. Because the pressure is constant, the heat released by the process, which is the total of the heat absorbed by the calorimeter and by the solution itself, is equal to ΔH.

SIGNIFICANT TERMS

thermodynamics
system
surroundings
thermochemistry
heat
exothermic
endothermic
internal energy
intermolecular forces
intramolecular forces
internal energy change
first law of thermodynamics
work
enthalpy
heat of reaction
thermochemical equation
standard state
standard enthalpy changes
standard enthalpy of formation
combustion
standard enthalpy of combustion
Hess's law
heat capacity
molar heat capacity
specific heat
calorimeter

THOUGHTS ON CHEMISTRY

An Inquiry on Heat

PHILOSOPHICAL TRANSACTIONS,
by Count Rumford

Being engaged lately in superintending the boring of cannon in the workshops of the military arsenal at Munich, I was struck with the very considerable degree of heat that a brass gun acquires in a short time in being bored, and with the still higher temperature (much higher than that of boiling water, as I found by experiment) of the metallic chips separated from it by the borer.

The more I meditated on these phenomena, the more they appeared to me to be curious and interesting. A thorough investigation of them seemed even to bid fair to give a farther insight into the hidden nature of heat; and to enable us to form some reasonable conjectures respecting the existence, or nonexistence, of an igneous fluid — a subject on which the opinions of philosophers have in all ages been much divided.

It would be difficult to describe the surprise and astonishment expressed in the countenances of the bystanders on seeing so large a quantity of cold water heated, and actually made to boil, without any fire. Though there was, in fact, nothing that could justly be considered as surprising in this event, yet I acknowledged fairly that it afforded me a degree of childish pleasure, which, were I ambitious of the reputation of a grave philosopher, I ought most certainly rather to hide than to discover.

It is hardly necessary to add that anything which any insulated body, or system of bodies, can continue to furnish without limitation, cannot possibly be a material substance; and it appears to me to be extremely difficult, if not quite impossible, to form any distinct idea of anything capable of being excited and communicated in the manner in which heat was excited and communicated in these experiments, except it be MOTION.

Count Rumford, "An Inquiry Concerning the Source of the Heat Which is Excited by Friction," in *Philosophical Transactions*, Vol. 88, p. 80, 1798. Quoted from *Harvard Case Histories in Experimental Science*, Vol. 1 (Cambridge: Harvard University Press, 1966).

QUESTIONS

Energy

7.1 Define the term "thermodynamic system." What types of interactions do we consider to take place between a system and its surroundings?

7.2 What will be the sign on the value of the heat transferred by a system if an endothermic process has occurred? What will be the sign for an exothermic process?

7.3 What is internal energy? What can happen to a system in which an internal energy change is occurring?

7.4 State the first law of thermodynamics in equation form. Explain this equation in your own words.

7.5 What is the sign convention for work being done on the surroundings by the system? What is the sign convention for work done by the surroundings on the system?

7.6 What happens to ΔE for a system during a process in which (a) $q > 0$ and $w > 0$, (b) $q = w = 0$, (c) $q < 0$ and $w > 0$?

7.7 What happens to ΔE for a system during a process in which (a) $q < 0$ and $w < 0$, (b) $q = 0$ and $w > 0$, (c) $q > 0$ and $w < 0$?

7.8 What is the special name given to the heat exchanged between a system and its surroundings under constant pressure conditions? What is the symbol used to represent this quantity?

7.9 During a process, the volume of a system remained constant. What is the value of the work for the process? Will the heat exchanged between the system and its surroundings be equal to ΔH or ΔE?

7.10 For each of the following chemical and physical changes carried out at constant pressure, decide whether work is done by the system (the substances undergoing the change) on the surroundings or by the surroundings on the system or whether the amount of work is negligible.

(a) $4HNO_3(l) + P_4O_{10}(s) \longrightarrow 2N_2O_5(s) + 4HPO_3(s)$

(b) $2MnO_4^- + 5H_2O_2(aq) + 6H^+ \longrightarrow$
$$2Mn^{2+} + 5O_2(g) + 8H_2O(l)$$

(c) $CO_2(g) + H_2O(l) + CaCO_3(s) \longrightarrow Ca^{2+} + 2HCO_3^-$

7.11 Repeat Question 7.10 for

(a) $C_6H_6(l) \longrightarrow C_6H_6(s)$

(b) $\frac{1}{2}N_2(g) + \frac{3}{2}H_2(g) \longrightarrow NH_3(g)$
(c) $3H_2S(g) + 2HNO_3(g) \longrightarrow 2NO(g) + 4H_2O(l) + 3S(s)$

7.12 The equation for the combustion of hydrazine under constant volume conditions is

$$H_2NNH_2(l) + O_2(g) \longrightarrow N_2(g) + 2H_2O(l)$$

Discuss the relationships among ΔE, ΔH, q_V, and w.

7.13 Repeat Question 7.12 for

$$3O_2(g) \xrightarrow{\Delta} 2O_3(g)$$

carried out under constant pressure conditions.

Heats of Reaction and Other Enthalpy Changes

7.14 Define the term "heat of reaction." If the chemical reaction occurs at constant pressure, to what is the value of q equal?

7.15 What is the standard state of water at (a) -5 °C, (b) 5 °C, (c) 93 °C, (d) 103 °C?

7.16 What is the standard state of chlorine at (a) -175 °C, (b) -100 °C, (c) -65 °C, (d) 25 °C, (e) 1275 °C? See Table 7.5 for the melting and boiling points of Cl_2.

7.17 Define the term "standard heat of formation" of a substance. Write the thermochemical equation for the formation of $Al_2O_3(s)$ from $Al(s)$ and $O_2(g)$.

7.18 Following is a list of the standard states at 25 °C of several elements: C(graphite), $Cl_2(g)$, Na(s), $Br_2(l)$, Ca(s), $S_8(s)$, and $O_2(g)$. Write chemical equations for the formation from the elements of (a) $CCl_4(l)$, (b) NaBr(s), and (c) $CaSO_4(s)$.

7.19 Define the term "standard heat of combustion" of a substance. Write the thermochemical equation for the combustion at 25 °C of ethyl alcohol, $CH_3CH_2OH(l)$.

7.20 Write chemical equations for the complete combustion of (a) benzene, $C_6H_6(l)$ and (b) methyl alcohol, $CH_3OH(l)$.

7.21 State Hess's law. Why is it important in thermochemistry?

7.22 As energy is added or removed during a phase change, what happens to the temperature of the system?

7.23 Which reaction will be more exothermic? Why?
(a) $A(g) + B(s) \longrightarrow C(l) + H_2O(g) \qquad \Delta H_1$
(b) $A(g) + B(s) \longrightarrow C(l) + H_2O(l) \qquad \Delta H_2$

7.24* Suppose it were possible to melt a substance and then vaporize it at the same temperature. What would be the relationship among the heats of fusion, vaporization, and sublimation?

Measuring Heat

7.25 What does the symbol ΔT represent? Will ΔT be positive or negative for a system which is getting hotter?

7.26 What does the term "heat capacity" mean? What do we call the heat capacity of a mole of a substance? What do we call the heat capacity of a gram of a substance?

7.27 What is the name of the device used for measuring the heat absorbed or released during a thermochemical process?

7.28 Define the term "heat capacity of the calorimeter." Why is this usually determined experimentally? Briefly explain two methods for determining the heat capacity of the calorimeter.

7.29* What is the advantage of designing a calorimeter so that the contribution by the heat capacity of the calorimeter to the calculation of the heat is negligible? What is the advantage if the contribution by the heat capacity of the calorimeter is so large that the heat capacities of the calorimeter's contents are negligible?

Answers to Selected Questions

7.7 (a) $\Delta E < 0$; (b) $\Delta E > 0$; (c) ΔE is > 0, $= 0$, or < 0 depending on the numerical values of q and w

7.11 (a) Work is negligible; (b) and (c) work is done by the surroundings on the system.

7.13 $\Delta H = q_P > 0$, $\Delta E > 0$, $w > 0$

7.15 (a) ice, (b) liquid, (c) liquid, (d) steam

7.18 (a) C(graphite) + $2Cl_2(g) \longrightarrow CCl_4(l)$, (b) Na(s) + $\frac{1}{2}Br_2(l) \longrightarrow$ NaBr(s), (c) Ca(s) + $\frac{1}{8}S_8(s) + 2O_2(g) \longrightarrow CaSO_4(s)$

7.20 (a) $C_6H_6(l) + \frac{15}{2}O_2(g) \longrightarrow 6CO_2(g) + 3H_2O(l)$, (b) $CH_3OH(l) + \frac{3}{2}O_2(g) \longrightarrow CO_2(g) + 2H_2O(l)$

7.23 ΔH_2 will be more exothermic because it includes heat that is released by the condensation of the steam.

7.24 $\Delta H_{sub} = \Delta H_{vap} + \Delta H_{fusion}$

PROBLEMS

Energy, Heat, and Work

7.1 A system performs 460. L atm of pressure-volume work (1 L atm $= 101.325$ J) on its surroundings and absorbs 6300 J of heat from its surroundings. What is the change in internal energy of the system? *Answer* $-40,300$ J

7.2 A system receives 45 J of electrical work, delivers 165 J of pressure-volume work, and releases 212 J of heat. What is the change in internal energy of the system?

7.3 One mole of an ideal gas will expand from 22.41 L to 22.49 L as it is heated from 0 °C to 1 °C at one atmosphere external pressure. The work for this process is given by $w = -P_{ext}\,\Delta V$. What is the work performed by this gas on the surroundings? (1 L atm $= 101.325$ J.)

7.4 What will be the volume change if 125 J of work is done on a system containing an ideal gas? The surroundings exert a constant pressure of 5.2 atm. *Answer* Volume will decrease by 0.24 L

7.5* The following processes were studied at 25 °C.
(a) $CaO(s) + CO_2(g) \longrightarrow CaCO_3(s)$
(b) $I_2(s) \longrightarrow I_2(g)$

Assuming molar quantities of reactants and products, the work that the system exchanges with its surroundings in each case can be calculated using $w = -RT$ (sum of n of gaseous products − sum of n of gaseous reactants). Calculate the work for each of the reactions assuming a constant external pressure of 1.00 atm.

7.6* Repeat Problem 7.5 for the following reactions:
(a) $CaSO_4 \cdot 5H_2O(s) \longrightarrow CaSO_4(s) + 5H_2O(g)$
(b) $2NH_3(g) + H_2SO_4(aq) \longrightarrow (NH_4)_2SO_4(aq)$
Answer (a) − 12.4 kJ, (b) 4.96 kJ

Heats of Reaction and Changes of State

7.7 Compare the quantities of heat liberated per mole of iron formed when the oxides of Fe_3O_4 and Fe_2O_3 react with aluminum.

$3Fe_3O_4(s) + 8Al(s) \longrightarrow 4Al_2O_3(s) + 9Fe(s) \Delta H° = -3347.6$ kJ

$Fe_2O_3(s) + 2Al(s) \longrightarrow Al_2O_3(s) + 2Fe(s)$ $\Delta H° = -851.4$ kJ

7.8 When a welder uses an acetylene torch, it is the combustion of acetylene that liberates the intense heat for welding metal together. The equation for this process is

$$2C_2H_2(g) + 5O_2(g) \longrightarrow 4CO_2(g) + 2H_2O(g)$$

The heat of combustion of acetylene is − 1300. kJ/mol. What amount of heat is liberated when 0.260 kg of C_2H_2 is burned? *Answer* 1.30×10^7 J

7.9 Write the chemical equation for the formation of one mole of methane, $CH_4(g)$, from the elements. Find the heat of formation of CH_4 at 20 °C from the following thermochemical equations and values of heats of combustion at 20 °C.

$H_2(g) + \frac{1}{2}O_2(g) \longrightarrow H_2O(l)$	$\Delta H° = -286.10$ kJ
$C(s) + O_2(g) \longrightarrow CO_2(g)$	$\Delta H° = -394.89$ kJ
$CH_4(g) + 2O_2(g) \longrightarrow CO_2(g) + 2H_2O(l)$	$\Delta H° = -882.0$ kJ

7.10 Find the heat of formation of liquid hydrogen peroxide at 25 °C from the following thermochemical equations.

$H_2(g) + \frac{1}{2}O_2(g) \longrightarrow H_2O(g)$	$\Delta H° = -241.818$ kJ
$2H(g) + O(g) \longrightarrow H_2O(g)$	$\Delta H° = -926.919$ kJ
$2H(g) + 2O(g) \longrightarrow H_2O_2(g)$	$\Delta H° = -1070.60$ kJ
$2O(g) \longrightarrow O_2(g)$	$\Delta H° = -498.340$ kJ
$H_2O_2(l) \longrightarrow H_2O_2(g)$	$\Delta H° = 51.46$ kJ

Answer − 187.79 kJ

7.11 Use the following thermochemical equations to find $\Delta H_f°$ for $CuCl_2(s)$.

$2Cu(s) + Cl_2(g) \longrightarrow 2CuCl(s)$	$\Delta H° = -274.5$ kJ
$2CuCl(s) + Cl_2(g) \longrightarrow 2CuCl_2(s)$	$\Delta H° = -165.7$ kJ

7.12 Find $\Delta H°$ for making chloroform ($CHCl_3$) from methane

$$CH_4(g) + 3Cl_2(g) \longrightarrow CHCl_3(l) + 3HCl(g)$$

using the following equations.

$\frac{1}{2}H_2(g) + \frac{1}{2}Cl_2(g) \longrightarrow HCl(g)$	$\Delta H° = -92.31$ kJ
$C(s) + 2H_2(g) \longrightarrow CH_4(g)$	$\Delta H° = -74.81$ kJ

$C(s) + \frac{1}{2}H_2(g) + \frac{3}{2}Cl_2(g) \longrightarrow CHCl_3(l)$ $\Delta H° = -134.47$ kJ
Answer − 336.58 kJ

7.13 Aragonite, a mineral, undergoes the following reaction in a very dilute solution of carbonic acid (CO_2 in H_2O).

$$CaCO_3(\text{aragonite}) + H_2CO_3(aq) \Longleftrightarrow Ca(HCO_3)_2(aq)$$

This means that the $CaCO_3$ can be dissolved in one place and transported to another in the form of $Ca(HCO_3)_2$—a very important step in the formation of stalagmites and stalactites. Calculate the heat of reaction at 25 °C given that the heat of formation is − 1207 kJ/mol for $CaCO_3$(aragonite), −699 kJ/mol for $H_2CO_3(aq)$, and − 1925 kJ/mol for $Ca(HCO_3)_2(aq)$.

7.14 Use the data given in Table 7.2 to calculate the heats of reaction at 25 °C for the following reactions.
(a) $2HI(g) + F_2(g) \longrightarrow 2HF(g) + I_2(s)$
(b) $2CaSO_4 \cdot 2H_2O(s) \longrightarrow (CaSO_4)_2 \cdot H_2O(s) + 3H_2O(l)$
(c) $2SO_2(g) + O_2(g) \longrightarrow 2SO_3(g)$

7.15 Repeat Problem 7.14 for
(a) $2Fe_3O_4(s) + \frac{1}{2}O_2(g) \longrightarrow 3Fe_2O_3$
(b) $KCl(s) + Na(s) \longrightarrow K(s) + NaCl(s)$
(c) $SO_3(g) + H_2O(l) \longrightarrow H_2SO_4(l)$
Answer (a) −235.8 kJ, (b) 24.87 kJ, (c) −132.44 kJ

7.16 The heat of formation at 1000 K for $Al(s)$ is −10.519 kJ/mol, for $Al(l)$ it is 0.000 kJ/mol, and for $Al(g)$ it is 310.114 kJ/mol. Find the heat of (a) fusion, (b) vaporization, and (c) sublimation at this temperature. *Answer* (a) 10.519 kJ/mol, (b) 310.114 kJ/mol, (c) 320.633 kJ/mol

7.17* A sample of coke contains 90.9% carbon by mass. Assuming that the heat produced by the burning of this coke comes from the combustion of C to CO_2, calculate the total quantity of heat obtainable at 25 °C through the burning of exactly 1 kg of the coke. If the coke sample contained 0.1% sulfur by mass and this sulfur burned completely to sulfur dioxide, SO_2, what is the total quantity of heat that would result from this source when the coke was burned? The heats of combustion of C and S are − 394 kJ/mol and −297 kJ/mol, respectively.

Heat Flow – Heat Capacity

7.18 What amount of heat must be added to one mole of ethyl alcohol (CH_3CH_2OH) to heat it from −5 °C to 35 °C? See Table 7.6 for heat capacity data.

7.19 What amount of heat must be removed from 15.0 g of red phosphorus to cool it from 25 °C to 23 °C? The molar heat capacity of red phosphorus is 21.21 J/K mol. *Answer* $q = -20$ J

7.20 The addition of 1698 J of heat to 30.0 g of acetic acid, CH_3COOH, caused a temperature increase of 27.32 °C. Calculate the molar heat capacity and the specific heat of acetic acid.

7.21 Exactly 250 J of energy was removed from one gram samples of oxygen and ozone. The O_2 cooled from 502 °C to 229 °C and the O_3 cooled from 498 °C to 192 °C. Which substance has the higher molar heat capacity? *Answer* O_3; heat capacity is 29.3 J/K mol for O_2 and 39.2 J/K mol for O_3

7.22* In 1819 Pierre Dulong and Alexis Petit recognized that for all solid metallic elements at room temperature (except for a few with very small atomic masses) the product of the atomic mass of the element and its specific heat is approximately a constant

(atomic mass)(specific heat) = 26 J/K mol

Using the following specific heat data, show that this empirical relationship is true.

Al	0.900 J/K g	Fe	0.452 J/K g
Be	1.824	Pb	0.130
Cr	0.460	Sn	0.226

7.23* A temperature increase of 54.0 °C was observed upon the addition of 76.5 J of heat to a 2.71 g sample of an unknown metal. Calculate the specific heat of the metal. Using the rule of Dulong–Petit (see Problem 7.22), identify the unknown metal. *Answer* 0.523 J/K g; Ti, V, or Cr

7.24 What is the final temperature of a system prepared by placing a 10.00 g block of aluminum (specific heat = 0.900 J/K g) originally at 75.0 °C on top of a 100.00 g block of aluminum originally at 25.0 °C? Assume that no heat escapes to the surroundings.

7.25 Find the final temperature of the system prepared by placing 100.0 g of hot copper metal (specific heat = 0.385 J/K g) originally at 98.8 °C into 100.00 g of water (specific heat = 4.184 J/K g) at 25.0 °C. Assume that no heat escapes to the surroundings. *Answer* 31.2 °C

7.26 A 45.2 g sample of water at 16.8 °C was poured into a glass beaker originally at 25.3 °C. The final temperature of the system was 18.6 °C. What is the specific heat of glass if the beaker has a mass of 47.9 g? Assume that no heat escapes to the surroundings. The specific heat of water is 4.184 J/K g.

7.27 Exactly 3000 J of heat was added to the system described in Problem 7.26 consisting of the beaker and water at 18.6 °C. What is the final temperature of the system? *Answer* 30 °C

Calorimetry

7.28 A calorimeter was calibrated by pouring 50.0 g of hot water into 100.0 g of cold water in the calorimeter. The original temperature of the hot water was 83.7 °C and of the cold water and calorimeter was 26.3 °C. The final temperature of the combined system was 41.2 °C. What is the value of the heat capacity of the calorimeter? The specific heat of water is 4.184 J/K g.

7.29 A calorimeter contained 75.0 g of water originally at 16.95 °C. A 75.2 g sample of iron at 63.14 °C was added, giving a final temperature of 19.68 °C for the system. Calculate the heat capacity of the calorimeter. The specific heat is 4.184 J/K g for H_2O and 0.450 J/K g for Fe. *Answer* 225 J/K

7.30 A calorimeter was calibrated by adding 100.0 g of dilute HCl to a like amount of dilute NaOH. The resulting temperature change of the calorimeter and of the NaCl solution formed as a result of the reaction (specific heat = 4.06 J/K g) was 0.627 °C. The amount of heat released by the reaction was 558.4 J. Find the heat capacity of the calorimeter.

7.31 A bomb calorimeter was constructed so that any contribution of the products to the heat flow could be neglected. A 1.298 g sample of benzoic acid was burned and the observed temperature change was 4.32 °C. The heat of combustion of benzoic acid is −26,440 J/g. What is the heat capacity of the calorimeter? *Answer* 7940 J/K

7.32 A 0.241 g piece of magnesium metal was added to 100.0 g of dilute hydrochloric acid in a calorimeter. A temperature increase of 10.89 °C was observed as a result of the reaction

$$Mg(s) + 2HCl(aq) \longrightarrow MgCl_2(aq) + H_2(g)$$

The specific heat of the $MgCl_2$-HCl solution is 4.21 J/K g and the heat capacity of the calorimeter is 2.74 J/K. Calculate the heat of reaction per mole of Mg that reacts. *Answer* −466 kJ

7.33* (a) A student heated a sample of a metal weighing 32.6 g to 99.83 °C and put it into 100.0 g of water at 23.62 °C in a calorimeter. The final temperature was 24.41 °C. The student calculated the specific heat of the metal, neglecting to use the heat capacity of the calorimeter. The specific heat is 4.184 J/K g for H_2O. What was his answer?

The metal was known to be either Cr, Mo, or W and by comparing the value of the specific heat to those of the metals (Cr, 0.460; Mo, 0.250; W, 0.135 J/K g), the student identified the metal. What was the metal?

(b) A student at the next laboratory bench did the same experiment, got the same data, and used the heat capacity of the calorimeter in his calculations. The heat capacity of the calorimeter was 410 J/K. Was his identification of the metal different? *Answer* (a) 0.13 J/K g, W; (b) 0.26 J/K g, Mo

Additional Problems

7.34 Calculate the enthalpy change for heating 10.0 g of water from −5.0 °C to 25.0 °C. The heat of fusion is 6009.5 J/mol and the specific heat is 2.1 J/K g for ice and 4.184 J/K g for water. *Answer* 4490 J

7.35* The heat of formation of HCl(g) is −92.307 kJ/mol at 25 °C. The value of ΔH_f° at 500. K can be found by (a) calculating the enthalpy change for cooling $\frac{1}{2}$ mol of $H_2(g)$ and $\frac{1}{2}$ mol of $Cl_2(g)$ from 500. K to 298 K; (b) adding the heat of reaction at 298 K to the answer to part (a); and (c) adding the enthalpy change for heating one mole of HCl(g) from 298 K to 500. K to the result of part (b).

$$\frac{1}{2}H_2(g) + \frac{1}{2}Cl_2(g) \xrightarrow{\Delta H_{500.}^\circ = ?} HCl(g)$$
$$\downarrow \Delta H_a^\circ \qquad\qquad \uparrow \Delta H_c^\circ$$
$$\frac{1}{2}H_2(g) + \frac{1}{2}Cl_2(g) \xrightarrow{\Delta H_{298.b}^\circ} HCl(g)$$

Find ΔH_f° at 500. K, given the heat capacities of 33.907 J/K mol for $Cl_2(g)$, 29.12 J/K mol for HCl(g), and 28.824 J/K mol for $H_2(g)$. Is the reaction more or less exothermic at 500. K than at 298 K? *Answer* −92.76 kJ; the reaction is more exothermic at 500. K

CHAPTER 8

Electronic Structure and the Periodic Table

Imagine the time when new elements were being discovered in nature and their properties investigated. Some elements were found to be very similar to each other, and others were very different. Lithium and sodium, for example, both have very similar properties. Fluorine and chlorine are also very similar to each other, but they are very different from lithium and sodium. Following the natural human desire to arrange things into categories, many individuals sought an organizing principle for the properties of the elements.

When the first 17 elements were arranged in the order of their atomic masses, seven elements were found to fall between lithium and sodium. What an exciting moment it must have been when it was recognized for the first time that seven elements also lie between fluorine and chlorine, and between other similar elements. The periodic table, in which elements with similar properties fall near each other, originated in such observations.

The periodic table is the most meaningful guide that we have to organizing the properties of the elements and their compounds. We now know that most of the properties of matter that are of interest in chemistry are intimately related to the arrangement of electrons in atoms. It is this arrangement that provides the explanation for the placement of elements in the periodic table. The goal of this chapter is to explain the connection between the electrons in atoms and the periodic table arrangement of the elements.

QUANTUM THEORY

The **periodic table** (see inside front cover) groups the elements in order of increasing atomic number in such a way that elements with similar properties fall near each other. As the atomic number increases, the number of electrons in each atom also increases (Section 3.9). A full appreciation of **electronic structure**—how the electrons are arranged in atoms—is essential for understanding the similarities and periodicities of the elements. Understanding electronic structure, in turn, requires a brief excursion into classical and modern physics. To begin, we must look at the behavior of light, the energy of light, and some aspects of the interaction of light with matter.

You may wonder why it is important to discuss light in order to understand the periodic table. It turns out that light and electrons in atoms have many properties in common. Only when what physicists had been learning about light and what chemists had been learning about atoms were brought together in the 1920s were both the arrangement of electrons in atoms and the arrangement of the elements in the periodic table fully explained.

In Sections 8.1–8.9 we concentrate on presenting the facts and theories that provide the basis for our modern picture of electronic structure. As we have said, the purpose of this material is to provide a foundation for our study of the periodic table. The topics are discussed mainly in a qualitative way. Except for understanding the meaning of some symbols and units, you will not be asked to use the mathematics related to either classical mechanics or quantum mechanics.

The word "classical" is generally used for anything that was established and important in the past. Physics, like all of the sciences, began with observations of the world around us. The major areas of interest that developed in classical physics were mechanics (the motion of objects), electricity and magnetism (the interactions of charged particles and charged particles in motion, which result in magnetic forces), thermodynamics (the study of heat and energy), and optics (the study of light). Experiments with large, easily observed objects led to laws explaining phenomena in each of these fields. Classical mechanics, for example, is based on Isaac Newton's laws of motion from the seventeenth century. One physicist of a later time (Werner Heisenberg) put it this way: "The concepts of classical physics are just a refinement of the concepts of daily life and are an essential part of the language which forms the basis of all natural science."

When something is described as "classical" it is almost certain that in modern times it has either been replaced or had added to it something new and quite different. The essential difference between classical physics and modern physics lies in the scale of what they deal with. In the late nineteenth century, physics and chemistry began to look at the behavior of tiny particles and at phenomena that are *not* part of daily life. The old laws were not in harmony with the new observations and a change became inevitable—a change that has been called "the greatest and most radical revolution in natural philosophy since the time of Newton." In the early 1900s a new physics was born.

Classical physics was not replaced. A new set of theories and laws was developed to deal with small particles like electrons that move at great speeds. The classical laws are not "wrong"—they are fine for apples falling out of trees. For electrons in atoms, modern physics is better.

In the following sections you will encounter the names of some of the scientists who played crucial roles in the transition from classical to modern physics. The Historical Aside at the end of Section 8.9 puts the contributions of these men in the context of their time.

8.1 LIGHT AS WAVES   Early physicists found that the description of light as a series of waves traveling through space successfully accounts for many of the properties of light. Generally, waves are set in motion by a vibrating body, just as you set water waves in motion by moving your hand in a pond. In the case of light, the vibrations were presumed to be those of electrons, atoms, or groups of atoms. The waves that result are waves of electromagnetic energy, in the form of fluctuating electric and magnetic fields.

The terminology and units of measurement that are used to describe light are based on the picture of waves traveling through space. **Wavelength** (λ, Greek lambda) is the distance between any two similar points on adjacent waves (Figure 8.1). The **frequency** (ν, Greek nu) of light is the number of complete waves, also

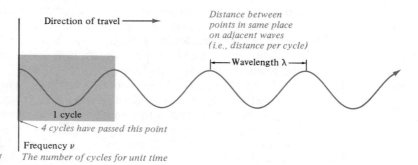

Figure 8.1
Wavelength and Frequency

Table 8.1

Units for Wavelength The preferred units for wavelength are those based on the meter. Although angstroms, millimicrons, and microns are no longer recommended, they are still seen in older publications. The use of the units marked * is being discontinued.

Unit Abbreviation	Unit	Unit equal to	
		Meters	Nanometers
m	meter	—	1×10^9 nm
cm	centimeter	1×10^{-2} m	1×10^7 nm
μm	micrometer	1×10^{-6} m	1×10^3 nm
μ	micron*	1×10^{-6} m	1×10^3 nm
nm	nanometer	1×10^{-9} m	—
mμ	millimicron*	1×10^{-9} m	—
Å	angstrom*	1×10^{-10} m	0.1 nm

known as the number of *cycles*, passing a given point in a unit of time (see Figure 8.1).

Wavelength has units of length. For light, wavelengths are now often given in nanometers, nm (see Table 8.1 for other units that are sometimes encountered). Frequency has units of cycles per unit time. Frequency is usually given in cycles per second. Since cycles is a dimensionless quantity, the unit is written as s^{-1}, reciprocal seconds, with the word "cycles" left out. In the SI system one cycle per second is a hertz, abbreviated Hz; 1 Hz = 1 s^{-1} (for the range of wavelengths and frequencies over the electromagnetic spectrum, see Tools of Chemistry: Electromagnetic Radiation and Spectra).

The speed of light in a vacuum is one of the fundamental constants of nature and does not vary with the wavelength or any other properties of the light

$$\underset{\substack{\text{speed of light} \\ \text{in a vacuum}}}{} c = 2.998 \times 10^8 \text{ m/s}$$

The speed of light in air is slightly less than the speed in a vacuum, but the difference is so small that the value given above can be used in most cases.

The wavelength and frequency of light are related to the speed of light by the equation

$$\underset{\substack{\text{speed of} \\ \text{light}}}{} c = \overset{\text{wavelength}}{\lambda} \nu \leftarrow \text{frequency} \qquad \textbf{(8.1)}$$

or, with the wavelength expressed in meters, the frequency in reciprocal seconds, and the speed of light given to three significant figures

$$3.00 \times 10^8 \text{ m/s} = \underset{\text{meters/second}}{\lambda} \quad \underset{\text{meters s}^{-1}}{\nu} \qquad \textbf{(8.1a)}$$

Equation (8.1) allows the calculation of frequency from wavelength or of wavelength from frequency. Another quantity used to characterize waves is the wave number.

$$\underset{\text{wave number}}{} \bar{\nu} = \frac{1}{\lambda}$$

The **wave number** is the number of wavelengths per unit of length covered. Its unit is the reciprocal of the wavelength unit, and it is often given in cm^{-1}. These relationships are illustrated in Table 8.2 for red and yellow light.

Table 8.2
Properties of Yellow and Red Light

	Yellow Light	Red Light
Wavelength (distance per cycle)		
	5.8×10^{-7} m	7×10^{-7} m
	5.8×10^{-5} cm	7×10^{-5} cm
	580 nm	700 nm
	5800 Å	7000 Å
Frequency (cycles per second), $\nu = \dfrac{c}{\lambda}$		
	$\dfrac{3.0 \times 10^8 \text{ m/s}}{5.8 \times 10^{-7} \text{ m}} = 5.2 \times 10^{14} \text{ s}^{-1}$	$\dfrac{3.0 \times 10^8 \text{ m/s}}{7 \times 10^{-7} \text{ m}} = 4 \times 10^{14} \text{ s}^{-1}$
	$= 5.2 \times 10^{14}$ Hz	$= 4 \times 10^{14}$ Hz
Wave number, $\bar{\nu} = \dfrac{1}{\lambda}$		
	$\dfrac{1}{5.8 \times 10^{-5} \text{ cm}} = 1.7 \times 10^4 \text{ cm}^{-1}$	$\dfrac{1}{7 \times 10^{-5} \text{ cm}} = 1 \times 10^4 \text{ cm}^{-1}$

EXAMPLE 8.1
Wave Nature of Light

Blue-green light has a wavelength of about 520 nm in the visible range of the spectrum. What is the frequency corresponding to this color?

Given the wavelength and wanting to know the frequency, we use the relationship between these two quantities and the speed of light given by Equation (8.1a).

$$\nu = \frac{c}{\lambda} = \frac{3.00 \times 10^8 \text{ m/s}}{(520 \text{ nm})(1 \text{ m}/10^9 \text{ nm})} = 5.8 \times 10^{14} \text{ s}^{-1} = 5.8 \times 10^{14} \text{ Hz}.$$

Note that the conversion factor based on 1 m $= 10^9$ nm must be used to convert the wavelength to meters. The frequency is 5.8×10^{14} Hz.

Exercise What is the wavelength of yellow light having a frequency of 5.2×10^{14} s^{-1}? *Answer* 580 nm

---

EXAMPLE 8.2
Wave Nature of Light

What is the wave number of the blue-green light of wavelength 520 nm described in Example 8.1? Express the value in units of cm^{-1}.

The wave number is simply the reciprocal of the wavelength

$$\bar{\nu} = \frac{1}{\lambda} = \frac{1}{(520 \text{ nm})(1 \text{ m}/10^9 \text{ nm})(10^2 \text{ cm/m})} = 1.9 \times 10^4 \text{ cm}^{-1}$$

The wave number of the blue-green light is 1.9×10^4 cm^{-1}.

Exercise What is the wavelength of yellow light having a wave number of 1.7×10^4 cm^{-1}? *Answer* 590 nm

---

Two properties characteristic of light waves are interference and diffraction, both of which can be seen in water waves on the surface of a pond. If you throw two stones into the pond, the two sets of wave patterns interfere with each other in the area where they meet. When identical waves meet in phase, that is, so that their high and low points match up, they reinforce each other. This is called *constructive interference* (Figure 8.2a). In the opposite situation, identical waves meet out of

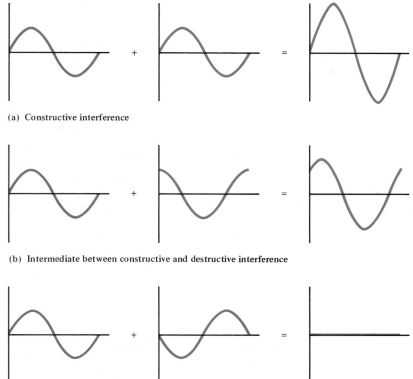

(a) Constructive interference

(b) Intermediate between constructive and destructive interference

Figure 8.2
Wave Interference (a) The waves are in phase and reinforce one another. (b) The waves are partly out of phase. (c) The waves are completely out of phase and cancel one another out.

(c) Destructive interference

phase, so that the high points of one exactly match the low points of the other, and they cancel each other. This is *destructive interference* (Figure 8.2c).

Diffraction is the spreading of waves as they pass obstacles or openings comparable in size to their wavelength (Figure 8.3). You can, for example, see waves spreading out as they pass between rocks at the edge of the pond. In circumstances where light passes through two slits, the diffracted light waves interfere with each other and produce a pattern of light and dark — a diffraction patern — on a screen placed in their path (Figure 8.4).

When interference and diffraction are observed, they are interpreted as proof that the passage of waves has taken place.

Figure 8.3
Diffraction The amount of spreading depends upon the size of the opening relative to the wavelength. If the opening is very much larger than the wavelength (as with a beam of visible light passing through a keyhole) the effect is undetectable.

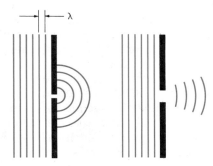

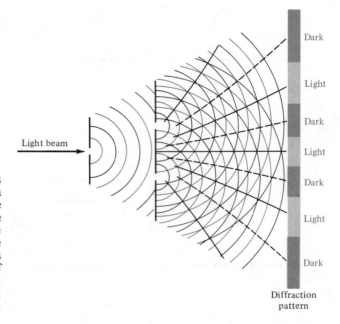

Light beam →

Dark

Light

Dark

Light

Dark

Light

Dark

Diffraction
pattern

Figure 8.4
A Diffraction Pattern Such a
pattern is produced by the
interference of light waves that have
passed though two or more
openings close in size to the
wavelength of the light. Dark bands
appear where waves arrive out of
phase and cancel one another out,
light bands where they arrive in
phase and reinforce one another.

8.2 LIGHT AS PARTICLES: THE
BIRTH OF QUANTUM THEORY

For a time, the description of light as waves was satisfactory in answering most of the
questions that were being asked about light. But then questions arose that could only
by answered in a different way—by describing light as consisting of separate
particles. You might think, as many scientists once did, that one description had to
be right and one wrong. Not true, for both are necessary to fully account for the
behavior of light. It was later found that electrons in atoms, as discussed in the next
section, can also be described as both waves and particles. This existence of two ways
of describing the behavior of light and small particles is referred to as *wave–particle
duality:* In some ways light behaves like continuous waves and in some ways it
behaves like individual particles. Similarly, in some ways matter behaves like
individual particles and in some ways it behaves like waves. Wave–particle duality
should not be thought of as something strange in the behavior of the natural world,
but as a result of the way that we observe and describe the world.

The shortcomings in the classical wave model of light first became apparent
when physicists began to study the energy of light. In classical theory, the energy of a
wave can have any value along a continuum. To make an analogy, your car can be
driven at any speed along a continuum. From standing still you can gradually
accelerate to the speed at which you choose to travel. Whether this speed is 40 km/h,
80 km/h, 80.5 km/h, or 80.501 km/h, any speed is possible.

The new description of light began with the realization that at each wavelength
light does not have available a continuum of energy values, as classical theory had
assumed. Rather, light can be regarded as made up of particles each of which carries a
definite amount of energy, referred to as a **quantum.**

A quantum is like a package or bundle of something that is available only in
specific and separate amounts. A quantum is somewhat like the scoops of ice cream
in an ice cream cone that you buy at a store. You can order one scoop, or two scoops,
or three scoops, but not 1.5 or 2.35 scoops. The amount of ice cream you get must be
one, two, three, or *n* times the size of the scoop (Figure 8.5). Something that is
quantized is restricted to amounts that are *whole-number multiples* of the basic unit,
or quantum, for the particular system. **Quantum theory** is a general term for the idea
that energy is quantized and the consequences of that idea. Like wave–particle
duality, quantum theory has also been extended to electrons in atoms (discussed in
the next section).

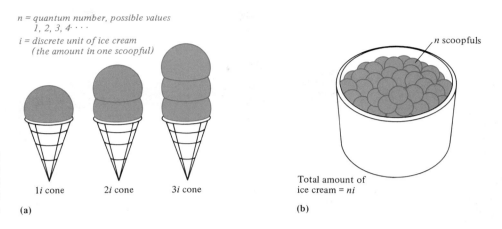

**Figure 8.5
If Ice Cream Were
Quantized . . .** (a) Quantized ice
cream in cones. (b) Quantized ice
cream in a tub.

The quantization of energy was introduced by Max Planck in 1900 to explain the emission of light by hot bodies at various temperatures. This effect can be seen in the change of color from orange to "red hot" to "white hot" as a piece of metal is heated. To account for the observed distribution of the frequencies of the emitted light, Planck found it necessary to abandon the view of radiation as waves with continuous energy. He proposed that the light was produced by vibrating groups of atoms.

The energy of these groups of atoms could be related to their frequency by a constant h, now called Planck's constant, according to the following equation:

Planck's equation: $E = h\nu$

$$E = h\nu \tag{8.2}$$

Planck proposed that radiation could only be absorbed or given off in amounts of $h\nu$. Like the scoops of ice cream, the radiation energy could, according to Planck, be transferred only in small-whole-number multiples of $h\nu$, that is, 1 $h\nu$, or 2 $h\nu$, or 3 $h\nu$, and so on.

Planck's constant, h, is a fundamental, universal constant. It has the units of energy × time and appears in the mathematical statements of many laws. A modern value for h is

$$h = 6.6262 \times 10^{-34}\ \text{J s} \tag{8.3}$$

The units in Equation (8.2) would be

$$E = h \qquad \nu$$
joules   *joule* ~~*second*~~ ~~*seconds*~~$^{-1}$

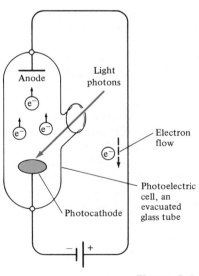

**Figure 8.6
A Photoelectric Cell** The
photocathode is made of a metal
that exhibits the photoelectric effect.
Such a photoelectric cell is an
essential part of an "electric eye"
device used for example, in
automatic door openers. When the
light beam is interrupted the
photoelectric current no longer
flows and this triggers opening of
the door.

In 1905 Albert Einstein extended the quantum concept to electromagnetic radiation. Not only is the energy of the radiator quantized, but, Einstein proposed, the energy of the radiation is also quantized in accordance with the relationship $E = h\nu$. This was a bit like proposing that the ice cream in the tub is already frozen in scoop-sized portions (see Figure 8.5b). Here was the first suggestion that radiation could behave like a wave, yet also be divided into packets of energy like a stream of particles.

By assuming that light is quantized, Einstein was able to explain the **photoelectric effect,** in which electrons are released by certain metals (particularly Cs and the other alkali metals, Li, Na, K, and Rb) when light shines on them. (The photoelectric effect is used in practical devices such as automatic door openers; Figure 8.6.) Previous attempts to explain the photoelectric effect had encountered a dilemma.

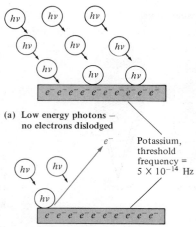

Figure 8.7
The Photoelectric Effect It takes energy equal to or greater than the $h\nu$ threshold to knock electrons out of a metal. (a) High-intensity red light, $\nu = 4.5 \times 10^{14}$ Hz; (b) low-intensity yellow light, $\nu = 5.2 \times 10^{14}$ Hz. Note that the intensity of the light is related only to the number of photons per unit time; it has no bearing on the amount of energy carried by each individual photon.

(a) Low energy photons — no electrons dislodged

Potassium, threshold frequency = 5×10^{-14} Hz

(b) Higher energy photons — electrons dislodged

According to classical theory, light of any frequency should deliver more energy to a surface as the intensity of the light increases (that is, as more light per unit area reaches the surface). Electrons should be able to accumulate energy from the light until they have acquired enough to break away from the metal. But, in reality, electrons do not leave the surface when exposed to light of just any frequency. For each metal there is a characteristic minimum frequency—the *threshold frequency* —below which the photoelectric effect does not occur.

A red light ($\nu = 4.3 - 4.6 \times 10^{14}$ Hz) of any brightness can shine on a piece of potassium for hours and no photoelectrons will be released. But as soon as even a very weak yellow light ($\nu = 5.1 - 5.2 \times 10^{14}$ Hz) shines on potassium, the photoelectric effects begins. The threshold frequency of potassium is 5×10^{14} Hz.

A quantum of radiant energy is called a **photon.** If the energy of the incoming radiation is quantized according to $E = h\nu$, then the energy of the photons is determined by the frequency of the light. Each photon has energy equal to $h\nu$. Individual photons of high-intensity light of a given frequency have no greater energy than individual photons of a low-intensity light of the same frequency. High-intensity light just has *more* photons, each with the *same* energy (Figure 8.7).

Each photon can act like a particle in a collision with a single electron and deliver to that electron a maximum of 1 $h\nu$ of energy. The amount of energy delivered by one photon can increase only if the frequency increases. This explains the threshold frequency. When the frequency, and therefore the energy of the incoming light, is too low, not even one electron can acquire enough energy to escape. Red light can never initiate the photoelectric effect in potassium, because each photon has too little energy. (The energy is dissipated by an increase in the temperature of the metal.)

EXAMPLE 8.3
Particle Nature of Light

What is the energy of a photon of the blue-green light described in Example 8.1, which has $\lambda = 520$ nm and $\nu = 5.8 \times 10^{14}$ Hz?

The energy of a photon depends on its frequency and is given by $E = h\nu$:

$$E = h\nu = (6.626 \times 10^{-34} \text{ J s})(5.8 \times 10^{14} \text{ s}^{-1}) = 3.8 \times 10^{-19} \text{ J}$$

The energy of the light is 3.8×10^{-19} J for each photon, or quantum, of blue-green light.

Exercise   What is the energy of a photon of yellow light having $\nu = 5.2 \times 10^{14}$ s^{-1}? *Answer* 3.4×10^{-19} J

Electromagnetic Radiation and Spectra

When a rainbow forms in the sky or gasoline produces colored patterns as it floats on a puddle of water, sunlight is being broken up into colored light of different frequencies. The spectrum of light that we can see ranges from violet at 8×10^{14} Hz to red at 4×10^{14} Hz. But visible light is just a small portion of the entire spectrum of electromagnetic radiation (Figure A).

As discussed in Section 8.2, the energy of light is directly proportional to its frequency ($E = h\nu$). The electromagnetic spectrum (Figure A) extends from short-wavelength, high-frequency gamma rays of 10^{20} Hz and beyond at the high-energy end, to long-wavelength, low-frequency radiowaves of 10^8 Hz and less at the low-energy end.

When electromagnetic radiation interacts with matter, energy is exchanged, and atoms and molecules may absorb energy. In returning to their normal, more stable lower energy states, the atoms and molecules may then emit radiation in various parts of the electromagnetic spectrum.

The spectrum of radiation emitted by a substance that has absorbed energy is called an **emission spectrum.** Atoms, molecules, or ions that have absorbed radiation are spoken of as "excited." To produce an emission spectrum, energy is supplied to a sample by heating it or passing radiation through it, and the wavelength (or frequency) of the radiation emitted as the sample gives up the absorbed energy is recorded.

An absorption spectrum is like the photographic negative of an emission spectrum. A continuum of radiation is passed through a sample, which absorbs radiation of certain wavelengths. The missing wavelengths leave dark spaces in the bright continuous spectrum. The radiation *not* absorbed by the sample is recorded to produce an **absorption spectrum.**

The study of spectra is referred to as *spectroscopy*. An instrument that records the intensity and frequency of absorbed or emitted radiation is called a spectrophotometer, or simply a **spectrometer.** A spectrometer usually has five basic sections (Figure B): (1) a source of the beam of radiation; (2) an analyzer, which divides up the beam according to the property or properties being analyzed; (3) the sample holder; (4) the detector, which measures the quantity or quantities being determined (e.g., the intensity of radiation absorbed or emitted); (5) a display device, which makes the results visible as a graph, chart, or photograph.

Some of the applications of spectroscopy in the various regions of the electromagnetic spectrum are listed in Table A.

There are three types of distribution of radiation that appear in spectra. The sun and heated solids (such as the filament in a light bulb) produce **continuous spectra** —spectra in which radiation is emitted at all of the wavelengths in a region. The rainbow is a continuous spectrum. **Line spectra** are produced when radiation is

Short wavelength

High frequency

Wavelength (meters)		Frequency
10^{-12}	Gamma rays	10^{20}
10^{-10}	x rays	10^{18}
10^{-8}	Ultraviolet	10^{16}
10^{-6}	Visible	
	Infrared	10^{14}
10^{-4}		10^{12}
10^{-2}	Microwave	10^{10}
1	Radio	10^8

Increasing energy →

Long wavelength

Low frequency

Figure A
The Electromagnetic Spectrum

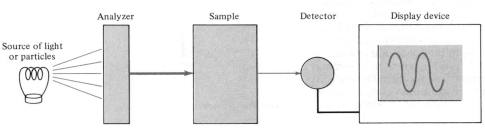

Source of light or particles

Analyzer

Sample

Detector

Display device

Figure B
A Spectrometer

Table A

Regions of the Electromagnetic Spectrum of Chief Interest to Chemistry

Gamma rays	Emitted in radioactive decay
x-Rays	Diffraction of x-rays used in determining crystal structure
Ultraviolet	Absorption spectra used for structure determination in organic and inorganic molecules
Visible	Emission and absorption spectra used for qualitative and quantitative identification of elements
Infrared	Absorption spectra used for structure determination in organic and inorganic molecules
Radiofrequency	Absorption at accurately measured frequencies; used in structure determination

emitted (or absorbed) only at specific wavelengths. Line emission spectra are of greatest interest to studies of electronic structure, for they are produced by electrons that have absorbed energy. Moseley was studying line emission spectra of atoms in the x-ray region when he discovered the significance of atomic numbers (see Section 3.8). Sodium vapor gives a line emission spectrum in the visible region, as does hydrogen in a gas-discharge tube (Figure C). The origin and production of line spectra is discussed in Section 8.5. In **band spectra,** which are produced by molecules that have become excited, groups of closely spaced lines form bands.

Much of our knowledge of the structure of matter is derived from spectroscopy. In addition, many theories of the structure of matter have had their experimental confirmation in the accurate prediction of where spectral absorption or emission will occur.

Tools of Chemistry sections later in the book discuss the various types of spectra in connection with the types of chemical species for which they are most useful. (See Table of Contents for Tools of Chemistry, at the beginning of the book.)

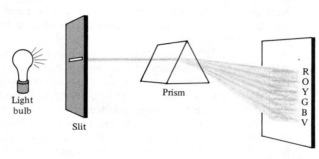

(a) Continuous emission spectrum

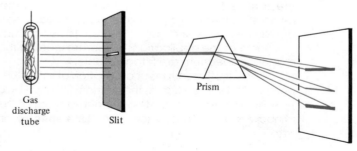

Figure C

Continuous and Line Spectra (a) Continuous spectra are emitted when solids, liquids, or very highly compressed gases have been heated to incandescence. (b) Line spectra are emitted by atoms in the gaseous state that have absorbed extra energy. (Molecules under similar conditions give band spectra — groups of lines spaced very close together.) (c) When a continuum of wavelengths is passed through a sample of unexcited atoms or molecules, certain wavelengths are absorbed, producing dark lines (or bands) in the continuous spectrum. This is known as an absorption spectrum. The wavelengths absorbed are the same ones that the sample would radiate when excited.

(b) Line emission spectrum

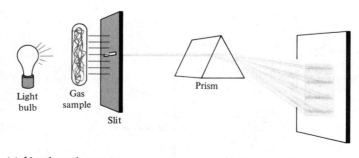

(c) Line absorption spectrum

8.3 ELECTRONS AS WAVES

de Broglie's equation:

$$\lambda = \frac{h}{mu}$$

After Planck and Einstein established that waves of light also behave like particles, Louis de Broglie, in 1923, turned up the other side of the coin. If radiation has particle-like properties, then particles in motion should have wave-like properties. De Broglie predicted that the wavelength of a moving particle could be calculated from the equation

$$\underset{\substack{\text{wavelength} \\ \text{of particle}}}{} \lambda = \frac{h \quad \text{Planck's constant}}{\underset{\substack{\text{mass of} \\ \text{particle}}}{mu} \quad \text{velocity of particle}} \tag{8.4}$$

Two American physicists at the Bell Telephone Laboratory, C. J. Davisson and L. H. Germer, soon did an experiment that proved that de Broglie was right. In 1927 Davisson and Germer found that what they had first observed as an unexpected result in an electron-scattering experiment was the diffraction of the electron beam. Diffraction, as we have explained, is clearly a wave property. When their electron beam was aimed at a nickel crystal, they obtained a diffraction pattern similar to the pattern obtained from the diffraction of x-rays by a crystal (Figure 8.8). The wavelength of the electron beam calculated from the diffraction pattern agreed to within 1% with the wavelength calculated from de Broglie's equation. Electrons can indeed behave like waves. (See Tools of Chemistry: Diffraction, in Chapter 13.)

The wavelength of a moving body of any mass can be calculated with the de Broglie equation, and presumably moving bodies of any mass have wavelengths. However, the wave properties of matter are observable only for particles of very small mass. An α-particle of mass 6.6×10^{-27} kg which is emitted from a radioactive source at a speed of 1.9×10^7 m/s has a wavelength of 5.3×10^{-6} nm, which is observable. A 2 g hummingbird flying at 160 km/h has a wavelength of 7×10^{-24} nm, much too small to be observed.

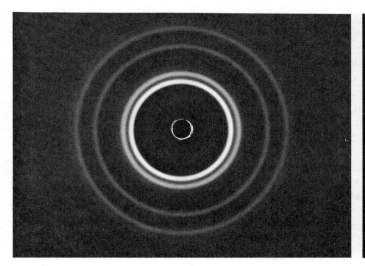 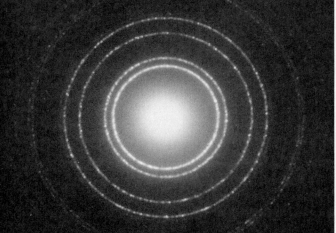

Figure 8.8
Diffraction of (a) X-rays and (b) An Electron Beam by the Same Thin Aluminum Foil The identical patterns of the rings demonstrate the wavelike nature of both x-rays and the electron beam. (Source: PSSC Physics film *Matter Waves,* Cambridge, Massachusetts: Education Development Center.)

EXAMPLE 8.4
Wave Nature of Particles

What is the wavelength corresponding to an electron of mass 9.11×10^{-31} kg, moving at one-tenth the speed of light?

The relationship between the wavelength, and the mass and velocity of a particle is given by the de Broglie equation (Equation 8.4). The velocity of the electron is $(0.100)(3.00 \times 10^8 \text{ m/s}) = 3.00 \times 10^7$ m/s. Note that we must include the conversion factor based on 1 kg m²/s² = 1 J so that units cancel appropriately.

$$\lambda = \frac{h}{mu} = \frac{(6.626 \times 10^{-34} \text{ J s})}{(9.11 \times 10^{-31} \text{ kg})(3.00 \times 10^7 \text{ m/s})} \times \left(\frac{1 \text{ kg m}^2/\text{s}^2}{1 \text{ J}}\right) = 2.42 \times 10^{-11} \text{ m}$$

The wavelength is 2.42×10^{-11} m = 0.0242 nm.

Exercise What is the wavelength corresponding to a neutron of mass = 1.67×10^{-27} kg moving at 2200 m/s? *Answer* 0.18 nm

8.4 QUANTUM MECHANICS:
THE HEISENBERG
UNCERTAINTY PRINCIPLE

"Mechanics" is the study of motion, and **quantum mechanics** refers to the study of the motion of entities that are small enough and move fast enough to have both observable wavelike and particlelike properties. When quantum mechanics is applied to large-scale, familiar phenomena, the effects are too small to be significant and we are left with the laws of classical mechanics intact. Classical mechanics and quantum mechanics are in a sense at the opposite ends of the same continuum.

The field of quantum mechanics began with efforts to explain spectra and the behavior of electrons in atoms. In Sections 8.5–8.9 we pick up the story of how the quantum mechanical model of the atom originated. First, we must mention a principle which is of central significance in the difference between classical mechanics and quantum mechanics. This principle, named for Werner Heisenberg who first enunciated it (see A Historical Aside: The Quantum Revolution), is viewed by some as an intrinsic property of nature, by some as a statement of the limits of our knowledge, and by others as a matter for philosophical thought.

Classical physics incorporates the assumption that if we are clever enough and careful enough we can continue indefinitely to improve the precision with which anything can be measured. Werner Heisenberg discovered that in the realm of photons and electrons this assumption does not hold up. What is called the **Heisenberg uncertainty principle** may be stated as follows: It is impossible to know simultaneously both the exact momentum and the exact position of an electron. (**Momentum** is mass times velocity. It expresses not only the tendency of a moving body to keep moving, but also, since velocity is a directional quantity, to maintain the *direction* of its motion.) As is discussed in Sections 8.7 and 8.8, the Heisenberg uncertainty principle has a profound influence on our picture of the distribution of electrons in atoms.

The Heisenberg principle, theoretically, holds for all objects, including those that we see around ourselves all the time. However, like the wavelength of particles, it becomes significant only at the subatomic level. Suppose you shine a flashlight into a dark closet and observe a mouse running across the floor. The light from the flashlight does not noticeably slow the mouse down or change the direction of his flight. Trying to look at an electron is a different story. Radiation is the only "yardstick" small enough to measure the properties of tiny particles like electrons. However, the electron is so small that no matter what kind of radiation we shine on it, the speed and direction of the electron will be changed the instant the radiation hits it.

In summary, light (and all electromagnetic radiation) is characterized by its wavelength and frequency, and displays the wave properties of interference and

*diffraction. On the other hand, the energy of radiation is quantized according to
$E = h\nu$. The energy of electrons is also quantized by $E = h\nu$. Electrons and
similar small particles obey quantum-mechanical laws, not classical-mechanical
laws, and exhibit the wave properties of interference and diffraction. It is not
possible to know simultaneously both the position and momentum of such
particles.*

**QUANTUM THEORY AND
THE ATOM**

8.5 ATOMIC SPECTRA

In the early 1900s atomic spectra seemed as hard to explain as the photoelectric
effect. Atoms excited by heat or by an electric discharge, that is, atoms that have
absorbed energy over and above their normal energy content, radiate energy at
specific wavelengths. All atoms in the gaseous state give line emission spectra, and
there is a characteristic line spectrum for each element (see Tools of Chemistry:
Electromagnetic Radiation and Spectra). This regularity in the line spectra, so
puzzling at first, was the key to understanding electronic structure.

The simplest line spectrum is that of hydrogen, the lightest element. Atomic
spectra become more and more complex for heavier atoms. The hydrogen spectrum
consists of five series of lines, named for the men who discovered them (Figure 8.9).
The first interpretation of the hydrogen spectrum was an empirical one, that is, it was
derived solely from the observed spectrum, without any theoretical justification. It
was found that the wave numbers of all of the lines in the hydrogen spectrum can be
calculated accurately from the equation

$$\bar{\nu} = \mathcal{R}\left(\frac{1}{n_1^2} - \frac{1}{n_2^2}\right) \tag{8.5}$$

where $\mathcal{R}$ is a constant called the Rydberg constant (named for spectroscopist
Johannes Rydberg), and n_1 and n_2 are whole numbers. There is a characteristic single
value of n_1 for each series of lines in the hydrogen emission spectrum, while for each
series n_2 can be any number greater than n_1, that is, $n_2 = n_1 + 1, n_1 + 2, \ldots$
J. J. Balmer in 1885 first developed this empirical relationship for the series bearing
his name, where $n_1 = 2$. For the four later-discovered series n_1 has the values 5, 4, 3,
and 1. The experimentally determined value of the Rydberg constant for the
hydrogen spectrum is 109,678 cm^{-1}.

Such regularity in the spectrum had to be related to some kind of regularity in
the structure of the atom. Here was another problem that begged to be solved.

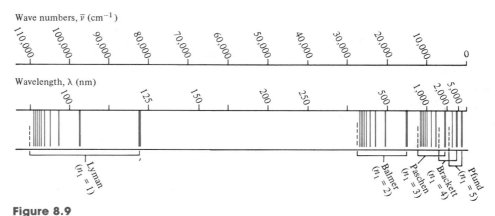

Figure 8.9

The Hydrogen Emission Spectrum A schematic drawing showing the five series of lines.
The dashed lines indicate the limits of each series. The Balmer series, which is in the visible
region, was the first to be discovered.

8.6 THE BOHR MODEL OF THE
HYDROGEN ATOM

The Rutherford nuclear atom (Section 3.6) left an inexact picture of how electrons are distributed about the nucleus. Rutherford knew that the electrons must be in motion or they would be pulled into the nucleus by the attraction between opposite charges. He suggested that the electrons might orbit the nucleus as planets orbit the sun. But this was not satisfactory. Electrons are charged, while planets are not. Classical physics predicted that charged particles moving in circles should emit radiation. As a result, the electrons would very quickly radiate away all of their energy and spiral into the nucleus.

The difficulties of the Rutherford atomic model were overcome in 1913 by Niels Bohr. The Bohr model of the hydrogen atom was the first atomic model based on the quantization of energy. Bohr made the following three assumptions:

1. The electron in the hydrogen atom can move about the nucleus in any one of several fixed circular orbits, but *only* in these orbits.

2. The angular momentum of the electron in a hydrogen atom is quantized; it is a whole number multiple of $h/2\pi$. This is why only certain fixed orbits are allowed. **Angular momentum,** which is given by mass times velocity times the radius of a body's motion, is a measure of the tendency of a body to keep moving on a curved path. For an electron in a Bohr atom

$$mur = n\left(\frac{h}{2\pi}\right) \tag{8.6}$$

where mur has *mass of electron*, *velocity*, *radius of Bohr orbit*, n is the *quantum number*, and $h/2\pi$ contains *Planck's constant*.

By this condition of quantization, it could be shown, using certain relationships from classical physics, that the electron can be assigned an energy for each orbit that is given by the following proportional relationship:

$$E \propto \frac{me^4}{n^2} \tag{8.7}$$

where m is the *mass of electron*, e is the *charge of electron*, and n is the *quantum number*.

No energies other than those governed by Equation (8.7) are possible. Each orbit in the Bohr hydrogen atom is called a *stationary state*. The lowest energy orbit, the one in which the single electron in a hydrogen atom

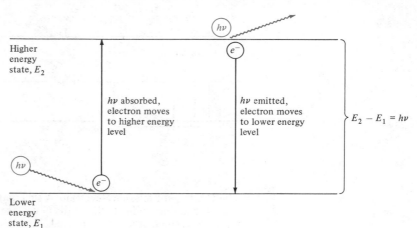

Figure 8.10
**Absorption and Emission of
Photons by an Electron in an Atom**

normally resides, is the **ground state** for that electron. The states of energy higher than the ground state are **excited states,** reached by the electron when the atom has absorbed extra energy.

3. The electron does not radiate energy as long as it remains in one of the orbits. When the electron drops from a higher energy state (E_2) to a lower one (E_1), a definite quantity of energy is emitted as one photon of radiation. The energy change and the frequency of this radiation are proportional to each other according to Planck's relationship:

$$\Delta E = E_2 - E_1 = h\nu \tag{8.8}$$

If the electron is to be raised from state 1 to state 2, the same quantity of energy must be absorbed (Figure 8.10).

The n in Equations (8.6) and (8.7) is a **quantum number,** a whole-number multiplier that specifies an amount of energy. When de Broglie proposed that particles can have wavelike properties (Section 8.3), he had in mind the Bohr model of the atom. He saw that the quantized energy of an electron moving in a circle about the nucleus could be explained as a wave property. To see how, picture a vibrating guitar string of length l, which is fixed at both ends. Only a certain number of wavelengths can fit into a fixed length. Thus the wavelength of the vibration of the string (and consequently of the sound that it produces) is quantized. The possible wavelengths are given by the expression $\lambda = 2l/n$, where n is a quantum number. When $n = 1$ (Figure 8.11a), the vibration of the string has the longest allowed wavelength. The fixed points, where there is no motion, are known as *nodes*. With $n = 1$, nodes exist only at the ends of the string. At higher values of n, additional nodes appear along the length of the string (see Figure 8.11a). Only waves with such fixed points—standing waves—are allowed for guitar strings.

As Figure 8.11b shows, the same conditions apply to electrons in atoms. For an electron in a Bohr orbit to have wavelike motion, the wave must be a standing wave (Figure 8.11b). Otherwise the wave would interfere with itself and cancel itself (Figure 8.11c). The allowable wavelengths are given by the expression

$$\lambda = \frac{2\pi r}{n}$$

where n is a whole number.

In the normal (or ground) state, the electron in a hydrogen atom is in the lowest energy level. The quantum number n for the ground state is 1. When the atom absorbs energy (for example, from the electric current in a gas-discharge tube), the atom becomes "excited," and the electron jumps to higher energy levels ($n > 1$). As

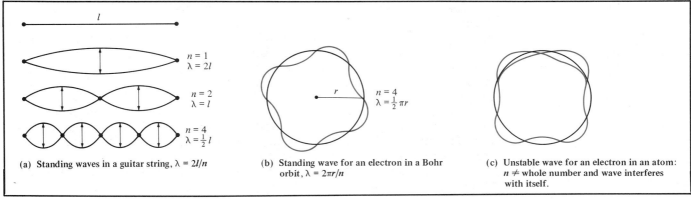

(a) Standing waves in a guitar string, $\lambda = 2l/n$

(b) Standing wave for an electron in a Bohr orbit, $\lambda = 2\pi r/n$

(c) Unstable wave for an electron in an atom: $n \neq$ whole number and wave interferes with itself.

Figure 8.11
Standing Waves

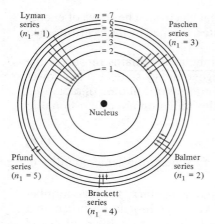

Figure 8.12

Energy Levels in the Bohr Hydrogen Atom (not drawn to scale) The single electron can reside in any circular orbit without emitting energy. The electron reaches orbits with $n > 1$ only when the atom is excited. The series of lines in the hydrogen spectrum arise from transitions of the electron from orbit to orbit. The n value for each series refers to the n_1 in Equation (8.5). The n_2 values are all of the n values greater than n_1 in each series. The lines of the Lyman series represent all the transitions in which an electron drops from a higher energy level to level 1 (the ground state). Similarly, the Balmer series lines represent transitions down to the second energy level, and so on.

it falls back to the ground state, the extra energy is emitted as electromagnetic radiation. This produces a line in the hydrogen spectrum. The wavelength of the line depends on the size of the energy jump, in accordance with the basic quantum relationship, $E = h\nu$ (or, using Equation 8.1, $E = hc/\lambda$).

From the mathematics of his theory, Bohr was able to calculate the wavelengths of the hydrogen spectral lines. How each of the five series of lines was explained by the Bohr theory of the hydrogen atom is shown in Figure 8.12. Bohr's calculated values agreed with the observed values. Furthermore, his theory led directly to Equation (8.5) and a value of the Rydberg constant close to that found experimentally.

Two of Bohr's ideas—quantization of energy levels for electrons in atoms, and energy radiation by the electron only when changing energy levels—have stayed with us. However, the Bohr model did not fully explain the spectra of atoms containing more than one electron. While starting from the "new" ideas of quantized energy, the Bohr atom was still based in part on classical physics. Also, it presumed exact knowledge of the location and momentum of the electron at the same moment, a violation of Heisenberg's uncertainty principle.

8.7 THE QUANTUM-MECHANICAL MODEL OF THE ATOM

Erwin Schrödinger, in developing a quantum-mechanical model for the atom, began with a classical equation for the properties of waves. He modified this equation to take account of the mass of a particle and the de Broglie relationship between mass and wavelength. The outcome—the Schrödinger equation—is the basis for a purely mathematical description of electrons in atoms. The electrons are treated as moving with wavelike motion in the three-dimensional space surrounding the nucleus, not just in planar orbits as in the Bohr atom. The wavelike motion, just as for the guitar string, naturally imposes the requirement for standing waves, nodes, and quantized energy. But when the waves associated with electrons in atoms are extended into three dimensions, *three* quantum numbers are needed in the equation.

The Schrödinger equation for the hydrogen atom successfully predicts all aspects of the hydrogen atom spectrum, including some phenomena that could not be explained by the Bohr model. In addition, the quantization of energy of the electrons arises as a natural consequence of the mathematics—it is not necessary to begin from an assumption of quantization. Application of the hydrogen atom wave equation to many-electron atoms requires modifications for the effect of electrons on each other and the effect of the nuclear charge on electrons. The mathematics is difficult, but very accurate approximations can be obtained with numerical methods programmed for digital computers. These approximate solutions allow the description of atoms other than hydrogen with good success (for example, the frequencies of spectral lines can be predicted to within 1%).

The important consequences of the quantum-mechanical view of atoms are the following:

1. The energy of electrons in atoms is quantized.
2. The number of possible energy levels for electrons in atoms of different

elements is a direct consequence of the wavelike properties of electrons.
3. The position and momentum of an electron cannot both be determined simultaneously (the Heisenberg uncertainty principle).
4. The region in space around the nucleus in which an electron is most probably located is what can be predicted for each electron in an atom. Electrons of different energies are likely to be found in different regions. The region in which an electron with a specific energy will most probably be located is called an **atomic orbital.**

Note the distinction between an orbit, as in the Bohr atom, and an orbital. An orbit is a clearly defined path through space, whereas an orbital is just a region of space. We can predict that the electron is somewhere within that region, but according to the Heisenberg principle, we cannot know its exact location at any instant.

The energies of the orbitals are reflected in the lines in atomic spectra for atoms in the gaseous state, just as was described for the Bohr model of the hydrogen atom (Section 8.6).

Our excursion into the wavelike properties of electrons has, as will become apparent in the following sections, brought us back to the periodic table. It turns out that electrons in similar energy levels impart similar properties to elements. To return to our earlier example, when the periodic table was first devised, no one knew *why* lithium and sodium are so different from fluorine and chlorine. Once we see how quantum numbers specify different types of atomic orbitals, we will find that the electrons that determine the properties of lithium and sodium have the same type of atomic orbitals. The same holds true for fluorine and chlorine. The similarities and differences among all of the elements in the periodic table are a result of their electronic structures.

8.8 ORBITALS AND QUANTUM NUMBERS

The designation of the orbital "location" of an electron requires four quantum numbers. Independent of any experimental evidence, three of them arise from solutions of the Schrödinger equation. A fourth quantum number, the spin quantum number, is needed to complete the designation of each individual electron within an atom.

Introducing the quantum numbers is difficult because there is no satisfactory physical description of them. So let's start by explaining why we need quantum numbers. Each electron in a many-electron atom has its own set of quantum numbers. By using quantum numbers we can identify which electron we are talking about and know to which atomic orbital the electron belongs. To make a rough analogy (rough because for electrons we deal only with their *probable* locations), suppose it is necessary to locate a person who is attending a performance in a large theater. We know that his ticket reads, "Second balcony, A104." Three "quantum numbers" identify his location. To find him we must look first for balcony number 2, then in row A, and then in seat 104.

Being able to specify the "location" of electrons is important. Many of the properties of atoms are determined by how many electrons are present and to which orbitals they belong. The orbitals may have different energies and occupy different regions in space—both properties that profoundly affect the way atoms combine and what the geometry of molecules will be.

The first quantum number, the *principal* quantum number, identifies the main energy levels (like the balconies). The second, the *subshell* quantum number (traditionally called either the angular momentum or azimuthal quantum number) identifies sublevels of energy within the main energy level (like the rows in each balcony). The third quantum number is the *orbital* quantum number (traditionally called the magnetic quantum number)—it pins down the location of individual

Table 8.3
Subshell Quantum Number (l)
Values The letters s, p, d, and f come from the designation of lines in emission spectra as belonging to the sharp, principal, diffuse, or fundamental series. The number of sublevels in each quantum level is equal to n.

For $n =$	$l = 0, 1, 2, \ldots,$ $(n-1)$ (Subshell Letters)
1	0 (s)
2	0, 1 (s, p)
3	0, 1, 2 (s, p, d)
4	0, 1, 2, 3 (s, p, d, f)

Principal quantum number,
$$n = 1, 2, 3, 4, \ldots$$
Subshell quantum number,
$$l = 0, 1, 2, \ldots \text{(up to } n-1)$$
Orbital quantum number,
$$m_l = -l \text{ to } +l$$
Spin quantum number,
$$m_s = -\tfrac{1}{2}, +\tfrac{1}{2}$$

electrons in orbitals (like the seats in each row). A fourth quantum number is needed because the electron can occupy the orbital in two different orientations.

1. **Principal quantum number, n.** The principal quantum number is roughly equivalent to the n of the energy levels in the Bohr atom. It has whole number values, $n = 1, 2, 3, 4, \ldots$, and designates the main energy levels in an atom. As n increases, electrons are generally further from the nucleus and have higher total energy. Values of n range from 1 to 7 in the unexcited states of the known elements. Values of n from 1 to ∞ are possible in the excited states of atoms (∞, infinity, corresponds to the complete removal of an electron, to form an ion).

2. **Subshell quantum number, l.** The second quantum number, l, designates the different energy subshells, or sublevels, within the main, or n, level. Only certain values of l are allowed. These depend on n: $l = 0, 1, 2, \ldots, (n-1)$. *The total number of possible subshells in each level is equal to n.* For example, the $n = 3$ shell has three l levels, $l = 0, 1,$ and 2. The first four subshells are identified by the letters s, p, d, and f (Table 8.3), which correspond to l values of 0, 1, 2, and 3. Higher values of l would be designated as g, h, i, $\ldots$ levels, but these occur only in excited states of atoms and we need not be concerned with them. The subshells "occupy" different regions of space and in this sense l is associated with the "shapes" of orbitals. Each type of subshell, s, p, d, and f, has a characteristic shape (discussed in the next section). Transitions between the subshells can be identified in spectra. In general, the energies of the subshells increase from s, to p, to d, to f, orbitals.

3. **Orbital quantum number, m_l.** In isolated atoms of the same element, electrons with the same values of n and l have the same energy. However, within the subshell, it is possible for these electrons to occupy different regions of space when the substance is exposed to a magnetic field. The number of allowed values of m_l is limited and depends upon l (and therefore also on n): $m_l = -l$ to $+l$. The number of orbitals in each subshell equals the number of values of m_l, which is given by $2l + 1$, resulting in one s orbital, three p orbitals, five d orbitals, and seven f orbitals, as shown in Table 8.4.

4. **Spin quantum number, m_s.** An electron within an orbital has angular momentum. Although the picture should not be taken too literally, we can imagine the electron as spinning on its own axis like the earth as it orbits the sun. This spinning causes each electron to behave like a tiny magnet. Electron spin has two possible orientations (Figure 8.13) and the two values of m_s are $m_s = +\tfrac{1}{2}, -\tfrac{1}{2}$.

Because only certain values of l and m_l are allowed, only a specific number of atomic orbitals are allowed within each main energy level. For the lowest energy level, where $n = 1$, l has only one possible value, $l = 0$, and m_l has only one possible value, $m_l = 0$. Therefore, at the $n = 1$ level, only a single atomic orbital is present, an s orbital.

Atomic orbitals are designated by the following notation:

Table 8.4
Orbital Quantum Number (m_l) Values

For $l =$	$m_l = -l, \ldots$ $-1, 0, 1, \ldots +l$ (Total)
0 (s)	0 (one s orbital)
1 (p)	$+1, 0, -1$ (three p orbitals)
2 (d)	$+2, +1, 0, -1, -2$ (five d orbitals)
3 (f)	$+3, +2, +1, 0, -1, -2, -3$ (seven f orbitals)

$$\underset{\substack{principal \\ quantum \\ number}}{} nl \underset{\substack{subshell\ quantum\ number, \\ expressed\ as\ s,p,d,\ or\ f}}{}$$

The single orbital in the s subshell of the lowest energy level is a $1s$ orbital. The one electron in a hydrogen atom normally occupies a $1s$ orbital.

Study of Tables 8.3 and 8.4 and a little thought show how the quantum numbers determine the number of available orbitals. When $n = 2$, four orbitals are possible

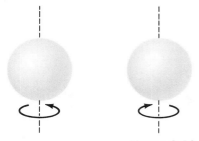

Figure 8.13
Electron Spin Two possible orientations of the spin of an electron about its own axis.

—one *s* orbital (for *l* = 0, the 2*s* orbital) and three *p* orbitals (for *l* = 1, the 2*p* orbitals). When *n* = 3, nine orbitals are possible, and when *n* = 4, sixteen orbitals are possible.

n = 1, *l* = 0	one *s* orbital
n = 2, *l* = 0, 1	one *s* orbital + three *p* orbitals
n = 3, *l* = 0, 1, 2	one *s* orbital + three *p* orbitals + five *d* orbitals
n = 4, *l* = 0, 1, 2, 3	one *s* orbital + three *p* orbitals + five *d* orbitals + seven *f* orbitals

In summary, four quantum numbers (n, l, m_l, and m_s) are needed to identify each electron in an atom. The energy of the main energy level increases with the value of n and the energy of the subshells increases with the value of l. The letters s, p, d, and f designate the l = 0, 1, 2, and 3 subshells. Electrons with the same n and l values have the same energy in isolated atoms of the same element. Excited electrons move to higher energy levels or sublevels. Spectra confirm that the energy emitted or absorbed equals that of transitions between the possible energy levels specified by the quantum numbers. An atomic orbital is the region in space in which an electron with a specific set of quantum numbers is most likely to be found. The number of possible atomic orbitals in each energy level is specified by the quantum numbers (see Table 8.5). Within an energy level, the number of types of orbitals equals n (e.g., the n = 2 level has two types of orbitals, s and p orbitals). There are one s, three p, five d, and seven f orbitals.

8.9 PICTURING ORBITALS

Unfortunately, we do not have a good way to draw pictures of atomic orbitals. Artists' best efforts at representing the three-dimensional electron clouds still convey the idea of distinct shapes. These "shapes," as we have said, are only regions in space within which electrons can be found with a certain probability, and the probability gradually trails off to zero in every direction. The shapes have no physical existence, nor are they independent of each other. The overall distribution of electron density for a given principal quantum level is close to a sphere for any isolated atom.

Having said this, we can look at some of the ways of picturing the location of electrons and the shapes of orbitals. First, let's look at the *relative locations* of electrons in the principal quantum levels.

An orbital with *l* = 0 is an *s* orbital. A plot of the probability of finding 1*s*, 2*s*, and 3*s* electrons at any distance from the nucleus is shown in Figure 8.14a. As you can see, a 1*s* electron is *most* likely to be found quite close to the nucleus, and the 2*s* and 3*s* electrons are successively further away. Similar plots for the 2*p* and 3*p* electrons (Figure 8.14b) show the same increasing distance from the nucleus with the value of *n*. Remember that total energy increases with distance from the nucleus. The probability plots for the 3*s*, 3*p*, and 3*d* orbitals are superimposed in Figure 8.14c to

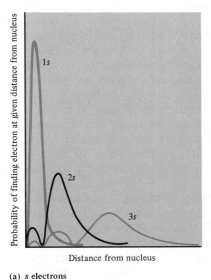

(a) *s* electrons

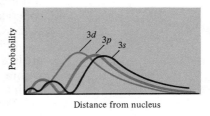

(b) *p* electrons

(c) *n* = 3 electrons

Figure 8.14
Probable Distances of *n* = 1, 2, and 3 Electrons from the Nucleus. (a) and (b) Plots for the *n* = 1–3 *s* and *p* electrons, which show that as *n* increases the electrons are generally further from the nucleus. (c) Plots for the *s*, *p*, and *d* electrons in the *n* = 3 energy level, which show that they occupy roughly the same region around nucleus.

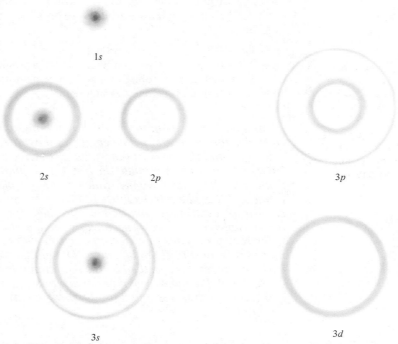

Figure 8.15

Electron Density Cross-Sections for $n = 1$, 2, and 3 Electrons These cross-sections are drawn to the same scale as the plots in Figure 8.14. Although not easily visible at this scale, the electron density falls to zero at the center of each orbital, indicating the electron has an insignificant probability of being found in the immediate vicinity of the nucleus.

show that electrons with the same n value are roughly the same distance from the nucleus and therefore have similar energies.

The probability of locating an electron can be represented by electron density drawings, in which shading indicates variations in the density. Where the density is greatest (shown by heavier shading) the probability of finding the electron is greatest. Electron density *cross sections* for $1s$, $2s$, $3s$, $2p$, $3p$, and $3d$ electrons are given in Figure 8.15.

Now let's turn our attention to the *shapes* of the atomic orbitals, which have practical significance because they influence the shapes of molecules. For each subshell, the number of orbitals is determined by the value of the orbital quantum number, m_l. The s subshell has only one orbital. All s orbitals have the form of spherical shells centered on the nucleus. As n increases, the shells increase in size, like successive layers in an onion.

Orbitals are often drawn as probability, or boundary, contours—surfaces which are like solid shapes viewed from a distance. The surface indicates the region of space within which the electron has a certain probability (usually 90%) of being found. Such a contour surface for an s orbital has the shape of a sphere (Figure 8.16).

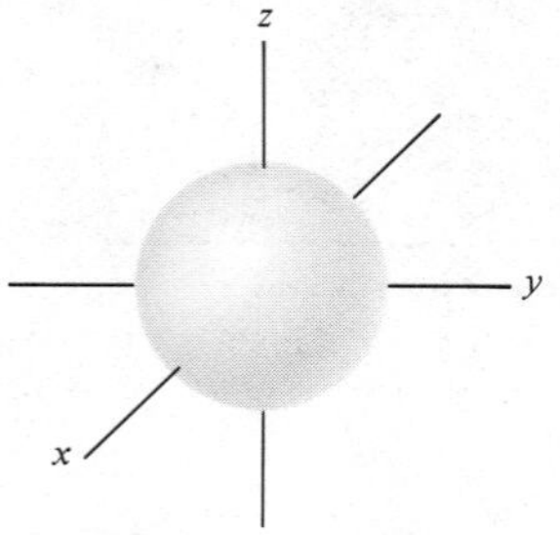

The p subshell at each energy level has three orbitals. Each p orbital has two lobes, one on each side of the nucleus, as shown in a "three-dimensional" electron density picture in Figure 8.17a. The lobes of the three different p orbitals can be thought of as directed along the x, or y, or z axes of a set of coordinates. Essentially, the electrons in each p orbital stay as far from the electrons in the other p orbitals as possible (Figure 8.17b). The shapes of the lobes of the p orbitals vary with the energy level, as you can see from Figure 8.17c, but the lobes always extend along the axes.

Figure 8.16
An s Orbital

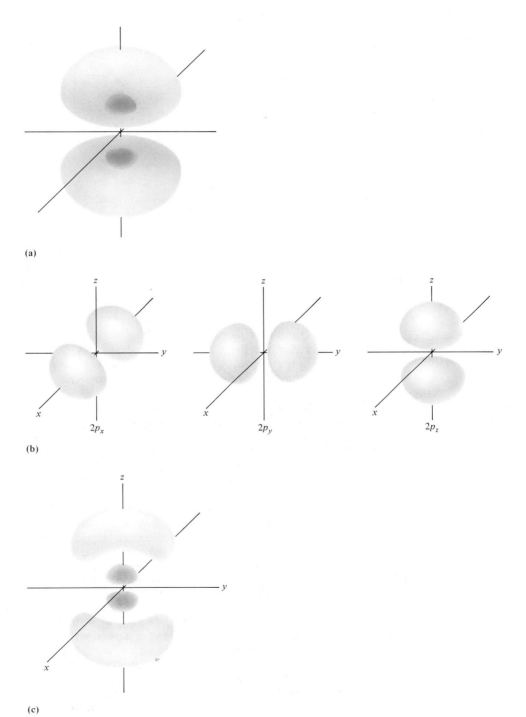

Figure 8.17
The *p* Orbitals (a) An electron density picture in three dimensions of a 2*p* orbital. (b) Contour surfaces for the three 2*p* orbitals. (c) The somewhat different shape of a 3*p* orbital.

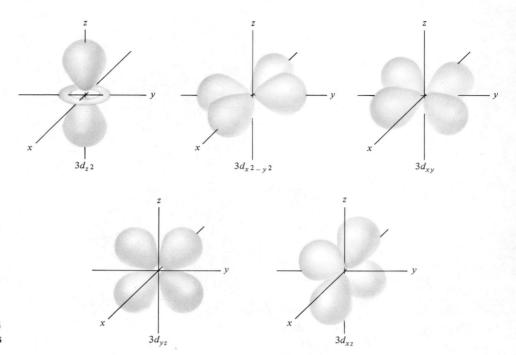

Figure 8.18
The 3d orbitals

The d orbitals—five of them for the five possible values of m_l—are more complex (Figure 8.18). [The f orbitals are still more complex.] One d orbital resembles the p orbital along the z axis, but with an additional doughnut-shaped volume in the center. The other four have four lobes each, extending in one case along the x and y axes and in the other cases, between the axes.

A HISTORICAL ASIDE

The Quantum Revolution

Toward the end of the nineteenth century, some scientists were ready to conclude that the era of discovery in physics was over. They felt that everything there was to know had been found out—an attitude that proved to be far from correct. The first 25 years of the twentieth century saw a revolution in physics that also had a profound effect upon chemistry. It gradually became clear that the laws that explain readily observable phenomena do not apply on the scale of electrons and radiation. The revolution was founded on the work of a number of European physicists who dared to depart from classical physics.

Table A relates the classical experiments on atomic structure discussed in Chapter 3 and the major events of the quantum revolution to historical events. The political and social turmoil caused in Europe by the rise to power of the Nazi party in Germany touched the lives of Planck, Einstein, and many of the physicists who were carrying forward the quantum revolution. Einstein was horrified by the Nazi preparations for war and, although a pacifist, urged that Europe take up arms. In 1933 when Hitler became Chancellor, Einstein renounced his German citizenship and moved to the United States. Bohr, a brilliant physicist, played a role in the development of the atomic bomb during World War II. He had fled from Denmark to Sweden in a fishing boat when it was learned that Hitler had ordered that he be kidnapped. Still in danger, he was then flown to England in a British bomber. In later years, Bohr was deeply troubled by the awful destructive potential of the atomic bomb and was outspoken on the need for peaceful coexistence among all nations.

For a superb description of the difficulties of coping with the new physics, from the viewpoint of a prominent physicist of today, we suggest that you read the Thoughts on Chemistry at the end of this chapter.

Table A
Historical Perspective — Atomic Structure

		1876	Custer's Last Stand
Cathode rays, William Crookes	1879		
"Electron," G. Johnstone Stoney	1881		
Hydrogen spectrum, Johann Balmer	1885		
Canal rays, Eugen Goldstein	1886		
Electron e/m, J.J. Thomson	1897	1897	Klondike gold rush
Canal ray e/m, W. Wien	1898	1898	Spanish–American War
$E = h\nu$, Max Planck	1900		
		1901	McKinley assassinated: Theodore Roosevelt becomes U.S. President
		1903	Wright Brothers flight at Kitty Hawk
Quantized radiation, Albert Einstein	1905		
Charge on electron, Robert A. Millikan	1909		
Nuclear atom model, Ernest Rutherford	1911		
		1912	Woodrow Wilson elected U.S. President
Hydrogen atom model, Niels Bohr	1913	1914	World War I begins
Meaning of atomic number, Henry Moseley			
		1917	Russian Bolshevik Revolution
		1919	Treaty of Versailles ends World War I
$\lambda = \dfrac{h}{mu}$, Louis de Broglie	1923		
Wave-mechanical atomic model, Erwin Schrödinger	1926		
Uncertainty principle, Werner Heisenberg			
Electron diffraction, C. J. Davisson and L. H. Germer	1927	1927	Transatlantic flight by Lindbergh
		1929	U.S. stock market crash; beginning of Depression
Neutron, James Chadwick	1932		
		1933	Hitler becomes dictator in Germany

ELECTRONS AND THE PERIODIC TABLE

8.10 ELECTRON CONFIGURATIONS

The **electron configuration** of an atom is the distribution among the subshells of all of the electrons in the atom. Electron configurations are designated by using the standard form of notation for subshells as follows:

$$nl^x$$

principal quantum number 1,2,3, . . .   *subshell quantum number*   *number of electrons in subshell*

Here n represents the principal quantum level as a number (1, 2, 3, . . .); l represents the subshell as a letter (s, p, d, f); and x indicates the number of electrons in the subshell. For example,

$$3d^8$$

In the n = 3 *level*   *the* d *orbitals*   *are occupied by 8 electrons*

The complete electron configuration for an atom is given by a series of symbols representing each occupied subshell. For example, the complete ground-state configuration of an argon atom is written

$$\text{Ar} \qquad 1s^2\,2s^2\,2p^6\,3s^2\,3p^6$$

showing that the 1s, 2s, and 3s subshells each contain two electrons, and that the 2p and 3p subshells each contain six electrons. For a neutral atom, the sum of all the x values is the atomic number (Z) of the element. Thus for argon (atomic number 18),

$$Z = 2 + 2 + 6 + 2 + 6 = 18$$

A good approach to understanding electron configurations is to start with hydrogen and consider how each successive electron is added as the atomic numbers of the elements increase in order. This is known as the *aufbau* process (from the German for "building up").

The single electron in hydrogen is a 1s electron. Where will the second electron needed to form helium go? There are three rules for building up electron configurations, and two of them apply here. The first is the *Pauli exclusion principle* (named for Wolfgang Pauli, who suggested it in 1925 on the basis of spectra): No two electrons can have the same four quantum numbers, n, l, m_l and m_s.

The maximum number of electrons that can go into each atomic orbital is given by this principle. Once all of its possible quantum number combinations have been used, an energy level, and each of its orbitals, is full. With this rule the spin quantum number takes on great significance, for it allows two electrons of opposite spin to occupy each atomic orbital. The maximum numbers of electrons for each principal quantum level and each sublevel are summarized in Table 8.5. (Note that the maximum number of electrons in each n level is $2n^2$.)

Based on the Pauli exclusion principle, the second electron needed to form a helium atom ($Z = 2$) could also be a 1s electron, but of opposite spin from the first. (The two sets of quantum numbers would be $n = 1$, $l = 0$, $m_l = 0$, $m_s = +\frac{1}{2}$ and $n = 1$, $l = 0$, $m_l = 0$, $m_s = -\frac{1}{2}$.)

But couldn't the second electron instead be an $n = 2$ electron, say a 2s electron? This is where the next rule applies, the *lowest energy principle*. Electrons occupy the lowest-energy orbitals available to them; they enter higher energy orbitals only when

> **Pauli exclusion principle: No two electrons can have the same quantum numbers.**

Table 8.5

Electron Distribution and Maximum Electron Population The number of s, p, d, and f orbitals is determined by the number of m_l values for each sublevel (see Table 8.4). Two electrons of opposite spin can reside in each orbital.

n	l	Number of l Orbitals	Maximum Number of Electrons per l Sublevel	Maximum Number of Electrons per n Level ($=2n^2$)
1	0(s)	One s orbital	2	2
2	0(s)	One s orbital	2	
	1(p)	Three p orbitals	6	8
3	0(s)	One s orbital	2	
	1(p)	Three p orbitals	6	
	2(d)	Five d orbitals	10	18
4	0(s)	One s orbital	2	
	1(p)	Three p orbitals	6	
	2(d)	Five d orbitals	10	
	3(f)	Seven f orbitals	14	32
5	0(s)	One s orbital	2	
	1(p)	Three p orbitals	6	
	2(d)	Five d orbitals	10	
	3(f)	Seven f orbitals	14	
	4("g")*	Nine "g" orbitals*	18*	50*

* No element has yet been found that uses an $l = 4$ ("g") energy sublevel in the ground state.

the lower energy orbitals are filled. This rule establishes that the second electron in helium must also be a $1s$ electron, not an electron in an $n = 2$ orbital, which is of higher energy. The electron configuration of the helium atom is written

$$\text{He} \qquad 1s^2 \qquad (Z = 2)$$

The configurations for atoms of the next three elements follow easily from the two rules given:

Li	$1s^2\,2s^1$	$(Z = 3)$
Be	$1s^2\,2s^2$	$(Z = 4)$
B	$1s^2\,2s^2\,2p^1$	$(Z = 5)$

What about the sixth electron to form a carbon atom? It should be another p electron. Does it make any difference to which of the three $2p$ atomic orbitals it belongs? They are of equal energy, so the lowest energy principle is of little help. The third rule for electron configurations, *Hund's principle,* applies here: <u>Orbitals of equal energy are each occupied by a single electron before a second electron, which will have the opposite spin quantum number, enters any of them.</u> For a carbon atom $(Z = 6)$ this means that the sixth electron enters a *different* p orbital from the first electron. Single electrons in orbitals in the same sublevel have parallel spins (i.e., spin in same direction). By using a box for each orbital and an arrow for each electron, with opposite directions indicating opposite spins, the boron and carbon configurations are written

Hund's principle: Orbitals of equal energy are each occupied by a single electron before any of them acquires a second electron.

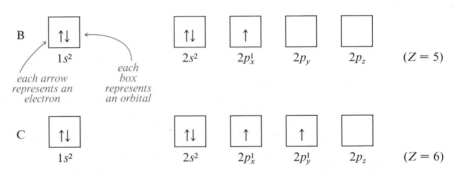

In nitrogen there is one electron in each of the three p orbitals.

The next three electrons pair up one by one with the unpaired $2p$ electrons, and at neon $(Z = 10)$ all of the orbitals in the $n = 2$ level are full.

The eleventh electron, in sodium, will be a $3s$ electron and the process will begin again.

As stated by Hund's principle, atoms or ions (or molecules) can have varying numbers of unpaired electrons. The presence or absence of unpaired electrons is

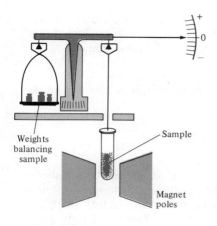

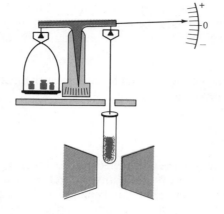

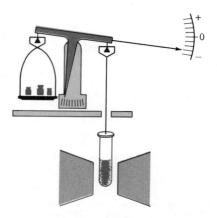

(a) No magnetic field

(b) Diamagnetic substance slightly repelled by magnetic field

(c) Paramagnetic substance attracted strongly in magnetic field

Figure 8.19

Experimental Determination of Magnetic Properties (a) The sample is first balanced exactly by weights in the absence of a magnetic field. (b) A diamagnetic substance—one with only paired electrons—is weakly repelled by the field, as shown by the pointer moving in the + direction. (c) A paramagnetic substance—one with one or more unpaired electrons—is more strongly attracted by the magnetic field, as shown by the pointer moving in the − direction.

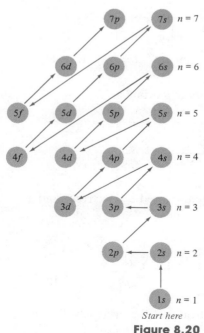

Figure 8.20

Orbital Occupancy Sequence — A Diagram.

found experimentally by the behavior of a substance in the presence of a magnetic field (Figure 8.19). **Paramagnetism** is the property of attraction to a magnetic field shown by substances containing unpaired electrons. **Diamagnetism** is the property of repulsion by a magnetic field and shows the absence of unpaired electrons. There can be one unpaired s electron and as many as three unpaired p electrons, or five unpaired d electrons, or seven unpaired f electrons.

The ground-state electron configurations—those of lowest energy—can be built up for atoms of all of the elements as we have illustrated (see Table 8.6, in which the configurations of all of the elements are given). With increasing atomic number, electrons occupy the subshells available in each main energy level in the following order:

$$1s\ 2s\ 2p\ 3s\ 3p\ 4s\ 3d\ 4p\ 5s\ 4d\ 5p\ 6s\ 4f\ 5d\ 6p\ 7s\ 5f\ 6d\ 7p$$

Figure 8.20 is an aid to remembering this sequence.

Note that up through the $3p$ level, the sequence given above is exactly as expected based upon the increase in energy for each main energy level (the n levels) and the increase in energy within a main energy level for each subshell. After $3p$, variations in the filling sequence begin to occur, the first being that the $4s$ subshell is fully occupied before electrons enter the $3d$ subshell. The reason for these variations is to be found in the greater complexity of atoms with higher atomic number. As the atomic number increases, nuclear charge increases. The electrons are drawn closer together and also closer to the nucleus, allowing electrons in different energy levels to influence each other to an increasing extent. The influences on each electron are unique. How strongly an electron is attracted to the nucleus and how strongly it is repelled by other electrons affect the energy of that electron. The configuration of each atom is the one that gives the lowest energy to the atom as a whole.

Table 8.6

Electron Configurations of the Elements Noble gases are shown against a color background. Unfilled orbitals are shown in color. Transition elements are shown against a gray background.

Atomic Number	Symbol	Electron Configuration
1	H	$1s^1$
2	He	$1s^2$
3	Li	$1s^2\ 2s^1$
4	Be	$1s^2\ 2s^2$
5	B	$1s^2\ 2s^2\ 2p^1$
6	C	$1s^2\ 2s^2\ 2p^2$
7	N	$1s^2\ 2s^2\ 2p^3$
8	O	$1s^2\ 2s^2\ 2p^4$
9	F	$1s^2\ 2s^2\ 2p^5$
10	Ne	$1s^2\ 2s^2\ 2p^6$
11	Na	$1s^2\ 2s^2\ 2p^6\ 3s^1$
12	Mg	$1s^2\ 2s^2\ 2p^6\ 3s^2$
13	Al	$1s^2\ 2s^2\ 2p^6\ 3s^2\ 3p^1$
14	Si	$1s^2\ 2s^2\ 2p^6\ 3s^2\ 3p^2$
15	P	$1s^2\ 2s^2\ 2p^6\ 3s^2\ 3p^3$
16	S	$1s^2\ 2s^2\ 2p^6\ 3s^2\ 3p^4$
17	Cl	$1s^2\ 2s^2\ 2p^6\ 3s^2\ 3p^5$
18	Ar	$1s^2\ 2s^2\ 2p^6\ 3s^2\ 3p^6$
19	K	$1s^2\ 2s^2\ 2p^6\ 3s^2\ 3p^6\ 4s^1$
20	Ca	$1s^2\ 2s^2\ 2p^6\ 3s^2\ 3p^6\ 4s^2$

Transition Metals, Period 4

Atomic Number	Symbol	Electron Configuration
21	Sc	$1s^2\ 2s^2\ 2p^6\ 3s^2\ 3p^6\ 3d^1\ 4s^2$
22	Ti	$1s^2\ 2s^2\ 2p^6\ 3s^2\ 3p^6\ 3d^2\ 4s^2$
23	V	$1s^2\ 2s^2\ 2p^6\ 3s^2\ 3p^6\ 3d^3\ 4s^2$
24	Cr	$1s^2\ 2s^2\ 2p^6\ 3s^2\ 3p^6\ 3d^5\ 4s^1$
25	Mn	$1s^2\ 2s^2\ 2p^6\ 3s^2\ 3p^6\ 3d^5\ 4s^2$
26	Fe	$1s^2\ 2s^2\ 2p^6\ 3s^2\ 3p^6\ 3d^6\ 4s^2$
27	Co	$1s^2\ 2s^2\ 2p^6\ 3s^2\ 3p^6\ 3d^7\ 4s^2$
28	Ni	$1s^2\ 2s^2\ 2p^6\ 3s^2\ 3p^6\ 3d^8\ 4s^2$
29	Cu	$1s^2\ 2s^2\ 2p^6\ 3s^2\ 3p^6\ 3d^{10}\ 4s^1$
30	Zn	$1s^2\ 2s^2\ 2p^6\ 3s^2\ 3p^6\ 3d^{10}\ 4s^2$
31	Ga	$1s^2\ 2s^2\ 2p^6\ 3s^2\ 3p^6\ 3d^{10}\ 4s^2\ 4p^1$
32	Ge	$1s^2\ 2s^2\ 2p^6\ 3s^2\ 3p^6\ 3d^{10}\ 4s^2\ 4p^2$
33	As	$1s^2\ 2s^2\ 2p^6\ 3s^2\ 3p^6\ 3d^{10}\ 4s^2\ 4p^3$
34	Se	$1s^2\ 2s^2\ 2p^6\ 3s^2\ 3p^6\ 3d^{10}\ 4s^2\ 4p^4$
35	Br	$1s^2\ 2s^2\ 2p^6\ 3s^2\ 3p^6\ 3d^{10}\ 4s^2\ 4p^5$
36	Kr	$1s^2\ 2s^2\ 2p^6\ 3s^2\ 3p^6\ 3d^{10}\ 4s^2\ 4p^6$
37	Rb	$5s^1$
38	Sr	$5s^2$

Transition Metals, Period 5 (Krypton Core)

Atomic Number	Symbol	Electron Configuration
39	Y	$4d^1\ 5s^2$
40	Zr	$4d^2\ 5s^2$
41	Nb	$4d^4\ 5s^1$
42	Mo	$4d^5\ 5s^1$
43	Tc	$4d^5\ 5s^2$
44	Ru	$4d^7\ 5s^1$
45	Rh	$4d^8\ 5s^1$
46	Pd	$4d^{10}$
47	Ag	$4d^{10}\ 5s^1$
48	Cd	$4d^{10}\ 5s^2$
49	In	$4d^{10}\ 5s^2\ 5p^1$
50	Sn	$4d^{10}\ 5s^2\ 5p^2$
51	Sb	$4d^{10}\ 5s^2\ 5p^3$
52	Te	$4d^{10}\ 5s^2\ 5p^4$
53	I	$4d^{10}\ 5s^2\ 5p^5$
54	Xe	$4d^{10}\ 5s^2\ 5p^6$

Atomic Number	Symbol	Electron Configuration
55	Cs	$4d^{10}\ 5s^2\ 5p^6\ 6s^1$
56	Ba	$4d^{10}\ 5s^2\ 5p^6\ 6s^2$

Lanthanides (Krypton Core)

Atomic Number	Symbol	Electron Configuration
57	La	$4d^{10}\ 5s^2\ 5p^6\ 5d^1\ 6s^2$
58	Ce	$4d^{10}\ 4f^1\ 5s^2\ 5p^6\ 5d^1\ 6s^2$
59	Pr	$4d^{10}\ 4f^3\ 5s^2\ 5p^6\ 6s^2$
60	Nd	$4d^{10}\ 4f^4\ 5s^2\ 5p^6\ 6s^2$
61	Pm	$4d^{10}\ 4f^5\ 5s^2\ 5p^6\ 6s^2$
62	Sm	$4d^{10}\ 4f^6\ 5s^2\ 5p^6\ 6s^2$
63	Eu	$4d^{10}\ 4f^7\ 5s^2\ 5p^6\ 6s^2$
64	Gd	$4d^{10}\ 4f^7\ 5s^2\ 5p^6\ 5d^1\ 6s^2$
65	Tb	$4d^{10}\ 4f^9\ 5s^2\ 5p^6\ 6s^2$
66	Dy	$4d^{10}\ 4f^{10}\ 5s^2\ 5p^6\ 6s^2$
67	Ho	$4d^{10}\ 4f^{11}\ 5s^2\ 5p^6\ 6s^2$
68	Er	$4d^{10}\ 4f^{12}\ 5s^2\ 5p^6\ 6s^2$
69	Tm	$4d^{10}\ 4f^{13}\ 5s^2\ 5p^6\ 6s^2$
70	Yb	$4d^{10}\ 4f^{14}\ 5s^2\ 5p^6\ 6s^2$

Transition Metals, Period 6 (Krypton Core)

Atomic Number	Symbol	Electron Configuration
71	Lu	$4d^{10}\ 4f^{14}\ 5s^2\ 5p^6\ 5d^1\ 6s^2$
72	Hf	$4d^{10}\ 4f^{14}\ 5s^2\ 5p^6\ 5d^2\ 6s^2$
73	Ta	$4d^{10}\ 4f^{14}\ 5s^2\ 5p^6\ 5d^3\ 6s^2$
74	W	$4d^{10}\ 4f^{14}\ 5s^2\ 5p^6\ 5d^4\ 6s^2$
75	Re	$4d^{10}\ 4f^{14}\ 5s^2\ 5p^6\ 5d^5\ 6s^2$
76	Os	$4d^{10}\ 4f^{14}\ 5s^2\ 5p^6\ 5d^6\ 6s^2$
77	Ir	$4d^{10}\ 4f^{14}\ 5s^2\ 5p^6\ 5d^7\ 6s^2$
78	Pt	$4d^{10}\ 4f^{14}\ 5s^2\ 5p^6\ 5d^9\ 6s^1$
79	Au	$4d^{10}\ 4f^{14}\ 5s^2\ 5p^6\ 5d^{10}\ 6s^1$
80	Hg	$4d^{10}\ 4f^{14}\ 5s^2\ 5p^6\ 5d^{10}\ 6s^2$

Krypton Core

Atomic Number	Symbol	Electron Configuration
81	Tl	$4d^{10}\ 4f^{14}\ 5s^2\ 5p^6\ 5d^{10}\ 6s^2\ 6p^1$
82	Pb	$4d^{10}\ 4f^{14}\ 5s^2\ 5p^6\ 5d^{10}\ 6s^2\ 6p^2$
83	Bi	$4d^{10}\ 4f^{14}\ 5s^2\ 5p^6\ 5d^{10}\ 6s^2\ 6p^3$
84	Po	$4d^{10}\ 4f^{14}\ 5s^2\ 5p^6\ 5d^{10}\ 6s^2\ 6p^4$
85	At	$4d^{10}\ 4f^{14}\ 5s^2\ 5p^6\ 5d^{10}\ 6s^2\ 6p^5$
86	Rn	$4d^{10}\ 4f^{14}\ 5s^2\ 5p^6\ 5d^{10}\ 6s^2\ 6p^6$
87	Fr	$4d^{10}\ 4f^{14}\ 5s^2\ 5p^6\ 5d^{10}\ 6s^2\ 6p^6\ 7s^1$
88	Ra	$4d^{10}\ 4f^{14}\ 5s^2\ 5p^6\ 5d^{10}\ 6s^2\ 6p^6\ 7s^2$

Actinides (Krypton Core)

Atomic Number	Symbol	Electron Configuration
89	Ac	$4d^{10}\ 4f^{14}\ 5s^2\ 5p^6\ 5d^{10}\ 6s^2\ 6p^6\ 6d^1\ 7s^2$
90	Th	$4d^{10}\ 4f^{14}\ 5s^2\ 5p^6\ 5d^{10}\ 6s^2\ 6p^6\ 6d^2\ 7s^2$
91	Pa	$4d^{10}\ 4f^{14}\ 5s^2\ 5p^6\ 5d^{10}\ 5f^2\ 6s^2\ 6p^6\ 6d^1\ 7s^2$
92	U	$4d^{10}\ 4f^{14}\ 5s^2\ 5p^6\ 5d^{10}\ 5f^3\ 6s^2\ 6p^6\ 6d^1\ 7s^2$
93	Np	$4d^{10}\ 4f^{14}\ 5s^2\ 5p^6\ 5d^{10}\ 5f^4\ 6s^2\ 6p^6\ 6d^1\ 7s^2$
94	Pu	$4d^{10}\ 4f^{14}\ 5s^2\ 5p^6\ 5d^{10}\ 5f^6\ 6s^2\ 6p^6\ 7s^2$
95	Am	$4d^{10}\ 4f^{14}\ 5s^2\ 5p^6\ 5d^{10}\ 5f^7\ 6s^2\ 6p^6\ 7s^2$
96	Cm	$4d^{10}\ 4f^{14}\ 5s^2\ 5p^6\ 5d^{10}\ 5f^7\ 6s^2\ 6p^6\ 6d^1\ 7s^2$
97	Bk	$4d^{10}\ 4f^{14}\ 5s^2\ 5p^6\ 5d^{10}\ 5f^9\ 6s^2\ 6p^6\ 7s^2$
98	Cf	$4d^{10}\ 4f^{14}\ 5s^2\ 5p^6\ 5d^{10}\ 5f^{10}\ 6s^2\ 6p^6\ 7s^2$
99	Es	$4d^{10}\ 4f^{14}\ 5s^2\ 5p^6\ 5d^{10}\ 5f^{11}\ 6s^2\ 6p^6\ 7s^2$
100	Fm	$4d^{10}\ 4f^{14}\ 5s^2\ 5p^6\ 5d^{10}\ 5f^{12}\ 6s^2\ 6p^6\ 7s^2$
101	Md	$4d^{10}\ 4f^{14}\ 5s^2\ 5p^6\ 5d^{10}\ 5f^{13}\ 6s^2\ 6p^6\ 7s^2$
102	No	$4d^{10}\ 4f^{14}\ 5s^2\ 5p^6\ 5d^{10}\ 5f^{14}\ 6s^2\ 6p^6\ 7s^2$
103	Lr	$4d^{10}\ 4f^{14}\ 5s^2\ 5p^6\ 5d^{10}\ 5f^{14}\ 6s^2\ 6p^6\ 6d^1\ 7s^2$
104	Unq	$4d^{10}\ 4f^{14}\ 5s^2\ 5p^6\ 5d^{10}\ 5f^{14}\ 6s^2\ 6p^6\ 6d^2\ 7s^2$
105	Unp	$4d^{10}\ 4f^{14}\ 5s^2\ 5p^6\ 5d^{10}\ 5f^{14}\ 6s^2\ 6p^6\ 6d^3\ 7s^2$
106	Unh	$4d^{10}\ 4f^{14}\ 5s^2\ 5p^6\ 5d^{10}\ 5f^{14}\ 6s^2\ 6p^6\ 6d^4\ 7s^2$

EXAMPLE 8.5
Writing Electron Configurations

What is the complete electron configuration of the zirconium atom ($Z = 40$)?

Forty electrons must be accommodated. The $n = 1$ and $n = 2$ energy levels are filled to maximum capacity first.

$$1s^2\ 2s^2\ 2p^6 \quad \text{(10 electrons)}$$

The next subshells in the filling sequence (see Figure 8.20) are $3s$, $3p$, $4s$, and $3d$. There are enough electrons to fill up all of these subshells, also. Now the $n = 1$, 2, and 3 levels have their maximum populations and $4s$ is also full.

$$1s^2\ 2s^2\ 2p^6\ 3s^2\ 3p^6\ 3d^{10}\ 4s^2 \quad \text{(30 electrons)}$$

[Note that complete configurations are written in this book in the order of the principal quantum number, not the filling order.]

Ten electrons remain to be placed. The next sublevel in the sequence is $4p$, which takes a maximum of six electrons; followed by $5s$, which takes two electrons. The remaining two electrons go into $4d$ orbitals. The total electron configuration of Zr is

$$\text{Zr} \quad 1s^2\ 2s^2\ 2p^6\ 3s^2\ 3p^6\ 3d^{10}\ 4s^2\ 4p^6\ 4d^2\ 5s^2 \quad \text{(40 electrons)}$$

The two $4d$ electrons are in separate orbitals and have parallel spins.

Exercise Write the complete electron configuration for the arsenic atom. *Answer* $1s^2\ 2s^2\ 2p^6\ 3s^2\ 3p^6\ 3d^{10}\ 4s^2\ 4p^3$

8.11 GROUPS, PERIODS, AND ELECTRON CONFIGURATIONS

A modern periodic table is given in Figure 8.21 (and inside the front cover). The symbol, atomic number, and atomic mass for each element are included in this version of the table, and also the outer electron configuration. As atomic number and nuclear charge increase, the electrons in lower energy levels are drawn closer to the nucleus and have a decreasing influence on properties. Most often, we are interested in the outer electron configuration, for the outer electrons determine many of the properties of the elements. It is most useful to be able to recognize the outer configuration of an element from its position in the periodic table and how this is done is discussed below.

The elements in a single vertical column in the table are referred to as members of a **group** or **family.** We have mentioned the similarity in properties of lithium and sodium. In the periodic table in Figure 8.21, you can see that these two elements and all of the elements in the same group have the same outer electron configuration. This explains their similar properties. The elements in *each* periodic table family have similar properties and have identical or very similar outer configurations.

The relationship of the subshell filling sequence to the periodic table is shown in Figure 8.22a. It is often convenient to refer to the elements of the s block, p block, or d block, as indicated in the figure. A horizontal row in the periodic table is called a **period.** Hydrogen and helium make up the first period (Figure 8.22b). For atoms with $n = 2$, a maximum of eight electrons can be accommodated (see Table 8.5) in the s and p subshells (the one s and three p orbitals). Filling these two subshells accounts for the eight elements of the second period. The third-period elements, for which $n = 3$, have outer configurations identical to those of the second-period elements.

With the fourth period, the periods become longer as electrons begin to enter d subshells. The $4s$ subshell is filled by two electrons in potassium and calcium (see the periodic table, Figure 8.21). At scandium ($Z = 21$) it is easier for an electron to enter an orbital in the $3d$ subshell than one in the $4p$ subshell. Continuing occupancy of the $3d$ level gives the ten elements of what is called the first d-transition series (Sc–Zn). The $4p$ subshell then fills, and the fourth period ends at krypton ($Z = 36$). After

Group (family): elements in a vertical column of the periodic table

Period: a horizontal row of the periodic table

Representative Elements

Representative Elements

Noble gases

d-Transition Elements

f-Transition Elements

Group numbers

| I | II |
| ns¹ | ns² |

ns^1 ns^2

Representative Elements

Noble gases $ns^2 np^6$

| | He 2 $1s^2$ 4.00260 |

III $ns^2 np^1$	IV $ns^2 np^2$	V $ns^2 np^3$	VI $ns^2 np^4$	VII $ns^2 np^5$	
B 5 $2s^2 2p^1$ 10.81	C 6 $2s^2 2p^2$ 12.011	N 7 $2s^2 2p^3$ 14.0067	O 8 $2s^2 2p^4$ 15.9994	F 9 $2s^2 2p^5$ 18.998403	Ne 10 $2s^2 2p^6$ 20.179
Al 13 $3s^2 3p^1$ 26.98154	Si 14 $3s^2 3p^2$ 28.0855	P 15 $3s^2 3p^3$ 30.97376	S 16 $3s^2 3p^4$ 32.06	Cl 17 $3s^2 3p^5$ 35.453	Ar 18 $3s^2 3p^6$ 39.948
Ga 31 $4s^2 4p^1$ 69.72	Ge 32 $4s^2 4p^2$ 72.59	As 33 $4s^2 4p^3$ 74.9216	Se 34 $4s^2 4p^4$ 78.96	Br 35 $4s^2 4p^5$ 79.904	Kr 36 $4s^2 4p^6$ 83.80
In 49 $5s^2 5p^1$ 114.82	Sn 50 $5s^2 5p^2$ 118.69	Sb 51 $5s^2 5p^3$ 121.75	Te 52 $5s^2 5p^4$ 127.60	I 53 $5s^2 5p^5$ 126.9045	Xe 54 $5s^2 5p^6$ 131.29
Tl 81 $6s^2 6p^1$ 204.383	Pb 82 $6s^2 6p^2$ 207.2	Bi 83 $6s^2 6p^3$ 208.9804	Po 84 $6s^2 6p^4$ (209)	At 85 $6s^2 6p^5$ (210)	Rn 86 $6s^2 6p^6$ (222)

d-Transition Elements

$(n-1)d^1 ns^2$	$(n-1)d^2 ns^2$	$(n-1)d^3 ns^2$	$(n-1)d^5 ns^1$	$(n-1)d^5 ns^2$	$(n-1)d^6 ns^2$	$(n-1)d^7 ns^2$	$(n-1)d^8 ns^2$	$(n-1)d^{10} ns^1$

Sc 21 $3d^1 4s^2$ 44.9559	Ti 22 $3d^2 4s^2$ 47.88	V 23 $3d^3 4s^2$ 50.9415	Cr 24 $3d^5 4s^1$ 51.996	Mn 25 $3d^5 4s^2$ 54.9380	Fe 26 $3d^6 4s^2$ 55.847	Co 27 $3d^7 4s^2$ 58.9332	Ni 28 $3d^8 4s^2$ 58.69	Cu 29 $3d^{10} 4s^1$ 63.546
Y 39 $4d^1 5s^2$ 88.9059	Zr 40 $4d^2 5s^2$ 91.22	Nb 41 $4d^4 5s^1$ 92.9064	Mo 42 $4d^5 5s^1$ 95.94	Tc 43 $4d^5 5s^2$ (98)	Ru 44 $4d^7 5s^1$ 101.07	Rh 45 $4d^8 5s^1$ 102.9055	Pd 46 $4d^{10}$ 106.42	Ag 47 $4d^{10} 5s^1$ 107.868
La* 57 $5d^1 6s^2$ 138.9055	Hf 72 $4f^{14} 5d^2 6s^2$ 178.49	Ta 73 $5d^3 6s^2$ 180.9479	W 74 $5d^4 6s^2$ 183.85	Re 75 $5d^5 6s^2$ 186.207	Os 76 $5d^6 6s^2$ 190.2	Ir 77 $5d^7 6s^2$ 192.22	Pt 78 $5d^9 6s^1$ 195.09	Au 79 $5d^{10} 6s^1$ 196.9665
Ac** 89 $6d^1 7s^2$ 227.0278	Unq 104 $6d^2 7s^2$ (261)	Unp 105 $6d^3 7s^2$ (262)	Unh 106 $6d^4 7s^2$ (263)					

$(n-1)d^{10} ns^2$
Zn 30 $3d^{10} 4s^2$ 65.38
Cd 48 $4d^{10} 5s^2$ 112.41
Hg 80 $5d^{10} 6s^2$ 200.59

Representative Elements

H 1 $1s^1$ 1.0079	
Li 3 $2s^1$ 6.941	Be 4 $2s^2$ 9.01218
Na 11 $3s^1$ 22.98977	Mg 12 $3s^2$ 24.305
K 19 $4s^1$ 39.0983	Ca 20 $4s^2$ 40.08
Rb 37 $5s^1$ 85.4678	Sr 38 $5s^2$ 87.62
Cs 55 $6s^1$ 132.9054	Ba 56 $6s^2$ 137.33
Fr 87 $7s^1$ (223)	Ra 88 $7s^2$ 226.0254

f-Transition Elements

| Ce 58 $4f^1 5d^1 6s^2$ 140.12 | Pr 59 $4f^3 5d^0 6s^2$ 140.9077 | Nd 60 $4f^4 5d^0 6s^2$ 144.24 | Pm 61 $4f^5 5d^0 6s^2$ (145) | Sm 62 $4f^6 5d^0 6s^2$ 150.36 | Eu 63 $4f^7 5d^0 6s^2$ 151.96 | Gd 64 $4f^7 5d^1 6s^2$ 157.25 | Tb 65 $4f^9 5d^0 6s^2$ 158.9254 | Dy 66 $4f^{10} 5d^0 6s^2$ 162.50 | Ho 67 $4f^{11} 5d^0 6s^2$ 164.9304 | Er 68 $4f^{12} 5d^0 6s^2$ 167.26 | Tm 69 $4f^{13} 5d^0 6s^2$ 168.9342 | Yb 70 $4f^{14} 5d^0 6s^2$ 173.04 | Lu 71 $4f^{14} 5d^1 6s^2$ 174.967 |
| Th 90 $5f^0 6d^2 7s^2$ 232.0381 | Pa 91 $5f^2 6d^1 7s^2$ 231.0359 | U 92 $5f^3 6d^1 7s^2$ 238.0289 | Np 93 $5f^4 6d^1 7s^2$ 237.0482 | Pu 94 $5f^6 6d^0 7s^2$ (244) | Am 95 $5f^7 6d^0 7s^2$ (243) | Cm 96 $5f^7 6d^1 7s^2$ (247) | Bk 97 $5f^9 6d^0 7s^2$ (247) | Cf 98 $5f^{10} 6d^0 7s^2$ (251) | Es 99 $5f^{11} 6d^0 7s^2$ (252) | Fm 100 $5f^{12} 6d^0 7s^2$ (257) | Md 101 $5f^{13} 6d^0 7s^2$ (258) | No 102 $5f^{14} 6d^0 7s^2$ (259) | Lr 103 $5f^{14} 6d^1 7s^2$ (260) |

*Lanthanides ~ $4f^n 5d^0 - 1 6s^2$

**Actinides ~ $5f^n 6d^0 - 1 7s^2$

Symbol

H	1
$1s^1$	
1.0079	

Atomic number
Outer configuration
Atomic mass

Period number, highest occupied electron level

Figure 8.21

The Modern Periodic Table The atomic number, atomic mass, and electron configuration are given here for each element. The information given in a periodic table varies with the purpose of the table and the amount of space available.

For three pairs of elements (Ar and K; Co and Ni; Te and I) the element with the larger atomic mass precedes the element with the smaller atomic mass. This is the result of varying isotope abundances. Values in parentheses are for longest-lived isotopes of radioactive elements.

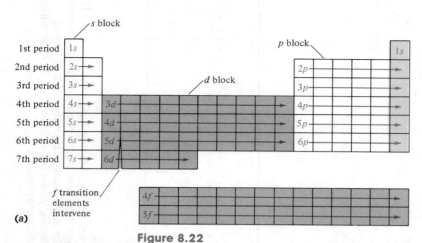

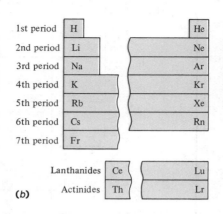

Figure 8.22

(a) Orbital Filling Sequence in the Periodic Table Transition element areas have a gray background. The noble gas column has a colored background. Representative element areas have no background color. **(b)** Periods of the periodic table.

krypton, a similar sequence is repeated in the fifth period as the $5s$ and then the $4d$ subshells are filled to give the second d-transition series, extending from yttrium to cadmium. The fourth and fifth periods contain 18 elements each, because in each an outer s subshell (2 electrons), the d subshell of the next lowest energy level (10 electrons), and the p outer subshell (6 electrons) are filling.

After the $6s$ subshell is filled in barium, the third transition series begins at lanthanum ($Z = 57$). However, the next electrons fill the $4f$ subshell (beginning with cerium, $Z = 58$) to give the first f-transition series, called the **lanthanides** (Ce to Lu). After lutetium ($Z = 71$), the third d-transition series is completed by addition of the $5d$ electrons, followed by addition of $6p$ electrons to complete the sixth period at radon ($Z = 86$).

The seventh period includes most of the man-made radioactive elements. The elements from Th ($Z = 90$) to Lr ($Z = 103$), in which the $5f$ subshell is filling, are called the **actinides.** The seventh period limit should be $Z = 118$, where the $5f$, $6d$, $7s$, and $7p$ subshells would be filled. (To date, the elements from 93 through 107 have been made in the laboratory, and the creation of a single atom of element 109 has been reported.) To save space, and also to confine elements with closely similar properties to a single column, the two f-transition series are generally placed at the bottom of the periodic table.

Each period ends with a **noble gas**—an element in which all energy sublevels that are occupied are completely filled (see Table 8.6, where the noble gas configurations are shown against a color background). Writing electron configurations can be simplified by using the symbol of the appropriate noble gas to represent the configuration of inner electrons. For the configuration of the outer electrons, the periodic table serves as our guide.

Suppose we want to know the configuration for phosphorus. It is in the third period, so its inner, or core, electrons have the same configuration as those in neon, the last element in the preceding period. Moving across the third period from left to right (see Figure 8.22a) to reach phosphorus shows that it has two $3s$ level electrons and, because it is the third element from the left in the p block, it has three p level electrons. The configuration of phosphorus is

P   [Ne] $3s^2 3p^3$

The s and p block elements all have exactly the configurations found in this way. In the d and f blocks there are some variations. For example, in the fourth period chromium and copper have, respectively, five and ten d level electrons, where four and nine would be predicted. (See the "ideal" family configurations at the top of each column in Figure 8.21.) The variations are thought to result from the somewhat greater stability of half-filled (5 electrons) and completely filled (10 electrons) d energy sublevels. For every d-transition element, however, the total number of s plus d electrons is equal to two (for the s subshell) plus one electron for each element counted from the left in the d block.

EXAMPLE 8.6
Writing Electron Configurations

What are the electron configurations of rubidium, molybdenum, and iodine? Write complete configurations using the noble gas symbols for the core electrons.

These three elements are all in the fifth period, and therefore all have an inner core of electrons in the krypton configuration. Rubidium is the first element in the s block and therefore has one s electron

$$Rb \quad [Kr]5s^1$$

Molybdenum is in the d block; because it is the fourth element from the left the sum of its $5s$ and $4d$ electrons must be six. The "ideal" configuration is

$$Mo \quad [Kr]4d^4\,5s^2$$

(The actual configuration is $[Kr]4d^5\,5s^1$; see Figure 8.21.) Iodine is the fifth p block element in the fifth period. As such, it has completely filled d sublevel and the following configuration

$$I \quad [Kr]4d^{10}\,5s^2\,5p^5$$

Exercise Write electron configurations using the noble gas symbols for the core electrons for (a) Se, (b) Fe, and (c) Hg. *Answer* (a) $[Ar]3d^{10}\,4s^2\,4p^4$, (b) $[Ar]3d^6\,4s^2$, (c) $[Xe]4f^{14}\,5d^{10}\,6s^2$

EXAMPLE 8.7
Writing Electron Configurations

Write the electron configurations for elements A, B, and C.

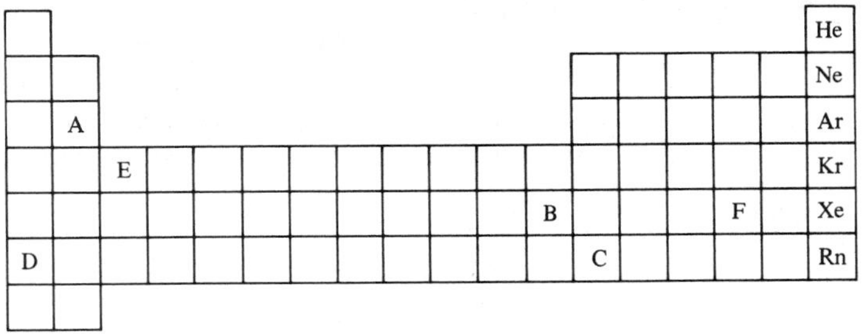

Element A is a third-period element and it is second in the s block. It has two s level electrons, giving

$$A \quad [Ne]3s^2$$

As a fifth-period, d block element, B has electrons in the $5s$ and $4d$ subshells (note that the d electrons are in the next lowest main energy level). Because it is the last d block element, it has 10 d level electrons, giving a configuration of

$$B \quad [Kr]4d^{10}\,5s^2$$

Element C is a sixth-period element and the first in the p block. It has two $6s$ electrons, ten $5d$ electrons, and one $6p$ electron, giving

$$C \quad [Xe]5d^{10}\,6s^2\,6p^1$$

Exercise Write the electron configurations for the elements (a) D, (b) E, and (c) F, given in the above periodic table. *Answer* (a) $[Xe]6s^1$, (b) $[Ar]3d^1\,4s^2$, (c) $[Kr]4d^{10}\,5s^2\,5p^4$

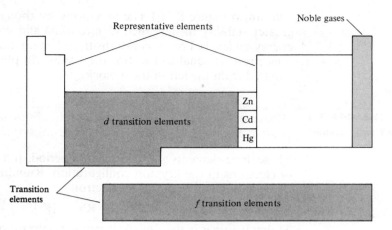

Figure 8.23
Representative and Transition Elements

8.12 CLASSIFICATION OF THE ELEMENTS

The elements are classified in two major ways relative to their positions in the periodic table and, as a result, relative to their electron configurations and properties. Every element is either a representative element or a transition element (Figure 8.23). Also, every element is either a metal, a semiconducting element, or a nonmetal (see Figure 8.25). These categories are used freely and often in discussions of chemical and physical properties. It is helpful to have a mental picture of where these types of elements fall in the periodic table.

Representative elements: s or p subshells filling
Transition elements: d or f subshells filling

---

a. Representative and transition elements The elements in which the s and p sublevels are filling are called the **representative elements** (Figure 8.23). These are the s block elements on the left and, with the exception of the noble gases, the p block element on the right. Zinc, cadmium, and mercury fall in the periodic table within the d block and are in a sense the last of the d-transition series. However, in their configurations and properties they are most like representative elements (each has a completely filled d subshell together with a complete s subshell of the next higher energy level) and so we include them in this category.

The groups of representative elements in the s and p blocks are given Roman numerals, starting at the left in the periodic table with I for Li–Fr (Figure 8.24).

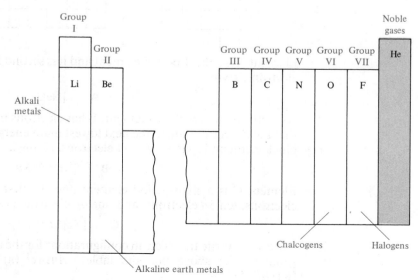

Figure 8.24
Groups, or Families, of the Periodic Table

Table 8.7
Named Element Groupings

Representative elements	
Alkali metals (Group I)	Li, Na, K, Rb, Cs, Fr
Alkaline earth metals (Group II)	Be, Mg, Ca, Sr, Ba, Ra
Chalcogens (Group VI)	O, S, Se, Te, Po
Halogens (Group VII)	F, Cl, Br, I, At
Noble gases	He, Ne, Ar, Kr, Xe, Rn
Transition elements	
Rare earth elements	Sc, Y, La–Lu
Lanthanides	Ce–Lu
Actinides	Th–Lr
Transuranium elements	Np, Pu, Am, . . .

(Hydrogen stands alone and is not a member of any group.) In this book we refer to Representative Group I, or the lithium family, Representative Group II or the beryllium family, and so on. (In many periodic tables representative element groups are indicated by the letter A after the Roman numeral; Be–Ra would be Group IIA. The letter B is then used for transition element families.)

Four of the representative element families have distinctive names (Table 8.7). The first two, the lithium (Group I) and beryllium (Group II) families, are known as the **alkali metals** and the **alkaline earth metals,** respectively. The elements of the oxygen family (Group VI) are sometimes called the *chalcogens* (a name less commonly used than the other group names). The fluorine family elements (Group VII) are virtually always referred to as the **halogens.**

Group I: alkali metals
Group II: alkaline earth metals
Group VII: halogens

The **transition elements** include all elements in which the d or f sublevels are filling. These are referred to as the d-transition elements and the f-transition elements. (The lanthanides and the actinides are f-transition elements.) Sometimes the f-transition elements are called the inner transition elements. Scandium, yttrium, and all of the sixth-period elements from lanthanum to lutetium are also known as the **rare earth elements.** Following uranium ($Z = 92$) come the **transuranium elements.**

Elements with each of four basic types of electron configurations fall together in the periodic table (Table 8.8).

Representative element configuration Outer configurations vary from ns^1 to $ns^2\ np^5$ with all occupied subshells in lower energy levels filled to capacity.

Table 8.8
The Four Basic Types of Electron Configurations

	Inner Levels	Outermost Level (n)	Outer Configuration
Representative elements e.g., Na, Sr, Br	Filled	s and p being filled	ns^1 to $ns^2\ np^5$
Noble gas elements e.g., He, Ne, Kr	Filled	s or s and p filled	$ns^2\ np^6$ (except He, $1s^2$)
d-Transition elements e.g., Sc, Pd, W	$(n-1)d$ being filled, others filled	s^1 or s^2	$(n-1)d^{1-10}\ ns^{1,2}$
f-Transition elements e.g., Nd, Tm, Pu	$(n-2)f$ being filled, $(n-1)d^{0-2}$, others filled	s^2	$(n-2)f^{1-14}$ $(n-1)d^{0-2}\ ns^2$

These are the s and p block elements, plus zinc, cadmium, and mercury.

Noble gas configuration: all occupied energy sublevels completely filled

---

Noble gas configuration   All of the subshells that are occupied by electrons are completely filled. Helium, the noble gas in the first row, has the $1s^2$ configuration. All other noble gases have the outer configuration of $ns^2\,np^6$, where n indicates the outer energy level.

d–Transition element configuration   The d subshell in the energy level just below the outermost energy level (the $n-1$ level) is being filled by electrons. Atoms of these elements generally have the outer configurations $(n-1)$ $d^{1-10}\,ns^{1-2}$, with all other subshells that are occupied filled to capacity.

f–Transition element configuration   The f subshell in the $n-2$ level is being filled. In atoms of such elements, the outer configurations are $(n-2)$ $f^{0-14}\,(n-1)d^{0-2}\,ns^2$ with all other subshells that are occupied completely filled.

EXAMPLE 8.8
Electron Configurations and the Periodic Table

From their configurations, identify the part of the periodic table from which the elements with the following configurations come.

(a) $[Xe]5d^{10}\,6s^2\,6p^2$ (c) $[Kr]4d^7\,5s^1$
(b) $1s^2\,2s^2\,2p^6\,3s^2$ (d) $[Kr]4d^{10}\,5s^2\,5p^6$

(a) The highest level configuration of $s^2\,p^2$, and the Xe core with filled d sublevel, both indicate that this is a representative element. The $s^2\,p^2$ configuration identifies this as an element from the carbon family, in the p block (Representative Group IV).
(b) All occupied orbitals below the highest level are full, showing this also to be a representative element. The two electrons in the highest level indicate that it is an alkaline earth metal, from the s block (Representative Group II).
(c) The incompletely filled d sublevel identifies this as a d–transition element.
(d) The outermost $s^2\,p^6$ configuration shows this element to be a noble gas.

Exercise   Identify the part of the periodic table from which the elements with the following configurations are found: (a) $[Ne]3s^2\,3p^5$, (b) $[Rn]5f^6\,7s^2$, and (c) $[Xe]4f^{14}\,5d^9\,6s^1$.   *Answer* (a) p-block representative element, halogen; (b) f-transition element, actinide; (c) d-transition element

---

b. Metals, nonmetals, and semiconducting elements   Based on their physical and chemical properties, elements are classified as metals, nonmetals, and semiconducting elements. More than three-fourths of the elements are metals. In the next chapter (Sections 9.5 and 9.6) and in subsequent chapters the properties of metals are discussed at length. The most characteristic property of metals, the one that distinguishes metals most clearly from nonmetals, is their ability to conduct electricity.

How the elements are divided into metals, nonmetals, and semiconducting elements is shown in Figures 8.25 and 8.26. All of the s block elements, all of the transition elements, and some of the p block elements are metals. At the left are two complete families of metals, the lithium family (Representative Group I, the alkali metals) and the beryllium family (Group II, the alkaline earth metals). Metallic properties persist further to the right in the table for the heavier elements than for the lighter ones. The four heaviest elements of the boron family (Al, Ga, In, and Tl) are

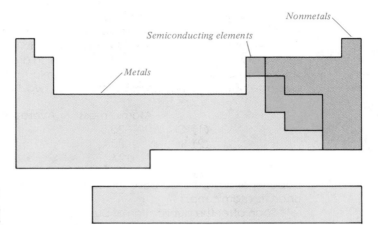

Figure 8.25
Metals, Semiconducting Elements, and Nonmetals

classified as metals, as are the two heaviest elements in the carbon family (Sn and Pb). Only the single heaviest elements in the nitrogen and oxygen families (Bi and Po) are metals.

Both in position in the periodic table and in properties, the **semiconducting elements** fall between the metals and the nonmetals. In appearance, the seven semiconducting elements—boron, silicon, germanium, arsenic, selenium, antimony, and tellurium—resemble metals. However, in chemical behavior and in their compounds they are more like nonmetals.

At the right in the periodic table are two complete families of elements that are nonmetals—the noble gases and the fluorine family (Group VII, the halogens). In the carbon family, only carbon, the lightest element, is a nonmetal. In both the nitrogen and oxygen families, the two lightest elements (N and P, and O and S, respectively) are nonmetals. In all, seventeen of the elements are nonmetals.

	Group I		Group II	Group III	Group IV	Group V	Group VI	Group VII	Noble Gases
Period 1	$_1$H $1s^1$								$_2$He $1s^2$
Period 2	$_3$Li $2s^1$		$_4$Be $2s^2$	$_5$B $2s^2 2p^1$	$_6$C $2s^2 2p^2$	$_7$N $2s^2 2p^3$	$_8$O $2s^2 2p^4$	$_9$F $2s^2 2p^5$	$_{10}$Ne $2s^2 2p^6$
Period 3	$_{11}$Na $3s^1$		$_{12}$Mg $3s^2$	$_{13}$Al $3s^2 3p^1$	$_{14}$Si $3s^2 3p^2$	$_{15}$P $3s^2 3p^3$	$_{16}$S $3s^2 3p^4$	$_{17}$Cl $3s^2 3p^5$	$_{18}$Ar $3s^2 3p^6$
Period 4	$_{19}$K $4s^1$		$_{20}$Ca $4s^2$	$_{31}$Ga $3d^{10} 4s^2 4p^1$	$_{32}$Ge $3d^{10} 4s^2 4p^2$	$_{33}$As $3d^{10} 4s^2 4p^3$	$_{34}$Se $3d^{10} 4s^2 4p^4$	$_{35}$Br $3d^{10} 4s^2 4p^5$	$_{36}$Kr $3d^{10} 4s^2 4p^6$
Period 5	$_{37}$Rb $5s^1$		$_{38}$Sr $5s^2$	$_{49}$In $4d^{10} 5s^2 5p^1$	$_{50}$Sn $4d^{10} 5s^2 5p^2$	$_{51}$Sb $4d^{10} 5s^2 5p^3$	$_{52}$Te $4d^{10} 5s^2 5p^4$	$_{53}$I $4d^{10} 5s^2 5p^5$	$_{54}$Xe $4d^{10} 5s^2 5p^6$
Period 6	$_{55}$Cs $6s^1$		$_{56}$Ba $6s^2$	$_{81}$Tl $4f^{14} 5d^{10} 6s^2 6p^1$	$_{82}$Pb $4f^{14} 5d^{10} 6s^2 6p^2$	$_{83}$Bi $4f^{14} 5d^{10} 6s^2 6p^3$	$_{84}$Po $4f^{14} 5d^{10} 6s^2 6p^4$	$_{85}$At $4f^{14} 5d^{10} 6s^2 6p^5$	$_{86}$Rn $4f^{14} 5d^{10} 6s^2 6p^6$
Period 7	$_{87}$Fr $7s^1$		$_{88}$Ra $7s^2$						

Metals • Semiconducting elements • Nonmetals

Transition elements, all metals, intervene

s block elements   *p* block elements

Figure 8.26
The Representative Elements and the Noble Gases The heavy lines separate the elements classified as metals, the semiconducting elements, and the nonmetals. First and second period elements have only *s*, or *s* and *p* orbitals. Third period elements have empty *3d* orbitals available. Fourth and higher period elements have $(n-1)d$ electrons close in energy to the *ns* electrons. (The electrons that participate in chemical bonds are shown in color.)

The Evolution of the Periodic Table

The pathway to the periodic table began with a search for numerical relationships among the atomic masses of similar elements. In 1829 the German chemist Johann Döbereiner (1780–1849) published a remarkable paper. He called attention to several sets of three elements — triads — which are similar in properties, which form similar compounds, and for which the atomic mass of one is approximately the average of the atomic masses of the other two. For example,

	Atomic mass	Average of (1) and (3)
(1) Cl	35.5	81
(2) Br	80	
(3) I	127	

Döbereiner drew the logical conclusion that the properties of an element depend upon its atomic mass.

Soon after the publication of Dumas's ideas, better methods for measurement of atomic masses were developed and the distinction between atoms and molecules was clarified (see A Historical Aside: Relative Atomic Masses, Chapter 4). This made possible a great step forward, which was taken by the English chemist John A.R. Newlands (1837–1898). In 1864, Newlands proposed that if the elements are arranged in the order of increasing atomic mass, the eighth is like the first, the ninth is like the second, and so on. He called this rule the "law of octaves" and set up a table to illustrate it. Unfortunately, the value of Newlands's work was not appreciated at first and he was even ridiculed when he presented his ideas at a meeting of the Chemical Society. Later, however, he was highly honored for his work.

The form of the periodic table in use today originated in 1869. A German chemist, Lothar Meyer, and a Russian chemist, Dmitri Mendeleev, published similar tables, although they had worked independently of each other. Meyer also illustrated the periodicity of properties by plotting properties that could be expressed as numbers versus atomic masses. A portion of the curve for atomic volume (the volume occupied by one mole of an element) looked something like the curve depicted in the margin.

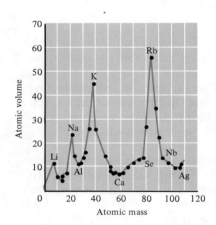

The alkali metals (Group I) are at the peaks and the more dense elements are in the troughs. Two other things should be observed: (1) The change in atomic mass in going from lithium to sodium and from sodium to potassium is about the same, but that between potassium and rubidium, and rubidium and cesium is much larger; (2) the omission of undiscovered elements does not change the general shape of the curve.

Mendeleev, like Newlands, proposed a table with columns of related elements. But Mendeleev's table was more nearly complete and left spaces for undiscovered elements. For example, in 1869, the next heaviest known element after zinc was arsenic. Arsenic is not much like aluminum or silicon — it is much more like phosphorus. So Mendeleev placed arsenic next to phosphorus and left spaces next to aluminum and silicon in his table for elements that he felt sure would be discovered later (Figure A). He was even able to predict the properties of these elements with considerable accuracy. Both were discovered a few years later and fulfilled his predictions.

Eventually, the growth of our knowledge of atomic structure indicated that after the first two horizontal rows, the next rows in the table should be made longer. This could have been predicted from Lothar Meyer's curves.

The discovery of helium and argon in the last decade of the nineteenth century raised some serious questions about the periodic table, for there was no place for them. Soon, however, other similar gases — neon, krypton, and xenon — were found. It was seen that these elements constitute an entirely new family in the periodic table. Indeed, in the light of our present knowledge of the electronic structure of atoms, these gases are extremely important. Had they not been discovered in nature, chemists would certainly be looking for them.

Figure A
Mendeleev's Periodic Table (as it was published in *Zeitschrift für Chemie* in 1869) The tables of Mendeleev and Meyer were very similar, although Mendeleev based his primarily on chemical properties and Meyer based his primarily on physical properties. Note the spaces for unknown elements, as indicated by question marks in the symbol column. Tellurium and iodine (symbolized by J here for German Jod), are out of atomic mass order because Mendeleev recognized that their chemical properties related them to selenium and bromine, respectively. In a later version, Mendeleev rearranged his table so that the vertical columns listed the groups as in the modern periodic table.

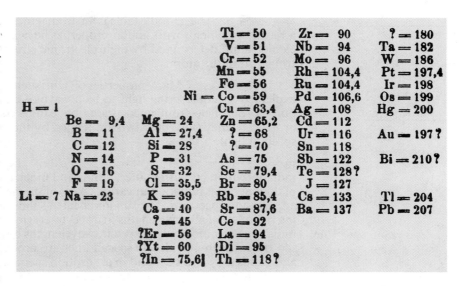

Even with the addition of the newly discovered elements and the expansion of the table into eighteen columns, some difficulties remained. In three cases, the order of increasing atomic masses did not put the elements in the proper chemical sequence (cobalt and nickel, argon and potassium, tellurium and iodine). Also, the rare earth elements (elements 57–71) all seemed to belong in a single space between barium and hafnium. The first of these difficulties was resolved when Henry Moseley found that the atomic number, rather than the atomic mass, is the fundamental property for the arrangement of the elements. The second was resolved in a practical way by relegating the rare earth elements to a space outside the table proper. Knowledge of electronic structure explained the similarities of these elements and showed that they do indeed all belong between barium and hafnium as the 4f orbitals are filled.

The four heaviest elements known for many years (elements 89–92, actinium-uranium) were assigned positions in the four columns of the table following radium. In terms of the properties of the elements, this assignment was only moderately satisfactory, but it was accepted. On the basis of this plan, elements 93 and 94 should resemble rhenium and osmium. However, when these elements were synthesized, it was found that they are not like rhenium and osmium, but instead *both* resemble uranium.

This similarity in properties brought to mind the rare earth series. In 1944 Glenn Seaborg at the University of California, where the new elements had been made, proposed that the elements after radium were misplaced in the periodic table. Instead they are part of a second "rare earth" series, which like the first, would contain fourteen elements, the last being element number 103. All of these elements have now been synthesized and found to fit into the scheme very well. Moreover, elements 104, 105, 106, 107, and 109 have been synthesized. So far, chemical studies have shown that 104 has properties that relate it to hafnium, as the periodic table would lead us to expect.

All of the synthetic elements are radioactive and, except for plutonium, have been prepared in only very small amounts. It is not yet known whether still heavier elements can be made. There is some speculation that elements in the region of number 114 will not be radioactive, but will be stable (see An Aside: Superheavy Elements, Chapter 31). However, that is an exciting possibility that remains to be demonstrated.

INTRODUCTION The periodic table is an arrangement of the chemical elements in such a way that elements with similar properties lie near each other. The properties of the elements are determined by their electronic structures—the arrangement of electrons within the atom.

8.1 LIGHT AS WAVES Many properties of light, such as diffraction and interference, are explained by considering light to be a wave of electromagnetic energy. Light, like other forms of electromagnetic radiation, can be characterized by its wavelength (λ) or its frequency (v). These two are related by the expression $c = \lambda v$, where c is the speed of light.

TOOLS OF CHEMISTRY: ELECTROMAGNETIC RADIATION AND SPECTRA When electromagnetic radiation interacts with matter, atoms and molecules may absorb energy. Emission of this energy as radiation in various parts of the electromagnetic spectrum produces an emission spectrum. The sun and heated solids emit continuous spectra containing radiation of all wavelengths in a spectral region. Line spectra are produced when radiation is emitted only at specific wavelengths by excited electrons in atoms. Band spectra consisting of closely spaced lines are produced by excited molecules. Lines and bands may also be found in absorption spectra, produced when a continuum of radiation is passed through a sample that absorbs certain wavelengths. A spectrometer records the intensity and frequency of absorbed or emitted radiation.

8.2 LIGHT AS PARTICLES; THE BIRTH OF QUANTUM THEORY Around the turn of the century physicists realized that some properties of light could be accounted for by regarding light as made up of particles (photons). Since each photon carries a fixed amount of energy, the energy of light is said to be quantized—limited to whole-number multiples of the fundamental unit, or quantum. The energy of a quantum is related to the frequency of the light by the expression $E = hv$, where h is Planck's constant. Light thus exhibits wave–particle duality; in some situations it has the properties of a wave, in others those of a particle.

8.3 ELECTRONS AS WAVES **8.4** QUANTUM MECHANICS: THE HEISENBERG UNCERTAINTY PRINCIPLE Electrons also exhibit wave–particle duality. For example, electrons can be diffracted from the atoms of a crystal. Quantum mechanics is the study of the motion of entities such as the electron which are small enough to exhibit both wave and particle properties. Basic to quantum mechanics is the Heisenberg uncertainty principle, which states that it is impossible to know both the exact momentum and the exact position of an electron at the same time.

8.5 ATOMIC SPECTRA **8.6** THE BOHR MODEL OF THE HYDROGEN ATOM Excited atoms in the gaseous state emit radiation at specific wavelengths which are characteristic for each element. By making the assumption that the electron in a hydrogen atom can occupy only certain discrete orbits with quantized angular momentum and energy, Bohr was able to explain the wavelengths of the hydrogen spectrum. Bohr proposed that electrons radiate only when they fall from one allowed orbit to another of lower energy; the energy of the photon emitted is equal to the difference in energy between the two orbits.

8.7 THE QUANTUM-MECHANICAL MODEL OF THE ATOM **8.8** ORBITALS AND QUANTUM NUMBERS The quantum-mechanical model of the atom treats electrons as three-dimensional waves occupying the space around the nucleus. The region in which an electron has the greatest probability of being found is its atomic orbital. The energy of the electron is quantized, and each orbital is defined by three quantum numbers. The principal quantum number, n, designates the main energy level of the electron (for ground states of known elements, $n = 1$–7). The subshell quantum number, l, designates the different subshells within each principal energy level ($l = 0$ to $n - 1$). The orbital quantum number, m_l, designates different orbitals within each subshell ($m_l = -l$ to $+l$). In addition, each orbital can be occupied by two electrons of opposite spin, designated by the spin quantum number, m_s, ($m_s = +\frac{1}{2}$ or $-\frac{1}{2}$). The quantum numbers designate the number of possible orbitals within each main energy level and each orbital may be occupied by two electrons of opposite spin (see Tables 8.3 and 8.4). Where they are allowed, there are one *s* orbital, three *p* orbitals, five *d* orbitals, and seven *f* orbitals.

8.9 PICTURING ORBITALS Pictures of orbitals should not be interpreted as "shapes" that have an actual physical existence; they depict regions of probable electron density. For s orbitals, the region is spherical (see Figure 8.16). For *p* orbitals, the regions are lobes that extend along the *x*, *y*, and *z* axes (see Figure 8.17). The regions for *d* and *f* orbitals have more complex "shapes"; for the *d* orbitals (see Figure 8.18), some have lobes extending along the axes and some have lobes that fall in between the axes.

8.10 ELECTRON CONFIGURATIONS Three principles govern the sequence in which orbitals are filled as the number of electrons per atom increases. The Pauli exclusion principle states that no two electrons can have the same four quantum numbers. The principle of lowest energy states that electrons occupy the lowest-energy orbitals available to them, entering higher-energy orbitals only when lower energy orbitals are filled. Hund's principle states that orbitals of equal energy are each occupied by a single electron before the second electron (with opposite spin quantum number) enters the orbital.

8.11 GROUPS, PERIODS, AND ELECTRON CONFIGURATIONS **8.12** CLASSIFICATION OF THE ELEMENTS The outermost electrons take part in chemical bonding and so determine the chemical properties of each element as reflected in the periodic table. Elements in a vertical column constitute a group or family. A horizontal row is called a period. The first two groups, collectively the *s* block, contain only *s* electrons in their outermost energy levels. Elements of Groups III–VII, in which *p* subshells are being filled, are called *p* block elements. The column at the extreme right contains the noble gases, elements for which all occupied energy subshells are completely filled. The rest of the elements are either *d*-transition elements (in which the *d* subshells are being filled) or *f*-transition elements (in which the *f* subshells are being filled). Elements of Groups I–VII, together with Zn, Cd, and Hg, are classified as representative elements. The elements can also be divided, based on their properties, into metals, semiconducting elements, and nonmetals.

THOUGHTS ON CHEMISTRY

The Character of Physical Law

THE CHARACTER OF PHYSICAL LAW,
by Richard P. Feynman

Electrons, when they were first discovered, behaved exactly like particles or bullets, very simply. Further research showed, from electron diffraction experiments for example, that they behaved like waves. As time went on there was a growing confusion about how these things really behaved — waves or particles, particles or waves? Everything looked like both.

This growing confusion was resolved in 1925 or 1926 with the advent of the correct equations for quantum mechanics. Now we know how the electrons and light behave. But what can I call it? If I say they behave like particles I give the wrong impression; also if I say they behave like waves. They behave in their own inimitable way, which technically could be called a quantum mechanical way. They behave in a way that is like nothing that you have ever seen before. Your experience with things that you have seen before is incomplete. The behaviour of things on a very tiny scale is simply different. An atom does not behave like a weight hanging on a spring and oscillating. Nor does it behave like a miniature representation of the solar system with little planets going around in orbits. Nor does it appear to be somewhat like a cloud or fog of some sort surrounding the nucleus. It behaves like nothing you have ever seen before.

There is one simplification at least. Electrons behave in this respect in exactly the same way as photons; they are both screwy, but in exactly the same way. . . .

The difficulty really is psychological and exists in the perpetual torment that results from your saying to yourself, `But how can it be like that?' which is a reflection of uncontrolled but utterly vain desire to see it in terms of something familiar. I will not describe it in terms of an analogy with something familiar; I will simply describe it. There was a time when the newspapers said that only twelve men understood the theory of relativity. I do not believe there ever was such a time. There might have been a time when only one man did, because he was the only guy who caught on, before he wrote his paper. But after people read the paper a lot of people understood the theory of relativity in some way or other, certainly more than twelve. On the other hand, I think I can safely say that nobody understands quantum mechanics. So do not take the lecture too seriously, feeling that you really have to understand in terms of some model what I am going to describe, but just relax and enjoy it. I am going to tell you what nature behaves like. If you will simply admit that maybe she does behave like this, you will find her a delightful, entrancing thing. Do not keep saying to yourself, if you can possibly avoid it, `But how can it be like that?' because you will get `down the drain', into a blind alley from which nobody has yet escaped. Nobody knows how it can be like that.

Richard P. Feynman, *The Character of Physical Law*, The Messenger Lectures, 1964 (Cambridge, Massachusetts: MIT Press, 1967), pp. 127–128.

QUESTIONS

Quantum Theory

8.1 Why is their wave nature important for particles that have very small masses? Why can we neglect the wave nature of objects that have large masses?

8.2 Which of the following exhibit quantization: (a) the length of a rope, (b) the energy of an electron in a hydrogen atom, (c) the seating arrangement in an auditorium, (d) the wavelength of light, (e) the seating arrangement in a classroom containing movable chairs, (f) grains of corn?

8.3 Describe what happens to a photoelectric surface when a low-intensity light of a frequency below the threshold energy shines on the surface. What happens if the intensity of the low-frequency light is increased by a factor of 1000? What happens if a low-intensity light of a frequency *above* the threshold frequency is used? What happens if the intensity of this light is increased?

8.4 What happens when quantum mechanics is applied to large-scale, familiar phenomena?

8.5 State the Heisenberg uncertainty principle. Is this principle significant at the atomic level? Why don't we worry about this principle when discussing everyday phenomena?

Quantum Theory and the Atom

8.6 Choose the atomic electronic transition which emits more energy than the $n = 3$ to $n = 1$ transition: (a) $n = 1$ to $n = 25$, (b) $n = 3$ to $n = 2$, (c) $n = 5$ to $n = 3$, (d) $n = 4$ to $n = 1$.

8.7 Name the five basic parts of a spectrometer. Briefly describe the function of each.

8.8 Prepare a sketch similar to Figure 8.10 that shows a ground energy state and two excited energy states. Using vertical arrows, indicate the transitions which would correspond to the absorption spectrum for this system.

8.9 State the three basic principles that make up the Bohr theory. Why is this theory no longer used as the working model of the atom?

8.10 How does the Bohr theory explain the line spectra that are observed for atomic hydrogen?

8.11 Your laboratory partner asks you to explain the subshell quantum number to him. You decide that the important things to cover include symbol, permitted values, and a physical interpretation. What do you tell him?

8.12 What are the permitted values of the principal quantum number? What is the range of values for the ground states of the known elements? What does $n = \infty$ mean? What physical interpretation can be given for n?

8.13 Briefly discuss the orbital quantum number. What are the permitted values of this quantum number?

8.14 What values of the spin quantum number are permitted?

8.15 What values of the subshell quantum number correspond to the (a) d, (b) f, (c) s, (d) p, and (e) g subshells?

8.16 What values can m_l take for (a) a $4d$ orbital, (b) a $1s$ orbital, and (c) a $3p$ orbital?

8.17 Choose the set of quantum numbers which could correctly describe an electron in an atom: (a) $n = 4$, $l = 4$, $m_l = 3$, $m_s = +\frac{1}{2}$; (b) $n = 3$, $l = 2$, $m_l = -3$, $m_s = -\frac{1}{2}$; (c) $n = 0$, $l = 0$, $m_l = 0$, $m_s = +\frac{1}{2}$; (d) $n = 3$, $l = 1$, $m_l = 0$, $m_s = -\frac{1}{2}$.

8.18 How many orbitals are in the (a) s, (b) p, (c) d, (d) f subshells? How many electrons can each orbital hold? How many electrons can each subshell hold?

8.19 Prepare sketches for the (a) $1s$, (b) $2p_x$, (c) $2p_y$, (d) $2p_z$, (e) $3d_{z^2}$, (f) $3d_{x^2-y^2}$, (g) $3d_{xy}$, (h) $3d_{yz}$, and (i) $3d_{xz}$ atomic orbitals.

8.20 Using Figure 8.14, place the following subshells in order of increasing distance from the nucleus (use the maximum in the curve for the basis of your ordering): $1s$, $2s$, $2p$, $3s$, $3p$, and $3d$.

8.21 Choose the set of quantum numbers that represents the electron of the lowest energy: (a) $n = 2$, $l = 0$, $m_l = 0$, $s = -\frac{1}{2}$; (b) $n = 2$, $l = 1$, $m_l = 0$, $s = +\frac{1}{2}$; (c) $n = 4$, $l = 0$, $m_l = 0$, $s = +\frac{1}{2}$; (d) $n = 4$, $l = 0$, $m_l = 0$, $s = -\frac{1}{2}$.

Electrons and the Periodic Table

8.22 State the Pauli exclusion principle. Do any of the following electron configurations violate this rule: (a) $1s^2$, (b) $1s^2\,2p^1$, (c) $1s^3$?

8.23 State the lowest energy principle. Do any of the following electron configurations violate this rule: (a) $1s^1\,2s^1$, (b) $1s^2\,2p^1$, (c) $1s^2\,2s^2\,2p_x^1\,2p_y^1$?

8.24 State the Hund principle. Do any of the following electron configurations violate this rule: (a) $1s^2$, (b) $1s^2\,2s^2\,2p_x^2$, (c) $1s^2\,2s^2\,2p_x^1\,2p_y^1$, (d) $1s^2\,2s^2\,2p_x^1\,2p_z^1$, (e) $1s^2\,2s^2\,2p_x^2\,2p_y^1\,2p_z^1$?

8.25 Using the rules given in Section 8.10, write reasonable electron configurations for atoms of (a) K, (b) Sc, (c) Si, (d) F, (e) U, and (f) Ag. Compare your answers to the known configurations given in Table 8.6. Which elements are paramagnetic?

8.26 Repeat Question 8.25 for (a) Mg, (b) Fe, (c) Pr, (d) Sn, (e) Ga, and (f) W.

8.27 Repeat Question 8.25 for (a) C, (b) Cr, (c) Zn, (d) P, (e) Ne, and (f) Au.

8.28 Identify the elements corresponding to the following electron configurations: (a) $1s^2\,2s^2\,2p^6\,3s^2\,3p^6\,3d^{10}\,4s^2\,4p^3$, (b) [Kr] $4d^{10}\,4f^{14}\,5s^2\,5p^6\,5d^{10}\,5f^{14}\,6s^2\,6p^6\,6d^2\,7s^2$, (c) [Kr] $4d^{10}\,4f^{14}\,5s^2\,5p^6\,5d^{10}\,6s^2\,6p^4$, (d) [Kr] $4d^5\,5s^2$, and (e) $1s^2\,2s^2\,2p^6\,3s^2\,3p^6\,3d^3\,4s^2$.

8.29 Repeat Question 8.28 for (a) $1s^2\,2s^2\,2p^6\,3s^2\,3p^6\,3d^5\,4s^1$, (b) [Kr] $4d^{10}\,4f^{14}\,5s^2\,5p^6\,5d^{10}\,6s^2\,6p^1$, (c) $1s^2\,2s^2\,2p^6\,3s^2\,3p^6$, and (d) [Kr] $4d^{10}\,4f^{14}\,5s^2\,5p^6\,5d^{10}\,6s^2\,6p^6\,7s^2$.

8.30 Predict and write the electron configuration for element 119. In what family of the periodic table would it fall?

8.31* Write the electron configuration for the Cu atom using the order of filling predicted by the aufbau principle. Because a configuration of d^{10} is very favorable, one of the $4s$ electrons is used to complete the $3d$ subshell. Write the electron configuration for this alternative arrangement of electrons. Do the different configurations predict a difference in the magnetic properties of Cu?

8.32 Identify the groups of the periodic table having outer electron configurations of (a) $ns^2\,np^5$, (b) ns^2, (c) $ns^2\,(n-1)d^{1-10}$, (d) $ns^2\,np^1$.

8.33 Repeat Question 8.32 for (a) $ns^2\,np^3$, (b) ns^1, (c) $ns^2\,(n-1)d^{0-2}\,(n-2)f^{1-14}$

8.34 Write the outer electron configurations for the (a) noble gases, (b) alkali metals, (c) f-transition metals, and (d) vanadium family.

8.35 Repeat Question 8.34 for the (a) alkaline earth metals, (b) d-transition metals, and (c) halogens.

8.36 What are the four basic types of elements in the modern periodic table? Write the outer electron configurations for these types.

8.37 Identify the part of the periodic table from which the elements with the following configurations are found: (a) $1s^2\,2s^2\,2p^6\,3s^2\,3p^6\,4s^2$, (b) [Kr]$4d^8\,5s^1$, (c) [Xe]$4f^{14}\,5d^6\,6s^2$, and (d) [Xe]$4f^{12}\,6s^2$.

8.38 Repeat Question 8.37 for (a) [Kr]$4d^{10}\,5s^2\,5p^6$, (b) [Kr]$4d^{10}\,4f^{14}\,5s^2\,5p^6\,5d^{10}\,6s^2\,6p^2$, (c) [Rn]$5f^7\,7s^2$, and (d) [Rn]$7s^2$.

8.39 Repeat Question 8.37 for (a) $1s^2\,2s^2\,2p^6\,3s^2\,3p^6\,3d^8\,4s^2$, (b) [Xe]$4f^{11}\,6s^2$, (c) [Kr]$4d^{10}\,5s^2\,5p^3$, and (d) [Rn]$7s^1$.

8.40 Use the location of the elements in the following periodic table to identify (a) the alkali metal, (b) the element with the outer configuration of $d^8\,s^2$, (c) the lanthanide, (d) the p-block representative elements, (e) the elements with incompletely filled f-subshells, (f) the halogen, (g) the s-block representative elements, (h) the actinide, (i) the d-transition elements, and (j) the noble gas.

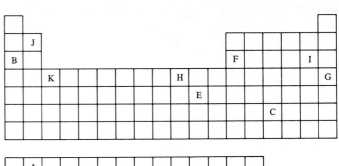

8.2 (b), (c), (f)

8.12 1,2,3, . . .; 1–7; electron removed from atom (ionization); n defines the energy of an atomic electron and its average distance from the nucleus.

8.15 (a) 2, (b) 3, (c) 0, (d) 1, (e) 4

8.17 (d)

8.21 (a)

8.23 Electrons first occupy the lowest energy subshell available; yes—(a) and (b)

8.29 (a) Cr, (b) Tl, (c) Ar, (d) Ra

8.33 (a) Group V, the nitrogen family; (b) Group I, the alkali metals; (c) the f-transition metals

8.35 (a) ns^2, (b) $ns^{1,2} (n-1)d^{1-10}$, (c) $ns^2 np^5$

8.37 (a) Ca, s-block representative element (alkaline earth); (b) Rh, d-transition element; (c) Os, d-transition element; (d) Er, f-transition element (lanthanide)

8.40 (a) B; (b) H; (c) A; (d) C, F, I; (e) A, D; (f) I; (g) B, J; (h) D; (i) E, H, K; (j) G

PROBLEMS

Wave-Particle Nature of Light and Particles

8.1 Orange light has a wavelength of about 605 nm in the visible range of the spectrum. Calculate (a) the frequency, (b) the wave number, and (c) the energy of a photon of this light. *Answer* (a) 4.96×10^{14} s^{-1}, (b) 1.65×10^4 cm^{-1}, (c) 3.29×10^{-19} J

8.2 Typical infrared frequencies are near 1×10^{13} Hz. What wavelength and wave number correspond to this frequency? What is the energy of a photon of this radiation?

8.3 Carbon dioxide absorbs energy at $v = 2.001 \times 10^{13}$ s^{-1}, 4.017×10^{13} s^{-1}, and 7.043×10^{13} s^{-1}. Calculate the wavelengths for these absorptions. In what spectral range do these absorptions occur? *Answer* 1.498×10^{-5} m, 7.463×10^{-6} m, 4.257×10^{-6} m; infrared

8.4 Find the de Broglie wavelength of (a) a 1.2 g bullet moving with a velocity of 1.5×10^4 cm/s, (b) a 2.6 ton automobile moving with a velocity of 55 miles/hr, and (c) an electron (mass $= 9.11 \times 10^{-31}$ kg) moving with a velocity of 3.00×10^7 m/s.

8.5* The energy of a photon in the x-ray region of the spectrum is 7×10^{-16} J. According to de Broglie's equation, what is the mass of this photon? *Answer* 7×10^{-30} g

Additional Problems

8.6 Calculate the wave number of the first six lines in the Lyman series for atomic hydrogen.

8.7 Use Equation 8.5 to calculate $\bar{v}$ for atomic hydrogen as an electron changes from the $n = 3$ level to the $n = 1$ level. To what wavelength does this value of $\bar{v}$ correspond? Is this wavelength in the visible region of the spectrum? *Answer* 97,491.6 cm^{-1}; 102.573 nm; no, it lies in the ultraviolet.

8.8* Light energy is emitted as an electron is "captured" by a hydrogen ion: $H^+ (g) + e^- \longrightarrow H(g)$. Assuming that the resulting hydrogen atom is in the ground electronic state after the capture, what is the wavelength of the emitted radiation?

8.9* Each of the ions formed by the elements in Representative Group I of the periodic table has a spectral line in the visible region of the spectrum which can be used to identify the element. Using the following data for the most intense lines, predict what color would be observed (violet, 400–450 nm; blue, 450–510 nm; green, 510–550 nm; yellow, 550–590 nm; orange, 590–620 nm; red, 620–700 nm); (a) Li, $\lambda = 6708$ Å for $2p \longrightarrow 2s$; (b) Na, $\bar{v} = 16980$ cm^{-1} for $3p \longrightarrow 3s$; (c) K, $v = 3.90 \times 10^{14}$ Hz for $4p \longrightarrow 4s$ and 7.41×10^{14} Hz for $5p \longrightarrow 4s$; (d) Rb, $\lambda = 7.9 \times 10^{-7}$ m for $5p \longrightarrow 5s$ and 4.2×10^{-7} m for $6p \longrightarrow 5s$; and (e) Cs, $v = 3.45 \times 10^{14}$ Hz for $6p \longrightarrow 6s$ and 6.53×10^{14} Hz for $7p \longrightarrow 6s$.

8.10* The following lines were observed in the spectrum of atomic hydrogen: 5331.5 cm^{-1}, 7799.3 cm^{-1}, 9139.8 cm^{-1}, and 9948.1 cm^{-1}. These lines all belong to the same spectroscopic series. Identify this series. *Answer* Paschen series

8.11 The average distance from the moon to the earth is 2.36×10^5 miles. How long will it take for a quantum of light energy to travel this distance? Does the amount of time depend on whether the photon is in the x-ray or infrared region of the spectrum? *Answer* 1.27 s; no

8.12 The energy of a photon of light must be 2.26 eV in order to produce the photoelectric effect in potassium. What is the wavelength of a photon having this energy? (1 eV $= 1.602 \times 10^{-19}$ J.) Would a photon having $\lambda = 700$ nm produce the photoelectric effect in potassium?

Among your friends, there are probably some whom you think of as cheerful, some as pessimistic, others as purposeful and always busy, and still others as lazy or devoted mainly to having fun. We put people in categories in many ways—leaders and followers, winners and losers, good guys and bad guys. Yet no collection of adjectives, no list of generalities, can give the whole picture of what a single individual is like. There isn't any substitute for getting to know people by talking with them, being in their company, and seeing how they react in different situations.

Here and in the next chapter we are going to deal with many generalities about atoms, ions, and molecules—about bonding types in this chapter and about the properties of the elements related to their placement in the periodic table in the next chapter. Understanding the generalities of bonding and properties is valuable and can lead to predictions about chemical behavior. But, as with human beings, generalities about elements and compounds are not sufficient. In later chapters the "personalities" of the elements and some of their compounds are considered individually and in more detail.

ELECTRONS AND CHEMICAL BONDS

9.1 DEFINITION OF THE CHEMICAL BOND

Few terms in chemistry are as difficult to define as "the chemical bond." It is apparent that a force of some kind holds atoms together. Historically, the difficult problem was in understanding the *nature* of the force of attraction between atoms in chemical compounds. We now believe that the attraction between electrons and atomic nuclei, and the different ways in which electrons are distributed among and around the nuclei, can account for all types of chemical bonding.

The chemical bond definitions given at the end of this chapter (see Thoughts on Chemistry) reflect the growing understanding of the nature of the chemical bond. In writing a definition of the chemical bond we must distinguish chemical bonding from other, weaker and less long-lasting forces. We choose to define the **chemical bond** as a force that acts strongly enough between two atoms or groups of atoms to hold them together in a different species that has measurable properties.

9.2 VALENCE ELECTRONS AND LEWIS SYMBOLS

Valence electrons: electrons available for chemical bonding

For representative elements: Number of valence electrons = group number

Valence electrons are the electrons that are available to take part in chemical bonding. We say that "The carbon atom has four valence electrons," meaning that each carbon atom has four electrons that can participate in the formation of chemical bonds.

In all of the representative elements, the *s* and *p* electrons in the highest occupied energy level (the *n* level) are the bonding electrons. Carbon is in Representative Group IV, and the $2s^2$ and $2p^2$ electrons are the valence electrons. *Each* Group IV element has four valence electrons, the $ns^2\,np^2$ electrons. The Representative Group I elements all have a single valence electron, the ns^1 electron. This relationship can be generalized for all the representative elements: The number of valence electrons in an atom of a representative element equals the group number of that element. For the representative elements, the electrons in the *d* subshell of the next to highest energy level, as well as all of the electrons of lower energy, are too deeply buried within the atoms to take part in bonding or to have any great influence on chemical properties.

The story for the *d*-transition elements is a bit different. The outer level *s* electrons and the *d* electrons of the next lowest level—the one that is being filled across each period of *d*-transition metals—have almost the same energy. As a result, in addition to the one or two *s* electrons that are present, one or more of the *d* electrons are often able to take part in bond formation. Therefore, for the *d*-transition elements, it is not possible to know from the electron configurations alone how many electrons other than the *s* electrons are valence electrons.

EXAMPLE 9.1
Valence Electrons of Representative Elements

How many valence electrons are present in (a) antimony, (b) bromine, and (c) barium atoms?

(a) Antimony is in the nitrogen family, which is Representative Group V, and therefore has five valence electrons: the two *s* and the three *p* electrons in the $n = 5$ energy level ($5s^2\,5p^3$).
(b) Bromine is in the fluorine family, which is Representative Group VII, and so has seven valence electrons: the two *s* and the five *p* electrons in the $n = 4$ level ($4s^2\,4p^5$).
(c) Barium is in the beryllium family, which is Representative Group II. Barium has two valence electrons in the $n = 6$ energy level ($6s^2$).

Exercise How many valence electrons are present in cesium, silicon, and sulfur?
Answer one, $6s^1$; four, $3s^2\,3p^2$; six, $3s^2\,3p^4$

The Lewis symbol is a convenient notation for showing both the outer electron configurations of atoms and the electrons involved in bonding in compounds. In this notation the symbol of the element represents the nucleus plus the underlying, normally filled, energy levels of the atom. In a **Lewis symbol** the outer electrons are indicated by dots (or circles, or x's, etc.) arranged around the atomic symbol. The pairing of two electrons in the same orbital is represented by two dots on the same side of the symbol; for example, for the phosphorus atom

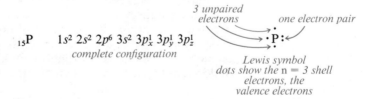

$_{15}P$ $1s^2\,2s^2\,2p^6\,3s^2\,3p_x^1\,3p_y^1\,3p_z^1$
complete configuration

Table 9.1 gives the Lewis symbols for atoms of the second-period elements. How Lewis symbols are used in writing chemical formulas is shown in later sections.

Table 9.1
Lewis Symbols for the Second-Period Elements

Element	Representative Group Number	Outer Electron Configuration	Number of Outer Electrons
Li·	I	$2s^1$	1
Be:	II	$2s^2$	2
Ḃ:	III	$2s^2\,2p^1$	3
·Ċ:	IV	$2s^2\,2p^2$	4
·N̈:	V	$2s^2\,2p^3$	5
·Ö:	VI	$2s^2\,2p^4$	6
·F̈:	VII	$2s^2\,2p^5$	7
:N̈e:	VIII	$2s^2\,2p^6$	8

<table>
<tr><td>**EXAMPLE 9.2**
Lewis Symbols of Representative Elements</td><td>Write the Lewis symbols for calcium and iodine.

Calcium is in Representative Group II and has two valence electrons that are paired ($4s^2$). Iodine is in Group VII and has seven valence electrons, six of them in pairs ($5s^2\,5p^5$).

 Ca: :I:

Exercise Write the Lewis symbols for B and S. *Answer* ·B: , ·S:</td></tr>
</table>

9.3 NOBLE GASES AND THE STABLE OCTET

The noble gases fall at the end of each period in the periodic table and as a group are the least reactive of all the elements (see Section 10.15). This resistance to chemical change, or **chemical stability,** is credited to the completely filled outer s and p subshells of the noble gases (Table 9.2).

Chemical reactions tend to occur in ways that lead to substances more stable than the original ones. A rule that accounts for the formation of many chemical compounds, although by no means all, is based upon the observed stability of compounds in which atoms are associated, as in the noble gas atoms (except helium), with eight valence electrons. According to the **octet rule,** atoms tend to combine by gain, loss, or sharing of electrons so that the outer energy level of each atom holds or shares four pairs of electrons. The octet rule—really just a summary of what has been observed—is useful in describing various compounds and in organizing compounds according to those that "obey" the rule and those that do not.

The next section is devoted to a general introduction to the three major types of chemical bonds and the properties associated with each of them. The rest of the chapter further examines the electron configurations and properties of substances with each type of bonding.

Table 9.2
The Noble Gases

Element	Period Number	Outer Electron Configuration	Lewis Symbol
He	1	$1s^2$	He:
Ne	2	$2s^2\,2p^6$	:Ne:
Ar	3	$3s^2\,3p^6$	:Ar:
Kr	4	$4s^2\,4p^6$	:Kr:
Xe	5	$5s^2\,5p^6$	:Xe:
Rn	6	$6s^2\,6p^6$	:Rn:

9.4 TYPES OF CHEMICAL BONDS

Gaseous chlorine and solid sodium react to form sodium chloride

$$2Na(s) + Cl_2(g) \longrightarrow 2NaCl(s) \tag{9.1}$$

This is a common type of reaction—the formation of an ionic compound (NaCl) from a metal (Na) and a nonmetal (Cl_2). We are going to use the substances involved in this particular reaction to illustrate the three basic types of chemical bonds—metallic, ionic, and covalent bonds—and the properties associated with them.

An examination of the properties of the reactants and the product in reaction

Table 9.3
Properties of Sodium, Chlorine, and Sodium Chloride

Property	Sodium Na (A Metal)	Chlorine Cl₂ (A Molecular Compound)	Sodium Chloride NaCl (An Ionic Compound)
Appearance	Silvery solid	Greenish yellow gas	White crystals
Molar mass (g)	22.99	70.90	58.44
Melting point (°C)	98	−101	808
Boiling point (°C)*	883	−34	1465
Density of solid (g/cm³)	0.967	1.9 (at −101 °C)	2.16
Heat of fusion at m.p.† (kJ/mol)	2.6	6.40	28.4
Heat of vaporization at b.p.† (kJ/mol)	81.2	20.4	171
Electrical conductivity			
Liquid	Very high	Very low	High
Solid	Very high	Very low	Very low

* Boiling point at atmospheric pressure.

† See Figure 7.9

(9.1) shows that these properties are very different (Table 9.3). Sodium is a silvery metal that has high **chemical reactivity,** that is, a tendency to undergo chemical reactions. (For instance, it reacts violently with water.) Although sodium is softer and less dense than most metals, it has a high boiling point. (Some *general* properties that distinguish metals and nonmetals are listed in Table 9.4. Chlorine, a nonmetallic element, is a yellow-green gas with a suffocating odor; it is a dangerous irritant to the lungs. Sodium chloride, the reaction product, is the stable, white, crystalline solid used as table salt. The melting and boiling points of sodium chloride are much higher than those of sodium or chlorine.

Because the force of chemical bonding is dependent upon the attraction between electrons and nuclei, experiments on the electrical conductivity of these substances provide some information about their bonding. Recall that for an electrical current to pass through a substance, charged particles, either electrons or ions, must be available to move through the substance (see Tools of Chemistry: Electricity and Magnetism, Chapter 3). The following observations can be made:

1. *Chlorine,* whether it is in the gaseous, liquid, or solid state, is an extremely poor conductor of electricity.

2. Solid *sodium* has a very high electrical conductivity. The conductivity is so high that the metal apparently offers almost no resistance to the flow of electrical current. Above its melting point sodium has a somewhat lower electrical conductivity (Figure 9.1), but it remains highly conductive. For both solid and liquid sodium, electrical conductivity decreases with increasing temperature.

3. Solid *sodium chloride* is a very poor conductor of electricity. At the melting point there is a dramatic increase in conductivity, although molten sodium chloride is about 10^5 times *less* conductive than solid sodium (see Figure 9.1). The electrical conductivities of both solid and molten sodium chloride increase with temperature, behavior opposite to that of sodium.

4. When direct current passes through molten sodium chloride, the reactants of Equation (9.1)—sodium and chlorine—are regenerated.

Chlorine in any state obviously contains neither freely mobile electrons nor freely mobile ions. Somehow, electrons are arranged so that the two chlorine atoms are held together in a Cl₂ molecule, but in such a way that neither ions nor free

Table 9.4
General Physical Properties of Metallic and Nonmetallic Elements The boiling point range for metals is approximately 650 °C to 6000 °C; for nonmetals it is approximately −250 °C to 450 °C (except for carbon, which is a network covalent substance; Section 9.17). Note that the properties of many elements do not agree with these general properties. For example, sodium melts below 100 °C, mercury melts at −38.87 °C, carbon as diamond melts at about 3700 °C and is the hardest of all substances, tin is brittle above 161 °C, lithium has a low density, carbon as graphite is a conductor, and iodine can also conduct electricity, although only weakly.

Metals	Nonmetals
Solids of high melting point, yielding high-boiling liquids	Gases or low-melting solids, yielding low-boiling liquids
Lustrous, reflecting light of many wavelengths	Dull, reflecting light poorly or absorbing strongly
High density	Low density
Often hard	Often soft
Malleable, ductile, strong	Brittle, weak
Conductors of heat and electricity	Insulators

electrons are present. This arrangement apparently does not change with a change in the state of chlorine.

The high electrical conductivity of sodium, by contrast, suggests that it contains highly mobile, charged particles in both the solid and liquid states. Electrons are much lighter than ions, and therefore are much more mobile than ions. So it seems reasonable to suppose that electrons are the current carriers in sodium.

Support for this conclusion is provided by the temperature dependence of conductivity in sodium (see Figure 9.1). In the passage of electrical current, electrons enter at one end of a piece of metal and come out at the other end. A metal wire is somewhat like a pipe full of water—water is ready to flow out one end when it is pushed in the other. Metals must contain electrons set free from the atoms so that they are ready to flow. This would leave behind positive metal ions. Increased vibration of these metal ions at higher temperatures would interfere with the flow of electrons, accounting for the decrease in conductivity with increasing temperature.

Solid sodium chloride apparently contains neither mobile electrons nor mobile ions. However, at the melting point current carriers are set free. Because the electrical conductivity is low relative to that of metallic sodium, it seems likely that ions rather than electrons have become mobile. As the temperature increases, the ions flow more easily and conductivity increases. The chemical change that occurs when current flows through the molten sodium chloride confirms the presence of both sodium and chloride ions. The sodium and chloride ions are converted to sodium atoms ($Na^+ + e^- \rightarrow Na$) and to chlorine molecules ($2Cl^- \rightarrow Cl_2 + 2e^-$).

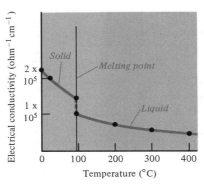

(a) Sodium

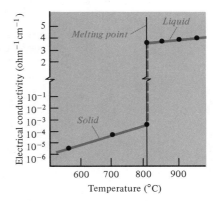

(b) Sodium chloride

Figure 9.1
Electrical Conductivity of Sodium and Sodium Chloride Note that the scales of these two graphs are quite different. At the melting point the conductivity of sodium chloride increases 10,000-fold. However, the conductivity of sodium at its lowest point in (a) is still 100,000 times greater than the conductivity of molten sodium chloride.

To summarize what these observations illustrate: Chlorine, a nonmetallic substance, contains no free electrons or ions. Sodium, a metal, contains mobile electrons in both the solid and liquid states. Sodium chloride, an ionic compound, contains neither mobile electrons nor mobile ions in the solid state. However, melting solid sodium chloride sets Na^+ and Cl^- ions free. A reasonable conclusion is that these ions are present in the solid state, but are not mobile.

In the following sections, we describe metallic bonding, which was illustrated here by sodium; ionic bonding, illustrated by sodium chloride; and covalent bonding, illustrated by chlorine. We discuss the electron configurations and properties associated with these three types of bonding separately. However, it should be understood before we begin that this separate discussion is done for simplicity. The bonding in most chemical compounds is not fully metallic, fully ionic, or fully covalent, but lies at some intermediate point in electron arrangement and properties. Later in the chapter (Section 9.19), we have more to say about the continua of bond types.

THE METALLIC BOND

9.5 BONDING IN METALS

Metal atoms contain outermost electrons that are much more easily removed than the outermost electrons in nonmetal atoms. The sodium atom

$$Na \qquad 1s^2\, 2s^2\, 2p^6\, 3s^1$$

has a single outer s valence electron. Look at Table 9.5, which gives configurations for some fifth-period metals, and notice that all but the p block metals have only one or two electrons in their highest energy levels.

In a metal, each atom gives up one or more valence electrons to become a cation. The valence electrons from all of the atoms form what has been called an "electron sea" that surrounds a network of metal cations. The freed valence electrons no longer "belong" to specific atoms. **Metallic bonding** is the attraction between positive metal ions and surrounding, freely mobile electrons (Figure 9.2). Representative metal atoms contribute their outermost s electrons or s and p electrons to the sea of free electrons. In transition metals some of the $(n-1)d$ electrons can also join the electron sea.

Table 9.5
Electron Configurations of Some Fifth-Period Metals

	Atomic Number	Configuration
s-block metals		
Rb	37	$[Kr]5s^1$
Sr	38	$[Kr]5s^2$
d-transition metals		
Y	39	$[Kr]4d^1\, 5s^2$
Ru	44	$[Kr]4d^7\, 5s^1$
Ag	47	$[Kr]4d^{10}\, 5s^1$
Cd	48	$[Kr]4d^{10}\, 5s^2$
p-block metals		
In	49	$[Kr]4d^{10}\, 5s^2\, 5p^1$
Sn	50	$[Kr]4d^{10}\, 5s^2\, 5p^2$

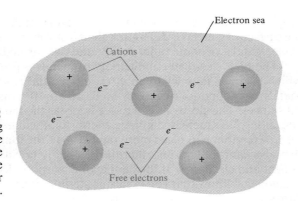

Figure 9.2
Metallic Bonding Metallic bonding is the attraction between positive ions and surrounding freely mobile electrons. Most metals contribute more than one mobile electron per atom.

9.6 PROPERTIES IMPARTED BY THE METALLIC BOND

Most substances that have metallic bonding are either metallic elements or alloys (mixtures of metals, or metals and nonmetals). Their general properties are those listed in Table 9.4 for the metallic elements. Some compounds, such as titanium nitride (TiN), also conduct electricity and apparently contain free electrons. (In recent years, an exciting area of new chemistry has opened up in the preparation of polymers that display metallic properties.)

The high boiling points and heats of vaporization of many metals (Table 9.6) show that it is difficult to liberate metal ions from the surrounding free electrons. Many metals are dense, but when a mechanical force is applied to a metal, the cations can move, sliding along on a "cushion" of free electrons (see Figure 9.5b). No specific bonds need be broken, the forces between the cation and the free electrons need not be disrupted, and no additional forces of repulsion are encountered. This explains the ease with which metals are hammered into shape (*malleability*) or drawn out into wires (*ductility*).

The free electrons are not limited to a few specific energy levels, but have a wide distribution of energies. Therefore, they are able to absorb and reemit visible light of many wavelengths, leading to the luster that is characteristic of metals and many alloys. As is demonstrated by sodium, pure metals (and also many alloys) retain the

Table 9.6
Properties of Some Metallic Elements

Property	Potassium K	Calcium Ca	Copper Cu	Molybdenum Mo	Tin* Sn
Appearance	Silvery, lustrous	Silvery, lustrous	Reddish, lustrous	Silvery, lustrous	White, lustrous
Atomic number	19	20	29	42	50
Melting point (°C)	63.4	851	1083	2610	232
Boiling point (°C)	757	1482	2582	5560	2270
Density of solid (g/cm³)	0.86	1.54	8.94	10.2	7.29
Heat of fusion at m.p. (kJ/mol)	2.3	8.5	13.3	27.8	7.1
Heat of vaporization at b.p. (kJ/mol)	76.9	155	304	589	259
Electrical conductivity					
Solid	Very high	Very high	Very high	Very high	Very high
Liquid	Very high	Very high	Very high	Very high	Very high

* In the form of white tin.

properties of high electrical conductivity and metallic luster in the liquid state. When the surface of a metal is dull rather than lustrous, it is usually because a layer of metal oxide, sulfide, or some other compound has formed on the surface.

The high electrical conductivity of metals is provided by the mobile electrons, which begin to flow when an electric potential is applied across a piece of metal. Metals also conduct heat very well, 10 to 10^5 times better than do most other substances. The electrons can move freely as the temperature rises, and they readily pass along their increased kinetic energy to other electrons. Also, the ions in a metal are free to vibrate in place more rapidly than the ions in an ionic compound, and so they also contribute to high thermal conductivity. Silver is one of the best conductors of heat and electricity. If the handle of a teaspoon feels hot as soon as you stir your tea, you will know that you are using sterling silver (92.5% Ag) and not silver-plated flatware.

THE IONIC BOND

9.7 BONDING IN IONIC COMPOUNDS

Ionic bonding is the attraction between positive and negative ions (Figure 9.3). Ionic compounds are simply collections of ions held together by the force of electrostatic attraction between cations and anions. Independent molecules do not exist in ionic compounds (Section 4.1b), and in the solid state the ions occupy fixed positions in a crystal (Figure 9.4).

The reaction between sodium and chlorine discussed in Section 9.4 is the combination of a metal and a nonmetal, a type of reaction that frequently produces ionic bonding. The result of the reaction is that sodium atoms have given up electrons to become sodium cations, and chlorine molecules have split into chlorine atoms, which have gained electrons to become chlorine anions. In terms of electron configurations what happens is that sodium and chlorine both form ions with octet configurations.

$$Na \odot \quad + \quad \cdot \ddot{\underset{\cdot\cdot}{Cl}} : \quad \longrightarrow \quad [Na]^+ \quad \left[: \ddot{\underset{\cdot\cdot}{Cl}} : \right]^-$$

$$(1s^2 2s^2 2p^6 (3s^1)) \quad (1s^2 2s^2 2p^6 3s^2 3p^5) \quad (1s^2 2s^2 2p^6) \quad (1s^2 2s^2 2p^6 3s^2 3p^6)$$

(The electron configurations of cations and anions are further discussed in Section 10.7.)

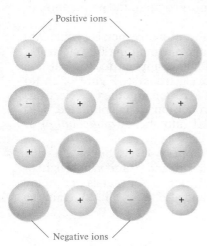

Positive ions

Negative ions

Figure 9.3
Ionic Bonding Ionic bonding is the attraction between positive and negative ions.

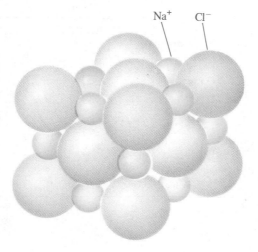

Na^+ Cl^-

Figure 9.4
Arrangement of Ions in Crystalline Sodium Chloride, NaCl

Table 9.7
General Properties of Ionic
Compounds The boiling point range
of ionic compounds is
approximately 700 ° – 3500 °C.

Crystalline solids	Good conductors of electricity when molten
Hard and brittle	Poor conductors of heat and electricity
High melting points	when solid
High boiling points	Many are soluble in water
High heats of vaporization	
High heats of fusion	

9.8 PROPERTIES IMPARTED BY THE IONIC BOND

Each ion in a solid ionic crystalline substance is surrounded by other ions of opposite charge. For example, in a sodium chloride crystal (see Figure 9.4) each Na^+ ion is surrounded by six Cl^- ions and each Cl^- ion is surrounded by six Na^+ ions. The electrostatic force of attraction holding the ions together is strong. Any changes that require disrupting the arrangement of ions in a crystalline ionic compound, therefore, require a large amount of energy. (It takes about 750 kJ per mole to separate the Na^+ and Cl^- ions in NaCl to "infinity," that is, to a distance at which they exert no force on each other.) As a result, ionic compounds have high melting points and boiling points, and high heats of vaporization and fusion (Tables 9.7, 9.8). For the same reasons, ionic crystalline substances are hard—a strong force is needed to break up the crystal lattice. However, such substances are brittle and when struck with sufficient force shatter along the planes between rows of ions (Figure 9.5).

The ratio of the numbers of different ions in a crystal is the ratio shown in the formula of the compound—the ratio necessary for electroneutrality. The geometrical arrangement of the ions is determined by the number of ions of each kind (Section 13.10) and by their sizes. The density of ionic compounds varies with the spacing of ions in the crystal and also, of course, with the masses of the ions. Ionic solids are generally less dense than metals.

Most solid ionic compounds are poor conductors of electricity because the ions are rigidly fixed in their positions. The ions become free to move and conduct electricity when ionic compounds melt or when they dissolve in water. Ionic solids

Table 9.8
Properties of Some Ionic Compounds

Property	Lithium Fluoride LiF	Potassium Bromide KBr	Calcium Nitrate Ca(NO₃)₂	Barium Sulfate BaSO₄	Praseodymium Iodide PrI₃
Appearance	White crystals	White crystals	White crystals, hygroscopic*	White crystals	Green crystals, hygroscopic*
Molar mass (g)	25.94	119.00	164.09	233.39	521.62
Melting point (°C)	870	730	561	1580	733
Boiling point (°C)	1670	1435	dec.†	dec.	1377
Density of solid (g/cm³)	2.64	2.75	2.36	4.5	2.31
Heat of fusion at m.p. (kJ/mol)	27.1	25.5	21	41	53.1
Heat of vaporization at b.p. (kJ/mol)	147	149	dec.	dec.	172
Electrical conductivity					
Liquid	High	High	High	High	High
Solid	Very low	Very low	Very low	Very low	Very low

* A *hygroscopic* substance takes up water from the air to become a wet solid.

† The abbreviation *dec.,* for decomposes, means that at the melting point or boiling point a chemical change takes place, usually a breakdown to simpler substances.

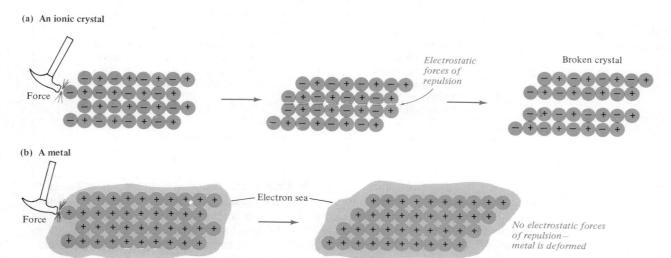

(a) An ionic crystal

Force

Electrostatic forces of repulsion

Broken crystal

(b) A metal

Force

Electron sea

No electrostatic forces of repulsion— metal is deformed

Figure 9.5
Shattering an Ionic Crystal; Bending a Metal.

are not very good conductors of heat, for the ions do not easily pass kinetic energy along to their neighbors.

THE COVALENT BOND

9.9 BONDING AND ELECTRON CONFIGURATION IN MOLECULAR COMPOUNDS

When a chemical bond forms between two atoms of a nonmetal, a molecule is produced, as in H_2 or Cl_2 or HCl. Elemental chlorine contains neither mobile electrons nor ions (Section 9.4). Instead the electrons of the two chlorine atoms are arranged to hold the atoms together in an electrically nonconducting substance.

The bond that holds atoms together in molecules is the result of the sharing of valence electrons, leading to the name "covalent" for such bonding. A chlorine atom is one electron short of an octet configuration. In the Cl_2 molecule, two $3p$ electrons are shared by the two chlorine atoms,

the shared pair of electrons

$$:\overset{\times\times}{\underset{\cdot\cdot}{Cl}} \overset{\times\times}{\underset{\times\times}{Cl}} \times $$

$1s^2 2s^2 2p^6 3s^2 3p^2 3p^2 \boxed{3p^1 \quad 3p^1} 3p^2 3p^2 3s^2 2p^6 2s^2 1s^2$

allowing each atom to achieve a stable octet configuration. Structures in which Lewis symbols are combined so that the bonding and nonbonding outer electrons are indicated are called **Lewis structures.** The dots and x's sometimes used in Lewis structures for compounds show the atomic origin of the electrons and aid in electron bookkeeping. However, the electrons in the bond are equivalent and indistinguishable from each other.

In an H_2 molecule the two $1s$ electrons are shared to give a stable two-electron configuration to each hydrogen atom. The sharing of a $1s$ electron from one hydrogen atom with the unpaired $3p$ electron from one chlorine atom gives a hydrogen chloride molecule in which the hydrogen and chlorine atoms both have noble-gas configurations

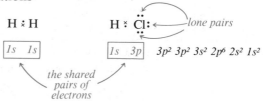

H $\overset{\times}{\cdot}$ H   H $\overset{\cdot\cdot}{\underset{\cdot\cdot}{\times}}$ Cl: ⟵ *lone pairs*

$\boxed{1s \quad 1s}$ $\boxed{1s \quad 3p}$ $3p^2\ 3p^2\ 3s^2\ 2p^6\ 2s^2\ 1s^2$

the shared pairs of electrons

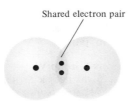

Shared electron pair

Figure 9.6
Covalent Bonding The bonded
atoms come close enough together
for their electron clouds to overlap.

Pairs of valence electrons not involved in bonding are called **nonbonding electron pairs,** or **lone pairs.** The chlorine atoms in Cl_2 and HCl each have three nonbonding electron pairs.

Covalent bonding: the attraction between atoms that share electrons

Covalent bonding is based upon electron-pair sharing and is the attraction between two atoms that share electrons (Figure 9.6). A **single covalent bond** is a bond in which two atoms are held together by sharing two electrons. The electrons in the bond spend enough time in the space between the two atoms to provide the "glue" that holds the atoms together. Each positive nucleus is attracted toward the region of high electron density between them.

Covalent bonds form between two atoms when ionic or metallic bonding is unlikely because the loss or gain of electrons requires a large amount of energy. The most obvious example is the bonding of nonmetal atoms with themselves (as in, e.g., Cl_2, H_2, O_2) and with each other (as in, e.g., HCl, H_2O, BrF_3). In bond formation, the semiconducting elements tend to behave like the nonmetals, forming covalent bonds in many compounds with nonmetals (e.g., BCl_3, SiF_4).

The number of valence electrons and the octet rule govern the formation of many covalent compounds. For second-period elements (Li to F), which have only s and p orbitals available, eight is the *maximum number* of valence electrons that can be accommodated.

Carbon, nitrogen, and oxygen form a great many covalent, or molecular, compounds that follow the octet rule. The Lewis structures for some compounds that obey the octet rule are given in Table 9.9. Recall that for the representative elements, the number of valence electrons equals the representative group number. As expected on this basis, a carbon atom, which has four valence electrons, forms four covalent bonds to achieve an octet. A nitrogen atom (five valence electrons) forms three covalent bonds and retains a lone pair of electrons to achieve an octet configuration, while oxygen (six valence electrons) forms two covalent bonds and retains two lone pairs of electrons. The fluorine family elements, with seven valence electrons, join in single covalent bonds in many compounds in order to complete their octets.

Table 9.9
Some Molecular Compounds Governed by the Octet Rule

H H
| |
H—C—N:
| |
H H

methylamine, CH₃NH₂
colorless gas, flammable
m.p. −93.5°C, b.p. −6°C

:Cl:
|
:Cl—Si—Cl:
|
:Cl:

silicon tetrachloride, SiCl₄
colorless liquid, fumes in air
m.p. −70°C, b.p. 59°C

H H
| |
H—C—C—H
| |
H H

ethane, C₂H₆
colorless gas, flammable
m.p. −183°C, b.p. −89°C

H
|
H—C—Ö—H
|
H

methanol, CH₃OH
colorless liquid, flammable and poisonous
m.p. −98°C, b.p. 65°C

The following two series of compounds illustrate simple covalent bonding to carbon, nitrogen, and oxygen by hydrogen and chlorine. As is usual, a line is drawn to indicate each shared electron pair.

C (Group IV)	N (Group V)	O (Group VI)
4 valence electrons	5 valence electrons	6 valence electrons
4 shared pairs 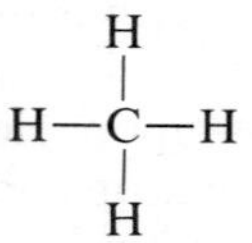	3 shared pairs 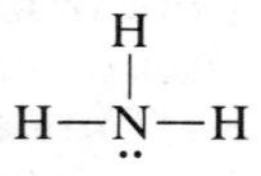	2 shared pairs 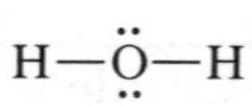

$$\text{H}-\underset{\underset{\text{H}}{|}}{\overset{\overset{\text{H}}{|}}{\text{C}}}-\text{H} \qquad \text{H}-\underset{..}{\overset{\overset{\text{H}}{|}}{\text{N}}}-\text{H} \qquad \text{H}-\overset{..}{\underset{..}{\text{O}}}-\text{H}$$

methane, CH_4
colorless gas, nonpoisonous
   and flammable
m.p. $-183\ °C$, b.p. $-161\ °C$

ammonia, NH_3

colorless gas, pungent odor
m.p. $-78\ °C$, b.p. $-33\ °C$

water, H_2O

colorless liquid
m.p. $0\ °C$, b.p. $100\ °C$

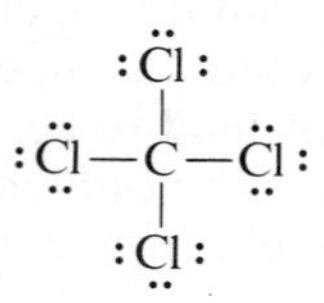

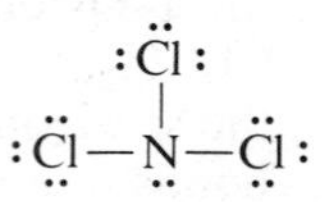

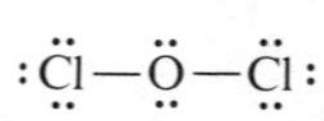

$$:\overset{..}{\underset{..}{\text{Cl}}}-\underset{\underset{:\overset{..}{\underset{..}{\text{Cl}}}:}{|}}{\overset{\overset{:\overset{..}{\text{Cl}}:}{|}}{\text{C}}}-\overset{..}{\underset{..}{\text{Cl}}}: \qquad :\overset{..}{\underset{..}{\text{Cl}}}-\underset{..}{\overset{\overset{:\overset{..}{\text{Cl}}:}{|}}{\text{N}}}-\overset{..}{\underset{..}{\text{Cl}}}: \qquad :\overset{..}{\underset{..}{\text{Cl}}}-\overset{..}{\underset{..}{\text{O}}}-\overset{..}{\underset{..}{\text{Cl}}}:$$

carbon tetrachloride, CCl_4

colorless liquid, dense
and nonflammable,
poisonous
m.p. $-23\ °C$, b.p. $77\ °C$

nitrogen trichloride, NCl_3

yellow, oily liquid,
very unstable and explosive

m.p. $-91.7\ °C$, b.p. $71\ °C$

chlorine   monoxide, Cl_2O
yellowish brown
gas, explosive

m.p. $-116\ °C$,
   b.p. $2\ °C$

Many stable compounds also exist in which the central atom is *not* surrounded by eight electrons. Most of these compounds fall into one of three categories:

1. *Certain molecular compounds of beryllium, boron, or aluminum* Beryllium, from Representative Group II, has two valence electrons ($2s^2$), and boron and aluminum, from Representative Group III, each have three valence electrons (B, $2s^2\,2p^1$; Al, $3s^2\,3p^1$). Therefore, these elements can form compounds with two or three covalent bonds, respectively, and no remaining unshared electron pairs, for example,

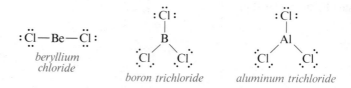

beryllium
chloride

boron trichloride   aluminum trichloride

2. *Certain molecular compounds of phosphorus, sulfur, chlorine, or other elements from the third period and beyond* In atoms with $n = 3$ or more, d orbitals are available (see Table 8.5). For elements of the third to sixth periods, the *outermost* d subshells are empty (remember that it is the next to outermost d subshells that are being filled in the d-transition elements).

Therefore, these elements can accommodate *more* than eight valence electrons if some of them utilize vacant outermost *d* subshells.

Compounds in which phosphorus, sulfur, or chlorine have more than an octet of electrons are commonly encountered. For example, in sulfur hexafluoride, SF_6, the sulfur atom shares six electron pairs. An isolated sulfur atom has six valence electrons in *s* and *p* subshells ($3s^2 3p^4$), and therefore room for only two more electrons in these occupied subshells. Of necessity, some of the shared electron pairs in the SF_6 molecule must utilize empty $3d$ subshells. In some cases, compounds with fewer than four covalent bonds to the central atom have more than an octet of electrons. In chlorine trifluoride, for example, the chlorine atom is surrounded by two unshared pairs of electrons and three shared pairs of electrons. To accommodate these 10 electrons, the empty *d* subshells must obviously also be utilized. (How the *d* subshells are involved in covalent bonding in such compounds is discussed in Section 11.6.)

12 electrons in outermost level of S ⟵ *10 electrons in outermost level of Cl* ⟶

sulfur(VI) fluoride, SF_6
colorless gas, m.p. $-50\ °C$
b.p. $64\ °C$

chlorine(III) fluoride, ClF_3
colorless gas,
m.p. $83\ °C$
b.p. $11.3\ °C$

3. *Compounds with unpaired electrons* Some compounds exist in which one or more electrons remain unpaired. In such cases the total of the valence electrons of the central atom and the atoms bonded to it is an odd number. Chlorine dioxide, for example, has a total of 19 valence electrons (6 from each of the two oxygen atoms and 7 from the chlorine atom). Measurements of the magnetism of this compound (see Figure 8.19) show the presence of one unpaired electron per molecule. The Lewis structure for such a compound must agree with the observed magnetic properties. A reasonable Lewis structure for chlorine dioxide is

$$:\ddot{O}:\dot{\underset{..}{Cl}}:\ddot{O}:$$

Most species that contain even numbers of electrons are diamagnetic (see Figure 8.9, Section 8.10). A notable exception is the O_2 molecule, which contains two unpaired electrons. (An explanation of the paramagnetism of O_2 must be deferred to Chapter 24.)

9.10 MULTIPLE COVALENT BONDS

More than one pair of electrons can be shared between the same two atoms, resulting in what is called a **multiple covalent bond**. In a **double covalent bond** two electron pairs are shared between the same two atoms.

ethylene, C_2H_4
colorless gas,
m.p. $-170\ °C$, b.p. $-104\ °C$

carbon dioxide, CO_2
solid goes directly to gas at
$-78\ °C$

In a **triple covalent bond** three electron pairs are shared between the same two atoms.

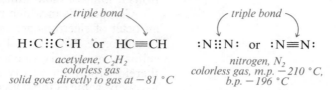

H : C :: C : H or HC≡CH   :N :: N: or :N≡N:

acetylene, C₂H₂
colorless gas
solid goes directly to gas at −81 °C

nitrogen, N₂
colorless gas, m.p. −210 °C,
b.p. −196 °C

Carbon, nitrogen, and oxygen are the most common participants in multiple covalent bonds. Carbon and nitrogen can form either double or triple bonds. Oxygen is doubly bonded in many compounds and triply bonded in a few cases, for example, carbon monoxide, C≡O, and nitrosyl ion, N≡O⁺. Phosphorus, sulfur, and selenium can also form multiple bonds in some compounds.

9.11 COORDINATE COVALENT BONDS

So far, we have considered mainly covalent bonds to which each atom contributes one electron. Sometimes, both electrons are provided to a bond by the same atom. A single covalent bond in which both electrons in the shared pair come from the same atom is called a **coordinate covalent bond.**

The **donor atom** provides both electrons to a coordinate covalent bond, and the **acceptor atom** accepts an electron pair for sharing in a coordinate covalent bond. For a coordinate covalent bond, as for any other kind of bond, it is impossible to distinguish among the electrons once the bond has formed. For example, a hydrogen ion unites with an ammonia molecule by a coordinate covalent bond to form the ammonium ion

but all four hydrogen atoms and all four nitrogen–hydrogen bonds in the ammonium ion are found by experiment to be equivalent.

Frequently nonmetal atoms that are already part of molecules or ions form coordinate covalent bonds with metal atoms or ions, usually those of transition metals. For example, the nitrogen atom in ammonia can "coordinate" with a silver cation to form what is called a *complex ion*

$$2H : \overset{\cdot\cdot}{\underset{H}{N}} : + Ag^+ \longrightarrow \left[H : \overset{H}{\underset{H}{N}} : Ag : \overset{H}{\underset{H}{N}} : H \right]^+ \quad \text{or} \quad [Ag(NH_3)_2]^+$$

Neutral compounds with similar coordinate covalent bonding can also be formed, notably by carbon monoxide and metal atoms.

$$4 : C \equiv O : + Ni \longrightarrow \left[\begin{array}{c} \overset{\cdot\cdot}{O} \\ \parallel \\ C \\ | \\ : O \equiv C : Ni : C \equiv O : \\ | \\ C \\ \parallel \\ \underset{\cdot\cdot}{O} \end{array} \right] \quad \text{or} \quad [Ni(CO)_4]$$

9.12 POLYATOMIC IONS The atoms in polyatomic ions such as hydroxide ion, ammonium ion, and sulfate ion, are held together by covalent bonds.

$$[:\ddot{O}:H]^- \qquad \left[:\ddot{O}:\underset{\underset{\textstyle :\ddot{O}:}{\textstyle ..}}{\overset{\overset{\textstyle :\ddot{O}:}{\textstyle ..}}{S}}:\ddot{O}: \right]^{2-} \qquad \left[\underset{\textstyle \ddot{H}}{\overset{\textstyle \ddot{H}}{H:N:H}} \right]^+$$

hydroxide ion, OH⁻   *sulfate ion, SO₄²⁻*   *ammonium ion, NH⁺*

Polyatomic ions are charged because they have fewer or more electrons than are needed to balance the positive charges of the nuclei present in the ion. In the hydroxide ion, the oxygen atom has six valence electrons and the hydrogen atom one, a total of seven valence electrons from the two atoms. The ion has gained an eighth electron from some other atom that can lose an electron, and as a result has one extra electron and a charge of -1. In the ammonium ion, one valence electron for each of four hydrogen atoms and the normal number of five valence electrons for the nitrogen atom would give a total of nine electrons. With eight electrons present, the ammonium ion is short one electron and thus has a $+1$ charge. Similarly, the sulfate ion has two more valence electrons (32) than the total for four oxygen atoms and one sulfur atom, and thus a -2 charge.

9.13 WRITING LEWIS STRUCTURES FOR MOLECULAR COMPOUNDS A stepwise approach to writing Lewis structures for molecular compounds is outlined below. In order to begin, it is necessary to know the arrangement of the atoms—which ones are connected to each other. Are the three atoms in N_2O, for example, arranged like this, N—N—O, or like this, N—O—N? In some cases the arrangement is obvious. For example, oxygen, hydrogen, and the elements of the fluorine family often surround central atoms in a symmetrical arrangement. In many cases only consulting reference books or performing experiments can give the answer.

1. Write down the correct arrangement of the atoms using single bonds.

2. Find the total number of valence electrons available by adding the number of valence electrons contributed by each atom. Remember that for representative elements, the number of valence electrons equals the group number. If the species is an ion, subtract one electron for each unit of positive charge or add one electron for each unit of negative charge.

3. Assign two electrons to each covalent bond.

4. Distribute the remaining electrons so that each atom has the appropriate number of nonbonded electrons. For representative elements from the second period, other than beryllium and boron, this is the number of electrons needed so that each atom is surrounded by an octet. For elements of the third period and beyond, except for aluminum, this is often the number of electrons needed to complete an octet, although extra electrons can also be placed around atoms of these elements when they are the central atoms in compounds. Remember that atoms bonded to the central atom usually obey the octet rule.

5. If there are not enough electrons to go around, change some single bonds to multiple bonds. Multiple bonds can be written to carbon, nitrogen, and oxygen atoms, and also to sulfur, selenium, and phosphorus atoms. (Note that beryllium, boron, and aluminum do *not* form multiple bonds.)

EXAMPLE 9.3
Lewis Structures

Write Lewis structures for (a) chlorous acid, $HClO_2$ (the arrangement of the atoms is HOClO), (b) chlorate ion, ClO_3^-, and (c) nitrosyl ion, NO^+.

(a) The arrangement of atoms in $HClO_2$ and the total number of valence electrons are as follows:

$$H-O-Cl-O$$
$$\text{Total valence electrons} = \underset{Cl}{7} + \underset{O}{(2 \times 6)} + \underset{H}{1} = 20$$

Of the valence electrons, 6 are used in the three bonds in the above structure, leaving 14 to be distributed. If we complete the octets on the O atoms and Cl atom, it works out just right:

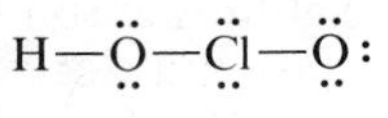

$$H-\overset{..}{\underset{..}{O}}-\overset{..}{\underset{..}{Cl}}-\overset{..}{\underset{..}{O}}:$$

(b) We can correctly assume that the three oxygen atoms are arranged around the chlorine atom

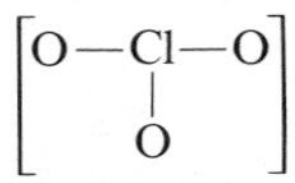

$$\left[\begin{array}{c} O-Cl-O \\ | \\ O \end{array} \right]$$

$$\text{Total valence electrons} = \underset{Cl}{7} + \underset{O}{(3 \times 6)} + \underset{\substack{charge \\ of-1}}{1} = 26$$

The three covalent bonds we have already put in the structure account for 6 electrons, leaving 20 electrons to be distributed. If we place 6 on each of the oxygen atoms and 2 on the chlorine atom, we find that all of the octets are filled using the available electrons:

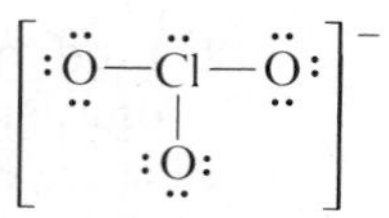

$$\left[\begin{array}{c} :\overset{..}{\underset{..}{O}}-\overset{..}{\underset{..}{Cl}}-\overset{..}{\underset{..}{O}}: \\ | \\ :\overset{..}{\underset{..}{O}}: \end{array} \right]^{-}$$

(c) The only possible arrangement of atoms in NO^+ is

$$N-O$$

In this structure we must distribute

$$\text{Total valence electrons} = \underset{N}{5} + \underset{O}{6} - \underset{\substack{charge \\ of+1}}{1} = 10$$

so that both octets are satisfied. A single bond between N and O would use 2 electrons and leave both the N and the O atoms 6 electrons short of an octet. A double bond would use 4 electrons and leave both N and O 4 electrons short of an octet. Since there are only 10 electrons available, neither of these structures can be correct. Only a triple bond between the atoms will allow an octet on each atom, so we have

$$[:N \equiv O:]^{+}$$

Exercise   Write Lewis structures for (a) IO_3^-, (b) H_2O_2 (HOOH), and (c) $[B(OH)_4]^-$.   *Answer*

(a) $\left[:\ddot{O}-\overset{\displaystyle ..}{\underset{\displaystyle :\ddot{O}:}{I}}-\ddot{O}: \right]^-$

(b) $H-\ddot{O}-\ddot{O}-H$

(c) $\left[\begin{array}{c} H \\ | \\ :O: \\ | \\ H-\ddot{O}-B-\ddot{O}-H \\ | \\ :O: \\ | \\ H \end{array} \right]^-$

EXAMPLE 9.4
Lewis Structures

Write Lewis structures for phosphorus pentachloride, PCl_5, and bromine trifluoride, BrF_3.

In both cases the halogen atoms must surround the central atom.

$$\begin{array}{c} F \\ | \\ F-Br-F \end{array} \qquad\qquad \begin{array}{c} Cl \quad\; Cl \\ \diagdown \; \diagup \\ Cl-P-Cl \\ | \\ Cl \end{array}$$

Total
valence = $7 + (3 \times 7) = 28 \qquad 5 + (5 \times 7) = 40$
electrons $Br \qquad F \qquad\qquad P \qquad Cl$

Distributing electrons as lone pairs to the halogen atoms gives

$$\begin{array}{c} :\ddot{F}: \\ | \\ :\ddot{F}-Br-\ddot{F}: \end{array} \qquad\qquad \begin{array}{c} \ddot{Cl}\;\; \ddot{Cl}. \\ \diagdown \; \diagup \\ :\ddot{Cl}-P-\ddot{Cl}: \\ | \\ :\ddot{Cl}: \end{array}$$

24 electrons   *40 electrons*

The PCl_5 structure is complete, but the BrF_3 structure needs four more electrons. Bromine is in the fourth period, and therefore can accommodate more than eight valence electrons. The correct structure is

$$\begin{array}{c} :\ddot{F}: \\ | \\ :\ddot{F}-\ddot{Br}-\ddot{F}: \end{array}$$

Exercise   Write Lewis structures for IF_5 and CS_2.   *Answer*

$$\begin{array}{c} \ddot{F}\;\; \ddot{F}. \\ \diagdown \; \diagup \\ :\ddot{F}-I-\ddot{F}: \\ | \\ :\ddot{F}: \end{array} \qquad\qquad \ddot{S}=C=\ddot{S}$$

9.14 RESONANCE The representation of bonding by Lewis structures runs into difficulty when more than one structure that agrees with the electronic requirements and the properties of a compound can be written. A typical example is nitrogen(I) oxide, N_2O, a diamagnetic molecule in which the two nitrogen atoms are bonded to each other. The 16 valence electrons of N_2O can be arranged in two reasonable ways, both of which satisfy the octet rule:

$$:\ddot{N}{=}N{=}\ddot{O}: \qquad :N{\equiv}N{-}\ddot{\underset{..}{O}}:$$

Each of these formulas accommodates the 16 valence electrons that are available, each formula gives to each atom eight valence electrons, each is electrically neutral, and in each, the atoms form numbers of bonds that might reasonably be expected (see Section 9.10). Two structures can also be written for ozone, O_3

In writing molecular structures, and also chemical equations, we must not lose sight of an essential point — the structures and equations are our way of trying to put down on paper what we have learned by experiment. Experimental investigation of properties of N_2O, O_3, and many other such molecules invariably reveals not one structure *or* another, but a structure that is a composite of the possible structures. For example, the two O—O bonds in ozone are identical — there is no evidence for both single and double bond properties in the molecule.

Many organic compounds also have structures intermediate between those that can be written with the lines and dots of Lewis formulas. The classic example is that of benzene, a six-membered ring of carbon atoms with the molecular formula C_6H_6. Each carbon atom in benzene has an octet of electrons in each of the following two formulas (called Kekulé structures for the man who first devised them)

In one structure there are double covalent bonds between three pairs of adjacent carbon atoms, and in the other structure there are single covalent bonds between the same pairs of carbon atoms. All experimental evidence, however, indicates that all of the carbon-carbon bonds in benzene are the same.

Obviously, no single structure that we can write accounts for the characteristic properties of compounds such as benzene, N_2O, and O_3. To deal with this problem, if two or more structures can be written for a molecule or ion that differ only in the position of the valence electrons, the molecule is said to exhibit resonance. **Resonance** refers to the arrangement of valence electrons in molecules or ions for which several Lewis structures can be written. That two Lewis structures are resonance structures of the same compound is indicated by a double-headed arrow, for example,

$$:\ddot{N}{=}N{=}\ddot{O}: \longleftrightarrow :N{\equiv}N{-}\ddot{\underset{..}{O}}:$$

[Note that this differs from the arrows used to indicate equilibrium, $\rightleftharpoons$.]

"Resonance" does *not* mean that the molecule constantly flips from one structure to another. The concept of resonance is necessary because of limitations in the way we *write* structures. The actual, single structure of a molecule or ion for which resonance structures can be written is called a **resonance hybrid,** since it has the characteristics of two or more of the possible structures. The *actual* molecule is always the same. A resonance hybrid is similar to the tangelo, a hybrid citrus fruit. You can pick up a tangelo and examine its characteristic properties—it is not a tangerine at one moment and a grapefruit at another moment.

Sometimes a dashed or dotted line in a single structure is used to indicate resonance, for example,

$$O\overset{\cdots}{----}O\overset{\cdots}{----}O$$

This structure shows that the oxygen–oxygen bonds are equivalent and are intermediate in their properties between single bonds and double bonds. For benzene we write

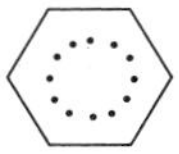

or, often,

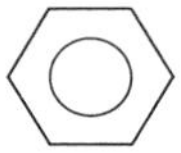

to emphasize that benzene has only one structure, the hybrid in which all carbon–carbon bonds are identical.

In writing resonance structures, the following rules apply:

1. The sequence of atoms in each resonance structure must be the same. That is, the same atoms must be connected to the same other atoms. For example,

$$:N\equiv C-\overset{\cdot\cdot}{\underset{\cdot\cdot}{O}}-H \text{ and } H-\overset{\cdot\cdot}{\underset{\cdot\cdot}{N}}=C=\overset{\cdot\cdot}{\underset{\cdot\cdot}{O}}:$$

are not resonance structures for the same compound; they are the structures of different compounds [cyanic acid and isocyanic acid, respectively].

2. All resonance structures for the same molecule must have the same number of paired or unpaired valence electrons. For example, the third structure written below

$$:\overset{\cdot\cdot}{N}=N=\overset{\cdot\cdot}{O}:\longleftrightarrow:N\equiv N-\overset{\cdot\cdot}{\underset{\cdot\cdot}{O}}:\overset{\longleftrightarrow}{\diagup\!\!\!\!}:\overset{\cdot\cdot}{N}=\overset{\cdot\cdot}{N}-\overset{\cdot\cdot}{\underset{\cdot\cdot}{O}}:$$

8e⁻ pairs   *8e⁻ pairs*   *9e⁻ pairs*

is not a correct resonance structure because it has an extra electron pair.

EXAMPLE 9.5
Resonance

Write the possible resonance forms of nitryl chloride, NO_2Cl, in which the atoms are arranged as follows:

$$\begin{array}{ccc} & & O \\ Cl & N & \\ & & O \end{array}$$

We begin by putting in single bonds

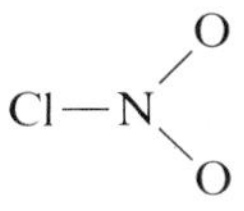

$$Cl-N\overset{\diagup O}{\diagdown_{O}}$$

The total number of valence electrons available is 7 for Cl, 5 for N, and 2×6 for the two O atoms, giving a total of 24 valence electrons. With 6 electrons in the single bonds, 18 electrons remain to be distributed. Putting enough lone pairs for complete octets into each atom would require 20 electrons (6 for Cl, 2 for N, and 6 each for the O atoms), two more than we have. Therefore, one double bond must be used. Nitrogen–oxygen double bonds are to be expected, while Cl—N double bonds are not. There are two equivalent possibilities for nitrogen–oxygen double bonds, giving the two resonance forms

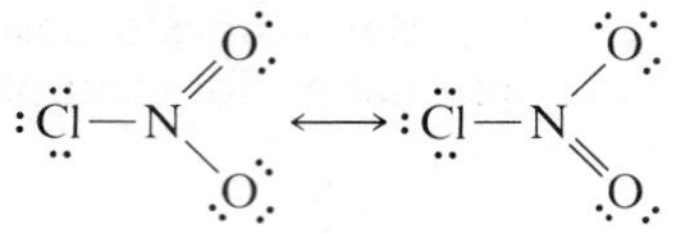

or, as a resonance hybrid

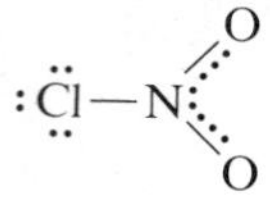

Exercise Write the Lewis structures for the possible resonance forms of the nitrite ion, NO_2^-. Also write the Lewis structure of the resonance hybrid. *Answer*

$$[:\ddot{O}-\ddot{N}=\ddot{O}]^-, \ [\ddot{O}=\ddot{N}-\ddot{O}:]^-; \ [O\cdots\ddot{N}\cdots O]^-$$

9.15 NONPOLAR AND POLAR COVALENT BONDS

In molecules such as H_2, Cl_2, and N_2, the electron density (the probability of finding the valence electrons in a given area) is equally divided between the two bonded atoms. In a covalent bond of this type—a **nonpolar covalent bond**—the electrons are shared equally (see Figure 9.7a).

Whenever atoms of two different elements are covalently bonded, the sharing of the electrons becomes unequal, because no two atoms of different elements have exactly the same electron-attracting ability. The electron density around one atom becomes greater than that around the other. How unequally the electrons are shared depends on the relative abilities of the two different atoms to attract electrons.

A covalent bond in which electrons are shared unequally is called a **polar covalent bond** (Figure 9.7b); one atom acquires a *partial* negative charge ($\delta-$; Greek delta and a minus sign) and the other acquires a *partial* positive charge ($\delta+$). These are not unit charges, but only represent a reorientation, a sort of pushing around, of the total electron density of the two bonded atoms. The entire molecule remains electrically neutral.

(a) Nonpolar covalent compound

(b) Polar covalent compound

Figure 9.7
Polar and Nonpolar Covalent Bonding

H—H   *nonpolar covalent bonds*   F—F

$\delta+$ H—F $\delta-$ *polar covalent bonds*   O

In the hydrogen fluoride and water molecules, electrons are attracted away from hydrogen atoms and toward fluorine and oxygen atoms, respectively. Polar covalent bonds are also found between atoms of the same element, if the rest of the molecule differs in electron-attracting ability. For example, the carbon–carbon bond in trifluoroethane is polar (although less so than a carbon–fluorine bond) because of the strong electron-attracting ability of fluorine atoms

$$\overset{\delta+}{H_3C}-\overset{\delta-}{CF_3}$$
trifluoroethane

A polar molecule is a **dipole** — a pair of opposite charges of equal magnitude at a specific distance from each other. The nonpolar covalent bond is at one end of a continuum of variation in bond polarity. At the other end of this continuum, which is discussed further in Section 9.19, one atom attracts electrons so strongly that the electrons depart completely from the other atom and the bonding is ionic. (In the next chapter we discuss the factors that influence the electron-attracting ability of different atoms.)

9.16 PROPERTIES IMPARTED BY THE COVALENT BOND

Covalent bonds hold atoms together in discrete molecules. The force of the covalent bond is highly directional, and individual molecules have distinctive geometries. Molecules usually retain their identity when a molecular compond melts, evaporates, or dissolves. As a result, many properties of molecular compounds are determined not by the covalent bonds themselves, but by the weaker forces that act between the molecules—the intermolecular forces. Because of their importance, molecular geometry and the intermolecular forces are discussed at length in Chapter 11.

Liquid and solid substances composed of covalently bonded molecules generally have lower melting and boiling points, and also lower heats of fusion and vaporization, than do substances with ionic or metallic bonding. (Compounds that are exceptions to this rule are described in the next section.) To melt or boil ionic or metallic substances requires more heat because the stronger bonding forces, rather than the weaker intermolecular forces, must be disrupted. Compare the values for these properties for the simple nonpolar molecular substances listed in Table 9.10 with those for the metallic and ionic substances in Tables 9.6 and 9.8. Solids

Table 9.10
Properties of Some Typical Nonpolar Molecular Substances

Property	Oxygen O_2	White Phosphorus P_4	Carbon Tetrachloride CCl_4	Silicon Tetrabromide $SiBr_4$
Appearance	Colorless gas	White waxy solid	Colorless liquid	Colorless fuming liquid
Molar mass (g)	32.00	123.90	153.82	347.72
Melting point (°C)	−218.4	44.1	−23	5.4
Boiling point (°C)	−183	280.5	77	154
Density (g/cm³)	1.429 (g/liter) (g, 0 °C)	1.83	1.59	2.77
Heat of fusion at m.p. (kJ/mol)	0.444	0.66	2.5	8.4
Heat of vaporization at b.p. (kJ/mol)	6.82	14.1	30.0	38.1
Electrical conductivity				
Solid	Very low	Very low	Very low	Very low
Liquid	Very low	Very low	Very low	Very low

Table 9.11

General Properties of Molecular Compounds Melting and boiling points and heats of vaporization and fusion all tend to increase with increasing molecular mass for similar covalent compounds. The boiling point range of covalent compounds is approximately −250 ° to 600 °C. The properties listed do not apply to network covalent compounds (Section 9.17).

Gases, liquids, or solids	Low densities
Solids brittle and weak, or soft and waxy	Poor conductors of heat and electricity
Low melting points	Nonpolar compounds generally soluble in nonpolar solvents
Low boiling points	
Low heats of vaporization	Polar compounds generally soluble in polar solvents
Low heats of fusion	

composed of molecules are usually either soft and waxy or brittle and easily broken up. The properties of molecular compounds are summarized in Table 9.11.

9.17 NETWORK COVALENT SUBSTANCES

Certain substances such as diamond (crystalline carbon), borazon (one form of boron nitride, BN), carborundum (silicon carbide, SiC), and quartz (silicon dioxide, SiO_2) have most of the characteristics of covalent compounds, except that they are very hard and have very high melting points (approximate range 2000 °C– 6000 °C). In these materials no discrete molecules are present. The diamond and the other materials like it are **network covalent substances** — three-dimensional arrays of covalently bonded atoms.

In diamond (Figure 9.8a) each carbon atom is covalently bonded to four other carbon atoms, each of which is bonded to three more carbon atoms, and so on throughout the entire diamond crystal under consideration. In quartz (Figure 9.8b), a form of silica, SiO_2, each Si atom is bonded to four O atoms and each O atom is bonded to two Si atoms in a three-dimensional array. Many covalent bonds must be broken to disrupt the crystals, resulting in the characteristic hardness, high melting and boiling points, and high heats of fusion and vaporization of these substances.

For network covalent substances as for ionic substances, the simplest formula represents only the stoichiometric composition. A piece of the substance is a giant molecule of molecular mass determined only by the size of the piece.

In summary, when metal atoms combine with metal atoms of the same or different elements, they are held together by metallic bonding. Free electrons surround cations in metallic substances, imparting the properties of high conductivity, luster, and ductility and malleability.

Metals often combine with nonmetals to give compounds usually thought of as ionic, although in most cases they have some covalent character. Ionic compounds conduct electricity only in solution or when they are molten. Solid ionic substances are crystalline, brittle, nonconducting, and often have relatively high melting and boiling points.

Nonmetals combine with nonmetals to give covalently bonded molecular compounds or network covalent substances. Where atoms of the same element are bonded together (e.g., in Cl_2), the bonds are nonpolar. Atoms of different nonmetals form bonds with varying degrees of polarity. Many properties of covalent compounds are determined by molecular geometry and intermolecular forces (discussed in Chapter 11).

The general properties of metals, nonmetals, ionic compounds, and molecular compounds are summarized in Tables 9.4, 9.7, and 9.11.

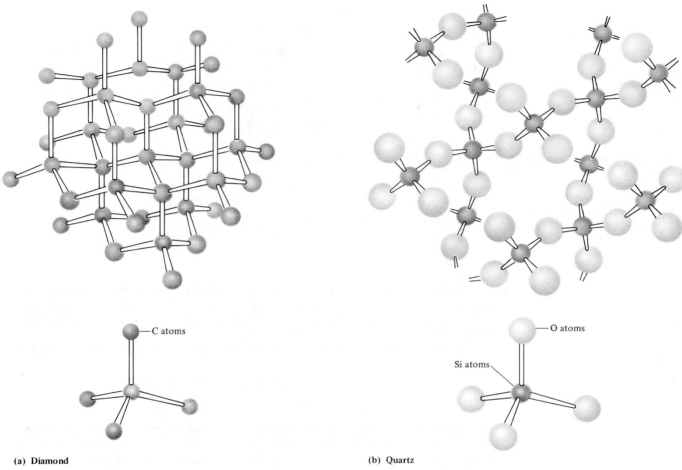

(a) Diamond

(b) Quartz

Figure 9.8
Network Covalent Substances These are three-dimensional arrays of covalently bonded
atoms. Diamond and quartz structures are shown as examples. On a hardness scale from 1
to 10 diamond has a hardness of 10 and quartz of 7. For comparison, rock salt has a
hardness of 2; marble, of 3; and iron, of 4-5 on the same scale.

PROPERTIES OF BONDS

9.18 BOND LENGTHS AND
BOND STRENGTHS

Suppose that we start with two atoms far enough apart to have no detectable
influence on one another, and see what happens as they approach along a straight
line. As this happens, the nucleus of each atom is attracted by the electron cloud of
the other. But there is also repulsion between the two nuclei and between the two
electron clouds. As the distance between the two atoms decreases (from right to left
on the graph in Figure 9.9) the attractive forces are initially stronger than the
repulsive forces, so the potential energy of the atoms decreases as they approach.
Within a certain distance, however, the repulsive forces start to predominate, and the
potential energy of the atoms increases again. Where the attractive and repulsive
forces balance, the atoms are at the bottom of an "energy well"—their potential
energy is at a minimum. The distance between the two atoms at this point is the **bond
length**—the distance between the nuclei of the two atoms in a stable molecule. (The
bond length is actually an *average* distance because bonded atoms or ions always
vibrate back and forth within the region of bond stability, as shown in
Figure 9.9.)

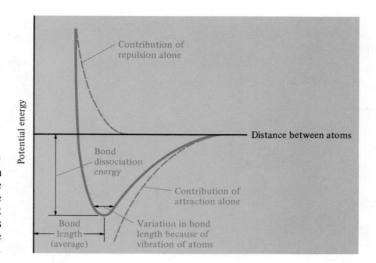

**Figure 9.9
Energy-Distance Relationship in
Bond Formation** The values of the
bond dissociation energy and the
bond length vary for different
molecules, but if bond formation is
to occur, the general shape of the
curve is as shown.

The heats of reactions in which bonds are broken are measures of the strengths of chemical bonds. Bond energies are determined by measuring the heats of reactions in the gaseous state, where the atoms formed are distinctly separate and free from attraction or repulsion by other atoms, molecules, or ions.

In some reactions it is possible to rupture a single chemical bond to give the free atoms.

$$H_2(g) \longrightarrow H(g) + H(g) \qquad \Delta H° = 436 \text{ kJ}$$

$$HI(g) \longrightarrow H(g) + I(g) \qquad \Delta H° = 298 \text{ kJ}$$

Bond dissociation energy is the enthalpy per mole required to break exactly one bond of the same type per molecule. When it is only possible to rupture several bonds in a single reaction, bond energies that are averages must be used. For example, four carbon–hydrogen bonds are broken in the gas-phase dissociation of methane.

$$CH_4(g) \longrightarrow C(g) + 4H(g) \qquad \Delta H° = 1663 \text{ kJ}$$

One-fourth of the enthalpy of the preceding reaction is the average bond energy of the C—H bond, 415.8 kJ/mol. **Bond energy** is the *average* enthalpy per mole for breaking one bond of the same type per molecule. Bond breaking is an endothermic process, and bond energies are positive enthalpies. In general, the larger the bond energy, the stronger the bond.

**EXAMPLE 9.6
Bond Energies**
Calculate the Sb—Cl bond energy, given $\Delta H_f° = -313.8$ kJ/mol for $SbCl_3(g)$, 262.3 kJ/mol for Sb(g), and 121.679 kJ/mol for Cl(g).

The equation for breaking three Sb—Cl bonds in $SbCl_3$ is

$$SbCl_3(g) \longrightarrow Sb(g) + 3Cl(g)$$

To find the heat of reaction for breaking these bonds, the data given for the heats of formation of the reactant and products can be used as follows (Equation 7.18):

$\Delta H° = [(1 \text{ mol})\Delta H_f°(Sb) + (3 \text{ mol})\Delta H_f°(Cl)] - [(1 \text{ mol})\Delta H_f°(SbCl_3)]$
$= [(1 \text{ mol})(262.3 \text{ kJ/mol}) + (3 \text{ mol})(121.679 \text{ kJ/mol})] - [(1 \text{ mol})(-313.8 \text{ kJ/mol})]$
$= 941.1 \text{ kJ}$

This heat for breaking three Sb—Cl bonds must be divided by three to get the average bond energy for breaking one mole of Sb—Cl bonds.

$$\frac{941.1 \text{ kJ}}{3 \text{ mol}} = 313.7 \text{ kJ/mol}$$

The average Sb—Cl bond energy is 313.7 kJ/mol.

Exercise   Calculate the Br—F bond energy given $\Delta H_f^\circ = -428.9$ kJ/mol for $BrF_5(g)$, 111.884 kJ/mol for $Br(g)$, and 78.99 kJ/mol for $F(g)$.   *Answer* 187.1 kJ/mol

The standard enthalpy of a reaction is equal to the sum of the energy required to break all of the bonds in the reactants and the energy released by the formation of all of the bonds in the products.

$$\Delta H^\circ = \left(\begin{matrix} \text{sum of heats of} \\ \text{breaking all bonds} \\ \text{in reactants} \end{matrix} \right) + \left(\begin{matrix} \text{sum of heats of} \\ \text{forming all bonds} \\ \text{in products} \end{matrix} \right) \qquad \textbf{(9.2)}$$

The first term in Equation (9.2) is the sum of the bond energies for all of the bonds in the reactants. Bond formation is an exothermic process and is the reverse of bond breaking, meaning that the heat of forming a bond has the same value as the bond energy, but is negative rather than positive. The second term in Equation (9.2) is, therefore, equivalent to − (sum of bond energies for all of the products). These relationships allow Equation (9.2) to be rewritten in the following useful form

$$\Delta H^\circ = \left(\begin{matrix} \text{sum of bond energies} \\ \text{of all bonds in reactants} \end{matrix} \right) - \left(\begin{matrix} \text{sum of bond energies} \\ \text{of all bonds in products} \end{matrix} \right) \qquad \textbf{(9.3)}$$

ΔH° = **(sum of bond energies of all bonds in reactants)** − **(sum of bond energies of all bonds in products)**

The accuracy of the calculation of ΔH° by using Equation (9.3) is limited. The strength of a chemical bond is not independent of its surroundings, that is, of the molecule in which it exists. Bonds between A and B in different compounds, or even in the same compound, may have different strengths, and the energy to break them may vary with the reaction sequence. For example,

$$NH_3(g) \longrightarrow NH_2(g) + H(g) \qquad \Delta H^\circ = 435 \text{ kJ}$$
$$NH_2(g) \longrightarrow NH(g)\ + H(g) \qquad \Delta H^\circ = 377 \text{ kJ}$$
$$NH(g) \longrightarrow N(g)\ \ + H(g) \qquad \Delta H^\circ = 356 \text{ kJ}$$

For single covalent bonds, bond lengths range from roughly 0.05 to 0.2 nm (Table 9.12) and the energies range from about 160 to 600 kJ/mol (Table 9.13). In general, stronger bonds are shorter. Multiple bonds, with much greater electron density between the atoms, are always stronger and shorter than single bonds. (Compare the values for C—C, C=C, and C≡C in Table 9.13.) Bonds in molecules in which resonance occurs have lengths intermediate between single and double bond lengths, or between double and triple bond lengths. For example, the carbon–carbon bonds in benzene have a bond length of 0.140 nm, compared to 0.154 nm for C—C bonds and 0.134 nm for C=C bonds.

EXAMPLE 9.7
Bond Energies

Estimate the heat released as one mole of *n*-butane burns. The necessary bond energies are given in Table 9.12.

$$
\begin{array}{cccc}
\text{H} & \text{H} & \text{H} & \text{H} \\
| & | & | & | \\
\text{H}-\text{C}-\text{C}-\text{C}-\text{C}-\text{H} \ (g) + \tfrac{13}{2}\,\text{O}=\text{O}\ (g) \longrightarrow \\
| & | & | & | \\
\text{H} & \text{H} & \text{H} & \text{H}
\end{array}
$$

$$4\,\text{O}=\text{C}=\text{O}(g) + 5\,\text{H}-\text{O}-\text{H}(g)$$

In this reaction we find that 3 C—C, 10 C—H and $\tfrac{13}{2}$ O=O bonds are being broken and 8 C=O and 10 O—H bonds are being formed. Thus

$$
\Delta H^\circ = \left[(3\ \text{mol})\left(\frac{331\ \text{kJ}}{1\ \text{mol}}\right) + (10\ \text{mol})\left(\frac{414\ \text{kJ}}{\text{mol}}\right) + \left(\frac{13}{2}\ \text{mol}\right)\left(\frac{498\ \text{kJ}}{1\ \text{mol}}\right) \right]
$$

$$
- \left[(8\ \text{mol})\left(\frac{803\ \text{kJ}}{1\ \text{mol}}\right) + (10\ \text{mol})\left(\frac{464\ \text{kJ}}{1\ \text{mol}}\right) \right]
$$

$$
= -2694\ \text{kJ/mol}
$$

The heat released is estimated to be 2694 kJ/mol. The experimental value of ΔH° is -2660 kJ for the reaction as written.

Exercise   Use the bond energies given in Table 9.12 to calculate the heat of reaction for

$$\text{NF}_3(g) + \text{H}_2(g) \longrightarrow \text{NF}_2\text{H}(g) + \text{HF}(g)$$

Answer -243 kJ

Table 9.12
Average Bond Energies in kJ/mol

	F	O	Cl	N	Br	I	S	C	H
H—	569	464	431	389	368	297	368	414	435
C—	490	326	326	285	272	218	289	331	
C=	—	803	—	515	—	—	582	590	
		(728 if						(506 if	
		O						alternating	
		‖						— and =)	
		—C—)							
C≡	—	1075	—	858	—	—	—	812	
S—	343	423	272	—	209	—	247		
S=	—	523	—	—	—	—			
I—	280	—	209	—	176	151			
Br—	285	—	218	163	192				
N—	280	230	201	159					
N=	—	590	—	473					
		(406 if							
		—NO₂)							
		(368 if							
		—NO₃)							
N≡	—	—	—	946					
Cl—	255	205	243						
O—	213	142							
O=	—	498							
F—	159								

Table 9.13
Some Bond Lengths and Bond Strengths

	Bond Length (nm)	Bond Energy (kJ/mol)
H—H	0.074	435
H—Cl	0.127	431
Cl—Cl	0.198	243
H—C	0.109	414
C—C	0.154	331
C=C	0.134	590
C≡C	0.120	812
C—O	0.143	326
C=O	0.120	803
C≡O	0.113	1075
N—N	0.145	159
N=N	0.125	473
N≡N	0.110	946

Because ionic compounds are aggregates of many ions, rather than discrete molecules, bond length and bond energy as described for molecular compounds have little meaning for ionic compounds. Instead, the distances between the ions within a crystal are of interest. In a crystal, each ion is attracted and repelled by many other ions. The geometry of the arrangement of ions (Section 13.10), the interionic distances, and the charges on the ions all influence the strength of ionic bonding. The thermodynamic quantity that expresses the sum of all of these effects and is used to measure the strength of ionic bonding is the **lattice energy**—the energy liberated when gaseous ions combine to give one mole of a crystalline ionic compound. For sodium chloride, the thermochemical equation that represents the lattice energy is

$$Na^+(g) + Cl^-(g) \longrightarrow NaCl(s) \qquad \Delta H = -769 \text{ kJ}$$

9.19 THE CONTINUA OF BOND TYPES

Although we often speak and write about "ionic compounds," or "covalent bonds," or "metallic bonding," the bonding in most chemical species is *not* 100% ionic, or 100% covalent, or 100% metallic. Instead, the bonding is somewhere in between—anywhere along a continuum of bonding from covalent to ionic, or from ionic to metallic, or from metallic to covalent. We speak of a bond as "covalent" if the properties expected for covalently bound atoms predominate, or we speak of an alloy as "metallic" if it exhibits mainly the properties we expect of metals.

The triangular diagram in Figure 9.10 gives examples of compounds that fall along the bond type continua. At the corners are lithium, a metal that is a good conductor of electricity and easily gives up its valence electron to form ionic compounds; cesium fluoride, CsF, a highly ionic compound between a reactive nonmetal and a reactive metal; and fluorine, F_2, a molecule with a 100% covalent bond between two small nonmetal atoms.

Only by determining many properties of a substance can the nature of its bonding be understood. Information about the sizes of atoms and ions, spectra, bond energies and lattice energies, interatomic distances, polarity, and structures of substances can be useful. In the next chapter some of these topics are discussed. But no single experimental method or type of calculation has yet proved totally reliable in determining or predicting quantitatively what type of bond exists in a particular compound.

The bonds in H_2 or Cl_2 are certainly 100% covalent. However, it is likely that the 100% ionic bond does not exist in any compound. A cation has an attraction for the electron cloud of an anion, causing it to be less than spherical (Figure 9.11), or *polarized* (Section 10.8). The more the electron cloud is distorted, the greater is the covalent character of the bond.

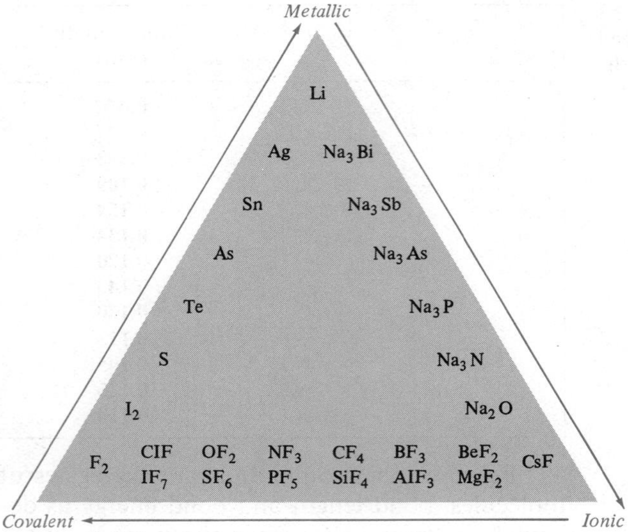

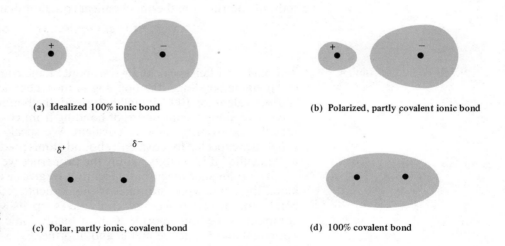

Figure 9.10
The Metallic-Covalent-Ionic Bonding Continua Examples of substances that exhibit the variation of bonding from purely metallic in lithium, to purely covalent in fluorine, to highly ionic in cesium fluoride. (Source: J. A. A. Ketelaar, *Chemical Constitution* Amsterdam: Elsevier, 1958, p. 21.)

Metallic

Li

Ag   Na$_3$Bi

Sn   Na$_3$Sb

As   Na$_3$As

Te   Na$_3$P

S   Na$_3$N

I$_2$ Na$_2$O

F$_2$ ClF OF$_2$ NF$_3$ CF$_4$ BF$_3$ BeF$_2$ CsF
   IF$_7$ SF$_6$ PF$_5$ SiF$_4$ AlF$_3$ MgF$_2$

Covalent   *Ionic*

As we discussed earlier, a covalent bond becomes polar when the atoms attract electrons to different degrees. Along the ionic to covalent continuum, there eventually comes an area in which there is only a semantic difference between whether a bond is viewed as a polar covalent bond or a polarized ionic bond.

+   −

(a) Idealized 100% ionic bond

+   −

(b) Polarized, partly covalent ionic bond

δ^+ δ^-

Figure 9.11
The Ionic-Covalent Bonding Continuum

(c) Polar, partly ionic, covalent bond

(d) 100% covalent bond

SUMMARY

9.1 DEFINITION OF THE CHEMICAL BOND   A chemical bond is a force that acts between two atoms or groups of atoms, holding them together in a distinct species with measurable properties. All chemical bonds are the result of the attraction between the electrons and the nuclei of atoms in chemical compounds

9.2 VALENCE ELECTRONS AND LEWIS SYMBOLS   The electrons that are available to take part in chemical bonding are called valence electrons. For representative elements, the number of valence electrons is equal to the group number. The outer electron configuration of an atom is shown by a Lewis symbol, in which electrons are represented by dots around the symbol for the element.

9.3 NOBLE GASES AND THE STABLE OCTET   **9.4** TYPES OF CHEMICAL BONDS   The chemical stability of the noble gases is attributed to filled outermost *s* and *p* subshells. Atoms of many elements tend to combine so that they, too, have outermost subshells filled by eight electrons (octet rule). The properties of sodium (a metal), chlorine (a molecular substance), and the ionic compound that they form, sodium chloride, illustrate the general properties imparted by metallic, covalent, and ionic bonding, respectively.

9.5 BONDING IN METALS **9.6** PROPERTIES IMPARTED BY THE METALLIC BOND Metals contain outermost electrons that are removed relatively easily. Each metal atom gives up one or more valence electrons to become a cation surrounded by an electron "sea." The attraction between positive metal ions and these freely mobile electrons results in metallic bonding. The general properties of substances with metallic bonding are summarized in Table 9.4.

9.7 BONDING IN IONIC COMPOUNDS **9.8** PROPERTIES IMPARTED BY THE IONIC BOND Ionic compounds consist of cations and anions held together by the electrical attraction, which gives rise to ionic bonding. Individual molecules are not present, but in the solid state the ions occupy fixed positions in a crystal. The general properties of ionically bonded substances are summarized in Table 9.7.

9.9 BONDING AND ELECTRON CONFIGURATION IN MOLECULAR COMPOUNDS **9.10** MULTIPLE COVALENT BONDS **9.11** COORDINATE COVALENT BONDS Covalent bonding is the attraction between two atoms that share one or more pairs of valence electrons. Pairs of valence electrons *not* involved in bonding are called nonbonding electron pairs, or lone pairs. The sharing of one pair of electrons creates a single covalent bond; two or three electron pairs may be shared, creating double and triple covalent bonds. Many elements, notably C, N, and O, form covalent bonds in accordance with the octet rule. Exceptions to the octet rule are found in compounds of B, Be, Al (less than 8 electrons), certain compounds of atoms from the third period and higher (more than 8 electrons), and compounds with unpaired electrons. A covalent bond in which both electrons of the shared pair come from the same atom is a coordinate covalent bond.

9.12 POLYATOMIC IONS Covalent bonds hold together the atoms in polyatomic ions, which are charged because they have more or fewer electrons than are needed to balance the positive charge of their atomic nuclei.

SIGNIFICANT TERMS

chemical bond
valence electrons
Lewis symbols
chemical stability
octet rule
chemical reactivity
metallic bonding
ionic bonding
Lewis structures
nonbonding electron pairs, lone pairs
covalent bonding
single covalent bond
multiple covalent bond
double covalent bond
triple covalent bond
coordinate covalent bond

9.13 WRITING LEWIS STRUCTURES FOR MOLECULAR COMPOUNDS **9.14** RESONANCE To determine the Lewis structure for a molecular compound or ion, it is necessary to know the arrangement of the atoms and distribute the valence electrons among them. Often oxygen, hydrogen, or halogen atoms surround a central atom in symmetrical arrangements. If several different correct Lewis structures can be written for a single compound, the compound is said to exhibit resonance. In such cases the actual structure is always a resonance hybrid—a composite of the possible structures.

9.15 NONPOLAR AND POLAR COVALENT BONDS Two atoms of the same element form a nonpolar covalent bond, in which electrons are shared equally. Because no two elements have exactly the same ability to attract electrons, the sharing of electrons between atoms of different elements is always somewhat unequal. The result is a polar covalent bond in which one atom has a partial positive charge and the other, a partial negative charge.

9.16 PROPERTIES IMPARTED BY THE COVALENT BOND **9.17** NETWORK COVALENT SUBSTANCES The covalent bond is highly directional, and covalently bonded molecules have distinctive geometries. Many properties of molecular compounds are determined not by the covalent bonds but by the weaker intermolecular forces. The general properties of covalently bonded substances are summarized in Table 9.11. Network covalent substances contain no discrete molecules, consisting instead of three-dimensional arrays of covalently bonded atoms. Such substances have many of the properties of covalent compounds, but are very hard and have high melting points.

9.18 BOND LENGTHS AND BOND STRENGTHS   Bond length is the average distance between the nuclei of two atoms in a stable compound. It corresponds to the distance at which the potential energy of the two atoms is at a minimum. The average enthalpy per mole for breaking bonds between the atoms of the same two elements is called the bond energy. The breaking of bonds is always endothermic, so bond energies are always positive enthalpies. The standard enthalpy of a reaction is equal to the sum of the bond energies of all bonds in the reactants minus the sum of the bond energies of all bonds in the products. In general, the stronger a bond is, the shorter it is. Multiple bonds are always stronger than single bonds.

9.19 THE CONTINUA OF BOND TYPES   No bonds are completely ionic or completely metallic, and the only bonds that are completely covalent are those between atoms of the same element. Actual bonds fall along a series of continua from covalent to ionic, from ionic to metallic, and from metallic to covalent.

THOUGHTS ON CHEMISTRY

Chemical Bond Definitions

It clearly follows that no rest is given to the atoms in their course through the depths of space. Driven along in an incessant but variable movement, some of them bounce far apart after a collision while others recoil only a short distance from the impact. From those that do not recoil far, being driven into a closer union and held there by the entanglement of their own interlocking shapes, are composed firmly rooted rock, the stubborn strength of steel and the like.

Lucretius, *De rerum natura.* 55 BC. Quoted from *Lucretius, On the Nature of the Universe,* translated by Ronald Latham (New York: Penguin Books, 1951), p. 63.

Particles attract one another by some force, which in immediate contact is exceeding strong, at small distances performs the chymical operations, and reaches not far from the particles with any sensible effect.

Sir Isaac Newton, *Opticks,* 1730. Quoted from J. R. Partington, *A Short History of Chemistry* (New York: Harper, 1937), p. 166.

It is clear that the intimate description of a chemical bond of which we have spoken, must be essentially electronic. It is the behaviour and distribution of electrons around the nucleus that gives the fundamental character of an atom: it must be the same for molecules. In one sense, therefore, the description of the bonds in any molecule is simply the description of the electron distribution in it.

C. A. Coulson, *Valence* (Oxford, England: Clarendon Press, 1952), p. 3.

There is a chemical bond between two atoms or groups of atoms in case that the forces acting between them are such as to lead to the formation of an aggregate with sufficient stability to make it convenient for the chemist to consider it as an independent molecular species.

Linus Pauling, *The Nature of the Chemical Bond,* 3rd ed. (Ithaca, New York: Cornell University Press, 1960), p. 6

From a chemical point of view the structure of a molecule is described primarily to specify the pairs of atoms which are presumed to stay, as a result of restraints upon their relative motions, at fairly definite short distances from each other. The two members of each such pair are then said to be joined by a bond.

Encyclopaedic Dictionary of Physics (New York: Pergamon Press, 1961), p 469.

Chemical bonds result when the electron structure of an atom is altered sufficiently to link it with the electron structure of another atom or atoms.

"Chemical Bonding," in the *Encyclopedia Britannica*, 15th ed., Vol. 4 (Chicago: Encyclopedia Britannica, Inc., 1974), p. 84.

QUESTIONS

Electrons and Chemical Bonds

9.1 Give a suitable definition of a chemical bond. What type of force holds the atoms together in a chemical bond?

9.2 What are valence electrons? Compare the energy level of valence electrons to the energy levels of the rest of the electrons in an atom. What is the relationship between the number of outermost electrons and the periodic table group number for representative elements?

9.3 How many valence electrons are present in atoms of the following elements: (a) Na, (b) Ga, (c) Xe, (d) O, and (e) Sr?

9.4 Repeat Question 9.3 for (a) Rb, (b) As, (c) S, (d) Ne, and (e) I.

9.5 Interpret the following Lewis symbols

(a) $\cdot \ddot{\underset{\cdot}{S}}:$; (b) $\cdot \dot{S}i:$; (c) Rb$\cdot$

9.6 Write the Lewis symbols for (a) Al, (b) Li, (c) Ar, (d) Te, and (e) S.

9.7 Write the Lewis symbols for (a) Tl, (b) As, (c) Mg, (d) F, and (e) O.

9.8 The outermost electron configuration of the alkali metals (lithium family elements) is ns^1. How can an atom of each of these metals attain a noble gas electron configuration?

9.9 Repeat Question 9.8 for the halogens (fluorine family elements) which have an outer electron configuration of $ns^2 np^5$.

9.10 List the three basic types of chemical bonding. Give an example of each. What are the differences among these types? What are some of the general properties that are associated with the three types of bonding?

9.11 What reservation should we keep in mind when we classify the bonding in a substance as metallic, covalent, or ionic?

The Metallic Bond

9.12 Describe how a metallic bond is formed. Why don't nonmetals form metallic bonds?

9.13 Why are metals malleable and ductile?

9.14 Why are metals excellent conductors of heat and electric-

ity? What happens to the electrical conductivity of a metal as the temperature is increased? Why?

The Ionic Bond

9.15 Describe what happens to the valence electron(s) as an ionic bond is formed between a metal atom and a nonmetal atom.

9.16 Why are most solid ionic compounds rather poor conductors of electricity? Why does conductivity increase when an ionic compound is melted?

9.17 Write the electron configurations for (a) K, (b) Zn, and (c) Sn. Predict the cations that these elements might form by the loss of the valence electrons and write the electron configurations for these ions.

9.18 Repeat Question 9.17 for (a) Mg, (b) Al, and (c) Sc.

9.19 Write the electron configurations for (a) F, (b) C, and (c) I. Predict the anions that these elements might form by the addition of electrons and write the electron configurations for these ions.

9.20 Repeat Question 9.19 for (a) N, (b) S, and (c) P.

The Covalent Bond

9.21 How many electrons are shared between two atoms in (a) a single covalent bond, (b) a double covalent bond, (c) a triple covalent bond, and (d) a coordinate covalent bond?

9.22 What is the maximum number of covalent bonds that second-period elements can form? Why can the representative elements beyond the second period form more than this number of covalent bonds?

9.23 Identify the species in which there are exceptions to the octet rule:

(a) $:\ddot{F}-\ddot{F}:$ (b) $:\ddot{O}-\ddot{\underset{\cdot\cdot}{C}l}-\ddot{O}:$ (c) $:\ddot{F}-\ddot{X}e-\ddot{F}:$

(d) $\left[\begin{array}{c} :\ddot{O}: \\ | \\ :\ddot{O}-S-\ddot{O}: \\ | \\ :\ddot{O}: \end{array} \right]^{2-}$ (e) $\begin{array}{c} :\ddot{C}l \\ \diagdown \\ C{=}\ddot{O} \\ \diagup \\ :\ddot{C}l \end{array}$ (f) $\begin{array}{c} :\ddot{F}: \\ | \\ :\ddot{F}-P-\ddot{F}: \\ | \\ :\ddot{F}: :\ddot{F}: \end{array}$

9.24 Repeat Question 9.23 for

(a)

$$\ddot{P}$$ structure with central P bonded to :P—P: and P below

(b) $\ddot{O}=C=\ddot{O}:$

(c)

$$\left[\begin{array}{c} :\ddot{O}: \\ | \\ :\ddot{O}-\overset{}{C}l-\ddot{O}: \end{array} \right]^{-}$$

(d) $:\ddot{C}l-B-\ddot{C}l:$
$\qquad | $
$\qquad :\ddot{C}l:$

(e)

$$\left[\begin{array}{c} H \\ | \\ H-\overset{}{O}-H \end{array} \right]^{+}$$

9.25 Identify the donor and acceptor atoms in each of the following:

(a)

$$H-\overset{\textstyle |}{\underset{\displaystyle}{\ddot{O}}}: + H^{+} \longrightarrow \left[\begin{array}{c} H \\ | \\ H-\overset{}{\ddot{O}}-H \end{array} \right]^{+}$$
where the O in the first has an H above it.

(b)

$$6\left[:\ddot{C}l:\right]^{-} + Pt^{4+} \longrightarrow \left[\begin{array}{ccc} & \overset{\cdot\cdot}{Cl} & \overset{\cdot\cdot}{Cl} \\ & | & | \\ :\ddot{C}l- & Pt & -\ddot{C}l: \\ & | & | \\ & \overset{\cdot\cdot}{Cl} & \overset{\cdot\cdot}{Cl} \end{array} \right]^{2-}$$

(c)

$$2H-\overset{H\ H}{\underset{H\ H}{\ddot{N}-C-C-\ddot{N}}}-H + Pt^{2+} \longrightarrow$$

$$\left[\begin{array}{cccc} H & H & H & H \\ | & | & | & | \\ H-C-N & & N-C-H \\ | & | \diagdown & \diagup | & | \\ H & H & Pt & H & H \\ | & | \diagup & \diagdown | & | \\ H-C-N & & N-C-H \\ | & | & | & | \\ H & H & H & H \end{array} \right]^{2+}$$

9.26 Describe the bonding in potassium chlorate, $KClO_3$

$$[K]^{+} \left[\begin{array}{c} :\ddot{O}: \\ | \\ :\ddot{O}-\overset{}{C}l-O: \end{array} \right]^{-}$$

9.27 Repeat Question 9.26 for ammonium sulfate, $(NH_4)_2SO_4$

$$2\left[\begin{array}{c} H \\ | \\ H-N-H \\ | \\ H \end{array} \right]^{+} \left[\begin{array}{c} :\ddot{O}: \\ | \\ :\ddot{O}-S-\ddot{O}: \\ | \\ :O: \end{array} \right]^{2-}$$

9.28 Repeat Question 9.26 for barium hydroxide, $Ba(OH)_2$

$$[Ba]^{2+} \quad 2[:\ddot{O}-H]^{-}$$

9.29 Write Lewis structures for (a) H_2S_2, (b) IO_4^-, (c) BeH_2, (d) NCl_3, and (3) CH_3COOH.

9.30 Repeat Question 9.29 for (a) ClO_4^-, (b) NOF, (c) XeF_4, (d) $CrCl_6^{3-}$, and (e) $COCl_2$.

9.31 Repeat Question 9.29 for (a) BCl_3, (b) SF_6, (c) CN^-, (d) AlH_4^-, and (e) N_2H_4.

9.32 Repeat Question 9.29 for (a) H_2NOH; (b) S_8, ring of eight atoms; (c) SiH_4; (d) F_2O_2, oxygen atoms in center and fluorine atoms on outside; and (e) CO.

9.33 What do we mean by the term "resonance"? Do the resonance structures that we draw actually represent the bonding in the substance? Explain your answer.

9.34 Write the Lewis structures for the formate ion, $HCOO^-$.

9.35 Repeat Question 9.34 for the sulfur dioxide molecule, SO_2.

9.36 There are two resonance structures for toluene, $C_6H_5CH_3$, which can be written

$$\text{(two benzene ring resonance structures with CH}_3\text{ group)}$$

How would you expect the carbon–carbon bond length in the six-member ring to compare with the carbon–carbon bond length between the CH_3 group and the carbon atom on the ring?

9.37 What causes a covalent bond to be polar? Choose the polar covalent bonds from the following list: (a) F—Xe, (b) O—O, (c) O=O, (d) C=O, (e) C—O, and (f) I—I.

9.38 Name two compounds that contain network covalent bonds. What kinds of properties are associated with these substances? How do we calculate the molar mass of these substances?

9.39* The following sketch represents a hydrogen molecule

electron 1
•

nucleus a   nucleus b

•
electron 2

Identify the four forces of attraction and the two forces of repulsion in the hydrogen molecule.

9.40* Write the Lewis structure for molecular $AlCl_3$. Note that the aluminum atom is an exception to the octet rule in this molecule. In the gaseous phase, two molecules of $AlCl_3$ are joined together (dimerized) to form Al_2Cl_6. Write the Lewis structure for this molecule.

Properties of Bonds

9.41 What does the term "bond length" refer to in a covalently bonded substance? Why is it necessary to discuss an average value for the bond length? How does the bond length change as the bonding increases from a single to a double to a triple covalent bond?

9.42 What does the term "bond energy" mean? How does the value change as the bonding increases from a single to a double to a triple covalent bond?

9.43 Would the value of $\Delta H°$ be the same for both of the following reactions if you used average bond energies to calculate the enthalpy change? Give a reason for your answer.

$$H-\underset{\underset{H}{|}}{\overset{\overset{H}{|}}{C}}-\underset{\underset{H}{|}}{\overset{\overset{H}{|}}{C}}-\underset{\underset{H}{|}}{\overset{\overset{H}{|}}{C}}-H + \tfrac{13}{2}O_2(g) \longrightarrow 4CO_2(g) + 5H_2O(l)$$

$$H-\underset{\underset{H}{|}}{\overset{\overset{H}{|}}{C}}-\underset{\underset{H}{|}}{\overset{\overset{H}{|}}{C}}-\underset{\underset{H}{|}}{\overset{\overset{H}{|}}{C}}-\underset{\underset{H}{|}}{\overset{\overset{H}{|}}{C}}-H + \tfrac{13}{2}O_2(g) \longrightarrow 4CO_2(g) + 5H_2O(l)$$

9.44* Even though values of bond energies are given for molecules and atoms in the gaseous phase, they are often used for calculations involving reactions in solid, liquid, and solution phases. What additional information is needed to perform such calculations correctly?

9.45 Classify the bonds that would form between the following pairs of atoms as (a) ionic, (b) polar covalent, or (c) nonpolar covalent: (i) Li, O; (ii) Br, I; (iii) Ca, H; (iv) O, O; and (v) H, O.

9.46 Repeat Question 9.45 for (i) Si, O; (ii) N, O; (iii) Sr, F, and (iv) As, As.

9.47 A common laboratory technique to remove oxygen from a gas is to pass the gas over hot, finely divided copper metal:

$$2Cu(s) + O_2(g) \xrightarrow{\Delta} 2CuO(s)$$

The copper can be regenerated for further use by allowing the CuO to react with hydrogen:

$$CuO(s) + H_2(g) \xrightarrow{\Delta} Cu(s) + H_2O(g)$$

What type of bonding would be found in (a) Cu, (b) O_2, (c) CuO, (d) H_2, and (e) H_2O? Write the Lewis structures for (f) O_2, (g) CuO, (h) H_2 and (i) H_2O. (j) Which of these substances would be relatively hard? (k) Which of these substances would

have relatively low melting and boiling points? (l) Which of these substances are good conductors of heat and electricity?

Answers to Selected Questions

9.4 (a) 1, (b) 5, (c) 6, (d) 8, (e) 7

9.7 (a) Tl: (b) ·Äs· (c) Mg: (d) ·F̈: (e) ·Ö:

9.18 (a) $[Ne]3s^2$, +2, [Ne]; (b) $[Ne]3s^2 3p^1$, +3, [Ne]; (c) $[Ar]3d^1 4s^2$, +3, [Ar]

9.20 (a) $[He]2s^2 2p^3$, −3, [Ne]; (b) $[Ne]3s^2 3p^4$, −2, [Ar]; (c) $[Ne]3s^2 3p^3$, −3, [Ar]

9.24 (d)

9.28 ionic bonding between Ba^{2+} and OH^-; polar covalent bonding between O and H atoms

9.30

(a), (b), (c), (d), (e)

9.32

(a), (b), (c), (d), (e)

9.35 :Ö—S̈=Ö ⟷ Ö=S̈—Ö:

9.36 It would be shorter.

9.40

9.43 Yes, there are the same number of C—C and C—H bonds in both compounds.

9.46 (a) iii, (b) i, ii; (c) iv

9.47 (a) metallic, (b) covalent, (c) ionic, (d) covalent, (e) polar covalent, (f) Ö=Ö, (g) $[Cu]^{2+}$ $[:Ö:]^{2-}$, (h) H—H, (i) H—Ö—H, (j) Cu and CuO, (k) H_2 and O_2, (l) Cu

PROBLEMS

Bond Energies

9.1 Calculate the S—F bond energy if $\Delta H_f^\circ = -1209$ kJ/mol for $SF_6(g)$, 278.805 kJ/mol for $S(g)$, and 78.99 kJ/mol for $F(g)$.

9.2 Calculate the O—H bond energy if $\Delta H_f^\circ = 249.170$ kJ/mol for $O(g)$, 217.965 kJ/mol for $H(g)$, and -241.818 kJ/mol for $H_2O(g)$. *Answer* 463.459 kJ/mol

9.3 Use the following heat of formation data to calculate ΔH° for each of the following reactions:

$$CH_4(g) \longrightarrow CH_3(g) + H(g)$$
$$CH_3(g) \longrightarrow CH_2(g) + H(g)$$
$$CH_2(g) \longrightarrow CH(g) + H(g)$$
$$CH(g) \longrightarrow C(g) + H(g)$$

$\Delta H_f^\circ = 716.682$ kJ/mol for $C(g)$, 595.8 kJ/mol for $CH(g)$, 392.0 kJ/mol for $CH_2(g)$, 138.9 kJ/mol for $CH_3(g)$, -74.81 kJ/mol for $CH_4(g)$, and 217.965 kJ/mol for $H(g)$. Calculate the average C—H bond energy.

9.4 Use the following heats of formation data to calculate ΔH° for each of the following reactions:

$$H_2S(g) \longrightarrow H(g) + HS(g)$$
$$HS(g) \longrightarrow H(g) + S(g)$$

$\Delta H_f^\circ = 217.965$ kJ/mol for $H(g)$, 113.30 kJ/mol for $HS(g)$, 278.805 kJ/mol for $S(g)$, and -20.63 kJ/mol for $H_2S(g)$. Calculate the average S—H bond energy. *Answer* 351.90 kJ, 383.47 kJ, 367.69 kJ/mol

9.5 Using the bond energies given in Table 9.12, predict the heats of reaction for

(a)

(b)

(c)

9.6 Using the bond energies given in Table 9.12, predict the heats of reaction for

(a) $2:C\equiv O:(g) + O=O(g) \longrightarrow 2:\ddot{O}=C=\ddot{O}:(g)$

(b)

(c)

$$2H-C\equiv N:(g) + 6H-\ddot{O}-H(g)$$

Answer (a) -560 kJ, (b) -62 kJ, (c) -970 kJ

9.7 Calculate the O—H bond energy using

$$H_2(g) + \tfrac{1}{2}O_2(g) \longrightarrow H_2O(g) \qquad \Delta H^\circ = -241.818 \text{ kJ}$$

and the values of the H—H and O=O bond energies given in Table 9.12.

9.8 Calculate the C=O bond energy using

$$CH_4(g) + 2O_2(g) \longrightarrow CO_2(g) + 2H_2O(g) \quad \Delta H^\circ = -802.32 \text{ kJ}$$

and the values of the O=O, O—H, and C—H bond energies given in Table 9.12. *Answer* 799 kJ/mol

9.9* Using the bond energies given in Table 9.12, predict the heats of combustion for the following fuels:

$$CH_4(g) + 2O_2(g) \longrightarrow CO_2(g) + 2H_2O(g)$$
methane
$$C_2H_4(g) + 3O_2(g) \longrightarrow 2CO_2(g) + 2H_2O(g)$$
ethylene
$$H_2(g) + \tfrac{1}{2}O_2(g) \longrightarrow H_2O(g)$$
hydrogen
$$C_2H_6(g) + \tfrac{7}{2}O_2(g) \longrightarrow 2CO_2(g) + 3H_2O(g)$$
ethane
$$C_2H_2(g) + \tfrac{5}{2}O_2(g) \longrightarrow 2CO_2(g) + H_2O(g)$$
acetylene
$$CH_3OH(g) + \tfrac{3}{2}O_2(g) \longrightarrow CO_2(g) + 2H_2O(g)$$
methyl alcohol

Which fuel delivers the most heat per gram of fuel? Which fuel delivers the most heat per gram of total reactants? *Answer* -810 kJ, -1330 kJ, -244 kJ, -1440 kJ, -1260 kJ, -680 kJ; H_2; H_2

Additional Problems

9.10 Use the following heats of formation data to calculate the heat of sublimation for LiI, Li, and I_2: -270.3 kJ/mol for LiI(s), -92 kJ/mol for LiI(g), 0 kJ/mol for Li(s) and $I_2(s)$, 160.7 kJ/mol for Li(g), and 62.442 kJ/mol for $I_2(g)$. Do your results reflect the general trends expected for the different bond types?

9.11 Use the following heat of formation data to calculate ΔH° for the reactions

$$Ca(g) \longrightarrow Ca^+(g) + e^-$$
$$Ca^+(g) \longrightarrow Ca^{2+}(g) + e^-$$

$\Delta H_f^\circ = 1939.87$ kJ/mol for $Ca^{2+}(g)$, 788.512 kJ/mol for $Ca^+(g)$, and 192.63 kJ/mol for $Ca(g)$. What conclusions can you make about the successive removal of electrons from a calcium atom?

CHAPTER 10

Periodic Perspective

Look at the world around you. That's how chemistry began — with the limitless curiosity of human beings about their surroundings. We examine and try to discover as much as possible about the materials and living things in our world. Inevitably, the outcome of such an examination is that questions are raised. It has been through seeking the answers to such questions that chemistry has grown.

Sometimes, however, chemistry becomes so theoretical that it is easy to forget its relationship to real substances that can be seen and touched. The periodic table provides the ideal focal point at which invisible electrons and orbitals can be related to visible, touchable matter — the elements. For example, the word "aluminum" refers to an element whose atoms have 13 protons, 14 neutrons (in its stable isotope), and 13 electrons. Each individual aluminum atom is described as having an outer electron configuration of $3s^2\,3p^1$ and each can readily form either ionic or covalent bonds. But "aluminum" also refers to a silvery white metal. Aluminum occurs naturally combined with oxygen and silicon in silicates. Aluminum is quite soft and light, and is used in making pots and pans, airplanes, and packaging materials. Its oxide, alumina, forms rubies and sapphires and is used in making glass and abrasives.

In individual chapters later in this book, we deal with the descriptive, or factual, chemistry of the elements — what the substances themselves look like and how they behave; what kinds of compounds they form and what the compounds look like and how they behave; and in what ways we can manipulate these substances and put them to use. Here, we pause to look up and down and across the columns and rows of the periodic table.

THE SIZES OF ATOMS AND IONS

To compare the sizes of atoms and ions, we compare their radii. This is not so simple as it seems, because measuring the radius of an atom or ion is not like measuring the radius of, say, a basketball. Atoms and ions are not rigid and they do not have clearly defined boundaries. Instead, the electron density drops off gradually and even at a great distance from the nucleus has a finite value. Also, atoms or ions cannot be isolated for measurement of their radii. Only the distance between nuclei in compounds can be measured. This distance depends upon the environment — the type and strength of the bonding in the substance under investigation.

The approach used, therefore, is to define sets of radii for different bonding situations. We have available tabulated values of covalent radii, ionic radii, and metallic radii. Our concern here is primarily with what are called atomic radii and ionic radii, together with the factors that influence them and their trends with respect to the periodic table.

10.1 ATOMIC AND IONIC RADII

We use the term **atomic radii** to refer to an internally consistent set of radii for the elements based on the size of their atoms in single bonds. (These might also be referred to as covalent-metallic radii, for the values are derived from single-bonded covalent radii for nonmetals and metallic radii for metals.) Atomic radii are found by

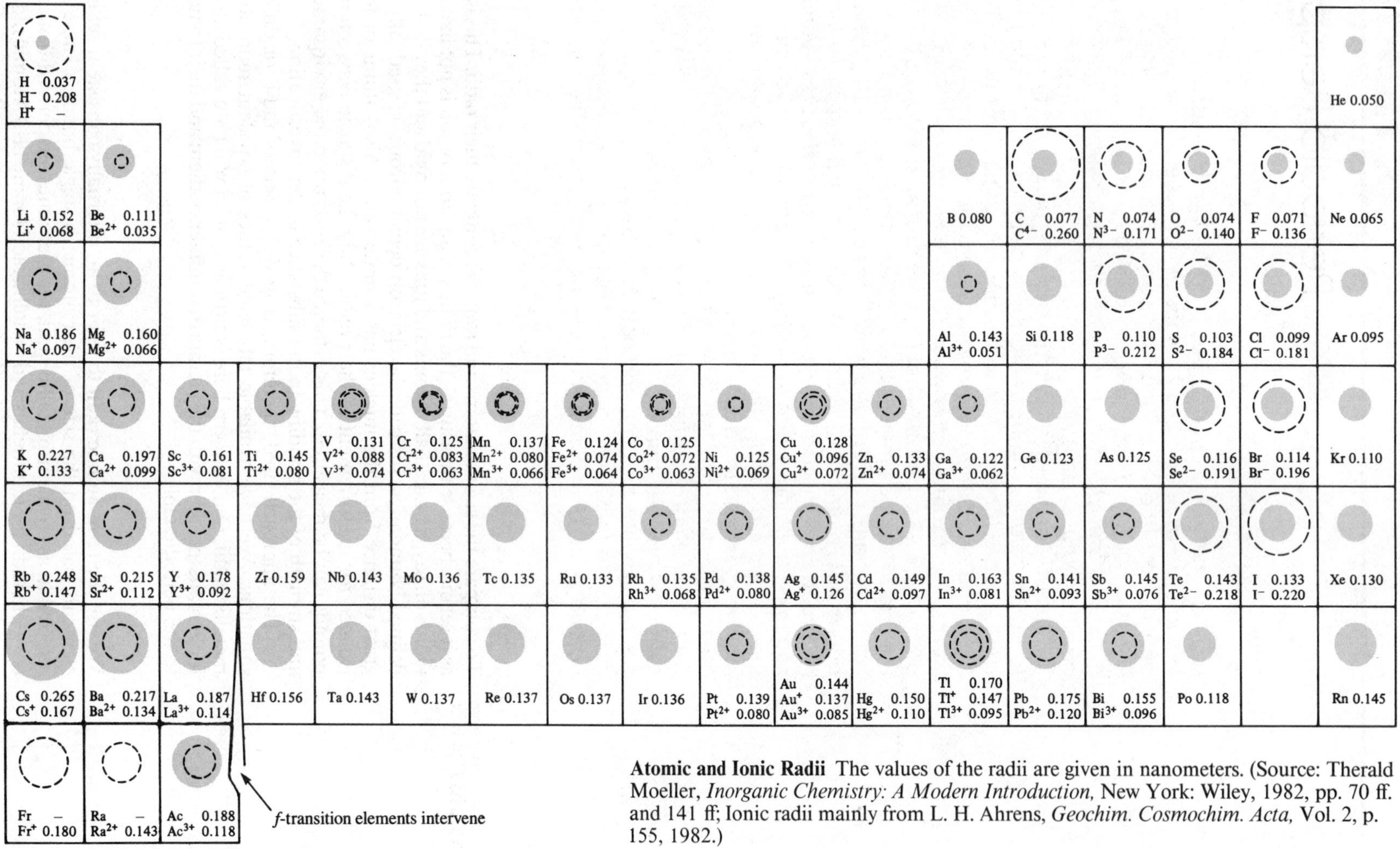

Atomic and Ionic Radii The values of the radii are given in nanometers. (Source: Therald Moeller, *Inorganic Chemistry: A Modern Introduction*, New York: Wiley, 1982, pp. 70 ff. and 141 ff; Ionic radii mainly from L. H. Ahrens, *Geochim. Cosmochim. Acta*, Vol. 2, p. 155, 1982.)

H 0.037, H+ 0.208, H- –

Li 0.152, Li+ 0.068
Be 0.111, Be2+ 0.035
B 0.080
C 0.077, C4- 0.260
N 0.074, N3- 0.171
O 0.074, O2- 0.140
F 0.071, F- 0.136
He 0.050
Ne 0.065

Na 0.186, Na+ 0.097
Mg 0.160, Mg2+ 0.066
Al 0.143, Al3+ 0.051
Si 0.118
P 0.110, P3- 0.212
S 0.103, S2- 0.184
Cl 0.099, Cl- 0.181
Ar 0.095

K 0.227, K+ 0.133
Ca 0.197, Ca2+ 0.099
Sc 0.161, Sc3+ 0.081
Ti 0.145, Ti2+ 0.080
V 0.131, V2+ 0.088, V3+ 0.074
Cr 0.125, Cr2+ 0.083, Cr3+ 0.063
Mn 0.137, Mn2+ 0.080, Mn3+ 0.066
Fe 0.124, Fe2+ 0.074, Fe3+ 0.064
Co 0.125, Co2+ 0.072, Co3+ 0.063
Ni 0.125, Ni2+ 0.069
Cu 0.128, Cu+ 0.096, Cu2+ 0.072
Zn 0.133, Zn2+ 0.074
Ga 0.122, Ga3+ 0.062
Ge 0.123
As 0.125
Se 0.116, Se2- 0.191
Br 0.114, Br- 0.196
Kr 0.110

Rb 0.248, Rb+ 0.147
Sr 0.215, Sr2+ 0.112
Y 0.178, Y3+ 0.092
Zr 0.159
Nb 0.143
Mo 0.136
Tc 0.135
Ru 0.133
Rh 0.135, Rh3+ 0.068
Pd 0.138, Pd2+ 0.080
Ag 0.145, Ag+ 0.126
Cd 0.149, Cd2+ 0.097
In 0.163, In3+ 0.081
Sn 0.141, Sn2+ 0.093
Sb 0.145, Sb3+ 0.076
Te 0.143, Te2- 0.218
I 0.133, I- 0.220
Xe 0.130

Cs 0.265, Cs+ 0.167
Ba 0.217, Ba2+ 0.134
La 0.187, La3+ 0.114
Hf 0.156
Ta 0.143
W 0.137
Re 0.137
Os 0.137
Ir 0.136
Pt 0.139, Pt2+ 0.080
Au 0.144, Au+ 0.137, Au3+ 0.085
Hg 0.150, Hg2+ 0.110
Tl 0.170, Tl+ 0.147, Tl3+ 0.095
Pb 0.175, Pb2+ 0.120
Bi 0.155, Bi3+ 0.096
Po 0.118
Rn 0.145

Fr 0.180, Fr+ 0.180
Ra –, Ra2+ 0.143
Ac 0.188, Ac3+ 0.118

f-transition elements intervene

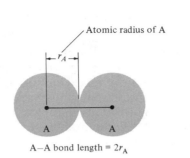

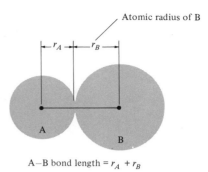

Figure 10.1
Atomic Radii

A–A bond length = $2r_A$ A–B bond length = $r_A + r_B$

measuring the distances between bonded atoms and assigning part of the distance to each atom.

One-half of the length of the single covalent bond between atoms of the same element is taken as the radius of atoms of that element (Figure 10.1). For example, the length of the chlorine–chlorine bond in Cl_2 is 0.198 nm. The atomic radius of chlorine is therefore taken as $\frac{1}{2}$ (0.198 nm) = 0.099 nm. Radii assigned in this way are used to determine the radii of atoms of other elements. Suppose the Sn—Cl bond length was measured to be 0.240 nm. Subtracting the known Cl radius of 0.099 nm from this value gives a radius of 0.141 nm for the tin atom.

The atomic radii of the representative and *d*-transition elements, together with the radii of their most common ions, are given in Figure 10.2. Adding together two atomic radii gives a reasonable estimate of the length of a single covalent bond between those two atoms. The exact bond length must be determined experimentally, for it will vary somewhat with the type of compound.

Ionic radii are the radii of the anions and cations in crystalline ionic compounds. The radius of a positive ion is always smaller than the radius of the atom from which it was formed. The loss of an electron leaves the same nuclear charge acting on a smaller number of electrons, and as a result, the electrons are pulled in toward the nucleus a bit more (Figure 10.3a). Also, in many of the common positive ions, the atom has lost all of its valence electrons and is smaller because it has one less occupied energy level.

The radius of a negative ion is always larger than the radius of the atom from which it was formed. An added electron repels other electrons, causing the electron cloud to spread out, and also adds to the screening effect described in the following section (Figure 10.3c).

Because the sizes of atoms strongly influence their properties, atomic radii are also useful in examining the periodic trends of properties (Section 10.13).

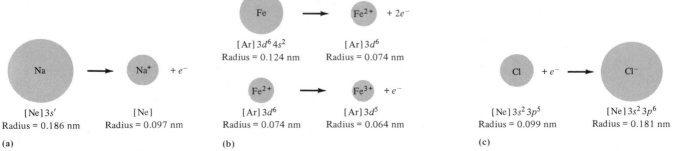

Na	Na⁺ + e^-	
[Ne]$3s'$	[Ne]	
Radius = 0.186 nm	Radius = 0.097 nm	

Fe ⟶ Fe^{2+} + $2e^-$
[Ar]$3d^6 4s^2$ [Ar]$3d^6$
Radius = 0.124 nm   Radius = 0.074 nm

Fe^{2+} ⟶ Fe^{3+} + e^-
[Ar]$3d^6$ [Ar]$3d^5$
Radius = 0.074 nm   Radius = 0.064 nm

Cl + e^- ⟶ Cl^-
[Ne]$3s^2 3p^5$ [Ne]$3s^2 3p^6$
Radius = 0.099 nm   Radius = 0.181 nm

(a)   (b)   (c)

Figure 10.3
Variations in Radii with Cation and Anion Formation

10.2 FACTORS THAT
INFLUENCE RADII

The radius of a given atom or ion is primarily the net result of two factors: the effective nuclear charge and the number of energy levels occupied by electrons. (The bonding environment of the atom, as we mentioned earlier, also has an effect.)

   a. *Effective nuclear charge*   The **effective nuclear charge** is the portion of the nuclear charge that acts on a given electron. As the actual nuclear charge increases, electrons are attracted more strongly to the nucleus. This effect, in isolation, would cause a continuous decrease in radii with increasing atomic number. However, electrons that pass between a given electron and the nucleus shield that electron from the full force of attraction of the nucleus. The **screening effect** is the decrease in the nuclear charge acting on an electron due to the effects of other electrons. A given outer energy level electron is screened slightly by other outer level electrons, somewhat more by the next highest energy level electrons, and to an even greater extent by the electrons closer to the nucleus than the $n - 1$ level. In addition, because of the different distributions of electron density in s, p, d, and f orbitals, the effectiveness of screening by electrons in different types of subshells varies. As a result, the effective nuclear charge is always less than the actual nuclear charge and varies somewhat with the number of electrons in each type of subshell. In general, the effective nuclear charge increases across a period.

   b. *Highest occupied energy level*   Earlier we described the energy levels of atoms as resembling the layers in an onion. The electrons in each energy level are somewhat further from the nucleus than the electrons in the next lowest energy level. The first electron to enter the s subshell in a new outer energy level moves into a region further from the nucleus and also, because it is screened by all of the electrons in what has become the $n - 1$ level, feels a smaller effective nuclear charge than an electron in the formerly outermost level. As a result, there is a big increase in radius from the last element in one period to the first element in the next period as well as an increase in size down a family.

10.3 PERIODIC TRENDS IN RADII

The representative elements decrease in atomic radius across a period, as shown in Figure 10.2 and in Figure 10.4, in which atomic radii are plotted versus atomic number. Across a period of representative elements, the effective nuclear charge is increasing, pulling electrons closer to the nucleus. Because s and p electrons are entering the same energy level, there is no change in the highest main occupied energy level. Therefore, the decrease in radii due to increased nuclear charge predominates.

In going *down* a family of representative elements, the atomic radii increase. Here the occupancy of higher energy levels has a greater influence on size than the increasing nuclear charge.

Beginning with the fourth period, the transition elements come between the s- and p-block elements. The transition elements decrease less in size across the periods than do representative elements. Here d or f electrons are being added to inner shells, where they are very effective at screening the outer s electrons from the nuclear charge. Thus the outer s electrons feel only a slightly increased nuclear charge, and the decrease in size across a transition element period is much more gradual than for the representative elements. The gradual decrease in size across the first of the two f-transition elements series from lanthanum to lutetium is referred to as the **lanthanide contraction.**

In Figure 10.2 note the increase in size from sodium to potassium and from calcium to magnesium in the s block. Then look across the table and in the p block compare the similar pairs of third and fourth period elements, aluminum and gallium, silicon and germanium, and so on. You can see that gallium is somewhat smaller than aluminum, and silicon and germanium are very close in size. This is the

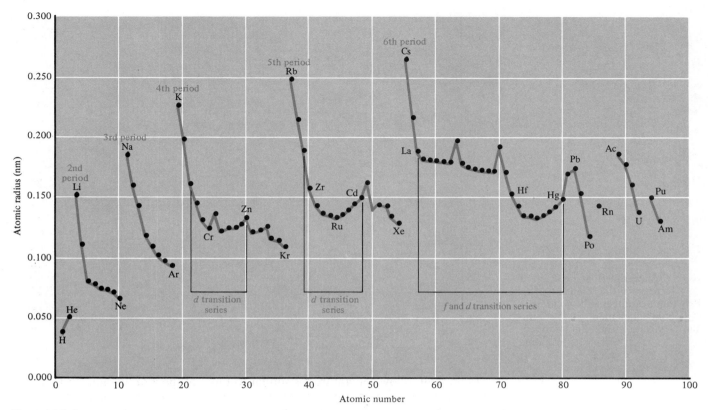

Figure 10.4
Variation of Atomic Radii with Atomic Number

result of the intervention of the *d*-transition elements and the accompanying increase in nuclear charge. The difference in nuclear charge between the third and fourth period *p*-block elements is much greater than that between the third and fourth period *s*-block elements. As a result, the electrons are held more closely than they would be in the absence of the *d*-transition elements.

A similar effect on the size of the *d*-transition elements results from the lanthanide contraction, the intervention of the lanthanides (La—Lu) between barium and hafnium. The expected increase in radii due to the higher outermost level that is occupied is just about balanced by the additional nuclear charge due to the intervention of the lanthanides. Consequently, the two heaviest elements in each *d*-transition element family have almost identical radii and very similar chemical properties.

In each family of representative elements the first member differs in many respects from the other elements in the family, partly due to its much smaller size. In their chemistry, lithium, beryllium, and boron bear many resemblances to the element diagonally below each of them in the next family.

$$_3\text{Li} \quad _4\text{Be} \quad _5\text{B} \quad _6\text{C}$$
$$_{11}\text{Na} \quad _{12}\text{Mg} \quad _{13}\text{Al} \quad _{14}\text{Si}$$

This diagonal relationship can be explained as follows: As the atomic radii decrease from left to right across a period, there is a general decrease in the ease with which electrons are lost (Section 10.4). This decrease in moving from one element to the next one at the right is at least partially compensated for by moving one step down to the next period, where the atoms are larger; thus the elements on the diagonal are similar to each other.

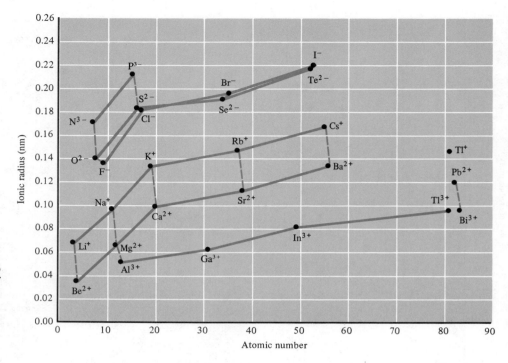

Figure 10.5
Variation of Ionic Radii of Representative Elements with Atomic Number The solid lines connect elements in the same families. The dashed lines connect isoelectronic ions.

Ionic radii follow general trends similar to those of the atomic radii. In Figure 10.5, the solid lines connect ions of elements in the same representative families and show the increase in ionic radii down a family. The dashed lines connect ions of elements in the same periods that are **isoelectronic**—they have identical electron configurations. For isoelectronic ions such as, for example, Na^+ and Mg^{2+} ($1s^2\,2s^2\,2p^6$), the increasing nuclear charge in the absence of any additional electrons causes a decrease in radius.

The trends in atomic and ionic radii are summarized in Table 10.1.

Table 10.1
Atomic and Ionic Radii

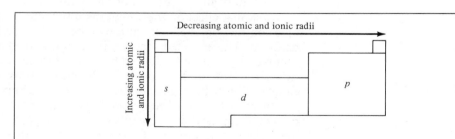

Radii generally decrease across the periods.

Radii generally increase down the families.

Cations are smaller and anions are larger than neutral atoms of the elements from which they are formed.

Cations are generally smaller than anions.

Effective nuclear charge increases across each period.

In *p*-block families, the second and third members are similar in size and properties, because of the intervention of the *d*-transition elements.

In *d*-transition element families, the two heaviest members are similar in size and properties because of the intervention of the lanthanides.

The first element in each representative element family differs from other elements in the family because of the much smaller size of its atoms.

EXAMPLE 10.1 **Atomic Radii**	Consulting only the periodic table (inside front cover), decide whether the first atom in each of the following pairs is larger, smaller, or similar in atomic radius to the second atom: (a) Si, Pb; (b) Cs, Pb; (c) Rh, Ir; and (d) Ti, V.

(a) Silicon is the second element in the carbon family, while lead is the fifth. Silicon atoms should be smaller as size increases down a representative element family.
(b) Cesium and lead are in the same period, with lead further to the right in the period. Size decreases across the periods, and therefore cesium atoms should be larger than lead atoms.
(c) Rhodium and iridium are the second and third members of a *d*-transition metal family. Because of the lanthanide contraction, the atomic radii of these elements should be similar.
(d) Titanium and vanadium are adjacent elements in the same *d*-transition period. Atoms of these two elements should be similar in atomic radius, for the decrease in size across the periods for transition elements is gradual.
[Check the conclusions reached here by consulting Figure 10.2.]

Exercise Choose the element from each set that has the larger atomic radius: (a) K, Na; (b) Na, Mg; and (c) As, S. *Answer* (a) K, (b) Na, (c) As

---

ELECTRON GAIN AND LOSS

The ease with which atoms gain and lose electrons strongly influences their properties—the ease with which they undergo chemical reactions and the types of chemical bonds that they form. In the following sections, several aspects of electron gain and loss are discussed. First we look at the thermodynamic quantities that are used to compare ease of electron gain and loss (ionization energies in Sections 10.4 and 10.5; electron affinities in Section 10.6). Measurements are made of the enthalpy changes due to electron gain and loss by isolated atoms and ions in the gas phase, for under these conditions they are free from the influence of other atoms or ions. The relationship of such enthalpy changes to atomic radii and electron configurations provides valuable information about periodic trends in the properties of the elements and their compounds. Also, these enthalpy changes provide evidence for the correlation between electron configuration and chemical reactivity. In Section 10.7 we examine periodic trends in the formation of the ions that are commonly found in ionic compounds and how these are related to electron configurations.

10.4 IONIZATION ENERGY

The **ionization energy** (sometimes called the ionization potential) is the enthalpy change for the removal of the least tightly bound electron from an atom or an ion in the gaseous state. Ionization energies are given per mole of atoms or ions of a given type. The *first* ionization energy is that required for the removal of one electron. For example, for sodium the first ionization energy is the enthalpy change for the reaction

$$Na(g) \longrightarrow Na^+(g) + e^- \qquad \Delta H_0^\circ = 495.8 \text{ kJ} \qquad \textit{1st ionization energy}$$

Such reactions are always endothermic and ionization energies are always positive —energy must be put into the system to pull an electron away from the nuclear charge. The energies for removal of successive electrons are the second ionization energy, the third ionization energy, and so on. For example,

$$Al(g) \longrightarrow Al^+(g) + e^- \qquad \Delta H_0^\circ = 578 \text{ kJ} \qquad \textit{1st ionization energy} \qquad \textbf{(10.1)}$$

$$Al^+(g) \longrightarrow Al^{2+}(g) + e^- \qquad \Delta H_0^\circ = 1817 \text{ kJ} \qquad \textit{2nd ionization energy} \qquad \textbf{(10.2)}$$

$$Al^{2+}(g) \longrightarrow Al^{3+}(g) + e^- \qquad \Delta H_0^\circ = 2745 \text{ kJ} \qquad \textit{3rd ionization energy} \qquad \textbf{(10.3)}$$

Removing electrons from ions of increasing positive charge is increasingly difficult.

Note that the ionization energy is defined as the energy required for the removal of *the least tightly bound* electron. In the total environment of the atom or ion under consideration, the electron removed is at the highest energy level. You might expect this to be the last electron that was added according to the building up order across the periodic table. This is not necessarily what happens. Electrons *always* come off in the order of the principal energy levels; for example, $n = 3$ electrons before $n = 2$ electrons, and $n = 2$ electrons before $n = 1$ electrons. Within the same main energy level, the order of electron loss in ionization is f, then d, then p, then s electrons. For example, in the d-transition elements, the d electrons enter last, but the s electrons leave first. For scandium

$$\text{Sc [Ar] } 3d^1 4s^2 \qquad \textit{last electron to be added}$$
$$\text{Sc}^+ \text{ [Ar] } 3d^1 4s^1 \qquad \textit{first electron to be lost}$$
$$\text{Sc}^{2+} \text{ [Ar] } 3d^1$$
$$\text{Sc}^{3+} \text{ [Ar]}$$

(Recall that the noble gas symbol in square brackets is used as a shorthand notation for the noble gas configuration.)

10.5 FACTORS THAT INFLUENCE IONIZATION ENERGY; PERIODIC TRENDS

Ionization energies, like radii, are influenced by the effective nuclear charge and the electron configuration. In general, a greater effective nuclear charge makes it more difficult to remove an electron, resulting in a higher value for the ionization energy. However, all other factors being equal, it is easier to remove an electron from a larger atom or ion than from a smaller one. In addition, certain electron configurations are more stable than others, and more energy is required for electron removal.

The removal of an electron from an atom or ion with a **noble gas configuration** —$ns^2 np^6$ (or $1s^2$)— is difficult, for this is a very stable configuration. Note in Table 10.2 the high ionization energies for the noble gases. (When the term "ionization energy" is used in this general way, the first ionization energy is usually meant.)

The stability of the noble gas configuration is dramatically illustrated by the successive ionization energies of the elements. For example, for aluminum, the fourth ionization requires the loss of an electron from an ion of noble gas configuration

$$Al^{3+}(g) \longrightarrow Al^{4+}(g) + e^- \qquad \Delta H_0^\circ = 11,577 \text{ kJ} \qquad \textit{4th ionization energy}$$
$$(1s^2\, 2s^2\, 2p^6) \qquad (1s^2\, 2s^2\, 2p^5)$$

Table 10.2
First Ionization Energies The values are given in kilojoules per mole at 0 K. To use these values in calculations with other enthalpies that are given for 298 K the values in this table must be converted to approximate values at 298 K by adding 6.19 kJ. [Adapted from Therald Moeller, *Inorganic Chemistry: A Modern Introduction* (New York: Wiley, 1982), pp. 76–79.]

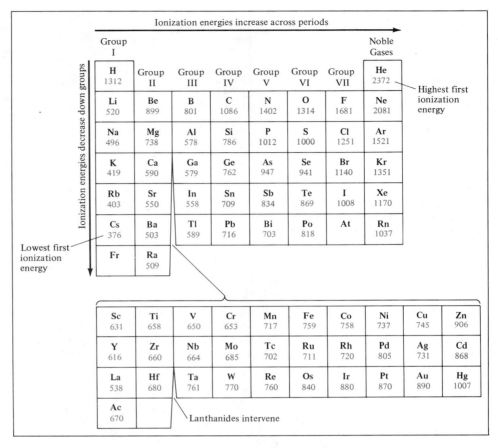

In Table 10.3, compare the first and second ionization energies of sodium, the second and third ionization energies of magnesium, and so on. The successive ionization energies provide a satisfying experimental verification of the existence of energy levels and the number of electrons expected, on the basis of the quantum

Table 10.3
Ionization Energies of Na-Ar Period Elements Energies for the removal of successive outer electrons are given in black, and for removal of inner shell electrons, in color. Values are in kilojoules per mole at 0 K. In the $n = 1$ and $n = 2$ energy levels each of these elements has a neon-like ($1s^2\, 2s^2\, 2p^6$) configuration. The screening effect across the period is approximately constant. To convert to approximate values at 298 K, add 6.19 kJ per electron removed. [Adapted from Therald Moeller, *Inorganic Chemistry: A Modern Introduction* (New York: Wiley, 1982), pp. 76–79.]

Ionization Energy	Na ($3s^1$)	Mg ($3s^2$)	Al ($3s^2\, 3p^1$)	Si ($3s^2\, 3p^2$)	P ($3s^2\, 3p^3$)	S ($3s^2\, 3p^4$)	Cl ($3s^2\, 3p^5$)	Ar ($3s^2\, 3p^6$)
1st	**496**	**738**	**578**	**786**	**1,012**	**1,000.**	**1,251**	**1,521**
2nd	4,562	**1,451**	**1,817**	**1,577**	**1,903**	**2,251**	**2,297**	**2,666**
3rd	6,912	7,733	**2,745**	**3,232**	**2,912**	**3,361**	**3,822**	**3,931**
4th	9,543	10,540.	11,577	**4,355**	**4,956**	**4,564**	**5,158**	**5,771**
5th	13,353	13,629	14,831	16,091	**6,274**	**7,013**	**6,540**	**7,238**
6th	16,610.	17,994	18,377	19,784	21,268	**8,495**	**9,362**	**8,781**
7th	20,114	21,703	23,294	23,776	25,397	27,106	**11,018**	**11,995**
8th	25,489	25,655	27,459	29,251	29,853	31,669	33,604	**13,841**

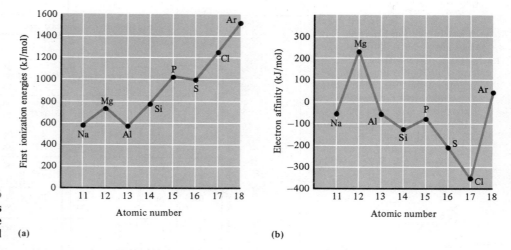

Figure 10.6
**Trends in First Ionization Energies
and Electron Affinities for the
Elements of the Third Period** (a)   (b)

numbers, to be in each level. The black numbers in Table 10.3 are the energies for removal of the outer electrons—one for sodium ($3s^1$) and up to eight for argon ($3s^2\,3p^6$).

First ionization energies generally increase across the periodic table and decrease down the families. These trends parallel what would be expected from atomic radii—less energy is required to remove electrons from larger atoms because the electrons are further away from the nucleus.

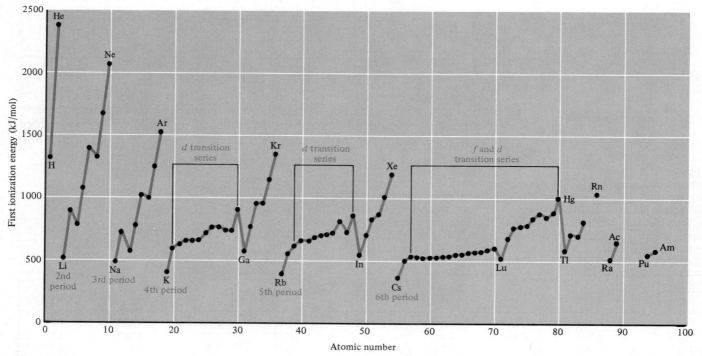

Figure 10.7
Variation of First Ionization Energies with Atomic Number In each period the lithium family element has the lowest ionization energy and the noble gas the highest ionization energy. Note the lack of variation for the transition elements. (Source: Therald Moeller, *Inorganic Chemistry: A Modern Introduction,* New York: Wiley, 1982, pp. 76–79.)

Table 10.4
Ionization Energy

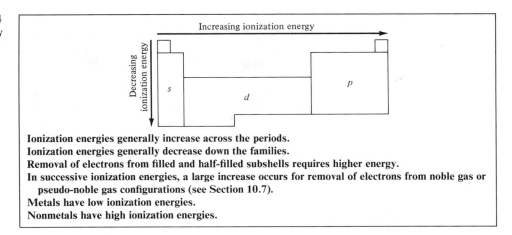

Ionization energies generally increase across the periods.
Ionization energies generally decrease down the families.
Removal of electrons from filled and half-filled subshells requires higher energy.
In successive ionization energies, a large increase occurs for removal of electrons from noble gas or
  pseudo-noble gas configurations (see Section 10.7).
Metals have low ionization energies.
Nonmetals have high ionization energies.

A plot of ionization energies for the third-period elements (Figure 10.6a) illustrates variations in the general trend caused by the extra stability of electron configurations in which subshells are completely filled or one-half filled. It is easier to remove a $3p$ electron from an aluminum atom ([Ne]$3s^2\,3p^1$) than to remove a $3s$ electron from the pair in an s subshell in a magnesium atom ([Ne]$3s^2$). Also, it is easier to remove the fourth p electron from a sulfur atom ([Ne]$3s^2\,3p^4$) than to remove a p electron from the half-filled p subshell in a phosphorus atom ([Ne]$3s^2\,3p^3$).

Similar variations for each period can be seen in the plot of ionization energies in Figure 10.7. The extra stability of the noble gas configuration is also apparent.

Metal atoms, which have larger radii than nonmetal atoms, form cations readily, and their ionization energies lie in the troughs of the curve—roughly below 1000 kJ/mol. The large and highly reactive atoms of lithium family elements have the lowest ionization energies. As expected from the small variation in their radii, the ionization energies of atoms of the transition elements do not vary greatly.

Nonmetals, which have smaller atomic radii than metals, do not form cations under ordinary conditions, and they have high ionization energies, roughly above 1000 kJ/mol.

The trends in ionization energies are summarized in Table 10.4.

EXAMPLE 10.2
Ionization Energy

The pairs of elements, Mg and Ca, and Al and Ga, occupy corresponding positions in the beryllium and boron families. The ionization energy for the removal of all of the valence electrons is much greater for Mg than for Ca [$\Delta H_0^\circ = 2188$ kJ/mol for Mg(g) $\rightarrow$ Mg^{2+}(g) $+ 2e^-$; 1735 kJ/mol for Ca(g) $\rightarrow$ Ca^{2+}(g) $+ 2e^-$], while the similar energy for Al is smaller than that for Ga [$\Delta H_0^\circ = 5139$ kJ/mol for Al(g) $\rightarrow$ Al^{3+}(g) $+ 3e^-$; 5521 kJ/mol for Ga(g) $\rightarrow$ Ga^{3+}(g) $+ 3e^-$]. Account for this difference.

The decrease in ionization energy from magnesium to calcium is not unexpected. The atoms of these elements have the same outer electron configurations, and although the nuclear charge of the calcium atom is larger than that of the magnesium atom, its size is also larger. The size factor is the predominant one in determining the trend in ionization energy.

The intervention of the $3d$ sequence of elements between aluminum and gallium (and the general decrease in atomic size along that sequence; Sections 10.1

and 10.3) makes atoms of these two elements more similar in size. This similarity in atomic size and the much larger nuclear charge of gallium give gallium atoms a greater effective nuclear charge than aluminum atoms and, correspondingly, a larger ionization energy.

Exercise The first ionization energy of Y is larger than that of La, but for the rest of the *d*-transition elements in these two periods the order is reversed, for example, the first ionization energy of Hf is greater than that of Zr and the first ionization energy of Ta is greater than that of Nb. Explain this trend. *Answer* Intervention of lanthanides makes atoms virtually identical in size and the much larger nuclear charge of Hf—Hg produces a larger ionization energy.

10.6 ELECTRON AFFINITY

The **electron affinity** is the enthalpy change for the addition of one electron to an atom or ion in the gaseous state. Electron affinity values are given per mole of atoms or ions. For example, for chlorine

$$\text{Cl}(g) + e^- \longrightarrow \text{Cl}^-(g) \qquad \Delta H_0^\circ = -349 \text{ kJ}$$

The chlorine atom, which is one electron short of a noble gas configuration, adds an electron readily in an exothermic reaction.

Unlike ionization energies, electron affinities can be either positive or negative. Energy is *required* to add an electron to an already stable configuration. The electron affinity values for the beryllium family elements, which have ns^2 configurations, and for the noble gases, with their $ns^2 np^6$ configurations, are positive (Table 10.5). In

Table 10.5

Electron Affinities of the Representative and *d*-Transition Elements Values are given in kilojoules/mole at 0 K. Values in parentheses have been calculated from theory; others are from experimental measurements. Only eight electron affinity values, mainly for the halogens, had been experimentally measured before 1970. Since then the development of more accurate measurement techniques and better methods of producing negative ions have provided the additional values given in this table. [From Therald Moeller, *Inorganic Chemistry: A Modern Introduction* (New York: Wiley, 1982), p. 81.]

Group I	Group II	Group III	Group IV	Group V	Group VI	Group VII	Noble gases
H −73							He (21)
Li 60	Be (240)	B −83	C −123	N 0.0	O −141	F −322	Ne (29)
Na −53	Mg (230)	Al (−50)	Si −120	P −74	S −200	Cl −349	Ar (35)
K −48	Ca (156)	Ga (−36)	Ge −116	As −77	Se −195	Br −325	Kr (39)
Rb −47	Sr (168)	In −34	Sn −121	Sb −101	Te −183	I −295	Xe (41)
Cs −46	Ba (52)	Tl −50	Pb −101	Bi −101	Po (−170)	At (−270)	Rn (41)
Fr (−44)	Ra						

		Ti −38	V −90	Cr −64		Fe −56	Co −90	Ni −123	Cu −123	
				Mo −96					Ag −126	
		Ta −80	W −50	Re −14				Pt −205	Au −223	

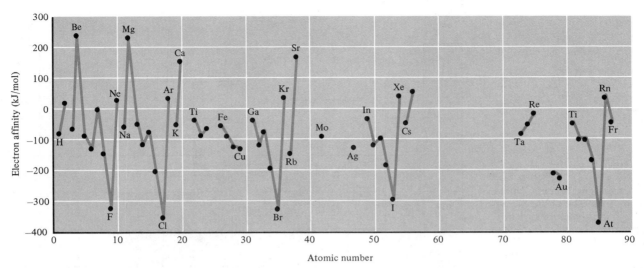

Figure 10.8
Variation in Electron Affinity with Atomic Number The halogens, which add electrons most readily of any of the elements, have the most negative electron affinities. (Source: Therald Moeller, *Inorganic Chemistry: A Modern Introduction,* New York: Wiley, 1982, p. 81.

atoms of these elements all of the occupied subshells are completely filled and the nuclei are well screened. The ability of such nuclei to bind electrons in unoccupied energy levels is extremely small, and the positive electron affinities suggest that negative ions of these elements would be unstable.

Second electron affinities are *all* positive, for it takes energy to overcome the repulsion between an electron and the already-negative ion; for example,

$$O^-(g) + e^- \longrightarrow O^{2-}(g) \qquad \Delta H_0^\circ = 880 \text{ kJ}$$

Adding the first electron would be expected to become easier across a period as the atoms become smaller and the effective nuclear charge increases. Although there are deviations, such a general trend does occur. The electron affinities of the third-period elements are plotted in Figure 10.6b. The large increase in electron affinity between sodium and magnesium occurs because the ns^2 electron level of magnesium is filled, and the next electron must enter the p subshell. The small increase between silicon and phosphorus is, like the ionization energy drop from phosphorus to sulfur, due to pairing of electrons of opposite spin. An electron added to a phosphorus atom enters a p orbital already occupied by one electron. This occurs less readily than addition of an electron to the remaining unoccupied p orbital of a silicon atom. Similar variations in the general trend for electron affinities for elements of other periods can be seen in Figure 10.8. Variations in electron affinity down a family are not so easily explained.

[Two things should be noted about electron affinities. First, they are difficult to measure; therefore, fewer are known than ionization energies and the accuracy of the values is not as great. Some of the values in Table 10.5 are based on calculations rather than experiments. Second, in some publications, electron affinities are defined differently and given the opposite signs from those in Table 10.5.]

10.7 ELECTRON
CONFIGURATIONS OF IONS

In ionic compounds, most of the representative elements form ions with noble gas configurations. To form cations, the representative metals of the s block (see Table 9.1) lose their s valence electrons to give singly or doubly charged cations with noble

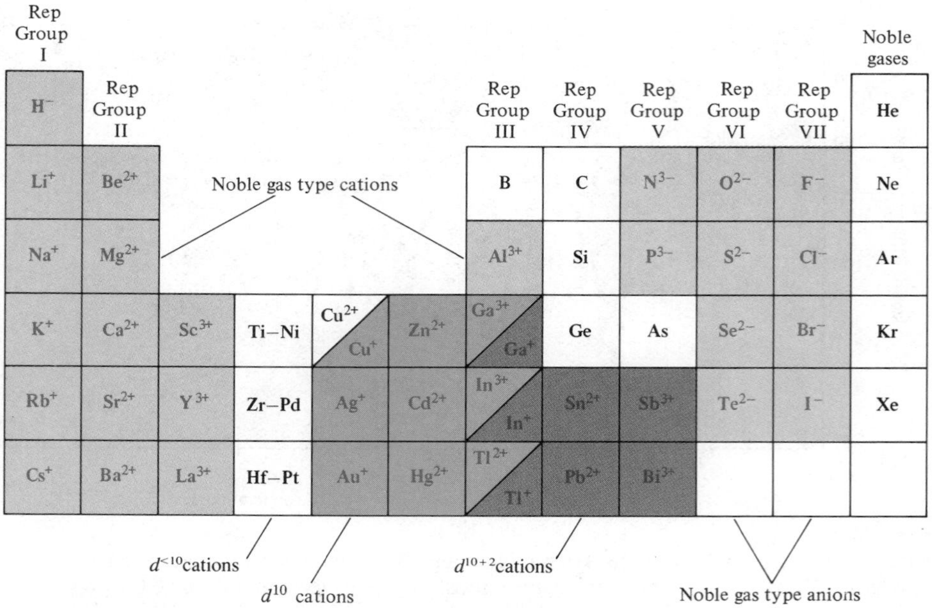

Figure 10.9
Configuration of Common Monatomic Ions The noble gas type ions have ns^2 or ns^2np^6, configurations. The d^{10} cations form by loss of s electrons to leave filled d subshells. The d^{10+2} cations form by loss of p electrons to leave $(n-1)d^{10}ns^2$ configurations. Atoms of elements that form $d < 10$ cations do so by loss of s or s plus d electrons.

Table 10.6
Monatomic Nonmetal Ions The Roman numerals are the representative group numbers. The outermost configurations are shown; lower levels are filled. All of these ions have noble gas configurations. In simple binary ionic compounds, the nonmetals always have the configuration shown here. Carbon forms C_2^{2-} ions. Astatine does form an ion (At$^-$, $6s^26p^6$), but it is a radioactive element and is so short-lived that very little of it can be accumulated.

H$^-$ (hydride)	VI
($1s^2$)	O^{2-} (oxide)
IV	($2s^22p^6$)
C^{4-} (methide)	S^{2-} (sulfide)
($2s^22p^6$)	($3s^23p^6$)
[in a few	VII
compounds]	F$^-$ (fluoride)
V	($2s^22p^6$)
N^{3-} (nitride)	Cl$^-$ (chloride)
($2s^22p^6$)	($3s^23p^6$)
P^{3-} (phosphide)	Br$^-$ (bromide)
($3s^23p^6$)	($4s^24p^6$)
	I$^-$ (iodide)
	($5s^25p^6$)

gas configurations, for example,

$$\text{Li} \quad [\text{He}]2s^1 \qquad\qquad \text{Li}^+ \quad [\text{He}]$$

electrons lost

$$\text{Ca} \quad [\text{Ar}]2s^2 \qquad\qquad \text{Ca}^{2+} \quad [\text{Ar}]$$

The electron configurations and charges of commonly encountered ions are summarized in periodic table form in Figure 10.9. Note that the charges on the Representative Group I and II metal ions are the same as the group number. Aluminum also forms an ion with a noble gas configuration and a charge equal to its group number (Al^{3+}).

The Group III metals of periods 4–6 form both +3 and +1 cations, for example, for gallium

$$\text{Ga } [\text{Ar}]3d^{10}\,4s^2\,4p^1$$
$$\text{Ga}^+ [\text{Ar}]3d^{10}\,4s^2 \qquad \text{Ga}^{3+} [\text{Ar}]3d^{10}$$

A noble gas core with an outer d^{10} **configuration**, as in Ga^{3+}, is sometimes known as a **psuedo-noble gas configuration.** A "d^{10} cation" like Ga^{3+} is stabilized by the presence of a highest principal energy level completely filled by 18 electrons, with 10 electrons in the d subshell. (The complete configuration of Ga^{3+} is $1s^2\,2s^2\,2p^6\,3s^2\,3p^6\,3d^{10}$.) The metals of Groups IV and V do not form d^{10} cations, but form only the +2 and +3 ions that result from loss of the valence electrons from the outer p subshells. For example, Bi^{3+} [Xe]$4f^{14}\,5d^{10}\,6s^2$, is what might be called a "$d^{10}\,s^2$ cation."

Among the p-block elements, boron, silicon, germanium, arsenic and the noble gases are never present as monatomic ions in ordinary compounds. Carbon in a *few* compounds forms C^{4-} ions. For the nonmetals that do form ions, it is easier to gain electrons to achieve noble gas configurations than it is to give up electrons. A sulfur atom, for example, would have to lose six electrons to form an ion with the neon configuration. Removing successive electrons from positive ions becomes increasingly more difficult and the energy needed to remove this many electrons is not

Table 10.7

Table 10.7
Some Fourth-Period Transition Metal Ions The Cu^{2+} ion is more common than the Cu^+ ion and the Ti^{2+} ion is rare.

Atom	Ion
Sc $[Ar]3d^14s^2$	Sc^{3+} $[Ar]$
Ti $[Ar]3d^24s^2$	Ti^{2+} $[Ar]3d^2$
	Ti^{3+} $[Ar]3d^1$
Cr $[Ar]3d^54s^1$	Cr^{2+} $[Ar]3d^4$
	Cr^{3+} $[Ar]3d^3$
Fe $[Ar]3d^64s^2$	Fe^{2+} $[Ar]3d^6$
	Fe^{3+} $[Ar]3d^5$
Cu $[Ar]3d^{10}4s^1$	Cu^+ $[Ar]3d^{10}$
	Cu^{2+} $[Ar]3d^9$

available in ordinary chemical reactions. (Adding successive electrons to anions is also increasingly difficult. Ions with charges greater than $+3$ or -3 are rarely formed.)

The nonmetals each form only one monatomic anion. These anions have negative charges equal to the number of electrons needed to give eight outer electrons. For example, for sulfur from Group VI and iodine from Group VII

$$S \quad [Ne]3s^23p^4 \qquad S^{2-} \quad [Ne]3s^23p^{4+2}$$
$$\text{added electrons}$$

$$I \quad [Kr]4d^{10}5s^25p^5 \qquad I^- \quad [Kr]4d^{10}5s^25p^{5+1}$$

Hydrogen gives an anion with the helium configuration (the hydride ion, H^-). The nonmetal anions are listed in Table 10.6. (Note that the negative charges are equal to the group number minus eight.) The semiconducting elements selenium and tellurium also form anions with noble gas configurations (see Figure 10.9).

Most d-transition elements give cations with $+2$ charges, although in many cases $+1$ or $+3$ ions are also formed. In Figure 10.9, note that the copper and zinc family transition metals form d^{10} cations. The electron configurations of some fourth-period transition metal ions are given in Table 10.7.

EXAMPLE 10.3
Electron Configuration of Ions

Show with Lewis symbols and electron configurations the changes that occur in the individual atoms (a) when strontium and oxygen combine to give strontium oxide and (b) when magnesium combines with nitrogen to give magnesium nitride. Both strontium oxide and magnesium nitride are ionic compounds. What are the formulas of the products?

(a) Strontium is in Representative Group II and forms Sr^{2+}. Oxygen is in Representative Group VI and forms O^{2-}.

$$Sr: \; + \quad \cdot \ddot{O}: \quad \longrightarrow \quad Sr^{2+} \qquad :\ddot{O}:^{2-}$$
$$[Kr]5s^2 \quad [He]2s^2\,2p^4 \qquad [Kr] \quad [He]2s^2\,2p^6 \; or \; [Ne]$$

Strontium oxide has the formula SrO.

(b) Magnesium is in Representative Group II and forms Mg^{2+}. Nitrogen is in Representative Group V and forms N^{3-}. The charges on these ions are not equal, and it takes three magnesium atoms to provide the six electrons needed to form two N^{3-} ions

$$3Mg: \; + \quad 2\cdot\ddot{N}\cdot \quad \longrightarrow \quad 3Mg^{2+} \qquad 2:\ddot{N}:^{3-}$$
$$[Ne]3s^2 \quad [He]2s^2\,2p^3 \qquad [Ne] \quad [He]2s^2\,2p^6 \; or \; [Ne]$$

The product, magnesium nitride, has the formula Mg_3N_2. [Note that Mg^{2+} and N^{3-} both have the same electron configuration, but, because of their different molar masses and charges, they are very different species.]

Exercise Barium reacts with chlorine to produce an ionic compound. What is the formula of the compound? Show with Lewis symbols and electron configurations the changes that occur in the individual atoms during this reaction. *Answer* $BaCl_2$;

$$Ba: \; + \quad 2\cdot\ddot{Cl}: \quad \longrightarrow \quad Ba^{2+} \qquad 2\left[:\ddot{Cl}:\right]^-$$
$$[Xe]6s^2 \quad [Ne]3s^2\,3p^5 \qquad [Xe] \qquad [Ar]$$

EXAMPLE 10.4
Electron Configurations of Ions

Write the electron configurations (above the Ar core) for the following ions, which are the common ions for these elements: Sc^{3+}, Cr^{3+}, Mn^{2+}, Fe^{2+}, Fe^{3+}, Ni^{2+}, Cu^+, Cu^{2+}.

Although the $3d$ level is filled after electrons enter the $4s$ level, the electrons from the $4s$ level are the first ones lost in the formation of ions of d-transition elements. To find the configurations of the d-transition metal ions, we must first take away s level electrons and, then, if more electrons must be removed to reach the appropriate positive charge, we must take away d electrons. For example

$$Sc \qquad [Ar]3d^14s^2 \overset{\curvearrowleft}{\underset{\substack{must\ be \\ removed\ to \\ give\ +3\ ion}}{}}$$

The configurations of the other ions are as follows:

Sc^{3+}	$3d^0$	Fe^{3+}	$3d^5$
Cr^{3+}	$3d^3$	Ni^{2+}	$3d^8$
Mn^{2+}	$3d^5$	Cu^+	$3d^{10}$
Fe^{2+}	$3d^6$	Cu^{2+}	$3d^9$

[Note that only scandium forms an ion with a noble gas configuration.]

Exercise   Write the electron configurations for the following ions: (a) Ba^{2+}, (b) Ag^+, (c) Cd^{2+}, and (d) Pb^{2+}.   *Answer* (a) [Xe], (b) $[Kr]4d^{10}$, (c) $[Kr]4d^{10}$, (d) $[Xe]4f^{14}\,5d^{10}\,6s^2$

EXAMPLE 10.5
Ionic Compounds

Write formulas for any ionic compounds that might form between (a) calcium and oxygen, (b) aluminum and silicon, (c) potassium and selenium, (d) iron and sulfur. Consult Figure 10.9 to find which of these elements forms ions.

(a) Ca + O. This is simply the combination of a metal and a nonmetal. The compound would be CaO.

(b) Al + Si. This is the combination of a metal and a semiconducting element. Silicon forms neither anions nor cations, so no ionic compound would be produced.

(c) K + Se. The representative metal K might combine with the semiconducting element Se, as Se forms a noble gas type of anion. The compound would be K_2Se.

(d) Fe + S. The transition metal Fe is known to form both Fe^{2+} and Fe^{3+} cations. Sulfur is a Group VI nonmetal and forms S^{2-} ions. Therefore, the two possible compounds would be FeS and Fe_2S_3.

[Note that only by consulting reference books or doing experiments can predictions about the existence and properties of chemical compounds be confirmed.]

Exercise   Write the formulas of any ionic compounds that might form between (a) F and Cl, (b) Na and F, and (c) Mg and As.   *Answer* (a) none, (b) NaF, (c) none

ATOMS AND IONS IN CHEMICAL COMPOUNDS

As we have pointed out (Section 9.19), few compounds are 100% ionically bonded or 100% covalently bonded. Various approaches are used to describe or predict the degree of covalent bonding in an "ionic" compound or the degree of polarity in a "covalent" compound. In Sections 10.8 and 10.9 two concepts that are useful for this purpose are introduced, one based on the influence of ions on each other (polarizability) and the other based on the ability of atoms in covalent bonds to attract electrons (electronegativity). Following that, in Sections 10.10 and 10.11, a bookkeeping system is introduced that is extremely useful for keeping track of the electron distribution in compounds—the assignment of oxidation states to all of the atoms in chemical compounds. Each of these concepts is used frequently in later chapters that deal with the reactions and properties of chemical compounds.

10.8 POLARIZATION

The **polarization of an ion** is the distortion of its electron cloud by an ion of opposite charge. (In the presence of ions, the electron clouds of atoms and molecules can also be polarized.) Cations are small and have a high charge density, while anions are larger and have lower charge density. Cations tend to attract the electron clouds of anions. The smaller a cation and the larger its charge, the greater is its polarizing ability.

Covalent bonding is the attraction of nuclei to a region of high electron density that lies between the nuclei. The greater the polarizing ability of a cation, the more it draws electron density into the region between itself and an anion. The result is an increase in the covalent character of the bond (see Figure 9.12).

The charge-to-size ratio of a cation—the absolute value of its charge divided by its ionic radius—is a *relative* measure of the polarizing ability of a cation, if it were to form. The larger the charge-to-size ratio of an ion, the greater the degree of covalent character in its bonds. The charge-to-size ratios for the beryllium and calcium +2 ions

$$Be^{2+} \quad 2/0.035 = 59 \qquad Ca^{2+} \quad 2/0.099 = 20$$

reflect what is known from experiment to be the case. The bonds to beryllium in most of its compounds are highly covalent, while calcium forms many ionic compounds. Note that the significance of the charge-to-size ratios is not in their numerical values, but in the relative magnitudes of the absolute values.

The relative effects of size and charge contribute to the diagonal similarity of the representative elements and their compounds mentioned in Section 10.3. The Be^{2+} ion is smaller than the Al^{3+} ion, but the size difference is compensated for by the larger charge of the aluminum ion (Be^{2+}, $2/0.035 = 57$; Al^{3+}, $3/0.051 = 59$). As a result, the ions have nearly identical polarizing abilities, and many analogous aluminum and beryllium compounds have very similar properties.

Larger charge/size ratio → bonds with more covalent character

The charge-to-size ratio concept is frequently used qualitatively in rationalizing the ionic or covalent bonding of the elements. For example, boron is the first element in Representative Group III and boron atoms are quite small. A noble gas type cation of boron would have a +3 charge. Based on what would be the high charge and small size of a boron +3 ion, we would not expect to find that, for example, BCl_3 is a highly ionic compound. (It isn't. It is a molecular compound.)

There is one significant effect on the polarizing ability of cations that is not reflected in the charge-to-size ratio. Cations with d^{10} electron configurations (see Section 10.7) cause greater polarization than cations with noble gas configurations. For example, the Na^+ and Cu^+ cations are of the same charge and almost identical size. However, they differ in their electron configurations. Because Cu^+ has only outer d level electrons, which shield the nuclear charge much less than the outer s and p level electrons of Na^+, the Cu^+ ion exerts a much stronger polarizing effect and forms compounds with greater covalent character.

EXAMPLE 10.6
Polarization

According to Figure 9.10, the following three compounds decrease in covalent character in the order shown: $ZnCl_2 > CaCl_2 > KCl$. Account for these differences in terms of the polarization of ions (ionic radii: Zn^{2+}, 0.074 nm; Ca^{2+}, 0.099 nm; K^+, 0.133 nm).

The K^+ cation is the least polarizing cation in the group — it is the largest and has only a $+1$ charge (1/0.133 nm = 7.5); therefore KCl is more highly ionic than the other two compounds. Because it is both smaller and of a higher charge than K^+, the Ca^{2+} ion (2/0.099 nm = 20.) is more polarizing than K^+ and $CaCl_2$ is more covalent than KCl. The Zn^{2+} cation, in addition to its still smaller radius and its $+2$ charge (2/0.074 nm = 27), also has a d^{10} configuration, making it the most polarizing cation in the group.

Exercise Which one of the following bonds will be the most ionic and which the least ionic: (a) Na—Cl, (b) Mg—Cl, and (c) Be—Cl? *Answer* (a) most, (c) least

10.9 ELECTRONEGATIVITY

Electronegativity is the ability of an atom in a covalent bond to attract electrons to itself. In a bond between two atoms of the same element, there is no electronegativity difference between the two atoms and the bond is nonpolar. At the other extreme of the ionic-to-covalent bonding continuum, the difference in electronegativity of two atoms is so great that it is as if one atom pulls one or more electrons completely away from the other to form an ionic bond.

Many different approaches have been made to assigning numerical values to electronegativity. Linus Pauling originated the term and derived an electronegativity scale based upon calculations using bond energies. The Pauling scale, which we use in this book, is adjusted so that fluorine, the most electronegative element, has an electronegativity of 4, the highest value (Table 10.8).

Table 10.8
The Complete Electronegativity Scale [Adapted from Linus Pauling, *The Nature of the Chemical Bond*, 3rd ed. (Ithaca, New York: Cornell University Press, 1960), p. 43.]

H 2.1																	
Li 1.0	Be 1.5											B 2.0	C 2.5	N 3.0	O 3.5	F 4.0	
Na 0.9	Mg 1.2											Al 1.5	Si 1.8	P 2.1	S 2.5	Cl 3.0	
K 0.8	Ca 1.0	Sc 1.3	Ti 1.5	V 1.6	Cr 1.6	Mn 1.5	Fe 1.8	Co 1.8	Ni 1.8	Cu 1.9	Zn 1.6	Ga 1.6	Ge 1.8	As 2.0	Se 2.4	Br 2.8
Rb 0.8	Sr 1.0	Y 1.2	Zr 1.4	Nb 1.6	Mo 1.8	Te 1.9	Ru 2.2	Rh 2.2	Pd 2.2	Ag 1.9	Cd 1.7	In 1.7	Sn 1.8	Sb 1.9	Te 2.1	I 2.5
Cs 0.7	Ba 0.9		Hf 1.3	Ta 1.5	W 1.7	Re 1.9	Os 2.2	Ir 2.2	Pt 2.2	Au 2.4	Hg 1.9	Tl 1.8	Pb 1.8	Bi 1.9	Po 2.0	At 2.2
Fr 0.7	Ra 0.9															

La–Lu 1.1–1.2				
Ac 1.1	Th 1.3	Pa 1.5	U 1.7	Np–Lr 1.3

Table 10.9
Electronegativity

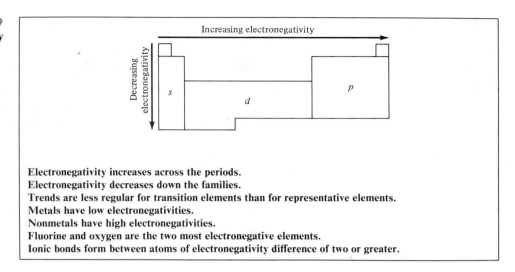

Electronegativity increases across the periods.
Electronegativity decreases down the families.
Trends are less regular for transition elements than for representative elements.
Metals have low electronegativities.
Nonmetals have high electronegativities.
Fluorine and oxygen are the two most electronegative elements.
Ionic bonds form between atoms of electronegativity difference of two or greater.

**Electronegativity difference >
2 → predominantly ionic bond
Electronegativity difference <
2 → predominantly covalent
bond**

The significance of electronegativity lies in its usefulness for predicting the types and properties of bonds, not in the specific numerical values. Pairs of atoms with moderate differences in electronegativity form polar covalent bonds. The magnitude of the electronegativity difference reflects the degree of polarity. In a polar bond, the more electronegative atom has the partial negative charge. With a large enough difference in electronegativity, an ionic bond can be expected to form. A commonly used rule of thumb is that if the electronegativity difference is 2 or greater, the bond between two atoms will be more ionic than covalent in character.

As shown in Figure 10.10, electronegativities are lowest for the metals at the bottom left in the periodic table and are highest for the nonmetals at the top right. Among the representative elements, electronegativities increase regularly across

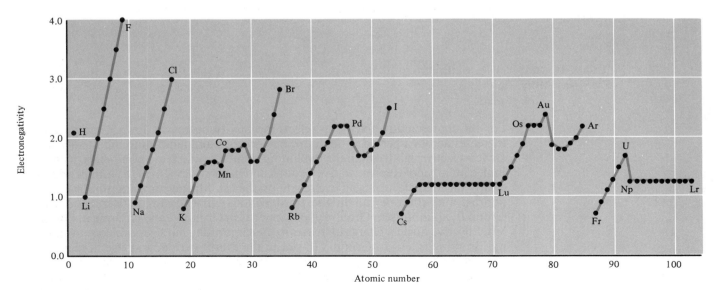

Figure 10.10

Variation of Electronegativity with Atomic Number In each period, the alkali metal (Group I) has the lowest electronegativity and the halogen (Group VI) has the highest electronegativity.

High electronegativity means high electron affinity and high ionization energy

each period and decrease, with a few exceptions, down each family. Comparison of Table 10.8 with Tables 10.2 and 10.5 shows that, as might be expected, increasing electronegativity is associated with increasingly difficult electron removal (increasing ionization energy) and increasing ease of electron addition (increasing electron affinity). Ionic compounds form most readily between large metal atoms of low electronegativity and small nonmetal atoms of high electronegativity.

Frequently "electronegative" and "electropositive" are used in a general way to describe the properties of atoms. An **electronegative atom** tends to acquire a partial negative charge in a covalent bond or to form a negative ion. Nonmetals are generally electronegative. An **electropositive atom** tends to acquire a partial positive charge in a covalent bond or to form a positive ion. Metals are generally electropositive. Of course, the terms are relative—in ICl the chlorine atom is the more electronegative atom and the iodine atom is the more electropositive atom.

Trends in electronegativity are not as regular among the transition metals, all of which have electronegativity values between 1.1 and 2.4. This smaller variation in electronegativity is in line with the smaller variations of atomic radii and ionization energies of these elements. Table 10.9 summarizes trends in electronegativity.

EXAMPLE 10.7
Electronegativity

With the use of the electronegativities in Table 10.8, arrange the following covalent bonds in order of increasing polarity: O—H, I—Br, C—F, P—H, S—Cl.

The polarity of a bond increases with increasing difference in electronegativity of the bonded atoms. The covalent bonds in question have the following order of increasing polarity, with the electronegativity differences shown:

P—H	I—Br	S—Cl	O—H	C—F
0.0	0.3	0.5	1.4	1.5

Exercise Arrange the following bonds in order of increasing polarity: (a) C—N, (b) S—O, (c) Si—N, and (d) B—O. *Answer* C—N, S—O, Si—N, B—O

EXAMPLE 10.8
Electronegativity

By consulting only the periodic table, arrange the following elements in order of increasing electronegativity: P, Al, Mg, Rb, Cl, Br. Give reasons for your arrangement.

For the representative elements, electronegativity decreases down a family and increases across a period. Rubidium, magnesium, and aluminum are metals and are less electronegative than the remaining elements, which are nonmetals. Rubidium, a member of Representative Group I and the first element in the fifth period, is clearly the least electronegative element on the list. Magnesium, aluminum, phosphorus, and chlorine fall in the third period—magnesium in Representative Group II, aluminum in Group III, phosphorus in Group V, and chlorine in Group VII. Effective nuclear charge increases in the same order and so does electronegativity. Bromine is also in Group VII, but in the fourth period, and therefore is less electronegative than chlorine. Even though bromine is one period farther down than phosphorus in the periodic table and its atomic size is slightly greater (0.114 nm vs 0.110 nm), it is the more electronegative element. The much greater nuclear charge on the bromine atom ($Z = 35$ for Br vs. $Z = 15$ for P) gives it a substantially larger effective nuclear charge. The order of increasing electronegativity is Rb < Mg < Al < P < Br < Cl.

Exercise Arrange the following elements in order of increasing electronegativity: K, N, As, F, and Sn. *Answer* K < Sn < As < N < F

10.10 OXIDATION STATE

In an "ionic compound," for example, NaCl, the sodium atoms have lost electrons and the chlorine atoms have gained electrons — we describe the electrons as having been transferred from one atom to the other. As we have said numerous times by now, chemical bonds are neither fully ionic nor fully covalent. It would be desirable to know to what extent the atoms in a compound have changed their share of "ownership" of the total number of valence electrons that they started with. Many properties could be related to this knowledge. A simple bookkeeping system for electrons allows assignment of numbers that, in many cases, indicate the *relative* change in electron ownership by each atom.

Oxidation numbers are assigned to atoms in compounds and are equal either to the charges of ions or to the charges atoms *would* have if the compound were ionic. The term **oxidation state** has the same meaning as "oxidation number."

Oxidation numbers *do not* convey information about chemical properties in the same way as, say, ionization energies. The closest they come to chemical significance is to show the relative differences in the shift of electrons toward or away from each atom. In some cases, they have *no* such significance. However, oxidation numbers are very useful in balancing equations (Section 17.7). They are also useful in predicting possible reaction products and in predicting the properties of chemical compounds. Such predictions can be made because the atoms of most elements can have more than one oxidation state, and there tend to be similarities among compounds of the same element in the same oxidation state.

The rules for assigning oxidation numbers are given in the following paragraphs. In each case, the objective of the rule is to assign a negative oxidation number to the most electronegative element in a compound. Table 10.10 summarizes the rules and gives examples. Study the table while you study the rules.

1. The oxidation number of any element in the free state is zero. Whether the element is polyatomic or not, the oxidation number of a free element is zero. For example, Cu in elemental copper and H in elemental hydrogen (H_2) are both assigned oxidation numbers of zero.

2. The oxidation number of a monatomic ion is equal to the charge on the ion. For example, in $CaCl_2$ the oxidation number of the chlorine (Cl^-) is -1 and the oxidation number of the calcium (Ca^{2+}) is $+2$.

3. Fluorine (the most electronegative element) always has the oxidation number -1.

4. Oxygen, with only a few exceptions, has an oxidation number of -2. Oxygen is assigned an oxidation number of -2 in all ionic and nonionic compounds except peroxides, superoxides, and ozonides, which contain O—O bonds, and the few compounds that contain O—F bonds (in which F has the negative oxidation number).

5. Hydrogen, except in metal hydrides, has an oxidation number of $+1$. In virtually all of its compounds, the oxidation number of hydrogen is $+1$. In the binary metal hydrides, such as NaH, hydrogen is assigned an oxidation number of -1.

6. For a neutral compound, the algebraic sum of the oxidation numbers of all the atoms must equal zero. By using the preceding rules together with this rule or rule 7, it becomes possible to calculate oxidation numbers for atoms in many compounds without any additional information.

Table 10.10

Rules for Assigning Oxidation Numbers In (6) and (7) the oxidation numbers calculated using the rules are shown in black.

(1) **Free elements, oxid. no. = 0**

$\overset{0}{Ca}$ $\overset{0}{O_2}$ $\overset{0}{S_8}$

(2) **Monatomic ions, oxid. no. = ionic charge**

$\overset{+1}{Na}\overset{-1}{Cl}$ $\overset{+2}{Ca}\overset{-1}{F_2}$ $\overset{+1}{Cu}\overset{-1}{Br}$ $\overset{+2}{Cu}\overset{-1}{Br_2}$

(3) **Fluorine, oxid. no. = -1, *always***

$\overset{-1}{Ba}\,F_2$ $H\overset{-1}{F}$ $Ba\,Si\,\overset{-1}{F_6}$ $\overset{-1}{Br}F$

(4) **Oxygen, oxid. no. = -2 (except, e.g., H_2O_2; OF_2)**

$\overset{+1\,-1}{}$ $\overset{+2\,-1}{}$

$\overset{-2}{H_2O}$ $\overset{-2}{BaO}$ $\overset{-2}{H_2SO_4}$ $\overset{-2}{CO_2}$

(5) **Hydrogen, oxid. no. = $+1$ (except hydride, e.g., NaH)**

$\overset{+1\,-1}{}$

$\overset{+1}{H_2O}$ $\overset{+1}{H_2SO_4}$ $\overset{+1}{Ba(OH)_2}$ $\overset{+1}{CH_4}$

(6) **Neutral compounds, sum of oxid. nos. = 0**

$\overset{2(+5)}{As_2}\overset{5(-2)}{O_5}$ $\overset{+1}{K}\overset{+7}{Cl}\overset{4(-2)}{O_4}$

$\overset{-3}{N}\overset{3(+1)}{H_3}$ $\overset{+4}{C}\overset{4(-1)}{Cl_4}$

(7) **Polyatomic ions, sum of oxid. nos. = charge of ion**

$\left(\overset{-2}{O}\overset{+1}{H}\right)^{-}$ $\left(\overset{+6}{S}\overset{4(-2)}{O_4}\right)^{2-}$

$\left(\overset{+3}{Cl}\overset{2(-2)}{O_2}\right)^{-}$ $\left(\overset{2(+5)}{P_2}\overset{7(-2)}{O_7}\right)^{4-}$

For free elements: oxidation state = 0

F: oxi. state *always* −1
O: oxi. state *usually* −2
H: oxi. state *usually* +1

For a neutral compound: sum of oxi. numbers of all atoms = 0

---

7. For a polyatomic ion, the algebraic sum of the oxidation numbers of the atoms must equal the charge on the ion. For example, in the carbonate ion, CO_3^{2-}, oxygen contributes a total oxidation number of $3 \times (-2)$, or -6; therefore to have a total charge of -2, the oxidation number of carbon must be $+4$.

If there are three types of atoms in a molecule or ion and if the rules give us the oxidation numbers of two atoms in a compound or ion, we can calculate the oxidation number for the third type of atom. For example, to find the oxidation number of Cl in perchloric acid, $HClO_4$, we use the assigned values of $+1$ for H and -2 for O.

$$\text{(Oxidation no. H)} + \text{(oxidation no. Cl)} + \text{(total oxidation no. O)} = 0$$
$$(+1) + \text{(oxidation no. Cl)} + [4(-2)] = 0$$
$$\text{(Oxidation no. Cl)} = -1 + 8 = +7$$

The oxidation number of Cl in $HClO_4$ is $+7$. Although we have written out an equation to illustrate this process, an equation is not necessary. Just by examining the formula and the known oxidation states, what is needed to maintain neutrality can be seen.

$$\overset{+1 \quad +7 \quad 4(-2)}{\text{H Cl O}_4}$$

EXAMPLE 10.9
Oxidation Numbers

Using the rules discussed above, find the oxidation states of sulfur in the following species: (a) S_8, (b) S, (c) S^{2-}, (d) H_2S, (e) SO_2, (f) SO_3, (g) HSO_4^-, (h) H_2SO_4, and (i) SO_3^{2-}.

(a) and (b) The oxidation number of S is zero in both S_8 and S, for these symbols both represent the free element (rule 1).
(c) The oxidation number of S in S^{2-} is -2, the charge on the ion (rule 2).
(d) Based on the oxidation number of $+1$ for hydrogen (rule 5) and the maintenance of an oxidation number sum of zero (rule 6), sulfur has an oxidation number of -2.

$$\overset{2(+1)-2}{\text{H}_2\text{S}}$$

(e) and (f) Based on an oxidation number of -2 for O (rule 4) and maintaining oxidation number sums of zero (rule 6), S has oxidation numbers of $+4$ and $+6$ in these compounds.

$$\overset{+4 \, 2(-2)}{\text{SO}_2} \qquad \overset{+6 \, 3(-2)}{\text{SO}_3}$$

(g), (h), and (i) Applying rules 4, 5, 6 and 7 (O, -2; H, $+1$; oxidation number total $= 0$ for neutral compound; oxidation number total $=$ total charge of polyatomic ion) gives oxidation numbers of $+6$, $+6$, and $+4$ to sulfur in these species.

$$\overset{+1+6 \, 4(-2)}{\text{HSO}_4^-} \qquad \underline{\text{check}}$$
$$(+1) + (+6) + 4(-2) = -1$$

$$\overset{2(+1)+6 \, 4(-2)}{\text{H}_2\text{SO}_4} \qquad 2(+1) + (+6) + 4(-2) = 0$$

$$\overset{+4 \, 3(-2)}{\text{SO}_3^{2-}} \qquad (+4) + 3(-2) = -2$$

Exercise Find the oxidation states of nitrogen in the following species: (a) HNO_3,

(b) HNO_2, (c) NO^+, (d) N^{3-}, (e) N_2, and (f) NH_3. *Answer* (a) $+5$, (b) $+3$, (c) $+3$, (d) -3, (e) 0, (f) -3

In binary compounds for which the rules do not specifically indicate the oxidation states of both of the atoms present, the element that usually forms negative ions or is more electronegative is assigned an oxidation number equal to the charge it would have *if* it were present as a negative ion (whether it is ionic or not). The other element is given the positive oxidation number that makes the molecule neutral. For example, in PCl_3 and PCl_5 chlorine is assigned an oxidation number of -1, resulting in oxidation numbers of $+3$ and $+5$ for phosphorus. An outcome of this procedure is that the halogens have oxidation numbers of -1 in almost all compounds except those with oxygen or other, more electronegative, halogens.

Oxidation numbers can easily be assigned to elements that always form positive ions of the same charge, for example, $+1$ for the Representative Group I elements and $+2$ for the Group II elements.

For some compounds, following the rules leads to fractional oxidation numbers. For example, Fe in Fe_3O_4 must have an oxidation number of $+2\frac{2}{3}$ ($3 \times 2\frac{2}{3} = +8$, to balance the -8 of the 4 O atoms). This seemingly strange result is explained by the fact that Fe_3O_4 contains Fe atoms of both $+2$ and $+3$ oxidation numbers, combined in what may be thought of as $FeO \cdot Fe_2O_3$. The oxidation number found in such a case is an average.

10.11 PERIODIC TRENDS IN OXIDATION STATE

Knowing which elements can display only one, or only two, or more than two oxidation states, and knowing the more common oxidation states is useful in many ways. For example, possible products of chemical reactions can be predicted from possible oxidation states of the elements involved. Also, in their higher oxidation states many elements are more electronegative, with a resulting influence on properties.

Table 10.11 summarizes the variability of the oxidation states of the representa-

Table 10.11

Variability of Common Oxidation States in Compounds This table is based upon the commonly encountered oxidation states of these elements. In some compounds, boron has oxidation state $+3$; in others, the bonding is unique and assigning oxidation states has little meaning.

tive elements. Table 10.12 lists common oxidation states and gives examples of compounds of the representative elements. The following guidelines are helpful in remembering the common oxidation states of the common elements:

1. For the representative elements, the maximum possible positive oxidation state equals the representative group number. What we might call the *group oxidation state* in a sense represents the involvement of all of the *s* and *p* electrons in bonding. Oxygen and fluorine are the *only* representative elements that *never* show the group oxidation state in any compounds.

2. The members of the *s* block and the scandium family show only one oxidation state in their compounds.

3. Most *p*-block elements show more than one oxidation state. Halogens other than fluorine have either oxidation states of −1 or positive oxidation states when combined with more electronegative elements. The most negative oxidation state in the nitrogen, oxygen, and fluorine families is for anions that have added enough electrons to give a noble gas configuration, for example, N^{3-}, O^{2-}, and F^- (also, in a few compounds, C^{4-}). With the notable exceptions of nitrogen, fluorine, and oxygen, many elements in these families show positive oxidation states that decrease from the group oxidation state by increments of 2 (see Table 10.12).

4. Variability of oxidation states is the rule for most transition elements. In most cases it is difficult to predict from the electron configurations which are the most common oxidation states of transition elements.

Table 10.12

Oxidation States and Typical Compounds for the Representative Elements Except for oxygen and fluorine, the most electronegative elements, the maximum oxidation state for each element is equal to its group number.

Group I	Group II	Group III	Group IV	Group V	Group VI	Group VII	Noble gases
$_1$H +1: HCl −1: Na^+H^-							$_2$He
$_3$Li +1: Li^+Cl^-	$_4$Be +2: $BeCl_2$	$_5$B +3: BCl_3	$_6$C −4: CH_4 +2: CO +4: CO_2; CCl_4	$_7$N −3: $(Li^+)_3 N^{3-}$; NH_3 +2: NO +3: N_2O_3 +4: NO_2 +5: N_2O_5	$_8$O −2: $(Na^+)_2 O^{2-}$; H_2O −1: $(Na^+)_2 O_2^{2-}$; H_2O_2	$_9$F −1: Na^+F^-; CF_4	$_{10}$Ne
$_{11}$Na +1: Na^+Cl^-	$_{12}$Mg +2: $Mg^{2+}(Cl^-)_2$	$_{13}$Al +3: Al_2Cl_6	$_{14}$Si −4: SiH_4; +4: $SiCl_4$	$_{15}$P −3: PH_3; Na_3P +3: PCl_3 +5: PCl_5, P_4O_{10}	$_{16}$S −2: $(Na^+)_2 S^{2-}$; H_2S +4: SO_2 +6: SO_3	$_{17}$Cl −1: Na^+Cl^-; CCl_4 +1: HOCl +3: $HClO_2$ +5: $HClO_3$ +7: $HClO_4$	$_{18}$Ar
$_{19}$K +1: K^+Cl^-	$_{20}$Ca +2: $Ca^{2+}(Cl^-)_2$	$_{31}$Ga +3: Ga_2Cl_6	$_{32}$Ge +2: $GeCl_2$ +4: $GeCl_4$	$_{33}$As −3: AsH_3; Na_3As +3: $AsCl_3$ +5: As_4O_{10}	$_{34}$Se −2: H_2Se +4: SeO_2 +6: SeO_3	$_{35}$Br −1: Na^+Br^-; HBr +1: HOBr +5: $HBrO_3$ +7: $HBrO_4$	$_{36}$Kr +2: KrF_2
$_{37}$Rb +1: Rb^+Cl^-	$_{38}$Sr +2: $Sr^{2+}(Cl^-)_2$	$_{49}$In +3: $InCl_3$	$_{50}$Sn +2: $Sn^{2+}(F^-)_2$; $SnCl_2$ +4: $SnCl_4$; SnO_2	$_{51}$Sb −3: SbH_3 +3: $Sb^{3+}(F^-)_3$, $SbCl_3$ +5: $SbCl_5$	$_{52}$Te −2: H_2Te +4: TeO_2 +6: TeO_3	$_{53}$I −1: Na^+I^-; HI +1: HOI +5: HIO_3 +7: HIO_4	$_{54}$Xe +2: XeF_2 +4: XeF_4 +6: XeF_6 +8: Na_4XeO_6
$_{55}$Cs +1: Cs^+Cl^-	$_{56}$Ba +2: $Ba^{2+}(Cl^-)_2$	$_{81}$Tl +1: Tl^+Cl^- +3: TlF_3	$_{82}$Pb +2: $Pb^{2+}(F^-)_2$ +4: PbO_2	$_{83}$Bi −3: BiH_3 +3: $Bi^{3+}(F^-)_3$ +5: Bi_2O_5	$_{84}$Po +4: PoO_2	$_{85}$At	$_{86}$Rn

EXAMPLE 10.10
Oxidation Numbers

Make use of your knowledge of periodic positions and trends in properties of the elements to determine the oxidation numbers of the elements in (a) $BaSiF_6$, barium fluorosilicate, and (b) $Mn_2(SiF_6)_3$, manganese fluorosilicate.

(a) Barium, silicon, and fluorine are representative elements. Barium, a member of Representative Group II, is a metal and forms the Ba^{2+} ion in its compounds. Barium, therefore, has an oxidation number of $+2$. The combination of silicon and fluorine must have a charge of -2 to balance the charge on the barium ion. Fluorine, the most electronegative element known, is a member of Representative Group VII and each fluorine atom is assigned an oxidation number of -1, the charge it would have if it were present in the compound as an ion. For the combination of silicon and fluorine to have a charge of -2, the silicon atom must be assigned an oxidation number of $+4$. This value is consistent with the position of silicon in the table, in Representative Group IV.
(b) Manganese is a transition metal that exhibits several different oxidation states. In part (a) we found that the SiF_6 group has a charge of -2. With this information at hand, we find that in $Mn_2(SiF_6)_3$, manganese must have an oxidation number of $+3$.

$$\underset{Mn_2}{\overset{2(+3)}{}}\,\underset{(SiF_6)_3}{\overset{3(-2)}{}}$$

Exercise Determine the oxidation numbers of the elements in $CaMg(SiO_3)_2$.
Answer Ca is $+2$, Mg is $+2$, Si is $+4$, O is -2

10.12 OXIDATION STATES IN FORMULAS AND NAMES

In Section 4.3 we introduced the Stock system for naming chemical compounds and illustrated its use for cations and binary ionic compounds such as

| Mn^{2+} | manganese(II) ion | $CuCl$ | copper(I) chloride |
| Mn^{3+} | manganese(III) ion | $CuCl_2$ | copper(II) chloride |

The Stock system is used to name molecular as well as ionic compounds. For molecular compounds the Roman numeral is simply the oxidation number. Binary molecular compounds may be named by the classical system *or* by the Stock system.

Classical System		Stock System	
N_2O	dinitrogen monoxide	nitrogen(I) oxide	$\overset{+1\,-2}{N_2O}$
N_2O_3	dinitrogen trioxide	nitrogen(III) oxide	$\overset{+3\,-2}{N_2O_3}$
N_2O_5	dinitrogen pentoxide	nitrogen(V) oxide	$\overset{+5\,-2}{N_2O_5}$
ICl	iodine monochloride	iodine(I) chloride	$\overset{+1\,-1}{ICl}$
ICl_3	iodine trichloride	iodine(III) chloride	$\overset{+3\,-1}{ICl_3}$

EXAMPLE 10.11
Chemical Nomenclature

Manganese forms oxides in which the metal exhibits oxidation states of $+2$, $+3$, $+4$, and $+7$. Write the formulas and give the names (Stock system) for these compounds.

Oxygen exhibits an oxidation number of -2 in these oxides. The formulas of the manganese compounds and their names are

MnO	manganese(II) oxide
Mn_2O_3	manganese(III) oxide
MnO_2	manganese(IV) oxide
Mn_2O_7	manganese(VII) oxide

Exercise Determine the oxidation state of gold in each of the following compounds and name the compounds using the Stock system of nomenclature: (a) $AuCl_3$, (b) Au_2S, and (c) Au_2O_3. *Answer* (a) $+3$, gold(III) chloride; (b) $+1$, gold(I) sulfide; (c) $+3$, gold(III) oxide

---

EXAMPLE 10.12
Chemical Nomenclature

Write the formulas of the following binary compounds: iodine(V) fluoride, tin(IV) sulfide, selenium(VI) oxide, nitrogen(IV) oxide, and phosphorus(III) oxide.

Based on their positions in the periodic table, fluorine (Representative Group VII), sulfur (Group VI), and oxygen (Group VI) would be expected to have the respective oxidation numbers -1, -2, and -2 in these binary compounds. The formulas for the compounds are IF_5, SnS_2, SeO_3, NO_2, and P_2O_3. The formulas for the last two compounds indicate one of the potential shortcomings of the Stock system of nomenclature for binary covalent compounds. The system relates to the empirical formulas of such compounds and gives no indication of situations where the molecules do not have the simplest formulas. The name nitrogen(IV) oxide does not distinguish between NO_2 and N_2O_4, both of which exist. The true molecular formula of phosphorus(III) oxide is P_4O_6, not P_2O_3. In this case the classical names for the nitrogen(IV) oxides — nitrogen dioxide and dinitrogen tetroxide — and for phosphorus(III) oxide — tetraphosphorus hexoxide — are more descriptive than the Stock names.

Exercise Write the formulas for the following compounds: (a) arsenic(III) fluoride, (b) bismuth(V) oxide, (c) cerium(IV) sulfate, (d) chromium(II) chloride. *Answer* (a) AsF_3, (b) Bi_2O_5, (c) $Ce(SO_4)_2$, and (d) $CrCl_2$

10.13 IN SUMMARY: TRENDS IN PROPERTIES OF THE ELEMENTS

The periodic table is our guide in making generalizations about the properties of the elements. At this point we can summarize the concepts that serve as a foundation for much of the descriptive chemistry of the elements that is covered in later chapters. Because generalizations apply most readily to the representative elements, this summary is directed mainly to these elements.

The chemical properties of the elements are determined to a large extent by their electron configurations and radii. Across the periods of representative elements, except for H and He, the outermost configurations build up from s^1 to s^2p^5, and each period ends with a noble gas of the s^2p^6 configuration. The effective nuclear charge increases across each period, causing a continuously greater attraction by the nuclei for the outer electrons and a decrease in atomic radii.

Along with the progression from s^1 to s^2p^6 configuration and the decrease in size, a progression from metallic to nonmetallic character is observed. Metallic properties in general are associated with larger radii and fewer valence electrons. Nonmetallic properties are associated with smaller size and larger numbers of valence electrons. The trend across the periods is reflected in a general increase in the energy needed to remove electrons (increasing ionization energy; Table 10.13). At the same time there

Table 10.13
Comparisons of Ranges of Ionization Energies, Electron Affinities, and Electronegativities For electron affinities we have considered only the experimentally determined values (see Table 10.5). The Representative Group II metals have calculated positive values ranging from 52 to 240 kJ/mol.

First ionization energies (kJ/mol)	
Nonmetals	1000–2372
Semiconducting elements	762–947
Metals	376–1007
Electron affinities (kJ/mol)	
Nonmetals	−349 to 0
Semiconducting elements	−195 to −77
Metals	−120 to −14
Electronegativities	
Nonmetals	2.1–4.0
Semiconducting elements	1.8–2.4
Metals	0.7–2.4

Nonmetals:
generally small radii
4 or more valence electrons
high ionization energies
high electron affinities

Metals:
generally large radii
few valence electrons
low ionization energies
low electron affinities

---

is an increasing tendency for isolated atoms to add electrons to form anions (increasing electron affinity) and also for atoms to attract electrons in chemical bonds (increasing electronegativity). The ability to gain or lose electrons almost disappears at the noble gases, with their stable $1s^2$ and s^2p^6 configurations.

Down a family of representative elements, nuclear charge increases and also new levels of electrons are added. The influence of the electrons added to new outer energy levels predominates, and atomic size generally increases down a family. As a result, the transition from metallic to nonmetallic character across a period moves further to the right with increasing period number. In Group IV, tin and lead in periods 5 and 6 are metals; in Groups V and VI, bismuth and polonium, the elements in the sixth period, are the only metals. In Group VII none of the elements are metals.

When representative metals combine with the nonmetals of Groups V, VI, and VII (with s^2p^3, s^2p^4, and s^2p^5 configurations) ionic compounds are usually formed. As a generalization, the combination of elements with large differences in electronegativity yields ionic compounds, and combination of elements with relatively small differences in electronegativity gives molecular compounds. Covalent bonds between atoms of differing electronegativity are polar, and the greater the difference in electronegativity, the greater the polarity.

The charge-to-size ratio of a cation is related to the degree of covalent character in its bonding. The smaller a cation and the higher its charge, the greater its polarizing ability. By drawing electron density from an anion into the region between the ions, small, highly charged cations form bonds with a high degree of covalent character.

There is a significant difference in behavior between the first member of each representative element family and the remaining family members. The primary reason for the difference in each case is the smaller atomic size of the first family member. Two first family members, oxygen and fluorine, are the most electronegative elements (see Table 10.8). In relative reactivity and the types and properties of the compounds formed, the first family members lithium, beryllium, and boron more closely resemble the second members of the groups to the right. This diagonal relationship is strongest for beryllium and aluminum, which have approximately the same charge-to-size ratio and the same electronegativity.

Some simple correlations between oxidation state and periodic table position can be made for the representative elements. The oxidation states of transition metals show few such correlations.

For the representative elements, the maximum positive oxidation states (except for oxygen and fluorine) equal the group numbers. Metals have *only* positive oxidation states, and those in Groups I and II show only the group number oxidation state. The maximum negative oxidation states of the nonmetals correspond to the number of electrons required to attain noble gas configurations. The *p*-block metals other than aluminum (Ga, In, Tl, Sn, Pb, Bi) can exhibit two oxidation states, one that corresponds to the loss of the *p* valence electrons (e.g., Tl^+, Sn^{2+}, Bi^{3+}) and the other that corresponds to the use of all valence electrons (e.g., $TlCl_3$, $SnCl_4$, BiF_5). Note that in higher oxidation states, these elements are more likely to form molecular compounds.

All of the nonmetals (except fluorine) and many of the semiconducting elements show a variety of oxidation states, but correlations with configurations for these states are not always possible.

For the *d*- and *f*-transition elements, gradually increasing ionization energies and electronegativities accompany the gradually decreasing size across the periods. Copper, silver, and gold are among the least electropositive metals, and they are relatively unreactive. Because of the decrease in atomic size across the 4*f* series (the lanthanide contraction), atoms of the two heaviest members of each transition metal family are very similar in size and in chemical properties.

In atoms of the *d*-transition elements, the $(n-1)d$ and ns levels differ relatively little in energy. Therefore, electrons in both levels are available for chemical bonding, and multiple oxidation states are common for the *d*-transition metals. In fact, only the members of the scandium family commonly show a single oxidation state.

In the introduction to Chapter 9, we drew an analogy between the personalities of individual human beings and the "personalities" of individual elements. This seems a good place to remind ourselves of the different elemental personalities. We organize and systematize descriptive chemistry as much as possible, for we need the guidelines in learning chemistry. But chemists have made many observations about the behavior of elements and compounds that do not fit into the framework of generalizations and theory (at least not yet). Such information is no less important to the science of chemistry.

In the next section we discuss the properties of the noble gases, which, with their stable electron configurations and lack of reactivity, provide reference points in the periodic table.

THE NOBLE GASES

10.14 DISCOVERY OF THE NOBLE GASES

Helium (He), neon (Ne), argon (Ar), krypton (Kr), xenon (Xe), and radon (Rn) make up the group of elements called the noble gases. All except radon are normally present in the atmosphere, although in such small concentration that they are sometimes called the "rare gases." Radon is radioactive (Chapter 12) and decomposes soon after it is formed from other radioactive elements.

Helium was the first of the noble gases to be discovered (1868). Its existence was recognized when sunlight was observed through a then relatively new instrument, the spectroscope. A pattern of lines not previously observed was identified. For a while this new gas (named for *helios,* the sun) was thought to be present only in the sun. Later it was observed on Earth in the gases formed by a radioactive mineral, and still later it was identified in the atmosphere.

Argon was discovered in 1894 by William Ramsay, a Scottish chemist, and Lord Rayleigh, a professor at Cambridge University. A sample of nitrogen from the atmosphere was allowed to react with magnesium to form magnesium nitride.

$$3Mg(s) + N_2(g) \xrightarrow{\Delta} Mg_3N_2(s)$$
magnesium nitride

A small amount of the gas did not react with the magnesium. Ramsay examined this gas in the spectroscope and found a pattern of lines different from that of nitrogen. At the suggestion of a friend, the new gas was named "argon," meaning "the lazy one," because it was so unreactive.

At the time, no place for helium and argon was allowed in the periodic table. Ramsay was convinced that other members of a new periodic table group were present in the atmosphere, and he began a search for the element that would fall between helium and argon. By carefully separating the components of liquid air, Ramsay and his assistant, William Travers, soon isolated from the atmosphere and identified with the spectroscope three additional members of the "zero" group—krypton (in May 1898), named from the Greek meaning "hidden"; neon (in June 1898), named from the Greek meaning "new"; and xenon (in July 1898), named from the Greek meaning "stranger." Radon, the radioactive noble-gas element, was discovered in 1900.

10.15 PROPERTIES AND COMPOUNDS OF THE NOBLE GASES

The physical properties of the noble gases are summarized in Table 10.14. The periodic trends that we have been describing are evident for these elements. Down the family from He to Rn, the atomic radii increase. Along with the increase in size goes a decrease in ionization energy. Melting point, boiling point, and gas density values also increase as the atomic masses increase.

Helium has the lowest boiling point of any known substance, only about four degrees above absolute zero. This property makes liquid helium valuable in the study of materials and reactions at very low temperatures. Helium itself at very low temperatures has some extraordinary properties. It develops such strong surface tension that the liquid will creep all the way up the sides of a container and out of it. Close to absolute zero, helium becomes superconductive, a condition in which a material offers no resistance to current flow.

For more than 60 years after the discovery of radon, it was believed by almost all chemists and taught in almost all chemistry courses that the "group zero" elements were inert, that because of their stable filled outer electron levels they neither gained, lost, nor shared electrons to form compounds. In fact, they were known as the "inert gases." Isaac Asimov has pointed out a fine semantic distinction: Chemists were thinking and writing, "The noble gases cannot form compounds under any condi-

Table 10.14
Properties of the Noble Gases All of the noble gases are colorless, odorless, and monatomic. Values of atomic radii for elements for which compounds are not known have been found by extrapolation.

	He	Ne	Ar	Kr	Xe	Rn
Melting point (°C)	$-272°$	$-249°$	$-189°$	$-157°$	$-112°$	$-71°$
Boiling point (°C)	$-269°$	$-246°$	$-186°$	$-153°$	$-108°$	$-62°$
Gas density (g/L; 0 °C, 1 atm)	0.179	0.900	1.78	3.75	5.90	—
Atomic radii (nm)	0.050	0.065	0.095	0.110	0.130	0.145
Ionization energy at 0 K (kJ/mol)	2372	2081	1521	1351	1170.	1037

tions," when they should have been saying, "As far as we know, the noble gases do not form compounds."

The preparation in 1962 of xenon platinum hexafluoride ($Xe[PtF_6]$), followed shortly thereafter by the preparation of xenon tetrafluoride (XeF_4), amazed many chemists. Obviously, they had forgotten to remain open to the possibility of the discovery of new facts.

The preparation of $Xe[PtF_6]$ came about when Neil Bartlett, who had just made $O_2[PtF_6]$, looked, "quite by chance" he said, at a chart of ionization energies plotted against atomic number (a similar chart appears in most general chemistry textbooks; see Figure 10.7). Bartlett saw that the ionization energy of xenon is almost equal to that of oxygen and had the thought that xenon might undergo the same type of reaction with PtF_6 as did O_2.

The rest is history. The experiment worked—Xe and PtF_6 combined. Furthermore, xenon tetrafluoride could be made quite simply by heating xenon and fluorine together at 750 °C for one hour. In fact, if xenon and fluorine are mixed in a flask and the flask is allowed to stand in the sunlight, some of the compound eventually forms. Xenon tetrafluoride turned out to be a quite ordinary crystalline substance which can be melted, recrystallized, and stored in a bottle on the shelf. A barrage of research was set off by the initial discoveries of xenon compounds, and within a year 50 publications on noble gas compounds had appeared in scientific journals.

Thus far, most of the known noble gas compounds are those in which xenon is bonded to oxygen or fluorine or both. This is reasonable, since xenon has a relatively low ionization energy, and fluorine and oxygen are highly electronegative.

Xenon combines with fluorine to give fluorides in which it has oxidation states of $+2$, $+4$, and $+6$ (Table 10.15).

$$Xe(g) + F_2(g) \longrightarrow XeF_2(s)$$
$$XeF_2(s) + F_2(g) \longrightarrow XeF_4(s)$$
$$XeF_4(s) + F_2(g) \longrightarrow XeF_6(s)$$

As far as we know, xenon does not combine directly with oxygen, but xenon–oxygen compounds are prepared from the xenon–fluorine compounds, for example,

$$XeF_6(s) + 3H_2O(l) \longrightarrow XeO_3(s) + 6HF(g)$$
highly
explosive

A few krypton compounds, notably KrF_2, have been prepared, as has a very small amount of a radon fluoride. Although radon has an even lower ionization energy than xenon and should form stable compounds, its radioactivity and scarcity

Table 10.15
Some Xenon Compounds

Compound	M.p. (°C)	Form; properties
XeF_2	129°	Colorless crystals; stable; reacts with H_2O
XeF_4	117°	Colorless crystals; stable
$XeOF_2$	31°	Colorless crystals; unstable
XeF_6	49.6°	Colorless crystals; stable; reacts with H_2O
Cs_2XeF_8	—	Yellow solid; stable to 400 °C
XeO_3	—	Colorless crystals; explosive
XeO_4	—	Colorless gas; explosive

make it very difficult to study. As yet, no comparable compounds of helium, neon, or argon have been prepared.

10.16 SOURCES AND USES OF THE NOBLE GASES

Natural gas from some wells contains up to 6% of helium (see An Aside: A Surprise for Dexter, Kansas). Helium is separated from the other components of natural gas by liquefaction, followed by fractional distillation (see Tools of Chemistry: Distillation, Chapter 15). Most of the helium used commercially is obtained from this source. The other noble gases (except for radon) are obtained from liquefied air.

Several of the major uses of the noble gases take advantage of their lack of reactivity. Helium and argon are used in various ways in metallurgy to protect metals that are being melted or heated from reacting with oxygen or nitrogen in the air. For example, argon is used as a shielding gas in welding. In laboratories, both helium and argon provide protection in working with highly reactive materials.

Common incandescent light bulbs are filled with an 88% argon-12% nitrogen mixture. Argon is better than nitrogen for this purpose in two ways: Because they are heavier, argon molecules move more slowly and conduct heat less readily than nitrogen molecules. Thus, the filament in the bulb reaches a higher temperature and glows more brightly in the presence of argon. Also, the life of the filament is prolonged because it sublimes more slowly in the heavier gas. Some nitrogen must be present in the bulb, however, or an electrical arc would be formed. Krypton is even better than argon for the purposes described because it is still heavier, but krypton is too expensive for routine use in light bulbs.

When an electric current is passed through neon under low pressure in a closed tube, the neon glows bright red. All signs made from such gas-filled tubes are called "neon" signs, though some contain mixtures of neon and argon or other gases. Helium produces a yellow-white light; argon a blue light; a helium–argon mixture, an orange light; and a neon–argon mixture, a deep lavender light. By using appropriate gas combinations, colored glass tubes, and the addition of a bit of mercury, almost any color can be produced.

Argon is of major importance in the steel industry, where an argon–oxygen mixture is used to help remove carbon impurities from the molten metal. Helium and argon provide the necessarily inert and very pure atmosphere needed for the growth of single crystals for semiconductors.

The largest use of helium is in a variety of applications that take advantage of its unusual properties at low temperatures. The possible importance of helium in future energy-related applications has caused concern over the need to conserve helium by separating it from natural gas before the gas is used as fuel. Otherwise, during combustion of the fuel helium goes up the chimney. Because helium is so light, it then escapes from the earth's atmosphere and cannot be reclaimed.

AN ASIDE

A Surprise for Dexter, Kansas

The people of Dexter, Kansas, had high hopes in 1903 when drilling began close to the end of Main Street. An oil or natural gas well would bring industry and prosperity to their small town.

It looked as though the town had a sure thing when at only 400 feet, the drilling brought in a "howling gasser." Nine million cubic feet of gas a day blew out of the $8\frac{1}{4}$-inch pipe at the well site. While preparations were made to cap the well, company officials rushed off to the larger town of Winfield to sell stock. In Dexter, the well became a sightseeing attraction for passing trains, and somebody made a big tin whistle to hold in the stream of rushing gas.

Soon a nasty rumor began to circulate—the natural gas from the Dexter well would not burn. The proud citizens of Dexter were determined to disprove the rumor, especially since some felt it had been started by their rivals from the town of Winfield.

An all-day picnic and barbecue was held, complete with a brass band and a parade. The climax of the day was to be the lighting of a huge torch of gas at a pipe leading from the well. The big moment came and a flaming bale of hay was thrust into the gas. Two times this was done. Not only did the gas fail to ignite, but it put out the flames.

The disappointed and humiliated citizens of Dexter probably did not much care what was in their well. However, a Kansas state geologist sent a sample of the gas to the chemistry department at the University of Kansas. An analysis showed that it contained 71% nitrogen and an additional "inert residue." Not until two years later did Dr. H. P. Cady make the connection between the Dexter gas and the new, inert gas that had been discovered several years earlier. In 1905, Dr. Cady showed that the gas from Dexter, Kansas contained 1.84% of helium. This was the first discovery of helium in gas wells, which were to become the major source of helium in this country. (This account based on Clifford W. Seibel, *Helium, Child of the Sun* (Lawrence, Kansas: University Press of Kansas, 1968).)

SUMMARY

10.1 ATOMIC AND IONIC RADII Atomic radii are assigned on the basis of the distances between atoms joined by single covalent or metallic bonds. Ionic radii are the radii of ions in crystalline ionic compounds. The radii of cations are always smaller, and those of anions larger, than the radii of the atoms from which they are derived.

10.2 FACTORS THAT INFLUENCE RADII Atomic or ionic radii decrease with increasing effective nuclear charge—the portion of the nuclear charge that acts on an electron. The effective nuclear charge is reduced by the screening effect—the shielding of electrons from the full force of nuclear attraction by other electrons. Atomic or ionic radii increase when a new energy level (farther from the nucleus) is occupied.

10.3 PERIODIC TRENDS IN RADII The atomic radii of representative elements increase down each family and decrease across each period. This decrease is smaller for transition elements. Because the *f*-transition elements intervene in the sixth period, the two heaviest elements in each *d*-transition family have very similar radii and chemical properties.

10.4 IONIZATION ENERGY **10.5** FACTORS THAT INFLUENCE IONIZATION ENERGY; PERIODIC TRENDS The ionization energy is the energy required to remove the least tightly bound electron from an atom or ion in the gaseous state. Ionization energies increase across periods (because of increasing effective nuclear charge) and decrease down families (because of increasing atomic or ionic radius). Thus metals generally have low ionization energies and nonmetals high ionization energies. It is especially difficult to remove an electron from an atom or ion with a noble gas configuration ($1s^2$ or ns^2np^6).

10.6 ELECTRON AFFINITY Electron affinity is the enthalpy for the addition of one electron to an atom or ion in the gaseous state. The first electron affinity may be positive or negative; the value for adding a second electron is always positive, since it takes energy to overcome the repulsion between an electron and a negative ion.

10.7 ELECTRON CONFIGURATIONS OF IONS In ionic compounds most representative elements form ions with noble gas configurations. Nonmetals generally form anions and metals generally form cations, but ions with charges greater than three are rarely found. The electron configurations and charges of common ions are shown in Figure 10.9.

10.8 POLARIZATION The polarization of an ion is the distortion of its electron cloud by an ion of opposite charge. Cations, which are small and have high charge density, tend to attract the electron clouds of anions. They draw electron density into the region between themselves and anions to which they are bonded, making the bond more covalent and less ionic in character.

10.9 ELECTRONEGATIVITY Electronegativity is the ability of an atom in a covalent bond to attract electrons to itself. If the electronegativity difference between two elements is 2.0 or greater, the bond between them will generally be more ionic than covalent. Elements at the upper right of the periodic table (nonmetals) have the highest electronegativities and those at the lower left (metals) the lowest electronegativities. Electronegative atoms (generally nonmetals) tend to acquire a partial negative charge in a covalent bond or to form a negative ion; electropositive atoms (generally metals) tend to acquire a partial positive charge in a covalent bond or to form a positive ion.

10.10 OXIDATION STATE **10.11** PERIODIC TRENDS IN OXIDATION STATE **10.12** OXIDATION STATES IN FORMULAS AND NAMES The oxidation state (oxidation number) of an atom in a compound is equal to its charge (if it is a monatomic ion) or to the charge it would have if the compound were ionic. The rules for assigning oxidation numbers are summarized in Table 10.10. For the representative elements, the maximum possible oxidation state is given by the representative group number. Most p-block and transition elements exhibit more than one oxidation state. The common oxidation states of the representative elements are listed in Table 10.12. When the Stock system (Section 4.3) is used to name molecular compounds, the oxidation number is given as a Roman numeral in parentheses for elements of variable oxidation number.

10.13 IN SUMMARY: TRENDS IN THE PROPERTIES OF THE ELEMENTS The chemical and physical properties of the elements can be correlated in many ways with their electron configurations, atomic radii, electronegativities, ionization energies, electron affinities, and oxidation states.

10.14 DISCOVERY OF THE NOBLE GASES **10.15** PROPERTIES AND COMPOUNDS OF THE NOBLE GASES **10.16** SOURCES AND USES OF THE NOBLE GASES The existence of helium was first detected in the solar spectrum. The next four family members (Ne, Ar, K, and Xe) were first isolated from air in the 1890s. Radon is radioactive. Until the 1960s it was thought that the noble gases formed no chemical compounds. Since then, numerous compounds of xenon, particularly with fluorine and oxygen, have been prepared, as well as some compounds of krypton and radon. Helium is present in natural gas found in the United States. In their uses, advantage is taken of the lack of reactivity of the noble gases, the colors they emit in "neon" signs, and, for helium, the very low temperatures that can be maintained.

SIGNIFICANT TERMS

atomic radii
ionic radii
effective nuclear charge
screening effect
lanthanide contraction
isoelectronic
ionization energy
noble gas configuration
electron affinity
pseudo-noble gas configuration, d^{10} configuration
polarization of an ion
electronegativity
electronegative atom
electropositive atom
oxidation number, oxidation state

THOUGHTS ON CHEMISTRY
The Grim Silence of Facts

THE GRIM SILENCE OF FACTS, by Derek A. Davenport, 1970

While grading a beginning graduate inorganic examination some time ago I was startled to discover that the student believed silver chloride to be a pale green gas. Now we all have our off days . . . and I read on willing to forgive and forget, if not to allow partial credit. A little later the student launched into a long, plausible explanation as to why silver chloride is a pale green gas. I was reminded of Dr. Johnson's: "I can give you the explanation, M'am, but not the understanding of it." . . .

That we should begin by setting up a skeleton of inorganic principles is undeniable. Without it the presentation of facts becomes inefficient and their accumulation a shapeless mass of protoplasm. But these principles should not be restricted to the narrowly structural. Instability and stability, lability and inertness, oxidation and reduction, acidity and basicity, and their relationship to position in the periodic table are as much a part of modern inorganic chemistry as is ligand field theory, though admittedly they are less fashionable. . . .

But, the arguments run, teaching the facts of inorganic chemistry is dull beyond conception. Leaving aside the implicit suggestion that molecular orbital theory is intrinsically hilarious, one must demur. Anyone who can bring life to a character table should not despair of lending a little color to the oxidation states of vanadium. It takes effort—what in teaching doesn't—but the effort must be made. For as Conrad urged: "Every sort of shouting is a transitory thing, after which the grim silence of facts remains."

Derek A. Davenport, *The Grim Silence of Facts.* Quoted from *Journal of Chemical Education,* Vol. 47, 1970, p. 271.

QUESTIONS

The Sizes of Atoms and Ions

10.1 What is the trend in atomic radii across a period for the representative elements? What is the trend down a family?

10.2 Why are the atomic radii of Al and Ga nearly the same? How does this similarity affect the chemical behavior of these elements?

10.3 What is the lanthanide contraction? How does this contraction affect the radii of the two heaviest elements in each *d*-transition element family?

10.4 Place the following species in order of increasing radius: Cl, Cl^-, and Cl^+.

10.5 How would the ionic radius of O^{2-} compare to that of O^-?

10.6 Compare the radii of Fe, Fe^{2+}, and Fe^{3+}.

10.7 On the basis of the arrangement of elements in the periodic table, match the following atomic radii—(i) 0.095 nm, (ii) 0.099 nm, (iii) 0.141 nm, and (iv) 0.175 nm—to the following elements: (a) Sn, (b) Ar, (c) Cl, (d) Pb.

10.8 Arrange the following ions in order of increasing radius: F^-, Mg^{2+}, Cl^-, Be^{2+}, S^{2-}, and Na^+.

10.9 Using the arrangement of elements in the periodic table, match the following ionic radii—(i) 0.068 nm, (ii) 0.136 nm, (iii) 0.196 nm, and (iv) 0.112 nm—to the following ions: (a) F^-, (b) Sr^{2+}, (c) Br^-, and (d) Li^+.

10.10* Arrange the following species in order of decreasing radius: Li, O, I, Li^+, O^{2-}, and I^-.

Electron Gain and Loss

10.11 The first ionization energy of oxygen is 1313.9 kJ/mol at 0 K. The second ionization energy is 3388.1 kJ/mol. Why is this second value much larger than the first?

10.12 Choose the electron which will be removed first in the ionization of a phosphorus atom: (a)$1s$, (b) $2p$, (c) $3d$, or (d) $3p$.

10.13 Choose the electron which will be removed first in the ionization of a chromium atom: (a) $1s$, (b) $4s$, (c) $3d$, or (d) $3p$.

10.14 What is the general trend of first ionization energies for atoms in the same period? What is the general trend within a family of representative elements?

10.15 How do the values of the ionization energies of the metals compare to those of the nonmetals? How do these values determine the chemical behavior of the metals and nonmetals?

10.16* Assume that the first ionization energy of Se is unknown, but that the values for the other elements given in Table 10.2 are known. Predict the value for Se by using both horizontal and vertical periodic trends.

10.17 Write a chemical equation showing the reaction associated with the ionization energy of element M. Write a similar chemical equation showing the reaction associated with the electron affinity of element X.

10.18 The enthalpy for the addition of one electron to an oxygen atom is − 141 kJ/mol, and for the addition of a second electron, 880 kJ/mol. Explain the difference between these numbers.

10.19 What would you predict as the general trend for values of electron affinity across a period?

10.20 Compare the cations formed by the *s*-block representative metals in the fourth through sixth periods to these formed by the Representative Group III elements in these periods.

10.21 What types of cations do the metals of Group IV and V form?

10.22 Write the Lewis symbols for K^+, Zn^{2+}, F^-, C^{4-}, and I^-.

10.23 Write the Lewis symbols for Mg^{2+}, Al^{3+}, Sc^{3+}, N^{3-}, and S^{2-}.

10.24 Show with Lewis symbols and electron configurations the changes that occur when (a) lithium and chlorine combine to form ionic lithium chloride, (b) magnesium and sulfur combine to form ionic magnesium sulfide, and (c) magnesium and chlorine combine to form ionic magnesium chloride.

10.25 Show with Lewis symbols and electron configurations the changes that occur when (a) zinc and chlorine combine to form ionic zinc chloride and (b) calcium and oxygen combine to form ionic calcium oxide.

10.26 Show with Lewis symbols and electron configurations the changes that occur when (a) Sc and Cl combine to form $ScCl_3$, (b)

Ag and O combine to form Ag_2O, (c) Be and C combine to form Be_2C, and (d) Li and N combine to form Li_3N.

10.27 Write the formulas for any ionic compounds that might form between (a) Ca and O_2 (b) Sc and O_2.

10.28 Write the formulas for any ionic compounds that might form between (a) La and Cl_2 and (b) Cu and F_2.

Atoms and Ions in Chemical Compounds

10.29 Briefly describe the concept of polarization of an ion by another ion. How does polarization of ions affect the ionic bonding in an ionic crystal?

10.30 Choose the cation that would be most effective in polarizing a given anion: K^+, ionic radius = 0.133 nm; Mg^{2+}, ionic radius = 0.066 nm; or Cs^+, ionic radius = 0.167 nm.

10.31 Choose the cation that would be most effective in polarizing a given anion: Na^+, ionic radius = 0.097 nm; Mg^{2+}, ionic radius = 0.066 nm; or Al^{3+}, ionic radius = 0.051 nm.

10.32 Arrange the following bonds in order of decreasing polarity: (a) C—F, (b) H—F, (c) F—F, and (d) O—F.

10.33 Arrange the following bonds in order of increasing polarity: (a) Li—O, (b) Li—N, (c) Li—F, and (d) Li—I.

10.34 What is meant by the term "electronegativity"? How does the difference in electronegativity between atoms of different elements affect the bonding between these atoms? What value of the electronegativity difference is usually considered necessary for the formation of an ionic bond?

10.35 In which part of the periodic table would we find the elements with the lowest values of electronegativity? Where would the elements with the highest values be?

10.36 Arrange the following elements in order of increasing electronegativity: (a) Rb, (b) Sn, (c) Si, and (d) O.

10.37 Arrange the following elements in order of increasing electronegativity: (a) I, (b) Te, (c) Bi, and (d) Ra.

10.38 Find the oxidation numbers of the atoms in the following species: (a)KH, (b) $MnCl_2$, (c)NH_4^+, (d) P_4, and (e) Cl^-.

10.39 Repeat Question 10.38 for the following species: (a) SO_3^{2-}, (b) Na_2O_2, (c) MnF_3, (d) ICl_3, and (e) H_2Se.

10.40 Repeat Question 10.38 for the following species: (a) Al^{3+}, (b) $Cr_2O_7^{2-}$, (c) $Mg(NO_3)_2$, (d) Al_2O_3, and (e) P_4O_{10}.

10.41 Repeat Question 10.38 for the following species: (a) $KHCO_3$, (b) $(NH_4)_2SO_4$, (c) $Fe(ClO_4)_3$, (d) H_2O_2, and (e) N_3^-.

10.42* Find the oxidation number of Cr in each of the following substances: (a)$K_2Cr_2O_7$, (b) Na_2CrO_4, (c) Cr, (d) Cr^{3+}, (e) $CrBr_2$, (f) $[Cr(H_2O)_6]I_3 \cdot 3H_2O$, (g) CrN, (h) CrO, (i) CrO_2, (j) Cr_2O_3, (k) CrO_2Cl_2, (l) CrS, and (m) $[Cr(OH)_4]^-$.

10.43 What is the maximum possible positive oxidation state for the representative elements? Which two representative elements

do not form species with the maximum possible values of their oxidation numbers?

10.44 Which elements in the periodic table have only one oxidation number (other than 0)? Which elements have oxidation numbers equal to the group number and the group number minus 2 as the two possible oxidation states?

10.45 What oxidation numbers might be expected for a nonmetal?

10.46 Name the following substances using the Stock system: (a) I_2O_5, (b)NO, (c)SF_6, (d)SO_3, and (e) ICl.

10.47 Repeat Question 10.46 for (a) CO, (b) IF_3, (c)N_2O_5, (d) $SiCl_4$, and (e) CCl_4.

10.48 Repeat Question 10.46 for (a) N_2O_3, (b) ICl_3, (c) CO_2, (d) SO_2, and (e) BF_3.

10.49 Write the formulas for the following compounds: (a) nitrogen(I) oxide, (b) silicon(IV) oxide, (c) phosphorus(III) chloride, (d) iodine(V) oxide, and (e) sulfur(II) chloride.

10.50 Repeat Question 10.49 for (a) sulfur(IV) fluoride, (b) nitrogen(II) oxide, (c) phosphorus(V) chloride, (d) bromine(III) fluoride, and (e) silicon(IV) sulfide.

10.51 Repeat Question 10.49 for (a) boron(III) nitride, (b) carbon(IV) selenide, (c) bromine(I) chloride, (d) nitrogen(III) oxide, and (e) oxygen(II) fluoride.

The Noble Gases

10.52 Write the chemical symbol and name for each of the noble gases. How do we isolate each of these elements? Identify one use for each of these gases.

10.53 Briefly discuss the discovery of each of the noble gases.

10.54 What are the general trends for the (a) atomic radii, (b) ionization energies, (c) gas densities, and (d) boiling points of the noble gases down a family?

10.55 Which noble gases are known to form chemical compounds? With which elements are the noble gas atoms bonded?

10.56 Write the electron configuration for Xe. Why might Xe be predicted to be "inert"? Write the Lewis structure for XeF_4. How can we explain this exception to the octet rule?

10.57 Write the Lewis structures for XeF_2 and XeF_6. Name these compounds using the Stock system.

Additional Questions

10.58 Identify the general trend across a period as (i) increasing, (ii) decreasing, or (iii) showing no significant change for the following properties: (a) atomic radius, (b) ionization energy, (c) electron affinity, (d) electronegativity, (e) positive charge on cation, and (f) negative oxidation state. Repeat this exercise identifying the trend down a family.

10.59* A neutral atom of element "E" has 15 electrons. Answer as many of the following questions as you can without looking at a periodic table: (a) What is the approximate atomic mass? (b) What is the atomic number? (c) What is the total number of s electrons? (d) Is the element a metal, nonmetal, or semiconducting element? (e) What is the empirical formula of the binary compound formed between sodium and this element? (f) What is the empirical formula of the binary compound formed between chlorine and this element? (g) What oxidation states can we normally expect for this element?

10.60* The following "message" was found in an alien spacecraft:

A chemist on Earth quickly recognized the "message" as a portion of the periodic table showing the elements important to the alien life form. Answer the following questions about the alien elements: (a) What is the symbol for the least active metal which forms a singly positive ion? (b) Which nonmetals form doubly negative ions? (c) Which halogen is important to their life form? (d) Which element forms a covalently bonded compound having the formula EX_2, where E and X are nonmetals and each atom of X gains two electrons? (e) Is their life form based on carbon or silicon?

Answers to Selected Questions

10.4 $Cl^+ < Cl < Cl^-$

10.6 $Fe^{3+} < Fe^{2+} < Fe$

10.7 (a) iii, (b) i, (c) ii, (d) iv

10.8 $Be^{2+} < Mg^{2+} < Na^+ < F^- < Cl^- < S^{2-}$

10.11 It is more difficult to remove an electron from a positively charged ion than from a neutral atom.

10.13 (b)

10.15 They are smaller; metals form cations and nonmetals do not.

10.21 They form ions with charges of $+2$ and $+3$, from loss of np electrons.

10.23 $[Mg]^{2+}$, $[Al]^{3+}$, $[Sc]^{3+}$, $\left[:\!\ddot{N}\!:\right]^{3-}$, $\left[:\!\ddot{S}\!:\right]^{2-}$

10.25 (a) $Zn:$ + $2:\dot{\underset{..}{Cl}}:$ $\longrightarrow$ Zn^{2+} $2\left[:\!\ddot{Cl}\!:\right]^-$

      $[Ar]3d^{10}\,4s^2$ $[Ne]3s^2\,3p^5$ $[Ar]3d^{10}$ $[Ar]$

(b) $Ca:$ + $\cdot\ddot{O}:$ $\longrightarrow$ Ca^{2+} $\left[:\!\ddot{O}\!:\right]^{2-}$

    $[Ar]4s^2$ $[He]2s^2\,2p^4$ $[Ar]$ $[Ne]$

10.28 (a) $LaCl_3$, (b) CuF and CuF_2

10.31 Al^{3+}

10.33 (d) < (b) < (a) < (c)

10.37 (d) < (c) < (b) < (a)

10.39 (a) $+4, -2$; (b) $+1, -1$; (c) $+3, -1$;(d) $+3, -1$;(e) $+1, -2$

10.41 (a) $+1, +1, +4, -2$; (b) $-3, +1, +6, -2$; (c) $+3, +7, -2$; (d) $+1, -1$; (e) $-\frac{1}{3}$

10.48 (a) nitrogen(III) oxide, (b) iodine(III) chloride, (c) carbon(IV) oxide, (d) sulfur(IV) oxide, (e) boron(III) fluoride

10.51 (a) BN, (b) CSe_2, (c) BrCl, (d) N_2O_3, (e) OF_2

10.57 $:\!\ddot{F}\!-\!\ddot{Xe}\!-\!\ddot{F}\!:$

xenon(II) fluoride, xenon(VI) fluoride

10.59 (a) 30 u, (b)15, (c) 6, (d) nonmetal, (e) Na_3E, (f) ECl_3 or ECl_5, (g) $0, \pm 3, +5$

10.60 (a) ⌐; (b) E, Ǝ; (c) ⊔; (d) ⊏; (e) carbon

PROBLEMS

Atomic and Ionic Radii

10.1 The bond lengths in F_2 and Cl_2 molecules are 0.142 nm and 0.198 nm, respectively. Calculate the atomic radii for these elements. Predict the Cl—F bond length. [The actual Cl—F bond length is 0.164 nm.]

10.2 The P—Cl bond length in PCl_3 is 0.204 nm. The bond length in Cl_2 is 0.198 nm. Calculate the atomic radii for these elements. Using the atomic radius for F given in Figure 10.2, predict the P—F bond length in PF_3. *Answer* Cl, 0.099 nm; P, 0.105 nm; P—F, 0.176 nm

10.3 The atoms in crystalline nickel are arranged so that they are touching each other as shown in the sketch

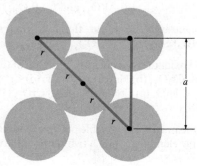

From plane geometry, we can see that $4r = a\sqrt{2}$. Calculate the radius of a nickel atom given that $a = 0.35238$ nm.

10.4* The ions in crystalline LiI are arranged as shown in the sketch

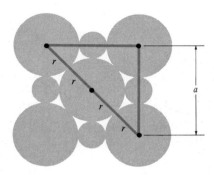

What is the relationship between a and the radius of the iodide ion, r_-? Calculate the ionic radius of the iodide ion given that $a = 0.600$ nm for LiI. *Answer* $4r = a\sqrt{2}$, 0.212 nm

10.5* The ions in crystalline KBr, KCl, and LiCl are arranged as shown in the sketch

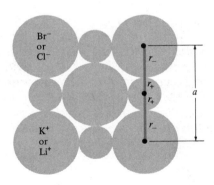

What is the relationship between a and the ionic radii? Using $a = 0.6578$ nm for KBr, 0.62931 nm for KCl, and 0.514 nm for LiCl, and 0.196 nm for the ionic radius for Br^-, calculate the ionic radii for K^+, Cl^-, and Li^+.

Ionization Energy, Electron Affinity, and Electronegativity

10.6 The ΔH_f° at 25 °C is 160.707 kJ/mol for Li(g) and 687.163 kJ/mol for Li^+(g). Calculate the ionization energy of lithium at this temperature.

10.7 The ΔH_f° at 25 °C is 78.99 kJ/mol for F(g) and −270.7 kJ/mol for F^-(g). Calculate the electron affinity for fluorine at this temperature. *Answer* −349.7 kJ/mol

10.8* One way to calculate the approximate amount of ionic character in a chemical bond between two atoms is by using the

following equation:

% ionic character = (16)(electronegativity difference)
$$+ (3.5)(\text{electronegativity difference})^2$$

Note that we always find the electronegativity difference by subtracting the value for the less electronegative element from the value for the more electronegative element. Calculate the % ionic character in chemical bonds between: (a) Cs and F, (b) Na and Cl, (c) S and O, (d) I and Cl, and (e) N and N using this equation. *Answer* (a) 91%, (b) 49%, (c) 20.%, (d) 9%, (e) 0%

10.9* Using the equation given in Problem 10.8, find the difference in electronegativity that is required to give a bond (a) 60% ionic and 40% covalent character and (b) 40% ionic and 60% covalent character. How do your answers agree with the "rule of thumb" given in Section 10.9 concerning the usual dividing line between ionic and polar covalent bonding?

Additional Problems

10.10 Using the data for radii of the ions given in Figure 10.3, calculate the charge to radius ratio for the following cations: (a) K^+, (b) Ca^{2+}, (c) Sc^{3+}, (d) Fe^{2+}, (e) Zn^{2+}, and (f) Ga^{3+}. Discuss the trend across this period. Which ion would polarize a given anion most?

10.11 Repeat the calculation in Problem 10.10 for (a) Cu^+ and (b) Cu^{2+}. Discuss the trend for ions of the same element. Which ion would polarize a given anion more? *Answer* (a) 10., (b) 28; a cation with a higher charge has a higher charge-to-radius ratio; Cu^{2+} would therefore polarize an anion more.

10.12 Repeat the calculation in Problem 10.10 for (a) Al^{3+}, (b) Ga^{3+}, (c) In^{3+}, and (d) Tl^{3+}. Discuss the trend for equally charged ions of elements in the same family of the periodic table. Which ion would polarize a given anion most?

10.13 Xenon(VI) fluoride can be produced from xenon(IV) fluoride by the addition of fluorine. Write a chemical equation for this reaction. What mass of XeF_6 will be produced from 3.62 g of XeF_4? *Answer* 4.29 g XeF_6

10.14 Xenon hexafluoride reacts rapidly with the SiO_2 in glass or quartz containers to form $XeOF_4$ (*l*) and SiF_4(g). What will be the pressure of SiF_4 in a 1.00 L container at 25 °C if 1.00 g of XeF_6 decomposes?

10.15 The heat of formation is −402 kJ/mol for XeF_6(s) and −285 kJ/mol for XeF_4(s). Calculate the heat of reaction at 25 °C for the preparation of XeF_6 from XeF_4 and F_2(g).

10.16* Using the data given in Table 10.3 for sodium, divide each value of the ionization energy by the total number of electrons that have been removed for each ion. Correlate your values with the energy levels and sublevels that are involved during the ionization process. *Answer* 496 kJ/mol for 3*s*; 2281 to 2386 kJ/mol for the first half of 2*p*; 2670.6 to 2873.4 kJ/mol for the second half of 2*p*; 3186.1 kJ/mol for 2*s*

CHAPTER 11

Molecular Bonding and Molecular Properties

Almost everyone has played with some kind of building toy. There are plain wooden blocks that slide together with grooves, or wooden balls connected by sticks. There are toys with snap-together plastic parts of many sizes and shapes. It is fun to create large, complex structures with these toys (and then to knock them down). The shapes of the structures are governed by the number of connecting points on each block or part, and by the angles at which connections can be made.

Atoms are built up into molecules in somewhat the same way. Some atoms have more "connecting points" than others. The angles of the connectors are determined by the electronic structures of the atoms. There is a major difference between inert toy parts and atoms, however. Atoms connected together influence each other's properties and change them. Electron clouds are distorted by the attraction and repulsion between atoms. Thus even within the limits of a specific molecular geometry, bond lengths and the angles between bonds can vary.

The shapes of molecules profoundly affect the materials of our world and the functioning of living things. If water molecules were linear instead of bent, many of their unique properties would disappear, and our climate, connected as it is to the water cycle, would be quite different. (Indeed, the chemistry of life itself would have to be very different.) We create plastics that are rigid or flexible, soft or hard, by tailor-making the shapes of their molecules. In biochemistry we are still discovering the many ways in which distinctive molecular shapes allow the chemical changes necessary to life.

MOLECULAR GEOMETRY

11.1 MOLECULAR GEOMETRY AND ELECTRON-PAIR REPULSION

Molecular geometry is the two- or three-dimensional arrangement in space of the atoms in a molecule. The geometry of a molecule is described by the lengths and angles of the bonds. A **bond angle** is the angle between the bonds that join two atoms to a third atom. The relationships among atomic radii (Section 10.1), bond length (Section 9.18), and bond angle are shown in Figure 11.1.

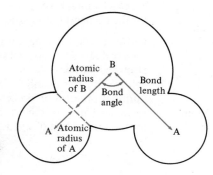

Figure 11.1
Bond Length, Bond Angle, and Atomic Radii

Experimental methods (including various types of spectroscopy; see Tools of Chemistry: Molecular Spectroscopy) allow the determination of the geometry of many molecules, both simple and complex. Given the knowledge that, for example, the mercury(II) chloride molecule is linear but the water molecule is bent

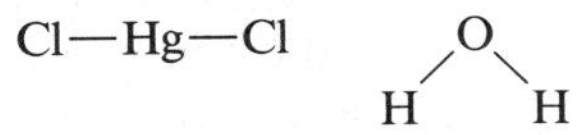

$$Cl—Hg—Cl \qquad \overset{\displaystyle O}{\underset{H \qquad H}{\diagup \diagdown}}$$

we then want to know why. Why should three atoms form a linear molecule in one case and a bent molecule in another case?

The valence-shell electron-pair repulsion theory (VSEPR) can be used to predict the general shapes of molecules. The basis for VSEPR is the repulsion that exists between particles of like charge. VSEPR describes molecular geometry as the result of the repulsion between the electron pairs in covalent bonds and in lone pairs. Sections 11.2 and 11.3 explain how VSEPR theory may be used to explain and predict the geometry of simple molecules.

11.2 VSEPR; MOLECULES WITHOUT LONE-PAIR ELECTRONS ON THE CENTRAL ATOM

Many simple molecules or polyatomic ions consist of a central atom to which a number of other atoms or groups are bonded, for example

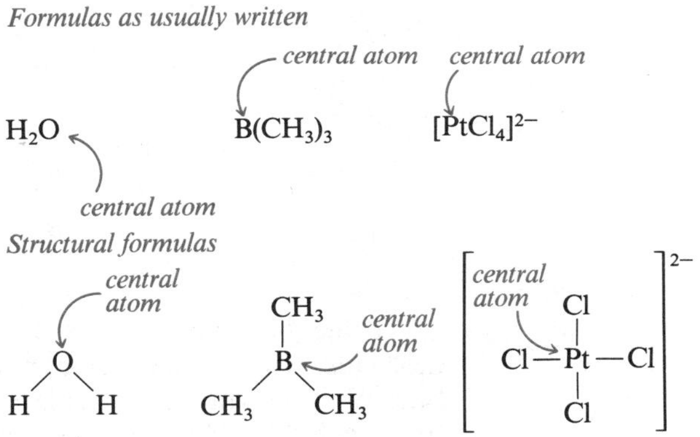

Formulas as usually written

$$H_2O \qquad B(CH_3)_3 \qquad [PtCl_4]^{2-}$$

central atom

Structural formulas

To apply VSEPR theory, molecules and ions are classified according to the number of bonding electron pairs and lone electron pairs surrounding the central atom. The electron pairs in the bonds and lone pairs are repelled by each other. The predicted molecular geometry is therefore the one that places the atoms or groups bonded to the central atom, as well as the lone pairs, as far apart as possible. In this section we focus our attention on molecules in which the central atom has no lone electron pairs. (Those with lone pairs are discussed in the next section.)

Consider a molecule AB_n in which A is the central atom. For $n = 1$ there is only one possible structure — a linear AB molecule (whether or not lone electron pairs are present).

$$n = 1 \qquad A—B \qquad \text{e.g.,} \qquad H—\overset{..}{\underset{..}{Cl}}:$$

hydrogen chloride

An AB_2 molecule contains two shared electron pairs. Obviously, they achieve the greatest distance from each other if the A—B bonds are on opposite sides of A in a linear molecule. The BAB bond angle is 180°.

$$n = 2 \quad \text{B—A—B} \quad \text{e.g., H—Be—H}$$
beryllium hydride

When three covalent bonds surround the central molecule, BAB angles of 120° place the bonding electron pairs at the greatest distance from each other. This gives a planar molecule with A at the center of an equilateral triangle and the B atoms at the corners.

$$n = 3 \qquad \text{e.g.,}$$ 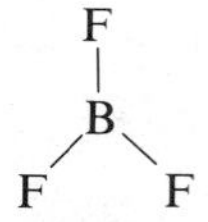
boron trifluoride

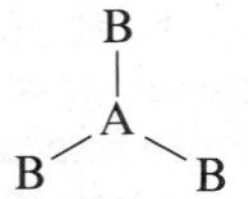

With $n = 4$ we reach molecules of the common type AB_4, with four substituents around a central atom that has formed enough bonds to obtain an octet of electrons in its outer energy level. (The word "substituent" refers to atoms or groups bonded to another atom or group, in this case to A.) The four substituents are at the corners of a regular tetrahedron, for in this arrangement the bonding electrons are as far apart as possible. Tetrahedral geometry occurs often, particularly in carbon compounds.

a tetrahedron

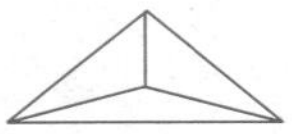

$$n = 4 \qquad \text{e.g.,}$$

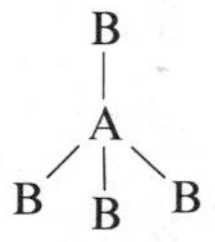

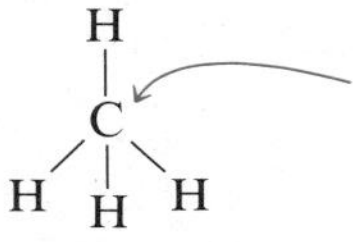

a tetrahedral carbon atom

methane

Table 11.1 summarizes the ideal geometries and ideal bond angles for AB_n molecules with 2 to 6 covalent bonds and no lone-pair electrons on the central atom. Each of these arrangements places the bonding electron pairs at maximum distances from each other. In real molecules, the bond angles often vary from the ideal values given in the table, but the overall geometry of the molecule is based on that shown.

In each structure in Table 11.1 except that for AB_5 molecules, the ideal BAB angles are equal to each other. A molecule with five covalent bonds in a triangular bipyramidal structure has two different types of BAB bond angles. The three equivalent B substituents all in the same plane with the central atom occupy what are called the *equatorial* positions and lie at 120° angles from each other. The two B substituents at opposite ends of the molecule, in what are referred to as the *axial* positions, are at angles of 90° from the B substituents in the equatorial positions. The result is that the three equatorial B substituents have an environment different from that of the axial B substituents. (In the next section we see the effect of this difference in the geometry of molecules with lone-pair electrons.)

In predicting molecular geometry by VSEPR theory, double and triple bonds are treated like single bonds. For example, the formaldehyde molecule, $H_2C{=}O$, is classified as an AB_3 molecule. And each carbon atom in ethylene, $H_2C{=}CH_2$, is the A atom in an AB_3 situation (one of the B's is ${=}CH_2$). Double bonds take up more space around A than single bonds because their greater electron density repels the other bonding electrons. As a result, the bond angles are distorted from the ideal

angles of Table 11.1, for example

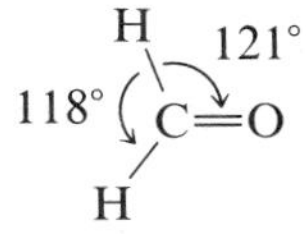

H 121°
118° C=O
H

formaldehyde
a triangular planar molecule

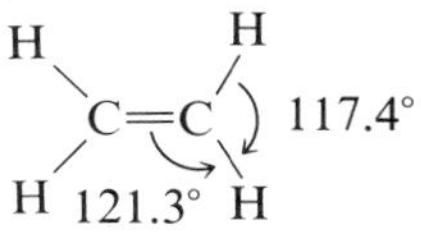

H   H
C=C   117.4°
H 121.3° H

ethylene
a planar molecule

Table 11.1

Geometry of Covalent Molecules with No Unshared Electron Pairs on the Central Atom In the molecules shown here all valence electrons on the central atom (A) participate in covalent bonds. Geometry could possibly be limited by the size of A and B. Only in AB_5 molecules are there different BAB angles within the molecule. Each B^e is separated by 120° from other B^e's. Each B^a is separated by 90° from the B^e's. Therefore, the B^e's have more room. Note: The geometry summarized here and in Table 11.2 applies to most cases where A is a representative element and often when A is a transition element. When d orbitals enter into bonding, there are additional geometric possibilities (Chapter 32).

Formula Type	Shared Electron Pairs	Arrangement of B Atoms Relative to A Atoms (Ideal BAB Bond Angle)	Molecular Structures
AB_2	2	Linear (180°)	
AB_3	3	Triangular planar (120°)	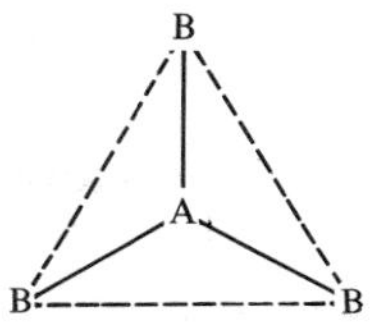
AB_4	4	Tetrahedral (109.47°)	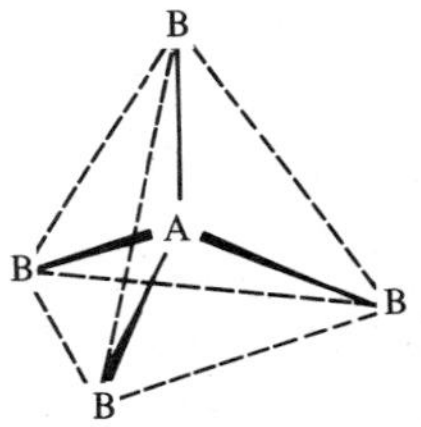
AB_5	5	Triangular bipyramidal (B^eAB^e, 120°) (B^eAB^a, 90°)	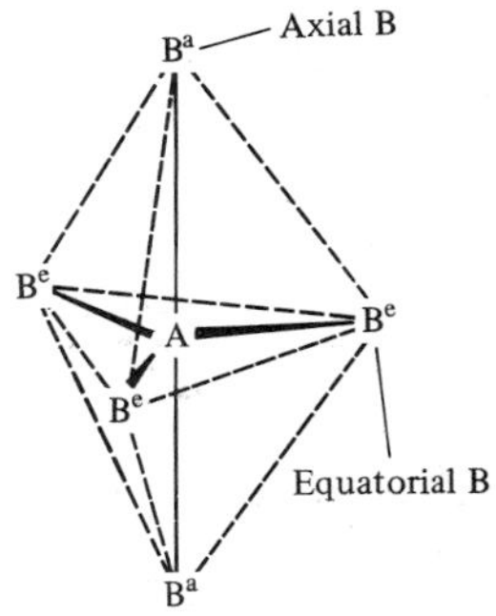
AB_6	6	Octahedral (90°)	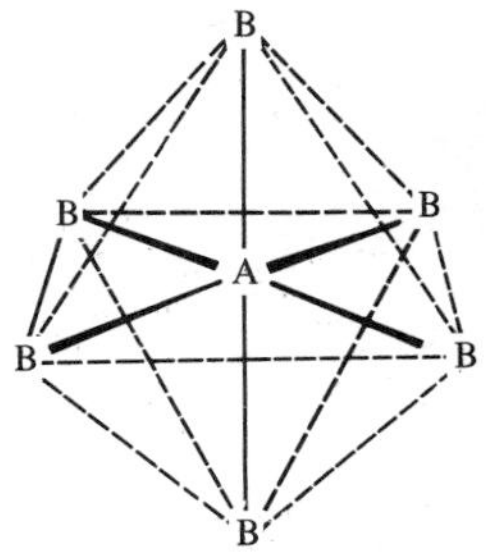

To use VSEPR theory, it is necessary to write the correct Lewis structure for the molecule and determine whether or not there are any lone electron pairs present on the central atom. If there are no lone pairs, the molecule is of the AB_n type and the geometry is expected to be based on that shown in Table 11.1.

EXAMPLE 11.1
VSEPR

Using VSEPR, show that the $BeCl_2(g)$ molecule is linear.

The beryllium atom has two valence electrons $(2s^2)$ and the Lewis structure shows no lone-pair electrons on the central beryllium atom.

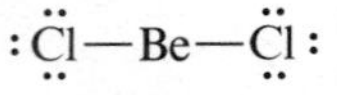

$$: \ddot{Cl} - Be - \ddot{Cl} :$$

Therefore, $BeCl_2$ is a linear, AB_2 type molecule.

Exercise Using VSEPR, predict the shape of the CO_2 molecule. *Answer* CO_2 is a linear molecule (type AB_2).

EXAMPLE 11.2
VSEPR

Use VSEPR to predict the geometry of (a) PF_5 and (b) SO_4^{2-}.

(a) Phosphorus is the third-period element of Group V and has five valence electrons. Because some bonding electrons can occupy vacant d orbitals in third and higher period elements (Section 9.9), the phosphorus atom can accommodate more than an octet of valence electrons. The Lewis structure shows that there are no lone-pair electrons on the phosphorus atom. Therefore, PF_5 is an AB_5 molecule and has triangular bipyramidal geometry.

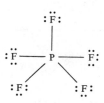

An AB_5 molecule

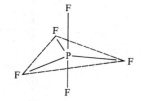

A triangular bipyramidal molecule

(b) Sulfur is a third-period element of Group VI. The Lewis structure shows no lone pairs on the sulfur atom, and therefore this AB_4 ion has tetrahedral geometry. Note that the VSEPR theory applies equally well to both ions and molecules.

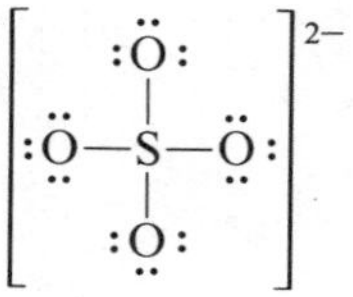

$$\begin{bmatrix} : \ddot{O} : \\ | \\ : \ddot{O} - S - \ddot{O} : \\ | \\ : \ddot{O} : \end{bmatrix}^{2-} \qquad \begin{bmatrix} O \\ | \\ S \\ O \quad O \end{bmatrix}^{2-}$$

An AB_4 ion 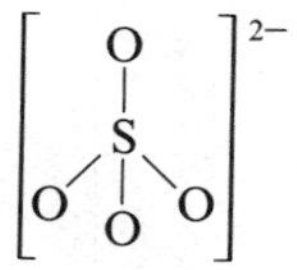   *A tetrahedral ion*

Exercise Using VSEPR, predict the geometry of SF_6 and NH_4^+. *Answer* SF_6 is an octahedral molecule (type AB_6); NH_4^+ is a tetrahedral ion (type AB_4).

11.3 VSEPR: MOLECULES
WITH LONE-PAIR ELECTRONS
ON THE CENTRAL ATOM

What happens when the central atom in a molecule has one or more lone electron pairs? Like bonding pairs, lone pairs repel each other. There is also repulsion between lone pairs and bonding pairs. This leads to arrangements in which all electron pairs—lone and bonding—are as far as possible from each other. Taken together, therefore, bonding and lone pairs assume the same general arrangements shown in Table 11.1. However, because the space of one or more bonding pairs is occupied only by lone pairs, rather than by bonds to other atoms, the resulting molecule has a different geometry. That is, because in molecular geometry we are looking only at the positions of *atoms,* replacing an atom with a lone pair changes the geometry.

For example, methane, ammonia, and water molecules each have four electron pairs around a central atom. Each has a different molecular geometry, but all derive their geometry from the AB_4 tetrahedron (Figure 11.2). The ammonia molecule has the geometry of a triangular pyramid, rather than a tetrahedron, because one place in AB_4 is filled by a lone pair. The general formula for such a molecule is AB_3E, where E represents a lone pair. Water, with two lone pairs, is a bent molecule represented by the general formula AB_2E_2. An unpaired electron has the same effect on geometry as a lone pair.

Nonbonding electron pairs spread out around atom A more than electron pairs in bonds, because nonbonding pairs are attracted by only one nucleus, not two. A lone pair on atom A repels the shared electron pairs of A—B bonds. Therefore, in most cases the BAB bond angles in compounds where atom A has one or more lone pairs are compressed and are smaller than the ideal angles given in Table 11.1. The effect of one lone pair is shown by comparing the bond angles in methane and ammonia (see Figure 11.2). Methane, with no lone pair, has the ideal tetrahedral angle, 109.47°. In ammonia, with one lone pair, the extra repulsion of the lone pair decreases the angle to 106.67°.

Two lone pairs repel each other more than a lone pair and a bonding pair. As a result, the bond angles in a molecule that has two lone pairs are more compressed than the bond angles in a similar molecule that has one lone pair. For example, compare the bond angle in ammonia (106.67°) with that in water (104.5°), which has two lone pairs rather than one. Note that a *single* unpaired electron on a central atom requires *less* space than either a bonding pair or a lone pair of electrons.

Because the lone, or nonbonding, electron pairs need more space, they enter AB_5

Figure 11.2
Methane, Ammonia, and Water Molecules The methane molecule has tetrahedral geometry; ammonia is a triangular pyramidal molecule; and water is a bent, or angular, molecule.

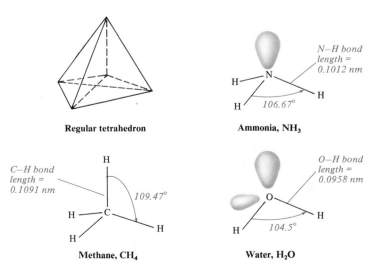

Regular tetrahedron

Ammonia, NH₃
N–H bond length = 0.1012 nm
106.67°

C–H bond length = 0.1091 nm
109.47°
Methane, CH₄

Water, H₂O
O–H bond length = 0.0958 nm
104.5°

and AB_6 molecules at specific positions. In Figure 11.3, which summarizes the effects of lone pairs on molecular shape, look at the rows beginning AB_5 and AB_6. As pointed out above, AB_5 molecules have two different bond angles between nearest neighbors. The equatorial positions have more space than the axial positions, and lone pairs occupy these equatorial positions (see Table 11.1). In AB_6 molecules, all the B positions are equivalent; the lone pairs can best stay separated from each other by entering positions opposite each other. Note that the smallest bond angle in AB_5 and AB_6 molecules is $90°$. Thus in each case, the lone pairs occupy the positions that minimize the number of lone pairs separated by $90°$. An excellent demonstration of the value of VSEPR was the correct prediction of the molecular structures of the previously unknown compounds of xenon shown in Figure 11.4.

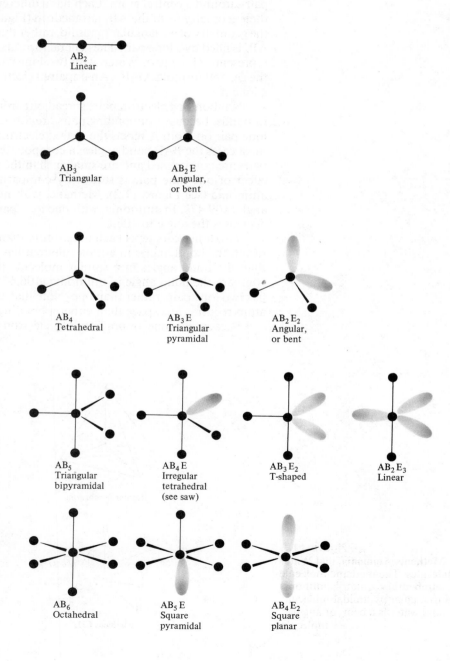

Figure 11.3
General Shapes of Covalent Molecules with Bonding and Nonbonding Electron Pairs A nonbonding electron pair is symbolized by E. With a nonbonded electron pair on A, the BAB bond angles tend to be smaller than ideal. (Source: R. J. Gillespie, *J. Chem. Educ.*, **40**, 295, 1963.)

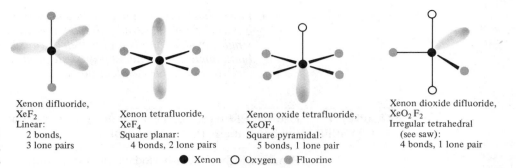

Figure 11.4
Structures of the Xenon Fluorides
and Oxofluorides

Xenon difluoride,
XeF_2
Linear:
2 bonds,
3 lone pairs

Xenon tetrafluoride,
XeF_4
Square planar:
4 bonds, 2 lone pairs

Xenon oxide tetrafluoride,
$XeOF_4$
Square pyramidal:
5 bonds, 1 lone pair

Xenon dioxide difluoride,
XeO_2F_2
Irregular tetrahedral
(see saw):
4 bonds, 1 lone pair

● Xenon ○ Oxygen ● Fluorine

In summary, VSEPR theory explains molecular geometry as based on the repulsion between electron pairs. Molecular geometry can be predicted from the number of bonding electron pairs and lone electron pairs on the central atom in a molecule. Table 11.2 summarizes the geometry of molecules with and without nonbonding electron pairs on the central atoms and gives further examples. The following steps are necessary in using VSEPR to predict molecular geometry:

1. Write the Lewis structure of the molecule.
2. Determine the number of bonding pairs and lone pairs of electrons around the central atom.
3. From Table 11.1 determine the ideal geometry. Then, if necessary taking into account the presence of lone pairs, use Table 11.1 or Table 11.2 to predict the actual shape of the molecule. (Remember that multiple bonds are treated like single bonds, and unpaired electrons are treated like lone electron pairs.)
4. Keep in mind that lone pairs occupy larger sites (equatorial in molecules derived from AB_5 geometry) or, when sites are equal, occupy sites opposite rather than next to each other.

Table 11.2
Geometry of Covalent Molecules AB_n and AB_nE_m E represents an unshared electron pair.
The observed molecular shape is derived from the geometry as shown in Figure 11.3. See Note in Table 11.1 caption.

Type Formula	Shared Electron Pairs	Unshared Electron Pairs	Ideal Geometry	Observed Molecular Shape	Examples
AB_2	2	0	**Linear**	**Linear**	$CdBr_2$
AB_2E	2	1	**Triangular planar**	**Angular, or bent**	$SnCl_2$, PbI_2
AB_2E_2	2	2	**Tetrahedral**	**Angular, or bent**	OH_2, OF_2, SCl_2, TeI_2
AB_2E_3	2	3	**Triangular bipyramidal**	**Linear**	XeF_2
AB_3	3	0	**Triangular planar**	**Triangular planar**	BCl_3, BF_3, GaI_3
AB_3E	3	1	**Tetrahedral**	**Triangular pyramidal**	NH_3, NF_3, PCl_3, $AsBr_3$
AB_3E_2	3	2	**Triangular bipyramidal**	**T-shaped**	ClF_3, BrF_3
AB_4	4	0	**Tetrahedral**	**Tetrahedral**	CH_4, $SiCl_4$, $SnBr_4$, ZrI_4
AB_4E	4	1	**Triangular bipyramidal**	**Irregular tetrahedral (or "seesaw")**	SF_4, $SeCl_4$, $TeBr_4$
AB_4E_2	4	2	**Octahedral**	**Square planar**	XeF_4
AB_5	5	0	**Triangular bipyramidal**	**Triangular bipyramidal**	PF_5, $PCl_5(g)$, SbF_5
AB_5E	5	1	**Octahedral**	**Square pyramidal**	ClF_5, BrF_5, IF_5
AB_6	6	0	**Octahedral**	**Octahedral**	SF_6, SeF_6, $Te(OH)_6$, MoF_6

5. *Variations from the ideal bond angles are caused by multiple covalent bonds and lone electron pairs, both of which require more room than single covalent bonds and therefore cause compression of surrounding bond angles. A single, unpaired electron requires* less *space than electrons in single covalent bonds or lone pairs.*

EXAMPLE 11.3
VSEPR

Use VSEPR to predict the molecular geometry of BrF_3 and BrF_5. Discuss in general the bond angles in these molecules.

Bromine is the fourth-period element in Group VII. The bromine atom has seven valence electrons and can accommodate more than an octet of electrons in its outermost energy level. The Lewis structures show the number of lone pairs and bonding pairs in BrF_3 and BrF_5 as follows:

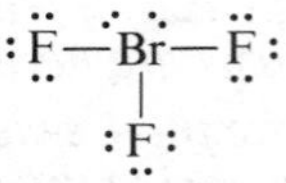

3 bonding pairs
2 lone pairs
An AB_3E_2 molecule

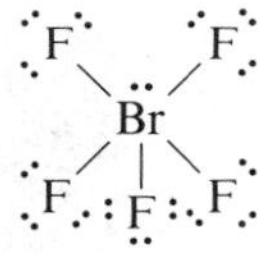

5 bonding pairs
1 lone pair
An AB_5E molecule

From Table 11.2 we predict that BrF_3 will be a T-shaped molecule and BrF_5 will have square pyramidal geometry.

The F—Br—F bond angles in BrF_3 should be less than the ideal 90° (see AB_3 in Table 11.1) because of the two lone pairs of electrons. Similarly, the angles in BrF_5 should also be compressed from the ideal 90° (AB_6 in Table 11.1), because there is one lone pair. (Experiment confirms this prediction—the F—Br—F bond angles are about 83.5°.)

Exercise Using VSEPR, predict the shape of $[I_3]^-$. *Answer* $[I_3]^-$ is a linear ion (type AB_2E_3).

EXAMPLE 11.4
VSEPR

Use VSEPR to predict the molecular geometry of NO_2. Discuss the bond angles in this molecule.

The Lewis structure for NO_2

shows that there are two substituents and one lone electron on the central nitrogen atom. Thus NO_2 fits the AB_2E pattern and should be an angular, or bent, molecule.

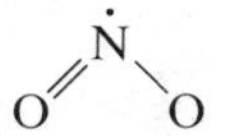

The repulsion between *one* lone electron and bonded electron pairs is not nearly as great as that between a lone pair or a bonded pair and other bonded pairs. Therefore, we would predict that the O—N—O bond angle would be somewhat *greater* than 120° because of the repulsion between the bonded pairs. (Experiment confirms this prediction—the O—N—O bond angle is 134.25°.)

Exercise Use VSEPR to predict the molecular geometry of ClO_2. Briefly explain the observed O—Cl—O bond angle of 117°. *Answer* ClO_2 is a bent molecule (type AB_2E_2); the O—Cl—O angle should be greater than the ideal tetrahedral angle of 109.47° because the central Cl atom has a single unpaired electron.

TOOLS OF CHEMISTRY

Molecular Spectroscopy

Spectroscopy in different regions of the electromagnetic spectrum gives different kinds of information about the structure and geometry of molecules. In this section we take an overview of what can be learned from molecular spectroscopy. (The spectroscopy of atoms was discussed in Section 8.5.)

Radiation at different wavelengths excites molecules in different ways, depending upon the match between the energy of the radiation and the energy of the various types of motion of the molecules and their atoms. The table summarizes the phenomena induced by radiation from different regions of the spectrum.

Over the years spectroscopic techniques have become increasingly sophisticated, allowing the accumulation of more and more knowledge about molecules. One major advance has been the coupling of computers to spectrometers, permitting the direct conversion of spectral data into whatever form is desired. Another major advance has been the advent of lasers as radiation sources in spectroscopy. A *laser* is a device that produces an intense beam of coherent radiation—radiation of a single wavelength with all of the waves in step with each other. The high light intensity and fine tuning available over a wide range of wavelengths have allowed the detection of single isotopes and even single atoms by laser spectroscopy.

Like electrons, nuclei have spin properties and thus, magnetic properties. At the low-energy (long-wavelength) end of the spectrum is a region where the magnetic component of radiation interacts with nuclei. Nuclear magnetic resonance (NMR) spectroscopy measures the absorption of radiofrequency radiation by nuclei and gives information about the location of the nuclei in molecules (see Tools of Chemistry: Nuclear Magnetic Resonance, Chapter 27).

Microwave radiation induces variations in how entire molecules rotate on their axes. Through correlation of microwave spectra with the components of molecular rotation, the bond lengths and bond angles for simple molecules have been determined. However, the major sources of information about bond angles and bond lengths are x-ray diffraction and electron diffraction (Tools of Chemistry, Chapter 13).

Changes in molecular vibrations—the motion of atoms in a molecule with respect to *each other*—are responsible for infrared spectra. Spectroscopy in this region is used to identify groups of atoms in polyatomic molecules or to identify the molecules themselves by comparing the entire spectrum—the "fingerprint" of the molecule—with the spectra of known molecules. (To a more limited extent, spectra in most other regions can also be used for "fingerprinting.") Infrared spectroscopy is especially valuable for the study of the carbon-containing molecules of organic chemistry and is discussed in Chapter 33 (Tools of Chemistry: Infrared and Ultraviolet Spectroscopy).

Ultraviolet and visible spectra result from transitions of valence electrons in molecules to and from higher energy levels. Spectra in this region are simpler and more limited in application than infrared spectra. For organic chemistry, transitions involving electrons are of interest because they show the presence of various groupings containing double and triple bonds. For inorganic chemistry, spectroscopy in this region is used in studying transition metals, for which the interactions of d and f electrons with the radiation can be observed.

In recent years, increasing use has been made of electron spectra in the x-ray region, in what is called ESCA (electron spectroscopy for chemical analysis). The high-energy x-radiation causes ionization by the loss of inner energy level electrons

Spectroscopy and the Electromagnetic Spectrum

Energy (J/mol)	Wavelength (m)	Regions	Phenomena Causing Absorption of Radiation
	10^{-11}	γ radiation	Nuclear transitions*
	10^{-10}	X-radiation	Inner electron transitions
	10^{-9}		
10^7	10^{-8}	Vacuum ultra-violet	Loss of valence electrons
10^6	10^{-7}		
10^5		Ultraviolet	
	10^{-6}	Visible	Valence electron transitions
10^4	10^{-5}	Infrared	Molecular vibrations
10^3	10^{-4}	Far infrared	
10^2	10^{-3}		
10	10^{-2}	Microwave	Molecular rotations, Electron spin
1	10^{-1}		
	1		
	10		
	10^2	Radiofrequency	Nuclear spin, Nuclear quadrupole
	10^3		
	10^4		

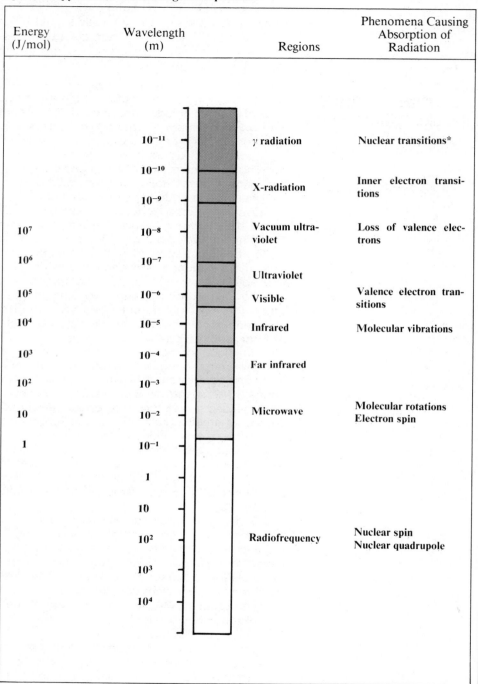

* The transitions of nucleons from one nuclear energy level to another (Section 12.6).

rather than valence electrons. While inner electrons do not participate in bonding, the energy with which they are held varies with their environment. ESCA can show, for example, whether two carbon atoms in the same molecule are in similar or different environments.

VALENCE BOND THEORY

11.4 BOND FORMATION

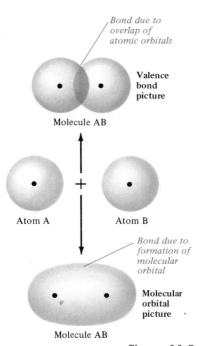

Bond due to overlap of atomic orbitals

Valence bond picture

Molecule AB

Atom A   +   Atom B

Bond due to formation of molecular orbital

Molecular orbital picture

Molecule AB

Figure 11.5
Comparison of Valence Bond and Molecular Orbital Approaches

The VSEPR theory presented in the preceding sections is a simple, practical tool that works well in predicting molecular geometry. However, there are several things that it does *not* do. It does not relate the shapes of molecules to the orbitals and energy levels of atoms. And it gives no picture of when, how, or why bonds form.

Two approaches are used to understand bonding in these terms—the valence bond theory and the molecular orbital theory. In both theories, nuclei are pictured as attracted to an area of high electron density located along the line between the two nuclei—the **bond axis.** At the same time, the bonding electrons are attracted by both nuclei.

So far we have pictured covalent bonding as the result of sharing of electron pairs. **Valence bond theory,** which we discuss in the following sections, describes bond formation as the interaction, or overlap, of atomic orbitals. The concept of shared electron pairs remains important in valence bond theory. The sharing occurs when the atomic orbitals from two atoms overlap so that a region of high electron density is possible between the bonded atoms. Two electrons jointly occupy this region and form the bond.

In molecular orbital theory, which is discussed in Chapter 24, atomic orbitals are pictured as combining to form molecular orbitals—new orbitals that "belong" to the entire molecule or to groups of atoms, rather than to individual atoms. Molecular orbital theory places less emphasis on shared electron pairs and more on the total electron density between bonded atoms. Both valence bond and molecular orbital theories are based on the mathematics of quantum mechanics. Both seek to explain experimental facts, such as the *observed* geometry of molecules, their molecular spectra, or their bond energies, and to correctly predict these properties.

Figure 11.5 presents a comparison of valence bond and molecular orbital theories. In the valence bond picture, the atomic orbitals maintain their identity and overlap to give an area of greater electron density between A and B. In the molecular orbital picture, the overlapping orbitals have combined and rearranged to give a bonding molecular orbital with greater electron density between A and B. (An antibonding orbital, not pictured in the figure, is also formed; see Section 24.3.)

11.5 SINGLE BONDS IN DIATOMIC MOLECULES

To describe when and how bonding will occur according to valence bond theory, we must consider the electron configurations and orbitals of the atoms that are about to combine. The possibility for bond formation exists when two atoms can approach each other in such a way that occupied orbitals which have similar energies and occupy similar regions in space can come into contact, or overlap. The greater the amount of overlap, the stronger the bond can be.

The simplest example of bond formation by atomic orbital overlap is given by the H_2 molecule. The single electron associated with each hydrogen atom occupies a spherical $1s$ orbital (configuration $1s^1$). Overlap of the two $1s$ orbitals allows pairing of the electron spins and formation of a single covalent bond.

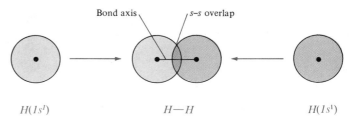

Bond axis   *s–s* overlap

$H(1s^1)$ $H—H$ $H(1s^1)$

All bonds such as this, in which the region of highest electron density surrounds the bond axis, are called **σ bonds** (sigma bonds). Only one sigma bond can form between any two atoms.

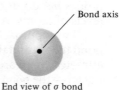

End view of σ bond

An *s* orbital and a *p* orbital each of which contains a single electron can also overlap to yield a σ bond. For example, a hydrogen atom ($1s^1$) can combine with a chlorine atom ($[Ne]3s^2\,3p^2\,3p^2\,3p^1$) to form an HCl molecule by overlap of the $1s$ orbital of the hydrogen atom and the $3p$ orbital of the chlorine atom that holds a single electron.

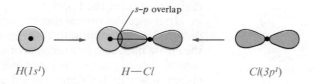

$H(1s^1)$ $H—Cl$ $Cl(3p^1)$

Similarly, two *p* orbitals can overlap to produce a σ bond, *if* the overlapping orbitals lie along the same axis. For example, the chlorine–chlorine bond in the Cl_2 molecule can be described by the overlap of two $3p$ orbitals, each containing one electron. To form a bond, the orbitals must approach end-on.

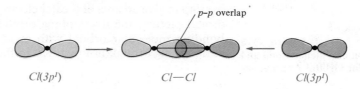

$Cl(3p^1)$ $Cl—Cl$ $Cl(3p^1)$

σ Bond:
s and/or p_x orbitals overlap
along bond axis
highest electron density along
bond axis

In general, overlapping orbitals, in order to form a bond, must have the same symmetry with respect to the bond axis. The three *p* orbitals on a single atom are oriented in space at 90° to each other, Therefore, geometry does not allow bond formation between *s* and *p* orbitals when two atoms approach each other in certain ways. A *p* orbital cannot overlap an *s* or another *p* orbital sufficiently to form a σ bond when they approach as follows:

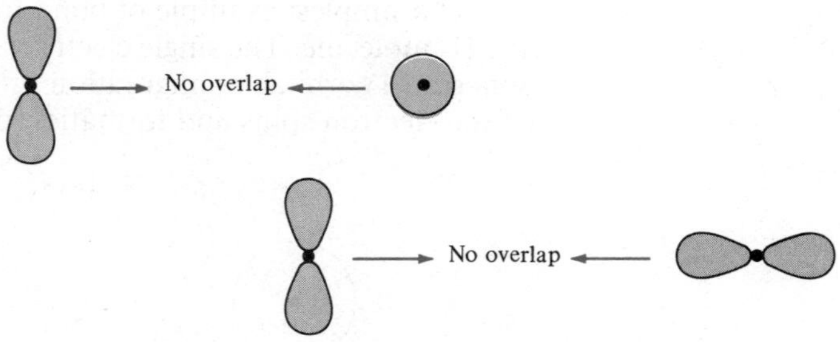

EXAMPLE 11.5
Valence Bond Theory

Describe the bonding in the hydroxide ion, OH^-, in terms of the valence bond theory. The Lewis structure for the hydroxide ion is

$$[:\ddot{O}—H]^-$$

The outer electron configuration of an oxygen atom is $2s^2\,2p^4$, which means that it has two p orbitals each occupied by one electron and one p orbital occupied by two electrons. A σ bond can form between an oxygen atom and a hydrogen atom by overlap of the s orbital from the hydrogen atom with one of the oxygen $2p$ orbitals that holds a single electron. The extra electron that allows oxygen to complete an octet, the electron that accounts for the -1 charge, can occupy the other p orbital that originally held one electron.

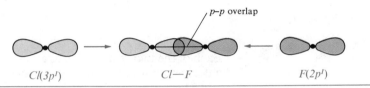

s–p overlap

$H(1s^1)$ $\qquad$ $H\!-\!O$ $\qquad$ $O(2p^1)$

Exercise Describe the bonding in ClF using the valence bond theory. *Answer* Overlap of a $3p$ electron from the Cl atom with a $2p$ electron from the F atom gives a σ bond.

p–p overlap

$Cl(3p^1)$ $\qquad$ $Cl\!-\!F$ $\qquad$ $F(2p^1)$

11.6 SINGLE BONDS IN
POLYATOMIC MOLECULES;
HYBRIDIZATION

Overlap of s and p orbitals as we have pictured it thus far cannot explain the bond lengths and bond angles in most molecules with more than two atoms. For example, consider the O—H and N—H bonds in H_2O and NH_3. If each bond resulted from overlap of the hydrogen $1s^1$ orbital with either a p orbital of an oxygen atom ($1s^2\,2s^2\,2p^4$) or a p orbital of a nitrogen atom ($1s^2\,2s^2\,2p^3$), the HOH or HNH bond angles should be about the same as the angles between the p orbitals, which are all $90°$. But in both compounds the angles are closer to the tetrahedral angle, as we have seen in our discussion of VSEPR theory (see Figure 11.2).

Furthermore, there are difficulties in explaining the observed geometry of a molecule that contains bonds derived from the overlap of different types of orbitals. In methane, CH_4, two s electrons and two p electrons from a carbon atom ($1s^2\,2s^2\,2p^2$) must each form a bond with a $1s$ electron from H. Differences in bond length and bond angle might be expected between C—H bonds from s–p overlap and those from s–s overlap. However, as far as we can tell from experimental measurements, the four C—H bonds in CH_4 are identical in length and form equal tetrahedral angles with each other.

The concept of hybridization was introduced to allow an explanation of molecular geometry in terms of atomic orbitals and valence bond theory. **Hybridization** is the mixing of the atomic orbitals on a single atom to give a new set of orbitals, called *hybrid orbitals,* on that atom.

Hybridization applies only to the orbitals of a single, covalently bonded atom in a molecule. In terms of quantum theory, hybridization represents a combination of the mathematical functions that describe the atomic orbitals involved in bonding. The result is a new description of the probable electron density about the atom. In terms of energy, hybridization represents the blending of higher energy and lower energy orbitals to form orbitals of intermediate energy. The hybrid orbitals are still atomic orbitals and remain oriented around a single nucleus.

Hybridization provides a connection between observed molecular geometry and

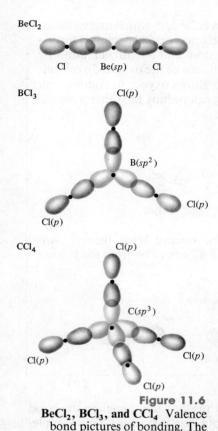

BeCl$_2$

Cl   Be(sp)   Cl

BCl$_3$ Cl(p)

B(sp^2)

Cl(p)

Cl(p)

CCl$_4$ Cl(p)

C(sp^3)

Cl(p)   Cl(p)

Cl(p)

Figure 11.6
BeCl$_2$, BCl$_3$, and CCl$_4$ Valence
bond pictures of bonding. The
hybrid orbitals are shown in color.

the electron configurations of the combining atoms. Consider, for example, the BeCl$_2$ molecule, which is known to be linear in the gas phase. A beryllium atom has two 2s electrons which are, of course, paired. How can *two* equivalent covalent bonds be formed by an atom that has only paired electrons? The 2s^2 valence electrons must in some way become unpaired. Hybridization pictures this as happening by combination of the s and p orbitals to give two equivalent hybrid orbitals, each containing one electron. These are known as sp hybrid orbitals, or simply sp orbitals. (The inner electrons, which are not involved in the hybridization, are not included in the following diagram.)

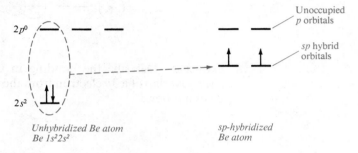

$2p^0$ ———— ———— ———— Unoccupied p orbitals

sp hybrid orbitals

$2s^2$ ⇅

Unhybridized Be atom *sp-hybridized*
Be 1s²2s² *Be atom*

Each of the two sp hybrid orbitals can be pictured as overlapping with a p orbital of a chlorine atom to give the two covalent bonds of BeCl$_2$ (Figure 11.6).

The number of hybrid orbitals formed always equals the number of atomic orbitals that have combined. Each sp hybrid orbital is asymmetrical, with a large lobe on one side of the nucleus and a smaller lobe on the other (Figure 11.7). For simplification, the smaller lobe is often omitted in drawings of sp hybrid orbitals. sp Hybrid orbitals form somewhat stronger bonds than p orbitals because they allow greater overlap.

Boron, with the 2s^2 2p^1 configuration, forms three equivalent bonds to chlorine in BCl$_3$. As predicted by VSEPR and as shown by experiment, this is a triangular planar molecule. In order to give three equivalent orbitals, hybridization in this case

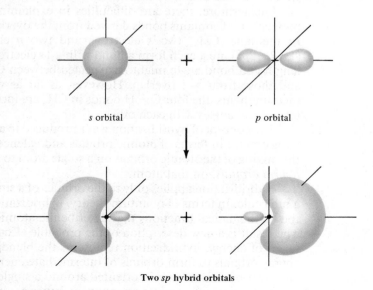

s orbital p orbital

Figure 11.7
Hybridization to Give sp Orbitals
The sp orbitals, shown separately for
clarity, are all from the same atom.

Two sp hybrid orbitals

involves one *s* orbital and two *p* orbitals and is termed sp^2 hybridization.

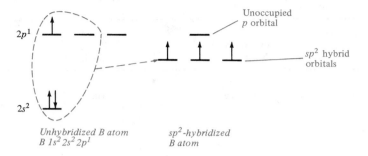

The three sp^2 orbitals of the boron atom can be pictured as overlapping with orbitals from chlorine atoms to form BCl_3 (see Figure 11.6).

A carbon atom, which has the $2s^2 2p^2$ configuration, forms four equivalent covalent bonds in CCl_4 (see Figure 11.6). This is accomplished by sp^3 hybridization, the combination of one *s* and three *p* orbitals.

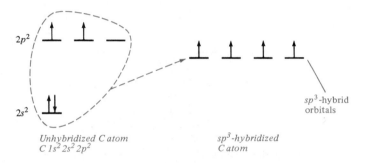

As is discussed in connection with multiple bonds in the next section, carbon atoms in various bonding situations can be *sp, sp^2,* or sp^3 hybridized.

Linear, triangular planar, and tetrahedral geometries (see Figure 11.6) are all accounted for by hybridization of *s* and *p* orbitals. Where lone-pair electrons are present on atoms with hybridized orbitals, they occupy one or more of the hybrid orbitals. For example, the carbon, nitrogen, and oxygen atoms in the methane, ammonia, and water molecules (see Figure 11.2) are all pictured in valence bond theory as having formed sp^3-hybridized orbitals. In ammonia, one sp^3 hybrid orbital is occupied by a lone pair, and in water two hybrid orbitals are occupied by lone pairs.

In this discussion of hybridization we have focused on the central atom as in VSEPR. The question arises as to whether or not the orbitals on other atoms in a molecule, for example, the chlorine atoms in $BeCl_2$, BCl_3, or CCl_4, should be hybridized. In Figure 11.6 we have shown the bonds as formed by overlap of hybrid orbitals with the unhybridized *p* orbitals on chlorine. These bonds could equally well be pictured as formed between hybrid orbitals on the central atom and hybrid orbitals on the chlorine atoms. There are some valid arguments for doing so, because the overlap and hence the bond strengths would be greater. The mathematical techniques upon which hybridization is based allow either complete or partial hybridization, so that the percentage of hybridization can be adjusted to match the observed bond strengths. Because our concern here is mainly with providing some insight into how observed molecular geometries are explained by bonding theories, we have, in most cases, considered only hybridization of the central atoms.

Table 11.3
Hybridized Orbitals These orbitals form σ bonds by overlap with other hybrid orbitals and with s and p orbitals.

Type	Constituent Orbitals	Ideal Bond Angle	Hybrid Orbitals	Geometry
sp	One s + one p orbital	180°		Linear
sp^2	One s + two p orbitals	120°		Triangular planar
sp^3	One s + three p orbitals	109.47°		Tetrahedral
sp^3d, dsp^3	One s + three p + one d orbital	180°, 120°, 90°*		Triangular bipyramidal
sp^3d^2, d^2sp^3	One s + three p + two d orbitals	90°		Octahedral

* See AB$_5$ in Table 11.1.

The s and p orbitals of any atom give a maximum of four hybrid orbitals. Atoms of second-period elements, which have *only* s and p orbitals, can form no more than four hybrid orbitals and no more than four covalent bonds. Beyond the second period, atoms can form a larger number of covalent bonds by involving d orbitals in hybridization. In Example 11.2, we found that PF$_5$ is a triangular bipyramidal molecule. This geometry for PF$_5$ is explained by sp^3d hybridization. A phosphorus atom has five valence electrons in four orbitals ($3s^2\,3p^3$). Hybridization that includes one vacant $3d$ orbital allows formation of five equivalent sp^3d hybrid orbitals.

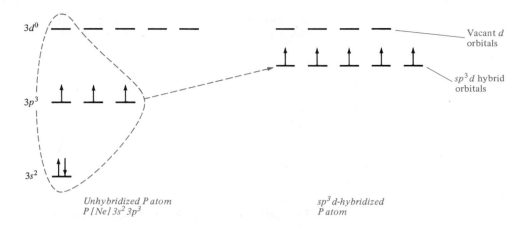

$3d^0$ — Vacant d orbitals

sp^3d hybrid orbitals

$3p^3$

$3s^2$

Unhybridized P atom
P [Ne] $3s^2 3p^3$

sp^3 d-hybridized P atom

The octahedral geometry of molecules with six covalent bonds is accounted for by sp^3d^2 hybridization. In some of the transition metals the d orbitals involved in hybridization come from the next-to-outermost energy level, rather than the outermost level, to give dsp^3 or $d^2 sp^3$ hybridization.

In summary, in sp *hybridization one* s *and one* p *orbital combine to give two* sp *hybrid orbitals that lie at 180° to each other. In* sp^2 *hybridization one* s *and two* p *orbitals combine to give three* sp^2 *hybrid orbitals that lie in a plane with 120° angles between them. In* sp^3 *hybridization one* s *and three* p *orbitals combine to give four* sp^3 *hybrid orbitals arranged in a tetrahedron. Including* d *orbitals from the outer energy level in hybridization gives* sp^{3}d *and* sp^{3}d^2 *hybridization, which account for triangular bipyramidal and octahedral geometry.*

To explain bonding by using hybrid orbitals, first decide how many σ bonds and lone pairs surround each atom. This indicates how many hybrid orbitals are needed and the type of hybridization. For example, an atom with two σ bonds and two lone pairs needs four hybrid orbitals and must be sp^3-hybridized. Table 11.3 summarizes the formation and geometry of hybrid orbitals. Comparison with Table 11.1 shows the equivalence of VSEPR and hybridization in describing molecular geometry.

EXAMPLE 11.6
Valence Bond Theory

Describe the bonding in BrF_3 in terms of the valence bond theory.

$$:\ddot{F}—\ddot{Br}—\ddot{F}:$$
$$:\ddot{F}:$$

The Lewis structure shows that BrF_3 is an AB_3E_2 type molecule and the bromine atom is surrounded by three σ bonds and two lone pairs. To explain bonding in this molecule, five equivalent hybridized orbitals on the bromine atom are necessary. The outer electron configuration for the bromine atom is $4s^2 4p^5$. By using the $4s$ orbital, the three $4p$ orbitals, and one of the empty $4d$ orbitals in sp^3d hybridization, five hybrid orbitals can be formed. Two of these hybrid orbitals contain lone pairs of electrons and three of the hybrid orbitals contain single electrons which will form the σ bonds with the fluorine atoms.

The five hybridized orbitals will be arranged in the shape of a triangular bipyramid (see Table 11.3). With lone pairs in two of the hybrid orbitals, the T shape predicted by VSEPR for BrF_3 is explained in terms of orbitals.

Exercise Describe the bonding in H_2O in terms of the valence bond theory. *Answer* There are four equivalent hybrid orbitals on the oxygen atom, formed by sp^3 hybridization; two contain lone pairs of electrons and two contain a single electron each, which will form the σ bonds with the hydrogen atoms.

EXAMPLE 11.7
Valence Bond Theory

Describe the bonding in ethane, C_2H_6, in terms of the valence bond theory.

$$H-\underset{\underset{H}{|}}{\overset{\overset{H}{|}}{C}}-\underset{\underset{H}{|}}{\overset{\overset{H}{|}}{C}}-H$$

We can see from the Lewis structure that each carbon atom must have four equivalent hybridized orbitals. These are formed by sp^3 hybridization. Three of the hybridized orbitals on each carbon atom contain a single electron which will form a σ bond with a hydrogen atom and one of the hybridized orbitals contains a single electron which will form a σ bond with the other carbon atom.

Exercise Describe the bonding in hydrogen peroxide, H_2O_2, in terms of the valence bond theory. *Answer* Each oxygen atom has four equivalent hybrid orbitals formed by sp^3 hybridization; two contain lone pairs of electrons, one contains a single electron which will form a σ bond with a hydrogen atom, and one contains a single electron which will form a σ bond with the other oxygen atom.

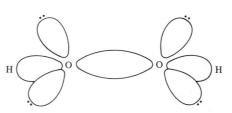

11.7 MULTIPLE COVALENT BONDS

a. π Bonds So far, we have dealt only with single covalent bonds, which are σ bonds and are symmetrical about the bond axis. Only one σ bond can form between any two atoms. Multiple covalent bonds arise when p or d orbitals on atoms that are σ-bonded to each other also overlap.

When p orbitals approach parallel to each other, both lobes can overlap.

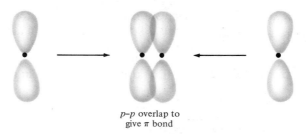

p–p overlap to give π bond

A bond formed in this way is called a π bond (pi bond). π **Bonds** concentrate electron density above and below the bond axis and always have a plane of zero electron density passing through the bond axis.

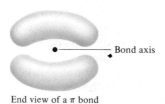

Bond axis

End view of a π bond

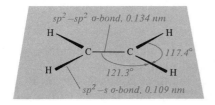

(a) Ethylene σ-bonded skeleton

sp^2–sp^2 σ-bond, 0.134 nm
117.4°
121.3°
sp^2–s σ-bond, 0.109 nm

p_z orbitals overlap to give π-bond

(b) Ethylene π bonds

Figure 11.8
Ethylene Molecule (a) Ethylene σ-bonded skeleton; (b) ethylene π bonds.

π-Bond formation can also result from the interaction of p and d orbitals, as well as d and d orbitals.

Multiple covalent bonds are the result of σ- and π-bond formation between the same two atoms. One σ bond plus one π bond form a double covalent bond, and one σ bond plus two π bonds form a triple covalent bond. The σ bonds are stronger and provide most of the force holding the atoms together. The overall geometry of the molecule is also determined by the σ bonds, for the π bonds simply lie above and below the geometrical framework of the σ-bonded atoms. This explains why double bonds can be treated like single bonds in using VSEPR theory.

Carbon–carbon multiple covalent bonds are explained by the hybridization of carbon atoms to form either sp or sp^2 hybrid orbitals. In ethylene, $CH_2{=}CH_2$, and in other molecules that contain carbon–carbon double bonds, each of the two carbon atoms in the double bonds is sp^2-hybridized and is able to form three σ bonds. This provides a planar skeleton of σ bonds for the molecule, with each carbon atom at the center of three σ bonds arranged in a planar triangle (Figure 11.8a). One electron occupies each of the three sp^2 orbitals on each carbon atom, leaving one

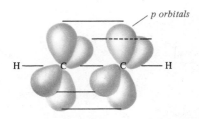

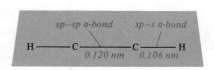

Figure 11.9
Acetylene Molecule (a) Acetylene
σ-bonded skeleton; (b) *p* orbitals,
approaching to form π orbitals.

(a) Acetylene σ-bonded skeleton

(b) *p* orbitals, approaching to form π orbitals

electron on each carbon atom in an unhybridized *p* orbital, which we picture as the p_z orbital. With the carbon–hydrogen skeleton in the x–y plane, the two valence electrons in the p_z orbitals can be shared by parallel overlap, creating a π bond (Figure 11.8b).

Acetylene, HC≡CH, like ethylene, has a linear carbon skeleton. In this case, each of the carbon atoms is *sp*-hybridized and can form two σ bonds. Each forms a σ bond with the other carbon atom and with one hydrogen atom (Figure 11.9). Sidewise overlap of the p_z and p_y orbitals leads to sharing of the remaining two electrons from each carbon atom to form a pair of π bonds. All carbon–carbon triple bonds, like the triple bond in acetylene, are combinations of one σ bond and two π bonds.

In determining the type of hybridization required for an atom that forms a multiple bond, remember that there is only one σ bond in a multiple covalent bond.

Double bond:
1 σ bond + 1 π bond
Triple bond:
1σ bond + 2 π bonds

EXAMPLE 11.8
Valence Bond Theory

Describe the bonding in formaldehyde, H_2CO, using the valence bond theory.

$$\overset{\displaystyle :\!\ddot{O}\!:}{\underset{\displaystyle H-C-H}{\|}}$$

The Lewis structure for the formaldehyde molecule shows that around the carbon atom there are two carbon–hydrogen single bonds and a carbon–oxygen double bond. The carbon atom is sp^2-hybridized to produce the three equivalent hybrid orbitals needed for the formation of the three σ bonds. The $2p_z$ orbital on the carbon atom is unhybridized and contains a single electron which forms the π bond by the parallel overlap with the unhybridized $2p_z$ orbital on the oxygen atom.

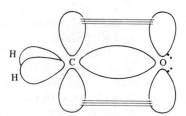

Exercise Describe the bonding in nitroxyl hydride, HNO, using the valence bond theory.

$$H-\ddot{N}=\ddot{O}:$$

Answer The nitrogen atom is sp^2-hybridized; the three hybridized orbitals are used for the N—H σ bond, the lone pair of electrons, and the N—O σ bond; the unhybridized $2p_z$ orbital is used to form the π bond by the parallel overlap of the unhybridized $2p_z$ orbital of the oxygen atom.

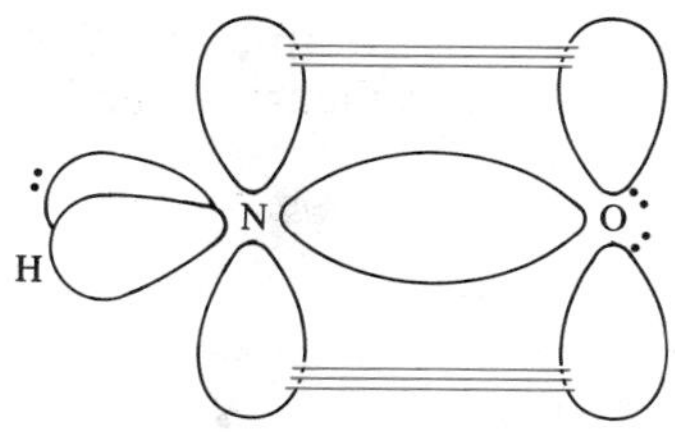

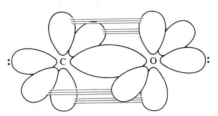

EXAMPLE 11.9
Valence Bond Theory

Describe the bonding in carbon monoxide using the valence bond theory. Assume that both the carbon atom and the oxygen atom are hybridized.

$$:C{\equiv}O:$$

If each atom is *sp*-hybridized, each will have two equivalent *sp* orbitals, one for the lone pair of electrons and one for the σ bond with the other atom. There will be two unhybridized *p* orbitals on each atom that can overlap with the two unhybridized *p* orbitals of the other atom, producing two π bonds.

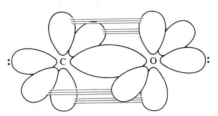

Exercise Using the valence bond theory, describe the bonding in hydrogen cyanide, HCN.

$$H{-}C{\equiv}N:$$

Answer The carbon atom is *sp*-hybridized; the two hybridized orbitals are used for the σ bonds between C and H, and C and N; the two unhybridized *p* orbitals form two π bonds with the two unhybridized *p* orbitals on the nitrogen atom.

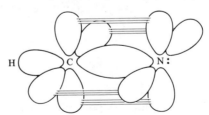

---

b. *Cis–trans* isomerism For the π bonds in a multiple covalent bond to remain intact, the orientation of the atoms must not change—the *p* orbitals have to be parallel to each other. Turning the atoms would break the π bond. Therefore, (1) the atoms attached to the multiply bonded atoms must lie in the same plane, and (2) the atoms in multiple bonds are not free to rotate about the bond axis. Because rotation about a double bond is restricted, the way in which other atoms or groups are attached to the double-bonded atoms makes a difference in the structure of the molecule.

Compounds that differ in molecular structure but have the same molecular formula are called **isomers**. Consider ethane

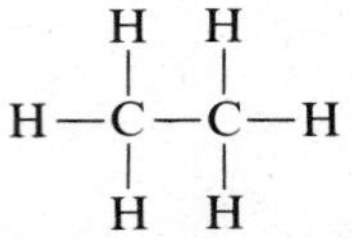

$$H-\underset{\underset{H}{|}}{\overset{\overset{H}{|}}{C}}-\underset{\underset{H}{|}}{\overset{\overset{H}{|}}{C}}-H$$

Two chlorine atoms can replace hydrogen atoms in ethane in two different ways.

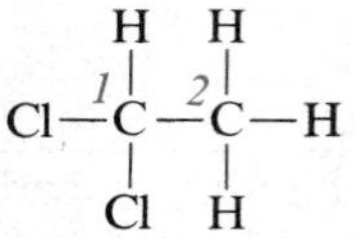

1,1-dichloroethane
m.p. − 97.0 °C, b.p. 57.3 °C

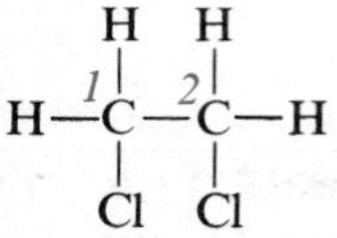

1,2-dichloroethane
m.p. − 35.4 °C, b.p. 83.5 °C

These two dichloroethanes are **structural isomers**—they have the same molecular formula, but differ in how the atoms are bonded to each other.

Introduction of a double bond into ethane to give ethylene introduces the possibility of another kind of isomerism. The placement of atoms or groups on the same or different sides of a double bond produces isomers.

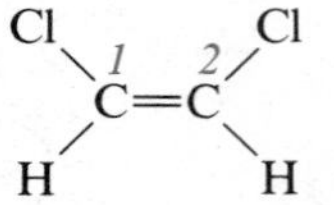

cis-dichloroethylene
m.p. − 80.5 °C, b.p. 60.3 °C

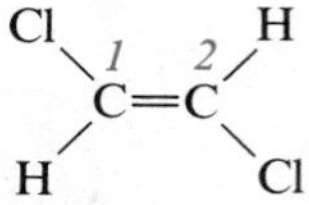

trans-dichloroethylene
m.p. − 50 °C, b.p. 47.5 °C

If rotation about the double bond were easy, these two compounds would be identical. In **cis–trans** **isomerism**, or **geometric isomerism**, atoms or groups are arranged in different ways on either side of a double bond or some other rigid bond, such as that in a cyclic compound. In **cis** **isomers** the groups under consideration are on the same side of a double bond or other rigid structure. In **trans** **isomers** the groups under consideration are on opposite sides. Note that in *cis–trans* isomerism involving double bonds, each doubly bonded carbon atom must have two *different* groups attached to it.

As you may have noticed, there is a third isomer of dichloroethylene.

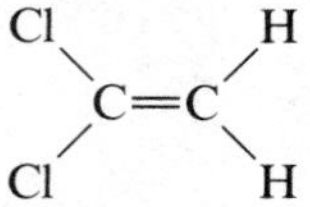

1,1-dichloroethylene

This compound is a *structural* isomer of the *cis* and *trans* compounds.

EXAMPLE 11.10
Isomerism

How many structural isomers are there for C_2Br_2HCl? How many *cis–trans* isomers are there for this compound?

The structural isomers have the bromine atoms either at the same end of the molecule or at opposite ends.

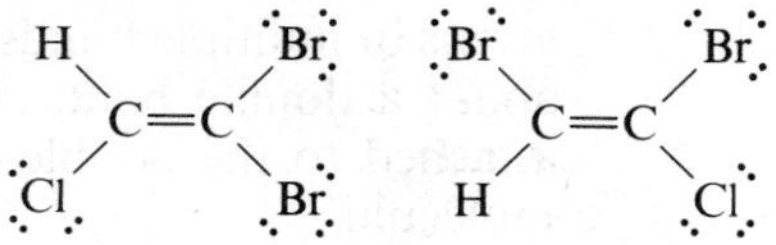

There are no *cis–trans* isomers of the first structural isomer. However, for the second we can write a structure in which the bromine atoms are *trans* instead of *cis* as shown above.

$$
\begin{array}{ccc}
\text{H} & & \text{Br} \\
 & \diagdown \quad / & \\
 & \text{C}{=}\text{C} & \\
 & / \quad \diagdown & \\
\text{Br} & & \text{Cl}
\end{array}
$$

There are two structural isomers of this compound and one structural isomer has *cis* and *trans* isomers.

Exercise Draw the *cis* and *trans* isomers of diimide, HNNH. *Answer*

$$
\begin{array}{cc}
\text{H} \quad\quad \text{H} & \text{H} \\
\diagdown \quad\quad \diagdown & \quad \diagdown \\
\text{N}{=}\text{N} \quad\quad \ddot{\text{N}}{=}\ddot{\text{N}} \\
& \diagup \\
& \text{H}
\end{array}
$$

c. Delocalization of electrons The valence bond picture of bonds formed by the overlap of orbitals on adjacent atoms must be modified to account for the bonding in molecules that exhibit resonance (Section 9.14). Consider the resonance forms of the nitrate ion and the single resonance hybrid that can be drawn

$$
\left[\begin{array}{c} :\text{O}: \\ \| \\ \text{N} \\ \diagup \diagdown \\ :\ddot{\text{O}}. \quad .\ddot{\text{O}}: \end{array} \right]^{-}
\longleftrightarrow
\left[\begin{array}{c} :\ddot{\text{O}}: \\ | \\ \text{N} \\ \diagup \diagdown \\ :\ddot{\text{O}}. \quad .\ddot{\text{O}}: \end{array} \right]^{-}
\longleftrightarrow
\left[\begin{array}{c} :\ddot{\text{O}}: \\ | \\ \text{N} \\ \diagup \diagdown \\ :\ddot{\text{O}}. \quad .\ddot{\text{O}}: \end{array} \right]^{-}
\quad \text{or} \quad
\left[\begin{array}{c} \text{O} \\ \| \\ \text{N} \\ \diagup \diagdown \\ \text{O} \quad\quad \text{O} \end{array} \right]^{-}
$$

It is known from experiment that the three nitrogen–oxygen bonds are equivalent (e.g., the bond lengths are the same). A simple valence bond description of this ion would give resonance forms in which the nitrogen atom is sp^2-hybridized and forms three σ bonds, leaving the electrons in unhybridized p orbitals to form π bonds as follows:

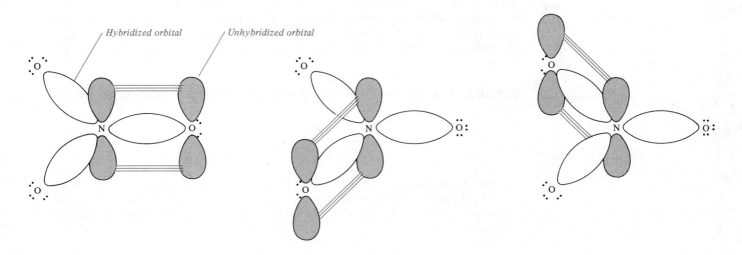

Hybridized orbital *Unhybridized orbital*

Here again, three structures are required.

To achieve a single structure for the nitrate ion, or any other such ion or molecule, we use the concept of **delocalized electrons**—electrons that occupy a space spread over three or more atoms. Merging the electrons in the π bonds shown above gives a picture of the delocalization of electrons in the nitrate ion.

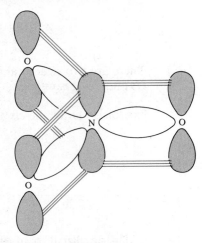

The delocalized electrons occupy a larger region of space than they do in localized bonds and their repulsion for each other is decreased. For this reason, molecules with delocalized electrons gain in stability.

Mathematically, in aspects of bonding theory that we need not pursue, delocalized electrons are a more natural consequence of molecular orbital theory (Chapter 24) than of valence bond theory. The important point is that the properties of equivalent bonds in molecules for which several resonance structures can be written are accounted for by the spreading of electron density over three or more atoms.

EXAMPLE 11.11
Delocalized Electrons

Use the concept of delocalization of electrons to describe the bonding in sulfur dioxide, SO_2.

$$:\ddot{O}-\ddot{S}=\ddot{O} \longleftrightarrow \ddot{O}=\ddot{S}-\ddot{O}:$$

The sulfur atom is sp^2-hybridized. The three sp^2 orbitals are used to form σ bonds between the sulfur atom and each of the oxygen atoms and for the lone pair of electrons on sulfur. The unhybridized p orbital on the sulfur atom overlaps with the unhybridized p orbitals on both of the oxygen atoms, giving delocalized bonding of the π electrons. Thus both S—O bonds are identical, as can be seen in the margin figure.

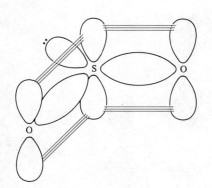

Exercise Use the concept of delocalization to describe the bonding in benzene, C_6H_6.

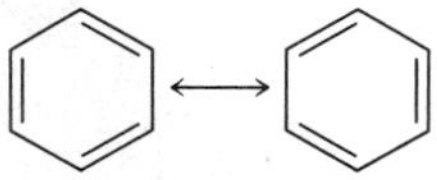

Answer Each carbon atom is sp^2-hybridized; one hybrid orbital is used for the C—H σ bond; two hybrid orbitals are used for the C—C σ bonds; the parallel unhybridized p orbitals allow delocalization of the π bonding over the entire carbon ring (Figure 24.12c).

In summary, in valence bond theory bonds are pictured as being formed by the overlap of atomic orbitals and emphasis is on the sharing of electron pairs between atoms. For bond formation to occur, two orbitals must have similar energies and the same symmetry with respect to the bond axis, so that they can overlap enough to allow interaction to occur. The combination of orbitals by hybridization is used to account for observed molecular geometry and properties. Second-period elements can form up to four covalent bonds by hybridization of s and p orbitals. Elements of the third period and beyond have d orbitals available for hybridization and can form five and six equivalent orbitals by sp³d and sp³d² hybridization.

σ Bonds give areas of high electron density that surround the bond axis. π Bonds, which are weaker than σ bonds, give areas of high electron density on opposite sides of the bond axis, but have no electron density along the bond axis. Double and triple covalent bonds include one σ bond and one and two π bonds, respectively. The concept of bonding by delocalized electrons is applied to molecules for which resonance forms can be written.

INTERMOLECULAR FORCES

Intermolecular forces act between molecules. They are much weaker than the forces of metallic, ionic, or covalent bonding. The strength of the intermolecular forces at a particular temperature determines whether a molecular substance is a gas, a liquid, or a solid at that temperature. Polarity, molecular mass, and molecular geometry all influence these forces.

There are three principal types of intermolecular forces: dipole–dipole forces, hydrogen bonding, and London forces. Collectively, these are called **van der Waals forces.** The stronger the van der Waals forces, the higher the boiling points and heats of vaporization and fusion (Section 7.11).

In the next two sections we discuss the van der Waals radii and the dipole moment, a molecular property that influences intermolecular forces. Then, the three types of intermolecular forces are discussed individually.

**van der Waals forces:
dipole–dipole forces
London forces
hydrogen bonds**

11.8 VAN DER WAALS RADII

The intermolecular distance between molecules in contact in a solid is determined by a balance between the van der Waals forces of attraction and the forces of repulsion that act between like charges. The intermolecular distances in solids are used to assign a set of van der Waals radii for atoms (Figure 11.10). For example, in solid bromine, the average distance between a bromine atom in one molecule and that in an adjacent molecule is 0.370 nm. Half of this value, 0.185 nm, is the value assigned as the van der Waals radius of a covalently bonded bromine atom. Values for some of the **van der Waals radii**—the radii of atoms not bonded to each other,

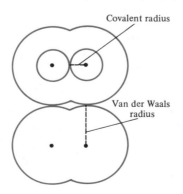

Covalent radius

Van der Waals
radius

**Figure 11.10
Relationship between Covalent
Radius and van der Waals Radius**

Table 11.4
Some van der Waals Radii
(in nanometers)

H 0.120				He 0.140
	C 0.170	N 0.155	O 0.152	F 0.147	Ne 0.154
	Si 0.210	P 0.180	S 0.180	Cl 0.175	Ar 0.188
		As 0.185	Se 0.190	Br 0.185	Kr 0.202
		Sb 0.22	Te 0.206	I 0.198	Xe 0.216

Source: A. Bondi, *J. Phys. Chem.* **68**, 441 (1964).

but in contact at the most stable distance from each other — are given in Table 11.4. These values are only averages and are not reliable to more than about 0.005 nm. Note that van der Waals radii are much larger than typical values of atomic radii (see Figure 10.2).

11.9 DIPOLE MOMENT

Covalent bonds between atoms of differing electronegativity are dipoles — they have a partial negative charge at one end and a partial positive charge at the other (Section 9.15). Whether or not a *molecule* is a dipole depends not only upon bond polarity, but also upon molecular geometry and the presence of lone-pair electrons.

The degree of polarity of a molecule is measured by its **dipole moment,** μ (Greek mu, pronounced "mew"). The common unit for dipole moments is the debye, D (pronounced "de-buy"). For a diatomic molecule in the gaseous state, the dipole moment (Figure 11.11) is a direct indication of the polarity of the bond. The decrease in bond polarity with decreasing electronegativity of the halogen atom is shown by the dipole moments of the hydrogen halides.

	$\delta+$ $\delta-$ H — F	$\delta+$ $\delta-$ H — Cl	$\delta+$ $\delta-$ H — Br	$\delta+$ $\delta-$ H — I
Dipole moment:	*1.9 D*	*1.04 D*	*0.79 D*	*0.38 D*
Electronegativity of halogen	*4.0*	*3.0*	*2.8*	*2.5*

The effect of molecular geometry on dipole moment is illustrated in Figure 11.12. The colored arrows show individual bonds that are polar. In the angular water molecule, negative charge is concentrated on the oxygen atom due to the lone-pair electrons and the bond polarity. The balancing positive charge is effectively centered between the two hydrogen atoms, leading to a large dipole moment for the water

Figure 11.11
Polar Molecules in an Electric Field The alignment of polar molecules in an electric field in the gas phase allows the dipole moment of the molecules to be measured.

No electric field

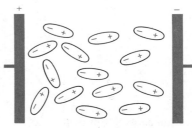

Electric field

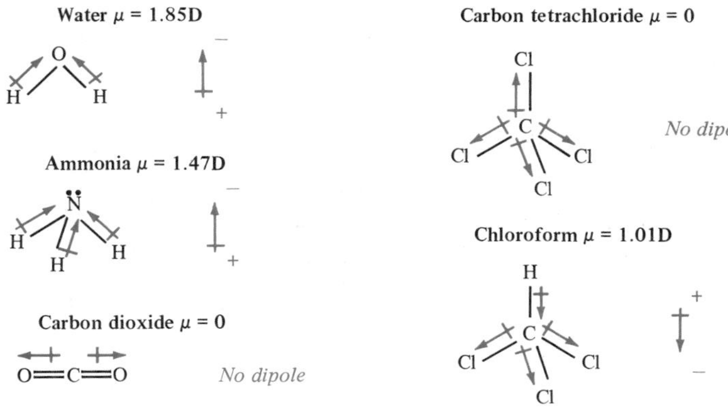

Figure 11.12
Dipole Moments of Some Gaseous Polyatomic Molcules The direction of the dipole for each bond and each molecule is shown by the arrow. In CO_2 and CCl_4 the individual bonds are polar. In both cases, however, the atoms with the partial negative charges (O and Cl) symmetrically surround the central carbon atom. Consequently the *center* of the negative charge coincides with the carbon atom, where the positive charge is also localized. With no net separation of charge, these molecules have no dipole moments.

Water $\mu = 1.85D$

Ammonia $\mu = 1.47D$

Carbon dioxide $\mu = 0$

$O = C = O$ *No dipole*

Carbon tetrachloride $\mu = 0$

No dipole

Chloroform $\mu = 1.01D$

molecule. The ammonia molecule, which has triangular pyramidal geometry, also has a large dipole moment.

In molecules with certain geometries, the internal compensation of partial charges can lead to an overall absence of polarity ($\mu = 0$) even though the individual bonds are themselves polar. For example, in the linear arrangement of atoms in carbon dioxide, one strongly polar carbon–oxygen double bond cancels the other (see Figure 11.12).

The symmetrical regular tetrahedral geometry of carbon tetrachloride (CCl_4) provides the same internal compensation (see Figure 11.12). However, in chloroform ($CHCl_3$), the hydrogen atom is both less electronegative than the carbon atom and markedly different in electronegativity, size, and electronic atmosphere from the chlorine atoms. Thus, a partial negative charge is concentrated among the chlorine atoms, and the molecule has a dipole moment.

EXAMPLE 11.12
Intermolecular Forces

Identify which of the following molecules would be polar: (a) SO_2, (b) BCl_3, (c) ClF_3, and (d) *trans*-$C_2H_2Cl_2$.

The structures of the molecules are shown below:

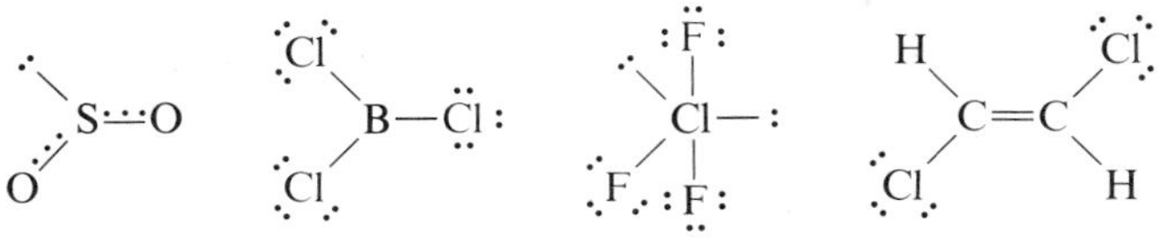

The geometries of BCl_3 and *trans*-$C_2H_2Cl_2$ are such that even though the bonding within the molecules is polar covalent, the overall effect of this bonding is cancelled and the molecules are not polar. The geometries of SO_2 and ClF_3 are such that the overall effect of the polar covalent bonding within the molecules is not cancelled. The polar molecules are (a) SO_2 and (c) ClF_3.

Exercise Identify which of the following molecules would be polar: (a) SO_3, (b) BCl_2F, (c) XeF_2, and (d) *cis*-$C_2H_2Cl_2$. *Answer* (b), (d)

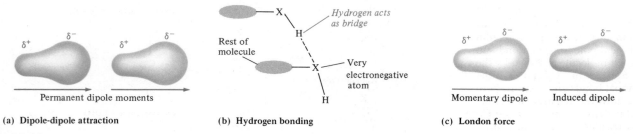

Figure 11.13
Intermolecular Forces

11.10 DIPOLE–DIPOLE FORCES   In **dipole–dipole interaction,** molecules with dipole moments attract each other electrostatically; the positive end of one molecule attracts the negative end of another molecule, and so on, leading to an alignment of the molecules (Figure 11.13a). The dipole–dipole attraction, along with other forces, must be overcome in melting a solid and it thereby influences the melting point and heat of fusion of the compound. Dipole–dipole forces persist in the liquid state, in this case influencing the boiling point and heat of vaporization. At ordinary temperatures and pressures in the gaseous state molecules are far apart, and dipole–dipole forces are not very effective. As temperature drops and/or pressure increases, molecules come closer together and the dipole attraction can pull them together into a liquid or a solid.

Comparison of the properties of compounds of similar molecular mass illustrates the effect of dipole–dipole forces. Look at the properties of SiH_4, PH_3, and H_2S in Table 11.5. Among these compounds of similar molecular mass, SiH_4 is nonpolar and has the lowest melting and boiling points, and the lowest heats of fusion and vaporization. Hydrogen sulfide, H_2S, has a dipole moment twice that of PH_3 and, as expected, has the highest melting and boiling points, and the highest heats of fusion and vaporization of the three compounds.

Table 11.5
Properties of Some Nonmetal Hydrides The data for the second-period elements are given in black, those for the third-period elements in color.

Property	Methane CH_4 (nonpolar)	Silane SiH_4 (nonpolar)	Ammonia NH_3 (polar, H bonded)	Phosphine PH_3 (polar)	Water H_2O (polar, H bonded)	Hydrogen sulfide H_2S (polar)	Hydrogen fluoride HF (polar, H bonded)	Hydrogen chloride HCl (polar)
Appearance	Colorless gas	Colorless gas	Colorless gas	Colorless gas	Colorless liquid	Colorless gas	Colorless fuming gas, or liquid	Colorless gas
Molecular mass (u)	16.04	32.09	17.03	34.00	18.02	34.08	20.01	36.46
Melting point (°C)	−182	−185	−78	−134	0.00	−85.6	−83.0	−114
Boiling point (°C)	−161	−111	−33	−87.8	100.	−60.8	19.5	−84.9
Density of liquid (g/mL)	0.42 (−164 °C)	0.68 (−185 °C)	0.68 (−33.4 °C)	0.75 (−87.78 °C)	0.96 (100 °C)	0.95 (−61.3 °C)	0.99 (19.5 °C)	1.19 (−84.9 °C)
Heat of fusion at m.p. (kJ/mol)	0.941	0.665	5.52	1.13	6.02	2.38	4.56	1.99
Heat of vaporization at b.p. (kJ/mol)	8.20	13	23.3	14.6	40.7	18.7	25.6	16.1
Dipole moment (D)	0	0	1.47	0.55	1.85	1.10	1.9	1.04

11.11 LONDON FORCES

London forces act on *all* atoms and molecules, polar or nonpolar. The London forces are responsible for the condensation, at low enough temperatures, of even the monatomic noble gases, which come closer to ideal behavior than any other gases. (London forces are among the forces represented by the constant *a* in the van der Waals equation for nonideal gases, Section 5.14. Sometimes the phrase "van der Waals attraction" is used incorrectly for the London forces alone. *All* of the forces that help to liquefy gases, taken together, are called van der Waals forces.)

London forces (also known as *dispersion forces*) are the result of momentary shifts in the symmetry of the electron cloud of a molecule. Recall that we spoke of the polarizability of the electron cloud—the ease with which it is distorted. In a large collection of molecules, at any given moment collisions are taking place, with resulting polarization of the molecules. As soon as a slight positive charge is produced at one end of one molecule, it induces a slight negative charge in one end of the molecule next to it—an *induced dipole*. For an instant, a force of attraction exists between these molecules. **London forces** are the forces of attraction between fluctuating dipoles in atoms and molecules that are very close together (see Figure 11.13c).

The strength of London forces is influenced by the size and geometry of the molecules involved and by the ease of polarization of the electron clouds. Close contact between the molecules over a larger region gives greater opportunity for dipole interaction than when only a small amount of contact is possible. In the series of pentanes in Table 11.6a, the London forces get weaker (as shown by the lower boiling points) as the molecules get closer to spherical in shape, because spheres can make contact at only one point. Among molecules of similar geometry (Table 11.6b), London forces increase with increasing number of electrons, that is, with increasing molecular mass. The difference in boiling point between CH_4 and SiH_4 (Table 11.5), which are both nonpolar, is due to the different strengths of the London forces. Melting points are affected by crystal geometry and other factors in addition to London forces, and therefore may not show as good a correlation with molecular mass and shape as do boiling points.

Table 11.6
London Forces and Boiling Points The decrease in boiling point in each of the series of compounds is due to decreasing London forces.

(a) Same molecular mass, increasingly compact shape	(b) Similar molecular geometry, increasing molecular mass
$CH_3CH_2CH_2CH_2CH_3$ *n*-pentane, C_5H_{12} b.p. 36°C	CH_4 Methane, CH_4 b.p. −161°C
$CH_3CH_2CHCH_3$ | CH_3 Isopentane, C_5H_{12} b.p. 28°C	CH_3CH_3 Ethane, C_2H_6 b.p. −88.6°C $CH_3CH_2CH_3$ *n*-Propane, C_3H_8 b.p. −44.5°C
CH_3 | CH_3-C-CH_3 | CH_3 Neopentane, C_5H_{12} b.p. 9.5°C	$CH_3CH_2CH_2CH_3$ *n*-Butane, C_4H_{10} b.p. −0.5°C

11.12 HYDROGEN BONDS

**Strongest hydrogen bonds:
between H and F, N, or O**

When a hydrogen atom is covalently bonded to an electronegative atom that strongly attracts the shared electron pair, the small hydrogen atom has little electron density around it. Under these circumstances, the hydrogen atom carries a partial positive charge, and can act as a bridge to another electronegative atom. A **hydrogen bond** is the attraction of a hydrogen atom covalently bonded to an electronegative atom for a second electronegative atom (Figure 11.13b). The strongest hydrogen bonds form between hydrogen atoms and fluorine, nitrogen, or oxygen atoms, which are small and have their negative charges highly concentrated in a small volume. Hydrogen bonds are the strongest intermolecular forces. It is the strength of the hydrogen bonds in water that is largely responsible for the unique properties of water and the resulting influence of water on the environment and the living things on earth (Sections 14.1 and 14.2).

The strongest hydrogen bond (100 kJ/mol) occurs between hydrogen and the most electronegative element, fluorine. Hydrogen fluoride crystals contain long chains in which each hydrogen atom can be thought of as covalently bonded to one fluorine atom and hydrogen-bonded to another.

$$\text{H} \underset{\substack{\\ \text{F} \\ \delta-}}{\overset{\delta+}{\diagdown}} \text{H} \underset{140°}{\overset{\delta+}{\diagup}} \overset{\overset{\delta-}{\text{F}}}{} \overset{\delta+}{\text{H}} \underset{\substack{\\ \text{F} \\ \delta-}}{\diagdown} \overset{\delta+}{\text{H}}$$

The hydrogen bond in hydrogen fluoride is strong enough to persist in the liquid state, where the chains are shorter and vary in length, and even in the gaseous state, where the chains are still shorter.

The effect of hydrogen bonding on the properties of compounds is clearly illustrated by the nonmetal hydrides (see Table 11.5). In Table 11.5, compare the properties of the hydrogen-bonded, second-period hydrides ammonia, water, and

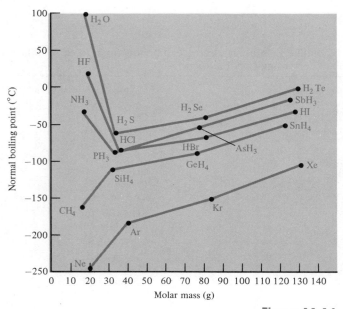

Figure 11.14
**Boiling Points of Simple Hydrides
and Noble Gas Elements**

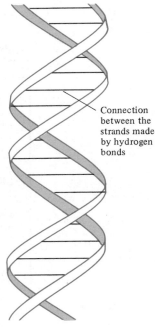

Connection between the strands made by hydrogen bonds

Figure 11.15
The DNA Double Helix

hydrogen fluoride, with the non-hydrogen-bonded third-period hydrides, phosphine, hydrogen sulfide, and hydrogen chloride. In each of the comparable pairs from the same periodic table families (NH_3–PH_3, H_2O–H_2S, HF–HCl), the compound with the smaller molecular mass is less volatile and has the higher melting point and the larger heats of fusion and vaporization. These differences, which are illustrated in Figure 11.14, are due to the extra energy needed to break the intermolecular hydrogen bonds in NH_3, H_2O, and HF.

Hydrogen bonds can form between atoms in different molecules or in the same molecule. The large molecules in living systems are often held in exactly the shape they need for their specific biochemical function by hydrogen bonds. DNA (deoxyribonucleic acid) is the molecule that embodies the genetic code. Hydrogen bonding is one of the two forces that hold the DNA molecule in its double helical shape (Figure 11.15). The ease and speed with which hydrogen bonds can be produced and re-formed makes them ideal for this purpose. Hydrogen bond energies, except for the very strong H—F hydrogen bonds, are about 20–40 kJ/mol. Because covalent bond energies range from roughly 150–900 kJ/mol, the energy required to make and break equivalent covalent bonds in these large, biochemically important molecules would be much too great for the two halves of DNA to untwine, as they must in duplication of the genetic material of a cell.

EXAMPLE 11.13
Intermolecular Forces

Which intermolecular forces influence the properties of BrF_5 (see Example 11.3)?

Bromine(V) fluoride is an AB_5E molecule and has square pyramidal geometry. The molecule is a dipole because of the unsymmetrical molecular geometry, and therefore its properties are influenced by dipole–dipole attraction. In addition, BrF_5 would have London forces (as do all molecules). There is no hydrogen bonding between molecules of BrF_5.

Exercise   List the intermolecular forces that influence the properties of PH_3.
Answer Dipole–dipole interactions and London forces

EXAMPLE 11.14
Intermolecular Forces

List the intermolecular forces that influence the properties acetone, CH_3COCH_3.

The Lewis structure of acetone is

$$\begin{array}{ccccc} H & & :O: & & H \\ | & & \| & & | \\ H-C & - & C & - & C-H \\ | & & & & | \\ H & & & & H \end{array}$$

The central carbon atom is surrounded by three σ bonds, which should be separated by two approximately 120° angles. The molecule will be a dipole because of the electronegativity of the oxygen atom and the geometry of the molecule. There is no hydrogen atom bonded to oxygen, and therefore there is no hydrogen bonding in this molecule. As in all molecules, London forces will be present. Therefore, the intermolecular forces that are important in determining the properties of acetone are dipole–dipole interactions and London forces.

Exercise   List the intermolecular forces that influence the properties of ethyl alcohol, CH_3CH_2OH. *Answer* Dipole–dipole interactions, London forces, and hydrogen bonding

11.1 MOLECULAR GEOMETRY AND ELECTRON-PAIR REPULSION   Molecular geometry refers to the spatial arrangement of atoms in a molecule. It is determined by the length of the various bonds and the angles between them. VSEPR (valence-shell electron-pair repulsion) theory helps to explain and predict the geometries of covalently bonded molecules.

11.2 VSEPR: MOLECULES WITHOUT LONE-PAIR ELECTRONS ON THE CENTRAL ATOM   The electron pairs in covalent bonds repel each other, as do nonbonding electron pairs (lone pairs). The geometry of a molecule in which atoms or groups are bonded to a central atom is therefore the one that places the atoms or groups and the lone pairs as far apart as possible. This principle gives rise to the molecular geometries shown in Table 11.1 for molecules in which there are no lone pairs on the central atom.

11.3 VSEPR: MOLECULES WITH LONE-PAIR ELECTRONS ON THE CENTRAL ATOM   When lone electron pairs take the place of one or more bonded pairs, the geometry of the resulting molecule is altered, as shown in Table 11.2 and Figure 11.3. Because lone pairs repel each other strongly, they occupy locations as far apart as possible (equatorial positions in AB_5 structures, positions opposite one another in AB_6 structures). Since lone pairs take up more space than bonded pairs, bond angles tend to be smaller than their ideal values when lone pairs are present.

11.4 BOND FORMATION   Valence bond theory describes bond formation as resulting from the overlap of atomic orbitals. For bond formation to take place, the orbitals forming the bond must be occupied by electrons of similar energy, have the same symmetry with respect to the bond axis (the line joining the two nuclei), and overlap enough to allow interaction.

11.5 SINGLE BONDS IN DIATOMIC MOLECULES   Bonds in which the region of highest electron density surrounds the bond axis are called σ (sigma) bonds. They can be formed by the overlap of two s orbitals, an s and a p orbital, or two p orbitals, but only one σ bond can form between any two atoms.

11.6 SINGLE BONDS IN POLYATOMIC MOLECULES; HYBRIDIZATION   Hybridization is the combination of atomic orbitals of slightly different energy levels on a single atom to give a new set of hybrid orbitals of intermediate energy. Second-period elements can form sp (linear), sp^2 (triangular planar), or sp^3 (tetrahedral) hybrid orbitals. Beyond the second period, sp^3d (triangular bipyramidal) and sp^3d^2 and d^2sp^3 (octahedral) hybridization can also occur (Table 11.3).

11.7 MULTIPLE COVALENT BONDS p Orbitals oriented parallel to one another can overlap to form a π (pi) bond, in which electron density is concentrated on either side of rather than along the bond axis. π Bonds are weaker than σ bonds. Multiple bonds consist of a σ bond together with one or two π bonds. Atoms joined by multiple covalent bonds cannot rotate about the bond axis, and groups or atoms joined to them must all lie in the same plane. Structural isomers are substances that have the same molecular formula but differ in how the atoms are bonded to each other. *Cis–trans* isomers contain atoms or groups arranged in different ways on either side of a rigid bond, such as a double bond or a bond in a ring. Molecular or ionic species for which several resonance structures can be written are best explained by assuming that some of the π-bonding electrons are delocalized—they occupy a space spread over three or more atoms.

11.8 VAN DER WAALS RADII   Intermolecular forces, though weaker than chemical bonds, are important in determining the physical properties of covalently bonded substances. They are known collectively as van der Waals forces. Van der Waals radii are the radii of atoms not bonded to each other but in contact at the most stable distance.

11.9 DIPOLE MOMENT   Whether or not a molecule is a dipole depends on both the

SIGNIFICANT TERMS

molecular geometry
bond angle
bond axis
valence bond theory
σ bond
hybridization
π bond
isomers

polarity of its bonds and its geometry. The degree of polarity of a molecule is given by its dipole moment. A symmetrical structure may cause a molecule to have no dipole moment even though its individual bonds are polar.

11.10 DIPOLE–DIPOLE FORCES **11.11** LONDON FORCES **11.12** HYDROGEN BONDS Electrical attraction between molecules with dipole moments is called dipole–dipole interaction; the positive end of one molecule attracts the negative end of another. London forces act on both polar and nonpolar molecules and increase with molecular mass. They result from the attraction between transient dipoles, in atoms or molecules that are very close together. A hydrogen bond is the attraction of a hydrogen atom covalently bonded to an electronegative atom for a second electronegative atom. Hydrogen bonds can form between atoms in different molecules or in the same molecule; they have a crucial influence on the properties of water and of many biologically important molecules.

THOUGHTS ON CHEMISTRY

Molecular Structure

THE ATOM AND THE MOLECULE,
by G. N. Lewis

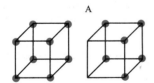

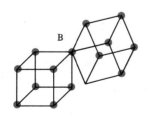

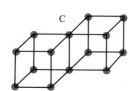

Great as the difference is between the typical polar and nonpolar substances, we may show how a single molecule may, according to its environment, pass from the extreme polar to the extreme nonpolar form, not per saltum, but by imperceptible gradations, as soon as we admit that an electron may be the common property of two atomic shells.

Let us consider first the very polar compounds. Here we find elements with but few electrons in their shells tending to give up these electrons altogether to form positive ions, and elements which already possess a number of electrons tending to increase this number to form the group of eight. Thus Na^+ and Ca^{++} are kernels without a shell, while chloride ion, sulfide ion, nitride ion (as in fused nitrides) may each be represented by an atom having in the shell eight electrons at the corners of a cube.

As an introduction to the study of substances of slightly polar type we may consider the halogens. In the figure I have attempted to show the different forms of the iodine molecule I_2. A represents the molecule as completely ionized, as it undoubtedly is to a measurable extent in liquid iodine. Without ionization we may still have one of the electrons of one atom fitting into the outer shell of the second atom, thus completing its group of eight as in B. But at the same time an electron of the second atom may fit into the shell of the first, thus satisfying both groups of eight and giving the form C which is the predominant and characteristic structure of the halogens. Now, notwithstanding the symmetry of the form C, if the two atoms are for any reason tending to separate, the two common electrons may cling more firmly sometimes to one of the atoms, sometimes to the other, thus producing some dissymmetry in the molecule as a whole, and one atom will have a slight excess of positive charge, the other of negative. This separation of the charges and the consequent increase in the polar character of the molecule will increase as the atoms become separated to a greater distance until complete ionization results. Thus between the perfectly symmetrical and nonpolar molecule C and the completely polar and ionized molecule represented by A there will be an infinity of positions representing a greater or lesser degree of polarity. Now in a substance like liquid iodine it must not be assumed that all of the molecules are in the same state, but rather that some are highly polar, some almost nonpolar, and others represent all gradations between the two. When we find that iodine in different *environments shows different degrees of polarity, it means merely that in one medium there is a larger percentage of the more polar forms. So bromine, although represented by an entirely similar formula, is less polar than iodine. In other words, in the average molecule the separation of the charge is less than in the case of iodine. Chlorine and fluorine are less polar than either and can be regarded as composed almost completely of molecules of the form C.*

"The Atom and the Molecule," by G. N. Lewis. Reprinted from the *Journal of the American Chemical Society*, Vol. 38, pp. 762–785. Published 1916 by the American Chemical Society.

QUESTIONS

Molecular Geometry

11.1 What geometrical structures would be predicted for molecules having the formulas (a) AB, (b) AB_2, (c) AB_3, and (d) AB_5?

11.2 Sketch the triangular biypyramidal geometrical structure. What are the values of the bond angles?

11.3 When using VSEPR theory to predict molecular geometry, how are double and triple bonds treated?

11.4 Use VSEPR to predict the geometries of each of the following species: (a) H_2Be, (b) molecular $AlCl_3$, (c) SiH_4, (d) SF_6, and (e) IO_4^-.

11.5 Repeat Question 11.4 for (a) CO_2, (b) $[AlH_4]^-$, (c) NH_4^+, and (d) $[Cr(H_2O)_6]^{3+}$.

11.6 Repeat Question 11.4 for (a) Cl_2CO, (b) PCl_5, (c) BCl_3, (d) ClO_4^-, and (e) molecular $MgCl_2$.

11.7 How does the presence of nonbonding pairs of electrons on an atom influence the bond angles around the atom?

11.8 What geometrical structures would be predicted for molecules having the following formulas: (a) AB_3E, (b) AB_2E_3, (c) AB_5E, and (d) $A_2B_2E_2$?

11.9 List, in decreasing order, the strength of electron-pair repulsions involving lone pairs (LP) and bonded pairs (BP of electrons: LP–BP, LP–LP, BP–BP.

11.10 When using VSEPR theory to predict molecular geometry, how is a single, nonbonding electron treated?

11.11 Sketch the three different possible arrangements of the three B atoms around the central atom A for the molecule AB_3E_2. Which of these structures correctly describes the molecular geometry? Why? What are the predicted ideal bond angles and how would the actual bond angles deviate from these values?

11.12 Sketch the three different possible arrangements of the two B atoms around the central atom A for the molecule AB_2E_3. Which of these structures correctly describes the molecular geometry?

11.13 Use VSEPR to predict the geometries of each of the following species: (a) F_2, (b) H_2S, (c) F_2O, (d) H_3O^+, and (e) XeF_4.

11.14 Repeat Question 11.13 for (a) CO, (b) NCl_3, (c) ClO_3^-, (d) SeF_6, and (e) ClO_2.

11.15 Repeat Question 11.13 for (a) $[I_3]^-$, (b) $[ICl_4]^-$, (c) NOCl, (d) OH^-, and (e) XeF_2.

11.16 Nitrogen forms the following series of compounds with hydrogen (the first two only at low temperatures): imidogen, NH; amidogen, NH_2; ammonia, NH_3; and ammonium ion, NH_4^+. Use VSEPR to discuss the geometry of these species.

Valence Bond Theory

11.17 Prepare sketches of the overlap of the following atomic orbitals: (a) s with s, (b) s with p along the bond axis, (c) p with p along the bond axis, and (d) p with p perpendicular to the bond axis.

11.18 Prepare a sketch of the cross section taken between two atoms that have formed a (a) single σ bond, (b) a double bond consisting of a σ and a π bond, and (c) a triple bond consisting of a σ bond and two π bonds.

11.19 Describe the bonding in the HCl molecule in terms of simple valence bond theory.

11.20 Describe the bonding in the F_2 molecule in terms of simple valence bond theory.

11.21 What are hybridized atomic orbitals? Why was the theory of hybridized orbitals introduced?

11.22 Prepare sketches of the orbitals around atoms which are (a) sp, (b) sp^2, (c) sp^3, (d) sp^3d, and (e) sp^3d^2 hybridized. Show in the sketches any unhybridized p orbitals that might participate in multiple bonding.

11.23 What types of hybridization would you predict for molecules having the following general formulas: (a) AB_3, (b) AB_2E_2, (c) AB_3E, (d) ABE_4, and (e) ABE_3?

11.24 Repeat Question 11.23 for (a) ABE_5, (b) AB_2E_4, (c) AB_4, (d) AB_3E_2, and (e) AB_5.

11.25 What is the hybridization of the central atom in each of the following: (a) H_2Be, (b) $AlCl_3$, (c) SiH_4, (d) SF_6, (e) IO_4^-, (f) NCl_3, and (g) ClO_3^-?

11.26 Repeat Question 11.25 for (a) $[AlH_4]^-$, (b) $AsCl_5$, (c) NH_4^+, (d) $[Cr(H_2O)_6]^{3+}$, (e) SeF_4, and (f) ClO_2.

11.27 Repeat Question 11.25 for (a) PCl_5, (b) BCl_3, (c) ClO_4^-, (d) molecular $MgCl_2$, (e) $[I_3]^-$, and (f) XeF_2.

11.28 What type of hybridization will the carbon atom have in (a) CO, (b) CO_2, and (c) CO_3^{2-}? In which species are there π bonds that are not delocalized? In which species will there be delocalized π bonding?

11.29 Prepare a sketch of the molecule $CH_3CH{-}CH_2$ showing orbital overlaps. Identify the type of hybridization of atomic orbitals for each carbon atom.

11.30 Draw the Lewis structures for molecular oxygen and ozone. Assuming that all of the oxygen atoms are hybridized, what will be the hybridization of the oxygen atoms in each substance? Prepare sketches of the molecules.

11.31* What type of hybridization does the nitrogen atom(s) have in each of the following molecules and ions: (a) NO; (b) N_2O_2, the dimer of NO; (c) N_2O_5; (d) NO_2; (e) N_2O_4, the dimer of NO_2; and (f) N_2O_3? (See Section 26.9 for the atomic arrangement in these species.)

Intermolecular Forces

11.32 What are van der Waals forces? What are the three types of van der Waals forces we consider in this chapter?

11.33 How do we determine the van der Waals radius for an atom? Is this radius larger or smaller than the atomic radius?

11.34 Briefly describe the interaction between two dipoles.

11.35 Choose the molecular geometries which would give rise to polar molecules: (a) AB_3E, (b) AB_2E_3, (c) AB_6, and (d) AB_3E_2.

11.36 Choose the polar molecules: (a) molecular $AlCl_3$, (b) molecular Al_2Cl_6, (c) SF_6, (d) Cl_2CO, (e) NO, and (f) SeF_4.

11.37 Repeat Question 11.36 for (a) SiH_4, (b) molecular $MgCl_2$, (c) NOCl, (d) NCl_3, and (e) F_2O.

11.38 What causes London forces? What factors determine the strength of London forces between molecules?

11.39 There are two different isomers of butane, C_4H_{10}.

Which would you expect to have the higher boiling point? Why?

11.40 What is a hydrogen bond? Which atoms can form strong hydrogen bonds?

11.41 Draw a likely structure for the dimer of acetic acid, which is formed as a result of two hydrogen bonds between the two individual molecules. The structural formula of acetic acid is

11.42 Why does HF have a lower boiling point and lower heat of vaporization than H_2O even though the molecular masses are nearly the same and the hydrogen bonds between molecules of HF are stronger?

11.43 Indicate which of the following molecules would exhibit hydrogen bonding: (a) H_2Be, (b) SiH_4, (c) NH_3, (d) HI, and (e) molecular $AlCl_3$.

11.44 Repeat Question 11.43 for (a) CH_4, (b) N_2H_4, (c) CH_3CH_2OH, and (d) H_2Se.

11.45 List the intermolecular forces that are present in liquid ammonia, NH_3, and methane, CH_4. Which of these compounds should have the lower freezing and boiling points? Which substance would you expect to be a liquid over a larger temperature range?

11.46 The structures for three molecules having the formula $C_2H_2Cl_2$ are

Describe the intermolecular forces present in each of these compounds.

11.47 List the intermolecular forces that would be important for (a) H_2Be, (b) molecular $AlCl_3$, (c) SiH_4, and (d) SF_6.

11.48 Repeat Question 11.47 for (a) CO_2, (b) $AsCl_5$, (c) Cl_2CO, and (d) molecular $MgCl_2$.

11.49 Repeat Question 11.47 for (a) BCl_3, (b) F_2, (c) XeF_4, (d) SeF_4, and (e) NOCl.

11.50 Choose which substance within each group has the greatest intermolecular force to overcome: (a) P_4, S_8, or Cl_2 (considering mass); (b) CO_2 or SO_2 (considering dipole moment); (c) F_2 or Ar (considering shape); (d) *n*-octane or isooctane—

n-octane   *isooctane*

(considering shape); and (e) CH_4 or CCl_4 (considering mass).

11.51* Assign each of the boiling points to the respective substances within each group on the basis of intermolecular forces: (a) Ne, Ar, Kr, -246.048 °C, -185.7 °C, -152.30 °C; (b) N_2, HCN, C_2H_6, -195.8 °C -88.63 °C, 26 °C; and (c) NH_3, H_2O, HF, -33.35 °C, 19.54 °C, 100.00 °C.

Additional Questions

11.52* The Lewis concept of atoms completing "octets" when forming chemical bonds predicts that Xe should form no compounds, and yet we know that XeF_2, XeF_4, and XeF_6 (as well as others) exist. (a) Prepare Lewis structures for these substances and decide what type of hybridization of the Xe atomic orbitals has taken place. (b) Draw all of the isomers of XeF_2 and discuss your choice of molecular geometry. (c) What shape do you predict for XeF_4? (d) What are the important intermolecular forces in XeF_2 and XeF_4?

11.53* Iodine and fluorine form a series of interhalogen molecules and ions. Among these are IF (minute quantities observed spectroscopically), IF_3, IF_4^-, IF_5, IF_6^-, and IF_7. (a) Draw Lewis structures for each of these species. (b) Identify the type of hybridization that the orbitals of the iodine atom have undergone in each substance. (c) Identify the shape of the molecule or ion. (d) What intermolecular forces are important for IF, IF_3, IF_5, and IF_7?

Answers to Selected Questions

11.6 (a) triangular planar; (b) triangular bypyramidal; (c) triangular planar; (d) tetrahedral; (e) linear

11.12 The molecule is linear (first sketch).

11.15 (a) linear; (b) square planar; (c) bent; (d) linear; (e) linear

11.20 A partially filled $2p$ orbital on one F atom overlaps with a similar orbital on the other to form a σ bond.

11.23 (a) sp^2; (b) sp^3; (c) sp^3; (d) sp^3d; (e) sp^3

11.27 (a) sp^3d; (b) sp^2; (c) sp^3; (d) sp; (e) sp^3d; (f) sp^3d

11.30 sp^2

11.37 (c), (d), (e)

11.42 Water forms two hydrogen bonds per molecule, HF only one.

11.44 (b), (c)

11.48 (a) London forces; (b) London forces; (c) London forces, dipole–dipole interactions; (d) London forces

11.50 (a) S_8; (b) SO_2; (c) F_2; (d) n-octane; (e) CCl_4

11.52 (a)

The geometry should be linear (first sketch) to minimize lone pair–lone pair interactions; (c) square planar; (d) London forces

PROBLEMS

Review of Principles

11.1 The enthalpy of vaporization is 18.673 kJ/mol for H_2S, 19.33 kJ/mol for H_2Se, and 23.22 kJ/mol for H_2Te. (a) Explain this general trend. (b) Plot the heat of vaporization against the atomic number of the central atom. (c) Extrapolate your plot and predict the heat of vaporization of water. (d) Why is there a large difference between your answer for part (c) and the measured value of 40.6563 kJ/mol?

11.2 Sulfur reacts with fluorine to form two gaseous compounds: SF_4 and SF_6. The respective heats of formation at 25 °C are −774.9 kJ/mol and −1209 kJ/mol. The heat of formation is 278.805 kJ/mol for $S(g)$ and 78.99 kJ/mol for $F(g)$. (a) Calculate the S—F bond energy in each compound. (b) How is the sulfur atom hybridized in each compound? *Answer* (a) 342.4 kJ/mol, 327 kJ/mol; (b) sp^3d, sp^3d^2

11.3* Calculate the C—O, C—O and C=O bond energies from the following heats of formation at 25 °C: 716.682 kJ/mol for $C(g)$, −110.525 kJ/mol for $CO(g)$ −393.51 kJ/mol for $CO_2(g)$, −200.66 kJ/mol for $CH_3OH(g)$, −74.81 kJ/mol for $CH_4(g)$, 217.965 kJ/mol for $H(g)$, −241.818 kJ/mol for $H_2O(g)$ and 249.170 kJ/mol for $O(g)$.

CHAPTER 12

Nuclear Chemistry

The story of the discovery of radioactivity and the exploitation of nuclear energy holds more high drama than any other area of science. We think of Pierre and Marie Curie, reducing several tons of ore to a few specks of previously unknown radioactive elements. And carrying out this laborious task in a shed once used by a medical school for dissecting cadavers, a shed freezing and damp in the winter, and hot and stinking in the summer. There are the honors that came to Pierre and Marie and to their daughter, Irène, and Irène's husband, Frédéric Joliot-Curie, who carried on the research; and there are the deaths of both Marie and Irène from leukemia, quite likely caused by radiation from their own experiments.

World War II thrust a generation of physicists, chemists, and engineers into what was for many of them a moral dilemma—rushing to build a weapon that, while certain to end the war, would unleash a force too terrible to comprehend. But there was also drama and excitement in the triumph of pure science surrounding the development of the bomb. For example, there was the day when Enrico Fermi supervised the start-up of the first nuclear chain reaction, when he ordered what he calculated to be the last control rod drawn out and then announced with a smile, "The reaction is self-sustaining."

Drama of another kind was there when the first bomb was exploded over the New Mexico desert, and J. Robert Oppenheimer, the brooding, intellectual physicist who had overseen the birth of the bomb, remarked that at the moment of the explosion there came to his mind these words from the Bhagavad Gita, the sacred book of the Hindus, "I am become Death, the Shatterer of Worlds."

Many benefits to mankind have developed from the application of radioactivity in medicine and industry, and from the utilization of nuclear energy for power. But the fear persists that the horror of nuclear weapons may fade from the minds of many people.

NUCLEAR STABILITY AND RADIOACTIVITY

12.1 THE NUCLEUS

To review briefly (Section 3.9), the mass number (A) is the sum of the atomic number (Z, equal to the number of protons in the nucleus) plus the number of neutrons in the nucleus (N), that is, $A = Z + N$. Atoms with the same number of protons but different numbers of neutrons are isotopes—atoms of the same element that have different masses. **Nuclide** is a general term used to refer to any isotope of any element.

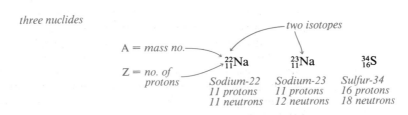

three nuclides

two isotopes

A = *mass no.*

Z = *no. of protons*

$^{22}_{11}\text{Na}$ $\qquad$ $^{23}_{11}\text{Na}$ $\qquad$ $^{34}_{16}\text{S}$

Sodium-22 $\qquad$ *Sodium-23* $\qquad$ *Sulfur-34*
11 protons $\qquad$ *11 protons* $\qquad$ *16 protons*
11 neutrons $\qquad$ *12 neutrons* $\qquad$ *18 neutrons*

Figure 12.1

Figure 12.1
Potential Energy Barrier between Nucleons (a) Coulombic repulsion acts between two protons until they reach a distance of about 10^{-13} cm. At this point the nuclear force of attraction takes over. (b) No forces act between a proton and a neutron (or between two neutrons) until a distance of 10^{-13} cm is reached.

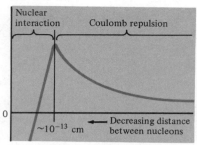

(a) Potential energy between pair of protons

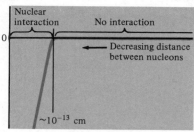

(b) Potential energy between proton and neutron

Nuclide: any isotope of any element
Nucleons: protons and neutrons

Protons and neutrons, collectively called **nucleons,** are packed tightly together in the nucleus. As a result, the volume of a nucleus is directly proportional to its mass. Most nuclei are either spherical or slightly football-like in shape. Nuclear radii are on the order of 10^{-13} cm—about 10,000 times smaller than atomic radii. Nuclei all have roughly the same, extremely high, density of about 10^{14} g/cm^3. By comparison, platinum, one of the densest of metals, has a density of about 22 g/cm^3. A pocket matchbox full of platinum weighs somewhat less than half a kilogram. A comparable volume of matter of the density of nuclei would weigh over 2.5×10^{12} kg.

The **nuclear force** is the force of attraction between nucleons; it acts between protons, between neutrons, and between protons and neutrons. A force that can hold positively charged protons and uncharged neutrons so closely together in the absence of any negative charge is very different from, and much stronger than, the Coulomb forces between electrons and protons. In fact, the nuclear force is the strongest force yet to be discovered.

The exact nature of the nuclear force is not known. Here, it is of interest mainly that the nuclear force is very strong (30–40 times the Coulomb repulsion at 10^{-13} cm) and very short in its range, extending only to a distance of about 10^{-13} cm.

Figure 12.1 shows the potential energy changes as a proton approaches a neutron or a proton. At distances greater than 10^{-13} cm two protons repel each other. Once they reach this distance the nuclear force of attraction takes over. A neutron and a proton neither repel nor attract each other until they reach the distance at which the nuclear force can act.

12.2 MASS, ENERGY, AND NUCLEAR BINDING ENERGY

The law of conservation of energy and the law of conservation of mass as they apply to "ordinary" chemical reactions have been discussed in Chapters 6 and 7. In "ordinary" reactions, atoms are rearranged but always maintain their identity. Before going on to further study of "ordinary" chemistry, we want to discuss **nuclear chemistry,** which deals with nuclei and reactions that cause changes in nuclei. The consequences of the uses of nuclear chemistry in weapons and in power plants are constantly debated in the press. For this reason, if for no other, everyone should have some understanding of nuclear chemistry.

Two aspects of nuclear chemistry make it notably different from other chemistry. First, the composition of nuclei, and therefore the identities of atoms, change in nuclear reactions. Second, in nuclear reactions, the relationship between mass and energy takes on a significance that it does not have in ordinary chemical reactions.

The law of conservation of mass and the law of conservation of energy are dealt with separately in ordinary chemistry and this causes no problems. In reality, however, mass and energy are equivalent to each other and are connected by a more fundamental law, which we might call the law of conservation of mass–energy: <u>The total of the mass and energy in the universe is a constant.</u> This relationship was first expressed by Albert Einstein (in 1905) in his now-famous equation (part of the special theory of relativity).

$$E = mc^2$$

(12.1)

energy → E = mc^2 ← *mass* *speed of light*

joules *kilograms* $\frac{meters^2}{seconds^2}$

[Recall that in the SI system, $1 J = 1 (kg\ m^2)/s^2$.]

(Energy plus mass) is conserved

A consequence of the mass–energy relationship is that mass and energy are interconvertible. For the energy of the universe to remain constant, every energy change must be accompanied by a change in mass ($\Delta E = \Delta m \times c^2$). This means that when energy is released during a chemical reaction, mass must be lost by the substances involved.

Your first thought may be that what we told you in Chapter 6 about the conservation of mass is not true, and very strictly speaking, it isn't. However, the amount of energy absorbed or released in ordinary chemical reactions is equivalent to a *very small* change in mass—too small to be detected. Therefore, in ordinary chemical reactions, we can expect the law of conservation of mass to be obeyed.

The difference between the mass–energy changes in ordinary chemical reactions and in nuclear reactions is one of magnitude. The energy of nuclear reactions is determined by the nuclear force, which is much stronger than the Coulomb force that holds electrons and nuclei together. In nuclear reactions the energy changes are so large that the accompanying mass changes *can* be detected.

The sum of the masses of the individual neutrons, protons, and electrons in any given atom is always greater than the mass of the atom. The difference between the sum of the masses of the individual nucleons and electrons and the mass of an atom is called the **mass defect**. The missing mass represents the **nuclear binding energy**— the energy that would be released in the combination of nucleons to form the nucleus (Figure 12.2). (The mass change due to the binding of the electrons is too small to be detected.)

While no way has been found to directly combine protons and neutrons, nuclear binding energy can be calculated from the mass defect. Nuclear binding energy is similar in nature to the standard enthalpy of formation of a chemical compound. Just as the enthalpy of formation is the heat of formation of one mole of the compound from the elements, the binding energy is the energy of formation of a single nucleus from the nucleons. Note that binding energy is expressed *per nucleus,* and not per mole. In this book we give nuclear binding energy as a negative number, showing that energy is released. (In some publications, nuclear binding energy is reported as a positive number.) The following example illustrates the calculation of the mass defect and the nuclear binding energy.

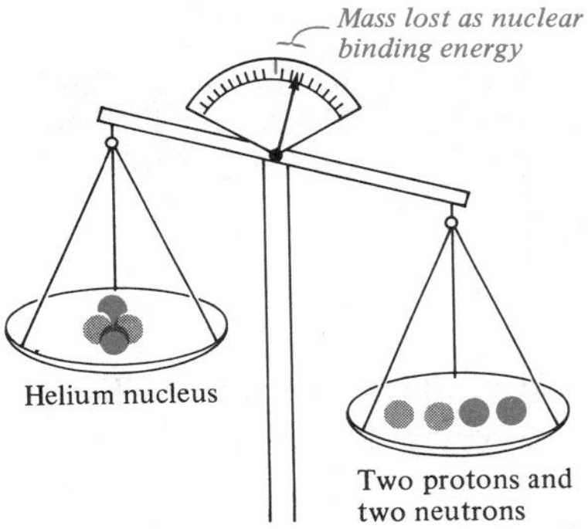

Figure 12.2
Nuclear Mass vs. Nucleon Mass The mass of a nucleus is always less than the mass of the uncombined neutrons and protons. The difference in mass has been converted to nuclear binding energy. (This difference could not, of course, be weighed on a balance.)

EXAMPLE 12.1
Nuclear Binding Energy

The atomic mass of $^{39}_{19}K$ is 38.96371 u. Calculate the binding energy for this nuclide using 1.008665 u for the mass of a neutron, 1.007276 u for the mass of a proton, 0.00054858 u for the mass of an electron, and 2.9979×10^8 m/s for the speed of light. (1 u = $1.6605655 \times 10^{-27}$ kg.) Calculate the total binding energy of one mole of $^{39}_{19}K$ atoms.

The symbol for the nuclide, $^{39}_{19}K$, tells us that there are 19 protons and $39 - 19 = 20$ neutrons.

The calculated mass of one atom of $^{39}_{19}K$ is

(19 protons)(1.007276 u/proton) + (19 electrons)(0.00054858 u/electron)
+ (20 neutrons)(1.008665 u/neutron) = 39.32197 u

The mass defect is the difference between the actual mass and the calculated mass:

$$\text{Mass defect} = 38.96371\ u - 39.32197\ u = -0.35826\ u$$

This loss of mass is equivalent to

$$(-0.35826\ u)\left(\frac{1.6605655 \times 10^{-27}\ kg}{1u}\right) = -5.9491 \times 10^{-28}\ kg$$

According to the Einstein mass–energy relationship, the energy equivalent to this mass is

$$E = mc^2$$

$$= (-5.9491 \times 10^{-28}\ kg)(2.9979 \times 10^8\ m/s)^2\left(\frac{1\ J}{1(kg\ m^2)/s^2}\right)$$

$$= -5.3467 \times 10^{-11}\ J$$

The binding energy for $^{39}_{19}K$ is -5.3467×10^{-11} J. For one mole of $^{39}_{19}K$ atoms, the total nuclear binding energy is this energy multiplied by Avogadro's number:

$$(-5.3467 \times 10^{-11}\ J/atom)(6.0220 \times 10^{23}\ atom/mol) = -3.2198 \times 10^{13}\ J/mol$$

Exercise Calculate the total binding energy of one mole of $^{81}_{35}Br$ atoms. The atomic mass of $^{81}_{35}Br$ is 80.9163 u. *Answer* -6.799×10^{13} J/mol

Note that because the magnitude of the unit is more convenient, energies are often expressed in millions of electron volts (MeV) instead of joules when dealing with nuclear processes. Using the conversion factor 1 MeV = $1.6021892 \times 10^{-13}$ J gives the following value for the binding energy of $^{39}_{19}K$:

$$(-5.3467 \times 10^{-11}\ J)\left(\frac{1\ MeV}{1.6021892 \times 10^{-13}\ J}\right) = -333.71\ MeV$$

The direct conversion of mass changes in atomic mass units to energy in millions of electron volts is a routine calculation; the conversion factor is 1 u = 931.5017 MeV. For the $^{39}_{19}K$ nuclide,

$$(-0.35826\ u)\left(\frac{931.5017\ MeV}{1\ u}\right) = -333.72\ MeV$$

The **binding energy per nucleon** (also called average binding energy) is the nuclear binding energy of a nucleus divided by the number of nucleons in that nucleus. For example, for $^{39}_{19}K$ from Example 12.1 the binding energy per nucleon is

$$\frac{-333.72\ MeV}{39\ nucleons} = \frac{8.5569\ MeV}{nucleon}$$

Binding energy per nucleon is more useful than the total nuclear binding energy for comparing one nucleus with another.

The binding energy per nucleon rises rapidly for the lighter elements (Figure 12.3), showing that as the number of nucleons increases in these elements, they are held together more strongly. Once carbon-12 is reached, there is much less variation in the binding energy per nucleon. Apparently, the strength of interaction of each additional nucleon with its neighbors is very similar beyond this point. A maximum in the curve occurs in the region of iron, showing that in iron nuclei, the nucleons are most strongly bound together.

Combination of two of the lightest nuclei to give a heavier nucleus further along on the curve releases energy. **Nuclear fusion** is the combination of two light nuclei to give a heavier nucleus. Nuclei at the heavier end of the curve have slightly *lower*

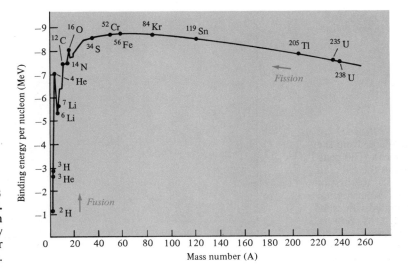

Figure 12.3
The Binding Energy per Nucleon vs. the Mass Number Nuclear fission and nuclear fusion release energy and form nuclei with greater binding energies per nucleon.

Nuclear fission: splitting of a heavy nucleus into two parts
Nuclear fusion: combination of two light nuclei

binding energies per nucleon than those in the middle. Thus the splitting of a heavy nucleus to give two lighter nuclei also releases energy. **Nuclear fission** is the splitting of a heavy nucleus into two lighter nuclei of intermediate mass numbers (and sometimes other particles as well). In both fission and fusion, nuclei are transformed into other nuclei in which the nucleons are more strongly bound together — those in the middle of the curve in Figure 12.3. The total mass of the nuclei involved decreases, and energy is released in both processes. Nuclear reactions have energies a million or more times greater than ordinary chemical reactions. In Sections 12.17– 12.19, we discuss the uses of fission and fusion as sources of energy.

12.3 RADIOACTIVITY: NATURAL AND ARTIFICIAL

Radioactivity is the spontaneous emission by unstable nuclei of particles, or electromagnetic radiation, or both. Nuclides that spontaneously break down, or *decay,* are called radioisotopes, radioactive nuclides, or **radionuclides.**

The discovery of radioactivity was made when radiation was observed being emitted by naturally occurring materials, notably pitchblende, a uranium-containing ore (see A Historical Aside: Radioactivity). It was later found possible to create in the laboratory radionuclides not found in nature. We speak of substances found on earth as "natural" and their radioactivity as "natural radioactivity." The word "artificial" is used to describe nuclides made in the laboratory and their radioactivity. Roughly one-third of the elements have natural radioisotopes. All of the isotopes of elements heavier than bismuth ($Z > 83$) are radioactive.

Most of the natural radionuclides have either been present since the earth was formed or are products of the decay of other, long-lived radionuclides. Some radionuclides are continuously produced on earth by the cosmic ray bombardment of stable natural nuclides. (Primary cosmic rays are high-energy particles from outer space — mainly protons — that continually bombard the earth. In the atmosphere they collide with atoms to produce secondary cosmic rays composed of photons, electrons, neutrons, and other particles that in turn collide with materials at the surface of the earth.)

More than 350 artificial radionuclides have been identified in the environment. Most of them were created during the period (1955–1962) when nuclear bombs were being tested by many nations (for example, see Figure 12.4). Some radionu-

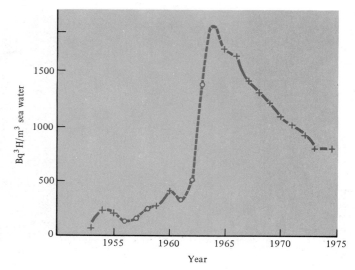

clides are also introduced into the environment during the operation of nuclear plants and facilities doing nuclear research.

12.4 PROPERTIES OF ISOTOPES

Nuclides of the same element—isotopes—have essentially the same physical and chemical properties. This is to be expected, for the number of electrons and the electronic structure are the same. Because of their similar properties, the separation of isotopes from each other is very difficult. Isotopes of the same element undergo all of the same chemical reactions. However, the speed, or rate, of the reactions may differ slightly. For a given element and a specific reaction, the difference in rate increases as the relative difference in mass number increases. Thus rate differences are greatest with isotopes of the lighter elements and are at a maximum with those of hydrogen ($A = 1, 2,$ and 3).

Sometimes differences in reaction rates can be used in the separation of light isotopes. Heavier isotopes must be separated by physical methods that depend upon small absolute differences in mass, as, for example, in the separation of uranium isotopes by gaseous diffusion of their hexafluorides (Section 5.13).

New and more economical isotope separation methods are being sought. Possibilities are gas-centrifuge separation, in which the heavier isotopes are spun to the outside in a powerful centrifuge, and laser separation. By the use of a finely tuned laser the atoms of one isotope can be excited. They can then be converted to ions and separated by an electric field from the nonionized atoms of a similar isotope, or they can be taken up in a chemical reaction that does not occur with the unexcited isotope.

The radioactivity of an isotope is largely unaffected by its chemical environment. For example, carbon-14 decays by the same nuclear reactions and at the same rate whether it is in a sample of coal or is incorporated in a complex biological molecule.

12.5 NEUTRON–PROTON RATIO

Why are some nuclides radioactive and others not radioactive? An answer to this question is suggested by a plot of the number of neutrons versus the number of protons in stable nuclei. In Figure 12.5 the solid line shows where nuclei with an equal number of neutrons and protons would fall. Along this line $Z = N$ and the neutron-to-proton ratio is $1:1$.

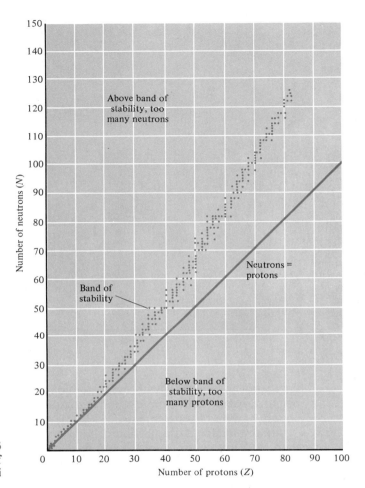

Figure 12.5
Number of Neutrons vs. Number of Protons for Stable Nuclei

Isotopes of the lighter elements, up to $^{40}_{20}$Ca, fall on or quite close to the line. For heavier elements, the number of neutrons increases faster than the number of protons and the neutron–proton ratio eventually reaches about 5:3. The additional neutrons apparently provide the additional nuclear force necessary to hold larger numbers of protons close together within the nucleus. Once the atomic number reaches 84, even extra neutrons are not sufficient to maintain stability and, as we have mentioned, all nuclides of $Z > 83$ are unstable and radioactive.

For each nuclear charge, only isotopes with a neutron–proton ratio within a specific range are stable, that is, are not radioactive. Essentially, radioactivity is the spontaneous transformation of unstable nuclei to nuclei with more favorable neutron–proton ratios (further discussed in Section 12.11). Nuclides with too many protons fall below the stable nuclei band in Figure 12.5. Such nuclides decay so that the net result is a decrease in the number of protons relative to the number of neutrons (greater n/p ratio). Nuclides with too many neutrons fall above the stable nuclei band in Figure 12.5. Such nuclides decay so that the net result is a decrease in the number of neutrons relative to the number of protons (smaller n/p ratio).

12.6 COSMIC ABUNDANCE AND NUCLEAR STABILITY

A plot of the cosmic abundance of the elements (Figure 12.6) — their abundance not on earth but in the universe — reveals some interesting relationships. Hydrogen and helium atoms are far more abundant in the universe than any other elements. Except

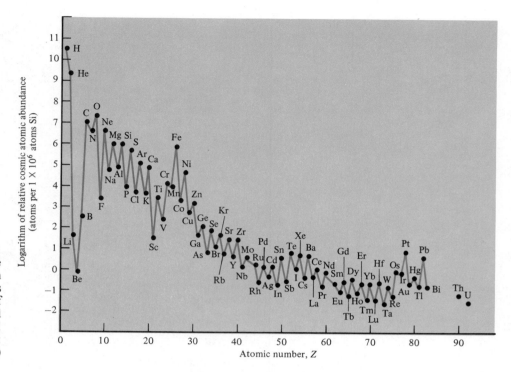

Figure 12.6
Relative Cosmic Abundances of the Elements Silicon is widespread in the crust of the Earth and its abundance is used as a standard of comparison. (Source: Therald Moeller, *Inorganic Chemistry: A Modern Introduction,* New York: Wiley, 1982, p. 28.)

for hydrogen, elements with even atomic numbers are more abundant than their neighbors with odd atomic numbers. And in general, light elements are more abundant than heavy elements.

If abundance is a reflection of nuclear stability—a reasonable assumption—then even numbers of protons and nuclear stability must be related in some way. Further examination reveals that of the ten most abundant elements (again with the exception of hydrogen) all have even numbers of both neutrons and protons. In addition, of all the nuclides in the earth's crust, 86% have even mass numbers.

Certain numbers of neutrons or protons—called **magic numbers**—impart particularly great nuclear stability. The magic numbers are 2, 8, 20, 28, 50, 82, and 126. Nuclides with magic numbers of *both* neutrons and protons are very stable and are abundant, for example, $^4_2$He, $^{16}_8$O, $^{40}_{20}$Ca, and $^{208}_{82}$Pb. The magic numbers were so named before enough was known about the nucleus to interpret their significance. Now, these relationships are explained by the existence of energy levels within the nucleus similar to the electron energy levels outside the nucleus. The magic numbers represent energy levels filled by nucleons. Nuclides with filled levels have greater nuclear stability, just as atoms with energy levels filled by electrons have greater chemical stability.

The elements originated, it is believed, in nuclear reactions within the stars. In stars like our sun, hydrogen is converted to helium by nuclear fusion. By successive fusion reactions, helium then yields the elements through iron and nickel. Because nuclear binding energy is at a maximum with the iron and nickel nuclides, continued fusion to produce heavier elements does not occur. The heavier elements are formed in smaller quantities by subsequent nuclear reactions of other types.

After the earth was formed and before it cooled, natural geochemical processes concentrated iron and nickel in its core and the light elements in its crust and atmosphere. Thus, the portion of the earth available to chemists and geologists offers an abundance and distribution pattern of the elements quite different from that in the universe as a whole (Table 12.1).

Table 12.1
Abundances of the Elements of the First Four Periods
Source: T. Moeller, *Inorganic Chemistry; A Modern Introduction.* (New York: Wiley, 1982), p. 24.

| Atomic Number | Symbol | Igneous Rocks of Crust of Earth* | | Cosmos*† Atomic Abundance (Si = 1×10^6) |
		Percent by Mass	Atoms/10^6 Atoms Si	
1	H			3.18×10^{10}
2	He	3×10^{-7}	7.6×10^{-2}	2.21×10^9
3	Li	6.5×10^{-3}	9.1×10^2	49.5
4	Be	6×10^{-4}	67	0.81
5	B	3×10^{-4}	28	350
6	C	3.2×10^{-2}	2.7×10^3	1.18×10^7
7	N	4.6×10^{-3}	3.3×10^2	3.74×10^6
8	O	46.6	2.96×10^6	2.15×10^7
9	F	$(6-9) \times 10^{-2}$	$(3.2-4.8) \times 10^3$	2.45×10^3
10	Ne	7×10^{-9}	3.5×10^{-4}	3.44×10^6
11	Na	2.83	1.24×10^5	6.0×10^4
12	Mg	2.09	8.76×10^4	1.061×10^6
13	Al	8.13	3.05×10^5	8.5×10^4
14	Si	27.72	1.00×10^6	1.00×10^6
15	P	0.118	3.8×10^3	9.60×10^3
16	S	5.2×10^{-2}	1.6×10^3	5.0×10^5
17	Cl	3.14×10^{-2}	9×10^2	5.70×10^3
18	Ar	4×10^{-6}	0.1	1.172×10^5
19	K	2.59	4.42×10^4	4.20×10^3
20	Ca	3.63	9.17×10^4	7.21×10^4
21	Se	5×10^{-4}	11	35
22	Ti	0.44	9.2×10^3	2.775×10^3
23	V	1.5×10^{-2}	3.0×10^2	262
24	Cr	2.0×10^{-2}	3.9×10^2	1.27×10^4
25	Mn	0.10	1.8×10^3	9.30×10^3
26	Fe	5.0	9.13×10^4	8.3×10^5
27	Co	2.3×10^{-3}	40	2.21×10^3
28	Ni	8.0×10^{-3}	1.4×10^2	4.80×10^4
29	Cu	7.0×10^{-3}	1.1×10^2	5.40×10^2
30	Zn	1.32×10^{-2}	2.0×10^2	1.244×10^3
31	Ga	1.5×10^{-3}	22	48
32	Ge	7×10^{-4}	9.5	1.15×10^2
33	As	5×10^{-4}	6.7	6.6
34	Se	9×10^{-6}	0.12	67.2
35	Br	1.6×10^{-4}	2.0	13.5
36	Kr			46.8

* 10^6 atoms of Si is a useful point of reference.

† *Source:* A. G. W. Cameron, *Space Sci. Rev.* **15**, 121 (1973).

12.7 HALF-LIFE   The radionuclides decompose at very different rates, as shown by the values of their half-lives. The **half-life** of a radionuclide, $t_{\frac{1}{2}}$, is the time it takes for one-half of the nuclei in a sample of that nuclide to decay. For example, consider a radionuclide with a half-life of ten years. Suppose 100 g of this nuclide is put away today. Ten years from today 50 g of the original nuclide will remain, along with the more stable decay products. Ten years after that, 25 g of the original nuclide will be left, and so on. For a given nuclide, the value of the half-life is always the same. The sample size has no influence on $t_{\frac{1}{2}}$. If 8 g of the nuclide with $t_{\frac{1}{2}} = 10$ yr were put away today, 4 g would be left unchanged ten years from today, 2 g would be unchanged in 20 years, and so on.

Figure 12.7
Radioactive Decay Curves (a) A general curve for radioactive decay. (You may recognize this as an exponential decay curve.) (b) Radioactive decay of a 100 g sample of $^{226}_{88}$Ra, which has a half-life of 1600 yr.

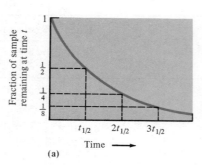

(a)

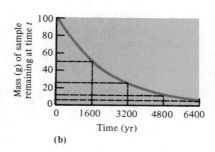

(b)

For *every* radioactive nuclide, the following relationships govern the rate of decay. Taking 1 as the amount of the original sample, we have

number of half-lives that have elapsed	amount of sample remaining
$1\ t_{\frac{1}{2}}$	$\frac{1}{2}$
$2\ t_{\frac{1}{2}}$	$\frac{1}{2} \times \frac{1}{2} = \frac{1}{4}$
$3\ t_{\frac{1}{2}}$	$\frac{1}{2} \times \frac{1}{2} \times \frac{1}{2} = \frac{1}{8}$
$4\ t_{\frac{1}{2}}$	$\frac{1}{2} \times \frac{1}{2} \times \frac{1}{2} \times \frac{1}{2} = \frac{1}{16}$
$\vdots$	$\vdots$

A plot of the amount of sample remaining versus the time elapsed — a radioactive decay curve — is shown in Figure 12.7.

Half-lives range from a few microseconds to 10^{15} yr (Table 12.2). The shorter the half-life, the less stable is the nuclide. The nuclides with short half-lives are highly radioactive — many nuclei are decaying per unit time. The more stable nuclides stay around longer, but their radioactivity is weaker — fewer nuclei decay per unit time.

Knowing the half-life of a nuclide allows us to find the amount of a given sample remaining after a specific time, or the age of a sample. The *activity* of a radionuclide — the number of nuclei that decay in a unit of time — is directly proportional to the size of the sample. Therefore, the rate of decrease in activity of a sample, measured in decays per minute or in some other way, is also governed by the half-life.

EXAMPLE 12.2
Half-Life

The number of nuclei decaying in a sample of $^{68}_{31}$Ga decreased by a factor of four over a 136.6 min period. What is the half-life of this nuclide?

In order for $\frac{1}{4}$ of the original sample to remain at the end of 136.6 min, two half-life periods must have passed ($\frac{1}{2} \times \frac{1}{2} = \frac{1}{4}$). The half-life is

$$\frac{136.6\ \text{min}}{2\ \text{half-lives}} = 68.3\ \text{min/half-life}$$

The half-life of $^{68}_{31}$Ga is 68.3 minutes.

Exercise The half-life of $^{60}_{27}$Co is 5.26 yr. How many half-life periods must pass in order for $\frac{7}{8}$ of a sample to decay? How many years is this? *Answer* 3 half-lives, 15.8 yr

---

In the preceding example we could deal easily with what happens in a time period that is an exact multiple of the half-life. Two mathematical relationships allow us to deal with the results in *any* time period. (These relationships are derived in Section 18.9.) The first equation relates the initial quantity, q_0, of a radionuclide

Isotope	Half-Life
Radioisotopes produced on earth by cosmic rays	
$^{3}_{1}H$ (tritium)	12.26 yr
$^{14}_{6}C$	5730 yr
Natural radioisotopes	
$^{40}_{19}K$	1.28×10^9 yr
$^{144}_{60}Nd$	5×10^{15} yr
$^{232}_{90}Th$	1.41×10^{10} yr
$^{235}_{92}U$	7.1×10^8 yr
$^{238}_{92}U$	4.51×10^9 yr
Artificial radioisotopes	
$^{24}_{11}Na$	15.0 h
$^{52}_{26}Fe$	8.2 h
$^{60}_{27}Co$	5.26 yr
$^{90}_{38}Sr$	28.1 yr
$^{87}_{35}Br$	55 s
$^{131}_{53}I$	8.070 day
$^{137}_{55}Cs$	30.23 yr
$^{239}_{94}Pu$	24,400 yr

(in any mass units or as the number of nuclei) to the quantity, q, after a period of time, t, has passed. The proportionality constant, k, called the *rate constant,* has a characteristic value for each nuclear decay reaction.

$$\log\left(\frac{q_0}{q}\right) = \frac{kt}{2.303} \tag{12.2}$$

where q_0 is the initial quantity, k is the rate constant, t is the time elapsed, and q is the quantity at time t.

The same relationship is valid for the activities of a radioactive nuclide.

$$\log\left(\frac{a_0}{a}\right) = \frac{kt}{2.303} \tag{12.3}$$

(At this point, you may want to review the use of logarithms, which is discussed in Appendix I.)

These relationships show that the half-life is independent of the quantity of a radionuclide and is dependent only on the rate constant k. At $t_{\frac{1}{2}}$, one-half of the original quantity ($0.5q_0$) remains, giving the following relationship between $t_{\frac{1}{2}}$ and k:

$$\log\left(\frac{q_0}{0.5q_0}\right) = \frac{kt_{\frac{1}{2}}}{2.303}$$

$$\log 2 = \frac{kt_{\frac{1}{2}}}{2.303}$$

$$0.301 = \frac{kt_{\frac{1}{2}}}{2.303}$$

$$t_{\frac{1}{2}} = \frac{0.693}{k} \tag{12.4}$$

EXAMPLE 12.3
Half-Life

What percentage of the $^{68}_{31}Ga$ sample described in Example 12.2 would remain at the end of 3.00 h?

The rate constant for the radioactive decay of this nuclide is

$$k = \frac{0.693}{t_{\frac{1}{2}}} = \frac{0.693}{68.3 \text{ min}} = 0.0101/\text{min}$$

With q_0 the initial amount of the isotope and q the amount remaining after 3.00 h, Equation (12.2) for $^{68}_{31}Ga$ is, using $t = (3.00 \text{ h})(60 \text{ min/h}) = 180.$ min and $k = 0.0101/\text{min}$,

$$\log\left(\frac{q_0}{q}\right) = \frac{kt}{2.303}$$

$$= \frac{(0.0101/\text{min})(180. \text{ min})}{(2.303)} = 0.789$$

The fraction of the isotope remaining after 3.00 h is q/q_0, which can be found from this equation as follows:

$$\log\left(\frac{q_0}{q}\right) = 0.789$$

$$\frac{q_0}{q} = 6.15 \text{ and therefore } \frac{q}{q_0} = \frac{1}{6.15} = 0.163$$

The fraction of $^{68}_{31}$Ga remaining after 3.00 h will be 0.163; the percentage remaining is therefore 16.3%.

Exercise What percentage of a $^{60}_{27}$Co sample remains at the end of 3.0 yr? The half-life of $^{60}_{27}$Co is 5.26 yr. *Answer* 67%

12.8 RADIOISOTOPE DATING

Ingenious use has been made of the natural radioactive isotope carbon-14 to determine the age of plant and animal relics. Carbon-14 is formed in the upper atmosphere by cosmic ray bombardment of nitrogen and is incorporated into CO_2. The amount of carbon-14 in the earth's environment is assumed to have been relatively constant over the centuries.

As long as a plant or animal lives, it contains the same proportion of $^{14}_{6}$C as its surroundings. But as soon as a plant stops utilizing CO_2 or an animal stops eating carbon-containing plants, its supply of $^{14}_{6}$C is no longer replenished and the ratio of radioactive $^{14}_{6}$C to nonradioactive $^{12}_{6}$C begins to decrease. From the half-life of carbon-14, which is 5730 yr, and the measured ratio of $^{14}_{6}$C to $^{12}_{6}$C, the age of the plant or animal remains can be calculated. Such a procedure is known as radiocarbon dating.

Radiocarbon dating is limited to objects less than about 50,000 to 75,000 years old. In older objects, the activity is too low for reliable measurements. Rocks that are older can be dated by measuring their ratio of uranium-238 to lead-206. It is assumed that the radioactive uranium and its decay products have been trapped in the rock since the time that the rock solidified. Ultimately, all uranium-238 decay products are converted to the stable isotope, lead-206 (Section 12.12).

Highly refined mass spectrometers and very careful experimental techniques have also been used in radioisotope dating. The actual relative numbers of atoms of the parent nuclide and its decay products are counted. Use of this technique for moon rocks established the age of the moon and the earth to be the same, 4.5×10^9 years.

EXAMPLE 12.4
Half-Life

Ptolemy V reigned in Egypt during the period 203 to 181 BC (about 2170 years ago). Could a piece of wood from an artifact that had a $^{14}_{6}$C activity of 11.8 disintegrations per minute per gram of carbon have come from this same time period? The half-life of $^{14}_{6}$C is 5730 years and the current $^{14}_{6}$C activity is 15.3 disintegrations per minute per gram of carbon.

The rate constant for the decay of $^{14}_{6}$C is

$$k = \frac{0.693}{t_{\frac{1}{2}}} = \frac{0.693}{5730 \text{ yr}} = 1.21 \times 10^{-4}/\text{yr}$$

Solving Equation (12.2) for the time and substituting $a = 11.8/\text{min g C}$, $a_0 = 15.3/\text{min g C}$, and $k = 1.21 \times 10^{-4}/\text{yr}$ gives the age of the wood as

$$t = \frac{(2.303) \log \left(\dfrac{a_0}{a}\right)}{k}$$

$$= \frac{(2.303) \log \left(\dfrac{15.3/\text{min g C}}{11.8/\text{min g C}}\right)}{1.21 \times 10^{-4}/\text{yr}} = 2150 \text{ yr}$$

The wooden artifact is 2150 years old and could have come from the reign of Ptolemy, about 2170 years ago.

Exercise A bone found in a cave was "dated" using carbon-14 analysis. A sample of the bone had an activity of 2.93 disintegrations per minute per gram of carbon. What is the age of the bone specimen? *Answer* 1.37×10^4 yr

---

NUCLEAR REACTIONS

The various types of **nuclear reactions**—reactions that lead to changes in the atomic number, mass number, or energy states of nuclei—are described below. Nuclear reactions result from (1) the spontaneous decay of radioactive nuclides, either artificial or natural, (2) **bombardment reactions,** in which electromagnetic radiation or fast-moving particles are captured by a nucleus to form an unstable nucleus that subsequently decays, (3) the fission of unstable heavy nuclei, or (4) the fusion of light nuclei, which occurs naturally only in the sun and other stars.

12.9 TYPES OF RADIATION

Soon after the discovery of radioactivity, three types of radiation were identified as coming from natural radionuclides. They were named by the first three letters of the Greek alphabet as α rays (alpha rays), β rays (beta rays), and γ rays (gamma rays). Each type of ray responds differently to an electric field. γ Rays, which have no mass or charge, are undeflected by the field. α Rays are positively charged and β rays are negatively charged, as shown by their deflection in opposite directions by the field (Figure 12.8). The difference in the amount of deflection shows α rays to have greater mass than β rays.

Although we now know the composition of the α, β, and γ rays, their names and the Greek letter symbols continue to be used in nuclear chemistry. α Rays are helium ions, $^4_2\text{He}^{2+}$, and β rays are electrons. γ Rays are not beams of particles of atomic origin, but of photons—electromagnetic radiation at the high-energy, short-wavelength end of the spectrum (see Tools of Chemistry: Electromagnetic Radiation, Chapter 8).

> Nuclear reactions:
> **(1) spontaneous decay**
> **(2) bombardment**
> **(3) fission**
> **(4) fusion**

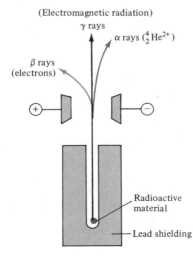

Figure 12.8
α, β, and γ Rays in an Electric Field The α rays have a positive charge and are heavier (they are less deflected) than β rays, which have a negative charge. γ Rays are neutral and are unaffected by the field. While this sketch illustrates the behavior of all three types of rays, they are not ordinarily produced simultaneously by the same radioactive source.

(Electromagnetic radiation)
γ rays
α rays ($^4_2\text{He}^{2+}$)
β rays (electrons)
Radioactive material
Lead shielding

Radioactivity was discovered quite by accident in 1896 by a French physicist, Henri Becquerel. He was studying a uranium salt (potassium uranyl sulfate, $K_2SO_4 \cdot UO_2SO_4 \cdot 2H_2O$) that was known to be phosphorescent — it reemitted radiation when it was exposed to light. Becquerel was looking for a relationship between x-rays, which had been discovered the year before by Röntgen, and the phenomenon of phosphorescence.

X-rays had been found to penetrate the black paper wrappers that kept ordinary light from exposing photographic plates. Becquerel had already discovered that radiation from the phosphorescing uranium salt exposed photographic plates in the same way. During several cloudy days some prepared experiments were left waiting in a drawer. Being curious, Becquerel developed the plates. He had quite a surprise. The image of the uranium salt appeared sharp and clear on the plates. The emission of radiation was obviously unrelated to exposure of the salt to any other radiation, but was a property of the uranium salt itself.

In 1897 Marie Curie began a systematic search for naturally radioactive elements. Among the elements known at that time, and with the methods of measurement available, she found only uranium and thorium to be radioactive. But a uranium-containing ore, pitchblende, was more radioactive then either the uranium or the thorium contained in it. Marie Curie correctly suspected that an undiscovered radioactive element might also be present in pitchblende. Using chemical methods, Marie and her physicist husband, Pierre, demonstrated the presence of two previously unknown radioactive elements in the ore. The first, which resembled barium in its chemical behavior, they named radium (from the Latin for "ray"). The other, which resembled bismuth in its chemical behavior, they named polonium (for Marie's native country, Poland). After almost four more years of physically exhausting labor, they succeeded in winning one-tenth of a gram of radium chloride from several tons of pitchblende ore.

Pierre Curie was killed tragically in 1906 when he was struck by a heavy horse-drawn wagon while crossing the street. Marie carried on their work with courage. In 1921 she traveled to the United States, where President Harding presented her with 1 gram of pure radium to aid in her ongoing research. The women of the United States, to honor this great woman scientist, had contributed $100,000 to finance the mining and purification of this radium.

The mystery of radioactivity deepened when it was found that not only radiation, but also atoms of other elements, were continuously produced in radioactive decay. It was Rutherford and Frederick Soddy who concluded in 1902 that in the process of radioactive decay, one element is transformed, or *transmuted,* into another element. To announce this conclusion to the scientific community must have taken a special form of courage. It was contrary to what had been firmly believed since the time of Dalton — that atoms of one element cannot be transformed into atoms of another element. (Rutherford is reported to have remarked "For Mike's sake, Soddy, don't call it transmutation. They'll have our heads off as alchemists.")

A further milestone in the understanding of radioactivity and its relationship to nuclear instability came in 1934 when Marie Curie's daughter, Irène, and son-in-law, Frédéric Joliot-Curie, discovered that radioactive substances not only existed in nature, but could be produced artificially (Section 12.13). The Joliot-Curies also played a role in the discovery of the neutron (Section 3.7), which became the key to unleashing the energy held in atomic nuclei.

Enrico Fermi used neutrons to bombard many elements, frequently producing isotopes of elements of the next highest atomic number. Neutron bombardment of uranium, however, led not to the expected next heaviest element, but to splitting of the uranium atom into two lighter atoms. Nuclear fission had been discovered. At this point, the history of radioactivity became entwined with the political events of World War II (see A Historical Aside: The Atomic Bomb).

12.10 WRITING EQUATIONS FOR NUCLEAR REACTIONS

α-particle $= {}_2^4\text{He}^{2+}$

β^--particle $=$ electron

β^+-particle $=$ positron

In order to write equations for nuclear reactions, we must add to our chemical notation some symbols for the particles that arise in nuclear reactions. These symbols are summarized in Table 12.3. Electrons, for example, are known as beta-particles in nuclear chemistry, and are given the symbol β^-. The neutrino and antineutrino, two massless, chargeless particles, and the positron, the positively charged twin of the electron, are new to us here. These particles are encountered only in nuclear reactions. The reactions in which they are formed are discussed in the following sections.

Mass number and often atomic number as well are written for all of the nuclides involved in a nuclear reaction. For the particles involved, the mass number and number of protons (2 for an α particle; 0 for a neutron; -1 for an electron, as described below) are not always included, but they are helpful in writing and balancing nuclear equations.

Following are the equations for some nuclear reactions of historical interest:

First recognized natural transmutation of an element (Rutherford and Soddy, 1902)

$$\underset{\substack{an\ atom\ of \\ radium\text{-}226}}{{}_{88}^{226}\text{Ra}} \xrightarrow[\substack{decays \\ to}]{} \underset{\substack{an \\ \alpha\text{-}particle}}{{}_2^4\alpha} + \underset{\substack{an\ atom\ of \\ radon\text{-}222}}{{}_{86}^{222}\text{Rn}} \tag{12.5}$$

First artificial transmutation of an element (Rutherford, 1919)

$$\underset{\substack{an\ atom \\ of \\ nitrogen\text{-}14}}{{}_7^{14}\text{N}} + \underset{\substack{bombarded \\ by\ an\ \alpha\text{-} \\ particle}}{{}_2^4\alpha} \xrightarrow{\ yields\ } \underset{\substack{an\ atom \\ of \\ oxygen\text{-}17}}{{}_8^{17}\text{O}} + \underset{\substack{a \\ proton}}{{}_1^1p} \tag{12.6}$$

Discovery of the neutron (Chadwick, 1932)

$$\underset{\substack{an\ atom \\ of \\ beryllium\text{-}9}}{{}_4^9\text{Be}} + \underset{\substack{bombarded \\ by\ an \\ \alpha\text{-}particle}}{{}_2^4\alpha} \xrightarrow{\ yields\ } \underset{\substack{an\ atom \\ of \\ carbon\text{-}12}}{{}_6^{12}\text{C}} + \underset{\substack{a \\ neutron}}{{}_0^1n} \tag{12.7}$$

Discovery of nuclear fission (Otto Hahn and Fritz Strassman, 1939)

$$\underset{\substack{an\ atom \\ of \\ uranium\text{-}235}}{{}_{92}^{235}\text{U}} + \underset{\substack{bombarded \\ by\ a \\ neutron}}{{}_0^1n} \xrightarrow{\ yields\ } \underset{\substack{an\ atom \\ of \\ barium\text{-}141}}{{}_{56}^{141}\text{Ba}} + \underset{\substack{an\ atom \\ of \\ krypton\text{-}92}}{{}_{36}^{92}\text{Kr}} + \underset{\substack{three \\ neutrons}}{3{}_0^1n} \tag{12.8}$$

Equation (12.8) shows only one of many possible combinations of products from this reaction.

Some of the species in nuclear reactions may be ions, for example, the α-particle, which is ${}_2^4\text{He}^{2+}$. However, because only the mass and atomic numbers are of concern in nuclear reactions, the charges need not be included in the symbols. As a nuclear reaction proceeds, excited electrons within an atom lose energy so as to return the atom to a stable state, and positive ions eventually pick up electrons to become neutral species.

A nuclear equation is correctly written when the following two rules are obeyed:

1. *Conservation of mass number.* The sum of the number of protons and neutrons in the reactants must equal the sum of the number of protons and neutrons in the products. This can be checked by comparing the sum of the mass numbers of the products with that of the reactants. For example, in Equation (12.7), $9 + 4 = 12 + 1$.
2. *Conservation of nuclear charge.* The total nuclear charge of the products must equal the total nuclear charge of the reactants. This can be checked by comparing the sum of the atomic numbers (equal to the nuclear charge) of the products with the sum of the atomic numbers of the reactants. For example, in Equation (12.7), $4 + 2 = 6 + 0$.

Table 12.3
Particles in Nuclear Reactions These are the particles and the symbols most commonly encountered in writing nuclear reactions. The superscripts are the mass numbers (neutrons + protons). The subscripts are the number of protons or, for the β-particles, values that compensate for the change in the number of protons (see Sections 12.11c, d).

Name	Symbols
Alpha-particle (helium nucleus)	$\alpha,\ {}_2^4\alpha,\ {}_2^4\text{He}$
Electron (beta-minus-particle)	$\beta^-,\ {}_{-1}^0\beta,\ {}_{-1}^0e$
Positron (beta-plus-particle)	$\beta^+,\ {}_{+1}^0\beta,\ {}_{+1}^0e$
Proton (hydrogen nucleus)	$p,\ {}_1^1p,\ {}_1^1\text{H}$
Neutron	$n,\ {}_0^1n$
Neutrino	$\nu,\ {}_0^0\nu$
Antineutrino	$\bar{\nu},\ {}_0^0\bar{\nu}$

If the atomic numbers and mass numbers of all but one of the atoms or particles in a nuclear reaction are known, the unknown particle can easily be identified by using the rules given.

EXAMPLE 12.5
Nuclear Equations

A nuclide of element 104 (for which the name unnilquadium has been suggested) with a mass number of 257, $^{257}_{104}$Unq, is formed by the nuclear reaction of $^{249}_{98}$Cf and $^{12}_{6}$C, with the emission of four neutrons. This new nuclide has a half-life of about 5 s and decays by emitting an α-particle. Write the equations for these nuclear reactions and identify the nuclide formed as $^{257}_{104}$Unq undergoes decay.

The problem gives all the information needed to write the equation for the formation of $^{257}_{104}$Unq.

$$^{249}_{98}\text{Cf} + {}^{12}_{6}\text{C} \longrightarrow {}^{257}_{104}\text{Unq} + 4^{1}_{0}n$$

Note that the totals of the mass numbers of the reactants and products are equal, $249 + 12 = 261 = 257 + 4(1)$, as are the totals of the atomic numbers, $98 + 6 = 104 = 104 + 4(0)$.

The equation for the radioactive decay of $^{257}_{104}$Unq can be written as

$$^{257}_{104}\text{Unq} \longrightarrow {}^{4}_{2}\alpha + {}^{A}_{Z}E$$

where E represents the unidentified element. To conserve mass number (A) and nuclear charge we see that

$$257 = 4 + A \quad \text{and} \quad 104 = 2 + Z$$

or

$$A = 257 - 4 = 253 \quad \text{and} \quad Z = 104 - 2 = 102$$

The unidentified element has atomic number 102 and the periodic table (inside front cover) shows it to be an isotope of nobelium. The complete equation is

$$^{257}_{104}\text{Unq} \longrightarrow {}^{4}_{2}\alpha + {}^{253}_{102}\text{No}$$

Exercise A $^{10}_{5}$B nucleus reacts with a neutron to form a $^{10}_{4}$Be nucleus and another particle. Write the equation for this nuclear process and identify the unknown particle. *Answer* $^{10}_{5}\text{B} + {}^{1}_{0}n \rightarrow {}^{10}_{4}\text{Be} + {}^{1}_{1}\text{H}$, proton

---

12.11 SPONTANEOUS RADIOACTIVE DECAY

a. γ Decay α Decay and β decay, described in the following sections, are the major routes by which radioactive nuclides decay spontaneously. Frequently, α or β decay leaves the nucleus above its ground-state nuclear energy level. To return to this most stable energy level the nucleus undergoes γ **decay** — the emission of a γ ray — thereby giving up the excess energy in the form of electromagnetic radiation. The wavelength range for both x-rays and γ rays is from roughly 1 to 0.001 nm. X-rays are at the longer wavelength end of this range and γ rays at the shorter wavelength end of the range. However, the terms refer not to wavelength, but to the origin of the radiation — "x-rays" from energy changes of electrons and "γ rays" from nuclear energy changes.

γ Rays travel with the speed of light and their energies are represented by the different frequencies of the radiation ($E = h\nu$). Support for the existence of discrete nuclear energy levels is provided by γ-ray emission, which is quantized. Only certain specific frequencies of γ rays are emitted by specific radionuclides. There is no change of mass number or nuclear charge in γ decay.

indicates excited state

$$^{A}_{Z}X^{*} \longrightarrow {}^{A}_{Z}X + h\nu \tag{12.9}$$

γ-Ray emission usually occurs within a nanosecond following an α or β decay—virtually at the same time. When the excited nuclide survives for a longer time it is called an "isomer" and its decay by delayed γ-ray emission is called an **isomeric transition** (see Table 12.5). These longer-lived excited nuclides are usually designated by adding the letter "m" to the name or symbol for the nuclide, for example, technetium-99m, ^{99m}Tc.

b. α Decay **α Decay** is the emission of an α-particle by a radionuclide. The mass number is decreased by 4 units and the atomic number by 2.

$$^{A}_{Z}X \longrightarrow ^{A-4}_{Z-2}Y + ^{4}_{2}\alpha \qquad (12.10)$$

Heavy nuclides for which the neutron–proton ratio is too low (see Figure 12.5) and those with $Z > 83$ undergo α decay. For example, you can see that the gold isotope with 79 protons and a mass number of 185, or 106 neutrons, lies below the stability band in Figure 12.5, and that the product nuclide with 77 protons and 104 neutrons is closer to the band and therefore more stable.

$$^{185}_{79}\text{Au} \longrightarrow ^{181}_{77}\text{Ir} + ^{4}_{2}\alpha$$

Sometimes several α-particle emissions must take place before a stable nuclear mass and charge are achieved. Many of the nuclides with $Z > 83$ decay by α-particle emission, for example, radium-226.

$$^{226}_{88}\text{Ra} \longrightarrow ^{222}_{86}\text{Rn} + ^{4}_{2}\alpha$$

α-Particles emitted from a given radionuclide have a single energy or one of a few specific energies (Figure 12.9), providing further evidence for the existence of energy levels within the nucleus. Emission of an α-particle can leave a nuclide in an excited state; it then emits γ radiation to reach the stable state. The total energy of the emitted α-particle and the γ ray is equal to the reaction energy. For example, in Figure 12.9 the energy of α_1 plus γ_2 plus γ_3, or α_1 plus γ_1, equals $E_1 - E_2$, the total reaction energy.

c. β Decay: electron emission The emission of electrons is one of three types of reactions now classified as β decay. **β Decay** includes electron emission, positron emission, and electron capture.

Explanation of how radioactive decay occurs by electron emission originally offered two difficulties. First, as there are no electrons in the nucleus, where does the electron come from? The answer is that the electron is created at the moment of its emission: A neutron within the nucleus decays to give a proton and an electron. The

α decay:
A decreases by 4
Z decreases by 2

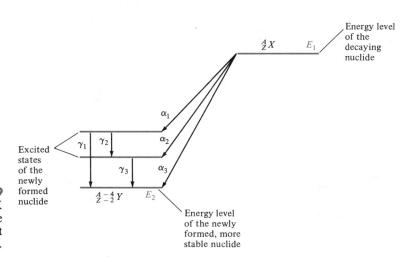

Figure 12.9
An α-Decay Scheme Isotope X yields α-particles with three different energies plus three different γ rays.

emission of an electron causes no change in the mass number of a nuclide, but *increases* the positive charge on the nucleus by 1 because a proton is left behind. To compensate for this increase in nuclear charge, a -1 is written for the "nuclear charge" of an electron, allowing conservation of nuclear charge to be indicated in writing the equations for nuclear reactions.

$$^{A}_{Z}X \longrightarrow {}^{A}_{Z+1}Y + {}^{0}_{-1}\beta$$

The net effect of electron emission is the conversion of a neutron to a proton (Table 12.4). Thus, in electron emission, the neutron–proton ratio decreases. Electron emission is the most common mode of decay for nuclides that are radioactive because they lie above the band of stability (too many neutrons; Figure 12.5). For example, carbon-14 undergoes electron emission to form nitrogen-14, which is not radioactive.

$$^{14}_{6}C \longrightarrow {}^{14}_{7}N + {}^{0}_{-1}\beta \qquad (12.11)$$

You can see that nuclear charge is conserved: $6 = 7 - 1$.

The electrons emitted in β decay have a continuous spectrum of energies from zero to a maximum that is characteristic of the decaying nuclide. Herein lies the second difficulty in explaining electron emission. Electron emission is accompanied by the emission of γ rays of quantized energies. The energies of the electrons plus the energies of the γ rays must equal the reaction energy, as for α-particle emission (see Figure 12.9). Suppose a given nuclide during β decay emits γ rays of six different energies from three different excited states (Figure 12.10). Conservation of energy would require that the energy of the electrons should also have only specific values so that the sum of each electron energy plus that of the appropriate γ rays equals $E_1 - E_2$ (see Figure 12.10). For example, the energies of β_1 plus γ_6, or β_1 plus γ_4 plus γ_5, or β_2 plus γ_3, and so on, would equal the total reaction energy. This is not what happens. The energy of the β-particles plus the specific energies of the γ rays do not equal the reaction energy. Where does the rest of the energy go? This dilemma was solved by the suggestion that a neutral massless particle is emitted simultaneously with an electron. The kinetic energy of such a particle would account for the missing energy.

The existence of two such particles has now been proved — they are the **antineutrino** ($\bar{\nu}$), a massless chargeless particle that is emitted with an electron, and the **neutrino** (ν), a massless chargeless particle that is emitted with a positron (see below). For example, as shown in Figure 12.10, a nuclide can reach the highest excited state by the emission of β_1^- and $\bar{\nu}_1$, which have a total energy equal to the difference between E_1 and this state. The energy of β_1^- plus $\bar{\nu}_1$, plus the appropriate combination of γ rays, equals the reaction energy, $E_1 - E_2$. (We note that in 1980 physicists reported the possibility that neutrinos may have mass and be unstable. Ongoing experiments are exploring this possibility and its consequences.)

β⁻ decay:
A unchanged
Z increases by 1

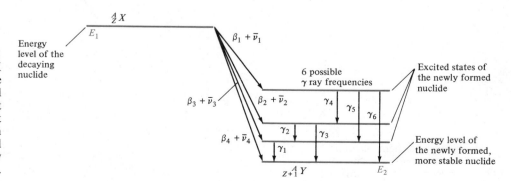

Figure 12.10
A β-Decay Scheme Isotope X decays by electron emission to give β rays with energies between 0 and $E_1 - E_2$, plus γ rays of six different frequencies, plus neutrinos that account for the difference between the β-ray energy and the total energy change in each β-ray emission.

d. β Decay: positron emission A **positron** is a particle identical to an electron in all of its properties except for the charge, which is $+1$ rather than -1. Positrons were first detected during an investigation of cosmic rays.

Positron emission causes a decrease of 1 in atomic number, but no change in mass number. In the equations for nuclear reactions, the positron is written with a $+1$ "nuclear charge" to compensate for the decrease in atomic number.

$$_Z^A X \longrightarrow {}_{Z-1}^A Y + {}_{+1}^0 \beta \qquad (12.12)$$

The net effect of positron emission is the conversion of a proton to a neutron (see Table 12.4). This increases the neutron–proton ratio.

Isotopes with too many protons (below the band in Figure 12.5) decay by positron emission. Positrons, like electrons, are emitted with a continuous range of energies, and they are accompanied by neutrinos that carry away the remaining energy. Only artificial radionuclides have been observed to undergo positron emission.

When a positron and an electron interact, they annihilate each other—all of their mass is converted to energy in the form of two 0.51 MeV γ rays traveling in opposite directions.

β^+ **(positron) emission or electron capture:**
A **unchanged**
Z **decreases by 1**

e. β Decay: electron capture The positive charge of an unstable nucleus can also be decreased by **electron capture**—the capture by the nucleus of one of its own inner orbital electrons. The mass number is again unchanged while the atomic number decreases by 1.

$$_Z^A X + {}_{-1}^0 \beta \longrightarrow {}_{Z-1}^A Y \qquad (12.13)$$

Here a proton captures an electron to produce a neutron (and a neutrino; Table 12.4). The result is an increase in the neutron–proton ratio. As the electrons rearrange themselves to compensate for the electron pulled into the nucleus, x-rays are emitted.

In summary, unstable nuclides undergo spontaneous radioactive decay (Table 12.5) by emitting subatomic particles and/or γ radiation (or by spontaneous fission; Section 12.14). The common modes of decay are α decay and β decay.

Table 12.5
Spontaneous Radioactive Decay An m following the mass number superscript, as in the isomeric transition reaction, indicates an excited, or isomeric, state of an isotope. (Sometimes an asterisk is used to designate an excited state.) As is usually done, neutrinos and antineutrinos are omitted.

Reaction	Reacting Nuclide	Reaction Symbol	Change in			Example
			A	*Z*	*n/p*	
γ Decay (isomeric transition)	Excited nuclear state	IT	0	0	—	$_{34}^{77m}\text{Se} \longrightarrow {}_{34}^{77}\text{Se} + \gamma \text{ ray}$
Spontaneous fission	Too heavy ($Z > 92$)	SF	—	—	—	$_{98}^{254}\text{Cf} \longrightarrow$ intermediate mass nuclides and neutrons
α Decay	$Z > 83$; n/p too low	α	-4	-2	Increase	$_{84}^{210}\text{Po} \longrightarrow {}_{82}^{206}\text{Pb} + {}_2^4\alpha$
β Decay						
Electron emission	n/p too high	$\beta-$	0	$+1$	Decrease	$_{89}^{227}\text{Ac} \longrightarrow {}_{90}^{227}\text{Th} + {}_{-1}^0\beta$
Positron emission	n/p too low	$\beta+$	0	-1	Increase	$_7^{13}\text{N} \longrightarrow {}_6^{13}\text{C} + {}_{+1}^0\beta$
Electron capture	n/p too low	EC	0	-1	Increase	$_{33}^{73}\text{As} + {}_{-1}^0\beta \longrightarrow {}_{32}^{73}\text{Ge}$

Of the three types of β decay, electron emission decreases the neutron–proton ratio, and positron emission and electron capture increase this ratio. The net effect of β decay is either conversion of a neutron to a proton ($_{-1}^{0}\beta$ emission) or the conversion of a proton to a neutron ($_{+1}^{0}\beta$ emission or electron capture). Nuclides that fall above the band of stability in Figure 12.5 undergo electron emission. Those that fall below the band of stability undergo positron emission, electron capture, or α decay (the heavier nuclides). Many nuclides with Z > 83 undergo α decay or (in the case of the heaviest nuclides) spontaneous fission.

12.12 NATURAL RADIOACTIVE SERIES

The heavy natural radioactive nuclides are members of one of three series. Each of these series has a long-lived parent and a stable isotope of lead as the end product. Decay from the parent to the final stable isotope proceeds through a sequence of reactions, most of which are α- or β-particle emission. The sequence for the series beginning with uranium-238 is given in Figure 12.11, and the three series are summarized in Table 12.6.

The ratio of lead-206 to uranium-238 in natural minerals, together with the half-life of the uranium isotope, has been used to calculate the age of the earth (Section 12.8).

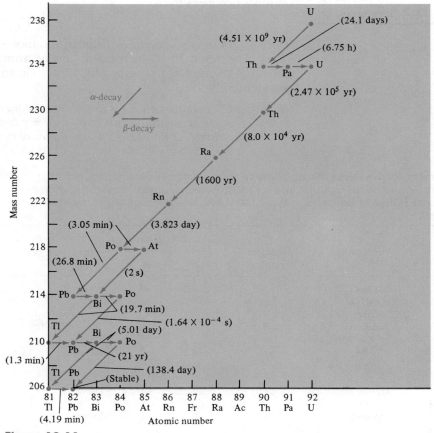

Figure 12.11
Uranium-238 Decay Series Some of the isotopes decay by both α- and β-particle emission. The half-lives of the nuclides are given in parentheses.

Table 12.6
The Natural Radioactive Decay Series The mass number of each member of the thorium series is given by 4 times a whole number (m); of the uranium series by 4 times a whole number plus 2; of the actinium series by 4 times a whole number plus 3. ^{241}Pu is the parent of a fourth series, which is the $4m + 1$ series that ends with ^{209}Bi. This series was discovered with the advent of artificial radioisotope production and makes only a very small contribution to the quantity of natural radioisotopes.

Designation	Parent	Half-Life of Parent (yr)	Final Product
Thorium series 4m	$^{232}_{90}$Th	1.39×10^{10}	$^{204}_{82}$Pb
Uranium series 4m + 2	$^{238}_{92}$U	4.49×10^{9}	$^{206}_{82}$Pb
Actinium series 4m + 3	$^{235}_{92}$U	7.13×10^{8}	$^{207}_{82}$Pb

12.13 BOMBARDMENT

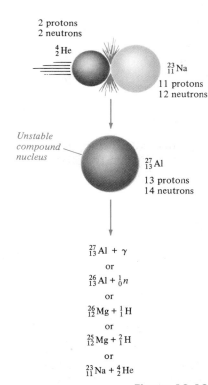

2 protons
2 neutrons

$^{4}_{2}$He

$^{23}_{11}$Na

11 protons
12 neutrons

Unstable compound nucleus

$^{27}_{13}$Al

13 protons
14 neutrons

$^{27}_{13}$Al + γ

or

$^{26}_{13}$Al + $^{1}_{0}n$

or

$^{26}_{12}$Mg + $^{1}_{1}$H

or

$^{25}_{12}$Mg + $^{2}_{1}$H

or

$^{23}_{11}$Na + $^{4}_{2}$He

Figure 12.12
Bombardment of Sodium-23 by α-Particles The compound nucleus may decay by one or several of the routes shown.

In *bombardment* a nucleus is struck by a moving particle. The particles used to bombard nuclei usually have energies of 10 MeV or more. The particle combines with the nucleus to form an unstable compound nucleus that decays either instantaneously or with a measurable half-life (Figure 12.12). If the bombarding particle has enough energy to overcome the nuclear force (in the billion electron volt range), it may smash the atom to bits. Physicists search among the debris from such reactions for information about nuclear particles and forces.

Early investigators were limited to bombardment with α-particles from naturally radioactive sources. To enter a nucleus, a particle must have enough energy to overcome any repulsive forces between itself and the nucleus. The α-particles from natural sources have energies of less than 10 MeV and can be captured only by relatively light nuclei.

Two English physicists, Sir John Cockcroft and E. T. S. Walton, in 1932 succeeded in accelerating protons in a vacuum tube. The first nuclear reaction produced by artificially accelerated particles was the splitting of lithium-7 into two α-particles.

$$^{7}_{3}\text{Li} + ^{1}_{1}p \longrightarrow ^{4}_{2}\alpha + ^{4}_{2}\alpha$$

Since the experiments of Cockcroft and Walton, accelerators have continued to grow in size and complexity. The cost of the big accelerators is now so great that only national governments can afford to pay for them. The latest proposal is for a proton accelerator, 60–120 miles in diameter, at a cost of 2 to 4 billion dollars.

The synthesis of the *transuranium elements* ($Z > 92$) was made possible by the advent of the big accelerators. The bombardment reactions by which the elements up to 106 were first prepared are listed in Table 12.7. Most of these elements were discovered at the famous Lawrence Radiation Laboratory of the University of California at Berkeley. Weighable amounts of elements 93–99 have been prepared. The remaining transuranium elements have been identified literally atom by atom, an impressive achievement. A West German research group has reported the synthesis of elements 107 and 109 (in 1981 and 1982, respectively) by bombardment reactions with iron-58 nuclei accelerated in a heavy-ion linear accelerator. After the bombardment of a bismuth target for one week a *single atom* of element 109 was identified on the basis of its predicted velocity and by identification of its decay products.

A shorthand notation is used for bombardment reactions. The bombarding particle and the product particle are written in parentheses between the symbols for the reactant and product nuclides. For example, for the second reaction in Table

Table 12.7
The Transuranium Elements up to
Z = 106 and The Reactions in
Which They Were First Observed

Atomic Number	Symbol	Name	Reaction
93	Np	Neptunium	$^{238}_{92}U + ^{1}_{0}n \longrightarrow ^{239}_{93}Np + ^{0}_{-1}\beta$
94	Pu	Plutonium	$^{238}_{92}U + ^{2}_{1}H \longrightarrow ^{238}_{93}Np + 2^{1}_{0}n$ $^{238}_{93}Np \longrightarrow ^{238}_{94}Pu + ^{0}_{-1}\beta$
95	Am	Americium	$^{239}_{94}Pu + ^{1}_{0}n \longrightarrow ^{240}_{95}Am + ^{0}_{-1}\beta$
96	Cm	Curium	$^{239}_{94}Pu + ^{4}_{2}He \longrightarrow ^{242}_{96}Cm + ^{1}_{0}n$
97	Bk	Berkelium	$^{241}_{95}Am + ^{4}_{2}He \longrightarrow ^{243}_{97}Bk + 2^{1}_{0}n$
98	Cf	Californium	$^{242}_{96}Cm + ^{4}_{2}He \longrightarrow ^{245}_{98}Cf + ^{1}_{0}n$
99	Es	Einsteinium	$^{238}_{92}U + 15^{1}_{0}n \longrightarrow ^{253}_{99}Es + 7^{0}_{-1}\beta$
100	Fm	Fermium	$^{238}_{92}U + 17^{1}_{0}n \longrightarrow ^{255}_{100}Fm + 8^{0}_{-1}\beta$
101	Md	Mendelevium	$^{253}_{99}Es + ^{4}_{2}He \longrightarrow ^{256}_{101}Md + ^{1}_{0}n$
102	No	Nobelium	$^{246}_{96}Cm + ^{12}_{6}C \longrightarrow ^{254}_{102}No + 4^{1}_{0}n$
103	Lr	Lawrencium	$^{252}_{98}Cf + ^{10}_{5}B \longrightarrow ^{257}_{103}Lr + 5^{1}_{0}n$
104	Unq	Unnilquadium	$^{249}_{98}Cf + ^{12}_{6}C \longrightarrow ^{257}_{104}Unq + 4^{1}_{0}n$
105	Unp	Unnilpentium	$^{249}_{98}Cf + ^{15}_{7}N \longrightarrow ^{260}_{105}Unp + 4^{1}_{0}n$
106	Unh	Unnilhexium	$^{249}_{98}Cf + ^{18}_{8}O \longrightarrow ^{263}_{106}Unh + 4^{1}_{0}n$

12.7 (d is used for deuterium, $^{2}_{1}H$)

$$\overset{\text{bombarding particle}}{\searrow} \quad \overset{\text{product particles}}{\swarrow}$$
$$^{238}_{92}U(d,\, 2n)\, ^{238}_{93}Np$$

EXAMPLE 12.6
Nuclear Equations

Many neutrons, α-particles, and other particles are produced in reactions between cosmic rays and nuclei near the top of the earth's atmosphere. Most of the neutrons produced then react with ^{14}N to produce ^{14}C, as shown by the shorthand notation

$$^{14}N(n,\, p)^{14}C$$

Write the nuclear equation for this reaction.

The shorthand notation indicates that the bombarding particle is a neutron, $^{1}_{0}n$, and the product particle is a proton, $^{1}_{1}H$. The reactant nuclide is ^{14}N and the product nuclide is $^{14}_{6}C$. The complete nuclear equation is

$$^{14}_{7}N + ^{1}_{0}n \longrightarrow ^{14}_{6}C + ^{1}_{1}H$$

Exercise Write the shorthand notation for the equation

$$^{242}_{96}Cm + ^{4}_{2}He \longrightarrow ^{245}_{98}Cf + ^{1}_{0}n$$

Answer $^{242}Cm(\alpha,\, n)^{245}Cf$

12.14 RADIATION AND MATTER

During the decay of a radioactive nuclide, mass is lost and energy is released. The energy is given up mainly as the kinetic energy of the particles and nuclei produced in the reaction. These particles and nuclei collide with the atoms and molecules of their surroundings, gradually losing energy. What happens to the atoms and molecules of the irradiated matter depends on several things, including the state and type of matter, the energy of the radiation, and the type of radiation. Valence electrons may be knocked out of atoms and molecules to produce ions, or they may be pushed up to excited states and then emit x-rays as they return to the ground state. Highly reactive free radicals (atoms or molecules with unpaired electrons) may be produced. In some

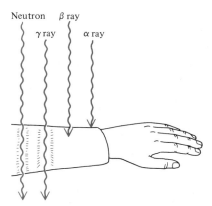

Neutron β ray

γ ray α ray

Figure 12.13
Penetration of Radiation

cases, anions are formed or chemical bonds are broken. Electromagnetic radiation (x-rays and γ rays) and subatomic particle radiation (α rays, β rays, neutrons, etc.) from radioactive sources are collectively referred to as *ionizing radiation.* The study of the interaction of ionizing radiation with matter is the concern of *radiation chemistry.*

The distance that ionizing radiation travels depends upon the medium that it encounters and the type of radiation. γ Rays are highly penetrating, and neutrons even more so. Aluminum 5 to 11 cm thick is required to stop most γ rays, which can penetrate deeply into the human body or even pass through it. β Rays are considerably less penetrating than γ rays. In air, β rays can travel for several meters, but they penetrate only a few millimeters into human tissue. α Rays, with their heavier, doubly charged particles, are the least penetrating natural radiation. Typical α-particles will travel only a few centimeters in air and are stopped by a sheet of paper or a layer of clothing (Figure 12.13).

If radiation originates outside the body, γ radiation and neutron radiation are most hazardous; the body is easily shielded from α- and β-particles. Neutron radiation is very damaging because the neutrons, being uncharged, collide with nuclei. High-energy neutrons cause recoil of nuclei that can break bonds; lower energy neutrons are captured to give radionuclides that release further radioactivity. If radioactive material is created in the body or enters the body through a wound or by being inhaled or swallowed, α-particles become more dangerous. Internally, they give up all of their energy to the tissue in a very small distance, causing great damage.

A variety of units are used to measure the interaction of radiation with matter. For reference they are summarized in Table 12.8. The roentgen measures x- or γ radiation by the number of ions it produces while passing through the air. Geiger counters (Figure 12.14), commonly used to detect the presence of radioactive materials, are often calibrated in roentgens.

Comparison of the amounts of radiation to which human beings are exposed is best done in terms of the rem (roentgen equivalent man). This unit takes into account not only the amount of energy delivered by the radiation, but also the variation in the biological effects of different types of radiation.

Everyone is exposed to radiation from the environment. Those who live at high elevations or travel often in jet planes receive more exposure to cosmic rays than

Table 12.8
Radiation Units

Unit	Quantity Measured	Definition of Unit
Roentgen (R)	Exposure to x-rays or γ rays	Radiation that produces 2×10^9 ion pairs in 1 cm³ of dry air at normal temperature and pressure
Rad (radiation adsorbed dose)	Energy absorbed by tissue	1×10^{-5} J absorbed per gram of tissue
Gray (Gy) (SI unit)	Energy absorbed by tissue	1 J/kg tissue (1 gray = 100 rad)
RBE (relative biological effectiveness)	Factor relating effects of different types of radiation	Comparison to γ rays from cobalt-60
Rem (roentgen equivalent man)	Dose to human beings	Rems = rads × RBE (1 rem = same effect in man as 1 roentgen)
Curie (Ci)	Activity	3.7×10^{10} disintegrations/s
Becquerel (Bq) (SI unit)	Activity	1 disintegration/s
Rutherford (Rd)	Activity	10^6 disintegrations/s
Linear energy transfer (LET)	Energy transferred	Energy lost per unit path length (varies with material irradiated)

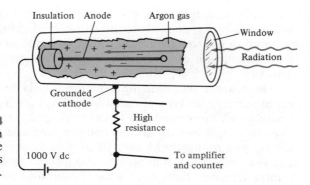

Figure 12.14
Geiger Counter The radiation ionizes the argon gas in the tube and the resulting electric current is measured.

those who pass their lives at sea level. Uranium and its decay products are present in natural building materials, and living in a stone or brick house increases radiation exposure compared to living in a wooden house. Smoking one pack of cigarettes a day yields 40 mrem/yr of exposure to radiation from radioactive isotopes that concentrate in tobacco leaves. Potassium is an essential element for plants and we take in small amounts of potassium-40 with all foods that contain potassium. (We note in passing that Brazil nuts and caviar have been reported to contain abnormally high levels of radioactive isotopes.) Table 12.9 summarizes radiation exposure as averaged over the whole population of the United States.

How seriously an organism is damaged by ionizing radiation depends on many factors and varies from individual to individual. An irradiated organism or plant may undergo *somatic effects*—changes in its own cell structure, immediate or delayed, that may be damaging but will not be passed on to future generations. It may also suffer *genetic effects*—changes in the genes that will produce physical changes in future generations.

Intense short-term exposure to radiation, as in an accident with radioactive materials, leads to immediate somatic damage. A 25 rem exposure, about the lowest level detectable by blood tests, raises the white blood cell count. In a few months the blood will return to normal. With exposure to 200 rem, nausea and fatigue are induced and infection-fighting capability is reduced. This level of radiation can cause death in six weeks or so. A dose of 400 rem will be fatal to 50% of those exposed by causing damage to the bone marrow and spleen.

Radionuclides that are incorporated into the body cause damage by exposure over a long time span. For example, cancer may be initiated by radioactive iodine that concentrates in the thyroid gland, or by radioactive calcium, strontium, and

Table 12.9
Background Radiation Estimated annual average whole-body dose rates from all sources of ionizing radiations in the United States. *Source:* From R. A. Bailey et al., *Chemistry of the Environment,* New York: Academic Press, 1978, p. 537.

Source	Dose Rate (mrem/yr)
Natural background	
Cosmic rays	45
Terrestrial radiation	
External	40
Internal (^{40}K)	17
Fallout (from weapons tests, 1955–1962)	4
Nuclear power (since 1970)	0.003–0.01
Medical (x-rays, tracer isotopes)	90
Occupational	1
Miscellaneous (color TV, air travel, etc.)	3
Total	**200**

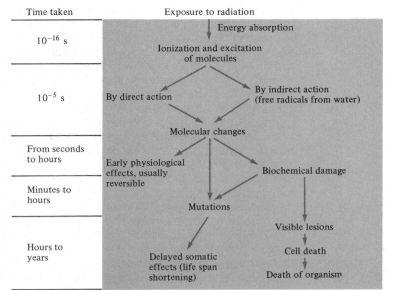

Figure 12.15
Effects of Radiation Exposure The time after radiation exposure at which various effects, depending on the degree of exposure, can occur. Molecular changes in cells are caused both directly by the radiation and indirectly by free radicals formed by irradiation of water molecules. (Source: P. N. Tiwari, *Fundamentals of Nuclear Science,* New Delhi, India: Wiley Eastern Limited, 1974, p. 131.)

radium that concentrate in bones. At one time, luminescent radium-containing paint was widely used in watch and instrument dials. However, the radiation from radium is hazardous and other materials have been substituted for it. In the 1920s, many women painting watch dials developed bone cancer because they were in the habit of pointing the tips of their paint brushes by licking them.

Longer term exposure to low levels of background radiation can lead to mutations—changes in the structure of the DNA molecule that carries the code of heredity. What percentage of mutations are due to background radiation is difficult to estimate, as there are other natural causes of such effects.

Figure 12.15 is a generalized summary of the possible effects of radiation exposure on plants and/or animals.

AN ASIDE

Uses of Radioisotopes

Each distinctive property of radioisotopes has been put to use in dozens of ways in fields ranging from chemical synthesis to medicine, to agriculture, to manufacturing and engineering.

We have already mentioned the dating of historical artifacts, a procedure based on the constancy of the rate of decay of isotopes. Many other applications arise simply because a radioisotope is continuously emitting radiation that can be detected and measured, making it possible to monitor the location of the isotope. Radioactive tracers have helped to follow the course of underground water supplies, and a large number of isotopes are used as diagnostic tools in medicine. Specific isotopes find their way in the body to specific organs, and by emitting radiation from these locations, make the organ visible to a radiation-detecting camera. For example, thallium-201 concentrates in normal heart muscle, allowing determination by the dark areas on the film of the amount of damage caused by a heart attack. Complementary information is obtained with technetium-99m, which is taken up by damaged heart cells, but not by healthy ones.

One of the first applications of radioisotopes was based on the ability of radiation to destroy cells—radiation therapy for cancer, in which the malignant cells are wiped out. In another application of this property, male insects have been irradiated to destroy their reproductive cells. For instance, millions of sterile flies were released near cattle farms, where they mated with female flies, who then produced no offspring. In this way, the screwworm fly, which does great damage to livestock, has been eliminated in several areas.

In chemistry and biochemistry, radioactive labeling of compounds has revealed much information about how reactions take place. By determining in which of the reaction products the radioactive atom winds up, the route of the atom through intermediate chemical and metabolic processes can be worked out. For example, in photosynthesis green plants convert water and carbon dioxide into carbohydrates and oxygen. Until the 1940s it was always assumed that the oxygen released in this reaction comes from the CO_2, while the carbon is combined with water to form carbohydrate. Use of a radioactive isotope of oxygen as a "tracer," however, showed, in fact, that all the oxygen released comes from the water. In the late 1940s and early 1950s the very complex series of reactions by which carbohydrates are made in photosynthesis was elucidated with the help of radioisotope labeling. Similarly, isotopic labeling revealed that, contrary to what had been believed, protein molecules in the liver, although their number remains unchanged, are constantly being synthesized and destroyed at equal rates.

The heat generated by radioactive decay can be converted to electricity in nuclear-powered batteries for use in remote locations, such as the moon. Plutonium-238 powers a tiny battery used in heart pacemakers implanted in the human body. The long life of the isotope allows the battery to function for almost 10 years before an operation must be performed to replace it.

The regular variation in the penetration by radiation of materials of various thicknesses has found many industrial and engineering applications. The thickness of a film of plastic passing over a set of rollers as it is formed can be monitored by radiation passing through the film. This information is then fed back electronically to control the machinery and regulate the thickness of the product.

We shall mention just one more item in this sampling of applications of radioactivity — neutron activation analysis, which is a valuable technique for measuring the concentration of small amounts of elements. The great advantage of neutron activation analysis is that the sample is not destroyed in the process. For example, irradiating an old Dutch painting with neutrons forms silver-110m from the traces of silver in white pigment. The amount of silver present can be found from the γ-ray spectrum of the isotope. A change in silver extraction methods in the mid-nineteenth century decreased the amount of silver impurity in the white pigment made after that time. Therefore, the amount of silver-110m present in the pigment reflects the date when a painting was made.

12.15 NUCLEAR FISSION

In a single nuclear fission event, one atom of a heavy fissionable isotope splits into two atoms of intermediate mass and several neutrons. Fission can be initiated by bombardment with many types of particles or by γ radiation, and many heavy nuclides can undergo fission. Some do so spontaneously. The neutron-induced fission of natural uranium-235 and of artificial plutonium-239 are fission reactions of practical importance.

The history of the discovery of nuclear fission is intertwined with the history of World War II (see A Historical Aside: The Atomic Bomb). Uranium-235 and plutonium-239 were the fissionable isotopes used in the first atomic bombs. Uranium-235 fission produces a wide array of nuclides, with many of mass numbers near 95 and 139 (Figure 12.16), together with varying amounts of energy. Most of the nuclides produced are radioactive and continue to decay through as many steps as are necessary to reach a stable neutron–proton ratio. These nuclides provide an ongoing source of radiation in the environment.

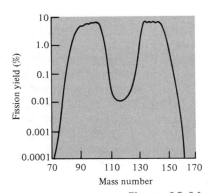

Figure 12.16
Distribution of Isotopes in the Slow-Neutron-Induced Fission of Uranium-235 On the average, 2.5 neutrons and 200 MeV per fission are also produced.

The single fact of greatest significance for the use of nuclear energy is that fission produces more than one neutron per fission event. Enough neutrons are thus available to keep the fission going. A series of reactions in which the products of the reactions initiate other similar reactions, so that the series can be self-sustaining, is called a **chain reaction.** Nuclear fission becomes a self-sustaining chain reaction when the number of neutrons emitted equals or is greater than the number of neutrons absorbed by fissioning nuclei plus those lost to the surroundings. The **critical mass** of a fissionable material is the smallest mass that will support a self-sustaining chain reaction under a given set of conditions.

Critical mass is affected by many factors, including the geometry of the sample of fissionable material. In the first atomic bomb to be exploded (the Trinity Test; see Thoughts on Chemistry: The Atomic Age Begins), a sphere of plutonium was compressed to a critical mass by the force of exploding TNT. The rapid chain reaction that is set off by assembly of a critical mass continues until the force of the explosion disperses the fuel (Figure 12.17a).

By controlling the rate of a chain reaction, energy can be produced slowly enough to allow its use for constructive rather than destructive purposes. The term **nuclear reactor** is usually applied to the equipment in which fission is carried out at a controlled rate (Figure 12.17b).

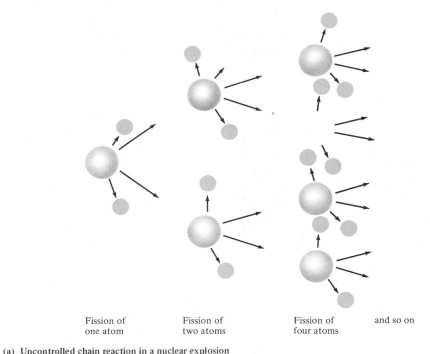

Fission of one atom   Fission of two atoms   Fission of four atoms   and so on

(a) Uncontrolled chain reaction in a nuclear explosion

Figure 12.17
Chain Reactions (a) In an uncontrolled chain reaction, the fission of each atom releases enough high-energy neutrons to initiate the fission of more than one new atom. Fission of all the fuel available takes place rapidly and with explosive force. (b) In a nuclear reactor the chain reaction is controlled so that each fission initiates the fission of only one more atom, and energy is released at a controlled rate.

(b) Controlled nuclear reaction in a nuclear reactor

12.16 NUCLEAR FUSION

So far, continuous nuclear fusion has been observed only in the sun and other stars. The conversion of hydrogen to helium in the sequence of fusion reactions shown in Table 12.10 is the main source of solar energy.

Nuclei must approach each other with a large amount of energy if they are to overcome the electrostatic repulsion between their positive charges and be able to fuse. Particles can be given enough energy in an accelerator to fuse with target atoms, and fusion was known and understood several years before the discovery of fission. However, in an accelerator bombardment reaction, only a random few atoms collide and fuse, while a large amount of energy is expended by the accelerator. Useful extraction of energy from nuclear fusion is not possible under these conditions.

The temperature in the center of the sun is about 1.5×10^7 K. At such a high temperature, atoms are stripped of electrons, forming a *plasma*—a neutral mixture of ions and electrons at a high temperature. Within a dense, very hot plasma, light nuclei are moving fast enough for large numbers of them to collide and fuse, releasing large amounts of energy in the process. Nuclear reactions at very high temperatures (roughly $> 10^6$ K) are called **thermonuclear reactions.**

To produce the temperature needed for thermonuclear fusion on earth once seemed impossible. But man-made nuclear fission, in the form of the atomic bomb, provided the match needed to light a large-scale fusion reaction. The result was the "H bomb" first tested at Bikini atoll in the Pacific Ocean in 1952.

In very general terms, a hydrogen bomb can be pictured as a fission bomb surrounded by the compound formed by deuterium (hydrogen-2) and lithium-6, $^6_3\text{Li}^2_1\text{H}$. The sequence of reactions is

$$\text{fission bomb} \longrightarrow \text{heat} + \text{neutrons} \tag{12.14}$$

$$^6_3\text{Li} + ^1_0n \longrightarrow ^4_2\text{He} + ^3_1\text{H} + 4.78 \text{ MeV} \tag{12.15}$$

$$^2_1\text{H} + ^3_1\text{H} \longrightarrow ^4_2\text{He} + ^1_0n + 17.6 \text{ MeV} \tag{12.16}$$

where the energy released is equivalent to the loss in mass in the reaction.

The reaction of lithium and neutrons is used to produce tritium for the fusion reaction between tritium and deuterium. The energy release per nuclear fusion is roughly one-tenth that released per nuclear fission event. (Compare 200 MeV per uranium-235 fission with 17.6 MeV per deuterium–tritium reaction.) However, the yield from a thermonuclear explosion for a given quantity of fuel is much greater than that from a fission explosion for several reasons: because of the smaller mass of lithium and deuterium compared to that of uranium, because new fusionable nuclei are produced in the explosion, and possibly also because a larger proportion of the fuel is consumed. Fortunately, thermonuclear weapons have so far been used only in tests.

Table 12.10

Nuclear Reactions in the Stars This sequence of reactions occurs in the sun and other stars of similar mass.

Overall reaction:
$4 \ ^1_1\text{H} \longrightarrow \ ^4_2\text{He} + 2 \ ^0_{+1}\beta + 26.7 \text{ MeV}$
$^1_1\text{H} + ^1_1\text{H} \longrightarrow \ ^2_1\text{H} + ^0_{+1}\beta$
$^2_1\text{H} + ^1_1\text{H} \longrightarrow \ ^3_2\text{He} + \gamma$
$^3_2\text{He} + ^3_2\text{He} \longrightarrow \ ^4_2\text{He} + 2 \ ^1_1\text{H}$

A HISTORICAL ASIDE

The Atomic Bomb

At the end of the 1930s, turmoil had come to Europe. Refugees were fleeing troubled countries and national energies were being turned to war and defense.

In 1938 Otto Hahn, a chemist at the Kaiser Wilhelm Institute in Berlin, identified barium in a sample of uranium that had been bombarded by slow neutrons. He dared to write of the discovery to Lise Meitner, a former colleague who had fled from Germany to Sweden. It was Christmas time and Lise Meitner's nephew Otto Frisch, a physicist working at Niels Bohr's Institute of Theoretical Physics in Copenhagen, was visiting her. They walked together in the snow near Gothenburg; while sitting on a log they figured out how fission of a heavy nucleus into smaller fragments could release a large amount of energy. Frisch went back to his laboratory, measured the speed of a barium nucleus released in uranium bombardment by neutrons, and found that it was what they had thought it would be—very fast.

Nuclear fission was announced on February 11, 1939. The news caused great excitement among physicists, and about a month later Leo Szilard made clear the implications of the discovery for a world heading for war. Szilard showed that in each fission of a uranium atom, two or three neutrons were released. This meant one thing—a terrible explosive force could be released in a nuclear fission chain reaction.

An extraordinary group of refugees in America, physicists all, drafted a letter to President Franklin Roosevelt. Szilard, Edward Teller, and Eugene Wigner, all Hungarians; Victor Weisskopf, an Austrian; and the brilliant Italian, Enrico Fermi, explained the potential of nuclear fission, and warned that Germany might already be working to build a nuclear bomb. So that their warning would carry more weight, they persuaded Albert Einstein, the world's most famous and respected scientist, to sign the letter.

President Roosevelt was impressed enough by the letter to authorize financial assistance to American universities studying nuclear reactions. The major problem was the production of the fissionable isotopes needed for a bomb. Progress was slow. Then, in December, 1941, the Japanese attacked Pearl Harbor and the United States was at war with Japan as well as with Germany. An all-out crash program to develop an atomic bomb—the Manhattan Project—was launched. So uncertain was the knowledge of what had to be done that it was decided to press ahead simultaneously on several different approaches to making fuel out of either uranium or plutonium, in the hope that one would work.

Under the direction of J. Robert Oppenheimer the design and construction of the bomb was undertaken by the most impressive collection of scientific talent ever assembled. The site was a ranch school in Los Alamos, New Mexico. A group of physicists that included numerous Nobel prize winners found themselves facing a new and different challenge. As one put it, they had to change from "probing the deep-seated secrets of nature to producing a device that worked."

Proceeding at an increasingly feverish pace, they succeeded. On July 16, 1945, the Trinity Test—the first explosion of a nuclear fission bomb—took place in the desert in New Mexico, in what the Spanish had called the Jornada del Muerto Valley—the Journey of Death Valley, a strangely appropriate name. The Trinity device was a plutonium bomb. A second bomb made from uranium leveled the Japanese city of Hiroshima on August 6, 1945, six years almost to the day after delivery of the letter to President Roosevelt. A third bomb was dropped on Nagasaki on August 9, 1945. Five days later Japan surrendered.

NUCLEAR ENERGY

Nuclear reactors provided 12% of the electrical energy generated in the United States in 1981. Early in 1981 the relative amount of power generated in nuclear power plants exceeded that generated by oil-fired power plants. Where nuclear power generation will be in the total United States and world energy picture in the year 2000, or even 10 years from now, is difficult to predict. A plethora of government agencies, private foundations, public interest groups, and industrial organizations are evaluating our energy needs and problems. Political, economic, and social issues, including the public perception of danger from nuclear power, make a significant contribution to decisions about developing nuclear power. In some cases, the scientific and technological facts bear heavily on the decisions, in others they appear to play only a minor role.

Virtually all commercial nuclear power in the United States is generated in light water reactors of two types, either pressurized water or boiling water reactors (Section 12.17). The future of nuclear power may lie with breeder reactors (Section 12.18) or with nuclear fusion reactors (Section 12.19).

12.17 FISSION REACTORS

A nuclear fission reactor cooled by light water has five essential parts (Figure 12.18):

1. *Fuel.* The fuel is a core of fissionable material. Light water reactors use enriched uranium oxide, U_3O_8, in which the natural 0.7% of uranium-235

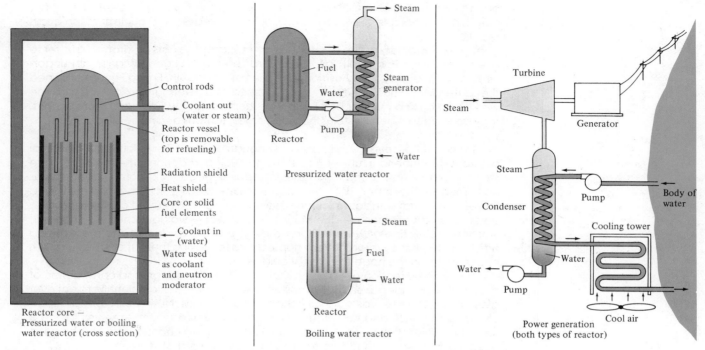

Figure 12.18

Light Water Nuclear Reactors Both boiling water and pressurized water reactors generate electricity from steam in the same way that it is generated in a coal-fired power station. Note that the coolant is in a closed system and does not come in contact with the outside body of water. Both nuclear and coal-fired power stations need cooling water; the thermal pollution (temperature rise in a natural body of water used for cooling) is somewhat greater for nuclear reactors. (Source: Glenn T. Seaborg and William R. Corliss, *Man and Atom: Building a New World through Nuclear Technology,* copyright © 1971 by Glenn T. Seaborg and William R. Corliss, reprinted by permission of the publishers, E. P. Dutton.)

has been raised to the 2%–3% uranium-235 needed for efficient operation. The fuel is formed into solid elements with a protective coating.

2. *Moderator.* The fast neutrons produced in fission must be slowed down to speeds at which they produce the fission reaction most efficiently (the slower moving neutrons are called *thermal neutrons*). Neutrons must be able to lose energy by colliding with the nuclei of the moderator, without being absorbed by or reacting with the moderator. Materials with a large proportion of hydrogen atoms are good moderators. Light water reactors are so called because they use ordinary water as the moderator (as opposed to "heavy" water, D_2O). Graphite is also a good moderator.

3. *Control system.* Just enough free slow neutrons are needed to carry on the chain reaction at a safe rate (see Figure 12.17). If too many neutrons initiate fission, more heat would build up than could be carried away. This condition could lead to the most serious type of nuclear reactor accident, a meltdown, in which the fuel core, and eventually its container, would melt.

In a light water reactor control rods containing boron are raised and lowered in between the fuel elements so that unneeded neutrons are removed by the reaction

$$^{10}_{5}B + ^{1}_{0}n \longrightarrow ^{7}_{3}Li + ^{4}_{2}\alpha$$

Enough control rods are available to completely stop the reaction by lowering all of them into the spaces between the radioactive rods.

4. *Cooling system.* The energy of the fission reaction must be carried away for transformation into electrical power and to keep the reactor from overheating as well. In *pressurized water reactors,* liquid water under pressure is the coolant; in *boiling water reactors* steam is the coolant (see Figure 12.18).

5. *Shielding.* Both the walls of the reactor and the personnel operating the reactor must be protected from heat and radiation. In addition, the entire nuclear reactor is enclosed in a heavy steel or concrete dome that is intended to contain the radioactive materials that might be set free in a serious reactor accident.

The major technological problems facing the present day nuclear power industry are in the fuel cycle:

1. *Isotope separation.* The process is costly in both dollars and energy. All enrichment in this country is presently done in three gaseous diffusion plants operated by the U.S. government. These plants, originally built to produce fuels for weapons, cost $2.3 billion to build and use very large amounts of electricity. As pointed out above (Section 12.4), less costly methods are being sought.

2. *Reprocessing of spent fuel.* Much slower progress has been made toward successful operation of reprocessing plants than toward successful reactor operation. Meanwhile, stockpiles of spent fuel are growing. As natural uranium ores are depleted, the need for reprocessing will become greater.

3. *Waste storage.* Permanent solutions to the storage of wastes that remain radioactive for thousands of years have not been found. The most practical approach to storing high-level waste appears to be conversion to a solid form (e.g., the very stable mineral monazite) and burial in a geologically stable location such as a salt mine.

AN ASIDE

Nature's Nuclear Reactor

A remarkable discovery in 1972 in the Gabon Republic in West Africa has shown that nature, not man, created the first nuclear fission reactor. Between 1.7 and 1.9 billion years ago, in what is now an open-pit uranium mine at a place called Oklo, a rich deposit of uranium ore began operating as a natural fission reactor.

The clue that led to discovery of the reactor was the finding in May, 1972, that the uranium-235 content of the uranium taken from the mine was significantly less than that generally encountered. The search for the cause of this discrepancy led to the conclusion that the uranium-235 has been depleted through nuclear fission.

Elements that are usually formed in the fission of uranium-235 were found in veins of the ore depleted in that isotope. Moreover, the quantities of these elements and their isotopic composition could be accounted for *only* by their origin in fission.

A truly extraordinary series of events had to occur for nature to have assembled the reactor. Uranium from an entire watershed had to be washed into the Oklo region to yield concentrated deposits. Operation of the nuclear chain reaction would have required a concentration of uranium in the ore of at least 10%, with a minimum of 1% of uranium-235. Since uranium-235 decays more rapidly ($t_{\frac{1}{2}} = 700$ million years) than uranium-238 ($t_{\frac{1}{2}} = 4.5$ billion years), uranium-235 must have been much more abundant in the past. It has been estimated that at the time of the formation of the earth the total natural abundance of uranium-235 was about 17% and that 1.7–1.9 billion years ago when the reactor began to function, the abundance was about 3%. On the basis of the necessary 1% of uranium-235, a natural fission reactor could have operated at Oklo up until about 400 million years ago.

To sustain an appropriate flow of neutrons required a seam of uranium ore at least 2 m thick. Also required was a natural mechanism for moderating the high-energy neutrons given off by the fissioning uranium nuclei. Such moderation was apparently provided by the hydrogen atoms of water. About 6% water by mass would give the optimum moderation for an ore about 2 billion years old. Water of crystallization (water chemically bound to the minerals in the ore) would have satisfied this condition. The ore deposit was probably also saturated with ground water, which might have slowed down the neutrons too much. However, once a chain reaction had begun, some loss of water by evaporation due to the heat released could have supplied conditions favorable for moderation.

The evidence indicates that besides the fission of uranium-235, conversion of uranium-238 to plutonium-239 through the same sequence of reactions used in modern breeder reactors (see Equations 12.18–12.20) also occurred at Oklo. Plutonium-239 decays by α-particle emission to uranium-235.

12.18 BREEDER REACTORS

A **breeder reactor** can produce at least as many fissionable atoms as it consumes. The primary advantages of a breeder reactor are that it is able to convert uranium-238 or thorium-232, both naturally more plentiful than uranium-235, into fissionable fuel, and that it is thermally more efficient than the light water reactors because it can operate at higher temperatures. Current light water reactors have a once-through fuel cycle — no fuel is reprocessed or re-used. Such reactors liberate only 0.6% of the fission energy available in the fuel. By using breeder reactors and also recycling fuel, up to 70% of the available energy might be set free. The excess fissionable artificial isotopes (uranium-233 or plutonium-239) produced in a breeder can be used as fuel for other reactors. The first prototype breeder reactor for power generation began operation in 1972 in the Soviet Union.

The type of breeder reactor closest to commercial development in the United States is the liquid metal fast breeder. It uses a liquid metal such as sodium as the coolant, and the neutrons need not be moderated (hence "fast breeder"). The following equations show the reaction cycle in a fast breeder reactor fueled by plutonium-239 bred from uranium-238.

$$^{238}_{92}\text{U} + {}^{1}_{0}n \longrightarrow {}^{239}_{92}\text{U} \tag{12.17}$$

$$^{239}_{92}\text{U} \xrightarrow{t_{\frac{1}{2}} = 24 \text{ min}} {}^{239}_{93}\text{Np} + {}^{0}_{-1}\beta \tag{12.18}$$

$$^{239}_{93}\text{Np} \xrightarrow{t_{\frac{1}{2}} = 2.4 \text{ days}} {}^{239}_{94}\text{Pu} + {}^{0}_{-1}\beta \tag{12.19}$$

$$^{239}_{94}\text{Pu} + {}^{1}_{0}n \longrightarrow \text{fission products} + (2-3){}^{1}_{0}n + \text{energy} \tag{12.20}$$

It has been predicted that breeder reactors could be available for commercial power generation in the United States by the year 2000. But a few major questions remain about the advisability of developing large-scale breeder reactors. First, do we need the power and fuel economy of the breeders enough to risk having to handle large amounts of plutonium-239, a material so poisonous that inhaling a tiny speck of it can be fatal? Second, how great a risk is incurred by making available in various parts of the country and in transit plutonium-239, which is much more readily used in nuclear weapons than enriched uranium? The answers to these questions lie as much in the realm of politics, economics, and philosophy as in the realms of science and technology.

12.19 FUSION REACTORS

The problem of igniting, controlling, and maintaining a fusion reaction in a power plant has been called the greatest technological challenge taken up by man. Light atoms must be held together in a vacuum at high density, at a high enough temperature, and for a long enough time for the thermonuclear fusion to take place.

Confinement of nuclear fusion in a vessel is not possible for two reasons: (1) the

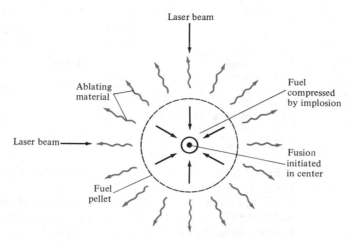

Laser beam

Ablating
material

Fuel
compressed
by implosion

Laser beam

Fusion
initiated
in center

Fuel
pellet

Figure 12.19
Nuclear Fusion by Inertial
Confinement in a Laser Beam The
synchronized laser beam rapidly
heats the pellet. In ablating, or
burning away of the surface, the
center of the pellet is compressed to
a pressure great enough to cause
fusion (10^{12} atm).

reacting nuclei and electrons, which have such high energy that they are traveling at several hundred miles per second, would lose their energy as soon as they struck the walls and before fusion could occur; (2) in striking the walls the particles would knock atoms out of the walls and these impurities would contribute to a loss of energy in the reaction system. Two major approaches to containing nuclear fusion are being investigated — magnetic confinement and inertial confinement.

If a large enough current is passed through a plasma parallel to the axis of a magnetic field, the plasma is pinched in and pulled away from the walls of the container, forming a so-called magnetic bottle. Plasma behavior in such a field has turned out to be very complex, but gradually it is being understood, and experiments are coming closer and closer to plasma confinement under the conditions needed for fusion. In 1980 the U.S. Congress passed the Magnetic Fusion Engineering Act, with the goal of having a demonstration fusion power plant in operation by the year 2000.

The basic concept of inertial confinement is that a small sphere of fuel is made to react before it has time to fly apart. In laser fusion, a powerful laser beam strikes a sphere of fuel with such energy that some of the surface material is vaporized. The resulting shock wave compresses the fuel at the center of the sphere, both bringing the nuclei close enough together and raising the temperature to the point where fusion can occur (Figure 12.19).

The fusion of deuterium and tritium to give helium (the reaction used in the hydrogen bomb; Equation 12.16) is the prime candidate for the major reaction in thermonuclear power plants (Table 12.11). Deuterium is available in huge quantities in the oceans and obtaining it would be easy and relatively inexpensive. Two reaction schemes have been proposed for fusion reactors, one involving lithium as a breeder for tritium, as in reactions (12.14) to (12.16) and the other involving only deuterium, as follows:

$$\frac{2}{1}H + \frac{2}{1}H \longrightarrow \frac{3}{1}H + \frac{1}{1}H + 4.0 \text{ MeV}$$
$$\frac{2}{1}H + \frac{2}{1}H \longrightarrow \frac{3}{2}He + \frac{1}{0}n + 3.3 \text{ MeV}$$
$$\frac{2}{1}H + \frac{3}{1}H \longrightarrow \frac{4}{2}He + \frac{1}{0}n + 17.6 \text{ MeV}$$
$$\overline{5 \frac{2}{1}H \longrightarrow \frac{4}{2}He + \frac{3}{2}He + \frac{1}{1}H + 2 \frac{1}{0}n + 24.9 \text{ MeV}}$$

The heat produced in fusion reactions can be converted to electricity by conventional turbines, as in light water reactors. However, converting fusion energy more directly and efficiently to other forms of energy is being considered. One plan is to use fusion energy directly to split water into hydrogen and oxygen, and then to produce methane (CH_4) from the hydrogen. Methane can be used as a fuel, or built up into larger carbon–hydrogen compounds like those derived from petroleum.

Table 12.11

Some Fusion Reactions The energy ratio compares the potential of the reactions for use in commercial energy production. The deuterium–tritium reaction is most favorable. The other combinations are spoken of as advanced fuels.

Reaction	Energy Produced (keV)	Energy Required for Ignition (keV)	Energy Ratio (Energy Produced/ Energy Required)
$^2_1H + {}^3_1H \longrightarrow {}^4_2He + {}^1_0n$	17,600	10	1,760
$^2_1H + {}^2_1H \longrightarrow {}^3_2He + {}^1_0n$	3,300	50	66
$^2_1H + {}^2_1H \longrightarrow {}^3_1H + {}^1_1p$	4,000	50	80
$^2_1H + {}^3_2He \longrightarrow {}^4_2He + {}^1_1p$	18,300	100	183
$^1_1p + {}^{11}_5B \longrightarrow 3{}^4_2He$	8,700	300	29

Another plan is to use hydrogen directly as fuel (see An Aside: The Hydrogen Economy, Chapter 16).

Fusion reactors would have a number of advantages over fission reactors, including (1) the lower cost and unlimited supply of the fuel; (2) the worldwide availability of the fuel, thereby avoiding international tensions over obtaining it; (3) the potential for production of energy at a lower cost.

SUMMARY

12.1 THE NUCLEUS The general term for an isotope of any element is a nuclide. Protons and neutrons—nucleons—are bound together in the extremely dense atomic nucleus by the nuclear force, the strongest known force in nature.

12.2 MASS, ENERGY, AND NUCLEAR BINDING ENERGY In nuclear reactions the compositions of nuclei, and thus the identities of atoms, are changed. Mass and energy are interconvertible ($E = mc^2$) and mass–energy is conserved. In nuclear reactions the energy absorbed or released is great enough for the corresponding changes in mass to be measured. The difference between the mass of an atom and the combined masses of its component particles is the mass defect; the missing mass represents the nuclear binding energy, the energy released in the combination of the nucleons to form the nucleus. Nuclear fusion is the combination of two light nuclei to give a heavier nucleus. Nuclear fission is the splitting of a heavy nucleus into two lighter nuclei. Both of these processes release energy.

12.3 RADIOACTIVITY: NATURAL AND ARTIFICIAL **12.4** PROPERTIES OF ISOTOPES Radioactivity is the spontaneous emission of particles and/or radiation by unstable nuclei. Nuclides that decay spontaneously are called radioisotopes or radionuclides. Some radionuclides are found in nature; others are man made. All elements with $Z > 83$ are radioactive. Nuclides of the same element (isotopes) have nearly identical physical and chemical properties, which makes separation of isotopes very difficult.

12.5 NEUTRON–PROTON RATIO **12.6** COSMIC ABUNDANCE AND NUCLEAR STABILITY Light nuclides are generally stable when their nuclei have about equal numbers of protons and neutrons (neutron–proton ratio $\simeq 1$). As the elements increase in atomic mass, the neutron–proton ratio necessary for stability increases. Unstable, radioactive nuclides decay in such a way as to achieve more stable neutron–proton ratios. Nuclides with even numbers of nucleons are more stable and abundant than those with odd numbers of nucleons; certain numbers of nucleons, called magic numbers, confer an especially high degree of stability.

12.7 HALF-LIFE **12.8** RADIOISOTOPE DATING The half-life ($t_{\frac{1}{2}}$) of a radionuclide is the time it takes for half the nuclei in any sample to decay. Knowing the half-life of a nuclide enables us to find the amount of a given sample remaining after a specific time, or the age of a sample. The constant rate of radioactive decay is the basis for radioisotope dating.

12.9 TYPES OF RADIATION **12.10** WRITING EQUATIONS FOR NUCLEAR REACTIONS γ Rays are high-energy, short-wavelength electromagnetic radiation. α Particles are helium nuclei, $^4_2He^{2+}$, symbolized $^4_2\alpha$ (see Table 12.3). β Particles are electrons, symbolized $^0_{-1}\beta$. In nuclear reactions, both mass numbers and nuclear charge must be conserved.

12.11 SPONTANEOUS RADIOACTIVE DECAY **12.12** NATURAL RADIOACTIVE SERIES In γ decay, excited nuclei return to their ground states by emitting γ rays—quantized electromagnetic radiation. In α decay, a radionuclide emits an α-particle. β Decay includes electron emission, positron emission, and electron capture. Conservation of energy is maintained in β decay because a variable amount of energy is carried away by massless, chargeless particles called neutrinos and antineutrinos. The effects of radioactive decay are summarized in Table 12.5. The heavy natural radionuclides are members of three series, each with a long-lived parent and a stable isotope of lead as the end product.

12.13 BOMBARDMENT Nuclear reactions can be produced by bombardment of nuclei with subatomic particles of high kinetic energy. This technique has been used to synthesize the transuranium elements: elements with atomic numbers above 92.

12.14 RADIATION AND MATTER High-energy electromagnetic radiation (x-rays and γ rays) and subatomic particles (α-particles, β-particles, protons, and neutrons) from radioactive decay are known collectively as ionizing radiation. Such radiation can cause a variety of chemical changes and do harm to living things. α and β Particles are not very penetrating, but α radiation from sources within the body is extremely destructive to the tissues. γ Rays and neutrons are much more penetrating and very dangerous. Neutrons cause nuclear reactions and produce radionuclides, which may in turn be sources of α, β, and γ radiation. The biological effects of radiation may be somatic (changes in body cells) or genetic (changes in genes, which may be passed on to succeeding generations).

12.15 NUCLEAR FISSION **12.16** NUCLEAR FUSION Neutrons can cause fission of ^{238}U or ^{239}Pu. These reactions release more neutrons, so a self-sustaining chain reaction can result. The critical mass of a fissionable substance is the smallest mass that will support a chain reaction under given conditions. Fission is carried out at a controlled rate in nuclear reactors. Fusion reactions take place in the extremely hot interior of the sun and other stars (thermonuclear reactions) and in hydrogen bomb explosions, where the necessary temperature and pressure are provided by a fission (atomic) bomb.

12.17 FISSION REACTORS **12.18** BREEDER REACTORS **12.19** FUSION REACTORS In a nuclear fission reactor, neutrons produced by reactions in the fuel are slowed by a moderator (often D_2O or graphite) to speeds at which they produce fission most effectively. A breeder reactor produces as much new fissionable material as it consumes. It is difficult to confine the reacting nuclei and electrons and to sustain the high temperatures needed for nuclear fusion. The two most promising approaches to utilizing nuclear fusion as a source of energy involve magnetic confinement and the use of lasers.

SIGNIFICANT TERMS

nuclide
nucleon
nuclear force
nuclear chemistry
mass defect
nuclear binding energy
binding energy per nucleon
nuclear fusion
nuclear fission
radioactivity
radionuclide
magic numbers
half-life
nuclear reaction
bombardment reaction
γ decay
isomeric transition
α decay
β decay
antineutrino
neutrino
positron
electron capture
chain reaction
critical mass
nuclear reactor
thermonuclear reaction
breeder reactor

THOUGHTS ON CHEMISTRY

The Atomic Age Begins

A description of the first atomic bomb explosion — the test explosion in New Mexico on July 16, 1945

MEN AND ATOMS, by William L. Laurence

Suddenly, at 5:29:50, as we stood huddled around our radio, we heard a voice ringing though the darkness, sounding as though it had come from above the clouds: "Zero minus ten seconds!" A green flare flashed out through the clouds, descended slowly, opened, grew dim, and vanished into the darkness.

The voice from the clouds boomed out again: "Zero minus three seconds!" Another green flare came down. Silence reigned over the desert. We kept moving in small groups in the direction of Zero. From the east came the first faint signs of dawn.

And just at that instant there rose as if from the bowels of the earth a light not of this world, the light of many suns in one. It was a sunrise such as the world had never seen, a great green supersun climbing in a fraction of a second to a height of more than eight thousand feet, rising even higher until it touched the clouds, lighting up earth and sky all around with a dazzling luminosity.

Up it went, a great ball of fire about a mile in diameter, changing colors as it kept shooting upward, from deep purple to orange, expanding, growing bigger, rising as it expanded, an elemental force freed from its bonds after being chained for billions of years. For a fleeting instant the color was unearthly green, such as one sees only in the corona of the sun during a total eclipse. It was as though the earth had opened and the skies had split.

A huge cloud rose from the ground and followed the trail of the great sun. At first it was a giant column, which soon took the shape of a supramundane mushroom. Up it went, higher and higher, quivering convulsively, a giant mountain born in a few seconds instead of millions of years. It touched the multicolored clouds, pushed its summit through them, and kept rising until it reached a height of 41,000 feet, 12,000 feet higher than the earth's highest mountain.

All through the very short but long-seeming time interval not a sound was heard. I could see the silhouettes of human forms motionless in little groups, like desert plants in the dark. The newborn mountain in the distance, a giant among the pygmies of the Sierra Oscuro range, stood leaning at an angle against the clouds, like a vibrant volcano spouting fire to the sky.

Then out of the great silence came a mighty thunder. For a brief interval the phenomena we had seen as light repeated themselves in terms of sound. It was the blast from thousands of blockbusters going off simultaneously at one spot. The thunder reverberated all through the desert, bounced back and forth from the Sierra Oscuro, echo upon echo. The ground trembled under our feet as in an earthquake. A wave of hot wind was felt by many of us just before the blast and warned us of its coming.

The big boom came about a hundred seconds after the great flash — the first cry of a newborn world.

QUESTIONS

Nuclear Stability and Radioactivity

12.1 What are nucleons? What is the relationship between the number of protons and the atomic number? What is the relationship among the number of protons, the number of neutrons, and the mass number?

12.2 Describe what happens to the energy of the system as a proton approaches another proton until they are closer than 10^{-13} cm. Repeat your description for a neutron approaching a proton.

12.3 What is the nuclear binding energy? How do we calculate this energy?

12.4 Define the term "binding energy per nucleon." How can we use this quantity to compare the stability of nuclei?

12.5 Describe how (a) nuclear fission, and (b) nuclear fusion generate more stable nuclei.

12.6 Why do the various isotopes of an element (such as ^1_1H, ^2_1H, and ^3_1H) undergo the same chemical reactions?

12.7 What does the half-life of a radionuclide represent? How do we compare the relative stabilities of radionuclides in terms of half-lives?

12.8 Briefly describe radiocarbon dating. What is the source of the radioactive carbon? What is the limit of its use?

Nuclear Reactions

12.9 What are the three types of radiation from natural radionuclides? What is the composition of each of these?

12.10 Write the symbol that would be used in a nuclear equation for (a) an α-particle, (b) a β-particle, (c) a positron, (d) a proton, and (e) a neutron.

12.11 Write the nuclear equations for the following processes: (a) $^{228}_{90}\text{Th}$ undergoing α decay, (b) $^{110}_{49}\text{In}$ undergoing positron emission, (c) $^{127}_{53}\text{I}$ being bombarded by a proton to form $^{121}_{54}\text{Xe}$ and 7 neutrons, (d) tritium and deuterium undergoing fusion to form an α-particle and a neutron, and (e) $^{95}_{42}\text{Mo}$ being bombarded by a proton to form $^{95}_{43}\text{Tc}$ and radiation (identify this radiation).

12.12 Write the nuclear equations for the following processes: (a) $^{110}_{49}\text{In}$ undergoing electron capture, (b) $^{10}_{5}\text{B}$ being bombarded by a neutron to form $^{10}_{4}\text{Be}$ and a proton, (c) $^{96m}_{43}\text{Tc}$ undergoing isomeric transition, and (d) $^{3}_{2}\text{He}$ and a deuterium ion undergoing fusion to form a proton and an α-particle.

12.13 Write the nuclear equations for the following processes: (a) $^{63}_{28}\text{Ni}$ undergoing β^- emission, (b) two deuterium ions undergoing fusion to give $^{3}_{2}\text{He}$ and a neutron, (c) a nuclide being bombarded by a neutron to form $^{7}_{3}\text{Li}$ and an α-particle (identify the unknown nuclide), and (d) $^{14}_{7}\text{N}$ being bombarded by a neutron to form 3 α-particles and an atom of tritium.

12.14 An alkaline earth element (Representative Group II) is radioactive. It undergoes decay by emitting three α-particles in succession. In what periodic table group is the resulting element found?

12.15 "Radioactinium" is produced in the actinium series from $^{235}_{92}\text{U}$ by the successive emission of an α-particle, a β^--particle, an α-particle, and a β^--particle. What nuclide is "radioactinium"?

12.16 Artificial radioactivity was discovered by the Joliot-Curies as the result of a bombardment reaction. A sample of $^{27}_{13}\text{Al}$ was bombarded by α-particles to give $^{30}_{15}\text{P}$ nuclei and neutrons. When the bombardment ceased, the $^{30}_{15}\text{P}$ continued to decay by giving off β^+ particles. Write the nuclear equations for these processes.

12.17 Describe what happens to the (a) atomic number, (b) mass number, and (c) n/p ratio during isomeric transition. (d) Write a nuclear equation for $^{91m}_{39}\text{Y}$ undergoing isomeric transition.

12.18 Describe what happens to the (a) atomic number, (b) mass number, and (c) n/p ratio during α decay. (d) Write the equation for the α decay of $^{205}_{84}\text{Po}$.

12.19 Describe what happens to the (a) atomic number, (b) mass number, and (c) n/p ratio during β^- decay. (d) Write the equation for the β^- decay of $^{215}_{83}\text{Bi}$. (e) What additional particle is involved in this process?

12.20 Describe what happens to the (a) atomic number, (b) mass number, and (c) n/p ratio during β^+ emission. (d) Write the equation for the β^+ decay of $^{148}_{63}\text{Eu}$. (e) What additional particle is involved in this process?

12.21 Describe what happens to the (a) atomic number, (b) mass number, and (c) n/p ratio during electron capture. (d) Write the equation for electron capture by $^{148}_{63}\text{Eu}$. (e) Compare the product nuclide of electron capture by $^{148}_{63}\text{Eu}$ with that produced by β^+ emission (see Question 12.20).

12.22 Consider a radioactive nuclide with a neutron–proton ratio that is larger than those for the stable isotopes of that element. What mode(s) of decay might be expected for this nuclide and why?

12.23 Repeat Question 12.22 for a neutron–proton ratio that is smaller than those for the stable isotopes.

12.24 What is a radioactive decay series? What is the end product of the three natural series?

12.25 What are bombardment reactions? Explain the shorthand notation used to describe bombardment reactions.

12.26 What particles were used by early investigators for bombardment reactions? Why were accelerated protons more useful than α-particles for bombardment reactions? What other types of particles can be used for bombarding particles?

12.27 Write the nuclear equation for each of the following bombardment processes: (a) $^{14}_{7}\text{N}(\alpha, p)^{17}_{8}\text{O}$, (b) $^{106}_{46}\text{Pd}(n, p)^{106}_{45}\text{Rh}$, and (c) $^{23}_{11}\text{Na}(n, \beta^-)\text{X}$, and identify X.

12.28 Repeat Question 12.27 for (a) $^{113}_{48}\text{Cd}(n, \gamma)^{114}_{48}\text{Cd}$, (b) $^{6}_{3}\text{Li}(n, \alpha)^{3}_{1}\text{H}$ and (c) $^{2}_{1}\text{H}(\gamma, p)\text{X}$, and identify X.

12.29 Write the shorthand notation for each of the following nuclear equations: (a) $^{6}_{3}\text{Li} + ^{1}_{0}n \rightarrow ^{4}_{2}\text{He} + ^{3}_{1}\text{H}$, (b) $^{31}_{15}\text{P} + ^{2}_{1}\text{H} \rightarrow ^{32}_{15}\text{P} + ^{1}_{1}\text{H}$, and (c) $^{238}_{92}\text{U} + ^{1}_{0}n \rightarrow ^{239}_{93}\text{Np} + ^{0}_{-1}\beta$.

12.30 Repeat Question 12.29 for (a) $^{253}_{99}\text{Es} + ^{4}_{2}\text{He} \rightarrow ^{256}_{101}\text{Md} + ^{1}_{0}n$, (b) $^{27}_{13}\text{Al} + ^{1}_{0}n \rightarrow ^{26}_{13}\text{Al} + 2^{1}_{0}n$, and (c) $^{37}_{17}\text{Cl} + ^{1}_{1}\text{H} \rightarrow ^{1}_{0}n + ^{37}_{18}\text{Ar}$.

12.31 Compare the general penetrating abilities of α-particles, β-particles, γ rays, and neutrons. Why are α-particles that are absorbed internally by the body particularly dangerous?

12.32 In what two ways can an organism be damaged by radiation? In which of these ways might the giant insects that so often threaten to destroy the world in science fiction movies be produced?

12.33 Briefly describe a nuclear fission process. What are the two most important fissionable materials?

12.34 What is a "chain reaction"? Why are nuclear fission processes considered chain reactions? What is the "critical mass" of a fissionable material?

12.35 Where have continuous nuclear fusion processes been observed? What is the main reaction that is taking place in these sources?

Nuclear Energy

12.36 List the five primary components of a nuclear reactor and briefly describe their functions. Do any of these components present ecological or environmental problems?

12.37 How does a breeder reactor operate? Write the nuclear equations for the production of $^{239}_{94}\text{Pu}$ from $^{238}_{92}\text{U}$.

12.38 Name some of the advantages that fusion reactors could have over fission reactors.

12.39* The first artificially produced element was technetium. (a) Write the equation for the production of $^{97}_{43}$Tc by the reaction of $^{96}_{42}$Mo with $^{2}_{1}$H and (b) identify the other product of the reaction.

All known isotopes of Tc are radioactive, and $^{97}_{43}$Tc decays by the process of electron capture. (c) Write the equation for this decay and (d) identify its product. (e) Is this decay an example of natural or artificial radiation? (f) In the process of electron capture, essentially what is happening to a proton? (g) How is the neutron–proton ratio changing in this process? The half-life of $^{97}_{43}$Tc is 2.6×10^6 yr. (h) If you paid \$100 for a gram of $^{97}_{43}$Tc, would you worry about your economic loss in a week's time?

All of the isotopes of Tc with mass numbers between 92 and 97 decay by electron capture or positron emission. (i) What element do all these isotopes form when they decay? All of the isotopes of Tc with mass numbers between 98 and 107 decay by electron emission. (j) What element do all these isotopes form upon decay?

Answers to Selected Questions

12.13 (a) $^{63}_{28}$Ni $\longrightarrow$ $^{0}_{-1}\beta$ + $^{63}_{29}$Cu; (b) 2 $^{2}_{1}$H $\longrightarrow$ $^{3}_{2}$He + $^{1}_{0}n$; (c) $^{10}_{5}$B + $^{1}_{0}n \longrightarrow$ $^{4}_{2}$He + $^{7}_{3}$Li, $^{10}_{5}$B; (d) $^{14}_{7}$N + $^{1}_{0}n \longrightarrow 3$ $^{4}_{2}$He + $^{3}_{1}$H

12.15 $^{227}_{90}$Th

12.19 (a) Z increases by 1; (b) A is unchanged; (c) n/p ratio decreases; (d) $^{215}_{83}$Bi $\longrightarrow$ $^{0}_{-1}\beta$ + $^{215}_{84}$Po, $\bar{\nu}$

12.21 (a) Z decreases by 1; (b) A is unchanged; (c) n/p ratio increases; (d) $^{148}_{63}$Eu + $^{0}_{-1}\beta \longrightarrow$ $^{148}_{62}$Sm; (e) the same nuclide is produced

12.23 β^+ Emission or electron capture could occur, increasing the n/p ratio by changing a proton into a neutron; for $Z > 83$ α decay could occur, increasing the n/p ratio by decreasing both the atomic and mass numbers

12.28 (a) $^{113}_{48}$Cd + $^{1}_{0}n \longrightarrow$ $^{114}_{48}$Cd + γ; (b) $^{6}_{3}$Li + $^{1}_{0}n \longrightarrow$ $^{3}_{1}$H + $^{4}_{2}$He; (c) $^{2}_{1}$H + $\gamma \longrightarrow$ $^{1}_{1}$H + $^{1}_{0}n$, n

12.30 (a) $^{253}_{99}$Es$(\alpha, n)^{256}_{101}$Md, (b) $^{27}_{13}$Al$(n, 2n)$ $^{26}_{13}$Al, (c) $^{37}_{17}$Cl$(p, n)^{37}_{18}$Ar

12.39 (a) $^{96}_{42}$Mo + $^{2}_{1}$H $\longrightarrow$ $^{97}_{43}$Tc + $^{1}_{0}n$; (b) n; (c) $^{97}_{43}$Tc + $^{0}_{-1}\beta \longrightarrow$ $^{97}_{42}$Mo; (d) $^{97}_{42}$Mo; (e) artificial; (f) a proton is changing to a neutron; (g) n/p ratio is increasing; (h) no; (i) Mo; (j) Ru

PROBLEMS

Nuclear Binding Energy

12.1 Calculate the nuclear binding energy for (a) ^{14}N, (b) $^{56}_{26}$Fe, and (c) $^{130}_{52}$Te. The respective atomic masses are 14.00307 u, 55.9349 u, and 129.9067 u. Which of these nuclides has the largest binding energy per nucleon?

12.2 Repeat Problem 12.1 for (a) $^{32}_{16}$S, (b) $^{45}_{21}$Sc, and (c) $^{64}_{30}$Zn. The atomic masses are 31.97207 u, 44.95592 u, and 63.9291 u, respectively. *Answer* (a) -4.3543×10^{-11} J, -1.3607×10^{-12} J/nucleon; (b) -6.2138×10^{-11} J, -1.3808×10^{-12} J/nucleon;

(c) -8.959×10^{-11} J, -1.400×10^{-12} J/nucleon; $^{64}_{30}$Zn has the greatest binding energy per nucleon

12.3 Calculate the binding energy per nucleon for the following isotopes: (a) $^{15}_{8}$O with a mass of 15.00300 u; (b) $^{16}_{8}$O with a mass of 15.99491 u; (c) $^{17}_{8}$O with a mass of 16.99913 u; (d) $^{18}_{8}$O with a mass of 17.99915 u; and (e) $^{19}_{8}$O with a mass of 19.0035 u. Which of these would you expect to be most stable?

Half-Life

12.4 The half-life of $^{193}_{81}$Tl is 23 min. Calculate the (a) rate constant, k, and (b) mass of radioactive material left if a 1.00 g sample is allowed to decay for 1.00 h.

12.5 The half-life of $^{19}_{8}$O is 29 s. What fraction of the isotope originally present would be left after 5.0 s? *Answer* 88.5%

12.6 A 3.50 mg sample of a new isotope was analyzed and found to contain 2.73 mg of the isotope after a period of 6.3 h. Calculate $t_{\frac{1}{2}}$.

12.7 The activity of a sample of tritium decreased by 5.5% over the period of a year. What is the half-life of $^{3}_{1}$H? *Answer* 12.2 yr

12.8 The half-life of $^{11}_{6}$C is 20.3 min. How long will it take for exactly 90% of a sample to decay? How long will it take for exactly 99% of the sample to decay?

12.9 A piece of wood from a burial site was analyzed using $^{14}_{6}$C dating and was found to have an activity of 13.4/(min)(g C). Using the data given in Example 12.4 for $^{14}_{6}$C dating, determine the age of this piece of wood.

12.10 The $^{14}_{6}$C activity of an artifact from the tomb of Hemaka (2930 $\pm$ 200 BC) was 8.3/(min)(g C). Using the data given in Example 12.4 for $^{14}_{6}$C dating, determine the age of this artifact. *Answer* 5100 yr

Reaction Energy

12.11 The last step in the uranium decay series is

$$^{210}_{84}\text{Po} \longrightarrow {}^{206}_{82}\text{Pb} + {}^{4}_{2}\text{He}$$

The respective masses of the nuclides are 209.9829 u, 205.9745 u, and 4.00260 u. Find the energy released by this reaction.

12.12 The reaction that occurred in the first fusion bomb was $^{7}_{3}$Li(p, α)X. (a) Write the complete equation for the process and identify the other product, X. (b) The atomic masses are 1.007825 u for $^{1}_{1}$H, 4.00260 u for α, and 7.01600 u for $^{7}_{3}$Li. Find the energy for the reaction. *Answer* (a) $^{7}_{3}$Li + $^{1}_{1}$H $\longrightarrow 2$ $^{4}_{2}$He; (b) -2.781×10^{-12} J

12.13 Which reaction produces the larger amount of energy per atomic mass unit of material reacting?

$$\text{fission: } ^{235}_{92}\text{U} + {}^{1}_{0}n \longrightarrow {}^{94}_{40}\text{Zn} + {}^{140}_{58}\text{Ce} + 6 {}^{0}_{-1}\beta + 2 {}^{1}_{0}n$$

$$\text{fusion: } 2 {}^{2}_{1}\text{H} \longrightarrow {}^{3}_{1}\text{H} + {}^{1}_{1}\text{H}$$

The atomic masses are 235.0439 u for $^{235}_{92}$U, 1.00867 u for $^{1}_{0}n$, 93.9061 u for $^{94}_{40}$Zn, 139.9053 u for $^{140}_{58}$Ce, 0.00055 u for $^{0}_{-1}\beta$, 3.01605 u for $^{3}_{1}$H, 1.007825 u for $^{1}_{1}$H, and 2.0140 u for $^{2}_{1}$H.

12.14* Consider the following reactions which are possible when $^{27}_{13}Al$ is bombarded with neutrons:

$$^{27}_{13}Al + ^{1}_{0}n \longrightarrow {}^{28}_{13}Al \longrightarrow \begin{cases} ^{26}_{13}Al + 2\ ^{1}_{0}n \\ ^{28}_{13}Al + \gamma \\ ^{27}_{12}Mg + ^{1}_{1}H \\ ^{24}_{11}Na + ^{4}_{2}He \end{cases}$$

The nuclide masses are 26.98153 u for $^{27}_{13}Al$, 1.008665 u for $^{1}_{0}n$, 25.9858 u for $^{26}_{13}Al$, 27.98193 u for $^{28}_{13}Al$, 26.98437 u for $^{27}_{12}Mg$, 1.007825 u for $^{1}_{1}H$, 23.99102 u for $^{24}_{11}Na$, and 4.00260 u for $^{4}_{2}He$. Which reaction releases the most energy and is therefore most favorable? *Answer* Formation of $^{28}_{13}Al$ is the most favorable reaction.

Additional Problems

12.15 Using Graham's law (see Section 5.13), calculate the ratio of the rates of effusion for $^{2}_{1}H_2(g)$ and $^{1}_{1}H_2(g)$. The atomic masses are 1.007825 u and 2.0140 u for $^{1}_{1}H$ and $^{2}_{1}H$, respectively.

12.16 Repeat Problem 12.17 for $^{235}_{92}UF_6(g)$ and $^{238}_{92}UF_6(g)$. The atomic masses of the uranium isotopes are 235.0439 u and 238.0508 u, respectively. *Answer* (rate of $^{235}_{92}UF_6$)/(rate of $^{238}_{92}UF_6$) = 1.004298

12.17 Calculate the neutron–proton ratio for the following radioactive nuclides and predict how each of the nuclides might decay: (a) $^{13}_{5}B$ (stable mass numbers for B are 10 and 11), (b) $^{81}_{38}Sr$ (stable mass numbers for Sr are between 84 and 88), and (c) $^{212}_{82}Pb$ (stable mass numbers for Pb are between 204 and 208).

12.18 Repeat Problem 12.17 for (a) $^{193}_{79}Au$ (stable mass number for Au is 197), (b) $^{184m}_{75}Re$ (stable mass numbers for Re are 185 and 187), and (c) $^{142}_{59}Pr$ (stable mass number for Pr is 141). *Answer* (a) 1.443, β^+ emission and/or electron capture; (b) 1.453, β^+ emission and/or electron capture after isomeric transition; (c) 1.407, β^- emission

12.19* Predict the mode of decay for $^{159}_{64}Gd$. The energies of the radiation are 0.59 MeV, 0.95 MeV, and 0.89 MeV. The energies of the accompanying γ radiation are 0.362 MeV and 0.058 MeV. Prepare a decay scheme (like Figure 12.9) consistent with these data.

12.20* The nuclide $^{19}_{8}O$ is radioactive. (a) Predict the mode of decay for this isotope. (b) Particles with a maximum energy of 4.60 MeV are emitted followed by 0.20 MeV γ radiation, along with particles with a maximum energy of 3.25 MeV followed by 1.37 MeV and 0.20 MeV γ radiation. Prepare a decay scheme (like Figure 12.9) for this nuclide. *Answer* (a) The nuclide is a β^- emitter; (b)

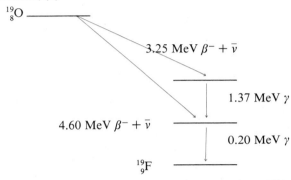

12.21* The thickness, X, of a shielding material which will decrease the amount of γ radiation from a_0 to a is given by

$$X = \frac{2.303 \log (a_0/a)}{\mu}$$

where μ is a parameter that depends on the substance being used as the shielding material and on the energy of the radiation. If $\mu = 48.9/m$ for stopping 3.0 MeV γ radiation in Pb, calculate the thickness needed to decrease a_0 to $(0.500)a_0$. Repeat the calculation to find X for decreasing a_0 to $(0.010)a_0$.

CHAPTER 13

Liquid and Solid States; Changes of State

The word "solid" is another word like "heat" and "temperature," which we discussed in the introduction to Chapter 7. Everyone has an intuitive feeling for what a solid is. But the word has a subtly different significance to a mineralogist, a crystallographer, an electronics engineer, and a civil engineer.

In the popular sense, anything that is obviously not a gas and obviously not a liquid—anything that does not flow or take the shape of its container—is a solid. To many scientists, the term "solid" is appropriate only for crystalline substances, with their orderly internal structure. The fine distinction that window glass, which certainly appears to be solid, is truly just a very viscous liquid, is of practical importance to very few people. However, an understanding of the difference will aid in the study of chemistry.

Another popular use of the word "solid" was born with the revolution in the electronics industry caused by the replacement of vacuum tubes with transistors. The term "solid state" is freely applied to anything that contains a transistor or other semiconducting device. (These are discussed in Chapter 30, which deals with the semiconducting elements.)

The growing understanding of the electronic properties of solids has stimulated investigations of other properties of solids. Since the late 1950s, several new branches of science and technology have emerged, such as solid-state physics, solid-state chemistry, and materials science and engineering. Engineers now can predict the properties of materials not just on the basis of past experience, but also on the basis of an understanding of the internal structures of the substances involved. This chapter on liquids and solids can barely scratch the surface of what has been learned about the solid state in recent years.

RELATIONSHIPS BETWEEN PHASES

13.1 KINETIC-MOLECULAR THEORY FOR LIQUIDS AND SOLIDS

We have discussed the kinetic-molecular theory as it applies to gases (Section 5.2). The atoms, molecules, or ions in liquids and solids, like those in gases, are in constant motion. In a gas the molecules are far apart, are relatively independent of each other, and move in straight lines until they collide with something. In solids and liquids the particles are close together and there is comparatively little empty space. As a result, the motion of the particles is restricted. However, with the exception of the first statement, concerning the large distance between molecules (see Section 5.2), the kinetic-molecular theory applies to liquids and solids as well. The distribution of the kinetic energy of the particles in a liquid, or their speed, follows a curve similar to that of the molecules in a gas (Figure 13.1; see also Figure 5.4). The higher the temperature, the higher the average kinetic energy of the particles. Within the limits of their rigidly fixed positions, the particles in a solid have a similar distribution of energies.

The state in which a substance exists is dependent to a great extent on the balance between the kinetic energies of the particles, which tend to keep them moving, and the intermolecular or bonding forces, which tend to pull them together.

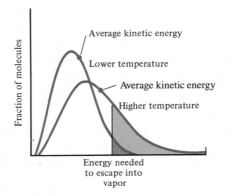

Figure 13.1
Change in Kinetic Energy with Temperature The colored areas represent the relative numbers of molecules of a substance that can enter the vapor at higher and lower temperatures.

With decreasing temperature, particles move more slowly. Eventually the interparticle forces of attraction exceed the kinetic energy and pull the particles together—a gas becomes a liquid, or a liquid becomes a solid. Raising the temperature sets the particles free from the forces of attraction and causes a phase change in the opposite direction.

In a liquid, the motion of a particle is restricted and it collides often with other particles. Each of the colliding particles rebounds, but the distance that either one can move away from the other is very small. However, the particles in a liquid, individually or in random groups, can easily slide past each other, allowing a liquid to take the shape of its container (Figure 13.2).

Particles in a solid, unlike those in liquids and gases, are held rigidly in place by the surrounding particles. In crystalline solids, the positions of the atoms, molecules, or ions are highly ordered. Most particles in a solid can only vibrate about their fixed positions. The rigid structure in which the particles of a solid are held prevents solids from spreading out.

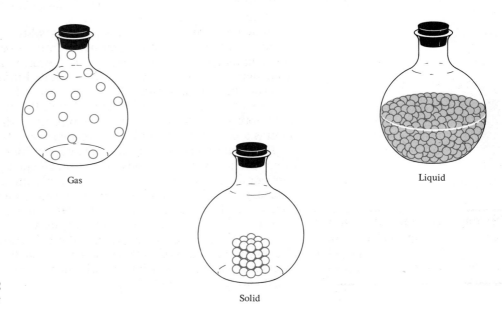

Gas

Liquid

Solid

Figure 13.2
The Three States of Matter

13.2 CHANGES OF STATE

Figure 13.3

Camphor—A Solid that Sublimes at Room Temperature Camphor is an organic compound used in some mothballs. Frequently you will find camphor crystals sublimed onto clothing stored over mothballs.

Molecules near the surface of a liquid can escape into the gaseous phase if they have enough kinetic energy to overcome the attraction of other molecules. Many such escaping molecules strike molecules of the gas above the liquid, lose energy, and return to the liquid phase. However, if the vessel is open to the air all the molecules eventually escape from the liquid. We call this process **evaporation**—the escape of molecules from a liquid in an open container to the gas phase. **Vaporization** is the more general term for escape of molecules from the liquid or solid phase to the gas phase.

The escaping molecules are the "hottest" molecules—the ones at the high-kinetic-energy end of the curve (see Figure 13.1). Therefore evaporation is faster when the temperature is higher, for a larger fraction of molecules have energy high enough to escape. The rate of evaporation is also dependent on surface area—the larger the surface area, the larger the number of "hot" molecules that reach the surface. Escape of the highest energy molecules leaves behind a collection of molecules with a lower average kinetic energy and, therefore, a lower temperature. When evaporation is rapid—for example, when you get out of a swimming pool on a windy day—the cooling effect of evaporation is obvious. It is less noticeable in slow evaporation of a liquid from a noninsulated container because the loss of heat is gradually made up from the surroundings as evaporation occurs.

Particles with a high enough kinetic energy can also escape from the surface of a solid. **Sublimation** is the vaporization of a solid (Figure 13.3). The reverse transition, from the gas phase directly to the solid phase, is called "deposition." A solid can be purified by first heating it so that the pure material sublimes away from the impurities, and then cooling the vapor. ("Sublimation" is also sometimes used to mean the vaporization *and* redeposition of the same solid.)

If a liquid is in a tightly closed container, molecules escape from the liquid into the space above, but can go no further. Some of the molecules, in bouncing around the enclosed space, hit the liquid surface and reenter the liquid phase. This process is **condensation**—the movement of molecules from the gaseous phase to the liquid phase. We also speak of the transformation of a gas into a liquid as **liquefaction.** (Note the *e* in liquefaction—to use *i* in its place is wrong.) Eventually, the concentration of molecules in the vapor is so great that the number of them going back into the liquid equals the number escaping from the liquid. At this point, a dynamic equilibrium has been established and the partial pressure of the vapor over the liquid equals its vapor pressure (Section 5.12).

When a solid is heated, the particles vibrate faster and faster in their fixed positions until they are no longer held firmly in place and are thus free enough to form a liquid. The **melting point** of a solid is the temperature at which the solid and liquid phases of a substance are at equilibrium. **Fusion** is a term also used in scientific publications to mean melting. (Remember that "fusion" means melting, *not* solidification.) The freezing point is identical with the melting point but is thought of as being approached from the opposite temperature direction. In other words, freezing point is a property of a liquid, melting point a property of a solid.

The terminology for changes of state is summarized in Figure 13.4. In Chapter 7, in connection with our study of thermochemistry, we discussed the changes in temperature and enthalpy during changes of state (Section 7.11). All such enthalpy changes refer to the changes of state at constant temperatures, which are the boiling points or melting points of the substances at atmospheric pressure, or the temperatures at which the solids go directly to the vapor state. Fusion and vaporization always require the addition of heat and the ΔH values for these processes are positive. The reverse processes of condensation and crystallization (see Figure 13.4) have ΔH values of equal magnitude but opposite sign. (Some values for enthalpies for changes of state are given in Table 7.5.)

Strong intermolecular forces:
high melting point
high boiling point
high ΔH_{fus} and ΔH_{vap}

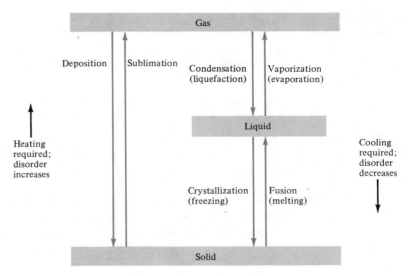

Figure 13.4
Changes of State The alternate names for changes of state are given in parentheses.

13.3 VAPOR PRESSURE

The vapor pressure of a liquid or solid is the pressure at which vaporization and condensation, or sublimation and deposition, are at equilibrium (Figure 13.5b). Vapor pressure increases as temperature increases and decreases as temperature decreases. If air or some mixture of gases is in contact with the liquid, the partial pressure of the vapor in the mixture is equal to its vapor pressure. The vapor pressure obeys Dalton's law of partial pressures and is independent of whatever other gases are present (Section 5.12). It is also independent of the volume or shape of the container and the ratio of liquid to empty space. If the volume occupied by the vapor is increased, more molecules leave the surface, the volume of the liquid or solid decreases, and the vapor pressure remains unchanged (Figure 13.5c).

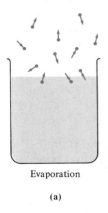

Evaporation

(a)

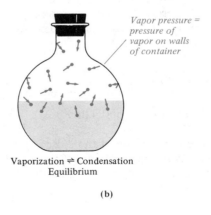

Vaporization ⇌ Condensation
Equilibrium

(b)

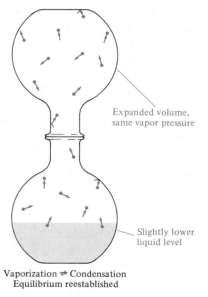

Vaporization ⇌ Condensation
Equilibrium reestablished

(c)

Figure 13.5
Evaporation, Vaporization, Condensation, and Vapor Pressure

EXAMPLE 13.1
Vapor Pressure

The vapor pressure of liquid bromine at room temperature is 168 Torr. Suppose that bromine is introduced drop by drop into a closed system containing air at 745 Torr and room temperature. If the bromine is added until no more vaporizes and a few drops of liquid are present in the flask, what will the total pressure in the flask be?

The total pressure of the mixture of gases in the flask will be that given by Dalton's law as

$$P_{total} = p_{air} + p_{Br_2}$$
$$= 745 \text{ Torr} + 168 \text{ Torr} = 913 \text{ Torr}$$

The pressure in the flask will be 913 Torr.

Exercise A closed flask contained liquid water at 73.2 °C. The total pressure of the air and water vapor mixture was 627.4 Torr. The vapor pressure of water at this temperature is 268.0 Torr. What was the partial pressure of the air? *Answer* 359.4 Torr

EXAMPLE 13.2
Vapor Pressure

Suppose that the volume of the closed system containing air and bromine that is described in Example 13.1 can be decreased to one-half its original value. What will happen to the pressure in the system? (Assume the temperature is constant.)

To solve this problem, we must treat the air and the bromine in different ways. The air can be treated as an ideal gas and the new pressure for the air calculated by using Boyle's law

$$p_{air} = (P_1) \frac{V_1}{V_2} = (745 \text{ Torr}) \left(\frac{V_1}{0.5\, V_1} \right) = 1490 \text{ Torr}$$

The vapor pressure of the bromine will remain constant at 168 Torr because the temperature has not changed and because the vapor is in equilibrium with the liquid. Some of the bromine that was present as a gas will condense to form additional liquid bromine because the volume of the system has decreased.

The total pressure of the mixture of gases in the flask after the volume change will be

$$P_{total} = p_{air} + p_{Br_2}$$
$$= 1490 \text{ Torr} + 168 \text{ Torr} = 1660 \text{ Torr}$$

The pressure will increase to 1660 Torr.

Exercise Suppose the volume of the closed system containing air and bromine that is described in Example 13.1 can be decreased to one-fifth of its original value. What will be the pressure in the system after the change? *Answer* 3.90×10^3 Torr

The magnitude of the vapor pressure, like the state of a substance, is determined to a great extent by the interplay between the kinetic energy of the particles and the forces of attraction between them. At a given temperature, a substance with strong intermolecular forces has a lower vapor pressure than a substance of the same molar mass with relatively weaker intermolecular forces. As temperature increases, more molecules have enough kinetic energy to escape from the surface and the vapor

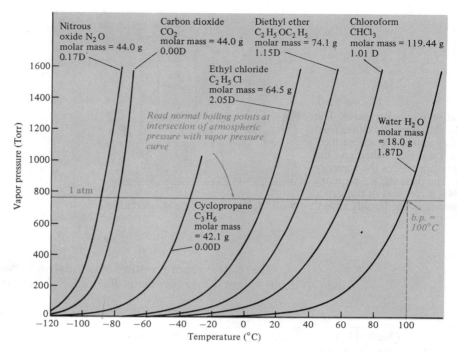

Figure 13.6
Vapor Pressure vs. Temperature Curves With the exception of water and carbon dioxide, which are included for comparison, each of these liquids is an anesthetic. The molar mass and dipole moment of each substance are given on the curves.

pressure of the substance increases. The vapor pressure versus temperature curves given in Figure 13.6 all increase similarly with temperature. Water, with its strong hydrogen bonds, has a low vapor pressure. The substances with the lower molar masses and either no dipole moment (CO_2 and C_3H_6) or a very small dipole moment (N_2O) have higher vapor pressures.

Table 13.1 gives the heats of vaporization of the substances for which vapor pressures are plotted in Figure 13.6. Comparison of Table 13.1 and Figure 13.6 shows the similar influence of intermolecular forces on both heats of vaporization and vapor pressure.

Table 13.1
Vaporization Data for Substances in Figure 13.6

	Substance	ΔH_{vap} (kJ/mol)	B.P. (°C)
N_2O	Nitrous oxide	16.5	−88.5
CO_2	Carbon dioxide	—	—*
$H_2C\!\!-\!\!CH_2$ $\quad CH_2$	Cyclopropane	24.7	−33
C_2H_5Cl	Ethyl chloride	25	12.3
$C_2H_5OC_2H_5$	Diethyl ether	29.1	35
$CHCl_3$	Chloroform	29.4	61.2
H_2O	Water	40.7	100

* Carbon dioxide sublimes at atmospheric pressure.

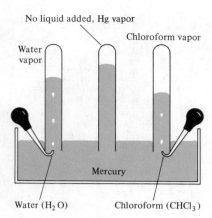

Figure 13.7
Relative Vapor Pressures The liquids added are less dense than mercury and rise to the surface. Equilibrium is established and the vapor pressure pushes the mercury down. The distance the mercury falls is a measure of the vapor pressure of the liquids added.

The relative vapor pressures of liquids can be demonstrated by introducing a few drops of liquid into barometer-like tubes of mercury (Figure 13.7).

EXAMPLE 13.3
Intermolecular Forces

Each of the following substances is a liquid at −100 °C:

ethane   dimethyl ether   ethyl alcohol

Place these liquids in order of increasing vapor pressure, basing your argument on the strengths of intermolecular forces (Sections 11.10–11.12).

London forces are expected in all molecules and are present in each substance. Both dimethyl ether and ethyl alcohol molecules should be bent at the electronegative oxygen atoms (AB_2E_2; see Table 11.2), which means that dipole–dipole attraction will be significant. In addition, ethyl alcohol has a polar OH group and will be relatively strongly hydrogen-bonded in the liquid state. There is no possibility for hydrogen bonding in either dimethyl ether or ethane. The intermolecular attraction should be strongest in ethyl alcohol and weakest in ethane, giving the predicted order of increasing vapor pressures at −100 °C as

ethyl alcohol < dimethyl ether < ethane

which is in excellent agreement with the respective measured vapor pressure values of 4×10^{-4} Torr, 6 Torr, and 360 Torr at −100 °C.

Exercise Which of the following substances

trans-*1,2-dichloroethylene*   cis-*1,2-dichloroethylene*

will have the higher vapor pressure at a given temperature? *Answer* trans-1,2-dichloroethylene

13.4 BOILING POINT

We have all seen bubbles rising to the surface in a pot of boiling water. The first small bubbles, when heating begins, are bubbles of air which is driven out of solution by the rising temperature. When the water has come to a boil, larger bubbles continuously form and rise to the surface. These bubbles contain water vapor.

As water (or any other liquid) is heated, the average kinetic energy of the molecules increases, the rate of evaporation increases, and the vapor pressure increases. Eventually the point is reached where the vapor pressure of the liquid equals the pressure of the atmosphere pushing down on the surface of the liquid and a great many molecules have acquired enough energy to escape from the attraction by their neighbors. At this point bubbles of vapor can form in the liquid, whereas previously they would have been collapsed by the pressure from above. As the bubbles form they rise to the surface and boiling commences. The temperature at which this happens is the **boiling point**—the temperature at which the vapor pressure of a liquid equals the pressure of the gases above the liquid and bubbles of vapor form throughout the liquid.

If the pressure of the gases above a liquid is lowered, the vapor pressure will reach this pressure at a lower temperature and the liquid will boil at a lower temperature. A boiling point given without any mention of pressure can be assumed to be a **normal boiling point**—the boiling point at 760 Torr, the average atmospheric pressure at sea level.

Plots of the variation of the vapor pressure with the temperature like those in Figure 13.6 also show the variation of the boiling point with pressure. Below atmospheric pressure, boiling points are lower than the normal boiling point. For example, you can see from Figure 13.6 that at 600 Torr ethyl chloride boils at about 0 °C. At 9000 ft above sea level, where the pressure is about 550 Torr, water boils at 91 °C. At this altitude an egg must be boiled for about 5 min to reach the same consistency as a 3 min egg at sea level, and a hard-boiled egg requires about 18 minutes of cooking time. An experiment that demonstrates the boiling of water at lower temperatures under reduced pressure is shown in Figure 13.8.

It is possible for a liquid to be **superheated**—heated to a temperature above the boiling point without the occurrence of boiling. Superheating occurs when it is difficult for molecules with enough kinetic energy to get together to form a bubble.

> **Normal boiling point: b.p. at 760 Torr**
> **Normal freezing point: f.p. at 760 Torr**

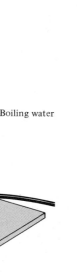
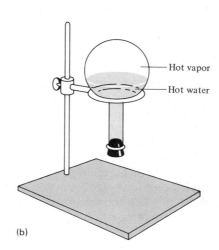
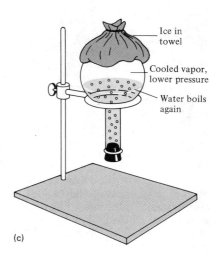

(a)　　　　　　　(b)　　　　　　　(c)

Figure 13.8
Lowering of Boiling Point by Lowering Vapor Pressure (a) Water is brought to a boil. (b) Heat is removed, stopper added, and flask inverted. (c) Vapor is cooled, lowering pressure and bringing water back to boil.

Bubble formation is encouraged by the presence of "boiling chips"—pieces of broken porcelain, or something similar, that release tiny air bubbles during heating. The boiling liquid evaporates into the bubble, which grows in size, and smooth boiling is encouraged. A superheated liquid is hazardous, for it can start to boil suddenly and with great violence.

13.5 PHASE DIAGRAMS

A phase diagram is used to show the relationships between the physical state of a substance and the pressure and temperature. To construct a phase diagram for a three-phase solid–liquid–gas system, the vapor pressure–temperature curve for the liquid phase (like those in Figure 13.6) is combined with the vapor pressure–temperature curve for the solid phase. This second curve represents the temperatures and pressures at which molecules can escape directly from the solid into the vapor phase, in other words, at which solid and vapor are in equilibrium. The general shape of such curves is shown in Figure 13.9a.

The vapor–liquid equilibrium curve in Figure 13.9a would continue upward, if there were space, until it reached the **critical temperature**—the temperature above which a substance cannot exist as a liquid no matter how great the pressure. The **critical pressure** is the pressure that will cause liquefaction of a gas *at* the critical temperature. The vapor–liquid equilibrium curve terminates at the **critical point,** at which the densities of the liquid and the vapor have become equal, and the boundary between the two phases disappears.

The curve for the vapor pressure of the solid ends at its intersection with the liquid curve—at this point the solid melts. A liquid can be **supercooled**—cooled below its freezing point without the occurrence of freezing—as shown by the dashed line in Figure 13.9a. In this condition, crystallization will sometimes start if a "seed crystal" of the substance is added to provide a surface on which crystals begin to form. Once crystallization is triggered in this way, supercooled liquids often crystallize very rapidly, with the noticeable evolution of heat.

To complete the simple phase diagram, the line representing the relationship between pressure and melting point is added (Figure 13.9b). In most cases, the melting point increases with pressure; either way, increase or decrease, the effect is usually quite small, so this line is usually almost vertical.

At any point not on a line in the phase diagram, only a single phase of the substance can exist. At any point along a line, two phases are in equilibrium. At the point where three lines intersect—called a **triple point**—three phases are in equilibrium. Phase diagrams for carbon dioxide and water are given in Figure 13.10. (The scale and shape of the lines have been adjusted to make the relationships more easily visible.) Note the different slopes of the solid–liquid equilibrium lines. The freezing point of water *decreases* with increasing pressure.

The **normal freezing point** of a liquid is the temperature at which the liquid freezes at 760 Torr pressure, that is, the temperature at which solid and liquid are in equilibrium at 760 Torr pressure. The temperatures of the normal freezing point and the triple point are usually not the same. At the triple point the solid and liquid phases are both also in equilibrium with the *pure* vapor. Therefore, the pressure at the triple point can be quite different from 760 Torr.

The triple point for water lies *below* atmospheric pressure, while the triple point for carbon dioxide lies above atmospheric pressure. The significance of this difference is apparent when a block of ice and a block of dry ice, which is solid carbon dioxide, stand side by side on a hot day. The water ice melts to a liquid; the dry ice disappears—it sublimes directly to a gas. For the few substances like CO_2, with triple points above atmospheric pressure, the vapor pressure reaches atmospheric pressure *before* a liquid forms. Liquid carbon dioxide exists only at pressures greater than 5.11 atm, the pressure at the triple point.

At critical point: liquid and gas phases no longer distinct

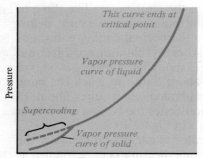

Figure 13.9

Phase Diagram for a Solid-Liquid-Gas System To the vapor pressure curves of the solid and liquid (a) are added the melting point–vapor pressure curve of the solid (b). The colored arrows show the phase changes at constant pressure that occur in crossing the lines at various points.

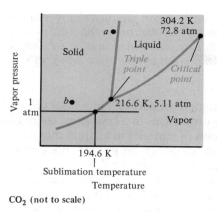 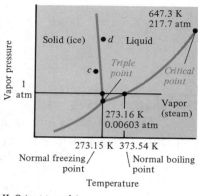

Figure 13.10
Phase Diagrams for CO₂ and H₂O The temperature and pressure scales are not linear and the slope of the solid–liquid line is greatly exaggerated. (The lettered points are used in various examples and exercises in this chapter.)

The boiling point of water (see Figure 13.10) decreases with decreasing pressure along the line connecting the normal boiling point and the triple point. Below the triple point, the temperature of sublimation decreases with decreasing pressure. Practical use is made of this effect. At lower pressure, it is possible to remove water safely from a substance that would be damaged by heating for a long time at 100 °C. Coffee and many kinds of food are preserved by "freeze-drying." The coffee or food is first frozen and the ice then vaporized by lowering the pressure. The complex organic compounds that give food its flavor and texture are unharmed at the low temperature and pressure.

It is important to note that it is the *partial pressure* of the vapor that is plotted in a phase diagram, not the total pressure above a substance. On a dry winter day the partial pressure of water vapor in the air can drop low enough to allow ice to sublime. The gradual disappearance of snow during a bitter cold period is due to sublimation.

| **Triple point:** T **and** P **at which three phases are in equilibrium** |

EXAMPLE 13.4
Interpretation of a Phase Diagram

Describe what happens to a sample of CO_2 originally at point a in the phase diagram (Figure 13.10) as the pressure is decreased at constant temperature.

For a change at constant temperature, the CO_2 will follow a vertical path on the diagram. (See the figure for this example.) Along this path, five different conditions occur: (1) The CO_2 remains a solid as the pressure decreases. At the most, a very slight expansion in volume might occur. (2) The solid becomes a liquid. (3) The CO_2 remains liquid as the pressure decreases. As for the solid, a very slight expansion might occur. (4) The liquid CO_2 vaporizes. (5) With further decrease in pressure, the gas volume increases in accordance with the gas laws.

Exercise Would liquid CO_2 form upon heating at constant pressure a sample of dry ice originally at point a in the accompanying figure? What about point b? *Answer* yes, no

---

In summary, the kinetic energy of particles in the liquid and solid states, as in the gaseous state, is dependent upon the temperature. Particles are held together in solids and liquids by the interparticle forces of chemical bonding or the weaker intermolecular forces (see Tables 13.2 and 13.3). Those particles with high enough kinetic energy can leave the surface of a liquid or a solid and enter the gas phase. At equilibrium between a solid or liquid and its vapor, the vapor pressure is a constant at a given temperature. Changes in temperature and/or changes in pressure can produce changes of state. The curves for the changes with pressure of the melting point, boiling point, and sublimation temperature of a substance are combined in a phase diagram, from which the state of a substance at a given temperature and pressure can be determined.

THE LIQUID STATE AND THE SOLID STATE

13.6 GENERAL PROPERTIES OF LIQUIDS

The arrangement of particles in a liquid is neither completely random, as in a gas, nor strictly ordered, as in a crystalline solid. Liquids have what is called short-range order. Groups of particles in a liquid might be closely packed together or associated in chains or rings. These groups move past each other with equal ease in any direction, accounting for the fluidity of liquids and the way that they take the shape of their container. The particles in a liquid are affected by interparticle forces, which vary in magnitude and direction. A single, comprehensive model for the structure and behavior of all liquids is, therefore, not to be expected.

Most substances that immediately come to mind as examples of liquids, such as water, alcohol, cleaning fluids, or antifreeze, are composed of rather simple molecules, containing up to about 20 atoms per molecule. Substances that are solid at ordinary temperatures, such as metals, some salts, and some polymers of moderate molecular mass, become liquids when the temperature is raised sufficiently (Table 13.2). Because the particles in liquids are close enough to touch each other, there is little room to squeeze them together, so liquids are only slightly compressible.

The difference in density between the solid and liquid states of pure substances is not great, and pressure changes have only a small effect on the volume and density of liquids and solids. For most liquids, and for water above 4 °C (Section 14.2), raising the temperature causes a slight increase in volume and a slight decrease in density.

The resistance of a substance to flow is **viscosity** — the opposite of fluidity. Most often viscosity is a property of concern for liquids. "Molasses in January" has a high viscosity; it will not run downhill easily or quickly. Internal forces that keep liquid particles from flowing past each other are responsible for viscosity.

Like most other properties of liquids, viscosity is dependent upon the size, shape, and chemical nature of the molecules. In general, higher intermolecular forces mean higher viscosity, and for similar types of compounds, higher molar mass also means higher viscosity. As illustrated by molasses, viscosity increases as the temperature decreases.

Lubricating oils are classified by their viscosity. The Society of Automotive Engineers assigns numbers to motor oils based on their relative viscosities. The SAE numbers range from 5 to 50 at a given temperature — 0 °F for winter (W) oils and

Table 13.2
Types of Liquids

Substances	Examples	Particles in Liquid	Major Interparticle Forces
Monatomic species at low temperatures	Noble gases at low temperatures (e.g., He, Ne)	Atoms	London forces
Hydrogen-bonded liquids	H_2O, C_2H_5OH, NH_3	Associated molecules	Hydrogen bonding (plus other intermolecular forces)
Non-hydrogen-bonded liquids	Benzene, Br_2, chloroform ($CHCl_3$)	Molecules	London forces; dipole–dipole forces for polar molecules
Molten salts	Molten NaCl, $Na_3[AlF_6]$ (cryolite)	Ions	Attraction between + and − ions
Molten metals and Hg	Molten Fe, Cu	Atoms*	Metallic bond

* Neither "atoms" nor "ions" is an exact description, for each electron in the "electron sea" is associated with several electron-deficient atoms.

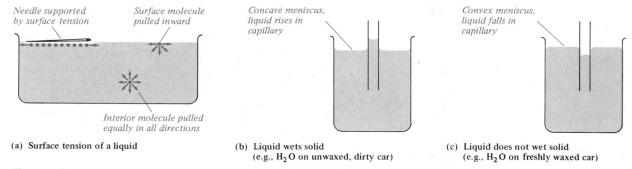

Figure 13.11
Surface Tension and Wetting The curved shape of the surface of a liquid in a narrow tube
is called a *meniscus.*

210 °F for oils that are usable at summer temperatures. The larger the number, the
greater the viscosity. Oils with a double number contain additives that moderate the
change of viscosity with temperature so that they are neither too thin in summer nor
too thick in winter. For example, SAE 10W/40 oil has an SAE number of 10 at 0 °F
and of 40 at 210 °F.

In the interior of a liquid each molecule is subjected to equal forces of attraction
from other molecules on all sides. Molecules at the surface feel these forces only on
the liquid side, however, and as a result are pulled inward and closer together (Figure
13.11). The surface of a liquid can be thought of as behaving like a stretched
membrane trying to contract to the smallest possible surface area. **Surface tension** is
the property of a surface that imparts membrane-like behavior to the surface; it is
formally defined as the amount of energy required to expand the surface of a liquid
by a unit area.

Surface tension causes a tiny suspended liquid droplet to take the shape of a
sphere — the shape with the smallest surface-to-volume ratio. It is surface tension
that supports a steel needle on the surface of a glass of water (Figure 13.11a). (The
needle is denser than water, and if pushed under, it sinks.) The surface tension at a
liquid–solid interface is responsible for whether or not the liquid "wets" the solid.
"Wetting" occurs when the attraction between the liquid and solid molecules is
greater than the internal cohesive forces in the liquid (Figure 13.11b,c). The rise of a
liquid in a narrow tube due to wetting of the walls — *capillary action* — contributes
to the rise of water in the stems of plants.

13.7 TYPES OF SOLIDS Solids were once described as "those parts of the material world which support when
sat on, which hurt when kicked, which kill when shot." In terms of their chemical
and physical properties, there are two types of solids — crystalline solids and amorphous solids. A **crystalline solid,** also called a *true solid,* is a substance in which the
atoms, molecules, or ions have a characteristic, regular, and repetitive three-dimensional arrangement. Sugar and salt are crystalline solids. An **amorphous solid** is a
substance in which the atoms, molecules, or ions have a random and nonrepetitive
three-dimensional arrangement. Tar is an amorphous solid. The gemstone opal and
volcanic glass (obsidian) are two of the very few parts of the earth's crust that are
amorphous.

**Amorphous solid: random
arrangement of atoms, ions,
or molecules
Crystalline solid: regular
repeated structural pattern**

Everyone is familiar with the beautiful and varied crystalline forms of the
gemstones formed in nature and collected by mineralogists (Figure 13.12). A **crystal**
is a solid that has a shape bounded by plane surfaces intersecting at fixed angles. To a
chemist, a crystal is an array of atoms, molecules, or ions in which a structural

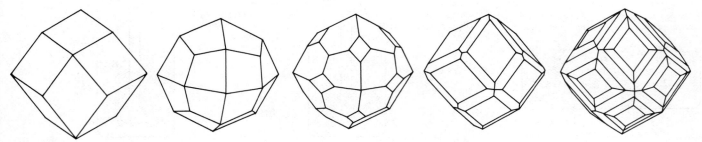

Figure 13.12
Natural Crystal Forms of Garnet (Source: C. S. Hurlburt, Jr., *Dana's Manual of Mineral-ogy,* 18th ed., New York; John Wiley & Sons, 1971.)

pattern is repeated periodically in three dimensions. The regular geometrical shape of a crystal is the large-scale expression of the internal order of its atoms, molecules, or ions. Perfectly symmetrical single crystals of pure substances form only when the crystals have the opportunity to grow slowly in all directions. Most crystalline materials are *polycrystalline*—composed of small regions with plane faces and the characteristic internal order, but randomly oriented toward each other (Figure 13.13c).

Crystalline substances, because of their internal order, may be *anisotropic*—they may have certain physical and chemical properties that vary with direction. For example, electrical conductivity may be greater in one direction than another. One way to identify a crystalline substance is by its cleavage, when struck sharply, into smaller pieces with planar faces. Amorphous substances are generally *isotropic*—their physical properties are the same in all directions. Cleavage of an amorphous material gives smaller pieces with nonplanar faces.

Amorphous and crystalline materials are also quite different in their melting behavior. Crystalline solids generally have sharp melting points—as the crystal is heated, all of the particles are released from their fixed positions at the same temperature. Amorphous solids soften gradually as the temperature rises. Glass, tar, and many polymers are, in fact, often classified not as solids, but as liquids of such high viscosity at ordinary temperatures that their flow is not normally observable. In a sheet of glass taken from an old window, there is a significant (though small) difference in thickness between the bottom and the top. The bottom is thicker because the glass has flowed slightly over the years. Most glasses are mixtures of

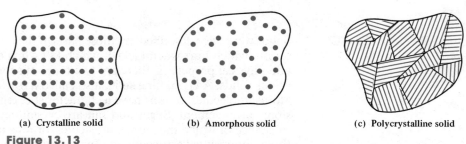

(a) Crystalline solid   (b) Amorphous solid   (c) Polycrystalline solid

Figure 13.13
Three Types of Solids, Classified According to Atomic Arrangement (a) Crystalline and (b) amorphous materials are illustrated by microscopic views of the atoms, whereas (c) polycrystalline structure is illustrated by a more macroscopic view of adjacent single-crys-talline regions, which are called *crystallites.* (Source: B. Streetman, *Solid State Electronic Devices,* Englewood Cliff, N.J.: Prentice-Hall, 1980, p. 4.)

Table 13.3
Types of Crystalline Solids Keep in mind that both covalent and ionic contributions to bonding often exist in the same substance.

Substances	Examples	Particles in Crystal Lattice	Major Interparticle Forces
Pure metals	**Fe, Cu, Al**	**Atoms***	**Metallic bond**
Alloys	**AuAg**	**Atoms***	**Metallic bond**
Ionic crystals	**All salts (e.g., NaCl, BaSO₄)**	**Monatomic or polyatomic ions**	**Ionic bond**
Molecular crystals	**All covalent compounds (e.g., CO₂, ice, organic compounds)**	**Neutral molecules**	**Intermolecular forces**
Network covalent materials	**Silicon, diamond, quartz, germanium, boron nitride**	**Atoms**	**Covalent bonds**

* Neither "atoms" nor "ions" is an exact description, for each electron in the "electron sea" is associated with many electron-deficient atoms.

oxygen-containing compounds that have cooled from a molten state without crystallizing.

In many scientific contexts, the word "solid" is used strictly for crystalline materials. Table 13.3 summarizes the types of crystalline solids. Network covalent substances, in which all of the atoms are continuously joined by covalent bonds, were described previously (Section 9.17). Molecular crystals include almost all organic compounds in the solid state. The intermolecular forces acting in such substances were discussed in Chapter 11 (see Sections 11.7–11.9). Hydrogen bonding is particularly important in determining the arrangement in space of the molecules in many crystalline organic compounds, such as in urea (Figure 13.14).

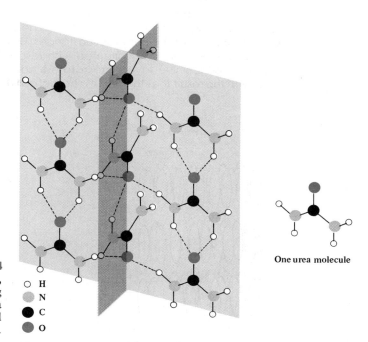

One urea molecule

○ H
● N
● C
● O

Figure 13.14
Crystal Structure of Urea, (NH₂)₂C═O This drawing represents the arrangement of urea molecules in a crystal. The dashed lines represent hydrogen bonds.

AN ASIDE

Liquid Crystals

The liquid crystalline state is intermediate between the solid state and the liquid state. Liquid crystals have become familiar through the advertising for LCD — liquid crystal display — wrist watches, calculators and other items with digital displays (i.e., displays of numbers). A liquid crystal display in, for example, a watch, usually shows black numbers against a silvery background. (The displays that show red digits against a black background have LED — light-emitting diode — displays. These are semiconducting devices; Section 30.10).

Liquid crystals can be formed by heating certain solids or by mixing controlled amounts of solvent with certain solid substances. Liquid crystals flow like liquids, but exhibit some of the optical properties of crystals. In the liquid crystalline state, substances have lost the three-dimensional order typical of crystals, but retain two-dimensional order and are therefore more ordered than liquids. The optical mechanical, and electrical properties of liquid crystals are anisotropic, that is, they vary with the direction in which they are observed. This variation is essential to the use of liquid crystals in display devices.

The molecules of typical substances that display liquid crystallinity are long and narrow, rigid, and contain benzene rings or other similar rings, for example,

$$CH_3O \overset{}{\underset{}{\bigcirc}} - N = \overset{O^-}{\underset{+}{N}} - \bigcirc OCH_3$$

p-azoxyanisole

Three basic types of molecular arrangement have been identified in liquid crystals. *Smectic liquid crystals* are turbid, viscous substances with parallel molecules in planes that can slip past each other (Figure A). (The curious name comes from the Greek word for soap; soap films are smectic substances.) *Nematic liquid crystals* are less turbid and more mobile than smectic liquid crystals. In the nematic state the molecules are parallel to each other but are not ordered into planes (Figure B). ("Nematic" comes from the Greek word meaning thread and refers to a threadlike optical pattern seen in films of such substances.) Frequently a smectic substance is transformed into a nematic substance — a further decrease in order — during the course of heating to a higher temperature.

Cholesteric liquid crystals, sometimes called twisted nematic crystals, have order similar to that of the nematic substances. However, the molecules in successive layers are not randomly oriented with respect to each other. Instead, the molecules in successive layers are rotated about axes perpendicular to their centers, with the result that they form a helical coil (Figure C). A complete 360° turn

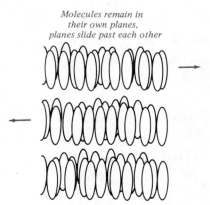

Molecules remain in their own planes, planes slide past each other

Figure A
Smectic Liquid Crystalline Substance

Parallel molecules slide past each other

Figure B
Nematic Liquid Crystalline Substance

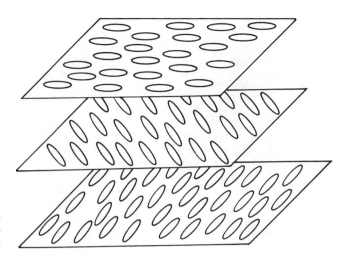

Figure C
Cholesteric Liquid Crystalline
Substance

in such a substance frequently occurs within the distance of the wavelength of visible light.

Cholesteric substances have the remarkable property of reflecting light of different colors at different temperatures because of the sensitivity of this helical structure to temperature. The color observed is the result of reflection of visible light in the same way as x-rays are reflected by the layers of ions or molecules in a crystal (Bragg reflection; see Tools of Chemistry: Diffraction, this chapter). The variation in color of cholesteric liquid crystals with changing temperature can be exploited in a variety of ways. For example, thin films incorporating these substances are used to map skin temperature (as an aid to the diagnosis of diseased tissue) and electrical circuit temperatures.

A typical LCD consists of a thin flat cell in which the long liquid crystals are held in a specific orientation (Figure D). When an electric field is applied to certain regions of the cell (regions in the shape of digits), various optical properties in those regions, such as reflection of light, are changed, making them visible.

The potential of liquid crystals, both in studies of molecular order and phase transitions and in practical applications, is great, and much remains to be discovered. Liquid crystalline substances have been found in numerous living systems, and a better understanding of their behavior is therefore also of importance in biochemistry.

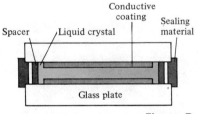

Figure D
A Liquid Crystal Display Device

13.8 CLOSEST PACKING; METALS

A pure metal is a crystalline solid made of identical atoms. Many metals have high densities, showing that in their crystal structures empty spaces are small. To visualize the crystal structures of metals, think of each metal atom as a solid sphere. The simplest way to pack spheres of the same radius into a single layer as closely as possible is in a hexagonal arrangement. Each sphere touches six other spheres (Figure 13.15a). This arrangement, called closest packing, can continue indefinitely in a single layer, and a crystal can be built up by superimposing one such layer over another.

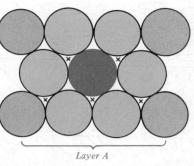

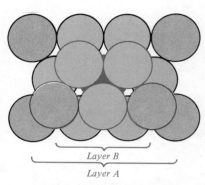

Figure 13.15
Closest Packing in Layers The light-colored spheres all touch the dark-colored spheres.

(a) Closest packing of spheres of equal radius in a single layer. Here and in (b), all of the spheres that touch the dark central spheres are shown in light color.

(b) Another closest-packed layer, layer B, has been added above layer A. Layer B spheres cover the layer A spaces marked x in (a). Three spheres in layer B touch the dark central sphere of layer A.

Two types of superimposition maintain closest packing in three dimensions. In each, the second layer (B) is placed over the first layer (A) so that three spheres of layer B touch the same sphere of layer A (Figure 13.15b). The third layer can then be superimposed in one of two ways. In the first, each atom in the third layer lies directly above an atom in the first layer. In this arrangement, called **hexagonal closest packing,** closest packed layers of atoms are arranged in an ABABAB. . . sequence (Figure 13.16).

In the second way of adding the third layer (layer C), the layer is displaced so that its atoms are not directly above those of either layer A or layer B. In this arrangement,

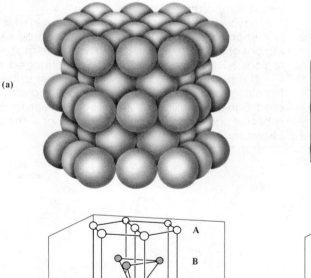

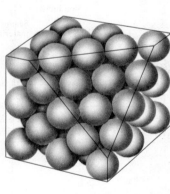

Figure 13.16
Hexagonal and Cubic Closest Packing (a) Stacked planes of spheres. (b) Exploded views of stacking of planes of spheres showing 12 nearest neighbors about one sphere.

(b)

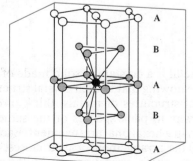

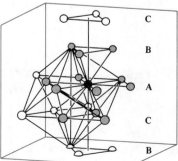

called **cubic closest packing,** closest packed layers of atoms are arranged in an ABCABCABC. . . sequence (see Figure 13.16).

In both hexagonal and cubic closest packing, each sphere touches six other spheres in its own layer, plus three in the layer above and three in the layer below. This gives each sphere twelve nearest neighbors (see Figure 13.16b). The **coordination number** of an atom, ion, or molecule in a particular crystal structure is the number of nearest neighbors of that atom, ion, or molecule. In metals with either of the two closest packed structures, 74% of the available space is occupied.

> **Coordination number: number of nearest neighbors in crystal structure**

13.9 CRYSTAL SYSTEMS; UNIT CELLS

To talk and write about crystal structure is a difficult problem of a type that we have mentioned more than once. How do you use words and two-dimensional pictures to describe three-dimensional things that you cannot see? In this section we introduce a few of the terms used by crystallographers and spectroscopists in coping with this problem. They have developed elaborate methods for classifying crystals according to their geometry. We need only study a few of the definitions upon which these methods are based.

The infinite repetition of an orderly arrangement of particles in a crystal means that beginning at any given atom and moving in a specific direction will lead to another atom with an identical environment. A **space lattice** is a system of points representing sites with identical environments in the same orientation in a crystal. A simple cubic space lattice is shown in Figure 13.17. The **crystal structure** of a substance is the complete geometrical arrangement of the particles that occupy the space lattice.

A **unit cell** is the most convenient small part of a space lattice that, if repeated in three dimensions, will generate the entire lattice. The cube outlined in color in Figure 13.17 is a simple cubic unit cell. Each cracker box in a supermarket display is like a unit cell in the display. The overall shape of the display is governed to a certain extent by the shape of the box, with variations possible depending on how the boxes are stacked.

A **primitive unit cell** is a unit cell in which only the corners are occupied. In some cases, unit cells are chosen that contain other lattice points in addition to those at the corners; these are called **multiple unit cells.** A primitive cubic unit cell and two cubic unit cells that include other points in addition to those at the corners are shown in Figure 13.18. Together these cubic unit cells comprise an example of a crystal system—the cubic crystal system. The crystal structure of every substance, once it has been studied, is assigned to one of a number of different crystal systems. The assignment is made on the basis of symmetry operations—different ways of turning groups of lattice points in space that help to identify their symmetry. (We need not be concerned with symmetry operations here. The designation of unit cells and crystal

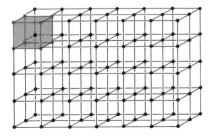

Figure 13.17
A Simple Cubic Space Lattice The unit cell is shaded in color.

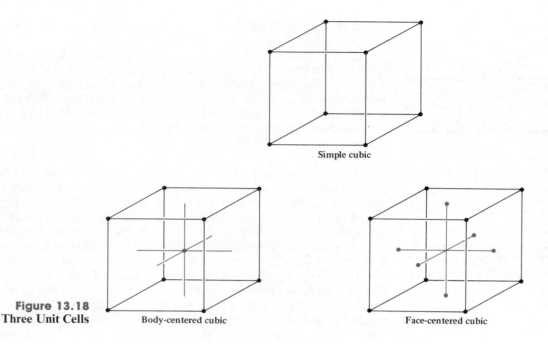

Figure 13.18
Three Unit Cells

Simple cubic

Body-centered cubic

Face-centered cubic

systems based on crystal structure data is best left to those with experience in this field.)

In a perfect crystal of diamond, the arrangement of the carbon atoms has the symmetry characteristics of a cube, and diamond belongs to the cubic crystal system. Information from x-ray analysis (see Tools of Chemistry: Diffraction: X-rays, Neutrons, and Electrons) shows that, in addition to the atoms that occupy the face-centered lattice points, the unit cell of diamond contains four interior carbon atoms arranged in a tetrahedron (Figure 13.19).

The unit cell diagrams in Figure 13.18 are misleading because they suggest that each cell contains a lot of empty space. The packing of atoms in a crystal is more realistically shown by the sphere-based packing models given in Figure 13.20. Most metals have one of these unit cells. A cubic closest packed array of atoms is assigned a face-centered cubic unit cell. (The parallel planes of closest packed atoms pass through the unit cell at an angle.) The unit cell for a hexagonal closest packed array of atoms is the hexagonal unit cell, which includes one interior point.

About two-thirds of all elemental metals have either the face-centered cubic or hexagonal unit cells shown in Figure 13.20. Many of the remaining metals crystallize

Figure 13.19
A Diamond Unit Cell Each sphere represents a carbon atom. The unit cell belongs to the cubic crystal system, and the atoms that form the face-centered cube that defines this unit cell are shown in the dark color. The solid lines are the C—C bonds. This unit cell also contains four interior carbon atoms, shown in the lighter color.

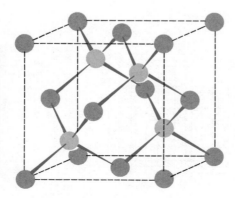

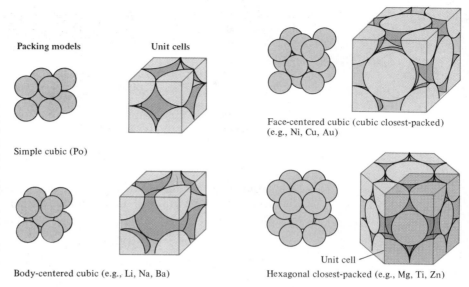

**Figure 13.20
Crystal Structure of Metals:
Packing Models and Unit Cells for
Cubic and Hexagonal Crystal
Systems** One metal, polonium, has
a simple cubic structure. Most other
metals have one of the remaining
three structures shown. The number
of atoms per unit cell for hexagonal
closest packing, which is two, is not
so obvious as it is in the other cases.
The unit cell for hexagonal closest
packing is the hexagonal cell with
one additional interior point.

with the body-centered cubic structure, an arrangement in which the coordination number of the central atom is eight, the layers are not closest packed, and space is not quite as efficiently filled.

The concepts of space lattices, symmetry operations, and unit cells are applied to all types of crystals. When the points of a space lattice are occupied by ions of different sizes (discussed in the next section) or molecules, the total structure of the unit cell becomes more complex. The unit cell of carbon dioxide (dry ice) is a simple example of the structure of a molecular crystal (Figure 13.21).

Crystallographers specify the number of atoms per unit cell. At first glance, you might think that there are eight atoms occupying the simple cubic unit cell shown in Figure 13.18, but this is not the case. Even though eight lattice points outline the cubic unit cell, an atom at each point is part of seven other units cells that are adjacent to the cell under consideration (Figure 13.22). To find the number of atoms

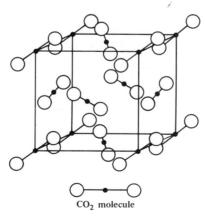

**Figure 13.21
The CO$_2$ Unit Cell** (Source: Arthur W. Adamson, *A Textbook of Physical Chemistry*, Academic Press, 1979, p. 854.)

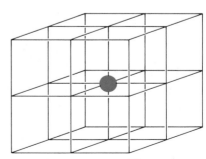

**Figure 13.22
Sharing of a Corner Atom by Eight
Unit Cells**

that belong to *each* unit cell, the atoms must be sliced along the faces of the cube. In the simple cubic unit cell, only one-eighth of each corner atom is contained within the individual cell. Therefore, the simple, or primitive, cubic unit cell "contains" one atom:

$$(8 \text{ corners})\left(\frac{1/8 \text{ atom}}{\text{corner}}\right) = 1 \text{ atom}$$

The body-centered cubic unit cell has one complete atom in the interior in addition to the corner atoms, to give a unit cell with two atoms:

$$(8 \text{ corners})\left(\frac{1/8 \text{ atom}}{\text{corner}}\right) + (1 \text{ center atom}) = 2 \text{ atoms}$$

An atom at a face-centered point is divided between two unit cells, giving the face-centered cubic unit cell a total of four atoms.

$$(8 \text{ corners})\left(\frac{1/8 \text{ atom}}{\text{corner}}\right) + (6 \text{ faces})\left(\frac{1/2 \text{ atom}}{\text{face}}\right) = 4 \text{ atoms}$$

Once the number of atoms in the unit cell is known, the mass of the unit cell can be calculated. To do this, we multiply the mass of one atom by the number of atoms in the unit cell. (The mass of one atom can be found by dividing the molar mass of the substance by Avogadro's number.)

EXAMPLE 13.5
Unit Cell — Number of Atoms

(a) How many atoms occupy the diamond unit cell shown in Figure 13.19?
(b) What is the mass of a diamond unit cell?

(a) From the sketch of the unit cell, we can see that there are eight corner atoms, six atoms at face-centered points, and four atoms at points in the interior of the cell. The number of atoms in the unit cell is

$$(8 \text{ corners})\left(\frac{1/8 \text{ atom}}{\text{corner}}\right) + (6 \text{ faces})\left(\frac{1/2 \text{ atom}}{\text{face}}\right) + (4 \text{ atoms in interior}) = 8 \text{ atoms}$$

There are eight carbon atoms in the diamond unit cell.
(b) The mass of a carbon atom is found by dividing the molar mass by Avogadro's number.

$$\frac{(12.01 \text{ g/mol})}{(6.022 \times 10^{23} \text{ C atoms/mol})} = 1.994 \times 10^{-23} \text{ g/C atom}$$

Thus, for the eight carbon atoms in the unit cell,

$$(8 \text{ C atoms})(1.994 \times 10^{-23} \text{ g/C atom}) = 1.595 \times 10^{-22} \text{ g}$$

The mass of a unit cell of diamond is 1.595×10^{-22} g.

Exercise   The unit cell of metallic gold is face-centered cubic. (a) How many atoms occupy the gold unit cell? (b) What is the mass of a gold unit cell? *Answer* (a) 4; (b) 1.308×10^{-21} g

---

The lengths of the sides of a unit cell can be found by x-ray diffraction (see Tools of Chemistry: Diffraction: X-rays, Neutrons, and Electrons). For a cubic unit cell the lengths of the sides are identical. The volume of the cubic unit cell can be calculated by cubing the length of the edge of the unit cell.

The density of any piece of metal can be calculated by dividing the mass of the piece by its volume (Section 2.8d). Density is one of the properties that does not depend upon the size of the sample. For this reason, the density of a metal can be found from the smallest solid sample possible — the unit cell. The mass of the unit cell divided by its volume gives the density of the metal.

Density calculated in this way for a unit cell is sometimes called the **theoretical density.** The theoretical density differs from the actual density because most crystals have defects (Section 13.12). Vacancies, for example, would lead to an actual density less than the theoretical density. The presence of impurities could make the actual density either greater or less than the theoretical density, depending on the relative masses of the metal atoms and he impurity atoms.

EXAMPLE 13.6
Unit Cell — Volume and Density

The unit cell length of diamond was measured as 0.3567 nm. (a) Calculate the volume of this cubic unit cell in cubic centimeters. (b) Using the mass found in Example 13.5b for the diamond unit cell, find the theoretical density of diamond.

(a) To find the unit cell length expressed in centimeters, the conversion factors based on the meaning of the prefixes "nano" and "centi" must be used:

$$(0.3567 \text{ nm})\left(\frac{1 \text{ m}}{10^9 \text{ nm}}\right)\left(\frac{10^2 \text{ cm}}{\text{m}}\right) = 3.567 \times 10^{-8} \text{ cm}$$

The volume of the cubic unit is found by cubing the length of the side

$$(3.567 \times 10^{-8} \text{ cm})^3 = 4.538 \times 10^{-23} \text{ cm}^3$$

The volume of the diamond unit cell is 4.538×10^{-23} cm³.

(b) Dividing the mass found in Example 13.5b by the volume gives the density as

$$\frac{1.595 \times 10^{-22} \text{ g}}{4.538 \times 10^{-23} \text{ cm}^3} = 3.515 \text{ g/cm}^3$$

The theoretical density of diamond is found from the unit cell data to be 3.515 g/cm³. [The measured density of diamond is 3.513 at 25 °C.]

Exercise The unit cell length of gold is 0.4079 nm. (a) Calculate the volume of this cubic unit cell in cubic centimeters. (b) The mass of the gold unit cell is 1.308×10^{-21} g. Calculate the theoretical density of gold. *Answer* (a) 6.787×10^{-23} cm³, (b) 19.27 g/cm³

TOOLS OF CHEMISTRY

Diffraction: X-rays, Neutrons, and Electrons

Two beams of light that come from two different sources and meet at the same point can reinforce or cancel each other. These effects represent constructive and destructive interference, respectively (see Figure 8.2). If the waves are in phase and reinforce each other, a bright light appears. If the waves are partially or completely out of phase, a dimmer light or no light at all is visible. A diffraction pattern of light and dark lines is produced when light is split by passing through two or more slits (see Figure 8.4). To be diffracted, waves must have a wavelength comparable in size to the width of the slits.

The regularly spaced rows of atoms, ions, or molecules in a crystal can diffract radiation with wavelengths on the order of 0.1 nm. X-rays, neutron beams, and electron beams that fulfill this requirement are used in studying both crystal structure and molecular structure.

X-ray diffraction is a valuable tool in the determination of crystal structure. Only after 1912, when the German physicist Max von Laue found that x-rays could be

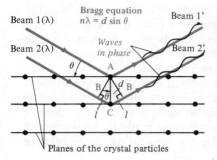

Figure A

X-ray Diffraction, as Interpreted by the Bragg Equation Beams 1 and 2 of monochromatic x-radiation are reflected by the successive planes of the crystal to give beams 1' and 2' with their waves in phase.

diffracted by crystals, was proof of the orderly structures of crystals possible. X-rays interact with the orbital electrons of the atoms in a crystal and x-ray diffraction shows where electron density is concentrated in a crystal. X-ray diffraction patterns are interpreted by a method developed by the English scientists William and Laurence Bragg. If x-rays of the same wavelength arrive at a given point in phase, the distance they have traveled must be a whole-number multiple of their wavelength. Picture two x-ray beams as reflected by successive planes of atoms in a crystal (Figure A). The rays from the lower plane travel a distance $2l$ further than the rays reflected by the upper plane. If this distance is a whole-number multiple of the wavelength, beams 1' and 2' are in phase and reinforce each other. Mathematically this condition is stated

$$n\lambda = 2l$$

whole number   *wavelength*

The angle of incidence of the beam θ is equal to the angle BAC and the triangle BAC is a right triangle, with AC equal to d, the distance between the planes. Therefore

$$l = d \sin \theta$$

Combining the two preceding equations gives the *Bragg equation,* or Bragg's law,

$$n\lambda = 2d \sin \theta$$

In the original Bragg method a single crystal is rotated through many values of θ. Using x-rays of a known single wavelength, the value of d and the dimensions of the unit cell in a crystal can be found. The intensity of the diffracted radiation varies with the type and location of atoms or ions in the unit cell. Information about the structure of molecules in a molecular crystal or the arrangement of ions in an ionic crystal is derived by studying these variations. Polycrystalline samples can also be studied, using the technique called x-ray powder diffraction (Figure B, next page).

An electron does not penetrate as far past a crystalline surface as an x-ray beam does. Therefore, low-energy electron diffraction (LEED) is useful for studying atomic arrangements and electron densities at surfaces. In electron diffraction, scattering, or reemission, of the radiation is the result of interaction with both orbital electrons and nuclei. Electron diffraction studies of thin foils yield information both about the regularity of the crystal structure and about its defects.

In neutron diffraction, an incident neutron beam is scattered solely by the nuclei, not by the orbital electrons. This makes neutron diffraction useful in two cases where x-ray diffraction will not work. Neutron diffraction can (1) locate very light atoms in the presence of heavier ones (e.g., H atoms in the presence of carbon atoms in organic compounds), and (2) distinguish between atoms with similar numbers of electrons, such as those combined in intermetallic compounds. In x-ray diffraction, scattering is proportional to the number of orbital electrons, and it fails in case (1) because the relative contribution of the light atoms is too small, and in case (2) because the contributions of the two types of atoms are too similar.

By combining information on electron density from x-ray studies and information on the positions of nuclei from neutron diffraction, it is possible to find the pattern of electron density about two atoms in a given bond. The diffraction of a neutron beam is influenced by magnetic fields as well as by nuclei, and most of what we know about the magnetic structures of materials has been found by neutron diffraction.

The interpretation of diffraction patterns is complex. Often, particularly for x-ray diffraction, substances are identified by comparison of their diffraction patterns with those of substances that have been studied earlier.

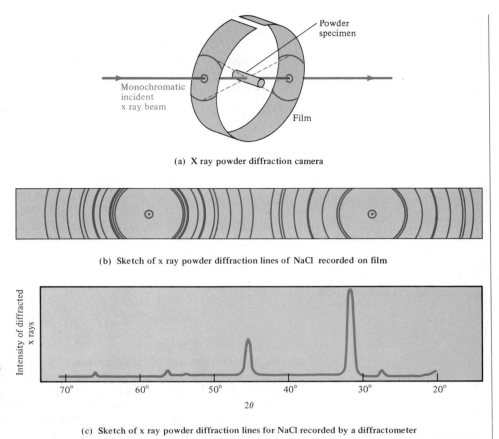

(a) X ray powder diffraction camera

(b) Sketch of x ray powder diffraction lines of NaCl recorded on film

(c) Sketch of x ray powder diffraction lines for NaCl recorded by a diffractometer

Figure B
X-ray Powder Diffraction The diffraction pattern is recorded on a cylindrical film. Each line in (b) and each peak in (c) represents reflection from a different set of planes.

13.10 CRYSTAL STRUCTURE OF IONIC COMPOUNDS

Closest packing of spheres of the same size leaves two types of open spaces, or "holes," between the layers. One approach to visualizing the crystal structure of ionic compounds is to picture a closest packed array of larger ions, with smaller ions occupying the holes. Usually anions, which are commonly larger than cations, form the closest packed array, with cations in the holes, but in some cases the situation is reversed.

A *tetrahedral hole* lies at the center of a cluster of four spheres that form a tetrahedron (Figure 13.23). In a closest packed array there are two tetrahedral holes per closest packed sphere. An *octahedral hole,* larger than the tetrahedral hole, lies at the center of a cluster of six spheres that form an octahedron (Figure 13.23). One octahedral hole is present for every sphere in a closest packed array.

An array of anions may open up and depart somewhat from closest packing in order to accommodate cations in the holes. For example, in a sodium chloride crystal, the Na^+ cations occupy octahedral holes in a slightly expanded Cl^- cubic closest packed array. There is one octahedral hole per Cl^- ion, all of these holes are occupied by Na^+ ions, and thus the 1-to-1 NaCl stoichiometry is achieved. The six Cl^- ions that comprise one octahedron are shown in color in Figure 13.24. Each Na^+ ion in an octahedral hole is surrounded by six Cl^- ions and has a coordination number of six. Similarly, each Cl^- ion has a coordination number of six. Figure 13.25

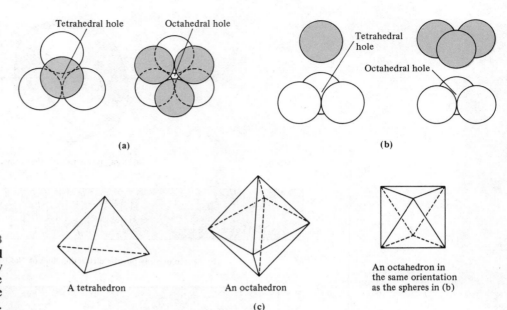

Figure 13.23
Tetrahedral and Octahedral Holes (a) Top view; (b) side view with top layer lifted; (c) the geometric figures formed by the spheres.

A tetrahedron   An octahedron   An octahedron in the same orientation as the spheres in (b)

(a)   (b)

(c)

shows how the sodium chloride crystal structure fits into the cubic crystal system. Although we do not pursue the topic here, all ionic crystal structures are assigned to crystal systems as discussed in the preceding section on metals.

Titanium dioxide (TiO_2) is an example of a compound that is **polymorphous**—able to crystallize in more than one crystal structure. The anatase form of TiO_2 has a crystal structure related to that of NaCl. The O^{2-} ions form a cubic close-packed array and the Ti^{4+} cations occupy octahedral holes. To maintain the proper stoichiometry, one-half of the holes are occupied in the manner shown in Figure 13.26a. Rutile (see Figure 13.27), the other crystalline form of TiO_2, is based on a hexagonal closest packed array of anions, with one-half of the octahedral holes occupied as shown in Figure 13.26b: In both crystalline forms, the Ti^{4+} ions have a crystal coordination number of six and the O^{2-} ions have a crystal coordination number of three.

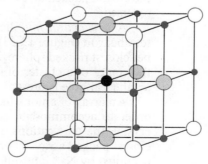

Figure 13.24
Ions in a Sodium Chloride Crystal The larger Cl^- ions outline the cube. The colored Cl^- ions form one octahedron. The Na^+ ion in the hole at the center of this octahedron is shown in black.

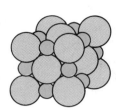
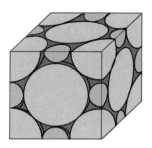

(a) NaCl packing model

(b) NaCl unit cell (one Na⁺ ion is concealed in the center of the cell)

Figure 13.25
Sodium Chloride Crystal Structure You can see that the Na^+ ions are each surrounded by six Cl^- ions, and the Cl^- ions are each surrounded by six Na^+ ions.

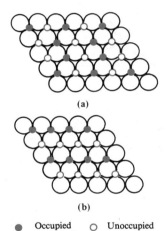

(a)

(b)

● Occupied   ○ Unoccupied
   octahedral   octahedral
   hole   hole

Figure 13.26
Occupation of $\frac{1}{2}$ of the Octahedral Holes (a) Pattern followed in the anatase form of TiO_2; (b) pattern followed in the rutile form of TiO_2. Other patterns are possible.

Tetrahedral holes are smaller than octahedral holes, and an ion in a tetrahedral hole always has a coordination number of four. There are two tetrahedral holes per anion in a closest packed array of anions. In compounds with a 2-to-1 stoichiometry such as Li_2O and Na_2S, every tetrahedral hole is occupied by a cation. In compounds with a 1-to-1 stoichiometry, such as ZnS, the cations occupy one-half of the tetrahedral holes in the closest packed array of anions (see Figure 13.27).

Crystal structure is influenced by the relative sizes of the cations and anions, as well as by their charges. When the cation is large relative to the anion, it may not fit into the tetrahedral *or* octahedral holes in a closest packed array of anions. In such a case, a simple cubic array of anions (each layer of anions directly above another layer of anions; see Figure 13.20, top) leaves cubic holes that provide enough space for the larger cations. A cation in a cubic hole has a coordination number of eight.

The **radius ratio** — the ratio of cation to anion radii, r_+/r_- — needed for an ion to fit into a specific type of hole can be calculated from simple geometry. The upper limits of r_+/r_- for tetrahedral and octahedral hole occupation are 0.414 and 0.732, respectively (Table 13.4). These are radius ratios at which maximum stability is achieved by the cation just touching the surrounding anions. For example, cesium bromide has a radius ratio of 0.852. This is larger than the upper limit for a cation with a coordination number of six, and, as expected, Cs^+ ions in a CsBr crystal structure occupy cubic holes. The Mg^{2+} cations in magnesium fluoride, MgF_2 ($r_+/r_- = 0.49$), occupy octahedral holes and have coordination number six. Stoichiometry requires that in MgF_2 one-half of the octahedral holes be occupied.

Table 13.4
Radius Ratio and Crystal Structure The upper limit of the radius ratio for each arrangement is that in which the cation is in contact with its nearest neighbor anions. Once r_+/r_- reaches unity, the reverse of the radius ratio is used. r_-/r_+ is calculated and the choice of structure fits the corresponding geometry, except that the larger cations form the lattice and the smaller anions fit in the holes.

Range of Radius Ratio, r_+/r_-	Cation Coordination Number	Hole Geometry
0.225–0.414	4	Tetrahedral
0.414–0.732	6	Octahedral
>0.732	8	Cubic

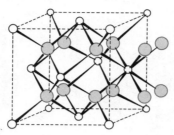
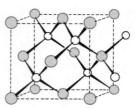
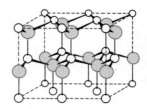

Fluorite, CaF$_2$
Simple cubic packed
anions with cations in
1/2 of cubic holes
cation C.N. 8
anion C.N. 4

Zincblende, ZnS
Cubic closest-packed
anions with cations in
1/2 of tetrahedral holes
cation C.N. = 4
anion C.N. = 4

Wurtzite, ZnS
Hexagonal closest packed
anions with cations in
1/2 of tetrahedral holes
cation C.N. = 4
anion C.N. = 4

Figure 13.27
Some Simple Crystal Structures
These are common types of crystal
structures adopted by many
different compounds and referred to
by the name of the compound given
here. The large colored circles
represent anions; the smaller open
circles represent cations. An
antifluorite structure in which the
cations and anions are reversed is
adopted in some compounds where
cations are larger than anions.

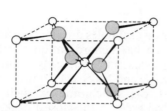
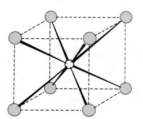

Rutile, TiO$_2$
Hexagonal closest packed
anions with cations in
1/2 of octahedral holes
cation C.N. = 6
anion C.N. = 3

Cesium chloride, CsCl
Simple cubic packed anions
with cations in all cubic holes
cation C.N. = 8
anion C.N. = 8

EXAMPLE 13.7
Unit Cell — Radius Ratio

The ionic radii for Co^{2+} and O^{2-} are 0.072 nm and 0.140 nm, respectively. Calculate the radius ratio for these ions and predict the crystal structure of cobalt(II) oxide, CoO.

The radius ratio is

$$\frac{r_+}{r_-} = \frac{0.072 \text{ nm}}{0.140 \text{ nm}} = 0.51$$

According to Table 13.4, this radius ratio fits into the range for octahedral hole geometry. Therefore CoO should have a structure in which Co^{2+} cations fit into the octahedral holes in a closest packed array of O^{2-} anions. Because the stoichiometry is 1 to 1, all of the holes should be occupied. [CoO has the same structure as NaCl.]

Exercise The ionic radii of Zn^{2+} and Se^{2-} are 0.074 nm and 0.191 nm, respectively. Calculate the radius ratio for these ions and predict the crystal structure for ZnSe. *Answer* 0.39, Zn^{2+} cations in one-half of the tetrahedral holes [a zincblende structure]

Predictions of crystal structure based on radius ratio are sometimes correct and sometimes not, for there are several factors other than ionic radii that influence crystal structure. In particular, the calculated ranges of radius ratio values are for spherical ions. This is a limitation when ions are polarized and bonding is other than 100% ionic. In addition, because of difficulties in making the measurements, reliable values are not available for all ionic radii.

Some of the more common ionic crystal structures are illustrated in Figure 13.27, and described in terms of anion packing and hole geometry.

Substances that have the same crystal structure are said to be **isomorphous.** Some such substances can crystallize together to give a mixed product. For example, sodium nitrate ($NaNO_3$) and calcium carbonate ($CaCO_3$) form mixed crystals, although in terms of other physical properties and all chemical properties, they are quite different.

In summary, the atoms, molecules, or ions in crystalline substances have a regular, repetitive three-dimensional arrangement. In a single layer, atoms or ions of the same size are arranged most efficiently in a closest packed layer with each atom surrounded by six others. Most metals have crystal structures based on the stacking of closest packed layers in either hexagonal closest packing (AB AB. . . layers) or cubic closest packing (ABC ABC. . . layers).

Crystal structures are classified by assigning the spatial arrangement of atoms, ions, or molecules to crystal systems identified by the type of space lattice and unit cell that are occupied. Examples are given in Section 13.10 of the simple cubic lattice and some unit cells based upon it. Other similar crystal systems, not discussed here, are used in classifying all types of crystals, whether made up of atoms, molecules, or ions.

Ionic crystals can be pictured as arrays of the larger ions, usually anions, with the smaller ions occupying holes. In cubic and hexagonal closest-packed arrays there are two types of holes — tetrahedral holes and octahedral holes. The octahedral holes are the larger of the two. Still larger holes — cubic holes — are formed in simple cubic arrays of anions, which are not closest packed. The radius ratio, r_+/r_-, is an indicator of what type of hole will be occupied.

13.11 LATTICE ENERGIES; THE BORN–HABER CYCLE

Lattice energy is a thermodynamic quantity defined as the energy liberated when gaseous ions combine to give one mole of a crystalline ionic compound (Section 9.18). Lattice energy is essentially the enthalpy of formation of an ionic compound from ions in the gas phase. As illustrated by the values given in Table 13.5, lattice

Table 13.5

Lattice Energies In the two series of halides, the lattice energy decreases as the size of the anion or the cation increases. The pairs of Fe and Na salts show the effect of higher charges in increasing the lattice energy.

Halide	Lattice Energy (kJ/mol)	Interionic Distance (nm)
NaF	−910	0.2317
NaCl	−769	0.282
NaBr	−732	0.297
NaI	−682	0.323
LiCl	−834	0.257
NaCl	−769	0.282
KCl	−701	0.315
RbCl	−680	0.329
CsCl	−657	—
FeCl$_2$	−2525	—
FeCl$_3$	−5364	—
Na$_2$SO$_4$	−1827	—
FeSO$_4$	−2983	—
Na$_2$CO$_3$	−2301	—
FeCO$_3$	−3121	—

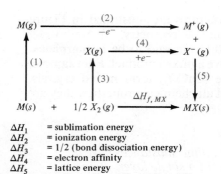

ΔH_1 = sublimation energy
ΔH_2 = ionization energy
ΔH_3 = 1/2 (bond dissociation energy)
ΔH_4 = electron affinity
ΔH_5 = lattice energy
$\Delta H_{f, MX} = \Delta H_1 + \Delta H_2 + \Delta H_3 + \Delta H_4 + \Delta H_5$

Figure 13.28

Born-Haber Cycle for the Formation of MX(s) from M(s) and $\frac{1}{2}X_2$ (g)
[This type of thermochemical cycle was introduced by M. Born, K. Fajans, F. Haber in 1919. For reasons that are not known, the cycle is commonly called the "Born-Haber" cycle rather than, more correctly, the Born-Fajans-Haber cycle.]

energies vary with interionic distances in the crystal and the charges of the ions. The closer together the ions and the larger their charges, the greater the lattice energy.

Lattice energies may be calculated by the application of Hess's law (Section 7.9c) to a standard cycle of reactions known as the Born–Haber cycle. The reactions in the cycle for the formation of a metal halide of formula MX represent conversion of the solid metal to cations in the gas phase (steps 1 and 2 in Figure 13.28), conversion of halogen molecules to anions in the gas phase (steps 3 and 4), and combination of the gaseous ions to give the solid compound (step 5). The enthalpy for the last step (step 5) is the lattice energy.

Sublimation energies (step 1), ionization energies (step 2), and bond energies (step 3) are generally known from experimental measurements. Electron affinities (step 4) and lattice energies (step 5), both of which are difficult to measure experimentally, are often determined by Born–Haber cycle calculations.

Steps (1), (2), and (3) all require the input of energy and have positive ΔH values. Electron affinity (step 4) is negative for the halogens and ranges from -349 kJ to -295 kJ. Lattice energy values (step 5) are always negative. When the lattice energy and electron affinity combined provide the energy required by steps (1) to (3), the formation of the ionic compound in question is exothermic and therefore is more favorable than if it were endothermic

In the following example, the Born–Haber cycle is used to answer a question frequently posed by students of chemistry.

EXAMPLE 13.8

Born–Haber Cycle

Even though much less energy is required to remove one valence electron from a magnesium atom than both electrons ($_{12}$Mg, $1s^2\,2s^2\,2p^6\,3s^2$), the element forms compounds containing Mg^{2+} ion rather than Mg^+. With the use of the thermochemical information given below (at 25 °C) show that the reaction

$$Mg(s) + Cl_2(g) \longrightarrow MgCl_2(s)$$

is more favorable energetically than

$$Mg(s) + \tfrac{1}{2}Cl_2(g) \longrightarrow MgCl(s)$$

Assign the known data to Born–Haber cycle steps according to Figure 13.28 for the formation of MgCl. Note that the stoichiometry of the steps must be modified for the formation of $MgCl_2$.

Reaction	$\Delta H°$(kJ)
$Mg(s) \longrightarrow Mg(g)$	150.2
$Mg(g) \longrightarrow Mg^+(g) + e^-$	743.8
$Mg(g) \longrightarrow Mg^{2+}(g) + 2e^-$	2200.3
$Cl_2(g) \longrightarrow 2Cl(g)$	243.4
$Cl(g) + e^- \longrightarrow Cl^-(g)$	-367.8
$Mg^+(g) + Cl^-(g) \longrightarrow MgCl(s)$	-676.1
$Mg^{2+}(g) + 2Cl^-(g) \longrightarrow MgCl_2(s)$	-2500.1

For the formation of MgCl(s) from the elements, we have, using the Born–Haber cycle steps in Figure 13.28,

Reaction	$\Delta H°$(kJ)	
$Mg(s) \longrightarrow Mg(g)$	150.2	(Step 1, sublimation energy)
$Mg(g) \longrightarrow Mg^+(g) + e^-$	743.8	(Step 2, ionization energy)
$\tfrac{1}{2}Cl_2(g) \longrightarrow Cl(g)$	121.7	(Step 3, $\tfrac{1}{2} \times$ bond dissociation energy)
$Cl(g) + e^- \longrightarrow Cl^-(g)$	-367.8	(Step 4, electron affinity)
$Mg^+(g) + Cl^-(g) \longrightarrow MgCl(s)$	-676.1	(Step 5, lattice energy)
$Mg(s) + \tfrac{1}{2}Cl_2(g) \longrightarrow MgCl(s)$	-28.2 kJ $= \Delta H_f°$, MgCl(s)	

For the formation of $MgCl_2(s)$, the thermochemical steps are as follows:

Reaction	$\Delta H°(kJ)$	
$Mg(s) \longrightarrow Mg(g)$	150.2	(Step 1, sublimation energy)
$Mg(g) \longrightarrow Mg^{2+}(g) + 2e^-$	2200.3	(Step 2, ionization energy)
$Cl_2(g) \longrightarrow 2Cl(g)$	243.4	(Step 3, bond dissociation energy)
$2Cl(g) + 2e^- \longrightarrow 2Cl^-(g)$	-735.6	(Step 4, $2\times$ electron affinity)
$Mg^{2+}(g) + 2Cl^-(g) \longrightarrow MgCl_2(s)$	-2500.1	(Step 5, lattice energy)
$Mg(s) + Cl_2(g) \longrightarrow MgCl_2(s)$	-641.8 kJ $= \Delta H_f°$, $MgCl_2(s)$	

The energy released in the formation of $MgCl_2(s)$ from its elements is much greater than that which would be released if $MgCl(s)$ were formed. Thermochemically, in terms of $\Delta H_f°$ values, $MgCl_2(s)$ is the much more stable species. It is clear from the data that the much greater lattice energy of $MgCl_2(s)$ is the major factor contributing to this greater stability. The smaller size and greater charge of Mg^{2+} compared to Mg^+ contribute to the greater lattice energy of $MgCl_2$.

Exercise The heat of formation of $KF(s)$ at 25 °C is -562.58 kJ/mol. Use the following thermodynamic data at 25 °C to calculate the lattice energy of $KF(s)$: $\Delta H° = 424.93$ kJ/mol for the ionization of $K(g)$, $\Delta H° = -349.7$ kJ/mol for the electron affinity of $F(g)$, $\Delta H° = 90.00$ kJ/mol for the sublimation of $K(s)$, and $\Delta H° = 157.99$ kJ/mol for the bond dissociation energy of $F_2(g)$. *Answer* -806.8 kJ/mol

13.12 DEFECTS

Except for single crystals grown under special conditions, real crystalline substances are seldom perfect. A perfect crystal is chemically pure and structurally perfect, with every lattice point occupied as specified by the unit cell.

Many physical and chemical properties of solids *depend* upon the presence of defects in the solid state. Perfect crystals are very strong, whereas most solids contain enough defects to allow them to yield more easily to mechanical forces. Also, chemical reactions in the solid state require the motion of atoms or ions through a solid. In a perfect crystal there is no available pathway for such motion, whereas in real crystals, atoms or ions can move from defect to defect. The defect structure plays an essential role in determining the properties of semiconductors (Section 30.8).

Solid-state defects can be classified as point defects, line defects, planar defects, or three-dimensional (spatial) defects.

Point defects are variations in the occupation of the lattice or interstitial sites in the crystal. Three basic types of point defects occur (Figure 13.29): (1) vacancies— unoccupied lattice sites; (2) interstitial atoms or ions—atoms or ions in the spaces among lattice sites; and (3) impurity defects—foreign ions in regular lattice sites or interstitial sites. In ionic crystals neutrality must be maintained by the establishment of an equilibrium between positively and negatively charged defects.

The tendency of some substances to incorporate point defects in their crystal structures accounts for the occurrence of **nonstoichiometric compounds**—compounds in which atoms of different elements combine in other than whole-number ratios. Such compounds exist only in the solid state and in some cases have variable compositions. For example, in wüstite, $Fe_{<1}O$, up to 14% of the normal cation sites can be empty. To maintain neutrality, two Fe^{2+} ions are converted to Fe^{3+} for every missing Fe^{2+}. As prepared in the laboratory at atmospheric pressure, neither iron(II) oxide nor copper(II) sulfide has a stoichiometric composition. And in titanium oxide of the stoichiometric composition TiO, 15% of the sites of each type are vacant. Therefore, there exists a wide range of nonstoichiometric titanium oxide compositions, TiO_x, where x can be less than or greater than one depending upon the oxygen pressure during preparation of the sample.

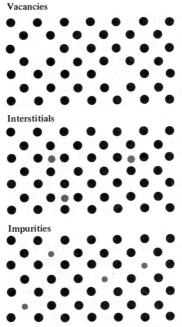

Vacancies

Interstitials

Impurities

Figure 13.29
Point Defects

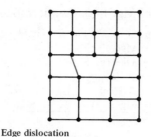

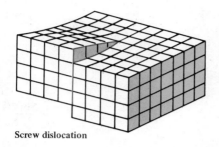

Figure 13.30
Line Defects The edge dislocation is the insertion of an incomplete plane of atoms. The screw dislocation forms a spiral around the dislocation.

Edge dislocation

Screw dislocation

Dislocations are line defects; they represent the displacement of rows of particles in a crystal. Edge and screw dislocations—the two types of line defects—usually occur together (Figure 13.30). Line defects account for the ease of mechanical deformation of a solid.

Planar defects include grain boundaries in polycrystalline materials, phase boundaries in multiphase solids, and stacking faults, in which the stacking sequence of crystal layers is not regular (for example, the occurrence of a sequence such as ABCABABC. . . in a face-centered cubic crystal).

The *three-dimensional defects* include pores—open spaces within the solid—or the presence of macroscopic regions of impurities within the solid.

SUMMARY

13.1 KINETIC-MOLECULAR THEORY FOR LIQUIDS AND SOLIDS   In solids and liquids the particles are close together, so their motion is restricted. In other respects, however, the kinetic-molecular theory (Section 5.2) applies to solids and liquids as well as gases. The state in which any substance exists depends upon the balance between the kinetic energies of the particles and the intermolecular and/or bonding forces acting between them.

13.2 CHANGES OF STATE   The escape of molecules from the liquid or solid to the gas phase is called vaporization; the transition from the gas to the liquid phase is condensation. Those molecules that escape from the surface of a liquid or solid are those with the most kinetic energy; thus evaporation becomes faster as the temperature increases. Evaporation from a solid is called sublimation. Equilibrium between the liquid and solid phases occurs at the melting point. Fusion is the technical term for melting. Fusion and vaporization always require heat, so ΔH for these processes is positive.

13.3 VAPOR PRESSURE   **13.4** BOILING POINT   The vapor pressure over a liquid (or solid) is the pressure at which vaporization and condensation (or sublimation and deposition) are in equilibrium. Vapor pressure increases with increasing temperature and is lower for substances with strong intermolecular forces. The boiling point of a liquid is the temperature at which the vapor pressure of a liquid equals the pressure of the gases above the liquid. Boiling point thus varies with pressure; the normal boiling point is the boiling temperature at 760 Torr.

13.5 PHASE DIAGRAMS   A phase diagram is used to show the relationship between the state of a substance and the temperature and pressure. A phase diagram combines the plots of melting point, boiling point, and sublimation temperature against pressure for a given substance. The boiling point curve, which marks the equilibrium between liquid and gaseous phases, ends at the critical point. Above the temperature at this point (the critical temperature), no amount of pressure is sufficient to cause liquefaction. At a triple point, three phases are in equilibrium. A liquid can be supercooled to a temperature below its freezing point without freezing.

13.6 GENERAL PROPERTIES OF LIQUIDS The arrangement of particles in a liquid is neither completely random nor completely ordered. Groups of particles are organized by intermolecular forces, but these groups can still slide past each other easily. Intermolecular forces are responsible for viscosity (the resistance to flow) and surface tension (the membrane-like behavior of a liquid surface).

13.7 TYPES OF SOLIDS An amorphous solid is one in which the particles have a random, nonrepetitive spatial arrangement. A crystalline (or true) solid is one in which the particles have a characteristic, regular, and repetitive spatial arrangement. On the molecular level a crystal is an array of atoms, molecules, or ions in which a single structural pattern is repeated periodically in three dimensions. Crystalline solids can be cleaved along planes, have sharp melting points, and are sometimes anisotropic (that is, some of their properties may vary with direction).

13.8 CLOSEST PACKING; METALS A pure metal is a crystalline solid made of identical atoms. Spaces in the crystal structure of metals are small, so metals generally have high densities. The crystal coordination number of an atom, molecule, or ion in a crystal is the number of nearest neighbors that it has. In both hexagonal closest packing and cubic closest packing arrangements, atoms are packed together as tightly as possible and each atom has a crystal coordination number of 12.

13.9 CRYSTAL SYSTEMS; UNIT CELLS A space lattice is a system of points representing sites with identical environments in a crystal. The crystal structure of a substance is the complete geometrical arrangement of the particles that occupy the space lattice. A unit cell is part of a space lattice that, if repeated in three dimensions, will generate the entire lattice. Most metals have either face-centered cubic unit cells (cubic closest packing), hexagonal unit cells (hexagonal closest packing), or body-centered cubic unit cells, in which the packing is less dense. The mass of a unit cell divided by its volume gives the theoretical density of the substance.

TOOLS OF CHEMISTRY: DIFFRACTION The regularly spaced atoms, ions, or molecules in a crystal can diffract beams of x-rays, electrons, and neutrons, providing information about the structure of crystals and of individual molecules. From the x-ray diffraction studies the distance between planes of atoms in the crystal can be calculated, and the dimensions of the unit cell found. The intensity of the diffracted radiation varies with the type and location of atoms or ions in the unit cell, providing information about the structure of molecules in molecular crystals or the arrangement of ions in ionic crystals. Low-energy electron diffraction (LEED) can be used to study atomic arrangements and electron densities at surfaces. Beams of neutrons are scattered solely by atomic nuclei and not by orbital electrons. This technique also yields information about the magnetic structures of materials.

13.10 CRYSTAL STRUCTURE OF IONIC COMPOUNDS Since anions are generally larger than cations, we can imagine anions defining the crystal structure with cations occupying the spaces, or holes. In closest packing arrangements there are two kinds of holes. Ions in tetrahedral holes have a crystal coordination number of four; ions in the larger octahedral holes have a crystal coordination number of six. In simple cubic crystals (which are not closest packed) there are still larger holes in which an atom has a crystal coordination number of eight. The cation-to-anion radius ratio determines whether ions can fit into specific holes, and thus which structures are possible for different compounds.

13.11 LATTICE ENERGIES; THE BORN–HABER CYCLE Lattice energy can be calculated by applying Hess's law (Section 7.13) to a sequence of reactions known as the Born–Haber cycle if the enthalpies of the individual steps are known.

13.12 DEFECTS Real crystals are seldom perfect. Defects that may occur include point defects, line defects (dislocations), planar defects, and three-dimensional defects. Defects contribute to the physical and chemical properties of substances.

SIGNIFICANT TERMS

evaporation
vaporization
sublimation
condensation,
liquefaction
melting point
fusion
boiling point
normal boiling point
superheated
critical temperature
critical pressure
critical point
supercooled
triple point
normal freezing point
viscosity
surface tension
crystalline solid
amorphous solid
crystal
hexagonal closest packing
cubic closest packing
coordination number (crystal)
space lattice
crystal structure
unit cell
primitive unit cell
multiple unit cell
theoretical density
polymorphous
radius ratio
isomorphous
nonstoichiometric compound

THOUGHTS ON CHEMISTRY

The Importance of Crystals

NEEDS AND OPPORTUNITIES IN CRYSTAL GROWTH, by Stanley Mroczkowski

Crystals are the unacknowledged pillars on which our advanced technology rests. The manufacture of crystals and the devices that they have made possible is now a large and expanding industrial enterprise. A multitude of objects that we use daily, but rarely pause to consider, would not be available today were it not for an industry centered on growing single crystals. Most watches contain "jewels" made of synthetic rubies. Radios, televisions, record players, hearing aids, and automobile ignition systems all contain solid-state components. The ubiquitous chip — a small single crystal with a complex history — is the emblem of the information of communication networks that serve as the nerves and brain of our complex social organism.

The applications of crystals include (1) power regulation for cities, (2) management of bank accounts and credit cards, (3) telephone communications, (4) direction of air and rail traffic and reservations, (5) diagnosis of disease. The everyday business of technologically developed countries is profoundly dependent on crystals; yet very few people are aware of either the utility of crystals or the industries that produce them. This consumer ignorance, a natural result of the packaging of crystal-incorporating products, ought to be dispelled without delay. The crystal industry is today worth millions of dollars, without it modern society could not function. . . .

In the early days of materials science (the 1950s), advances were frequently made by the "brute force" method. The brute force method was "try it first; if it works, let's figure out why afterwards." By means of the brute force method and exhaustive testing of many materials, technologists developed crystals with outstanding characteristics for specific applications. When a suitable material was found a growth technique was perfected that would yield crystals of the desired size and quality. Growth and testing were continued until all reasonable combinations had been tried, and the one best fitted to the particular function was chosen. Then, for each type of compound, there was usually one (or at most a few) that was considered superior. The less immediately impressive compounds were shelved and seldom mentioned in the literature. By this trial and error system, crystal growers were slowly learning how to predict the properties of new materials.

Today the brute force method has largely been replaced by efforts to understand the physical principles that determine chemical bonding, molecular structures, and electronic properties. We owe much to the Edisonian ingenuity, labor, and sweat of the early researchers, but as materials science becomes more complex we must improve the predictability of our approach. Without better predictive models the task of testing new materials will exceed the resources available.

Stanley Mroczkowski, Needs and Opportunities in Crystal Growth, *J. Chem. Educ.* **57,** 537–539 (1980).

QUESTIONS

Relationships between Phases

13.1 Briefly compare the models for the gaseous, liquid, and solid states.

13.2 If you pour ether on your hand, your hand will feel cold. Explain this effect in terms of the kinetic-molecular theory.

13.3 Is the equilibrium that is established between two physical states of matter an example of static or dynamic equilibrium? Explain your answer.

13.4 The three major components of air are N_2 (b.p. $-$ 196 °C, O_2 (b.p. $-$ 183 °C), and Ar (b.p. $-$ 186 °C). Suppose we had a sample of liquid air at -200 °C. In what order would these gases evaporate as the temperature is raised?

13.5 Choose the variable(s) that influence the vapor pressure of a substance: (a) ratio of liquid or solid to empty space, (b) temperature, (c) pressure of air above liquid, and (d) composition of gas above liquid.

13.6 The equilibrium vapor pressure of water at 17.2 °C is 14.7 Torr. Describe what happens as a warm, wet air mass having a partial pressure of water vapor equal to 22.4 Torr is cooled to 17.2 °C.

13.7 Choose from each pair the substance that in the liquid state would have the greater vapor pressure at a given temperature: (a) $BiBr_3$ or $BiCl_3$, (b) CO or CO_2, (c) Li or Au, (d) N_2 or NO, and (e) CH_3COOH or $HCOOCH_3$. Base your choice on the strength of the intermolecular forces.

13.8 Repeat Question 13.7 for (a) C_6H_6 or C_6Cl_6, (b) $H_2C{=}O$ or CH_3OH, (c) Ga or Cu, and (d) He or H_2.

13.9 The vapor pressure of solid carbon dioxide is 35 Torr at -110 °C and 1485 Torr at -70 °C (see Figure 13.6). A student predicted that at -90 °C, which is halfway between -110 °C and -70 °C, the vapor pressure would be (35 Torr $+$ 1485 Torr)/2 $=$ 760. Torr. He was amazed to find that the value was only 280. Torr at this temperature. What was wrong with his prediction?

13.10 Why is it necessary to specify the atmospheric pressure over a liquid when measuring a boiling point? What is the definition of the normal boiling point?

13.11 What is "superheating"? How can we avoid superheating a liquid?

13.12 What is the critical point? Will a substance always be a liquid below the critical temperature? Why or why not?

13.13 Are samples of supercooled and superheated liquids examples of stable states? Explain.

13.14 How many phases exist at a triple point? Describe what would happen if a small amount of heat were added under constant-volume conditions to a sample of water at the triple point. Assume a negligible volume change during fusion.

13.15 Most chemists are careful to measure boiling points at 1 atm pressure or to report boiling points corrected to 1 atm pressure. Yet, chemists seldom worry about this for melting points. Why?

13.16 Describe what would happen to a sample of CO_2 originally at point b in Figure 13.10 if it undergoes a sudden isothermal (constant temperature) decrease in pressure. Compare your answer to that for a sample originally at point b being heated at constant pressure.

13.17 The pressure on a sample of CO_2 at point a and on a sample of H_2O at point c in Figure 13.10 is greatly increased under constant-temperature conditions. Compare the effect on the samples.

13.18 Describe the physical state of a sample of water originally at point d in Figure 13.10. (a) Describe the changes on the sample as the pressure is decreased at constant temperature. (b) Prepare a heating curve (see Figure 7.7) for a second sample of water originally at point d as it is heated at constant pressure. (c) Prepare a cooling curve for a third sample of water originally at point d as it is cooled at constant pressure.

The Solid State

13.19 Compare some of the properties of crystalline and amorphous substances.

13.20 Briefly describe how layers of closest packed atoms can be arranged to give hexagonal and cubic closest packing.

13.21 What does the term "crystal coordination number" mean? What is the value of the coordination number for an atom in either hexagonal or cubic closest packing?

13.22 What is a space lattice? How does this differ from a crystal structure?

13.23 Define the term "unit cell." Prepare sketches of the primitive, body-centered, and face-centered cubic unit cells.

13.24 Choose two different unit cells in the two-dimensional lattice shown. Make one as simple as possible and the other orthogonal (containing right angles). Which of these is simpler to use to calculate area, etc.?

13.25* Draw several equilateral triangles so that they fit together as tightly as possible. Do the same for squares, hexagons, and octagons. Are all equally close packed?

13.26 What is diffraction? What must be the relationship between the wavelength of incident radiation and the spacing of the particles in a crystal in order for diffraction to occur? What types of waves are suitable for diffraction studies of crystals?

13.27 Prepare sketches of tetrahedral and octahedral holes. Why do anions usually form the closest packed array and cations occupy holes in this array?

13.28 Which type of hole—cubic, octahedral, or tetrahedral—is the largest? Which would be preferred by a substance having a small radius ratio, r_+/r_-?

13.29* Sketch the Born–Haber cycle for the formation of $MO(s)$ from $M(s)$ and $O_2(g)$. Write the expression for ΔH_f° in terms of the various enthalpy changes involved.

PROBLEMS

Vapor Pressure

13.1 The apparatus shown in the sketch can be used to determine the vapor pressure of a liquid. A very small amount of liquid is injected and allowed to evaporate. More liquid is added until a small amount of liquid remains and establishes equilibrium with the vapor. The difference between the heights of the liquid in the U-shaped tube, h, measured in mm is the vapor pressure in Torr if the tube contains mercury. At 15 °C the values read at a and b were 26.9 and 22.5 mm, and at 32 °C the values were 47.6 and 1.7 mm. Find the vapor pressure at each temperature.

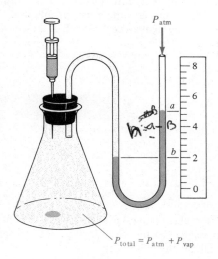

13.2 The vapor pressure of solid iodine at room temperature is 0.466 Torr. What mass of iodine will sublime into a 1.0 L container? If the atmospheric pressure in the container is 763 Torr, what will be the total pressure in the container? *Answer* 0.0063 g, 763 Torr

13.3 The atmospheric pressure in a closed flask was 716 Torr. Liquid formic acid was added dropwise and the pressure in the flask was recorded after the addition of each drop. Calculate the vapor pressure of formic acid at this temperature from the following pressure data: 720 Torr, 725 Torr, 729 Torr, 732 Torr, 736 Torr, 741 Torr, 745 Torr, 749 Torr, 754 Torr, 757 Torr, 758 Torr, 758 Torr, 758 Torr.

13.4 The vapor pressure of $CH_3CH_2CH_2Cl$ at room temperature

is 385 Torr. The total pressure of $CH_3CH_2CH_2Cl$ and air in a container is 745 Torr. What will happen to the pressure if the volume of the container is doubled at constant temperature? Assume that a small amount of liquid $CH_3CH_2CH_2Cl$ is present in the container at all times.

13.5 The total pressure in a flask containing dry air and silicon tetrachloride, $SiCl_4$, was 988 Torr at 25 °C. The volume of the flask was halved and the pressure changed to 1742 Torr while the temperature was held constant. What is the vapor pressure of $SiCl_4$ at this temperature? Assume that a small amount of liquid $SiCl_4$ is present in the container at all times. *Answer* 234 Torr

13.6 The relative humidity is defined as the actual partial pressure of water present in air divided by the equilibrium vapor pressure at that temperature. What is the relative humidity of air containing 14.3 Torr water vapor at 22 °C given that the equilibrium vapor pressure of water is 19.8 Torr at this temperature? Express your answer as a percentage.

13.7 What is the partial pressure of water in air that has a relative humidity (see Problem 13.6) equal to 82% at 28 °C? The vapor pressure of water at 28 °C is 28.3 Torr. What would happen as this air sample is cooled to 22 °C? The vapor pressure of water at 22 °C is 19.8 Torr. *Answer* 23 Torr; water vapor would condense (rain).

Unit Cell

13.8 Polonium crystallizes in a primitive cubic unit cell with an edge length of 0.336 nm. (a) What is the mass of the unit cell? (b) What is the volume of the unit cell? (c) What is the theoretical density of Po?

13.9 Below 1000 °C, iron crystallizes in a body-centered cubic unit cell with an edge length of 0.28664 nm. (a) What is the mass of the unit cell? (b) What is the volume of the unit cell? (c) What is the theoretical density of Fe? *Answer* (a) 1.8548×10^{-22} g, (b) 2.3551×10^{-23} cm³, (c) 7.8757 g/cm³

13.10 Above 1000 °C, iron changes from the body-centered cubic unit cell described in Problem 13.9 to a face-centered cubic unit cell with an edge length of 0.363 nm. Repeat the calculations of Problem 13.9 for this unit cell. Compare the densities.

13.11 Crystalline silicon has the same structure as diamond, with an edge length of 0.54305 nm. What is the theoretical density of Si? *Answer* 2.3297 g/cm³

13.12 Platinum crystallizes in a cubic unit cell with an edge length of 0.39231 nm. The density of Pt is 21.45 g/cm³. Determine the type of cubic unit cell that Pt forms and calculate the value of Avogadro's number from these data.

13.13 Silver crystallizes in a face-centered cubic unit cell. The density of Ag is 10.5 g/cm³. Calculate the length of the edge of the unit cell. *Answer* 0.409 nm

13.14* Magnesium crystallizes in the hexagonal closest packed unit cell with $a = 0.3203$ nm and $c = 0.5196$ nm, as shown in the sketch. (a) What is the mass contained in the unit cell? The volume of the unit cell is given by $a^2 c \sin 60°$. (b) Calculate the volume of the unit cell. (c) Calculate the theoretical density of Mg.

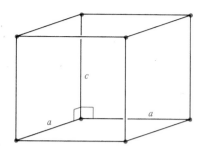

13.15 A unit cell consists of a cube in which there are cations at each corner and anions at the center of each face. (a) Sketch the unit cell. How many (b) cations and (c) anions are present? (d) What is the simplest formula of the compound?

13.16 A unit cell consists of a cube in which there are anions at each corner and one at the center of the unit cell and cations at the center of each face. How many cations and anions make up the unit cell? What is the simplest formula for this compound? *Answer* 3, 2; C_3A_2

13.17 Ammonium iodide crystallizes in the cubic crystal system. The ionic radii are 0.148 nm for NH_4^+ and 0.220 nm for I^-. Calculate the radius ratio and describe the crystal structure of NH_4I.

13.18 Magnesium oxide crystallizes in the cubic crystal system. The ionic radii are 0.066 nm for Mg^{2+} and 0.140 nm for O^{2-}. Calculate the radius ratio and describe the crystal structure of MgO. *Answer* 0.47, Mg^{2+} ions occupy octahedral holes in the O^{2-} lattice (NaCl type structure).

13.19* Using quarters, derive a two-dimensional radius ratio rule as follows: (i) place three quarters in a triangle so that each is touching two others and measure the radius of the small hole; (ii) place four quarters so that the centers form a square, so that again each is touching two others, and measure the radius of the small hole; (iii) place five quarters in the shape of a pentagon and measure the radius of the hole; and (iv) place six coins in the shape of a hexagon and measure the radius of the hole. Divide the measured radii by the radius of a quarter and prepare a table similar to Table 13.4.

13.20* Show that the limiting radius ratio for a tetrahedral arrangement of large spherical anions about a smaller spherical cation is 0.225. Hint: Assume that the tetrahedron is fitted into a cube of edge a with anion sphere of radius r_- at alternate corners contacting each other and the cation sphere of radius r_+ at the center.

Born–Haber Cycle

13.21 The lattice energy for RbF is $-770.$ kJ/mol. Combine this value with appropriate values of the ionization energy (Table 10.2), electron affinity (Table 10.5), and the bond dissociation energy (Table 9.12). The heat of sublimation for Rb is 88.7 kJ/mol. Find ΔH_f° for RbF at 0 K.

13.22 Use the following heat of formation data at 25 °C to calculate the lattice energy for NaCl and KCl: -233.9 kJ/mol for $Cl^-(g)$, 514.197 kJ/mol for $K^+(g)$, 609.839 kJ/mol for $Na^+(g)$, -411.12 kJ/mol for NaCl(s), and -436.68 kJ/mol for KCl(s). Both of these ionic compounds have the same charges on the ions and have the same crystal geometry. What conclusion can you make, based on your results, about the value of lattice energy and interionic distance? *Answer* -787.1 kJ/mol for NaCl, -717.0 kJ/mol for KCl; the lattice energy increases with decreasing interionic distance.

13.23 The ΔH_f° at 25 °C is 2350.521 kJ/mol for $Mg^{2+}(g)$, 803 kJ/mol for $O^{2-}(g)$, and -601.83 kJ/mol for MgO(s). (a) Calculate the lattice energy for MgO. The ΔH_f° at 25 °C is 610.927 kJ/mol for $Na^+(g)$, -332.6 kJ/mol for $F^-(g)$, and -569.0 kJ/mol for NaF(s). (b) Calculate the lattice energy for NaF. (c) Why is there such a large difference between these lattice energies even though both substances crystallize in the same pattern and there is only about a 10% difference in the distance between the ions? *Answer* (a) -3755 kJ/mol; (b) -847.3 kJ/mol; (c) the ionic charges are greater in MgO than in NaF.

Additional Problems

13.24 How much heat is required to (a) melt one gram of ice at 0 °C and (b) boil one gram of water at 100 °C? See Table 7.5 for molar values of heats of transition.

13.25 The heat of formation of BeF_2 at 700 K is -1023 kJ/mol for the solid and -797 kJ/mol for the gas. Calculate the heat of sublimation of BeF_2 at 700 K. *Answer* 226 kJ/mol

13.26 The heat of formation of ICl at 25 °C is -35.1 kJ/mol for the solid, -23.89 kJ/mol for the liquid, and 17.8 kJ/mol for the gas. Calculate the heats of fusion, vaporization, and sublimation for ICl at this temperature.

13.27 Water can be cooled in hot climates by the evaporation of water from the surface of canvas bags. What mass of water (heat capacity = 75 J/K mol) can be cooled from 35 °C to 20. °C by the evaporation of one gram of water (heat of vaporization = 44 kJ/mol)? *Answer* 38 g

13.28 A scald from steam is much more severe than a burn from hot water. To illustrate this, calculate the amount of heat released as one gram of steam at 100.0 °C condenses and cools to 35 °C and compare it to the heat released as one gram of water at 100.0 °C undergoes the same cooling. The heat capacity of water is 75 J/K mol and the heat of vaporization is 40.7 kJ/mol.

13.29* A common technique for measuring the viscosity, η, of a liquid is to observe the time t required for a sphere to drop through it. If the same sphere is dropped through water and another liquid,

$$\frac{\eta_{\text{liq}}}{\eta_{\text{water}}} = \frac{(d_{\text{sphere}} - d_{\text{liq}})t_{\text{liq}}}{(d_{\text{sphere}} - d_{\text{water}})t_{\text{water}}}$$

where d is the density and η is the viscosity in centipoises. How much longer would a pearl (density = 3.0 g/cm³) take to fall through a sample of shampoo ($d = 1.03$ g/cm³) having $\eta = 6.23$ centipoise than through water ($d = 1.00$ g/cm³) having $\eta = 0.89$ centipoise? *Answer* 7.0

Oxygen, water, and the compounds of hydrogen and oxygen with other elements are abundant in our surroundings. All of the life forms on earth are dependent upon these substances. It is not surprising that the chemistry of water, hydrogen, and oxygen illustrates some of the most important principles that govern chemistry on our planet.

In this chapter we have two purposes. The first is to present the descriptive chemistry of water: What are its physical properties? Its chemical properties? The second is to introduce some general types of chemical compounds and chemical reactions that are encountered again and again in both simple and complex chemical systems, especially those that include water. A consideration of the chemistry of water leads naturally into a definition of chemical equilibrium and a brief look at ions in aqueous solutions. These are areas of broad significance that are expanded upon in later chapters. After a discussion of the properties of solutions in the next chapter, this twofold approach continues in Chapter 16. The descriptive chemistry of hydrogen, oxygen, and some of their compounds is covered in Chapter 16, and oxidation–reduction, another broad and very important aspect of chemistry, is introduced.

From a chemical viewpoint, the most fascinating thing about water is that it is unique. In many of its properties water differs from similar compounds and has values outside the normal range. It is just these differences that make water so ideally suited for its role in the earth's life support system.

Water is a simple triatomic molecule, but its behavior is very complex. No chemist, biologist, or physicist would dare to say that water has been thoroughly studied or that how it functions on a molecular scale in either living or nonliving systems is completely understood.

THE CHEMISTRY OF WATER

14.1 THE WATER MOLECULE AND ITS AGGREGATES

In the water molecule two hydrogen atoms are joined to an oxygen atom by covalent bonds, and two lone pairs of electrons remain on the oxygen atom. (In the VSEPR classification, H_2O is an AB_2E_2 molecule; see Figures 11.2 and 11.3.)

$$2H\cdot \; + \; \cdot \ddot{O} \cdot \longrightarrow H-\ddot{O}-H$$

The repulsion of the lone pairs for each other and for the electrons in the O—H bonds results in an H—O—H angle of 104.5° (Figure 14.1), less than the regular tetrahedral angle of 109.47°.

Oxygen is second only to fluorine in electronegativity. Consequently, the covalent bonds in water are highly polar. The combined effects of molecular geometry and bond polarity give the water molecule a fairly large dipole moment (Figure 14.1c). The oxygen atom has a partial negative charge and the hydrogen atoms, partial positive charges—exactly the situation in which hydrogen bonding can occur (Section 11.12).

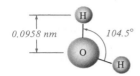

(a) An isolated water molecule

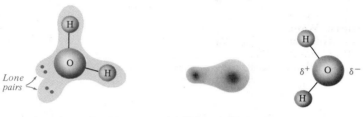

Lone pairs

(b) Electron density

(c) Water as a dipole, dipole moment = 1.84D

Figure 14.1
The Water Molecule Compare the water dipole moment of 1.84D with that of H_2S, which is 0.89 D.

In liquid water, hydrogen bonding holds groups of water molecules together. Each oxygen atom can form two hydrogen bonds—one through each of the lone pairs. Although much remains to be learned about the structure of liquid water, it is certain that aggregates of varying numbers of water molecules held together by hydrogen bonds exist throughout liquid water. Some uncombined water molecules are also present (Figure 14.2). The "flickering cluster" theory of the structure of liquid water pictures a dynamic equilibrium between aggregates and single molecules, with the aggregates continually forming and breaking up. The half-life of hydrogen bonds in liquid water (the time in which one-half of them break) is reported to be 10^{-11} s.

In ice, each oxygen atom is covalently bonded to two hydrogen atoms and hydrogen-bonded to two other hydrogen atoms. Each hydrogen atom is covalently

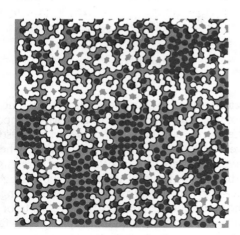

Figure 14.2
The Structure of Liquid Water at 20 °C and 1 atm The water clusters are outlined and the "free" water molecules are shaded. (Source: R. A. Courant, B. J. Ray, and R. A. Horne, *Zh. Struk. Khim.,* **4,** 581, 1972.)

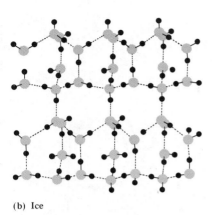

Figure 14.3
Aggregates of Water
Molecules The O - - - H hydrogen
bonds in ice are about 0.177 nm in
length.

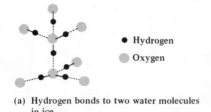

(a) Hydrogen bonds to two water molecules
    in ice

(b) Ice

● Hydrogen

● Oxygen

Water is densest at 4 °C

bonded to one oxygen atom and hydrogen-bonded to another oxygen atom. The
result is a structure in which each oxygen atom is connected to four other oxygen
atoms through hydrogen atoms (Figure 14.3a). These units build up a big, honey-
comb-like lattice containing large open spaces (Figure 14.3b). When water molecules
arrange themselves into this pattern they occupy more space than they do in the less
organized form of liquid water. The result is that water expands when it freezes, a
phenomenon observed when the freezing of water in a bottle breaks the bottle.
Another familiar effect of the increased volume of ice is that ice floats. At 0 °C the
density of ice is 0.9168 g/cm³ and the density of liquid water is 0.99984 g/cm³. Most
liquids contract and become more dense on freezing, so most freezing solids sink in
the liquid.

A curious phenomenon occurs when air-free water is warmed from 0 °C to
3.98 °C. The water gradually becomes *more* dense in this temperature range,
reaching a maximum density at 3.98 °C (Figure 14.4). Very few liquids become
more dense upon heating in any temperature range. Apparently the melting of ice
does not break all the hydrogen bonds, and the honeycomb structure only partially
collapses. The average number of hydrogen bonds per oxygen atom in liquid water at
0 °C is estimated at 1.8, as compared to 2.0 in ice. A further increase in temperature
breaks more hydrogen bonds and causes further collapse; the volume decreases, and
there is a corresponding increase in density. The temperature of maximum density,
3.98 °C, is the temperature at which contraction, as a result of collapse of the ice
structure, is exactly balanced by normal thermal expansion caused by the increased
energy of individual molecules. The transformation of solid ice to liquid water and
then to water vapor can be summarized as passing through the following stages:

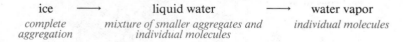

ice   ⟶   liquid water   ⟶   water vapor
complete   *mixture of smaller aggregates and*   *individual molecules*
aggregation   *individual molecules*

The weathering of rocks and the formation of holes in streets are hastened by the
expansion of freezing water inside cracks. More importantly, because ice stays at the
top of a lake, pond, or other body of water, and also because it acts as an insulator,
fish can live through the winter at the bottom, where the water does not freeze. If
water behaved like most liquids, lakes and streams would freeze solid as ice that
formed at the top continually sank to the bottom. As a result aquatic life would be
nonexistent—or very different. The seasonal changes in temperature in temperate
climates and the resulting changes in the density of water allow the water in many
lakes to turn over completely each spring and fall. This leads to the uniform
distribution of oxygen and nutrients throughout the water (Figure 14.5).

Super-
cooled
water

Maximum density,
3.98°C

1.000

0.999

0.998

0.997

0.996

0.995

Absolute density (g/mL)

−10 −5   0   5   10 15 20 25 30
Temperature (°C)

Figure 14.4
The Effect of Temperature on the
Density of Water

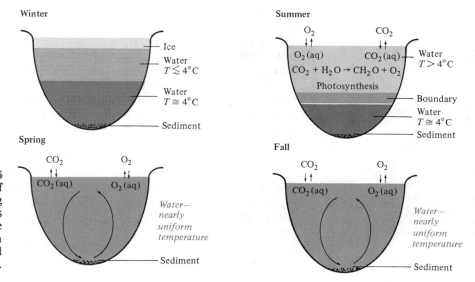

Figure 14.5
Lake Turnover as a Result of Changes in Water Density During the spring thaw, surface water sinks as it is warmed and becomes more dense. During the fall freeze, warm surface water sinks as it is cooled and becomes more dense.

EXAMPLE 14.1
Properties of Water

Why is the hydrogen bonding in H_2O stronger than that in H_2S?

The electronegativity of an oxygen atom (3.5) is considerably greater than the electronegativity of a sulfur atom (2.5). As a result, the covalent bonds in water are much more polar than they are in hydrogen sulfide, and stronger hydrogen bonds are formed between the water molecules. Hydrogen bonding in liquid H_2S is of little importance. [This is one of the reasons why H_2S is a gas at room temperature.]

14.2 PROPERTIES OF WATER

Water molecules are simple, but the behavior of water is complex.

Water is found naturally on earth in all three states—gaseous, liquid, and solid. Furthermore, water is the only naturally occurring inorganic liquid that is found in abundance. The physical properties of water are very different from those of similar simple substances.

Many of the unusual properties of water result, as we have seen, from its high degree of hydrogen bonding, a consequence of the <u>polarity</u> of water molecules. The freezing point, boiling point, heat of vaporization, and heat of fusion of water (Table 14.1) are all high relative to those of the hydrides of other oxygen family elements

---

Table 14.1
Properties of Water

Molar mass	18.02 g/mol
Melting point	0.0 °C
Boiling point (1 atm)	100.0 °C
Density (g/cm³)	
0 °C	0.9168 g/cm³ (ice)
	0.99984 g/cm³ (liquid)
3.98 °C	0.99997 g/cm³
25 °C	0.99704 g/cm³
Vapor pressure (25 °C)	23.756 Torr
Triple point	0.0100 °C and 4.58 Torr
Dipole moment	1.84 D
Surface tension (25 °C)	0.07197 N/m
Heat capacity (25 °C)	75.2 J/K mol
Heat of formation (of liquid) (25 °C)	−286 kJ/mol
Heat of fusion (0 °C)	6.01 kJ/mol
Heat of vaporization (100 °C)	40.7 kJ/mol

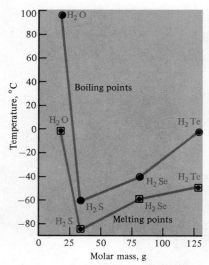

Figure 14.6
Melting and Boiling Points of the Hydrides of the Oxygen Family

(H₂S, H₂Se, H₂Te; Figure 14.6). As explained in the preceding section, the geometry of water molecules and the effect of hydrogen bonding combine to give ice a lower density than liquid water. Water has a higher heat capacity, thermal conductivity, and surface tension than almost any other liquid. These properties all contribute to the role of water in our environment (Table 14.2).

The high surface tension of water, a result of the strong attraction of water molecules for each other through hydrogen bonding, helps water to rise in the narrow vessels in plant stems and roots by capillary action. The high surface tension also helps to hold water in the small spaces between soil particles.

Because water is an excellent solvent, it is the ideal medium for transporting the ions and molecules needed for plant and animal metabolism. Ions do not readily recombine in dilute aqueous solutions because the water molecules that surround them cut down the attractive force between them.

Because of the high heat capacity of water, the lakes and oceans, or the body fluids, can absorb or release large quantities of heat while undergoing only small changes in temperature. Because of its high thermal conductivity, water readily transports heat to and from its surroundings. These properties allow large bodies of water to moderate the temperature of the atmosphere and thereby affect the climate. The hottest and coldest regions on earth are all inland regions, those farthest from the moderating effects of the oceans. In addition, warm-blooded animals maintain their necessary narrow ranges of body temperatures with the aid of both the high specific heat of water and its high heat of vaporization — excess heat is expended in evaporating water from the skin. Also, because of the high heat of vaporization of water, less liquid evaporates with the addition of a given amount of heat than for most other liquids. This keeps water loss to a minimum, making it easier for plants and animals to stay alive in environments where water is scarce.

Table 14.2
Some of the Unusual Physical–Chemical Properties of Water and Their Environmental and Biological Significance Source: Adapted from R. A. Horne, *The Chemistry of Our Environment* (New York: Wiley-Interscience, 1978), p. 237. (Copyright © 1978 by John Wiley and Sons, Inc.)

Property	Comparison with Normal Liquids	Significance
Heat capacity	Very high	Moderates environmental temperatures, good heat transport medium
Heat of fusion	Very high	Has moderating effect, tends to stabilize liquid state
Heat of vaporization	Very high	Has moderating effect important in atmospheric physics and in precipitation–evaporation balance
Density	Anomalous maximum at 3.98 °C (for pure water)	Allows freezing from the surface and controls temperature distribution and circulation in bodies of water
Surface tension	Very high	Is important in surface phenomena, droplet formation in the atmosphere, and many physiological processes including transport through biomembranes
Dipole moment	Very high	Provides good solvent properties
Hydration*	Very extensive	Provides good solvent properties and allows mobilization of environmental pollutants and alteration of the biochemistry of solutes
Ionization	Very small	Provides a neutral medium but with some availability of both H^+ and OH^- ions
Thermal conductivity	Very high	Can provide an important heat transfer mechanism in stagnant systems such as cells

* See Section 14.3.

Table 14.3
Solubilities of Various Substances in Liquid Water

Substance			Solubility (g/100 g H$_2$O)	
Name	Formula	Type of Solute	20 °C	50 °C
Silver nitrate	AgNO$_3$	Ionic	222	455
Aluminum sulfate	Al$_2$(SO$_4$)$_3$	Ionic	36.4	52.2
Ammonium nitrate	NH$_4$NO$_3$	Ionic	192	344
Barium sulfate	BaSO$_4$	Ionic	2.5×10^{-4}	3.4×10^{-4}
Calcium acetate	Ca(CH$_3$COO)$_2$	Ionic	34.7	33.0
Copper(II) sulfate	CuSO$_4$	Ionic	20.7	33.3
Lead(II) chloride	PbCl$_2$	Ionic	0.99	1.70
Potassium chlorate	KClO$_3$	Ionic	7.4	19.3
Sodium chloride	NaCl	Ionic	36.0	37.0
Zinc iodide	ZnI$_2$	Ionic	200.	273
Hydrogen*	H$_2$	Nonpolar covalent	1.6×10^{-4}	1.3×10^{-4}
Ethane*	CH$_3$CH$_3$	Nonpolar covalent	0.006	0.003
Diethyl ether	(C$_2$H$_5$)$_2$O	Polar covalent	7.5	—
Ethyl alcohol	CH$_3$CH$_2$OH	Polar covalent	∞	∞
Ethylene glycol	HOCH$_2$CH$_2$OH	Polar covalent	∞	∞
Cane sugar	C$_{12}$H$_{22}$O$_{11}$	Polar covalent	204	260.

* Gas at 760 Torr total pressure.

14.3 WATER AS A SOLVENT

Water is a remarkably versatile solvent. Although it may stretch our imaginations a bit to conclude, as some have done, that every chemical is at least slightly soluble in water, a great many substances certainly are water soluble in varying degrees. The substances most likely to be highly soluble in water are those with ionic or polar covalent bonds (Table 14.3). Such substances dissolve as their ions or molecules respond to the attractive forces of the polar water molecules.

Figure 14.7 illustrates the dissolution of an ionic compound. The positive ions are attracted to the negative ends of the water dipoles and the negative ions are attracted to the positive ends of the water dipoles. Similar Coulomb forces draw

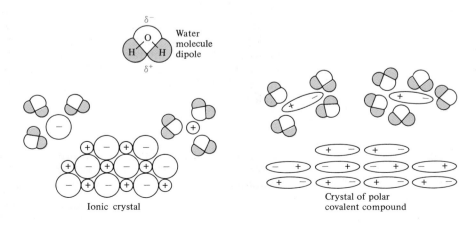

Figure 14.7
Dissolution of Ionic and Polar Covalent Substances

Polarity of water molecule: makes water a good solvent for ionic and polar covalent substances	water molecules to the charged regions in polar molecules. The bonding of an ion or molecule to water molecules is called **hydration.** (A more general term for the bonding of the molecules or ions of a dissolved substance to solvent molecules is **solvation.**)

All ions in aqueous solution are assumed to be hydrated. In some cases the number of water molecules associated with an ion is known with certainty; in other cases the number is indefinite. A hydrated ion and its associated water molecules are written together within square brackets, for example, $[Cu(H_2O)_4]^{2+}$. (This is a *complex ion* — see Section 14.10.) However, the water molecules in the formulas of ions in solution are generally omitted unless their role is under discussion.

The strength of the attraction of water molecules to ions in solution increases with *decreasing size* of the ion and increases with *increasing charge* of the ion. In other words, water molecules are more strongly attracted to ions with higher charge-to-size ratios.

The heat of hydration — the heat released when an ion becomes hydrated — reflects these trends. For example, the fluoride ion has a greater heat of hydration than the much larger iodide ion.

	ionic radius	*charge/size ratio*	ΔH_{hydr}
F^-	0.136 nm	$1/0.136 = 7.35$	-483 kJ/mol
I^-	0.220 nm	$1/0.220 = 4.55$	-273 kJ/mol

The effect of charge is shown by comparing the heat of hydration of the magnesium(II) ion with that of the lithium ion, which is comparable in size.

	ionic radius	*charge/size ratio*	ΔH_{hydr}
Li^+	0.068 nm	$1/0.068 = 15$	-543 kJ/mol
Mg^{2+}	0.066 nm	$2/0.066 = 30.$	-1921 kJ/mol

You should not assume that all ionic or highly polar substances are highly soluble in water. This is clearly shown in Table 14.3. The extent to which such substances are soluble in water varies widely. The force of attraction to the water molecules must exceed the interparticle forces of a liquid or solid, or must be strong enough to hold a gas in solution.

EXAMPLE 14.2 **Properties of Water**	If water molecules were linear instead of bent, would H_2O be as good a solvent as it is? Why or why not?

Water definitely would not be as good a solvent if the molecules were linear. A linear H—O—H molecule, even though it had polar hydrogen–oxygen bonds, would not be a dipole and could not dissolve substances by the mechanisms shown in Figure 14.7. The nonlinear shape of the water molecule produces a polar molecule which will interact with either positively or negatively charged parts of the solute. In fact, life on earth would be quite different if the water molecule were linear, for many of its unusual properties depend on the polar nature of the molecule.

14.4 THE IONIZATION OF WATER: A CHEMICAL EQUILIBRIUM

The concept of a dynamic equilibrium was introduced earlier in connection with vapor pressure (Section 5.12). In a closed vessel a liquid and its vapor reach a state of dynamic equilibrium in which evaporation and condensation occur at the same rate.

$$\text{Liquid} \rightleftharpoons \text{vapor}$$

A double arrow is used to indicate that changes in both directions are taking place simultaneously.

The ionization of water is an example of a *chemical* equilibrium. Recall that the term "ionization" is usually reserved for the formation of ions from a substance that does not contain ions. Experiments show that a very small percentage of hydrogen ions and hydroxide ions are always present in liquid water. The ions form by ionization of the water:

$$H_2O \longrightarrow H^+ + OH^-$$

and can also combine to give water molecules.

$$H^+ + OH^- \longrightarrow H_2O$$

Left undisturbed, these two reactions establish a dynamic chemical equilibrium.

$$H_2O \underset{\substack{\text{reverse} \\ \text{reaction}}}{\overset{\substack{\text{forward} \\ \text{reaction}}}{\rightleftharpoons}} H^+ + OH^- \qquad (14.1)$$

At equilibrium: rates of forward and reverse reactions are equal; amounts of reactants and products are constant

In **chemical equilibrium** the rates of the forward and the reverse chemical reactions are the same and the amounts of the species present do not change with time. Chemical equilibria are possible in solution, in all phases, and between species in different phases.

The chemical equation for a reaction that establishes chemical equilibrium, it should be noted, gives *no* indication of the amounts of the substances that are present at equilibrium. Do not make the common error of assuming that the amounts of the species on the two sides of the arrow are equal. In the ionization of pure water, which is a *very* slightly ionized substance, only 1.8×10^{-7} % of the water molecules (at 25 °C) are ionized at any given moment. The amounts of the species present at equilibrium vary greatly for different types of reactions, different substances, and different reaction conditions. (The quantitative aspects of chemical equilibrium reactions are examined in Chapters 19–21.)

The question arises of how to represent the hydrogen ion when it is involved in reactions in aqueous solution. The hydrogen ion is the smallest positive ion. As might be expected, it is very strongly attracted to the negative end of the water dipole and therefore the presence of hydrogen ions free from association with water molecules is unlikely. In aqueous solution, hydrogen ions—whether from the ionization of water or from some other source—are always strongly bonded to one or more water molecules. To emphasize the association of the hydrogen ion with water molecules, the hydronium ion, H_3O^+, is frequently written instead of H^+. This allows the ionization of hydrogen-containing molecules or ions to be pictured as the transfer of a hydrogen ion to a water molecule to form a hydronium ion plus a hydroxide ion:

$$H_2O(l) + H_2O(l) \rightleftharpoons H_3O^+ + OH^- \qquad (14.2)$$

Even the hydronium ion is not a fully accurate representation, for protons are probably surrounded by several and possibly varying numbers of water molecules (see An Aside: The Hydronium Ion, Chapter 20).

14.5 CHEMICAL REACTIONS OF WATER

The chemical reactions in which water participates are many and varied. Because the reactions of water are included where appropriate in later chapters on chemical reactions (Chapter 17), acids and bases (Chapter 20), ions in aqueous solution (Chapter 21), and the descriptive chemistry of the elements and their compounds (Chapters 25–31), these reactions need not be studied here. A few examples will illustrate the varied reactions of water.

Equilibria with ions in aqueous solution:

$$CN^- + H_2O(l) \rightleftharpoons HCN(aq) + OH^- \tag{14.3}$$

$$NH_4^+ + H_2O(l) \rightleftharpoons NH_3(aq) + H_3O^+ \tag{14.4}$$

Reactions in which one or both hydrogen–oxygen bonds are broken and new compounds formed:

$$Al_2S_3(s) + 6H_2O(l) \longrightarrow 2Al(OH)_3(s) + 3H_2S(g) \tag{14.5}$$

$$SiI_4(s) + 2H_2O(l) \xrightarrow{H_2O} SiO_2(s) + 4H^+ + 4I^- \tag{14.6}$$

Reactions in which elemental hydrogen is produced:

$$2Na(s) + 2H_2O(l) \longrightarrow 2Na^+ + 2OH^- + H_2(g) \tag{14.7}$$

Reactions in which water combines with another substance:

$$SO_3(g) + H_2O(l) \longrightarrow H_2SO_4(aq) \tag{14.8}$$

A general term for reactions such as (14.3), (14.5), and (14.6), in which the water molecule is split, is **hydrolysis.**

14.6 HYDRATES

Hydration is the bonding of water molecules to other substances *without* the splitting of the water molecule. We have already discussed the hydration of ions in aqueous solution (Section 14.3). In many cases intact water molecules are incorporated into compounds. Chemical compounds that include water molecules are called **hydrates.** Hydrates can be found in all three physical states; many are crystalline solids.

The formulas of hydrates are often written with a centered dot between the water molecules and the compound that has been hydrated, for example,

$$Ba(OH)_2 \cdot 8H_2O \qquad\qquad CuSO_4 \cdot 5H_2O$$
barium hydroxide octahydrate   *copper sulfate pentahydrate*

The formula of a hydrate written in this way does not show *how* the water molecules are incorporated into the compound.

Each hydrate listed in Table 14.4 contains a fixed quantity of water and has a definite composition. Each may lose its water of hydration upon heating and may be reformed by reaction of the *anhydrous* (water-free) substance with water.

The forces holding the water molecules in hydrates are often not very strong, as shown by the ease with which water is lost and regained. The water molecules can (1) be held to a central atom by coordinate covalent bonds between oxygen and a metal atom or ion (*coordination water*); (2) be held to anions in the crystal by hydrogen bonds (*anion water*); or (3) simply occupy either fixed or random positions within the crystal structure (either *lattice water* or if it is in openings in a zeolite structure, *zeolitic water*, Section 14.11).

Not all of the water molecules in a given hydrate need be held in the same way. The pentahydrate of copper(II) sulfate is a good example of a crystalline hydrate in which water molecules are bound in different ways. If solid copper(II) sulfate is dissolved in water and the solution allowed to evaporate by standing in air, blue crystals are deposited. After careful drying at room temperature, these crystals have the chemical composition $CuSO_4 \cdot 5H_2O$, and remain unchanged in normally moist

Table 14.4
Some Hydrates The common names are given in parentheses.

$CuSO_4 \cdot 5H_2O$	Copper sulfate pentahydrate (blue vitriol)
$KAl(SO_4)_2 \cdot 12H_2O$	Potassium aluminum sulfate dodecahydrate (alum)
$Na_2B_4O_7 \cdot 10H_2O$	Sodium tetraborate decahydrate (borax)
$FeSO_4 \cdot 7H_2O$	Iron(II) sulfate heptahydrate (green vitriol)
$H_2SO_4 \cdot H_2O$	Sulfuric acid monohydrate (m.p. 8.6 °C)

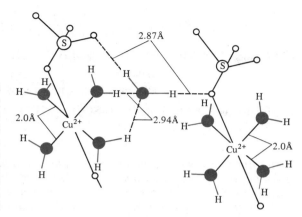

Figure 14.8
The Environment of the Water Molecules in Copper(II) Sulfate Pentahydrate The water molecules are shown in color. Four of them are held by each Cu^{2+} ion. One in the center, is held by hydrogen bonds. (Source: Arlo D. Harris and Lee H. Kalbus, *J. Chem. Educ.* **56**, 417, June 1979.)

air. Careful heating causes loss of four water molecules to give a monohydrate, while stronger heating drives off the fifth water molecule.

$$CuSO_4 \cdot 5H_2O(s) \xrightarrow{140\ °C} CuSO_4 \cdot H_2O(s) + 4H_2O(g)$$

$$CuSO_4 \cdot H_2O(s) \xrightarrow{400\ °C} CuSO_4(s) + H_2O(g)$$

Studies of the crystal structure of $CuSO_4 \cdot 5H_2O$ (Figure 14.8) have shown that four water molecules are held to Cu^{2+} by coordinate covalent bonds and one is held in place by hydrogen bonds. A better formula for this compound might be $[Cu(H_2O)_4]SO_4(H_2O)$.

The loss of water by a hydrate on exposure to air is called **efflorescence.** Many hydrates have appreciable water vapor pressure because the water molecules are held loosely. If the vapor pressure of a hydrate is greater than that of the water vapor in the air, the hydrate will effloresce until a state of equilibrium has been reached. For example, $Na_2SO_4 \cdot 10H_2O$ has a vapor pressure of 30.8 Torr at room temperature. The partial pressure of water vapor at room temperature and average humidity is about 20 Torr. Therefore, $Na_2SO_4 \cdot 10H_2O$ is normally an efflorescent hydrate. With the loss of water, the crystal structure of a hydrated substance collapses and a powder appears on the surface.

Some compounds are **hygroscopic**—they take up water from the air. In some cases the result may be the formation of a hydrate. Compounds that take up enough water from the air to dissolve in the water they have taken up are called **deliquescent.** For example, calcium chloride ($CaCl_2$) and sodium hydroxide (NaOH) are deliquescent. Water is often removed from gases or liquids by "drying agents" that are anhydrous salts, such as Na_2SO_4, $CaCl_2$, or $MgSO_4$. Of course, the drying agent should not react with the substance being dried.

EXAMPLE 14.3
Formula of a Hydrate

A 1.83 g sample of a hydrate of $Al_2(SO_4)_3$ was heated until no more water vapor was driven off. The anhydrous material weighed 0.94 g. Determine the formula of the hydrate.

The mass of water driven off by the heating process was

$$1.83\ g - 0.94\ g = 0.89\ g$$

The number of moles of water and of anhydrous $Al_2(SO_4)_3$ are

$$(0.89\ g\ H_2O)\left(\frac{1\ mol\ H_2O}{18.02\ g\ H_2O}\right) = 0.049\ mol\ H_2O$$

$$(0.94 \text{ g Al}_2(\text{SO}_4)_3)\left(\frac{1 \text{ mol Al}_2(\text{SO}_4)_3}{342.14 \text{ g 1 mol Al}_2(\text{SO}_4)_3}\right) = 0.0027 \text{ mol Al}_2(\text{SO}_4)_3$$

The ratio of moles of water to moles of $\text{Al}_2(\text{SO}_4)_3$ is

$$\frac{0.049 \text{ mol H}_2\text{O}}{0.0027 \text{ mol Al}_2(\text{SO}_4)_3} = \frac{18 \text{ mol H}_2\text{O}}{1 \text{ mol Al}_2(\text{SO}_4)_3}$$

The formula of the hydrate is $\text{Al}_2(\text{SO}_4)_3 \cdot 18\text{H}_2\text{O}$.

In summary, water is an angular molecule with a large dipole moment. Water molecules are strongly hydrogen-bonded to each other and this is the basis for many of the unusual properties of water. Ice, which has an open crystal structure, floats on liquid water, which attains its maximum density at 3.98 °C. Water has a high heat capacity, high thermal conductivity, and high heat of vaporization, all properties important to the role of water in the environment and in living things. A great many ionic and polar covalent substances are soluble in water, being attracted in varying degrees to the polar water molecules. Water is very slightly ionized to H⁺ and OH⁻ in a dynamic chemical equilibrium, $H_2O \rightleftharpoons H^+ + OH^-$. Often the hydronium ion, H_3O^+, is written instead of the hydrogen ion to emphasize that hydrogen ions are always associated with water molecules in aqueous solution.

Ions and molecules dissolved in water are hydrated—surrounded by water molecules. Compounds in which intact water molecules are incorporated are called hydrates. The water of hydration may be bound by coordinate covalent or by hydrogen bonds, or may simply occupy spaces in the crystal structure. Efflorescence is the loss of water of hydration. Hygroscopic substances take up water from the air, and deliquescent substances dissolve in the water that they take up from the air.

IONS IN AQUEOUS SOLUTION

14.7 ELECTROLYTES AND NONELECTROLYTES

When an ionic compound such as sodium chloride melts, it can conduct electricity because mobile ions are available to carry the current (Section 9.4). Dissolving an ionic compound in water, like melting, frees the ions from their fixed positions in the solid. As a result, aqueous solutions of ionic compounds also conduct electricity. When a direct current is passed through a solution that contains ions, the positive ions are attracted to the negative electrode and the negative ions to the positive electrode (Figure 14.9). Pure substances and substances which in solution conduct electricity by the movement of ions are called **electrolytes.** All compounds that yield ions in aqueous solution are electrolytes. Compounds which are 100% dissociated or

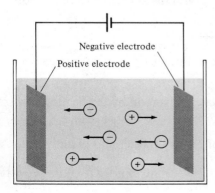

Figure 14.9
Conduction of Electricity by a Solution Containing Ions

Table 14.5
Ions Present in Common Strong Electrolytes Salts containing the ions listed are 100% dissociated into ions in aqueous solution, to the extent that they are soluble.

Li^+
Na^+
K^+
Mg^{2+}
Ca^{2+}
Sr^{2+}
Ba^{2+}
La^{3+}
NH_4^+
Cl^-
Br^-
I^-
ClO_4^-
BrO_3^-
IO_3^-
SO_4^{2-}
HSO_4^-
NO_3^-
CO_3^{2-}
HCO_3^-

ionized in aqueous solution are called **strong electrolytes.** Whatever the *amount* of a strong electrolyte dissolved in a given volume of water, virtually all of the compound dissociates or ionizes. (Recall that ionic compounds are said to "dissociate" and molecular compounds are said to "ionize"; Section 4.4.)

Most salts are strong electrolytes. If a salt that is a strong electrolyte is only slightly soluble in water, a chemical equilibrium is established between any remaining undissolved salt and the ions in aqueous solution. For example, for mercury(II) sulfide, one of the *least soluble* of salts, the equilibrium is written

$$HgS(s) \xrightleftharpoons{H_2O} Hg^{2+} + S^{2-} \qquad \textbf{(14.9)}$$

As with the soluble strong electrolytes, the only species dissolved in the water are ions. Table 14.5 is a list of the ions most commonly found in strong electrolytes. For example, salts containing Na^+, whatever the anion, or salts containing IO_3^-, whatever the cation, are strong electrolytes.

Molecular compounds as well as ionic compounds can be strong electrolytes in aqueous solution. The molecular electrolytes are generally highly polar compounds such as hydrogen chloride. The negatively charged (oxygen) ends of the water dipoles attract the positively charged (hydrogen) ends of HCl molecules. Similarly, the positive (hydrogen) ends of the water molecules attract the negative (chloride) ends of the HCl molecules (Figure 14.10). The strength of the attraction by the water molecules is strong enough to break the hydrogen–chlorine bond and produce ions in aqueous solution.

$$HCl(g) + H_2O(l) \longrightarrow H_3O^+ + Cl^- \qquad \textbf{(14.10)}$$

Hydrogen chloride and other molecular compounds that are strong electrolytes are 100% ionized when they are present in any concentration in aqueous solutions.

Many polar molecular compounds dissolve in water with only partial, rather than complete, ionization. An equilibrium is established between the molecules and ions, all of which are dissolved in the water. For example, acetic acid is soluble in water, but only four out of every 1000 molecules of the acetic acid are ionized in a 1 M solution at 25 °C.

Strong electrolytes: 100% ionized or dissociated in aqueous solution

$$\underset{\text{acetic acid}}{CH_3COOH(aq)} + H_2O(l) \rightleftharpoons \underset{\text{acetate ion}}{CH_3COO^-} + H_3O^+ \qquad \textbf{(14.11)}$$

Acetic acid and other substances like it that are only partially ionized in aqueous solution are called **weak electrolytes.** The extent to which different weak electrolytes ionize under similar conditions varies widely.

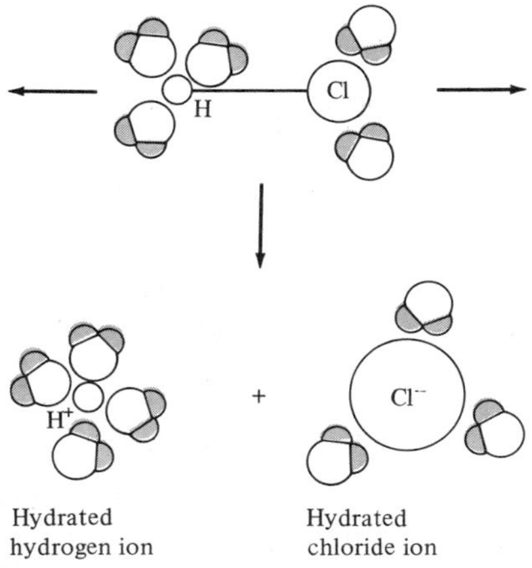
H
Cl
H+
+
Cl−
Hydrated hydrogen ion
Hydrated chloride ion

Figure 14.10
Ionization of Hydrogen Chloride in Aqueous Solution

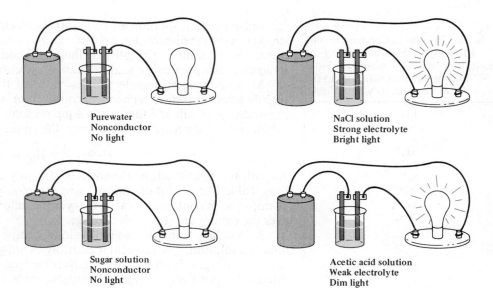

Figure 14.11
Electrolytes and Nonelectrolytes Pure water contains so few ions that it is a nonconductor in this type of experiment. Tap water contains many ions in solution and is conductive.

Purewater
Nonconductor
No light

NaCl solution
Strong electrolyte
Bright light

Sugar solution
Nonconductor
No light

Acetic acid solution
Weak electrolyte
Dim light

Substances that dissolve in water to give solutions that do not conduct electricity are called **nonelectrolytes.** Nonelectrolytes remain as molecules in solution and their solutions do not conduct electricity. Some examples are ethyl alcohol (C_2H_5OH), acetone (CH_3COCH_3, a common laboratory solvent), and sucrose (table sugar).

Figure 14.11 illustrates a demonstration of the conduction of electricity by electrolytes. Pure water is so slightly ionized that its conductance is only detected by very sensitive instruments. Tapwater, however, is seldom pure; it usually contains various ions (Section 14.11) and so conducts electricity quite well. (That is why you should never touch electrical equipment when your hands are wet or while you are standing on a wet floor.)

EXAMPLE 14.4
Electrolytes and Nonelectrolytes

Write chemical equations for what happens when each of the following substances is mixed with water: (a) gaseous hydrogen iodide; (b) solid calcium nitrate; (c) solid magnesium hydroxide; and (d) *n*-propyl alcohol (a liquid with the structure $CH_3CH_2CH_2OH$).

(a) Based on what we know about HCl—that it is a strong electrolyte (Equation 14.10)—we would expect HI(*g*) to behave in a similar fashion and be 100% ionized in aqueous solution.

$$HI(g) + H_2O(l) \longrightarrow H_3O^+ + I^-$$

(b) Nitrates (see Table 6.3) are generally soluble salts. Also, Ca^{2+} and NO_3^- are ions found in strong electrolytes (see Table 14.4). Therefore, calcium nitrate should be a strong electrolyte and should be soluble and 100% dissociated in aqueous solution.

$$Ca(NO_3)_2(s) \xrightarrow{H_2O} Ca^{2+} + 2NO_3^-$$

(c) Only the alkali metal hydroxides are soluble (see Table 6.3). Therefore, solid $Mg(OH)_2$ establishes an equilibrium with ions in solution.

$$Mg(OH)_2(s) \overset{H_2O}{\rightleftharpoons} Mg^{2+} + 2OH^-$$

(d) By analogy with what we know of ethyl alcohol, we would expect *n*-propyl alcohol to be soluble in water and to be a nonelectrolyte (which indeed it is).

$$CH_3CH_2CH_2OH(l) \xrightarrow{H_2O} CH_3CH_2CH_2OH(aq)$$

Exercise Write chemical equations describing the dissolution of the following substances in water: (a) gaseous oxygen, O_2; (b) solid potassium bromide, KBr; (c) solid sodium hydroxide, NaOH; and (d) solid silver chloride, AgCl. *Answer* (a) $O_2(g) \xrightarrow{H_2O} O_2(aq)$, (b) $KBr(s) \xrightarrow{H_2O} K^+ + Br^-$, (c) $NaOH(s) \xrightarrow{H_2O} Na^+ + OH^-$, (d) $AgCl(s) \underset{}{\overset{H_2O}{\rightleftharpoons}} Ag^+ + Cl^-$

14.8 ACIDS AND BASES; H^+ AND OH^-

Acids and bases were first recognized as specific classes of compounds because of the distinctive properties exhibited by their aqueous solutions. The classic acid and base properties and a few common acidic and basic substances are listed in Table 14.6.

In the 1880s Svante Arrhenius, a Swedish chemist, developed a theory for ionization in aqueous solutions. Part of his theory explains that the classic acid properties are imparted to an aqueous solution by the hydrogen ion, H^+, and the basic properties by the hydroxide ion, OH^-. An **acidic aqueous solution** contains a greater concentration of H^+ ions than of OH^- ions. A basic aqueous solution, better called an **alkaline aqueous solution,** contains a greater concentration of OH^- ions than H^+ ions. (The term "alkaline" is preferable because "basic" also has other

Table 14.6

Acids and Bases Early chemists blithely tasted their chemicals. Experience has shown that this can be a fatal mistake. *Never* taste any laboratory chemicals. The acidity of vinegar is due to acetic acid (CH_3COOH). Fruits and vegetables derive their acidity from various organic acids. Gastric juice contains hydrochloric acid (HCl). Carbonated beverages are acidic because of the reaction of CO_2 with water. Aspirin and vitamin C are organic acids, acetylsalicylic acid and ascorbic acid, respectively. Household ammonia is alkaline because of the reaction of ammonia gas (NH_3) with water, and milk of magnesia contains magnesium hydroxide [$Mg(OH)_2$]. Soap and detergents contain various organic and inorganic bases.

Acids	*Bases*
Sour taste	Bitter taste
Change colors of indicators, e.g., litmus turns from blue to red; phenolphthalein turns from red to colorless	Slippery feeling
	Change colors of indicators, e.g., litmus turns from red to blue; phenolphthalein turns from colorless to red
React with active metals to give hydrogen, e.g., Zn(s) + 2H$^+$⟶Zn^{2+} + H$_2$(g)	
	Basic properties disappear in reaction with an acid
Acidic properties disappear in reaction with a base	

Some Acidic Substances	*Some Alkaline Substances*
Vinegar	Household ammonia
Tomatoes	Baking soda
Citrus fruits	Soap
Carbonated beverages	Detergents
Black coffee	Milk of magnesia
Gastric fluid	Oven cleaners
Vitamin C	Lye
Aspirin	Drano
Saniflush	

Table 14.7

Common Acids and Bases Nitrous acid is known only in solution.

Strong acids	
HCl	Hydrochloric acid
HBr	Hydrobromic acid
HI	Hydroiodic acid
HNO_3	Nitric acid
H_2SO_4	Sulfuric acid
$HClO_4$	Perchloric acid
Weak acids	
CH_3COOH	Acetic acid
HF	Hydrofluoric acid
H_3PO_4	Phosphoric acid
HNO_2	Nitrous acid
Strong bases	
NaOH	Sodium hydroxide
KOH	Potassium hydroxide
Weak base	
NH_3	Ammonia

Water-ion definitions:

Acid: H compound $\xrightarrow{H_2O}$ H^+

Base: OH compound $\xrightarrow{H_2O}$ OH^-

---

meanings. "Alkaline" derives from "alkali," an old name for substances with the classic properties of bases.)

The Arrhenius definitions of acids and bases, derived as they are from the presence of hydrogen and hydroxide ions in aqueous solutions, can be called the *water-ion* definitions. An **acid (water-ion)** is a substance that contains hydrogen and yields hydrogen ions in aqueous solution. The common *strong acids* are all water-ion acids. They are molecular compounds that are strong electrolytes and are 100% ionized in aqueous solution. Some are binary acids like hydrochloric acid (Equation 14.10) and others are oxo acids, such as nitric acid:

$$HNO_3(l) + H_2O(l) \longrightarrow H_3O^+ + NO_3^- \tag{14.12}$$

A **base (water-ion)** is a compound that contains hydroxide ions and when it dissolves in water dissociates to give hydroxide ions. The bases defined in this way are all ionic compounds and strong electrolytes. Those hydroxides that are soluble or moderately soluble (the alkali metal hydroxides, and calcium, strontium, and barium hydroxide) give high concentrations of hydroxide ions in solution and are referred to as *strong bases*. The most common strong bases are sodium and potassium hydroxide:

$$NaOH(s) \xrightarrow{H_2O} Na^+ + OH^- \tag{14.13}$$

$$KOH(s) \xrightarrow{H_2O} K^+ + OH^- \tag{14.14}$$

The majority of metal hydroxides, although they are all strong electrolytes, are only slightly soluble (see Table 6.3), and therefore give lower concentrations of OH^- in aqueous solution.

Many hydrogen-containing molecular compounds are weak electrolytes and therefore *weak acids,* for they are less than 100% ionized. For example, acetic acid (Equation 14.11) and hydrogen cyanide, known in its aqueous solution as hydrocyanic acid, are both weak acids and weak electrolytes.

$$HCN(aq) + H_2O(l) \rightleftharpoons H_3O^+ + CN^- \tag{14.15}$$

You should become familiar with the names and formulas of the common acids and bases listed in Table 14.7.

Sulfuric acid and phosphoric acid (see Table 14.7), and other acids like them that contain more than one ionizable hydrogen atom, are known as **polyprotic acids.** Such acids ionize in steps, for example, for phosphoric acid:

$$H_3PO_4(aq) \rightleftharpoons H_2PO_4^- + H^+ \tag{14.16}$$

$$H_2PO_4^- \rightleftharpoons HPO_4^{2-} + H^+ \tag{14.17}$$

$$HPO_4^{2-} \rightleftharpoons PO_4^{3-} + H^+ \tag{14.18}$$

Broader definitions of acids and bases than those of Arrhenius have been introduced over the years as it became desirable to categorize more types of substances as acids and bases. To give a simple example of a substance that is clearly a base although not an ionic hydroxide, consider ammonia, which yields hydroxide ions in solution according to the following equilibrium:

$$NH_3(g) + H_2O(l) \rightleftharpoons NH_4^+ + OH^- \tag{14.19}$$

Ammonia is the most common weak base. (A useful way of defining acids and bases that includes ammonia as a base is discussed at length in Chapter 20.)

EXAMPLE 14.5
Acids and Bases

Write equations for the interaction of water with (a) perchloric acid; (b) nitrous acid (*aq*); and (c) the weak base aniline, $C_6H_5NH_2$.

(a) Perchloric acid, a strong acid, is completely ionized.

$$HClO_4(l) + H_2O(l) \longrightarrow H_3O^+ + ClO_4^-$$

(b) Nitrous acid is a weak acid and establishes an equilibrium with water molecules.

$$HNO_2(aq) + H_2O(l) \rightleftharpoons H_3O^+ + NO_2^-$$

(c) Given that aniline is a weak base, we can assume that it enters into an equilibrium that yields OH^- ions.

$$C_6H_5NH_2(aq) + H_2O(l) \rightleftharpoons C_6H_5NH_3^+ + OH^-$$

Exercise Write equations showing the interaction of water with (a) formic acid, HCOOH, a weak acid like acetic acid; (b) hydrogen bromide; and (c) cesium hydroxide. *Answer* (a) $HCOOH(aq) + H_2O(l) \rightleftharpoons HCOO^- + H_3O^+$; (b) $HBr(g) + H_2O(l) \longrightarrow H_3O^+ + Br^-$; (c) $CsOH(s) \xrightarrow{H_2O} Cs^+ + OH^-$

14.9 NEUTRALIZATION

Neutralization is the reaction of a strong acid with a strong base. Here are the equations for two neutralization reactions.

$$HCl(aq) + NaOH(aq) \longrightarrow NaCl(aq) + H_2O(l) \qquad \textbf{(14.20)}$$
$$HNO_3(aq) + KOH(aq) \longrightarrow KNO_3(aq) + H_2O(l) \qquad \textbf{(14.21)}$$

The products of a neutralization reaction between a water-ion acid and base are water and an ionic compound—a salt. The salts formed by the strong acids and bases shown above are soluble in water and remain in solution as dissociated ions.

Neutralization: Strong acid + strong base→H$_2$O + a salt

Crystalline sodium chloride and potassium nitrate would be obtained if the water were evaporated.

The term "neutralization" arises from the fact that if *stoichiometric amounts* of a strong acid and a strong base are mixed, both the "acidic" and "basic" properties of the original solutions disappear—they are "neutralized." How this occurs is made apparent by writing the net ionic equations for neutralization reactions. In reactions (14.20) and (14.21) the acids, bases, and salts are all soluble strong electrolytes. Writing these compounds as ions and canceling to give the net ionic equations

$$H_3O^+ + Cl^- + Na^+ + OH^- \longrightarrow Na^+ + Cl^- + 2H_2O(l)$$
$$H_3O^+ + OH^- \longrightarrow 2H_2O(l)$$
$$H_3O^+ + NO_3^- + K^+ + OH^- \longrightarrow K^+ + NO_3^- + 2H_2O(l)$$
$$H_3O^+ + OH^- \longrightarrow 2H_2O(l)$$

reveals that the result is the same in both cases. In the reaction between a strong acid and a strong base, the net ionic reaction is the reverse of the ionization of water. When the H^+ and OH^- ions combine to give water, the original acidic and basic properties of the solutions can no longer be detected.

In a general sense, any reaction between an acid and a base can be referred to as neutralization. However, when weak acids or weak bases are involved in the reaction, as is discussed in Section 21.10, the acidic or basic properties of the solution are not completely neutralized.

EXAMPLE 14.6
Neutralization

What mass of solid NaOH would be required to neutralize (that is, to react completely with) the H^+ present in 4.3×10^{-3} mol of HCl in an aqueous solution?

The equation for the reaction is

$$NaOH(s) + HCl(aq) \longrightarrow NaCl(aq) + H_2O(l)$$

We can see from the equation that the amount of NaOH needed is

$$(4.3 \times 10^{-3} \text{ mol HCl})\left(\frac{1 \text{ mol NaOH}}{1 \text{ mol HCl}}\right) = 4.3 \times 10^{-3} \text{ mol NaOH}$$

This corresponds to

$$(4.3 \times 10^{-3} \text{ mol NaOH})\left(\frac{40.00 \text{ g NaOH}}{1 \text{ mol NaOH}}\right) = 0.17 \text{ g NaOH}$$

A 0.17 g sample of NaOH would be required to neutralize the HCl.

In summary, substances that conduct electricity by the movement of ions are called electrolytes, and all compounds that dissolve in water with the formation of ions are electrolytes. Strong electrolytes are 100% ionized or dissociated into ions, and their solutions contain only ions (Table 14.8). Weak electrolytes establish equilibria between ions and molecules in aqueous solution. Compounds that dissolve in water but form no ions and give solutions that do not conduct electricity are nonelectrolytes.

Strong acids (water-ion) and strong bases (water-ion) are strong electrolytes and in aqueous solutions yield hydrogen ions and hydroxide ions, respectively, that impart acidic and basic properties to their solutions. In the reaction between stoichiometric amounts of such strong acids and bases, the acidic and basic properties of the solutions are "neutralized." The products of neutralization are a salt and water. Weak acids are weak electrolytes and their solutions contain varying proportions of ions and molecules depending upon the individual acids and the conditions. As is discussed in Chapter 20, the original water-ion definitions of acids and bases have been expanded in various ways to include many more types of compounds.

Table 14.8
Electrolytes and Nonelectrolytes in Aqueous Solutions Besides weak acids or weak bases, many compounds of other types are also weak electrolytes.

Type of Compound	Species Present in Pure Compound	Species Present in Aqueous Solution	Examples
Strong electrolytes			
Strong acids (water-ion)	Polar molecules	Ions only	$HCl(g) + H_2O(l) \longrightarrow H_3O^+ + Cl^-$
Strong bases (water-ion)	Ions	Ions only	$NaOH(s) \xrightarrow{H_2O} Na^+ + OH^-$
Salts	Ions	Ions only	$NaCl(s) \xrightarrow{H_2O} Na^+ + Cl^-$
Weak electrolytes			
Weak acids	Polar molecules	Ions and molecules in equilibrium	$HF(aq) + H_2O(l) \rightleftharpoons H_3O^+ + F^-$
Weak bases	Polar molecules	Ions and molecules in equilibrium	$NH_3(aq) + H_2O(l) \rightleftharpoons NH_4^+ + OH^-$
Nonelectrolytes			
Water-soluble molecular compounds	Molecules	Molecules only	$CH_3CH_2OH(l) \xrightarrow{H_2O} CH_3CH_2OH(aq)$

14.10 FORMATON OF
COMPLEX IONS

A **complex ion,** or "complex," consists of a central metal atom or cation to which are bonded one or more molecules or anions. Transition metals, in particular, form complex ions readily. The molecules or ions bonded to the central atom or cation are called **ligands.**

The charge of a complex ion equals the sum of the charge of the cation and the charges of any ligands that are anions. For example, with ammonia, a neutral ligand, the charge of the complex ion equals that of the cation.

$$
\underset{\text{ligand charge}\,=\,0}{\overset{\overset{\text{cation}}{\text{charge}\,=\,+2}\quad\overset{\text{charge of}}{\text{complex ion}}}{[\text{Ni}(\text{NH}_3)_4]^{2+}}}
$$

With anionic ligands, the charge of a complex ion is found as follows:

$$
\underset{\text{total ligand}\atop\text{charge}\,=\,(4\times-1)\,=\,-4}{\overset{\overset{\text{cation}}{\text{charge}\,=\,+2}\quad\overset{\text{charge of complex ion}}{=\,(+2)+(-4)=-2}}{[\text{Cd}(\text{CN})_4]^{2-}}}
\qquad
\underset{\text{total ligand}\atop\text{charge}\,=\,(6\times-1)\,=\,-6}{\overset{\overset{\text{cation}}{\text{charge}\,=\,+3}\quad\overset{\text{charge of complex ion}}{=\,(+3)+(-6)=-3}}{[\text{CoF}_6]^{3-}}}
$$

Anionic and molecular ligands can be present in the same complex, and in some cases the total charge of a complex is zero.

$$
\underset{\text{total ligand}\atop\text{charge}\,=\,0+(-2)\,=\,-2}{\overset{\overset{\text{cation}}{\text{charge}\,=\,+3}\quad\overset{\text{charge of complex ion}}{=\,(+3)+(-2)=+1}}{[\text{Co}(\text{NH}_3)_4(\text{CO}_3)]^{+}}}
\qquad
\underset{\text{total ligand charge}\atop=\,0+(2\times-1)\,=\,-2}{\overset{\overset{\text{cation}}{\text{charge}\,=\,+2}\quad\overset{\text{charge of complex ion}}{=\,(+2)+(-2)=0}}{[\text{Pt}(\text{NH}_3)_2(\text{Cl})_2]^{0}}}
$$

A hydrated metal cation is a complex ion with water molecules as ligands, for example, $[\text{Cu}(\text{H}_2\text{O})_n]^{2+}$. The stepwise displacement of water molecules leads to the formation of other complex ions, for example,

$$[\text{Cu}(\text{H}_2\text{O})_n]^{2+} + \text{NH}_3(aq) \rightleftharpoons [\text{Cu}(\text{H}_2\text{O})_{n-1}(\text{NH}_3)]^{2+} + \text{H}_2\text{O}(l)$$
$$[\text{Cu}(\text{H}_2\text{O})_{n-1}(\text{NH}_3)]^{2+} + \text{NH}_3(aq) \rightleftharpoons [\text{Cu}(\text{H}_2\text{O})_{n-2}(\text{NH}_3)_2]^{2+} + \text{H}_2\text{O}(l)$$

Like slightly soluble salts, complex ions in solution are in equilibrium with their cations and ligands. In writing equations, the water molecules are generally omitted, and the overall equilibrium in the solution of a complex ion is represented, for example, as follows:

$$\text{Ag}^+ + 2\text{NH}_3(aq) \rightleftharpoons [\text{Ag}(\text{NH}_3)_2]^+ \qquad\qquad \textbf{(14.22)}$$

The formation of a complex ion is often useful when it is desirable to dissolve a precipitate. A precipitate of silver chloride

$$\text{Ag}^+ + \text{Cl}^- \longrightarrow \text{AgCl}(s)$$

can be dissolved by the addition of a solution containing NH_3 or by the addition of excess chloride ion to give complex ions in solution.

$$AgCl(s) + 2NH_3(aq) \rightleftharpoons [Ag(NH_3)_2]^+ + Cl^- \qquad \textbf{(14.23)}$$

$$AgCl(s) + Cl^- \rightleftharpoons [AgCl_2]^- \qquad \textbf{(14.24)}$$

Complex ion equilibria are dealt with quantitatively in Chapter 21, and bonding and other aspects of complex ion chemistry are discussed in Chapter 32.

14.11 HARD WATER

Hard water: contains Ca²⁺, Mg²⁺, Fe²⁺

The presence of certain metal ions in water destined for domestic or industrial use causes practical problems. Water containing these ions is called "hard" water. It can be recognized by the grayish white scum it forms with soap, the dull appearance of clothes washed in it using soap, the hard scale it forms in boilers and tea kettles, and, sometimes, by an unpleasant taste. **Hard water** contains metal ions (principally Ca^{2+}, Mg^{2+}, and Fe^{2+}) that form precipitates with soap or upon boiling.

The properties of hard water are partly determined by what anions accompany the metal cations. To the extent that water contains HCO_3^- anions together with the Ca^{2+}, Mg^{2+}, and Fe^{2+} ions, it displays what is called **carbonate hardness** (or **temporary hardness**). Boiling hard water that contains hydrogen carbonate ions drives off carbon dioxide, leaving behind carbonate ions that form insoluble salts with the metal cations present.

$$M^{2+} + 2HCO_3^- \xrightarrow{\Delta} MCO_3(s) + CO_2(g) + H_2O(g) \qquad \textbf{(14.25)}$$

Carbonate hardness is undesirable because the insoluble carbonates form a hard coating known as "boiler scale" that collects on the walls of tea kettles, hot water pipes, and other vessels. (Have you ever seen a domestic hot water pipe that was choked off by such a deposit?) Boiler scale is a poor conductor of heat and the efficiency of industrial boilers (and tea kettles) is decreased by its presence.

Water softening is the removal of the ions that cause hardness in water. If a sufficient concentration of hydrogen carbonate ions is present, water can be softened by boiling (as shown above); hence the name "temporary" hardness. Water that contains Ca^{2+}, Mg^{2+}, and Fe^{2+} ions but no HCO_3^- ion has what is referred to as **noncarbonate hardness** (or **permanent hardness**). Such water cannot be "softened" by boiling. However, it also contributes to boiler scale to the extent that it contains sulfate ion. Calcium sulfate is less soluble in hot water than in cold water. Therefore, it too collects on the walls of vessels or pipes that continually hold hot water.

Hard water is effectively softened for use in homes or in industrial operations either by removing the metal ions or by tieing them up chemically. Chemicals may be added to precipitate the metal ions. This was accomplished in home laundries for many years by adding washing soda ($Na_2CO_3 \cdot 10H_2O$) to the water before putting in the soap. This causes calcium, iron(II), and magnesium ions to precipitate out as carbonates. Modern synthetic detergents (Section 15.20) contain *builders*—compounds that, among other functions, prevent the formation of precipitates in hard water by tieing up the metal ions in soluble complexes.

Another method for softening water involves the replacement of the objectionable cations by sodium ions, which do not give a precipitate with soap or form scales. The process of replacement of one ion by another is known as **ion exchange.** Water is passed over naturally occurring zeolites or similar synthetic materials. The zeolites, which are complex sodium aluminum silicates (Section 30.16), possess a three-dimensional open structure, with a negatively charged aluminosilicate framework and sodium ions in the openings of the framework. When hard water is passed through a column of a zeolite, the Ca^{2+}, Mg^{2+}, and Fe^{2+} ions present in the water change places with the sodium ions and are thus removed from the liquid phase.

$$M^{2+} + 2NaZ(s) \longrightarrow 2Na^+ + M(Z)_2(s) \qquad (Z = \text{anion of zeolite})$$

People on restricted diets should be aware that water softened in this way contains a high concentration of sodium ions.

Synthetic organic materials known as *ion-exchange resins* are even better water softeners than the zeolites. The resins have a hydrocarbon framework to which are chemically bonded either negatively charged groups, such as sulfonate, $-SO_3^-$, or positively charged groups, such as $-NR_3^+$ (where R = a group containing only hydrogen and carbon). The former are counterbalanced by positive ions, usually Na^+ or H^+, and the latter by anions, for example, OH^-. It is possible to remove virtually all the unwanted ions from water by passing it through a mixture of a cation-exchange resin containing H^+ as the positive ion and an anion-exchange resin having OH^- as the negative ion. The H^+ replaced from one resin by cation impurities in the water combines with the OH^- replaced from the other by anionic impurities. Water with almost all ions removed (except, of course, the H^+ and OH^- ions normally present from the H_2O ionization equilibrium) is called *deionized water.*

EXAMPLE 14.7
Water Hardness

Water from a certain reservoir is "hard" because it contains dissolved $CaSO_4$. Remembering that $BaSO_4$ is insoluble, a student suggested that the water could be softened by adding a solution of $Ba(OH)_2$. What is wrong with the suggestion?

The reaction

$$CaSO_4(aq) + Ba(OH)_2(aq) \longrightarrow BaSO_4(s) + Ca(OH)_2(aq)$$

would remove the SO_4^{2-} ion from solution, but not the Ca^{2+} ion, which is the ion that causes the hardness in the water.

SUMMARY

14.1 THE WATER MOLECULE AND ITS AGGREGATES   Water is an AB_2E_2 molecule with two lone electron pairs on the oxygen atom. The H—O—H bond angle is 104.5°, and since the O—H bonds are highly polar, water has a large dipole moment. Hydrogen bonding holds groups of water molecules together in shifting groups that constantly break up and reform. The crystal structure of ice is very open, so water (unlike most liquids) becomes less dense when it freezes, and ice floats on liquid water. Water reaches its maximum density at about 4 °C.

14.2 PROPERTIES OF WATER   Water has many unusual properties, most of which are related to the polarity of water molecules and their extensive hydrogen bonding. The freezing point, boiling point, heat of fusion, heat of vaporization, heat capacity, thermal conductivity, and surface tension are all uncommonly high in comparison with similar compounds. The central role of water in the environment and in living systems depends upon these properties.

14.3 WATER AS A SOLVENT   Water is an excellent solvent, especially for ionic or polar covalent substances. The association of an ion or molecule in solution with water molecules is called hydration. All ions in aqueous solution are assumed to be hydrated.

14.4 THE IONIZATION OF WATER: A CHEMICAL EQUILIBRIUM   Liquid water always contains a small fraction, about $1.8 \times 10^{-7}\%$, of H^+ and OH^- ions. The ionization of water and the recombination of the ions establish a dynamic chemical equilibrium: The rates of the forward and reverse reactions are the same, and the amounts of the various species present do not change with time. An H^+ ion in aqueous solution is normally associated with one or more water molecules, and is often represented by H_3O^+, which is a hydronium ion.

14.5 CHEMICAL REACTIONS OF WATER   **14.6** HYDRATES   Water takes part in a wide variety of chemical reactions. The general term for reactions in which the water molecule is split is hydrolysis. Chemical compounds that include water molecules are called hydrates. The forces that hold water molecules in hydrates are not usually very strong, and water can be easily lost and regained.

14.7 ELECTROLYTES AND NONELECTROLYTES Substances that conduct electricity by the movement of ions are called electrolytes. Strong electrolytes are 100% ionized or dissociated in aqueous solution. Most salts, as well as some molecular compounds, are strong electrolytes. Substances that are only partially ionized in aqueous solution are weak electrolytes; they establish equilibria between molecules and ions. Substances that dissolve in water to give solutions that do not conduct electricity are nonelectrolytes.

14.8 ACIDS AND BASES; H⁺ AND OH⁻ An acidic aqueous solution contains a greater concentration of H^+ ions than of OH^- ions; the reverse is true of an alkaline aqueous solution. According to the water-ion definitions, an acid is a substance that contains hydrogen and yields H^+ ions in aqueous solution; a base is a compound that contains hydroxide ions and dissociates in aqueous solution to give OH^- ions. The common strong acids are all molecular compounds that are strong electrolytes (100% ionized in aqueous solution). Some hydrogen-containing molecular compounds are weak acids because they are weak electrolytes (less than 100% ionized in aqueous solution). The most common strong bases are NaOH and KOH. Acids that contain more than one ionizable hydrogen atom per molecule are called polyprotic acids.

14.9 NEUTRALIZATION The reaction of a strong acid with a strong base is called neutralization. The products of a neutralization reaction between a water-ion acid and base are water and an ionic compound called a salt.

14.10 FORMATION OF COMPLEX IONS A complex ion, or complex, consists of a central metal atom or cation to which are bonded one or more molecules or anions known as ligands. The charge on a complex ion is the sum of the charges on the constituent ions. Often a precipitate can be dissolved by incorporating the cation into a complex ion.

14.11 HARD WATER Hard water contains metal ions (chiefly Ca^{2+}, Mg^{2+}, and Fe^{2+}) that form precipitates with soap or upon boiling. The removal of such ions is called water softening. Water that contains HCO_3^- anions along with metal cations exhibits carbonate or temporary hardness. If the concentration of HCO_3^- is high enough, such water can be softened by boiling, which drives off CO_2 and leaves behind insoluble carbonate salts of the metal cations. Hard water that lacks HCO_3^- exhibits noncarbonate or permanent hardness. Such water is softened by use of chemicals that precipitate the metal ions as insoluble compounds or tie them up in soluble complexes. Another method is ion exchange, in which the metal ions are replaced by Na^+ ions.

SIGNIFICANT TERMS

hydration
solvation
chemical equilibrium
hydrolysis
hydrates
efflorescence
hygroscopic
deliquescent
electrolytes
strong electrolytes
weak electrolytes
nonelectrolytes
acidic aqueous solution
alkaline aqueous solution
acid (water-ion)
base (water-ion)
polyprotic acids
neutralization
complex ion
ligands
hard water
carbonate hardness, temporary hardness
water softening
noncarbonate hardness, permanent hardness
ion exchange

THOUGHTS ON CHEMISTRY

The Ocean System

WHY BIG FIERCE ANIMALS ARE RARE,
by Paul Colinvaux

The oceans are cruel deserts, and the things they lack are the soluble plant nutrients. But this is a strange conclusion for one who broods about the history of the earth. The oceans have existed since almost the beginnings of earthly time, changing in shape, shoved from one part of the planet to another before the drifting continents, but always present in roughly the volume we know. And all the time soluble nutrients have been washed into them by the rivers coming from the land. The sea has been made salty by this process. And yet it lacks the nutrients needed for life. Strange.

Some details of the answer to this riddle still escape us, but the outlines are clear. The chemistry of the sea is controlled by its mud. Even as the endless-flowing rivers discharge their chemicals into the ocean, so the mud at the bottom soaks them up. The mud is selective. It has compli-

cated minerals similar to the clays of temperate soils that hold metallic cations like calcium, potassium, and sodium. In its medium of salt, the surface of the mud allows slow crystals to grow, like the nodules of manganese that some mining corporations plan to dredge for. There are sites where calcium carbonate precipitates and collects into reefs of limestone, dragging with it other elements such as magnesium. The mud contains organic debris on which bacteria do their strange feeding, fixing some elements to their corpses and discarding others. . . .

Chemicals are removed from the ocean basins as fast as they arrive from the rivers. They flow back to the land with the writhing of the earth's crust. Every thrust of a mountain range and every emergence of a coastline from the sea brings the chemical-rich mud back to the land. All the sedimentary rocks, from limestone and sandstone to shale and schist, were once part of the ocean's mud. When they were lifted out of the sea, they took with them the chemical nutrients stored in them. At once these nutrients began to be washed out of the rocks again by rain, to be caught in the roots of land plants and held for a while in land ecosystems, then to escape in a slow leak to the rivers, and to be sent on another journey to the sea, another spreading through the fluid mass, and another sorting on the sea's bottom.

It is an enormous chemical machine that keeps the sea a desert. All the chemicals in the sea are cycled slowly through it. They come from the rivers, they spend a time in the oceans, diluted and in suspense, then they are taken in by the mud, held for a brief few million years, and then thrust back onto the land in a prison of rock. This is a system that holds the chemistry of the sea constant from eon to eon. It is not an ecosystem, for all that bacteria and other forms of life do some of the chemical things on the way, particularly influencing the deposition of carbonates. It is a passive physical and chemical system, driven by the sun because the sun is there, but not organized by life.

QUESTIONS

The Chemistry of Water

14.1 Draw the Lewis structure of a water molecule. What type of bonding exists between the oxygen and hydrogen atoms within the molecule?

14.2 Draw a three-dimensional sketch of a water molecule. Describe the geometry of the molecule. Describe the hybridization of the atomic orbitals on the oxygen atom.

14.3 What is the value of the predicted bond angle in water? Is the actual value greater or less than this value? Why is there a difference? Would you predict a water molecule to be a dipole?

14.4 What types of intermolecular forces are present in water?

14.5* The hydrogen bond formed between two molecules of hydrogen fluoride is slightly stronger than that formed between two molecules of water. Yet the physical properties of water are significantly more dependent on hydrogen bonding than those of hydrogen fluoride. Why?

14.6 Why is liquid water less dense at temperatures both higher and lower than 3.98 °C? Why is liquid water more dense than ice?

14.7 What properties of water make it useful as a cooling agent, for example, in automobile radiators and in industrial processes?

14.8 Why is water a much better solvent for ionic and polar substances than for nonpolar substances? Are all ionic and highly polar substances highly soluble in water? Prepare sketches showing how ionic and polar substances dissolve in water.

14.9 What does the term "solvation" mean? What do we call the solvation process that occurs in an aqueous solution?

14.10 What two factors determine the strength of the attraction of water molecules to ions during hydration? Will Na^+ or Zn^{2+} have the greater enthalpy of hydration?

14.11 Write the chemical equation for the self-ionization of water. Do a large percentage of water molecules undergo ionization?

14.12 How do we usually write the chemical formula for the hydrated hydrogen ion? Draw a Lewis structure for this cation.

14.13* Would you expect OH^- to be highly hydrated? Draw a Lewis structure for $H_3O_2^-$.

14.14 Define the term "hydrolysis." Write two chemical equations illustrating hydrolysis reactions.

14.15 Describe three ways in which water molecules can be held in a hydrate.

14.16 Name the following compounds: (a) $Cr(CH_3COO)_3 \cdot H_2O$, (b) $Cd(NO_3)_2 \cdot 4H_2O$, (c) $(NH_4)_2C_2O_4 \cdot H_2O$ ($C_2O_4^{2-}$ is oxalate ion), and (d) $LiBr \cdot 2H_2O$.

14.17 Write the formulas of the following compounds: (a) sodium acetate trihydrate, (b) aluminum iodide hexahydrate, (c) magnesium bromate hexahydrate (bromate ion is BrO_3^-), and (d) thallium(III) chloride tetrahydrate.

Ions in Aqueous Solution
14.18 Is water a very weak electrolyte? Why?

14.19 What are strong electrolytes? Write chemical equations illustrating how $NaBr(s)$, $NaOH(s)$, and $HBr(g)$ act as strong electrolytes.

14.20 Are slightly soluble ionic compounds considered to be strong or weak electrolytes? Why?

14.21 What types of substances are weak electrolytes in aqueous solution? Write a chemical equation showing that hydrogen fluoride is a weak electrolyte when dissolved in water.

14.22 Write chemical equations describing what happens as each of the following substances is mixed with water: (a) $HNO_3(l)$; (b) $KOH(s)$; (c) $KF(s)$; (d) $MgCO_3(s)$, a slightly soluble salt; and (e) $Ca(ClO_4)_2(s)$.

14.23 Write chemical equations describing what happens as each of the following substances is mixed with water: (a) $H_2SO_4(l)$, (b) $NH_4I(s)$, (c) $Sr(OH)_2(s)$, (d) $HCN(g)$, and (e) $AgCl(s)$.

14.24 Name four classic properties of aqueous solutions of acids. Contrast these with the properties of bases.

14.25 What does the word "acid" mean in terms of the water-ion acid–base definition? Name and write the formulas for some of the common strong and weak acids.

14.26 What does the term "polyprotic" mean? Write the formula for a common polyprotic acid. Write the chemical equations showing the stepwise ionization of the acid.

14.27 Write the chemical equations for the interaction with water of (a) hydrogen bromide, HBr; (b) hypobromous acid, HBrO; and (c) phosphorous acid, H_3PO_3, in which only two of the protons are ionizable.

14.28 Repeat Question 14.27 for (a) oxalic acid, HOOCCOOH(s); (b) hydrogen cyanide, HCN(g); and (c) nitric acid, $HNO_3(l)$.

14.29 What does the term "base" mean in terms of the water-ion acid–base definition? Name and write the formula for one strong base.

14.30 What is a neutralization reaction? Write a chemical equation for the neutralization of any strong acid by any strong base. Write the net ionic equation for the reaction.

14.31 How does the net ionic equation for a "neutralization" reaction involving a weak acid and a strong base differ from that for the reaction involving a strong acid and a strong base?

14.32* Write chemical equations showing the various stages of ionization of phosphoric acid, H_3PO_4, a triprotic acid. Write chemical equations for all possible reactions of H_3PO_4 with calcium hydroxide, $Ca(OH)_2$.

14.33 What is a complex ion? What is the term for the molecules or ions that bond to the central metal atom or cation?

14.34 Determine the charges on the following complex ions: (a) $[Cr(H_2O)_6]^?$, where the ionic charge on Cr is $+3$; (b) $[Fe(H_2O)_5Cl]^?$, where the ionic charge on Fe is $+3$; and (c) $[Co(NH_3)_5Cl]^?$, where the ionic charge on Co is $+3$.

14.35 Repeat Question 14.34 for (a) $[AuCl_4]^?$, where the ionic charge on Au is $+3$; (b) $[Cr(H_2O)_4Cl_2]^?$, where the ionic charge on Cr is $+3$; and (c) $[Al(OH)_4]^?$, where the ionic charge on Al is $+3$.

14.36 What is meant by the term "hard water"? What are the two types of hard water and how do they differ from each other?

14.37 What is the general name for the process in which the undesirable ions in hard water are removed? Name several ways in which these ions can be removed.

14.38 What does the term "ion exchange" mean? Briefly describe how ion-exchange resins are used in a home water softener.

Answers to Selected Questions
14.3 109.47°; the actual value is less (104.5°); repulsions between lone pairs of electrons and between lone pairs and bonded pairs reduce the bond angle; yes

14.10 ionic size, ionic charge; Zn^{2+}

14.17 (a) $Na(CH_3COO) \cdot 3H_2O$, (b) $AlI_3 \cdot 6H_2O$, (c) $Mg(BrO_3)_2 \cdot 6H_2O$, (d) $TlCl_3 \cdot 4H_2O$

14.18 Yes; relatively few ions are formed by self-ionization in pure water.

14.20 Strong; dissociation into ions is complete to the extent that the compound dissolves.

14.23 (a) $H_2SO_4(l) \xrightarrow{H_2O} H^+ + HSO_4^-$, (b) $NH_4I(s) \xrightarrow{H_2O} NH_4^+ + I^-$, (c) $Sr(OH)_2(s) \underset{H_2O}{\rightleftharpoons} Sr^{2+} + 2OH^-$, (d) $HCN(g) \underset{H_2O}{\rightleftharpoons} H^+ + CN^-$, (e) $AgCl(s) \rightleftharpoons Ag^+ + Cl^-$

14.28 (a) HOOCCOOH(s) $\xrightarrow{H_2O}$ HOOCCOO$^-$ + H$^+$, HOOCCOO$^-$ $\xrightarrow{H_2O}$ H$^+$ + OOCCOO^{2-}; (b) HCN(g) $\xrightarrow{H_2O}$ H$^+$ + CN$^-$; (c) HNO$_3$(l) $\xrightarrow{H_2O}$ H$^+$ + NO$_3^-$

14.29 A base is a substance that contains OH$^-$ and yields OH$^-$ in aqueous solution; NaOH (or KOH).

14.35 (a) -1, (b) $+1$, (c) -1

14.37 The removal of unwanted ions is called water softening; it can be accomplished by precipitation, complexation, or ion exchange.

PROBLEMS

Neutralization

14.1 What mass of NaOH is needed to neutralize 1.00 g of (a) HBr and (b) HClO$_4$?

14.2 What mass of each of the following acids is needed to neutralize 1.00 g of KOH: (a) HCl and (b) HNO$_3$? *Answer* (a) 0.649 g HCl and (b) 1.12 g HNO$_3$

14.3 What mass of NaOH is needed to neutralize 50.0 mL of 0.1036 M HCl? If the NaOH is available as a 0.0937 M aqueous solution, what volume will be required?

14.4 What volume of 0.1123 M HCl is needed to neutralize 16.9 g of Ca(OH)$_2$? *Answer* 4.06 L

14.5 The net ionic equation for the neutralization of a strong acid by a strong base is

$$H^+ + OH^- \longrightarrow H_2O(l)$$

The standard state heats of formation at 25 °C are 0 kJ/mol for H$^+$(aq), -229.99 kJ/mol for OH$^-$(aq), and -285.830 kJ/mol for H$_2$O(l). Calculate the heat of neutralization for this reaction. *Answer* -55.84 kJ

Hydrates

14.6 Calculate the mass percent of water in (a) gypsum, CaSO$_4\cdot$2H$_2$O, and (b) natrolite, Na$_2$Al$_2$Si$_3$O$_{10}\cdot$2H$_2$O.

14.7 Calculate the mass percent of water in (a) epsomite, MgSO$_4\cdot$7H$_2$O, and (b) turquoise, CuAl$_6$(PO$_4$)$_4$(OH)$_8\cdot$4H$_2$O. *Answer* (a) 51.17%, (b) 8.861%

14.8 A student needed anhydrous calcium chloride, CaCl$_2$, to use as a drying agent in an experiment. The stockroom had only one-pound bottles of the hexahydrate. Upon consulting a reference book, the student found that the hexahydrate could be converted to the anhydrous compound by heating at 200 °C. The student heated the contents of one of the bottles at that temperature until the mass no longer decreased to ensure that all of the water had been driven off. What was the final mass of anhydrous salt obtained? *Answer* 230. g

14.9 A 23.4 g sample of a hydrate of CuCl$_2$ was heated at 100 °C until no additional water was driven off. The anhydrous sample weighed 18.5 g. What is the formula of the hydrate?

14.10 A 1.563 g sample of a hydrate of LiClO$_3$ was heated at 95 °C until no additional water was driven off. The anhydrous sample weighed 1.421 g. What is the formula of the hydrate? *Answer* LiClO$_3\cdot\frac{1}{2}$H$_2$O

Additional Problems

14.11 The vapor pressure of water at 25 °C over a sample of CuSO$_4\cdot$5H$_2$O(s) is 7.8 Torr. This vapor pressure is the result of the reaction

$$CuSO_4\cdot5H_2O(s) \longrightarrow CuSO_4\cdot3H_2O(s) + 2H_2O(g)$$

What is the minimum amount of CuSO$_4\cdot$5H$_2$O needed to produce a partial pressure of 7.8 Torr in a 1.00 L container of dry air at 25 °C?

14.12 The heat of combustion of a typical coal is 31 kJ/g. Utilizing this heat, calculate the mass of steam at 125 °C that can be prepared from water at 25 °C for each gram of coal burned. Assume the heat of vaporization of water to be 2260 J/g, the specific heat of water to be 4.184 J/kg, and the specific heat of steam to be 2.1 J/kg. *Answer* 12 g

14.13 A solution that contains hydroiodic acid, HI(aq), can be made by the treatment of phosphorus(III) iodide with water:

$$PI_3(s) + 3H_2O(l) \longrightarrow 3HI(aq) + H_3PO_3(aq)$$

A 30.0 g sample of PI$_3$ was dissolved in water and the resulting solution was diluted to exactly 500 mL. What is the molarity of the hydroiodic acid in the solution?

14.14 One of the sources of elemental magnesium is seawater, where the magnesium occurs to the extent of 1300 mg/L in the form of the chloride and sulfate. The magnesium is recovered from the seawater as MgCl$_2\cdot$H$_2$O and the molten hydrate is decomposed to give the metal. What volume of seawater would have to be processed in order to produce 1.00 g of the metal? Assume that the entire process is 80.% efficient. *Answer* 0.96 L

14.15* What will be the final temperature of the mixture prepared from 100.0 g of ice at 0 °C and 100.0 g of steam at 100 °C? For water, the heat of vaporization is 2256.2 J/g, the heat of fusion is 333.5 J/g, and the specific heat is 4.184 J/kg.

14.16* The scum-producing reaction between soap and Ca^{2+} represented by Ca^{2+} + 2Na(C$_{17}$H$_{35}$COO) $\longrightarrow$ 2Na$^+$ + Ca(C$_{17}$H$_{35}$COO)$_2$ can be used to determine water hardness quantitatively. A standardized soap solution is slowly added to a water sample until a lasting sudsing effect is observed. A soap solution was treated with 20.0 mL of a solution that contained 495 ppm of Ca^{2+} (1 ppm = 10^{-6} g Ca^{2+}/mL of hard water). Express the concentration of the soap solution in terms of grams of Ca^{2+}/mL soap solution if 35.2 mL of the soap solution were required for the reaction.

A 25.0 mL sample of well water required 3.0 mL of the soap solution before a lasting suds was formed. What is the concentration of Ca^{2+} in the well water (expressed in ppm)?

14.17* The crystal structure of ordinary ice is a hexagonal unit cell with volume given by (0.4535 nm)^2(0.741 nm)(sin 60°). The number of molecules in the unit cell is four. Calculate the theoretical density of ice.

CHAPTER 15

Solutions and Colloids

Enclosed within your skin is a very complex system—a biological–physical–chemical system that we are just beginning to understand in detail. Your body consists of more than a trillion cells, most of them highly specialized. Each cell contains an elaborate array of structures called organelles—complex "machines" made up largely of giant molecules. Each performs a specific function that helps to keep the cell alive and/or enables it to perform its role in the organism as a whole.

All this machinery functions in a fluid environment, for the interior of a cell is mostly water. Individual cells and groups of cells—tissues and organs—are bathed in a fluid known as lymph. Cells are supplied with oxygen and nutrients, and get rid of their wastes, by means of another fluid: the blood, which also carries chemical messengers and the body's defense forces. Wastes leave the body via yet another fluid, called urine. Each of these fluids is a complex mixture of ions, molecules, and molecular aggregates in an aqueous medium.

The interior of a living cell is a colloidal dispersion of large protein molecules and fat globules. It is also a true solution, containing dozens of ions and small molecules (for example, amino acids and simple sugars). Since the earliest life forms almost certainly evolved in the oceans, it is not surprising that the concentrations of ions in the body fluids of most organisms are similar to those of seawater. Na^+ and Cl^- ions are most abundant, and K^+, Ca^{2+}, and Mg^{2+} are always present, though in varying amounts.

Ions and molecules of many kinds pass into and out of cells by osmosis. Osmosis is the transport of solvent molecules through a membrane—in this case, the membrane that surrounds each living cell. Osmosis is a process of vital importance to organisms, and its operation depends on the concentration of solutes in the liquids on either side of the membrane. Medicine to be administered intravenously must be dissolved in physiological saline solution, an aqueous solution of the same ionic concentration as blood (an "isotonic" solution). Blood cells bathed in a solution that is not isotonic can swell up and explode (if the ionic concentration of the solution is less than that of the cells' interior) or shrivel up and collapse (if the ionic concentration of the solution is greater than that of the cells' interior).

GENERAL PROPERTIES OF SOLUTIONS

15.1 SOME DEFINITIONS

Solution: a single-phase mixture

Any mixture with only a single phase is a solution. We are used to dealing with liquid solutions, but solutions are also found in the gas phase (e.g., air) or in the solid phase (some types of metal alloys; Section 28.11). Most of this chapter is devoted to solutions in the liquid phase, especially to those in which various solutes are dissolved in water.

The process of one substance dissolving in another is referred to as *dissolution*. In reporting the amount of one substance that can dissolve in another, the temperature must be specified, because temperature influences to what extent dissolution will occur. Dissolution is also influenced by the nature of the solute and the solvent, the pressure (if the solute is a gas), and, in some cases, the presence of additional solutes.

The *concentration* of a solution is the amount of solute in a given amount of solvent or solution. For example, the concentration of a solution might be given as grams of solute per 100 g of solution or as moles of solute per liter of solution (Section 4.7). (Units of concentration are discussed in Sections 15.6–15.10.)

Suppose a soluble salt is gradually added to water at a given temperature. Beyond a certain point, no more seems to dissolve. In reality, it is still dissolving, but at the same time, an equal amount of salt is coming out of solution and crystallizing on the surface of the solid salt or on the sides of the container. A condition of dynamic equilibrium has been reached—the processes of dissolution and crystallization are proceeding at the same rate, so that each exactly offsets the other (Figure 15.1).

Figure 15.1
Crystals in a Saturated Solution The mass of the crystals remains the same as long as the temperature is unchanged. Molecules or ions join and leave the crystal surface in a dynamic equilibrium.

$$\text{Solid salt} \rightleftharpoons \text{salt in solution}$$

This equilibrium can be demonstrated by placing a broken, irregular crystal of salt in the solution. As ions from the crystal go into solution, ions from the solution precipitate on the crystal surface. These ions precipitate onto areas which will give a more symmetrical crystal. Over a period of several days (at constant temperature), the broken corners fill in and a more perfect crystal of the same mass as the broken crystal is produced.

A **saturated solution** is a solution in which the concentration of dissolved solute is equal to that which would be in equilibrium with undissolved solute under the given conditions (solvent, temperature, and for a gas, pressure). The undissolved solute need not actually be there—a solid could have been filtered off, or the solution could have been made by dissolving exactly the right amount of solute for saturation. The **solubility** of a substance is the concentration of a solution that is saturated under the given conditions. When the temperature is not specified, it may be assumed that solubility data are given for 25 °C. An **unsaturated solution** is a solution that can still dissolve more solute.

The terms "dilute" and "concentrated" are used very loosely to indicate solutions with relatively little solute, or a relatively large amount of solute. There is no definite line of demarcation between them. These terms should never be confused with "unsaturated" and "saturated," for they refer to quite different properties of the solution. A *saturated* aqueous solution of barium sulfate is extremely *dilute* (0.002 g of solute per liter of water at 18 °C), because barium sulfate is not very soluble. But a *saturated* aqueous solution of sodium thiosulfate is very *concentrated* (500 g of solute per liter of water at 25 °C), because sodium thiosulfate is very soluble.

Students often make the mistake of defining a saturated solution as one in which "the solution holds all of the solute that it can." This is not correct. It is quite possible to have a **supersaturated solution**—a solution that holds more dissolved solute than would be in equilibrium with undissolved solute. Many solids are more soluble at higher temperatures than at lower temperatures. Sometimes when a solution of such a material dissolved at a higher temperature is then allowed to cool slowly and without disturbance, all of the solute remains dissolved. Honey is essentially a supersaturated solution of various sugars in water. It is produced in the beehive when some of the water of an unsaturated solution evaporates. Honey does not quickly revert to saturation, but on long standing it may do so and become at least partly crystalline.

The more complex the crystal structure of a particular compound and the more soluble the compound, the more apt that compound is to form a supersaturated solution. If a crystal with a similar or identical crystal structure is introduced into a supersaturated solution, the solute molecules or ions can orient themselves on the

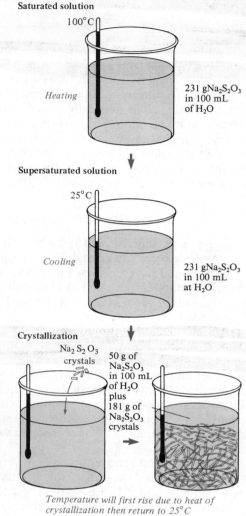

Saturated solution

100°C

Heating

231 gNa$_2$S$_2$O$_3$
in 100 mL
of H$_2$O

Supersaturated solution

25°C

Cooling

231 gNa$_2$S$_2$O$_3$
in 100 mL
at H$_2$O

Crystallization

Na$_2$S$_2$O$_3$
crystals

50 g of
Na$_2$S$_2$O$_3$
in 100 mL
of H$_2$O
plus
181 g of
Na$_2$S$_2$O$_3$
crystals

Figure 15.2
Sodium Thiosulfate
Solution During careful cooling of a
saturated solution no solid
crystallizes out, and the solution
becomes supersaturated. "Seeding"
the solution by adding a few crystals
of the solute (or a substance with
similar crystal structure) causes the
excess solute to precipitate out.

Temperature will first rise due to heat of
crystallization then return to 25°C

surface of the crystal and precipitation begins (Figure 15.2). The solid precipitates until a saturated solution is formed. Inducing crystallization in a supersaturated solution by adding a crystal is called "seeding."

15.2 THE NATURE OF
SOLUTIONS IN THE LIQUID PHASE

In liquid solutions the solvent and solute molecules or ions are mobile and come in close contact with each other. (This explains why many chemical reactions are most effective when the reactants are in solution.) Dissolving a solute in a liquid involves (1) interactions of solvent molecules with each other (solvent–solvent), (2) interactions of solute molecules or ions with each other (solute–solute), and, most importantly, (3) interactions between the solvent molecules and the ions or molecules of the solute (solute–solvent). If the solute–solvent interaction is not sufficiently strong, the molecules or ions of solute will remain attracted to each other and dissolution will not occur.

a. Liquid–liquid solutions The mutual solubility of two substances in the same phase (both liquids, both solids, or both gases) is called **miscibility.** Substances that

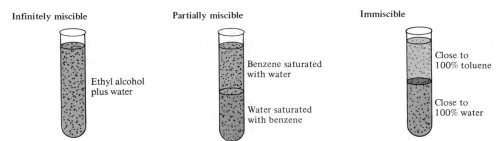

Infinitely miscible

Ethyl alcohol plus water

Partially miscible

Benzene saturated with water

Water saturated with benzene

Immiscible

Close to 100% toluene

Close to 100% water

Figure 15.3
Miscibility of Liquids Very few liquids are totally immiscible.

All gases are infinitely miscible in each other

Like generally dissolves like

---

are completely soluble in each other are **infinitely miscible.** All gases are infinitely miscible in each other. Some liquids and solids are also infinitely miscible.

There is an old adage that "like dissolves like," meaning that substances with similar bonding, structures, and intermolecular forces will be mutually soluble. This is true for many liquids. Their miscibility depends upon the similarity of their molecules. The more similar the intermolecular forces within each of the two liquids, the more likely it is that their molecules will be able to mingle together. Ethyl alcohol (CH_3CH_2OH) and water (HOH) are infinitely miscible because the primary intermolecular force in each pure liquid is hydrogen bonding. On mixing, the CH_3CH_2OH and HOH molecules readily form strong hydrogen bonds with each other.

Another infinitely miscible pair is benzene and toluene.

benzene   *toluene* —CH_3

Here London forces are the most important attractive forces between the molecules in the pure liquids, meaning that the attraction of benzene and toluene molecules for each other (the solute–solvent interaction) will be similar in strength to that of benzene molecules for each other and that of toluene molecules for each other.

Benzene and water are partially miscible, however, because the intermolecular forces in each are different (London forces in benzene, and the stronger forces of hydrogen bonding in water; Figure 15.3). A demonstration of the partial miscibility of ethyl ether and water is illustrated in Figure 15.4.

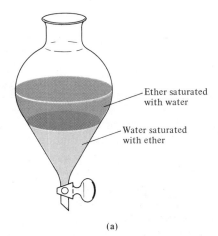

Ether saturated with water

Water saturated with ether

(a)

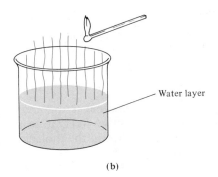

Water layer

(b)

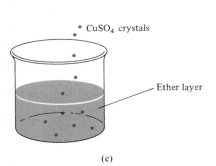

CuSO$_4$ crystals

Ether layer

(c)

Figure 15.4
Partial Miscibility Ether and water are shaken together in a separatory funnel and the layers allowed to separate. The presence of some ether in a sample of the water layer is shown by igniting the ether vapor. The presence of some water in a sample of the ether layer is shown by the solubility of anhydrous $CuSO_4$, which is *not* soluble in pure ether.

Liquids that are mutually insoluble, or very nearly so, are referred to as **immiscible.** Toluene and water are considered to be immiscible, as are vinegar and oil. No matter how hard you shake a bottle of vinegar and oil salad dressing, the water droplets are soon drawn back together by their strong intermolecular forces, squeezing out the nonpolar oil droplets.

As with most old adages, "like dissolves like" must be applied with care because there are always exceptions. For example, insolubility may result if the molecules of a liquid solvent are so strongly attached to each other that they cannot let go to attach themselves to the molecules of a potential solute. Thus, hydrogen chloride will not dissolve in liquid hydrogen fluoride, even though the two are closely related in structure and properties. Hydrogen fluoride has strong hydrogen bonds, and the hydrogen fluoride molecules show little tendency to separate from each other in order to attach themselves to hydrogen chloride molecules.

b. Solid–liquid solutions The dissolution of a solid occurs at the interface between the solid and the liquid. Sodium chloride will not dissolve in liquids like benzene, because the benzene is nonpolar and does not attract the sodium and chloride ions. Even though alcohol is somewhat polar, sodium chloride will not dissolve in it to any great extent because the polar attractions are not great enough to overcome the attraction of the sodium ions and chloride ions in the crystal for each other.

Many ionic compounds are water soluble, but here also, generalities must not be overextended. Although barium sulfate is an ionic compound, not much of it will dissolve in water. The attraction of the barium and sulfate ions for each other in the crystal is so great that the attraction of the water molecules cannot overcome it.

A finely divided solid presents a much larger surface area to a solvent than a large piece of the same solid. Therefore, crushing a solid will hasten dissolution. For example, confectioner's sugar dissolves much more rapidly than rock candy. Shaking a mixture of a solid solute and a solvent will also hasten dissolution. But note that while the *rate* of dissolution varies with the shaking or size of the pieces of solid, the *solubility* of the solid is unaffected. Whether it takes a few seconds with shaking or weeks without shaking, dissolution will appear to stop when saturation for that solute–solvent combination at that temperature is reached.

EXAMPLE 15.1
Mutual Solubility

Decide whether each of the following substances is more likely to be soluble in water or in benzene: (a) KCl; (b) C_8H_{18} (*n*-octane; the *n* indicates that the carbon atoms are attached to each other in a linear manner; see Section 27.5); (c) [Ag(NH$_3$)$_2$]Cl; and (d) HOCH$_2$CH$_2$OH (ethylene glycol).

(a) Potassium chloride is an ionic compound that is soluble in water (most chlorides are) and is unlikely to be soluble in a nonpolar solvent like benzene.

(b) Hydrocarbons like *n*-octane, which contain no strongly electronegative atoms, are essentially nonpolar. Octane is more likely to be soluble in benzene than in water.

(c) This is an ionic compound that contains the complex ion [Ag(NH$_3$)$_2$]$^+$ combined with Cl$^-$. It is more likely to be soluble in water than in benzene.

(d) With two —OH groups in the molecule, ethylene glycol [the main ingredient in antifreeze] should be able to form hydrogen bonds with water. It is more likely to be soluble in water than in benzene.

Exercise Decide whether each of the following substances is more likely to be soluble in water or in *n*-hexane (*n*-C$_6$H$_{14}$): (a) K$_3$[Fe(CN)$_6$]; (b) CCl$_4$ (carbon tetrachloride); (c) C$_{10}$H$_{22}$ (*n*-decane); and (d) Ca(NO$_3$)$_2$. *Answer* (a) water; (b) *n*-hexane; (c) *n*-hexane; (d) water

15.3 IDEAL VERSUS NONIDEAL SOLUTIONS

Real atoms, ions, and molecules influence each other, and their behavior rarely is exactly what theory predicts. It is useful to have a convenient way to compare real to theoretical behavior.

Ideal gas molecules are thought of as far enough apart to be independent of each other's influence. A different approach to ideality is needed for liquid solutions, where the solvent and solute particles are intimately mixed and in contact with each other. An **ideal solution of a molecular solute** is defined as one in which the forces between all particles of both solvent and solute are identical. In other words, in an ideal solution of A and B the forces between particles of A and A, or A and B, or B and B are the same. If A and B form an ideal solution and both substances are liquids, interparticle forces in pure A are so similar to those in pure B that particles of one added to the other find themselves in a virtually identical environment. Benzene and toluene (Section 15.2a) are so similar that they form solutions that are close to ideal.

An **ideal solution of an ionic solute** is defined as one in which the ions in solution are independent of each other and attracted only to solvent molecules. The electrostatic attraction between positive and negative ions is considered negligible in such a solution. Very dilute solutions of ionic substances approach ideal behavior because the ions are so far apart that electrostatic attraction is weak.

Components in an ideal solution make a fully effective contribution to the concentration. Think of a lone swimmer in a swimming pool. He can go anywhere in the pool he wants to at any speed he chooses. He makes a fully effective contribution to the concentration of swimmers in the pool (1 swimmer/pool). Now put 24 other swimmers in the pool with him. The effectiveness of each is decreased by bumping into or going around the others. The effective concentration is less than 25 swimmers/pool. Furthermore, if three sea lions were thrown into the pool, the effective concentrations of the swimmers would change drastically.

In a nonideal solution, forces between atoms, ions, and molecules must be taken into account. Consider, for example, the electrical conductivity of an aqueous solution of a strong electrolyte, say, a salt. If the electrolyte solution is very dilute—about 0.01 M or less—the conductivity is just about what we would expect on the basis of complete dissociation of a salt into ions. But the difference between the expected and observed values becomes greater and greater as the concentration of the solution is increased. For many years, such behavior was interpreted to mean that dissociation or ionization of strong electrolytes was not complete except in dilute solutions. We know now, however, that a solution of a strong electrolyte contains only ions. Another explanation has been found, and it is quite simple—ions of opposite charge attract each other, and this mutual attraction increases as the ions come closer together, as they must in more concentrated solutions. Each ion becomes surrounded by ions of opposite charge; these tend to hold the original ion back and so retard its journey toward the electrode (Figure 15.5), causing a lower conductivity than expected. The effect is larger if the solution is more concentrated or if the ions have charges greater than one, for example, for $MgSO_4$, as compared with NaCl.

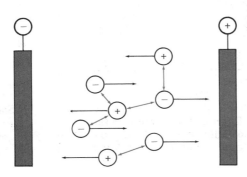

Figure 15.5
Ions in Solution in an Electrical Field The black arrows show the force on the ions due to the electrical field. The colored arrows show the interionic forces holding the ions back.

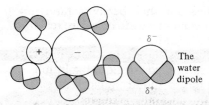

The
water
dipole

Figure 15.6
**Pairing of Ions in Aqueous
Solution** The formation of such ion
pairs contributes to the nonideal
behavior of solutions.

In quite concentrated solutions, or for highly charged ions, or for ions in solvents other than water, ion pairing may also occur. Individual pairs of ions held together by electrostatic attraction contribute to the nonideal behavior of such solutions (Figure 15.6).

For extremely accurate experimental work, for the mathematics of physical chemistry, or for work with quite concentrated solutions, it is necessary to deal with effective concentrations rather than actual concentrations. [Physical chemists define a quantity called "activity" for this purpose.] In our study of chemistry and in many aspects of everyday laboratory work in chemistry, this is not necessary and actual concentrations may be used.

15.4 THE EFFECT OF
TEMPERATURE AND PRESSURE
ON SOLUBILITY

a. Temperature and solubility   The effect of temperature on the solubility of salts in water, a type of solubility in which we are often interested, is quite variable (Figure 15.7).

The solubility in water of most inorganic salts increases with temperature, but there are also many which become less soluble as temperature increases. One study has noted that the following anions are present in most such salts: SO_4^{2-}, SeO_4^{2-}, SO_3^{2-}, AsO_4^{3-}, and PO_4^{3-}. Sodium chloride (see Figure 15.7) is unusual because the various forces balance out so that there is almost no change in solubility with temperature.

The effect of temperature on the solubility of gases is, by contrast, much more predictable. The solubility of gases in liquids decreases with rising temperature (Figure 15.8), although the decrease is not at the same rate for all gases or all solvent liquids. Gases that dissolve without ionizing can always be driven out of solution by boiling. However, the gases that ionize in aqueous solution, such as HCl or NH_3, are the most soluble gases. The rapid ionization and great solubility of ammonia in water are demonstrated by the experiment described in Figure 15.9.

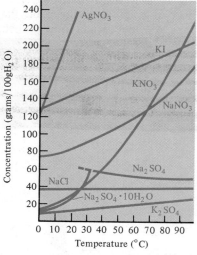

Figure 15.7
**The Effect of Temperature on the
Solubility of Several Inorganic
Substances in Water**

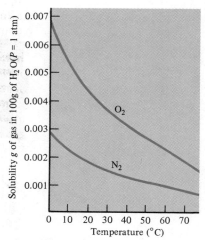

Figure 15.8
**Solubility of Nitrogen and Oxygen
in Water at 1 atm** Data for
solubility at pure oxygen or pure
nitrogen pressure.

b. Pressure and the solubility of gases The solubility of gases in liquids or solids varies not only with the temperature but also with the pressure. (The solubility of liquids and solids in liquids does not vary significantly with pressure.) Recall that partial pressure is the pressure of a gas in a mixture and that the total pressure over an aqueous solution of a gas is the sum of the vapor pressure of the water and the partial pressure of the gas (Section 5.12). The relationship between the partial pressure of a solute gas and its solubility is expressed by **Henry's law:** At constant temperature, the partial pressure of a gas over a solution is directly proportional to the solubility of the gas in that solution. In other words, increasing the pressure increases the solubility of a gas. Doubling the oxygen pressure, for example, doubles the amount of oxygen that will dissolve in a given amount of solvent. Henry's law is most closely followed by dilute solutions of gases that do not react with the solvent.

Mathematically, Henry's law is expressed as

$$p_A = kC \qquad (15.1)$$

partial pressure of solute gas; constant; gas concentration in solution

where k is a constant characteristic of the specific combination of solvent and gas, p_A is the partial pressure of the solute gas in the gas phase over the solution, and C is the concentration of the gas in the solution.

A variety of units can be used in Henry's law, for example,

$$p_A = kC \qquad (15.2a)$$

atmospheres; $\dfrac{\text{liter atmospheres}}{\text{mole}}$; $\dfrac{\text{moles}}{\text{liter}}$

$$p_A = kC \qquad (15.2b)$$

atmospheres; atmospheres; mole fraction

The mole fraction is a dimensionless number (see Section 15.9).

Probably the most familiar gas–liquid solution is carbon dioxide in water. In manufacturing soft drinks the sweetened and flavored water is saturated at a carbon dioxide pressure greater than that in the atmosphere. The carbon dioxide does not escape immediately when the pressure is relieved, for carbon dioxide readily forms supersaturated solutions in water. If the solution is stirred or shaken, however, most of the gas escapes rapidly, leaving a solution that is saturated at the newly established partial pressure of the carbon dioxide above the solution. This is in accordance with Henry's law and Dalton's law of partial pressures ($P_{total} = p_1 + p_2 + p_3 + \cdots$; Section 5.12). Since carbon dioxide in the atmosphere has a partial pressure of only 4×10^{-4} atm, a soft drink winds up tasting "flat" when it has come to equilibrium with the carbon dioxide in the atmosphere.

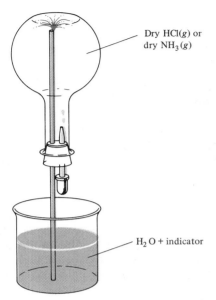

Dry HCl(g) or dry NH₃(g)

H₂O + indicator

Figure 15.9
Solubility of NH₃ (or HCl) A flask (2L) filled with dry NH₃ gas (or dry HCl gas) is closed with a stopper fitted with a long glass tube drawn to a nozzle at the end in the flask and a medicine dropper filled with water. The flask is up-ended with the end of the glass tube in a large beaker of water containing an indicator—a substance that changes color in the presence of OH⁻ (or H⁺ for the experiment with HCl). Squirting a few drops of water into the flask dissolves so much gas that the reduction in pressure causes a fountain to flow. The color change of the water in the fountain shows that the reaction to produce OH⁻ ions (or H⁺ ions) has occurred.

EXAMPLE 15.2
Solubility: Henry's Law

During bottling, a carbonated beverage was made by saturating water with CO_2 at 0 °C and a pressure of 4.0 atm. Later, the bottle was opened and the soft drink allowed to come to equilibrium at 25 °C with air containing CO_2 at a partial pressure of 4.0×10^{-4} atm. Find the concentration of CO_2 in the freshly bottled soda and in the soda after it had stood open and come to equilibrium with the air. The Henry's law constants for aqueous solutions of CO_2 are $k = 13.0$ L atm/mol at 0 °C and 32 L atm/mol at 25 °C.

We know the partial pressures of CO_2 over the aqueous solutions during the bottling process (4.0 atm) and after the bottle was opened (4.0×10^{-4} atm). These pressures can be used in Henry's law to find the concentration of the CO_2 in the bottled soft drink and in the soft drink in the opened bottle:

$$C = \frac{p_{CO_2}}{k} = \frac{4.0 \text{ atm}}{13.0 \text{ L atm/mol}} = 0.31 \text{ mol/L}$$

$$C = \frac{4.0 \times 10^{-4} \text{ atm}}{32 \text{ L atm/mol}} = 1.3 \times 10^{-5} \text{ mol/L}$$

The concentration of CO_2 decreased from 0.31 mol/L to 1.3×10^{-5} mol/L, a decrease of more than 99.99%. [The drink had definitely become "flat."]

Exercise Calculate the solubility of argon in water at 0 °C at a pressure of 2.16 atm. The value of the Henry's law constant for Ar in H_2O at 0 °C is 396 L atm/mol. *Answer* 5.45×10^{-3} mol/L

15.5 HEATS OF SOLUTION

The process of dissolution can be exothermic or endothermic. Before solute and solvent particles can mingle, the solute–solute and solvent–solvent forces of attraction must be broken. Like bond breaking, these processes are endothermic—they require the input of energy. Once dissolution begins, new forces of attraction pull solute and solvent molecules together in a process that, like bond formation, is exothermic, releasing energy. The overall heat of solution depends upon the relative magnitudes of these endothermic and exothermic processes.

In calculating enthalpies, any processes can be combined so long as their sum is the desired chemical change or change of state (Section 7.9c). For the purpose of calculating the heats of solution of ionic crystalline substances, dissolution is divided into two theoretical steps: First, the ions of the solute must be set free from their positions in a crystal. This is the reverse of crystal formation and has an enthalpy that has the same value as the lattice energy (Section 9.18) but is of opposite sign. Recall that the lattice energy is always negative, so this term is always positive; it takes an input of energy to break apart a crystal lattice. For example, for potassium chloride

$$KCl(s) \xrightarrow{\Delta} K^+(g) + Cl^-(g) \qquad \Delta H = -[KCl \text{ lattice energy}] = 701 \text{ kJ}$$

The second step is the hydration of the ions in a large amount of water (large enough that the ions do not influence each other).

$$K^+(g) + Cl^-(g) \xrightarrow{H_2O} K^+(aq) + Cl^-(aq) \qquad \Delta H_{hydr} = \text{hydration energy} = -685 \text{ kJ}$$

(Like lattice energies, heats of hydration are given in compilations of thermodynamic data.) Combination of the endothermic dissociation of the solid compound and the exothermic hydration of ions gives the heat of solution of potassium chloride:

$$KCl(s) \xrightarrow{\Delta} K^+(g) + Cl^-(g) \qquad \Delta H = 701 \text{ kJ} \qquad \textbf{(15.3)}$$

$$\underline{K^+(g) + Cl^-(g) \xrightarrow{H_2O} K^+(aq) + Cl^-(aq) \qquad \Delta H_{hydr} = -685 \text{ kJ} \qquad \textbf{(15.4)}}$$

$$KCl(s) \xrightarrow{H_2O} K^+(aq) + Cl^-(aq) \qquad \Delta H_{soln} = 16 \text{ kJ}$$

Heats of solution vary with the concentration of the solution and are recorded either for a specific number of moles of solvent per mole of solute, as shown in the following equations, or, as calculated above, for a very large quantity of solvent (the heat of solution at infinite dilution, as given in Table 15.1).

$$AgNO_3(s) \xrightarrow[\substack{H_2O}]{50 \text{ moles}} Ag^+(aq) + NO_3^-(aq) \qquad \Delta H = 20.17 \text{ kJ}$$

$$Ca(NO_3)_2(s) \xrightarrow[\substack{H_2O}]{10 \text{ moles}} Ca^{2+}(aq) + 2NO_3^-(aq) \qquad \Delta H = -22.93 \text{ kJ}$$

Table 15.1
Heats of Solution of Some Halides These are heats of solution at infinite dilution. Note that the salts of dipositive cations have greater heats of solution than do the salts of monopositive cations (i.e., their dissolution is more exothermic).

Salt	ΔH_{soln} (kJ/mol)
LiCl	−37.15
NaCl	3.891
LiI	−63.30
$MgCl_2$	−155.06
$CaCl_2$	−82.9
MgI_2	−214.0
CaI_2	−120.1

Table 15.2

Heats of Solution, Calculated and Experimental Lattice energy, hydration energy, and heats of solution are given for selected alkali metal halides. The calculated heats of solution were found by adding the hydration energy and the heat for the formation of gaseous ions from the solid, which has the same value as the lattice energy, but the opposite sign (see Equations 15.3 and 15.4).

Compound	Lattice Energy (kJ/mol)	Hydration Energy (kJ/mol)	Calculated Heat of Solution (kJ/mol)	Experimental Heat of Solution (kJ/mol)
LiCl	−834	−884	−50	−37.15
NaCl	−769	−769	0	3.891
KCl	−701	−685	16	17.24
RbCl	−680	−664	16	16.7
CsCl	−657	−640	17	18.0
KF	−808	−827	−19	−17.74
KBr	−671	−658	13	20.04
KI	−632	−617	15	20.5

Lattice energies and hydration energies tend to be of similar magnitude. Their combined effect results in heats of solution that are either positive or negative and of small magnitude (Table 15.2).

In summary, solutions can form in all three phases. Solutions in the liquid phase are governed by the strength of solute–solute, solvent–solvent, and solute–solvent forces. The first two must be disrupted by the latter in the process of dissolution. Liquids with similar intermolecular forces are most likely to be miscible. Solutions are considered ideal if forces between all particles of both molecular solute and solvent are identical, or if ions in solution are independent of each other.

Pressure has only a small effect on the solubility of liquids and solids. The solubility of gases varies with pressure according to Henry's law, $p_A = kC$, where p_A is the partial pressure of solute gas A and C is the concentration of the gas in solution. The majority of inorganic salts increase in solubility with increasing temperature (but there are many exceptions).

The relative magnitudes of the lattice energy and the heat of hydration determine whether the dissolution of a solid is exothermic or endothermic.

CONCENTRATION OF SOLUTIONS

15.6 STANDARD SOLUTIONS

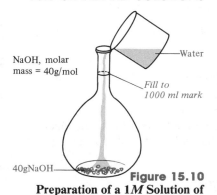

NaOH, molar mass = 40g/mol

Water

Fill to 1000 ml mark

40gNaOH

Figure 15.10
Preparation of a 1M Solution of NaOH

A solution of known concentration is called a **standard solution.** Standard solutions can be prepared by mixing weighed or measured amounts of solvents and solutes (Figure 15.10). The concentration of a solute in a solvent is most often expressed in units that indicate the mass or volume of solute in a given mass or volume of solution or of solvent. Various ways of expressing concentration are used in various circumstances — in some cases because the units are most convenient, in other cases just by convention.

The following sections describe some of the more common concentration units. Molarity — moles of solute per liter of solution — is based on the mole and is often the unit of choice for solutions to be used in chemical reactions. Molarity was introduced in Section 4.7 and is reviewed in Section 15.8. The mole fraction was introduced in the discussion of vapor pressure (Section 5.12) and is reviewed in Section 15.9.

Density is a quantity that is often useful in calculations involving the concentration of solutions. The units of density for a liquid or a solution are those of mass per unit volume, usually grams per milliliter (Section 2.8d). Knowing the density of a liquid or a solution allows conversion from mass to volume or from volume to mass for a specific amount of that liquid or solution (see Equation 2.7).

15.7 MASS PERCENT   The concentration of a solution can be given in **mass percent (weight percent).**

$$\text{Mass percent} = \frac{\text{mass of solute}}{\text{mass of solution}} \times 100\% \qquad (15.5)$$

The mass of the solution is equal to the sum of the masses of the solute (or solutes) and the solvent. Concentrations in units based only upon masses, such as mass percent, do not vary with temperature—an advantage in some applications.

EXAMPLE 15.3
Solution Concentration:
Mass Percent

What is the mass percent of methanol in a solution of 2.0 L of methanol in 3.5 L of diethyl ether? The density of methanol is 0.79 g/mL and the density of diethyl ether is 0.71 g/mL.

To find the mass percent of methanol, we must know the masses of all of the components in the solution. The known densities allow conversion of the known volumes to the masses of methanol and diethyl ether.

$$(2.0 \text{ L methanol})\left(\frac{1000 \text{ mL}}{\text{L}}\right)\left(\frac{0.79 \text{ g}}{\text{mL}}\right) = 1600 \text{ g methanol}$$

$$(3.5 \text{ L diethyl ether})\left(\frac{1000 \text{ mL}}{\text{L}}\right)\left(\frac{0.71 \text{ g}}{\text{mL}}\right) = 2500 \text{ g diethyl ether}$$

Mass % =

$$\frac{\text{mass of solute}}{\text{mass of solution}} \times 100\%$$

The mass of the solution is

$$\text{Mass of solution} = 1600 \text{ g} + 2500 \text{ g} = 4100 \text{ g}$$

The mass percent of the methanol in the solution is

$$\text{Mass \%} = \frac{\text{mass methanol}}{\text{mass solution}} \times 100\% = \frac{1600 \text{ g}}{4100 \text{ g}} \times 100\% = 39\%$$

The solution is 39 mass % methanol.

Exercise   The solubility of $CoSO_4$ in water is 36.2 g $CoSO_4$/100 g H_2O at 20 °C. What is the mass percent of $CoSO_4$ in this solution?   *Answer* 26.6 mass %

15.8 MOLARITY   The expression of concentration in terms of the number of moles of solute per liter of solution is called *molarity* (Section 4.7; see Examples 4.18–4.20).

$$\text{Molarity} = \frac{\text{moles of solute}}{\text{liter of solution}} \qquad (15.6)$$

Knowing the molarity of a solution allows calculation of the number of moles of solute or the number of grams of solute in a given volume of solution.

Molarity = $\dfrac{\text{moles of solute}}{\text{liters of solution}}$

$$(\text{Molarity})(\text{volume}) = \text{moles of solute} \qquad (15.7)$$
$$\underset{\text{liter}}{\overset{\text{moles}}{}} \qquad \text{liters} \qquad \text{moles}$$

$$(\text{Molarity})(\text{volume})(\text{molar mass of solute}) = \text{mass of solute} \qquad (15.8)$$
$$\underset{\text{liter}}{\overset{\text{moles}}{}} \qquad \text{liters} \qquad \underset{\text{mole}}{\overset{\text{grams}}{}} \qquad \text{grams}$$

Care must be exercised in dealing with the molarity of solutions of strong electrolytes. For example, a solution of cobalt(II) iodide that is 1 M in CoI_2 contains *three* moles of ions and is 1 M in Co^{2+}, but 2 M in I^-.

$$CoI_2(s) \xrightarrow{H_2O} Co^{2+} + 2I^-$$
$$\textit{1 mol} \qquad\qquad \textit{1 mol} \quad \textit{2 mol}$$

EXAMPLE 15.4
Solution Concentration: Solution Preparation

How would 500. mL of 0.10 M $CuSO_4$ be prepared from the hydrate, $CuSO_4 \cdot 5H_2O$?

For 500. mL of 0.10 M solution, the required number of moles of $CuSO_4$ is

$$(0.500 \text{ L})(0.10 \text{ mol/L}) = 0.050 \text{ mol}$$

From the formula of the hydrate, we can see that each mole of hydrate contains 1 mol of $CuSO_4$. Therefore, the solution can be prepared from 0.050 mol of $CuSO_4 \cdot 5H_2O$. The mass of the hydrate needed is

$$(0.050 \text{ mol CuSO}_4 \cdot 5H_2O)\left(\frac{249.68 \text{ g CuSO}_4 \cdot 5H_2O}{1 \text{ mol CuSO}_4 \cdot 5H_2O}\right) = 12 \text{ g CuSO}_4 \cdot 5H_2O$$

The solution is prepared by adding sufficient water to 12 g of $CuSO_4 \cdot 5H_2O$ to make 500. mL of solution. [Once the solution is prepared, the water molecules weighed along with the $CuSO_4$ are, of course, indistinguishable from the water molecules added in liquid form.]

Exercise What is the molarity of chloride ion in a solution prepared by dissolving 16.7 g of $CaCl_2$ in sufficient water to obtain 400. mL of solution? *Answer* 0.750 M Cl^-

15.9 MOLE FRACTION

The mole fraction, symbolized by X, is the ratio of the number of moles of one component to the total number of moles of all components of a solution (Section 5.12). The sum of the mole fractions of all solution components is 1.

For a two-component solution, where n represents number of moles,

mole fraction of A
$$X_A = \frac{\text{moles of A}}{\text{moles of A} + \text{moles of B}} = \frac{n_A}{n_A + n_B} \tag{15.9}$$

mole fraction of B
$$X_B = \frac{n_B}{n_A + n_B} \tag{15.10}$$

$$X_A + X_B = 1 \tag{15.11}$$

Mole fraction of B =

$$\frac{\textbf{moles of solute B}}{\textbf{total moles, solute + solvent}}$$

The mole fraction expresses the ratio of the number of particles of one component to the total number of particles in a solution. Mole fraction, like mass percent, is independent of temperature.

EXAMPLE 15.5
Solution Concentration: Mole Fraction

Find the mole fraction of table sugar (sucrose, $C_{12}H_{22}O_{11}$) in an aqueous solution containing 30.0 g of the sugar (molar mass, 342.3 g) and 70.0 g of water.

First, we must find the number of moles of each component

$$(30.0 \text{ g sucrose})\left(\frac{1 \text{ mol sucrose}}{342.3 \text{ g}}\right) = 0.0876 \text{ mol sucrose}$$

$$(70.0 \text{ g water})\left(\frac{1 \text{ mol water}}{18.015 \text{ g water}}\right) = 3.89 \text{ mol water}$$

The mole fraction of the sugar is given by

$$X_{\text{sucrose}} = \frac{n_{\text{sucrose}}}{n_{\text{sucrose}} + n_{\text{water}}} = \frac{0.0876 \text{ mol}}{0.0876 \text{ mol} + 3.89 \text{ mol}} = 0.0220$$

The mole fraction of sugar in the solution is 0.0220.

Exercise A solution contained 5.0 g NaCl, 15.0 g KCl, and 80.0 g H_2O. Calculate the mole fraction of water. *Answer* $X_{H_2O} = 0.939$

15.10 MOLALITY   **Molality** is defined as the number of moles of solute per kilogram of solvent.

$$\text{Molality} = \frac{\text{moles of solute}}{\text{kilogram of solvent}} \qquad (15.12)$$

> **Molality =**
>
> **moles of solute**
> ―――――――――
> **kilograms of solvent**

A 1 molal solution of NaOH would be prepared by dissolving 40 g (1 mol) of NaOH in 1000 g of water, or 20 g (0.5 mol) of NaOH in 500 g of water, or any other combination that maintains this proportion. On the outside of this bottle we would write 1 m NaOH. (Note the different abbreviations—lowercase m for "molal" and uppercase M for "molar.") Molality is another concentration unit which, because it is defined only in terms of masses, is independent of temperature. Usually molality is chosen as the concentration unit for solutions in which one component is clearly the solvent and another the solute.

The molarity and molality of *dilute* aqueous solutions have very similar values. Frequently one can be substituted for the other in calculations without introducing significant error. As aqueous solutions become more concentrated, this approximation becomes less valid. Why? The density of water is 1 g/mL or 1 kg/L. A dilute aqueous solution has a density close to that of pure water and contains close to 1 kg of solvent per liter of solution. But as the concentration increases, the mass of the solute begins to make a significant contribution to the density of the solution. (Remember that molarity is moles per liter of *solution,* not of solvent.) Therefore in concentrated solutions the density of the solution differs significantly from 1 kg/L and the molarity and molality no longer have similar values.

EXAMPLE 15.6
Solution Concentration: Molality

What is the molality of a 6.0 M nitric acid solution for which 298 g of solution contains 95 g, or 1.5 mol, of HNO_3?

To find the molality we must know the mass in kilograms of water, which is the difference between the mass of solution and of HNO_3:

$$298 \text{ g} - 95 \text{ g} = 203 \text{ g } H_2O \quad \text{or} \quad 0.203 \text{ kg } H_2O$$

The molality is

$$\text{Molality} = \frac{\text{moles } HNO_3}{\text{kg } H_2O} = \frac{1.5 \text{ mol}}{0.203 \text{ kg}} = 7.4 \text{ mol/kg}$$

The concentration of this solution is 7.4 m.

Exercise Express the concentration of the sugar solution described in Example 15.5 in terms of molality. *Answer* 1.25 m

---

In summary, a standard solution is a solution of known concentration, prepared by mixing weighed or measured amounts of solvents and solutes. For a given solution, the density of the solution provides the connection between the mass and volume of a given amount of that solution. The major ways of expressing the concentrations of solutions are mass percent, molarity, mole fraction, and

Table 15.3
Summary of Concentration Units A is the solvent and B is the solute. The second column shows how to calculate the concentration from known quantities of A and B.

Unit	Calculation
Mass %	$\dfrac{\text{mass of B}}{\text{mass of A + mass of B}} \times 100\%$
Molarity (moles/liter)	$\dfrac{\text{moles of B}}{\text{volume of solution (L)}}$
Mole fraction, X	$\dfrac{\text{moles of B}}{\text{moles of A + moles of B}}$
Molality (moles/kg of solvent)	$\dfrac{\text{moles of B}}{\text{mass of A (kg)}}$

molality. How to find the concentration of a solution in these units is summarized in Table 15.3.

Example 15.7 allows comparison of different ways of expressing the concentration of the same solution. In problems that do not involve specific volumes as either knowns or unknowns, we must choose a mass or volume of one of the solutions as the basis for calculations which require converting from one concentration unit to another.

EXAMPLE 15.7
Solution Concentration

Commercial vinegar is an aqueous solution that must contain at least 4 mass percent of acetic acid (CH_3COOH, molar mass, 60.05 g). The density of such a solution is 1.0058 g/mL. Express the concentration of acetic acid in terms of (a) mol fraction, (b) molality, and (c) molarity.

This problem does not specify a given mass or volume as a known quantity. We are free to choose any convenient sample of solution for our calculations. One obvious choice is 100.00 g of solution, which contains 4.00 g of CH_3COOH and 96.00 g of H_2O.

(a) The numbers of moles of solute and solvent in 100.00 g of solution are

$$(4.00 \text{ g } CH_3COOH)\left(\frac{1 \text{ mol } CH_3COOH}{60.05 \text{ g } CH_3COOH}\right) = 0.0666 \text{ mol } CH_3COOH$$

$$(96.00 \text{ g } H_2O)\left(\frac{1 \text{ mol } H_2O}{18.015 \text{ g } H_2O}\right) = 5.329 \text{ mol } H_2O$$

The mole fraction of acetic acid in vinegar is

$$X_{CH_3COOH} = \frac{0.0666 \text{ mol}}{0.0666 \text{ mol} + 5.329 \text{ mol}} = 0.0123$$

(b) The molality of the solution is

$$\frac{0.0666 \text{ mol } HC_3COOH}{0.09600 \text{ kg } H_2O} = 0.694 \text{ mol/kg } H_2O$$

(c) The volume of the 100.00 g of solution is

$$(100.00 \text{ g})\left(\frac{1 \text{ mL}}{1.0058 \text{ g}}\right) = 99.42 \text{ mL}$$

giving the molarity as

$$\frac{0.0666 \text{ mol } CH_3COOH}{0.09942 \text{ L}} = 0.670 \text{ mol/L}$$

To summarize, the concentration of acetic acid in commercial vinegar which is 4 mass percent acetic acid can be expressed as $X_{CH_3COOH} = 0.0123$, 0.694 m, or 0.670 M.

Exercise A solution of acetone, CH_3COCH_3, in water contains 0.500 g of CH_3COCH_3 dissolved in 99.500 g of H_2O. The density of this solution is 0.9993 g/mL. Express the concentration of this solution in terms of (a) molarity, (b) molality, and (c) mole fraction of acetone. *Answer* (a) 0.0860 M, (b) 0.0865 *m*, (c) 1.56×10^{-3}

15.11 DILUTION OF SOLUTIONS

In the laboratory it is often necessary to prepare a solution of a desired concentration from a more concentrated solution, or to know the concentration of a solution that has been diluted. When solvent is added to a solution, the *concentration* of the solution changes, but the *amount* of solute remains the same. For example, suppose that 0.35 L of a 12 M solution of HCl was diluted to 1.5 L and we want to know the molarity of the new solution. From the given volume and molarity, we first find the number of moles of HCl present.

$$(0.35 \text{ L})\left(\frac{12 \text{ mol HCl}}{1 \text{ L}}\right) = 4.2 \text{ mol HCl}$$

In the new solution, the same amount of HCl, 4.2 mol, is now present in 1.5 L of solution, for a concentration of

$$\frac{4.2 \text{ mol HCl}}{1.5 \text{ L}} = 2.8 \text{ mol HCl/L}$$

EXAMPLE 15.8
Solution Concentration: Dilution

An analytical procedure required that 13.2 mL of a 0.1016 M solution of sodium hydroxide be diluted to exactly 25.00 mL. What was the molarity of the diluted solution?

The number of moles of NaOH in the original solution is

$$(13.2 \text{ mL})\left(\frac{0.1016 \text{ mol NaOH}}{1000 \text{ mL}}\right) = 0.00134 \text{ mol NaOH}$$

giving a new molarity in the dilute solution of

$$\left(\frac{0.00134 \text{ mol NaOH}}{25.00 \text{ mL}}\right)\left(\frac{1000 \text{ mL}}{1 \text{ L}}\right) = 0.0536 \text{ mol NaOH/L}$$

The concentration of the new sodium hydroxide solution is 0.0536 M.

Exercise A 0.250 *m* NaCl solution contained 14.6 g NaCl and 996 g H_2O. An additional 225 g of H_2O was added. What is the concentration of the diluted solution? *Answer* 0.205 *m*

In deciding how to dilute a concentrated solution to a desired concentration, it is necessary to first know the amount of solute needed in the new solution.

EXAMPLE 15.9
Solution Concentration: Dilution

What volume of commercially available concentrated H_2SO_4, which has a concentration of 18.0 M, must be diluted to give 1.00 L of 6.0 M H_2SO_4?

One liter of the desired dilute acid will contain 6.0 mol of H_2SO_4. The volume of concentrated acid that contains 6.0 mol of H_2SO_4 is

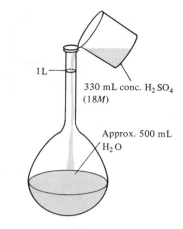 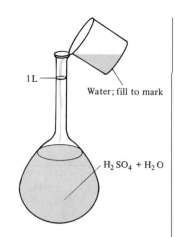

1 L —
330 mL conc. H_2SO_4
(18M)

Approx. 500 mL
H_2O

1 L —
Water; fill to mark

$H_2SO_4 + H_2O$

Figure 15.11
Dilution of Concentrated Sulfuric Acid

(a) Add acid to water

(b) Dilute to exact volume desired

$$(6.0 \text{ mol } H_2SO_4)\left(\frac{1 \text{ L}}{18.0 \text{ mol } H_2SO_4}\right) = 0.33 \text{ L}$$

A volume of 0.33 L of 18.0 M H_2SO_4 must be diluted to 1.00 L. [The procedure, illustrated in Figure 15.11, is as follows: (a) First, 330 mL of concentrated acid is added slowly to about 500 mL of water. Sulfuric acid is always added to water because a considerable amount of heat is released when H_2SO_4 is dissolved in water and the bulk of the water helps to dissipate the heat. This solution is mixed thoroughly and then (b) diluted with additional water until the volume is 1.00 L.]

Exercise What volume of commercially available concentrated nitric acid, which has a concentration of 15.6 M, must be diluted to give 1.00 L of 6.0 M HNO_3?
Answer 0.38 L

VAPOR PRESSURES OF LIQUID SOLUTIONS AND RELATED PROPERTIES

15.12 LIQUID–LIQUID SOLUTION VAPOR PRESSURES: RAOULT'S LAW

The molecules in a liquid are in rapid constant motion. This motion causes molecules to escape from the surface into the vapor phase, creating a vapor pressure above the liquid. If more than one liquid is present in a solution, the total vapor pressure of the solution is the sum of the vapor pressures of each liquid. Molecules of each liquid are present at the solution surface. For an ideal liquid–liquid solution, where the forces between all molecules are identical, the tendency of either type of molecule to escape depends only on the relative numbers of each (Figure 15.12b), which are given by their mole fractions.

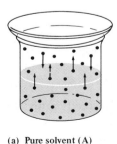 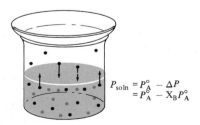

(a) Pure solvent (A)

(b) Liquid (B) in solution in solvent (A)
$P_{soln} = X_A P_A^\circ + X_B P_B^\circ$

(c) Nonvolatile solute (B) in solution in solvent (A)
$P_{soln} = P_A^\circ - \Delta P$
$= P_A^\circ - X_B P_A^\circ$

Figure 15.12
Vapor Pressure over Solutions In (b) and (c) fewer solvent molecules are available at the surface to evaporate.

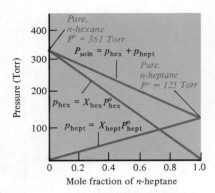

Figure 15.13
Vapor Pressure of a Solution that Follows Raoult's Law The top line is the total vapor pressure of the hexane-heptane solution. The other two lines are the partial vapor pressures of each component of the solution.

The effect on vapor pressure of mixing two liquids to form an ideal solution is shown in Figure 15.13. Adding either liquid to the other (i.e., starting at either side of Figure 15.13) causes a decrease from the vapor pressure of that pure liquid because fewer molecules of the original liquid are at the surface. The partial vapor pressure of either liquid is equal to its concentration in the solution, expressed as the mole fraction, times the vapor pressure of the pure liquid. For an ideal solution of liquids A and B at a given temperature,

$$p_A = X_A P_A^\circ \qquad\qquad p_B = X_B P_B^\circ \qquad\qquad (15.13)$$

partial vapor pressure of A over solution — mole fraction of A in solution — vapor pressure of pure A

Equation (15.13) is a mathematical statement of **Raoult's law:** <u>The vapor pressure of a liquid in a solution is equal to the mole fraction of that liquid in the solution times the vapor pressure of the pure liquid.</u>

The total vapor pressure of the solution is the sum of the partial pressures of all of the components of the solution (see Dalton's law, Section 5.12). For a solution of A and B

$$P_{soln} = p_A + p_B \qquad\qquad (15.14)$$

total vapor pressure of solution

Substituting the relationship of partial pressure to vapor pressure given by Raoult's law (Equation 15.13) into Dalton's law gives

$$P_{soln} = X_A P_A^\circ + X_B P_B^\circ \qquad\qquad (15.15)$$

An ideal solution of two liquids would obey Raoult's law perfectly. There are a few miscible liquids that form solutions that come quite close to ideality. Solutions that obey Raoult's law are formed, for example, by

ethyl bromide, C_2H_5Br
+
ethyl iodide, C_2H_5I
} *form close to ideal solutions* {
n-hexane, $CH_3(CH_2)_4CH_3$
+
n-heptane, $CH_3(CH_2)_5CH_3$

It is apparent that the forces between the molecules in these pairs are similar, for the molecules are very similar in molecular mass, structure, and the types of intermolecular forces that act between them.

EXAMPLE 15.10
Solution Properties: Vapor Pressure

What is the vapor pressure of a benzene–toluene solution of composition $X_{benz} = 0.30$ and $X_{tol} = 0.70$? The vapor pressures of the pure substances are 73 Torr for benzene (C_6H_6) and 27 Torr for toluene (C_7H_8). Assume that benzene and toluene form an ideal solution.

The partial pressure of each component in the vapor phase is directly proportional to its mole fraction in the solution, according to Raoult's law,

$$p_{benz} = X_{benz}\, P_{benz}^\circ = (0.30)(73\ \text{Torr}) = 22\ \text{Torr}$$
$$p_{tol} = X_{tol}\, P_{tol}^\circ = (0.70)(27\ \text{Torr}) = 19\ \text{Torr}$$

and the total vapor pressure of the solution is the sum of the partial pressures.

$$P_{soln} = p_{benz} + p_{tol} = 22 \text{ Torr} + 19 \text{ Torr} = 41 \text{ Torr}$$

The vapor pressure of the solution is 41 Torr.

Exercise Calculate the vapor pressure at 25 °C of the benzene–toluene solution of composition $X_{benz} = 0.70$ and $X_{tol} = 0.30$. *Answer* 59 Torr

The composition of the vapor over a solution of two liquids is not the same as the composition of the solution. The vapor composition depends upon the relative vapor pressures of the two liquids. The vapor over a solution of any composition and at any temperature is always richer in the more volatile (i.e., lower boiling) component than is the solution.

For example, benzene (b.p. 80.1 °C) is more volatile than toluene (b.p. 110.6 °C). Using the relationship between the partial and total pressures of a mixture of gases, $p_A = X_A P_{total}$ (Section 5.12), we can find the composition of the vapor over the solution described in Example 15.10 by taking the total pressure as the solution vapor pressure:

$$p_{benz} = X_{benz} P_{soln}$$
$$22 \text{ Torr} = X_{benz}(41 \text{ Torr})$$
$$X_{benz} = \frac{22 \text{ Torr}}{41 \text{ Torr}} = 0.54$$

The vapor contains almost twice as great a concentration of benzene as the liquid phase.

Nonideal liquid–liquid solutions show either positive or negative deviations from Raoult's law. When the different molecules of two liquids (A--B) attract each other less than they do other molecules of the same kind (A--A, B--B), molecules of either A or B escape from solution more easily than from the pure liquids. This causes *positive* deviation from Raoult's law. Heat is absorbed when A and B are mixed (Table 15.4), and the partial vapor pressures of both A and B are greater than those predicted by Raoult's law. Ethanol and *n*-hexane form such a solution. Most liquid–liquid solutions behave in this way.

Negative deviations from Raoult's law occur when the different molecules attract each other more strongly than they do other molecules of the same kind. The molecules have a smaller tendency to escape from the solution surface than from their pure liquid surfaces and their partial vapor pressures are lower than predicted by Raoult's law. Formic acid (HCOOH) and water form this type of solution. The solution process is exothermic for solutions that deviate negatively from Raoult's law.

Table 15.4
Properties of Real Solutions of Two Liquids, A and B Positive deviation is the more common situation.

Positive Deviation from Raoult's Law	Negative Deviation from Raoult's Law
A–B forces less than A–A or B–B forces	A–B forces greater than A–A or B–B forces
Solution process endothermic	Solution process exothermic
Heating increases solubility	Heating decreases solubility

Distillation

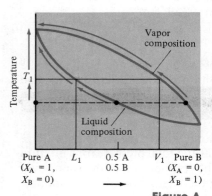

Figure A
Boiling Point Diagram for a Solution of Two Liquids A and B (at Atmospheric Pressure) The dots mark the beginning of distillation of a 50–50 mixture of A and B. For a mixture boiling at T_1, the composition of the liquid is given by the mole fractions of A and B at L_1 and the composition of the vapor is given by the mole fractions of A and B at V_1.

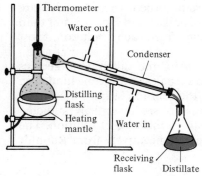

Figure B
Laboratory Apparatus for Simple Distillation

The liquids in a solution can be separated from each other by making use of the fact that the vapor above the solution is always richer in the more volatile component of the mixture than is the solution. **Distillation** involves heating a liquid or a solution to boiling, and collecting and condensing the vapors. As a mixture of liquids is distilled, the composition of the liquid phase, the composition of the vapor phase, and the boiling point of the solution change continuously. Figure A illustrates these changes for an ideal mixture of liquids A and B. The three dots mark the temperature, vapor composition, and liquid composition at the beginning of the distillation of a 50–50 mixture of A and B in which B is the more volatile component. The colored arrows mark the directions of change during distillation. The composition of the vapor at any temperature is read from the top curve and the composition of the liquid solution is read from the bottom curve.

The objective of distillation is to separate individual components from mixtures. The components may be pure liquids, substances that are solid at ordinary temperatures but can be melted and then distilled, or pure gases (which can be distilled from mixtures of liquefied gases). When the mixture is a solution of nonvolatile impurities in a liquid to be purified, simple distillation is sufficient. A laboratory scale set up for simple distillation is shown in Figure B. This type of apparatus might be used, for example, to prepare distilled water. The mixture to be distilled is heated, the vapor condenses in the water-cooled condenser, and the **distillate**—the product of distillation—is collected in a receiving flask.

From the boiling point diagram in Figure A it is apparent that a single simple distillation cannot completely separate two or more volatile liquids from each other. The vapor collected as the temperature rises, while richer in the more volatile component (B) of the mixture, is still a mixture of the two vapors at all temperatures up to the boiling point of A. A *series* of simple distillations would provide distillates richer and richer in the more volatile component, but the repeated distillations would be tedious.

Fractional distillation is a process that separates liquid mixtures into fractions that differ in boiling points. A fractionating column is designed so that a series of simple distillations is achieved over its length. The column might have an internal structure of projections or trays or perforated plates, or it may be packed with small pieces of ceramic, metal, or glass in the shape of rings, or beads, or saddles. The purpose of all these items is to provide surfaces at which the rising vapor meets descending liquid and exchanges heat with it. Vapor moves up the column and some of it condenses on the packing. This condensate is richer in the less volatile components of the mixture. The condensate trickles down the column, where it meets rising hotter vapor. A heat exchange occurs—more of the more volatile component leaves the condensate and joins the rising vapor, while more of the less volatile component leaves the vapor and joins the descending liquid. The net result is that pure vapor can be collected at the top of the column and pure liquid at the bottom of the column. The process of vapor moving up the column, condensing, and trickling down the column is called **refluxing.**

A laboratory-scale fractional distillation apparatus is shown in Figure C. During distillation some of the condensing vapor is returned to the column and some is collected as product. Batch distillation—the distillation of one batch of the mixture at a time—is carried out in such an apparatus.

In most industrial-scale distillations, continuous operation is more economical than batch distillation. A simple continuous distillation column for separating two liquids is shown in Figure D. The material to be distilled (the feed) is added continuously at the middle of the column, at a point where the composition of the liquid phase in the column is similar to that of the feed. The more volatile product is collected continuously at the top (the overhead product), and the less volatile product at the bottom (the bottoms product). Distillation may be carried out at atmospheric pressure, or at either reduced or increased pressure, depending on the properties of the materials involved.

When a several-component mixture is fractionally distilled, fractions that differ

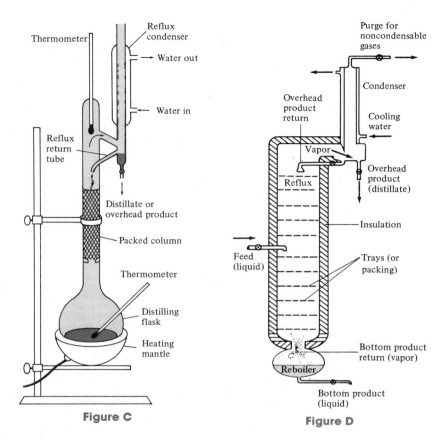

Figure C
**Laboratory Apparatus for Batch
Fractional Distillation**

Figure D
**Column for Continuous Fractional
Distillation** Source: Gerhard A.
Cook, *Survey of Modern Industrial
Chemistry* (Ann Arbor: Michigan
Ann Arbor Science, 1977), p. 29.

Figure C

Figure D

in boiling point are collected in the order of increasing boiling point, either one by
one at the top of the column or continuously at successively higher points along the
column.

Solutions that deviate sufficiently from Raoult's law cannot be totally separated
by fractional distillation. At some definite composition they form **azeotropes**—constant-boiling mixtures that distill without change in composition. A minimum boiling
point azeotrope has a boiling point below that of either component, and a maximum boiling point azeotrope has a boiling point above that of either component
(Figure E). If A and B can form an azeotrope, the best separation possible from
distillation of a mixture of A and B is to obtain pure A *or* pure B plus the azeotrope.
Distillation of a mixture with *exactly* an azeotropic composition would yield no
separation at all.

Figure E
**Boiling Point Diagrams for
Azeotropic Solutions (at 760 Torr)**

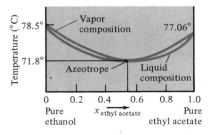

(a) Minimum boiling point azeotrope —
ethyl acetate ($CH_3CO_2C_2H_5$) +
ethanol (C_2H_5OH)

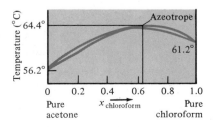

(b) Maximum boiling point azeotrope —
acetone (CH_3COCH_3) + chloroform
($CHCl_3$)

15.13 VAPOR PRESSURE LOWERING BY NONVOLATILE NONELECTROLYTE SOLUTES

In this section we confine our discussion to solutes that have essentially no vapor pressure and are not electrolytes—nonvolatile nonelectrolytes. Such solutes decrease the vapor pressure of the solvent by allowing fewer solvent molecules to escape from the surface (see Figure 15.12c), but do not contribute to the vapor pressure. From Raoult's law (Equation 15.13), therefore, where A is the solvent

$$P_{soln} = X_A P_A^\circ \qquad (15.16)$$

This equation shows that, because the mole fraction of the solvent will be less than one, the vapor pressure of the solution will be less than that of the pure solvent—it is lowered by adding the solute.

The **vapor pressure lowering**, ΔP, is the difference between the vapor pressure of a pure solvent and the total vapor pressure over a solution of a nonvolatile solute. Introducing the mole fraction of the solute B into Equation (15.16) and rearranging gives an expression for the vapor pressure lowering in terms of the mole fraction of the *solute* (B).

$$X_A + X_B = 1, \quad \text{so} \quad X_A = 1 - X_B$$
$$P_{soln} = X_A P_A^\circ = (1 - X_B) P_A^\circ \qquad (15.17)$$

$$\Delta P = P_A^\circ - P_{soln} = P_A^\circ - (P_A^\circ - X_B P_A^\circ)$$

$$\underset{\substack{vapor \\ pressure \\ lowering}}{} \Delta P = X_B P_A^\circ \underset{\substack{vapor\ pressure \\ of\ pure\ solvent}}{} \qquad (15.18)$$

$$\underset{mole\ fraction\ of\ solute}{}$$

When the solute molecules do not interact with each other or the solvent molecules and have no tendency to escape from the solution (i.e., the ideal solution of a nonvolatile nonelectrolyte), the vapor pressure lowering is dependent only on the relative number of solute and solvent molecules.

Once ΔP is known, the vapor pressure of such a solution can be found by subtracting ΔP from the vapor pressure of the pure solvent.

$$P_{soln} = P_A^\circ - \Delta P \qquad (15.19)$$

EXAMPLE 15.11
Solution Properties: Vapor Pressure

What is the vapor pressure at 25 °C above the aqueous sucrose solution described in Example 15.5 for which $X_{sucrose} = 0.0220$? Assume that the vapor pressure of the sucrose is negligible and that the vapor pressure of pure water at 25 °C is 23.756 Torr.

The unknown in this problem is the vapor pressure over the solution of a nonvolatile solute. To find this, we must first find the vapor pressure lowering of the solvent, ΔP. Using $X_{sucrose} = 0.0220$, the vapor pressure lowering is

$$\Delta P = X_{sucrose} P_{H_2O}^\circ = (0.0220)(23.756\ \text{Torr}) = 0.523\ \text{Torr}$$

The solution vapor pressure is the difference between the vapor pressure of the pure water and the vapor pressure lowering.

$$P_{soln} = P_{H_2O}^\circ - \Delta P = 23.756\ \text{Torr} - 0.523\ \text{Torr} = 23.233\ \text{Torr}$$

The vapor pressure of the sugar solution is 23.233 Torr, about 2% less than that of the pure solvent.

Exercise Find the vapor pressure at 45 °C of a solution which contains 0.083 mol of urea (NH_2CONH_2) in 1000.0 g H_2O. The vapor pressure of water at 45 °C is 71.88 Torr. *Answer* 71.77 Torr

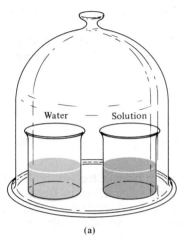
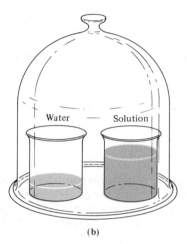
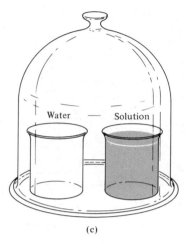

(a)   (b)   (c)

Figure 5.14
Demonstration of Vapor Pressure Lowering (a) Molecules evaporate from the surface of the pure water in the beaker. If the beaker containing a solution were not also present, a state of equilibrium would eventually be attained when the partial pressure of water vapor in the bell jar reached the vapor pressure of pure water at this temperature. (b) The vapor pressure of the solution, however, is always *lower* than that of pure water (Equation 15.16). As soon as the partial pressure of water vapor in the bell jar rises higher than the vapor pressure of the *solution,* water molecules start to enter the solution beaker more rapidly than they evaporate from it. There is a continuous net movement of water molecules into the solution, preventing the vapor pressure of pure water from ever being reached. (c) Since equilibrium can never be attained, *all* of the water will eventually end up in the solution beaker except for those molecules that remain in the gaseous state. (The final partial pressure of water vapor will be that given by Equations 15.18 and 15.19.) If this experiment is done with two solutions, transfer of solvent stops when the solution concentrations reach the point at which the solvent vapor pressures are equal.

The effect of vapor pressure lowering can be seen in the transfer of a solvent in the closed system illustrated in Figure 15.14. The vapor pressure of the solution is always lower than that of the pure water, and equilibrium between water molecules in the gas phase and those in the two beakers is not possible. More molecules leave the surface of the water than reenter it, because some enter the solution beaker. *All* of the water molecules eventually migrate to the solution beaker.

Any property of a solution that depends on the relative numbers of solute and solvent particles is called a **colligative property** (from the Latin *colligare,* to bind together). Vapor pressure lowering is a colligative property. The three phenomena discussed in the following sections—boiling point elevation, freezing point depression, and osmosis—are also colligative properties.

15.14 BOILING POINT
ELEVATION AND FREEZING
POINT DEPRESSION

Recall that the normal boiling point of a liquid is the temperature at which its vapor pressure equals the atmospheric pressure. Figure 15.15 shows the effect of vapor pressure lowering on the boiling point and also the freezing point of pure water. The solution–vapor equilibrium curve lies *below* the curve for pure water at all points. As a result of this vapor pressure lowering, the solution must be heated to a higher temperature to reach a vapor pressure equal to atmospheric pressure, and therefore to boil. The boiling point has been elevated—the solution boils at a higher temperature than the solvent. As shown in Figure 15.15, the lowering of the vapor pressure also causes the freezing point to be lowered—the solution freezes at a lower temperature than the solvent.

Ideally one mole of any nonvolatile nonelectrolyte solute in a given amount of solvent will have the *same* effect on colligative properties as one mole of any other nonvolatile nonelectrolyte solute. Each contains the *same* number of particles—equal to Avogadro's number. In working with colligative properties *molality* (or mole fraction) is used as the concentration unit because it gives the ratio of molecules

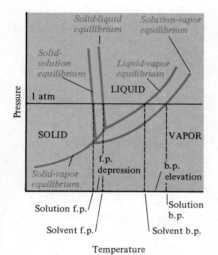

Pressure

Solid-liquid equilibrium

Solution-vapor equilibrium

Solid-solution equilibrium

Liquid-vapor equilibrium

LIQUID

1 atm

SOLID

VAPOR

f.p. depression

b.p. elevation

Solid-vapor equilibrium

Solution f.p.

Solution b.p.

Solvent f.p.

Solvent b.p.

Temperature

Figure 15.15
Comparison of Phase Diagrams of Pure Water and an Aqueous Solution of a Nonvolatile Solute The solution freezing point is the point at which crystals of pure *solvent* appear. If a compound or solid solution formed between the solvent and solute as cooling occurred, the phase diagram would be more complex.

of solute to a fixed number of molecules of solvent and also because it is independent of temperature changes.

The boiling point elevation, ΔT_b (= b.p. solution − b.p. solvent), and the freezing point depression, ΔT_f (= f.p. solvent − f.p. solution), are directly proportional to the molality of a solution.

b.p. elevation

molal b.p. elevation constant

f.p. depression

molal f.p. depression constant

$$\Delta T_b = K_b m \qquad \Delta T_f = K_f m \qquad \text{(15.20a,b)}$$

A 1 molal aqueous solution of any nonvolatile nonelectrolyte boils at 100.512 °C, a boiling point elevation of 0.512 °C. This same solution freezes at −1.86 °C, a freezing point lowering of 1.86 °C. These values provide the constants used in Equations (15.20a) and (15.20b) for aqueous solutions. The units for the constants are derived as follows:

molal b.p. elevation constant

$$K_b = \frac{0.512\,°C}{1\,m\ \text{solution}} = 0.512\,°C\left(\frac{1\ \text{kg}}{1\ \text{mol}}\right) = 0.512\,\frac{°C\ \text{kg}}{\text{mol}} \qquad \text{(15.21a)}$$

molal f.p. depression constant

$$K_f = \frac{1.86\,°C}{1\,m\ \text{solution}} = 1.86\,°C\left(\frac{1\ \text{kg}}{1\ \text{mol}}\right) = 1.86\,\frac{°C\ \text{kg}}{\text{mol}} \qquad \text{(15.21b)}$$

and the complete equations for aqueous solutions are

$$\Delta T_b = \left(0.512\,\frac{°C\ \text{kg}}{\text{mol}}\right) m \qquad \Delta T_f = \left(1.86\,\frac{°C\ \text{kg}}{\text{mol}}\right) m$$

$$°C \qquad \frac{°C\ \text{kg}}{\text{mol}} \qquad \frac{\text{mol}}{\text{kg}} \qquad °C \qquad \frac{°C\ \text{kg}}{\text{mol}} \qquad \frac{\text{mol}}{\text{kg}}$$

The values of K_b and K_f are different for each solvent (Table 15.5).

To find the boiling or freezing point of a solution, the tabulated value of K_b or K_f for the solvent and the known molality of the solution are used in Equation (15.20a) or (15.20b) to find the boiling point elevation or the freezing point lowering. Then the boiling point (T_b) or freezing point (T_f) of the given solution is found from the following relationships:

$$T_{b,\text{solution}} = T_{b,\text{solvent}} + \Delta T_b \qquad T_{f,\text{solution}} = T_{f,\text{solvent}} - \Delta T_f \qquad \text{(15.22a, b)}$$

Table 15.5
Molal Boiling Point Elevation (K_b) and Molal Freezing Point Lowering (K_f) Constants for Several Solvents

Solvent	K_b (°C kg/mol)	K_f (°C kg/mol)
Water	0.512	1.86
Benzene	2.53	4.90
Nitrobenzene ($C_6H_5NO_2$)	5.24	7.00
Biphenyl	—	8.00
Ethylene dibromide	—	11.80
Naphthalene	—	6.8
Carbon disulfide	2.34	—
Carbon tetrachloride	5.03	32
Ethyl alcohol	1.22	—
Methyl alcohol	0.83	—

Because ΔT_b represents a boiling point *elevation* it is *added* to the boiling point of the solvent. Because ΔT_f represents a *depression,* or lowering of the freezing point, it is *subtracted* from the freezing point of the solvent. Think of it this way—the freezing point moves toward a colder temperature, the boiling point moves toward a higher temperature. Do not make the common error of disregarding or confusing the $+$ and $-$ signs in Equations (15.22a) and (15.22b).

EXAMPLE 15.12
Solution Properties: Colligative Properties

A solution contained a mixture of sugars: 0.50 mol of fructose, 0.50 mol of glucose, 0.50 mol of lactose, 0.50 mol of maltose, and 0.50 mol of sucrose dissolved in 1.00 kg of water. What are the freezing point and boiling point of this solution?

The freezing point depression and boiling point elevation are colligative properties which depend on the total number of solute particles present, not on the nature of these particles. The total number of moles of solute is 2.50 mol (for the five sugars) and the total concentration of solute is

$$\text{Molality} = \frac{\text{moles of solute}}{\text{kg of solvent}} = \frac{2.50 \text{ mol}}{1.00 \text{ kg H}_2\text{O}} = 2.50 \text{ mol/kg}$$

Using 1.86 °C kg/mol as the freezing point depression constant for water, we have

$$\Delta T_f = K_f m = (1.86 \text{ °C kg/mol})(2.50 \text{ mol/kg}) = 4.65 \text{ °C}$$

and

$$T_{f,\text{solution}} = T_{f,\text{solvent}} - \Delta T_f = 0.00 \text{ °C} - 4.65 \text{ °C} = -4.65 \text{ °C}$$

Using 0.512 °C kg/mol as the boiling point elevation constant, we obtain

$$\Delta T_b = K_b m = (0.512 \text{ °C kg/mol})(2.50 \text{ mol/kg}) = 1.28 \text{ °C}$$
$$T_{b,\text{solution}} = T_{b,\text{solvent}} + \Delta T_b = 100.00 \text{ °C} + 1.28 \text{ °C} = 101.28 \text{ °C}$$

The solution containing the mixture of sugars will freeze at -4.65 °C and boil at 101.28 °C.

Exercise What are the boiling and freezing points of a 0.125 m aqueous solution of sucrose? *Answer* 100.0640 °C, -0.233 °C

15.15 MOLAR MASS DETERMINATION

Any of the colligative properties can be used to determine the molar masses of nonvolatile nonelectrolytes. A weighed amount of a substance of unknown molar mass is dissolved in a weighed amount of solvent. The colligative property, say boiling point elevation, is measured. The molality of the solution can then be calculated from the relationship $\Delta T_b = K_b m$ rearranged to give $m = \Delta T_b/K_b$. Once the molality is known, the molar mass can be found.

Experimentally, freezing point lowering is the colligative property easiest to measure and it is used most often in molar mass determinations of relatively low molecular mass substances. However, molar masses over 1000 are difficult to determine by using vapor pressure lowering, ΔT_b, or ΔT_f because of the large mass of material that must be dissolved in order to produce significant changes in the vapor pressure, freezing point, or melting point. Osmotic pressure measurements (next section) offer a better method for determining high molar masses. It should be pointed out that the boiling point elevation constant and the freezing point depression constant, like many so-called scientific constants, are not really constant. The values of K_b and K_f vary slightly with the nature of the solute and the concentration of the solution. A great many scientific "constants" are in actuality subject to minor variations with changing conditions, and the results of calculations involving such constants are therefore only approximate, as shown by the result in Example 15.13.

EXAMPLE 15.13
Solution Properties: Colligative
Properties
Either camphor ($C_{10}H_{16}O$, molar mass $= 152.24$ g) or naphthalene ($C_{10}H_8$, molar mass $= 128.19$ g) can be used in mothballs. A 5.0 g sample of mothballs was dissolved in 100.0 g of ethyl alcohol and the resulting solution had a boiling point of 78.91 °C. Determine whether the mothballs were made of camphor or naphthalene. Pure ethyl alcohol has a boiling point of 78.41 °C and $K_b = 1.22$ °C kg/mol for this solvent.

The boiling point elevation is

$$\Delta T_b = T_{b,\text{solution}} - T_{b,\text{solvent}} = 78.91\ °C - 78.41\ °C = 0.50\ °C$$

Using $\Delta T_b = 0.50$ °C and $K_b = 1.22$ °C kg/mol, we can calculate the molality of the solution as

$$\text{Molality} = \frac{\Delta T_b}{K_b} = \frac{0.50\ °C}{1.22\ °C\ \text{kg/mol}} = 0.41\ \text{mol/kg}$$

The number of moles of solute in the 100.0 g, or 0.1000 kg, of solvent is

$$(0.41\ \text{mol/kg})(0.1000\ \text{kg}) = 0.041\ \text{mol}$$

The molar mass of the solute is found by dividing the known mass by the number of moles of solute.

$$\text{Molar mass} = \frac{5.0\ \text{g}}{0.041\ \text{mol}} = 120\ \text{g/mol}$$

The value of 120 g/mol for the molar mass indicates that naphthalene was used to make mothballs.

Exercise A solution contained 15.00 g of urea dissolved in 85.00 g of water. The freezing point of this solution was -5.02 °C. What is the molar mass of urea? $K_b = 1.86$ °C kg/mol for H_2O. *Answer* 65.2 g/mol (actual molar mass $= 60.06$ g)

15.16 OSMOTIC PRESSURE

Liquids can diffuse through skin and other biological membranes, as well as through parchment, cellophane, and polyvinyl chloride membranes. **Semipermeable membranes** are membranes that allow the passage of some molecules but not others. The passage of *solvent* molecules through a semipermeable membrane from a more dilute solution into a more concentrated solution is called **osmosis.** Osmosis is one of the ways in which water molecules move in and out of living cells. If red blood cells are placed in a solution containing a lower concentration of inorganic ions than the fluid inside the cells, the cells swell up and burst as more and more water molecules enter the cells from the solution.

[Note that *osmosis* specifically refers to conditions under which only *solvent* molecules pass through a membrane. There are other processes in which membranes selectively allow passage of particles in a particular size range while retaining larger particles. For example, in the purification of commercially produced enzymes (biological catalysts; Section 33.21), the enzymes are retained by membranes which allow the passage of water, small organic molecules, and inorganic impurities.]

Osmosis, like vapor pressure, is dependent upon the relative numbers of solute and solvent molecules in a solution. To visualize the process of osmosis, consider a vessel divided by a semipermeable membrane (Figure 15.16). With the same pure liquid in both halves of the vessel, molecules of the liquid diffuse through the membrane with equal freedom in both directions, and there is no apparent change. When a solute that will not pass through the membrane is dissolved in the solvent on one side of the membrane, the effective concentration of the solvent on that side is lowered. Fewer solvent molecules make contact with the membrane and diffuse

Figure 15.16
Osmosis (a) Diffusible molecules of solvent pass through a semipermeable membrane separating two chambers. Because chamber 2 contains molecules of a nondiffusible solvent (dark circles), the effective solvent concentration there is lower than in chamber 1. Consequently more molecules diffuse from left to right than from right to left. (b) Equilibrium is reached when the pressure in chamber 2 has increased enough to make the rate of diffusion from right to left equal to that in the opposite direction. The additional pressure needed to equalize the rates of diffusion is the *osmotic pressure* of the solution in chamber 2.

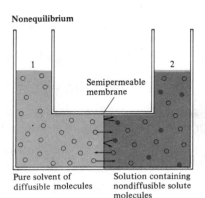

Nonequilibrium

Semipermeable membrane

Pure solvent of diffusible molecules

Solution containing nondiffusible solute molecules

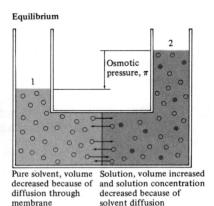

Equilibrium

Osmotic pressure, π

Pure solvent, volume decreased because of diffusion through membrane

Solution, volume increased and solution concentration decreased because of solvent diffusion

through it. (The situation is similar to the evaporation of solvent molecules shown in Figure 15.12.) The molecules on the other side of the membrane can still diffuse freely, however, with the result that the rates of diffusion of liquid in the two directions are unequal.

The liquid level on the solution side rises as more water molecules enter than leave. Consequently the pressure exerted by the solution against the membrane increases, slowing down the diffusion of solvent molecules. Eventually the pressure increases to the point at which the rates of diffusion of solvent molecules in the two directions are once again equal. The pressure exerted by the solution at this point is equal to the *osmotic pressure*—a colligative property exhibited when a pure solvent and a solution, or solutions of two different concentrations, are separated by a semipermeable membrane. **Osmotic pressure** is defined as the external pressure exactly sufficient to oppose osmosis and stop it. Osmosis can be reversed by applying a pressure *greater* than the osmotic pressure, a principle utilized in the desalination of seawater (see An Aside: Desalination of Water).

The mathematical expression for osmotic pressure, Π, in dilute solution is as follows:

$$\underset{\substack{osmotic-\\pressure\\ \text{atm}}}{\Pi} = \underset{\substack{\frac{mol}{L}\frac{L\ atm}{K\ mol}K}}{\left(\frac{n_B}{V}\right)\ RT} = \overset{\substack{molarity\ of\ solution}}{MRT} \tag{15.23}$$

where n_B is moles of solute, V is solution volume in liters, R is the ideal gas constant (0.0821 L atm/K mol for Π in atmospheres), T is the absolute temperature, and M is the molarity of the solution. [You may have noticed that this equation has the same form as the ideal gas law. The behavior of solute molecules in dilute solutions is not unlike the behavior of gas molecules.]

EXAMPLE 15.14
Solution Properties: Colligative Properties

An aqueous solution contained 77.1 g of inulin, $(C_6H_{10}O_5)_x$, per liter of solution. (Inulin is a high molecular mass sugar.) The osmotic pressure at 20 °C of this solution was 0.58 atm. Calculate the molar mass of inulin. What is the value of x in the formula for inulin?

The molarity of the solution can be found from the osmotic pressure.

$$\Pi = MRT$$

$$M = \frac{\Pi}{RT} = \frac{(0.58 \text{ atm})}{(0.0821 \text{ L atm/K mol})(293 \text{ K})} = 0.024 \text{ mol/L}$$

The molar mass of the solute, as found from the mass and molarity, is

$$\left(\frac{77.1 \text{ g}}{1 \text{ L}}\right)\left(\frac{1 \text{ L}}{0.024 \text{ mol}}\right) = 3200 \text{ g/mol}$$

The mass of the formula unit, $C_6H_{10}O_5$, is 162 g/mol, so the value of x is found by dividing 3200 g/mol by 162 g/mol and rounding off to the nearest integer.

$$x = \frac{3200 \text{ g/mol}}{162 \text{ g/mol}} = 20$$

The molar mass of inulin is 3200 g and with $x = 20$ the formula for inulin is $(C_6H_{10}O_6)_{20}$.

Exercise What pressure would have to be applied to the solution side of a semipermeable membrane separating pure water from a 0.25 M aqueous solution of sucrose to prevent solvent flow from taking place? Assume the temperature to be 25 °C. *Answer* 6.1 atm

15.17 COLLIGATIVE PROPERTIES OF ELECTROLYTE SOLUTIONS

In a 0.1 m solution of sodium chloride (NaCl)—a strong electrolyte—there are twice as many solute particles (Na^+, Cl^-) as in a 0.1 m solution of a nonelectrolyte such as sucrose. The effect of sodium chloride on the colligative properties of a 1 m solution—if such a solution were ideal—would be twice that of sucrose. Experimentally, it is found that the value of the freezing point depression of a 0.1 m NaCl solution is 1.87 times that predicted from Equation (15.20b) for a nonelectrolyte, and for a 0.001 m solution it is 1.97 times the expected value.

These data illustrate the general trend in the colligative properties of solutions of strong electrolytes. As the solution becomes more dilute, and therefore approaches ideality, the values of the colligative properties approach those expected based on the number of ions per formula unit of solute. For NaCl, the values approach two times the expected values; for K_2SO_4, they approach three times the expected values; and so on. The second of the following two examples illustrates how the effect on colligative properties of a weak electrolyte can be used to find the extent of ionization of the electrolyte.

EXAMPLE 15.15
Solution Properties: Colligative Properties

Upon dissolution, Na_2HPO_4 forms two Na^+ ions and one HPO_4^{2-} ion. Assuming an ideal solution, what is the predicted freezing point depression of a 0.010 m aqueous solution of $NaHPO_4$? $K_f = 1.86$ °C kg/mol for H_2O.

Because each formula unit of Na_2HPO_4 that dissolves forms three ions, the concentration of ions in a 0.010 m solution of Na_2HPO_4 is 0.030 m. The freezing point depression is, therefore,

$$\Delta T_f = K_f m = (1.86 \text{ °C kg/mol})(0.030 \text{ mol/kg}) = 0.056 \text{ °C}$$

The predicted freezing point depression is 0.056 °C.

Exercise A compound was known to be either K_2SO_4, which forms two K^+ ions and one SO_4^{2-} ion upon dissolution, or $KHSO_4$, which forms one K^+ ion and one HSO_4^- ion upon dissolution. The osmotic pressure of a 0.010 M solution of this compound at 25 °C was 0.50 atm. Which substance was present? *Answer* $KHSO_4$—only two ions per formula unit.

EXAMPLE 15.16
Solution Properties: Colligative
Properties

Hydrofluoric acid (HF) is a weak electrolyte—only a small number of the HF molecules ionize to form H^+ ions and F^- ions. The observed freezing point depression of a $0.100 \, m$ HF solution is $0.197 \, °C$. What percentage of the HF molecules are ionized in this solution? $K_f = 1.86 \, °C \, kg/mol$ for H_2O.

In this solution there are three types of solute particles: H^+ ions, F^- ions, and non-ionized HF molecules. If we let X represent the fraction of molecules that are ionized, the concentration of each species is

$$\left(\frac{0.100 \text{ mol HF}}{kg}\right)\left(\frac{X \text{ mol } H^+}{1 \text{ mol HF}}\right) = (0.100 \, X) \text{ mol } H^+/kg$$

$$\left(\frac{0.100 \text{ mol HF}}{kg}\right)\left(\frac{X \text{ mol } F^-}{1 \text{ mol HF}}\right) = (0.100 \, X) \text{ mol } F^-/kg$$

$$\left(\frac{0.100 \text{ mol HF}}{kg}\right)\left(\frac{(1 - X) \text{ mol non-ionized HF}}{1 \text{ mol HF}}\right)$$

$$= (0.100 - 0.100 \, X) \text{ mol non-ionized HF/kg}$$

The total concentration of solute particles is

$$(0.100 \, X) + (0.100 \, X) + (0.100 - 0.100 \, X) = (0.100 + 0.100 \, X) \text{ mol/kg}$$

The freezing point depression for this solution in terms of the total concentration of solute particles is

$$\Delta T_f = K_f m = (1.86 \, °C \, kg/mol)[(0.100 + 0.100 \, X) \text{ mol/kg}]$$
$$= (1.86)(0.100 + 0.100 \, X) \, °C$$

Equating this predicted freezing point depression to the observed value gives

$$(1.86)(0.100 + 0.100 \, X) \, °C = 0.197 \, °C$$

$$X = 0.06$$

The fraction of HF molecules that are ionized is 0.06 or 6%.

Exercise Benzoic acid, C_6H_5COOH, is a weak electrolyte—only 2.6% of it ionizes in a $0.100 \, m$ aqueous solution to form H^+ ions and $C_6H_5COO^-$ ions. Calculate the total concentration of solute particles in this solution. What is the predicted freezing point depression? $K_f = 1.86 \, °C \, kg/mol$ for H_2O. *Answer* 0.1026 mol/kg, 0.191 °C

In summary, the total vapor pressure for a mixture of volatile liquids is governed by Raoult's law, $P_{soln} = X_A P_A° + X_B P_B°$, where $P_A°$ and $P_B°$ are the vapor pressures of the pure liquids. Nonvolatile solutes lower the vapor pressure from that of the pure solvent. Vapor-pressure lowering and the properties dependent upon it—freezing-point depression, boiling-point elevation, and osmotic pressure— are called colligative *properties. These properties are dependent more on the number of nonvolatile particles than on the nature of the particles.*

Any of the colligative properties can be used to find the molality of a solution and from the molality the molar mass of the solute. In dilute solutions of strong electrolytes, the number of ions per formula unit determines the colligative properties. Because of the interaction of ions of opposite charge, electrolytes in more concentrated solutions deviate from the theoretical, or ideal, colligative behavior.

AN ASIDE

Desalination of Water

The removal of ions, especially Na^+ and Cl^-, from water is called *desalination*. Desalination is necessary to obtain very pure water from ordinary tap water, to obtain drinking water from seawater or brackish water (less salty than seawater), and to remove excessively high concentrations of ions in purifying industrial or municipal wastewater.

Desalination methods utilize one of several different principles. In *distillation processes*, the salty water is boiled and the pure water vapor condensed. Distillation has long been used to make small quantities of water of high purity in laboratories. It is also the basis for the majority of the large-scale seawater desalination plants. To get the maximum efficiency out of the energy input needed to vaporize the water, the vapor is passed back over the incoming seawater and the heat of condensation given up by the vapor aids in heating the seawater (Figure A).

Desalination by *crystallization* also utilizes a phase change. Salty water is partially frozen to a slurry, then the ice crystals are separated and melted. Seawater desalination by crystallization is still in the experimental stage.

Several processes utilize membranes that in essence filter out the ions. *Reverse osmosis* is just what it says—when a pressure greater than the osmotic pressure is applied (Section 15.16) on the solution side of a semipermeable membrane, the water molecules diffuse through the membrane to the freshwater side. (The pressures used are from 200 to 1500 psig.) This is the opposite of the direction in which water molecules move in osmosis. Reverse osmosis is being used in small-scale units for the desalination of brackish water. The process will retain solutes of molecular mass below 500. (It does not work well with seawater; the ion concentration is too high.)

In *electrodialysis* (Figure B), ion-selective membranes—membranes that let only positive or only negative ions pass through—are combined with an electrochemical cell. A few seawater desalination plants and municipal wastewater treatment plants use this process.

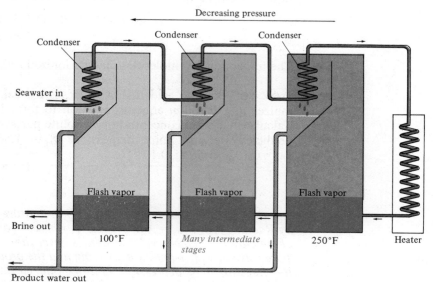

Figure A

Seawater Desalination by Multistage Flash Distillation This is the process most widely used for seawater desalination. A plant at Key West, Florida, produces 2.6 million gallons/day by this method. Hot seawater enters a chamber where the pressure is low enough to cause some water to vaporize instantly—to "flash" into steam. The temperature of the remaining seawater drops as it moves over to the next chamber, where low pressure causes more water to flash distill. The Key West plant takes water from 250 °F to 100 °F in 50 stages.

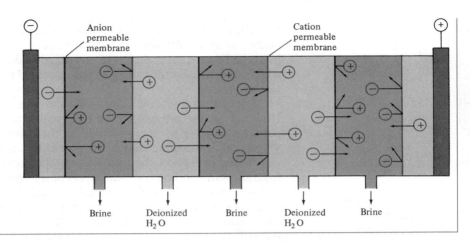

Figure B
An Electrodialysis Cell Anions move to the right and cations to the left under the influence of a strong electric field. By alternating anion- and cation-permeable membranes, ions collect in some subcells, while all ions leave other subcells.

COLLOIDS

15.18 PROPERTIES OF COLLOIDS

A sample of mud may be kept in suspension in water by stirring. As soon as the stirring is stopped, the larger particles will fall to the bottom of the vessel. Some smaller particles may remain in suspension for a while, but most of them will settle out before long. There are usually some particles, however, that remain suspended in the water for several days, or perhaps indefinitely. These make the mixture cloudy, but the individual particles cannot be seen even under powerful magnification, and the mixture cannot be clarified by passing it through a conventional filter.

A mixture in which small particles remain dispersed almost indefinitely is called a **colloidal dispersion,** or simply a colloid. Rather than use the terms "solute" and "solvent" for a colloid, we speak of the dispersing medium and the dispersed substance or dispersed phase. As illustrated in the next section, all three states of matter may serve in either capacity.

Strictly speaking, a **colloid** is a substance made up of suspended particles larger than most molecules, but too small to be seen in an optical microscope. The size range of colloidal particles is not clearly defined, but is usually set as somewhere between 1 nm and 1000 nm. Colloidal dispersions can be produced by suspending particles, or breaking up larger aggregates, or by condensation of smaller particles.

When a colloidal dispersion is brightly illuminated by a beam of light at right angles to the line of sight and examined under a microscope, the individual particles cannot be seen, but they are detected as tiny flashes of light dancing in the liquid. This motion, called *Brownian motion* after its discoverer, Robert Brown (1773–1858), is constant but quite irregular. For many years after its discovery, the cause of the Brownian motion was not known. Several theories were advanced to explain it, Brown himself suggesting that the dancing particles were alive. Recognition that the movement of the suspended particles is due to bombardment by rapidly moving molecules and that the speed increases with temperature led to the development of the kinetic-molecular theory.

When a strong beam of light passes through a colloid, the scattering of light by the suspended particles makes the beam clearly visible. This is called the *Tyndall effect* and is frequently used to distinguish between true solutions and colloids (Figure 15.17). The Tyndall effect can be seen when a beam of light passes through a cloud of smoke or a glass of soapy water.

At the center of each colloidal particle can be a small crystal or a single large molecule. Many biochemical molecules are of colloidal dimensions. Intermolecular forces between the molecules of the dispersing medium and the molecules or portions of molecules on the surfaces of the colloidal particles play an important role in the behavior of colloids (a role not fully understood).

Tyndall effect

Colloidal suspension

Solution

Figure 15.17
Light and Colloids

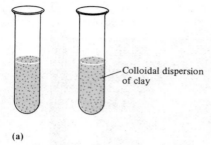

(a)

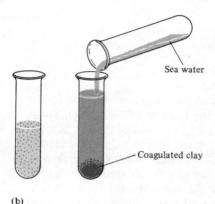

Sea water

Colloidal dispersion of clay

Coagulated clay

(b)

Figure 15.18
Coagulation of a Colloid Clay is dispersed in water by vigorously shaking the test tubes. Sea water (or $0.5\ M$ NaCl + $0.05\ M$ $MgCl_2$ — "artificial" sea water) added to one test tube causes the colloidal dispersion to coagulate as the negative charge on the colloid particles is neutralized by Na^+ and Mg^{2+} ions.

The properties of colloids in which water is the dispersing medium, such as clays, paints, gelatins, and the colloids present in many biological systems, are of great interest. To get a general picture of such colloids, consider a solid suspended in water which, as is usually the case, also has dissolved in it varying concentrations of strong electrolytes.

Like all macroscopic substances, the colloidal dispersion as a whole is neutral. However, in the presence of an electrical field it is found that all of the colloidal particles migrate to one electrode or the other. The particles themselves are obviously all of the same charge. How does this come about?

At the centers of the particles are chemically similar molecules which attract from the surrounding medium layers of ions all of the same charge. (The attraction of a substance to the surface of a solid is called **adsorption.** An adsorbed layer can be held to a surface by intermolecular forces, the forces of chemical bonding, or a combination of the two.) As a colloidal particle with its charged surface layer drifts through the water, it attracts a more loosely held "atmosphere" made up of ions bearing the opposite charge. The charge on the particle is exactly neutralized by these ions, which cluster around the particle, forming a thin, diffuse layer of ions intermingled with water molecules. The ions are kept from adhering to the surface of the particle by the motion of the intervening water molecules. As the colloidal particles approach each other, their surrounding diffuse layers merge and strong repulsion arises between the charged surface layers. It is this electrical repulsion that keeps colloidal particles in suspension. If the central molecules in the colloidal particles could collide, they would adhere to each other as a result of van der Waals attractions.

The thickness of the diffuse layer containing the ions required for electrical neutrality is determined by the concentration of ions in the suspending medium. If there are few ions, the diffuse layer is large and the colloidal particles experience maximum repulsion. When the concentration of ions is large, the diffuse layer becomes very thin and two colliding particles can collide with sufficient energy to overcome all forces of repulsion, allowing them to come close enough to each other to stick together because of van der Waals attractions. For this reason, colloidal particles may be coagulated by adding electrolytes. Deltas form where rivers meet the ocean partly because the electrolyte concentration in seawater is higher than that in the river (Figure 15.18), causing the colloidal clay particles to coagulate and settle.

Colloidal particles have very large surface areas in comparison with their diameters, a geometrical property characteristic of small objects. As a result, colloidal particles are very efficient at adsorbing other substances on their surfaces, a property useful in the role of many colloidal substances as catalysts.

15.19 TYPES OF COLLOIDS

Colloids are categorized by the states of the dispersed phase and the dispersing medium. Examples of the various types of colloids are given in Table 15.6.

Mud or clay consists of solid particles suspended in a liquid—a type of colloid called a **sol.** Sols are very common and examples of them are easily prepared in the laboratory. If, for example, a small amount of a solution of iron(III) chloride is poured slowly into a large volume of boiling water, and the boiling is continued for some time, a clear red sol of hydrated iron(III) oxide particles is formed:

$$2FeCl_3(aq) + (x + 3)H_2O(l) \longrightarrow Fe_2O_3 \cdot xH_2O(\text{red sol}) + 6HCl(aq)$$

A **gel** is a special type of colloid in which solid particles, usually very large molecules, unite in a random and intertwined structure that gives rigidity to the mixture. For example, the carbohydrate pectin from fruit is the dispersed substance that stiffens grape jelly. Many gels can be converted into sols by changes in temperature, pH, or other conditions. Jello dessert is a colloid that undergoes sol–gel interconversion—the gel form from the refrigerator "melts" to a sol in a warm room.

Table 15.6
Types of Colloids

Dispersing Medium	Dispersed Substance	Type of Colloid	Examples
Liquid	Gas	Foam*	Soap suds, whipped cream, beer foam
	Liquid	Emulsion*	Mayonnaise, milk, face cream
	Solid	Sols, gels†	Protoplasm, starch, gelatin and jelly, clay
Gas	Liquid	Liquid aerosol	Fog, mist, aerosol spray
	Solid	Solid aerosol	Smoke, airborne bacteria and viruses
Solid	Gas	Solid foam	Aerogels, polyurethane foam
	Liquid	Solid emulsions, some gels	Cheese
	Solid	Solid sol	Ruby glass, some alloys

* Stable foams and emulsions are usually formed only when an emulsifying agent, such as a soap, is present in addition to the pure liquid and gas.

† Sols contain individual dispersed particles; in gels the particles link together in a structure of some strength.

Many of the unusual properties of proteins in aqueous media are due to sol–gel interconversion.

A colloid in which particles of a liquid are suspended in another liquid is called an **emulsion.** Colloidal suspensions of immiscible liquids, such as oil in water, and water in oil, are emulsions. Such colloids form only in the presence of an emulsifying agent which forms a protective layer on the surface of each colloidal particle. Without the emulsifying agent the droplets would combine and the two liquids would separate. Soap molecules (next section) emulsify droplets of oily dirt. Mayonnaise is a familiar example of an emulsion — the dispersed phase is oil, the dispersing medium is water, and egg yolk is the emulsifying agent.

Foam is a colloid consisting of tiny bubbles of gas suspended in a liquid. Most foams in which the liquid phase is pure water are short-lived, but if the surface tension of the water is reduced by the addition of a surface-active agent, very stable foams may be generated. Common substances that can be added to water to produce this effect are soap and licorice, both of which lower the surface tension of water. Whipped cream is both an emulsion and a foam, for in it both butterfat and air bubbles are colloidally suspended.

Smoke is a colloidal suspension of solid particles in air, and fog is a colloid consisting of suspended droplets of water in the air. A colloidal suspension in which air (or any gas) is the suspending medium is called an **aerosol.**

The precipitation of colloidal particles is illustrated by the operation of electrostatic smoke and dust removers. In the Cottrell precipitator, for example, metal plates carrying a strong electrostatic charge are mounted in a smokestack. Because of their electrical charge, the colloidal smoke particles that pass through the stack are attracted to the plate of opposite charge and, upon contact with it, lose their charge and precipitate (Figure 15.19).

Many colloids are known in which the dispersing medium is a liquid, and the dispersed particles are either gaseous or solid. A very efficient device for cleaning grease spots from clothes consists of a can containing colloidal silica suspended in a mixture of a volatile oil and a pressurized gas. When the pressure is released by opening the valve, a jet of fluid is ejected from the can and is directed on the grease spot. The liquefied gas immediately evaporates; the oil dissolves the grease in the spot and this solution is adsorbed on the silica. The oil evaporates in a few minutes, and the silica with the adsorbed grease is brushed from the garment.

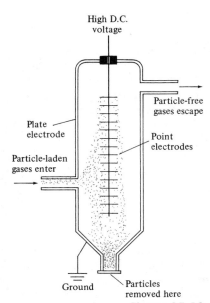

Figure 15.19

The Cottrell Precipitator Installed near the top of the smokestack, the precipitator removes charged colloidal particles from the smoke.

15.20 THE SOAP AND DETERGENT OPERA

Hydrolysis of natural fats and oils in the presence of a base, usually sodium hydroxide, produces a soap. Long before the chemical structure of the reactants was known, soaps were made by the treatment of animal fats with lye. What we call soap, once used in bar or flake form for all household cleaning and laundry, is a mixture of the salts of straight-chain organic acids. A soap has two parts: (1) a long, straight hydrocarbon chain that is oil soluble and (2) the water-soluble sodium or potassium salt of an acid. For example, a common soap is sodium stearate,

$$CH_3CH_2CH_2CH_2CH_2CH_2CH_2CH_2CH_2CH_2CH_2CH_2CH_2CH_2CH_2CH_2C\overset{\displaystyle O}{\overset{\|}{}}{}-O^-Na^+$$

Oily or greasy dirt adheres firmly to clothing and is undisturbed by washing in tap water, in which oil and grease are insoluble. Soap acts as an emulsifying agent and brings the dirt into colloidal dispersion. The hydrocarbon end of the soap molecule is soluble in the oil or grease. The anionic end is not soluble in the oil or grease, but protrudes from the colloidal droplets, making them water soluble and repelling other similar droplets, thus preventing coalescence (Figure 15.20).

The great disadvantage of soap is that in hard water (Section 14.11) the sodium ion is replaced by magnesium or calcium ions from the water to give insoluble compounds. These compounds precipitate to form bathtub scum and a dull film on laundry washed with soap in hard water.

Synthetic detergents, often simply called detergents, are synthetic cleaning agents (not made directly from animal fats) used as substitutes for soap. Most laundry detergents contain a surface-active agent that, like a soap, consists of a long hydrocarbon chain with a water-soluble group at the end of the chain; for example,

$$CH_3CH_2CH_2CH_2CH_2CH_2CH_2CH_2CH_2CH_2CH_2CH_2-\langle \bigcirc \rangle-SO_3^-Na^+$$

a straight-chain sodium alkylbenzenesulfonate

The calcium and magnesium salts of such compounds are soluble in hard water.

Synthetic detergents were introduced in 1945 and quickly became very popular. These compounds are more effective cleaning agents than soap, and they can be used in hard water as well. In the first generation of detergents, however, the hydrocarbon side chains were not straight (as they are in soap and in the sodium alkylbenzenesulfonate written above), but branched; for example,

$$\underset{\quad\quad CH_3 \quad\ CH_3 \quad\ CH_3 \quad\ CH_3}{CH_3CHCH_2CHCH_2CHCH_2CH}-\langle \bigcirc \rangle-SO_3^-Na^+$$

a branched-chain sodium alkylbenzenesulfonate

It was soon discovered that these compounds were not biodegradable, that is, they could not be broken down by organisms in the environment. A major reason was that the bacteria in natural bodies of water and in municipal wastewater treatment plants rejected a branched-chain diet. The detergents remained effective, and sudsy water was found in streams and even ran out of faucets. This problem was solved by a second generation of detergents with straight hydrocarbon chain surface-active agents, a more acceptable diet to bacteria.

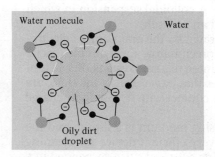

Water-soluble anionic end — Oil-soluble end

(a) A molecule of soap or synthetic detergent

Detergent molecules / Oily dirt
H₂O / H₂O
Fiber

(b) Action of soap or synthetic detergent on oily dirt on clothing

Water molecule / Water
Oily dirt droplet

(c) Oily dirt in wash water

Figure 15.20
The Action of Soap and Synthetic Detergents on Oily and Greasy Dirt

SUMMARY

15.1 SOME DEFINITIONS In a saturated solution the concentration of dissolved solute is equal to that which would be in equilibrium with undissolved solute under the given conditions. The solubility of a substance is the concentration of a saturated solution (at 25 °C if not otherwise stated). An unsaturated solution is one that can dissolve more solute. A supersaturated solution holds more solute than would be in equilibrium with undissolved solute.

15.2 THE NATURE OF SOLUTIONS IN THE LIQUID PHASE The mutual solubility of two substances in the same phase is known as miscibility. Substances that are similar in structure, bonding, and especially in intermolecular forces tend to be highly or even infinitely miscible ("like dissolves like"). A solid dissolves in a liquid if the interaction between the two substances is stronger than the forces holding the ions or molecules of the solid together.

15.3 IDEAL VS. NONIDEAL SOLUTIONS In an ideal solution of a molecular solute the forces between all particles of both solvent and solute are identical. In an ideal solution of an ionic solute the ions in solution are independent of each other and attracted only to solvent molecules. In a nonideal solution the forces between atoms, ions, and molecules are significant, and lower the effective concentration of the solute.

15.4 THE EFFECT OF TEMPERATURE AND PRESSURE ON SOLUBILITY **15.5** HEATS OF SOLUTION The solubility of most inorganic salts in water increases with temperature, but to widely varying degrees. The solubility of gases in liquids decreases with rising temperature. An increase in pressure increases the solubility of a gas in a liquid, in accordance with Henry's law ($p_A = kC$, where C = gas concentration). Dissolution can be exothermic or endothermic.

15.6 STANDARD SOLUTIONS **15.7** MASS PERCENT **15.8** MOLARITY **15.9** MOLE FRACTION **15.10** MOLALITY **15.11** DILUTION OF SOLUTIONS A solution of known concentration is called a standard solution. Solution concentrations can be expressed as mass percent, molarity, mole fraction, or molality. These are summarized in Table 15.3. For dilute aqueous solutions, the molarity and molality have similar values. When more solvent is added to a solution, the concentration of the solution is lowered but the amount of solute is unchanged.

15.12 LIQUID–LIQUID SOLUTION VAPOR PRESSURES: RAOULT'S LAW Raoult's law states that the vapor pressure of a liquid in an ideal solution is equal to the mole fraction of that liquid in the solution times the vapor pressure of the pure liquid. The composition of the vapor over a solution is always richer in the more volatile (lower boiling) component. Nonideal solutions exhibit positive deviations (greater partial pressures) or negative deviations (lower partial pressures) from Raoult's law.

TOOLS OF CHEMISTRY: DISTILLATION Distillation involves heating a liquid or solution to boiling and collecting and condensing the vapor; it is used to separate liquid components of a solution that differ in boiling point. Fractional distillation consists of a continuous series of simple distillations which progressively increase the separation of components. Solutions that deviate sufficiently from Raoult's law cannot be totally separated by distillation. At some definite composition they form azeotropes —mixtures of constant boiling point that distill without change of composition.

15.13 VAPOR PRESSURE LOWERING BY NONVOLATILE NONELECTROLYTE SOLUTES Nonvolatile nonelectrolyte solutes decrease the vapor pressure of a solvent by allowing fewer solvent molecules to escape from the surface. The amount of the decrease, ΔP, is equal to the vapor pressure of the pure solvent times the mole fraction of solute present. Vapor pressure lowering and the other properties that depend on the relative numbers of solute and solvent particles are colligative properties.

15.14 BOILING POINT ELEVATION AND FREEZING POINT DEPRESSION **15.15** MOLAR MASS DETERMINATION Because the presence of a solute lowers the vapor pressure of a solution it also *lowers* its freezing point ($\Delta T_f = K_f m$) and *raises* its boiling point ($\Delta T_b = K_b m$).

Experimentally, freezing point lowering is often used to determine the molar masses of substances. (For substances with molar masses over 1000, osmotic pressure measurements are more practical.)

15.16 OSMOTIC PRESSURE   Semipermeable membranes allow the passage only of certain molecules. The passage of solvent molecules through a semipermeable membrane from a more dilute to a more concentrated solution is called osmosis. The external pressure sufficient to oppose and halt osmosis is the osmotic pressure.

15.17 COLLIGATIVE PROPERTIES OF ELECTROLYTE SOLUTIONS   As the solution of a strong electrolyte becomes more dilute it approaches ideality, and the values of its colligative properties approach those expected on the basis of the number of ions per formula unit of solute.

15.18 PROPERTIES OF COLLOIDS   A mixture in which particles generally between 1 nm and 1000 nm in diameter remain dispersed almost indefinitely is called a colloidal dispersion or colloid. Colloidal particles in aqueous solution are usually surrounded by layers of ions which prevent them from coalescing.

15.19 TYPES OF COLLOIDS   A sol consists of solid particles suspended in a liquid. In a gel the solid particles, usually very large molecules, unite in a random, intertwined structure, producing greater rigidity. Particles of a liquid colloidally dispersed in another liquid constitute an emulsion. A foam consists of tiny gas bubbles suspended in a liquid. A colloid in which a gas is the suspending medium is an aerosol.

15.20 THE SOAP AND DETERGENT OPERA   Soaps are mixtures of the salts of straight-chain organic acids. The long hydrocarbon chains dissolve in droplets of oil or grease; the anions at the ends of the chains protrude from the droplets and interact with water molecules, preventing coalescence of the droplets and creating a colloidal dispersion. Synthetic detergents also consist of long hydrocarbon chains with water-soluble groups at the end. The Ca and Mg salts of synthetic detergents, unlike those of soaps, are water soluble.

THOUGHTS ON CHEMISTRY

Second-hand Molecules

SIZING UP SCIENCE, by R. Houwink

Inspector Veryfit of the Public Health Department was having a drink with his old friend Dr. Pure, who was in charge of the Waterworks. Veryfit was worried. `I have an uncomfortable feeling,' he said, `that sometimes I am drinking water that has been drunk before.' Dr. Pure consulted his note-book and replied that things looked very bad indeed; the total number of people ever to have lived he estimated at a hundred thousand million (10^{11}), and their average lifespan was only 25 years (— the infant mortality rate was high until very recently). If all these people excreted two litres of water every day of their lives, roughly one molecule in every million has been excreted by someone at some time. `Assuming,' Dr Pure added, `that all the water on the Earth is thoroughly mixed up.'

`So the number of ``dirty'' molecules in your glass of beer, my dear Veryfit, is in the region of 15 million million million — far more than you can imagine. To give you some idea of the numbers involved, think of the cavity in a hollow tooth: it could contain $10^{20}$ molecules, which means more than $10^{14}$ ``dirty'' ones — 200,000 molecules each for everyone now living.

`Of course,' he went on, `some of these molecules have been excreted more than once, so there are ``double-dirty'' ones; and on top of that, the ``dirty'' water is not distributed evenly over the Earth and it is likely to be much dirtier in densely-populated areas like this.'

The Inspector poured his beer down the sink, calculating that if there was one `dirty' molecule per million there would be enough in his pint to *provide every living person with a hundred million of them! A young scientist had been listening to this conversation from behind his newspaper, but this waste of beer prompted him to point out to Inspector Veryfit that the concentration of dirty molecules was really very low — the same, for instance, as the amount of fluoride added to the water to prevent tooth decay. 'In the air you breathe,' he continued, 'about one molecule in every 500 has been exhaled by someone else: this is 2000 times the concentration of the dirty molecules in the Inspector's beer.*

'And in every breath you inhale about half a litre of air, or 10^{22} molecules, so about 300 million of these molecules have previously been exhaled by some particular person who lived to the age of 40 — Socrates, Shakespeare or Einstein, for example. Isn't it rather wonderful to think that we are breathing the same air as these people?'

'Another round!' said Inspector Veryfit, encouraged by these inspiring words, 'but nothing for Dr. Pure, who has made no attempt to size up his knowledge!'

R. Houwink, *Sizing Up Science* (London: John Murray (Publishers) Ltd., 1975), p. 135.

QUESTIONS

General Properties of Solutions

15.1 A solution may be defined as "a homogeneous mixture of two or more substances." What does the word "homogeneous" mean? Does a mixture have variable or fixed composition? What is the name given to the substance in a solution that is usually present in the larger amount?

15.2 What terms do we give to solutions in which the concentration of solute is (a) greater than, (b) equal to, or (c) less than the solubility?

15.3 Two liquids, A and B, which do not react chemically, are completely miscible. What happens as one is poured into the other? What would happen in the case of two completely immiscible liquids or two partially miscible liquids?

15.4 Briefly describe the equilibrium between a saturated solution and undissolved solute. How might you prove that your description is correct?

15.5 Describe the processes by which NaCl, HCl, and CH_3OH dissolve in water. Prepare sketches showing how these compounds exist in aqueous solution.

15.6* The cleansing action of soaps and detergents (see Section 15.20) illustrates how an insoluble material can be suspended in a solvent. Prepare a sketch showing this mechanism.

15.7 Compare the relative magnitude of the solvent–solvent, solute–solute, and solvent–solute interactions (a) for a solution having positive heat of solution (endothermic) and (b) for a solution having a negative heat of solution (exothermic).

15.8 We can see from Table 15.2 that for the dissolution of ionic solids, the lattice energy is a large negative number, the hydration energy is a large negative number, and the calculated heat of solution is a relatively small number. Describe the effect on the calculated heat of solution that would be caused by a small error (say, 5%) in either the lattice energy or the hydration energy.

15.9* Using Hess's law, show that ΔH(solution) $= \Delta H$(vaporization) $+ \Delta H$(solvation) for the dissolution of a liquid in another liquid.

15.10 How does the solubility of a gas in a liquid vary with increasing (a) temperature and (b) pressure?

15.11 (a) Does the solubility of a solid in a liquid exhibit an appreciable pressure dependence? (b) Is the same true for the solubility of a liquid in a liquid?

Concentrations of Solutions

15.12 Concentration units that are based on the volume of solution, solvent, solute, etc., are dependent on temperature. Which of these units depends on temperature: molality, molarity, mole fraction, and mass %?

15.13 What physical quantity provides the connection between concentration units based on mass (mole fraction, molality, mass %, etc.) and those based on volume (molarity, etc.)?

15.14 Define the concentration unit "mass percent." Many handbooks list solubilities in units of (g solute/100 g H_2O). How would you convert from this unit to mass percent?

15.15 Define molarity and molality. Under what conditions are concentrations in these units nearly the same? Which concentration unit is more useful when using burets, pipets, and volumetric flasks in the laboratory? Why?

15.16 Write an equation which defines the mole fraction of solute. What is the relationship between the mole fraction of solute and the mole fraction of solvent in a binary solution?

Vapor Pressures of Liquid Solutions and Related Properties

15.17 Is the composition of the vapor over a solution the same as the composition of the solution?

15.18 A solution shows positive deviation from Raoult's law for both components A and B. What can be inferred about the intermolecular forces between A and A, B and B, and A and B?

15.19 Define the term "colligative property." What colligative properties do we consider in this chapter? How do colligative properties depend on the nature of the solute particles?

15.20 Is the vapor pressure of a solution containing a nonvolatile solute greater or less than that of the pure solvent? How does this change in vapor pressure affect the boiling point of the solution?

15.21 Describe what happens as a solution begins to freeze. How does the freezing point of a solution compare to that of the pure solvent?

15.22 What is meant by the term "osmotic pressure of a solution?" How is it related to the concentration of the solution?

15.23 Compare the number of solute particles present in solutions of equal concentrations of strong electrolytes, weak electrolytes, and nonelectrolytes.

Colloids

15.24 Define the term "colloid." How does a colloidal dispersion differ from a true solution?

15.25 What is the usual reason that colloidal particles do not coalesce into larger particles upon collision? How can colloids be coagulated?

15.26 What special name is given to colloids (a) in which the *dispersing* phase is a gas, and (b) in which the *dispersed* phase is a gas?

Additional Questions

15.27 Toluene and water are essentially immiscible. If a flask containing the two liquids is heated, the system begins to boil at a temperature which is below the boiling point of either liquid. Why?

15.28* A chemist wanted to remove traces of chlorine from a sample of air. In his first attempt he bubbled the gaseous mixture through a technical grade sample of carbon tetrachloride, which contained chloroform (m.p. -63.5 °C, b.p. 61.7 °C) and naphthalene (m.p. 80.55 °C) as impurities. After smelling the "purified" gas, the chemist noted that a faint smell of chlorine was still present, so he next passed the gas through a stainless steel (18% Cr, 77% Fe) column containing "activated" charcoal. After the second process, the air was essentially chlorine free.

There are at least seven different solutions involved in the above procedures—for example, the chlorine-free air is a solution of a gas (oxygen, the major solute) dissolved in a gas (nitrogen, the solvent). Identify solutions that are examples of (a) a gas dissolved in a gas, (b) a gas dissolved in a liquid, (c) a gas dissolved in a solid, (d) a liquid dissolved in a liquid, (e) a solid dissolved in a liquid, and (f) a solid dissolved in a solid. In each case, specify which component is the solvent and which is the solute.

Answers to Selected Questions

15.11 (a) No; (b) yes

15.12 Molarity

15.14 Mass percent = [(mass of solute)/(mass of solution)](100%) = [(mass of solute)/(mass of solute + 100 g H_2O)](100%)

15.16 $X_B = n_B/(n_A + n_B)$, $X_B = 1 - X_A$

15.18 The forces between A and A and between B and B are both stronger than those between A and B

15.20 Less; the boiling point is raised

15.26 (a) Aerosol; (b) foam

PROBLEMS

Solubility

15.1 A handbook lists the value of the Henry's law constant as 3.02×10^4 atm for ethane, C_2H_6, dissolved in water at 25 °C. The absence of concentration units on k means that the constant is meant to be used with concentration expressed as mole fraction. Calculate the mole fraction of ethane in water at an ethane pressure of 0.15 atm.

15.2 The mole fraction of methane, CH_4, in water can be calculated from the Henry's law constants of 4.13×10^4 atm at 25 °C and 5.77×10^4 atm at 50 °C. Calculate the solubility of methane at these temperatures for a methane pressure of 15 atm above the solution. Does the solubility increase or decrease with increasing temperature? *Answer* 3.6×10^{-4}, 2.6×10^{-4}; solubility decreases

15.3 Use the following solubility data for SO_2 in water at 0 °C to calculate the Henry's law constant for this system:

P_{SO_2} (Torr)	0.25	0.60	1.2	1.9
solubility (g SO_2/100 g H_2O)	0.02	0.05	0.10	0.15

15.4 Henry's law constants at 25 °C for N_2 and O_2 in water are 4.34×10^5 Torr/(g N_2/100 g H_2O) and 1.93×10^5 Torr/(g O_2/100 g H_2O), respectively. Assume the partial pressure of N_2 to be 608 Torr and of oxygen to be 152 Torr above the solution. Find the solubility of these gases in water. Is the ratio of the mass of O_2 to N_2 greater or less in water than in air? *Answer* 1.40×10^{-3} g N_2/100 g H_2O, 7.88×10^{-4} g O_2/100 g H_2O; greater

Solution Concentration

15.5 Sodium fluoride has a solubility of 4.22 g in 100.0 g of water at 18 °C. Express the concentration in mass percent.

15.6 What masses of NaCl and H_2O are present in 160. g of a 12 mass % aqueous solution of NaCl? *Answer* 19 g NaCl, 141 g H_2O

15.7 A solution that is 37.2 mass % HCl has a density of 1.19 g/mL. What mass of HCl is contained in 30.0 mL of this solution?

15.8 How would you prepare 150. g of a 6 mass % solution of KOH in water? *Answer* 9 g KOH dissolved in 141 g H_2O

15.9 A 40.0 mL sample of ethyl ether, $(C_2H_5)_2O$, is dissolved in enough methyl alcohol, CH_3OH, to make 250. mL of solution. The density of the ether is 0.714 g/mL. What is the molarity of this solution? *Answer* 1.54 M

15.10* Hydrogen chloride and water form an azeotrope at 1 atm containing 20.2 mass % HCl. This azeotrope has a density of 1.102 g/cm³. What is the molarity of this solution?

15.11 Given a sufficient quantity of 4.38 M NaOH, describe how you would prepare exactly 250 mL of 0.876 M NaOH.

15.12 A solution contained 5.0 g KI and 10.0 g KCl dissolved in 85.0 g H_2O. What is the mole fraction of KI in this solution?

15.13 The solubility of K_2ZrF_6 at 100 °C in 100 g of H_2O is 25 g. Express this concentration in terms of mole fraction of solute. *Answer* 0.016

15.14 What is the concentration of KCl expressed in molality for the solution described in Problem 15.12?

15.15 What is the concentration of K_2ZrF_6 expressed in molality for the solution described in Problem 15.13? *Answer* 0.88 *m*

15.16* The solubility of $BeSO_4 \cdot 4H_2O$ in water at 25 °C is 42.5 g/100 g H_2O. What is the molality of this solution?

15.17 Describe how to prepare 1.000 L of 0.250 *m* NaCl. The density of this solution is 1.011 g/mL. *Answer* 14.8 g NaCl in 996 g H_2O

15.18* The density of a solution containing 10.00 g K_2SO_4 in 100.00 g solution is 1.0825 g/mL. Calculate the concentration of this solution in molarity, molality, mass percent of K_2SO_4, and mole fraction of solvent.

15.19* An aqueous ammonium chloride solution contains 6.50 mass % NH_4Cl. The density of the solution is 1.0201 g/mL. Express the concentration of this solution in molarity, molality, and mole fraction of solute. *Answer* 1.24 M, 1.30 *m*, $X_{NH_4Cl} = 0.0230$

15.20* The density of a sulfuric acid solution taken from a car battery is 1.225 g/cm³. This corresponds to a 3.75 M solution. Express the concentration of this solution in molality, mole fraction of H_2SO_4, and mass % of water.

15.21* Which aqueous solution has the highest Cl⁻ concentration: 0.05 *m* HCl, 15 mass % NaCl, or a $CaCl_2$ solution that has a mole fraction of 0.10 for $CaCl_2$? *Answer* The $CaCl_2$ solution has the highest concentration of Cl⁻.

Solution Properties
15.22 Using Raoult's law, predict the partial pressures over a solution containing 0.300 mol acetone ($P° = 345$ Torr) and 0.200 mol chloroform ($P° = 295$ Torr). What is the total pressure over this solution?

15.23 At 60 °C, the vapor pressure of pure ethyl alcohol, CH_3CH_2OH, is 353 Torr and that of methyl alcohol, CH_3OH, is 625 Torr. Using Raoult's law, predict the vapor pressure of each component of the solution and the total pressure for a solution in which $X_{CH_3OH} = 0.500$. Is the vapor richer or poorer in CH_3OH than the liquid? *Answer* $p_{CH_3OH} = 313$ Torr, $p_{CH_3CH_2OH} = 177$ Torr, $p_t = 490.$ Torr; the vapor is richer in CH_3OH.

15.24 What is the vapor pressure (at 25 °C) above a solution containing 100.00 g of water and 10.0 g of urea, $CO(NH_2)_2$, a nonvolatile solute? The vapor pressure of pure water (at 25 °C) is 23.76 Torr.

15.25 Methyl alcohol, CH_3OH, and ethylene glycol, HOH_2CCH_2OH, are both used to prevent the freezing of water in automobile radiators in cold weather. (a) Which will be more effective in a given radiator, 25 g of methyl alcohol or 25 g of ethylene glycol? (b) Which will be more effective, a 5 *m* solution of methyl alcohol or a 5 *m* solution of ethylene glycol? *Answer* (a) Methyl alcohol; (b) effectiveness will be the same.

15.26 The molal freezing point constant for copper is 23 °C kg/mol. If pure copper melts at 1083 °C, what will be the melting point of a brass made of 10. mass % Zn and 90. mass % Cu?

15.27* An 11.5 qt automobile cooling system containing water and ethylene glycol antifreeze (molar mass = 62.07 g) is "safe" to −20 °F. A very cold night is expected and the owner decides to change the protection limit to −40 °F by replacing some of the solution with pure ethylene glycol. What should he do? The density of the original solution is 1.063 g/cm³ and that of pure antifreeze is 1.116 g/cm³. *Answer* He should replace 2 qt of the original solution with an equal amount of pure ethylene glycol.

15.28 A solution was made by dissolving 3.75 g of a nonvolatile solute in 95.0 g of acetone. The solution boiled at 56.58 °C. The boiling point of pure acetone is 55.95 °C and $K_b = 1.71$ °C kg/mol. Calculate the molar mass of the solute.

15.29 The molar mass of an organic compound was determined by measuring the freezing point depression of a benzene solution. A 0.500 g sample was dissolved in 50.0 g of benzene ($K_f = 2.53$ °C kg/mol) and the resulting depression was 0.42 °C. What is the approximate molar mass? The compound gave the following elemental analysis: 40.0 mass % C, 6.67 mass % H, and 53.3 mass % O. Determine the formula and exact molar mass of the substance. *Answer* 59 g/mol, $C_2H_4O_2$, 60.052 g/mol

15.30 The freezing point of a 1.00 mass % aqueous solution of acetic acid, CH_3COOH, is −0.31 °C. What is the approximate molar mass of acetic acid in water? A 1.00 mass % solution of acetic acid in benzene ($K_f = 4.90$ °C kg/mol) has a freezing point depression of 0.441 °C. What is the molar mass of acetic acid in this solvent? Explain the difference.

15.31 What is the osmotic pressure associated with a 0.001 M solution of a nonvolatile nonelectrolyte solute at 75 °C?

15.32 The osmotic pressure of a solution of a nonvolatile nonelectrolyte solute was 14.7 atm at 0 °C. What is the concentration of the solution? *Answer* 0.656 M

15.33 At what temperature would a 1.00 M solution of sugar have an osmotic pressure of 1.00 atm? Is this answer reasonable?

15.34 The public works departments of many cities are replacing NaCl by $CaCl_2$ for use on icy streets. The solubility of $CaCl_2$ in water at 0 °C is 59.5 g/100 g H_2O and of NaCl is 35.7 g/100 g H_2O. Which solution has the lower freezing point? Assume complete dissociation of the salts. *Answer* −22.7 °C for NaCl, −29.9 °C for $CaCl_2$

15.35 One gram each of NaCl, NaBr, and NaI was dissolved in 100.0 g water. What is the vapor pressure above the solution at 100 °C?

15.36 A 0.050 *m* aqueous solution of $K_3Fe(CN)_6$ has a freezing point of −0.2800 °C. Calculate the total concentration of solute particles in this solution and interpret your results. *Answer* 0.151 mol/kg; the substance forms four ions in solution.

15.37* The freezing point depression for a 1.00 *m* aqueous solution of NH_3 is 1.94 °C. What fraction of ammonia molecules react with water in this solution?

$$NH_3(aq) + H_2O(l) \rightleftharpoons NH_4^+ + OH^-$$

15.38* An aqueous solution contained 1.00 g each of acetic acid (CH_3COOH, a weak electrolyte that is 4% ionized into H^+ ions and CH_3COO^- ions), ammonium sulfate [$(NH_4)_2SO_4$, a strong electrolyte], and formic acid (HCOOH, a weak electrolyte that is 6% ionized into H^+ ions and $HCOO^-$ ions) in 100.0 g H_2O. What is the freezing point of this solution? *Answer* −1.17 °C

15.39* The major components of seawater are 18,980. ppm Cl^-, 10,561 ppm Na^+, 2652 ppm SO_4^{2-}, 1272 ppm Mg^{2+}, 400. ppm Ca^{2+}, 380. ppm K^+, 142 ppm HCO_3^-, and 65 ppm Br^-. A ppm (part per million) means 1 g solute in 10^6 g of solution. Calculate the molality of seawater with respect to each ion. What would be the predicted freezing and boiling points? Assuming molarity and molality to be equal, what pressure would be required at 25 °C in order to obtain pure water by reverse osmosis? *Answer* 0.55446 *m* Cl^-, 0.47576 *m* Na^+, 0.02859 *m* SO_4^{2-}, 0.05419 *m* Mg^{2+}, 0.0103 *m* Ca^{2+}, 0.0101 *m* K^+, 0.00241 *m* HCO_3^-, 0.00084 *m* Br^-, −2.11 °C, 100.582 °C, 27.8 atm

Additional Problems

15.40 At 1.000 atm the solubility of CO in water at 25 °C is 0.002603 g/100 g H_2O and of SO_2 in water it is 9.41 g/100 g H_2O. What is the Henry's law constant for each gas? What is the molality of each solution? What would be the freezing point of each solution? Why is there such a large difference in the solubility of these gases?

15.41 The heat of formation at 25 °C is −887 kJ/mol for H_2SO_4 (1 M) and −866 kJ/mol for H_2SO_4(16 M). As for chemical reactions and changes of state, the process of dilution of a solution can be exothermic or endothermic. How much heat is

absorbed or released in the dilution of 16 M H_2SO_4 to 1 M H_2SO_4?

$$H_2SO_4(16\ M) \xrightarrow{H_2O} H_2SO_4(1\ M)$$

If the solution cannot gain or lose this heat fast enough to remain at 25 °C, what sensation would you feel if you touched the beaker in which this reaction was performed?

15.42 The heat of formation at 25 °C is −365.56 kJ/mol for $NH_4NO_3(s)$, −343.1 kJ/mol for NH_4NO_3(1 M), and −339.7 kJ/mol for NH_4NO_3(0.1 M). Calculate the heat of solution for preparing a 1 M solution

$$NH_4NO_3(s) \xrightarrow{H_2O} NH_4NO_3(1\ M)$$

If the solution cannot gain or lose this heat fast enough to remain at 25 °C, what sensation would you feel if you touched the beaker in which this reaction was performed? Also calculate the heat absorbed or released in preparing a 0.1 M solution from a 1 M solution

$$NH_4NO_3(1\ M) \xrightarrow{H_2O} NH_4NO_3(0.1\ M)$$

Answer 22.5 kJ; the beaker would feel cool to the touch; 3.4 kJ

15.43* The heat of formation of Al(*g*) is 326.4 kJ/mol, the ionization energy of Al(*g*) to $Al^{3+}(g)$ is 5157.6 kJ/mol, and the heat of hydration of $Al^{3+}(g)$ is −6015 kJ/mol. Write the equation for the formation of $Al^{3+}(aq)$ from Al(*s*) and use the above data to predict $\Delta H°$ for this reaction.

The heat of sublimation of $I_2(s)$ is 62.438 kJ/mol, the bond dissociation energy of $I_2(g)$ is 151.240 kJ/mol, the electron affinity of I(*g*) is −303.5 kJ/mol, and the hydration energy of $I^-(g)$ is 141.5 kJ/mol. Write the equation for the formation of $I^-(aq)$ from $I_2(s)$ and use the above data to predict $\Delta H°$ for this reaction.

Combine your two results to predict $\Delta H°$ for the reaction

$$Al(s) + \tfrac{3}{2}I_2(s) \xrightarrow{H_2O} Al^{3+}(aq) + 3I^-(aq)$$

15.44* The density of one brand of commercial vinegar (5.00 mass % CH_3COOH) is 1.0055 g/cm³. (a) Express the concentration of the solute in molarity, molality, and mole fraction.

The freezing point of vinegar is −1.65 °C. Acetic acid is a weak electrolyte that forms H^+ ions and CH_3COO^- ions. (b) Calculate the fraction of molecules that ionize. (c) Calculate the osmotic pressure of the solution at 25 °C.

Assuming an ideal solution, use Raoult's law to calculate (d) the total vapor pressure of the vinegar. The vapor pressure of water is 23.8 Torr and of acetic acid is 15.5 Torr at 25 °C.

The heat of formation is −484.5 kJ/mol for $CH_3COOH(l)$ and −485.54 kJ/mol for CH_3COOH (5.00 mass %) at 25 °C. (e) Calculate the heat of solution. *Answer* (a) 0.838 M, 0.877 *m*, $X_{CH_3COOH} = 0.0156$, (b) 0.01, (c) 20.5 atm, (d) 23.6 Torr, (e) −1.0 kJ

CHAPTER 16

Hydrogen and Oxygen, Oxidation–Reduction Reactions

Hydrogen has been known since the eighteenth century and oxygen has been known for much longer. Credit for the discovery of hydrogen is usually given to Henry Cavendish, who recognized it as a distinct substance in 1766. Earlier, in 1671, Robert Boyle had observed hydrogen as a flammable gas produced by the reaction of zinc and hydrochloric acid. And Nicholas Lémery in 1700 made it from iron and sulfuric acid. Lémery was so impressed by the way the gas exploded when ignited that he thought he had discovered the cause of thunder and lightning.

One of the earliest descriptions of the properties of oxygen came from Leonardo da Vinci in the fifteenth century. In what is a model of simple writing about scientific facts, da Vinci reported that "Where flame cannot live no animal that draws breath can live." Oxygen was independently "discovered," in the sense of being prepared, collected, and recognized as an element, by two men, Wilhelm Scheele and Joseph Priestley, in the 1770s. Scheele probably performed his experiments earlier, but his publisher was slow to process the manuscript of his book, "Fire and Air," which did not appear until 1777. In the meantime, Joseph Priestley prepared oxygen from mercuric oxide on August 1, 1774 (see A Historical Aside, Chapter 6). Priestley went on to become the more famous chemist. A group of American chemists met in 1874 to celebrate the one-hundredth anniversary of the discovery of oxygen by Priestley. At that meeting the need for an organization of chemists was discussed. As a result, the American Chemical Society, now the largest organization of chemists in the world, was founded in New York City in 1876.

As was the case in Chapter 14 on the chemistry of water, we have two purposes in this chapter. The first is to present the descriptive chemistry of hydrogen and oxygen. The second is to introduce another of the major types of chemical reactions, oxidation–reduction reactions.

16.1 ORIGIN AND ABUNDANCE OF HYDROGEN AND OXYGEN

Hydrogen is the most abundant element in the cosmos (see Figure 12.6) and oxygen is the most abundant element in the crust of the earth.

Oxygen makes up almost 50% by mass of the earth's solid crust, where it is present in the oxides, silicates, and carbonates of the metals and semiconducting elements. Water, a compound that is 11.19% by mass hydrogen and 88.81% by mass oxygen, covers 70% of the earth's surface as oceans, rivers, lakes, and other bodies of water. The atmosphere of the earth contains about 20% by volume of oxygen (see Figure 27.14).

90% of the atoms in the universe are hydrogen

Very little molecular hydrogen is present in the atmosphere of the earth today. Most of the hydrogen present on earth is combined with other elements in chemical compounds, most importantly, in water and in the three main classes of biological substances: proteins, fats, and carbohydrates. Hydrogen is also a component of the fossil fuels—coal, petroleum, and natural gas. In our sun and other stars, the fusion of hydrogen nuclei to produce helium gives rise to enormous quantities of energy (see Table 12.10) and provides all of the energy necessary for life here on earth.

In the atmosphere of the primitive earth, hydrogen and helium were more abundant than any of the other elements, as is still true in the cosmos. Hydrogen and helium are the lightest gases. As we have seen (Section 5.2), all gases have distributions of velocities, and the lightest gases have the highest velocities. A significant fraction of the hydrogen and helium molecules have velocities sufficiently high to escape from the force of the earth's gravity. The atmospheric concentration of these gases has been decreasing steadily with time, and today there is very little of either in the atmosphere, although some hydrogen is produced in the decay of organic matter, and the outgassing of volcanoes, and by the photochemical dissociation of water.

OXIDATION AND REDUCTION

16.2 OXIDATION–REDUCTION REACTIONS

Oxidation: increase in oxidation number
Reduction: decrease in oxidation number

In Chapter 10 we presented the rules for assigning oxidation numbers to all of the atoms or ions in chemical compounds. One of the major ways in which chemical reactions are classified is based on whether or not the oxidation numbers of atoms and ions change during a reaction. Any process in which an oxidation number *increases* algebraically is **oxidation**. Any process in which an oxidation number *decreases* algebraically is **reduction**. (An algebraic increase is a change in the direction of a more positive number. Oxidation number changes of $-4 \rightarrow -2$, or $-1 \rightarrow +1$, or $+2 \rightarrow +3$ represent oxidation. Similarly, changes of $+5 \rightarrow +2$, or $+2 \rightarrow -1$, or $-1 \rightarrow -2$ represent reduction.) These definitions of "oxidation" and "reduction" have been adopted as the most general and useful meanings of the terms. [Here is a simple mnemonic trick: **O**xidation and **i**ncrease in oxidation number both begin with vowels; **r**eduction and **d**ecrease in oxidation number both begin with consonants.]

As is the case for "acids" and "bases," the original meanings have been extended to apply to many more compounds and reactions than were originally covered. The early definitions of oxidation and reduction, like those of acids and bases (Section 14.8), were derived from common, easily observed reactions and properties. As you might guess, there was a relationship between "oxygen" and "oxidation." Oxidation was first known as the addition of oxygen to another substance. The equation for the oxidation of copper is

$$\overset{0}{2Cu}(s) + O_2(g) \longrightarrow \overset{+2}{2CuO}(s) \tag{16.1}$$

Oxygen combines with copper, and we say that copper is oxidized to copper(II) oxide. In the process the oxidation number of copper has been increased ($0 \rightarrow +2$).

The word "reduction" was first used to refer to the production of a free metal from its ore. Many ores are oxides, and "reduction" came to mean the *removal* of oxygen from a substance—the opposite of oxidation. ("The processes of oxidation and deoxidation . . . give a degree of activity even to the world of rocks." Dana's *Manual of Geology*, 1862.) Tin, for example, is found naturally as the mineral cassiterite, which is SnO_2. Metallic tin is prepared by reduction with coke (coke is coal that has been heated in the absence of air to leave behind mostly carbon).

$$\overset{+4}{SnO_2}(s) + 2C(s) \overset{\Delta}{\longrightarrow} \overset{0}{Sn}(l) + 2CO(g) \tag{16.2}$$

The tin(IV) oxide is reduced by carbon. In modern terms, the reduction of the tin is shown by the decrease in oxidation number ($+4 \rightarrow 0$).

What happens to the carbon in reaction (16.2)?

$$SnO_2(s) + \overset{0}{2C}(s) \overset{\Delta}{\longrightarrow} Sn(l) + \overset{+2}{2CO}(g) \tag{16.3}$$

In both the original and the modern meanings of the term, carbon has been oxidized — oxygen has been added and the oxidation number increased $(0 \rightarrow +2)$.

Equations (16.2) and (16.3) illustrate an important point. Oxidation and reduction *always* occur together. If the oxidation number of one atom or ion increases in a reaction, the oxidation number of another atom or ion *must* decrease. Reactions in which oxidation and reduction take place are known as **oxidation–reduction reactions,** or, frequently, as **redox reactions.**

In a redox reaction the total increase in oxidation number for all atoms or ions must equal the total decrease in oxidation number for all atoms or ions. The increase of four for carbon in the reduction of tin(IV) oxide is balanced by the decrease of four for tin. In the reaction of copper with oxygen, copper is oxidized and oxygen is reduced:

$$\overset{0}{2Cu}(s) + \overset{0}{O_2}(g) \longrightarrow \overset{+2\,-2}{2CuO}(s) \tag{16.4}$$

The total oxidation number increase (for the two Cu atoms) is $(2) \times (+2) = +4$; the total oxidation number decrease (for the two O atoms) is $(2) \times (-2) = -4$. To give another example, in the combination of hydrogen and oxygen to form water, hydrogen is oxidized $(0 \rightarrow +1)$ and oxygen is reduced $(0 \rightarrow -2)$.

$$\overset{0}{2H_2}(l) + \overset{0}{O_2}(g) \longrightarrow \overset{+1\,-2}{2H_2O}(l)$$

The change in oxidation number is $+1$ for each hydrogen atom and -2 for each oxygen atom. But here, as in every redox reaction, the total oxidation number gain and loss is equal — for the four hydrogen atoms, $(4) \times (+1) = +4$, and for the two oxygen atoms, $(2) \times (-2) = -4$.

In classifying chemical reactions, every reaction is either a redox reaction or *not* a redox reaction. For example, oxidation and reduction do *not* occur in partner-exchange reactions (Section 6.3d). You can see that the oxidation numbers in the following example of a partner-exchange reaction do not change:

$$\overset{+2\,-1}{ZnCl_2}(aq) + \overset{+1\,-2}{H_2S}(aq) \longrightarrow \overset{+2\,-2}{ZnS}(s) + \overset{+1\,-1}{2HCl}(aq)$$

Therefore, this is *not* a redox reaction.

EXAMPLE 16.1
Redox Reactions

Are either or both of the following, redox reactions?

$$Zn(s) + HgO(s) \longrightarrow ZnO(s) + Hg(l)$$
$$NaOH(aq) + HCl(aq) \longrightarrow NaCl(aq) + H_2O(l)$$

To determine whether or not these are redox reactions we can put in all of the oxidation numbers.

$$\overset{0}{Zn}(s) + \overset{+2\,-2}{HgO}(s) \longrightarrow \overset{+2\,-2}{ZnO}(s) + \overset{0}{Hg}(l)$$

This is a redox reaction — zinc has been oxidized $(0 \rightarrow +2)$ and mercury has been reduced $(+2 \rightarrow 0)$.

$$\overset{+1\,-2\,+1}{NaOH}(aq) + \overset{+1\,-1}{HCl}(aq) \longrightarrow \overset{+1\,-1}{NaCl}(aq) + \overset{+1\,-2}{H_2O}(l)$$

This is not a redox reaction — no changes in oxidation number have occurred. [It is a neutralization reaction and also a partner-exchange reaction.]

Exercise Determine whether or not the following reactions are redox reactions:
(a) $\quad I^- + ClO^- \rightarrow IO^- + Cl^-,\quad$ (b) $\quad H_2O(l) \rightleftharpoons H^+ + OH^-,\quad$ (c) $4HNO_3(l) \rightarrow 2N_2O_4(g) + O_2(g) + 2H_2O(l)$, and (d) $C_6H_6(l) \rightarrow C_6H_6(s)$. *Answer* Reactions (a) and (c) are redox reactions.

16.3 OXIDIZING AGENTS AND
REDUCING AGENTS

**Oxidizing agent:
contains atom in an oxidized
state;
causes increase in the
oxidation state of another
substance**

**Reducing agent:
contains atom in a reduced
state;
causes decrease in the
oxidation state of another
substance**

An atom, molecule, or ion that causes an *increase* in the oxidation state of another substance and is itself reduced is called an **oxidizing agent**. In the reaction with copper (Equation 16.4), oxygen is the oxidizing agent. The expansion from the original meaning of oxidation that we discussed above is shown by comparing that reaction with the reaction of copper and fluorine:

$$\overset{0}{Cu}(s) + \overset{0}{F_2}(g) \longrightarrow \overset{+2\ -1}{CuF_2}(s) \tag{16.5}$$

Oxygen has not been added, but this reaction is clearly of the same type as that in Equation (16.4). As you can see, the oxidation number of fluorine, the oxidizing agent in this reaction, decreases — *the oxidizing agent is reduced.*

An atom, molecule, or ion that causes a *decrease* in the oxidation state of another substance and is itself oxidized is called a **reducing agent**. In the reaction of tin(IV) oxide with carbon (Equation 16.3), carbon is the reducing agent. During the course of a reaction, *the reducing agent is oxidized.*

Obviously, because oxidation and reduction always occur together, each redox reaction includes both an oxidizing agent and a reducing agent. In the reaction between ammonia and oxygen to give nitrogen(II) oxide and water,

$$\overset{-3}{4\,NH_3}(g) + \overset{0}{5\,O_2}(g) \longrightarrow \overset{+2\ -2}{4\,NO}(g) + \overset{-2}{6\,H_2O}(l) \tag{16.6}$$

oxidizing agent

reducing agent

ammonia is the reducing agent and oxygen is the oxidizing agent. (Note that the entire molecule or ion — not just the atom that changes oxidation number — is called the oxidizing or reducing agent.) Whether a reaction is commonly thought of as "oxidation" or "reduction," or as caused by the oxidizing agent or by the reducing agent, usually depends only on what aspect of the reaction we are most interested in.

How can an atom, molecule, or ion be recognized as a *potential* oxidizing or reducing agent? A clue lies in the statements made above — oxidizing agents are reduced and reducing agents are oxidized. An oxidizing agent must contain an atom in an oxidized state — an atom that in other species is assigned a lower oxidation number. Otherwise, no reduction is possible. We have seen that molecular oxygen is an oxidizing agent. The free element has oxidation state 0 and in *most* compounds oxygen is assigned an oxidation number of -2. Reduction of molecular oxygen when it enters into a reaction is therefore quite likely.

**In a redox reaction:
— oxidizing agent is reduced
— reducing agent is oxidized**

Similarly, a reducing agent must contain an atom in a reduced state — an atom that in other species is assigned a higher oxidation number. In Equation (16.6) ammonia is the reducing agent. It contains nitrogen in oxidation state -3. We know that nitrogen can have many different oxidation states more positive than -3. As you might expect, elements with variable oxidation states can be present in both oxidizing and reducing agents.

The conditions under which redox reactions occur are examined quantitatively in Chapter 23. For now, we want you to learn to recognize redox reactions, particularly those of hydrogen and oxygen, which are discussed in this chapter. In Chapter 17, we summarize and further discuss various types of redox reactions.

Table 16.1
**Vocabulary of Oxidation and
Reduction** Oxidizing agents are also
sometimes referred to as *oxidants*
and reducing agents as *reductants.*

In:	Oxidation Number:
oxidation	increases
reduction	decreases
the oxidized substance	increases
the reduced substance	decreases
the oxidizing agent	decreases
the reducing agent	increases

In summary, oxidation is an increase in oxidation number and reduction is a decrease in oxidation number. Oxidation and reduction always occur together. The total increase in oxidation number equals the total decrease in oxidation number for all atoms or ions that are oxidized or reduced in a given reaction.

An oxidizing agent causes another substance to be oxidized and is itself reduced. A reducing agent causes another substance to be reduced and is itself oxidized. Table 16.1 summarizes the vocabulary of oxidation and reduction.

EXAMPLE 16.2
Redox Reactions

Identify the oxidizing and reducing agents in the following reactions:

$$I_2(s) + H_2S(aq) \longrightarrow S(s) + 2HI(aq)$$
$$2HNO_3(aq) + SO_2(g) \longrightarrow H_2SO_4(aq) + 2NO_2(g)$$

In the first reaction elemental iodine is reduced to an iodide ion, and therefore iodine is the oxidizing agent. Sulfur from hydrogen sulfide is oxidized to elemental sulfur, and therefore hydrogen sulfide is the reducing agent.

reducing agent (→ H_2S); *oxidizing agent* (→ I_2)

$$\overset{0}{I_2}(s) + H_2\overset{-2}{S}(aq) \longrightarrow \overset{0}{S}(s) + 2H\overset{-1}{I}(aq)$$

In the second reaction both reactants contain elements that can be either oxidized or reduced—nitrogen in HNO_3 and sulfur in SO_2. Examination of the oxidation number changes in the reaction shows that HNO_3 is the oxidizing agent (N, $+5 \rightarrow +4$) and SO_2 is the reducing agent (S, $+4 \rightarrow +6$).

oxidizing agent (→ HNO_3); *reducing agent* (→ SO_2)

$$2H\overset{+5}{N}O_3(aq) + \overset{+4}{S}O_2(g) \longrightarrow H_2\overset{+6}{S}O_4(aq) + 2\overset{+4}{N}O_2(g)$$

Exercise Identify the oxidizing and reducing agents in the following reactions: (a) $I^- + ClO^- \rightarrow IO^- + Cl^-$ and (b) $4HNO_3(l) \rightarrow 2N_2O_4(g) + O_2(g) + 2H_2O(l)$. *Answer* (a) I^- is reducing agent, ClO^- is oxidizing agent; (b) HNO_3 is both the oxidizing and reducing agent (O is oxidized, N is reduced).

HYDROGEN

16.4 PROPERTIES OF HYDROGEN

Hydrogen is not properly a member of any group or family in the periodic table. It has similarities to both the lithium and fluorine family elements—it forms positive ions (H^+), although normally only in solution, and negative ions (H^-). But hydrogen is sufficiently different from the elements in these families that it must stand alone.

Under ordinary conditions, elemental hydrogen occurs as the diatomic molecule, H_2. Molecular hydrogen is a colorless, odorless gas. It can be liquefied and solidified only at temperatures close to absolute zero. The low boiling and melting points (Table 16.2) show that there are only weak intermolecular forces acting between the hydrogen molecules.

Table 16.2
Properties of Hydrogen

		For Comparison	
Molecular properties			
Melting point (°C)	−260	He	−272
Boiling point (°C)	−253	He	−269
Density (g/L, at STP)	0.090	He	0.18
Bond length (nm)	0.074	N_2	0.110
Bond dissociation energy (kJ/mol)	436	N_2	946
Atomic properties			
Ionization energy (kJ/mol)	1312	Na	496
Electron affinity (kJ/mol)	−73	O	−141
Electronegativity	2.1	O	3.5
Atomic radius (nm)	0.037	O	0.074

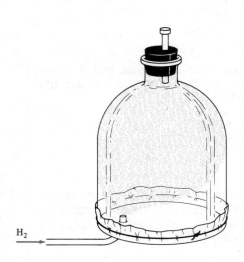

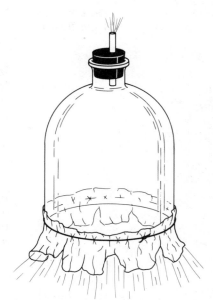

(a) Bell jar is filled with hydrogen through a hole in a piece of paper tied across the bottom of the bell jar.

(b) The top is opened and the escaping pure hydrogen ignited. It burns quietly at the opening as hydrogen rises in the jar.

(c) As hydrogen escapes at the top, air comes in at the bottom of the jar and mixes with the hydrogen. When enough air has mixed with the hydrogen, the mixture explodes violently, rupturing the paper at the bottom.

Figure 16.1
Properties of Hydrogen (a) The jar can be filled from the bottom because hydrogen is lighter than air and rises. The jar must be supported above the table top and not rest on the table. (b) Pure hydrogen burns without exploding. (c) It is the hydrogen-air mixture that is explosive. [CAUTION: The bell jar has been known to crack in this experiment.]

The high flammability of hydrogen requires that it be handled with care. Hydrogen burns with a very hot, nearly invisible flame in mixtures with air of from 4% to 74% H_2 by volume. Air containing from 18% to 60% of hydrogen by volume is potentially explosive and can be ignited by a spark or static electricity. However, hydrogen, like many other hazardous materials (for example, natural gas), is routinely handled and transported with safety. It is shipped by rail as a liquid held at low temperatures in tank cars equipped with specially designed insulation.

The density of gaseous hydrogen is low, about $\frac{1}{14}$ that of air, and it provides excellent buoyancy to balloons. In 1937 on its 22nd crossing of the Atlantic Ocean, a hydrogen-filled airship, the Hindenburg, caught fire after passing through an electrical storm and was destroyed, with the loss of many lives. This disaster permanently impressed upon the public that hydrogen is a dangerous material and led to the use of helium instead of hydrogen in airships. An experiment that demonstrates the flammability and explosive properties of hydrogen is illustrated in Figure 16.1.

The electron configuration of the hydrogen atom is $1s^1$ (Table 16.3). The hydrogen atom, with its one electron, is the simplest atom, and the hydrogen molecule, in which the two atoms are covalently bonded, is the simplest neutral, diatomic molecule. Hydrogen is of intermediate electronegativity (see Table 10.8). In bonding, it can achieve the stable helium configuration either by sharing an electron in a covalent bond or by gaining an electron to form a hydride ion, H^-. The hydrogen atom shares electrons easily and forms many covalent compounds. It gains electrons less readily, but does so in combination with metals that easily lose

Table 16.3
Hydrogen

Normal hydrogen, or protium, ^1_1H	*Deuterium, D,* ^2_1H
Hydrogen atom H	**Deuterium atom**
$1s^1$ configuration	1 electron
1 electron	1 proton
1 proton	1 neutron
Hydrogen molecule, H_2, H:H	
2 electrons	*Tritium, T,* ^3_1H
2 protons	**Tritium atom**
Hydride ion, H^-, $(H:)^-$	1 electron
$1s^2$ configuration	1 proton
2 electrons	2 neutrons
1 proton	(radioactive)
Proton, H^+	
1 proton only	

electrons. Hydrogen is assigned a $+1$ <u>oxidation state</u> in all of its compounds, except for the ionic hydrides (e.g., Na^+H^-), where it has an oxidation state of -1.

Hydrogen forms <u>compounds</u> with almost all of the other elements and these compounds range over the entire continuum from ionic to covalent. Molecules in which hydrogen is bonded to small, highly electronegative atoms (e.g., F, O, N) exhibit <u>hydrogen bonding</u> (Section 11.12).

The H^+ ion is a proton. No other positive ion is so small or has such a high concentration of charge. With the single electron gone, the charge of the proton is completely unshielded. As a result, the hydrogen atom does not give up an electron to form H^+ unless it can simultaneously share electrons with some other group, as in aqueous solution, where it is associated with water molecules (Section 14.4). Although free H^+ ions have been observed in outer space and at high temperatures, we normally find them only in the hydrated form in aqueous solutions, which we indicate by writing H_3O^+ (see An Aside: The Hydronium Ion, Chapter 20).

The <u>bond dissociation energy</u> of the hydrogen–hydrogen bond in H_2 is relatively high and the hydrogen molecule is thermally quite stable. Because of the large amount of energy needed to rupture the H—H bond, the <u>chemical reactivity</u> of molecular hydrogen is moderate. High temperatures and/or catalysts, which in many cases serve to split the molecule into atoms, are often required to carry out the reactions of hydrogen effectively. Hydrogen *atoms* are highly reactive.

Hydrogen oxidation states:
-1 in ionic hydrides
$+1$ in all other compounds

16.5 ISOTOPES OF HYDROGEN

The most abundant of the three isotopes of hydrogen is the species of mass number 1 (see Table 16.3). Deuterium, the isotope of mass number 2, has a nucleus of one proton and one neutron and is represented by the symbol ^2_1H or D. This isotope constitutes 1 part in 5000 of naturally occurring hydrogen. The isotope of mass number 3, tritium, is symbolized as ^3_1H or T. Tritium is radioactive, in contrast to ordinary hydrogen and deuterium, which have stable nuclei. Tritium occurs to only an extremely small extent in nature (about 1 part in 10^{14}).

In general, ordinary hydrogen undergoes reactions more rapidly than deuterium, and the latter, in turn, more rapidly than tritium. It must be emphasized, however, that the products formed with any particular element or compound have the same molecular compositions, because each of the isotopic atoms has the same

---

Deuterium: ^2_1H or D
Heavy water: D_2O

Table 16.4
**Comparison of Properties of H$_2$ and
D$_2$, and of H$_2$O and D$_2$O** D$_2$O is
commonly called heavy water.

	H$_2$	D$_2$
Melting point (°C)	−260	−254
Boiling point (°C)	−253	−250
Bond length (nm)	0.074	0.074
Bond dissociation energy (kJ/mol)	435	442
Heat of fusion (J/mol)	117	197
Heat of vaporization (J/mol)	904	1226
	H$_2$O	**D$_2$O**
Melting point (°C)	0.0	3.8
Boiling point (°C)	100.0	101.4
Density at 25 °C (g/mL)	0.997	1.10
Heat of fusion (J/mol)	6010.	6276
Heat of vaporization (J/mol)	40,656	41,606
Heat of formation of liquid at 25 °C (kJ/mol)	−286	−295

electronic structure. The physical properties of H$_2$ and D$_2$, and H$_2$O and D$_2$O—
heavy water—are compared in Table 16.4.

Deuterium and tritium have proved to be extremely valuable in the study of
chemical reactions of compounds containing hydrogen. Some of the ordinary
hydrogen in a compound under investigation is replaced with deuterium or tritium.
The chemical behavior of the compounds is altered very little by the substitution. If
the locations of the atoms in the reactants are known, the course of a chemical
reaction can often be inferred from their locations in the products. Deuterium and
tritium can be located by mass spectrometric analysis (see Tools of Chemistry: Mass
Spectrometer, in Chapter 3) and tritium by its radioactivity as well.

16.6 REACTIONS OF HYDROGEN

a. Hydrogen as a reducing agent Hydrogen is assigned a positive oxidation
state in all of its compounds except the ionic hydrides. What does this tell us about
molecular hydrogen? Is it likely to be an oxidizing agent or a reducing agent? In
reacting to form compounds other than ionic hydrides, molecular hydrogen undergoes an *increase* in oxidation number ($0 \rightarrow +1$) and is therefore a reducing agent.

Here are some examples of the reduction of metal oxides by hydrogen.

$$\overset{+2}{\text{CuO}}(s) + \text{H}_2(g) \overset{\Delta}{\longrightarrow} \overset{0}{\text{Cu}}(s) + \text{H}_2\text{O}(g)$$

$$\overset{+6}{\text{WO}_3}(s) + 3\text{H}_2(g) \overset{\Delta}{\longrightarrow} \overset{0}{\text{W}}(s) + 3\text{H}_2\text{O}(g)$$

As shown in the activity series (Table 6.2), hydrogen is not a strong enough reducing
agent to reduce the very stable oxides of the more active metals. (By *active metals* we
generally mean those at the top of the activity series—the strongly electropositive
metals of the *s* block in the periodic table.)

Hydrogen also reduces some nonmetal oxides. For example,

$$\overset{+4}{\text{SO}_2}(g) + 3\text{H}_2(g) \longrightarrow \overset{-2}{\text{H}_2\text{S}}(g) + 2\text{H}_2\text{O}(g)$$

$$\overset{+4}{\text{SO}_2}(g) + 2\text{H}_2(g) \longrightarrow \overset{0}{\text{S}}(s) + 2\text{H}_2\text{O}(g)$$

$$2\overset{+2}{\text{NO}}(g) + 2\text{H}_2(g) \longrightarrow \overset{0}{\text{N}_2}(g) + 2\text{H}_2\text{O}(g)$$

Hydrogen is a reducing agent in all of the reactions described in the following sections except for those with active metals.

b. Combination of hydrogen with oxygen Hydrogen burns in air or oxygen to give water. Like many reactions, the combination of hydrogen and oxygen, although it has a favorable, negative $\Delta H°$,

$$2H_2(g) + O_2(g) \longrightarrow 2H_2O(g) \qquad \Delta H° = -484 \text{ kJ}$$

proceeds at an insignificant rate at ordinary temperatures and pressures. Left undisturbed, a mixture of hydrogen and oxygen will stand without reacting. Even at 400 °C in the presence of a catalyst, the reaction is extremely slow. However, once the reaction is initiated by temperatures above 600 °C or by a spark or a flame, the combination occurs with explosive violence. The flame temperature of hydrogen burning in air is about 2000 °C, and temperatures up to 2800 °C are achieved in the oxyhydrogen torch, which is used in cutting metals. Even higher temperatures (up to 5000 °C) are achieved in a torch in which hydrogen molecules are split into hydrogen atoms in an electrical arc before they are burned. The higher torch temperature is possible because none of the energy from the combination of hydrogen with oxygen in the flame is taken up by breaking the hydrogen–hydrogen bonds.

c. Combination of hydrogen with nonmetals other than oxygen Hydrogen combines directly with all of the halogens.

$$\begin{aligned}
H_2(g) + F_2(g) &\longrightarrow 2HF(g) & \Delta H° &= -542 \text{ kJ} \\
H_2(g) + Cl_2(g) &\longrightarrow 2HCl(g) & \Delta H° &= -185 \text{ kJ} \\
H_2(g) + Br_2(l) &\longrightarrow 2HBr(g) & \Delta H° &= -73 \text{ kJ} \\
H_2(g) + I_2(s) &\longrightarrow 2HI(g) & \Delta H° &= +53 \text{ kJ}
\end{aligned}$$

The vigor of these reactions decreases in the order shown, which parallels the order of the elements in the periodic table family. The reaction with fluorine is rapid and was once considered useful in rocket propulsion. Hydrogen will burn in chlorine, and an explosive reaction of hydrogen and chlorine is initiated by exposure of the mixture to light. (Hydrogen–chlorine mixtures should be kept in the dark or under red light, since they are very sensitive to short-wavelength radiation and are thus extremely dangerous to handle.)

Ammonia, a commercially very important chemical, is produced by the combination of nitrogen with hydrogen at elevated temperature and pressure, in the presence of a catalyst:

$$N_2(g) + 3H_2(g) \xrightarrow[\text{pressure}]{\overset{\Delta}{\text{catalyst}}} 2NH_3(g)$$
$$\textit{ammonia}$$

Also at elevated temperature, hydrogen unites with sulfur vapor to form hydrogen sulfide. The reaction is much less exothermic than that with oxygen, which precedes sulfur in the same periodic table family.

$$H_2(g) + S(g) \xrightarrow{\Delta} H_2S(g) \qquad \Delta H° = -20.6 \text{ kJ}$$

There is essentially no reaction with selenium and tellurium, the semiconducting elements in the same family.

d. Combination of hydrogen with active metals Hydrogen combines directly with the active metals of Representative Group I and Representative Group II (except for Be) to give ionic hydrides, also known as *saline* or *saltlike hydrides*. The metal atoms give up electrons to hydrogen to form hydride ions in reactions such as

$$2\text{Li}(s) + \text{H}_2(g) \xrightarrow{725\ °C} 2\text{LiH}(s) \qquad \Delta H° = -181 \text{ kJ} \qquad \textbf{(16.7)}$$
$$\textit{lithium hydride}$$

$$\text{Ba}(s) + \text{H}_2(g) \longrightarrow \text{BaH}_2(s) \qquad \Delta H° = -171 \text{ kJ} \qquad \textbf{(16.8)}$$
$$\textit{barium hydride}$$

EXAMPLE 16.3
Properties of Hydrogen

In the reaction of hydrogen with an active metal, as shown in Equations (16.7) and (16.8), which reactant is oxidized and which is reduced?

We know that the compounds of hydrogen with active metals are ionic, and we also know the hydrogen as H^- is assigned an oxidation state of -1. Therefore, elemental hydrogen is reduced — the oxidation state change is from 0 to -1. The active metal changes in oxidation state from 0 to $+1$ or $+2$ and is therefore oxidized. Contrary to the situation in most reactions, hydrogen is the "oxidizing agent" in combination with active metals.

---

e. Interaction of hydrogen with transition metals The interaction of hydrogen with transition metals is an area of chemistry that is under active investigation and is not fully understood. In some cases, the bonding is intermediate between metallic and ionic bonding. In other cases, it is difficult to make the distinction between the formation of nonstoichiometric compounds (Section 13.12) and the formation of what are simply solid solutions.

A number of the transition metal hydrides, particularly those of d transition metals, are nonstoichiometric compounds. To give just one example, zirconium reacts with hydrogen to form compounds with two different crystal structures, one with the composition range $\text{ZrH}_{1.73}-\text{ZrH}_{2.00}$ and the other with the composition range $\text{ZrH}_{1.50}-\text{ZrH}_{2.00}$.

The hydrides of the $4f$ transition metals and some $5f$ transition metals have considerable ionic character, but also resemble metals in their appearance and electrical conductivity. Hydrides that retain the properties of metals are sometimes called "metallic" hydrides. The crystal structure of the metal may be expanded to accommodate the hydrogen atoms or ions, or the crystal structure may be different from that of the metal. The "metallic" hydrides are less dense than the parent metals and tend to be brittle. The formation of brittle metal hydrides contributes to the deterioration of metal pipes and vessels that are exposed to hydrogen.

Hydrogen is absorbed by many metals. **Absorption** is the incorporation of one substance into another at the molecular level. Palladium, amazingly, can absorb 800 to 900 times its own volume of hydrogen. The hydrogen enters the crystal structure of the metal to form what is essentially a solution. One method of purifying hydrogen consists of putting it in a thin-walled palladium vessel under slight pressure. The hydrogen dissolves in the metal and escapes on the other side of the wall, where the pressure is less. Other gases are not dissolved by palladium and remain behind. Several other heavy metals and their alloys will also dissolve hydrogen. Apparently H_2 dissociates into atoms at the metal surface. The atoms then diffuse into the metal and occupy interstitial or vacant lattice positions, forming what are called *interstitial hydrides*.

f. Hydrogenation **Hydrogenation** is the addition of hydrogen atoms to molecular compounds. Hydrogenation reactions generally require catalysts and are usually carried out under pressure.

Often the purpose of hydrogenation is to add hydrogen to the carbon–carbon multiple bond in an organic compound or a mixture of organic compounds. A simple example is the hydrogenation of ethylene.

Vegetable oils, such as soybean, cottonseed, and coconut oils, are hydrogenated to produce solid fats for shortening and margarine.

The need for new sources of fuel has focused attention on the hydrogenation of carbon monoxide and carbon dioxide. Under appropriate conditions hydrocarbons can be produced from mixtures of hydrogen and the oxides of carbon. (The production of "synfuels" by such reactions is discussed in Sections 27.11–27.14.)

16.7 HYDRIDES OF REPRESENTATIVE ELEMENTS

As illustrated in Table 16.5, most of the representative elements form simple hydrides with the structures that are expected based upon the electron configurations of the elements to which hydrogen is bonded.

The ionic hydrides are highly reactive compounds. When decomposed by heat they yield the free metals and elemental hydrogen, for example,

$$2NaH(s) \xrightarrow{\Delta} 2Na(s) + H_2(g) \tag{16.9}$$

Table 16.5
Binary Compounds of Hydrogen with the Common Representative Elements The Group I–III compounds, and also SbH_3, BiH_3, SeH_2, and TeH_2, are named as hydrides, e.g., lithium hydride, although SeH_2 and TeH_2 are also called hydrogen selenide and hydrogen telluride. The other compounds are named as follows (going from the top down within the groups): Group IV, methane, silane, germane, stannane, plumbane; Group V, ammonia, phosphine, arsine; Group VI, water, hydrogen sulfide; Group VII, the hydrogen halides, e.g., hydrogen fluoride.

Group	I	II	III	IV	V	VI	VII
Valence Electron Configuration	s^1	s^2	s^2p^1	s^2p^2	s^2p^3	s^2p^4	s^2p^5
	Li$^+$H:$^-$	(BeH$_2$)$_x$*	(BH$_3$)$_2$†	H:C̈:H†	:N̈:H†	:Ö:H†	H:F̈:
	Na$^+$H:$^-$	Mg^{2+}2H:$^-$	(AlH$_3$)$_x$*	H:S̈i:H†	:P̈:H†	:S̈:H†	H:C̈l:
	K$^+$H:$^-$	Ca^{2+}2H:$^-$	(GaH$_3$)$_x$*	H:G̈e:H†	:Äs:H	:S̈e:H	H:B̈r:
	Rb$^+$H:$^-$	Sr^{2+}2H:$^-$	(InH$_3$)$_x$*	H:S̈n:H†	:S̈b:H	:T̈e:H	H:Ï:
	Cs$^+$H:$^-$	Ba^{2+}2H:$^-$		H:P̈b:H	:B̈i:H		

* The subscript x indicates that the actual molecule consists of a number of recurring units of the formula shown.
† Formula of most simple compound; others of a more complicated nature (e.g., C_2H_6, C_3H_8, C_4H_{10}, Si_2H_6) are known.

With water, they react instantaneously, also with the formation of free hydrogen:

$$NaH(s) + H_2O(l) \longrightarrow NaOH(aq) + H_2(g) \qquad \textbf{(16.10)}$$

Note that the ionic hydrides are strong bases — they increase the OH^- concentration in an aqueous solution. The reaction of calcium hydride with water to form hydrogen is utilized both for drying organic liquids and to generate hydrogen for filling weather balloons in the field.

The hydride ion is a very strong reducing agent, stronger than elemental hydrogen. This difference is illustrated by the lack of reaction between molecular hydrogen and water, as compared to the vigorous reaction of hydride ion and water (Equation 16.10).

Hydrogen forms covalent bonds with nonmetals and semiconducting elements, and the hydrides of these elements are molecular compounds. Most of the molecular hydrides listed in Table 16.5 are gases at room temperature. (Only the simplest of the many compounds with hydrogen of the elements of the carbon family are included in the table.) Some of the molecular hydrides are quite stable both thermally and chemically (e.g., CH_4). Others are very reactive (e.g., SiH_4 and GeH_4 are spontaneously flammable in air). The hydrides of beryllium and the elements of the boron family are neither ionic nor simple molecular hydrides. The boron hydrides (Section 30.11) have structures that are not readily explained by the common concepts of bonding.

In addition to the binary hydrides, more complex hydrides of the representative elements are known. Two such compounds are sodium borohydride, $NaBH_4$, and lithium aluminum hydride, $LiAlH_4$, which contain, respectively, the tetrahedral anions, BH_4^- and AlH_4^-. These compounds are widely used as reducing agents in organic chemistry. They are particularly valuable for the selective reduction of the carbonyl groups, $\diagdown C{=}O$ (Section 33.8), in certain types of organic compounds.

The hydrides react by breaking the carbon–oxygen double bond and adding hydrogen across the bond, a necessary step in the syntheses of many organic compounds.

EXAMPLE 16.4
Redox Reactions   In the reaction of sodium hydride with water (Equation 16.10), which reactant is oxidized and which reduced?

We can best answer this question by inserting the oxidation numbers for each element in each substance in the reaction.

$$\overset{+1\,-1}{NaH}(s) + \overset{+1-2+1}{HOH}(l) \longrightarrow \overset{+1-2+1}{NaOH}(aq) + \overset{0}{H_2}(g)$$

Neither sodium nor oxygen has undergone any change in oxidation number. The hydrogen from NaH has increased in oxidation number and therefore NaH is the reactant that has been oxidized. One of the hydrogen atoms from water has decreased in oxidation number from $+1$ to 0, and therefore water is the reactant that has been reduced.

16.8 PREPARATION AND USES OF HYDROGEN

The main industrial sources of hydrogen are water and hydrocarbons, both abundant and relatively inexpensive raw materials. At present, the major hydrogen-producing processes use various combinations of catalysts and elevated temperatures, with the overall result that hydrocarbons in the presence of steam and/or oxygen are converted to hydrogen plus carbon dioxide and/or carbon monoxide.

In the industrial process called *steam reforming,* gaseous or vaporized hydrocarbons react with steam over a bed of nickel catalyst at temperatures of 600° to 1000 °C and pressures of 8–50 atm. The product is a mixture of hydrogen, carbon monoxide, and carbon dioxide. At the present time, the steam reforming of natural gas, which is mostly methane, is the major industrial source of hydrogen.

$$CH_4(g) + H_2O(g) \xrightarrow[\text{pressure}]{\overset{\Delta}{\text{catalyst}}} CO(g) + 3H_2(g) \qquad (16.11)$$

$$CH_4(g) + 2H_2O(g) \xrightarrow[\text{pressure}]{\overset{\Delta}{\text{catalyst}}} CO_2(g) + 4H_2(g) \qquad (16.12)$$

The partial oxidation of hydrocarbons from petroleum also yields mixtures of hydrogen and the oxides of carbon. An older method for producing hydrogen was by the action of steam on coke.

$$C(s) + H_2O \xrightarrow{1000\ °C} H_2(g) + CO(g) \qquad (16.13)$$

Hydrogen of great purity can be prepared by the *electrolysis of water* (an experiment that demonstrates this preparation is shown in Figure 16.2). *Electrolysis* is a process in which electrical energy is used to cause a redox reaction to occur (further discussed in Chapter 23). A small amount of a substance that provides ions as current carriers must be added to the water, which then decomposes as follows:

$$2H_2O(l) \xrightarrow[\substack{\text{NaOH or} \\ H_2SO_4}]{\substack{\text{electrical} \\ \text{energy}}} 2H_2(g) + O_2(g) \qquad (16.14)$$

This process is too expensive to use on a large scale because it consumes a large amount of electricity. However, new, less expensive methods of electrolysis are being developed, and the process may become economically possible.

Hydrogen is also produced industrially in large quantities as a by-product in the manufacture of gasoline. Hydrocarbons of higher molecular mass are converted to mixtures of hydrogen and lower molecular mass compounds more suitable for gasoline. These decomposition reactions require a catalyst and elevated temperatures. Additional hydrogen is available as a by-product of the chloralkali industry (Section 29.8a).

The industrial process for manufacturing ammonia—the largest consumer of hydrogen—requires a 1:3 mixture (by volume) of nitrogen and hydrogen as the starting material, and the industrial process for manufacturing methanol requires a 1:2 mixture of carbon monoxide and hydrogen (Section 27.3). By adjusting the conditions of steam reforming of hydrocarbons (air is added when a source of nitrogen is needed), the gaseous reaction mixtures for these two processes are produced directly. Most commercially produced hydrogen is used within the chemical industry. Table 16.6 summarizes the uses of hydrogen. Well over 100 billion cubic feet of hydrogen is produced for industrial use each year (and this figure does not include hydrogen used directly where it is produced).

At one time, all hydrogen and other gases needed in the laboratory had to be generated at the time of use. The common method for laboratory preparation of hydrogen (Figure 16.3) is by *displacement from dilute acids by metals,* most often by zinc.

$$Zn(s) + 2HCl(aq) \rightarrow H_2(g) + ZnCl_2(aq)$$

In this and all such displacement reactions, the metal is the reducing agent. Gases are now available in small tanks that are safer and more convenient to use than the classical gas-producing reactions.

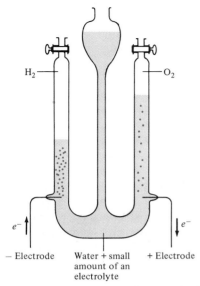

Figure 16.2
Electrolysis of Water Hydrogen is produced at one electrode and oxygen at the other. The volume of H_2 *produced* is twice that of O_2. (The ratio of the volumes of gases *collected* is effected by the relative solubilities of H_2 and O_2 at the temperature of the experiment.)

Table 16.6
Uses of Hydrogen

Major
Ammonia manufacture
Hydrogenation
   of petroleum products
   of vegetable oils
   of CO to give CH_3OH
      (methanol)
   of CO and CO_2 to give
      hydrocarbons
Manufacture of plastics, pesticides,
   and industrial chemicals

Others
Fuel (including rocket fuel)
Reduction of oxide-containing ores to
   give free metals
Welding

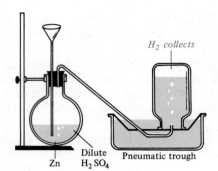

Figure 16.3
Laboratory Preparation of Hydrogen

EXAMPLE 16.5
Redox Reactions

One does not ordinarily regard water as an oxidizing agent, but there are a number of industrially important reactions in which it functions as such an agent. Two such reactions have been described in this section. Pick out those reactions and show the changes in oxidation state that occur.

In the production of hydrogen from hydrocarbons or coke by reaction with steam, water acts as an oxidizing agent. It should be noted that the reactions are carried out at elevated temperatures and in the presence of catalyst. They will not take place under ordinary conditions.

$$\overset{-4+1}{CH_4(g)} + \overset{+1}{H_2O(g)} \xrightarrow[\text{catalyst}]{\Delta} \overset{+2}{CO(g)} + 3\overset{0}{H_2(g)}$$
methane

$$\overset{0}{C(s)} + \overset{+1}{H_2O(g)} \xrightarrow{\Delta} \overset{+2}{CO(g)} + \overset{0}{H_2(g)}$$
coke

[Note that in the first reaction the hydrogen from methane as well as from water is reduced.]

Table 16.7
Outstanding Properties of Hydrogen and Some of Its Compounds

H 1s	Lightest atom; one proton, one electron
strong *bond* H—H	Most reactions of H_2 require high temperature and/or catalysts
+1 H—	Oxidation state +1 in all compounds except ionic hydrides
0 +1 $H_2 \rightarrow H$	Reducing agent
H_3O^+ *hydronium ion*	H^+ hydrated in aqueous solution
M^+H^-, $M^{2+}(H^-)_2$	Ionic hydrides with Li family elements, Mg–Ba
hydride ion $H^- + H_2O(l) \rightarrow OH^- + H_2(g)$ $H^- \rightarrow H, H_2$	H^- is a base and a very strong reducing agent
EH, EH_2, EH_3, EH_4	Molecular hydrides with representative elements of Groups III–VII
transition metal M_aH_b	*a*, *b* not always whole numbers and may vary for same hydride

Table 16.8
Some Reactions of Hydrogen and Its Compounds

With nonmetals	
$2H_2(g) + O_2(g) \longrightarrow 2H_2O(l)$	Can occur with explosive force; used in oxyhydrogen torch
$H_2(g) + X_2(g) \longrightarrow 2HX(g)$	$X_2 = F_2, Cl_2, Br_2, I_2$
$3H_2(g) + N_2(g) \rightleftharpoons 2NH_3(g)$	An important industrial process; catalyst, high pressure, and moderately high temperature needed
With active metals	
$2M(s) + H_2(g) \longrightarrow 2M^+H^-$	M = Li, Na, K, Rb, Cs
$M(s) + H_2(g) \longrightarrow M^+(H^-)_2$	M = Mg, Ca, Sr, Ba
Reduction of metal oxides	
$CuO(s) + H_2(g) \xrightarrow{\Delta} Cu(s) + H_2O(g)$	No reaction with Li and Be family oxides
Reduction of nonmetal oxides	
$2NO(g) + 2H_2(g) \longrightarrow N_2(g) + 2H_2O(g)$	—
With compounds containing multiple bonds (hydrogenation)	

With many compounds containing C=C bonds. Preparation of saturated fats

Reductions of saltlike hydrides	
$2M^+H^- \xrightarrow{\Delta} 2M(s) + H_2(g)$	—
$M^+H^- + H_2O(l) \longrightarrow MOH(aq\ or\ s) + H_2(g)$	—

The outstanding properties and principal reactions of hydrogen and its compounds are summarized in Tables 16.7 and 16.8.

The Hydrogen Economy

An economy based upon the chemical energy stored in hydrogen is one possible alternative to our present fossil fuel-based economy. Only about 10% of the energy needs in the United States are met directly by electricity. For the remainder, we require a fuel that can be transported, stored, and consumed at the site where energy is needed. Hydrogen might fill this role and might also replace electricity in some uses.

It is proposed that energy from nuclear power plants or conventional power plants be used to convert water to hydrogen during periods when demand for electricity is low. Solar energy might also be used. The hydrogen could be transported directly to homes and factories in pipelines as is done with natural gas. In processes that regenerate water, the energy stored in the hydrogen would be utilized to produce electricity in fuel cells (Section 23.16),

$$2H_2(g) + O_2(g, \text{from air}) \xrightarrow{\text{fuel cell}} 2H_2O(l) + \text{electrical energy}$$

or it could be burned.

$$2H_2(g) + O_2(g, \text{from air}) \longrightarrow 2H_2O(l) + \text{thermal energy}$$

Hydrogen-burning automobile engines are also under development. The hydrogen supply might be carried as a liquid or stored in a metal alloy. As noted earlier, many transition metals absorb hydrogen. This hydrogen can be released as needed by heating the alloy. One hydrogen storage system utilizes iron-titanium hydride, $FeTiH_{1-2}$.

The hydrogen for a hydrogen-based economy might be produced by improved methods of electrolysis. Another possibility is the use of thermal energy in a

Table A
Two Proposed Thermochemical Cycles for Hydrogen Production

1. $CaBr_2 + 2H_2O \xrightarrow{730\ °C} Ca(OH)_2 + 2HBr$

2. $2HBr + Hg \xrightarrow{250\ °C} HgBr_2 + H_2$

3. $HgBr_2 + Ca(OH)_2 \xrightarrow{100\ °C} CaBr_2 + H_2O + HgO$

4. $HgO \xrightarrow{600\ °C} Hg + \frac{1}{2}O_2$

- - -

1. $2HI \xrightarrow{425\ °C} I_2 + H_2$

2. $2H_2O + SO_2 + I_2 \xrightarrow{90\ °C} H_2SO_4 + 2HI$

3. $H_2SO_4 \xrightarrow{850\ °C} SO_2 + H_2O + \frac{1}{2}O_2$

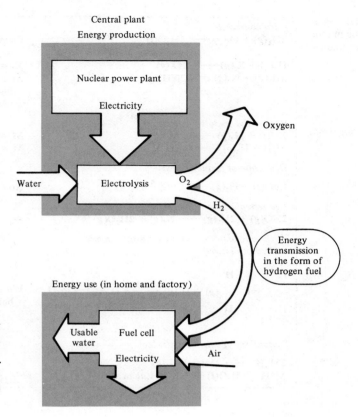

Central plant
Energy production

Figure A
The Hydrogen Economy
One view of how a hydrogen economy might work. (Source: R. A. Horne, *The Chemistry of Our Environment,* New York: Wiley-Interscience, 1978.)

thermochemical cycle—a series of chemical reactions in which only heat and water are consumed and only hydrogen and oxygen are produced. The thermal energy might be the waste heat from a nuclear power plant. All reactants other than hydrogen and oxygen are recycled. Two possible thermochemical cycles are given in the table. (Check for yourself by cancelling like reactants and products that the overall reaction in each case is $H_2O \longrightarrow H_2 + \frac{1}{2}O_2$.)

A hydrogen economy (summarized in Figure A) would have numerous advantages. Hydrogen can be continuously generated, stored, and called upon when needed. Water, the source of the fuel, is widely distributed—nations would not have to fight over it. Moreover, water is regenerated—a homeowner could collect more than 10 L of pure water as the by-product of an average day's production of electricity by fuel cells. Hydrogen combustion and the use of fuel cells produce far less pollution than burning fossil fuels. And the hydrogen would also be available for use in the chemical industry. How, when, and whether or not a hydrogen economy becomes operative depends primarily upon the costs of the processes involved relative to the cost of using other possible fuels.

OXYGEN

16.9 PROPERTIES OF OXYGEN

Oxygen is the first element of Representative Group VI. Molecular oxygen, O_2, is a colorless, odorless, tasteless gas; it boils at $-183\,°C$, 70 Celsius degrees above the boiling point of hydrogen (Table 16.9). Pure gaseous oxygen is slightly more dense than air. Liquid oxygen is pale blue.

The solubility of oxygen in water is low—about 30 mL dissolves in 1 L of water at 20 °C and 1 atm. Both aquatic life and the destruction of organic waste in bodies of water (see An Aside: Water Pollution and Sewage Treatment) are made possible by this solubility, even though it is slight.

The electron configuration of atomic oxygen is $1s^2\,2s^2\,2p^4$—there are six va-

Table 16.9
Properties of Oxygen

		For Comparison	
Molecular properties			
Melting point (°C)	−219	H_2	−260
Boiling point (°C)	−183	H_2	−253
Density (g/L)	1.43	Air	1.29
Bond length (nm)	0.12	H_2	0.0742
Bond dissociation	498	H_2	436
energy (kJ/mol)		N_2	946
Atomic properties			
Ionization energy (kJ/mol)	1314	Na	496
Electron affinity (kJ/mol)	−141	F	−322
Electronegativity	3.5	F	4.0
Atomic radius (nm)	0.074	F	0.071
Ionic radius (O^{2-}) (nm)	0.140	F^-	0.136

lence electrons. Molecular oxygen, despite its even number of electrons (16), has two of them unpaired and is paramagnetic (this exception to the usual pairing of electrons is discussed in Section 24.7). In bonding, the oxygen atom readily shares electrons with nonmetal atoms and with metal atoms that do not lose electrons easily. Oxygen forms single, double, and triple covalent bonds. With metals that lose electrons easily, oxygen gains electrons to form ionic compounds. The following compounds illustrate different types of bonding by oxygen.

$$Ca^{2+} : \ddot{O} :^{2-} \qquad H-\ddot{O}-H \qquad H-\ddot{O}-Cl-\ddot{O}: \qquad CH_3HC=\ddot{O} \qquad :C\equiv O:$$

calcium oxide   *water*   *perchloric acid*   *acetaldehyde*   *carbon monoxide*

The oxidation state of oxygen in such compounds is −2.

Oxygen is second only to fluorine in electronegativity and therefore is assigned a positive oxidation number in its compounds with fluorine (e.g., OF_2, in which fluorine has oxidation number −1 and oxygen therefore has +2). The only other compounds in which oxygen has an oxidation number other than −2 are those in which two or three oxygen atoms are bonded to each other (peroxides, e.g., H_2O_2; superoxides, e.g., KO_2; and ozonides, e.g., KO_3; see Sections 16.13–16.15).

Like most nonmetals, oxygen has a high ionization energy and a negative value for its electron affinity, showing that it gives up electrons with difficulty and gains them easily.

The oxygen–oxygen bond in molecular oxygen is quite stable, with a bond dissociation energy similar to that in molecular hydrogen. The chemical reactivity of molecular oxygen, like that of hydrogen, is moderate. Some reactions of oxygen, notably the rusting of iron, are spontaneous, although slow at ordinary temperatures. In the laboratory and in industry elevated temperatures and also elevated pressures are required to carry out most chemical reactions of oxygen rapidly.

Oxygen forms compounds with all of the elements except (so far as is known) helium, neon, argon, and krypton.

In our perspective view of the periodic table (Section 10.13) we noted that the first element in a representative element family is frequently quite different in its properties from the other family members. Atoms of these first elements are lighter and smaller, and do not have *d* orbitals available for octet expansion. Oxygen is followed in Group VI by the nonmetal sulfur, the two semiconducting elements selenium and tellurium, and the radioactive metal, polonium. The significant

Property	Comments
The only element of the group that is a gas at room temperature.	The free element is a diatomic molecule, O_2, at room temperature. The common forms of sulfur and selenium are octa-atomic molecules, S_8 and Se_8, whereas tellurium has metallic bonding.
Exhibits positive oxidation states only when bound to fluorine.	Positive oxidation states of +4, and +6, e.g., SO_2, H_2SO_4, SF_6, SeO_2, H_2SeO_4, H_6TeO_6, are common for other elements in the group.
Next to fluorine, oxygen has the highest electronegativity of any element.	The high electronegativity accounts for the hydrogen bonding of H_2O in the liquid and solid states. The analogous hydrides of S, Se, and Te do not exist as hydrogen-bonded species.
Formation of compounds with more than two covalent bonds to O is rare.	Because O has six valence electrons and only s and p orbitals available for bonding, it generally forms two covalent bonds. (One exception is H_3O^+.) Compounds with four and six covalent bonds to S, Se, and Te are common.
The oxide ion, O^{2-}, and covalent species where oxygen exhibits a −2 oxidation state, e.g., H_2O, OH^-, are oxidized only with difficulty.	A reflection of the high electronegativity of oxygen. S, Se, and Te in the −2 oxidation state are easily oxidized (good reducing agents).
Forms no chains containing more than three oxygen atoms, e.g., O_3 (ozone), O_3^- (ozonide ion).	Salts containing polysulfide (e.g., S_6^{2-}) and polyselenide (Se_5^{2-}) chains are readily prepared. Polytellurides are also known, but are not very stable. Relative ability to form chains is consistent with element–element bond energies: O—O, 138; S—S, 264; Se—Se, 193; Te—Te, 138 kJ/mol.

differences between oxygen and these elements are summarized in Table 16.10, which we urge you to read thoroughly, for it summarizes some very interesting chemistry.

16.10 REACTIONS OF OXYGEN   **a. Oxygen as an oxidizing agent** In Sections 16.2 and 16.3 it was demonstrated that molecular oxygen is an oxidizing agent. All of the reactions discussed in the following sections are redox reactions in which molecular oxygen is the oxidizing agent and is reduced, in most cases, to oxidation state −2.

b. Combination of oxygen with lithium family elements The reaction of oxygen with lithium gives a compound containing the oxide ion, O^{2-}. Reaction with sodium yields a salt of the less common peroxide ion, $(O_2)^{2-}$, and the larger and heavier family elements, potassium, rubidium, and cesium give salts that contain the still less common superoxide ion $(O_2)^-$:

$$4Li(s) + O_2(g) \longrightarrow 2Li_2O(s)$$
lithium oxide

$$2Na(s) + O_2(g) \longrightarrow Na_2O_2(s)$$
sodium peroxide

$$K(s) + O_2(g) \longrightarrow KO_2(s)$$
(also Rb, Cs)   *potassium superoxide*

These oxides and other compounds that contain oxygen–oxygen bonds are discussed further in Section 16.15.

c. Combination of oxygen with other than lithium family elements Oxygen combines directly with all of the elements except the noble gases, the halogens, and some of the less active metals such as silver, gold, and platinum. Except in the reactions with the lithium family elements described above, the products contain oxygen in the -2 oxidation state.

The compounds formed with nonmetals contain covalent oxygen–nonmetal bonds. The compounds of oxygen with metals may be anywhere on the continuum from ionic to covalent, depending upon the metal and its oxidation state.

Some typical reactions of oxygen with metals and nonmetals are shown in Table 16.11. The properties of oxides are discussed in Section 16.11.

d. Oxidation of compounds Exposure to heat and an ample supply of oxygen can be used to oxidize the lower oxides of elements that can exhibit more than one oxidation state. For example,

$$2Cu_2O(s) + O_2(g) \xrightarrow{\Delta} 4CuO(s)$$
$$\text{\textit{copper(I) oxide}} \qquad\qquad\qquad \text{\textit{copper(II) oxide}}$$

$$2SO_2(g) + O_2(g) \underset{\text{catalyst}}{\overset{\overset{\Delta}{\text{pressure}}}{\rightleftharpoons}} 2SO_3(g)$$
$$\text{\textit{sulfur dioxide}} \qquad\qquad\qquad\qquad \text{\textit{sulfur trioxide}}$$

The combustion of fossil fuels is the reaction of hydrocarbons with oxygen to produce water and carbon dioxide (Section 7.8). For example, methane, the major component of natural gas, yields almost 900 kJ of energy for each mole that is burned.

$$CH_4(g) + 2O_2(g) \longrightarrow CO_2(g) + 2H_2O(l) \qquad \Delta H^\circ = -890. \text{ kJ}$$

The reactions of oxygen with ammonia and carbon disulfide are further examples of reactions in which, as in combustion of hydrocarbons, each of the elements of

Table 16.11
Direct Combination Reactions of Oxygen Carbon monoxide and copper(I) oxide are produced rather than carbon dioxide or copper(II) oxide when the oxygen supply is limited.

Reactions with nonmetals

$$S_8(s) + 8O_2(g) \longrightarrow 8SO_2(g)$$
$$\text{\textit{sulfur}} \qquad\qquad\qquad \text{\textit{sulfur dioxide}}$$

$$P_4(s) + 5O_2(g) \longrightarrow P_4O_{10}(s)$$
$$\text{\textit{phosphorus}} \qquad\qquad\qquad \text{\textit{phosphorus(V) oxide}}$$

$$C(s) + O_2(g) \longrightarrow CO_2(g)$$
$$\text{\textit{carbon}} \qquad\qquad\qquad \text{\textit{carbon dioxide}}$$

$$2C(s) + O_2(g) \longrightarrow 2CO(g)$$
$$\qquad\qquad\qquad\qquad \text{\textit{carbon monoxide}}$$

$$N_2(g) + O_2(g) \longrightarrow 2NO(g)$$
$$\text{\textit{nitrogen}} \qquad\qquad\qquad \text{\textit{nitrogen(II) oxide}}$$

Reactions with metals

$$2Mg(s) + O_2(g) \longrightarrow 2MgO(s)$$
$$\text{\textit{magnesium}} \qquad\qquad\qquad \text{\textit{magnesium oxide}}$$

$$2Cu(s) + O_2(g) \longrightarrow 2CuO(s)$$
$$\text{\textit{copper}} \qquad\qquad\qquad \text{\textit{cupric oxide}}$$
$$\qquad\qquad\qquad\qquad \text{\textit{(copper(II) oxide)}}$$

$$4Cu(s) + O_2(g) \longrightarrow 2Cu_2O(s)$$
$$\qquad\qquad\qquad\qquad \text{\textit{cuprous oxide}}$$
$$\qquad\qquad\qquad\qquad \text{\textit{(copper(I) oxide)}}$$

$$4Al(s) + 3O_2(g) \longrightarrow 2Al_2O_3(s)$$
$$\text{\textit{aluminum}} \qquad\qquad\qquad \text{\textit{aluminum oxide}}$$

the compounds combines with oxygen.

$$4NH_3(g) + 5O_2(g) \xrightarrow{\text{catalyst}} 4NO(g) + 6H_2O(g)$$
$$CS_2(g) + 3O_2(g) \longrightarrow CO_2(g) + 2SO_2(g)$$

The human body uses about 500 L of oxygen each day to "burn" fats and carbohydrates with the production of energy, CO_2, and H_2O. Many materials that will not burn, such as glass, ceramics, clays, and water, contain elements that are already fully combined with oxygen and are at their highest oxidation states.

16.11 OXIDES AND HYDROXIDES

With elements to the left in the periodic table, oxygen forms ionic oxides. With elements to the right, the oxides are molecular compounds (Table 16.12). With elements between these extremes, the bonding in the oxides is intermediate between ionic and covalent. Many oxides can be characterized as either "acidic" or "basic" by the products formed in their reactions with water.

a. Nonmetal oxides Covalent bonding in the nonmetal oxides is indicated by their low melting and boiling points (Table 16.13). Most nonmetal oxides combine with excess water to give oxygen-containing acids, for example,

$$SO_2(g) + H_2O(l) \rightleftharpoons \underset{\textit{sulfurous acid}}{H_2SO_3(aq)}$$

$$SO_3(g) + H_2O(l) \longrightarrow \underset{\textit{sulfuric acid}}{H_2SO_4(aq)}$$

$$P_4O_6(s) + 6H_2O(l) \longrightarrow \underset{\textit{phosphorous acid}}{4H_3PO_3(aq)}$$

A nonmetal oxide that combines with water to give an acid is known as an **acidic anhydride** (anhydride meaning "without water"), or an **acidic oxide.** Acidic oxides react with aqueous bases to give solutions of salts, for example,

$$CO_2(g) + 2NaOH(aq) \longrightarrow Na_2CO_3(aq) + H_2O(l)$$
$$SiO_2(s) + 4NaOH(aq) \longrightarrow Na_4SiO_4(aq) + 2H_2O(l)$$

b. Metal and semiconducting element oxides; amphoteric oxides Oxides derived from cations with large radii are ionic crystalline substances. The most common examples of such oxides are those of the Representative Group I and

Table 16.12
Some Binary Compounds of Oxygen with the Common Representative Elements Elements whose symbols are shown in color form ionic oxides.

Group	I	II	III	IV	V	VI	VII
Valence Shell Configuration	s^1	s^2	s^2p^1	s^2p^2	s^2p^3	s^2p^4	s^2p^5
General Formula	$(M^+)_2O^{2-}$	$M^{2+}O^{2-}$	M_2O_3	MO MO_2	M_2O_3 M_2O_5	MO_2 MO_3	M_2O_5 M_2O_7
	Li	Be	B	C	N*	—	F†
	Na	Mg	Al	Si	P*	S	Cl†
	K	Ca	Ga	Ge	As	Se	Br†
	Rb	Sr	In	Sn	Sb	Te	I†
	Cs	Ba		Pb	Bi	Po	

* Nitrogen also forms N_2O, NO, NO_2, and N_2O_4. Phosphorus forms P_4O_6 and P_4O_{10}.

† Fluorine forms OF_2, O_2F_2, O_3F_2, and O_4F_2, but not F_2O_5 or F_2O_7. Chlorine also forms Cl_2O and ClO_2. Bromine forms various oxides such as Br_2O and BrO_2, but Br_2O_5 and Br_2O_7 are not known. Iodine forms I_2O_4, I_2O_5, I_2O_7, and I_4O_9. The last of these appears to be saltlike.

Table 16.13
Melting and Boiling Points of Some Nonmetal Oxides

Formula of Compound	Name	M.p. (°C)	B.p. (°C)
SO_2	Sulfur dioxide	−75.5	−10.0
SO_3	Sulfur trioxide	16.9	44.8
NO	Nitric oxide (nitrogen(II) oxide)	−161	−151
NO_2	Nitrogen dioxide (nitrogen(IV) oxide)	−11.2	21.2
P_4O_6	Phosphorus(III) oxide	23.8	175
CO	Carbon monoxide	−207	−192
CO_2	Carbon dioxide	−78.5 (sublimes)	—

Group II metals (except for beryllium) and those of certain d-transition elements in their lower oxidation states. Ionic oxides react with water to form metal ions and hydroxide ions:

$$K_2O(s) + H_2O(l) \longrightarrow 2K^+OH^-(aq)$$
$$MgO(s) + H_2O(l) \longrightarrow Mg^{2+}(OH^-)_2(s)$$
$$Na_2O(s) + H_2O(l) \longrightarrow 2Na^+OH^-(aq)$$

A metal oxide that yields a hydroxide base with water is known as a **basic anhydride,** or a **basic oxide.** Basic oxides, including many that are only slightly soluble in water, react with aqueous acids to form cations and water, for example,

$$Na_2O(s) + 2H_3O^+ \longrightarrow 2Na^+ + 3H_2O(l)$$
$$MnO(s) + 2H_3O^+ \longrightarrow Mn^{2+} + 3H_2O(l)$$
$$Fe_2O_3(s) + 6H_3O^+ \longrightarrow 2Fe^{3+} + 9H_2O(l)$$

Not all oxides of metals or semiconducting elements are ionic, basic oxides. Whether a particular oxide might be ionic, covalent, or intermediate in its bonding is generally indicated by the charge-to-size ratio of the cation that would be present if the compound were ionic. Consider, for example, the elements sodium, magnesium, aluminum, and silicon. The information of interest in predicting the nature of their oxides is as follows:

	Valence Electrons	Ion Formed by Loss of Valence Electrons	Atomic Radius (nm)	Ionic Radius (nm)	Charge-to-Size Ratio of Ion
Na	$3s^1$	Na^+	0.186	0.097	10.
Mg	$3s^2$	Mg^{2+}	0.160	0.066	30.
Al	$3s^23p^1$	Al^{3+}	0.143	0.051	59
Si	$3s^23p^2$	$[Si^{4+}]$	0.118	0.026	154

+4 ion not
likely to
form

Recall that the larger the charge-to-size ratio, the greater the polarizing ability of the cation and the greater the covalent character of the bond. On the basis of the information given above, silicon(IV) oxide, SiO_2, must surely have covalent bonding and thus must be an acidic oxide (which it is). The large charge-to-size ratio indicates that aluminum oxide, Al_2O_3, should have a greater degree of covalent character in its bonding than either sodium oxide, Na_2O, or magnesium oxide, MgO. This prediction is borne out by the chemical properties of the oxides. Both Na_2O and MgO are basic oxides, showing that they are ionic compounds. On the other hand, Al_2O_3 exhibits basic properties in the presence of strong acids and acidic properties in the presence of strong hydroxide bases,

$$Al_2O_3(s) + 6H^+ \longrightarrow 2Al^{3+} + 3H_2O(l) \qquad (16.15)$$
$$Al_2O_3(s) + 2OH^- + 3H_2O(l) \longrightarrow 2[Al(OH)_4]^- \qquad (16.16)$$

Substances like aluminum oxide that can act as either acids or bases are described as **amphoteric.** The common amphoteric oxides are listed in Table 16.14. [Formulation of the aluminate ion as a complex ion, $[Al(OH)_4]^-$, best represents its properties. However, this anion is also sometimes written AlO_2^-, which is related to $[Al(OH)_4]^-$ by the loss of two molecules of water. This type of dehydration formula can be written for the anion formed by any of the amphoteric oxides.]

For oxides of the same metal in various oxidation states, the covalent character of the oxide increases with the increasing oxidation state of the metal. This variation can be attributed to the greater polarizing ability of the more highly charged, smaller cation. The increase in covalent character is shown by an increase in the acidic nature of the oxide. For example, in each of the following pairs of oxides, the second is less basic than the first: FeO, Fe_2O_3; Mn_2O_3, MnO_2; Ce_2O_3, CeO_2; UO_2, UO_3. A decrease in basic properties is accompanied by an increase in acidic properties. Thus, although MnO is basic, MnO_3 is completely acidic and reacts with water to give an acidic solution.

$$MnO_3(s) + H_2O(l) \longrightarrow MnO_4^{2-} + 2H^+$$

Most metal oxides are quite stable and are unaffected by high temperatures. The few oxides that do decompose upon heating to yield oxygen are those of the least active metals — mercury, silver, gold, and platinum (see Table 6.2), for example,

$$2HgO(s) \xrightarrow{\Delta} 2Hg(l) + O_2(g)$$

Some oxides of metals in their less stable, higher oxidation states decompose with heat to give oxygen and an oxide of the metal in a lower oxidation state,

$$2PbO_2(s) \xrightarrow{>500\ ^\circ C} 2PbO(s) + O_2(g)$$

c. Metal hydroxides   In writing chemical equations, the precipitates produced when solutions containing metal ions are treated with hydroxide ions are usually formulated as hydroxides; for example,

$$Al^{3+} + 3OH^- \longrightarrow Al(OH)_3(s)$$

**Table 16.14
Amphoteric Oxides and Hydroxides**

Compound	Reaction with H^+ Produces	Reaction with OH^- Produces*
Sb_2O_3 or $Sb(OH)_3$	Sb^{3+} or SbO^+	$[Sb(OH)_4]^-$ or SbO_2^-
SnO or $Sn(OH)_2$	Sn^{2+}	$[Sn(OH)_4]^{2-}$ or SnO_2^{2-}
PbO or $Pb(OH)_2$	Pb^{2+}	$[Pb(OH)_4]^{2-}$ or PbO_2^{2-}
SnO_2 or $Sn(OH)_4$	Sn^{4+}	$[Sn(OH)_6]^{2-}$ or SnO_3^{2-}
Al_2O_3 or $Al(OH)_3$	Al^{3+}	$[Al(OH)_4]^-$ or AlO_2^-
Cr_2O_3 or $Cr(OH)_3$	Cr^{3+}	$[Cr(OH)_4]^-$ or CrO_2^-
ZnO or $Zn(OH)_2$	Zn^{2+}	$[Zn(OH)_4]^{2-}$ or ZnO_2^{2-}
Ga_2O_3 or $Ga(OH)_3$	Ga^{3+}	$[Ga(OH)_4]^-$ or GaO_2^-
TiO_2 or $Ti(OH)_4$	TiO^{2+}	$[Ti(OH)_6]^{2-}$ or TiO_3^{2-}

* Written as hydroxo complex ions or as their dehydration products.

Many metal ions yield precipitates with hydroxide ions, and the compounds formed are referred to as insoluble hydroxides, as opposed to those oxides which are water soluble — the ionic hydroxides of the alkali metals and barium. The precipitates — for example, the substances formulated as $Cu(OH)_2$, $Fe(OH)_3$, $Mg(OH)_2$, and $Cr(OH)_3$ — are almost always gelatinous in nature. All such precipitates contain varying numbers of water molecules. Some, such as $Mg(OH)_2$, are true insoluble hydroxides accompanied by water molecules. Others are simply insoluble *oxides* with water molecules trapped in the solid in stoichiometry equivalent to that of hydroxides. For example, "$Cr(OH)_3$" and "$Ti(OH)_4$" are equivalent to Cr_2O_3 plus three water molecules and to TiO_2 plus two water molecules, respectively. Still other gelatinous "hydroxide" precipitates are oxides combined with water molecules, but *not* in the correct stoichiometry for simple hydroxides; $Fe_2O_3 \cdot H_2O$, sometimes written $FeOOH$, is such a compound ($Fe_2O_3 \cdot H_2O = 2FeOOH$). Although formulating a precipitate as a hydroxide may not always be correct, it is convenient, especially because the actual structures of many "hydroxide" precipitates are not known.

Whatever their structures, however, the hydroxides are chemically equivalent to the oxides. The "hydroxides" are acidic, basic, or amphoteric, like the oxides from which they are derived. Therefore, the following equations

$$Al(OH)_3(s) + 3H^+ \longrightarrow Al^{3+} + 3H_2O(l) \qquad \textbf{(16.17)}$$

$$Al(OH)_3(s) + OH^- \longrightarrow [Al(OH)_4]^- \qquad \textbf{(16.18)}$$

represent the same chemical reactions as Equations (16.15) and (16.16).

EXAMPLE 16.6
Properties of Oxides

Of the three oxides BaO, SeO_3, and Ga_2O_3, one is acidic, one amphoteric, and one basic. Predict which oxide fits into each category and describe simple tests that will either confirm or contradict your predictions.

The highest oxidation state of the elements bonded to oxygen in these three oxides is $+6$ for selenium. The oxide SeO_3 is most likely to be the acidic one — the bonding of Se to O must be covalent, for a $+6$ ion is not likely to form. The lowest oxidation is $+2$ for barium and the charge-to-size ratio for Ba^{2+} is $2/0.134 = 14.9$. Barium oxide is probably ionic and basic. This leaves Ga_2O_3 as the amphoteric oxide, as might be predicted from the large charge-to-size ratio for Ga^{3+}, $3/0.062 = 48$. Barium oxide should react with acids such as aqueous HCl, but not with aqueous bases. Gallium(III) oxide should react with solutions of both strong acids and strong bases. Selenium(VI) oxide should react with solutions of strong bases but not with solutions of acids.

Exercise Of the three oxides P_4O_{10}, Cs_2O, and ZnO, one is acidic, one amphoteric, and one basic. Identify which oxide fits each category. *Answer* P_4O_{10}, acidic; Cs_2O, basic; ZnO, amphoteric

---

16.12 PREPARATION AND USES OF OXYGEN

The composition of clean dry air is given in Table 16.15. Air is the major industrial source of oxygen, as well as nitrogen, argon, neon, krypton, and xenon. Helium can also be separated from air, but at the present time helium is available more cheaply from natural gas; Section 10.16).

Modern liquid air plants utilize a combination of cooling by allowing compressed gas to do expansion work, fractional distillation, and the adsorption of krypton and xenon to fully separate air into its components.

A large percentage of the annual output of oxygen (more than 400 billion cubic feet per year) is produced on the site of its use. Liquid-air plants stand beside steel

Table 16.15
Average Composition of Clean, Dry Air *Source:* S. S. Butcher and R. J. Charlson, *An Introduction to Air Chemistry,* (New York: Academic Press, 1972), pp. 4, 5.

Symbol or Formula	Name	Percent by Volume
N_2	Nitrogen	78.084
O_2	Oxygen	20.946
Ar	Argon	0.934
CO_2	Carbon dioxide	0.0325
Ne	Neon	1.818×10^{-3}
He	Helium	5.24×10^{-4}
Kr	Krypton	1.14×10^{-4}
Xe	Xenon	8.7×10^{-6}
CH_4	Methane	1.6×10^{-4}
H_2	Hydrogen	5×10^{-5}
CO	Carbon monoxide	8×10^{-6} to 5×10^{-5}
N_2O	Nitrous oxide	2 to 4×10^{-7}
SO_2	Sulfur dioxide	7×10^{-7} to $>1 \times 10^{-4}$
NO	Nitric oxide	10^{-6} to 10^{-4}
NO_2	Nitrogen dioxide	10^{-6} to 10^{-4}
HCHO	Formaldehyde	$\leq 10^{-5}$
NH_3	Ammonia	$\leq 10^{-4}$
O_3	Ozone	0 to 5×10^{-5}

mills, the single largest users of oxygen, and beside metal fabricating plants. The oxygen goes directly to the mill or plant, where it is used to speed combustion and raise the combustion temperature (Section 28.9). A relatively new use for on-site-generated oxygen is in wastewater treatment, where it replaces air in the activated sludge process (see An Aside: Water Pollution and Sewage Treatment in this chapter).

Oxygen is also transported to industrial users in cylinders, tanks, or tank cars. The greatest outlet for such oxygen is the chemical industry, where oxygen is consumed in oxidation reactions and the production of oxygen-containing compounds. Other uses are summarized in Table 16.16.

On a laboratory-scale, preparation of oxygen can be carried out by heating an oxygen-containing compound, which gives up all or part of its oxygen. The thermal decomposition of potassium chlorate, the classic laboratory method for oxygen preparation, is aided by a catalyst.

$$2KClO_3(l) \xrightarrow[\text{Fe}_2\text{O}_3]{\Delta, \text{ MnO}_2 \text{ or}} 3O_2(g) + 2KCl(s)$$

potassium
chlorate

This is a hazardous reaction and can lead to explosions, particularly if the hot reaction mixture comes in contact with rubber stoppers, hoses, wood, or other combustible materials.

Table 16.16
Uses of Oxygen

Major Uses	Other Uses
Combustion aid	Life support
In steelmaking	Medical
In metal fabricating	Aerospace
Production of oxygen-containing	Wastewater treatment
chemicals	Oxidizer
	Liquid oxygen (LOX) in rockets
	Oxyacetylene torch (3000 °C)

EXAMPLE 16.7
Preparation of Oxygen

When heated, lead(IV) oxide loses half of its oxygen content, potassium chlorate loses all of its oxygen content, and potassium nitrate loses one-third of its oxygen content. Write a balanced equation for each reaction. Neglecting the cost of heat energy, determine by calculation which compound would be the cheapest laboratory source of oxygen, given the following prices per pound: PbO_2, $24.94; $KClO_3$, $18.81; KNO_3, $12.60.

The equations for the decomposition reactions are

$$2PbO_2(s) \longrightarrow 2PbO(s) + O_2(g)$$
$$2KClO_3(s) \longrightarrow 2KCl(s) + 3O_2(g)$$
$$2KNO_3(s) \longrightarrow 2KNO_2(s) + O_2(g)$$

To compare the cost, we take as the basis the preparation of 1.00 g of O_2 from each source. The cost to produce 1.00 g of O_2 is found by dimensional calculations, as follows:

For PbO_2:

$$\text{Cost of } O_2 = (1.00 \text{ g } O_2)\left(\frac{1 \text{ mol } O_2}{32.0 \text{ g } O_2}\right)\left(\frac{2 \text{ mol } PbO_2}{1 \text{ mol } O_2}\right)\left(\frac{239.2 \text{ g } PbO_2}{1 \text{ mol } PbO_2}\right)$$
$$\times \left(\frac{1 \text{ lb } PbO_2}{454 \text{ g}}\right)\left(\frac{\$24.94}{1 \text{ lb } PbO_2}\right) = \$0.821$$

For $KClO_3$:

$$\text{Cost of } O_2 = (1.00 \text{ g } O_2)\left(\frac{1 \text{ mol } O_2}{32.0 \text{ g } O_2}\right)\left(\frac{2 \text{ mol } KClO_3}{3 \text{ mol } O_2}\right)\left(\frac{122.6 \text{ g } KClO_3}{1 \text{ mol } KClO_3}\right)$$
$$\times \left(\frac{1 \text{ lb } KClO_3}{454 \text{ g}}\right)\left(\frac{\$18.81}{1 \text{ lb } KClO_3}\right) = \$0.106$$

For KNO_3:

$$\text{Cost of } O_2 = (1.00 \text{ g } O_2)\left(\frac{1 \text{ mol } O_2}{32.0 \text{ g } O_2}\right)\left(\frac{2 \text{ mol } KNO_3}{1 \text{ mol } O_2}\right)\left(\frac{101.1 \text{ g } KNO_3}{1 \text{ mol } KNO_3}\right)\left(\frac{1 \text{ lb } KNO_3}{454 \text{ g}}\right)$$
$$\times \left(\frac{\$12.60}{1 \text{ lb } KNO_3}\right) = \$0.175$$

The least expensive compound to use is $KClO_3$.

SUBSTANCES WITH OXYGEN–OXYGEN BONDS

16.13 OZONE

Ozone, O_3, is oxygen in the form of gaseous, triatomic molecules. Oxygen and ozone are **allotropes**—different forms of the same element in the same state (in this case, both gases). Most of the nonmetals tend to "self-link" in this way—that is, to form chains. (The bonding of many atoms of the same element to each other in chains or rings is called *catenation*.)

Earlier we discussed the molecular and electronic structure of ozone. It is a bent, or angular, molecule that can be pictured as having resonance forms (Section 9.14).

Pure ozone is a pale blue gas which condenses to a dark blue liquid that boils at −111.5 °C. Ozone is formed when energy is supplied to gaseous oxygen in the form of radiation, electricity, or heat.

$$3O_2(g) \longrightarrow 2O_3(g) \qquad \Delta H° = 285 \text{ kJ} \qquad \textbf{(16.19)}$$

The characteristic odor of ozone is often noticeable near a sparking electric motor.

Usually, the preparation of ozone is accomplished by passing gaseous oxygen through an electrical field under high voltage. The yield of ozone is low. Equation (16.19) shows that ozone has a much higher energy content than molecular oxygen.

As might be expected, the stability and reactivity of ozone differ from those of oxygen. Ozone is more reactive than oxygen. In general, substances formed in endothermic reactions are reactive, releasing the energy stored in their formation. Ozone tends to decompose to oxygen, in a reversal of reaction (16.19). The decomposition, slow at low temperatures, increases rapidly with rising temperature, is catalyzed by a variety of substances such as platinum and manganese dioxide, MnO_2, and can be explosive.

Ozone is a much more powerful oxidizing agent than ordinary oxygen. When ozone functions as an oxidizing agent, only one oxygen atom from each molecule is reduced; the other two form molecular oxygen, as, for example, in the oxidation of lead sulfide.

$$PbS(s) + 4\overset{0}{O}_3(g) \longrightarrow Pb\overset{-2}{S}\overset{0}{O}_4(s) + 4\overset{0}{O}_2(g)$$

In this reaction, sulfur is oxidized from its lowest oxidation state (-2) to its highest ($+6$).

The oxidation of potassium iodide by ozone is often used as a test for ozone. The iodine liberated from KI is detected by the deep blue color it gives to a suspension of starch in water.

$$2KI(aq) + O_3(g) + H_2O(l) \longrightarrow 2KOH(aq) + I_2(aq) + O_2(g)$$
$$I_2(aq) + \text{starch} \longrightarrow \text{blue complex}$$

(Other oxidizing agents also liberate iodine from KI.)

Ozone performs a vital role in protecting living things on earth from ultraviolet radiation from the sun. In the stratosphere (11–50 km above the earth's surface) ozone is formed from oxygen in a two-step process initiated by radiation.

$$O_2(g) \xrightarrow{hv} O(g) + O(g)$$
$$O(g) + O_2(g) + M(g) \longrightarrow O_3(g) + M(g)$$

(M represents a "third body," usually a nonreactive atom, needed to carry excess energy away from the reactions so that O and O_2 can "stick" together when they collide; see Figure 18.5.)

The ozone cycle in the stratosphere is completed by ozone's absorbing ultraviolet radiation and breaking down into an oxygen molecule and an oxygen atom. Heat is given off in this reaction and serves to warm the stratosphere.

$$O_3 \xrightarrow{hv} O_2 + O + \text{heat}$$

Concern has arisen in recent years over pollutants such as nitrogen oxides (see An Aside: Air Pollution, Smog, and Acid Rain, Chapter 26) and the Freons used as refrigerants and propellants in aerosol cans (see Section 25.4a). These substances can find their way into the stratosphere and destroy ozone there. The primary reason for concern is that a decrease in stratospheric ozone would allow more ultraviolet radiation to pass through the stratosphere and reach the surface of the earth. This type of radiation is known to be a cancer-causing agent, and the occurrence of skin cancer has been shown to increase with increased exposure to ultraviolet radiation. The chemistry of the stratosphere is quite complex and the effects of pollutants that reach the stratosphere are still being evaluated.

Most uses of ozone are dependent upon its strength as an oxidizing agent or its reactions with various organic compounds. Ozone bleaches paper or cloth and destroys harmful chemicals and bacteria in water (see An Aside: Water Pollution and Sewage Treatment). In large amounts, ozone is toxic. Restaurant kitchens once used machines to generate ozone; the ozone could react with and destroy airborne particles of fat and smoke from the cooking. This practice was stopped years ago when it was discovered that ozone is toxic.

16.14 HYDROGEN PEROXIDE

Hydrogen peroxide, H_2O_2, is a colorless, somewhat unstable liquid (m.p. $-0.4\ ^\circ$C, b.p. 151 $^\circ$C) that is harmful to the skin. The two oxygen atoms are joined by a single covalent bond (Figure 16.4), and the reactivity of the compound is reflected in the relatively low O—O bond energy of 142 kJ/mol. The molecules are polar and associated through hydrogen bonding. Hydrogen peroxide is completely miscible with water and is an extremely weak acid, yielding two hydrogen ions per molecule.

$$H_2O_2(aq) \rightleftharpoons H^+ + \quad HO_2^-$$
$$\text{\textit{hydroperoxide ion}}$$

$$HO_2^- \rightleftharpoons H^+ + \quad O_2^{2-}$$
$$\text{\textit{peroxide ion}}$$

The decomposition of either pure hydrogen peroxide or concentrated aqueous solutions of the compound occurs readily, often explosively, with the liberation of oxygen.

$$2H_2O_2(l) \xrightarrow{\text{heat or catalyst}} 2H_2O(l) + O_2(g) \qquad \Delta H^\circ = -196\ \text{kJ} \qquad \textbf{(16.20)}$$

The decomposition is catalyzed by traces of impurities, such as certain metal ions (e.g., Fe^{2+}), finely divided metals (e.g., Pt, Au), various metal oxides (e.g., MnO_2), and also blood and saliva.

The oxygen in a peroxide ion, which is assigned an oxidation state of -1, can be both oxidized to the zero state (in O_2) and reduced to the -2 state (in H_2O), as in reaction (16.20). Therefore, hydrogen peroxide is both an oxidizing and a reducing agent. Actually it is an extremely powerful oxidizing agent and a rather poor reducing agent, acting in the latter role only with very strong oxidizing agents and usually in acidic solution. The reactions with arsenous acid and lead(II) sulfide illustrate the behavior of hydrogen peroxide as an oxidizing agent.

$$\overset{+3}{H_3}\text{AsO}_3(aq) + \overset{-1}{H_2O_2}(aq) \longrightarrow \overset{+5}{H_3}\text{AsO}_4(aq) + \overset{-2}{H_2O}\ (l)$$
$$\overset{-2}{Pb}\overset{}{S}(s) + 4\overset{-1}{H_2O_2}(aq) \longrightarrow \overset{+6}{Pb}\overset{}{SO_4}(s) + 4\overset{-2}{H_2O}\ (l)$$

The conversion of permanganate ion, MnO_4^-, to manganous ion, Mn^{2+}, is an example of reduction by hydrogen peroxide.

$$2\overset{+7}{Mn}O_4^- + 5\overset{-2}{H_2}\overset{}{O}_2(aq) + 6H^+ \longrightarrow 2\overset{+2}{Mn}^{2+} + 5\overset{0}{O}_2(g) + 8H_2O(l)$$

In general, when hydrogen peroxide acts as a reducing agent, *both* water and oxygen are products, with one mole of oxygen formed for each mole of hydrogen peroxide consumed. When hydrogen peroxide acts as an oxidizing agent, water is also a product, but oxygen is not.

The major industrial preparation of hydrogen peroxide is the reaction of oxygen with an organic compound of a type that readily gives up two hydrogen atoms.

Commercial hydrogen peroxide solutions have a concentration of about 30% H_2O_2 by mass. A 3% solution of H_2O_2 is sometimes used medically as an antiseptic. A stabilizer must be added to such solutions to prevent the decomposition of H_2O_2 during storage.

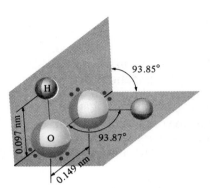

93.85°

93.87°

0.097 nm

0.149 nm

H

O

Figure 16.4
The Configuration of the H_2O_2 Molecule

EXAMPLE 16.8
Properties of Hydrogen Peroxide

Shown below are two reactions of hydrogen peroxide. In which reaction is hydrogen peroxide an oxidizing agent and in which is it a reducing agent? What oxidation state changes occur?

$$HgO(s) + H_2O_2(aq) \longrightarrow Hg(l) + H_2O(l) + O_2(g)$$
$$\textit{mercury(II) oxide}$$
$$N_2H_4(l) + 2H_2O_2(aq) \longrightarrow N_2(g) + 4H_2O(g)$$
$$\textit{hydrazine}$$

In the first reaction, H_2O_2 is a reducing agent, converting mercury from the $+2$ oxidation state to the zero state. The oxygen from H_2O_2, oxidation state -1, is oxidized to the zero state in molecular oxygen. In the second reaction, hydrogen peroxide is an oxidizing agent. Nitrogen in the -2 state in hydrazine is converted to the zero state in molecular nitrogen and the peroxide oxygen is reduced from the -1 state to the -2 state in water. The second reaction occurs with the release of large amounts of energy ($\Delta H° = -642.33$ kJ/mol) and finds use in rocket propulsion.

16.15 PEROXIDES, SUPEROXIDES, AND OZONIDES

The formation of peroxides and superoxides by direct combination of oxygen with lithium family metals was discussed earlier (Section 16.10b). Reactions between strong bases and hydrogen peroxide also yield metallic peroxides, usually as the hydrates; for example,

$$Ba(OH)_2(aq) + H_2O_2(aq) + 6H_2O(l) \longrightarrow BaO_2 \cdot 8H_2O(s)$$

Peroxides are known for all of the lithium family elements and for calcium, strontium, and barium—all very active metals. The peroxides react with acid to produce hydrogen peroxide. This reaction can be used to prepare hydrogen peroxide in the laboratory.

$$BaO_2(s) + H_2SO_4(aq) \longrightarrow H_2O_2(aq) + BaSO_4(s)$$

Peroxide and superoxide ions both contain two covalently bonded oxygen atoms. The peroxide ion has one more electron than the superoxide ion (Table 16.17).

Table 16.17
Types of Metal Oxides All metals form normal oxides. Sodium and barium peroxide are the two most common peroxides. The most stable superoxides and ozonides are those of the heavier alkali metals.

Type	Ion	Average Oxidation State of Oxygen
Normal oxides e.g., Na_2O, MgO	$\left[:\ddot{O}: \right]^{2-}$	-2
Peroxides e.g., Na_2O_2, BaO_2	$\left(:\ddot{O}:\ddot{O}: \right)^{2-}$	-1
Superoxides e.g., KO_2	$\left[:\ddot{O}:\ddot{O}: \right]^{-}$ ↕ $\left[:\ddot{O}:\ddot{O}: \right]^{-}$	$-\frac{1}{2}$
Ozonides e.g., KO_3	$\left[:\ddot{O}:\ddot{O}:\ddot{O}: \right]^{-}$ ↕ $\left[:\ddot{O}:\ddot{O}:\ddot{O}: \right]^{-}$ ↕ $\left[:\ddot{O}:\ddot{O}:\ddot{O}: \right]^{-}$	$-\frac{1}{3}$

Table 16.18
Some Reactions of Oxygen and Its Compounds

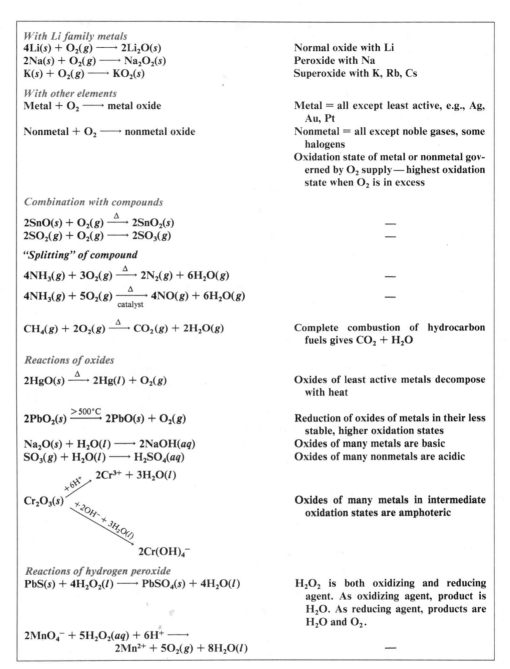

With Li family metals	
$4Li(s) + O_2(g) \longrightarrow 2Li_2O(s)$	Normal oxide with Li
$2Na(s) + O_2(g) \longrightarrow Na_2O_2(s)$	Peroxide with Na
$K(s) + O_2(g) \longrightarrow KO_2(s)$	Superoxide with K, Rb, Cs
With other elements	
Metal + $O_2 \longrightarrow$ metal oxide	Metal = all except least active, e.g., Ag, Au, Pt
Nonmetal + $O_2 \longrightarrow$ nonmetal oxide	Nonmetal = all except noble gases, some halogens
	Oxidation state of metal or nonmetal governed by O_2 supply — highest oxidation state when O_2 is in excess
Combination with compounds	
$2SnO(s) + O_2(g) \xrightarrow{\Delta} 2SnO_2(s)$	—
$2SO_2(g) + O_2(g) \longrightarrow 2SO_3(g)$	—
"Splitting" of compound	
$4NH_3(g) + 3O_2(g) \xrightarrow{\Delta} 2N_2(g) + 6H_2O(g)$	—
$4NH_3(g) + 5O_2(g) \xrightarrow[\text{catalyst}]{\Delta} 4NO(g) + 6H_2O(g)$	—
$CH_4(g) + 2O_2(g) \xrightarrow{\Delta} CO_2(g) + 2H_2O(g)$	Complete combustion of hydrocarbon fuels gives $CO_2 + H_2O$
Reactions of oxides	
$2HgO(s) \xrightarrow{\Delta} 2Hg(l) + O_2(g)$	Oxides of least active metals decompose with heat
$2PbO_2(s) \xrightarrow{>500°C} 2PbO(s) + O_2(g)$	Reduction of oxides of metals in their less stable, higher oxidation states
$Na_2O(s) + H_2O(l) \longrightarrow 2NaOH(aq)$	Oxides of many metals are basic
$SO_3(g) + H_2O(l) \longrightarrow H_2SO_4(aq)$	Oxides of many nonmetals are acidic
$Cr_2O_3(s)$ $\xrightarrow{+6H^+}$ $2Cr^{3+} + 3H_2O(l)$ $\xrightarrow{+2OH^- + 3H_2O(l)}$ $2Cr(OH)_4^-$	Oxides of many metals in intermediate oxidation states are amphoteric
Reactions of hydrogen peroxide	
$PbS(s) + 4H_2O_2(l) \longrightarrow PbSO_4(s) + 4H_2O(l)$	H_2O_2 is both oxidizing and reducing agent. As oxidizing agent, product is H_2O. As reducing agent, products are H_2O and O_2.
$2MnO_4^- + 5H_2O_2(aq) + 6H^+ \longrightarrow$ $\qquad 2Mn^{2+} + 5O_2(g) + 8H_2O(l)$	—

Ozonides of potassium, rubidium, and cesium are produced by the reaction of ozone with the hydroxides, for example,

$$6CsOH(s) + 4O_3(g) \longrightarrow 4CsO_3(s) + 2CsOH \cdot H_2O(s) + O_2(g)$$

The outstanding properties and principal reactions of oxygen and its compounds are summarized in Tables 16.18 and 16.19.

To demonstrate that analyzing a problem according to what is known and unknown is useful for purely chemical problems as well as those involving mathe-

Table 16.19
Outstanding Properties of Oxygen and Its Compounds

O $2s^2 2p^4$	A member of Representative Group VI; six valence electrons
O_2	Oxygen molecule has two unpaired electrons
O_3	Ozone, an allotrope of oxygen and a strong oxidizing agent
$\overset{-2}{O}$	Oxidation state -2 except in compounds with F (e.g., $+2$ in OF_2), peroxides (-1), superoxides ($-\frac{1}{2}$), and ozonides ($-\frac{1}{3}$)
$\overset{0}{O_2} \longrightarrow \overset{-2}{O}$	Oxidizing agent
$\overset{\delta-}{O} \overset{polar\ covalent\ bond}{\underset{}{\rightharpoonup}} \overset{\delta+}{E}$	Second-most electronegative element
M_2O, MO	Ionic oxides with Li and Be family elements
E_2O, E_2O_3, . . . , E_2O_5, E_2O_7	Binary oxides with all elements except He, Ne, Ar, Kr
Fossil fuels, carbohydrates, fats $\xrightarrow{O_2}$ $CO_2 + H_2O$	Essential to combustion of fuels and to living things

matics, the second of the following two examples is worked by the problem-solving method introduced in Chapter 2. At first glance, this may look like a very long solution to a simple problem. Remember that this method illustrates a way of *thinking* about the problem. (Also, without mathematics, more words are necessary.) We have set the problem up assuming a knowledge only of facts that we have discussed thus far. (With greater or different knowledge of descriptive chemistry, other approaches would, of course, be possible.)

EXAMPLE 16.9
Redox Reactions

Oxygen is known to form four anions: O^{2-}, oxide ion; O_2^{2-}, peroxide ion; O_2^-, superoxide ion; and O_3^-, ozonide ion. Show how the oxidation number of oxygen in each of the anions is found, and predict which of them can behave as oxidizing agents, knowing that these are the only anions oxygen forms.

In the oxide ion, O^{2-}, the oxidation number of oxygen is simply the charge, -2. For the peroxide ion, O_2^{2-}, it is the charge divided by 2, or -1; for the superoxide ion, O_2^-, it is the charge divided by 2, which gives an oxidation state of $-\frac{1}{2}$; and for the ozonide ion, O_3^-, it is the charge divided by 3, or $-\frac{1}{3}$.

The peroxide, superoxide, and ozonide ions can all act as oxidizing agents. In each of them the oxidation number of oxygen lies above -2, the lowest state known for the element. Therefore, in a redox reaction oxygen in these ions can decrease in oxidation state, allowing the increase in oxidation state — the oxidation — of another substance. [In fact, all three ions are strong oxidizing agents.] Oxide ion, which is oxygen in it lowest oxidation state, cannot be an oxidizing agent.

EXAMPLE 16.10
Oxides

Based on what you have learned, how do $Na_2O_2(s)$ and $MnO_2(s)$ differ in structure and bonding?

1. Study the problem and be sure you understand it.
   (a) What is unknown?
   The structure and bonding of the two oxides. Are they ionic or covalent compounds? Which atoms shown in the formulas are con-

nected to which other atoms? Are the compounds similar or different in structure and bonding?

(b) What is known?

What the formulas show — that in each compound a metal and oxygen have combined — two oxygen atoms with two sodium atoms, and two oxygen atoms with one manganese atom.

Whatever you know about the chemistry of sodium, manganese, and oxygen.

2. Decide how to solve the problem.

It is necessary to review the facts that you know about the chemistry of the elements involved and choose those facts that apply to the problem at hand.

3. Set up the problem and solve it.

(a) Review the known chemistry that is relevant to structure and bonding.

Sodium is a lithium family element of large atomic radius and is an active metal. Sodium atoms lose electrons readily to give Na^+ ions, and $+1$ is the only common oxidation state of sodium, which is one of the least electronegative elements (0.9).

Manganese is a transition metal and as such has several oxidation states. It is more electronegative (1.5) than sodium.

Oxygen is the second most electronegative element (3.5). It is assigned the oxidation state of -2 in most compounds, but also forms the peroxide ion, $(O\!-\!O)^{2-}$, where it has oxidation state -1. Peroxides form with active metals, which include sodium. Normal oxides of a given metal tend to be ionic for the lower oxidation state of the metal and covalent for the higher oxidation states.

(b) Choose the appropriate structures and give the best prediction for the type of bonding.

First, we must decide whether Na_2O_2 and MnO_2 are oxides or peroxides. If Na_2O_2 were a normal oxide, sodium would have an oxidation state of $+2$. Sodium is a Group I metal and has only one oxidation state, which is $+1$. For this reason, and also because sodium is one of the most active metals, which we know form peroxides, we can conclude that Na_2O_2 is sodium peroxide, and is an ionic compound that contains Na^+ and O_2^{2-} ions.

On the other hand, because manganese is a transition metal and therefore not one of the most active metals, the formation of manganese peroxide seems unlikely. Moreover, if MnO_2 is a normal oxide, the manganese must have an oxidation state of $+4$, which for a transition metal of variable oxidation state is reasonable. Therefore, we conclude that MnO_2 is probably a normal oxide.

It remains to decide whether the bonding in MnO_2 is ionic or covalent, or intermediate between the two. We have learned several different ways to examine this problem. If the compound is ionic, the formation of Mn^{4+} is necessary. Removal of four electrons requires a large amount of energy and the formation of $+4$ ions is not common. Also, the Mn^{4+} ion would have quite a large charge-to-size ratio, as transition metal atoms are not very large to begin with (see Figure 10.4). Therefore, if it existed, Mn^{4+} would be a highly polarizing ion. This suggests that the manganese–oxygen bond is probably covalent. The electronegativity difference between manganese and oxygen is 2, which is right on the borderline between covalent (<2) and ionic (>2) bonding, according to the usual rule of thumb. The best prediction, then, is that in MnO_2 the two oxygen atoms are joined to the manganese atom by highly polar covalent bonds.

Water Pollution and Sewage Treatment

Municipal sewage is what drains from our sinks, washing machines, bathtubs, and toilets, combined with industrial wastewater and, in some places, with the water that runs into storm sewers. Surprisingly, average domestic sewage is 99.94% pure water and only 0.06% dissolved and suspended solids. Taking out as much of that 0.06% as possible before returning the water to the hydrosphere is increasingly important as the population increases.

The pollutants in sewage, as well as in many polluted natural bodies of water, include (1) pathogens—the viruses and bacteria that can cause illness, (2) oxygen-demanding organic wastes, and (3) the by-products of our advanced industrial society—heavy metals, pesticides, fertilizers, and detergents.

The oxygen-demanding wastes are organic materials that come from plants and animals, living and dead. A host of bacteria and other microorganisms are able to destroy these wastes, and do so in both natural waters and sewage treatment plants. The large organic molecules, which contain primarily carbon, hydrogen, nitrogen, oxygen, sulfur, and phosphorus, are broken down by microorganisms to simple harmless molecules and ions. Decomposition of organic matter by bacteria in the presence of oxygen is called *aerobic decomposition*.

aerobic decomposition

$$\text{Organic molecules containing C, H, N, O, S, P} \xrightarrow[O_2]{\text{aerobic bacteria}}$$
$$CO_2,\ H_2O,\ NO_3^-,\ SO_4^{2-},\ HPO_4^{2-},\ H_2PO_4^-$$

As long as enough oxygen is available to decompose all of the organic matter present, natural microorganisms can keep a body of water sparkling and clean.

If the oxygen supply is cut down, or if the supply of organic material increases to the point where aerobic decomposition cannot keep up with it, drastic changes take place. Bacteria that depend upon oxygen die, other bacteria switch to oxygen-containing ions such as NO_3^- for their oxygen supply, and anaerobic bacteria, which require oxygen-free conditions, thrive. Decomposition by bacteria in the absence of oxygen is called *anaerobic decomposition*. The products are as simple as those in aerobic decomposition, but much less pleasant.

anaerobic decomposition

$$\text{Organic molecules containing C, H, N, O, S, P} \xrightarrow[\text{no } O_2]{\text{anaerobic bacteria}}$$
$$CH_4,\ NH_3,\ NH_4^+,\ H_2S,\ HPO_4^{2-},\ H_2PO_4^-,\ \text{sometimes } PH_3$$

In a body of water that has "gone anaerobic," gas bubbles are visible and the smell of rotten eggs characteristic of hydrogen sulfide (H_2S) is in the air, sometimes combined with the smell of phosphine (PH_3), which is equally noxious. The water appears black and is filled with slime. Fish and other oxygen-consuming residents of ponds or lakes that have gone anaerobic eventually die.

Nitrogen- and phosphorus-containing wastes, which include fertilizers and detergents, play a role in upsetting the balance of living organisms and destroying oxygen-demanding pollutants in natural waters. The outcome is what is referred to as eutrophication, or the "death" of, say, a lake or pond. *Eutrophication* is a natural process in which a lake grows rich in nutrients and subsequently gradually fills with organic sediment and aquatic plants. The lake becomes shallower as undecomposed sediment builds up, and plant life thrives within the lake and at its boundaries. The end result of eutrophication, a very slow process when unaffected by man's activities, is the transformation of the lake first to a marsh and then to dry land.

Before water that has been used in households is returned to natural bodies of water, it must be purified. Sewage treatment, with the overall goal of reducing all types of pollutants, takes place in three stages—primary, secondary, and advanced, or tertiary, wastewater treatment.

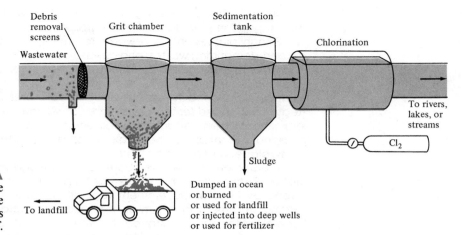

Figure A
Primary Sewage Treatment The sludge is partially digested and the water partly removed before it is disposed of.

The first step in *primary sewage treatment* (Figure A) is to filter out obvious debris such as pieces of paper and wood, and then to get rid of sand, cinders, and gravel (collectively called "grit") that might clog or damage pipes and machinery further along in the treatment plant. Next, organic and inorganic solids are allowed to settle out in large sedimentation tanks. Sometimes chemicals are added to speed up settling and sometimes provision is made for further purification of the *sludge* (the solids that settle out of sewage) by sludge digestion, which utilizes anaerobic decomposition. At the end of primary treatment 40%–60% of the suspended solids and 25%–35% of the oxygen-demanding wastes have been removed.

Secondary sewage treatment (Figure B) goes on to remove up to 90% of the oxygen-demanding wastes. Two methods are used, both of which expose the sewage to a vigorous population of aerobic bacteria and a plentiful supply of oxygen. In the trickling filter method, which doesn't really filter anything, the water runs over a bed of stones 5–10 cm in diameter. Aerobic bacteria and other microorganisms attach themselves to the stones and take organic matter out of the water as it trickles past, while oxygen from the air mixes into the running water. The other method relies on vigorously mixing air (or oxygen generated on site) with the sewage and adding *activated sludge*—sludge from previous batches of sewage that has developed a high population of microorganisms. This is necessary

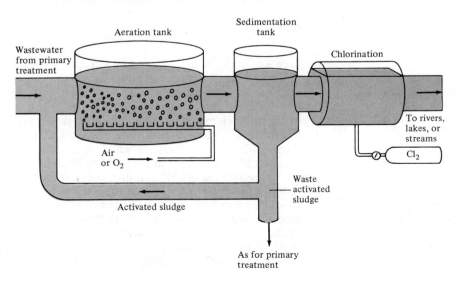

Figure B
Secondary Sewage Treatment

because one batch of sewage cannot produce enough microorganisms during a short stay in the plant to purify itself sufficiently.

Primary plus secondary sewage treatment does a good job of removing solids, oxygen-demanding wastes, and disease-causing organisms. Dissolved ions, including heavy metals and plant nutrients, still remain, as do organic compounds, such as pesticides that are nonbiodegradable and also radioactive materials. Sewage treatment designed to remove specific pollutants that remain after secondary treatment is called *tertiary, or advanced, wastewater treatment.* The major problem currently being attacked by tertiary treatment is the removal of nitrogen- and phosphorus-containing chemicals, which are growth accelerators for microorganisms, algae, and aquatic plants.

There eventually will be about 22,000 sewage treatment plants in the United States. Communities that once discharged untreated sewage are now being forced by Federal Government regulations to build treatment plants. Also, all existing treatment plants must, if necessary, upgrade their treatment to meet Federal water pollution standards. When all plants are in conformance with the government requirements, 57% of the plants will have secondary treatment and 43% will have tertiary treatment. Primary treatment alone is no longer sufficient.

Before its return to natural bodies of water, the treated water is disinfected to kill any remaining pathogens. Chlorine is the usual disinfectant. However, ozone is even more effective, being a stronger oxidizing agent than chlorine. Many plants in Europe generate ozone on site for use in disinfecting the effluent from sewage treatment plants, and this use is expected to grow in the United States.

SUMMARY

OXIDATION AND REDUCTION (Sections **16.2** and **16.3**) Any process in which an oxidation number increases algebraically constitutes oxidation. Any process in which an oxidation number decreases algebraically constitutes reduction. Reactions involving oxidation and reduction, which must always occur together, are known as redox reactions. In such reactions the total increase in oxidation number for all atoms or ions must equal the total decrease in oxidation number for all atoms or ions. An atom, ion, or molecule that causes an increase in the oxidation state of another substance is an oxidizing agent; one that causes a decrease in the oxidation state of another substance is a reducing agent. In a redox reaction, the oxidizing agent is always reduced and the reducing agent is always oxidized (Table 16.1). Therefore an oxidizing agent must contain at least one atom in an oxidized state (i.e., an atom that could have a lower oxidation number), and a reducing agent must contain at least one atom in a reduced state (i.e., an atom that could have a higher oxidation number).

HYDROGEN (Sections **16.4**–**16.8**) Although hydrogen has similarities to elements of both the lithium and fluorine families, it is not a member of any Representative Group. It occurs naturally as the diatomic molecule H_2 (Table 16.2). Heat, high pressure, and catalysts are needed to bring about many of the reactions of H_2, which commonly behaves as a reducing agent. Hydrogen forms compounds with many other elements; these compounds range over the entire continuum from ionic to covalent. The oxidation state of hydrogen is $+1$ in all of its compounds except those with active metals, in which it is assigned the -1 oxidation state. In these compounds it is present as the hydride ion, H^-, which is a very strong reducing agent. (Hydrogen forms the H^+ ion only when it can also share electrons with some other group, as in the H_3O^+ ion in aqueous solution.)

The ionic hydrides are decomposed by heat and react vigorously with water to give alkaline solutions; in both of these reactions hydrogen is produced. Hydrogen forms molecular hydrides with representative elements of Groups III–VII (Table 16.5). With many transition metals, hydrogen forms nonstoichiometric hydrides that have metallic properties. The major industrial preparation of hydrogen is by steam reforming of methane (Equations 16.11 and 16.12). Some uses of hydrogen are given in Table 16.6. The outstanding properties and reactions of hydrogen and its compounds are summarized in Tables 16.7 and 16.8.

OXYGEN; SUBSTANCES WITH OXYGEN–OXYGEN BONDS (Sections 16.9–16.15) Oxygen occurs naturally as the diatomic molecule O_2 (Table 16.9). The molecule is unusual in having two unpaired electrons. In almost all of its reactions, molecular oxygen is an oxidizing agent; its ionization energy, electronegativity, and electron affinity are all high. Oxygen is assigned an oxidation state of -2 in all of its compounds except those with fluorine and those containing O—O bonds: ozone, peroxides, superoxides, and ozonides (Table 16.17). Oxygen, as the first member of Representative Group VI, exhibits many differences in properties from the other members of the family (Table 16.10).

Oxygen forms compounds with all of the elements except (so far as we know) helium, neon, argon, and krypton. It combines directly with many elements (Table 16.11), forming ionic compounds with electropositive metals and molecular compounds with other elements (Table 16.12).

Many ionic oxides are basic anhydrides, yielding OH^- ions in reactions with water. Oxides of nonmetals are molecular compounds and are frequently acidic anhydrides, yielding H^+ ions in reactions with water. Many oxides of metals in their intermediate oxidation states are amphoteric (Table 16.14). The major industrial source of oxygen is liquefied air. Important uses of oxygen are listed in Table 16.15. The outstanding properties and chief reactions of oxygen and its compounds are summarized in Tables 16.18 and 16.19.

SIGNIFICANT TERMS

fossil fuels
oxidation
reduction
oxidation–reduction reactions,
redox reactions
oxidizing agent
reducing agent
heavy water
absorption
hydrogenation
acidic anhydride, acidic oxide
basic anhydride, basic oxide
amphoteric oxide
allotropes

THOUGHTS ON CHEMISTRY
The Chemical History of a Candle

From a lecture given in 1860 by Michael Faraday

There is another experiment which I must give you before you are fully aquainted with the general nature of carbonic acid (CO_2). Being a compound body, consisting of carbon and oxygen, carbonic acid is a body that we ought to be able to take asunder. And so we can. As we did with water, so we can with carbonic acid—take the two parts asunder. The simplest and quickest way is to act upon the carbonic acid by a substance that can attract the oxygen from it, and leave the carbon behind. You recollect that I took potassium and put it upon water or ice, and you saw that it could take the oxygen from the hydrogen. Now, suppose we do something of the same kind here with this carbonic acid. . . . Let me take a piece of potassium, a substance which, even at common temperatures, can act upon carbonic acid, though not sufficiently for our present purpose, because it soon gets covered with a protecting coat; but if we warm it up to the burning point in air, as we have a fair right to do, you will see that it can burn in carbonic acid; and if it burns, it will burn by taking oxygen, so that you will see what is left behind. I am going, then, to burn this potassium in the carbonic acid, as a proof of the existence of oxygen in the carbonic acid . . . you perceive that it burns in the carbonic acid—not so well as in the air, because the carbonic acid contains the oxygen combined; but it does burn, and takes away the oxygen. If I now put this potassium into water, I find that, besides the potash formed (which you need not trouble about), there is a quantity of carbon produced. . . .

I do not know that there is any other elementary substance besides carbon that burns with these conditions; and if it had not been so, what would happen to us? Suppose all fuel had been like iron, which, when it burns, burns into a solid substance. We could not then have such a combustion as you have in this fireplace. . . .

If, when the carbon burned, the product went off as a solid body, you would have had the room filled with an opaque substance, as in the case of the phosphorus; but when carbon burns, everything passes up into the atmosphere. It is in a fixed, almost unchangeable condition before the combustion; but afterwards it is in the form of gas, which it is very difficult (though we have succeeded) to produce in a solid or a liquid state. . . .

It is a striking thing to see that the matter which is appointed to serve the purpose of fuel waits in its action: it does not start off burning, like the lead and many other things that I could show you; but it waits for action. This waiting is a curious and wonderful thing. Candles do not start into action at once, like the lead or iron (for iron finely divided does the same thing as lead), but there they wait for years, perhaps for ages, without undergoing any alteration.

Michael Faraday, *The Chemical History of a Candle: A Series of Lectures Given in 1860,* (as reprinted by Crowell, New York, 1957), pp. 132ff.

QUESTIONS

Oxidation and Reduction

16.1 Define the terms "oxidation" and "reduction." Which of the following changes in oxidation number represent oxidation: (a) $0 \rightarrow +2$, (b) $-3 \rightarrow -2$, (c) $+1 \rightarrow -1$, (d) $0 \rightarrow -2$, (e) $+3 \rightarrow 0$, (f) $-2 \rightarrow +1$, and (g) $+2 \rightarrow +1$?

16.2 What is an oxidizing agent? What is a reducing agent? What happens to each during a chemical reaction?

16.3 What must occur together with any oxidation process? What is the relationship between the total increase and decrease in oxidation number for all atoms in an oxidation–reduction reaction?

16.4 Identify which of the following are redox reactions. Identify the oxidizing and reducing agents in each of the redox reactions.
(a) $LiAlH_4(s) + 4H^+ \longrightarrow Li^+ + Al^{3+} + 4H_2(g)$
(b) $Cr_2O_7^{2-} + 2OH^- \longrightarrow 2CrO_4^{2-} + H_2O(l)$
(c) $3KClO(s) \longrightarrow 2KCl(s) + KClO_3(s)$
(d) $24Cu_2S(s) + 128H^+ + 32NO_3^- \longrightarrow$
$\qquad 48Cu^{2+} + 32NO(g) + 3S_8(s) + 64H_2O(l)$

16.5 Repeat Question 16.4 for the following equations:
(a) $2Na_2O_2(s) + 2H_2O(l) \longrightarrow O_2(g) + 4NaOH(aq)$
(b) $Sn(s) + 2HCl(aq) \longrightarrow SnCl_2(aq) + H_2(g)$
(c) $CaO(s) + H_2O(l) \longrightarrow Ca(OH)_2(aq)$
(d) $N_2O_5(s) + H_2O(l) \longrightarrow 2HNO_3(aq)$

16.6 For each of the following reactions, choose the oxidizing agent and the reducing agent. Show the change in oxidation number which occurs for each substance:
(a) $4Al(s) + 3O_2(g) \longrightarrow 2Al_2O_3(s)$
(b) $Cr_2O_7^{2-} + 3SO_3^{2-} + 8H^+ \longrightarrow 2Cr^{3+} + 3SO_4^{2-} + 4H_2O(l)$
(c) $Fe_3O_4(s) + 4H_2(g) \longrightarrow 3Fe(s) + 4H_2O(g)$
(d) $3PbO_2(s) \xrightarrow{\Delta} Pb_3O_4(s) + O_2(g)$

16.7 Repeat Question 16.6 for the following equations:
(a) $Sn^{2+} + 2Fe^{3+} \longrightarrow Sn^{4+} + 2Fe^{2+}$
(b) $MnO_2(s) + 4HCl(aq) \longrightarrow MnCl_2(aq) + Cl_2(g) + 2H_2O(l)$
(c) $2XeF_2(s) + 2H_2O(l) \longrightarrow 2Xe(g) + O_2(g) + 4HF(g)$

16.8 Aqueous ammonia and nitric acid react to form ammonium nitrate:

$$HNO_3(aq) + NH_3\,(aq) \longrightarrow NH_4NO_3(aq)$$

Is this an oxidation–reduction reaction? The resulting solution can be evaporated to yield the white crystalline ammonium nitrate, and upon further heating NH_4NO_3 undergoes decomposition:

$$NH_4NO_3(s) \xrightarrow{\Delta} N_2O(g) + 2H_2O(g)$$

Is this an oxidation–reduction reaction? Prove your answers by showing any changes in oxidation numbers that occur.

16.9* Potassium permanganate, $KMnO_4$, was once prepared commercially using the two-step process

$MnO_2(s) + KOH(aq) + O_2(g) \longrightarrow K_2MnO_4(aq) + H_2O(l)$
$K_2MnO_4(aq) + O_3(g) + H_2O(l) \longrightarrow$
$\qquad\qquad\qquad KMnO_4(aq) + O_2(g) + KOH(aq)$

(a) Balance these equations. (b) What are the oxidizing agents in the reactions? (c) Combine both balanced equations into an overall equation.

Hydrogen

16.10 Write the electron configuration for atomic hydrogen. What oxidation states would you predict for this element?

16.11 How do the chemical properties of the isotopes of hydrogen differ? How do the physical properties differ?

16.12 The boiling and melting points of molecular hydrogen are very low. Explain this observation in terms of intermolecular forces.

16.13 Many of the reactions of molecular hydrogen described in this chapter do not occur at ordinary temperatures. Why?

16.14 Write the chemical equations for the reaction of $H_2(g)$ as (a) a reducing agent with $WO_3(s)$, $Br_2(g)$, and $C_2H_4(g)$ and (b) an oxidizing agent with $Na(s)$.

16.15 Complete and balance chemical equations for the reaction of $H_2(g)$ with (a) $N_2(g)$, (b) $I_2(g)$, (c) $Ca(s)$, and (d) $SnO(s)$. In which reactions is hydrogen acting as an oxidizing agent and in which is it acting as a reducing agent?

16.16 Write the formula of a binary hydride for each element in the third period (Na–Cl) of the periodic table. Specify the type of bonding in each compound.

16.17 What type of chemical reaction is common for the hydride ion? How does the reaction between $NaH(s)$ and water illustrate this?

16.18 Write chemical equations illustrating the laboratory preparations of molecular hydrogen from a dilute aqueous solution of an acid and from water.

Oxygen

16.19 Write the electron configuration for atomic oxygen. What oxidation states would you predict for this element?

16.20 Draw a Lewis structure for the oxygen molecule using a double bond between the atoms. Does this structure correctly show that the O_2 molecule is paramagnetic?

16.21 What are the important intermolecular forces present in liquid and solid molecular oxygen? Would you expect O_2 to have high melting and boiling points? Why?

16.22 Write chemical equations for the reactions of the elements in the lithium family with molecular oxygen. Name the compounds that are formed.

16.23 Write the chemical equations for the reactions between molecular oxygen (in excess) and (a) $S_8(s)$, (b) $Mg(s)$, (c) $Cu_2O(s)$, and (d) $CH_4(g)$.

16.24 Repeat Question 16.23 for (a) phosphorus, (b) carbon, (c) sulfur dioxide, and (d) tin(II) oxide.

16.25 Write the formula of an oxide for each element in the third period (Na–Cl) of the periodic table. What type of bonding would you expect in each compound?

16.26 Repeat Question 16.25 for elements in the second period (Li–F) of the periodic table.

16.27 Each of the following compounds is a basic anhydride or acidic anhydride: (a) $MgO(s)$, (b) $P_4O_6(s)$, (c) $CO_2(g)$, (d) $SO_2(g)$, and (e) $Na_2O(s)$. Write the chemical equation for the reaction between each substance and water.

16.28 Classify each of the following oxides as (i) probably basic, (ii) probably acidic, or (iii) probably amphoteric: (a) Cl_2O_7, (b) SrO, (c) MnO, (d) Mn_2O_7, (e) Sb_2O_3, and (f) Cl_2O.

16.29 The metallic element M forms a series of oxides: MO, M_2O_3, and M_2O_5. One of these oxides will dissolve only in an acidic solution while the others will dissolve in alkaline or neutral solutions. How can you choose the oxide that is different?

16.30 Write the chemical equation for a laboratory method of preparation of oxygen.

Substances with Oxygen–Oxygen Bonds

16.31 Write the Lewis structure(s) for the ozone molecule. Describe the geometry of the molecule.

16.32 What types of intermolecular forces are present in liquid ozone? Would you expect the boiling point of ozone to be higher or lower than that of oxygen? Why?

16.33 Write the chemical equation for the formation of ozone from oxygen. Is this reaction endothermic or exothermic?

16.34 Write the chemical equations showing the reactions of ozone with (a) $PbS(s)$, (b) $Ag(s)$, and (c) $KOH(s)$.

16.35 Write the Lewis structure for the hydrogen peroxide molecule. Describe the geometry of the molecule. What intermolecular forces are present in liquid and solid hydrogen peroxide?

16.36 Write chemical equations showing the stepwise ionization of hydrogen peroxide as a weak acid. Name all ions formed.

16.37 Is the decomposition of H_2O_2 an example of an oxidation–reduction reaction? What is undergoing oxidation and what is undergoing reduction? Write the chemical equation for the reaction.

16.38* Paintings in which Pb^{2+} salts were used as white paint pigments become dark upon aging because of the presence of hydrogen sulfide in the air. Write a chemical equation for this reaction and explain why the color darkens. How can hydrogen peroxide be used to restore the whiteness? Write the chemical equation for this process.

16.39 Write the chemical equation for the laboratory preparation of hydrogen peroxide from barium peroxide.

Additional Questions

16.40 A student was given two unmarked test tubes, one containing hydrogen and one containing oxygen. A glowing wooden splint was inserted into the mouth of each tube; it burst into flame in the first tube and was extinguished in the second tube. A burning splint was held near the mouth of the second tube and a minor explosion occurred which sounded similar to a sharp bark. Which gas did the student decide was in each of the test tubes?

16.41* Arrange the metals that participate in the following reactions in an activity series: (a) $Li_2O + H_2 \xrightarrow{\Delta} NR$, (b) $2Cu + O_2 \xrightarrow{\Delta} 2CuO$, (c) $Ag + O_2 \xrightarrow{\Delta} NR$, (d) $NiO + H_2 \xrightarrow{\Delta} Ni + H_2O$, (e) $4Li + O_2 \xrightarrow{\Delta} 2Li_2O$, (f) $CuO + H_2 \xrightarrow{\Delta} Cu + H_2O$, (g) $2Ag_2O \xrightarrow{\Delta} 4Ag + O_2$, and (h) $2Ni + O_2 \xrightarrow{\Delta} 2NiO$. NR signifies that no reaction takes place. Where a judgment cannot be made, so indicate.

16.42* Does the activity series given in Table 6.2 predict that the reaction given by the equation

$$Cu(s) + 2H^+ \longrightarrow Cu^{2+} + H_2(g)$$

will occur? We can easily verify in the laboratory that copper will react with nitric and sulfuric acids according to the equations

$$3Cu(s) + 8HNO_3(aq) \longrightarrow$$
$$3Cu(NO_3)_2(aq) + 2NO(g) + 4H_2O(l)$$
$$Cu(s) + 2H_2SO_4(conc) \longrightarrow CuSO_4(s) + SO_2(g) + 2H_2O(g)$$

How can you explain this behavior?

16.43* A chemistry graduate student used the following series of reactions to prepare diborane, B_2H_6:

$$2Na + H_2 \longrightarrow 2NaH \qquad \text{(i)}$$
$$4NaH + B(OCH_3)_3 \longrightarrow NaBH_4 + 3NaOCH_3 \qquad \text{(ii)}$$
$$2NaBH_4 + H_2SO_4 \longrightarrow B_2H_6 + 2H_2 + Na_2SO_4 \qquad \text{(iii)}$$

However, a small amount of oxygen was present in the system used in the experiments. The oxygen reacted with the B_2H_6 and the H_2 formed in reaction (iii).

$$2H_2 + O_2 \longrightarrow 2H_2O \qquad \text{(iv)}$$
$$B_2H_6 + 3O_2 \longrightarrow B_2O_3 + 3H_2O \qquad \text{(v)}$$

caused a serious explosion. Answer the following questions about the substances and the reactions given above. What are the oxidation states of (a) H and (b) O each of the above compounds? (c) Which reactions involve oxidation–reduction? In which reaction is H_2 (d) an oxidizing agent and (e) a reducing agent? Which of the above compounds are (f) ionic and (g) molecular? Into which classification of hydrides do (h) NaH, (i) B_2H_6, and (j) H_2O fall? (k) Would deuterium undergo these same reactions? Which of the above reactions are examples of (l) hydrogenation and (m) combustion reactions?

Answers to Selected Questions

16.3 reduction, same

16.5 (a), (b); oxidizing agents: (a) Na_2O_2, (b) H^+; reducing agents: (a) Na_2O_2, (b) Sn

16.7 (a) Fe^{3+}, Sn^{2+}, Sn from $+2$ to $+4$, Fe from $+3$ to $+2$; (b) MnO_2, HCl, Mn from $+4$ to $+2$, Cl from -1 to O; (c) XeF_2, H_2O, Xe from $+2$ to 0, O from -2 to 0

16.8 no, no change in oxidation number; yes, nitrogen from $+5$ in NO_3^- and -3 in NH_4^+ to $+1$ in N_2O

16.15 (a) $N_2(g) + 3H_2(g) \rightarrow 2NH_3(g)$, reducing agent; (b) $I_2(g) + H_2(g) \rightarrow 2HI(g)$, reducing agent; (c) $Ca(s) + H_2(g) \rightarrow CaH_2(s)$, oxidizing agent; (d) $SnO(s) + H_2(g) \rightarrow Sn(s) + H_2O(g)$, reducing agent

16.24 (a) $P_4(s) + 5O_2(g) \rightarrow P_4O_{10}(s)$, (b) $C(s) + O_2(g) \rightarrow CO_2(g)$, (c) $2SO_2(g) + O_2(g) \rightarrow 2SO_3(g)$, (d) $2SnO(s) + O_2(g) \rightarrow 2SnO_2(s)$

16.26 Li_2O, BeO, B_2O_3, CO_2, NO (or others), none for oxygen, OF_2; Li_2O, ionic bonding and others, polar covalent bonding.

16.28 (a) ii, (b) i, (c) i, (d) ii, (e) iii, (f) ii

16.32 London forces, dipole–dipole interactions; higher

16.37 yes, O from -1 to 0 and from -1 to -2, $2H_2O_2(l) \rightarrow 2H_2O(l) + O_2(g)$

16.40 O_2 in first tube, H_2 in second tube

16.43 (a) 0 in H_2, -1 in NaH and $NaBH_4$, $+1$ in rest; (b) 0 in O_2, -2 in rest; (c) i, iii, iv, v; (d) i; (e) iv; (f) NaH, $NaBH_4$, $NaOCH_3$, Na_2SO_4; (g) H_2, $B(OCH_3)_3$, H_2SO_4, B_2H_6, O_2, H_2O, B_2O_6; (h) saltlike; (i) covalent; (j) covalent; (k) yes; (l) none, (m) iv, v

PROBLEMS
Review of Principles

16.1 Calculate the density of molecular hydrogen at 25 °C and 0.85 atm. What mass can one liter of hydrogen lift under these conditions? Assume the density of the air to be 1.10 g/L.

16.2 What is the ratio of the rates of effusion of gaseous $^1H_2{}^{16}O$ to $^2H_2{}^{18}O$? Use 1 u, 2 u, 16 u, and 18 u as the atomic masses. *Answer* 1.1/1.0

16.3 The half-life of tritium is 12.26 yr. What fraction of a sample of tritium will remain at the end of one year?

16.4 The average atomic mass of naturally occurring hydrogen is 1.00797 u. Assuming only ^1_1H (1.007825 u) and ^2_1H (2.0140 u) to be present, find the percentage of natural abundance of ^2_1H. *Answer* 0.015%

16.5 The crust of the earth is estimated to be about 95% silicate minerals. Calculate the mass percent of oxygen in silica, SiO_2, and in a typical feldspar, $KAlSi_3O_8$. Do these values confirm that the crust is roughly 50 mass % oxygen? (The feldspars and silica make up about 75% of the silicate minerals.)

16.6 The analysis of an ionic compound of sodium showed that it contained 59% by mass of Na and 41% by mass of O. Determine the simplest formula of the compound. Using your knowledge of the oxidation states of sodium and oxygen, determine the true formula and name the compound. *Answer* NaO, Na_2O_2, sodium peroxide

16.7 Molecular hydrogen was prepared by adding 4.0 g Zn to 30.0 mL of 6 M H_2SO_4. The evolved gas was collected over water at 20. °C. The barometric pressure was 738 Torr. What volume of "dry" gas was collected? The vapor pressure of water at 20. °C is 17.5 Torr.

16.8 A sample of barium hydride weighing 10.0 g reacted with water and the resulting solution was diluted to a volume of 400. mL. What is the molarity of the barium hydroxide solution formed? *Answer* 0.180 M

16.9 What volume of dry O_2 at 37 °C and 1.007 atm can be produced from the decomposition of 25 g of $KClO_3$ by the following reaction?

$$2KClO_3(s) \xrightarrow{\text{MnO}_2} 2KCl(s) + 3O_2(g)$$

16.10 A mixture of ozone and oxygen was bubbled through an excess of potassium iodide solution. The mass of the liberated elemental iodine was 101.6 mg. What mass of ozone reacted with the potassium iodide? Assume that the iodide ion does not react with molecular oxygen. *Answer* 19.21 mg

16.11 Silver will not react directly with oxygen at room temperature to form Ag_2O (even though the reaction is slightly exothermic), but will react with ozone according to the equation

$$2Ag(s) + O_3(g) \longrightarrow Ag_2O(s) + O_2(g)$$

Calculate the enthalpy of reaction given that the $\Delta H°$ of formation at 25 °C is -31.05 kJ/mol for $Ag_2O(s)$ and 142.7 kJ/mol for $O_3(g)$.

16.12 Torches using hydrogen and oxygen can produce very high temperatures. Those that electrically decompose the hydrogen molecules into atomic hydrogen before mixing the fuel with the oxygen generate even higher temperatures. The heat of formation at 25 °C is -242 kJ/mol for $H_2O(g)$ and 218 kJ/mol for $H(g)$. Calculate $\Delta H°$ for the reaction

$$2H(g) + \tfrac{1}{2}O_2(g) \longrightarrow H_2O(g)$$

and compare the value to that for

$$H_2(g) + \tfrac{1}{2}O_2(g) \longrightarrow H_2O(g)$$

Answer -678 kJ, 2.80 times as great

16.13 Using the bond energies given in Table 9.12, calculate $\Delta H°$ for the reactions below and predict which form of molecular oxygen would be preferred:

(a) $O(g) \rightarrow \tfrac{1}{8}$
(b) $O(g) \rightarrow \tfrac{1}{2}[O{=}O]$
Answer (a) -142 kJ, (b) -249 kJ; $O{=}O$ favored

16.14 Following are some heats of formation at 25 °C: $H_2O(g)$, -241.818 kJ/mol; $H_2O(l)$, -285.83 kJ/mol; $H_2O_2(g)$, -136.31 kJ/mol; and $H_2O_2(l)$, -187.78 kJ/mol. Calculate the heat of vaporization of both compounds at this temperature and compare the strengths of the intermolecular forces present.

16.15* Pure, dry oxygen was passed through an ozonizer (a commercial instrument for converting oxygen to ozone by means of an electrical discharge) at a gas pressure of 750 Torr, a temperature of 22 °C, and a flow rate of about 30 mL/min. Analysis of the gas coming from the ozonizer showed it to contain 4.5% by volume ozone. What mass of ozone was produced in the passage of 125.0 L of oxygen? *Answer* 10 g

16.16* Aqueous solutions of H_2O_2 undergo the following decomposition:

$$2H_2O_2(aq) \longrightarrow 2H_2O(l) + O_2(g)$$

This is the reaction that makes H_2O_2 an important disinfectant and bleach.

What are the oxidation numbers of (a) H and (b) O in each of the substances? Identify the (c) oxidizing agent and (d) reducing agent.

What types of intermolecular forces are present between molecules of (e) H_2O_2, (f) H_2O_2 and H_2O, (g) H_2O, and (h) O_2?

The oxygen formed from the decomposition of 1.00 g of H_2O_2 is confined to a volume of 25 mL at 25 °C. (i) What will be the pressure?

The enthalpy of formation at 25 °C is -191.17 kJ/mol for $H_2O_2(aq)$ and -285.830 kJ/mol for $H_2O(l)$. (j) What is the heat of reaction?

The heat of formation of $H_2O_2(g)$ is -136.31 kJ/mol and of $H_2O(g)$ is -241.818 kJ/mol. The bond energy of $H{-}H$ is 435.93 kJ/mol and of $O{=}O$ is 498.17 kJ/mol. Calculate the (k) $O{-}H$ and (l) $O{-}O$ bond energies. *Answer* (a) $+1$ in H_2O_2 and H_2O; (b) 0 in O_2, -1 in H_2O_2, -2 in H_2O; (c) H_2O_2; (d) H_2O_2; (e) London forces, dipole–dipole interactions, hydrogen bonding; (f) same as (e); (g) same as (e); (h) London forces; (i) 14 atm; (j) -189.32 kJ; (k) 463.42 kJ/mol; (l) 143.57 kJ/mol

CHAPTER 17

Chemical Reactions in Perspective

The prediction of the products of chemical reactions is an essential part of inorganic and organic chemistry. The purpose of this chapter is to review what we have learned about chemical reactions, add to it, and look forward to what lies ahead.

How do we predict what the products of a chemical reaction might be? To answer this question requires factual knowledge. Many students look upon the prediction of what might happen when chemicals are brought together as a formidable task. With more than 100 elements, all of their possible compounds, and all of the possible reactions of those compounds, how can the study of chemical reactions be organized?

We cannot offer a systematic classification of all possible chemical reactions. There is nothing in chemistry comparable to the kingdoms, phyla, classes, and orders that biologists use to classify living things. What we do have is a body of knowledge based on years of observation of chemical reactions. We also have generalities about chemical properties based on electron configurations and on the positions of the elements in the periodic table. We come to expect that the compounds of certain elements or compounds with certain structures will react in certain ways. For example, we expect an oxide of a metal from the lithium family to give a strongly alkaline solution in water, and we would be quite surprised if it did not do so.

A person studying or using chemistry every day becomes familiar with the properties of the substances that he or she works with regularly. An experienced chemist acquires knowledge based upon direct experience and also develops a good "chemical intuition" that allows the prediction of what might happen in untried circumstances. One of the authors of this book has spent many years studying the chemistry of complex ions and their compounds. He can predict with reasonable certainty the outcome of hundreds of reactions involving complex ions. Another author is an organic chemist. He can make predictions about hundreds of reactions of organic compounds. But given the need to predict, say, the outcome of a reaction between free atoms in the upper atmosphere, each would have to consult books in the library or experts on atmospheric chemistry.

Whatever their specialties within chemistry and whatever the success rate of their predictions, wise chemists soon learn two important lessons. First, careful experiments are always necessary to test predictions. Second, the possibility always exists that what has been accepted as "true" must be revised if new information is uncovered. We have seen an example of this in the discovery that some of the noble gases, long thought to be inert, can indeed form chemical compounds.

17.1 THE STUDY OF CHEMICAL REACTIONS

At the beginning of a study of chemical reactions, limits must be set. Our goal is to review *the most common types of reactions of the simplest types of common compounds*. The emphasis is on inorganic chemistry. Within inorganic chemistry, the emphasis is on reactions in aqueous solution, particularly the behavior of ions in aqueous solution. As you learn more of the facts of chemistry, you will find it easier and easier to make reasonable and correct predictions. Some concentrated effort at memorizing *representative examples* of the simple reactions described in this chapter will be well worthwhile. Note that we said "representative examples" (such as those collected in the tables in this chapter). Do not think that you need memorize *all* of the reactions in the following sections. What is important is to learn to recognize the possible simple *types* of chemical reactions and then, by analogy with some examples, conclude what products are possible in a given reaction.

You have already learned more about chemical reactions and the properties of chemical compounds that govern chemical reactions than you may realize. In Section 6.3 we introduced four general types of chemical reactions—combination, decomposition, displacement, and partner exchange. Based solely upon the qualitative observations summarized in the activity series of metals (Section 6.3c) and the solubility rules for ionic compounds (Section 6.4), it is possible to predict the products of many such reactions. In Chapter 10, we discussed the periodic trends that influence the behavior of the elements in chemical reactions. Chapters 14 and 16 introduced chemical equilibria, the reactions of water, the reactions of ions in aqueous solution, redox reactions, and the reactions of hydrogen and oxygen and some of their compounds. We suggest that you take a few moments now to review some of the chemistry that is summarized in these earlier chapters—the general types of reactions (Table 6.1), the activity series of metals (Table 6.2), the solubility rules (Table 6.3), periodic trends in the properties of the elements (Section 10.13), the rules for assigning oxidation numbers (Table 10.10), the ions present in common strong electrolytes (Table 14.5), the common strong acids and bases (Table 14.7), and the chemistry of water (Sections 14.3, 14.4), hydrogen, and oxygen (Tables 16.7, 16.8, 16.10, 16.11, and 16.18). The chemistry that you have already studied, plus the further exploration of chemical reactions in this chapter, provide the foundation for our stated goal—a knowledge of the most common reactions of the simplest types of common inorganic compounds.

All chemical reactions fall into two major categories—those in which oxidation numbers do not change (nonredox reactions) and those in which oxidation numbers do change (redox reactions). Recognizing the difference and learning to predict the products of simple reactions of each type are important. In Sections 17.3 and 17.4, we use the types of reactions introduced in Section 6.3 to organize reviews of common nonredox and redox reactions. Section 17.5 describes the most common oxidizing and reducing agents.

First, however, because of the importance of knowing when the establishment of equilibrium is significant and when it is not, in the next section we address the question, Is equilibrium established in all chemical reactions?

The six chapters following this one build upon the qualitative understanding of chemical reactions and expand it to include quantitative methods for predicting what will happen in chemical reactions.

17.2 IS EQUILIBRIUM ESTABLISHED IN ALL CHEMICAL REACTIONS?

In discussing the chemistry of water in Chapter 14, we introduced several types of chemical equilibria: the ionization of water (see Equation 14.1), the equilibria of slightly soluble strong electrolytes (Equation 14.9), and the equilibria of weak electrolytes (Equation 14.11). Any chemical reaction that can proceed in either direction is thought of as reversible and is potentially capable of establishing equilibrium.

The classic example of a reversible reaction involves iron and iron oxide (Fe_3O_4), and hydrogen and water. In 1766, Sir Henry Cavendish discovered the element hydrogen by passing steam through a red-hot iron gun barrel.

$$3Fe(s) + 4H_2O(g) \xrightarrow{\Delta} Fe_3O_4(s) + 4H_2(g) \qquad (17.1)$$

When the hydrogen is removed from the reaction system, the reaction proceeds in the direction shown by the arrow in Equation (17.1).

If instead, hydrogen gas is passed over hot iron oxide, the reaction that occurs is exactly the reverse of the one that Cavendish carried out.

$$Fe_3O_4(s) + 4H_2(g) \xrightarrow{\Delta} 3Fe(s) + 4H_2O(g) \qquad \textbf{(17.2)}$$

Here also the reaction proceeds in the direction shown when one of the products—in this case the steam—is removed from the reaction system.

However, if iron and steam are heated together in a closed vessel, the situation is different (Figure 17.1). As soon as traces of iron oxide and hydrogen have formed, they begin to react with each other to form iron and steam; reactions (17.1) and (17.2) proceed simultaneously.

At first, the concentration of steam is relatively high and reaction (17.1) is faster than reaction (17.2). As steam is consumed, this reaction slows down. At the same time, since a supply of hydrogen is building up, the reverse reaction (17.2) between H_2 and Fe_3O_4 speeds up. Eventually, both reactions proceed with equal speed. Once this point is reached, the amounts of the substances present do not change. The reactions have not ceased, but each exactly opposes the other. A state of chemical equilibrium has been established.

The *theoretically* correct answer to the question posed in the heading to this section is, Yes, every chemical reaction is potentially an equilibrium reaction. A finite chance always exists that under the appropriate conditions some product atoms, molecules, or ions will undergo the reverse of the reaction by which they were formed to yield some of the original reactant atoms, molecules, or ions. The more practical question that we can pose is, Are there any circumstances in which chemical equilibrium is relatively unimportant in considering the outcome of a reaction?

To some extent, of course, whether equilibrium is "important" or not depends upon the situation under consideration. For example, cadmium sulfide (CdS) is sparingly soluble in water. If it is to be prepared in the laboratory by precipitation from a solution that contains cadmium ion, an almost 100% yield can be expected and the reaction is thought of as "going to completion."

$$Cd^{2+} + S^{2-} \longrightarrow CdS(s) \qquad \textbf{(17.3)}$$

However, cadmium compounds are poisonous. If we are considering the effect of dumping cadmium sulfide near a public water supply, the concentration of cad-

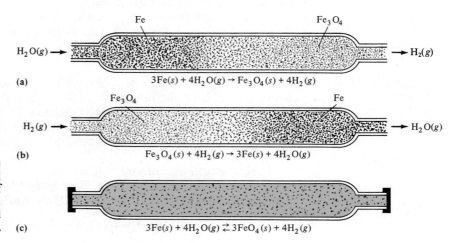

Figure 17.1
A Reversible Reaction The direction of the reaction in (a) and (b) is determined by the removal of a component of the reaction system. Equilibrium is reached in the closed system (c).

(a) $3Fe(s) + 4H_2O(g) \rightarrow Fe_3O_4(s) + 4H_2(g)$

(b) $Fe_3O_4(s) + 4H_2(g) \rightarrow 3Fe(s) + 4H_2O(g)$

(c) $3Fe(s) + 4H_2O(g) \rightleftarrows 3FeO_4(s) + 4H_2(g)$

mium ions that will dissolve due to the reverse of reaction (17.3) and the establishment of the equilibrium

$$CdS(s) \underset{H_2O}{\rightleftharpoons} Cd^{2+} + S^{2-} \tag{17.4}$$

though exceedingly small, might be *very* important.

Reactions that appear to "go to completion" continue until practically all of the reactants have been converted to products (as governed by the stoichiometry of the reaction). Such reactions *do* reach equilibrium, but one set of reactants is present in so much smaller concentration than the other that upon superficial examination it looks as though the reaction has gone only one way.

Many reactions that appear to go to completion are driven by the formation of a product that by its nature is "removed" from the system by becoming unavailable for the reverse reaction. One way in which this happens is the formation of one or more products no longer intimately in contact with the other products. For example, if a reaction takes place in a liquid or solid phase and a product escapes as a gas, the reverse reaction cannot occur to any significant extent. Each of the following reactions is driven in the forward direction by the escape of one product as a gas.

$$NH_4Cl(aq) + NaOH(aq) \longrightarrow NaCl(aq) + H_2O(l) + NH_3(g)$$

$$CaF_2(s) + H_2SO_4(conc) \xrightarrow{\Delta} CaSO_4(s) + 2HF(g)$$

Similarly, the formation of an insoluble precipitate removes ions from aqueous solution so that the reverse of a reaction cannot occur to any significant extent. For example, if solutions of silver nitrate and sodium chloride are mixed, silver chloride will precipitate,

$$Ag^+ + Cl^- \longrightarrow AgCl(s)$$

thereby removing most of the ions from solution.

A general principle that we will have occasion to refer to frequently applies to all chemical equilibria, as well as to all equilibria of other types. Known as **Le Chatelier's principle,** it is stated as follows: If a system at equilibrium is subjected to a stress, the system will react in a way that tends to relieve the stress. The formation of a product that is unavailable for the reverse reaction is a stress to a chemical equilibrium. In response more of that product is formed, meaning that more of the reactant or reactants are used up. In this way, reactions are driven toward completion. Le Chatelier's principle can be utilized by purposefully removing a reaction product with the intention of upsetting an equilibrium and driving a reaction to the formation of more of that product.

A reaction can also be driven to completion by the formation of products so stable with respect to the reverse reaction that the tendency for that reaction to occur is very small. The reactions of strong oxidizing agents or strong reducing agents (Section 17.6) are often "irreversible." For example, lead sulfate and water, the products of the reaction of the oxidizing agent hydrogen peroxide with lead(II) sulfide,

$$\overset{\underset{\displaystyle reducing\ agent}{\downarrow}}{PbS(s)} + 4\overset{\underset{\displaystyle oxidizing\ agent}{\downarrow}}{H_2O_2}(aq) \longrightarrow PbSO_4(s) + 4H_2O(l)$$

are such poor oxidizing and reducing agents that the reverse reaction is of little significance. In other words, a mixture of lead(II) sulfate and water is very stable with respect to the reaction to form lead sulfide and hydrogen peroxide.

One general objective in studying chemical reactions is to recognize reactions that are likely to go to completion. To do so in a qualitative way, we look for gaseous products, products that are insoluble, products that remove ions from an aqueous solution, and the reactions of strong oxidizing agents or strong reducing agents (to be discussed in Section 17.5).

EXAMPLE 17.1
Equilibrium in Chemical Reactions

Which of the following reactions are likely to "go to completion"? For what reason would they do so?

(a) $Pb(NO_3)_2(aq) + 2NaOH(aq) \longrightarrow 2NaNO_3(aq) + Pb(OH)_2(s)$

(b) $2NaHCO_3(s) \xrightarrow[\substack{in\ open \\ vessel}]{\Delta} Na_2CO_3(s) + H_2O(g) + CO_2(g)$

(c) $2KCl(aq) + MgSO_4(aq) \longrightarrow K_2SO_4(aq) + MgCl_2(aq)$

(d) $H_2O_2(aq) + 2Fe^{2+} + 2H^+ \longrightarrow 2Fe^{3+} + 2H_2O(l)$

(a) This is a partner-exchange reaction driven by the formation of a slightly soluble product, lead(II) hydroxide. Formation of a solid phase removes lead and hydroxide ions from solution. Completion is likely.

(b) In this thermal decomposition reaction, two gaseous products can escape, preventing the reverse reaction. Completion is likely.

(c) The reactants and possible products are all strong electrolytes. No reaction will occur and all ions will remain in solution.

(d) This is a redox reaction—hydrogen peroxide is an oxidizing agent (Section 16.14) and iron is oxidized from +2 to +3. Water is not easily reduced (Section 14.2), so we can conclude that this reaction is likely to go to completion.

Exercise Which of the following reactions are likely to go to completion? For what reasons?

(a) $Zn(CN)_2(s) + 2HCl(aq) \longrightarrow ZnCl_2(aq) + 2HCN(g)$

(b) $K_2CrO_4(aq) + 2AgNO_3(aq) \longrightarrow 2KNO_3(aq) + Ag_2CrO_4(s)$

(c) $2KCl(aq) + Mg(NO_3)_2(aq) \longrightarrow 2KNO_3(aq) + MgCl_2(aq)$

Answer (a) Completion. HCN is a gaseous product. (b) Completion. Ag_2CrO_4 is insoluble. (c) No reaction. All reactants and products are strong electrolytes.

17.3 A REVIEW OF NONREDOX REACTIONS

Many common reactions of acids, bases, salts, and simple covalent compounds such as CO_2, SO_2, or NH_3 are nonredox reactions—reactions in which no changes in oxidation number take place.

In the following sections several simple types of nonredox reactions are reviewed, all of which fit into the reaction categories introduced in Section 6.3: combination, decomposition, displacement, and partner exchange. Note that free elements are never reactants or products in nonredox reactions—to undergo a chemical change an element must be oxidized or reduced. [The sole exception is the formation of a complex between a metal and a ligand, such as $Ni(CO)_4$, in which the metal maintains its oxidation state of zero.] Many of the reactions of ions in aqueous solution are nonredox reactions.

The goal of the following sections is to acquaint you with typical, simple reaction patterns: An acid plus a base gives a salt and water, a salt decomposes when heated if a gas can form, and so on. To learn to recognize the possible types of reactions, "read" each equation by thinking about the kinds of chemical compounds that are involved. We have given a labeled example of each type of reaction. Then at the end of the section we have given further examples for additional practice in recognizing reaction patterns. Memorizing all of these equations is *not* necessary. By recognizing reaction patterns you will be able to predict the possible products of many simple chemical reactions without memorizing equations. You will probably not be exactly right every time. But after you have studied this chapter and later ones in this book you should be able to avoid outrageous mistakes like writing equations that include oxidation but no reduction, or not recognizing when no reaction can occur in aqueous solution because all possible products are soluble strong electrolytes.

a. Combination of compounds   Some chemical compounds combine with each other with no change in oxidation number. This occurs when one compound has acidic properties and the other has basic properties. Included in this category are a number of reactions involving water-ion acids and bases (Section 14.8), and acidic and basic oxides (Section 16.11).

The reactions of acidic and basic oxides with water,

$$B_2O_3(s) + 3H_2O(l) \longrightarrow 2H_3BO_3(aq) \tag{17.5}$$

acidic nonmetal oxide   *boric acid*

$$BaO(s) + H_2O(l) \longrightarrow Ba(OH)_2(aq) \tag{17.6}$$

basic metal oxide   *barium hydroxide*

and with each other,

basic metal oxide   *acidic nonmetal oxide*   *salt*

$$CaO(s) + CO_2(g) \longrightarrow CaCO_3(s) \tag{17.7}$$

calcium carbonate

are examples of the nonredox combination of compounds. Similarly, ammonia, a weak base (Equation 14.19), combines with acids to give ammonium salts:

base   *acid*   *salt*

$$NH_3(aq) + HCl(aq) \longrightarrow NH_4Cl(aq) \tag{17.8}$$

ammonium chloride

Acidic oxides combine with bases to give acid salts or salts plus water. [An **acid salt** is formed by a metal cation and a hydrogen-containing anion from a polyprotic acid.]

acidic nonmetal oxide   *base*   *acid salt*

$$SO_2(g) + NaOH(aq) \longrightarrow NaHSO_3(aq) \tag{17.9}$$

sodium hydrogen sulfite

acidic nonmetal oxide   *base*   *salt*

$$SO_3(g) + 2KOH(aq) \longrightarrow K_2SO_4(aq) + H_2O(l) \tag{17.10}$$

potassium sulfate

Take a few moments to think about the further examples given below. Read them thoroughly. Which are the acidic and the basic oxides?

Further Examples of Nonredox Combination

$$SO_2(g) + H_2O(l) \longrightarrow H_2SO_3(aq) \qquad CaO(s) + H_2O(l) \longrightarrow Ca(OH)_2(aq)$$

$$SO_3(g) + H_2O(l) \longrightarrow H_2SO_4(aq) \qquad Na_2O(s) + SO_2(g) \longrightarrow Na_2SO_3(s)$$

$$P_4O_{10}(s) + 6H_2O(l) \longrightarrow 4H_3PO_4(aq) \qquad BaO(s) + SiO_2(s) \xrightarrow{\Delta} BaSiO_3(l)$$

$$CO_2(g) + NaOH(aq) \longrightarrow NaHCO_3(aq)$$

b. Thermal decomposition to give compounds Heating the product of a combination reaction may cause the reaction to go in the opposite direction, especially if a product of the reverse reaction is a gas. Salts of ammonium ion with anions that cannot be reduced (*nonoxidizing anions*) yield ammonia. For example, ammonium chloride decomposes when heated to give ammonia and hydrogen chloride.

$$\overset{\substack{ammonium\ salt,\\ nonoxidizing\ anion}}{NH_4Cl(s)} \xrightarrow{\Delta} \overset{ammonia}{NH_3(g)} + HCl(g) \qquad \textbf{(17.11)}$$

Most carbonates decompose to give carbon dioxide and the metal oxide.

$$\overset{carbonate}{ZnCO_3(s)} \xrightarrow{\Delta} \overset{metal\ oxide}{ZnO(s)} + \overset{carbon\ dioxide}{CO_2(g)} \qquad \textbf{(17.12)}$$

The temperature required for such reactions depends upon the basic and acidic strengths of the two products and upon their volatility. (A *volatile substance* is one that is easily converted to a gas.) The carbonates of the active metals (those metals which form strongly basic oxides) decompose only at very high temperatures, if at all. And because neither BaO nor SiO_2 is volatile, $BaSiO_3$ does not decompose, even at white heat. (Note that the decomposition reactions of ammonium salts of anions that *can* be reduced take a different course. These are redox reactions and are discussed in Section 17.5c.)

Many acid salts also decompose to give gaseous oxides of the nonmetals plus the normal salts and water, for example,

$$\overset{acid\ salt}{2NaHSO_3(s)} \xrightarrow{\Delta} \overset{normal\ salt}{Na_2SO_3(s)} + \overset{water}{H_2O(g)} + \overset{nonmetal\ oxide}{SO_2(g)} \qquad \textbf{(17.13)}$$
$$\underset{\substack{sodium\ hydrogen\\ sulfite}}{} \quad \underset{\substack{sodium\\ sulfite}}{} \quad \underset{sulfur\ dioxide}{}$$

and many hydroxides yield oxides and water when heated.

$$\overset{hydroxide}{Mg(OH)_2(s)} \xrightarrow{\Delta} \overset{metal\ oxide}{MgO(s)} + \overset{water}{H_2O(g)} \qquad \textbf{(17.14)}$$

Take a few moments to think about the further examples given below. Read them thoroughly. Which are the volatile products?

$$(NH_4)_2S(s) \xrightarrow{\Delta} 2NH_3(g) + H_2S(g)$$

$$CaCO_3(s) \xrightarrow{\Delta} CaO(s) + CO_2(g)$$

$$2NaHCO_3(s) \xrightarrow{\Delta} Na_2CO_3(s) + H_2O(g) + CO_2(g)$$

$$2Al(OH)_3(s) \xrightarrow{\Delta} Al_2O_3(s) + 3H_2O(g)$$

c. Nonredox displacement reactions One type of nonredox displacement reaction is the displacement from a compound of one oxide by another. The displaced oxide must be the more volatile oxide, that is, it must be more easily converted to a gas. For example, silicon dioxide (b.p. 2000 °C) displaces carbon dioxide from calcium carbonate.

Less volatile oxide displaces more volatile oxide.

$$\underset{\substack{\text{calcium carbonate}}}{CaCO_3(s)} + \underset{\substack{\text{silicon}\\\text{dioxide}}}{\overset{\substack{\text{less volatile}\\\text{oxide}}}{SiO_2(s)}} \xrightarrow{\Delta} \underset{\substack{\text{calcium}\\\text{silicate}}}{CaSiO_3(l)} + \overset{\text{more volatile oxide}}{CO_2(g)} \qquad \textbf{(17.15)}$$

The formation of one complex ion from another can occur by the displacement of ligands by other ligands if the product is more stable to dissociation than the reactant. For example, many CN^- complex ions are quite stable.

$$\overset{\text{complex ion}}{[HgCl_4]^{2-}} + 4\overset{\text{ligand}}{CN^-} \longrightarrow \overset{\substack{\text{more stable}\\\text{complex ion}}}{[Hg(CN)_4]^{2-}} + 4\overset{\text{displaced ligand}}{Cl^-} \qquad \textbf{(17.16)}$$

Take a few moments to think about the further examples given below. Read them thoroughly. Which are the displaced ligands or volatile oxides?

$$Na_2CO_3(s) + SiO_2(s) \xrightarrow{\Delta} Na_2SiO_3(l) + CO_2(g)$$

$$2Ca_3(PO_4)_2(s) + 6SiO_2(s) \xrightarrow{\Delta} 6CaSiO_3(s \text{ or } l) + P_4O_{10}(g)$$

$$[PtCl_4]^{2-} + 2NH_3(aq) \longrightarrow [PtCl_2(NH_3)_2](s) + 2Cl^-$$

$$[Cu(H_2O)_4]^{2+} + 4NH_3(g) \longrightarrow [Cu(NH_3)_4]^{2+} + 4H_2O(l)$$

EXAMPLE 17.2
Nonredox Reactions The boiling point of boron oxide, B_2O_3, lies above 1500 °C, and phosphorus(V) oxide, P_4O_{10}, sublimes at about 250 °C. Will the following reaction occur?

$$6Na_2B_4O_7(s) + P_4O_{10}(s) \xrightarrow{\Delta} 4Na_3PO_4(s) + 12B_2O_3(s)$$

This reaction is the displacement of one oxide by another. It will not occur because phosphorus(V) oxide is much more volatile than boron oxide, and a more volatile

As vinegar upon nitre,
so is the singer of songs
to a weary heart.
Proverbs 25:20

$$Na_2CO_3(s) + 2CH_3COOH(aq) \rightarrow$$
$$CO_2(g) + 2Na(CH_3COO)(aq) + H_2O(l)$$

Figure 17.2
Biblical Chemistry Vinegar
contains acetic acid. The name
"nitre" was used in biblical times
for sodium carbonate as it is found
in nature. (The word "nitre" has
also been used to refer to potassium
nitrate, which is used in making gun
powder.)

Reactions that go to
completion:

→ **gas**
→ **precipitate**
→ **weak electrolyte**
→ **water**

---

oxide will not displace a less volatile one to form a compound. [Instead, the more volatile oxide will vaporize out of the mixture.]

Exercise   Will the following reaction occur?

$$HgSO_4(s) + 2NaCl(s) \longrightarrow Na_2SO_4(s) + HgCl_2(g)$$

Answer Yes, because the chloride formed is volatile. (This reaction is used in the preparation of $HgCl_2$.)

---

d. Partner-exchange reactions   Partner-exchange reactions follow the pattern

$$AC + BD \longrightarrow AD + BC$$

and occur with no oxidation or reduction of A, B, C, or D. Partner-exchange reactions are most often thought of in connection with the reactions of ions in aqueous solution. In fact, when aqueous solutions of *soluble* ionic compounds are combined and no redox reaction can occur, there are only two possible results: no reaction or partner exchange.

For a partner-exchange reaction to occur, at least one of the products (i.e., AD or BC or both) must remove ions from solution. This can occur in three ways:

1. *Formation of a gas that escapes from solution*

    Carbonates (Figure 17.2), sulfites, and many sulfides react with acids to produce gases—CO_2, SO_2, and H_2S, respectively. The first products of the reactions of carbonates and sulfites are carbonic acid (H_2CO_3) and sulfurous acid (H_2SO_3), which are unstable acids that immediately decompose to give carbon dioxide (CO_2) and sulfur dioxide (SO_2) plus water. For example,

$$\overset{\textit{sulfite}}{CaSO_3(aq)} + \overset{\textit{acid}}{2HCl(aq)} \longrightarrow CaCl_2(aq) + \overset{\substack{\textit{unstable}\\\textit{acid}}}{H_2SO_3(aq)} \qquad \textbf{(17.17a)}$$

$$H_2SO_3(aq) \longrightarrow H_2O(l) + \overset{\textit{gas}}{SO_2(g)} \qquad \textbf{(17.17b)}$$

The overall equation is

$$CaSO_3(aq) + 2HCl(aq) \longrightarrow CaCl_2(aq) + SO_2(g) + H_2O(l) \qquad \textbf{(17.17c)}$$

and the net ionic equation is

$$SO_3{}^{2-} + 2H^+ \longrightarrow SO_2(g) + H_2O(l) \qquad \textbf{(17.17d)}$$

When carbonates, sulfites, or sulfides react with acids, the gases released bubble out of solution and clearly cannot take part in any chemical reactions in the solution. The reactions continue until all of one of the reactants is used up.

2. *Formation of an insoluble product that precipitates*

$$\overset{\substack{\textit{strong}\\\textit{electrolytes}}}{AgNO_3(aq) + NaCl(aq)} \longrightarrow \overset{\substack{\textit{precipitate}\\\textit{slightly soluble salt}}}{AgCl(s)} + NaNO_3(aq) \qquad \textbf{(17.18)}$$
$$Ag^+ + Cl^- \longrightarrow AgCl(s)$$
$$\underset{\substack{\textit{net}\\\textit{ionic equation}}}{}$$

The formation of precipitates in reactions of this type can be predicted by using the solubility rules (Table 17.1) or by quantitative methods (Sections 21.10–21.13).

Generally Soluble
All Na^+, K^+, and NH_4^+ compounds
All Cl^-, Br^-, and I^- compounds
Except those of Ag^+, Pb^{2+}, Hg_2^{2+}, insol.
$PbCl_2$ sol. in hot water
$HgBr_2$, mod. sol.
I^- with heavier metals, insol.
All SO_4^{2-} compounds
Except those of Sr^{2+}, Ba^{2+}, Pb^{2+}, insol.
$CaSO_4$, Ag_2SO_4, mod. sol.
All NO_3^- and NO_2^- compounds
Except $AgNO_2$, mod. sol.
All ClO_3^-, ClO_4^-, MnO_4^- compounds
Except $KClO_4$, mod. sol.
All CH_3COO^- compounds
Except $AgCH_3COO$, mod. sol.

Generally Insoluble
All S^{2-} compounds
Except those of NH_4^+, Li^+, Na^+, K^+, sol.
All O^{2-}, OH^- compounds
Except those of Li^+, Na^+, K^+, sol.
BaO, $Ba(OH)_2$, CaO, $Ca(OH)_2$, SrO, $Sr(OH)_2$, mod. sol.
All CO_3^{2-}, PO_4^{3-}, CN^-, SO_3^{2-} compounds
Except those of NH_4^+, Li^+, Na^+, K^+

3. *Formation of water or a weak electrolyte*

All reactions between water-ion acids and bases are driven by the removal of H^+ and OH^- through the formation of water:

$$\overset{\text{strong base}}{NaOH(aq)} + \overset{\text{strong acid}}{HCl(aq)} \longrightarrow \overset{\text{salt}}{NaCl(aq)} + \overset{\text{water}}{H_2O(l)} \qquad (17.19)$$

(Think of water as HOH to see the partner-exchange pattern of neutralization.)

Many slightly soluble salts dissolve in strong aqueous acids because ions are removed from solution by the formation of molecules of weak acids, for example,

$$\overset{\text{slightly soluble salt}}{Mg_3(BO_3)_2(s)} + \overset{\text{strong acid}}{6HCl(aq)} \longrightarrow 3MgCl_2(aq) + \overset{\text{weak acid}}{2H_3BO_3(aq)} \qquad (17.20)$$

Neither the water in reaction (17.19) nor the weak acid in reaction (17.20) is removed from the solution. However, water and weak acids are weak electrolytes and are so slightly ionized that the ions from which they were formed are no longer available for the reverse reactions.

The partner-exchange type of nonredox reaction is not limited to reactions of ions in aqueous solution. Among the many reactions that can be classified as partner exchange are the reactions of metal sulfides with acids to give hydrogen sulfide,

$$\overset{\text{sulfide}}{Al_2S_3(s)} + \overset{\text{acid}}{6HCl(aq)} \overset{\Delta}{\longrightarrow} 2AlCl_3(aq) + \overset{\text{hydrogen sulfide}}{3H_2S(g)} \qquad (17.21)$$

and the reactions of metal chlorides with concentrated sulfuric acid to give the hydrogen sulfate salt and hydrogen chloride,

$$\overset{\text{chloride}}{NaCl(s)} + H_2SO_4(conc) \overset{\Delta}{\longrightarrow} \overset{\text{acid salt}}{NaHSO_4(s)} + HCl(g) \qquad (17.22)$$

Both of these reactions are driven by the formation of gases. Both can be thought of as the displacement of a volatile acid by a less volatile acid: H_2S by HCl, and HCl by H_2SO_4.

Reactions in which the water molecule is split—hydrolysis reactions—also follow the pattern of partner-exchange reactions. Many compounds consisting of two nonmetals (other than oxygen) or a nonmetal and a semiconducting element react with water to give two acids (or an acid plus an oxide). When this takes place an OH group from the water molecule combines with the less electronegative element of the other compound and the remaining hydrogen atom combines with the more electronegative atom. For example,

$$\overset{\text{binary compound of two nonmetals}}{BCl_3(l)} + 3H_2O(l) \longrightarrow \overset{\text{two acids}}{H_3BO_3(aq)} + 3HCl(aq) \qquad (17.23)$$
$$\underset{\text{boric acid}}{}$$

Boric acid, which is formed from the boron atom and three OH groups, could be written $B(OH)_3$, but in writing the formulas of acids, it is customary to put the symbol for hydrogen at the left of the formula.

Take a few moments to think about the further examples given below. Read them thoroughly. Which is the product that by its formation drives the reaction to completion?

Further Examples of Partner-Exchange Reactions

ionic compounds in aqueous solution

$BaCl_2(aq) + (NH_4)_2CO_3(aq) \longrightarrow BaCO_3(s) + 2NH_4Cl(aq)$

or $Ba^{2+} + CO_3^{2-} \longrightarrow BaCO_3(s)$

$PbCl_2(aq) + Na_2CrO_4(aq) \longrightarrow PbCrO_4(s) + 2NaCl(aq)$

$BaS(aq) + ZnSO_4(aq) \longrightarrow BaSO_4(s) + ZnS(s)$

$Na_2SO_3(aq) + 2HCl(aq) \longrightarrow 2NaCl(aq) + SO_2(g) + H_2O(l)$

$Ba(OH)_2(aq) + 2HNO_3(aq) \longrightarrow Ba(NO_3)_2(aq) + 2H_2O(l)$

others

$AlPO_4(s) + 3HCl(aq) \longrightarrow AlCl_3(aq) + H_3PO_4(aq)$

$CuS(s) + 2HCl(aq) \longrightarrow CuCl_2(aq) + H_2S(g)$

$SiBr_4(l) + 3H_2O(l) \longrightarrow H_2SiO_3(s) + 4HBr(aq)$

EXAMPLE 17.3
Nonredox Reactions

Will the following partner-exchange reactions take place? Give reasons for your answers.

(a) $H_2SO_4(aq) + 2KOH(aq) \longrightarrow K_2SO_4(aq) + 2H_2O(l)$
(b) $H_2SO_4(aq) + 2NaNO_3(aq) \longrightarrow 2HNO_3(aq) + Na_2SO_4(aq)$
(c) $HNO_3(aq) + NaF(aq) \longrightarrow HF(aq) + NaNO_3(aq)$
(d) $Cs_2CO_3(aq) + H_2SO_4(aq) \longrightarrow Cs_2SO_4(aq) + H_2CO_3(aq)$
  $H_2CO_3(aq) \longrightarrow CO_2(g) + H_2O(l)$

(a) Water, a very slightly ionized substance, is formed, thus effectively removing H^+ (from H_2SO_4) and OH^- (from KOH). The reaction will take place.
(b) The reactants and products here are all strong electrolytes and are soluble in water. No reaction will occur.
(c) The formation of the weak acid HF ties up the H^+ and F^- ions from the reactants. The reaction will take place.
(d) The carbonic acid decomposes to yield a gas that escapes, driving the reaction to continue to form carbonic acid. The reaction will take place.

Exercise Will the following partner-exchange reactions occur?

(a) $K_2SO_3(aq) + 2HCl(aq) \longrightarrow SO_2(g) + H_2O(l) + 2KCl(aq)$

(b) $SnSO_4(aq) + H_2S(aq) \xrightarrow{H^+} SnS(s) + H_2SO_4(aq)$
(c) $BaSO_4(s) + 2CH_3COOH(aq) \longrightarrow Ba(CH_3COO)_2(aq) + H_2SO_4(aq)$

Explain your reasoning.
Answer (a) Yes, formation of a gas; (b) yes, formation of a precipitate; (c) no, this would be formation of a soluble salt from an insoluble salt.

EXAMPLE 17.4
Nonredox Reactions

You have a white water-soluble substance which you think contains silver ion, Ag^+. To test for that ion, you dissolve a small amount of the material in water and add some dilute hydrochloric acid solution. A white precipitate forms. Your textbook describes silver chloride, AgCl, as a white insoluble compound. On the basis of your information, you conclude that the original material indeed does contain silver ion. Is this conclusion justified?

No, because other ions (e.g., Hg_2^{2+}, Pb^{2+}, Cu^+) also give white insoluble chlorides. You have shown that Ag^+ *may* be present. To *prove* that it is present you must fnd a more specific test for Ag^+ or prove that other ions that give white insoluble chlorides (such as Hg_2^{2+}, Pb^{2+}, or Cu^+) are *not* present.

Exercise You have a mixture of the salts $BaCO_3$ and $PbSO_4$, both of which are insoluble in water. By what simple partner-exchange reaction can these salts be separated? *Answer* Reaction with dilute strong acid (e.g., HCl, HNO_3); carbonate will react to give H_2CO_3, which decomposes to CO_2 and H_2O:

$$BaCO_3(s) + 2HNO_3(aq) \longrightarrow Ba(NO_3)_2(aq) + CO_2(g) + H_2O(l)$$

Sulfate will not react.

EXAMPLE 17.5
Nonredox Reactions

Predict the products of each of the following nonredox reactions, write the balanced equations, and identify the type of reaction that occurs. If no reaction can occur, give a reason.

(a) $NH_3(g) + HNO_3(aq) \longrightarrow$ (d) $Na_2O(s) + H_2O(l) \longrightarrow$

(b) $Na_2SO_3(s) + SiO_2(s) \xrightarrow{\Delta}$ (e) $Pb(NO_3)_2(aq) + Na_2S(aq) \longrightarrow$

(c) $SO_2(g) + Ba(OH)_2(aq) \longrightarrow$

(a) Ammonia, a basic substance, combines with acids to give ammonium salts:

$$NH_3(g) + HNO_3(aq) \longrightarrow NH_4NO_3(aq)$$

This is a combination reaction.

(b) Silicon dioxide, which is not volatile, displaces the volatile oxide SO_2 from sodium sulfite:

$$Na_2SO_3(s) + SiO_2(s) \longrightarrow Na_2SiO_3(s) + SO_2(g)$$

This is a displacement reaction.

(c) Sulfur dioxide, the oxide of a nonmetal, is an acidic oxide, and can react with a base:

$$SO_2(g) + Ba(OH)_2(aq) \longrightarrow BaSO_3(s) + H_2O(l)$$

Formation of a salt from an acidic oxide plus a base is classified as a combination reaction. The insolubility of the salt is also a driving force for this reaction.

(d) The oxides of the active metals are basic and react with water to give hydroxides in solution:

$$Na_2O(s) + H_2O(l) \longrightarrow 2NaOH(aq)$$

This is a combination reaction.

(e) A reaction between two soluble salts can occur only if partner exchange removes ions from solution. In this case, a precipitate of an insoluble sulfide will form.

$$Pb(NO_3)_2(aq) + Na_2S(aq) \longrightarrow PbS(s) + 2NaNO_3(aq)$$

This is a partner-exchange reaction.

Exercise Predict the products of each of the following nonredox reactions:

(a) $H_2SO_4(conc) + NaCl(s) \rightarrow$ (b) $BaSO_4(s) + HCl(aq) \rightarrow$ (c) $[Zn(NH_3)_4]^{2+} + CN^- \rightarrow$

Write the balanced equations and identify the type of reaction that occurs. If no reaction occurs, give a reason. *Answer* (a) $H_2SO_4(conc) + NaCl(s) \rightarrow$ $NaHSO_4(s) + HCl(g)$, partner exchange, formation of a gas; (b) no reaction (the reverse reaction is favorable because $BaSO_4$ is quite insoluble); (c) $[Zn(NH_3)_4]^{2+} + 4CN^- \longrightarrow [Zn(CN)_4]^{2-} + 4NH_3(aq)$, partner-exchange, formation of more stable complex ion.

Table 17.2 summarizes and gives examples of the simple types of nonredox reactions discussed in this section.

Table 17.2
Inorganic Reactions in Which No Changes in Oxidation Number Occur

Combination of Compounds	
$SO_3(g) + H_2O(l) \longrightarrow H_2SO_4(l)$	Acidic oxide + water $\longrightarrow$ acid
$CaO(s) + H_2O(l) \longrightarrow Ca(OH)_2(s)$	Basic oxide + water $\longrightarrow$ base
$SO_3(g) + CaO(s) \longrightarrow CaSO_4(s)$	Acidic oxide + basic oxide $\longrightarrow$ salt
$NH_3(g) + HCl(g) \longrightarrow NH_4Cl(s)$	Ammonia + acid $\longrightarrow$ salt
$SO_2(g) + NaOH(aq) \longrightarrow NaHSO_3(aq)$	Acidic oxide + base $\longrightarrow$ salt

Decomposition to Give Compounds	
$NH_4Cl(s) \xrightarrow{\Delta} NH_3(g) + HCl(g)$	Ammonium salts containing *nonoxidizing* anions
$CaCO_3(s) \xrightarrow{\Delta} CaO(s) + CO_2(g)$	Except carbonates of Na, K, Rb, Cs, which form the most basic oxides.
$2NaHSO_3(s) \xrightarrow{\Delta} Na_2SO_3(s) + H_2O(g) + SO_2(g)$	All hydrogen sulfites
$2NaHCO_3(s) \xrightarrow{\Delta} Na_2CO_3(s) + H_2O(g) + CO_2(g)$	All hydrogen carbonates
$Mg(OH)_2(s) \xrightarrow{\Delta} MgO(s) + H_2O(g)$	Except hydroxides of Na, K, Rb, Cs

Nonredox Displacement	
$CaCO_3(s) + SiO_2(s) \xrightarrow{\Delta} CaSiO_3(l) + CO_2(g)$	Of a more volatile oxide by a less volatile oxide
$[HgCl_4]^{2-} + 4CN^- \longrightarrow [Hg(CN)_4]^{2-} + 4Cl^-$	Of a ligand in a complex ion to give a more stable complex ion.

Partner-Exchange Reactions between Ions in Aqueous Solution	
$Na_2CO_3(aq) + 2HCl(aq) \longrightarrow$ $2NaCl(aq) + CO_2(g) + H_2O(l)$	*Formation of a gas* — reaction of metal carbonates, sulfites, and sulfides with acids
$Na_2SO_3(aq) + 2HCl(aq) \longrightarrow$ $2NaCl(aq) + SO_2(g) + H_2O(l)$	
$Na_2S(aq) + 2HCl(aq) \longrightarrow 2NaCl(aq) + H_2S(g)$	
$AgNO_3(aq) + NaCl(aq) \longrightarrow AgCl(s) + NaNO_3(aq)$	*Formation of a precipitate*
$HCl(aq) + NaOH(aq) \longrightarrow NaCl(aq) + H_2O(l)$	*Formation of water* — all neutralizations of H^+ acid and OH^- base
$Mg_3(BO_3)_2(s) + 6HCl(aq) \longrightarrow$ $3MgCl_2(aq) + 2H_3BO_3(aq)$	*Formation of a weak electrolyte* — salt of weak acid + stronger acid $\rightarrow$ soluble salt + weak acid

Other Partner-Exchange Reactions	
$Al_2S_3(s) + 6HCl(aq) \longrightarrow 2AlCl_3(aq) + 3H_2S(g)$	Slightly soluble sulfide + acid $\rightarrow$ metal salt + H_2S (except with *very* slightly soluble sulfides, e.g., HgS)
$NaCl(s) + H_2SO_4(conc) \longrightarrow NaHSO_4(s) + HCl(g)$	Solid chloride + conc. sulfuric acid $\rightarrow$ metal hydrogen sulfate + HCl
$BCl_3(l) + 3H_2O(l) \longrightarrow H_3BO_3(aq) + 3HCl(aq)$	Hydrolysis, compound of two nonmetals $\rightarrow$ two acids.

17.4 A REVIEW OF REDOX REACTIONS

One way to recognize a redox reaction is by the presence of a free element as a reactant or product. Another way is by recognizing the presence of a reactant that is an oxidizing or reducing agent. Recall that an oxidizing agent contains an element that can have a lower oxidation state and a reducing agent contains an element that can have a higher oxidation state. Of course, the most certain way to recognize a redox reaction, *if* all of the reactants and products are known, is by determining whether changes in oxidation number have in fact occurred.

Given the need to predict the products of a redox reaction, we can look for elements or oxidizing or reducing agents among the reactants, determine what changes in oxidation number are possible, and then choose the most likely products. It is very useful to know the products usually formed by the more common oxidizing and reducing agents. These are discussed in Section 17.5.

Reactions involving free elements:
always redox
Partner-exchange reactions:
never redox

Many simple redox reactions are combination, decomposition, or displacement reactions, and many of these involve free elements as reactants or products. Such reactions are reviewed below. (Note that partner-exchange reactions can *never* be redox reactions.) A great many redox reactions are quite complex, however, and there is no value in attempting to categorize such reactions here.

A knowledge of the common oxidation states of the common elements in their typical compounds is of great value in understanding redox reactions and in predicting their outcome. Table 17.3 summarizes these common oxidation states, and we recommend that you learn them. In using the table, it is helpful to keep in mind the relationship between the positions of the elements in the periodic table and their oxidation states. For the representative elements (except for oxygen and fluorine, which are the most electronegative elements), the highest positive oxidation state equals the group number. The negative oxidation states of the nonmetals, you may have noticed, are equal to the group number minus 8. In general, the *p*-block elements have more than one positive oxidation state, and these states decrease by increments of 2 from the group oxidation state (except for nitrogen). The *d*-transition elements also tend to have more than one common oxidation state.

Knowing the relative activities of the elements as oxidizing and reducing agents is also very useful in the study of redox reactions. Metals, because they have only

Table 17.3
Common Oxidation States of Common Elements The semiconducting elements Si and As are included with the metals.

One Common Oxidation State (other than zero)	
Metals	*Nonmetals*
Na $+1$	F -1
K $+1$	
Mg $+2$	
Ca $+2$	
Ag $+1$	
Zn $+2$	
Al $+3$	
Si $+4$	
Ni $+2$	

More Than One Common Oxidation State (other than zero)	
Metals	*Nonmetals*
Cr $+3, +6$	N $-3, +1, +2, +3, +4, +5$
Mn $+2, +4, +7$	P $-3, +1, +3, +5$
Fe $+2, +3$	O $-2, -1$ (in peroxides)
Co $+2, +3$	S $-2, +4, +6$
Cu $+1, +2$	Cl $-1, +1, +3, +5, +7$
Au $+1, +3$	Br $-1, +5, +7$
Hg $+1, +2$	I $-1, +5, +7$
Sn $+2, +4$	
Pb $+2, +4$	
As $-3, +3, +5$	

positive oxidation states, can function only as reducing agents. The activity series used earlier in our discussion of displacement reactions (Section 6.3c) is a list of metals in decreasing order of reactivity as reducing agents. (For convenience Table 17.4 duplicates Table 6.2.)

The nonmetals and semiconducting elements, which can have either positive or negative oxidation states, can function as either oxidizing or reducing agents. All are oxidizing agents in at least some of their reactions.

In general, the oxidizing strength of the elements decreases down a periodic table family (see the margin for an example). Although it is less generally applicable than that for metals, a short activity series can be assembled for the nonmetals (Table 17.5). Fluorine, at the top, is the most reactive nonmetal and a very strong oxidizing agent. The strength of these nonmetals as oxidizing agents decreases down the series. (In the presence of stronger oxidizing agents each of these elements except fluorine can react as a reducing agent.)

a. Combination reactions of elements The simplest combination reactions are those between two different elements. The more electronegative element, usually a nonmetal, is the oxidizing agent. The more electropositive element, which may be a metal or a nonmetal, is the reducing agent.

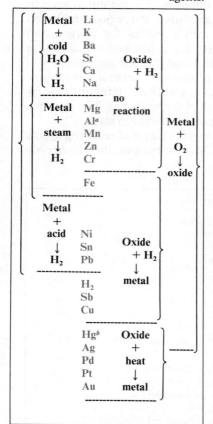

decrease in oxidizing strength — O, S, Se, Te, Po — increase in reducing strength

nonmetal, oxidizing agent

$$\overset{metal,\ reducing\ agent}{\overset{0}{Mg}(s)} + \overset{0}{Cl_2}(g) \longrightarrow \overset{+2\ -1}{MgCl_2}(s) \qquad (17.24)$$

$$\overset{0}{S}(s) + 3\overset{0}{F_2}(g) \longrightarrow \overset{+6\ -1}{SF_6}(g) \qquad (17.25)$$

less electronegative nonmetal, reducing agent ... *more electronegative nonmetal, oxidizing agent*

You should be able to write equations for all of the possible combinations of the elements in Table 17.3 with each other.

As shown in Table 17.3, a number of the common metals have two oxidation states. To which state a metal will be oxidized in a combination reaction depends to a great extent upon the relative strength of the other reactant as an oxidizing agent. Consider some reactions of iron, which commonly has oxidation states of $+2$ or $+3$. With chlorine, either $FeCl_2$ or $FeCl_3$ can be formed, but since chlorine is a very reactive element, the formation of $FeCl_3$ is preferred. The reactions of iron with iodine or sulfur, however, which are weaker oxidizing agents than chlorine (see Table 17.5), lead to compounds of iron in its lower oxidation state. The products are FeI_2 or FeS. With copper, the case is even more striking. Reaction with fluorine, chlorine, or bromine gives CuF_2, $CuCl_2$, or $CuBr_2$, but with iodine only CuI is formed.

$$\overset{0}{Cu}(s) + \overset{0}{X_2}(g) \longrightarrow \overset{+2\ -1}{CuX_2}(s) \qquad (X = F, Cl, \text{ or } Br)$$

$$2\overset{0}{Cu}(s) + \overset{0}{I_2}(g) \longrightarrow 2\overset{+1\ -1}{CuI}(s)$$

In some cases, there is more than one correct answer in predicting the products of combination reactions. Which product will form may depend upon the relative amounts of the reactants, the temperature, and other conditions. For example, the combination of carbon with oxygen can give either CO or CO_2 (or both), depending upon the supply of oxygen.

The more reactive nonmetallic elements at the top of Table 17.5 can also combine with compounds. At least one element in the compound must have a higher

Table 17.4

Activity Series of Metals The metals are listed in the order of decreasing strength as reducing agents.

Metal + cold H₂O ↓ H₂	Li, K, Ba, Sr, Ca, Na	Oxide + H₂ ↓
		no reaction
Metal + steam ↓ H₂	Mg, Al[a], Mn, Zn, Cr	Metal + O₂ ↓ oxide
	Fe	
Metal + acid ↓ H₂	Ni, Sn, Pb	Oxide + H₂ ↓ metal
	H₂, Sb, Cu	
	Hg[b], Ag, Pd, Pt, Au	Oxide + heat ↓ metal

[a] Pure aluminum forms a protective oxide coating in air. When cleaned of this oxide, aluminum will react with water.

[b] Mercury adds O₂ to give HgO, and HgO undergoes thermal decomposition.

possible oxidation state. In the following examples, note again that iodine is less reactive than chlorine and oxygen.

Table 17.5

Activity Series of Nonmetals The strength of the nonmetals as oxidizing agents decreases down this series.

F_2
Cl_2
O_2
Br_2
I_2
S
Se
P(red)

$$\text{can have higher ox. state} \quad 2FeCl_2(s) + Cl_2(g) \longrightarrow 2FeCl_3(s) \tag{17.26}$$
$$2CO(g) + O_2(g) \longrightarrow 2CO_2(g) \tag{17.27}$$
$$CO(g) + Cl_2(g) \longrightarrow COCl_2(g) \tag{17.28}$$
$$CO(g) + I_2(s) \longrightarrow \text{no reaction} \tag{17.29}$$

Take a few moments to think about the further examples given below. Read them thoroughly. Which elements are oxidized and which reduced?

Further Examples of Combination Reactions of Elements

$$ZnS(s) + 2O_2(g) \longrightarrow ZnSO_4(s) \qquad Zn(s) + S(s) \longrightarrow ZnS(s)$$

$$SnS(s) + S(s) \longrightarrow SnS_2(s) \qquad 2SO_2(g) + O_2(g) \longrightarrow 2SO_3(g)$$

$$H_2(g) + Cl_2(g) \longrightarrow 2HCl(g) \qquad SO_2(g) + Cl_2(g) \longrightarrow SO_2Cl_2(g)$$

$$2Al(s) + N_2(s) \longrightarrow 2AlN(s) \qquad SO_2(g) + I_2(s) \longrightarrow \text{no reaction}$$

EXAMPLE 17.6
Redox Reactions

Describe what happens in each of the following combination reactions in terms of oxidation and reduction. Predict the products of the reactions by referring to the common oxidation states given in Table 17.3. Write the balanced equations.

(a) $Al(s) + S(s) \xrightarrow{\Delta}$ (b) $Na(s) + P(s) \xrightarrow{\Delta}$ (c) $Sn(s) + O_2(g) \longrightarrow$

In each case, the metal is the reducing agent and the nonmetal is the oxidizing agent. The metal increases in oxidation state and the nonmetal decreases in oxidation state. Note that in binary compounds between a metal and a nonmetal, the nonmetal has the negative oxidation state.
(a) Aluminum will have a $+3$ oxidation state and sulfur a -2 oxidation state.

$$2Al(s) + 3S(s) \xrightarrow{\Delta} Al_2S_3(s)$$

(b) Sodium can have only a $+1$ oxidation state and phosphorus will have a -3 oxidation state.

$$3Na(s) + P(s) \xrightarrow{\Delta} Na_3P$$

(c) Tin is a metal that has more than one common oxidation state, $+2$ and $+4$. There are two possible products, SnO and SnO_2.

$$2Sn(s) + O_2(g) \longrightarrow 2SnO(s)$$
$$Sn(s) + O_2(g) \longrightarrow SnO_2(s)$$

Without specific knowledge of the chemistry of tin, it would be difficult to predict which oxide forms. If tin were in excess, SnO might form; if oxygen were in excess SnO_2 might form.

Exercise Describe what happens in each of the following combination reactions in terms of oxidation and reduction. Predict the products and write the balanced equations.

(a) $Mg(s) + N_2(g) \xrightarrow{\Delta}$ (b) $K(s) + Br_2(l) \longrightarrow$ (c) $P(s) + Cl_2(g) \longrightarrow$

Answer (a) and (b) The metals are the reducing agents (undergoing oxidation) and the nonmetals are the oxidizing agents (undergoing reduction):

$$3Mg(s) + N_2(g) \xrightarrow{\Delta} Mg_3N_2(s)$$
$$2K(s) + Br_2(l) \longrightarrow 2KBr(s)$$

(c) The more electronegative of the two nonmetals, Cl_2, is the oxidizing agent; P is the reducing agent and would be oxidized to either the $+3$ or $+5$ oxidation state:

$$2P(s) + 3Cl_2(g) \longrightarrow 2PCl_3$$
$$2P(s) + 5Cl_2(g) \longrightarrow 2PCl_5$$

b. Decomposition with oxidation–reduction

Many of the oxides and halides of the least active metals—the noble metals—decompose when heated to give the metal plus oxygen or the free halogen, for example,

$$\underset{\substack{noble \\ metal \\ oxide}}{} \overset{+2\,-2}{2PdO(s)} \xrightarrow{\Delta} \overset{0}{2Pd(s)} + \overset{0}{O_2(g)} \quad \text{(17.30)}$$

with labels *free metal* and *oxygen*

Such decomposition reactions are **internal redox reactions**—the oxidized and reduced elements originate in the same compound.

Metal nitrates undergo thermal decomposition to give oxygen and other products which depend upon the nature of the metal. Lithium and beryllium family nitrates are reduced to nitrites,

$$\underset{\substack{active \\ metal \\ nitrate}}{} \overset{+5\,-2}{2KNO_3(s)} \xrightarrow{\Delta} \overset{+3}{2KNO_2(s)} + \overset{0}{O_2(g)} \quad \text{(17.31)}$$

with label *nitrite*

while nitrates of less active metals yield oxides plus nitrogen dioxide and oxygen.

$$\underset{\substack{less \\ active \\ metal \\ nitrate}}{} \overset{+5\,-2}{2Pb(NO_3)_2(s)} \xrightarrow{\Delta} \overset{+4}{2PbO(s)} + \overset{}{4NO_2(g)} + \overset{0}{O_2(g)} \quad \text{(17.32)}$$

with label *oxide*

All ammonium salts decompose when heated. Ammonia is produced by salts with anions that cannot be reduced—halides, for example (see Equation 17.11). Heating an ammonium salt of an **oxidizing anion** (Section 17.5a)—an anion capable of being reduced—produces a different result. An internal redox reaction takes place in which the ammonium ion is oxidized and the anion is reduced. For example, the nitrate ion is an oxidizing anion because it contains nitrogen in the $+5$ oxidation state, from which it can be reduced to lower oxidation states.

$$\overset{-3\ \ +5}{NH_4NO_3(s)} \xrightarrow{\Delta} \overset{+1}{N_2O(g)} + 2H_2O(g) \quad \text{(17.33)}$$

Ammonium nitrite undergoes a similar reaction:

$$\overset{-3\ \ +3}{NH_4NO_2(s)} \xrightarrow{\Delta} \overset{0}{N_2(g)} + 2H_2O(g) \quad \text{(17.34)}$$

Take a few moments to think about the further examples given on the next page. Read them thoroughly. Which elements are oxidized and which are reduced? Which are the noble metals? Which are the oxidizing anions?

Further Examples of Decomposition with Oxidation–Reduction

$$2HgO(s) \xrightarrow{\Delta} 2Hg(l) + O_2(g)$$

$$(NH_4)_2Cr_2O_7(s) \xrightarrow{\Delta} N_2(g) + Cr_2O_3(s) + 4H_2O(g)$$

$$2Mg(NO_3)_2(s) \xrightarrow{\Delta} 2Mg(NO_2)_2(s) + O_2(g)$$

$$2AuCl_3(s) \xrightarrow{\Delta} 2Au(s) + 3Cl_2(g)$$

c. Displacement of one element from a compound by another element

Reactions in which one element is displaced from a compound by another element make up a large group of simple redox reactions. The displacement reactions discussed in connection with the activity series of metals are all redox reactions of elements (Section 6.3c). A stronger reducing agent can displace a weaker one from a compound, for example,

$$\overset{0}{Zn}(s) + \overset{+2}{Cu}SO_4(aq) \longrightarrow \overset{+2}{Zn}SO_4(aq) + \overset{0}{Cu}(s) \qquad (17.35)$$

(stronger reducing agent than Cu; weaker reducing agent than Zn)

Other examples of the displacement reactions of metals and hydrogen discussed earlier are given below and in Table 17.7. Reactions that follow the displacement pattern occur not only in solution, but in other phases as well, for example,

$$2\overset{0}{Mg}(l) + \overset{+4}{Ti}Cl_4(g) \xrightarrow{\Delta} \overset{0}{Ti}(s) + 2\overset{+2}{Mg}Cl_2(l) \qquad (17.36)$$

Within limits, the short nonmetal activity series can be used to predict the displacement of nonmetals by other nonmetals that are stronger oxidizing agents. The halogens, in general, displace each other in the order shown in the table. For example, chlorine displaces bromine from bromides.

$$\overset{0}{Cl_2}(g) + 2\overset{-1}{K}Br(aq) \longrightarrow 2\overset{-1}{K}Cl(aq) + \overset{0}{Br_2}(aq) \qquad (17.37)$$

(stronger oxidizing agent than Br$_2$; weaker oxidizing agent than Cl$_2$)

Also, as is predicted by the activity series, oxygen and iodine both displace sulfur.

$$\overset{0}{O_2}(g) + 2\overset{-2}{H_2S}(aq) \longrightarrow 2\overset{-2}{H_2O}(l) + 2\overset{0}{S}(s)$$

$$\overset{0}{I_2}(g) + \overset{-2}{H_2S}(aq) \longrightarrow 2\overset{-1}{HI}(aq) + \overset{0}{S}(s)$$

The reactivity of the nonmetals and metals under conditions other than reactions in aqueous solution can sometimes be quite different from that reflected in the activity series. For example, from Table 17.5 we would predict that the displacement of chlorine by oxygen is not possible because chlorine stands above oxygen in the activity series. However, the reaction does occur at a high temperature in the presence of a catalyst and indeed at one time was the basis for an industrial method for the production of chlorine.

$$4HCl(g) + O_2(g) \xrightarrow[\text{catalyst}]{350-400\ °C} 2H_2O(g) + 2Cl_2(g)$$

Note the conditions indicated by the reaction as written above—it is a high temperature reaction in the gas phase. In comparing chemical reactivity we *must* compare reactions under similar conditions. In aqueous solution, chlorine is definitely a stronger oxidizing agent than oxygen.

Take a few moments to think about the further examples given below. Read them thoroughly. Which elements are oxidized and which reduced? Which elements are more active oxidizing and reducing agents?

Further Examples of Displacement of One Element from a Compound by Another

$$H_2(g) + NiO(s) \longrightarrow H_2O(l) + Ni(s)$$

$$Ni(s) + H_2O(l) \longrightarrow \text{no reaction}$$

$$Ni(s) + 2HCl(aq) \longrightarrow NiCl_2(aq) + H_2(g)$$

$$Zn(s) + Na_2SO_4(aq) \longrightarrow \text{no reaction}$$

$$Ca(s) + 2H_2O(l) \longrightarrow Ca(OH)_2(s) + H_2(g)$$

$$Cd(s) + NiCl_2(aq) \longrightarrow Ni(s) + CdCl_2(aq)$$

EXAMPLE 17.7
Redox Reactions

Some information about the reactions of four metals is given below. On the basis of this information, arrange the metals in the order of decreasing strength as reducing agents.

(a) $Sn(s) + H_2O(g) \longrightarrow \text{no reaction}$

(b) $Zn(s) + H_2O(g) \xrightarrow{\Delta} ZnO(s) + H_2(g)$

(c) $Ca(s) + 2H_2O(l) \longrightarrow Ca(OH)(s) + H_2(g)$

(d) $Zn(s) + H_2O(l) \longrightarrow \text{no reaction}$

(e) $3Fe(s) + 4H_2O(g) \xrightarrow{\Delta} 4H_2(g) + Fe_3O_4(s)$

(f) $Fe(s) + H_2O(l) \longrightarrow \text{no reaction}$

(g) $4H_2(g) + Fe_3O_4(s) \xrightarrow{\Delta} 3Fe(s) + 4H_2O(g)$

(h) $H_2(g) + ZnO(s) \longrightarrow \text{no reaction}$
(i) $H_2(g) + SnO(s) \longrightarrow Sn(s) + H_2O(l)$

The most reactive metals displace hydrogen from cold water. Calcium (reaction c) is thus the most reactive metal in the group. The least active metals will not displace hydrogen from water even at the temperature of steam. Tin (reaction a) therefore appears to be the least reactive metal in the group. Metals of activities intermediate between calcium and tin would displace hydrogen from steam but not from cold water. Zinc (reactions b and d) and iron (reactions e and f) fall into this category. To distinguish between them we can examine the reactions of their oxides with hydrogen. Hydrogen is able to reduce the oxides of less active metals, but not those of more active metals. Reactions (g), (h), and (i) show that zinc is a more active metal than either tin or iron. The order of decreasing strength as reducing agents for these metals is therefore

$$Ca > Zn > Fe > Sn$$

[For a long period in the history of chemistry, reasoning like that demonstrated above was the *only* way to derive information on the relative reactivity of chemical substances.]

Exercise On the basis of the information given in the following reactions, arrange the metals in order of decreasing strength as reducing agents.

(a) $Cu(s) + Pd^{2+} \longrightarrow Pd(s) + Cu^{2+}$ (c) $Pd(s) + Rh^{3+} \longrightarrow \text{no reaction}$
(b) $Pt(s) + Pd^{2+} \longrightarrow \text{no reaction}$ (d) $Rh(s) + Cu^{2+} \longrightarrow \text{no reaction}$

Answer $Cu > Rh > Pd > Pt$

EXAMPLE 17.8
Redox Reactions

Will the following reactions occur? Justify your answers.

(a) $Cu(s) + Sn^{2+} \longrightarrow Cu^{2+} + Sn(s)$

(b) $Fe(s) + 2HCl(aq) \longrightarrow FeCl_2(aq) + H_2(g)$

(c) $Zn(s) + CaO(s) \xrightarrow{\Delta} ZnO(s) + Ca(g)$

(d) $Zn(s) + CaCl_2(aq) \longrightarrow ZnCl_2(aq) + Ca(s)$

(e) $2NaF(aq) + Br_2(l) \longrightarrow 2NaBr(aq) + F_2(g)$

(f) $H_2S(aq) + Cl_2(g) \longrightarrow S(s) + 2HCl(aq)$

These are all reactions involving displacement of one element from a compound by another element. Examination of the activity series for metals in Table 17.4 indicates that reaction (a) will not occur (copper is not more active than tin) and reaction (b) will occur (iron is above hydrogen in the series). The important thing to note first about reaction (c) is that it does *not* take place in aqueous solution, and therefore the activity series may not apply. We can predict that the reaction will occur, however, because the temperature is apparently meant to be high enough for the calcium to escape as a vapor. By contrast, reaction (d), also a displacement of calcium by zinc, will not take place in aqueous solution because zinc is a less active metal than calcium. Reaction (e) will not take place because it would be a displacement of fluorine, the most active nonmetal, by bromine, which is less active than fluorine. Reaction (f), however, will take place, for chlorine is a more active nonmetal than sulfur.

Exercise Will the following reactions occur? Justify your answers.

(a) $2Cl^- + I_2(aq) \longrightarrow Cl_2(aq) + 2I^-$
(b) $ZnCl_2(aq) + Pb(s) \longrightarrow Zn(s) + PbCl_2(aq)$
(c) $Cu(s) + 2Ag^+ \longrightarrow Cu^{2+} + 2Ag(s)$

Answer (a) No, Cl_2 is a stronger oxidizing agent than I_2; (b) no, Zn is a stronger reducing agent than Pb; (c) yes, Cu is a stronger reducing agent than Ag.

Disproportionation: same element oxidized *and* reduced.

Table 17.6
Elements Most Commonly Involved in Disproportionation Reactions Note that the maximum oxidation states of the nonmetals equal their periodic table group numbers.

	Possible Oxidation States
N	$-3, 0, +1, +2, +3, +4, +5$
P	$-3, 0, +3, +5$
S	$-2, 0, +4, +6$
Cl	$-1, 0, +1, +3, +5, +7$
Br	$-1, 0, +1, +3, +5, +7$
I	$-1, 0, +1, +3, +5, +7$
Mn	$0, +2, +3, +4, +5, +6, +7$
Cu	$0, +1, +2$
Au	$0, +1, +3$
Hg	$0, +1, +2$

d. Disproportionation reactions In a **disproportionation reaction** an element in one oxidation state is both oxidized and reduced. One reactant must contain an element that is capable of having at least three oxidation states—that in the reactant plus one higher and one lower oxidation state. The halogens, with their many common oxidation states, can undergo disproportionation in many ways. For example, the reaction of chlorine with water to give hydrochloric acid and hypochlorous acid is a disproportionation reaction,

$$Cl_2(g) + H_2O(l) \longrightarrow HCl(aq) + HOCl(aq) \tag{17.38}$$

The elements most commonly encountered in disproportionation reactions are listed in Table 17.6. Sulfites, copper(I) compounds, and manganates are common examples of compounds that disproportionate. The thermal decomposition of sulfites is a disproportionation reaction:

$$4Na_2SO_3(s) \xrightarrow{\Delta} Na_2S(s) + 3Na_2SO_4(s) \tag{17.39}$$

Soluble copper(I) compounds, when they dissolve, immediately disproportionate to give the free metal and a copper(II) compound

$$\overset{+1}{Cu_2SO_4}(s) \xrightarrow{H_2O} \overset{0}{Cu}(s) + \overset{+2}{CuSO_4}(aq) \tag{17.40}$$
copper(I) sulfate   copper(II) sulfate

(except for insoluble compounds or compounds in which Cu^+ is stabilized by formation of a complex ion). Manganate ion disproportionates in acidic solution:

$$3\overset{+6}{MnO_4^{2-}} + 4H^+ \longrightarrow \overset{+4}{MnO_2}(s) + 2\overset{+7}{MnO_4^-} + 2H_2O(l) \tag{17.41}$$
manganate ion   manganese(IV)   permanganate
                                  oxide   ion

Generally, we must know the chemistry of a specific element and its compounds in order to predict the products of a disproportionation reaction.

Take a few moments to think about the further examples below. Read them thoroughly. Which elements disproportionate?

Further Examples of Disproportionation Reactions

$$2H_2O_2(l) \xrightarrow{\Delta} 2H_2O(l) + O_2(g)$$

$$3HNO_2(aq) \longrightarrow 2NO g) + NO_3^- + H_3O^+$$

$$3AuCl(s) \xrightarrow[H_2O]{\Delta} 2Au(s) + AuCl_3(aq)$$

$$4KClO_3(s) \xrightarrow{\Delta} 3KClO_4(s) + KCl(s)$$

$$Br_2(l) + H_2O(l) \longrightarrow HBr(aq) + HBrO(aq)$$

e. Electron transfer between monatomic ions in aqueous solution Direct transfer of electrons from one ion to another can occur in aqueous solution. For example,

$$2FeCl_3(aq) + SnCl_2(aq) \longrightarrow 2FeCl_2(aq) + SnCl_4(aq) \tag{17.42a}$$

The anions play no part in this reaction, and the net ionic equation for the reaction between a soluble iron(III) compound and a soluble tin(II) compound is

gains   loses
electrons   electrons

$$2Fe^{3+} + Sn^{2+} \longrightarrow 2Fe^{2+} + Sn^{4+} \tag{17.42b}$$
oxidizing   reducing
agent   agent

Nonmetal ions can also participate in electron-transfer reactions, for example,

electrons   electrons
gained   lost

$$2Cu^{2+} + 2I^- \longrightarrow 2Cu^+ + I_2(aq)$$
oxidizing   reducing
agent   agent

To predict with certainty when such reactions will occur requires the use of quantitative methods for evaluating the oxidizing and reducing strengths of ions (Section 23.10).

f. Other types of redox reactions Many redox reactions do not fit any of the "classes" of reactions described in the preceding sections. In general, redox reactions involving oxygen-containing redox agents in acidic or alkaline solution are not easily categorized. In most such reactions, the participation of water and hydrogen ion or hydroxide ion as reactants or products is a necessity. One example is the oxidation of copper by nitric acid,

$$\overset{0}{3Cu(s)} + \overset{+5}{8HNO_3}(dil) \longrightarrow \overset{+2}{3Cu(NO_3)_2}(aq) + \overset{+2}{2NO}(g) + 4H_2O(l)$$

or, written as a net ionic equation,

$$3Cu(s) + 8H^+ + 2NO_3{}^- \longrightarrow 3Cu^{2+} + 2NO(g) + 4H_2O(l)$$

The participation of water and H^+ or OH^- in redox reactions contributes to the complexity of the equations and the difficulty of balancing them (one method of doing so is discussed in Section 17.8). It also means that the concentration of an acid or a base can influence the course of a reaction. For example, if concentrated instead of dilute nitric acid is used to dissolve copper, the reduction product formed from the nitric acid is different from that shown above.

$$\overset{0}{Cu(s)} + \overset{+5}{4HNO_3}(conc) \longrightarrow \overset{+2}{Cu(NO_3)_2}(aq) + \overset{+4}{2NO_2}(g) + 2H_2O(l)$$

Some further examples of redox reactions that do not fit into simple categories are the combination of oxygen with each of the elements in a binary compound:

$$\overset{-2}{2ZnS(s)} + \overset{0}{3O_2}(g) \overset{\Delta}{\longrightarrow} 2ZnO(s) + \overset{+4 -2}{2SO_2}(g)$$

$$\overset{-4}{CH_4}(g) + \overset{0}{2O_2}(g) \longrightarrow \overset{+4}{CO_2}(s) + \overset{-2}{2H_2O}(l)$$

and reactions between gaseous, liquid, or solid compounds such as

$$\overset{-3}{2NH_3}(g) + \overset{+2}{3CuO(s)} \longrightarrow \overset{0}{N_2}(g) + \overset{0}{3Cu(s)} + 3H_2O(g)$$

$$\overset{+4}{3CO_2}(g) + \overset{-4}{CH_4}(g) \overset{\Delta}{\longrightarrow} \overset{+2}{4CO}(g) + 2H_2O(g)$$

EXAMPLE 17.9
Redox Reactions

Predict the products of the following reactions. Explain your reasoning.

(a) $Mn(s) + HCl(aq) \longrightarrow$
(b) $Al(s) + O_2(g) \longrightarrow$
(c) $Cl_2(g) + NaBr(aq) \longrightarrow$
(d) $Ni(s) + CaCl_2(aq) \longrightarrow$

(a) Manganese lies above hydrogen in the activity series and should displace it. Manganese would probably be oxidized to its lowest oxidation state of $+2$. Products: $MnCl_2(aq) + H_2(g)$
(b) Aluminum is an active metal and will combine with oxygen. The $+3$ oxidation state is most common for aluminum. Product: $Al_2O_3(s)$.
(c) Chlorine is a more active nonmetal than bromine and should displace it. Products: $Br_2 + NaCl(aq)$
(d) Nickel is a less active metal than calcium. No reaction will occur.

Exercise Predict the products of the following reactions. Explain your reasoning.

(a) $PCl_3(l) + Cl_2(g)$
(b) $Co(s) + Cl_2(l)$
(c) $Br_2(l) + NaCl(aq)$

Answer (a) PCl_5—phosphorus can be oxidized to the +5 oxidation state; (b) $CoCl_2$ or $CoCl_3$—cobalt has two common oxidation states; (c) no reaction—bromine is less active than chlorine

---

EXAMPLE 17.10
Nonredox and Redox Reactions

Classify each of the following reactions as a nonredox or a redox reaction. Further classify each reaction according to type of nonredox or redox reaction where possible.

(a) $\underset{\text{sodium hydroxide}}{3NaOH(aq)} + \underset{\text{phosphoric acid}}{H_3PO_4(aq)} \longrightarrow \underset{\text{sodium phosphate}}{Na_3PO_4(aq)} + 3H_2O(l)$

(b) $\underset{\text{sodium hypochlorite}}{3NaOCl(s)} \overset{\Delta}{\longrightarrow} \underset{\text{sodium chlorate}}{NaClO_3(s)} + \underset{\text{sodium chloride}}{2NaCl(s)}$

(c) $\underset{\text{phosphorus(III) chloride}}{PCl_3(l)} + 3H_2O(l) \longrightarrow \underset{\text{phosphorous acid}}{H_3PO_3(aq)} + \underset{\text{hydrochloric acid}}{3HCl(aq)}$

(a) This is the reaction of an acid and a base to give a salt and water. Nonredox. Partner-exchange reaction—neutralization, driven by the formation of water.
(b) Heating a single substance causes a decomposition reaction. Chlorine, an element of variable oxidation state, is +1 in $NaOCl$, +5 in $NaClO_3$, and −1 in $NaCl$. Redox. A decomposition reaction that is also a disproportionation reaction.
(c) Phosphorus trichloride is a compound between two nonmetals. The water molecule is split in this reaction. Nonredox. Partner-exchange—a hydrolysis reaction driven by formation of a weak electrolyte.

Exercise Classify each of the following reactions as a nonredox or a redox reaction. Further classify each reaction according to type of nonredox or redox reaction where possible.

(a) $KCl(l) + Na(g) \overset{\Delta}{\longrightarrow} K(g) + NaCl(l)$

(b) $2Na(s) + O_2(g) \overset{\Delta}{\longrightarrow} \underset{\text{sodium peroxide}}{Na_2O_2(s)}$

(c) $\underset{\text{boron oxide}}{2B_2O_3(s)} + Na_2CO_3(s) \overset{\Delta}{\longrightarrow} \underset{\text{sodium tetraborate}}{Na_2B_4O_7(s)} + CO_2(g)$

(d) $\underset{\text{dichromate ion}}{Cr_2O_7^{2-}} + 6I^- + 14H^+ \longrightarrow 2Cr^{3+} + 3I_2(s) + 7H_2O(l)$

Answer (a) Redox, displacement of one element from a compound by another element; (b) redox, combination of elements; (c) nonredox, displacement of a more volatile oxide by a less volatile oxide; (d) redox, a reaction of an oxygen-containing anion (We cannot further classify this reaction.)

A summary and examples of the simple inorganic redox reactions discussed in this section are given in Table 17.7.

Table 17.7
Simple Inorganic Redox Reactions

Combination of Two Elements to Give a Compound

$2Mg(s) + O_2(g) \longrightarrow 2MgO(s)$ Most metals with O_2

$Ti(s) + 2Cl_2(g) \longrightarrow TiCl_4(l)$ Most metals with halogens

$2H_2(g) + O_2(g) \longrightarrow 2H_2O(l)$ Oxygen with nonmetals except halogens and noble gases

Combination of an Element with a Compound to Give Another Compound

$4FeO(s) + O_2(g) \longrightarrow 2Fe_2O_3(s)$

$2CO(g) + O_2(g) \longrightarrow 2CO_2(g)$ { Element oxidized can exhibit more than one positive oxidation state.

$CO(g) + Cl_2(g) \longrightarrow COCl_2(g)$

Decomposition

$2HgO(s) \xrightarrow{\Delta} 2Hg(l) + O_2(g)$

$PtCl_4(s) \xrightarrow{\Delta} Pt(s) + 2Cl_2(g)$ { Of oxides and halides of least active metals to give the metal and elemental O_2 or halogen

$2KNO_3(s) \xrightarrow{\Delta} 2KNO_2(s) + O_2(g)$ Of Li and Be family nitrates (except Be)

$2Pb(NO_3)_2(s) \xrightarrow{\Delta} 2PbO(s) + 4NO_2(g) + O_2(g)$ Of less active metal nitrates

$NH_4NO_3(s) \xrightarrow{\Delta} N_2O(g) + 2H_2O(g)$

$(NH_4)_2Cr_2O_7(s) \xrightarrow{\Delta} N_2(g) + Cr_2O_3(s) + 4H_2O(g)$ { Of ammonium salts with oxidizing anions

Displacement of One Element from a Compound by Another Element

$2Na(s) + 2H_2O(l) \longrightarrow H_2(g) + 2NaOH(aq)$ Of H_2 from H_2O by an active metal

$Zn(s) + 2HCl(aq) \longrightarrow H_2(g) + ZnCl_2(aq)$ Of H_2 from a nonoxidizing acid by metals above H_2 in the activity series

$Zn(s) + CuSO_4(aq) \longrightarrow ZnSO_4(aq) + Cu(s)$ Of a metal from a compound by a more active metal

$CuO(s) + H_2(g) \xrightarrow{\Delta} Cu(s) + H_2O(g)$ Of a metal from an oxide by hydrogen

$2NaI(aq) + Br_2(aq) \longrightarrow 2NaBr(aq) + I_2(aq)$ Of a halogen by a more active halogen

$I_2(aq) + H_2S(aq) \longrightarrow S(s) + 2HI(aq)$ Of a nonmetal by a more active nonmetal

Disproportionation

$Cl_2(g) + H_2O(l) \longrightarrow HCl(aq) + HOCl(aq)$ Conversion of an element from one oxidation state to two other oxidation states, one higher and one lower

Electron Transfer between Metal Ions in Aqueous Solution

$2Fe^{3+} + Sn^{2+} \longrightarrow 2Fe^{2+} + Sn^{4+}$ Prediction of whether such reactions can occur must be by quantitative methods (Section 23.10)

17.5 OXIDIZING AND REDUCING AGENTS

In general, a reactant containing an element in its lowest oxidation state can function only as a reducing agent. A reactant containing an element in its highest oxidation state can function only as an oxidizing agent. When an element is present in an intermediate oxidation state, the substance may be able to act as either an oxidizing agent or a reducing agent. Which way it does react depends upon the relative oxidizing and reducing strengths of that substance and the other reactant.

To place all oxidizing and reducing agents on a continuum from strong to weak requires the quantitative methods discussed in Chapter 23. Without resorting to numbers, however, it is practical and useful to become familiar with the substances, in addition to the free elements, most often encountered as oxidizing and reducing agents.

a. Common oxidizing agents Some common oxidizing agents are listed in Table 17.8, with their usual reduction products. Fluorine is the strongest of the common oxidizing agents. Where more than one product is listed, the one formed depends upon the relative oxidizing and reducing strengths of the reactants and the other conditions of the reaction.

Many oxidizing agents contain oxygen combined with other elements in their higher oxidation states. In any reaction of a compound or anion containing oxygen plus an element of variable oxidation state, it is reasonable to consider the possibility of an oxidation–reduction reaction, in which the element in its higher oxidation state is reduced.

Among the *nonmetal–oxygen compounds or anions,* nitrogen (Group V), sulfur (Group VI), and chlorine, bromine, and iodine (Group VII) are found in common oxidizing agents. These are all elements of variable oxidation state, with the highest oxidation state equal to the group number. In addition, hydrogen peroxide is an oxidizing agent (Section 16.14).

HNO$_3$, concentrated H$_2$SO$_4$: oxidizing acids

Acids that are oxidizing agents are referred to as **oxidizing acids.** Two of the common strong acids, sulfuric acid and nitric acid, are oxidizing acids, sulfuric acid only when it is concentrated. Concentrated perchloric acid (HClO$_4$) is, as you might guess, also an oxidizing acid. At room temperature it is a weak oxidizing agent, but when concentrated and hot it is a very strong oxidant. However, perchloric acid is not commonly used as an oxidizing agent because its reactions can be violent, particularly if the acid comes into contact with any organic material.

Nitrous acid (HNO$_2$) and hypochlorous acid (HClO) are weak acids that are oxidizing agents. These two acids exist only in aqueous solution.

The oxoanions of chlorine, bromine, and iodine are all oxidizing agents in

Table 17.8

Common Oxidizing Agents In the presence of a sufficiently strong oxidizing agent, the species on the right can be oxidized to give the species on the left. It is not possible to predict the products of specific reactions in which nitric acid, nitrous acid, nitrate ion, or concentrated sulfuric acid are the oxidizing agents.

Oxidizing Agent	Usual Reduction Product
F$_2$	**F$^-$**
Cl$_2$	**Cl$^-$**
Br$_2$	**Br$^-$**
O$_2$	**O^{2-}**
S	**S^{2-}**
Cu$^+$, Cu^{2+}	**Cu**
Ag$^+$	**Ag**
Fe^{3+}	**Fe^{2+}**
conc. H$_2$SO$_4$	**SO$_2$, H$_2$S, S**
conc. HNO$_3$	**NO$_2$, various others***
dil. HNO$_3$	**NO, NO$_2$, N$_2$O, various others***
HNO$_2$ (nitrous acid)	**NO, N$_2$O**
HClO (hypochlorous acid)	**Cl$^-$, Cl$_2$**
NO$_3^-$ (nitrate ion, in acidic solution)	**HNO$_2$, NO, N$_2$O$_4$**
ClO$_3^-$ (chlorate ion)	**Cl$^-$, Cl$_2$**
ClO$^-$ (hypochlorite ion)	**Cl$^-$, Cl$_2$**
BrO$_3^-$ (bromate ion)	**Br$^-$, Br$_2$**
IO$_3^-$ (iodate ion)	**I$^-$, I$_2$**
H$_2$O$_2$ (hydrogen peroxide)	**H$_2$O**
MnO$_4^-$ (permanganate ion)	
in acidic solution	**Mn^{2+}**
in neutral or alkaline solution	**MnO$_2$(s)**
Cr$_2$O$_7^{2-}$ (dichromate ion, in acidic solution)	**Cr^{3+}**
BiO$_3^-$ (bismuthate ion, in acidic solution)	**Bi(III)**
PbO$_2$(s) (lead(IV) oxide, in acidic solution)	**Pb^{2+}**
MnO$_2$(s) (manganese(IV) oxide, in acidic solution)	**Mn^{2+}**

* Other possible products, such as NH$_3$, NH$_4^+$, and HNO$_2$, depending upon acid concentration and nature of the reducing agent.

varying degrees. Those that are strongest and most often used are listed in Table 17.8 (ClO^-, ClO_3^-, BrO_3^-, and IO_3^-). These ions are stronger oxidizing agents in acidic than in alkaline solutions.

Metal–oxygen compounds or anions are also found among the common oxidizing agents. The metals of Representative Groups III–V exhibit two oxidation states in compounds, one equal to the group number and one equal to the group number minus 2. The lower oxidation state corresponds to the use in bonding of the outermost p electrons and the higher one to the use of both the s and p electrons from the outermost energy level. For the heaviest metals in these three groups—thallium, lead, and bismuth—the lower of the two states is by far the more stable. As a result, compounds containing these elements in the higher oxidation states are all *strong* oxidizing agents, with the metals being readily reduced to the lower oxidation states. Lead(IV) appears on the list of common oxidizing agents in PbO_2 and bismuth(V) in the bismuthate ion, BiO_3^-.

Among the $3d$-transition metals, the highest oxidation states are found for chromium ($+6$), manganese ($+7$), and iron ($+6$). The oxoanions of these elements in these states (chromate ion, CrO_4^{2-}; dichromate ion, $Cr_2O_7^{2-}$; permanganate ion, MnO_4^-; and ferrate ion, FeO_4^{2-}) are all powerful oxidizing agents, whether in solid compounds or in solutions. Permanganate ion, usually from potassium permanganate solutions (which are a beautiful deep purple), and dichromate ion, usually from potassium dichromate solutions (which are deep orange), are frequently used as oxidizing agents in the laboratory.

b. Common reducing agents Free metals dominate the list of common reducing agents (Table 17.9). Lithium is the strongest common reducing agent, and all of the other metals of the lithium and beryllium families are also strong reducing agents. Of the metals above hydrogen in the activity series (Table 17.4), all of which are reducing agents, aluminum and tin (representative metals) and iron and zinc (transition metals) are most often utilized for their reducing properties. The Fe^{2+} ion—the iron(II) or ferrous ion—is also a useful reducing agent.

We might expect nonmetals in their lowest oxidation states to be good reducing agents. The hydride ion (H^-) is the strongest reducing agent of this type. The reducing strength of the halide ions increases down the fluorine family and only I^- is a reducing agent of significance. Sulfur in its -2 oxidation state, while not a strong reducing agent, is useful in this capacity, and sulfide ion (S^{2-}) and hydrogen sulfide (H_2S) are encountered as reducing agents. The sulfite ion (SO_3^{2-}), also a common reducing agent, contains sulfur in the $+4$ state and is oxidized to sulfate ion, with sulfur in the $+6$ state.

Take a few moments to think about the examples of redox reactions below. Read them thoroughly and compare them with Tables 17.8 and 17.9. Which are the common oxidizing and reducing agents? What are their products? Note that many of these reactions occur in acidic solutions. (How to balance complex redox equations like these is discussed in Section 17.8.)

Down Representative Groups III–V: lower oxidation states become more stable

Table 17.9
Common Reducing Agents

Reducing Agent	Usual Oxidation Product
Li, Na, K	Li^+, Na^+, K^+
Mg, Ca	Mg^{2+}, Ca^{2+}
Al, Sn	Al^{3+}, Sn^{2+}, Sn^{4+} (most often)
Fe, Zn	Fe^{2+} (sometimes Fe^{3+}), Zn^{2+}
Fe^{2+}	Fe^{3+}
Sn^{2+}	Sn^{4+}
H_2	H^+
H^-	H_2 or H^+
I^-	I_2
S^{2-}, H_2S	S
SO_3^{2-}	SO_4^{2-}
HPO_3^{2-}	H_3PO_4
NH_3	N_2
N_2H_4	N_2

Some Examples of Redox Reactions of Common Oxidizing and Reducing Agents

$$SO_3^{2-} + Br_2(l) + H_2O(l) \longrightarrow SO_4^{2-} + 2Br^- + 2H^+$$

$$IO_3^- + 3SO_2(g) + 3H_2O(l) \xrightarrow{H^+} I^- + 3SO_4^{2-} + 6H^+$$

$$5PbO_2(s) + 2Mn^{2+} + 4H^+ \longrightarrow 2MnO_4^- + 5Pb^{2+} + 2H_2O(l)$$

$$4I^- + 2Cu^{2+} \longrightarrow 2CuI(s) + I_2(s)$$

$$6Fe^{2+} + Cr_2O_7^{2-} + 14H^+ \longrightarrow 6Fe^{3+} + 2Cr^{3+} + 7H_2O(l)$$

$$2MnO_4^- + 5SO_2(g) + 2H_2O(l) \xrightarrow{H^+} 2Mn^{2+} + 5SO_4^{2-} + 4H^+$$

EXAMPLE 17.11
Redox Reactions

Referring to Tables 17.8 and 17.9, predict the oxidation and reduction products of each of the following reactions. Do not be concerned with other possible products or with writing balanced equations. (These reactions all take place.)

(a) $Al(s) + H^+ \longrightarrow$ (d) $Cr_2O_7^{2-} + Sn^{2+} \xrightarrow{H^+}$

(b) $Fe^{2+} + MnO_4^- \xrightarrow{H^+}$ (e) $BiO_3^- + Mn^{2+} \xrightarrow{H^+}$

(c) $SO_3^{2-} + Cl_2 \longrightarrow$ (f) $H_2S(g) + BrO_3^- \xrightarrow{H^+}$

(a) Aluminum can act as a reducing agent and will displace hydrogen ion from an acid in solution.

$$Al(s) + H^+ \xrightarrow{\overset{not}{balanced}} Al^{3+} + H_2$$

(b) Permanganate ion is a common oxidizing agent that is reduced to Mn^{2+} in acidic solution. The Fe^{2+} ion is commonly oxidized to Fe^{3+}.

$$Fe^{2+} + MnO_4^- \xrightarrow{not\ balanced} Fe^{3+} + Mn^{2+}$$

(c) Sulfite ion is a common reducing agent and chlorine is a common oxidizing agent.

$$SO_3^{2-} + Cl_2 \xrightarrow{not\ balanced} SO_4^{2-} + Cl^-$$

(d) Dichromate ion in acidic solution is an oxidizing agent and yields Cr^{3+} as its reduction product. The Sn^{2+} ion should go to the next highest oxidation state, Sn^{4+}.

$$Cr_2O_7^{2-} + Sn^{2+} \xrightarrow{not\ balanced} Cr^{3+} + Sn^{4+}$$

(e) The bismuthate ion is a very strong oxidizing agent in acidic solution. The common species in which manganese occurs in higher oxidation states are MnO_2 (Mn +4) or MnO_4^- (Mn +7). Because bismuthate is a strong oxidizing agent we predict that it would give MnO_4^-.

$$BiO_3^- + Mn^{2+} \xrightarrow{not\ balanced} Bi^{3+} + MnO_4^-$$

(f) Hydrogen sulfide is a reducing agent and gives free sulfur as its usual oxidation product. Bromate ion is an oxidizing agent which in acidic solution is reduced to bromide ion or bromine.

$$H_2S(g) + BrO_3^- \xrightarrow{not\ balanced} S(s) + Br^-\ or\ Br_2$$

Exercise Predict the products of each of the following reactions:

(a) $HNO_2(aq) + HI(aq) \longrightarrow$

(b) $Cr_2O_7^{2-} + Fe^{2+} \xrightarrow{H^+}$

(c) $PbO_2(s) + SO_3^{2-} \xrightarrow{H^+}$

Answer (a) $NO(g) + I_2(aq)$, (b) $Cr^{3+} + Fe^{3+}$, (c) $PbSO_4(s)$

17.6 PREDICTING REACTION
PRODUCTS

The types of chemical reactions that we have described in this chapter are organized into a flow chart in Table 17.10. By examining the reactants and identifying them in the order of the numbered questions in Table 17.10, it is possible to narrow down the choice of the types of reactions that might occur. Once this is done, general and specific information can be utilized to predict reaction products. For example, if a partner-exchange reaction is found to be a possible type of reaction, general infor-

Table 17.10
A Guide to Some Simple Types of Chemical Reactions

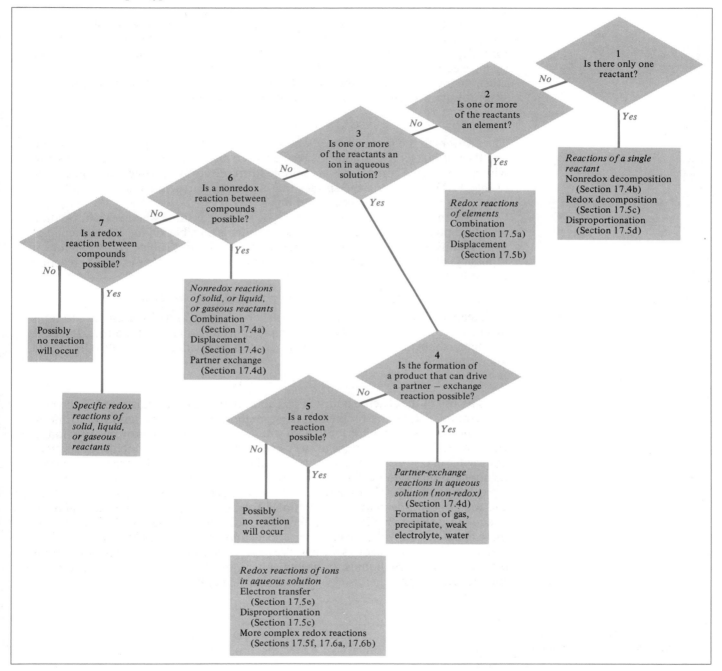

mation about solubilities (see Table 17.1) can be used to predict whether or not a precipitate might form.

To use Table 17.10, answer the questions in numerical order until you come to a box listing the types of reactions that are possible for the reactants under consideration. At that point, call upon your knowledge and the tables in this book to predict what the reaction products might be. The result may be a reasonably firm prediction of the reaction products (or that no reaction can occur); prediction of the type of reaction that is possible, if not the exact products; or the conclusion that no prediction can be made without additional knowledge.

In all cases, note must be taken of the reaction conditions, the states of the reactants, whether or not water is present as a solvent, and how the reactants are formulated. For reactions in aqueous solution it is important to recognize soluble strong electrolytes, as well as slightly soluble compounds and weak electrolytes. To illustrate these points, and the use of Table 17.10 in general, consider the reaction of silver nitrate with sodium chloride in aqueous solution.

$$AgNO_3 + NaCl \xrightarrow{H_2O}$$

The answers to the first two questions are "no"—there is not just a single reactant and there is no element among the reactants. To answer question 3, you must know whether or not the compounds are soluble strong electrolytes, which they indeed are (Table 17.1). Therefore, the species that are possible reactants are the Na^+, Ag^+, NO_3^-, and Cl^- ions in aqueous solution.

Next, in order to answer question 4, you must determine whether the formation of a gas, a precipitate, a weak electrolyte, or water is possible. Of the ions present Ag^+ and Cl^- can combine to give a precipitate of silver chloride (Table 17.1). Therefore, it is possible to predict that the reaction will be a nonredox, partner-exchange reaction driven by the formation of a precipitate.

$$AgNO_3(aq) + NaCl(aq) \longrightarrow AgCl(s) + NaNO_3(aq)$$

Keep in mind that the patterns of partner-exchange and displacement reactions in aqueous solution are based on the complete formulas of the compounds. It takes a moment's thought to recognize the partner-exchange pattern if we write only the net ionic equation

$$Ag^+ + Cl^- \longrightarrow AgCl(s)$$

The use of the scheme outlined in Table 17.10 is further illustrated in the next two examples. Like the problem-solving method that we have used from time to time, the table is a guide meant to help you in deciding how to answer a question. It will not lead you to the right answer every time, nor is it all inclusive. As your knowledge of chemistry increases, more and more questions will arise for which you do not need such a guide. (Perhaps you did not need it to recognize immediately that a precipitate of silver chloride would be the product of the reaction of silver nitrate and sodium chloride in aqueous solution.) The behavior of ions and acids and bases in aqueous solution is discussed extensively in Chapters 19–21, and after studying those chapters you will have a greater understanding of the possible products of the reactions of ions in aqueous solution. We have not yet studied many redox reactions between pure solids, liquids, or gases—reactions of this type are best covered in connection with the chemistry of the specific elements.

EXAMPLE 17.12
Predicting Reaction Products

For each of the following reactions, identify the most likely type of reaction and predict which are the most likely reaction products. Follow the guide in Table 17.10.

(a) $Cu(s) + Cl_2(g) \longrightarrow$ (c) $NO(g) + O_2(g) \longrightarrow$

(b) $ZnCO_3(s) \xrightarrow{\Delta}$ (d) $N_2H_4(l) + H_2O_2(l) \longrightarrow$

(a) The first "yes" answer is for question 2, indicating that a redox reaction of an element is likely. In this case, both reactants are elements, one a metal and the other a reactive nonmetal, making a redox combination reaction likely. Copper can have oxidation states of $+1$ or $+2$ (Table 17.3) and chlorine is an active oxidizing agent (Table 17.8). We therefore predict that the reaction will be the combination of the two elements to give copper(II) chloride because chlorine is a strong enough oxidizing agent to take copper to its higher oxidation state.

$$Cu(s) + Cl_2(g) \longrightarrow CuCl_2(s)$$

(b) With one reactant, the first "yes" answer is for question 1. The compound is to be heated, as shown by the Δ over the arrow. In a thermal decomposition reaction, carbonates form carbon dioxide and the metal oxide (Section 17.3b). Therefore, the most likely reaction is a nonredox thermal decomposition.

$$ZnCO_3(s) \xrightarrow{\Delta} ZnO(s) + CO_2(g)$$

(c) Because the first "yes" answer is for question 2, a redox reaction of an element is possible. Nitrogen, which in NO is in the $+2$ oxidation state, has several higher oxidation states, and oxygen is a good oxidizing agent, making a combination reaction appear likely. Without specific knowledge of the chemistry of nitrogen compounds, we cannot predict with certainty to which oxidation state nitrogen will be oxidized. One reasonable guess would be that it is oxidized to the next highest multiple of 2 state, to give nitrogen(IV) oxide.

$$2NO(g) + O_2(g) \longrightarrow 2NO_2(g)$$

(d) The answers to questions 1, 2, and 3 are all "no." There is not only a single reactant, nor is there an element or an ion in aqueous solution present. This leads us to question 6. None of the simple nonredox reactions between compounds that we have studied—combination, displacement, or partner exchange—appears likely. To answer question 7, we consider whether the reactants are known as oxidizing and reducing agents. This is the case—N_2H_4 (hydrazine) is a reducing agent (Table 17.9) and H_2O_2 is an oxidizing agent (Table 17.8). We predict that a redox reaction will occur between these two liquids to give nitrogen and water.

$$N_2H_4(l) + 2H_2O_2(l) \longrightarrow N_2(g) + 4H_2O(g)$$

Exercise For each of the following, identify the most likely type of reaction and predict the most likely products.

(a) $BrO_3^- + Br^- \xrightarrow{H^+}$ (b) $P_4(s) + I_2(g) \xrightarrow{\Delta}$ (c) $KMnO_4(aq) + H_2S(g) \xrightarrow{OH^-}$

Answer (a) complex redox reaction of ions in aqueous solution, $Br_2(aq) + H_2O(l)$; (b) redox combination of elements, $PI_3(s)$; (c) complex redox reaction (common oxidizing agent plus common reducing agent), $MnO_2(s) + S(s)$

EXAMPLE 17.13
Predicting Reaction Products

Will reactions occur when the following combinations of reactants are brought together in aqueous solution? If so, what type of reaction can take place and what might the products be? Follow the guide in Table 17.10.

(a) $ZnS + NaNO_3 \longrightarrow$ (c) $KMnO_4(aq) + Na_2SO_3(aq) \xrightarrow{OH^-}$
(b) $I^- + Br_2 \longrightarrow$ (d) $Na_2SO_3 + HCl \longrightarrow$

(a) Both questions 1 and 2 are answered by "no" and it is next necessary to decide whether ions in aqueous solution are present. Sodium nitrate is soluble (Table 17.1), so the answer is "yes." However, zinc sulfide is not soluble (Table 17.1). Therefore no partner exchange will occur, because the least soluble product is already present as a solid. Of the species present, $ZnS(s)$, Na^+, NO_3^-, none is likely to act as an oxidizing or reducing agent (Table 17.8; NO_3^- is an oxidizing agent only in acid solution), and therefore we predict that no chemical reaction will occur.

(b) One reactant is an element (question 2), making a redox reaction of an element possible. Bromine is a more active nonmetal than iodine (Table 17.4), and thus it can oxidize iodide ion. Although the cation is not written, it is apparent that this will be what we have categorized as a redox displacement reaction.

$$2I^- + Br_2(aq) \longrightarrow I_2(aq) + 2Br^-$$

(c) Here again, "no" answers to questions 1 and 2 lead us to question 3. We are shown that these are soluble compounds by the (aq) in the formulas, and therefore the answer to question 3 is "yes." Partner exchange is unlikely, since Na^+ and K^+ salts are generally water soluble, and the formation of a gas or a weak electrolyte does not appear likely. However, the answer to question 5 is "yes," because permanganate ion is an oxidizing agent (Table 17.8) and sulfite ion is a reducing agent (Table 17.9). We predict that the reaction will occur and that the major products will be $MnO_2(s)$ and SO_4^{2-}. [The net ionic equation for this reaction is

$$2MnO_4^- + 3SO_3^{2-} + H_2O(l) \longrightarrow 2MnO_2(s) + 3SO_4^{2-} + 2OH^-$$

The balancing of complex equations is discussed in the next section.]

(d) Seeing that questions 1 and 2 are answered by "no," we must decide whether ions are present. They are, for sodium sulfite is a soluble salt (Table 17.1) and an aqueous solution of hydrogen chloride is the strong acid, hydrochloric acid. To answer question 4, we must determine whether any possible products could drive a partner-exchange reaction. The answer is "yes." Partner exchange will result in the formation of sulfurous acid, H_2SO_3, which immediately decomposes to give gaseous sulfur dioxide, thereby driving the reaction to completion.

$$Na_2SO_3(aq) + 2HCl(aq) \longrightarrow 2NaCl(aq) + SO_2(g) + H_2O(l)$$

Exercise Will reactions occur when the following combinations of reactants are brought together in aqueous solution? If so, what types of reactions can take place and what might the products be?

(a) $AgCl + Cu$
(b) $Fe^{3+} + I^-$
(c) $SiCl_4(l) + H_2O(l)$

Answer (a) No reaction, AgCl is not soluble; (b) can't be sure, possible electron transfer to give Fe^{2+} and I_2; (c) nonredox partner exchange (hydrolysis), HCl plus oxide or hydroxide of Si(IV).

17.7 CHEMICAL STABILITY   Earlier in this chapter we posed the question, How do we predict what the products of a chemical reaction might be? We have now demonstrated one possible approach to answering this question for some simple reactions. Knowing the possible products of a chemical reaction, however, does not necessarily tell us whether the reaction will take place. Understanding chemical reactions also requires knowing how to answer a second question: How do we predict whether or not a chemical reaction will actually occur when specific chemicals are brought together under a given set of conditions?

Two areas of physical chemistry are devoted to providing a quantitative basis for the prediction of whether or not reactions will occur. The energy changes that accompany a specific reaction and the rate of the reaction must both be examined.

Predicting energy relationships is the business of thermodynamics, which we have introduced in our discussion of heats of reaction (Chapter 7), and which we discuss further in Chapter 22. Thermodynamics allows us to predict whether or not a reaction is favorable so far as energy changes are concerned. However, thermodynamics does not reveal how *fast* a reaction takes place. To be certain that reactants will interact within a reasonable time after they are mixed requires knowing the *rate* of the reaction under the given conditions. This is the concern of chemical kinetics, which is introduced in the next chapter.

Chemists frequently describe a substance or mixture as "stable." Strictly speaking, there are two kinds of stability—thermodynamic stability and kinetic stability. Thermodynamic stability is energy dependent. A *thermodynamically stable* substance is not likely to undergo chemical changes because it is already in a state of reasonably low energy. A *kinetically stable* substance might have the potential of reaching a lower energy state by chemical change, but the change would take place too slowly to be useful or interesting. General references to "stability" in discussing chemical properties almost always relate to thermodynamic stability.

A description of something as "stable" means that it is likely to remain unchanged *under a certain set of conditions.* Whether the conditions are specified or not, we must always ask ourselves, Stable in what way? Stable with respect to what? The conditions referred to might be temperature (thermal stability), pressure, acidity or alkalinity, an oxidative or reductive environment, concentration, or the presence of other substances. Often a substance is described as "stable" simply because it can be handled and stored without special precautions to protect it from reacting with water or oxygen in the air. Also, "stable" often refers to thermal stability and is used to describe a substance that does not decompose easily when heated.

In the preceding sections of the chapter we have referred to the "stability" of a number of compounds in various ways that are common:

1. "The formation of one complex ion from another can occur . . . if the product is more stable to dissociation than the reactant" (see Equation 17.16). The concept of stability is frequently applied to substances that establish equilibria in aqueous solution. Here we referred to the fact that complex ions are present in solution in equilibrium with their dissociation products.

$$[HgCl_4]^{2-} \rightleftharpoons Hg^{2+} + 4Cl^-$$
$$[Hg(CN)_4]^{2-} \rightleftharpoons Hg^{2+} + 4CN^-$$

The $[Hg(CN)_4]^{2-}$ complex is the "more stable" of these two complexes because it dissociates less. In solutions of these two complex ions of comparable concentration, the concentration of simple Hg^{2+} ions would be lower in the solution of the cyanide complex.

2. "A mixture of lead(II) sulfate and water is very stable with respect to reaction to form lead sulfide and hydrogen peroxide." Here we were referring specifically to stability toward oxidation and reduction. Lead(II) sulfate is *not* a strong enough oxidizing agent and water is *not* a strong enough reducing agent. No redox reaction is possible.

3. "For . . . thallium, lead, and bismuth, the lower of the two [oxidation] states is by far the more stable." What is meant here is that these elements in their higher oxidation states will react as oxidizing agents and become reduced whenever the opportunity presents itself.

    Following are some further examples of reference to stability from later chapters.

4. "Nitric oxide [nitrogen(II) oxide], NO, is not stable in air." Here, the lack of stability refers to the ready oxidation of the oxide by atmospheric oxygen to give nitrogen dioxide [nitrogen(IV) oxide], NO_2. Nitric oxide is a product of

combustion of fossil fuels, and the conversion to the dioxide contributes to the pollution of the atmosphere.

5. "Manganate(VI) ion (MnO_4^{2-}) is stable only in alkaline solution." This statement obviously means that the manganate(VI) ion can be prepared and handled in alkaline solution, but undergoes a chemical change if the solution is made neutral or acidic. This ion, which contains a transition metal in an intermediate oxidation state, undergoes a disproportionation reaction (Section 17.4d) in acid solution.

$$\overset{+6}{3MnO_4^{2-}} + 4H^+ \longrightarrow \overset{+4}{MnO_2}(s) + \overset{+7}{2MnO_4^-} + 2H_2O(l)$$

6. "Chlorous acid ($HClO_2$), which forms when an alkaline solution of chlorite ion (ClO_2^-) is treated with acid, is an *extremely unstable substance*." When "unstable" is used with strong emphasis it means "watch out." In this case, it appears that the substance is unstable with respect to its very existence in acidic solution and that it is not likely to stay around very long. The reason is that as soon as it is formed, chlorous acid undergoes a redox disproportionation reaction (Section 17.4d) that is sometimes accompanied by explosion of the chlorine dioxide (ClO_2) that is produced.

$$\underset{\text{chlorite ion}}{ClO_2^-} + H^+ \rightleftharpoons \underset{\text{chlorous acid}}{HClO_2(aq)}$$

$$\overset{+3}{4\ HClO_2}(aq) \longrightarrow 2H^+ + \underset{\underset{\text{dioxide}}{\text{chlorine}}}{\overset{+4}{2ClO_2}(g)} + \overset{+5}{ClO_3^-} + \overset{-1}{Cl^-} + H_2O(l)$$

17.8 BALANCING REDOX EQUATIONS: OXIDATION NUMBER METHOD

The equations for many redox reactions are difficult to balance by inspection. Step-by-step methods must be used to balance such equations. The method discussed here is based on the total oxidation number changes in the reaction. (A second method, based on electron "gain" and "loss," is discussed in Section 23.2.)

The *total* increase in oxidation number in a redox reaction is the increase in oxidation number times the number of atoms that undergo the increase. In the reaction

$$\overset{0}{2H_2}(g) + \overset{0}{O_2}(g) \longrightarrow \overset{+1\ -2}{2H_2O}(l)$$

each H atom is oxidized from 0 to +1 and the total oxidation number increase is $(4)(+1) = +4$. Similarly, for the two oxygen atoms that are reduced, the total oxidation number decrease is $(2)(-2) = -4$. Notice that these changes are equal and of opposite sign. In a redox reaction, the total increase in oxidation number always equals the total decrease in oxidation number.

To balance a redox reaction by the oxidation number method requires five steps. These steps are given below and are illustrated for the reaction between dichromate ion and iron(II) ion to give chromium(III) ion and iron(III) ion in an acidic solution.

Step A. *Write the unbalanced equation for major reactants and products. Determine total oxidation number changes.*

$$\overset{+6}{Cr_2O_7^{2-}} + \overset{+2}{Fe^{2+}} \longrightarrow \overset{+3}{Cr^{3+}} + \overset{+3}{Fe^{3+}}$$

To find the total oxidation number increase and decrease, use partial "equations" in which the *numbers of the atoms* oxidized and reduced are balanced. Here, for example, since there are two Cr atoms in $Cr_2O_7^{2-}$, there must also be two Cr^{3+} ions produced.

$$\overset{+6}{Cr_2O_7{}^{2-}} \longrightarrow 2\overset{+3}{Cr^{3+}} \qquad \textit{total decrease in oxidation}$$
$$\qquad\qquad\qquad\qquad \textit{number is } (2)(-3) = -6$$
$$\overset{+2}{Fe^{2+}} \longrightarrow \overset{+3}{Fe^{3+}} \qquad \textit{total increase in oxidation}$$
$$\qquad\qquad\qquad\qquad \textit{number is } (1)(+1) = +1$$

Step B. *Add coefficients to balance change in oxidation number.* The total increase in oxidation number must equal the total decrease in oxidation number. If necessary, multiply the species oxidized and reduced by factors that equalize the change in oxidation number. In this case, with a total decrease of -6 (for Cr) and a total increase of $+1$ (for Fe), both Fe^{2+} and Fe^{3+} must be multiplied by 6 to equalize the change.

$$\overset{(2)(-3)\,=\,-6}{Cr_2O_7{}^{2-} + 6Fe^{2+} \longrightarrow 2Cr^{3+} + 6Fe^{3+}}$$
$$(6)(+1) = +6$$

Step C. *If necessary, balance the charges.* To balance charge, H^+ may be added for reactions in acidic solution and OH^- may be added for reactions in alkaline solution. After Step B, the equation has a total charge of $(-2) + (6)(+2) = +10$ on the left and $(2)(+3) + (6)(+3) = +24$ on the right. To balance the charge for this reaction in acidic solution, $14\ H^+$ ions must be added on the left.

$$Cr_2O_7{}^{2-} + 6Fe^{2+} + 14H^+ \longrightarrow 2Cr^{3+} + 6Fe^{3+}$$

Note: In balancing the charge in a redox equation, and also in checking the charge balance, be sure that you use the *charges on ions.* Do not make the <u>common error</u> of confusing oxidation numbers and ionic charges.

Step D. *Complete balancing by inspection, using water to balance oxygen* (for reactions in aqueous solution). Seven oxygen atoms are needed on the right in this case, so seven water molecules are added.

$$Cr_2O_7{}^{2-} + 6Fe^{2+} + 14H^+ \longrightarrow 2Cr^{3+} + 6Fe^{3+} + 7H_2O(l)$$

Inspection shows that the hydrogen atoms are now balanced and no other atoms need to be balanced.

Step E. *Check to be sure that both atoms and charge are balanced.* On each side of the equation there are 2 Cr, 7 O, 6 Fe, and 14 H atoms. On each side the total charge is $+24$. The equation is balanced.

As the following examples demonstrate, this method applies equally well to reactions in alkaline solution and to molecular rather than net ionic equations.

EXAMPLE 17.14
Balancing Redox Equations

Write the balanced chemical equation for the oxidation of iodate ion ($IO_3{}^-$) to periodate ion ($IO_4{}^-$) by permanganate ion in alkaline solution.

Step A. *Write the unbalanced equation for major reactants and products. Determine total oxidation number changes.* From Table 17.8 we see that when permanganate ion, $MnO_4{}^-$, acts as an oxidizing agent in alkaline solution, the reduction product is manganese(IV) oxide, $MnO_2(s)$.

$$\overset{+7}{MnO_4^-} + \overset{+5}{IO_3^-} \longrightarrow \overset{+4}{MnO_2} + \overset{+7}{IO_4^-}$$

$$\overset{+7}{MnO_4^-} \longrightarrow \overset{+4}{MnO_2} \qquad (1)(-3) = -3$$

$$\overset{+5}{IO_3^-} \longrightarrow \overset{+7}{IO_4^-} \qquad (1)(+2) = +2$$

Step B. *Add coefficients to balance change in oxidation number.*

$$\overset{(2)(-3)=-6}{\overbrace{2MnO_4^- + 3IO_3^- \longrightarrow 2MnO_2 + 3IO_4^-}}$$
$$\underset{(3)(+2)=+6}{\underbrace{}}$$

Step C. *If necessary, balance charge.* The total charge on the left is $(2)(-1) + (3)(-1) = -5$ and the total charge on the right is $(3)(-1) = -3$. Hydroxide ion must be added on the right to balance charge, since this is a reaction in alkaline solution.

$$2MnO_4^- + 3IO_3^- \longrightarrow 2MnO_2 + 3IO_4^- + 2OH^-$$

Step D. *Complete balancing by inspection, using water to balance oxygen.* There are $(2)(4) + (3)(3) = 17$ oxygen atoms on the left and $(2)(2) + (3)(4) + (2)(1) = 18$ oxygen atoms on the right. One water molecule must be added on the left to balance oxygen.

$$2MnO_4^- + 3IO_3^- + H_2O(l) \longrightarrow 2MnO_2(s) + 3IO_4^- + 2OH^-$$

Step E. *Check atom and charge balance.* On each side there are 2 Mn, 18 O, 3 I, and 2 H atoms. On each side the charge is -5. The equation is balanced.

Exercise Balance the following redox equation:

$$MnO_2(s) + PbO_2(s) \xrightarrow{H^+} MnO_4^- + Pb^{2+}$$

Answer $2MnO_2(s) + 3PbO_2(s) + 4H^+ \longrightarrow 2MnO_4^- + 3Pb^{2+} + 2H_2O(l)$

EXAMPLE 17.15
Balancing Redox Equations

The products of the thermal decomposition of nickel nitrate are nickel(II) oxide, nitrogen dioxide, and oxygen. Write a balanced equation for this reaction.

Step A. *Write the unbalanced equation for major reactants and products. Determine total oxidation number changes.*

$$\overset{+5-2}{Ni(NO_3)_2(s)} \xrightarrow{\Delta} NiO(s) + \overset{+4}{NO_2(g)} + \overset{0}{O_2(g)}$$

$$\overset{+5}{Ni(NO_3)_2} \longrightarrow \overset{+4}{2NO_2} \qquad (2)(-1) = -2$$

$$\overset{-2}{Ni(NO_3)_2} \longrightarrow \overset{0}{3O_2} \qquad (6)(+2) = +12$$

Step B. *Add coefficients to balance change in oxidation number.*

$$(6)(-2) = -12$$

$$6Ni(NO_3)_2(s) \xrightarrow{\Delta} NiO(s) + 12NO_2(g) + 3O_2(g)$$

$$(6)(+2) = +12$$

(Not all of the oxygen atoms are oxidized.)

Step C. *If necessary, balance the charges.* Not needed.
Step D. *Complete balancing by inspection.* In this case, water is not involved in balancing the equation, for the reaction does not take place in aqueous solution. It is apparent that 6 Ni atoms and 6 O atoms are needed on the right.

$$6Ni(NO_3)_2(s) \xrightarrow{\Delta} 6NiO(s) + 12NO_2(g) + 3O_2(g)$$

Step E. *Check atom and charge balance.* There are 6 Ni, 12 N, and 36 O atoms on each side and there are no ions present. The equation is balanced. Occasionally a stepwise method leads, as in this case, to an equation balanced with coefficients that have a common denominator. This equation could be written as

$$2Ni(NO_3)_2(s) \xrightarrow{\Delta} 2NiO(s) + 4NO_2(g) + O_2(g)$$

Exercise Sulfite ion, SO_3^{2-}, reacts with chromate ion, CrO_4^{2-}, in alkaline solution to give $[Cr(OH)_4]^-$ and SO_4^{2-}. Write the balanced chemical equation for this redox reaction. *Answer* $3SO_3^{2-} + 2CrO_4^{2-} + 5H_2O(l) \longrightarrow 3SO_4^{2-} + 2[Cr(OH)_4]^- + 2OH^-$

SUMMARY

17.1 THE STUDY OF CHEMICAL REACTIONS **17.2** IS EQUILIBRIUM ESTABLISHED IN ALL CHEMICAL REACTIONS? In theory, all chemical reactions reach equilibrium. In practice, many reactions "go to completion"—they proceed so far that the reactants are almost entirely converted to products. This will occur when one or more products are removed from the system and so are unavailable for the reverse reaction. For example, the product may be a gas which escapes, or precipitate that removes ions from solution. Le Chatelier's principle states that if a system at equilibrium is subjected to a stress, it will react so as to relieve the stress. The formation of a product that is unavailable for the reverse reaction is a stress that results in more of that product being formed, driving the reaction further toward completion. In addition, some products are so stable with respect to the reverse reaction that in practice the reaction goes in only one direction. This is often the case with reactions of strong oxidizing or reducing agents.

17.3 A REVIEW OF NONREDOX REACTIONS In a nonredox reaction there is no change in oxidation numbers. Elements can never be reactants or products in such reactions. Many nonredox reactions of common substances can be classified as combination, decomposition, displacement, or partner exchange. Table 17.2 gives examples of these types of nonredox reactions. Compounds may combine to give other compounds. Compounds may decompose with heat to give other compounds, particularly if the products are gases. Less volatile oxides displace more volatile oxides, and ligands displace other ligands to form more stable complex ions. Partner-exchange reactions between ions in solution take place when ions are removed from solution as gases, precipitates, weak electrolytes, or water.

17.4 A REVIEW OF REDOX REACTIONS Many of the simple types of redox reactions involve free elements as reactants or products. Examples of such reactions are given in Table 17.7. More active metals—those metals that are stronger reducing agents—displace less active metals from compounds. The metal activity series (Table 17.4) allows prediction of the outcome of many such reactions. A short activity series (Table 17.5) can be used to predict some reactions of some of the nonmetals. Elements combine to give compounds. In such reactions, the more electronegative element is the oxidizing agent. Thermal decomposition is undergone by oxides and halides of the least active metals, by metal nitrates, and by ammonium salts with oxidizing anions. In disproportionation reactions, an element in one oxidation state is both oxidized and reduced. Many redox reactions, notably those of oxygen-containing redox agents in acidic or alkaline solutions, and reactions of gaseous, liquid, and solid compounds with each other, are not easily categorized.

17.5 OXIDIZING AND REDUCING AGENTS   A number of common oxidizing agents are listed in Table 17.8. Many oxidizing agents contain oxygen combined with other elements in their higher oxidation states. Among the common oxidizing agents are the oxoanions of the halogens, and the permanganate and dichromate ions. Nitric and concentrated sulfuric acids are important oxidizing acids. The free halogens are also strong oxidizing agents. Some common reducing agents are listed in Table 17.9. A number of free metals, especially the active metals of Groups I and II, are reducing agents.

17.6 PREDICTING REACTION PRODUCTS   **17.7** CHEMICAL STABILITY   A flow chart useful for predicting possible reaction products is given in Table 17.10. Not all reactions that are possible, however, will actually take place. The energy change of the reaction and its rate must both be taken into consideration. A thermodynamically stable substance is not likely to undergo a chemical change because it is already in a state of relatively low energy. A kinetically stable substance is one that will undergo a particular chemical change only at an insignificantly slow rate. In discussions of chemical properties, the word "stable" generally refers to thermodynamic stability. Stability is generally a function of specific conditions such as temperature, pH, and so on.

17.8 BALANCING REDOX EQUATIONS: OXIDATION NUMBER METHOD   In a redox reaction, the total increase in oxidation number always equals the total decrease in oxidation number. This fact is the basis for the method of balancing redox equations given in Section 17.8.

SIGNIFICANT TERMS

Le Chatelier's principle
acid salt
internal redox reaction
oxidizing anion
disproportionation reaction
oxidizing acid

THOUGHTS ON CHEMISTRY

Chemicals: How Many Are There?

CHEMICALS: HOW MANY ARE THERE?
by Thomas H. Maugh II

Like it or not, the world around us is filled with chemicals. The clothes we wear, the foods we eat, the magazines we read, and virtually all of the other things that nurture our civilization are made possible by the use of chemicals. Recognition of these facts, and of some of the potential dangers of chemicals, often prompts the question How many chemicals are there? A definitive answer to that question has proved elusive, but one measure of the answer is provided by the American Chemical Society's Chemical Abstracts Service (CAS). As of November 1977, CAS's unique computer registry of chemicals contained 4,039,907 distinct entities. The number of chemicals in the register, moreover, has been growing at an average rate of about 6000 per week. . . . The registry contains all compounds that have been mentioned in the literature since 1965.

The system is not set up to provide a detailed breakdown of different classes of chemicals. Some broad generalizations can be made, though. About 96 percent of the chemicals, for example, contain carbon. The average compound in the registry, if it is possible to define such a thing as an average compound, contains 43 atoms, 22 of which are hydrogen. The fictitious average compound also contains one and a half ring systems with eight atoms per ring.

About 3.4 million of the chemicals are organic or inorganic chemicals whose structures are fully defined. About 59,000 are organic compounds whose structures are not completely defined. About 120,000 entries are listed only by name or molecular formula; these are specifically identified substances for which not enough is known or has been disclosed about structure to permit machine structure registration. The registry also lists 72,000 alloys, 120,000 polymers, and 10,000 mixtures with specific names. . . .

The vast majority of chemicals in the registry are esoteric materials that have been isolated from natural products or synthesized for research purposes. A more interesting problem, then, might be to define the number of chemicals that are in everyday use. . . .

. . . The best estimate is that there are about 63,000 chemicals in common use.

Thomas H. Maugh II, "Chemicals: How Many Are There?" *Science* **199**, 162 (13 January 1978). (Copyright 1978 by the American Association for the Advancement of Science.)

QUESTIONS

Chemical Equilibrium

17.1 When a chemical reaction reaches equilibrium, does that mean that there are equal amounts of reactants and products? Have all chemical reactions stopped at equilibrium? Explain your answers.

17.2 Name the general principle that governs the displacement of equilibria. State this principle in words.

17.3 Which of the following reactions are likely to "go to completion"? Explain your reasoning.
(a) $CaC_2(s) + 2H_2O(l) \longrightarrow C_2H_2(g) + Ca(OH)_2(aq)$
(b) $H_2AsO_3^- + 3Ag^+ \longrightarrow Ag_3AsO_3(s) + 2H^+$
(c) $CaCO_3(s) + 2HCl(aq) \longrightarrow CaCl_2(aq) + CO_2(g) + H_2O(l)$
(d) $AgCl(s) \xrightarrow{H_2O} Ag^+ + Cl^-$

17.4 Repeat Question 17.3 for the following reactions:
(a) $2NaCl(s) + H_2SO_4(conc) \longrightarrow Na_2SO_4(aq) + 2HCl(g)$
(b) $2Fe^{3+} + 3Cu^{2+} \longrightarrow 2Fe(s) + 3Cu(s)$
(c) $UO_2(NO_3)_2(aq) + (NH_4)_2SO_3(aq) \longrightarrow$
$$UO_2SO_3(s) + 2NH_4NO_3(aq)$$
(d) $H_3AsO_3(aq) + H_2O_2(aq) \longrightarrow H_3AsO_4(aq) + H_2O(l)$

Nonredox Reactions

17.5 Write chemical equations for the nonredox combination of (a) $NH_3(g)$ with $H_2SO_4(aq)$ and (b) $CaO(s)$ with $SiO_2(l)$. (The first reaction produces a useful nitrogen fertilizer and the second occurs during the production of glass.)

17.6 A common superphosphate fertilizer consists of a mixture of $CaSO_4(s)$ and $Ca(H_2PO_4)_2(s)$. This fertilizer is produced by the nonredox reaction of $Ca_3(PO_4)_2(s)$ with sulfuric acid. Write the chemical equation for this reaction.

17.7 What are the usual products produced by the nonredox thermal decomposition of (a) ammonium salts, (b) carbonates, except those of the most active metals, (c) many hydroxides, and (d) acid salts?

17.8 Complete and balance the following nonredox displacement reactions:
(a) $Na_2CO_3(l) + SiO_2(s) \longrightarrow$
(b) $[Cu(H_2O)_4]^{2+} + NH_3(aq) \longrightarrow$
(c) $[AgCl_2]^- + NH_3(aq) \longrightarrow$

17.9 Choose the nonredox partner-exchange reactions which will take place:
(a) $Pb(NO_3)_2(aq) + H_2SO_4(aq) \longrightarrow PbSO_4(s) + 2HNO_3(aq)$
(b) $Hg_2Cl_2(s) + 2KNO_3(aq) \longrightarrow Hg_2(NO_3)_2(aq) + 2KCl(aq)$
(c) $BaCrO_4(s) + 2KNO_3(aq) \longrightarrow Ba(NO_3)_2(aq) + K_2CrO_4(aq)$
(d) $HCl(aq) + KHSO_3(aq) \longrightarrow SO_2(g) + H_2O(l) + KCl(aq)$
(e) $Ni(OH)_2(s) + 2HCl(aq) \longrightarrow NiCl_2(aq) + 2H_2O(l)$
Give reasons for your answers.

17.10 Repeat Question 17.9 for
(a) $FeS(s) + 2HCl(aq) \longrightarrow FeCl_2(aq) + H_2S(g)$
(b) $BaSO_4(s) + 2KCl(aq) \longrightarrow BaCl_2(aq) + K_2SO_4(aq)$
(c) $2NaOH(aq) + H_2S(aq) \longrightarrow Na_2S(aq) + 2H_2O(l)$

17.11 Predict the products of each of the following nonredox partner-exchange reactions:
(a) $Ba(NO_3)_2(aq) + H_2SO_4(aq) \longrightarrow$
(b) $CaI_2(aq) + AgNO_3(aq) \longrightarrow$
(c) $Ca_3(PO_4)_2(s) + H_2SO_4(l) \longrightarrow$
(d) $NH_4Cl(aq) + KOH(aq) \longrightarrow$
(e) $CaCl_2(aq) + Na_2C_2O_4(aq) \longrightarrow$

17.12 Repeat Question 17.11 for
(a) $Na_2S(aq) + HCl(aq) \longrightarrow$
(b) $CdSO_4(aq) + Na_2S(aq) \longrightarrow$
(c) $(NH_4)_2CrO_4(aq) + Pb(CH_3COO)_2(aq) \longrightarrow$
(d) $AsCl_3(aq) + H_2S(aq) \longrightarrow$

Redox Reactions

17.13 Complete and balance the following redox combination reactions between free elements:

(a) $C(s) + O_2(g, \text{excess}) \longrightarrow$
(b) $P_4(s) + Cl_2(g, \text{excess}) \longrightarrow$
(c) $Ti(s) + Cl_2(g) \longrightarrow$
(d) $Mg(s) + N_2(g) \longrightarrow$

17.14 Identify the products of the following redox combination reactions:

(a) $FeO(s) + O_2(g) \longrightarrow$
(b) $NO(g) + O_2(g) \longrightarrow$
(c) $P_4O_6(s) + O_2(g) \longrightarrow$

17.15 Complete and balance the following redox displacement reactions:

(a) $K(s) + H_2O(l) \longrightarrow$
(b) $Mg(s) + HBr(aq) \longrightarrow$
(c) $NaBr(aq) + Cl_2(aq) \longrightarrow$
(d) $WO_3(s) + H_2(g) \longrightarrow$
(e) $H_2S(aq) + Cl_2(aq) \longrightarrow$

17.16 Using the activity series, predict whether or not the following reactions in aqueous solution will occur:

(a) $Mg(s) + Cu^{2+} \longrightarrow Mg^{2+} + Cu(s)$
(b) $Pb(s) + 2H^+ \longrightarrow H_2(g) + Pb^{2+}$
(c) $2Ag^+ + Cu(s) \longrightarrow 2Ag(s) + Cu^{2+}$
(d) $2Al^{3+} + 3Zn(s) \longrightarrow 3Zn^{2+} + 2Al(s)$

Explain your reasoning.

17.17 Repeat Question 17.16 for the following reactions:

(a) $Mg(s) + Ca(s) \longrightarrow Mg^{2+} + Ca^{2+}$
(b) $2Al^{3+} + 3Pb^{2+} \longrightarrow 2Al(s) + 3Pb(s)$
(c) $H_2(g) + Zn^{2+} \longrightarrow 2H^+ + Zn(s)$
(d) $2KI(aq) + Br_2(aq) \longrightarrow 2KBr(aq) + I_2(aq)$

17.18* Complete and balance the equations for the following redox displacement reactions: (a) the preparation of chlorine by heating hydrogen chloride with oxygen in the presence of copper chloride as catalyst (the Deacon process) and (b) the preparation of finely divided elemental iron by passing hydrogen over heated solid iron(III) oxide.

17.19 What are the usual products formed by the thermal decomposition of (a) nitrates of Representative Group I and II metals, and (b) nitrates of less active metals?

17.20 What is a disproportionation reaction? How can we recognize the possibility of a given compound undergoing such a reaction?

17.21 Identify the products of the following disproportionation reactions:

(a) $Cu_2SO_4(aq) \longrightarrow$
(b) $Hg_2Cl_2(s) \longrightarrow$
(c) $KClO_3(l) \longrightarrow$
(d) $Cl_2(g) + H_2O(l) \longrightarrow$

17.22 The sulfite ion is a good reducing agent. Predict the products of the redox reactions between SO_3^{2-} and (a) $Br_2(aq)$, (b) $O_2(g)$, (c) $H_2O_2(aq)$, and (d) MnO_4^- in acidic solution.

17.23 Zinc metal is a good reducing agent. Predict the products of the redox reactions between $Zn(s)$ and (a) $O_2(g)$, (b) H^+, and (c) $I_2(aq)$.

17.24 Lithium metal is a good reducing agent. Predict the products of the reactions between $Li(s)$ and (a) $H_2O(l)$, (b) $O_2(g)$, (c)

$F_2(g)$, (d) $H_2(g)$, and (e) $N_2(g)$.

17.25 The permanganate ion is a good oxidizing agent. Predict the products of the redox reactions between MnO_4^- and (a) $SO_2(g)$, (b) Cl^-, and (c) Sn^{2+}, assuming all reactions take place in an acidic solution.

17.26 Gaseous chlorine is a good oxidizing agent. Predict the products of the redox reactions between $Cl_2(g)$ and (a) $P_4(s)$, (b) $PCl_3(l)$, (c) $CuCl(s)$, and (d) I^-.

17.27 Determine which of the following are redox reactions. Identify the oxidizing and reducing agent in each of the redox reactions.

(a) $Ti(s) + 2Cl_2(g) \xrightarrow{\Delta} TiCl_4(l)$
(b) $NH_4Br(s) \longrightarrow NH_3(g) + HBr(g)$
(c) $3CuO(s) + 2NH_3(g) \xrightarrow{\Delta} 3Cu(s) + N_2(g) + 3H_2O(g)$
(d) $K_2Cr_2O_7(aq) + 14HCl(aq) \longrightarrow$
$\qquad 2KCl(aq) + 2CrCl_3(aq) + 7H_2O(l) + 3Cl_2(g)$

17.28 Repeat Question 17.27 for:

(a) $NaOH(aq) + H_3PO_4(aq) \longrightarrow NaH_2PO_4(aq) + H_2O(l)$
(b) $NH_3(g) + CO_2(g) + H_2O(l) \longrightarrow NH_4HCO_3(aq)$
(c) $TiCl_4(g) + 2Mg(l) \xrightarrow{\Delta} Ti(s) + 2MgCl_2(l)$
(d) $NaCl(s) + NaHSO_4(s) \xrightarrow{\Delta} HCl(g) + Na_2SO_4(s)$

Predicting Reaction Products

17.29 Predict the major products of the following reactions:

(a) $SO_3(g) + H_2O(l) \longrightarrow$
(b) $Sr(s) + H_2(g) \longrightarrow$
(c) $Mg(s) + H_2SO_4(aq, \text{dilute}) \longrightarrow$
(d) $Na_3PO_4(aq) + AgNO_3(aq) \longrightarrow$
(e) $Li_2O(s) + SO_2(g) \longrightarrow$
(f) $Ca(HCO_3)_2(s) \xrightarrow{\Delta}$
(g) $P_4O_6(s) + O_2(g) \longrightarrow$

17.30 Repeat Question 17.29 for:

(a) $Li(s) + H_2O(l) \longrightarrow$
(b) $Ag_2O(s) \xrightarrow{\Delta}$
(c) $Li_2O(s) + H_2O(l) \longrightarrow$
(d) $H_2O(l) \xrightarrow{\text{electrolysis}}$
(e) $I_2(s) + Cl^-(aq) \longrightarrow$
(f) $Cu(s) + HCl(aq) \longrightarrow$
(g) $NaNO_3(s) \xrightarrow{\Delta}$

17.31 Write balanced equations for the following chemical reactions:

(a) $Al(s) + H_2SO_4(aq) \longrightarrow$
(b) $NO_2(g) + H_2O(l) \longrightarrow$
(c) $Pb_3O_4(s) \xrightarrow{\Delta}$
(d) $N_2(g) + H_2(g) \longrightarrow$

17.32 Repeat Question 17.31 for:

(a) $NH_4NO_3(s) \xrightarrow{\Delta}$

(b) $H_2S(g) + Pb(CH_3COO)_2(aq) \longrightarrow$

(c) $Ba(OH)_2(aq) + H_2SO_4(aq) \longrightarrow$

(d) $Fe^{3+} + Sn^{2+} \longrightarrow$

Chemical Stability

17.33 Briefly define "thermodynamic stability" and "kinetic stability." If a substance is thermodynamically unstable, does that mean that the substance will react readily? Why? A substance can be described as "stable" with respect to a number of conditions. Name some of them.

17.34 Write a sentence describing the stabilities of the chromate ion and dichromate ion as a function of the concentration of H^+. The relevant chemical equation is

$$2CrO_4^{2-} + 2H^+ \rightleftharpoons Cr_2O_7^{2-} + H_2O(l)$$

17.35 Compare the relative stabilities of ozone and oxygen, given the following data:

$$2O_3(g) \longrightarrow 3O_2(g) \qquad \Delta H^\circ = -285.3 \text{ kJ}$$

17.36 Compare the relative stabilities of $AgCl$ and $[Ag(NH_3)_2]^+$. The relevant chemical equation is

$$AgCl(s) + 2NH_3(aq) \xrightarrow{\text{excess } NH_3} [Ag(NH_3)_2]^+ + Cl^-$$

Balancing Redox Equations Using Oxidation Numbers

17.37 Using the oxidation number method, balance the equations for the following reactions:

(a) $SiO_2(s) + Al(s) \longrightarrow Si(s) + Al_2O_3(s)$

(b) $I_2(s) + H_2S(aq) \longrightarrow I^- + S(s) + H^+$

(c) $PbO_2(s) + HCl(aq) \longrightarrow Cl_2(g) + PbCl_2(s) + H_2O(l)$

(d) $Cu(s) + Br_2(aq) + OH^- \longrightarrow Cu_2O(s) + Br^- + H_2O(l)$

(e) $S^{2-} + Cl_2(g) + OH^- \longrightarrow SO_4^{2-} + Cl^- + H_2O(l)$

17.38 Repeat Question 17.37 for:

(a) $H_2O_2(aq) + HI(aq) \longrightarrow I_2(s) + H_2O(l)$

(b) $H_2S(g) + O_2(g) \longrightarrow SO_2(g) + H_2O(g)$

(c) $NH_3(g) + O_2(g) \longrightarrow NO(g) + H_2O(g)$

(d) $MnO_4^- + IO_3^- + H_2O(l) \longrightarrow MnO_2(s) + IO_4^- + OH^-$

(e) $Sn(s) + OH^- + H_2O(l) \longrightarrow [Sn(OH)_4]^{2-} + H_2(g)$

17.39 Repeat Question 17.37 for:

(a) $SO_2(g) + H_2S(g) \longrightarrow S_8(s) + H_2O(g)$

(b) $Ca_3(PO_4)_2(s) + C(s) + SiO_2(s) \longrightarrow$
$$CaSiO_3(l) + P_4(g) + CO(g)$$

(c) $SO_2(g) + Cr_2O_7^{2-} + H^+ \longrightarrow Cr^{3+} + H_2SO_4(aq) + H_2O(l)$

(d) $Cl_2(g) + OH^- \longrightarrow ClO_3^- + Cl^- + H_2O(l)$

(e) $S(s) + OH^- \longrightarrow S^{2-} + SO_3^{2-} + H_2O(l)$

17.40* Identify the products, complete the equation, and balance the equation for the following:

(a) bismuth + concentrated nitric acid $\longrightarrow$ brown gas

(b) tin(II) chloride(aq) + mercury(II) chloride(aq) $\longrightarrow$ white precipitate

(c) zinc + dilute nitric acid $\longrightarrow$ ammonium ion

Additional Questions

17.41 Classify each of the following reactions according to the reaction types listed in Tables 17.2 and 17.7:

(a) $MgO(s) + 2HCl(aq) \longrightarrow MgCl_2(aq) + H_2O(l)$

(b) $WO_3(s) + 3H_2(g) \longrightarrow W(s) + 3H_2O(l)$

(c) $2NaHCO_3(s) \xrightarrow{\Delta} Na_2CO_3(s) + CO_2(g) + H_2O(g)$

(d) $CaO(s) + SO_2(g) \longrightarrow CaSO_3(s)$

17.42 Repeat Question 17.41 for:

(a) $BaO(s) + H_2O(l) \longrightarrow Ba(OH)_2(aq)$

(b) $CaH_2(s) + 2H_2O(l) \longrightarrow Ca(OH)_2(aq) + 2H_2(g)$

(c) $2SO_2(g) + O_2(g) \longrightarrow 2SO_3(g)$

(d) $2KClO_3(s) \xrightarrow{\Delta} 2KCl(s) + 3O_2(g)$

17.43 Repeat Question 17.41 for:

(a) $Zn(s) + 2AgNO_3(aq) \longrightarrow 2Ag(s) + Zn(NO_3)_2(aq)$

(b) $BaO(s) + SO_3(g) \longrightarrow BaSO_4(s)$

(c) $[Ni(H_2O)_4]^{2+} + 4CN^- \longrightarrow [Ni(CN)_4]^{2-} + 4H_2O(l)$

(d) $CaCO_3(s) + 2HCl(aq) \longrightarrow CaCl_2(aq) + H_2O(l) + CO_2(g)$

17.44 Repeat Question 17.41 for:

(a) $Na_2CO_3(l) + SiO_2(s) \xrightarrow{\Delta} Na_2SiO_3(l) + CO_2(g)$

(b) $3Cu(s) + 8HNO_3(aq) \longrightarrow$
$$3Cu(NO_3)_2(aq) + 2NO(g) + 4H_2O(l)$$

(c) $2NO(g) + O_2(g) \longrightarrow 2NO_2(g)$

(d) $(NH_4)_2Cr_2O_7(s) \xrightarrow{\Delta} N_2(g) + Cr_2O_3(s) + 4H_2O(g)$

17.45 A piece of magnesium ribbon was placed in a crucible and was strongly heated in air to give a mixture of magnesium oxide and magnesium nitride. A small amount of water was added to convert the magnesium nitride to gaseous ammonia and magnesium hydroxide. The sample was heated again to convert the magnesium hydroxide to magnesium oxide. Write chemical equations for each of these reactions. Classify each reaction as nonredox or redox. Within each classification, identify the type of reaction.

17.46* A piece of copper was allowed to react in hot concentrated sulfuric acid to give a solution. This solution was added slowly to a large volume of water, giving a blue solution. Addition of aqueous sodium sulfide to the blue solution produced a black precipitate. Addition of nitric acid dissolved the precipitate, forming a blue solution. Addition of a small amount of ammonia gave a light blue precipitate which dissolved upon addition of more ammonia, giving a blue-purple solution. A blue solution was formed upon the addition of sulfuric acid. A blue precipitate was produced by the addition of sodium hydroxide solution. This precipitate was removed by filtering and heated to give a black solid. The black solid dissolved in sulfuric acid. Upon addition of zinc, copper was regenerated. Write a net ionic equation for each of these reactions. Classify each as nonredox or redox. Within each classification, identify the type of reaction.

17.47* A laboratory experiment called for the following tests: (a) addition of Br^- to VO_2^+, (b) addition of I^- to VO_2^+ and extraction of $I_2(aq)$, (c) addition of Zn to VO_2^+, and (d) addition of V to

Zn^{2+}. No evident reaction was observed in test (a). After the I_2 extraction, a light blue-green solution remained in test (b). In test (c) a blue-green solution was formed which eventually changed to an indigo solution. An indigo solution was formed in test (d). Vanadium has several oxidation states. In acidic solution these are $+2$ as V^{2+}, indigo; $+3$ as V^{3+}, blue-green; $+4$ as VO^{2+}, light blue-green; and $+5$ as VO_2^+, yellow. Using the results of the four tests, create an activity series for Zn, I^-, Br^-, V, V^{2+}, V^{3+}, and VO^{2+}.

Answers to Selected Questions

17.4 (a) completion—formation of a gas; (b) reaction cannot occur—two reductions, no oxidation; (c) completion—insoluble precipitate removes ions from solution; (d) completion—H_2O_2 is a strong oxidizing agent, water is not a reducing agent

17.6 $Ca_3(PO_4)_2 + 2H_2SO_4 \longrightarrow Ca(H_2PO_4)_2 + 2CaSO_4$

17.7 (a)NH_3; (b) CO_2; (c) oxides and H_2O; (d) gaseous oxides of the nonmetals, the normal salts, and H_2O

17.10 (a) yes—formation of a gas; (b) no—$BaSO_4$ is highly insoluble; (c) yes—formation of H_2O, which is less ionized than H_2S

17.12 (a) $H_2S(g) + NaCl(aq)$, (b) $CdS(s) + Na_2SO_4(s)$, (c) $PbCrO_4(s) + NH_4(CH_3COO)(aq)$, (d) $As_2S_3(s) + HCl(aq)$

17.17 (a) no, cannot have two oxidations with no reduction; (b) no, cannot have two reductions with no oxidation; (c) no, Zn is a better reducing agent than H_2; (d) yes, Br_2 is a better oxidizing agent than I_2

17.18 (a) $4HCl(g) + O_2(g) \xrightarrow{\Delta}{}_{CuCl_2} 2H_2O(g) + 2Cl_2(g)$, (b) $Fe_2O_3(s) + 3H_2(g) \xrightarrow{\Delta} 2Fe(s) + 3H_2O(g)$

17.23 (a) $ZnO(s)$, (b) $Zn^{2+} + H_2(g)$, (c) $ZnI_2(aq)$

17.26 (a) $PCl_3(l)$ or $PCl_5(s)$, (b) $PCl_5(s)$, (c) $CuCl_2(s)$, (d) $I_2(aq) + Cl^-$

17.28 (c) oxidizing agent: $TiCl_4$; reducing agent: Mg

17.30 (a) $LiOH(aq)$, $H_2(g)$; (b) $Ag(s)$, $O_2(g)$; (c) $LiOH(aq)$; (d) $H_2(g)$, $O_2(g)$; (e) no reaction; (f) no reaction; (g) $NaNO_2$, $O_2(g)$

17.32 (a) $NH_4NO_3(s) \xrightarrow{\Delta} N_2O(g) + 2H_2O(g)$, (b) $H_2S(g) + Pb(CH_3COO)_2(aq) \longrightarrow PbS(s) + 2CH_3COOH(aq)$, (c) $Ba(OH)_2(aq) + H_2SO_4(aq) \longrightarrow BaSO_4(s) + 2H_2O(l)$, (d) $2Fe^{3+} + Sn^{2+} \longrightarrow 2Fe^{2+} + Sn^{4+}$

17.36 in the presence of excess ammonia, $[Ag(NH_3)_2]^+$ is more stable than AgCl

17.39 (a) $8SO_2 + 16H_2S \longrightarrow 3S_8 + 16H_2O$, (b) $2Ca_3(PO_4)_2 + 10C + 6SiO_2 \longrightarrow 6CaSiO_3 + P_4 + 10CO$, (c) $3SO_2 + Cr_2O_7^{2-} + 8H^+ \longrightarrow 2Cr^{3+} + 3H_2SO_4(aq) + H_2O$, (d) $3Cl_2 + 6OH^- \longrightarrow ClO_3^- + 5Cl^- + 3H_2O$, (e) $3S + 6OH^- \longrightarrow 2S^{2-} + SO_3^{2-} + 3H_2O$

17.41 (a) nonredox—partner exchange, (b) redox—displacement of one element from a compound by another element, (c) nonredox—decomposition to give compounds, (d) nonredox—combination of compounds

17.44 (a) nonredox—displacement, (b) redox—does not fit into any of the categories listed, (c) redox—combination of an element with a compound to give another compound, (d) redox—decomposition

17.47 V, Zn, V^{2+}, V^{3+}, I^-, VO^{2+}, Br^-

PROBLEMS

Review of Principles

17.1 More sulfuric acid is produced each year than any other synthetic chemical. One process for the production of H_2SO_4 can be represented by the following equations:

$$S(s) + O_2(g) \longrightarrow SO_2(g) \qquad \text{(i)}$$
$$SO_2(g) + \tfrac{1}{2}O_2(g) \longrightarrow SO_3(g) \qquad \text{(ii)}$$
$$SO_3(g) + H_2SO_4(l) \longrightarrow H_2S_2O_7(l) \qquad \text{(iii)}$$
$$H_2S_2O_7(l) + H_2O(l) \longrightarrow 2H_2SO_4(l) \qquad \text{(iv)}$$

Answer these questions about the chemicals and reactions involved in the above process. What is the oxidation state of S in (a) S, (b) SO_2, (c) SO_3, (d) H_2SO_4, and (e) $H_2S_2O_7$, and of O in (f) O_2, (g) SO_2, (h) SO_3, (i) H_2SO_4, and (j) $H_2S_2O_7$? (k) Which reactions involve oxidation–reduction? (l) Identify the oxidizing agents in the reactions involving oxidation–reduction. (m) If the process is 100% efficient, how many moles of H_2SO_4 are produced—net—for each mole of S atoms? [Note that some H_2SO_4 is used in reaction (iii).]

17.2 How many grams of $K_2Cr_2O_7$ are required to oxidize 50.0 g of HCHO to HCOOH? Assume Cr^{3+} is the preferred reduction product of $Cr_2O_7^{2-}$ in acidic medium. *Answer* 163 g

17.3 A 0.500 g sample of a powder containing $SnCl_2$ was oxidized using 0.103 M Ce^{4+} (in HCl solution). Find the mass % $SnCl_2$ in the powder, given that 35.72 mL of the Ce^{4+} solution was used. The reduction product of Ce^{4+} is Ce^{3+}. (HCl is not reduced.)

17.4* Which solution can oxidize more of a given reducing agent in an acidic solution: 1 L of 1 M $K_2Cr_2O_7$ or 1 L of 1 M $KMnO_4$? Assume that the oxidation products in both cases are the same. *Answer* $K_2Cr_2O_7$

CHAPTER 18

Chemical Kinetics

Chemical kinetics provides information about how fast a reaction takes place. This information has great practical value. For one thing, chemical engineers need to consult data on reaction rates in deciding how best to design chemical plants. Chemical kinetics also provides information about how individual molecules interact with each other, a topic of intense interest to those in pursuit of a deeper understanding of chemical reactions.

The scene of action in the modern study of kinetics is computer modeling of complex systems, computer-aided solution of equations that describe the variation in reactant concentrations with time, and the experimental observation of very fast reactions. The determination of reaction rates for very fast reactions and the detection of short-lived reaction intermediates present formidable experimental challenges. Modern techniques are meeting these challenges and making it possible to observe lower and lower concentrations of reactive intermediates and to study faster and faster reactions (see Thoughts on Chemistry: A Conversation with Manfred Eigen, which appears at the end of this chapter). The frontiers of study in kinetics were once reaction times on the order of milliseconds (10^{-3} s). Now kineticists are looking at reaction times of nanosecond (10^{-9} s) and even picosecond (10^{-12} s) duration. The limiting factor in studying fast reactions by laser spectroscopy is becoming the speed with which electrons can pass through the instrumentation.

These state-of-the-art techniques are beyond the scope of our present discussion. The best way of introducing you to this complex topic is to provide some insight into the molecular level, or micro, view of chemical reactions, together with a description of some of the simpler techniques used to study the macro aspects of kinetics.

CHEMICAL KINETICS AT THE MOLECULAR LEVEL

18.1 CHEMICAL KINETICS: RATES AND MECHANISMS

Given a correct, balanced chemical equation, we can derive useful information about the reaction represented by the equation. We can apply our knowledge of atomic masses and mole relationships to determine the amounts of reactants and products involved. We can use our knowledge of bond energies and heats of formation to determine the amount of heat absorbed or released by the reaction under different conditions. This information can all be derived from the chemical equation without our knowing anything about what happens to individual atoms, molecules, or ions *during* the reaction — the pathway from reactants to products is of no concern.

In chemical kinetics, we come to the area of chemistry that deals with what happens *while* a reaction is under way, not just with the final result. Ideally, we would like to sit back and observe the progress of each atom or ion from its position in the reactants to its position in the products. In fact, looking even more closely is desirable. Because chemical reactions take place by the transfer of electrons or by changes in the way electrons are shared, we would like to know the fate of every valence electron.

At one time, such close observation seemed an impossibility. Today, ingenious experimental techniques allow studies of individual reacting molecules, transient intermediate states of reactants, and very fast reactions. However, such experiments are difficult to perform and are often limited to specific types of reactions. Therefore, chemical reactions are usually studied by observing the overall behavior of larger quantities of reactants, which are easier to handle experimentally. Then mathematical models and prior knowledge about other reactions are used to deduce reasonable descriptions of the reaction pathway at the molecular and electron level.

The best way to get information about the pathway of a chemical reaction is to study how fast it happens — the *rate* of the reaction. Once the reaction rate is known, pathways can be proposed that are consistent with the rate information.

Perhaps an analogy will demonstrate the relationship between how fast a reaction takes place and what the pathway might be. Suppose you had several hundred textbooks in the basement of your house and wanted to move them to your study on the second floor. One possible pathway, or "reaction mechanism," might require the following steps: (1) put ten books (the maximum number you can lift) into a carton, (2) walk up one flight of stairs to the first floor, (3) rest a bit, (4) walk up another flight of stairs to the second floor, (5) empty the carton, and (6) return for another load. Another "reaction mechanism" might involve a different series of steps: (1) fill three cartons with books, (2) push the three full cartons into the elevator, (3) ride up to the second floor, (4) push the cartons off the elevator, (5) empty the cartons, and (6) ride down for another load. How fast the reaction — moving all of the books — is accomplished obviously is going to be dependent upon the pathway.

A typical pathway for a chemical reaction includes several simple steps called elementary reactions. An **elementary reaction** is a reaction that occurs in a single step exactly as written. The equation for an elementary reaction shows the actual species that must interact at the molecular level for the reaction to take place. It often does not represent what can be observed as the overall final result of a chemical reaction.

A **reaction mechanism** consists of all of the elementary steps in a single reaction pathway. These steps show all of the changes that take place at the molecular level. The sum of the reaction steps is the stoichiometric equation for the reaction. For example, the reaction of iodine monochloride and hydrogen,

$$2ICl(g) + H_2(g) \longrightarrow I_2(g) + 2HCl(g)$$

is proposed to have a two-step mechanism. One ICl molecule and one H_2 molecule first react to give HI and HCl. The HI molecule then reacts with another molecule of ICl. The HI molecule in this mechanism is an **intermediate** — a reactive species that is produced during the course of a reaction but always reacts further and is not among the final products of the reaction.

$$
\begin{array}{l}
ICl(g) + H_2(g) \longrightarrow HI(g) + HCl(g) \\
\underline{HI(g) + ICl(g) \longrightarrow I_2(g) + HCl(g)} \\
2ICl(g) + H_2(g) \longrightarrow I_2(g) + 2HCl(g)
\end{array}
$$

Chemical kinetics is the study of the rates and mechanisms of chemical reactions. We can use the book-moving analogy to illustrate another important point — an essential difference between chemical kinetics and chemical thermodynamics. The reaction rate, a kinetic property, is dependent upon the mechanism, but the thermodynamic properties of a reaction are independent of the mechanism. Earlier we studied the heats of chemical reactions without needing to know anything about reaction rates or mechanisms. Similarly, we could calculate the change in potential energy of the books as a result of their move from the basement to the second floor without knowing by which "mechanism" they got there. Thermodynamics (Chapters 7 and 22) can tell us whether or not a reaction is possible, but kinetics is needed to tell us if the reaction happens *fast enough* to be of any interest or value.

18.2 HOW REACTANTS
GET TOGETHER

What is necessary for two molecules to react with each other? In considering this question, let's look at the usual simplest case — some isolated molecules in the gas phase. Ozone and nitric oxide react with each other in the upper atmosphere as follows:

$$O_3(g) + NO(g) \longrightarrow NO_2(g) + O_2(g) \tag{18.1}$$

This is one of the reactions that may contribute to depletion of the ozone layer (Section 25.4).

Suppose we have mixed small amounts of these two gases and can study the reaction by watching the individual molecules. We would see the molecules flying about in random paths, as expected from kinetic-molecular theory (Section 5.2). Some molecules move faster and have more kinetic energy than others — the distribution of speeds and energies is determined by the temperature. The molecules also have internal energy, represented by the vibration of the individual atoms and the rotation of the molecule (Section 7.6).

Ozone and nitric oxide molecules often collide with each other as they fly about. The frequency of collisions between O_3 and NO clearly depends on their relative *concentrations*. At 1 atm and 0 °C, for equal concentrations of O_3 and NO, there are about 10^{29} O_3–NO collisions per cubic centimeter per second. Each collision presents an opportunity for a reaction to occur between the two molecules that collide. We can think of a "collision" as having three parts: (1) the approach of the molecules, (2) interaction between the molecules, and (3) separation.

Two molecules approach each other from a distance, each with its own kinetic energy. When they get close enough together, their electrons "see" each other and repulsion builds up between the molecules. If their kinetic energies are not great enough to overcome this repulsion, the molecules just veer away from each other. The only results of this interaction are changes in the kinetic energy and direction of the molecules after they separate. No chemical reaction occurs.

On the other hand, the energy of the approaching molecules may be sufficient to drive them together in spite of the forces of repulsion, allowing the molecules to stay together for a brief time. In our imagined observation of such a collision, we would see the electron clouds of the two molecules interpenetrate each other, allowing a redistribution of electron density to take place. The molecules merge into a temporary intermediate "molecule." During this interaction phase of the collision, the kinetic energy of the colliding molecules is also available for redistribution within the temporary intermediate. The internal energy of this "molecule" can increase to the point where the vibrations of some atoms become so strong that bonds break.

Suppose the nitrogen atom from the NO molecule collides with an oxygen atom at one end of the O_3 molecule and their electron clouds merge. Enough energy from the collision can be converted into vibrational energy in the oxygen–oxygen bond in O_3 to weaken it. For a brief moment there is only a partial bond between the oxygen atoms as electron density shifts away from the bond that is about to break. At the same time, electron density shifts toward the nitrogen atom, and a partial bond forms between the oxygen and nitrogen atoms. Electron density in the other bonds in these two molecules is also shifted.

The short-lived combination of reacting atoms, molecules, or ions that is intermediate between reactants and products is called the **transition state,** or **activated complex.** The transition state breaks up either to give the products of the reaction, which then separate, or to give back the reactants. The overall result of an *effective* collision of an NO molecule and an O_3 molecule—a collision that leads to a reaction—is the breaking of an O—O bond, the formation of an N—O bond, and distribution of the internal and kinetic energies of the reactant molecules among the internal and kinetic energies of the product molecules. (The *total* energy of the system is unchanged.)

Of all the collisions that occur, only a small fraction are effective and result in a chemical change. There are three requirements for effective collisions:

1. The orientation of ions or molecules when they collide must be such that the atoms directly involved in the transfer or sharing of electrons come into contact.
2. The collision must take place with enough energy that the outer electron shells of the atoms concerned penetrate each other to some extent and bonding electrons are rearranged.
3. The transfer or sharing of electrons must give a structure that is capable of existence under the conditions of the collision; that is, stable bonds or new stable species must be formed.

We have already discussed the second condition: that the collisions must take place with sufficient energy so that the molecules do not fly apart unchanged. The third condition is straightforward—no reaction can occur if there is no possible product.

The first condition becomes apparent if we examine our example, the reaction between nitric oxide and ozone. If the molecules approach one another so that the *oxygen* atom in the NO molecule makes contact with the one of the oxygen atoms in ozone, the possibility of rearrangement into any new substance is very limited. Condition 2 might be met but condition 3 would not be met.

Condition 3 becomes more important as the reacting species become larger. For example, molecules of hydrogen chloride and ammonia (both gases) have a much better chance to react if they collide as in (a) in Figure 18.1 than if they collide when they are in other relative positions, such as (b) or (c). The hydrogen atom of the HCl molecule must present itself to the unshared pair of electrons on the nitrogen atom. No other approach is apt to lead to reaction. This effect is more pronounced in the reaction of hydrogen chloride with tri-*n*-propylamine, $N(CH_2CH_2CH_3)_3$. Here the bulky hydrocarbon groups further hinder the approach of the HCl molecule to the nitrogen atom (Figure 18.1d). The HCl molecule must approach through a narrow "window" for an effective collision to take place.

The process of collision that we have described is fundamental to kinetics. Two major mathematical models for the advanced study of kinetics are the "collision theory" and the "transition state theory." You may see these terms in other books. The differences between these theories lie in the emphasis placed on different aspects of the collision and in the mathematics of the models. There is no essential difference between these two theories in what is proposed as happening to individual atoms, molecules, or ions during a reaction.

Because of the three requirements that we have discussed, only a small fraction of all collisions are effective for most reactions. In a few types of chemical reactions, however, almost every collision produces products. Mostly, these are reactions of ions in aqueous solution, such as

$$H^+ + OH^- \longrightarrow H_2O(l) \tag{18.2}$$
$$H^+ + NH_3(aq) \longrightarrow NH_4^+ \tag{18.3}$$
$$H^+ + HS^- \longrightarrow H_2S(aq) \tag{18.4}$$

or they are reactions between radicals. A radical, or **free radical,** is a highly reactive species that contains an unpaired electron. For example, hydrogen and chlorine atoms are radicals, as is any fragment of a compound containing a carbon atom with three bonds and one unpaired electron. A reaction between a radical and a molecule,

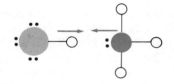

(a) Effective collision, HCl + NH_3

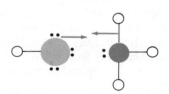

(b) Ineffective collision, HCl + NH_3

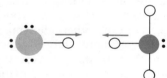

(c) Ineffective collision, HCl + NH_3

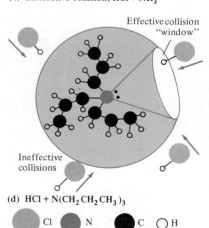

(d) HCl + $N(CH_2CH_2CH_3)_3$

⬤ Cl ⬤ N ⬤ C ○ H

Figure 18.1
Collisions of Hydrogen Chloride with Ammonia and Tripropylamine

such as reaction (18.5) or (18.6), almost always yields another radical and a molecule.

$$H \cdot (g) + Br_2(g) \longrightarrow HBr(g) + Br \cdot (g) \qquad \textbf{(18.5)}$$
$$Cl \cdot (g) + HCl(g) \longrightarrow Cl_2(g) + H \cdot (g) \qquad \textbf{(18.6)}$$

A reaction between two radicals generally produces a nonradical.

$$\cdot CH_3(g) + \cdot CH_3(g) \longrightarrow CH_3CH_3(g) \qquad \textbf{(18.7)}$$

Reactions such as these are very fast.

18.3 THE ENERGY PATHWAY OF A CHEMICAL REACTION

The energy relationship *during* the course of a chemical reaction can be represented by a diagram like that in Figure 18.2. At the left, the curve begins with the internal energy possessed by the reactants, in this case ozone and nitric oxide. At the right, the curve ends with the internal energy possessed by the products. The reaction between ozone and nitric oxide is exothermic. The products possess less energy than the reactants and heat (kinetic energy) is released during the reaction.

$$O_3(g) + NO(g) \longrightarrow O_2(g) + NO_2(g) \qquad \Delta H° = -199.6 \text{ kJ}$$

In Figure 18.2 the total energy change in the reaction is represented by the difference between the reactant and product energies. [For this reaction $\Delta E° = \Delta H°$ because there is no change in the number of moles of gases present, that is, no PV work is done. Recall that $\Delta H = \Delta E + \Delta(PV)$, or at constant pressure, $\Delta H = \Delta E + P \Delta V$; Section 7.4. For the purpose of the general discussion in this section, we assume that $P \Delta V$ is negligible and $\Delta E = \Delta H$ in all cases.]

The horizontal axis in Figure 18.2 is called the reaction coordinate. The progress of the reaction is represented by moving from left to right along this coordinate. As the reactants approach each other, the potential energy rises—repulsion is taking effect. The highest point in the curve represents formation of the transition state. Only collisions that have enough energy to bring the reactants to this point can lead to reaction. It takes about 1.7×10^{-23} kJ to form the transition state between one O_3 molecule and one NO molecule. The **activation energy,** E_a, is defined as the minimum energy that reactants must have for reaction to occur. Customarily, activation energy is reported as the energy needed for the formation of one mole of the transition state. The activation energy for the ozone–nitric oxide reaction is 10.29 kJ. (This is a relatively low activation energy and the reaction is a relatively fast one.)

Activation energy is a characteristic property of a reaction and is found by experiment (Section 18.12). Whenever bonds are broken in a chemical reaction, there must be an activation energy. In only a few types of reactions, such as the rapid reactions of ions or radicals mentioned above, is there no activation energy. Most

Figure 18.2
Energy Pathway in the Reaction of O_3 with NO (not drawn to scale) The heat of reaction, $\Delta H°$ (with no $P\Delta V$ work) is the difference between the energy of the reactants and the energy of the products.

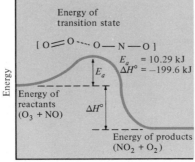

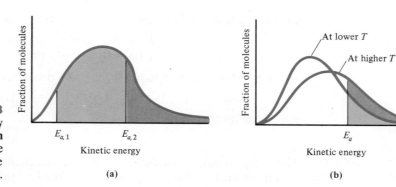

Figure 18.3
Relationship of Activation Energy (a) and Temperature (b) to Fraction of Molecules that can React The areas under the curves represent the total number of molecules.

Greater activation energy → slower reaction

---

values of E_a fall in the range of 40 to 200 kJ. The magnitude of E_a depends on the nature of the reacting atoms, molecules, or ions—their bond energies, structures, and so on.

The larger the activation energy, the slower a reaction will tend to be. The smaller the activation energy, the faster a reaction will tend to be. These relationships can be explained by referring to the curve in Figure 18.3a. The total area under the curve represents the total number of molecules of all possible energies. Suppose $E_{a,1}$ is the activation energy for a particular reaction. The entire shaded area represents the number of molecules that have enough energy to react. However, if the activation energy is higher, say $E_{a,2}$, then only a much smaller number of the molecules, shown by the darkly shaded area, have sufficient energy to react. In other words, there will be fewer effective collisions.

In general, reaction rates increase with temperature. An old rule of thumb states that the rate of a chemical reaction is doubled for each 10 Celsius degree rise in temperature. This is a rough approximation. Reactions with very small activation energies have only a small temperature dependence, while the rates of other reactions are much more than doubled by a 10 Celsius degree temperature increase.

The effect of changing the temperature of a reacting system is twofold. As the temperature is increased, the molecules move more rapidly, so collisions are more frequent. However, calculations show that only a small percentage of the rate increase with temperature can be accounted for by the larger number of collisions. The energy distribution curve provides the explanation for most of the increase in rate. Figure 18.3b shows how the curve changes as the temperature increases. The area under both curves is the same, but as the curve flattens out with increasing temperature, a larger number of molecules occupy the high-energy end of the distribution, as shown by the darkly shaded portion of the area under the curve. More molecules have higher energy and can undergo effective collisions.

The energy changes for exothermic and endothermic reactions are compared in Figure 18.4. The heat of reaction in both cases is the difference between the energy of

---

Figure 18.4
Energy Pathways for Exothermic (a) and Endothermic (b) Reactions Note that the activation energy for an endothermic reaction is always greater than that for the reverse, exothermic reaction.

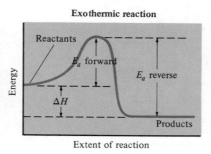

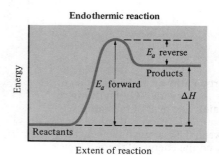

E_a for endothermic reaction:
always greater than E_a for
reverse (exothermic) reaction

---

the products and the energy of the reactants. Take a moment to think about the relationships represented by these curves. Note that the reverse of an exothermic reaction is an endothermic reaction, and that the endothermic reaction always has the larger activation energy.

As we have pointed out, thermodynamics is concerned only with the initial and final states of a chemical reaction, which are represented in Figure 18.4 by the energy levels of the reactants and products. The existence of the activation energy explains why some reactions that are spontaneous according to the calculations of thermodynamics do not take place rapidly as soon as the reactants are mixed. Look at Figure 18.4a and imagine a situation in which, although the products have lower energy than the reactants (which is thermodynamically favorable), very little reaction occurs because the activation energy "hill" is too high and very few effective collisions can occur.

The first step in the mechanism for the oxidation of carbon monoxide is such a reaction.

$$CO(g) + O_2(g) \longrightarrow CO_2(g) + O(g) \qquad \begin{matrix} \Delta H° = -33 \text{ kJ} \\ E_a = 213 \text{ kJ} \end{matrix} \qquad \textbf{(18.8)}$$

The reaction is exothermic—the products have less energy than the reactants. But carbon monoxide is certainly not oxidized by oxygen in the air as soon as it is formed. You can die from the carbon monoxide that collects when an automobile engine is left running in a closed garage. The activation energy of reaction (18.8) is high and the temperature must be raised to over 2000 °C before CO and O_2 molecules collide with enough energy to get over the energy barrier. (One purpose of the catalytic converter in an automobile exhaust system is to allow this reaction to take place at a lower temperature.)

Some reactions keep going once a few molecules gather the energy needed to react. This occurs when the overall reaction is exothermic. The products carry away much of the energy released by the reaction in the form of kinetic energy, raising the temperature of the entire system. As a result, more and more reactants have sufficient energy to react as time proceeds. The classic example of this type of reaction is the combination of hydrogen and oxygen. In a clean, undisturbed flask, a mixture of hydrogen and oxygen will stand indefinitely virtually without reaction. A single spark which heats only a few molecules can set off an explosive reaction of the entire contents of the flask.

18.4 ELEMENTARY REACTIONS

An elementary reaction represents what happens at the molecular level. The reactants are the particles that must come together in the interaction phase of an effective collision. Elementary reactions are categorized in terms of their **molecularity**—the number of reactant particles involved in an elementary reaction. The reactants in elementary reactions are often highly reactive species—atoms and free radicals, or ionic fragments of larger molecules—that do not appear in stoichiometric equations.

The reaction of nitric oxide and ozone is a **bimolecular reaction**—an elementary reaction that has two reactant particles. The reactants in a bimolecular reaction can be the same or different—the point is that two particles must collide.

elementary bimolecular reactions

$$A + A \longrightarrow \text{products} \qquad \textbf{(18.9)}$$
$$A + B \longrightarrow \text{products} \qquad \textbf{(18.10)}$$

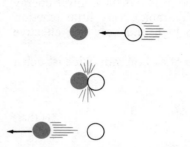

Two bodies cannot stay together after impact

(a) Two-body collision

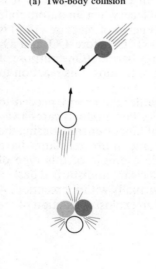

Two bodies can stay together after impact because third carries excess energy away

(b) Three-body collision

Figure 18.5

Two-Body and Three-Body Collisions (Such collisions between molecules have similarities to collisions between billiard balls.) A successful three-body collision between molecules occurs when the third molecule arrives before the other two have flown apart.

Gas phase

$$O + O_3 \longrightarrow O_2 + O_2$$
$$N + NO \longrightarrow N_2 + O$$
$$K + HBr \longrightarrow KBr + H$$
$$CH_3 + CCl_4 \longrightarrow CH_3Cl + CCl_3$$
$$CO + NO_2 \longrightarrow CO_2 + NO$$
$$CO + O_2 \longrightarrow CO_2 + O$$

Solution phase

$$H^+ + HS^- \xrightarrow{H_2O} H_2S$$
$$H^+ + NH_3 \xrightarrow{H_2O} NH_4^+$$
$$H^+ + OH^- \xrightarrow{H_2O} H_2O$$
$$CH_3Br + Cl^- \xrightarrow{acetone} CH_3Cl + Br^-$$
$$CH_3I + C_6H_5N(CH_3)_2 \xrightarrow{CH_3OH} C_6H_5N(CH_3)_3^+ + I^-$$
$$\text{hemoglobin} \cdot 3O_2 + O_2 \longrightarrow \text{hemoglobin} \cdot 4O_2$$

By far the majority of elementary reactions are bimolecular. Some examples are given in Table 18.1.

A **termolecular reaction** is an elementary reaction that requires the interaction of three reactant particles. Termolecular reactions are rare, for the probability of three reacting particles coming together at the same time to form a transition state is low. The following reactions are thought to be termolecular elementary reactions:

$$2NO(g) + O_2(g) \longrightarrow 2NO_2(g)$$
$$2NO(g) + Br_2(g) \longrightarrow 2NOBr(g)$$

In the recombination of atoms in the gas phase to give diatomic molecules, however, a third participant is *necessary*. Suppose two atoms come together with sufficient energy to combine in an activated complex, [A—A]*. To form the molecule A—A, the activated complex must lose some energy. Otherwise, all of the kinetic energy of the two original atoms will be converted to vibrational energy in the A—A bond, and this bond will break. Instead of settling down into a stable molecule, the atoms will fly apart again. Only if a third body carries away some of the energy can the two atoms remain combined (Figure 18.5). Following are some examples of recombination reactions in the gas phase that require a third body (M):

$$Br(g) + Br(g) + M(g) \longrightarrow Br_2(g) + M(g)$$
$$O(g) + O_2(g) + M(g) \longrightarrow O_3(g) + M(g)$$

The third body may also be another atom of the same type:

$$H(g) + H(g) + H(g) \longrightarrow H_2(g) + H(g)$$

The question next arises as to whether or not there are unimolecular reactions. These would be elementary reactions in which one reactant gives one or more products. But there is a problem. We know that most reactions have an activation energy. How can a single reactant in a unimolecular reaction become activated? The answer is that in most cases, reactions involving only a single reactant are *not* really elementary unimolecular reactions. The reactions proceed by a simple mechanism in which the first step is activation of the reactant: by radiation or by collision with something that does not become part of the product. The collision might be with an inert atom or molecule or even with the wall of the container. The activated molecule does not react immediately. The energy it has gained must be distributed among the various rotational and vibrational motions of the molecule. The decomposition or isomerization occurs when sufficient energy reaches the bond that will break, usually the weakest bond in the molecule, and reaction occurs. The mechanism is

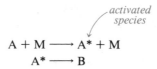

$$A + M \longrightarrow A^* + M$$
$$A^* \longrightarrow B$$

activated species

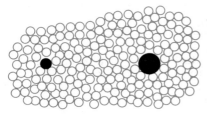

Separated reactant molecules

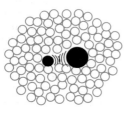

Reactant molecules in same solvent cage

Figure 18.6
Reactants in Solution The reactant molecules collide frequently while they are in the same solvent cage.

What we have said about elementary reactions also applies in general to reactions in solution—there are bimolecular and occasionally termolecular reactions. However, at the molecular level reactions in solution differ from gas-phase reactions because of the solvation of the reactants. Reactants cannot simply come together, interact briefly, and then separate. Their coming together is slowed down by surrounding solvent molecules, called the solvent cage, and the frequency of collisions between isolated molecules is lower than in the gas phase But once the reactants get close together, they are trapped in the same solvent cage and collide with each other many times in a short space of time (Figure 18.6). Interestingly, these two effects sometimes offset each other. Where there is little attraction or repulsion between solvent molecules and reactants, the same reactions can have similar rates in the gas phase and in solution.

The reactions of ions in aqueous solution are generally very fast. Many such reactions are "diffusion controlled" because the activation energy is close to zero. In such cases, the rate of the reaction is limited only by the time it takes for the ions to diffuse through the water until they encounter each other. For example, the formation of water from H^+ and OH^- is diffusion controlled.

REACTION RATES

18.5 DEFINITION OF REACTION RATE

A → B

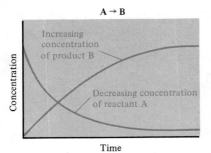

Increasing concentration of product B

Decreasing concentration of reactant A

Concentration

Time

Figure 18.7
Change in Reactant and Product Concentrations with Time

The rate of a process is expressed as the amount of change per unit of time. A car may travel at a rate of 88 km/h. Water may flow through a pipe at a rate of 32 L/min. In a chemical reaction the quantities that are changing are the amounts of reactants and products. The concentration of reactants decreases with time and the concentration of products increases (Figure 18.7). **Reaction rate** is defined as the change in concentration of a reactant or a product in a unit of time.

$$\text{Rate} = \frac{\text{change of concentration}}{\text{time period of change}} = \frac{\Delta C}{\Delta t}$$

Reaction rates are expressed in units of concentration per time unit, most commonly moles per liter per time unit—seconds, minutes, days, and so on, depending upon how slow the reaction is. The units are written, for example, mol/L s (s is the abbreviation for seconds), or mol L^{-1} s^{-1} (where the -1 superscript indicates the reciprocal of the unit: $s^{-1} = 1/s$), or sometimes M/s (where M is the abbreviation for mol/L). In this book we write mol/L s, mol/L h, and so on. For reactions of gases, reaction rates are sometimes expressed in units of partial pressure change per unit time.

A significant difference exists between, say, the rate of flow of water through a pipe and the rate of a chemical reaction. The flow rate of water can be held constant, but in most cases a reaction rate is not constant. The rate of a chemical reaction is a smoothly changing quantity because it is dependent upon concentration, which changes as reactants are consumed and products are formed.

18.6 DETERMINATION OF REACTION RATE

The study of the kinetics of a chemical reaction begins with the experimental determination of the variation of the concentration of reactants or products with

Table 18.2
Kinetic Data for the Decomposition of N₂O₅ at 45 °C in CCl₄ Solution (*Source:* H. Eyring and F. Daniels, *J. Am. Chem. Soc.* **52,** 1472 (1930).)

		$2N_2O_5 \xrightarrow{CCl_4} 4NO_2 + O_2$	
t (s)	Concentration of N_2O_5 (mol/L)	Average Reaction Rate in Each Time Interval (mol/L s)	Instantaneous Reaction Rate at t (mol/L s)
0	2.33		1.42×10^{-3}
184	2.07	1.41×10^{-3}	1.27×10^{-3}
319	1.91	1.19×10^{-3}	1.17×10^{-3}
526	1.68	1.11×10^{-3}	1.02×10^{-3}
867	1.35	0.97×10^{-3}	0.83×10^{-3}
1198	1.11	0.76×10^{-3}	0.68×10^{-3}
1877	0.72	0.57×10^{-3}	0.44×10^{-3}
2315	0.55	0.39×10^{-3}	0.34×10^{-3}
3144	0.34	0.25×10^{-3}	0.21×10^{-3}

time. A typical set of data for the following reaction is given in Table 18.2 and plotted in Figure 18.8.

$$2N_2O_5 \xrightarrow[45\ °C]{\text{in } CCl_4} 4NO_2 + O_2$$

The average rate of reaction during each measured time period was found from the data by using the following relationship:

$$\text{Rate} = -\left(\frac{\Delta C}{\Delta t}\right) = -\left(\frac{C_2 - C_1}{t_2 - t_1}\right) \tag{18.11}$$

change in reactant concentration / *reactant concentration at t_1* / *change in time* / *reactant concentration at t_2*

The reactant concentration decreases with time, making $C_2 - C_1$ a negative

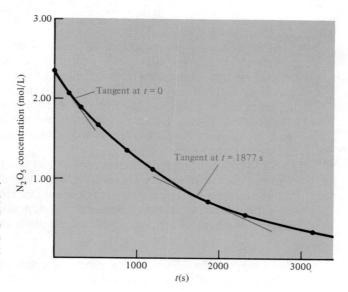

Figure 18.8
Plot of Kinetic Data for $2N_2O_5(g) \rightarrow 4NO_2(g) + O_2(g)$ at 45 °C in CCl₄ Solution (Table 18.2) Tangents are drawn at two points. The slope of the tangent to such a concentration vs. time plot at any value of t equals the reaction rate at that instant.

number. The minus sign is used in $-\Delta C/\Delta t$ because we wish the rate to be a positive number. The reaction rate could equally well be calculated from the change in concentration with time of the product of a reaction, for which the equation is Rate $= +\Delta C/\Delta t$.

For example, between the 319th second and the 526th second, the concentration of reactant N_2O_5 decreased from 1.91 mol/L to 1.68 mol/L and the average reaction rate during this period was

$$\text{Average rate} = -\frac{\Delta C}{\Delta t} = -\frac{(1.68 - 1.91)\ \text{mol/L}}{(526 - 319)\ \text{s}} = 1.11 \times 10^{-3}\ \frac{\text{mol}}{\text{L s}}$$

Keep in mind that the reaction rate is a constantly changing quantity. The value found above is the *average* reaction rate during the time interval from $t = 319$ s to $t = 526$ s. The reaction rate at any given instant, a more useful quantity in chemical kinetics, can be found from the plot of concentration versus time in Figure 18.8. The slope of the tangent to the curve at any given time is equal to the reaction rate at that time, called the instantaneous reaction rate. Tangents are drawn in Figure 18.8a at two points during the reaction, $t = 0$ s and $t = 1877$ s. The instantaneous reaction rate at $t = 0$ s, the instant when the reaction begins, is called the **initial reaction rate.** This and the instantaneous reaction rates for each data point in Figure 18.8 are given in the last column in Table 18.2. (The method for calculating the slope of a curve is described in Appendix IB.)

EXAMPLE 18.1
Reaction Rate

How might the "rate of reaction" be defined for the following reaction?

$$H_2(g) + I_2(g) \longrightarrow 2HI(g)$$

The rate of reaction can be defined in terms of the changes in concentration of either reactants or products with time. From the stoichiometry of the reaction we can see that a molecule of I_2 reacts every time a molecule of H_2 reacts. So, in terms of the reactants, we could define the rate of reaction as

$$\text{Rate} = -\frac{\Delta C_{H_2}}{\Delta t} = -\frac{\Delta C_{I_2}}{\Delta t}$$

For a definition in terms of the product,

$$\text{Rate} = \frac{\Delta C_{HI}}{\Delta t}$$

Note that two molecules of HI are produced for each molecule of H_2 and I_2 that react. The rate of reaction defined as $\Delta C_{HI}/\Delta t$ will be twice as large as the rate of reaction defined as $-\Delta C_{H_2}/\Delta t$ or $-\Delta C_{I_2}/\Delta t$.

Exercise How might the rate of reaction be defined for the following reaction: $2Al(s) + 3I_2(\text{in CS}_2) \rightarrow 2AlI_3(s)$? *Answer* Rate $= -(\Delta C_{I_2}/\Delta t)$

CONCENTRATION AND REACTION RATE: RATE EQUATIONS

18.7 SIMPLE RATE EQUATIONS AND REACTION ORDER

Having gathered concentration versus time data, the next step in the study of the kinetics of a reaction is to fit the data to a **rate equation,** which gives the mathematical relationship between the reaction rate and the concentration of one or more of the reactants. Remember that in most kinetics experiments and in the determination of rate equations, it is the overall, macroscopic result of the reaction that is under study.

The rate of a reaction is dependent upon the number of collisions between reactant particles. The number of collisions, in turn, is dependent upon the concentration of the reactants. A rate equation expresses the relationship between rate and concentration; it is always some function of one or more constants and the concentrations of the species present during the reaction raised to various powers. Frequently, although by no means always, experimentally determined rate equations have the following form:

$$\text{Rate} = k[A]^m[B]^n[C]^p \cdots \qquad (18.12)$$

rate constant   *reactant concentrations in moles/liter*

[A] = concentration of A in moles/liter

---

where the square brackets in [A], [B], [C], . . . denote reactant concentrations in moles per liter and k is the standard notation for a proportionality constant. The exponents $m, n, p, \ldots$ are most often 1 or 2. Sometimes they have values of 3 or of 0, or they may have values that are fractions. On occasion they may be negative.

The proportionality constant k that relates reaction rate to some function of reactant concentrations raised to various powers is called the **rate constant**. The value of a rate constant is characteristic of a specific reaction. It reflects the fraction of collisions that are effective in producing a reaction at a given temperature. Because k varies with the temperature (Section 18.12), the temperature at which a rate constant applies must always be stated. For fast reactions k is large; for slow reactions k is small. <u>Both the value of the rate constant and the form of the "reactant concentrations" part of the rate equation must be determined by experiment.</u>

The kinetics of a chemical reaction is categorized by the "order" of the reaction, a term that refers to the exponents on the concentration terms in the rate equation for the reaction. The **overall reaction order** is defined as the sum of the exponents of the concentration terms in the rate equation. For example, a reaction with the rate equation

$$\text{Rate} = k[A]^2[B]$$

is described as a third-order reaction overall, because the sum of the exponents on [A] and [B] is 3. The **reactant reaction order** is the exponent on the term for that reactant in the rate equation. The reaction with the rate equation given above is described as "second order in A" and "first order in B."

It is often convenient to describe a reaction as "first order" or "second order" overall. However, for reactions that have complex rate equations, overall reaction order has little meaning. Some further examples of the order of generalized rate equations for simple reactions are given in Table 18.3.

Table 18.3
Rate Equations and Reaction Order for Simple Reactions Because any number raised to the zero power equals 1, $k[A]^0 = k$. For complex rate equations, the concept of overall reaction order has little meaning.

Rate Equation Rate =	Overall Reaction Order
$k[A]^0 = k$	zero
$k[A]$	first
$k[A]^2$	second
$k[A][B]$	second
$k[A]^3$	third
$k[A]^2[B]$	third
$k[A][B][C]$	third
$k[A]^{\frac{3}{2}}[B]$	5/2

EXAMPLE 18.2
Reaction Order

The reaction between $NO(g)$ and $H_2(g)$,

$$2NO(g) + 2H_2(g) \longrightarrow N_2(g) + 2H_2O(g)$$

is second order with respect to NO and first order with respect to H_2. Write the rate equation for this reaction, assuming that it is of the form of Equation (18.12). What is the overall order of this reaction?

The rate reaction will take the general form

$$\text{Rate} = k[NO]^m[H_2]^n$$

when m is the order of reaction with respect to NO and n is the order of reaction with respect to H_2. We have been told that $m = 2$ and $n = 1$, so the rate equation is

$$\text{Rate} = k[NO]^2[H_2]$$

The reaction is an overall third-order reaction ($m + n = 2 + 1 = 3$). [Note that the order of reaction for a given substance is not necessarily equal to the stoichiometric coefficient for the substance in the chemical equation, as is discussed in Section 18.11a.]

Exercise The decomposition of hydrogen peroxide,

$$2H_2O_2(aq) \xrightarrow{I^-} 2H_2O(l) + O_2(g)$$

is known to be first order with respect to H_2O_2 and first order with respect to I^-. Write the rate equation for this reaction. What is the overall order of the reaction? *Answer* Rate $= k[H_2O_2][I^-]$, second order overall

---

EXAMPLE 18.3
Reaction Order

The rate equation for the oxidation of SO_2 to SO_3 in excess O_2 is as follows:

$$2SO_2(g) + O_2(g) \xrightarrow{Pt} 2SO_3(g) \qquad \text{Rate} = k[SO_2][SO_3]^{-\frac{1}{2}}$$

What is the order of the reaction with respect to each reactant? What happens to the rate of reaction as $[SO_3]$ increases?

The order of the reaction for each substance is given by the exponent on the concentration term in the rate equation. The reaction is first order with respect to SO_2 and negative one-half order with respect to SO_3. As the concentration of SO_3 increases, the reaction rate decreases.

Exercise The rate equation for the production of phosgene is

$$CO(g) + Cl_2(g) \longrightarrow COCl_2(g) \qquad \text{Rate} = k[Cl_2]^{\frac{3}{2}}[CO]$$

What is the order of the reaction with respect to each reactant? What happens to the reaction rate as $[CO]$ decreases? *Answer* three-halves order with respect to Cl_2 and first order with respect to CO; as the concentration of CO decreases, the reaction rate decreases

---

18.8 RATE EQUATIONS FOR FIRST-ORDER REACTIONS

The rate of a first-order reaction is dependent on the concentration of only one reactant.

$$\text{Rate} = k[A] \qquad \qquad \textbf{(18.13)}$$

$$\underbrace{\frac{mole}{(liter)(time\ unit)}}_{} \quad \underbrace{\frac{1}{time\ unit}}_{} \quad \underbrace{\frac{mole}{liter}}_{}$$

For rate expressed in the usual units of moles per liter per unit of time (Section 18.5), the rate constant of a first-order reaction has reciprocal time units, for example

$$\frac{1}{s} \text{ or } s^{-1} \qquad \frac{1}{min} \text{ or } min^{-1} \qquad \frac{1}{h} \text{ or } h^{-1}$$

Rate constants for some first-order reactions are given in Table 18.4.

Recalling that the rate of any reaction can be expressed as the change in concentration of any reactant or product with time (Section 18.5), we can write

$$\text{Rate} = -\frac{\Delta[A]}{\Delta t} \qquad \qquad \textbf{(18.14)}$$

By equating Equations (18.13) and (18.14), we find that for a first-order reaction,

$$k[A] = -\frac{\Delta[A]}{\Delta t} \qquad \qquad \textbf{(18.15)}$$

Using the mathematical methods of calculus, we can transform this equation into the following one, which relates concentration and time for a first-order reaction.

$$\log[A] = \log[A]_0 - \frac{kt}{2.303} \qquad \qquad \textbf{(18.16)}$$

Table 18.4

Rate Constants for Some First-Order Reactions The reactions given here are all gas-phase reactions. Because they are easier to study than condensed-phase reactions, the kinetics of more gas-phase reactions are known.

Reaction	k at 1000 °C (s^{-1})
$CO_2 \longrightarrow CO + O$	1.8×10^{-13}
$CS_2 \longrightarrow CS + S$	2.8×10^{-7}
$\begin{array}{c} H_2 \\ C \\ / \backslash \\ H_2C\text{---}CH_2 \end{array} \longrightarrow CH_2{=}CHCH_3$	9.2
$\begin{array}{c} H_2C\text{---}CH_2 \\ \mid \quad\quad \mid \\ H_2C\text{---}CH_2 \end{array} \longrightarrow 2H_2C{=}CH_2$	87

or, in another useful form

$$\log \frac{[A]}{[A]_0} = -\frac{kt}{2.303} \qquad (18.17)$$

where $[A]_0$ is the concentration of A at the beginning of the reaction when $t = 0$. Equations (18.16) and (18.17) are known as *integrated rate equations.*

[Calculus gives these and other similar equations in terms of the natural logarithm, usually abbreviated, for example, ln [A]. The factor 2.303 enters into the equation in order to convert natural logarithms to base 10 logarithms, log [A] = ln [A]/2.303. It is customary to work with logarithms to base 10, but with an appropriate calculator, there is no difference in the ease of using either type of logarithm. It is necessary to use logarithms frequently in this and later chapters. At this point, you may want to review logarithms, which are discussed in Appendix I.]

**First-order reaction:
Rate = k [A]**

If k is known, Equations (18.16) and (18.17) allow the calculation of the time needed to reach a given concentration of reactant or the concentration of reactant remaining after a given amount of time. Alternatively, k can be found by measuring these times and concentrations. Because the units of log $[A]/[A]_0$ cancel out in Equation (18.17), for a first-order reaction the concentrations of [A] and $[A]_0$ can be replaced by any quantity that is proportional to the concentration in moles per liter. For example, if the volume remains constant, the concentrations might be replaced by mass in grams, or amount of absorbed radiation, or for radioactive substances, by number of nuclei or even counts per minute per gram measured by a Geiger counter (see Figure 12.14).

**EXAMPLE 18.4
Rate Equations**

The decomposition of N_2O_5 in CCl_4 at 45 °C,

$$2N_2O_5 \xrightarrow{\ CCl_4\ } 4NO_2 + O_2$$

is first order with $k = 6.32 \times 10^{-4}$ s^{-1}. Find the concentration of N_2O_5 remaining after 1.0 h (3600 s) when the initial concentration of N_2O_5 was 0.40 mol/L. What percentage of the N_2O_5 has reacted?

The equation relating time and concentration for a first-order reaction, Equation (18.16), is used with $[N_2O_5]_0 = 0.40$ mol/L and $t = 3600$ s to find $[N_2O_5]$.

$$\log [N_2O_5] = \frac{-kt}{2.303} + \log [N_2O_5]_0$$

$$= \frac{(-6.32 \times 10^{-4} \text{ s}^{-1})(3600 \text{ s})}{(2.303)} + \log (0.40)$$

$$= (-0.988) + (-0.40) = -1.39$$

Taking antilogarithms of both sides gives

$$[N_2O_5] = 0.041 \text{ mol/L}$$

The concentration of N_2O_5 remaining is 0.041 mol/L. Therefore, (0.40 mol/L − 0.041 mol/L) = 0.36 mol/L of the N_2O_5 has reacted, giving

$$\left(\frac{0.36 \text{ mol/L}}{0.40 \text{ mol/L}}\right) (100\%) = 90.\%$$

Ninety percent of the N_2O_5 has reacted.

Exercise The decomposition of gaseous PH_3 at 600 °C, $4PH_3(g) \rightarrow P_4(g) + 6H_2(g)$, is first order with $k = 0.023$ s^{-1}. Find the partial pressure of PH_3 remaining after one minute when the initial partial pressure of PH_3 was 275 Torr. What percentage of the PH_3 has reacted? *Answer* 69 Torr, 74.9% of the PH_3 has reacted

EXAMPLE 18.5
Rate Equations

Given the same initial concentration of N_2O_5 (0.40 M) as in the reaction described in Example 18.4, find the time it would take for 95% of the N_2O_5 to decompose.

Equation (18.16), which relates time and concentration for a first-order reaction, can also be used to solve this problem. Rearranging the equation to solve for time gives

$$t = \frac{2.303 \, (\log [N_2O_5]_0 - \log [N_2O_5])}{k}$$

The values of k ($6.32 \times 10^{-4} \, \text{s}^{-1}$) and $[N_2O_5]_0$ are known. To find $[N_2O_5]$, the concentration of N_2O_5 unreacted at time t, we must take 5% (100% minus the 95% that has reacted) of the initial concentration, or $(0.05)(0.40 \, \text{mol/L}) = 0.02 \, \text{mol/L}$. Substituting these values into the equation for t and solving gives

$$t = \frac{(2.303)[\log (0.40) - \log (0.02)]}{6.32 \times 10^{-4} \, \text{s}^{-1}} = 4.7 \times 10^3 \, \text{s}$$

The time required for 95% of the N_2O_5 to react is 4.7×10^3 s, which is 79 min. [Note that this is 19 min longer than the time required for 90% to react; Example 18.4.]

Exercise Given initial partial pressure of PH_3 as 275 Torr, find the time required for the partial pressure to drop to 1 Torr (see Exercise following Example 18.4). For this first-order reaction, $k = 0.023 \, \text{s}^{-1}$ at 600 °C. *Answer* 240 s

18.9 HALF-LIFE OF FIRST-ORDER REACTIONS

Half-life, which is often used to characterize the relative stabilities of radioactive materials (Section 12.7), is the time it takes for one-half of a reactant to undergo a reaction. In terms of kinetics, radioactive decay is a first-order process. The equation that we used earlier to relate the initial mass of a radioactive nuclide (q_0) and the mass at time t (see Equation 12.2),

$$\log \frac{q_0}{q} = \frac{kt}{2.303} \qquad (18.18)$$

is the integrated rate equation for a first-order reaction (Equation 18.17) with concentration replaced by mass in grams. The expression for half-life derived from this relationship (Section 12.7),

Half-life for first-order reaction:
$$t_{\frac{1}{2}} = \frac{0.693}{k}$$

$$t_{\frac{1}{2}} = \frac{0.693}{k} \qquad (18.19)$$

applies to all first-order reactions, from which it is apparent that the half-life is *independent* of the concentration of the reactant.

EXAMPLE 18.6
Rate Equations: Half-Life

After two hours, a solution originally containing 1.30×10^{-6} mol/L of $^{240}AmCl_3$ contained only 1.27×10^{-6} mol/L of the radioactive substance. What is the half-life of ^{240}Am?

Before we can find the half-life, we must find the first-order rate constant by solving the integrated first-order rate equation, Equation (18.16), for k.

$$k = \frac{(2.303)(\log [^{240}Am]_0 - \log [^{240}Am])}{t}$$

$$= \frac{(2.303)[\log (1.30 \times 10^{-6}) - \log (1.27 \times 10^{-6})]}{2.00 \, \text{h}}$$

$$= 1.17 \times 10^{-2} \, \text{h}^{-1}$$

Now we can find $t_{\frac{1}{2}}$ from the equation for the half-life of a first-order reaction, Equation (18.19).

$$t_{\frac{1}{2}} = \frac{0.693}{k} = \frac{(0.693)}{(1.17 \times 10^{-2} \text{ h}^{-1})} = 59 \text{ h}$$

The half-life of ^{240}Am is 59 h.

Exercise The decomposition of gaseous PH_3 at 600 °C is known to be first order. After exactly 2 min, the partial pressure of PH_3 decreased from 262 Torr to 16 Torr. Using these data, calculate the half-life of this reaction at this temperature. *Answer* 29.7 s

18.10 RATE EQUATIONS FOR ZERO-ORDER AND SECOND-ORDER REACTIONS

The rate of a second-order reaction can be dependent upon the concentration of either one or two reactants.

$$\text{Rate} = k \, [A]^2 \qquad \text{(18.20)}$$

$$\text{Rate} = k[A][B] \qquad \text{(18.21)}$$

$$\underbrace{\frac{mole}{(liter)(time\ unit)}}_{} \qquad \underbrace{\frac{\cancel{liter}}{(\cancel{mole})(time\ unit)}\ \frac{\cancel{mole}}{\cancel{liter}}\ \frac{mole}{liter}}_{}$$

Second-order rate constants have units of reciprocal concentration (liters/mole) times reciprocal time (Table 18.5).

The rate of a zero-order reaction is *not* dependent on the reactant concentration, and therefore the rate is a constant.

$$\text{Rate} = k[A]^0 = k(1) = k$$

By using the methods of calculus, equations relating the variation of concentration with time (integrated rate equations) can be derived for zero- and second-order reactions. These equations and also the half-life equations are given in Table 18.6. Second-order reactions include those in which the rate is dependent upon the concentration of one reactant, or on the *equal* concentrations of two different reactants, or the *different* concentrations of two reactants.

The half-life equations demonstrate the interesting fact that it is only the half-lives of first-order reactions which are independent of the concentration.

The equations in Table 18.6 for zero- and second-order reactions can be used to solve the types of problems illustrated for first-order reactions in Examples 18.4–18.6.

In summary, rate equations express the proportionality of reaction rate to the concentrations of reactants raised to various powers. The form of the rate equation is dependent upon the reaction mechanism and must be determined by

---

Second-order reaction:
Rate = $k \, [A]^2$ or $k \, [A][B]$

Zero-order reaction:
Rate = constant

Table 18.5

Rate Constants for Some Second-Order Reactions These are all gas-phase reactions.

Reaction	k at 25 °C (L/mol s)
$H_2 + I_2 \longrightarrow 2HI$	1.7×10^{-18}
$2HI \longrightarrow H_2 + I_2$	2.4×10^{-21}
$2NO_2 \longrightarrow 2NO + O_2$	1.4×10^{-10}
$O_3 + NO \longrightarrow NO_2 + O_2$	2.2×10^{7}
$O_3 + NO_2 \longrightarrow NO_3 + O_2$	8.4×10^{4}
$NO + Cl_2 \longrightarrow NOCl + Cl$	7.3×10^{-6}
$CO + Cl_2 \longrightarrow COCl + Cl$	1.3×10^{-28}
$Cl + COCl \longrightarrow Cl_2 + CO$	9.3×10^{10}

Table 18.6
Equations for the Variation of Rate with Concentration, the Variation of Concentration with Time, and Half-Life Concentration at $t = 0$ is shown by $[A]_0$, $[B]_0$; concentration at t is shown by $[A]$, $[B]$.

Type of Reaction	Rate Equation	Integrated Rate Equation	Half-Life
Zero order	**Rate = k**	$[A] = [A]_0 - kt$	$\dfrac{[A]_0}{2k}$
First order	**Rate = $k[A]$**	$\log \dfrac{[A]}{[A]_0} = -\dfrac{kt}{2.303}$ or $\log [A] = \log [A]_0 - \dfrac{kt}{2.303}$	$\dfrac{0.693}{k}$
Second order	**Rate = $k[A]^2$** or **Rate = $k[A][B]$** with $[A] = [B]$	$\dfrac{1}{[A]} = \dfrac{1}{[A]_0} + kt$	$\dfrac{1}{k[A]_0}$
	Rate = $k[A][B]$ with $[A] \neq [B]$	$\log \dfrac{[A][B]_0}{[A]_0[B]} = ([A]_0 - [B]_0)\dfrac{kt}{2.303}$	—

experiment. Many reactions have rate equations of the general form Rate = k $[A]^m[B]^n[C]^p$. . . . Reactions are characterized as first order, second order, and so on, in each reactant, according to the exponent of the concentration for that reactant. The overall order is determined by $(m + n + p + \cdots)$. The relationship of reactant concentrations to time is given by integrated rate equations, derived from the rate equations. Expressions for the half-life of a reaction—the time in which one-half of the reactant is converted to product— are also derived from rate equations. Radioactive decay is a first-order process and, as for all first-order reactions, the half-life is independent of the amount of reactant. The equations that describe zero-, first-, and second-order reactions are summarized in Table 18.6.

18.11 FINDING RATE EQUATIONS

With a set of data at hand giving the concentration of reactants or products at different times, what can be done to find the rate equation? The first step is to determine if the data fit any of the rate equations given in Table 18.6. In this section we describe two simple methods for doing this. First, however, the relationships among the elementary reactions, the overall reaction, and the rate equations must be discussed.

a. Elementary reactions, overall reactions, and rate equations *If* a reaction is known to be an elementary reaction, its rate equation can be written based solely on the chemical equation for the reaction. In the general rate equation, Rate = $k[A]^m[B]^n \cdots$, A and B are the reactants and m and n are the coefficients of those reactants in the equation for an *elementary reaction*. For example,

$$A + 2B \longrightarrow C \qquad \text{Rate} = k[A][B]^2$$

or for our bimolecular reaction of ozone with nitric oxide,

$$O_3(g) + NO(g) \longrightarrow O_2(g) + NO(g) \qquad \text{Rate} = k[O_3][NO]$$

Writing a rate equation by inspection of the chemical equation is possible *only* for an elementary reaction, because the reactants in this case represent the actual species whose concentrations determine the reaction rate. The most common misunderstanding of kinetics by students is to assume that the exponents in a rate equation are necessarily equal to the coefficients in the chemical equation for the reaction. The exponents show how rate varies with collisions of individual reactant particles, and this is determined by the reaction mechanism and what is happening at the molecular level. Experimental rate equations usually apply to overall reactions, *not* elementary reactions.

Consider the reaction

$$2NO_2(g) + F_2(g) \longrightarrow 2NO_2F(g) \qquad (18.22)$$

for which the experimentally determined rate equation is

$$\text{Rate} = k[NO_2][F_2] \qquad (18.23)$$

Note that the exponent of $[NO_2]$ is *not* 2. A proposed mechanism for reaction (18.22) includes two steps:

$$NO_2(g) + F_2(g) \xrightarrow{\text{slow}} NO_2F + F \qquad (18.24)$$

$$\frac{NO_2(g) + F(g) \xrightarrow{\text{fast}} NO_2F}{2NO_2(g) + F_2(g) \longrightarrow 2NO_2F(g)} \qquad (18.25)$$

Reaction (18.24) is the **rate-determining step**—the slowest step in the reaction mechanism. Like all steps in a mechanism, reaction (18.24) is an elementary reaction. In this case of a reaction with a two-step mechanism, the rate is determined solely by collisions between NO_2 and F_2 and the formation of an activated complex between them. Further reaction depends on the presence of a product of this reaction, atomic fluorine, and the overall reaction cannot go any faster than the rate at which atomic fluorine is produced. Knowing only the experimentally determined rate equation (18.23), we could suspect that the rate of the reaction might well be determined by the formation of an activated complex between one NO_2 molecule and one F_2 molecule. However, while experimental rate equations do provide clues to reaction mechanisms by showing the species involved in the activated complex, the relationship between the rate equation and the mechanism is not always as simple as in this example.

For *elementary* reactions, the exponents in the rate equation *do* equal the coefficients in the chemical reaction. Equation (18.23) is the rate equation for the overall reaction represented by Equation (18.22), which is the sum of the separate steps of the reaction mechanism. Equation (18.23) is also the rate equation for reaction (18.24), which happens to be the elementary reaction step that governs the rate of the overall reaction. As we have said, the relationship is not always so simple.

The essential point is that neither the rate equation nor the mechanism of a reaction can be deduced from the overall stoichiometric chemical equation. Do not make the common error of assuming that the exponents in the rate equation are the same as the coefficients in the overall equation.

Rate equation: can be derived directly from balanced chemical equation *only* for *elementary* reactions

---

EXAMPLE 18.7
Rate Equations

Each of the reactions listed below is thought to occur in the upper atmosphere. *Assuming that these are all elementary reactions,* write rate equations for these reactions.

(a) $CH_3 + O_2 + M \longrightarrow CH_3O_2 + M$ (c) $2O + M \longrightarrow O_2 + M$
(b) $CH_3 + O_3 \longrightarrow CH_2O + O_2 + H$ (d) $2NO_3 \longrightarrow 2NO_2 + O_2$

For *elementary* reactions, the rate equations are of the form Rate $= k[A]^m[B]^n[C]^p \cdots$ with exponents equal to the coefficients.

(a) Rate $= k[CH_3][O_2][M]$ (c) Rate $= k[O]^2[M]$
(b) Rate $= k[CH_3][O_3]$ (d) Rate $= k[NO_3]^2$

These rate equations can be assumed to apply to reactions (a)–(d) *only* if these are elementary reactions. Rate equations cannot be written based on overall chemical equations.

Exercise Each of the following elementary reactions is part of a mechanism by which Fe^{3+} catalyzes the decomposition of aqueous hydrogen peroxide: (a) $Fe^{3+} + HO_2^- \rightarrow Fe^{2+} + HO_2(aq)$, (b) $Fe^{3+} + HO_2(aq) \rightarrow Fe^{2+} + O_2(g) + H^+$, (c) $Fe^{3+} + O_2^- \rightarrow Fe^{2+} + O_2(g)$, (d) $Fe^{2+} + H_2O_2(aq) \rightarrow Fe^{3+} + OH^- + OH(aq)$, (e) $Fe^{2+} + OH(aq) \rightarrow Fe^{3+} + OH^-$. Write the rate equations for these reactions. *Answer* (a) Rate $= k[Fe^{3+}][HO_2^-]$, (b) Rate $= k[Fe^{3+}][HO_2]$, (c) Rate $= k[Fe^{3+}][O_2^-]$, (d) Rate $= k[Fe^{2+}][H_2O_2]$, (e) Rate $= k[Fe^{2+}][OH]$

b. Method of initial rates for finding rate equations To find the experimental rate equation by the method of initial rates, it is necessary to gather concentration–time data in a series of separate experiments. Each experiment must have a different initial concentration of one or more reactants. (The experiments must be run at the same temperature.) The initial rate for each experiment can be found from the concentration versus time curve, as described in Section 18.6.

Suppose a reaction of the type A $\rightarrow$ products is under study. The data are inspected to find how the initial rate varies with $[A]_0$, the initial concentration of A. The objective is to find the value of the exponent in the rate equation, rate $= k[A]^m$. For a first-order reaction, $m = 1$ and the rate varies directly with $[A]_0$—if $[A]_0$ is doubled, the rate is doubled; if $[A]_0$ is tripled, the rate is tripled; and so on (Table 18.7). For a second-order reaction, $m = 2$ and the rate is increased by a factor of 2^2, or 4, if $[A]_0$ is doubled, and so on. If the reaction is zero order in A, changes in the concentration of A have no effect on the reaction rate.

The order for each of several reactants can be found by varying one initial concentration at a time, while keeping the others constant. For example, the kinetics of the reaction

$$2NO(g) + O_2(g) \longrightarrow 2NO_2(g) \tag{18.26}$$

was studied (at 80 K) by varying the initial pressures of the reactants individually and finding the initial reaction rates. The following data are typical of such a study.

Experiment	$p_{init}(NO)$ (Torr)	$p_{init}(O_2)$ (Torr)	Rate of NO_2 Formation (Torr/s)
(a)	1630	1630	6.13×10^{-8}
(b)	3260	1630	24.5×10^{-8}
(c)	1630	3260	12.2×10^{-8}

Holding the O_2 pressure constant while doubling the NO pressure quadrupled the rate, indicating that the reaction is second order in NO. With constant NO pressure, doubling the O_2 pressure caused the rate to double, showing that the reaction is first order in O_2. The rate equation is, therefore,

$$\text{Rate of } NO_2 \text{ formation} = k p_{NO}^2 p_{O_2}$$

Table 18.7
Change in Initial Rate with Change in $[A]_0$ for Rate $= k[A]^m$

For a Reaction of	If $[A]_0$ Is Doubled	If $[A]_0$ Is Tripled
Zero order ($m = 0$)	rate is unchanged	rate is unchanged
First order ($m = 1$)	rate is doubled	rate is tripled
Second order ($m = 2$)	rate is quadrupled ($\times 2^2$)	rate is 9 times greater ($\times 3^2$)

The experimental data can be used in the rate equation to find the value of k. For the data from experiment (a), for example,

$$k = \frac{\text{Rate of } NO_2 \text{ formation}}{p_{NO}^2 p_{O_2}} = \frac{6.13 \times 10^{-8} \text{ Torr/s}}{(1630 \text{ Torr})^2 (1630 \text{ Torr})} = 1.42 \times 10^{-17} \text{ Torr}^{-2} \text{ s}^{-2}$$

The best value for k is taken as an average of the k values calculated for each run; in this case, it is 1.41×10^{-17} Torr^{-2} s^{-1}.

In studying reaction (18.26) and the experiments described above, the value of the exponent in the rate equation was found by inspecting the data. Where this is not possible, other methods, such as the graphic method described in the next section, must be tried. Once it is proven that the data do not fit any of the simple rate equations, then a more complex rate equation must be sought.

EXAMPLE 18.8
Reaction Order

The rate law for the reaction of iodide ion with hypochlorite ion in an alkaline solution,

$$I^- + OCl^- \xrightarrow{OH^-} Cl^- + IO^-$$

was thought to be of the form

$$\text{Rate} = k\,[I^-]^m[OCl^-]^n[OH^-]^p$$

The reaction was studied using the method of initial rates and the following data collected at 25 °C:

Experiment	$[ClO^-]_0$	$[I^-]_0$	$[OH^-]_0$	Initial rate (mol/L s)
(a)	2.00×10^{-3}	2.00×10^{-3}	1.00	2.42×10^{-4}
(b)	4.00×10^{-3}	2.00×10^{-3}	1.00	4.82×10^{-4}
(c)	2.00×10^{-3}	4.00×10^{-3}	1.00	5.02×10^{-4}
(d)	2.00×10^{-3}	2.00×10^{-3}	0.500	4.64×10^{-4}

What is the order of reaction with respect to each reactant and what is the value of the rate constant?

We can see from the data for experiments (a) and (b) that the reaction rate essentially doubles as the concentration of ClO^- doubles. Thus the reaction is first order with respect to $[OCl^-]$ and $n = 1$. Likewise we can see from the data for experiments (a) and (c) that the reaction rate essentially doubles as the concentration of I^- doubles. Thus the reaction is first order with respect to $[I^-]$ and $m = 1$.

Upon comparison of the rate for experiment (d) with that of experiment (a), we can see that the rate essentially doubles as the concentration of OH^- is halved. This means that there is an inverse relationship between the rate and $[OH^-]$. The reaction is negative first order with respect to $[OH^-]$.

The complete rate equation is

$$\text{Rate} = k[I^-][OCl^-][OH^-]^{-1} = k\,\frac{[I^-][OCl^-]}{[OH^-]}$$

We can find the value of k by substituting the values of the rate and the respective concentrations into the rate law. For example, for experiment (a),

$$k_1 = \frac{\text{rate}_1[OH^-]_1}{[I^-]_1[OCl^-]_1} = \frac{(2.42 \times 10^{-4}\ \text{mol/L s})(1.00\ \text{mol/L})}{(2.00 \times 10^{-3}\ \text{mol/L})(2.00 \times 10^{-3}\ \text{mol/L})} = 60.5\ \text{s}^{-1}$$

Likewise, for the other experiments, $k_2 = 60.3\ \text{s}^{-1}$, $k_3 = 62.8\ \text{s}^{-1}$, and $k_4 = 58.0\ \text{s}^{-1}$, giving an average of $k = 60.4\ \text{s}^{-1}$.

Exercise The data below were obtained for the following reaction: A + B → products.

Experiment	(a)	(b)	(c)
Initial Rate (mol/L s)	0.030	0.059	0.060
$[A]_0$	0.10	0.20	0.20
$[B]_0$	0.20	0.20	0.30

Write the rate equation for this reaction. Evaluate k. *Answer* Rate = k [A], $k = 0.30\ \text{s}^{-1}$

c. Graphic method for finding rate equations Whether a reaction is zero, first, or second order in a specific reactant can be found by plotting data appropriately (Appendix I). The general equation for a straight-line plot of y versus x is

constant = slope of y vs. x plot

$$y = mx + b \qquad\qquad (18.27)$$

constant, intercept of y axis (y value at x = 0)

The integrated rate equations of zero-, first-, and second-order reactions can be arranged into this form. For example, for a first-order reaction

plot on x axis

$$\log [A] = -\frac{kt}{2.303} + \log [A]_0 \qquad\qquad (18.28)$$

plot on y axis   *slope*   *y intercept*

In Table 18.2 we give data for the decomposition of N_2O_5. Plotting $\log [N_2O_5]$ versus t (Figure 18.9) gives a straight line, showing that this reaction is first order in N_2O_5. The value of k is found from the slope of the line to be $6.17 \times 10^{-4}\ \text{s}^{-1}$ (at 45 °C).

Figure 18.9
Plot of Kinetic Data for Decomposition of N_2O_5 at 45 °C in CCl_4 Solution (Table 18.2), a First-Order Reaction

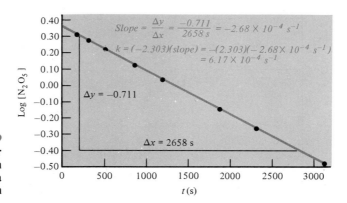

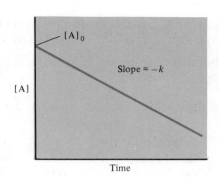

Figure 18.10
Plot for a Zero-Order Reaction

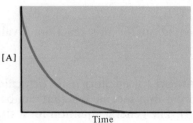
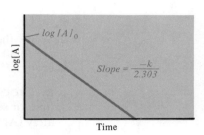

Figure 18.11
Plots for a First-Order Reaction

(a) Concentration vs. time for a first-order reaction

(b) Plot of the equation
$$\log [A] = -\frac{kt}{2.303} + \log [A]_0$$
for a first-order reaction

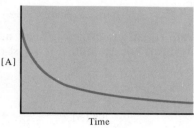
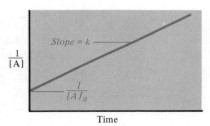

Figure 18.12
Plots for a Second-Order Reaction

(a) Concentration vs. time for a second-order reaction

(b) Plot of the equation $\frac{1}{[A]} = kt + \frac{1}{[A]_0}$ for a second-order reaction

As shown in Table 18.8, straight lines are obtained for a plot of [A] versus t for a zero-order reaction (Figure 18.10), of log [A] versus t for a first-order reaction (Figure 18.11), and of 1/[A] versus t for a second-order reaction (Figure 18.12). In each case the value of k can be found from the slope of the straight line.

Table 18.8
Equations for Plotting Kinetic Data

Type of Reaction	Equation for Straight Line $y = ax + b$	Linear Plot	Slope	y Intercept
Zero order (rate = k)	$[A] = -kt + [A]_0$	[A] vs. t	$-k$	$[A]_0$
First order (rate = $k[A]$)	$\log [A] = -\frac{kt}{2.303} + \log [A]_0$	log [A] vs. t	$-\frac{k}{2.303}$	$\log [A]_0$
Second order (rate = $k[A]^2$)	$\frac{1}{[A]} = kt + \frac{1}{[A]_0}$	$\frac{1}{[A]}$ vs. t	k	$\frac{1}{[A]_0}$

As we have discussed (Section 18.3), the number of molecules with sufficient energy to react increases with temperature. In 1889 Svante Arrhenius, the same Swedish chemist who gave us the classical, water-ion, definitions of acids and bases, observed that there is a mathematical relationship that connects activation energy, temperature, and the rate constant. This relationship, now known as the Arrhenius equation, is

$$k = Ae^{-E_a/RT}$$

(18.29)

with labels: *activation energy*, *ideal gas constant*, *rate constant at t*, *a constant*, *natural log base*.

or, taking logarithms of both sides,

$$\log k = - \frac{E_a}{2.303RT} + \log A$$

(18.30)

These equations show that reactions with larger activation energies have smaller values of k (the exponent is negative) and are, therefore, slower. This is what we would expect from our earlier discussion of effective collisions and energy relationships. Also, for a given value of the activation energy, the equations show that as the temperature increases, the value of the rate constant increases, meaning that the reaction is faster.

In terms of collision theory, $e^{-E_a/RT}$ in Equation (18.29) is the fraction of collisions in an elementary reaction in which the particles have enough energy to react. The constant A corrects for the frequency of collisions, the necessity for the proper orientation in effective collisions, and all factors other than activation energy that are significant in effective collisions.

The Arrhenius equation and the equations derived from it can be applied both to data for overall reactions and to data for elementary reactions. (Some complex reactions, such as explosions and certain catalyzed reactions, have non-Arrhenius temperature dependence.) When found by using the rate constant for an overall reaction, the activation energy value represents the net effect of the activation energies of *all of the steps* in the reaction mechanism. In this way, *effective* activation energies can be found even though reaction mechanisms are unknown.

Equation (18.30) is the equation for a straight line (see Table 18.8).

$$\log k = \left(- \frac{E_a}{2.303R}\right)\left(\frac{1}{T}\right) + \log A$$

(18.31)

with labels: *plot on y axis*, *slope*, *plot 1/T on x axis*, *y intercept*.

The value of E_a can be found from the slope of a plot of $\log k$ versus T, $E_a = -2.303R \times$ (slope).

Also, by combining the equations for values of k at two different temperatures for the same reaction, a relationship is obtained that allows for the calculation of E_a.

$$\log \frac{k_2}{k_1} = \frac{E_a}{2.303R}\left(\frac{T_2 - T_1}{T_1T_2}\right)$$

or

(18.32)

$$\log \frac{k_2}{k_1} = \frac{E_a}{2.303R}\left(\frac{1}{T_1} - \frac{1}{T_2}\right)$$

Alternatively, if E_a and three of the four values k_1, k_2, T_1, and T_2 are known, the fourth can be found. In using the Arrhenius equation, the energy is customarily expressed in joules, temperature must be in kelvins, and R is 8.314 J/K mol or 1.987 cal/K mol.

EXAMPLE 18.9
Activation Energy and Temperature

The thermal decomposition of $CH_3N{=}NCH_3$ in the gas phase to give nitrogen and methyl radicals,

$$CH_3N{=}NCH_3(g) \xrightarrow{\Delta} N_2(g) + 2 \cdot CH_3(g)$$

has an activation energy of 2.14×10^5 J/mol and, at 600. K, $k = 1.99 \times 10^8$ s^{-1}. Does the rule of thumb that a reaction rate doubles with a ten degree rise in temperature hold for this reaction?

To answer the question, we must calculate k at 610. K by using the appropriate form of the Arrhenius equation, Equation (18.32). The knowns are E_a, k_1 at $T_1 =$ 600. K, and $T_2 = 610$. K. The unknown is k_2 at 610. K.

$$\log \frac{k_2}{k_1} = \frac{E_a}{2.303R} \left(\frac{T_2 - T_1}{T_1 T_2} \right)$$

$$\log \frac{k_2}{1.99 \times 10^8 \text{ s}^{-1}} = \left(\frac{2.14 \times 10^5 \text{ J/mol}}{(2.303)(8.314 \text{ J/K mol})} \right) \left(\frac{610. \text{ K} - 600. \text{ K}}{(610. \text{ K})(600. \text{ K})} \right) = 0.31$$

Taking antilogarithms of both sides gives

$$\frac{k_2}{1.99 \times 10^8 \text{ s}^{-1}} = 2.0$$

$$k_2 = (2.0)(1.99 \times 10^8 \text{ s}^{-1}) = 4.0 \times 10^8 \text{ s}^{-1}$$

Comparison of k_1 with k_2 shows that for this reaction, the rate constant is doubled by a ten degree rise in temperature. (This is not always the case.)

Exercise The thermal decomposition of CH_3CHF_2,

$$CH_3CHF_2(g) \longrightarrow CH_2CHF(g) + HF(g)$$

has an activation energy of 260 kJ/mol. The reported value of the rate constant at 462 °C is 5.8×10^{-6} s^{-1}. What is the value of the rate constant at 487 °C? *Answer* 2.4×10^{-5} s^{-1}

EXAMPLE 18.10
Activation Energy and Temperature

The rate constant for the decomposition of N_2O_5 in chloroform,

$$2N_2O_5 \xrightarrow{CHCl_3} 4NO_2 + O_2$$

was measured at two different temperatures: $T_1 = 25$ °C, $k_1 = 5.54 \times 10^{-5}$ s^{-1} and $T_2 = 67$ °C, $k_2 = 9.30 \times 10^{-3}$ s^{-1}. Find the activation energy for this reaction.

The solution of this problem requires solving Equation (18.32) for E_a,

$$E_a = \log \frac{k_2}{k_1} (2.303R) \left(\frac{T_1 T_2}{T_2 - T_1} \right)$$

and then just substituting the known values of k_1 and k_2, and T_1 and T_2.

$$E_a = \left[\log \left(\frac{9.30 \times 10^{-3} \text{ s}^{-1}}{5.54 \times 10^{-5} \text{ s}^{-1}} \right) \right] (2.303) \left(8.314 \frac{\text{J}}{\text{K mol}} \right) \frac{(298 \text{ K})(340. \text{ K})}{(340. \text{ K} - 298 \text{ K})}$$

$$= (2.245)(2.303) \left(8.314 \frac{\text{J}}{\text{K mol}} \right) (2400 \text{ K})$$

$$= 1.0 \times 10^5 \text{ J/mol}$$

The activation energy is 1.0×10^5 J/mol.

Exercise The rate constant for the decomposition of gaseous CH_3CHF_2,

$$CH_3CHF_2(g) \longrightarrow CH_2CHF(g) + HF(g)$$

is 7.9×10^{-7} s^{-1} at 429 °C and 1.7×10^{-4} s^{-1} at 522 °C. Calculate the activation energy for this reaction. *Answer* 270 kJ/mol

---

18.13 HOMOGENEOUS AND HETEROGENEOUS REACTIONS

In a reaction between substances in the same gaseous or liquid phase—a **homogeneous reaction**—the question of contact between the reactive molecules is not an important one, for the molecules and ions are free to move and collisions are frequent. However, for reactions between substances in different phases—**heterogeneous reactions**—bringing the reacting molecules or ions together may be difficult. For example, the reaction between steam and red hot iron,

$$3Fe(s) + 4H_2O(g) \longrightarrow Fe_3O_4(s) + 4H_2(g)$$

proceeds very slowly if the iron is in one large block, but goes rapidly if the metal is powdered and spread out so as to expose a large surface to the steam. [Heterogeneous reactions involving the catalysis of reactions of gases by solids (Section 18.14) have been studied extensively.]

The rates at which solids react with each other are often limited by the amount of contact between them. The reaction of mercury(II) chloride and potassium iodide is a good illustration.

$$HgCl_2(s) + 2KI(s) \longrightarrow HgI_2(s) + 2KCl(s)$$
$$\text{white} \qquad \text{white} \qquad \text{red} \qquad \text{white}$$

If large crystals of the two solids are shaken together, there is no sign of reaction; if the crystals are ground together, reaction takes place fairly rapidly, as shown by the appearance of the bright red mercury(II) iodide. If the reactants are dissolved separately in water and the solutions are mixed, the insoluble red mercury iodide precipitates almost instantly. In general, for reactions between solids the reaction rate is proportional to the area of surface in contact.

There are many practical examples of how the degree of contact influences the rate of reaction, such as dust explosions in flour mills, grain elevators, and coal mines, or the effect of tetraethyllead in preventing "knock" in automobile engines. Knock—premature ignition of the fuel–air mixture—hinders smooth engine performance. When the volatile liquid tetraethyllead is drawn into the hot cylinder, it decomposes, giving an extremely fine suspension of metallic lead. This exposes a very large surface to the burning gases. Reaction on the surface of the metallic lead tends to slow down the combustion process and distribute the burning evenly throughout the cylinder, preventing knock. Placing a sheet of lead in the cylinder would not have a noticeable effect, because the sheet would not have enough surface in contact with the gases in the cylinder.

18.14 CATALYSIS

Catalysts do not change reaction equilibrium

A catalyst increases the rate of a chemical reaction, but can be recovered in its original form when the reaction is finished. A catalyst cannot assist a reaction that could not proceed in its absence. Nor can a catalyst change the concentrations in an equilibrium mixture; it can only lessen the *time* needed to reach equilibrium.

A catalyst works by providing an alternate and easier pathway from reactants to products. Catalysts accomplish this by a variety of mechanisms, but in each case the sole function of a catalyst is to lower the activation energy of a reaction. The role of a catalyst is highly specific to a particular reaction. A substance that catalyzes one reaction may well have no effect on another reaction, even if that reaction is very

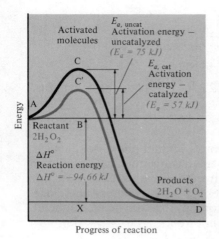

Figure 18.13
Energy Path of the Decomposition of H₂O₂, Catalyzed by I⁻ and Uncatalyzed

similar. Many of the most highly specific catalysts are those designed by nature. The chemical reactions in living things are controlled by biochemical catalysts—the enzymes.

Catalysts are classified as homogeneous or heterogeneous. **Homogeneous catalysts** are present in the same phase as the reactants. They function by combining with reacting molecules or ions to form unstable intermediates. These intermediates combine with other reactants to give the desired product and to regenerate the catalyst.

The energy pathway from reactants to products for the decomposition of hydrogen peroxide,

$$2H_2O_2(aq) \longrightarrow 2H_2O(l) + O_2(g) \qquad \Delta H° = -94.66 \text{ kJ}$$

is shown in Figure 18.13. The upper curve is for the uncatalyzed reaction. The lower curve shows the change in the energy pathway after the addition of iodide ion, I⁻, which serves as a homogeneous catalyst by the mechanism

$$H_2O_2 + I^- \longrightarrow H_2O + IO^-$$
$$\underline{IO^- + H_2O_2 \longrightarrow H_2O + O_2 + I^-}$$
$$2H_2O_2 \longrightarrow 2H_2O + O_2$$

The distance BC represents the activation energy of the uncatalyzed reaction and the distance BC′, the activation energy of the catalyzed reaction. Note that a catalyst decreases the energies of activation of both the forward and reverse reactions by an equal amount. Note also that the overall energy change in the reaction (BX) remains the same. The catalyst I⁻ takes part in the mechanism of the reaction, but is regenerated in its original state and can be recovered. Do not make the common error of saying that a catalyst "changes the rate of a reaction without taking part in it."

Heterogeneous catalysts are present in a phase different from that of the reactants and products. They are usually solids in the presence of gaseous or liquid reactants. Reactions occur at the surface of heterogeneous catalysts. For this reason the catalysts are usually finely divided solids or have particle shapes that provide a high surface-to-volume ratio—a property of importance in heterogeneous catalysis. Table 18.9 lists catalysts and conditions that are effective in controlling the products of the reaction between carbon monoxide and hydrogen.

One or both reactants are chemically adsorbed at the surface of a heterogeneous catalyst (Figure 18.14). Adsorption is the adherence of atoms, molecules, or ions (the adsorbate) to a surface. It is called **physical adsorption,** or physisorption, when the forces between surface and adsorbate are van der Waals forces, and it is called **chemical adsorption,** or chemisorption, when the forces between adsorbate and surface are of the magnitude of chemical bond forces. The process of chemisorption

Table 18.9
Reactions between Carbon Monoxide and Hydrogen (*Source:* R. L. Burwell, Jr., "Heterogeneous Catalysts," in *Survey of Progress in Chemistry,* A. F. Scott (ed.), Vol. 8, Academic Press, New York, 1977, p. 2.)

Catalyst	Conditions	Products
Ni*	100–200 °C, 1–10 atm	CH₄ + H₂O
ZnO·Cr₂O₃	400 °C, 500 atm	CH₃OH + H₂O
Co/ThO₂	190 °C, 1–20 atm	CH₄, C₂H₆, and higher hydrocarbons + H₂O
Ru	200 °C, 200 atm	High-molecular-mass hydrocarbons + H₂O
ThO₂	400 °C, 200 atm	Branched-chain hydrocarbons + H₂O

* This is the *methanation* reaction of current interest in the manufacture of *synthetic natural gas.* It converts carbon monoxide, which has a relatively low heat of combustion, to methane, which has a high one (Section 16.6f).

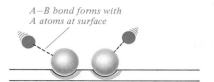

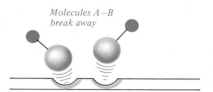

A—A bond breaks as A atoms are attracted to active sites

Active site on catalyst surface

A—B bond forms with A atoms at surface

Molecules A—B break away

Figure 18.14
How the Reaction A—A + 2B → 2AB Might Take Place at a Catalyst Surface

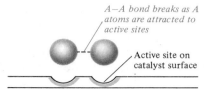

Figure 18.15
Some Examples of Chemisorption on Catalyst Surfaces (Source: Burwell, *op. cit.* Table 18.)

on a catalyst can alter the structure and activity of a reactant in the same way as the formation of an activated complex—by weakening some bonds and allowing the formation of others. Figure 18.15 shows some of the ways in which small molecules are chemisorbed at catalyst surfaces. A heterogeneously catalyzed reaction occurs in the following steps: (1) Reactants diffuse from the fluid phase to the catalyst surface; (2) one or more reactants are chemisorbed; (3) reaction occurs between adsorbed reactants or between a reactant in the fluid phase and an adsorbed reactant; (4) products are desorbed; and (5) products diffuse back into the fluid phase.

Heterogeneous catalysts can be recovered readily by filtration (say, when they need purification). They are much more widely used in industry than are homogeneous catalysts. The cracking of petroleum and the reforming of hydrocarbons (Section 27.10), and the preparation of ammonia (see An Aside: The Haber Process for the Manufacture of Ammonia, Chapter 19) are carried out with the aid of heterogeneous catalysts, as is the control of pollution in automobile exhaust.

One difficulty in the use of heterogeneous catalysts is that most of them are readily "poisoned"—that is, impurities in the reactants coat the catalyst with unreactive material or modify its surface, so that the catalytic activity is lost. Frequently, but not always, the poisoned catalyst can be purified and used again.

Inhibitors are substances that slow down a catalyzed reaction—usually by tieing up the catalyst, possibly also by tying up a reactant. For example, the development of rancidity in butter is greatly retarded by the addition of very small amounts of certain organic substances. The added organic materials apparently combine with the traces of copper ion that get into nearly all butter from the processing equipment. The copper ion catalyzes the development of rancidity, but in combination with the organic material, the copper ion does not exert a catalytic effect.

Promoters are substances that make a catalyst more effective. In the case of solid catalysts, a small amount of a promoter may encourage the formation of lattice defects, which are often the active sites on a catalyst surface.

REACTION MECHANISMS

18.15 REACTION MECHANISMS AND RATE EQUATIONS

Once an experimental rate equation has been established, the time has come to propose a mechanism for the reaction. In order to check the validity of a proposed mechanism, a rate equation based on the mechanism is worked out. (If the mechanism is complex, this is often done with the aid of a computer.) Remember that rate equations can be written by inspection of a chemical equation for *elementary* reactions (Section 18.11). Algebraic combination of the rate equations for the steps in a reasonably simple reaction mechanism gives an overall rate equation.

If the rate equation based on a proposed mechanism *is not* the same as the experimental rate equation, then the mechanism is wrong. If the rate equation based on a mechanism *is* the same as the experimental rate equation, the mechanism *might* be the correct one. The remaining uncertainty arises because two quite different mechanisms can sometimes lead to the same rate equation. A chemist studying kinetics tries to eliminate as many possible explanations for a reaction as he can. A reaction mechanism is often arrived at by a negative approach that first proves what the mechanism cannot be. One hopes that after the elimination process, there will be only one remaining mechanism. If there is more than one, the most probable mechanism must be selected. Different chemists may have different opinions as to which mechanism is most probable, a fact that sometimes leads to lively controversy in chemical publications. Writing possible reaction mechanisms based on experimental rate equations is an exercise best left to the experts. What we can do here is explore a few generalities about the relationship between mechanisms and overall rate equations.

The rate of a zero-order reaction is independent of the concentration of the reactants. This means that the rate is controlled by something other than collisions that involve reactants. The controlling factor might be the amount of light available in a photochemical reaction or the amount of catalyst present. Many reactions that occur on the surface of a metal (heterogeneous catalysis; Section 18.14) are zero order—the rate is controlled by the interaction of the reactant with the surface and the availability of active sites on the surface, for example,

$$2NH_3(g) \xrightarrow{\text{tungsten}} N_2(g) + 3H_2(g) \qquad \text{Rate} = k$$

One of the simplest types of reaction mechanism involves a single, rate-determining step upon which the rate equation is based. This occurs when the first step in the mechanism is the rate-determining step. In general, the rate of a reaction may be affected by reaction steps that precede the rate-determining step, but it is not influenced by steps that follow it. The overall third-order reaction of nitrogen(II) oxide (NO) with hydrogen,

$$2NO(g) + 2H_2(g) \longrightarrow N_2(g) + 2H_2O(g) \qquad \text{Rate} = k[NO]^2[H_2] \qquad \textbf{(18.33)}$$

is believed to occur by a two-step mechanism in which the first step is rate determining.

$$2NO(g) + H_2(g) \xrightarrow{\text{slow}} N_2(g) + H_2O_2(g) \qquad \textbf{(18.33a)}$$

$$H_2O_2(g) + H_2(g) \xrightarrow{\text{fast}} 2H_2O(g) \qquad \textbf{(18.33b)}$$

The following is an overall second-order reaction:

$$2ICl(g) + H_2(g) \longrightarrow I_2(g) + 2HCl(g) \qquad \text{Rate} = k[ICl][H_2] \qquad \textbf{(18.34)}$$

with a similar two-step mechanism,

$$ICl(g) + H_2(g) \xrightarrow{\text{slow}} HI(g) + HCl(g) \qquad \textbf{(18.34a)}$$

$$HI(g) + ICl(g) \xrightarrow{\text{fast}} I_2(g) + HCl(g) \qquad \textbf{(18.34b)}$$

Note that for overall reactions (18.33) and (18.34) the single elementary reaction steps that determine the overall reaction order are third- and second-order reactions (Equations 18.33a and 18.34a, respectively.) This is to be expected, for as we have seen, all collisions are either bimolecular or (in a few cases) termolecular. This means that a reaction for which the experimental, overall rate equation is other than second order or third order must proceed by a more complex mechanism in which the rate is not dependent on a single elementary reaction.

As an example of a reaction with a fairly common type of more complex rate equation and mechanism, we can consider the decomposition of acetic anhydride in the gas phase into acetic acid and ketene.

$$(CH_3CO)_2O(g) \longrightarrow CH_3COOH(g) + CH_2{=}C{=}O(g) \qquad \textbf{(18.35)}$$
$$\text{\textit{acetic anhydride}} \qquad \text{\textit{acetic acid}} \qquad \text{\textit{ketene}}$$

The proposed mechanism is as follows (where the asterisk indicates the activated acetic anhydride molecule, and k_{-1} is used to show that the second step is the reverse of the first step):

step 1

$$(CH_3CO)_2O(g) + (CH_3CO)_2O(g) \xrightarrow{k_1} (CH_3CO)_2O^*(g) + (CH_3CO)_2O(g) \qquad \textbf{(18.35a)}$$

step −1

$$(CH_3CO)_2O^*(g) + (CH_3CO)_2O(g) \xrightarrow{k_{-1}} (CH_3CO)_2O(g) + (CH_3CO)_2O(g) \qquad \textbf{(18.35b)}$$

step 2

$$(CH_3CO)_2O^*(g) \xrightarrow{k_2} CH_3COOH(g) + CH_2{=}C{=}O(g) \qquad \textbf{(18.35c)}$$

What this means is that the reaction can only begin when two molecules of acetic anhydride collide and one of the molecules is activated by the collision (step 1). Once this occurs, there are two possible outcomes. The activated molecule can be deactivated by another collision before it has a chance to react (step − 1); or it can react to give the products before being deactivated (step 2). The rate equation derived for this reaction from the mechanism, which agrees with experimental observations, is (in terms of the k's in Equations 18.35a, b, and c)

$$\text{Rate} = \frac{k_1 k_2 [A]^2}{k_{-1}[A] + k_2} \qquad \overset{\displaystyle\frown}{\quad}\textit{acetic anhydride} \qquad \textbf{(18.36)}$$

At high pressure, step 2 is the rate-determining step. Because k_2 is small relative to the values of k_1, k_{-1}, and [A], it can be neglected in the denominator of the rate equation. This expression therefore reduces to a first-order rate equation:

$$\text{Rate} = \frac{k_1 k_2}{k_{-1}}\,[A] = k'[A]$$

Since k_1, k_2, and k_{-1} are all constants, $k_1 k_2 / k_{-1}$ is also a constant. Note that the *overall* first-order rate constant, k', includes the rate constants of steps that *precede* the rate-determining step.

At low pressure, [A] is small; the $k_{-1}[A]$ term in the denominator in Equation (18.36) is therefore small compared to k_2 and can be dropped. The rate equation thus becomes

$$\text{Rate} = k_1 [A]^2$$

The reaction is second order, with a rate determined solely by step 1.

In summary, the sequence in a study of the kinetics of a chemical reaction is (1) experiments that yield concentration versus time data, (2) determination of the experimental rate equation and evaluation of the rate constant, and (3) the proposal of possible reaction mechanisms. A limited number of generalities can be drawn about the relationship between reaction mechanisms and rate equations: (1) The sum of the steps in a reaction mechanism must be the equation for the overall chemical reaction; (2) the concentrations of short-lived, activated intermediates do not appear in overall rate equations, (3) the experimental overall rate equation is derivable by some combination of the rate equations for the steps in a possible reaction mechanism, (4) it is not always feasible to eliminate all but one proposed mechanism for a reaction, (5) steps that follow the rate-determining step in a mechanism do not generally influence the rate equation, and (6) reactions that are other than second order or third order overall must *have rates dependent on more than one elementary step.*

SUMMARY   **18.1** CHEMICAL KINETICS: RATES AND MECHANISMS   A typical pathway for a chemical reaction includes several elementary reactions — reactions that occur in a single step exactly as written. The equation for an elementary reaction shows the actual species that must interact at the molecular level. A reaction mechanism consists of all the elementary steps in a single reaction pathway; the sum of these steps is the stoichiometric equation for the overall reaction. A reaction mechanism may involve one or more intermediates — species that are produced during the course of a reaction but always react further and so are not among the final products.

18.2 HOW REACTANTS GET TOGETHER A reaction between atoms, ions, or molecules can only occur if they collide with enough kinetic energy to form a short-lived transition state or activated complex, which quickly breaks up to give either the products of the reaction or the original reactants again. For a collision to result in a chemical change, the colliding species must be oriented so that the atoms directly involved in the transfer or sharing of electrons come into direct contact, the collision must be energetic enough for their electron clouds to interpenetrate, and stable new bonds must be formed. In general, only a small fraction of collisions are effective in producing a reaction. However, in some reactions, such as those involving ions in solution or free radicals (reactive species containing unpaired electrons), nearly every collision is effective.

18.3 THE ENERGY PATHWAY OF A CHEMICAL REACTION The minimum energy that the reactants must have for a reaction to occur is called the activation energy, E_a. The greater the activation energy, the slower the reaction. When the activation energy is very large, only a small fraction of molecules will have enough energy to react when they collide. In general, reaction rates increase with temperature, because higher temperature increases both the frequency of collisions and the number of molecules possessing enough energy to undergo effective collision. The reverse of an exothermic reaction is an endothermic reaction, which always has the larger activation energy.

18.4 ELEMENTARY REACTIONS Elementary reactions are categorized in terms of their molecularity — the number of reactant particles that they involve. Many reactions are bimolecular; only a few are termolecular. Some reactions in the gas phase require a third body to carry away some of the energy of the reactants, allowing them to form a stable molecule. In reactions involving a single reactant, the first step is often the activation of the reactant by collision with an inert species. Reactions of ions in solution are often very fast, limited only by the time it takes the ions to diffuse through the solvent and encounter each other.

18.5 DEFINITION OF REACTION RATE **18.6** DETERMINATION OF REACTION RATE **18.7** SIMPLE RATE EQUATIONS AND REACTION ORDER Reaction rate is the change in concentration of a reactant or product per unit time. The rate of a chemical reaction is generally not constant because it often depends on concentration, which changes as reactants are consumed and products formed. The rate at the instant when the reaction begins is the initial reaction rate. Rate data must be fitted to a rate equation, which gives the mathematical relationship between the reaction rate and the concentration of one or more of the reactants. Rate equations often take the form rate = $k[A]^m[B]^n[C]^p$ . . . where [A], [B], [C], . . . represent the concentrations of reactants in mol/L, and k is the rate constant. The value of k is characteristic of a specific reaction, but varies with temperature. The reactant reaction order is the exponent on the term for that reactant in the rate equation; the overall reaction order is the sum of the exponents on all of the concentration terms in the rate equation.

18.8 RATE EQUATIONS FOR FIRST-ORDER REACTIONS **18.9** HALF-LIFE OF FIRST-ORDER REACTIONS **18.10** RATE EQUATIONS FOR ZERO-ORDER AND SECOND-ORDER REACTIONS The rate of a first-order reaction depends on the concentration of only one reactant, from which it follows that $k[A] = -\Delta[A]/\Delta t$ and $\log[A] = \log[A]_0 - kt/2.303$. For all first-order reactions, such as radioactive decay (Section 12.7), the half-life of any quantity of reactant is given by $t_{\frac{1}{2}} = 0.693/k$. The rate of a second-order reaction can depend upon the concentration of one reactant, rate = $k[A]^2$, or of two reactants, rate = $k[A][B]$. The rate of a zero-order reaction does not depend on reactant concentration and is therefore constant.

18.11 FINDING RATE EQUATIONS If a reaction is known to be elementary, its rate equation can be written directly from the balanced chemical equation for the reaction. The exponents on the concentration terms in the general rate equation are then the coefficients of those reactants in the balanced equation. For reactions that are *not* elementary reactions, neither the rate equation nor the reaction mechanism can be deduced from the equation. The rate equation for nonelementary reactions must be found experimentally, e.g., by the method of initial rates or by graphic methods. In such a reaction the rate-determining step is the slowest step in the reaction mechanism.

18.12 EFFECT OF TEMPERATURE ON REACTION RATE The activation energy, temperature, and rate constant of a reaction are connected by the Arrhenius equation, $\log k = -(E_a/2.303RT) + \log A$, where A is a constant. This equation applies to overall reactions as well as elementary reactions, and allows us to find E_a if the values of k at two different temperatures are known.

18.13 HOMOGENEOUS AND HETEROGENEOUS REACTIONS A homogeneous reaction is one between substances in the same gaseous or liquid phase; a heterogeneous reaction involves substances in different phases. In general, for reactions between solids, the reaction rate is proportional to the area of surface in contact. Similarly, a reaction between a gas and a solid is accelerated if the solid is finely divided so as to increase its surface area.

18.14 CATALYSIS A catalyst increases the rate of a chemical reaction but can be recovered in its original form when the reaction is finished. A catalyst cannot drive a thermodynamically unfavorable reaction nor shift the equilibrium point of a reaction; it can only lessen the time needed to reach equilibrium. A catalyst functions by providing an alternate pathway, with lower activation energy, for the reaction. Many catalysts are highly specific to particular reactions. Homogeneous catalysts—ones that are present in the same phase as the reactants—function by combining with reactant species to form unstable intermediates. Heterogeneous catalysts are present in a phase different from that of the reactants and products; often they are finely divided solids. One or more of the reactants are chemically adsorbed on the surface of such a catalyst, where the reaction takes place. Inhibitors are substances that slow down a catalyzed reaction, often by tieing up the catalyst; promoters make a catalyst more effective.

18.15 REACTION MECHANISMS AND RATE EQUATIONS When an experimental rate equation has been determined, a plausible mechanism for the reaction can be proposed. The sum of the steps in the proposed reaction mechanism must be the equation for the overall reaction, and combination of the rate equations for these steps must yield an overall rate equation identical to that determined by experiment. Steps that follow the rate-determining step do not usually affect the rate equation. Sometimes more than one reaction mechanism can give the same rate equation.

SIGNIFICANT TERMS

elementary reaction
reaction mechanism
intermediate
chemical kinetics
transition state, activated complex
free radical
activation energy
molecularity
bimolecular reaction
termolecular reaction
reaction rate
initial reaction rate
rate equation
rate constant
overall reaction order
reactant reaction order
rate-determining step
homogeneous reaction
heterogeneous reaction
homogeneous catalyst
heterogeneous catalyst
physical adsorption
chemical adsorption
inhibitors
promoters

THOUGHTS ON CHEMISTRY

A Conversation with Manfred Eigen

THE SEARCH FOR SOLUTIONS, By Horace Freeland Judson

Perhaps the most delightful kind of chance encounter occurs when two apparently unrelated problems meet and annihilate each other in the mind of the right person. . . . When he was a research student, in the early fifties, (Manfred) Eigen solved for his doctorate a problem in the mechanisms by which molecules or their components associate when they are in solution. . . . "That was looking at the chemistry of electrolytes more or less as a static picture," he said to me recently. "But then I became interested in the dynamics of these reactions—exactly how they progress physically to reach equilibrium. And how fast. And, naturally, I looked up in textbooks how to measure the speed of chemical reactions.

"I found in one textbook the remark that certain types of chemical reactions, say in the behavior of chemicals combining when they are in solution, are infinitely fast. 'Infinitely' means, of course, so fast that there is no hope ever to measure the speed. I looked up the time scale and thought a little about the chemical mechanisms; and I realized that they called everything 'infinitely fast' that was faster than, say one-thousandth of a second. But I could easily estimate that the fastest possible reactions one could think of would require only one-billionth of a second. So here there was a time scale of six to nine orders of magnitude unexplored. . . . A gap like this is a challenge to a scientist," Eigen said, with a cock of an eyebrow and a quick smile. *"You say that perhaps, if you find the right trick, you could still measure those processes and fill up that gap."* . . .

"So this was the other thing," Eigen said. *"People at that time were measuring the sound absorption of sea water. And they found that sea water has a very large absorption coefficient for sound waves. And physicists were wondering why sea water absorbed sound much more efficiently than ordinary water or distilled water. I thought I had an answer for this.*

"Because I had investigated the properties of electrolyte solutions, I saw that this was a particular kind of mechanism. . . . I suggested it must be the magnesium sulfate—another salt—which causes this. Sea water contains quite a lot of magnesium sulfate. And in solution the magnesium ions complex with sulfate ions; I had studied that and knew the mechanisms. So my proposal was that the energy of the sound was used to cause a dissociation of these complexes and an association of the ions—so that part of the energy was being put into chemical energy. And that was causing the loss, causing the sound absorption. We carried out experiments; and it turned out that magnesium and sulfate were the correct ions, and the answer."

Antiproblem met problem in Eigen's mental cloud chamber and the two vanished in a flash of understandings. *"At that moment I saw immediately that this was the answer to the problem of measuring fast reactions. Because with sound, you can get frequencies of a thousand cycles, which you can hear, up to megacycles (millions of cycles) or hundreds of megacycles. And so with sound waves at the right frequency and energy, you can perturb the existing chemical equilibrium for the briefest instant —for that billionth of a second. And then see by simultaneous measurement of other parameters what difference the pulse of disturbance made in the physical chemistry.*

The absorption of sound proved, indeed, to be a way to pulse energy very briefly into a chemical reaction under study, so that dissociation and reassociation, departure from and return to equilibrium, can be watched. These are called *"relaxation techniques."* . . . For the invention of relaxation techniques for measuring ultrafast chemical reactions, Eigen shared the Nobel Prize in Chemistry in 1967 with George Porter and Ronald G. W. Norrish, two English chemists who had independently explored some related methods.

QUESTIONS

Chemical Kinetics at the Molecular Level

18.1 What information can be derived from a balanced chemical equation about the stoichiometry, thermodynamics, and kinetics of the reaction?

18.2 What is an "elementary reaction"? How are elementary reactions used to construct a reaction mechanism?

18.3 What is meant by the term "intermediate" as applied to one or more of the species in a reaction mechanism?

18.4 What is the first requirement if two molecules are to react chemically? How do we describe the initial species which these molecules might form? What can subsequently happen to this species?

18.5 What are the three conditions for effective collisions between reacting species? Which of these conditions is influenced most by (a) temperature, (b) molecular geometry, and (c) relative bond energies?

18.6 Define "activation energy" for a chemical reaction. How does the value of the activation energy affect the rate of reaction? How does the rate of reaction vary with temperature? Why?

18.7 Using the numbers from the diagram shown below, identify (a) the reactant(s), (b) the product(s), (c) the energy change of reaction, (d) the activation energy for the forward reaction, and (e) the activation energy for the reverse reaction.

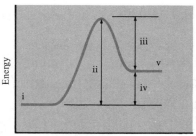

Extent of Reaction

18.8 The activation energy for the reaction

$$2HI(g) \longrightarrow H_2(g) + I_2(g) \qquad \Delta E^\circ = 9.47 \text{ kJ}$$

is 179 kJ. Construct a diagram similar to Figure 18.2 for this reaction.

18.9 From the plots of energy versus extent of reaction shown below, identify the diagram for (a) a highly endothermic reaction with a low activation energy, (b) a reaction in which a stable intermediate is formed, (c) an exothermic reaction with a low activation energy, (d) an endothermic reaction with a high activation energy, and (e) a highly exothermic reaction with a high activation energy.

18.10 Explain how elementary reactions are categorized in terms of molecularity. What are the usual molecularities of reactions? Why are termolecular reactions rare?

18.11 Are there any truly unimolecular reactions (excluding nuclear decay processes)? What is the usual explanation given for the mechanisms of gas-phase decomposition and isomerization reactions that one might believe to be unimolecular?

18.12 How do molecular collisions in aqueous solution differ from those in the gas phase?

18.13 A proposed mechanism for the decomposition of hydrogen peroxide in the presence of H_3O^+ and Br^-,

$$2H_2O_2(aq) \xrightarrow{H_3O^+,\ Br^-} 2H_2O(l) + O_2(g)$$

consists of the following elementary reactions:

$$H_2O_2(aq) + H_3O^+ + Br^- \longrightarrow HOBr(aq) + 2H_2O(l)$$
$$H_2O_2(aq) + HOBr(aq) \longrightarrow H_3O^+ + O_2 + Br^-$$

Discuss these elementary reactions in terms of their molecularity.

18.14 A proposed mechanism for the neutralization of acetic acid by the hydroxide ion:

$$CH_3COOH(aq) + OH^- \longrightarrow CH_3COO^- + H_2O(l)$$

consists of the following elementary reactions:

$$CH_3COOH(aq) + H_2O(l) \longrightarrow CH_3COO^- + H_3O^+$$
$$H_3O^+ + OH^- \longrightarrow 2H_2O(l)$$

What is the molecularity of each of these elementary reactions?

Reaction Rates

18.15 What is the definition of "reaction rate"? What are typical units for this physical quantity?

18.16 How does the rate of reaction vary with time for most reactions? Why?

18.17 How might the "rate of reaction" be defined for the following reactions:

(a) $2H_2O_2(aq) \longrightarrow 2H_2O(l) + O_2(g)$
(b) $CH_3COOH(aq) + OH^- \longrightarrow CH_3COO^- + H_2O(l)$
(c) $I^- + ClO^- \longrightarrow IO^- + Cl^-$
(d) $2K^+ + 2Fe^{3+} + 2[Fe(CN)_6]^{3-} + 2I^- \longrightarrow$
$$2KFe[Fe(CN)_6](s) + I_2(aq)$$
(e) $C_2H_4(g) + Br_2(g) \longrightarrow C_2H_4Br_2(g)$

18.18 Repeat Question 18.17 for

(a) $2HgO(s) \longrightarrow 2Hg(l) + O_2(g)$
(b) $CaCO_3(s) + 2HCl(aq) \longrightarrow CaCl_2(aq) + CO_2(g) + H_2O(l)$
(c) $S^{2-} + H_2O(l) \longrightarrow HS^- + OH^-$
(d) $2KClO_3(l) \longrightarrow 2KCl(s) + 3O_2(g)$

Concentration and Reaction Rate: Rate Equations

18.19 What is the name of the proportionality constant that relates reaction rate to concentration and what is its usual symbol? Does this constant always have the same set of units? Is it independent of temperature?

18.20 The oxidation of nitrogen(II) oxide,

$$2NO(g) + O_2(g) \longrightarrow 2NO_2(g)$$

is known to be second order with respect to NO and first order with respect to O_2. Write the rate equation for this reaction. What is the overall order of the reaction?

18.21 The hydrogenation of ethene,

$$C_2H_4(g) + H_2(g) \xrightarrow{Cu} C_2H_6(g)$$

is known to be first order with respect to H_2 and negative first order with respect to C_2H_4. Write the rate equation for this reaction.

18.22 The rate equation for the synthesis of urea from ammonium cyanate,

$$NH_4^+ + CNO^- \longrightarrow (NH_2)_2CO$$

is

$$Rate = k[NH_4^+][CNO^-]$$

What is the order of reaction with respect to each reactant and what is the overall order? What happens to the reaction rate as $[NH_4^+]$ increases?

18.23 Under certain conditions, the rate equation for

$$H_2(g) + Br_2(g) \longrightarrow 2HBr(g)$$

is

$$Rate = k[H_2][Br_2]^{\frac{3}{2}}[HBr]^{-1}$$

What is the order of the reaction with respect to each reactant? What happens to the rate of reaction as the concentrations of hydrogen and bromine decrease and the concentration of hydrogen bromide increases?

18.24 Briefly explain why the rate equation exponents for concentrations cannot be assumed to be equal to the respective coefficients in the overall chemical equation.

18.25 Write the rate equation for the overall first-order reaction

$$A \longrightarrow products$$

What are the units of k? What is the integrated rate equation? What would you plot so that the concentration–time data would be linear?

18.26 Repeat Question 18.25 for the overall second-order reaction

$$2A \longrightarrow products$$

18.27 Define the term "half-life." What is wrong with the statement, "After one half-life, there is one-half of the original amount of reactant remaining and after the second half-life period, all of the reactant has reacted"?

Factors That Influence Reaction Rates

18.28 Write the mathematical equation that describes the temperature dependency of the rate constant. What is the name of this equation?

18.29 Describe how you would determine the activation energy for a chemical reaction.

18.30 Briefly describe how physical contact between reactants affects reaction rate.

18.31 What is a catalyst? Explain how a catalyst increases the reaction rate. Will a catalyst change the relative amounts of reactants and products once equilibrium has been attained? Can a catalyst change a thermodynamically nonspontaneous reaction into a spontaneous reaction?

Reaction Mechanisms

18.32 What can be said about a proposed mechanism for which the derived rate equation does not agree with the experimental rate equation? What if they agree?

18.33 What does the term "rate-determining step" mean?

18.34* Given the following steps in the mechanism for a chemical reaction:

$$A + B \xrightarrow{fast} C$$
$$B + C \xrightarrow{slow} D + E$$
$$D + F \xrightarrow{fast} A + E$$

Identify which species, if any, are (a) catalysts and (b) intermediates in this reaction. (c) Write the rate equation for the rate-determining step. The concentration of C is directly proportional to [A]. (d) Rewrite the rate equation so that it includes concentration terms for only reactants and products, not intermediates. (e) What is the overall order of the reaction?

18.35* A proposed mechanism for the aqueous reaction given by the equation

$$I^- + ClO^- \longrightarrow IO^- + Cl^-$$

consists of the following steps:

$$ClO^- + H_2O \xrightarrow{rapid} HClO + OH^-$$
$$HClO + OH^- \xrightarrow{rapid} ClO^- + H_2O$$
$$I^- + HClO \xrightarrow{slow} HIO + Cl^-$$
$$OH^- + HIO \xrightarrow{rapid} H_2O + IO^-$$
$$H_2O + IO^- \xrightarrow{rapid} OH^- + HIO$$

(a) Write the rate equation for the rate-determining step. The concentration of HClO in a dilute aqueous solution is proportional to $[ClO^-]/[OH^-]$. (b) Rewrite the rate equation in terms of $[ClO^-]$, $[OH^-]$, and $[I^-]$. (c) What is the overall order of the reaction? (d) What would happen to the reaction rate if the concentration of OH^- were doubled?

Answers to Selected Questions

18.9 (a) iii, (b) v, (c) i, (d) iv, (e) ii

18.14 Both are bimolecular reactions.

18.18 (a) Rate $= \Delta C_{O_2}/\Delta t$; (b) Rate $= -\Delta C_{HCl}/\Delta t$ or Rate $= \Delta C_{CaCl_2}/\Delta t = \Delta C_{CO_2}/\Delta t$; (c) Rate $= -\Delta C_{S^{2-}}/\Delta t = \Delta C_{HS^-}/\Delta t = \Delta C_{OH^-}/\Delta t$; (d) Rate $= \Delta C_{O_2}/\Delta t$

18.21 Rate $= k[H_2][C_2H_4]^{-1}$

18.23 first order with respect to H_2, three-halves order with respect to Br_2, negative first order with respect to HBr; decreases

18.26 Rate $= k[A]^2$, $(concentration)^{-1}(time)^{-1}$, $1/[A] = 1/[A]_0 + kt$, $1/[A]$ vs. t

18.35 (a) Rate $= k[I^-][HClO]$, (b) Rate $= k''[I^-][ClO^-]/[OH^-]$, (c) first order overall, (d) the rate would decrease by a factor of two

PROBLEMS

Reaction Rate

18.1 For a hypothetical reaction

$$A + 2B \xrightarrow{C} D + E$$

the rate equation is

$$Rate = \frac{k[A][B][C]}{[D]}$$

What will happen to the reaction rate if (a) [A] is doubled, (b) [B] is doubled, (c) more catalyst is added, (d) D is removed as it is formed to keep [D] at a small value, (e) [A] and [B] are both doubled, and (f) the temperature is increased?

18.2 The rate equation for the decomposition of hydrogen peroxide in 0.02 M KI is

$$Rate = k[H_2O_2]$$

where $k = 5.21 \times 10^{-3}$ min^{-1} at 25 °C. What is the initial rate of decomposition of hydrogen peroxide in (a) a 0.10 M and (b) a 0.010 M solution of hydrogen peroxide?

18.3 The rate equation for the decomposition of N_2O_5 in CCl_4 is

$$Rate = k[N_2O_5]$$

where $k = 6.32 \times 10^{-4}$ min^{-1} at 45 °C. What is the initial rate of decomposition of N_2O_5 in (a) a 0.10 M and (b) a 0.010 M solution of N_2O_5? *Answer* (a) 6.3×10^{-5} mol/L min, (b) 6.3×10^{-6} mol/L min

18.4* The following concentration–time data were obtained for the decomposition of N_2O_5 at 45 °C:

$t(s)$	0	423	753	1116	1582	1986	2343
$[N_2O_5]$ (mol/L)	1.40	1.09	0.89	0.72	0.54	0.43	0.35

(a) Prepare a plot of concentration against time. (b) Estimate the concentrations of N_2O_5 at 600 s, 1200 s, 1800 s from your plot. (c) Determine the rate of reaction at 600 s by calculating the slope of a line drawn tangent to the curve at 600 s. (d) Repeat the calculation of (c) at 1200 and 1800 s. Does the rate seem to depend on concentration? (e) Divide your answers for (c) and (d) by the respective values of $[N_2O_5]$ and $[N_2O_5]^2$. Is the reaction first or second order?

Reaction Order

18.5 The first-order rate constant for the reaction

$$CS_2(g) \longrightarrow CS(g) + S(g)$$

is 2.8×10^{-7} s^{-1} at 1000 °C. What will be the concentration of CS_2 at $t = 2.0$ days given that the initial concentration is 1.30×10^{-2} mol/L? What is the half-life of this reaction?

18.6 The first-order rate constant for the reaction

cyclopropane

is 9.2 s^{-1} at 1000 °C. How long will it take for one-half of the cyclopropane to react? How long will it take for 95% of the cyclopropane to react? *Answer* 0.075 s, 0.33 s

18.7* The second-order rate constant for the reaction

$$2HI(g) \longrightarrow H_2(g) + I_2(g)$$

is 2.4×10^{-21} L/mol s at 25 °C. What will be the concentration of HI at $t = 1.0$ yr, given that the initial concentration is 5.2×10^{-3} mol/L? What is the half-life of the reaction for this initial value of concentration? *Answer* 5.2×10^{-3} mol/L, 2.5×10^{15} yr

Rate Equations and Half-Life

18.8 Consider the reaction

$$A + B \longrightarrow products$$

The following table gives the initial rates of reaction at various initial concentrations of A and B:

Experiment	(a)	(b)	(c)	(d)
Initial rate (mol/L s)	0.0090	0.036	0.018	0.027
$[A]_0$ (mol/L)	0.10	0.20	0.10	0.10
$[B]_0$ (mol/L)	0.10	0.10	0.20	0.30

Find the order of the reaction with respect to A and B and the overall order. *Answer* Rate $= k[A]^2[B]$, third order overall

18.9 The following initial rate data were obtained at 0 °C for the reaction

$$2ClO_2(aq) + 2OH^- \longrightarrow ClO_3^- + ClO_2^- + H_2O(l)$$

Experiment	(a)	(b)
Initial rate (mol/L s)	3.88×10^{-4}	1.55×10^{-3}
$[ClO_2]_0$ (mol/L)	1.5×10^{-2}	3.0×10^{-2}
$[OH^-]_0$ (mol/L)	1.5×10^{-2}	1.5×10^{-2}

Experiment	(c)	(d)
Initial rate (mol/L s)	7.76×10^{-4}	3.11×10^{-3}
$[ClO_2]_0$ (mol/L)	1.5×10^{-2}	3.0×10^{-2}
$[OH^-]_0$ (mol/L)	3.0×10^{-2}	3.0×10^{-2}

Determine the order of reaction with respect to $[ClO_2]$ and $[OH^-]$. Calculate k at this temperature.

18.10 The following data were obtained for the decomposition of diazomethane, CH_2N_2, at 600 °C:

t (min)	0	5	10	15	20	25
$[CH_2N_2]$ (mol/L)	0.100	0.076	0.058	0.044	0.033	0.025

Show graphically that the reaction is first order and determine the rate constant.

18.11* By graphical means, determine the order of reaction and the rate constant for the reaction

$$2Br(g) \xrightarrow{SF_6} Br_2(g)$$

from the following data:

t (μs)	120	220	320	420	520	620
[Br] (μmol)	25.8	15.1	10.4	8.0	6.7	5.6

Answer Rate = $k[Br]^2$, $k = 2.8 \times 10^8$ L/mol s

Activation Energy and Temperature

18.12 The activation energy for the reaction between O_3 and NO is 9.6 kJ/mol.

$$O_3(g) + NO(g) \longrightarrow NO_2(g) + O_2(g)$$

At 25 °C, the heat of formation is 33.2 kJ/mol for $NO_2(g)$, 90.25 kJ/mol for NO(g), and 142.7 kJ/mol for $O_3(g)$. Calculate the heat of reaction. Prepare an activation energy plot similar to Figure 18.2 for this reaction. (For this reaction, $\Delta E° = \Delta H°$.)

18.13 The rate constant for the reaction

$$\begin{matrix} H_2C-C=O \\ | \quad\quad | \\ H_2C-CH_2 \end{matrix} (g) \longrightarrow C_2H_4(g) + H_2C=C=O(g)$$

at 361 °C is 4.6×10^{-4} s^{-1} and at 371 °C is 7.2×10^{-4} s^{-1}. What is the energy of activation for this reaction?

18.14 The rate constant for the decomposition of N_2O,

$$2N_2O(g) \longrightarrow 2N_2(g) + O_2(g)$$

is 2.6×10^{-11} s^{-1} at 300. °C and 2.1×10^{-10} s^{-1} at 330. °C. What is the activation energy for this reaction? Prepare a plot of energy versus extent of reaction using -164.1 kJ as the energy of reaction. *Answer* 2.0×10^5 J

18.15 The activation energy for the reaction

$$2C_6H_5CHO(aq) \xrightarrow{CN^-} C_6H_5CH(OH)COC_6H_5$$

is 54.8 kJ. At 25 °C, the rate constant is 1.40×10^{-4} L^2/mol^2 s. Calculate the rate constant at 60. °C.

18.16 How much faster would a reaction proceed at 25 °C than at 0 °C if the activation energy is 65 kJ? *Answer* 10 times faster

18.17 The rate constant for the decomposition of A in solvent X is 4.7×10^{-5} s^{-1} at 60.0 °C and 1.60×10^{-4} s^{-1} at 70.0 °C; in solvent Y it is 7.0×10^{-5} s^{-1} at 65.0 °C and 2.30×10^{-4} s^{-1} at 75.0 °C. Calculate the energy of activation for the reaction in each solvent. Is one solvent acting as a stronger catalyst than the other (as determined by a lower value of E_a)? *Answer* 120 kJ in X, 120 kJ in Y, no

18.18* The rate constant for the decomposition of N_2O_5 was studied as a function of temperature:

T (°C)	0	25	35	45
k (s^{-1})	7.36×10^{-7}	3.33×10^{-5}	1.29×10^{-4}	4.58×10^{-4}
	55	65		
	1.51×10^{-3}	4.64×10^{-3}		

Prepare a plot of log k against the inverse of the absolute temperature. The slope of the straight line through the data is related to E_a by $E_a = -2.303R \times$ (slope). Calculate E_a for this reaction.

Additional Problems

18.19* A convenient experimental method for determining the order of reaction involves measuring the time necessary for a reaction to proceed by a fixed amount. This procedure is known as the "clock method." For example, the decomposition of gaseous PH_3 was studied at 600 °C:

$$4PH_3(g) \longrightarrow P_4(g) + 6H_2(g)$$

using the clock method. The time required for the partial pressure of PH_3 to decrease by 5.00 Torr was recorded at three different initial partial pressures of PH_3. The data were

$p_{PH_3,0}$ (Torr)	262.40	65.60	16.31
t(s)	0.83	3.42	15.81

The equation relating the time to the initial pressure (or concentration) is

$$\log (1/t) = K + n \log p_0$$

where K is a constant and n is the order of reaction. Prepare a plot of log $(1/t)$ versus log p_0 and determine the reaction order.

18.20* An important gas-phase reaction, which occurs in the atmosphere, is described by the equation

$$2O_3(g) \longrightarrow 3O_2(g) \qquad \Delta H°_{298} = -285.3 \text{ kJ}$$

A set of experiments gave the following data.

Initial p_{O_3} (Torr)	0.20	0.20	0.40
Initial p_{O_2} (Torr)	0.50	1.0	1.0
Initial rate (Torr/s)	6.0	3.0	12

(a) What are the values of x and y in the rate equation

$$\text{Rate} = kp_{O_3}^x \, p_{O_2}^y$$

(b) The reaction was investigated in the presence of CO_2 to determine any catalytic effect that CO_2 might have on the reaction rate. The results of two such experiments at 50 °C are:

$p_{CO_2} = 100$ Torr

t(s)	0	1800	3600	7200
p_{O_3} (Torr)	200	140	100	50

$p_{CO_2} = 180$ Torr

t(s)	0	1800	3600
p_{O_3} (Torr)	220	120	70

The complete rate equation for the catalyzed reaction is

$$\text{Rate} = k' p_{O_3}^m \, p_{CO_2}$$

Find the order of reaction with respect to p_{O_3} for each experiment and the rate constant in each case. (c) Does the catalyzed reaction have a mechanism different from that of the uncatalyzed reaction? The rate constants found in part (b) are equal to $k' p_{CO_2}$. (d) Find k'. *Answer* (a) $x = 2$, $y = -1$; (b) plots of log p_{O_3} against t are both linear, reaction is first order with respect to O_3 in both experiments, rate constants = 1.9×10^{-4} s^{-1} and 3.1×10^{-4} s^{-1}; (c) yes—mechanism must be different because the order of the reaction with respect to O_3 is different (that is, $x \neq m$); (d) 1.9×10^{-6} s^{-1} Torr^{-1}

CHAPTER 19

Chemical Equilibrium

Picture a large chicken house divided into two parts by a chicken-wire wall. On one side live 200 white chickens. On the other side live 200 brown chickens. What would happen if someone left the connecting door open? Gradually the brown and white chickens would mix together as their random paths took them through the door. How fast this happens — the "reaction rate" — would depend upon how fast the chickens are moving. The process might be quicker in the morning than just before sundown when the chickens are drowsy.

Eventually, we can assume, a state of dynamic equilibrium would be reached. The brown and white chickens would be pretty well mixed together on each side, and at any given moment some brown and some white chickens would be going through the door in each direction. There would be a roughly unchanging number of chickens on each side.

If we knew how long it would take to reach this equilibrium, we would still know nothing about how many chickens were on each side at equilibrium. It might be an equal number, or it might be any combination adding up to 400, depending upon the "conditions" of the "reaction." Suppose the water buckets on one side were empty. Then at equilibrium there might be only 50 chickens on that side and 350 on the other.

The purpose of this analogy, about which you are probably wondering by now, is to point out that the "rate" of a reaction and the equilibrium state of a reaction are different concepts. A thorough understanding of any chemical reaction must include quantitative knowledge about both the rate of the reaction and the conditions at which it reaches equilibrium.

THE LAW OF CHEMICAL EQUILIBRIUM

19.1 A CLOSE LOOK AT AN EQUILIBRIUM REACTION

As a chemical reaction proceeds, the concentration of reactants decreases and the concentration of products increases. If the reaction goes to "completion," the concentration of reactants, say A and B in the combination reaction

$$A + B \longrightarrow C$$

approaches zero, while the concentration of product C approaches the amount determined by the stoichiometry of the reaction and the initial amounts of A and B (Figure 19.1a).

If, instead, a dynamic equilibrium is reached, some molecules of A, B, and C will all remain at equilibrium. Equilibrium might be reached at a point where the number of reactant molecules remaining is much larger than the number of product molecules (Figure 19.1b). In such a case the reaction can be described as "not going very far toward completion." On the other hand, the reaction might come to equilibrium at a point where few reactant molecules remain and the system contains mainly products (Figure 19.1c). Such a reaction is described as "favorable in the forward direction" or as going "to the right."

Suppose some PCl_3 and Cl_2 are confined in a closed vessel at 500 K. As soon as the gases are mixed, the formation of PCl_5 — the forward reaction — begins.

$$PCl_3(g) + Cl_2(g) \longrightarrow PCl_5(g)$$

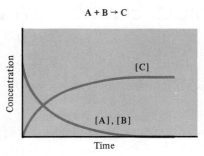

A + B → C

(a) Reaction goes to completion

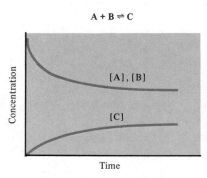

A + B ⇌ C

(b) Equilibrium with many reactant molecules unchanged

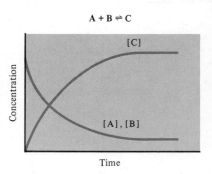

A + B ⇌ C

(c) Equilibrium with few reactant molecules remaining

Figure 19.1
Concentration Change with Time for Reactions that go to Completion or Reach Equilibrium The initial concentrations of A and B are equal.

At this temperature PCl_5 can decompose. As soon as some PCl_5 has formed, the reverse reaction begins — PCl_5 molecules decompose to give PCl_3 and Cl_2 molecules.

$$PCl_5(g) \longrightarrow PCl_3(g) + Cl_2(g)$$

The concentratons of the three gases will continue to change in one of the two general ways shown in Figure 19.1b and c. As the concentrations of PCl_3 and Cl_2 decrease, whatever collisions precede the formation of PCl_5 occur less often, and the rate of the forward reaction decreases. The rate of the reverse reaction depends upon the concentration of PCl_5 molecules; the more of these that are present in a given volume, the more there are that decompose. Thus, as more PCl_5 is formed, the rate of the reverse reaction increases (Figure 19.2). The rates of the forward and the reverse reactions, and the concentrations of the three gases continue to change until equilibrium is reached. At this point the rates of the forward and reverse reactions are equal (see Figure 19.2),

$$PCl_3(g) + Cl_2(g) \rightleftharpoons PCl_5(g)$$

with the net result that the concentrations of the three gases remain constant.

The system is in a state of dynamic, chemical equilibrium. Each time one PCl_5 molecule is formed, one PCl_3 and one Cl_2 molecule disappear. Each time a PCl_5 molecule decomposes, one PCl_3 and one Cl_2 molecule are formed. As long as the temperature and pressure remain constant and nothing is added to or taken from the mixture, the equilibrium state remains unchanged. The reaction could, of course, be driven to completion if PCl_5 were removed from the system (Le Chatelier's principle, Section 17.2).

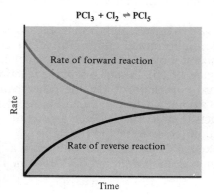

$PCl_3 + Cl_2 \rightleftharpoons PCl_5$

Rate of forward reaction

Rate of reverse reaction

Figure 19.2
Variation of Forward and Reverse Reaction Rates in an Equilibrium Reaction

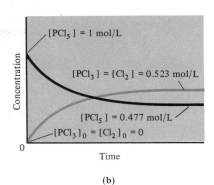

Figure 19.3
Equilibrium for
$PCl_3(g) + Cl_2(g) \rightarrow PCl_5(g)$
Approached from the (a) Forward and (b) Reverse Directions The concentrations at equilibrium are the same in these two reactions.

The variation in concentration with time for an experment beginning with 1 mol/L of PCl_3 and 1 mol/L of Cl_2 confined at 500 K is shown in Figure 19.3a. At equilibrium $[PCl_3] = [Cl_2] = 0.52$ mol/L and $[PCl_5] = 0.48$ mol/L. What would happen if an experiment was begun with 1 mol/L of PCl_5 and *no* PCl_3 or Cl_2? As Figure 19.3b shows, equilibrium would be reached at exactly the same concentrations.

Now let's consider what happens if more PCl_3 or Cl_2 molecules are introduced into the reaction vessel. With more reactant molecules available, more collisions occur in a given amount of time, and the rate of formation of PCl_5 increases. Once again, as the concentration of PCl_5 increases, the rate of its decomposition also increases. These changes in the rates of the forward and reverse reactions continue until equilibrium has been reached.

If one additional mole of PCl_3 and one mole of Cl_2 per liter were added, the equilibrium concentrations of reactants and products would be found to be $[PCl_3] = [Cl_2] = 0.82$ mol/L and $[PCl_5] = 1.18$ mol/L. If, instead, one additional mole per liter of Cl_2 only were added, the equilibrium concentrations would be found to be $[Cl_2] = 1.30$, $[PCl_3] = 0.30$, and $[PCl_5] = 0.70$. As you can see, the reactants and products in an equilibrium reaction need not be present in equal concentrations. This happens rarely. Most often the substances written on one side of the equation are present in greater concentrations than the substances written on the other side. It can be either side. As is discussed further in following sections, the reaction conditions and the characteristics of the particular reaction determine whether reactants or products are favored.

19.2 EQUILIBRIUM CONSTANTS

The concept of dynamic chemical equilibrium grew out of observations that changing the concentrations of one or more reactants or products involved in a chemical reaction leads to changes in the equilibrium concentrations of other reactants or products. Both experimental and theoretical approaches eventually led to the same general mathematical relationship for the equilibrium concentrations of reactants and products. In this section we present some experimental results and show how they reveal this relationship.

Nitrogen dioxide (NO_2) and dinitrogen tetroxide (N_2O_4) form an equilibrium mixture by the following reaction:

$$2NO_2(g) \rightleftharpoons N_2O_4(g) \tag{19.1}$$

The concentrations of these two gases have been measured after equilibrium was reached in a closed vessel at constant temperature (about 21 °C). In each of four experiments the initial concentrations of the two gases were different. Once equilibrium was reached, the following concentrations were found:

	At Equilibrium	
Experiment No.	$[NO_2]$ (mol/L)	$[N_2O_4]$ (mol/L)
1	0.052	0.595
2	0.024	0.127
3	0.068	1.02
4	0.101	2.24

It would be satisfying to find a mathematical relationship that brings some meaning to these numbers. The table shows that the concentrations of the reactant and product are *not* equal to each other at equilibrium. A little arithmetic shows that these concentrations do not maintain a constant ratio, either.

Experiment No.	$[N_2O_4]/[NO_2]$
1	11
2	5.3
3	15
4	22

We might try several dozen manipulations with such data before coming up with a meaningful relationship. Let's move ahead by skipping directly to the right one. Dividing the concentration of N_2O_4 by the square of the concentration of NO_2 gives a constant.

Experiment No.	$[N_2O_4]/[NO_2]^2$
1	220
2	220
3	220
4	220

Remember that the initial concentrations of the gases were different in each experiment. The existence of this mathematically constant relationship shows that whatever the initial conditions, the forward and reverse reactions adjust in reaching equilibrium so that $[N_2O_4]/[NO_2]^2$ remains the same.

Experiments with many different equilibrium reactions over the years and a theoretical derivation based on the principles of thermodynamics both give the same result. It is possible to formulate an expression for the relationships among equilibrium concentrations for any reaction. For the general reaction

$$aA + bB + \cdots \rightleftharpoons rR + sS + \cdots \qquad (19.2)$$

the "equilibrium constant," K, is given by the following expression:

$$K = \frac{[R]^r[S]^s \cdots}{[A]^a[B]^b \cdots} \quad \begin{array}{l} \textit{product concentrations} \\ \textit{reactant concentrations} \end{array} \qquad (19.3)$$

For reaction at equilibrium
$aA + bB + \cdots \rightleftharpoons$
$rR + sS + \cdots$
$K = \dfrac{[R]^r[S]^s \cdots}{[A]^a[B]^b \cdots}$

where [R], [S], [A], [B], and so on represent the concentrations of the reactants and products, at equilibrium, in moles per liter. It is more difficult to define the equilibrium constant in words than with an equation: The **equilibrium constant** is equal to the product of the concentrations of the reaction products, each raised to the power equal to its stoichiometric coefficient, divided by the product of the concentrations of the reactants, each raised to the power equal to its stoichiometric coefficient. (Note that K is used for the *equilibrium constant expression*, or the equilibrium constant, and k for the rate constant.)

The NO_2–N_2O_4 reaction fits into the general scheme of Equations (19.2) and (19.3) as

$$aA \rightleftharpoons rR \qquad 2NO_2 \rightleftharpoons N_2O_4$$

k = rate constant
K = equilibrium constant

and

$$K = \frac{[R]^r}{[A]^a} = \frac{[N_2O_4]}{[NO_2]^2} \qquad \text{(19.4)}$$

Some carefully gathered experimental data on the reaction between hydrogen and iodine,

$$H_2(g) + I_2(g) \rightleftharpoons 2HI(g) \qquad \text{(19.5)}$$

illustrate several additional important points about chemical equilibrium. In one set of experiments, the amount of hydrogen in the initial mixture was held relatively constant (at about 0.01 mol/L), while the amount of iodine was varied. The concentrations of H_2, I_2, and HI at equilibrium were measured (at 425.4 °C). These concentrations and the values of K calculated from

$$K = \frac{[HI]^2}{[H_2][I_2]} \qquad \text{(19.6)}$$

were as follows (data from A. H. Taylor and R. H. Crist, *J. Amer. Chem. Soc.* **63**, 1377, 1941):

	At Equilibrium		
[H$_2$]	[I$_2$]	[HI]	$K = \dfrac{[HI]^2}{[H_2][I_2]}$
0.001831	0.003129	0.01767	54.5
0.003560	0.001250	0.01559	54.6
0.004565	0.0007378	0.01354	54.4

The small variations in the value of K are due to small variations in the precision of the experiment and are not significant. Clearly, changes in the initial concentration of one of two reactants do not alter the constancy of K. Additional experiments show that K remains constant with simultaneous variations in the concentrations of both reactants. An infinite number of combinations of the concentrations of reactants and products is possible, but at equilibrium at a specific temperature and pressure, there is only one value for K.

However, similar experiments show that the value of K does vary with *temperature*. For example, at a temperature of 490.65 °C (instead of 425.4 °C) the value of K is constant at 45.6 (instead of 54.5).

In further experiments with this same system, hydrogen iodide was placed in a sealed vessel and allowed to reach equilibrium with its decomposition products hydrogen and iodine — the same reaction but approached from the reverse direction. Similar data and calculations (for 425.4 °C also) show by the constancy of K that the equilibrium state is the same, no matter from which direction it is approached.

At Equilibrium

$[H_2]$	$[I_2]$	$[HI]$	$K = \dfrac{[HI]^2}{[H_2][I_2]}$
0.0004789	0.0004789	0.003531	54.3
0.001141	0.001141	0.008410	54.3

In summary, we have used experimental data to show the following:
1. *The equilibrium concentrations of reactants and products in a reversible reaction are related by the law of chemical equilibrium*

$$K = \frac{[R]^r[S]^s \cdots}{[A]^a[B]^b \cdots} \qquad \text{where } a\text{A} + b\text{B} + \cdots \Longleftrightarrow r\text{R} + s\text{S} + \cdots$$

   where [ ] indicates concentration in moles per liter at equilibrium.
2. *An initial mixture of reactants of any concentrations will reach equilibrium (at a specific temperature and pressure) so that the concentrations of reactants and products are related by the law of chemical equilibrium.*
3. *The value of K is dependent upon the temperature.*
4. *Approaching equilibrium from either direction, at the same temperature, leads to equilibrium concentrations determined by the same value of K.*

EXAMPLE 19.1
Writing Equilibrium Constant Expressions

Write the equilibrium constant expression for each of the following gas-phase reactions:

(a) $N_2(g) + O_2(g) \Longleftrightarrow 2NO(g)$
(b) $2NO(g) + Br_2(g) \Longleftrightarrow 2NOBr(g)$

For chemical equation (a), there is only one product and it has a stoichiometric coefficient of 2; therefore the numerator of the equilibrium constant expression (Equation 19.3) consists of one term, $[NO]^2$. There are two reactants, each with stoichiometric coefficients of 1; therefore the denominator of the equilibrium constant expression consists of the product of these concentrations, each raised to the first power, $[N_2][O_2]$. The complete expression for K is

$$K = \frac{[NO]^2}{[N_2][O_2]}$$

For chemical equation (b), the numerator is $[NOBr]^2$ and the denominator is $[NO]^2[Br_2]$, giving

$$K = \frac{[NOBr]^2}{[NO]^2[Br_2]}$$

Exercise Write the equilibrium constant expression for each of the following gas-phase reactions:

(a) $2NO(g) + O_2(g) \Longleftrightarrow 2NO_2(g)$
(b) $2HF(g) \Longleftrightarrow H_2(g) + F_2(g)$

Answer (a) $K = [NO_2]^2/[NO]^2[O_2]$, $K = [H_2][F_2]/[HF]^2$

19.3 UNITS AND EQUILIBRIUM CONSTANT VALUES

In the discussion of K for the hydrogen–iodine reaction, we bypassed the subject of units. The units of K would be determined by the form of the K expression. For the hydrogen–iodine reaction,

$$K = \frac{[HI]^2}{[H_2][I_2]} = \frac{(\cancel{mol/L})^2}{(\cancel{mol/L})(\cancel{mol/L})}$$

K is dimensionless. This is true for any reaction in which the number of reactant molecules equals the number of product molecules.

Table 19.1 gives some additional examples of K for gas-phase reactions. For reaction (a) the units would be $(L/mol)^2$; for reaction (b) they would be L/mol; and for reaction (c) they would be mol/L. The confusion that might be caused by this diversity can be handled very simply—it is customary to omit the units with K values.

The values of equilibrium constants are usually given in scientific notation, and they range greatly in magnitude. In Table 19.2, compare the values for the gas-phase reactions of hydrogen plus oxygen and the decomposition of carbon dioxide. The reaction of hydrogen with oxygen, once it is initiated, can proceed with explosive violence. When the reaction is finished, very little hydrogen and oxygen remain unreacted. The high concentration of product when this reaction has come to equilibrium leads to a very large value for K (at 298 K).

$$K = \frac{[H_2O]^2}{[H_2]^2[O_2]} = 3.1 \times 10^{81}$$

On the other hand, carbon dioxide at 298 K dissociates to only a very small extent. The very low concentrations of the products at equilibrium lead to a very small value for K (at 298 K).

$$K = \frac{[CO]^2[O_2]}{[CO_2]^2} = 3.0 \times 10^{-92}$$

Large values of K indicate that large concentrations of products are present at equilibrium. Small values of K indicate the opposite—at equilibrium the concentrations of products are small. Table 19.2 gives equilibrium constant values for examples of some of the types of equilibrium reactions that we have discussed earlier (Section 14.7). Note that the K values for the ionization of weak electrolytes and for the solubilities of slightly soluble substances have values that are less than 1.

Strictly speaking, equilibrium constants expressed in terms of concentration (or pressure, as discussed below) are truly constant only for ideal gases or ideal solutions. In its theoretically correct form, the equilibrium constant expression is given in terms of the *activities* of the reactants and products, rather than the concentrations.

Table 19.1
Equilibrium Expressions for Homogeneous Gas-Phase Reactions (Brackets indicate concentration in moles per liter.)

$N_2(g) + 3H_2(g) \rightleftharpoons 2NH_3(g)$ (a)
$K = \dfrac{[NH_3]^2}{[N_2][H_2]^3}$
$2NO_2(g) \rightleftharpoons N_2O_4(g)$ (b)
$K = \dfrac{[N_2O_4]}{[NO_2]^2}$
$COCl_2(g) \rightleftharpoons CO(g) + Cl_2(g)$ (c)
$K = \dfrac{[CO][Cl_2]}{[COCl_2]}$

$K > 1$, **products favored**
$K < 1$, **reactants favored**

Table 19.2
Some Equilibrium Constants

	K_c at 25 °C
Gas-phase reactions	
$2H_2(g) + O_2(g) \rightleftharpoons 2H_2O(g)$	3.1×10^{81}
$H_2(g) + I_2(g) \rightleftharpoons 2HI(g)$	8.7×10^2
$2CO_2(g) \rightleftharpoons 2CO(g) + O_2(g)$	3.0×10^{-92}
Ionization of weak acids in water	
$CH_3COOH(aq) \rightleftharpoons CH_3COO^- + H^+$	1.8×10^{-5}
$HCN(aq) \rightleftharpoons H^+ + CN^-$	6.2×10^{-10}
Solubility of precipitates	
$CaSO_4(s) \rightleftharpoons Ca^{2+} + SO_4^{2-}$	2.5×10^{-5}
$AgCl(s) \rightleftharpoons Ag^+ + Cl^-$	1.8×10^{-10}
$Ag_2S(s) \rightleftharpoons 2Ag^+ + S^{2-}$	7.1×10^{-50}

However, as explained earlier (Section 15.3), except in highly accurate work or when dealing with concentrated solutions, concentrations are not significantly different from activities and may be used instead.

EXAMPLE 19.2
Evaluation of K

The reaction between nitrogen and oxygen to form $NO(g)$ is represented by the chemical equation

$$N_2(g) + O_2(g) \rightleftharpoons 2NO(g)$$

The equilibrium concentrations of the gases at 1500 K are 1.7×10^{-3} mol/L for O_2, 6.4×10^{-3} mol/L for N_2, and 1.1×10^{-5} mol/L for NO. Calculate the value of the equilibrium constant at 1500 K from these data.

The equilibrium constant expression for this chemical equation is

$$K = \frac{[NO]^2}{[N_2][O_2]}$$

Substituting the respective concentrations gives the numerical value of K as

$$K = \frac{[NO]^2}{[N_2][O_2]} = \frac{(1.1 \times 10^{-5})^2}{(6.4 \times 10^{-3})(1.7 \times 10^{-3})} = 1.1 \times 10^{-5}$$

The equilibrium constant at 1500 K is 1.1×10^{-5}.

Exercise   At elevated temperatures, BrF_5 establishes the following equilibrium:

$$2BrF_5(g) \rightleftharpoons Br_2(g) + 5F_2(g)$$

The equilibrium concentration of the gases at 1500 K are 0.0064 mol/L for BrF_5, 0.0018 mol/L for Br_2, and 0.0090 mol/L for F_2. Calculate the value of the equilibrium constant.   *Answer* 2.6×10^{-9}.

19.4 EQUILIBRIUM CONSTANTS FOR REACTIONS OF GASES

When the reactants and products of a reaction are all gases, partial pressures, which are directly proportional to concentrations, can be used in the law of chemical equilibrium instead of concentrations in moles per liter, giving K_p for the general reaction of Equation (19.2),

$$K_p = \frac{p_R{}^r p_S{}^s \cdots}{p_A{}^a p_B{}^b \cdots} \qquad \text{partial pressures in atm} \tag{19.7}$$

*indicates
K for partial
pressures of
reactants and products*

For example, for the reaction

$$PCl_3(g) + Cl_2(g) \longrightarrow PCl_5(g) \qquad K_p = \frac{p_{PCl_5}}{p_{PCl_3} p_{Cl_2}}$$

Note that partial pressures in equilibrium expressions are always given in atmospheres. The value of K_p for a given reaction is related to the equilibrium constant in terms of concentrations, K_c, by the ideal gas law. For substance A,

$$p_A V_A = n_A RT \qquad \text{and therefore} \qquad p_A = \frac{n_A RT}{V_A}$$

Because n/V is moles per liter, this expression can be written as

$$p_A = [A]RT \tag{19.8}$$

Substituting relationships such as that in Equation (19.8) into the expression for K_p gives

$$K_p = \frac{([R]RT)^r([S]RT)^s \cdots}{([A]RT)^a([B]RT)^b \cdots} = \frac{[R]^r[S]^s \cdots}{[A]^a[B]^b \cdots} \times (RT)^{(r+s+\cdots)-(a+b+\cdots)}$$

which yields the general expression

$$K_p = K_c(RT)^{\Delta n} \qquad \qquad \textbf{(19.9)}$$

where Δn for the balanced chemical equation is given by

$$\Delta n = \text{(moles of gaseous products)} - \text{(moles of gaseous reactants)}$$
$$= (r + s + \cdots) - (a + b + \cdots)$$

Note that if $\Delta n = 0$, that is, when the number of moles of reactants equals the number of moles of products in the balanced equation for the reaction being considered, then K_c has the same value as K_p [because $(RT)^0 = 1$].

EXAMPLE 19.3
Evaluation of K

Methyl alcohol can be prepared commercially by the reaction of hydrogen with carbon monoxide:

$$CO(g) + 2H_2(g) \rightleftharpoons CH_3OH(g)$$

Under equilibrium conditions at 700. K, $[H_2] = 0.072$ mol/L, $[CO] = 0.020$ mol/L, and $[CH_3OH] = 0.030$ mol/L. What are the values of K_c and K_p at this temperature?

Writing the equilibrium expression for K_c and then substituting the concentrations into it, we get

$$K_c = \frac{[CH_3OH]}{[CO][H_2]^2} = \frac{(0.030)}{(0.020)(0.072)^2} = 290$$

We must determine the value of Δn, the change in the number of moles of gaseous reactants and products, in order to convert the value of K_c to K_p. For this reaction

$$\Delta n = \text{(moles of gaseous products)} - \text{(moles of gaseous reactants)}$$
$$= (1) - (1 + 2) = -2$$

Thus

$$K_p = K_c(RT)^{\Delta n} = (290)[(0.0821)(700)]^{-2} = 0.088$$

The values of the equilibrium constants are $K_c = 290$ and $K_p = 0.088$.

Exercise $K_c = 2.6 \times 10^{-9}$ at 1500. K for the reaction

$$2BrF_5(g) \rightleftharpoons Br_2(g) + 5F_2(g)$$

Evaluate K_p at this temperature. *Answer* 0.60

EXAMPLE 19.4
Equilibrium Concentrations

The equilibrium constant for the reaction

$$I_2(g) + F_2(g) \rightleftharpoons 2IF(g)$$

is $K_p = 1.15 \times 10^7$ at 2000 K. If the system is at equilibrium, and the partial pressure of IF is 0.32 atm and the partial pressure of F_2 is 1.9×10^{-2} atm, find the partial pressure of I_2.

The expression for K_p for this reaction is

$$K_p = \frac{p_{IF}^2}{p_{I_2} p_{F_2}}$$

The pressure of the I_2 is found by solving the K_p expression for p_{I_2} and substituting the numerical data.

$$p_{I_2} = \frac{p_{IF}^2}{K_p p_{F_2}} = \frac{(0.32)^2}{(1.15 \times 10^7)(1.9 \times 10^{-2})} = 4.7 \times 10^{-7} \text{ atm}$$

The equilibrium pressure of I_2 is 4.7×10^{-7} atm. (Note that in K_p expressions, as in those for K_c, we do not include the units — as long as all pressures are expressed in the units of atmospheres.)

Exercise For the reaction

$$2BrF_5(g) \rightleftharpoons Br_2(g) + 5F_2(g)$$

the value of K_p at 1000 K is 7.4×10^{-16}. Calculate the partial pressure of F_2 at equilibrium with BrF_5 at a partial pressure of 1.2×10^{-3} atm and Br_2 at a partial pressure of 3.8×10^{-5} atm. *Answer* 4.9×10^{-4} atm

19.5 HETEROGENEOUS AND SOLUTION EQUILIBRIA

Reversible reactions can take place and equilibrium is established no matter what the physical state of the materials involved. In the iron–steam reaction (Section 17.2),

$$3Fe(s) + 4H_2O(g) \rightleftharpoons Fe_3O_4(s) + 4H_2(g) \qquad \textbf{(19.10)}$$

a solid and a gas are in equilibrium with another solid and gas. In the reaction of phosphorus(III) chloride with chlorine at elevated temperature,

$$PCl_3(g) + Cl_2(g) \rightleftharpoons PCl_5(g) \qquad \textbf{(19.11)}$$

the reactants and product are all gases. The solid substances, lead(II) oxide and tin, when both are finely powdered and heated to just below the melting point, slowly reach equilibrium with lead and tin(II) oxide according to the equation

$$PbO(s) + Sn(s) \rightleftharpoons Pb(s) + SnO(s) \qquad \textbf{(19.12)}$$

Some commercially important equilibria of different types are shown in Table 19.3.

In *homogeneous equilibria* all of the reactants and products are present in the same phase, as in the gas-phase reactions given in Table 19.1. In *heterogeneous equilibria* the reactants and products are *not* all in the same phase, for example, as in reactions (b) and (c) in Table 19.3.

The question arises of how to deal with solids and pure liquids in writing equilibrium constant expressions. Consider the iron–steam reaction (Equation 19.10). As the reaction proceeds, the concentrations of water and hydrogen in the gas

**Table 19.3
Some Equilibrium Reactions
Important to the Chemical Industry**

Haber process for ammonia production	
$N_2(g) + 3H_2(g) \rightleftharpoons 2NH_3(g)$	**(a)**
Lime (CaO) from limestone	
$CaCO_3(s) \rightleftharpoons CaO(s) + CO_2(g)$	**(b)**
Preparation of ammonium sulfate (a fertilizer)	
$2NH_3(g) + H_2SO_4(l) \rightleftharpoons (NH_4)_2SO_4(s)$	**(c)**
Preparation of ethyl acetate (a solvent for organic chemicals)	
$CH_3COOH(l) + C_2H_5OH(l) \rightleftharpoons CH_3COOC_2H_5(l) + H_2O(l)$	**(d)**
acetic acid *ethyl alcohol* *ethyl acetate*	

phase vary as the reaction approaches equilibrium. What about the "concentrations" of iron and iron oxide, the solids? As long as *some* of a solid reactant is always present, equilibrium is reached in the same way. For a solid (or a pure liquid), whether the amount is large or small, the *concentration* — the *mass per unit volume* — is always the same. How much iron or iron oxide is present during the time the reaction is coming to equilibrium has no influence on the equilibrium state that is eventually reached. Furthermore, adding or taking away some of either solid will cause no change in the equilibrium state once it is established.

For these reasons (and also for theoretical reasons that we need not discuss), the concentration terms for solids or pure liquids do not appear in equilibrium constant expressions. For the iron–steam reaction we can write

$$K_c = \frac{[H_2]^4}{[H_2O]^4} \quad \text{or} \quad K_p = \frac{p_{H_2}{}^4}{p_{H_2O}{}^4}$$

For the reaction

$$CaCO_3(s) \rightleftharpoons CaO(s) + CO_2(g)$$

the equilibrium constant expressions are

$$K_c = [CO_2] \quad \text{or} \quad K_p = p_{CO_2}$$

These expressions for K indicate that as long as both $CaCO_3$ and CaO are present, the pressure of carbon dioxide cannot vary (at a given temperature). If the CO_2 pressure is increased, then CO_2 combines with CaO until the equilibrium pressure of CO_2 is restored.

Many reactions with which we are concerned occur in dilute aqueous solutions. Frequently, water is a "participant" in the reactions in the sense that ions in solution are hydrated or formed by reaction with water. Water is present in such solutions in great excess compared to the other "reactants." The solvent water is considered to be virtually a pure liquid, and changes in the amount of water have little influence on the position of the equilibrium. Therefore, for reactions in dilute aqueous solution, the concentration of water need not appear in the equilibrium constant expression. For example, for the equilibria of weak electrolytes in water, such as ammonia and acetic acid,

$$NH_3(aq) + H_2O(l) \rightleftharpoons NH_4^+ + OH^-$$

$$CH_3COOH(aq) + H_2O(l) \rightleftharpoons CH_3COO^- + H_3O^+$$

we write

$$K = \frac{[NH_4^+][OH^-]}{[NH_3]} \quad \text{and} \quad K = \frac{[CH_3COO^-][H_3O^+]}{[CH_3COOH]}$$

> *Not* included in expression for *K*: concentrations of pure solids, pure liquids, solvents in dilute solutions

Note, however, that when water is a reactant or product but is *not* present in excess as the solvent, its concentration must be included in the equilibrium constant expression, as was done above for the iron–steam reaction. Do not make the common error of leaving [H_2O] out of an equilibrium expression for a reaction in which the variation in the concentration of water is of significance.

It is possible to have both pure substances and solutions as reactants and products in the same heterogeneous reaction. Consider, for example, the reaction of hydrochloric acid with calcium carbonate:

$$CaCO_3(s) + 2HCl(aq) \rightleftharpoons CaCl_2(aq) + CO_2(g) + H_2O(l)$$

The equilibrium constant expression for this reaction can be written as follows, where [CO_2] is the concentration of CO_2 in the gas phase:

$$K_c = \frac{[CaCl_2][CO_2]}{[HCl]^2}$$

Although at first it seems strange, an equilibrium constant expression for this heterogeneous reaction can also be written as follows:

$$K_p = \frac{[CaCl_2]p_{CO_2}}{[HCl]^2}$$

In dealing with heterogeneous reactions that include a gas, it must be made clear how the expression for K has been formulated.

The dissolution of any slightly soluble salt in water is another example of a heterogeneous equilibrium. The participants in the equilibrium are the solid salt, the solvent water, and the ions in aqueous solution. Only the concentrations of the ions in solution need appear in the equilibrium constant expression, for example,

$$Ag_2S(s) \xrightleftharpoons{H_2O} 2Ag^+ + S^{2-} \qquad K_c = [Ag^+]^2[S^{2-}]$$

EXAMPLE 19.5
Writing Equilibrium Constant Expressions

Sulfur reacts with fluorine to form sulfur hexafluoride:

$$S(s) + 3F_2(g) \rightleftharpoons SF_6(g)$$

Write the equilibrium constant expressions for this reaction.

The concentration of solid sulfur need not appear in K_p and K_c for this reaction. The expressions are

$$K_c = \frac{[SF_6]}{[F_2]^3} \qquad K_p = \frac{p_{SF_6}}{p_{F_2}^{3}}$$

Exercise Hydrogen gas can be produced from the action of an acid on magnesium metal.

$$2H^+ + Mg(s) \rightleftharpoons Mg^{2+} + H_2(g)$$

Write the equilibrium constant expressions for this reaction. *Answer* $K_c = [Mg^{2+}][H_2]/[H^+]^2$, $K_p = [Mg^{2+}]p_{H_2}/[H^+]^2$

EXAMPLE 19.6
Equilibrium Concentrations

Anhydrous calcium chloride is often used as a desiccant—a substance that removes water vapor from an enclosed volume of air. In the presence of excess calcium chloride, the amount of water taken up is governed by $K_p = 1.28 \times 10^{85}$ for the following reaction, at room temperature.

$$CaCl_2(s) + 6H_2O(g) \rightleftharpoons CaCl_2 \cdot 6H_2O(s)$$

What is the equilibrium vapor pressure of water in a closed vessel that contains $CaCl_2(s)$?

The equilibrium expression is

$$K_p = \frac{1}{p_{H_2O}^{6}}$$

Rearranging gives

$$p_{H_2O} = \sqrt[6]{1/K_p} = \sqrt[6]{1/1.28 \times 10^{85}} = 6.54 \times 10^{-15} \text{ atm}$$

The partial pressure of water in the enclosed volume will be reduced until it reaches 6.54×10^{-15} atm.

Exercise For the reaction

$$2Cs(s) + F_2(g) \longrightarrow 2CsF(s)$$

$K_p = 1.24 \times 10^{184}$ at 298 K. What is the partial pressure of fluorine in equilibrium with solid Cs and CsF_2? *Answer* 8.06×10^{-185} atm [This is a *very* favorable reaction.]

19.6 EQUILIBRIUM CONSTANTS AND REACTION EQUATIONS

In order to write the equilibrium constant expression for a given reaction, the balanced chemical equation for the reaction must be known. How the reaction equation is written determines the form of the expression for K. There are different ways of writing the chemical equations for the same reaction, and these lead to different equilibrium constant expressions. The equilibrium constant values for the various ways of writing the same chemical reaction are related mathematically.

For example, two ways of writing the combination of carbon monoxide and oxygen are

$$2CO(g) + O_2(g) \rightleftharpoons 2CO_2(g) \qquad K_{13} = \frac{[CO_2]^2}{[CO]^2[O_2]} \qquad \textbf{(19.13)}$$

$$CO(g) + \tfrac{1}{2}O_2(g) \rightleftharpoons CO_2(g) \qquad K_{14} = \frac{[CO_2]}{[CO][O_2]^{\frac{1}{2}}} \qquad \textbf{(19.14)}$$

Equation (19.13) has been divided by 2 to give Equation (19.14). The value of the equilibrium constant for reaction (19.14), K_{14}, is the square root of the value of K_{13},

$$K_{14} = \frac{[CO_2]}{[CO][O_2]^{\frac{1}{2}}} = \left(\frac{[CO_2]^2}{[CO]^2[O_2]}\right)^{\frac{1}{2}} \qquad \text{or} \qquad K_{14} = K_{13}^{\frac{1}{2}}$$

In general, if a chemical equation has been divided by n, the new K value is the $\dfrac{1}{n\text{th}}$ root of the original K value.

If an equation is multiplied by n, its equilibrium constant becomes the original equilibrium constant raised to the nth power. In the following example, for instance, $n = 2$:

$$\tfrac{1}{2}N_2(g) + \tfrac{3}{2}H_2(g) \rightleftharpoons NH_3(g) \qquad \textbf{(19.15)}$$

$$N_2(g) + 3H_2(g) \rightleftharpoons 2NH_3(g) \qquad \textbf{(19.16)}$$

> **If equilibrium constant for a reaction $= K$, equilibrium constant for the reverse reaction $= 1/K$**

$$K_{16} = \frac{[NH_3]^2}{[N_2][H_2]^3} = \left(\frac{[NH_3]}{[N_2]^{\frac{1}{2}}[H_2]^{\frac{3}{2}}}\right)^2 \qquad \text{or} \qquad K_{16} = K_{15}^2$$

If we write an equation in reverse, the new equilibrium constant is the reciprocal of the equilibrium constant for the original equation.

$$2NO_2(g) \rightleftharpoons N_2O_4(g) \qquad \textbf{(19.17)}$$

$$N_2O_4(g) \rightleftharpoons 2NO_2(g) \qquad \textbf{(19.18)}$$

$$K_{18} = \frac{[NO_2]^2}{[N_2O_4]} = \left(\frac{[N_2O_4]}{[NO_2]^2}\right)^{-1} \qquad \text{or} \qquad K_{18} = \frac{1}{K_{17}}$$

> **Adding reactions 1 & 2: K for combined reaction $= K_1 \times K_2$**

When the equations for two reactions are added together, the equilibrium constant for the total reaction is the product of the equilibrium constants of the original reactions. Consider the reaction

$$2SO_2(g) + O_2(g) + 2H_2O(g) \rightleftharpoons 2H_2SO_4(g) \qquad \textbf{(19.19)}$$

The equilibrium constant for this reaction is

$$K_{19} = \frac{[H_2SO_4]^2}{[SO_2]^2[O_2][H_2O]^2} \qquad \textbf{(19.20)}$$

However, it is highly unlikely that reaction (19.19) proceeds in a single step. A possible two-step mechanism is

$$2SO_2 + O_2 \rightleftharpoons 2SO_3 \qquad \text{(19.21)}$$
$$\underline{2SO_3 + 2H_2O \rightleftharpoons 2H_2SO_4} \qquad \text{(19.22)}$$
$$2SO_2 + O_2 + 2H_2O \rightleftharpoons 2H_2SO_4$$

The equilibrium constants for Equations (19.21) and (19.22) are

$$K_{21} = \frac{[SO_3]^2}{[O_2][SO_2]^2} \qquad K_{22} = \frac{[H_2SO_4]^2}{[H_2O]^2[SO_3]^2}$$

Multiplying K for Equation (19.21) by K for Equation (19.22) and canceling common terms gives the equilibrium constant expression for the reaction given in Equation (19.19).

$$K_{21}K_{22} = \left(\frac{[SO_3]^2}{[O_2][SO_2]^2}\right) \times \left(\frac{[H_2SO_4]^2}{[H_2O]^2[SO_3]^2}\right)$$

$$K_{19} = \frac{[H_2SO_4]^2}{[SO_2]^2[O_2][H_2O]^2}$$

This is the same as Equation (19.20), which was written without assuming two steps in the overall reaction. We can see, therefore, that the overall equilibrium constant is equal to the product of the equilibrium constants of the steps in the mechanism.

This brings us to a very important point: The equilibrium constant is independent of the number of steps in the reaction mechanism. Whether reaction (19.19) proceeds by two steps or by 50 steps, its equilibrium expression remains Equation (19.20). For this reason, equilibrium constant expressions can be written from the balanced overall equations. Rate equations, on the other hand, *do* depend upon the reaction pathway and, it bears saying once more, must be found by experiment.

K **is independent of the number of steps in the reaction mechanism**

EXAMPLE 19.7
Evaluation of *K*

A handbook of chemical properties lists $K_p = 644$ at 3000 K for the reaction

$$Li(g) + \tfrac{1}{2}I_2(g) \rightleftharpoons LiI(g) \qquad \text{(i)}$$

Rather than writing the chemical equation using fractional coefficients, a chemist wrote

$$2Li(g) + I_2(g) \rightleftharpoons 2LiI(g) \qquad \text{(ii)}$$

What is the value of K_p that the chemist should use for the second chemical equation?

The equilibrium constant expression for the first chemical equation is

$$K_{p,i} = \frac{p_{LiI}}{p_{Li}p_{I_2}^{\frac{1}{2}}}$$

The equilibrium constant expression for the second equation is

$$K_{p,ii} = \frac{p_{LiI}^2}{p_{Li}^2 p_{I_2}} = \left(\frac{p_{LiI}}{p_{Li}p_{I_2}^{\frac{1}{2}}}\right)^2 = (K_{p,i})^2$$

The value of the equilibrium constant for the second equation is

$$K_{p,ii} = (K_{p,i})^2 = (644)^2 = 4.15 \times 10^5$$

The chemist should use the value of K_p as 4.15×10^5 for his chemical equation.

Exercise For the reaction

$$2Cs(s) + F_2(g) \rightleftharpoons 2CsF(s)$$

$K_p = 1.24 \times 10^{184}$ at 298 K. What is the value of K_p for the reaction

$$Cs(s) + \tfrac{1}{2}F_2(g) \rightleftharpoons CsF(s)$$

Answer 1.11×10^{92}

EXAMPLE 19.8
Evaluation of K

Use the following chemical equations and values of K_p at 1000 K:

$$C(s) + \tfrac{1}{2}O_2(g) \rightleftharpoons CO(g) \qquad K_p = 2.9 \times 10^{10} \qquad \text{(i)}$$

$$C(s) + O_2(g) \rightleftharpoons CO_2(g) \qquad K_p = 4.8 \times 10^{20} \qquad \text{(ii)}$$

to predict K_p for the chemical equation

$$CO(g) + \tfrac{1}{2}O_2(g) \longrightarrow CO_2(g) \qquad \text{(iii)}$$

To combine Equations (i) and (ii) to give the desired equation (Section 7.9c), we must add the reverse of the reaction (i) to reaction (ii).

$$CO(g) \rightleftharpoons C(s) + \tfrac{1}{2}O_2(g) \qquad K_p = \frac{1}{2.9 \times 10^{10}} = 3.4 \times 10^{-11}$$

$$\underline{C(s) + O_2(g) \rightleftharpoons CO_2(g) \qquad K_p = 4.8 \times 10^{20}}$$

$$CO(g) + \tfrac{1}{2}O_2(g) \rightleftharpoons CO_2(g)$$

Note that because reaction (i) has been reversed, the equilibrium constant for the new reaction is the reciprocal of the original one. The equilibrium constant for the desired reaction is the product of the equilibrium constants for the two reactions.

$$K_{p,\text{iii}} = (3.4 \times 10^{-11})(4.8 \times 10^{20}) = 1.6 \times 10^{10}$$

The equilibrium constant for reaction (iii) is 1.6×10^{10}.

Exercise Use the following chemical equations and values of K_p at 2000 K:

$$\tfrac{1}{2}Br_2(g) + \tfrac{1}{2}F_2(g) \rightleftharpoons BrF(g) \qquad K_p = 148$$

$$\tfrac{1}{2}Br_2(g) + \tfrac{3}{2}F_2(g) \rightleftharpoons BrF_3(g) \qquad K_p = 2.3$$

to calculate K_p for

$$BrF_3(g) \rightleftharpoons BrF(g) + F_2(g)$$

Answer $K_p = 64$

19.7 THE REACTION QUOTIENT

The equilibrium constant expression and the numerical values of K provide a means of predicting what will happen when substances with the potential for reacting with each other are mixed. To do this, nonequilibrium concentrations are used to calculate the **reaction quotient,** Q, a value found from an expression which takes the same form as the equilibrium constant but is used for reactions not at equilibrium. For

$$a\text{A} + b\text{B} + \cdots \longrightarrow r\text{R} + s\text{S} + \cdots \tag{19.23}$$

$$Q = \frac{[\text{R}]^r[\text{S}]^s \cdots}{[\text{A}]^a[\text{B}]^b \cdots}$$

$Q < K$, forward reaction occurs

$Q > K$, reverse reaction occurs

The value of Q indicates what changes will occur in reaching equilibrium:

1. *Q less than K.* To establish equilibrium, the concentrations of the reactants will decrease and those of the products will increase. The reaction will proceed toward equilibrium in the forward direction.
2. *Q is larger than K.* To establish equilibrium the concentrations of the products will decrease and those of the reactants will increase. The reaction will approach equilibrium from the direction of the reverse reaction.

For example, at 425.4 °C, $K = 54.5$ for the combination of hydrogen and iodine to give hydrogen iodide (Equation 19.5). Suppose that 0.02 mol of H_2, 0.02 mol of I_2, and 0.04 mol of HI are introduced into a 1 L flask at this temperature. Would more HI form or would the reverse reaction occur to give more $H_2 + I_2$? The reaction quotient is

$$Q = \frac{[HI]^2}{[H_2][I_2]} = \frac{[0.04]^2}{[0.02][0.02]} = 4$$

This value of Q is smaller than K. Equilibrium will be established by the forward reaction proceeding, allowing [HI] to increase and [H_2] and [I_2] to decrease until $Q = K$.

EXAMPLE 19.9
Reaction Quotient

Cyclohexane undergoes a molecular rearrangement in the presence of $AlCl_3$ to form methylcyclopentane:

cyclohexane   *methylcyclopentane*

The equilibrium constant for the reaction is 0.143 at 25 °C. Describe what will happen if a solution is prepared so that it is 0.200 M in cyclohexane and 0.100 M in methylcyclopentane.

The reaction quotient for the solution is

$$Q = \frac{[\text{methylcyclopentane}]}{[\text{cyclohexane}]} = \frac{0.100}{0.200} = 0.500$$

Because $Q > K$, some of the methylcyclopentane will react to form cyclohexane. The respective concentrations will change until they are in a ratio of 0.143, at which point dynamic equilibrium will be established.

Exercise For the reaction

$$BrF_3(g) \rightleftharpoons BrF(g) + F_2(g)$$

$K_p = 64$ at 2000 K. Calculate the value of the reaction quotient and describe what will happen if a mixture containing $p_{F_2} = 1.36$ atm, $p_{BrF} = 0.01$ atm, and $p_{BrF_3} = 0.52$ atm is prepared. *Answer* $Q = 0.03$, some of the BrF_3 will decompose.

Table 19.4

Variation of Equilibrium Constant with How the Reaction Equation Is Written K_0 is the original equilibrium constant.

When the equation is	The new equilibrium constant is
Multiplied by n	$K_0{}^n$
Divided by n	$K_0{}^{1/n}$
Reversed	$K_0{}^{-1}$
Divided into 2 steps (a and b)	$K_0 = K_a K_b$

In summary, the concentrations of solids, pure liquids, and the solvents in dilute solutions need not appear in the equilibrium constant expressions.

The form of the equilibrium constant expression is determined by how the chemical equation is written. The value of K and the equilibrium constant expression for chemical equations for the same reaction written in different ways are related mathematically as shown in Table 19.4.

The equilibrium constant in terms of partial pressures, K_p, may be used when all reactants and products represented in the K expression are present in the gas phase. The values of K_c and K_p are related by the ideal gas law (Equation 19.9).

The reaction quotient, Q, takes the same form as K but is written for reactions not at equilibrium. If Q is greater than K, the reverse reaction is favored; if Q is smaller than K, the forward reaction is favored. When Q = K the reaction is at equilibrium.

FACTORS THAT INFLUENCE EQUILIBRIA

19.8 LE CHATELIER'S PRINCIPLE

Le Chatelier's principle: A system at equilibrium will change to relieve any imposed stress

---

The general principle that underlies all changes in equilibria is Le Chatelier's principle (Section 17.2): If a system at equilibrium is subjected to a stress, the system will react in a way that tends to relieve the stress. In the chemical sense, the stresses that can be applied to a system at equilibrium are changes in temperature, concentration, and pressure.

Catalysts can increase the speed with which equilibrium is reached, but they cause no change in the equilibrium constant or in the concentrations at equilibrium. The rates of both the forward and reverse reactions are increased equally by a catalyst (by lowering E_a; see Figure 18.14).

The effects of changes in reaction conditions on equilibrium constants, rate constants, and rates are summarized in Table 19.5. We suggest you consult this table as you read Sections 19.9–19.11. The Aside on the Haber process for the manufacture of ammonia later in this chapter illustrates the interaction of these factors in a single chemical reaction.

Table 19.5

Comparison of Variations in Equilibrium Constants, Rate Constants, and Rates The effects summarized here occur in most cases, although exceptions can be found.

When	Equilibrium Constant (K)	Rate Constant (k)	Rate
Temperature			
Increases	**Changes**	**Increases**	**Increases**
Decreases	**Changes**	**Decreases**	**Decreases**
Catalyst is added	**Does not change**	**Increases**	**Increases**
Concentration of reactants			
Increases	**Does not change**	**Does not change**	**Increases**
Decreases	**Does not change**	**Does not change**	**Decreases**

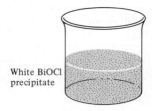

White BiOCl precipitate

$BiCl_3(aq) + H_2O(l) \rightleftharpoons BiOCl(s) + 2HCl(aq)$

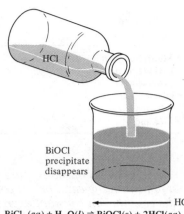

BiOCl precipitate disappears

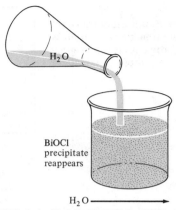

BiOCl precipitate reappears

Figure 19.4
Demonstration of Change in Equilibrium with Change in Concentration of Reactant or Product

$\xleftarrow{\hspace{2cm}}$ HCl
$BiCl_3(aq) + H_2O(l) \rightleftharpoons BiOCl(s) + 2HCl(aq)$

H_2O $\xrightarrow{\hspace{2cm}}$
$BiCl_3(aq) + H_2O(l) \rightleftharpoons BiOCl(s) + 2HCl(aq)$

19.9 CONCENTRATION

When the concentration of a reactant or product in a system in chemical equilibrium is changed, the system is put out of balance and the rates of the forward and reverse reactions become temporarily unequal. The system is stressed and must change to relieve the stress.

The reaction of bismuth(III) chloride with water to give bismuth(III) oxochloride can be used to demonstrate visibly the effect of changing concentration on chemical equilibrium. The experiment begins (Figure 19.4) with a mixture in which the white precipitate of BiOCl is in equilibrium with $BiCl_3$ in solution.

$$BiCl_3(aq) + H_2O(l) \rightleftharpoons BiOCl(s) + 2HCl(aq)$$
bismuth(III) chloride   *bismuth oxochloride*

When HCl is slowly added, some of the BiOCl disappears, showing that the reverse reaction is occurring at a greater rate than the forward reaction. As more $BiCl_3$ and H_2O are formed, the rate of the forward reaction increases until a new equilibrium position is established. If more H_2O is now added, the precipitate reappears as the forward reaction is once again favored. In each case, as would be predicted from Le Chatelier's principle, increasing the concentration of a substance has shifted the equilibrium in the direction that decreases that concentration.

$\xleftarrow{\hspace{2cm}}$ *HCl*
$$BiCl_3(aq) + H_2O(l) \rightleftharpoons BiOCl(s) + 2HCl(aq)$$
H₂O $\xrightarrow{\hspace{2cm}}$

A *decrease* in a concentration causes a shift in the direction that increases that concentration. Thus the continuous removal of a product—a *continuous decrease* in concentration—allows a reaction to be driven to completion. The forward reaction continues to occur in order to relieve the stress of the decreasing concentration. (The continuous displacement of solubility equilibria is utilized in separating substances by chromatography; see Tools of Chemistry: Chromatography.)

EXAMPLE 19.10
Factors That Influence Equilibria: Concentration

A mixture of $K_2CrO_4(aq)$ and $HCl(aq)$ was allowed to come to equilibrium:

$$2CrO_4^{2-} + 2H^+ \rightleftharpoons Cr_2O_7^{2-} + H_2O(l)$$
chromate ion   *dichromate ion*
yellow   *orange*

Describe the changes that will occur in the equilibrium system as (a) additional acid is added; (b) additional $K_2CrO_4(s)$ is added; (c) $K_2Cr_2O_7(s)$ is added; (d) Zn^{2+} is added—note that $ZnCrO_4$ is highly insoluble and $ZnCr_2O_7$ is very soluble; (e) NaOH is added.

(a) Some of the additional H$^+$ will react with some of the remaining chromate ion to produce more dichromate ion and water; [CrO$_4^{2-}$] will decrease and [Cr$_2$O$_7^{2-}$] will increase.

(b) Some of the additional chromate ion will react with some of the H$^+$ to produce more dichromate ion and water and the concentration of H$^+$ will decrease.

(c) Some of the additional dichromate ion will react to form chromate ion, and the concentration of CrO$_4^{2-}$ will increase.

(d) Addition of Zn^{2+} will remove some of the chromate ion as ZnCrO$_4$, lowering the concentration of chromate ion. Thus some of the dichromate ion will react to form additional chromate ion and H$^+$.

(e) Addition of OH$^-$ will remove some of the H$^+$ as a result of an acid–base reaction. The decrease in H$^+$ concentration will cause the reaction of additional Cr$_2$O$_7^{2-}$ with H$_2$O; [Cr$_2$O$_7^{2-}$] will decrease and [CrO$_4^{2-}$] will increase.

Exercise Describe the changes that will occur in the equilibrium system

$$2BrF_5(g) \rightleftharpoons Br_2(g) + 5F_2(g)$$

as (a) p_{BrF_5} (or [BrF$_5$]) is increased, (b) p_{F_2} (or [F$_2$]) is decreased, (c) p_{Br_2} and p_{F_2} (or [Br$_2$] and [F$_2$]) are both increased, and (d) a catalyst is added. *Answer* (a) Additional Br$_2$ and F$_2$ are formed; (b) additional Br$_2$ is formed by the further decomposition of BrF$_5$; (c) additional BrF$_5$ is formed; (d) no changes are observed.

TOOLS OF CHEMISTRY

Chromatography

Biochemical fluids, inorganic salts, organic compounds, polymers—mixtures of all kinds of substances can be separated by chromatography. It is a technique of special value because it can be used to analyze very complex mixtures and works effectively with very small amounts of material. In addition, the separated substances can be isolated, allowing chromatography to be used as a preparative method.

The basis of chromatography is the distribution of a solute between two immiscible solvents, as illustrated by the simple separations performed using separatory funnels. Suppose we have an aqueous solution of A, a fairly nonpolar substance. Most likely A is also soluble in a nonpolar solvent such as hexane. When the aqueous solution of A and hexane are shaken together in a separatory funnel (Figure A), an

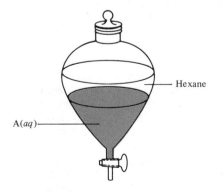
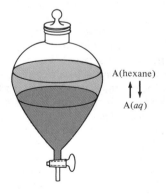
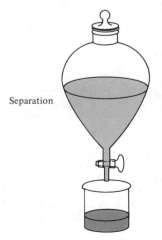

Figure A
Extraction in a Separatory Funnel In this method of separation a solute is distributed between two immiscible solvents.

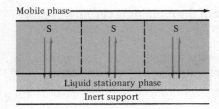

Partition chromatography

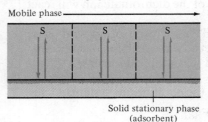

Adsorption chromatography

Figure B
Equilibria in Partition and
Adsorption Chromatography S
represents the solute.

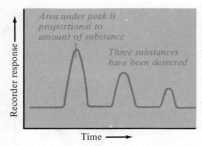

Figure C
A Chromatogram This type of
record of the results of
chromatography is obtained in any
type of chromatography when the
mobile phase is monitored by
instrumentation.

equilibrium is established, as some A is transferred from the aqueous solution to the hexane.

$$A(aq) \rightleftharpoons A(hexane)$$

The equilibrium constant for the distribution of a solute between two immiscible solvents is called the **distribution coefficient.** For the equilibrium above

$$K = \frac{[A]_{hexane}}{[A]_{aq}}$$

The value of the distribution coefficient expresses the relative affinity of the solute for hexane and water. If K is large, most of the A dissolved in the water can be transferred to hexane by extraction in a separatory funnel as shown in Figure A. If some other solute, B, that is less soluble in hexane than A were also present in the aqueous solution, A and B could be separated from each other by extraction.

In chromatography a *series* of extractions like the one just described is set up and equilibrium is constantly displaced by fresh solvent. **Chromatography** is the distribution of a solute between a stationary phase and a mobile phase. The stationary phase may be a solid or a liquid that is supported as a thin film on the surface of an inert solid — the *support.* The mobile phase flowing over the surface of the stationary phase may be a gas or a liquid.

Substances are separated in chromatography according to their relative affinities for the stationary and mobile phases. Suppose a mixture of A and B is adsorbed on a solid support and a solvent flows over the solid. The solutes will continuously move into the solvent because fresh solvent is continuously available and equilibrium can never be reached. The solute which has the greater affinity for the solvent will dissolve more quickly in the fresh solvent as it flows by than will the other solute. This more soluble solute, say A, will move down the column faster than B and thus be separated from it.

Chromatographic methods in which the stationary phase is a solid are classified as adsorption chromatography. A substance leaves the mobile phase to become adsorbed on the surface of the solid phase, called the adsorbent (Figure B). The equilibria in adsorption chromatography are governed by the weak intermolecular forces of physical adsorption such as London forces and hydrogen bonding. The adsorbent must have a large surface area. Alumina (Al_2O_3) and silica (SiO_2) in various forms are common adsorbents.

Chromatography based on solubility properties is called partition chromatography. In partition chromatography of any type the stationary phase is a liquid, and the substances being separated are distributed throughout both the stationary and the mobile phases.

In gas–liquid chromatography (GLC) there is a stationary liquid and a mobile gas phase. Gas chromatography is a general term for chromatography in which the mobile phase is a gas. GLC is useful for studying complex mixtures (up to 50 components have been separated), for detecting very small amounts of impurities, and because it is a relatively rapid method.

Any mixture of substances that can be vaporized below about 400 °C without decomposition can be examined by GLC. The sample is vaporized into a stream of inert gas that carries it past the stationary phase, which is packed in a tube, or column. The different components in the mixture are retained on the column for different, characteristic time periods and then appear at the column outlet. Changes in the composition of the gas flowing from the column are monitored in many different ways. However, each involves the same principle, the change in some property of the gaseous mixture such as thermal conductivity, density, or some type of absorption spectrum is monitored by means of instruments that produce a graphic record of what happens beginning from the time the sample is injected. A chromatogram is a plot of the response of the detector to whatever property is being measured versus time (Figure C). The area under the peak in a

Adsorption column chromatography	Distribution of solute between a solid and liquid phase on a column
Partition column chromatography	Distribution of a solute between two liquids on a column
Thin-layer chromatography	Adsorption or partition on an open thin sheet
Paper chromatography	Partition on a paper sheet
High-pressure liquid chromatography	Column liquid chromatography under high inlet pressure
Ion-exchange chromatography	Exchange of ions
Gas chromatography	Distribution of a gaseous solute between a gas and liquid or solid phase
Zone electrophoresis	Separation on a sheet in the presence of an electrical field
Molecular sieves	Separation is based on size of solute and absorption
Gel permeation (filtration)	Separation is based on size of solute and absorption

chromatogram is proportional to the amount of the substance in a mixture.

The various types of chromatography are summarized in Table A. In column chromatography, which includes most gas chromatography, the stationary phase is held in a tube. In paper chromatography, a stationary liquid phase is supported in the pores of a piece of paper. The end product of paper chromatography is a dried piece of paper with spots of the components of the mixture spread out across the paper. In thin-layer chromatography the adsorbent is spread on an inert support such as a piece of glass.

Gel permeation chromatography and molecular sieves allow separation of substances according to differences in molecular size. These techniques utilize supports that incorporate openings, or pores, of specific sizes — three-dimensional networks of polymers in the case of gel permeation chromatography, and the natural or synthetic minerals known as zeolites or molecular sieves (Section 30.16). The ease with which the substances being analyzed pass through openings of various sizes is added to the differences in adsorption as a factor in determining the rate at which separation occurs.

19.10 PRESSURE

Changes in pressure displace equilibria in gas-phase reactions in which the number of moles of reactant is different from the number of moles of product. An increase in pressure shifts the reaction equilibrium in the direction that produces the smaller number of molecules in the gas phase. For example, in the phosphorus(III) chloride–chlorine reaction

$$\xrightarrow{\text{pressure}}$$
$$PCl_3(g) + Cl_2(g) \rightleftharpoons PCl_5(g)$$
2 moles of gas   *1 mole of gas*

The stress of greater pressure can be relieved by an increase in the rate of the forward reaction, which decreases the number of molecules in the gas phase by forming one mole of gas from two. On the other hand, for the decomposition of iodopropane to give propene plus hydrogen iodide we have the opposite situation.

$$\xleftarrow{\qquad\qquad\qquad\qquad\text{pressure}}$$
$$CH_3CH_2CH_2I(g) \rightleftharpoons CH_3CH{=}CH_2(g) + HI(g)$$
1 mole of gas   *2 moles of gas*

The reverse reaction is favored by increasing pressure. A change in pressure is essentially a change in concentration and it does not change the value of K. The effect of pressure changes on reactions involving only liquids and solids is very small.

The displacement of an equilibrium in the gas phase can be demonstrated visibly with the reaction of the oxides of nitrogen discussed in Section 19.2. Nitrogen dioxide, NO_2, is a brown gas that is always in equilibrium with dinitrogen tetroxide, N_2O_4, a colorless gas.

$$2NO_2(g) \rightleftharpoons N_2O_4(g)$$
$$\text{brown} \qquad \text{colorless}$$

Increasing pressure favors the formation of N_2O_4, and the change in the concentration at equilibrium is observable by the gradual decrease in intensity of the brown color of NO_2.

EXAMPLE 19.11
Factors That Influence Equilibria: Pressure

What would be the effect on an equilibrium mixture of carbon, oxygen, and carbon dioxide if the total pressure of the system was decreased?

The chemical equation

$$2C(s) + O_2(g) \rightleftharpoons 2CO_2(g)$$

shows us that there are two moles of gaseous products and one mole of gaseous reactant. (Any substances in the solid, liquid, or liquid solution phases are neglected because the effect of a pressure change in these phases is negligible.) Decreasing the total pressure on the equilibrium mixture favors the reaction which has the larger number of moles of gaseous substances—in this case, the formation of CO_2.

Exercise   What would be the effect on an equilibrium mixture of Br_2, F_2, and BrF_5 if the total pressure of the system were increased?

$$2BrF_5(g) \rightleftharpoons Br_2(g) + 5F_2(g)$$

Answer   Additional BrF_5 would form.

19.11 TEMPERATURE

Every equilibrium reaction involves one exothermic reaction and one endothermic reaction (see Figure 18.4). When the temperature is increased, the equilibrium shifts so that the endothermic reaction—the one that requires heat—is favored. It can be the forward or the reverse reaction. Note that, unlike changes in concentration and pressure, changes in temperature cause changes in the *value* of K.

If we think of heat as a reactant or a product, it is easy to visualize, based on Le Chatelier's principle, which direction is favored by a temperature change. For example, the reaction between hydrogen and iodine to give hydrogen iodide is an overall exothermic reaction; that is, heat is a product ($\Delta H^\circ = -52.7$ kJ). This means that the reverse reaction is endothermic. In Section 19.2 we saw that K varied with temperature as follows:

$$\overset{\longleftarrow \text{ heat}}{H_2(g) + I_2(g) \rightleftharpoons 2HI + 52.7 \text{ kJ}} \qquad K = \frac{[HI]^2}{[H_2][I_2]}$$
$$K = 54 \text{ at } 425.4 \text{ °C}$$
$$K = 45.6 \text{ at } 490.65 \text{ °C}$$

An increase in temperature causes the decomposition of additional hydrogen iodide. The concentration of hydrogen iodide becomes smaller and the concentrations of hydrogen and iodine become larger. The result is a decrease in the value of K.

In an overall endothermic reaction, the reverse reaction is exothermic. Here we may think of heat as a reactant. The endothermic reaction of oxygen to form ozone ($\Delta H° = 285.3$ kJ) is at equilibrium at room temperature with very little ozone present. Increasing the temperature increases ozone formation and the equilibrium constant becomes larger.

$$\text{heat} \longrightarrow$$
$$285.3 \text{ kJ} + 3O_2(g) \rightleftharpoons 2O_3(g) \quad K = 6.2 \times 10^{-58} \text{ at 25 °C}$$
$$K = 2.6 \times 10^{-56} \text{ at 35 °C}$$

In general, K for exothermic reactions increases with lower temperatures and decreases with higher temperatures. The opposite is true for endothermic reactions, for which K decreases with lower temperatures and increases with higher temperatures.

In summary, Le Chatelier's principle predicts the response of a system at equilibrium to a stress that upsets the equilibrium. An increase in the concentration of a specific substance causes a change that decreases the concentration of that substance (Table 19.6). A decrease in a concentration favors a change that increases that concentration.

An increase in temperature favors whichever reaction requires heat (the endothermic reaction, which may be either the forward or the reverse reaction) and a decrease in temperature favors the reaction that liberates heat (the exothermic reaction). The value *of the equilibrium constant varies with changes in temperature, but not with pressure. Changes in pressure cause significant changes only in equilibria in which the number of moles of gaseous products and reactants differ.*

Table 19.6
Effect of Changing Conditions on a Chemical Reaction at Equilibrium Note that the *value* of K changes only with changes in temperature.

Change	Effect
Concentration	
Increase reactant concentration or decrease product concentration	Shift toward product formation
Decrease reactant concentration or increase product concentration	Shift toward reactant formation
Temperature	
Increase	*Exothermic reaction*—shift toward reactant formation. K decreases.
	Endothermic reaction—shift toward product formation. K increases.
Decrease	*Exothermic reaction*—shift toward product formation. K increases.
	Endothermic reaction—shift toward reactant formation. K decreases.
Pressure (for gas-phase reactions with unequal numbers of product and reactant molecules)	
Increase	Shift toward decrease in number of molecules
Decrease	Shift toward increase in number of molecules

EXAMPLE 19.12
Factors That Influence Equilibria:
Temperature

For the reaction

$$2Hg(l) + O_2(g) \rightleftharpoons 2HgO(s)$$

$\Delta H° = -180.7$ kJ over the temperature range 298 K to 500 K. $K_p = 3.2 \times 10^{20}$ at 298 K. Is the value of K_p at 500 K larger or smaller than this value?

For an exothermic reaction we can write

$$2Hg(l) + O_2(g) \rightleftharpoons 2HgO(s) + 180.7 \text{ kJ}$$

An increase in temperature favors the endothermic reaction—the reverse reaction in this case—and the equilibrium will be shifted toward the reactants side as the temperature is increased. The value of K_p at 500 K should be smaller than 3.2×10^{20}. [The value at 500 K is 5.1×10^7.]

Exercise   For the reaction

$$2BrF_5(g) \rightleftharpoons Br_2(g) + 5F_2(g)$$

$\Delta H° = 858$ kJ over the temperature range 1000 K to 1500 K. $K_p = 7.4 \times 10^{-16}$ at 1000 K. Is the value of K_p at 1500 K larger or smaller than this value? *Answer* The value would be larger ($K_p = 0.60$).

AN ASIDE

The Haber Process for the Manufacture of Ammonia

The Haber process for the manufacture of ammonia is the classic example of the role of kinetics and equilibrium in an industrial process. The reaction of nitrogen and hydrogen to give ammonia is exothermic, occurs in the gas phase, and involves a decrease in pressure at a given temperature.

$$N_2(g) + 3H_2(g) \rightleftharpoons 2NH_3(g)$$

4 moles   2 moles

$\Delta H_{25°C} = -92.22$ kJ
$\Delta H_{400°C} = -108$ kJ
$K_{p,25°C} = 5.5 \times 10^5$, $K_{p,400°C} = 1.8 \times 10^{-4}$

Le Chatelier's principle indicates that higher pressure will favor the formation of ammonia. Since the overall equilibrium is exothermic, higher temperatures will favor the decomposition of ammonia, an undesirable result, and lower temperatures will favor ammonia production.

However, a low temperature and a high pressure are not the easy answer to industrial production of ammonia by this reaction. The rate of the reaction at room temperature is very, very small. In commercial practice, both yield and rate must be considered, for a process is practical only if the plant produces a reasonable amount of the product per day.

The industrial process relies on a suitable catalyst, which increases the rate of attainment of equilibrium and permits the use of moderate temperatures. In modern industry the compromise among temperature, pressure, and yield of ammonia is struck by carrying out the reaction at about 250 atm (a pressure obtained economically with efficient centrifugal compressors) and 400 °C, the lowest temperature at which the catalyst is sufficiently effective. Under these conditions about 20% ammonia is present in the gases that come off the catalytic reactor on each pass. Unconverted reactants are recycled, as shown in Figure A, a simplified schematic diagram of NH_3 production from N_2 and H_2.

The catalyst is iron oxide, "doubly promoted" (that is, with the activity increased by two additives) by the addition of about 0.4% potassium oxide and 0.8% aluminum oxide. As is so often the case, the mechanism of the catalytic reaction is not known exactly. However, ammonia is formed at the catalyst surface, for the rate of ammonia formation is approximately proportional to the rate of nitrogen adsorption by the catalyst.

Fritz Haber, a German chemist, developed the industrial ammonia process

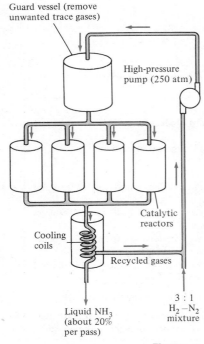

Guard vessel (remove unwanted trace gases)

High-pressure pump (250 atm)

Catalytic reactors

Cooling coils

Recycled gases

Liquid NH₃ (about 20% per pass)

3 : 1
H₂ –N₂ mixture

Figure A

named for him just before World War I. Had he not done so the war might have ended much sooner. Germany's trade was cut off by a blockade, and sodium nitrate from Chile was not available. Traditionally, nitric acid for explosives had been made from sodium nitrate, but ammonia from the Haber process provided another route to nitric acid. The success of the Haber process allowed the German chemical industry to produce the explosives and fertilizers needed for the war effort despite the blockade. (The importance of the Haber process in fertilizer manufacture is discussed in An Aside: Chemical Fertilizers, Chapter 26.)

EQUILIBRIUM PROBLEMS

19.12 HOW TO SOLVE EQUILIBRIUM PROBLEMS

The relationship between K and the equilibrium concentrations allows us to answer many questions about equilibrium reactions, such as, What are the concentrations of all species present at equilibrium? Given one concentration at equilibrium, what are the others? How must one concentration be changed to obtain a desired change in another concentration? The unknowns in equilibrium problems are most often the concentrations of one or more reactants or products. Whatever the unknown quantity in an equilibrium problem, it is most successfully obtained by careful and accurate bookkeeping. An excellent way to organize the solution is outlined below and illustrated for the following typical problem:

For the reaction $A \rightleftharpoons B + C$, what is the concentration of C at equilibrium when at the beginning of the reaction only 5.0 mol/L of A was present? Assume that $K = 3.0 \times 10^{-6}$.

Write the balanced equation.

$$A \rightleftharpoons B + C$$

Write the corresponding equilibrium expression.

$$K = \frac{[B][C]}{[A]}$$

Identify what is unknown. Often this will be a single concentration, or the equal concentrations of several substances, or several concentrations that are related to each other algebraically. Select a single quantity for which to solve the problem. This might be an equilibrium concentration or a change in concentration. Write down the unknown — you may forget what you solved for. It is customary to let x equal this unknown. For this problem, let x equal the equilibrium concentrations of B and C; $x = [B] = [C]$.

Prepare a table. The table has four lines: (1) the chemical equation; (2) initial concentrations, written under the reactants and products; (3) changes in concentration — use your knowledge of stoichiometry here. In this example, to reach equilibrium [A] must decrease while [B] and [C] increase. Therefore, the change in [A] is $-x$ and the changes in [B] and [C] are $+x$; and (4) equilibrium concentrations — the sum of lines (2) and (3).

		A	$\rightleftharpoons$	B	+	C
(2)	Initial	5.0		0		0
(3)	Change	$-x$		$+x$		$+x$
(4)	Equilibrium	$5.0 - x$		x		x

Substitute the equilibrium concentrations from the table (bottom line) into the equilibrium expression

$$K = \frac{(x)(x)}{5.0 - x} = 3.0 \times 10^{-6} \qquad \textbf{(19.24)}$$

<u>Solve for the quantity represented by x.</u> Use aproximations to simplify the expression that must be solved wherever the error introduced by doing so is negligible.

The usual approximation is to neglect x in addition or subtraction (e.g., in $5.0 - x$ or $5.0 + x$) when the value of x will be small relative to the known concentrations. This is likely to occur when the value of K is significantly smaller than the values of the known concentrations. Here 3.0×10^{-6} is quite small relative to 5.0 mol/L. Therefore, x may be dropped in $5.0 - x$ to give the simplified mathematical expression. (Note that x as a *multiplier* or *divisor* can-*not* be neglected.)

$$K = \frac{x^2}{5.0 - x} \approx \frac{x^2}{5.0} = 3.0 \times 10^{-6}$$

$$x^2 = (5.0)(3.0 \times 10^{-6}) = 15 \times 10^{-6}$$

$$x = 3.9 \times 10^{-3} \text{ mol/L}$$

<u>If an approximation was made, check it for validity.</u> If including x in the original sum or difference makes very little change in the expression, the aproximation is valid. In this case, since 5.0 mol/L minus 3.9×10^{-3} mol/L is very little different from 5.0 mol/L, the approximation looks good. Where it is difficult to decide, calculate the percentage by which the number would change if the approximation had not been made. If x was neglected in $(A + x)$ or in $(A - x)$

$$\% \text{ error} = \left(\frac{\text{value of } x}{\text{value of A}} \right) \times 100\% \qquad \textbf{(19.25)}$$

In this case

$$\% \text{ error} = \left(\frac{3.9 \times 10^{-3}}{5.0} \right) \times (100\%) = 0.078\%$$

Up to a 5% error is usually considered acceptable, so the aproximation is valid. If the aproximation is not valid, the expression must be solved exactly. The use of the quadratic formula in exact solutions is discussed in Section 19.14.

<u>Answer the questions in the problem.</u> At equilibrium, $[C] = 3.9 \times 10^{-3}$ mol/L.

In summary, the steps for solving equilibrium constant problems are given in Table 19.7.

Table 19.7
Solution of Equilibrium Constant Problems

1. Write balanced chemical equation.
2. Write equilibrium expression.
3. Identify the unknown and assign x.
4. Make a table:
    line 1   balanced chemical equation
    line 2   initial concentrations
    line 3   changes in concentrations
    line 4   equilibrium concentrations (line 2 + line 3)
5. Substitute results of line 4 into equilibrium expression.
6. Solve for x
    Decide what approximations can be made.
    Write the simplified expression when approximations can be made.
    Solve the simplified expression.
7. Check the approximations for validity. If the error is greater than 5%, solve the mathematical equation by an exact method.
8. Answer the questions in the problem.

19.13 SOME SIMPLE
EQUILIBRIUM PROBLEMS

Examples 19.13–19.16 represent some simple types of equilibrium problems. Example 19.13 illustrates the application of the problem-solving method of Section 2.13 to an equilibrium problem. The equilibrium constant expression provides the connection for almost all equilibrium problems.

EXAMPLE 19.13
Solving an Equilibrium Problem

For the reaction

$$H_2(g) + I_2(g) \rightleftharpoons 2HI(g)$$

$K = 29.1$ at 1000 K. What is the concentration of $I_2(g)$ under equilibrium conditions if the system originally contained only [HI] = 10.0 mol/L?

1. Study the problem and be sure you understand it.
   (a) What is unknown?
       The concentration of $I_2(g)$ at equilibrium.
   (b) What is known?
       Four things are known:
       (1) The chemical equation

$$H_2(g) + I_2(g) \rightleftharpoons 2HI(g)$$

   and from the equation the mole ratios of reactants and products.
       (2) The value of the equilibrium constant, $K = 29.1$.
       (3) The initial concentration of HI, 10.0 mol/L.
       (4) The initial concentrations of H_2 and I_2, which are zero.
2. Decide how to solve the problem.
   (a) What is the connection between the knowns and the unknown?
       The equilibrium expression, which we must write by using the known chemical equation.

$$K_c = \frac{[HI]^2}{[H_2][I_2]}$$

   (b) What is necessary to make the connection?
       It is necessary to substitute the known concentration and the unknown concentrations into the equilibrium constant expression. To do this, the information given by the chemical equation and the known concentration must be used to assign values to all of the terms in the equilibrium constant expression. In this problem, the equilibrium concentrations of H_2 and I_2 are both unknown. From the stoichiometry of the reaction we can see that H_2 and I_2 will be present in equal concentrations at equilibrium, and so we set $x = [H_2] = [I_2]$. The equilibrium concentration of HI will be the initial concentration *minus* the change due to conversion to H_2 and I_2. Because two moles of HI are required for every mole of H_2 and I_2 that form, the change in the concentration of HI will be $-2x$. The table format is best for using all of this information to determine what substitutions to make in the equilibrium constant expression

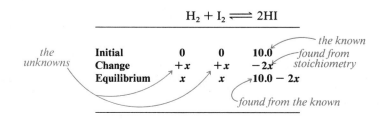

		H_2	$+$ I_2	$\rightleftharpoons$ 2HI
the unknowns	**Initial**	0	0	10.0
	Change	$+x$	$+x$	$-2x$
	Equilibrium	x	x	$10.0 - 2x$

the known found from stoichiometry

found from the known

3. Set up the problem and solve it.

$$K_c = \frac{(10.0 - 2x)^2}{(x)(x)} = 29.1$$

At this point, inspect the expression to determine how it can be solved. This expression is a special case because the terms containing x are all squared. The problem can be solved by taking the square root of both sides.

$$\frac{(10.0 - 2x)^2}{x^2} = 29.1$$

$$\frac{10.0 - 2x}{x} = \sqrt{29.1} = 5.39$$

$$10.0 - 2x = 5.39x$$

$$-2x - 5.39x = -10.0$$

$$7.39x = 10.0$$

$$x = 1.35 \text{ mol/L}$$

At equilibrium 1.35 mol/L of I_2 (and also of H_2) is present.

4. Check the result. Checking back over the algebra above shows that it is correct. No approximations were made, so no check of an introduced error is needed. Since K_c is greater than 1, we can expect a relatively large amount of HI to remain at equilibrium, and this is the case; [HI] = 10.0 − 2x = 10.0 − 2.70 = 7.3 mol/L. The answer is reasonable.

EXAMPLE 19.14
Equilibrium Concentrations

What is the concentration of CO in equilibrium at 25°C in a sample of gas originally containing 1.00 mol/L of CO_2? For the dissociation of CO_2 at 25°C (see Table 19.2), $K = 2.96 \times 10^{-92}$.

The reaction and K expression are

$$2CO_2(g) \rightleftharpoons 2CO(g) + O_2(g) \qquad K = \frac{[CO]^2[O_2]}{[CO_2]^2}$$

The equilibrium concentrations of both CO and O_2 are unknown; $[O_2]$ at equilibrium is a good choice for x.

	$2CO_2(g)$	$\rightleftharpoons$ $2CO(g)$	$+ O_2(g)$
Initial	1.00	0	0
Change	−2x	+2x	+x
Equilibrium	1.00 − 2x	2x	x

$$K = \frac{(2x^2)(x)}{(1.00 - 2x)^2} = 2.96 \times 10^{-92}$$

Because the value of K is much smaller than the known concentration, we can assume $1.00 - 2x \approx 1.00$.

$$\frac{(2x)^2(x)}{(1.00 - 2x)^2} \approx \frac{4x^3}{1.00} = 2.96 \times 10^{-92}$$

$$4x^3 = 2.96 \times 10^{-92}$$

$$x = \left(\frac{2.96 \times 10^{-92}}{4}\right)^{1/3} = 1.95 \times 10^{-31} \text{ mol/L}$$

The approximation is valid because $1.00 - 2(19.5 \times 10^{-31}) \approx 1.00$. At equilibrium

$$[CO] = 2(1.95 \times 10^{-31}) = 3.90 \times 10^{-31} \text{ mol/L}$$

Exercise What is the concentration of Br_2 in equilibrium at 1500 K in a sample of gas originally containing 1.00 mol/L of BrF_5?

$$2BrF_5(g) \rightleftharpoons Br_2(g) + 5F_2(g) \qquad K_c = 2.6 \times 10^{-9}$$

Answer $[Br_2] = 9.7 \times 10^{-3}$ mol/L

EXAMPLE 19.15
Evaluation of K

A solution of 0.100 M HIO_4 at 25 °C was found to contain 0.038 M H^+. Using this information, find K for the reaction

$$HIO_4(aq) \rightleftharpoons H^+ + IO_4^-$$

In this problem there is no question about what is unknown — it is K. Water is the solvent and its concentration does not enter into the equilibrium expression. The 0.100 M concentration refers to how the HIO_4 solution was prepared, not the concentration at equilibrium. Note that the stoichiometry of the reaction is such that $[H^+] = [IO_4^-]$ and that the concentration of HIO_4 that reacts is equal to the concentration of H^+ formed.

$$HIO_4(aq) \rightleftharpoons H^+ + IO_4^- \qquad K = \frac{[H^+][IO_4^-]}{[HIO_4]} \qquad K \text{ is unknown}$$

	$HIO_4(aq) \rightleftharpoons$	H^+	$+ \; IO_4^-$
Initial	0.100	0	0
Change	−0.038	+0.038	+0.038
Equilibrium	0.062	0.038	0.038

$$K = \frac{(0.038)(0.038)}{(0.062)} = 2.3 \times 10^{-2}$$

The equilibrium constant is 2.3×10^{-2}.

Exercise A gaseous mixture originally contained $[Br_2] = [F_2] = 0.100$ mol/L. After equilibrium was established for the system

$$Br_2(g) + F_2(g) \rightleftharpoons 2BrF(g)$$

at 2000 K, the concentration of bromine was 1.35×10^{-3} mol/L. Calculate K_c for this reaction. *Answer* 2.15×10^4

EXAMPLE 19.16
Equilibrium Concentrations

What are the concentrations of cyclohexane and methylcyclopentane once equilibrium has been established in a solution which was initially 0.200 M in cyclohexane and 0.100 M in methylcyclopentane? $K = 0.143$ at 25 °C for the reaction in which cyclohexane rearranges to methylcyclopentane. Q for these initial concentrations is 0.500 (see Example 19.9).

The equilibrium concentrations of the single reactant and the single product are unknown. To find these concentrations, we must know in which direction the equilibrium

$$\text{cyclohexane} \xrightarrow{\text{AlCl}_3} \text{methylcyclopentane}$$

will proceed. Given that $Q = 0.500$ and $K = 0.143$, we know that some methylcyclopentane will react to form cyclohexane. Therefore, the problem can be solved by letting $-x$ equal the decrease in concentration of methylcyclopentane and letting

$+x$ equal the increase in concentration of cyclohexane.

	cyclohexane $\rightleftharpoons$	methylcyclopentane
Initial	0.200	0.100
Change	$+x$	$-x$
Equilibrium	$(0.200 + x)$	$(0.100 - x)$

$$K_c = \frac{[\text{methylcyclopentane}]}{[\text{cyclohexane}]} = \frac{0.100 - x}{0.200 + x} = 0.143$$

$$0.100 - x = (0.143)(0.200 + x) = 0.0286 + 0.143x$$

$$1.143x = 0.071 \qquad x = \frac{0.071}{1.143} = 0.062 \text{ mol/L}$$

$$[\text{cyclohexane}] = 0.200 + 0.062 = 0.262 \text{ mol/L}$$

$$[\text{methylcyclopentane}] = 0.100 - 0.062 = 0.038 \text{ mol/L}$$

The concentrations will change until the solution is 0.038 M in methylcyclopentane and 0.262 M in cyclohexane.

Exercise For the extraction of $FeCl_3$ from aqueous solution by ether,

$$FeCl_3(aq) \rightleftharpoons FeCl_3(ether)$$

$K = 50.3$ at 25 °C. What are the equilibrium concentrations of $FeCl_3$ in each solvent if the initial concentration of $FeCl_3$ in water was 0.135 mol/L? *Answer* 0.132 mol/L in the ether phase, 0.003 mol/L in the aqueous phase

---

19.14 SOLVING EQUILIBRIUM PROBLEMS WITH THE QUADRATIC FORMULA

Solving equilibrium expressions for unknowns requires the use of algebra. In real laboratory and industrial situations the algebra can become very complex. In this book we restrict ourselves to problems that can be solved by using approximations and simple algebra, or to problems involving quadratic equations that can be solved completely. For such problems, once the equilibrium expression is rearranged into the quadratic form,

$$ax^2 + bx + c = 0 \tag{19.26}$$

the quadratic formula may be used to solve for x:

$$x = \frac{-b \pm \sqrt{b^2 - 4ac}}{2a} \tag{19.27}$$

> **The quadratic formula: for quadratic equation $ax^2 + bx + c = 0$,**
> $$x = \frac{-b \pm \sqrt{b^2 - 4ac}}{2a}$$

In Section 19.12 we illustrated the method for solving equilibrium problems by finding [C] at equilibrium for

$$A \rightleftharpoons B + C$$

with $K = 3.0 \times 10^{-6}$, the initial $[A] = 5.0$ mol/L, and $[B] = [C] = 0$. Suppose that instead of $K = 3.0 \times 10^{-6}$, we set $K = 0.30$, a value closer to the initial concentration of A of 5.0 mol/L. The expression

$$K = \frac{(x)(x)}{(5.0 - x)} = 0.30 \tag{19.28}$$

(see Equation 19.24) will have to be solved. If we assume $(5.0 - x) \approx 5.0$,

$$K = \frac{x^2}{5.0 - x} \approx \frac{x^2}{5.0} = 0.30$$

$$x^2 = (5.0)(0.30) = 1.5$$

$$x = \sqrt{1.5} = 1.2$$

In this case the error in the approximation,

$$\% \text{ error} = \left(\frac{1.2}{5.0}\right) \times (100\%) = 24\%$$

is much too large and the value of x will be in error. Therefore, the shortcut of neglecting x in the denominator of Equation (19.28) does not work; we must solve this equation by using the quadratic formula. First, Equation (19.28) must be rearranged into the form of Equation (19.26).

$$\frac{x^2}{5.0 - x} = 0.30$$

$$x^2 = (0.30)(5.0 - x) = 1.5 - 0.30x$$

$$x^2 + 0.30x - 1.5 = 0$$

where $a = 1$, $b = 0.30$, and $c = -1.5$ (see Equation 19.26). Therefore, using the quadratic formula (Equation 19.27), we have

$$x = \frac{-0.30 \pm \sqrt{(0.30)^2 - (4)(1)(-1.5)}}{2(1)}$$

$$= \frac{-0.30 \pm 2.5}{2}$$

$$x = 1.1 \text{ or } -1.4$$

The negative value of x is discarded because a negative concentration has no physical meaning. The equilibrium concentration of C is 1.1 mol/L.

EXAMPLE 19.17
Equilibrium Concentrations

At 3000 K chlorine gas dissociates into chlorine atoms in an equilibrium reaction for which $K = 0.37$. What is the concentration of chlorine atoms in a vessel that originally contained 1.0 mol/L of molecular chlorine?

The reaction is

$$Cl_2(g) \rightleftharpoons 2Cl(g)$$

The unknown is [Cl] at equilibrium and we choose the concentration of Cl_2 that dissociates into Cl as x. The algebraic expression that must be solved is found by arranging the known and unknown information in the usual way.

	$Cl_2(g)$	$\rightleftharpoons$	$2Cl(g)$
Initial	1.0		0
Change	$-x$		$+2x$
Equilibrium	$1.0 - x$		$2x$

$$K = \frac{[Cl]^2}{[Cl_2]} = \frac{(2x)^2}{(1.0 - x)} = 0.37$$

Inspection shows that the values of K and the known concentration are similar in magnitude. Therefore, this problem should be solved by using the quadratic formula (see Equations 19.26 and 19.27).

$$4x^2 = (0.37)(1.0 - x)$$

$$4x^2 + 0.37x - 0.37 = 0$$

with $a = 4$, $b = 0.37$, and $c = -0.37$

$$x = \frac{-0.37 \pm \sqrt{(0.37)^2 - (4)(4)(-0.37)}}{(2)(4)}$$

$$= \frac{-0.37 \pm (2.5)}{8} = 0.27 \text{ or } -0.36$$

Therefore,

$$[Cl] = 2x = (2)(0.27 \text{ mol/L}) = 0.54 \text{ mol/L}$$

The concentration of chlorine atoms at equilibrium is 0.54 mol/L.

Exercise Chlorous acid establishes the following equilibrium:

$$HClO_2(aq) \rightleftharpoons H^+ + ClO_2^- \qquad K = 1.1 \times 10^{-2}$$

What is the concentration of H^+ in a solution that originally contained 0.100 mol/L of $HClO_2$? *Answer* $[H^+] = 0.028$ mol/L

SUMMARY

19.1 A CLOSE LOOK AT AN EQUILIBRIUM REACTION **19.2** EQUILIBRIUM CONSTANTS **19.3** UNITS AND EQUILIBRIUM CONSTANT VALUES For any reaction at equilibrium, $aA + bB + \cdots \rightleftharpoons rR + sS + \cdots$, the equilibrium constant, K, is given by the expression

$$K = \frac{[R]^r[S]^s \cdots}{[A]^a[B]^b \cdots}$$

The value of K depends on the temperature but is independent of the initial concentrations; at a given temperature, the value of K for a particular reaction will always be the same. A large value of K means that at equilibrium the concentrations of products will be high; a small value of K indicates that at equilibrium the concentrations of reactants will be high.

19.4 EQUILIBRIUM CONSTANTS FOR REACTIONS OF GASES **19.5** HETEROGENEOUS AND SOLUTION EQUILIBRIA When the reactants and products of a reaction are all gases, partial pressures (in atm) can be used in the expression for the equilibrium constant:

$$K_p = \frac{p_R^r p_S^s \cdots}{p_A^a p_B^b \cdots} = K_c(RT)^{\Delta n}$$

where K_p is the equilibrium constant expressed in terms of partial pressures and K_c is the equilibrium constant expressed in terms of concentrations. In writing equilibrium constants, the concentrations of pure solids, pure liquids, and solvents in dilute solutions need not appear.

19.6 EQUILIBRIUM CONSTANTS AND REACTION EQUATIONS If a reaction equation is multiplied by n, its equilibrium constant is raised to the nth power. If the equilibrium constant for a reaction is K, the equilibrium constant for the reverse reaction is $1/K$. When the equations for two reactions are added together, the equilibrium constant for the total reaction is the product of the equilibrium constants of the original reactions. The equilibrium constant for an overall reaction is independent of the number of steps by which it takes place.

19.7 THE REACTION QUOTIENT The reaction quotient, Q, has the same form as the expression for K; however, it uses *nonequilibrium* concentrations. If Q is less than K, the reaction will move forward toward equilibrium. If Q is greater than K, the *reverse* reaction will occur until equilibrium is reached.

19.8 LE CHATELIER'S PRINCIPLE **19.9** CONCENTRATION **19.10** PRESSURE **19.11** TEMPERATURE Increasing the concentration of a product or reactant shifts the reaction equilibrium so as to decrease the concentration of that substance (in accordance with Le Chatelier's principle). Continuous removal of a product therefore drives a reaction toward completion. An increase in pressure shifts an equilibrium in the direction that produces the smaller number of molecules in the gas phase. (Changes in pressure have little effect on reactions involving only liquids and solids, or those in which no change in numbers of gaseous molecules occurs.) If the temperature is increased, the equilibrium shifts so that the endothermic reaction is favored. Thus K for exothermic reactions decreases with rising temperature, and K for endothermic reactions increases with rising temperature.

TOOLS OF CHEMISTRY: CHROMATOGRAPHY Chromatography is the distribution of a solute between a stationary and a mobile phase. It allows substances to be separated on the basis of their relative affinities for the two phases. Generally the stationary phase is a solid or a liquid, while the moving phase is a liquid or a gas. There are many versions of this technique. All depend on the fact that because one phase is in motion, equilibrium can never be reached, and so dissolved material moves continuously from the stationary into the mobile phase.

19.12 HOW TO SOLVE EQUILIBRIUM PROBLEMS **19.13** SOME SIMPLE EQUILIBRIUM PROBLEMS **19.14** SOLVING EQUILIBRIUM PROBLEMS WITH THE QUADRATIC FORMULA To solve equilibrium problems, a stepwise method utilizing a table to summarize initial concentrations, changes in concentrations, and equilibrium concentrations is recommended. In many equilibrium problems the change from initial to final concentration of one or more of the substances is small enough to be neglected in addition or subtraction (*not* multiplication or division) when solving the problem. This is usually the case when the value of K is substantially smaller than the values of the known concentrations. When the error introduced by such a simplification is greater than about 5%, it is necessary to solve the problem exactly. For a quadratic equation of the form $ax^2 + bx + c = 0$,

$$x = \frac{-b \pm \sqrt{b^2 - 4ac}}{2a}$$

THOUGHTS ON CHEMISTRY

On the Education of a
Chemist (circa 1830)

*CONSULTATIONS IN TRAVEL, OR THE
LAST DAYS OF A PHILOSOPHER, by Sir
Humphrey Davy*

However difficult it may have been to have given you a definition of chemistry, it is still more difficult to give you a detail of all the qualities necessary for a chemical philosopher. . .

The person who wishes to understand the higher departments of chemistry, or to pursue them in their most interesting relations to the economy of nature, ought to be well grounded in elementary mathematics; he will oftener have to refer to arithmetic than algebra, and to algebra than to geometry. But all these sciences lend their aid to chemistry: arithmetic, in determining the proportions of analytical results, and the relative weights of the elements of bodies; algebra, in ascertaining the laws of the pressure of elastic fluids, the force of vapour as dependent upon temperature, and the effects of masses and surfaces on the communication and radiation of heat; the applications of geometry are principally limited to the determination of the crystalline forms of bodies, which constitute the most important type of their nature, and often offer useful hints for analytical researches respecting their composition. . . .

With respect to the higher qualities of intellect necessary for understanding and developing the general laws of the science, the same talents I believe are required as for making advancement in every other department of human knowledge; I need not be very minute. The imagination must be active and brilliant in seeking analogies; yet entirely under the influence of the judgment in applying them. The memory must be extensive and profound; rather however calling up general views of things than minute trains of thought; the mind must not be like an ency-

clopedia, a burden of knowledge, but rather a critical dictionary which abounds in generalities, and points out where more minute information may be obtained.

In detailing the results of experiments and in giving them to the world, the chemical philosopher should adopt the simplest style and manner; he will avoid all ornaments as something injurious to his subject, and should bear in mind the saying of the first king of Great Britain respecting a sermon which was excellent in doctrine but overcharged with poetical allusions and figurative language "that the tropes and metaphors of the speaker were like the brilliant wild flowers in a field of corn, very pretty, but which did very much hurt the corn."

Sir Humphrey Davy, "Consultations in Travel, or the Last Days of a Philosopher" (London: John Murray, 1830), pp. 248–254. Quoted from *The Chemist*, May, 1981, p. 11.

QUESTIONS

The Law of Chemical Equilibrium

19.1 What is the relationship between the rates of the forward and reverse reactions at chemical equilibrium? Does this mean that all concentrations are equal?

19.2 Consider the reaction

$$H_2O(l) \rightleftharpoons H^+ + OH^-$$

What is the forward reaction in this case? What is the reverse reaction? What is the relationship between rates of the forward and reverse reactions at equilibrium?

19.3 Consider a system containing SO_2, O_2, and SO_3 at equilibrium for the reaction

$$SO_2(g) + \tfrac{1}{2}O_2(g) \rightleftharpoons SO_3(l)$$

Describe what happens as a small amount of radioactive O_2 is added.

19.4 Write the equilibrium constant expression for each of the following reactions:

(a) $SO_3(g) + H_2(g) \rightleftharpoons SO_2(g) + H_2O(g)$
(b) $4NH_3(g) + 5O_2(g) \rightleftharpoons 4NO(g) + 6H_2O(g)$
(c) $C_3H_8(g) + 5O_2(g) \rightleftharpoons 3CO_2(g) + 4H_2O(g)$

19.5 Repeat Question 19.4 for

(a) $MnO_4^- + 5Fe^{2+} + 8H^+ \rightleftharpoons 5Fe^{3+} + Mn^{2+} + 4H_2O(l)$
(b) $CH_3COOH(aq) \rightleftharpoons H^+ + CH_3COO^-$
(c) $3NaClO(aq) \rightleftharpoons NaClO_3(aq) + 2NaCl(aq)$
(d) $Ag^+ + Cl^- \rightleftharpoons AgCl(s)$

19.6 Repeat Question 19.4 for

(a) $H_2O(g) \rightleftharpoons H(g) + OH(g)$
(b) $H_2CCH_2(g) + Cl_2(g) \rightleftharpoons H_2ClCCClH_2(g)$
(c) $2O_3(g) \rightleftharpoons 3O_2(g)$
(d) $IF(g) \rightleftharpoons \tfrac{1}{2}I_2(g) + \tfrac{1}{2}F_2(g)$

19.7 Repeat Question 19.4 for

(a) $CO(g) + 2H_2(g) \rightleftharpoons CH_3OH(l)$
(b) $Cl_2(g) + H_2O(l) \rightleftharpoons H^+ + Cl^- + HOCl(aq)$
(c) $2Fe^{2+} + Cl_2(g) \rightleftharpoons 2Fe^{3+} + 2Cl^-$

19.8 A student attempted to prepare and isolate thiosulfuric acid, $H_2S_2O_3$, using the following sequence of reactions:

$$S(s) + O_2(g) \rightleftharpoons SO_2(g) \qquad \text{(a)}$$
$$SO_2(g) + H_2O(l) \rightleftharpoons H_2SO_3(aq) \qquad \text{(b)}$$
$$H_2SO_3(aq) + 2OH^- \rightleftharpoons SO_3^{2-} + 2H_2O(l) \qquad \text{(c)}$$
$$SO_3^{2-} + S(s) \rightleftharpoons S_2O_3^{2-} \qquad \text{(d)}$$
$$S_2O_3^{2-} + 2H^+ \rightleftharpoons H_2S_2O_3(aq) \qquad \text{(e)}$$

but found that the desired acid immediately decomposed:

$$H_2S_2O_3(aq) \rightleftharpoons H_2SO_3(aq) + S(s) \qquad \text{(f)}$$

Write the equilibrium constant expressions for reactions (a) through (f).

19.9 What is the relationship between K_p and K_c for gases? If there are more moles of gaseous products than of gaseous reactants, will K_p be larger, smaller, or equal to K_c?

19.10 How does the form of the reaction quotient compare to that for the equilibrium constant? What is the difference between these two expressions?

19.11 If the reaction quotient is larger than the equilibrium constant, what will happen to the reaction? What will happen if $Q < K$?

Factors That Influence Equilibria

19.12 State Le Chatelier's principle. What factors do we usually consider to have an effect on equilibrium?

19.13 How does the presence of a catalyst or an inhibitor affect a system at chemical equilibrium? Explain your answer.

19.14 How will a reaction relieve a stress brought about by (a) the addition of more of one of the reactants, (b) the removal of one of the products, (c) the addition of more of one of the products, or (d) the removal of one of the reactants?

19.15 Will increasing the temperature always increase the yield of products in a reaction at equilibrium? If not, what determines how the amounts of reactants and products will change?

19.16 What will be the effect of increasing the total pressure on the equilibrium conditions for (a) a reaction that has more moles of gaseous products than gaseous reactants, (b) a reaction that has more moles of gaseous reactants than gaseous products, (c) a reaction that has the same number of moles of gaseous reactants and gaseous products, and (d) a reaction in which all reactants and products are pure solids, pure liquids, or are in solution?

19.17 A weather indicator can be made by coating an object with $CoCl_2$, which changes color as a result of the following reaction

$$[Co(H_2O)_6]Cl_2(s) \rightleftharpoons [Co(H_2O)_4]Cl_2(s) + 2H_2O(g)$$
$$\text{pink} \qquad\qquad\qquad \text{blue}$$

Does a pink color indicate "moist" or "dry" air?

19.18 Silver chloride is a very slightly soluble substance, but because of the equilibrium

$$AgCl(s) \rightleftharpoons Ag^+(aq) + Cl^-(aq)$$

small amounts of Ag^+ and Cl^- are present in the aqueous phase in contact with pure AgCl. Describe what happens as a soluble salt such as $AgNO_3$ is added to such a mixture.

19.19 Consider the reaction

$$CaCO_3(s) \rightleftharpoons CaO(s) + CO_2(g)$$

Will the mass of $CaCO_3$ at equilibrium (i) increase, (ii) decrease, or (iii) remain the same if (a) CO_2 is removed from the equilibrium system? (b) the pressure is increased? (c) solid CaO is added?

19.20 The reaction between NO and O_2 is exothermic.

$$2NO(g) + O_2(g) \rightleftharpoons 2NO_2(g) \qquad \Delta H^\circ_{1000} = -116.86 \text{ kJ}$$

Will the concentration of NO_2 at equilibrium (i) increase, (ii) decrease, or (iii) remain the same if (a) additional O_2 is introduced, (b) additional NO is introduced, (c) the total pressure is increased, (d) the temperature is decreased?

19.21 Predict whether the equilibrium for the photosynthesis reaction described by the equation

$$6CO_2(g) + 6H_2O(l) \rightleftharpoons C_6H_{12}O_6(s) + 6O_2(g)$$
$$\Delta H^\circ = 2801.69 \text{ kJ}$$

would (i) shift to the right, (ii) shift to the left, or (iii) remain unchanged if (a) $[CO_2]$ was increased, (b) p_{O_2} was increased, (c) one-half of the $C_6H_{12}O_6$ was removed, (d) the total pressure was increased, (e) the temperature was increased, and (f) a catalyst was added.

<u>Answers to Selected Questions</u>

19.6 (a) $\quad K_p = p_H p_{OH}/p_{H_2O} \quad$ or $\quad K_c = [H][OH]/[H_2O]$,
(b) $\quad K_p = p_{C_2H_4Cl_2}/p_{C_2H_4}p_{Cl_2} \quad$ or $\quad K_c = [C_2H_4Cl_2]/[C_2H_4][Cl_2]$,
(c) $K_p = p_{O_2}{}^3/p_{O_3}{}^2$ or $K_c = [O_2]^3/[O_3]^2$, (d) $K_p = p_{F_2}{}^{\frac{1}{2}}p_{I_2}{}^{\frac{1}{2}}/p_{IF}$ or $K_c = [F_2]^{\frac{1}{2}}[I_2]^{\frac{1}{2}}/[IF]$

19.7 (a) $\quad K_p = 1/p_{CO}p_{H_2}{}^2 \quad$ or $\quad K_c = 1/[CO][H_2]^2$,
(b) $K_p = [H^+][Cl^-][HOCl]/p_{Cl_2}$ or $K_c = [H^+][Cl^-][HOCl]/[Cl_2]$,
(c) $\quad K_p = [Fe^{3+}]^2[Cl^-]^2/[Fe^{2+}]^2 p_{Cl_2} \quad$ or $\quad K_c = [Fe^{3+}]^2[Cl^-]^2/[Fe^{2+}]^2[Cl_2]$

19.8 (a) $K_p = p_{SO_2}/p_{O_2}$ (or $K_c = [SO_2]/[O_2]$), (b) $K_p = [H_2SO_3]/p_{SO_2}$ (or $K_c = [H_2SO_3]/[SO_2]$), (c) $K = [SO_3{}^{2-}]/[H_2SO_3][OH^-]^2$, (d) $K = [S_2O_3{}^{2-}]/[SO_3{}^{2-}]$, (e) $K = [H_2S_2O_3]/[S_2O_3{}^{2-}][H^+]^2$, (f) $K = [H_2SO_3]/[H_2S_2O_3]$

19.18 more AgCl precipitates

19.21 (a) i, (b) ii, (c) iii, (d) iii, (e) i, (f) iii

PROBLEMS

Evaluation of K

19.1 The reaction

$$PCl_3(g) + Cl_2(g) \rightleftharpoons PCl_5(g)$$

has come to equilibrium at a temperature at which the concentrations of PCl_3, Cl_2, and PCl_5 are 10, 9, and 12 mol/L, respectively. Calculate the value of the equilibrium constant, K_c, for this reaction at that temperature.

19.2 Nitrogen reacts with hydrogen as follows:

$$N_2(g) + 3H_2(g) \rightleftharpoons 2NH_3(g)$$

An equilibrium mixture at a given temperature was found to contain 0.31 mol/L N_2, 0.50 mol/L H_2, and 0.14 mol/L NH_3. Calculate the equilibrium constant K_c at the given temperature. *Answer $K_c = 0.51$*

19.3 Ethyl acetate, a solvent used in lacquers, reacts with water to form acetic acid and ethyl alcohol.

$$CH_3COOC_2H_5(aq) + H_2O(l) \rightleftharpoons$$
$$CH_3COOH(aq) + C_2H_5OH(aq)$$

Under certain conditions it was observed that 0.33 mol of ethyl acetate remained at equilibrium after 1.00 mol of ethyl acetate was mixed with enough water to make 1.00 L of solution. Calculate K_c.

19.4 The reversible reaction

$$2SO_2(g) + O_2(g) \rightleftharpoons 2SO_3(g)$$

has come to equilibrium in a vessel of specific volume and at a given temperature. Before the reaction the concentrations of the reactants were 0.060 mol/L of SO_2 and 0.050 mol/L of O_2. After equilibrium was reached, the concentration of SO_3 was 0.040 mol/L. What is the concentration of O_2 at equilibrium? What is the value of K_c? *Answer $[O_2] = 0.030$ mol/L, $K_c = 130$*

19.5 $K_p = 6.41 \times 10^{50}$ for the reaction

$$B(s) + \tfrac{3}{2}F_2(g) \rightleftharpoons BF_3(g)$$

at 1100. K. What is the value of K_c for this reaction?

19.6 $K_p = 2550$ for the reaction

$$Br_2(g) \rightleftharpoons 2Br(g)$$

at 4000. K. What is the value of K_c for this reaction? *Answer $K_c = 7.76$*

19.7 $K_c = 193$ for the reaction

$$H_2(g) + Cl_2(g) \rightleftharpoons 2HCl(g)$$

at 2500. K. What is the value of K_p for this reaction?

19.8 $K_c = 2.27 \times 10^{15}$ for the reaction
$$W(s) + 3Cl_2(g) \rightleftharpoons WCl_6(g)$$
at 1000. K. What is the value of K_p for this reaction? *Answer* $K_p = 3.37 \times 10^{11}$

19.9 Suppose the chemical equation in Problem 19.5 had been written
$$2B(s) + 3F_2(g) \rightleftharpoons 2BF_3(g)$$
What is the value of K_p for this reaction?

19.10 What is K_p for the chemical reaction
$$2Br(g) \rightleftharpoons Br_2(g)$$
See Problem 19.6 for data. *Answer* $K_p = 3.92 \times 10^{-4}$

19.11 What is K_c for the chemical reaction
$$HCl(g) \rightleftharpoons \tfrac{1}{2}H_2(g) + \tfrac{1}{2}Cl_2(g)$$
See Problem 19.7 for data.

19.12 Citric acid reacts with water to lose H^+ in three steps:
$$(C_3H_4OH)(COOH)_3(aq) \rightleftharpoons (C_3H_4OH)(COOH)_2(COO)^- + H^+$$
$$K_1 = 7.10 \times 10^{-4}$$
$$(C_3H_4OH)(COOH)_2(COO)^- \rightleftharpoons (C_3H_4OH)(COOH)(COO)_2^{2-} + H^+$$
$$K_2 = 1.68 \times 10^{-5}$$
$$(C_3H_4OH)(COOH)(COO)_2^{2-} \rightleftharpoons (C_3H_4OH)(COO)_3^{3-} + H^+$$
$$K_3 = 4.11 \times 10^{-7}$$
What is K_c for the overall reaction,
$$(C_3H_4OH)(COOH)_3 \rightleftharpoons (C_3H_4OH)(COO)_3^{3-} + 3H^+$$
Answer $K_c = 4.90 \times 10^{-15}$

19.13* Express the equilibrium constant $K_{(i)}$ for the reaction
$$2NH_3(aq) + CO_2(g) + H_2O(l) \rightleftharpoons 2NH_4^+ + CO_3^{2-} \quad (i)$$
in terms of the equilibrium constants for the following equations:
$$NH_3(aq) + H_2O(l) \rightleftharpoons NH_4^+ + OH^- \quad (ii)$$
$$CO_2(g) + H_2O(l) \rightleftharpoons H_2CO_3(aq) \quad (iii)$$
$$H_2CO_3(aq) \rightleftharpoons 2H^+ + CO_3^{2-} \quad (iv)$$
$$H_2O(l) \rightleftharpoons H^+ + OH^- \quad (v)$$

19.14* Following are the concentrations of ions at equilibrium in three different experiments:

	$[Fe^{2+}]$	$[SCN^-]$	$[Fe(SCN)_x^{2-x}]$
Expt. 1	0.012	0.012	0.0012
Expt. 2	0.027	0.056	0.012
Expt. 3	0.039	0.016	0.0050

Use these data to determine the value of x in the equation
$$Fe^{2+} + xSCN^- \rightleftharpoons [Fe(SCN)_x]^{2-x}$$
Answer $x = 1$

19.15* Solvent extraction is based on the equilibrium established for a solute between two mutually insoluble solvents. For example, when an aqueous HCl solution of $FeCl_3$ is shaken with twice its volume of ether (also containing HCl), the following

equilibrium is established:
$$FeCl_3(aq) \rightleftharpoons FeCl_3(ether)$$
and 99% of the $FeCl_3$ is transferred to the ether phase. Find the equilibrium constant (commonly called the distribution ratio) for the extraction. *Answer* 50

Equilibrium Concentrations

19.16 In the production of ammonium sulfate, which is used in fertilizer, NH_3 is in equilibrium with H_2SO_4 and $(NH_4)_2SO_4$.
$$2NH_3(g) + H_2SO_4(l) \rightleftharpoons (NH_4)_2SO_4(s)$$
If $K_p = 2.23 \times 10^{31}$ for the reaction at 25 °C, what is the pressure due to the NH_3? In order to produce ammonium sulfate, would you change the pressure of NH_3 so that it was larger than, equal to, or smaller than this value?

19.17 The equilibrium constant for the reaction
$$CO(g) + H_2O(g) \rightleftharpoons CO_2(g) + H_2(g)$$
is $K_c = 4.0$ at a given temperature. An equilibrium mixture contains 0.80 mol of CO, 0.35 mol of water, and 2.2 mol of CO_2. How many moles of H_2 are present? Note that the volume is not important in this calculation. Why not? *Answer* 0.51 mol; the volume terms cancel in the expression for K.

19.18 For the reaction
$$\text{cyclohexane} \rightleftharpoons \text{methylcyclopentane}$$
$K = 0.143$ at 25 °C. What are the equilibrium concentrations of these substances at equilibrium if the reaction was started with the concentration of cyclohexane equal to 0.100 mol/L?

19.19 For the reaction
$$PCl_3(g) + Cl_2(g) \rightleftharpoons PCl_5(g)$$
$K_c = 96.2$ at 400 K. What is the concentration of Cl_2 at equilibrium if the initial concentrations were 0.10 mol/L for PCl_3 and 3.5 mol/L for Cl_2? *Answer* $[Cl_2] = 3.4$ mol/L

19.20 For the reaction
$$C_6H_{10}(\text{in } CCl_4) + I_2(\text{in } CCl_4) \rightleftharpoons C_6H_{10}I_2(\text{in } CCl_4)$$
$K = 20.$ at 25 °C. If the initial concentrations of C_6H_{10} and I_2 are 0.10 mol/L and 0.25 mol/L, respectively, what is the concentration of $C_6H_{10}I_2$ at equilibrium?

19.21 The equilibrium constant for the reaction
$$\alpha\text{-D-glucose}(aq) \rightleftharpoons \beta\text{-D-glucose}(aq)$$
is 1.75 at 25 °C. What are the concentrations of these sugars at equilibrium if the initial concentration of α-D-glucose was 0.0100 mol/L? *Answer* [β-D-glucose] = 0.00636 mol/L, [α-D-glucose] = 0.0036 mol/L

19.22 For the reaction
$$\text{glutamate}(aq) + NH_4^+ \rightleftharpoons \text{glutamine}(aq)$$
$K = 2.24 \times 10^{-3}$ at 37 °C. What is the equilibrium concentration of glutamine if the initial concentrations of NH_4^+ and glutamate were 0.10 mol/L and 0.010 mol/L, respectively?

19.23 At 43.9 °C, $K = 3.7 \times 10^{-3}$ for the reaction
$$(C_6H_5COOH)_2(\text{in } C_6H_6) \rightleftharpoons 2C_6H_5COOH \ (\text{in } C_6H_6)$$

What is the concentration of C_6H_5COOH at equilibrium if the initial concentration of $(C_6H_5COOH)_2$ was 0.45 mol/L? *Answer* $[C_6H_5COOH] = 0.042$ mol/L

19.24* The hydroxide ion concentration in a sample of river water is 5×10^{-8} M. What is the maximum concentration of iron (both Fe^{2+} and Fe^{3+}) that can exist in the water if $K_c = 1.64 \times 10^{-14}$ for the reaction

$$Fe(OH)_2(s) \rightleftharpoons Fe^{2+}(aq) + 2OH^-(aq)$$

and $K_c = 1.1 \times 10^{-36}$ for the reaction

$$Fe(OH)_3(s) \rightleftharpoons Fe^{3+}(aq) + 3OH^-(aq)$$

19.25* Chloromethane, CH_3Cl, is produced by the reaction of Cl_2 with methane, CH_4, as follows:

$$CH_4(g) + Cl_2(g) \rightleftharpoons CH_3Cl(g) + HCl(g)$$

Assuming that equal amounts of CH_4 and Cl_2 were placed in a reaction vessel so that their initial partial pressures were identical and equilibrium was allowed to be established, what is p_{CH_3Cl}/p_{CH_4} if $K_p = 7.4 \times 10^{17}$? (It is not necessary to find the individual pressures of the gases at equilibrium to calculate this ratio.) *Answer* 8.6×10^8

19.26* The equilibrium constant for the reaction

$$Fe^{3+} + 3C_2O_4^{2-} \rightleftharpoons [Fe(C_2O_4)_3]^{3-}$$

is 1.67×10^{20}. What is the concentration of Fe^{3+} left in solution if equal volumes of 0.0010 M $Fe(NO_3)_3$ and 1.000 M $K_2C_2O_4$ are mixed? (The calculations are simplified if you assume that all of the Fe^{3+} has reacted and write the "changes" on the basis of $[Fe(C_2O_4)_3]^{3-}$ undergoing decomposition.)

19.27* Adenosine triphosphate (ATP) reacts with water to form adenosine diphosphate (ADP) and produces an inorganic phosphate (P_i) such as HPO_4^{2-}.

$$ATP(aq) + H_2O(l) \rightleftharpoons ADP(aq) + P_i \qquad K = 4 \times 10^6$$

Both ATP and ADP are found in living cells and are important in the storage of energy for many chemical reactions in the body. What is the concentration of ATP at equilibrium if the original solution contained 1×10^{-7} mol/L ATP? (The calculations may be simplified by assuming that practically all of the ATP reacts and only a small portion of ATP is left, so that $x = [ATP]$ and $[ADP] = [P_i] = [(1 \times 10^{-7}) - x]$.) *Answer* $[ATP] = 3 \times 10^{-21}$ mol/L

Reaction Quotient

19.28 What must be the pressure of hydrogen so that the reaction

$$WCl_6(g) + 3H_2(g) \rightleftharpoons W(s) + 6HCl(g)$$

will occur if $p_{WCl_6} = 0.012$ atm and $p_{HCl} = 0.10$ atm? $K_p = 1.37 \times 10^{21}$ at 900 K.

19.29 $K_c = 19.9$ at 2500 K for the reaction

$$Cl_2(g) + F_2(g) \rightleftharpoons 2ClF(g)$$

What will happen in a reaction mixture containing $[Cl_2] = 0.2$ mol/L, $[F_2] = 0.1$ mol/L, and $[ClF] = 3.65$ mol/L? *Answer* ClF will decompose.

19.30 What is the value of the reaction quotient for the reaction

$$PbSO_4(s) \rightleftharpoons Pb^{2+}(aq) + SO_4^{2-}(aq)$$

if 25.0 mL of 2.0×10^{-4} M $Pb(NO_3)_2$ is mixed with 75.0 mL of 1.0×10^{-4} M Na_2SO_4? $K_c = 1.06 \times 10^{-8}$ for this reaction. Will a precipitate form?

19.31 A solution that contains $[Ba^{2+}] = 1.0 \times 10^{-3}$ mol/L is mixed with an equal amount of a solution that contains $[CO_3^{2-}] = 2.0 \times 10^{-6}$ mol/L. (a) Calculate the reaction quotient for the equation

$$Ba^{2+} + CO_3^{2-} \rightleftharpoons BaCO_3(s)$$

(b) If $K = 5 \times 10^8$ at 25 °C for this reaction, will a precipitate form? *Answer* (a) $Q = 2.0 \times 10^9$, (b) no

Additional Problems

19.32 The value of K_p at 25 °C for

$$2CO(g) \rightleftharpoons C(graphite) + CO_2(g)$$

is 1.11×10^{21}. What is the value of K_c? Describe what will happen if 2 mol of CO and 1 mol of CO_2 are mixed in a 1 liter container with a suitable catalyst to make the reaction "go" at this temperature.

19.33* There are equilibrium constants other than K_c that may be used for homogeneous gas-phase reactions. One of these is defined in terms of mole fractions, K_X. Write the expression for K_X and find its value for the reaction

$$2SO_2(g) + O_2(g) \rightleftharpoons 2SO_3(g)$$

when an equilibrium mixture contains 56.5% SO_2, 10.2% O_2, and 33.3% SO_3 by mass. *Answer* $K_X = X_{SO_3}^2 / X_{SO_2}^2 X_{O_2} = 1.13$

CHAPTER 20

Acids and Bases

You should learn a few practical things about acids and bases, if you have not already experienced them. (How Ira Remsen, who later founded the chemistry department at Johns Hopkins University, discovered the properties of nitric acid in the 1800s is described in the Thoughts on Chemistry at the end of this chapter.) Acids and bases can hurt you — from the stinging sensation when you accidentally squirt lemon juice (citric acid) in your eye to very severe and persistent burns if you spill battery acid (sulfuric acid) or lye (sodium hydroxide) on your skin and do not immediately flush it with water.

One of the classical properties by which acids were first identified is a sour taste. Bases were identified by their bitter taste. That acids and bases can be distinguished by how they taste has been well established. So we caution you not to test it by tasting any acids or bases in the laboratory. Think of vinegar, tomatoes, or lemon juice — that should convince you that acids are sour. And think of soap to convince yourself that bases are bitter.

Acids and bases can also eat holes in clothing. You might first realize that an acidic or basic solution has splashed on you when your shirt or blouse comes out of the washing machine with little holes where the fabric was weakened. If you spill concentrated acid or base directly on your clothing, the effect will be immediately noticeable and the garment probably ruined. The conclusion is obvious — acids and bases must be handled with care.

BRØNSTED-LOWRY ACIDS AND BASES

20.1 PROTON DONORS AND ACCEPTORS

In Section 14.8 the classical definitions of acids and bases in terms of the ions of water were introduced. A water-ion acid yields hydrogen ions in aqueous solution and a water-ion base yields hydroxide ions in aqueous solution. An acid–base reaction results in the formation of water and a salt. Over the years many other definitions of acids and bases were introduced as it became desirable to include more types of molecules and ions in the categories of acids and bases. For reactions in aqueous solution, the aspect of chemistry upon which we concentrate in this book, the Brønsted-Lowry definitions are the most useful.

The Brønsted-Lowry acid–base concept emphasizes the role of the proton. Any molecule or ion that can act as a proton donor is a **Brønsted-Lowry acid.** Any molecule or ion that can act as a proton acceptor is a **Brønsted-Lowry base.** In the reaction of hydrogen chloride with water to form a solution of hydrochloric acid,

$$\underset{\substack{proton \\ donor}}{} HCl(g) + H_2O(l) \longrightarrow H_3O^+ + Cl^-$$

(with *proton acceptor* labeling H_2O)

Brønsted-Lowry: acid, proton donor base, proton acceptor

HCl is a strong Brønsted-Lowry acid: Virtually all the HCl molecules give up their protons to water molecules. In this case the water molecule is the base and attracts H^+ to form an ion that we write as H_3O^+, the hydronium ion (see An Aside: The Hydronium Ion). A **Brønsted-Lowry acid–base reaction** is the transfer of a proton from a proton donor to a proton acceptor.

When a Brønsted-Lowry acid loses a proton, it forms what is called the *conjugate base* of that acid, for example,

acid (proton donor)		*proton*		*conjugate base*	
HCl	$\longrightarrow$	H^+	+	Cl^-	**(20.1)**
H_2SO_4	$\longrightarrow$	H^+	+	HSO_4^-	**(20.2)**
HSO_4^-	$\longrightarrow$	H^+	+	SO_4^{2-}	**(20.3)**
HNO_3	$\longrightarrow$	H^+	+	NO_3^-	**(20.4)**
H_2O	$\longrightarrow$	H^+	+	OH^-	**(20.5)**
NH_4^+	$\longrightarrow$	H^+	+	NH_3	**(20.6)**

water as an acid

When a Brønsted-Lowry base adds a proton, it forms what is called the *conjugate acid* of that base, for example,

Brønsted-Lowry acid → H⁺ + conjugate base
Brønsted-Lowry base + H⁺ → conjugate acid

base (proton acceptor)		*proton*		*conjugate acid*	
OH^-	+	H^+	$\longrightarrow$	H_2O	**(20.7)**
CN^-	+	H^+	$\longrightarrow$	HCN	**(20.8)**
CO_3^{2-}	+	H^+	$\longrightarrow$	HCO_3^-	**(20.9)**
HCO_3^-	+	H^+	$\longrightarrow$	H_2CO_3	**(20.10)**
NH_3	+	H^+	$\longrightarrow$	NH_4^+	**(20.11)**
H_2O	+	H^+	$\longrightarrow$	H_3O^+	**(20.12)**

water as a base

Note that water can be either an acid or a base.

Equations (20.1)–(20.6) and Equations (20.7)–(20.12) represent only half of what takes place in acid–base reactions. An acid does not give up a proton to form its conjugate base unless another base is present to accept the proton. Similarly, a base cannot add a proton to form its conjugate acid unless another acid is present to provide the proton. In the reaction of hydrogen chloride with water, as in all Brønsted-Lowry acid–base reactions, there are two acid–base pairs. The products of the reaction are the conjugate base of hydrogen chloride (chloride ion) and the conjugate acid of water (hydronium ion). In each of the following reactions, $acid_1$ gives up a proton to yield $base_1$, and $base_2$ adds a proton to form $acid_2$.

acid₁	*+ base₂*		*base₁*	*+ acid₂*	
HCl	$+ H_2O$	$\rightleftharpoons$	Cl^-	$+ H_3O^+$	**(20.13)**
HNO_3	$+ H_2O$	$\rightleftharpoons$	NO_3^-	$+ H_3O^+$	**(20.14)**
NH_4^+	$+ CO_3^{2-}$	$\rightleftharpoons$	NH_3	$+ HCO_3^-$	**(20.15)**
H_3O^+	$+ OH^-$	$\rightleftharpoons$	H_2O	$+ H_2O$	**(20.16)**
H_2O	$+ NH_3$	$\rightleftharpoons$	OH^-	$+ NH_4^+$	**(20.17)**

Table 20.1 is a list of conjugate acid–base pairs. All substances that fit the classical water-ion definitions of acids are also Brønsted-Lowry acids, or what can be called *protonic acids,* because they give up protons. In addition, ions such as HSO_4^- or NH_4^+ that contain ionizable protons are included in the definition of Brønsted-Lowry acids.

In the presence of an acid stronger than itself, water is a base (Equation 20.14). In the presence of a base stronger than itself, water is an acid (Equation 20.17). Ammonia (see Table 20.1) can also act as either an acid or a base. Water, ammonia, and other such substances that can act as either acids or bases are called *amphoteric.* (We have discussed amphoteric oxides in Section 16.11b.)

Protonic acids can be *monoprotic*—capable of losing one proton,

$$HCl(aq) + H_2O(l) \longrightarrow H_3O^+ + Cl^-$$

or *diprotic*—capable of losing two protons,

$$H_2SO_4(aq) + H_2O(l) \longrightarrow HSO_4^- + H_3O^+$$
$$HSO_4^- + H_2O(l) \rightleftharpoons SO_4^{2-} + H_3O^+$$

or *triprotic*—capable of losing three protons,

$$H_3PO_4(aq) + H_2O(l) \rightleftharpoons H_2PO_4^- + H_3O^+$$
$$H_2PO_4^- + H_2O(l) \rightleftharpoons HPO_4^{2-} + H_3O^+$$
$$HPO_4^{2-} + H_2O(l) \rightleftharpoons PO_4^{3-} + H_3O^+$$

[Confusingly, the terms monobasic, dibasic, and tribasic are sometimes used in the same sense as the terms monoprotic, diprotic, and triprotic.]

The hydrogen-containing anions derived from diprotic and triprotic acids are amphoteric. As illustrated by the hydrogen sulfide ion, HS^-, they can be either

Table 20.1
Conjugate Acid–Base Pairs

		Acid		Base		
Increasing acid strength	Strong acids	Perchloric acid	$HClO_4$ — ClO_4^-	Perchlorate ion	Very weak bases	Increasing base strength
		Sulfuric acid	H_2SO_4 — HSO_4^-	Hydrogen sulfate ion (bisulfate)		
		Hydriodic acid	HI — I^-	Iodide ion		
		Hydrobromic acid	HBr — Br^-	Bromide ion		
		Hydrochloric acid	HCl — Cl^-	Chloride ion		
		Nitric acid	HNO_3 — NO_3^-	Nitrate ion		
		Hydronium ion	H_3O^+ — H_2O	Water		
		Trichloroacetic acid	Cl_3CCOOH — Cl_3CCOO^-	Trichloroacetate ion	Weak bases	
		Hydrogen sulfate ion	HSO_4^- — SO_4^{2-}	Sulfate ion		
		Phosphoric acid	H_3PO_4 — $H_2PO_4^-$	Dihydrogen phosphate ion		
		Nitrous acid	HNO_2 — NO_2^-	Nitrite ion		
		Hydrofluoric acid	HF — F^-	Fluoride ion		
		Formic acid	$HCOOH$ — $HCOO^-$	Formate ion		
		Acetic acid	CH_3COOH — CH_3COO^-	Acetate ion		
		Carbonic acid	H_2CO_3 — HCO_3^-	Hydrogen carbonate ion (bicarbonate)	Stronger weak bases	
		Hydrosulfuric acid	H_2S — HS^-	Hydrogen sulfide ion		
		Ammonium ion	NH_4^+ — NH_3	Ammonia		
		Hydrogen cyanide	HCN — CN^-	Cyanide ion		
		Hydrogen sulfide ion	HS^- — S^{2-}	Sulfide ion		
		Water	H_2O — OH^-	Hydroxide ion		
		Ammonia	NH_3 — NH_2^-	Amide ion	Strong bases	
		Hydrogen	H_2 — H^-	Hydride ion		
		Methane	CH_4 — CH_3^-	Methide ion		

proton donors or proton acceptors.

$$\begin{array}{cccc} acid_1 & base_2 & base_1 & acid_2 \end{array}$$
$$HS^- + OH^- \rightleftharpoons S^{2-} + H_2O$$
$$HCl + HS^- \rightleftharpoons Cl^- + H_2S$$

EXAMPLE 20.1
Identifying Acids and Bases

Consider the following reactions of the hydrogen sulfate ion:

$$HSO_4^- + H_3O^+ \rightleftharpoons H_2SO_4(aq) + H_2O(l)$$

and

$$HSO_4^- + H_2O(l) \rightleftharpoons SO_4^{2-} + H_3O^+$$

In which reaction is HSO_4^- an acid and in which reaction is it a base?

In the first reaction HSO_4^- acts as a proton acceptor and is therefore a base. In the second reaction HSO_4^- acts as a proton donor and is therefore an acid.

Exercise Consider the following reactions of the hydrogen sulfide ion:

$$HS^- + H_2O(l) \rightleftharpoons H_3O^+ + S^{2-} \qquad \text{(i)}$$
$$HS^- + H_3O^+ \rightleftharpoons H_2S(aq) + H_2O(l) \qquad \text{(ii)}$$

In which reaction is HS^- acting as (a) an acid and as (b) a base? *Answer* (a) i, (b) ii

---

EXAMPLE 20.2
Identifying Acids and Bases

Identify the Brønsted-Lowry acid which is a reactant and its conjugate base which is a product in each of the following reactions:

(a) $HNO_3(l) + H_2O(l) \longrightarrow H_3O^+ + NO_3^-$
(b) $H_3O^+ + HS^- \rightleftharpoons H_2S(aq) + H_2O(l)$
(c) $HF(aq) + OH^- \rightleftharpoons H_2O(l) + F^-$

The acid is the species that donates the proton in each reaction: (a) HNO_3, (b) H_3O^+, and (c) HF. The conjugate base is the species formed by the removal of a proton from the acid: (a) NO_3^-, (b) H_2O, and (c) F^-.

Exercise Identify the Brønsted-Lowry base which is a reactant and its conjugate acid which is a product in each of the following reactions:

(a) $H_2PO_4^- + HSO_4^- \rightleftharpoons H_3PO_4(aq) + SO_4^{2-}$
(b) $H_3O^+ + HCOO^- \rightleftharpoons H_2O(l) + HCOOH(aq)$
(c) $HI(g) + H_2O(l) \rightleftharpoons H_3O^+ + I^-$

Answer The bases are (a) $H_2PO_4^-$, (b) $HCOO^-$, and (c) H_2O and the conjugate acids are (a) H_3PO_4, (b) HCOOH, and (c) H_3O^+.

20.2 RELATIVE STRENGTHS OF ACIDS AND BASES

A Brønsted-Lowry acid–base reaction is the competition between two bases for a proton. In each of the reactions in Equations (20.13)–(20.17), $base_1$ and $base_2$ are competing for the proton. Chloride ion, for example, is a *very* weak base. Because water is so much stronger a base than chloride ion, the reaction of hydrogen chloride with water (Equation 20.13) goes so far toward formation of H_3O^+ that for all practical purposes, ionization is complete. The chloride ions are unable to attract protons away from the water molecules to any significant extent. Whether a given acid–base reaction goes virtually to completion or reaches equilibrium with significant amounts of both reactants and products present is dependent upon the relative strengths of the two bases.

Remember that in using the Brønsted-Lowry acid–base definitions to refer to reactions in aqueous solution, the reference point is the extent to which a substance reacts with water. The acids above the hydronium ion in Table 20.1 are strong electrolytes—their aqueous solutions contain only hydrogen ions and anions. The anions of these acids are such weak bases that they are unable to attract hydrogen ions to re-form the acids. In the competition for the proton, water is the winner, driving reactions such as (20.13) and (20.14) to the right.

By contrast, in reactions of weaker acids with water—acids below hydronium ion in Table 20.1—equilibrium is established with some undissociated acid still present. The anions of weak acids are stronger bases than water and win back some of the protons in equilibrium reactions such as

$$HF(aq) + H_2O(l) \rightleftharpoons F^- + H_3O^+$$
$$HCN(aq) + H_2O(l) \rightleftharpoons CN^- + H_3O^+$$

Looking down the list of bases in Table 20.1 you can see that all anions are Brønsted-Lowry bases, because they are potentially proton acceptors. To think in Brønsted-Lowry terms, you must get used to the idea that the OH^- *ion,* and not (say) NaOH, is the base. For bases, as for acids, the reaction with water is the reference point. The three anions below hydroxide ion in Table 20.1, because they are stronger bases than the hydroxide ion, react immediately and virtually completely with water; they win the competition for the protons and give up practically none of them.

$$H_2O(l) + NH_2^- \longrightarrow OH^- + NH_3(g) \tag{20.18}$$
$$H_2O(l) + H^- \longrightarrow OH^- + H_2(g) \tag{20.19}$$
$$H_2O(l) + CH_3^- \longrightarrow OH^- + CH_4(g) \tag{20.20}$$

Bases above hydroxide ion but below water in Table 20.1 are weaker bases than hydroxide ion, but strong enough to establish equilibria in the competition with hydroxide ion for the proton. These anions can, in the *absence* of H_3O^+ or other competing species, react with water to form hydroxide ion, establishing equilibria such as

$$H_2O(l) + F^- \rightleftharpoons OH^- + HF(aq) \tag{20.21}$$
$$H_2O(l) + CN^- \rightleftharpoons OH^- + HCN(aq) \tag{20.22}$$

As shown in Table 20.1, the weak bases fall into two groups, with those in one group significantly stronger than those in the other group. The anions above water in Table 20.1 are such weak bases that they do not react measurably with water; they are unable to take protons away from water molecules to any significant extent.

Examine the following reactions with reference to Table 20.1 and the competition between bases for the proton. $Base_2$ is stronger than $base_1$ in each case and the reactions are most favorable in the directions written.

$$\underset{acid_1}{NH_4^+} + \underset{base_2}{OH^-} \rightleftharpoons \underset{acid_2}{H_2O(l)} + \underset{base_1}{NH_3(aq)}$$
$$HI(g) + CN^- \rightleftharpoons HCN(aq) + I^-$$

EXAMPLE 20.3
Identifying Acids and Bases; Relative Strengths of Acids and Bases

Write the equation for the equilibrium reaction between acetic acid and ammonia in aqueous solution. Identify the species acting as acids. From experience we know that the reaction is most favorable in the direction written. Which of the two bases present is weaker?

The chemical equation for the reaction is

$$CH_3COOH(aq) + NH_3(aq) \rightleftharpoons NH_4^+ + CH_3COO^-$$

The species that lose protons are CH_3COOH and NH_4^+; therefore these are the acids. The species that gain protons are NH_3 and CH_3COO^-; therefore these are the bases. Because the forward reaction is favored, NH_3 must be the stronger base and CH_3COO^- must be the weaker base.

Exercise Write the equation for the equilibrium between hydrofluoric acid and sulfate ion in aqueous solution. Identify the species that are acting as acids. From experience we know that this reaction is not favorable. Which of the two bases present is stronger? *Answer* $HF(aq) + SO_4^{2-} \rightleftharpoons HSO_4^- + F^-$, HF and HSO_4^- are the acids, F^- is the stronger base.

In summary, the Brønsted-Lowry acid–base definitions emphasize the role of the proton in reactions in aqueous solution. An acid is a proton donor. A base is a proton acceptor. Anions are always Brønsted-Lowry bases, but those containing hydrogen (e.g., $H_2PO_4^-$) can also react as Brønsted-Lowry acids. Remembering the following simple concepts will help you to understand and use the Brønsted-Lowry definitions of acids and bases:

1. *A strong Brønsted-Lowry acid gives up its proton easily.*
2. *A strong Brønsted-Lowry base attracts a proton strongly.*
3. *Any acid–base reaction is a competition between two bases for the proton.*
4. *When one base is much stronger than the other, the reaction of that base to form its conjugate acid is favored to the extent that it is virtually complete.*
5. *When both bases are of moderate strength, equilibria are established in which significant amounts of both reactants and products are present.*

AN ASIDE

The Hydronium Ion, H_3O^+

A moderate ambiguity exists over how to write and speak about the "hydrogen ion." It is simple and easy to write H^+, and that is the traditional way. But their high charge density (Sections 14.4, 16.4) makes it unlikely that free H^+ ions stay around very long. In using the Brønsted-Lowry acid–base definitions we write H_3O^+ to represent the hydrogen ion because it emphasizes that a proton is transferred from an acid to water. However, in speaking about, say, the acidity of a solution, a chemist is most likely to refer to "hydrogen ion concentration." In this book, we deal with the "hydrogen ion" by writing "H_3O^+" in chemical equations and, because it is simpler, writing $[H^+]$ in equilibrium constant expressions.

But what about the scientific evidence? What really does exist in water, or in the solid or gaseous states when a hydrogen atom has lost an electron?

X-ray analysis (see Tools of Chemistry: Diffraction, Chapter 13) gives strong evidence that the H_3O^+ ion is present in the solid state in some compounds. The solid monohydrate of perchloric acid ($HClO_4 \cdot H_2O$) and solid ammonium perchlorate (NH_4ClO_4) are shown by x-ray studies to have the same structure. There is no doubt that crystals of NH_4ClO_4 consist of NH_4^+ and ClO_4^- ions. The similar structure demonstrates that the solid perchloric acid hydrate must also be composed of two ions, H_3O^+ and ClO_4^-.

The x-ray pattern attributed to H_3O^+ has also been found at low temperatures in other solid acid hydrates, such as $H_3O^+F^-$, $H_3O^+Cl^-$, $H_3O^+NO_3^-$, and $H_3O^+HSO_4^-$. This is taken as evidence that in each case H_3O^+ ions are present in the liquid state of the acid and are trapped in the crystalline state as the acid is cooled.

The existence of H_3O^+ in the gas phase is supported by analysis of mass spectra (see Tools of Chemistry: Mass Spectrometer, Chapter 3). When water vapor is ionized, mass peaks for H_3O^+ and also for H^+ associated with two, three, or more water molecules ($H_5O_2^+$, $H_7O_3^+$, and so on) are observed.

The structure of the hydronium ion itself has been investigated by nuclear magnetic resonance studies of solid acid monohydrates (see Tools of Chemistry: Nuclear Magnetic Resonance, Chapter 27). It has the shape of a triangular pyramid (a) and is similar in overall size to the K^+ ion, which is one of the larger monatomic ions. In aqueous solution the hydronium ion is surrounded by four water molecules (b), three held by hydrogen bonding and a fourth attracted to the positive charge on the hydronium ion through the negative end of the water dipole (called ion–dipole interaction).

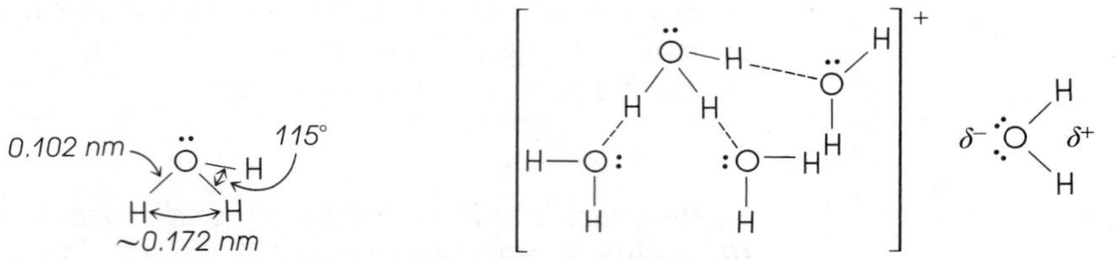

0.102 nm   115°

~0.172 nm

(a) H_3O^+ structure

(b) H_3O^+ in aqueous solution

"Hydrogen ions" are known to move very rapidly through aqueous solutions, accounting in part for the rapid rate of reactions involving them. If H_3O^+ were the mobile species, the ions should move at about the same speed as the K^+ ion of similar dimensions. This is not the case — the hydrogen ions move about twice as fast. Therefore, it has been proposed that H^+ moves rapidly through aqueous solutions by a "jump," or "pass the proton," mechanism.

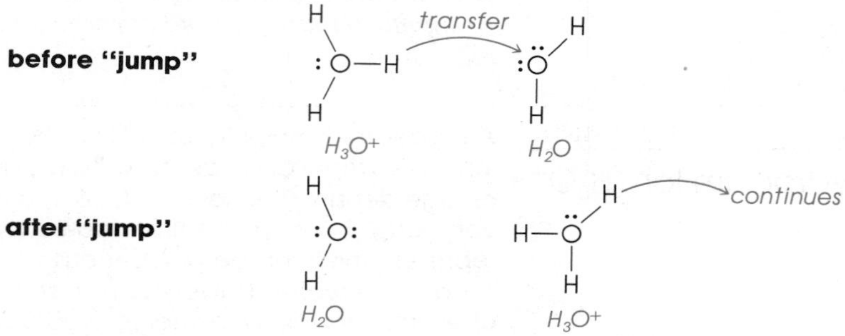

before "jump"   transfer

H_3O^+ H_2O

after "jump"   continues

H_2O H_3O^+

The lifetime of a given hydronium ion in aqueous solution is about 10^{-13} second. Support for the jump mechanism is provided by experiments in which methanol (CH_3OH) is added to acid–water solutions. The mobility of the hydrogen ions drops to a value comparable to that for K^+ ions in the same solution. This evidence suggests that when the jump mechanism is not possible because the methanol molecules come between the hydronium ions and water molecules, then hydronium ions become the mobile species.

BINARY ACIDS AND OXOACIDS

20.3 NAMING BINARY ACIDS

The binary acids are compounds of hydrogen and another element, such as HCl or H_2S, that ionize to give hydrogen ion and an anion. These compounds are hydrides of nonmetals or certain semiconducting elements. The names, as acids, are, for example,

HF(aq) H_2S(aq)   HI(aq)
hydrofluoric acid   *hydrosulfuric acid*   *hydroiodic acid*

Each name consists of three parts: (1) the prefix "hydro," which refers to the hydrogen atoms; (2) the name of the second element modified with the ending "ic"; (3) and the word "acid."

EXAMPLE 20.4
Nomenclature of Acids

Write the formula for hydrotelluric acid.

The form of the name shows that this is a binary acid. The two elements are hydrogen and tellurium. Tellurium is in the same periodic table group as sulfur (Group VI), and its negative oxidation state is −2. Therefore, hydrotelluric acid must be $H_2Te(aq)$.

Exercise Write the formula for the binary acid of bromine. Name this compound. *Answer* $HBr(aq)$, hydrobromic acid

20.4 STRENGTHS OF BINARY ACIDS

The strength of a binary acid depends upon the strength of the bond between the hydrogen atom and the second atom in the hydride. The two most important factors influencing this bond strength are the radius of the second atom and its electronegativity.

Electronegativity is the ability of an atom in a bond to attract electrons (Section 10.9). The ionic character of a bond increases with increasing electronegativity of the nonmetal atom. In the bond H—E, where E is a nonmetal atom, the greater the electronegativity of E, the more strongly it will attract electrons from H, thereby allowing H^+ to separate more readily. We therefore expect <u>acid strength to increase with increasing electronegativity of E in H—E bonds</u>.

The strength of the H—E bond will *decrease* as the atomic radius of E becomes larger. This decreasing bond strength will allow the proton to separate more easily. Thus we expect <u>acid strength to increase with increasing size of E in H—E bonds.</u>

In general, in going *down* a periodic table family, the acidity of the hydrides increases because the effect of increasing atomic radius predominates. For example, in the oxygen family, the strength of the binary acids increases with increasing radius down the family, despite the decrease in electronegativity down the family:

down a periodic table family:

$$H_2O \quad H_2S \quad H_2Se \quad H_2Te$$

———→

increasing acid strength with increasing radius

On the other hand, in going *across* a period in the periodic table, electronegativity becomes the predominating factor, despite the generally decreasing radii across the table. For example, the hydrides of the second-row elements nitrogen, oxygen, and fluorine display increasing acid strength.

across a periodic table period

$$NH_3 \quad H_2O \quad HF$$

———→

increasing acid strength with increasing electronegativity

20.5 NAMING OXOACIDS AND OXOANIONS

Oxoacids, for example, H_2SO_4 or HNO_3, contain hydrogen, oxygen, and a third, central element. Some oxoacids can be isolated as pure compounds. Others are known only in aqueous solution. Still others are known only by salts containing oxoanions.

The common names of the oxoacids were assigned when knowledge of chemistry was less developed than it is now. A name ending in "ic" was given to the acid that was best known or most common at the time. Other oxoacids of the same element were named according to the number of oxygen atoms surrounding the central element relative to this "most common" acid. The names assigned in this way remain in use, although in some cases one might argue that the "ic" named acid is not the most common one.

In the following table, n represents the number of oxygen atoms in the "most common," or reference, acid of a given element. The names of the other acids of the central element are derived from this name by adding suffixes and prefixes as shown in the table.

no. of oxygen atoms	*name*
$(n + 1)$	per . . . ic acid
n	. . . ic acid
$(n - 1)$	. . . ous acid
$(n - 2)$	hypo . . . ous acid

For example, HNO_3 is named nit*ric* acid. The acid with one less oxygen atom, HNO_2, is named nit*rous* acid. The nomenclature of some acids of the representative elements is illustrated in Table 20.2. The existence of a number of these acids as compounds that can be isolated is questionable. However, salts are known for many of them.

Table 20.2
Some Examples of Oxoacid Nomenclature The existence of some of these acids as substances that can be isolated is questionable, but some are known by their salts.

H_3BO_3 Boric acid	H_2CO_3 Carbonic acid	HNO_3 Nitric acid HNO_2 Nitrous acid $H_2N_2O_2$ Hyponitrous acid		
H_3AlO_3 Aluminic acid	H_4SiO_4 Silicic acid	H_3PO_4 Phosphoric acid H_3PO_3 Phosphorous acid H_3PO_2 Hypophosphorous acid	H_2SO_4 Sulfuric acid H_2SO_3 Sulfurous acid	$HClO_4$ Perchloric acid $HClO_3$ Chloric acid $HClO_2$ Chlorous acid $HClO$ Hypochlorous acid
H_3GaO_3 Gallic acid		H_3AsO_4 Arsenic acid H_3AsO_3 Arsenous acid	H_2SeO_4 Selenic acid H_2SeO_3 Selenous acid	$HBrO_4$ Perbromic acid $HBrO_3$ Bromic acid $HBrO$ Hypobromous acid
	H_4SnO_4 Stannic acid	H_3SbO_4 Antimonic acid H_3SbO_3 Antimonous acid	H_6TeO_6 Telluric acid H_2TeO_3 Tellurous acid	HIO_4 Periodic acid HIO_3 Iodic acid HIO Hypoiodous acid
	H_4PbO_4 Plumbic acid	H_3BiO_3 Bismuthic acid		

The oxoanions formed by the removal of all acidic hydrogen atoms from the oxoacid are named as follows:

per . . . ic acid	gives	per . . . ate ion
. . . ic acid	gives	. . . ate ion
. . . ous acid	gives	. . . ite ion
hypo . . . ous acid	gives	hypo . . . ite ion

For instance, some of the ions generated from the oxoacids in Table 20.2 would be

periodic acid	HIO_4	gives	IO_4^-	periodate ion
bromic acid	$HBrO_3$	gives	BrO_3^-	bromate ion
hypobromous acid	$HBrO$	gives	BrO^-	hypobromite ion
phosphoric acid	H_3PO_4	gives	PO_4^{3-}	phosphate ion
phosphorous acid	H_3PO_3	gives	HPO_3^{2-}	phosphite ion (one H is not ionizable)

Occasionally, you may see acid names that begin with "ortho," "meta," or "pyro." These prefixes come from another naming system, which began with the prefix "ortho" for the acid with the largest number of OH groups. For example, H_3PO_4,

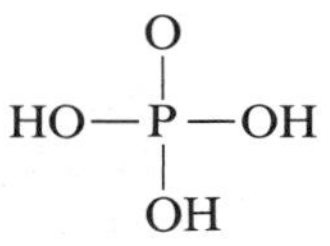

$$
\begin{array}{c}
\quad\ O \\
\quad\ \| \\
HO-P-OH \\
\quad\ | \\
\quad\ OH
\end{array}
$$

contains more OH groups than any other phosphoric acid and was known as "orthophosphoric acid." An "ortho" acid that has "lost" one or more water molecules yields a "meta" acid, and an acid produced by the loss of one water molecule between two molecules of the acid is called a "pyro" acid (Table 20.3).

The substitution of a sulfur atom for an oxygen atom in an oxoacid gives a "thio" acid; for example,

H_2SO_4	sulfuric acid
$H_2S_2O_3$	thiosulfuric acid

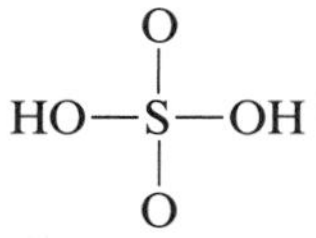

Thiosulfuric acid has not been identified, but salts of this acid are known. The presence of an oxygen–oxygen bond gives rise to "peroxo" acids, for example,

Table 20.3
"Ortho" Nomenclature for Acids A better name for pyrophosphoric acid is diphosphoric acid.

H_3PO_4
orthophosphoric acid
H_3PO_4 minus H_2O
HPO_3
metaphosphoric acid
$2H_3PO_4$ minus H_2O
$H_4P_2O_7$
pyrophosphoric acid

H_2SO_4 sulfuric acid
$$
\begin{array}{c}
\quad\ O \\
\quad\ \| \\
HO-S-OH \\
\quad\ \| \\
\quad\ O
\end{array}
$$

H_2SO_5 peroxomonosulfuric acid
$$
\begin{array}{c}
\quad\ O \\
\quad\ \| \\
HO-S-OOH \\
\quad\ \| \\
\quad\ O
\end{array}
$$

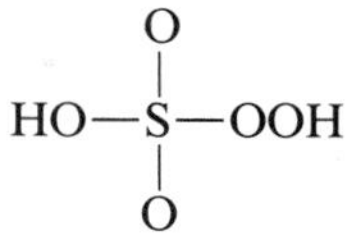

$H_2S_2O_8$ peroxodisulfuric acid
$$
\begin{array}{c}
\quad\ O \qquad\qquad O \\
\quad\ \| \qquad\qquad \| \\
HO-S-O-O-S-OH \\
\quad\ \| \qquad\qquad \| \\
\quad\ O \qquad\qquad O
\end{array}
$$

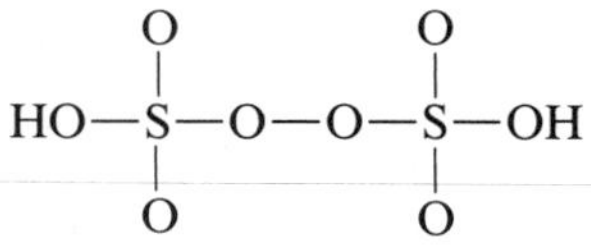

To identify peroxo acids it is necessary to know something about the structures of the compounds.

EXAMPLE 20.5
Nomenclature of Acids

Suppose we have discovered a remarkable new stable element and named it foxium, Fx. It readily forms a stable acid, $HFxO_3$, and three other less easily available acids, $HFxO_4$, $HFxO_2$, and $HFxO$. Salts of each of these acids can be isolated. Name the acids and their oxoanions.

Assuming that $HFxO_3$ is the most common acid and is named foxic acid, the names of the acids and the anions are as follows:

	oxoacid	oxoanion
$HFxO_4$	perfoxic acid	perfoxate ion
$HFxO_3$	foxic acid	foxate ion
$HFxO_2$	foxous acid	foxite ion
$HFxO$	hypofoxous acid	hypofoxite ion

Exercise Name the following oxoacids of sulfur and their respective oxoanions: (a) H_2SO_3, (b) H_2SO_4, (c) $H_2S_2O_7$, and (d) $H_2S_2O_3$. *Answer* (a) sulfurous acid, sulfite ion; (b) sulfuric acid, sulfate ion, (c) pyrosulfuric acid, pyrosulfate ion; (d) thiosulfuric acid, thiosulfate ion

20.6 STRENGTHS OF OXOACIDS

As we saw in Chapter 16, compounds containing oxide or hydroxide groups can be acidic, basic, or amphoteric. The deciding factors are the position in the periodic table, the electronegativity, and the oxidation state of the element to which the oxygen atoms are bonded. In oxides and hydroxides of the active metals of low electronegativity, such as sodium or barium, the bonding is ionic and the compounds are basic (Section 16.11). With more electronegative elements, the bonding is covalent and the oxides are often acidic.

Covalent compounds containing hydroxide groups are protonic acids if their hydrogen atoms can be attracted away by water molecules. This is possible when the oxygen atom is bonded to a highly electronegative atom. The electron density in the compound is drawn toward the electronegative atom and away from the hydrogen atom or atoms. The result is that the hydrogen atoms have partial positive charges and are more easily attracted away by the oxygen atom at the negative end of the water dipole; for example, in hypochlorous acid,

$$\underset{\substack{\delta+ \ \delta- }}{H_2O(l)} + \underset{\substack{\delta+ \ \delta- \\ \text{hypochlorous acid} \\ \text{(usually written HClO)}}}{HOCl(aq)} \;\rightleftharpoons\; H_3O^+ + OCl^- \qquad (20.23)$$

Although we are not accustomed to thinking of the formulas in this way, most oxoacids contain oxygen atoms and OH groups around a central atom. For example, H_2SO_4 could be written $O_2S(OH)_2$ and H_3PO_4 could be written $OP(OH)_3$. All oxoacids fit the general formula $O_nE(OH)_m$.

For a series of oxoacids of a given element, where m is the same and n can vary, the acid strength increases with the number of oxygen atoms bonded to the central element, as shown in Table 20.4 for the oxochlorine acids, $O_{0-3}Cl(OH)$. In other words, the acid strength increases with the oxidation state of the central atom. The bonding of each additional strongly electronegative oxygen atom to the central chlorine atom increases the displacement of electrons away from the hydrogen atom in the OH group. As a result, the hydrogen–oxygen bond becomes more polar, the hydrogen atom is more readily attracted by the negative end of a water molecule, and the strength of the acid increases.

Table 20.4
Oxochlorine Acids Oxygen content, the oxidation state of chlorine, and the acidity all increase in this series.

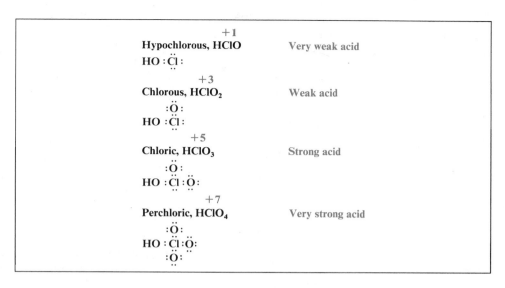

For a series of oxoacids of the same structure, for example, HOI, HOBr, and HOCl, the acid strength increases with increasing electronegativity and decreasing size of the atom bonded to the oxygen atom or atoms. Thus, the order of acidity for the acids noted is

$$HOCl > HOBr > HOI$$

In general, the polarity of the O—H bond in the EOH group (where E is any element), and thus the acidity of the hydrogen atom, increases with decreasing size and increasing electronegativity of E. Where E is of relatively large size and low electronegativity, the E—OH bond is ionic and the compound is basic. Where E is of intermediate electronegativity and size, amphoterism is encountered. For acids E is of small size and high electronegativity. These general trends are illustrated by the following series of compounds:

Periodic table row: increasing acidity with increasing
oxidation state and increasing electronegativity

NaOH	Mg(OH)$_2$	Al(OH)$_3$	Si(OH)$_4$
strongly basic	*basic*	*amphoteric*	*weakly acidic*

OP(OH)$_3$	O$_2$S(OH)$_2$	O$_3$Cl(OH)
acidic	*strongly acidic*	*very strongly acidic*

Periodic table family: decreasing acidity with increasing radii (same
oxidation state; similar electronegativity, except B)

B(OH)$_3$	Al(OH)$_3$	Ga(OH)$_3$	In(OH)$_3$	Tl(OH)$_3$
acidic	*amphoteric*	*amphoteric*	*basic*	*basic*

Same element in different oxidation states: increasing acidity
with increasing oxidation state

+2	+3	+4	+5
Mn(OH)$_2$	Mn(OH)$_3$	MnO$_2$	OMn(OH)$_3$
basic	*weakly basic*	*amphoteric*	*acidic*

+6	+7
O$_2$Mn(OH)$_2$	O$_3$Mn(OH)
strongly acidic	*very strongly acidic*

EXAMPLE 20.6
Relative Strengths of Acids and Bases

Compare the acid strength of $H_2SO_3(aq)$ to that of $H_2SO_4(aq)$, $H_2SeO_3(aq)$, and $HClO_3(aq)$.

For a series of oxoacids of a given element, the acid strength increases with the number of oxygen atoms bonded to the central element. Thus $H_2SO_3(aq)$ will be a weaker acid than $H_2SO_4(aq)$.

Acid strength increases with increasing electronegativity of the nonmetal. Thus we would expect $H_2SO_3(aq)$ to be a stronger acid than $H_2SeO_3(aq)$, but a weaker acid than $HClO_3(aq)$.

Exercise Compare the acid strength of $HClO(aq)$, $HBrO(aq)$, and $HClO_2(aq)$. *Answer* HClO is stronger than HBrO and $HClO_2$ is stronger than HClO.

20.7 EQUIVALENT MASS AND NORMALITY FOR ACIDS AND BASES

The concept of equivalents played an important role in the early history of chemistry. The relative amounts of two elements or two compounds that reacted with each other in a particular reaction were considered "chemically equivalent." Information about chemical equivalents eventually led to our understanding of atomic mass, mass in chemical combination, and stoichiometry. For example, Jeremias Richter and Ernst Fischer in the early 1800s published tables of equivalents of acids and bases. They knew that 1000 parts by mass of sulfuric acid or 1405 parts of nitric acid are each neutralized by 672 parts of ammonia. These quantities of sulfuric acid, nitric acid, and ammonia are chemically equivalent in neutralization reactions, although Richter and Fischer did not know why.

Our present knowledge of stoichiometry and the concept of the mole has made the use of equivalents unnecessary in most circumstances. The molar mass of a substance is more useful, for it is based solely on the identity of the substance and has only one value, no matter what the fate of the substance in a chemical reaction. Equivalent mass, however, is based on the behavior of a substance in a particular type of reaction. The definition of equivalent mass depends upon the type of reaction, and the equivalent mass of the same substance may be different in different reactions.

Equivalent masses are most likely to be encountered today in connection with acid–base reactions. The **equivalent mass of an acid** is the mass of the acid that donates one mole of H^+. For an acid the number of equivalents per mole is the number of ionizable protons in the acid: HCl has one equivalent per mole, H_2SO_4 has two equivalents per mole, and so on. The **equivalent mass of a base** is the mass of the base that donates one mole of hydroxide ions. A base has one equivalent per mole if it contains one hydroxide ion, as in NaOH; it has two equivalents per mole if it contains two hydroxide ions, for example, $Mg(OH)_2$, and so on.

The equivalent mass of acid or a base is the molar mass divided by the number of equivalents of H^+ or OH^- ions that the compound supplies per mole in an acid–base reaction.

$$\text{Equiv. mass (g/equiv)} = \frac{\text{molar mass (g/mol)}}{\text{no. of equiv. per mole}}$$

For example, hydrochloric acid supplies one mole of H^+ for each mole of HCl:

$$HCl(aq) \longrightarrow H^+ + Cl^-$$

Therefore, the equivalent mass of HCl is the same as the molar mass.

$$\text{Equiv. mass} = \frac{36.46 \text{ g/mol}}{1 \text{ equiv/mol}} = 36.46 \text{ g/equiv}$$

Sodium hydroxide donates one mole of OH^- and its equivalent mass is also the same as its molar mass (40.00 g/equiv). One mole of $Ca(OH)_2$ usually supplies two moles of OH^-:

$$Ca(OH)_2(s) \xrightarrow{H_2O} Ca^{2+} + 2OH^- \qquad \frac{74.09 \text{ g/mol}}{2 \text{ equiv/mol}} = 37.05 \text{ g/equiv}$$

and one mole of H_2SO_4 usually supplies two moles of H^+,

$$H_2SO_4(aq) \longrightarrow 2H^+ + SO_4^{2-} \qquad \frac{98.07 \text{ g/mol}}{2 \text{ equiv/mol}} = 49.04 \text{ g/equiv}$$

One equivalent of any strong acid will react completely with one equivalent of any strong base, for example,

$$H_2SO_4(aq) \quad + \quad 2NaOH(aq) \quad \longrightarrow Na_2SO_4(aq) + 2H_2O(l) \qquad \textbf{(20.24)}$$

1 equiv = 49.04 g   *1 equiv = 40.00 g*
(0.5 mol)   *(1.0 mol)*

The number of equivalents per mole can vary with the reaction under consideration, as shown by these reactions of phosphoric acid.

$$H_3PO_4(aq) + 3NaOH(aq) \longrightarrow Na_3PO_4(aq) + 3H_2O(l)$$
3 equiv/mol   *1 equiv/mol*

$$H_3PO_4(aq) + 2NaOH(aq) \longrightarrow Na_2HPO_4(aq) + 2H_2O(l)$$
2 equiv/mol   *1 equiv/mol*

$$H_3PO_4(aq) + NaOH(aq) \longrightarrow NaH_2PO_4(aq) + H_2O(l)$$
1 equiv/mol   *1 equiv/mol*

A solution containing one equivalent of a substance in one liter of solution is called a "one normal solution," written 1 N. **Normality** is the concentration of a solution expressed as the number of equivalents of solute per liter of solution. A solution containing 2 equivalents per liter is a 2 N solution, and 0.5 L of a 2 N solution contains one equivalent of solute.

The factor that connects the normality of a given solution to its molarity is the number of equivalents per mole in the reaction under consideration. The relationship is

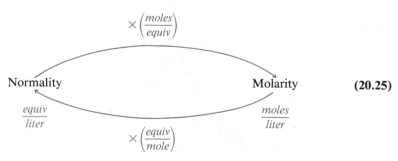

$$\textbf{(20.25)}$$

EXAMPLE 20.7
Equivalents

What are the relationships between the molar masses and the equivalent masses of HNO_3 and of $Ba(OH)_2$ in the following reaction?

$$2HNO_3(aq) + Ba(OH)_2(aq) \longrightarrow 2H_2O(l) + Ba(NO_3)_2(aq)$$

Each mole of HNO_3 donates one mole of H^+— 1 equiv/mol —and so the equivalent mass is the same as the molar mass.

Each mole of $Ba(OH)_2$ donates two moles of OH^-— 2 equiv/mol —and so the equivalent mass is one-half of the molar mass.

Exercise What are the relationships between the molar masses and the equivalent masses of H_2SO_3 and NaOH in the following reaction?

$$H_2SO_3(aq) + 2NaOH(aq) \longrightarrow 2H_2O(l) + Na_2SO_3(aq)$$

Answer 2 equiv/mol for H_2SO_3, 1 equiv/mol for NaOH

EXAMPLE 20.8
Equivalents

A commercially available concentrated sulfuric acid is 35.9 N. Assuming H_2SO_4 to donate two moles of H^+ per mole of H_2SO_4, express this concentration in terms of molarity.

The connecting ratio between normality and molarity is 2 equiv/mol. The molarity of the solution is

$$\left(\frac{35.9 \text{ equiv}}{1 \text{ L}}\right)\left(\frac{1 \text{ mol}}{2 \text{ equiv}}\right) = 18.0 \text{ mol/L}$$

Concentrated sulfuric acid is 18.0 M.

Exercise An old handbook listed various physical properties for a 0.5 N solution of lithium hydroxide. Express this concentration in terms of molarity. *Answer* 0.5 M

EXPRESSING THE STRENGTHS OF ACIDS AND BASES

20.8 IONIZATION EQUILIBRIUM OF WATER

Pure water, as we have learned (Section 14.4), is a slightly ionized substance:

$$H_2O(l) \rightleftharpoons H^+ + OH^- \quad \text{or} \quad H_2O(l) + H_2O(l) \rightleftharpoons H_3O^+ + OH^- \quad \text{(20.26)}$$

One liter of water contains 55.5 mol of H_2O molecules. The ionization of water is so slight that in each liter of water there is roughly one H^+ and one OH^- for each 555 million H_2O molecules. Water is ionized to such a small extent that the nonionized water molecules can be considered as part of a pure liquid. Thus their concentration is constant and need not appear in the equilibrium expression (see Section 19.5). The equilibrium expression for reaction (20.26), called the **ion product constant for water,** is therefore

$$K_w = [H^+][OH^-] \quad \text{(20.27)}$$

Measurements show that at 25 °C the value of K_w is 1.008×10^{-14}. The value increases with temperature; for example, at 60 °C it is 9.6×10^{-14}. With little introduction of error, the value of K_w at 25 °C (and frequently at other temperatures) is usually taken as

$$K_w = [H^+][OH^-] = 1.00 \times 10^{-14} \quad \text{(20.28)}$$

$K_w = 1 \times 10^{-14}$

From Equation (20.26) we know that the concentrations of hydrogen and hydroxide ions in pure water must be equal. Letting $x = [H^+] = [OH^-]$, we can see that at 25 °C the concentrations of these ions are equal to 1.00×10^{-7} mol/L.

$$[H^+][OH^-] = 1.00 \times 10^{-14}$$
$$(x)(x) = 1.00 \times 10^{-14}$$
$$x^2 = 1.00 \times 10^{-14}$$
$$x = 1.00 \times 10^{-7} \text{ mol/L}$$

Pure water is neutral — neither acidic nor alkaline — because the concentrations of hydrogen and hydroxide ions are equal. In an acidic solution the concentration of hydrogen ion is greater than 1×10^{-7} mol/L. By using Le Chatelier's principle (Section 17.2) we can predict that adding H^+ to a neutral solution should cause the equilibrium of Equation (20.26) to shift so that the concentration of OH^- decreases to less than that in pure water as the equilibrium is driven in the reverse direction. In an alkaline solution, the concentration of hydroxide ion is greater than 1×10^{-7} mol/L. The addition of a substance that increases the hydroxide ion concentration should also shift the equilibrium so that the concentration of hydrogen ion decreases.

The ion product constant expression is valid for all aqueous solutions — acidic, alkaline, or neutral. By using Equation (20.28), $[OH^-]$ can be found for any solution for which $[H^+]$ is known, and vice versa. The following example illustrates that, as predicted, increasing the hydrogen ion concentration decreases the hydroxide ion concentration from that in pure water.

EXAMPLE 20.9
Ion Product Constant of Water

What is the concentration of OH^- in a 0.01 M HCl solution? Because HCl is a strong acid and is 100% ionized, the H^+ concentration equals the molarity of the HCl solution.

The relationship between the concentrations of H^+ and OH^- in an aqueous solution is

$$K_w = [H^+][OH^-]$$

Solving this for $[OH^-]$ and substituting the known values of K_w and $[H^+]$ gives

$$[OH^-] = \frac{K_w}{[H^+]} = \frac{1.00 \times 10^{-14}}{0.01} = 1 \times 10^{-12}$$

The OH^- concentration in a 0.01 M HCl solution is 1×10^{-12} mol/L.

Exercise What is the concentration of H^+ in a 0.5 M solution of KOH? Because KOH is a strong, soluble base and is 100% dissociated, the OH^- concentration equals the molarity of the solution. *Answer* 2×10^{-14} mol/L

20.9 pH, pOH, AND pK_w

$$pH = -\log [H^+] = \log \frac{1}{[H^+]}$$

$$pOH =$$
$$-\log [OH^-] = \log \frac{1}{[OH^-]}$$

The concentrations of hydrogen ion and hydroxide ion in aqueous solutions are frequently of interest. These concentrations are often such small numbers that they are best expressed as exponential numbers (that is, in scientific notation). However, because they are in such common use, a more convenient way for expressing hydrogen and hydroxide ion concentrations has been devised. The expressions used, **pH** and **pOH**, are defined as follows:

$$pH = -\log [H^+] = \log \frac{1}{[H^+]} \qquad (20.29)$$

$$pOH = -\log [OH^-] = \log \frac{1}{[OH^-]} \qquad (20.30)$$

(Logarithmic notation is discussed in Appendix I.)

The values of pH or pOH for dilute solutions usually fall between 1 and 14 and are therefore easier to cope with than the small H^+ or OH^- concentrations. [For concentrated solutions, pH or pOH values are negative (e.g., pH < 0 for $[H^+] > 1$ M) or greater than 14 (e.g., pH > 14 for $[OH^-] > 1$ M). However, the use of pH and pOH is usually limited to dilute solutions where the values are between 1 and 14.]

The same notation (p . . .) can be used for the negative logarithm of any quantity, allowing pH and pOH to be combined with the ion product constant.

$$K_w = [H^+][OH^-]$$
$$\log K_w = \log ([H^+][OH^-])$$
$$= \log [H^+] + \log [OH^-]$$
$$-\log K_w = -\log [H^+] - \log [OH^-]$$
$$pK_w = pH + pOH \qquad (20.31)$$

Table 20.5
Acidity, Neutrality, and Alkalinity
in Aqueous Solutions (at 25 °C)

[H⁺] (mol/L)	pH	[OH⁻] (mol/L)	pOH		
10^1	−1	10^{-15}	15		
10^0	0	10^{-14}	14		
10^{-1}	1	10^{-13}	13		
10^{-2}	2	10^{-12}	12		Acidity increases
10^{-3}	3	10^{-11}	11	Acidic	
10^{-4}	4	10^{-10}	10		
10^{-5}	5	10^{-9}	9		
10^{-6}	6	10^{-8}	8		
10^{-7}	7	10^{-7}	7	Neutral	Neutral
10^{-8}	8	10^{-6}	6		
10^{-9}	9	10^{-5}	5		
10^{-10}	10	10^{-4}	4		
10^{-11}	11	10^{-3}	3		Alkalinity increases
10^{-12}	12	10^{-2}	2	Alkaline	
10^{-13}	13	10^{-1}	1		
10^{-14}	14	10^0	0		
10^{-15}	15	10^1	−1		

---

pH < 7, acidic solution
pH > 7, alkaline solution

Numerically, from Equation (20.28)

$$pK_w = -\log (1.00 \times 10^{-14}) = 14.000$$

so that

$$pH + pOH = 14.000$$
$$pH = 14.000 - pOH \qquad (20.32)$$
$$pOH = 14.000 - pH \qquad (20.33)$$

(Note that in a logarithm the digits after the decimal point are the significant digits; $pK_w = 14.000$ has three significant digits; see Appendix I.)

Equation (20.33) provides the very useful reference point that for a neutral solution,

$$pH = pOH = 7.000$$

If the pH is smaller than 7, the solution is an *acidic aqueous solution;* if the pH is larger than 7, the solution is an *alkaline aqueous solution.* (Remember that this is strictly accurate only at 25 °C.) The larger the departure from 7, the more acidic or the more alkaline the solution is (Table 20.5). In general, a solution is acidic when pH > pOH and alkaline when pOH > pH. Although both pH and pOH are useful, it is common practice to use pH to indicate both the acidity and the alkalinity of an aqueous solution. The pH values of some well-known substances are given in Table 20.6.

We stress that the pH and pOH scales are logarithmic, not linear, scales. For example, a solution of pH 1 has ten times the concentration of hydrogen ion that a solution of pH 2 has, not twice the concentration. A solution of pH 12 has 100 times the concentration of hydroxide ion that a solution of pH 10 has.

Table 20.6
Approximate pH Values of Some Well-Known Substances

0.1 M HCl	1.0
Gastric juice	1.4
Lemon juice	2.3
Vinegar	2.9
Orange juice	3.5
Tomatoes	4.2
Coffee	5.0
Rainwater	6.2
Pure water	7.0
Blood	7.4
Seawater	8.5
Bar soap	11.0
Household ammonia	11.5
0.1 M NaOH	13.0

EXAMPLE 20.10
pH and pOH

What is the pH of a 0.01 M solution of HCl?

Hydrochloric acid, a strong acid, is 100% ionized and so [H⁺] = 0.01 M. The pH for this concentration of H⁺ is

$$pH = -\log [H^+]$$
$$= -\log (1 \times 10^{-2}) = -(-2.0)$$
$$= 2.0$$

The pH of 0.01 M HCl is 2.0, written "pH 2.0."

Exercise The concentration of hydrogen ion in a cup of black coffee is 1.3×10^{-5} M. Find the pH of the coffee. Is this coffee acidic or alkaline? *Answer* 4.89, acidic

---

EXAMPLE 20.11
pH and pOH

What is the hydrogen ion concentration in a solution of pH 1.5?

We need to rearrange the definition of pH:

$$\log [H^+] = -pH = -1.5$$

To solve such an expression requires either using logarithm tables to find the antilogarithm of -1.5, which is equivalent to finding the antilogarithm of $(0.5 - 2)$ (see Appendix I), or finding $10^{-1.5}$ on a calculator. The answer must be rounded to one significant figure. The answer is

$$[H^+] = 3 \times 10^{-2} \text{ mol/L}$$

The hydrogen ion concentration is 0.03 mol/L.

Exercise The pH of blood serum is 7.4. What is the hydrogen ion concentration of blood serum? Is blood acid or alkaline? *Answer* 4×10^{-8} mol/L, alkaline

---

EXAMPLE 20.12
pH and pOH

Express the pOH of a 0.01 M solution of KOH. What is the pH of the solution?

Because KOH is a strong base, $[OH^-] = 0.01$ mol/L, giving

$$pOH = -\log [OH^-] = -\log (0.01) = 2.0$$

The pOH is 2.0, written "pOH 2.0."

The pH of the solution is found by using the relationship between pH and pOH found from pK_w (Equation 20.32).

$$pH = 14.000 - pOH$$
$$= 14.000 - 2.0 = 12.0$$

The pH of the KOH solution is 12.0.

Exercise What are the (a) pOH and (b) pH of a solution which contains $[OH^-] = 0.35$ mol/L? *Answer* (a) 0.46, (b) 13.54

EXAMPLE 20.13
pH and pOH

What are the pH and $[H^+]$ of a solution that has $[OH^-] = 3.5 \times 10^{-5}$ mol/L?

The pOH of the solution is

$$pOH = -\log [OH^-] = -\log (3.5 \times 10^{-5}) = 4.46$$

giving

$$pH = 14.00 - pOH = 14.00 - 4.46 = 9.54$$

which corresponds to

$$\log [H^+] = -pH = -9.54$$
$$[H^+] = 2.9 \times 10^{-10} \text{ mol/L}$$

The pH of this solution is 9.54 and the concentration of H^+ is 2.9×10^{-10} mol/L.

Exercise The pH of an alkaline solution is 8.36. What are the values of (a) pOH, (b) $[OH^-]$, and (c) $[H^+]$ for this solution? *Answer* (a) 5.64, (b) 2.3×10^{-6} mol/L, (c) 4.4×10^{-9} mol/L

EXAMPLE 20.14
pH and pOH

Which is the most acidic, a solution with (a) $[H^+] = 0.3$ mol/L, (b) $[OH^-] = 0.5$ mol/L, (c) pH 1.2, or (d) pOH 5.9? Acidities can be compared by comparing any one of the four quantities, $[H^+]$, $[OH^-]$, pH, or pOH. [We shall convert all of the given information to $[H^+]$ to make the comparison.]

Solution (a) has $[H^+] = 0.3$ mol/L. The $[H^+]$ concentration for solution (b) can be found by using the expression for K_w:

$$K_w = [H^+][OH^-]$$

$$[H^+] = \frac{K_w}{[OH^-]} = \frac{1.00 \times 10^{-14}}{0.5} = 2 \times 10^{-14} \text{ mol/L}$$

Finding $[H^+]$ from the pH for solution (c) gives

$$\log [H^+] = -pH = -(1.2)$$
$$[H^+] = 0.06 \text{ mol/L}$$

For solution (d) we first find the pH,

$$pH = 14.0 - pOH = 14.0 - 5.9 = 8.1$$

and then use this value to find $[H^+]$:

$$\log [H^+] = -pH = -(8.1)$$
$$[H^+] = 8 \times 10^{-9} \text{ mol/L}$$

We see that solution (a) is the most acidic.

Exercise Which is the most alkaline, a solution with (a) $[H^+] = 0.0025$ mol/L, (b) $[OH^-] = 0.0025$ mol/L, (c) pH = 3.65, or (d) pOH = 9.26? *Answer* (b)

20.10 THE ACID IONIZATION CONSTANT, K_a

The strength of a protonic acid is measured by the extent to which it ionizes in aqueous solution,

$$HA(aq) + H_2O(l) \rightleftharpoons H_3O^+ + A^- \quad \text{or} \quad HA(aq) \rightleftharpoons H^+ + A^- \quad \text{(20.34)}$$

The equilibrium constant for this reaction is called the **acid ionization constant, K_a**.

$$K_a = \frac{[H^+][A^-]}{[HA]} \quad \text{(20.35)}$$

The larger the value of K_a, the stronger is the acid. The strong acids that are virtually 100% ionized have K_a values greater than 1 because [HA] is very small. Weak acids, on the other hand, are less than 100% ionized. For weak acids, the predominant direction of reaction (20.34) is toward the formation of HA, and the K_a values are less than 1.

Since K_a values for weak acids are, like hydrogen ion concentrations for dilute solutions, frequently very small numbers, they can also be treated very conveniently as negative logarithms. The pK_a is defined as follows:

$$pK_a = -\log K_a \quad \text{(20.36)}$$

Table 20.7 gives the K_a and pK_a values for some weak acids in the order of decreasing acid strength, as shown by the *decreasing* K_a values and *increasing* pK_a values. (A more extensive list of K_a values is given in Appendix VA.)

Table 20.7
Ionization Constants of Weak Acids
at 25 °C for the Reaction
$HA(aq) \rightleftharpoons A^- + H^+$

	K_a	pK_a
Hydrogen sulfate ion HSO_4^-	1.0×10^{-2}	2.00
Phosphoric acid H_3PO_4	7.5×10^{-3}	2.12
Nitrous acid HNO_2	7.2×10^{-4}	3.14
Hydrofluoric acid HF	6.5×10^{-4}	3.19
Acetic acid CH_3COOH	1.754×10^{-5}	4.7560
Carbonic acid H_2CO_3	4.5×10^{-7}	6.35
Hydrosulfuric acid H_2S	1.0×10^{-7}	7.00
Ammonium ion NH_4^+	6.3×10^{-10}	9.20
Hydrogen sulfide ion HS^-	3×10^{-13}	12.5
Chromium(III) hydroxide $Cr(OH)_3$	9×10^{-17}	16.0
Copper(II) hydroxide $Cu(OH)_2$	1×10^{-19}	19.0
Zinc hydroxide $Zn(OH)_2$	1.0×10^{-29}	29.00

Equilibrium problems concerned with the concentrations of acids and their ions (or bases and their ions; Section 20.12) are solved by the same methods as any other equilibrium problems. If the concentration of any of the species present in the solution of an acid is changed, the equilibrium shifts according to Le Chatelier's principle, and the concentrations of the other species change so that the value of the equilibrium constant expression remains constant. The second of the following examples illustrates finding the concentration of an anion in the presence of additional hydrogen ion.

EXAMPLE 20.15
Acid Ionization Constants

A solution of iodic acid, HIO_3, was found to have, at equilibrium, a hydrogen ion concentration of 0.06 mol/L and an HIO_3 concentration of 0.02 mol/L. What is the value of K_a for this acid? Would HIO_3 be considered a "strong" or a "weak" acid? How does it compare in acid strength with the acids listed in Table 20.7?

The ionization equilibrium and the ionization constant expression for HIO_3 are

$$HIO_3(aq) \rightleftharpoons H^+ + IO_3^- \qquad K_a = \frac{[H^+][IO_3^-]}{[HIO_3]}$$

At equilibrium $[H^+] = [IO_3^-]$, allowing K_a to be found from the known $[H^+]$ and $[HIO_3]$.

$$K_a = \frac{[H^+][IO_3^-]}{[HIO_3]} = \frac{(0.06)(0.06)}{(0.02)} = 0.18$$

Because iodic acid has a K_a value less than 1, it is considered to be a weak acid. Comparison with the K_a values in Table 20.7 shows that it is one of the stronger of the weak acids.

Exercise   The chemical equation for the ionization of benzoic acid, C_6H_5COOH, is

$$C_6H_5COOH(aq) + H_2O(l) \rightleftharpoons H_3O^+ + C_6H_5COO^-$$

A solution of benzoic acid was found to contain $[H^+] = 2.6 \times 10^{-3}$ mol/L and $[C_6H_5COOH] = 0.100$ mol/L at equilibrium. What is the value of K_a for this acid? *Answer* 6.8×10^{-5}

EXAMPLE 20.16
Acid Ionization Constants

Hydrogen peroxide can act as a weak acid:

$$H_2O_2(aq) + H_2O(l) \rightleftharpoons H_3O^+ + HO_2^- \qquad K_a = 2.2 \times 10^{-12}$$

Assuming that additional acid (e.g., hydrochloric acid) has been added to a hydrogen peroxide solution, giving, at equilibrium, $[H^+] = 0.036$ mol/L and $[H_2O_2] = 0.100$ mol/L, what is the concentration of HO_2^- present at equilibrium?

The equilibrium constant expression for this reaction is

$$K_a = \frac{[H^+][HO_2^-]}{[H_2O_2]}$$

The unknown is the $[HO_2^-]$ that is in equilibrium with a known amount of $[H^+]$ and $[H_2O_2]$. (Note that in this solution, because of the added acid, $[HO_2^-] \neq [H^+]$.) Solving the acid ionization constant expression for $[HO_2^-]$ and substituting the data gives

$$[HO_2^-] = \frac{K_a[H_2O_2]}{[H^+]} = \frac{(2.2 \times 10^{-12})(0.100)}{(0.036)} = 6.1 \times 10^{-12} \text{ mol/L}$$

The concentration of the hydroperoxide ion is 6.1×10^{-12} mol/L.

Exercise   A solution contains formic acid and hydrochloric acid. At equilibrium, $[H^+] = 0.15$ mol/L and $[HCOOH] = 0.037$ mol/L. What is the concentration of the formate ion under these conditions? $K_a = 1.77 \times 10^{-4}$ for formic acid.   *Answer* 4.4×10^{-5} mol/L

EXAMPLE 20.17
Acid Ionization Constants

Find the concentrations of the various species present in a 0.10 M solution of nitrous acid, $HNO_2 \cdot K_a = 7.2 \times 10^{-4}$ for HNO_2. What is the pH of this solution?

Nitrous acid establishes the equilibrium

$$HNO_2(aq) + H_2O(l) \rightleftharpoons H_3O^+ + NO_2^- \qquad K_a = \frac{[H^+][NO_2^-]}{[HNO_2]}$$

From the mole ratios, we can see that $[H^+] = [NO_2^-]$ at equilibrium. We choose $x = [H^+] = [NO_2^-]$.

	$HNO_2(aq) \rightleftharpoons$	H^+	$+ NO_2^-$
Initial	0.10	0	0
Change	$-x$	$+x$	$+x$
Equilibrium	$0.10 - x$	x	x

Substituting into the expression for K_a gives

$$K_a = \frac{[H^+][NO_2^-]}{[HNO_2]} = \frac{(x)(x)}{(0.10 - x)} = 7.2 \times 10^{-4}$$

We first attempt to solve this expression for x by using the approximation $(0.10 - x) \approx 0.10$, which gives

$$x^2 = (7.2 \times 10^{-4})(0.10) = 7.2 \times 10^{-5}$$
$$x = 0.0085$$

The approximation is not valid because the error,

$$\frac{0.0085}{0.10} \times 100\% = 8.5\%$$

exceeds our permitted 5% error. Therefore we must use the quadratic formula to find the solution:

$$x^2 = (7.2 \times 10^{-4})(0.10 - x) = 7.2 \times 10^{-5} - (7.2 \times 10^{-4})x$$
$$x^2 + (7.2 \times 10^{-4})x - 7.2 \times 10^{-5} = 0$$

$$x = \frac{-(7.2 \times 10^{-4}) \pm \sqrt{(7.2 \times 10^{-4})^2 - (4)(1)(-7.2 \times 10^{-5})}}{2}$$

$$= 0.0081$$

Thus at equilibrium $[H^+] = [NO_2^-] = x = 0.0081$ mol/L and $[HNO_2] = (0.10 - x) = (0.10 - 0.0081) = 0.09$ mol/L. The pH of the solution is pH $= -\log [H^+] = -\log (0.0081) = 2.09$.

Exercise Find the concentrations of the various species present in a 0.0108 M solution of hypochlorous acid. $K_a = 2.90 \times 10^{-8}$ for HClO. *Answer* $[H^+] = [ClO^-] = 1.77 \times 10^{-5}$ mol/L, $[HClO] = 0.0108$ mol/L

20.11 PERCENT IONIZATION OF WEAK MONOPROTIC ACIDS

The percent of ionization of a weak acid is found from the concentration of hydrogen ion at equilibrium and the *initial* concentration of the acid. In general, for a monoprotic acid,

$$\text{Percent ionization} = \frac{[H^+]_{\text{equilibrium}}}{[HA]_{\text{initial}}} \times 100\% \qquad (20.37)$$

For example, at equilibrium the hydrogen ion concentration in an initially 0.10 M acetic acid solution is 0.0013 M, giving a percent ionization of 1.3%:

$$\text{Percent ionization} = \left(\frac{0.0013 \text{ mol/L}}{0.10 \text{ mol/L}}\right) \times 100\% = 1.3\%$$

The percentages of ionization for some weak acids are given in Table 20.8. Although it may not be immediately obvious, there is an important difference

Table 20.8
Percent Ionization of Some Weak Acids in Aqueous Solution at 25 °C The initial concentration of the acid is given in parentheses.

$H_3PO_4(aq) \rightleftharpoons H^+ + H_2PO_4^-$ *phosphoric acid* (0.5 M)	17%
$HF(aq) \rightleftharpoons H^+ + F^-$ *hydrofluoric acid* (1.0 M)	7.0%
$CH_3COOH(aq) \rightleftharpoons H^+ + CH_3COO^-$ *acetic acid* (1.0 M)	0.4%
$H_2O + CO_2 \rightleftharpoons H^+ + HCO_3^-$ *"carbonic acid"* (H_2CO_3) (0.1 M)	0.17%
$H_2S(aq) \rightleftharpoons H^+ + HS^-$ *hydrosulfuric acid* (0.1 M)	0.07%

between K_a values and percent ionization values. For a given acid (at the same temperature), K_a is always the same. However, the percentage of ionization of a weak acid or base varies with the initial concentration of the solution. The more dilute the solution, the larger is the percent ionization. For example, acetic acid in a 0.1 M solution is 1.3% ionized, but in a 0.01 M solution it is 4.3% ionized. This increase in ionization is a consequence of Le Chatelier's principle. The increasing dilution is equivalent to the addition of water to the following equilibrium system:

$$HA(aq) + H_2O(l) \rightleftharpoons H_3O^+ + A^-$$

The increase in the amount of water causes the equilibrium to shift in the direction of further ionization of HA. However, that is not the whole story. The greater dilution also decreases the *concentration* of the hydrogen, or hydronium, ions. Therefore, the solution becomes *less* acidic as it is made more dilute, even though the *percentage of ionization* is increased. For acetic acid solutions:

$$CH_3COOH(aq) + H_2O(l) \rightleftharpoons CH_3COO^- + H_3O^+$$

Concentration	% ionization	$[H^+]$	pH	
0.10 M	1.3%	0.0013 M	2.88	
0.010 M	*more* 4.3% *ionized*	0.00043 M	3.88	*less acidic*

The pH of solutions of strong acids can be found directly from the concentration of the solution (see Example 20.10), but this is not the case for weak acids. Because weak acids are less than 100% ionized, it is necessary to know, in addition to the concentration of the solution, one of the three quantities K_a, pH, or percent ionization. The following examples illustrate the relationships among these quantities.

EXAMPLE 20.18
Acid Ionization Constants

Electrical conductivity measurements show that 0.050 M acetic acid is 1.9% ionized at 25 °C. Calculate K_a.

The chemical equation is

$$CH_3COOH(aq) + H_2O(l) \rightleftharpoons CH_3COO^- + H_3O^+$$

The concentration of acetic acid that ionizes is $(0.019)(0.050 \text{ mol/L}) = 9.5 \times 10^{-4}$ mol/L. From the stoichiometry, we see that the concentrations of H^+ and CH_3COO^- formed will be 9.5×10^{-4} mol/L. Entering these values into our usual table gives

	$CH_3COOH(aq) \rightleftharpoons$	$CH_3COO^- +$	H^+
Initial	0.050	0	0
Change	−0.00095	+0.00095	+0.00095
Equilibrium	0.049	0.00095	0.00095

The value of K_a will be

$$K_a = \frac{[CH_3COO^-][H^+]}{[CH_3COOH]} = \frac{(9.5 \times 10^{-4})(9.5 \times 10^{-4})}{(0.049)} = 1.8 \times 10^{-5}$$

The ionization constant of acetic acid is 1.8×10^{-5}.

Exercise A 0.0202 M solution of chloroacetic acid, $ClCH_2COOH(aq)$, is 24.1% ionized at 25 °C. Calculate K_a for this acid. *Answer* 1.55×10^{-3}

EXAMPLE 20.19
Acid Ionization Constants

Find the percent ionization of hypobromous acid, HBrO, in a 0.025 M solution. What is the pH of this solution?

$$HBrO(aq) \rightleftharpoons H^+ + BrO^- \qquad K_a = 2.2 \times 10^{-9}$$

First it is necessary to find $[H^+]$ at equilibrium. Letting $x = [H^+]$, we have

	$HBrO(aq) \rightleftharpoons H^+ + BrO^-$		
Initial	0.025	0	0
Change	$-x$	$+x$	$+x$
Equilibrium	$0.025 - x$	x	x

$$K_a = \frac{[H^+][BrO^-]}{[HBrO]} = \frac{(x)(x)}{(0.025 - x)} = 2.2 \times 10^{-9}$$

Assuming that $(0.025 - x) \simeq 0.025$, we get

$$x^2 = (0.025)(2.2 \times 10^{-9}) = 5.5 \times 10^{-11}$$
$$x = 7.4 \times 10^{-6} = [H^+]$$

which corresponds to

$$pH = -\log [H^+] = -\log (7.4 \times 10^{-6}) = 5.13$$

The percentage of ionization is

$$\left(\frac{[H^+]_{equilibrium}}{[HBrO]_{,initial}}\right)(100\%) = \left(\frac{7.4 \times 10^{-6} \text{ mol/L}}{0.025 \text{ mol/L}}\right)(100\%) = 0.030\%$$

In a 0.025 M HBrO solution, the acid is 0.030% ionized.

Exercise Find the percent ionization of hypobromous acid in a 0.020 M solution. What is the pH of this solution? *Answer* 0.033%, 5.18

20.12 THE BASE IONIZATION CONSTANT, K_b

The equilibrium between a proton-accepting base and water can be represented by

$$B(aq) + H_2O(l) \rightleftharpoons BH^+ + OH^-$$

and the **base ionization constant** for this equilibrium is

$$K_b = \frac{[BH^+][OH^-]}{[B]} \tag{20.38}$$

The base B may be a neutral molecule, commonly ammonia,

$$NH_3(aq) + H_2O(l) \rightleftharpoons NH_4^+ + OH^-$$

for which

$$K_b = \frac{[NH_4^+][OH^-]}{[NH_3]} \tag{20.39}$$

or an anion

$$F^- + H_2O(l) \rightleftharpoons HF(aq) + OH^-$$

for which

$$K_b = \frac{[HF][OH^-]}{[F^-]} \tag{20.40}$$

Table 20.9
Ionization Constants for Some
Weak Bases at 25 °C

	K_b	pK_b		K_b	pK_b
Hydroxide ion OH$^-$	1	0	Ammonia NH$_3$	1.6×10^{-5}	4.80
Sulfide ion S^{2-}	3×10^{-2}	1.5	Aniline C$_6$H$_5$NH$_2$	4.2×10^{-10}	9.38
Triethylamine (C$_2$H$_5$)$_3$N	5.2×10^{-4}	3.28	Acetate ion CH$_3$COO$^-$	5.7×10^{-10}	9.24
Carbonate ion CO$_3^{2-}$	2.1×10^{-4}	3.68	Fluoride ion F$^-$	1.5×10^{-11}	10.82
Trimethylamine (CH$_3$)$_3$N	6.3×10^{-5}	4.20	Nitrate ion NO$_3^-$	5×10^{-17}	16.3
Cyanide ion CN$^-$	1.6×10^{-5}	4.80	Chloride ion Cl$^-$	3×10^{-23}	22.5

As with K_a, the larger the value of K_b, the stronger is the base; also, the larger the pK_b value, the weaker is the base. Table 20.9 gives the K_b and pK_b values of some common weak bases. You can see from the pK_b values that the anions of the weak acids H_2S, HCN, and H_2CO_3 are all relatively strong bases. As we would predict, the anions of the strong acids such as HNO_3 and HCl are relatively weak bases.

EXAMPLE 20.20
Base Ionization Constants

What is the pH of a 0.15 M solution of NH_3? What is the percent ionization of the NH_3?

$$NH_3(aq) + H_2O(l) \rightleftharpoons NH_4^+ + OH^- \qquad K_b = 1.6 \times 10^{-5}$$

To find the pH from the known K_b, we first find $[OH^-]$ and then use this to find the pOH, from which we can find the pH.

The concentration of OH^- can be found in the usual way.

$NH_3(aq) + H_2O(l) \rightleftharpoons$		$NH_4^+ +$	OH^-
Initial	0.15	0	0
Change	$-x$	$+x$	$+x$
Equilibrium	$0.15 - x$	x	x

$$K_b = \frac{[NH_4^+][OH^-]}{[NH_3]} = \frac{(x)(x)}{(0.15 - x)} = 1.6 \times 10^{-5}$$

$$x = [OH^-] = 1.5 \times 10^{-3} \text{ mol/L}$$

The percentage of ammonia that is ionized is

$$\frac{1.5 \times 10^{-3} \text{ mol/L}}{0.15 \text{ mol/L}} \times 100\% = 1.0\%$$

Now, solving for pOH and pH, we obtain

$$pOH = -\log [OH^-] = -\log (1.5 \times 10^{-3}) = 2.82$$
$$pH = 14.00 - pOH = 14.00 - 2.82 = 11.18$$

The ammonia is 1.0% ionized and the pH of the solution is 11.18.

Exercise What is the pH of a 0.015 M solution of NH_3? What is the percentage of ammonia that is ionized in this solution? Compare this to the 1.0% ionization of a 0.15 M NH_3 solution. *Answer* pH 10.69, 3.3%, larger percentage of ionization in more dilute solution

20.13 RELATIONSHIP OF K_a
AND K_b TO K_w

The product of the ionization constant for an acid and the ionization constant of its conjugate base is the ion product constant of water.

$$K_a \times K_b = K_w \qquad\qquad (20.41)$$

$$\overline{K_a \times K_b = K_w}$$

For example, for hydrofluoric acid

$$HF(aq) + H_2O(l) \rightleftharpoons F^- + H_3O^+ \qquad K_a = \frac{[F^-][H^+]}{[HF]}$$

and for fluoride ion, its conjugate base,

$$F^- + H_2O(l) \rightleftharpoons HF(aq) + OH^- \qquad K_b = \frac{[HF][OH^-]}{[F^-]}$$

The product of K_a and K_b is shown to be K_w as follows:

$$K_a \times K_b = \frac{[F^-][H^+]}{[HF]} \times \frac{[HF][OH^-]}{[F^-]} = [H^+][OH^-] = K_w$$

EXAMPLE 20.21
Ion Product Constant of Water

The value of K_a for hydrocyanic acid, HCN, is 6.2×10^{-10}. What is the value of K_b for the conjugate base?

From the equation

$$HCN(aq) + H_2O(l) \rightleftharpoons H_3O^+ + CN^-$$

we can see that the conjugate base is the cyanide ion, CN^-. The value of K_b for the reaction of CN^- as a base with water,

$$CN^- + H_2O(l) \longrightarrow HCN(aq) + OH^-$$

$$K_b = \frac{K_w}{K_a} = \frac{1.00 \times 10^{-14}}{6.2 \times 10^{-10}} = 1.6 \times 10^{-5}$$

The base ionization constant of CN^- is $K_b = 1.6 \times 10^{-5}$.

Exercise The value of K_b for NH_3 is 1.6×10^{-5}. What is the value of K_a for the conjugate acid? *Answer* 6.3×10^{-10}

In summary, for water, K_w, the ion product constant, equals $[H^+][OH^-]$. The acidity or alkalinity of aqueous solutions is expressed as pH or pOH, which are the negative logarithms of $[H^+]$ and $[OH^-]$, respectively. Pure water is neutral and has pH 7. A pH > 7 indicates an alkaline solution; a pH < 7 indicates an acidic solution. The relative strengths of acids and bases are shown by the K_a and K_b values—the equilibrium constants for the production of H^+ and OH^- ions in aqueous solution. The pK_a, the negative logarithm of the K_a, is also used to compare acid strengths, and pK_b, the negative logarithm of K_b, to compare basic strengths. The equilibrium constants K_a and K_b for conjugate acid–base pairs are related to K_w by $(K_a)(K_b) = K_w$.

LEWIS ACIDS AND BASES

20.14 ELECTRON-PAIR
DONORS AND ACCEPTORS

The Brønsted-Lowry acid–base definitions are entirely satisfactory for interpreting acid–base reactions that involve proton transfer. And since we are mainly concerned with acid–base behavior in water as a solvent, those are the definitions that we have emphasized. However, there are many important reactions that take place in solvents other than water, or in the absence of a solvent, which can be looked upon as acid–base reactions. Of the many other acid–base definitions that have been proposed over the years, the most generally useful has been that of G. N. Lewis.

Lewis observed that substances classified as acids and bases meet four experimental criteria:

1. Acids and bases combine rapidly with each other.
2. Acids and bases may be titrated against each other with the use of an indicator to identify an end point.
3. An acid or base will usually displace a weaker acid or base from a compound.
4. Acids and bases often act as catalysts in chemical reactions.

Lewis applied these criteria (which are met by water-ion and Brønsted-Lowry acids and bases) and introduced acid–base definitions that emphasize the role of electron pairs rather than protons.

A **Lewis acid** is a molecule or ion that can accept one or more electron pairs. A **Lewis base** is a molecule or ion that can donate an electron pair. The "donated" electron pair is shared between the acid and base (not physically transferred from one to the other). For example, in the following reaction, which occurs in the gas phase, boron trifluoride is an electron-pair acceptor and ammonia is an electron-pair donor:

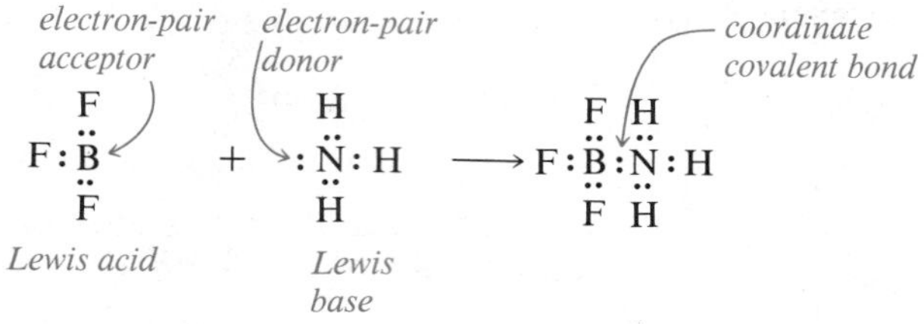

Lewis:
acid, electron-pair acceptor
base, electron-pair donor

$$
\underset{\substack{\text{Lewis acid}}}{\underset{\substack{electron\text{-}pair\\acceptor}}{\overset{F}{\underset{F}{F:\ddot{B}}}}} \;+\; \underset{\substack{\text{Lewis}\\\text{base}}}{\underset{\substack{electron\text{-}pair\\donor}}{\overset{H}{\underset{H}{:\ddot{N}:H}}}} \longrightarrow \overset{F\ \ H}{\underset{F\ \ H}{F:\ddot{B}:\ddot{N}:H}} \quad (coordinate\ covalent\ bond)
$$

The result of this reaction is the formation of a coordinate covalent bond between the boron and nitrogen atoms. A **Lewis acid–base reaction** is the donation of an electron pair from one atom to a covalent bond formed with another atom.

Because boron and aluminum are Representative Group III elements, they are surrounded in their compounds by only six outer shell electrons. These elements can complete their octets by accepting an electron pair, allowing their compounds to function as Lewis acids. Boron and aluminum compounds are active as catalysts in many reactions, presumably by temporarily forming electron-pair bonds to produce reactive intermediates. Metal atoms in which vacant d orbitals are available for occupancy by electron pairs are also found in Lewis acids [see reaction (d) in Table 20.10].

Several types of reactions that we have discussed earlier can also be classified as Lewis acid–base reactions. In the formation of complex ions, the ligands are Lewis bases and the metal cations are Lewis acids [reaction (f), Table 20.10]. The hydration of metal cations can also be viewed as Lewis acid–base reactions—an electron pair is donated from the oxygen atom of a water molecule to a cation. All M^{3+} cations and also Li^+, Be^{2+}, and Mg^{2+} are active as Lewis acids. The strength of a metal cation as a Lewis acid increases with its polarizing ability. The smaller cations with the higher charge-to-size ratios are the stronger Lewis acids.

The combination of an acidic oxide and a basic oxide is shown to be a Lewis acid–base reaction by writing out the Lewis structures of the two oxides [reaction (c), Table 20.10].

The Lewis definitions are especially useful in organic chemistry. In many reactions electron-deficient carbon atoms act as electron-pair acceptors. Carbon atoms are electron deficient when bonded to electronegative atoms and/or when electron density is withdrawn due to resonance in multiply bonded structures [reaction (g), Table 20.10].

Table 20.10
Lewis Acid–Base Reactions The shared electron pair is shown in color.

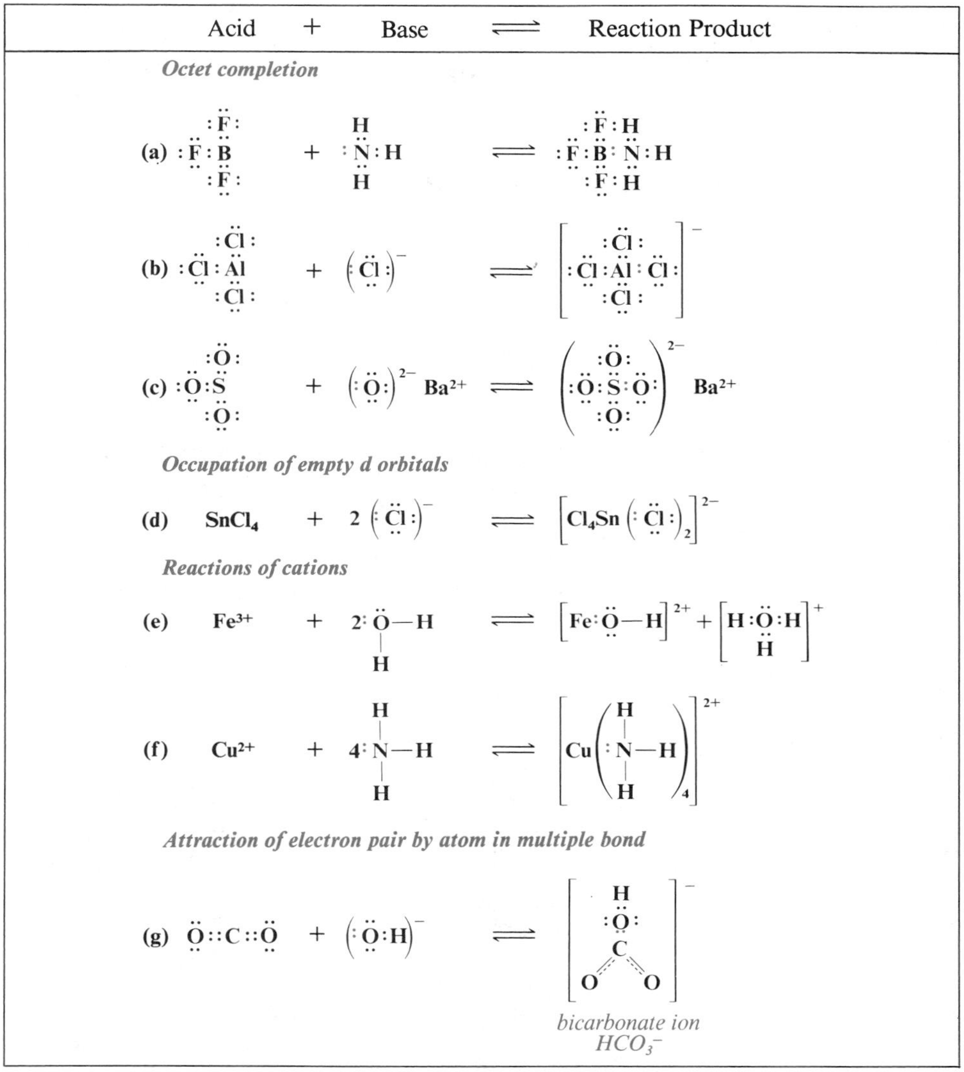

Acid	+	Base	⇌	Reaction Product

Octet completion

(a) $:F:B$ with $:F:$ above and $:F:$ below $\quad + \quad$ $:N:H$ with H above and H below $\quad ⇌ \quad$ $:F:B:N:H$ with $:F:H$ above and $:F:H$ below

(b) $:Cl:Al$ with $:Cl:$ above and $:Cl:$ below $\quad + \quad (:Cl:)^-$ $\quad ⇌ \quad$ $\left[:Cl:Al:Cl: \text{ with } :Cl: \text{ above and } :Cl: \text{ below} \right]^-$

(c) $:O:S$ with $:O:$ above and $:O:$ below $\quad + \quad (:O:)^{2-} Ba^{2+}$ $\quad ⇌ \quad$ $\left(:O:S:O: \text{ with } :O: \text{ above and } :O: \text{ below} \right)^{2-} Ba^{2+}$

Occupation of empty d orbitals

(d) $SnCl_4 \quad + \quad 2(:Cl:)^- \quad ⇌ \quad \left[Cl_4Sn(:Cl:)_2 \right]^{2-}$

Reactions of cations

(e) $Fe^{3+} \quad + \quad 2:O-H$ with H below $\quad ⇌ \quad \left[Fe:O-H \right]^{2+} + \left[H:O:H \text{ with H below} \right]^+$

(f) $Cu^{2+} \quad + \quad 4:N-H$ with H above and H below $\quad ⇌ \quad \left[Cu\left(:N-H \text{ with H above and H below} \right) \right]^{2+}_4$

Attraction of electron pair by atom in multiple bond

(g) $O::C::O \quad + \quad (:O:H)^- \quad ⇌ \quad \left[\begin{array}{c} H \\ :O: \\ C \\ O \quad O \end{array} \right]^-$

bicarbonate ion
HCO_3^-

Examination of the reactions given in Table 20.10 shows that all of the bases are also Brønsted-Lowry bases, but the Lewis definition includes many species that contain no protons and therefore are not Brønsted-Lowry acids. Protonic acids are traditionally also considered to be Lewis acids, and the hydrogen ion itself can be thought of as the electron-pair acceptor. [This causes no problems, although, strictly speaking, only free H^+ ions, which we know do not exist in aqueous solution, could *directly* accept electron pairs.]

EXAMPLE 20.22
Lewis Acids and Bases

Each of the following is a Lewis acid–base reaction:

(a) $Ni(s) + 4CO(g) \longrightarrow Ni(CO)_4(g)$ [An Ni—C bond is formed.]
(b) $NH_3(aq) + H^+ \longrightarrow NH_4^+$
(c) $BF_3(aq) + F^- \longrightarrow [BF_4]^-$

Identify the base in each reaction.

(a) In this reaction the carbon monoxide is the base, for an electron pair is donated by the carbon atom to the nickel atom.

$$Ni \frown :C\equiv O:$$

(b) In Lewis acid–base terms, the free hydrogen ion is thought of as the electron-pair acceptor and therefore NH_3 is the base and the electron-pair donor.

$$H^+ \frown :NH_3$$

(c) The fluoride ion donates a pair of electrons to the boron atom and is therefore the base.

$$F_3B \frown :\overset{..}{\underset{..}{F}}:$$

Exercise In each of the following Lewis acid–base reactions:

(a) $SO_3 + (C_2H_5)_2O \longrightarrow (C_2H_5)_2OSO_3$
(b) $SiF_4 + 2F^- \longrightarrow [SiF_6]^{2-}$
(c) $S + S^{2-} \longrightarrow [S_2]^{2-}$

identify the acid. *Answer* (a) SO_3, (b) SiF_4, (c) S

SUMMARY

20.1 PROTON DONORS AND ACCEPTORS Any molecule or ion that can act as a proton donor is a Brønsted-Lowry acid. Any molecule or ion that can act as a proton acceptor is a Brønsted-Lowry base. A Brønsted-Lowry acid–base reaction is the transfer of a proton from a proton donor to a proton acceptor. When a Brønsted-Lowry acid loses a proton it forms the conjugate base of that acid. When a Brønsted-Lowry base gains a proton it forms the conjugate acid of that base.

20.2 RELATIVE STRENGTHS OF ACIDS AND BASES A Brønsted-Lowry acid–base reaction is a competition of two bases for a proton. All anions are Brønsted-Lowry bases because they are potential proton acceptors. (Anions that contain ionizable hydrogens may also act as Brønsted-Lowry acids.) When two bases of quite different strengths compete for a proton, the stronger base is the winner and is converted almost entirely to its conjugate acid. When the two bases are of relatively equal strength, equilibrium is established with both bases and both conjugate acids present. Table 20.1 gives the relative strengths of acids and bases in some common acid–base pairs.

20.3 NAMING BINARY ACIDS **20.4** STRENGTHS OF BINARY ACIDS Binary acids are compounds of hydrogen and another element; they ionize to give hydrogen ion and an anion. The name of a binary acid consists of the prefix "hydro" and the name of the element modified with the ending "ic," followed by the word "acid." Usually the weaker the bond between the two elements in a binary acid, the stronger the acid.

20.5 NAMING OXO ACIDS AND OXO ANIONS **20.6** STRENGTHS OF OXO ACIDS Oxo acids contain hydrogen, oxygen, and a third, central element. The rules for naming oxo acids and their anions are given in Section 20.5. The strength of an oxo acid is determined by the electronegativity, oxidation state, and position in the periodic table of the element to which the oxygen atoms are bonded. In general, the more electronegative the central atom and the higher its oxidation state, the stronger the acid.

20.7 EQUIVALENT MASS AND NORMALITY FOR ACIDS AND BASES The equivalent mass of an acid is the mass of the acid that donates one mole of H^+. The number of equivalents per mole is the number of ionizable protons in the acid. The equivalent mass of a base is the mass of the base that donates one mole of OH^-. Normality, N, is the concentration of a solution expressed as the number of equivalents of solute per liter of solution.

20.8 IONIZATION EQUILIBRIUM OF WATER **20.9** pH, pOH, AND pK_w The ion product constant for water is $K_w = [H^+][OH^-] = 1.00 \times 10^{-14}$. In a neutral solution at 25 °C, $[H^+] = [OH^-] = 1.00 \times 10^{-7}$. The concentrations of H^+ and OH^- in solution are given in terms of pH and pOH: $pH = -\log[H^+] = \log 1/[H^+]$, $pOH = -\log[OH^-] = \log 1/[OH^-]$. For a neutral solution, $pH = pOH = 7.000$. An acidic aqueous solution has a pH smaller than 7; an alkaline aqueous solution has a pH greater than 7.

20.10 THE ACID IONIZATION CONSTANT, K_a **20.11** PERCENT IONIZATION OF WEAK MONOPROTIC ACIDS **20.12** THE BASE IONIZATION CONSTANT, K_b **20.13** THE RELATIONSHIP OF K_a AND K_b TO K_w The equilibrium constant for the reaction of a protonic acid in aqueous solution, $HA(aq) \rightleftharpoons H^+ + A^-$, is the acid ionization constant, $K_a = [H^+][A^-]/[HA]$. The larger the value of K_a, the stronger the acid; strong acids (100% ionized) have values of $K_a > 1$. The percent ionization of a weak monoprotic acid is equal to $([H^+]_{equilibrium}/[HA]_{initial}) \times 100\%$. The equilibrium constant for the reaction of a proton-accepting base with water, $B(aq) + H_2O(l) \rightleftharpoons BH^+ + OH^-$, is the base ionization constant, $K_b = [BH^+][OH^-]/[B]$. The more dilute the solution of a weak acid or base, the greater its percent ionization. The product of the ionization constant of an acid and that of its conjugate base is the ion product constant of water: $K_a \times K_b = K_w$.

20.14 ELECTRON-PAIR DONORS AND ACCEPTORS A Lewis acid is a molecule or ion that can accept one or more electron pairs. A Lewis base is a molecule or ion that can donate an electron pair. A Lewis acid–base reaction is the donation of an electron pair from one atom to a covalent bond formed with another atom. For example, in the formation of complex ions, the ligands are Lewis bases and the metal cations are Lewis acids. Among metals, Li^+, Be^{2+}, Mg^{2+}, and all M^{3+} cations are active as Lewis acids.

SIGNIFICANT TERMS

Brønsted-Lowry acid
Brønsted-Lowry base
Brønsted-Lowry acid–base reaction
oxoacid
equivalent mass of an acid
equivalent mass of a base
normality
ion product constant for water
pH
pOH
acid ionization constant
base ionization constant
Lewis acid
Lewis base
Lewis acid–base reaction

THOUGHTS ON CHEMISTRY

Ira Remsen Investigates Nitric Acid

THE LIFE OF IRA REMSEN, by Frederick H. Getman

"While reading a textbook of chemistry," said he, "I came upon the statement, 'nitric acid acts upon copper.' I was getting tired of reading such absurd stuff and I determined to see what this meant. Copper was more or less familiar to me, for copper cents were then in use. I had seen a bottle marked 'nitric acid' on a table in the doctor's office where I was then 'doing time!' I did not know its peculiarities, but I was getting on and likely to learn. The spirit of adventure was upon me. Having nitric acid and copper, I had only to learn what the words 'act upon' meant. Then the statement, 'nitric acid acts upon copper,' would be something more than mere words. All was still. In the interest of knowledge I was even willing to sacrifice one of the few copper cents then in my possession. I put one of them on the table; opened the bottle marked 'nitric acid'; poured some of the liquid on the copper; and prepared to make an observation. But what was this wonderful thing which I beheld? The cent was already changed, and it was no small change either. A greenish blue liquid foamed and fumed over the cent and over the table. The air in the neighborhood of the performance became colored dark red. A great colored cloud arose. This was disagreeable and suffocating—how should I stop this? I tried to get rid of the objectionable mess by picking it up and throwing it out of the window, which I had meanwhile opened. I learned another fact—nitric acid not only acts upon copper but it acts upon fingers. The pain led to another unpremeditated experiment. I drew my fingers across my trousers and another fact was discovered.

Nitric acid acts upon trousers. Taking everything into consideration, that was the most impressive experiment, and, relatively, probably the most costly experiment I have ever performed. I tell of it even now with interest. It was a revelation to me. It resulted in a desire on my part to learn more about that remarkable kind of action. Plainly the only way to learn about it was to see its results, to experiment, to work in a laboratory.''

Frederick H. Getman, *The Life of Ira Remsen* (Easton, Pennsylvania: Journal of Chemical Education, 1940), pp. 9, 10.

QUESTIONS

Brønsted-Lowry Acids and Bases

20.1 Define a Brønsted-Lowry acid. Why are all water-ion acids considered to be Brønsted-Lowry acids?

20.2 Write the chemical equation for the ionization of each of the following Brønsted-Lowry acids: (a) HNO_3, (b) HSO_4^-, (c) H_2SO_4, (d) HCl, and (e) H_2O. Identify the respective conjugate bases.

20.3 Define a Brønsted-Lowry base. Are all water-ion bases considered to be Brønsted-Lowry bases? Explain your answer.

20.4 Write the chemical equation for the addition of a proton by each of the following Brønsted-Lowry bases: (a) NH_3, (b) H_2O, (c) HCO_3^-, (d) CO_3^{2-}, (e) CN^-, and (f) OH^-. Identify the respective conjugate acids.

20.5 Write chemical equations showing (a) HSO_4^- acting as a base, (b) H_2O acting as an acid, (c) $Al(OH)_3(H_2O)_3$ acting as an acid, and (d) NH_4^+ acting as an acid.

20.6 The bicarbonate ion, HCO_3^-, is amphoteric. (a) Illustrate this property by writing typical Brønsted-Lowry acid–base reactions. (b) Identify the conjugate acid–base pairs.

20.7 Define a Brønsted-Lowry acid–base reaction. Write a chemical equation illustrating the reaction in terms of the acid, base, conjugate acid, and conjugate base.

20.8 Write the chemical equations for the following Brønsted-Lowry acid–base reactions: (a) H_2O and NH_3; (b) H_3O^+ and OH^-; (c) NH_4^+ and CO_3^{2-}; (d) HNO_3 and H_2O. Identify the respective conjugate acid–base pairs in each reaction.

20.9 Based on the relative strengths of acid–base pairs given in Table 20.1, predict what will happen if (a) HI is added to SO_4^{2-}, (b) H_2S is added to CN^-, and (c) HCOOH is added to Cl^-. Write the appropriate equations.

20.10 Repeat Question 20.9 for the following substances: (a) HF and Cl^-, (b) H_2S and OH^-, and (c) H_2SO_4 (6 M) and I^-.

20.11 Repeat Question 20.9 for the following substances: (a) HNO_2 and F^-, (b) HCOOH and CH_3COO^-, and (c) Cl_3CCOOH and NO_3^-.

20.12 List (a) all Brønsted-Lowry acids and (b) all Brønsted-Lowry bases from among the following: (i) SO_3^{2-}, (ii) $AlCl_3$, (iii) Cl^-, (iv) NH_4^+, (v) NH_3, (vi) H_2O, and (vii) HBr.

20.13 Indicate which of the following substances—(i) HCl, (ii) $H_2PO_3^-$, (iii) H_2CaO_2, (iv) $ClO_3(OH)$, and (v) $Sb(OH)_3$—are (a) Brønsted-Lowry acids or (b) Brønsted-Lowry bases. (Note: Do not be confused by the way the formulas are written.)

Binary Acids and Oxoacids

20.14 Which effect—electronegativity or nonmetal radius—is more important for determining the acid strength of binary hydrides of elements belonging to the same family of the periodic table? Which is the stronger acid: H_2Se or H_2Te?

20.15 Which effect—electronegativity or nonmetal radius—is more important for determining the acid strength of binary hydrides of elements in the same row of the periodic table? Which is the stronger acid: H_2Se or H_3As?

20.16 Predict which acid is stronger in each pair: (a) NH_3 or CH_4, (b) HI or HCl, (c) H_2S or HBr, and (d) H_2S and HS^-.

20.17 List the following acids in order of increasing strength: (a) hydrosulfuric, hydroselenic, and hydrotelluric; (b) HCl, H_2S, and PH_3; and (c) NH_3, H_2S, and HBr.

20.18 Name the following binary acids: (a) HF, (b) HBr, (c) H_2S, and (d) H_2Se.

20.19 Write the formulas for the following binary acids: (a) hydrochloric acid, (b) hydroiodic acid, and (c) hydrotelluric acid.

20.20 Name the following oxo acids: (a) HNO_2, (b) H_2SO_3, (c) HClO, (d) $HClO_4$, (e) HIO_3, and (f) H_2SeO_4.

20.21 Write the formulas for the following oxo acids: (a) tellurous acid, (b) bromic acid, (c) hyponitrous acid, and (d) phosphorous acid.

20.22 Why does NaOH behave as a base in water while ClOH behaves as an acid? Explain clearly this behavior and the general principles involved for any E—O—H compound.

20.23 How does the acid strength of a series of oxo acids of a given element depend on the oxidation state of the central atom? Which is the stronger acid, H_2SO_4 or H_2SO_3?

20.24 How does the acid strength of a series of oxo acids of elements in the same family of the periodic table in the same oxidation state depend on the electronegativity of the central atoms? Which is the stronger acid, $HBrO_2$ or $HClO_2$?

20.25 Predict which acid is stronger: (a) HIO_2 or HIO_3, (b) $As(OH)_3$ or $Sb(OH)_3$, and (c) H_2S or HNO_3.

20.26 List the acids in each group in order of increasing strength: (a) sulfuric, phosphoric, and perchloric; (b) HIO_3, HIO_2, HIO, and HIO_4; (c) selenous, sulfurous, and tellurous.

20.27 Name the following oxo anions: (a) BO_3^{3-}, (b) AsO_3^{3-}, (c) NO_2^-, (d) BiO_3^{3-}, (e) SeO_3^{2-}, (f) IO^-, and (g) ClO_4^-.

20.28 Write the formulas for the following oxo anions: (a) aluminate ion, (b) carbonate ion, (c) antimonite ion, (d) hypophosphite ion, (e) sulfate ion, (f) chlorite ion, and (g) hypobromite ion.

20.29 Name the following salts of oxo acids: (a) $Ga_2(SeO_4)_3$, (b) $Co_3(PO_4)_2$, (c) $Zn(BrO_3)_2$, (d) $TlNO_3$, and (e) $Th(SO_4)_2$.

20.30 Name the following salts of oxo acids: (a) $NaIO_4$, (b) $AlPO_4$, (c) $Ca(NO_2)_2$, and (d) $PbCrO_4$.

20.31 Write formulas for the following salts of oxo anions: (a) lead selenate, (b) cobalt(II) sulfite, (c) cadmium iodate, (d) cesium perchlorate, and (e) copper(I) sulfate.

20.32 Write formulas for the following salts of oxo anions: (a) mercury(II) chromate, (b) manganese(III) phosphate, (c) nickel(II) carbonate, (d) silver sulfate, (e) iron(III) nitrate.

20.33 What is the relationship between "ortho" oxo acids and "meta" oxo acids? Write a chemical equation representing the formation of metaphosphoric acid from orthophosphoric acid.

20.34 What is the relationship between "pyro" oxo acids and "ortho" oxo acids? Write a chemical equation representing the formation of pyrosulfuric acid from orthosulfuric acid.

20.35 How do we define the equivalent mass of an acid or base? Can the equivalent mass of a substance vary from reaction to reaction?

20.36 Define the concentration term *normality*. How can we convert from normality to molarity?

20.37 What is the relation between the molar mass and the equivalent mass in acid–base reactions for (a) HBr, (b) H_3PO_4, and (c) $Ca(OH)_2$? Assume complete reaction of all of the H^+ or OH^-.

20.38 What are the relationships between the molar masses and the equivalent masses of H_2CO_3 and $Ca(OH)_2$ in the following reaction?

$$2H_2CO_3(aq) + Ca(OH)_2(aq) \longrightarrow Ca(HCO_3)_2(aq) + 2H_2O(l)$$

Expressing the Strengths of Acids and Bases

20.39 Write a chemical equation showing the ionization of water. Write the equilibrium constant expression for this equation. What is the special symbol used for this equilibrium constant?

20.40 What is the relationship between $[H^+]$ and $[OH^-]$ in pure water? How can this relationship be used to define the terms "acidic" and "alkaline"?

20.41 Write mathematical definitions for pH and pOH. What is the relationship between pH and pOH? How can pH be used to define the terms "acidic" and "alkaline"?

20.42 A teacher once mistakenly told a class that the $[H^+]$ increased as the pH increased. Explain what was wrong with the statement.

20.43 Write a chemical equation representing the ionization of the acid HA. Write the equilibrium constant expression for this equation. What is the special symbol used for this equilibrium constant?

20.44 What is the relationship between the strength of an acid and the numerical value of K_a? What is the relationship between the acid strength and the value of pK_a?

20.45 Explain why the pH of a solution of a weak acid increases as the concentration of the solution decreases, even though the fraction of molecules that ionizes increases.

20.46 Write a chemical equation representing the ionization of the base MOH. Write the equilibrium constant expression for this equation. What is the special symbol used for this equilibrium constant?

20.47 Write a chemical equation representing the equilibrium between water and the proton-accepting base B. Write the equilibrium constant expression for this equation.

20.48 What is the relationship between base strength and the value of K_b? What is the relationship between base strength and the value of pK_b?

20.49 What is the relationship between the ionization constant for an acid and the ionization constant of its conjugate base?

20.50* Prove that $K_w = K_a K_b$ by writing the expressions for K_a for the acid HA, K_b for the base A^-, and K_w, and then multiplying the K_a and K_b expressions together to obtain the expression for K_w.

Lewis Acids and Bases

20.51 Define a Lewis acid. Prepare sketches showing how the following types of substances can act as Lewis acids: (a) cations, (b) molecules with unfilled octets, and (c) nonmetal atoms which can accommodate more than an octet.

20.52 Define a Lewis base. Prepare sketches showing how the following types of substances can act as Lewis bases: (a) anions and (b) molecules with two or fewer pairs of unshared electrons.

20.53 Define a Lewis acid–base reaction. Which of the following are Lewis acid–base reactions? (a) $Ag^+ + 2NH_3 \rightarrow [Ag(NH_3)_2]^+$, (b) $I^- + I_2 \rightarrow I_3^-$, (c) $H_3O^+ + OH^- \rightarrow 2H_2O$, and (d) $H^- + H_2O \rightarrow H_2 + OH^-$. Identify the Lewis acid in each of the acid–base reactions.

20.54 Which of the following are Lewis acid–base reactions? (a) $H_2O + SO_3 \rightarrow H_2SO_4$, (b) $O^{2-} + SO_3 \rightarrow SO_4^{2-}$, and (c) $AlCl_3 + CH_4 \rightarrow AlCl_3H^- + CH_3^+$. Identify the Lewis base in each of the acid–base reactions.

Additional Question

20.55 In many laboratories there are large bottles labeled "FIRST AID FOR ACID BURNS—Rinse area of burn thoroughly with water. Rinse with this 5% $NaHCO_3$ solution. Rinse again with water. Seek medical attention," and "FIRST AID FOR BASE BURNS—Rinse area of burn thoroughly with water. Rinse with this 5% CH_3COOH solution. Rinse again with water. Seek medical attention." (a) What is the purpose of the thorough water rinse? (b) What is the purpose of the $NaHCO_3$ rinse? Write a chemical equation to illustrate this purpose, assuming that a typical laboratory acid such as HCl was spilled. (c) What is the purpose of the CH_3COOH rinse? Write a chemical equation to illustrate this purpose, assuming that a typical laboratory base such as NaOH was spilled. (d) What is the purpose of the second rinse with water? (e) What is the main reason that $NaHCO_3$ and CH_3COOH were chosen over NaOH and HCl to be put in these bottles? (f) Why should the accident be reported and additional medical attention sought? (g) Why not use the $NaHCO_3$ solution for both acid and base burns?

Answers to Selected Questions

20.1 Any substance that can act as a proton donor is a Brønsted-Lowry acid; all water-ion acids are proton donors.

20.4 (a) $NH_3 + H^+ \rightarrow NH_4^+$, NH_4^+; (b) $H_2O + H^+ \rightarrow H_3O^+$, H_3O^+; (c) $HCO_3^- + H^+ \rightarrow H_2CO_3$, H_2CO_3; (d) $CO_3^{2-} + H^+ \rightarrow HCO_3^-$, HCO_3^-; (e) $CN^- + H^+ \rightarrow HCN$, HCN; (f) $OH^- + H^+ \rightarrow H_2O$, H_2O

20.6 (a) $HCO_3^- + H_2O \rightarrow H_3O^+ + CO_3^{2-}$, $HCO_3^- + H_3O^+ \rightarrow H_2CO_3 + H_2O$; (b) CO_3^{2-} is the conjugate base of HCO_3^-, H_2CO_3 is the conjugate acid of HCO_3^-.

20.11 (a) $HNO_2 + F^- \rightarrow NO_2^- + HF$, (b) $HCOOH + CH_3COO^- \rightarrow HCOO^- + CH_3COOH$, (c) $Cl_3CCOOH + NO_3^- \rightarrow NR$

20.12 (a) iv, v, vi, vii; (b) i, iii, v, vi

20.15 electronegativity, H_2Se

20.17 (a) $H_2S < H_2Se < H_2Te$; (b) $PH_3 < H_2S < HCl$, (c) $NH_3 < H_2S < HBr$

20.19 (a) HCl, (b) HI, (c) H_2Te

20.21 (a) H_2TeO_3, (b) $HBrO_3$, (c) $H_2N_2O_2$, (d) H_3PO_3

20.24 Acid strength increases with increasing electronegativity; $HClO_2$

20.26 (a) $H_3PO_4 < H_2SO_4 < HClO_4$, (b) $HIO < HIO_2 < HIO_3 < HIO_4$, (c) $H_2TeO_3 < H_2SeO_3 < H_2SO_3$

20.28 (a) AlO_3^{3-}, (b) CO_3^{2-}, (c) SbO_3^{3-}, (d) $H_2PO_2^-$, (e) SO_4^{2-}, (f) ClO_2^-, (g) BrO^-

20.30 (a) sodium periodate, (b) aluminum phosphate, (c) calcium nitrite, (d) lead(II) chromate

20.32 (a) $HgCrO_4$, (b) $MnPO_4$, (c) $NiCO_3$, (d) Ag_2SO_4, (e) $Fe(NO_3)_3$

20.34 A pyro acid is formed by removal of a water molecule from two molecules of ortho acid, $2H_2SO_4 \rightarrow H_2O + H_2S_2O_7$.

20.38 1 equiv/1 mol for H_2CO_3, 2 equiv/1 mol for $Ca(OH)_2$

20.44 Acid strength increases with increasing K_a, acid strength increases with decreasing pK_a.

20.54 (a) H_2O, (b) O^{2-}, (c) CH_4

20.55 (a) to wash off the spilled acid or base as well as cool the burn; (b) to neutralize any remaining acid: $HCO_3^- + H^+ \rightarrow H_2O + CO_2$; (c) to neutralize any remaining base: $CH_3COOH + OH^- \rightarrow H_2O + CH_3COO^-$; (d) to remove neutralization products; (e) a strong acid or base would release more heat during reaction than will the weak acid or base; (f) chemical burns are very serious; (g) HCO_3^- is too weak an acid to effectively neutralize the base

---

PROBLEMS

Ion Product Constant of Water

20.1 Calculate $[OH^-]$ that is in equilibrium with $[H^+] = 1.3 \times 10^{-4}$ mol/L.

20.2 Calculate $[H^+]$ that is in equilibrium with $[OH^-] = 4.21 \times 10^{-6}$ mol/L. *Answer* 2.38×10^{-9} mol/L

20.3 Calculate $[OH^-]$ that is in equilibrium with $[H^+] = 7 \times 10^{-9}$ mol/L.

20.4 The value of K_a for hypobromous acid, HBrO, is 2.2×10^{-9}. What is the value of K_b for the conjugate base?

20.5 The value of K_b for HPO_4^{2-} is 1.5×10^{-7} and the value of $K_a = 1 \times 10^{-12}$. Calculate K_b for PO_4^{3-} and K_a for $H_2PO_4^-$. *Answer* 1×10^{-2}, 6.7×10^{-8}

20.6 The value of K_b for the sulfide ion is 3×10^{-2} and for the hydrogen sulfide ion is 1.0×10^{-7}. What are the values of the K_a's for the conjugate acids of these ions?

20.7* The value of K_w is 9.614×10^{-14} at 60 °C. Find $[H^+]$ in water at this temperature and calculate the pH. Is pure water an acid at 60 °C? *Answer* 3.101×10^{-7} mol/L, 6.5085, no

pH and pOH

20.8 Convert each of the following values of $[H^+]$ into pH: (a) 9.5×10^{-6} mol/L, (b) 0.0001472 mol/L, (c) 0.00203 mol/L, (d) 12×10^{-12} mol/L, and (e) 1.0×10^1 mol/L. Which solutions are acidic?

20.9 Convert each of the following pH values into $[H^+]$: (a) 4.67, (b) 9.05, (c) 0.0, (d) 15.97, and (e) 0.153. Which solutions are acidic? *Answer* (a) 2.1×10^{-5} mol/L, (b) 8.9×10^{-10} mol/L, (c) 1 mol/L, (d) 1.1×10^{-16} mol/L, (e) 0.703 mol/L; (a), (c), (e)

20.10 Convert each of the following values of $[OH^-]$ into pH: (a) 0.00035 mol/L, (b) 11×10^{-13} mol/L, (c) 4.5×10^{-7} mol/L, and (d) 10 mol/L. Which solutions are alkaline?

20.11 Convert each of the following pOH values into $[H^+]$: (a) 13.97, (b) 0.12, (c) 5.04, and (d) 11.021. Which solutions are acidic? *Answer* (a) 0.93 mol/L, (b) 1.3×10^{-14} mol/L, (c) 1.1×10^{-9} mol/L, (d) 1.05×10^{-3} mol/L; (a) and (d)

20.12 Calculate the pH of each of the following solutions of strong acids and bases: (a) 0.2374 M NaOH, (b) 0.0365 M HCl, (c) 4.2×10^{-5} M HNO_3, and (d) 0.0826 M KOH.

20.13 Calculate the pH of each of the following solutions: (a) 0.0010 M HNO_3, (b) 0.103 M NaOH, (c) 0.5 M KOH, and (d) 0.104 M HCl. Assume all solutes are completely ionized or dissociated. *Answer* (a) 3.00, (b) 13.013, (c) 13.7, (d) 0.983

20.14 The reagent bottles labeled "Dilute NaOH" and "Dilute HCl" that are commonly found in the laboratory usually contain 6 M solutions of the substances. Calculate the $[H^+]$, $[OH^-]$, pH, and pOH for each reagent, assuming that the solutes are completely ionized or dissociated.

Acid Ionization Constant

20.15 What is the concentration of IO^- in equilibrium with $[H^+] = 0.035$ mol/L and $[HIO] = 0.427$ mol/L? $K_a = 2.3 \times 10^{-11}$ for HIO.

20.16 What is the concentration of HF in equilibrium with $[H^+] = 0.327$ mol/L and $[F^-] = 2.6 \times 10^{-3}$ mol/L? $K_a = 6.5 \times 10^{-4}$ for HF. *Answer* 1.3 mol/L

20.17 What is the concentration of CN^- in equilibrium with $[HCN] = 0.0123$ mol/L and pH 3.56? $K_a = 6.2 \times 10^{-10}$ for HCN.

20.18 Calculate the concentrations of all the species present in a 0.100 M solution of HIO. $K_a = 2.3 \times 10^{-11}$ for hypoiodous acid. *Answer* $[H^+] = [IO^-] = 1.5 \times 10^{-6}$ mol/L, $[HIO] = 0.100$ mol/L

20.19 Find the concentrations of the various species present in a 0.025 M solution of hydrofluoric acid, HF. What is the pH of the solution? $K_a = 6.5 \times 10^{-4}$ for HF.

20.20 Calculate the concentrations of all the species present in a 0.35 M benzoic acid solution. $K_a = 6.6 \times 10^{-5}$ for C_6H_5COOH. *Answer* $[H^+] = [C_6H_5COO^-] = 4.8 \times 10^{-3}$ mol/L, $[C_6H_5COOH] = 0.35$ mol/L

20.21* The ionization constant for acetic acid,
$$CH_3COOH(aq) + H_2O(l) \rightleftharpoons CH_3COO^- + H_3O^+$$
is 1.754×10^{-5} at 25 °C. What is the extent of ionization of the molecules in (a) a 0.100 M solution and (b) a 0.0100 M solution?

20.22* What is the percent ionization in a 0.0500 M solution of formic acid? $K_a = 1.772 \times 10^{-4}$ for HCOOH.

20.23* Calculate the percent ionization and the pH for each of the following solutions of nitrous acid: (a) 1.0 mol/L, (b) 0.10 mol/L, (c) 0.010 mol/L, and (d) 0.0010 mol/L. $K_a = 7.2 \times 10^{-4}$ for HNO_2. *Answer* (a) 2.7%, 1.57; (b) 8.1%, 2.09; (c) 23%, 2.64; (d) 54%, 3.27

20.24 Calculate the ionization constant K_a for an acid that is 1.25% ionized in a 0.250 M solution of the acid.

20.25 A 0.4000 M solution of oxalic acid, $H_2C_2O_4$, is 27.0%

ionized into H^+ and $HC_2O_4^-$ ions. Neglect the second ionization of $HC_2O_4^-$ to give H^+ and $C_2O_4^{2-}$. (a) What is the pH of the solution? (b) Calculate K_1 from the above data. *Answer* (a) 0.967, (b) 3.99×10^{-2}

20.26* Which solution will have the lowest pH: (a) 0.10 M $HClO_2$ ($pK_a = 1.96$); (b) 0.10 M HCN ($pK_a = 9.21$); (c) 0.10 M HF ($pK_a = 3.19$); or (d) 0.10 M HClO ($pK_a = 7.538$)?

Base Ionization Constant

20.27 What is the value of K_b for CN^-, given the following equilibrium concentrations: $[CN^-] = 0.37$ mol/L, $[HCN] = 1.3 \times 10^{-3}$ mol/L, and $[OH^-] = 4.6 \times 10^{-3}$ mol/L?

20.28 What is the concentration of $[OH^-]$ in equilibrium with $[CH_3COO^-] = 7.5 \times 10^{-3}$ mol/L and $[CH_3COOH] = 0.092$ mol/L? $K_b = 5.701 \times 10^{-10}$ for CH_3COO^-.

20.29 Calculate the pH of a solution containing $[HNO_2] = 3.2 \times 10^{-6}$ mol/L and $[NO_2^-] = 0.36$ mol/L. $K_b = 1.4 \times 10^{-11}$ for NO_2^-. *Answer* 8.20

20.30 What is the pH of a 0.13 M CN^- solution? $K_b = 1.6 \times 10^{-5}$ for CN^-.

20.31 Calculate the pH of a 0.50 M F^- solution. $K_b = 1.5 \times 10^{-11}$ for F^-. *Answer* 8.43

20.32 Calculate the values of K_b for the conjugate base of (a) HF, $K_a = 6.5 \times 10^{-4}$ for HF; (b) HNCS, $K_a = 69$ for the acid; and (c) HIO_4, $K_a = 5.6 \times 10^{-9}$ for HIO_4.

20.33 Which ion, Cl^- or CN^-, has the larger value of K_b? $K_a = 3 \times 10^8$ for HCl and 6.2×10^{-10} for HCN. *Answer* CN^-

20.34 A weak base, B, reacts only to the extent of 3.2% with water in a 0.100 M solution. Calculate K_b for this base.

20.35* Electrical conductance measurements at 18 °C show that the weak base $NH_3(aq)$ is 1.4% ionized in a 0.1000 M solution, 4.0% ionized in a 0.01000 M solution, and 12% ionized in a 0.0010 M solution. (a) Find the pH of each solution. (b) Calculate K_b for each solution. *Answer* (a) 11.15, 10.60, 10.08; (b) 2.0×10^{-5}, 1.7×10^{-5}, 2×10^{-5}

Additional Problems

20.36 What is the molarity of a 0.13 N solution of (a) H_2SO_4, (b) KOH, and (c) HNO_3? Assume complete reaction of all of the H^+ or OH^-. *Answer* (a) 0.065 mol/L, (b) 0.13 mol/L, (c) 0.13 mol/L

20.37 If 100.00 g of $Ba(OH)_2 \cdot 8H_2O$ is dissolved in enough water to make 1.000 L of solution, what is the normality of the solution? Assume that the $Ba(OH)_2$ will release both OH^- ions in an acid–base reaction. *Answer* 0.6340 equiv./L

20.38 Given the following heats of formation at 25 °C, 0 for H^+, -332.63 kJ/mol for F^-, -246.0 kJ/mol for Cl^-, -167.16 kJ/mol for $HCl(aq)$, and -320.08 kJ/mol for $HF(aq)$, calculate $\Delta H°$ for the ionization of $HCl(aq)$ and of $HF(aq)$. Which acid would yield more heat if equal molar amounts were allowed to react with solutions of sodium hydroxide? *Answer* -12.55 kJ/mol HF, -78.8 kJ/mol HCl, HCl

20.39* At 25 °C, the value of pK for the following reaction of deuterium oxide (heavy water):

$$2D_2O(l) \rightleftharpoons D_3O^+ + OD^-$$

is 14.869. (a) What is the value of K? (b) Under equilibrium conditions, what are the values of $[D_3O^+]$ and $[OD^-]$? (c) What is the pD of pure D_2O? (d) What is the relation between pD and pOD? (e) Give a suitable definition in terms of pD for an acidic solution in this solvent system.

Consider the following acid–base reactions taking place in pure D_2O:

$$CH_3COOH + D_2O \rightleftharpoons HD_2O^+ + CH_3COO^-$$
$$NH_3 + D_2O \rightleftharpoons NH_3D^+ + OD^-$$

Which substances are acting as (f) water-ion acids, (g) classical bases, (h) Brønsted-Lowry acids, (i) Brønsted-Lowry bases?

The equilibrium constant for the reaction

$$D_2O(l) + H_2O(l) \rightleftharpoons 2HDO(l)$$

is 3.56 at 25 °C. (j) If we prepare an equimolar solution of D_2O and H_2O, which is essentially 27.7 M in each, what will be the concentration of HDO once equilibrium has been established? *Answer* (a) 1.35×10^{-15}; (b) 3.67×10^{-8} mol/L; (c) 7.435; (d) pD + pOD = pK = 14.869; (e) the solution is acidic if pD < 7.435; (f) CH_3COOH, HD_2O^+; (g) none; (h) CH_3COOH, HD_2O^+; (i) D_2O, CH_3COO^-; (j) 28 mol/L

CHAPTER 21

Ions and Ionic Equilibria

Over the years, many people surely have been drawn to the study of chemistry by the sights and smells of a chemistry laboratory. It seems likely that this will always be the case. There is a fascination to the changing colors when solutions are mixed, the sudden appearance of solids where there were no solids, the rapid bubbling up of a gas. Such events are all part of one of the oldest areas of chemistry—the subject of this chapter— ions in solution.

"Wet chemistry," as it is sometimes called, once provided the only way to identify the metals in an alloy or the ions in a mineral. For such an analysis, the substance under study is dissolved in an appropriate acidic or alkaline solution. Then the ions present are separated and identified by the ingenious application of the principles of equilibrium, so that one ion or group of ions can be precipitated or dissolved, while others remain either in solution or undissolved. Some of you may have the opportunity to follow such a qualitative analysis scheme in laboratory work associated with this or another chemistry course.

Today analysis is often performed by electronic instruments. However, wet methods are quick and reliable, and remain in use in many applications. To mention just a few, methods based on the fundamentals presented in this chapter are used to determine the concentration of CO_2 in the atmosphere, the acetic acid content of vinegar, the HCO_3^- concentration in antacid tablets such as Alka Seltzer, the strength of paint removal and rust removal solutions, the ions present in hard water, and the concentration of metal ions in minerals, blood, and urine.

ACID–BASE EQUILIBRIA

21.1 REACTIONS OF IONS WITH WATER

Let's think for a moment of what happens when ions are added to pure water. The ions enter an environment in which water molecules are in equilibrium with hydrogen ions and hydroxide ions. Additional equilibria dependent on the interactions of the added ions with water will be established.

All ions in aqueous solution are hydrated—surrounded by water molecules— as a result of attraction between the ions and the polar water molecules (Section 14.3). For example, the hydration of potassium ion can be represented as follows:

$$K^+ + nH_2O(l) \rightleftharpoons [K(H_2O)_n]^+ \qquad (21.1)$$

The number of water molecules varies and is usually not known. The strength of the forces of attraction between the ion and the water molecules that surround it also varies. Some ions undergo only hydration in aqueous solution. Others enter into Brønsted-Lowry acid–base equilibria that result in the formation of acidic or alkaline solutions.

The three types of ions, (a) those that are simply hydrated, (b) those that react to give H_3O^+, and (c) those that react to give OH^-, are discussed below. The types of salts formed by these ions are discussed in Section 21.2. Table 21.1 gives examples of the various types of ions and salts. We suggest that you refer to this table as you read the following sections.

a. Anions or cations that simply become hydrated   Anions are potentially proton acceptors, that is, Brønsted-Lowry bases (Section 20.1). The anions that are simply hydrated in aqueous solution are all weaker bases than water—they cannot take protons away from water molecules. These are the anions above water as a base in Table 20.1 (Section 20.1); they are the conjugate bases of strong acids. We think of these anions as undergoing no reaction with water. Nitrate ion, for example, is simply hydrated and has no effect on the pH of an aqueous solution.

$$NO_3^- + nH_2O(l) \rightleftharpoons [NO_3(H_2O)_n]^- \qquad (21.2)$$

The hydration of a cation occurs by attraction of the negative end of the water dipole to the cation. Cations with low polarizing ability—the large cations of low charge—hold their associated water molecules loosely and so are simply hydrated (e.g., K^+, Equation 21.1). These are the same cations that form ionic hydroxides—those of elements from the lithium family, the larger members of the beryllium family (Ca, Sr, Ba, and Ra), and also the lanthanides and actinides.

b. Anions that react with water to give OH^-   The anions that give alkaline aqueous solutions are stronger bases than water (below H_2O as a base in Table 20.1). They are the conjugate bases of weak acids and establish equilibria because they are able to attract protons away from water molecules. These anions are the winners in the competition for the protons, and in their presence water reacts as an acid. By taking protons from the water molecules they leave behind OH^- ions that can make the solution alkaline.

For example,

anions that are stronger bases than water $\longrightarrow$ *alkaline solutions*

$$F^- + H_2O(l) \rightleftharpoons HF(aq) + OH^- \qquad K_b = 1.5 \times 10^{-11} \qquad (21.3)$$

$$CN^- + H_2O(l) \rightleftharpoons HCN(aq) + OH^- \qquad K_b = 1.6 \times 10^{-5} \qquad (21.4)$$

$$S^{2-} + H_2O(l) \rightleftharpoons HS^- + OH^- \qquad K_b = 3 \times 10^{-2} \qquad (21.5)$$

$\text{base}_1 \qquad \text{acid}_2 \qquad \text{acid}_1 \qquad \text{base}_2$

As you can see from the K_b values for F^-, CN^-, and S^{2-}, there is a wide variation in the strengths of these anionic bases. The weaker the acid, the stronger its conjugate base.

Table 21.1
Types of Ions and Salts in Aqueous Solution   Common examples of each type of ion and salt are given.

Cations / Anions	*Cations that simply become hydrated* Li^+, Na^+, K^+, Mg^{2+}, Ca^{2+}, Ba^{2+}	*Cations that react with water to give H_3O^+* NH_4^+, Be^{2+}, Zn^{2+}, Al^{3+}, Fe^{3+}, Cr^{3+}, Cu^{2+}
Anions that simply become hydrated ClO_4^-, I^-, Br^-, Cl^-, ClO_3^-, NO_3^-	*Salts give neutral solutions* NaCl $CaCl_2$ KNO_3	*Salts give acidic solutions* NH_4Cl NH_4NO_3 $AlCl_3$ $Fe(NO_3)_3$
Anions that react with water to give OH^- NO_2^-, F^-, CH_3COO^-, HCO_3^-, CO_3^{2-}, CN^-, S^{2-}, PO_4^{3-}	*Salts give alkaline solutions* $Ba(CH_3COO)_2$ K_2CO_3 NaF KCN	*pH of salt solution varies—weakly acidic or weakly alkaline* NH_4CH_3COO NH_4NO_2 NH_4CN

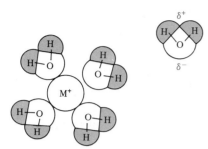

Figure 21.1
A Hydrated Metal Cation

c. Cations that react with water to give H_3O^+ The ammonium ion gives up a proton to a water molecule to yield an acidic solution. The ammonium ion and all other cations that give acidic solutions are stronger acids than water, and in reacting with these cations water is the proton acceptor — the base.

cation that is a stronger acid than water ⟶ *acidic solution*
$$NH_4^+ + H_2O \rightleftharpoons NH_3 + H_3O^+ \qquad K_a = 6.3 \times 10^{-10} \qquad \textbf{(21.6)}$$
acid₁   base₂   base₁   acid₂

A hydrated metal cation that gives an acidic aqueous solution does so by donating a proton from an associated water molecule; for example,

hydrated cations that are stronger acids than water ⟶ *acidic solutions*
$$[Al(H_2O)_6]^{3+} + H_2O(l) \rightleftharpoons [Al(H_2O)_5(OH)]^{2+} + H_3O^+ \qquad \textbf{(21.7)}$$
acid₁   base₂   base₁   acid₂

For simplicity, the bound water molecules are often omitted in writing the equations.

$$Al^{3+} + 2H_2O(l) \rightleftharpoons [AlOH]^{2+} + H_3O^+ \qquad K_a = 1.4 \times 10^{-5} \qquad \textbf{(21.8)}$$

In a hydrated metal cation, the electrons on the oxygen atoms of the water molecules are attracted to the positively charged metal ion (Figure 21.1). This attraction results in general displacement of electron density toward the metal ion and enhances the polarity of the oxygen–hydrogen bonds in the water molecule, exactly as for an oxo acid (Section 20.6).

Any property of the metal ion that increases its attraction for electrons favors this displacement and increases the polarity of the O—H bond. The most important of these properties are small radius and large positive charge — in other words, a high charge-to-size ratio and thereby, a high polarizing ability. These properties are increasingly evident in metal ions further to the right in the periodic table. As a consequence, cations such as $[Cu(H_2O)_4]^{2+}$, $[Al(H_2O)_6]^{3+}$, and $[Fe(H_2O)_6]^{3+}$ behave as weak acids toward water.

Anions that are stronger bases than H_2O ⟶ alkaline aqueous solutions
Cations that are stronger acids than H_2O ⟶ acidic aqueous solutions

---

EXAMPLE 21.1
Reactions of Ions with Water

How will the following ions react with water: I^-, NO_2^-, K^+, Bi^{3+}, and Be^{2+}? Write chemical equations showing the reactions that take place. Will the resulting solutions be neutral, acidic, or alkaline?

The I^- ion is the conjugate base of a strong acid (see Table 20.1), HI, and therefore is a weaker base than water and will simply be hydrated in aqueous solution. The NO_2^- ion is the conjugate base of a weak acid, HNO_2, and would be expected to react as a base, to give an alkaline solution (in the absence of other ions that influence the pH).

$$NO_2^- + H_2O(l) \rightleftharpoons HNO_2(aq) + OH^-$$

The hydrated ions of metals of small radius and high charge are stronger acids than water and donate protons to water molecules. The larger K^+ ion [charge-to-size ratio, 7.5], from the lithium family, does not react with water except to become hydrated, while the smaller, highly charged Bi^{3+} ion [charge-to-size ratio, 31] would be expected to react to give an acidic solution.

$$Bi^{3+} + 2H_2O(l) \rightleftharpoons [BiOH]^{2+} + H_3O^+$$

The beryllium ion is the smallest of the cations of elements in its family [charge-to-size ratio for Be^{2+}, 57], and can be expected to give an acidic solution.

$$Be^{2+} + 2H_2O(l) \rightleftharpoons [BeOH]^+ + H_3O^+$$

Exercise Describe how the following ions will react with water: (a) CH_3COO^-, (b) NO_3^-, (c) Ca^{2+}, and (d) Zn^{2+}. Write chemical equations showing the reactions that occur. Will these reactions produce neutral, acidic, or alkaline solutions?

Answer (a) $CH_3COO^- + H_2O(l) \rightleftharpoons CH_3COOH(aq) + OH^-$, alkaline; (b) hydration only; (c) hydration only; (d) $Zn^{2+} + H_2O(l) \rightarrow [Zn(OH)]^+ + H^+$, acidic

The reactions of ions or ionic compounds with water to give acidic or alkaline solutions have traditionally been called *hydrolysis reactions.* "Hydrolysis" is a general term for reactions in which the water molecule is split. The **hydrolysis of an ion** is the reaction of an ion with water to give either H_3O^+ or OH^-, plus whatever reaction product is formed by the ion.

In summary, anions that are the conjugate bases of strong acids, as well as cations of the metals of the lithium family and the larger members of the beryllium family (as well as the actinides and lanthanides), simply become hydrated in aqueous solution and do not cause a change in the pH. Anions that are stronger bases than water—the conjugate bases of weak acids—yield OH⁻ in reactions with water. Ammonium ion and small, highly charged cations of metals yield H₃O⁺ upon reaction with water.

21.2 THE BEHAVIOR OF SALTS TOWARD WATER

Keeping in mind the various possibilities for the behavior of individual ions toward water, we can now examine what happens when salts are dissolved in water. On the basis of the acidity or alkalinity of their solutions, there are four types of salts. (Examples of each type are given in Table 21.1.)

1. *Salts of cations and anions neither of which react with water—neutral solutions.* Since neither ion reacts significantly with water, only hydration of the ions occurs and the solutions are neutral. Common salts of this type are the perchlorates, chlorates, nitrates, chlorides, bromides, and iodides of the lithium family and larger beryllium family metal cations.

2. *Salts of cations that do not react with water and anions that are stronger bases than water—alkaline solutions.* Only the anions react with water to a significant extent. The resulting solutions are alkaline, with the anion reacting as illustrated in Equations (21.3)–(21.5). Common salts of this type are those carbonates, sulfides, and cyanides of the lithium and beryllium family cations that are soluble. Because the sulfate, nitrite, and fluoride ions are significantly weaker bases, their salts give very slightly alkaline solutions.

3. *Salts of the ammonium ion or cations which when hydrated are stronger acids than water, with anions that do not react with water—acidic solutions.* The hydrated cations are proton donors and react with water to give H_3O^+. The ammonium ion reacts according to Equation (21.6) and the metal cations as illustrated in Equation (21.7). Salts of this type are the perchlorates, chlorates, nitrates, chlorides, bromides, and iodides of the ammonium ion and most metals *other* than those mentioned in paragraph (1).

4. *Salts of cations and anions both of which react with water—pH varies with salt.* A limited number of ammonium salts containing anions more basic than water dissolve in water to give essentially neutral solutions. The cations and anions of these salts react to about the same extent with water, which is an indication that the ions are about equal in strength, one as an acid and the other as a base. The most common example is ammonium acetate, $NH_4(CH_3COO)$, which contains ions of about equal K values. The overall reaction is the sum of the following equilibria:

$$NH_4^+ + H_2O(l) \rightleftharpoons NH_3(aq) + H_3O^+ \qquad K = 6.3 \times 10^{-10} \quad \textbf{(21.9)}$$
$$CH_3COO^- + H_2O(l) \rightleftharpoons CH_3COOH(aq) + OH^- \qquad K = 5.7 \times 10^{-10} \quad \textbf{(21.10)}$$
$$H_3O^+ + OH^- \rightleftharpoons 2H_2O(l) \qquad K = 1 \times 10^{14} \quad \textbf{(21.11)}$$
$$\overline{NH_4^+ + CH_3COO^- \rightleftharpoons CH_3COOH(aq) + NH_3(aq)} \qquad \textbf{(21.12)}$$

(The ionization constants for such reactions are discussed further in the next section.)

A soluble salt formed by an anion and cation that both react with water, but differ in the extent to which they react, can give either an acidic or an alkaline solution. The ion which reacts to the greatest extent determines the pH. For example, an ammonium cyanide solution is slightly alkaline because cyanide ion ($K = 1.6 \times 10^{-5}$, Equation 21.4) reacts with water to a greater extent than ammonium ion ($K = 6.3 \times 10^{-10}$, Equation 21.6).

Note that the reactions of some salts of this type are driven to completion by the formation of solid hydroxides and gases. For example, aluminum sulfide reacts with water to give aluminum hydroxide and hydrogen sulfide, leaving few ions in solution.

$$Al_2S_3(s) + 6H_2O(l) \longrightarrow 2Al(OH)_3(s) + 3H_2S(g)$$

In summary, based upon the reactions of their ions with water there are four types of salts: (1) those that give neutral solutions because neither ion reacts with water to a significant extent, (2) those that give alkaline solutions because only the anion reacts with water, (3) those that give acidic solutions because only the cation reacts with water, and (4) those in which both ions react with water and the result depends upon the relative extent of the reactions of the two ions. (Examples of these four types of salts are given in Table 21.1.)

EXAMPLE 21.2
Reactions of Ions with Water

Predict whether aqueous solutions of the following salts would be acidic, alkaline, or close to neutral: (a) KCl, (b) NH_4NO_2, (c) $AlBr_3$, and (d) Na(HCOO), a salt of formic acid, HCOOH, a weak organic acid.

(a) Potassium chloride, KCl, is a salt of a cation, K^+, that is a weaker acid than water and an anion, Cl^-, that is a weaker base than water. Because neither ion reacts with water to any appreciable extent, a KCl solution will be neutral.

(b) Ammonium nitrite, NH_4NO_2, is the salt of a cation and an anion both of which react with water. A solution of this salt will be close to neutral and whether it is slightly alkaline or slightly acidic will depend upon the extent to which the individual ions react with water. [The solution will be slightly acidic.]

(c) Aluminum bromide, $AlBr_3$, is the salt of a cation that will react with water because it is a stronger acid than water and an anion that will not react because it is a weaker base than water. Therefore, the solution will be acidic.

(d) Sodium formate, Na(HCOO), is the salt of a cation that does not react with water and an anion that is a stronger base than water (because it is the anion of a weak acid). The solution produced will therefore have an excess of OH^- and will be alkaline.

Exercise Predict whether aqueous solutions of the following salts would be acidic, alkaline, or close to neutral: (a) $Fe(NO_3)_3$, (b) NH_4CN, (c) KI, and (d) $LiCH_3COO$. *Answer* (a) acidic, (b) close to neutral, (c) close to neutral, (d) alkaline

---

21.3 EQUILIBRIUM CONSTANTS FOR THE REACTIONS OF IONS AND SALTS WITH WATER; pH OF SALT SOLUTIONS

The equilibrium constants for the reactions of ions with water are simply K_a's and K_b's for acids and bases that happen to be ions. For example, for the reaction of an anion that gives an alkaline aqueous solution,

$$A^- + H_2O(l) \rightleftharpoons HA(aq) + OH^- \qquad K_b = \frac{[HA][OH^-]}{[A^-]}$$

For acetate ion, for example,

$$CH_3COO^- + H_2O(l) \rightleftharpoons CH_3COOH(aq) + OH^- \qquad K_b = \frac{[CH_3COOH][OH^-]}{[CH_3COO^-]}$$

The equilibrium constants for the reactions of an acid and its conjugate base with water are related to the ion product constant of water by the expression $K_w = K_a K_b$ (Section 20.13). The K_b for acetate ion can be found from K_w and the value of K_a for acetic acid as follows:

$$K_b = \underset{\substack{\text{for} \\ \text{acetate} \\ \text{ion}}}{\underbrace{\frac{[CH_3COOH][OH^-]}{[CH_3COO^-]}}} = \frac{K_w}{\underset{\substack{\text{for acetic} \\ \text{acid}}}{K_a}} = \frac{1.00 \times 10^{-14}}{1.75 \times 10^{-5}} = 5.70 \times 10^{-10} \quad \textbf{(21.13)}$$

This type of relationship is particularly useful because K_a values are more likely to be found tabulated than are the K_b values for anions.

The K_a and K_b values for the reactions of an acidic cation and its conjugate base with water are related by a similar equation. For ammonium ion

$$\underset{\text{for } NH_4^+}{} NH_4^+ + H_2O(l) \rightleftharpoons NH_3(aq) + H_3O^+$$

$$K_a = \frac{[NH_3][H^+]}{[NH_4^+]} = \frac{K_w}{\underset{\text{for } NH_3}{K_b}} = \frac{1.00 \times 10^{-14}}{1.6 \times 10^{-5}} = 6.3 \times 10^{-10} \quad \textbf{(21.14)}$$

$$K_{\substack{\text{basic} \\ \text{anion}}} = \frac{K_w}{K_{\substack{\text{conjugate} \\ \text{acid}}}}$$

The pH of a solution of a salt in which only one ion reacts with water can be found from the known concentration of the solution and the K_a or K_b for the ion that reacts with water. Equations like (21.13) or (21.14) are used, if necessary, to find the equilibrium constant that is needed.

EXAMPLE 21.3
Reactions of Ions with Water

What is the pH of a 0.10 M KCN solution? For HCN, $K_a = 6.2 \times 10^{-10}$.

For this salt of a cation that does not react with water and an anion that does react with water, the only reaction of importance is that of the cyanide ion. Consequently, we would expect the solution to be alkaline due to the reaction

$$CN^- + H_2O(l) \rightleftharpoons HCN(aq) + OH^-$$

First, we find K_b for the CN^- ion from the K_a for HCN.

$$K_b = \frac{[HCN][OH^-]}{[CN^-]} = \frac{K_w}{K_a} = \frac{1.00 \times 10^{-14}}{6.2 \times 10^{-10}} = 1.6 \times 10^{-5}$$

Letting $x = [OH^-]$, we set up our usual equilibrium problem table.

	CN^- + H_2O $\rightleftharpoons$ HCN + OH^-		
Initial	0.10	0	0
Change	$-x$	$+x$	$+x$
Equilibrium	$0.10 - x$	x	x

Substitution into the equilibrium expression gives

$$K_b = \frac{(x)(x)}{0.10 - x} \simeq \frac{x^2}{0.10} = 1.6 \times 10^{-5}$$

$$x = 1.3 \times 10^{-3} \text{ mol/L} = [OH^-]$$

The approximation $0.10 - (1.3 \times 10^{-3}) \simeq 0.10$ is valid and the OH^- ion concentration is 1.3×10^{-3} mol/L. Next we find the pOH and the pH.

$$pOH = -\log [OH^-] = -\log (1.3 \times 10^{-3}) = 2.89$$
$$pH = 14.00 - pOH = 14.00 - 2.89 = 11.11$$

The pH of the solution is 11.11. As we predicted, the solution is alkaline.

Exercise What is the pH of a 0.10 M NH_4Cl solution? $K_b = 1.6 \times 10^{-5}$ for NH_3. *Answer* 5.10

The equilibrium constant for the reaction with water of a salt of two ions, both of which react with water, is determined by three equilibria (Section 21.2). For NH_4A, a salt of ammonia with any anion that reacts with water,

$$NH_4^+ + H_2O(l) \rightleftharpoons NH_3(aq) + H_3O^+ \qquad K_a = \frac{K_w}{K_{b,NH_3}}$$

$$A^- + H_2O(l) \rightleftharpoons HA(aq) + OH^- \qquad K_b = \frac{K_w}{K_{a,HA}}$$

$$\underline{H_3O^+ + OH^- \rightleftharpoons 2H_2O(l) \qquad K = \frac{1}{K_w}}$$

$$NH_4^+ + A^- \rightleftharpoons NH_3(aq) + HA(aq)$$

The equilibrium constant for the overall reaction is equal to the product of the equilibrium constants for the three reactions:

$$K = \left(\frac{K_w}{K_{a,HA}}\right)\left(\frac{K_w}{K_{b,NH_3}}\right)\left(\frac{1}{K_w}\right) = \frac{K_w}{K_{a,HA}K_{b,NH_3}} \qquad (21.15)$$

This expression applies to ammonium acetate (see Equations 21.9–21.12) or to any ammonium salt with a basic anion. A similar relationship applies to any salt in which both ions react with water to give products that remain in solution.

$$\underbrace{K}_{\substack{K\ for \\ reaction \\ of\ salt \\ with \\ water}} = \frac{K_w}{\underbrace{K_a}_{\substack{For\ conjugate \\ acid\ of\ anion \\ in\ salt}} \underbrace{K_b}_{\substack{For\ conjugate \\ base\ of\ cation \\ in\ salt}}} \qquad (21.16)$$

When $K_b > K_a$ the solution will be alkaline; when $K_a > K_b$ the solution will be acidic.

EXAMPLE 21.4
Reactions of Ions with Water

What is the value of the equilibrium constant for the reaction of NH_4CN with water? Would the resulting solution be acidic or alkaline? $K_a = 6.2 \times 10^{-10}$ for HCN and $K_b = 1.6 \times 10^{-5}$ for NH_3.

The equilibria involved are

$$NH_4^+ + H_2O(l) \rightleftharpoons NH_3(aq) + H_3O^+ \qquad K_a = \frac{K_w}{K_{b,NH_3}}$$

$$CN^- + H_2O(l) \rightleftharpoons HCN(aq) + OH^- \qquad K_b = \frac{K_w}{K_{a,HCN}}$$

$$\underline{H_3O^+ + OH^- \rightleftharpoons 2H_2O(l) \qquad K = \frac{1}{K_w}}$$

$$NH_4^+ + CN^- \rightleftharpoons NH_3(aq) + HCN(aq)$$

and the equilibrium constant is

$$K = \frac{K_w}{K_{a,HCN}K_{b,NH_3}} \frac{(1.00 \times 10^{-14})}{(6.2 \times 10^{-10})(1.6 \times 10^{-5})} = 1.0$$

The value of the equilibrium constant is 1.0. We would predict a solution of NH_4CN to be somewhat alkaline because K_a for HCN is less than K_b for NH_3. [A 0.01 M solution of NH_4CN has a pH of 9.2.]

Exercise What is the value of the equilibrium constant for the reaction of ammonium formate, $NH_4(HCOO)$, with water? Would the resulting solution be acidic or alkaline? $K_a = 1.77 \times 10^{-4}$ for HCOOH and $K_b = 1.6 \times 10^{-5}$ for NH_3. *Answer* 3.5×10^{-6}, acidic

21.4 THE COMMON ION EFFECT

Aqueous solutions that contain a number of different types of ions are commonly encountered in practical chemistry. The concentrations of all of the ions present must simultaneously satisfy the equilibrium constant expressions for whatever equilibria are possible in a given solution. If more of a particular ion is introduced into a solution, whatever equilibria that it can participate in will be disturbed and will change in accordance with Le Chatelier's principle until the equilibrium constant expressions are once again satisfied. To understand how this happens, we can consider the simple case in which more of one ion is added to a solution in which a single equilibrium involving that ion has been established.

An ion added to a solution that already contains some of that ion is called a **common ion.** What happens if a small amount of sodium hydroxide is added to a saturated solution of magnesium hydroxide? The equilibrium in the solution will be displaced by the added hydroxide ions. The Na^+ ion is not a common ion, nor does it react with water; therefore, it is a spectator ion and has no effect on the equilibrium. The added hydroxide ions combine with magnesium ions until equilibrium is restored. As a result, the concentration of Mg^{2+} will decrease and more solid magnesium hydroxide will form.

$$\overset{\overleftarrow{\qquad \underset{a\ common\ ion}{OH^-} \qquad}}{Mg(OH)_2(s) \rightleftharpoons Mg^{2+} + 2OH^-}$$

The addition of the common ion has decreased the solubility of magnesium hydroxide. This change is an example of the **common ion effect:** a displacement of an ionic equilibrium by an excess of one or more of the ions involved.

The common ion effect is frequently used to control the pH of a solution of a weak acid or base. The common ion may be added as a soluble salt with another ion that does not react with water (such as Na^+ or Cl^-). For example, consider the addition of ammonium chloride to a solution of ammonia:

$$\overset{\overleftarrow{\qquad NH_4^+ \qquad}}{NH_3(aq) + H_2O(l) \rightleftharpoons NH_4^+ + OH^-}$$

The chloride ion does not react with water and is thus a spectator ion. The NH_4^+ from the salt increases the total concentration of NH_4^+ and displaces the equilibrium toward the formation of NH_3. Therefore, the solution becomes less alkaline because the concentration of OH^- is reduced by its reaction with NH_4^+.

The addition of sodium acetate, $Na(CH_3COO)$, to an acetic acid solution similarly displaces the equilibrium toward the formation of acetic acid and makes the solution less acidic.

$$\overset{\overleftarrow{\qquad CH_3COO^- \qquad}}{CH_3COOH(aq) + H_2O(l) \rightleftharpoons CH_3COO^- + H_3O^+}$$

EXAMPLE 21.5
Common Ion Effect

What is the pH of a solution which is 0.10 M in NH_3 and 0.10 M in NH_4NO_3? $K_b = 1.6 \times 10^{-5}$ for NH_3.

The pH of the solution is controlled by the ammonia–water equilibrium:

$$NH_3(aq) + H_2O(l) \rightleftharpoons NH_4^+ + OH^- \qquad K_b = \frac{[NH_4^+][OH^-]}{[NH_3]}$$

Let $x = [OH^-]$. The ammonium ion concentration at equilibrium is the amount formed by the above reaction plus the amount added as ammonium nitrate (because ammonium nitrate is soluble and is a strong electrolyte).

	NH_3	+ H_2O $\rightleftharpoons$	NH_4^+	+ OH^-
Initial	0.10		0.10	0
Change	$-x$		$+x$	$+x$
Equilibrium	$0.10 - x$		$0.10 + x$	x

These values can be used in the equilibrium constant expression.

$$K_b = \frac{(0.10 + x)(x)}{(0.10 - x)} = 1.6 \times 10^{-5}$$

The equilibrium reaction is shifted toward the reactants side by the added ammonium ion. Therefore, we can assume that x is small relative to the initial NH_3 and NH_4^+ concentrations, so that $(0.10 + x) \simeq 0.10$ and $(0.10 - x) \simeq 0.10$, giving

$$\frac{(0.10)(x)}{(0.10)} = 1.6 \times 10^{-5}$$

$$x = 1.6 \times 10^{-5} \text{ M} = [OH^-]$$

The approximation is valid. The pOH and pH of the solution are

$$pOH = -\log [OH^-] = -\log (1.6 \times 10^{-5}) = 4.80$$
$$pH = 14.00 - pOH = 14.00 - 4.80 = 9.20$$

The pH of the solution is 9.20. [For comparison — the pH of a 0.1 M NH_3 solution is 11.1, showing that the alkalinity of the solution has been decreased by the added NH_4^+ ion.]

Exercise What is the pH of a solution which is 0.100 M in KClO and 0.050 M in HClO? $K_a = 2.90 \times 10^{-8}$ for HClO. *Answer* 7.82

21.5 BUFFER SOLUTIONS

A **buffer solution** is a solution that resists changes in pH when small amounts of acid or base are added to it. The combination in solution of similar concentrations of a weak acid and the anion which is its conjugate base produces a buffer solution. Small amounts of added base react with the non-ionized acid,

$$OH^- + HA(aq) \rightleftharpoons A^- + H_2O(l)$$

and small amounts of added acid react with the basic anion,

$$H_3O^+ + A^- \rightleftharpoons HA(aq) + H_2O(l)$$

A solution of a base, say ammonia, plus the cation which is its conjugate acid (the ammonium ion in this case) can similarly act as a buffer:

$$OH^- + NH_4^+ \rightleftharpoons NH_3(aq) + H_2O(l)$$

$$H_3O^+ + NH_3(aq) \rightleftharpoons NH_4^+ + H_2O(l)$$

Such a combination of a weak acid and its conjugate base (HA/A$^-$) or of a weak base and its conjugate acid (e.g., NH_3/NH_4^+) is known as a *buffer pair*. The common anion or cation (that is, the conjugate base or acid) is added as a salt with an ion that does not react with water.

By rearranging the K_a expression for a weak acid and the K_b expression for ammonia, we can see that the ratio of the concentrations of the two members of the buffer pair determines the pH of a buffered solution.

$$K_a = \frac{[H^+][A^-]}{[HA]} \qquad K_b = \frac{[NH_4^+][OH^-]}{[NH_3]}$$

$$[H^+] = \frac{[HA]}{[A^-]} K_a \qquad [OH^-] = \frac{[NH_3]}{[NH_4^+]} K_b$$

$$\text{(21.17a,b)}$$

Weak acid/conjugate base buffer pairs give solutions buffered in the acid pH range. Weak base/conjugate acid buffer pairs give solutions buffered in the alkaline pH range.

The narrow pH ranges necessary in the body fluids of animals are maintained by buffer systems. The H_2CO_3/HCO_3^- buffer pair plays a vital role in maintaining human blood at an almost constant pH of 7.4. Excess acid in the blood reacts with the HCO_3^- ion to form H_2CO_3. This acid decomposes into water and carbon dioxide, which is exhaled.

$$H^+ + HCO_3^- \rightleftharpoons H_2CO_3(aq) \rightleftharpoons H_2O(l) + CO_2(g)$$

Deep breathing, which is stimulated by excess acid in the blood, helps to drive the equilibria toward CO_2 formation and a decrease in $[H^+]$, while shallow breathing, which is stimulated by decreased acid in the blood, drives the equilibria in the opposite direction, causing an increase in $[H^+]$.

To demonstrate how a buffer works, we can calculate the change in pH when an acid or a base is added to a solution that contains a buffer pair. Let's consider a buffer solution that is 0.100 M in acetic acid and 0.100 M in potassium acetate. First we must find the pH of this solution, which we can do by using the rearranged K_a expression of Equation (21.17a).

Assume that the equilibrium concentrations of CH_3COOH and CH_3COO^- are essentially equal to their initial concentrations. [Since acetic acid is a weak acid and the added acetate ion shifts the equilibrium toward the acid, this is a reasonable assumption. The acid concentration remains essentially unchanged and almost all of the acetate ion comes from the added potassium acetate. In using Equations (21.17a) and (21.17b) for buffer solutions this type of assumption is always valid. An equivalent assumption was made in taking x as negligible in Example 21.5.]

$$[H^+] = \frac{[CH_3COOH]}{[CH_3COO^-]} \times 1.75 \times 10^{-5}$$

$$= \frac{0.100}{0.100} \times 1.75 \times 10^{-5} = 1.75 \times 10^{-5} \text{ mol/L}$$

$$pH = -\log(1.75 \times 10^{-5}) = 4.757$$

If 0.005 mol of potassium hydroxide (assume the volume does not change) is added to 1 L of this solution, what happens? The added base reacts with 0.005 mol of acetic acid.

$$\underset{0.005 \; mol}{CH_3COOH(aq)} + \underset{0.005 \; mol}{OH^-} \longrightarrow \underset{0.005 \; mol}{CH_3COO^-} + H_2O(l)$$

Table 21.2
**Effects of Added Potassium
Hydroxide and Hydrochloric Acid
on the pH of 0.100 M CH₃COOH/
0.100 M K(CH₃COO) Solution**

Table 21.2
**Effects of Added Potassium
Hydroxide and Hydrochloric Acid
on the pH of 0.100 M CH_3COOH/
0.100 M $K(CH_3COO)$ Solution**

KOH Added (mol/L)	$[H^+]$ (mol/L)	pH
0	1.75×10^{-5}	4.757
0.0001	1.75×10^{-5}	4.757
0.001	1.7×10^{-5}	4.77
0.005	1.6×10^{-5}	4.80
0.010	1.4×10^{-5}	4.85
0.050	0.58×10^{-5}	5.24

HCl Added (mol/L)	$[H^+]$ (mol/L)	pH
0	1.75×10^{-5}	4.757
0.0001	1.75×10^{-5}	4.757
0.001	1.8×10^{-5}	4.74
0.005	1.9×10^{-5}	4.72
0.010	2.1×10^{-5}	4.68
0.050	5.3×10^{-5}	4.28

The result is to decrease the concentration of acetic acid to 0.095 mol/L,

$$[CH_3COOH] = (0.100 - 0.005) \text{ mol/L} = 0.095 \text{ mol/L}$$

and increase the concentration of acetate ion to 0.105 mol/L,

$$[CH_3COO^-] = (0.100 + 0.005) \text{ mol/L} = 0.105 \text{ mol/L}$$

Using these concentrations of the buffer pair in Equation (21.17a) allows calculation of the pH:

$$[H^+] = \frac{0.095}{0.105} \times (1.75 \times 10^{-5}) = 1.6 \times 10^{-5} \text{ mol/L}$$
$$pH = -\log (1.6 \times 10^{-5}) = 4.80$$

The addition of 0.005 mol of KOH to the buffer solution has changed the pH by only 0.04. The pH of pure water would have changed from 7.00 to 9.30 if the same amount of KOH were added. A similar calculation for the addition of 0.005 mol of hydrochloric acid to 1 L of this buffer solution shows a decrease in pH from 4.757 to 4.72. A series of similar calculations for the addition of acid and base to this system (Table 21.2) further illustrates its resistance to pH change.

EXAMPLE 21.6
Common Ion Effect: Buffers

What ratio of $[HCOO^-]/[HCOOH]$ is needed to make a sodium formate–formic acid buffer solution of pH 3.80? $K_a = 1.77 \times 10^{-4}$ for formic acid, $HCOOH$.

The equilibrium is

$$HCOOH(aq) + H_2O(l) \rightleftharpoons H_3O^+ + HCOO^-$$

A pH of 3.80 corresponds to $[H^+] = 1.6 \times 10^{-4}$ mol/L. The ratio of acid to common ion in a buffer is given by Equation (21.17a). In this case

$$[H^+] = \frac{[HCOOH]}{[HCOO^-]} \times (1.77 \times 10^{-4}) = 1.6 \times 10^{-4}$$

$$\frac{[HCOO^-]}{[HCOOH]} = \frac{1.77 \times 10^{-4}}{1.6 \times 10^{-4}} = 1.1$$

The $[HCOO^-]/[HCOOH]$ ratio must be 1.1 to 1 to attain pH 3.80 with this buffer system. For example, if 1 M HCOOH is used, the solution must be 1.1 M in sodium formate.

Exercise What must be the concentration of fluoride ion in an NaF/HF buffer to give pH 4.00? Assume that solid NaF is added to a 0.10 M solution of HF without volume change. $K_a = 6.5 \times 10^{-4}$ for HF. *Answer* 0.65 mol/L

EXAMPLE 21.7
Common Ion Effect: Buffers

What is the pH of the 0.10 M NH_3/0.10 M NH_4NO_3 solution described in Example 21.5, which had a pH of 9.20, after 0.10 g (0.0025 mol) of solid NaOH has been added to 100.0 mL of the buffer? (Assume that the volume has not changed.) $K_b = 1.6 \times 10^{-5}$ for NH_3.

First we must determine the changes in the concentrations of NH_3 and NH_4^+ present after the addition of the NaOH. Then we can calculate $[OH^-]$ by using the

$[NH_3]/[NH_4^+]$ ratio in Equation (21.17b). Note that we are working with 100.0 mL, or 0.1000 L, of the solution, which therefore initially contains 0.010 mol of NH_4^+ and 0.010 mol of NH_3.

The 0.0025 mol of NaOH reacts with the NH_4^+, forming additional ammonia,

$$NH_4^+ \;\; + \;\; OH^- \;\; \longrightarrow \;\; NH_3(aq) \;+ H_2O(l)$$
$$\text{0.010 mol} \quad \text{0.0025 mol} \quad\quad \text{0.0025 mol}$$

and leaving 0.008 mol of unreacted NH_4^+,

$$(0.010 - 0.0025) \text{ mol } NH_4^+ = 0.008 \text{ mol } NH_4^+$$

giving $[NH_4^+] = 0.08$ mol/L. The total amount of NH_3 in the solution is increased to 0.013 mol,

$$(0.010 + 0.0025) \text{ mol } NH_3 = 0.013 \text{ mol } NH_3$$

giving $[NH_3] = 0.13$ mol/L. Using these values of $[NH_4^+]$ and $[NH_3]$ in Equation (21.17b) gives an OH^- concentration of

$$[OH^-] = \frac{[NH_3]}{[NH_4^+]} (1.6 \times 10^{-5}) = \left(\frac{0.13}{0.08}\right)(1.6 \times 10^{-5})$$
$$= 3 \times 10^{-5} \text{ mol/L}$$

or

$$pOH = -\log [OH^-] = -\log (3 \times 10^{-5}) = 4.5$$
$$pH = 14.00 - pOH = 14.00 - 4.5 = 9.5$$

The pH has changed from 9.20 to 9.5. [Pure water would have changed from pH 7.00 to pH 12.40.]

Exercise   What is the pH of the 0.10 M NH_3/0.10 M NH_4NO_3 buffer described above after 0.040 g (0.0010 mol) of solid NaOH is dissolved in 100.0 mL of the buffer?   *Answer* 9.3

A convenient relationship between pK_a and pH for a buffer solution can be derived from Equation (21.17a):

$$[H^+] = \frac{[HA]}{[A^-]} K_a$$

$$-\log [H^+] = -\log K_a - \log \frac{[HA]}{[A^-]}$$

$$pH = pK_a - \log \frac{[HA]}{[A^-]} \tag{21.18}$$

This is known as the Henderson-Hasselbach equation. It is an alternative way of expressing the relationship of Equation (21.17a) and is frequently used in the biological sciences.

Both the pH range in which a buffer is effective and the capacity of a buffer to resist changes in pH are limited. A buffer is best able to maintain a constant pH in the range of $pH = pK_a \pm 1$. In order to maintain a specified pH, often a concern in the biological sciences, an acid with a pK_a in the range indicated by the Henderson-Hasselbach equation can be selected. Note that for buffers in which the acid and anion concentrations are equal, $pH = pK_a$. For a base, the comparable relationship is

$$pOH = pK_b - \log \frac{[B]}{[BH^+]} \tag{21.19}$$

As for Equations (21.17a) and (21.17b) in using Equations (21.18) and (21.19) it is assumed that the equilibrium concentrations of the conjugate acid–base pair of the buffer are the same as their initial concentrations, usually a reasonable assumption.

In summary, the addition of a common ion to a solution that already contains some of that ion displaces any equilibria in which that ion participates. This effect, called the common ion effect, can be used to decrease the solubility of a salt or to control the pH of a solution of a weak acid or base. A solution of a weak acid becomes less acidic if the concentration of its anion is increased. Similarly, a solution of a weak base becomes less alkaline if the concentration of the cation derived from that base is increased. A buffer solution—a solution that maintains a reasonably constant pH despite the addition of small amounts of acid or base—contains roughly equal concentrations of a weak acid and its conjugate base or of a weak base and its conjugate acid. An acid buffer is most effective in the range of $pH = pK_a \pm 1$ ($pOH = pK_b \pm 1$ for an alkaline buffer).

21.6 LIMITATIONS ON THE USE OF EQUILIBRIUM CONSTANTS

The equilibrium calculations in a book such as this one and in the practical applications of chemistry frequently have similar goals: to verify what chemical intuition tells us will happen in a given chemical reaction or to predict to what extent a chemical change will occur. For example, chemical intuition tells us that the anions of weak acids should give alkaline solutions. Equilibrium calculations using K_a and K_b values verify this prediction and allow comparison of the alkalinity of various solutions of various anions. Our focus is on the chemistry, and, like practicing chemists in many situations, we would rather avoid lengthy and complicated calculations.

The mathematics of equilibrium problems can be simplified in many cases by limiting the systems under consideration to those in which complications are minimized. One way to avoid the necessity for complex mathematics is to avoid very dilute or very concentrated solutions. Most examples and exercises in this book deal with ions at the 0.01 M to 1 M concentrations most often encountered in the laboratory.

As solutions become more concentrated, the ions are less and less isolated from each other, and the solutions become less ideal. The use of concentrations rather than activities in equilibrium expressions then gives results further and further from the true equilibrium concentrations of the ions. What is known as the *salt effect* is one result of this influence of ions on each other. The total concentration of ions in solution, common or not, has a small influence on the solubility of a salt. Silver chloride, for example, is slightly more soluble in a potassium nitrate solution than in pure water. In accurate analytical chemistry and in biochemistry the salt effect must be taken into account for solutions of *any* concentration.

In very dilute solutions of acidic or basic ions, the contribution of the H^+ and OH^- ions from the ionization of water cannot be ignored. For example, the rigorous calculation of the concentrations of *all* of the ions present in a very dilute solution of a weak acid requires solving four equations in four unknowns. Make no mistake—the exact equilibrium calculations based on purely mathematical considerations are always possible. One professor was fond of telling his general chemistry class that if one of them could earn a million dollars by such a calculation, he or she would be able to do it.

Without such motivation, we instead utilize our chemical knowledge to make assumptions that allow us to simplify the necessary mathematics. For example, when the ions in a given solution can participate simultaneously in several equilibria, each equilibrium constant must be satisfied. However, it is often possible to simplify the calculations by identifying one equilibrium as most important because it yields much larger concentrations of products. This allows us to treat contributions from other equilibria as negligible.

You will see in the following section, which deals with polyprotic acids, and in the later section on complex ions (Section 21.14) that we simplify the problems both by specifying certain reaction conditions and by assuming that the contributions from certain reactions can be ignored.

21.7 POLYPROTIC ACIDS

A polyprotic acid contains more than one ionizable hydrogen atom per molecule. Such an acid ionizes or reacts with a base in separate steps for each proton, with different equilibrium constants for each step. Each successive proton is released less readily than the preceding proton because each proton is held more strongly by the increasingly negative anion. (K_a values for some common polyprotic acids are given in Table 21.3.) For example, for carbonic acid

$$H_2CO_3(aq) + H_2O(l) \rightleftharpoons HCO_3^- + H_3O^+ \qquad K_{a_1} = 4.5 \times 10^{-7}$$
$$HCO_3^- + H_2O(l) \rightleftharpoons CO_3^{2-} + H_3O^+ \qquad K_{a_2} = 4.8 \times 10^{-11}$$

Equilibrium calculations for polyprotic acids are complex because the concentrations of the ions are determined by the overall result of the successive equilibria. This complexity is dealt with by making simplifying assumptions.

In general, a stepwise approach is used. The concentrations of the ions formed in the first ionization are found. Because the first step is always more extensive than the subsequent steps ($K_1 > K_2 > K_3$), it is assumed that the subsequent steps make a negligible change in the concentrations of these ions. This assumption allows the concentrations found in the first step to be used in the equilibrium constant expressions for subsequent steps to find the concentrations of the other anions.

a. Sulfuric acid Sulfuric acid is unique among the common polyprotic acids because it is a strong electrolyte in its first ionization and a moderately weak one in its second ionization.

$$H_2SO_4(aq) + H_2O(l) \longrightarrow H_3O^+ + HSO_4^- \qquad \text{complete in dilute solution}$$
$$HSO_4^- + H_2O(l) \rightleftharpoons H_3O^+ + SO_4^{2-} \qquad K_{a_2} = 1.0 \times 10^{-2}$$

The other common polyprotic acids are weak electrolytes in each ionization step, including the first.

As for all polyprotic acids, in a sulfuric acid solution the hydrogen ion concentration and the relative concentrations of the anions present are dependent upon each other. The H_3O^+ from the first reaction is a common ion for the second reaction:

$$\overset{\longleftarrow H_3O^+}{HSO_4^- + H_2O(l) \rightleftharpoons H_3O^+ + SO_4^{2-}}$$

The result is to decrease the SO_4^{2-} concentration and increase the HSO_4^- concentration relative to the concentrations that would be formed by HSO_4^- alone.

The pH in a concentrated sulfuric acid solution is less than 0. As shown in Figure 21.2, virtually the only anion in such a solution is HSO_4^-. If the concentration of H_3O^+ is decreased, more and more SO_4^{2-} is formed, until beyond pH 4, virtually all of the original HSO_4^- has been converted to SO_4^{2-}.

Because HSO_4^- is a weak acid, it is not fully dissociated in a sulfuric acid solution. As a result the concentration of H_3O^+ in a sulfuric acid solution is *not* equal to twice the molar concentration of the acid, as is shown in the following example. Do not make the <u>common error</u> of assuming that a sulfuric acid solution, because it is a strong acid, contains a concentration of hydrogen ion equal to twice the concentration of the sulfuric acid.

Table 21.3
K_a Values for Polyprotic Acids

Hydrosulfuric	
H_2S	1.0×10^{-7}
HS^-	3×10^{-13}
Sulfuric	
H_2SO_4	Large
HSO_4^-	1.0×10^{-2}
Carbonic	
H_2CO_3	4.5×10^{-7}
HCO_3^-	4.8×10^{-11}
Arsenic	
H_3AsO_4	6.5×10^{-3}
$H_2AsO_4^-$	1.1×10^{-7}
$HAsO_4^{2-}$	3×10^{-12}
Pyrophosphoric	
$H_4P_2O_7$	1.2×10^{-1}
$H_3P_2O_7^-$	7.9×10^{-2}
$H_2P_2O_7^{2-}$	2.0×10^{-7}
$HP_2O_7^{3-}$	4.8×10^{-10}
Phosphoric	
H_3PO_4	7.5×10^{-3}
$H_2PO_4^-$	6.6×10^{-8}
HPO_4^{2-}	1×10^{-12}

Figure 21.2
Effect of pH on Ionization of Sulfuric Acid in Aqueous Solution Sulfuric acid is 100% ionized to HSO_4^-. The "fraction" plotted represents the fraction of the original HSO_4^- ion present as HSO_4^- and SO_4^{2-}. Beyond pH 4, virtually all of the original HSO_4^- has been converted to SO_4^{2-}. (Note that curves such as this do not show very low fractions of the species that are present.)

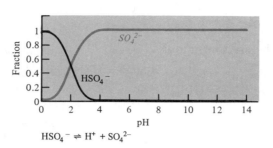

$$HSO_4^- \rightleftharpoons H^+ + SO_4^{2-}$$

EXAMPLE 21.8
Polyprotic Acids

Find $[H^+]$, $[HSO_4^-]$, $[H_2SO_4]$, and $[SO_4^{2-}]$ in equilibrium in a 0.100 M solution of H_2SO_4. $K_{a_2} = 1.0 \times 10^{-2}$.

Because $H_2SO_4(aq)$ is a strong acid in the first ionization step,

$$H_2SO_4(aq) + H_2O(l) \longrightarrow H_3O^+ + HSO_4^-$$

we can safely state that $[H_2SO_4] \simeq 0$ and that $[H_3O^+]$, or simply $[H^+]$, $= [HSO_4^-] =$ 0.100 mol/L before the second ionization step occurs. For the second step, letting $x = [SO_4^{2-}]$,

	HSO_4^-	$\rightleftharpoons$	H^+	$+ SO_4^{2-}$
Initial	0.100		0.100	0
Change	$-x$		$+x$	$+x$
Equilibrium	$0.100 - x$		$0.100 + x$	x

$$K_{a_2} = \frac{[H^+][SO_4^{2-}]}{[HSO_4^-]} = \frac{(0.100 + x)(x)}{(0.100 - x)} = 1.0 \times 10^{-2}$$

This equation must be solved by the exact method, using the quadratic equation, because the concentrations and K_{a_2} are of similar magnitude. Solving for x gives $[SO_4^{2-}] = 8.4 \times 10^{-3}$ mol/L. Thus

$$[HSO_4^-] = 0.100 - x = 0.100 - 0.0084 = 0.092 \text{ mol/L}$$

and

$$[H^+] = 0.100 + x = 0.100 + 0.0084 = 0.108 \text{ mol/L}$$

At equilibrium, $[H_2SO_4] \simeq 0$, $[HSO_4^-] = 0.092$ mol/L, $[SO_4^{2-}] = 0.0084$ mol/L, and $[H^+] = 0.108$ mol/L in a 0.100 M solution of H_2SO_4.

Exercise Find the molar concentrations of H^+, HSO_4^-, H_2SO_4, and SO_4^{2-} in equilibrium in a 0.0100 M solution of H_2SO_4. $K_{a_2} = 1.0 \times 10^{-2}$. *Answer* $[H_2SO_4] \simeq 0$, $[HSO_4^-] = 0.006$ mol/L, $[SO_4^{2-}] = 0.004$ mol/L, $[H^+] = 0.014$ mol/L

---

b. Hydrosulfuric acid Hydrosulfuric acid, H_2S, is a weak diprotic acid:

$$H_2S(aq) + H_2O(l) \rightleftharpoons H_3O^+ + HS^- \qquad K_{a_1} = 1.0 \times 10^{-7}$$
$$HS^- + H_2O(l) \rightleftharpoons H_3O^+ + S^{2-} \qquad K_{a_2} = 3 \times 10^{-13}$$

The second ionization constant of the acid is so much smaller than the first that in calculating the hydrogen ion concentration in a solution of the acid alone, the second step ionization may be neglected, and $[H^+]$ and $[HS^-]$ equated to each other.

EXAMPLE 21.9
Polyprotic Acids

A saturated aqueous hydrosulfuric acid solution at 1 atm pressure and room temperature has a concentration of approximately 0.1 M H_2S. Find the concentrations of all of the ions present in this solution. For H_2S, $K_{a_1} = 1.0 \times 10^{-7}$; $K_{a_2} = 3 \times 10^{-13}$.

For the first ionization,

$$H_2S(aq) + H_2O(l) \longrightarrow H_3O^+ + HS^-$$

Let $x = [H^+] = [HS^-]$.

	H_2S	$\rightleftharpoons$ H^+	$+ HS^-$
Initial	0.1	0	0
Change	$-x$	$+x$	$+x$
Equilibrium	$0.1 - x$	x	x

$$K_{a_1} = \frac{[H^+][HS^-]}{[H_2S]} = \frac{(x)(x)}{(0.1 - x)} \simeq \frac{x^2}{0.1} = 1.0 \times 10^{-7}$$

Since K_{a_1} is very small, we can make the approximation that $(0.1 - x) \simeq 0.1$.

$$x^2 = 1 \times 10^{-8}$$
$$x = 1 \times 10^{-4} \text{ mol/L} = [H^+] = [HS^-]$$

The value found for the concentration of H^+ and HS^- ions must satisfy the second-step equilibrium, $HS^- \rightleftharpoons H^+ + S^{2-}$. Because K_{a_2} is much smaller than K_{a_1}, we assume that the contribution to $[H^+]$ from this equilibrium is negligible. Therefore, the S^{2-} ion concentration may be calculated using $[H^+]$ and $[HS^-]$ from the first ionization as follows:

	HS^-	$\rightleftharpoons$ H^+	$+ S^{2-}$
Initial	1×10^{-4}	1×10^{-4}	0
Change	$-x$	$+x$	$+x$
Equilibrium	$1 \times 10^{-4} - x$	$1 \times 10^{-4} + x$	x

$$K_{a_2} = \frac{[H^+][S^{2-}]}{[HS^-]} = \frac{(1 \times 10^{-4} + x)(x)}{(1 \times 10^{-4} - x)} \approx \frac{(1 \times 10^{-4})(x)}{(1 \times 10^{-4})} = 3 \times 10^{-13}$$

$$x = [S^{2-}] = 3 \times 10^{-13} \text{ mol/L}$$

In a 0.1 M aqueous H_2S solution, the concentrations of the ions present are $[H^+] = [HS^-] = 1 \times 10^{-4}$ mol/L and $[S^{2-}] = 3 \times 10^{-13}$ mol/L.

Exercise Find the molar concentrations of H^+, HS^-, S^{2-}, and H_2S in a 0.010 M solution of H_2S. $K_{a_1} = 1.0 \times 10^{-7}$ and $K_{a_2} = 3 \times 10^{-13}$ for H_2S. *Answer* $[H^+] = [HS^-] = 3.2 \times 10^{-5}$ mol/L, $[S^{2-}] = 3 \times 10^{-13}$ mol/L, $[H_2S] \approx 0.010$ mol/L

From the preceding example we can conclude that in a solution of H_2S alone, the molar concentration of the sulfide ion is equal to the value of K_{a_2}. Indeed, for most weak diprotic acids, the molar concentration of the ions formed by the loss of both protons is equal to the second ionization constant (in the absence of added common ions).

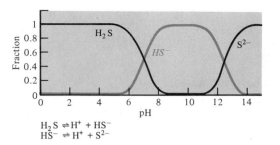

Effect of pH on Ionization of Hydrosulfuric Acid in Aqueous Solution The "fraction" plotted is the fraction of the original H_2S present as HS^- and S^{2-}. The sulfide ion concentration is high in alkaline solution.

$$H_2S \rightleftharpoons H^+ + HS^-$$
$$HS^- \rightleftharpoons H^+ + S^{2-}$$

Overall K_a values for polyprotic acids can be found from the K_a values for individual steps. For example, multiplying the equilibrium constant expressions for the two ionization steps of aqueous H_2S gives

$$K_a(\text{overall}) = \frac{[H^+][HS^-]}{[H_2S]} \times \frac{[H^+][S^{2-}]}{[HS^-]} = (1.0 \times 10^{-7})(3 \times 10^{-13})$$

$$= \frac{[H^+]^2[S^{2-}]}{[H_2S]} = 3 \times 10^{-20}$$

(21.20)

which represents the reaction

$$H_2S(aq) + 2H_2O(l) \rightleftharpoons 2H_3O^+ + S^{2-}$$

Ordinarily an overall equilibrium constant cannot be used to calculate the concentrations of the ions present in a solution of a polyprotic acid. In using such an equilibrium constant the assumption is implicit that the concentration of hydrogen ion produced in each step is the same. This is not correct, for at each step the acid ionizes to a lesser extent.

However, an expression that is very useful for finding concentrations in a saturated H_2S solution can be derived from Equation (21.20). For a 0.1 M saturated solution

$$\frac{[H^+]^2[S^{2-}]}{(0.1)} = 3 \times 10^{-20}$$

$$[H^+]^2[S^{2-}] = 3 \times 10^{-21}$$

(21.21)

This equation allows for the calculation of the hydrogen ion concentration in a solution of known sulfide ion concentration, or of sulfide ion concentration in a solution of known hydrogen ion concentration.

The variation with pH of the fraction of the original H_2S present as HS^- and S^{2-} is shown in Figure 21.3. The sulfide ion concentration is high in alkaline solutions and low in acidic solutions. By controlling the pH, the sulfide ion concentration can be controlled, a technique that is used in qualitative analysis to separate cations by precipitation of their sulfides (Section 21.15).

EXAMPLE 21.10
Polyprotic Acids

To what pH must a saturated, 0.1 M H_2S solution be adjusted so that $[S^{2-}] = 1 \times 10^{-9}$ M?

For a saturated H_2S solution, the relationship

$$[H^+]^2[S^{2-}] = 3 \times 10^{-21}$$

is valid. This relationship can be solved for the hydrogen ion concentration necessary to achieve a desired sulfide concentration.

$$[H^+]^2(1 \times 10^{-9}) = 3 \times 10^{-21}$$

$$[H^+] = \sqrt{\frac{3 \times 10^{-21}}{1 \times 10^{-9}}} = 2 \times 10^{-6} \text{ mol/L}$$

which corresponds to

$$pH = -\log[H^+] = -\log(2 \times 10^{-6}) = 5.7$$

The pH must be adjusted to 5.7.

Exercise To what pH must a 0.01 M solution of H_2S be adjusted so that $[S^{2-}] = 1 \times 10^{-9}$ mol/L? *Answer* 6.3

c. Phosphoric acid

Phosphoric acid is a triprotic acid that releases protons in three steps.

$$\begin{aligned} H_3PO_4(aq) &\rightleftharpoons H^+ + H_2PO_4^- & K_{a_1} &= 7.5 \times 10^{-3} \\ H_2PO_4^- &\rightleftharpoons H^+ + HPO_4^{2-} & K_{a_2} &= 6.6 \times 10^{-8} \\ HPO_4^{2-} &\rightleftharpoons H^+ + PO_4^{3-} & K_{a_3} &= 1 \times 10^{-12} \end{aligned}$$

The ionization constant for the first step in the ionization of phosphoric acid is large relative to the ionization constants for the second and third steps. It can therefore be assumed that $[H^+]$ and $[H_2PO_4^-]$ at equilibrium in a phosphoric acid solution are determined by the first ionization. As in Example 21.9 for hydrosulfuric acid, the concentrations of the products of the first ionization step can be used in the equilibrium expressions for subsequent steps to find the concentrations of all ions in the solution. Such a calculation for 0.010 M H_3PO_4 gives the following results:

$$\begin{aligned} [H_3PO_4] &= 4.3 \times 10^{-3} \text{ mol/L} & [HPO_4^{2-}] &= 6.6 \times 10^{-8} \text{ mol/L} \\ [H^+] = [H_2PO_4^-] &= 5.7 \times 10^{-3} \text{ mol/L} & [PO_4^{3-}] &= 1 \times 10^{-17} \text{ mol/L} \end{aligned}$$

The pH in this 0.010 M H_3PO_4 solution is 2.2. Figure 21.4 shows that most of the original H_3PO_4 in a solution at this pH is present as H_3PO_4 or $H_2PO_4^-$. (The fractions of the other two anions shown above are too small to appear in the figure.) The figure also illustrates that the concentration of PO_4^{3-} can be increased by making the solution alkaline.

Figure 21.4
Effect of pH on Ionization of Phosphoric Acid The "fraction" plotted is the fraction of the original H_3PO_4 converted to $H_2PO_4^-$, HPO_4^{2-}, and PO_4^{3-}. (See Figure 21.3 caption.)

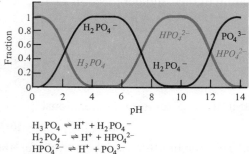

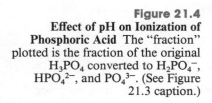

TOOLS OF CHEMISTRY
Measuring pH

Figure A
Phenolphthalein, an Acid-Base Indicator The pink color arises from an anion with three resonance structures.

The pH of a solution is usually measured by one of two methods. The first is the observation of the color change of an indicator. The second is the use of a pH meter—an instrument that employs electrodes to measure the potential difference between solutions of known and unknown hydrogen ion concentration. Because of their accuracy and speed, pH meters have superseded the older indicator method in many applications. However, the indicator method remains in use because it is simple and convenient.

An indicator is an organic acid or base that has in its structure a group that reacts with hydrogen or hydroxide ion so that the color of the compound changes. Letting HInd represent an indicator acid, its ionization, like that of any acid, is

$$HInd(aq) \rightleftharpoons Ind^- + H^+$$

The HInd and Ind$^-$ forms must have different colors. For the color change of an indicator to be visible, the concentration of one colored form must be about ten times greater than the concentration of the other. Most indicators have a useful color change over a 2 pH unit range.

The commonly encountered indicator phenolphthalein (Figure A), for example, changes from colorless to pink in the pH range from 8.3 to 10.0. Indicators are available for the entire pH range (Table A).

One way to improve the accuracy of using indicators is by comparing the color of the indicator in a solution of unknown pH with the color of the indicator in a solution of known pH. Paper impregnated with an organic pH indicator is very convenient to use. Litmus paper and its pink and blue colors may be familiar to many of you. A "universal" pH paper combines several different indicators in the same paper. This paper will show a characteristic color for any point in the pH range.

The essential parts of a pH meter are (1) a glass electrode, (2) a reference electrode, and (3) a voltmeter calibrated to read in pH units rather than in volts. (In some instruments, for convenience the two electrodes are combined into one

Table A
Common pH Indicators and Their Color Changes

Indicator	Color at Lower pH	pH Range	Color at Higher pH
Methyl violet	Yellow	0–2	Violet
Malachite green (acidic)	Yellow	0–1.8	Blue-green
Thymol blue (acidic)	Red	1.2–2.8	Yellow
Bromphenol blue	Yellow	3.0–4.6	Purple
Methyl orange	Red	3.1–4.4	Yellow-orange
Bromcresol green	Yellow	3.8–5.4	Blue
Methyl red	Red	4.4–6.2	Yellow
Litmus	Red	4.5–8.3	Blue
Bromcresol purple	Yellow	5.2–6.8	Purple
Bromthymol blue	Yellow	6.0–7.6	Blue
Phenol red	Yellow	6.4–8.2	Red
m-Cresol purple	Yellow	7.6–9.2	Purple
Thymol blue (alkaline)	Yellow	8.0–9.6	Blue
Phenolphthalein	Colorless	8.3–10.0	Red
Thymolphthalein	Colorless	9.3–10.5	Blue
Alizarin yellow	Yellow	10.1–11.1	Lilac
Malachite green (alkaline)	Green	11.4–13.0	Colorless
Trinitrobenzene	Colorless	12.0–14.0	Orange

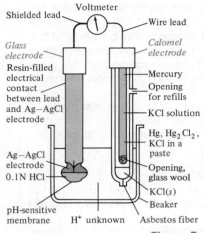

Shielded lead

Voltmeter

Wire lead

Glass electrode

Calomel electrode

Resin-filled electrical contact between lead and Ag–AgCl electrode

Mercury

Opening for refills

KCl solution

Hg, Hg_2Cl_2, KCl in a paste

Ag–AgCl electrode 0.1N HCl

Opening, glass wool

KCl(s)

Beaker

pH-sensitive membrane H^+ unknown

Asbestos fiber

Figure B
Electrodes Used for Measuring pH

probe.)The glass electrode is based upon a unique property of a thin membrane (about 0.5 mm) made of special glass. An electric potential develops across the membrane when its two sides are in contact with solutions of different hydrogen ion concentrations. The potential arises because of ion exchange between Na^+ ions in the glass and H^+ ions in the solutions, aided by a thin layer of hydrated glass on the membrane surface.

The glass membrane is formed into a bulb that is filled with a solution of known and constant pH (Figure B, left electrode). Sealed into the glass electrode and dipping into the solution with which the bulb is filled is an electrode, usually a silver wire coated with silver chloride. The entire glass electrode is placed in the solution of unknown pH during use, thereby putting the membrane in contact with the solutions of known and unknown pH. The reference electrode most often used is a calomel electrode, which contains a mixture of Hg, Hg_2Cl_2 (known as calomel), and KCl.

The arrangement is such that the potential difference measured by the voltmeter is due only to the difference in the hydrogen ion concentration of the two solutions. This potential is (see Section 23.13)

$$E = \text{a constant} + 0.0592 \text{ pH}$$

In practice, a pH meter must be calibrated before each use by placing the electrodes in a solution of known pH and setting the meter to read correctly. This is necessary because the value of the "constant" in the above equations varies slightly with conditions.

Electrodes based, like the glass electrode, on the movement of ions across a membrane have recently been developed for substances other than H^+. Such electrodes, called ion-selective electrodes, can directly determine the concentrations of, for example, Ca^{2+}, Pb^{2+}, Br^-. F^-, Cl^-, S^{2-}, and SO_2. Among the many practical uses of such electrodes are the monitoring of F^- concentrations in water supplies; monitoring of NH_3, NO_x, SO_2, H_2S, HF, HCl, and HCN in stack gases; the measurement of Cl^- in sweat as a diagnostic test for cystic fibrosis; the measurement of Ca^{2+} in beer, wine, and milk; and the measurement of CN^- in metal plating baths and wastewater.

21.8 ACID–BASE REACTIONS AND TITRATION IN AQUEOUS SOLUTIONS

Titration of an acid and a base is a technique used to determine accurately the concentration of an acid or a base in aqueous solution. The practical need for such information arises frequently.

Suppose we have 50 mL of a 0.10 M solution of HCl. The number of moles of HCl present is 0.005 mol. From the stoichiometry of the reaction between HCl and a base, say NaOH,

$$NaOH(aq) + HCl(aq) \longrightarrow NaCl(aq) + H_2O(l)$$

we know that when exactly 0.005 mol of NaOH has been added to the original solution containing 0.005 mol of HCl, all of the acid will have reacted. This is called the **equivalence point**—the point at which the chemically equivalent, or stoichiometric, amounts of reactants have reacted. For the HCl solution we started with, the equivalence point could be reached by the addition of 50 mL of 0.1 M NaOH, or 25 mL of 0.2 M NaOH, or 100 mL of 0.05 M NaOH, or any other combination of concentration and volume that equals 0.005 mol of NaOH.

Titration is the measurement of the volume of a solution of one reactant that is required to react completely with a measured amount of another reactant. Frequently both reactants are in solution and the titration is the measurement of the volume of one solution that must be added to a known volume of the other solution.

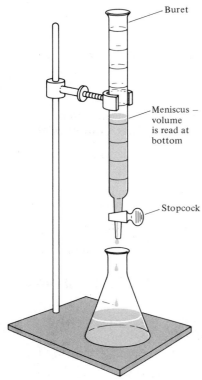

- Buret

- Meniscus —
volume
is read at
bottom

- Stopcock

Figure 21.5
Titration One solution is added
from the buret to another in the
flask. The volume of solution that
must be added to reach the end
point is carefully measured.

Usually the concentration of one solution — a standard solution — is known (Figure 21.5).

For example, if the HCl solution described above was of unknown concentration, we could take exactly 50 mL of that solution and gradually add a standard 0.10 M NaOH solution until the equivalence point was reached. This would occur when exactly 50 mL of the base was added, which would indicate that the original solution contained an equal molar amount of the acid and was therefore 0.10 M.

In acid–base titrations, the relative amounts of acid and base needed to reach the equivalence point are governed by the mole ratios of acid and base that react. In the reaction of sodium hydroxide with hydrochloric acid, a one-to-one mole ratio of the acid to the base is required to reach the equivalence point. For sulfuric acid,

$$H_2SO_4(aq) + 2NaOH(aq) \longrightarrow Na_2SO_4(aq) + 2H_2O(l)$$

each mole of sulfuric acid requires two moles of sodium hydroxide.

In an acid–base titration the pH changes very little until all of the H^+ or OH^- available has reacted with OH^- or H^+. At the equivalence point a small additional amount of acid, or base, causes a large rapid change in pH. This large change in pH is often detected by the presence in the solution of an **indicator** — a compound that changes color in a specific pH range (see Tools of Chemistry: Measuring pH). The point at which an indicator changes color in a titration is usually referred to as the **end point** of the titration. *Sometimes* the end point and the equivalence point are the same. But more often there is an end point error — a slight discrepancy between the end point and the exact equivalence point. In most titrations this error is considered negligible because an indicator is chosen that will change color as close to the equivalence point as possible.

All problems concerned with acid–base titrations can be solved by using the concepts of stoichiometry and solution concentration based on moles, mole ratios, and molarity that we have already studied. (The stoichiometry of acid–base reactions can also be described by using equivalents and normality, discussed in Section 20.7. Although the use of these quantities is not necessary and has fallen out of favor, some laboratories continue to express acid and base concentrations in normality. You should be aware of this.)

EXAMPLE 21.11
Acid–Base Reactions

Exactly 23.6 mL of a 0.131 M HCl solution was required to completely react with 25.0 mL of an NaOH solution. What was the concentration of the NaOH solution?

The chemical equation for the acid–base reaction is

$$NaOH(aq) + HCl(aq) \longrightarrow H_2O(l) + NaCl(aq)$$

The number of moles of HCl that reacted is

$$(23.6 \text{ mL}) \left(\frac{1 \text{ L}}{1000 \text{ mL}} \right) \left(\frac{0.131 \text{ mol HCl}}{\text{L}} \right) = 0.00309 \text{ mol HCl}$$

which corresponds to

$$(0.00309 \text{ mol HCl}) \left(\frac{1 \text{ mol NaOH}}{1 \text{ mol HCl}} \right) = 0.00309 \text{ mol NaOH}$$

The concentration of NaOH is

$$\left(\frac{0.00309 \text{ mol NaOH}}{25.0 \text{ mL}} \right) \left(\frac{1 \text{ L}}{1000 \text{ mL}} \right) = 0.124 \text{ mol/L}$$

Note that the individual steps can be combined.

$$(23.6 \text{ mL}) \left(\frac{1 \text{ L}}{1000 \text{ mL}} \right) \left(\frac{0.131 \text{ mol HCl}}{\text{L}} \right) \left(\frac{1 \text{ mol NaOH}}{1 \text{ mol HCl}} \right)$$

$$\times \left(\frac{1}{25.0 \text{ mL}} \right) \left(\frac{1000 \text{ mL}}{1 \text{ L}} \right) = 0.124 \text{ mol/L}$$

The concentration of the NaOH solution is 0.124 M.

Exercise   A volume of 42.6 mL of 0.0972 M NaOH was required to completely react with 50.0 mL of an $HClO_4$ solution. What was the concentration of the perchloric acid? *Answer* 0.0828 mol/L

EXAMPLE 21.12
Acid–Base Reactions

An approximately 0.1 M HCl solution was standardized (its exact concentration found) by titrating it into a solution containing 0.1223 g of 99.95% pure Na_2CO_3:

$$Na_2CO_3(aq) + 2HCl(aq) \longrightarrow 2NaCl(aq) + H_2O(l) + CO_2(g)$$

The equivalence point was reached when 22.65 mL of the HCl solution had been used. What was the exact concentration of the acid?

In this case, the known solution is that containing Na_2CO_3. The number of moles of Na_2CO_3 that reacted was

$$(0.1223 \text{ g impure } Na_2CO_3) \left(\frac{99.95 \text{ g } Na_2CO_3}{100.00 \text{ g impure } Na_2CO_3} \right) \left(\frac{1 \text{ mol } Na_2CO_3}{105.99 \text{ g } Na_2CO_3} \right)$$

$$= 0.001153 \text{ mol } Na_2CO_3$$

The chemical equation tells us that 2 mol of HCl react for every mole of Na_2CO_3, so the stoichiometric amount of HCl required to react with the Na_2CO_3 was

$$(0.001153 \text{ mol } Na_2CO_3) \left(\frac{2 \text{ mol HCl}}{1 \text{ mol } Na_2CO_3} \right) = 0.002306 \text{ mol HCl}$$

The molarity of the solution is

$$\frac{0.002306 \text{ mol}}{0.02265 \text{ L}} = 0.1018 \text{ mol/L}$$

The concentration of the acid is 0.1018 M.

Exercise   A 0.1 M NaOH solution was standardized by titrating it against pure potassium acid phthalate (commonly abbreviated KHP), a monoprotic acid.

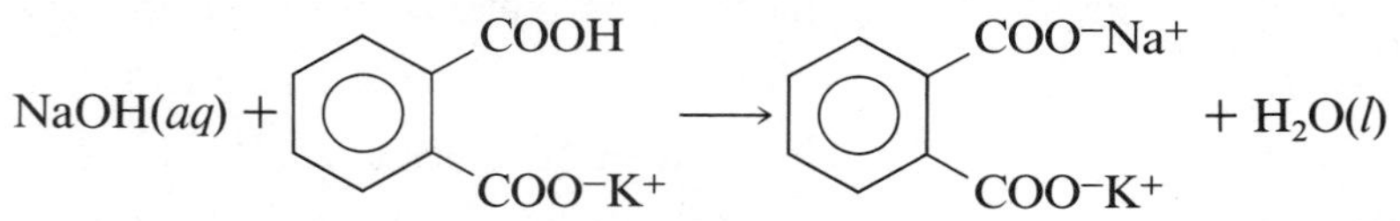

$$NaOH(aq) + \underset{\text{COO}^-\text{K}^+}{\overset{\text{COOH}}{\bigcirc}} \longrightarrow \underset{\text{COO}^-\text{K}^+}{\overset{\text{COO}^-\text{Na}^+}{\bigcirc}} + H_2O(l)$$

A 0.4963 g sample of the KHP was neutralized by 19.61 mL of the base. What is the exact concentration of the base? The molar mass of KHP is 204.23 g/mol. *Answer* 0.1239 mol/L

All acid–base titrations go essentially to completion; weak acids are driven to complete reaction as the H_3O^+ ion is removed by reaction with the added OH^- ion. The products of the reaction of an acid and base are a salt and water. The pH at the equivalence point in any acid–base reaction depends upon which of the four types of salts discussed earlier (see Table 21.1) has been formed. For example, in the titration of a hydrocyanic acid solution with sodium hydroxide,

$$HCN(aq) + NaOH(aq) \rightleftharpoons NaCN(aq) + H_2O(l)$$

a solution of sodium cyanide in water is present at the equivalence point. The solution will be alkaline because sodium cyanide is a soluble compound of a cation that does not react with water and an anion that reacts to give hydroxide ion (Section 21.2).

Many students make the common error of assuming that in *any* acid–base reaction in aqueous solution, all acidic and basic character is destroyed, leaving a solution with pH 7. This is *not* the case. The solution at the equivalence point in an acid–base reaction is exactly the same as a solution produced by dissolving a salt in water. Stoichiometric amounts of the cation and anion are present in aqueous solution in both cases. Basic anions and acidic cations react with water whenever they are able to do so. The solution will therefore *not* necessarily be neutral.

21.9 TITRATION CURVES

The change of the pH throughout the course of an acid–base titration can be represented by a **titration curve** — a plot of pH versus volume of acid or base added. The curves have different characteristic shapes that depend on the concentrations of reagents and on whether strong or weak acids and bases are involved. The calculation of the pH at various points in some representative titrations is discussed in the following sections and provides a review of pH calculations.

a. Strong acid–strong base titration

Figure 21.6 is the titration curve for the reaction of 40.0 mL of 0.100 M HCl with 0.100 M NaOH. We review here how the pH at different stages of the titration can be calculated.

The pH of the solution before the addition of any base is determined by the initial concentration of the strong acid and is 1.000 (pH $= -\log [H^+] = -\log 0.100$).

The pH of the solution before the equivalence point is determined by how much of the strong acid has not yet reacted with base. The amount of HCl originally present in 40.0 mL of the 0.100 M solution is 0.00400 mol. After, say, 10.0 mL of base has been added, the amount of HCl that has reacted is

$$\left(\frac{0.100 \text{ mol NaOH}}{1 \text{ L}}\right)(10.0 \text{ mL})\left(\frac{1 \text{ L}}{1000 \text{ mL}}\right)\left(\frac{1 \text{ mol HCl}}{1 \text{ mol NaOH}}\right) = 0.00100 \text{ mol HCl}$$

and the amount of HCl that has not yet reacted, which determines the pH, is

$$0.00400 \text{ mol HCl} - 0.00100 \text{ mol HCl} = 0.00300 \text{ mol HCl}$$

In calculations involving titrations, it is important to remember that the volume of the solution is changing. The 0.00300 mol of HCl is present in (40.0 + 10.0) mL of solution, for a concentration and pH of

$$\left(\frac{0.00300 \text{ mol}}{40.0 + 10.0 \text{ mL}}\right)\left(\frac{1000 \text{ mL}}{\text{L}}\right) = 0.0600 \text{ mol/L, or pH } 1.222$$

Table 21.4 gives the pH of the solution as this titration proceeds.

At the equivalence point, there is no excess of HCl or NaOH and the solution is neutral because neither the Na^+ nor the Cl^- ions react with water. Thus the pH at the equivalence point is 7.000. [Suitable indicators for strong acid–strong base titrations include litmus (pH 4.5–8.3), bromthymol blue (pH 6.0–7.6), and phenol red (pH 6.4–8.2).]

The pH of the solution after the equivalence point is determined by how much excess NaOH has been added. For example, after the addition of 45.0 mL, or 0.00450 mol, of base the amount of base in excess is

$$(0.00400 \text{ mol HCl})\left(\frac{1 \text{ mol NaOH}}{1 \text{ mol HCl}}\right) = 0.00400 \text{ mol NaOH reacted}$$

$$0.00450 \text{ mol NaOH} - 0.00400 \text{ mol NaOH} = 0.00050 \text{ mol NaOH}$$

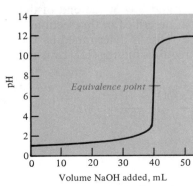

Figure 21.6
Strong Acid–Strong Base Titration Titration of 40.0 mL of 0.100 M HCl by 0.100 M NaOH.

Table 21.4
pH during the Acid–Base Titrations

Volume of NaOH Added, mL	Strong Acid–Strong Base* pH		Weak Acid–Strong Base† pH
0.0	1.000		2.879
5.0	1.109		3.911
10.0	1.222		4.279
15.0	1.342		4.534
20.0	1.477		4.756
25.0	1.637		4.978
30.0	1.845		5.233
35.0	2.176		5.601
36.0	2.279		5.710
37.0	2.409		5.847
38.0	2.591		6.035
39.0	2.898		6.347
39.3	3.076		6.505
39.7	3.378		6.878
40.0	7.000	⟵ equivalence ⟶ point	8.728
40.3	10.62		10.62
40.7	10.92		10.92
41.0	11.09		11.09
42.0	11.39		11.39

* 40.0 mL of 0.100 M HCl with 0.100 M NaOH.

† 40.0 mL of 0.100 M CH₃COOH with 0.100 M NaOH.

in excess, which corresponds to a concentration of

$$\left(\frac{0.00050 \text{ mol NaOH}}{(40.0 + 45.0) \text{ mL}}\right)\left(\frac{1000 \text{ mL}}{1 \text{ L}}\right) = 0.0059 \text{ mol/L}$$

or a pH of 11.77.

As illustrated in Figure 21.7, the shape of a strong acid–strong base curve changes slightly with the concentration of the acid. However, the equivalence point remains at pH 7.

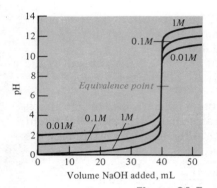

Figure 21.7
Strong Acid–Strong Base Titration Titration of 40.0 mL of HCl by NaOH of equal concentrations.

b. Weak acid–strong base or strong acid–weak base titration Figure 21.8 illustrates the curve for the titration of 40.0 mL of 0.100 M CH₃COOH with 0.100 M NaOH.

$$CH_3COOH(aq) + NaOH(aq) \longrightarrow Na(CH_3COO)(aq) + H_2O(l)$$

A comparable strong acid–weak base titration would give a curve with the identical shape in reverse. The pH would be high at the outset and low at the end of the titration. The pH in each region would be calculated as described in this section.

The pH of the solution before the addition of any base is determined by the initial concentration of the weak acid. To find the pH requires finding [H⁺] by using the K_a of acetic acid. Let $x = [H^+]$.

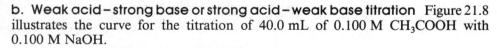

	CH₃COOH ⇌ CH₃COO⁻ + H⁺		
Initial	0.100	0	0
Change	$-x$	$+x$	$+x$
Equilibrium	$0.100 - x$	x	x

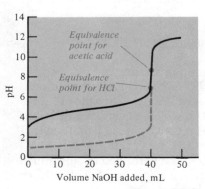

Figure 21.8
Weak Acid–Strong Base Titration Titration of 40.0 mL of 0.100 M CH₃COOH by 0.100 M NaOH. Dashed line is for HCl—NaOH titration for comparison.

$$K_a = \frac{[H^+][CH_3COO^-]}{[CH_3COOH]} = \frac{(x)(x)}{(0.100 - x)} \approx \frac{x^2}{0.100} = 1.75 \times 10^{-5}$$

$$x = 1.32 \times 10^{-3} \text{ mol/L} = [H^+]$$

$$pH = -\log(1.32 \times 10^{-3}) = 2.879$$

From the addition of the first drops of base and before the equivalence point, the solution in a weak acid–strong base titration contains a buffer pair—in this case, the solution contains acetic acid plus acetate ion. The Henderson-Hasselbach equation (Equation 21.19) can be used to calculate the pH of the solution up to the equivalence point. As an example, we calculate the pH of the solution after the addition of 10.0 mL of base. The original amount of acetic acid present in 40.0 mL of 0.100 M CH_3COOH was 0.00400 mol. The amount of CH_3COOH that reacted was

$$\left(\frac{0.100 \text{ mol NaOH}}{1 \text{ L}}\right)(10.0 \text{ mL})\left(\frac{1 \text{ L}}{1000 \text{ mL}}\right)\left(\frac{1 \text{ mol } CH_3COOH}{1 \text{ mol NaOH}}\right) = 0.00100 \text{ mol } CH_3COOH$$

which means that the amount of CH_3COO^- formed is 0.00100 mol and the amount of unreacted CH_3COOH is

$$0.00400 \text{ mol } CH_3COOH - 0.00100 \text{ mol } CH_3COOH = 0.00300 \text{ mol } CH_3COOH$$

The concentrations of CH_3COO^- and unreacted CH_3COOH are

$$[CH_3COO^-] = \left(\frac{0.00100 \text{ mol } CH_3COO^-}{(40.0 + 10.0) \text{ mL}}\right)\left(\frac{1000 \text{ mL}}{1 \text{ L}}\right) = 0.0200 \text{ mol/L}$$

$$[CH_3COOH] = \left(\frac{0.00300 \text{ mol } CH_3COOH}{(40.0 + 10.0) \text{ mL}}\right)\left(\frac{1000 \text{ mL}}{1 \text{ L}}\right) = 0.0600 \text{ mol/L}$$

The $[H^+]$ of the solution is (see Equation 21.17a)

$$[H^+] = \left(\frac{0.0600}{0.0200}\right)(1.75 \times 10^{-5}) = 5.25 \times 10^{-5} \text{ mol/L}$$

giving a pH of 4.279. Table 21.4 gives the pH at various points throughout this titration.

At the equivalence point, the acetic acid has been neutralized by the sodium hydroxide and the 80.0 mL of solution contains 0.00400 mol of $Na(CH_3COO)$, for an acetate ion concentration of

$$[CH_3COO^-] = \left(\frac{0.00400 \text{ mol}}{80.0 \text{ mL}}\right)\left(\frac{1000 \text{ mL}}{1 \text{ L}}\right) = 0.0500 \text{ mol/L}$$

The solution is not neutral because the acetate ion reacts with water. Let $x = [OH^-]$.

$$CH_3COO^- + H_2O \longrightarrow CH_3COOH + OH^-$$

	CH_3COO^-	CH_3COOH	OH^-
Initial	0.0500	0	0
Change	$-x$	$+x$	$+x$
Equilibrium	$0.0500 - x$	x	x

$$K_b = \frac{[CH_3COOH][OH^-]}{[CH_3COO^-]} = \frac{K_w}{K_a} = \frac{1.00 \times 10^{-14}}{1.75 \times 10^{-5}} = 5.71 \times 10^{-10}$$

$$\frac{(x)(x)}{(0.0500 - x)} \simeq \frac{x^2}{0.0500} = 5.71 \times 10^{-10}$$

$$x = 5.34 \times 10^{-6} \text{ mol/L} = [OH^-]$$

$$pOH = -\log (5.34 \times 10^{-6}) = 5.272 \qquad pH = 14.000 - 5.272 = 8.728$$

The pH at the equivalence point is in the alkaline range. [An indicator such as *m*-cresol purple (pH 7.6–9.2), thymol blue (pH 8.0–9.6), or phenolphthalein (pH 8.3–10.0) should be used for this titration.]

After the equivalence point the pH of the solution is controlled primarily by the excess NaOH. The calculation of the pH is the same as for points after the equivalence point in the titration of a strong acid with a strong base. From Table 21.4 you

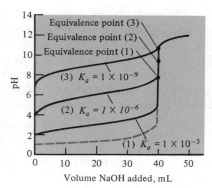

Figure 21.9
**Weak Acid–Strong Base
Titration** Titration of 40.0 mL of
0.100 M solutions of various weak
acids with 0.100 M NaOH. Dashed
line is for HCl for comparison.

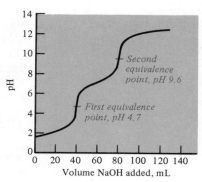

Figure 21.10
**Triprotic Acid–Strong Base
Titration** Titration of 40.0 mL of
0.100 M H_3PO_4 with 0.100 M
NaOH.

can see that beyond the equivalence point the titrations of a strong acid or a weak
acid with a strong base are identical.

The pK_a of a weak acid can be experimentally determined from a titration curve.
At the "half-equivalence" point, one-half of the acid has been neutralized and
[HA] = [A$^-$], which upon substitution into the Henderson-Hasselbach equation
gives

$$pH = pK_a - \log \frac{[HA]}{[A^-]} = pK_a - \log (1) = pK_a$$

The change in the pH at the equivalence point becomes less and less dramatic
the weaker the acid is, as illustrated by Figure 21.9. The curves show that the
equivalence point is very difficult to observe for acids with K_a values less than 10^{-8}.
For this reason, it is not practical to titrate a weak acid with a weak base; the
equivalence point is too difficult to detect.

c. Titration of a polyprotic acid with a strong base Figure 21.10 illustrates the
titration curve for the reaction of 40.0 mL of 0.100 M H_3PO_4 with 0.100 M NaOH.

$$H_3PO_4(aq) + NaOH(aq) \longrightarrow NaH_2PO_4(aq) + H_2O(l)$$
$$NaH_2PO_4(aq) + NaOH(aq) \longrightarrow Na_2HPO_4(aq) + H_2O(l)$$
$$Na_2HPO_4(aq) + NaOH(aq) \longrightarrow Na_3PO_4(aq) + H_2O(l)$$

Only the equivalence points for the first two reactions appear in the titration curve.
The third is not detectable (HPO_4^{2-} has $K_a = 1 \times 10^{-12}$). The pH before the first
equivalence point is governed by the $H_3PO_4/H_2PO_4^-$ buffer pair and the pH between
the first and second equivalence points is governed by the $H_2PO_4^-/HPO_4^{2-}$ buffer
pair.

SOLUBILITY EQUILIBRIA

The application of the principles of chemical equilibria to the solubility of ionic
compounds is, like the application of these principles to acid–base equilibria, of
importance in many aspects of chemistry. In particular, the ability to control the
precipitation or dissolution of solids is utilized in analytical chemistry in the
separation of mixtures and the determination of their compositions.

21.10 SOLUBILITY PRODUCT

K_{sp} : K for dissolution of a solid electrolyte

Many salts do not dissolve in water to a great extent. However, no salt is completely insoluble—at least a few ions always manage to escape into solution. Therefore, any salt can form a saturated solution—a solution in which the solid is in equilibrium with ions in solution.

The equilibrium constant for a solid electrolyte in equilibrium with its ions in solution is called the **solubility product,** or solubility product constant, K_{sp}. For example, for silver sulfate

$$Ag_2SO_4(s) \rightleftharpoons 2Ag^+ + SO_4^{2-}$$

the solubility product is

$$K_{sp} = [Ag^+]^2[SO_4^{2-}]$$

As for any equilibrium, the term for concentration of the solid is meaningless and need not appear in the solubility product constant. Some representative K_{sp} values are given in Table 21.5. (A more extensive table is given in Appendix V.3.) Substances that have $K_{sp} < 10^{-4}$ are considered "insoluble" in the general sense of the word. (Compare Table 21.5 with the general solubility rules, Table 6.3.)

Table 21.5
Solubility Products, K_{sp}, for Ionic Solids in Saturated Aqueous Solution (at 25 °C) (A more extensive table of K_{sp} values is given in Appendix V.3.)

Bromides
| $PbBr_2 \rightleftharpoons Pb^+ + 2Br^-$ | 3.9×10^{-5} |
| $AgBr \rightleftharpoons Ag^+ + Br^-$ | 4.9×10^{-13} |

Carbonates
$MgCO_3 \rightleftharpoons Mg^{2+} + CO_3^{2-}$	1×10^{-5}
$BaCO_3 \rightleftharpoons Ba^{2+} + CO_3^{2-}$	2.0×10^{-9}
$Ag_2CO_3 \rightleftharpoons 2Ag^+ + CO_3^{2-}$	8.1×10^{-12}
$PbCO_3 \rightleftharpoons Pb^{2+} + CO_3^{2-}$	7.4×10^{-14}

Chlorides
| $PbCl_2 \rightleftharpoons Pb^{2+} + 2Cl^-$ | 2×10^{-5} |
| $AgCl \rightleftharpoons Ag^+ + Cl^-$ | 1.8×10^{-10} |

Chromates
| $BaCrO_4 \rightleftharpoons Ba^{2+} + CrO_4^{2-}$ | 1.2×10^{-10} |
| $PbCrO_4 \rightleftharpoons Pb^{2+} + CrO_4^{2-}$ | 2.8×10^{-13} |

Fluorides
| $BaF_2 \rightleftharpoons Ba^{2+} + 2F^-$ | 1.0×10^{-6} |
| $CaF_2 \rightleftharpoons Ca^{2+} + 2F^-$ | 2.7×10^{-11} |

Hydroxides
$Ba(OH)_2 \rightleftharpoons Ba^{2+} + 2OH^-$	1.3×10^{-2}
$Be(OH)_2 \rightleftharpoons Be^{2+} + 2OH^-$	4×10^{-13}
$Ni(OH)_2 \rightleftharpoons Ni^{2+} + 2OH^-$	3×10^{-16}
$Co(OH)_2 \rightleftharpoons Co^{2+} + 2OH^-$	2×10^{-16}
$Fe(OH)_3 \rightleftharpoons Fe^{3+} + 3OH^-$	3×10^{-39}

Iodides
| $PbI_2 \rightleftharpoons Pb^{2+} + 2I^-$ | 7.1×10^{-9} |
| $HgI_2 \rightleftharpoons Hg^{2+} + 2I^-$ | 3×10^{-26} |

Phosphates
$Li_3PO_4 \rightleftharpoons 3Li^+ + PO_4^{3-}$	3×10^{-13}
$AlPO_4 \rightleftharpoons Al^{3+} + PO_4^{3-}$	5.8×10^{-19}
$Mg_3(PO_4)_2 \rightleftharpoons 3Mg^{2+} + 2PO_4^{3-}$	1×10^{-32}

Sulfates
| $Ag_2SO_4 \rightleftharpoons 2Ag^+ + SO_4^{2-}$ | 1.5×10^{-5} |
| $BaSO_4 \rightleftharpoons Ba^{2+} + SO_4^{2-}$ | 1.7×10^{-10} |

Sulfides
$FeS \rightleftharpoons Fe^{2+} + S^{2-}$	4.2×10^{-17}
$CdS \rightleftharpoons Cd^{2+} + S^{2-}$	2×10^{-28}
$HgS \rightleftharpoons Hg^{2+} + S^{2-}$	4×10^{-53}

21.11 K_{sp} AND SOLUBILITY   For salts of ions that do not react with water to a great extent, it is possible to find K_{sp} values from solubility data or to find solubilities from known K_{sp} values. In doing so, the relationships among solubility, the concentration of ions in solution, and the value of K_{sp} must be clearly understood. (And it must be remembered that the data will be valid only for the stated temperatures.) The solubility of a salt is usually expressed as mass per given volume of water, meaning the amount of the salt that will dissolve in that volume to produce a saturated solution. Converting solubility data to moles per liter gives the equilibrium concentrations needed in calculations involving K_{sp} expressions.

Suppose we know the solubility of barium sulfate in grams per liter and convert this to solubility in moles per liter. The concentrations of the ions in solution are shown by the chemical equation to be

$$BaSO_4(s) \rightleftharpoons \underset{x}{Ba^{2+}} + \underset{x}{SO_4^{2-}} \qquad (21.22)$$

Because one mole of each of the ions is formed for every mole of the salt that dissolves, the concentrations in solution are both equal to x, which is the "molar solubility."

Suppose we also know the solubility of cobalt(II) hydroxide, convert it to moles per liter, and represent this value by x. The concentrations of the ions in solution, as shown by the chemical equation, will be

$$Co(OH)_2(s) \rightleftharpoons \underset{x}{Co^{2+}} + \underset{2x}{2OH^-} \qquad (21.23)$$

Because two moles of the hydroxide ion are formed for each mole of the salt that dissolves, its concentration is $2x$, twice the molar solubility.

Remember that the solubility is the concentration of the ions in solution at *equilibrium*. Therefore, the concentrations found from the solubilities of these two salts can be used in the K_{sp} expressions. Observe closely what happens:

$$K_{sp} = [Ba^{2+}][SO_4^{2-}] = (x)(x) = x^2$$

note that both *are required*

$$K_{sp} = [Co^{2+}][OH^-]^2 = (x)(2x)^2 = 4x^3$$

The K_{sp} values represent very different functions of the molar solubilities of these two salts. There are two important points to be made here:

First, the stoichiometry of Equation (21.23) requires that $[OH^-]$ be squared in the K_{sp} for $Co(OH)_2$. Second, because $[OH^-]$ is the *total* molar concentration of OH^-, the concentration of the OH^- ion is *twice* the solubility in moles per liter. Do not make the common error of forgetting to take both of these factors into account in calculating K_{sp} values from solubilities.

Furthermore, note that K_{sp} values give different information than solubility data. The K_{sp} values provide information on the relative solubilities of different salts *only* if the values being compared are for salts of the same type (e.g., an AB salt with an AB salt, or an AB_2 salt with an AB_2 salt).

EXAMPLE 21.13
Solubility Product

The solubility of silver iodide at room temperature is 2.1×10^{-6} g/L. What is the solubility product for this salt? (Assume that neither ion reacts appreciably with water to form H^+ or OH^-.)

In a saturated solution equal amounts of Ag^+ and I^- are present. Letting $x =$ solubility in moles per liter gives, at equilibrium, $x = [Ag^+] = [I^-]$.

$$AgI(s) \rightleftharpoons Ag^+ + I^-$$
$$ x \quad\quad x$$

$$K_{sp} = [Ag^+][I^-] = (x)(x) = x^2$$

The value of the solubility in moles per liter is

$$x = \left(\frac{2.1 \times 10^{-6} \text{ g AgI}}{1 \text{ L}}\right)\left(\frac{1 \text{ mol AgI}}{234.77 \text{ g AgI}}\right) = 8.9 \times 10^{-9} \text{ mol/L}$$

and thus

$$K_{sp} = x^2 = (8.9 \times 10^{-9})^2 = 7.9 \times 10^{-17}$$

The solubility product of silver iodide is 7.9×10^{-17}.

Exercise   The solubility of magnesium hydroxide is 0.0070 g/L. What is the solubility product for this base? (Assume that the magnesium ion does not react appreciably with water to form H^+.) *Answer* 6.9×10^{-12}

EXAMPLE 21.14
Solubility Product

The solubility product of Ag_2SO_4 is 1.5×10^{-5}. Calculate the solubility of this salt. (Assume that neither ion reacts appreciably with water to form H^+ or OH^-.)

If $x =$ solubility in moles per liter, then at equilibrium

$$Ag_2SO_4(s) \rightleftharpoons 2Ag^+ + SO_4^{2-}$$
$$ 2x \quad\quad x$$

The K_{sp} expression can be solved to find the solubility as follows:

$$K_{sp} = [Ag^+]^2[SO_4^{2-}] = (2x)^2(x) = 4x^3 = 1.5 \times 10^{-5}$$
$$x = \sqrt[3]{(1.5 \times 10^{-5})/4} = 0.016 \text{ mol/L}$$

The solubility of Ag_2SO_4 is 0.016 mol/L or 5.0 g/L.

Exercise   The solubility product of strontium sulfate is 3.5×10^{-7}. Calculate the solubility of this salt in water. (Assume that neither ion reacts appreciably with water to form H^+ or OH^-.) *Answer* 5.9×10^{-4} mol/L or 0.11 g/L

The solubility of a salt, in accordance with Le Chatelier's principle, is decreased by a common ion. K_{sp} values can be used to calculate solubilities in the presence of common ions.

EXAMPLE 21.15
Solubility Product

The solubility product of Ag_2SO_4 is 1.5×10^{-5}. Calculate the solubility of this salt in an aqueous solution that is 0.20 M Na_2SO_4. (Assume that none of the ions react appreciably with water to form H^+ or OH^-.)

Let x represent the molar solubility of Ag_2SO_4. From the chemical equation

$$Ag_2SO_4(s) \rightleftharpoons 2Ag^+ + SO_4^{2-}$$
$$ 2x \quad\quad x$$

we can see that the concentration of Ag^+ from the dissolution of Ag_2SO_4 will be equal to $2x$. However, there are two sources of SO_4^{2-} in this solution, the dissolved Ag_2SO_4 and the initial Na_2SO_4 in the solution. Therefore

$$K_{sp} = [Ag^+]^2[SO_4^{2-}] = (2x)^2(0.20 + x) = 1.5 \times 10^{-5}$$

Assuming $(0.20 + x) \approx 0.20$ gives

$$x = \sqrt{\frac{1.5 \times 10^{-5}}{(4)(0.20)}} = 0.0043 \text{ mol/L}$$

The approximation is valid, so the molar solubility is 0.0043 mol/L or 1.3 g/L. Note that the common ion effect has reduced the solubility from 5.0 g/L for Ag_2SO_4 in pure water (see Example 21.14) to 1.3 g/L in the Na_2SO_4 solution.

Exercise Calculate the solubility of $SrSO_4$ in a solution that is 0.10 M in Sr^{2+}. $K_{sp} = 3.5 \times 10^{-7}$ for $SrSO_4$. Compare this solubility to 0.11 g/L, which represents the solubility of $SrSO_4$ in pure water. (Assume that neither of the ions reacts appreciably with water to form H^+ or OH^-.) *Answer* 0.00064 g/L, solubility reduced to about 0.6% of the original value

---

The solubility of a salt can also be influenced by the reaction of its ions with water. Any reaction of the cation or anion with water—for example, reaction of a basic anion with water to give OH^-—will increase the solubility of the salt. Consider lead(II) sulfide, which is the salt of an anion of a weak diprotic acid. When lead(II) sulfide dissolves,

$$PbS(s) \rightleftharpoons Pb^{2+} + S^{2-} \qquad K_{sp} = [Pb^{2+}][S^{2-}] = 1 \times 10^{-28}$$

the following additional equilibria are established in the same solution:

$$S^{2-} + H_2O(l) \rightleftharpoons HS^- + OH^- \qquad K_{b_2} = \frac{[HS^-][OH^-]}{[S^{2-}]} = 3 \times 10^{-2} \quad \textbf{(21.24)}$$

$$HS^- + H_2O(l) \rightleftharpoons H_2S(aq) + OH^- \qquad K_{b_1} = \frac{[H_2S][OH^-]}{[HS^-]} = 1.0 \times 10^{-7} \quad \textbf{(21.25)}$$

Using the K_{sp} alone, the solubility of lead(II) sulfide is found to be 1×10^{-14} mol/L. However, most of the sulfide ion goes on to react with water. If reactions (21.24) and (21.25) are taken into account, the solubility of PbS is found to be 7×10^{-12} mol/L, 700 times greater than the solubility found without considering the reaction of sulfide ion with water. A slightly greater solubility would be found if the reaction of Pb^{2+} with water to give OH^- were also taken into account. In general, molar solubility cannot be calculated from K_{sp}, and vice versa, for salts containing ions that react with water.

21.12 K_{sp} AND PRECIPITATION

Table 21.6
Ion Product (Q_i) and Precipitation

$Q_i < K_{sp}$	All ions in solution
$Q_i = K_{sp}$	Equilibrium—a saturated solution
$Q_i > K_{sp}$	Precipitation occurs until $Q_i = K_{sp}$

The product of the concentrations of ions in a nonsaturated, or nonequilibrium, solution is called the ion product. The **ion product** is equivalent to the reaction quotient (Section 19.7) for the dissolution of an ionic solid, Q_i. For example, $[Ca^{2+}][SO_4^{2-}]$ is the ion product for any solution containing calcium and sulfate ions. The ion product equals the K_{sp} when the solution is saturated. If the ion product is smaller than the K_{sp}, all the Ca^{2+} and SO_4^{2-} ions present are in solution. If the ion product is larger than the K_{sp}, solid calcium sulfate precipitates until equilibrium between the solid and a solution saturated with ions is established—in other words, precipitation continues until the ion product of the ions in solution equals the K_{sp} (Table 21.6).

EXAMPLE 21.16
Solubility Product

A solution is 0.10 M in Ba^{2+} and 0.10 M in Sr^{2+}. $K_{sp} = 1.7 \times 10^{-10}$ for $BaSO_4$ and 3.5×10^{-7} for $SrSO_4$. Describe what happens as solid Na_2SO_4 is added to the solution.

To answer this question we first write the chemical equations and the related equilibrium expressions:

$$BaSO_4(s) \rightleftharpoons Ba^{2+} + SO_4^{2-} \quad K_{sp} = [Ba^{2+}][SO_4^{2-}] = 1.7 \times 10^{-10}$$
$$SrSO_4(s) \rightleftharpoons Sr^{2+} + SO_4^{2-} \quad K_{sp} = [Sr^{2+}][SO_4^{2-}] = 3.5 \times 10^{-7}$$

The Na_2SO_4 will dissolve as it is added, giving Na^+ and SO_4^{2-} ions in solution. The concentration of SO_4^{2-} increases until it reaches 1.7×10^{-9} mol/L, at which point the ion product for $BaSO_4$ is equal to K_{sp} $[(0.10) \times (1.7 \times 10^{-9}) = 1.7 \times 10^{-10}]$ and $BaSO_4$ begins to precipitate. The $BaSO_4$ continues to precipitate as SO_4^{2-} is added. When the concentration of SO_4^{2-} reaches 3.5×10^{-6} mol/L, the ion product for $SrSO_4$ is equal to the K_{sp} $[(0.10) \times (3.5 \times 10^{-6}) = 3.5 \times 10^{-7}]$, and as more Na_2SO_4 is added, both $SrSO_4$ and $BaSO_4$ precipitate.

Exercise A solution is 0.00010 M in Ba^{2+} and 0.75 M in Sr^{2+}. $K_{sp} = 1.7 \times 10^{-10}$ for $BaSO_4$ and 3.5×10^{-7} for $SrSO_4$. Describe what happens as solid Na_2SO_4 is added to the solution. *Answer* $SrSO_4$ begins to precipitate at $[SO_4^{2-}] = 4.7 \times 10^{-7}$ mol/L and $BaSO_4$ begins to precipitate at $[SO_4^{2-}] = 1.7 \times 10^{-6}$ mol/L

EXAMPLE 21.17
Solubility Product

What percentage of the Ba^{2+} remains in solution at the point where the precipitation of $SrSO_4$ begins in the solution described in Example 21.16?

At $[SO_4^{2-}] = 3.5 \times 10^{-6}$ mol/L, the amount of Ba^{2+} remaining in solution is found from the expression for the solubility product:

$$1.7 \times 10^{-10} = [Ba^{2+}](3.5 \times 10^{-6})$$
$$[Ba^{2+}] = 4.9 \times 10^{-5} \text{ mol/L}$$

Thus

$$\frac{4.9 \times 10^{-5} \text{ M}}{0.10 \text{ M}} \times 100\% = 0.049\%$$

Of the original Ba^{2+}, 0.049% remains.

Exercise What percentage of the Sr^{2+} remains in solution at the point at which precipitation of $BaSO_4$ begins in the solution described in the exercise that follows Example 21.16? *Answer* 28%

21.13 K_{sp} AND THE DISSOLUTION OF IONIC PRECIPITATES

Ionic substances that are slightly soluble can be brought into solution by the application of Le Chatelier's principle. Any process that will remove, say, a calcium ion from a saturated calcium sulfate solution,

$$\xrightarrow{\text{remove } Ca^{2+}}$$
$$CaSO_4(s) \rightleftharpoons Ca^{2+} + SO_4^{2-}$$

will cause more of the calcium sulfate to dissolve. Removal of an ion causes the ion product to drop to less than the K_{sp} value; more of the salt dissolves until the equilibrium is reestablished and $Q_i = K_{sp}$ once more.

Most often, when it is necessary to increase the solubility of a salt, ions in solution are "removed" by nonredox reactions that produce weak electrolytes such as water, weak acids, or complex ions. Redox reactions are also sometimes used to bring precipitates into solution. All of these ways of dissolving precipitates are important in the separation and identification of cations in qualitative analysis (Section 21.15; most of the examples given here are drawn from the qualitative analysis scheme).

a. Solubility and pH The solubility of any salt that contains a basic anion is influenced by pH. Many of the more common insoluble salts are hydroxides, carbonates, or sulfides. The hydroxide, carbonate, and sulfide anions—OH^-, CO_3^{2-}, and S^{2-}—are Brønsted-Lowry bases and combine with hydrogen ions to give weakly ionized conjugate acids: H_2O; HCO_3^- and H_2CO_3; HS^- and H_2S.

Practically all water-insoluble metal hydroxides that are basic or amphoteric dissolve readily in solutions of strong acid, for example,

$$Fe(OH)_3(s) + 3H_3O^+ \longrightarrow Fe^{3+} + 6H_2O(l)$$
$$Al(OH)_3(s) + 3H_3O^+ \longrightarrow Al^{3+} + 6H_2O(l)$$

Dissolution occurs because the hydrogen ion from the acid reacts with the hydroxide ion from the salt to form water, a very weak electrolyte.

Recall that all possible equilibria are established simultaneously in any solution. Therefore, the hydroxide ion concentration in all aqueous solutions must satisfy the ion product constant for water, and the OH^- concentration in any solution of known H^+ concentration can be found from

$$K_w = [H^+][OH^-] = 1.00 \times 10^{-14}$$

For example, in a solution 1 M each in Fe^{3+} and H^+, we know from K_w that $[OH^-] = 1.00 \times 10^{-14}$, giving for the ion product of $Fe(OH)_3$ in this solution

$$[Fe^{3+}][OH^-]^3 = (1)(1 \times 10^{-14})^3 = 1 \times 10^{-42}$$

Because this value is smaller than the solubility product (3×10^{-39}), no solid $Fe(OH)_3$ will form in a solution that is 1 M in both Fe^{3+} and H^+.

The dissolution of slightly soluble metal carbonates in acid solution is governed by the transformations

$$CO_3^{2-} \xrightarrow{H^+} HCO_3^- \xrightarrow{H^+} H_2CO_3(aq) \longrightarrow CO_2(aq \text{ or } g) + H_2O(l)$$

The HCO_3^- ion and H_2CO_3 are weak electrolytes. Moreover, H_2CO_3 is unstable; decomposition to CO_2 and H_2O is favored by high hydrogen ion concentration. All insoluble metal carbonates dissolve in acid solutions, even solutions of such weak acids as acetic acid.

$$MCO_3(s) + 2H_3O^+ \longrightarrow M^{2+} + CO_2(g) + 3H_2O(l)$$

where M = dipositive metal ion.

The metal sulfides with *relatively* large solubility products (e.g., MnS, 2.3×10^{-13}; FeS, 4.2×10^{-17}; ZnS, 2×10^{-24}) are readily soluble in hydrochloric acid because of the formation of weakly ionized and volatile H_2S.

$$FeS(s) + H_3O^+ \longrightarrow Fe^{2+} + H_2S(aq \text{ or } g) + 2H_2O(l)$$

Such sulfides will not precipitate in an acidic solution because the presence of H^+ ion from the strong acid represses the ionization of H_2S and keeps the sulfide ion concentration in solution too low (see Figure 21.3). Sulfides that are even less soluble will precipitate from such a solution, however, allowing separation of cations by separation of their more and less soluble sulfides.

Writing the complete equation shows that the dissolution of a salt by an acid is a partner-exchange type of reaction, for example,

$$FeS(s) + 2HCl(aq) \longrightarrow FeCl_2(aq) + H_2S(aq)$$

EXAMPLE 21.18
Solubility Product

A 0.010 mol sample of $Fe(OH)_3(s)$ was added to 1.0 L of water, and a strong acid was added until the precipitate dissolved (assume negligible volume change due to added acid). At what pH was all of the solid $Fe(OH)_3$ dissolved? $K_{sp} = 3 \times 10^{-39}$ for $Fe(OH)_3$.

When all of the $Fe(OH)_3$ had dissolved, 0.010 mol of Fe^{3+} was present in 1 L of solution. The concentration of OH^- at the point where dissolution was complete can be found from the solubility product expression for $Fe(OH)_3$:

$$Fe(OH)_3(s) \rightleftharpoons Fe^{3+} + 3OH^- \qquad K_{sp} = [Fe^{3+}][OH^-]^3 = 3 \times 10^{-39}$$

$$[OH^-] = \sqrt[3]{\frac{K_{sp}}{[Fe^{3+}]}} = \sqrt[3]{\frac{3 \times 10^{-39}}{0.010}} = 7 \times 10^{-13} \text{ mol/L}$$

This $[OH^-]$ corresponds to

$$pOH = -\log [OH^-] = -\log (7 \times 10^{-13}) = 12.2$$
$$pH = 14.0 - pOH = 14.0 - 12.2 = 1.8$$

The pH at which all of the $Fe(OH)_3$ was dissolved was 1.8.

Exercise A 0.010 mol sample of $Fe(OH)_2(s)$ was added to 1.0 L of water and a strong acid was added until the solid dissolved (assume negligible volume change due to added acid). At what pH did all of the solid $Fe(OH)_2$ dissolve? $K_{sp} = 8 \times 10^{-16}$ for $Fe(OH)_2$. *Answer 7.5*

b. Solubility and complex ion formation The formation and dissolution of precipitates can sometimes be controlled by complex ion formation (Section 14.10). For example, the distinctive reactions of nickel and zinc ions with ammonia play a role in detecting the presence of these ions in solution. The hydroxides first precipitate upon addition of the aqueous ammonia solution, but then dissolve by the formation of complexes with the excess ammonia.

$$Ni^{2+} \xrightarrow{NH_3(aq)} \underset{pale\ green}{Ni(OH)_2(s)} \xrightarrow{NH_3(aq,\ xs)} \underset{deep\ blue}{[Ni(NH_3)_6]^{2+}}$$

$$Zn^{2+} \xrightarrow{NH_3(aq)} \underset{white}{Zn(OH)_2(s)} \xrightarrow{NH_3(aq,\ xs)} \underset{colorless}{[Zn(NH_3)_4]^{2+}}$$

In some instances, less soluble metal sulfides are brought into solution by hydrochloric acid, because both the cations and the sulfide ions are converted to weak electrolytes, the cations forming complex ions, for example,

$$Sb_2S_3(s) + 6H^+ + 8Cl^- \longrightarrow 2[SbCl_4]^- + 3H_2S(aq)$$
$$SnS_2(s) + 4H^+ + 6Cl^- \longrightarrow [SnCl_6]^{2-} + 2H_2S(aq)$$

c. Solubility and redox reactions Some very slightly soluble metal sulfides (e.g., CuS, $K_{sp} = 6 \times 10^{-36}$; HgS, $K_{sp} = 4 \times 10^{-53}$) furnish so little S^{2-} in saturated solutions that they cannot be dissolved by aqueous HCl. (HgS dissolves very slowly in concentrated HCl, S^{2-} being converted to H_2S and Hg^{2+} to the weakly dissociated $[HgCl_4]^{2-}$ complex.) In these cases S^{2-} can be effectively removed by oxidation to elemental sulfur. For PbS and CuS, 0.3 M nitric acid serves as the oxidizing agent, for example,

$$3PbS(s) + 8H^+ + 2NO_3^- \longrightarrow 3Pb^{2+} + 3S(s) + 2NO(g) + 4H_2O(l)$$

The much less soluble HgS does not furnish sufficient S^{2-} in saturated solution for oxidation with 0.3 M nitric acid to occur, and *aqua regia* (concentrated HCl and concentrated HNO_3 in a ratio of 3:1 by volume) is used. This reagent converts S^{2-} to the free element and at the same time ties up Hg^{2+} as the $[HgCl_4]^{2-}$ complex.

COMPLEX ION EQUILIBRIA

21.14 DISSOCIATION OF
COMPLEX IONS; K_d

Like polyprotic acids, complex ions in aqueous solution dissociate by stepwise equilibria. The ligands separate from the metal ion one by one, and equilibrium constants can be determined for each dissociation step, for example,

$$[Ag(NH_3)_2]^+ \rightleftharpoons [Ag(NH_3)]^+ + NH_3(aq)$$

$$K_1 = \frac{[NH_3][Ag(NH_3)^+]}{[Ag(NH_3)_2{}^+]} = 1.45 \times 10^{-4} \qquad \textbf{(21.26)}$$

$$[Ag(NH_3)]^+ \rightleftharpoons Ag^+ + NH_3(aq)$$

$$K_2 = \frac{[NH_3][Ag^+]}{[Ag(NH_3)^+]} = 4.3 \times 10^{-4} \qquad \textbf{(21.27)}$$

Equilibrium constants for the dissociation of complex ions are called **dissociation constants,** K_d. Some representative K_d values are given in Table 21.7 (Others are given in Table 32.5 and in Appendix V.4.) The tabulated dissociation constants are overall constants, like the overall acid dissociation constants for polyprotic acids (Section 21.7b). For the silver–ammonia complex ion

$$[Ag(NH_3)_2]^+ \rightleftharpoons Ag^+ + 2NH_3(aq)$$

$$K_d = K_1 \times K_2 = (1.45 \times 10^{-4})(4.3 \times 10^{-4}) = 6.2 \times 10^{-8}$$

$$= \frac{[NH_3][Ag(NH_3)^+]}{[Ag(NH_3)_2{}^+]} \times \frac{[NH_3][Ag^+]}{[Ag(NH_3)^+]}$$

$$= \frac{[NH_3]^2[Ag^+]}{[Ag(NH_3)_2{}^+]} \qquad \textbf{(21.28)}$$

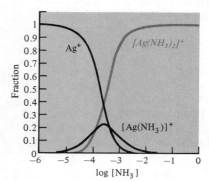

Figure 21.11

Effect of [NH₃] on the Complexation of Ag⁺ by NH₃ The "fraction" plotted is the fraction of the Ag⁺ present as the uncomplexed ion and the ions with one and two ligands. You can see that the concentration of Ag[NH₃]⁺ initially rises as [NH₃] increases, and then falls as both Ag⁺ and Ag[NH₃]⁺ are converted to Ag[NH₃]₂⁺. (Note that NH₃ concentration increases from left to right in this plot of log [NH₃].)

The similarity of complex ion equilibria and polyprotic acid equilibria extends to the relationships among the various possible ions that may be formed and also to the limitations on the use of overall equilibrium constants. Rearrangement of, for example, Equation (21.26), shows the relationship between the concentration of the ligand, ammonia, and the relative amounts of the ions present.

$$[NH_3] = \frac{[Ag(NH_3)_2{}^+]}{[Ag(NH_3)^+]} K_1$$

Figure 21.11 illustrates this relationship for the silver–ammonia complex. As the concentration of ammonia increases, the fraction of uncomplexed silver ion decreases, in accordance with Le Chatelier's principle — the dissociation equilibria are driven toward complex ion formation.

Overall dissociation constants for complex ions can be used for calculation of the equilibrium concentrations of metal ion and final complex ion only when excess

Table 21.7
Dissociation Constants, K_d, for Complex Ions in Aqueous Solution (at 25 °C)

$[Ag(NH_3)_2]^+ \rightleftharpoons Ag^+ + 2NH_3$	6.2×10^{-8}
$[AgCl_2]^- \rightleftharpoons Ag^+ + 2Cl^-$	9×10^{-6}
$[Au(CN)_2]^- \rightleftharpoons Au^{3+} + 2CN^-$	5×10^{-39}
$[Cd(CN)_4]^{2-} \rightleftharpoons Cd^{2+} + 4CN^-$	8.2×10^{-18}
$[CdI_4]^{2-} \rightleftharpoons Cd^{2+} + 4I^-$	8×10^{-7}
$[Cu(NH_3)_4]^{2+} \rightleftharpoons Cu^{2+} + 4NH_3$	1×10^{-13}
$[Cu(OH)_4]^{2-} \rightleftharpoons Cu^{2+} + 4OH^-$	7.6×10^{-17}
$[Fe(CN)_6]^{4-} \rightleftharpoons Fe^{2+} + 6CN^-$	1.3×10^{-37}
$[Fe(CN)_6]^{3-} \rightleftharpoons Fe^{3+} + 6CN^-$	1.3×10^{-44}
$[HgCl_4]^{2-} \rightleftharpoons Hg^{2+} + 4Cl^-$	2×10^{-16}
$[Zn(OH)_4]^{2-} \rightleftharpoons Zn^{2+} + 4OH^-$	5×10^{-21}

Note: Equilibrium expressions for complex ions are sometimes given as stability, or formation, constants, K_f, which represent the reverse of the reactions in this table and are equal to $1/K_d$.

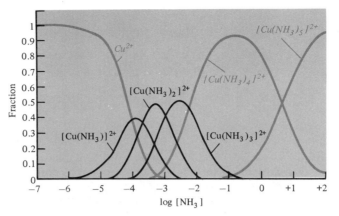

Figure 21.12

Effect of [NH₃] on the Complexation of Cu²⁺ by NH₃ The "fraction" plotted is the fraction of the Cu²⁺ present as the uncomplexed ion and the complexes with one, two, three, four, and five ligands. [Cu(NH₃)₅]²⁺ forms only when [NH₃] > 1 M and is not of concern at lower [NH₃].

ligand is present. Look at the curves for a complex ion that includes four ligands, [Cu(NH₃)₄]²⁺ (Figure 21.12). At any ammonia concentration less than 0.1 M (log [NH₃] = −1) there are from two to five ions of unknown concentration present in the solution. Calculation of these curves requires the solution of five equations in five unknowns. (At ammonia concentrations > 1 M a fifth ligand is added.)

IDENTIFICATION OF IONS IN AQUEOUS SOLUTION

21.15 INORGANIC QUALITATIVE ANALYSIS

The properties of ions in aqueous solution are determined to a great extent by their strengths as Brønsted-Lowry acids and bases, the solubilities of their salts, the stabilities of their complex ions, and their strengths as oxidizing and reducing agents. By taking advantage of similarities and differences in such properties, the methods of **inorganic qualitative analysis** allow the identification of the cations and anions present in an aqueous solution of unknown composition.

You may have the opportunity to do some qualitative chemical analysis in the laboratory. Anions in solution are identified by their general and specific chemical properties. Cations are first separated into groups by precipitating those in one group while leaving the cations of other groups in solution. For example, the addition of hydrochloric acid will precipitate Hg_2^{2+}, Pb^{2+}, and Ag^+ as chlorides, while other ions, for example Fe^{3+}, Cu^{2+}, Sb^{3+}, or Sn^{2+}, are left in solution. The cations precipitated as a group are further separated and then identified by specific reactions known as confirmatory tests.

To illustrate how the chemical properties of cations in aqueous solution are utilized in qualitative analysis, the reactions of Fe^{2+} during an analysis in the presence of other ions are shown below. At each step except the last (the confirmatory tests), the Fe^{2+} is being separated from other ions that react in different ways or do not react. At each step concentrations are adjusted so that the appropriate equilibrium is achieved.

Precipitation: governed by $K_{sp} = 8 \times 10^{-16}$ for $Fe(OH)_2$. The OH⁻ concentration is increased sufficiently to cause precipitation.

$$Fe^{2+} + 2OH^-(xs) \rightleftharpoons Fe(OH)_2(s)$$

Conversion to less soluble precipitate: governed by $K_{sp} = 4.2 \times 10^{-17}$ for FeS. The sulfide ion concentration necessary for precipitation is controlled by controlling the OH⁻ concentration in a saturated H₂S solution.

$$Fe(OH)_2(s) + S^{2-} \xrightleftharpoons[\substack{\text{(high} \\ [S^{2-}])}]{OH^-} FeS(s) + 2OH^-$$

Dissolution in acid: driven by reaction of basic anion with acid to give H₂S.

$$FeS(s) + 2H_3O^+ \longrightarrow Fe^{2+} + H_2S(g) + 2H_2O(l)$$

Oxidation: driven by strength of NO_3^- in acid solution as oxidizing agent.

$$3Fe^{2+} + NO_3^- + 4H^+ \longrightarrow 3Fe^{3+} + NO(g) + 2H_2O(l)$$

Confirmatory tests: Only Fe^{3+} gives these characteristic colors.

$$Fe^{3+} + K^+ + [Fe(CN)_6]^{4-} \rightleftharpoons KFe[Fe(CN)_6](s)$$
dark blue

$$Fe^{3+} + NCS^- \rightleftharpoons [Fe(NCS)]^{2+}$$
blood red

SUMMARY

21.1 REACTIONS OF IONS WITH WATER All ions in aqueous solution are hydrated. Anions that are weaker bases than water—the conjugate bases of strong acids—become hydrated without undergoing any reaction with water. The same is true of cations of low charge-to-size ratio. Such ions do not affect the pH of a solution. Anions that are stronger bases than water—the conjugate bases of weak acids—are able to attract protons away from water molecules, producing alkaline aqueous solutions. Cations that are stronger acids than water—the ammonium ion and metal ions of high charge-to-size ratio—give acidic aqueous solutions. These ions donate protons: the ammonium ion directly, the hydrated metal cations from associated water molecules.

21.2 THE BEHAVIOR OF SALTS TOWARD WATER An aqueous solution of a salt may be neutral, acidic, or alkaline. If neither ion reacts with water the solution will be neutral. If only the anion reacts, the solution will be alkaline; if only the cation reacts, the solution will be acidic. If both ions react, the pH of the solution will depend on the relative extents of the two reactions.

21.3 EQUILIBRIUM CONSTANTS FOR THE REACTIONS OF IONS AND SALTS WITH WATER; pH OF SALT SOLUTIONS The K_b for a basic anion is related to the ion product constant for water, K_w, and the K_a for its conjugate acid by the equation $K_b = K_w/K_a$. Similarly, the K_a for an acidic cation is given by $K_a = K_w/K_b$, where K_b is the ionization constant of its conjugate base. If only one ion of a salt reacts with water, the pH of a solution can be calculated from the K_a or K_b of the ion that reacts. The equilibrium constant for the reaction with water of a salt containing two ions that react with water is given by the equation $K = K_w/K_aK_b$, where K_a is the ionization constant for the conjugate acid of the basic anion in the salt and K_b is the ionization constant for the conjugate base of the acidic cation in the salt. When $K_a > K_b$ the solution is acidic; when $K_b > K_a$ the solution is alkaline.

21.4 THE COMMON ION EFFECT **21.5** BUFFER SOLUTIONS The common ion effect is the displacement of an ionic equilibrium by an excess of one or more of the ions involved in the equilibrium. One use of the common ion effect is to control the pH of a solution of a weak acid or base. A combination of a weak acid and its conjugate base, or of a weak base and its conjugate acid, constitutes a buffer solution. Such a solution resists changes in pH when acid or base is added to it. Weak acid/conjugate base buffer pairs give solutions buffered in the acid pH range; weak base/conjugate acid buffer pairs give solutions buffered in the alkaline pH range. The pH of an acidic buffer solution is related to the pK_a of the acid in the solution by the Henderson-Hasselbach equation: $pH = pK_a - \log [HA]/[A^-]$. A buffer is best able to maintain a constant pH in the range $pH = pK_a \pm 1$.

21.6 LIMITATIONS ON THE USE OF EQUILIBRIUM CONSTANTS **21.7** POLYPROTIC ACIDS The mathematics of equilibrium problems is simplest when solutions are neither extremely concentrated nor extremely dilute. (In concentrated solutions activities rather than concentrations must be used; in dilute solutions the ionization of water must be taken into account.) When one equilibrium in a complex situation yields much higher concentrations of products than others, the contributions of the other equilibria can often be ignored, simplifying the calculations. Such simplifying assumptions are illustrated in the discussion of the polyprotic acids H_2SO_4, H_2S, and H_3PO_4 in Section 21.7.

TOOLS OF CHEMISTRY: MEASURING pH   The pH of solutions is commonly measured by means of an indicator or with a pH meter. An indicator is an organic acid or base containing a group that reacts with H^+ or OH^- ion in such a way that the compound changes color. Most indicators have a useful color change over a range of 2 pH units. A pH meter employs electrodes to measure the potential difference between solutions of known and unknown pH.

21.8 ACID–BASE REACTIONS AND TITRATION IN AQUEOUS SOLUTIONS   **21.9** TITRATION CURVES
Titration of an acid and a base is a technique used to determine the concentration of acids or bases in solution. It involves measurement of the volume of a solution of one reactant that is required to react completely with a measured amount of another reactant. The point at which equivalent amounts of acid and base have reacted is the equivalence point. All acid–base titrations go essentially to completion; however, the resulting solution is not necessarily neutral. The change of pH in the course of an acid–base titration can be represented by a titration curve. The shape of such a curve varies with the concentrations of the reactants and the strengths of the acid and base involved.

21.10 SOLUBILITY PRODUCT, K_{sp} **21.11** K_{sp} AND SOLUBILITY   The equilibrium constant for a solid electrolyte in equilibrium with its ions is called the solubility product. For salts of ions that do not react significantly with water, it is possible to find K_{sp} values from solubilities or vice versa. K_{sp} values can also be used to calculate solubilities in the presence of common ions, which decrease solubility (Le Chatelier's principle).

21.12 K_{sp} AND PRECIPITATION   **21.13** K_{sp} AND THE DISSOLUTION OF IONIC PRECIPITATES   The ion product is the reaction quotient for the dissolution of an ionic solid. If the ion product is larger than K_{sp}, the solid will precipitate out until the two values are equal, at which point the solid will be in equilibrium with a solution saturated with ions. Ionic substances that are slightly soluble can be brought into solution by means of reactions that remove an ion — e.g., by formation of a weak electrolyte such as water, a weak acid, or a complex ion, or by a redox reaction.

21.14 DISSOCIATION OF COMPLEX IONS; K_d **21.15** INORGANIC QUALITATIVE ANALYSIS
Complex ions, like polyprotic acids, dissociate in aqueous solution by stepwise equilibria. Equilibrium constants for the dissociation of complex ions are called dissociation constants, K_d. Inorganic qualitative analysis exploits the similarities and differences in the properties and equilibria of ions, their compounds, and their complexes to identify the cations and anions present in an aqueous solution of unknown composition.

SIGNIFICANT TERMS

hydrolysis of an ion
common ion
common ion effect
buffer solution
equivalence point
titration
indicator
end point
titration curve
solubility product
ion product
dissociation constants (complex ions)
inorganic qualitative analysis

THOUGHTS ON CHEMISTRY

Signs of Solubility

CHEMICAL MANIPULATION, being instructions to students in chemistry, on the methods of performing experiments of demonstration or of research with accuracy and success, by Michael Faraday, 1827

333. There are two great and general objects to be gained by solution, which render it a process of constant occurrence in the laboratory. The first is that of preparing substances for the exertion of chemical action; and from the perfect manner in which it separates the particles one from another, every obstacle dependant upon the attraction of aggregation is removed, at the same time that other advantages are obtained. The second object is that of separating one substance from another; this being continually effected by the use of such fluids as have a solvent power over one or more of the substances present.

338. If the substance appear to be insoluble, or if it be necessary to know whether it be soluble in alcohol, ether, oils, or any other body, for the purpose of selecting a solvent from among them, a portion should be pulverized finely, and introduced into a small tube with a little of the

fluid to be tried, and heated; if the substance disappear, it is of course soluble. But if it be supposed to be a mixed body, and partly soluble, though not altogether so, then the presumed solution should be poured from the tube into an earthenware or platina capsule, and evaporated carefully and slowly; if any substance remain, it of course indicates a degree of solubility. Trials by evaporation cannot be made with oil unless the body be fixed and will allow the oil to be burned off; nor can trials of very volatile bodies be made in this manner. It is almost needless to add, that cases may occur requiring much chemical skill and judgment; and that it would be impossible to give directions for every possible case.

339. Indications of solution dependant upon chemical action are obtained from the changed appearance of the substance. A body not soluble in water except by the use of acids or alkalies, is generally, though not always, rendered so by chemical action, and has its properties changed. It is rarely that these chemical agents are applied with any other liquid than water. Indications of their power may be obtained in the manner before directed.

341. It may here be proper to warn the student of an appearance which sometimes takes place during mere solution, which has been frequently misconstrued into an indication of chemical action. Common salt, and several other salts, as well as their strong solutions, and also alcohol or spirit added to common or even distilled water, which has been exposed to air, frequently causes the evolution of a number of small air bubbles; these have the appearance of being the direct result of some chemical action, but are occasioned merely by the expulsion of the air dissolved in the water, which being incompatible with the substances added, is separated. Some of those solutions which dissolve air, produce the same appearances when added to the bodies mentioned.

Michael Faraday, *Chemical Manipulation* (London, 1827). Quoted from Halsted Press edition (New York: Wiley, 1974).

QUESTIONS

Acid–Base Equilibria

21.1 Some anions, upon dissolution, undergo no significant reaction with water molecules. What is the relative base strength of such an anion compared to water? What will be the effect on the pH of the solution upon dissolution of these anions?

21.2 Some cations, upon dissolution, undergo no significant reactions with water molecules. What is the relative acid strength of such a cation compared to water? What will be the effect on the pH of the solution upon dissolution of these cations?

21.3 Some anions, upon dissolution, react with water molecules. What is the relative base strength of such an anion compared to water? What will be the effect on the pH of the solution upon dissolution of these anions?

21.4 Some cations, upon dissolution, react with water molecules. What is the relative acid strength of such a cation compared to water? What will be the effect on the pH of the solution upon dissolution of these cations?

21.5 Choose the anions that will react with water to form OH^-: (a) S^{2-}, (b) HS^- (c) F^-, (d) ClO_4^-, and (e) NO_2^-. Write chemical equations for the hydrolysis reactions.

21.6 Repeat Question 21.5 for (a) I^-, (b) SO_4^{2-}, (c) HSO_4^-, (d) NO_3^-, and (e) NH_2^-. Write chemical equations for the hydrolysis reactions.

21.7 Choose the cations that will react with water to form H^+: (a) K^+, (b) NH_4^+, (c) $[Al(H_2O)_6]^{3+}$, (d) $[Fe(H_2O)_6]^{3+}$, and (e) $[Sr(H_2O)_6]^{2+}$. Write chemical equations for the reactions.

21.8 Repeat Question 21.7 for (a) $[Zn(H_2O)_6]^{2+}$, (b) $[Ca(H_2O)_6]^{2+}$, (c) $[Be(H_2O)_4]^{2+}$, and (d) $[Na(H_2O)_n]^+$. Write chemical equations for the reactions.

21.9 Classify aqueous solutions of the following salts as (a) acidic, (b) alkaline, or (c) essentially neutral: (i) $(NH_4)HSO_4$; (ii) $(NH_4)_2SO_4$, $K_a > K_b$; (iii) KCl; (iv) $LiCN$; and (v) $Al(NO_3)_3$.

21.10 Repeat Question 21.9 for (i) $NaClO_4$; (ii) $K_2C_2O_4$; (iii) $(NH_4)_2S$, $K_a < K_b$; (iv) NaH_2PO_4; and (v) NH_4CN, $K_a < K_b$.

21.11 Consider the reaction of cyanide ion with water:

$$CN^- + H_2O(l) \rightleftharpoons HCN(aq) + OH^-$$

Give some examples of substances that you could add that would illustrate the common ion effect. How would each of these substances affect the equilibrium?

21.12 Write the chemical equation for the ionization of formic acid, HCOOH. Give some examples of substances that you could add that would illustrate the common ion effect. How would each of these substances affect the equilibrium?

21.13 Briefly describe why the pH of a buffer solution remains nearly constant upon the addition of small amounts of acid or base. Over what pH range do we observe the best buffering action (nearly constant pH)?

21.14 Write chemical equations showing the stepwise ionization of sulfuric acid. Which anion(s) of sulfuric acid will react with water to change the pH?

21.15 Write chemical equations for the stepwise ionization of phosphoric acid. Which anion(s) of phosphoric acid will react with water to change the pH? Compare the base strengths of the various anions.

21.16 Repeat Question 21.15 for hydrosulfuric acid.

21.17 Will a solution always be neutral when stoichiometric amounts of acid and base have been mixed? Explain your answer.

21.18 Write the net ionic equation and equilibrium constant expression for the reaction between a strong monoprotic acid and a strong monohydroxo base which form a completely soluble salt.

21.19 Write the net ionic equation and corresponding equilibrium constant expression for the neutralization of a weak monoprotic acid by a strong monohydroxo base. Will the value of the equilibrium constant be as large as that for the reaction described in Question 21.18?

21.20 What is an acid–base indicator? Write the chemical equation showing the equilibrium involved for the indicator "HInd." Why do we limit the amount of indicator added to a titration solution?

21.21 Using Table A, Tools of Chemistry, choose one or more indicators that could be used to "signal" reaching a pH of (a) 2.4, (b) 7, (c) 10.3, (d) 5.1.

21.22 A "universal" indicator was prepared by mixing methyl red with thymolphthalein. What color would be observed at a pH value of (a) 3, (b) 7, (c) 11?

21.23 Make a rough sketch of the titration curve expected for the titration of a strong acid with a strong base. What determines the pH of the solution at the following points: (a) no base added, (b) half-equivalence point, (c) equivalence point, and (d) excess base?

21.24 Repeat Question 21.23 for the titration of a weak acid with a strong base.

21.25* Make a rough sketch of the titration curve expected for the titration of a diprotic acid with a strong base. What determines the pH of the solution at each of the following points: (a) no base added, (b) first half-equivalence point, (c) first equivalence point, (d) second half-equivalence point, (e) second equivalence point, and (f) excess base?

Solubility Equilibria

21.26 For each of the following chemical equations, write the expression for the solubility product: (a) $Ag_2SO_4(s) \rightleftharpoons 2Ag^+ + SO_4^{2-}$, (b) $Fe_2S_3 \rightleftharpoons 2Fe^{3+} + 3S^{2-}$, and (c) $SrCrO_4(s) \rightleftharpoons Sr^{2+} + CrO_4^{2-}$.

21.27 Repeat Question 21.26 for (a) $Hg_2Br_2(s) \rightleftharpoons Hg_2^{2+} + 2Br^-$, (b) $CdCO_3(s) \rightleftharpoons Cd^{2+} + CO_3^{2-}$, and (c) $Mn_3(PO_4)_2 \rightleftharpoons 3Mn^{2+} + 2PO_4^{3-}$.

21.28 What is meant by the term "ion product"? What will happen in a solution in which the ion product is (a) larger than K_{sp}, (b) smaller than K_{sp}, or (c) equal to K_{sp}?

21.29 How can most water-insoluble metal hydroxides be dissolved? Write a chemical equation for the dissolution of $Fe(OH)_3$.

21.30 How does the presence of excess H_3O^+ aid in the dissolution of slightly soluble metal carbonates? Write the chemical equation for the dissolution of $MnCO_3$.

21.31 Write chemical equations for the dissolution of FeS and of SnS_2 in HCl solution.

Complex Ion Equilibria

21.32 Write the chemical equations and the expressions for the dissociation constants for the stepwise dissociation of the $[Fe(C_2O_4)_3]^{3-}$ complex. What is the relationship between the overall dissociation constant and the stepwise constants?

21.33 Repeat Question 21.32 for $[Ag(CN)_2]^-$.

Answers to Selected Questions

21.2 The cation is a weaker acid than water; it has no effect on pH.

21.4 The cation is a stronger acid than water; it will decrease pH.

21.6 SO_4^{2-}, NH_2^-; (b) $SO_4^{2-} + H_2O \rightleftharpoons HSO_4^- + OH^-$, (e) $NH_2^- + H_2O \longrightarrow NH_3 + OH^-$

21.8 $[Zn(H_2O)_6]^{2+}$, $[Be(H_2O)_4]^{2+}$; (a) $[Zn(H_2O)_6]^{2+} + H_2O \rightleftharpoons [Zn(OH)(H_2O)_5]^+ + H_3O^+$, (c) $[Be(H_2O)_4]^{2+} + H_2O \rightleftharpoons [Be(OH)(H_2O)_3]^+ + H_3O^+$

21.10 (b) ii, iii, iv, v; (c) i

21.12 $HCOOH(aq) + H_2O(l) \rightleftharpoons H_3O^+ + HCOO^-$; a soluble formate salt such as Na(HCOO) or an acid such as HCl; they would reduce the extent of ionization of HCOOH.

21.16 $H_2S(aq) + H_2O(l) \rightleftharpoons HS^- + H_3O^+$, $HS^- + H_2O(l)$ $\rightleftharpoons S^{2-} + H_3O^+$, HS^- and S^{2-} will react with water to form OH^-, K_b for $S^{2-} > K_b$ for HS^-

21.22 (a) red, (b) yellow, (c) green

21.27 (a) $K_{sp} = [Hg_2^{2+}][Br^-]^2$, (b) $K_{sp} = [Cd^{2+}][CO_3^{2-}]$, (c) $K_{sp} = [Mn^{2+}]^3[PO_4^{3-}]^2$

21.33 $[Ag(CN)_2]^- \rightleftharpoons AgCN(s) + CN^-$, $AgCN(s) \rightleftharpoons Ag^+ + CN^-$; $K_{d_1} = [CN^-]/[Ag(CN)_2^-]$, $K_{d_2} = [Ag^+][CN^-] = K_{sp}$; $K_d = (K_{d_1})(K_{sp})$

PROBLEMS

Reactions of Ions with Water

21.1 Calculate the equilibrium constant for the reaction of fluoride ion with water. $K_a = 6.5 \times 10^{-4}$ for HF.

21.2 Calculate the equilibrium constant for the reaction of hypoiodite ion with water. $K_a = 2.3 \times 10^{-11}$ for HIO. *Answer* 4.3×10^{-4}

21.3 Calculate the equilibrium constant for the reaction of ammonium ion with water. $K_b = 1.6 \times 10^{-5}$ for NH_3.

21.4 What is the value of the equilibrium constant for the reaction of ammonium fluoride with water? $K_a = 6.5 \times 10^{-4}$ for HF and $K_b = 1.6 \times 10^{-5}$ for NH_3.

21.5 What is the value of the equilibrium constant for the reaction of ammonium hypoiodite with water? $K_a = 2.3 \times 10^{-11}$ for HIO and $K_b = 1.6 \times 10^{-5}$ for NH_3. *Answer* 27

21.6 What is the pH of a 0.10 M solution of KF? $K_b = 1.5 \times 10^{-11}$ for F^-.

21.7 What is the pH of a 0.10 M solution of KIO? $K_b = 4.3 \times 10^{-4}$ for IO^-. *Answer* 11.80

21.8 What is the pH of a 0.10 M solution of NH_4NO_3? $K_a = 6.3 \times 10^{-10}$ for NH_4^+.

21.9 Repeat the calculations of Problem 21.6 for 0.050 M and 0.010 M solutions. What is the trend of the pH with concentration?

21.10 A weak acid, HA, is too unstable to be isolated in pure form. However, the sodium salt of the acid, NaA, is stable and dissociates completely in aqueous solution. Calculate the K_a for the acid if a 0.10 M solution of NaA has a pH of 8.64. *Answer* 5.3×10^{-5}

Common Ion Effect

21.11 What is the pH of a solution that is 0.050 M in sodium acetate and 0.010 M in acetic acid? $K_a = 1.754 \times 10^{-5}$ for CH_3COOH.

21.12 What is the pH of a solution that is 0.025 M in NH_4Cl and 0.010 M in NH_3? $K_b = 1.6 \times 10^{-5}$ for NH_3.

21.13 What is the pH of a solution that is 0.50 M in HCN and 0.25 M in KCN? Why is this an alkaline solution? $K_a = 6.2 \times 10^{-10}$ for HCN. *Answer* 8.92, K_b for $CN^- > K_a$ for HCN

21.14 What is the concentration of acetate ion in a solution that is 0.10 M HCl and 0.10 M CH_3COOH? $K_a = 1.754 \times 10^{-5}$ for CH_3COOH. *Answer* 1.8×10^{-5} mol/L

21.15 What concentration of benzoate ion, $C_6H_5COO^-$, should be added to a 0.010 M benzoic acid, C_6H_5COOH, solution to prepare a buffer that has pH 5.00? $K_a = 6.6 \times 10^{-5}$ for C_6H_5COOH.

21.16 What concentration of ClO^- should be added to a 0.050 M HClO solution to prepare a buffer that has pH 8.00? $K_a = 2.90 \times 10^{-8}$ for HClO. *Answer* 0.15 mol/L

21.17 What concentration of NH_4^+ should be added to a 0.050 M NH_3 solution to prepare a buffer which has pH 8.80? $K_b = 1.6 \times 10^{-5}$ for NH_3.

21.18 Repeat the calculations of Problem 21.17 for a buffer solution having a pH of 7.00. Why might this buffer solution be impractical? *Answer* 8.0 mol/L, most ammonium salts are not this soluble

21.19* A buffer solution was made by mixing exactly 500 mL of 1.00 M acetic acid and 500 mL of 0.500 M calcium acetate solutions. Assume no volume change upon mixing. What is the concentration of each of the following in the buffer solution: (a) CH_3COOH, (b) Ca^{2+}, (c) CH_3COO^-, and (d) H^+? (e) What is the pH? $K_a = 1.754 \times 10^{-5}$ for CH_3COOH.

21.20 What is the pH of the 0.10 M NH_3/0.10 M NH_4NO_3 solution described in Example 21.5 after 0.0010 mol of HCl has been added to 100.0 mL of the buffer?

21.21 A buffer is made of 0.200 M NH_4Cl and 0.100 M NH_3. (a) What is the pH of this solution? $K_b = 1.6 \times 10^{-5}$ for NH_3. (b) What is the pH after the addition of 0.001 mol KOH to one liter of the buffer? *Answer* 8.90, 8.91

21.22 One liter of a solution contains 0.100 mol of $NaNO_2$ and 0.050 mol of HCl. What is the pH of this solution? If the solution is diluted twofold with water, what is the pH? $K_a = 7.2 \times 10^{-4}$ for HNO_2. *Answer* 3.14, 3.14

21.23* What is the pH of a solution that is a mixture of HBrO, HClO, and HIO, each at 0.10 M concentration? For HBrO, $K_a = 2.2 \times 10^{-9}$; for HClO, $K_a = 2.90 \times 10^{-8}$; and for HIO, $K_a = 2.3 \times 10^{-11}$.

Polyprotic Acids

21.24 Find $[H^+]$, $[HSO_3^-]$, $[H_2SO_3]$, and $[SO_3^{2-}]$ at equilibrium in a 0.100 M solution of H_2SO_3. $K_{a_1} = 1.43 \times 10^{-2}$ and $K_{a_2} = 5.0 \times 10^{-8}$ for H_2SO_3.

21.25 Calculate the concentration of all species (except water) present in a 0.010 M solution of H_3AsO_4. $K_{a_1} = 6.5 \times 10^{-3}$, $K_{a_2} = 1.1 \times 10^{-7}$, and $K_{a_3} = 3 \times 10^{-12}$ for arsenic acid. *Answer* $[H^+] = 5.3 \times 10^{-3}$ mol/L, $[H_2AsO_4^-] = 5.3 \times 10^{-3}$ mol/L, $[H_3AsO_4] = 0.005$ mol/L, $[HAsO_4^{2-}] = 1.1 \times 10^{-7}$ mol/L, $[AsO_4^{3-}] = 6 \times 10^{-17}$ mol/L

21.26 Find the pH of a solution of 0.25 M $H_2C_2O_4$ (oxalic acid). $K_{a_1} = 5.60 \times 10^{-2}$ and $K_{a_2} = 6.2 \times 10^{-5}$ for $H_2C_2O_4$. *Answer* 1.04

21.27 Calculate the pH of a 0.10 M solution of $NaHSO_4$. $K_{a_2} = 1.0 \times 10^{-2}$ for H_2SO_4.

21.28 What is the concentration of S^{2-} present in a saturated hydrosulfuric acid solution that has a pH of 5.3? $[H^+]^2[S^{2-}] = 3 \times 10^{-21}$ for a saturated solution of H_2S.

21.29 To what pH must a saturated solution of H_2S be adjusted so that $[S^{2-}] = 1 \times 10^{-20}$ M? $[H^+]^2[S^{2-}] = 3 \times 10^{-21}$ for a saturated H_2S solution. *Answer* 0.3

Acid–Base Reactions

21.30 Calculate the value of the equilibrium constant for the neutralization of aqueous ammonia with hydrochloric acid. $K_b = 1.6 \times 10^{-5}$ for NH_3.

21.31 Calculate the value of the equilibrium constant for the neutralization of hypoiodous acid with sodium hydroxide. $K_a = 2.3 \times 10^{-11}$ for HIO. *Answer* 2.3×10^3

21.32 What would be the pH at the equivalence point in the titration of 0.10 M NaOH with (a) 0.10 M HNO_3; (b) 0.10 M HNO_2, $K_a = 7.2 \times 10^{-4}$; and (c) 0.10 M HIO, $K_a = 2.3 \times 10^{-11}$? (Hint: Remember the effect of dilution.) What is the trend in pH with K_a? *Answer* (a) 7.00, (b) 7.92, (c) 11.65; pH at equivalence point approaches 7 as K_a increases

21.33 A 25.0 mL sample of 0.250 M HNO_3 is titrated with 0.100 M NaOH. Calculate the pH of the solution (a) before the addition of NaOH and after the addition of (b) 10.0 mL, (c) 25.0 mL, (d) 50.0 mL, (e) 62.5 mL, and (f) 75.0 mL of NaOH.

21.34 A 15.00 mL sample of 0.1063 M KOH is titrated with 0.1077 M HCl. Calculate the pH of the solution (a) before the addition of HCl and after the addition of (b) 10.00 mL, (c) 15.00 mL, and (d) 20.00 mL of HCl. *Answer* (a) 13.0265, (b) 12.316, (c) 3.15, (d) 1.796

21.35* Repeat the calculations in Problem 21.33 assuming the acid was 0.250 M HCOOH. $K_a = 1.772 \times 10^{-4}$ for formic acid.

21.36* Repeat the calculations of Problem 21.34 assuming the base was aqueous NH_3 instead of KOH. $K_b = 1.6 \times 10^{-5}$ for NH_3. *Answer* (a) 11.11, (b) 8.89, (c) 3.15, (d) 1.796

21.37 Sulfamic acid, HSO_3NH_2, is a strong monoprotic acid that can be used to standardize a strong base:

$$HSO_3NH_2(aq) + KOH(aq) \rightleftharpoons KSO_3NH_2(aq) + H_2O(l)$$

A 0.179 g sample of HSO_3NH_2 required 19.35 mL of an aqueous solution of KOH for complete reaction. What was the molar concentration of the solution of the base?

21.38 A 2.1734 g sample of Na_2CO_3 required 23.69 mL of a hydrochloric acid solution for complete reaction. What is the concentration of the acid solution? *Answer* 1.731 mol/L

21.39 The percent of Na_2CO_3 in a sample of impure soda ash was determined by titration with 0.107 M HCl. A 0.253 g sample of soda ash required 13.72 mL of HCl to reach the equivalence point. What was the percentage of Na_2CO_3 present? Assume that the impurities do not react with the acid.

21.40 The percentage of acetic acid in a vinegar sample was determined by titration with 0.103 M NaOH:

$$CH_3COOH(aq) + NaOH(aq) \rightleftharpoons$$
$$Na(CH_3COO)(aq) + H_2O(l)$$

A 10.13 g sample of vinegar required 67.43 mL of NaOH to reach the equivalence point. Did the vinegar meet the minimum specifications of 4 mass % acetic acid? *Answer* 4.12 mass %, yes

21.41 A student prepared a soluton of HCl having an approximate concentration of 0.15 M. To find the exact concentration, he observed that 22.37 mL of HCl was needed to completely react with 0.1870 g of pure Na_2CO_3. (a) Calculate the exact concentration of the acid. He then used his acid to determine the percent of Na_2CO_3 in an unknown, impure sample. From the data given: 0.3940 g of the unknown required 13.72 mL of HCl solution, (b) calculate the fraction of Na_2CO_3 present in the sample. *Answer* (a) 0.1577 mol/L, (b) 29.11%

21.42* The molar mass of a metal carbonate, $MeCO_3$, was determined by adding excess acid to the carbonate and then titrating the excess acid with a base (called "back titrating"). (a) Write the chemical equations for the reaction of HCl with $MeCO_3$ and HCl with NaOH. Exactly 50.00 mL of 0.800 M HCl was poured into a 0.844 g sample of $MeCO_3$. The excess acid was determined by back titrating with 14.30 mL of 1.400 M NaOH. (b) Calculate the molar mass of the carbonate.

Solubility Product

21.43 Calculate the K_{sp} for each of the following substances from the given solubilities: (a) AgCl, 1.9×10^{-3} g/L; (b) $PbBr_2$, 7.8 g/L; and (c) $Co(OH)_2$, 3.4×10^{-4} g/L.

21.44 Repeat Problem 21.43 for (a) AgBr, 1.3×10^{-4} g/L, and (b) PbI_2, 0.56 g/L. *Answer* (a) 4.8×10^{-13}, (b) 6.9×10^{-9}

21.45 Calculate the solubility in grams per liter for each of the following substances from the given values of K_{sp}: (a) $Ba(OH)_2$, $K_{sp} = 1.3 \times 10^{-2}$, and (b) PbI_2, $K_{sp} = 7.1 \times 10^{-9}$.

21.46 Repeat Problem 21.45 for (a) $Ni(OH)_2$, $K_{sp} = 3 \times 10^{-16}$, and (b) $Cu(OH)_2$, $K_{sp} = 1.3 \times 10^{-20}$. *Answer* (a) 4×10^{-4} g/L, (b) 1.5×10^{-5} g/L

21.47* Magnesium hydroxide is a slightly soluble substance. The pH of a saturated solution of $Mg(OH)_2$ is 10.38. Find the K_{sp}. Calculate the solubility in units of g/100 g of water. *Answer* 6.9×10^{-12}, 7.0×10^{-4} g/100 g H_2O

21.48 The K_{sp} for AgBr is 4.9×10^{-13} at 25 °C. What is the concentration of Ag^+ in a solution in which the concentration of Br^- is 0.010 M?

21.49 Calculate the solubility of $PbCl_2$ in (a) pure water and in (b) a 0.10 M NaCl solution. $K_{sp} = 2 \times 10^{-5}$ for lead chloride. *Answer* (a) 0.02 mol/L, (b) 0.002 mol/L

21.50 If 1.0 g of $AgNO_3$ is added to 50 mL of 0.050 M NaCl, will a precipitate form? $K_{sp} = 1.8 \times 10^{-10}$ for AgCl.

21.51 What pH could be used to separate Mn^{2+} from Zn^{2+} by selective precipitation of 0.010 mol of ZnS in 1 L of a saturated solution of H_2S? Assume that $[Mn^{2+}]$ is also 0.010 mol/L. $K_{sp} = 2.3 \times 10^{-13}$ for MnS and 2×10^{-24} for ZnS and $[H^+]^2[S^{2-}] = 3 \times 10^{-21}$ for a saturated solution of H_2S. *Answer* $-0.6 < pH < 5.0$

21.52 In a student-designed qualitative analysis scheme, Pb^{2+} is to be separated as PbC_2O_4 from Cu^{2+} by the addition of $Na_2C_2O_4$. To what value must the concentration of $C_2O_4^{2-}$ be adjusted so that only PbC_2O_4 will form in a solution that is roughly 0.01 M in each of these cations? $K_{sp} = 4.8 \times 10^{-12}$ for PbC_2O_4 and 3×10^{-8} for CuC_2O_4.

21.53* The solubility product of iron(III) hydroxide is 3×10^{-39}. (a) At what pH will a 0.001 M $Fe(NO_3)_3$ solution just begin to form the hydroxide precipitate? (b) If the source of the OH^- is a weak base having $K_b = 3.0 \times 10^{-6}$, what is the maximum concentration of that base which is permitted before $Fe(OH)_3$ forms? *Answer* (a) 2.0, (b) 1×10^{-12} mol/L

21.54 A strong acid is added to a solid mixture of 0.010 mol samples of $Fe(OH)_2$ and $Cu(OH)_2$ placed in 1 L of water. At what values of pH will the dissolution of each hydroxide be complete? $K_{sp} = 8 \times 10^{-16}$ for $Fe(OH)_2$ and 1.3×10^{-20} for $Cu(OH)_2$. (Assume no change in volume.)

Complexes

21.55 Use the overall dissociation constant for $[Ag(CN)_2]^-$ to find the concentration of Ag^+ in equilibrium with 0.25 M CN^- and 0.10 M $[Ag(CN)_2]^-$. $K_1 = 0.13$ and $K_2 = 1 \times 10^{-21}$.

21.56 Use the overall dissociation constant for $[Ni(NH_3)_6]^{2+}$ to calculate the concentration of Ni^{2+} in equilibrium with 6 M NH_3 and 0.05 M $[Ni(NH_3)_6]^{2+}$. $K_1 = 1$, $K_2 = 0.17$, $K_3 = 0.05$, $K_4 = 0.02$, $K_5 = 0.005$, $K_6 = 0.0017$. *Answer* 1×10^{-15} mol/L

21.57 What is the concentation of Ag^+ in a 0.10 M solution of $Na[Ag(CN)_2]$? $K_1 = 0.13$ and $K_2 = 1 \times 10^{-21}$ for $[Ag(CN)_2]^-$.

21.58* What is the concentration of Pb^{2+} in a solution that is saturated with $Pb(SCN)_2$? $K_1 = 0.04$ and $K_2 = 0.08$ for $Pb(SCN)_2$. *Answer* 0.05 mol/L

21.59 A solution is 0.010 M with respect to Cd^{2+} and also with respect to Pd^{2+}. Solid KBr is added to the solution (assume no change in volume) until $[Br^-] = 1.0$ M. Use the overall dissociation constants of the complexes shown below to calculate the concentrations of Cd^{2+} and Pd^{2+} once equilibrium is reached. $K_d = 2 \times 10^{-4}$ for $[CdBr_4]^{2-}$ and 8.0×10^{-14} for $[PdBr_4]^{2-}$.

21.60* Calculate the concentration of Ag^+ in equilibrium with 0.010 M $[Ag(NH_3)_2]^+$. $K_1 = 1.45 \times 10^{-4}$ and $K_2 = 4.3 \times 10^{-4}$. Use these values to calculate the ion product for AgCl if the solution is also 0.010 M in Cl^-. Will any AgCl form? $K_{sp} = 1.8 \times 10^{-10}$ for AgCl. *Answer* $[Ag^+] = 3 \times 10^{-4}$ mol/L, $Q_i = 3 \times 10^{-6}$, yes

21.61* Zinc(II) ion forms a complex with $EDTA^{4-}$,

$$Zn^{2+} + EDTA^{4-} \rightleftharpoons [Zn(EDTA)]^{2-} \qquad K = 3.9 \times 10^{16}$$

where $EDTA^{4-}$ represents the ethylenediaminetetraacetate ion. Will ZnS form in a solution originally containing 0.100 M $EDTA^{4-}$, 0.01 M S^{2-}, and 0.010 M Zn^{2+}? $K_{sp} = 2 \times 10^{-24}$ for ZnS.

21.62* It is possible to dissolve a precipitate of AgCl but not a precipitate of AgI by adding concentrated aqueous NH_3. To demonstrate this, calculate the ion product for (a) a solution containing 0.010 M Ag^+, 0.010 M Cl^-, 5.0 M NH_3 and (b) a solution containing 0.010 M Ag^+, 0.010 M I^-, and 5.0 M NH_3. (c) In which solution will the ion product exceed the K_{sp}? $K_{sp} = 8.3 \times 10^{-17}$ for AgI, $K_{sp} = 1.8 \times 10^{-10}$ for AgCl, and $K_d = 6.2 \times 10^{-8}$ for $[Ag(NH_3)_2]^+$.

Additional Problems

21.63 What is the pH of a solution prepared by adding 10.0 mL of 0.100 M HCl to (a) 5.0 mL of 0.100 M NaOH, (b) 10.0 mL of 0.100 M NaOH, (c) 15.0 mL of 0.100 M NaOH, (d) 5.0 mL of 0.100 M NH_3, (e) 10.0 mL of 0.100 M NH_3, and (f) 15.0 mL of 0.100 M NH_3? $K_b = 1.6 \times 10^{-5}$ for NH_3.

21.64 A solution contains 0.015 M CH_3COOH and 0.0030 M Ag^+. Will a precipitate form? $K_a = 1.754 \times 10^{-5}$ for acetic acid and $K_{sp} = 4.4 \times 10^{-3}$ for $Ag(CH_3COO)$. *Answer* $Q_i = 1.5 \times 10^{-6}$, no

CHAPTER 22

Thermodynamics

The word "spontaneous" is applied to physical and chemical changes in a very specific way related to the thermodynamics of a system. The meaning is somewhat different from what most of us think of as "spontaneous." Perhaps we think of a crowd jumping up when the home team scores a touchdown, or the hug a mother gives a child who has fallen down. These are impulsive reactions — they are immediate and quick.

We know that the rate, or quickness, of a chemical reaction is dependent upon the reaction mechanism and must be studied by the methods of kinetics. "Spontaneity" as a thermodynamic concept is unrelated to speed. A "spontaneous" chemical reaction or physical change is one that can happen without any continuing outside influence. (We could say "thermodynamically favorable" instead, but this is cumbersome.) A spontaneous change, whether slow or fast, has a natural direction, like the melting of ice at room temperature, the reaction of an acid with a base, or the rusting away of a piece of iron.

The first law of thermodynamics — the law of conservation of energy — deals only with the total energy in chemical reactions. It tells only part of the story about spontaneity. In this chapter we introduce two additional thermodynamic quantities — entropy and free energy. Entropy and enthalpy together allow the calculation of free energy, the quantity which tells us unequivocally whether or not a chemical reaction will take place spontaneously under a given set of reaction conditions.

DISORDER, SPONTANEITY, AND ENTROPY

22.1 ENTROPY: A QUANTITATIVE MEASURE OF RANDOMNESS

In Chapter 7 we found that when a chemical reaction or a change of state occurs, a change in the energy of the system occurs too. Although it is less obvious, something else also changes in most cases. When a liquid evaporates, what is happening to the molecules? They are gaining energy and moving into a larger space. When silver chloride precipitates from a solution, what is happening to the silver and chloride ions? Instead of moving randomly through the water, the ions assume fixed positions in a crystal.

In both of these changes, the amount of *order* among the particles in the system has changed. Molecules are more disordered in the gas phase — their motion and their arrangement in space are more random. Ions are more ordered in the solid phase — their motion is less random. In most physical and chemical changes there is a change in the order of the particles in the system as well as a change in energy.

A chemical or physical change that is exothermic is *often* spontaneous, but not always. A chemical or physical change that is endothermic is *most likely* not spontaneous, but not always.

To illustrate a case in which exothermic changes are not spontaneous, consider the three beakers of water shown in Figure 22.1. Each beaker holds a large reservoir of water maintained at a constant temperature. Ice cubes of equal size are dropped into each beaker. After a few minutes, the ice cube in the beaker containing water supercooled to $-1\ °C$ increases in size because some of the water freezes. No visible

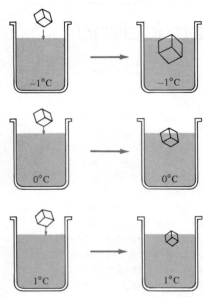

Figure 22.1
Changes in an Ice Cube at Different Temperatures At −1 °C the ice cube grows larger, at 0 °C it is unchanged, and at 1 °C it melts a bit.

change occurs in the second beaker, and the ice cube in the third beaker decreases in size because some of the ice melts.

The standard enthalpy changes for the process

$$H_2O(l, 1 \text{ atm}) \longrightarrow H_2O(s, 1 \text{ atm})$$

at each of the three temperatures of the water in the beakers can be calculated. The values are

$$\Delta H°_{272.15} = -5972.2 \text{ J/mol}$$
$$\Delta H°_{273.15} = -6009.5 \text{ J/mol}$$
$$\Delta H°_{274.15} = -6046.7 \text{ J/mol}$$

Based on the negative $\Delta H°$ values alone, the water should freeze in all three beakers, not just in one. Thus, we must conclude that the favorable enthalpy change is opposed by some other force. At −1 °C, this second force is not strong enough to counteract the enthalpy change. At 1 °C, it is strong enough to overcome the enthalpy change, and at 0 °C, it must be equal in magnitude to the enthalpy change, but opposite in effect, so that an equilibrium condition exists.

Could this second driving force toward spontaneity be related to order and disorder? You might think intuitively that it is, and your intuition would be correct. An ordered state is not generally expected to occur spontaneously. If you dropped a piggy bank and the coins landed in separate stacks of pennies, nickels, and dimes, it would be quite a shock. Similarly, if two gases were mixed in a flask, you would not expect to find later that all the molecules of one had migrated to the left half of the container and all the molecules of the other occupied the right half.

In fact, just the opposite is true: It is *disorder* that tends to increase spontaneously. If two bulbs, each containing a different gas, were connected to each other and the gases did *not* eventually mix, you would check the opening to see if it was stopped up.

Experience has also shown us that a process that is spontaneous in one direction is not spontaneous in the other. Left to themselves, the broken pieces of a piggy bank will not reunite, nor will the coins fly back into it. In Chapter 7 we discussed the spontaneous flow of heat from a hot block of metal to a reservoir of water. No one has yet seen a hot metal block get hotter when immersed in cold water.

Many practical circumstances arise in which it is desirable to know the natural direction of spontaneity of a physical or chemical change. To determine this natural direction of spontaneity it is necessary to take into account both the change in enthalpy and the change in the disorder of a system.

To deal quantitatively with the drive toward disorder, a thermodynamic property called **entropy,** which is a measure of disorder, is introduced. Entropy is symbolized by S; a change in entropy is symbolized in the usual way:

$$\text{change in entropy} \longrightarrow \Delta S = \overset{\text{final entropy}}{S_2} - \underset{\substack{\text{initial} \\ \text{entropy}}}{S_1}$$

The change in entropy of a system is a function both of the heat that flows into or out of the system and of the temperature.

The next four sections explore the meaning of entropy for chemical systems and demonstrate the calculation of ΔS for physical and chemical changes. Knowing the entropy change for a given change of a given system, however, does not allow for the reliable prediction of spontaneity. The thermodynamic property that makes such predictions possible, which is introduced in the second half of this chapter, incorporates *both* the change in enthalpy and the change in entropy for the system under study. It is referred to as the change in free energy.

Positive ΔS: **increase in disorder**
Negative ΔS: **decrease in disorder**

Table 22.1
Statements of the Second Law of Thermodynamics

> All systems tend to approach a state of equilibrium.
> Entropy is time's arrow.*
> The state of maximum entropy is the most stable state for an isolated system.†
> Every system which is left to itself will, on the average, change toward a condition of maximum probability.‡
> It is impossible in any way to diminish the entropy of a system of bodies without thereby leaving behind changes in other bodies.§
> Die Energie der Welt ist constant; die Entropie der Welt strebt einem Maximum zu.‖
> Things are getting more screwed up every day.#
> You can't break even.

* Sir Arthur Eddington.   † Enrico Fermi.   ‡ G. N. Lewis.

§ Max Planck. This and three preceding statements are quoted from J. Arthur Campbell, *Chemical Systems: Energetics, Dynamics, Structure* (San Francisco: W. H. Freeman, 1970).

‖ R. J. E. Clausius, quoted by J. W. Gibbs to head his classic memoir, *The Equilibrium of Heterogeneous Substances*.

Anonymous; with thanks to A. Truman Schwarz, *Chemistry: Imagination and Implication* (New York: Academic Press, 1973).

22.2 THE SECOND LAW OF THERMODYNAMICS

The role that the drive to disorder plays in every natural process is expressed in the second law of thermodynamics, which has profound implications that reach well beyond chemistry. Like the first law, the second law is based on observation of and experience with the real world. A straightforward statement of the second law is, The entropy of the universe is constantly increasing. Many other ways have been found to express the second law of thermodynamics (Table 22.1).

> **Second law of thermodynamics: The entropy of the universe is constantly increasing.**

The second law means that *every* spontaneous chemical and physical change increases the entropy of the *universe as a whole.* Conversely, a change can be spontaneous only when the entropy of the universe increases as a result of it. In a series of spontaneous changes over the course of time, entropy must always increase. The direction of all natural events is toward disorder—this is why entropy is sometimes referred to as "time's arrow" (see Table 22.1).

Fortunately, it is not necessary to measure the entropy of the universe as a whole. Recall that it is customary in thermodynamics (Section 7.2) to divide the universe into the *system* (the part of the universe under study) and the *surroundings* (everything else). We concentrate on studying entropy changes in chemical systems, just as we do in the study of enthalpy changes. The condition expressed by the second law of thermodynamics for a spontaneous process becomes

$$\Delta S_{\text{universe}} = \Delta S_{\text{system}} + \Delta S_{\text{surroundings}} > 0 \qquad (22.1)$$

The entropy of a *system* can either increase or decrease. If ΔS_{system} decreases (has a negative sign) in a spontaneous change, this change *must* be accompanied by a simultaneous and larger increase in $\Delta S_{\text{surroundings}}$. (Can you see how the entropy of the universe increases in the natural processes in Figure 22.2?)

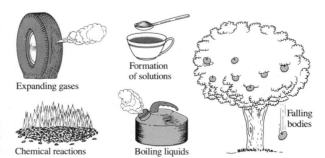

Expanding gases

Formation of solutions

Chemical reactions

Boiling liquids

Falling bodies

Figure 22.2
Spontaneous Natural Processes in which the Entropy of the Universe Increases

At this point students often ask, "So what is entropy, *really?*" On a microscopic, atom for atom, molecule for molecule level, entropy represents the number of possible ways the particles can be arranged — the statistical probability for disorder.

One way that the entropy of a system can be increased is by raising the temperature. The kinetic energy of the molecules increases, they move around more rapidly, and there is greater disorder within the system. You might be wondering how it can be that an exothermic reaction, during which the internal energy of a system decreases, can be spontaneous. Remember that the second law deals with the entropy of the *universe.* The energy released in an exothermic reaction is transferred to the surroundings. The temperature of the surroundings increases, contributing to the overall increase of the entropy of the universe required for spontaneous change.

There are mathematical techniques for dealing with probability, and applied to the calculation of entropy they yield results that agree with what is observed. The entropy of a system increases with the number of ways in which the individual atoms, molecules, or ions can be arranged with respect to each other. It also increases with the number of possible states available to each individual particle, for example, with how many different ways a molecule can rotate or vibrate (see Figure 7.2). In dynamic chemical systems, entropy increases when the number of particles increases, when the particles can move around more freely, faster, or in more different ways, and when they are more randomly mixed.

22.3 ENTROPY IN PHYSICAL CHANGES

Entropy increases (positive ΔS):
— **increase in temperature**
— **vaporization, melting**
— **mixing of substances**
— **expansion of a gas**

With other conditions held constant, significant increases in the entropy of a chemical system accompany four types of physical change (Figure 22.3): (1) an increase in temperature, as discussed above, (2) a change of state — vaporization or melting, (3) mixing of two or more substances, and (4) expansion of a gas.

An increase in the entropy of a system accompanies a change of state that allows greater freedom of motion to atoms, molecules, or ions. When a solid melts or a liquid evaporates, the *temperature* of the system does not increase, but the entropy increases because the particles have more freedom to move.

Consider a sample of argon for which equilibrium has been established between the liquid state and the gaseous state at the normal boiling point of argon,

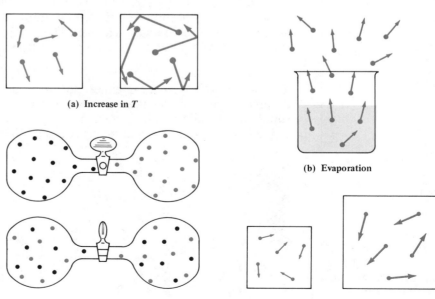

(a) Increase in T

(b) Evaporation

(c) Mixing

(d) Expansion of a gas

Figure 22.3
Changes in which Entropy Increases

−185.7 °C. Each atom in the liquid can move around freely in a space about 0.32 nm in diameter. However, the atom has only a small chance of getting out of one space and into another one in a different place. An atom in the gas phase moves much further—about 20 nm—before hitting another atom. The difference between these distances illustrates the significantly greater degree of randomness or disorder in the gaseous than in the liquid state.

On a molar basis, the entropy change for this or any change of state is given by

$$\Delta S \;=\; \frac{\Delta H}{T}$$

(enthalpy change for change of state)

(absolute temperature of the change of state)

$$\frac{joules}{kelvin\ mole} \qquad \frac{joules/mole}{kelvins}$$

(22.2)

For phase changes, $\Delta S = \dfrac{\Delta H}{T}$

Typical units for ΔS are joules per kelvin or calories per kelvin. When ΔS is expressed on a molar basis, the units are, for example, joules per kelvin per mole (J/K mol). (Note that because of its smaller magnitude, the energy unit used for ΔS is commonly joules rather than kilojoules, or calories rather than kilocalories.) For an entropy increase, ΔS for the given system has a positive value; for an entropy decrease, ΔS has a negative value.

Entropy changes for substances in their standard states at 1 atm pressure and a specified temperature are designated standard state entropy changes, $\Delta S°$. If no other temperature is indicated, the temperature can be assumed to be 25 °C. When $\Delta H°$ (the standard state enthalpy change) is used in Equation (22.2), the entropy change found is $\Delta S°$.

The following example illustrates the calculation of $\Delta S°$ for a change of state. In this example the system is one mole of argon. Keep in mind that $\Delta S°$ alone is not a criterion for spontaneity. As we would intuitively predict, vaporization is accompanied by an entropy increase. But vaporization is not spontaneous—it takes place only as a result of the continuous absorption of heat from the surroundings.

EXAMPLE 22.1
Entropy in Physical Changes

Calculate the standard state entropy change for the vaporization of one mole of argon at the normal boiling point. $\Delta H°$ (vaporization) = 6519 J/mol for Ar at 87.5 K. Is this an increase or decrease in entropy?

The entropy change for this change of state is

$$\Delta S°_{87.5}\ (\text{vaporization}) = \frac{\Delta H°_{87.5}(\text{vaporization})}{T} = \frac{6519\ \text{J/mol}}{87.5\ \text{K}} = 74.5\ \text{J/K mol}$$

The positive value of $\Delta S°$ tells us that the entropy of argon has increased by 74.5 J/K mol.

Exercise The normal boiling point of cesium is 690. °C and the heat of vaporization is 68.28 kJ/mol. Calculate $\Delta S°$ for the condensation of cesium vapor. Is this an increase or decrease in entropy for the cesium? *Answer* $\Delta S° = -70.9$ J/K mol, decrease

---

Figure 22.3c illustrates mixing, a physical process in which, unlike a change of state, there is a change in entropy but *no* change in enthalpy. Two ideal gases (no intermolecular forces) that do not react with each other are allowed to mix slowly while the temperature and pressure are held constant. The *only* driving force in this spontaneous change is the increase in entropy. In general, whenever two or more substances are mixed, or dissolution occurs, entropy increases. Entropy also increases when a gas (Figure 22.3d) expands at constant temperature.

If a process results in an increase in the entropy of a system, the reverse of that process causes an equal *decrease* in entropy. Entropy decreases (a) when the temperature of a system becomes lower, (b) when a gas condenses or a liquid freezes, (c) when a dissolved substance crystallizes out of solution, or (d) when a gas is compressed into a smaller volume.

The ice cubes of the experiment in Figure 22.1 demonstrate that entropy is not the sole criterion for spontaneity of a change in a chemical system. The entropy changes for freezing water at the three temperatures of the water in the beakers can be calculated and are found to be

$$\Delta S°_{272.15} = -21.8640 \text{ J/K mol}$$
$$\Delta S°_{273.15} = -22.0007 \text{ J/K mol}$$
$$\Delta S°_{274.15} = -22.1369 \text{ J/K mol}$$

Based on entropy alone, water would not be predicted to freeze in *any* of the three beakers, for the entropy value is negative in each case. In Section 22.6, we discuss how the effects of enthalpy and entropy changes can be combined to predict spontaneity.

EXAMPLE 22.2
Entropy for Physical Changes

Would you predict an increase or a decrease in entropy for the systems in which the following changes occur?
(a) The "disappearance" of the contents of a bottle of ethyl ether that was left open. (System = the ether)
(b) Making rock candy (crystalline sugar) from a saturated sugar solution. (System = candy + solution)
(c) Putting cream in your coffee. (System = coffee + cream)

(a) The evaporation of the ether would be an increase in the entropy, with entropy increasing due to both the phase change and expansion of the vapor.
(b) The crystallization of the sugar would be a decrease in entropy. The molecules are more ordered in a crystal than in solution.
(c) An increase in entropy would result from mixing the cream and the coffee solution. The randomness of the liquids combined is greater than that of the liquids in separate containers. (A slight decrease in entropy might result from cooling the coffee.)

Exercise   Would you predict an increase or a decrease in entropy for the systems in which the following physical changes occur: (a) the formation of a rain drop in a cloud (system = water), (b) the crystallization of the metal alloy from the molten state in molding a bookend (system = alloy), and (c) the beating of an egg for an omelet (system = egg)? *Answer* (a) decrease, (b) decrease, (c) increase

---

EXAMPLE 22.3
Entropy in Physical Changes

When solid sodium chloride is cooled from 25 °C to 0 °C, the entropy change is −4.4 J/K mol. Is this an increase or decrease in randomness? Explain this entropy change in terms of what is happening at the molecular level in the solid.

The decrease in entropy, indicated by the negative sign, is the result of the ions in the crystal structure having less kinetic energy at the lower temperature. As a result of the smaller amount of energy, the average vibrational motion of the ions in the lattice decreases and hence there is less chaotic motion in the crystal. Less chaotic motion means less entropy.

Exercise When a one mole sample of argon gas at 0 °C is compressed to one-half of its original volume, the entropy change is −5.76 J/K. Is this an increase or a decrease in randomness? Explain this entropy change in terms of what is happening at the molecular level in the gas. *Answer* decrease; the smaller volume restricts the random motion of atoms, reducing the randomness of the system

22.4 ABSOLUTE ENTROPIES

Only *changes* in energy (ΔE) and enthalpy (ΔH) can be measured experimentally. Entropy is different. Exactly how much disorder is possible in a given amount of any pure substance can be determined experimentally. This is known as **absolute entropy,** S, the entropy of a pure substance. The determination of absolute entropies is possible because there is a natural reference state for the entropy of a pure substance—the entropy at absolute zero. (It is not possible to determine absolute energy or enthalpy.)

Consider two separate 1 mol samples of neon and argon that are cooled at 1 atm pressure to the point where they liquefy and then to the point where they solidify. Assume that they form perfect crystals. The amount of disorder in the crystals decreases in both samples as the temperature continues to decrease. What happens as the temperature approaches absolute zero? The vibrational kinetic energy of the atoms in both samples is decreasing (Figure 22.4), and the atoms are becoming more and more confined to their positions in the crystal. At absolute zero, the atoms no longer vibrate in their crystal positions, and both substances have the same amount of disorder. The standard state entropy at absolute zero, S_0°, is zero for perfect crystalline substances. This is the third law of thermodynamics: The entropy of a perfect crystal at absolute zero is zero. In this context, a "perfect crystal" is one in which there are no crystal defects and, in addition, there is only one possible arrangement of particles and the particles are all of equivalent energy.

What about a substance more complicated than argon or neon—say, one composed of diatomic molecules AB? If the substance forms a perfect crystal with all molecules completely ordered (Figure 22.5a), again $S_0^\circ = 0$. On the other hand, if the substance forms a crystal with the molecules oriented in a random way (Figure 22.5b), the entropy is not zero, but is larger than zero and is dependent upon the number of possible arrangements of the molecules. (The statistics of probability can be applied to calculate S_0° for such a crystal.)

The absolute entropy of a substance at a given temperature above absolute zero is the sum of the following contributions: (1) the entropy of the substance at absolute zero (calculated on the basis of the complexity of the molecule and the number of possible arrangements), (2) the entropy increases for any phase changes that the substance undergoes between absolute zero and the desired temperature, and (3) the entropy increases during the heating of each phase over the temperature range in

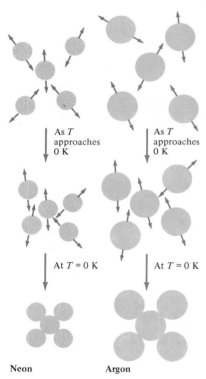

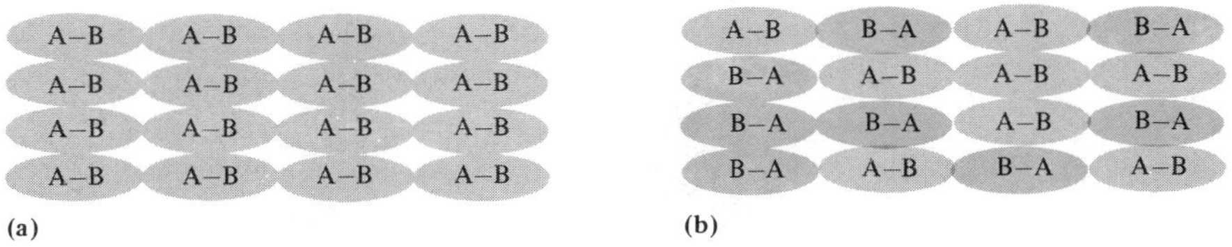

Figure 22.4
Decrease in Randomness as Absolute Zero is Approached The randomness of all perfect crystalline substances is the same at absolute zero and is $S_0^\circ = 0$. Note that this does not mean that the crystal structures of all substances are the same at absolute zero.

Figure 22.5
Order and Disorder in an A—B Crystal at Absolute Zero (a) Perfect order in a perfect crystal. (b) Random disorder.

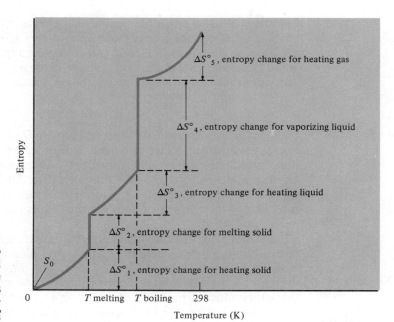

Figure 22.6
Contributions to the Standard
Absolute Entropy of a Substance
that is a Gas at 298 K For this
substance $S_{298}^\circ = S_0^\circ + \Delta S_1^\circ + \Delta S_2^\circ + \Delta S_3^\circ + \Delta S_4^\circ + \Delta S_5^\circ$

Table 22.2
Some Thermodynamic Data (at
25 °C) See Appendix IV for
additional values of thermodynamic
quantities.

Substance	ΔH_f° (kJ/mol)	ΔG_f° (kJ/mol)	S° (J/K mol)
O(g)	249.17	231.75	160.95
O$_2$(g)	0	0	205.03
O$_3$(g)	142.7	163.2	238.82
H(g)	217.97	203.26	114.60
H$^+$(g)	1536.20		
H$^+$(aq)	0*	0*	0*
H$_2$(g)	0	0	130.57
OH$^-$(g)	−140.88	—	—
OH$^-$(aq)	−229.99	−157.29	−10.75
H$_2$O(l)	−285.83	−237.18	69.91
H$_2$O(g)	−241.82	−228.59	188.72
H$_2$O$_2$(l)	−187.78	−120.42	109.6
He(g)	0	0	126.04
Ne(g)	0	0	146.22
F$_2$(g)	0	0	202.67
HF(g)	−271.1	−273.2	173.67
Cl$_2$(g)	0	0	222.96
HCl(g)	−92.31	−95.30	186.80
HCl(aq)	−167.16	−131.260	56.5
Br$_2$(l)	0	0	152.23
HBr(g)	−36.40	−53.43	198.59
Fe(α-solid)	0	0	27.3
Fe^{2+}(aq)	−89.1	−78.87	−137.7
Fe^{3+}(aq)	−48.5	−4.6	−315.9
FeO(s)	−272.0	—	—
Fe$_2$O$_3$(s)	−824.2	−742.2	87.40
Fe$_3$O$_4$(s)	−1118.4	−1015.5	146.4
FeCl$_2$(s)	−341.79	−302.34	117.95
FeCl$_2$(aq)	−423.4	−341.37	−24.7
FeCl$_3$(s)	−399.49	−334.05	142
FeCl$_3$(aq)	−550.2	−398.3	−146

* Chosen by convention to be zero. This choice sometimes gives negative values for S° for substances in aqueous solution, which means not that the entropy is negative, but that the entropy is negative with respect to the actual value for H$^+$.

Entropy (S):
gases > liquids > solids

Entropy (S):
large, complex
molecules > small, simple
molecules

which it is stable. Figure 22.6 illustrates the contributions to the entropy of a pure substance.

Table 22.2 includes the standard enthalpies of formation and the standard absolute entropies for a number of common substances at 25 °C (the $\Delta G°$ values are discussed in Sections 22.6 and 22.7). In general, the data demonstrate the following: (a) Gases have greater entropies than liquids. [Compare $H_2O(l)$ and $H_2O(g)$]. (b) Substances with more complex molecular or crystalline structures have greater entropies than more simple substances. [Compare $H_2O(l)$ and $H_2O_2(l)$; or Fe, Fe_2O_3, and Fe_3O_4.]

The values given in Table 22.2 are standard state absolute entropy values at 298 K. Note that at this temperature the standard state entropies of pure elements, including those that might form perfect crystals at absolute zero, are *not* zero, because the entropy is higher at the higher temperature. The standard state heats of formation [and also the values of $\Delta G_f°$; Section 22.7] for the elements are *defined* as zero at 298 K because, since absolute values of these quantities cannot be measured, it is necessary to set a reference point with respect to which changes are measured. For ions in aqueous solution, however, a reference entropy must be defined, and, as explained in the footnote to Table 22.2, this is chosen to be $S° = 0$ for $H^+(aq)$.

EXAMPLE 22.4
Absolute Entropy

The absolute entropy of HCl(g) at 25 °C is given in Table 22.2 as 186.80 J/K mol. Explain the contributions to this value, given that (a) at 0 K, HCl exists in a solid phase called solid-II (assume that this is not a perfect crystal); (b) at 98.38 K, solid-II changes to solid-I; (c) at 158.94 K, solid-I melts; and (d) at 188.11 K, the liquid evaporates.

There are eight contributions to the value of $S°$ for gaseous HCl. The first contribution is the result of the disorder of absolute zero because HCl does not form a perfect crystal. The second contribution is the entropy increase that results as solid-II is heated from 0 K to 98.38 K. The third contribution is the entropy increase that results as solid-II changes to solid-I at 98.38 K. The fourth and fifth contributions are for heating solid-I from 98.38 K to 158.94 K and for the fusion process at 158.94 K. The sixth and seventh contributions are for heating the liquid from 158.94 K to 188.11 K and for vaporization at 188.11 K. The last contribution is the entropy increase for heating the gas from 188.11 K to 298.15 K.

Exercise The absolute entropy of $F_2(g)$ at 25 °C is given in Table 22.2 as 202.67 J/K mol. Identify the contributions to this value given that (a) at 0 K, F_2 exists as a perfect crystal; (b) at 55.19 K, $F_2(s)$ melts; and (c) at 85.23 K and 1 atm, $F_2(l)$ boils *Answer* There are six contributions to the value of $S°$: (1) $S_0° = 0$, (2) heating solid from 0 K to 55.19 K, (3) fusion at 55.19 K, (4) heating liquid from 55.19 K to 85.23 K, (5) vaporization at 85.23 K, and (6) heating gas from 85.23 K to 298 K

22.5 ENTROPY IN CHEMICAL REACTIONS

Entropy can change in chemical reactions because of (1) a change in the number of atoms, ions, or molecules in a system; (2) a change in the phase in which the species in the system are present; or (3) a change in the complexity of the substances involved.

The thermal decomposition of potassium chlorate,

$$2KClO_3(s) \xrightarrow{\Delta} 2KCl(s) + 3O_2(g)$$

can easily be predicted to result in a very large increase in entropy. Two moles of reactant have been converted into five moles of products, including three moles of gas where originally there were none. For this reaction $\Delta S° = 808.14$ J/K.

In the combination of nitrogen and hydrogen to give ammonia,

$$N_2(g) + 3H_2(g) \longrightarrow 2NH_3(g)$$

it is apparent that the entropy will decrease. Four moles of gas have been converted to 2 mol of gas. For this reaction, $\Delta S° = -198.55$ J/K.

In the following reaction, there is no change in the number of moles of substances, nor in the phases of the substances.

$$Cu^{2+} + Zn(s) \longrightarrow Zn^{2+} + Cu(s)$$

One mole of solid plus one mole of ions in solution have been converted to one mole of solid and one mole of ions in solution. For such reactions, it is difficult to predict whether entropy will increase or decrease. Contributions to the entropy change could be made by differences in the crystal structure of copper as compared to zinc, and differences in the hydration of the two ions. We can, however, predict that the entropy change will be small. In fact, it is -21.0 J/K.

EXAMPLE 22.5
Entropy in Chemical Reactions

Predict whether the entropy change for each of the following reactions will be large and negative, large and positive, or small:

(a) $H_2(g) + Cl_2(g) \longrightarrow 2HCl(g)$

(b) $2ZnS(s) + 3O_2(g) \xrightarrow{\Delta} 2ZnO(s) + 2SO_2(g)$

(c) $2N_2O(g) \longrightarrow 2N_2(g) + O_2(g)$

(a) Two moles of gas react to form two moles of gas. We would expect only a small change in randomness for this reaction. (The actual value is 20.07 J/K.)

(b) Two moles of solid react with three moles of gas to produce two moles of solid and two moles of gas. The net loss of one mole of gas represents a decrease in randomness, so we would predict a large, negative value for $\Delta S°$. (The actual value is -147.1 J/K.)

(c) Two moles of gas produce three moles of gas—a net gain of one mole of gas. Thus we would predict a large, positive value for $\Delta S°$. (The actual value is 148.54 J/K.)

Exercise Classify the entropy change for each of the following reactions as (i) large and negative, (ii) large and positive, or (iii) small:

(a) $C(graphite) + 2H_2(g) + \frac{1}{2}O_2(g) \longrightarrow CH_3OH(l)$
(b) $3NO_2(g) + H_2O(l) \longrightarrow 2HNO_3(aq) + NO(g)$
(c) $NH_3(g) + H_2O(l) \longrightarrow NH_4^+ + OH^-$
(d) $2C(graphite) + O_2(g) \longrightarrow 2CO(g)$

Answer (a) i, (b) i, (c) i, (d) ii

The standard state entropy changes for chemical reactions can be calculated from known standard state entropies in two ways. In the first (Example 22.6), tabulated values for the *absolute* entropies of the reactants and products are used. The entropy change in the reaction is equal to the difference between the total entropy of the products (the final entropy) minus the total entropy of the reactants (the initial entropy).

$$\Delta S° = [\text{sum of } S°(\text{products})] - [\text{sum of } S°(\text{reactants})] \qquad (22.3)$$

The second method (Example 22.7) is the same as the method that we have used for finding heats of reaction (Section 7.9). Like enthalpy changes, entropy changes depend only on the initial and final states, and not on the sequence of changes that have taken place. Known standard entropies of formation and/or known entropy changes for other chemical reactions, and their respective equations, can be combined algebraically as is done in Hess's law calculations of enthalpy changes.

EXAMPLE 22.6
Entropy in Chemical Reactions

Find the standard state entropy of formation of $HCl(g)$ at 25 °C from the following absolute standard state entropies at 25 °C: 186.80 J/K mol for $HCl(g)$, 130.57 J/K mol for $H_2(g)$, and 222.96 J/K mol for $Cl_2(g)$.

The chemical equation for the formation of $HCl(g)$ is

$$\tfrac{1}{2}H_2(g) + \tfrac{1}{2}Cl_2(g) \longrightarrow HCl(g)$$

The entropy change is found by subtracting the sum of the absolute entropies of the reactants from the sum of the absolute entropies of the products:

$$\Delta S° = [(1 \text{ mol}) \times S°(\text{HCl})] - [(\tfrac{1}{2} \text{ mol}) \times S°(\text{H}_2) + (\tfrac{1}{2} \text{ mol}) \times S°(\text{Cl}_2)]$$
$$= [(1 \text{ mol})(186.80 \text{ J/K mol})]$$
$$\quad - [(\tfrac{1}{2} \text{ mol})(130.57 \text{ J/K mol}) + (\tfrac{1}{2} \text{ mol})(222.96 \text{ J/K mol})]$$
$$= 10.04 \text{ J/K}$$

For $HCl(g)$, $\Delta S°_f = 10.04$ J/K mol.

Exercise Using the values of absolute standard state entropies at 25 °C given in Table 22.2, find the $\Delta S°$ for each of the following reactions.

(a) $2O_3(g) \longrightarrow 3O_2(g)$
(b) $O_3(g) \longrightarrow O_2(g) + O(g)$

Which reaction has the larger increase in $\Delta S°$? *Answer* (a) $\Delta S° = 137.45$ J/K, (b) $\Delta S° = 127.16$ J/K; reaction (a) has the higher value of $\Delta S°$

EXAMPLE 22.7
Entropy in Chemical Reactions

Using the $\Delta S°$ values at 25 °C given for the following reactions:

$$C(\text{graphite}) + 2Cl_2(g) \longrightarrow CCl_4(l) \qquad \Delta S° = -235.27 \text{ J/K}$$
$$C(\text{graphite}) + \tfrac{3}{2}Cl_2(g) + \tfrac{1}{2}H_2(g) \longrightarrow CHCl_3(l) \qquad \Delta S° = -203.80 \text{ J/K}$$
$$\tfrac{1}{2}H_2(g) + \tfrac{1}{2}Cl_2(g) \longrightarrow HCl(g) \qquad \Delta S° = 10.04 \text{ J/K}$$

find $\Delta S°$ for the reaction

$$CCl_4(l) + H_2(g) \longrightarrow HCl(g) + CHCl_3(l)$$

The desired reaction can be obtained by adding the reverse of the first equation to the second and third equations as written:

$$
\begin{array}{ll}
CCl_4(l) \longrightarrow C(\text{graphite}) + 2Cl_2(g) & \Delta S° = 235.27 \text{ J/K} \\
C(\text{graphite}) + \tfrac{3}{2}Cl_2(g) + \tfrac{1}{2}H_2(g) \longrightarrow CHCl_3(l) & \Delta S° = -203.8 \text{ J/K} \\
\tfrac{1}{2}H_2(g) + \tfrac{1}{2}Cl_2(g) \longrightarrow HCl(g) & \Delta S° = 10.04 \text{ J/K} \\
\hline
CCl_4(l) + H_2(g) \longrightarrow HCl(g) + CHCl_3(l) & \Delta S° = 41.51 \text{ J/K}
\end{array}
$$

The entropy change for the reaction is 41.51 J/K under standard state conditions.

Exercise Combine the equations and values of $\Delta S°$ given in the exercise that follows Example 22.6 to calculate $\Delta S°$ for the reaction

$$O_3(g) + O(g) \longrightarrow 2O_2(g)$$

Answer 10.29 J/K

Table 22.3
Processes That Cause Entropy to Change

Entropy increases	Entropy decreases
Increasing temperature	Decreasing temperature
Melting a solid	Freezing a liquid
Evaporating a liquid	Condensing a gas
Mixing two substances in the same phase	Confining a gas in a smaller volume
Dissolving a solid or a gas in a liquid	Decreasing the number of moles of gas during a reaction
Expanding a gas	Decreasing the total moles of atoms, ions, or molecules during a reaction
Increasing the number of moles of gas during a reaction	Precipitation of a product in solution
Increasing the total moles of atoms, ions, or molecules during a reaction	

In summary, entropy changes and enthalpy changes are the two driving forces that influence the spontaneity of chemical reactions. Entropy is a quantitative measure of the degree of randomness, or disorder, in a system. The second law of thermodynamics says that the entropy of the universe must increase in any spontaneous process. The entropy of a specific system *can either increase or decrease. Entropy increases as the number of possible ways for the atoms, molecules, or ions of a chemical system to be arranged increases. Absolute entropies for individual pure substances can be determined. Both physical and chemical changes can cause increases or decreases in entropy. Entropy increases with increasing temperature, with the evaporation of a liquid, the melting of a solid, or the increase of the number of particles during a chemical reaction. The reverse of these changes cause decreases in entropy. Some of the processes that cause entropy changes are listed in Table 22.3.*

FREE ENERGY

22.6 FREE ENERGY: THE CRITERION FOR SPONTANEITY

The natural direction of many physical and chemical changes, as we have seen, is toward minimum energy or toward maximum disorder of the system under consideration. When both enthalpy and entropy change in a favorable direction (negative ΔH and positive ΔS), we can correctly predict that a process will be spontaneous. And when both change in an unfavorable direction (positive ΔH and negative ΔS) we can correctly predict that a process will be nonspontaneous. However, when these driving forces oppose each other, it is necessary to determine which predominates.

The combination of these two criteria for spontaneity into a single function was accomplished in 1876 by J. Willard Gibbs, a professor of mathematical physics at Yale. Gibbs published a lengthy, highly abstract paper that covered many aspects of thermodynamics in the *Transactions of the Connecticut Academy of Sciences*. The paper went unnoticed for years, but today Gibbs is recognized as having been one of America's most brilliant scientists. In his honor, the important thermodynamic function that we are about to discuss is called the Gibbs free energy and given the symbol G.

For the type of system of greatest interest in chemistry, a system at constant temperature and pressure, the following relationship is valid:

$$\underset{G_2 - G_1}{\Delta G} = \underset{H_2 - H_1}{\Delta H} - \underset{absolute}{T} \underset{S_2 - S_1}{\Delta S} \qquad (22.4)$$

The **free energy change**, ΔG, is the energy that is available, or *free*, to do useful work as the result of a chemical or physical change. Here we are most interested in chemical reactions rather than in ways of harnessing energy for useful work such as driving steam engines, although calculations of the change in free energy can be used for that purpose.

$$\Delta G = \Delta H - T \Delta S$$

We noted earlier that reactions for which ΔH is negative are *often* spontaneous. From Equation (22.4) we can see why this is so. When the change in entropy is quite small and $T \Delta S$ is also quite small, the change in free energy is almost equal to the heat of a chemical reaction. In a spontaneous change, a system moves toward a state of minimum free energy. Free energy is released and the change in free energy, ΔG, has a negative value.

As is the case for enthalpy and energy, only *changes* in free energy can be measured. And as for these other quantities, the change in free energy is independent of the number of steps taken in a chemical or physical change and depends only on the initial and final states of the system. Free energy changes for processes involving substances in their standard states at a specified temperature are designated as standard free energy changes, $\Delta G°$, giving

$$\underset{\frac{kilojoules}{mole}}{\Delta G°} = \underset{\frac{kilojoules}{mole}}{\Delta H°} - \underset{kelvins}{T} \underset{\frac{kilojoules}{kelvin\ mole}}{\Delta S°} \tag{22.5}$$

Like $\Delta H°$ and $\Delta S°$, for a given chemical reaction or physical change $\Delta G°$ has a constant value.

To demonstrate how Equation (22.5) predicts spontaneity, let's return to the ice cubes of Figure 22.1. At all three temperatures the $\Delta H°$ values are negative (Section 22.1), favoring the process under consideration, the freezing of water,

$$H_2O(l,\ 1\ atm) \longrightarrow H_2O(s,\ 1\ atm)$$

but the $\Delta S°$ values are negative (Section 22.3), making the process unfavorable from the viewpoint of entropy changes. Combining the $\Delta H°$ and $\Delta S°$ values in the calculation of $\Delta G°$ shows which drive to spontaneity dominates at each temperature.

$$\Delta G°_{272.15} = \left(-5972.2\ \frac{J}{mol}\right) - (272.15\ K)\left(-21.8640\ \frac{J}{K\ mol}\right) = -21.9\ \frac{J}{mol}$$

$$\Delta G°_{273.15} = \left(-6009.5\ \frac{J}{mol}\right) - (273.15\ K)\left(-22.0007\ \frac{J}{K\ mol}\right) = 0.0\ \frac{J}{mol}$$

$$\Delta G°_{274.15} = \left(-6046.7\ \frac{J}{mol}\right) - (274.15\ K)\left(-22.1369\ \frac{J}{K\ mol}\right) = 22.1\ \frac{J}{mol}$$

At -1 °C, $\Delta H°$ is the more significant driving force, $\Delta G°$ has a negative value, and the process is spontaneous—water freezes. At 0 °C, the effects of enthalpy and entropy are in balance and $\Delta G° = 0$. We know that at the freezing point ice and water are in equilibrium and no spontaneous change occurs. The value of the free energy change for a system at equilibrium is zero. The system is at the point of minimum free energy.

At $+1$ °C, $\Delta S°$ is the more important driving force, $\Delta G°$ has a positive value, and the process is nonspontaneous. Like $\Delta H°$, the sign of $\Delta G°$ is reversed for a change in the reverse direction. A positive value of $\Delta G°$ indicates that under the given conditions a process is *spontaneous in the reverse direction*. Ice does indeed melt above 0 °C.

The three possible relationships between the free energy change and spontaneity illustrated by these calculations hold for *all* chemical and physical changes (Table 22.4).

Table 22.4
Free Energy and Spontaneity

$\Delta G < 0$	Spontaneous
$\Delta G = 0$	Equilibrium; no change
$\Delta G > 0$	Nonspontaneous; reverse change is spontaneous

In summary, the free energy change is the unequivocal criterion for the spontaneity of a chemical reaction or a physical change at constant temperature and pressure. *If ΔG has a negative value, a chemical or physical change is spontaneous. When the system is at equilibrium, no "free energy" is available and $\Delta G = 0$. If ΔG has a positive value, the change is not spontaneous, but the reverse process is spontaneous.*

22.7 $\Delta G°$ FOR CHEMICAL REACTIONS

As discussed in the introduction to this chapter, a **spontaneous chemical change** takes place without any continuing outside influence. When the pure reactants are mixed, the reaction proceeds spontaneously to form products until equilibrium is established. A reaction is considered to be spontaneous in the forward direction if equilibrium is reached at a point where products are favored over reactants. In other words, a reaction for which the value of the equilibrium constant is greater than 1 is described as a spontaneous chemical reaction. For such a reaction, the value of $\Delta G°$ is negative. It must be kept in mind that free energy relationships are not in any way indicators of *kinetic* stability or instability—they give no indication of the *rate* of a chemical reaction.

The magnitude of $\Delta G°$ is an indication of the *extent* to which a chemical reaction proceeds under standard state conditions—how far the reaction goes toward the formation of products before equilibrium is reached. The greater the magnitude of a negative $\Delta G°$ value, the more favorable is the formation of products. The reactions that we think of as going to "completion" generally have large negative values of $\Delta G°$. The greater the magnitude of a positive $\Delta G°$, the more favorable is the *reverse* reaction. As you might expect, there is a quantitative relationship between the values of $\Delta G°$ and K; this relationship is discussed in the next section.

Free energy data, like enthalpy data, are usually tabulated for the standard states of substances at 1 atm and a specified temperature. Where no temperature is given, the temperature is assumed to be 25 °C. Values for the standard free energies of formation, $\Delta G_f°$, are included in Table 22.2. As for $\Delta H_f°$, the reference point for the data is chosen by designating $\Delta G_f° = 0$ for elements in their standard states.

The magnitude of the standard free energy of formation of a given species is an indicator of its *thermodynamic* stability. Species with large negative $\Delta G_f°$ values can be expected not to decompose into their elements unless they encounter vigorous reaction conditions. Look at the iron oxides in Table 22.2; it is not easy to win free iron from its oxide ores. On the other hand, a positive $\Delta G_f°$ is a good indicator that a compound will readily return to the free elements. Ozone, and hydrogen and oxygen atoms in the gas phase (the species in Table 22.2 that have positive free energies of formation) are highly reactive, yielding O_2 and H_2 in many reactions.

Depending upon the type of data available, there are three ways to calculate the value of $\Delta G°$ for a chemical reaction: (1) If $\Delta H°$ and $\Delta S°$ are known, $\Delta G°$ can be found from Equation (22.4), which defines the free energy change (Example 22.8). (2) If $\Delta G°$ values are known for an appropriate series of reactions, the equations and $\Delta G°$ values can be combined by algebraic addition and subtraction according to Hess's law (Section 7.9c) to give $\Delta G°$ (Example 22.9). (3) If standard free energies of formation of the reactants and products are available, $\Delta G°$ can be found (Example 22.10) by using the following relationship, similar to that for $\Delta H°$ (Section 7.10).

$$\Delta G° = \text{(sum of } \Delta G_f° \text{ of products)} - \text{(sum of } \Delta G_f° \text{ of reactants)}$$

It is customary to tabulate $\Delta H_f°$ and $\Delta G_f°$ in units of *kilo*joules per mole (or kilocalories per mole). The $S°$ values are customarily given in *joules* (or calories) per kelvin per mole. *This means* that when $\Delta H_f°$ and $\Delta G_f°$ data are used together with S, it is usually necessary to convert kilojoules to joules or vice versa. Do not make the common error of assuming that $\Delta H°$ and $S°$ data have the same energy units.

EXAMPLE 22.8
$\Delta G°$ **of Reaction**

Determine whether the reaction

$$CCl_4(l) + H_2(g) \longrightarrow HCl(g) + CHCl_3(l)$$

is spontaneous at 25 °C under standard state conditions. At 25 °C, $\Delta H° = -91.34$ kJ and $\Delta S° = 41.51$ J/K for this reaction.

The value of $\Delta G°$ is

$$\Delta G° = \Delta H° - T\,\Delta S°$$

$$= (-91.34 \text{ kJ}) - (298.15 \text{ K})\left(41.51\,\frac{J}{K}\right)\left(\frac{1 \text{ kJ}}{1000 \text{ J}}\right)$$

$$= -103.72 \text{ kJ}$$

The negative value of $\Delta G°$ indicates that the reaction will be spontaneous at this temperature and under standard state conditions. [Note the necessary conversion factor in the $T\,\Delta S°$ term.]

Exercise For the reaction

$$O_3(g) + O(g) \longrightarrow 2O_2(g)$$

$\Delta H° = -391.9$ kJ and $\Delta S° = 10.29$ J/K at 25 °C. Calculate $\Delta G°$ at this temperature and state whether the reaction is spontaneous or not. *Answer* $\Delta G° = -395.0$ kJ; the reaction is spontaneous.

EXAMPLE 22.9
$\Delta G°$ **of Reaction**

Use the following thermochemical equations:

$$S(\text{rhombic}) + O_2(g) \longrightarrow SO_2(g) \qquad \Delta G° = -300.19 \text{ kJ}$$
$$S(\text{monoclinic}) + O_2(g) \longrightarrow SO_2(g) \qquad \Delta G° = -300.29 \text{ kJ}$$

to find $\Delta G°$ for the change of state

$$S(\text{monoclinic}) \longrightarrow S(\text{rhombic})$$

The free energy change for the sulfur change of state can be found by adding the second equation to the reverse of the first equation,

$S(\text{monoclinic}) + O_2(g) \longrightarrow SO_2(g)$	$\Delta G° = -300.29 \text{ kJ}$
$SO_2(g) \longrightarrow S(\text{rhombic}) + O_2(g)$	$\Delta G° = 300.19 \text{ kJ}$
$S(\text{monoclinic}) \longrightarrow S(\text{rhombic})$	$\Delta G° = -0.10 \text{ kJ}$

This phase change is spontaneous at 25 °C under standard state conditions with $\Delta G° = -0.10$ kJ/mol, but the small value of $\Delta G°$ indicates that the extent of the reaction is not great. Monoclinic sulfur and rhombic sulfur will both be present in an equilibrium mixture in appreciable quantities. [The kinetic factor is also very significant in this solid-state crystal structure change.]

Exercise Use the following thermochemical equations:

$$2FeO(s) + \tfrac{1}{2}O_2(g) \longrightarrow Fe_2O_3(s) \qquad \Delta G° = -252.7 \text{ kJ}$$
$$3FeO(s) + \tfrac{1}{2}O_2(g) \longrightarrow Fe_3O_4(s) \qquad \Delta G° = -281.2 \text{ kJ}$$

to find $\Delta G°$ for the reaction

$$3Fe_2O_3(s) \longrightarrow 2Fe_3O_4(s) + \tfrac{1}{2}O_2(g)$$

Answer $\Delta G° = 195.7$ kJ

EXAMPLE 22.10
$\Delta G°$ **of Reaction**

The standard state free energies of formation at 25 °C are -78.87 kJ/mol for $Fe^{2+}(aq, 1 \text{ M})$, -4.6 kJ/mol for $Fe^{3+}(aq, 1 \text{ M})$, and 0 kJ/mol for $Fe(s)$. Calculate $\Delta G°$ for the disproportionation reaction

$$3Fe^{2+}(aq, 1 \text{ M}) \longrightarrow 2Fe^{3+}(aq, 1 \text{ M}) + Fe(s)$$

Is the reaction spontaneous under these conditions?

The $\Delta G°$ for this reaction can be found by subtracting the free energy of formation of the reactant from the sum of the free energies of formation of the products:

$$\begin{aligned}
\Delta G° &= [(2 \text{ mol}) \times \Delta G_f°(Fe^{3+}) + (1 \text{ mol}) \times \Delta G_f°(Fe)] - [(3 \text{ mol}) \times \Delta G_f°(Fe^{2+})] \\
&= [(2 \text{ mol})(-4.6 \text{ kJ/mol}) + (1 \text{ mol})(0 \text{ kJ/mol})] - [(3 \text{ mol})(-78.87 \text{ kJ/mol})] \\
&= 227.4 \text{ kJ}
\end{aligned}$$

With $\Delta G° = 227.4$ kJ, under standard state conditions at 25 °C, this disproportionation reaction is not spontaneous.

Exercise The standard state free energies of formation at 1000 K are -139.13 kJ/mol for $BrF_3(g)$, -78.58 kJ/mol for $BrF(g)$, and -144.85 kJ/mol for $BrF_5(g)$. Calculate $\Delta G°$ for the disproportionation reaction

$$2BrF_3(g) \longrightarrow BrF(g) + BrF_5(g)$$

Is the reaction spontaneous under these conditions? *Answer* $\Delta G° = 54.83$ kJ; the reaction is not spontaneous.

EXAMPLE 22.11
Free Energy as Criterion for Spontaneity

A student had just finished studying thermodynamics in his chemistry class and had been impressed by the fact that of the two forms of carbon, graphite is more stable than diamond:

$$C(\text{diamond}) \longrightarrow C(\text{graphite}) \qquad \Delta G° = -2.90 \text{ kJ}$$

When he became engaged to be married, he presented his fiancée with a ring in which a pellet of graphite was mounted where there would ordinarily have been a diamond. He informed her of the difference in stability of the two forms of carbon and pointed out that since a diamond would only change to graphite with time anyway, graphite was just as good. What common error had he made regarding the significance of the thermodynamic data?

Thermodynamics cannot predict *rates* of reaction. The rate at which diamond changes to graphite at 298 K is, fortunately, very, very slow.

22.8 RELATIONSHIPS BETWEEN FREE ENERGY AND EQUILIBRIUM; CONDITIONS OTHER THAN STANDARD STATE

Figure 22.7 illustrates schematically the relationships between free energy and equilibrium in a chemical reaction as the reaction proceeds from pure reactants to pure products in the standard state. The value of $\Delta G°$ is the difference between the free energy content of the products and that of the reactants:

$$\Delta G° = G°_{\text{products}} - G°_{\text{reactants}}$$

At equilibrium, no further net transformation of reactants to products takes place and the free energy of the system is at a minimum.

It can be shown that the relationship between the standard state free energy change and the equilibrium constant is as follows:

$$\boxed{\Delta G° = -2.303 \, RT \log K}$$

ln to log conversion factor — *gas constant* — *absolute temp.*

$$\Delta G° = -2.303 \, RT \log K \qquad (22.6)$$

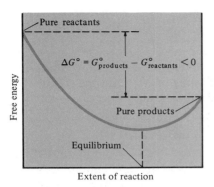

(a) **Spontaneous in forward direction,**
$\Delta G° < 0, K > 1$.

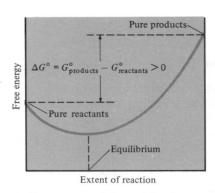

(b) **Nonspontaneous in forward direction,**
$\Delta G° > 0, K < 1$.

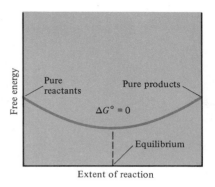

(c) **Equilibrium**

Figure 22.7
Free Energy and Equilibrium The reactions progress from left to right. The equilibrium points correspond to the concentrations of reactants and products at which $\Delta G = 0$.

From this equation you can see that when $\Delta G°$ is negative K will be greater than one (because log K must be positive), showing that products are favored over reactants. This is illustrated in Figure 22.7a. Because the reactants have a greater total free energy than the products, free energy is released in reaching the free energy minimum at equilibrium. When $\Delta G°$ is positive, the opposite is the case — K is less than one (because log K must be negative), showing that reactants are favored over products. This type of reaction (Figure 22.7b) is nonspontaneous in the forward direction, but spontaneous in the reverse direction. In the relatively rare case that $\Delta G° = 0$ (Figure 22.7c), then $K = 1$ and the numerator and the denominator in the equilibrium constant expression must be equal (i.e., $[R]^r[S]^s \cdots = [A]^a[B]^b \cdots$; Section 19.2). These relationships are summarized in Table 22.5.

Equation (22.6) makes it possible to calculate $\Delta G°$ when K is known and to calculate K when $\Delta G°$ is known (both at the specified temperature). (See Example 22.12.)

Many chemical reactions are carried out under conditions other than standard state conditions, frequently with gases at partial pressures other than 1 atm or aqueous solutions at other than 1 M. The nonstandard-state free energy change is related to $\Delta G°$ as shown by the following equation:

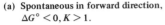

$$\Delta G = \Delta G° + 2.303 \, RT \log Q \qquad (22.7)$$

where R is the ideal gas constant (8.314 J/K mol), T is the absolute temperature, and Q, the reaction quotient, is expressed as before (Section 19.7) in terms of partial pressures of gases in atmospheres or concentrations of aqueous solutions in moles per liter. As demonstrated in numerous ways in our study of equilibrium (Chapters 19–21), with a change in the concentration of the reactants, a reaction may become more or less favorable and the direction of spontaneity may change.

Table 22.5
Relationship between Standard Free Energy Change and Equilibrium Constant

$\Delta G°$	K	Product Formation
$\Delta G° < 0$	$K > 1$	**Products are favored over reactants at equilibrium**
$\Delta G° = 0$	$K = 1$	**Equilibrium at** $[R]^r[S]^s \cdots = [A]^a[B]^b \cdots$
$\Delta G° > 0$	$K < 1$	**Reactants are favored over products at equilibrium**

EXAMPLE 22.12
ΔG° and Equilibrium

Calculate the equilibrium constant at 25 °C for the reaction

$$CCl_4(l) + H_2(g) \rightleftharpoons HCl(g) + CHCl_3(l)$$

given that $\Delta G° = -103.72$ kJ for this reaction at 25 °C.

Equation (22.6) gives the relationship between the value of $\Delta G°$ and the equilibrium constant. Solving this equation for $\log K$ and substituting values gives

$$\log K = \frac{-\Delta G°}{(2.303)\,RT} = \frac{-(-103.72 \text{ kJ})(1000 \text{ J/kJ})}{(2.303)(8.314 \text{ J/K mol})(298 \text{ K})}$$
$$= 18.18$$

Taking antilogarithms gives $K = 1.5 \times 10^{18}$. Under standard state conditions at 25 °C this reaction is spontaneous and products are greatly favored over reactants at equilibrium.

Exercise At 1000. K, $\Delta G° = 54.83$ kJ for

$$2BrF_3(g) \rightleftharpoons BrF(g) + BrF_5(g)$$

Calculate the equilibrium constant for this reaction at this temperature. *Answer* 1.37×10^{-3}

EXAMPLE 22.13
ΔG under Nonstandard State Conditions

Calculate ΔG for the reaction

$$CCl_4(l) + H_2(g) \rightleftharpoons HCl(g) + CHCl_3(l)$$

given that $\Delta G° = -103.72$ kJ at 25 °C and $p_{H_2} = 10$ atm and $p_{HCl} = 0.1$ atm. Will this reaction be more or less favorable under these nonstandard state conditions compared to standard state conditions?

The reaction quotient for the equation is

$$Q = \frac{p_{HCl}}{p_{H_2}} = \frac{0.1 \text{ atm}}{10 \text{ atm}} = 0.01$$

Using Equation (22.7) to calculate ΔG gives

$$\Delta G = \Delta G° + (2.303)\,RT \log Q$$

$$= (-103.71 \text{ kJ}) + (2.303)(8.314 \text{ J/K mol})(298 \text{ K})\left(\frac{1 \text{ kJ}}{1000 \text{ J}}\right) \log (0.01)$$

$$= -115 \text{ kJ}$$

The value of ΔG has become slightly more negative, meaning that the reaction is slightly more favorable under these conditions.

Exercise Calculate ΔG at 1000. K for the reaction

$$2BrF_3(g) \rightleftharpoons BrF(g) + BrF_5(g)$$

given that $\Delta G°_{1000} = 54.83$ kJ and $p_{BrF} = p_{BrF_5} = 0.0010$ atm and $p_{BrF_3} = 5.2$ atm. Will this reaction be more or less favorable under these nonstandard state conditions compared to standard state conditions? *Answer* -87 kJ; the reaction is more favorable and under these conditions is spontaneous in the forward direction.

22.9 VARIATIONS OF ΔG° AND K WITH TEMPERATURE; INTERPRETING THERMODYNAMIC DATA

The value of $\Delta G°$ varies with the temperature, as shown by the equation $\Delta G° = \Delta H° - T\,\Delta S°$. How temperature changes affect the direction and extent of a reaction depends upon the signs of $\Delta H°$ and $\Delta S°$. [Recall that the standard state is defined for any *specified* temperature. Because we commonly tabulate data for

Table 22.6
Relations among $\Delta H°$, $\Delta S°$, and $\Delta G°$ of Reaction at 298 K, and Reaction Spontaneity

Reaction	$\Delta H°$(kJ)	$\Delta S°$(J/K)	$\Delta G°$(kJ)
(a) $H_2(g) + Br_2(l) \longrightarrow 2HBr(g)$	-72.80	$+114.37$	-106.86
	favorable	favorable	spontaneous
(b) $2H_2(g) + O_2(g) \longrightarrow 2H_2O(g)$	-483.64	-88.75	-457.18
	favorable	unfavorable	spontaneous
(c) $Br_2(l) + Cl_2(g) \longrightarrow 2BrCl(g)$	$+29.28$	$+104.76$	-1.92
	unfavorable	favorable	spontaneous
(d) $N_2(g) + 2F_2(g) \longrightarrow N_2F_4(g)$	-7.2	-295.77	$+81.2$
	favorable	unfavorable	not spontaneous
(e) $H_2(g) \longrightarrow 2H(g)$	$+435.93$	$+98.63$	$+406.53$
	unfavorable	favorable	not spontaneous
(f) $2HCl(g) \longrightarrow H_2(g) + Cl_2(g)$	$+184.61$	-20.07	$+190.60$
	unfavorable	unfavorable	not spontaneous

25 °C, there is a tendency to forget that the standard state data can be calculated and reported for whatever temperature we choose to specify.]

When $\Delta H°$ and $\Delta S°$ have opposite signs, the outcome of a chemical reaction is predictable—it is either always spontaneous at all temperatures (negative $\Delta H°$, positive $\Delta S°$) or always nonspontaneous at all temperatures (positive $\Delta H°$, negative $\Delta S°$). Reactions (a) and (f) in Table 22.6 are reactions of these types. Consider the free energy variation with temperature for reaction (a):

$$\Delta G° = \Delta H° - T\,\Delta S°$$
$$\Delta G° = (-72.80 \text{ kJ}) - (T)(0.11437 \text{ kJ/K}) \tag{22.8}$$

In general, the value of $\Delta H°$ does not vary greatly with moderate temperature changes and $\Delta H°$ can be taken to be constant for most reactions. The entropy change, $\Delta S°$, is also reasonably constant with changes in temperature. However, the $T\,\Delta S°$ term is directly dependent upon temperature. From Equation (22.8) you can see that for a reaction of this type, no matter how the temperature changes, $\Delta G°$ will remain negative, and so the reaction will always be spontaneous. However, as illustrated below, the *extent* of such a reaction will increase with temperature.

For reaction (f), no matter what the temperature, $\Delta G°$ will always be positive,

$$\Delta G° = (+184.61 \text{ kJ}) - (T)(-0.02007 \text{ kJ/K}) \tag{22.9}$$

and the reaction will not be spontaneous.

When $\Delta H°$ and $\Delta S°$ are of the *same* sign, spontaneity depends upon the relative magnitudes of the $\Delta H°$ and $T\,\Delta S°$ terms in the free energy equation. Under these circumstances, the value of $\Delta G°$ can change from positive to negative, or vice versa, with changes in temperature. As an example, look at reaction (e) in Table 22.6, for which both $\Delta H°$ and $\Delta S°$ are positive. A strong bond, the H—H bond, is broken, and as expected this is an endothermic process. However, the entropy change is favorable because two moles of gas are created from one mole of gas. At 25 °C the large value of $\Delta H°$ outweighs the $T\,\Delta S°$ term, $\Delta G°$ is positive, and the reaction is not spontaneous. You can see, though, that increasing the value of T to the point where $T\,\Delta S° > \Delta H°$,

$$\Delta G° = (+435.93 \text{ kJ}) - (T)(0.09863 \text{ kJ/K})$$

will lead to a reversal in the sign of $\Delta G°$. (This is reasonable: At a high enough temperature, we know that the bond will break.)

A similar argument would show that reaction (d), for which both $\Delta H°$ and $\Delta S°$ are negative, becomes spontaneous in the direction written at a *lower* temperature (unless phase changes counteract the free energy change). The effects of the relative

Table 22.7
Variation of $\Delta G°$ with Temperature

$\Delta H°$	$\Delta S°$	$\Delta G°$	Examples in Table 22.6
−	+	− at all T	**Reaction (a)**
+	−	+ at all T	**Reaction (f)**
−	−	+ or −, depends on T **Becomes more favorable** **at lower temperatures**	**Reactions (b) and (d)**
+	+	+ or −, depends on T **Becomes more favorable** **at higher temperatures**	**Reactions (c) and (e)**

signs of $\Delta H°$ and $\Delta S°$ with respect to changes in temperature are summarized in Table 22.7.

EXAMPLE 22.14
$\Delta G°$ of Reaction

Discuss reactions (b) and (c) in Table 22.6 and the meaning of the thermodynamic data for these reactions.

Reaction (b) is the formation of water vapor by combination of the elements. We know that water is a thermodynamically stable compound. The large increase in the stability of the system when water is formed from its elements is shown by the large negative value of $\Delta H°$. The drive to minimum energy is opposed in this reaction by a decrease in entropy due to the formation of two moles of gas from three moles of gas. However, the $T \Delta S$ term in $\Delta G° = \Delta H° - T \Delta S°$ is small relative to the enthalpy change, and the reaction is spontaneous at 298 K. With negative $\Delta H°$ and negative $\Delta S°$, this is the type of reaction that will remain spontaneous and become more favorable at lower temperatures (see Table 22.7).

Reaction (c) is the formation of bromine(I) chloride by combination of the elements. As would be expected because of the need to break the reasonably strong Br—Br and Cl—Cl bonds, the reaction is endothermic. However, a relatively large entropy increase occurs, presumably due to the change from A—A type molecules to A—B type molecules. The entropy increase is sufficiently large that the $T \Delta S°$ term just barely prevails, giving the reaction a very small negative change in free energy. With a positive $\Delta H°$ and a positive $\Delta S°$, this is the type of reaction that should remain spontaneous and become more favorable at higher temperatures.

Exercise For the reaction

$$2O_2(g) \longrightarrow O_3(g) + O(g)$$

$\Delta H° = 391.9$ kJ and $\Delta S° = -10.29$ J/K at 25 °C. Briefly discuss the temperature dependence of $\Delta G°$ for this reaction. *Answer* $\Delta H°$ and $\Delta S°$ are both unfavorable; therefore $\Delta G°$ will remain positive and the reaction will remain nonspontaneous with changes in temperature.

A relationship that allows calculation of the standard state free energy change for a reaction at one temperature from a known $\Delta G°$ at another temperature can be derived from Equation (22.8) if $\Delta H°$ and $\Delta S°$ are assumed to be constant with changing temperature, a reasonable assumption. For an initial temperature T_1 and a final temperature T_2,

$$\Delta G_1° = \Delta H° - T_1 \Delta S° \qquad \Delta G_2° = \Delta H° - T_2 \Delta S°$$

$$\frac{\Delta G_1°}{T_1} = \frac{\Delta H°}{T_1} - \Delta S° \qquad \frac{\Delta G_2°}{T_2} = \frac{\Delta H°}{T_2} - \Delta S°$$

Combining these equations gives an equation that is valid for all but extreme temperature changes:

$$\frac{\Delta G_2^\circ}{T_2} - \frac{\Delta G_1^\circ}{T_1} = \Delta H^\circ \left(\frac{1}{T_2} - \frac{1}{T_1} \right) \tag{22.10}$$

(This relationship also allows the calculation of the temperature at which a non-spontaneous reaction becomes spontaneous; see Example 22.16.)

EXAMPLE 22.15
ΔG° as a Function of Temperature

How does the value of ΔG° change for the reaction

$$CCl_4(l) + H_2(g) \longrightarrow HCl(g) + CHCl_3(l)$$

if the reaction is carried out at 65 °C rather than at 25 °C? At 25 °C, $\Delta G^\circ = -103.72$ kJ and $\Delta H^\circ = -91.34$ kJ for this reaction.

To find the answer to this question, we must calculate ΔG_{338}° and compare it to ΔG_{298}°. We use Equation (22.8), which relates ΔG° to T:

$$\frac{\Delta G_{338}^\circ}{338 \text{ K}} = \frac{\Delta G_{298}^\circ}{298 \text{ K}} + \Delta H^\circ \left(\frac{1}{338 \text{ K}} - \frac{1}{298 \text{ K}} \right)$$

$$= \frac{(-103.72 \text{ kJ})}{298 \text{ K}} + (-91.34 \text{ kJ}) \left(\frac{1}{338 \text{ K}} - \frac{1}{298 \text{ K}} \right)$$

$$= -0.312 \text{ kJ/K}$$

$$\Delta G_{338}^\circ = (338 \text{ K})(-0.312 \text{ kJ/K}) = -105 \text{ kJ}$$

The value of ΔG_{338}° is more negative than that of ΔG_{298}°, so the reaction is more favorable at the higher temperature.

Exercise For the reaction

$$3Fe_2O_3(s) \longrightarrow 2Fe_3O_4(s) + \tfrac{1}{2}O_2(g)$$

$\Delta G^\circ = 195.7$ kJ and $\Delta H^\circ = 235.8$ kJ at 25 °C. Assuming ΔH° to be independent of temperature, calculate ΔG° at 1000. K. *Answer* $\Delta G_{1000}^\circ = 102$ kJ

Combining the equation that relates ΔG° to K (Equation 22.7) with the equation that defines ΔG° (Equation 22.5) gives

$$\Delta G^\circ = \Delta H^\circ - T \, \Delta S^\circ = -(2.303) \, RT \log K \tag{22.11}$$

A convenient relationship between the equilibrium constants at two different temperatures can be derived from this equation. First, Equation (22.11) is solved for $\log K$.

$$\log K = -\frac{\Delta H^\circ}{2.303 \, RT} + \frac{\Delta S^\circ}{2.303 \, RT}$$

If we assume that ΔH° and ΔS° are constant between T_1 and T_2, then the first of the following two equations:

$$\log K_1 = -\frac{\Delta H^\circ}{2.303 \, RT_1} + \frac{\Delta S^\circ}{2.303 \, RT_1}$$

$$\log K_2 = -\frac{\Delta H^\circ}{2.303 \, RT_2} + \frac{\Delta S^\circ}{2.303 \, RT_2}$$

can be subtracted from the second to give

$$\log\left(\frac{K_2}{K_1}\right) = -\frac{\Delta H°}{2.303\,R}\left(\frac{1}{T_2} - \frac{1}{T_1}\right) \tag{22.12}$$

This equation can be used to find the equilibrium constant at any desired temperature from the known equilibrium constant at a different temperature.

From Le Chatelier's principle, we expect that for an exothermic reaction, an increase in temperature will favor the reverse reaction and the value of K should be smaller. Similarly, for a endothermic reaction, the forward reaction is favored by a temperature increase and the value of K should be larger. The following example illustrates such a change in the value of K with temperature.

EXAMPLE 22.16
$\Delta G°$ and Equilibrium

For the reaction

$$BeSO_4(s) \rightleftharpoons BeO(s) + SO_3(g)$$

$K = 3.87 \times 10^{-16}$ at 400. K. Calculate K at 600. K assuming that the value of $\Delta H° = 175$ kJ for the reaction is constant over this temperature range.

To find K at 600. K, we use Equation (22.12).

$$\log\left(\frac{K_2}{K_1}\right) = \frac{-\Delta H°}{(2.303)\,R}\left(\frac{1}{T_2} - \frac{1}{T_1}\right)$$

$$\log\left(\frac{K}{3.87 \times 10^{-16}}\right) = \frac{-(175\text{ kJ/mol})(1000\text{ J/kJ})}{(2.303)(8.314\text{ J/K mol})}\left(\frac{1}{600.\text{ K}} - \frac{1}{400.\text{ K}}\right) = 7.62$$

Taking antilogarithms of both sides gives

$$\frac{K}{3.87 \times 10^{-16}} = 4.2 \times 10^7$$

$$K = 1.6 \times 10^{-8}$$

The equilibrium constant is 1.6×10^{-8} at 600. K. As expected for an endothermic reaction, an increase in temperature favors product formation, as shown by the increase in the value of K.

Exercise Calculate K for the reaction

$$3Fe_2O_3(s) \rightleftharpoons 2Fe_3O_4(s) + \tfrac{1}{2}O_2(g)$$

at 500. K given that $\Delta H° = 235.8$ kJ and $K = 5.0 \times 10^{-35}$ at 25 °C. (Assume that the $\Delta H°$ value is constant over this temperature range.) *Answer* $K = 3 \times 10^{-18}$

The preceding example shows that increasing the temperature for the decomposition of beryllium sulfate by 200 K shifts the equilibrium in the direction of product formation. Under standard state conditions, this reaction would still not be spontaneous in the forward direction. As the next example demonstrates, it is possible to calculate the temperature above which a reaction that is not spontaneous will become spontaneous under standard state conditions. The basis for this calculation is the knowledge that the direction of spontaneity changes at the point where $\Delta G° = 0$ because at this point $K = 1$. The equation that relates ΔG values at different temperatures (Equation 22.10) is used to find the temperature at which $\Delta G° = 0$.

The second of the following examples illustrates how the thermodynamic data for a reaction can be developed from knowledge of the equilibrium constant at two different temperatures.

EXAMPLE 22.17
$\Delta G°$ and Equilibrium

Find the temperature above which the decomposition of beryllium sulfate will become spontaneous under standard state conditions.

$$BeSO_4(s) \xrightarrow{\Delta} BeO(s) + SO_3(g) \qquad K = 1.6 \times 10^{-8} \text{ at } 600.\text{ K} \qquad \Delta H° = 175 \text{ kJ}$$

This reaction is of the type that becomes more favorable as the temperature increases, as shown in Example 22.16. The reaction will become spontaneous above the temperature at which $\Delta G° = 0$. First, we must find $\Delta G°$ at a known temperature. Using the known value of K at 600. K, we obtain

$$\Delta G°_{600} = -2.303\ RT \log K = -2.303 \left(8.314 \frac{J}{K\ mol}\right)(600.\ K)(\log 1.6 \times 10^{-8})$$

$$= 89{,}600 \text{ J}$$

With this value of $\Delta G°$ at 600. K and $\Delta G°_2 = 0$, we solve Equation (22.10) for T_2.

$$\frac{\Delta G°_2}{T_2} - \frac{\Delta G°_1}{T_1} = \Delta H° \left(\frac{1}{T_2} - \frac{1}{T_1}\right)$$

$$\frac{0}{T_2} - \frac{89.6 \text{ kJ}}{600.\ K} = 175 \text{ kJ} \left(\frac{1}{T_2} - \frac{1}{600.\ K}\right)$$

$$-\frac{89.6 \text{ kJ}}{(600.\ K)(175 \text{ kJ})} + \frac{1}{600.\ K} = \frac{1}{T_2}$$

$$T_2 = 1230 \text{ K}$$

Under standard conditions, the thermal decomposition of beryllium sulfate will be spontaneous above 1230 K.

Exercise Find the temperature above which the reaction

$$3Fe_2O_3(s) \longrightarrow 2Fe_3O_4(s) + \tfrac{1}{2}O_2(g)$$

will become spontaneous under standard state conditions. At 25 °C, $\Delta G° = 195.7$ kJ and $\Delta H° = 235.8$ kJ for this reaction. *Answer* 1800 K

EXAMPLE 22.18
$\Delta G°$ and Equilibrium

Usually it is relatively easy to measure the equilibrium constant for a chemical reaction. A great deal of thermodynamic information can be obtained concerning the reaction from the value of K at two different temperatures. To illustrate how this is done, we will use data for a biochemical reaction, the conversion of L-aspartate ion into fumarate ion and ammonium ion.

$$\begin{bmatrix} \begin{matrix} O \\ \diagdown \\ O \diagup \end{matrix} CCH_2CHC \begin{matrix} \diagup O \\ \diagdown O \end{matrix} \\ \qquad\quad | \\ \qquad\quad NH_3 \end{bmatrix}^{-} \rightleftharpoons \begin{bmatrix} \begin{matrix} O \\ \diagdown \\ O \diagup \end{matrix} CCH{=}CHC \begin{matrix} \diagup O \\ \diagdown O \end{matrix} \end{bmatrix}^{2-} + NH_4^{+}$$

L-aspartate ion   *fumarate ion*

This reaction, which is catalyzed by an enzyme, is part of a series of reactions that breaks down larger molecules in human and animal metabolism so that they can be eliminated as waste products. The overall result of the reaction cycle in which the aspartate–fumarate conversion takes part is the removal of NH_2 groups from amino acids and their conversion to urea, which is eliminated in urine.

The equilibrium constant for the reaction is 7.4×10^{-3} at 29 °C and 1.60×10^{-2} at 39 °C. From this set of data, calculate $\Delta H°$, K, $\Delta G°$, and $\Delta \bar{S}°$ at

37 °C (approximate human body temperature, used as the standard state temperature for biochemical data).

From the temperature dependence of K, Equation (22.12) gives us

$$\Delta H° = \frac{-(2.303)\ R \log (K_2/K_1)}{(1/T_2) - (1/T_1)}$$

$$= \frac{-(2.303)(8.314\ \text{J/K mol})(1\ \text{kJ}/1000\ \text{J}) \log (1.60 \times 10^{-2}/7.4 \times 10^{-3})}{(1/312\ \text{K}) - (1/302\ \text{K})}$$

$$= 60.4\ \text{kJ}$$

Using this value of $\Delta H°$ and the value of K at 39 °C, we can find K at 37 °C.

$$\log\left(\frac{K_2}{K_1}\right) = \frac{-\Delta H°}{(2.303)\ R}\left(\frac{1}{T_2} - \frac{1}{T_1}\right)$$

$$\log\left(\frac{K_2}{1.60 \times 10^{-2}}\right) = \frac{-(60.4\ \text{kJ})(1000\ \text{J/kJ})}{(2.303)(8.314\ \text{J/K mol})}\left(\frac{1}{310.\ \text{K}} - \frac{1}{312\ \text{K}}\right)$$

$$= -6.5 \times 10^{-2}$$

$$\frac{K_2}{1.60 \times 10^{-2}} = 0.86$$

$$K_2 = 1.38 \times 10^{-2}$$

The value of $\Delta G°$ is calculated using Equation (22.6).

$$\Delta G° = -(2.303)\ RT \log K$$

$$= -(2.303)(8.314\ \text{J/K mol})\left(\frac{1\ \text{kJ}}{1000\ \text{J}}\right)(310.\ \text{K}) \log (1.38 \times 10^{-2})$$

$$= 11.0\ \text{kJ}$$

Once $\Delta G°$ and $\Delta H°$ are known, we use Equation (22.4) to obtain the value of $\Delta S°$.

$$\Delta S° = \frac{\Delta H° - \Delta G°}{T} = \frac{[(60.4\ \text{kJ}) - (11.0\ \text{kJ})](1000\ \text{J/kJ})}{310.\ \text{K}} = 159\ \text{J/K}$$

From the value of K at two different temperatures, we have found the following thermodynamic data at 37 °C: $\Delta H° = 60.4$ kJ, $K = 1.38 \times 10^{-2}$, $\Delta G° = 11.0$ kJ, and $\Delta S° = 159$ J/K. At body temperature, this reaction has a favorable entropy change that is offset by an unfavorable enthalpy change. The result is a small but unfavorable $\Delta G°$ and an equilibrium point at which reactants are somewhat favored over products. [Like most biochemical reactions, this is but one reaction in a series of reactions linked by common reactants and products. The energy needed to drive the unfavorable reactions is derived from the favorable reactions (Section 33.23).]

Exercise The equilibrium constant is 3.66×10^{24} at 500. K and 2.58×10^{14} at 700. K for the reaction

$$P(s) + \tfrac{5}{2}Cl_2(g) \rightleftharpoons PCl_5(g)$$

Calculate $\Delta G_f°$, $\Delta H_f°$, and $\Delta S_f°$ for $PCl_5(g)$ at 600. K from these data. *Answer* $\Delta G_f° = -214$ kJ/mol, $\Delta H_f° = -340$ kJ/mol, $\Delta S_f° = -210$ J/K mol

Equation (22.12) provides a relationship that is useful in the study of vaporization equilibria.

$$A(s\text{ or }l) \rightleftharpoons A(g) \qquad \Delta H° = \Delta H°_{\text{sublimation or vaporization}}$$

Substituting the equilibrium constant expression for this change of state,

$$K_p = p_A$$

into Equation (22.12) gives an equation which relates the vapor pressure of a substance to the temperature:

$$\log\left(\frac{p_2}{p_1}\right) = \frac{-\Delta H^\circ_{\text{sublimation or vaporization}}}{2.303\ R}\left(\frac{1}{T_2} - \frac{1}{T_1}\right) \qquad \textbf{(22.13)}$$

Equation (22.13) (known as the Clausius-Clapeyron equation) can be used (1) to predict the value of the vapor pressure of a substance at a given temperature if the heat of vaporization and the vapor pressure at another temperature are known, (2) to calculate the heat of vaporization if two vapor pressures at two temperatures are known, or (3) to predict the temperature at which the vapor pressure has a certain value if the heat of vaporization and the vapor pressure at another temperature are known.

EXAMPLE 22.19
ΔG° **and Equilibrium**

The heat of sublimation of carbon dioxide is 25,800 J/mol and the vapor pressure is 35 Torr at −110. °C. Assuming that the heat of sublimation is constant, calculate the vapor pressure of dry ice at −90. °C.

The vapor pressure at −90.0 °C (= 183.2 K) is found from Equation (22.13).

$$\log\left(\frac{p}{35\ \text{Torr}}\right) = \frac{-(25{,}800\ \text{J/mol})}{(2.303)(8.314\ \text{J/K mol})}\left(\frac{1}{183\ \text{K}} - \frac{1}{163\ \text{K}}\right) = 0.90$$

Taking antilogarithms of both sides gives

$$\frac{p}{35\ \text{Torr}} = 7.9$$

which gives

$$p = (7.9)(35\ \text{Torr}) = 280\ \text{Torr}$$

The calculated vapor pressure at −90.0 °C is 280 Torr.

Exercise The vapor pressure of liquid tungsten is 1.00 Torr at 3990. °C and 100.0 Torr at 5168 °C. Calculate the heat of vaporization. *Answer* 754 kJ/mol

In summary, ΔG° for a chemical reaction can be calculated from ΔH° and ΔS°, from a series of ΔG° values for other reactions by using Hess's law, or from ΔG°_f (standard free energy of formation) values for the reactants and products. The magnitude of ΔG° indicates the extent of a reaction, in the forward direction for a reaction with a negative ΔG° and in the reverse direction for a reaction with a positive ΔG°. The value of ΔG° and the value of the equilibrium constant are related mathematically (Equation 22.6). The free energy change for a reaction beginning from reactant and product concentrations other than those specified for the standard state can be found from the reaction quotient (Equation 22.7). Unlike the values of ΔH° and ΔS°, the values of ΔG° and the equilibrium constant vary significantly with temperature. Equations can be derived which allow the calculation of ΔG° (Equation 22.10) or K (Equation 22.12) for one temperature from the known values of ΔG° or K at another temperature. It is also possible to find the temperature at which (under standard state conditions) a nonspontaneous reaction becomes spontaneous (by using Equation 22.10 with $\Delta G^\circ = 0$ for the unknown temperature).

22.1 ENTROPY: A QUANTITATIVE MEASURE OF RANDOMNESS Experience shows that disorder tends to increase spontaneously, whereas a more highly ordered state never arises spontaneously. Whether a given physical or chemical change can take place spontaneously depends both on the enthalpy change, ΔH (i.e., whether the change is exothermic or endothermic) and on the increase or decrease in order that the change entails. The degree of disorder in a system is given quantitative expression as the entropy, S; a change in entropy is represented by ΔS.

22.2 THE SECOND LAW OF THERMODYNAMICS The universal tendency toward increasing disorder is expressed in the second law of thermodynamics: The entropy of the universe is constantly increasing. Consequently, a process can be spontaneous only if it causes an increase in the entropy of the universe. On the micro level, entropy is related to the number of possible ways in which the particles of a system can be arranged and the number of states available to each individual particle. Entropy increases when the number of particles increases, when the particles can move about more freely, in more different ways, or faster (increasing temperature), and when the particles are more randomly oriented.

22.3 ENTROPY IN PHYSICAL CHANGES A change of state that allows greater freedom of motion to atoms, molecules, or ions (melting or vaporization) represents an increase in entropy. The entropy change for a change of state is given by $\Delta S = \Delta H/T$. Entropy also increases when two substances are mixed or one dissolves in the other, and when a gas expands at constant temperature. Entropy changes for substances in their standard states at 1 atm pressure and specified temperature (usually 25 °C) are called standard state entropy changes, $\Delta S°$.

22.4 ABSOLUTE ENTROPIES At 0 K, the absolute entropy, S, of a perfect crystal is 0 (the third law of thermodynamics). Most substances do not form perfectly ordered crystals and therefore have absolute entropies that are greater than 0 at 0 K. At any temperature above absolute zero, the absolute entropy of a substance is the sum of its absolute entropy at 0 K, the entropy increases for any phase changes that it undergoes in reaching the specified temperature, and the entropy increase during the heating of each phase over the temperature range in which it is stable. In general, gases have greater entropies than liquids, and substances with complex structures have greater entropies than simpler substances.

22.5 ENTROPY IN CHEMICAL REACTIONS In chemical reactions, entropy can change because of a change in the number of particles in the system, a change in phase of one or more species present, or a change in the complexity of the substances involved. An increase in the number of particles as the result of a chemical reaction — especially an increase in the number of moles of gas — generally produces a large increase in S. In a chemical reaction, $\Delta S° =$ (sum of $S°$ of the products) − (sum of $S°$ of reactants). The value of $\Delta S°$ for a reaction can also be found by algebraic combination of reactions of known $\Delta S°$.

22.6 FREE ENERGY: THE CRITERION FOR SPONTANEITY The free energy change of a reaction is given by $\Delta G = \Delta H - T \Delta S$. It corresponds to the amount of energy that is available to do useful work. As with $\Delta H°$ and $\Delta S°$, the standard free energy change is designated $\Delta G°$. A negative value of ΔG means that the reaction releases free energy and is spontaneous. A positive value of ΔG means that the reaction is nonspontaneous and that the *reverse* reaction will be spontaneous. For a reaction at equilibrium, $\Delta G = 0$.

22.7 $\Delta G°$ FOR CHEMICAL REACTIONS The greater the magnitude of a negative ΔG, the more favorable is the formation of products. The greater the magnitude of a positive ΔG, the more favorable is the *reverse* reaction. The magnitude of $\Delta G°$ is an indication of how far a chemical reaction will proceed under standard state conditions. The magnitude of the standard free energy of formation, $\Delta G_f°$, for a given species is an indication of its thermodynamic stability. The value of $\Delta G°$ for a chemical reaction can be calculated (a) from the equation $\Delta G° = \Delta H° - T \Delta S°$, (b) by algebraic combination of reactions with known $\Delta G°$ values, or (c) from the relationship $\Delta G° = $ (sum of $\Delta G_f°$ of products) $-$ (sum of $\Delta G_f°$ of reactants).

22.8 RELATIONSHIPS BETWEEN FREE ENERGY AND EQUILIBRIUM; CONDITIONS OTHER THAN STANDARD STATE $\Delta G°$ is related to the equilibrium constant, K, for a reaction by the equation $\Delta G° = -2.303\ RT \log K$. Under nonstandard state conditions, the free energy change of a reaction is given by $\Delta G = \Delta G° + 2.303\ RT \log Q$, where Q is the reaction quotient.

22.9 VARIATION OF $\Delta G°$ AND K WITH TEMPERATURE; INTERPRETING THERMODYNAMIC DATA The value of $\Delta G°$ varies with temperature depending upon the signs of the $\Delta H°$ and $\Delta S°$ terms in $\Delta G° = \Delta H° - T \Delta S°$ (summarized in Table 22.7). Some reactions are either favorable or unfavorable at all temperatures ($\Delta H°$ and $\Delta G°$ of opposite signs). Other reactions become more favorable with increasing temperature ($\Delta H°$ and $\Delta S°$ both positive) or with decreasing temperature ($\Delta H°$ and $\Delta S°$ both negative). It is possible to calculate $\Delta G°$ at one temperature from a known $\Delta G°$ at another temperature (Equation 22.10) or to calculate the equilibrium constant at one temperature from the equilibrium constant at another temperature (Equation 22.21), if $\Delta H°$ for the reaction is also known.

SIGNIFICANT TERMS

entropy
absolute entropy
free energy change
spontaneous chemical change

THOUGHTS ON CHEMISTRY

From the Preface to a Classic Book on Thermodynamics

THERMODYNAMICS, by G. N. Lewis and M. Randall

There are ancient cathedrals which, apart from their consecrated purpose, inspire solemnity and awe. Even the curious visitor speaks of serious things, with hushed voice, and as each whisper reverberates through the vaulted nave, the returning echo seems to bear a message of mystery. The labor of generations of architects and artisans has been forgotten, the scaffolding erected for their toil has long since been removed, their mistakes have been erased, or have become hidden by the dust of centuries. Seeing only the perfection of the completed whole, we are impressed as by some superhuman agency. But sometimes we enter such an edifice that is still partly under construction; then the sound of hammers, the reek of tobacco, the trivial jests bandied from workman to workman, enable us to realize that these great structures are but the result of giving to ordinary human effort a direction and a purpose.

Science has its cathedrals, built by the efforts of a few architects and of many workers. In these loftier monuments of scientific thought a tradition has arisen whereby the friendly usages of colloquial speech give way to a certain severity and formality. While this may sometimes promote precise thinking, it more often results in the intimidation of the neophyte. . . .

There are several kinds of audience to which . . . thermodynamics might be addressed. There is the beginner who, in order that he may decide whether the subject will meet his needs or arouse his interest, asks what thermodynamics is and what sorts of problems in physics, chemistry and engineering can be solved by its aid; there is the reader who looks for the philosophical implications of such concepts as energy and entropy; above all there is the investigator who, attacking problems of pure or applied science, seeks the specific thermodynamic methods which are applicable to his problem and the data requisite for its solution. Perhaps we have been over-ambitious in attempting, within the confines of a single volume, to meet all these demands—to lead the be-

ginner through the intricacies of thermodynamic theory and to guide the experienced investigator to the extreme limits now set by existing methods and data.

G. N. Lewis and M. Randall, *Thermodynamics* (Copyright © 1923. Used with permission of Mc-Graw Hill Book Company.)

QUESTIONS

Disorder, Spontaneity, and Entropy

22.1 What do we call the quantitative measure of the randomness or disorder in a system? Place the following systems in order of increasing randomness: (a) 1 mol of gas A, (b) 1 mol of solid A, and (c) 1 mol of liquid A.

22.2 Why would you expect a decrease in entropy as a gas condenses? Would this change be as large a decrease as when a liquid sample of the same substance crystallizes?

22.3 Briefly explain why heating a gas increases its entropy.

22.4 Would you expect a positive or negative ΔS for the system as the pressure on an ideal gas is increased under constant temperature conditions? Why?

22.5 What value do we assign to the entropy of a perfect crystalline substance at absolute zero? How does this value change for substances that do not form perfect crystals at absolute zero?

22.6 A flask containing nitrogen and a flask containing oxygen are connected by a small tube with a stopcock. After the stopcock is opened, the gases eventually mix so that a uniform composition is attained even though there is no enthalpy change. What is the driving force of this process?

22.7 Given the following information, specify the contributions to the absolute entropy of $O_2(g)$ at 298 K: (a) O_2 exists as the γ-solid at 0 K, (b) the γ-solid changes to the β-solid at 24 K, (c) the β-solid changes to the α-solid at 44 K, (d) the α-solid melts at 54 K, and (e) the liquid boils at 90.2 K.

22.8 Repeat Question 22.7 for $H_2S(g)$ using the following data: (a) H_2S exists as solid-III, an imperfect crystal, at 0 K; (b) solid-III changes to solid-II at 104 K; (c) solid-II changes to solid-I at 126 K; (d) solid-I melts at 188 K; and (e) the liquid boils at 213 K.

22.9* Why is the value of $S°$ for $Cl_2(g)$ given in Table 22.2 greater than that for $Br_2(l)$?

22.10* Why is the value of $S°$ for $H(g)$ given in Table 22.2 less than that for $H_2(g)$?

22.11 Classify the entropy change for each of the following reactions as (i) large and negative, (ii) large and positive, or (iii) small:

(a) $2Au(s) + 3Cl_2(g) \longrightarrow 2AuCl_3(s)$
(b) $Cd(s) + Ni_2O_3(s) + 3H_2O(l) \longrightarrow$
$$Cd(OH)_2(s) + 2Ni(OH)_2(s)$$
(c) $Cu^{2+} + H_2(g) \longrightarrow Cu(s) + 2H^+$
Explain each of your answers.

22.12 Repeat Question 22.11 for

(a) $S(s) + 3F_2(g) \longrightarrow SF_6(g)$
(b) $2NaCl(aq) + 2H_2O(l) \xrightarrow{\text{electrical energy}}$
$$Cl_2(g) + H_2(g) + 2NaOH(aq)$$
(c) $2HCl(aq) + Mg(s) \longrightarrow MgCl_2(aq) + H_2(g)$
(d) $SO_2(g) + Br_2(g) + 2H_2O(g) \xrightarrow{\Delta} 2HBr(g) + H_2SO_4(aq)$

22.13 Repeat Question 22.11 for

(a) $CaCO_3(\text{calcite}) \longrightarrow CaCO_3(\text{aragonite})$
(b) $Ag(s) + \frac{1}{2}Cl_2(g) \xrightarrow{\Delta} AgCl(l)$
(c) $ClO_4^- \longrightarrow Cl^- + 2O_2(g)$
(d) $2NH_4NO_3(s) \longrightarrow 2N_2(g) + 4H_2O(g) + O_2(g)$

22.14 Repeat Question 22.11 for

(a) $Mg(s) + Br_2(l) \longrightarrow MgBr_2(s)$
(b) $2I^- + Cl_2(g) \longrightarrow I_2(s) + 2Cl^-$
(c) $NaHSO_4(s) + NaCl(s) \longrightarrow HCl(g) + Na_2SO_4(s)$
(d) $Cl_2(g) + H_2O(l) \longrightarrow HCl(aq) + HClO(aq)$

Free Energy

22.15 Define "free energy" in terms of enthalpy and entropy. Characterize ΔG for (a) a spontaneous process, (b) a nonspontaneous process, and (c) a process at equilibrium?

22.16 What is the relationship between the enthalpy and the entropy changes for a process at equilibrium?

22.17 How is the free energy change related to the standard state free energy change and the reaction quotient? Will a large or a small value of the reaction quotient tend to make a chemical reaction more favorable?

22.18 What is the relationship between $\Delta G°$ and the equilibrium constant for a chemical reaction?

22.19 Which of the following conditions would predict a process that is (a) always spontaneous, (b) always nonspontaneous, or (c) spontaneous or nonspontaneous depending on the temperature and magnitudes of ΔH and ΔS: (i) $\Delta H > 0$, $\Delta S > 0$; (ii) $\Delta H > 0$, $\Delta S < 0$; (iii) $\Delta H < 0$, $\Delta S > 0$; (iv) $\Delta H < 0$, $\Delta S < 0$?

22.20 Why might we say that at absolute zero an exothermic reaction will always be spontaneous, but at temperatures above absolute zero we have to consider both enthalpy and entropy before we can predict spontaneity?

22.21 The standard enthalpy change at 25 °C for dissolving sodium chloride in water is 3810 J/mol,
$$NaCl(s) + nH_2O \longrightarrow NaCl(aq, 1 \text{ M})$$

which implies that the process is not spontaneous; yet we know that salt readily dissolves in water (think of the oceans!). (a) For this spontaneous process, is $\Delta G°$ positive or negative? (b) If the enthalpy change is unfavorable, what is the driving force for this reaction? (c) Is $\Delta S°$ positive or negative? (d) Does this sign represent an increase or decrease in randomness? (e) Does the formation of a mixture (in which the sodium and chloride ions are freely moving around in water) from a highly ordered crystal structure and a pure liquid confirm your answer to (d)?

Answers to Selected Questions

22.4 ΔS would be negative; the gas molecules would be closer together and so have less freedom of movement, creating a less disordered condition.

22.8 The contributions to $S_{298}°$ are: (1) $S_0°$, (2) $\Delta S°$ for heating solid-III from 0 K to 104 K, (3) $\Delta S°$ for solid-III changing to solid-II at 104 K, (4) $\Delta S°$ for heating solid-II from 104 K to 126 K, (5) $\Delta S°$ for solid-II changing to solid-I at 126 K, (6) $\Delta S°$ for heating solid-I from 126 K to 188 K, (7) $\Delta S°$ for melting at 188 K, (8) $\Delta S°$ for heating liquid from 188 K to 213 K, (9) $\Delta S°$ for boiling at 213 K, and (10) $\Delta S°$ for heating the gas from 213 K to 298 K.

22.10 H_2 has additional rotational and intramolecular vibrational contributions to $S°$ that are not possible for H.

22.12 (a) i, 1 mol solid + 3 mol gas → 1 mol gas; (b) ii, 4 mol liquid or solute → 2 mol solute + 2 mol gas; (c) ii, 3 mol solid or solute → 1 mol solute + 1 mol gas; (d) i, 4 mol gas → 2 mol gas + 1 mol solute

22.14 (a) iii, 1 mol solid + 1 mol liquid → 1 mol solid; (b) i, 2 mol solute + 1 mol gas → 1 mol solid + 2 mol solute; (c) ii, 2 mol solid → 1 mol gas + 1 mol solid; (d) i, 1 mol gas + 1 mol liquid → 2 mol solute

22.19 (a) iii, (b) ii, (c) i, iv

22.21 (a) negative, (b) an increase in entropy, (c) positive, (d) increase, (e) yes

PROBLEMS

Entropy in Physical Changes

22.1 Compare the entropy change for melting one mole of water at 273 K ($\Delta H_{273}° = 6010$ J/mol for fusion) with that for vaporizing a mole of water at 373 K ($\Delta H_{373}° = 40{,}660$ J/mol for vaporization). Why is the second value so much larger?

22.2 Gallium undergoes a solid–solid phase transformation at 275.6 K for which $\Delta H_{275.6}° = 2100$ J/mol. Calculate $\Delta S°$ for this change.

22.3 Gray tin changes at 291 K to white tin ($\Delta H_{291}° = 2500$ J/mol), white tin changes to tin-I at 476.0 K ($\Delta H_{476}° = 8$ J/mol), and tin-I melts at 505.1 K ($\Delta H_{505.1}° = 7070$ J/mol). Calculate $\Delta S°$ for these phase changes. Why are all three values of the same order of magnitude? *Answer* 8.6 J/K mol, 0.02 J/K mol, 14.0 J/K mol; all three transitions involve solids and liquids, which do not differ greatly in randomness

22.4* The stable form of $Na_2SO_4(s)$ at absolute zero is solid-V. At 298 K, solid-V changes to solid-III with $\Delta H° = 3.00$ kJ/mol. The entropy change for heating solid-V from 0 K to 298 K is 149.58 J/K mol and for cooling solid-III from 298 K to 0 K is -154.92 J/K mol. What is the value of $S_0°$ for solid-III?

22.5* The value of $\Delta S°$ for vaporizing a sample of a substance at the normal boiling point is usually about 88 J/K mol, no matter what the substance (as long as there is no hydrogen bonding in the liquid and/or dimers are not formed in the gaseous phase). (a) Confirm this value by calculating $\Delta S°$ for the evaporation of the following substances:

(i) $Xe(l) \longrightarrow Xe(g)$ $\Delta H_{165.1}° = 12.64$ kJ/mol
(ii) $SO_2(l) \longrightarrow SO_2(g)$ $\Delta H_{263.14}° = 24.92$ kJ/mol
(iii) $CCl_4(l) \longrightarrow CCl_4(g)$ $\Delta H_{349.9}° = 30.0$ kJ/mol

(b) Would you predict $\Delta S°$ for vaporizing a mole of water to be greater or less than 88 J/K mol? Why? Confirm your answer using $\Delta H_{373.15}° = 38{,}372$ J/mol. (c) Would you predict $\Delta S°$ for vaporizing a mole of methyl alcohol, CH_3OH, to be as large as for water, since the amount of hydrogen bonding in it is about the same as in water? Confirm your answer using $\Delta H_{337.9}° = 35{,}270$ J/mol. (d) Predict the boiling point of lead, given that $\Delta H°$ of vaporization is 179.9 kJ/mol. *Answer* (a) 76.56 J/K mol, 94.70 J/K mol, 85.7 J/K mol, average = 85.7 J/K mol; (b) greater, $\Delta H°$ (vaporization) is large because of H-bonding in liquid, 102.83 J/K mol; (c) yes, 104.4 J/K mol; (d) 2.0×10^3 K

Entropy in Chemical Reactions

22.6 Calculate the entropy changes for the sublimation of iodine and for the formation of gaseous iodine atoms from gaseous iodine molecules,

(a) $I_2(s) \longrightarrow I_2(g)$
(b) $I_2(g) \longrightarrow 2I(g)$

given $S° = 180.68$ J/K mol for $I(g)$, 116.14 J/K mol for $I_2(s)$, and 260.58 J/K mol for $I_2(g)$. Why are these entropy changes similar in sign and magnitude?

22.7 The standard state absolute entropy at 500 K in J/K mol is 219.681 for $F_2(g)$, 264.307 for $Br_2(g)$, 246.609 for $BrF(g)$, 329.394 for $BrF_3(g)$, and 381.129 for $BrF_5(g)$. Calculate the entropy change for each of the following reactions:

(a) $Br_2(g) + F_2(g) \longrightarrow 2BrF(g)$
(b) $Br_2(g) + 3F_2(g) \longrightarrow 2BrF_3(g)$
(c) $Br_2(g) + 5F_2(g) \longrightarrow 2BrF_5(g)$
Answer (a) 9.230 J/K, (b) -264.562 J/K, (c) -600.454 J/K

22.8 Using the data for absolute entropies given in Table 22.2, calculate $\Delta S°$ for the reactions

(a) $2Fe(\alpha\text{-solid}) + \tfrac{3}{2}O_2(g) \longrightarrow Fe_2O_3(s)$
(b) $3Fe(\alpha\text{-solid}) + 2O_2(g) \longrightarrow Fe_3O_4(s)$
Which of these reactions have a favorable entropy change?

22.9 Repeat Problem 22.8 for
(a) $Fe_2O_3(s) + 6HCl(g) \longrightarrow 2FeCl_3(s) + 3H_2O(g)$
(b) $2HBr(g) + Cl_2(g) \longrightarrow 2HCl(g) + Br_2(l)$
(c) $H_2O_2(l) \longrightarrow H_2O(l) + \tfrac{1}{2}O_2(g)$
Answer (a) -358 J/K; (b) -94.31 J/K; (c) 62.8 J/K, favorable

22.10 Combine your answers for Problem 22.6 to obtain $\Delta S°$ for the reaction

$$I_2(s) \longrightarrow 2I(g)$$

Is this a favorable entropy change?

22.11 Combine your answers for Problem 22.7 to obtain $\Delta S°$ for the reaction

$$2BrF_3(g) \longrightarrow BrF(g) + BrF_5(g)$$

Is this a favorable entropy change? *Answer* -31.050 J/K, no

22.12 Combine your answers for Problem 22.8 to obtain $\Delta S°$ for the reaction

$$3Fe_2O_3(g) \longrightarrow 2Fe_3O_4(s) + \tfrac{1}{2}O_2(g)$$

Is this a favorable entropy change?

$\Delta G°$ of Reaction

22.13 The heat of formation of gaseous hydrogen bromide is -36.40 kJ/mol and the entropy of formation is 57.183 J/K mol under standard state conditions at 25 °C. Calculate the standard state free energy of formation.

22.14 The free energy of formation of gaseous water at 25 °C under standard state conditions is -228.589 kJ/mol and the heat of reaction is -241.818 kJ/mol. What is the entropy of formation?

22.15 Calculate $\Delta G°$ at 25 °C for the reaction

$$FeCl_2(aq) + \tfrac{1}{2}Cl_2(g) \longrightarrow FeCl_3(aq)$$

given that $\Delta H° = -127.2$ kJ and $\Delta S° = -233$ J/K. *Answer* -57.7 kJ

22.16 Use the following thermochemical equations:

$$HF(aq) \longrightarrow H^+ + F^- \qquad \Delta G° = 18.03 \text{ kJ}$$
$$H_2O(l) \longrightarrow H^+ + OH^- \qquad \Delta G° = 79.89 \text{ kJ}$$

to calculate $\Delta G°$ for the neutralization of hydrofluoric acid by a strong base:

$$HF(aq) + OH^- \longrightarrow H_2O(l) + F^-$$

22.17 Use the following thermochemical equations:

$$CH_4(g) + 2O_2(g) \longrightarrow CO_2(g) + 2H_2O(l)$$
$$\Delta G° = -817.96 \text{ kJ}$$
$$CH_3OH(l) + \tfrac{3}{2}O_2(g) \longrightarrow CO_2(g) + 2H_2O(l)$$
$$\Delta G° = -702.36 \text{ kJ}$$

to calculate $\Delta G°$ for the partial oxidation of methane to form methyl alcohol:

$$CH_4(g) + \tfrac{1}{2}O_2(g) \longrightarrow CH_3OH(l)$$

22.18 Use the following thermochemical equations:

$$Br_2(l) \longrightarrow Br_2(g) \qquad \Delta G° = 3.14 \text{ kJ}$$
$$HBr(g) \longrightarrow H(g) + Br(g) \qquad \Delta G° = 339.12 \text{ kJ}$$
$$Br_2(g) \longrightarrow 2Br(g) \qquad \Delta G° = 161.72 \text{ kJ}$$
$$H_2(g) \longrightarrow 2H(g) \qquad \Delta G° = 406.53 \text{ kJ}$$

to predict the $\Delta G°$ of formation of HBr(g) at 25 °C. *Answer* -53.43 kJ/mol

22.19 Calculate $\Delta G°$ for the reduction of the oxides of iron and copper by carbon at 700 K represented by the reactions

$$2Fe_2O_3(s) + 3C(s) \longrightarrow 4Fe(s) + 3CO_2(g)$$
$$2CuO(s) + C(s) \longrightarrow 2Cu(s) + CO_2(g)$$

given that the standard free energy of formation is -92 kJ/mol for CuO(s), -637 kJ/mol for Fe$_2$O$_3$(s), and -395 kJ/mol for CO$_2$(g). Which oxide can be reduced using carbon in a wood fire (which has a temperature of about 700 K) assuming standard state conditions?

22.20 The standard state free energy of formation at 25 °C is 0 for O$_2$(g), 86.57 kJ/mol for NO(g), 51.30 kJ/mol for NO$_2$(g), 104.18 kJ/mol for N$_2$O(g), 139.41 kJ/mol for N$_2$O$_3$(g), and 115.1 kJ/mol for N$_2$O$_5$(g). Calculate $\Delta G°$ for each of the following reactions and predict which one is most favorable under standard state conditions at 25 °C:

(a) $N_2O(g) + \tfrac{1}{2}O_2(g) \longrightarrow 2NO(g)$
(b) $N_2O(g) + O_2(g) \longrightarrow N_2O_3(g)$
(c) $N_2O(g) + \tfrac{3}{2}O_2(g) \longrightarrow 2NO_2(g)$
(d) $N_2O(g) + 2O_2(g) \longrightarrow N_2O_5(g)$

Answer (a) 68.96 kJ; (b) 35.23 kJ; (c) -1.58 kJ, most favorable; (d) 10.9 kJ

ΔG at Conditions Other than 25 °C or Standard State

22.21 At 25 °C, $\Delta G° = -95.3$ kJ/mol for the formation of HCl(g):

$$\tfrac{1}{2}H_2(g) + \tfrac{1}{2}Cl_2(g) \longrightarrow HCl(g)$$

What is the value of ΔG for the process if the partial pressure of H$_2$ is 3.5 atm, of Cl$_2$ is 1.5 atm, and of HCl is 0.31 atm? Is the process more or less favorable under these conditions than under standard state conditions?

22.22 The standard state free energy of formation at 25 °C is -134.10 kJ/mol for H$_2$O$_2$(aq), 0 for O$_2$(g), and -237.18 kJ/mol for H$_2$O(l). Calculate $\Delta G°$ for the reaction

$$2H_2O_2(aq) \longrightarrow 2H_2O(l) + O_2(g)$$

This spontaneous reaction can be stopped by increasing the pressure of the oxygen. Find the value of the pressure necessary to stop the reaction. *Answer* -206.16 kJ, 1.3×10^{36} atm

22.23 The standard state free energy of formation at 25 °C is 0 for H$^+$, -157.293 kJ/mol for OH$^-$, and -237.178 kJ/mol for H$_2$O(l). Find ΔG for the reaction

$$H_2O(l) \longrightarrow H^+ + OH^-$$

under conditions such that $[H^+] = [OH^-] = 1.0 \times 10^{-7}$ M.

22.24 The standard heat of formation of O$_3$(g) at 298 K is 142.7 kJ/mol and it varies negligibly with temperature up to 6000 K. Calculate the $\Delta G°$ of formation of ozone at 1000. K given that the $\Delta G°$ of formation is 163.1 kJ/mol at 298 K.

22.25 The heat of reaction under standard state conditions at 25 °C for the combustion of CO,

$$CO(g) + \tfrac{1}{2}O_2(g) \longrightarrow CO_2(g)$$

is -282.985 kJ/mol and $\Delta G°$ for the reaction at 25 °C is -257.207 kJ/mol. At what temperature will this reaction no longer be spontaneous under standard state conditions? *Answer* 3273 K

$\Delta G°$ and Equilibrium

22.26 For the reaction:

$$2NO_2(g) \rightleftharpoons N_2O_4(g)$$

$\Delta G° = -4.77$ kJ at 25 °C. Calculate the value of K at 25 °C for this reaction. Would you have expected a value larger than unity? Why?

22.27 For this reaction

$$AgCl(s) \rightleftharpoons Ag^+ + Cl^-$$

$K = 1.8 \times 10^{-10}$ at 25 °C. Calculate the value of $\Delta G°$ for this reaction. Would you have expected a positive value? Why? *Answer* 55.6 kJ, yes, the small value of K indicates an unfavorable reaction

22.28 At 25 °C, the $\Delta G°$ of formation is -237.178 kJ/mol for $H_2O(l)$, 0 for H^+ (*aq*, 1 M), and -157.293 kJ/mol for OH^-(*aq*, 1 M). Find $\Delta G°$ for the reaction

$$H_2O(l) \rightleftharpoons H^+(aq, 1 M) + OH^-(aq, 1 M)$$

and calculate the value of equilibrium constant, K_w.

22.29 The standard free energy of formation at 25 °C is -202.97 kJ/mol for $NH_4Cl(s)$, -16.48 kJ/mol for $NH_3(g)$, and -95.299 kJ/mol for $HCl(g)$. (a) What is $\Delta G°$ for the reaction

$$NH_4Cl(s) \rightleftharpoons NH_3(g) + HCl(g)$$

(b) What is the equilibrium constant for this decomposition? (c) Calculate the equilibrium partial pressure of HCl above a sample of NH_4Cl. *Answer* (a) 91.19 kJ, (b) 1.1×10^{-16}, (c) 1.0×10^{-8} atm

22.30 The equilibrium constant for the reaction

$$Cl_2(g) + F_2(g) \rightleftharpoons 2ClF(g)$$

is 2.10×10^{18} at 298 K and 1.35×10^{11} at 500. K. Find $\Delta H°$ for the reaction.

22.31 For the reaction

$$CO(g) + Cl_2(g) \rightleftharpoons COCl(g) + Cl(g)$$

$\Delta H° = 168.778$ kJ and $K_p = 9.12 \times 10^{-30}$ at 25 °C. What is the value of K_p at 500. K? Has the equilibrium shifted to the reactants or products side by increasing the temperature? *Answer* 9×10^{-18}, products

22.32 At the normal boiling point the heat of vaporization of water (100.00 °C) is 40,656 J/mol and of heavy water (101.41 °C) is 41,606 J/mol. Use these data to calculate the vapor pressure of each liquid at 75.00 °C.

22.33 What is the boiling point of water at a typical laboratory pressure of 745 Torr? The heat of vaporization of water at 100.00 °C and 760.0 Torr is 40,656 J/mol. *Answer* 99.5 °C

22.34 The sublimation pressure of tungsten is 9.08×10^{-8} atm at 3000. K and 7.42×10^{-6} atm at 3500. K. Find the heat of sublimation of tungsten. Predict the sublimation pressure of tungsten at 3200. K. How many atoms of tungsten are in a cubic centimeter in the gaseous state near the filament in a light bulb at 3200. K?

22.35* A plot of the logarithm of the vapor pressure against the inverse of the absolute temperature is predicted by the Clausius-Clapeyron equation to be a straight line. Prepare such a plot for

mercury from the following data:

P, Torr	1.00	10.0	40.0	100.0	400.0	760.0
T, °C	126.2	184.0	228.8	261.7	323.0	357.0

The slope of the straight line is equal to $-\Delta H_{vaporization}/2.303\,R$. Calculate the value of $\Delta H_{vaporization}$ from your graph.

22.36* Prepare plots of the logarithm of the vapor pressure against the inverse of the absolute temperature for the solid and liquid forms of ammonia using the following data:

state	solid			liquid		
P, Torr	1.00	10.0	40.0	100.0	400.0	760.0
T, °C	-109.1	-91.9	-79.2	-68.4	-45.4	-33.6

The slopes of the lines through these data are equal to $-\Delta H_{sublimation}/2.303\,R$ and $-\Delta H_{vaporization}/2.303\,R$, respectively. Calculate these heats of transformation. Predict the vapor pressure of ammonia at the melting point, -77.8 °C. *Answer* $\Delta H_{sublimation} = 32.7$ kJ/mol, $\Delta H_{vaporization} = 23.7$ kJ/mol, 49 Torr

Additional Problems

22.37 Calculate $\Delta S°$ for the production of ozone from oxygen,

$$3O_2(g) \longrightarrow 2O_3(g)$$

given that $S° = 205$ J/K mol for $O_2(g)$ and 239 J/K mol for $O_3(g)$ at 25 °C. Is this an increase or decrease in randomness? The heat of formation at 25 °C is 142.7 kJ/mol for $O_3(g)$ and is 0 for $O_2(g)$. Calculate $\Delta G°$ for this reaction and the $\Delta G°$ of formation for $O_3(g)$. Is this reaction spontaneous under standard conditions?

22.38* Chlorine and fluorine react to form the interhalogen compound ClF according to the equation

$$Cl_2(g) + F_2(g) \longrightarrow 2ClF(g)$$

(a) What is $\Delta H°$ for this reaction given that the heat of formation of ClF(g) at 25 °C is -54.48 kJ/mol? (b) Calculate $\Delta G°$ for this reaction given that the free energy of formation at 25 °C is -55.94 kJ/mol for ClF(g), 0 for $Cl_2(g)$, and 0 for $F_2(g)$. (c) Using your values of $\Delta H°$ and $\Delta G°$, calculate $\Delta S°$ for the reaction at 25 °C. (d) Compare your answer for (c) to that calculated using absolute entropies of 217.78 J/K mol for ClF(g), 222.96 J/K mol for $Cl_2(g)$, and 202.67 J/K mol for F_2. (e) What would be the value of ΔG if the partial pressure of Cl_2 is 1.52 atm, of F_2 is 1.78 atm, and of ClF is 0.10 atm? Is the reaction more or less favorable under these nonstandard state conditions? *Answer* (a) -109.0 kJ; (b) -111.9 kJ; (c) 9.7 J/K; (d) 9.93 J/K; (e) -125.8 kJ, more favorable

22.39* The standard state heat of formation at 25 °C is -285.830 kJ/mol for $H_2O(l)$, 0 for H^+(*aq*, 1 M), and -229.994 kJ/mol for OH^-(*aq*, 1 M). (a) Calculate $\Delta H°$ for the reaction represented by the equation

$$H_2O(l) \rightleftharpoons H^+(aq, 1 M) + OH^-(aq, 1 M)$$

The standard state free energy of formation at 25 °C is -237.178 kJ/mol for $H_2O(l)$, 0 for H^+(*aq*, 1 M), and -157.293 kJ/mol for OH^- (*aq*, 1 M). (b) Calculate $\Delta G°$ for the above reaction. What is the value of K (c) at 25 °C and (d) at 35 °C? (e) What is the pH of water at 35 °C? Does this mean that water becomes acidic at 35 °C? Explain your answer.

CHAPTER 23

Oxidation–Reduction and Electrochemistry

Electrochemistry is of great practical value. Think of the number of batteries we have to buy to satisfy the needs of our flashlights, portable shavers and hedge clippers, radios and tape recorders, toys, calculators, and watches. Pure metals are produced from ores, inorganic and organic compounds are synthesized, metal surfaces are coated with other metals or even with paint, and items such as the flared ends of brass musical instruments are manufactured by electrochemical processes.

Such processes are attractive because they are clean and produce very pure materials. One imaginative suggestion for applying electrochemistry is in a pollution-free method for getting rid of junked cars. Reclamation of the metals in a car requires that the metals be separated from other materials. A car can't just be cut up and fed back into a steel mill. It has been estimated that a whole car could be dissolved in an electrochemical bath in about one week. Once all the metals were in solution as ions, the pure metals could be recovered one by one by deposition on the electrodes at varying electrical potentials.

You may know the story of Luigi Galvani and his accidental discovery about electricity. One day in 1791 Galvani casually placed a dissected frog on a table near an "electric machine." An assistant observed that the frog's muscle twitched when the machine discharged electricity. What we might call "bioelectrochemistry" is still a frontier of electrochemical science. We are only beginning to understand the electrical potentials of cell membranes and the function of electrical messages in biochemistry.

REDOX REVISITED

23.1 ELECTRON GAIN AND LOSS IN REDOX REACTIONS

Oxidation and reduction were defined in Sections 16.2 and 17.4, in terms of changes in oxidation numbers. These definitions hold for substances with bonding of any type. It is also possible to define oxidation and reduction in terms of electron gain and loss. But it must be clearly understood that the *actual* electron gain and loss to form ions is not a requirement for oxidation and reduction to occur.

When a piece of zinc is dropped into a solution of copper(II) sulfate, a chemical reaction occurs (Figure 23.1). The deep blue color of the copper(II) sulfate solution

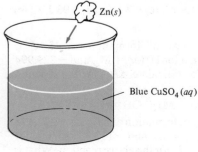

Zn(s)

Blue CuSO$_4$(aq)

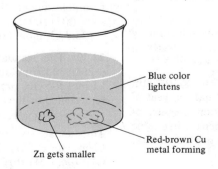

Blue color lightens

Zn gets smaller

Red-brown Cu metal forming

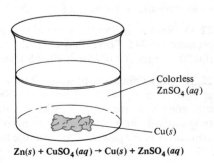

Colorless ZnSO$_4$(aq)

Cu(s)

$$Zn(s) + CuSO_4(aq) \rightarrow Cu(s) + ZnSO_4(aq)$$

Figure 23.1
The Redox Displacement of Copper by Zinc

grows lighter and the piece of zinc grows smaller. Writing the chemical equation

$$Zn(s) + CuSO_4(aq) \longrightarrow Cu(s) + ZnSO_4(aq) \tag{23.1}$$

shows this to be a redox displacement reaction. Because copper(II) sulfate and zinc sulfate are soluble strong electrolytes we can write the net ionic equation as

$$Zn(s) + Cu^{2+} \longrightarrow Cu(s) + Zn^{2+} \tag{23.2}$$

To convert zinc metal to Zn^{2+} ions, each zinc atom must *lose* two electrons.

$$Zn(s) \longrightarrow Zn^{2+} + 2e^- \tag{23.3}$$

The zinc has lost electrons and has thus been oxidized (its oxidation number has increased from 0 to $+2$). To convert copper ions into copper metal, each copper ion must *gain* two electrons.

$$Cu^{2+} + 2e^- \longrightarrow Cu(s) \tag{23.4}$$

The copper ion has gained electrons and has thus been *reduced* (its oxidation number has decreased from $+2$ to 0).

Gain of electrons: reduction
Loss of electrons: oxidation

Every oxidation–reduction reaction can be divided into two **half-reactions**—reactions representing either oxidation only or reduction only. The sum of the half-reactions of Equations (23.3) and (23.4),

$$Zn(s) \longrightarrow Zn^{2+} + 2e^-$$
$$\underline{Cu^{2+} + 2e^- \longrightarrow Cu(s)}$$
$$Zn(s) + Cu^{2+} \longrightarrow Cu(s) + Zn^{2+}$$

is the net ionic equation for the redox reaction. In this reaction and in every redox reaction involving ions, oxidation is electron loss and reduction is electron gain.

Equations (23.3) and (23.4) are **ion-electron equations**—balanced equations that include only the electrons and other species directly involved in the oxidation or reduction of a given atom, molecule, or ion. Like net ionic equations, ion-electron equations must be balanced as to both number of atoms and charge.

The oxidized and reduced species that appear in an ion-electron equation are sometimes called a **redox couple**, or just a couple. In Equations (23.3) and (23.4) the redox couples are $Zn^{2+}/Zn(s)$ and $Cu^{2+}/Cu(s)$ (both written, as we will do throughout the text, with the oxidized form first).

EXAMPLE 23.1
Ion-Electron Equations

Write the ion-electron equations for the reduction of iron(III) ion to iron(II) ion by tin(II) ion:

$$Sn^{2+} + 2Fe^{3+} \longrightarrow 2Fe^{2+} + Sn^{4+}$$

Write the redox couples for these ion-electron equations.

Each iron(III) ion gains one electron during reduction.

$$Fe^{3+} + e^- \longrightarrow Fe^{2+}$$

The redox couple for this ion-electron equation is Fe^{3+}/Fe^{2+}.
Each tin(II) ion loses two electrons during oxidation.

$$Sn^{2+} \longrightarrow Sn^{4+} + 2e^-$$

The redox couple for this ion-electron equation is Sn^{4+}/Sn^{2+}.

Exercise Write the ion-electron equations for the oxidation of bromide ion by chlorine:

$$Cl_2(g) + 2Br^- \longrightarrow 2Cl^- + Br_2(l)$$

> Write the redox couples for these ion-electron equations. *Answer*
> $Cl_2(g) + 2e^- \rightarrow 2Cl^-$, $2Br^- \rightarrow Br_2(l) + 2e^-$; $Cl_2(g)/Cl^-$, $Br_2(l)/Br^-$

Like any other chemical equation, an ion-electron equation must always describe an actual chemical change. The element undergoing a change in oxidation number must appear as part of the formula of the substance being oxidized or reduced. For reactions in aqueous solution, only species that exist as ions in solution during the reaction are written as ions. For example, when hydrogen sulfide acts as a reducing agent, the sulfur in the −2 oxidation state is oxidized to free sulfur. The balanced ion-electron equation for the oxidation of hydrogen sulfide in acidic aqueous solution is

$$H_2S(g) \longrightarrow S(s) + 2H^+ + 2e^- \tag{23.5}$$

not $S^{2-} \longrightarrow S(s) + 2e^-$, because sulfide ions are not involved.

Similarly, when nitrate ion acts as an oxidizing agent in acidic solution, one possible product is nitrogen(II) oxide. Nitrogen appears in the ion-electron equation as the nitrate ion and the molecular oxide,

$$NO_3^- + 4H^+ + 3e^- \longrightarrow NO(g) + 2H_2O(l) \tag{23.6}$$

not as $N^{5+} + 3e^- \longrightarrow N^{2+}$. Nitrogen never forms such ions. The error here is in confusing the *oxidation states* of nitrogen in NO_3^- and NO with the *charges* on monatomic ions. Do not make the common error of writing nonexistent species in ion-electron equations; in particular, do not confuse oxidation states and ionic charges.

Note that H^+ ions and water appear in Equations (23.5) and (23.6). For redox reactions which occur in aqueous systems, whatever hydrogen or oxygen atoms are required to balance the equations must come from water and either H_3O^+ or OH^-. Whether or not a reaction will occur and the type of product obtained often depend upon the pH of the system. Hydrogen ions and hydroxide ions never show up in the same ion-electron equation because, obviously, a solution cannot be both alkaline and acidic.

23.2 BALANCING REDOX EQUATIONS: HALF-REACTION METHOD

The oxidation number method of balancing redox equations has as its basis the equality of the increase and decrease in oxidation numbers. The half-reaction method is based on electron gain and loss. In a redox reaction, the number of electrons "gained" must equal the number of electrons "lost." This means that the number of electrons in two ion-electron equations must be made equal before the equations can be added to give an overall redox equation.

In redox reactions: electron gain in one half-reaction = electron loss in other half-reaction

In order to balance a complete redox equation by the half-reaction method, it is necessary to first balance the ion-electron equations for the oxidation and reduction half-reactions that are involved. A procedure for doing so is outlined below and illustrated by balancing the ion-electron equations for the reduction of ClO_4^- to Cl_2 in either acidic or alkaline solution. As is illustrated, different approaches must be taken to balancing ion-electron equations for reactions in acidic and alkaline solutions.

a. *Write the oxidized and reduced species on opposite sides of the equation and balance atoms other than oxygen and hydrogen by inspection.*

$$2ClO_4^- \xrightarrow[\text{balanced}]{\text{not}} Cl_2$$

b. *Balance oxygen atoms by adding H_2O to the side that is deficient in oxygen.*

$$2ClO_4^- \xrightarrow{\text{not balanced}} Cl_2 + 8H_2O$$

c. *Balance hydrogen atoms.* For reactions in <u>acidic solution</u> add H^+ ions to the side that is deficient in hydrogen.

$$2ClO_4^- + 16H^+ \xrightarrow{\text{not balanced}} Cl_2 + 8H_2O \qquad (23.7)$$

For reactions in <u>alkaline solution,</u> it is necessary to add OH^- to balance hydrogen atoms, but this also introduces more oxygen atoms. A method that overcomes this complication in many cases is to add OH^- ions equal in number to the deficiency in hydrogen atoms on the *same side* as the H_2O was added in step b,

$$2ClO_4^- \xrightarrow{\text{not balanced}} Cl_2 + 8H_2O + 16OH^- \qquad (23.8)$$

and then add the *same number* of H_2O molecules (as OH^- ions) on the opposite side,

$$2ClO_4^- + 16H_2O \xrightarrow{\text{not balanced}} Cl_2 + 8H_2O + 16OH^-$$

and cancel the excess water molecules.

$$2ClO_4^- + 8H_2O \xrightarrow{\text{not balanced}} Cl_2 + 16OH^- \qquad (23.9)$$

Both Equations (23.7) and (23.9) are now balanced with regard to atoms.

d. *Balance charge by adding electrons.* The two balanced ion-electron equations are as follows:

$$2ClO_4^- + 16H^+ + 14e^- \longrightarrow Cl_2(g) + 8H_2O(l)$$
$$2ClO_4^- + 8H_2O(l) + 14e^- \longrightarrow Cl_2(g) + 16OH^-$$

EXAMPLE 23.2
Ion-Electron Equations

Write the balanced ion-electron equations for the reduction of NO_3^- to (a) $HNO_2(aq)$ in acidic solution and to (b) NO_2^- in alkaline solution.

(a) The oxidized and reduced species are

$$NO_3^- \longrightarrow HNO_2$$

This equation is already balanced with respect to the N atoms. The oxygen atoms are balanced by adding one H_2O molecule to the products side to obtain

$$NO_3^- \longrightarrow HNO_2 + H_2O$$

The H atoms are balanced in this acidic solution by adding three H^+ ions to the reactants side, which gives

$$NO_3^- + 3H^+ \longrightarrow HNO_2 + H_2O$$

The charge is balanced by adding two e^- to the reactants side.

$$NO_3^- + 3H^+ + 2e^- \longrightarrow HNO_2(aq) + H_2O(l)$$

The total charge on the left in this equation is $(-1) + (3)(+1) + (2)(-1) = 0$, and the total charge on the right is also zero. The equation is balanced.

(b) For the reduction reaction in alkaline solution, the oxidized and reduced species are

$$NO_3^- \longrightarrow NO_2^-$$

This equation is already balanced with respect to the N atoms. The oxygen atoms are balanced by adding one H_2O molecule to the products side to obtain

$$NO_3^- \longrightarrow NO_2^- + H_2O$$

The H atoms are balanced in this alkaline solution by adding two OH^- ions to the product side (the same number as the H atom deficiency),

$$NO_3^- \longrightarrow NO_2^- + H_2O + 2OH^-$$

adding two H_2O molecules to the reactants side (the same number as the OH^- ions),

$$NO_3^- + 2H_2O \longrightarrow NO_2^- + H_2O + 2OH^-$$

and cancelling the excess H_2O molecules to obtain

$$NO_3^- + H_2O \longrightarrow NO_2^- + 2OH^-$$

The charge is balanced by adding two e^- to the reactants side.

$$NO_3^- + H_2O(l) + 2e^- \longrightarrow NO_2^- + 2OH^-$$

The total charge on each side in this equation is $(-1) + (0) + (2)(-1) = (-1) + (2)(-1) = -3$. The equation is balanced.

Exercise   Write the balanced ion-electron equations for the reduction of MnO_4^- to (a) Mn^{2+} in acidic solution and to (b) $MnO_2(s)$ in alkaline solution.   *Answer* (a) $MnO_4^- + 8H^+ + 5e^- \rightarrow Mn^{2+} + 4H_2O(l)$,   (b) $MnO_4^- + 2H_2O(l) + 3e^- \rightarrow MnO_2(s) + 4OH^-$

Earlier we gave the balanced ion-electron equations for the reactions of hydrogen sulfide as a reducing agent and nitrate ion in acidic solution as an oxidizing agent (Equations 23.5 and 23.6). To find the balanced overall equation for the oxidation of hydrogen sulfide by nitrate ion in acidic solution, the two equations must be multiplied by three and two, respectively, so that six electrons are gained and six are lost. Then the two ion-electron equations are added together and any species that appear on both sides are cancelled to obtain the overall equation.

$$(3)[H_2S(g) \longrightarrow S(s) + 2H^+ + 2e^-] = \qquad 3H_2S(g) \longrightarrow 3S(s) + \cancel{6H^+} + \cancel{6e^-}$$

$$2H^+$$

$$(2)[NO_3^- + 4H^+ + 3e^- \longrightarrow NO(g) + 2H_2O(l)] = \quad \underline{2NO_3^- + \cancel{8H^+} + \cancel{6e^-} \longrightarrow 2NO(g) + 4H_2O(l)}$$

$$3H_2S(g) + 2NO_3^- + 2H^+ \longrightarrow 3S(s) + 2NO(g) + 4H_2O(l)$$

The complete set of rules (summarized in Table 23.1) for balancing overall redox equations by the half-reaction method is as follows:

1. *Write the overall equation, unbalanced, including all species that actually undergo a change in the redox reaction. Do not include spectator ions.*
2. *Identify the oxidized and reduced substances and write the two unbalanced ion-electron equations.* If it is not immediately obvious what has been oxidized or reduced, determine the oxidation numbers for all species and identify those for which the numbers have changed. Use ions only if they are

Table 23.1
Balancing Redox Equations by the Half-Reaction Method

1. Write the overall unbalanced equation.
2. Identify oxidized and reduced substances and write the unbalanced ion-electron equations.
3. Balance each ion-electron equation for atoms and charge:
   a. Balance for atoms other than O or H.
   b. Balance O atoms by adding H_2O on side deficient in O atoms.
   c. Balance H atoms by adding H^+ for acidic solutions or OH^- and H_2O for alkaline solutions.*
   d. Balance charge by adding electrons.
4. Multiply the ion-electron equations by appropriate factors so that electrons gained equals electrons lost.
5. Add the ion-electron equations, cancelling where appropriate.

* For reactions in alkaline solution, add OH^- ions equal in number to the deficiency in hydrogen atoms to *same* side as H_2O was added in step b, then add equal number of H_2O molecules to opposite side and cancel excess H_2O.

present as such, usually as ions in solution. Substances that are present as solid reactants or as products that precipitate out during a reaction in aqueous solution are represented by their molecular formulas in the ion-electron equation. Gases that are reactants or products are represented by their molecular formulas.

3. *Balance each ion-electron equation for atoms and charge.* Follow the procedure outlined above, taking note of whether the reaction occurs in acidic or alkaline solution.

4. *If necessary, multiply the half-reactions by appropriate factors so that electrons gained equal electrons lost.*

5. *Add the ion-electron equations to get the overall equation.* The electrons should automatically cancel. Be sure to cancel any other species that appear on both sides of the equation and to check that atoms and charges are both balanced.

EXAMPLE 23.3
Half-Reaction Method

Bismuthate ion, BiO_3^-, a strong oxidizing agent, can oxidize Mn^{2+} to permanganate ion, MnO_4^-, in acidic solution. The BiO_3^- ion is reduced to Bi^{3+}. Balance the equation for this reaction by the half-reaction method.

Step 1. Write the overall unbalanced equation.

$$BiO_3^- + Mn^{2+} \longrightarrow Bi^{3+} + MnO_4^-$$

Step 2. Write the unbalanced ion-electron equations.

$$BiO_3^- \longrightarrow Bi^{3+} \qquad Mn^{2+} \longrightarrow MnO_4^-$$

Step 3. Balance each ion-electron equation for atoms and charge. The reaction occurs in acidic solution, so H^+ and H_2O may be used to balance atoms.

$$BiO_3^- + 6H^+ \longrightarrow Bi^{3+} + 3H_2O$$
$$Mn^{2+} + 4H_2O \longrightarrow MnO_4^- + 8H^+$$

Balancing for charge gives

$$BiO_3^- + 6H^+ + 2e^- \longrightarrow Bi^{3+} + 3H_2O$$
$$Mn^{2+} + 4H_2O \longrightarrow MnO_4^- + 8H^+ + 5e^-$$

Step 4. Multiply the ion-electron equations by appropriate factors so that electrons gained equal electrons lost.

$$(5)[BiO_3^- + 6H^+ + 2e^- \longrightarrow Bi^{3+} + 3H_2O]$$
$$= 5BiO_3^- + 30H^+ + 10e^- \longrightarrow 5Bi^{3+} + 15H_2O(l)$$

$$(2)[Mn^{2+} + 4H_2O \longrightarrow MnO_4^- + 8H^+ + 5e^-]$$
$$= 2Mn^{2+} + 8H_2O \longrightarrow 2MnO_4^- + 16H^+ + 10e^-$$

Step 5. Add the two equations to get the overall equation, cancelling where appropriate.

$$\begin{array}{c} \qquad\qquad 14H^+ \qquad\qquad\qquad 7H_2O \\ 5BiO_3^- + \cancel{30H^+} + \cancel{10e^-} \longrightarrow 5Bi^{3+} + \cancel{15H_2O} \\ 2Mn^{2+} + \cancel{8H_2O} \longrightarrow 2MnO_4^- + \cancel{16H^+} + \cancel{10e^-} \\ \hline 5BiO_3^- + 2Mn^{2+} + 14H^+ \longrightarrow 5Bi^{3+} + 2MnO_4^- + 7H_2O(l) \end{array}$$

Checking shows that the atoms are all balanced and the charge on the left, $(5)(-1) + (2)(+2) + 14(+1) = +13$, equals the charge on right, $(5)(+3) + (2)(-1) = +13$. The equation is balanced.

Exercise In acidic solution, hydrogen peroxide is reduced to water by chlorate ion, which is oxidized to perchlorate ion. Write the ion-electron equations describing these processes and balance the overall equation for the redox process using the half-reaction method. *Answer* $H_2O_2(aq) + 2H^+ + 2e^- \rightarrow 2H_2O(l)$, $ClO_3^- + H_2O(l) \rightarrow ClO_4^- + 2H^+ + 2e^-$, $H_2O_2(aq) + ClO_3^- \rightarrow ClO_4^- + H_2O(l)$

EXAMPLE 23.4
Half-Reaction Method

The nitrate ion is reduced to ammonia by elemental aluminum under alkaline conditions with the formation of $[Al(OH)_4]^-$. Using the half-reaction method, find the balanced overall equation.

Step 1. Write the overall unbalanced equation.

$$Al(s) + NO_3^- + OH^- \longrightarrow NH_3(aq) + [Al(OH)_4]^-$$

Step 2. Write the unbalanced ion-electron equations.

$$\overset{0}{Al} \longrightarrow \overset{+3}{[Al(OH)_4]^-} \qquad \overset{+5}{NO_3^-} \longrightarrow \overset{-3}{NH_3}$$

Step 3. Balance each ion-electron equation for atoms and charge. Inspection shows that only OH^- ions need be added to balance atoms in the oxidation half-reaction.

$$Al + 4OH^- \longrightarrow [Al(OH)_4]^-$$

Balancing charge gives

$$Al(s) + 4OH^- \longrightarrow [Al(OH)_4]^- + 3e^-$$

The procedure given above for reactions in alkaline solution can be used to balance atoms in the reduction half-reaction.

$$NO_3^- \longrightarrow NH_3 + 3H_2O$$
$$NO_3^- \longrightarrow NH_3 + 3H_2O + 9OH^-$$
$$NO_3^- + 9H_2O \longrightarrow NH_3 + 3H_2O + 9OH^-$$
$$NO_3^- + 6H_2O \longrightarrow NH_3 + 9OH^-$$

The atoms are balanced. Balancing charge gives

$$NO_3^- + 6H_2O(l) + 8e^- \longrightarrow NH_3(aq) + 9OH^-$$

Step 4. Multiply the ion-electron equations by appropriate factors, so that electrons gained equal electrons lost.

$$(8)[Al + 4OH^- \longrightarrow [Al(OH)_4]^- + 3e^-]$$
$$(3)[NO_3^- + 6H_2O + 8e^- \longrightarrow NH_3 + 9OH^-]$$

Step 5. Add the two equations to get the overall equation, cancelling where appropriate.

$$5OH^-$$
$$8Al(s) + \cancel{32OH^-} \longrightarrow 8[Al(OH)_4]^- + \cancel{24e^-}$$
$$3NO_3^- + 18H_2O(l) + \cancel{24e^-} \longrightarrow 3NH_3(aq) + \cancel{27OH^-}$$
$$\overline{8Al(s) + 3NO_3^- + 5OH^- + 18H_2O(l) \longrightarrow 8[Al(OH)_4]^- + 3NH_3(aq)}$$

Exercise Magnesium metal will be oxidized to magnesium hydroxide by chromate ion in an alkaline solution. The chromate ion is reduced to $Cr(OH)_3(s)$. Write the ion-electron equations describing these processes and balance the overall equation for the redox process using the half-reaction method. *Answer* $Mg(s) + 2OH^- \rightarrow Mg(OH)_2(s) + 2e^-$, $CrO_4^{2-} + 4H_2O(l) + 3e^- \rightarrow Cr(OH)_3(s) + 5OH^-$, $3Mg(s) + 2CrO_4^{2-} + 8H_2O(l) \rightarrow 3Mg(OH)_2(s) + 2Cr(OH)_3(s) + 4OH^-$

EXAMPLE 23.5
Half-Reaction Method

In an alkaline solution, aqueous sodium hypochlorite disproportionates into sodium chloride and sodium chlorate. Write the ion-electron equations and overall redox equations for this process. Use the half-reaction method to balance the overall equation.

Once the stepwise method of balancing redox equations is learned, it is no longer necessary to write out each step. It is common practice to write the steps in the more condensed format shown below.

$$ClO^- + 4OH^- \longrightarrow ClO_3^- + 2H_2O + 4e^-$$
$$(2)[ClO^- + H_2O + 2e^- \longrightarrow Cl^- + 2OH^-]$$
$$\overline{3ClO^- \longrightarrow ClO_3^- + 2Cl^-}$$

By adding the spectator ions, the overall equation can be written from the net ionic equation:

$$3NaClO(aq) \longrightarrow NaClO_3(aq) + 2NaCl(aq)$$

Exercise In an acidic solution, aqueous hydrogen peroxide disproportionates into water and oxygen. Write the ion-electron equations and overall redox equation for this process. Use the half-reaction method to balance the overall equation. *Answer* $H_2O_2(aq) \rightarrow O_2(g) + 2H^+ + 2e^-$, $H_2O_2(aq) + 2H^+ + 2e^- \rightarrow 2H_2O(l)$, $2H_2O_2(aq) \rightarrow 2H_2O(l) + O_2(g)$

FUNDAMENTALS OF ELECTROCHEMISTRY

23.3 ELECTROCHEMICAL CELLS

Electrons flowing through a wire constitute an electrical current, and ions flowing through an aqueous solution also constitute an electrical current. If the electrons lost and gained in a spontaneous reaction are able to flow through a wire on their pathway from the substance that is being oxidized to the substance that is being reduced, the energy of the reaction is released as electrical energy rather than thermal energy. Conversely, a *non*spontaneous redox reaction can be driven forward by the introduction of electrical energy into the system.

Electrochemistry deals with oxidation–reduction reactions that either produce or utilize electrical energy. Any device in which an electrochemical reaction occurs is called an **electrochemical cell.**

In Section 23.1 we used the spontaneous oxidation of metallic zinc by copper(II) ions as an example of a redox reaction in which actual electron gain and loss occur (see Figure 23.1). An electrochemical cell in which this reaction takes place (Figure 23.2) illustrates the essential components of every electrochemical cell.

Two electrodes connected by an external conductor carry the electrons out of and into the cell. The electrodes are conductors and may or may not take part in the **cell reaction**—the overall chemical reaction that occurs in an electrochemical cell. The cell reaction is the sum of the half-reactions. In this cell the zinc of the electrode is a reactant.

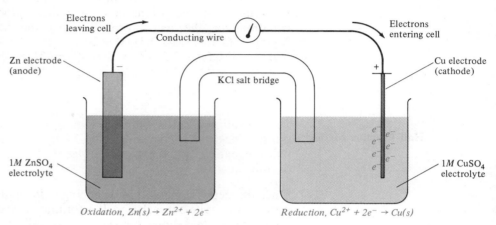

(a) **Beginning of reaction, showing electron flow**

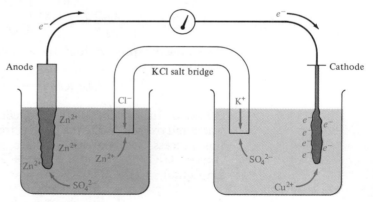

(b) **Intermediate point, showing ion flow**

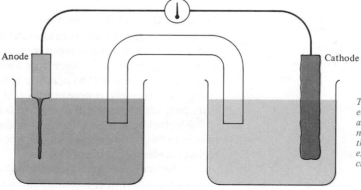

Figure 23.2
The Zinc-Copper Voltaic Cell   (c) **Complete reaction; copper electrode covered with deposited copper and zinc electrode dissolved**

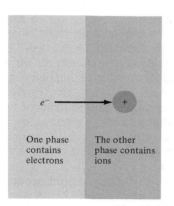

Figure 23.3
"The Fundamental Act in Electrochemistry" (Source: J. O. M. Bockris and A. K. N. Reddy, *Modern Electrochemistry,* New York: Plenum, 1970, p. 4.)

Each electrode is immersed in an *electrolyte*—a medium through which ions can flow. The electrolytes in the zinc–copper cell are aqueous solutions of zinc sulfate and copper(II) sulfate. Electrolytes may also be molten salts, solids, or other media (for example, a paste). Although it is usually desirable to keep the electrolytes separated, for the electrical circuit to be complete a pathway must be provided for ions to flow within the cell. As is discussed below, the salt bridge which connects the two electrolyte solutions permits this to happen.

Each electrode and its surrounding electrolyte, e.g., the copper electrode and the copper sulfate solution on the right in Figure 23.2, make up a **half-cell.** The half-reaction that occurs in a half-cell is an **electrode reaction**—in this case, $Cu^{2+} + 2e^- \rightarrow Cu(s)$.

When the electrical circuit is complete, current is carried in the electrodes and the external circuit by electrons, and in the electrolytes and salt bridge by ions. The chemical reaction occurs at the surfaces of the electrodes (Figure 23.3), where electron gain and loss must occur to allow current to flow. The spontaneous reaction in an electrochemical cell continues until the reactants and products have come to equilibrium.

In the cell of Figure 23.2, oxidation occurs at the zinc electrode, where zinc atoms lose electrons to form Zn^{2+} ions. Reduction occurs at the copper electrode, where Cu^{2+} ions from the electrolyte gain electrons to form metallic copper. As the reaction proceeds, the zinc electrode erodes away, electrons flow from the zinc electrode through the external circuit to the copper electrode, and the copper(II) solution loses its blue color as fresh copper is deposited on the copper electrode. The current flowing in the external circuit could, in principle, be used to perform work—for example, to drive a motor.

Within the cell, current is carried by the flow of ions (Figure 23.2b). As Zn^{2+} ions accumulate at the zinc electrode, negative ions from the salt bridge are attracted into the zinc half-cell solution. Similarly, positive ions from the salt bridge are attracted into the copper half-cell to replace the Cu^{2+} ions that are consumed there. Salt bridges commonly are filled with a salt such as KCl, KNO_3, NH_4Cl, or NH_4NO_3 in an aqueous gel. Overall electrical neutrality in the cell is maintained by positive ions flowing from left to right in the cell as drawn in Figure 23.2, while negative ions flow from right to left.

There are two types of electrochemical cells. The first is called a "voltaic" cell after Alessandro Volta, an Italian professor of natural philosophy who constructed the first battery, the "voltaic pile" (Figure 23.4), in about 1800. Voltaic cells are also

Figure 23.4
Some Early Cells In the voltaic pile zinc was oxidized by water with the evolution of hydrogen. In the Daniell cell, zinc was oxidized by copper ion.

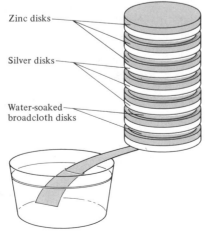

(a) **Voltaic pile**

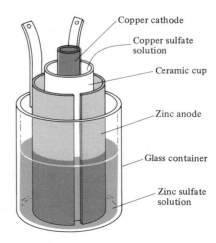

(b) **Daniell cell**

Anode	Cathode
Oxidation	Reduction
Anions generally migrate to anode	Cations generally migrate to cathode
Electrons leave cell	Electrons enter cell
Negative in voltaic cell	Negative in electrolytic cell

Anode: oxidation
Cathode: reduction

Anions move toward anode
Cations move toward cathode

---

sometimes called "galvanic" cells after Luigi Galvani (see introduction to this chapter). A **voltaic cell** generates electrical energy from a spontaneous redox reaction. The zinc–copper cell we have been discussing is a voltaic cell. (A "battery" is defined as two or more voltaic cells combined to provide electrical current for a practical purpose. However, the term is commonly used for any device that converts chemical energy into electrical energy.)

In the other type of cell, a *non*spontaneous redox reaction is caused to occur by the addition of electrical energy from a direct current source such as a generator or a battery. An **electrolytic cell** uses electrical energy from outside the cell to cause a redox reaction to occur. The process of driving a nonspontaneous redox reaction to occur by means of electrical energy is called **electrolysis.**

By definition, in any cell the **anode** is the electrode at which oxidation occurs, and the **cathode** is the electrode at which reduction occurs (see Figure 23.2a). A good memory trick is this—oxidation and anode both begin with vowels, and reduction and cathode with consonants. [Also by definition, in a voltaic cell the anode is labeled as the negative electrode and in an electrolytic cell the cathode is labeled as the negative electrode.]

Figure 23.5 is a simple diagram of a cell for the electrolysis of molten sodium chloride. In this cell, the electrodes are inert—they do not take part in the cell reaction. Electrons enter the cell from the outside source at the cathode, where they attract sodium ions and cause their reduction. As the sodium ions are consumed at the cathode, more cations are attracted into the vicinity of the cathode. At the anode, chloride ions are oxidized to give chlorine molecules, and the electrons that they lose leave the cell. More chloride ions move toward the anode and the reaction continues.

Note that in *both* the voltaic cell of Figure 23.2 and the electrolytic cell of Figure 23.5, cations move from left to right and anions move from right to left as the cells are drawn. That is, in general, in both voltaic and electrolytic cells, *anions* move toward the *anode,* and *cations* move toward the *cathode.* Table 23.2 summarizes what happens at the electrodes in both types of cells.

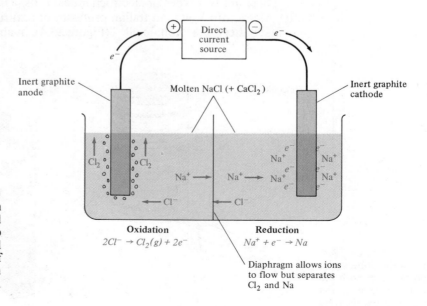

Figure 23.5
The Electrolysis of Molten Sodium Chloride Addition of $CaCl_2$ to NaCl lowers the melting point enough to make the cell workable. (Pure NaCl melts at about the boiling point of metallic sodium.) The cell reaction is $2Na(l) + Cl_2(g) \rightarrow 2NaCl(l)$.

Oxidation
$2Cl^- \rightarrow Cl_2(g) + 2e^-$

Reduction
$Na^+ + e^- \rightarrow Na$

Diaphragm allows ions to flow but separates Cl_2 and Na

23.4 ELECTRODES AND CELL NOTATION

Figure 23.6 illustrates schematically some of the types of electrodes used in simple electrochemical cells. Electrodes of different types can be combined. The metal electrodes of the zinc–copper cell (see Figure 23.2) were of type a. A gas electrode (type b) requires that the gas be continuously bubbled into the half-cell, where it is oxidized or reduced at an inert electrode to give anions or cations in solution. For example, in a hydrogen electrode the redox couple is H^+/H_2, and in a chlorine electrode the redox couple is Cl_2/Cl^-.

A standard notation is used to describe voltaic cells. The pattern of the notation is as follows

anode|anode electrolyte‖cathode electrolyte|cathode

A single vertical line indicates physical contact between species in different phases. The double line indicates a salt bridge, porous divider, or similar means of permitting ion flow while preventing the electrolytes from mixing. The zinc-copper cell would be written

phase boundary　　*salt bridge*　　*phase boundary*

$$Zn|Zn^{2+}‖Cu^{2+}|Cu$$

anode　　　*cathode*

The symbol for an inert electrode, like the platinum electrode in the hydrogen half-cell, is often written in parentheses. For example,

inert electrode

$$Mg|Mg^{2+}‖H^+|H_2|(Pt)$$

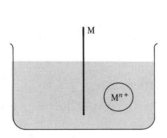

(a) Metal electrode, electrolyte containing the metal cation
M/M^{n+} (e.g., Zn/Zn^{2+})

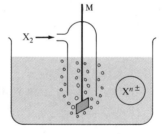

(b) Gas electrode with inert conductor, electrolyte containing anion or cation formed from the gas
$(M)/X_2(g)/X^{n\pm}$ (e.g., $Cl_2(g)/Cl^-$)

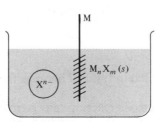

(c) Metal electrode coated with precipitate (e.g., Ag + AgCl), electrolyte contains anion of the salt
$M/M_nX_m(s)/X^{n-}$ (e.g., $Ag/AgCl(s)/Cl^-$)

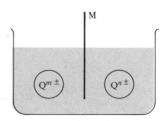

(d) "Redox" electrode with inert conductor, electrolyte containing two different species which include oxidized and reduced forms of same element
(Q = monatomic or polyatomic species)
$(M)/Q^{m\pm}, Q^{n\pm}$ (e.g., $(C)/Fe^{2+}, Fe^{3+}$)

Figure 23.6
Schematic Drawings of Some Simple Types of Electrodes Species in circles are in solution.

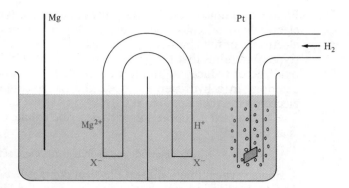

Figure 23.7
A Magnesium-Hydrogen Voltaic Cell The cell reaction is Mg(s) + 2H$^+$ ⟶ Mg^{2+} + H$_2$(g).

The anode, cathode, and cell reactions for this cell, drawn schematically in Figure 23.7, are

$$
\begin{array}{ll}
\textit{anode} & \text{Mg}(s) \longrightarrow \text{Mg}^{2+} + 2e^- \\
\textit{cathode} & 2\text{H}^+ + 2e^- \longrightarrow \text{H}_2(g) \\
\hline
\textit{cell reaction} & \text{Mg}(s) + 2\text{H}^+ \longrightarrow \text{Mg}^{2+} + \text{H}_2(g)
\end{array}
$$

Species in the same phase in a cell are separated by commas, as in the notation for this zinc–iron(II)/iron(III) cell,

$$\text{Zn}|\text{Zn}^{2+}\|\overbrace{\text{Fe}^{3+}, \text{Fe}^{2+}}^{\textit{in same phase}}|(\text{C})\underset{\textit{inert graphite electrode}}{\nearrow}$$

in which the cell reaction is

$$\text{Zn}(s) + 2\text{Fe}^{3+} \longrightarrow \text{Zn}^{2+} + 2\text{Fe}^{2+}$$

Frequently, the concentration of ions in solution and the pressure of gases are included, in parentheses, in the cell notation, for example,

$$\underbrace{(\text{Pt})|\text{H}_2(g, 1\text{ atm})|\text{H}^+(1\text{ M}),}_{\textit{hydrogen gas anode}} \underbrace{\text{Cl}^-(1\text{ M})|\text{AgCl}(s)|\text{Ag}}_{\textit{metal-precipitate cathode}}$$

No salt bridge is needed in this cell because the reactants are not soluble and do not mix.

Note that an electrode reaction may go in either direction and the electrode may be the anode or the cathode, depending upon the overall cell reaction. In Figure 23.8a, the hydrogen electrode is the anode, while in Figure 23.8b, the hydrogen electrode is the cathode. Table 23.3 lists some of the types of reactions most commonly encountered as anode reactions and cathode reactions.

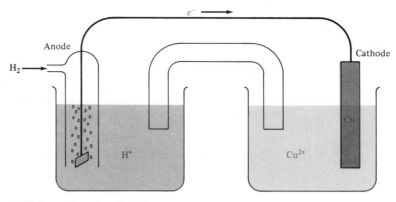

(a) Hydrogen electrode — Cu^{2+}/Cu cell

Figure 23.8
Hydrogen Electrode as Anode or Cathode In cell (a) oxidation occurs at the H_2 electrode and the cell reaction is $Cu^{2+} + H_2(g) \rightarrow 2H^+ + Cu(s)$. In cell (b) reduction occurs at the H_2 electrode and the cell reaction is $Zn(s) + 2H^+ \rightarrow Zn^{2+} H_2(g)$.

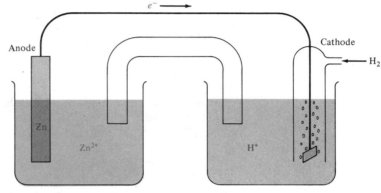

(b) Zn^{2+}/Zn — hydrogen electrode cell

Table 23.3
Some Typical Electrode Reactions

Anode reactions
1. **Oxidation of an anion to a free element**
   (a) $2Cl^- \longrightarrow Cl_2(g) + 2e^-$
   (b) $4OH^- \longrightarrow O_2(g) + 2H_2O + 4e^-$
2. **Oxidation of an anion or a cation to another species in solution**
   (a) $ClO^- + 2H_2O \longrightarrow ClO_3^- + 4H^+ + 4e^-$
   (b) $Sn^{2+} \longrightarrow Sn^{4+} + 2e^-$
   (c) $2Cr^{3+} + 7H_2O \longrightarrow Cr_2O_7^{2-} + 14H^+ + 6e^-$
3. **Oxidation of a metal anode**
   (a) $Cu(s) \longrightarrow Cu^{2+} + 2e^-$
   (b) $Au(s) + 4Cl^- \longrightarrow AuCl_4^- + 3e^-$
4. **Oxidation of water**
   $2H_2O \longrightarrow O_2(g) + 4H^+ + 4e^-$ (Solution becomes acidic.)

Cathode reactions
5. **Reduction of a cation or a metal in a complex ion to a free metal**
   (a) $Zn^{2+} + 2e^- \longrightarrow Zn(s)$
   (b) $Ag(CN)_2^- + e^- \longrightarrow Ag(s) + 2CN^-$
6. **Reduction of an anion or cation**
   (a) $NO_3^- + 3H^+ + 2e^- \longrightarrow HNO_2 + H_2O$
   (b) $Ce^{4+} + e^- \longrightarrow Ce^{3+}$
   (c) $2H^+ + 2e^- \longrightarrow H_2$
7. **Reduction of an elemental nonmetal to an anion**
   $I_2 + 2e^- \longrightarrow 2I^-$
8. **Reduction of water**
   $2H_2O + 2e^- \longrightarrow H_2(g) + 2OH^-$ (Solution becomes alkaline.)

EXAMPLE 23.6
Electrochemical Cell Notation

The notation for a voltaic cell is

$$Ag(s)|AgCl(s)|Cl^-\|Br^-|Br_2(g)|(C)$$

Write the ion-electron equations for the electrode reactions and the overall chemical equation for the cell reaction.

The notation on the left represents the half-cell in which oxidation takes place — the anode. The ion-electron equation for the anode reaction is

$$Ag(s) + Cl^- \longrightarrow AgCl(s) + e^-$$

The notation on the right represents the half-cell in which reduction takes place — the cathode. The cathode reaction is

$$Br_2(g) + 2e^- \longrightarrow 2Br^-$$

Combining these half-reactions gives the overall cell reaction as

$$(2)[Ag + Cl^- \longrightarrow AgCl + e^-]$$
$$\underline{Br_2 + 2e^- \longrightarrow 2Br^-}$$
$$2Ag(s) + Br_2(g) + 2Cl^- \longrightarrow 2Br^- + 2AgCl(s)$$

Exercise   The notation for a voltaic cell is

$$Fe(s)|Fe^{2+}\|Sn^{2+}, Sn^{4+}|(Pt)$$

Write the ion-electron equations for the electrode reactions and the overall chemical equation for the cell reaction.   *Answer* anode: $Fe(s) \rightarrow Fe^{2+} + 2e^-$, cathode: $Sn^{4+} + 2e^- \rightarrow Sn^{2+}$, overall: $Fe(s) + Sn^{4+} \rightarrow Fe^{2+} + Sn^{2+}$

23.5 ELECTROCHEMICAL STOICHIOMETRY

In an electrochemical reaction, there must obviously be a relationship between the amount of electricity that passes through a cell and the amount of chemical change that takes place. This relationship can be demonstrated by comparing the effect of a given amount of electrical current on several different electrolytic reactions.

Figure 23.9 illustrates an experiment for the simultaneous electrolyses of aqueous solutions of four different substances. Enough direct current is passed through the system to deposit 1 mol of silver (107.87 g). Using the mole ratios of the reduction half-reaction as for any chemical reaction shows that liberation of 1 mol of silver has required the passage of 1 mol of electrons.

$$Ag^+ + e^- \longrightarrow Ag(s) \quad (1 \text{ mol Ag})\left(\frac{1 \text{ mol } e^-}{1 \text{ mol Ag}}\right) = 1 \text{ mol } e^-$$

Simultaneously with the deposition of the silver, it is found that $\frac{1}{2}$ mol of copper, $\frac{1}{3}$ mol of gold, and $\frac{1}{2}$ mol of hydrogen have been produced. The formation of these amounts of products is explained by the stoichiometry of the half-reactions and the passage of 1 mol of electrons through each solution, as follows:

$$Cu^{2+} + 2e^- \longrightarrow Cu(s) \quad (1 \text{ mol } e^-)\left(\frac{1 \text{ mol Cu}}{2 \text{ mol } e^-}\right) = \frac{1}{2} \text{ mol Cu}$$

$$Au^{3+} + 3e^- \longrightarrow Au(s) \quad (1 \text{ mol } e^-)\left(\frac{1 \text{ mol Au}}{3 \text{ mol } e^-}\right) = \frac{1}{3} \text{ mol Au}$$

$$2H^+ + 2e^- \longrightarrow H_2(g) \quad (1 \text{ mol } e^-)\left(\frac{1 \text{ mol H}_2}{2 \text{ mol } e^-}\right) = \frac{1}{2} \text{ mol H}_2$$

The quantitative relationship between the amount of electricity and the amount of chemical change was first recognized by Michael Faraday, an English chemist, and is now known as Faraday's law. From his experiments in 1833 Faraday drew the following conclusion (in his own words): "The chemical power of a current of electricity is in direct proportion to the absolute quantity of electricity which passes." In modern terminology, "chemical power" is the extent to which the electrochemical reaction occurs and the "absolute quantity of electricity" is the number of moles of electrons transferred.

Clearly, we can treat the quantity of electrons involved in an electrochemical reaction exactly as we do the quantity of any other reactant or product. But we measure electrical current, not the masses of electrons, so some unit conversions are necessary to do electrochemical stoichiometry calculations.

The quantity of electrical charge is equal to the current that has flowed multiplied by the time. In the SI system of units, the coulomb (C) is the unit of electrical charge, the ampere (A) is the unit of current, and time is expressed in seconds.

$$\underset{\substack{charge \\ coulombs}}{\,} q = \underset{\substack{current \\ time \\ amperes\ seconds}}{I\,t} \qquad (23.10)$$

The relationships among the units are as follows:

$$1\ \text{ampere} = \frac{1\ \text{coulomb}}{1\ \text{second}} \qquad 1\ \text{coulomb} = 1\ \text{ampere second}$$

or, as a conversion factor,

$$\frac{1\ \text{coulomb}}{1\ \text{ampere second}}$$

Using the most accurate values, the charge on 1 mol of electrons is found to be

$$1.6021892 \times 10^{-19}\ \frac{\text{coulomb}}{\text{electron}} \times 6.022045 \times 10^{23}\ \frac{\text{electrons}}{\text{mol}} = 96{,}484.56\ \frac{\text{coulombs}}{\text{mol}\ e^-}$$

Because of its usefulness to chemistry, this quantity of electricity is defined as a unit—the **faraday**—which is equivalent to 96,485 C, or the amount of electrical charge represented by 1 mol of electrons. For most calculations, the value of the faraday, also called the Faraday constant and symbolized by F, can be rounded to 96,500 C.

The stoichiometric amount of electrical charge required by a given half-reaction is the moles of electrons transferred times the faraday.

$$\begin{array}{c}
\times\dfrac{1}{faraday} \\[4pt]
\text{Amount of} \xrightarrow{\hspace{3cm}} \text{No. of} \\
\text{electrical} \qquad\qquad \text{moles of} \\
\text{charge} \xleftarrow{\hspace{3cm}} \text{electrons} \\[4pt]
\times\,faraday
\end{array} \qquad (23.11)$$

For example, for $Mg^{2+} + 2e^- \rightarrow Mg(s)$, the stoichiometric amount of charge is

$$(2\ \text{mol}\ e^-)\left(\frac{96{,}500\ \text{C}}{1\ \text{mol}\ e^-}\right) = 1.93 \times 10^5\ \text{C}$$

(which is 1.93×10^5 ampere seconds, or 53.6 ampere hours).

The faraday provides the connection between the amount of electrical charge and stoichiometry. To know the amount of electrical charge we must know the current flow (in amperes) and the length of time for which the current has flowed.

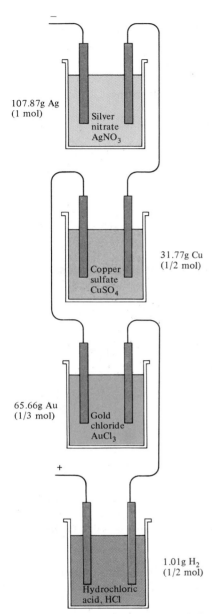

107.87g Ag
(1 mol)

Silver nitrate AgNO₃

31.77g Cu
(1/2 mol)

Copper sulfate CuSO₄

65.66g Au
(1/3 mol)

Gold chloride AuCl₃

1.01g H₂
(1/2 mol)

Hydrochloric acid, HCl

Figure 23.9
Simultaneous Electrolysis Experiment This experiment illustrates chemical equivalence as the basis for Faraday's laws. The stoichiometric amount of each substance equivalent to 1 mol of electrons is produced.

This can be converted into the amount of charge. For example, a 100 ampere current flowing for 60 s is equivalent to 6000 coulombs of charge:

$$q = It = (100 \text{ A})(60 \text{ s})\left(\frac{1 \text{ C}}{1 \text{ A s}}\right) = 6000 \text{ C}$$

The faraday allows conversion from coulombs to moles of electrons.

$$(6000 \text{ C})\left(\frac{1 \text{ mol } e^-}{96,500 \text{ C}}\right) = 0.06 \text{ mol } e^-$$

A 100 A direct current flowing for 60 s delivers 0.06 mol of electrons to an electrolytic cell. Conversely, the transfer of 0.06 mol of electrons in a voltaic cell would be required (ideally) to produce a 100 A current for 60 s.

EXAMPLE 23.7
Electrochemical Stoichiometry

What mass of elemental copper can be produced by the electrolysis of a copper(II) sulfate solution for 1.00 h at a steady direct current of 100. A?

First, we must use the current and the time to find the amount of electrical charge that has entered the cell.

$$(100. \text{ A})\left(\frac{1 \text{ C}}{1 \text{ A s}}\right)(1.00 \text{ h})\left(\frac{3600 \text{ s}}{1 \text{ h}}\right) = 3.60 \times 10^5 \text{ C}$$

The number of moles of electrons is found from the amount of charge.

$$(3.60 \times 10^5 \text{ C})\left(\frac{1 \text{ mol } e^-}{96,500 \text{ C}}\right) = 3.73 \text{ mol } e^-$$

Using the mole ratios from the reduction half-reaction

$$Cu^{2+} + 2e^- \longrightarrow Cu(s)$$

shows that the amount of copper produced will be

$$(3.73 \text{ mol } e^-)\left(\frac{1 \text{ mol Cu}}{2 \text{ mol } e^-}\right)\left(\frac{63.55 \text{ g Cu}}{1 \text{ mol Cu}}\right) = 119 \text{ g Cu}$$

The electrolysis will produce 119 g of copper metal. [This assumes, of course, that the reduction reaction is 100% efficient. In practice, as for example in a copper refinery, the reaction is not 100% efficient because of loss of current through competing electrochemical reactions.]

Exercise What mass of zinc will be oxidized in a voltaic cell if the cell is to produce a direct current of 0.015 A for a period of 15 min? *Answer* 0.0049 g Zn

---

23.6 CELL POTENTIAL

The spontaneous flow of electrons in the external circuit in a voltaic cell shows that electrons are attracted more strongly by one half-cell than by the other. There is an electrical potential difference between the two electrodes (see Tools of Chemistry: Electricity and Magnetism, Chapter 3). The anode has a higher negative potential than the cathode and electrons flow from the anode to the cathode.

The **cell potential** (E or E_{cell}), also called the **electromotive force** or **emf** of a cell, is a measure of the potential difference between the two half-cells. We think of the emf as the chemical driving force of the cell reaction, or of any redox reaction.

Electrical potential is measured in volts (V). The cell potential, or cell voltage, is the voltage measured in the external circuit when no current is flowing (called the open-circuit voltage). Under these conditions, the cell potential is a direct measure of the tendency of electrons to flow from one half-cell to the other. The potential varies with the nature of the chemical reaction, the temperature, and the concentration of the reactants. It is independent of the size of the electrodes or the volume of electrolyte in the cell.

The potential of the zinc–copper cell of Figure 23.2 is 1.10 V when the temperature is 25 °C and the concentration of ions is 1 M in each half-cell. The 1.10 V is a measure of the net effect of the tendency of Zn atoms to lose electrons and of Cu^{2+} ions to gain electrons under the given conditions.

Just as a cell reaction can be divided into two half-reactions, so a cell potential can be divided into two potentials. An **electrode potential** is the potential for one half-reaction. Because only the potential of a complete cell can be measured, electrode potentials, as discussed in the next section, are determined relative to a standard reference electrode. Knowing electrode potentials makes possible the comparison of the strengths of oxidizing and reducing agents, the prediction of reaction spontaneity, and the development of much useful thermodynamic data (Sections 23.8–23.13).

Volts (the unit of electrical potential) are related to joules (the unit of energy) and coulombs (the unit of charge) as follows:

---
1 faraday (F) = 96,500 C = charge on 1 mol of electrons

$$1 \text{ volt} = \frac{1 \text{ joule}}{1 \text{ coulomb}} \qquad 1 \text{ coulomb} = \frac{1 \text{ joule}}{1 \text{ volt}}$$

or, as a conversion factor,

$$\frac{1 \text{ joule}}{1 \text{ volt coulomb}}$$

---
1 faraday (F) = 96.5 kJ/V mol e⁻

Note that the faraday, 96,500 C/mol e^-, is equal to 96.5 kJ/V mol e^-.

EXAMPLE 23.8
Thermodynamics of Electrochemical Cells

The amount of electrical work produced by a voltaic cell is given by the product of the cell potential and the amount of electrical charge delivered by the cell.

$$w = -Eq$$

Calculate the electrical work done by a cell that has delivered 645 C of charge at a potential of 1.35 V.

Introducing $E = 1.35$ V and $q = 645$ C into the expression for w gives

$$w = -(1.35 \text{ V})(645 \text{ C})\left(\frac{1 \text{ J}}{1 \text{ V C}}\right) = -871 \text{ J}$$

The cell has generated 871 J of electrical work.

Exercise A voltaic cell is designed to deliver 1.0 kJ of electrical work during each minute of operation. If the operating potential of the cell is 1.52 V, what amount of electrical charge must be generated by the cell reaction each minute? *Answer* 660 C

23.7 ELECTROMOTIVE FORCE AND FREE ENERGY

The electromotive force, like the free energy change, is a measure of whether or not a chemical reaction is spontaneous and to what extent the reaction will occur. As you might expect, the two quantities are related mathematically. The free energy change is equal to the maximum amount of electrical work that can be performed (under ideal conditions) when n moles of electrons are transferred.

$$\Delta G = -nFE \qquad\qquad (23.12)$$

$$\underset{kilojoules}{} \quad \underset{moles\ e^-}{} \quad \underset{\frac{kilojoules}{volt\ moles\ e^-}}{} \quad \underset{volts}{}$$

Table 23.4
Electrical Potential and ΔG

	ΔG	E
Spontaneous reaction (voltaic cell)	Negative	Positive
Equilibrium	0	0
Nonspontaneous reaction (electrolytic cell)	Positive	Negative

Positive $E°$: reaction spontaneous in direction written

When the value of the cell potential is that for the usual standard state conditions, as discussed in the next section, then the standard state free energy change for the cell reaction can be found from the cell potential.

$$\Delta G° = -nFE° \qquad \text{(23.13)}$$

(This equation is also valid for the free energy changes and potentials of electrode reactions, Section 23.8.)

The zinc–copper voltaic cell (see Figure 23.2) has a *positive* cell potential. The cell potential is positive for all spontaneous redox reactions and all voltaic cells. You can see that a positive cell potential gives a negative value for the free energy change in Equation (23.12). Nonspontaneous redox reactions and electrolytic cells have negative cell potentials, which give positive values for the change in free energy according to Equation (23.12). When an electrochemical cell has reached equilibrium, electron flow ceases. If the cell was in a flashlight battery, we would say that the battery was dead. At equilibrium both the free energy change and the cell potential are equal to zero. These relationships are summarized in Table 23.4 and discussed further in Section 23.14.

The value of n needed in Equation (23.13) is most easily found from the oxidation and reduction half-reactions. This means essentially going backward in the half-reaction method for balancing redox reactions.

EXAMPLE 23.9
Thermodynamics of Electrochemical Cells

Find the standard cell potential for an electrochemical cell in which the following reaction takes place spontaneously:

$$Cl_2(g) + 2Br^- \longrightarrow Br_2(aq) + 2Cl^- \qquad \Delta G° = -52.5 \text{ kJ}$$

First, we must find the value of n, the moles of electrons transferred, by writing the half-reactions for reduction of Cl_2 and oxidation of Br^-.

$$Cl_2(g) + 2e^- \longrightarrow 2Cl^-$$
$$\underline{2Br^- \longrightarrow Br_2(aq) + 2e^-}$$
$$Cl_2(g) + 2Br^- \longrightarrow Br_2(aq) + 2Cl^-$$

The value of n is 2.

The cell potential is found by solving Equation (23.13) for $E°$ and substituting $n = 2$ and the known value of $\Delta G°$.

$$E° = \frac{-\Delta G°}{nF} = \frac{-(-52.5 \text{ kJ})}{(2 \text{ mol } e^-)(96.5 \text{ kJ/V mol } e^-)} = 0.272 \text{ V}$$

The cell potential at standard state conditions is 0.272 V.

Exercise The cell potential for an electrochemical cell in which the following reaction occurs:

$$2Fe^{3+} + 2I^- \longrightarrow 2Fe^{2+} + I_2(s)$$

is $E° = 0.236$ V. Calculate the value of $\Delta G°$ for this reaction. *Answer* -45.5 kJ

In summary, three things happen in an electrochemical cell: (1) An oxidation reaction occurs at the surface of one electrode (the anode) and a reduction reaction at the surface of the other electrode (the cathode), (2) electrons flow through an external circuit, and (3) ions flow in the electrolytes. All three of these processes must take place simultaneously, or current will not flow through the completed circuit. Although the two half-reactions are physically separated, they too can only occur simultaneously.

The electrical potential, or emf, of a cell is a measure of the tendency of the cell reaction to occur. In a voltaic cell, electrical energy is produced by a spontaneous redox reaction and cell potential has a positive value. In an electrolytic cell, a nonspontaneous redox reaction is made to occur by the introduction of electrical energy and cell potential has a negative value. Cell potentials and electrode potentials are related to the free energy change by the equation $\Delta G = -nFE$, where n is the number of electrons transferred and F is the faraday, the charge of one mole of electrons.

STANDARD REDUCTION POTENTIALS

23.8 $E°$ Defined

The potentials of electrochemical cells are easily measured and their values allow the calculation of other thermodynamic data. As is customary for thermodynamic data, electrochemical potentials are reported for substances in the standard states that are taken as approximating unit activities: all aqueous solutions at 1 M concentrations, all gases at 1 atm partial pressure, and all pure solids and liquids in their most stable forms at 1 atm. The symbol for redox potentials measured under these conditions is $E°$ and as usual we assume the temperature to be 25 °C unless it is stated otherwise.

Any redox couple can be described by an ion-electron equation written either as oxidation or reduction, for example,

$$Fe^{2+} \longrightarrow Fe^{3+} + e^-$$
$$Fe^{3+} + e^- \longrightarrow Fe^{2+}$$

The potentials for such redox half-reactions, which are the electrode potentials, by international agreement are given for reduction—the addition of electrons.

In a by-now-familiar situation, a reference point must be chosen for electrode potential values because individual electrode potentials cannot be measured. (It is not possible to have oxidation without reduction or vice versa.) The proton–hydrogen gas redox couple is chosen as the reference point for the relative scale of electrode potentials. This electrode is assigned a standard potential of 0.000 V at 298 K.

$$2H^+(1 \text{ M}) + 2e^- \longrightarrow H_2(g, 1 \text{ atm}) \qquad E° = 0.000 \text{ V}$$

H^+/H_2: $E° = 0.000$ V

The entire cell potential of a cell that includes an H^+/H_2 electrode plus a second electrode is assigned to the second electrode. The potential of 0.000 V for the H^+/H_2 couple and all other potentials established relative to it under the standard state conditions are called **standard electrode potentials,** or **standard reduction potentials.**

Table 23.5A is a list of standard reduction potentials in order from the most negative to the most positive values (a more extensive list is given in Appendix VI). Where hydrogen ion is a participant in the half-reaction, the hydrogen ion concentration must be 1 M (the standard state), giving a pH of 0. Table 23.5B is a similar list of half-reactions that occur in the presence of hydroxide ion, which at a concentration of 1 M gives a pH of 14. (The potentials of half-reactions in which neither H^+ nor OH^- are participants are unaffected by pH.)

23.9 RELATIVE STRENGTHS OF OXIDIZING AND REDUCING AGENTS

To illustrate standard reduction potentials and how they can be used, we begin by comparing two voltaic cells, one in which the standard hydrogen electrode is combined with a Cu^{2+}/Cu half-cell and one in which it is combined with a Zn^{2+}/Zn half-cell. In the cell with the copper electrode (see Figure 23.8a) the reactions would be

anode $\qquad\qquad H_2(g) \rightarrow 2H^+ + 2e^-$

cathode $\qquad \underline{Cu^{2+} + 2e^- \rightarrow Cu(s)}$ $\qquad\qquad$ measured cell voltage

$\qquad\qquad Cu^{2+} + H_2(g) \rightarrow 2H^+ + Cu(s)$ $\qquad$ 0.337 V

The entire cell voltage is assigned to the Cu^{2+}/Cu half-cell. The cell reaction is spontaneous in the direction written, copper is *reduced,* and, assuming the measurements have been made at standard state conditions, the measured voltage is the standard reduction potential of copper:

$$Cu^{2+} + 2e^- \longrightarrow Cu(s) \qquad E^\circ = 0.337 \text{ V}$$

In the cell in which the hydrogen electrode and the Zn^{2+}/Zn half-cell are combined (see Figure 23.8b), the hydrogen electrode acts as the *cathode:*

anode	$Zn(s) \rightarrow Zn^{2+} + 2e^-$	*measured*
cathode	$2H^+ + 2e^- \rightarrow H_2(g)$	*cell voltage*
	$Zn(s) + 2H^+ \rightarrow Zn^{2+} + H_2(g)$	0.763 V

Here again the reaction is spontaneous as written and the entire cell voltage is assigned to the Zn^{2+}/Zn couple. *However,* because by convention it is chosen to report standard *reduction* potentials, the anode reaction and the sign of the measured voltage are reversed. Again assuming measurements at standard state conditions, the standard reduction potential of the Zn^{2+}/Zn couple is

$$Zn^{2+} + 2e^- \longrightarrow Zn(s) \qquad E^\circ = -0.763 \text{ V}$$

As noted when we discussed the equation which relates standard free energy change and standard reduction potentials, $\Delta G^\circ = -nFE^\circ$, a positive E° value indicates a reaction that, under standard state conditions, is spontaneous as written (negative ΔG°). Standard reduction potential values tell us that Cu^{2+} is more easily reduced than either H^+ or Zn^{2+} (because E° for the Cu^{2+}/Cu is positive). Looked at the other way, zinc is more easily oxidized and is therefore a stronger reducing agent than either hydrogen or copper.

A table of standard reduction potentials like Table 23.5 is a list of reactants in the order of increasing strength as oxidizing agents. The reactants at the top of the table—those in the couples with the most negative standard reduction potentials—are the *weakest oxidizing agents,* and the reactants at the bottom of the table are the *strongest oxidizing agents.* Compare the position of Na^+, which is very stable to reduction and is therefore a very weak oxidizing agent, with the positions of ozone and fluorine, which are strong oxidizing agents (and are easily reduced). Conversely, the products at the top of the tables are the *strongest reducing agents*—the common alkali and alkaline earth metals—and the products at the bottom are the *weakest reducing agents.*

A spontaneous redox reaction (at standard state conditions) occurs between a species that is a *product* in a given couple and a species that is a *reactant* in any couple below it in a table like Table 23.5. For example, from their relative positions in the table, it can be predicted that cadmium metal ($Cd^{2+}/Cd(s)$, $E^\circ = -0.403$ V) will reduce Sn^{2+} ($Sn^{2+}/Sn(s)$, $E^\circ = -0.136$ V). The greater the difference between the potentials of two couples, the greater the extent to which the reaction will occur (at standard state conditions).

Comparison of Table 23.5A with Table 17.4 shows the basis of the activity series of metals, which we used in Sections 6.3c and 17.4c for qualitative predictions of the occurrence of redox displacement reactions. The metals appear in the activity series in the order of increasingly positive standard reduction potentials, and therefore of decreasing activity as reducing agents.

The following examples illustrate a few ways in which a table of standard reduction potentials can be used to provide qualitative information about the relative strengths of oxidizing and reducing agents in their reactions at standard state conditions. The calculation of E° for specific reactions is discussed in the next section.

Large positive E°: reactant is good oxidizing agent
Large negative E°: product is good reducing agent

Table 23.5
Standard State Reduction Potentials A more extensive table is given in Appendix VI.
(*Source*: Therald Moeller, *Inorganic Chemistry: A Modern Introduction,* Appendix IV, New York: Wiley, 1982 © 1982 by John Wiley & Sons, Inc.)

A. Acidic Solution	$E°$ (V)	A. Acidic Solution	$E°$ (V)
$Li^+ + e^- \longrightarrow Li(s)$	-3.045	$Pt^{2+} + 2e^- \longrightarrow Pt(s)$	~ 1.2
$K^+ + e^- \longrightarrow K(s)$	-2.925	$ClO_3^- + 3H^+ + 2e^- \longrightarrow HClO_2(aq) + H_2O(l)$	1.21
$Ba^{2+} + 2e^- \longrightarrow Ba(s)$	-2.906	$O_2(g) + 4H^+ + 4e^- \longrightarrow 2H_2O(l)$	1.229
$Sr^{2+} + 2e^- \longrightarrow Sr(s)$	-2.888	$MnO_2(s) + 4H^+ + 2e^- \longrightarrow Mn^{2+} + 2H_2O(l)$	1.23
$Ca^{2+} + 2e^- \longrightarrow Ca(s)$	-2.866	$2HNO_2(aq) + 4H^+ + 4e^- \longrightarrow N_2O(g) + 3H_2O(l)$	1.29
$Na^+ + e^- \longrightarrow Na(s)$	-2.714	$Cr_2O_7^{2-} + 14H^+ + 6e^- \longrightarrow 2Cr^{3+} + 7H_2O(l)$	1.33
$Mg^{2+} + 2e^- \longrightarrow Mg(s)$	-2.363	$Cl_2(g) + 2e^- \longrightarrow 2Cl^-$	1.360
$H_2(g) + 2e^- \longrightarrow 2H^-$	-2.25	$PbO_2(s) + 4H^+ + 2e^- \longrightarrow Pb^{2+} + 2H_2O(l)$	1.455
$Al^{3+} + 3e^- \longrightarrow Al(s)$	-1.662	$Au^{3+} + 3e^- \longrightarrow Au(s)$	1.498
$Mn^{2+} + 2e^- \longrightarrow Mn(s)$	-1.185	$MnO_4^- + 8H^+ + 5e^- \longrightarrow Mn^{2+} + 4H_2O(l)$	1.51
$Zn^{2+} + 2e^- \longrightarrow Zn(s)$	-0.763	$2HClO(aq) + 2H^+ + 2e^- \longrightarrow Cl_2(g) + 2H_2O(l)$	1.63
$Cr^{3+} + 3e^- \longrightarrow Cr(s)$	-0.744	$HClO_2(aq) + 2H^+ + 2e^- \longrightarrow HClO(aq) + H_2O(l)$	1.645
$Fe^{2+} + 2e^- \longrightarrow Fe(s)$	-0.440	$H_2O_2(aq) + 2H^+ + 2e^- \longrightarrow 2H_2O(l)$	1.776
$Cr^{3+} + e^- \longrightarrow Cr^{2+}$	-0.408	$O_3(g) + 2H^+ + 2e^- \longrightarrow O_2(g) + H_2O(l)$	2.07
$Cd^{2+} + 2e^- \longrightarrow Cd(s)$	-0.403	$F_2(g) + 2e^- \longrightarrow 2F^-$	2.87
$PbSO_4(s) + 2e^- \longrightarrow Pb(s) + SO_4^{2-}$	-0.359	$F_2(g) + 2H^+ + 2e^- \longrightarrow 2HF(aq)$	3.06
$PbCl_2(s) + 2e^- \longrightarrow Pb(s) + 2Cl^-$	-0.268		
$Ni^{2+} + 2e^- \longrightarrow Ni(s)$	-0.250	**B. Alkaline Solution**	$E°$ (V)
$Sn^{2+} + 2e^- \longrightarrow Sn(s)$	-0.136		
$Pb^{2+} + 2e^- \longrightarrow Pb(s)$	-0.126		
$2H^+ + 2e^- \longrightarrow H_2(g)$	0.000	$Mg(OH)_2(s) + 2e^- \longrightarrow Mg(s) + 2OH^-$	-2.690
$S(s) + 2H^+ + 2e^- \longrightarrow H_2S(aq)$	0.142	$Al(OH)_3(s) + 3e^- \longrightarrow Al(s) + 3OH^-$	-2.30
$Sn^{4+} + 2e^- \longrightarrow Sn^{2+}$	0.15	$Zn(OH)_2(s) + 2e^- \longrightarrow Zn(s) + 2OH^-$	-1.245
$Sb_2O_3(s) + 6H^+ + 6e^- \longrightarrow 2Sb(s) + 3H_2O(l)$	0.152	$Fe(OH)_2(s) + 2e^- \longrightarrow Fe(s) + 2OH^-$	-0.877
$Cu^{2+} + e^- \longrightarrow Cu^+$	0.153	$2H_2O(l) + 2e^- \longrightarrow H_2(g) + 2OH^-$	-0.828
$SO_4^{2-} + 4H^+ + 2e^- \longrightarrow H_2SO_3(aq) + H_2O(l)$	0.172	$Cd(OH)_2(s) + 2e^- \longrightarrow Cd(s) + 2OH^-$	-0.809
$AgCl(s) + e^- \longrightarrow Ag(s) + Cl^-$	0.222	$Ni(OH)_2(s) + 2e^- \longrightarrow Ni(s) + 2OH^-$	-0.72
$Cu^{2+} + 2e^- \longrightarrow Cu(s)$	0.337	$Fe(OH)_3(s) + e^- \longrightarrow Fe(OH)_2(s) + OH^-$	-0.56
$SO_4^{2-} + 8H^+ + 6e^- \longrightarrow S(s) + 4H_2O(l)$	0.357	$S(s) + 2e^- \longrightarrow S^{2-}$	-0.447
$H_2SO_3(aq) + 4H^+ + 4e^- \longrightarrow S(s) + 3H_2O(l)$	0.450	$Cu_2O(s) + H_2O(l) + 2e^- \longrightarrow 2Cu(s) + 2OH^-$	-0.358
$I_2(s) + 2e^- \longrightarrow 2I^-$	0.536	$CrO_4^{2-} + 4H_2O(l) + 3e^- \longrightarrow Cr(OH)_3(s) + 5OH^-$	-0.13
$MnO_4^- + e^- \longrightarrow MnO_4^{2-}$	0.564	$MnO_2(s) + 2H_2O(l) + 2e^- \longrightarrow Mn(OH)_2(s) + 2OH^-$	-0.05
$[PtCl_6]^{2-} + 2e^- \longrightarrow [PtCl_4]^{2-} + 2Cl^-$	0.68	$NO_3^- + H_2O(l) + 2e^- \longrightarrow NO_2^- + 2OH^-$	0.01
$O_2(g) + 2H^+ + 2e^- \longrightarrow H_2O_2(aq)$	0.682	$HgO(s) + H_2O(l) + 2e^- \longrightarrow Hg(l) + 2OH^-$	0.098
$Fe^{3+} + e^- \longrightarrow Fe^{2+}$	0.771	$PbO_2(s) + H_2O(l) + 2e^- \longrightarrow PbO(s) + 2OH^-$	0.247
$Hg_2^{2+} + 2e^- \longrightarrow 2Hg(l)$	0.788	$IO_3^- + 3H_2O(l) + 6e^- \longrightarrow I^- + 6OH^-$	0.26
$Ag^+ + e^- \longrightarrow Ag(s)$	0.799	$ClO_3^- + H_2O(l) + 2e^- \longrightarrow ClO_2^- + 2OH^-$	0.33
$2NO_3^- + 4H^+ + 2e^- \longrightarrow N_2O_4(g) + 2H_2O(l)$	0.803	$Ag_2O(s) + H_2O(l) + 2e^- \longrightarrow 2Ag(s) + 2OH^-$	0.345
$2Hg^{2+} + 2e^- \longrightarrow Hg_2^{2+}$	0.920	$ClO_4^- + H_2O(l) + 2e^- \longrightarrow ClO_3^- + 2OH^-$	0.36
$NO_3^- + 3H^+ + 2e^- \longrightarrow HNO_2(aq) + H_2O(l)$	0.94	$O_2(g) + 2H_2O(l) + 4e^- \longrightarrow 4OH^-$	0.401
$NO_3^- + 4H^+ + 3e^- \longrightarrow NO(g) + 2H_2O(l)$	0.96	$NiO_2(s) + 2H_2O(l) + 2e^- \longrightarrow Ni(OH)_2(s) + 2OH^-$	0.490
$Pd^{2+} + 2e^- \longrightarrow Pd(s)$	0.987	$MnO_4^- + 2H_2O(l) + 3e^- \longrightarrow MnO_2(s) + 4OH^-$	0.588
$Br_2(l) + 2e^- \longrightarrow 2Br^-$	1.065	$BrO_3^- + 3H_2O(l) + 6e^- \longrightarrow Br^- + 6OH^-$	0.61
$Br_2(aq) + 2e^- \longrightarrow 2Br^-$	1.087	$ClO^- + H_2O(l) + 2e^- \longrightarrow Cl^- + 2OH^-$	0.89
$ClO_4^- + 2H^+ + 2e^- \longrightarrow ClO_3^- + H_2O(l)$	1.19	$O_3(g) + H_2O(l) + 2e^- \longrightarrow O_2(g) + 2OH^-$	1.24
$2IO_3^- + 12H^+ + 10e^- \longrightarrow I_2(s) + 6H_2O(l)$	1.195		

Note: In some chemistry texts, particularly older American ones, you may find *standard oxidation potentials.* Such potentials are for the same standard state conditions relative to 0.000 V for the H_2/H^+ couple. The differences are that the ion-electron equations are written as oxidations (electrons on the other side) and the *signs* of the potentials are opposite. In 1953 the International Union of Pure and Applied Chemistry chose to recommend the uniform, worldwide use of standard reduction potentials, which had previously been more common in Europe. The numerical values for both sets of potentials are the same; only the signs are different.

EXAMPLE 23.10

Relative Strengths of Oxidizing and Reducing Agents

Earlier, we included nitric acid and the three chlorine-containing oxo anions— perchlorate ion, chlorate ion, and hypochlorite ion—in our list of common oxidizing agents (see Table 17.8). Using the $E°$ values for the couples in the ion-electron equations in Table 23.5A, arrange these species in order of increasing strength as oxidizing agents at standard state conditions in acid solution (ClO^- is present in strongly acid solution as $HClO$).

The more positive the standard reduction potential values, the stronger the oxidizing agent. In the nitric acid solution we can assume that the nitrate ion is the reactant. Scanning Table 23.5A shows three possible reactions for NO_3^-. The order of the $E°$ values for the possible reactions of the species under consideration is as follows:

Couples	$E°$ (V)
$NO_3^-/NO(g)$, $NO_3^-/HNO_2(aq)$, $NO_3^-/N_2O_4(g)$	0.96, 0.94, 0.803
ClO_4^-/ClO_3^-	1.19
$ClO_3^-/HClO_2(aq)$	1.21
$HClO(aq)/Cl_2(g)$	1.63

At standard state conditions, nitrate ion is the weakest oxidizing agent and hypochlorous acid is the strongest. The order of strength as oxidizing agents is

$$NO_3^- < ClO_4^- < ClO_3^- < HClO(aq)$$

Exercise Arrange ClO_4^-, ClO_3^-, ClO^-, and NO_3^- in order of increasing strength as oxidizing agents at standard state conditions in alkaline solution. Use the $E°$ values given in Table 23.5B. *Answer* $NO_3^- < ClO_3^- < ClO_4^- < ClO^-$

EXAMPLE 23.11

Relative Strengths of Oxidizing and Reducing Agents

What simple conclusion can be drawn from the $E°$ data for nitrate ion used in the preceding example, plus the following additional data: $HNO_2(aq)/NO(g)$, $E° = 1.00$ V; $HNO_2(aq)/N_2O(g)$, $E° = 1.29$ V; $N_2O_4(g)/NO(g)$, $E° = 1.03$ V; $N_2O_4(g)/HNO_2(aq)$, $E° = 1.07$ V?

The data show that within a narrow range of $E°$ values nitric acid can form several different products and these products can undergo various further redox reactions. One must conclude that it would be very difficult to make qualitative predictions of what the products will be when nitric acid reacts as an oxidizing agent.

Exercise Use the data given in Table 23.5A to discuss the reduction of ClO_4^- in an acidic solution. *Answer* Reduction of ClO_4^- should produce very little ClO_3^-, $HClO_2(aq)$, or $HClO(aq)$ because these substances are stronger oxidizing agents than ClO_4^-. Thus ClO_4^- will be reduced to Cl_2. If conditions are right, the $Cl_2(g)$ will continue to form Cl^-.

EXAMPLE 23.12

Relative Strengths of Oxidizing and Reducing Agents

Arrange the following less commonly encountered metals in an activity series from most active to least active: radium ($Ra^{2+}/Ra(s)$, $E° = -2.9$ V), rhodium ($Rh^{3+}/Rh(s)$, $E° = 0.80$ V), europium ($Eu^{2+}/Eu(s)$, $E° = -3.4$ V), and plutonium ($Pu^{3+}/Pu(s)$, $E° = -2.0$ V). How do these metals compare in reducing ability with the active metal lithium ($Li^+/Li(s)$, $E° = -3.0$ V), with hydrogen, and with gold ($Au^{2+}/Au(s)$, $E° = 1.5$ V), which is a noble metal and one of the least active of the metals?

The strongest reducing agents have the most negative $E°$ values. The activity series in order of decreasing activity as reducing agents is

$$Eu > Ra > Pu > Rh$$

Europium is a more active metal than lithium (more negative $E°$ value). Europium, radium, and plutonium are all more active reducing agents than hydrogen (all negative $E°$ values). Rhodium is a less active reducing agent than hydrogen but not as "noble" a metal — not as unreactive — as gold.

Exercise Arrange the following metals in an activity series from most active to least active: nobelium ($No^{3+}/No(s)$, $E° = -2.5$ V), cobalt ($Co^{2+}/Co(s)$, $E° = -0.28$ V), gallium ($Ga^{3+}/Ga(s)$, $E° = -0.53$ V), thallium ($Tl^+/Tl(s)$, $E° = -0.34$ V), and polonium ($Po^{2+}/Po(s)$, $E° = 0.65$ V). *Answer* $No > Ga > Tl > Co > Po$

23.10 CALCULATING $E°$ VALUES FOR REDOX REACTIONS FROM ELECTRODE POTENTIALS

The standard potential of a redox reaction can be calculated from the standard electrode potentials of the two half-cell reactions. A positive value of the potential for a redox reaction means that the reaction will be spontaneous in the direction written (under standard state conditions) *either* as a reaction in solution or as a cell reaction in which the two specific half-cells are combined. The standard potential calculated for the reaction will be the cell voltage for the reaction when it takes place under standard state conditions in a voltaic cell.

Since electrode potentials are all given for half-reactions going in the reduction direction, one of the half-reactions must be reversed in direction and the *sign* of its $E°$ changed before the electrode reactions and their potentials can be added. The reaction that is reversed is always that of the couple *higher* in tables such as Table 23.5A. This is the reaction that will be the oxidation (anode) half of the overall redox reaction. For example, to calculate the standard state potential for a zinc–copper cell, the ion-electron equations and the potentials,

reduction	$Zn^{2+} + 2e^- \longrightarrow Zn(s)$	$E° = -0.763$ V
reduction	$Cu^{2+} + 2e^- \longrightarrow Cu(s)$	$E° = 0.337$ V

are combined as follows:

oxidation	$Zn(s) \longrightarrow Zn^{2+} + 2e^-$	$E° = 0.763$ V
reduction	$Cu^{2+} + 2e^- \longrightarrow Cu(s)$	$E° = 0.337$ V
	$Zn(s) + Cu^{2+} \longrightarrow Zn^{2+} + Cu(s)$	$E° = 1.100$ V

Earlier, on the basis of qualitative knowledge of the chemistry of the substances involved, we predicted that the following reaction would occur (Example 17.8):

$$H_2S(aq) + Cl_2(g) \longrightarrow S(s) + 2HCl(aq)$$

By combining $E°$ values we can verify this prediction by showing that the reaction potential is positive.

$H_2S(aq) \longrightarrow S(s) + 2H^+ + 2e^-$	$E° = -0.142$ V
$Cl_2(g) + 2e^- \longrightarrow 2Cl^-$	$E° = 1.360$ V
$H_2S(aq) + Cl_2(g) \longrightarrow S(s) + 2HCl(aq)$	$E° = 1.218$ V

The displacement of sulfur from aqueous hydrogen sulfide by chlorine will be spontaneous under standard state conditions. [The standard free energy change of the reaction would be $\Delta G° = -nFE° = -(2$ mol $e^-)(96.485$ kJ/V mol $e^-)(1.218$ V$) = -235.0$ kJ.] With the appropriate electrodes and electrolytes, this reaction would take place in a voltaic cell, with a cell voltage of 1.218 V. The oxidation of hydrogen sulfide would be the anode reaction and the reduction of chlorine would be the cathode reaction.

In combining ion-electron equations to get the overall equation for a redox reaction, it is often necessary to multiply the equations by whole numbers to equalize the number of electrons gained and lost. The $E°$ values *are not* multiplied by these same factors when a cell potential is calculated from electrode potentials. The standard state potential difference is, by definition, the potential difference between 1 M solutions, pure substances, or gases at 1 atm partial pressure. The *amount* of the substances does not change the voltage. Think about the common batteries: A, AA, C, and D. These batteries of the same type differ in size, but they each have a 1.5 V potential. Do not make the common errors of (1) multiplying the value of $E°$ by the factors used to equalize the number of electrons in the ion-electron equations, or (2) forgetting to reverse the sign of the $E°$ value (from Table 23.5) for the oxidation half-reaction.

Also, in using standard potential values it must always be remembered that, like $\Delta G°$ values, they only allow predictions of whether or not a reaction is thermodynamically favorable (that is, thermodynamically spontaneous under standard state conditions). As for all thermodynamic quantities (e.g., ΔH or K values), the potentials have no bearing on *how fast* a possible reaction will proceed.

> **In combining half-reactions $E°$ values are not multiplied by the same factors as equations**

EXAMPLE 23.13
Thermodynamics of Electrochemical Cells

Show that $E° = -1.662$ V for the reduction of Al^{3+} to $Al(s)$, regardless of whether the reaction is written

$$\tfrac{1}{3}Al^{3+} + e^- \longrightarrow \tfrac{1}{3}Al(s) \qquad \Delta G° = 160.4 \text{ kJ} \qquad \textbf{(i)}$$

or

$$Al^{3+} + 3e^- \longrightarrow Al(s) \qquad \Delta G° = 481.2 \text{ kJ} \qquad \textbf{(ii)}$$

The $E°$ values for these reactions can be calculated from the $\Delta G°$ values that are given. For reaction (i)

$$E° = \frac{-\Delta G°}{nF} = \frac{-(160.4 \text{ kJ})}{(1 \text{ mol } e^-)(96.485 \text{ kJ/V mol } e^-)} = -1.662 \text{ V}$$

For reaction (ii)

$$E° = \frac{-(481.2 \text{ kJ})}{(3 \text{ mol } e^-)(96.485 \text{ kJ/V mol } e^-)} = -1.662 \text{ V}$$

That both $E°$ values are the same shows that the electromotive force of a reaction, unlike $\Delta G°$, is independent of the quantities or molar amounts of the reactants.

Exercise Calculate $\Delta G°$ for the half-reaction

$$\tfrac{1}{2}H_2O_2(aq) + H^+ + e^- \longrightarrow H_2O(l)$$

given that $E° = 1.776$ V for the $H_2O_2(aq)/H_2O(l)$ couple. *Answer* -171.4 kJ

EXAMPLE 23.14
Calculating $E°$

The standard reduction potentials are 0.771 V for the Fe^{3+}/Fe^{2+} couple and 0.536 V for the $I_2(s)/I^-$ couple. Write the reaction for the reduction of Fe^{3+} by I^-. Calculate $E°$ for this reaction. Would this reaction be spontaneous under standard state conditions?

The oxidation and reduction half-reactions would be

$$\begin{array}{ll} \textit{oxidation} & 2I^- \longrightarrow I_2(s) + 2e^- \\ \textit{reduction} & Fe^{3+} + e^- \longrightarrow Fe^{2+} \end{array}$$

To equalize the number of electrons, the reduction equation must be multiplied by two, but the $E°$ value is *not* multiplied by this factor.

$$
\begin{aligned}
2I^- &\longrightarrow I_2(s) + 2e^- & E° &= -0.536 \text{ V} \\
(2)[Fe^{3+} + e^- &\longrightarrow Fe^{2+}] & E° &= 0.771 \text{ V} \\
\hline
2Fe^{3+} + 2I^- &\longrightarrow 2Fe^{2+} + I_2(s) & E° &= 0.235 \text{ V}
\end{aligned}
$$

The positive value of the emf tells us that the reaction will be spontaneous under standard state conditions.

Exercise Use the standard reduction potentials given in Table 23.5 to calculate $E°$ for the reaction

$$3Zn(s) + IO_3^- + 3H_2O(l) \longrightarrow I^- + 3Zn(OH)_2(s)$$

Answer $E° = 1.51$ V

EXAMPLE 23.15
Calculating $E°$

There is a significant difference in the way some metals react with oxidizing and nonoxidizing acids. Using data from Table 23.5A, compare the reactions of zinc and copper with hydrochloric acid and nitric acid under standard state conditions.

To react with an acid a metal must be oxidized. For zinc and copper the half-reactions are

$$
\begin{aligned}
\textit{oxidation} \quad Zn(s) &\longrightarrow Zn^{2+} + 2e^- & E° &= 0.763 \text{ V} \\
\textit{oxidation} \quad Cu(s) &\longrightarrow Cu^{2+} + 2e^- & E° &= -0.337 \text{ V}
\end{aligned}
$$

With hydrochloric acid, only H^+ is available to be reduced. Combining the electrode potentials for zinc and copper oxidation with that for the H^+/H_2 couple,

$$
\begin{aligned}
Zn(s) &\longrightarrow Zn^{2+} + 2e^- & E° &= 0.763 \text{ V} \\
2H^+ + 2e^- &\longrightarrow H_2(g) & E° &= 0.000 \text{ V} \\
\hline
Zn(s) + 2H^+ &\longrightarrow Zn^{2+} + H_2(g) & E° &= 0.763 \text{ V} \\
Cu(s) &\longrightarrow Cu^{2+} + 2e^- & E° &= -0.337 \text{ V} \\
2H^+ + 2e^- &\longrightarrow H_2(g) & E° &= 0.000 \text{ V} \\
\hline
Cu(s) + 2H^+ &\longrightarrow Cu^{2+} + H_2(g) & E° &= -0.337 \text{ V}
\end{aligned}
$$

shows that under standard state conditions zinc will react with hydrochloric acid, but copper will not.

In the reaction of nitric acid with metals, the nitrate ion is available to be reduced. Selecting from Table 23.5A the NO_3^- couple with the most positive $E°$, the reaction potentials are found to be

$$
\begin{aligned}
(3)[Zn(s) &\longrightarrow Zn^{2+} + 2e^-] & E° &= 0.763 \text{ V} \\
(2)[NO_3^- + 4H^+ + 3e^- &\longrightarrow NO(g) + 2H_2O(l)] & E° &= 0.96 \text{ V} \\
\hline
3Zn(s) + 2NO_3^- + 8H^+ &\longrightarrow 3Zn^{2+} + 2NO(g) + 4H_2O(l) & E° &= 1.72 \text{ V} \\
(3)[Cu(s) &\longrightarrow Cu^{2+} + 2e^-] & E° &= -0.337 \text{ V} \\
(2)[NO_3^- + 4H^+ + 3e^- &\longrightarrow NO(g) + 2H_2O(l)] & E° &= 0.96 \text{ V} \\
\hline
3Cu(s) + 2NO_3^- + 8H^+ &\longrightarrow 3Cu^{2+} + 2NO(g) + 4H_2O(l) & E° &= 0.62 \text{ V}
\end{aligned}
$$

Both zinc and copper will dissolve in nitric acid at standard state conditions and 25 °C. The reaction with zinc is more favorable. [Note that for zinc in nitric acid, the hydrogen reduction reaction as well as the nitrate reduction will be more favorable.]

Exercise Can iodide ion be oxidized to iodate ion by reaction with chromate ion in alkaline solution under standard state conditions? Will the reaction occur using dichromate ion in acidic solution under standard state conditions? See Table 23.5

for values of $E°$. *Answer* no, $E° = -0.39$ V for $2CrO_4^{2-} + 5H_2O(l) + I^- \rightarrow IO_3^- + 2Cr(OH)_3(s) + 4OH^-$; yes, $E° = 0.79$ V for $6I^- + Cr_2O_7^{2-} + 14H^+ \rightarrow 3I_2(s) + 2Cr^{3+} + 7H_2O(l)$ and $E° = 0.14$ V for $5Cr_2O_7^{2-} + 34H^+ + 3I_2(s) \rightarrow 6IO_3^- + 10Cr^{3+} + 17H_2O(l)$

Often, not all of the oxidation states of a given element are represented in tables of standard reduction potentials. The electrode potentials for two couples can be combined to give the electrode potential for a different couple.

However, it is important to see that an unknown electrode potential *cannot* be found by simply adding known electrode potentials along with equations, as was done to find cell potentials. It is necessary to take into account the *number of electrons* transferred in each of the half-reactions. This can be demonstrated by combining two half-reactions and their $\Delta G°$ values in a Hess's law calculation.

$$\begin{array}{ll} A + 2e^- \longrightarrow B & \Delta G_1 = -2FE_1° \\ B + 3e^- \longrightarrow D & \Delta G_2 = -3FE_2° \\ \hline A + 5e^- \longrightarrow D & \Delta G_{1+2} = (-2FE_1°) + (-3FE_2°) \end{array}$$

The number of electrons in the new half-reaction is five, and the expression for the new electrode potential must be found as follows:

$$\Delta G_{1+2}° = -5FE_{1+2}°$$

$$-2FE_1° - 3FE_2° = -5FE_{1+2}°$$

$$E_{1+2}° = \frac{2E_1° + 3E_2°}{5}$$

To find an unknown electrode potential by combining two known electrode potentials, multiply each known $E°$ by the number of electrons in the electrode reaction, add these two $E°$ values together (algebraically) and divide by the total number of electrons in the new electrode reaction. [If you wish, you can prove for yourself by using $-nFE°$ in place of $\Delta G°$ in a Hess's law calculation that the number of electrons cancels out when electrode potentials are combined to give a cell potential, although, as shown above, they do not when two half-reactions are combined to produce a third half-reaction.]

EXAMPLE 23.16
Calculating $E°$

The standard reduction potentials are -1.798 V and -0.607 V for the couples $U^{3+}/U(s)$ and U^{4+}/U^{3+}, respectively. Calculate $E°$ for the $U^{4+}/U(s)$ couple.

The number of electrons gained in the two known half-reactions and the new half-reactions are

$$\begin{array}{ll} U^{3+} + 3e^- \longrightarrow U(s) & E° = -1.798 \text{ V} \\ U^{4+} + e^- \longrightarrow U^{3+} & E° = -0.607 \text{ V} \\ \hline U^{4+} + 4e^- \longrightarrow U(s) & \end{array}$$

Multiplying each known $E°$ by the number of electrons in the half-reaction, adding them, and dividing by the number of electrons in the new half-reaction gives

$$E° = \frac{(3)(-1.798 \text{ V}) + (1)(-0.607 \text{ V})}{(4)} = -1.500 \text{ V}$$

The standard reduction potential of the $U^{4+}/U(s)$ couple is -1.500 V.

Exercise The standard reduction potential is 0.536 V for the I_2/I^- couple and 1.195 V for the IO_3^-/I_2 couple. Calculate $E°$ for the IO_3^-/I^- couple. *Answer* $E° = 1.085$ V

23.11 ELECTROLYSIS

In the electrolysis of molten sodium chloride (Figure 23.5), the only possible electrode reactions are the reduction of sodium ions and the oxidation of chloride ions. When electrical energy is introduced into an aqueous solution, however, the possibility of reactions of water, and (if their concentration is high) of H^+ and OH^-, must also be considered. In general, the anode reaction should be the one with the least positive reduction potential and the cathode reaction should be the one with the most positive potential.

However, there are limitations to predicting the products of electrolysis. The voltage required to cause a particular reaction to occur is frequently greater than shown by the standard potential because of **overvoltage**—a collective term for several effects that add to the voltage required by an electrochemical reaction.

For example, the electrolysis of acidified zinc sulfate solution results in deposition of elemental zinc at the cathode ($Zn^{2+} + 2e^- \rightarrow Zn$, $E° = -0.763$ V) rather than the liberation of hydrogen gas ($2H^+ + 2e^- \rightarrow H_2$, $E° = 0.000$ V), even though the reduction potential data predict the opposite. Predictions are further complicated when several possible electrode reactions have the same or nearly the same potential values. Under these conditions, two or more reactions may occur simultaneously. This may be desirable (e.g., in the simultaneous electrodeposition of several metals) or undesirable (e.g., in the simultaneous liberation of hydrogen during deposition of a metal).

Electrolysis is used in many ways in industry. Metals are freed from their ores by electrolysis (Section 28.5), and objects are coated, or *plated,* with thin layers of metal. A major area of industrial chemistry—the chloralkali industry (Section 29.8a)—is based on the electrolysis of concentrated sodium chloride solutions. The two possible anode reactions in an aqueous sodium chloride solution are the oxidation of chloride ion or the oxidation of water:

$$2Cl^- \longrightarrow Cl_2(g) + 2e^- \qquad E° = -1.36 \text{ V}$$
$$2H_2O(l) \longrightarrow O_2(g) + 4H^+ + 4e^- \qquad E° = -1.23 \text{ V}$$

When the concentration of chloride ion is high the first reaction takes place to the greater extent, producing chlorine, which is a large-volume industrial chemical. In dilute solutions the second reaction is favored.

The two possible cathode reactions are the reduction of sodium ion or the reduction of water.

$$Na^+ + e^- \longrightarrow Na(s) \qquad E° = -2.71 \text{ V}$$
$$2H_2O(l) + 2e^- \longrightarrow H_2(g) + 2OH^- \qquad E° = -0.83 \text{ V}$$

The reduction of water is much more favorable and the cathode products in the electrolysis of concentrated sodium chloride are hydrogen and a solution of sodium hydroxide, both also valuable industrial chemicals.

23.12 CONDITIONS OTHER THAN STANDARD STATE

The free energy change at concentrations other than those chosen for the standard state (Section 22.8) is

$$\Delta G = \Delta G° + 2.303RT \log Q$$

Substitution of $\Delta G = -nFE$ and $\Delta G° = -nFE°$ into this equation gives the relationship between the potential at nonstandard and standard state conditions:

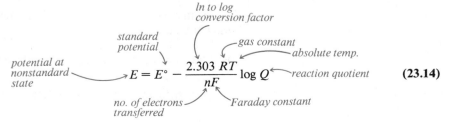

$$E = E° - \frac{2.303 \, RT}{nF} \log Q \qquad \textbf{(23.14)}$$

Nernst equation:
$E = E° - \dfrac{0.0592}{n} \log Q$

This is known as the Nernst equation, named for Walther Nernst, a German chemist who in the early 1900s studied electrochemistry and was also the first person to state the third law of thermodynamics. The Nernst equation is valid both for the potentials of half-reactions and for overall redox reactions. When $T = 298.15$ K, the value for the factor $2.303 \, RT/F$ is 0.0592 and Equation (23.14) becomes

$$E = E° - \frac{0.0592}{n} \log Q \qquad (23.15)$$

EXAMPLE 23.17
Calculating E

The standard reduction potential for the MnO_4^-/Mn^{2+} couple in acidic solution is 1.51 V at 25 °C. Will the permanganate ion become a stronger or weaker oxidizing agent in a solution which contains $[MnO_4^-] = 0.10$ mol/L, $[H^+] = 1.3 \times 10^{-2}$ mol/L, and $[Mn^{2+}] = 2.5 \times 10^{-5}$ mol/L?

The reduction half-reaction is

$$MnO_4^- + 8H^+ + 5e^- \longrightarrow Mn^{2+} + 4H_2O(l) \qquad E° = 1.51 \text{ V}$$

The reaction quotient is

$$Q = \frac{[Mn^{2+}]}{[MnO_4^-][H^+]^8} = \frac{(2.5 \times 10^{-5})}{(0.10)(1.3 \times 10^{-2})^8} = 3.1 \times 10^{11}$$

The Nernst equation gives the cell potential under these conditions as

$$E = E° - \frac{0.0592}{n} \log Q = (1.51 \text{ V}) - \frac{0.0592}{5} \log (3.1 \times 10^{11}) = 1.37 \text{ V}$$

Because $E < E°$, MnO_4^- under these conditions is a weaker oxidizing agent.

Exercise   The standard reduction potential for the $F_2(g)/F^-$ couple is 2.87 V. What must the pressure of fluorine gas be in order to produce a half-cell potential of 2.85 V in a solution that contains 0.10 M F⁻?   *Answer* 0.002 atm

---

EXAMPLE 23.18
Calculating E

Under standard state conditions the reaction

$$3Zn(s) + 2Cr^{3+} \longrightarrow 3Zn^{2+} + 2Cr(s) \qquad E° = 0.019 \text{ V}$$

is spontaneous. Will the above reaction occur if $[Cr^{3+}] = 0.010$ mol/L and $[Zn^{2+}] = 5.3$ mol/L?

The value of the reaction quotient is

$$Q = \frac{[Zn^{2+}]^3}{[Cr^{3+}]^2} = \frac{(5.3)^3}{(0.010)^2} = 2.8 \times 10^5$$

and the cell potential is

$$E = E° - \frac{0.0592}{n} \log Q$$

$$= 0.019 - \frac{0.0592}{6} \log (2.8 \times 10^5) = -0.035 \text{ V}$$

The negative cell potential implies that the reaction will not be spontaneous under these conditions.

Exercise   Under standard state conditions the following reaction is not spontaneous:

$$Br^- + 2MnO_4^- + H_2O(l) \longrightarrow BrO_3^- + 2MnO_2(s) + 2OH^- \qquad E° = -0.022 \text{ V}$$

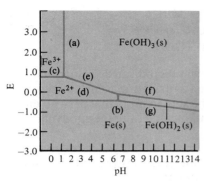

Figure 23.10
**pH-Potential Diagram for the
Iron-Water System** The various
species are thermodynamically
stable in the areas indicated.

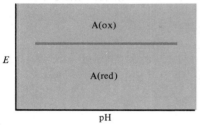

pH-dependent non-redox equilibrium

$$A \xrightleftharpoons[\text{OH}^- \text{ or H}^+]{\text{H}^+ \text{ or OH}^-} B$$

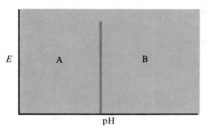

pH-independent redox equilibrium

$$A(\text{ox}) \rightleftharpoons A(\text{red})$$

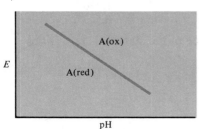

pH-dependent redox equilibrium

$$A(\text{ox}) \xrightleftharpoons[\text{OH}^- \text{ or H}^+]{\text{H}^+ \text{ or OH}^-} A(\text{red})$$

Figure 23.11
**Interpretation of pH-Potential
Diagrams**

The reaction conditions are adjusted so that $E = 0.100$ V by making $[\text{Br}^-] = [\text{MnO}_4^-] = 1.5$ mol/L and $[\text{BrO}_3^-] = 0.5$ mol/L. What is the concentration of hydroxide ion in this cell? *Answer* 2×10^{-6} mol/L

A change in the pH has a profound effect upon the value of the reduction potential for any couple that contains the H^+ or OH^- ion. For example, for the reference couple

$$2\text{H}^+ + 2e^- \longrightarrow \text{H}_2(g)$$

where $[\text{H}^+] = 1$ mol/L, $E°$ is 0.000 V. A change to pure water, where $[\text{H}^+] = 1.00 \times 10^{-7}$ mol/L, while keeping the pressure of H_2 at 1.00 atm, decreases the potential for the reaction.

$$E = E° - \frac{0.0592}{n} \log \frac{p_{\text{H}_2}}{[\text{H}^+]^2}$$

$$= 0.000 - \frac{0.0592}{n} \log \frac{1.00}{(1.00 \times 10^{-7})^2} = 0.000 - \frac{0.0592}{2}(14.00) = -0.414 \text{ V}$$

The negative E value shows that the reverse of the reaction as written is spontaneous. For the same couple in a 1.00 M NaOH solution, where $[\text{OH}^-] = 1.00$ mol/L and $[\text{H}^+] = 1.00 \times 10^{-14}$ mol/L,

$$E = 0.000 - \frac{0.0592}{2} \log \frac{1.00}{[1.00 \times 10^{-14}]^2} = -0.829 \text{ V}$$

Figure 23.10 illustrates the effects of variation of pH and potential on a system containing iron and water. Such pH–potential diagrams (also called Pourbaix diagrams) provide a very useful summary of the possible equilibria in a given system.

We can use the simple pH–potential diagram of Figure 23.10 to illustrate how pH–potential diagrams are interpreted. (For systems in which several pH- and potential-dependent equilibria occur simultaneously, the diagrams can become exceedingly complicated.) A vertical line represents an equilibrium that is independent of potential—a nonredox equilibrium (Figure 23.11). The iron–water system has two such equilibria (lines a and b), between the cations and the hydroxides that form in alkaline solution.

$$\text{Fe}^{3+} \xrightleftharpoons[\text{H}^+]{\text{OH}^-} \text{Fe(OH)}_3(s) \qquad [a]$$

$$\text{Fe}^{2+} \xrightleftharpoons[\text{H}^+]{\text{OH}^-} \text{Fe(OH)}_2(s) \qquad [b]$$

To the left of the vertical lines (lower pH) the cations are favored, to the right (higher pH) the hydroxides are favored.

Horizontal lines represent redox equilibria that are independent of pH. In a pH–potential diagram the oxidized species appear above the horizontal (or diagonal) lines and reduced species below the lines. For the iron–water system, two such equilibria (lines c and d) occur.

$$\text{Fe}^{3+} + e^- \rightleftharpoons \text{Fe}^{2+} \qquad [c]$$
$$\text{Fe}^{2+} + 2e^- \rightleftharpoons \text{Fe}(s) \qquad [d]$$

Both lie to the left of the points at which the pH becomes sufficiently alkaline for hydroxides to precipitate.

Diagonal lines show equilibria that depend upon both pH and potential—redox equilibria in which hydrogen or hydroxide ions are participants. Lines e, f, and g, respectively, represent the following equilibria of this type:

$$Fe(OH)_3(s) + e^- \rightleftharpoons Fe^{2+} + 3OH^- \qquad [e]$$

$$Fe(OH)_3(s) + e^- \rightleftharpoons Fe(OH)_2(s) + OH^- \qquad [f]$$

$$Fe(OH)_2(s) + 2e^- \rightleftharpoons Fe(s) + 2OH^- \qquad [g]$$

Within the spaces enclosed by the solid lines, the species indicated are thermodynamically stable. Species high in the diagram can react as oxidizing agents; those low in the diagram can react as reducing agents. It must be kept in mind that pH–potential diagrams are based on thermodynamic data and include only thermodynamically stable species.

Also, a reminder about thermodynamic versus kinetic stability is in order with respect to pH–potential diagrams. In some cases, the reactions presented in the diagrams come to equilibrium too slowly to be of consequence.

23.13 REDOX EQUILIBRIA: FINDING K FROM $E°$

Just as $\Delta G°$ is directly related to the equilibrium constant (Section 22.8), so also is the standard potential of a reaction. At equilibrium, $E = 0$ and $Q = K$. Introducing these values into the Nernst equation (Equation 23.15) provides a simple relationship between the equilibrium constant and the standard potential.

$$E = E° - \frac{0.0592}{n} \log K = 0 \qquad \textbf{(23.16)}$$

$$\log K = \frac{n}{0.0592} E° \qquad \textbf{(23.17)}$$

[Equation (23.17) can also be derived from $\Delta G° = -nFE° = -2.303RT \log K$.] Equation (23.17) shows that the magnitude of K for a redox reaction is directly proportional to the number of electrons involved and to the standard potential for the reaction. Values of K can be calculated from the standard potential for an overall redox reaction. Once K is known, it may be used in any of the usual ways to determine concentrations in either redox reactions or electrochemical cells at equilibrium.

EXAMPLE 23.19
Thermodynamics of Electrochemical Cells

The standard reduction potentials are 1.229 V for the $O_2(g)/H_2O(l)$ couple and 1.776 V for the $H_2O_2(aq)/H_2O(l)$ couple in acidic solution. Find $E°$, $\Delta G°$, and K for the decomposition of hydrogen peroxide.

$$2H_2O_2(aq) \rightleftharpoons 2H_2O(l) + O_2(g)$$

The standard state potential of the cell is

$$
\begin{array}{ll}
2H_2O(l) \longrightarrow O_2(g) + 4H^+ + 4e^- & E° = -1.229 \text{ V} \\
\underline{(2)[H_2O_2(aq) + 2H^+ + 2e^- \longrightarrow 2H_2O(l)]} & \underline{E° = 1.776 \text{ V}} \\
2H_2O_2(aq) \longrightarrow O_2(g) + 2H_2O(l) & E° = 0.547 \text{ V}
\end{array}
$$

Using this value of $E°$, we obtain the following value of the standard state Gibbs free energy change:

$$\Delta G° = -nFE° = -(4 \text{ mol } e^-)(96.5 \text{ kJ/V mol } e^-)(0.547 \text{ V})$$
$$= -211 \text{ kJ}$$

and the equilibrium constant is

$$\log K = \frac{n}{0.0592} E° = \frac{4}{0.0592}(0.547) = 37.0$$

$$K = 1 \times 10^{37}$$

For this spontaneous reaction (at standard state conditions), $E° = 0.547$ V, $\Delta G° = -211$ kJ, and $K = 1 \times 10^{37}$.

Exercise The standard reduction potentials are 2.87 V for the $F_2(g)/F^-$ couple and 3.06 V for the $F_2(g)/HF(aq)$ couple. Find $E°$, $\Delta G°$, and K_a for the reaction

$$HF(aq) \rightleftharpoons H^+ + F^-$$

Answer $E° = -0.19$ V, $\Delta G° = 18$ kJ, $K_a = 6 \times 10^{-4}$

In summary, standard electrochemical potentials are reported for reactions in which the reactants and products are in the usual standard states. The hydrogen ion–hydrogen gas electrode is chosen as a reference electrode and its electrode potential set as zero. Standard electrode potentials are measured relative to this electrode and reported for reduction half-reactions.

A table of standard reduction potentials is a list of redox couples in the order of their strength as oxidizing and reducing agents. The more negative the standard reduction potential, the stronger is the product *in the couple as a reducing agent [those at the top in tables like Table 23.5]. The more positive is the standard reduction potential, the stronger is the* reactant *in the couple as an oxidizing agent [those at the bottom in tables like Table 23.5]. At standard state conditions a spontaneous reaction should occur between a product in a given couple and a reactant in any couple with a more positive standard reduction potential.*

The standard potentials for redox reactions may be calculated from the tabulated standard electrode potentials. An unknown electrode potential can also be calculated; account must be taken of the differing numbers of electrons transferred in each half-reaction.

Redox potentials for nonstandard-state concentrations may be calculated from a knowledge of the reaction quotient (Q) and the number of moles of electrons transferred (Equations 12.14 and 12.15). At equilibrium $\Delta G = 0$, $Q = K$, and the value of K can be calculated from a known value of $E°$ and the number of moles of electrons transferred (Equation 23.17).

PRACTICAL ELECTROCHEMISTRY

23.14 DRY CELL BATTERIES

Zinc–copper cells based on the early designs shown in Figure 23.4 were used to provide direct current for many years. But sealed cells that contain no free liquid are more compact, portable, and practical. The best known and still the most common of these *dry cells* is the Leclanché cell, which has been in use for over 100 years.

The zinc anode in a Leclanché cell doubles as the cell container (Figure 23.12). There is a moist ammonium chloride–zinc chloride electrolyte which is thickened to

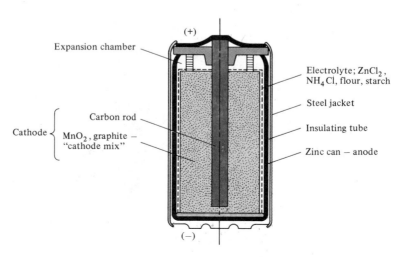

Figure 23.12
Leclanché Dry Cell

a paste, and the reactant at the carbon cathode is manganese dioxide. The anode reaction is the oxidation of zinc. The zinc ions produced go on to combine with the electrolyte to form compounds such as $Zn(NH_3)Cl_2$ and $ZnCl_2 \cdot 4Zn(OH)_2$. The cathode reaction, the reduction of MnO_2, is influenced by variations in the physical state of the MnO_2 and the pH within the cell; the reaction is complicated and not fully understood. It is a solid-state reaction that is thought to begin with the reaction of electrons and protons as they diffuse into the crystal.

$$MnO_2(s) + H^+ + e^- \longrightarrow MnOOH(s)$$

The Mn^{2+} ion and $Zn(MnO_2)_2$ are also found among the reduction products. An approximation to the cell reaction that roughly agrees with the current-producing capacity of the cell is

$$Zn(s) + 2MnO_2(s) + 2H_2O(l) \longrightarrow Zn(OH)_2(s) + 2MnOOH(s)$$

The Leclanché cell has a potential of 1.5 V. Combining more than one of these cells in series (anode to cathode, cathode to anode) gives batteries with voltages that are multiples of 1.5 V. If energy is withdrawn too rapidly from a Leclanché cell, the voltage drops because by-products that hinder the cathode reaction accumulate. A cell in this condition regains its voltage on standing. Unused Leclanché cells deteriorate because of a slow reaction between zinc and the ammonium ion. Common flashlight batteries are Leclanché cells.

The alkaline manganese(IV) oxide–zinc cell, which is illustrated in Figure 23.13, has replaced the Leclanché cell in many applications because it has several advantages: It yields a sustained operating voltage at large current drains, operates at low temperatures, has a longer shelf-life, and can, within limits, be recharged. Since the standard voltage of "alkaline batteries" is 1.54 V, they can be used in place of the Leclanché cell without problems.

As in the Leclanché cell, the anode and cathode reactions in alkaline batteries are the oxidation of zinc and the reduction of MnO_2. The electrolyte is potassium hydroxide, and the anode is a gel-thickened mixture of zinc dust and potassium

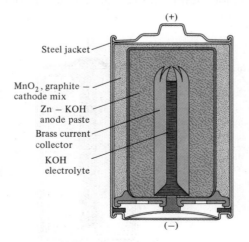

Steel jacket

MnO_2, graphite —
cathode mix
Zn – KOH
anode paste
Brass current
collector
KOH
electrolyte

(+)

(−)

Figure 23.13
Alkaline Manganese(IV) Oxide-
Zinc Cell

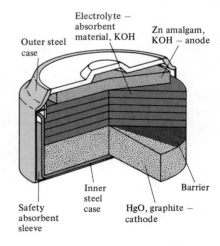

Electrolyte –
absorbent
material, KOH

Zn amalgam,
KOH – anode

Outer steel
case

Safety
absorbent
sleeve

Inner
steel
case

HgO, graphite –
cathode

Barrier

Figure 23.14
A "Button" Type Ruben-Mallory,
Mercury Battery

hydroxide. Either $[Zn(OH)_4]^{2-}$ or ZnO is formed at the anode and the final product of the complicated cathode reaction is $Mn(OH)_2$.

The solid-state revolution (Section 30.1) and the rapid growth in the availability of electronic watches and other small devices has stimulated the development of batteries that permit the use of smaller volumes of reactants and deliver larger currents at various potentials. A particularly successful battery of this type is the mercury cell, or Ruben-Mallory cell. This cell, also an alkaline cell, contains a zinc anode and a mercury(II) oxide cathode. The anode and cathode materials are both compacted powders. The space between these electrodes is filled with an absorbent material containing a sodium or potassium hydroxide electrolyte (Figure 23.14). The cell delivers electrical energy by the following reactions:

$$\textit{anode} \qquad Zn(s) + 2OH^- \longrightarrow ZnO(s) + H_2O + 2e^-$$
$$\textit{cathode} \qquad HgO(s) + H_2O(l) + 2e^- \longrightarrow Hg(l) + 2OH^-$$

at a potential of 1.35 V. No gaseous products result. Spent cells should be reprocessed for mercury recovery or treated to prevent mercury or mercury compounds from reentering the environment and causing contamination. A similar "button" type battery utilizes zinc and silver oxide.

23.15 STORAGE BATTERIES

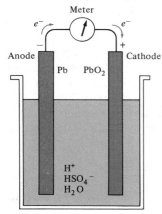

Discharging cell

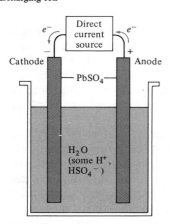

Charging cell

Figure 23.15
The Principles and Operation of the Lead Storage Cell during Discharge and Charge

Batteries that can be recharged by using electrical energy from an external source to reverse the initial oxidation–reduction reactions are called **storage batteries** (or accumulators, or secondary cells). They are particularly useful in applications that require electrical energy at one time but generate energy at another time, notably in the automobile. A storage battery provides electrical energy for starting the automobile and is then recharged by energy from a generator or alternator while the engine is running.

The most widely used storage cell is the lead storage cell. It is constructed of electrodes that are lead alloy grids packed with either finely divided spongy elemental lead or finely divided lead(IV) oxide. These electrodes are arranged alternately, separated by thin wooden or fiberglass sheets, and suspended in dilute sulfuric acid solution (about 6 M).

When the external circuit is closed in the discharging cell, the spongy lead is oxidized and forms lead(II) sulfate that adheres to the electrode.

$$\textit{anode} \qquad Pb(s) + HSO_4^- \underset{\text{charge}}{\overset{\text{discharge}}{\rightleftharpoons}} PbSO_4(s) + H^+ + 2e^- \qquad \textbf{(23.18)}$$

The released electrons reduce lead(IV) oxide preferentially, and in the presence of hydrogen ions and sulfate ion, adherent lead(II) sulfate forms here also, this time on the lead(IV) oxide cathode.

$$\textit{cathode} \qquad PbO_2(s) + 3H^+ + HSO_4^- + 2e^- \underset{\text{charge}}{\overset{\text{discharge}}{\rightleftharpoons}} PbSO_4(s) + 2H_2O(l) \qquad \textbf{(23.19)}$$

The net results of discharge are the conversion of the active chemicals on both electrodes to lead(II) sulfate and a decrease in the concentration of the sulfuric acid solution, as indicated by a decrease in the specific gravity of the solution. (When the service station attendant checks the charge of a battery, he measures the specific gravity of the sulfuric acid solution.) Reactions (23.18) and (23.19) are reversed when the battery is charged (Figure 23.15). Sulfuric acid is regenerated, and the specific gravity of the solution increases. During the charging operation, the cell becomes an electrolytic cell. The overall reaction in the lead storage battery is

$$Pb(s) + PbO_2(s) + 2H_2SO_4(aq) \underset{\text{charge}}{\overset{\text{discharge}}{\rightleftharpoons}} 2PbSO_4(s) + 2H_2O(l) \qquad \textbf{(23.20)}$$

Each lead storage cell develops a potential of 2 V. In practice, a number of these cells are connected in *parallel* (anode to anode, cathode to cathode) to increase the current that can be generated, and three or six such blocks of cells are connected in *series* to increase the voltage to 6 V or 12 V. The resulting lead storage batteries give excellent service for long periods of time, providing their liquid levels are maintained, they are never permitted to discharge completely, they are not allowed to freeze, and they are not subjected to frequent "quick charge" procedures. (A quick charge reverses the reactions so rapidly that the regenerated Pb and PbO_2 may not adhere completely to the electrodes and may fall off. The Pb and PbO_2 can build up to form a short-circuiting sludge if the quick charge procedure is repeated frequently. The same problem results if the car is driven over roads rough enough to dislodge the Pb and PbO_2.)

The nickel–cadmium alkaline storage cell (used in "ni-cad" batteries) has a longer life and delivers a more nearly constant potential than the lead storage cell. In this cell, a cadmium electrode and a metal grid containing a mixture of nickel oxides in various oxidation states are immersed in a potassium hydroxide solution. The chemical reactions during discharge and charge can be summarized by the equations

$$Cd(s) + 2OH^- \underset{\text{charge}}{\overset{\text{discharge}}{\rightleftharpoons}} Cd(OH)_2(s) + 2e^-$$

$$[NiOOH] + H_2O(l) + e^- \underset{\text{charge}}{\overset{\text{discharge}}{\rightleftharpoons}} Ni(OH)_2(s) + OH^-$$

where [NiOOH] represents a mixture of oxides and hydrates. No change in concentration of the electrolyte occurs in the overall cell reaction. This cell delivers current at a potential of about 1.4 V. Nickel–cadmium batteries are light and are often used in cordless appliances.

Much effort has been expended recently to develop compact storage cells that will deliver exceptionally large quantities of energy. This type of cell would be particularly useful for an electrically powered automobile that would avoid the pollution problems of the internal combustion gasoline engine. One such cell is the Weber-Kummer cell of the Ford Motor Company, a liquid sodium–sulfur cell. This cell is based upon molten sodium, separated by a sodium-ion-conducting porous ceramic barrier from molten sulfur contained in a porous electrode. The reactions occurring during discharge and charge are as follows:

$$2Na(l) \underset{\text{charge}}{\overset{\text{discharge}}{\rightleftharpoons}} 2Na^+ + 2e^- \qquad S(l) + 2e^- \underset{\text{charge}}{\overset{\text{discharge}}{\rightleftharpoons}} S^{2-}$$

To produce energy, this cell must be heated initially to 250–300 °C to melt the reactants; it then operates at this temperature.

23.16 FUEL CELLS   Burning fuel to obtain thermal energy that is then converted into electrical energy is a wasteful process. Heat is inevitably lost to the surroundings, and there are also thermodynamic limits to the amount of useful energy that can be produced. The best conventional power plant can operate at only about 40% efficiency. Theoretically, the electrochemical conversion of traditional fuels such as hydrocarbons to combustion products could be 100% efficient. While perfect efficiency seems unattainable, 60% has been called possible.

Much research is being devoted to the development of **fuel cells,** cells that produce electrical energy directly from the air oxidation of a fuel continuously supplied to the cell. The technical, economic, and practical problems to be overcome are great. These problems include difficulties in providing contact among the three phases needed in a fuel cell (the gaseous fuel, the liquid electrolyte, and the solid conductor), the corrosiveness of acid electrolyte systems or the buildup of carbonates in alkaline systems (from CO_2 in the air), the high cost of catalysts needed for the electrode reactions (metals such as platinum, palladium, and silver), and the problems of handling gaseous fuels containing hydrogen at either low temperatures or high pressures.

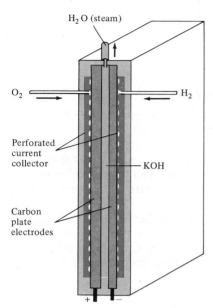

H₂O (steam)

O₂

H₂

Perforated current collector

KOH

Carbon plate electrodes

+   −

Figure 23.16
A Hydrogen-Oxygen Fuel Cell

A few test vehicles that run on energy from fuel cells have been operated. Fuel cells in which hydrogen is the fuel and oxygen is the oxidant have been built into a van by General Motors. Tanks of liquid hydrogen and liquid oxygen are carried in the back of the van and 32 fuel cells ride beneath the floorboards.

In alkaline hydrogen–oxygen fuel cells (Figure 23.16), the electrode reactions are

$$\text{anode} \qquad 2H_2(g) + 4OH^- \longrightarrow 4H_2O(l) + 4e^-$$
$$\text{cathode} \qquad O_2(g) + 2H_2O + 4e^- \longrightarrow 4OH^-$$

The cell reaction

$$2H_2(g) + O_2(g) \longrightarrow 2H_2O(l)$$

is simply the same reaction as the combustion of hydrogen.

Catalysts are necessary to facilitate the breaking of hydrogen–hydrogen bonds at the anode and oxygen–oxygen bonds at the cathode. In one fuel cell design, porous carbon electrodes are "activated" by the presence of metallic catalysts. The electrolyte is a concentrated aqueous potassium hydroxide solution, and the product water is removed as vapor in an excess of hydrogen. The cell operating temperature is 70–140 °C and each cell delivers about 0.9 V.

A partly "reformed" gaseous hydrocarbon fuel—a mixture of light hydrocarbons and hydrogen—is the fuel in one of the actively studied and promising fuel cell systems. Ammonia is also under investigation for use in fuel cells. The oxidation reaction and the overall cell reaction in an ammonia fuel cell are

$$2NH_3(g) + 6OH^- \longrightarrow N_2(g) + 6H_2O(l) + 6e^-$$
$$4NH_3(g) + 3O_2(g) \longrightarrow 2N_2(g) + 6H_2O(l)$$

23.17 CORROSION

Corrosion is the blanket name applied to a large variety of deterioration processes undergone by manufactured materials when they experience material loss and/or weakening during exposure to their environments. We are interested here in the corrosion of metals, which is an electrochemical phenomenon.

The corrosion of metals may appear as a general material loss all over the surface (often with discoloration and scaling, as in rusted iron), deep gouge formation (usually found in bends in pipes), uncontrolled enlargement of cracks and crevices, or apparently inexplicable pinhole formation. Weakening may be due not only to material loss, but also to embrittlement and cracking under conditions of stress, or selective leaching of constituents from an alloy (e.g., the loss of zinc from brass).

Corrosion is the principal route by which manufactured materials are reclaimed by the ever-increasing entropy of the universe, and it has been likened to the death and decay of living things. Corrosion serves the useful function of making room for new generations of improved equipment, although by the same token it is desirable to postpone it as long as possible. Therefore, corrosion has been studied extensively.

By far the bulk of corrosion occurs in materials exposed to the atmosphere, where complex interactions with particulates, atmospheric moisture, and gaseous sulfur compounds complicate the problem. The important aspects of corrosion can be illustrated by considering the corrosion of metals in the presence of aqueous electrolytes.

All metallic corrosion involves an anodic process, which is an oxidation reaction that releases electrons into the metal, and a cathodic process, which is a reduction reaction that consumes electrons at exactly the same rate. The anodic process is oxidation of the metal to its ions.

The cathodic process most often occurs on the same piece of metal as the anodic process, but it may also occur on an electrically connected, "more noble" metal (one that is less easily oxidized). The cathodic process is the reduction of hydrogen ions or oxygen from the environment. Hydrogen ions are reduced to hydrogen atoms, which are then catalytically combined on the metal surface to give hydrogen gas. The potentials for hydrogen ion reduction,

$$2H^+ + 2e^- \rightleftharpoons 2H \rightleftharpoons H_2(g)$$

and also oxygen molecule reduction,

$$O_2(g) + 4H^+ + 4e^- \rightleftharpoons 2H_2O(l)$$

(and hence the free energy or driving force) are clearly pH dependent (see Section 23.13). The higher the pH, the less favorable the reaction in each case.

The connection between the metal and the cathode may be direct, in which case the metal and the cathode together in their environment are called a *couple* and the corrosion is referred to as **couple action.** When couple action results from inadvertent contact with impurities or other metals, it can cause a dramatic and unexpected acceleration of corrosion.

In couple action a voltaic cell is formed by direct contact between two different substances. While the presence of two different substances is not necessary for corrosion to occur, couple action does accelerate the process. Consider a piece of zinc—when placed in an acidic aqueous medium it tends to liberate electrons:

$$Zn(s) \longrightarrow Zn^{2+} + 2e^- \tag{23.21}$$

This reaction proceeds only to a slight extent, for the electrons stay on the metal surface and the Zn^{2+} ions that have gone into solution remain close to the surface, preventing further reaction. If some of the electrons are removed from the zinc metal, then the Zn^{2+} ions can wander off into the solution and reaction (23.21), the corrosion of zinc, will continue to occur.

If a bit of graphite is embedded in the zinc surface, some of the electrons generated on the zinc move over to the graphite, which is a conductor. Hydrogen ions in the solution are attracted by the electrons, and the reaction

$$2H^+ + 2e^- \longrightarrow H_2(g)$$

occurs. The hydrogen seems to come from the carbon particle, but actually it is the result of the redox reaction, $Zn(s) + 2H^+ \longrightarrow Zn^{2+} + H_2(g)$, with zinc as the anode, and carbon as the inert cathode. If a piece of pure zinc immersed in an acid solution is touched with, say, a piece of platinum wire, the same thing happens. Some of the electrons leave the zinc surface for the other metal, and hydrogen forms on the platinum wire. In this case, the platinum wire is the inert cathode.

Investigation of the relationship between pH and potential for metals in the presence of hydrogen ion and oxygen, and the construction of pH–potential diagrams (like Figure 23.10, but usually much more complex) reveal regions of potential and pH where the metal and one of (usually) several possible impervious oxides are the thermodynamically favored species. In these regions the metal will not corrode. A material with an impervious oxide coating is called *passivated.* Some materials, such as stainless steels, have exceptionally wide passive potential–pH regions.

In other pH–potential regions, a metal is in equilibrium with its ions at finite concentrations, the anodic reaction will take place, and the metal will dissolve. For example, in acid solutions at moderate potentials, iron is in equilibrium with Fe^{2+} ions (see Figure 23.10) and so it dissolves. In aerated solutions, the Fe^{2+} ions are quickly oxidized to Fe_2O_3, which is the familiar red rust. Since Fe_2O_3 is not an impervious oxide, the oxidation continues.

Left to itself, a metal or metal couple in an aqueous environment will go to its "rest" or "corrosion" potential, at which the rates of the anode and cathode reactions are equal. If this falls in an unfavorable place on the pH–potential diagram, the metal will corrode. Corrosion control consists of interfering with the anode or cathode reaction. Most commonly, this is done by applying coatings. Also, the

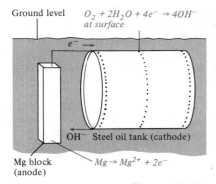

Ground level

$O_2 + 2H_2O + 4e^- \rightarrow 4OH^-$
at surface

$e^- \rightarrow$

OH^- Steel oil tank (cathode)

Mg block
(anode)

$Mg \rightarrow Mg^{2+} + 2e^-$

Figure 23.17
Cathodic Protection of an Oil Tank The magnesium is embedded in sand to aid flow of ions away from the surface. The electrons used at the surface of the oil tank come through the conductor from the magnesium and the tank is undisturbed.

potential can be forced into a more favorable region in the pH–potential relationship by an external power supply inserted between the equipment and an inert electrode. Such protection is usually cathodic—the potential is lowered, making the anodic reaction less favorable. For example, in pulp and paper mills, where strongly corrosive conditions prevail, expensive filter presses are continuously protected in this way. As a variation of this principle, protection is sometimes provided by what are called sacrificial anodes. For example, large magnesium blocks—the sacrificial anodes—are attached to the steel of an off-shore oil drilling platform or an underground oil tank (Figure 23.17). Because the magnesium is much more active than the steel, the anode reaction, oxidation of the metal, occurs at the magnesium instead of the steel, and the steel becomes the inert cathode. Massive sacrificial anodes are consumed fairly rapidly. Galvanizing—coating steel with zinc—works on the same principle. In the iron–zinc couple, zinc is the anode and iron the cathode.

Under some conditions, a coating can accelerate rather than deter corrosion. Iron cans used to be coated with tin. However, tin is more noble than iron. Any imperfections in the coating provide a metal couple with a very large cathode (the tin) to anode (the iron) area ratio, excellent conditions for rapid localized corrosion. Organic lacquers and plastics are now used to protect the metal. Household water pipes provide another example. Given conventional hardness and pH in water, we can usually rely on a shell of calcium carbonate to form in iron or copper pipes and protect them from corrosion. But if the pH is not quite right or the water is a little too soft, the coating may not be complete. Because a calcium carbonate coating does not interfere with the cathode reaction, the result is a very small active anode (the metal exposed where the coating is incomplete) connected to a large cathode. Here again are the conditions for very rapid localized corrosion, the formation of a pinhole in the pipe, and a leak in the basement. Water that creates such conditions is referred to as *aggressive water*.

SUMMARY

23.1 ELECTRON GAIN AND LOSS IN REDOX REACTIONS Every redox reaction can be divided into two half-reactions—an oxidation half-reaction and a reduction half-reaction—the sum of which is the net ionic equation for the total reaction. In any redox reaction involving ions, oxidation is the loss of electrons and reduction is the gain of electrons. Ion-electron equations include only the electrons and other species directly involved in the oxidation or reduction of a given atom, ion, or molecule. Such equations must be balanced as to number of atoms and charge. In writing ion-electron equations it is important not to show species as ions unless they actually exist in that form, and to avoid confusing oxidation numbers with ionic charges.

23.2 BALANCING REDOX EQUATIONS: HALF-REACTION METHOD To produce a balanced overall equation for a redox reaction, the number of electrons in the two ion-electron equations must be made equal before they are added. This fact is the basis for the half-reaction method for balancing redox equations which is summarized in Table 23.1.

23.3 ELECTROCHEMICAL CELLS **23.4** ELECTRODES AND CELL NOTATION Any device in which reaction that either produces or utilizes electrical energy occurs is called an electrochemical cell. Electrodes connected by an external conductor carry electrons into and out of a cell. The electrodes may or may not take part in the actual cell reaction. Each electrode and its surrounding electrolyte make up a half-cell; the half-reaction that occurs in a half-cell is an electrode reaction. Half-cells are connected by a salt bridge, which allows current to flow by means of mobile ions. A voltaic cell generates electrical energy by means of a spontaneous redox reaction. An electrolytic cell uses electrical energy from outside the cell to drive a nonspontaneous redox reaction. In both types of cells, the electrode at which oxidation occurs is the anode, and the electrode at which reduction occurs is the cathode. In both, anions move toward the anode and cations move toward the cathode. Notation for an electrochemical cell takes the form anode|anode electrolyte‖cathode electrolyte| cathode, where a single vertical line indicates physical contact between species in different phases and a double vertical line indicates a salt bridge or other means of permitting current flow while preventing mixing. Species in the same phase are separated by commas.

23.5 ELECTROCHEMICAL STOICHIOMETRY   **23.6** CELL POTENTIAL   **23.7** ELECTROMOTIVE FORCE AND FREE ENERGY   The charge on 1 mol of electrons, 96,485 C, is the faraday (F). The amount of electrical charge required by a given half-reaction is the number of moles of electrons transferred times the faraday. The cell potential (E), or electromotive force (emf), of a cell is the potential difference between the two half-cells. It is measured in volts (1 V = 1 J/C). Cell potential varies with the nature of the chemical reaction, the temperature, and the concentration of the reactants. The potential for one half-reaction is an electrode potential. The potential of a cell is related to the free energy change by the equation $\Delta G = -nFE$.

23.8 $E°$ DEFINED   **23.9** RELATIVE STRENGTHS OF OXIDIZING AND REDUCING AGENTS   **23.10** CALCULATING $E°$ VALUES FOR REDOX REACTIONS FROM ELECTRODE POTENTIALS   The H^+/H_2 redox couple is assigned a potential of exactly 0 V, and the redox potentials for other couples under standard state conditions are defined with respect to this reference point. Such potentials, called standard electrode potentials or standard reduction potentials, $E°$, are always given for the reaction written as reduction. A positive value of $E°$ indicates a spontaneous reaction (negative $\Delta G°$). Reactants in those couples with the most positive $E°$ values are the strongest oxidizing agents; products in those couples with the most negative $E°$ values are the strongest reducing agents (Table 23.5). Under standard state conditions, a spontaneous redox reaction will occur between a product in a given couple and a reactant in any couple with a more positive value of $E°$. The $E°$ value of a redox reaction can be calculated by adding the $E°$ values of the two half-cell reactions that it comprises. However, the half-reaction of the couple with the more negative standard reduction potential must first be reversed and the sign of its $E°$ value changed. The electrode potentials for two couples can be combined to give the electrode potential for a different couple, provided the number of electrons transferred in each half-reaction is taken into account.

23.11 ELECTROLYSIS   In electrolysis reactions in aqueous solution, reactions of H_2O, H^+, and OH^- are possible in addition to reactions of whatever other species are present. Theoretically, the anode reaction should be the one with the most negative reduction potential, and the cathode reaction should be the one with the most positive reduction potential. In practice, numerous effects, combined in what is called overvoltage, influence the voltage and the reactions that occur, and the outcome may be different.

23.12 CONDITIONS OTHER THAN STANDARD STATE   **23.13** REDOX EQUILIBRIA: FINDING K FROM $E°$ The cell potential under conditions other than standard state is given by the Nernst equation, $E = E° - (0.0592/n) \log Q$. Conditions under which different species are stable, and the equilibria between different species, as functions of pH and reduction potential are shown graphically in pH–potential diagrams. The standard reduction potential of a reaction is related to its equilibrium constant by the equation $\log K = (n/0.0592) E°$.

23.14 DRY CELL BATTERIES   **23.15** STORAGE BATTERIES   **23.16** FUEL CELLS   Common flashlight batteries are Leclanché cells, the overall reaction of which can be approximated as $Zn(s) + 2MnO_2(s) + 2H_2O(l) \rightarrow Zn(OH)_2(s) + 2MnOOH(s)$. Alkaline batteries also oxidize Zn and reduce MnO_2, but via somewhat different reactions. Mercury cells produce energy by oxidation of Zn and reduction of HgO to Hg and OH^-. Batteries that can be recharged by using electrical energy from an external source to reverse the redox reaction are called storage batteries. Among these is the lead storage battery (Equation 23.18). Nickel–cadmium alkaline storage batteries are light, long-lived, and deliver quite constant potential. Fuel cells produce electrical energy directly from the air oxidation of a fuel. Several such cells, utilizing fuels such as hydrogen, hydrocarbons, or ammonia, have been developed, but their technical and economic problems are still great.

23.17 CORROSION The corrosion of metals is an electrochemical process. It involves oxidation of the metal in conjunction with reduction of hydrogen ions or oxygen from the environment, processes favored by low pH. Under certain conditions, some materials tend to form impervious oxide coatings, which prevent corrosion. Corrosion may be avoided by the use of an externally applied potential, or by a sacrificial anode—a more active metal which is consumed instead of the metal being protected.

THOUGHTS ON CHEMISTRY

Volta Describes His Discoveries

ON THE ELECTRICITY EXCITED BY THE MERE CONTACT OF CONDUCTING SUBSTANCES OF DIFFERENT KINDS, by Alexander Volta

After a long silence, for which I shall offer no apology, I have the pleasure of communicating to you . . . some striking results I have obtained in pursuing my experiments on electricity excited by the mere mutual contact of different kinds of metal. . . .

I provide a few dozens of small round plates or disks of copper, brass, or rather silver, an inch in diameter more or less (pieces of coin, for example), and an equal number of plates of tin, or, what is better, of zinc, nearly of the same size and figure . . . I prepare also a pretty large number of circular pieces of pasteboard, or any other spongy matter capable of imbibing and retaining a great deal of water or moisture, with which they must be well impregnated in order to ensure success to the experiments. . . .

Having all these pieces ready in a good state . . . I have nothing to do but to arrange them, a matter exceedingly simple and easy. . . . I place them horizontally, on a table or any other stand, one of the metallic pieces, for example one of silver, and over the first I adapt one of zinc; on the second I place one of the moistened disks, then another plate of silver followed immediately by another of zinc, over which I place another of the moistened disks. In this manner I continue coupling a plate of silver with one of zinc and always in the same order, that is to say, the silver below and the zinc above it, or vice versa, according as I have begun, and interpose between each of these couples a moistened disk. I continue to form, of several of these stories, a column as high as possible without any danger of its falling. . . .

If, by means of an ample contact of the hand (well moistened) I establish on one side a good communication with one of the extremities of my electro-motive apparatus (we must give new names to instruments that are new not only in their form, but in their effects on the principle on which they depend); and on the other I apply the forehead, eye-lid, tip of the nose, also well moistened, or any other part of the body where the skin is very delicate: if I apply, I say, with a little pressure, any one of these delicate parts, well moistened, to the point of a metallic wire, communicating properly with the other extremity of the said apparatus, I experience, at the moment that the conducting circle is completed, at the place of the skin touched, and a little beyond it, a blow and a prick, which suddenly passes, and is repeated as many times as the circle is interrupted and restored. . . .

What proof more evident of the continuation of the electric current as long as the communication of the conductors forming the circle is *continued? — and that such a current is only suspended by interrupting that communication? This endless circulation of the electric fluid (this perpetual motion) may appear paradoxical and even inexplicable, but it is no less true and real, and you feel it, as I may say, with your hands.*

Alexander Volta, *On the Electricity Excited by the Mere Contact of Conducting Substances of Different Kinds*, Alexander Volta's letter to the Royal Society of London, March 20, 1800. Quoted from an English translation, *Philosophical Magazine*, September 1800, as reproduced in *Galvani-Volta*, by Bern Dibner (Burndy Library, Norwalk, Connecticut, 1952), pp. 42 ff.

QUESTIONS

Redox Revisited

23.1 Define oxidation and reduction in terms of electron gain or loss. What is the relationship between the number of electrons gained and lost in a redox reaction?

23.2 What is a redox couple? How is the symbol for a redox couple constructed?

23.3 Identify the two redox couples for each of the following reactions:

(a) $I_2(s) + H_2S(aq) \longrightarrow I^- + S(s) + H^+$
(b) $H_2O_2(aq) + I^- + H^+ \longrightarrow I_2(s) + H_2O(l)$
(c) $I^- + H^+ + NO_2^- \longrightarrow NO(g) + H_2O(l) + I_2(s)$
(d) $Al(s) + H_2SO_4(conc) + H^+ \longrightarrow Al^{3+} + H_2O(l) + SO_2(g)$
(e) $Zn(s) + OH^- + NO_3^- + H_2O(l) \longrightarrow$
$$NH_3(aq) + [Zn(OH)_4]^{2-}$$

23.4 Repeat Question 23.3 for

(a) $HNO_3(aq) + Cu(s) \longrightarrow Cu(NO_3)_2(aq) + NO(g) + H_2O(l)$
(b) $I_2(s) + OH^- \longrightarrow I^- + IO_3^- + H_2O(l)$
(c) $H_2S(aq) + Cr_2O_7^{2-} + H^+ \longrightarrow Cr^{3+} + H_2O(l) + S(s)$

23.5 For each reaction given in Question 23.3, write the ion-electron equations and balance the overall equations using the half-reaction method.

23.6 For each reaction given in Question 23.4, write the ion-electron equations and balance the overall equations using the half-reaction method.

23.7 Balance the following equations using the half-reaction method. [Note that in most cases H^+ or OH^- and H_2O are not shown. You should be able to decide whether the system is neutral, acidic, or alkaline with a little detective work, and add H^+ or OH^- and H_2O as needed to balance the equation.]

(a) $[Fe(CN)_6]^{4-} + CrO_4^{2-} \longrightarrow [Fe(CN)_6]^{3-} + Cr_2O_3(s)$
(b) $ClO^- + I_2(s) \longrightarrow Cl^- + IO_3^-$
(c) $Mn(OH)_2(s) + H_2O_2(aq) \longrightarrow MnO_2(s)$
(d) $CN^- + [Fe(CN)_6]^{3-} \longrightarrow CNO^- + [Fe(CN)_6]^{4-}$
(e) $N_2H_4(aq) + Cu(OH)_2(s) \longrightarrow N_2(g) + Cu(s)$

23.8 Repeat Question 23.7 for

(a) $Zn(s) + NO_3^- \longrightarrow Zn^{2+} + NH_4^+$
(b) $Cu(s) + NO_3^- \longrightarrow NO(g) + Cu^{2+}$
(c) $P_4(s) + NO_3^- \longrightarrow H_3PO_4(aq) + NO(g)$
(d) $H_2S(aq) + NO_3^- \longrightarrow S(s) + NO(g)$
(e) $Fe(s) + NO_3^- \longrightarrow Fe^{3+} + N_2(g)$

23.9 Manganese(IV) oxide and lead(IV) oxide react in the presence of nitric acid to give permanganic acid ($HMnO_4$) and lead(II) nitrate. Write the balanced chemical equation for this reaction using the half-reaction method.

23.10* Write the ion-electron equation for each half-reaction described. [You may need to do a little detective work to determine the actual species that are involved in each case. For example, Cl in the +3 oxidation state exists as the weak acid $HClO_2$ in neutral and acidic solutions but as ClO_2^- in alkaline solutions.] (a) Br, +5 to −1 in acidic solution; (b) Co, +3 to +2 in alkaline solution; (c) Cl, +5 to −1 in alkaline solution; (d) Pb, +4 to +2 in acidic solution; and (e) Pb, +4 to +2 in alkaline solution.

Fundamentals of Electrochemistry

23.11 What are the two classifications of electrochemical cells? What is the difference between them?

23.12 Distinguish clearly between the terms "anode" and "cathode." In writing the notation for an electrochemical cell, where do the anode and the cathode half-cells appear?

23.13 In writing the notation for an electrochemical cell, what does (a) a vertical line, (b) a comma, (c) the formula of a substance in parentheses, and (d) a double vertical line represent?

23.14 What is the purpose of a salt bridge?

23.15 Prepare a simple sketch of a voltaic cell showing the anode, the cathode, the signs of the electrodes, and the direction of electron and ion flow for the cell represented by the notation

$$Ag(s)|AgCl(s)|HCl(aq)|Cl_2(g)|(C)$$

Is a salt bridge necessary for this reaction?

23.16 Repeat Question 23.15 for a voltaic cell in which the following reaction occurs:

$$Mg(s) + F_2(g) \longrightarrow MgF_2(l)$$

Write the cell notation for this electrochemical cell.

23.17 Write the ion-electron equations for the half-reactions and overall cell equation for the electrochemical cell represented by

$$(Pt)|H_2(g)|HCl(aq)||Fe^{3+}, Fe^{2+}|(Pt)$$

23.18 The Edison cell, represented by
$Fe(s)|Fe(OH)_2(s)|LiOH(aq),$
$$KOH(aq)|Ni(OH)_2(s)|[NiOOH](s)|(inert)$$

is sometimes used in place of lead storage batteries when weight considerations are important. Write the ion-electron equations for the half-reactions describing the oxidation and reduction processes and write the overall cell equation.

23.19 What is Faraday's law? How do we calculate the number of moles of electrons from the electrical charge? How do we calculate the amount of electrical charge from electrical current?

23.20 Whether we perform a redox reaction electrochemically or not, the same chemical change will occur. What is the advantage of carrying out the process electrochemically?

23.21 Describe the operation of an electrochemical cell.

23.22 Write the equation relating the potential of an electrochemical cell or half-reaction to the free energy change. Define all symbols.

23.23 What is the sign convention for potential used to describe the spontaneity of a reaction?

Standard Reduction Potentials
23.24 How would a list of standard oxidation potentials differ from Table 23.5?

23.25 How does the numerical value of an electrode potential reflect the strength of a reducing agent?

23.26 The standard reduction potential is 2.9 V for $F_2(g)/F^-$, 0.8 V for $Ag^+/Ag(s)$, 0.5 for $Cu^+/Cu(s)$, 0.3 V for $Cu^{2+}/Cu(s)$, -0.4 V for $Fe^{2+}/Fe(s)$, -2.7 V for Na^+/Na, and -2.9 V for $K^+/K(s)$. (a) Arrange these oxidizing agents in order of increasing strength. (b) Which oxidizing agents will oxidize Cu under standard state conditions?

23.27 The standard reduction potential is 1.455 V for the $PbO_2(s)/Pb(s)$ couple, 1.360 V for $Cl_2(g)/Cl^-$, 3.06 V for $F_2(g)/HF(aq)$, and 1.776 V for $H_2O_2(aq)/H_2O(l)$. Under standard state conditions, (a) which is the strongest oxidizing agent, (b) which oxidizing agent(s) could oxidize lead to lead(IV) oxide, and (c) which oxidizing agent(s) could oxidize fluorine in an acidic solution?

23.28 The standard reduction potential is -1.245 V for the $Zn(OH)_2(s)/Zn(s)$ couple, -2.690 V for $Mg(OH)_2(s)/Mg(s)$, -0.877 V for $Fe(OH)_2(s)/Fe(s)$, and -2.30 V for $Al(OH)_3(s)/Al(s)$. Under standard state conditions, (a) which is the strongest reducing agent, (b) which reducing agent(s) could reduce $Zn(OH)_2(s)$ to $Zn(s)$, and (c) which reducing agent(s) could reduce $Fe(OH)_2(s)$ to $Fe(s)$?

23.29 Using Table 23.5, identify an oxidizing agent for each case that, under standard state conditions, will oxidize (a) $I_2(s)$ to IO_3^-, but not Cl^- to $Cl_2(g)$; (b) $Fe(s)$ to Fe^{2+}, but not $Pb(s)$ to Pb^{2+}; (c) $Zn(s)$, but not $Cd(s)$, in alkaline solution.

23.30 When using $E°$ values to predict the course of a given oxidation–reduction reaction, what restrictions on reaction conditions must a chemist keep in mind?

23.31 How do we combine standard reduction potentials for half-reactions to find the potential of a redox reaction? How do we combine standard reduction potentials for half-reactions to find the potential of a new half-reaction?

23.32 What is the relationship between the potential at nonstandard state conditions and $E°$ and the reaction quotient?

23.33 What happens to an electrochemical cell once equilibrium has been reached? How can the equilibrium constant be calculated from $E°$?

23.34 The equilibrium constants of the following reactions:
$$A + B^+ \longrightarrow A^+ + B \qquad \text{(i)}$$
$$A + B^{2+} \longrightarrow A^{2+} + B \qquad \text{(ii)}$$
$$A + B^{3+} \longrightarrow A^{3+} + B \qquad \text{(iii)}$$
all have the same numerical values. Choose the correct statement concerning $E°$ for these reactions: (a) reaction (i) has the largest $E°$ and reaction (iii) has the smallest value, (b) reaction (iii) has the largest value of $E°$, (c) the $E°$ values cannot be determined unless the identities of A and B are known, (d) all three reactions have the same value of $E°$.

23.35 How do we predict which of several reduction reactions will take place at the cathode during electrolysis? What about the oxidation processes at the anode?

23.36 On the basis of standard reduction potentials, the reaction
$$Cu(s) + 2K^+ \longrightarrow Cu^{2+} + 2K(s)$$
is predicted to be unfavorable (see Table 23.5). To make this reaction "go," a chemist supplied electrical energy from an external source, but to his amazement a flame burst out in the cell. What had the chemist forgotten to consider?

23.37 An examination question concerned the half-reactions in the electrolysis of a sodium chloride solution:
$$2NaCl(aq) + 2H_2O(l) \xrightarrow{\text{electrolysis}} 2NaOH(aq) + H_2(g) + Cl_2(g)$$
A student wrote that chlorine is liberated at the anode and sodium at the cathode, followed by a second reaction:
$$2Na(s) + 2H_2O(l) \longrightarrow 2NaOH(aq) + H_2(g)$$
What is wrong with this answer?

23.38* Write the balanced equation for the half-reaction that takes place at each electrode as an electrical current is passed through a 1 M aqueous solution of each of the following substances using inert electrodes: (a) $AgNO_3$, (b) $CuBr_2$, and (c) H_2SO_4. (You may want to refer to Table 23.5 to decide which half-reactions are most favorable.)

Practical Electrochemistry
23.39 Does the physical size of a commercial cell govern the potential that it will deliver? What will the size govern?

23.40 Briefly describe how a storage cell works.

23.41 How does a fuel cell differ from a dry cell or a storage battery?

23.42* Why do we measure "open-circuit" potentials for electrochemical cells? What happens to the potential of a cell if an appreciable current is being drawn from the cell?

23.43 Many electronic calculators use rechargeable nickel–cadmium batteries. The overall equation for the spontaneous reaction in these cells is

$$Cd(s) + 2[NiOOH](s) + 2H_2O(l) \xrightarrow{KOH}$$
$$Cd(OH)_2(s) + 2Ni(OH)_2(s)$$

What are the oxidation states of Cd in (a) Cd and (b) $Cd(OH)_2$ and of Ni in (c) [NiOOH] and (d) $Ni(OH)_2$? What is the (e) oxidizing agent, (f) reducing agent, (g) substance oxidized, and (h) substance reduced? Write the shorthand notation for (i) the reduction couple and (j) the overall cell. During the middle of an examination, the battery in a student's calculator failed. (k) What happened chemically? (l) Write the overall cell equation for the recharge cycle of this cell.

Answers to Selected Questions

23.4 (a) $NO_3^-/NO(g)$, $Cu^{2+}/Cu(s)$; (b) $I_2(s)/I^-$, $IO_3^-/I_2(s)$; (c) $Cr_2O_7^{2-}/Cr^{3+}$, $S(s)/H_2S(aq)$

23.6 (a) $NO_3^- + 4H^+ + 3e^- \rightarrow NO(g) + 2H_2O(l)$, $Cu(s) \rightarrow Cu^{2+} + 2e^-$, $3Cu(s) + 8HNO_3(aq) \rightarrow 2NO(g) + 4H_2O(l) + 3Cu(NO_3)_2(aq)$, (b) $I_2(s) + 2e^- \rightarrow 2I^-$, $I_2(s) + 12OH^- \rightarrow 2IO_3^- + 6H_2O(l) + 10e^-$, $3I_2(s) + 6OH^- \rightarrow 5I^- + IO_3^- + 3H_2O(l)$; (c) $H_2S(aq) \rightarrow S(s) + 2H^+ + 2e^-$, $Cr_2O_7^{2-} + 14H^+ + 6e^- \rightarrow 2Cr^{3+} + 7H_2O(l)$, $3H_2S(aq) + Cr_2O_7^{2-} + 8H^+ \rightarrow 2Cr^{3+} + 7H_2O(l) + 3S(s)$

23.8 (a) $4Zn(s) + NO_3^- + 10H^+ \rightarrow NH_4^+ + 4Zn^{2+} + 3H_2O(l)$, (b) $3Cu(s) + 2NO_3^- + 8H^+ \rightarrow 3Cu^{2+} + 2NO(g) + 4H_2O(l)$, (c) $3P_4(s) + 20NO_3^- + 20H^+ + 8H_2O(l) \rightarrow 12H_3PO_4(aq) + 20NO(g)$, (d) $3H_2S(aq) + 2NO_3^- + 2H^+ \rightarrow 3S(s) + 2NO(g) + 4H_2O(l)$, (e) $10Fe(s) + 6NO_3^- + 36H^+ \rightarrow 3N_2(g) + 10Fe^{3+} + 18H_2O(l)$

23.9 $2MnO_2(s) + 3PbO_2(s) + 6HNO_3(aq) \rightarrow 2HMnO_4(aq) + 3Pb(NO_3)_2(aq) + 2H_2O(l)$

23.13 (a) physical contact between two different phases, (b) two substances in the same phase, (c) an inert electrode, (d) a salt bridge or membrane

23.18 $Fe(s) + 2OH^- \rightarrow Fe(OH)_2(s) + 2e^-$,
$[NiOOH](s) + H_2O(l) + e^- \rightarrow Ni(OH)_2(s) + OH^-$,
$Fe(s) + 2[NiOOH](s) + 2H_2O(l) \rightarrow Fe(OH)_2(s) + 2Ni(OH)_2(s)$

23.19 The extent to which an electrochemical reaction occurs is related to the number of moles of electrons transferred; divide the total charge by Faraday's constant; multiply current (expressed in A) by time (expressed in s) to give charge.

23.24 Each half-reaction would be reversed, values of $E°$ would be the same but with opposite sign.

23.27 (a) $F_2(g)$, (b) $H_2O_2(aq)$ and $F_2(g)$, (c) none will

23.29 (a) $Cr_2O_7^{2-}$, (b) Ni^{2+}, (c) $H_2O(l)$

23.34 (a)

23.37 H^+ is reduced at the cathode, not Na^+.

23.39 No, potential is dependent only on the half-reactions; size determines the amount of electrical work that will be produced.

23.43 (a) 0, (b) +2, (c) +3, (d) +2, (e) [NiOOH](s), (f) Cd, (g) Cd, (h) [NiOOH](s), (i) [NiOOH](s)/Ni(OH)$_2$(s), (j) $Cd(s)|Cd(OH)_2(s)|OH^-|Ni(OH)_2(s)|[NiOOH](s)|(inert)$, (k) equilibrium was reached, (l) $Cd(OH)_2(s) + 2Ni(OH)_2(s) \xrightarrow{electricity} Cd(s) + 2[NiOOH](s) + 2H_2O(l)$

PROBLEMS

Electrochemical Stoichiometry

23.1 What mass of zinc(II) ion will be reduced by one mole of electrons?

23.2 How many moles of electrons would be required to reduce 0.100 g of Eu^{3+} to the metal? *Answer* 1.97×10^{-3} mol e^-

23.3 The same quantity of electrical charge that deposited 0.583 g of silver was passed through a solution of a gold salt and 0.355 g of gold was formed. What is the oxidation state of gold in this salt?

23.4 What mass of molten sodium would be produced by electrolyzing molten sodium bromide using a current of 15 A for 3.0 h? *Answer* 39 g

23.5 Calculate the current required to deposit 0.50 g of elemental platinum from a solution containing the $[PtCl_6]^{2-}$ ion within a period of 5.0 h.

23.6 What time would be required to plate an iron platter with 5.0 g of silver using a solution containing the $[Ag(CN)_2]^-$ ion and a current of 1.5 A? *Answer* 3.0×10^3 s

23.7 A sample of Al_2O_3 dissolved in a molten fluoride bath is electrolyzed using a current of 1.00 A. (a) What is the rate of production of Al in grams per hour? (b) The oxygen liberated at the positive carbon electrode reacts with the carbon to form CO_2. What mass of CO_2 is produced per hour?

Calculating $E°$

23.8 The standard reduction potential is -0.76 V for the $Zn^{2+}/Zn(s)$ couple and 1.36 V for the $Cl_2(g)/Cl^-$ couple. Write the equation for the oxidation of $Zn(s)$ by $Cl_2(g)$. Calculate the potential of this reaction under standard state conditions. Is this a spontaneous reaction?

23.9 Using the standard reduction potentials given for the appropriate couples, calculate $E°$ for each reaction and indicate whether or not each of the reactions described below will be spontaneous under standard state conditions:
(a) $E° = -0.809$ V for $Cd(OH)_2(s)/Cd(s)$ and $E° = 0.098$ V for $HgO(s)/Hg(l)$

$$Cd(s) + HgO(s) + H_2O(l) \longrightarrow Hg(l) + Cd(OH)_2(s)$$

(b) $E° = -0.036$ V for $Fe^{3+}/Fe(s)$ and $E° = 0.0000$ V for $H^+/H_2(g)$

$$2Fe(s) + 6H^+ \longrightarrow 2Fe^{3+} + 3H_2(g)$$

23.10 Repeat Problem 23.9 for the following:
(a) $E° = 1.36$ V for $Cl_2(g)/Cl^-$ and $E° = 1.33$ V for $Cr_2O_7^{2-}/Cr^{3+}$

$$6Cl^- + 14H^+ + Cr_2O_7^{2-} \longrightarrow 2Cr^{3+} + 3Cl_2(g) + 7H_2O(l)$$

(b) $E° = 0.17$ V for $SO_4^{2-}/H_2SO_3(aq)$ and $E° = 0.96$ V for $NO^{3-}/NO(g)$

$$3H_2SO_3(aq) + 2NO_3^- \longrightarrow$$
$$2NO(g) + 4H^+ + H_2O(l) + 3SO_4^{2-}$$

Answer (a) -0.03 V, nonspontaneous; (b) 0.79 V, spontaneous

23.11 An electrochemical cell was needed in which hydrogen and oxygen would react to form water. Using the following standard reduction potentials for the couples given, determine which set of reactions gives the maximum output potential: $E° = -0.828$ V for $H_2O(l)/H_2(g),OH^-$; $E° = 0.0000$ V for $H^+/H_2(g)$; $E° = 1.229$ V for $O_2(g),H^+/H_2O(l)$; and $E° = 0.401$ V for $O_2(g),H_2O(l)/OH^-$.

23.12 The element ytterbium forms both $+2$ and $+3$ cations in aqueous solution. $E° = -2.797$ V for $Yb^{2+}/Yb(s)$ and -2.267 V for $Yb^{3+}/Yb(s)$. What is the standard state reduction potential for the Yb^{3+}/Yb^{2+} couple?

23.13 The standard reduction potential for Cu^+ to $Cu(s)$ is 0.521 V and for Cu^{2+} to $Cu(s)$ is 0.337 V. Calculate $E°$ for Cu^{2+}/Cu^+. *Answer* 0.153 V

23.14 The standard reduction potential for $Cu^+/Cu(s)$ is 0.521 V and $K_{sp} = 5.2 \times 10^{-9}$ for $CuBr(s)$ at 25 °C. Calculate $E°$ for the reduction of $CuBr(s)$:

$$CuBr(s) + e^- \longrightarrow Cu(s) + Br^-$$

23.15 At 25 °C, $E° = 0.071$ V for the reduction of AgBr and 0.799 V for the reduction of Ag^+. Calculate K_{sp} for $AgBr(s)$.

23.16 At 25 °C, $E° = 0.142$ V for the reduction of S from 0 to -2 in acidic media and -0.447 V in alkaline media. Calculate K for the reaction

$$H_2S(aq) \rightleftharpoons 2H^+ + S^{2-}$$

Answer 1.2×10^{-20}

Calculating E

23.17 Calculate the potential associated with the half-reaction

$$Co(s) \longrightarrow Co^{2+} + 2e^-$$

given that the concentration of the cobalt(II) ion is 1×10^{-4} M. The standard reduction potential for the $Co^{2+}/Co(s)$ couple is -0.277 V.

23.18 Calculate the reduction potential for hydrogen ion in a system having a perchloric acid concentration of 1×10^{-4} M and a hydrogen pressure of 2 atm. (Recall that $HClO_4$ is a strong acid in aqueous solution.) *Answer* -0.25 V

23.19 What is the concentration of Ag^+ in a half-cell if the reduction potential of the Ag^+/Ag couple is changed from $E° = 0.80$ V to 0.35 V?

23.20 The potential of the cell for the reaction

$$M(s) + 2H^+(1.0\ M) \longrightarrow H_2(g, 1.0\ atm) + M^{2+}(0.10\ M)$$

is 0.500 V. What is the standard reduction potential for the $M^{2+}/M(s)$ couple? *Answer* -0.470 V

23.21 The standard reduction potentials for the $H^+/H_2(g)$ and $O_2(g),H^+/H_2O(l)$ couples are 0.0000 V and 1.229 V, respectively. Write the half-reactions, the overall reaction, and calculate $E°$ for the reaction

$$2H_2(g) + O_2(g) \longrightarrow 2H_2O(l)$$

Calculate E for the cell when the pressure of H_2 is 5.0 atm and of O_2 is 9.0 atm.

23.22 Consider the cell represented by the notation

$$Zn(s)|ZnCl_2(aq)|Cl_2(g,\ 1\ atm)|(C)$$

The standard reduction potentials are -0.763 V for $Zn^{2+}/Zn(s)$ and 1.360 V for $Cl_2(g)/Cl^-$ at 25 °C. Calculate $E°$ and E for the cell when the concentration of the $ZnCl_2$ is 0.10 mol/L.

23.23 Consider the following unbalanced equation:

$$Hg(l) + Fe^{3+}(aq) \longrightarrow Hg_2^{2+}(aq) + Fe^{2+}(aq)$$

(a) Write the ion-electron equations for the half-reactions and the overall cell equation. (b) Write the shorthand notation for this cell. The standard reduction potential at 25 °C is 0.788 V for $Hg_2^{2+}/Hg(l)$ and 0.771 V for Fe^{3+}/Fe^{2+}. (c) Find $E°$ for the reaction. Is the reaction spontaneous under standard state conditions? (d) When $[Hg_2^{2+}] = 0.0010$ mol/L $[Fe^{2+}] = 0.10$ mol/L, and $[Fe^{3+}] = 1.00$ mol/L, what is E for the cell? Is the reaction more, less, or identically favorable under these conditions compared to standard state conditions? *Answer* (a) $2Hg(l) \rightarrow Hg_2^{2+} + 2e^-$, $Fe^{3+} + e^- \rightarrow Fe^{2+}$, $2Hg(l) + 2Fe^{3+} \rightarrow 2Fe^{2+} + Hg_2^{2+}$; (b) (inert)$|Hg(l)|Hg_2^{2+}||Fe^{2+},Fe^{3+}|$ (inert); (c) -0.017 V, nonspontaneous; (d) 0.131 V, more favorable

Thermodynamics of Electrochemical Cells

23.24 At 1000 K, $\Delta G° = -81.06$ kJ for the reaction

$$Ag(s) + \tfrac{1}{2}Cl_2(g) \longrightarrow AgCl(l)$$

What is the potential of an electrochemical cell based on this reaction? *Answer* 0.8401 V

23.25 $E° = -0.036$ V for the $Fe^{3+}/Fe(s)$ reduction couple. Calculate $\Delta G°$ for the reactions

$$Fe^{3+} + 3e^- \longrightarrow Fe(s)$$
$$\tfrac{1}{3}Fe^{3+} + e^- \longrightarrow \tfrac{1}{3}Fe(s)$$

23.26 $E° = -1.529$ V for the reduction of Zr^{4+}:

$$Zr^{4+} + 4e^- \longrightarrow Zr(s)$$

Calculate $\Delta G°$ for this reaction. *Answer* 590.1 kJ

23.27 The standard free energy of formation of water at 25 °C is -237.2 kJ/mol. What potential would be expected from a fuel cell consuming hydrogen and oxygen that is operating under standard state conditions?

23.28 Calculate the value of the equilibrium constant for the reaction

$$2K(s) + 2H_2O(l) \rightleftharpoons 2K^+ + 2OH^- + H_2(g)$$

The standard reduction potential is -2.925 V for $K^+/K(s)$ and -0.8281 V for $H_2O(l)/H_2(g),OH^-$.

23.29 The standard reduction potential is 1.087 V for $Br_2(aq)/Br^-$ and 1.360 V for $Cl_2(g)/Cl^-$. Calculate the equilibrium constant for the reaction

$$2Br^- + Cl_2(g) \rightleftharpoons Br_2(aq) + 2Cl^-$$

Answer 1.7×10^9

23.30 Using the following half-reaction and $E°$ data at 25 °C:

$$PbSO_4(s) + 2e^- \longrightarrow Pb(s) + SO_4^{2-} \qquad E° = -0.359 \text{ V}$$
$$PbI_2(s) + 2e^- \longrightarrow Pb(s) + 2I^- \qquad E° = -0.365 \text{ V}$$

calculate the equilibrium constant for the reaction

$$PbSO_4(s) + 2I^- \rightleftharpoons PbI_2(s) + SO_4^{2-}$$

23.31* Assuming $K = 1.00 \times 10^{-14}$ for the reaction

$$H_2O(l) \rightleftharpoons H^+ + OH^-$$

determine $E°$ for this reaction and write the notation for an electrochemical cell that could generate this value of emf. *Answer* -0.829 V, $(Pt)|H_2(g)|H^+\|OH^-, H_2O(l)|H_2(g)|(Pt)$

Additional Problems

23.32 A particular electrochemical cell consists of one half-cell in which a silver wire coated with $AgCl(s)$ dips into a 1 M KCl solution and another half-cell in which a piece of platinum dips into a solution that is 0.1 M in $CrCl_3$, 0.001 M in $K_2Cr_2O_7$, and 1 M in HCl. In the cell described, the following reaction takes place:

$$Ag(s) + Cr_2O_7^{2-} + Cl^- + H^+ \longrightarrow AgCl(s) + Cr^{3+} + H_2O(l)$$

The standard reduction potentials are 1.33 V and 0.22 V for the $Cr_2O_7^{2-}/Cr^{3+}$ and $AgCl(s)/Ag,Cl^-$ couples, respectively. Write (a) the ion-electron equations for the half-reactions for this cell and the overall cell equation. Determine (b) the standard state potential and (c) the potential of the cell under the above nonstandard state conditions. (d) Calculate the equilibrium constant for the reaction.

23.33 The following reaction takes place in an electrochemical cell:

$$Sn(s) + 2AgCl(s) \longrightarrow SnCl_2(aq) + 2Ag(s)$$

For $AgCl(s)/Ag(s),Cl^-$, $E° = 0.222$ V and for $Sn^{2+}/Sn(s)$, $E° = -0.136$ V. (a) Determine $E°$ for this cell at 25 °C. (b) What is the cell potential given that the concentration of the $SnCl_2$ is 0.10 mol/L? (c) What would be the resulting cell potential if the $SnCl_2$ solution were diluted tenfold? (d) At equilibrium, the cell potential assumes a unique value. What is this value? (e) From the result in (d), calculate the equilibrium constant. (f) What is the equilibrium concentration of Sn^{2+}? *Answer* (a) 0.358 V, (b) 0.429 V, (c) 0.518 V, (d) 0 V, (e) 1×10^{12}, (f) 6×10^3 mol/L

23.34 Consider the electrochemical cell represented by $Zn(s)|Zn^{2+}\|Fe^{3+}|Fe(s)$. (a) Write the ion-electron equations for the half-reactions and overall cell equation. (b) The standard reduction potentials for $Zn^{2+}/Zn(s)$ and $Fe^{3+}/Fe(s)$ are -0.763 V and -0.036 V, respectively, at 25 °C. Determine the standard potential for the reaction. (c) Determine E for the cell when the concentration of Fe^{3+} is 10 mol/L and that of Zn^{2+} is 1×10^{-3} mol/L. (d) If 150 mA is to be drawn from this cell for a period of 15 min, what is the minimum mass for the zinc electrode?

23.35* The production of uranium metal from purified uranium dioxide ore consists of the following steps:

$$UO_2(s) + 4HF(g) \longrightarrow UF_4(s) + 2H_2O(l)$$
$$UF_4(s) + 2Mg(s) \longrightarrow U(s) + 2MgF_2(aq)$$

What is the oxidation number of U in (a) UO_2, (b) UF_4, and (c) U? Identify (d) the reducing agent and (e) the substance reduced. (f) If the second reaction were performed electrochemically, predict $E°$ for the reaction given $E° = -1.50$ V for $U^{4+}/U(s)$ and -2.363 V for $Mg^{2+}/Mg(s)$. (g) What current could the second reaction produce if 1.00 g of UF_4 reacted each minute? (h) What volume of $HF(g)$ at 25 °C and 10.0 atm would be required to produce 1.00 g of U? (i) Would 1.00 g of Mg be enough to produce 1.00 g of U? *Answer* (a) $+4$, (b) $+4$, (c) 0, (d) $Mg(s)$, (e) $UF_4(s)$, (f) 0.86 V, (g) 20.5 A, (h) 0.0411 L, (i) yes

CHAPTER 24

Molecular Orbital Theory

Erwin Schrödinger was one of the architects of quantum mechanics (Chapter 8). The description of bonding by molecular orbital theory, discussed in this chapter, grows out of the mathematics of quantum mechanics. Schrödinger is most often remembered for the "Schrödinger equation," one of the first fundamental mathematical expressions of quantum theory — for the hydrogen atom with its one electron the equation is

Planck's constant

variation in probability of finding electron in a three-dimensional space

quantized energy levels of electron

$$\frac{h^2}{8\pi^2 m}\left(\frac{\partial^2 \psi}{\partial x^2} + \frac{\partial^2 \psi}{\partial y^2} + \frac{\partial^2 \psi}{\partial z^2}\right) + (V - E)\psi = 0$$

electron mass

potential energy of electron

Schrödinger was an individual with, in his own words, a "keen longing for unified, all embracing knowledge." In response to this longing, he set out, in a book called What Is Life? to explore the question, "How can the events in space and time which take place within the spatial boundary of a living organism be accounted for by physics and chemistry?" (See Thoughts on Chemistry at the end of this chapter.)

Eventually, he felt, there was no doubt that physics and chemistry would achieve an understanding of life in terms of energy and molecules. But first these sciences would have to recognize an essential difference between living organisms and the systems they had been studying. Many of the laws of physics are based on the average behavior of large collections of identical particles. Living organisms, on the other hand, are unique. The code that leads, say, one egg to grow into a frog while another egg grows into a white rabbit must, Schrödinger concluded, lie in a "well-ordered association of atoms." Specific differences in the arrangement of the atoms in a small number of molecules must determine the distinctive features of different organisms.

Writing before the mechanism of heredity was understood, Schrödinger had anticipated the field of molecular genetics. Francis H. C. Crick, who was a physicist, read What Is Life? a few years after it was written. The book helped to inspire a change in the direction of Crick's career: He moved into biology. In 1962, Crick shared a Nobel prize for the discovery, with James D. Watson and Maurice H. F. Wilkins, of the structure of DNA (Section 33.22), which carries the coded message of heredity from one generation to the next.

So far we have used Lewis structures, valence-shell electron-pair repulsion theory, and valence bond theory to describe molecular structures and covalent bonds. We are about to introduce molecular orbital theory for the same purposes. Why are there so many ways of describing the same phenomena? As is often the case in science, each of several different approaches is useful, while each has its limitations. Lewis structures and VSEPR are simple and nonmathematical, while valence bond and molecular orbital theories relate bonding to electronic structure and quantum theory. Those who are interested in such things can push valence bond and molecular orbital theories to greater and greater levels of mathematical sophistication. For our purposes, it is sufficient to understand in a general way the differences between the valence bond and molecular orbital theories of bonding.

PRINCIPLES OF MOLECULAR ORBITAL THEORY

24.1 VALENCE BOND THEORY VERSUS MOLECULAR ORBITAL THEORY

Molecular orbital theory explains bond formation as the occupation by electrons of orbitals characteristic of bonded atoms rather than individual atoms. As in valence bond theory, molecular orbital theory begins with atomic orbitals of similar energy that are able to overlap enough to allow interaction. One approach to simplifying the mathematics is to begin with the functions that describe the individual atomic orbitals and then combine them. The result is a mathematical description and a physical picture of a new orbital — a molecular orbital.

A **molecular orbital** is the space in which an electron with a specific energy is most likely to be found in the vicinity of two or more nuclei that are bonded together. The electron can be closer to one nucleus at one instant and closer to the other nucleus at another instant. The difference between bonds in the molecular orbital and valence bond theories is a little bit like the difference between scrambled eggs and two fried eggs that have run together at the edges in the frying pan. In forming molecular orbitals the atomic orbitals, like the scrambled eggs, lose their individuality.

Molecular structure and geometry are more easily pictured in terms of the VSEPR and valence bond theories (Chapter 11) than in terms of molecular orbitals. Atomic orbital overlap diagrams such as Figure 11.6 indicate how geometry and bonding are interrelated. However, the valence bond theory does not clarify the relative energy levels of the orbitals involved in the bonding — something that can be done by using molecular orbitals. An understanding of energy levels is important — for one reason, because we derive much of our information about molecules from spectroscopy. To interpret spectra, a knowledge of the number of possible excited states for electrons and of the energy of the transitions to and from these states is needed (see An Aside: Molecular Spectroscopy, Chapter 11). One of the great successes of molecular orbital theory is the prediction and explanation of electronic spectra. Molecular orbital theory also permits a clearer understanding of multiple bonds, molecules for which resonance must be used to write Lewis structures, and molecules with unpaired electrons.

The molecular orbital approach, like the valence bond approach, is based on quantum theory and the use of the Schrödinger equation (Section 8.7). The energies of electrons in bonds, like those in isolated atoms, are quantized. For molecules, not only the interactions of electrons with each other and with nuclei must be accounted for, but also the interactions of nuclei with each other. As for the atomic orbitals of many-electron atoms, approximations are used to reduce the complexity of the mathematical treatment of molecular orbitals.

Molecular orbital calculations can be used to develop electron density maps of molecules like those in the Aside in this chapter. Energy-level diagrams for the molecular orbitals can also be drawn and electrons distributed among the energy levels as we did in determining the electron configurations of atoms (Section 8.10). From the configuration of the electrons in the molecular orbitals, predictions can be made about whether or not a bond between two specific atoms will form and whether or not a molecule will be paramagnetic — information that is not easily available from valence bond theory. For example, molecular orbital theory explains why Be_2 molecules have only a brief existence and it can account for the magnetic properties of O_2 molecules, neither of which can be done easily by valence bond theory. In reading the following sections, keep in mind that we are describing a mathematical process for representing bonding as it is observed.

24.2 MOLECULAR ORBITALS AND THEIR ENERGY LEVELS

Number of molecular orbitals = number of atomic orbitals that have combined

The orbitals of two atoms that are about to form a bond are thought of as rearranging themselves as the electrons and nucleus of each atom come under the influence of the electrons and nucleus of the other. The number of molecular orbitals formed must equal the number of atomic orbitals that have combined. For example, when two atoms that each have two atomic orbitals combine, there will be four molecular orbitals in the area of the bonded atoms. This does not mean that all of these molecular orbitals will be filled with electrons. To use molecular orbital theory we first determine the number of possible molecular orbitals. Then we find out how many electrons are available in the atoms that have combined. Finally, we assign the electrons to molecular orbitals, writing an electron configuration for the molecule, somewhat as we wrote *spdf* configurations for atoms.

The process is a little like assigning dormitory rooms to freshmen in college. The person in charge of housing first has to figure out how many rooms are available and on what floors in a particular building. But the Office of Admissions has to decide how many freshmen there will be to occupy the rooms. Once this is known, the students are assigned to the empty rooms. Maybe there will be fewer students than rooms, but the empty rooms—like the vacant molecular orbitals—are still there to be occupied if someone else comes along.

Bonding molecular orbital:
—lower energy than either atomic orbital
— electron density concentrated between nuclei
—contributes to bond

The combination of two atomic orbitals must produce two molecular orbitals and in the process energy must be conserved. The two molecular orbitals result from the combination of the atomic orbitals in such a way that the electron waves either reinforce each other (constructive interference; see Figure 8.2a) or cancel each other (destructive interference; see Figure 8.2c). In the first case, a **bonding molecular orbital**—an orbital in which most of the electron density is located between the nuclei of the bonded atoms—is formed. A bonding molecular orbital is always of lower energy than either of the atomic orbitals that have combined—formation of a bond creates a more stable situation. In the second case an **antibonding molecular orbital**—an orbital in which most of the electron density is located away from the space between the nuclei—is formed. The energy of the antibonding orbital is raised above the energy of the atomic orbitals that have combined by an amount equal to that by which the energy of the bonding orbital has been lowered. In this way, the two molecular orbitals have the same total energy as the two original atomic orbitals. Mathematically, the formation of bonding and antibonding orbitals is most commonly described by the addition and subtraction of the wave functions of the individual atomic orbitals. A generalized energy-level diagram for the formation of a molecular orbital is given in Figure 24.1, which shows atomic orbitals of equal energy from two different atoms combining to give one antibonding and one bonding molecular orbital.

Antibonding molecular orbital:
—higher energy than either atomic orbital
—low electron density between nuclei
—weakens existing bond

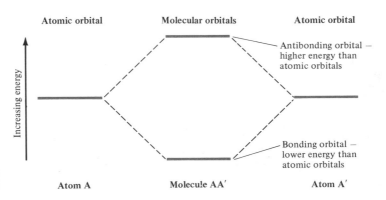

Figure 24.1
Energy Levels in Formation of a Molecular Orbital

24.3 TYPES OF MOLECULAR ORBITALS

The redistribution of electron density in the formation of a bonding and an anti-bonding molecular orbital is illustrated in Figure 24.2, which depicts the combination of two $1s$ atomic orbitals. The boundary contours in the figure show the regions in which the electrons are most likely to be found. A *node*, which is a region of zero electron density, lies between the nuclei in the antibonding orbital. (A *nodal plane*—a plane that encounters no electron density—intersects the bond axis in an antibonding molecular orbital.) The nuclei are mutually repelled by each other's positive charges, rather than held together. Electrons in antibonding orbitals do not form bonds; rather, they can weaken bonds formed between the same two atoms by other electrons.

In Chapter 11, we learned that bonds in which the electron density surrounds the bond axis are called σ bonds and those that leave an area of zero electron density around the bond axis are called π bonds. The σ and π notation is used similarly for molecular orbitals.

The bonding molecular orbital formed from two $1s$ atomic orbitals (see Figure 24.2) is a bonding σ molecular orbital. It is symbolized as follows and the symbol is read as "sigma one ess":

a sigma bonding molecular orbital $\longrightarrow \sigma_{1s} \longleftarrow$ *formed from 1s atomic orbitals*

Antibonding molecular orbitals are symbolized by adding a "star" to the bonding molecular orbital symbol. The antibonding orbital from two $1s$ atomic orbitals is a "sigma star one ess" orbital:

a sigma antibonding molecular orbital $\longrightarrow \sigma_{1s}^{*} \longleftarrow$ *formed from 1s atomic orbitals*

In valence bond theory, we talk of π bonds as formed by parallel overlap of p orbitals. The molecular orbital picture is similar. The parallel combination of p atomic orbitals forms π bonding and π antibonding molecular orbitals.

The three p orbitals from each of two atoms must yield six molecular orbitals. Two pairs of p orbitals combine in parallel fashion to give four π molecular orbitals, two bonding (π_p) and two antibonding (π_p^{*}) orbitals. The two π_p orbitals lie at 90° to each other, as do the two π_p^{*} orbitals. The third pair of p orbitals combines in end-on fashion to give σ molecular orbitals (σ_p, σ_p^{*}).

When their energy levels are similar, an s and a p orbital can also combine to give molecular orbitals (σ_{sp}, σ_{sp}^{*}). The formation of σ and π molecular orbitals from s and p atomic orbitals is summarized in Figure 24.3. Note that each antibonding molecular orbital has an area of zero electron density between the nuclei.

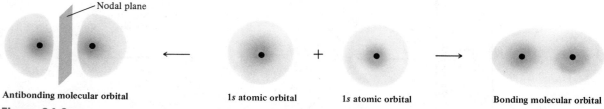

Nodal plane

Antibonding molecular orbital $1s$ atomic orbital $1s$ atomic orbital   Bonding molecular orbital

Figure 24.2
Combination of s Atomic Orbitals to give Antibonding and Bonding Molecular Orbitals

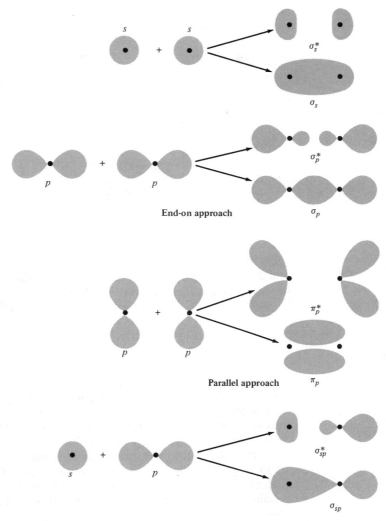

Figure 24.3
**Molecular Orbitals from *s* and *p*
Atomic Orbitals** The direction of
approach is chosen as along the x
axis. The antibonding molecular
orbitals are higher in energy and the
bonding molecular orbitals are
lower in energy than the atomic
orbitals from which they arise.

24.4 RULES FOR FILLING
MOLECULAR ORBITALS

Just as for atomic orbitals, there are rules that determine the order in which
molecular orbitals are filled. Electrons are pictured as entering the orbitals one by
one according to the following rules:

1. Electrons first occupy the molecular orbitals of lowest energy; they enter
   higher energy molecular orbitals only when the lower energy orbitals are
   filled.
2. Each molecular orbital can accommodate a maximum of two electrons
   (Pauli exclusion principle).
3. Molecular orbitals of equal energy are occupied by single electrons before
   electron pairing begins (Hund principle).

**HOMONUCLEAR
DIATOMIC MOLECULES**

24.5 H₂ AND ''He₂''

As in our discussion of valence bond theory (Section 11.3), we look first at the
simplest neutral, stable molecule, the hydrogen molecule. To derive the molecular
orbital description of the hydrogen molecule we begin with two isolated hydrogen
atoms, each with one electron in a $1s$ orbital. For this simple case, the two $1s$ atomic
orbitals combine to give one lower energy, bonding σ molecular orbital and one

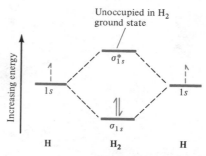

Figure 24.4
Relative Energy Levels in Formation of H_2

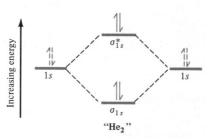

Figure 24.5
Relative Energy Levels of Molecular Orbitals in "He_2" The equal numbers of bonding and antibonding electrons cancel each other.

higher energy, antibonding σ^* molecular orbital. The ground state H_2 molecule has a total of two molecular orbitals available to be filled. Following the rules given above, the two electrons pair up to occupy the lowest level molecular orbital available, the σ_{1s} orbital (Figure 24.4). Two electrons in a σ orbital formed from atomic $1s$ orbitals are symbolized as

$$H_2 \qquad \sigma_{1s}{}^2 \overset{\frown}{\quad} \textit{two electrons in a } \sigma_{1s} \textit{ orbital}$$

The antibonding σ_{1s}^* orbital is unoccupied in the ground state of the H_2 molecule.

The energy-level diagram for the combination of two He atoms into an He_2 molecule is the same as that for H_2. As for the hydrogen atoms, two atomic $1s$ orbitals yield a σ_{1s} and a σ_{1s}^* orbital. But here there are two more electrons to be accommodated. Both the σ and σ^* orbitals are filled by the four available electrons, and the molecular electron configuration is $\sigma_{1s}{}^2 \sigma_{1s}^{*2}$ (Figure 24.5). The net result of an equal number of electrons in bonding and antibonding orbitals is that the effect of the bonding orbital is offset by the antibonding orbital. This molecular orbital theory prediction agrees with what has been observed—gaseous helium is monatomic and He_2 molecules are unstable.

24.6 BOND ORDER

Earlier, we discussed double and triple bonds as the sharing of two or three pairs of electrons. Molecular orbital theory sets us free from the consideration of Lewis structures in order to determine how many pairs of electrons are shared between two atoms. Whether a bond is, for example, single or double is determined by the relative numbers of electrons in the bonding and antibonding orbitals formed between the atoms in question.

The **bond order** of a covalent bond between two atoms is the number of effective bonding electron pairs shared between the two atoms. The repulsion due to electrons in antibonding orbitals cancels the attraction due to bonding electrons. Therefore, to find bond order, the number of electrons in antibonding orbitals must be subtracted from the number of electrons in bonding orbitals and the difference divided by 2.

Bond order = $\frac{1}{2}$ (number of bonding electrons − number of antibonding electrons)

Bond order = $\frac{1}{2}$[(the number of bonding electrons) − (the number of antibonding electrons)]

For the H_2 molecule

Bond order = $\frac{1}{2}(2 - 0) = 1$

Bond order zero: no bond between atoms

Increasing bond order:
— stronger bond
— shorter bond

The hydrogen molecule has a single covalent bond.
For the "He_2" molecule

$$\text{Bond order} = \tfrac{1}{2}(2 - 2) = 0$$

A bond order of zero tells us that a stable bond does not form. In general, the strength of a bond increases with increasing bond order and the length of the bond decreases with increasing bond order. As shown in Example 24.1, it is possible to have fractional bond orders.

EXAMPLE 24.1
Bond Order

We have found that H_2 is a stable molecule and "He_2" is not. Would the formation of H_2^+ and He_2^+ be possible?

To form H_2^+ from H_2, which has the σ_{1s}^2 configuration, one electron would be removed to give one electron in a bonding orbital and a configuration of σ_{1s}. The bond order of H_2^+ is found as follows:

$$\text{Bond order} = \tfrac{1}{2}(1 - 0) = \tfrac{1}{2}$$

A bond order of $\tfrac{1}{2}$ indicates that H_2^+ should exist, but would be less stable than H_2.
The He_2^+ ion would have three electrons, one less than the "He_2" molecule, which has the $\sigma_{1s}^2 \sigma_{1s}^{*2}$ configuration. This would give two electrons in the σ_{1s} orbital and one in the σ_{1s}^* orbital. Therefore, He_2^+ has a configuration of $\sigma_{1s}^2 \sigma_{1s}^*$ and a bond order of

$$\text{Bond order} = \tfrac{1}{2}(2 - 1) = \tfrac{1}{2}$$

We conclude that the He_2^+ ion can also exist. [H_2^+ and He_2^+ have both been observed to exist in the gas phase; their bond dissociation energies are 255 kJ/mol and 300 kJ/mol, respectively, while that of H_2 is 435 kJ/mol.]

Exercise Write the molecular orbital configuration and calculate the bond order for H_2^-. Would the formation of H_2^- be possible? *Answer* $\sigma_{1s}^2 \sigma_{1s}^*, \tfrac{1}{2}$, yes

---

AN ASIDE

Electron Density Diagrams

The elegant electron density diagrams presented here were plotted by a computer from quantum-mechanical calculations. The electron density in a cross-sectional plane passing through a molecule is plotted at right angles to that plane. These plots show the electron densities of the σ_{1s}, σ_{2s}, σ_{2p}, and π_{2p} bonding and antibonding molecular orbitals of a homonuclear diatomic molecule. To save space, the peaks of some of the plots have been cut off. Note the areas of zero electron density between the atoms in the antibonding orbitals. The chemists who produced these diagrams (John R. Van Wazer and Ilyas Absar, *Electron Densities in Molecules and Molecular Orbitals*, New York: Academic Press, 1975) cite the Confucian maxim that "one picture is worth ten thousand words."

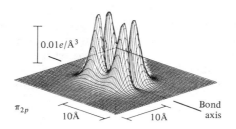

π_{2p} 0.01e/Å³   10Å   10Å   Bond axis

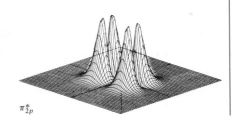

π_{2p}^*

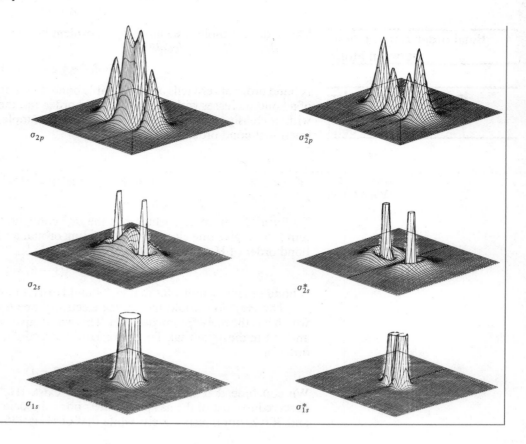

σ_{2p} σ_{2p}^*

σ_{2s} σ_{2s}^*

σ_{1s} σ_{1s}^*

24.7 MOLECULAR ORBITALS FOR DIATOMIC MOLECULES OF SECOND-PERIOD ELEMENTS, Li–Ne

Atoms of second-period elements have two main energy levels ($n = 1, 2$) and five orbitals—one $1s$, one $2s$, and three $2p$. The $1s$ electrons are core electrons. They are drawn close to the nucleus and remain essentially atomic in character. The $1s$ orbitals need not be considered in constructing molecular orbitals. In general, only valence electrons are placed into molecular orbitals.

Homonuclear: atoms of same element

In this section we consider how the molecular orbitals are filled for homonuclear diatomic molecules of the elements lithium through neon. **Homonuclear** means literally "the same nucleus"; the term refers to atoms of the same element. The value of molecular orbital theory in predicting whether or not a bond will form and in explaining the magnetic properties, bond energies, and bond lengths of molecules is well illustrated by these molecules.

The energy-level diagram for the molecular orbitals formed by the second-period element diatomic molecules is shown in Figure 24.6. Note that the three p orbitals form two π molecular orbitals (by parallel approach of $2p_y$ and $2p_z$ orbitals) and one σ molecular orbital (by end-on approach of $2p_x$ orbitals; see Figure 24.3). For the molecules of the first five elements of the period ($Li_2 - N_2$), experiment shows that the π_{2p} orbitals are of slightly lower energy than the σ_{2p} orbitals. For O_2 and F_2, the positions are reversed, and the σ_{2p} orbital is of lower energy than the π_{2p} orbitals.

What determines the relative energies of molecular orbitals? The situation is similar to that which we encountered with the ns and $(n - 1)d$ energy levels for electrons in many-electron atoms (Section 8.10). The relative energy levels in each atom or molecule depend upon the specific interactions possible in that atom or molecule.

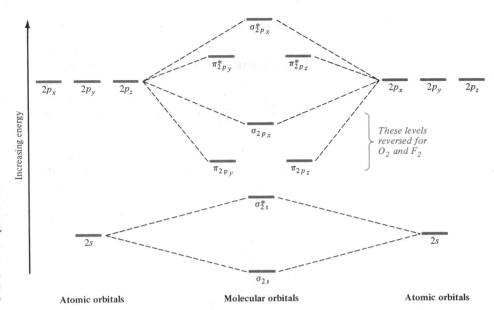

Figure 24.6
Relative Energy Levels for Atomic and Molecular Orbitals of Second-Period Elements The $n = 1$ electrons are the nonbonding, or "core" electrons and are not included in consideration of molecular orbitals. Each heavy line represents an orbital that can accommodate two electrons. (This and other energy level diagrams are not drawn to scale.)

Figure 24.7 shows the relative positions of the molecular orbital energy levels for the diatomic molecules Li_2 to F_2. The electron configurations of the individual molecules (Table 24.1) are discussed in the following paragraphs. Note that in each case we are discussing orbitals and the possible formation of bonds in diatomic molecules in the gaseous state. *Elemental* lithium and beryllium are metals; *elemental* carbon is a network covalent substance.

Lithium, $1s^2 2s^1$. An Li_2 molecule will contain six electrons. The first four electrons, as for all of the second-period elements, are the nonbonding $1s$ electrons (the core electrons). The remaining two electrons come from the $2s$ orbitals of the two lithium atoms. Just as in H_2, the s orbitals combine to give one bonding and one antibonding σ molecular orbital. The lower energy σ_{2s} orbital is occupied by the two electrons (see Figure 24.7), giving Li_2 a bond order of $\frac{1}{2}(2 - 0) = 1$.

The diatomic Li_2 molecules can be detected in the gaseous state. They are much less stable than H_2 molecules because of the larger size of the lithium atoms and the

Table 24.1
Electron Configurations of the Diatomic Molecules of Second-Period Elements The nonbonding $1s$ electrons are not included.

Li_2	σ_{2s}^2
B_2	$\sigma_{2s}^2 \sigma_{2s}^{*2} \pi_{2p_y}^1 \pi_{2p_z}^1$
C_2	$\sigma_{2s}^2 \sigma_{2s}^{*2} \pi_{2p_y}^2 \pi_{2p_z}^2$
N_2	$\sigma_{2s}^2 \sigma_{2s}^{*2} \pi_{2p_y}^2 \pi_{2p_z}^2 \sigma_{2p_x}^2$
O_2	$\sigma_{2s}^2 \sigma_{2s}^{*2} \sigma_{2p_x}^2 \pi_{2p_y}^2 \pi_{2p_z}^2 \pi_{2p_y}^{*1} \pi_{2p_z}^{*1}$
F_2	$\sigma_{2s}^2 \sigma_{2s}^{*2} \sigma_{2p_x}^2 \pi_{2p_y}^2 \pi_{2p_z}^2 \pi_{2p_y}^{*2} \pi_{2p_z}^{*2}$

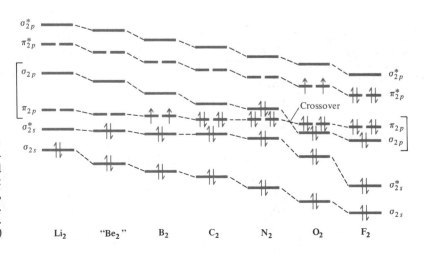

Figure 24.7
Molecular Orbital Diagram for the Second-Period Elements Li_2–F_2 Note the reversal of the σ_{2p} and π_{2p} orbitals for O_2 and F_2. (Source: F. A. Cotton and G. Wilkinson, *Advanced Inorganic Chemistry*, Fig. 3.12, New York: Wiley, 1976 p. 66. © 1976 John Wiley and Sons, Inc.)

greater nuclear repulsion between them. Compare the bond dissociation energies of H_2 and Li_2 in Table 24.2.

Beryllium, $1s^2 2s^2$. Of the eight electrons available for a Be_2 molecule, the first four are the nonbonding inner electrons. The next four fill the σ_{2s} and σ_{2s}^* orbitals. This gives a bond order of $\frac{1}{2}(2 - 2) = 0$. As predicted, Be_2 molecules are not stable.

Boron, $1s^2 2s^2 2p^1$. The B_2 molecule has six outer electrons to be distributed in molecular orbitals. Four electrons fill the σ_{2s} and σ_{2s}^* orbitals, leaving two electrons for the π orbitals. Following the Hund principle, the two electrons enter the π_{py} and π_{pz} orbitals singly. This gives B_2 a bond order of one.

The conclusions that may be drawn from the molecular orbital diagram for B_2 (see Figure 24.7) are that it will exist and that it will exhibit a paramagnetism showing the presence of two unpaired electrons. Both of these predictions are correct. Note that the two-electron paramagnetism of boron is evidence for the lower energy of the π_{2p} orbitals. If the σ_{2p} orbital had lower energy, the last two electrons would be paired and B_2 would be diamagnetic.

Carbon, $1s^2 2s^2 2p^2$. Eight electrons must be placed into the molecular orbitals for the C_2 molecule. In addition to the pairs of electrons in the σ_{2s} and σ_{2s}^* orbitals, pairs of electrons are also placed in the π_{2p_y} and π_{2p_z} orbitals. The C_2 molecule has a bond order of $\frac{1}{2}(6 - 2) = 2$, and the higher bond order is reflected in a high bond dissociation energy (see Table 24.2). All electrons are paired, and C_2 is diamagnetic. The C_2 molecule exists at high temperatures or in the presence of an electrical discharge.

Nitrogen, $1s^2 2s^2 2p^3$. A nitrogen molecule has ten outer electrons to be placed in molecular orbitals. The first eight assume the same configuration as in C_2, and the remaining two enter the σ_{2p_x} orbital (see Table 24.1). With eight bonding electrons and two antibonding electrons, the bond order is three, in agreement with the Lewis formula that we have been writing for N_2, which is $:N{\equiv}N:$. All electrons are paired, in agreement with the observed diamagnetism of the N_2 molecule. The very large bond dissociation energy results from the large bond order.

Oxygen, $1s^2 2s^2 2p^4$. One of the early successes of molecular orbital theory was in explaining the paramagnetism of oxygen. The theory also nicely accounts for the relative bond dissociation energies of O_2 and $O_2{}^+$. The first ten outer electrons from the oxygen atoms fill the molecular orbitals up to the π_{2p} orbitals as in N_2, but note that the π_{2p} and σ_{2p} orbitals are reversed in order (see Figure 24.7). The next highest energy level has two equal π_{2p}^* antibonding orbitals available. The final two electrons

Table 24.2
Diatomic Molecules of First- and Second-Period Elements In general, bond length decreases and bond energy increases with bond order. Note these trends in the series B_2, C_2, N_2, and $O_2{}^+$, O_2, $O_2{}^-$.

Species	Total Number of Electrons	Bond Order	Bond Length (nm)	Bond Dissociation Energy, (kJ/mol)
H_2	2	1	0.074	432
"He_2"	4	0	—	—
Li_2	6	1	0.267	108
"Be_2"	8	0	—	—
B_2	10	1	0.159	292
C_2	12	2	0.124	590.
N_2	14	3	0.109	942
$O_2{}^+$	15	$2\frac{1}{2}$	0.112	636
O_2	16	2	0.121	494
$O_2{}^-$	17	$1\frac{1}{2}$	0.130	394
F_2	18	1	0.141	154
"Ne_2"	20	0	—	—
CO	14	3	0.113	1070
NO	15	$2\frac{1}{2}$	0.115	628

Figure 24.8
Paramagnetism of Oxygen Liquid oxygen (b.p. -183 °C) is held between the poles of a strong magnet (9 kilogauss) until it evaporates. Liquid nitrogen (b.p. -196 °C) is not held by such a magnet. Note that these liquefied gases must be handled with great care. (Source: For details of this demonstration, see Bassam Z. Shakhashiri et al., *Chemical Demonstrations*, University of Wisconsin Press, 1983.)

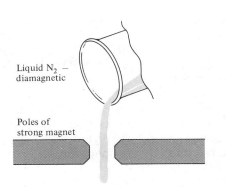

Liquid N$_2$ — diamagnetic

Poles of strong magnet

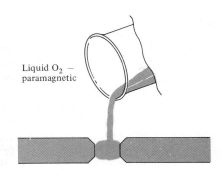

Liquid O$_2$ — paramagnetic

of O$_2$ should enter these π^*_{2p} orbitals singly. The paramagnetism of O$_2$ shows that this does indeed happen—two unpaired electrons are present in an oxygen molecule. Only the molecular orbital theory was able to explain both the paramagnetism and the bond order of O$_2$, which is two. A demonstration of the paramagnetism of O$_2$ and the diamagnetism of N$_2$ is illustrated in Figure 24.8.

Removal of one electron from O$_2$ to give O$_2{}^+$ increases the O—O bond energy (see Table 24.2). Taking away an antibonding electron has strengthened the bond, which is exactly what molecular orbital theory predicts.

Fluorine, $1s^2\,2s^2\,2p^5$. In the F$_2$ molecule, the 14 available electrons are placed in the molecular orbitals of increasing energy up to the π^*_{2p} energy level (see Figure 24.7). All electrons are paired and the bond order, in agreement with the Lewis formula, $:\!\ddot{F}\!-\!\ddot{F}\!:$, is one.

Neon, $1s^2\,2s^2\,2p^6$. The Ne$_2$ molecule is not stable. All electrons are paired, and with all of the molecular orbitals in Figure 24.6 filled, the bond order is zero.

EXAMPLE 24.2
Molecular Orbital Electron Configuration

Using the molecular orbital energy diagram given in Figure 24.6, write the electron configuration for O$_2{}^+$.

In the O$_2{}^+$ molecule there is a total of 15 electrons. The four $1s$ electrons will not be involved in the bonding because they lie very close to the oxygen nuclei and we simply write the atomic configurations for these four electrons:

$$1s^2\,1s^2$$

The remaining 11 electrons are placed in the orbitals shown in the figure using the usual rules for filling orbitals.

$$\sigma_{2s}{}^2\,\sigma^{*2}_{2s}\sigma^2_{2p_x}\,\pi^2_{2p_y}\,\pi^2_{2p_z}\,\pi^{*1}_{2p_y}$$

The molecular orbital electron configuration for O$_2{}^+$ is

$$1s^2\,1s^2\,\sigma_{2s}{}^2\,\sigma^{*2}_{2s}\sigma^2_{2p_x}\,\pi^2_{2p_y}\,\pi^2_{2p_z}\,\pi^{*1}_{2p_y}.$$

Exercise Using the molecular orbital energy diagram given in Figure 24.6, write the electron configuration for O$_2{}^-$. *Answer* $1s^2\,1s^2\,\sigma_{2s}{}^2\,\sigma^{*2}_{2s}\sigma^2_{2p_x}\,\pi^2_{2p_y}\,\pi^2_{2p_z}\,\pi^{*2}_{2p_y}\,\pi^{*1}_{2p_z}$

EXAMPLE 24.3
Molecular Orbital Electron Configuration; Bond Order

Discuss the electron configuration of O$_2{}^-$. Comment on the relative bond orders, magnetic properties, bond lengths, and bond dissociation energies of O$_2{}^-$, O$_2$, and O$_2{}^+$ (discussed above).

To form O$_2{}^-$ from O$_2$, an additional electron must enter one of the π^*_{2p} orbitals. This reduces the paramagnetism from that of two unpaired electrons in O$_2$ to that of one unpaired electron, the same as for O_2^+. The bond order of O_2^- is $\frac{1}{2}(8-5) = 1\frac{1}{2}$. This decrease in bond order from that of O_2 should lead to an increase in bond length and a decrease in bond strength. For O_2^+, with a bond order of $2\frac{1}{2}$, the bond length should be less than that in O_2 and the bond strength greater. The data in Table 24.2 confirm these predictions.

Exercise Comment on the (a) relative bond orders, (b) magnetic properties, (c) bond lengths, and (d) bond dissociation energies of N_2, N_2^+, and N_2^-. *Answer* (a) 3 for N_2, $2\frac{1}{2}$ for N_2^+ and N_2^-; (b) N_2 is diamagnetic, N_2^+ and N_2^- are paramagnetic; (c) N_2 is less, N_2^+ and N_2^- are about the same; (d) N_2 is largest, N_2^+ and N_2^- are about the same.

EXAMPLE 24.4
Bond Energy

Using the following heat of formation data at 0 K, calculate the bond dissociation energy for O_2^+:

$$O_2^+(g) \qquad \Delta H_{0,f}^\circ = 1172 \text{ kJ/mol}$$
$$O^+(g) \qquad \Delta H_{0,f}^\circ = 1561 \text{ kJ/mol}$$
$$O(g) \qquad \Delta H_{0,f}^\circ = 247 \text{ kJ/mol}$$

The bond dissociation energy for O_2^+ is the ΔH_0° for the reaction

$$O_2^+(g) \longrightarrow O^+(g) + O(g)$$

The data given for the heats of formation for each species can be combined as follows:

$$\Delta H_0^\circ = [(1 \text{ mol}) \times \Delta H_{0,f}^\circ(O^+) + 1 \text{ mol}) \times \Delta H_{0,f}^\circ(O)] - [(1 \text{ mol}) \times \Delta H_{0,f}^\circ(O_2^+)]$$
$$= [(1 \text{ mol})(1561 \text{ kJ/mol}) + (1 \text{ mol})(247 \text{ kJ/mol})] - [(1 \text{ mol})(1172 \text{ kJ/mol})]$$
$$= 636 \text{ kJ}$$

The bond dissociation energy for O_2^+ is 636 kJ/mol.

Exercise The standard state heat of formation at 0 K is 1503 kJ/mol for $N_2^+(g)$, 471 kJ/mol for $N(g)$, and 1874 kJ/mol for $N^+(g)$. Calculate the bond dissociation energy for N_2^+. *Answer* 842 kJ/mol

---

TOOLS OF CHEMISTRY: THE COMPUTER

Computer-Generated Views of an Amino Acid On the following two pages, the tryptophan molecule is

COO$^-$
|
H$_2$N—CH$_2$
|
C

shown in three different orientations in space. The structures on the bottom of each set, which are based on the van der Waals radii, show the surfaces of the molecules. The structures on the top of each set are

It is widely believed that we are in the midst of an information revolution that will change society as profoundly as the industrial revolution did nineteenth century Europe and America. The digital computer is both the tool and the symbol of this revolution. Every scientific discipline has been affected by advances in computer technology, and chemistry is no exception.

The earliest applications of computational methods in chemistry were made by quantum theorists, who were trying to find accurate methods of calculating the electronic structure of molecules. Both the internal electronic energy of molecules and the distribution of electronic charge in a molecule are obtained by solving the Schrödinger equation (see the introduction to this chapter). This equation can be solved exactly only for a few very simple problems of interest in chemistry, for example, the electronic structure of the hydrogen atom. It is from these exact solutions that our insight into chemical structure has developed; the concept of atomic orbitals comes directly from the solutions of the Schrödinger equation for the hydrogen atom. But even for the hydrogen molecule, an exact solution of the Schrödinger equation is impossible without the use of numerical methods. Chemists during the 1930s were using analog computers (and even mechanical desk calculators) to solve the Schrödinger equation numerically, and they were able to

based on atomic radii. (Molecular graphics courtesy of Richard J. Feldmann, Division of Computer Research and Technology, National Institutes of Health).

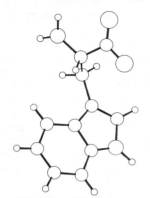

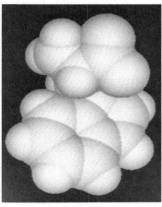

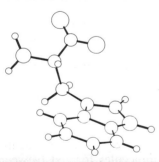

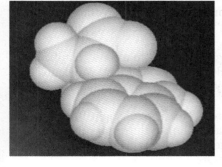

determine the bond energy of the hydrogen molecule to within 10 percent of the presently accepted experimental value.

For any molecule heavier than the hydrogen molecule, the Schrödinger equation is complex enough to render numerical computations very tedious if done by hand. As digital computers became available in universities during the 1950s, computational methods for solving Schrödinger's equation for molecules with many electrons were developed. There are now many research groups in both universities and industries that have computers dedicated entirely to electronic structural calculations, and accurate studies can be done on large, chemically interesting molecules. For example, it is now possible to compute the interaction energies between two molecules such as the biochemically important cyclic bases adenine and thymine when they are hydrogen-bonded, as in the double-helix form of DNA (Section 33.22).

Of course, molecular structure can be determined by many experimental methods as well, for example, by x-ray diffraction, molecular spectroscopy, or magnetic resonance (see Tools of Chemistry, Chapters 13, 11, and 27, respectively). In each of these experimental methods, the availability of computer-based methods of analyzing data has made possible the determination of structures far more complex than could have been done 20 years ago. For example, the complete three-dimensional structures of biologically significant molecules such as myoglobin, an oxygen-carrying protein that is similar to hemoglobin and contains more than one hundred atoms, has been completely worked out using x-ray diffraction and computer reduction of data.

Complex molecular structures can also be displayed on a variety of output devices, using the techniques of computer graphics. By representing the positions of all atoms within a molecule by vectors, each atom can be located in space with three numbers. Atoms themselves can be depicted in many ways: as points, as spheres with radii equal to the van der Waals radii of the atoms (Section 11.8), or even as contour diagrams of electron density (Section 8.9). Devices such as high resolution graphics terminals or plotters can then be used to draw a picture of the molecule, viewed from any angle at any distance. The viewing perspective can be changed until a particular structural feature of interest comes into view. The figures in the margin show examples of such computer-generated structures.

In addition, chemists have found that microcomputers can be used for more than driving beasties around video screens in arcade games; they can also be used very effectively in the laboratory to control experimental equipment and to help record data. For example, the pH electrode you read about in Chapter 21 (Tools of Chemistry: Measuring pH) can be interfaced with a microcomputer to produce an instrument that will record the pH every second during a titration. With another electronic interface and some flow control valves, the microprocessor can be used to add specific volumes of titrant at regular intervals. With some additional programming, the two functions—data acquisition and experimental control—can be combined so that the volume of titrant added decreases as the endpoint is approached. It is then a simple matter to have the microcomputer calculate the molarity of the unknown acid. Now that a machine can do this much of your acid–base titration lab, what do you think the next step will be?

The real power of computer-based chemical instrumentation is seen in more complex experiments than titrations, however. For example, the tools of gas chromatography (Chapter 19) and mass spectrometry (Chapter 3) can be combined, with the aid of a minicomputer, to produce an analytical instrument of great sensitivity and specificity. A mixture of many different chemical compounds can be separated with chromatography, but simple detectors cannot identify the compounds as they are eluted from the column. A mass spectrometer can be used to read the "fingerprint" of each compound as it emerges. Instruments that combine mass spectrometers with chromatographs require delicate adjustments both before and during an experiment. Minicomputers are used to control the acquisition

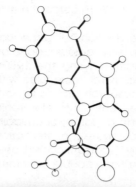

and analysis of the data, allowing specific compounds present in the original sample in concentrations of less than one part per million to be detected.

In the chemical industry, many chemical processes also require elaborate control of conditions such as temperature, pressure, flow rate, and catalyst condition, as well as immediate analyses of the process stream for the desired product. Computers are an essential tool used by chemical engineers in the design and operation of chemical plants.

The ability of computers to search through huge data bases for desired information is also making significant changes in the field of chemistry. From the graphical input of the structure of a molecule, the data base of existing compounds can be checked to see if a molecule of interest has been made. It is also possible to search the data base for other compounds containing structural features similar to those of the compound originally entered. With the knowledge gained in learning to deal with complex chemical structures in this way, another interesting use of computers has emerged. There are now programs that will aid organic chemists in designing successful syntheses of compounds that have not yet been made. Several of these programs use concepts developed in the field of artificial intelligence to guide the synthesis design.

EXAMPLE 24.5
Molecular Orbital Electron Configuration

Assume that the molecular orbital diagram given in Figure 24.6 is valid for BO. Write the electron configuration for this molecule.

There are 13 electrons in this molecule. The complete configuration is

$$1s^2 1s^2 \sigma_{2s}^2 \sigma_{2s}^{*2} \pi_{2p_y}^2 \pi_{2p_z}^2 \sigma_{2p_x}^1$$

where we have written $1s^2 1s^2$ for the four $1s$ electrons that are not involved in the bonding.

HETERONUCLEAR AND POLYATOMIC MOLECULES

24.8 HETERONUCLEAR DIATOMIC MOLECULES

Heteronuclear: atoms of different elements

Within limits, the energy-level diagram of Figure 24.6 can be used to determine the molecular orbital configuration of gaseous diatomic molecules formed between atoms of different elements—heteronuclear diatomic molecules—in the second period. **Heteronuclear** means "of different nuclei"; that is, it refers to atoms of different elements.

The elements C and O, and N and O are not very different in atomic number, and the energies with which these atoms hold electrons are similar. Molecular orbitals can therefore form between these atoms by overlap of comparable atomic orbitals (as illustrated by Figure 24.6).

Consider carbon monoxide, CO, with 14 electrons (six from C, eight from O). Placing these electrons in the energy levels in order according to the usual rules gives a molecule with the same configuration as the nitrogen molecule (see Figure 24.7 and Table 24.1), and therefore a bond order of 3, :C≡O: .

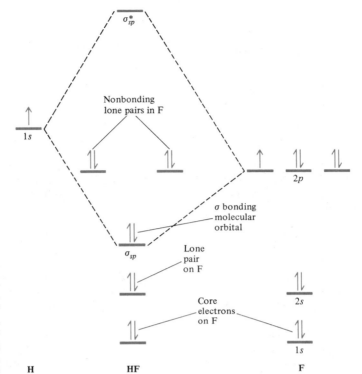

Figure 24.9
Molecular Orbital Energy Diagram
for HF Drawn for unhybridized
orbitals on fluorine. (Only the $2p$
orbitals of F are sufficiently close in
energy to the hydrogen $1s$ orbital to
allow overlap and molecular orbital
formation. Of these only the $2p_z$
orbital has the proper symmetry.)

The nitric oxide molecule, NO, has a total of fifteen electrons. Its configuration should be like that of nitrogen (see Figure 24.7), but with one more electron added in a π_{2p}^* orbital. Nitric oxide does indeed have the paramagnetism of a molecule with one unpaired electron. Like the $O\!-\!O^+$ case described above, removal of an antibonding electron (the π_{2p}^* electron) from NO produces a positive ion, NO^+, more stable than its neutral parent.

When the atoms in a heteronuclear diatomic molecule have large differences in atomic number and in ionization energies, overlap occurs between orbitals of similar energy level but not necessarily of similar description (i.e., not necessarily $1s$ with $1s$, $2p$ with $2p$). Such a situation is illustrated for HF in Figure 24.9. The $1s$ orbital of hydrogen has approximately the same energy as a $2p$ orbital of fluorine, allowing the formation of a σ_{sp} molecular orbital.

24.9 SIMPLE POLYATOMIC
MOLECULES

As the number of atoms in a molecule increases, the molecular orbital energy diagrams become more and more complex. Even the diagrams for simple polyatomic molecules like water, ammonia, and methane are not so simple.

To construct a molecular orbital energy diagram for a polyatomic molecule, it is customary to begin with the description of the electrons in the molecule according to the valence bond theory. For example, to depict the molecular orbital energy levels for water, the orbitals from an sp^3-hybridized oxygen atom are combined with two $1s$ orbitals from the hydrogen atoms (Figure 24.10). Two of the sp^3-hybridized atomic orbitals overlap with the two $1s$ atomic orbitals of the hydrogen atoms to form two bonding and two antibonding σ molecular orbitals. One bonding and one antibonding orbital are associated with each oxygen–hydrogen bond. The remaining two sp^3-hybridized atomic orbitals are not involved in the formation of molecular orbitals and each holds one of the two lone electron pairs on the oxygen atom.

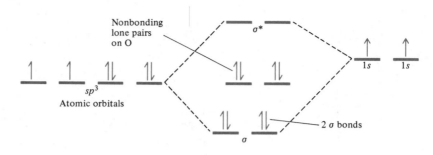

Figure 24.10
**Molecular Orbital Energy Diagram
for Water** Drawn for hybridized
orbitals on oxygen.

24.10 MULTIPLE BONDS AND DELOCALIZED ORBITALS

The molecular orbital picture of ethylene (Figure 24.11) is not very different from the valence bond picture (see Figure 11.8). σ Bonds determine the geometry of the carbon–hydrogen skeleton, and π bonds lie above and below the carbon–carbon bond axis. Three valence electrons from each carbon atom enter the σ orbitals, leaving one valence electron from each carbon atom for the π orbitals. Two p orbitals, one from each carbon atom, form two π molecular orbitals, one bonding and occupied by the two electrons, and one antibonding and unoccupied in the ground state of ethylene.

When a molecule or ion has more than one multiple bond, it is often possible to write several Lewis structures that are in agreement with the known properties of the molecule or ion. We have dealt with such species by the concept of resonance (Section 9.17) or the concept of delocalization of π electrons. In molecular orbital theory, the π molecular orbitals are delocalized—spread over the entire molecule.

Previously (Section 9.14) we described the bonding in benzene in terms of the classical resonance structures,

that account for the equivalence of the carbon–carbon bonds. To build up a molecular orbital picture of a benzene molecule, a total of 42 electrons from the six

Figure 24.11
**Molecular Orbital Views of
Ethylene** (a) Conventional drawing
of ethylene π and π^* molecular
orbitals; (b) π-bonding orbital
electron density distribution in
ethylene. The plot, viewed from two
different angles, shows electron
density in a plane perpendicular to
the plane of the C—H skeleton.
(See An Aside: Electron Density
Diagrams. The C atoms lie in the
"valleys," as indicated; the H atoms
(not shown) would be above and
below the plane of the plot. Source:
J. R. Van Wazer and I. Absar, New
York: Academic Press, 1975, p. 33.)

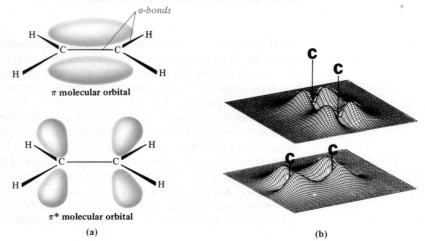

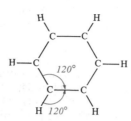

(a) σ-bonded C–H skeleton

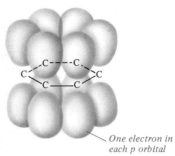

One electron in each p orbital

(b) p atomic orbitals available for molecular orbitals

Figure 24.12
The Benzene Molecule The six atomic orbitals (b) combine to give three bonding and three antibonding molecular orbitals. One bonding orbital is shown in (c). The sum of the molecular orbitals, or delocalized bonding, is represented by (d).

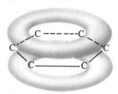

(c) Lowest energy molecular orbital

(d) Symbol for benzene that emphasizes delocalized bonding

carbon atoms and six hydrogen atoms must be placed in orbitals. The first 12 electrons remain in $1s$ atomic orbitals on the carbon atoms. The next 24 electrons occupy the orbitals that form the carbon–hydrogen skeleton of benzene—12 in carbon–hydrogen bonds and 12 in carbon–carbon bonds. This leaves six electrons for the next highest energy level molecular orbitals, which must be formed from the single p orbital on each carbon atom not involved in σ bonds. These six p orbitals combine to form three π orbitals and three π* orbitals. The three π orbitals add up to a region of uniform electron density above and below the ring of carbon atoms (Figure 24.12) and are occupied by the six electrons in pairs. The three π* orbitals remain unoccupied.

This bonding picture accounts for the equivalence of all the carbon–carbon bonds in benzene and for the thermal stability of the molecule. As we have pointed out, electron energy is lowered when an electron is given a larger space to move about in. The six electrons in the delocalized π orbitals can be anywhere within the electron cloud shown in Figure 24.12.

SUMMARY

24.1 VALENCE BOND THEORY VERSUS MOLECULAR ORBITAL THEORY   Molecular orbital theory explains bond formation as the occupation by electrons of orbitals characteristic of bonded atoms rather than individual atoms. A molecular orbital is the space in which an electron with a specific energy is most likely to be found in the vicinity of two or more nuclei that are bonded together. In forming molecular orbitals, atomic orbitals lose their individuality. Molecular orbital theory permits a clearer understanding of the relative energy levels of orbitals involved in bonding, of multiple bonds and resonance, and of which molecules will have unpaired electrons and so exhibit paramagnetism. It also helps make accurate predictions about whether or not a bond will form between two specific atoms. (Keep in mind that the descriptions in this chapter are based on a *mathematical* representation of what occurs in bonding.)

24.2 MOLECULAR ORBITALS AND THEIR ENERGY LEVELS   The combination of two atomic orbitals produces two molecular orbitals: a bonding molecular orbital, in which most of the electron density is located between the nuclei of the bonded atoms, and an antibonding molecular orbital, in which most of the electron density is located away from the space between the two nuclei. The bonding molecular orbital has a lower energy than that of the atomic orbitals from which it was created, while the antibonding molecular orbital has a higher energy than that of the atomic orbitals. The two molecular orbitals have the same total energy as the two original atomic orbitals.

24.3 TYPES OF MOLECULAR ORBITALS **24.4** RULES FOR FILLING MOLECULAR ORBITALS **24.5** H_2 AND "He_2" Electrons in bonding orbitals form chemical bonds. Electrons in antibonding orbitals do not form bonds; rather, they can weaken bonds formed between the same atoms by other electrons. Molecular orbitals can be formed from two s atomic orbitals (σ_s and σ_s^*), two p atomic orbitals that approach one another end-on (σ_p and σ_p^*), or (if their energy levels are similar) an s and a p atomic orbital (σ_{sp} and σ_{sp}^*). Two pairs of p atomic orbitals can combine in parallel fashion to give four molecular orbitals, two bonding (π_p) and two antibonding (π_p^*). Electrons are placed in molecular orbitals one by one according to a set of rules: (a) Electrons first occupy molecular orbitals of lowest energy; (b) each molecular orbital can accommodate two electrons; (c) molecular orbitals of equal energy are occupied by single electrons before pairing of electrons in orbitals begins.

24.6 BOND ORDER The bond order of a covalent bond between two atoms is the number of effective bonding electron pairs shared between them. It is equal to the number of bonding electrons minus the number of antibonding electrons, divided by two. In general, the strength of a bond increases and its length decreases with increasing bond order. A bond order of 0 means that no bonding will take place.

24.7 MOLECULAR ORBITALS FOR DIATOMIC MOLECULES OF SECOND-PERIOD ELEMENTS, Li–Ne **24.8** HETERONUCLEAR DIATOMIC MOLECULES **24.9** SIMPLE POLYATOMIC MOLECULES **24.10** MULTIPLE BONDS AND DELOCALIZED ORBITALS The value of molecular orbital theory in predicting the formation of bonds, their energies, and their lengths, as well as the magnetic properties of the resulting molecules, is illustrated in Section 24.7 for homonuclear diatomic molecules (molecules comprising two atoms of the same element). For example, molecular orbital theory explains why the O_2 molecule has two unpaired electrons, making it strongly paramagnetic, and also makes it clear why this molecule has a bond order of 2. When the atoms in a heteronuclear diatomic molecule (one comprising two atoms of different elements) differ considerably in atomic number and ionization energies, molecular orbitals can be formed from atomic orbitals of similar energy level, though these may differ in designation (e.g., $1s$ may combine with $2p$). The concept of delocalized π orbitals has its basis in the formation of molecular orbitals that encompass a number of atoms.

SIGNIFICANT TERMS

molecular orbital theory
molecular orbital
bonding molecular orbital
antibonding molecular orbital
bond order
homonuclear
heteronuclear

TOOLS OF CHEMISTRY: THE COMPUTER The impact of computers on chemistry is profound. Computers allow the theoretical calculation of electronic structures, the analysis of experimental data used in the study of molecular structure, and the graphical representation of molecular structures. Computers can control analytical instruments used in, for example, titration or gas chromatography and can also collect and analyze the data. Computers are also used to control industrial processes and to search data bases for desired information.

THOUGHTS ON CHEMISTRY

Is Life Based on the Laws of Physics?

WHAT IS LIFE? by Erwin Schrödinger

What I wish to make clear is, in short, that from all we have learnt about the structure of living matter, we must be prepared to find it working in a manner that cannot be reduced to the ordinary laws of physics. And that not on the ground that there is any 'new force' or what not, directing the behaviour of the single atoms within a living organism, but because the construction is different from anything we have yet tested in the physical laboratory. . . . Contrary to the common belief, the regular course of events, governed by the laws of physics, is never the consequence of one well-ordered configuration of atoms—not unless that configuration of atoms repeats itself a great number of times, either as in the periodic crystal or as in a liquid or in a gas composed of a great number of identical molecules.

Even when the chemist handles a very complicated molecule in vitro he is always faced with an enormous number of like molecules. To them his laws apply.

In biology we are faced with an entirely different situation. A single group of atoms existing only in one copy produces orderly events, marvellously tuned in with each other and with the environment according to most subtle laws. I said, existing only in one copy, for after all we have the example of the egg and of the unicellular organism. In the following stages of a higher organism the copies are multiplied, that is true. But to what extent? Something like 10^{14} in a grown mammal, I understand. What is that? Only a millionth of the number of molecules in one cubic inch of air. Though comparatively bulky, by coalescing they would form but a tiny drop of liquid. And look at the way they are actually distributed. Every cell harbours just one of them (or two, if we bear in mind diploidy). Since we know the power this tiny central office has in the isolated cell, do they not resemble stations of local government dispersed through the body, communicating with each other with great ease, thanks to the code that is common to all of them?

Well, this is a fantastic description, perhaps less becoming a scientist than a poet. However, it needs no poetical imagination but only clear and sober scientific reflection to recognize that we are here obviously faced with events whose regular and lawful unfolding is guided by a 'mechanism' entirely different from the 'probability mechanism' of physics. For it is simply a fact of observation that the guiding principle in every cell is embodied in a single atomic association existing only in one copy (or sometimes two)—and a fact of observation that it results in producing events which are a paragon of orderliness. Whether we find it astonishing or whether we find it quite plausible that a small but highly organized group of atoms be capable of acting in this manner, the situation is unprecedented, it is unknown anywhere else except in living matter. The physicist and the chemist, investigating inanimate matter, have never witnessed phenomena which they had to interpret in this way. The case did not arise and so our theory does not cover it—our beautiful statistical theory of which we were so justly proud because it allowed us to look behind the curtain, to watch the magnificent order of exact physical law coming forth from atomic and molecular disorder.

Erwin Schrödinger, *What Is Life?* 1944 (New York and London: Cambridge University Press combined reprint, 1980), pp. 81–85.

QUESTIONS

Principles of Molecular Orbital Theory

24.1 What is a molecular orbital? What two types of information can be obtained from molecular orbital calculations? How do we use such information to describe the bonding within a molecule?

24.2 What is the relationship between the number of molecular orbitals and the number of atomic orbitals from which they are formed?

24.3 What two types of molecular orbitals are formed by addition and subtraction of atomic orbitals? How do the electron waves interact with each other in these new orbitals?

24.4 What is the relationship between the energy of a bonding molecular orbital and the energies of the original atomic orbitals? What is the relationship between the energy of an antibonding molecular orbital and the energies of the original atomic orbitals?

24.5 Draw an energy-level diagram for the formation of molecular orbitals from two atomic orbitals of equal energy. Identify the bonding and antibonding molecular orbitals.

24.6 Prepare sketches of the bonding and antibonding molecular orbitals formed by combining (a) two s atomic orbitals, (b) two p atomic orbitals in end-on approach, (c) two p atomic orbitals in parallel approach, and (d) an s atomic orbital and a p atomic orbital interacting so that they approach along the axis of the p orbital (e.g., p_z along the z axis).

24.7 Interpret the symbol σ_{1s}. Write the symbol for the corresponding antibonding molecular orbital.

24.8 Describe the two different types of molecular orbitals that are formed by the overlap of two $2p$ orbitals. Write the symbols for the bonding and antibonding orbitals of each type.

24.9* Complete the following energy-level diagram for the formation of molecular orbitals:

$$\overline{2_{p_x}}\ \overline{2_{p_y}}\ \overline{2_{p_z}} \qquad\qquad \overline{2_{p_x}}\ \overline{2_{p_y}}\ \overline{2_{p_z}}$$
atomic orbitals   molecular orbitals   atomic orbitals

Assume the bonding axis to be the x axis. Be sure to identify the bonding and antibonding molecular orbitals that are formed.

Homonuclear Diatomic Molecules

24.10 State the three rules for placing electrons in molecular orbitals.

24.11 What is meant by the term "bond order"? How is the value of the bond order calculated?

24.12 Using the molecular orbital energy diagram given in Figure 24.4, write the electron configuration for each of the following molecules and predict which molecules would exist: (a) H_2^+, (b) H_2, (c) H_2^-, and (d) H_2^{2-}.

24.13 Write the electron configuration for He_2^+ and He_2 using the molecular orbital energy diagram given in Figure 24.4. Which of these would you predict to exist?

24.14 Briefly discuss the energies of the π_{2p} orbitals with respect to the σ_{2p} orbital for the diatomic molecules of the second-period elements.

24.15 Using the molecular orbital energy diagram given in Figure 24.6, write the electron configurations for (a) Be_2, (b) C_2, and (c) Ne_2. Which of these molecules are predicted to exist?

24.16 Repeat Question 24.15 for (a) Li_2, (b) B_2, and (c) F_2.

24.17 List the following species in order of decreasing bond strength: O_2, O_2^+, O_2^-, O_2^{2+}, and O_2^{2-}. Which has the shortest bond length?

24.18* The molecular orbitals formed by the $3s$ and $3p$ atomic orbitals have the same pattern as those formed by the $2s$ and $2p$ orbitals. Write the electron configurations and discuss the bonding, if any, in the following gaseous homonuclear diatomic molecules: (a) Na_2, (b) Mg_2, (c) Al_2, (d) Si_2, (e) P_2, (f) S_2, (g) Cl_2, and (h) Ar_2. Are any of the molecules paramagnetic?

Heteronuclear and Polyatomic Molecules

24.19 We have assumed that the molecular orbital energy diagram given in Figure 24.6 can be used to describe gaseous heteronuclear diatomic molecules. How reasonable is this assumption for the molecule NO? How reasonable is this assumption for the molecule BeO?

24.20 Assuming the molecular orbital diagram given in Figure 24.6 is valid for NO, write the molecular orbital description for this molecule. Would NO be paramagnetic? Would you predict that NO^+ would be more stable? Why?

24.21 Arrange these species in order of increasing bond length: CN, CN^+, and CN^-.

24.22* Prepare a molecular orbital energy diagram similar to Figure 24.9 for HF using a fluorine atom that has undergone sp^3 hybridization. Compare this diagram with Figure 24.9. Is there any difference in the number of bonding or antibonding orbitals? Is there any difference in the number of nonbonding orbitals? Is there a difference in the pattern of the nonbonding orbitals?

24.23* Complete this molecular orbital energy diagram similar to Figure 24.10 for ammonia, NH_3. Assume that the electrons of the nitrogen atom are sp^3 hybridized.

24.24* Complete this molecular orbital energy diagram similar to Figure 24.10 for methane, CH_4. Assume that the carbon atom is sp^3 hybridized.

Answers to Selected Questions

24.13 $\sigma_{1s}^2\ \sigma_{1s}^*$, exists; $\sigma_{1s}^2\ \sigma_{1s}^{*2}$, does not exist

24.16 (a) $\sigma_{1s}^2\,\sigma_{1s}^{*2}\,\sigma_{2s}^2$, exists; (b) $\sigma_{1s}^2\,\sigma_{1s}^{*2}\,\sigma_{2s}^2\,\sigma_{2s}^{*2}\,\pi_{2p_y}^1\,\pi_{2p_z}^1$, exists; (c) $\sigma_{1s}^2\,\sigma_{1s}^{*2}\,\sigma_{2s}^2\,\sigma_{2s}^{*2}\pi_{2p_y}^2\,\pi_{2p_z}^2\,\sigma_{2p_x}^2\,\pi_{2p_y}^{*2}\,\pi_{2p_z}^{*2}$, exists

24.21 $CN^- < CN < CN^+$

24.24

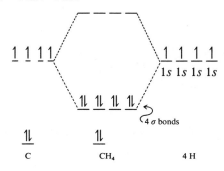

C   CH₄   4 H

24.4 Calculate the bond order of each of the species in Question 24.17.

Bond Energy

24.5 The heats of formation are 218.0 kJ/mol for H(g), 79.0 kJ/mol for F(g), 121.7 kJ/mol for Cl(g), -271.1 kJ/mol for HF(g), and -92.3 kJ/mol for HCl(g). Calculate the H—F and H—Cl bond energies.

24.6 The standard state heats of formation at 0 K are 155 kJ/mol for $N_2^-(g)$, 478 kJ/mol for $N^-(g)$, and 471 kJ/mol for N(g). Calculate the bond energy of N_2^-.

24.7* The heat of formation is 67 kJ/mol for $CN^-(g)$, 1797 kJ/mol for $CN^+(g)$, and 435 kJ/mol for CN(g). Calculate the carbon–nitrogen bond energy in CN^-, CN, and CN^+. Use the following:

$$CN^-(g) \longrightarrow C(g) + N^-(g)$$
$$CN(g) \longrightarrow C(g) + N(g)$$
$$CN^+(g) \longrightarrow C^+(g) + N(g)$$

as bond dissociation reactions. The heats of formation are 715 kJ/mol for C(g), 471 kJ/mol for N(g), 1809 kJ/mol for $C^+(g)$, and 478 kJ/mol for $N^-(g)$. *Answer* 1126 kJ/mol for CN^-, 751 kJ/mol for CN, 483 kJ/mol for CN^+

PROBLEMS

Bond Order

24.1 Calculate the bond order of each of the species given in Question 24.12.

24.2 Calculate the bond order of the species given in Question 24.15. *Answer* (a) 0, (b) 2, (c) 0

24.3 Calculate the bond order of each of the species given in Question 24.16. *Answer* (a) 1, (b) 1, (c) 1

CHAPTER 25

Nonmetals: The Halogens

In chemistry textbooks, the types of interactions possible in dynamic chemical systems are taken up one at a time. This is the only way it can be done—examine the principles of heats of reaction; then turn to how gases, liquids, and solids dissolve in each other; then go on to, say, kinetics and the various types of equilibria, and so on. The order in which the topics are taken up varies, but each is considered somewhat in isolation from the others.

When it comes to chemistry in the "real world" the circumstances change. All of chemistry applies simultaneously. Acid–base reactions, redox reactions, dissolution and precipitation, evaporation and condensation, corrosion, reactions at interfaces—anything can happen, and many things often do. For example, one list of the redox processes that might be important in a natural body of water includes twenty-three equilibria. The chemistry of such systems is fascinating, but complicated.

As we proceed in our study of the chemistry of the elements, we look briefly at examples of some complex systems. The chemistry of the halogens, the subject of this chapter, provides a good opportunity for this. By their nature, systems containing halogen oxoacids are not simple. Among the many practical applications of halogens that could be described, we have emphasized two—bleaching and swimming pool chemistry—that illustrate some of the varied interactions of such acids and their ions.

PHYSICAL AND CHEMICAL PROPERTIES OF THE HALOGENS

25.1 GENERAL PROPERTIES OF THE HALOGENS

The members of the fluorine family—fluorine (F), chlorine (Cl), bromine (Br), iodine (I), and astatine (At)—are collectively called the halogens. The word "halogen" comes from the Greek words meaning "salt-former."

The group electron configuration, ns^2np^5, is one electron short of an octet (Table 25.1). In the free elemental state the halogens all form diatomic molecules in which they complete octets by sharing their single unpaired electrons

$$:\ddot{X}-\ddot{X}:$$

At room temperature and pressure, fluorine and chlorine are gases, bromine is a liquid (the only liquid nonmetallic element), and iodine is a metallic-appearing, low-melting solid that sublimes readily. The intensity of color increases from a very pale yellow for fluorine to violet-black for iodine.

Bromine and iodine have high vapor pressures, and even at room temperature dark red vapor is always present above liquid bromine and violet vapor above solid iodine. The halogens all have pungent and irritating odors, and attack the skin and flesh. Bromine is particularly nasty; it causes burns that are very slow to heal. Astatine is radioactive and its most stable isotope has a half-life of 8.3 h.

Fluorine, perhaps more so than any other element, illustrates the *differences* in properties expected of first family members compared to other elements in the family (Table 25.2). For fluorine these differences are largely due to the small size and

Table 25.1
Configurations of Halogen Atoms

Fluorine, F
[He]$2s^22p^5$
Chlorine, Cl
[Ne]$3s^23p^5$
Bromine, Br
[Ar]$3d^{10}4s^24p^5$
Iodine, I
[Kr]$4d^{10}5s^25p^5$
Astatine, At
[Xe]$4f^{14}5d^{10}6s^26p^5$

Table 25.2
Differences between Fluorine and the Other Members of the Fluorine Family (Cl, Br, I)

Property	Comments
Strongest chemical oxidizing agent known	No other element has as great a tendency to add electrons.
The only element that combines directly with some of the noble gases	Forms fluorides with Kr, Xe, and Rn
Low bond dissociation energy compared to Cl_2 and Br_2; value out of line with family trend	Large repulsive forces between small, highly electronegative atoms allow easy breaking of F—F bond
F^-, the only halide ion that cannot function as a reducing agent	F^- must be oxidized to F_2 electrolytically
No positive oxidation states	No oxohalo anions comparable to, e.g., ClO^- and ClO_4^- are known.
HF strongly hydrogen bonded, causing high m.p., b.p., and heats of fusion and vaporization	Hydrogen bonding also partly accounts for hydrofluoric acid being a weak acid.

high electronegativity of the fluorine atom, which combine to make fluorine the most reactive of all of the nonmetals.

The trends in properties expected in periodic table families are especially apparent for the halogens. The ionic and covalent radii increase down the family with increasing atomic number and added electrons. The melting points and boiling points, as expected, also increase down the family (Table 25.3).

The free halogen molecules are quite stable to dissociation. Breaking the X—X bond becomes easier in going down the family from Cl_2 to Br_2 to I_2, reflecting the larger size of the atoms (Table 25.4). The surprisingly low bond dissociation energy

Table 25.3
Properties of the Halogens

	Fluorine, F_2	Chlorine, Cl_2	Bromine, Br_2	Iodine, I_2
Color and state	Pale yellow gas	Yellow-green gas	Red-brown liquid	Violet-black solid
Melting point (°C)	−220	−101	−73	113
Boiling point (°C)	−188	−34	59	184
Atomic radius (nm)	0.071	0.099	0.114	0.133
Ionic radius, X^- (nm)	0.136	0.181	0.196	0.220

Table 25.4
Bond Energies of X_2, HX, and AlX_3

	Bond Energies (kJ/mol)		
	XX	HX	AlX_3
F	159	569	582
Cl	243	431	427
Br	192	368	360
I	151	297	285

Table 25.5
**Electronic Properties of
the Halogens**

	Fluorine	Chlorine	Bromine	Iodine
Ionization energy (0 K) $X(g) \longrightarrow X^+(g) + e^-$ (kJ/mol)	1681	1251	1140	1008
Electronegativity	4.0	3.0	2.8	2.5
Electron affinity (0 K) $X(g) + e^- \longrightarrow X^-(g)$ (kJ/mol)	−322	−349	−325	−295
Standard reduction potential, $E°$ (V) $X_2 + 2e^- \longrightarrow 2X^-$	2.87	1.36	1.07	0.536

of fluorine is thought to be due mainly to the large repulsive forces between electrons in the small, highly electronegative fluorine atoms. These forces make the bond easy to break, a property which contributes to the extraordinary reactivity of fluorine. However, bonds between fluorine and other types of atoms are stronger than comparable bonds of other halogens (see Table 25.4).

The outstanding chemical characteristics of the halogens are their high reactivities and the large number of compounds they form with other elements. In bonding, halogen atoms readily accept single electrons to form singly charged negative ions, X^-, in ionic compounds. They also readily share their single unpaired electrons with other atoms to form covalent bonds.

The ease with which halogen atoms add electrons is shown by the large negative values of their electron affinities (Table 25.5), larger than those of any other elements. The difficulty of removing an electron from a halogen atom results in high values for the ionization energies, which decrease down the group, with the largest decrease between fluorine and chlorine. Only the noble gases have larger ionization energies than the halogens.

The high electronegativities of the halogens show their strong ability to attract electrons toward themselves in compounds. Covalent bonds to halogen atoms are often polar, with a partial negative charge on the halogen atom. Even in OF_2, the fluorine has a partial negative charge, because fluorine is *more* electronegative than oxygen. Fluorine is the most electronegative element and is, therefore, assigned a negative oxidation state (-1) in all compounds. The other halogens, in addition to the -1 state in ionic compounds, have positive oxidation states $(+1, +3, +5,$ or $+7)$ in covalent compounds with more electronegative elements (Table 25.6).

EXAMPLE 25.1
Physical Properties: Halogens

What is responsible for the increasing melting and boiling points in going down the halogen family?

Increasing melting and boiling points indicate that greater intermolecular forces are present. The halogens form diatomic molecules that are symmetrical and do not have dipole moments. Therefore, the increasing force of attraction between the molecules of the successive halogens must be due solely to the increased induced dipole forces (London forces) that go with larger size, increased polarizability, and greater numbers of electrons.

Table 25.6
Oxidation States and Some Compounds and Ions of Chlorine, Bromine, and Iodine

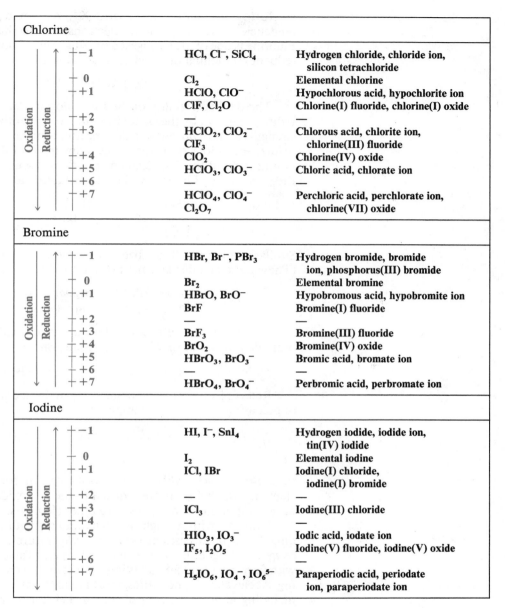

		Chlorine	
	-1	HCl, Cl$^-$, SiCl$_4$	Hydrogen chloride, chloride ion, silicon tetrachloride
	0	Cl$_2$	Elemental chlorine
	$+1$	HClO, ClO$^-$	Hypochlorous acid, hypochlorite ion
		ClF, Cl$_2$O	Chlorine(I) fluoride, chlorine(I) oxide
	$+2$	—	—
	$+3$	HClO$_2$, ClO$_2^-$	Chlorous acid, chlorite ion,
		ClF$_3$	chlorine(III) fluoride
	$+4$	ClO$_2$	Chlorine(IV) oxide
	$+5$	HClO$_3$, ClO$_3^-$	Chloric acid, chlorate ion
	$+6$	—	—
	$+7$	HClO$_4$, ClO$_4^-$	Perchloric acid, perchlorate ion,
		Cl$_2$O$_7$	chlorine(VII) oxide

		Bromine	
	-1	HBr, Br$^-$, PBr$_3$	Hydrogen bromide, bromide ion, phosphorus(III) bromide
	0	Br$_2$	Elemental bromine
	$+1$	HBrO, BrO$^-$	Hypobromous acid, hypobromite ion
		BrF	Bromine(I) fluoride
	$+2$	—	—
	$+3$	BrF$_3$	Bromine(III) fluoride
	$+4$	BrO$_2$	Bromine(IV) oxide
	$+5$	HBrO$_3$, BrO$_3^-$	Bromic acid, bromate ion
	$+6$	—	—
	$+7$	HBrO$_4$, BrO$_4^-$	Perbromic acid, perbromate ion

		Iodine	
	-1	HI, I$^-$, SnI$_4$	Hydrogen iodide, iodide ion, tin(IV) iodide
	0	I$_2$	Elemental iodine
	$+1$	ICl, IBr	Iodine(I) chloride, iodine(I) bromide
	$+2$	—	—
	$+3$	ICl$_3$	Iodine(III) chloride
	$+4$	—	—
	$+5$	HIO$_3$, IO$_3^-$	Iodic acid, iodate ion
		IF$_5$, I$_2$O$_5$	Iodine(V) fluoride, iodine(V) oxide
	$+6$	—	—
	$+7$	H$_5$IO$_6$, IO$_4^-$, IO$_6^{5-}$	Paraperiodic acid, periodate ion, paraperiodate ion

(The left side of each panel shows an arrow labeled "Oxidation" pointing up and "Reduction" pointing down.)

EXAMPLE 25.2
Bonding: Halides

The bonding in tin(IV) fluoride is much more ionic than the bonding in tin(IV) chloride, as indicated by the temperatures at which these two substances vaporize (SnF$_4$ sublimes at 705 °C; SnCl$_4$ boils at 114 °C). How can this be explained?

The electronegativity of tin is 1.7, while that of fluorine, the most electronegative element, is 4.0 and that of chlorine is 3.0. The highly electronegative fluorine atom attracts electrons so strongly that they are given up by tin atoms. With chlorine the electrons are shared in a polar covalent bond. The difference in degree of ionic bonding is reflected in the electronegativity differences. For tin and fluorine it is greater than 2 ($4.0 - 1.7 = 2.3$) while for tin and chlorine it is less than 2 ($3.0 - 1.7 = 1.3$).

a. Redox reactions of X_2 and X^- As would be expected from their strong tendencies to react by adding electrons, the free halogens are all oxidizing agents. Fluorine is one of the strongest oxidizing agents known and has the highest standard reduction potential of the elemental halogens.

$$F_2(g) + 2e^- \longrightarrow 2F^- \qquad E° = 2.87 \text{ V}$$

The oxidizing ability of the free halogens decreases regularly from fluorine to iodine, as shown by the standard reduction potentials (see Table 25.5). The relative strengths of the halogens as oxidizing agents make it possible for each free halogen to oxidize the anions of the halogens following it in the family. (The activity series of nonmetals and the displacement reactions discussed in Section 17.4 are based on these reactions.) Fluorine will oxidize chloride ions:

$$
\begin{array}{lr}
F_2(g) + 2e^- \longrightarrow 2F^- & E° = 2.87 \text{ V} \\
2Cl^- \longrightarrow Cl_2(g) + 2e^- & E° = -1.36 \text{ V} \\
\hline
F_2(g) + 2Cl^- \longrightarrow Cl_2(g) + 2F^- & E° = 1.51 \text{ V}
\end{array}
$$

Similarly chlorine will oxidize bromide ions, and bromine will oxidize iodide ions. (These are redox displacement reactions.)

$$
\begin{array}{lr}
Cl_2(g) + 2Br^- \longrightarrow Br_2(aq) + 2Cl^- & E° = 0.29 \text{ V} \\
Br_2(l) + 2I^- \longrightarrow 2Br^- + I_2(s) & E° = 0.53 \text{ V}
\end{array}
$$

In the presence of excess halogen, further oxidation takes place; for example, bromide ion can be oxidized to bromate ion.

$$3Cl_2(g) + Br^- + 3H_2O(l) \longrightarrow BrO_3^- + 6HCl(aq)$$

Redox reactions in which one halogen displaces another can be used as methods of preparing halides, for example,

$$CaCl_2(s) + F_2(g) \longrightarrow CaF_2(s) + Cl_2(g)$$

b. Combination with other elements In combination reactions with other elements, the halogens are reduced to the -1 oxidation state to give *halides*—binary compounds of halogens with other elements.

Fluorine, with its high reactivity and strength as an oxidizing agent, combines directly, in most cases at ordinary temperatures, with all of the elements except oxygen, nitrogen, helium, neon, and argon (Table 25.7). When placed in contact with fluorine, charcoal bursts into flame; hydrogen–fluorine mixtures are self-igniting. At elevated temperatures, most metals burn in fluorine. However, some metals, including aluminum, copper, and nickel, form protective fluoride films on their

Table 25.7
Combination of the Halogens with Other Elements Compounds of fluorine and chlorine with oxygen and nitrogen, and of chlorine with carbon, do form by other methods.

	With Metals	With Semiconducting Elements	With Nonmetals
F_2	All	All	All except O_2, N_2, He, Ne, Ar
Cl_2	Most	All	All except O_2, N_2, C, and noble gases
Br_2	Most	Most	Only halogens, H_2, P, S
I_2	Most	Most	Only halogens, H_2, P

surfaces, inhibiting further reaction. This property allows fluorine to be shipped and handled in containers made of these metals. Because fluorine is such a strong oxidizing agent and also because the small size of the fluorine atoms allows more of them to fit together around another atom, many elements show their highest oxidation states in compounds with fluorine — for example, for arsenic from Group V and sulfur from Group VI:

$$2As(s) + 5F_2(g) \xrightarrow[\text{temperature}]{\text{room}} 2AsF_5(g)$$

$$S(s) + 3F_2(g) \xrightarrow{\text{bluish flame}} SF_6(g)$$

Chlorine is also very reactive (see Table 25.7) and many metals and semiconducting elements burn on contact with chlorine (e.g., copper, iron, antimony, boron).

Bromine and iodine are less vigorous in their combination reactions, and tend to take other elements to lower oxidation states than do fluorine and in some cases chlorine. The variations in reactivity of the halogens are shown in their combination reactions with arsenic. The products are AsF_5 (see above), $AsCl_3$, $AsBr_3$, and AsI_3. Note the increasing difficulty of reaction.

$$2As(s) + 3Cl_2(g) \xrightarrow[\text{burns}]{\text{As usually}} 2AsCl_3(l)$$

$$2As(s) + 3Br_2(g) \xrightarrow[\substack{\text{initiate} \\ \text{reaction}}]{\text{heat to}} 2AsBr_3(s)$$

$$2As(s) + 3I_2(CS_2) \xrightarrow{\Delta} 2AsI_3(s)$$

c. Combination with molecular compounds A **halogenation** reaction is the introduction of a halogen atom or atoms into a covalent compound. The free halogens react with many compounds in this way. In each of the following examples the free halogen acts as an oxidizing agent.

$$\overset{+4}{S}\overset{}{O_2}(g) + \overset{0}{X_2} \longrightarrow \overset{+6 \ -1}{SO_2X_2} \qquad X = F, Cl$$

sulfur dioxide   *sulfuryl halide*

$$\overset{+2}{C}O(g) + \overset{0}{X_2} \longrightarrow \overset{+4 \ -1}{COX_2} \qquad X = Cl, Br$$

carbon monoxide   *carbonyl halide*

Not every halogen takes part in every one of the many possible halogenation reactions. Fluorine is so reactive that it often behaves differently and gives other products than those shown in the preceding equations.

Halogenation reactions are of great importance in the chemical industry in the production of halogen-substituted hydrocarbons. Halogens add across carbon–carbon double bonds,

$$H_2C{=}CH_2(g) + X_2(g) \longrightarrow CH_2X{-}CH_2X \qquad X = Cl, Br$$

ethylene   *dihaloethane*

or replace hydrogen atoms, for example,

$$CH_4(g) + Cl_2(g) \longrightarrow CH_3Cl(g) + HCl(g)$$

methane   *methyl chloride*

A series of chlorinated compounds, all of which are industrially important, is produced by successive replacement of all four hydrogen atoms in methane (Figure 25.1).

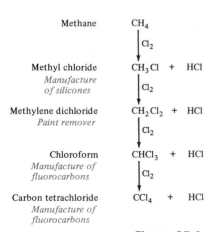

Methane	CH_4		
Methyl chloride *Manufacture of silicones*	CH_3Cl	+	HCl
Methylene dichloride *Paint remover*	CH_2Cl_2	+	HCl
Chloroform *Manufacture of fluorocarbons*	$CHCl_3$	+	HCl
Carbon tetrachloride *Manufacture of fluorocarbons*	CCl_4	+	HCl

Figure 25.1
Chlorination of Methane, CH₄ An example of an industrial halogenation reaction. The products are separated by distillation.

d. Reactions of halogens with water and bases   Fluorine reacts rapidly with water at room temperature, displacing oxygen.

$$2F_2(g) + 2H_2O(l) \longrightarrow 4HF(aq) + O_2(g) \tag{25.1}$$

Other oxidation products of water, such as oxygen difluoride (OF_2) and hydrogen peroxide (H_2O_2), are also formed.

Chlorine, bromine, and iodine disproportionate in aqueous solution to give the hydrohalic (HX) and hypohalous (HXO) acids, for example,

$$\overset{0}{Cl_2}(aq) + H_2O(l) \longrightarrow \overset{-1}{HCl}(aq) + \overset{+1}{HClO}(aq) \tag{25.2}$$
$$\underset{\substack{\text{hydrochloric}\\ \text{acid}}}{} \quad \underset{\substack{\text{hypochlorous}\\ \text{acid}}}{}$$

In such reactions, the halogen is both oxidized to the $+1$ and reduced to the -1 oxidation states. The extent of disproportionation decreases from chlorine to iodine.

$$K = \frac{[H^+][X^-][HXO]}{[X_2]}$$

At 25 °C for Cl_2, $K = 4.4 \times 10^{-4}$
Br_2, $K = 7.2 \times 10^{-9}$
I_2, $K = 2.0 \times 10^{-13}$

As a result, in a saturated solution at 25 °C chlorine is 30% converted to hypochlorous acid, whereas with bromine and iodine much smaller amounts of hypobromous and hypoiodous acid are present under similar conditions.

Aqueous solutions of chlorine and bromine are usually stored in brown bottles because the decomposition of the hypohalous acids is accelerated by sunlight:

$$2HXO(aq) \xrightarrow{hv} O_2(g) + 2H^+ + 2X^- \tag{25.3}$$

Iodine dissolves readily in solutions that contain the iodide ion because of the formation of the brown triiodide ion, I_3^-.

Two reactions can occur when chlorine, bromine, or iodine is dissolved in an alkaline solution. The first is disproportionation to give the hypohalite and halide ions:

$$X_2 + 2OH^- \longrightarrow X^- + XO^- + H_2O(l) \tag{25.4}$$

The second is the disproportionation of the hypohalite ion:

$$3XO^- \longrightarrow 2X^- + XO_3^- \tag{25.5}$$

Because of differences in the relative rates of reactions (25.4) and (25.5), at *room temperature* an aqueous alkaline solution of chlorine contains mainly hypochlorite and chloride ions, a bromine solution contains a mixture of all three possible ions, and an iodine solution contains mainly iodate and iodide ion.

major products

$$Cl_2 \xrightarrow{OH^-} Cl^- + ClO^-$$
$$Br_2 \xrightarrow{OH^-} Br^- + BrO^- + BrO_3^-$$
$$I_2 \xrightarrow{OH^-} I^- + IO_3^-$$

e. Ions in aqueous solution   The halide ions are all found in many soluble salts. The Cl^-, Br^-, and I^- anions simply become hydrated in aqueous solution. The F^- ion reacts to give weakly alkaline solutions ($K_b = 1.5 \times 10^{-11}$).

Of the possible anions of the known halogen oxoacids (see Table 25.14), those most commonly encountered are the hypochlorite ion (ClO^-); the anions with halogens in the +5 state, namely the chlorate (ClO_3^-), bromate (BrO_3^-), and iodate (IO_3^-) ions; and the perchlorate ion (ClO_4^-). The basicity of the anions—their attraction for protons—decreases with increasing oxidation number of the halogen. Hypochlorous acid is a weak acid and the hypochlorite ion can hydrolyze to give a weakly alkaline solution:

$$ClO^- + H_2O(l) \rightleftharpoons HClO(aq) + OH^- \qquad \textbf{(25.6)}$$

(In the presence of additional OH^-, the ClO^- ion disproportionates; Equation 25.5.) Chloric acid ($HClO_3$) and perchloric acid ($HClO_4$) are strong acids, and their anions do not react with water to a significant extent.

ClO_4^- perchlorate ion
ClO_3^- chlorate ion
ClO_2^- chlorite ion
ClO^- hypochlorite ion

f. Thermal decomposition of compounds containing halogen oxoanions

Metal chlorates and perchlorates decompose when heated to liberate oxygen and form the halides, for example,

$$2NaClO_3(s) \xrightarrow{\Delta} 2NaCl(s) + 3O_2(g) \qquad \textbf{(25.7)}$$

$$KClO_4(s) \xrightarrow{\Delta} KCl(s) + 2O_2(g) \qquad \textbf{(25.8)}$$

At moderate temperatures the perchlorate is an intermediate in the decomposition of chlorates, for example,

$$4KClO_3(s) \xrightarrow{\Delta} 3KClO_4(s) + KCl(s) \qquad \textbf{(25.9)}$$

Alkali metal bromates and iodates also thermally decompose to oxygen and the halide, while compounds of less active metals give other products, often the halogen and oxygen, for example,

$$2Zn(BrO_3)_2(s) \xrightarrow{\Delta} 2ZnO(s) + 2Br_2(g) + 5O_2(g)$$

EXAMPLE 25.3
Thermodynamics: Halogen Compounds

Determine whether or not the reaction described by the equation

$$2KIO_3(s) + Cl_2(g) \longrightarrow 2KClO_3(s) + I_2(s)$$

is feasible under standard state conditions at 25 °C, given that for $KClO_3(s)$, $\Delta H_f^\circ = -391.2$ kJ/mol and for $KIO_3(s)$, $\Delta H_f^\circ = -508.4$ kJ/mol; and that for $KClO_3(s)$, $S^\circ = 143.0$ J/K mol; for $KIO_3(s)$, $S^\circ = 151.5$ J/K mol; for $Cl_2(g)$, $S^\circ = 223.0$ J/K mol, and for $I_2(s)$, $S^\circ = 116.1$ J/K mol.

To determine whether or not this reaction is thermodynamically spontaneous under standard state conditions at 25 °C, the data given can be used to calculate ΔG°.

The enthalpy of the reaction is given by

$$\Delta H^\circ = [\text{sum of } \Delta H_f^\circ(\text{products})] - [\text{sum of } \Delta H_f^\circ(\text{reactants})]$$
$$= [(2 \text{ mol})(-391.2 \text{ kJ/mol}) + (1 \text{ mol})(0 \text{ kJ/mol})]$$
$$\quad - [(2 \text{ mol})(-508.4 \text{ kJ/mol}) + (1 \text{ mol})(0 \text{ kJ/mol})]$$
$$= 234.4 \text{ kJ}$$

The entropy change is given by

$$\Delta S^\circ = [\text{sum of } S^\circ(\text{products})] - [\text{sum of } S^\circ(\text{reactants})]$$
$$= [(2 \text{ mol})(143.0 \text{ J/K mol}) + (1 \text{ mol})(116.1 \text{ J/K mol})]$$
$$\quad - [(2 \text{ mol})(151.5 \text{ J/K mol}) + (1 \text{ mol})(223.0 \text{ J/K mol})]$$
$$= -123.9 \text{ J/K} = -0.1239 \text{ kJ/K}$$

Finally, $\Delta G°$ can be found from $\Delta H°$ and $\Delta S°$,

$$\Delta G° = \Delta H° - T \Delta S°$$
$$= (234.4 \text{ kJ}) - (298.15 \text{ K})(-0.1239 \text{ kJ/K})$$
$$= 271.3 \text{ kJ}$$

The positive value for $\Delta G°$ shows that under standard state conditions at 25 °C solid potassium iodate is not a strong enough oxidizing agent to convert chlorine to perchlorate.

EXAMPLE 25.4
Chemical Equilibria: Halogens

How might the concentration of HBrO in a saturated aqueous bromine solution be (a) increased, (b) decreased?

In a saturated bromine solution the equilibrium is

$$Br_2(l) + H_2O(l) \rightleftharpoons HBrO(aq) + H^+ + Br^-$$

(a) The concentration of HBrO could be increased by adding OH^- to react with the H^+ to form water, or by adding a cation that forms a slightly soluble salt with Br^-, for example,

$$Br_2(l) + H_2O(l) + AgNO_3(aq) \longrightarrow HBrO(aq) + AgBr(s) + H^+ + NO_3^-$$

(b) The concentration of HBrO could be decreased by adding an acid to increase the H^+ concentration or a soluble bromide to increase the Br^- concentration, in either case displacing the equilibrium in favor of $Br_2(l)$ and $H_2O(l)$.

PREPARATION AND USES OF THE HALOGENS

25.3 SOURCES OF THE HALOGENS

Because of their great reactivity, the halogens are never found in the free state in nature, but commonly occur in deposits of various salts or in solutions of these salts in the oceans or in natural brine wells. The sources of the halogens are summarized in Table 25.8.

Table 25.8
Natural Occurrence of the Halogens

	Percent in Earth's Crust	Sources
Fluorine	$6-9 \times 10^{-2}$	Fluorspar, CaF_2 Cryolite, $Na_3(AlF_6)$ Fluorapatite, $Ca_5(PO_4)_3F$
Chlorine	3.14×10^{-2}	NaCl Salt beds, brine wells, seawater (2.8%) Carnallite, $KCl \cdot MgCl_2 \cdot 6H_2O$
Bromine	1.6×10^{-4}	NaBr, KBr, $MgBr_2$ Brine wells Seawater
Iodine	3×10^{-5}	$NaIO_3$, $NaIO_4$ $NaNO_3$ deposits in Chile Iodides Brine wells

25.4 FLUORINE

a. Preparation and uses of fluorine No chemical oxidizing agent is strong enough to oxidize fluoride ion to elemental fluorine. Since all natural sources of fluorine contain fluoride ions, elemental fluorine must be prepared by electrolysis. First, hydrogen fluoride is obtained by treating the mineral fluorspar, which is calcium fluoride, with concentrated sulfuric acid:

$$CaF_2(s) + H_2SO_4(conc) \xrightarrow{\Delta} CaSO_4(s) + 2HF(g) \qquad \text{(25.10)}$$

There are numerous partner-exchange reactions of this type—reactions driven by the formation of a volatile acid from salt and a less volatile acid.

Elemental fluorine is produced by the electrolysis of hydrogen fluoride dissolved in molten potassium fluoride (the reaction must be carried out in the absence of water):

$$2HF(in\ KF) \xrightarrow[\text{energy}]{\text{electrical}} H_2(g) + F_2(g)$$

The electrolytic vessel is usually constructed of one of the metals, such as nickel, copper, or the nickel–copper–iron alloy known as Monel metal, which quickly becomes protected by a metal fluoride coating. The K^+ and HF_2^- ions are formed in the HF–KF solution and conduct the current. The anode is graphite and the cathode is Monel metal or steel.

Before the 1940s there was no commercial production of free fluorine, and fluorine-containing chemicals were just beginning to find uses as refrigerants. The great reactivity of fluorine had made chemists reluctant to handle it. Fluorine technology developed when, in the drive to produce the atomic bomb, it was found that the uranium isotopes ^{238}U and ^{235}U could be separated by diffusion of their hexafluorides (Section 5.13). Isotope separation remains the principal use of gaseous fluorine. Some of the products that incorporate fluorine compounds are listed in Table 25.9.

b. Fluorine–carbon compounds "Fluorochlorocarbon" is a general term for hydrocarbons in which some or all of the hydrogen atoms have been replaced by fluorine and chlorine atoms. The low molecular mass fluorochlorocarbons, known by the trade name Freons, are nontoxic, stable at high temperatures, inert, odorless, and nonflammable. They are ideal for use as refrigerants and aerosol propellants because they are easily liquefied by pressure alone and have large enthalpies of vaporization.

The discovery of the useful properties of the Freons is an outstanding example of problem-solving scientific research. Each of the early refrigerants was unsatisfactory. Ethylene was flammable; sulfur dioxide and ammonia were corrosive and poisonous; carbon dioxide, although a harmless gas, required cumbersome, high-pressure equipment. At General Motors (they also make refrigerators) in the 1920s a group set out to devise a better refrigerant by plotting periodic table trends of toxicity, flammability, and boiling point. The first compound they picked to try was dichlorodifluoromethane, the first Freon.

In the 1970s concern arose over the possible destruction of ozone in the stratosphere (Section 16.13) by reactions of two of the Freons that were being released during their use as propellants in aerosol spray cans (Figure 25.2). Dichlorodifluoromethane and trichlorofluoromethane are thought to yield chlorine atoms by photodecomposition in the stratosphere.

$$CF_2Cl_2(g) \xrightarrow{h\nu} CF_2Cl(g) + Cl(g)$$
$$CFCl_3(g) \xrightarrow{h\nu} CFCl_2(g) + Cl(g)$$

The reactive chlorine atoms may then destroy ozone in the following reaction sequence, which can be repeated over and over, since the chlorine atoms are

Table 25.9
Some Fluorine-Containing End Products

Refrigerants
Aerosol propellants
Polyfluorocarbon resins
  (e.g., Teflon)
Textile finishes
  (e.g., Scotchgard)
Toothpaste
Electrical insulating
  medium (SF_6)

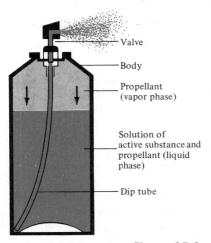

Figure 25.2
An Aerosol Spray Can The pressure of the volatile propellant forces the liquid out when the valve is opened.

Valve
Body
Propellant (vapor phase)
Solution of active substance and propellant (liquid phase)
Dip tube

regenerated in the second reaction with oxygen atoms that are always present in the stratosphere.

$$Cl(g) + O_3(g) \longrightarrow ClO(g) + O_2(g)$$
$$ClO(g) + O(g) \longrightarrow Cl(g) + O_2(g)$$

After extensive investigation and debate, the use of these two Freons in aerosol sprays in the United States was banned. (Similar bans are not in effect in other countries and the concern remains.)

Polymers made from fluorocarbons, such as Teflon, are also inert and resistant to high temperatures, and they can be used in contact with very reactive chemicals. Teflon is polytetrafluoroethylene:

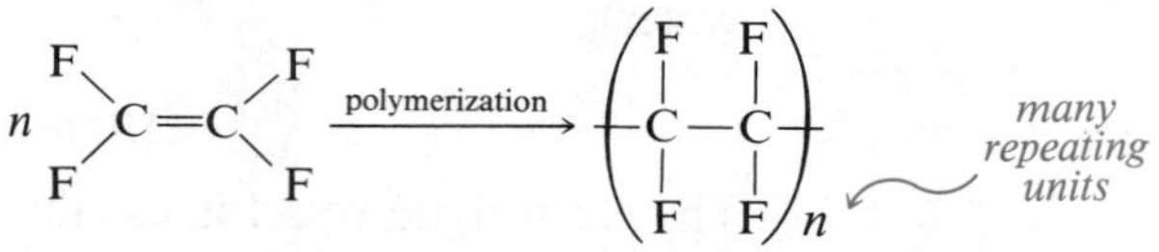

Teflon

It is interesting to note that tetrachloroethylene does not give polymers in a similar manner. Apparently the much larger size of the chlorine atoms inhibits the polymerization reaction.

In one of the more fascinating uses for any chemical, perfluorocarbons (organic compounds with all hydrogen atoms replaced by fluorine atoms) are being developed as "blood substitutes." Aqueous emulsions containing the fluorine derivatives are able to transport oxygen and carbon monoxide just as blood does. Rats have lived out normal life spans with all of their blood replaced by perfluorocarbon "blood," and a blood substitute containing perfluorodecalin, $C_{10}F_{18}$,

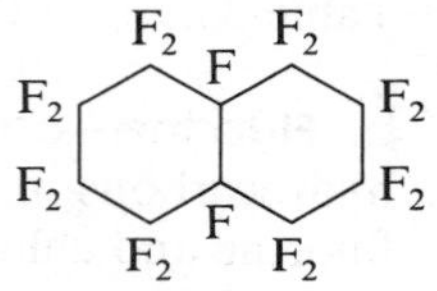

perfluorodecalin

has been safely tested on more than 500 human patients. The perfluorocarbons have a longer storage life than blood, can be used in individuals with any blood type, and, because the molecules are smaller than blood cells, can more easily enter damaged tissue.

c. Fluoridation of water

Thanks to the advertising industry, it seems impossible for anyone in the United States not to know that fluorides fight dental cavities. Discovery of the cavity-fighting property of fluorides was made when the cause of the spotted and darkened teeth of residents of several towns in the western United States was investigated. Fluoride ion was found to be dissolving from natural mineral deposits into the town water supplies. Persistent U.S. Public Health Service dentists soon found that along with the discolored teeth went an unusually low rate of tooth decay, and this too was attributed to fluoride ion.

At a concentration of 1 part per million in the drinking water, fluoride ion prevents decay without causing discoloration. For discoloration to occur, the fluoride ion concentration must be greater than 1.5 ppm. When this was learned, an obvious suggestion was made — add 1 ppm of fluoride ion to the water wherever it doesn't occur naturally and protect everyone's teeth. In 1945, Grand Rapids, Michigan, became the first city to do so.

Teeth contain calcium in the form of the mineral apatite (Figure 25.3),

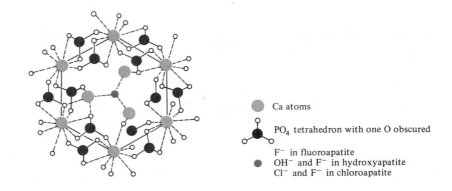

Figure 25.3
The Crystal Structure of Apatite Apatite [$Ca_5(PO_4)_3OH$] is a mineral and also occurs in teeth as hydroxyapatite. Fluoride replaces OH^- in the structure of teeth when it is available in the diet. In the structure the F^- or OH^- is surrounded in the same plane by three Ca^{2+} ions. The six Ca^{2+} ions that delineate the hexagon are in two different planes.

○ Ca atoms

PO₄ tetrahedron with one O obscured

F^- in fluoroapatite
OH^- and F^- in hydroxyapatite
Cl^- and F^- in chloroapatite

$Ca_5(PO_4)_3OH$. Fluoride ions replace the hydroxide ions in the apatite structure and make it resistant to attack by the acids which cause tooth decay. Fluoride toothpastes reach the surface of teeth and can build a protective coating there. But fluoride provides the greatest benefits when it is incorporated throughout the entire tooth as it forms. This is achieved when fluoride is ingested by children and gets carried to the growing teeth by the bloodstream.

The compounds used to maintain 1 ppm of fluoride ion in the water supply are sodium fluoride, NaF; sodium hexafluorosilicate, Na_2SiF_6; hexafluorosilicic acid, H_2SiF_6, which is formed only in solution; or Na_2PO_3F, sodium monofluorophosphate.

25.5 CHLORINE

a. Preparation and uses of chlorine The major industrial preparation of chlorine, one of the top ten industrial chemicals (Table 25.10), is by electrolysis of concentrated sodium chloride solutions. Sodium hydroxide is an equally important co-product in this process, which is discussed in Section 29.6a on the chloralkali industry. More than 50% of the chlorine produced is utilized in the manufacture of other chemicals. Some of the types of products that incorporate chlorine compounds are herbicides and pesticides, poly (vinyl chloride) plastics, drycleaning fluids, pharmaceuticals, and refrigerants. Other major uses for free chlorine are as a bleach for textiles and paper (discussed in the next section), in sanitizing and disinfecting municipal water supplies, and in wastewater and sewage treatment.

Table 25.10
The Top Ten Industrial Chemicals These data are for 1982. Frequently, nitric acid* is a top ten industrial chemical.

Rank		Billions of Kilograms Produced
1	Sulfuric acid	29.36
2	Nitrogen	15.87
3	Ammonia	14.05
4	Oxygen	13.25
5	Lime (CaO)	12.88
6	Ethylene	11.18
7	Sodium hydroxide	8.37
8	Chlorine	8.29
9	Phosphoric acid	7.76
10	Sodium carbonate	7.16

* In 1982, the next five largest volume industrial chemicals were 11, toluene; 12, nitric acid; 13, ammonium nitrate; 14, propylene; 15, urea.

EXAMPLE 25.5
Stoichiometry: Preparation of Chlorine

In plants where industrial chemicals are manufactured, concentrations are not ordinarily expressed in molar terms. For example, the concentration of the sodium chloride solution (brine) electrolyzed to produce chlorine is given as 25.50 mass percent NaCl (essentially a saturated solution at room temperature). The density of such a solution is 1.195 g/mL. Calculate its molarity.

The mass of 1 L of solution is 1195 g. The mass of NaCl in this volume of solution is

$$\left(1195 \text{ g solution}\right)\left(\frac{25.50 \text{ g NaCl}}{100.00 \text{ g solution}}\right) = 304.7 \text{ g NaCl}$$

The number of moles of NaCl per liter, the molarity, is

$$\left(\frac{304.7 \text{ g NaCl}}{1 \text{ L solution}}\right)\left(\frac{1 \text{ mol NaCl}}{58.44 \text{ g NaCl}}\right) = 5.214 \text{ mol/L}$$

The brine solution used in the electrolysis is 5.214 M.

EXAMPLE 25.6
Electrochemistry: Sodium Chloride

If a 1 M solution of sodium chloride were electrolyzed, would the products be the same as in electrolysis of a concentrated brine? The following are the reduction potential values for the possible electrode reactions:

$$
\begin{array}{ll}
\text{Na}^+ + \text{e}^- \longrightarrow \text{Na} & E^\circ = -2.71 \text{ V} \\
2\text{H}_2\text{O} + 2\text{e}^- \longrightarrow \text{H}_2 + 2\text{OH}^-(10^{-7} \text{ M}) & E = -0.41 \text{ V} \\
\text{O}_2 + 4\text{H}^+(10^{-7} \text{ M}) + 4\text{e}^- \longrightarrow 2\text{H}_2\text{O} & E = 0.82 \text{ V} \\
\text{Cl}_2 + 2\text{e}^- \longrightarrow 2\text{Cl}^- & E^\circ = 1.36 \text{ V}
\end{array}
$$

The reduction reactions that might take place at the cathode are

$$
\begin{array}{ll}
\text{Na}^+ + \text{e}^- \longrightarrow \text{Na} & E^\circ = -2.71 \text{ V} \\
2\text{H}_2\text{O} + 2\text{e}^- \longrightarrow \text{H}_2 + 2\text{OH}^-(10^{-7} \text{ M}) & E = -0.41 \text{ V}
\end{array}
$$

The likely reaction will be the second one, for it has the more positive reduction potential.

The oxidation reactions possible at the anode are

$$
\begin{array}{ll}
2\text{H}_2\text{O} \longrightarrow \text{O}_2(g) + 4\text{H}^+(10^{-7} \text{ M}) + 4\text{e}^- & E = -0.82 \text{ V} \\
2\text{Cl}^- \longrightarrow \text{Cl}_2 + 2\text{e}^- & E^\circ = -1.36 \text{ V}
\end{array}
$$

Here, the first reaction is the one with the greater thermodynamic likelihood of occurring. The overall reaction expected on the basis of the thermodynamic data is simply the decomposition of water.

$$2\text{H}_2\text{O}(l) \xrightarrow[\substack{\text{electrical} \\ \text{energy}}]{\text{Na}^+\text{Cl}^-} 2\text{H}_2(g) + \text{O}_2(g)$$

b. Chlorine bleaching and disinfecting Chlorine and oxo compounds of chlorine in its lower oxidation states are valuable chemicals in a number of applications that require bleaching, removing undesirable odors, and destroying disease-causing, or pathogenic, bacteria (disinfecting). When chlorine, hypochlorites, or organic compounds containing chlorine bonded to nitrogen are used as bleaching agents, hypochlorous acid, which is formed in solution, is the active species.

$$
\begin{array}{lr}
\text{Cl}_2(g) + \text{H}_2\text{O}(l) \rightleftharpoons \text{H}^+ + \text{Cl}^- + \text{HClO}(aq) & \textbf{(25.11)} \\
\text{NaClO}(aq) + \text{H}_2\text{O}(l) \rightleftharpoons \text{Na}^+ + \text{OH}^- + \text{HClO}(aq) & \textbf{(25.12)} \\
\text{RR}'\text{NCl}(s) + \text{H}_2\text{O}(l) \rightleftharpoons \text{RR}'\text{NH}(aq) + \text{HClO}(aq) & \textbf{(25.13)}
\end{array}
$$

(In RR′NCl, the R and R′ represent the rest of the organic molecule.)

Unwanted color in paper pulp, textiles, household laundry, and swimming pools is most often due to the presence of colored organic compounds. The color is often the result of absorption of light in the visible region by structures that contain alternating single and double carbon–carbon bonds (Section 27.6). When some of the double bonds are broken, this light is no longer absorbed and the objectionable color disappears.

Bleaches attack double bonds in various ways. The hypochlorous acid molecule splits so that OH is added to one carbon atom and Cl to the other in a double bond, producing a single bond and thereby breaking up the color-absorbing system. Household bleach (for example, Clorox) is an alkaline solution of sodium hypochlorite. Solutions of sodium hypochlorite are generated at the site of their use in, for example, sewage treatment plants or large swimming pools, by the electrolysis of cold concentrated aqueous sodium chloride solutions. The chlorine produced at one electrode and the hydroxide ion produced at the other,

$$\textit{cathode} \quad 2H_2O + 2e^- \longrightarrow 2OH^- + H_2$$
$$\textit{anode} \quad\quad\quad 2Cl^- \longrightarrow Cl_2 + 2e^-$$

are allowed to react with each other:

$$Cl_2(g) + 2OH^- \longrightarrow ClO^- + Cl^- + H_2O(l)$$

The overall reaction in the electrolysis of concentrated sodium chloride under these conditions is

$$Cl^- + H_2O(l) \xrightarrow[\text{cold}]{\text{electrolysis}} ClO^- + H_2(g)$$

(In the electrolytic production of chlorine, the products formed at the electrodes must be kept separated so that this reaction does not occur; Section 29.8a.) Calcium hypochlorite, $Ca(ClO)_2$, one of the few stable solid hypochlorites (the others are those of lithium, strontium, and barium), is also an important commercial bleach.

Hypochlorous acid is a wonderfully useful chemical because it not only bleaches and oxidizes, but also acts as a disinfectant. Contrary to popular opinion, it is not chlorine, but hypochlorous acid that kills bacteria in city water or swimming pools (see An Aside: Swimming Pool Chemistry).The acid is thought to act by diffusing through the cell walls and destroying enzymes essential to the health of the bacteria. Epidemics of such water-borne diseases as dysentery, hepatitis, and typhoid are rare in areas where water is chlorinated.

AN ASIDE

Swimming Pool Chemistry

A freshly filled swimming pool is an aqueous equilibrium system open to the atmosphere and (if it is outdoors) to sunlight. When swimmers enter the pool, bacteria, dirt, and organic by-products are mixed into the system. To maintain a healthy and beautifully clear swimming pool requires careful balancing of the pool chemistry.

The majority of pools are treated with chemicals that release hypochlorous acid (Equations 25.11–25.13). As this acid is the active ingredient for oxidizing odor-causing organic chemicals, bleaching, and disinfecting, it is desirable to keep the concentration of the acid high. Because hypochlorous acid (and hypochlorite ion) participates in several equilibria in aqueous solution (Equations 25.2, 25.4–25.6), its concentration is clearly pH dependent.

The pool pH is, in turn, dependent upon the natural "alkalinity" of the water—the concentration of hydrogen carbonates, carbonates, and hydroxides dissolved in the water. Hydrogen carbonates can provide a buffering action that helps to maintain a constant pH. In a pool with low alkalinity, very small additions of acid or base can cause undesirably wide swings in pH, and in such cases sodium hydrogen carbonate must be added to the pool to correct this condition. A pH range of 7.2–7.6 is ideal, for in this range hypochlorous acid has its maximum bactericidal effect.

Each pool has its own "chlorine demand" based on the amount of contaminants brought into it, the temperature, the alkalinity, and the amount of sunlight it receives, for sunlight accelerates the decomposition of hypochlorous acid (Equation 25.3). In regions where sunlight exposure is high, pools can be "chlorinated" and protected from sunlight by the same chemical. For example, trichloroisocyanuric acid yields hypochlorous acid and cyanuric acid upon hydrolysis.

trichloroisocyanuric acid   cyanuric acid

The cyanuric acid absorbs ultraviolet radiation (note the double bonds alternating with single bonds), thereby screening the hypochlorous acid in a swimming pool from the sun.

An additional factor that influences swimming pool chemistry is the hardness of the water (Section 14.11). A bad balance among alkalinity, temperature, pH, and water hardness can lead at one extreme to precipitation of calcium carbonate on the pool walls and filtering system, or at the other extreme, to corrosion of metal equipment exposed to the pool water (Section 23.17). These conditions are corrected by adding hydrochloric acid or sodium hydrogen carbonate to adjust the pH and the alkalinity as needed.

One more interesting bit of swimming pool chemistry—an unpleasant odor and eye irritation are often attributed to too much chlorine in a pool. The cause of this condition is actually *too little* "chlorine" in the pool. The irritating chemicals are chloramines (compounds with nitrogen–chlorine bonds), which are formed by the reaction of hypochlorous acid with amines and urea (from sweat and urine), for example,

$$NH_3(aq) + HClO(aq) \longrightarrow \underset{\text{monochloramine}}{NH_2Cl(aq)} + H_2O(l)$$

In the presence of additional hypochlorous acid, the chloramines are destroyed by oxidation to nitrogen, for example,

$$2NH_2Cl(aq) + HClO(aq) \longrightarrow N_2(g) + H_2O(l) + 3HCl(aq)$$

The next time you dive into a sparkling swimming pool, you might remember that you are about to disturb a number of simultaneous aqueous equilibria.

25.6 BROMINE

Bromine is prepared by oxidation of the bromide ions in natural brine or seawater. The primary source of bromine in the United States, the natural brines from Arkansas, contain about 4000 ppm of bromine. The oxidizing agent used in industry for bromide ion is chlorine (Section 25.2a).

The major industrial use of bromine has been in ethylene dibromide, $C_2H_4Br_2$, which is added to leaded gasoline. The ethylene dibromide reacts with lead oxide and lead sulfate, combustion products that would otherwise be deposited in the engine. The lead bromide formed is volatile and is carried away with the exhaust. As antipollution laws that limit the use of lead in gasoline go into effect, this use of bromine is declining. Other uses of bromine compounds take advantage of their fireretarding properties, their high density (e.g., in hydraulic fluids), their activity as fungicides, and the sensitivity to light of silver bromide (see An Aside: The Photographic Process, Chapter 31).

25.7 IODINE One source of iodine is the liquid containing sodium iodate left after removal of sodium nitrate from Chilean ores. Reduction with hydrogen sulfite ion, HSO_3^-, yields free iodine in a two-step process:

$$2NaIO_3(aq) + 6NaHSO_3(aq) \longrightarrow 2NaI(aq) + 3Na_2SO_4(aq) + 3H_2SO_4(aq)$$
$$5NaI(aq) + NaIO_3(aq) + 3H_2SO_4(aq) \longrightarrow 3I_2(s) + 3Na_2SO_4(aq) + 3H_2O(aq)$$

(What are the oxidizing and reducing agents in the second reaction above?)

Iodine is also made from brines or from seaweed, which concentrates iodide ion from seawater. The seaweed is burned to yield an ash that may contain from 0.5–1.5% of iodide ion. The iodide is oxidized by chlorine or other oxidizing agents to yield free iodine.

The major uses of iodine are in animal feed, pharmaceutical chemicals, catalysts, and chemicals for photography. Iodide ion is necessary for the production of thyroxine in the thyroid gland. Insufficient iodide ion in the diet leads to a condition known as goiter, which is an enlargement of the thyroid gland. To assure the presence of iodide ion in the diet, sodium or potassium iodide is added to table salt, which is sold as "iodized" salt.

COMPOUNDS OF THE HALOGENS

25.8 HYDROGEN HALIDES AND THEIR AQUEOUS SOLUTIONS

a. Properties of the hydrogen halides and the hydrohalic acids At room temperature and pressure, all of the hydrogen halides are colorless gases. They fume in moist air as they react to form droplets of the hydrohalic acids. The hydrogen halides are strong irritants to the mucous membranes, and hydrogen fluoride is a particularly dangerous material in this respect.

There is a regular increase in the melting and boiling points and also in the heats of fusion and vaporization from the chloride to the iodide (Table 25.11). Hydrogen fluoride has much higher values for these properties because of hydrogen bonding between hydrogen and fluorine. In the solid and liquid states, and even in the gaseous state if the temperature is not too high, HF molecules remain hydrogen-bonded in chains and rings (Section 11.12).

The strength of the hydrogen–halogen bond is very high in hydrogen fluoride; it decreases with increasing size of the halogen atom. The bond strength is reflected in the increasing ease of dissociation of the hydrogen halides at elevated temperatures (see Table 25.11).

The hydrogen halides other than hydrogen fluoride can all act as reducing agents, their strength increasing in the order HCl < HBr < HI. Hydrogen iodide is a strong reducing agent. In redox reactions the hydrogen halides are oxidized to elemental halogens.

Table 25.11
Properties of the Hydrogen Halides

Property	HF	HCl	HBr	HI
Melting point (°C)	−83.1	−114.8	−86.9	−50.7
Boiling point (°C)	19.5	−84.9	−66.8	−35.4
Heat of fusion at melting point (kJ/mol)	4.58	1.99	2.41	2.87
Heat of vaporization at boiling point (kJ/mol)	30.3	16.2	17.6	19.7
Percent dissociation into elements at 1000 °C	0	0.014	0.5	33
H—X bond length (nm)	0.0917	0.127	0.141	0.161
Bond dissociation energies HX(g) ⟶ H(g) + X(g) (kJ/mol)	568	432	356	298

The hydrogen halides are extremely soluble in water, giving the solutions that we know as hydrofluoric, hydrochloric, hydrobromic, and hydroiodic acids. In large part because of the strength of the hydrogen–fluorine bond, hydrofluoric acid is a weak acid, with a K_a of 6.5×10^{-4} (comparable to that of acetic acid, 1.75×10^{-5}). The other three hydrohalic acids are strong nonoxidizing acids.

In what is unique behavior among weak acids, hydrofluoric acid is more highly ionized in concentrated than in dilute aqueous solutions. In dilute solutions, the principal hydrogen-bonded species is HF $\cdots$ HOH. This is a weaker acid than the HF $\cdots$ HF species present in more concentrated solutions, which can ionize as follows:

$$\text{HF} \cdots \text{HF} \rightleftharpoons \text{H}^+ + \text{HF}_2^-$$

The hydrogen–fluorine hydrogen bond is sufficiently strong that stable salts containing the HF_2^- anion are formed.

$$\text{KOH}(s) + 2\text{HF}(aq) \longrightarrow \underset{\substack{\textit{potassium hydrogen} \\ \textit{fluoride}}}{\text{KHF}_2(s)} + \text{H}_2\text{O}(l)$$

The HF_2^- anion can be pictured as a resonance hybrid with one covalent bond and one hydrogen bond, $[\text{F} \cdots \text{H}—\text{F}] \leftrightarrow [\text{F}—\text{H} \cdots \text{F}]$.

Hydrochloric acid, while not used in as great a volume as the big three industrial acids (Section 26.6), has many applications in industrial chemistry. It is also commonly used in the laboratory, particularly when a strong acid without any oxidizing properties is needed. Over 90% of the hydrochloric acid produced is obtained as a by-product of the chlorination of organic compounds (see Figure 25.1). The major consumption of hydrochloric acid is in the production of inorganic and organic chlorine-containing compounds.

b. Preparation of the hydrogen halides The combination of hydrogen with fluorine to give hydrogen fluoride is violent, even at room temperature. Commercially, hydrogen fluoride is prepared by the reaction of fluorspar with sulfuric acid (Equation 25.10).

Hydrogen chloride can be produced in a two-step process known as the salt–sulfuric acid process. The first reaction, a partner exchange, proceeds to completion at a low temperature as hydrogen chloride escapes from the reaction mixture.

$$\text{NaCl}(s) + \text{H}_2\text{SO}_4(conc) \longrightarrow \text{HCl}(g) + \text{NaHSO}_4(s) \tag{25.14}$$

Adding more sodium chloride and heating to a high temperature gives additional hydrogen chloride.

$$\text{NaHSO}_4(s) + \text{NaCl}(s) \overset{\Delta}{\longrightarrow} \text{HCl}(g) + \text{Na}_2\text{SO}_4(s) \tag{25.15}$$

The reactions of bromine and iodine with hydrogen are slow at room temperature but can be made to go at practical rates at elevated temperatures in the presence of a catalyst such as platinum. Hydrogen bromide and hydrogen iodide can also be prepared by reduction of the elemental halogens by phosphorus or sulfur in aqueous solution, for example,

$$\text{S}(s) + 3\text{Br}_2(l) + 4\text{H}_2\text{O}(l) \longrightarrow \text{H}_2\text{SO}_4(aq) + 6\text{HBr}(g)$$

Note that the sulfuric acid produced is present in a dilute solution and therefore does not oxidize the hydrogen bromide. Hydrogen bromide and hydrogen iodide cannot be prepared by the salt–sulfuric acid method because in the presence of concentrated sulfuric acid the hydrogen halide is oxidized, for example,

$$\text{H}_2\text{SO}_4(conc) + 2\text{HBr}(g) \longrightarrow \text{Br}_2(g) + \text{SO}_2(g) + 2\text{H}_2\text{O}(l)$$

Hydroiodic acid is produced directly by the reduction of an elemental iodine suspension by hydrogen sulfide or hydrazine, for example,

$$N_2H_4(g) + 2I_2(s) \xrightarrow{H_2O} 4HI(aq) + N_2(g)$$

(What are the oxidation number changes in this reaction?)

25.9 METAL HALIDES

Halides are known for all of the metals, and preparation of most of them is possible by the direct combination of the elements. Other preparative methods include partner-exchange reactions or displacement of hydrogen from halogen acids by active metals.

Since the metals vary considerably in electropositive character and the halogens vary in electronegative character, <u>bonding</u> in metal halides varies with the nature of both the metal and the halogen. The metal halides, therefore, span the entire continuum from ionic to covalent bonding and have a wide range of physical and chemical properties.

In general, metals that have low ionization energies (such as the alkali metals) form ionic halides. These are the metals with low charge-to-size ratios. But if the energy for removal of all the valence electrons of the metal is high, and if the charge-to-size ratio of the cations that might form is high, the bonds between metal and halogen (particularly for chlorine, bromine, or iodine) will be covalent. Fluorine, the smallest and most electronegative of the halogens, frequently forms predominately ionic compounds even with metals that have high ionization energies and high polarizing abilities. For example, AlF_3 is an ionic compound, whereas the other halides of aluminum have predominately covalent bonding.

In most cases, the <u>thermal stability</u> of ionic halides decreases regularly and markedly from the fluoride to the iodide salts of the same cation. This order, illustrated in Table 25.12 with some thermochemical values for the sodium halides, is a direct reflection of changes in ionic size. Interaction between the cation and the halide ion in the crystal is strongest with fluoride ion, the smallest of the halide ions, and weakest with iodide, the largest.

The greater the ionic character of the metal–halogen bond, the higher the <u>melting and boiling points</u> of the halides. This reflects the fact that the forces between ions in a crystal are stronger than those between covalent molecules. If a metal has two or more oxidation states, the halide with the metal in the lower state is the more ionic and has the higher melting and boiling points.

Frequently the <u>solubility in water</u> of a fluoride differs considerably from that of the corresponding chloride, bromide, or iodide. For example, whereas the fluorides of lithium, magnesium, calcium, strontium, barium, and the lanthanides are relatively insoluble in water, the other halides of these elements are quite soluble. Most metal chlorides, bromides, and iodides are soluble (see Table 17.1).

Table 25.12
Some Thermochemical Values for the Sodium Halides

	Lattice Energy, ΔH, 25 °C (kJ/mol)	Standard Enthalpy of Formation, ΔH_f° (kJ/mol)
NaF	−912	−569.0
NaCl	−774	−411.0
NaBr	−736	−359.9
NaI	−703	−288.0

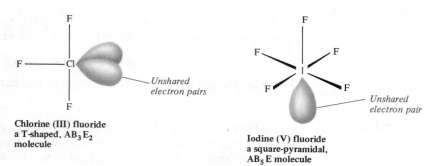

Figure 25.4
Geometry of Representative Interhalogen Molecules

Chlorine (III) fluoride
a T-shaped, AB_3E_2 molecule

Iodine (V) fluoride
a square-pyramidal, AB_5E molecule

25.10 INTERHALOGENS

Table 25.13
Interhalogen Compounds

ClF	BrF
colorless gas	*red gas*
ClF$_3$	BrF$_3$
colorless gas	*colorless liquid*
ClF$_5$	BrF$_5$
colorless gas	*colorless liquid*
	BrCl
	red gas
IF$_3$	
yellow solid	
IF$_5$	
colorless liquid	
IF$_7$	
colorless gas	
ICl	
dark red liquid;	
black crystals	
ICl$_3$	
yellow solid	
IBr	
brown-black solid	

Molecular compounds formed by the combination of two different halogens are known as **interhalogens**. The interhalogens are either diatomic molecules (e.g., ICl) or molecules of the type AB_n, where A is the larger halogen atom and is surrounded by three, five, or seven atoms of the smaller halogen. Note in Table 25.13 that in compounds with the small fluorine atom, chlorine, bromine, and iodine are able to form more than four covalent bonds by utilizing d orbitals. In interhalogens, the smaller, more electronegative halogen is assigned an oxidation state of -1, giving the central atom a positive oxidation state.

The geometry of the interhalogen molecules is what would be expected from our previous study of molecular geometry and electron-pair repulsion (Figure 25.4).

The interhalogens are all volatile, reactive compounds. Several of them are very corrosive and actively attack the skin. They are also all strong oxidizing agents. Mixtures of halides are produced in reactions between interhalogens and most other elements. With water, in a partner-exchange reaction, the more electronegative halogen forms the hydrohalic acid and the less electronegative element, the oxoacid, for example,

$$BrCl(g) + H_2O(l) \longrightarrow HCl(aq) + HBrO(aq)$$

Bromine chloride has been introduced as a water-treatment chemical, apparently because the hypobromous acid formed in the above reaction is as effective a disinfectant as hypochlorous acid.

A large number of anions in which several halogen atoms have combined — **polyhalide ions** — are also known. To give just a few examples of the many polyhalide ions that form stable crystalline salts, there are I_2Br^-, $IClBr^-$, ICl_4^-, BrF_2^-, and several polyiodide ions, I_3^-, I_5^-, and I_7^-.

EXAMPLE 25.7
Oxidation Numbers: Halogens

In ICl, what oxidation numbers should be assigned to chlorine and iodine? What reaction illustrates that these oxidation number assignments are correct?

The more electronegative element, in this case chlorine, is always assigned the negative oxidation number, so in ICl, Cl is assigned -1 and I is assigned $+1$. In the hydrolysis of this compound,

$$\overset{+1\ -1}{ICl(s)} + H_2O(l) \longrightarrow \overset{-1}{HCl(aq)} + \overset{+1}{HIO(aq)}$$

chlorine forms the hydrohalic acid and iodine the hypohalous acid with no change in the oxidation numbers of the halogens, demonstrating that the chlorine is indeed the more electronegative element.

Table 25.14
Oxoacids of Halogens (Other than Fluorine)

Oxidation No. of Halogen	Known Acids	Can be Isolated	Aqueous Acid Strength	Salts (Example of Common Stable Salt)
+1	*Hypohalous acids*			
	HClO	No	Weak ($K_a = 2.9 \times 10^{-8}$)	Hypochlorites (Ca(OCl)$_2$)
	HBrO	No	Weak ($K_a = 2.2 \times 10^{-9}$)	Hypobromites*
	HIO	No	Weak ($K_a = 2.3 \times 10^{-11}$)	Hypoiodites*
+3	*Halous acids†*			
	HClO$_2$	No	Moderately strong ($K_a = 1.1 \times 10^{-2}$)	Chlorites*
+5	*Halic acids*			
	HClO$_3$	No	Strong	Chlorates (KClO$_3$)
	HBrO$_3$	No	Strong	Bromates (AgBrO$_3$)
	HIO$_3$	Yes	Moderately strong ($K_a = 1.6 \times 10^{-1}$)	Iodates (Ba(IO$_3$)$_2$)
+7	*Perhalic acids*			
	HClO$_4$	Yes	Strong	Perchlorates (KClO$_4$)
	HBrO$_4$	No	Strong	Perbromates (KBrO$_4$)
	HIO$_4$	Yes	Weak	Periodates (KIO$_4$)
	H$_5$IO$_6$	Yes	Weak	Paraperiodates (Na$_5$IO$_6$)

* Salts are not stable. Chlorites explode readily.

† The bromine and iodine acids are not known. Bromites (e.g., NaBrO$_2 \cdot$H$_2$O) have been prepared.

25.11 OXOACIDS OF THE HALOGENS AND THEIR SALTS

Oxoacids are known for all of the halogens except fluorine; their properties are summarized in Table 25.14. Only iodic acid (HIO$_3$), perchloric acid (HClO$_4$), and the two periodic acids (HIO$_4$ and H$_5$IO$_6$) can be isolated. The others are known in solution and by their salts. All but paraperiodic acid (H$_5$IO$_6$) are monoprotic acids. They contain one hydrogen atom in an OH group bonded to the halogen atom (Figure 25.5). Because of π bonding between p electrons and d electrons, the halogen–oxygen bonds all have double bond character.

Oxoacids and oxoanions of the halogens in their lower oxidation states disproportionate to varying degrees, particularly in alkaline solutions. The acids in the higher oxidation states are stable to disproportionation.

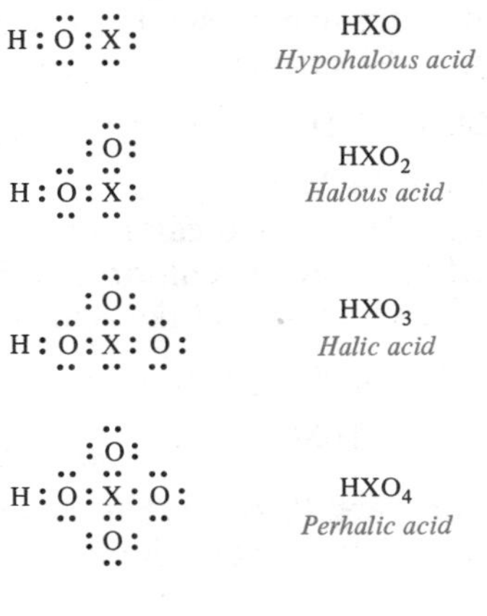

Figure 25.5
Lewis Structures of Halogen Oxoacids Fluorine does not form oxoacids.

H:Ö:X: HXO   *Hypohalous acid*

H:Ö:X: HXO$_2$ *Halous acid*

H:Ö:X:Ö: HXO$_3$ *Halic acid*

H:Ö:X:Ö: HXO$_4$ *Perhalic acid*

Table 25.15
Standard Reduction Potentials for
Oxochloro Species

Reaction	E°_{298} (V)
Acidic media	
$ClO_4^- + 2H^+ + 2e^- \rightleftharpoons ClO_3^- + H_2O$	1.19
$ClO_3^- + 3H^+ + 2e^- \rightleftharpoons HClO_2 + H_2O$	1.21
$HClO + H^+ + e^- \rightleftharpoons \frac{1}{2}Cl_2 + H_2O$	1.63
$HClO_2 + 2H^+ + 2e^- \rightleftharpoons HClO + H_2O$	1.65
Alkaline media	
$ClO_3^- + H_2O + 2e^- \rightleftharpoons ClO_2^- + 2OH^-$	0.33
$ClO_4^- + H_2O + 2e^- \rightleftharpoons ClO_3^- + 2OH^-$	0.36
$ClO_2^- + H_2O + 2e^- \rightleftharpoons ClO^- + 2OH^-$	0.66
$ClO^- + H_2O + 2e^- \rightleftharpoons Cl^- + 2OH^-$	0.89

a. Oxochloro acids and their salts All of the oxochloro acids and their anions can act as oxidizing agents, as shown by the standard reduction potentials in Table 25.15. Note that the weaker acids ($HClO$ and $HClO_2$) are present in acidic solution as the undissociated acids and in alkaline solution as the anions. (The standard reduction potentials for transformations between other oxidation states are given in Appendix VI.)

Comparisons of oxidizing strength at standard state conditions, that is, in terms of the E° values, reveal a trend toward decreasing oxidizing strength with increasing halogen oxidation state. Hypochlorous acid and chlorous acid (which is less often encountered) are the strongest oxidizing agents. Aqueous perchlorate ion is the weakest oxidizing agent at room temperature under standard state conditions. However, such comparisons are misleading because the oxidizing strength of these species is strongly dependent upon pH, concentration, and the reaction conditions. At high temperatures or in concentrated solutions, perchloric acid becomes a very strong oxidizing agent and a hazardous material, frequently exploding on contact with oxidizable substances. A classic laboratory accident is a fire or explosion caused by hot perchloric acid coming into contact with a rubber stopper or some rubber tubing. One should be aware that vigorous oxidation reactions are a possibility in any system containing halogen oxoacids or oxoanions.

Many preparations of the oxochloro acids are either disproportionation reactions or reactions of salts with nonvolatile acids, often sulfuric acid. At room temperature about 30% of the chlorine in an aqueous Cl_2 solution is present as hypochlorous acid. Larger concentrations of this acid can be produced by the addition of mercury(II) oxide. The reaction is driven toward hypochlorous acid by the removal of chloride ion from solution.

$$2Cl_2(g) + 2HgO(s) + H_2O(l) \longrightarrow HgCl_2 \cdot HgO(s) + 2HClO(aq)$$

Chlorous acid, an extremely unstable substance, is formed along with chloric acid when chlorine dioxide is passed into water:

$$2ClO_2(g) + H_2O(l) \longrightarrow HClO_2(aq) + H^+ + ClO_3^-$$

(What type of reaction is this?)

Chloric acid and perchloric acid can both be prepared by the reactions of salts with concentrated sulfuric acid. Perchloric acid is distilled at low pressure from a mixture of potassium perchlorate and the acid:

$$Ba(ClO_3)_2(aq) + H_2SO_4(conc) \longrightarrow 2HClO_3(aq) + BaSO_4(s)$$

$$KClO_4(s) + H_2SO_4(conc) \xrightarrow[\text{low pressure}]{\Delta} KHSO_4(s) + HClO_4(g)$$

(What type of reactions are these? What drives them to "completion"?) Pure perchloric acid, a colorless hygroscopic liquid (m.p. $-112\ ^\circ$C), is a highly unstable and dangerous substance. By contrast, salts of perchloric acid (the perchlorates) and of chloric acid (the chlorates) are more stable substances, and most are water-soluble compounds.

Chlorates can be prepared in solution by the reaction of chlorine with hot concentrated hydroxides, for example,

$$3Cl_2(g) + 6NaOH(aq) \longrightarrow NaClO_3(aq) + 5NaCl(aq) + 3H_2O(l)$$

Most likely, the hypochlorite ion is formed first and then disproportionates (Equation 25.5).

Commercially, perchlorates are prepared by the electrolysis of hot concentrated chloride solutions, for example,

$$KCl(aq) + 4H_2O(l) \xrightarrow[\text{electrolysis}]{\Delta} KClO_4(aq) + 4H_2(g)$$

As we have mentioned (Section 25.5b), only a few stable solid hypochlorites are known.

b. Oxobromo and oxoiodo compounds

Hypobromous acid (HBrO) and bromic acid ($HBrO_3$) are both strong oxidizing agents and bromic acid is a strong acid. Solid hypobromites slowly disproportionate to bromides and bromates (Equation 25.4). Many bromates are more stable compounds and can be utilized as oxidizing agents.

The first preparation of perbromic acid and perbromates provides an interesting contrast with the discovery of noble gas compounds (Section 10.15). The noble gas compounds were not expected to exist, and for a long time they were not actively sought. However, by analogy with perchlorates, it seemed reasonable that perbromates should form and be relatively stable compounds. Repeated attempts were therefore made to prepare them, and some elaborate explanations were put forth to rationalize the failure of these efforts.

In 1968 it was found that perbromic acid and perbromates *could* be prepared from bromates under strongly oxidizing conditions. Interestingly, xenon difluoride was one of the first strong oxidizing agents utilized to produce a perbromate.

$$NaBrO_3(aq) + XeF_2(aq) + H_2O(l) \longrightarrow \underset{\text{\textit{sodium perbromate}}}{NaBrO_4(aq)} + 2HF(aq) + Xe(g)$$

The reaction also proceeds with fluorine, demonstrating the strength of fluorine as an oxidizing agent.

$$NaBrO_3(aq) + F_2(g) + 2NaOH(aq) \longrightarrow NaBrO_4(aq) + 2NaF(aq) + H_2O(l)$$

Once produced, the perbromates were indeed found to be reasonably stable. They are strong oxidizing agents, but the reactions are slow. It has been suggested that these compounds were elusive for kinetic reasons—their formation appears to have a large energy of activation.

Hypoiodous acid and hypoiodite ion can be formed in solution, but both rapidly disproportionate, and stable hypoiodites cannot be isolated. Iodic acid and many iodates are stable. The acid can be prepared by oxidation of iodine by fuming nitric acid.

Two periodic acids (see Table 25.14) are sufficiently stable to be isolated—HIO_4, often called periodic acid and systematically named as metaperiodic acid, and H_5IO_6, paraperiodic acid. Various anions are present in solutions of both of these acids (IO_4^-, $H_3IO_6^{2-}$, $H_4IO_6^-$) and stable salts of IO_4^-, $H_3IO_6^{2-}$, and IO_6^{5-} are known. Paraperiodic acid is a weak, polyprotic acid and a strong oxidizing agent.

Table 25.16

Outstanding Properties of the Halogens and Some of Their Compounds

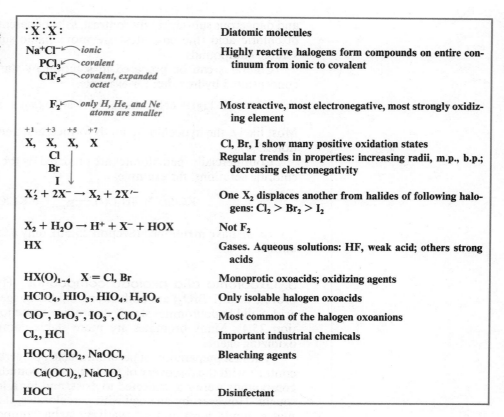

$:\overset{..}{\underset{..}{X}}:\overset{..}{\underset{..}{X}}:$	Diatomic molecules
Na^+Cl^- — *ionic*	Highly reactive halogens form compounds on entire continuum from ionic to covalent
PCl_3 — *covalent*	
ClF_5 — *covalent, expanded octet*	
F_2 — *only H, He, and Ne atoms are smaller*	Most reactive, most electronegative, most strongly oxidizing element
$\overset{+1}{X}, \overset{+3}{X}, \overset{+5}{X}, \overset{+7}{X}$	Cl, Br, I show many positive oxidation states
Cl Br I ↓	Regular trends in properties: increasing radii, m.p., b.p.; decreasing electronegativity
$X_2' + 2X^- \rightarrow X_2 + 2X'^-$	One X_2 displaces another from halides of following halogens: $Cl_2 > Br_2 > I_2$
$X_2 + H_2O \rightarrow H^+ + X^- + HOX$	Not F_2
HX	Gases. Aqueous solutions: HF, weak acid; others strong acids
$HX(O)_{1-4}$ X = Cl, Br	Monoprotic oxoacids; oxidizing agents
$HClO_4, HIO_3, HIO_4, H_5IO_6$	Only isolable halogen oxoacids
$ClO^-, BrO_3^-, IO_3^-, ClO_4^-$	Most common of the halogen oxoanions
Cl_2, HCl	Important industrial chemicals
HOCl, ClO_2, NaOCl, Ca(OCl)$_2$, NaClO$_3$	Bleaching agents
HOCl	Disinfectant

The outstanding properties of the halogens and their compounds are summarized in Table 25.16.

SUMMARY

PHYSICAL AND CHEMICAL PROPERTIES OF THE HALOGENS (Sections **25.1, 25.2**)   The halogens (Representative Group VII) are reactive elements which combine with most other elements (Table 25.7) and form many compounds, which range from ionic to covalent. Trends expected within a periodic table family are uniformly displayed by the halogens (Tables 25.3–25.5). Fluorine atoms are small and highly electronegative. As a result, fluorine is the most reactive nonmetal and a very strong oxidizing agent; it differs in many ways from the other halogens (Table 25.2). The other halogens are also quite electronegative (Table 25.5), and covalent bonds to halogens are generally polar.

Each halogen can oxidize the halide ions of the elements below it in the family, displacing halide ions from compounds. In aqueous solution, chlorine, bromine, and iodine disproportionate to X^- and XO^-. Except for fluorine, the halogens exhibit positive oxidation states ($+1, +3, +5, +7$) in addition to the -1 state in the halide ions (Table 25.6). Fluoride ion and hypochlorite ion (ClO^-) hydrolyze to give alkaline solutions.

PREPARATION AND USES OF THE HALOGENS (Sections **25.3–25.7**)   Elemental fluorine, because it is such a strong oxidizing agent, must be made by electrolysis in the absence of water. Freons (which are fluorochlorocarbons, e.g., CF_2Cl_2, $CFCl_3$) have been used as refrigerants and aerosol propellants, but their use has been curtailed because of fear that they destroy stratospheric ozone, which protects the earth from ultraviolet radiation. Teflon is polytetrafluoroethylene. Fluoride ion prevents tooth decay by replacing OH⁻ in the hydroxyapatite in teeth.

Chlorine, a "top ten" industrial chemical (Table 25.10), is made by electrolysis of concentrated sodium chloride solutions. The major use of chlorine is in the production of other chemicals. Chlorine and hypochlorites are used extensively for bleaching, disinfecting, and sanitizing. Bromine is obtained from natural brines and iodine from brines or seaweed by oxidizing of their − 1 ions by chlorine.

COMPOUNDS OF THE HALOGENS (Sections **25.8 – 25.11**) The hydrogen halides (Table 25.11) are all gases that dissolve in water to give acidic solutions. Hydrofluoric acid is a weak acid; the other HX acids are strong and nonoxidizing. Except for hydrogen fluoride, the hydrogen halides are reducing agents, with strength increasing down the family. The metal halides of cations with low charge-to-size ratios are ionic compounds, while those of what would be cations of high charge-to-size ratios have predominately covalent bonding.

The halogens combine with each other to form numerous highly reactive compounds—the interhalogens (Table 25.13). Because they have available d orbitals, the larger halogens can expand their octets to accommodate more than four small fluorine atoms in such compounds.

The oxoacids and oxoanions of chlorine, bromine, and iodine (Table 25.14) are oxidizing agents, with strongly pH-dependent properties (Table 25.15). (Fluorine forms no oxoanions.) Most of the oxoacids are known only in solution. The lower acids are weak acids and the higher acids of chlorine and iodine are strong acids. Hypochlorous acid is a bleaching agent and a disinfectant. The properties of the halogens and their compounds are summarized in Table 25.16.

SIGNIFICANT TERMS

halogenation
interhalogens
polyhalide ions

THOUGHTS ON CHEMISTRY

''Oxymuriatic Acid''

OBSERVATION ON THE HALOGENS,
by John Dalton

(What is oxymuriatic acid? Try to decide as you read Dalton's observations of its properties.)

The highly interesting compound, now denominated oxymuriatic acid, was discovered by Scheele, in 1774. It may be procured by applying a moderate heat to a mixture of muriatic acid (HCl) and oxide of manganese or red lead; a yellowish coloured gas ascends, which may be received over water; it is oxymuriatic acid gas. But this gas, which is largely obtained for the purposes of bleaching, is usually got from a mixture of equal weights of common salt (muriate of soda), oxide of manganese, and a dilute sulphuric acid of the strength 1.4; . . . .

Some of its properties are:
1. It has a pungent and suffocating smell, exceeding most other gases in these respects, and it is highly deleterious. . . .
2. Oxymuriatic acid gas is absorbed by water, but in a very small degree compared with muriatic acid gas. . . .
3. Water impregnated with the gas is called liquid oxymuriatic acid. It has the same odour as the gas, and an astringent, not acid, taste. When exposed to the light of the sun, the liquid acid is gradually decomposed, as was first observed by Berthollet, into its elements, muriatic acid and oxygenous gas; the former remains combined with the water, and the latter assumes the gaseous form. Neither light nor heat has been found to decompose the acid gas.
4. This acid, in the gaseous state or combined with water, has a singular effect on colouring matter. Instead of converting vegetable blue into red, as other acids do, it abstracts colours in general from bodies,

leaving them white or colourless. The oxygen combines with the colouring principle, and the muriatic acid remaining dissolves the compound. Hence the use of this acid in bleaching. . . .

6. Oxymuriatic acid seems to combine readily with the fixed alkalis and the earths when dissolved in water; but it decomposes ammonia. . . .

7. . . .Upon mixing hydrogen and oxymuriatic acid in a strong phial capable of containing 600 grams of water, and exposing the mixture to the solar rays, an explosion almost instantly took place with a loud report, just as if it had received an electric spark. If the stopper was well closed, a vacuum nearly was formed, which was instantly filled with water when the stopper was drawn out under water; but it generally happened that the stopper was expelled with violence.

It remains now to point out the constitution of this acid. All experience shews, that it is a compound of muriatic acid and oxygen; but the exact proportion has not hitherto been ascertained.

John Dalton, *A New System of Chemical Philosophy* (London: Bickestaff, Strand, 1808), pp. 297ff.

QUESTIONS

Physical and Chemical Properties of the Halogens

25.1 Name the elements known as the halogens and write the chemical symbol for each. Describe the physical state of each molecular halogen at room temperature and pressure.

25.2 Write the electron configuration for each of the atomic halogens. How do these change in the formation of the negative ions?

25.3 Choose the properties that increase in going down the fluorine family in the periodic table: (a) atomic radius, (b) melting and boiling points, (c) bond dissociation energies of X_2, (d) ionic radius of X^-, (e) electron affinities, (f) ionization energies, (g) electronegativities, and (h) values of the standard reduction potential for X_2.

25.4 What is the usual oxidation state of each of the halogens in direct combination with metals, semiconducting elements, and most nonmetals?

25.5 Consider an element that can exhibit multiple oxidation states such as iron or phosphorus. Compare the oxidation states that result when the element combines with the various halogens.

25.6 What is a "halogenation reaction"? Write chemical equations for X_2 reacting with SO_2, PX_3, CO, and $H_2C{=}CH_2$.

25.7 Compare the reactivities of the halogens with water. Write chemical equations for the reactions. Which halogen is quite different from the others in its reaction?

25.8 Iodine is not very soluble in water, but readily dissolves in solutions containing I^-. Why?

25.9 Choose the ions which will react with water to give an alkaline solution: (a) F^-, (b) Cl^-, (c) Br^-, (d) I^-, (e) ClO^-, (f) ClO_3^-, (g) BrO_3^-, (h) IO_3^-, and (i) ClO_4^-. Write chemical equations for those that react.

25.10 Write chemical equations describing the two different reactions that can happen when chlorine, bromine, or iodine is dissolved in an alkaline solution. Briefly compare the products of the reactions for the various halogens.

25.11 Briefly compare the products formed by the thermal decomposition of alkali metal and less reactive metal salts containing halogen oxoanions.

Preparation and Uses of the Halogens

25.12 Table 25.8 shows that the halogens occur in nature as the halide ions, except for iodine, which also occurs in nature as $NaIO_3$. Explain this difference.

25.13 Write chemical equations representing the commercial preparations of F_2, Cl_2, Br_2, and I_2.

25.14 Fluorine is considered to be a highly reactive substance. Why can it be safely stored in certain metal containers?

25.15 What are Freons, perfluorocarbons, and Teflon?

25.16 Briefly discuss the use of "fluoride" in drinking water to prevent tooth decay.

25.17 In what forms is chlorine valuable as a bleach? Briefly discuss the bleaching process.

25.18 What is "iodized salt"? What role does iodine play in human nutrition?

Compounds of the Halogens

25.19 Predict the type of bonding between atoms of (a) Al and I, (b) Na and F, (c) Ca and F, (d) I and Cl, and (e) Br and Br.

25.20 Briefly describe the chemical and physical properties of gaseous and aqueous HCl, HBr, and HI. How does HF differ significantly in behavior from the other hydrogen halides?

25.21 Because there is considerable hydrogen bonding in HF, hydrogen fluoride is polymeric. Draw a Lewis structure illustrating this behavior. Also illustrate the structure of the $[HF_2]^-$ anion.

25.22 The rate of formation of HBr(g) from $H_2(g)$ and $Br_2(g)$ between 200 °C and 300 °C is given by the equation

$$\text{rate} = \frac{k[H_2][Br_2]^{\frac{1}{2}}}{1 + k' \dfrac{[HBr]}{[Br_2]}}$$

How would you adjust the concentrations in order to make the reaction proceed as fast as possible?

25.23 Hydrogen chloride can be produced by treating a metal chloride with concentrated sulfuric acid. Write the chemical equations for this process. What happens when concentrated sulfuric acid reacts with metal bromides and iodides? Write chemical equations illustrating these reactions.

25.24 Aluminum fluoride is an ionic substance, but aluminum iodide is molecular. Explain this difference.

25.25 Iron(II) chloride is an ionic compound, but iron(III) chloride is a volatile, molecular compound. Explain this difference.

25.26 List the general solubility rules for metal halides in water.

25.27 Write balanced equations for any reactions that occur in aqueous mixtures of (a) NaI and Cl_2, (b) NaCl and Br_2, (c) NaI and Br_2, (d) NaBr and Cl_2, and (e) NaF and I_2.

25.28 What is the oxidation number of Cl in each of the following interhalogens: (a)ClF, (b) BrCl, (c) ICl, (d) ClF_3, (e) ClF_5, (f) ICl_3, (g) ClF_2^-, (h) ClF_4^-, (i) ICl_2^-, (j) ICl_4^-, (k) $BrCl_2^-$, (l) $IClBr^-$, and (m) $IFCl_3^-$?

25.29 Draw the Lewis structure and a three-dimensional sketch for I_3^-. Discuss the geometry of this ion.

25.30 What is the oxidation number of bromine in each of the following compounds: (a) BrF, (b) BrF_3, (c) BrF_5, (d) BrCl, and (e) IBr?

25.31 Draw the Lewis structures and three-dimensional sketches for the molecules listed in Question 25.30. Identify which of the molecules are polar.

25.32 Describe the geometry of the (a) ClF_2^- and (b) ClF_4^- ions.

25.33 Unlike the other halogens, fluorine forms no oxoacids nor oxoanions. Why?

25.34 Choose the strongest acid from each group: (a) HClO, HBrO, and HIO; (b) HClO, $HClO_2$, $HClO_3$, and $HClO_4$; (d) HIO, $HBrO_3$, and $HClO_4$.

25.35 Do the oxochloro acids and anions generally act as oxidizing or reducing agents? What is the trend in reduction potential with increasing oxidation state?

25.36* Arrange the oxoanions of chlorine in order of increasing thermal stability and write chemical equations describing the decomposition of the sodium salt of each ion as the salt is heated.

Additional Questions

25.37 What intermolecular forces are present in (a) Cl_2, (b) HI, (c) HF, (d) $HClO_4$, (e) ICl_3, (f) HBrO, and (g) Cl_2O_7?

25.38 An aqueous solution contains either NaBr or a mixture of NaBr and NaI. Using only aqueous solutions of I_2, Br_2, and Cl_2 and a small amount of CCl_4, describe how you might determine what is in the unknown solution.

25.39 Based on your knowledge of halogen chemistry, suggest a reaction for preparing (a) $KBrO_3(aq)$ from $Br_2(l)$; (b) $KBrO_3(aq)$ from $KBrO(aq)$; (c) $BrF_5(g)$ from $Br_2(l)$; and (d) $Br_2(aq)$ from Br^-. Write a balanced ionic equation (or equations) for each of the preparations.

25.40 Identify which of the following are redox reactions. Identify the oxidizing and reducing agent in each of the redox reactions.

(a) $4NaClO_3(s) \xrightarrow{\Delta} 3NaClO_4(s) + NaCl(s)$

(b) $3Br_2(l) + 6OH^- \longrightarrow BrO_3^- + 5Br^- + 3H_2O(l)$

(c) $2NaF(s) + H_2SO_4(conc) \xrightarrow{\Delta} Na_2SO_4(s) + 2HF(g)$

(d) $2Cl_2(g) + HgO(s) + H_2O(l) \longrightarrow HgCl_2(aq) + 2HOCl(aq)$

25.41 Repeat Question 25.40 for:

(a) $BrO_3^- + 5Br^- + 6H^+ \longrightarrow 3Br_2(l) + 3H_2O(l)$

(b) $I^- + Br_2(aq) \longrightarrow IBr(aq) + Br^-$

(c) $NaHSO_4(s) + NaCl(s) \xrightarrow{\Delta} Na_2SO_4(s) + HCl(g)$

(d) $2KClO_3(l) \xrightarrow{\Delta} 2KCl(s) + 3O_2(g)$

25.42 Classify each of the following reactions according to the reaction types listed in Tables 17.2 and 17.7:

(a) $HBrO_4(aq) + KOH(aq) \longrightarrow KBrO_4(aq) + H_2O(l)$

(b) $2KClO(s) \xrightarrow{\Delta} 2KCl(s) + O_2(g)$

(c) $3KClO(s) \xrightarrow{\Delta} KClO_3(s) + 2KCl(s)$

(d) $TiI_4(g) \xrightarrow{\Delta} Ti(s) + 2I_2(g)$

25.43 Repeat Question 25.42 for:

(a) $Cl_2(g) + 2I^- \longrightarrow I_2(s) + 2Cl^-$

(b) $K_2CO_3(s) + 2HClO_4(aq) \longrightarrow$
$$2KClO_4(s) + H_2O(l) + CO_2(g)$$

(c) $Hg(NO_3)_2(aq) + 2KI(aq) \longrightarrow HgI_2(s) + 2KNO_3(aq)$

(d) $S_8(s) + 24F_2(g) \longrightarrow 8SF_6(g)$

25.44 Predict the major products of the following reactions:

(a) $Sn(s) + Cl_2(g) \longrightarrow$

(b) $Cl_2(g) + F_2(g) \xrightarrow{\Delta}$

(c) $KI(s) + H_2SO_4(aq, conc) \xrightarrow{\Delta}$

(d) $Cl_2(g) + KOH(aq, conc) \longrightarrow$

25.45 Repeat Question 25.44 for:

(a) $KHF_2(l) \xrightarrow[\text{energy}]{\text{electrical}}$

(b) $S_8(s) + Br_2(l) + H_2O(l) \longrightarrow$

(c) $IO_3^- + I^- + H^+ \longrightarrow$

(d) $Fe(s) + Cl_2(g) \longrightarrow$

25.46 Write balanced equations for the following chemical reactions: (a) preparation of Cl_2 from aqueous KCl by electrolysis, (b) any reaction of Br_2 as an oxidizing agent, (c) disproportionation of KClO when it is heated, (d) displacement of one halogen by another in aqueous solution, and (e) formation of an iodine chloride from the elements.

25.47* Only one stable isotope of iodine is found in nature, $^{127}_{53}I$. Calculate the neutron–proton ratio for this stable isotope. The artificial radioisotope $^{131}_{53}I$, in the form of I^-, is commonly used to decrease thyroid gland activity. What mode of decay would be predicted for this isotope? Write the nuclear equation for the decay.

25.48 Commercial bleaching powder is a mixture of Ca(OCl)Cl, $CaCl_2$, and $Ca(OCl)_2$ in approximately equimolar quantities. (a) Name these substances.

The powder is prepared by passing chlorine over dry calcium oxide,

$$CaO(s) + Cl_2(g) \longrightarrow Ca(OCl)Cl(s)$$
$$2CaO(s) + 2Cl_2(g) \longrightarrow Ca(OCl)_2(s) + CaCl_2(s)$$

leaving a small amount of CaO as an impurity. (b) Determine the oxidation state of chlorine in the compounds given in the above equations and identify the (c) oxidizing agent and (d) reducing agent in each reaction.

The chlorine needed for bleaching is produced in aqueous solution by the reaction between water, OCl^-, and Cl^-, represented by the equation

$$OCl^- + Cl^- + H_2O(l) \longrightarrow Cl_2(g) + 2OH^-$$

What element in the above equation is being (e) oxidized and (f) reduced? (g) What happens to the pH of the solution as the chlorine is being generated?

Answers to Selected Questions

25.7 F_2 forms HF and O_2:
$2F_2(g) + 2H_2O(l) \longrightarrow 4HF(aq) + O_2(g)$; Cl_2, Br_2, and I_2 form $HX(aq)$ and $HOX(aq)$:
$X_2 + H_2O(l) \longrightarrow H^+ + X^- + HOX(aq)$

25.24 The two major factors are the large electronegativity of F compared to the smaller electronegativity of I and the larger lattice energy of AlF_3 compared to the smaller lattice energy of AlI_3.

25.27 (a)$2NaI(aq) + Cl_2(aq) \longrightarrow 2NaCl(aq) + I_2(aq)$ (further oxidation of I_2 is possible); (c) $2NaI(aq) + Br_2(aq) \longrightarrow 2NaBr(aq) + I_2(aq)$; (d) $2NaBr(aq) + Cl_2(aq) \longrightarrow 2NaCl(aq) + Br_2(aq)$

25.28 -1 in (b), (c), (f), (i), (j), (k), (l), and (m); $+1$ in (a) and (g); $+3$ in (d) and (h); $+5$ in (e)

25.32 (a) linear, (b) square planar

25.37 (a) London; (b) dipole and London; (c) hydrogen bond-

ing, dipole, and London; (d) dipole, London, hydrogen bonding; (e) dipole and London; (f) dipole, London, hydrogen bonding; (g) dipole and London

25.39 (a) $3Br_2(l) + 6OH^- \rightarrow BrO_3^- + 5Br^- + 3H_2O(l)$; (b) $3BrO^- \xrightarrow{\Delta} BrO_3^- + 2Br^-$; (c) $Br_2(l) + 5F_2(g) \rightarrow 2BrF_5(g)$; (d) $2Br^- + Cl_2(aq) \rightarrow Br_2(aq) + 2Cl^-$

25.41 (a), (b), (d); oxidizing agents: (a) BrO_3^-, (b) Br_2, (d) $KClO_3$; reducing agents: (a) Br^-, (b) I^-, (d) $KClO_3$

25.43 (a) redox—displacement of one element from a compound by another element; (b) nonredox—partner exchange; (c) nonredox—partner exchange between ions in aqueous solution; (d) redox—combination of two elements to give a compound

25.45 (a) $H_2(g)$, $F_2(g)$, $KF(s)$; (b) $H_2SO_4(aq)$, $HBr(g)$; (c) $I_2(s)$, $H_2O(l)$; (d) $FeCl_3(s)$

25.48 (a) calcium chloride, calcium hypochlorite chloride, calcium hypochlorite; (b) $+1$ in OCl^- of Ca(OCl)Cl and $Ca(OCl)_2$, -1 in Cl^- of Ca(OCl)Cl and $CaCl_2$, 0 in Cl_2; (c) Cl_2 in both; (d) Cl_2 in both; (e) Cl; (f) Cl; (g) pH increases

---

PROBLEMS

Review of Principles

25.1 The vapor pressure of $Br_2(l)$ at 25 °C is 204 Torr. What mass of bromine vapor would be found in a liter of air saturated with bromine at 25 °C?

25.2 The average concentration of bromine in seawater is 75 ppm, calculated as Br^- ion. Calculate (a) the volume of seawater in cubic feet that is required to produce one ton of liquid bromine and (b) the volume of chlorine gas, in liters, measured at STP, required to displace all of this bromine. The density of seawater is 64.5 lb/ft³. *Answer* (a) 4.13×15^5 ft³, (b) 1.27×10^5 L

25.3 When powdered antimony is sprinkled into a bottle containing chlorine, tiny sparkles are generated. The white powder formed contains 47 mass % chlorine. Find the empirical formula of the chloride and write an equation for the reaction.

25.4 The solubility in water at 0 °C is 59.5 g/100 g H_2O for $CaCl_2$ and 35.7 g/100 g H_2O for NaCl. In a saturated solution, which salt is more effective in lowering the freezing point of water? $K_f = 1.86$ K/m for water. *Answer* $CaCl_2$

25.5 A convenient laboratory preparation of chlorine, bromine, or iodine is to allow a metal halide or hydrohalic acid to react with $MnO_2(s)$ in an acidic solution:

$$MnO_2(s) + 4H^+ + 4X^- \longrightarrow Mn^{2+} + 2X^- + X_2(g) + 2H_2O(l)$$

An excess of concentrated hydrochloric acid is added to 0.100 mol MnO_2. Calculate the mass and volume of chlorine collected at 27 °C and 765 Torr.

25.6 Determine the mass of $KClO_3$ theoretically obtained by the reaction of 50.0 L of $Cl_2(g)$, measured at 25 °C and 1.00 atm, with hot, concentrated KOH(aq). What mass of KClO would be theoretically obtainable by the reaction of the same quantity of $Cl_2(g)$ with cold, dilute KOH(aq)?

25.7 The standard state enthalpy of formation at 25 °C is −320.1 kJ/mol for HF(*aq*), −230.0 kJ/mol for OH⁻, −332.6 kJ/mol for F⁻, and −285.8 kJ/mol for $H_2O(l)$. Find the enthalpy of neutralization of hydrofluoric acid.

$$HF(aq) + OH^- \longrightarrow F^- + H_2O(l)$$

Using the following thermochemical equation:

$$H^+ + OH^- \longrightarrow H_2O(l) \qquad \Delta H^\circ = -55.8 \text{ kJ}$$

find the enthalpy change for the reaction

$$HF(aq) \longrightarrow H^+ + F^-$$

Answer −68.3 kJ, −12.5 kJ

25.8 The standard free energy of formation at 25 °C is −95.3 kJ/mol for HCl(*g*) and −228.6 kJ/mol for $H_2O(g)$. Determine whether the reaction

$$4HCl(g) + O_2(g) \longrightarrow 2Cl_2(g) + 2H_2O(g)$$

is spontaneous or not.

25.9 In acidic solution, the dichromate ion, $Cr_2O_7^{2-}$, oxidizes iodide ion to elemental iodine and is itself reduced to chromic ion, Cr^{3+}. (a) Write the equations for the half-reactions and calculate E° for the reaction using the following half-cell potentials: 0.5355 V for the I_2/I^- couple and 1.33 V for the $Cr_2O_7^{2-}/Cr^{3+}$ couple. (b) Would the reaction become more or less favorable if the concentrations of all ions were 0.1 M instead of 1 M? *Answer* (a) $Cr_2O_7^{2-} + 14H^+ + 6e^- \longrightarrow 2Cr^{3+} + 7H_2O$, $2I^- \longrightarrow I_2 + 2e^-$, $Cr_2O_7^{2-} + 14H^+ + 6I^- \longrightarrow 3I_2(s) + 2Cr^{3+} + 7H_2O(l)$, $E^\circ = 0.79$ V; (b) less favorable

25.10 The equilibrium constant at 25 °C for the reaction

$$Cl_2(g) + H_2O(l) \rightleftharpoons H^+ + Cl^- + HClO(aq)$$

is 4.4×10^{-4}. Assuming that the HClO does not ionize appreciably, what will be the pH of a solution of "chlorine water" at a chlorine pressure of 0.5 atm?

CHAPTER 26

Nonmetals: Nitrogen, Phosphorus, and Sulfur

The story of the discovery of phosphorus is worth retelling. In the seventeenth century in Hamburg, Germany, Hennig Brand, a physician and alchemist, had what seems a very curious idea. He would try to obtain from urine a liquid with which he could convert silver into gold. Brand evaporated fresh urine and let the residue stand until it had putrefied. Then he heated this potent substance vigorously and collected in water the vapors that were given off. We have no way of knowing what he expected to see, but the white, flammable, waxy solid which glowed in the dark must surely have been a surprise. Brand was the first to discover an element not among those known since antiquity—he had distilled pure white phosphorus.

Sulfur is an element that occurs in nature in elemental form and was undoubtedly known before recorded history. "Brimstone" and "sulfur" are mentioned in the Bible and in Homer's Odyssey. The alchemists sometimes used the term "sulfur" to describe anything that was combustible.

To complete the historical background of the nonmetals discussed in this chapter, we note that nitrogen was discovered in 1772 by Daniel Rutherford. He described it as the "noxious air" left after first a mouse had died in a confined volume of air and then the "fixed air" (carbon dioxide) had been absorbed by caustic potash. Scheele, Priestley, and Cavendish all did experiments with nitrogen at about the same time.

26.1 GENERAL PROPERTIES OF NITROGEN, PHOSPHORUS, AND SULFUR

Nitrogen and phosphorus are the nonmetallic members of the nitrogen family (Representative Group V), and oxygen and sulfur are the nonmetallic members of the oxygen family (Representative Group VI). (The chemistry of oxygen was discussed in Chapter 16.)

As expected for nonmetals, relative to metals these elements have high electronegativities, high ionization energies, and small atomic radii (Table 26.1). The first element in Representative Group V—nitrogen—differs significantly from phosphorus and other members of the group (Table 26.2), as do most first members of periodic table groups. Some of these differences are accounted for by the smaller size and greater electronegativity of the nitrogen atom. Others arise because nitrogen atoms are limited to eight valence electrons, while the other elements in the group can accommodate more than eight electrons in their outer energy levels by utilizing d orbitals.

Nitrogen and phosphorus atoms have five valence electrons in the ns^2np^3 configuration, while the sulfur atom has six valence electrons in the ns^2np^4 configuration. Consequently, the maximum oxidation state for both nitrogen and phosphorus is $+5$, while for sulfur it is $+6$. All three elements exhibit negative oxidation states in their compounds with hydrogen (NH_3, PH_3, and H_2S) and in compounds in which they complete octets by forming ions—nitride ion, N^{3-}; phosphide ion, P^{3-}; and sulfide ion, S^{2-}. The most common oxidation states of nitrogen are -3, $+3$, and $+5$,

Most common oxidation states	
N:	$-3, +3, +5$
P:	$+3, +5$
S:	$-2, +4, +6$

Table 26.1
Properties of Nitrogen, Phosphorus, and Sulfur

Property	Nitrogen	Phosphorus	Sulfur
Configuration	[He]$2s^2 2p^3$	[Ne]$3s^2 3p^3$	[Ne]$3s^2 3p^4$
Formula of molecule	N_2	P_4	S_8
Melting point (°C)	−210.0	44.1 (white)	112.8 (rhombic)
			119.0 (monoclinic)
Boiling point (°C)	−195.8	280 (white)	444.6
Atomic radius (nm)	0.074	0.110	0.103
Bond dissociation energy (kJ/mol)	946	209	264
Ionization energy (0 K) (kJ/mol)	1402	1012	1000
Electronegativity	3.0	2.1	2.5

but nitrogen is unique among the elements in forming compounds in all oxidation states from −3 to +5 (see Table 26.10). Because of the numerous possible oxidation states of nitrogen, its compounds undergo a number of disproportionation reactions. The +3 and +5 oxidation states are most common for phosphorus (see Table 26.14), while for sulfur, in addition to the negative oxidation state, the +4 and +6 states are most important (see Table 26.18).

In their positive oxidation states, nitrogen, phosphorus, and sulfur form cova-lent bonds. Nitrogen and phosphorus utilize their unpaired p electrons in forming three covalent bonds, as in :PCl_3 or :NH_3, leaving a lone electron pair on the central atom. In NH_4^+ the bonding electrons are pictured as occupying four sp^3 hybrid orbitals. Sulfur forms two covalent single bonds by sharing its two unpaired electrons, as in H_2S or SCl_2. It also forms SO_4^{2-} or SO_3^{2-}, utilizing four equivalent sp^3 hybrid orbitals. Phosphorus and sulfur atoms can also enter into five and six covalent

Table 26.2
Differences between Nitrogen and the Other Members of the Nitrogen Family (P, As, Sb, Bi)

Property	Comments
Occurs free in nature to a large extent	A reflection of the relative inertness of N_2 at ordinary temperatures; other elements in the group occur chiefly in combined forms.
A gas at ordinary temperatures	Other elements form a variety of solid allo-tropes at ordinary temperatures; the simplest form of phosphorus is P_4, and no discrete molecules are present in solid forms of the other elements.
N_2 molecule has a very high bond dissociation energy	Other elements have lower bond energies. Because of the thermal stability of N_2, many compounds containing more than one nitrogen atom decompose to give N_2, some explosively; certain nitrogen-rich compounds find use in explosives.
Can form no more than four covalent bonds	Only s and p orbitals available for bonding. Other elements in the family can use d orbitals, for example, in PF_5, PF_6^-.
Only element of the group that combines directly with H_2	$N_2 + 3H_2 \rightleftharpoons 2NH_3$
Only element of the group that forms a stable cation with hydrogen	NH_4^+, the ammonium ion; PH_4^+ is known, but is unstable in aqueous solution, immediately reacting to form PH_3.
All possible oxidation states from −3 to +5 are well defined	For P, As, Sb, and Bi the +3 and +5 states are most common. (The −3 and +1 states are of some importance for phosphorus.)

bonds by utilizing vacant d orbitals in sp^3d or sp^3d^2 hybrid orbitals, as in PCl_5 or SF_6.

Nitrogen, phosphorus, and sulfur each form a variety of compounds in which multiple bonding and resonance play important roles. The nitrogen oxides and the oxoacids of all three elements are particularly interesting in this respect. In compounds containing nitrogen–oxygen bonds, π bonding is contributed by overlap of p orbitals of oxygen with p orbitals of nitrogen. In compounds containing bonds between sulfur or phosphorus and oxygen, π bonding is contributed by interaction of the oxygen p orbitals with d orbitals of sulfur or phosphorus atoms. Often the bonds of nitrogen, sulfur, or phosphorus with oxygen have properties intermediate between those of single and double covalent bonds. As a result, the structures of compounds containing such bonds, although they can be written correctly with single bonds, are often seen written with double bonds between the central elements and oxygen.

Elemental phosphorus and sulfur in their most common allotropic forms (Sections 26.3a and 26.4a) are composed of P_4 and S_8 molecules. (In chemical equations for the reactions of these elements, we generally write P and S in order to simplify the coefficients in the equations.)

ELEMENTAL NITROGEN, PHOSPHORUS, AND SULFUR

26.2 ELEMENTAL NITROGEN

$:N\equiv N:$
Extremely strong bond, very stable molecule

Nitrogen is a colorless, odorless, nontoxic, and low-boiling gas. Gaseous nitrogen constitutes about 78% of the atmosphere (by volume), and this is the major source of nitrogen, which is obtained industrially from liquefied air (Section 16.12).

The nitrogen atoms in molecular nitrogen, N_2, are joined by a triple bond, $:N\equiv N:$. This bond is the second strongest bond in a diatomic molecule (only CO has a stronger bond). Consequently, molecular nitrogen is chemically very unreactive at ordinary temperatures despite the high electronegativity of nitrogen atoms. Because of the great thermal stability of the nitrogen molecule, some nitrogen compounds have positive heats of formation and decompose rapidly to produce molecular nitrogen. The great rates of decomposition and the expansion of the hot gaseous nitrogen ideally suit certain nitrogen compounds to be explosives (see An Aside: Explosives).

The major use of nitrogen is in the manufacture of ammonia by the Haber process (see An Aside: The Haber Process, Chapter 19). Nitrogen for this purpose is generally obtained directly from the atmosphere.

Elemental nitrogen is used in a variety of ways (Table 26.3) dependent upon either its lack of reactivity or its low boiling point. Chemicals that would react violently with oxygen or decompose in the presence of moist air are often "blan-

Table 26.3
Uses of Elemental Nitrogen

Major use		
Manufacture of ammonia		
Other uses	Blanketing applications, e.g.,	Low-temperature applications, e.g.,
Manufacture of nitrogen compounds, e.g.,	**For reactive chemicals**	
	For foods	**Condensing gases**
Calcium cyanamide (a fertilizer)	**For electrical equipment**	**Preserving biological materials**
Nitrides (used in cutting and grinding tools)	**For blowing bubbles into foamed polymers**	**Cryosurgery (selective destruction of tissue)**
Hydrazine (a rocket fuel)		**Freezing food**
		Shrink fitting molded parts
		Embrittling

keted" with nitrogen to protect them from chemical change. Nitrogen is frequently swept through equipment to drive out air before oxygen- or moisture-sensitive chemicals are admitted. In the food industry, replacing air with nitrogen prevents the breakdown of food by oxidation, and also prevents mold growth and kills dormant insect eggs. The low temperatures provided by liquid nitrogen are used to fast-freeze foods and for the refrigeration of both food and biological specimens. The brittleness of materials frozen in liquid nitrogen allows, for example, spices to be ground more finely and unwanted sharp edges to be broken off molded plastic parts.

26.3 ELEMENTAL PHOSPHORUS

a. Allotropic forms There are three allotropic forms of phosphorus, known as white phosphorus, red phosphorus, and black phosphorus. They decrease in chemical reactivity in the order given, white phosphorus being a highly reactive substance, and black phosphorus quite unreactive.

White phosphorus is a soft, low-melting waxy solid that is white to yellow, depending upon its purity. (It often appears yellow, and is called "yellow phosphorus," because of the formation of small amounts of red phosphorus on its surface.) White phosphorus can ignite spontaneously in air and is usually stored under water, in which it is insoluble. When the supply of oxygen is extremely limited and moisture is present, oxidation of white phosphorus is slow and is accompanied by phosphorescence.

White phosphorus is highly toxic. Small amounts can cause severe irritation of the lungs and gastrointestinal tract and about 50 mg inhaled or ingested can be fatal. It should *never* be touched, for its ignition temperature is about the same as the temperature of the skin, and it can cause painful, slow-healing burns.

White P: P_4, highly reactive
Red P: polymeric, less reactive
Black P: crystalline, least reactive

White phosphorus is moderately soluble in diethyl ether and benzene and is very soluble in carbon disulfide. As a solid, in solution, and in the vapor state below 800 °C, it exists in the form of covalently bonded P_4 molecules with a phosphorus atom at each corner of a regular tetrahedron (Figure 26.1a). Above 800 °C some P_2 molecules form.

The second allotropic form of phosphorus—red phosphorus—is obtained when the white variety is heated to about 250 °C in the absence of air or is exposed to light. Red phosphorus differs radically from the white allotrope. It is relatively nonpoisonous, is insoluble in those solvents that dissolve the white form, and melts at about 600 °C. Red phosphorus is stable toward atmospheric oxidation at ordinary temperatures, but it ignites when heated to about 400 °C. In general, red phosphorus undergoes the same reactions as white phosphorus, but requires higher temperatures. Red phosphorus has a complex polymeric structure.

Black phosphorus (Figure 26.1b), which is crystalline and metallic in appearance, forms when white phosphorus is heated under extremely high pressure (35,000 atm) for a number of days in the presence of a catalyst.

Figure 26.1
Forms of Phosphorus Black phosphorus is an electrical conductor, as is graphite, which has a similar structure.

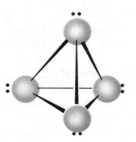

(a) The P_4 molecule of white phosphorus

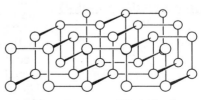

(b) The crystal structure of black phosphorus

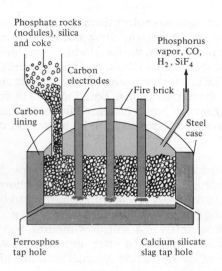

Figure 26.2
An Electric Phosphorus Furnace A high voltage electric arc produces temperatures of 1200°–1450 °C in the furnace. Molten ferrophos is heavy and sinks to the bottom, where it can be drawn off. Molten calcium silicate is less dense than the ferrophos and forms a second liquid layer that can be drawn off separately. (Source: A. D. F. Toy, *Phosphorus Chemistry in Everyday Living,* Washington, D.C.: American Chemical Society, 1976.)

b. Sources, preparation, and uses of phosphorus Phosphorus is the tenth most abundant element (see Table 28.1). It occurs only in combined form, mainly as phosphates in various minerals. The most common phosphate-bearing minerals are fluorapatite, $Ca_5(PO_4)_3F$, and phosphorite, which is hydroxyapatite, $Ca_5(PO_4)_3OH$ (see Figure 25.3).

Elemental phosphorus is produced by treating **phosphate rock,** as the mineral deposits containing the calcium phosphates and silica are called, with coke in electric furnaces (Figure 26.2). In the overall reaction, phosphate is reduced to elemental phosphorus and coke is oxidized to carbon monoxide, with calcium being removed as calcium silicate slag.

$$2Ca_3(PO_4)_2(s) + 6SiO_2(s) + 10C(s) \xrightarrow{1200-1450\ °C} 6CaSiO_3(l) + 10CO(g) + P_4(g)$$
$$\Delta H = 3050\ kJ$$

Table 26.4
Uses of Elemental Phosphorus

Major use
Manufacture of P_4O_{10} and H_3PO_4
Other uses
Synthesis of other chemicals
Matches, bombs, and fireworks
Rodent poisons
Alloying agent

At the same time, the fluoride ion usually present in phosphate rock is converted by reaction with SiO_2 to volatile SiF_4, a toxic gas that must be removed from the vapor stream. Iron oxide, usually also present in phosphate rock to a small extent, reacts with phosphorus to give iron phosphide, known as "ferrophos."

Most phosphate rock is used directly in the manufacture of phosphate fertilizers rather than in the production of the element (see An Aside: Plant Nutrients and Chemical Fertilizers). Only about 5% of all phosphorus used in a year is in elemental form (Table 26.4). Most of it is burned to give phosphorus(V) oxide, which is converted to pure phosphoric acid (Section 26.6b) and other chemicals.

26.4 ELEMENTAL SULFUR

S: many allotropic forms

a. Allotropic forms Like phosphorus, sulfur is a solid at room temperature and exists in various allotropic forms. Although elemental sulfur is reactive and combines directly with most elements, in none of its forms is it as difficult to handle or as toxic as white phosphorus. Elemental sulfur has been used medically as a laxative and in various preparations applied to the skin.

The form of sulfur stable at ordinary temperatures is rhombic sulfur (Figure 26.3), which is crystalline, bright yellow in color, odorless, and tasteless. It is practically insoluble in water, but dissolves freely in carbon disulfide, CS_2. When heated to 95.6 °C rhombic sulfur undergoes a slow transition to monoclinic sulfur. The change is so slow that if rhombic sulfur is heated rapidly to its melting point of 112.8 °C, little conversion to the monoclinic modification occurs. Like the rhombic

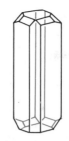

Figure 26.3
Rhombic and Monoclinic Sulfur Crystals

Rhombic sulfur   Monoclinic sulfur

form, monoclinic sulfur is bright yellow, odorless, tasteless, and insoluble in water. Its crystals are long, yellow needles. In both forms sulfur exists as S_8 molecules (Figure 26.4). (We have mentioned here only the more important sulfur allotropes — over thirty are known.)

The changes on melting and heating of sulfur are complicated and interesting. The true melting point of rhombic sulfur is 112.8 °C and that of the monoclinic form 119.0 °C. When solid sulfur is heated, it melts to give a mobile yellow liquid. The melting process is accompanied to a very small extent by the breaking of S_8 rings. Between the melting point and about 160 °C there is little change in the mobility of the liquid sulfur, but between 160 °C and 187 °C, there is a *10,000-fold increase* in viscosity and the material turns brown. The increased viscocity is due to the formation of long chains of sulfur atoms that entangle each other. Above 200 °C, the viscosity decreases, probably as a result of the breaking of the long chains, and at 444.6 °C, the normal boiling point, the sulfur is again a mobile liquid. If the liquid material at about 200 °C is cooled very rapidly by pouring it into cold water, a soft rubbery substance known as plastic sulfur forms. In plastic sulfur, the long chains of sulfur atoms are in the form of coils, and the rubbery character is due to the ability of these chains to uncoil and coil again under stress. On standing, plastic sulfur slowly reverts to the rhombic allotrope.

Sulfur vapor contains S_8, S_6, S_4, and S_2 molecules, with the relative amounts varying with temperature and pressure. The proportion of S_2 in the vapor increases, as would be expected, with increasing temperature. Like O_2, S_2 molecules contain two unpaired electrons. The same tendency of sulfur atoms to bond to each other in short chains and small rings is exhibited in species such as S_2Cl_2, S_2^{2-}, S_4^{2-}, and H_2S_6.

S atoms:
tend to form chains and rings

Figure 26.4
The S_8 Molecule (a) S_8 ring structure; (b) packing of rings in rhombic sulfur. (Source: J. Donohue, *The Structure of the Elements,* New York: Wiley, 1974, p. 335.)

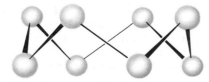

(a) S_8 ring structure

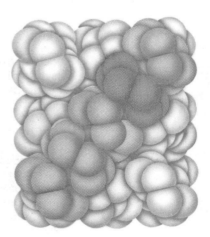

(b) Packing of rings in rhombic sulfur

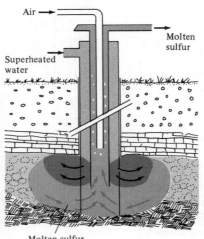

Figure 26.5
The Frasch Process for Sulfur Extraction Three concentric pipes are sunk from the surface into the bed of sulfur. Water at a temprature of about 170 °C and a pressure of 100 lb/sq inch is forced down the outer pipe to melt the sulfur. Hot compressed air is pumped down the innermost pipe and mixes with the molten sulfur, forming a froth of water, air, and sulfur. This froth rises to the surface through the middle pipe and is collected in large bins. Removal of the water leaves sulfur with a purity of about 99.5%.

b. Sources, preparation, and uses of sulfur Sulfur is much less abundant than oxygen and one-half as abundant as phosphorus, making up 0.052% (by mass) of the earth's crust. It is found mainly as the free element, in heavy metal sulfides (e.g., PbS, ZnS, $CuFeS_2$), and in light metal sulfates (e.g., $MgSO_4$, $CaSO_4$). Much of the sulfur currently utilized in this country is obtained from the vast deposits of the free element found in Texas and Louisiana. The sulfur occurs in veins and pockets in beds of limestone and is covered with several hundred feet of quicksand and rock. It is brought to the surface by a process developed at the turn of this century and called the *Frasch process* after its inventor, the engineer Herman Frasch (the process is described in Figure 26.5; see also Thoughts on Chemistry in this chapter).

Growing concern over pollution by sulfur dioxide (see An Aside: Air Pollution, Smog, and Acid Rain in this chapter) has led to the removal of sulfur from natural gas and petroleum. In addition, sulfur-containing compounds are being removed from the effluent and stack gases of metal-smelting plants that process sulfide ores. Elemental sulfur from these operations is now coming into the market in increasing quantities. The major use of sulfur is in the manufacture of sulfuric acid (Table 26.5; Section 26.6a).

Table 26.5
Uses of Elemental Sulfur

Major use
  Manufacture of sulfuric acid
  —roughly 90% of all elemental sulfur goes into sulfuric acid.
Other uses
  Pulp and paper industry
  Manufacture of carbon disulfide
  Rubber
  Fungicides, insecticides, and medicine

AN ASIDE

The Nitrogen, Phosphorus, and Sulfur Cycles

Each element circulates in a cycle governed by the properties of the element and its natural sources and compounds. The primary forces in these natural cycles are the uptake of nutrients by plants and animals and the decay of dead plants and animals, the solution by runoff water of soluble materials, and the return of solids to dry land by the upwelling of mountains from the ocean floor.

The atmosphere is a primary reservoir for nitrogen, oxygen, carbon (in the form of CO and CO_2), and hydrogen (in the form of water). Sulfur spends part of its time as gaseous compounds in the atmosphere (hydrogen sulfide and sulfur oxides), but the major sulfur reservoir is as soluble sulfate in the oceans. No gaseous phosphorus compound plays a significant role in the phosphorus cycle, the primary source of phosphorus being phosphate rock.

Oxidation and reduction are important in the nitrogen cycle (Figure A). In plants and animals, nitrogen is present in the reduced form primarily as ammonium

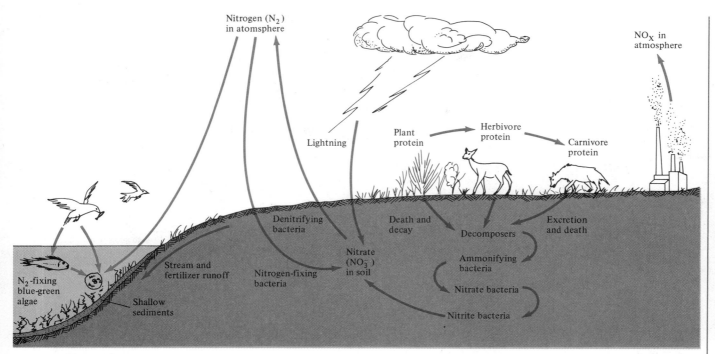

Figure A
The Nitrogen Cycle

ion or as —NH_2 groups in organic compounds. But plants cannot use atmospheric nitrogen, presumably because of the large amount of energy needed to break the nitrogen–nitrogen bond. Molecular nitrogen must undergo **nitrogen fixation** — the combination of molecular nitrogen with other atoms — before it can be taken up by plants from the soil, usually in the form of nitrate ion. In nature, bacteria and algae that live free in soil, ponds, and lakes, or that live in a mutually dependent relationship with specific plants, fix nitrogen by converting it to ammonia. Other microorganisms convert ammonia to nitrites and nitrates — a process called nitrification. The conversion of nitrites and nitrates to elemental nitrogen is called denitrification. Denitrification occurs during the decay of organic matter. Mankind's role in the nitrogen cycle is through the industrial fixation of nitrogen and its return to the land and water as fertilizer, and through the formation of nitrogen oxides in the combustion of fossil fuels.

Sulfur is taken up by plants as sulfate ion. Sulfate ion enters the soil in precipitation (see An Aside: Air Pollution, Smog, and Acid Rain) and from sea spray. Also, the sulfur in decaying organic matter is converted to hydrogen sulfide by "decomposer" bacteria and then oxidized to sulfate ion by other bacteria. The sulfur cycle is represented in simplified form in Figure B.

The phosphorus cycle comprises only movement from land to the hydrosphere, to plants and animals, and back to the land and hydrosphere. The primary source of phosphorus is phosphate rock, which is not very soluble. Man plays an important role in the phosphorus cycle by mining large quantities of phosphate rock and returning it to the land and water as fertilizer and detergents. Phosphates are deposited in ocean sediment and after many, many years may return to dry land in the upwelling of mountains. The organic phosphate of plants and animals returns to the soil and the ocean as inorganic phosphate. The phosphorus cycle is represented in Figure C.

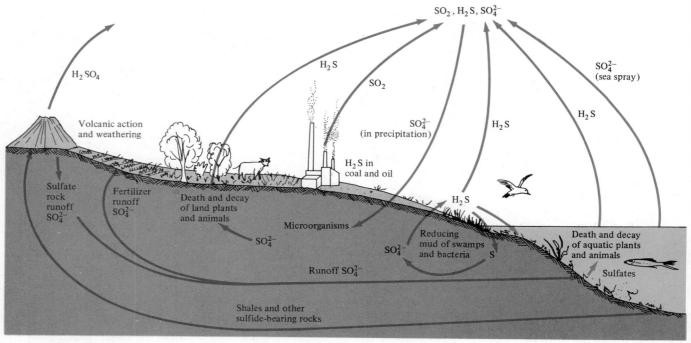

Figure B
The Sulfur Cycle

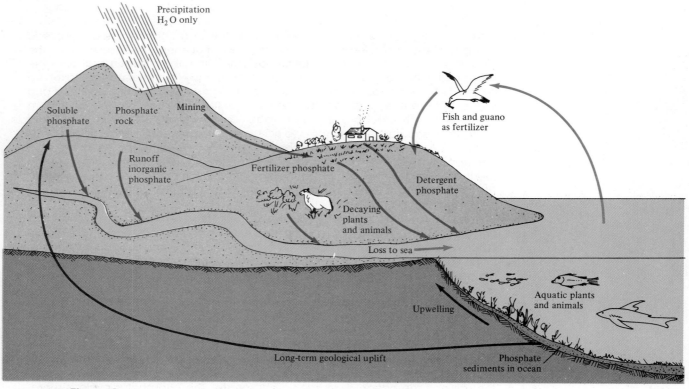

Figure C
The Phosphorus Cycle

CHEMICAL REACTIONS OF NITROGEN, PHOSPHORUS, AND SULFUR; INDUSTRIAL ACIDS

26.5 SOME CHEMICAL REACTIONS OF NITROGEN, PHOSPHORUS, AND SULFUR AND THEIR COMPOUNDS

a. Combination with other elements The only element with which nitrogen combines at room temperature is lithium, the strongest elemental reducing agent.

$$6Li(s) + N_2(g) \longrightarrow 2Li_3N(s) \qquad (26.1)$$

At higher temperatures, presumably because it is partially dissociated into atoms, nitrogen is more reactive. It combines with active metals of Group II and certain p block elements (B, Al, Si, Ge) to give binary nitrides such as magnesium nitride, Mg_3N_2, boron nitride, BN, and silicon nitride, Si_3N_4 (Section 26.7). Combustion reactions in air all produce NO by the reaction of atmospheric nitrogen and oxygen at the temperature of the flame. Nitrogen also reacts with the halogens at elevated temperatures, but the reactions and the products are of little utility and are not commonly encountered.

Phosphorus and sulfur combine with most elements. White phosphorus reacts vigorously with oxygen, the halogens, and other nonmetals. Red phosphorus requires higher temperatures for such reactions, for example,

$$4P(s) + 5O_2(g, xs) \xrightarrow[\substack{\text{white P, spontaneous in air} \\ \text{red P, ignites when heated} \\ \text{to 400 °C}}]{} P_4O_{10}(s)$$
$$\textit{phosphorus(V) oxide}$$

With a limited amount of oxygen, P_4O_6 rather than P_4O_{10} is formed. In reactions with the halogens, phosphorus yields either PX_3 or PX_5, except that the pentaiodide is not known. Apparently five large iodine atoms cannot fit around the small phosphorus atom.

Sulfur combines at room temperature with the active metals lithium, sodium, and potassium, and also with copper, silver, and mercury, to form sulfides, for example,

$$Hg(l) + S(s) \longrightarrow HgS(s)$$
$$\textit{mercury(II) sulfide}$$

Sulfur burns in air to produce mainly sulfur dioxide, along with some sulfur trioxide (further discussed in Section 26.6a).

$$S(s) + O_2(g)) \longrightarrow SO_2(g) \qquad \Delta H° = -296.8 \text{ kJ} \qquad (26.2)$$
$$2SO_2(g) + O_2(g) \longrightarrow 2SO_3(g) \qquad \Delta H° = -197.8 \text{ kJ} \qquad (26.3)$$

The products of the combination of sulfur with the halogens vary with the conditions; frequently the products contain sulfur–sulfur bonds, for example,

$$2S(s) + Cl_2(g) \xrightarrow{\Delta} S_2Cl_2(l)$$
$$\textit{disulfur dichloride (Cl—S—S—Cl)}$$

Oxides of N, P, S: all acidic

b. Reactions of oxides The oxides of nitrogen, phosphorus, and sulfur are all molecular compounds with covalent bonding, and they are all acidic oxides (Section 16.11a). They combine with water in nonredox reactions to give acids, for example,

$$SO_3(s) + H_2O(l) \longrightarrow H_2SO_4(aq)$$

and react with bases and basic oxides to give salts (see also Table 17.2), for example,

$$SO_3(s) + 2NaOH(aq) \longrightarrow Na_2SO_4(aq) + H_2O(l)$$

The nitrogen(IV) oxide, NO_2, is an exception—with water it undergoes a disproportionation reaction (a redox reaction) rather than a nonredox combination reaction:

$$\overset{+4}{3NO_2(g)} + H_2O(l) \longrightarrow \overset{+5}{2HNO_3(aq)} + \overset{+2}{NO(g)} \qquad (26.4)$$
$$\textit{nitrogen dioxide} \qquad\qquad \textit{nitric acid} \quad \textit{nitric oxide}$$

c. Nitric acid as an oxidizing agent

In any concentration greater than about 2 M, nitric acid, HNO_3, can function as an oxidizing agent. The product to which it is reduced depends on the concentration of the acid, the temperature, and the nature of the reducing agent. The most common reduction products are nitrogen(IV) oxide and nitrogen(II) oxide.

$$\overset{+5}{NO_3^-} + 2H^+ + e^- \longrightarrow \overset{+4}{NO_2} + H_2O \qquad E° = 0.81 \text{ V}$$

$$\overset{+5}{NO_3^-} + 4H^+ + 3e^- \longrightarrow \overset{+2}{NO} + 2H_2O \qquad E° = 0.96 \text{ V}$$

Other possible reduction products are NH_4^+, N_2, HNO_2, and N_2O.

All metals except the least reactive ones, such as gold and platinum, are oxidized by nitric acid. In some cases the reaction must be initiated by heat, but once started it proceeds vigorously. In general, the stronger the reducing agent and the more dilute the acid, the lower will be the oxidation state of the nitrogen in the reduction product. For example, zinc, a reasonably active metal, reduces dilute nitric acid all the way to ammonium ion.

$$4Zn(s) + 10H^+ + \overset{+5}{NO_3^-} \longrightarrow 4Zn^{2+} + \overset{-3}{NH_4^+} + 3H_2O(l) \qquad \textbf{(26.5)}$$

In somewhat less dilute acid, elemental nitrogen is produced in the reaction of zinc with nitric acid. With *concentrated* nitric acid, nitrogen dioxide is the main reduction product in reactions with both active metals and less active metals, such as copper.

$$Cu(s) + 4H^+ + 2\overset{+5}{NO_3^-} \longrightarrow Cu^{2+} + 2\overset{+4}{NO_2}(g) + 2H_2O(l) \qquad \textbf{(26.6)}$$

With warm dilute nitric acid, the main reduction product in the reaction with copper is nitrogen(II) oxide, NO (Section 26.9).

A number of metals that are attacked by dilute nitric acid—for example, iron and chromium—are inert to the concentrated acid. These metals are said to be *passive* toward the acid; they are protected by oxide coatings.

A 3-to-1 by volume mixture of concentrated HCl and HNO_3 is known as **aqua regia** ("royal water") because of its ability to dissolve such noble metals as gold and platinum, which are inert to either acid alone. The redox reaction between concentrated nitric and hydrochloric acids gives water, elemental chlorine, and nitrosyl chloride.

$$3HCl(aq) + HNO_3(aq) \longrightarrow Cl_2(g) + \underset{\substack{nitrosyl \\ chloride}}{NOCl(g)} + 2H_2O(l) \qquad \textbf{(26.7)}$$

The solvent action of aqua regia probably results mainly from the action of the nitrosyl chloride and chlorine, which convert the metals initially to chlorides. The metal chlorides are then transformed to stable complex anions by reaction with chloride ion. The overall reaction for gold is

$$Au(s) + 4H^+ + 4Cl^- + NO_3^- \longrightarrow [AuCl_4]^- + NO(g) + 2H_2O(l) \qquad \textbf{(26.8)}$$

d. Thermal decomposition of ammonium salts and nitrates

All ammonium salts decompose on heating, the manner of decomposition depending on the nature of the anion of the salt. Salts containing anions that do not act as oxidizing agents decompose into ammonia and the parent acids (nonredox decomposition, Section 17.3b), for example,

$$\underset{\substack{ammonium\ hydrogen \\ carbonate}}{NH_4HCO_3(s)} \xrightarrow{\Delta} NH_3(g) + CO_2(g) + H_2O(g) \qquad \textbf{(26.9)}$$

Aqua regia: HCl + HNO$_3$
(3:1 by volume)

Decomposition of NH_4HCO_3 occurs to some extent even at room temperature, and for this reason the compound is used in smelling salts, once popular for reviving ladies prone to fainting spells. In general, ammonium salts of weak acids are much less stable thermally than those of strong acids.

Ammonium salts containing anions which are oxidizing agents undergo internal oxidation–reduction when heated (redox decomposition, Section 17.4b), for example,

$$\overset{-3}{N}H_4\overset{+5}{N}O_3(s) \xrightarrow{170-260\ ^\circ C} \overset{+1}{N_2}O(g) + 2H_2O(g) \qquad \textbf{(26.10)}$$
ammonium nitrate

In this reaction, the nitrogen in the ammonium ion is oxidized, whereas that in the nitrate ion is reduced. Ammonium nitrate is a dangerous solid and should be handled with great care. Decomposition, particularly in a limited space or at higher temperatures, may occur with explosive violence, with N_2O being reduced to elemental nitrogen (see Equation 26.15) in the overall reaction

$$2NH_4NO_3(s) \xrightarrow{>300\ ^\circ C} 2N_2(g) + 4H_2O(g) + O_2(g) \qquad \textbf{(26.11)}$$

Mixtures of ammonium nitrate and oxidizable materials are potentially dangerous. Accidental exposure to elevated temperatures may initiate oxidation, and this in turn may increase the temperature to the point of detonation.

In April 1947, an explosion due to the decomposition of ammonium nitrate touched off a series of explosions that took the lives of 576 persons at Texas City, Texas. The ammonium nitrate, intended for use as a fertilizer, was being loaded onto a ship in the harbor. Apparently, explosion of the ship occurred because the sacks of the material were piled so high and so tightly that heat built up within the pile. With proper precautions, however, ammonium nitrate can be shipped safely and is widely used as a fertilizer.

All nitrates decompose with heat by redox reactions (see Table 17.7). The active metal nitrates give up oxygen and form nitrites, while the nitrates of the less active metals yield nitrogen(IV) oxide as the nitrate reduction product (see Table 17.8).

> **All NH_4^+ salts,
> all NO_3^- salts:
> decompose when heated**

$$Mg(NO_3)_2(s) \xrightarrow{\Delta} Mg(NO_2)_2(s) + O_2(g) \qquad \textbf{(26.12)}$$
$$2Pb(NO_3)_2(s) \xrightarrow{\Delta} 2PbO(s) + 4NO_2(g) + O_2(g) \qquad \textbf{(26.13)}$$

e. Additional redox reactions of nitrogen compounds Frequently, molecular nitrogen is released when species containing nitrogen in a higher and lower oxidation state are brought together. Warming an aqueous solution saturated with both ammonium chloride and sodium nitrite has been used as a laboratory preparation of nitrogen.

$$NH_4^+ + NO_2^- \xrightarrow{\Delta} N_2(g) + 2H_2O(g) \qquad \textbf{(26.14)}$$

This reaction goes slowly even at room temperature. Nitrogen(I) oxide at high temperatures decomposes to give nitrogen and oxygen, a reaction which can occur with explosive force:

$$2N_2O(g) \xrightarrow{\Delta} 2N_2(g) + O_2(g) \qquad \Delta H^\circ = -164.1\ kJ \qquad \textbf{(26.15)}$$

Anhydrous hydrazine, H_2NNH_2 (Figure 26.6), is a fuming colorless liquid and a potent reducing agent. It is converted mainly to nitrogen by strong oxidizing agents such as hydrogen peroxide, liquid oxygen, or nitrogen tetroxide (N_2O_4). These redox reactions release large amounts of energy,

$$H_2NNH_2(l) + O_2(g) \longrightarrow N_2(g) + 2H_2O(g) \qquad \Delta H^\circ = -543.3\ kJ \quad \textbf{(26.16a)}$$
$$2H_2NNH_2(l) + N_2O_4(g) \longrightarrow 3N_2(g) + 4H_2O(g) \qquad \Delta H^\circ = -1252\ kJ \quad \textbf{(26.16b)}$$

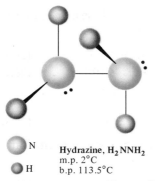

○ N
● H
Hydrazine, H_2NNH_2
m.p. 2°C
b.p. 113.5°C

Figure 26.6

Reaction (26.16b) was used in propulsion of the Apollo lunar excursion module. [Note that both hydrazine and nitrogen(I) oxide, which decompose vigorously, are compounds that have positive heats of formation.]

f. Sulfuric acid as a dehydrating agent and an oxidizing agent   The dehydrating ability of concentrated sulfuric acid results from the ease with which it forms hydrates (e.g., $H_2SO_4 \cdot H_2O$, $H_2SO_4 \cdot 2H_2O$). This ability makes sulfuric acid an extremely effective drying agent for wet gases and liquids, provided that the gas or liquid does not react with the acid. Sulfuric acid can also remove the elements of water from organic compounds that themselves contain no free water. Table sugar, or sucrose, has the formula $C_{12}H_{22}O_{11}$. Although no water is present in the compound, the hydrogen-to-oxygen ratio is the same as that in water. When concentrated sulfuric acid is added to sugar, these elements are removed in the form of water, and a residue of carbon is left.

$$C_{12}H_{22}O_{11}(s) + 11H_2SO_4(conc) \longrightarrow 12C(s) + 11(H_2SO_4 \cdot H_2O) \qquad (26.17)$$

The same type of reaction accounts for the charring of wood, paper, cotton, and wool and the destruction of skin by the concentrated acid.

Hot concentrated sulfuric acid is a moderately strong oxidizing agent, although not as strong as nitric acid. The sulfur atom is usually (though not always) reduced from its oxidation state of $+6$ to $+4$, for example,

$$Cu(s) + 2H_2SO_4(conc) \longrightarrow CuSO_4(aq) + SO_2(g) + 2H_2O(l) \qquad (26.18)$$
$$C(s) + 2H_2SO_4(conc) \longrightarrow CO_2(g) + 2SO_2(g) + 2H_2O(l) \qquad (26.19)$$

Zinc, which stands above copper in the activity series and is a stronger reducing agent, reduces concentrated sulfuric acid to elemental sulfur or hydrogen sulfide. At lower temperatures concentrated sulfuric acid is a weaker oxidizing agent.

In dilute solutions of sulfuric acid (as in solutions of all nonoxidizing acids) it is the hydrogen ion from the ionization of the acid that is the oxidizing agent, not the sulfate ion. For example, dilute H_2SO_4 solutions attack metals above hydrogen in the activity series, with the liberation of hydrogen.

$$Zn(s) + 2H^+ \longrightarrow Zn^{2+} + H_2(g) \qquad (26.20)$$

N^{3-}, P^{3-}: strong bases
S^{2-}, HS^-: weak bases
NH_4^+: weak acid

g. Ions in aqueous solution   The nitride and phosphide ions are such strong bases that they react vigorously and completely with water to give ammonia and phosphine, respectively, and strongly alkaline solutions.

$$N^{3-} + 3H_2O(l) \longrightarrow NH_3(aq) + 3OH^- \qquad (26.21)$$
$$P^{3-} + 3H_2O(l) \longrightarrow PH_3(g) + 3OH^- \qquad (26.22)$$

The sulfide ion and the hydrogen sulfide ion are weaker bases. These anions of weak acids give alkaline solutions due to the following equilibria:

$$S^{2-} + H_2O(l) \rightleftharpoons HS^- + OH^- \qquad K_b = 3 \times 10^{-2} \qquad (26.23)$$
$$HS^- + H_2O(l) \rightleftharpoons H_2S(aq) + OH^- \qquad K_b = 1.0 \times 10^{-7} \qquad (26.24)$$

Ammonium ion, NH_4^+, is weakly acidic,

$$NH_4^+ + H_2O(l) \rightleftharpoons NH_3(aq) + H_3O^+ \qquad K_a = 6.3 \times 10^{-10} \qquad (26.25)$$

while the phosphonium ion, PH_4^+, which is less stable than ammonium ion, is completely decomposed in water,

$$PH_4^+ + H_2O(l) \longrightarrow PH_3(g) + H_3O^+ \qquad (26.26)$$

Table 26.6
Oxoanions of N, P, and S in Their Common Oxidation States; Redox Properties

Nitrogen

+3	NO_2^- nitrite ion	Oxidizing agent in H^+
+5	NO_3^- nitrate ion	Oxidizing agent in H^+; poor oxidizing agent in OH^-

Phosphorus

+3	$H_2PO_3^-$ dihydrogen phosphite ion	Reducing agent in H^+ or OH^-
	HPO_3^{2-} hydrogen phosphite ion	Reducing agent in H^+ or OH^-
+5	PO_4^{3-} phosphate ion	—
	HPO_4^{2-} hydrogen phosphate ion	—
	$H_2PO_4^-$ dihydrogen phosphate ion	—

Sulfur

+4	SO_3^{2-} sulfite ion	Mild reducing agent
	HSO_3^- hydrogen sulfite ion	Mild reducing agent
+6	SO_4^{2-} sulfate ion	Oxidizing agent only in concentrated acid
	HSO_4^- hydrogen sulfate ion	—

Table 26.7
Acidity and Basicity of N, P, and S Oxoanions

Moderately basic
PO_4^{3-} $K_b = 5.1 \times 10^{-2}$

Weakly basic
HPO_4^{2-} $K_b = 1.5 \times 10^{-7}$
SO_3^{2-} $K_b = 2 \times 10^{-7}$
HPO_3^{2-} $K_b = 6.3 \times 10^{-8}$
NO_2^- $K_b = 1.4 \times 10^{-11}$
$H_2PO_3^{2-}$ $K_b = 3 \times 10^{-13}$

Neutral
NO_3^- —
SO_4^{2-} —

Weakly acidic
HSO_3^- $K_a = 5.0 \times 10^{-8}$
$H_2PO_4^-$ $K_a = 6.6 \times 10^{-8}$

Moderately acidic
HSO_4^- $K_a = 1.0 \times 10^{-2}$

The oxoanions of nitrogen, phosphorus, and sulfur in their common oxidation states are listed in Table 26.6. Nitrate and nitrite ions are both oxidizing agents, while the oxoanions of +3 phosphorus and +4 sulfur usually react as reducing agents.

As shown in Table 26.7, many of the oxoanions of nitrogen, phosphorus, and sulfur are weakly basic. The phosphate ion is more strongly basic than the others and the nitrate ion does not undergo hydrolysis to any significant extent.

Upon acidification with dilute, nonoxidizing acids, two of the oxoanions yield unstable acids that decompose to evolve gases (partner-exchange reactions, Section 17.3d).

$$SO_3^{2-} + 2H^+ \longrightarrow \underset{\text{sulfurous acid}}{H_2SO_3(aq)} \longrightarrow SO_2(g) + H_2O(l) \qquad (26.27)$$

$$2NO_2^- + 2H^+ \longrightarrow \underset{\text{nitrous acid}}{2HNO_2(aq)} \longrightarrow NO(g) + NO_2(g) + H_2O(l) \qquad (26.28)$$

Sulfide ion, when similarly acidified, forms hydrogen sulfide.

$$S^{2-} + 2H^+ \longrightarrow H_2S(aq) \qquad (26.29)$$

EXAMPLE 26.1
Disproportionation: Nonmetals

Many nonmetals react with aqueous sodium hydroxide and in the reaction are both oxidized and reduced (i.e., they disproportionate). For example,

$$Cl_2(g) + 2NaOH(aq) \longrightarrow NaCl(aq) + NaClO(aq) + H_2O(l)$$
$$P_4(s) + 3NaOH(aq) + 3H_2O(l) \longrightarrow PH_3(g) + 3NaH_2PO_2(aq)$$
$$3S(s) + 6NaOH(aq) \longrightarrow 2Na_2S(aq) + Na_2SO_3(aq) + 3H_2O(l)$$

Nitrogen and oxygen do not react with sodium hydroxide in this way. For each element, give a reason why the reaction does not take place.

Nitrogen does not react because the two nitrogen atoms in the nitrogen molecule are so strongly bonded to each other that elemental nitrogen is inert. Oxygen does not react because it is so strongly electronegative that it cannot achieve a positive oxidation state, except in combination with fluorine, the only element that is more electronegative than oxygen.

EXAMPLE 26.2
Chemical Reactions: S Compounds

The combustion of coal in power plants often gives rise to sulfur dioxide, formed by the oxidation of sulfur impurities. One method of preventing the emission of sulfur dioxide is to mix limestone (calcium carbonate) with the coal as it is fed into the combustion chamber. The products of this overall process, which results in removing sulfur dioxide from the combustion products, are calcium sulfate, calcium sulfite, and carbon dioxide. Write equations for a series of reactions that could result in the formation of these products.

To solve such a problem it is necessary to review what reactions are possible. First, what happens to coal, sulfur, and calcium carbonate in the hot furnace? The carbon from the coal and sulfur combine with oxygen. In the presence of excess oxygen, CO_2 is formed from carbon. The principal product formed by sulfur is sulfur dioxide, but some sulfur trioxide is also formed by combination of the sulfur dioxide with oxygen:

$$C(s) + O_2(g) \longrightarrow CO_2(g)$$
$$S(s) + O_2(g) \longrightarrow SO_2(g)$$
$$2SO_2(g) + O_2(g) \longrightarrow 2SO_3(g)$$

Calcium carbonate when heated decomposes to give calcium oxide and carbon dioxide.

$$CaCO_3(s) \xrightarrow{\Delta} CaO(s) + CO_2(g)$$

Now we must ask what further reactions of these substances can take place to yield the known products of the reaction. As the oxides of nonmetals, the sulfur oxides are acidic. As the oxide of an active metal, CaO is a basic oxide. The known products can be formed by combination of the oxides present as follows:

$$CaO(s) + SO_2(g) \longrightarrow CaSO_3(s)$$
$$CaO(s) + SO_3(g) \longrightarrow CaSO_4(s)$$

The formation of carbon dioxide is accounted for both by the combustion of coal and the decomposition of $CaCO_3$.

26.6 INDUSTRIAL ACIDS

Acids and bases are essential industrial chemicals. They are used both for adjusting the pH in industrial processes and for reactions specific to the individual acids. The three most common acids derived from nitrogen, phosphorus, and sulfur—nitric acid, phosphoric acid, and sulfuric acid—are important industrial chemicals (see Table 25.10). (Industrial alkalis are discussed in Section 29.8.) Sulfuric acid is perennially the largest volume industrial chemical. It is the least expensive nonvolatile acid. The amount of sulfuric acid used by a country is, it is often said, a direct measure of that country's industrial progress and prosperity.

a. Sulfuric acid Pure sulfuric acid (Figure 26.7) is a viscous, oily liquid which begins to boil at 290 °C with decomposition into sulfur trioxide (which escapes as a gas) and water (some of which remains in the solution). Once the composition of 98.3% H_2SO_4 and a boiling point of 338 °C are reached, the composition remains unchanged, giving the usual concentrated laboratory acid, which is 18 M. When the concentrated acid is added to water, a large amount of heat is evolved, partly due to the exothermic formation of low-melting hydrates (e.g., $H_2SO_4 \cdot H_2O$, m.p. 8.5 °C). (The danger of boiling and splattering is minimized by pouring the acid slowly into water with constant stirring.) Sulfuric acid is a strong acid in its first dissociation (Table 26.8).

The crucial step in the production of sulfuric acid is the catalytic oxidation of

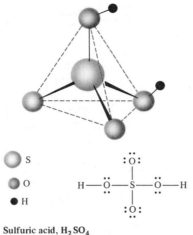

S
O
H

H—Ö—S—Ö—H

Sulfuric acid, H_2SO_4
m.p. 10.36°C
b.p. ~290°C (dec)

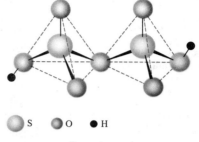

S   O   H

Pyrosulfuric acid, $H_2S_2O_7$
m.p. 35°C

**Figure 26.7
Sulfur(VI) Oxacids**

sulfur dioxide to sulfur trioxide (Equation 26.3). The usual catalyst is vanadium(V) oxide, V_2O_5. The sulfur dioxide is obtained by burning sulfur, or may be a by-product from the production of metals (Section 28.6).

The oxidation of sulfur dioxide provides an excellent example of the need to consider both thermodynamic and kinetic factors in predicting chemical behavior. Since the union of sulfur dioxide and oxygen is exothermic and the reaction reaches a state of equilibrium, it would be predicted on the basis of Le Chatelier's principle that

**Table 26.8
Properties of Sulfuric Acid,
Phosphoric Acid, and Nitric Acid**

Sulfuric acid

$$H_2SO_4(aq) + H_2O(l) \longrightarrow HSO_4^- + \underset{\text{strong acid}}{H_3O^+}$$

$$HSO_4^- + H_2O(l) \rightleftharpoons SO_4^{2-} + H_3O^+ \quad K_a = 1.0 \times 10^{-2}$$

M.p.: pure acid 10.4 °C; 98% acid, 3 °C
B.p.: ~ 290 °C with decomposition ($SO_3 + H_2O$)
Density of 98% acid: 1.84 g/mL
Concentrated acid: 18 M, 98% H_2SO_4 by mass
Hot, concentrated H_2SO_4 is a strong oxidizing agent. Dilute H_2SO_4 is
    not an oxidizing acid.

Phosphoric acid

$$H_3PO_4(aq) + H_2O(l) \rightleftharpoons H_2PO_4^- + H_3O^+ \quad K_a = 7.5 \times 10^{-3}$$
$$H_2PO_4^- + H_2O(l) \rightleftharpoons HPO_4^{2-} + H_3O^+ \quad K_a = 6.6 \times 10^{-8}$$
$$HPO_4^{2-} + H_2O(l) \rightleftharpoons PO_4^{3-} + H_3O^+ \quad K_a = 1 \times 10^{-12}$$

M.p.: 42.35 °C At 200 °C $\longrightarrow H_4P_2O_7(l)$
Density: 100% acid, 1.87 g/mL; 85% acid, 1.69 g/mL
Concentrated acid: 14.8 M, 85% H_3PO_4 by mass
H_3PO_4 is *not* an oxidizing agent.

Nitric acid

$$HNO_3(aq) + H_2O(l) \longrightarrow NO_3^- + \underset{\text{strong acid}}{H_3O^+}$$

M.p.: −41.6 °C
B.p.: 83 °C Decomposes in sunlight (to NO_2)
Density: pure acid 1.50 g/mL; 70.4% acid, 1.42 g/mL
Concentrated acid: 15.9 M, 70.4% HNO_3 by mass
In any concentration > 2 M HNO_3 can be an oxidizing agent.

Table 26.9

Uses of Sulfuric Acid There are hundreds of ways of using sulfuric acid.

| *Major uses* |
| Manufacture of fertilizers, |
| e.g., |
| Ammonium sulfate |
| Superphosphates |
| *Other uses* |
| Synthesis of other chemicals |
| Pigments and paints |
| Petroleum refining |
| Iron and steel |
| Storage batteries |
| Metal and ore refining |

HNO₃: strong acid, strong oxidizing agent

H₂SO₄: strong acid, oxidizing agent when concentrated, dehydrating agent

H₃PO₄: moderately strong acid, poor oxidizing agent

low temperatures would favor the formation of sulfur trioxide in high yield. This is true, but the rate at which combination occurs at low temperatures, even in the presence of a catalyst, is too low for the reaction to be economically practical. Therefore, the temperature employed must be high enough to effect a rapid union between sulfur dioxide and oxygen, but not so high that the equilibrium is driven toward decomposition of sulfur trioxide.

Experimental data show that at temperatures between 400° and 450 °C, approximately 97% conversion to sulfur trioxide occurs; at 900 °C essentially none of the compound is formed. The maximum yield can be obtained in the shortest time by carrying out the reaction by two or more passes over catalyst beds. First SO_2 and O_2 are passed over the catalyst at a temperature at which the rate is high (575 °C) to convert about 80% of the SO_2 to SO_3. In subsequent passes at lower temperatures at which the percentage of conversion is higher, the overall yield is raised to 99%.

The sulfur trioxide is not converted to sulfuric acid by direct addition to water. Gaseous sulfur trioxide reacts with water to form a mist of sulfuric acid, which is absorbed only slowly in the liquid water. The sulfur trioxide is actually passed into 98% sulfuric acid, in which it is extremely soluble, to form pyrosulfuric acid, $H_2S_2O_7$ (also called disulfuric acid). By addition of water, sulfuric acid of the desired concentration is obtained.

$$\underset{\text{sulfur trioxide}}{SO_3(g)} + \underset{\text{sulfuric acid}}{H_2SO_4(l)} \rightleftharpoons \underset{\text{pyrosulfuric acid}}{H_2S_2O_7(l)} \qquad \textbf{(26.30)}$$

$$H_2S_2O_7(l) + H_2O(l) \longrightarrow 2H_2SO_4(aq) \qquad \textbf{(26.31)}$$

The major use of sulfuric acid is in the production of fertilizers (see An Aside: Plant Nutrients and Chemical Fertilizers in this chapter). A few other important uses, of which there are many, are listed in Table 26.9.

b. Phosphoric acid Pure phosphoric acid (also called orthophosphoric acid; Figure 26.8a) is a white solid that melts at 42.35 °C to a viscous liquid with a strong tendency to supercool. Phosphoric acid is a moderately strong acid, but a much weaker acid than sulfuric acid or nitric acid. It is a poor oxidizing agent and is useful in applications in which oxidizing properties are undesirable.

Two major industrial processes are in use for the production of phosphoric acid. They differ in giving products of quite different purity. Thermal process phosphoric

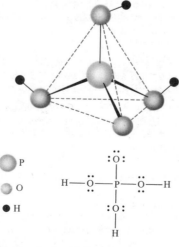

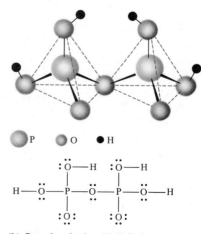

Figure 26.8
Phosphorus(V) Oxoacids

(a) Phosphoric acid, H_3PO_4
m.p. 42.35°C

(b) Pyrophosphoric acid, $H_4P_2O_7$
m.p. 61°C

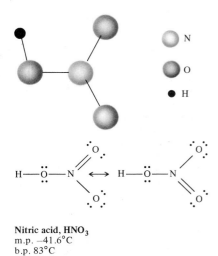

Nitric acid, HNO_3
m.p. $-41.6°C$
b.p. $83°C$

Figure 26.9

acid is manufactured from phosphorus produced by the electric furnace method, which has been distilled and is therefore quite pure. In the two-step process the elemental phosphorus is oxidized and then the oxide is allowed to react with water.

$$4P(s) + 5O_2(g) \longrightarrow P_4O_{10}(s)$$
$$P_4O_{10}(s) + 6H_2O(l) \longrightarrow 4H_3PO_4(aq)$$

The phosphoric acid produced in this way is pure enough for most industrial uses, although small amounts of arsenic present as H_3AsO_4 must be removed if the acid is destined for use in food or pharmaceuticals.

A less pure product, wet process phosphoric acid, is made by the reaction between the calcium phosphate in phosphate rock and sulfuric acid.

$$Ca_3(PO_4)_2(s) + 3H_2SO_4(aq) \longrightarrow 2H_3PO_4(aq) + 3CaSO_4(s)$$

The acid from this process is generally concentrated by boiling off water to give an 85% aqueous solution, which is known as "syrupy" phosphoric acid because of its viscous nature. Wet process phosphoric acid, which represents over 90% of the phosphoric acid produced worldwide, is used directly in the production of fertilizers.

Thermal process phosphoric acid is used in metal treatment, in refractories (substances that withstand high temperature), in catalysts, and in foods and beverages. Dilute phosphoric acid is not toxic and has a pleasant sour taste similar to that of the citric acid and acetic acid present in many foods. For this reason it is widely used as a tart flavoring agent, especially in carbonated beverages. It has a number of other applications in the food industry, for example, as a buffer in jams and jellies, and as a cleaning agent for dairy equipment.

c. Nitric acid Nitric acid (Figure 26.9) is a colorless, fuming liquid with a choking odor. The pure acid (as opposed to its aqueous solutions) is rarely encountered, as it is difficult to prepare and decomposes rapidly. Both the pure acid and its solutions decompose in sunlight to give nitrogen dioxide.

$$4HNO_3(aq) \xrightarrow{hv} 4NO_2(aq) + 2H_2O(l) + O_2(g) \qquad \text{(26.32)}$$

Old solutions of nitric acid are usually yellow or brown because of the presence of dissolved nitrogen dioxide.

Nitric acid is miscible in all proportions with water and is both a strong acid and a strong oxidizing agent in aqueous solutions. The usual concentrated nitric acid is about 70% HNO_3 by mass (see Table 26.8).

Almost all nitric acid is produced by the oxidation of ammonia. Anhydrous ammonia and air are the sole raw materials in the three-step process.

$$4NH_3(g) + 5O_2(g) \xrightarrow[\sim 900\ °C]{Pt-Rh\ catalyst} 4NO(g) + 6H_2O(l) \qquad \text{(26.33)}$$
$$2NO(g) + O_2(g) \longrightarrow 2NO_2(g) \qquad \text{(26.34)}$$
$$3NO_2(g) + H_2O(l) \longrightarrow 2HNO_3(aq) + NO(g) \qquad \text{(26.35)}$$

The first step, the catalytic oxidation of ammonia, is rapid. Once the reaction has been initiated, the ammonia burns spontaneously to give a 90% yield of nitrogen(II) oxide. The second step is a reaction that becomes less favorable at high temperatures. The hot gases from reaction (26.33) are cooled and more air is added to produce nitrogen dioxide in this step. In the third step, the nitrogen dioxide is absorbed by water to produce nitric acid in a disproportionation reaction. The nitrogen(II) oxide formed in this step is recycled. In modern plants the entire process is carried out under pressure.

Like so many of the chemicals discussed in this chapter, nitric acid has its major use in the manufacture of fertilizers. It is also important in the nitration reactions that produce many organic nitrates used in explosives, plastics, dyes, and lacquers.

Table 26.10
Oxidation States and Some
Compounds and Ions of Nitrogen

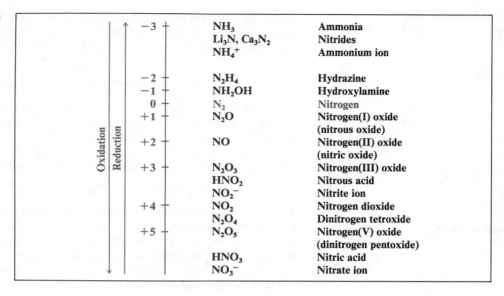

−3	NH_3	Ammonia
	Li_3N, Ca_3N_2	Nitrides
	NH_4^+	Ammonium ion
−2	N_2H_4	Hydrazine
−1	NH_2OH	Hydroxylamine
0	N_2	Nitrogen
+1	N_2O	Nitrogen(I) oxide (nitrous oxide)
+2	NO	Nitrogen(II) oxide (nitric oxide)
+3	N_2O_3	Nitrogen(III) oxide
	HNO_2	Nitrous acid
	NO_2^-	Nitrite ion
+4	NO_2	Nitrogen dioxide
	N_2O_4	Dinitrogen tetroxide
+5	N_2O_5	Nitrogen(V) oxide (dinitrogen pentoxide)
	HNO_3	Nitric acid
	NO_3^-	Nitrate ion

(Oxidation ↑ / Reduction ↓)

COMPOUNDS OF NITROGEN

Table 26.10 gives examples of the compounds of nitrogen in all of its oxidation states from −3 to +5.

26.7 NITRIDES

Nitrides have widely different properties. The so-called saltlike nitrides are ionic compounds that contain the nitride ion, N^{3-}. Lithium and the active metals of the beryllium family, as well as cadmium and zinc, form saltlike nitrides. These are white, crystalline, high-melting solids. Their most characteristic property is their vigorous reaction with water to give ammonia and the metal hydroxide (Equation 26.21).

Some covalent nitrides are molecular compounds formed with nonmetals. Many of these compounds are volatile and unstable (e.g., Cl_3N, which is very unstable, and S_4N_4, which is detonated by shock or temperatures greater than 30 °C). Other covalent nitrides are very hard, high-melting network covalent compounds known as diamondlike nitrides. Silicon, boron, and the other boron family elements form diamondlike nitrides. Boron nitride, BN, is nearly identical in structure with graphite (see Figure 27.2), with boron and nitrogen atoms alternating throughout. Just as graphite can be converted to diamond (Section 27.2), boron nitride is converted by heat and pressure to a very hard, diamondlike material called borazon.

The interstitial nitrides formed by many of the d-transition metals (e.g., titanium, iron, tungsten) are hard, high-melting alloys (Section 28.11) that retain the metallic properties of luster and conductivity. As in the interstitial hydrides (Section 16.7) and carbides (Section 27.4e), the small nonmetal atoms occupy holes in the metal crystal structure. The metal nitrides and the diamondlike nitrides have many applications that make use of their properties of hardness and resistance to temperature and chemical attack.

26.8 AMMONIA AND AMMONIUM SALTS

Ammonia, a top ten industrial chemical (see Table 25.10), is a colorless gas with a characteristic pungent odor. It is a powerful heart stimulant, and excessive inhalation may produce serious effects—even death.

In the gaseous state, ammonia exists as discrete polar molecules of pyramidal

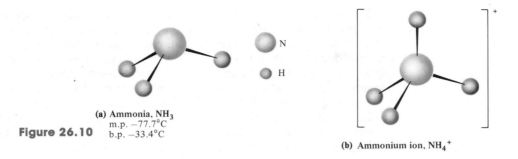

Figure 26.10

(a) Ammonia, NH$_3$
m.p. −77.7°C
b.p. −33.4°C

(b) Ammonium ion, NH$_4^+$

structure (Figure 26.10a). In the liquid and solid states, ammonia is extensively associated through <u>hydrogen bonding</u>, as would be expected from the high electronegativity of nitrogen.

Many of the chemical properties of ammonia arise from the presence on the nitrogen atom of an unshared pair of electrons. This permits ammonia to act as a <u>Lewis base</u>, that is, an electron-pair donor. It is a ligand in many complex ions. The ammonium ion (Figure 26.10b) is formed by the donation of the unshared electron pair from ammonia to a hydrogen ion.

Ammonia is, as we have seen, a weak Brønsted-Lowry base (Section 20.12). Although aqueous ammonia solutions are often labeled "ammonium hydroxide," the compound NH$_4$OH has never been isolated and has not been observed in aqueous solution. Ammonia reacts with acids to give ammonium salts, for example,

NH$_3$: Lewis base, ligand in complex ions (unshared electron pair on N)

$$NH_3(g) + HCl(g) \longrightarrow NH_4Cl(s)$$

Most simple ammonium salts are very soluble in water and all undergo thermal decomposition (Section 26.5d). Aqueous solutions of ammonium salts of strong acids—NH$_4$Cl, NH$_4$NO$_3$, (NH$_4$)$_2$SO$_4$, for example—are acidic due to hydrolysis of the ammonium ion. The potassium ion (K$^+$, radius 0.133 nm) and the ammonium ion are similar in size and their comparable compounds often have similar properties.

Ammonia can act as a <u>reducing agent</u>, particularly at elevated temperatures; the nitrogen-containing oxidation products vary with the reaction conditions, elemental nitrogen being the most common product. The industrial chemistry of nitrogen, ammonia, and other nitrogen-containing compounds is based to a great extent upon the Haber process for the manufacture of ammonia by the direct combination at elevated temperatures of hydrogen and nitrogen (see An Aside: The Haber Process, Chapter 19).

Table 26.11
Uses of Ammonia

Second in importance to the Haber process as a commercial method for the production of ammonia is the destructive distillation of bituminous, or soft, coal. Bituminous coal is mainly a mixture of hydrocarbons with moderate amounts of chemically bound oxygen and nitrogen. When coal is heated in the absence of air, gases are driven off to leave a residue of coke. In the gases liberated, nitrogen is present as the free element and as ammonia.

The single greatest outlet for ammonia (Table 26.11) and for the compounds made from it is as fertilizers.

Major uses
  Preparation of nitric acid
  Direct use as fertilizer
  Synthesis of other fertilizers
Other uses
  Synthesis of dyes, polymers, drugs, explosives, and synthetic fibers
  Refrigerant
  Household cleaning agent

26.9 NITROGEN OXIDES

There is an oxide of nitrogen for each of the five oxidation states from +1 to +5. All but one (N$_2$O$_5$) are gases, two (NO and NO$_2$) have unpaired electrons, and two (NO and NO$_2$) play a significant role in air pollution (see An Aside: Air Pollution, Smog, and Acid Rain).

<u>Nitrogen(I) oxide</u>, N$_2$O, known as nitrous oxide, was the first synthetic anes-

thetic to be discovered and is still in use as a light anesthetic, especially in dentistry. When inhaled in low concentrations, the gas produces mild euphoria — the basis for its common name, laughing gas. Nitrous oxide was also the first aerosol propellant. It was introduced before World War II in whipped cream dispensers. We have seen that nitrous oxide can be prepared by the thermal decomposition of ammonium nitrate (Equation 26.10) and can decompose with explosive force (Equation 26.15).

Nitrogen(II) oxide, NO, also known as nitric oxide, is an intermediate in the production of nitric acid (Section 26.6c). In the presence of oxygen at ordinary temperatures, it is oxidized to the nitrogen(IV) oxide (Equation 26.34). Nitric oxide can be prepared by the redox reaction between copper and *dilute* nitric acid.

$$3Cu(s) + 8H^+ + 2NO_3^- \longrightarrow 3Cu^{2+} + 2NO(g) + 4H_2O(l)$$

It is a fairly reactive substance and combines with all of the halogens except iodine to give nitrosyl halides, NOX. Loss of the unpaired electron from NO gives the NO$^+$ ion (Section 24.8).

Nitrogen(IV) oxide, or nitrogen dioxide, NO$_2$, under ordinary conditions is always in equilibrium with its dimer, dinitrogen tetroxide:

$$2NO_2(g) \rightleftharpoons N_2O_4(g) \qquad \Delta H° = -57.20 \text{ kJ}$$
nitrogen dioxide   *dinitrogen tetroxide*
red-brown gas   *colorless gas*

(A **dimer** is a molecule formed by combination of two identical molecules.) The dimerization occurs by pairing of the unpaired electrons on two molecules (see structures, Table 26.12). The formation of N$_2$O$_4$ is favored at low temperatures, as shown by the negative ΔH value for the dimerization. In the solid state, only the dimer is present. The nitrogen(IV) oxides are strong oxidizing agents. Their most

Nitrogen(IV) oxides:
$$2NO_2 \rightleftharpoons N_2O_4$$

Table 26.12
The Common Oxides of Nitrogen

Nitrogen(I) oxide, N$_2$O (nitrous oxide)

$$:N\equiv N-\ddot{O}: \longleftrightarrow :\ddot{N}=N=\ddot{O}:$$

Colorless gas. M.p. $-90.8°$C; b.p., $-88.8°$C
Laughing gas. Quite stable.

Nitrogen(II) oxide, NO (nitric oxide)

$$:\dot{N}=\ddot{O}:$$

Colorless gas. M.p. $-163.6°$C; b.p. $-151.8°$C
One unpaired electron. Fairly reactive. An air pollutant.

Nitrogen(IV) oxides, NO$_2 \rightleftharpoons$ N$_2$O$_4$
Nitrogen dioxide, NO$_2$

Red-brown gas, always in equilibrium with N$_2$O$_4$
B.p. 21.15°C
One unpaired electron. Air pollutant. Reactive.

Dinitrogen tetroxide

3 other $\longleftrightarrow$ resonance forms

Colorless gas, always in equilibrium with NO$_2$, amount of N$_2$O$_4$ increases with decreasing temperature.

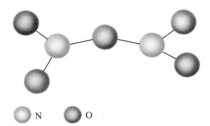

N ◯ O

Nitrogen pentoxide, N_2O_5
m.p. 30°C
b.p. 47°C (dec)

$[NO_2]^+[NO_3]^-$
crystalline solid

Figure 26.11

significant reaction is the one with warm water to yield nitric acid and nitric oxide (Equation 26.35).

The less commonly encountered nitrogen oxides are nitrogen(III) oxide, N_2O_3, and nitrogen(V) oxide, N_2O_5 (Figure 26.11), which is a solid. These oxides are the anhydrides of nitrous acid and nitric acid, respectively. Nitrogen(III) oxide, or dinitrogen trioxide, is the least stable nitrogen oxide. It can be obtained as a blue liquid by the union of equimolar quantities of nitric oxide and nitrogen dioxide at -20 °C

$$NO(g) \ + \ NO_2(g) \ \underset{\longleftarrow}{\overset{-20\ °C}{\longrightarrow}} \ N_2O_3(l)$$
nitric oxide   nitrogen dioxide   dinitrogen trioxide

The compound is never pure, for even in the liquid state it is in equilibrium with NO and NO_2. At 25 °C and 1 atm pressure, the equilibrium mixture of gases contains only about 10% N_2O_3. When the trioxide, or, more precisely, an equimolar mixture of NO and NO_2, is passed into cold water, nitrous acid (HNO_2) is formed.

$$NO(g) + NO_2(g) + H_2O(l) \longrightarrow 2HNO_2(aq)$$

Nitrogen(V) oxide is prepared by the dehydration of nitric acid by phosphorus(V) oxide:

$$4HNO_3(l) + P_4O_{10}(s) \longrightarrow 2N_2O_5(s) \ + \ 4HPO_3(s)$$
$$\qquad\qquad\qquad\qquad \textit{nitrogen(V)} \quad \textit{metaphosphoric}$$
$$\qquad\qquad\qquad\qquad \textit{oxide} \qquad\quad \textit{acid}$$

As might be expected, N_2O_5 reacts exothermically with water to regenerate nitric acid.

26.10 NITROGEN OXOACIDS AND THEIR SALTS

a. Nitrous acid and nitrites Nitrous acid, HNO_2, is a weak acid:

$$HNO_2(aq) \rightleftharpoons H^+ + NO_2^- \qquad K_a = 7.2 \times 10^{-4} \text{ at } 25 \text{ °C}$$

and even in cold solutions, some decomposition occurs to give nitric acid and nitric oxide, another nitrogen disproportionation reaction.

$$3HNO_2(aq) \longrightarrow HNO_3(aq) + 2NO(g) + H_2O(l) \qquad \textbf{(26.36)}$$

Because of the intermediate, $+3$, oxidation state of the nitrogen, nitrous acid may act as either an oxidizing or a reducing agent. In acidic solution, it is a strong oxidizing agent, the reduction product depending upon the strength of the reducing agent. Nitrous acid is a relatively weak reducing agent and is oxidized (to nitric acid) only by such strong oxidizing agents as chlorine and permanganate ion.

Nitrites, the salts of nitrous acid, are colorless or pale yellow solids that are stable to heat (note the difference from nitrates). The alkali metal nitrites are very soluble in water, and those of calcium, strontium, and barium are moderately soluble in water. The nitrites are made either by passing an equimolar mixture of nitric oxide and nitrogen dioxide into a solution of metal hydroxide, for example,

$$NO(g) + NO_2(g) + 2KOH(aq) \longrightarrow 2KNO_2(aq) + H_2O(l) \qquad \textbf{(26.37)}$$

or by reduction at elevated temperatures of a metal nitrate by a reducing agent such as lead or iron powder.

$$NaNO_3(s) + Pb(s) \overset{\Delta}{\longrightarrow} NaNO_2(l) + PbO(l) \qquad \textbf{(26.38)}$$

In alkaline solution the nitrite ion (Figure 26.12) is a rather strong reducing agent.

b. Nitric acid and nitrates Nitric acid is a strong acid, a large-volume industrial chemical (Section 26.6c), and an oxidizing agent (Section 26.5c).

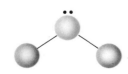

Nitrite ion, NO_2^-

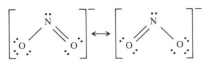

Figure 26.12

Table 26.13
Outstanding Properties of Nitrogen and Some of Its Compounds

N [He] $2s^2 2p^3$ *5 valence electrons*	Member of Representative Group V. Cannot form more than four covalent bonds.
:N≡N: (g) *very strong bond*	Second highest bond dissociation energy for any diatomic molecule (only C≡O is higher). Unreactive molecule at ordinary temperatures.
-3 $+5$ N to N	Forms compounds in all possible oxidation states from -3 to $+5$.
N⋯O	Many N—O bonds are intermediate between single and double bonds.
H—N̈—H	*lone pair* H	A Lewis base. A reducing agent at elevated temperatures. Weakly basic in aqueous solution. A "top 10" industrial chemical; important in fertilizer manufacture.
N^{3-}	Unstable in H_2O; forms NH_3 + OH^-.
Li_3N	Only compound formed by combination of N_2 with another element at room temperature.
NH_4^+	Acidic in aqueous solution. Most NH_4^+ salts are water soluble.
N_2H_4	Powerful reducing agent. Used in rocket fuels.
N_2O	"Laughing gas"—a light anesthetic.
NO, NO_2	Intermediates in production of nitric acid. Play important roles in air pollution.
HNO_2	Known only in solution. Strong oxidizing agent and weak reducing agent.
NO_2^-	Moderately strong reducing agent in alkaline solution.
HNO_3	An oxidizing agent. A strong acid. An industrial chemical.

Nitrates, the salts of nitric acid, are easily prepared by the reaction between nitric acid and metal oxides, hydroxides, or carbonates. With oxides and hydroxides, the reaction is simply neutralization and goes to completion because of the formation of water. With carbonates, the reaction is complete because of the evolution of carbon dioxide gas, for example,

$$CaCO_3(s) + 2HNO_3(aq) \longrightarrow Ca(NO_3)_2(aq) + CO_2(g) + H_2O(l)$$

Metal nitrates are very soluble in water. The few that appear to be insoluble, such as bismuth nitrate, $Bi(NO_3)_3$, and mercury(II) nitrate, $Hg(NO_3)_2$, actually react with water with the formation of insoluble basic salts that contain the O or OH group.

$$Bi(NO_3)_3(s) + H_2O(l) \rightleftharpoons BiO(NO_3)(s) + 2HNO_3(aq)$$
bismuth nitrate   *basic bismuth nitrate (bismuthyl nitrate)*

The properties of nitrogen and its compounds are summarized in Table 26.13.

EXAMPLE 26.3
Chemical Reactions: N Compounds

Predict the products of the following reactions of nitrogen compounds.

(a) $Ba_3N_2(s) + H_2O(l) \longrightarrow$

(b) $Ca(NO_2)_2(s) \xrightarrow{\Delta}$

(c) $NO(g) + Br_2(l) \longrightarrow$

(d) $TiN(s) + H_2O(l) \longrightarrow$

(e) $AgNO_3(s) \xrightarrow{\Delta}$

(a) This is a reaction between two compounds. Barium is an active metal. Therefore barium nitride is a saltlike nitride and contains the strongly basic nitride ion N^{3-}, which reacts completely with water.

$$Ba_3N_2(s) + 6H_2O(l) \longrightarrow 3Ba(OH)_2(aq) + 2NH_3(aq)$$

(b) Thermal decomposition is the only possible reaction. However, *nitrites*, as opposed to nitrates, do not decompose when heated. No reaction will occur.

(c) This is a reaction between an element and a compound. Combination is possible because nitrogen can have a higher oxidation state.

$$2NO(g) + Br_2(l) \longrightarrow 2NOBr(l)$$

(d) Like (a) this is a reaction between two compounds. However, titanium is *not* an active metal and titanium nitride is most likely an interstitial nitride. No reaction will take place because the nitride ion is not present.

(e) As in (b) a thermal decomposition is possible, and nitrates of heavy metals like silver react to form oxygen, nitrogen(IV) oxide, and the metal oxide. However, because the oxides of the least active metals also decompose thermally to form the metal and oxygen, the overall reaction is as follows:

$$2AgNO_3(s) \xrightarrow{\Delta} 2Ag(s) + 2NO_2(g) + O_2(g)$$

AN ASIDE

Explosives

A big bang, heat, the power to shatter solid objects, possibly flames—these are the effects that we associate with explosions. In chemical terms, just what are explosions and explosives?

All chemical explosions are very fast redox reactions which result in the release of large volumes of gases. A chemical explosion can be initiated by high temperatures, a sudden increase in pressure, or a physical shock. Once the activation energy has been provided, a sufficient amount of heat is generated for the explosive reaction to be self-sustaining.

Not all chemical compounds that explode—in fact, very few—are suitable for practical use as explosives. A substance that explodes with the slightest shock or temperature increase cannot be fabricated into an artillery shell or transported to the blasting site where a road is being built. The components of military and industrial explosives are substances that are safe to handle, and explode only under controlled conditions. Millions of kilograms of such substances are produced annually with an accident rate no higher than that in other industrial operations.

The essential characteristic of an explosion-causing redox reaction is a rapid reaction rate. The release of a large amount of energy as heat is less important. A comparison of the combustion of gasoline and the explosion of gunpowder illustrates this difference. Burning 1 g of gasoline in an internal combustion engine produces about 46 kJ of thermal energy and requires about 0.01 s. One gram of gunpowder releases only 3.3 kJ in propelling an artillery shell, but does so in 0.0005 s.

Explosives are divided into two general classes based on the way in which the chemical reaction moves through the mass of the material while it is exploding. *High explosives* undergo detonation—the redox reaction moves directly through the body of a solid at a rapid rate (2000 to 9000 m/s) as the reaction, thought to be carried by a chain mechanism, spreads. *Low explosives* "burn" by a more slow-moving reaction of material close to the surface (less than 0.25 m/s) rather than by detonation. Neither high nor low explosives react with oxygen from the air. The oxidized and reduced atoms are either part of the same compound, which undergoes an internal redox reaction, or they are present in an intimate mixture of oxidizing agent and fuel.

Most high explosives are compounds that contain nitrogen, combined with oxygen, hydrogen, and/or carbon. During the explosion, the combined nitrogen is reduced to elemental nitrogen. In addition, the other elements are all converted to gases—carbon to carbon dioxide or carbon monoxide, and hydrogen and oxygen to water or to molecular hydrogen and oxygen. The rapidly produced large volume of hot gases is responsible for the surge of pressure and the damaging shock wave that accompany an explosion.

High explosives are described as either primary or secondary, depending upon their sensitivity. Primary explosives can be set off by a spark or a blow and must be handled with great care. They have lower detonation rates and produce less energy than secondary explosives. Most primary explosives are inorganic salts. Secondary explosives, such as nitroglycerin, are less sensitive than primary explosives, but more powerful. Once set off, they react with great heat and shattering power (known as *brisance*). The explosion of a secondary explosive is often initiated by a primary explosive in, for example, a detonator cap. Alfred Nobel's idea that the detonation of a small amount of mercury fulminate could trigger the explosion of nitroglycerin was the first step in the development of modern high explosives.

$$Hg(ONC)_2(s) \longrightarrow Hg(l) + 2CO(g) + N_2(g)$$
mercury fulminate
(a primary explosive)

Heat of explosion at constant volume: **1.8 kJ/g**
Specific pressure (the pressure exerted by explosion of 1 kg in a 1 L volume): **5212 kg/cm²**
Velocity of detonation wave: **3920 m/s**
Explosion temperature: **4105 °C**

$$\begin{array}{c} H_2C-ONO_2 \\ | \\ HC-ONO_2(l) \\ | \\ H_2C-ONO_2 \end{array} \longrightarrow 3CO_2(g) + \tfrac{5}{2}H_2O(g) + \tfrac{3}{2}N_2(g) + \tfrac{1}{4}O_2(g)$$
nitroglycerin
(a secondary explosive)

Heat of explosion at constant volume: **6.4 kJ/kg**
Specific pressure: **9835 kg/cm²**
Velocity of detonation wave: **8500 m/s**
Explosion temperature: **3360 °C**

Dynamite is a mixture of nitroglycerin with a solid inert support and other reactive substances.

Most secondary high explosives are organic compounds that contain nitro groups (NO_2). TNT is trinitrotoluene.

$$(s) \longrightarrow 6CO(g) + C(s) + \tfrac{5}{2}H_2(g) + \tfrac{3}{2}N_2(g)$$
TNT
(trinitrotoluene)

A mixture of TNT and ammonium nitrate (which explodes via the reaction of Equation 26.11) is almost as powerful an explosive as TNT alone and is much cheaper. Such mixtures are used in military bombs and shells. Ammonium nitrate is also used in a mixture with organic matter as a substitute for dynamite in open-pit mining.

Table 26.14
Oxidation States and Some
Compounds and Ions of Phosphorus

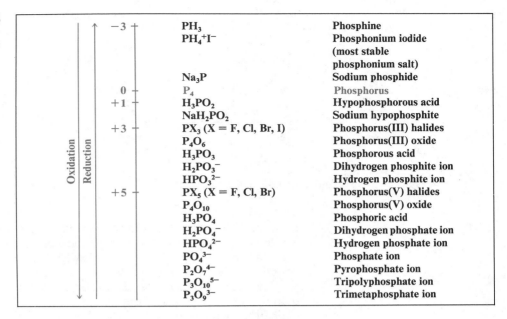

−3	PH₃	Phosphine
	PH₄⁺I⁻	Phosphonium iodide (most stable phosphonium salt)
	Na₃P	Sodium phosphide
0	P₄	Phosphorus
+1	H₃PO₂	Hypophosphorous acid
	NaH₂PO₂	Sodium hypophosphite
+3	PX₃ (X = F, Cl, Br, I)	Phosphorus(III) halides
	P₄O₆	Phosphorus(III) oxide
	H₃PO₃	Phosphorous acid
	H₂PO₃⁻	Dihydrogen phosphite ion
	HPO₃²⁻	Hydrogen phosphite ion
+5	PX₅ (X = F, Cl, Br)	Phosphorus(V) halides
	P₄O₁₀	Phosphorus(V) oxide
	H₃PO₄	Phosphoric acid
	H₂PO₄⁻	Dihydrogen phosphate ion
	HPO₄²⁻	Hydrogen phosphate ion
	PO₄³⁻	Phosphate ion
	P₂O₇⁴⁻	Pyrophosphate ion
	P₃O₁₀⁵⁻	Tripolyphosphate ion
	P₃O₉³⁻	Trimetaphosphate ion

COMPOUNDS OF PHOSPHORUS

Table 26.14 gives examples of compounds of phosphorus in its oxidation states of −3, +1, +3, and +5.

26.11 PHOSPHIDES AND PHOSPHINE

The compounds of phosphorus in the −3 oxidation state, the phosphides and phosphine, are similar in some ways to the comparable nitrogen compounds, the nitrides and ammonia. In other oxidation states the compounds of these two elements are quite different.

Ionic phosphides are known for most of the lithium and beryllium family metals. These phosphides are attacked vigorously by water with the liberation of phosphine, PH_3, a volatile molecular compound (Equation 26.22). Phosphine is a colorless gas that has an offensive, garliclike odor and is extremely toxic. The pure compound ignites when heated in air at about 150 °C. However, phosphine frequently also contains diphosphine (P_2H_4), which is very reactive and renders the mixture spontaneously flammable. Phosphine is much less soluble in water than ammonia and does not form alkaline solutions. Like ammonia, phosphine is an electron-pair donor and can function as a ligand in complex ions.

26.12 PHOSPHORUS HALIDES AND OXIDES

The phosphorus(III) halides are simple molecular substances and have the same pyramidal molecular geometry as ammonia and phosphine (Figure 26.13a). At room temperature, the fluoride is a colorless gas, the chloride and bromide are volatile, fuming liquids (PCl_3, b.p. 74.2 °C; PBr_3, b.p. 175.3 °C), and the iodide is a red, low-melting (m.p. 61.0 °C) solid that is not stable.

The trihalides are unstable in water, being completely and irreversibly hydrolyzed (PF_3 reacts quite slowly).

$$PX_3 + 3H_2O(l) \longrightarrow \underset{phosphorous\ acid}{H_3PO_3(aq)} + 3HX(aq) \qquad (26.39)$$

All of the phosphorus(V) halides except the iodide are known. In the vapor and the liquid states, the pentahalides are covalent, the PF_5 and PCl_5 molecules in the vapor having a triangular bipyramidal structure (Figure 26.13b), considered to be the

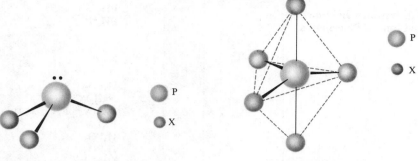

Figure 26.13
Phosphorus Halides   (a) Phosphorus trihalides, PX$_3$ (b) Phosphorus pentahalides, PX$_5$

result of bonding by electrons in hybridized sp^3d orbitals on the phosphorus atom. There is excellent evidence that in the solid state the pentachloride is a saltlike substance consisting of tetrahedral [PCl$_4$]$^+$ and octahedral [PCl$_6$]$^-$ ions. The solid pentabromide apparently is also ionic and is made up of the ions [PBr$_4$]$^+$ and Br$^-$.

Like the trihalides, the pentahalides react rapidly with water. With a limited quantity of water, two of the halogen atoms in the molecule are removed, and oxohalides of the formula POX$_3$—phosphoryl halides or phosphorus(V) oxohalides —are formed, along with hydrohalic acids.

$$PX_5 + H_2O(l) \longrightarrow POX_3 + 2HX(aq) \qquad (26.40)$$

With an excess of water, all of the halogen atoms react and the pentahalides are converted to phosphoric acid.

$$PX_5 + 4H_2O(l) \longrightarrow H_3PO_4(aq) + 5HX(aq) \qquad (26.41)$$

The oxidation of white phosphorus at about 100 °C in a limited supply of air gives phosphorus(III) oxide, P$_4$O$_6$, a white, crystalline substance, as the main product. The P$_4$O$_6$ molecule is a tetrahedron in which an oxygen atom has been added between each pair of phosphorus atoms (Figure 26.14a).

With an excess of air, the phosphorus(V) oxide, P$_4$O$_{10}$, is formed. It is a white solid that exists in a number of crystalline modifications. When heated, it sublimes as discrete P$_4$O$_{10}$ molecules (Figure 26.14b), which are related in structure to the P$_4$O$_6$ molecules by addition of an oxygen atom to each phosphorus atom. (Sometimes this

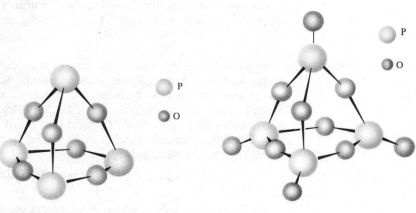

Figure 26.14
Phosphorus Oxides   (a) Phosphorus(III) oxide, P$_4$O$_6$
                           m.p. 23.8°C
                           b.p. 175.4°C   (b) Phosphorus(V) oxide, P$_4$O$_{10}$
                                                              sublimes at 358°C

oxide is incorrectly referred to as phosphorus pentoxide and given the formula P_2O_5.) Phosphorus(V) oxide is the anhydride of phosphoric acid and its most important chemical property is its tremendous affinity for water. It reacts with water to form the acid and is one of the most useful drying agents. When phosphorus burns in air, P_4O_{10} is produced as a cloud of very white particles of colloidal dimensions. The particles are kept in suspension in the air by Brownian motion (Section 15.18) and the resulting very dense smoke has been used as a military smoke screen.

26.13 PHOSPHORUS
OXOACIDS AND THEIR SALTS

Phosphorous acid, H_3PO_3, is commonly prepared by hydrolysis of phosphorus trichloride (Equation 26.39). [Note one of the great pitfalls in the study of chemistry: the extra *"o"* appears *only* in the spelling of the P(I) and P(III) acids.] In the H_3PO_3 molecule one hydrogen atom is bonded directly to the phosphorus atom (Figure 26.15). Because the hydrogen–phosphorus bond is essentially nonpolar (P and H have about the same electronegativities), this hydrogen atom is not acidic and therefore phosphorous acid is a *diprotic acid*. It is a moderately strong acid with respect to its first dissociation ($K_{a1} = 3 \times 10^{-2}$; $K_{a2} = 1.6 \times 10^{-7}$). Phosphorous acid is a strong reducing agent, forming phosphoric acid as its oxidation product. Phosphites are salts of phosphorous acid containing either the dihydrogen phosphite ion, $H_2PO_3^-$, or the hydrogen phosphite ion, HPO_3^{2-} (see Tables 26.6 and 26.7 for the properties of these anions).

The formulas and names of the phosphorus(V) acids are included in Table 26.15. In all of these acids and their salts, each phosphorus atom is surrounded by four oxygen atoms and in none is a phosphorus atom bonded directly to another phosphorus atom. The octet rule is satisfied by the four single, or σ, bonds around phosphorus in both phosphorous and the phosphoric acids. However, greater bond strengths and shorter bond lengths than those expected for single bonds show that there is π-bond, or multiple-bond, character to the bonds between phosphorus atoms and oxygen atoms (those not bonded to hydrogen). The π bonding is contributed by overlap of oxygen p orbitals with phosphorus d orbitals.

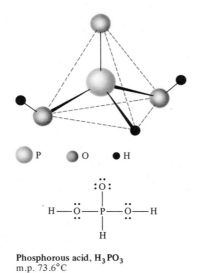

P ⬤ O ⬤ H

Phosphorous acid, H_3PO_3
m.p. 73.6°C
b.p. 200°C (dec)

Figure 26.15

**Table 26.15
Phosphorus Acids**

Phosphorus(I)	
H_3PO_2	Hypophosphorous acid, monoprotic
Phosphorus(III)	
H_3PO_3	Phosphorous acid, diprotic
Phosphorus(V)	
H_3PO_4	Phosphoric acid (orthophosphoric acid), triprotic
$H_4P_2O_7$	Pyrophosphoric acid (diphosphoric acid) tetraprotic
$H_5P_3O_{10}$	Triphosphoric acid (tripolyphosphoric acid) pentaprotic
$(HPO_3)_n$	Metaphosphoric acid ($n = 3$, 4, . . .)

The simplest phosphorus(V) acid is phosphoric acid, H_3PO_4, a major industrial chemical (Section 26.6b). The other phosphoric acids are the products of the elimination of water between successive molecules of phosphoric acid. The elimination of one molecule of water from two molecules of phosphoric acid yields pyrophosphoric, or diphosphoric, acid

$$\text{(26.42)}$$

phosphoric acid   *pyrophosphoric acid, $H_4P_2O_7$*

Triphosphoric acid, also called tripolyphosphoric acid, is formed similarly from three molecules of phosphoric acid. Theoretically this process can go on indefinitely. Pyrophosphoric acid, $H_4P_2O_7$ (see Figure 26.8b), a colorless, glassy solid, is extremely soluble in water, in which it slowly reverts to phosphoric acid. "Metaphosphoric acid" is a mixture of polymeric acids of empirical formula HPO_3, obtained when phosphoric acid is heated.

$$n\,H_3PO_4(l) \xrightarrow{\;325-350°C\;} (HPO_3)_n + n\,H_2O(g) \qquad \text{(26.43)}$$

$n = $ *a variety of whole numbers*

The metaphosphoric acids are difficult to separate. They contain either rings or long chains of PO_4 tetrahedra. (The structures of two simple cyclic metaphosphates are shown in the margin.) Salts of metaphosphoric acid are also polymeric. Sodium metaphosphate, $(NaPO_3)_n$, which forms stable complexes with the $+2$ metal ions in hard water, has been used as a water softener.

The possibilities for making phosphates with desirable properties are extensive — any or all of the hydrogen atoms in any of the phosphoric acids can be replaced by metal ions. Some phosphates yield acidic aqueous solutions, others yield alkaline aqueous solutions, and others are only slightly soluble — all properties that have been put to use. Like phosphoric acid, many phosphates are nontoxic and therefore can be used in the food industry, where their ability to act as buffers is often desirable.

The sodium salts derived from phosphoric acid,

NaH_2PO_4	Na_2HPO_4	Na_3PO_4
sodium dihydrogen phosphate	*disodium monohydrogen phosphate*	*trisodium phosphate*
(or monosodium phosphate)	*(or disodium phosphate)*	*(or normal sodium phosphate)*

trimetaphosphoric acid, $H_3P_3O_9$

tetrametaphosphoric acid, $H_4P_4O_{12}$

all have numerous and varied uses. Sodium dihydrogen phosphate, NaH_2PO_4, which gives an acidic aqueous solution, is used in acidic cleaning agents. The monohydrogen phosphate, Na_2HPO_4, can prevent separation of fat and water, and serves this purpose in pasteurized process cheese. In addition, it is used in cured hams, instant cereals, and evaporated milk. By contrast, trisodium phosphate is not appropriate for use in foods because it gives a strongly alkaline aqueous solution; it appears in heavy-duty alkaline cleaning agents and in water-softening agents, where it functions in the removal of $+2$ metal ions by precipitation of insoluble phosphates. The hydrate $Na_3PO_4 \cdot 12H_2O$ is a crystalline compound sold as a cleaning compound and paint remover.

Calcium phosphates, in contrast to the sodium phosphates, are not very soluble in water. The dihydrate of calcium monohydrogen phosphate is widely used as a polishing agent in toothpaste.

Table 26.16
Uses of Phosphates In food applications, the calcium phosphates are most common. In cleaning applications, the sodium phosphates are most common.

Food uses	*Cleaning agents*	*Other uses*
Food supplements for humans and animals	Builders in detergents	Water softeners
Carbonated beverages (for tartness)	Strongly alkaline cleaning agents	Flame retardants
Leavening agents	Acidic cleaning agents	In ore flotation
Quick-cooking cereals	Abrasives in toothpastes	In plating plastics with metals
Emulsifiers		Dishwasher detergents
Buffers		
Consistency control		

Sodium tripolyphosphate (a salt of tripolyphosphoric acid),

sodium tripolyphosphate

dominates the market as a *builder* in synthetic detergents. The purpose of a builder is to sequester, that is, to form complex ions, with the metal ions that cause hardness in water, thereby decreasing their concentration and preventing their precipitation. The use of sodium tripolyphosphate as a builder is the largest volume application for any phosphate other than applications related to fertilizers. In addition to its sequestering action, the compound also buffers and adds to the alkalinity of the detergent solution, aids in removal of dirt, and prevents the redeposition of dirt. The nonfertilizer uses of phosphates are summarized in Table 26.16.

EXAMPLE 26.4
Thermochemistry: Matches

The reactive chemicals on the tip of a "strike anywhere" match are usually P_4S_3 and an oxidizing agent such as potassium chlorate. When the tip strikes a rough surface, the heat generated by friction ignites the P_4S_3, and the oxidizing agent brings about rapid combustion. The head of the match, which is coated with a combustible substance such as sulfur and an oxidizing agent, then catches fire, and finally the stick of the match burns.

The products of combustion of P_4S_3 are P_4O_{10} and SO_2. Given the following standard enthalpies of formation: P_4S_3, -154.4; P_4O_{10}, -2984; SO_2, -296.8 kJ/mol; calculate the standard enthalpy for the combustion of P_4S_3.

The equation for the reaction is

$$P_4S_3(s) + 8O_2(g) \longrightarrow P_4O_{10}(s) + 3SO_2(g)$$

The heat of reaction can be found from the standard enthalpies of formation:

$$\Delta H^\circ = [(1 \text{ mol}) \times \Delta H_f^\circ(P_4O_{10}) + (3 \text{ mol}) \times \Delta H_f^\circ(SO_2)]$$
$$- [(1 \text{ mol}) \times \Delta H_f^\circ(P_4S_3) + (8 \text{ mol}) \times \Delta H_f^\circ(O_2)]$$
$$= [(1 \text{ mol})(-2984 \text{ kJ/mol}) + (3 \text{ mol})(-296.8 \text{ kJ/mol})]$$
$$- [(1 \text{ mol})(-154.4 \text{ kJ/mol}) + (8 \text{ mol})(0)]$$
$$= -3720. \text{ kJ}$$

The reaction is strongly exothermic and it is clear why P_4S_3 is used on the tip of the match.

The properties of phosphorus and its compounds are summarized in Table 26.17.

Table 26.17
Outstanding Properties of Phosphorus and Some of Its Compounds

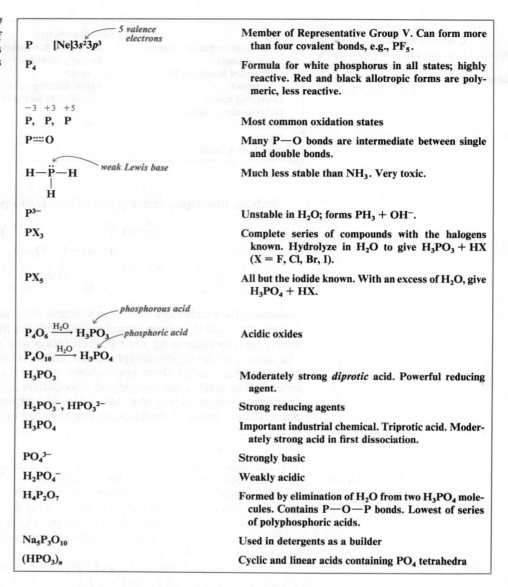

P [Ne]$3s^23p^3$ *5 valence electrons*	Member of Representative Group V. Can form more than four covalent bonds, e.g., PF_5.
P_4	Formula for white phosphorus in all states; highly reactive. Red and black allotropic forms are polymeric, less reactive.
$\overset{-3}{P}$, $\overset{+3}{P}$, $\overset{+5}{P}$	Most common oxidation states
P⚌O	Many P—O bonds are intermediate between single and double bonds.
H—P̈—H *weak Lewis base* | H	Much less stable than NH_3. Very toxic.
P^{3-}	Unstable in H_2O; forms $PH_3 + OH^-$.
PX_3	Complete series of compounds with the halogens known. Hydrolyze in H_2O to give $H_3PO_3 + HX$ (X = F, Cl, Br, I).
PX_5	All but the iodide known. With an excess of H_2O, give $H_3PO_4 + HX$.
$P_4O_6 \xrightarrow{H_2O} H_3PO_3$ *phosphorous acid* $P_4O_{10} \xrightarrow{H_2O} H_3PO_4$ *phosphoric acid*	Acidic oxides
H_3PO_3	Moderately strong *diprotic* acid. Powerful reducing agent.
$H_2PO_3^-$, HPO_3^{2-}	Strong reducing agents
H_3PO_4	Important industrial chemical. Triprotic acid. Moderately strong acid in first dissociation.
PO_4^{3-}	Strongly basic
$H_2PO_4^-$	Weakly acidic
$H_4P_2O_7$	Formed by elimination of H_2O from two H_3PO_4 molecules. Contains P—O—P bonds. Lowest of series of polyphosphoric acids.
$Na_5P_3O_{10}$	Used in detergents as a builder
$(HPO_3)_n$	Cyclic and linear acids containing PO_4 tetrahedra

EXAMPLE 26.5
Structure and Bonding: Halides

The "highest" chlorides of the third-period elements form an interesting series: Al_2Cl_6, $SiCl_4$, $PCl_5(gas)$, $[PCl_4^+][PCl_6^-](solid)$, SCl_4. Discuss the variations in the compositions and structures of these compounds.

In aluminum chloride, $AlCl_3$, the aluminum atom forms three covalent bonds and so has six electrons in its outer energy level. When two $AlCl_3$ molecules combine to give Al_2Cl_6, each aluminum atom forms a coordinate covalent bond with one of the chlorine atoms that is covalently bonded to the other aluminum atom (see Figure 29.5). In this way, both aluminum atoms achieve octet configurations and tetrahedral geometry. Silicon is in Group IV and has four valence electrons; in silicon tetrachloride eight electrons surround the silicon atom and the molecule is tetrahedral. The five equivalent bonds in $PCl_5(gas)$ are attributed to the sp^3d hybridization of the $n = 3$ orbitals of phosphorus, and the molecule has a triangular bipyramidal structure (see Figure 26.13b). When phosphorus(V) chloride crystallizes, one chlorine atom is transferred between two PCl_5 molecules to give a tetrahedral PCl_4^+ ion and an octahedral PCl_6^- ion. Apparently these ions combine in a more stable crystal than would be formed by molecular PCl_5. The highest chloride of sulfur is the tetrachloride because the sulfur atom is not large enough to accommodate five or six chloride atoms.

Plant Nutrients and Chemical Fertilizers

The major end uses of nitrogen, phosphorus, and sulfur, and of their most important industrial products, ammonia, phosphoric acid, and sulfuric acid, are in the production of chemical fertilizers.

Nitrogen and phosphorus are two of the three major nutrients (Table A) supplied to plants through the soil. Sulfur plays a double role in the fertilizer industry—it is necessary to plants, although in smaller amounts than nitrogen and phosphorus, and it is vitally important in the manufacture of other chemical fertilizers (Table B), particularly the superphosphates. Ammonia, also essential to fertilizers, is manufactured by the reaction of nitrogen and hydrogen in the Haber process—an important industrial method of fixing nitrogen. Because natural gas and oil are the sources of hydrogen for the Haber process, countries rich in supplies of these fossil fuels are potentially big producers of fertilizers.

Nitrogen atoms are needed for amino acids—the building blocks of proteins—and for chlorophyll, as well as for many other biochemically important molecules. The rate of growth and yield from crops is directly influenced by the nitrogen available, and it has been shown that the amount of protein in, for example, corn is increased by nitrogen fertilizers.

About 50 years ago there was, in some places, a thriving business in supplying bacteria that farmers plowed into the soil where clover or other legumes were growing. The business died out when chemical fertilizers became available at lower prices. But now interest is reviving in bacterial nitrogen fixation, and it has become an active area of research. With greater understanding of the natural fixation process, it is hoped that bacteria can again be put directly to work in the fields, cutting down the need for chemical fertilizers, which require large amounts of energy in their manufacture. Possibly better plant–microorganism combinations might be designed, or possibly a nonbiological system for nitrogen fixation that resembles the natural process might be developed.

The primary role of phosphorus in biological systems is in energy transfer—plants and animals store energy in the phosphorus–oxygen bonds. Good suppliers of phosphorus in the soil hasten the growth of young plants. Most of the phosphorus used by plants is in the form of phosphate ions, particularly the dihydrogen phosphate ion, $H_2PO_4^-$.

The raw material for phosphate fertilizers is phosphate rock. The rock is converted directly to single superphosphate—a mixture of monocalcium phosphate and calcium sulfate (gypsum),

$$2Ca_5(PO_4)_3F(s) + 7H_2SO_4(aq) + 17H_2O(l) \longrightarrow$$
$$3Ca(H_2PO_4)_2 \cdot H_2O(s) + 7CaSO_4 \cdot 2H_2O + 2HF(g)$$

or it is converted directly to triple superphosphate, which contains no calcium sulfate and therefore delivers a higher percentage of phosphorus,

$$Ca_5(PO_4)_3F(s) + 7H_3PO_4(aq) + 5H_2O(l) \longrightarrow 5Ca(H_2PO_4)_2 \cdot H_2O(s) + HF(g)$$

Finely ground phosphate rock can also be used as a fertilizer, or phosphoric acid can be produced and soluble salts made from the acid (Table B). The ammonium phosphates, $(NH_4)H_2PO_4$ (MAP) and $(NH_4)_2HPO_4$ (DAP), are manufactured economically from wet process phosphoric acid, and in the 1970s became the leading phosphate fertilizers.

Table A

Plant Nutrients Carbon, hydrogen, and oxygen are obtained by plants from the air and the soil. All other nutrients are obtained only from the soil. Primary nutrients are needed in largest amounts (up to 200 pounds per acre), secondary nutrients are needed in smaller amounts (up to 50 pounds per acre), and others are needed only in small amounts (<1 pound per acre).

Needed in large amounts
Carbon
Hydrogen
Oxygen
Nitrogen
Phosphorus
Potassium

Needed in moderate amounts
Calcium
Magnesium
Sulfur

Some of those needed in trace amounts
Boron
Copper
Iron
Manganese
Zinc
Molybdenum
Chlorine

Just a word about how the other essential nutrients are delivered to crops. Most of them, including the important nutrient potassium, are available in mineral deposits. The mineral need only be mined and added in suitable amounts to nitrogen- and phosphorus-containing chemical fertilizers.

Table B
Manufacture of Major Chemical Fertilizers Natural raw materials appear in black and manufactured raw materials in color in the left-hand column.

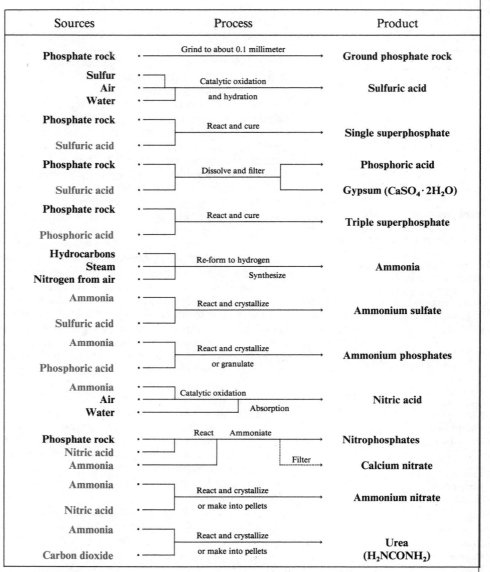

Sources	Process	Product
Phosphate rock	Grind to about 0.1 millimeter	**Ground phosphate rock**
Sulfur / Air / Water	Catalytic oxidation and hydration	**Sulfuric acid**
Phosphate rock / Sulfuric acid	React and cure	**Single superphosphate**
Phosphate rock / Sulfuric acid	Dissolve and filter	**Phosphoric acid** / **Gypsum (CaSO$_4 \cdot$ 2H$_2$O)**
Phosphate rock / Phosphoric acid	React and cure	**Triple superphosphate**
Hydrocarbons / Steam / Nitrogen from air	Re-form to hydrogen / Synthesize	**Ammonia**
Ammonia / Sulfuric acid	React and crystallize	**Ammonium sulfate**
Ammonia / Phosphoric acid	React and crystallize or granulate	**Ammonium phosphates**
Ammonia / **Air** / **Water**	Catalytic oxidation / Absorption	**Nitric acid**
Phosphate rock / Nitric acid / Ammonia	React Ammoniate / Filter	**Nitrophosphates** / **Calcium nitrate**
Ammonia / Nitric acid	React and crystallize or make into pellets	**Ammonium nitrate**
Ammonia / **Carbon dioxide**	React and crystallize or make into pellets	**Urea (H$_2$NCONH$_2$)**

Source: Adapted from Christopher J. Pratt, "Chemical Fertilizers," *Scientific American,* **212**(6), June 1965. (Copyright © by Scientific American, Inc. All rights reserved.)

COMPOUNDS OF SULFUR

Table 26.18 gives examples of compounds and ions of sulfur in its oxidation states of -2, $+4$, and $+6$.

Table 26.18
Oxidation States and Some Compounds and Ions of Sulfur

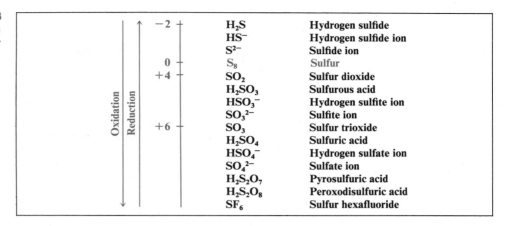

	-2	H_2S	Hydrogen sulfide
		HS^-	Hydrogen sulfide ion
		S^{2-}	Sulfide ion
	0	S_8	Sulfur
	$+4$	SO_2	Sulfur dioxide
		H_2SO_3	Sulfurous acid
		HSO_3^-	Hydrogen sulfite ion
		SO_3^{2-}	Sulfite ion
	$+6$	SO_3	Sulfur trioxide
		H_2SO_4	Sulfuric acid
		HSO_4^-	Hydrogen sulfate ion
		SO_4^{2-}	Sulfate ion
		$H_2S_2O_7$	Pyrosulfuric acid
		$H_2S_2O_8$	Peroxodisulfuric acid
		SF_6	Sulfur hexafluoride

26.14 HYDROGEN SULFIDE AND OTHER SULFIDES

Hydrogen sulfide (Figure 26.16), H_2S, is an extremely poisonous colorless gas with an obnoxious odor resembling that of rotten eggs. A few breaths of the concentrated gas can be fatal. At lesser concentrations, headaches and dizziness are produced. Hydrogen sulfide is especially hazardous because it deadens the sense of smell so that increasing concentrations are not detected.

Many metal sulfides are only slightly soluble (Table 26.19). The precipitation of metal sulfides plays an important role in qualitative analysis schemes (Section 21.15) for the identification of the elements present in a sample of unknown composition. By controlling the hydrogen ion concentration, the sulfide ion concentration can be controlled (Section 21.7b) and sulfides can be selectively precipitated according to their solubilities.

At one time, many qualitative analysis laboratories were recognizable from great distances by the strong smell of H_2S in the air as it leaked from generators that produced the gas. However, H_2S is now more safely generated directly in solution. This is accomplished by heating an aqueous solution of thioacetamide.

$$CH_3CSNH_2(aq) + 2H_2O(l) \xrightarrow{\Delta} CH_3COO^- + NH_4^+ + H_2S(aq) \quad \textbf{(26.44)}$$
$$\underset{\text{thioacetamide}}{} \qquad\qquad \underset{\text{acetate ion}}{} \underset{\substack{\text{ammonium} \\ \text{ion}}}{} \underset{\text{hydrogen sulfide}}{}$$

Hydrogen sulfide is a good reducing agent both in the pure state and in aqueous solution. In an excess of oxygen (or air), hydrogen sulfide burns, when ignited, to give sulfur dioxide and water.

$$2H_2S(g) + 3O_2(g) \longrightarrow 2SO_2(g) + 2H_2O(g)$$

If the amount of air is limited, the oxidation product is elemental sulfur.

The only appreciably soluble sulfides are those of the alkali metals and the ammonium ion. They give solutions that are distinctly alkaline as a result of the hydrolysis of the sulfide ion.

Table 26.19
Solubility Product Constants (K_{sp}) of Some Metal Sulfides

Metal Sulfide	K_{sp}
MnS *manganese(II) sulfide*	2.3×10^{-13}
FeS *iron(II) sulfide*	4.2×10^{-17}
ZnS *zinc sulfide*	2×10^{-24}
SnS *tin(II) sulfide*	3×10^{-27}
CdS *cadmium sulfide*	2×10^{-28}
PbS *lead sulfide*	1×10^{-28}
CuS *copper(II) sulfide*	6×10^{-36}
HgS *mercury(II) sulfide*	4×10^{-53}

Hydrogen sulfide, H_2S
m.p. $-85.5°C$
b.p. $-60.7°C$

Figure 26.16

Elemental sulfur dissolves in a solution containing sulfide ion due to formation of polysulfide ions, S_n^{2-}, demonstrating the tendency of sulfur atoms to self-link. Adding acid to a solution containing polysulfide ions precipitates white, finely divided sulfur and liberates H_2S.

26.15 SULFUR OXIDES AND HALIDES

Sulfur dioxide, SO_2 (Figure 26.17a), is a colorless gas which has a characteristic suffocating odor, and is very irritating to the eyes and respiratory tract. It is formed in the combustion of sulfur-containing fuels and in the smelting of sulfide ores, and it is a primary air pollutant (see An Aside: Air Pollution, Smog, and Acid Rain).

Sulfur dioxide is a strong reducing agent. In addition to its essential role in the production of sulfuric acid (Section 26.6a), it is extensively used as a bleach for textiles and food, a disinfectant, a mold inhibitor in dried fruits, and in the production of paper pulp.

Sulfur trioxide, SO_3 (Figure 26.17b), is usually gaseous when formed, but solidifies on cooling. It has three different solid modifications (m.p.'s, 62.3 °C, 32.5 °C, 16.8 °C). Liquid sulfur trioxide fumes in moist air as it forms sulfuric acid.

Sulfur hexafluoride, SF_6, is the most stable of the sulfur–halogen compounds. It is a colorless, odorless gas and is one of the most chemically unreactive compounds known. It does not react with water, but most other sulfur–halogen compounds do so with sufficient vigor to make these substances hazardous to handle. For example, sulfur tetrafluoride hydrolyzes rapidly upon exposure to moist air,

$$SF_4(g) + 2H_2O(l) \longrightarrow 4HF(g) + SO_2(g) \tag{26.45}$$

The halides with sulfur–sulfur bonds, S_2X_2 (X = F, Cl, Br, I), are all known.

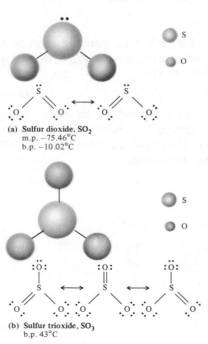

(a) **Sulfur dioxide, SO_2**
m.p. −75.46°C
b.p. −10.02°C

(b) **Sulfur trioxide, SO_3**
b.p. 43°C

Figure 26.17
Sulfur Oxides

26.16 SULFUR OXOACIDS AND THEIR SALTS

Sulfur dioxide is very soluble in water. Its aqueous solutions are acidic and this acidity is traditionally described as the result of the following equilibria:

$$SO_2(g) + H_2O(l) \rightleftharpoons H_2SO_3(aq) \tag{26.46}$$

$$H_2SO_3(aq) + H_2O(l) \rightleftharpoons HSO_3^- + H_3O^+ \qquad K_a = 1.43 \times 10^{-2} \tag{26.47}$$

$$HSO_3^- + H_2O(l) \rightleftharpoons SO_3^{2-} + H_3O^+ \qquad K_a = 5.0 \times 10^{-8} \tag{26.48}$$

Sulfurous acid, H_2SO_3, is thus considered to be a diprotic acid. In reality, most of the dissolved sulfur dioxide is simply in solution as a hydrate and there is no clear-cut evidence for the existence of sulfurous acid. However, stable salts containing both the hydrogen sulfite and sulfite ions are well known. Like sulfur dioxide, the sulfites and hydrogen sulfites are reducing agents.

The properties and preparation of sulfuric acid, which is a strong acid and the number one industrial chemical, have already been discussed (Section 26.6a).

Pyrosulfuric acid, $H_2S_2O_7$, is also known as "oleum" or "fuming sulfuric acid," because it evolves white fumes on contact with moist air. The fumes are caused by the immediate reaction of the escaping SO_3 with water to form ordinary sulfuric acid as a mist. Pyrosulfuric acid is a more powerful oxidizing agent than sulfuric acid. It is formed by dissolving SO_3 in H_2SO_4. As is true for phosphorus in its $+5$ oxoacids and salts, each sulfur atom in the $+6$ oxygen acids and salts is surrounded tetrahedrally by four oxygen atoms (see Figure 26.7).

Peroxosulfuric acids contain the peroxo groups $—\overset{..}{\underset{..}{O}}—\overset{..}{\underset{..}{O}}—$ (as in hydrogen peroxide). The Lewis structures of the two such acids that have been characterized— peroxomonosulfuric acid, H_2SO_5, and peroxodisulfuric acid, $H_2S_2O_8$—are shown in Figure 26.18. As you might expect, these acids are strong oxidizing agents. They are also potentially explosive and their salts are unstable, for example,

$$2K_2S_2O_8(s) \xrightarrow{\Delta} 2K_2SO_4(s) + 2SO_3(g) + O_2(g) \tag{26.49}$$

When an aqueous solution containing sulfite ion is boiled with elemental sulfur, the thiosulfate ion is produced.

$$SO_3^{2-} + S(s) \longrightarrow \underset{\substack{thiosulfate \\ ion}}{S_2O_3^{2-}} \tag{26.50}$$

The two sulfur atoms in the thiosulfate ion are not chemically equivalent, and the ion has a tetrahedral configuration that is, in a formal sense, derived from the tetrahedral sulfate ion by replacement of an oxygen atom with a sulfur atom.

Thiosulfates can be thought of as salts of thiosulfuric acid, $H_2S_2O_3$, which (like sulfurous acid) is of doubtful existence. The most common thiosulfate is the sodium salt, which is obtained from solution as the pentahydrate, $Na_2S_2O_3 \cdot 5H_2O$. This substance is known as "hypo" and is used in photography (see An Aside: The Photographic Process, Chapter 29).

The thiosulfate ion is unstable in acidic solution, immediately decomposing to give free sulfur and sulfur dioxide.

$$S_2O_3^{2-} + 2H^+ \longrightarrow S(s) + SO_2(g) + H_2O(l) \tag{26.51}$$

The ion is a fairly strong reducing agent. Strong oxidizing agents, such as chlorine, oxidize thiosulfate to sulfate ion.

$$S_2O_3^{2-} + 4Cl_2(g) + 5H_2O(l) \longrightarrow 2SO_4^{2-} + 10H^+ + 8Cl^- \tag{26.52}$$

Moderately strong oxidizing agents, such as iodine, convert $S_2O_3^{2-}$ to $S_4O_6^{2-}$.

$$2S_2O_3^{2-} + I_2(s) \longrightarrow S_4O_6^{2-} + 2I^- \tag{26.53}$$

This reaction occurs quantitatively and rapidly, and is useful for the analytical determination of iodine and in other analytical procedures.

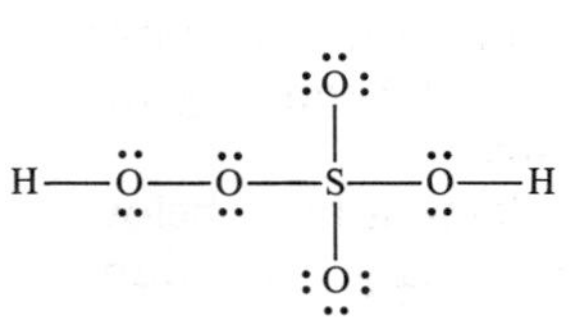

The properties of sulfur and its compounds are summarized in Table 26.20.

Peroxomonosulfuric acid, H_2SO_5

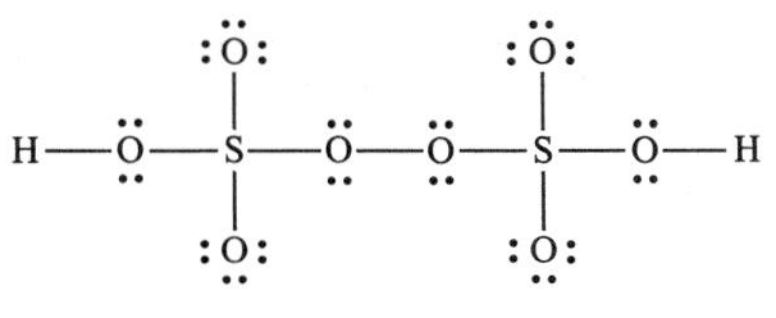

Peroxodisulfuric acid, $H_2S_2O_8$

Figure 26.18
Peroxo Acids of Sulfur

Table 26.20
Outstanding Properties of Sulfur and Some of Its Compounds

S [Ne] $3s^2 3p^4$ ← 6 valence electrons	Member of Representative Group VI. Can form more than four covalent bonds, e.g., SF_6
S_8 ← cyclic	Many allotropic forms, some with S_8 rings. Strong tendency of sulfur atoms to self-link.
$\overset{-2\ +4\ +6}{S, S, S}$	Most common oxidation states
S⋯O	Many S—O bonds are intermediate between single and double bonds.
H_2S	A weak diprotic acid. Very poisonous.
S^{2-} ion	Gives alkaline aqueous solution. Many metal sulfides are insoluble and give H_2S with acids.
S_x^{2-}	Polysulfides formed by union of sulfide ion with elemental sulfur.
SO_2	Formed in combustion of sulfur and sulfur-containing fuels and smelting of sulfide ores. Air pollutant. Strong reducing agent.
HSO_3^-	Weakly acidic. Reducing agent.
SO_3^{2-}	Reducing agent. Salts give SO_2 with acid.
H_2SO_4	The largest volume industrial chemical. Strong acid in first dissociation. Hot, concentrated acid is strong oxidizing agent and dehydrating agent.
HSO_4^-	Acidic in aqueous solution.
$H_2S_2O_7$ ← pyrosulfuric acid	Intermediate in production of H_2SO_4.
$H_2SO_5, H_2S_2O_8$ ← peroxosulfuric acids	Contain the —O—O— linkage. Strong oxidizing agents.
$Na_2S_2O_3 \cdot 5H_2O$	"Hypo," used in photography.

EXAMPLE 26.6
Chemical Properties: SF_6

Sulfur hexafluoride, SF_6, is a remarkable compound. In spite of its rather high molar mass (146.05 g), this covalent substance is a gas at room temperature. Despite the fact that sulfur is in its maximum oxidation state of $+6$, the compound is chemically inert at ordinary temperatures and is not an oxidizing agent even at red heat. These properties make it useful as an insulator in high-voltage generators. What reasons can be given for the properties described?

Here is an excellent case where properties can be related to structure. The SF_6 molecule is octahedral, and the sizes of the sulfur and fluorine atoms are such that the latter essentially envelop the sulfur atom completely. As a result, attractions between individual molecules are weak (the solid sublimes at -63 °C) and reagents cannot penetrate the fluoride barrier to react with the sulfur atom.

[It is worth noting that the hexafluoride of selenium, the element lying below sulfur in Representative Group VI, is more reactive than SF_6. The larger selenium atom is less well shielded by the six fluorine atoms.]

EXAMPLE 26.7
Chemical Reactions: P and S Compounds

Categorize the following reactions of phosphorus and sulfur compounds.

(a) $P_4O_6(s) + 6H_2O(l) \longrightarrow 4H_3PO_3(aq)$
(b) $H_2S(g) + 2NaOH(aq) \longrightarrow Na_2S(aq) + 2H_2O(l)$
(c) $2ZnS(s) + 3O_2(s) \longrightarrow 2ZnO(s) + 2SO_2(g)$
     (reaction used in smelting metals; produces pollution)
(d) $Ca_3(PO_4)_2(s) + 3H_2SO_4(aq) \longrightarrow 2H_3PO_4(aq) + 3CaSO_4(s)$
     (preparation of wet process phosphoric acid)

(a) This is a nonredox combination of compounds and the reaction of an acidic oxide with water.

(b) An acid (H_2S) and a base (NaOH) combine to give water and a salt (Na_2S). This is a neutralization reaction — a partner-exchange reaction driven by the formation of water.

(c) This reaction of an element and a compound is the redox displacement of a nonmetal (S) by a more active nonmetal (O). Elemental oxygen is reduced and sulfide ion from ZnS is oxidized to the +4 state in SO_2.

(d) While not a reaction between ions in aqueous solution, this reaction follows the pattern of a partner-exchange reaction. In this case a strong acid reacts with a salt to produce a weaker acid.

EXAMPLE 26.8
Chemical Reactions: P and S Compounds

Predict the products of the following reactions:

(a) $ZnS(s) + HCl(aq) \longrightarrow$
(b) $Ba(H_2PO_2)_2(aq) + H_2SO_4(aq) \longrightarrow$
(c) $Na_3PO_4(s) + H_2O(l) \longrightarrow$

(a) Metal sulfides dissolve in strong acid solutions with the formation of hydrogen sulfide (Equation 26.29).

$$ZnS(s) + 2HCl(aq) \longrightarrow ZnCl_2(aq) + H_2S(aq)$$

This is a partner-exchange reaction.

(b) This is a reaction between ionic compounds in aqueous solution. A partner-exchange reaction can be driven by the formation of slightly soluble barium sulfate. The other product is hypophosphorous acid. [This reaction is a preparative method for hypophosphorous acid.]

$$Ba(H_2PO_2)_2(aq) + H_2SO_4(aq) \longrightarrow BaSO_4(s) + 2H_3PO_2(aq)$$

(c) Like all sodium salts, sodium phosphate is water soluble. The PO_4^{3-} anion, the anion of a weak acid (HPO_4^{2-}), will react with water and the solution will be alkaline.

$$Na_3PO_4(s) \xrightarrow{H_2O} 3Na^+ + PO_4^{3-}$$
$$PO_4^{3-} + H_2O(l) \rightleftharpoons HPO_4^{2-} + OH^-$$

AN ASIDE

Air Pollution, Smog, and Acid Rain

A pollutant is an undesirable substance added to the environment, usually by the activities of earth's human inhabitants. Some pollutants, such as the insecticide DDT, are unknown in nature. Others, such as NO, occur naturally (NO is formed in lightning flashes and bacterial decay), but are considered to be pollutants when they are added to the environment in excessive amounts by human activities. Still other substances, known as secondary pollutants, are harmful materials formed by chemical reactions in the atmosphere or hydrosphere, for example, the sulfuric acid formed in the atmosphere from the oxides of sulfur.

The five major air pollutants are carbon monoxide, hydrocarbons, the nitrogen oxides, the sulfur oxides, and particulates — airborne solid particles and liquid droplets. The sources and effects of the nitrogen and sulfur oxides are considered here. The other air pollutants are discussed in An Aside: Carbon Compounds in the Atmosphere, in Chapter 27.

Nitric oxide (NO) and nitrogen dioxide (NO_2) — referred to as NO_x, "nox" — are produced by oxidation of atmospheric nitrogen (and nitrogen-containing compounds, as in coal).

$$N_2 + O_2 \xrightarrow{\Delta} \underset{\textit{nitric oxide}}{2NO} \qquad 2NO + O_2 \xrightarrow{\Delta} \underset{\textit{nitrogen dioxide}}{2NO_2}$$

The first of these reactions takes place at high temperatures (about 1200–1750 °C); therefore, NO is a by-product of any high-temperature combustion in the presence of air. Most fossil fuel combustion in both motor vehicles and stationary sources achieves the necessary temperatures and almost 90% of the pollutant NO is introduced in this way. Pollution by NO_x reaches its highest levels over highly industrialized cities with high automobile populations.

Sulfur dioxide, SO_2, is produced when sulfur-containing coal and fuel oil are burned. Very little sulfur dioxide pollution can be blamed on the automobile, because in the production of gasoline most of the sulfur is removed. One-half of the annual sulfur dioxide emission comes from power plants, and the second most substantial contribution is made by industrial processes, especially metal smelting, in which sulfur is removed from sulfide ores by oxidation (Section 28.6). Sulfur trioxide is formed in the air by oxidation of the lower oxide (Equation 26.3).

On their own, neither of the nitrogen oxides is a health hazard at present pollution levels. Nitrogen dioxide is potentially the more dangerous of the two, and in high enough concentration can damage the lungs. Sulfur dioxide and sulfur trioxide—referred to as SO_x, "sox"—are both strongly irritating to the respiratory tract. At SO_2 concentrations of 5 ppm almost everyone suffers throat and eye irritation, and SO_3 at a concentration of 1 ppm can cause severe discomfort. Elderly persons and those with respiratory diseases are most seriously affected.

The hazards from NO_x and SO_x of greatest concern are twofold—the smog produced when high concentrations accumulate over industrial areas, and the acid rain resulting from the generally rising concentrations of these pollutants throughout the atmosphere.

Nitrogen oxides are essential to the unpleasant mixture of gases and particulates that make up photochemical smog. The ingredients of **photochemical smog** are sunlight, nitrogen oxides, and hydrocarbons. This is the type of smog for which Los Angeles is famous.

The intervention of hydrocarbons in the natural cycle of NO_2 reactions in the atmosphere starts the trouble (Figure A). Hydrocarbons react with oxygen atoms to form highly reactive free radical intermediates which contain unpaired electrons. The free radicals (symbolized here by a dot on the formula, e.g., $RCO\cdot$) initiate a variety of reactions, among which may be the following:

$$RCO\cdot + O_2 \longrightarrow RCO_3\cdot$$
$$RCO_3\cdot + \text{hydrocarbons} \longrightarrow R_2C{=}O, RCHO$$
$$RCO_3\cdot + NO \longrightarrow RCO_2\cdot + NO_2$$
$$RCO_3\cdot + O_2 \longrightarrow RCO_2\cdot + O_3$$
$$RCO_3\cdot + NO_2 \longrightarrow \underset{\textit{peroxyacylnitrates (PAN)}}{RCO_3NO_2}$$

As a result, concentrations of ozone, the peroxyacylnitrates (PAN), and aldehydes (RCHO) build up. These substances are all irritants to the respiratory system and can also damage many materials. Ozone is particularly destructive to rubber and fabrics, and is harmful to crops and ornamental plants. Nitrogen dioxide also accumulates and is responsible for the characteristic brown color of photochemical smog. Airplane pilots are familiar with the sight of a brown pall hanging over cities.

The word "smog" is a combination of "smoke" and "fog." It is something of a misnomer for photochemical smog, which includes nitrogen oxides, ozone, PAN, aldehydes, hydrocarbons, and carbon monoxide, but not smoke or fog. The term "smog" is more accurate for **London smog**, or gray smog, which is initiated by a mixture of sulfur oxides, particulates, and high humidity. Many of the chemicals in particulates can catalyze the formation of SO_3 from SO_2, and high humidity assures

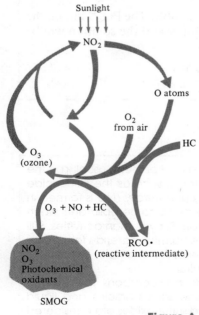

Figure A
Interaction of Hydrocarbons (HC) with Natural NO_2 in Photochemical Reaction Cycle The natural cycle is shown in black.

(a) Acid rain
containing
H_2SO_4 falls

(b) Crust forms as
calcite ($CaCO_3$) is
transformed to
gypsum
($CaSO_4 \cdot 2H_2O$)

(c) Crust washes
off as the more
soluble gypsum
dissolves

(d) Layer of stone
is removed

Figure B
Effect of Acid Rain on Limestone

the formation of a fog containing many sulfuric acid droplets formed by reaction of SO_3 with water. The sulfuric acid also coats the surface of particulates and is drawn into the lungs with them. The smog of 1952 in London is blamed for 4000 deaths.

Unlike smog, acid rain is a global rather than an urban problem, affecting the wildlife in remote wilderness areas as well as stone buildings and monuments. The disappearance of trout from lakes in the Adirondack Mountains has only recently been recognized as the result of the rising acidity of the lakes.

"Pure" rainwater is defined as having a pH of 5.6—slightly acid due to equilibrium with the natural concentration of carbon dioxide in the atmosphere. With rising air pollution has come rising acid concentration that is washed out of the atmosphere by rain. Today, rainfall in the entire eastern half of the United States has a pH of 5 or below. In the Northeast, rain of pH 4.2 or less is commonplace. (The pH of tomato juice is 4.2.)

Nitric acid and sulfuric acid in varying proportions are present in acid rain. According to current studies, the formation of nitric acid is linked to photochemical reactions of hydroxyl radicals, $\cdot OH$, generated by reaction of photochemically excited oxygen atoms with water.

$$O_3(g) \xrightarrow{h\nu} O^*(g) + O_2(g)$$
$$O^*(g) + H_2O(g) \longrightarrow 2 \cdot OH(g)$$
$$\cdot OH(g) + NO_2(g) \longrightarrow HNO_3(g)$$

Sulfuric acid is formed by the oxidation of SO_2 by ozone or hydrogen peroxide. The reactions are believed to occur while the gases are also dissolved in water droplets.

Nitric and sulfuric acids are deposited not only by rainfall, but also by fog and snow, as well as on the surface of particulates that fall to the ground. Some of the worrisome effects of the resultant rising acidity of natural waters are declining fish populations (70% of Norwegian lakes with pH levels of less than 4.5 have *no* fish); the dissolution by acid runoff and the transportation into natural waters of metals such as aluminum (toxic to fish) and mercury (toxic to humans by concentration up the food chain); possible destructive effects on plants in wilderness areas as well as on farms; and problems in the lumber industry due to the deaths of trees. Also, stone buildings and monuments weather rapidly under acidic conditions (Figure B).

SUMMARY

GENERAL PROPERTIES OF NITROGEN, PHOSPHORUS, AND SULFUR (Section **26.1**) Nitrogen, phosphorus, and sulfur have the relatively high electronegativities, high ionization energies, and small atomic radii typical of nonmetals (Table 26.1). Nitrogen, the first member of Group V, differs from the other elements of the group (Table 26.2). Nitrogen is unique in having eight oxidation states (-3 to $+5$) in its compounds. Nitrogen, phosphorus, and sulfur form ionic compounds containing the N^{3-}, P^{3-}, and S^{2-} ions. In their positive oxidation states these elements form covalent bonds and molecular compounds. In many compounds of nitrogen, phosphorus, and sulfur, especially those with oxygen, multiple bonding and resonance play important roles.

ELEMENTAL NITROGEN, PHOSPHORUS, AND SULFUR (Sections **26.2–26.4**) The $N \equiv N$ triple bond in elemental nitrogen is very strong, making the N_2 molecule quite stable. As a result, many nitrogen compounds have positive heats of formation and decompose (sometimes explosively) to give N_2. Nitrogen is obtained directly from liquefied air; its major use is in the manufacture of ammonia (Table 26.3).

The three allotropic forms of phosphorus are quite different. White phosphorus ignites spontaneously in air and is highly toxic. Red phosphorus (polymeric) is much less reactive and much less toxic. Black phosphorus is crystalline and made under high pressure. Elemental phosphorus is obtained from phosphate rock by reduction with coke in electric furnaces. Phosphate rock is used directly in the manufacture of fertilizer (Table 26.4).

Elemental sulfur, best known in the rhombic and monoclinic crystalline forms which consist of S_8 molecules, has many allotropes that exhibit complex phase relationships. Sulfur atoms have a marked tendency to self-link in chains and small rings. Elemental sulfur is obtained by the Frasch process, in which sulfur is melted by superheated water and forced to the surface by compressed air. The major use of sulfur is in the manufacture of sulfuric acid (Table 26.5).

CHEMICAL REACTIONS OF NITROGEN, PHOSPHORUS, AND SULFUR; INDUSTRIAL ACIDS (Sections **26.5, 26.6**)   In combination with other elements at ordinary temperatures, white phosphorus is highly reactive and nitrogen is unreactive. At elevated temperatures nitrogen forms nitrides with reactive metals and oxides with oxygen, while phosphorus and sulfur combine with most other elements. The oxides of nitrogen, phosphorus, and sulfur are all acidic oxides, but note that NO_2 undergoes disproportionation with water. Nitric acid is a strong oxidizing agent; its reduction products vary, but most commonly are NO_2 or NO. Aqua regia, which dissolves noble metals, is a 3-to-1 mixture of concentrated HCl and concentrated HNO_3. Because of the many oxidation states of nitrogen, nitrogen compounds participate in numerous redox reactions and disproportionation reactions. Sulfuric acid is a strong oxidizing acid and a dehydrating agent.

The N^{3-} and P^{3-} ions are strong bases and react completely with water. The S^{2-} and HS^- ions are weaker bases, and the ammonium ion, NH_4^+, is weakly acidic. Many of the oxoanions of nitrogen, phosphorus, and sulfur are weakly basic (Tables 26.7, 26.8). The NO_2^-, SO_3^-, and S^{2-} ions react in solution with dilute nonoxidizing acids to give NO, NO_2, SO_2, and H_2S, respectively.

Nitric acid, phosphoric acid, and sulfuric acid (Table 26.8) are among the top industrial chemicals. Sulfuric acid is produced by catalytic oxidation of SO_2 to SO_3 and reaction of the SO_3 with water (via $H_2S_2O_7$). Phosphoric acid is a moderately strong triprotic acid and a poor oxidizing agent. It is made by oxidation of phosphorus and reaction of the oxide with water or, in less pure form, directly from phosphate rock. The major use of both sulfuric and phosphoric acids is in the production of fertilizers. Nitric acid decomposes easily to give NO_2, O_2, and H_2O. It is miscible in all proportions with water, and is both a strong acid and a strong oxidizing agent in aqueous solutions. It is produced by catalytic oxidation of ammonia, using air. Its chief use is in the manufacture of fertilizers, explosives, plastics, and dyes.

COMPOUNDS OF NITROGEN (Sections **26.7 – 26.10**)   The most common oxidation states of nitrogen are -3, $+3$, and $+5$ (Table 26.10). Saltlike nitrides are ionic compounds containing the nitride ion. Some covalent nitrides are molecular compounds formed with nonmetals; others are hard, high-melting network covalent compounds (the diamondlike nitrides). With many of the d-transition metals, nitrogen forms interstitial nitrides with metallic properties. In the gaseous state, ammonia exists as discrete, pyramidal molecules; in the liquid and solid states the molecules are extensively linked by hydrogen bonding. The ammonia molecule has an unshared electron pair, which allows it to act as a Lewis base and a ligand in many complex ions. Ammonia is a weak base and reacts with acids to form ammonium salts, most of which are soluble. Ammonium nitrate is important as a fertilizer and as a component in explosives. Ammonia can act as a reducing agent. It is made by direct combination of hydrogen and nitrogen at high temperature and pressure (the Haber process). There are oxides of nitrogen for each of its oxidation states from $+1$ to $+5$ (Table 26.12). Nitric oxide (NO) and nitrogen dioxide (NO_2) are acid-forming air pollutants. Nitrous acid, HNO_2, is a weak acid that can act as either an oxidizing or a reducing agent. Nitrite ion is a strong reducing agent. The outstanding properties of nitrogen and its compounds are summarized in Table 26.13.

COMPOUNDS OF PHOSPHORUS (Sections **26.11 – 26.13**)   The common oxidation states of phosphorus are -3, $+3$, and $+5$ (Table 26.14). The compounds of phosphorus in the -3 oxidation state—phosphine, PH_3, and the phosphides—are similar to the comparable compounds of nitrogen. All phosphorus $+3$ and $+5$

halides are known except for the $+5$ iodide. The halides all react vigorously with water. Phosphorous acid is a moderately strong diprotic acid, and the acid and its ions are strong reducing agents, yielding phosphoric acid and phosphate ions. The outstanding properties of phosphorus and its compounds are summarized in Table 26.17.

COMPOUNDS OF SULFUR (Sections **26.14–26.16**)   The common oxidation states of sulfur are -2, $+4$, and $+6$ (Table 26.18). Hydrogen sulfide, H_2S, is a very toxic gas which in aqueous solution is a weak diprotic acid. Many metal sulfides are insoluble (Table 26.19), but will dissolve in acidic solutions with the formation of hydrogen sulfide. Fewer sulfur–halogen compounds than phosphorus–halogen compounds are known. Sulfur dioxide is a primary air pollutant. It is very soluble in water. Although H_2SO_3 probably does not exist in solution, salts containing the sulfite (SO_3^{2-}) and hydrogen sulfite (HSO_3^-) ions are known. Like SO_2, they are generally good reducing agents. Loss of a molecule of water between two sulfuric acid molecules yields pyrosulfuric acid, $H_2S_2O_7$, which is an intermediate in sulfuric acid production and is a stronger oxidizing agent than sulfuric acid. Thiosulfate ion, $S_2O_3^{2-}$, which forms when sulfite ion in solution reacts with sulfur, is a fairly strong reducing agent. Thiosulfate salts include $Na_2S_2O_3 \cdot 5H_2O$, the "hypo" used in photographic processing. The outstanding properties of sulfur and its compounds are summarized in Table 26.20.

SIGNIFICANT TERMS

phosphate rock
nitrogen fixation
aqua regia
dimer
photochemical smog
London smog

THOUGHTS ON CHEMISTRY

Frasch Describes His First Success

FRASCH DESCRIBES HIS FIRST SUCCESS, by Herman Frasch

After permitting the melting fluid to go into the ground for twenty-four hours, I decided that sufficient material must have been melted to produce some sulphur. The pumping engine was started on the sulphur line, and the increasing strain against the engine showed that work was being done. More and more slowly went the engine, more steam was supplied, until the man at the throttle sang out at the top of his voice, "She's pumping." A liquid appeared on the polished rod, and when I wiped it off I found my finger covered with sulphur. Within five minutes the receptacles under pressure were opened and a beautiful stream of the golden fluid shot into the barrels we had ready to receive the product. After pumping for about fifteen minutes, the forty barrels we had supplied were seen to be inadequate. Quickly we threw up embankments and lined them with boards to receive the sulphur that was gushing forth; and since that day no further attempt has been made to provide a vessel or a mold into which to put the sulphur.

When the sun went down we stopped the pump to hold the liquid sulphur below until we could prepare to receive more in the morning. The material on the ground had to be removed, and willing hands helped to make a clean slate for the next day. When everything had been finished, the sulphur all piled up in one heap, and the men had departed, I enjoyed all by myself this demonstration of success. I mounted the sulphur pile and seated myself on the very top. It pleased me to hear the slight noise caused by the contraction of the warm sulphur, which was like a greeting from below—proof that my object had been accomplished. Many days and many years intervened before financial success was assured, but the first step towards the ultimate goal had been achieved. We had melted the mineral in the ground and brought it to the surface as a liquid. We had demonstrated that it could be done.

Herman Frasch, *The Journal of Industrial and Engineering Chemistry*, February 1912 (with thanks to *Chemtech*, February 1976).

QUESTIONS

The Elements: N, P, and S

26.1 What is meant by the term "allotropy"? Describe some of the allotropic forms of phosphorus and sulfur. List some of the physical properties of N_2, P_4, and S_8.

26.2 Describe the commercial preparations of elemental nitrogen, phosphorus, and sulfur. Be sure to give any pertinent equations.

26.3 Although nitrogen and phosphorus are in the same periodic table family, phosphorus forms a pentachloride, PCl_5, but the analogous nitrogen compound, NCl_5, does not exist. Why is this not surprising?

26.4 List some of the major uses of elemental nitrogen, phosphorus, and sulfur.

26.5* The phase diagram for sulfur is shown in the accompanying figure. Describe what happens to a sample of sulfur (a) that is heated very slowly at 1 atm from 25 °C to 500 °C; (b) that is heated at 1420 atm from 25 °C to 153 °C; (c) that has been melted and is then poured slowly into boiling water at 1 atm; (d) that is in the gaseous phase between 95.31 °C and 115.18 °C and that has the pressure upon it increased to 2000 atm; and (e) in the monoclinic form between 5.1×10^{-6} atm and 3.2×10^{-5} atm when it is heated.

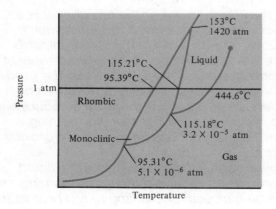

Temperature

N, P, S Chemical Reactions; Industrial Acids

26.6 Compare the reactivity of N, P, and S in combination reactions with other elements. Does the existence of allotropic forms of phosphorus make a difference in the reactivity of this element?

26.7 Write chemical equations illustrating the acidic nature of the oxides of nitrogen, phosphorus, and sulfur.

26.8 Briefly discuss the oxidizing properties of nitric acid. What determines the oxidation state of the nitrogen in the reduction product?

26.9 Describe the chemical behavior of ammonium salts upon heating. Contrast the reaction products of ammonium salts containing anions that can act as oxidizing agents with the reaction products of those salts containing anions that do not act as oxidizing agents.

26.10 Compare the chemical reactivity of the nitride, phosphide, and sulfide ions toward water. Write chemical equations describing these reactions.

26.11 Briefly describe the industrial preparations of sulfuric, nitric, and phosphoric acids.

Compounds of Nitrogen

26.12 Name three classes of nitrides and briefly discuss the bonding in each.

26.13 Describe the molecular geometry of the ammonia molecule. How does this geometry affect the physical properties of the substance? Will ammonia act as a Lewis acid or base? Illustrate this acid–base behavior by completing the following equations: (a) $NH_3(aq) + H^+ \rightarrow$ and (b) $AgCl(s) + NH_3(aq) \rightarrow$.

26.14 Write the Lewis structures for (a) N_2O, (b) NO, (c) HNO_2, (d) HNO_3, (e) NO_2^-, and (f) NO_3^-. Name each species and identify the hybridization of the outermost orbitals of the nitrogen atom in each species.

26.15 Why can nitrous acid act as both an oxidizing agent and a reducing agent? Write the chemical equation for the disproportionation of nitrous acid.

26.16 Why does NO_2, a brown gas, lose its color when cooled to 0 °C?

Compounds of Phosphorus

26.17 What structural feature do molecules of P_4, P_4O_6, and P_4O_{10} have in common? What is the common structural feature for all of the acids containing phosphorus(V)?

26.18 Draw Lewis structures for (a) PCl_3, (b) $[PCl_4]^+$, (c) PCl_5, and (d) $[PCl_6]^-$. What is the hybridization of the phosphorus atom in each species? Prepare three-dimensional sketches of these species and identify the molecular geometry.

26.19 Phosphoric acid, H_3PO_4, forms sodium salts corresponding to replacement of all three hydrogen atoms—NaH_2PO_4, Na_2HPO_4, and Na_3PO_4—but only two analogous salts for phosphorous acid, H_3PO_3, can be obtained—NaH_2PO_3 and Na_2HPO_3. Give a reasonable explanation for this difference in the behavior of the two acids.

Compounds of Sulfur

26.20 Write Lewis structures for the following species: (a) sulfur dioxide, (b) sulfuric acid, (c) sulfur trioxide, (d) pyrosulfuric acid, (e) peroxodisulfuric acid, (f) sulfite ion, (g) sulfate ion, (h) thiosulfate ion, (i) sulfide ion, and (j) molecular sulfur. What is the oxidation number of sulfur in each of these species?

26.21 Are all metal sulfides highly insoluble in water? Which ones are considered soluble? Will solutions containing the soluble sulfides be alkaline, neutral, or acidic?

26.22* A sample of powdered sulfur was divided into two parts — one about twice the size of the other. The smaller sample was heated until the sulfur melted and began to burn. The gaseous product (a) of this reaction was collected and mixed with water to form (b). The larger sulfur sample was mixed with iron filings and heated in a crucible, producing a dark solid (c). This solid was placed in a container, and HCl was added, producing a gas (d), which was allowed to mix with (b), giving a yellow to white finely divided precipitate (e). Identify the five substances mentioned above and write chemical equations describing the reactions.

Additional Questions

26.23 Which of the following are redox reactions? Identify the oxidizing and reducing agent in each of the redox reactions.

(a) $2Ca_3(PO_4)_2(s) + 6SiO_2(s) + 10C(s) \xrightarrow{\Delta}$
$$6CaSiO_3(l) + 10CO(g) + P_4(g)$$

(b) $P_4O_{10}(s) + 6H_2O(l) \longrightarrow 4H_3PO_4(aq)$

(c) $Au(s) + 4H^+ + 4Cl^- + NO_3^- \longrightarrow$
$$[AuCl_4]^- + NO(g) + 2H_2O(l)$$

(d) $3H_3PO_4 \longrightarrow H_5P_3O_{10} + 2H_2O(l)$

26.24 Repeat Question 26.23 for:

(a) $P_4(s) + 3OH^- + 3H_2O(l) \longrightarrow 3H_2PO_2^- + PH_3(g)$

(b) $3NO_2(g) + H_2O(l) \longrightarrow 2HNO_3(aq) + NO(g)$

(c) $2S_2O_3^{2-} + I_3^- \longrightarrow S_4O_6^{2-} + 3I^-$

(d) $3S_8(s) + 48OH^- \longrightarrow 16S^{2-} + 8SO_3^{2-} + 24H_2O(l)$

26.25 Classify each of the following reactions according to the reaction types listed in Tables 17.2 and 17.7:

(a) $HNO_3(l) + H_2O(l) \longrightarrow H_3O^+ + NO_3^-$

(b) $Mg_3N_2(s) + 6H_2O(l) \longrightarrow 3Mg(OH)_2(s) + 2NH_3(g)$

(c) $2NaNO_3(s) \xrightarrow{\Delta} 2NaNO_2(s) + O_2(g)$

(d) $3S_8(s) + 48OH^- \longrightarrow 8SO_3^{2-} + 16S^{2-} + 24H_2O(l)$

26.26 Repeat Question 26.25 for:

(a) $4NH_3(g) + 5O_2(g) \xrightarrow{\Delta} 4NO(g) + 6H_2O(g)$

(b) $Cu^{2+} + H_2S(g) \longrightarrow CuS(s) + 2H^+$

(c) $Na_2SO_3(s) + S(s) + 5H_2O(l) \longrightarrow Na_2S_2O_3 \cdot 5H_2O(s)$

(d) $(NH_4)_2Cr_2O_7(s) \xrightarrow{\Delta} Cr_2O_3(s) + 4H_2O(g) + N_2(g)$

26.27 Predict the major products of the following reactions:

(a) $HNO_3(l) + P_4O_{10}(s) \longrightarrow$

(b) $Cu(s) + HNO_3(6\ M) \longrightarrow$

(c) $PBr_3(l) + H_2O(l) \longrightarrow$

(d) $HSO_3^- + H_2O(l) \longrightarrow$

26.28 Repeat Question 26.27 for:

(a) $Li_3N(s) + H_2O(l) \longrightarrow$

(b) $NH_4NO_3(s) \xrightarrow{\Delta}$

(c) $HNO_2(aq) + I^- + H^+ \longrightarrow$

(d) $H_2SO_4(18\ M) + H_2S(g) \longrightarrow$

26.29 Write balanced equations for the following chemical reactions: (a) formation of sulfur hexafluoride; (b) combustion of hydrogen sulfide, using excess oxygen; (c) laboratory preparation of nitric oxide; and (d) thermal decomposition of solid disodium monohydrogen phosphate.

Answers to Selected Questions

26.5 (a) rhombic solid warms up, rhombic solid changes to monoclinic solid at 95.39 °C, monoclinic solid warms up, solid melts at 115.21 °C, liquid warms up, liquid vaporizes at 444.6 °C, gas warms up; (b) some rhombic solid melts, and some of the liquid crystallizes in the monoclinic form; all three phases remain in contact, as this is a triple point; (c) monoclinic sulfur forms; (d) gas condenses to monoclinic solid, monoclinic solid changes to rhombic solid; (e) monoclinic solid sublimes

26.13 trigonal pyramid, one lone pair of electrons; strong intermolecular forces because of hydrogen bonding and dipole–dipole interactions; Lewis base, $NH_3(aq) + H^+ \rightarrow NH_4^+$, $AgCl(s) + 2NH_3(aq) \rightarrow [Ag(NH_3)_2]^+ + Cl^-$

26.17 the phosphorus atoms are in a tetrahedral arrangement; oxygen atoms are arranged tetrahedrally about each phosphorus atom

26.22 $S(l) + O_2(g) \rightarrow SO_2(g)$, (a) is SO_2; $SO_2(g) + H_2O(l) \rightarrow H_2SO_3(aq)$, (b) is H_2SO_3; $S(s) + Fe(s) \rightarrow FeS(s)$, (c) is FeS; $FeS(s) + 2HCl(aq) \rightarrow H_2S(g) + FeCl_2(aq)$, (d) is H_2S; $H_2SO_3(aq) + 2H_2S(g) \rightarrow 3S(s) + 3H_2O(l)$, (e) is S

26.24 all four reactions are redox; oxidizing agents: (a) P_4, (b) NO_2, (c) I_3^-, (d) S_8; reducing agents: (a) P_4, (b) NO_2, (c) $S_2O_3^{2-}$, (d) S_8

26.26 (a) redox — combination of an element with a compound to give other compounds, (b) nonredox — partner-exchange between ions in aqueous solution; (c) redox — combination of an element with a compound to give another compound, and nonredox — combinations of compounds, (d) redox — decomposition

26.28 (a) $LiOH(s)$ and $NH_3(g)$; (b) $N_2O(g)$ and $H_2O(g)$ or $N_2(g)$, $H_2O(g)$, and $O_2(g)$; (c) $I_2(s)$, $NO(g)$, and $H_2O(l)$; (d) $S(s)$, $SO_2(g)$, and $H_2O(l)$

PROBLEMS

Review of Principles

26.1 The average atomic mass of N is 14.0067 u. There are two isotopes which contribute to this average: $^{14}_{7}N$ (14.00307 u) and $^{15}_{7}N$ (15.00011 u). Calculate the percentage of $^{15}_{7}N$ atoms in a sample of naturally occurring nitrogen.

26.2 A sample of phosphorus was burned in air and produced a product containing 56 mass % P and 44 mass % O. Find the simplest formula of the oxide formed. The density of this gaseous oxide at 200 °C and 1 atm pressure is 5.7 g/L. What is the molecular formula of this oxide? *Answer* P_4O_6

26.3 At 502 Torr and 750 °C, exactly 1 L of sulfur vapor is found to weigh 0.5350 g. What is the major component of the vapor? *Answer* S_2.

26.4 The detonator-induced thermal explosion of ammonium nitrate yields $N_2(g)$, $H_2O(g)$, and $O_2(g)$. Calculate the total volume of gas, measured at 1.00 atm and 827 °C, theoretically released in the explosive decomposition of 1.00 kg of $NH_4NO_3(s)$.

26.5 Which solution has a larger mole fraction of solute: concentrated H_2SO_4 (which is 96.0 mass % H_2SO_4) or concentrated "ammonium hydroxide" (which is 58.6 mass % NH_3)?

26.6 A gaseous mixture at 300 °C in a 1.00 L vessel originally contained 1.00 mol SO_2 and 5.00 mol O_2. Once equilibrium conditions were attained, 81% of the SO_2 had been converted to SO_3. What is the value of the equilibrium constant (K_c) for this reaction at this temperature? *Answer* 4.0

26.7 Calculate the pH of each of the following solutions: (a) 0.05 M HNO_3; (b) 1 M NH_3, $K_b = 1.6 \times 10^{-5}$, and (c) 0.1 M HNO_2; $K_a = 7.2 \times 10^{-4}$.

26.8 What would be the pH of a buffer solution prepared using equal volumes of 0.20 M HNO_2 and 0.20 M KNO_2? $K_a = 7.2 \times 10^{-4}$ for HNO_2. *Answer* 3.14

26.9 The enthalpy change for dissolving sulfur in six moles of CS_2 at 25 °C

$$S(s) + 6CS_2(l) \longrightarrow S(\text{in } 6CS_2)$$

is 1695 J/mol for rhombic sulfur and 1360. J/mol for monoclinic sulfur. Calculate $\Delta H°$ for the phase transformation

$$S(\text{rhombic}) \longrightarrow S(\text{monoclinic})$$

Which form of sulfur would you predict to be more stable at this temperature?

26.10* A careless stockroom attendant prepared a liter each of the following solutions: 0.1 M Na_3PO_4, 0.1 M Na_2HPO_4, and 0.1 M NaH_2PO_4, but forgot to label the containers. Quickly the attendant realized that each solution had a unique value of pH and all that was needed was to calculate the theoretical values of pH from the values of K_a ($K_{a1} = 7.5 \times 10^{-3}$, $K_{a2} = 6.6 \times 10^{-8}$, $K_{a3} = 1 \times 10^{-12}$), measure the pH values of the solutions using a pH meter, and properly label each container. What were the values of pH that the attendant calculated? *Answer* 12.5 for Na_3PO_4, 10.0 for Na_2HPO_4, 4.1 for NaH_2PO_4

26.11* Using molecular orbital notation, (a) write the electron configuration for a molecule of nitrogen. (b) What types of bonds and how many of each would you predict the molecule to have? (c) Prepare a Lewis structure and a three-dimensional sketch of a molecule of N_2. (d) Will the molecule be paramagnetic or diamagnetic?

The N≡N bond energy is 946 kJ/mol and the N—N bond energy is about 159 kJ/mol. (e) Predict whether four gaseous nitrogen atoms would form two nitrogen molecules or a tetrahedral molecule similar to P_4, basing your prediction on the amount of energy released as the molecules are formed. (f) Repeat part (e) for phosphorus using 485 kJ/mol for P≡P and 243 kJ/mol for P—P.

CHAPTER 27

Nonmetals: Carbon and Hydrocarbons

Carbon is an element with many facets to its personality. As diamond it sparkles brilliantly. As graphite it lubricates bearings, is slippery and black, and makes a mess if you get it on your clothes. As soot, it is deposited on cold surfaces from smoky flames. Carbon is one of the elements known from antiquity, and the manufacture of charcoal by heating wood in the absence of air was described in the first century A.D.

The geometry of the bonding of carbon atoms, combined with their ability to link with each other in endless arrays, is the basis for the entire field of organic chemistry. And, of course, organic compounds, with their carbon atom-to-carbon atom skeletons, are the basis for living matter, at least as it is known on this planet.

It is scarcely possible to pick up a newspaper or a magazine without encountering news of carbon compounds that are vitally important to our society—the fossil fuels and their possible replacements, the "synfuels." Despite schemes for the use of solar power, wind power, or wave power, we are and will remain for many years to come dependent upon burning hydrocarbon fuels for most of our energy.

In still another facet of its personality, carbon forms many compounds other than those of organic chemistry and biochemistry. In this chapter we discuss the inorganic chemistry of carbon and introduce organic chemistry.

CARBON AND ITS INORGANIC COMPOUNDS

27.1 PROPERTIES OF CARBON

Carbon is the first member of Representative Group IV and is the only nonmetal in the group. The electron configuration of carbon is $1s^2 2s^2 2p^2$ (Table 27.1).

In most of its compounds, carbon atoms form four equivalent single bonds, which are attributed to sp^3 hybridization. Carbon can also form a double covalent bond (along with two single bonds) through sp^2 hybridization, and a triple covalent bond (with one single bond) through sp hybridization. A double bond is composed of one σ bond and one π bond, a triple bond of one σ bond and two π bonds (Sections 11.6, 11.7). Carbon has a high ionization energy and only in compounds with the

Table 27.1
Properties of Carbon

Melting point (°C)		Density (g/cm³)	
Diamond	>3550	Diamond	3.51
Graphite	3652–3697 (sublimes)	Graphite	2.25
Ionization energy (kJ/mol, 0 K)	1086	C—C single bond length (nm)	0.154
Electron affinity (kJ/mol, 0 K)	123	Atomic radius (nm)	0.077
Electronegativity	2.5	Bond energy (kJ/mol)	C—C 331
			C=C 590
			C≡C 812

Table 27.2
Differences between Carbon and the Other Members of the Carbon Family (Si, Ge, Sn, Pb)

Property	Comments
Only nonmetal in the family	Silicon and germanium are semiconducting elements; tin and lead are metals.
Can form no more than four covalent bonds	The $n = 2$ energy level can hold only 8 electrons and only s and p orbitals are available for bonding. Other elements have d orbitals available and can form species such as SiF_6^{2-}, $SnCl_6^{2-}$.
Only family member to form anions containing only the element; C_2^{2-} and C^{4-} are known.	Such anions form by combination of carbon with very reactive metals, e.g., in Be_2C, CaC_2, Al_4C_3.
Has the greatest tendency of all elements to self-link	Gives rise to the realm of organic chemistry.
C—C bond is strong (331 kJ/mol).	Strongest nonmetal–nonmetal single bond except for H_2 (other family members, Si—Si, 209 kJ/mol; Ge—Ge, 160 kJ/mol; Sn—Sn, 140 kJ/mol).
Forms multiple bonds with itself, oxygen, nitrogen, sulfur, and phosphorus	Very few multiple bonds formed by other family members (Si=Si bonds are known).

4 single bonds: sp^3 hybridization

1 double bond, 2 single bonds: sp^2 hybridization

1 triple bond, 1 single bond: sp hybridization

most electropositive metals does it form the C_2^{2-} anion and, in a few compounds, the C^{4-} anion. In its inorganic compounds, carbon has oxidation states of -4 (in C^{4-}), -1 (in C_2^{2-}), $+2$ (in CO), or $+4$. [In organic compounds it may have any oxidation state from -4 to $+4$.]

Like most first members of periodic table families, carbon differs significantly from the other members of its family (Table 27.2). The single most outstanding difference between carbon atoms and those of all other elements is the extent to which they undergo **catenation** — the formation of bonds between atoms of the same element. Silicon atoms have some tendency to catenate (as do sulfur atoms), but they do not come close to carbon in this respect. In polymers (Section 33.13) carbon atoms form chains thousands of atoms long.

The reactivity of elemental carbon is rather low and reactions of elemental carbon require high temperatures. Carbon is less electronegative than nitrogen, oxygen, fluorine, chlorine, and bromine, other nonmetals with which it forms many compounds. With respect to other members of its own family, however, carbon has the highest ionization energy and is the most electronegative element.

Two *allotropic forms* of carbon — diamond and graphite — are discussed in the next section.

27.2 DIAMOND, GRAPHITE, AND OTHER FORMS OF CARBON: THEIR USES

Carbon is found naturally in two allotropic forms that are both crystalline — diamond and graphite. There are also numerous natural and man-made amorphous forms of carbon, including coke and many varieties of finely divided industrial carbon known as, for example, carbon black, lampblack, animal charcoal, and activated carbon.

Diamond and graphite differ greatly in properties as a result of the differences in their crystal structures. Diamond is clear and colorless and is the hardest substance known. It has a very high melting point, is extremely brittle, and when struck, breaks into many pieces. It does not conduct electricity. These properties reflect the strength of network covalent bonding (Section 9.17) — each carbon atom in the crystal shares its four valence electrons with four other carbon atoms, which surround it tetrahedrally (Figures 27.1, 27.2a).

The ability of diamond to refract light rays is high, and when properly cut and polished, a diamond reflects light in an array of many colors. On this account, and

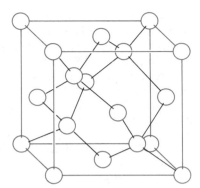

Figure 27.1
The Crystal Structure of Diamond

because of its durability, diamond is highly prized as a gemstone. Impure samples are often black; these have no value as gems, but when crushed, they are used in abrasives. In rare cases a diamond has an attractive color because of traces of impurities; such a diamond, because it is unique, is especially valuable as a gem. The famous Hope diamond, for example, is blue. (The blue color may be due to the presence of a small amount of boron.)

Diamonds have been found in North and South America and in Australia, but nearly all of the world's supply comes from South Africa. Diamonds are found there in "blue clay" from which they may be separated by washing the clay away in a stream of water.

Graphite is black and soft, and is much less dense than diamond (see Table 27.1). Like diamond, graphite melts only at an extremely high temperature. It feels smooth and slippery to the touch and is an excellent lubricant. The carbon atoms are arranged in planar layers in the graphite crystal (Figure 27.2b). Within each layer, each carbon atom is bonded to three other carbon atoms by covalent single bonds. The fourth valence electron of each carbon atom participates in delocalized π bonding. The atoms in each layer are tightly bonded together (bond order, ~ 1.3; bond energy, 477 kJ/mol), but the binding force between layers is weak (17 kJ/mol), allowing the layers to slip over each other. The delocalized electrons give graphite metallic properties. It has a dull luster and conducts electricity moderately well. The lubricating properties of graphite depend not only on slippage between the planes, but also on a film of moisture or of gas molecules adsorbed on the surface of the graphite layers. The adsorbed substance decreases friction as the layers slide past each other. (Dry graphite in a vacuum is not slippery.)

Figure 27.2
Comparison of the Crystal Structures of Diamond and Graphite, Showing the "Layers" in Each

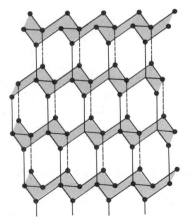

(a) Diamond

(b) Graphite

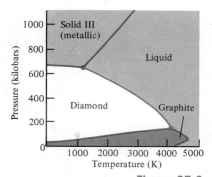

Figure 27.3
Phase Diagram for Carbon One kilobar is approximately equal to 1000 atm.

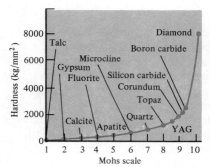

Figure 27.4
Hardness of Diamond and Other Materials The Mohs scale for hardness is based on the properties of a series of minerals. A value of 10 is assigned to diamond (hardest) and 1 to talc (softest). (Corundum is aluminum oxide.) Note that the Mohs scale is nearly linear for values from 1 to 8, but deviates sharply for higher values.

In addition to its use as a lubricant, graphite is employed on a large scale in electrodes, in molds and crucibles to be used with hot metal, and in fabricated parts for the aerospace industry (e.g., nose cones). The control rods in nuclear reactors are also made of graphite. Graphite is the black ingredient in pencils, a pencil "lead" being a baked rod of graphite mixed with clay.

Comparison shows that the crystal structures of graphite and diamond are closely related (see Figure 27.2). If alternate carbon atoms in each layer of graphite could be raised above the plane of the layer and the others depressed below it, and the layers could then be pushed a little closer together, the diamond structure would result. According to the phase diagram for carbon (Figure 27.3), this should be possible at a high enough temperature and pressure. The difficulty of compressing graphite, however, was recognized by the famous physicist Percy Bridgeman, who said, "Graphite is nature's strongest spring," and by an unidentified scientist who put it this way: "It is easy to squeeze carbon atoms together, but very difficult to keep them squz."

After much effort, synthetic diamonds were first made in 1955 at the General Electric Company laboratory. The process requires chambers able to maintain, at the minimum, a 50 kbar pressure and 1500 K for long periods of time. A molten metal catalyst enhances the reaction rate. Synthetic diamonds have a variety of industrial applications that mainly utilize the properties of hardness and abrasiveness in various cutting and polishing tools. For example, concrete can be cut like wood with a blade coated with tiny diamond crystals.

Gem-quality diamonds have not yet been made synthetically. The diamondlike synthetic gems sold at less-than-diamond prices are "cubic zirconia" (ZrO_2), titanium dioxide (TiO_2), strontium titanate ($SrTiO_3$), or yttrium aluminum garnet ($Y_3Al_5O_{12}$), called "YAG." Titanium dioxide and strontium titanate give stones of fiery brilliance, but they are softer than diamond. "YAG" is less brilliant than the others, but is harder (Figure 27.4). Cubic zirconia is the closest to diamond in its properties.

The most familiar amorphous forms of carbon are coke, made by heating coal at a high temperature to drive off volatile inorganic and organic substances, and charcoal. The charcoal burned in stoves and fireplaces is made from wood by heating it in the absence of air. Finely powdered forms of carbon, sometimes also referred to as charcoal of various types, are made similarly from such materials as animal bones, coconut shells, or sugar. Finely divided carbon "activated" by heating with steam to clean its surface is an excellent adsorbent. Such activated carbon has a very high surface area—ranging from 600 to 2000 m^2/g. Activated carbon is used to remove bad-smelling or dangerous vapors from the air and to remove colored or bad-tasting impurities from water or other liquids. For example, many municipal water-treatment plants pass water through beds of activated carbon, and it is used to purify soft drinks, fruit juices, and honey.

Carbon black, usually made by the thermal decomposition of hydrocarbons in an open flame, is a very finely divided, very pure form of carbon. The human eye can distinguish 260 shades of black, and 10 nm particles of carbon black are the blackest of substances. Carbon black is used in printing ink and as a paint pigment, and large quantities are used to reinforce and color rubber—an automobile tire is one-fourth carbon black.

27.3 SOME CHEMICAL REACTIONS OF CARBON AND INORGANIC CARBON COMPOUNDS

Many of the chemical reactions of carbon and carbon compounds that are common in inorganic chemistry have been discussed in earlier chapters. These and the additional reactions discussed here are summarized in Table 27.3

Only fluorine among the halogens combines with elemental carbon and it does so at ordinary temperatures (reaction a, Table 27.3). At elevated temperatures, the reactivity of carbon depends upon its form. Diamond combines with oxygen above

Table 27.3
Some Reactions of Carbon and Its
Compounds and Ions

Elemental carbon

(a) $C(s) + 2F_2(g) \xrightarrow[\text{temperature}]{\text{room}} CF_4(g)$

(b) $C(s) + 2S(s) \xrightarrow[\substack{\text{slightly} \\ >1 \text{ atm}}]{700-900 \text{ °C}} CS_2(g)$

(c) $C(s) + W(s) \xrightarrow[\text{H}_2]{1400-1600 \text{ °C}} WC(s)$

(d) $2C(s) + O_2(g) \xrightarrow{\Delta} 2CO(g)$ $\Delta H° = -221 \text{ kJ}$

(e) $C(s) + O_2(g) \xrightarrow{\Delta} CO_2(g)$ $\Delta H° = -394 \text{ kJ}$

(f) $C(s) + 2H_2SO_4(conc) \xrightarrow{\Delta} CO_2(g) + 2SO_2(g) + 2H_2O(g)$

(g) $C(s) + 4HNO_3(conc) \xrightarrow{\Delta} CO_2(g) + 4NO_2(g) + 2H_2O(g)$

Hydrocarbon combustion

(h) $CH_4(g) + 2O_2(g) \xrightarrow{\Delta} CO_2(g) + 2H_2O(g)$ $\Delta H° = -803 \text{ kJ}$

Carbon and carbon monoxide as reducing agents

(i) $C(s) + H_2O(g) \xrightarrow{1000 \text{ °C}} H_2(g) + CO(g)$

(j) $CO(g) + H_2O(g) \xrightarrow[\text{catalyst}]{250 \text{ °C}} H_2(g) + CO_2(g)$

(k) $C(s) + ZnO(s) \xrightarrow{\Delta} Zn(g) + CO(g)$

(l) $3CO(g) + Fe_2O_3(s) \xrightarrow{\Delta} 3CO_2(g) + 2Fe(s)$

Ions in aqueous solution

(m) $CO_3^{2-} + H_2O(l) \rightleftharpoons HCO_3^- + OH^-$ $K_b = 2.1 \times 10^{-4}$

(n) $HCO_3^- + H_2O(l) \rightleftharpoons H_2CO_3(aq) + OH^-$ $K_b = 2.2 \times 10^{-8}$

(o) $CN^- + H_2O(l) \rightleftharpoons HCN(aq) + OH^-$ $K_b = 1.6 \times 10^{-5}$

800 °C, while natural graphite oxidizes slowly above 450 °C. A number of carbides (Section 27.4e) are made by the combination of finely divided carbon with metals at high temperatures (e.g., reaction c, Table 27.3). (Hydrogen is often added so that it will react with any oxygen present and prevent the oxidation of carbon.)

<u>Carbon monoxide and carbon dioxide</u> are the products of the reaction of carbon with oxygen (reactions d, e), and the combustion of methane (reaction h) is representative of the complete combustion of hydrocarbons. Such reactions are the primary sources of thermal energy in the combustion of fossil fuels. The combustion of carbon, hydrocarbons, and fossil fuels is exothermic and thermodynamically spontaneous (negative ΔG values). Why is it then that coal, petroleum, and dead trees do not burst into flames? These substances are *kinetically stable*—their reactions with oxygen have large energies of activation. Carbon monoxide also burns at elevated temperatures.

$$2CO(g) + O_2(g) \longrightarrow 2CO_2(g) \qquad \Delta H° = -566.1 \text{ kJ} \qquad (27.1)$$

The relative amounts of the two oxides formed in the combustion of carbon compounds depend on the temperature and the supply of oxygen. With a limited oxygen supply, carbon monoxide is favored; with an excess of oxygen, carbon dioxide is favored. At high temperatures the reduction of carbon dioxide by carbon, an endothermic reaction, can also take place.

$$CO_2(g) + C(s) \longrightarrow 2CO(g) \qquad \Delta H° = 172.4 \text{ kJ} \qquad (27.2)$$

C, CO: reducing agents at
high temperatures

Carbon and carbon monoxide are both good *reducing agents* at elevated temperatures. In reactions that are important in the synthesis of fuels (Sections 27.11, 27.12), carbon or carbon monoxide can reduce water to hydrogen (reactions i, j).

The reducing properties of carbon (often as coke) and carbon monoxide are valuable in freeing metals from their oxide ores (e.g., reactions k, l).

With variations in the conditions, the combination of carbon monoxide and hydrogen can be used to manufacture methanol (CH_3OH), as well as methane (CH_4) and other hydrocarbons. These reactions are discussed in Section 27.12 in connection with their use in the production of synthetic fuels.

In sunlight, or in the presence of an appropriate catalyst, carbon monoxide combines with chlorine to give the highly toxic gas carbonyl chloride, $COCl_2$, better known as phosgene.

By sharing the electron pair on the carbon atom, carbon monoxide forms coordinate covalent bonds with many metals. In the resulting coordination compounds, such as $Fe(CO)_5$ and $Cr(CO)_6$, carbon monoxide is a ligand (as in complex ions; Section 14.10).

The commonly encountered carbon-containing anions are the carbonate and hydrogen carbonate ions (CO_3^{2-} and HCO_3^-) and the cyanide ion (CN^-), which are anions of weak acids and give alkaline aqueous solutions.

The addition of acid to solutions of CO_3^{2-} or HCO_3^- generates carbon dioxide and addition of acid to CN^- in solution generates (very poisonous) hydrogen cyanide.

Cyanide ion forms complex ions with many metals, in some cases by first forming an insoluble cyanide which then goes into solution due to complex formation, for example,

$$Ag^+ + CN^- \longrightarrow AgCN(s)$$
$$AgCN(s) + CN^- \longrightarrow [Ag(CN)_2]^- \tag{27.3}$$

27.4 INORGANIC COMPOUNDS OF CARBON

Some of the simple, inorganic compounds of carbon are listed in Table 27.4. Note that the properties of the carbon tetrahalides vary as would be expected with increasing mass and decreasing electronegativity of the halogen atoms. Melting and boiling points increase from the fluoride to the bromide, and thermal stability decreases.

a. Carbon monoxide Carbon monoxide is a colorless, odorless gas which is insoluble in water and most other liquids. It is toxic because, when inhaled, it combines with the hemoglobin of the blood, displacing oxygen needed by the cells. In many of its physical properties carbon monoxide closely resembles nitrogen, with which it is isoelectronic.

strongest bond in a diatomic molecule

$:C{\equiv}O:$
bond energy, 1075 kJ/mol

$:N{\equiv}N:$
bond energy, 946 kJ/mol

Like nitrogen, carbon monoxide is unreactive at ordinary temperatures. When heated in air, it burns, with the liberation of heat and the formation of carbon dioxide (Equation 27.1). The current importance of carbon monoxide as an industrial raw material lies primarily in its reactions with hydrogen in the preparation of numerous organic compounds (Section 27.12). Mixtures of hydrogen and carbon monoxide result from the steam reforming of hydrocarbons and the partial oxidation of hydrocarbons (Section 16.8), and also from coal gasification (Section 27.13). Pure carbon monoxide is prepared by the purification of gas streams from these or other industrial processes.

Table 27.4
Some Simple Inorganic
Carbon Compounds

Compound	M.p. (°C)	B.p.(°C)	Remarks
CF_4	−185	−128	Very stable
CCl_4	−23	77	Moderately stable
CBr_4	90	190	Decomposes slightly on boiling
CI_4	171	—	Decomposes before boiling
$COCl_2$	−118	8	"Phosgene," highly toxic
$COBr_2$	—	65	Fumes in air
CO	−199	−192	Odorless and toxic
CO_2	−57 (6.2 atm)	−79	Acidic oxide
CS_2	−111	46	Flammable and toxic
$(CN)_2$	−28	−21	Colorless, water soluble, very toxic, and instantly fatal
HCN	−14	26	Very toxic and instantly fatal

b. Carbon dioxide, carbonic acid, and carbonates <u>Carbon dioxide</u> is a colorless, nontoxic gas with what has been described as a "faintly pungent" odor. The carbon dioxide molecule is linear, with double bonds between the carbon and oxygen atoms, $\ddot{O}=C=\ddot{O}$. The gas is readily condensed to the liquid state by cooling and compression, and upon further cooling the liquid freezes to a white solid ("dry ice"). This substance does not melt upon warming, but sublimes at −78.5 °C. Solid CO_2 leaves no trace when it evaporates (except for the water that condenses on its surface). It is very convenient for use in cooling ice cream, reactive chemicals, and many other things. At high temperatures (above 1700 °C) carbon dioxide decomposes to give carbon monoxide and oxygen (an endothermic reaction which is the reverse of reaction 27.1).

The atmosphere contains only 0.0325% carbon dioxide by volume, but atmospheric carbon dioxide plays an important role in photosynthesis and the carbon and oxygen cycles. On the other hand, life is impossible in an atmosphere that contains too much carbon dioxide, because CO_2 reduces the capacity of the hemoglobin in the blood to bind and transport oxygen. A CO_2 concentration of 1% by volume in air causes headaches, 10% causes severe distress, and over 30% causes unconsciousness and death.

Because carbon dioxide is inert and does not support combustion, and because it is heavier than air, allowing it to blanket a fire, it is an excellent fire-extinguishing agent. Liquid carbon dioxide (held in tanks at elevated pressure) is used in fire-extinguishing systems in airplanes and ships, and in chemical plants and other industrial installations. Hand-held extinguishers also may contain carbon dioxide under pressure. When the pressure is released by opening a valve, the liquid carbon dioxide escapes and immediately evaporates. Expansion of the gas causes a dramatic drop in temperature. As a result, the CO_2 freezes and forms a blanket of CO_2 "snow."

$$CO_2 + H_2O \longrightarrow \text{acidic solution}$$
$$CO_3{}^{2-} \text{ or } HCO_3{}^- + H_2O \longrightarrow \text{alkaline solution}$$

Like carbon monoxide, carbon dioxide is present as a by-product in the gaseous streams exiting from many industrial processes. Pure carbon dioxide for dry ice and other applications (Table 27.5) is made by purifying such gaseous mixtures.

In pure water a saturated CO_2 solution at 1 atm pressure and 25 °C contains about 0.034 mol/L of CO_2 gas, most of which is simply dissolved in the water. Only approximately one out of every 400 CO_2 molecules in solution reacts with a water molecule to give <u>carbonic acid</u>, H_2CO_3. This acid cannot be isolated, but does exist in small concentrations in aqueous CO_2 solutions. In writing the first ionization constant expression for H_2CO_3, it is customary to include both the dissolved CO_2 and the small amount of CO_2 converted to H_2CO_3 by using the sum of their concentrations as the reactant concentration. That is, in the K expression $[H_2CO_3]$ is equivalent to $[CO_2] + [H_2CO_3]$,

Table 27.5
Some Uses of Carbon Dioxide

Raw material in production of organic chemicals
Recovery of oil from depleted wells*
Refrigeration
Beverage carbonation
Fire extinguishing

* Carbon dioxide is forced into wells, dislodging some of the remaining petroleum.

$$H_2CO_3(aq) \rightleftharpoons HCO_3^- + H^+$$

$$K = \frac{[H^+][HCO_3^-]}{[H_2CO_3]} = \frac{[H^+][HCO_3^-]}{[CO_2] + [H_2CO_3]} = 4.5 \times 10^{-7}$$

The salts derived from carbonic acid are the carbonates, such as Li_2CO_3 and $CaCO_3$, and the hydrogen carbonates, such as $NaHCO_3$. Carbonates other than those of the alkali metals and ammonium ions are generally insoluble in water.

Minerals containing carbonate ions are plentiful in the earth's crust, and more than half of the rock mined each year contains carbonates. The principal carbonate minerals are calcite ($CaCO_3$), which we know as limestone and marble, magnesite ($MgCO_3$), siderite ($FeCO_3$), and dolomite, which is a calcite with about half of the calcium ions replaced by magnesium ions [$(Ca,Mg)CO_3$]. Calcium carbonate is also the major component of animal by-products such as pearls, eggshells, and coral.

c. Carbon disulfide Carbon disulfide, CS_2, is a volatile, flammable liquid. It is made by the combination of hardwood charcoal and sulfur or the reaction of methane (CH_4) with sulfur at high temperatures. Carbon disulfide is important to the chemical industry because it is an excellent solvent for waxes, greases, hydrocarbons, and other nonpolar substances, and because of its role in the manufacture of rayon. The major disadvantages to its use are its toxicity and high flammability (carbon disulfide vapor has been known to ignite upon contact with a hot steam pipe).

d. Carbon tetrachloride Carbon disulfide reacts with chlorine to give carbon tetrachloride and disulfur dichloride (a compound that is sometimes erroneously called sulfur monochloride).

$$CS_2(l) + 3Cl_2(g) \longrightarrow \underset{\substack{carbon \\ tetrachloride}}{CCl_4(l)} + \underset{\substack{disulfur \\ dichloride}}{S_2Cl_2(l)}$$

The products of reaction are readily separated by distillation.

At one time, carbon tetrachloride was widely used as a solvent for greases, a dry-cleaning agent, and in fire extinguishers. However, increasing awareness of its toxicity led eventually, in 1970, to a government ban on carbon tetrachloride in consumer products. The major use of carbon tetrachloride is now as a reactant and solvent within the chemical industry.

e. Carbides The binary compounds of carbon with metals and semiconducting elements are called carbides. There are three types of carbides. The ionic, or saltlike, carbides are formed between cations of the alkali and alkaline earth metals, the most reactive metals, and in most cases contain the C_2^{2-} ion, $[:C{\equiv}C:]^{2-}$. Carbides containing the C_2^{2-} ion react readily with water to produce acetylene (Section 27.6),

$$\underset{calcium\ carbide}{CaC_2(s)} + 2H_2O(l) \longrightarrow Ca(OH)_2(aq) + \underset{acetylene}{HC{\equiv}CH(g)} \qquad \textbf{(27.4)}$$

and are sometimes referred to as *acetylides*.

Calcium carbide, CaC_2 (Figure 27.5), which is a typical saltlike carbide, is a colorless crystalline material prepared industrially by the reduction of calcium oxide (quicklime) with coke at a very high temperature.

$$\underset{\substack{calcium\ oxide \\ (quicklime)}}{CaO(s)} + \underset{coke}{3C(s)} \longrightarrow \underset{calcium\ carbide}{CaC_2(s)} + CO(g) \qquad \textbf{(27.5)}$$

Calcium carbide produced by this reaction is the starting material in a commercial method for the production of acetylene via reaction (27.4).

The C^{4-} ion is found in beryllium carbide, Be_2C, and aluminum carbide, Al_4C_3. These compounds react with water to form methane.

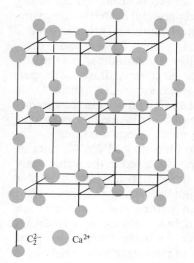

C_2^{2-} ● Ca^{2+}

Figure 27.5
The Crystal Structure of CaC₂

Interstitial carbides, or metallic carbides, result when carbon atoms fill open spaces in the cubic or hexagonal close-packed structures of transition metals (these compounds are analogous to the interstitial nitrides, Section 26.7). Such interstitial carbides as those of titanium, tungsten, tantalum, and niobium are very hard, heat-resistant materials and are used in cutting tools. Interstitial carbides are unreactive, and the ability of the metal to conduct electricity is retained.

Boron and silicon form extremely hard and inert carbides in which the bonding is fully covalent (the covalent carbides). Silicon carbide is a network covalent substance similar to diamond, in which alternate atoms of carbon are replaced by silicon atoms. Boron carbide (B_4C) is composed of groups of three covalently bonded carbon atoms that fit into the crystal lattice of boron. Boron carbide and silicon carbide (also known as carborundum) come close to diamond in hardness (see Figure 27.4), and like industrial diamonds, are used in abrasives and cutting tools.

f. Cyanides Hydrogen cyanide, HCN, is an extremely poisonous, highly volatile liquid (b.p. 26 °C), which has an odor of bitter almonds. Hydrogen cyanide is made by passing a mixture of methane, ammonia, and air over a catalyst at 800 °C.

$$\underset{\text{methane}}{2CH_4(g)} + 2NH_3(g) + 3O_2(g) \xrightarrow[\text{catalyst}]{800°} \underset{\substack{\text{hydrogen} \\ \text{cyanide}}}{2HCN(g)} + 6H_2O(g)$$

Aqueous solutions of HCN are known as hydrocyanic acid. Neutralization with a base (for example, NaOH) gives cyanide salts (for example, NaCN). The cyanide ion, like the C_2^{2-} ion, contains triply bonded carbon, $[\,:C \equiv N:\,]^-$.

The cyanide ion forms very stable complex ions with most of the d-transition elements (e.g., Equation 27.3).

Hydrogen cyanide and all cyanides are highly toxic. They inactivate enzymes essential to the production of energy by cellular oxidation.

The properties of carbon and its inorganic compounds are summarized in Table 27.6.

Table 27.6
Outstanding Properties of Carbon and Some Common Inorganic Carbon Compounds

$-\overset{\displaystyle \mid}{\underset{\displaystyle \mid}{C}}-$ $>C=C<$ $-C\equiv C-$	Forms 4 single covalent bonds; also double and triple bonds
$-C-C-C-C-$ C—C / C \ C \ C—C / (ring structure)	Catenates (self-bonds) more readily than any other element; basis of organic chemistry; C—C bond is strong
Diamond, graphite	Very different allotropes
C(s), ordinary temperatures	Not very reactive at room temperature; attacked only by F_2 and oxidizing acids
$C(s) + O_2(g) \rightarrow CO, CO_2$ Hydrocarbons + $O_2 \rightarrow CO, CO_2, H_2O$	Thermal energy sources
C(s) and CO(g) at high temperatures	Good reducing agents; used in metallurgy
CO_2, acidic oxide	H_2CO_3 formed in H_2O, but only by small percentage of molecules
CO_3^{2-}, HCO_3^-, CN^-	Weakly basic anions
HCN, all cyanides	*Very* poisonous; instantly fatal
$M(CO)_m$, $[M(CN)_n]^{x+}$	CO and CN^- form many complexes and complex ions with transition metals
$Ca^{2+}C_2^{2-}$, WC, SiC and B_4C *ionic metallic covalent*	Three types of carbides; B_4C and SiC, only covalent carbides, are very hard

EXAMPLE 27.1
Chemical Reactions: C Compounds

Following are the descriptions of three qualitative chemical tests. Write chemical equations for the reactions that occur in each test. Identify the reactions as either redox or nonredox reactions. (a) Test for elemental carbon: A solid sample is melted together with a small piece of elemental sodium. Cooling gives a white solid. Addition of water causes evolution of a gas which ignites spontaneously as a result of the heat developed. (b) Test for CO: A piece of filter paper moistened with a dilute, acidic solution of palladium(II) chloride, when held in the stream of gas to be tested, turns black. (c) Test for CO_3^{2-}: Dilute sulfuric acid is added to a crystalline solid. A gas evolves. Passage of the gas into a solution containing barium hydroxide yields a white precipitate.

(a) Carbon and the active metal sodium combine to form sodium carbide (a redox combination reaction). Addition of water yields acetylene (nonredox, reaction of C_2^{2-} with water), which burns in air (redox, combination of oxygen with a compound).

$$2Na(s) + 2C(s) \longrightarrow Na_2C_2(s)$$
$$Na_2C_2(s) + 2H_2O(l) \longrightarrow 2NaOH(aq) + C_2H_2(g)$$
$$2C_2H_2(g) + 5O_2(g) \longrightarrow 4CO_2(g) + 2H_2O(g)$$

(b) Carbon monoxide is a reducing agent; the black stain is elemental palladium (redox reaction).

$$PdCl_2(aq) + CO(g) + H_2O(l) \longrightarrow Pd(s) + CO_2(g) + 2HCl(aq)$$

(c) Addition of acid to a carbonate produces carbon dioxide (nonredox, partner exchange). The carbon dioxide, an acidic oxide, reacts with the alkaline solution to form an insoluble salt and water (nonredox).

$$CO_3^{2-} + H_2SO_4(aq) \longrightarrow SO_4^{2-} + H_2O(l) + CO_2(g)$$
$$CO_2(g) + Ba(OH)_2(aq) \longrightarrow BaCO_3(s) + H_2O(l)$$

AN ASIDE

Carbon Compounds in the Atmosphere

Carbon monoxide and hydrocarbons are primary pollutants added to the atmosphere by the activities of civilization. The major source of both is the internal combustion engine. The concentration of carbon monoxide in automobile exhaust rises when the mixing of fuel and oxygen is poor and when the temperature of combustion is lower than it should be. Levels of carbon monoxide as high as 100 ppm have been measured in downtown urban areas at peak traffic hours. Since concentrations of 50–100 ppm are sufficient to slow human responses, and higher concentrations lead to headaches and nausea, rising carbon monoxide concentrations are clearly undesirable.

Hydrocarbons enter the atmosphere as partially unburned fuel emitted with the exhaust, and gasoline also escapes from fuel tanks and engines. Little hydrocarbon pollution comes from stationary fuel-burning sources, since the combustion temperatures are usually higher and the combustion more complete. However, hydrocarbons are also lost to the atmosphere during handling in industrial processes. Harmful physiological effects from hydrocarbon pollutants are not likely at present concentrations. Several thousand times larger amounts would be necessary to cause such effects in human beings. The potential for damage due to hydrocarbons comes from the crucial role that they play in the formation of photochemical smog (see An Aside: Air Pollution, Smog, and Acid Rain, Chapter 26).

The Clean Air Act of 1970 called for a 90% reduction in automobile emission of three pollutants—hydrocarbons, carbon monoxide, and nitrogen(II) oxide—between 1970 and 1975. The amounts of emission of each pollutant were to be decreased in stages, with the toughest standard enforceable in 1976 model automobiles. A variety of problems has caused continuing postponement of enforcement of the final set of standards. However, some reductions have been achieved. By changing engine design to improve combustion efficiency and to better control the air-to-fuel ratio, losses of unburned gasoline have been cut back. To decrease the concentration of hydrocarbons and carbon monoxide in the exhaust gases major reliance thus far has been placed upon catalytic converters. Exhaust gases pass over a catalyst containing a metal such as platinum or rhodium, and carbon monoxide and hydrocarbons are oxidized to carbon dioxide and water by additional air taken in at the converter.

Particulates, the fifth of the five major air pollutants (the others are CO, hydrocarbons, NO_x, and SO_x) are airborne solid particles and liquid droplets, which often contain carbon or carbon compounds. They range greatly in size, origin, and composition. There are tiny particles of soot (amorphous carbon) and droplets of sulfuric acid mist. Particles produced in burning coal, called *fly ash*, can be up to 500,000 nm in diameter; they consist chiefly of oxides, such as SiO_2, Al_2O_3, MgO, Fe_2O_3, and TiO_2. Man-made particulates are contributed to the atmosphere in roughly equal amounts by stationary fuel combustion, industrial processes, and fires, such as forest fires and agricultural burning of wastes.

Persistent irritation of the lungs by particulates may be a contributing factor in the rising incidence of emphysema, although the causes of the disease are not completely understood. Chronic bronchitis is also aggravated by particulates. And some particulates, notably those of certain heavy metals, may exert long-term toxic effects specific to their individual chemistry.

An untold amount of damage is done each year by particulates settling out on buildings and within homes. Costs of cleaning go up and corrosion is often accelerated. Particulates are also suspected of influencing weather patterns by serving as nuclei for cloud formation, and by altering the amount of radiation reaching the earth's surface.

To decrease pollution by particulates, the particles must be captured before they enter the atmosphere. Various devices are in use to wash out, settle out, or precipitate out pollutants before waste gases leave power plants or industrial plants. As is usually the case with pollution control measures, they add to the cost of the process or the product being manufactured, a factor that retards the introduction of such measures.

Carbon dioxide is not an air pollutant in the sense that it causes damage to living or material things. However, the potential effect of rising carbon dioxide levels on the climate is a matter of concern. Carbon dioxide and water vapor in the atmosphere play an essential role in regulating the temperature at the surface of the earth by trapping heat between the surface and the upper atmosphere. The surface of the earth is warmed by absorption of solar radiation of many wavelengths, including those of the visible region. Because the earth is so much cooler than the sun, it reradiates this thermal energy at longer wavelengths, chiefly in the infrared region of the spectrum. Carbon dioxide and water vapor, however, absorb infrared radiation very effectively. Thus a great deal of energy is trapped in the atmosphere instead of being radiated away into space. The result of this effect, known as the greenhouse effect, is maintenance of the energy balance and the surface temperature of the earth to which we are accustomed.

Mainly as the result of the combustion of fossil fuels, atmospheric carbon dioxide increased 7% between 1958 and 1981. Sophisticated mathematical modeling of the climate predicts that doubling the concentration of carbon dioxide will result in an increase of 3 °C ($\pm$ 1.5 °C) in the global mean temperature. The rates of both evaporation and precipitation would increase with increased CO_2 concentration. While debate continues on the specific effects of rising carbon dioxide levels and the resultant temperature increase, there is no doubt that major changes in the variation of the seasons with latitude will accompany such a temperature change.

HYDROCARBONS

During the early part of the nineteenth century the compounds found in living organisms were thought to be formed only through a subtle "vital force" present in such organisms. "Organic" chemistry was named on this basis and distinguished from "inorganic" chemistry, which covered all compounds not found in living matter. It was noted that all of the organic compounds then known contained carbon.

In 1828 a German chemist, Friedrich Wöhler, converted ammonium cyanate, a compound that had never been found in any living organism, into urea, a substance known to be produced by animals.

$$NH_4OCN \xrightarrow{\Delta} H_2N-\overset{\overset{\displaystyle O}{\|}}{C}-NH_2$$

ammonium   *urea*
cyanate

This crucial experiment freed organic chemistry from its link to living organisms. The vital force concept gradually faded away, and organic chemistry became the chemistry of the compounds of carbon and the carbon–carbon bond. The number of organic compounds now known is in the millions. Many organic compounds do, of course, occur in nature, but even more have been made synthetically.

All organic compounds contain carbon atoms and, with a few exceptions, hydrogen atoms. Oxygen, nitrogen, the halogens, sulfur, phosphorus, silicon, and a few other elements may be present also, their frequency of occurrence in organic compounds decreasing roughly in the order given. All organic compounds can be thought of as based upon the structures of the hydrocarbons, which are introduced in the following sections. Organic compounds containing other elements are discussed in Chapter 33.

27.5 SATURATED HYDROCARBONS

a straight carbon chain

butane
(b.p. −0.5 °C)

a branched carbon chain

isobutane
(b.p. −12 °C)

Saturated hydrocarbons contain only covalent single bonds. Each tetrahedral carbon atom in a saturated hydrocarbon is joined to four other atoms, and each hydrogen atom is joined by one bond to a carbon atom. With this arrangement, it is easy to write down collections of atoms that represent actual compounds. An uninhibited approach to such an activity, limited only by the number of bonds to carbon and to hydrogen atoms, allows some chemical doodling, that can be quite instructive.

For example, it is possible to arrange the atoms of C_4H_{10} in more than one way, as shown in the structures in the margin. Butane and isobutane, both well-known compounds, are isomers—they have the same molecular formula but are different compounds that are not readily converted into each other under ordinary conditions. Each can be isolated essentially free of the other. Saturated hydrocarbons with more than three carbon atoms all exhibit *structural isomerism*—the existence of compounds with the same molecular formula but with the atoms joined in a different order. The number of possible structural isomers increases rapidly as the number of carbon atoms in a hydrocarbon increases. One could write 75 different structures for $C_{10}H_{22}$ and over 62 trillion for $C_{40}H_{82}$.

Because the saturated hydrocarbons are composed of only tetrahedral carbon atoms combined with hydrogen atoms, the bond angles are all close to 109.5° (the tetrahedral angle), the C—C bond lengths are all close to 0.154 nm, and the C—H bond lengths are all close to 0.109 nm. As a result, a continuous chain of carbon atoms with attached hydrogen atoms has a staggered, or zigzag, configuration.

(a) configuration of
atoms in butane

$CH_3CH_2CH_2CH_3$

(b) condensed formula
of butane

In the atoms in butane formula (a), the dotted bonds point toward the back of the plane of the paper and the wedge-shaped bonds point toward the viewer. Since each carbon atom can rotate about its bonds, it is possible for a long continuous chain to assume many shapes. The atoms are usually written in straight lines, as shown in (b), with the understanding that the carbon atoms are bonded to each other.

Saturated hydrocarbons can have straight-chain carbon skeletons (as in butane), branched-chain carbon skeletons (as in isobutane), or cyclic, or ring-shaped, carbon chains (as in compounds 7–9, Table 27.7). The straight and branched saturated

Table 27.7
Simple Saturated Hydrocarbons For the first four compounds, the common names are accepted by IUPAC.

Structure	Boiling Point (°C)	Common Name (IUPAC Name)	Structure and Common Name of R Groups
(1) CH_4	−162	Methane	$CH_3—$, methyl
(2) CH_3CH_3	−89	Ethane	$CH_3CH_2—$, ethyl
(3) $CH_3CH_2CH_3$	−42	Propane	$CH_3CH_2CH_2—$, n-propyl
			CH_3CHCH_3, isopropyl
(4) $CH_3(CH_2)_2CH_3$	−0.5	Butane	$CH_3CH_2CH_2CH_2—$, n-butyl
			$CH_3CH_2CHCH_3$, sec-butyl
(5) CH_3CHCH_3 $\quad\ \ CH_3$	−12	Isobutane (2-methylpropane)	$CH_3CHCH_2—$, isobutyl $\quad\ \ CH_3$ CH_3CCH_3, tert-butyl $\quad\ \ CH_3$
(6) $CH_3(CH_2)_3CH_3$	36	Pentane	$CH_3(CH_2)_4—$, n-pentyl (two other $C_5H_{11}—$ groups*)
(7) $H_2C\!\!-\!\!CH_2$ $\quad\ C$ $\quad\ H_2$	−33	Cyclopropane	$H_2C\!\!-\!\!CH—$, cyclopropyl $\quad\ C$ $\quad\ H_2$
(8) $H_2C\!\!-\!\!CH_2$ $H_2C\!\!-\!\!CH_2$	13	Cyclobutane	$H_2C\!\!-\!\!CH—$, cyclobutyl $H_2C\!\!-\!\!CH_2$
(9) $\quad\ H_2$ $\quad\ C$ $H_2C\quad CH_2$ $H_2C\quad CH_2$ $\quad\ C$ $\quad\ H_2$	81	Cyclohexane	$\quad\ H_2$ $\quad\ C$ $H_2C\quad CH—$, cyclohexyl $H_2C\quad CH_2$ $\quad\ C$ $\quad\ H_2$

* The other $C_5H_{11}—$ groups are not usually named as pentane-derived groups.

hydrocarbons are called alkanes. **Alkanes** are saturated hydrocarbons with the general molecular formula C_nH_{2n+2}. Alkanes are also sometimes referred to as *paraffin hydrocarbons.*

As n increases, a sequence of compounds is generated in which each member differs from its immediate neighbor by a CH_2 group. Such a series of compounds that can be represented by a general formula is called a **homologous series.** The first four members of the alkane series are methane, ethane, propane, and butane (1–4, Table 27.7). Note that each name ends in *ane,* indicating an alk*ane.*

It is often convenient to have a name for the group that results when one of the hydrogen atoms in a hydrocarbon molecule, say, a methane molecule, is replaced by another atom or a group of atoms. Thus, CH_3Cl could be called a chloride if the CH_3 group had a name. Such names are obtained by dropping the *ane* of the hydrocarbon name and adding *yl.* Methane becomes *methyl,* ethane becomes *ethyl,* and so on. These groups containing one less hydrogen than an alkane are called **alkyl groups.** Collectively, they are very often represented by the letter R, so that R—H stands for any member of the homologous series of alkanes. Therefore, CH_3Cl is called *methyl chloride,* and RCl represents any unspecified alkyl chloride. Starting with the propyl ($n = 3$) group, isomeric R groups are possible (Table 27.7).

A systematic nomenclature for organic compounds has been formulated by the International Union of Pure and Applied Chemistry. This is known as IUPAC ("eye-you-pack") nomenclature. Two simple rules will introduce you to the IUPAC procedure for naming alkanes with more than four carbon atoms.

1. A prefix (penta, C_5; hexa, C_6; hepta, C_7; octa, C_8; nona, C_9; deca, C_{10}) indicates the longest continuous chain of carbon atoms; the suffix *ane* is added to this prefix (one of the two "a's" is dropped).

$$CH_3CH_2CH_2CH_2CH_3 \quad \text{or} \quad CH_3(CH_2)_3CH_3$$
pentane

$$CH_3CH_2CH_2CH_2CH_2CH_3 \quad \text{or} \quad CH_3(CH_2)_4CH_3$$
hexane

2. The position and name of branches from the main chain, or of atoms other than hydrogen, are added as prefixes to the name of the longest hydrocarbon chain. The position of attachment to the longest continuous chain is given by a number obtained by numbering the longest chain from the end nearest the branch. In this way, the groups attached to the chain are designated by the lowest numbers.

Some examples of this alkane nomenclature are given in Table 27.8. If there is a choice, the number at the beginning of the name should be the lowest number possible, for example,

$$H-\overset{\overset{\displaystyle H}{|}}{\underset{\underset{\displaystyle H}{|}}{C}}-\overset{\overset{\displaystyle Cl}{|}}{\underset{\underset{\displaystyle Cl}{|}}{C}}-\overset{\overset{\displaystyle H}{|}}{\underset{\underset{\displaystyle H}{|}}{C}}-\overset{\overset{\displaystyle H}{|}}{\underset{\underset{\displaystyle H}{|}}{C}}-\overset{\overset{\displaystyle H}{|}}{\underset{\underset{\displaystyle H}{|}}{C}}-\overset{\overset{\displaystyle Cl}{|}}{\underset{\underset{\displaystyle H}{|}}{C}}-H$$

is named 1,5,5-trichlorohexane, not 2,2,6-trichlorohexane, because 1 is smaller than 2. Common, or trivial, names—names not based on the currently recommended system of nomenclature—persist for many compounds, such as isooctane (Table 27.8). We often give both systematic and common names.

Compounds in which the carbon atoms of a saturated hydrocarbon are joined together in a ring are called cycloalkanes (also alicyclic hydrocarbons or cycloparaffins). **Cycloalkanes** are cyclic saturated hydrocarbons that have the general molecular formula C_nH_{2n}. The nomenclature of cycloalkanes follows the same pattern used

Table 27.8
Examples of Systematic Alkane Nomenclature

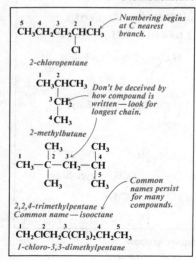

for the noncyclic alkanes. If there are substituents, one is given the number 1 and others are given the lowest possible numbers.

cyclopropane   abbreviated as

1,2-dichlorocyclohexane   abbreviated as

In the abbreviated expressions, we understand without writing them that there is a carbon atom at each corner and that sufficient hydrogen atoms are present to complete four bonds to each carbon atom.

At this point, close examination of Tables 27.7 and 27.8 will be very helpful. The principles of nomenclature illustrated there are used repeatedly. Note that a carbon atom joined to only one other carbon atom is called a *primary carbon atom,* often designated by 1°; one joined to two other carbon atoms, a *secondary (2°) carbon atom* (as in the *sec*-butyl group); and one joined to three carbon atoms, a *tertiary (3°)* carbon atom (as in the *tert*-butyl group). A carbon atom joined to four other carbon atoms is a *quarternary (4°) carbon atom.*

Unbranched hydrocarbons are referred to as **normal hydrocarbons,** as in "normal hexane," written *n*-hexane. When the letter *n* is omitted, it is assumed that the normal structure is meant.

$$CH_3CH_2CH_2CH_2CH_2CH_3$$
n-hexane or hexane

(Nuclear magnetic resonance spectroscopy is a technique that yields information about the structure of hydrocarbons and other organic compounds; see Tools of Chemistry: Nuclear Magnetic Resonance.)

EXAMPLE 27.2
Organic Nomenclature: Alkanes

Write the structural formula for 2,3-dimethylbutane. Indicate the primary, secondary, tertiary, and quaternary carbon atoms.

The "butane" part of this name tells us that the longest straight carbon chain in this compound consists of four carbon atoms:

$$C—C—C—C$$

The prefix "2,3-dimethyl" indicates that there are methyl groups, CH_3—, attached to the second and third carbon atoms:

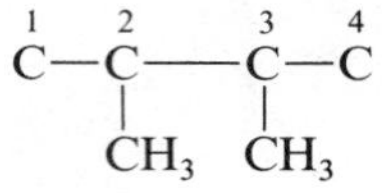

$$\overset{1}{C}-\overset{2}{\underset{\underset{CH_3}{|}}{C}}-\overset{3}{\underset{\underset{CH_3}{|}}{C}}-\overset{4}{C}$$

Filling in hydrogen atoms so that each carbon atom has four covalent bonds gives

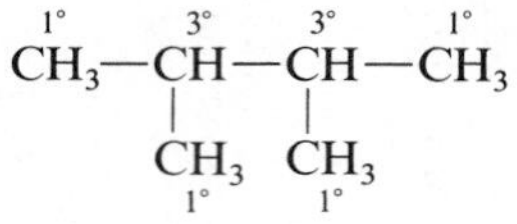

$$\overset{1°}{CH_3}-\overset{3°}{\underset{\underset{1°}{\underset{CH_3}{|}}}{CH}}-\overset{3°}{\underset{\underset{1°}{\underset{CH_3}{|}}}{CH}}-\overset{1°}{CH_3}$$

As indicated above, there are four primary carbon atoms — carbon atoms joined to only one other carbon atom — and two tertiary carbon atoms — carbon atoms joined to three other carbon atoms.

Exercise Write the structural formula for 2,2-dimethylpropane. Indicate the primary, secondary, tertiary, and quaternary carbon atoms. *Answer*

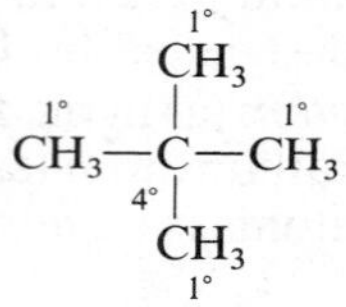

$$\overset{1°}{\underset{\underset{4°}{|}}{CH_3}}\atop{CH_3-\underset{\underset{\underset{1°}{CH_3}}{|}}{C}-CH_3}$$

EXAMPLE 27.3
Organic Nomenclature: Alkanes

Give the IUPAC name for

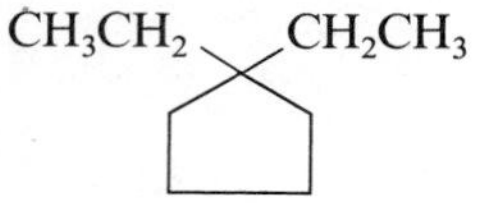

$$CH_3CH_2 \diagdown \quad \diagup CH_2CH_3$$

Indicate the primary, secondary, tertiary, and quarternary carbon atoms in this compound.

The "parent" hydrocarbon in this structure is the ring containing five carbon atoms — the *cyclopentane ring*. The two groups attached to the ring each have two carbon atoms; these are ethyl groups, indicating that this compound is a *diethylcyclopentane*. Both ethyl groups are attached to the same carbon atom, which we give the number 1. The complete name is *1,1-diethylcyclopentane*. The molecule contains two primary, six secondary, and one quarternary carbon atoms.

$$\overset{1°}{CH_3}-\overset{2°}{CH_2}\qquad\overset{2°}{CH_2}-\overset{1°}{CH_3}$$

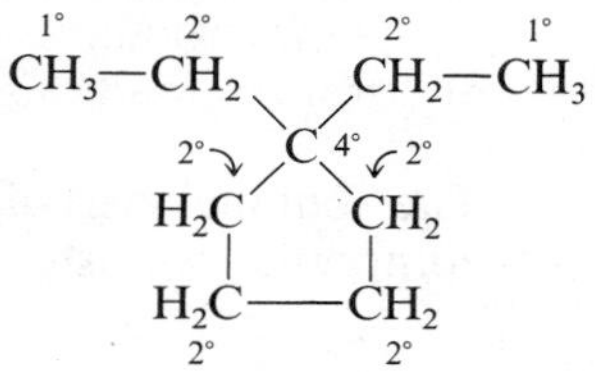

Exercise Give the IUPAC name for

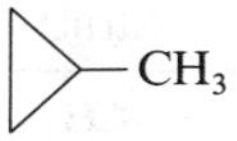

$$\triangleright\!-\!CH_3$$

Indicate the primary, secondary, tertiary, and quarternary carbon atoms in this compound. *Answer* methylcyclopropane

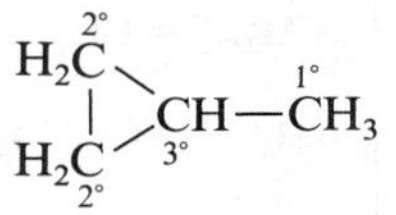

$$\begin{array}{c} \overset{2°}{H_2C} \\ | \quad \overset{1°}{CH}\!-\!CH_3 \\ \underset{2°}{H_2C} \quad {}_{3°} \end{array}$$

27.6 UNSATURATED HYDROCARBONS

a. Nomenclature Hydrocarbons that possess covalent double bonds or covalent triple bonds between carbon atoms are said to be **unsaturated hydrocarbons.** This term arises from the ability of the atoms in such bonds to accept additional atoms, or groups of atoms.

Hydrocarbons with covalent double bonds are called **olefins** or **alkenes** (IUPAC). Hydrocarbons with covalent triple bonds are called **acetylenes** or **alkynes** (IUPAC). To derive the systematic names of the individual alkenes, the *ane* of the corresponding saturated hydrocarbon name is dropped and *ene* is added if one double bond is present, *adiene* is added if two double bonds are present, and so on. For example,

CH_3CH_3	$CH_2\!=\!CH_2$	$CH_2\!=\!CHCH\!=\!CH_2$
ethane	*ethene*	*1,3-butadiene*

Similarly, the individual alkynes are named by dropping the *ane* and adding *yne, adiyne, atriyne,* and so on. In either case, the position of the multiple bond is indicated by numbering from the end of the chain, starting at the end that will assign the lower number to the first carbon atom of the multiple bond. For example,

$$CH_3CH_2CH_2CH_2CH_3 \qquad \overset{5}{C}H_3\overset{4}{C}\!\equiv\!\overset{3}{C}\!-\!\overset{2}{C}\!\equiv\!\overset{1}{C}H$$
pentane   *1,3-pentadiyne*

In the common system of nomenclature, the *ane* ending of the saturated hydrocarbon name is replaced by *ylene* for the olefins. Compounds containing triple bonds are sometimes named as substituted acetylenes. (Because of the triple bond between the carbon atoms in acetylene, each carbon can have only one group attached to it.) Table 27.9 illustrates these naming systems. Study the table and be sure you understand how the names were assigned.

Cycloalkenes are common, but cycloalkynes exist only for C_8 or larger rings. The triple bond is not flexible enough to fit easily into smaller rings.

Beginning with propylene, alkenes of the homologous series of molecular formula C_nH_{2n} are isomeric with cycloalkanes.

Saturated: only single bonds
Unsaturated: contains double and/or triple bonds

Alkanes: C_nH_{2n+2}
Cycloalkanes: C_nH_{2n}
Alkenes: C_nH_{2n}
Cycloalkenes: C_nH_{2n-2}
Alkynes: C_nH_{2n-2}

$$CH_3CH\!=\!CH_2 \qquad\qquad \begin{array}{c} H_2C\!-\!\!-\!\!-\!CH_2 \\ \diagdown\;\diagup \\ C \\ H_2 \end{array}$$
propene, C_3H_6   *cyclopropane, C_3H_6*

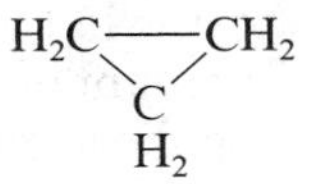

Table 27.9
Simple Unsaturated Hydrocarbons

Structure	Boiling Point (°C)	Common Name (IUPAC Name)	Structure and Common Name of R Group
$CH_2{=}CH_2$	-102	Ethylene (ethene)	$CH_2{=}CH-$, vinyl
$CH_3CH{=}CH_2$	-48	Propylene (propene)	$CH_2{=}CHCH_2-$, allyl
$CH_3CH_2CH{=}CH_2$	-7	α-Butylene (1-butene)	—
$(CH_3)_2C{=}CH_2$	-7	Isobutylene (2-methylpropene)	—
$CH_3CH{=}CHCH_3$	-4 (cis)	β-Butylene (2-butene)	$CH_3CH{=}CHCH_2-$, crotyl
$HC{\equiv}CH$	-83	Acetylene (ethyne)	$HC{\equiv}C-$, ethynyl
$CH_3C{\equiv}CH$	-23	Methylacetylene (propyne)	$HC{\equiv}CCH_2-$, propargyl
$CH_2{=}CH-C{\equiv}CH$	3	Vinylacetylene (1-buten-3-yne)	—

Acetylenes of the series of molecular formula C_2H_{2n-2} with $n > 2$ are isomeric with cycloalkenes.

$$CH_3C{\equiv}CH$$

propyne

$$HC{=\!=\!=}CH$$
$$C$$
$$H_2$$

cyclopropene

b. Properties associated with double bonds The two carbon atoms in a double bond and the four other atoms to which they are bonded all lie in the same plane. This configuration is attributed to the planar sp^2 hybrid orbitals which form the three σ bonds at each carbon atom. The region of the double bond in any molecule is thus flat.

Covalent double bonds that alternate with single covalent bonds are said to be **conjugated double bonds.** For example, the long straight chain in the natural pigment β-carotene, which gives carrots their orange color, contains a series of conjugated double bonds (Figure 27.6). The color in such compounds arises because of the extensive delocalized π bonding present in the system of conjugated double bonds. In terms of molecular orbital theory, the color is explained as due to the absorption of light by electrons in the highest π bonding molecular orbitals, which may be excited to the lowest π antibonding orbitals. In general, the gap between these molecular orbitals becomes smaller as the delocalization is extended over a larger number of atoms. As a result, the wavelength of light absorbed is shifted into the visible region and the compound appears colored. (Color in chemical compounds is further discussed in Section 32.11.)

The rotation relative to one another of two carbon atoms joined by a double bond is inhibited by the π bond which lies above and below the plane of the σ bonds. The π bond must be broken if rotation of the carbon atoms is to take place. As pointed out in our discussion of bonding (Section 11.7), this restricted rotation means that *cis–trans* isomerism can occur. For example, 2-butene (Figure 27.7) exists in two forms that are not interconvertible without supplying the considerable amount of energy needed to break the π bond. The form with the two methyl groups on the same side of the double bond is the *cis* form, that with the two methyl groups on opposite sides is the *trans* form. When the groups are large enough to get in each

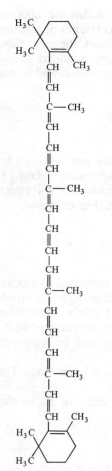

Figure 27.6
β-Carotene, the Pigment in Carrots

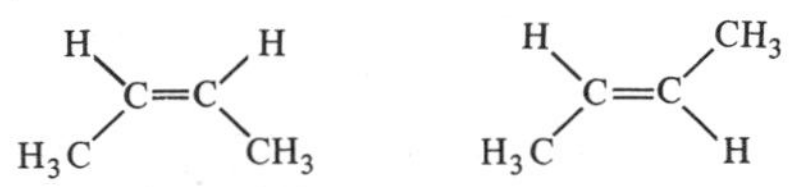

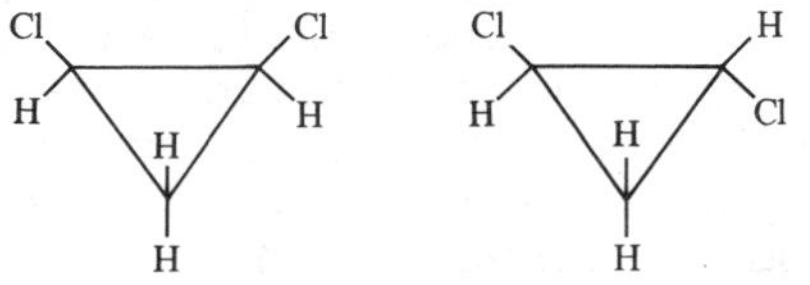

Figure 27.7
Cis-Trans Isomerism

cis-2-butene   trans-2-butene

cis-1,2-dichloro-   trans-1,2-dichloro-
cyclopropane   cyclopropane

other's way—called **steric hindrance**—the *trans* form is normally more stable than the *cis* form. In cycloalkanes the carbon atoms also cannot rotate, so *cis–trans* isomerism exists in such compounds too, as in *cis*-1,2-dichlorocyclopropane and *trans*-1,2-dichlorocyclopropane (see Figure 27.7).

EXAMPLE 27.4
Organic Nomenclature: Alkenes and Alkynes

Write the structural formula for 3,4-dimethyl-3-hexene. Write the structural formula for any *cis* or *trans* isomer that might exist.

The "3-hexene" part of the name tells us that the longest straight carbon chain in this compound consists of six carbon atoms with one double bond between the third and fourth carbon atoms.

$$\overset{1}{C}-\overset{2}{C}-\overset{3}{C}=\overset{4}{C}-\overset{5}{C}-\overset{6}{C}$$

The "3,4-dimethyl" prefix indicates that there are two methyl groups, one attached to the third carbon atom and one attached to the fourth carbon atom.

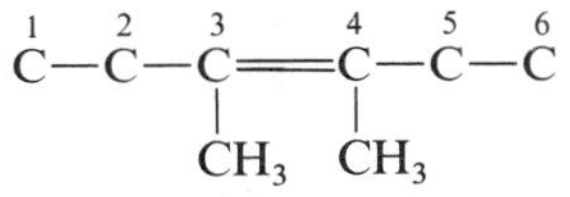

$$\overset{1}{C}-\overset{2}{C}-\overset{3}{C}=\overset{4}{C}-\overset{5}{C}-\overset{6}{C}$$
$$\qquad\qquad | \qquad |$$
$$\qquad\quad CH_3 \quad CH_3$$

Filling in hydrogen atoms so that each carbon atom has four covalent bonds gives

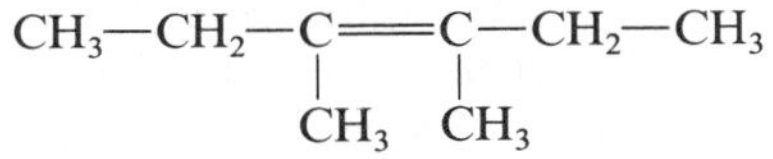

$$CH_3-CH_2-C=C-CH_2-CH_3$$
$$\qquad\qquad | \quad |$$
$$\qquad\quad CH_3 \ CH_3$$

As we have written this structural formula, it is a *cis* isomer. A *trans* isomer is also possible:

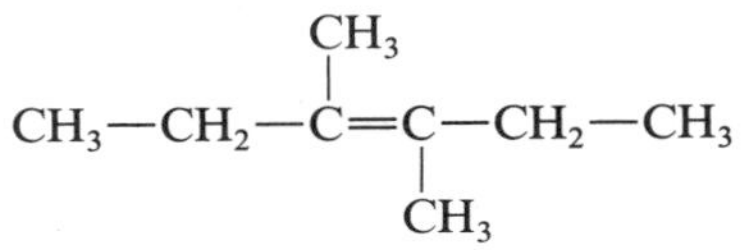

$$\qquad\qquad\qquad CH_3$$
$$\qquad\qquad\qquad |$$
$$CH_3-CH_2-C=C-CH_2-CH_3$$
$$\qquad\qquad\qquad |$$
$$\qquad\qquad\qquad CH_3$$

Exercise Write the IUPAC name for $CH_3C\equiv CCH_2CH_3$. Give the structural formulas for any *cis–trans* isomers that might exist. *Answer* 2-pentyne, no *cis–trans* isomers possible

A proton spins about its axis in the same way that an electron does, and the spinning produces a small magnetic moment. Because of this magnetic moment, the proton behaves like a tiny magnet: In an external magnetic field the proton aligns itself either parallel to the field or opposite, called antiparallel, to the field. Being parallel to the field is a somewhat lower energy condition than being antiparallel to the field. By allowing protons in a magnetic field to absorb energy in the radio frequency (rf) range of the electromagnetic spectrum, they can be made to change their alignment. This absorption is the basis for a spectroscopic technique.

Nuclear magnetic resonance (NMR) spectroscopy is the study of the structure of molecules as revealed by the absorption of radio frequency radiation by nuclei. When the nuclei being studied are protons, the technique is referred to as proton magnetic resonance (PMR). Some of the other nuclei that have net spin and can also be studied by nuclear magnetic resonance are deuterium (^2H), boron (^{11}B), carbon (^{13}C), and oxygen (^{17}O). Here we are interested only in the proton and what can be learned from its magnetic resonance.

The spectrum is measured by placing the sample, in solution, in an rf field of constant frequency and varying the strength of an applied magnetic field. At certain values of the applied magnetic field absorption of rf energy occurs, the alignment of the spin changes, and the energy absorption is detected and recorded.

The primary use of proton magnetic resonance spectroscopy is in the determination of the structure of organic compounds. The magnetic field strength at which a proton absorbs rf energy varies with the chemical environment of that proton.

Consider the methane and ethane molecules. The four protons in methane all have the same chemical environment, and so do the six protons in ethane. In propane, however, the protons have two different types of surroundings.

propane

Six protons have environment a (part of a CH_3 group) and two protons have environment b (part of a $-CH_2-$ group). In a nuclear magnetic resonance spectrum, methane and ethane each give only one peak, but propane gives two peaks. And, making NMR an even more useful technique, the areas under the two peaks in the propane spectrum are proportional to the number of protons of each type — they have the ratio 6:2.

The variation in applied magnetic field at which protons in different environments absorb rf energy is called the *chemical shift*. Since it is not possible to measure the absorption of rf energy by a free proton, chemical shift must be measured relative to a specific standard. Most often the standard is tetramethylsilane, TMS,

a compound with only one type of H environment and a peak that appears conveniently near one end of the spectrum. The chemical shift of a particular peak is the difference between its absorption and that of TMS (the zero of the chemical shift scale). It is reported in parts per million, and called δ (delta):

$$\delta \text{ (in ppm)} = \frac{B_r - B}{B_r} \times 10^6$$

where B_r is the reference magnetic field strength (that at which absorption by TMS occurs) and B is the magnetic field strength at which absorption by the substance being studied is observed.

As an example of the kinds of information that can be obtained from an NMR spectrum, we examine the spectrum of 3-methyl-1-butene, given in Figure A. Ignoring for a moment the splitting, or small peaks, in each group—the four areas of absorption show that there are four proton environments in the molecule, which is as it should be.

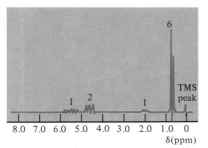

Figure A
Nuclear Magnetic Resonance Spectrum of 3-Methy-1-Butene

$$\overset{a}{CH_3}\overset{b}{CH}\overset{c}{CH}=\overset{d}{CH_2}$$
$$\underset{a}{|}$$
$$\underset{a}{CH_3}$$

3-methyl-1-butene

The relative areas of 1 : 2 : 1 : 6 under the four groups of peaks show, as we can see in the structure, that there are six H's of one type (*a*), two of a second type (*d*), and one each of two other types (*b,c*). From the study of many spectra, the chemical shift ranges for different types of protons are known. Compare the following values with the spectrum: CH_3—C, 0.95–0.85; CH—, 1.6–1.4; HC=C, 4.8–6.2. With this information the complete structure of the compound could be worked out. The splitting into several peaks of the absorption peak for protons in each type of chemical environment is caused by the influence of the magnetic moment of the protons on *adjacent* atoms. With experience, additional information about structure can be obtained from the splitting.

The chemical shift values for hydrogen bonded to atoms other than carbon and in different types of chemical environments have been extensively tabulated. Since its discovery in 1946, NMR spectroscopy has rapidly become an important tool in organic structure determination and also for studying many types of inorganic compounds.

27.7 AROMATIC HYDROCARBONS

Benzene, C_6H_6, is the parent of a large family of compounds known as aromatic hydrocarbons. In Sections 11.7c and 24.10, we described the bonding in benzene in terms of two resonance structures and the delocalization of electrons in molecular orbitals, respectively.

benzene, resonance structures

benzene, structure emphasizing delocalized electrons

Aromatic hydrocarbons are unsaturated hydrocarbons containing planar ring systems stabilized by delocalized electrons, as in benzene. The pleasant odor of compounds containing such ring systems originally suggested the name "aromatic," but many not-so-sweet-smelling "aromatic" compounds are now known. Instead, their similar structures and chemical reactions are the basis for treating aromatic compounds as a group. Aromatic hydrocarbons are so distinct and different from other hydrocarbons that we have a general term for the others too. **Aliphatic hydrocarbons** are hydrocarbons that contain no aromatic rings. Saturated, unsaturated, and cyclic hydrocarbons with no aromatic rings are all aliphatic compounds.

Aromatic: rings with delocalized π bonding
Aliphatic: no aromatic rings

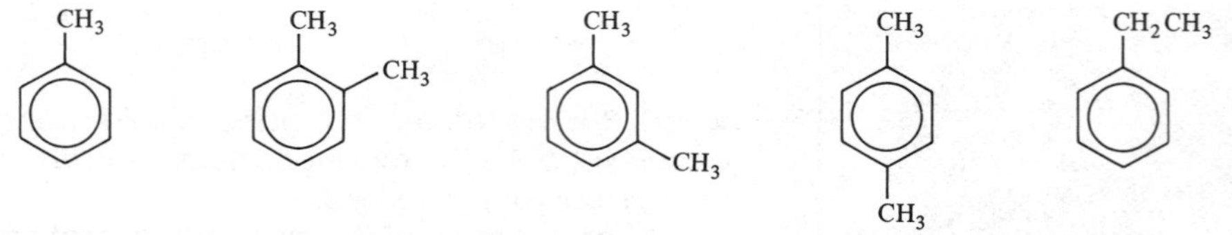

Figure 27.8
Some Simple Substituted Benzene Hydrocarbons

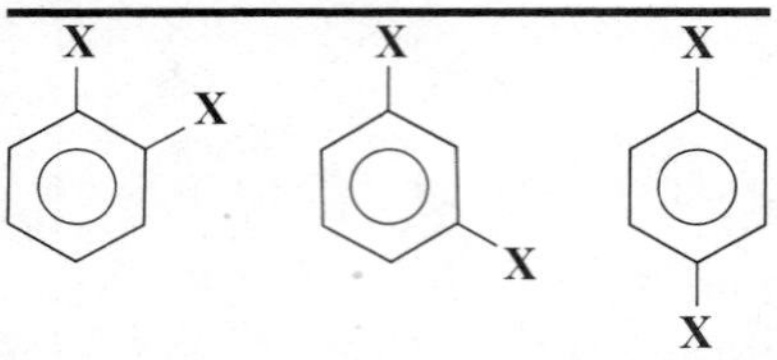

toluene b.p. 111°C   *o-xylene* b.p. 144°C   *m-xylene* b.p. 139°C   *p-xylene* b.p. 138°C   *ethylbenzene* b.p. 136°C

ortho   *meta*   *para*

Benzene is a colorless liquid, b.p. 80 °C, that burns with a very sooty flame, a property that is characteristic of aromatic hydrocarbons. Figure 27.8 illustrates some aromatic hydrocarbons derived from benzene. The added groups are referred to as *substituents*. The name of a single substituent is added to "benzene" as a prefix, as in ethylbenzene. Three structurally isomeric forms are possible for a disubstituted benzene, whether or not the substituents are the same. The three possibilities are designated *ortho* (abbreviated *o-*), *meta* (abbreviated *m-*), and *para* (abbreviated *p-*), as shown below and for the xylenes in Figure 27.8.

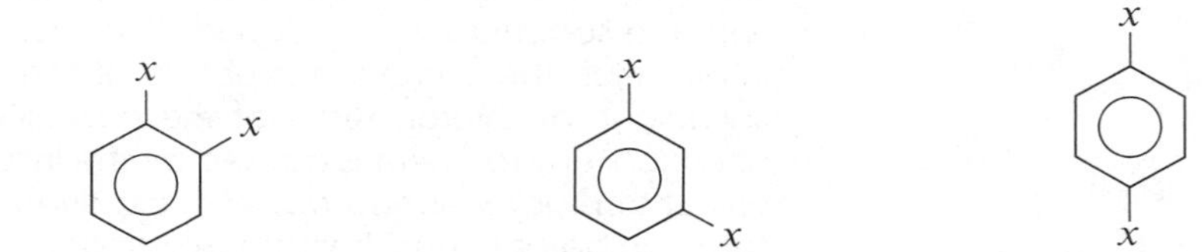

ortho substitution   *meta substitution*   *para substitution*

Numbers are also used to show the positions of substituents in aromatic compounds. Unless there is no question of what the structure is, as in hexachloro-benzene, numbers are always used to locate the substituents when three or more are present in the ring.

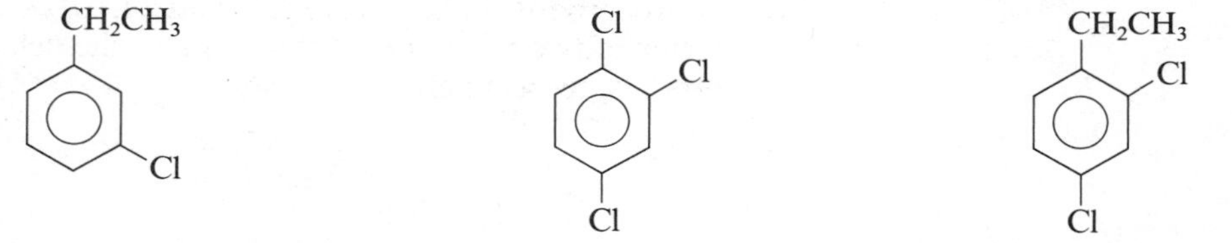

m-chloroethylbenzene or 3-chloroethylbenzene   *1,2,4-trichlorobenzene*   *2,4-dichloroethylbenzene*

The benzene molecule less one hydrogen atom is known as the *phenyl group*, C_6H_5. Diphenylmethane, for example, is $(C_6H_5)_2CH_2$.

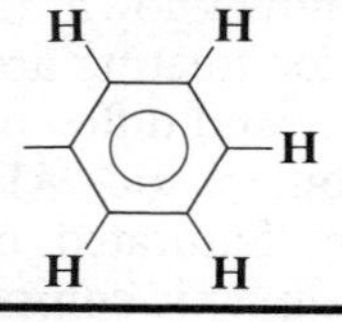

Polycyclic aromatic hydrocarbons contain two or more aromatic rings fused together. ("Fused" rings have in common a bond between the same two atoms.) Some examples are given in Figure 27.9. Several resonance forms can be written for each of these compounds. Numbers are assigned by convention to carbon atoms in fused ring systems (except to those at the points of fusion, where substitution is not possible). The locations of substituents are identified by the assigned numbers, as shown in the figure for naphthalene.

Phenyl group:

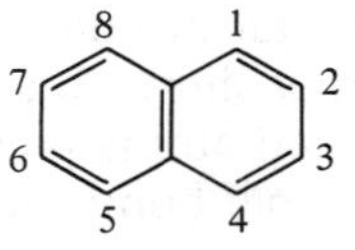

Figure 27.9
Some Simple Polycyclic Aromatic Hydrocarbons The positions on the rings are numbered by convention as shown. Numbers are not assigned to the positions where rings are joined because substituents do not bond at these positions (there are no replaceable hydrogen atoms).

naphthalene
m.p. 80°C

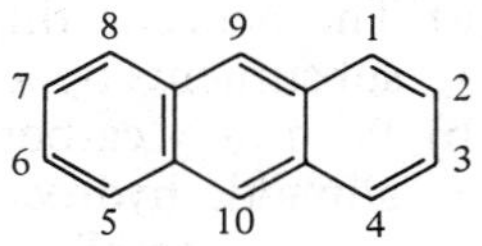

anthracene
m.p. 218°C

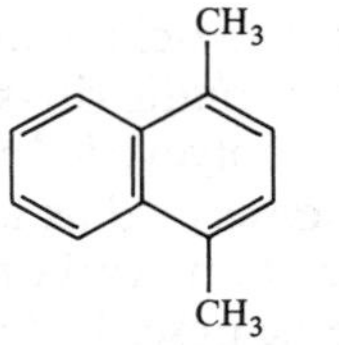

1,4-dimethylnaphthalene
m.p. 7.6°C

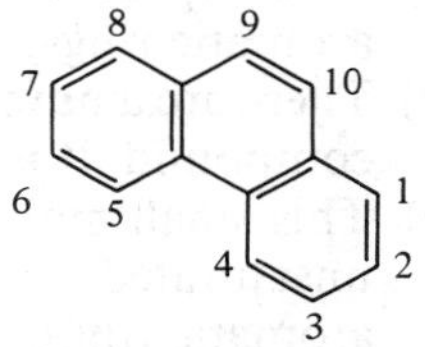

phenanthrene
m.p. 100°C

EXAMPLE 27.5
Organic Nomenclature: Aromatic Hydrocarbons

Give a name for

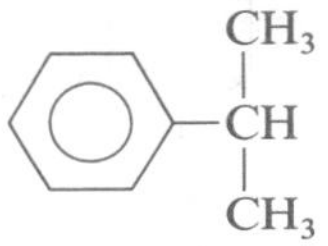

A benzene ring with a single alkyl substituent is named by adding the alkyl group name as a prefix. The common name for this group is "isopropyl" (see Table 27.7) and the compound is named isopropylbenzene.

Exercise Write the structural formula for 1-methylnaphthalene (see Figure 27.9). *Answer*

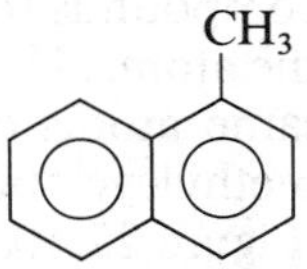

EXAMPLE 27.6
Structure of Organic Molecules

Are the following compounds aromatic or aliphatic; saturated or unsaturated; alkanes, alkenes, or alkynes; branched or straight chains? In what other ways, if any, might these compounds each be described (other than by their names)?

(a)

(b) $HC \equiv C - CH_2CH_2CH_3$

(c) $CH_3CH_2CH_2CHCH_3$
$|$
CH_2
$|$
CH_2
$|$
CH_3

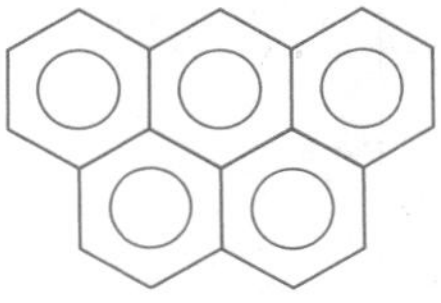

(e) $CH_3CH = CH_2$

(d)

(a) The benzene ring makes this an aromatic compound. The location of the substituents opposite each other shows this to be a para-substituted benzene.

(b) With only carbon and hydrogen atoms present in a straight chain, this is an aliphatic hydrocarbon. The triple bond makes it an unsaturated compound which is an alkyne, or an acetylene. The compound can also be described as a straight-chain compound.

(c) This hydrocarbon is saturated (no double or triple bonds) and aliphatic (no aromatic rings), and is a branched-chain alkane.

(d) There are a number of fused aromatic rings with no substituents present in this compound. It is an aromatic, polycyclic hydrocarbon.

(e) This small molecule can be described as a straight-chain hydrocarbon that is unsaturated (it contains a carbon–carbon double bond). It is aliphatic (no aromatic rings) and can also be described as an olefin or an alkene.

Exercise Use the terms given above to describe the following molecules:

(a)

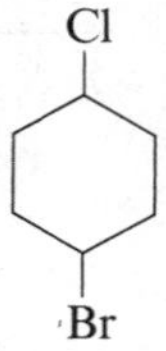

(b) $CH_3CH_2CH_2CH_3$

(c) $CH_3CH=CHCH=CHCH_3$

Answer (a) aliphatic, saturated, substituted cycloalkane; (b) aliphatic, saturated, alkane, straight chain; (c) aliphatic, unsaturated, alkene, straight chain (also a conjugated diene)

27.8 OPTICAL ISOMERISM

To review for a moment, we have thus far encountered two types of isomers, that is, compounds that have the same molecular formula but differ in the arrangement of the atoms. In *structural isomerism* the atoms are arranged in a different order — the same atoms are not attached to each other. Examples of structural isomers are methylcyclobutane and cyclopentane, or the three possible isomeric diethylbenzenes (Figure 27.10a).

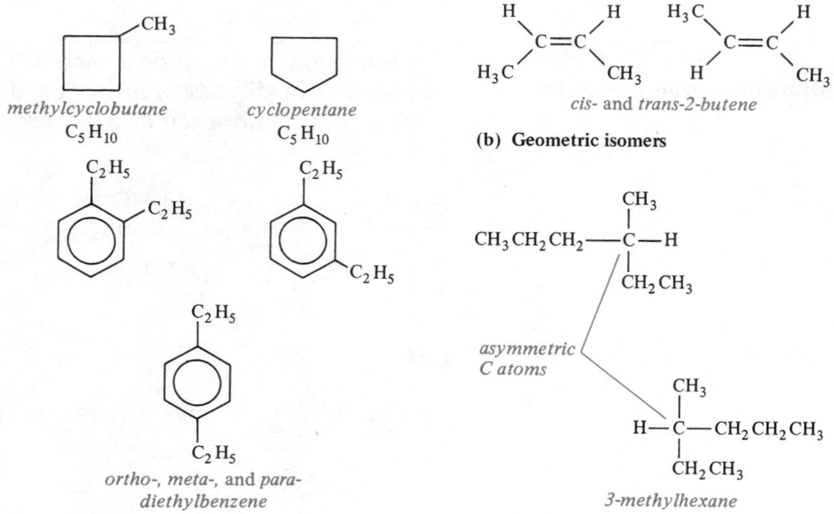

Figure 27.10
Isomers Examples of the three types of isomerism.

methylcyclobutane
C_5H_{10}

cyclopentane
C_5H_{10}

ortho-, meta-, and para-diethylbenzene

(a) Structural isomers

cis- and *trans-2-butene*

(b) Geometric isomers

asymmetric C atoms

3-methylhexane

(c) Optical isomers

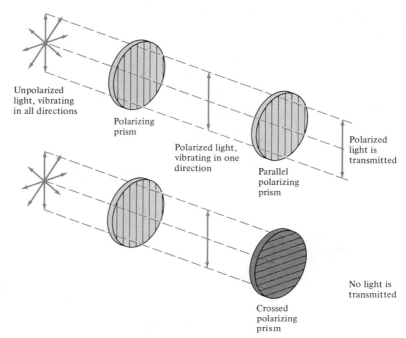

Figure 27.11
Polarized Light The effect of parallel and crossed polarizers can be observed with a pair of lenses from polarizing sunglasses.

cis: **groups on same side**
trans: **groups on opposite sides**

Structural isomers: atoms bonded in different order

Cis – trans **(geometrical) isomers: groups arranged differently with respect to double bond**

Optical isomers (enantiomers): mirror image structures

In *cis – trans,* or *geometric, isomerism* (Section 11.7b), the same kinds of atoms are bonded to each other. However, the groups are arranged in different ways on either side of a covalent double bond, as in *cis-* and *trans*-2-butene (Figure 27.10b), or some other rigid structure such as a ring (see Figure 27.6). The physical properties of structural isomers and of *cis – trans* isomers are usually different.

There is a third kind of isomerism in which the isomers are almost identical in their properties and as a result are difficult to separate. This type of isomerism is detected by the use of polarized light and is called optical isomerism. All classes of organic compounds and many inorganic compounds can exhibit this type of isomerism. **Optical isomerism** is the occurrence of pairs of molecules of the same molecular formula that rotate plane-polarized light in opposite directions.

Ordinary light rays vibrate in all planes perpendicular to the direction of travel of the rays. When such light is passed through a polarizing prism or a piece of polarizing plastic like that used in Polaroid sunglasses, the part of the light that is transmitted vibrates in one plane only and is called **plane-polarized light** (Figure 27.11). When a beam of plane-polarized light passes through certain substances or their solutions, the plane of vibration of the light is rotated. The amount of rotation varies from compound to compound and is measured by an instrument called a polarimeter (Figure 27.12).

What is the nature of organic substances that rotate the plane of vibration of plane-polarized light? A simple example of an optically active substance is one in which a single atom is bonded to four different kinds of atoms or groups. For example, in 3-methylhexane,

$$
\begin{array}{c}
\text{H} \\
| \\
\text{CH}_3\text{CH}_2\text{CCH}_2\text{CH}_2\text{CH}_3 \\
| \\
\text{CH}_3
\end{array}
$$

an asymmetric carbon atom

3-methylhexane

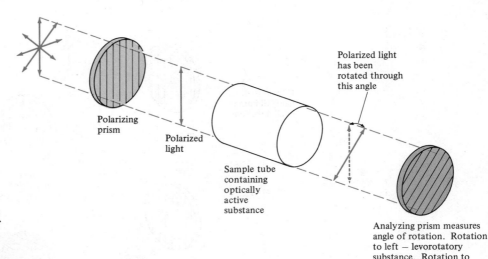

Polarizing prism

Polarized light

Sample tube containing optically active substance

Polarized light has been rotated through this angle

Analyzing prism measures angle of rotation. Rotation to left — levorotatory substance. Rotation to right — dextrorotatory substance.

Figure 27.12
Principle of a Polarimeter The extent to which the plane of polarization has been rotated by the sample is determined by rotating the analyzing prism until transmission of the beam is maximized.

Asymmetric carbon: bonded to four different groups

the number 3 carbon atom in the hexane chain is bonded to an ethyl group, a methyl group, a hydrogen atom, and a propyl group. Such an atom bonded to four different kinds of atoms or groups is said to be an **asymmetric atom.** One cannot cut a molecule containing such an atom—or indeed, any asymmetric structure—into two halves that are identical as one might, say, cut a Frisbee into two identical halves.

If an object is asymmetric, it has a nonsuperimposable mirror image. A most familiar example of an asymmetric object is your left or right hand. Hold your two hands up, palms facing each other. You can imagine that each is the mirror image of the other. Now try to place one hand on top of the other so that *all* parts coincide— you will find that it can't be done.

An asymmetric carbon atom in a molecule causes the molecule to rotate the plane of vibration of plane-polarized light. Such a molecule is said to be **optically active.** (The carbon atom itself is not asymmetric, of course; it is the molecule containing a tetrahedral carbon atom with four different kinds of attached groups that is asymmetric. The carbon atom is *asymmetrically substituted.*)

As with your left and right hands, for every asymmetric molecule there exists a nonsuperimposable mirror image isomer that is also optically active. An asymmetric molecule cannot be placed over its mirror image and have all parts coincide. The two forms have different *spatial configurations.* Figure 27.13 represents the mirror image configuration of 3-methylhexane in two dimensions. (Looking at three-dimensional models will help in seeing the difference.) **Chirality** is the property of having two forms which are nonsuperimposable mirror images. A molecule that has a nonsuperimposable mirror image and is therefore optically active is spoken of as a *chiral* molecule.

One optically active isomer rotates plane-polarized light counterclockwise, or to the left, and is called *levorotatory.* The other isomer rotates plane-polarized light clockwise, or to the right, and is called *dextrorotatory.* The members of such pairs are called **enantiomers** or **optical isomers.** In solutions of equal concentrations, optical isomers rotate plane-polarized light equally in opposite directions. The individual molecules are referred to as the L-isomer and the D-isomer. In most properties, such as melting point, boiling point, and solubility, two optical isomers behave identically and appear to have the same molecular structure. However, the dextro and levo forms can differ greatly in their reactivity toward other optically active substances.

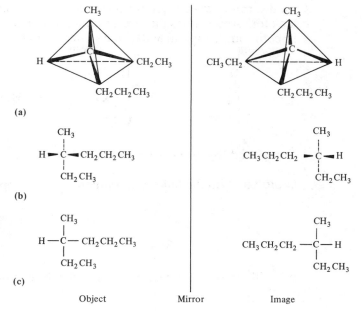

Figure 27.13
Enantiomeric Forms of 3-methylhexane (a) Three-dimensional representation; (b) simulated three-dimensional models; (c) Fischer projections of the models in (b). In a Fischer projection, horizontal lines represent bonds that project outward toward the reader and vertical lines represent bonds that project away from the reader.

Object   Mirror   Image

A mixture of equal parts of the levorotatory isomer and the dextrorotatory isomer of the same substance—a **racemic mixture**—shows no net rotation of polarized light as a result of the cancellation of the equal and opposite rotation of the isomers. Such a mixture is optically inactive.

A laboratory synthesis in which a compound with an asymmetric center is formed from one or more nonchiral compounds gives a racemic mixture. The separation of the optical isomers in a racemic mixture, a process called **resolution,** can often be accomplished by converting the isomers temporarily into derivatives that are no longer mirror images, and hence have different solubilities. Once the compounds are separated the isomers can be regenerated.

Many naturally occurring substances exist only as one or the other member of an enantiomeric pair. This implies that the plants or animals producing these substances must synthesize them by methods very different from those that are used in the chemistry laboratory. Furthermore, living systems are often able to distinguish between optical isomers that are administered to them. For example, *only* the dextrorotatory form of an optically active drug might be effective in a specific case, while the levorotatory isomer might have little or no effect or even be toxic. It is this biological specificity that often requires considerable ingenuity in the synthesis of compounds that duplicate complex natural products. Often several asymmetric atoms are present in a single molecule and the number of possible optically active isomers is quite large. [Molecular asymmetry also occurs in molecules with no asymmetrically substituted atoms.]

EXAMPLE 27.7
Optical isomerism

Which of the following compounds can exhibit optical isomerism? Draw structural formulas (like the "Fischer projections" in Figure 27.13) which show the asymmetric carbon atoms.

(a) $CH_3CHBrCH_2CH_3$
(b) $CH_2BrCH_2CH_2CH_3$
(c) $CH_2ClCHBrCH_3$

To determine whether or not these compounds can have optical isomers, we can look for carbon atoms that are asymmetric — that have four different substituents. In both compounds (a) and (c) the second carbon atom from the left is asymmetric.

$$
\text{(a)} \quad CH_3-\underset{\underset{CH_2CH_3}{|}}{\overset{\overset{H}{|}}{C}}-Br \qquad Br-\underset{\underset{CH_2CH_3}{|}}{\overset{\overset{H}{|}}{C}}-CH_3 \qquad \text{(c)} \quad ClCH_2-\underset{\underset{Br}{|}}{\overset{\overset{H}{|}}{C}}-CH_3 \qquad CH_3-\underset{\underset{Br}{|}}{\overset{\overset{H}{|}}{C}}-CH_2Cl
$$

Compound (b) has no asymmetric carbon atom.

Exercise Will the following compound exhibit optical isomerism?

$$
CH_2=CHCHCH_3 \\
\quad\quad\quad\quad | \\
\quad\quad\quad\quad Cl
$$

If it will, draw the Fischer projections for the enantiomeric pair. *Answer* yes

$$
CH_2=CH-\underset{\underset{Cl}{|}}{\overset{\overset{H}{|}}{C}}-CH_3 \qquad\qquad CH_3-\underset{\underset{Cl}{|}}{\overset{\overset{H}{|}}{C}}-CH=CH_2
$$

27.9 PROPERTIES AND REACTIONS OF HYDROCARBONS

**Hydrocarbons:
insoluble in water
soluble in each other**

The properties of hydrocarbons are to a large extent those imparted by the covalent bond (Section 9.16) in combination with those imparted by intermolecular forces (Section 11.8–11.12). In solubility, the behavior of hydrocarbons reflects the fact that they are nonpolar. Hydrocarbons are virtually insoluble in water but are soluble in each other. Most hydrocarbons are less dense than water and float on the surface. Within any series of similar alkanes, alkenes, or aromatic hydrocarbons, melting points and boiling points generally increase with increasing molecular mass (as shown by the boiling points given in Tables 27.7 and 27.9). Alkanes containing eighteen or more carbon atoms are waxy solids at room temperature (the paraffins).

All hydrocarbons, as we know, burn readily. Otherwise, the reactivity of hydrocarbons varies with the presence or absence of multiple covalent bonds and with whether or not the compound is aromatic.

A polar bond in a molecule presents a likely site for a chemical reaction (this is further discussed in Section 33.2). Since the bond polarity of the C—H bond is relatively small, saturated hydrocarbons do not show a high degree of chemical reactivity at the C—H bonds. The C—C bond is also unreactive, as might be predicted. The alkanes are not attacked at room temperature by acids, bases, or oxidizing agents such as potassium permanganate or potassium dichromate.

One reaction of alkanes that does occur readily is the replacement of a hydrogen atom by reaction with a halogen atom, a halogenation reaction. This type of reaction is typical of halogen atoms generated by the absorption of energy, for example, from light (see Section 25.2c).

$$
Cl_2 \underset{}{\overset{light}{\rightleftharpoons}} 2Cl\cdot
$$
$$
Cl\cdot + CH_4 \longrightarrow HCl + CH_3\cdot
$$
$$
CH_3\cdot + Cl_2 \longrightarrow CH_3Cl + Cl\cdot
$$
$$
\underset{\substack{methyl \\ chloride}}{}
$$

Table 27.10
Reactions of Unsaturated Hydrocarbons

Addition to an alkene
Oxidation of an alkene
$CH_3CH{=}CH_2$
Br_2
CH_3CHCH_2 (Br Br)
propylene dibromide
(1,2-dibromopropane)
HBr
CH_3CHCH_3 (Br)
isopropyl bromide
(2-bromopropane)
H_2SO_4
CH_3CHCH_3 (OSO_3H)
isopropyl hydrogen sulfate
$CH_3CH{=}CHCH_3$
excess $KMnO_4$
H_2O
$2CH_3COH$ (O)
acetic acid

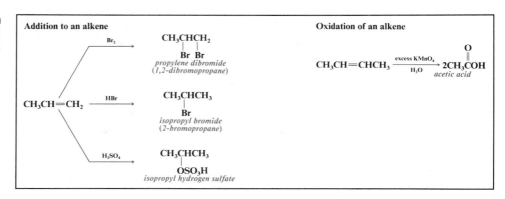

(This is an example of a chain reaction—the chlorine atom produced in the third step reacts with another methane molecule as in the second step.)

Reactive sites in aliphatic compounds: double bonds, polar bonds

The reactivity of double and triple bonds between carbon atoms in *nonaromatic* compounds is greater than that of similar single bonds. **Addition reactions**—the addition of atoms or groups to the carbon atoms in a covalent double bond or a covalent triple bond—occur readily for unsaturated hydrocarbons (Table 27.10).

Alkenes and alkynes also react with oxidizing agents, eventually leading to cleavage of the double or triple covalent bond (Table 27.10). Both the reaction with bromine and that with potassium permanganate shown in Table 27.10 are useful to test for the presence of double and triple bonds in a molecule. The reddish color of the bromine and the purple color of aqueous permanganate are observed to disappear in the presence of unsaturated compounds.

Unsaturated hydrocarbons: undergo addition reactions
Aromatic hydrocarbons: undergo substitution reactions

The reactivity of aromatic compounds differs from that of nonaromatic unsaturated compounds. In contrast to the addition reactions of olefins and acetylenes, aromatic compounds undergo **substitution reactions**—replacement of one or more hydrogen atoms of the aromatic ring with reagents such as bromine or sulfuric acid (Table 27.11). The aromatic ring is so strongly stabilized by resonance that the ring is

Table 27.11
Reactions of Aromatic Compounds The reactions shown here are typical of all aromatic compounds.

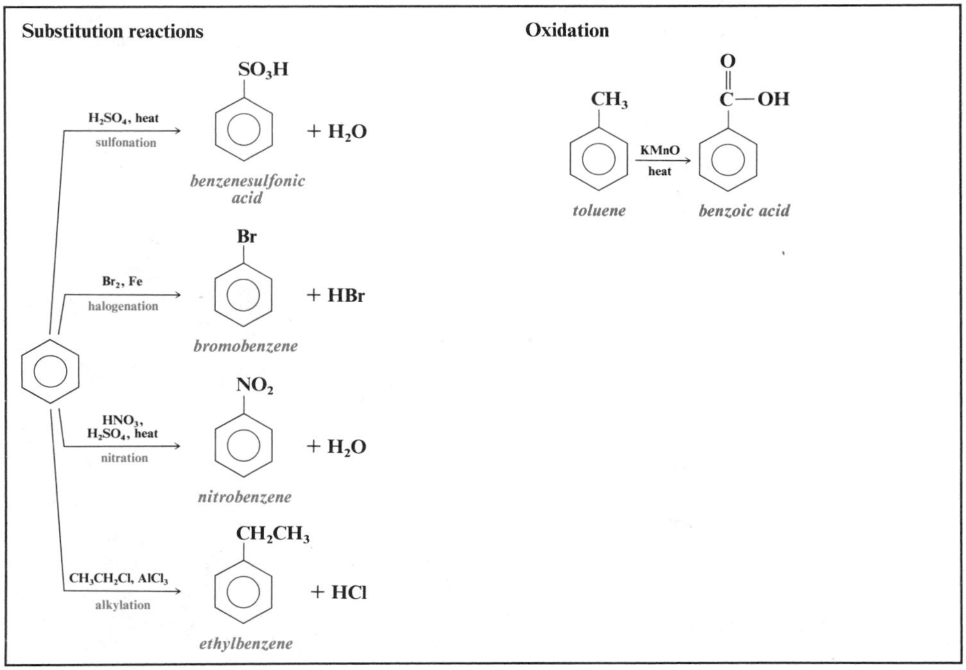

Substitution reactions
Oxidation
SO_3H
H_2SO_4, heat
sulfonation
$+ H_2O$
benzenesulfonic acid
Br
Br_2, Fe
halogenation
+ HBr
bromobenzene
NO_2
HNO_3, H_2SO_4, heat
nitration
$+ H_2O$
nitrobenzene
CH_2CH_3
CH_3CH_2Cl, $AlCl_3$
alkylation
+ HCl
ethylbenzene
CH_3
C—OH
O
KMnO
heat
toluene
benzoic acid

preserved. The ring is also quite stable to oxidation reactions such as that with potassium permanganate (Table 27.11). The stability to oxidation and the reaction by substitution instead of addition together contribute to what is called *aromatic character*.

HYDROCARBONS AND ENERGY

Fossil fuels: natural gas, petroleum, coal

Carbon, the nineteenth most abundant element, makes up only 0.032% of the earth's crust. Its importance far outweighs its abundance. In nature, elemental carbon is found as both diamond and graphite. Naturally occurring inorganic carbon compounds include carbon dioxide cycling through the atmosphere and hydrosphere, hydrogen carbonate ion dissolved in natural waters, and limestone, dolomite, and other carbonate-bearing minerals. Marine and land plants and animals are reservoirs of organic carbon compounds (Figure 27.14).

The major sources of hydrocarbons and carbon are the fossil fuels—natural gas, petroleum, and coal—formed by the decay of plants and animals over a period of millions of years. The major use of hydrocarbons and carbon is as fuel. Approximately 75% of the energy consumed in the United States is derived from natural gas and petroleum. The energy available to a society determines what that society can do and may determine what that society will do. Both the availability and the economics of hydrocarbons are changing. How long the current dominant role of naturally occurring hydrocarbons as an energy source can, or will, continue is a question that is open to debate. That they will all eventually be gone is certain.

Within the United States, the rising cost of imported oil and the cutback in its availability during the 1970s focused attention on alternative energy resources. Numerous long-term energy scenarios have been developed which examine possible new and changing sources of energy as the United States attempts to become less

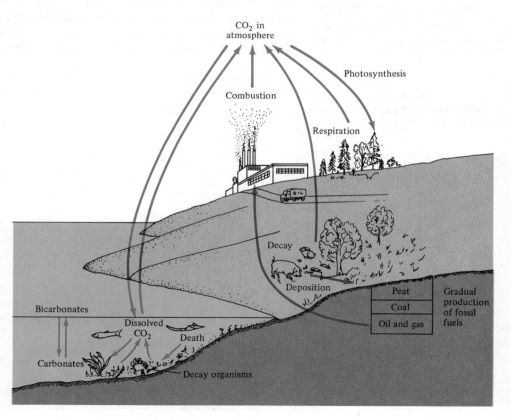

Figure 27.14
The Oxygen-Carbon Cycle Through most of the cycle, oxygen and carbon are chemically combined. In photosynthesis, CO_2 and H_2O, with the aid of chlorophyll and sunlight, combine in the green parts of plants to form carbohydrates. The plants are consumed by animals, which breathe in oxygen and reverse the photosynthesis reaction, breaking down organic matter to release energy, CO_2, and H_2O. Organic matter is present in the land mass as fossil fuels. Carbon dioxide is continually being absorbed and given up by the oceans. Almost all carbon that passes through organic matter eventually returns as CO_2 to the air or water.

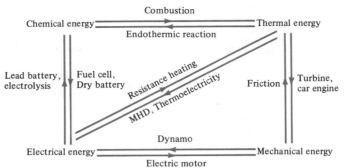

Figure 27.15
**Some Energy Conversion
Pathways** MHD refers to
magnetohydrodynamics, by which
electricity is generated by a
conductive fluid flowing in a
magnetic field. (Source: J. H. Harker
and J. R. Backhurst, *Fuel and
Energy,* New York: Academic Press,
1981, p. 4.)

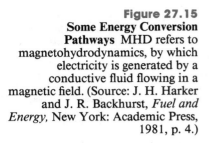

dependent on foreign oil and as the existing supplies of fossil fuels are used up. Predictions about the energy future belong as much to the realm of politics and economics as to the realm of science and technology. Here we look briefly at the traditional sources of hydrocarbon fuels and at some possible new and different sources.

Figure 27.15 shows some of the ways in which energy is converted from one form to another. The pathway for utilization of hydrocarbon fuels is from chemical to thermal to mechanical to electrical energy. Hydrocarbon fuels from new sources would enter the cycle of energy conversion as stored chemical energy and be utilized in the same way as the traditional fossil fuels.

27.10 FOSSIL FUELS

Natural gas is a mixture of gaseous substances trapped along with petroleum in the earth's crust. The composition of natural gas varies widely (Table 27.12), but methane is always the major constituent. Natural gas is recovered from oil wells and isolated gas wells, where the gas has migrated through the rock. The "calorific" value of an average natural gas is about 38 MJ/m³ (megajoules per cubic meter; the calorific value is the heat released when one unit — in this case one cubic meter — of the fuel undergoes complete combustion at 1 atm). Pipelines carry natural gas from large producing fields to major industrial and population centers, where it is used directly as fuel or as a chemical raw material.

Petroleum, as it is pumped from underground reservoirs, is a dark, thick, smelly liquid. Up to 95% of crude petroleum (Table 27.13) is a mixture of hydrocarbons, including alkanes, cycloalkanes, and aromatics, but no alkenes. A use has been found for virtually every component of petroleum.

Table 27.12
**Composition of Natural Gas
(by Volume)**

Methane, CH_4	70–90%
Ethane, C_2H_6	0–7%
Propane, C_3H_8	0–20%
Butane, C_4H_{10}	0–1%
Hydrogen, H_2	nil
Carbon dioxide, CO_2	0–8%
Oxygen, O_2	0–0.2%
Nitrogen, N_2	0–5%
Hydrogen sulfide, H_2S	0–5%
Noble gases, Ar, He, Ne, Xe	0–2%

Table 27.13
Approximate Composition of Crude Petroleum

Hydrocarbons Alkanes, cycloalkanes, and aromatics	50–95%
Oxygen, nitrogen, and sulfur-containing compounds	0.5–8%
Resins and asphalts Polymers and polycyclic aromatics, among others	5–15%

Table 27.14
Important Products from Crude Petroleum

	Boiling Range (K)	Composition	Source	Principal Uses
Natural gas	—	Mainly methane, some nitrogen depending on source	Natural sources	Fuel gas, also reformed to synthesis gas
Liquefied petroleum gas (LPG)	—	Propane, butane	Stripped from "wet" natural gas or from cracking operations	Domestic and industrial fuel— production of coal gas, synthetic chemicals
Primary flash distillate (PFD)	varies	Propane and butane dissolved in gasoline–kerosene range of liquids	Preliminary distillation of crude petroleum	Manufacture of synthesis gas
Gasoline	300–450	Complex mixture of materials. Contains additives to improve performance but no sulfur or polymerizable components	Primary distillation, cracking and reforming processes	Spark ignition internal combustion engines
Kerosene	410–575	Paraffinic hydrocarbons with substantial proportion of aromatics, low sulfur content	Distillation, cracking	Agricultural tractors, lighting, heating and aviation gas turbines
Gas oil	450–620	Saturated hydrocarbons	Distillation, hydrodesulfur-ization	Diesel fuel, heating and furnaces. Feed to cracking units
Diesel fuel	450–650	Saturated hydrocarbons, often with high sulfur	Distillation cracking	Diesel engines, furnace heating
Fuel oils	500–700+	—	Residue of primary distillation, blended with distillates	Large-scale industrial heating
Lubricating oils	wide range	Three types: mainly aromatic, mainly aliphatic or mixed	Vacuum distillation of primary distillation residue; solvent extraction	Lubrication
Wax	—	Paraffins	Chilling residue from vacuum distillation	Toilet preparations, food, candles, petroleum jelly
Bitumen	—	Wide variation	Residue from vacuum distillation or oxidation of residue from primary distillation ("blown" bitumen)	Road surfacing, waterproofing

Source: J. H. Harker and J. R. Backhurst, *Fuel and Energy* (New York: Academic Press, 1981), p. 86.

The first step toward manufacture of petroleum products is separation of the crude petroleum by distillation and extraction into fractions possessing various boiling points and molecular masses. These fractions can be used as indicated in Table 27.14 or treated further by a variety of processes to convert the initial fractions into more desirable mixtures or pure compounds. For example, at least two-thirds of the molecules in the gasoline that you obtain at a service station were not present as such when the petroleum was pumped from the oil well. Isomerization, cracking, alkylation, and reforming are processes used to increase the yield of products such as gasoline from the crude oil and to improve its quality. **Petroleum isomerization,** accomplished by heat and catalysts, converts straight-chain alkanes into branched alkanes. The latter perform better as fuels. **Petroleum cracking,** also via heat and catalysts, breaks large molecules above the gasoline range into smaller molecules (alkanes and also alkenes) that are in the gasoline range. **Petroleum alkylation** combines lower molecular weight alkanes and alkenes to form molecules in the gasoline range. **Petroleum reforming** employs catalysts in the presence of hydrogen to convert noncyclic hydrocarbons to aromatic compounds. The molecules are "reformed" as, for example, in the following reaction.

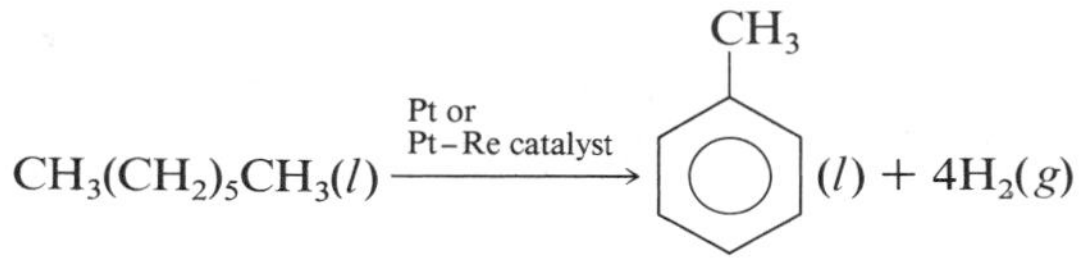

$$CH_3(CH_2)_5CH_3(l) \xrightarrow[\text{Pt-Re catalyst}]{\text{Pt or}} \underset{\textit{toluene}}{\overset{CH_3}{\bigcirc}} (l) + 4H_2(g)$$

n-heptane

These processes also are used to supply higher yields of hydrocarbons needed for purposes other than gasoline. Further treatment of petroleum products depends upon their ultimate use. For example, liquid products that will be burned must be treated to remove hydrogen sulfide and sulfur-containing organic compounds.

Petroleum is the source of compounds that serve as starting materials for the syntheses of a major portion of the industrial organic chemicals, particularly those used in plastics, coatings, and synthetic rubber. However, only 10% of the petroleum processed each year goes to the chemical industry in the form of raw materials. The remaining 90% is eventually burned.

Coal, like natural gas, can be burned directly as a fuel. Coal contains carbon, hydrogen, nitrogen, oxygen, and sulfur in varying amounts, as well as traces of heavy metals. The carbon content of coal ranges from 45% to 95%. The second most important use of coal is in production of coke for the iron and steel industry. Coke is made by heating coal in the absence of air to drive off volatile materials, a process called carbonization. Ammonia and coal tar, from which organic chemicals, particularly aromatics, can be obtained are important by-products of this operation.

$$\text{Coal} \xrightarrow{\text{heat, no air}} NH_3 + \text{other gases } (H_2, CH_4, CO, CO_2) +$$
$$\text{coke} + \text{coal tar (source of aromatic compounds)}$$

27.11 SYNFUELS

The first problem in discussing "synfuels" is to explain what the term means. Strictly speaking, it should mean a synthetic fuel—one that is man made. By this definition, gasoline is a synthetic fuel, for most of its molecules have been synthesized from other molecules. However, "synfuel" has come to mean any hydrocarbon fuel derived in a nontraditional way either from natural resources *or* by chemical synthesis. In other words, a synfuel is one that has been obtained by methods different from those we have been using with fossil fuels and hydrocarbons over the years.

As the term is used, liquid synfuels include liquid fuel produced from coal (the liquefaction of coal), alcohol made from sugar cane or corn (an example of a fuel from biomass), or natural hydrocarbon liquids extracted from oil-bearing shale. Gaseous synthetic fuels include substitute natural gas (SNG) derived from coal (the gasification of coal) and methane from the reaction of hydrogen with carbon monoxide and carbon dioxide.

Under appropriate conditions, hydrocarbons can be produced from mixtures of hydrogen and carbon monoxide. In order to illustrate the possible routes to synfuels, we describe here two of the more well-studied processes based on carbon monoxide–hydrogen mixtures—the Lurgi process for the gasification of coal and the Fischer–Tropsch synthesis of hydrocarbons. At first glance, it may seem strange to be making carbon monoxide and hydrogen from coal in order to synthesize hydrocarbons to replace fossil fuels. However, natural resources of coal are much more abundant than those of natural gas or petroleum, and most of our vehicles, houses, and industrial plants are designed to consume gaseous and liquid fuels. Also, gaseous or liquid fuels are much more easily transported—for example, in pipelines—than is coal. It is also possible that synfuels may provide necessary raw materials for the chemical industry.

27.12 CARBON MONOXIDE–HYDROGEN MIXTURES

Mixtures of carbon monoxide and hydrogen go by different names, depending upon their sources and uses. The name "water gas" is based on the reaction of coal or coke with steam.

$$C(s) \underset{\textit{coal or coke}}{} + H_2O(g) \xrightarrow{1000\ °C} CO(g) + H_2(g)$$

This reaction, the water gas reaction, was once used to provide household cooking gas, but the availability of natural gas made it obsolete. Water gas, not necessarily a mixture of pure gases, has a calorific value of about 11 MJ/m³.

The reaction of carbon monoxide and water to give hydrogen and carbon dioxide (reaction j, Table 27.3), known as the water gas shift reaction, is used to increase the hydrogen content of water gas. The ratio of carbon monoxide to hydrogen in a gaseous mixture can be controlled by controlling the degree of "shifting."

A carbon monoxide–hydrogen mixture destined for use in the production of other compounds is known as synthesis gas. For example, a 2-to-1 hydrogen–carbon monoxide mixture is the synthesis gas used for methanol production. (Some of the uses of CO–H₂ mixtures are summarized in Table 27.15.)

**Table 27.15
Uses of Carbon Monoxide–
Hydrogen Mixtures**

As a fuel (water gas)

$$2H_2(g) + O_2(g) \xrightarrow{\Delta} 2H_2O(g)$$

$$2CO(g) + O_2(g) \xrightarrow{\Delta} 2CO_2(g)$$

Methanol production

$$CO(g) + 2H_2(g) \xrightarrow[\substack{300\ \text{atm} \\ \text{Ag or Cu catalyst}}]{230-400\ °C} CH_3OH(l)$$

Methane production (methanation; SNG production)

$$CO(g) + 3H_2(g) \xrightarrow[\substack{1-100\ \text{atm} \\ \text{Ni or Co} \\ \text{catalyst}}]{230-450\ °C} CH_4(g) + H_2O(g)$$

Hydrocarbon synthesis (Fischer–Tropsch synthesis)

$$mCO(g) + (2m+1)H_2(g) \xrightarrow[\substack{1\ \text{to several hundred atm} \\ \text{catalyst}}]{150-350\ °C} C_mH_{2m+2} + mH_2O(g)$$

Aldehyde production (oxo process)

$$RCH{=}CH_2 + H_2(g) + CO(g) \xrightarrow{200-250\ °C} RCH_2CH_2CHO$$

27.13 THE LURGI PROCESS
FOR COAL GASIFICATION

The Lurgi process was developed in Germany during the 1930s, and today is a fully commercial process in use in several countries other than the United States. A unit for carrying out the process is depicted in Figure 27.16. Lump coal enters the gasifier at the top and feeds downward. The coal is held on a rotating grate and steam and oxygen enter from beneath. Ash falls through the grate and is removed at the bottom. By operating under pressure, a Lurgi gasifier produces its product gases at a faster rate than units which operate at atmospheric pressure.

There are three major reaction zones in the gasifier. Immediately above the grate is the combustion zone. Here the coal is oxidized to carbon dioxide at 1200 °C. The combustion in this zone produces most of the heat needed for the entire gasification operation.

In the second zone — the reduction zone — carbon dioxide and water are reduced by carbon at 900 °C.

$$CO_2(g) + C(s) \longrightarrow 2CO(g)$$
$$H_2O(g) + C(s) \longrightarrow CO(g) + H_2(g)$$

In the third zone, actually the first encountered by the entering coal, volatile products such as methane, some hydrocarbons, and hydrogen are formed at 600 °C. Here, some carbon reacts with hydrogen to form methane,

$$C(s) + 2H_2(g) \longrightarrow CH_4(g)$$

and the water gas shift reaction also takes place.

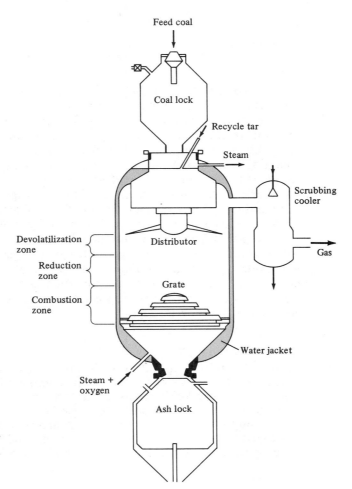

Figure 27.16
A Lurgi Coal Gasifier This gasifier is designed to run at elevated pressures.

The gas that exits from the Lurgi gasifier contains mainly hydrogen, carbon monoxide, carbon dioxide, and methane. Removal of the carbon dioxide increases the calorific value to about 16 MJ/m^3. The resulting gas contains about 30% carbon monoxide, 55% hydrogen, and 15% methane. It can be burned as a fuel or, after suitable removal of contaminants, it can be used as a synthesis gas for methanol or hydrocarbon production (see next section).

When the production of substitute natural gas is the goal, the gas from the Lurgi process is "methanated."

$$3H_2(g) + CO(g) \xrightarrow[400\ °C]{Fe_2O_3\ or\ Ni} CH_4(g) + H_2O(g)$$

This process increases the calorific value of the gas by 2 to 3 times, making it about equal to that of natural gas. Before methanation can take place, the relative amounts of carbon monoxide and hydrogen must be adjusted to give the best yield of methane. This is accomplished by adding hydrogen from an outside source, usually from a water gas shift reaction.

27.14 FISCHER–TROPSCH HYDROCARBON SYNTHESIS

The Fischer–Tropsch synthesis, like the methanation reactions, produces hydrocarbons by the catalyzed reaction of carbon monoxide with hydrogen. By varying the pressure, temperature, and catalysts, hydrocarbons ranging from light oils to heavy waxes can be produced. The reaction can be summarized as follows:

$$mCO(g) + (2m + 1)H_2(g) \xrightarrow[\substack{hundred\ atm \\ catalyst}]{\substack{150\text{–}350\ °C \\ 1\ to\ several}} C_mH_{2m+2} + mH_2O(g)$$

For example,

$$8CO(g) + 17H_2(g) \xrightarrow{\hspace{3cm}} \underset{octane}{C_8H_{18}(g)} + 8H_2O(g)$$

In a commercial installation running a "medium pressure" Fischer–Tropsch synthesis, typical conditions are 7 atm pressure, 175°–195 °C, with a cobalt oxide–thorium oxide–magnesium oxide catalyst and 1-to-2 carbon monoxide–hydrogen reactant stream. The product is 35% gasoline range hydrocarbons, 35% diesel oil range hydrocarbons, and 30% soft paraffins. A multitude of variations on the conditions and the possible products are under study and development as a result of the growing need for alternate energy sources.

The Fischer–Tropsch synthesis, like the Lurgi gasification process, was developed in the 1930s in Germany. During World War II, Germany, a country with no oil wells, fueled its vehicles with synthetic petroleum products from Fischer–Tropsch plants. Today the major industrial installation is in South Africa. In a huge complex next to the coal fields, coal is fed to Lurgi gasifiers, the product gas is purified to provide synthesis gas for Fischer–Tropsch reactors producing various hydrocarbon mixtures, and the hydrocarbon products are separated by distillation as necessary. When a planned expansion is complete, this installation will consume over 50,000 tons of coal each day.

SUMMARY

CARBON AND ITS INORGANIC COMPOUNDS (Sections **27.1–27.4**)   Carbon, the first member of Representative Group IV, is the only nonmetal in the group, and usually exhibits covalent bonding in its compounds. It can form four equivalent single bonds (sp^3 hybridization), a double bond and two single bonds (sp^2 hybridization), or one triple bond and one single bond (sp hybridization). Carbon differs significantly (Table 27.2) from other elements in the extent to which its atoms undergo catenation—bonding to one another. The C—C bond is strong and stable, allowing carbon to form ring compounds as well as polymeric chains thousands of atoms long. Carbon has two crystalline allotropes, diamond and graphite, and also exists in various amorphous forms such as charcoal (Table 27.1).

Carbon burns to form CO_2 or (in limited oxygen) the poisonous CO, and also combines with sulfur to give CS_2 and with fluorine to give carbon tetrafluoride. At elevated temperatures, both carbon and CO are reducing agents. The common carbon-containing anions are CO_3^{2-}, HCO_3^-, and CN^-, all three of which give alkaline aqueous solutions. In a saturated solution of CO_2 in water, one out of some 400 molecules of CO_2 forms H_2CO_3, producing an acidic solution. The binary compounds of carbon with metals and semiconducting elements are called carbides; they may be covalent, interstitial, or ionic (Tables 27.3 and 27.6).

HYDROCARBONS (Sections **27.5–27.9**) All organic compounds can be regarded as based on the structures of hydrocarbons. Saturated hydrocarbons (Table 27.7) contain only single covalent bonds; they may consist of straight or branched carbon chains (alkanes) or rings (cycloalkanes). All hydrocarbons with more than three carbon atoms exhibit structural isomerism. Groups containing one less hydrogen atom than an alkane are called alkyl groups. Unsaturated hydrocarbons (Table 27.9) are those containing double bonds (alkenes) or triple bonds (alkynes). Rotation of two carbon atoms joined by a double bond is inhibited by the π bond, and carbon atoms in rings are similarly unable to rotate. In both cases, *cis–trans* isomerism is therefore possible (Section 11.7). A carbon–carbon double bond creates a planar region in a molecule. Compounds that contain conjugated double bonds—double bonds that alternate with single bonds—are often colored. Aromatic hydrocarbons are unsaturated compounds with planar ring systems stabilized by delocalized π bonding, as in benzene. Hydrocarbons that do not contain aromatic rings are termed aliphatic. The preferred system of nomenclature for organic compounds is that formulated by the International Union of Pure and Applied Chemistry, IUPAC (Table 27.8).

Pairs of molecules with the same molecular formula that rotate plane-polarized light in opposite directions are called optical isomers or enantiomers. They are mirror images of one another and are usually very similar in their properties, and so are difficult to separate. Optical isomers may arise when four different groups are bonded to one carbon atom, producing an asymmetric molecule. The property of having optical isomers is called chirality. A mixture of equal parts of the levorotatory and dextrorotatory isomers of a substance—a racemic mixture—causes no net rotation of polarized light.

The reactivity of saturated hydrocarbons is generally low, although hydrogen atoms are readily replaced by halogen atoms (halogenation). Double bonds or polar bonds provide sites where reaction is more likely to occur. Unsaturated hydrocarbons readily undergo addition reactions (Table 27.10); aromatic compounds tend to undergo substitution reactions (Table 27.11).

HYDROCARBONS AND ENERGY (Sections **27.10–27.14**) The combustion of fossil fuels, which contain carbon and hydrocarbons, is our primary source of energy. Natural gas is a mixture of substances, with methane the chief component; it is recovered from oil wells and isolated natural gas wells. Petroleum is largely a mixture of hydrocarbons of various types (Table 27.13). Ninety percent of all petroleum is burned for energy and ten percent is used in the manufacture of industrial organic chemicals, including plastics and rubber (Table 27.14). Distillation is used to separate crude petroleum into fractions of different boiling points and molecular masses. In the production of gasoline or other useful substances, these components are modified in various ways (by isomerization, cracking, alkylation, and reforming). Coal contains carbon, hydrogen, nitrogen, oxygen, and sulfur in varying proportions. Coke is made by heating coal in the absence of air, a process that also yields ammonia and coal tar, from which other important organic compounds can be obtained. Synfuels are hydrocarbon fuels obtained by chemical synthesis or from natural sources by novel methods. They include liquid fuel made from coal, alcohol

SIGNIFICANT TERMS

catenation
saturated hydrocarbons
alkanes
homologous series
alkyl groups
cycloalkanes
normal hydrocarbons
unsaturated hydrocarbons
olefins, alkenes
acetylenes, alkynes
steric hindrance
conjugated double bonds
nuclear magnetic resonance (NMR) spectroscopy
aromatic hydrocarbons
aliphatic hydrocarbons
optical isomerism
plane-polarized light
asymmetric atom
optically active
chirality
enantiomers, optical isomers
racemic mixture
resolution
addition reactions
substitution reactions
petroleum isomerization
petroleum cracking
petroleum alkylation
petroleum reforming

derived from biomass, hydrocarbons extracted from oil-bearing shale, substitute natural gas derived from coal, and methane produced by reaction of hydrogen with CO and CO_2. In the Lurgi process, coal reacts with steam and oxygen to produce a gas consisting of hydrogen, methane, carbon monoxide, and carbon dioxide. In Fischer–Tropsch synthesis, various hydrocarbons can be produced by the catalyzed reaction of hydrogen with carbon monoxide.

THOUGHTS ON CHEMISTRY

Fuel's Paradise

FUEL'S PARADISE, by Art Buchwald

Every time you pick up the newspapers you read of some newfangled thing that is going to save us from the oil crisis. One day it's methane made from garbage; the next day it's hot springs underneath Montana. Then it's ocean waves that can be tamed, and then, of course, there are energy-producing windmills.

I can't keep up with all of it, but Carbuncle can and does.

A month ago he told me, "Did you hear they have a new synthetic fuel that can save a million barrels of oil a day?"

"No," I said. "What is it?"

"After-shave lotion. Some professor at MIT discovered that after-shave lotion contains alcohol. He devised a method of taking the perfume out of it through a cracking process, and what's left can be burned in a car."

"Great," I said. "When will they start making it?"

"Right now the price is too high. A half liter of Faberge after-shave will cost you $25, but if the OPEC countries keep raising their rates the prices will soon be competitive."

A few days later he came back. "Well, it's all over for the Arabs. A geologist in Colorado has just developed a method for squeezing oil out of asphalt roads. He was able to get one liter of crude out of a kilometer of asphalt. He figures with all the asphalt roads in America we should be self-sufficient by 1989."

"I knew they'd come up with something. . . . Wait a minute! If they dig up all the asphalt roads in the U.S. there will be nothing for the cars to drive on."

"Exactly! That's where the big conservation savings will come. He's just applied for a grant from the Department of Energy."

"To continue his research?"

"No, for bail money. They arrested him for digging up a stretch of U.S. Highway 70."

I didn't hear from Carbuncle for a week. Then he called me excitedly on the phone.

"There's a man in New Jersey who has perfected a system to make coal out of gold. One ton of gold will give you one ton of soft-burning coal."

"Great! How does it work?"

"Once you get the gold, you put it in a blast furnace at 1500 degrees. This produces a gas which you siphon off. The residue at the bottom of the furnace hardens and looks just like coal. You scrape it up and shape it into pellets. A ton of it can get you through the winter. The beauty is that coal made from gold doesn't pollute the air."

"It sounds like the answer," I said.

A few days later the phone rang again. Carbuncle said, "You been watching television?"

"No."

"There's a guy on the 'Today' show who runs his car on Tabasco

sauce. He says he mixes three parts Tabasco with one part no-lead, and a tank of fuel lasts him a month. He told Tom Brokaw all the oil companies know about it, but won't use it because they're afraid it will cut into their profits."

Yesterday Carbuncle called again. "The energy crisis is over. A 14-year-old boy scout in Pasadena rubbed two sticks together and managed to get a fire out of it. The National Academy of Sciences duplicated the experiment and it works. This country has enough sticks to light every home in the U.S. for 2000 years."

"Yeah, but what do you burn after the fire gets started?" I asked.

Carbuncle replied, "Furniture. It's cheaper now than heating oil."

Art Buchwald, "Fuel's Paradise," 1979. Reprinted with permission of the author.

QUESTIONS

Carbon and Its Inorganic Compounds

27.1 Write the electron configurations of the C and Si atoms. What would you predict for the formulas of the compounds formed between these elements and fluorine? Although silicon can form the $[SiF_6]^{2-}$ ion, the analogous ion for carbon, $[CF_6]^{2-}$, is unknown. Why?

27.2 Discuss the possible ways in which the carbon atom can form covalent bonds. Draw Lewis structures for each of the possibilities and predict the angles between the bonds around the carbon atom.

27.3 Name the two allotropic forms of carbon. Briefly compare some of their properties.

27.4 Briefly describe the reactivity of carbon with (a) the halogens, (b) sulfur, (c) metals, and (d) oxygen.

27.5 Describe some of the types of reactions in which C and CO serve as reducing agents at elevated temperatures.

27.6 Name the oxo anions of carbon and write their formulas. Will solutions of salts of these anions be acidic, alkaline, or neutral? Why?

27.7 Draw Lewis structures for CO, CO_2, and CO_3^{2-}. Predict which substance has (a) the strongest carbon–oxygen bond and (b) the shortest bond.

27.8 What is the shape of a CO_2 molecule? What is the hybridization of the carbon atom orbitals? What intermolecular forces will be found in CO_2?

27.9 How will the concentration of CO_2 in water depend on the temperature? How does it depend on the partial pressure of the CO_2 above the solution?

27.10 Before silicon carbide was first prepared, would it have been possible to predict that it would be very hard? Why?

27.11* Write Lewis structures for N_2, CN^-, CO, and C_2^{2-}. Assuming that the available molecular orbitals on CN^- and CO are similar to those on N_2 and C_2^{2-}, write the electron configurations for all four species. What type of hybridization is present?

27.12 Which of the following are redox reactions? Identify the oxidizing and reducing agent in each of the redox reactions.

(a) $2KHCO_3(s) \xrightarrow{\Delta} K_2CO_3(s) + CO_2(g) + H_2O(g)$

(b) $CS_2(l) + 3Cl_2(g) \longrightarrow CCl_4(l) + S_2Cl_2(l)$

(c) $Fe_2O_3(s) + 3CO(g) \xrightarrow{\Delta} 2Fe(s) + 3CO_2(g)$

(d) $C(s) + 4HNO_3(aq, conc) \xrightarrow{\Delta}$
$$CO_2(g) + 4NO_2(g) + 2H_2O(l)$$

27.13 Repeat Question 27.12 for:

(a) $2CH_4(g) + 2NH_3(g) + 3O_2(g) \xrightarrow{800\ °C} 2HCN(g) + 6H_2O(g)$

(b) $AgCN(s) + CN^- \longrightarrow [Ag(CN)_2]^-$

(c) $4Au(s) + 8CN^- + O_2(g) + 2H_2O(l) \longrightarrow$
$$4[Au(CN)_2]^- + 4OH^-$$

(d) $Pd^{2+} + CO(g) + H_2O(l) \longrightarrow Pd(s) + CO_2(g) + 2H^+$

27.14 Classify each of the following reactions according to the reaction types listed in Tables 17.2 and 17.7:

(a) $CaCO_3(s) \xrightarrow{\Delta} CaO(s) + CO_2(g)$

(b) $MgCO_3(s) + H_2SO_4(aq) \longrightarrow MgSO_4(aq) + CO_2(g) + H_2O(l)$

(c) $CH_4(g) + 2O_2(g) \longrightarrow CO_2(g) + 2H_2O(g)$

(d) $HCO_3^- + OH^- \longrightarrow CO_3^{2-} + H_2O(l)$

27.15 Repeat Question 27.14 for:

(a) $CO(g) + Cl_2(g) \longrightarrow COCl_2(g)$

(b) $2CH_3OH(l) + 3O_2(g) \xrightarrow{\Delta} 2CO_2(g) + 4H_2O(g)$

(c) $Na_2CO_3(s) + SiO_2(s) \xrightarrow{\Delta} Na_2SiO_3(l) + CO_2(g)$

(d) $CdO(s) + C(s) \xrightarrow{\Delta} Cd(g) + CO(g)$

27.16 Predict the major products of the following reactions:

(a) $Fe_3O_4(s) + CO(g) \xrightarrow{\Delta}$

(b) $CaCO_3(s) + H_2O(l) + CO_2(g) \longrightarrow$

(c) $CN^- + H_2O(l) \rightleftharpoons$

27.17 Repeat Question 27.16 for:

(a) $CaC_2(s) + H_2O(l) \longrightarrow$

(b) $Ag(s) + CN^- + O_2(g) + H_2O(l) \longrightarrow$

(c) $CH_4(g) + O_2(g) \xrightarrow{\Delta}$

(d) $C(s) + H_2SO_4(conc) \xrightarrow{\Delta}$

27.18 Write balanced equations for the following chemical reactions: (a) formation of $CaSiO_3(l)$ from $CaCO_3(s)$, (b) reaction of CO_3^{2-} with water, (c) formation of a metal carbonyl, (d) reaction of a solid carbonate with an aqueous acid, and (e) formation of carbon monoxide from carbon dioxide.

Hydrocarbons

27.19 What are alkanes? Write the general molecular formula for an alkane. Could a substance having the molecular formula C_6H_{14} be an alkane? Explain your answer.

27.20 What are cycloalkanes? Write the general molecular formula for a cycloalkane. Could a substance having the molecular formula C_5H_{12} be a cycloalkane? Explain your answer.

27.21 What is the name of the international body that devised the systematic nomenclature used for organic compounds? In this system what is the suffix that is used to indicate a saturated hydrocarbon? How is the number of carbon atoms indicated in the name of a saturated hydrocarbon? Is 2-dimethylpentane a correct name?

27.22 Write the structural formulas for the three isomeric saturated hydrocarbons having the molecular formula C_5H_{12}. Name each by the IUPAC system. Which one of these isomers would show a single peak in its proton NMR spectrum?

27.23 Repeat Question 27.22 for the five isomers of C_6H_{14}.

27.24 What is an alkyl group? What are the general molecular formulas for the alkyl groups derived from an alkane and a cycloalkane? How is the name of an alkyl group derived from the name of an alkane?

27.25 What is an alkene? Write the general molecular formula for the homologous series beginning with ethene (ethylene). Is C_6H_{12} a possible molecular formula for an alkene? Explain your answer.

27.26 What is a diene? What are conjugated double covalent bonds?

27.27 One objective of a satisfactory system of nomenclature is to give each different molecular structure a specific name; a correct name should describe a specific molecular structure. In what respect are the names "butene" and "butadiene" deficient?

27.28 What is an alkyne? Write the general molecular formula for the homologous series beginning with ethyne (acetylene). Is C_6H_{10} a possible molecular formula for an alkyne? Explain your answer.

27.29 Draw the molecular structures of the following compounds: (a) 3-hexyne, (b) 1,3-pentadiene, (c) cyclobutene, and (d) 3,4-diethylhexane.

27.30 Draw the molecular structures of the following compounds: (a) 1-butyne, (b) 2-methylpropene, (c) 2-ethyl-3-methyl-1-butene, and (d) 3-methyl-1-butyne.

27.31 Write the IUPAC names for the following compounds:

(a)

(b) $CH_3CHCH_2CH_3$
         |
        CH_3

(c) $CH_3C{\equiv}CCH_3$

(d) $CH_3C{=}CHCH_3$
          |
         CH_3

(e) $CH_3CH_2CHCH_3$
              |
            CH_2CH_3

(f) $CH_3CHCH_2CH_3$
         |
       CH_2CH_3

27.32 Repeat Question 27.31 for:

(a) CH_3
          |
    $CH_3CCH_2CH_3$
          |
         CH_3

(b) $CH_2{=}CBr_2$

(c) CH_3
          |
    $CH_3CHCHCH_3$
              |
             CH_3

(d)

27.33 What is an aromatic hydrocarbon? How does an aromatic hydrocarbon differ from an aliphatic hydrocarbon?

27.34 How do the chemical properties of benzene differ from those of an alkene?

27.35 There are three possible isomeric trimethylbenzenes. Write their molecular structures and name each of them.

27.36 How many isomeric dibromobenzenes are possible? What names are used to designate these isomers?

27.37 Is ethylbenzene a structural isomer of o-xylene (1,2-dimethylbenzene)?

27.38 What is a phenyl group? How many isomeric monophenylnaphthalenes are possible?

27.39 Write the molecular structures for the following compounds: (a) p-dinitrobenzene, (b) n-propylbenzene, (c) 1,3,5-tribromobenzene, and (d) 1,3-diphenylbutane.

27.40 Write the IUPAC names for the following compounds:

(a)

(b)

(c)

(d)

27.41 Define plane-polarized light. What is a polarimeter? To what do the terms levorotatory and dextrorotatory refer?

27.42 What are Fischer projections (see Figure 27.13)? How are they used to show enantiomers?

27.43 What type of isomerism is not disclosed in the name 2-hexene? How is the name for 2-hexene modified to show this isomerism?

27.44 Which of the following compounds can exist as cis and trans isomers: (a) 1-butene, (b) 2-bromo-1-butene, (c) 2-bromo-2-butene, (d) 2,3-dimethyl-2-butene, and (e) 2,3-dichloro-2-butene?

27.45 Which of the following compounds would exhibit optical isomerism?

(a) CH_3CHCH_3
     |
     Br

(b) $CH_3CHCH_2CH_3$
     |
     OH

(c) $HO-\bigcirc-\overset{\overset{H}{|}}{\underset{\underset{Cl}{|}}{C}}-\bigcirc$

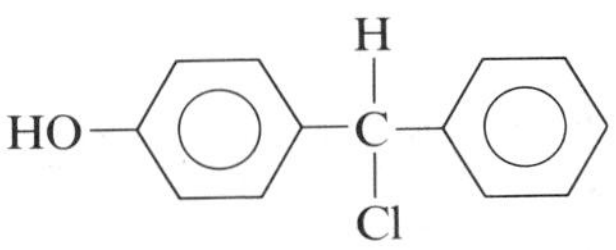

(d) $CH_3CH=CHCH_3$

Draw the Fischer projections for the enantiomeric pairs.

27.46 Suppose a series of test tubes each contained 2 mL of one of the following pairs of compounds: (a) hexane or 2-hexene, (b) benzene or styrene ($C_6H_5CH=CH_2$), and (c) cyclohexene or 2-bromopropane. Describe a simple chemical test that would enable you to determine visually which compound was present in each test tube.

27.47 Show the molecular structure of the organic compound formed in each of the following reactions:

(a) 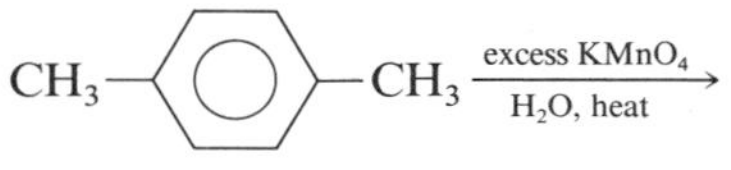 $CH_3-\bigcirc-CH_3 \xrightarrow[\text{H}_2\text{O, heat}]{\text{excess KMnO}_4}$

(b) $CH_3CH=CHCH_3 \xrightarrow{HBr}$

(c) $C_6H_5CH=CH_2 \xrightarrow{Br_2}$

(d) 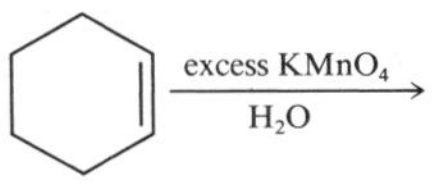 $\bigcirc \xrightarrow[\text{H}_2\text{O}]{\text{excess KMnO}_4}$

Hydrocarbons and Energy

27.48 What are the combustion products of a hydrocarbon in (a) excess oxygen and (b) limited oxygen?

27.49 Name some of the major components of natural gas.

27.50 Discuss the following processes in the petroleum industry: (a) isomerization, (b) cracking, (c) alkylation, and (d) reforming.

27.51 What does the term "synfuel" mean? Give some examples of synfuels.

27.52 Briefly describe the chemical reactions that occur in the gasification of coal by the Lurgi process. Why is the product gas often methanated?

27.53 What are the products of the Fischer–Tropsch synthesis? Write a general chemical equation representing this process.

Answers to Selected Questions

27.8 linear; sp; London forces

27.13 a, c, d; oxidizing agents: (a) O_2, (c) O_2, (d) Pd^{2+}; reducing agents: (a) NH_3, (c) Au, (d) CO

27.15 (a) redox—combination of an element with a compound to form another compound, (b) redox—combination of an element with a compound to form other compounds, (c) nonredox—displacement, (d) redox—displacement of one element from a compound by another element

27.17 (a) $Ca(OH)_2(s)$, $C_2H_2(g)$; (b) $[Ag(CN)_2]^-$, OH^-; (c) $CO_2(g)$ or $CO(g)$, $H_2O(g)$; (d) $CO_2(g)$, $SO_2(g)$, $H_2O(l)$

27.22 $CH_3CH_2CH_2CH_2CH_3$, n-pentane; $CH_3CH_2CHCH_3$,
                                                                                                      |
                                                                                                    CH_3

$\qquad$ 2-methylbutane; $\quad CH_3\overset{\overset{CH_3}{|}}{\underset{\underset{CH_3}{|}}{C}}CH_3$, $\quad$ 2,2-dimethylpropane;

2,2-dimethylpropane would have only one NMR peak

27.27 location of the C=C bond is not clear—could be between the first and second carbon atoms or between the second and third carbon atoms; location of the C=C bonds is not clear—could be between the first and second and second and third carbon atoms, or between the first and second and third and fourth carbon atoms

27.30 (a) $CH\equiv C-CH_2-CH_3$, $\qquad$ (b) $CH_3-\overset{\overset{}{\underset{\underset{CH_3}{|}}{C}}}{}=CH_2$,

(c) $CH_2=\overset{}{\underset{\underset{H_2C}{|}}{C}}-\overset{}{\underset{\underset{CH_3}{|}}{CH}}-CH_3$, $\qquad$ (d) $CH_3-\overset{}{\underset{\underset{CH_3}{|}}{CH}}-C\equiv CH$

27.32 (a) 2,2-dimethylbutane, (b) 1,1-dibromoethene, (c) 2,3-dimethylbutane, (d) 1,3-cyclohexadiene

27.36 3; 1,2-dibromobenzene, 1,3-dibromobenzene, 1,4-dibromobenzene

27.38 C_6H_5-, two

27.40 (a) 1,2-dichlorobenzene, (b) 1-methyl-4-chlorobenzene, (c) 1,7-dichloronaphthalene, (d) 1,2,3,4,5-pentachlorobenzene

27.44 (c), (e)

27.46 2-hexene, styrene, and cyclohexene will all undergo addition reactions with Br_2 in which the red-brown color of bromine will disappear

27.48 (a) H_2O and CO_2, (b) H_2O and CO

27.53 hydrocarbons and water; $mCO(g) + (2m + 1) H_2(g) \longrightarrow C_mH_{2m+2} + mH_2O(g)$

PROBLEMS

Review of Principles

27.1 The largest diamond ever discovered was the Cullinan diamond, which weighed 3106 carats. Calculate the volume of this stone in cm^3. The density of diamond is 3.51 g/cm^3. One carat is equal to 200 mg.

27.2 Pieces of dry ice were mixed with 100. mL of 5.0 M NaOH. Write the chemical equation for the reaction to form sodium carbonate. What mass of sodium carbonate would be formed from 2.2 g of CO_2 reacting with the NaOH solution? *Answer* $2NaOH(aq) + CO_2(aq) \longrightarrow Na_2CO_3(aq) + H_2O(l)$, 5.3 g Na_2CO_3

27.3 The production of "water gas" is represented by the equation

$$C(s) + H_2O(g) \longrightarrow CO(g) + H_2(g)$$

At 1000 K, $K_p = p_{CO}p_{H_2}/p_{H_2O} = 3.2$. What are the partial pressures of CO and H_2 at this temperature if $p_{H_2O} = 15.6$ atm?

27.4 What is the pH of a 0.010 M solution of $NaHCO_3$? $K_{a_1} = 4.5 \times 10^{-7}$ for H_2CO_3. *Answer* 9.18

27.5 The heat of combustion at 25 °C is −395.4 kJ/mol for diamond and −393.5 kJ/mol for graphite. The absolute entropies are 2.38 J/K mol and 5.74 J/K mol, respectively. Determine which allotropic form of carbon is more stable under room conditions.

27.6 The heat of formation at 25 °C is −75 kJ/mol for $CH_4(g)$, 717 kJ/mol for $C(g)$, and 218 kJ/mol for $H(g)$. (a) Calculate the average C—H bond energy. The heat of formation at 25 °C is −85 kJ/mol for $C_2H_6(g)$, 52 kJ/mol for $C_2H_4(g)$, and 227 kJ/mol for $C_2H_2(g)$. Calculate the (b) C—C, (c) C=C, and (d) C≡C bond energies. *Answer* (a) 416 kJ/mol, (b) 330 kJ/mol, (c) 590 kJ/mol, (d) 810 kJ/mol

27.7* The heat of combustion at 20 °C is −3.487 MJ/mol for n-C_5H_{12}, −4.141 MJ/mol for n-C_6H_{14}, −4.811 MJ/mol for n-C_7H_{16}, and −5.450 MJ/mol for n-C_8H_{18}. Using −286 kJ/mol for the heat of formation of $H_2O(l)$ and −395 kJ/mol for $CO_2(g)$, calculate the heat of formation of each of the alkanes. Prepare a plot of $\Delta H_{f,293}^{\circ}$ against the number of carbon atoms in these molecules and predict the heat of formation of n-C_9H_{20}.

$$C_nH_{2n+2}(l) + \frac{(3n + 1)}{2} O_2(g) \longrightarrow nCO_2(g) + (n + 1)H_2O(l)$$

CHAPTER 28

Metals and Metallurgy

In the 1960s we were reminded of the limits to our natural resources by a series of Whole Earth catalogs. In 1970 R. Buckminster Fuller gave us an "Operating Manual For Spaceship Earth," another reminder that the vast and beautiful spaces of our planet are part of a finite system.

Each year the Bureau of Mines of the U.S. Department of the Interior publishes a large volume of "Mineral Facts and Problems." Turning its data-filled pages also brings to mind a picture of the Whole Earth that is our resource. The minerals needed for production of essential metals are buried all over the globe, some in countries that rarely come to our attention.

Most of the nickel is in New Caledonia and Zimbabwe. Most of the chromium is in Botswana and Turkey. Our industrialized society dictates the interdependence of countries on all continents. For example, almost all of the titanium that is essential for our jet engines, space vehicles, and missiles is imported into the United States from Australia and India. And 97% of the manganese that we use, a metal necessary for steelmaking, comes from Gabon, Brazil, the Republic of South Africa, France, and a few other countries. It is obvious that there are very practical, political, and economic, as well as scientific, implications in such data.

METALS

28.1 GENERAL PROPERTIES OF METALS

When we think of the term "metal" we are inclined to consider substances that are dense, high melting, malleable and ductile (Section 9.6), and good conductors of heat and electricity. The metals with which we are most familiar have these characteristics. However, the common metals are not representative of all metals. More than three-fourths of the elements are metals. They appear in all of the families of the periodic table except the halogen and noble gas families. Metals, therefore, should show a wide range of properties, and indeed they do. The density of lithium is 0.534 g/cm^3, whereas that of platinum is 21.45 g/cm^3. Mercury is a liquid at ordinary temperatures, but osmium melts at 3045 °C. Sodium and potassium are soft enough to be cut easily with a knife, but iron and chromium are very hard. Sodium reacts violently with water, but platinum and gold do not react even with hot hydrochloric acid.

Yet the metals do have certain properties in common. All of them have a tendency (though in quite varying degrees) to form positive ions, and thus to form salts. All of them, when freshly cut, have a bright luster. (Many metals lose their luster quickly when exposed to air because oxides, carbonates, or sulfides form on their surfaces by reaction of the metal with oxygen, carbon dioxide, or hydrogen sulfide in the air.) Metals are good conductors of heat and electricity, though, again, to quite different degrees. These common properties of metals all depend upon the availability of the electrons of the metal atoms. We have discussed ionization in terms of valence electron configurations, ionization energies, and relative electronegativities (Sections 10.6–10.9). The electrical and thermal conductivities as well as the luster of metals depend upon the presence of electrons that are not bound to

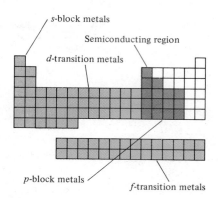

Figure 28.1
Metals in the Periodic Table

individual atoms, but move freely through the metal (Sections 9.5 and 9.6). The molecular orbital description of bonding provides the best picture of the behavior of these mobile electrons. Metallic bonding from the molecular orbital viewpoint, and the distinctions among conductors, insulators, and semiconductors, are discussed in Section 30.7.

In studying the properties of metals, it must be kept in mind that there is no sharp line separating metals from nonmetals. The semiconducting elements are neither distinctly metallic nor distinctly nonmetallic (Figure 28.1). In general, as one proceeds to the left of the semiconductor region of the periodic table, the metallic behavior of the elements becomes more marked, although correlations of metallic behavior with position in the periodic table are not always entirely reliable. Aluminum is certainly a metal, but it has a few of the chemical characteristics of nonmetals (for example, its anhydrous chloride is volatile and soluble in benzene). The *d*-transition metals include those elements such as copper, iron, gold, and silver that best represent the properties commonly thought of as metallic.

28.2 THE WHOLE EARTH

The planet earth is, at least at the present time, the only source we have for all of the raw materials needed to sustain life and support our lifestyle. We draw gases from the atmosphere, water and some elements and chemical compounds from the hydrosphere, and fossil fuels, metals, and structural materials from the lithosphere (Figure 28.2).

The portion of the solid earth that is available to us is a very small part of the whole (less than 1% by mass). The deepest mine extends only 3.8 km beneath the surface. Geologists define the earth's crust (by studying earthquake waves) as the

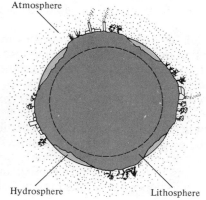

Figure 28.2
The Three Regions of the Earth
(Not drawn to scale.) The atmosphere includes all of the gases that surround the Earth. The hydrosphere includes all of the water on the surface of the planet. The lithosphere is the strong and rigid outer portion of the solid Earth.

Table 28.1
Average Composition of the Crust of the Earth (Igneous Rocks)

	Mass %
Element*	
Oxygen	46.6
Silicon	27.72
Aluminum	8.13
Iron	5.0
Calcium	3.63
Sodium	2.83
Potassium	2.59
Magnesium	2.09
Titanium	0.44
Phosphorus	0.118
Manganese	0.10
Other nonmetals (excluding noble gases)	$\sim 10^{-2} - 10^{-4}$ each
Other metals (nonradioactive)	$\sim 10^{-2} - 10^{-7}$ each
As oxides†	
SiO_2	61.9
Al_2O_3	15.6
CaO	5.7
FeO	3.9
Fe_2O_3	2.6
Na_2O	3.1
MgO	3.1
K_2O	2.9
TiO_2	0.8
P_2O_5	0.3
MnO	0.1

* *Source:* Therald Moeller, *Inorganic Chemistry: A Modern Introduction* (New York: Wiley, 1982), pp. 24, 25.

† *Source:* I. G. Gass, P. J. Smith, R. C. L. Wilson (eds.), *Understanding the Earth: A Reader in the Earth Sciences* (2nd ed., published for the Open University by The Artemis Press Ltd., Horsham, Sussex, 1972), p. 56.

region about 30 to 50 km deep that lies over the mantle, which is a region of much greater density (Figure 28.3).

Three major types of rocks are found in the earth's crust: igneous rocks, formed by solidification of molten substances; sedimentary rocks, formed by deposition of material by the oceans and rivers; and metamorphic rocks, formed by the action of heat and pressure on existing rocks. The most abundant substances in rocks are silicates, which are composed of metal cations and SiO_4 tetrahedra combined in many different ways (Section 30.16). Table 28.1 gives the average composition of the earth's crust reported as mass percentages of the elements and, as is the custom of geochemists, as mass percentage of oxides of the principal elements.

A **mineral** is a naturally occurring inorganic substance with a characteristic crystal structure and composition. The compositions of many minerals, particularly the silicates, vary within the limits set by their crystal structures, because a variety of metal cations can occupy similar sites in the anionic framework.

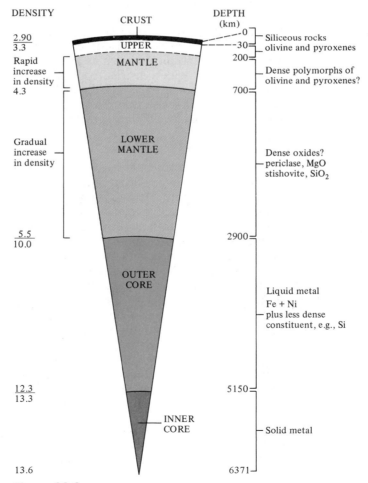

Figure 28.3
A Schematic Section through the Earth (Source: I. G. Gass et al., (eds.), *Understanding the Earth*, Cambridge: M.I.T. Press, 1971, p. 59.)

28.3 THE OCCURRENCE OF METALS

The form in which metals occur in the earth's crust depends chiefly upon the solubilities of their salts and the ease with which they react with water or are oxidized. Very unreactive metals, such as gold, silver, and platinum, are usually found in nature in the elemental state. If, early in their geological history, these metals were present in the form of compounds, these compounds were unstable and have long since decomposed. The somewhat more reactive metals are still present in the form of sulfides (e.g., CuS, PbS, ZnS) which, because of their extremely low solubility, have resisted both oxidation and reactions with water. The still more reactive metals have been converted to oxides (e.g., MnO_2, Al_2O_3, TiO_2) and are mined in that form.

The highly reactive metals of the beryllium family, along with aluminum, have formed salts. Calcium and magnesium occur widely as carbonates, sulfates, and silicates (often containing both Ca and Mg). Magnesium sulfate is readily soluble in water and is found in many mineral springs. Calcium sulfate ($CaSO_4 \cdot 2H_2O$, gypsum) is only slightly soluble, but enough so to contribute to the hardness of natural waters (Section 14.11; noncarbonate hardness). In the presence of dissolved carbon dioxide, calcium carbonate is dissolved as the hydrogen carbonate, also contributing to the hardness of water (carbonate hardness). Aluminum, which has about the same reactivity as magnesium, occurs largely in the form of aluminosilicates such as muscovite, $KAl_2(OH)_2Si_3AlO_{10}$ (one form of mica), and kaolin, $H_4Al_2Si_2O_9$ (a clay). Sometimes it occurs as the insoluble oxide, $Al_2O_3 \cdot 2H_2O$, and the complex fluoride, $Na_3[AlF_6]$.

The most reactive metals, such as sodium and potassium, are found in nature either as soluble salts in the ocean and mineral springs or in very insoluble, unreactive aluminosilicates such as albite, $NaAlSi_3O_8$, and orthoclase, $KAlSi_3O_8$. These silicates are widely distributed in all parts of the world, but since they are very stable, they are not used as sources of the metals which they contain. The slow weathering of orthoclase is important, however, for it liberates potassium ions, which are essential for all plant growth.

THE PREPARATION OF METALS

28.4 METALLURGY

Metallurgy is the science and technology of metals—their production from the compounds in which they occur in nature, their purification, and the study of their properties. Here we are interested in how pure or relatively pure metals are produced from their ores (extractive metallurgy).

Most metals occur in nature as minerals found as crystals scattered through the surrounding rock or in veins in the rock. If the combination of rocky matrix and mineral can profitably be mined and treated for extraction of the metal it is called an **ore**. The percentages of metals in ores vary over a wide range—a typical ore of iron may contain 50% iron, whereas some valuable copper ores contain less than 1% of the metal. The determining factor is a balance between the economic value of the metal in the ore and the ease with which the metal can be won from the ore. As the supplies of ores that contain higher percentages of metals are exhausted, industry must turn to lower and lower grade ores.

The procedures needed to produce pure metals from ores fall into three general categories: (1) concentration of the ore; (2) extraction of the metal from the concentrated ore, which includes reduction of the metal from a positive oxidation state to the free metal; and (3) refining of the crude metal.

a. Concentration It is desirable to separate the valuable mineral from as much as possible of the unwanted rock, collectively called the **gangue** (pronounced "gang"). Usually the first step is crushing or grinding the ore into smaller pieces so that separating the mineral from the gangue will be easier.

The separation is commonly carried out by **flotation**—concentration of the metal-bearing mineral in a froth of bubbles that can be skimmed off. The finely crushed ore is placed in a large tank containing water, a wetting agent such as pine oil that will wet the metal-bearing mineral but not the unwanted silicate rock particles, a carefully selected surface-active agent, and possibly also a frothing agent. The surface-active agent functions like a soap or detergent molecule (Section 15.20); it has a polar end that is adsorbed on the mineral surface and a hydrophobic, hydrocarbon end that is drawn into the air bubble, carrying the mineral into the froth (Figure 28.4).

b. Extraction Extraction of the metal from the concentrated ore requires reduction of the metal from a positive oxidation state to the free metal. Before reduction to give the free metal, other operations may be necessary. A finely divided ore may undergo **sintering**—heating without melting to cause the formation of larger particles. An ore may undergo **calcining**—heating to drive off a gas, often to convert a carbonate to an oxide,

$$4FeCO_3(s) + O_2(g) \xrightarrow{\Delta} 2Fe_2O_3(s) + 4CO_2(g) \qquad \textbf{(28.1)}$$

or to convert a hydrate to an oxide,

$$Fe_2O_3 \cdot 2Fe(OH)_3 \xrightarrow{\Delta} 2Fe_2O_3(s) + 3H_2O(g) \qquad \textbf{(28.2)}$$

In **roasting,** a term usually applied to sulfide ores, the ore is heated below its melting point in air or oxygen to convert sulfides to oxides, for example,

$$2PbS(s) + 3O_2(g) \longrightarrow 2PbO(s) + 2SO_2(g) \qquad \textbf{(28.3)}$$

The processes for extracting and reducing metals, and also those used in metal refining, fall into three general areas of metallurgy: pyrometallurgy, electrometallurgy, and hydrometallurgy.

Since the beginning of civilization, most metals have been obtained from their ores by high-temperature methods. The processes of **pyrometallurgy** employ chemical reactions carried out at high temperatures. For example, in **smelting,** reduction of a mineral yields the molten metal, which in the process is separated from unwanted rock. The reducing agent in smelting is usually carbon or another metal. The oxides produced by roasting sulfide ores are generally reduced by smelting with carbon.

$$ZnO(s) + C(s) \xrightarrow{\Delta} Zn(l) + CO(g) \qquad \textbf{(28.4)}$$

Ordinarily, the concentration process does not make a complete separation of the gangue from the mineral. The remaining gangue is removed during smelting by

Figure 28.4
Froth Flotation Cell The mixture is vigorously stirred and a strong stream of air is blown through the tank carrying the coated mineral particles to the surface with the air bubbles. Most of the unwanted rock sinks to the bottom of the tank. A concentrated ore is obtained in this way. The flotation process has been so highly developed that it can even be used to separate very similar minerals; in the Arizona copper industry, molybdenum sulfide and copper sulfide are separated from each other by flotation.

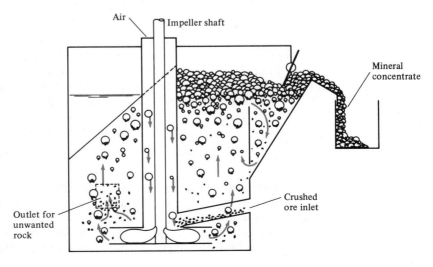

adding something that will react with it, called a **flux,** to give a material, called the **slag,** that is liquid at the temperature of the smelting furnace. Most slags are silicates, for example,

$$\underset{rock}{SiO_2(s)} + \underset{limestone}{\overset{flux}{CaCO_3(s)}} \overset{\Delta}{\longrightarrow} \underset{\substack{calcium \\ silicate}}{\overset{slag}{CaSiO_3(l)}} + CO_2(g) \qquad (28.5)$$

The molten metal and the slag form separate layers in the furnace and are drawn off at different points. The slag solidifies to a glassy mass that may be discarded or may be used to make Portland cement (Section 30.17c).

Electrometallurgy is a general term for processes that utilize electrical energy in the reduction of minerals or the refining of metals. For example, the metals of the lithium family are so reactive that their compounds cannot be reduced by heating with carbon, so they are often reduced by electrolysis of molten salts (Section 28.5).

Hydrometallurgy is the general term for processes that utilize aqueous solutions in the extraction and reduction of metals. As the richer ores have been depleted and it has become necessary to use poorer ones, pyrometallurgical methods have become less efficient. For some metals and some ores, they are being replaced by hydrometallurgical processes. In these, the metal or a compound of the metal is dissolved out of the ore by water or an aqueous solution in a process called **leaching.** After suitable purification of the solution, a pure compound of the metal may be isolated from it. Reduction to the metal may be carried out directly in the solution by a chemical or electrochemical reaction. Often, the leach solution is regenerated and can be used again.

Hydrometallurgy offers several advantages. First, the ore does not have to be concentrated. It is only broken into small pieces and the leach solution is allowed to run through it. Second, the use of large amounts of coal and coke to roast the ore and then to reduce it is avoided. Third, pollution of the atmosphere by such by-products of pyrometallurgy as sulfur dioxide, arsenic(III) oxide, and furnace dust is avoided.

Some typical reactions which take place in leaching processes are

$$2CuFeS_2(s) + H_2SO_4(aq) + 4O_2(g) \longrightarrow 2CuSO_4(aq) + Fe_2O_3(s) + 3S(s) + H_2O(l)$$
$$PbSO_4(s) + 4NaCl(aq) \longrightarrow Na_2[PbCl_4](aq) + Na_2SO_4(aq)$$

The leaching of native gold from its ores,

$$4Au(s) + 8CN^- + O_2(g) + 2H_2O(l) \longrightarrow 4[Au(CN)_2]^- + 4OH^-$$

was one of the first hydrometallurgical processes; it was introduced in the late nineteenth century. Some regions where "cyaniding" was practiced in earlier years still retain sufficient cyanide to be dangerous.

Chemical reduction of the solubilized compounds can be effected by displacement by a more reactive metal or by reaction with some other type of reducing agent, for example,

$$CuSO_4(aq) + Fe(s) \longrightarrow FeSO_4(aq) + Cu(s)$$
$$[Ni(NH_3)_4]SO_4(aq) + H_2(g) \overset{\Delta}{\longrightarrow} Ni(s) + (NH_4)_2SO_4(aq) + 2NH_3(aq)$$

c. Refining   The **refining,** or purification, of crude metals is important for two reasons: First, the impurities may make the metal unfit for use. For example, even a small fraction of a percent of arsenic (a common impurity) in copper lowers the electrical conductivity by 10% to 20%. Second, the impurities in the metal may be valuable. Lead sulfide ore often contains a small amount of silver sulfide, Ag_2S. The silver is carried along with the lead in the concentration, roasting, and smelting processes, and therefore appears in the final product. If silver is present in an appreciable amount, its removal more than pays for itself. Most of the silver of commerce is a by-product of the metallurgy of lead and copper.

Methods for refining crude metal include electrolytic purification (as for copper; Section 28.6), oxidation of impurities to be removed (as for iron; Section 28.7), or distillation of low-boiling metals such as mercury or zinc.

There are many variations on these metallurgical processes. The exact method used for each ore depends upon the nature of the ore, the metals it contains, and economic considerations. In recent years, many changes in metallurgical operations have been initiated because of the need to turn to lower grade ores and also by the desire to reduce environmental pollution.

In the following sections the extractive metallurgy of several industrially important metals is discussed. Sodium and aluminum are representative of active metals that are best reduced electrochemically. Copper and zinc are examples of metals that are won from stable sulfide minerals by pyrometallurgy combined with other types of processes. Iron and steel, which are essential to our industrial society, are also obtained by pyrometallurgical processes.

28.5 ELECTROMETALLURGY: SODIUM AND ALUMINUM

The alkali metals are the most electropositive of all elements. To obtain the free alkali metals from their compounds, the following reduction must be carried out in the absence of water:

$$M^+ + e^- \longrightarrow M$$

The reduction process requires the expenditure of much energy. One convenient way to supply this energy is with electricity. Most sodium is produced by electrolysis of molten sodium chloride by what is called the Downs process (Figure 28.5).

$$\text{cathode} \quad 2Na^+ + 2e^- \longrightarrow 2Na(l)$$
$$\text{anode} \quad 2Cl^- \longrightarrow Cl_2(g) + 2e^-$$

Because sodium chloride melts at 808 °C, which is close to the boiling point of sodium, calcium chloride is added to lower the melting point to about 600 °C. This also permits the electrolysis to be carried out more economically. Resistance to the flow of electric current is the source of the heat required to keep the salt mixture molten. Lithium is also produced by electrolysis of its chloride.

At present there is no economical method for the extraction of aluminum from the silicate minerals and clays, and the source of practically all of the metal is *bauxite,* an ore that contains a high concentration of hydrated aluminum oxide, $Al_2O_3 \cdot xH_2O$.

Bauxite is generally found associated with large amounts of silica (SiO_2) and iron(III) oxide (Fe_2O_3), and these substances must be removed before the aluminum can be obtained in metallic form. The purification of bauxite is accomplished by the Bayer process, which takes advantage of the differences in the acid–base properties of the oxides. Aluminum oxide is amphoteric, whereas iron(III) oxide is basic and silica is a relatively inert acidic oxide. The crude bauxite is digested under pressure with hot sodium hydroxide solution, which dissolves the aluminum oxide as sodium tetrahydroxoaluminate, $Na[Al(OH)_4]$, and leads to precipitation of silica as a complex sodium aluminum silicate. Iron(III) oxide and other impurities are unaffected by the sodium hydroxide treatment. Insoluble materials are removed by filtration, and the filtrate is then diluted with water and cooled, precipitating the aluminum hydroxide. The precipitate is separated by filtration and converted to the pure anhydrous oxide, Al_2O_3, by heating. The sodium hydroxide solution is concentrated and used again.

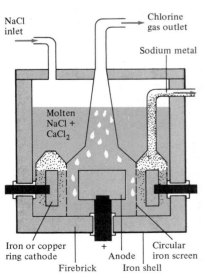

Figure 28.5
The Downs Cell for the Production of Sodium

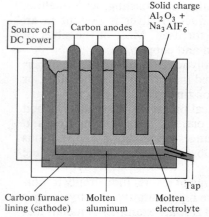

Source of DC power

Carbon anodes

Solid charge
Al₂O₃ +
Na₃AlF₆

Tap

Carbon furnace lining (cathode)   Molten aluminum   Molten electrolyte

Figure 28.6
Electrolytic Cell for Production of Aluminum

Aluminum metal is obtained from the anhydrous oxide by an electrolytic method known in this country as the Hall process. While he was a student at Oberlin College, Charles Martin Hall, inspired by a professor's remark that a fortune awaited the man who could invent a cheap process for producing aluminum, set this as his goal. In 1886 at the age of 21, shortly after he graduated, he succeeded. Hall did become a rich man, and a memorial to him in the form of an aluminum statue stands on the Oberlin campus. The Hall process is used today with only minor modifications. Before introduction of the Hall process, aluminum was rare and highly prized. Denmark's King Christian X wore an aluminum crown, and Napoleon III set the table with aluminum knives and forks for his most important guests.

In the electrolytic cells (Figure 28.6) for the Hall process, steel boxes lined with graphite are the cathodes. The electrolyte is molten cryolite (Na_3AlF_6, a mineral found only in Greenland) or a molten mixture of sodium, calcium, and aluminum fluorides. The purified aluminum oxide dissolves readily in such electrolytes. Carbon rods, which serve as anodes, are suspended in the molten solution, and electrolysis is carried out at temperatures in the neighborhood of 900°–1000 °C. During electrolysis, Al^{3+} ions from the oxide migrate toward the cell lining (the cathode) where they are reduced to the liquid metal, which collects at the bottom of the cell. (The AlF_6^{3-} of the electrolyte is not reduced because of its great stability.) At the carbon anodes, the main electrolytic reaction is the oxidation of O^{2-} ions to molecular oxygen. In addition, elemental fluorine is formed by oxidation of fluoride ions present in the melt. Both the oxygen and the fluorine react with the carbon anodes, which are gradually consumed and must be replaced periodically. The Hall process yields aluminum of a purity between 99.0 and 99.9%.

28.6 METALS FROM SULFIDE ORES: COPPER AND ZINC

After concentration by crushing and flotation, copper ore is roasted and smelted in a multi-step process that must accomplish the separation of the iron and copper sulfides that are present in most copper ores (chalcocite, Cu_2S; chalcopyrite, $CuFeS_2$). The ore may first be roasted to drive off some of the sulfur as sulfur dioxide and sulfur trioxide. Next, in a reverberatory furnace (Figure 28.7), partial separation of iron and copper is accomplished. Heating with a silica flux converts iron oxides and some of the iron sulfide to slag, but does not affect the copper. The product from the furnace is a molten mixture of copper and iron sulfides called the *matte*. The iron silicate slag floats on top of the matte. Some of the reactions that take place in the furnace are the following:

$$FeS_2(l) + O_2(g) \xrightarrow{\Delta} FeS(l) + SO_2(g)$$

$$3FeS(l) + 5O_2(g) \xrightarrow{\Delta} Fe_3O_4(l) + 3SO_2(g)$$

$$2CuFeS_2(l) + O_2(g) \xrightarrow{\Delta} Cu_2S(l) + 2FeS(l) + SO_2(g)$$

$$Fe_3O_4(l) + FeS(l) + 4SiO_2(s) + O_2(g) \xrightarrow{\Delta} 4FeSiO_3(l) + SO_2(g)$$
$$\text{iron silicate}$$
$$\text{slag}$$

The molten sulfide mixture is transferred to a converter where it is smelted with silica in the presence of oxygen that is blown through the mixture. Here, the remaining iron is separated in the iron silicate slag that forms and the final reduction to copper metal is accomplished.

$$2Cu_2S(l) + 3O_2(g) \longrightarrow 2Cu_2O(l) + 2SO_2(g)$$
$$2Cu_2O(l) + Cu_2S(l) \longrightarrow 6Cu(l) + SO_2(g)$$

If the sulfur dioxide produced in the smelting of copper and other sulfide minerals is allowed to escape into the atmosphere, it not only creates an unpleasant

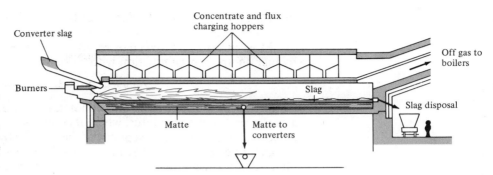

**Figure 28.7
Reverberatory Furnace Used in the
Smelting of Roasted Copper Ore
Concentrate** Slag from the converter
is returned for further separation of
copper.

odor, but also affects the health of those who inhale it. If it is present in high
concentration, it may kill growing plants for several miles downwind from the
smelter. Moreover, it is slowly converted in the air to sulfur trioxide, which, in turn,
reacts with moisture in the atmosphere to produce sulfuric acid (see An Aside: Air
Pollution, Smog, and Acid Rain, Chapter 26). Smelters in some localities in the
United States have been forced by government action to remove the sulfur dioxide
from stack gases and convert it to nonpolluting products. This can be done either by
catalytically oxidizing the sulfur dioxide in the stack to sulfuric acid (via sulfur
trioxide) or by reducing it to elemental sulfur by passing it over red hot carbon.

$$SO_2(g) + 2C(s) \longrightarrow S(l) + 2CO(g)$$

The products of these reactions (H_2SO_4 and S) are useful materials, but commonly
they cannot be sold for enough to pay for their recovery. However, the pollution
problem in the vicinity of smelters is so great that removal of the sulfur dioxide from
the stack gases is necessary.

The copper from smelting a sulfide ore is quite impure, the chief impurities
being silver, gold, iron, zinc, lead, arsenic, sulfur, copper(I) oxide, and bits of slag. By
heating the molten metal in a stream of air, most of the arsenic and sulfur are
converted to the volatile oxides and escape. The other impurities are removed by an
electrolytic process. Bars of the crude copper serve as anodes in the electrolysis and
plates of pure copper as the cathodes; a mixture of dilute sulfuric acid, sodium
chloride, and copper(II) sulfate is the electrolyte (Figure 28.8). By careful control of
the voltage across the cell, only copper and the more electropositive metal impurities
(e.g., iron, zinc, lead) in the anode are oxidized and dissolved. Metallic impurities less
electropositive than copper, such as silver and gold, are unaffected and drop from the
anode as it disintegrates. These anode sludges are worked over and valuable metal
by-products of the refining process are recovered. Voltage control is so maintained
that only copper, the least electropositive of the various metals that dissolve from the
anode, is plated out on the pure copper cathode. The refining process yields
electrolytic copper, which has a purity of greater than 99.9%.

The most common zinc ores are *sphalerite* or *zinc blende,* ZnS, and *smithsonite,*
$ZnCO_3$. Others of significance are *zincite,* ZnO, and *franklinite* $(Zn,Mn)O \cdot xFe_2O_3$.
[The expression $(Zn,Mn)O$ indicates that the zinc and manganese are not present in
any fixed ratio. Different samples of ore contain the metals in different ratios. The x
preceding the formula Fe_2O_3 indicates that the ratio of zinc and manganese to iron is
also variable.]

The property of zinc most significant for its extraction from ores is its low boiling
point, 907 °C, which allows it to be distilled away from molten rock and in some
cases refined by distillation. The metallurgy of franklinite ore is interesting, for upon
reduction at a high temperature, it yields zinc, manganese, and iron. The zinc distills

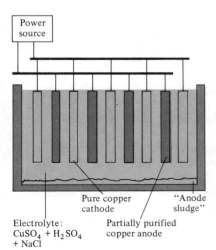

**Figure 28.8
Electrolytic Cell for Refining Copper**

from the mixture and is condensed outside the furnace. The manganese–iron alloy that remains is used directly in the manufacture of alloy steels.

Most zinc ores are treated by roasting to convert the sulfide to the oxide, followed by high-temperature reduction with carbon,

$$ZnO(s) + C(s) \xrightarrow{\Delta} Zn(g) + CO(g)$$

At the temperature at which the reaction takes place, zinc is a gas, and it escapes into a cooler part of the apparatus, where it condenses. The zinc usually contains specks of carbon that have been swept out of the furnace by the escaping carbon monoxide gas and zinc vapor. The irregulary shaped pieces of zinc, called "mossy zinc" and often used for reactions in the laboratory, are formed by pouring molten zinc into water.

Zinc is also extracted by hydrometallurgical methods. For example, a solution of zinc sulfate can be obtained by leaching the sulfide ore with sulfuric acid in the presence of oxygen.

$$2ZnS(s) + O_2(g) + 2H_2SO_4(aq) \longrightarrow 2ZnSO_4(aq) + 2S(s) + 2H_2O(l)$$

Zinc dust is stirred into the solution of zinc sulfate to reduce and precipitate any metals which may be present that are more easily reduced than zinc, for example,

$$Zn(s) + CdSO_4(aq) \longrightarrow ZnSO_4(aq) + Cd(s)$$
$$3Zn(s) + Sb_2(SO_4)_3(aq) \longrightarrow 3ZnSO_4(aq) + 2Sb(s)$$

The solution of zinc sulfate is then filtered and electrolyzed to give pure metallic zinc:

$$\begin{aligned} cathode \qquad & Zn^{2+} + 2e^- \longrightarrow Zn(s) \\ anode \qquad & 2H_2O(l) \longrightarrow 4H^+ + O_2(g) + 4e^- \end{aligned}$$

The overall reaction is

$$2ZnSO_4(aq) + 2H_2O(l) \xrightarrow{electrolysis} 2Zn(s) + O_2(g) + 2H_2SO_4(aq)$$

EXAMPLE 28.1
Chemical Reactions: Compounds of Metals

The following reactions take place in the roasting and hydrometallurgical extraction of zinc:

(a) $ZnS(s) + 2O_2(g) \longrightarrow ZnSO_4(s)$
(b) $2ZnS(s) + 3O_2(g) \longrightarrow 2ZnO(s) + 2SO_2(g)$
(c) $ZnO(s) + H_2SO_4(aq) \longrightarrow ZnSO_4(aq) + H_2O(l)$
(d) $Zn(s) + CdSO_4(aq) \longrightarrow ZnSO_4(aq) + Cd(s)$

How can each of these reactions be classified? (Consult Table 17.10.)

(a) One of the reactants is an element. This is therefore a redox reaction—the combination of an element and a compound.
(b) This is also a redox reaction of an element; elemental oxygen combines with both elements in a binary compound.
(c) One of the reactants, aqueous sulfuric acid, contains sulfate ions. The reaction is a nonredox partner-exchange reaction between a basic oxide and an acid to form water as a product.
(d) Elemental zinc is a reactant. This is a redox displacement reaction in which a more active metal displaces a less active metal.

EXAMPLE 28.2
Redox Reactions: Copper Metallurgy

The following reactions take place in the copper converter:

(a) $2Cu_2S(l) + 3O_2(g) \longrightarrow 2Cu_2O(l) + 2SO_2(g)$
(b) $2Cu_2O(l) + Cu_2S(l) \longrightarrow 6Cu(l) + SO_2(g)$

Identify the oxidizing and reducing agents. Show that each equation is correctly balanced by demonstrating that the increase and decrease in oxidation numbers are equal.

(a) Oxygen is the oxidizing agent ($\overset{0}{O_2} \longrightarrow S\overset{-2}{O_2}$) and sulfide ion in the molten salt is the reducing agent ($\overset{-2}{S^{2-}} \longrightarrow S\overset{+4}{O_2}$)

$$\overset{(6)(-2) = -12}{\boxed{}}$$
$$2Cu_2S + 3O_2 \longrightarrow 2Cu_2O + 2SO_2$$
$$\underset{(2)(+6) = +12}{\boxed{}}$$

The total decrease in oxidation number (-12) and the total increase ($+12$) are equal.

(b) All of the copper is reduced and the copper(I) in the molten salts is the oxidizing agent ($\overset{+1}{Cu} \longrightarrow \overset{0}{Cu}$). As in reaction (a), the sulfide ion is the reducing agent ($\overset{-2}{S^{2-}} \longrightarrow S\overset{+4}{O_2}$).

$$\overset{(6)(-1) = -6}{\boxed{}}$$
$$2Cu_2O + Cu_2S \longrightarrow 6Cu + SO_2$$
$$\underset{(1)(+6) = +6}{\boxed{}}$$

The increase ($+6$) and decrease (-6) in the oxidation numbers are equal.

EXAMPLE 28.3
Electrochemistry: Copper
Metallurgy

In electrorefining copper, the copper is separated from iron, lead, zinc, gold, and silver. The electrolytic cells employ anodes of impure copper and cathodes of pure copper. Based on the following standard reduction potentials, discuss what happens in this type of cell:

$$
\begin{array}{ll}
 & E° \\
Zn^{2+} + 2e^- \longrightarrow Zn & -0.763 \text{ V} \\
Pb^{2+} + 2e^- \longrightarrow Pb & -0.126 \text{ V} \\
Cu^{2+} + 2e^- \longrightarrow Cu & +0.337 \text{ V} \\
Ag^+ + e^- \longrightarrow Ag & +0.799 \text{ V} \\
Au^+ + e^- \longrightarrow Au & +1.691 \text{ V}
\end{array}
$$

We know that oxidation—the loss of electrons—takes place at an anode. The series of electrode potentials is written above in the order of increasing ease of reduction and decreasing ease of oxidation. The voltage must be such that copper is dissolved from the impure copper anode,

$$Cu \longrightarrow Cu^{2+} + 2e^-$$

which means that lead and zinc, which are more easily oxidized than copper, will also be oxidized to cations and dissolve. Gold and silver are less readily oxidized than the other metals, and at the appropriately controlled voltage they will be unaffected. As the anode dissolves these metals drop to the bottom as the anode sludge.

Reduction—the gain of electrons—occurs at the cathode. Of the metal ions in solution—Cu^{2+}, Zn^{2+}, and Pb^{2+}—the copper(II) ion has the most positive standard reduction potential and is most readily reduced. Therefore, the voltage can be controlled so that only copper will be deposited at the cathode.

IRON AND STEEL

28.7 SOURCES AND USES
OF IRON

Like copper and zinc, iron occurs in nature as the sulfide (FeS_2, "pyrite" or "fool's gold"), but this mineral is not used as an ore because it is difficult to remove the last traces of sulfur during the metallurgical processes, and sulfur makes the steel brittle. Fortunately, iron also occurs in large amounts in the form of oxides. Of these, *hematite,* Fe_2O_3, is the most abundant. *Magnetite,* Fe_3O_4 (which is $FeO \cdot Fe_2O_3$), is a valuable ore, for it contains a higher percentage of iron than does iron(III) oxide. As the name implies, magnetite is attracted by a magnet; some samples, in fact, act as magnets. These are called *lodestone.*

Iron(II) carbonate, or *siderite,* $FeCO_3$, is a good source of iron, for it is converted by heat to oxides, which can be reduced to metal. Siderite is present in many soils and contributes to hardness in water through its ready conversion to the soluble hydrogen carbonate.

$$FeCO_3(s) + CO_2(g) + H_2O(l) \rightleftharpoons Fe(HCO_3)_2(aq)$$

In air, iron(II) hydrogen carbonate in solution is oxidized to the insoluble iron(III) oxide.

$$4Fe(HCO_3)_2(aq) + O_2(g) \longrightarrow 2Fe_2O_3(s) + 8CO_2(g) + 4H_2O(l)$$

This accounts for the brown stain so often seen under dripping faucets and in other places where hard water is in contact with air.

Taconite ores, which are chiefly iron oxides containing silica, are now increasingly used in the United States as sources of iron. They are extremely hard and difficult to handle, but metallurgical research has overcome most of the problems.

The term **steel** is used for alloys (Section 28.10) of iron that contain carbon (up to ~ 1.5%), and often other metals as well. Without carbon, iron is not strong enough or hard enough for many modern applications. The properties of steel depend upon the percentage of carbon present, the heat treatment of the steel, and the alloying metals present. Low-carbon, or mild, steel contains up to 0.2% carbon. It is malleable and ductile and is used in making wire, pipe, and sheet steel. Medium steel (0.2–0.6% carbon) is used in rails, boiler plate, and structural pieces. High-carbon steel (0.6–1.5% carbon) is hard, but lacks ductility and flexibility. It is used for tools, springs, and cutlery.

Almost all of the metallic iron produced is used in steel or other alloys. Some of the nonsteel alloys of iron are cast iron (> 1.5% C), nickel–iron, and iron–silicon alloys.

28.8 IRONMAKING: THE BLAST
FURNACE

The raw materials for ironmaking are (1) iron ore that has been concentrated by crushing, grinding, washing, sintering, and so on, (2) coke, and (3) limestone, which serves as a flux. Crude iron, called pig iron or cast iron, is produced in a blast furnace—a tower about 100 ft high and 25 ft in diameter that is lined with special refractory (heat-resistant) brick.

The furnace is charged from the top with a mixture of iron ore, coke, and limestone (Figure 28.9). A strong (about 350 mph) blast of very hot air (or oxygen) is blown in at the bottom, where the coke is converted to carbon monoxide, which is the reducing agent. The charge is heated gradually as it descends. First the moisture is driven off. Then the ore is partially reduced by carbon monoxide. In the hotter part of the furnace the reduction of the ore to metallic iron is completed, and the limestone loses CO_2 and reacts with the impurities in the ore (mainly silicon dioxide, but also manganese and phosphorus oxides) to produce the molten slag. The molten iron and slag are immiscible and form separate layers at the bottom of the furnace.

The reduction reactions are reversible, and complete reduction takes place only if the carbon dioxide formed is destroyed. This is effected by reduction to carbon monoxide with an excess of coke.

$$CO_2(g) + C(s) \longrightarrow 2CO(g)$$

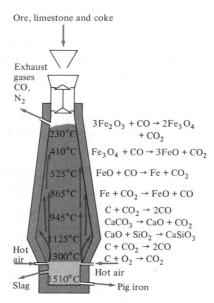

Ore, limestone and coke

Exhaust
gases
CO,
N_2

230°C $3Fe_2O_3 + CO \rightarrow 2Fe_3O_4$
                          $+ CO_2$

410°C $Fe_3O_4 + CO \rightarrow 3FeO + CO_2$

525°C $FeO + CO \rightarrow Fe + CO_2$

865°C $Fe + CO_2 \rightarrow FeO + CO$

               $C + CO_2 \rightarrow 2CO$
945°C $CaCO_3 \rightarrow CaO + CO_2$
               $CaO + SiO_2 \rightarrow CaSiO_3$
1125°C $C + CO_2 \rightarrow 2CO$
Hot $C + O_2 \rightarrow CO_2$
air   1300°C   Hot air
1510°C
Slag   Pig iron

Figure 28.9
The Blast Furnace

The gas that escapes from the top of the furnace consists largely of carbon monoxide and the nitrogen that was introduced in the air blast. This hot nitrogen–carbon monoxide mixture is combined with air so that the carbon monoxide can burn, and the products of this combustion pass through a heat exchanger to help heat the incoming gas.

Relatively pure oxygen can be used in place of air in blast furnaces. This allows for a smaller furnace and somewhat higher temperatures, and the carbon monoxide formed is a much better fuel than a carbon monoxide–nitrogen mixture. The advantages largely overcome the obvious disadvantage of the cost of the oxygen.

EXAMPLE 28.4
Chemical Reactions: Ironmaking

The following are some of the reactions that take place in the iron blast furnace:

(a) $C(s) + O_2(g) \longrightarrow CO_2(g)$
(b) $C(s) + CO_2(g) \longrightarrow 2CO(g)$
(c) $CaO(s) + SiO_2(s) \longrightarrow CaSiO_3(s)$
(d) $CaCO_3(s) \longrightarrow CaO(s) + CO_2(g)$
(e) $FeO(s) + CO(g) \longrightarrow Fe(l) + CO_2(g)$

How can each of these reactions be classified?

(a) Combination of elements. Redox reaction.
(b) Combination of element and compound. Redox reaction.
(c) Combination of compounds. Nonredox reaction.
(d) Thermal decomposition of a single compound. Nonredox reaction.
(e) Redox reaction between compounds. (Carbon monoxide is the reducing agent.)

28.9 STEELMAKING

The pig iron withdrawn from the blast furnace contains small amounts of carbon, sulfur, phosphorus, silicon, manganese, and other impurities. At this stage, the iron is so brittle that it is useless for most purposes. Ironmaking is a reduction process: The iron oxide ore is reduced. Steelmaking is an oxidation process: The impurities are oxidized. The two objectives in steelmaking are to burn out the unwanted impurities from pig iron and to add the exact amounts of alloying materials desired.

Ironmaking: reduction of iron ore
Steelmaking: oxidation of impurities

The manganese, phosphorus, and silicon in molten pig iron are converted by air or oxygen to oxides, which react with appropriate fluxes to give slags. Sulfur enters the slag as a sulfide and carbon is burned to carbon monoxide or carbon dioxide. If the chief impurity is manganese, an acidic flux — the oxide of a nonmetal — must be used. Silicon dioxide is the usual acidic flux.

$$MnO(s) + SiO_2(s) \longrightarrow MnSiO_3(l)$$

If the chief impurity is silicon or phosphorus (the more common case), a basic flux must be used. This is usually magnesium oxide or calcium oxide, which give reactions such as

$$SiO_2(s) + MgO(s) \xrightarrow{\Delta} MgSiO_3(l)$$

$$P_4O_{10}(s) + 6CaO(s) \xrightarrow{\Delta} 2Ca_3(PO_4)_2(l)$$

The steelmaking furnace is lined with brick made of the fluxing material, and this lining absorbs part of the oxide to be removed.

More than one-half of the steel in the United States is now made by the basic oxygen process, which can provide 300 tons of steel in an hour from one furnace. The older open hearth process was introduced in the late 1800s and was the major steelmaking process for many years.

The essential feature in the <u>open hearth process</u> furnace (Figure 28.10) is a large, dish-shaped container into which 100 or 200 tons of molten iron is placed. This dish is underneath a concave roof which reflects heat onto the surface of the metal. A blast of oxygen is passed over the surface of the molten crude iron to burn out the impurities. The impurities beneath the surface are brought to the top by convection and diffusion — a process which requires up to 8 h. Some iron is also oxidized, of course, but the iron oxide so formed is recovered and returned to the blast furnace.

The <u>basic oxygen process</u> of removing the impurities from iron follows the same chemical principles as the open hearth method, but is quite different in engineering design and is much faster (Figure 28.11). The molten pig iron, along with scrap iron and the materials needed to form a slag, is contained in a barrel-shaped furnace that may hold up to 300 tons of material. A blast of high-purity oxygen under a pressure of 150–180 lb/sq. inch is directed against the surface of the liquid, and the barrel can be tipped and rotated to bring fresh material to the surface. The oxidation of the impurities is very rapid, and the escape of gaseous products so agitates the mass that even the iron at the bottom of the vessel is brought into reaction. The temperature of the material rises almost to the boiling point of the iron without the application of any external heat. At such a temperature, the reactions are extremely rapid, and the

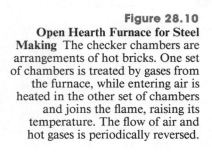

Figure 28.10
Open Hearth Furnace for Steel Making The checker chambers are arrangements of hot bricks. One set of chambers is treated by gases from the furnace, while entering air is heated in the other set of chambers and joins the flame, raising its temperature. The flow of air and hot gases is periodically reversed.

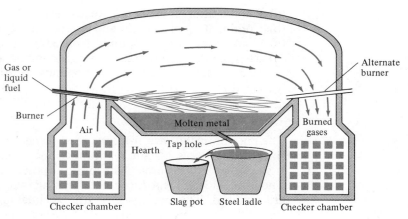

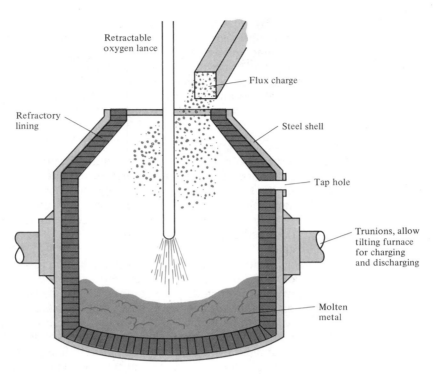

Retractable
oxygen lance

Flux charge

Refractory
lining

Steel shell

Tap hole

Trunions, allow
tilting furnace
for charging
and discharging

Molten
metal

Figure 28.11
Basic Oxygen Process Steelmaking
Furnace

whole process is completed in an hour or less, leaving a product that is uniform and of high quality.

The molten purified iron is converted to steel by addition of the correct amount of carbon and alloying metals such as vanadium, chromium, titanium, manganese, and nickel.

The electric arc method, once used only for making small amounts of specialty steels, can now be carried out on a larger scale and is also increasing in use. An electric arc between carbon electrodes in the roof over a large saucer containing the molten metal provides the heat. Oxygen is added in controlled amounts and also released from impurities and oxides of alloying metals that are added at the beginning of the process. The advantages of this process are that the amount of oxide impurities in the steel can be controlled and that there is less loss of alloying materials, some of which are quite expensive.

28.10 HEAT TREATMENT
OF STEEL

At high temperatures, iron and carbon combine to form iron carbide, Fe_3C, called cementite. The reaction of formation is reversible, but unlike most reactions of combination, it is endothermic. As the equation

$$3Fe + C + heat \rightleftharpoons Fe_3C$$

indicates, the stability of cementite increases as the temperature rises, at least in the temperature range involved in the heat treatment of steel. When steel containing cementite is cooled slowly, the equilibrium shifts toward the formation of iron and carbon, and the carbon separates as minute flakes of graphite. These give the metal a gray color. If, however, the steel is cooled very rapidly, equilibrium is not attained and the carbon remains largely in the form of cementite, which is light in color. At ordinary temperatures the decomposition of cementite is so slow that, for all practical purposes, it does not take place at all. Steel containing cementite is harder and much more brittle than that containing graphite.

By "tempering," that is, by heating the steel to a suitable temperature for a short time and then cooling it rapidly, the ratio of carbon present as graphite and as cementite can be adjusted within rather wide limits. It is also possible to vary the total amount of carbon in different parts of a single piece of steel, and thus modify its properties. Ball bearings, for example, are made of a medium steel to give them toughness and strength, but the surface is *case hardened* by heating the bearings in a bed of carbon to give a thin surface coating containing cementite.

ALLOYS

28.11 PROPERTIES AND USES OF ALLOYS

When two or more metals, or metals plus nonmetals, are intimately mixed to yield a substance with metallic properties, they have formed an **alloy.** Although we commonly think of alloys as consisting only of metals, there are a few alloys that contain small proportions of light nonmetals, such as carbon, nitrogen, or boron. Alloys are usually prepared by melting the constituents together, but sometimes they are obtained by the simultaneous deposition of metals on electrodes in an electrolytic cell.

Alloys are extremely important in an industrial civilization because of their great diversity of properties. These are usually *not* the average of the properties of the metals of which they are composed. The melting points of many alloys are lower or higher than the average of the melting points of the component metals. For example, solder (tin–lead) melts at a lower temperature than either tin or lead. The so-called fusible alloys, many with melting points below 100 °C, have a diversity of uses. For example, the cavities in metal parts are filled with a fusible alloy which is allowed to harden. The parts can be machined while the alloy prevents distortion of the shape; the parts are then immersed in hot water to remove the alloy, which can be reused. Fusible alloys are also present in automatic fire extinguishers and electrical fuses.

An alloy may show greater resistance to corrosion or other chemical attack than its constituents. Stainless steel, which is chiefly iron, chromium (about 18%), and nickel (about 8%), and smaller amounts of other elements, is not attacked by hydrochloric acid, although the individual metals in it are easily dissolved.

Some alloys have much greater electrical resistance than their components. This property makes nichrome and chromel (both largely nickel and chromium) useful in electrical resistance heaters (for example, in toasters, space heaters, and a myriad of other devices). It should be noted that these alloys also resist atmospheric corrosion —they do not "rust away" even when heated to redness many times.

Other alloys have remarkable magnetic properties. Highly magnetic devices are now usually made of Alnico (chiefly iron, aluminum, nickel, and cobalt).

Steel is greatly hardened by alloying it with manganese, vanadium, and other metals. These alloys and similar ones are used in armor plate, the jaws of rock crushers, safes, and bank vaults.

The color of an alloy may also be quite different from the colors of its component metals. Alloys of gold with copper are red or yellow, those with palladium or nickel are white, those with silver or cadmium are green, those with iron are blue, and those with aluminum are purple.

28.12 TYPES OF ALLOYS

The wide ranges of properties of alloys are due, in part, to the fact that alloys are of many different kinds. Some alloys are simple heterogeneous mixtures—polycrystalline materials with small areas of different metals in contact. Other alloys are solid solutions—homogeneous mixtures in which the atoms of one metal are randomly distributed among the atoms of another metal. Still others are actually intermetallic compounds.

Alloys that are heterogeneous mixtures result when crystals of more than one composition form as a mixture of molten metals cools. Melted metals, like other liquids, may dissolve in each other to only a limited extent. In such a case, the solubility of one metal in the other will vary with the temperature. If we think of melted metal A being dissolved in melted metal B, A may crystallize out as the temperature is lowered, leaving B (and some A) still liquid. On further cooling, this, too, will solidify. A heterogeneous alloy formed in this way will contain microscopic crystals of A embedded in a matrix of B. Alternatively, the first crystals which separate may contain both A and B, but not in the same proportion as they are in the liquid. If the surface of such an alloy is "etched" by treatment with an acid, microscopic examination will show the different types of crystals. Lead – tin solder is an alloy of this type.

The requirements for solid solution formation are (1) similar chemical properties, (2) similar crystal structures, and (3) appropriate radius ratios. A **substitutional solid solution** is an alloy in which atoms of one metal replace atoms in the crystal lattice of the other. Metals with radii that differ from each other by no more than 15% (e.g., Ni, 0.125 nm, and Cu, 0.128 nm) are completely soluble in each other in all proportions. For example, the United States "nickel" coin is 25% nickel and 75% copper. This alloy is harder and less easily corroded than either nickel or copper. Although it is mostly copper, it is white. As metal atoms become more different in size, solid solubility decreases and ultimately disappears. Silver (0.145 nm) and copper have only limited solubility in each other.

In **interstitial solid solutions** small atoms occupy the holes in the crystal structure of a metal. A series of very high-melting, extremely hard, brittle, electrically conducting, and chemically inert alloys results when various d-transition metals (e.g., Ti, Zr, Hf, V, Nb, Ta, Cr, Mo, W, or Fe) are united with nitrogen, carbon, or boron at elevated temperatures. The nitrides and carbides often have or closely approach 1:1 atomic ratios. Structural analyses show that they are formed by distortions of the metallic crystal structure by the entry of the small atoms (N, radius = 0.074 nm; C, 0.077 nm) into holes (Sections 13.9, 13.10). The borides often have structures with parallel layers of metal and boron atoms. Hydrogen combines with a number of the transition metals to give interstitial hydrides (Section 16.6e).

Some metals, when melted together, react to form alloys known as **intermetallic compounds.** These compounds have reproducible stoichiometry not based on the usual concepts of ionic or covalent bonding, but upon maintaining a constant (or nearly constant) ratio of the total number of valence electrons to the total number of atoms. For example, copper and zinc form three distinct compounds—$CuZn$, Cu_5Zn_8, and $CuZn_3$. These rather surprising formulas are rationalized by the Hume-Rothery rule (so named from the British scientist who suggested it). This rule relates the formulas of the compounds to the ratio between the total number of valence electrons and the total number of atoms in the compound. Counting one valence electron for copper and two for zinc, for the three compounds listed, these valence electron/atom ratios are as follows in terms of the formulas of the compounds or in terms of the number of atoms for every 21 electrons.

$CuZn$ (*β-brass*)	3 electrons/2 atoms	or	21 electrons/14 atoms
Cu_5Zn_8 (*γ-brass*)	21 electrons/13 atoms	or	21 electrons/13 atoms
$CuZn_3$ (*ε-brass*)	7 electrons/4 atoms	or	21 electrons/12 atoms

Compounds of these compositions are known as β-brass, γ-brass, and ϵ-brass, respectively. As the ratio of electrons to atoms increases, the metal atoms are bound more tightly together, so hardness increases and malleability and ductility decrease. ϵ-Brass is so brittle that it shatters like glass when it is struck with a hammer.

There are many alloys to which these ratios apply. All of those in which the ratio is $3:2$ are called β-alloys. They all crystallize in the same system. Examples are $AgZn$, Ag_3Al, Cu_5Sn, and Cu_5Si. Similarly, there are many γ-alloys: Au_5Zn_8, Cu_9Al_4, $Cu_{31}Si_8$, $Cu_{31}Sn_8$, $Na_{31}Pb_8$, and $Cu_8Al_3Zn_2$. These, too, all crystallize in the same system as γ-brass. The ϵ-alloys are exemplified by $AgZn_3$, Ag_5Al_3, Cu_3Sn, and Cu_3Si. At this time there is no adequate explanation for these exact ratios.

SUMMARY

28.1 GENERAL PROPERTIES OF METALS   More than three-fourths of the elements are metals, and they vary widely in properties. Nevertheless, all metals have a tendency to lose electrons (i.e., to form positive ions) and thus to form salts. All metals have a bright luster when freshly cut, and are good conductors of heat and electricity. These properties are related to the presence of electrons that are not bound to individual atoms, but move freely through the metal.

28.2 THE WHOLE EARTH   **28.3** THE OCCURRENCE OF THE METALS   The earth's crust, which extends to a depth of some 30 to 50 km, contains three kinds of rock: igneous, sedimentary, and metamorphic. The most abundant substances in rocks are silicates, composed of metal cations and SiO_4 tetrahedra. A mineral is a naturally occurring inorganic substance with a characteristic crystal structure and composition. Very unreactive metals (e.g., Au, Ag, Pt) are usually found in the elemental state. The somewhat more reactive metals (e.g., Cu, Pb, Zn) exist as sulfides of very low solubility. The still more reactive metals (e.g., Mn, Cr, Ti) are usually present as oxides. The highly reactive elements of the beryllium family (e.g., Mg, Ca) and also aluminum are found as carbonate, silicate, and sulfate salts. The most reactive metals (e.g., Na, K) occur either as soluble salts in the oceans and mineral springs or in very insoluble, unreactive aluminosilicates.

28.4 METALLURGY   An ore is a deposit of rock that contains enough of a given metal to make extraction profitable. After being crushed or ground, the metal or mineral can often be separated from much of the unwanted rock (gangue) by flotation. The crushed ore may then be heated to cause formation of larger particles (sintering), to drive off a gas (calcining), or to convert sulfides to oxides (roasting). To be extracted from minerals in the ore, a metal must be reduced from a positive oxidation state to the free metal. Many metals can be obtained by pyrometallurgy — processes involving chemical reactions carried out at high temperatures. An example is smelting, the reduction of a mineral with carbon or another metal to produce free molten metal. A flux, such as $CaCO_3$, may be added to react with the remaining gangue, forming a slag which can be separated from the molten metal. Electrometallurgy comprises those processes that use electrical energy for the reduction or refining of metals. Hydrometallurgy includes processes such as leaching that utilize water or aqueous solutions to extract or reduce metals. Once a metal has been extracted, it is refined, or purified, by electrolytic methods, oxidation of impurities, or distillation.

28.5 ELECTROMETALLURGY: SODIUM AND ALUMINUM   Most sodium is produced by electrolysis of molten sodium chloride (the Downs process). Aluminum hydroxide is extracted from bauxite, an ore containing a high concentration of $Al_2O_3 \cdot xH_2O$. After the aluminum hydroxide is purified it is heated to produce anhydrous Al_2O_3. Pure aluminum metal is then obtained by the Hall process, in which the aluminum is electrolytically reduced while dissolved in molten salt.

28.6 METALS FROM SULFIDE ORES: COPPER AND ZINC   Copper ores contain Cu_2S mixed with iron sulfides. The iron is removed by smelting with silica in the presence of oxygen to produce iron silicate; the Cu_2S is reduced to free copper, with liberation of SO_2. The metal is purified in an electrolytic cell. Zinc ores are roasted to convert zinc sulfide to zinc oxide and reduced at high temperature by carbon to give gaseous zinc. Zinc is also produced by oxidizing and dissolving ZnS to form $ZnSO_4$, which is then reduced to free zinc by electrolysis.

The common natural sources of iron include carbonate and oxide ores. Iron is produced in a blast furnace from iron ore, coke, and limestone, $CaCO_3$ (the flux). Very hot air is used to convert coke to CO, which reduces the iron oxides. $CaCO_3$ is decomposed by the heat to CaO, which reacts with impurities such as SiO_2 and oxides of other metals to form slag. The molten iron and the slag, being immiscible, are easily separated. Steels are alloys of iron that contain up to 1.5% carbon and often other metals as well. The presence of the carbon imparts strength and hardness. In steelmaking, unwanted impurities are burned out and the desired amounts of alloying materials added. In both the open hearth process and the newer, faster basic oxygen process, oxygen under pressure is used to oxidize Mn, P, Si, and other impurities; the resulting oxides react with fluxes (SiO_2 for Mn, MgO or CaO for Si or P) to form phosphates or silicates. Sulfur forms sulfides, which also become part of the slag, while carbon is oxidized to CO or CO_2.

28.10 HEAT TREATMENT OF STEEL At high temperatures, iron and carbon combine to form iron carbide, or cementite, Fe_3C. Steel containing cementite is harder and more brittle than steel containing graphite. By heating steel to a high temperature for a short time and then cooling it quickly, the ratio of graphite to cementite can be adjusted, and even varied in different parts of a single piece of steel.

28.11 PROPERTIES AND USES OF ALLOYS **28.12** TYPES OF ALLOYS An alloy is a substance with metallic properties that is formed by the intimate mixture of two metals or a metal with a nonmetal. The properties of alloys vary widely; often they are quite different from those of their components. Some alloys are heterogeneous mixtures with polycrystalline structures. Others are solid solutions—homogeneous mixtures in which the atoms of the two components are randomly distributed. In a substitutional solid solution, atoms of one metal replace atoms in the crystal lattice of the other metal. In an interstitial solid solution, small atoms occupy the holes in the crystal structure of a metal. Some metals can be melted together to form intermetallic compounds. Such compounds exhibit characteristic ratios of the total number of valence electrons to the total number of atoms.

SIGNIFICANT TERMS

mineral
metallurgy
ore
gangue
flotation
sintering
calcining
roasting
pyrometallurgy
smelting
flux
slag
electrometallurgy
hydrometallurgy
leaching
refining
steel
alloy
substitutional solid solution
interstitial solid solution
intermetallic compound

THOUGHTS ON CHEMISTRY

Smelting in the 16th Century

OF THINGS METALLIC (in 1556) by Georgius Agricola

This, indeed, is the custom of many most excellent smelters, who know how to govern the four elements (earth, air, water, fire). They combine in right proportion the ores, which are part earth, placing no more than is suitable in the furnaces; they pour in the needful quantity of water; they moderate with skill the air from the bellows; they throw the ore into that part of the fire which burns fiercely. The master sprinkles water into each part of the furnace to dampen the charcoal slightly, so that the minute parts of ore may adhere to it, which otherwise the blast of the bellows and the force of the fire would agitate and blow away with the fumes. But as the nature of the ores to be smelted varies, the smelters have to arrange the hearth now high, now low, and to place the pipe in which the nozzles of the bellows are inserted sometimes on a great and sometimes at a slight angle, so that the blast of the bellows may blow into the furnace in either a mild or a vigorous manner. For those ores which heat and fuse easily, a low hearth is necessary for the work of the smelters, and the pipe must be placed at a gentle angle to produce a mild blast from the bellows. On the contrary, those ores that heat and fuse slowly must have a high hearth, and the pipe must be placed at a steep incline in order to blow a strong blast of the bellows, and it is necessary, for this kind of ore, to have a very hot furnace in which slags, or cakes melted from pyrites, or stones which melt easily in the fire, are first melted, so that the ore should not settle in the hearth of the furnace and obstruct and choke up the tap-hole, as the minute metallic particles that have been washed from the ores are wont to do. . . .

After a quarter of an hour, when the lead which the assistant has placed in the forehearth is melted, the master opens the tap-hole of the furnace with a tapping-bar. . . . The slag first flows from the furnace into the forehearth, and in it are stones mixed with metal or with the metal adhering to them partly altered, the slag also containing earth and solidified juices. After this the material from the melted pyrites flows out, and then the molten lead contained in the forehearth absorbs the gold and silver. When that which has run out has stood for some time in the forehearth, in order to be able to separate one from the other, the master first either skims off the slags with the hooked bar or else lifts them off with an iron fork; the slags, as they are very light, float on the top. He next draws off the cakes of melted pyrites, which as they are of medium weight hold the middle place; he leaves in the forehearth the alloy of gold or silver with the lead, for these being the heaviest, sink to the bottom. . . . He repeats the same operation until a certain and definite part of the ore has been smelted, and the day's work is at an end; if the ore was rich the work is finished in eight hours; if poor, it takes a longer time.

Georgius Agricola, *De Re Metallica*, 1556. Translated by Herbert C. Hoover and Lou H. Hoover, 1912 (New York: Dover, 1950), pp,. 379ff.

QUESTIONS

Metals

28.1 What are some of the physical properties that we usually associate with metals? What are some of the chemical properties?

28.2 What do we call the elements that separate the metals from the nonmetals in the periodic table? In which portion of the periodic table is each category of elements located?

28.3 Name and write the chemical symbols for a few of the (a) *s* block metals, (b) *d*-transition metals, (c) *f*-transition metals, and (d) *p* block metals.

28.4 Name the three major types of rocks that are found in the earth's crust. How was each type formed? What is the most abundant kind of chemical compound in rocks?

28.5 What are the three mineralogical regions of the earth? What types of raw materials do we obtain from each region?

28.6 Define a "mineral." Does every mineral have a definite, fixed composition? Explain.

28.7 In what types of minerals do we generally find (a) unreactive metals, (b) the slightly reactive metals, (c) the more reactive metals, (d) the highly reactive metals, and (e) the most reactive metals?

The Preparation of Metals

28.8 Define the term "metallurgy." What does the study of metallurgy include?

28.9 How does an ore differ from a mineral? What determines whether a given mineral-rock mixture will be used for the production of a metal?

28.10 Name the three general categories of procedures needed to produce pure metals from ores.

28.11 Briefly describe one method by which gangue may be separated from the desired mineral during the concentration of an ore.

28.12 What preliminary treatment steps might be used before a concentrated ore undergoes extraction? What does each of these steps accomplish? Name three general ways in which a metal can be extracted from an ore.

28.13 How does pyrometallurgy differ from the other ways of reducing minerals? What substances are commonly used as the reducing agents in smelting? What happens to the remaining gangue during smelting?

28.14 Briefly describe a leaching process. Name some of the advantages of hydrometallurgy over other methods of extraction.

28.15 Give two reasons for refining crude metals. Name some of the processes used for purification.

28.16 Why must alkali metals be produced by the electrolysis (in the absence of water) of their compounds or by redox reactions involving other very active metals? Briefly describe how metallic sodium is produced.

28.17 In the preparation of sodium by the Downs process, calcium chloride is added to the sodium chloride to lower the melting point. A student raised the question as to why calcium metal does not form instead of sodium, since calcium is below sodium in the electromotive series. What did he overlook?

28.18 What is the name of the ore which contains a high concentration of hydrated aluminum oxide? What are the usual impurities that are found in this ore? Briefly describe how the ore is purified.

28.19 What is the name of the electrochemical process used to obtain aluminum metal from anhydrous aluminum oxide? Briefly describe this process.

28.20 Even though clays and other minerals are more abundant sources of aluminum than bauxite, they are not of commercial importance. Why?

28.21 What metal sulfide is the common impurity in copper ores? How is this impurity removed during the production of copper metal?

28.22 Name the undesirable gaseous product formed during the smelting of copper and other sulfide minerals. Why is it undesirable? How can this substance be eliminated as a pollutant?

28.23 What are the common impurities in copper metal produced by smelting? How is each of these eliminated?

28.24 What would happen during the electrolytic purification of copper if the voltage across the cell were (a) too high or (b) too low?

28.25 Write chemical equations describing the roasting of sphalerite and the subsequent high-temperature reduction by carbon to give zinc metal.

28.26 Briefly describe the hydrometallurgical method used to produce zinc metal from zinc sulfide. Write the chemical equations for the various steps.

Iron and Steel

28.27 Name some of the common minerals that contain iron. Write the chemical formula for the iron compound in each. What is the oxidation number of iron in each substance?

28.28 What does the term "steel" mean? List a few types of steel and some of their properties and uses.

28.29 Briefly describe the operation of a blast furnace. What are the raw materials and major products of the process?

28.30 What are some of the usual impurities found in pig iron? How is each of these removed from the iron? Write the chemical equations for reactions of "fluxes" with MnO, SiO_2, and P_4O_{10}.

28.31 What is the formula of cementite? Briefly discuss the equilibrium between Fe, C, and cementite.

28.32 What are the properties of steels that contain cementite? How can "tempering" give steel desirable properties?

Alloys

28.33 Define the term "alloy." Based on structure, give three classifications of alloys. Compare the general properties of alloys to those of the individual metals.

28.34 What properties are important for the metals which form substitutional solid solutions?

28.35 What characterizes interstitial solid solutions? Name some of the properties of the alloys formed between d-transition metals and small nonmetal atoms such as N, C, or B.

28.36 What criterion can be used to determine the empirical formula of possible intermetallic compounds? Show that Au_3Sn can be classified as an ϵ-alloy.

28.37 Pure copper and pure zinc are both relatively soft metals, but the alloy $CuZn_3$ is very hard. Suggest a reason.

Additional Questions

28.38 The following equations represent the chemistry involved in important metallurgical processes:

(a) $Fe_3O_4(s) + CO(g) \longrightarrow Fe(l) + CO_2(g)$
(b) $MgCO_3(s) + SiO_2(s) \longrightarrow MgSiO_3(l) + CO_2(g)$
(c) $Au(s) + CN^- + H_2O(l) + O_2(g) \longrightarrow [Au(CN)_2]^- + OH^-$

Balance each of these equations and classify each as (i) roasting, (ii) calcining, (iii) leaching, (iv) adding a flux, or (v) reduction.

28.39 Repeat Question 28.38 for

(a) Al_2O_3 (cryolite solution) $\xrightarrow{\text{electrolysis}}$ $Al(l) + O_2(g)$
(b) $PbSO_4(s) + PbS(s) \longrightarrow Pb(l) + SO_2(g)$
(c) $TaCl_5(g) + Mg(l) \longrightarrow Ta(s) + MgCl_2(l)$

28.40* Using a suitable reference source, look up the principal mineral which serves as the source for (a) antimony, (b) barium, (c) beryllium, (d) bismuth, (e) platinum, (f) tantalum, and (g) thorium.

28.41* After many years of controversy, element 41 was officially named niobium in 1950. (Many metallurgists and U.S. commercial producers still refer to it as columbium.) The major mineral is columbite (or niobite), $(Fe, Mn)(Nb, Ta)_2O_6$. The metal was first prepared by formation of the chloride by reaction of the ore with $HCl(g)$ and subsequent heating of the chloride with hydrogen gas. Write chemical equations for these processes.

Answers to Selected Questions

28.7 (a) native or free state, (b) sulfides, (c) oxides, (d) salts, (e) soluble salts.

28.17 the electromotive series is valid only for aqueous solutions under standard state conditions at 25 °C—reactions under other conditions may be different

28.20 Al is present in clays and other minerals as very stable aluminosilicates; the processing of these substances for metal production currently is not economically feasible

28.24 (a) Ag and Au might also be oxidized, or water might be decomposed to H_2 and O_2; (b) Cu would not be oxidized

28.31 Fe_3C; Fe_3C is favored at high temperatures, Fe and C are favored at low temperatures

28.38 (a) $Fe_3O_4(s) + 4CO(g) \longrightarrow 3Fe(l) + 4CO_2(g)$, reduction; (b) balanced as written, adding a flux; (c) $4Au(s) + 8CN^- + 2H_2O(l) + O_2(g) \longrightarrow 4[Au(CN)_2]^- + 4OH^-$, leaching

28.41 $(Fe,Mn)(Nb,Ta)_2O_6(s) + 12HCl(g) \longrightarrow 2(Nb,Ta)Cl_5(s) + (Fe,Mn)Cl_2(s) + 6H_2O(g)$, $2NbCl_5(s) + 5H_2(g) \longrightarrow 10HCl(g) + 2Nb(s)$

PROBLEMS

Review of Principles

28.1 Assuming complete recovery of metal, identify which ore would yield the larger quantity of copper on a mass basis: (a) an ore containing 3.80 mass % azurite, $Cu(OH)_2 \cdot 2CuCO_3$, or (b) an ore containing 4.85 mass % chalcopyrite, $CuFeS_2$.

28.2 The principal iron ore in Minnesota is hematite, Fe_2O_3. This ore is calcined to magnetite, Fe_3O_4, before being shipped to the mills in Illinois, Indiana, Michigan, Ohio, and Pennsylvania. Write the chemical equation for the calcination step. What mass of magnetite can be obtained from a metric ton of hematite?

Why is the calcination step desirable? *Answer* $6Fe_2O_3(s) \longrightarrow 4Fe_3O_4(s) + O_2(g)$; 0.967 metric ton Fe_3O_4; it is more economical to transport Fe_3O_4 (72.4% Fe) than Fe_2O_3 (69.9% Fe)

28.3* During the operation of a blast furnace, coke reacts with the oxygen in air to produce carbon monoxide, which, in turn, serves as the reducing agent for the iron ore. Assuming the formula of the iron ore to be Fe_2O_3, calculate the mass of air needed for each ton of iron produced. Assume air to be 21% O_2 by mass.

28.4 What mass of copper could be electroplated from a solution of $CuSO_4$ using an electrical current of 3.00 A flowing for 5.00 h? (Assume 100% efficiency.)

28.5 Write a balanced ion-electron equation for each electrode reaction in the Hall process for producing aluminum metal. What amount of time is needed to produce 1.00 kg of molten aluminum using a current of 1015 A? (Assume the process to be 91% efficient.) *Answer* $Al^{3+} + 3e^- \longrightarrow Al(l)$, $2O^{2-} \longrightarrow O_2(g) + 4e^-$; 3.3 h

28.6 Silver and cadmium form three intermetallic compounds. Analysis shows these compounds to contain 24.2% Ag, 49.0% Ag, and 37.5% Ag by mass, respectively. Determine the empirical formulas of these compounds and label each as a β-, γ-, or ϵ-alloy.

CHAPTER 29

The Representative Metals

The course of history has been significantly influenced by the use of metals. No doubt exists about this. Many history books open with definitions of the Stone Age, the Copper and Bronze Ages, and the Iron Age. The line of reasoning goes like this: Each time a better material was discovered, the people who had it developed faster because they could make stronger tools and more effective weapons. Copper can be worked more easily than stone, bronze is harder than copper, and so on. The introduction of the metals in the order cited paralleled the advance of civilization.

Few records of very early metallurgy exist. The designation of the Bronze and Iron Ages is based upon artifacts found in tombs and other archeological sites of known dates, and also upon some speculation about the known properties of the metals.

Bronze is a tin-copper alloy; it may have been discovered in some areas as the direct product of smelting ores that contained both metals. The argument is sometimes presented that the Iron Age followed the Bronze Age because iron has a much higher melting point than copper. It is reasoned that iron could not be utilized until ways were found to introduce air into the flames and raise the temperature of the metallurgists' furnaces. On the other hand, it may be that decorative copper and bronze objects survived in tombs, giving the impression that these were the most commonly used metals, while iron tools used by workmen in the same era simply oxidized out of existence. Perhaps a future historian among the chemistry students of today will find the answer.

29.1 METALS IN THE GROUPS OF REPRESENTATIVE ELEMENTS; THE ZINC FAMILY

The representative metals fall into Representative Groups I through V in the periodic table (see Figure 28.1). The *s* **block metals** are those of Groups I and II, which have ns^1 and ns^2 electron configurations, respectively. The *p* **block metals** appear in Groups III to V and have $ns^2 np^1$, $ns^2 np^2$, and $ns^2 np^3$ configurations. The trends to less metallic behavior across the periodic table and to more metallic behavior down each family are evident in the *p* block. In Group III, all the elements except the first (B) are metals (Al, Ga, In, Tl). In Group IV the two heaviest elements (Sn and Pb) are metals, while in Group V only the heaviest element (Bi) is a metal. The *s* and *p* block metals have in common electron configurations in which only *s* and *p* electrons are available for bonding.

Zinc, cadmium, and mercury fall in the periodic table at the end of the *d*-transition series—the final *d* electron takes its place in the $(n - 1)$ energy levels of these elements to give $(n - 1)d^{10} ns^2$ configurations. Only the outermost *s* electrons of zinc, cadmium, and mercury atoms become involved in chemical bonding. For this reason, these elements more closely resemble the representative metals than the transition metals. Therefore, the chemistry of the zinc family elements is included in this chapter.

**GENERAL PROPERTIES
AND REACTIONS OF THE
REPRESENTATIVE METALS
AND THEIR COMPOUNDS**

29.2 GENERAL PROPERTIES
OF THE s BLOCK METALS

The lithium family, or alkali, metals are the most reactive metals. They have the largest atomic radii (Table 29.1; see also Figures 10.3 and 10.4) and the lowest ionization energies (see Figure 10.7) of all of the elements in their respective periods. These are the most electropositive metals. Of all the metals, they form cations most readily, losing their single ns electrons to give large $+1$ cations, which have low charge-to-size ratios and therefore low polarizing ability (Section 10.8). The bonding in all of the common simple compounds of these elements is ionic. However, because of its small size, Li^+ has a slightly greater polarizing ability and therefore a greater covalent character in its compounds, causing certain differences in properties. For example, although most compounds of these elements are water-soluble, some salts of lithium (such as LiF, Li_2CO_3, Li_3PO_4) are only slightly soluble.

Calcium, strontium, and barium are second only to the alkali metals in reactivity. Their ionization energies are higher than those of the alkali metals but are lower than those of most other metals. The common compounds of calcium, strontium, and barium, like those of the alkali metals, are ionic, the metals having lost their two outermost s electrons. The alkali metals have only oxidation state $+1$ and the beryllium family, or alkaline earth metals, have only oxidation state $+2$.

Beryllium atoms are the smallest metal atoms, and the chemistry of beryllium is significantly different from that of the other s block metals, resembling more closely the chemistry of its diagonal neighbor, aluminum (Table 29.2). The beryllium ion, Be^{2+}, has a high polarizing ability and thus beryllium forms many simple molecular, rather than ionic, compounds. Also, the beryllium ion attracts electron pairs from other molecules or ions strongly enough to form stable complex ions, a property not shared by cations of most of the other s block elements.

Table 29.1
Properties of the s Block Metals

Configuration: Group I, [noble gas]ns^1 Group II, [noble gas]ns^2					
	Li Be	Na Mg	K Ca	Rb Sr	Cs Ba
Melting point (°C)	179 1283	97.5 650	63.5 851	39.0 757	28.4 704
Boiling point (°C)	1372 ~1500	892 1107	774 1487	679 1384	690 1640
Density (g/cm³)	0.53 1.85	0.70 1.74	0.86 1.54	1.53 2.58	1.87 3.65
Atomic radius (nm)	0.152 0.111	0.186 0.160	0.227 0.197	0.248 0.215	0.265 0.217
Ionic radius (nm) M⁺ **M²⁺**	0.068 0.035	0.097 0.066	0.133 .099	0.147 0.112	0.167 0.134
First ionization energy **(kJ/mol, 0 K)**	520 900	496 738	419 590	403 550	376 503
Electronegativity	1.0 1.5	0.9 1.2	0.8 1.0	0.8 1.0	0.7 0.9
Standard reduction **potential (V)*** **Mⁿ + ne⁻ → M(s)**	−3.05 −1.85	−2.71 −2.36	−2.93 −2.87	−2.93 −2.89	−2.92 −2.91

* $n = 1$ for alkali metals, $n = 2$ for beryllium family elements.

Property	Comments
Covalent in most binary compounds	A result of smaller size and stronger attraction for electrons
A weaker reducing agent than other family members	In this, as in other properties, Be resembles its diagonal neighbor, Al.
Oxide and hydroxide are amphoteric.	Be is the least "metallic," most electronegative element in the family.
Hydrated cation is hydrolyzed to give acidic aqueous solution.	Another consequence of small size and stronger attraction for electrons
Able to form stable complexes	Although all metals form complexes, other Be family metals form less stable complexes than Be^{2+} because cations are larger.

The polarizing ability of magnesium ions is much lower than that of beryllium ions, but sufficiently high that in some compounds magnesium forms covalent or partially covalent bonds. (In organic compounds known as Grignard reagents, e.g., C_2H_5MgBr, magnesium is covalently bonded to one carbon atom and one halogen atom.)

The s block metals are all strong reducing agents. In Table 29.1, compare the atomic radii, ionization energies, and reduction potentials. As might be expected, ease of electron loss and strength as reducing agents generally increase with atomic radius. However, lithium is an exception—it has a small atomic radius but is a powerful reducing agent. To explain this, we must remind ourselves that reduction potentials measure reactivity in aqueous solution. The contributions to the energy of electron loss in aqueous solution are represented by the following steps. (M = a metal atom.)

$$M(s) \longrightarrow M(g) \qquad \text{\textit{sublimation}} \qquad \textbf{(29.1)}$$
$$M(g) \longrightarrow M^{n+}(g) + ne^- \qquad \text{\textit{ionization}} \qquad \textbf{(29.2)}$$
$$\underline{M^{n+}(g) + ne^- \xrightarrow{H_2O} M^{n+}(aq) + ne^-(aq) \quad \text{\textit{hydration}}} \qquad \textbf{(29.3)}$$
$$M(s) \longrightarrow M^{n+}(aq) + ne^-(aq) \qquad \textbf{(29.4)}$$

Sublimation and ionization are always endothermic, and hydration—the process of an ion attracting and being surrounded by water molecules—is always exothermic. The more strongly an ion attracts the water molecules, the greater the hydration energy. Because of its high charge-to-size ratio, hydration of the small lithium ion releases a larger amount of energy than hydration of the other alkali metal ions. This factor makes reaction (29.4) more favorable, accounting for the greater strength of lithium as a reducing agent.

The alkali metals have lower melting and boiling points and are less dense than most metals (see Figure 31.1). In addition, they are soft; all except lithium can be cut with a knife. The beryllium family metals have considerably higher melting and boiling points, and also greater densities than the alkali metals (see Table 29.1). All the s block metals are excellent conductors of electricity. The loosely held outer electrons of the alkali metal atoms can be set free by light of the correct wavelength, in what is called the photoelectric effect (Section 8.2). Cesium, the most electropositive of all the elements, releases electrons most readily of all the alkali metals and is frequently used in devices that depend upon the photoelectric effect.

29.3 GENERAL PROPERTIES OF THE p BLOCK METALS

The p block metals fall into three different periodic table families. Consequently their properties vary more than those of the s block metals. In compounds, aluminum has only one positive oxidation state of significance, while the other elements are known in the group oxidation state and the group oxidation state minus two (Table 29.3).

Aluminum is of low density but has typically metallic properties of conductivity and luster. Thallium and lead are the most dense of the representative metals (Tables 29.4 and 29.5). Bismuth, the least "metallic" metal in its physical properties, is brittle rather than malleable, and has the lowest electrical conductivity of all metals except mercury.

Collectively, the p block elements exclusive of aluminum are known as the **post-transition metals.** These elements have higher effective nuclear charges than the lighter elements in their families due to the intervention of the transition elements. As a result, gallium has a small atomic radius (see Table 29.4), and the post-transition elements, especially thallium, lead, and bismuth (which follow *both* the d and f transition elements), hold onto their electrons strongly. Thallium, lead, and bismuth are each more stable in their lower oxidation states, and species containing these elements in their higher oxidation states are strong oxidizing agents (e.g., Tl^{3+}, PbO_2,

Table 29.3
Common Oxidation States of the p Block Metals The more stable oxidation states are shown in color.

Al	+3
Ga	+3, +1
In	+3, +1
Tl	+3, **+1**
Sn	+2, +4
Pb	**+2**, +4
Bi	**+3**, +5

Table 29.4
Properties of the Representative
Group III Metals

	Al	Ga	In	Tl
	Configuration: $ns^2\,np^1$			
Melting point (°C)	658	29.75	155	303.5
Boiling point (°C)	1800	1700	>1450	1650
Density (g/cm³)	2.70	5.9 (solid)	7.30	11.5
Atomic radius (nm)	0.143	0.122	0.163	0.170
Ionic radius, M^{3+} (nm)	0.051	0.062	0.081	0.095 (Tl^+ 0.147)
First ionization energy (kJ/mol, 0 K)	578	579	558	590
Electronegativity	1.5	1.8	1.5	1.4
Standard reduction potential (V) $M^{3+} + 3e^- \rightarrow M(s)$	−1.66	−0.53	−0.343	0.719*

* $Tl^{3+} + 2e^- \rightleftharpoons Tl^+$ $E° = 1.25$ V

BiO_3^-). [In describing certain oxidation states as more "stable" than others, we mean that compounds or ions containing elements in these states are both oxidized and reduced with difficulty.]

Al(III) compounds $\xrightarrow{H_2O}$ Al^{3+} ions

The ionization energies for removal of three electrons from aluminum, gallium, and indium are very high (all >2500 kJ/mol) and compounds of these elements in the +3 oxidation state have predominantly covalent bonding. Nevertheless, the Al^{3+}, Ga^{3+}, and In^{3+} ions form readily in aqueous solutions because they have high heats of hydration. Thallium, however, is more stable in both aqueous solutions and compounds as the thallium(I) ion, in which only the single p valence electron has been lost. Gallium and indium form a few compounds in the +1 oxidation state, but the +1 ions are not stable in aqueous solution.

Tin and lead form compounds in the +2 and +4 oxidation states, which represent involvement of only the np^2 electrons or both ns^2 and np^2 electrons in bonding, respectively. As is shown in the discussion of the halides of these elements (Section 29.10b), the +2 and +4 states are equally stable for tin, while for lead the +4 state is less stable and less common.

Table 29.5
Properties of Tin, Lead,
and Bismuth

	Sn	Pb	Bi
Configuration	$[Kr]4d^{10}\,5s^2\,5p^2$	$[Xe]4f^{14}\,5s^2\,5p^6\,5d^{10}$ $6s^2\,6p^2$	$[Xe]4f^{14}\,5s^2\,5p^6\,5d^{10}$ $6s^2\,6p^3$
Melting point (°C)	232	327	271
Boiling point (°C)	2270	1620	1560
Density (g/cm³)	5.75 (gray) 7.28 (white) 6.52 (brittle)	11.29	9.80
Atomic radius (nm)	0.141	0.175	0.155
Ionic radius (nm)	0.093 (Sn^{2+})	0.120 (Pb^{2+})	0.096 (Bi^{3+})
First ionization energy (at 0 K) (kJ/mol)	709	716	703
Electronegativity	1.7	1.6	1.9
Standard reduction potential (V)			
$M^{2+} + 2e^- \rightarrow M(s)$	−0.136	−0.126	—
$BiO^+ + 2H^+ + 3e^- \rightarrow$ $Bi(s) + H_2O$	—	—	0.32

Table 29.6
Properties of Zinc, Cadmium, and Mercury

	Configuration: $(n-1)d^{10} ns^2$		
	Zn	Cd	Hg
Melting point (°C)	419.5	320.9	−38.87
Boiling point (°C)	907	767	357
Density (g/cm³)	7.14	8.64	13.59
Atomic radius (nm)	0.133	0.149	0.150
Ionic radius, M^{2+} (nm)	0.074	0.097	0.110

Table 29.7
Comparison of the Properties of Alkaline Earth and Zinc Family Elements

	$_{20}Ca$ / $_{30}Zn$	$_{38}Sr$ / $_{48}Cd$	$_{56}Ba$ / $_{80}Hg$
Standard reduction potential (V) $M^{2+} + 2e^- \rightarrow M$	−2.87 / −0.763	−2.89 / −0.403	−2.91 / 0.851
Electronegativity	1.0 / 1.6	1.0 / 1.7	0.9 / 1.9
Atomic radii (nm)	0.197 / 0.133	0.215 / 0.149	0.217 / 0.150
Boiling points (°C)	1487 / 907	1384 / 767	1640 / 357

29.4 GENERAL PROPERTIES OF ZINC, CADMIUM, AND MERCURY

Only the two outer s electrons are employed in bonding by atoms of zinc, cadmium, and mercury (Table 29.6). Therefore, these elements exhibit no oxidation state higher than +2, and for zinc and cadmium this is the only stable state known. Mercury has a +2 oxidation state in the Hg^{2+} cation and a +1 oxidation state in the Hg_2^{2+} cation, in which the two Hg^+ ions, each formed by the loss of an s electron, are covalently joined through the remaining s electron of each, $Hg^+:Hg^+$.

Atoms of these elements are smaller than those of the alkali and alkaline earth metals; they give up electrons less easily and are more electronegative (Table 29.7). In their electronegativities and standard reduction potentials, zinc, cadmium, and mercury resemble gallium, indium, and thallium (see Table 29.4). Zinc is a reasonably strong reducing agent, while cadmium is a poor reducing agent. Mercury, as shown by the positive value of its reduction potential, is, like thallium, not easily oxidized. Cadmium and zinc are generally more reactive than mercury.

Zn^{2+}, Cd^{2+}: oxidation state +2
Hg^{2+}: oxidation state +2
Hg_2^{2+}: oxidation state +1

29.5 SOME CHEMICAL REACTIONS OF REPRESENTATIVE METALS AND THEIR COMPOUNDS

In considering the reactions of elemental metals, it must be kept in mind that several factors other than the reactivity of the pure metals themselves can influence the outcome of the reactions. The bulk of a metal can be prevented from reacting if a protective coating of a compound of the metal forms on its surface. Often such a coating is an oxide or a carbonate formed by reaction with oxygen or carbon dioxide from the atmosphere. For example, magnesium and aluminum are both quite active metals. However, both are protected by the formation of oxides on the surfaces. With the oxide coating in place, these elements do not react with water; without it both can displace hydrogen from water.

Often the reactivity of a metal in combination reactions is greatly increased when the metal is finely divided. For example, zinc is a moderately active metal which, based on the activity series, would be expected to displace hydrogen from steam. Finely divided zinc, however, will slowly displace hydrogen even from *cold* water. Also, sufficiently high temperatures bring about many combination reactions of metals that are relatively unreactive at room temperature.

a. Combination with other elements The s block metals all combine directly with the halogens and oxygen, most of them in reactions that are vigorous at room temperature. At elevated temperatures many compounds with other nonmetals can be formed by combination. In general, the reactivity of the metals increases down each family. With oxygen, sodium and barium form peroxides (which contain O_2^{2-}) and potassium, rubidium, and cesium give the superoxides (which contain O_2^-) (Section 16.10b). The other s block metals form the expected oxides containing the oxide ion, O^{2-}.

Zinc, cadmium, and mercury, and the p block metals except for thallium, are generally stable in dry air (i.e., they do not corrode or rust away), either because of the formation of a protective coating or lack of reactivity. Thallium exposed to the atmosphere builds up a layer of thallium(I) oxide which continues to spread (like the rust on an iron surface). These elements all combine with oxygen, the halogens, and various other nonmetals at high temperatures. Mercury gives the mercury(I) halides (Hg_2X_2) when the metal is in excess and the mercury(II) halides (HgX_2) when the halogens are in excess. With sulfur and oxygen, mercury is oxidized to the $+2$ state. The metals of the boron family (Al, Ga, In, Tl) give the M_2O_3 and MX_3 oxides and halides, with the exception that thallium tends to be oxidized only to the $+1$ state (with iodine it forms both TlI and $Tl(I_3)$).

Tin is oxidized to the $+4$ state by halogens and oxygen to give SnX_4 and SnO_2. Lead reacts with oxygen to give PbO at lower temperatures (< 500 °C) and to give Pb_3O_4 at higher temperatures (> 500 °C). Red lead, as Pb_3O_4 is known, contains both lead(II) and lead(IV). Lead and bismuth are oxidized only to their lower oxidation states of $+2$ and $+3$, respectively, by the halogens to give PbX_2 and BiX_3. With oxygen, bismuth forms the $+3$ oxide, Bi_2O_3. Only fluorine among the halogens is a strong enough oxidizing agent to take bismuth to its less common $+5$ oxidation state, to give BiF_5 (the reaction is carried out with the molten metal at 600 °C).

b. Reactions with water and acids The alkali metals and calcium, strontium, and barium are sufficiently active to displace hydrogen from water at room temperature [e.g., $2Na(s) + 2H_2O(l) \longrightarrow 2NaOH(aq) + H_2(g)$]. With most alkali metals, the reaction is so exothermic that it may occur with explosive violence as a result of the ignition of the hydrogen that is liberated. Beryllium does not react with water, and magnesium (free of its protective oxide coating) reacts with boiling water. All of the s block metals displace hydrogen from acids. It should be emphasized that the very active metals of the lithium family react even more violently with solutions of acids than they do with water.

Among zinc, cadmium, mercury, and the p block metals, aluminum and zinc are the most reactive elements. Both will displace hydrogen from water [if freed of their protective coatings of Al_2O_3 and $Zn_2(OH)_2CO_3$, respectively]. All of these metals except for mercury and bismuth, the least reactive among them, react with nonoxidizing acids to give salts and hydrogen, for example,

$$Zn(s) + 2HCl(aq) \longrightarrow ZnCl_2(aq) + H_2(g)$$
$$2Al(s) + 6HCl(aq) \longrightarrow 2AlCl_3(aq) + 3H_2(g)$$

Pure aluminum reacts very slowly with such acids. The presence of small amounts of metal impurities increases the rate of reaction through couple action (Section 23.17). Lead reacts only superficially with dilute sulfuric acid because the lead(II) sulfate produced is insoluble in the acid and forms a protective coating on the metal.

Zinc, cadmium, mercury, and the p block metals all react with oxidizing acids. However, the reaction with aluminum is not extensive because the metal is soon protected by an oxide layer. (The activity of pure aluminum can be demonstrated by first washing a piece of aluminum in dilute acid to dissolve the oxide, then dipping the aluminum into a solution of $HgCl_2$ to form an amalgam coating to which Al_2O_3 does not adhere. Whiskers of Al_2O_3 grow rapidly from the surface of aluminum treated in this way and the temperature of the system increases sharply. The treated aluminum will also liberate hydrogen from water and react with acids.)

Tin is oxidized to the $+4$ state by oxidizing acids, while lead and bismuth are oxidized to their lower oxidation states of $+2$ and $+3$, respectively. Some examples of the reactions of these metals with oxidizing acids are as follows:

$$Zn(s) + 2H_2SO_4(conc) \xrightarrow{\Delta} ZnSO_4(aq) + SO_2(g) + 2H_2O(l)$$
$$Sn(s) + 4HNO_3(aq) \longrightarrow SnO_2(s) + 4NO_2(g) + 2H_2O(l)$$
$$Hg(l) + 2H_2SO_4(conc, xs) \xrightarrow{\Delta} HgSO_4(aq) + SO_2(g) + 2H_2O(l)$$
$$2Hg(l, xs) + 2H_2SO_4(conc) \xrightarrow{\Delta} Hg_2SO_4(aq) + SO_2(g) + 2H_2O(l)$$

c. Reactions of oxides and hydroxides Recall that ionic oxides are basic, covalent oxides are acidic, and oxides with intermediate bonding are amphoteric. The oxides of the representative metals are all either basic or amphoteric; none are acidic.

The alkali metal oxides react vigorously with water to give strongly alkaline solutions.

$$M_2O(s) + H_2O(l) \longrightarrow 2MOH(aq) \qquad M = Li, Na, K, Rb, Cs$$

These solutions of alkali metal hydroxides absorb carbon dioxide from the air to form carbonates or hydrogen carbonates.

$$2MOH(aq) + CO_2(g) \longrightarrow M_2CO_3(aq) + H_2O(l) \qquad M = Li, Na, K, Rb, Cs$$
$$MOH(aq) + CO_2(g, xs) \longrightarrow MHCO_3(aq)$$

Magnesium oxide reacts slowly and not very energetically with water. The oxides of calcium, strontium, and barium combine with water with progressively greater vigor:

$$MO(s) + H_2O(l) \longrightarrow M(OH)_2 \qquad M = Mg, Ca, Sr, Ba$$

The oxides of beryllium, zinc, aluminum, gallium, tin, and lead are all amphoteric. They form hydrated cations in acidic solutions and hydroxo anions in alkaline solution (Section 16.11), for example, for beryllium oxide (the only amphoteric oxide of an *s* block metal)

$$BeO(s) + 2H^+ \longrightarrow Be^{2+} + H_2O(l)$$
$$BeO(s) + 2OH^- + H_2O(l) \longrightarrow [Be(OH)_4]^{2-}$$

Oxides of Be, Zn, Al, Ga, Sn, Pb: all amphoteric

Bismuth(III) oxide is a basic oxide. It is not soluble in water, but reacts with acids to give salts plus water.

d. Reactions with bases The representative metals that form amphoteric oxides and hydroxides (beryllium, zinc, aluminum, gallium, tin, and lead) all react with strongly alkaline aqueous solutions to form the hydroxo anions and hydrogen, for example,

$$2Al(s) + 2OH^- + 6H_2O(l) \longrightarrow 2[Al(OH)_4]^- + 3H_2(g)$$

Such reactions can be thought of as occurring by reaction of the amphoteric oxides of these metals with the hydroxide ion.

$$2Al(s) + 3H_2O(l) \longrightarrow Al_2O_3(s) + 3H_2(g)$$
$$Al_2O_3(s) + 2OH^- + 3H_2O(l) \longrightarrow 2[Al(OH)_4]^-$$

e. Thermal decomposition of hydroxides and carbonates There is a significant difference between the thermal decomposition of the carbonates and hydroxides of the alkali metals and those of most other metals. Except for lithium hydroxide, alkali metal hydroxides do not decompose when heated.

Lithium carbonate undergoes some decomposition to give carbon dioxide when heated, but the carbonates of sodium through cesium are thermally very stable. The temperature required for thermal decomposition to CO_2 increases from magnesium to barium in the beryllium family (Be forms other products).

$$M(OH)_2(s) \xrightarrow{\Delta} MO(s) + H_2O(g) \qquad M = Be, Mg, Ca, Sr, Ba$$

$$MCO_3(s) \xrightarrow{\Delta} MO(s) + CO_2(g) \qquad \begin{aligned} M = &\text{ Mg (400 °C),} \\ &\text{Ca (900 °C),} \\ &\text{Sr (1175 °C),} \\ &\text{Ba (1500 °C)} \end{aligned}$$

Zn family and *p* block element hydroxides and carbonates: decompose on heating

The known hydroxides and carbonates of zinc, cadmium, and the *p* block metals decompose to give metal oxides, plus water and carbon dioxide, respectively.

f. Ions in aqueous solution Only the beryllium ion, among the ions of the *s* block metals, reacts with water to give acidic solutions (Section 21.1c)

$$[Be(H_2O)_4]^{2+} + H_2O(l) \rightleftharpoons [Be(OH)(H_2O)_3]^+ + H_3O^+$$

or

$$Be^{2+} + H_2O(l) \rightleftharpoons BeOH^+ + H^+$$

Similarly, only for the beryllium ion is the formation of complexes significant.

For ions of the lithium family elements, there are very few precipitation reactions with simple anions because most of the salts are water soluble. In qualitative analysis, the ions of the lithium family elements must be precipitated as large, complex compounds such as sodium zinc uranyl acetate, $Na[Zn(UO_2)_3(CH_3COO)_9]$, or potassium tetraphenylborate, $K[B(C_6H_5)_4]$ (the phenyl group, C_6H_5, is derived from benzene; Section 27.7).

Of the ions formed by the representative metals of the zinc family and the *p* block, Zn^{2+}, Cd^{2+}, Al^{3+}, and Sn^{2+} establish equilibria with water to give acidic solutions. The simple Bi^{3+} ion is not found in aqueous solution, for it immediately reacts with water to give the bismuthyl ion, BiO^+, which forms what are known as bismuthyl compounds.

$$Bi^{3+} + H_2O(l) \longrightarrow BiO^+ + 2H^+$$
$$BiO^+ + Cl^- \longrightarrow BiOCl(s)$$
$$\qquad\qquad\qquad\qquad \textit{bismuthyl chloride}$$

Tin(IV), lead(IV), and bismuth(V) are not found as ions in aqueous solution; their water-soluble compounds immediately undergo hydrolysis or reduction.

The addition of OH^- to solutions containing Be^{2+}, Zn^{2+}, Al^{3+}, Ga^{3+}, Sn^{2+}, or Pb^{2+} first precipitates hydroxides, which then dissolve in excess base to form the hydroxo anions, for example,

$$Pb^{2+} \xrightarrow{OH^-} Pb(OH)_2(s) \xrightarrow{OH^-} [Pb(OH)_4]^{2-}$$

The ions that undergo this reaction sequence are, you may have noticed, the ions of the elements that also form amphoteric oxides and hydroxides.

In aqueous solution, mercury(I) ions establish a disproportionation equilibrium,

$$Hg_2^{2+} \rightleftharpoons Hg^{2+} + Hg(l)$$

$Hg_2^{2+} \rightleftharpoons Hg^{2+} + Hg(l)$

which is easily shifted in either direction according to Le Chatelier's principle. Mercury(I) disproportionates in the presence of any reagent that gives a slightly soluble or slightly dissociated mercury(II) compound, for example,

$$Hg_2^{2+} + 2OH^- \longrightarrow Hg(l) + HgO(s) + H_2O(l)$$
$$Hg_2^{2+} + 4CN^- \longrightarrow Hg(l) + [Hg(CN)_4]^{2-}$$
$$Hg_2^{2+} + H_2S(aq) \longrightarrow Hg(l) + HgS(s) + 2H^+$$

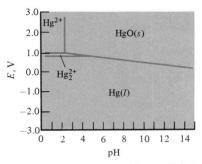

Figure 29.1
pH–Potential Diagram for Mercury

The small region of stability of Hg_2^{2+} is shown in the pH–potential diagram for mercury (Figure 29.1).

g. Aluminothermic reactions At high temperatures, aluminum burns in air to form the oxide in a strongly exothermic reaction.

$$4Al(s) + 3O_2(g) \longrightarrow 2Al_2O_3(s) \qquad \Delta H° = -3350 \text{ kJ}$$

The large heat of this reaction makes finely divided aluminum an excellent reducing agent for many metal oxides that must be reduced at high temperatures. The reactions of aluminum with metal oxides are called **aluminothermic reactions.** So much heat is liberated in such reactions that the reduced metal is often obtained in the molten state. The Thermit process utilizes the reaction of iron(III) oxide with aluminum to provide both the high temperature and the molten iron needed for welding.

$$Fe_2O_3(s) + 2Al(s) \longrightarrow 2Fe(l) + Al_2O_3(s) \qquad \Delta H° = -851.4 \text{ kJ}$$

EXAMPLE 29.1
Chemical Reactions: Elemental Sn

Write equations for the reactions of metallic tin with dilute hydrochloric acid, hot concentrated sulfuric acid, and concentrated sodium hydroxide.

Tin is a sufficiently active metal to displace hydrogen from dilute hydrochloric acid (Table 17.4). We would expect the formation of tin(II) rather than tin(IV) with this "nonoxidizing" acid.

$$Sn(s) + 2HCl(aq) \longrightarrow SnCl_2(aq) + H_2(g)$$

With a strong oxidizing acid tin would be oxidized to tin(IV). The usual products of the oxidation of a metal by sulfuric acid are the metal sulfate and sulfur dioxide.

$$Sn(s) + 4H_2SO_4(conc) \xrightarrow{\Delta} Sn(SO_4)_2(aq) + 2SO_2(g) + 4H_2O(l)$$

Tin is one of the metals that forms amphoteric oxides and reacts with hydroxide bases to form hydroxo ions and hydrogen. With no strong oxidizing agent present, tin(II) will be formed. Specific knowledge would be required to predict how many hydroxide ions would be present in the hydroxo ion that is formed.

$$Sn(s) + (n-2)OH^- + 2H_2O(l) \longrightarrow [Sn(OH)_n]^{(n-2)-} + H_2(g)$$

METALS OF REPRESENTATIVE GROUPS I AND II: THE *s* BLOCK METALS

29.6 *s* BLOCK METALS: PREPARATION, PROPERTIES, AND USES

Four of the metals in Groups I and II (Ca, Na, K, Mg) are among the ten most abundant metals in the crust of the earth (see Table 28.1). All of the elements in these two groups occur in the earth's crust in combination with other elements. They are too reactive ever to be found free. Lithium, sodium, potassium, magnesium, and calcium are also found as dissolved salts in seawater, brine wells, and a few salt lakes. Many compounds of these metals are recovered directly from seawater and natural brines or artificial brines (formed by flushing water through salt deposits).

The preparation of Group I and Group II metals requires large amounts of energy—their positive ions are difficult to reduce. Sodium and lithium are produced by electrolysis of molten salts (the production of sodium was discussed in Section 28.5). Potassium is made by reaction of molten potassium chloride with sodium vapor in the absence of air.

$$KCl(l) + Na(g) \xrightarrow{\Delta} K(g) + NaCl(l)$$

Li, Na, K, Mg, Ca: soluble salts in seawater

The lithium family metals when freshly cut have a characteristic metallic luster, but on exposure to air they soon tarnish rapidly by reacting with atmospheric oxygen

Li	Lithium–magnesium alloys	Na	Tetraethyllead production
	Lithium battery		Coolant (liquid)
	Aluminum production (in electrolyte)		Na vapor light
			Reducing agent
Rb and Cs	Photoelectric cells	K	KO$_2$ (superoxide) production (for gas masks)
	Scavengers		Reducing agent

Be	Alloys (Small amounts as a hardening agent; in nonsparking tools)	Mg	Structural metal aircraft portable tools industrial machinery
	Shielding nuclear reactors (captures neutrons)		Deoxidizer and desulfurizer
	Heat sink for aerospace vehicles		Batteries
Ba	Alloys		Flares, rocket propellants
	Scavenger (vacuum and TV tubes)		Cathodic protection of other metals
		Ca	Deoxidizer
			Reducing agent

and water vapor. To prevent these reactions, which can be quite vigorous, these metals are stored under oxygen-free organic liquids such as kerosene or mineral oil (a mixture of hydrocarbons). The major uses of the lithium family metals are listed in Table 29.8.

The alkaline earth metals are all silvery metals that are malleable and ductile. Pure calcium is crystalline in appearance. Barium, the most reactive metal in the family, is spontaneously flammable and must be stored under an inert liquid.

The major use of magnesium is in the production of alloys (Table 29.9). Magnesium is the lightest metal that can be used for structural applications. Its alloys are easily fabricated and welded. Magnesium "desulfurizes" steel by combining with sulfur present in the molten metal to give magnesium sulfide, which is removed with the slag.

Calcium, barium, and strontium are similar in their properties and uses. Since calcium is the least expensive, more of it is used than of either of the other metals.

29.7 s BLOCK METALS: COMPOUNDS

Some of the many commercially important compounds of the Group I and Group II metals are listed in Table 29.10 with some of their uses. Those that are among the "top ten" industrial chemicals in terms of the quantity produced each year (CaO, Ca(OH)$_2$, NaOH, Na$_2$CO$_3$) are discussed in the next section on industrial alkalis.

The Group I hydroxides are white, water-soluble solids. The Group II hydroxides are much less soluble than those of the Group I metals, the solubility increasing from Be(OH)$_2$ to Ba(OH)$_2$, in line with the decreasing attraction between cation and hydroxide ion in the crystal. The alkalinity of solutions of these hydroxides is limited by their solubilities.

Potassium hydroxide (KOH), or caustic potash, is made by electrolysis of potassium chloride solutions in diaphragm or mercury cells similar to those used for sodium hydroxide (Section 29.8a).

Sodium peroxide (Na$_2$O$_2$) and, to a lesser extent, potassium superoxide (KO$_2$) are compounds of industrial significance. They are powerful oxidizing and bleaching agents and form hydrogen peroxide on contact with cold solutions of acids or with an excess of cold water.

$$Na_2O_2(s) + 2H_2O(l, xs) \longrightarrow H_2O_2(aq) + 2NaOH(aq)$$
$$2KO_2(s) + 2H_2O(l, xs) \longrightarrow H_2O_2(aq) + O_2(g) + 2KOH(aq)$$

Potassium superoxide is employed in "breathing" apparatus as a quick source of oxygen. Such apparatus is used in rescue work in mines and other areas where the air is so deficient in oxygen that an artificial atmosphere must be generated. The moisture of the breath reacts with the oxide to liberate oxygen, and at the same time the potassium hydroxide formed removes carbon dioxide as it is exhaled.

$$4KO_2(s) + 2H_2O(l) \longrightarrow 4KOH(s) + 3O_2(g)$$
$$2KOH(s) + CO_2(g) \longrightarrow K_2CO_3(s) + H_2O(l)$$

The alkali metal carbonates, except for lithium carbonate, are quite soluble in water, while the carbonates of the elements of Group II (and most other carbonates) are practically insoluble in water. Insoluble carbonates are brought into solution in

Table 29.10
Some Commercially Important Alkali and Alkaline Earth Metal Compounds and Their Uses Common names are given in parentheses.

NaOH* (lye, caustic soda)	Industrial chemical
	Pulp and paper industry
	Extraction of Al from ores
	S removal from petroleum
	Soaps and detergents
	Food processing
Na_2CO_3* (soda ash)	Glass
	Industrial chemicals
	Detergents and cleansers
	Water softening
	Pulp and paper industry
$NaHCO_3$ (baking soda)	Food industry
	Household use
	Industrial chemical
	Fire extinguishers
CaO* (lime, quicklime) and $Ca(OH)_2$ (slaked lime)	Metallurgy
	Mortar, plaster, and cement
	Industrial alkali
	Pulp and paper industry
	Bleaching powder
	Pollution control
	Water treatment
KOH (caustic potash)	K_2CO_3 manufacture
	Liquid soaps
	Tetrapotassium pyrophosphates (detergent builders)
K_2CO_3 (potash)	Glass
KNO_3	Gunpowder
KCl (muriate of potash)	Fertilizer
	Salt substitute
MgO (magnesia)	Refractory
	Insulation
	Paper manufacture
	Animal food
	Flocculant
$MgSO_4 \cdot 7H_2O$ (epsom salt)	Leather tanning
	Mordant
	Medicine

* A top ten industrial chemical.

water containing dissolved carbon dioxide by the following reaction, which is the reverse of the thermal decomposition of solid metal hydrogen carbonates:

$$MCO_3(s) + H_2O(l) + CO_2(g) \longrightarrow M^{2+} + 2HCO_3^-$$

Groundwater always contains carbon dioxide, and therefore can dissolve limestone and dolomite, for example,

$$\underset{dolomite}{CaCO_3 \cdot MgCO_3(s)} + 2H_2O(l) + 2CO_2(aq) \rightleftharpoons Ca^{2+} + Mg^{2+} + 4HCO_3^-$$

The calcium and magnesium ions thus brought into solution make the water "hard" (Section 14.11).

The dissolution of carbonate minerals in groundwater has another interesting effect — if the mineral is below the surface of the earth and is covered by rocks that do not dissolve, a cave may be formed. Groundwater may then seep into the cave through cracks in the walls or roof. The water contains calcium and magnesium hydrogen carbonates that it has dissolved elsewhere, and when it enters the cave, because the partial pressure of the carbon dioxide is lower, the carbon dioxide escapes from solution by a reversal of the reaction shown above. Insoluble calcium and magnesium carbonates are thus produced and deposit around the opening through which the water is trickling into the cave, forming an icicle-like structure called a *stalactite*. Some of the hydrogen carbonate remains in solution until drops of water fall from the tip of the stalactite. As the drops fall, the hydrogen carbonate decomposes and forms carbonate deposits on the floor of the cave, building up another "icicle," called a *stalagmite*. After many centuries, the tips of the stalactite and stalagmite meet and the two "icicles" grow into a column that one might think was left there to support the roof of the cave.

Sodium carbonate forms a number of hydrates, the most common of which is the decahydrate, $Na_2CO_3 \cdot 10H_2O$, known as washing soda. Solutions of this salt are effective cleaning agents because of the alkalinity resulting from hydrolysis of the carbonate ion. Sodium hydrogen carbonate, or bicarbonate of soda, is made from pure sodium carbonate.

$$Na_2CO_3(aq) + H_2O(l) + CO_2(g) \longrightarrow 2NaHCO_3(s)$$

It is used in baking powders as a *leavening agent,* a substance that produces gas bubbles in dough. This gives rise to its common name, baking soda. An acid substance must be present in the dough to liberate carbon dioxide by the following reaction:

$$HCO_3^- + H^+ \longrightarrow CO_2(g) + H_2O(l)$$

The liberation of gas causes the dough to rise and gives the product the appropriate lightness and texture. Sour milk can be the source of the acid. Some recipes call for use of a baking *powder*. These powders are mixtures of sodium hydrogen carbonate and an acidic substance, for example, sodium alum (sodium aluminum sulfate), $NaAl(SO_4)_2 \cdot 12H_2O$ (acidic due to reaction of hydrated Al^{3+} with water); calcium dihydrogen phosphate, $Ca(H_2PO_4)_2$; or potassium hydrogen tartrate, $K(HC_4H_4O_6)$. "Double acting" baking powder is made possible by coated crystals of $Ca(H_2PO_4)_2$ that release about half of their hydrogen ion during mixing and half during baking.

EXAMPLE 29.2
Chemical Reactions: Alkali Metal Compounds

Complete the following equations (a reaction does occur in each case):

(a) $K_2CO_3(s) + C(s) \xrightarrow{\;>1000\;°C\;}$

(b) $NaHCO_3(s) \xrightarrow{\;\Delta\;}$

(c) $Li^+ + HPO_4^{2-} + OH^- \longrightarrow$

(a) One of the reactants is an element, so this will be a redox reaction. Combination is not possible. At elevated temperature elemental carbon is a reducing agent and can be expected to "displace" potassium to yield elemental potassium. The carbon will be oxidized, most likely to carbon monoxide at this high temperature. (Recall that CO_2 is reduced to CO by C at high temperatures; Section 27.3.)

$$K_2CO_3(s) + 2C(s) \longrightarrow 2K(g) + 3CO(g)$$

(b) With one reactant, this could be a redox or a nonredox decomposition reaction, or a disproportionation. Hydrogen carbonates undergo nonredox decomposition upon heating to form carbonates, carbon dioxide, and water.

$$2NaHCO_3(s) \longrightarrow Na_2CO_3(s) + CO_2(g) + H_2O(g)$$

Sodium carbonate, like most of the alkali metal carbonates, will not undergo further thermal decomposition.

(c) This is a reaction of ions in aqueous solution. Although with three ions present, the reaction pattern will not be exactly that of a partner-exchange reaction, we should still first look for the possibility of the formation of the types of products that cause such reactions to occur. The OH^- ion can react with the acidic HPO_4^{2-} ion.

$$HPO_4^{2-} + OH^- \longrightarrow PO_4^{3-} + H_2O(l)$$

A further reaction is possible because lithium, unlike the other members of its family, forms several only slightly soluble salts, including the phosphate. The overall reaction should be

$$3Li^+ + HPO_4^{2-} + OH^- \longrightarrow Li_3PO_4(s) + H_2O(l)$$

EXAMPLE 29.3
Chemical Reactions: Ca salts

In chemical handbooks in the column listing solubility in water, d or dec (meaning decomposition) appears for certain compounds, including calcium carbide, calcium nitride, and calcium sulfide. Explain why these compounds "decompose" rather than dissolving in aqueous solution.

Neither the nitride ion nor the carbide ion exists in aqueous solution. Both react completely, the nitride ion to give ammonia (Section 26.5g) and the carbide ion to give acetylene (Section 27.4e).

$$CaC_2(s) + 2H_2O(l) \longrightarrow Ca(OH)_2(aq) + C_2H_2(g)$$
$$Ca_3N_2(s) + 6H_2O(l) \longrightarrow 3Ca(OH)_2(aq) + 2NH_3(g)$$

The sulfide ion is one of the more basic anions (Section 21.1b) and reacts with water as follows:

$$S^{2-} + 2H_2O(l) \rightleftharpoons H_2S(aq) + 2OH^-$$

We might expect that in aqueous solution calcium sulfide establishes the following equilibrium to an extent dependent upon the concentrations of the species involved.

$$CaS(s) + 2H_2O(l) \rightleftharpoons Ca(OH)_2(aq) + H_2S(aq)$$

In each equation above we have written (aq) for calcium hydroxide. However, we note that this is one of the moderately insoluble hydroxides. In each reaction it might precipitate if the concentrations of the ions are great enough.

29.8 INDUSTRIAL ALKALIS   The hydroxides, oxides, and carbonates of sodium, potassium, magnesium, and calcium are interrelated industrial chemicals of practical and economic importance. In the chemical industry, "alkali" is a general term for any compound that produces hydroxide ion in aqueous solution. Sodium hydroxide and chlorine are co-produced by the electrolysis of saturated aqueous sodium chloride solutions and are two of the primary products of what is referred to as the *chloralkali industry*. The third major chloralkali chemical is sodium carbonate, which, as you should recall, gives alkaline solutions by the hydrolysis of the carbonate ion.

$$CO_3^{2-} + H_2O(l) \rightleftharpoons HCO_3^- + OH^-$$

Chemicals derived from limestone, most importantly calcium oxide and calcium hydroxide, are central to another segment of the alkali industry. Many chemicals are known commercially by common names. The term **lime** refers to either calcium oxide, specifically known as **quicklime** (or **unslaked lime**), or calcium hydroxide, specifically known as **hydrated lime** (or **slaked lime**).

a. The chloralkali industry   The overall chemical reaction in the electrolysis of saturated sodium chloride solutions (known as "brines") produces chlorine, hydrogen, and an aqueous sodium hydroxide solution.

$$2NaCl(aq) + 2H_2O(l) \xrightarrow{\text{electrolysis}} 2NaOH(aq) + H_2(g) + Cl_2(g)$$

Sodium hydroxide and chlorine are seventh and eighth in the list of the top ten industrial chemicals (see Table 25.10). (In 1973 the chloralkali industry consumed 0.5% of the electricity produced in the United States.)

Three major types of electrochemical cells are used in this industry — diaphragm cells, membrane cells, and mercury cells — the objective in each being to keep chlorine, which is produced at the anodes, from mixing with either hydrogen or sodium hydroxide. The reactions that would result,

$$2NaOH(aq) + Cl_2(g) \longrightarrow NaOCl(aq) + NaCl(aq) + H_2O(l)$$
$$H_2(g) + Cl_2(g) \longrightarrow 2HCl(g)$$

are undesirable because product is lost, and also because hydrogen–chlorine mixtures can explode.

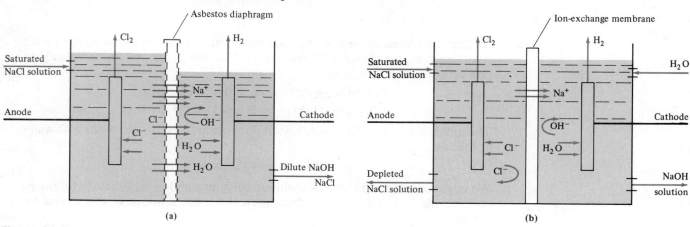

Figure 29.2
Schematic Drawings of the Diaphragm (a) and Membrane (b) Cells for the Electrolysis of Sodium Chloride Solutions (a) Sodium and chloride ions can pass through the wet-asbestos diaphragm, but hydrogen and chlorine gases cannot pass through. A positive pressure of the solution on the anode side prevents the return flow of hydroxide ions from the cathode compartment. The sodium hydroxide solution produced is contaminated with unreacted salt, which precipitates as the solution is concentrated and can be removed by filtration. (b) The ion exchange membrane allows the passage of sodium ions, but prevents the passage of both chloride and hydroxide ions (and also, of course, hydrogen and chlorine gases). The product solution is not contaminated by chloride ions and is more concentrated than that from the diaphragm cells.

In diaphragm and membrane cells the electrode reactions are

$$\begin{array}{lll} \textit{cathode} & 2H_2O + 2e^- \longrightarrow H_2 + 2OH^- & E° = -0.83 \text{ V} \\ \textit{anode} & 2Cl^- \longrightarrow Cl_2 + 2e^- & E° = 1.36 \text{ V} \end{array}$$

The cathode in a diaphragm cell is a metal mesh that supports an asbestos diaphragm (Figure 29.2a). In membrane cells (Figure 29.2b), the products of a newer technology, the asbestos diaphragm is replaced by an ion-exchange membrane. The sodium ions from the anode compartment are allowed by the membrane to enter the cathode compartment, where OH^- ions are being generated. But the Cl^- ions are *not* allowed to pass by the membrane. In this way a more concentrated sodium hydroxide solution can be produced.

Flowing mercury is used as the cathode in the mercury cells (Figure 29.3). Sodium ion is reduced at the mercury cathode and forms sodium amalgam

$$Na^+ + e^- + xHg(l) \longrightarrow NaHg_x(l)$$

which reacts with water in a separate vessel to give a concentrated sodium hydroxide solution that is free from NaCl.

$$2NaHg_x(l) + 2H_2O(l) \longrightarrow H_2(g) + 2NaOH(aq) + 2xHg(l)$$

The mercury is recycled. However, some of the mercury inevitably escapes into the surrounding air and bodies of water, and such cells have contributed to the mercury pollution problem. For this reason, the use of mercury cells is being discontinued.

Caustic soda, as sodium hydroxide is known in the industry, is sold as a 50% solution, or as more concentrated solutions, and also in various solid, anhydrous forms such as pellets and flakes. The addition of water to concentrated or solid sodium hydroxide releases heat and must be done with caution. Half of the caustic soda manufactured each year is used in the production of other chemicals. Five percent is consumed in the production of alumina from bauxite ores (Section 28.5). A small but growing application of caustic soda is in commercial food processing—caustic soda solutions are used to peel vegetables. (Similarly, hominy is made from corn by heating the corn with sodium hydroxide. The coating on the corn is dissolved, leaving the starch, which is washed thoroughly to free it from sodium hydroxide.) Other uses of caustic soda are listed in Table 29.10.

Anhydrous sodium carbonate is known industrially as **soda ash.** On a worldwide basis, the principal method for making sodium carbonate is the Solvay process, a multi-step process that uses limestone (predominantly calcium carbonate), salt, and ammonia as the raw materials. The *overall* reaction is

$$\underset{\textit{limestone}}{CaCO_3} + \underset{\textit{brine}}{2NaCl} \longrightarrow \underset{\textit{soda ash}}{Na_2CO_3} + CaCl_2$$

In the United States the production of "natural soda ash" has replaced the Solvay process. In 1938 very large deposits of the relatively rare mineral *trona*, $Na_2CO_3 \cdot NaHCO_3 \cdot 2H_2O$, were discovered in the residue from a huge lake that 50 million years ago covered southwestern Wyoming. The trona is either purified first by crystallization and then heated to convert the sodium hydrogen carbonate to sodium carbonate, or the mineral is heated first and then the impure soda ash is purified. More than half of the soda ash produced is used in making glass. Other important uses are in the pulp and paper industry and in soaps and detergents. Most dishwasher detergents contain soda ash.

b. Lime Lime is the cheapest source of alkalinity and an industrial chemical with a great diversity of uses. It is fifth in the list of large-volume industrial chemicals.

Limestone is the raw material for the production of quicklime and hydrated lime. A bewildering array of types of "lime" are sold. They contain varying propor-

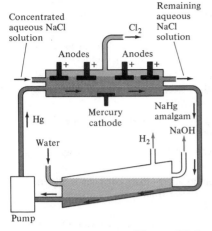

Figure 29.3
The Mercury Cell for the Electrolysis of Sodium Chloride This cell is more expensive to build and operate than the diaphragm or membrane cells. The toxic nature of the mercury released to the environment is another drawback. Like the membrane cell, this cell produces a more pure and more concentrated sodium hydroxide solution.

Industrial alkalis:
quicklime, CaO
hydrated (slaked) lime,
Ca(OH)₂
caustic soda, NaOH
soda ash, Na₂CO₃ (anhydrous)

Table 29.11
Outstanding Properties of the *s* Block Metals and Their Compounds

Li–Cs, ns^1 Be–Ba, ns^2	Valence electrons in *s* orbitals only
Li^+–Cs^+ Be^{2+}–Ba^{2+}	One oxidation state only; ions in all compounds (except some Mg compounds)
Li, Na, K, Rb, Cs Ca, Sr, Ba	Most reactive metals; combine with all nonmetals (except, in Group I, only Li + $N_2 \longrightarrow$ nitride)
Li–Cs	Not stable in air; soft, low-melting, least dense metals.
$M \longrightarrow M^+ + e^-$ $M \longrightarrow M^{2+} + 2e^-$	Strong reducing agents; Li *very* strong
Be(II)	Covalent in many binary compounds; differs in properties from other family members (Table 29.2)
M_2O, $M'O$ MOH, $M'(OH)_2$ (M = Li–Cs; M′ = Mg–Ba)	Strongly basic oxides and hydroxides; MOH, water soluble and thermally stable; $M'(OH)_2$, slightly soluble and less thermally stable.
M_2CO_3 (M = Na–Cs) $M_n{}^+A^{n-}$; (M = Na–Cs; A = common anions)	Very stable thermally Water-soluble compounds; hydrated cations not hydrolyzed
NaOH(caustic soda) Na_2CO_3 (soda ash) $Ca(OH)_2$ (hydrated lime) CaO (quicklime)	Top ten industrial chemicals and alkalis

tions of hydroxides, oxides, carbonates, and water. Many are derived from dolomitic limestone and contain magnesium compounds as well as calcium compounds. The following equations represent the major classifications of lime and their preparation. The addition of water to quicklime is called "slaking"; it is a very exothermic reaction.

$$\underset{\text{high-calcium limestone}}{CaCO_3(s)} \xrightarrow{\Delta} \underset{\text{high-calcium quicklime}}{CaO(s)} + CO_2(g)$$

$$\underset{\text{dolomitic limestone}}{CaCO_3 \cdot MgCO_3(s)} \xrightarrow{\Delta} \underset{\text{dolomitic quicklime}}{CaO \cdot MgO(s)} + 2CO_2(g)$$

$$CaO(s) + H_2O(l) \longrightarrow \underset{\text{high-calcium hydrated lime}}{Ca(OH)_2(s)}$$

$$CaO \cdot MgO(s) + 2H_2O(l) \xrightarrow{\text{pressure}} \underset{\text{dolomitic hydrated lime}}{Ca(OH)_2 \cdot Mg(OH)_2(s)}$$

Forty-five percent of the lime produced is used in metallurgy, mainly as a flux in steelmaking (Section 28.9). (The other *major* uses are listed in Table 29.10.)

The outstanding properties of the s block metals and their compounds are summarized in Table 29.11.

METALS OF REPRESENTATIVE GROUPS III–V: THE *p* BLOCK METALS

a. The Group III metals Aluminum is the third most abundant element in the earth's crust, following only oxygen and silicon, with which it is associated in aluminosilicate granites and clays. The extraction of aluminum from bauxite ore and its production by electrometallurgy have been discussed in Section 28.5.

29.9 *p* BLOCK METALS: PREPARATION, PROPERTIES, AND USES

Bauxite is an abundant mineral, but the best deposits are rapidly being exhausted or are far from the United States. Because of this, efforts are being made to develop alternate sources of aluminum. None of these are now in commercial use, but as the supplies of bauxite become less attractive, new sources will be needed.

Most of the aluminosilicates, such as the feldspars and clays, are very stable, but they are attacked and disintegrated by strong, hot acids, forming soluble aluminum salts and insoluble silicon dioxide. For kaolinite, which is the most promising of the clays for extraction by hydrometallurgy, the reaction is

$$H_4Al_2Si_2O_9(s) + 6H^+ \longrightarrow 2Al^{3+}(aq) + 2SiO_2(s) + 5H_2O(l)$$

Aluminum is a silvery white metal of low density. When pure, it is rather soft and weak, but its strength can be increased considerably by alloying with other metals, such as copper or magnesium. The pure metal is a good conductor of heat and electricity. Its electrical conductivity is comparable, weight for weight, with that of copper, and it has been used in electrical wiring. Without proper installation, however, aluminum wiring can be hazardous. It must not be connected to standard brass terminals, because couple action results in corrosion of the aluminum and formation of an oxide on its surface. Oxide also forms if the insulation wears away, exposing the pure aluminum wire. The outcome of oxide formation is an increase in electrical resistance, the generation of heat, and the possibility of igniting surrounding materials.

Aluminum has a host of end uses (Table 29.12) that take advantage of its many desirable properties, especially its combination of lightness and strength. Aluminum can be cast in massive, complex shapes, drawn into fine wires, or rolled into thin sheets. Anodized aluminum has a thick, durable coating of aluminum oxide, a coating that can be permanently colored by introduction of a dye.

Gallium, indium, and thallium are also typical silvery white metals, similar in appearance to aluminum. These elements all have high boiling points, but note the low melting point of gallium (see Table 29.4), which gives it an extremely large liquid temperature range (gallium melts in the hand). Gallium is also unusual because, like water, it is one of the few substances that expand on freezing.

Gallium is widely distributed in the crust of the earth, often as a minor constituent of aluminum minerals, in which Ga^{3+} replaces Al^{3+}. Gallium is recovered by electrolysis from the concentrated sodium hydroxide solutions used to digest the bauxite from which aluminum is obtained. Both indium and thallium occur in lead- and zinc-bearing ores, and they are obtained by extraction from flue dust and other by-products of lead and zinc smelting and refining. Gallium is in much greater supply than indium or thallium, but none of these elements has large-scale applications.

Gallium and indium are, however, important to the solid-state electronics industry. They are used primarily in compound semiconductors—compounds between Representative Group III and Representative Group V elements that have semiconducting properties, for example, gallium arsenide or indium antimonide (Sections 30.9, 30.10). The intense red light in the numerical display in some hand-held calculators is provided by gallium–arsenic–phosphorus light-emitting diodes. Over 80% of all gallium and indium produced is used in the electronics industry.

Thallium compounds are useful as rat and ant poisons, but care must be exercised, because thallium and its compounds are also *highly toxic* to human beings. Thallium finds other uses in low-melting glasses and, to a much lesser extent than indium and gallium, in semiconductors.

b. Tin, lead, and bismuth The ancient Egyptians and Babylonians were familiar with tin and lead. A record of bismuth goes back to the 1400s, but it may have been known long before that time and confused with lead. The aqueducts that brought

Table 29.12

End Uses of Aluminum In 1934 aluminum was proclaimed to be the "theme metal of the twentieth century."

Structural material
  Buildings
  Airplanes
  Boats
Electrical wire
Kitchen utensils
Foil wrap
Alloys
  Alnico (magnetic)
  Duraluminum (light, but strong)
Welding (thermite reaction)
Pigments
Fireworks, flares, and rocket fuel
Alumina (Al_2O_3) (α-alumina, γ-alumina)
  Watch bearings (synthetic ruby or sapphire)
  Dehydrating agent ("activated")
  Refractory bricks
  Catalyst support (catalyst deposited on surface of finely divided alumina)
Aluminum sulfate
  Water purification
  Pulp and paper sizing

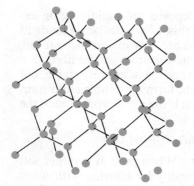

Gray tin

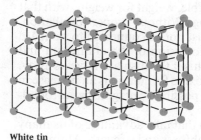

White tin

Figure 29.4
Crystal Structures of Gray and White Tin

Table 29.13
Major End Products of Tin, Lead, and Bismuth

Sn

Tinplate for beverage cans
Alloys, e.g.,
   soft solders (Sn, Pb)
   Babbit metal (Sn, Cu, Pb) used in
      bearings
   bronzes (Cu, Sn)

Pb

Alloys, e.g., in lead storage batteries
Tetraethyllead (antiknock)
Litharge, PbO, used in rubber,
   ceramics, etc.
Red lead, Pb_3O_4, rust-inhibiting
   pigment

Bi

Acoustical barriers
Radiation shields
Low-melting alloys, e.g.,
   Wood's metal, m.p. 70–72 °C
   (50% Bi, 25% Pb, 12.5% Sn,
   12.5% Cd) used in, e.g., electrical
   fuses, automatic sprinklers, safety
   plugs in gas cylinders

---

water to ancient Rome were lined with lead. Even though they have been known and used for so long, these elements are not abundant in nature.

Tin is obtained by heating cassiterite with charcoal or coke.

$$SnO_2(s) + 2C(s) \longrightarrow Sn(l) + 2CO(g)$$
cassiterite

The crude tin obtained from the reduction is partially purified by placing it on a hot sloping table and permitting the molten metal to flow away from the higher melting impurities. Further refinement is carried out by an electrolytic method in which impure tin, serving as the anode, is oxidized into solution and electrolytically plated out on a pure tin cathode.

Tin is a soft, low-melting metal that exists in three allotropic forms. The form stable at ordinary temperatures is white tin (Figure 29.4), which is distinctly metallic in character. Below 13.2 °C, it changes slowly into an amorphous gray powder, gray tin, which is a semiconductor and is less dense than the metallic form (see Table 29.5). The gradual crumbling away of tin as it changes to gray tin when exposed to low temperatures is called "tin disease." When the metal is heated to 161 °C it changes to brittle tin, a material that shatters when it is struck with a hammer.

The major uses of tin are in the manufacture of tinplate—low-carbon steel with a thin coating of tin—and alloys (Table 29.13). Tinplate is made by electrolytic deposition of tin on the steel; the coating improves such properties of the metal as its workability and ease of soldering, and protects it from corrosion.

The extractive metallurgy of lead is a multistep process similar in many ways to that of copper (Section 28.6). The sulfide ore is sintered, roasted, and smelted. The crude lead may be refined by pyrometallurgical or electrometallurgical methods. At all steps, the methods used must be designed to separate lead from the other elements (e.g., As, Sb, Sn, Bi, Ag, Au, Pt) usually also present in its ores, many of them metals worthy of recovery because of their own value. One method of separating silver and gold from crude lead takes advantage of the immiscibility of lead and zinc, and the solubility of silver and gold in zinc. In what is called the Parkes process, lead and a small amount of zinc are melted together. The silver and gold, along with some lead, dissolve in the zinc and the mixture rises to the surface and solidifies. Further refining is necessary to separate the silver and gold.

Lead, like tin, is soft and easily melted. It is quite dense. When freshly cut, lead has a high luster, but upon exposure to the air, it quickly becomes dull as the result of the formation of a thin coating of oxide or carbonate. This coating adheres tightly to the metal and protects it from further corrosion. For this reason, the metal has long been used for roofing, gutters, downspouts, and sewer lines. It should never be used to conduct water intended for human consumption, for lead is slowly corroded and dissolved by water (particularly by soft water), and it is toxic (see An Aside: Metals as Poisons).

The recovery of bismuth from its native ores is a simple process. The ore is heated at least to the melting point of bismuth (271 °C) and the metal is permitted to flow away from the impurities. Oxide and sulfide ores are roasted in the air and then reduced with carbon. A large amount of bismuth is obtained in the United States as a by-product of copper and lead smelting and refining.

Most of the bismuth that is used commercially appears in low-melting alloys for electrical fuses, automatic sprinkler systems, safety plugs in compressed gas cylinders, and other such devices. Bismuth alloys, for which dimensional changes during casting are predictable, are useful where accurate dimensions in the product are important. Bismuth and gallium are the only metals that increase in volume upon solidification.

29.10 *p* BLOCK METALS:
COMPOUNDS

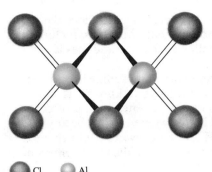

Cl   Al

Figure 29.5
Aluminum Chloride, Al₂Cl₆, in the
Vapor State

O²⁻

Al³⁺

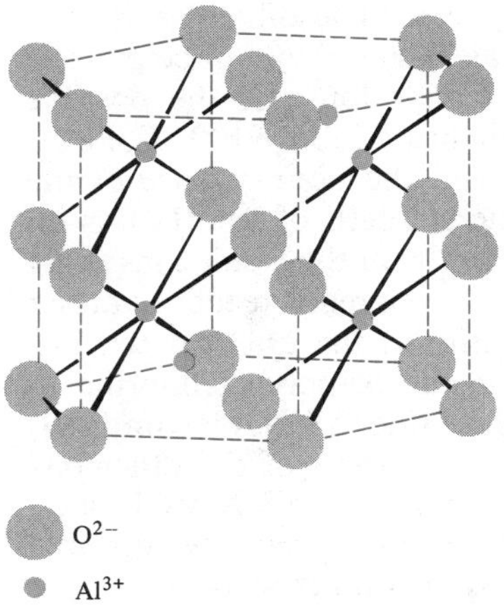

Figure 29.6
Crystal Structure of Al₂O₃ in the
Form of Corundum, also known as
α-Alumina

a. Compounds of aluminum   Salts of aluminum with strong acids are obtained as hydrates from aqueous solution under ordinary conditions (e.g., $AlCl_3 \cdot 6H_2O$, $Al_2(SO_4)_3 \cdot 18H_2O$) a reflection of the strong tendency of the aluminum ion to combine with water. These salts contain the $[Al(H_2O)_6]^{3+}$ ion. Any additional water molecules are associated with the anions or held in crystal lattices.

Anhydrous aluminum chloride, $AlCl_3$, is a white, deliquescent substance. It fumes in moist air as it hydrolyzes to HCl and it reacts vigorously with water. The compound is prepared by reaction of molten aluminum with chlorine. The aluminum chloride sublimes out of the hot reaction mixture. Many organic reactions are catalyzed by anhydrous aluminum chloride.

In benzene solution and in the vapor state, the anhydrous chloride, bromide, and iodide form Al_2X_6 molecules in which each aluminum atom is surrounded tetrahedrally by four halogen atoms, with two of them common to both tetrahedra (Figure 29.5).

Aluminum oxide, Al_2O_3, known as alumina, occurs in nature in the hydrated form as *bauxite* and in the anhydrous form as *corundum*. Corundum is used as an abrasive and a *refractory* (a material that is unchanged by high temperatures); it is hard and comparatively inert toward chemical attack. Some deposits of corundum include crystals that are colored by the presence of small amounts of oxides of other metals and are of value as gemstones. In the ruby the impurity is Cr_2O_3; in the sapphire, FeO and TiO_2; in the oriental amethyst, Mn_2O_3; and in the oriental topaz, Fe_2O_3. Synthetic alumina gemstones that are practically identical with the natural ones are manufactured by melting aluminum oxide and the appropriate metal oxides in an oxyhydrogen flame and allowing the melts to crystallize.

Treatment of an aqueous solution of an aluminum salt with a weak base, such as aqueous ammonia, yields a white gelatinous precipitate usually formulated as $Al(OH)_3$ and referred to as aluminum hydroxide. Sometimes the formula of the product is written as $Al_2O_3 \cdot xH_2O$. A number of hydrates of aluminum oxide are known, and at least one of them contains OH groups. The hydroxide is converted to the anhydrous oxide at about 800 °C.

Corundum (Figure 29.6) and the anhydrous aluminum oxide obtained by dehydrating the hydroxide have the same formula, Al_2O_3, but they have different crystal structures, which impart different properties. As noted above, corundum — the form of the oxide called **α-alumina,** α-Al_2O_3— is quite inert. However, the other form of the oxide is, like the hydroxide, an amphoteric substance that will dissolve in either acids or strong hydroxide bases. This reactive form of the oxide is known as **γ-alumina,** or γ-Al_2O_3. Heating γ-alumina above 1000 °C converts it to α-alumina. Finely divided alumina has a very high surface area, a property that makes it useful as a support for catalysts and as a dehydrating agent. For some uses of the aluminas, see Table 29.12.

Aluminum sulfate, $Al_2(SO_4)_3$, which can be obtained directly from bauxite by the action of sulfuric acid,

$$Al_2O_3 \cdot xH_2O(s) + 3H_2SO_4(aq) \longrightarrow Al_2(SO_4)_3(aq) + (3 + x)H_2O(l)$$

is the aluminum salt of greatest commercial use. The major consumer of aluminum sulfate is the pulp and paper industry, where it is used in the sizing process (in which rosin renders paper resistant to water), to adjust the pH of the stock, and to treat waste effluent. Because the Al^{3+} ion is an astringent (it causes body tissues to contract, thereby cutting down on secretions such as blood or perspiration), the aluminum sulfate hydrate is used in styptic pencils and aluminum chloride hexahydrate is used in antiperspirants.

The second most important use of aluminum sulfate is in the treatment of municipal water supplies and sewage. An essential step in water treatment is the precipitation of aluminum hydroxide by an alkaline substance, such as lime, naturally present in the water or added with the aluminum sulfate, for example,

$$Al_2(SO_4)_3(aq) + 3Ca(OH)_2(aq) \longrightarrow 2Al(OH)_3(s) + 3CaSO_4(aq)$$
$$Al_2(SO_4)_3(aq) + 3Na_2CO_3(aq) + 3H_2O(l) \longrightarrow 2Al(OH)_3(s) + 3Na_2SO_4(aq) + 3CO_2(g)$$

The aluminum hydroxide is gelatinous and highly polymeric. It acts as a flocculant, a substance that adsorbs and entangles suspended and colloidal impurities, including bacteria. The "floc" of hydroxide plus impurities is allowed to settle and the clarified water is filtered to remove any remaining particles.

When solutions containing aluminum sulfate and potassium sulfate in equimolar concentrations are permitted to evaporate, a double salt known as alum, $KAl(SO_4)_2 \cdot 12H_2O$, crystallizes. This substance is one of a general class of compounds, the alums, of the formula $M^+M^{3+}(SO_4)_2 \cdot 12H_2O$, where M^+ can be any one of a large number of singly charged cations and M^{3+} one of several triply charged ions. Alums of Na^+, K^+, and NH_4^+ and of Al^{3+}, Cr^3, and Fe^{3+} are the most common.

b. Compounds of tin, lead, and bismuth The known halides of tin, lead, and bismuth clearly illustrate the influence of electronegativity and polarizing ability on bonding and properties. All of the possible tin(II) and tin(IV) halides are known. The tin(IV) halides, except for SnF_4, are volatile compounds—$SnCl_4$ is a fuming liquid (b.p. 114 °C), and $SnBr_4$ and SnI_4 boil at 202 °C and 340 °C, respectively. These compounds are more molecular than ionic, as we would expect from the large charge-to-size ratio that an Sn^{4+} ion would have. They undergo complete reaction with water, rather than dissolution. (The existence of the Sn^{4+} ion in any compound or in solution is doubtful.) The high electronegativity of fluorine contributes to the lesser volatility of SnF_4 (it sublimes at 705 °C).

The tin(II) halides are all significantly less volatile than the comparable tin(IV) compounds; all but the iodide are water soluble, and these are considered to be ionic compounds. Tin(II) chloride, a common laboratory chemical, is a weak reducing agent. Its aqueous solutions are slowly oxidized by air and often some of the free metal is kept in contact with the solution to maintain the tin in the +2 state. We note that SnF_2, stannous fluoride by its older name, is the "fluoristan" of toothpaste fame.

Among the lead halides, the dihalides are all known compounds. They are much less volatile than any of the tin halides (all boil above 900 °C), and molten $PbCl_2$ conducts electricity—a demonstration of its ionic nature. The dihalides are not soluble in water (except that $PbCl_2$ dissolves in hot water), and they can be precipitated by combining solutions containing lead and halide ions. Of the possible lead(IV) halides, only PbF_4 and $PbCl_4$ are known. When heated above 100 °C, $PbCl_4$ decomposes to give $PbCl_2$ and Cl_2. This behavior and the nonexistence of the lead(IV) bromide and iodide are consistent with the strength of lead(IV) as an oxidizing agent and the increasing ability down their family for the halide ions to act as reducing agents. Lead(IV) and Br^- and I^- ions will undergo redox reactions rather than combine to form lead(IV) halides. Similarly, BiF_5 is the only known bismuth(V) halide. It is a potent fluorinating agent, readily supplying fluorine in chemical reactions and being itself converted to the trifluoride. All four bismuth(III) halides are known, but only BiF_3 is a true salt. The structures of the other bismuth(III) halides in the solid state are complex and show no discrete BiX_3 molecules.

Lead(II) oxide, known as *litharge,* is used in the glaze for decorative ceramic objects (it should not be used for objects that come into contact with food). The molten oxide is an excellent solvent medium for growing garnet crystals useful in electronic devices and as gems. Also, a paste of litharge and glycerine hardens on standing and yields a cement that is stable toward water and is often employed to seal drain pipes to sinks.

Lead(IV) oxide, PbO_2, does not exist in nature. It may be obtained as a dark brown material by the oxidation of lead(II) in alkaline solution with very strong

---

Sn(IV) halides: covalent
Sn(II) halides: ionic

Table 29.14
Some Compounds of Tin, Lead, and Bismuth

$SnCl_2$	Tin(II) chloride tinplating
SnF_2	Tin(II) fluoride toothpaste
$SnCl_4$	Tin(IV) chloride a fuming liquid
$SnCl_4 \cdot 5H_2O$	Tin(IV) chloride pentahydrate perfume and soap
SnO_2	Tin(IV) oxide white enamel, white glass
SnO	Tin(II) oxide
PbO	Lead(II) oxide "litharge," pottery glaze
$Pb(C_2H_3O_2)_2 \cdot 3H_2O$	Lead acetate trihydrate
PbO_2	Lead(IV) oxide a nonstoichiometric compound; lead storage battery
Pb_3O_4	Red lead anticorrosion paint for structural steel
$PbCrO_4$	Lead chromate chrome yellow pigment
BiF_3	Bismuth(III) fluoride
BiF_5	Bismuth(V) fluoride
Bi_2O_3	Bismuth(III) oxide yellow enamel
$Bi(NO_3)_3 \cdot 5H_2O$	Bismuth(III) nitrate pentahydrate
$BiOCl$	Bismuthyl chloride

oxidizing agents such as hypochlorite ion. The compound isolated never has the stoichiometric formula PbO_2, the atomic ratio of oxygen to lead ordinarily being about 1.888. This is an example of a compound with a lattice defect. In this case, the crystal has some vacancies at lattice points where there should be oxygen atoms. Because of this defect, lead(IV) oxide is able to conduct electricity as the oxide ions move from hole to hole. This property allows PbO_2 to function as an electrode in the lead storage battery (Section 23.15).

For many years, white lead, a basic carbonate of the approximate composition $Pb_3(OH)_2(CO_3)_2$, was the most important white paint pigment, largely because of its excellent covering power and protection of wood. However, small children who tend to eat flaking paint can develop lead poisoning from it. Moreover, the compound darkens on exposure to air as a result of the formation of black lead sulfide. It has therefore been replaced by less toxic and more stable compounds such as titanium dioxide. White lead is also used as a component of glazes for ceramic vessels — though not, of course, those to be used for food.

Other lead compounds that see service as pigments include the yellow chromate $PbCrO_4$, the red compound $PbO \cdot PbCrO_4$, and the red oxide Pb_3O_4, known as red lead, a component of paints used to protect structural steel from corrosion.

Some of the compounds of tin, lead, and bismuth are listed in Table 29.14.

EXAMPLE 29.4
Chemical Properties: Tin

The pipes of pipe organs are commonly made of tin, which has the proper resonant qualities. The story is told that some years ago a pipe organ was installed in a church in northern Russia. In only one year the new organ had become unusable. Can you explain what happened?

The organ was exposed to lower temperatures than most organs. The tin in the pipes changed to gray tin and crumbled away.

EXAMPLE 29.5
Chemical Properties: BiO^+ Compounds

At one time, bismuthyl nitrate, which is a soft, white powder, was used as a face powder. What disadvantages do you see in this?

If this powder becomes moist, the salt will hydrolyze to give bismuthyl hydroxide and nitric acid,

$$BiO(NO_3)(s) + H_2O(l) \longrightarrow BiO(OH)(s) + HNO_3(aq)$$

The nitric acid is hardly good for a lady's complexion.

AN ASIDE

Metals as Poisons

Evaluating the danger from metals in the environment is difficult for several reasons. The concentrations involved may be small and difficult to measure. There are wide variations in amount of exposure and the reaction to exposure of different individuals. Also, the only testing possible is with animals, and much is yet to be learned about how much a human reaction will be like that of, for example, a rat. In addition, as experiences with mercury have shown, the natural cycles of metals must be better understood before the fate of metals in the environment can be predicted.

In this section we discuss three representative metals under suspicion as environmental poisons — lead, mercury, and cadmium. Other metals that have been detected in the environment and that may be of concern are beryllium and nickel, particularly as nickel carbonyl, $Ni(CO)_4$.

a. Lead.   Some historians believe that lead poisoning contributed to the fall of the Roman Empire. The Romans stored their wine in pottery vessels glazed with lead compounds, creating acidic conditions that were sure to leach lead into the wine. They also received their water from lead-lined aqueducts. Upper-class Romans, who could afford glazed pottery vessels, apparently suffered from high rates of stillbirth and brain damage, which may have contributed to their downfall. The use of lead glazes is now banned in the United States, but care must be taken with old pottery or pottery made in other countries where such glazes are still in use.

Since soluble lead salts are cumulative poisons, the indiscriminate use of the metal and its compounds represents a serious health hazard. A daily intake of more than 1 mg of the element for a prolonged period apparently can be dangerous. Early stages of lead poisoning are characterized by constipation, anemia, loss of appetite, and pain in the joints. Unfortunately, these symptoms may not immediately be associated with lead poisoning. Later stages of the disease include paralysis of the extremities and mental damage.

Concentrations of environmental lead rose dramatically beginning in the 1940s (see Figure A), mainly because of the use of tetraethyllead in gasoline. Studies have shown that with the decrease in the use of "leaded" gasoline, there has been a decrease in blood lead levels in children.

b. Mercury.   Pure metallic mercury is not as toxic as mercury vapor and soluble mercury compounds, which are highly poisonous. However, mercury metal as well as its compounds must be handled with care.

Mercury poisoning is most often a local problem where mercury concentrations are high. The mercury reaches human beings mainly in food. It was thought for years that the discharge of metallic mercury into, say, a lake, was harmless because the mercury would sink and remain at the bottom as part of the sediment. Now it is known that bacteria can convert metallic mercury into methylmercury (CH_3Hg^+), a form in which it is soluble and highly poisonous. Mercury is concentrated up the food chain as, for example, bigger fish eat smaller fish that have eaten still smaller fish that contained mercury.

The symptoms of mercury poisoning (which, like lead poisoning, is hard to diagnose in its early stages), include loss of muscle control and blurred vision, leading ultimately to paralysis and kidney failure. Erratic behavior and mental deterioration are also likely to occur. (You probably remember the "Mad Hatter" from *Alice in Wonderland*. This character is based on experience, not fantasy. In the 19th century, mercury compounds were used to process felt in the manufacture of hats. As a result, it was not unusual for hatters to develop mercury poisoning, and the phrase "mad as a hatter" was in common use.) Because the body has a natural mechanism for eliminating mercury, mercury is not a great threat as a low-level cumulative poison.

c. Cadmium.   Cadmium compounds are exceedingly poisonous, and several tragic events have resulted from cadmium poisoning. The most notable of these took place in Toyama Prefecture, Japan, where the poisoning went on for several years before the cause was discovered, and where several hundred people died of cadmium poisoning. A smelter handling large amounts of cadmium-rich ore discharged wastes into the Jintsu River, the waters of which were used to irrigate the rice fields downstream. The cadmium in this water was absorbed into the rice, and so was introduced into the diet. The body has no mechanism for eliminating cadmium, which in this instance rapidly accumulated and caused serious kidney trouble and disintegration of the bones.

Recently, fear has been expressed that enough cadmium gets into the atmosphere to cause health problems. For example, as an automobile tire wears, the zinc oxide and the associated cadmium oxide in the rubber are liberated as fine dusts, which may not settle for some time and so may be drawn into the lungs. Tobacco contains a small amount of cadmium, which in smoking is carried into the lungs of both smokers and those around them. The human body, at birth, does not contain cadmium, but as we grow older, cadmium compounds accumulate from our use of galvanized kitchen utensils (the zinc used in galvanizing always contains some cadmium), from galvanized water pipes, from automobile tires, and in other ways. Eventually, this may bring on chronic disease.

Figure A
Environmental Lead. Lead levels in isolated Greenland glaciers have been growing since 800 B.C. The actual data are a series of scattered points, and the curve represents the best average line through these points. In addition, there is considerable seasonal variation in lead levels. The trend is significant, however. (Source: G. Tyler Miller, Jr. *Living in the Environment*, Belmont, California: Wadsworth, 1975, p. 97.)

THE ZINC FAMILY

29.11 THE ZINC FAMILY
METALS: PREPARATION,
PROPERTIES, AND USES

Zinc is one of the four workhorse metals of our modern civilization (the others being iron, copper, and lead). The metallurgy of zinc was discussed in Section 28.6. Zinc is used in coating iron to prevent rusting (galvanized iron) and in many important alloys, of which the most widely used are brasses, bronzes, and bearing metals (Table 29.15). Other uses of zinc, together with uses of cadmium and mercury, are listed in Table 29.16.

The largest use of metallic cadmium is in alloys (see Table 29.15), especially those that melt at low temperatures. Wood's metal and Lipowitz metal, both of which melt at 70 °C, are used in automatic fire extinguishers and fire alarms. Cerrolow alloy, which also contains indium, melts at 47 °C. Cadmium rods are used in nuclear reactors to absorb neutrons, and thus, by moderating neutron flux, to control the chain reaction.

Mercury is less abundant in the earth's crust than is cadmium, it is not as widely distributed, and it is not obtained as a by-product. Yet there are important uses for mercury for which there are no adequate substitutes. Hence, mercury is an expensive metal. Most of the mercury used in the United States is imported from Spain, though some is mined in California. The chief ore is the red *cinnabar*, HgS. Roasting in the presence of oxygen yields elemental mercury.

There are, it has been estimated, more than three thousand uses of mercury (a few are given in Table 29.16). Many of them depend upon its liquid nature. The relatively great change in volume of the metal with changes in temperature makes it useful in thermometers. Its liquidity and high density account for its use in barometers, and its electrical conductivity for its use in electric switches. Mercury also conducts electricity in the vapor state, emitting the bright blue light of mercury arc lights. With most of the metals, mercury forms alloys called **amalgams.** One is used in dentistry. When the intermetallic compound Ag_3Sn is ground with mercury, it dissolves to form a semisolid amalgam which, on standing, sets to form a hard, solid mixture of the intermetallic compounds Ag_5Hg_8 (a γ intermetallic compound; Section 28.12) and Sn_7Hg. During the formation of these compounds, the amalgam expands slightly and fits the walls of a cavity so tightly that bacteria cannot easily get in. These amalgams are not toxic, apparently because the intermetallic compounds are extremely stable.

Table 29.15
Some Alloys of Zinc and Cadmium The numbers are percentages by mass of the metals in the alloy.

	Zn	Cd	Cu	Bi	Pb	Sn	Ni	In
Brass	18–40	—	60–82	—	—	—	—	—
Lead–tin–yellow brass	24.0	—	72.0	—	1.0	3.0	—	—
Bronze	1–25	—	70–95	—	—	1–18	—	—
Lead–nickel–brass	20.0	—	57.0	—	9.0	2.0	12.0	—
Nickel silver (German silver)	24.0	—	64.0	—	—	—	12.0	
Wood's metal	—	12.5	—	50.0	25.0	12.5	—	—
Lipowitz metal	—	10	—	50.0	26.7	13.3	—	—
Cerrolow	—	5.3	—	44.7	22.6	8.3	—	19.1

Table 29.16
Some End Uses of Zinc, Cadmium, and Mercury

Zn	Cd	Hg
Electroplating	Electroplating	Fungicides
Alloys	Alloys, for brazing and low-melting alloys	Pulp and paper industry
Galvanized iron		Batteries
Pigments, e.g., ZnO, ZnS (both white)	Ni–Cd batteries	Pigment, e.g., HgS (red)
	Pigments, e.g., CdS (yellow)	Tanning leather
Rubber	Fungicides	Thermometers and scientific instruments
Zinc oxide ointment (antiseptic)		Hg vapor lights
Batteries (dry cells) and Ni–Zn batteries		Electrical switches
		Amalgams for dentistry

29.12 THE ZINC FAMILY METALS: COMPOUNDS

Some compounds of zinc, cadmium, and mercury are listed in Table 29.17.

Mercury(II) oxide, HgO, is either red or yellow, depending upon its method of preparation. The red and yellow forms have identical crystal structures and differ only in particle size, the yellow form being more finely divided than the red. Mercury(I) oxide is not known.

Zinc oxide, ZnO, is white at ordinary temperatures, but turns yellow when heated. On cooling, it turns white again. Cadmium oxide, CdO, varies in color from green-yellow to black, depending upon the temperature at which it is obtained. Both cadmium and zinc oxides are only slightly soluble in water.

Mercury(I) chloride, Hg_2Cl_2, known as *calomel*, has been used in medicine for a long time. It is a diuretic, a cathartic, and an antiseptic. It also kills intestinal worms and cabbage and onion maggots. The extremely poisonous nature of mercury compounds is masked in calomel by its very small solubility.

Mercury(II) chloride, $HgCl_2$, or *corrosive sublimate* is, by contrast, quite soluble in water and is a *violent* poison, being corrosive to mucous membranes. In very dilute solution, it can be used as a disinfectant. The compound is prepared by combination of mercury with excess chlorine or by heating a mixture of mercury(II) sulfate and sodium chloride.

$$HgSO_4(s) + 2NaCl(s) \longrightarrow HgCl_2(g) + Na_2SO_4(s)$$

The $HgCl_2$ sublimes away from the solid reactants and the sodium sulfate.

Mercury(II) sulfide, HgS, is the least soluble sulfide and one of the least soluble of all simple binary compounds.

The outstanding properties of the p block and zinc family metals are summarized in Table 29.18.

Table 29.17
Some Compounds of Zinc, Cadmium, and Mercury

ZnO	Zinc oxide
	Chinese white, a pigment; photo-conductor in copying machine; ointment base
ZnS	Zinc sulfide
	in lithopone, a white pigment; TV tube phosphor
$ZnCl_2$	Zinc chloride
	deodorant; wood preservative
CdO	Cadmium oxide
	Ni–Cd battery electrodes
CdS	Cadmium sulfide
	yellow to red pigment
CdSe	Semiconductor
CdTe	Semiconductor
HgO	Mercury(II) oxide
	red and yellow forms
Hg_2Cl_2	Mercury(I) chloride
	calomel, a drug
$HgCl_2$	Mercury(II) chloride
	corrosive sublimate, antiseptic in dilute solution

Table 29.18
Outstanding Properties of the *p* Block and Zinc Family Metals

+2 +2 +3 +3 +3 **Zn Cd Al Ga In**	One common oxidation state
+1 +2 +2 +4 **Hg Sn**	Two common oxidation states; Hg(I) in Hg_2^{2+}
+1 +3 +2 +4 +3 +5 ← *lower state more stable* **Tl Pb Bi**	
+4 +5 Tl^{3+}, PbO_2, BiO_3^-	Strong oxidizing agents
Hg_2^{2+}	Disproportionates to Hg(*l*) and Hg(II) with OH^-, other reagents
Al Zn	Most reactive of *p* block and Zn family elements
Bi Hg	Least reactive of *p* block and Zn family elements
Halides	Lesser ionic character in higher oxidation states. Only Pb(IV) fluoride and chloride and only Bi(V) fluoride are known.
M + strong hydroxide base ⟶ **dissolution** **M + O_2** ⟶ **amphoteric oxides**	M = Zn, Al, Ga, Sn, Pb

EXAMPLE 29.6
Metallurgy: Zinc

Zinc can be recovered from sphalerite (ZnS) by roasting, dissolution of the product of roasting in dilute sulfuric acid, and electrolysis. (A) Write a balanced equation for each chemical reaction. (B) Calculate the amount of electricity (in coulombs) required to recover the zinc from 100. kg of ore containing 90.% by mass of ZnS. Assume that the process is 100% efficient.

1. Study the problem and be sure you understand it.
    (a) What is unknown?
       The two parts of this problem are connected. In (A) the balanced equations for the three steps in the metallurgical process are unknown. Writing them requires knowing what "roasting" and "electrolysis" mean in the treatment of a zinc sulfide ore. In (B), the quantity of electrical energy is unknown. This depends upon the amount of material present at the outset of the process and on the stoichiometry of the unknown equations.
    (b) What is known?
       In (A) the description of the three-step process and in (B) the mass of ore and the fact that it is only 90% zinc sulfide.
2. Decide how to solve the problem.
       For (A), review in your mind the chemistry of the steps described and be sure you know what the description means. For (B), consider what the connection is between the known mass of ore and the electrical energy needed to produce zinc from it. Recall from electrochemistry (Section 23.5) that the faraday provides the connection between the amount of electricity required and the number of moles of electrons required in an electrolysis reaction. The relationship of 96,500 C/mol e^- provides the connection needed here. To solve this problem requires (i) writing the balanced equations, (ii) finding the number of moles of ZnS present at the outset, (iii) finding the number of moles of electrons required to produce metallic zinc, taking into account the stoichometry of the reactions, and (iv) finding the amount of electricity required.
3. Set up and solve the problem.
    (i) Balanced equations
       "Roasting" means heating in air to convert a sulfide to an oxide plus sulfur dioxide

$$2ZnS(s) + 3O_2 \xrightarrow{\Delta} 2ZnO(s) + 2SO_2(g)$$

The dissolution of zinc oxide in dilute sulfuric acid is the reaction of an oxide with a nonoxidizing acid.

$$ZnO(s) + H_2SO_4(dil) \longrightarrow ZnSO_4(aq) + H_2O(l)$$

Electrolysis of the zinc sulfate solution under the appropriate conditions will result in reduction of zinc ions at the cathode.

$$Zn^{2+} + 2e^- \longrightarrow Zn(s)$$

   (ii) Initial moles of ZnS   (Remember that only 90% of the ore is ZnS.)

$$\left(\frac{90. \text{ kg ZnS}}{100. \text{ kg ore}}\right)\left(100. \text{ kg ore}\right)\left(\frac{1000 \text{ g}}{\text{kg}}\right)\left(\frac{1 \text{ mol ZnS}}{97.4 \text{ g ZnS}}\right) = 920 \text{ mol ZnS}$$

   (iii) Moles of electrons required   (The foolproof method is to write out all of the mole ratios)

$$\left(920 \text{ mol ZnS}\right)\left(\frac{2 \text{ mol ZnO}}{2 \text{ mol ZnS}}\right)\left(\frac{1 \text{ mol ZnSO}_4}{1 \text{ mol ZnO}}\right)\left(\frac{1 \text{ mol Zn}^{2+}}{1 \text{ mol ZnSO}_4}\right)\left(\frac{2 \text{ mol } e^-}{1 \text{ mol Zn}^{2+}}\right)$$

$$= 1800 \text{ mol } e^-$$

(iv) Amount of electricity required

$$\left(\frac{96,500 \text{ C}}{1 \text{ mol } e^-}\right)\left(1800 \text{ mol } e^-\right) = 1.7 \times 10^8 \text{ C}$$

4. Check the result.

Are significant figures and the final units correct? Yes. Is the answer reasonable? At first glance, this is a large quantity of electricity, but remember that we started with 100. kg of ore. [No industrial process is 100% efficient. More than 1.7×10^8 C would undoubtedly be required.]

SUMMARY

METALS IN THE GROUPS OF REPRESENTATIVE ELEMENTS: THE ZINC FAMILY (Section **29.1**) GENERAL PROPERTIES AND REACTIONS OF THE REPRESENTATIVE METALS (Sections **29.2–29.5**) The representative metals fall into Groups I through V of the periodic table. The s block metals of Groups I and II have ns^1 and ns^2 electron configurations, while the p block metals of Groups III–V have $ns^2 np^1$, $ns^2 np^2$, and $ns^2 np^3$ configurations. Metallic behavior decreases across the periods and increases down each family. In zinc, cadmium, and mercury, at the end of the d-transition series, only the outermost s electrons are involved in bonding, so these elements tend to resemble the representative metals rather than the transition metals.

The lithium family metals are the most reactive metals; they have the largest atomic radii and lowest ionization energies. The most electropositive of the elements, they easily lose their single s electrons to form $+1$ cations, and exhibit the $+1$ oxidation state in all their compounds. Calcium, strontium, and barium are second only to the lithium family elements in reactivity, and like them form ionic bonds in all their common compounds. The chemistry of beryllium differs from that of the other s block elements (Table 29.2), resembling more closely that of aluminum. Because of its small size, the Be^{2+} ion has a high polarizing ability; consequently Be forms many molecular compounds. It also forms many stable complex ions. Magnesium also tends to form bonds with more covalent character than do the other s block metals. The beryllium family metals exhibit the $+2$ oxidation state in all their common compounds. The s block metals are good reducing agents; the great hydration energy of the small Li^+ ion makes Li an unusually strong reducing agent. The lithium family elements are softer, less dense, and have lower melting points than most metals. All the s block metals are good conductors of electricity. (See Table 29.1.)

The only significant oxidation state of aluminum is $+3$. All other p block metals have two positive oxidation states—the group state and the group state minus 2 (Table 29.3). Thallium, lead, and bismuth are more stable in their lower oxidation states; species containing these elements in their higher oxidation states are strong oxidizing agents. Compounds of aluminum, gallium, and indium in their $+3$ oxidation states are predominantly covalent, but the Al^{3+}, Ga^{3+}, and In^{3+} ions form readily in solution because of their high heats of hydration. The only stable oxidation state for Zn and Cd is $+2$. Hg, less reactive, forms the Hg^{2+} cation and also the Hg_2^{2+} cation (oxidation state $+1$), in which two Hg^+ ions are covalently joined. (See Tables 29.4, 29.5, and 29.6.)

The s block metals all combine directly with the halogens and oxygen; Zn, Cd, Hg, and all the p block metals except Tl are generally stable in dry air, but combine with oxygen, halogens, and other nonmetals at high temperatures. The alkali metals, Ca, Sr, Ba, and Al, and Zn (if the surfaces are clean) all displace hydrogen from water. All s block metals displace hydrogen from acids, as do Zn, Cd, and all the p block elements except bismuth. Zinc, cadmium, and mercury and all the p block metals react with oxidizing acids; Be, Zn, Al, Ga, Sn, and Pb all react with strongly alkaline solutions to form hydroxo anions and hydrogen. The oxides of these six elements are amphoteric. The hydroxides and carbonates of Zn, Cd, and the p block metals decompose on heating to give the metal oxide plus water or CO_2. Lithium hydroxide and (to some extent) lithium carbonate also decompose on heating; the hydroxides and carbonates of the other Group I metals are thermally stable, while those of the Group II metals exhibit varying degrees of stability. The Be^{2+}, Zn^{2+}, Cd^{2+}, Al^{3+}, and Sn^{2+} ions react with water to give acidic solutions. The Be^{2+}, Zn^{2+}, Al^{3+}, Ga^{3+}, Sn^{2+}, and Pb^{2+} ions react with excess base to form hydroxo anions. In aqueous solutions, $Hg_2{}^{2+}$ ions are in equilibrium with Hg^{2+} and elemental Hg; anything that removes Hg^{2+} from solution causes the $Hg_2{}^{2+}$ to disproportionate. Aluminum is an excellent reducing agent for many metal oxides because of the high temperature produced by the reduction reactions (aluminothermic reactions).

METALS OF REPRESENTATIVE GROUPS I AND II: THE *s* BLOCK METALS (Sections **29.6–29.8**)   Ca, Na, K, and Mg are among the most abundant elements in the earth's crust. Soluble salts of these elements and of lithium are also found in seawater and brines. Because their positive ions are difficult to reduce, production of Group I and II metals requires a great deal of energy. Group I metals are so reactive that they must be stored under organic liquids such as kerosene. The Group I hydroxides and carbonates (except that of Li) are very soluble; those of the Group II metals are much less soluble. Electrolysis of saturated NaCl solutions to produce NaOH, H_2, and Cl_2 is carried out in several different types of cells designed to keep the chlorine produced at the anode from mixing with the other products. Important industrial alkalis include NaOH (caustic soda); anhydrous Na_2CO_3 (soda ash), made by the Solvay process or extracted from the mineral trona; CaO (quicklime); and $Ca(OH)_2$ (hydrated or slaked lime). The latter two alkalis are made from limestone, $CaCO_3$. (See Table 29.11.)

METALS OF REPRESENTATIVE GROUPS III–V: THE *p* BLOCK METALS (Sections **29.9, 29.10**)   THE ZINC FAMILY (Sections **29.11, 29.12**)   Aluminum is light, strong, and a good conductor of electricity. The most reactive of the zinc family and *p* block metals, it readily acquires a coating of oxide which protects it from further reaction. Gallium and indium are important in the solid-state electronics industry. Tin is a soft, low-melting metal with three allotropes; it is used in alloys and tinplate. Lead is soft, dense, and easily melted; on exposure to air it forms a protective coating of oxide or carbonate. Salts of Al with strong acids are hydrates that contain the $[Al(H_2O)_6]^{3+}$ ion. Al_2O_3, known as alumina, exists in two different forms with different crystal structures; the α form, called corundum and used as an abrasive and refractory, is quite inert, but the γ form is a reactive, amphoteric substance. $Al(OH)_3$ is a gelatinous, hydrated, polymeric substance. The tin(IV) halides are volatile, predominantly covalent compounds. Lead(IV) oxide, PbO_2, is a nonstoichiometric compound. Zinc and cadmium are used in many alloys; Zn is also used in galvanizing iron. Mercury has a large number of uses. Compounds of Cd and Hg, like those of Be, Tl, and Pb, are generally toxic. (See Table 29.18.)

SIGNIFICANT TERMS

s block metals
p block metals
post-transition metals
aluminothermic reactions
lime
quicklime, unslaked lime
hydrated lime, slaked lime
caustic soda
soda ash
α-alumina
γ-alumina
amalgams

THOUGHTS ON CHEMISTRY

The Centennial of Chemistry in 1874

THE CENTURY'S PROGRESS IN CHEMISTRY, by J. Lawrence Smith

Chemistry was an art long before it was a science. But it was not until Priestley had discovered oxygen, and Lavoisier became the interpreter of chemistry with his great analytical mind, and the balance in his hand, did the daylight of chemistry truly dawn upon the world; previous to that time all was dim twilight little better than darkness. When Lavoisier made the study of quantity an important element in chemistry, followed by Dalton's discovery of chemical proportions, then the inventive genius of mankind made chemistry a useful and certain servant, and built up one industry after another. . . . All that is asked of me on this occasion is a review of a century's progress in industrial chemistry. . . .

Industrial chemistry links itself with every modern art in such an intimate manner, that were we to take away the influence and results of chemistry, it would be almost like taking away the laws of gravitation from the universe. Industrial chaos would result in one case, as material chaos would in the latter. . . . No one can paint in too vivid colors the sum of the indebtedness the civilized world is already under to the chemist, and no enthusiast can transcend in his wildest speculations what we are yet to realize. The chemical arts in their strictest sense do not simply aid the other arts, but they keep in activity a vast amount of capital, and consequently give employment to a large number of individuals, skilled and unskilled. [There follows a lengthy review of American chemistry from oxygen to medicine.]

But I must not detain you longer, and shall conclude by congratulating you that we are living in an age in which an industry requires but a few years for its creation or development.

In our days a useful discovery is scarcely made, or a happy application of one found out, before it is published, described in the scientific journals, or other technical periodicals, and especially in the specifications of patents. It then becomes the starting-point of a thousand researches and new experiments, entered into by the philosopher in the hope of advancing scientific progress, and by the manufacturer with the expectation of reaping a material benefit. From these multiplied and diverse efforts — these incessant labors of an army of workers — arises an industry which has no sooner sprung into existence than it becomes important and prosperous.

Prof. J. Lawrence Smith, "The Century's Progress in Industrial Chemistry" (a lecture at the centennial celebration of American Chemistry on August 1, 1874), *American Chemist*, August/September 1874, pp. 61ff.

QUESTIONS

General Properties and Reactions of the Representative Metals, the Zinc Family Metals, and Their Compounds

29.1 Briefly describe the physical properties of the elements in Groups I and II.

29.2 Write the general outer electron configurations for atoms of (a) the s block metals, (b) the p block metals, and (c) the zinc family metals. What oxidation state(s) would you predict for each group of elements? What types of bonding would you expect in most of the compounds of these elements? Why are the zinc family metals sometimes considered transition elements and sometimes representative metals? Explain why the p block metals have more than one positive oxidation state.

29.3 Write the electron configurations of Hg, Hg^+, and Hg^{2+}. Which of these should be diamagnetic? One piece of evidence that mercury(I) exists as Hg_2^{2+} is that solutions containing mercury(I) are diamagnetic. Sketch the Lewis structure for Hg_2^{2+} and explain why this ion is diamagnetic.

29.4 Lithium and its compounds resemble magnesium and its compounds in many respects. Why is this true? Is this kind of diagonal behavior shown by beryllium?

29.5 There is less difference in physical and chemical properties between Zn and Cd than between Cd and Hg. Examine the periodic table and explain this fact.

29.6 Where do the metals of Groups I and II fall in the activity series with respect to H_2? What does this tell us about their reactivity with water and acids? Repeat this question for the metals in the zinc family and for aluminum.

29.7 Write chemical equations describing the reactions of O_2 with each of the alkali and alkaline earth metals.

29.8 Although aluminum is a reactive metal, it is not noticeably corroded in air. Why? Why is this property important in determining various uses for the metal?

29.9 The metals in Groups I and II (represented by M and M′, respectively) react vigorously with the halogens. Complete the following equations for the reactions with the hypothetical halogen X: (a) $M(s) + X_2 \rightarrow$ and (b) $M'(s) + X_2 \rightarrow$

29.10* Metallic tin reacts with concentrated nitric acid to form SnO_2 and lead reacts to form $Pb(NO_3)_2$. Write the chemical equations for these reactions and explain this difference.

29.11 What type of solution is formed by dissolving the oxides of Groups I and II in water? How does BeO differ from the others in this behavior?

29.12 Zinc hydroxide is amphoteric, but cadmium hydroxide is not. Explain why.

29.13 Contrast the behavior upon heating of the hydroxides and carbonates of Group I elements to that of the hydroxides and carbonates of Group II elements.

The s Block Metals

29.14 Are the elements in Groups I and II found in the free state in nature? What are the primary sources for these elements? How are the metals obtained?

29.15 Write the chemical equation for the electrolysis of a saturated sodium chloride solution. Why are the electrochemical cells used for this electrolysis designed to keep the products separate?

29.16 Write balanced equations and give the experimental conditions necessary for preparing solid (a) $NaOH$, (b) Na_2CO_3, (c) $NaHCO_3$, (d) CaO, and (e) $Ca(OH)_2$.

29.17 Write and discuss the chemical equations describing the formation of limestone caverns and the growth of stalagmites and stalactites in these caverns.

29.18* Polychlorinated biphenyls (PCB's) are carcinogenic substances that are often found in fluids used with electrical equipment. These compounds are chlorinated hydrocarbons which can be destroyed by treatment with finely divided sodium metal. Why does sodium react with these substances?

29.19* Approximately three-fourths of the common inorganic salts of lithium and sodium exist as hydrates. Only one-fourth of the inorganic compounds of potassium exist as hydrates and nearly all of the rubidium and cesium salts are anhydrous. Give a reasonable explanation for these facts.

The *p* Block Metals
29.20 As a student added a solution of NaOH dropwise to a test tube containing a solution of Al^{3+}, he noticed that a gelatinous precipitate was formed that disappeared upon the addition of more of the alkaline solution. Explain his observations and write the chemical equations for the reactions involved.

29.21 Choose which of the following halides are essentially molecular and prepare three-dimensional sketches of their molecular structures: (a) $PbCl_2$, (b) $BiCl_3$, (c) SnF_4, (d) BiF_3, (e) $SnCl_2$, and (f) SnI_4.

29.22 Briefly mention some uses of (a) $Al(s)$, (b) $AlCl_3$, (c) Al_2O_3, and (d) $Al_2(SO_4)_3$.

29.23 Write the formula for lead(IV) oxide. How is this compound prepared? Why can it conduct electricity? What is the major use of this compound?

The Zinc Family
29.24 Compare the bonding in compounds of the zinc family to that in compounds of the alkaline earth family. Why is there a difference?

29.25 Compare the behavior of Zn^{2+}, Cd^{2+}, Hg^{2+}, and Hg_2^{2+} as sodium hydroxide is added until an excess is present.

29.26 Explain why HgF_2 is more ionic than HgI_2.

29.27 When zinc sulfide ore is roasted, the major products are ZnO and $ZnSO_4$. However, when mercury(II) sulfide, cinnabar, is treated in the same way, metallic mercury is formed. Explain this difference.

Additional Questions
29.28 An abbreviated activity series for some of the representative metals studied in this chapter is $Mg/Zn/Sn/Pb/H_2/Hg$ with the most "active" metal on the left and the least "active" metal on the right. Use this series to predict whether each of the following reactions will occur or not under the same conditions

that prevailed when the series was determined:

(a) $Sn + HCl \longrightarrow$ (c) $Hg + HCl \longrightarrow$
(b) $Pb^{2+} + Mg \longrightarrow$ (d) $Zn^{2+} + Mg^{2+} \longrightarrow$

For those that you predicted to occur, complete and balance the equations.

29.29 Which of the following are redox reactions? Identify the oxidizing and reducing agents in each of the redox reactions.

(a) $Al_2O_3(s) + 2NaOH(aq) + 3H_2O(l) \longrightarrow 2NaAl(OH)_4(aq)$
(b) $2Al(s) + 3MnO(s) \xrightarrow{\Delta} 3Mn(l) + Al_2O_3(s)$
(c) $Mg(OH)_2(s) + 2HCl(aq) \longrightarrow MgCl_2(aq) + 2H_2O(l)$
(d) $2NaCl(l) \xrightarrow{electrolysis} 2Na(l) + Cl_2(g)$

29.30 Repeat Question 29.29 for:
(a) $Sn(s) + O_2(g) \longrightarrow SnO_2(s)$
(b) $MgCO_3(s) \longrightarrow MgO(s) + CO_2(g)$
(c) $2K(s) + 2H_2O(l) \longrightarrow 2KOH(aq) + H_2(g)$
(d) $NaOH(aq) + CO_2(g) \longrightarrow NaHCO_3(aq)$

29.31 Classify each of the following reactions according to the reaction types listed in Tables 17.2 and 17.7:
(a) $Cl_2(g) + H_2O(l) \longrightarrow HOCl(aq) + H^+ + Cl^-$
(b) $Na(g) + KCl(l) \longrightarrow NaCl(l) + K(g)$
(c) $NH_4HCO_3(aq) + NaCl(aq) \longrightarrow NaHCO_3(s) + NH_4Cl(aq)$
(d) $Hg_2^{2+} + 2OH^- \longrightarrow HgO(s) + Hg(l) + H_2O(l)$

29.32 Repeat Question 29.31 for:
(a) $2NaHCO_3(s) \longrightarrow Na_2CO_3(s) + CO_2(g) + H_2O(g)$
(b) $CaO(s) + H_2O(l) \longrightarrow Ca(OH)_2(s)$
(c) $HgSO_4(s) + 2NaCl(s) \xrightarrow{\Delta} HgCl_2(g) + Na_2SO_4(s)$
(d) $Al_2O_3(s) + 2NaOH(aq) + 3H_2O(l) \longrightarrow 2NaAl(OH)_4(aq)$

29.33 Predict the major products of the following reactions:
(a) $PbO(s) + H_2O(l) + NaOH(aq) \longrightarrow$
(b) $BiCl_3(aq) + H_2O(l) \longrightarrow$
(c) $Al_2O_3(s) + H_2SO_4(aq) \longrightarrow$
(d) $Pb(s) + O_2(g) \xrightarrow{\Delta}$

29.34 Repeat Question 29.33 for:
(a) $NaOH(aq) + H_2O(l) + CO_2(g, \text{excess}) \longrightarrow$
(b) $Cl_2(g) + NaOH(aq) \longrightarrow$
(c) $MgCO_3 \cdot CaCO_3(s) \xrightarrow{\Delta}$
(d) $Na_2O(s) + H_2O(l) \longrightarrow$

29.35 Write balanced equations for the following chemical reactions:

(a) $NaOH(s) \xrightarrow{\Delta}$
(b) $BeO(s) + NaOH(s) + H_2O(l) \longrightarrow$
(c) $NaCl(aq, conc) + H_2O(l) \xrightarrow{electrolysis}$
(d) $NH_4Cl(aq) + Ca(OH)_2(s) \longrightarrow$

29.36* Devise a procedure by which the ions in each of the following groups can be separated from each other: (a) Zn^{2+}, Cd^{2+}, Hg^{2+}, Hg_2^{2+}; (b) Zn^{2+}, Ba^{2+}, Al^{3+}; and (c) Na^+, Be^{2+}, Mg^{2+}.

29.37 First-year students in chemistry laboratories are usually surprised to find that metals in Group I such as Na are stored under oil, that metals in Group II such as Ca, when stored in the presence of air, become coated with white powders, and that Al reacts with H_2O and HCl much more slowly than expected. Explain these observations.

Answers to Selected Questions

29.14 no; seawater, brines, and soluble salts; electrolysis of molten chlorides

29.26 F is more electronegative and forms a more ionic bond with Hg than does iodine.

29.30 a, c; oxidizing agents: (a) O_2, (c) H_2O; reducing agents: (a) Sn, (c) K

29.32 (a) nonredox—decomposition to give compounds, (b) nonredox—combination of compounds, (c) nonredox—partner exchange, (d) nonredox—combination of compounds

29.34 (a) $NaHCO_3(aq)$; (b) $NaOCl(aq)$, $NaCl(aq)$, $H_2O(l)$; (c) $MgO(s)$, $CaO(s)$, $CO_2(g)$; (d) $NaOH(aq)$

29.37 Metals form oxides upon exposure to the atmosphere—oil protects the metals of Group I, the white powder is the oxide of the Group II metal, Al forms a protective oxide coating which decreases its activity.

PROBLEMS

Review of Principles

29.1 Seawater contains 0.13 mass % Mg^{2+}. How much water would have to be processed to yield 1.0 ton of the metal if the recovery process is 75% efficient?

29.2 Brines from Searles Lake in southeastern California are processed commercially for the recovery of trona ($Na_2CO_3 \cdot NaHCO_3 \cdot 2H_2O$) and borax ($Na_2B_4O_7 \cdot 10H_2O$). In terms of its sodium content, which compound would be more economical to transport commercially? *Answer* trona

29.3* A sample containing 40 g of Ca and 60 g of Al is thoroughly mixed and heated to 1200 °C, resulting in the formation of a liquid solution. The solution is cooled to about 1050 °C and crystals that contain 43 mass % Ca and 57 mass % Al start to form. As the mixture is cooled further, a second solid phase appears at 72.5 °C, and it contains 32 mass % Ca and 68 mass % Al. Each of these solid phases corresponds to an intermetallic compound formed between aluminum and calcium. Find the empirical formulas of these substances.

29.4 What mass of "white lead," $Pb(OH)_2 \cdot 2PbCO_3$, can be made from 10.0 g of Pb? *Answer* 12.5 g

29.5 The standard state free energy of formation at 25 °C is 0 for $Hg(l)$, 164.43 kJ/mol for $Hg^{2+}(aq)$, and 153.55 kJ/mol for $Hg_2^{2+}(aq)$. Calculate $\Delta G°$ and the equilibrium constant for the reaction

$$Hg(l) + Hg^{2+} \rightleftharpoons Hg_2^{2+}$$

Explain why a drop of Hg is added to a solution of Hg_2^{2+} to "stabilize" it toward air oxidation.

29.6 Write the chemical equation for a thermit-type reaction of PbO_2 with Al. $\Delta H_f° = -277.4$ kJ/mol for PbO_2 and -1675.7 kJ/mol for Al_2O_3. Calculate $\Delta H°$ for this reaction. Is the energy change favorable? *Answer* $3PbO_2(s) + 4Al(s) \longrightarrow 3Pb(s) + 2Al_2O_3(s)$, $\Delta H° = -2519.2$ kJ, yes

29.7 The vapor pressure of mercury is 0.0012 Torr at 20.0 °C and 0.2729 Torr at 100.0 °C. Calculate the heat of vaporization of liquid mercury.

29.8* Lead is known to crystallize in the cubic system with a unit cell length of 0.495 nm. The density of lead is 11.29 g/cm³. Is the unit cell primitive, body centered, or face centered? *Answer* face centered

29.9 The standard heat of formation is -426.73 kJ/mol for $NaOH(s)$, -469.23 kJ/mol for $NaOH(aq, 6 M)$, and -469.10 kJ/mol for $NaOH(aq, 0.1 M)$. (a) Calculate the heat of solution to form a 6 M NaOH solution from solid NaOH and water. Comment on your answer. (b) Calculate the heat of dilution to prepare 0.1 M NaOH from 6 M NaOH. *Answer* (a) -42.50 kJ, the solution will increase in temperature by about 50 °C unless the heat of solution is dissipated; (b) 130 J

29.10 A voltaic cell consists of a tin electrode dipping into a 1 M $Sn(NO_3)_2$ solution and a lead electrode dipping into a 1 M $Pb(NO_3)_2$ solution. The half-cells are connected by a $NaNO_3$ salt bridge. Which electrode is the anode? The standard state reduction potentials are -0.136 V for Sn^{2+} and -0.126 V for Pb^{2+}. What voltage will the cell generate? How can the cell voltage be increased?

29.11 Write the equation that describes the electrolysis of a brine solution to form NaOH, Cl_2, and H_2. What mass of each substance will be produced in an electrolysis cell for each mole of electrons passed through the cell? *Answer* 35.46 g Cl_2, 1.01 g H_2, 40.00 g NaOH

29.12 What is the pH of a saturated $Mg(OH)_2$ solution? $K_{sp} = 7.1 \times 10^{-12}$.

29.13 To what pH range must a solution containing 0.01 M Zn^{2+} and 0.01 M Sn^{2+} be adjusted so that $Sn(OH)_2$ will precipitate, but not $Zn(OH)_2$? $K_{sp} = 3.3 \times 10^{-17}$ for $Zn(OH)_2$ and 6×10^{-23} for $Sn(OH)_2$.

29.14* In many qualitative analysis schemes, Pb^{2+}, Ag^+, and Hg_2^{2+} are separated from other ions by adding hydrochloric acid and precipitating the cations as insoluble chlorides. However, a large excess of HCl cannot be used, because AgCl and $PbCl_2$ will form soluble complex compounds and a complete separation will not occur. Assuming that no chloro complexes have formed, what is the concentration of each cation at equilibrium in a solution containing Cl^- at 0.3 mol/L? $K_{sp} = 2 \times 10^{-5}$ for $PbCl_2$, 1.8×10^{-10} for AgCl, and 1.3×10^{-18} for Hg_2Cl_2. If the cation concentrations remaining in solution are greater than 1×10^{-4} mol/L, the various tests used in the schemes may be in error. Are any of the concentrations of Pb^{2+}, Ag^+, or Hg_2^{2+} large enough that errors might occur in subsequent tests?

CHAPTER 30

Semiconducting Elements

A recent gift catalog advertises LCD (liquid crystal display) watches, LED (light-emitting diode) alarm clocks, programmable calculators, and even a pocket calculator that translates a foreign language. None of these items has been around for very long. They are all products of the solid-state revolution.

What does "solid state" really mean? In electronics, it means that the electric signals are generated or amplified or controlled by tiny devices made of semiconducting elements — semiconductor devices. These transistors, rectifiers, diodes, and so on have no moving parts nor heated wires and need no vacuum. They perform their functions because of properties imparted by their internal electronic structures.

The solid state revolution began in 1947 with the discovery of the transistor by Walter Brattain, John Bardeen, and William Shockley of the Bell Telephone Laboratories in Murray Hill, New Jersey. Time magazine (July 12, 1948) described the transistor as a "little brain cell." Newsweek (September 6, 1948) hailed it as "an innovation which may revolutionize electronics and communication as the original three-element vacuum tube did 35 years ago." Today we have space vehicles, computers, word processors, video games, and even talking cars to prove that this statement was correct.

The semiconducting elements would be important and valuable for their role in the electronics industry alone. However, their bonding and structural properties make these elements special in many other ways. The bonding in many boron compounds is unique. Naturally occurring silicon–oxygen compounds form much of the crust of the earth. Furthermore, we reshape silicon–oxygen compounds to give structural materials such as glass and cement, and to make beautiful objects of cut glass, pottery, and fine china.

THE SEVEN SEMICONDUCTING ELEMENTS

30.1 GENERAL PROPERTIES OF THE SEMICONDUCTING ELEMENTS

Semiconducting elements: B, Si, Ge, As, Sb, Se, Te

The properties of the semiconducting elements, like their positions in the periodic table, are intermediate between those of the metals and those of the nonmetals. Often called *metalloids* or *semimetals,* these seven elements are boron (from Representative Group III), silicon and germanium (Group IV), arsenic and antimony (Group V), and selenium and tellurium (Group VI). Some of the properties of these elements are given in Table 30.1.

These elements resemble metals in appearance but are more like nonmetals in their chemical reactions. The semiconducting elements conduct electric current, but much less effectively than metals. It is the nature of the <u>electrical conductivity</u> of the semiconducting elements that puts them in a class by themselves; their conductivity increases under conditions that decrease the conductivity of metals. This distinctive property is explained in terms of bonding (Section 30.8).

Boron and silicon each have a single positive <u>oxidation state</u> (Table 30.2). These

Table 30.1
Properties of the Semiconducting Elements

Element	Configu- ration	Atomic Radius (nm)	Melting Point (°C)	Boiling Point (°C)	Ionization Energy (kJ/mol)	Electro- negativity
B	$[He]2s^2 2p^1$	0.080	2300	2500	801	2.0
Si	$[Ne]3s^2 3p^2$	0.118	1420	2355	786	1.8
Ge	$[Ar]3d^{10}4s^2 4p^2$	0.123	958	2700(?)	762	1.8
As	$[Ar]3d^{10}4s^2 4p^3$	0.125	814 (32 atm)	610 (sublimes)	947	2.0
Sb	$[Kr]4d^{10}5s^2 5p^3$	0.145	630.5	1325	834	1.9
Se	$[Ar]3d^{10}4s^2 4p^4$	0.116	217 (gray form)	685	941	2.4
Te	$[Kr]4d^{10}5s^2 5p^4$	0.143	450	1390	869	2.1

Table 30.2
Common Oxidation States of the Semiconducting Elements The most stable states are shown in color. For many of the unusual boron compounds the concept of oxidation state has little meaning.

Group III
B
−3, +3

Group IV
Si
−4, +4
Ge
+2, +4

Group V
As
−3, +3, +5
Sb
−3, +3, +5

Group VI
Se
−2, +4, +6
Te
−2, +4, +6

states, +3 for boron and +4 for silicon, are the group oxidation states; they represent involvement of the outermost s and p electrons in bonding. Germanium has both +2 and +4 oxidation states. The elements of Group V (As, Sb) and Group VI (Se, Te) commonly form compounds in both the group oxidation states (+5 and +6) and the oxidation states two less than the group oxidation states (+3 and +4, respectively). The Group V and Group VI elements in their +5 and +6 oxidation states are present in oxidizing agents, the elements being reduced to the lower states in redox reactions. The semiconducting elements are all assigned negative oxidation states in their compounds with hydrogen or with more electropositive metals.

The atomic radii and ionization energies of these elements follow the general trends expected from their positions in the periodic table and are intermediate between those of the metals and the nonmetals (see Tables 30.1, 10.2, and 10.13; Figures 10.3, 10.4, and 10.7). Their electronegativities all fall between 1.9 and 2.4.

The bonding of semiconducting elements in compounds is generally covalent. The covalent nature of the halides of these elements, for example, is shown by their volatilities and low melting points (see Tables 30.6–30.9) relative to those of the ionic halides of many metals.

Germanium, arsenic, antimony, and selenium all exist in a number of allotropic forms, both amorphous and crystalline. In their pure crystalline forms, the metallic nature of these elements is evident in the dark metallic luster of the crystals. The amorphous forms tend to show greater chemical reactivity than the crystalline forms, although none of the semiconducting elements are highly reactive at ordinary temperatures and pressures.

30.2 SOME CHEMICAL REACTIONS OF THE SEMICONDUCTING ELEMENTS AND THEIR COMPOUNDS

a. Combination with other elements All of the semiconducting elements react with the halogens and oxygen. As is to be expected, the reactions with fluorine are the most vigorous and those with iodine are the least vigorous. The elements that show more than the one oxidation state best achieve their higher oxidation state in reactions with fluorine (unless the amount of fluorine is deficient). In general, the reactions with oxygen require elevated temperatures. Some reactions which illustrate these principles are the following:

$$2B(s) + 3F_2(g) \longrightarrow 2BF_3(g) \qquad Se(s) + O_2(g) \overset{\Delta}{\longrightarrow} SeO_2(s)$$

$$2B(s) + 3I_2(s) \overset{\Delta}{\longrightarrow} 2BI_3(s) \qquad Te(s) + 3F_2(g) \longrightarrow TeF_6(g)$$

Combination reactions of the semiconducting elements with metals produce binary compounds called borides, arsenides, silicides, and so on. In some cases, the products are true compounds in which the semiconducting elements are assigned the negative oxidation numbers, for example,

$$2K(s) + Se(s) \xrightarrow[\text{liq. NH}_3]{\text{in}} \overset{+1\ -2}{K_2Se}(s)$$

potassium
selenide

Such compounds are formed by arsenic, selenium, and tellurium with the most electropositive metals. In other cases, solid solutions or various types of alloys are formed. For example, in many borides the small boron atoms occupy interstices in the metal lattice.

b. Reactions with water, acids, and bases   Unlike the more metallic elements, none of the semiconducting elements react with water or with nonoxidizing acids. With oxidizing acids, they give oxoacids or oxides, usually in their higher oxidation states, although hot *dilute* nitric acid oxidizes arsenic and antimony to H_3AsO_3 (arsenous acid) and Sb_2O_3, in which the elements are in the $+3$ rather than the $+5$ oxidation states. Some examples of the oxidation of the semiconducting elements by oxidizing acids are the following:

$$B(s) + 3HNO_3(conc) \longrightarrow H_3BO_3(s) + 3NO_2(g)$$
$$2As(s) + 5H_2SO_4(conc) \xrightarrow{\Delta} 2H_3AsO_4(aq) + 5SO_2(g) + 2H_2O(l)$$
$$2Sb(s) + 10HNO_3(conc) \longrightarrow Sb_2O_5(s) + 10NO_2(g) + 5H_2O(l)$$

Silicon does not react with concentrated nitric acid, but it does dissolve in a mixture of nitric and hydrofluoric acids to form fluorosilicic acid.

$$Si(s) + 4HNO_3(conc) + 6HF(aq) \longrightarrow H_2SiF_6(aq) + 4NO_2(g) + 4H_2O(l)$$

Boron reacts with molten alkali metal hydroxides, with the liberation of hydrogen,

$$2B(s) + 6NaOH(l) \xrightarrow{\Delta} 2Na_3BO_3(s) + 3H_2(g)$$

Silicon and germanium, like tin and lead (the metals that follow them in Group IV), both react similarly with molten alkali metal hydroxides to give hydrogen and silicates or germanates, respectively.

c. Reactions of oxides   The oxides of the semiconducting elements are either amphoteric (As_2O_3, Sb_2O_3, TeO_2) or acidic. None are basic, again demonstrating the chemical similarity of these elements to the nonmetals. The oxides of boron and selenium react with water to give acids (these are nonredox combination reactions).

$$B_2O_3(s) + 3H_2O(l) \longrightarrow 2H_3BO_3(aq)$$

boric acid

$$SeO_3(s) + H_2O(l) \longrightarrow H_2SeO_4(aq)$$

selenic acid

The amphoteric oxides react with both acid and base, as illustrated by the reactions of antimony (III) oxide (also nonredox reactions):

$$Sb_2O_3(s) + 3H_2SO_4(aq) \longrightarrow Sb_2(SO_4)_3(aq) + 3H_2O(l)$$
$$Sb_2O_3(s) + 6NaOH(aq) \longrightarrow 2Na_3SbO_3(aq) + 3H_2O(l)$$

All of the oxides of the semiconducting elements react with strong bases to give salts plus water.

d. Hydrolysis of halides   All of the halides of the semiconducting elements react rapidly with water. The final products are oxoacids or oxides, depending upon the

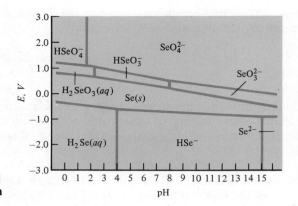

Figure 30.1
pH–Potential Diagram for Selenium

solubility of the oxide and the amount of water present. Some of the reactions are quite violent.

$$SiX_4 + 2H_2O(l) \longrightarrow SiO_2(hydrated)(s) + 4HX(aq)$$
$$AsX_3 + 3H_2O(l) \longrightarrow H_3AsO_3(aq) + 3HX(aq)$$
$$AsF_5 + 4H_2O(l) \longrightarrow H_3AsO_4(aq) + 5HF(aq)$$

Antimony trichloride gives an insoluble oxochloride which then slowly reacts with additional water to give the oxide.

$$SbCl_3(s) + H_2O(l) \longrightarrow SbOCl(s) + 2HCl(aq)$$
$$2SbOCl(s) + H_2O(l) \longrightarrow Sb_2O_3(s) + 2HCl(aq)$$

The hydrolyses of halides are all nonredox partner-exchange reactions. (The partner-exchange pattern is somewhat obscured by the way that we write the formulas of acids and by the formation of oxides rather than oxoacids in some cases.)

e. Ions in aqueous solution   Unlike the metals and more like the nonmetals, the semiconducting elements are not found as hydrated monatomic cations in aqueous solution. Aside from the oxocation of antimony, SbO^+, and a few complex ions (e.g., $[BF_4]^-$, $[SiF_6]^{2-}$, $[SbCl_4]^-$), the semiconducting elements are always present in aqueous solutions as oxoanions or monatomic anions (Se^{2-}, Te^{2-}). Some of these oxoanions have a variety of forms containing varying amounts of hydrogen and oxygen (for example, see Figure 30.1, the pH–potential diagram for selenium). Most of them give alkaline solutions because, as the anions of weak acids, they react to a certain extent with water. For example, soluble salts containing the tetraborate ion, $B_4O_7{}^{2-}$, in aqueous solution give boric acid:

$$B_4O_7{}^{2-} + 7H_2O(l) \rightleftharpoons 4H_3BO_3(aq) + 2OH^-$$

Note the reverse of this reaction: When a boric acid solution reacts with a base, the tetraborate ion, rather than the borate ion, $BO_3{}^{3-}$, is formed.

Sodium silicate, which is present in glass, also reacts slowly with water to give a mixture of various hydrated silicic acids:

$$Na_4SiO_4(s) + 3H_2O(l) \rightleftharpoons H_2SiO_3(hydrated) + 4NaOH(aq)$$

EXAMPLE 30.1
pH–Potential Diagram;
Nomenclature

Name all of these species in the pH–potential diagram for selenium (Figure 30.1) and indicate the oxidation state of selenium in each. Write equations for each of the pH-dependent equilibria represented in the diagram.

Selenium species in oxidation states −2, 0, +4, and +6 are represented in the diagram.

Oxidation state −2
H₂Se   hydroselenic acid
HSe⁻   hydrogen selenide ion
Se²⁻   selenide ion

Oxidation state 0
Elemental selenium

Oxidation state +4
H₂SeO₃   selenous acid
HSeO₃⁻   hydrogen selenite ion
SeO₃²⁻   selenite ion

Oxidation state +6
HSeO₄⁻   hydrogen selenate ion
SeO₄²⁻   selenate ion

There are five pH-dependent equilibria represented in the diagram:

$$H_2Se(aq) \rightleftharpoons H^+ + HSe^- \qquad HSeO_3^- \rightleftharpoons H^+ + SeO_3^{2-}$$
$$HSe^- \rightleftharpoons H^+ + Se^{2-} \qquad HSeO_4^- \rightleftharpoons H^+ + SeO_4^{2-}$$
$$H_2SeO_3(aq) \rightleftharpoons H^+ + HSeO_3^-$$

30.3 BORON   Boron occurs in the crust of the earth mainly as boric acid (H_3BO_3), known as the mineral *sassolite,* and borates. The borates most important as boron ores are *borax* ($Na_2B_4O_7 \cdot 10H_2O$), *kernite* ($Na_2B_4O_7 \cdot 4H_2O$), and *colemanite* ($Ca_2B_6O_{11} \cdot 5H_2O$).

The free element is obtained as an impure microcrystalline brown powder, "amorphous" boron, by the reduction of boric oxide, B_2O_3, with magnesium at high temperatures.

$$B_2O_3(s) + 3Mg(s) \longrightarrow 2B(s) + 3MgO(s)$$

Pure boron, in the form of black lustrous crystals, can be prepared by reduction of boron trichloride with hydrogen above 1000 °C.

$$2BCl_3(g) + 3H_2(g) \xrightarrow{\Delta} 2B(s) + 6HCl(g)$$

Elemental crystalline boron is an extremely hard, high-melting (2300 °C) substance that exists in at least three allotropic forms. All three forms have giant-molecule structures in which the fundamental structural unit is an icosahedral (twenty-faced) arrangement of twelve boron atoms (Figure 30.2) united by strong covalent single bonds. Weaker covalent bonds join the icosohedra to each other (these are three-center bonds, explained in Section 30.11).

Boron, like other first elements in representative groups, differs significantly from the other group members (Table 30.3) and tends to resemble its diagonal neighbor, which is silicon. Boron is an unusual element, and the structure and bonding in many boron compounds (Section 30.11) are not predictable on the basis of what is known of any other elements and their compounds.

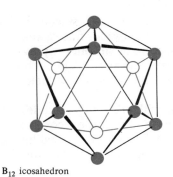

B₁₂ icosahedron

Figure 30.2
Elemental Boron

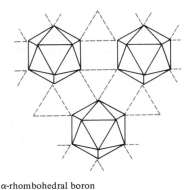

α-rhombohedral boron

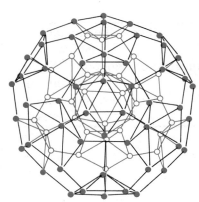

84-atom unit of β-rhombohedral boron

Table 30.3
Differences between Boron and the Other Members of the Boron Family (Al, Ga, In, Tl)

Property	Comments
The only nonmetal in the boron family	Boron is a semiconducting element; its chemical behavior is essentially that of a nonmetal. Other family members are all metals.
Resembles Si more than Al in its chemistry	A consequence of similar electronegativity and effective nuclear charge
Oxide (B_2O_3) is acidic.	Al_2O_3 and Ga_2O_3 are amphoteric, In_2O_3 and Tl_2O_3, basic. B_2O_3 is the anhydride of a number of boric acids, the best characterized being H_3BO_3 and HBO_2.
Forms a series of unique hydrides (e.g., B_2H_6, B_4H_{10})	The hydrides are covalent compounds with unusual, three-center bonding. Aluminum forms a polymeric hydride. There is little evidence for hydrides of other family members.

Boron is added in small amounts to aluminum and to steel, where it aids in hardening. The element has a high affinity for oxygen and is used as an oxygen scavenger in the production of metals. A newer application of boron is the production of fibers for use in fiber-reinforced materials. Pure boron fibers or boron-coated tungsten fibers embedded in aluminum or magnesium produce a light, very stiff, and strong material used in aircraft parts.

Boron reacts readily with neutrons,

$$^{10}_{5}B + ^{1}_{0}n \longrightarrow ^{7}_{3}Li + ^{4}_{2}He$$

and boron rods control the flux of neutrons in light water nuclear reactors (Section 12.17).

Boron is less used in electronic devices than are the other semiconducting elements. It is limited to use as an additive in low concentrations (a dopant; Section 30.8).

30.4 SILICON AND GERMANIUM

Silicon is the second most abundant element in the earth's crust, while germanium is among the less abundant elements. Silicon is not found naturally as the free element, but it is widely distributed in the form of **silica,** SiO_2, or **silicates,** compounds containing silicon–oxygen groups and metals. Roughly 85% of the earth's crust is composed of silica and silicate minerals (described further in Sections 30.15 and 30.16). Elemental silicon of about 98% purity is obtained by reduction of sand, which is largely SiO_2, with coke in an electric furnace.

$$SiO_2(s) + 2C(s) \xrightarrow{3000\ °C} Si(l) + 2CO(g)$$

Silicon: the element, Si
Silica: SiO_2
Silicates: compounds of Si, O, and metals
Silicones: polymers of Si, O, C, and H

Silicon made in this way is used in alloys, for example, in spring steel (22% silicon), in corrosion-resistant iron alloy (about 15%), and in aluminum alloys for fine casting (about 17%). It is also the starting material in the manufacture of **silicones**—polymers composed of silicon, carbon, hydrogen, and oxygen (Section 30.18). The preparation of the ultrapure silicon and germanium needed in semiconductor devices is discussed in Section 30.9.

Germanium is found mainly as a sulfide in association with other metal sulfides, for example, those of lead and zinc (see Example 30.2). Germanium is also recovered from coal ashes and flue dust. Pure germanium, which has several crystalline allotropes, is metallic in appearance, but brittle, like glass. Both silicon and germanium have the diamond crystal structure (see Figure 27.1).

The first semiconductor devices were made of germanium and today the major use of germanium is in the electronics industry. Germanium is ideally suited for fabricating semiconducting devices. It can be prepared in very pure form with clearly defined crystal structure and crystal defects. It has been said that because of the interest in its electronic properties, germanium is the best understood of all of the elements. Certainly this is true of its solid-state properties. Applications of germanium outside the electronics industry include infrared-transmitting glass, low-melting gold–germanium alloys (sometimes used in dental work), and substances that exhibit red fluorescence when struck by light of appropriate wavelengths.

EXAMPLE 30.2
Chemical Reactions: Germanium Compounds

A process for the production of elemental germanium includes the following steps: (a) Ore containing germanium(IV) sulfide is treated with a mixture of concentrated sulfuric acid and nitric acid to convert the sulfide to germanium(IV) oxide. (b) The oxide-containing product is dispersed in hydrochloric acid, and upon heating, germanium(IV) chloride distills out of the mixture. (c) Treating the chloride with water yields the pure oxide. (d) Elemental germanium is produced by the reaction between the oxide and hydrogen. How does each step in this process take advantage of the distinctive properties of the substances involved? Where possible, write chemical equations.

(a) A mixture of concentrated sulfuric acid and nitric acid is a strongly acidic and strongly oxidizing medium. Many sulfides are soluble in acids. The sulfide ion is oxidized, but it would be difficult to write a single equation for the reaction in this mixture of acids and ore.

(b) Halides of the semiconducting elements are covalent and many of them are volatile [$GeCl_4$, b.p. 83.1 °C]. The reaction

$$GeO_2(s) + 4HCl(aq) \xrightarrow{\Delta} GeCl_4(g) + 2H_2O(l)$$

takes advantage of the removal of a volatile product to allow a nonredox partner-exchange reaction to proceed in the direction desired.

(c) This reaction takes advantage of a property common to halides of the semiconducting elements—their ready reaction with water, in this case to form an oxide:

$$GeCl_4(l) + 2H_2O(l) \longrightarrow GeO_2(s) + 4HCl(aq)$$

(d) Hydrogen reduces oxides of many elements other than those in the lithium and beryllium families to the free elements (Table 16.7):

$$GeO_2(s) + 2H_2(g) \xrightarrow{\Delta} Ge(s) + 2H_2O(g)$$

30.5 ARSENIC AND ANTIMONY

Arsenic and antimony are not abundant elements. Their principal minerals are sulfides, including As_2S_3, *orpiment,* which was known to the alchemists. Arsenic and antimony are also found in the free state in nature—like bismuth, the heaviest element in Group V, but unlike the lighter phosphorus, which is more reactive.

Elemental arsenic and antimony each have two allotropes. The common semiconducting forms, often referred to as the metallic forms, are gray, lustrous, and crystalline, while the amorphous allotropes are yellow. Yellow arsenic, which is obtained on the rapid cooling of arsenic vapor, is very unstable and reverts quickly to the semiconducting form. Like white phosphorus, yellow arsenic is soluble in carbon disulfide. In solution in this solvent it exists as tetrahedral molecules, As_4.

Yellow arsenic and arsenic compounds are highly poisonous, leading quickly in high doses to convulsions and death. Chronic arsenic poisoning causes fatigue and a variety of unpleasant effects, including hair loss, visual disturbances and blindness, a garlic odor on the breath, paralysis, and anemia. By taking small doses of arsenic over an extended period, tolerance to arsenic can be built up. "Arsenic eating" was once thought to increase the vigor of persons living in high altitudes. The "arsenic" of detectives stories is the oxide, As_2O_3, which is soluble, odorless, tasteless, and fatal in doses of 0.1 g or more.

Arsenic and antimony are both of use in hardening lead alloys destined for lead shot, bullets, bearings, battery grids, and cable sheathings. Antimony has been a component of the metal used to make type for printing since the fifteenth century. Because it expands on solidifying, antimony helps to produce type and that has sharp edges and prints clear images.

"Arsenicals" is a general term for arsenic compounds used in human and veterinary medicine, in agriculture, and as pesticides. The major use of arsenic compounds is in agriculture, especially in the defoliation of cotton bolls before the cotton is harvested. *Paris green* [copper acetoarsenite, $Cu(CH_3COO)_2 \cdot 3Cu(AsO_2)_2$] and various other arsenites and arsenates were once widely used as plant insecticides and in livestock dips. However, their highly poisonous nature led to some unfortunate accidents and they have been replaced in many uses by other substances. A number of organic arsenicals are valuable in the treatment of chronic skin diseases.

Antimony compounds are much less toxic than arsenic compounds, but more so than bismuth compounds. Antimony compounds played a role in the early history of medicine, sometimes with disastrous results, as antimony and arsenic compounds were often confused with each other. "Antimonials," like the arsenicals, are used in medicine and as pesticides. They provided the first cures for two quite dreadful parasitic diseases prevalent in tropical climates, schistosomiasis and leishmaniasis, bringing them under control as they had never been before.

30.6 SELENIUM AND TELLURIUM

Selenium and tellurium are among the ten or fifteen rarest elements. No ores are mined specifically for their selenium or tellurium content. These elements generally occur as selenides (e.g., PbSe, $(AgCu)_2Se$, Ag_2Se) and tellurides (e.g., PbTe, Cu_4Te_3, Ag_3AuTe_2) associated with sulfide ores of such heavy metals as copper and lead. They are obtained commercially as by-products of the metallurgy of heavy metals. The principal commercial source of both selenium and tellurium is the anode mud formed in electrolytic copper refining (Section 28.6).

Selenium, like sulfur, which precedes it in Representative Group VI, is known in several allotropic forms, including two crystalline forms. One is red selenium (m.p. 170–180 °C), which is soluble in carbon disulfide and does not conduct electricity. It is generally obtained when selenium compounds are reduced to the free element in solution. The selenium molecule is octaatomic and has the same puckered ring structure as the S_8 molecule. When red selenium is heated below its melting point, it changes to the more stable gray semiconducting form (m.p. 217.4 °C), called metallic selenium. This substance consists of spiral chains of selenium atoms held by covalent bonds; the chains are parallel to each other in the crystal (Figure 30.3). The electrical conductivity of gray selenium increases with the intensity of the light striking it. This property makes selenium valuable in photosensitive semiconducting devices.

Crystalline tellurium, unlike sulfur and selenium, has no allotropic forms. It is a silvery white solid that has the same crystal structure as gray selenium (see Figure 30.3). The electrical conductivity of tellurium is little affected by light.

Selenium has a variety of uses in alloys. It is a decolorizer for glass at low concentrations, a coloring agent for ruby glass at high concentrations, and a vulcanizing agent for rubber. Tellurium is also a component of many different alloys, including various steels, malleable cast iron, and copper, lead, and tin alloys used in automotive bearings.

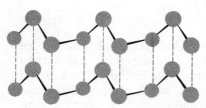

Figure 30.3
Gray Selenium, Elemental Tellurium Both have this structure.

EXAMPLE 30.3
Physical and Chemical Properties: H_2Se

Oxygen, sulfur, and selenium are in the same family in the periodic table. Considering what we have learned about H_2O and H_2S, what properties might be expected of H_2Se?

Water is a liquid with many unusual properties dependent upon the strong hydrogen bonding that results from the high electronegativity of oxygen and the resulting polar nature of the angular water molecule. Because selenium is slightly less electronegative than sulfur, we can expect H_2Se to be more similar to H_2S than to H_2O. Hydrogen selenide should be a colorless gas with a higher boiling point than hydrogen sulfide, since the molecule has a greater mass. As in liquid H_2S, hydrogen bonding should be of little importance in liquid H_2Se. Hydrogen selenide, like H_2S, should be an acid in aqueous solution. It would be a somewhat stronger acid, since the H—Se bond is weaker than the H—S bond. Hydrogen sulfide is a reducing agent and we might expect that hydrogen selenide can also act as a reducing agent. Familiarity with the terrible odor and toxicity of H_2S would lead to the suspicion that H_2Se is also foul in odor and toxic. [It is.]

EXAMPLE 30.4
Chemical Reactions: Halide Preparations

Given below are the incomplete equations for several reactions (other than combination) by which some of the halides of the semiconducting elements can be prepared in the laboratory. Classify these reactions as best you can, identify any oxidizing and reducing agents, and complete the equations. Why are none of these reactions carried out in aqueous solutions?

(a) $Te(OH)_6(conc) + HI(fuming) \longrightarrow TeI_4(s) + \cdots$
   telluric acid

(b) $BaGeF_6(s) \xrightarrow[N_2]{>700\,°C} GeF_4(g) + \cdots$

(c) $As_2O_3(s) + S(s) + Br_2(l) \xrightarrow[7\,h]{\Delta} AsBr_3(s) + \cdots$

(d) $AlBr_3(s) + BF_3(g) \xrightarrow{\Delta} BBr_3(g) + \cdots$

(a) Tellurium is reduced in this reaction from $+6$ to $+4$. Therefore telluric acid is the oxidizing agent. Hydrogen iodide is the reducing agent and it can be expected to form elemental iodine as its oxidation product. Adding water to balance the equation gives

$$Te(OH)_6(conc) + 6HI(fuming) \longrightarrow TeI_4(s) + I_2(s) + 6H_2O(l)$$

This reaction does not fit into one of the simple classes of redox reactions.

(b) Germanium is in the $+4$ oxidation state in both $BaGeF_6$ and GeF_4. Therefore this is a nonredox thermal decomposition reaction in which a gaseous product is formed. Driving off the GeF_4 by heating will leave BaF_2, a high-melting salt.

$$BaGeF_6(s) \longrightarrow GeF_4(g) + BaF_2(s)$$

(c) Arsenic is in the $+3$ state in both As_4O_6 and the product $AsBr_3$, but bromine has been reduced to bromide ion. Therefore this is a redox reaction, clearly not a simple one. Bromine is the oxidizing agent. Sulfur must be the reducing agent, which indicates that an oxidation product of sulfur must also be formed, most likely SO_2.

$$2As_2O_3(s) + 3S(s) + 6Br_2(l) \longrightarrow 4AsBr_3(s) + 3SO_2(g)$$

(d) No oxidation numbers change here. This nonredox reaction between pure compounds must follow the pattern of a partner-exchange reaction, indicating that the other product will be AlF_3.

$$AlBr_3(s) + BF_3(g) \longrightarrow BBr_3(g) + AlF_3(s)$$

The halides of the semiconducting elements cannot be prepared in aqueous solution, for they would immediately undergo hydrolysis in the presence of water.

BONDING IN METALS AND SEMICONDUCTORS

30.7 METALLIC BONDING

Many of the characteristic properties of metals depend upon the presence of freely mobile electrons with a continuous distribution of energies (Sections 9.5 and 9.6). The molecular orbital description of bonding (Chapter 24) provides a picture of how these free electrons become available.

When many atoms are brought together in a metal, many molecular orbitals are possible. Instead of electrons being confined to orbitals that encompass two, or three, or a dozen atoms in a molecule, some electrons reside in orbitals that encompass a great many atoms.

Consider the combination of lithium atoms. Two lithium atoms, each of configuration $1s^2 2s^1$ combine to give four molecular orbitals occupied by six electrons as shown at the left in Figure 30.4a. Three lithium atoms produce six molecular orbitals, three at the lower energy level and three at the upper energy level. The process of combination is pictured as continuing up to N lithium atoms that combine to give N molecular orbitals in each energy level.

As the energy levels are divided into more and more molecular orbitals, the energy differences between any two orbitals get smaller and smaller. The point is reached where the molecular orbitals in an energy level are so close together that they are essentially continuous. A continuous energy level produced by a large number of molecular orbitals is called a band, or **energy band.**

The bands formed by the lithium $1s$ and $2s$ atomic orbitals are delocalized over a great many atoms, much as six atomic orbitals are delocalized over a whole benzene molecule. The lower energy band in lithium metal is full, just as the $1s$ atomic orbital in a gaseous lithium atom is full. The upper band, to which each lithium atom contributes only one electron, is one-half full. Such delocalized orbitals in metals hold the electrons of the electron sea on which our earlier explanation of metallic bonding was based.

The highest energy electrons within the half-full energy band of elemental lithium are close to empty levels in the other half of the band that are not much higher in energy. Therefore, they can easily move from their own energy level to another that is only slightly higher. Once in an energy level that is not full, these electrons are available as current carriers. An energy band in which electrons are free

Figure 30.4
Formation of Electron Bands by Lithium and Magnesium The band structures of all alkali metals resemble that of lithium, and the band structures of all alkaline earth metals resemble that of magnesium. Metallic conduction requires the presence of either (a) a partially filled conduction bond (as in lithium) or (b) a valence band that overlaps an empty conduction band (as in magnesium).

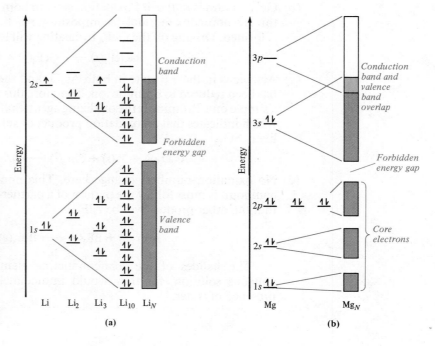

to flow and therefore to conduct electricity is a **conduction band.** The electrons in a conduction band that have enough energy so that they are not held back by attraction to the positive ions are the conduction electrons. The electrons at lower levels in a conduction band need a larger amount of energy to reach empty orbitals and in general do not participate in conduction. When an electric field is applied, the conduction electrons are accelerated in the direction of the field, and the net result is a flow of electrons.

Electrons contribute to conduction only if they are in a partially filled band. In a full band with no adjacent empty orbitals, all that the electrons can do, if they have enough energy to move, is to change places with each other. The net result in the presence of an electric field is no conduction, since equal numbers of electrons are going in both directions.

At first glance, an element such as magnesium (Figure 30.4b) looks as if it should be a nonconductor, since the highest energy band is filled by two $3s$ electrons contributed by each atom. However, magnesium (and beryllium, calcium, zinc, and other metals that form 2+ ions) is metallic and does conduct electricity. The empty $3p$ orbitals form an energy band that, because of the closeness of the atoms, overlaps the $3s$ band (Figure 30.4b). Therefore, electrons can move up out of the full $3s$ band and travel in the empty $3p$ band. The highest completely filled band in a metal is called the **valence band.** In divalent metals, the valence and conduction bands overlap. Electrons below the valence band, such as the $1s$, $2s$, and $2p$ electrons of magnesium, are the *core electrons.* They are held tightly by the nuclei.

A **forbidden energy gap,** or **energy gap**—an area of forbidden electron energies—can lie between energy bands. The energy gap is a consequence of the quantum mechanical nature of electrons. As discussed in the next section, the energy gap between the valence and conduction band plays an important role in the differences among conductors, semiconductors, and insulators.

> **Metallic conduction: partly filled conduction band, or valence band overlapping empty conduction band**

30.8 BONDING AND SEMICONDUCTIVITY

The energy band picture of bonding can be applied to the solid state of any material, for in the solid state the orbitals of the many individual atoms are brought close enough to overlap. The size of the energy gap between the valence band and the conduction band varies in different materials. In an **insulator**—a substance that does not conduct electricity—the energy gap is so large that electrons from the valence band cannot cross it (Figure 30.5). And since the valence band is full, no conduction occurs in an insulator, because no net flow of electrons is possible.

In a semiconducting element, an energy gap between the valence band and the conduction band is also present, but it is smaller than in an insulator. Even at room

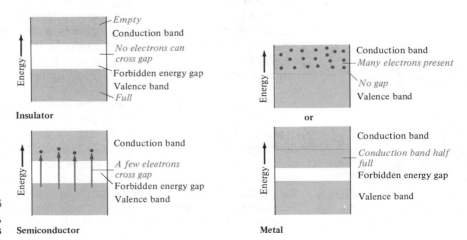

Figure 30.5
Energy Bands in Insulators, Semiconductors, and Metals

Table 30.4

Energy Gaps The energy gap for diamond is 502 kJ/mol.

	Energy gap (kJ/mol)
Semiconducting elements	
B	320
Si	100
Ge	67
As (gray)	120
β-Sb	10
Te	37
Some semiconducting compounds	
InP	130
GaAs	140
InSb	20
CdTe	140

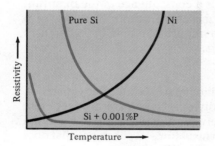

Figure 30.6
Variation of Resistivity with Temperature Note the large change in resistivity with the addition of only 0.001% of an impurity.

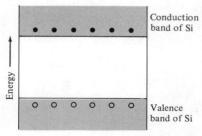

Figure 30.7
Electron–Hole Pairs in an Intrinsic Semiconductor

temperature, a few electrons have enough energy to jump the gap and enter the conduction band, where they are free to move. Some energy gaps are given in Table 30.4.

A **semiconductor** is a solid, crystalline material with an electrical conductivity intermediate between that of a metal and that of an insulator. Semiconductors are not as conductive as metals, because fewer electrons are available in conduction bands. Put another way, we say that semiconductors are more resistive to the passage of electrical current. Electrical resistance is measured in ohms. The *resistivity* of a substance is the electrical resistance per centimeter of a conductor of 1 cm^2 cross-sectional area and has units of ohm-centimeters (ohm-cm). *Conductivity* is the reciprocal of resistivity and has units of ohm^{-1}-cm^{-1}.

Aluminum, a typical metal, has an electrical resistivity of 2.7×10^{-6} ohm-cm at 20 °C. Pure silicon has a resistivity of 10^5 ohm-cm, while pure diamond, an insulator, is highly resistive — 10^{14} ohm-cm at 15 °C. The resistivity range for semiconductors is roughly 10^{-3} to 10^8 ohm-cm.

An increase in temperature causes the ions in a metallic crystal lattice to vibrate more within their lattice positions. This increases the chances for an electron moving through the metal under the influence of an electric field to collide with the ions. For a metal, the net result of an increase in temperature is an *increase* in resistivity (Figure 30.6).

Now we come to the essential difference between metals and semiconductors. With an increase in temperature, more electrons in a semiconductor gain the energy needed to jump out of the valence band and into the conduction band. Therefore, with rising temperature, the resistivity of a semiconductor *decreases* (Figure 30.6). The amount of decrease is different for each semiconductor. At low enough temperatures, the conductivity of semiconductors is the same as that of insulators, and at high enough temperatures it is like that of metals.

The conductance of a semiconductor is aided both by the free flow of electrons in the conduction band and by what is thought of as the migration of holes in the valence band in a direction opposite to that of the electron flow. Understanding this may take a moment's thought. Look at it this way. An electron jumping out of the valence band leaves behind a hole, in the same way as a person getting up from his seat in a theater leaves a vacant seat. Suppose that the empty seat is on the end of a row. The person in the second seat can move over to the end seat. Then the person in the third seat from the end can decide to move into the second seat. If everyone in the row moves over by one seat the vacant seat — the hole — will have moved across the entire row. Under the influence of an electric field, holes move in this way through the valence band. The net effect of the motion of the holes is that of positive charges moving in the opposite direction from the conduction electrons. The positive charge is the result of the electron deficiency.

In a pure semiconductor at room temperature, the number of electrons in the conduction band and the number of holes in the valence band are equal. An **intrinsic semiconductor** contains equal numbers of current-carrying holes and electrons; the conduction is an intrinsic property of the material (Figure 30.7). At high enough temperatures, even insulators such as diamond can become intrinsic semiconductors.

In an **extrinsic semiconductor** the number of current-carrying holes and electrons is not equal, and conduction depends on extrinsic materials — on the addition of appropriate impurities. The impurities are of two types — donors and acceptors. A donor provides electrons in the following way. In pure silicon and germanium, each atom is joined to four neighboring atoms by covalent bonds. An atom of a Representative Group V element — for example, phosphorus, arsenic, or antimony — enters the germanium or silicon crystal lattice without distorting the lattice very much and bonds to its four germanium atom neighbors. Since the atoms of the Group V element have the ns^2np^3 configuration, one electron is left over for every atom. These

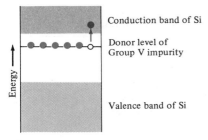

n-type

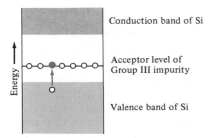

p-type

Figure 30.8
***n*- and *p*-Type Semiconductors**

extra electrons enter an occupied valence band, called a **donor level,** that usually lies slightly below the conduction band of the host semiconductor (Figure 30.8). Electrons in the donor level are easily promoted to the host semiconductor conduction band. This greatly increases the conductivity.

In a semiconductor, a **donor impurity** contributes electrons to the conduction band and it does so without leaving holes in the valence band. The addition of controlled amounts of impurities to semiconducting elements is called **doping.** The impurity, called a **dopant,** is usually added at concentrations of 100 to 1000 parts per million. A crystal doped with a donor impurity is called an ***n*-type semiconductor** — negative electrons are the majority of the current carriers. In an *n*-type semiconductor, for each electron that enters the conduction band, a positive ion is left in the crystal structure.

An atom of a Representative Group III element — for example, boron, aluminum, or indium — has the ns^2np^1 configuration, and therefore when added to silicon or germanium can bond to only three of its neighboring atoms. One neighboring atom is left with only three bonds and a single electron that has no partner. This situation contributes an electron deficiency, in other words, a hole. An **acceptor impurity** contributes holes to a vacant **acceptor level** of energy, which is slightly above the valence band (Figure 30.8). The acceptor level is created when electrons from the valence band move to fill the vacancies in the acceptor atoms, leaving behind a band of holes. Electrons are easily promoted from the valence band to the acceptor level. In such a semiconductor, called a ***p*-type semiconductor,** positive holes are the majority of the current carriers. In a *p*-type semiconductor, for each acceptor atom, a negative ion is left in the crystal structure.

30.9 PREPARATION OF SEMICONDUCTOR MATERIALS

Silicon and germanium are the elements most extensively used as host semiconductors. As starting materials for semiconductor device manufacture, the elements must contain less than 1 part per *billion* of impurities. This is comparable to one pinch of salt in 10 tons of potato chips. Conversion of the elements as they are first isolated to materials of such purity requires exacting procedures.

The 98% pure metallurgical silicon (Section 30.4) is purified by a series of chemical and physical processes such as the following. The crude silicon is converted to the chloride, $SiCl_4$, by reaction with elemental chlorine. The chloride is purified by repeated fractional distillation and is then reduced to elemental silicon by means of pure magnesium or zinc. In the process, the reducing agent is converted to its chloride ($MgCl_2$ or $ZnCl_2$), which is sublimed from the silicon. For further purification, the iodide, SiI_4, is prepared from the silicon and then decomposed by heat. The silicon is then formed into ingots for the remaining steps in the purification process. Elemental germanium ingots ready for further purification are obtained directly from the preparation of the free metal as described in Example 30.2.

Zone refining, or zone melting, of the ingots is the next step. **Zone refining** is a method for purifying solids in which a melted zone carries impurities out of the solid. A rod of the solid is heated at a point near one end until it melts. The melted zone is moved slowly along the rod (either the heater or the rod is moved). Because dissolved impurities lower the melting point of the solid, the melt is always less pure than the solid. Impurities therefore collect in the molten zone and eventually are concentrated at the end of the rod.

Not only must materials for semiconducting devices be ultrapure, but they must also be free of crystalline imperfection. Boundaries between microcrystals would act as barriers to the desired free flow of electrons and holes. A semiconducting device is usually made from a piece of a single crystal. Among the many techniques of growing single crystals, one of the most successful is the "pulling" of a large crystal from a melt of the same composition as the crystal. A small seed crystal is touched to the melt and gradually withdrawn at such a rate that the melt solidifies slowly onto the seed crystal (Figure 30.9). Single crystals of germanium 5 cm in diameter and 25 cm

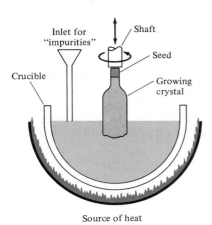

Figure 30.9
Apparatus for Pulling a Single Crystal

Table 30.5
Some Common Semiconductor Materials The designation of zinc family metals as "Group II" metals is based on their similar electron configurations [Group II, or Be family, $(n - 1)p^6ns^2$; Zn family, called Group II B in some versions of the periodic table, $(n - 1) d^{10}ns^2$].

Elements	III–V compounds	II–VI compounds
Si	AlP	ZnS
Ge	AlAs	ZnSe
	AlSb	ZnTe
	GaP	CdS
	GaAs	CdSe
	GaSb	CdTe
	InP	
	InAs	
	InSb	

in length and even larger silicon crystals are made by this technique.

Compound semiconductor materials are often prepared by what is called epitaxial growth — the deposition of a thin crystalline layer on top of another crystal, the substrate (Figure 30.10). The epitaxial layer can be deposited from either the liquid or vapor phase and assumes a crystal structure similar to that of the substrate.

The common semiconductor materials (Table 30.5) are silicon, germanium, and a number of binary intermetallic compounds between elements from Groups III and V (the III–V compounds) or between elements from the zinc family and Group VI (called II–VI compounds because zinc, cadmium, and mercury atoms, like those of the Group II elements, have two s valence electrons). In a III–V compound, for example, the Group III element contributes three electrons per atom and the Group V element contributes five electrons per atom, giving an average of four electrons per atom. These compounds form crystals with a diamondlike structure similar to that of silicon and germanium, and can be doped with the same results as the elemental semiconducting materials.

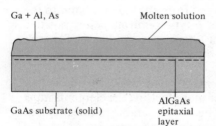

Ga + Al, As   Molten solution

GaAs substrate (solid)   AlGaAs epitaxial layer

Figure 30.10
Liquid-Phase Epitaxial Growth of an AlGaAs Layer on a GaAs Substrate

Among the properties of interest in semiconducting materials are the size of the energy gap; the concentration of charge carriers, either electrons or holes; the mobility, or speed with which the charge carriers can move; and the lifetime of a charge carrier before it is annihilated by the combination of an electron with a hole. By varying the concentrations of dopants, the wide range of properties needed to create the various types of semiconductor devices is made available.

30.10 SEMICONDUCTOR DEVICES

In their operation, most semiconducting devices depend upon the properties imparted by adjacent p-type and n-type semiconductors. A **p–n junction** is the boundary between n-type and p-type semiconductors. The p–n junction is created by different doping of adjacent areas in the same crystal.

Electrons from the n-type semiconductor and holes from the p-type semiconductor at first migrate toward the junction, where they combine (Figure 30.11). Their combination leaves excess positive ions on the n-type side of the junction and excess negative ions on the p-type side of the junction. Before long, no further migration of electrons and holes occurs, because each would have to move toward a region with a charge the same as its own. The result is a potential barrier, which makes the resistance at the p–n junction greater than in the bulk of the material. By varying the characteristics of the p–n junction, the current-carrying capability of the junction can be varied.

Figure 30.11
Formation of a p-n Junction The resistance of the material at the junction is increased because electrons must approach a region of negative charge and holes must approach a region of positive charge.

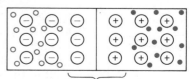

p-type semiconductor with mobile holes and stationary negative ions

n-type semiconductor with mobile electrons and stationary positive ions

p-n junction

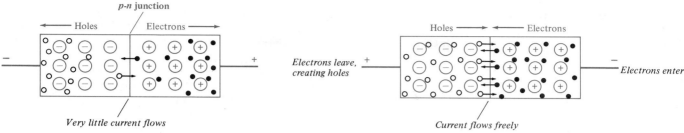

Figure 30.12

Operation of a *p-n* Junction as a Rectifier Alternating current is converted to direct current because current can flow freely in only one direction.

A diode is a semiconducting device that incorporate a *p–n* junction and can perform many different functions. For example, a diode can act as a *rectifier,* converting alternating to direct current. Electrodes are attached to the ends of a rectifying diode and alternating current is passed through it. During part of the current cycle electrons from the *n*-type (electron-rich) part of the semiconductor are attracted to one electrode and the positive holes of the *p*-type part are attracted to the other electrode, leaving the junction region bare of electrical carriers and thus effectively stopping current flow. During the other part of the current cycle, when the polarity of the electrodes is reversed, electrons are repelled from the pole to which they were previously attracted and are now pulled to the other electrode, while the positive "holes" are attracted to the electrode from which the electrons are repelled. Now the two processes reinforce each other with respect to flow of current. The rectifier thus prevents flow of current in one direction and offers a low resistance to flow in the other (Figure 30.12).

A photodiode responds to the absorption of light of energy equal to the band gap of the semiconducting material from which the diode is fabricated. Absorption of a photon raises an electron into the conduction band, creating a free electron and a hole which can migrate and allow current to flow. In a light-emitting diode, an external current causes current to flow so that electrons and holes meet at the *p–n* junction and combine. As the electrons "fall" into the holes they emit visible radiation of energy equal to that of the band gap.

Transistors consist of two diodes, back to back. The main functions performed by transistors are switching and amplifying current. Integrated circuits, in which diodes, transistors, and other necessary circuit components are combined in a single semiconductor chip, have set instrument designers free from the use of discrete components. As a result, for example, computers that filled several large cabinets have shrunk to the size of typewriters.

COMPOUNDS OF THE SEMICONDUCTING ELEMENTS

30.11 COMPOUNDS OF BORON

From the $2s^2 2p^1$ configuration of a boron atom, a hydride of the composition BH_3 would be expected. However, the actual compositions of the boron hydrides are not predictable—they are unique compounds. The simplest of the boron hydrides is diborane, B_2H_6 (Table 30.6). Diborane is the first member of a series of **boranes**—boron–hydrogen compounds—among them B_4H_{10}, B_5H_9, B_5H_{11}, $B_{10}H_{14}$, and 15 or so others that have been prepared so far.

The boranes are generally volatile substances (B_2H_6, b.p. -92.5 °C; B_4H_{10}, b.p. 17.6 °C; B_5H_{11}, b.p. 65 °C) and they are highly reactive. They decompose when heated in the absence of air to give boron and hydrogen, many of them are spontaneously flammable, and they are decomposed by water to yield hydrogen and boric acid.

The nature of the bonding in the boron hydrides has been a matter of great interest. Although the boranes are covalent compounds, they are sometimes referred to as **electron-deficient compounds**—they possess too few valence electrons for the atoms to be held together by ordinary electron-pair covalent bonds. In the diborane molecule, for example, there are 12 valence electrons, 3 from each of the 2 boron

Table 30.6
Some Compounds of Boron

B_2H_6	Diborane (m.p. −166 °C, b.p. −92.5 °C)	B_4C	Boron carbide (m.p. 2350 °C, b.p. >3500 °C; very hard)
H_3BO_3	Boric acid (at 169 °C ⟶ HBO_2)	BN	Boron nitride (∼3000 °C, sublimes; very hard)
HBO_2	Metaboric acid (m.p. 236 °C)	$Na_2B_4O_7 \cdot 10H_2O$	Sodium tetraborate decahydrate (borax) (m.p. 320 °C)
B_2O_3	Boric oxide (m.p. 460 °C, b.p. ∼1860 °C)	CaB_6	Calcium boride (m.p. 2235 °C, very hard)
BCl_3	Boron trichloride (m.p. −107 °C, b.p. 13 °C)		

atoms and 1 from each of the 6 hydrogen atoms. For each boron atom to be joined covalently to 3 hydrogen atoms and to the other boron atom by covalent single bonds would require 14 electrons. Therefore, the configuration

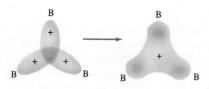

Figure 30.13
Structure of Diborane

$$\begin{array}{ccc} H & & H \\ | & & | \\ H{-}B & {-}B & {-}H \\ | & & | \\ H & & H \end{array}$$

not a possible configuration

which is found in the organic compound ethane, C_2H_6, is impossible in diborane.

The experimentally determined molecular structure of diborane is shown in Figure 30.13. The boron atoms and the 4 terminal hydrogen atoms lie in one plane; the 2 remaining hydrogen atoms lie above and below the plane and connect the 2 boron atoms. The 4 terminal hydrogen atoms are bonded to the boron atoms by ordinary covalent single bonds. Each "bridging" hydrogen atom is bonded to the 2 boron atoms by a **three-center bond**—a bond in which a single pair of electrons bonds 3 atoms covalently.

Three-center bond: 3 atoms, 2 bonding electrons

The B—H—B bond is described in terms of molecular orbital theory as follows: One sp^3 hybrid orbital from each of the two boron atoms and the $1s$ orbital from the hydrogen atom combine to form three molecular orbitals. One is a bonding molecular orbital that is occupied by the two available electrons to form what is known as a three-center, two-electron bond. One nonbonding molecular orbital and one antibonding molecular orbital are also formed, but remain unoccupied. Boron atoms form both B—H—B and B—B—B three-center bonds (Figure 30.14). The pentaborane molecule (Figure 30.15), for example, has four B—H—B bonds and one B—B—B bond in addition to two conventional B—B bonds.

<u>Boric acid</u>, which structurally is $B(OH)_3$, is a weak *mono*protic acid which yields hydrogen ion by the following reaction:

$$H_3BO_3(aq) + 2H_2O(l) \rightleftharpoons [B(OH)_4]^- + H_3O^+$$

A boric acid solution is a mild antiseptic, so mild that it can be used as an eyewash. Boric acid is produced by acidification of a cold aqueous solution of the mineral borax, $Na_2B_4O_7 \cdot 10H_2O$. (The reaction amounts to driving the hydrolysis of the tetraborate ion to completion as the OH^- ion reacts with the acid; see Section 30.2e.)

Borax has long been used as a cleansing agent and water softener because of the alkalinity of its solutions, which is due to hydrolysis of the tetraborate anion. Borax is also necessary in the manufacture of Pyrex glass (Section 30.17a).

Only a few simple salts containing the borate anion, BO_3^{3-}, are known. Most borates contain planar BO_3 units or tetrahedral BO_4 units in complex polymeric structures.

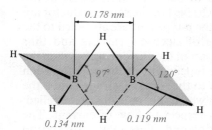

B—B—B three-center bond

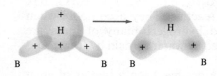

B—H—B three-center bond

Figure 30.14
Boron 3-Center Bonds

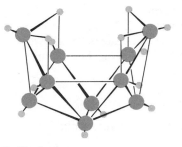

$B_{10}H_{14}$ decaborane

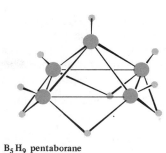

$B_5 H_9$ pentaborane

$B_4 H_{10}$ tetraborane

● B
● H

Figure 30.15
Structures of a Few Boranes

As would be expected for molecules with three shared pairs and no unshared pairs of electrons, the boron halide molecules are planar. Because the boron atom has only six electrons, the boron halides can function as electron-pair acceptors, that is, as Lewis acids. Reactions of boron trifluoride with fluoride ion and ammonia illustrate the Lewis acid–base reactions of the boron halides.

$$
\ddot{\underset{\textstyle :\ddot{F}:}{\overset{\textstyle :\ddot{F}:}{:\ddot{F}-B}}} + :\ddot{F}:^- \longrightarrow \left[\ddot{\underset{\textstyle :\ddot{F}:}{\overset{\textstyle :\ddot{F}:}{:\ddot{F}-B-\ddot{F}:}}} \right]^-
$$

tetrafluorobrate ion

$$
\ddot{\underset{\textstyle :\ddot{F}:}{\overset{\textstyle :\ddot{F}:}{:\ddot{F}-B}}} + :\overset{\textstyle H}{\underset{\textstyle H}{N-H}} \longrightarrow \ddot{\underset{\textstyle :\ddot{F}:}{\overset{\textstyle :\ddot{F}:}{:\ddot{F}-B}}}\overset{\textstyle H}{\underset{\textstyle H}{-N-H}}
$$

30.12 COMPOUNDS OF SILICON AND GERMANIUM

Silicon and germanium form both monoxides and dioxides, but only the dioxides are stable. The natural and man-made silicon–oxygen compounds are so numerous and important that they are discussed separately (Sections 30.16 to 30.18). Germanium dioxide, GeO_2, the major commercially available germanium compound, is a solid that exists in two crystalline forms, one more inert and less soluble than the other (Table 30.7).

Silicon and germanium atoms, like the carbon atom, the nonmetallic member of Group IV, can form four covalent single bonds using the four ns^2np^2 valence electrons in each atom. In compounds, atoms of these elements do not self-link to the great extent that carbon atoms do.

Silicon–hydrogen compounds are called **silanes.** The simplest compound is monosilane, SiH_4, and other members of the series that have been definitely

Table 30.7
Some Compounds of Silicon and Germanium

SiH_4	Silane (m.p. -185 °C, b.p. -112 °C)	$SiCl_4$	Silicon tetrachloride (m.p. -70 °C, b.p. 57.6 °C)
Si_2H_6	Disilane (m.p. -132.5 °C, b.p. -14.5 °C)	Si_2Cl_6	Disilicon hexachloride (m.p. -1 °C, b.p. 145 °C)
Si_3H_8	Trisilane (m.p. -117.4 °C, b.p. 52.9 °C)	GeH_4	Germane (m.p. -165 °C, b.p. -89 °C)
SiO_2	Silica (silicon dioxide) (quartz, m.p. 1610 °C, b.p. 2230 °C)	GeO_2	Germanium dioxide (insoluble, m.p. 1087 °C; soluble, m.p. 1115 °C)
SiF_4	Silicon tetrafluoride (m.p. -90.2 °C, b.p. -86 °C)	$GeCl_4$	Germanium tetrachloride (m.p. -49.5 °C, b.p. 84 °C)

characterized include Si_2H_6, Si_3H_8, and Si_4H_{10}, all compounds which contain silicon–silicon bonds. The general formula for the series is Si_nH_{2n+2}, with compounds known up to $n = 10$. The higher silanes are unstable and decompose. Most silanes are quite flammable and must be handled in the absence of air. For example, silane itself is a gas and is spontaneously flammable in air,

$$SiH_4(g) + 2O_2(g) \longrightarrow SiO_2(s) + 2H_2O(l)$$
silane

and violently decomposed by water in a reaction like that of the silicon halides with water (Section 30.2):

$$SiH_4(g) + (2 + x)H_2O(l) \longrightarrow SiO_2 \cdot xH_2O(aq) + 4H_2(g)$$

The germanium hydrides, Ge_nH_{2n+2}, called **germanes,** are known up to about $n = 10$ also. The germanes are generally less flammable and less easily hydrolyzed than the silanes.

The tetrahalides of silicon and germanium are volatile substances; their boiling points increase with the atomic mass of the halogen in each series. Silicon also forms a number of halides of the composition Si_nX_{2n+2} in which, as in the silanes, there are silicon–silicon bonds. For example, molecular species such as Si_2Cl_6, Si_2Br_6, Si_2I_6, Si_5Cl_{12}, and $Si_{10}Cl_{22}$ have been characterized.

30.13 COMPOUNDS OF ARSENIC AND ANTIMONY

Arsine, AsH_3, and stibine, SbH_3 (which takes its name from the Latin name for antimony), are unstable gases that are easily decomposed into their elements by heat (Table 30.8). They are much less thermally stable than ammonia and phosphine, the hydrides of the nonmetallic members of their periodic table family. Neither arsine nor stibine appears to be significantly basic, and cations analogous to the ammonium and phosphonium ions are not known. Arsine and stibine are both very poisonous.

Arsenic and antimony combine with oxygen to give the amphoteric $+3$ oxides, which in the gaseous state are molecular compounds of the formulas As_4O_6 and Sb_4O_6.

In arsenic(III) oxide the acidic character is predominant. Aqueous solutions of the oxide are definitely acidic and contain arsenous acid, H_3AsO_3, a compound which undergoes both acidic and basic dissociation.

$$H_3AsO_3 \rightleftharpoons H^+ + H_2AsO_3^- \qquad K_{a_1} = 5.08 \times 10^{-10}$$
$$H_3AsO_3 \rightleftharpoons AsO^+ + OH^- + H_2O(l) \qquad K_{b_1} = 5 \times 10^{-15}$$

and is known only in aqueous solution.

Table 30.8
Some Compounds of Arsenic and Antimony

AsH_3	Arsine (m.p. -116 °C, b.p. -55 °C)	Sb_2O_3	Antimony(III) oxide (m.p. 656 °C, b.p. 1550 °C)
As_2O_3	Arsenic(III) oxide (sublimes at 193 °C)	Sb_2O_5	Antimony(V) oxide (loses O_2 at 930 °C)
As_2O_5	Arsenic(V) oxide (m.p. 315 °C, dec, amorphous)	$SbCl_5$	Antimony(V) chloride (m.p. 2.8 °C, b.p. 79 °C)
$AsCl_3$	Arsenic(III) chloride (m.p. -8.5 °C, b.p. 63 °C)	$SbOCl$	Antimonyl(III) oxochloride (m.p. 170 °C, dec)
$AsOCl$	Arsenic(III) oxochloride (dec)	$NaSb(OH)_6$	Sodium hydroxo-antimonate(V) (difficultly soluble in water)
SbH_3	Stibine (m.p. -88 °C, b.p. -17 °C)		

Arsenic(V) oxide, As_2O_5, and antimony(V) oxide, Sb_2O_5, are acidic oxides obtained by oxidation of the lower oxides with concentrated nitric acid. The arsenic compound dissolves in water to give a solution from which arsenic acid, H_3AsO_4, can be isolated. This acid, like phosphoric acid, is decomposed by heat to give pyro ($H_4As_2O_7$) and meta ($HAsO_3$) acids. Salts of these acids, the arsenates (e.g., Na_3AsO_4), are similar to the corresponding phosphates. Antimony(V) oxide is relatively insoluble in water, and no free antimony(V) acid has been prepared. However, the oxide reacts with alkaline substances to give solid salts known as antimonates which contain the octahedral $Sb(OH)_6^-$ ion. [Note the difference in formulas of oxoanions corresponding to the $+5$ state: AsO_4^{3-} and $Sb(OH)_6^-$. This difference is a reflection of the difference in size of the arsenic and antimony atoms; the latter, being larger, can accommodate more surrounding oxygen atoms without crowding.]

In acidic solution, arsenic(V) and the antimony(V) are moderately strong oxidizing agents, but, as expected, not so strong as bismuth(V).

$$H_3AsO_4(aq) + 2H^+ + 2e^- \rightleftharpoons HAsO_2 + 2H_2O(l) \qquad E_{298}^\circ = 0.56 \text{ V}$$
$$Sb_2O_5(s) + 6H^+ + 4e^- \rightleftharpoons 2SbO^+ + 3H_2O(l) \qquad E_{298}^\circ = 0.58$$

Arsenic and antimony form complete series of trihalides which are liquids or low-melting solids, and in the vapor state, at least, exist as simple molecules with trigonal pyramidal structures. They are rapidly hydrolyzed (Section 30.2d).

Only three pentahalides—AsF_5, SbF_5, and $SbCl_5$—have been prepared and characterized unequivocally. The inability of these elements to form the other possible pentahalides is probably due to their strong oxidizing power in the $+5$ oxidation state.

30.14 COMPOUNDS OF SELENIUM AND TELLURIUM

The semiconducting elements of Group VI, selenium and tellurium, form the hydrides hydrogen selenide, H_2Se, and hydrogen telluride, H_2Te. In their chemistry, these compounds have a close resemblance to hydrogen sulfide (Section 26.14). The compounds are gaseous, have vile odors, and are poisonous.

Hydrogen selenide and telluride are stronger reducing agents than hydrogen sulfide, with the reducing power increasing in the order H_2S, H_2Se, H_2Te, in line with the decreasing thermal stability of the hydrides.

Selenium and tellurium form dioxides and trioxides. In contrast to SO_2, which is a colorless gas at room temperature, SeO_2 and TeO_2 are white solids (Table 30.9). Selenium dioxide has a molecular structure of polymeric chains:

Tellurium dioxide is known in several allotropic modifications, none of which is based upon discrete molecules.

Selenium dioxide is very soluble in water, and selenous acid, H_2SeO_3, can be isolated from the aqueous solutions. Tellurium dioxide is only slightly soluble in water, and no acid derived from the oxide is known. Both selenites, such as $NaHSeO_3$ and Na_2SeO_3, and tellurites, such as Na_2TeO_3, have been prepared by reaction of the dioxides with solutions of alkali metal hydroxides.

Selenic acid, H_2SeO_4, has been obtained by the reaction of selenous acid with strong oxidizing agents. The corresponding acid of tellurium, telluric acid, correctly written as either H_6TeO_6 or $Te(OH)_6$, is made in a similar manner. This acid may be dehydrated to TeO_3 by heating. Both selenic and telluric acids are diprotic acids, with the former being much stronger than the latter (K_{a_1}: $H_2SeO_4 > 1$; $H_6TeO_6 \sim 10^{-7}$). Both acids are much stronger oxidizing agents than sulfuric acid. Salts corresponding

Table 30.9
Some Compounds of Selenium
and Tellurium

H_2Se	Hydrogen selenide (m.p. −60 °C, b.p. −41.5 °C)	H_2Te	Hydrogen telluride (m.p. −49 °C, b.p. −2.2 °C)
SeO_2	Selenium(IV) oxide (sublimes at ∼ 345 °C)	TeO_2	Tellurium(IV) oxide (m.p. 733 °C, b.p. 1245 °C)
SeO_3	Selenium(VI) oxide (m.p. 118 °C, b.p. 180 °C, dec)	TeO_3	Tellurium(VI) oxide (m.p. 395 °C, dec)
H_2SeO_3	Selenous acid (m.p. 70 °C, dec)	TeI_4	Tellurium(IV) iodide (m.p. 280 °C)
$SeBr_4$	Selenium tetrabromide (m.p. 75 °C, dec)	H_6TeO_6, or $Te(OH)_6$	Telluric acid (m.p. 136 °C, weak acid)
H_2SeO_4	Selenic acid (m.p. 58 °C, strong acid)		

to the replacement of both one and two hydrogen atoms are known, for example, $NaHSeO_4$, Na_2SeO_4, $Na(H_5TeO_6)$, $Na_2H_4TeO_6$. Many such salts, as well as other compounds of selenium and tellurium, are quite toxic; for example, about 5 mg of sodium selenate, Na_2SeO_4, is a fatal dose.

The difference in the formulas of selenic and telluric acids is worth noting. Here, as in the case of the arsenate and antimonate ions (see above), size factors are important. The tellurium atom is large enough to bind six—OH groups in an octahedral fashion; the smaller selenium atom can accommodate only four oxygen atoms, and selenic acid, like sulfuric acid, has a tetrahedral structure of oxygen atoms around the central atom.

SILICON−OXYGEN COMPOUNDS

30.15 NATURAL SILICA

The common crystalline form of silica, SiO_2, is quartz, which is present in most igneous, sedimentary, and metamorphic rocks. Sand, flint, and agate are other familiar natural forms of silica. All of the crystalline modifications of silica are three-dimensional polymeric substances consisting of linked SiO_4 tetrahedra, with each silicon atom joined to 4 oxygen atoms and each oxygen atom attached to 2 silicon atoms. Indeed, all silicon-containing substances in the earth's crust have the SiO_4 tetrahedron as the fundamental structural unit.

At high temperatures (about 1600 °C for quartz), silica melts to a viscous liquid that has a strong tendency to supercool and form a glass (Section 30.17). Quartz glass undergoes very small changes in volume with changes in temperature and is highly transparent to both ultraviolet and visible light. Because of these properties, it is useful for chemical apparatus where large temperature changes occur and for optical instruments where transparency to ultraviolet radiation is necessary. (Ordinary glass absorbs ultraviolet light.)

Silica is a substance of considerable chemical stability [ΔH_f° (quartz) = −910.94 kJ/mol; ΔG_f° = −856.67 kJ/mol]. It is inert toward all of the halogens except fluorine and all acids but hydrofluoric. The following is one of the reactions by which glass is etched by hydrofluoric acid.

$$SiO_2(s) + 4HF(aq\ or\ g) \longrightarrow SiF_4(g) + 2H_2O(l)$$

At high temperatures, silica is reduced by active metals and also by carbon, with which it gives either elemental silicon or silicon carbide, SiC, a very hard, diamond-like substance known as *carborundum* and used as an abrasive.

$$\underset{\text{silica}}{SiO_2(s)} + 3C(s) \longrightarrow \underset{\text{carborundum}}{SiC(s)} + 2CO(g)$$

Hot concentrated sodium hydroxide slowly converts silica to water-soluble silicates.

$$x\text{SiO}_2(s) + 2\text{NaOH}(aq) \longrightarrow \text{Na}_2\text{O} \cdot x\text{SiO}_2(aq) + \text{H}_2\text{O}(l)$$

In the mixture of silicates formed, the ratio of sodium to silicon ranges from 0.5 to 4. Concentrated, syrupy solutions of the silicate mixtures are sold under the name of *water glass*. The solutions are useful as adhesive, cleansing, waterproofing, and fireproofing agents. Treatment of a solution of a soluble silicate with dilute acid yields a gelatinous material, $\text{SiO}_2 \cdot x\text{H}_2\text{O}$, called silicic acid. Although silica is an acidic oxide, no protonic acids derived from it have been definitely characterized.

A variety of anions have been detected in the soluble silicates, including SiO_4^{4-}, $\text{Si}_2\text{O}_7^{6-}$, $\text{Si}_3\text{O}_{10}^{8-}$, and others. The soluble silicates are relatively simple substances compared with the insoluble silicates.

30.16 NATURAL SILICATES

The simplest naturally occurring silicates contain SiO_4^{4-} ions and are known as orthosilicates. For example, the gemstone zircon, ZrSiO_4, is an orthosilicate. In SiO_4^{4-} ions, the silicon atom is at the center of a tetrahedron of oxygen atoms (Figure 30.16).

The ions of many different metals occur in natural silicates. The most common ones are Al^{3+}, Fe^{3+}, Ti^{4+}, Mg^{2+}, Ca^{2+}, Fe^{2+}, Mn^{2+}, Li^+, Na^+, and K^+. Few silicate minerals are homogeneous substances, one reason being that metal ions of appropriate sizes can substitute for each other in the crystal lattices. For example, olivine, $(\text{Mg,Fe})_2\text{SiO}_4$, also a simple silicate, can be found with magnesium and iron present in all proportions.

In structure, most silicates are polymeric. They are easily classified according to the way SiO_4 tetrahedra are linked to each other. Beginning with the disilicate ion, $\text{Si}_2\text{O}_7^{6-}$, in which two tetrahedra have a common oxygen corner,

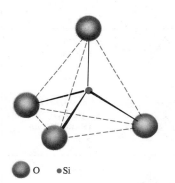

Figure 30.16
A Silicate Anion, SiO_4^{2-}

O   ● Si

and which occurs naturally in the rare scandium mineral thortveitite, $\text{Sc}_2\text{Si}_2\text{O}_7$, they range through rings, chains, and sheets to three-dimensional networks like that of silica. These variations are simply represented by drawing the SiO_4 tetrahedra as in Table 30.10, which summarizes some of the varieties of silicate minerals.

Benitoite, $\text{BaTiSi}_3\text{O}_9$, contains a ring structure made up of three SiO_4 tetrahedra (Figure 30.17). Beryl, known as a gemstone, has a larger ring (Table 30.10).

Natural silicates: structures based on linked SiO_4 tetrahedra

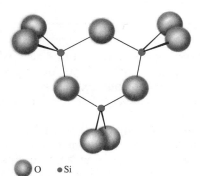

Figure 30.17
The $\text{Si}_3\text{O}_9^{6-}$ Ion This ion contains 3 SiO_4 tetrahedra.

O   ● Si

Table 30.10
Silicate Structures (*Source:* P. Powell and P. L. Timms, *The Chemistry of the Non-Metals,* London: Chapman & Hall, 1974, p. 115.)

Structurual Type	Number of Vertices Shared	Anion Composition	General Class	Anion Structure	Examples
Discrete anionic groups	**0**	SiO_4^{4-}	**Orthosilicates**		Be_2SiO_4 (phenacite) $(Mg, Fe)_2SiO_4$ (olivine)
	1	$Si_2O_7^{6-}$	**Pyrosilicates**		$Sc_2Si_2O_7$ (thortveitite)
	2	$Si_3O_9^{6-}$ $Si_6O_{18}^{12-}$	**(Rings)**		$BaTiSi_3O_9$ (benitoite) $Be_3Al_2Si_6O_{18}$ (beryl)
One-dimensional chains	**2**	$[SiO_3]_n^{2n-}$	**Pyroxenes (linear chains)**		$CaMgSi_2O_6$ (diopside)
	2	$[(Si_4O_{11})_n]^{6n-}$	**Amphiboles (double chains)**		$Ca_2(OH)_2Mg_5$ $(Si_4O_{11})_2$ (tremolite, an asbestos)
Two-dimensional sheets	**3**	$[Si_2O_5]^{2-}$	**Mica and talc; clays**		$Mg_3[Si_4O_{10}](OH)_2$ (talc) $Al_2[Si_4O_{10}](OH)_2$ (pyrophyllite)
Three-dimensional networks	**4**	SiO_2	**Silica**	—	Quartz, tridymite, cristobalite
	4	$[AlSi_3O_8]^-$ $[Al_2Si_2O_8]^{2-}$	**Feldspars and zeolites**	—	$NaAlSi_3O_8$ (albite) $CaAl_2Si_2O_8$ (anorthite)

Since the oxygen atoms that surround each silicon atom are arranged tetrahedrally, the SiO_4 chains are not straight, but zigzag (Figure 30.18). Although each silicon atom is attached to four oxygen atoms, the composition of the chain is expressed by the formula $(SiO_3)_n^{2n-}$, for two of the four oxygen atoms are shared with other silicon atoms.

Double silicate chains are also known (see Table 30.10). In these, half of the silicon atoms share three oxygen atoms with other silicon atoms, whereas the other half share only two. The repeating anionic silicate unit is $(Si_4O_{11})^{6-}$. Minerals containing this group, the *amphiboles,* are complex in structure, for most of them

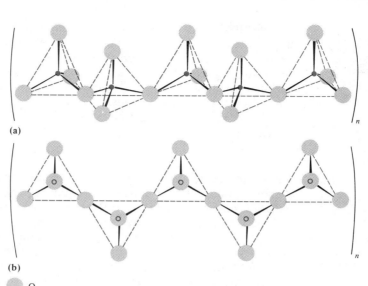

Figure 30.18
Silicon–Oxygen Chain View (b) is
90° from view (a).

⬤ O

• Si

contain two or more cations, and all of them have hydroxide groups linked to the cations. The *asbestos* minerals, such as tremolite, $Ca_2(OH)_2Mg_5(Si_4O_{11})_2$, are typical members of the amphibole family. The internal structure of these minerals is reflected in their highly fibrous nature. The strong Si—O bonds in the chains remain intact, but the weaker bonds to the ions between the chains can be broken. Asbestos is not flammable and the fibers are incorporated in many materials, ranging from wallboard to fireproof fabrics. However, airborne asbestos fiber is a cancer-causing agent and care must be exercised that the asbestos material is not worn down so that minute fibers can be released to the atmosphere.

There are many silicate minerals in which the anions are in sheets formed by extension of the double silicate chains. Each silicon atom shares three of its four oxygen atoms with adjacent silicon atoms. Talc, some clay minerals, and some micas contain sheets of this sort, but the structures of these minerals are complicated by the presence of hydroxide groups, which are bonded to the silicate sheets through magnesium or aluminum ions. The bonds between the hydroxide groups and the metal ions are rather weak and easily broken. This accounts for the ease with which these minerals can be split into thin layers.

The mica phlogopite is an **aluminosilicate,** a silicate in which aluminum atoms replace some of the silicon atoms. Many clays and feldspars are also aluminosilicates. The replacement of silicon atoms by aluminum atoms leaves a charge imbalance, for each aluminum atom has only three valence electrons rather than four. For each aluminum atom a +1 cation must also enter the aluminosilicate structure, or for every two aluminum atoms, one +2 cation must be added. The ratio of aluminum atoms to silicon atoms may vary over a wide range, but the ratio of positive ions to aluminum atoms is fixed by the requirement for neutrality. Typical natural aluminosilicates are $KAlSi_3O_8$ (orthoclase) and $CaAl_2Si_2O_8$ (anorthite).

The **zeolites** are a family of aluminosilicates with much more open structures than the clays and feldspars. The crystals contain channels which are from 0.5 to 0.13 nm in diameter. Sodium ions or other cations reside in the channels and are not attached to the rigid aluminosilicate structure. The diameters of the openings in zeolites vary with the sizes of the cations. If structures with openings of the correct size are chosen, zeolites can be used to selectively absorb small molecules, a property

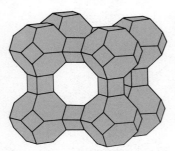

Figure 30.19
A Synthetic Zeolite The polyhedra are units containing a total of 24 aluminum and silicon atoms and the lines connect the aluminum and silicon atoms. An oxygen atom (not shown) lies between each aluminum and silicon atom (see Figure 30.18). The molecular formula of this "molecular sieve" is $Na_{12}(Al_{12}Si_{12}O_{48}) \cdot 27H_2O$.

for which zeolites are referred to as *molecular sieves*. Such small molecules as ammonia, carbon dioxide, and ethyl and methyl alcohols are reversibly absorbed by zeolites. Molecular sieves are used industrially in drying gases and liquids, in separating nitrogen from air, and in separating straight and branched-chain hydrocarbons. Synthetic zeolites (Figure 30.19) can be produced with the properties needed for specific applications.

The ions in a zeolite can be replaced readily by other ions of equivalent charge, for example,

$$2NaZ + Ca^{2+} \rightleftharpoons CaZ_2 + 2Na^+ \quad (Z = \text{zeolite})$$

These displacement reactions are reversible, and an important use of zeolites depends upon this fact. When hard water is passed through a bed of a zeolite, the calcium, magnesium, and iron(II) ions take the place of the sodium ions, thereby softening the water. (Zeolites are now being added to synthetic detergents for the same purpose.) A fixed bed of spent zeolite can be regenerated by passing a concentrated solution of sodium chloride through it.

Zeolites are also extremely important in the chemical industry because the sodium ions can be replaced by ions which are catalytically active, such as those of various transition metals. Zeolite catalysts are used in petroleum refining, in making gasoline from a hydrogen–methane mixture, and in other ways.

30.17 MAN-MADE SILICATE MATERIALS

a. Glass Many of the silicate minerals, once melted, do not crystallize readily when cooled, but form hard, noncrystalline, transparent substances called glasses. (Other materials also form glasses, but the term is most often used for the silicate glass of everyday use.) Since glasses are extremely viscous, rearrangement of the structure into the more stable crystalline forms proceeds only very slowly, and may require centuries.

Glass: noncrystalline, supercooled liquid silicates

Common window glass is a mixture of sodium and calcium silicates. It is made by melting sodium carbonate, calcium carbonate (or oxide), and silicon dioxide together.

$$x\,Na_2CO_3(l) + x\,SiO_2(s) \longrightarrow Na_{2x}(SiO_3)_x(l) + x\,CO_2(g)$$
$$x\,CaCO_3(s) + x\,SiO_2(s) \longrightarrow Ca_x(SiO_3)_x(l) + x\,CO_2(g)$$

White sand serves as the source of the silica. Even the best grade of sand contains a small proportion of iron(III) compounds, which give it a yellow or brown shade. When this sand is made into glass, the iron is converted into a mixture of light green iron(II) silicates. The undesirable color of these compounds may be offset by the inclusion of manganese dioxide (MnO_2) in the glass mix. The manganese dioxide is reduced to form manganese(II) silicates, the pink color of which balances the green color due to the iron. This makes the glass appear to be colorless.

Countless variations in glass composition are possible. For example, the replacement of part of the sodium by potassium makes the glass harder and raises the temperature at which it softens. The addition of transition metal compounds to the glass mix forms silicates that are colored—chromium(III) oxide gives a deep green glass, cobalt(II) oxide gives a blue one, and so on. The inclusion of colloidal materials may give a glass a color (Au gives ruby glass) or make it translucent or opaque (SnO_2 gives opaque glass). The addition of lead(II) oxide increases the refractive index of the glass so that it gives a play of colors when exposed to the rays of white light. Lead glass (flint glass) is used for cut-glass dishes, lenses, and artificial gems.

If part of the silicon dioxide is replaced by boric oxide in the form of borax, the resultant glass has a very low coefficient of expansion and can undergo rapid changes in temperature without breaking. Pyrex, the trade-marked glass common in laboratories, is a borosilicate glass.

Ordinary glass is only slightly soluble in water, but it is soluble enough that water that has stood in a vessel of such glass for some time gives an alkaline reaction and, upon evaporation, yields a weighable residue. Alkali and alkaline earth metal hydroxides attack glass markedly, for the polymeric silicate anions are degraded by alkalies. Acids, except hydrofluoric, are almost without action on most glasses. Hydrofluoric acid attacks glass rather rapidly and is used for etching designs on objects made of glass.

$$CaSiO_3(s) + 6HF(aq) \longrightarrow CaF_2(s) + SiF_4(g) + 3H_2O(l)$$

A very interesting glass, which is only slightly etched by hydrofluoric acid, contains a large proportion of aluminum phosphate, $AlPO_4$. Aluminum and phosphorus flank silicon in the periodic table, the aluminum atom having one proton and one electron less than the silicon atom and the phosphorus atom having one more of each. Aluminum phosphate is, therefore, isoelectronic with silicon dioxide. Indeed, it has the same crystal structure as quartz, with alternate silicon atoms replaced by aluminum and phosphorus atoms.

b. Ceramics Glass is noncrystalline and has sand as its major silicate ingredient. In contrast, most of the products that we think of as ceramics — brick, tile, earthenware, pottery, and porcelain — have clay as their major ingredient and are mixtures of crystalline and glass phases. The term "ceramics" is hard to define precisely. One encyclopedia includes as ceramics all solid materials that are not organic or metallic. A common definition is materials made from clay.

Clays are formed by the weathering of aluminosilicate minerals and generally contain the original mineral and sand as impurities. Most clays also have iron(III) oxide as an impurity, and the reddish color of many clays and ceramic products is due to this oxide. Clays of greatest importance to the ceramics industry contain kaolin group minerals [$Al_2Si_2O_5(OH)_4$, for example] as the main components.

Ceramic objects are made by shaping, drying, and then heating to high temperature plastic mixtures of clay, additives such as other silicate minerals or quartz, and water. The changes that occur on firing are complex and have not been studied in a truly scientific manner.

A vitreous coating or glaze is often put on ceramic pieces after a preliminary period of firing. The glaze material — it may be a metal oxide or a salt, or a metal silicate, or a mixture of these — is applied to the surface, and the object is reheated to a temperature at which the additive either melts or reacts with clay to form a glassy coating. The appearance and properties of ceramic ware may vary widely depending upon the type of clay employed, the nature and quantity of the additives, the nature of the glaze material, the time and temperature of firing, and the presence of an oxidizing or reducing atmosphere during firing.

c. Cement The main raw materials of cement, a mixture often called Portland cement (because of its similarity to a stone native to the Isle of Portland in England) or hydraulic cement (because it sets even under water), are limestone ($CaCO_3$) and clay. A powdered mixture of these materials is heated in a rotary kiln to 1400–1600 °C. Carbon dioxide is evolved from the limestone, and the resulting mixture sinters together into small lumps called "clinker." This material, a mixture of calcium aluminates and silicates with lime (CaO), is mixed with a little gypsum ($CaSO_4 \cdot 2H_2O$) and powdered.

When cement is mixed with water, hydrates are formed. This gives a plastic mass. When the material first hardens, within about 24 hours, it is still reasonably soft and can even be cut with a knife for a day or two. The gypsum extends the hardening time, permitting a longer period for working with the cement. The process of hardening appears to involve hydrolysis of the calcium aluminate to give calcium hydroxide and hydrated aluminum oxide, which react with the calcium silicates to form calcium aluminosilicates. Hardening continues for many years. The compounds first formed when cement sets apparently undergo slow hydration, followed by crystallization of the hydrates.

In quick-hardening cements, aluminum oxide in the form of bauxite is substituted for some of the clay. These cements set more slowly but harden much more rapidly than Portland cement. In use, cement is usually mixed with sand and gravel or crushed rock. This prevents excessive shrinkage and gives a hard, strong material known as *concrete*.

30.18 SILICONES

linear silicone

cross-linked silicone

The usefulness of the mineral silicates and similar man-made substances is largely attributable to their high stability to heat and their relative inertness toward the action of other chemicals—properties related to the great strength of the silicon–oxygen bond (368 kJ/mol). Polymeric substances that combine the —Si—O—Si— framework with hydrocarbon groups have been synthesized and have found many valuable applications. Silicones are polymers of the general formula $(R_2SiO)_n$, where R is a hydrocarbon group such as —CH_3 (methyl), —C_2H_5 (ethyl), or —C_6H_5 (phenyl). The simplest silicones are linear molecules. However, they may be cyclic or there may be cross-linking of the linear polymers, as illustrated by the structures in the margin. By varying the nature of the hydrocarbon groups, the degree of cross-linking, and the length of the chains, a great variety of silicone polymers is obtained.

These polymers have properties that are to a considerable extent a combination of those of hydrocarbons and of the —Si—O—Si— framework. They are resistant to heat and to attack by chemical agents. They are not susceptible to atmospheric oxidation and are not wet by water. Their inertness has made silicones useful in surgical applications. Those silicones that are liquid are used as brake fluids and as water repellants, those that are greaselike are good lubricants, the plastic ones have special applications in place of rubber and also in chewing gum, and the cross-linked, rigid ones are employed as insulators.

The outstanding properties of the semiconducting elements and their compounds are summarized in Tables 30.11 and 30.12.

Table 30.11
Outstanding Properties of the Semiconducting Elements

"Metalloids"	Intermediate in properties between metals and nonmetals; form mostly covalent bonds
B(III), Si(IV), Ge(IV)	One common positive oxidation state
As, Sb (III,V) Se, Te (IV,VI)	Two common positive oxidation states; higher states, oxidizing agents (e.g., H_3AsO_4, Sb_2O_5)
SiH_4, AsH_3, . . . , Na_3Se, Mg_2Si, . . .	Negative oxidation states in compounds with electropositive elements
As, Se, Te, and their compounds	All toxic, As and its compounds *highly* toxic
Si, Ge, III–V compounds (GaAs, . . .), II–VI compounds (ZnSe, . . .)	Semiconductors; conductivity increases with temperature.
Free elements + H_2O or + HX $\not\longrightarrow$ NR	Inert to water and nonoxidizing acids
Free elements + HNO_3, H_2SO_4(*conc*) $\longrightarrow$ oxoanions, oxides	React with oxidizing acids
Si(s) + F_2 $\longrightarrow$ SiF_4(s)	Vigorous at room temperature
Si	Second most abundant element; SiO_4 tetrahedra form framework for many rocks and minerals.

Table 30.12
Outstanding Properties of Compounds of the Semiconducting Elements E represents these elements.

As_2O_3, Sb_2O_3, TeO_2	Amphoteric oxides; other oxides acidic
EX_n ($n = 3-6$)	Halides covalent, formed by combination of elements, many are volatile.
$EX_n \xrightarrow{H_2O}$ oxides, oxoacids	Halides readily hydrolyzed.
$B_4O_7{}^{2-}(aq)$, $HAsO_3{}^{2-}(aq)$, $AsO_4{}^{3-}(aq)$, . . .	In aqueous solution, various oxoanions, no cations except SbO^+; a few complex ions.
"$SiO_4{}^{4-}$"	In aqueous solution, mixture of ions with varying H^+ and H_2O content.
Silica, silicates $(SiO_2)_x$, $(SiO_3)_x{}^{n-}$	Polymeric; composed of SiO_4 tetrahedra
B_nH_m *boranes*	Volatile, highly reactive, have unusual three-center bonds
BX_3	Strong Lewis acids

SUMMARY

SIGNIFICANT TERMS

silica
silicates
silicones
energy band
conduction band
valence band
forbidden energy gap, energy gap
insulator
semiconductor
intrinsic semiconductor
extrinsic semiconductor
donor level
donor impurity
doping
dopant
n-type semiconductor
acceptor impurity
acceptor level
p-type semiconductor
zone refining
p–n junction
boranes
electron-deficient compounds
three-center bond
silanes
germanes
aluminosilicate
zeolites

THE SEVEN SEMICONDUCTING ELEMENTS (Sections **30.1–30.6**) The semiconducting elements (B, Si, Ge, As, Sb, Se, Te) resemble nonmetals in their chemical behavior and metals in their physical appearance. Many of their properties (radii, ionization energies, electronegativities) are intermediate between those of metals and nonmetals (Table 30.1). The free elements are generally stable in air and not highly reactive. At elevated temperatures they all combine with halogens and oxygen and in many cases with metals, forming borides, silicides, and so on, which may or may not be true stoichiometric compounds. Common oxidation states of the semiconducting elements are listed in Table 30.2. The elements are inert to water and nonoxidizing acids, but react with oxidizing acids to give oxoacids and oxides. The oxides are acidic or amphoteric, never basic. The halides are covalent, often volatile, and undergo hydrolysis in water.

Like most first elements of families, boron resembles its diagonal neighbor, silicon (Table 30.3). Many of its compounds are very unusual in structure and bonding. Silicon is the second most abundant element on earth. Several of the semiconducting elements (Ge, As, Sb, Se) have various allotropic forms. Arsenic and its compounds are highly toxic. All of these elements have numerous specialized uses; all but boron are important in semiconducting devices. Outstanding properties of the semiconducting elements are summarized in Table 30.11.

BONDING IN METALS AND SEMICONDUCTORS (Sections **30.7–30.10**) The property unique to the semiconducting elements is an increase in electrical conductivity with increasing temperature. This is explained as due to excitation of electrons out of the valence band, across an energy gap, and into the conduction band. An insulator has an energy gap so large that no electrons can cross it; a metal has no energy gap (Figures 30.4, 30.5). *n*-Type semiconductors are doped so that they contain an excess of electrons as charge carriers. *p*-Type semiconductors contain an excess of "positive" holes. Semiconducting devices are made from extremely pure single crystals. Diodes contain *p–n* junctions produced by differently doping areas of the same crystal; they can function as rectifiers, light emitters, and photoactive conductors. Silicon, germanium, and III–V and II–VI compounds (where the "II" elements are from the zinc family) are used in most diodes, transistors, and integrated circuits (Table 30.5).

COMPOUNDS OF THE SEMICONDUCTING ELEMENTS (Sections **30.11–30.14**) Boranes are electron-deficient compounds which contain two-electron, three-center covalent bonds. Boron trihalides are strong Lewis acids. Silanes (Si_nH_{2n+2}) and germanes (Ge_nH_{2n+2}) are known up to $n = 10$. Many of the silanes are flammable and very easily hydrolyzed; the germanes are less reactive. Arsenic and antimony, as well as selenium and tellurium, form oxides and halides in both of their common oxidation states, and various oxygen-containing anions in aqueous solution. (See Tables 30.6–30.9, 30.12.)

SILICON–OXYGEN COMPOUNDS (Sections **30.15–30.18**) Silicon is present in most rocks and minerals, in which SiO_4 tetrahedra, by sharing oxygen atoms, are connected in various ways (Table 30.10). Zeolites are aluminosilicates that, because of their open channels and replaceable cations, can be used as molecular sieves, catalysts, and in water softening. Glass, ceramics of all types, and cement are man-made silicate materials. Silicones are polymers of the general formula $(R_2SiO)_n$, which have widely varying properties and a vast number of applications.

THOUGHTS ON CHEMISTRY

Nonsense

THE DANCING WU LI MASTERS,
by Gary Zukov

The importance of nonsense hardly can be overstated. The more clearly we experience something as "nonsense," the more clearly we are experiencing the boundaries of our own self-imposed cognitive structures. "Nonsense" is that which does not fit into the prearranged patterns which we have superimposed on reality. There is no such thing as "nonsense" apart from a judgmental intellect which calls it that. . . .

Nonsense is only that which, viewed from our present point of view, is unintelligible. Nonsense is nonsense only when we have not yet found that point of view from which it makes sense.

In general, physicists [and chemists] do not deal in nonsense. Most of them spend their professional lives thinking along well-established lines of thought. Those scientists who establish the established lines of thought, however, are those who do not fear to venture boldly into nonsense, into that which any fool could have told them is clearly not so. This is the mark of the creative mind; in fact, this is the creative process. It is characterized by a steadfast confidence that there exists a point of view from which the "nonsense" is not nonsense at all—in fact, from which it is obvious.

In physics, as elsewhere, those who most have felt the exhilaration of the creative process are those who best have slipped the bonds of the known to venture far into the unexplored territory which lies beyond the barrier of the obvious. This type of person has two characteristics. The first is a childlike ability to see the world as it is, and not as it appears according to what we know about it. . . .

The second characteristic of true artists and true scientists is the firm confidence which both of them have in themselves. This confidence is an expression of an inner strength which allows them to speak out, secure in the knowledge that, appearances to the contrary, it is the world that is confused and not they. The first man to see an illusion by which men have flourished for centuries surely stands in a lonely place. In that moment of insight he, and he alone, sees the obvious which to the uninitiated (the rest of the world) yet appears as nonsense or, worse, as madness or heresy. This confidence is not the obstinacy of the fool, but the surety of him who knows what he knows, and knows also that he can convey it to others in a meaningful way.

QUESTIONS

The Seven Semiconducting Elements

30.1 Name the seven semiconducting elements and write the chemical symbol for each. Briefly discuss the appearance, electrical conductivity, and chemical behavior of these elements.

30.2 List the common oxidation states of the semiconducting elements. How are these values related to their respective electron configurations?

30.3 Aluminum, silicon, and phosphorus occupy adjacent positions on the periodic table. List similarities and differences in the properties of these elements.

30.4 Complete the following equations:
(a) $Te(s) + O_2(g) \longrightarrow$
(b) $Te(s) + F_2(g) \longrightarrow$
(c) $Te(s) + Na(s) \xrightarrow{\text{liq NH}_3}$
Name the compounds that are formed.

30.5 Describe the reactivities of the semiconducting elements with water and nonoxidizing acids. What are the products formed upon reaction with oxidizing acids?

30.6* Write the formulas of the oxides of the seven semiconducting elements discussed in this chapter. Write an equation for the reaction each undergoes with water. Name each substance that is formed.

30.7 Write chemical equations illustrating how the halides of the semiconducting elements resemble the nonmetallic halides in their behavior toward water much more than they do the metallic halides.

30.8 Write the chemical equation describing the preparation of elemental silicon from sand using coke? What are some of the uses for the silicon prepared in this way?

Bonding in Metals and Semiconductors

30.9 What term is used for a continuous energy level produced by a large number of closely spaced molecular orbitals? If electrons partially fill this energy level, what properties can be expected for the element?

30.10 How does the size of the energy gap between the valence band and the conduction band determine whether a substance is an insulator, a metal, or a semiconductor?

30.11 Compare the variation of electrical resistance with temperature of a metal to that of a semiconducting element.

30.12 Which elements are commonly used as donor impurities? Which elements are used as acceptor impurities?

30.13 Briefly describe how an n-type semiconductor device operates and how this differs from the operation of a p-type device.

30.14 Describe how the silicon from ordinary metallurgical reduction is treated to produce silicon suitable for semiconductor devices.

Compounds of the Semiconducting Elements

30.15 What elements make up the class of compounds known as the "boranes"? What is the formula of the simplest known borane? Draw the molecular structure for this compound.

30.16 What does the term "three-center bond" mean? How is it different from our ordinary concept of covalent bonding?

30.17 Write the Lewis structures for BCl_3 and $[BCl_4]^-$. What are the geometries of these species?

30.18 What are compounds that contain only silicon and hydrogen called? Write the general formula for this series of compounds.

30.19 Monosilane reacts vigorously with water. Write the chemical equation for this reaction. Explain why monosilane reacts vigorously with water and methane does not.

30.20 What kind of intermolecular forces would you predict to be present in the tetrahalides of silicon? Briefly describe the resulting physical properties of these compounds.

30.21 Sulfur dioxide is a gas, but selenium dioxide is a solid. Explain the difference in terms of molecular structure.

30.22 Sulfuric and selenic acids have the formulas H_2SO_4 and H_2SeO_4, respectively. The formula of telluric acid, however, is H_6TeO_6. How do you account for this difference?

Silicon–Oxygen Compounds

30.23 What is the fundamental building unit in all silicon-containing substances in the crust of the earth? How is this building block modified to form the various types of natural silicates?

30.24 How is carborundum produced? Write the equation for the reaction.

30.25 Discuss the chemical reactivity of silica with strong aqueous acids, with strong bases, and with hydrofluoric acid. Write equations illustrating any reactions.

30.26 What is a zeolite? Name some of the properties and uses of this class of compounds.

30.27 What properties does a glass have in common with a crystalline solid and with a liquid?

30.28 Describe the processes involved in making ordinary glass from Na_2CO_3, $CaCO_3$, and SiO_2. Write chemical equations for any reactions that take place. List some of the substances that are added to glass and the properties that result from their presences.

30.29 How are clays formed? What is a common impurity in most clays? Briefly discuss the production of a ceramic object and subsequent glazing.

30.30 Briefly discuss the chemistry of cement.

30.31 Many times concrete is poured during the winter even though the air temperature is expected to drop below freezing (32 °F) that night. The workers simply cover the fresh concrete with straw and there is no problem with it freezing. Why?

30.32 What are silicones? How do they differ from silicates?

Additional Questions

30.33 Which of the following are redox reactions? Identify the oxidizing and reducing agent in each of the redox reactions.

(a) $BCl_3(l) + 3H_2O(l) \longrightarrow H_3BO_3(s) + 3HCl(aq)$

(b) $SiO_2(s) + 3C(s) \xrightarrow{\Delta} SiC(s) + 2CO(g)$

(c) $2B(s) + 6NaOH(l) \xrightarrow{\Delta} 3H_2(g) + 2Na_3BO_3(s)$

(d) $SiH_4(g) + 2O_2(g) \longrightarrow SiO_2(s) + 2H_2O(l)$

30.34 Repeat Question 30.33 for:

(a) $Si(s) + 4HNO_3(aq) + 6HF(aq) \longrightarrow$
$H_2SiF_6(aq) + 4NO_2(g) + 4H_2O(l)$

(b) $3Na(s) + As(s) \xrightarrow{\Delta} Na_3As(s)$

(c) $B_2O_3(s) + 3H_2O(l) \longrightarrow 2H_3BO_3(s)$

(d) $SbCl_3(s) + H_2O(l) \longrightarrow SbOCl(s) + 2HCl(aq)$

30.35 Classify each of the following reactions according to the reaction types listed in Tables 17.2 and 17.7:

(a) $B(s) + 3HNO_3(aq, conc) \longrightarrow H_3BO_3(s) + 3NO_2(g)$
(b) $SbCl_3(s) + HCl(aq) \longrightarrow H^+ + [SbCl_4]^-$
(c) $SeCl_4(s) + 3H_2O(l) \longrightarrow 4HCl(aq) + H_2SeO_3(s)$
(d) $Te(s) + 3F_2(g) \longrightarrow TeF_6(g)$

30.36 Repeat Question 30.35 for:

(a) $2BCl_3(g) + 3H_2(g) \xrightarrow{\Delta} 2B(s) + 6HCl(g)$

(b) $GeO_2(s) + 4HCl(aq) \xrightarrow{\Delta} GeCl_4(g) + 2H_2O(l)$

(c) $BaGeF_6(s) \xrightarrow[N_2]{\Delta} GeF_4(g) + BaF_2(s)$

(d) $Te(OH)_6(aq, conc) + 6HI(aq, conc) \longrightarrow$
$TeI_4(s) + I_2(s) + 6H_2O(l)$

30.37 Predict the major products of the following reactions:

(a) $AlBr_3(s) + BF_3(g) \xrightarrow{\Delta}$

(b) $GeO_2(s) + H_2(g) \xrightarrow{\Delta}$

(c) $SiO_2(g) + NaOH(aq) \longrightarrow$

(d) $Na_2B_4O_7(s) + H_2O(l) \longrightarrow$

30.38 Repeat Question 30.37 for:

(a) $BBr_3(g) + H_2O(l) \longrightarrow$
(b) $BF_3(g) + NaF(aq) \longrightarrow$
(c) $Ge(s) + Cl_2(g) \longrightarrow$
(d) $SeO_2(s) + H_2O(l) \longrightarrow$

30.39 Write balanced equations for the following chemical reactions:

(a) $H_3BO_3(s) \xrightarrow{\Delta}$

(b) $SiO_2(s) + HF(aq) \longrightarrow$

(c) $Na_2CO_3(s) + SiO_2(s) \xrightarrow{\Delta}$

(d) $B(s) + O_2(g) \xrightarrow{\Delta}$

(e) $AsCl_3(l) + H_2O(l) \longrightarrow$

30.40* In a student-designed qualitative analysis scheme, As^{3+} and Sb^{3+} are separated from other ions in the form of highly insoluble sulfide precipitates by adding $H_2S(aq)$ to the solution. After filtering, these two elements are separated from each other by adding excess $HCl(aq)$ to the precipitate. The basis of this separation is that the Sb_2S_3 reacts with HCl to form the soluble $[SbCl_4]^-$ anion, whereas the As_2S_3 does not react with the HCl and remains as a precipitate. After filtering, the presence of As^{3+} in the precipitate is confirmed by forming AsO_4^{3-} by adding $H_2O_2(aq)$ in the presence of OH^- to the precipitate, and then forming the red precipitate Ag_3AsO_4 by adding Ag^+. The presence of Sb^{3+} is confirmed by adding NH_3 to remove enough H^+ to allow the orange sulfide Sb_2S_3 to precipitate again. Write chemical equations describing the above reactions.

30.41* A manufacturer wanted to prepare some semiconductor devices by using radioactive isotopes of Ge as dopants to form the Ga and As impurities upon decay. To one sample of ultrapure Ge, a sufficient amount of ^{69}Ge (a β^+ emitter) was added so that its concentration was 4 ppm. (a) Write the equation for the nuclear decay process and (b) identify the doping impurity formed by this radioisotope. (c) Will this sample of Ge be used for a p- or n-type semiconductor? To the second sample of ultrapure Ge, a sufficient amount of ^{77}Ge (a β^- emitter) was added so that its concentration was 2 ppm. (d) Write the equation for the nuclear decay process and (e) identify the doping impurity resulting from this radioisotope.

Answers to Selected Questions

30.20 London forces; volatile substances, soluble in nonpolar solvents

30.21 SO_2 exists as discrete molecules, SeO_2 exists in polymeric chains.

30.31 The hardening process is exothermic; the straw acts as an insulator to retain the heat, so the concrete does not freeze.

30.34 (a), (b); oxidizing agents: (a) HNO_3, (b) As; reducing agents: (a) Si, (b) Na

30.36 (a) redox—displacement of one element from a compound by another element; (b) nonredox—partner exchange; (c) nonredox—decomposition to give compounds; (d) redox—does not fit into any of the categories

30.38 (a) $H_3BO_3(s)$, $HBr(aq)$; (b) $NaBF_4(aq)$; (c) $GeCl_4(l)$; (d) $H_2SeO_3(aq)$

30.41 (a) $^{69}_{32}Ge \longrightarrow {}^{0}_{+1}\beta + {}^{69}_{31}Ga$, (b) Ga, (c) p-type, (d) $^{77}_{32}Ge \longrightarrow {}^{0}_{-1}\beta + {}^{77}_{33}As$, (e) As

PROBLEMS

Review of Principles

30.1 A gaseous sample of a boron hydride had a density of 0.57 g/L at 25 °C and 0.500 atm. What is the molar mass of the compound?

30.2 A sample of arsenic was burned in a limited amount of oxygen to form an oxide containing 76 mass % As. (a) What is the empirical formula of this oxide? The true molar mass of this compound is 200 g/mol. (b) What is the molecular formula of the oxide? This oxide was dissolved in water to form an acid that contained 59.5 mass % As, 38.1 mass % O, and 2.4 mass % H. (c) What is the empirical formula of this acid? (d) Write chemical equations for both reactions. *Answer* (a) As_2O_3; (b) As_2O_3; (c) H_3AsO_3; (d) $4As(s) + 3O_2(g) \longrightarrow 2As_2O_3(s)$, $As_2O_3(s) + 3H_2O(l) \longrightarrow 2H_3AsO_3(aq)$

30.3* What is the mass of silicon in the crust of the earth? Assume that the radius of the earth is 6400 km, the crust is 50 km thick, the density of the crust is 3.5 g/cm³, and 25.7 mass % of the crust is silicon.

30.4 A lead sulfide ore from the western United States contains 0.02 mass % As. What quantity of the ore must be processed to give two metric tons of As_2O_3? Assume the conversion process to be 90% efficient and that 98% of the As_2S_3 is recoverable from the ore. *Answer* 1×10^4 metric tons of ore

30.5 The lead content of a decorative glass was determined by allowing it to react with excess HF. The resulting suspension was evaporated to remove all of the silicon as $SiF_4(g)$. The fluoride residue was then dissolved in $HNO_3(aq)$, and the lead content determined by precipitation titration with 0.0503 M K_2CrO_4 solution. Assuming that the molecular composition of the glass is $K_2O \cdot SiO_2 \cdot PbO$, (a) write equations for all the chemical reactions involved and on the basis of a 1.0000 g sample of the glass calculate (b) the volume of $SiF_4(g)$ liberated at 25 °C and 740 Torr and (c) the volume of K_2CrO_4 solution used in the titration.

30.6 A graduate student prepared some diborane using the reaction

$$4BF_3(g) + 3LiAlH_4(s) \xrightarrow{\text{ether}} 2B_2H_6(g) + 3LiF(s) + 3AlF_3(s)$$

Assuming 100% yield, what mass of B_2H_6 could be produced from the reaction of 5.0 g of BF_3 with 10.0 g of $LiAlH_4$? The student used ether that had not been carefully dried and lost some diborane to the following reaction:

$$B_2H_6(g) + 6H_2O(l) \longrightarrow 2H_3BO_3(\text{ether}) + 6H_2(g)$$

How much of the diborane would react with 0.01 g of water? *Answer* 1.0 g B_2H_6, 0.003 g B_2H_6

30.7 The equation for the carbon reduction of SiO_2 is

$$SiO_2(l) + 2C(s) \xrightarrow{3300 \text{ K}} Si(l) + 2CO(g)$$

The standard state heats of formation at 3300 K are zero for the elements, -128.8 kJ/mol for $CO(g)$, and -910.1 kJ/mol for $SiO_2(l)$. (a) Calculate ΔH°_{3300} for this reaction. Based on energy alone, would you expect this reaction to be favorable? The standard state entropies at 3300 K are 277.1 J/K mol for $CO(g)$, 109.8 J/K mol for $Si(l)$, 53.2 J/K mol for $C(s)$ and 215.7 J/K mol for $SiO_2(l)$. (b) Calculate ΔS°_{3300} for this reaction. Based on entropy alone, would you expect this reaction to be favorable? Using your values of ΔH°_{3300} and ΔS°_{3300}, (c) calculate ΔG°_{3300} for this reaction and discuss your result.

30.8 The standard state free energy of formation at 25 °C is -27.87 kJ/mol for $H_2S(aq)$, 0 for H^+, 12.05 kJ/mol for HS^-, 22.2 kJ/mol for $H_2Se(aq)$, and 43.9 kJ/mol for HSe^-. Calculate ΔG° and K for the reactions

$$H_2S(aq) \rightleftharpoons H^+ + HS^-$$
$$H_2Se(aq) \rightleftharpoons H^+ + HSe^-$$

Which of these substances is the stronger acid? *Answer* For the H_2S reaction, $\Delta G^\circ = 39.92$ kJ and $K = 1.02 \times 10^{-7}$; for the H_2Se reaction, $\Delta G^\circ = 21.7$ kJ and $K = 1.6 \times 10^{-4}$; H_2Se is the stronger acid.

30.9 Choose the solution which will have the highest pH; (a) 0.10 M H_3AsO_4, $K_{a_1} = 6.5 \times 10^{-3}$ for H_3AsO_4; (b) 0.35 M KHS, $K_{a_2} = 3 \times 10^{-13}$ for H_2S, $K_b = 1.0 \times 10^{-7}$ for HS^-; (c) 0.0015 M H_3BO_3, $K_a = 6.0 \times 10^{-10}$.

CHAPTER 31

Transition Metals

Some of the transition elements are native metals. Iron, copper, and silver can be found among the rocks of the earth's crust and these elements have been known since antiquity. Other transition elements, because of their great similarity in properties, were among the most elusive of the elements. The story of the separation of the rare earth elements from the minerals in which they naturally occur is a monument to the curiosity and persistence of those who pursue chemical research.

Over 100 years of confusion and hard work were associated with the "discovery" of the rare earths: the transition elements from lanthanum to lutetium. The story began in 1764 and 1803 with the separation from two different Swedish ores of two substances, each thought to be the oxide of a newly discovered element. The oxides were named ceria and yttria.

Because ceria and yttria had different properties when prepared by different investigators, the suspicion arose that neither was a single substance. In 1841, after two years of work in his basement laboratory, Carl Mosander, a Swedish chemist and mineralogist, announced that ceria contained the oxides of two additional substances. He named these oxides lanthana (the hidden one) and didymia (the twin brother of lanthanum). Two years later Mosander produced three new oxides from yttria.

The secrets of the two original Swedish minerals were just beginning to unfold. There followed a period of intense interest during which time several investigators claimed that they had isolated new substances from Mosander's oxides, only to have others show that these also were mixtures. The poor communication of the times and the use of names such as "old terbia" and "new erbia" added to the confusion.

We can imagine that at each step of the way in the laborious separation process, some small clue of color or solubility or, in later years, of spectra guided the investigators in their research. Eventually ceria proved to be a mixture of the oxides of seven of the lighter rare earths (from lanthanum to gadolinium, with the exception of promethium). Yttria was found to be a mixture of the oxides of the eight heaviest rare earths (gadolinium through lutetium) and of those of scandium and yttrium.

d-TRANSITION METALS

31.1 ELECTRON CONFIGURATIONS OF d-TRANSITION METALS

The outermost electron configurations of the d-transition elements are given in Table 31.1. Atoms of each d-transition element, with the exception of palladium ($4s^2\, 4p^6\, 4d^{10}$), contain one or two s electrons in the outermost main energy level (the n level). These elements are all metals. Except for elements near the ends of the series, each transition metal atom also has an incompletely filled $(n-1)d$ shell.

Zinc, cadmium, and mercury in a sense conclude the d-transition series. However, because of their $d^{10}\, s^2$ configurations, the properties of zinc, cadmium, and mercury are those of the representative metals (Sections 29.11, 29.12).

Lanthanum can be thought of as the first member of the third transition series, but its chemistry more closely resembles that of the 4f-transition elements (Sections

Table 31.1

Outermost Electron Configurations of *d*-Transition Elements Deviations from the idealized configuration occur when a different configuration is more stable.

Idealized Configuration:	$(n-1)d^1ns^2$	$(n-1)d^2ns^2$	$(n-1)d^3ns^2$	$(n-1)d^4ns^2$	$(n-1)d^5ns^2$	$(n-1)d^6ns^2$	$(n-1)d^7ns^2$	$(n-1)d^8ns^2$	$(n-1)d^{10}ns^1$
First Series:	$_{21}$Sc $3d^14s^2$	$_{22}$Ti $3d^24s^2$	$_{23}$V $3d^34s^2$	$_{24}$Cr $3d^54s^1$	$_{25}$Mn $3d^54s^2$	$_{26}$Fe $3d^64s^2$	$_{27}$Co $3d^74s^2$	$_{28}$Ni $3d^84s^2$	$_{29}$Cu $3d^{10}4s^1$
Second Series:	$_{39}$Y $4d^15s^2$	$_{40}$Zr $4d^25s^2$	$_{41}$Nb $4d^45s^1$	$_{42}$Mo $4d^55s^1$	$_{43}$Tc $4d^55s^2$	$_{44}$Ru $4d^75s^1$	$_{45}$Rh $4d^85s^1$	$_{46}$Pd $4d^{10}$	$_{47}$Ag $4d^{10}5s^1$
Third Series:	$_{57}$La $5d^16s^2$	$_{72}$Hf $4f^{14}5d^26s^2$	$_{73}$Ta $4f^{14}5d^36s^2$	$_{74}$W $4f^{14}5d^46s^2$	$_{75}$Re $4f^{14}5d^56s^2$	$_{76}$Os $4f^{14}5d^66s^2$	$_{77}$Ir $4f^{14}5d^76s^2$	$_{78}$Pt $4f^{14}5d^96s^1$	$_{79}$Au $4f^{14}5d^{10}6s^1$

31.13 and 31.14). Following barium and the addition of the 5*d* electron to form the lanthanum atom ($5d^1\,6s^2$), the next fourteen electrons enter the 4*f* energy levels in cerium through lutetium (see Section 8.11). It is only after that energy level is filled that electrons enter the 5*d* energy level again at hafnium ($4f^{14}\,5d^2\,6s^2$).

Electrons in the $(n-1)d$ and *ns* energy levels in transition metal atoms are close to each other (recall the variation in how successive electrons add across the series; Section 8.10). The electrons in the partially filled *d* energy levels are therefore close to the outer regions of the electron cloud and are available to interact with their surroundings. The ready availability of the *d* electrons is responsible for many of the characteristic properties of the *d*-transition metals and their ions and molecules. Also, because of the influence of the *d* electrons, generalizations about the properties of the transition metals and their compounds are much more difficult to make than for the representative elements and their compounds.

31.2 GENERAL PROPERTIES OF *d*-TRANSITION METALS

The *d*-transition elements are all typically metallic in their physical properties. Most of them are hard and strong, and they are, with the exception of the members of the scandium family, among the densest of the elements (Figure 31.1). In the absence of surface coatings of oxides or other compounds, the transition metals all display a

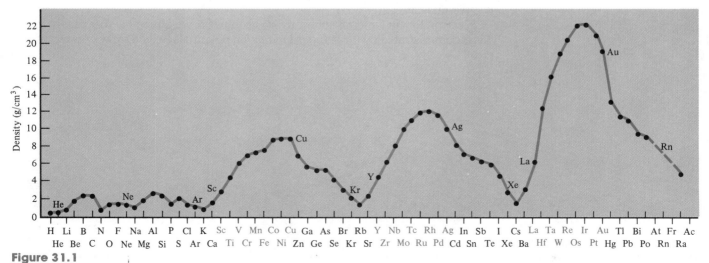

Figure 31.1
Densities of the Elements

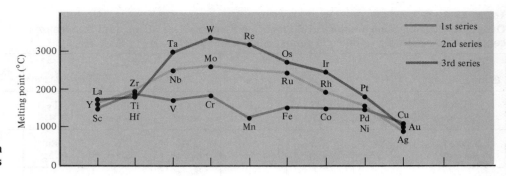

Figure 31.2
Melting Points of the *d*-Transition Elements

metallic luster. They have high melting points (Figure 31.2) and boiling points and are good conductors of heat and electricity.

The members of the <u>first family</u>—scandium, yttrium, and lanthanum—are reactive metals. They resemble the beryllium family metals in their chemical properties more than they resemble other transition metals. <u>Technetium</u> is a radioactive element. It has been made by nuclear reactions in kilogram quantities and has been detected in stars, but it has never been found in the earth's crust.

As we saw in Chapter 10, the transition metals vary less in radii, ionization energy, and electronegativity than do the representative elements.

Comparison of the atomic <u>radii</u> of the three *d*-transition series shows a gradual but not regular decrease in size, with minima about halfway across each series (Figure 31.3; see also Figures 10.3 and 10.4). In atoms of the heavier elements to the right, the influence of interactions among the increasing number of *d* electrons slightly outweighs the increasing effective nuclear charge across the series, causing a small *increase* in radius. As is strikingly shown in Figure 31.3, the second and third series elements have virtually identical atomic radii, the result of the lanthanide contraction (Section 10.3).

The general trend of decreasing radii across a period is followed by transition metal ions, as shown by the radii of ions of comparable charge for the first transition series, plotted in Figure 31.4.

The increasing difficulty of electron loss across the *d*-transition series is shown by the plot of the energy for the loss of two electrons in Figure 31.5. Note the effect of the intervention of the lanthanides: The 5*d* series elements hafnium through gold have generally higher <u>ionization energies</u> (because they are of similar size but greater effective nuclear charge).

Electron loss in aqueous solution also becomes more difficult across each series. This is demonstrated by the standard *reduction* potentials (which show how electron

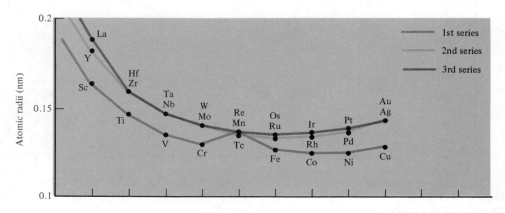

Figure 31.3
Radii of *d*-Transition Metal Atoms

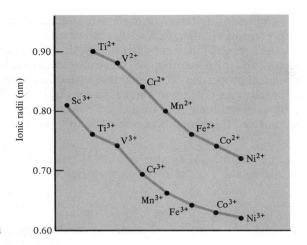

Figure 31.4
Radii of 3d-Transition Metal Ions

gain becomes *more favorable* across the series):

$Sc^{3+} + 3e^- \longrightarrow Sc$	$E° = -2.08$ V		$Cu^{2+} + 2e^- \longrightarrow Cu$	$E° = 0.337$ V
$Y^{3+} + 3e^- \longrightarrow Y$	$E° = -2.37$ V		$Ag^+ + e^- \longrightarrow Ag$	$E° = 0.799$ V
$La^{3+} + 3e^- \longrightarrow La$	$E° = -2.52$ V		$Au^{3+} + 3e^- \longrightarrow Au$	$E° = 1.50$ V

The elements at the left in the *d*-transition series are reasonably strong <u>reducing</u> <u>agents</u>, while those at the right are very weak reducing agents.

The <u>electronegativities</u> of all of the *d*-transition metals fall between 1.1 (La) and 2.4 (Au), with most between 1.6 and 2.2 (see Table 10.8). The electronegativities, in line with the other properties that we have discussed, range from lower values at the

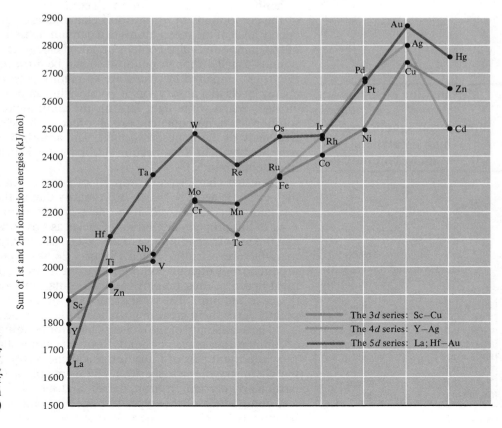

Figure 31.5
Energy Required for Formation of $M^{2+}(g)$ **by** *d*-**Transition Metals,** $M(g) \rightarrow M^{2+}(g) + 2e^-$ (The sum of the first and second ionization energies.)

left (representing larger, more easily ionized atoms) to higher values at the right (representing smaller, less easily ionized atoms) in each series.

As a result of their similarities in both atomic size and electron configuration, the second and third members of each transition metal family are similar in physical and chemical properties. They resemble each other more than they do the first members of the families. The resemblance is strongest for the families at the left in the periodic table and gradually diminishes across the series. Comparable compounds of the second and third members of each family also tend to be similar.

EXAMPLE 31.1
Reduction Potentials: Mn^{3+} and Fe^{3+}

As the following reduction potentials indicate, the Mn^{3+} ion is a much stronger oxidizing agent in aqueous solution than the Fe^{3+} ion.

$$Mn^{3+} + e^- \longrightarrow Mn^{2+} \qquad E° = 1.51 \text{ V}$$
$$Fe^{3+} + e^- \longrightarrow Fe^{2+} \qquad E° = 0.771 \text{ V}$$

The difference in ease of gaining electrons cannot be attributed to differences in ionic radii (Mn^{3+}, 0.066 nm; Fe^{3+}, 0.064 nm). In fact, one would expect that the Fe^{3+} ion, with its larger nuclear charge and slightly smaller size, would gain electrons more easily than the Mn^{3+} ion. What electronic factors are probably significant in accounting for the difference in oxidizing power of the two species?

The Mn^{3+} ion has a $3d^4$ electron configuration (see Table 31.1) and the gain of an electron to form Mn^{2+} gives the relatively more stable $3d^5$ configuration (see Section 8.11). On the other hand, to convert Fe^{3+} to Fe^{2+} requires a change from a stable $3d^5$ configuration to a less stable $3d^6$ configuration.

31.3 CHARACTERISTIC PROPERTIES OF d-TRANSITION METALS AND THEIR COMPOUNDS

d-transition elements and compounds: often paramagnetic, colored high catalytic activity many complex ions

In contrast to inorganic compounds containing only representative elements, many of the compounds of d-transition elements are paramagnetic and colored. The d energy level of the metal atoms can contain up to five unpaired electrons and many of the compounds also contain unpaired electrons. Color in transition metal compounds usually (though not always) can be attributed to the presence of unpaired electrons. Unpaired electrons are so readily promoted from the d level to higher energy levels that absorption of visible light can provide enough energy to cause this change. When white light falls on the compound, either in the solid state or in solution, certain frequencies are absorbed, and we see a color corresponding to the frequency of the unabsorbed light. The absorbed energy is dispersed as heat, not reemitted as light. (See Section 32.11 for further discussion of color in transition metal compounds.)

Another characteristic property of d-transition metals and their compounds is high catalytic activity, which is ordinarily due to the ease with which electrons are lost and gained or moved from one energy level to another. Some typical applications of this property are the use of nickel as a hydrogenation catalyst (Section 16.6f) and the use of vanadium(V) oxide, V_2O_5, as a catalyst in the contact process for the manufacture of sulfuric acid (Section 26.6a). Many industrial processes for the production of organic compounds from hydrocarbons, particularly from unsaturated hydrocarbons, employ catalysts containing cobalt, platinum, palladium, rhodium, or titanium. The catalytic activity of the d-transition metals and their compounds gives them great importance in the chemical industry.

The availability of the d energy level for bonding electrons makes the formation of complex ions and compounds in which ligands share electrons with metal atoms a very important part of transition metal chemistry. (The next chapter is devoted to the chemistry of such species.) The elements of the first d-transition series, and particularly chromium, iron, cobalt, and nickel, form a great many complex ions and compounds of this type. In aqueous solution, the cations of these elements become hydrated and impart characteristic colors to their solutions (Table 31.2).

Table 31.2
Some Hydrated 3d-Transition Metal Cations

$[Ti(H_2O)_6]^{3+}$*	violet
$[V(H_2O)_6]^{3+}$*	green
$[Cr(H_2O)_6]^{3+}$	violet
$[Mn(H_2O)_6]^{2+}$	pale pink
$[Fe(H_2O)_6]^{2+}$	pale green
$[Co(H_2O)_6]^{2+}$	pink
$[Ni(H_2O)_6]^{2+}$	green
$[Cu(H_2O)_4]^{2+}$	blue

* Easily oxidized.

31.4 OXIDATION STATES AND BONDING OF *d*-TRANSITION METALS

Sc, Y, La: oxidation state +3

Because electrons in both the $(n - 1)d$ and ns energy levels are available for bonding, all of the *d*-transition metals (except those of the scandium family) exhibit a variety of oxidation states. In oxidation states as in other properties, the scandium family elements differ from other transition elements. They have only one oxidation state, $+3$. Most compounds of scandium, yttrium, and lanthanum are ionic and contain the metals as $+3$ ions, which have noble gas configurations, as do representative metal ions. This accounts for the similarity of these elements to the representative elements rather than the transition elements.

The number of well-characterized oxidation states for the remaining *d*-transition metals generally increases with the number of unpaired *d* electrons, reaching maxima with the members of the manganese and iron families. In the first series, manganese ($3d^5 4s^2$), with five unpaired electrons, has the largest number of well-defined oxidation states of any transition element ($+2, +3, +4, +5, +6, +7$).

For the scandium family through the manganese family the *maximum* oxidation state equals the sum of the number of 3*d* and 4*s* electrons, for example,

Sc	Ti	V	Cr	Mn
$3d^1 4s^2$	$3d^2 s^2$	$3d^3 s^2$	$3d^5 s^1$	$3d^5 s^2$
$+3$	$+4$	$+5$	$+6$	$+7$

Beyond the manganese family, there is no correlation between maximum oxidation state and electron configuration. The highest known oxidation state, $+8$, is found for ruthenium and osmium, members of the iron family. The only simple compounds containing these elements in the $+8$ state are the oxides RuO_4 and OsO_4.

In most cases, it is not possible to predict from the electron configuration of a *d*-transition element what its *most stable,* and therefore most common, oxidation state will be. For members of the titanium and vanadium families, the maximum oxidation states of $+4$ and $+5$, respectively, are most stable (Table 31.3). Beyond the vanadium family the most stable oxidation states of the 3*d*-series elements are lower than the maximum states, a fact closely related to the increasing energy required for involving larger numbers of electrons in bonding. Starting at the manganese family, the $+2$ state is common.

A word regarding the term "stable" is pertinent here. We are using the term in its thermodynamic rather than its kinetic sense in this discussion of oxidation states (Section 17.7). For example, the statement that the Ni^{2+} ion is stable in aqueous solution signifies that the ion is oxidized with difficulty and reduced with difficulty, as measured by the potentials for the appropriate reactions.

Within the families of elements that exhibit a large number of oxidation states (notably the Cr, Mn, and Fe families), the maximum oxidation state is *least* stable for the first element in each family. In acidic solution, the dichromate ion ($Cr_2O_7^{2-}$, with $+6$ chromium) and the permanganate ion (MnO_4^-, with $+7$ managanese) are both strong oxidizing agents. Also, the ferrate ion (FeO_4^{2-}, with $+6$ iron) is a very strong oxidizing agent.

It is not surprising to find the *d*-transition metals in their higher oxidation states bonded mainly to highly electronegative, not easily oxidized elements, often oxygen or fluorine. Some examples of common species containing the higher oxidation states of metals from these central transition metal families are CrO_4^{2-}, CrO_3, CrO_2F_2, MoF_6, WF_6, MnO_4^-, MnO_3F, and $ReOF_5$.

Do transition elements in their most common oxidation states form ionic or covalent bonds when combined with nonmetals? An important point to remember is that the *s* electrons are always lost first in the ionization of transition metal atoms. We know that the removal of successive electrons requires the expenditure of increasing amounts of energy. Therefore, ionic compounds are most likely to be formed when the elements are in *low* oxidation states. Indeed, there are many ionic compounds containing $+2$ ions of the first series elements—Mn^{2+}, Fe^{2+}, Co^{2+}, Ni^{2+}, and Cu^{2+}. However, in most binary compounds of iron(III) and chromium(III), the

Table 31.3
Common Oxidation States of the *d*-Transition Metals Grouped by families: Note that for the Sc through the Mn families, the maximum oxidation state equals the sum of the number of $(n - 1)d$ and ns electrons. The most frequently encountered states are shown in color.

Sc	+3	Fe	+2, +3
Y	+3	Ru	+2, +3, +4
La	+3	Os	+2, +3, +4
Ti	+3, +4	Co	+2, +3*
Zr	+4	Rh	+2, +3
Hf	+4	Ir	+3, +4
V	+3, +4, +5	Ni	+2, +3
Nb	+3, +5	Pd	+2, +4
Ta	+5	Pt	+2, +4
Cr	+2, +3, +6	Cu	+1, +2
Mo	+4, +6	Ag	+1
W	+4, +6	Au	+1, +3
Mn	+2, +4, +7		
Tc	+4, +7		
Re	+4, +7		

* In complexes or insoluble compounds only.

bonding is essentially covalent. Iron(III) chloride, for example, exists as the dimeric Fe_2Cl_6 molecule in the vapor state.

In general, binary compounds containing transition metals in oxidation states of $+3$ or higher are molecular compounds.

Except for the elements of the copper family, the chemistry of the lower oxidation states of the $4d$- and $5d$-transition metals is much less well known than that of the $3d$ metals.

31.5 METALS OF THE $3d$-TRANSITION SERIES

The $3d$-series metals titanium, vanadium, chromium, manganese, iron, cobalt, and nickel have a great deal in common economically and industrially, as well as chemically. All of them are used in alloys in which strength, hardness, and resistance to corrosion are important. Iron, cobalt, nickel, and also gadolinium (a $4f$-transition metal) are the only elements that are **ferromagnetic,** that is, they can exhibit magnetism in the absence of an external magnetic field. In a ferromagnetic material, large numbers of paramagnetic ions are grouped into "domains" in which their magnetic moments are aligned in the same direction. The domains, once the material has been "magnetized" by exposure to a strong magnetic field, also have their magnetic moments permanently aligned in the same direction.

Titanium is ninth in abundance of the elements in the earth's crust and was found in a high percentage (12%) in rocks brought back from the moon by Apollo 11. The pure metal possesses excellent structural characteristics, an unusual resistance to corrosion under ordinary conditions, and a relatively low density ($4.5 \ g/cm^3$). (For comparison, the density of iron is $7.8 \ g/cm^3$ and the density of platinum is $21.5 \ g/cm^3$.)

Most titanium is used in military and aerospace applications—there is no other metal that is a satisfactory substitute for titanium in these applications. Titanium is also widely used as titanium carbide in cutting tools. A form of titanium dioxide called rutile is the most important titanium compound; it is a bright white substance used as a pigment in paint, paper, and many other products. The compound has great covering power and, in contrast to the once common pigment white lead, $Pb(OH)_2 \cdot 2PbCO_3$, it is not toxic. The minerals ilmenite ($FeO \cdot TiO_2$) and rutile (TiO_2) are converted directly to pure TiO_2 for commercial use.

The outstanding use of vanadium metal is in high-strength steels, in which small percentages of vanadium impart desirable mechanical properties.

Cu, Ag, Au: coinage metals

The chemistry and uses of chromium, manganese, iron, cobalt, and nickel are discussed in later sections of this chapter. Also discussed is the chemistry of copper, silver, and gold, which together make up the family that is sometimes called the **coinage metals** because of their use in coins since ancient times.

31.6 METALS OF THE $4d$- AND $5d$-TRANSITION SERIES

Typically metallic in appearance, the second and third series metals range from the bluish gray tantalum, through platinum (which is a beautiful, silvery white metal that takes a high polish), to the familiar silver and gold. Whether it be hardness, corrosion resistance, temperature resistance, activity as a catalyst, or electrical properties, almost every one of these metals possesses some property that makes it desirable and useful in practical applications.

Hafnium, which immediately follows the lanthanide elements, is amazingly similar to zirconium, largely as a consequence of their nearly identical radii. Hafnium and zirconium always occur together in nature, and their separation has been called the most difficult in chemistry. It can now be accomplished in various ways, including by means of fractional solvent extraction or the fractional distillation of similar compounds of the elements that have slightly different boiling points. Pure hafnium finds commercial use, for example, as the filament in some flashbulbs.

Niobium and tantalum are also very similar to each other, although slightly less so than zirconium and hafnium. (Commercially and in metallurgical publications, niobium is still referred to as *columbium.* This older name commemorates the discovery of the element, in England, in a sample of ore that had been sent from America.) In moving to the right across the periodic table, the second and third series elements in each family gradually become more different from each other.

Because of their great resistance to high temperatures, zirconium and zirconium oxide, along with alloys of niobium and molybdenum, are used in space vehicles that must reenter the atmosphere. Niobium and molybdenum are also important in steelmaking. Molybdenum sulfide is used as a lubricant, for example, in wheel bearings and gear oils. Tantalum is very resistant to body fluids and is used as a bone replacement; a tantalum plate can be put into the skull to replace a piece of bone that has been crushed or surgically removed.

Horizontal similarities also exist in these series, as they did in the first series. The three elements following technetium and the three following rhenium are all quite alike and occur together in various combinations in nature. Ruthenium, osmium, rhodium, iridium, palladium, and platinum are collectively called the **platinum metals.** All six of the platinum metals are valuable as catalysts in a wide variety of reactions.

Ru, Os, Rh, Ir, Pd, Pt: platinum metals

31.7 SOME CHEMICAL REACTIONS OF *d*-TRANSITION METALS

As is true for all of their physical properties, fewer generalizations can be made about the chemical properties of the *d*-transition metals than can be made about the representative metals. The following sections give an overview of some of the types of reactions that are significant in transition metal chemistry.

a. Combination with elements The reactivity of the elemental transition metals in combination reactions is affected in many ways by the formation of protective coatings on the metal surfaces. In general, the combination reactions that do occur require high temperatures. For example, manganese, once an oxide coating has formed, reacts no further with oxygen at room temperature. At elevated temperatures, manganese combines with fluorine, chlorine, nitrogen, and oxygen. As for all metals, reactions are frequently accelerated if the metal is finely divided. (A very fine form of iron, known as pyrophoric iron, spontaneously bursts into flame when exposed to air.) Many transition metals combine directly with nitrogen, carbon, and boron to form compounds that are in some cases true stoichiometric compounds and in other cases are solid solutions or interstitial compounds (Section 28.12).

b. Reactions with acids and bases The reactivity of many transition metals with acids is also inhibited by the formation of protective coatings. For example, concentrated nitric acid renders iron, cobalt, and nickel passive to further chemical attack by oxidizing the surface of the metals. Some transition metals react with nonoxidizing acids (e.g., Cr and Mn), others with oxidizing acids only (e.g., Cu), and some with concentrated aqueous alkaline solutions (e.g., Cr). The platinum metals (Ru, Os, Rh, Ir, Pd, and Pt) are all quite resistant to reactions with acids and aqueous bases. Platinum, gold, and ruthenium are attacked only by aqua regia (a mixture of hydrochloric and nitric acids). Some of the least reactive *d*-transition metals can be oxidized in the presence of molten alkali metal hydroxides (e.g., Ru, and Os).

c. Ions in aqueous solution   The most significant aqueous chemistry of the transition metal ions involves the formation of complex ions (to which the next chapter is devoted). The redox reactions of the oxoanions of manganese and chromium are of importance and are discussed in the sections on these metals.

To varying degrees the hydrated cations of transition metals react with water to form H^+ and, in the absence of other ions that influence the pH, give acidic solutions.

A characteristic sequence of reactions for many transition metal ions is the precipitation of a salt followed by its dissolution to give a complex ion in aqueous solution. For example, the addition of aqueous ammonia to a solution containing nickel(II) ion gives an apple green precipitate of nickel(II) hydroxide, which dissolves upon the addition of excess aqueous ammonia to yield the deep blue *hexaammine-nickel* (II) ion, $[Ni(NH_3)_6]^{2+}$.

$$Ni^{2+} + 2OH^- \rightleftharpoons Ni(OH)_2(s)$$
$$Ni(OH)_2(s) + 6NH_3(aq) \rightleftharpoons [Ni(NH_3)_6]^{2+} + 2OH^-$$

Note that these are equilibria, and the process of complex formation can be reversed by the introduction of an acid.

PROPERTIES OF SELECTED d-TRANSITION METALS

31.8 CHROMIUM

a. Elemental chromium   Chromium is a bluish white, hard, and brittle metal that does not tarnish, is very resistant to corrosion, and takes a high polish. Its principal uses are in alloys, particularly steel, and in *chrome plating*—the electrolytic deposition of a layer of chromium on another metal (Table 31.4). Chrome plating produces a shiny, attractive surface with high resistance to wear and corrosion. Because the chromium layer itself always has pinholes, which would allow corrosion to occur, an object is first plated with copper, which provides an adherent surface, then with nickel, which imparts corrosion resistance, and then with the chromium. The chromium surface is protected by a thin layer of oxide.

The chief ore of chromium is chromite, $FeCr_2O_4$. Each iron atom is surrounded tetrahedrally by four oxygen atoms, and each chromium atom is surrounded octahedrally by six oxygen atoms. Several naturally occurring minerals have this same structure, which is indicative of its great stability. Such minerals are known as *spinels*—they are all represented by the general formula $M^{2+}M_2^{3+}O_4$.

For the manufacture of stainless steel, which is mainly iron, chromium, and nickel, separation of the metals in the chromite ore is not necessary. An alloy of iron and chromium called *ferrochrome* is produced from chromite by reduction with carbon or silicon in an electric furnace and is used directly in steelmaking.

Chromium metal is obtained by reduction of the oxide with carbon, silicon, or aluminum (an aluminothermic reaction; Section 29.5g) as follows:

$$2Al(s) + Cr_2O_3(s) \longrightarrow 2Cr(l) + Al_2O_3(l) \qquad \Delta H° = -527 \text{ kJ}$$

The chromium melts and is separated from the molten aluminum oxide by the difference in their densities (Figure 31.6).

Table 31.4
Uses of Chromium and Chromium Compounds

Chromium
  Steel
  Other alloys
  Chrome plating
  Nickel chromium
    heating elements
Chromium (VI) oxide (CrO₃)
  Chrome plating baths
  Other metal treatment
  Oxidizing agents,
    pigments
Sodium chromate (Na₂CrO₄) and sodium dichromate (Na₂Cr₂O₇) and other chromates
  Pigments
  Leather tanning
  Corrosion inhibitors
  Aluminum anodizing
  Pigment manufacture
Chromite, FeCr₂O₄
  Refractories

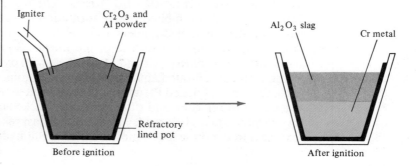

Figure 31.6
Aluminothermic Production of Chromium

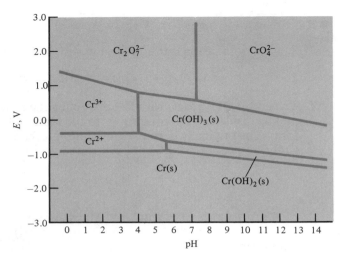

Figure 31.7
pH–Potential Diagram for Chromium

b. Chromium oxidation states and equilibria

Chromium is known in all positive oxidation states from +2 to +6. Its most common oxidation states are +2, +3, and +6; as shown in the pH–potential diagram (Figure 31.7), these are the thermodynamically stable states. The +3 state is the most common. Chromium(II) compounds are reducing agents (shown by their appearance in the negative potential region on the pH–potential diagram) and chromium(VI) compounds are oxidizing agents (shown by their appearance in the positive region on the diagram). Dichromates in acidic solution are common oxidizing agents, being reduced to Cr^{3+}, for example,

$$Cr_2O_7{}^{2-} + 6Br^- + 14H^+ \longrightarrow 2Cr^{3+} + 3Br_2(aq) + 7H_2O(l)$$

$$Cr_2O_7{}^{2-} + 3CH_3CHO(aq) + 8H^+ \longrightarrow 2Cr^{3+} + 3CH_3COOH(aq) + 4H_2O(l)$$
acetaldehyde   *acetic acid*

The conditions necessary for some of the equilibria of chromium and its ions are shown in Figure 31.8. Vigorous oxidation is required to convert chromium(III), the most stable state of chromium, to oxoanions containing chromium(VI).

Chromate ion, $CrO_4{}^{2-}$, and dichromate ion, $Cr_2O_7{}^{2-}$ (Figure 31.9), exist in solution in an equilibrium dependent upon the pH (see Figure 31.7).

$$H^+ + CrO_4{}^{2-} \rightleftharpoons HCrO_4{}^- \qquad 2HCrO_4{}^- \rightleftharpoons Cr_2O_7{}^{2-} + H_2O(l)$$
chromate   *hydrogen*   *dichromate*
ion   *chromate ion*   *ion*
(yellow)   *(deep orange)*

or

$$2CrO_4{}^{2-} + 2H^+ \underset{OH^-}{\overset{H^+}{\rightleftharpoons}} Cr_2O_7{}^{2-} + H_2O(l)$$

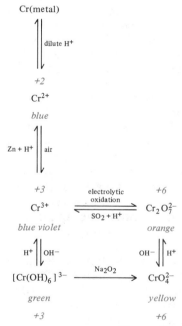

Figure 31.8
Oxidation and Reduction of Chromium

The shifting of the chromate ion–dichromate ion equilibrium with changing pH is readily observed as a change in color.

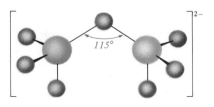

Figure 31.9
Dichromate Ion

EXAMPLE 31.2
**Equilibria of Oxoanions: Chromate–
Dichromate Ions**

Discuss what happens as OH^- is added to a solution containing dichromate ion.

The dichromate ion is in equilibrium with hydrogen chromate and chromate ions.

$$Cr_2O_7^{2-} + H_2O(l) \rightleftharpoons 2HCrO_4^- \rightleftharpoons 2H^+ + 2CrO_4^{2-}$$

The added OH^- reacts with H^+, disrupting the equilibrium (Le Chatelier's principle) by displacing the equilbrium to the right and causing more chromate ion to form. The originally deep orange solution turns yellow as $Cr_2O_7^{2-}$ is converted to CrO_4^{2-}.

**Table 31.5
Some Compounds of Chromium**

$Cr(C_2H_3O_2)_2 \cdot H_2O$	Chromium(II) acetate monohydrate (dark red)
$CrCl_3 \cdot 6H_2O$	Chromium(III) chloride hexahydrate (hydrate isomers)
Cr_2O_3	Chromium(III) oxide (green; a pigment)
$Cr(OH)_3$	Chromium(III) hydroxide (blue-green; polymeric, variable composition)
$PbCrO_4$	Lead chromate (bright yellow; a pigment)
$BaCrO_4$	Barium chromate (yellow; a pigment)
K_2CrO_4	Potassium chromate (yellow)
$K_2Cr_2O_7$	Potassium dichromate (orange-red)

c. Compounds of chromium Many chromium compounds are colored and are used as pigments (Table 31.5). Chromium(III) oxide, Cr_2O_3, is a green stable amphoteric oxide. It is used as a pigment in glass and porcelain, in fabrics, and in printing. Chromium(III) salts are prepared by reaction of the oxide with acids or by reduction of chromium(VI) compounds in the presence of the appropriate acid.

The crystalline chromium(III) chloride of commerce is commonly labeled $CrCl_3 \cdot 6H_2O$. It is either $[Cr(H_2O)_5Cl]Cl_2 \cdot H_2O$ or $[Cr(H_2O)_4Cl_2]Cl \cdot 2H_2O$ or a mixture of the two, depending upon the method of manufacture. In each case, six groups (those shown inside the square brackets) have formed coordinate bonds with the chromium ion. Coordinated chloride ions are precipitated only slowly by silver ion, whereas noncoordinated chloride ions (shown outside the bracket) are precipitated at once. The two compounds can be distinguished from one another by their different shades of green and more certainly by the fact that when solutions of the two are treated with silver ion, one of them immediately precipitates one-third of its chlorine, and the other one, two-thirds of its chlorine. The coordinated water molecules are bound tightly to the chromium ion, but the others are not bound at all; they evidently fit into holes in the crystal lattice in a stoichiometric way without being attached.

The violet chloride $[Cr(H_2O)_6]Cl_3$ is also well known, but it is more difficult to prepare in crystalline form than either of the green chlorides. It is precipitated as fine crystals when an ice-cold, saturated solution of either of the green forms is treated with hydrogen chloride gas. These three chromium(III) chlorides are examples of a type of isomerism known as **hydrate isomerism** — isomerism involving coordinated and noncoordinated water molecules (Table 31.6).

Chromium(III) hydroxide, $Cr(OH)_3$, is a highly polymeric, hydrated material in which each OH group is coordinated to two chromium atoms (Figure 31.10). Such bridges often, but not always, occur in pairs. Each chromium atom is coordinated to six oxygen atoms. Theoretically, chromium(III) hydroxide is $[Cr(OH)_3(H_2O)_3]$, but part of the water is lost upon exposure to air or heating, making the composition somewhat variable. Chromium(III) hydroxide is amphoteric.

Chromium(VI) oxide, CrO_3, or chromium trioxide, is a red crystalline compound that is a strong oxidizing agent and is used in chrome plating. It is made commercially from sodium dichromate.

**Table 31.6
Hydrate Isomerism of
Chromium(III) Chloride,
$CrCl_3 \cdot 6H_2O$**

$[Cr(H_2O)_6]Cl_3$	violet
$[Cr(H_2O)_5Cl]Cl_2 \cdot H_2O$	bluish green
$[Cr(H_2O)_4Cl_2]Cl \cdot 2H_2O$	green

$$\underset{\substack{sodium \\ dichromate}}{Na_2Cr_2O_7(s)} + H_2SO_4(conc) \longrightarrow \underset{\substack{chromium(VI) \\ oxide}}{2CrO_3(s)} + H_2O(l) + Na_2SO_4(aq) \quad \textbf{(31.1)}$$

This and other chromium (VI) compounds are highly toxic and are irritants to the skin and respiratory tract.

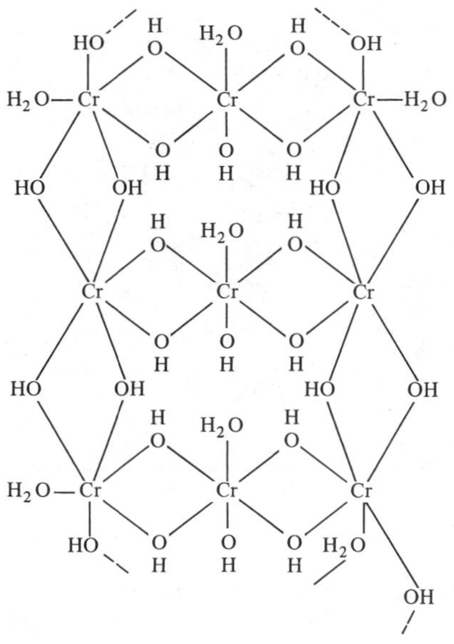

Figure 31.10
Chromium(III) Hydroxide A suggested structure. The amount of water incorporated into the polymeric structure is variable.

31.9 MANGANESE

Table 31.7
Uses of Manganese and Its Compounds

Manganese
  Steel
  Other alloys
Manganese dioxide (MnO₂, black)
  Glassmaking
  Paint (drying agent)
  Dry cell batteries
Potassium permanganate (KMnO₄, purple)
  Metal treatment
  Medicine and pharmaceuticals
  Water and waste treatment
  Chemical oxidizing agent

**Common Cr oxidation states:
+2, +3, +6**

**Common Mn oxidation states:
+2, +4, +7**

a. Elemental manganese Manganese is a silvery, brittle metal with a slightly pink appearance. It has several allotropic forms that vary in brittleness and ductility. Unlike chromium, manganese corrodes in moist air. Manganese compounds are much less toxic than those of chromium. Manganese is one of the essential trace elements for both plants and animals, and manganese sulfate is added to some fertilizers.

Manganese compounds are widely distributed on earth (see Table 28.1). The primary ore is the mineral known as pyrolusite, $MnO_2 \cdot xH_2O$. An intriguing possible source of manganese is nodules that have been found on the ocean floor. These nodules, 1–15 cm across, contain a high percentage of manganese, together with compounds of other metals, such as iron, nickel, copper, and cobalt. The nodules are apparently laid down very slowly in concentric layers, perhaps at the rate of 1–100 mm per million years. Microorganisms are thought to play a role in depositing MnO_2 in the nodules. Whether the sea floor can be successfully mined for manganese nodules is not yet known.

Manganese imparts hardness and strength to steel and is essential to the production of almost all types of steel. It is also used in other alloys, such as manganese bronze (copper and manganese) and a nonconducting alloy (with nickel and copper) called *manganin* (Table 31.7). For steelmaking, production of pure manganese is not necessary. Instead, mixed iron and manganese oxides are reduced by carbon to give ferromanganese, an iron–manganese carbide (25–30% Mn), which is used directly.

b. Manganese oxidation states and equilibria Compounds are known containing manganese in all oxidation states from +2 to +7. The +2, +4, and +7 states are the most common ones (Table 31.8). Manganese(III) is stable only in complex ions or in compounds of small solubility.

Manganese is most stable in its +2 oxidation state (Figure 31.11). The pale pink manganese(II) salts are formed when manganese in any higher oxidation state is reduced in acidic solution. Manganese in its higher oxidation states is best known as the dark green manganate(VI) ion, MnO_4^{2-}, and the deep purple permanganate, or manganate(VII), ion, MnO_4^-, which are both strong oxidizing agents.

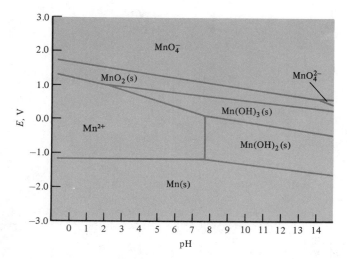

Figure 31.11
pH–Potential Diagram for Manganese

When permanganate ion acts as an oxidizing agent in very strongly alkaline solution, the manganate(VI) ion is formed, for example,

$$2MnO_4^- + OH^- + HCOO^- \longrightarrow 2MnO_4^{2-} + CO_2(g) + H_2O(l)$$

permanganate ion (purple)   *formate ion*   *manganate ion (dark green)*

Table 31.8
Some Compounds of Manganese

Mn(OH)$_2$	Manganese(II) hydroxide (pink)
MnS	Manganese(II) sulfide (salmon colored)
MnSO$_4$	Manganese(II) sulfate (reddish)
MnCl$_2$	Manganese(II) chloride (pink)
MnCl$_2\cdot$4H$_2$O	Manganese(II) chloride tetrahydrate (rose colored)
MnO$_2$	Manganese(IV) oxide (black; nonstoichiometric)
K$_2$MnO$_4$	Potassium manganate(VI) (deep green)
KMnO$_4$	Potassium permanganate (purple; oxidizing agent)

As can be seen in the pH–potential diagram for manganese (Figure 31.11), the manganate(VI) ion is thermodynamically stable *only* in strongly alkaline solution. When a solution containing this ion is acidified, disproportionation immediately takes place to give manganese(IV) oxide and permanganate ion:

$$3MnO_4^{2-} + 4H^+ \longrightarrow 2MnO_4^- + MnO_2(s) + 2H_2O(l)$$

In less strongly alkaline solution or in neutral solution, the reduction product of permanganate ion is manganese(IV) oxide

$$2MnO_4^- + 3H_2S(g) \longrightarrow 2MnO_2(s) + 3S(s) + 2OH^- + 2H_2O(l)$$

When permanganate ion acts as an oxidizing agent in weakly acidic solutions containing excess fluoride or phosphate, manganese(III) complex ions are formed, for example,

$$MnO_4^- + 2C_2O_4^{2-} + 2H_2PO_4^- + 4H^+ \longrightarrow [Mn(PO_4)_2]^{3-} + 4CO_2(g) + 4H_2O(l)$$

oxalate ion

In the absence of species that can stabilize manganese(III), manganese(II) is obtained, for example,

$$2MnO_4^- + 5H_2S(g) + 6H^+ \longrightarrow 2Mn^{2+} + 5S(s) + 8H_2O(l)$$
$$2MnO_4^- + 5C_2O_4^{2-} + 16H^+ \longrightarrow 2Mn^{2+} + 10CO_2(g) + 8H_2O(l)$$

c. Compounds of manganese Manganese(IV) oxide, MnO$_2$, is a dark brown or black powdery substance. It dissolves slowly in solutions of strong bases or rapidly in molten alkali hydroxides to form manganate(IV) salts,

$$MnO_2(s) + 2OH^- \longrightarrow MnO_3^{2-} + H_2O(l)$$

manganate (IV)ion

Stoichiometric manganese dioxide is extremely rare, if it exists at all. Analysis of the material found in nature as well as of that prepared in the laboratory shows a Mn to O ratio of 1:1.85 (approximately), the exact ratio depending on the mode of preparation. (Compare with lead dioxide; Section 29.10.) X-ray analysis shows that this material has the crystal structure calculated for pure manganese dioxide, but that several percent of the oxygen atoms are missing, leaving holes in the crystal structure. Oxide ions from adjacent sites are able to move into these holes, thus leaving new holes; this process makes the oxide conductive. It is both the oxidizing power and conductivity of the manganese(IV) oxide that make it valuable in dry cells. The compound has many other uses, including as an additive in fertilizer and animal feed, and as a decolorant in glass, where it oxidizes green Fe^{2+} to Fe^{3+}.

Potassium manganate(VI), K_2MnO_4, is an intermediate in the preparation of potassium permanganate, $KMnO_4$. Potassium manganate(VI) is prepared by fusing a compound in which manganese is in a lower oxidation state with a basic material (e.g., KOH or K_2CO_3) and an oxidizing agent (e.g., KNO_3, $KClO_3$, or air):

$$MnO_2(s) + 2KOH(l) + KNO_3(l) \xrightarrow{\Delta} K_2MnO_4(s) + KNO_2(s) + H_2O(g)$$

Potassium manganate(VII), $KMnO_4$, usually called potassium permanganate, crystallizes in dark purple, almost black, needles, which dissolve in water to give a purple solution. Permanganates are usually prepared from manganate(VI) compounds by acidification in the presence of a strong oxidizing agent, for example,

| MnO_4^-: strong oxidizing agent |

$$2MnO_4^{2-} + O_3(g) + 2H^+ \longrightarrow 2MnO_4^- + O_2(g) + H_2O(l)$$

Even in acidic solution permanganate ion slowly decomposes, especially when exposed to light, producing a residue of MnO_2 in the bottom of its container. The uses of potassium permanganate in treating athlete's foot and rattlesnake bite and as an antidote for poisons depend upon its strong oxidizing ability. It is also widely employed as an oxidant in organic chemistry, in quantitative analysis, and in the treatment of polluted air and water by oxidation of impurities. Because of its instability, solutions that are to be used in quantitative work must be freshly prepared and standardized by titration with a pure, stable reducing agent, often sodium oxalate, $Na_2C_2O_4$ (Section 31.9b).

EXAMPLE 31.3
Chemical Reactions: Ions of Cr and Mn

Predict the major products of the following reactions (which do take place). Do not be concerned with balancing the equations.

(a) $Cr^{3+} + H_2O_2(aq) \xrightarrow{OH^-}$

(b) $Cr_2O_7^{2-} + Fe^{2+} \xrightarrow{H^+}$

(c) $MnO_4^- + Cr^{3+} \xrightarrow{OH^- \text{ (mildly alkaline)}}$

(a) We recognize that hydrogen peroxide is an oxidizing agent; water is its reduction product (Table 17.8). Chromium has only two common oxidation states, $+3$ and $+6$. We can expect it to be oxidized to a $+6$ oxoanion. The question arises as to whether to write CrO_4^{2-} or $Cr_2O_7^{2-}$ as the product. Because the reaction takes place in alkaline solution, the product must be CrO_4^{2-} (see Example 31.2).

$$Cr^{3+} + H_2O_2(aq) \xrightarrow[\text{not balanced}]{} CrO_4^{2-} + H_2O(l)$$

(b) Dichromate ion is a strong oxidizing agent and is reduced to Cr^{3+}. Iron has only two common oxidation states, $+2$ and $+3$, so it will probably be oxidized to iron(III)

$$Cr_2O_7^{2-} + Fe^{2+} \xrightarrow[\substack{\text{not} \\ \text{balanced}}]{H^+} Cr^{3+} + Fe^{3+}$$

(c) Like (a), this is a reaction of Cr^{3+} with an oxidizing agent. In this mildly alkaline solution permanganate ion will be reduced to manganese(IV) oxide and Cr^{3+} will form predominantly CrO_4^{2-}:

$$MnO_4^- + Cr^{3+} \xrightarrow[\substack{not \\ balanced}]{OH^- \text{ (mildly alkaline)}} MnO_2(s) + CrO_4^{2-}$$

31.10 IRON

In many respects, our industrial civilization is built upon iron. It is fourth in abundance of all the elements (see Table 28.1). The plentiful ores are readily reduced to the metal. Pure iron, which we rarely see, is silvery white and relatively soft. By metallurgical working, iron can be made extremely strong. It can also be made soft or hard, flexible or stiff, malleable or brittle, depending on the treatment to which it is subjected. The sources and metallurgy of iron and the process of steelmaking are discussed in Sections 28.7–28.9. The corrosion of iron is discussed in Section 23.17.

Fe oxidation states: +2, +3

Iron is most stable and most common in the +2 (ferrous) and +3 (ferric) states (see Figure 23.10). The most common of the soluble iron(II) salts is iron(II) sulfate, which crystallizes from water in the form of large, light green crystals, $FeSO_4 \cdot 7H_2O$ (Table 31.9). It is a by-product of the steel industry, for sheet steel that is to be plated or enameled is often cleaned of corrosion products by treatment with dilute sulfuric acid. Cleaning metal in an acid bath is called *pickling* (the leftover acid is called pickle liquor). In this process some of the metal is dissolved, along with the rust. The iron(II) sulfate that forms is recovered as the green hydrate, which is the iron compound with the largest number of commercial uses. It is the starting material for the preparation of most other iron compounds and is widely used as a reducing agent, as a disinfectant, in the dyeing industry, and in such products as weed killers and wood preservatives. On exposure to air, its solutions soon become turbid and deposit a precipitate of hydrated iron(III) compounds.

There are three iron oxides—FeO, Fe_2O_3, and Fe_3O_4—all of which are found in nature and all of which tend to be nonstoichiometric. In these oxides the oxygen atoms form a lattice and iron atoms occupy the holes. The crystal structures and uses of the iron oxides are summarized in Table 31.10. In Fe_3O_4, +2 and +3 ions occupy different sites in the crystal lattice. Like chromite ore, this compound is a spinel; it can be written $Fe^{2+}Fe_2^{3+}O_4$.

Iron pyrite, FeS_2, a mineral, is often called "fool's gold" because of its yellow color and bright metallic luster. Upon heating, pyrite (which contains S_2^{2-}) decomposes to iron(II) sulfide, FeS, and sulfur, and it is sometimes used as a source of elemental sulfur.

Iron(II) and iron(III) salts with the common anions are generally soluble. Unlike iron(II) chloride, which is a salt, iron(III) chloride is covalent, volatile, and somewhat soluble in nonpolar solvents (see Section 31.3). Many iron salts form crystalline hydrates. In both the +2 and +3 states, iron forms many complex ions. The addition of cyanide ion to a solution of an iron(II) salt gives a gray, slimy precipitate of iron(II) cyanide, which dissolves when excess cyanide is added to form a clear yellow solution:

$$Fe^{2+} + 2CN^- \longrightarrow Fe(CN)_2(s)$$
$$Fe(CN)_2(s) + 4CN^- \longrightarrow \underset{\textit{hexacyanoferrate(II) ion}}{[Fe(CN)_6]^{4-}}$$

Potassium hexacyanoferrate(II), $K_4Fe(CN)_6 \cdot 3H_2O$, is a common laboratory chemical (sometimes called potassium ferrocyanide). Oxidizing agents readily change potassium hexacyanoferrate(II) to potassium hexacyanoferrate(III), $K_3Fe(CN)_6$ (also called potassium ferricyanide).

When $K_4Fe(CN)_6$ reacts with an iron(III) salt in aqueous solution *or* when $K_3Fe(CN)_6$ reacts with an iron(II) salt, a precipitate of $KFe[Fe(CN)_6]$ is formed. This

Table 31.9
Some Compounds of Iron

$FeSO_4 \cdot 7H_2O$	Iron(II) sulfate heptahydrate (light green; from pickle liquor; green vitriol)
FeO	Iron(II) oxide (black; nonstoichiometric)
FeS	Iron(II) sulfide (brownish black)
$FeCl_3$	Iron(III) chloride (anhydrous; brown black)
Fe_2O_3	Iron(III) oxide (red-brown, nonstoichiometric)
$K_4Fe(CN)_6$	Potassium ferrocyanide (yellow)
$K_3Fe(CN)_6$	Potassium ferricyanide (red)
$Fe(SCN)_3$	Iron(III) thiocyanate (bright red)
FeS_2	Iron pyrite ("fool's gold")

Table 31.10
Iron Oxides Fe_2O_3 occurs in two different crystal structures.

Oxide	Natural Mineral Name	Crystal Structure	Uses
FeO, Iron(II) oxide (black)	**Wüstite (an ore)**	**Sodium chloride structure, cubic close-packed** O^{2-} **anions with** Fe^{2+} **in all octahedral holes**	**Green glass, ceramics, catalysts**
Fe₂O₃, Iron(III) oxide (brown)	**Hematite, also limonite, (2Fe₂O₃·3H₂O, the most common ores)**	**Two structures:** **(a) Cubic close-packed** O^{2-} **anions with** Fe^{3+} **distributed in octahedral and tetrahedral holes** **(b) Hexagonal close-packed with** Fe^{3+} **in ⅔ of octahedral holes**	**Red paint pigment** **Magnetic recording tape**
Fe₃O₄, Iron(II, III) oxide	**Magnetite (an ore)**	**Cubic close-packed** O^{2-} **anions with** Fe^{2+} **ions in octahedral holes and** Fe^{3+} **ions half in octahedral and half in tetrahedral holes**	**Pigment in ceramics and glass** **Magnetic recording tape** **Corrosion-resistant coating on steel**

very slightly soluble, deep-blue compound is known as *Prussian blue*. The absorption of light by Prussian blue, resulting in its intense color, is facilitated by the ease with which electrons can migrate from one iron atom to another. This compound follows the general rule that a solid that contains atoms of the same metal in two different oxidation states is deeply colored—a phenomenon known as *interaction absorption.*

The formation of Prussian blue is utilized in making blueprints. Paper is moistened in total darkness with a solution containing iron(III) ion, hexacyanoferrate(III) ion, and ammonium citrate, a mild reducing agent. The paper is then dried and is ready for use. As long as it is kept in darkness, no reaction occurs, but upon exposure to light the citrate reduces part of the iron(III) to iron(II), and when the paper is moistened, the insoluble Prussian blue is formed. Any parts of the paper protected from the light remain unaffected. The soluble compounds that have not reacted are then washed away.

EXAMPLE 31.4
Chemical Reactions: Fe Compounds

What are the products of the following reactions?

(a) $Fe(NO_3)_2 \cdot 6H_2O(s) \xrightarrow{\text{gentle heat (140 °C)}}$

(b) Solid product of (a) $\xrightarrow{\text{strong heat, air}}$

(c) $FeCO_3(s) \xrightarrow{\text{200 °C, air}}$

These are all thermal decomposition reactions. We should consider what gases might form.

(a) *Gentle* heating of a hydrate is likely to drive off water, leaving behind iron(II) nitrate, $Fe(NO_3)_2$.
(b) Heating the nitrate of a metal such as iron (Table 17.7) causes thermal decomposition to give nitrogen(IV) oxide (NO_2), oxygen, and the metal oxide.

We might expect that strong heating in the presence of air would oxidize the iron present, resulting in the formation of Fe_2O_3, with iron oxidized to the $+3$ state.

(c) Heating a metal carbonate causes decomposition to give carbon dioxide and the metal oxide. We cannot be *sure* which iron oxide is the product; FeO would form first and at this moderate temperature might not be further oxidized. [The product is FeO.]

31.11 COBALT AND NICKEL

a. Elemental cobalt and nickel Cobalt and nickel are less abundant than chromium, manganese, or iron. The principal nickel ores are sulfides or oxides. Very few ores are valuable for their cobalt content alone. Cobalt and its salts are obtained chiefly as by-products in the metallurgy of nickel.

Cobalt is a component of many valuable alloys. Among these are Alnico (Fe, Al, Ni, Co), which is highly magnetic, Stellite (Cr, Co, W), used in surgical instruments because it is hard and corrosion resistant, and Hastelloy B (chiefly Co and Ni), which is very strong and hard, even at high temperatures.

Cobalt is much less reactive than iron and dissolves in acids only slowly. It corrodes very slightly in ordinary air. Cobalt compounds are widely used as catalysts. For example, cobalt naphthenate catalyzes the drying of paint. It is deep blue, but is used in such small concentration that, even in a white paint, the color is not perceptible. A cobalt–molybdenum–alumina catalyst is used in removing sulfur from crude oil. Also, cobalt catalysts are used in the Fischer–Tropsch synthesis of hydrocarbons (Section 27.14).

The importance of nickel in modern civilization can hardly be overestimated. It is widely used as a protective plate on iron, as a catalyst for hydrogenation and petroleum refining, and as a constituent of many valuable alloys, including steel (Table 31.11). The nickel steels are hard, tough, and corrosion resistant.

b. Compounds of cobalt and nickel. In most of their compounds, cobalt has the oxidation state of $+2$ or $+3$, and nickel has the oxidation state of $+2$. Both form many complex ions and $+3$ cobalt is stable in aqueous solution *only* as part of a complex ion. Most simple cobalt salts contain the pink, hydrated ion $[Co(H_2O)_6]^{2+}$ (Table 31.12). The water is expelled from most of these salts by heating somewhat above 100 °C. In general, cobalt(II) with four ligands is blue and cobalt(II) with six ligands is pink. The color change of a hydrated cobalt complex ion is used in devices

Table 31.11
Uses of Nickel and Nickel Compounds

Nickel
  Stainless steel
  Other alloys, e.g.,
    Nichrome (Ni, Cr)
    Monel metal (Ni, Cu)
    Modern coinage
  Hydrogenation catalyst
  Nickel plating
  Undercoat in chrome plating
  Magnets
Nickel compounds
  Catalysts
  Electroplating baths
  Magnets
  Ceramics
  Dyes

Co, Ni oxidation states:
+2, +3

Table 31.12
Some Compounds of Cobalt

CoF_3	Cobalt(III) fluoride (brown)	CoO	Cobalt(II) oxide (green-brown)
$CoSO_4$	Cobalt(II) sulfate (dark blue)	Co_2O_3	Cobalt(III) oxide (gray-black)
$[Co(H_2O)_6]Cl_2$	Hexaaquacobalt(II) chloride (pink)	$K_3[Co(CN)_6]$	Potassium hexacyanocobaltate(III) (yellow)
$[Co(H_2O)_6](NO_3)_2$	Hexaaquacobalt(II) nitrate (red)	$[Co(NH_3)_6]Cl_3$	Hexaaminecobalt(III) chloride (yellow)
CoS	Cobalt(II) sulfide (black)	$K_3[Co(NO_2)_6]$	Potassium hexanitrocobaltate(III) (yellow)

Table 31.13
Some Compounds of Nickel

NiCl$_2$	Nickel(II) chloride (yellow)
NiCl$_2 \cdot$ 6H$_2$O	Nickel(II) chloride hexa-hydrate (green)
NiO	Nickel(II) oxide (green-black)
NiS	Nickel(II) sulfide (green-black)
NiSO$_4 \cdot$ 6H$_2$O	Nickel(II) sulfate hexa-hydrate (green)
Ni(CO)$_4$	Nickel carbonyl (volatile, flammable liquid, poisonous)
[Ni(NH$_3$)$_6$](NO$_3$)$_2$	Hexaammine-nickel(II) nitrate (bright blue)

that are supposed to tell when it is going to rain. At high humidity, the blue complex ion takes up water and turns pink.

$$[Co(H_2O)_4]Cl_2(s) \xrightleftharpoons[\text{atmosphere}]{\text{H}_2\text{O in}} [Co(H_2O)_6]Cl_2(s)$$
$$\textit{blue} \qquad\qquad\qquad \textit{pink}$$

The best known of the cobalt(II) salts is the pink chloride, [Co(H$_2$O)$_6$]Cl$_2$, which dissolves in water to give a pink solution and in alcohol to give a blue solution of [Co(C$_2$H$_5$OH)$_4$]Cl$_2$. It is the source of most other cobalt salts.

When an aqueous solution containing the cobalt(II) ion is treated with potassium cyanide, a slimy gray precipitate of Co(CN)$_2$ is formed, but this dissolves upon addition of more cyanide. In a few moments, the solution grows warm, and bubbles of hydrogen gas escape. When this reaction is ended, yellow crystals of potassium hexacyanocobaltate(III) can be obtained from the solution:

$$Co^{2+} + 2CN^- \longrightarrow Co(CN)_2(s)$$
$$2Co(CN)_2(s) + 8KCN(aq) + 2H_2O(l) \longrightarrow 2K_3[Co(CN)_6](aq) + 2KOH(aq) + H_2(g)$$

In many soluble nickel(II) compounds nickel is present as the light green hydrated ion, [Ni(H$_2$O)$_6$]$^{2+}$ (Table 31.13). The halide salts, upon heating above 100 °C, are converted to the anhydrous salts NiCl$_2$ (yellow), NiBr$_2$ (yellow-brown), and NiI$_2$ (black). These dissolve readily in water, giving green solutions. Nickel(II) sulfate, nickel(II) nitrate, and other nickel(II) salts containing oxoanions retain their green color upon dehydration; this color must, therefore, be due to the coordination of oxygen atoms with the nickel(II) ion.

In nickel carbonyl, Ni(CO)$_4$, the metal shows an oxidation state of zero. This interesting compound, which long baffled theoretical chemists, is a volatile (b.p. 43 °C), *extremely toxic* liquid. It is obtained by the action of carbon monoxide gas on nickel powder at slightly elevated temperatures.

$$Ni(s) + 4CO(g) \longrightarrow Ni(CO)_4(g)$$
$$\textit{nickel} \\ \textit{carbonyl}$$

At somewhat higher temperatures, nickel carbonyl decomposes with the liberation of metallic nickel. This property once was employed in the separation of nickel from other metals, but nickel is now purified mainly by electrolytic refining. Several of the transition metals form carbonyls of this sort; all are volatile, highly poisonous, and soluble in nonpolar solvents.

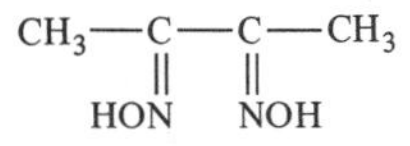

dimethylglyoxime

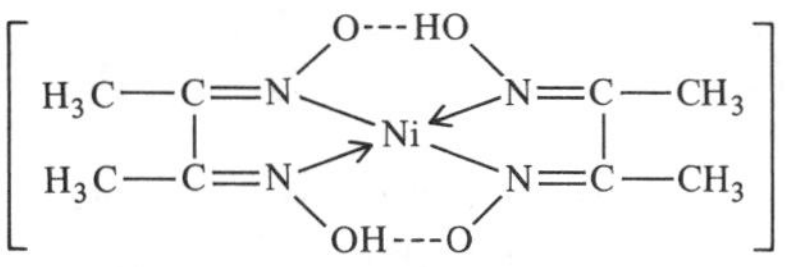

complex between nickel ion and two molecules of dimethylglyoxime

Figure 31.12
Nickel Complex with Dimethylglyoxime

One of the most striking of the nickel complexes is that formed with the organic compound dimethylglyoxime (DMG), which has the structural formula shown in Figure 31.12. When nickel(II) ion is added to a neutral solution of this material, it coordinates with the two nitrogen atoms in each of the two DMG molecules. At the same time one hydrogen ion escapes from each molecule of DMG, and the other forms a hydrogen bond with an oxygen atom of the other DMG molecule. This complex is only very slightly soluble in water and is bright red. Since no other common metal ion gives a precipitate with dimethylglyoxime, the formation of a red precipitate when DMG is added to a solution is a very strong indication that nickel(II) ion is present in that solution.

31.12 COPPER, SILVER, AND GOLD

a. Elemental copper, silver, and gold Typical metals, we have learned, are ductile, malleable, good conductors of heat and electricity, and have metallic luster. In these physical properties, copper, silver, and gold are the most "metallic" of all of the metals. If a heavy weight is hung on a fairly thin copper wire, the wire will continue to stretch slowly for several days until it is too small in diameter to support the weight. Gold is the most malleable of all metals; it can be rolled into sheets that

Table 31.14
Some Alloys of Copper, Silver, and Gold

Name	Composition (%)
Brass	Cu, 20–97; Zn, 2–80; Sn, 0–14; Pb, 0–12; Mn, 0–25
Bronze	Cu, 50–98; Sn, 0–35; Zn, 0–29; Pb, 0–50; P, 0–3
German silver	Cu, 46–93; Zn, 20–36; Ni, 6–30
Bell metal	Cu, 75–80; Sn, 20–25
Nickel coin	Cu, 75; Ni, 25
Sterling silver	Cu, 7.5; Ag, 92.5
Gold (18 karat)	Cu, 5–14; Au, 75; Ag, 10–20
Gold (14 karat)	Cu, 12–28; Au, 58; Ag, 4–30
Purple gold	Au, 78; Al, 22
White gold	Au with varying amounts of Pd, Ni, or Zn

Table 31.15
Uses of Copper, Silver, and Gold

Copper
Electrical applications
Pipes, plumbing, gutters
Industrial machinery
Coinage

Silver
Sterling silver tableware
Photography
Mirror backing
Heat-exchange equipment
Pharmaceuticals
Electronic devices
Coinage
Jewelry

Gold
Electronic devices
Photography
Jewelry
Reflective coating, e.g., on spaceships, windows

Common oxidation states
Cu: +1, +2
Ag: +1
Au: +1, +3

are so thin as to be transparent (they transmit green light). Gold leaf is used in signs on windows and office doors, and in covering the domes of capitol buildings.

Copper, silver, and gold are excellent conductors of electricity. Copper is used in cooking vessels because of its high thermal conductivity and in electrical wiring because of its high electrical conductivity. Both silver and gold are better conductors than copper, but their higher cost rules them out for most purposes.

All three of the metals in this family are relatively soft and are often alloyed with other metals to achieve hardness, rigidity, and other desirable properties (Table 31.14). Because of their beautiful luster and color, copper, silver, and gold have been used for many centuries in ornaments, jewelry, and tableware.

The major uses of copper, silver, and gold are summarized in Table 31.15. (The metallurgy of copper was discussed in Section 28.6.)

b. Chemical properties of copper, silver, and gold Copper, silver, and gold atoms each have one electron in the outer s subshell and ten electrons in the underlying d subshell (see Table 31.1). As would be expected, an atom of each of these elements can lose its s electron; under suitable conditions, each can also lose one or two of the d electrons. Thus, all show *oxidation states* of +1, +2, and +3. However, in most of its common compounds, copper is in the +2 state; silver rarely has any oxidation state but +1, and gold is practically always in the +1 or +3 state.

Copper, silver, and gold all lie below hydrogen in the electromotive series. They do not react with nonoxidizing acids such as hydrochloric acid and they are not readily attacked by oxygen at ordinary temperatures. On heating with air, copper, which is the most reactive of the three, forms copper(II) oxide, CuO; silver slowly forms silver(I) oxide, Ag_2O, which, however, decomposes into its elements on strong heating. Gold does not react with oxygen.

Copper and silver readily react with sulfur and sulfur-containing compounds, forming either Cu_2S or CuS and Ag_2S, respectively. This reaction is particularly evident in the case of silver, which darkens rapidly when left in contact with sulfur-containing substances such as eggs, rubber, or mustard. Both metals tarnish slowly when exposed to the atmosphere, for there are nearly always traces of hydrogen sulfide in the air.

Both copper and silver readily react with oxidizing acids, such as nitric acid, copper going to the +2 state, and silver to the +1 state. Gold does not tarnish noticeably in the air or when exposed to sulfur or its compounds. It is not attacked by nitric acid, but it is dissolved by aqua regia (HCl/HNO_3; Section 26.5c) with the formation of $[AuCl_4]^-$.

The formation of complex ions is of great importance in the chemistry of these metals; advantage is taken of it in the metallurgy and the electroplating of all three, in analysis, and, in the case of silver, in the developing of photographs (see An Aside: The Photographic Process).

c. Compounds of copper In most of its common compounds, copper is in the +2 oxidation state. Copper(II) oxide, CuO, is a black, insoluble substance formed by gentle heating of the metal in air or by the addition of an alkaline solution to a hot solution of a copper(II) salt. An interesting use of CuO is as a black surface coating in devices that collect solar energy. A thin layer of CuO transmits infrared radiation, but not shorter wavelength radiation.

The blue-green copper(II) hydroxide is obtained either as a gelatinous material with variable water content or as a crystalline substance of the composition $Cu(OH)_2$ when a base is added to a copper(II) solution maintained at room temperature. Both the oxide and the hydroxide are predominantly basic in character and react with most acids to give solutions of copper(II) salts. Such solutions are generally blue or blue-green, the color being due to the hydrated copper(II) ion.

Table 31.16
Some Compounds of Copper

Cu_2O	Copper(I) oxide (red)
Cu_2S	Copper(I) sulfide (black)
$CuCl$	Copper(I) chloride (white)
$CuCl_2 \cdot 2H_2O$	Copper(II) chloride di-hydrate (green)
$Cu(NO_3)_2 \cdot 6H_2O$	Copper(II) nitrate hexahydrate (blue)
$CuSO_4 \cdot 5H_2O$	Copper(II) sulfate pentahy-drate (blue)
CuO	Copper(II) oxide (black)

Copper(II) sulfide, CuS, usually obtained by the action of hydrogen sulfide on a solution of a copper(II) salt, is highly insoluble in water ($K_{sp} = 6 \times 10^{-36}$ at 25 °C) but dissolves readily in a solution of sodium sulfide because of the formation of the complex $[CuS_2]^{2-}$, which is even less dissociated than solid CuS.

$$Na_2S(aq) + CuS(s) \longrightarrow Na_2[CuS_2](aq)$$

This reaction is often used in analytical chemistry to separate copper from the ions of other heavy metals that do not form such complexes. Copper(II) ion has a great tendency to form both cationic and anionic complexes. The most familiar cation is the deep blue tetraamminecopper(II) ion, $[Cu(NH_3)_4]^{2+}$.

Copper(II) sulfate pentahydrate, $CuSO_4 \cdot 5H_2O$, commonly called blue vitriol, is the copper compound used commercially in the greatest quantity. Like most other hydrated copper(II) salts, this one is blue, which is characteristic of the $[Cu(H_2O)_4]^{2+}$ ion. The fifth molecule of water is held to the sulfate ion by hydrogen bonding. When the salt is dehydrated by gentle heating or placing it in a desiccator, the blue crystals crumble to a fine white powder of anhydrous copper sulfate, $CuSO_4$. On dissolution in water, this powder again gives a blue solution. Copper(II) sulfate is used to kill algae and fungi, in fertilizers, and as the starting material for the production of many other copper compounds.

Stable copper(I) compounds include the halides, the sulfide, and the cyanide (Table 31.16), all of which are anhydrous crystalline compounds. Copper(I) compounds containing oxoanions are known, but they are unstable. For example, Cu_2SO_4 can be prepared and stored in dry air, but upon exposure to moisture it disproportionates vigorously:

$$Cu_2SO_4(s) \longrightarrow Cu(s) + CuSO_4(s)$$

d. Compounds of silver and gold Silver nitrate, $AgNO_3$ (once referred to as "lunar caustic"; "lunar" because in alchemical lore, silver was related to the moon and "caustic" because in the solid form, it burns flesh) is made by the reaction of metallic silver with nitric acid. It can be crystallized from the resulting solution as large, white crystals that are readily soluble in water. It is the usual source of other silver compounds (Table 31.17).

Most of the other simple compounds of silver are insoluble in water and can be prepared by precipitation from a solution of silver nitrate. The formation of the white, curdy precipitate of silver chloride, AgCl, is a sensitive test for the presence of either Ag^+ or Cl^- in solution. The pale yellow bromide and yellow iodide are even less soluble than the chloride. Although silver chloride is not very soluble in water ($K_{sp} = 1.8 \times 10^{-10}$), it is dissolved by solutions of ammonia, with which it forms a stable soluble complex ($K_d = 6.2 \times 10^{-8}$), diamminesilver chloride, $[Ag(NH_3)_2]Cl$,

Table 31.17
Some Compounds of Silver and Gold

Ag_2O	Silver(I) oxide (brown)
$AgNO_3$	Silver(I) nitrate (white)
$AgCl$	Silver(I) chloride (white)
$AgCN$	Silver(I) cyanide (white)
$AuCl$	Gold(I) chloride (yellow)
$AuCl_3$	Gold(III) chloride (red)
Au_2S_3	Gold(III) sulfide (brown-black)

$$AgCl(s) + 2NH_3(aq) \longrightarrow [Ag(NH_3)_2]Cl(aq)$$

Upon addition of acid, this reaction is reversed:

$$[Ag(NH_3)_2]Cl(aq) + 2H^+(aq) \longrightarrow AgCl(s) + 2NH_4^+(aq)$$

As with copper, the simple compounds of gold in the +1 state are the halides, the sulfide, and the cyanide. All of these are insoluble and show a tendency to disproportionate into metallic gold and the gold(III) compound. All of them are readily reduced to metallic gold. The most important soluble compound of gold(I) is the cyano complex, $Na[Au(CN)_2]$, which is used in electroplating gold onto metallic objects. Among the gold(III) compounds, the commonest simple substance is red gold(III) chloride, usually written $AuCl_3$, but which is actually a dimer, Au_2Cl_6, in both the solid and vapor phases.

The properties of the d-transition metals and their compounds are summarized in Tables 31.18 and 31.19.

Table 31.18
Outstanding Properties of *d*-Transition Metals

$ns^{1,2}$	One or two s electrons (except Pd).
$(n-1)d$	Incomplete *d* levels (most elements); influence of *d* electrons important, leads to greater difficulties in generalizations about properties than for representative elements.
+1 to +8	Variable oxidation states.
Sc, Y, La	More like lanthanides and Be family metals.
Tc	Radioactive; not naturally occurring.
3*d* series (Ti–Cu)	Similar properties. Reducing strength decreases, ionization energy increases across series. Industrially important.
4*d* series (Zr–Ag) and 5*d* series (Hf–Au)	Due to lanthanide contraction, very similar in size and other properties. 4*d* and 5*d* similarities decrease across series.
Cr, Mo, Mn, Tc, Re	Stable $(n-1)d^5ns^{1,2}$ configurations. Maximum number of unpaired electrons. Largest number of oxidation states.
Ti family to Cu family	Down these families, density increases, ease of oxidation decreases, reducing strength decreases
$M \rightarrow M^{n+} + e^-$	Activity of metals as reducing agents decreases across periods.

Table 31.19
Outstanding Properties of *d*-Transition Metal Compounds

Many are paramagnetic, colored, and catalytically active	Unpaired *d* electrons; readily available *d* electrons.
$[M(L)_n]^{n+, 0, n-}$	Complex formation is common. Especially for Cr, Fe, Co, Ni; the Cu family; the Pt metals.
M^{2+}, M^{3+}	Ionic in lower oxidation states.
$[M^{2+,3+}(H_2O)_n]$	Hydrated ions in solution. Many crystalline hydrates.
$\overset{+3 \text{ to } +8}{M\text{——}A}$	More nearly covalent bonding as oxidation state increases.
$\overset{+6}{Cr}$ $\overset{+7}{Mn}$ $\overset{+6}{Fe}$	Strong oxidizing agents (e.g., $Cr_2O_7^{2-}$, MnO_4^-, FeO_4^{2-}).
MnO_2, FeO, Fe_2O_3, Fe_3O_4	Oxides usually nonstoichiometric.
Cobalt(III)	Stable in aqueous solution only in complex ions.
$M(OH)_n$	Many hydroxides polymeric, hydrated in varying degree; many are amphoteric in intermediate oxidation states and acidic in higher oxidation states.

AN ASIDE
The Photographic Process

When exposed to light of short wavelength, silver halides are "activated," after which they are more easily reduced to the metallic state than unactivated silver halides. This is the basis of the photographic process.

$$AgX(s) + \text{light energy} \longrightarrow AgX^* \text{ (activated silver halide)}$$
$$AgX^* + \text{reducing agent} \longrightarrow Ag(s)$$

The silver halide (usually a mixture of halides) is suspended in gelatin, which is spread in a uniform layer on the film. Exposure activates those parts of the coating on which light falls. The image is developed by placing the film in a solution of a weak organic reducing agent. This reduces the activated silver halide to metallic silver in a finely divided form, which is black. (If the reducing action is too strong or if the film is left in the reducing agent too long, both the activated and the unactivated silver halide are reduced and the entire film becomes black.) Once the film has been developed, the unreduced silver halide must be removed before the film is taken into the light; otherwise, it will slowly turn black. This silver halide is removed by washing the film in a solution of sodium thiosulfate, $Na_2S_2O_3$, which forms a stable, soluble complex with the silver halide. This is the fixing process, and sodium thiosulfate is called *hypo*.

$$AgX(s) + 2S_2O_3^{2-}(aq) \longrightarrow [Ag(S_2O_3)_2]^{3-}(aq) + X^-(aq)$$

After rinsing in water, the negative is dried. It is black where light fell on it and clear where no light struck it. To make a print, the negative is projected onto paper coated with silver halide–gelatin. Where the negative is black, no light passes through to the paper; where the negative is transparent, the paper is exposed. Once the paper is developed, fixed, and dried, the print is ready.

Portraits can be toned by converting the silver in the picture to some color other than black. This is done by immersing the picture in a solution of a material that will react with silver and leave a suitable deposit on the paper.

$$Ag(s) + [AuCl_2]^- \longrightarrow AgCl(s) + Cl^- + Au(s) \qquad \text{(sepia)}$$
$$2Ag(s) + PtCl_4^{2-} \longrightarrow 2AgCl(s) + 2Cl^- + Pt(s) \qquad \text{(gray)}$$

The silver chloride formed in toning with gold or platinum is removed by treatment with hypo.

The chemistry of color photography is extremely complex, but the initial steps rely on the photosensitivity of the silver halides, just as black and white photography does. The silver halide is most sensitive to light in the blue and ultraviolet regions. In color film, the halide surface may be coated with an organic compound that absorbs, say, red light. The dye transfers energy to the silver halide, allowing it to be exposed by light of colors that it does not ordinarily "see." There are three layers of AgX–gelatin suspension, one for blue light, one for green light, and one for red light. Each layer also contains an organic dye which reacts with the silver to give a characteristic color. The silver salt formed by reaction with the dye is later washed out, and the final picture contains dyes, but no silver.

f-TRANSITION ELEMENTS

31.13 ELECTRON CONFIGURATIONS AND GENERAL PROPERTIES OF *f*-TRANSITION METALS

The elements lanthanum ($Z = 57$) through lutetium ($Z = 71$) are collectively referred to as the *lanthanides*, or the *rare earth elements*. The former name emphasizes that all of these elements and their compounds closely resemble lanthanum and its compounds. The latter name, which is now less widely used, is based upon the original isolation of these elements as *oxides* (referred to by the Greeks as *earths*) from the relatively rare Scandinavian minerals *gadolinite* and *cerite*. That the term *rare* is not generally correct is shown by a comparison of the crustal abundances of the lanthanides with those of some better known elements in Table 31.20. The lanthanides are all shiny, silvery, reactive metals. Most tarnish readily in air by formation of oxides, although gadolinium and lutetium are quite stable.

Table 31.20

Comparison between the Crystal Abundances of the Lanthanide Elements and Certain Other More Familiar Elements (*Source:* T. Moeller, *The Chemistry of the Lanthanides*, Oxford: Pergamon Press, 1973, p. 46.)

Symbol	Abundance (ppm)	Symbol	Abundance (ppm)
La	18.3	N	46.3
Ce	46.1	Sn	40
Pr	5.53	Nb	24
Nd	23.9	Co	23
Pm	4.5×10^{-20}	Pb	16
Sm	6.47	Ga	15
Eu	1.06	Mo	2.5–15
Gd	6.36	Be	6
Tb	0.91	As	5
Dy	4.47	U	4
Ho	1.15	B	3
Er	2.47	Ta	2.1
Tm	0.20	Br	1.62
Yb	2.66	Sb	1
Lu	0.75	I	0.3
		Cd	0.15
Sc	5	Se	0.09
Y	28.1	Au	0.005

The elements actinium ($Z = 89$) through lawrencium ($Z = 103$) are collectively referred to as the *actinides*. This name derives from the position of actinium in the periodic table, which is similar to the position of lanthanum, and from observations that many of the properties of these elements and their compounds are similar to those of the lanthanides and their compounds.

The first six actinides (through plutonium) are present in the earth's crust. The actinides from americium to lawrencium are man-made radioactive isotopes produced in nuclear bombardment reactions. Because uranium was for many years the terminal element in the periodic table, the elements from neptunium on are known as the *transuranium elements*.

The electron configurations and atomic radii of the *f*-transition elements and their ions are given in Table 31.21. All energy levels below the $(n - 2)f$ level are filled to capacity and electrons from these levels are not available for bond formation. For the lanthanides, the $5d$ and $6s$ electrons, and for the actinides the $6d$ and $7s$ electrons, are most available. The *f* electrons do not participate in bonding as readily as do the *d* electrons from the incomplete energy levels in the *d*-transition elements. However, the $5f$ orbitals do project into the outer electron atmosphere more than the $4f$ orbitals, leading to greater variability of oxidation states for the actinides than for the lanthanides.

_f_-transition elements: lanthanides, $_{57}$La$-_{71}$Lu actinides, $_{89}$Ac$-_{103}$Lr

Table 31.21
Electron Configurations of the _f_-Transition Elements

Element	Symbol	Outermost Electron Configuration	Atomic Radius (nm)
4f-transition elements (lanthanides)			
		[Xe core]	
Lanthanum	$_{57}$La	$5d^1\, 6s^2$	0.187
Cerium	$_{58}$Ce	$4f^1\, 5d^1\, 6s^2$	0.183
Praseodymium	$_{59}$Pr	$4f^3\quad 6s^2$	0.182
Neodymium	$_{60}$Nd	$4f^4\quad 6s^2$	0.181
Promethium	$_{61}$Pm	$4f^5\quad 6s^2$	0.181
Samarium	$_{62}$Sm	$4f^6\quad 6s^2$	0.180
Europium	$_{63}$Eu	$4f^7\quad 6s^2$	0.199
Gadolinium	$_{64}$Gd	$4f^7\, 5d^1\, 6s^2$	0.179
Terbium	$_{65}$Tb	$4f^9\quad 6s^2$	0.176
Dysprosium	$_{66}$Dy	$4f^{10}\quad 6s^2$	0.175
Holmium	$_{67}$Ho	$4f^{11}\quad 6s^2$	0.174
Erbium	$_{68}$Er	$4f^{12}\quad 6s^2$	0.173
Thulium	$_{69}$Tm	$4f^{13}\quad 6s^2$	0.173
Ytterbium	$_{70}$Yb	$4f^{14}\quad 6s^2$	0.194
Lutetium	$_{71}$Lu	$4f^{14}\, 5d^1\, 6s^2$	0.172
5f-transition elements (actinides)			
		[Rn core]	
Actinium	$_{89}$Ac	$6d^1\, 7s^2$	0.188
Thorium	$_{90}$Th	$6d^2\, 7s^2$	0.180
Protactinium	$_{91}$Pa	$5f^2\, 6d^1\, 7s^2$	0.161
Uranium	$_{92}$U	$5f^3\, 6d^1\, 7s^2$	0.139
Neptunium	$_{93}$Np	$5f^4\, 6d^1\, 7s^2$	—
Plutonium	$_{94}$Pu	$5f^6\quad 7s^2$	0.151
Americium	$_{95}$Am	$5f^7\quad 7s^2$	—
Curium	$_{96}$Cm	$5f^7\, 6d^1\, 7s^2$	—
Berkelium	$_{97}$Bk	$5f^9\quad 7s^2$	—
Californium	$_{98}$Cf	$5f^{10}\quad 7s^2$	—
Einsteinium	$_{99}$Es	$5f^{11}\quad 7s^2$	—
Fermium	$_{100}$Fm	$5f^{12}\quad 7s^2$	—
Mendelevium	$_{101}$Md	$5f^{13}\quad 7s^2$	—
Nobelium	$_{102}$No	$5f^{14}\quad 7s^2$	—
Lawrencium	$_{103}$Lr	$5f^{14}\, 6d^1\, 7s^2$	—

The lanthanides and the actinides, like the *d*-transition elements, vary less in their properties than do the representative elements. The gradual decrease in atomic radii (and also in comparable ionic radii) referred to as the lanthanide contraction can be seen in the data in Table 31.21. The similar decrease in radii for actinium through lawrencium is sometimes called the *actinide contraction*. Within each series, this contraction is responsible for gradual changes in properties related to size and thus to attraction for electrons.

All of the *f*-transition elements are metals with electronegativities between 1 and 1.2 (comparable to those of magnesium or calcium) and of moderately high melting points (all between 650 °C and 1750 °C). The densities of the lanthanides are moderately high, comparable to those of the first *d* series elements. Those actinides for which data are available have greater densities than the lanthanides, more like those of the second *d* series elements.

31.14 OXIDATION STATES, CHARACTERISTIC PROPERTIES, AND COMPOUNDS OF THE *f*-TRANSITION METALS

The +3 oxidation state is the characteristic and most common oxidation state for the lanthanides (Table 31.22). The +2 ions of Eu, Yb, and Sm are easily oxidized, and cerium in the +4 state is easily reduced (it is a strong oxidizing agent).

Unlike the lanthanides, there is no single oxidation state characteristic of the actinides, although the +4 state is fairly common. The greater ease of involvement of the 5*f* electrons in reactions is no doubt related to the greater variability of oxidation state for these elements than for the lanthanides. As might be expected, there is much less similarity in properties among the actinides than among the lanthanides.

The regular decrease in ionic radius of the lanthanides (Figure 31.13) leads to a decrease in ionic character for compounds containing a given anion, an increase in the stabilities of complexes with a given ligand, and for many compounds, a general decrease in solubility. Because of the similar atomic radii of the lanthanides, many of their compounds with a given anion are isomorphous (of the same crystal structure). This means not only that all of the lanthanide +3 ions occur together in nature, but also that they are difficult to separate from each other. Separations by crystallization,

---

Lanthanide oxidation state:

+3

Table 31.22
Oxidation States of 4*f*-Transition Elements

Name	Common Oxidation States	Examples
Lanthanum	+3	La^{3+}, $La_2O_3(s)$
Cerium	+3	Ce^{3+}, $CeF_3(s)$
	+4	Ce^{4+}, $CeO_2(s)$
Praseodymium	+3	Pr^{3+}, $Pr_2O_3(s)$
	+4	$PrO_2(s)$
Neodymium	+3	Nd^{3+}, $Nd(NO_3)_3(s)$
Promethium	+3	Pm^{3+}, $Pm_2O_3(s)$
Samarium	+2	Sm^{2+}, $SmSO_4(s)$
	+3	Sm^{3+}, $Sm_2(SO_4)_3(s)$
Europium	+2	Eu^{2+}, $EuCl_2(s)$
	+3	Eu^{3+}, $Eu_2O_3(s)$
Gadolinium	+3	Gd^{3+}, $GdF_3(s)$
Terbium	+3	Tb^{3+}, $Tb(NO_3)_3(s)$
	+4	$TbO_2(s)$, $TbF_4(s)$
Dysprosium	+3	Dy^{3+}, $Dy_2O_3(s)$
Holmium	+3	Ho^{3+}, $HoCl_3(s)$
Erbium	+3	Er^{3+}, $Er_2(SO_4)_3(s)$
Thulium	+2	Tm^{2+}, $TmI_2(s)$
	+3	Tm^{3+}, $Tm_2O_3(s)$
Ytterbium	+2	Yb^{2+}, $YbI_2(s)$
	+3	Yb^{3+}, $YbF_3(s)$
Lutetium	+3	Lu^{3+}, $LuCl_3(s)$

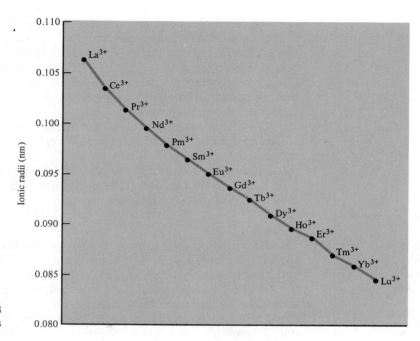

Figure 31.13
Radii of Ions of the Lanthanides

ion exchange, and solvent extraction are never effected in a few steps, but require many, many repetitions.

In a given oxidation state (e.g., +3), the lanthanide and actinide ions are so similar in size that they participate in similar reactions and are difficult to separate from each other. Indeed, much of the chemistry of the actinide ions was developed by analogy to the lanthanides.

In most oxidation states, the atoms and ions of the lanthanides and actinides contain electrons with unpaired spins. As a consequence, these ions are paramagnetic and usually colored. For example, among the lanthanide cations, only La^{3+}, Ce^{4+}, Yb^{2+}, and Lu^{3+} are diamagnetic. The only colorless lanthanide ions are La^{3+}, Ce^{3+}, Gd^{3+}, Yb^{3+}, and Lu^{3+}. The ions Ce^{3+}, Gd^{3+}, and Yb^{3+}, all of which contain one or more unpaired electrons, also absorb radiation, but in regions of the ultraviolet or infrared which the human eye cannot detect.

The f-transition metal ions form fewer complexes than do the d-transition metal ions. Those complexes that form dissociate to a greater extent than comparable d-transition metal complexes. The colors and magnetic properties of most lanthanide complexes are the same as those of the uncomplexed lanthanide +3 ions. Bonding in the lanthanide complexes is largely ionic in character. Involvement of $4f$ electrons in complex formation is unlikely.

31.15 SOURCES AND USES OF THE f-TRANSITION METALS

All fourteen lanthanides are present together in bastnasite, monazite, and xenotine, the major ores from which the elements are recovered. It is impractical both chemically and economically to extract only specific lanthanides from the ores. Therefore, the relative amounts of these metals and their compounds produced each year reflect their distribution in the ores.

As you might imagine, the discovery and identification of the very similar lanthanides took many years and had to overcome much confusion. The difficult separation of the lanthanides from each other was first accomplished by precipitation of individual salts of differing solubilities. The development of modern, highly effective separation methods was first inspired by the discovery in the 1950s that

Table 31.23
Outstanding Properties of *f*-Transition Metals and Their Compounds

La $\longrightarrow$ Lu	Lanthanides, or rare earths. Very similar in properties; occur together in nature. Relatively active metals. Radii decrease (lanthanide contraction).
a lanthanide ion	
Ln^{3+}	Only common oxidation state. All lanthanides form ionic compounds.
Ln $\longrightarrow$ Ln^{3+} + 3e^-	Easily oxidized. Not useful as structural metals.
Ac $\longrightarrow$ Lr	Actinides. All radioactive; less similar in properties than lanthanides. Radii decrease (actinide contraction).
an actinide n^+ An	Variable oxidation states.
Lanthanide and actinide compounds are commonly paramagnetic and colored.	Unpaired *f* electrons.
Lanthanides and actinides form fewer complexes than do *d*-transition metals.	4*f* electrons not involved in bonding; 5*f* electrons may be. Complexes that do form are less stable than those of *d* series elements.

cerium(IV) oxide is a superior polishing compound for plate glass and optical glass. In the 1960s further impetus was given to rare earth production by the demand for phosphors for color television tubes. (An yttrium–europium oxosulfide or oxide of very high purity is a bright red phosphor essential to color television.) Ion exchange or liquid–liquid extraction between water and an organic solvent containing a chelating agent (Section 32.3) are now used effectively to separate the ions from each other. The light rare earths can be reduced electrolytically; the heavy ones must be reduced by high-temperature reactions with active metals, often calcium.

One of the first uses of the lanthanides was in the production of *mischmetal* for the flints in cigarette lighters. Mischmetal is an alloy of a mixture of the light rare earths (La, Ce, Pr, Nd) with iron. Some very interesting new applications for lanthanides are on the horizon. A lanthanum–nickel intermetallic compound that can reversibly store more hydrogen per unit volume than liquid hydrogen may find use in a hydrogen economy (see An Aside: The Hydrogen Economy, Chapter 16).

$$\text{LaNi}_5(s) + 3\text{H}_2(g) \rightleftharpoons \text{LaNi}_5\text{H}_6(s)$$

Samarium–cobalt permanent magnets are five to ten times more powerful than common magnets and are making new devices possible. And monocrystals of very pure gadolinium–gallium garnets form the substrate for the bubble memory chip now being developed for calculators and other data-recording devices.

The outstanding properties of the f-transition metals and their compounds are summarized in Table 31.23.

AN ASIDE

Superheavy Elements

How far can the periodic table be extended? Is it possible that elements beyond 109 will be found in nature or produced by nuclear bombardment reactions? These are not fanciful questions. On the basis of nuclear theory, periodic table trends, and computer-assisted calculations, predictions have been made about the configurations and properties of elements all the way to atomic number 168.

The elements most recently produced, 104, 105, 106, 107, and 109, are very unstable, with half-lives of less than 1 second.

However, what has been termed an "island of stability" (Figure A) may lie ahead in the region of atomic number 114 and mass number 298. Nuclei of element $^{294}_{110}\text{X}$ will contain a magic number of neutrons (184), and nuclei of $^{298}_{114}\text{X}$ will be doubly

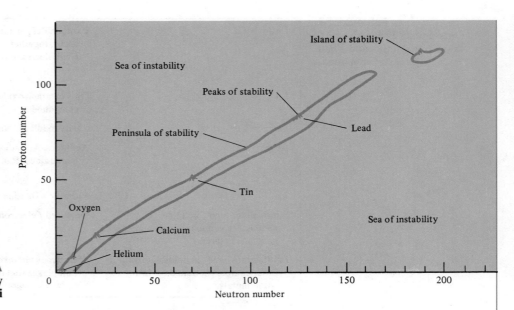

magic, with magic numbers of both neutrons (184) and protons (114). These nuclei will have the filled nuclear energy levels known to impart stability (Section 12.6). Half-lives of about 10^3 yr are thought possible for elements in the island of stability.

Calculations of possible electron configurations of the superheavy atoms suggest that after element 106 (probably of outer configuration $5f^{14} 6d^4 7s^2$) will be regular completion of $6d$, $7p$, and $8s$ orbitals. Next will come complete series of transition elements in which the $6f$ and $5g$ energy levels are being filled.

Element 114 would be a member of Representative Group IV and would resemble lead in its properties. Proposed similarities between known elements and the superheavy elements are being used in the examination of potential naturally occurring or artificial sources of these elements. Several flurries of excitement have been caused by tentative identification of superheavy elements in minerals and meteorites. Although conclusive proof of the existence of superheavy, stable elements has not yet been presented, it remains possible that they will eventually be found.

SUMMARY   *d*-TRANSITION METALS   (Sections **31.1–31.7**)   In their physical properties, many of the *d*-transition metals are among the most typically "metallic" elements— dense, hard, strong, malleable, and highly conductive. Nearly all have important industrial uses, especially the 3*d* series metals. The metals of all three series are more similar to each other in general properties such as radii, electronegativity, and ionization energy than are the representative elements. The 4*d* and 5*d* series metals are *very* similar in radii and properties that depend upon electron loss; this is due to the lanthanide contraction. However, prediction of oxidation state stability and other properties on the basis of electron configuration (Table 31.1) is difficult because of the ready availability of *d* electrons, which are close in energy to the outermost *s* electrons. The *d*-transition elements exhibit many oxidation states (Table 31.3), with the greatest number for the elements of the chromium and manganese families—the elements that have the maximum number of unpaired *d* electrons (d^5). Compounds of these elements become more nearly covalent as the oxidation state of the metal increases. Chromium, manganese, and iron in their higher oxidation states are strong oxidizing agents, and elements in this series beyond Cr all have stable +2 oxidation states. Transition metal compounds often contain unpaired electrons and as a result are colored and paramagnetic. Many of the metals and their compounds are catalytically active. The formation of complexes is a very important aspect of transition metal chemistry, especially for the $3d$ metals Cr, Fe, Co, and Ni; the copper family, or coinage metals (Cu, Ag, Au); and all of the platinum metals (Ru, Os, Rh, Ir, Pd, Pt). Titanium is unique in its combination of lightness, strength, and resistance to corrosion; it is used in the aerospace industry. There are striking similarities in the properties of Zr and Hf, Nb and Ta, Ru, Rh, and Pd, and Os, Ir, and Pt. Combination reactions involving transition metals are often inhibited by the formation of protective coatings and generally require high temperatures. Some transition metals react with oxidizing acids, others with nonoxidizing acids, and some with concentrated alkaline solutions. The platinum metals are resistant to both acids and bases; Pt, Au, and Ru are attacked only by aqua regia. The hydrated cations of transition metals react with water to varying degrees, producing acidic solutions. A reaction typical of many transition metal ions is the precipitation of a salt followed by its dissolution to give a complex ion in aqueous solution.

PROPERTIES OF SELECTED d-TRANSITION METALS (Sections **31.8–31.12**) Because of its great resistance to corrosion, Cr is used to plate other metals; Cr(II) compounds are reducing agents and Cr(VI) compounds are oxidizing agents. The chromate (CrO_4^{2-}) and dichromate ($Cr_2O_7^{2-}$) ions exist in solution in a pH-dependent equilibrium. Manganese imparts hardness and strength to steel. It exhibits all oxidation states from $+2$ to $+7$ (Figure 31.11). $KMnO_4$ is a common oxidizing agent with many uses. MnO_2 is a nonstoichiometric compound valuable for its electrical conductivity and its oxidizing properties. The three oxides of iron—FeO, Fe_2O_3, and Fe_3O_4—also tend to be nonstoichiometric (Table 31.10). Cobalt and nickel are used in many alloys, and also as catalysts. The Co(II) complex ion with four ligands is blue, while with six ligands it is pink.

f-TRANSITION ELEMENTS (Section **31.13–31.15**) The lanthanides and actinides, elements in which electrons are added to inner f orbitals (Table 31.21), are very similar in properties. Radii decrease only slightly across each series (the lanthanide and actinide contractions). The actinides are all radioactive and the elements beyond plutonium are not found in nature, but have been synthesized in nuclear reactions. The lanthanides are more active metals than the d-transition metals (except for scandium, yttrium, and lanthanum). They are not strong metals and are easily oxidized (comparable to magnesium). The lanthanides form $+3$ ions in most compounds (Table 31.22). With the same anion, the compounds are generally less ionic as the atomic number of the metal increases. Similarly, the stability of those complexes that do form increases across the series. However, the lanthanides form far fewer complexes than the d-transition metals; the f electrons do not participate in bonding in complexes. The actinides are more variable in oxidation state than the lanthanides. Their most stable oxidation states cannot be predicted from their electron configurations. The actinides are active metals, and are more dense than the lanthanides. Compounds of both the lanthanides and actinides are often colored and paramagnetic. All the lanthanides are usually present together in the same ores, and the individual elements are extremely difficult to separate.

SIGNIFICANT TERMS

ferromagnetic
coinage metals
platinum metals
hydrate isomerism

THOUGHTS ON CHEMISTRY

A President's Statement

SOME THOUGHTS ON CHEMISTRY,
by Robert W. Parry

Is chemistry really important to our future as a nation or is it a source of our problems? Why should anyone study chemistry? . . . These are all fair and common questions demanding a reasoned answer. Here is the way I see it.

As we all know, the population of the world continues to increase while the resources of planet Earth remain constant. Concentrated mineral ores are being scattered. The entropy of the system climbs. Clearly our hopes for a better life must involve better and more enlightened use of our resources. We must get needed materials from lower and lower grade raw materials. Our processes must get more and more efficient. Undesirable waste materials must be returned in suitable form to the use-cycle. Knowledge is the key to our hopes and dreams—knowledge about science and about the immutable natural laws that govern the world in which we live.

Chemistry is central to our quest for this scientific knowledge. It looks toward physics and mathematics on one hand and toward biology and medicine on the other. Almost any serious effort in science . . . must involve chemistry at some level. For example, the new field of molecular biology, with its promise in medicine, involves the chemistry of giant molecules that are taken apart and reconstructed to achieve a given goal. New techniques are being used, but standard chemical principles of structure and dynamics underlie the entire operation. Looking toward physics, the new field of optical communication is in commercial development today because of spectacular advances in the preparation of ultra-clear glass. Chemistry is truly the central science that offers fantastic opportunities for the future.

Those of us who have elected to study and practice chemistry have both a responsibility and an opportunity to serve mankind in a crucial period of the world's technological history. The benefits to humanity are large; failure is unthinkable.

Robert W. Parry, President, American Chemical Society 1982, "Some Thoughts on Chemistry and the American Chemical Society," *The Philter,* Student Affiliate Newsletter, American Chemical Society, **14,** No. 3 (Spring, 1982).

QUESTIONS

d-Transition Metals

31.1 Identify the energy levels that are being filled with electrons for each of the three d-transition series. Why do many chemists consider zinc, cadmium, and mercury to be representative metals?

31.2 Briefly describe some of the physical properties of the d-transition elements. Name some of the characteristic chemical properties of d-transition metals and their ions.

31.3 Zirconium and hafnium are very much alike in their chemical and physical properties even though they are in different periods in the periodic table. Why are they so similar?

31.4 What are the relationships between the maximum oxidation states and the electron configurations for the metals of the scandium, titanium, vanadium, chromium, and manganese families?

31.5 Compare the bonding in compounds formed by transition elements in their higher and lower common oxidation states.

31.6 Name some elements that are ferromagnetic. What does this term mean? How does ferromagnetism differ from paramagnetism?

31.7 Name the coinage metals. Why are these metals used for this purpose?

31.8 Name the platinum metals. Why are these metals grouped together even though they are not in the same periodic table family?

Properties of Selected d-Transition Metals

31.9 Name the chief ore of chromium. How is this ore treated to produce chromium metal?

31.10 What are the three most common oxidation states of chromium? Which of these is most common? What properties will chromium in the other two oxidation states have?

31.11 Define the term "hydrate isomerism." Illustrate this type of isomerism by writing three formulas of compounds all having the empirical formula $CrCl_3 \cdot 6H_2O$.

31.12 Write chemical equations illustrating the amphoteric behavior of chromium(III) hydroxide.

31.13 What is wrong with the statement "Chromate ion acts as a strong oxidizing agent in acidic solution"?

31.14 From its general reactivity and its position in the electromotive series, would you expect manganese to occur in nature as the sulfide or the oxide? Name the primary ore of manganese.

31.15 What are the most common oxidation states of manganese? What use is made of MnO_2 and MnO_4^-?

31.16 Why is solid MnO_2 an electrical conductor?

31.17 Outline the steps and write the chemical equations for the production of potassium permanganate from manganese dioxide.

31.18 Write the half-reactions and overall equation for the disproportionation of MnO_4^{2-} in an acidic solution.

31.19 What are the common oxidation states of iron? What are the common names for the simple cations having these oxidation states?

31.20 Write the formulas for the common oxides of iron. What is the oxidation state of iron in each of them?

31.21 Write the formula for iron pyrite. What is the oxidation number of iron in this compound? Explain.

31.22 Identify the oxidation state(s) of iron in the compound $KFe[Fe(CN)_6]$. Is there more than one answer to this question? Explain.

31.23 What are some of the commercial uses of cobalt and nickel?

31.24 Anhydrous nickel chloride is yellow. When this substance is dissolved in water, a green solution is formed. Upon addition of $NH_3(aq)$, an apple green precipitate forms which, upon addition of more ammonia, dissolves, giving a deep blue solution. Explain these changes.

31.25 Compare the relative reactivities of copper, silver, and gold by discussing briefly their reactions with air, nonoxidizing acids, and oxidizing acids.

31.26 To extract gold and silver from impure lead, the mixture is extracted with molten zinc. How can these metals be recovered from the zinc?

31.27 Write chemical equations describing the reaction between Cu^{2+} and $H_2S(aq)$ and the subsequent addition of $Na_2S(aq)$.

31.28 How is silver nitrate prepared? What are some of the uses for this compound?

f-Transition Elements

31.29 Write the chemical outershell electron configurations for atoms of the *f*-transition elements. Which electrons are primarily involved in chemical bonding?

31.30 What is the most common oxidation state for the lanthanides? Write the general formulas of the oxides, nitrides, and halides.

31.31 Compare the number of complexes formed by the *f*-transition elements to those formed by the *d*-transition elements. Why is there a significant difference? Would you expect lanthanum ion or lutetium ion to be more prone to form complexes?

Additional Questions

31.32 A student placed clean samples of Mn, Fe, Ni, and Cu into test tubes containing hydrochloric acid and observed gas bubbles being formed in the test tubes containing Mn, Fe, and Ni. (a) Write chemical equations for these reactions. A student with somewhat poorer laboratory technique performed the same experiment without cleaning the surfaces of the metals and reported gas bubbles in the test tubes containing Mn, Fe, and Ni and a change of color on the Cu surface. (b) What reaction did the second student see in the test tube containing the Cu? Write an equation describing this reaction.

A surprising number of students each year insist that Cu reacts with HCl. This is incorrect. However, Cu will react with an oxidizing acid such as HNO_3. (c) Write the chemical equation for this reaction and explain the difference in reactivity.

31.33 Which of the following are redox reactions. Identify the oxidizing and reducing agent in each of the redox reactions.
(a) $Cr(OH)_3(s) + 3OH^- \longrightarrow [Cr(OH)_6]^{3-}$
(b) $6Fe^{2+} + Cr_2O_7^{2-} + 14H^+ \longrightarrow 6Fe^{3+} + 2Cr^{3+} + 7H_2O(l)$
(c) $[Ag(NH_3)_2]^+ + Cl^- + 2H^+ \longrightarrow AgCl(s) + 2NH_4^+$
(d) $[Au(CN)_2]^- + e^- \longrightarrow Au(s) + 2CN^-$

31.34 Repeat Question 31.33 for:
(a) $3MnO_4^{2-} + 4H^+ \longrightarrow 2MnO_4^- + MnO_2(s) + 2H_2O(l)$
(b) $2[Co(CN)_6]^{4-} + 2H_2O(l) \longrightarrow$
$$2[Co(CN)_6]^{3-} + H_2(g) + 2OH^-$$
(c) $(NH_4)_2Cr_2O_7(s) \xrightarrow{\Delta} Cr_2O_3(s) + N_2(g) + 4H_2O(g)$
(d) $[Cu(H_2O)_4]^{2+} + 4NH_3(aq) \longrightarrow [Cu(NH_3)_4]^{2+} + 4H_2O(l)$

31.35 Classify each of the following reactions according to the reaction types listed in Tables 17.2 and 17.7:
(a) $Cr_2O_3(s) + 6OH^- + 3H_2O(l) \longrightarrow 2[Cr(OH)_6]^{3-}$
(b) $8Al(s) + 3Fe_3O_4(s) \xrightarrow{\Delta} 4Al_2O_3(s) + 9Fe(l)$
(c) $Fe_2O_3(s) + 3CCl_4(g) \xrightarrow{\Delta} Fe_2Cl_6(g) + 3COCl_2(g)$
(d) $Fe^{3+} + Cr^{2+} \longrightarrow Fe^{2+} + Cr^{3+}$

31.36 Repeat Question 31.35 for:
(a) $2Eu^{2+} + 2H^+ \longrightarrow 2Eu^{3+} + H_2(g)$
(b) $[Ag(NH_3)_2]^+ + 2CN^- \longrightarrow [Ag(CN)_2]^- + 2NH_3(aq)$
(c) $2La(s) + N_2(g) \xrightarrow{\Delta} 2LaN(s)$
(d) $Th(s) + 4H^+ \longrightarrow Th^{4+} + 2H_2(g)$

31.37 Predict the major products of the following reactions:
(a) $Pr(s) + HCl(aq) \xrightarrow{\Delta}$
(b) $MnO_2(s) + HBr(aq) \longrightarrow$
(c) $Fe_3O_4(s) + CO(g) \xrightarrow{\Delta}$
(d) $[Au(CN)_2]^- + Zn(s) \longrightarrow$

31.38 Repeat Question 31.37 for:
(a) $Cr_2O_7^{2-} + OH^- \longrightarrow$
(b) $Mn^{2+} + OCl^- + OH^- \longrightarrow$
(c) $FeS_2(s) + O_2(g) \xrightarrow{\Delta}$
(d) $MnO_4^- + Fe^{2+} + H^+ \longrightarrow$

31.39 Write balanced equations for the following chemical reactions: (a) chromate–dichromate equilibrium in aqueous solution, (b) preparation of $K_2MnO_4(s)$ from $MnO_2(s)$ at elevated temperature, (c) reaction of $Fe^{2+}(aq)$ with excess $CN^-(aq)$, and (d) reaction of neodymium(III) oxide(s) with aqueous HCl (net ionic).

31.40* The presence of Fe, Co, and Ni in an alloy can be confirmed by dissolving the alloy in a nonoxidizing acid to form Fe^{2+}, Co^{2+}, and Ni^{2+} and then performing the following series of qualitative analysis separations and tests on the resulting solution: (a) The metal ions are precipitated in alkaline solution as FeS, CoS, and NiS by H_2S; (b) dilute HCl is added to dissolve the more soluble FeS, and the Fe^{2+} is thus separated from the other cations; (c) the CoS and NiS are dissolved in concentrated HNO_3, forming Co^{2+} and Ni^{2+}; (d) the Fe^{2+} is oxidized to Fe^{3+} by HNO_3; (e) a red complex, $[Fe(CNS)]^{2+}$, is formed by adding a few crystals of NH_4CNS to Fe^{3+}; (f) ammonia is added to the solution containing Co^{2+} and Ni^{2+} to form the hexaammine complexes; (g) to half of the solution of the hexaammines, dimethylgloxime is added to form the red precipitate $[Ni(DMG)_2]$; and (h) to the other half of the solution of the hexaammines, HCl is added to destroy the complex and then a few crystals of NH_4CNS are added to form the blue complex $[Co(CNS)_4]^{2-}$. Write chemical equations for the reactions involved in these eight steps.

31.41* A sample of copper metal was treated as follows: (a) Concentrated nitric acid was poured on it, giving at first a green and then a blue solution and a brown gas, (b) a dilute solution of ammonia was added, forming a very dark blue solution, (c) zinc was added, producing a colorless solution and a slime of finely divided metal, (d) the metal slime was separated, dried, and then heated in the air to form a black powder, (e) the black powder was added to a dilute solution of HCl, forming a blue solution, (f) a solution of NaOH was added, forming a blue gelatinous precipitate, (g) the blue precipitate changed to a black precipitate upon boiling, (h) the black precipitate reacted with a solution of H_2SO_4 to form a blue solution, (i) the blue solution was slowly evaporated to form blue crystals, and (j) the blue crystals were heated to form very light blue, nearly white crystals. Identify the form of the copper after each process and write a chemical equation for each process.

Answers to Selected Questions

31.13 In acidic solution, the dichromate ion, which does act as a strong oxidizing agent, is the major species present.

31.21 FeS_2, $+2$, the sulfur is present as $[S_2]^{2-}$

31.27 $Cu^{2+} + H_2S(aq) \rightarrow CuS(s) + 2H^+$, $\quad CuS(s) + S^{2-} \rightarrow [CuS_2]^{2-}$

31.30 $+3$, M_2O_3, MN, MX_3

31.32 (a) $M(s) + 2HCl(aq) \rightarrow MCl_2(aq) + H_2(g)$ where M = Mn, Fe, Ni; (b) reaction of the oxide coating, $CuO(s) + 2HCl(aq) \rightarrow CuCl_2(aq) + H_2O(l)$, (c) $3Cu(s) + 8HNO_3(aq) \rightarrow 3Cu(NO_3)_2(aq) + 2NO(g) + 4H_2O(l)$

31.34 a, b, c; oxidizing agents: (a) MnO_4^{2-}, (b) H_2O, (c) $Cr_2O_7^{2-}$; reducing agents: (a) MnO_4^{2-}, (b) $[Co(CN)_6]^{4-}$, (c) NH_4^+

31.36 (a) redox—electron transfer between ions in aqueous solution, (b) nonredox—displacement, (c) redox—combination of two elements to give a compound, (d) redox—displacement of one element from a compound by another element

31.38 (a) CrO_4^{2-}, $H_2O(l)$; (b) $MnO_2(s)$, Cl^-, $H_2O(l)$; (c) $Fe_2O_3(s)$, $SO_2(g)$; (d) Mn^{2+}, Fe^{3+}, $H_2O(l)$

31.41 (a) Cu^{2+} or $[Cu(H_2O)_4]^{2+}$, $Cu(s) + 4HNO_3(aq) \rightarrow Cu^{2+} + 2NO_3^- + 2NO_2(g) + 2H_2O(l)$; (b) $[Cu(NH_3)_4]^{2+}$, $Cu^{2+} + 4NH_3(aq) \rightarrow [Cu(NH_3)_4]^{2+}$; (c) Cu, $[Cu(NH_3)_4]^{2+} + Zn(s) \rightarrow Cu(s) + [Zn(NH_3)_4]^{2+}$; (d) CuO, $2Cu(s) + O_2(g) \rightarrow 2CuO(s)$; (e) Cu^{2+}, $CuO(s) + 2HCl(aq) \rightarrow Cu^{2+} + 2Cl^- + H_2O(l)$; (f) $Cu(OH)_2$, $Cu^{2+} + 2OH^- \rightarrow Cu(OH)_2(s)$; (g) CuO, $Cu(OH)_2(s) \xrightarrow{\Delta} CuO(s) + H_2O(g)$; (h) Cu^{2+}, $CuO(s) + H_2SO_4(aq) \rightarrow Cu^{2+} + SO_4^{2-} + H_2O(l)$; (i) $CuSO_4 \cdot 5H_2O(s)$; (j) $CuSO_4$, $CuSO_4 \cdot 5H_2O(s) \xrightarrow{\Delta} CuSO_4(s) + 5H_2O(g)$

PROBLEMS

Review of Principles

31.1 A 1.00 g sample of iron combined with 215 mL of $O_2(g)$ measured at 762 Torr and 20.0 °C. Determine the formula of the oxide formed.

31.2 A photograph is toned with a solution of $[AuCl_2]^-$. Write the equation for the toning process and state what color the tone will be. If 2.1 mg of silver is oxidized to Ag^+, what mass of gold is reduced to metal? *Answer* $Ag(s) + [AuCl_2]^- \rightarrow AgCl(s) + Cl^- + Au(s)$, sepia, 3.8 mg

31.3 Iron(II) can be oxidized to iron(III) by MnO_4^- in acidic solution, the latter being reduced to Mn^{2+}. Write equations for the half-reactions for the oxidation and reduction processes and combine them to obtain the overall equation. A 0.302 g sample of iron ore is dissolved, the iron in it is reduced to Fe^{2+}, and the Fe^{2+} is oxidized using 42.79 mL of 0.0205 M $KMnO_4$. What is the percentage of iron in the sample?

31.4 In most activity series of metals, silver is listed above platinum. Show that the reaction between Ag and Pt^{2+} is favorable, given that standard reduction potentials for the Ag^+/Ag and Pt^{2+}/Pt couples are 0.799 V and 1.2 V, respectively. However, a student observed that Ag does not reduce Pt(II) in alkaline solution. Confirm this result using $E° = 0.16$ V for the $Pt(OH)_2/Pt$ couple and 0.345 V for the Ag_2O/Ag couple.

31.5 Air oxidation of solutions of Fe^{2+} presents a problem in keeping these solutions in the laboratory. Given that the $E° = -0.440$ V for the Fe^{2+}/Fe couple and 0.771 V for Fe^{3+}/Fe^{2+} couple, show that simply putting a piece of Fe in a solution of Fe^{2+} will maintain the iron in the $+2$ state.

31.6* The shorthand designation for the "alkaline accumulator" (or Edison or ferro–nickel cell) is

steel$|$Fe$(s)|$Fe(OH)$_2(s)|$KOH$(aq)|$Ni(OH)$_2(s)|$NiOOH$(s)|$steel

Write equations for the half-reactions for the oxidation and reduction processes and write the overall equation for the cell. The standard reduction potential for the $Fe(OH)_2/Fe$ couple is -0.877 V and the overall potential of the cell is 1.40 V. What is the standard reduction potential for the $NiOOH/Ni(OH)_2$ couple? *Answer* $Fe + 2OH^- \rightarrow Fe(OH)_2 + 2e^-$, $NiOOH + H_2O + e^- \rightarrow Ni(OH)_2 + OH^-$, $Fe(s) + 2NiOOH(s) + 2H_2O(l) \rightarrow Fe(OH)_2(s) + 2Ni(OH)_2(s)$; 0.52 V

31.7 The total surface area of a car bumper is 1750 sq inches. The bumper is to be chrome plated to a thickness of 0.0003 inch in a Cr(VI) solution in one hour. What must the current be to perform this plating assuming 20% efficiency? The density of Cr is 7.20 g/cm^3.

31.8 At 25 °C, $K_{sp} = 2.8 \times 10^{-13}$ for $PbCrO_4$. Calculate the solubility of this salt in pure water and in a solution containing 0.100 M Pb^{2+}. *Answer* 5.3×10^{-7} M, 2.8×10^{-12} M

31.9 What is the equilibrium concentration of Fe^{2+} in a solution that is 0.050 M in $[Fe(C_2O_4)_2]^{2-}$ and 0.050 M in $C_2O_4^{2-}$? $K_d = 2 \times 10^{-8}$ for $[Fe(C_2O_4)_2]^{2-}$.

31.10* The standard state free energy of formation at 25 °C is -727.9 kJ/mol for CrO_4^{2-}, -1301.2 kJ/mol for $Cr_2O_7^{2-}$, 0 for H^+, and -237.2 kJ/mol for $H_2O(l)$. What is the equilibrium constant for the reaction

$$2CrO_4^{2-} + 2H^+ \rightleftharpoons Cr_2O_7^{2-} + H_2O(l)$$

To what pH must a 0.100 M CrO_4^{2-} solution be adjusted so that the concentration of CrO_4^{2-} and $Cr_2O_7^{2-}$ are equal? *Answer* 3×10^{14}, 6.5

31.11 During 1.00 h, 3.4 mg of $^{95}_{43}Tc$ underwent radioactive decay by electron capture. The original sample size was 0.1000 g. Write the equation for the nuclear reaction for the decay process and calculate the half-life of this isotope.

CHAPTER 32

The Chemistry of Complexes

Platinum (II) chloride is a stable greenish powder that is not very soluble in water. Ammonia is a simple molecular compound with covalent nitrogen–hydrogen bonds. The fact that such compounds react with each other to give completely different stable compounds was once puzzling. None of the concepts of bonding which were then current could explain why compounds with all of their "valences" satisfied would combine with each other.

In 1893 Alfred Werner proposed that metal atoms had "principal" valences and "auxiliary" valences. In compounds then written, for example, $CoCl_3 \cdot 4NH_3$, Werner showed that substituents were held to cobalt by both types of valence. In modern terms, a "principal" valence is an ionic bond and an "auxiliary" valence is a coordinate covalent bond. Today the formula for this compound is written $[Co(NH_3)_4Cl_2]Cl$. One chlorine atom is held by a principal valence (ionic bond) and the remaining chlorine atoms and the ammonia groups are held by auxiliary valences (coordinate covalent bonds).

Werner's ideas initiated the modern study of the chemistry of complexes, or "coordination compounds," which in recent years has become a very active area of inorganic chemical research and discovery. Thirty years ago, a comprehensive inorganic chemistry textbook devoted one chapter to what was then known about complexes. Today's inorganic chemistry textbooks devote up to half of their many pages to the subject. Three of today's frontier areas in inorganic chemistry—bioinorganic chemistry, organometallic chemistry, and the study of how catalysts function—are dominated by coordination chemistry.

STRUCTURE, NOMENCLATURE, AND PROPERTIES OF COMPLEXES

32.1 SOME DEFINITIONS

To review, complex ions such as

Ag^+ ion

$[Ag(NH_3)_2]^+$

NH_3 molecule ligand

Co^{3+} ion

$[CoF_6]^{3-}$

F^- ion ligand

are formed by the combination of a central metal cation and one or more molecules or anions, referred to as ligands (Section 14.10). The formation or dissociation of complex ions in aqueous solution occurs by stepwise gain or loss of the ligands. For example,

$$[Ag(NH_3)_2]^+ \rightleftharpoons [Ag(NH_3)]^+ + NH_3(aq)$$
$$[Ag(NH_3)]^+ \rightleftharpoons Ag^+ + NH_3(aq)$$

overall dissociation

$$[Ag(NH_3)_2]^+ \rightleftharpoons Ag^+ + 2NH_3(aq)$$

The equilibrium constants for such reactions are referred to as dissociation constants of complex ions (Section 21.14).

The ligands in complex ions like those just above—the classical complex ions—can be thought of as joined to the central metal ion by coordinate covalent bonds. Recall that a coordinate covalent bond (Section 9.11) is formed between a donor atom or ion, which has an unshared pair of electrons, and an acceptor atom or ion that has unoccupied orbitals that can accommodate the electron pair.

$$2H \!:\! \overset{\text{H}}{\underset{\text{H}}{\ddot{\text{N}}}} \!:\! + Ag^+ \longrightarrow \left[H \!:\! \overset{\text{H}}{\underset{\text{H}}{\ddot{\text{N}}}} \!:\! Ag \!:\! \overset{\text{H}}{\underset{\text{H}}{\ddot{\text{N}}}} \!:\! H \right]^+ \quad \text{or} \quad [Ag(NH_3)_2]^+$$

Complex ions are members of a large and very important class of chemical compounds generally referred to as complexes. A **complex** is formed between a metal atom or ion that accepts one or more electron pairs, and ions or neutral molecules that contain nonmetal atoms which donate electron pairs. The entire complex can be charged or it can be neutral. Neutral complexes result when both the metal and the ligands are uncharged, or when the positive charge on the metal ion is balanced by oppositely charged ligands. The term "complex" is usually reserved for metals combined with donors that also can exist *independently*, either in the pure state or as ions in solution. Most metal atoms or ions can accept more than one pair of electrons, for example,

$$4 \!:\! NH_3 + Ni^{2+} \longrightarrow [Ni(\!:\!NH_3)_4]^{2+} \tag{32.1}$$

$$4 \!:\! CO + Ni \longrightarrow [Ni(\!:\!CO)_4] \tag{32.2}$$

$$4 \!:\! \ddot{\underset{..}{C}}l \!:\!^- + Pt^{2+} \longrightarrow [Pt(\!:\!\ddot{\underset{..}{C}}l\!:\!)_4]^{2-} \tag{32.3}$$

$$2 \!:\! \ddot{\underset{..}{C}}l \!:\!^- + 2 \!:\! NH_3 + Pt^{2+} \longrightarrow [(\!:\!\ddot{\underset{..}{C}}l\!:\!)_2 Pt(\!:\!NH_3)_2] \tag{32.4}$$

$$4 \!:\! NO_2^- + Pt^{2+} \longrightarrow [Pt(\!:\!NO_2)_4]^{2-} \tag{32.5}$$

The donor atom may be part of a molecule (Equations 32.1, 32.2), it may be an ion (Equations 32.3 and 32.4), or it may be part of an ion (Equation 32.5). The charge on a complex is the sum of the charges of the constituent parts. For example, in $[PtCl_4]^{2-}$ the charge is found by adding $+2$ (for the platinum) and $4 \times (-1)$ for the four Cl^- ions to obtain the charge of -2 that the complex carries.

The ligand in a complex is said to be "coordinated to" the atom which is in the center of the new structure. In the nickel–ammonia complex ion shown in Equation (32.1), the ammonia molecules are the ligands, and they are coordinated to the nickel(II) ion. We might point out here that the terminology of complexes derives from coordinate covalent bonding, but, as with all types of compounds, bonds in complexes cover the range from covalent to ionic.

Any neutral compound that contains a metal atom and its associated ligands is called a **coordination compound.** Such a compound may be formed between a complex ion and other ions, for example, $[Ag(NH_3)_2]^+Cl^-$ or $(K^+)_2[Pt(NO_2)_4]^{2-}$. Or the complex itself may be neutral, for example, $[Pt(NH_3)_2(NO_2)_2]$, in which platinum has oxidation state $+2$, or $[Ni(CO)_4]$, in which nickel has oxidation state zero. The formula of the complex is usually enclosed in square brackets.

The **coordination number** of the central metal atom or ion in a complex is the number of nonmetal atoms bonded to that atom or ion (Table 32.1). The most common coordination numbers are two, four, and six. A number of complexes in which the metal has a coordination number of five are known. Coordination numbers of three are rare. Other odd coordination numbers, particularly seven and nine, are less common than even ones. Coordination numbers of ten and twelve are also rare.

Table 32.1
Common Coordination Numbers of Cations

Ag^+	2	Hg^{2+}	4	Al^{3+}	4, 6	Pd^{4+}	6
Au^+	2, 4	Ca^{2+}	6	Au^{3+}	4	Pt^{4+}	6
Cu^+	2, 4	Co^{2+}	4, 6	Co^{3+}	6	Zr^{4+}	8
Li^+	4	Cu^{2+}	4, 6	Cr^{3+}	6	Hf^{4+}	8
Tl^+	2	Fe^{2+}	6	Fe^{3+}	6	Th^{4+}	8
		Ni^{2+}	4, 5, 6	Ir^{3+}	6		
		Pb^{2+}	4	Os^{3+}	6		
		Pd^{2+}	4	Sc^{3+}	6		
		Pt^{2+}	4				
		V^{2+}	6				
		Zn^{2+}	4				

To give a few examples—for Ag^+, the coordination number is commonly two, as in $[Ag(CN)_2]^-$, but sometimes it is three, as in $[Ag(CN)_3]^{2-}$. Nickel(II) can have coordination numbers of four, five, or six, as in $[Ni(CN)_4]^{2-}$, $[Ni(CN)_5]^{3-}$, and $[Ni(NH_3)_6]^{2+}$. With cobalt(III), the coordination number is almost invariably six; and with zirconium(IV) and hafnium(IV), it is often eight, as in $[ZrF_8]^{4-}$ and $[HfF_8]^{4-}$. [We note that a few species, such as $[PF_6]^-$ or $[ICl_4]^-$, are of the same type, and differ only in having a central nonmetal.]

EXAMPLE 32.1
Structure of Complexes

How would you describe each species listed below? For each species listed, identify the ligands and give the coordination number and oxidation number of the central atom or ion.

(a) $[Co(NH_3)_5(SO_4)]Br$ (c) $[Ir(NH_3)_3Cl_3]$
(b) $[Ag(CN)_2]^-$

(a) This is a coordination compound with the complex ion $[Co(NH_3)_5(SO_4)]^+$ as the cation. The ligands are five ammonia molecules and a sulfate ion, so the coordination number of the central cobalt ion is 6. To give the complex ion its +1 charge, the cobalt must be in its +3 oxidation state.

$$\overset{+3}{[Co(NH_3)_5}\overset{-2}{(SO_4^{2-})]^+}$$

[Note that SO_4^{2-}, although it has a charge of -2, occupies only one coordination position; see Table 32.2.]

(b) This is a complex ion. There are two CN^- ions as ligands, so the coordination number of the silver ion is 2. Silver has only one common oxidation state, +1, and this gives the complex ion its -1 charge.

$$\overset{+1}{[Ag}\overset{2\times(-1)}{(CN)_2]^-}$$

(c) This is a coordination compound. The absence of any other species (or of a charge) outside the bracket shows that this is a neutral molecule, not an ion. The ligands are ammonia molecules and chloride ions. The coordination number of the iridium is six, and it must have a +3 oxidation number.

$$\overset{+3}{[Ir(NH_3)_3}\overset{3\times(-1)}{Cl_3]}$$

Exercise Identify each of the following, (a) $[Pt(NH_3)_5Cl]Cl_3$, (b) $[Mn(H_2O)_6]^{3+}$, and (c) $[CoF_6]^{3-}$; also identify the ligands and give the coordination number and the oxidation number for the central atom or ion. *Answer* (a) coordination compound containing complex cation, NH_3 and Cl^-, 6, +4; (b) complex cation, H_2O, 6, +3; (c) complex anion, F^-, 6, +3

32.2 NOMENCLATURE OF COMPLEXES

A few simple rules will cover what you need to know about naming complexes:

1. The ligands are named first; the prefixes di, tri, tetra, and so on are used to indicate the number of each kind of ligand present. [Sometimes the prefixes bis (2 ligands), tris (3 ligands), and tetrakis (4 ligands) are also used, especially when the ligand name is complicated or already includes di, etc.] Negative ligands are given names that end in -o.

2. The ligand names are given in alphabetical order. (In an older system, negative ligands were named first, neutral ones second, and positive ones last.) Some ligands have familiar names also used in naming other types of compounds (e.g., chloro, cyano); others have names special to complexes (e.g., carbonato, CO_3^{2-}; aqua, H_2O). Table 32.2 lists the names of the most common ligands. Note that the ammine group — two m's — is NH_3.

3. The name of the central metal atom or ion followed by its oxidation state in parentheses is given after the ligand names. The metal name is *not* separated from the ligand names by a space.

4. When a complex ion has a negative charge, the name of the central metal atom is given the ending *ate*. For some of the elements, the ion name is based on the Latin name from which the symbol is derived, for example, ferrate for iron, Fe; plumbate for lead, Pb. When naming only the ion, the word "ion" is always used in the name.

Using these rules, the complexes formed in reactions (32.1)–(32.5) receive the following names:

$[Ni(NH_3)_4]^{2+}$	tetraamminenickel(II) ion
$[PtCl_4]^{2-}$	tetrachloroplatinate(II) ion
$[Pt(NH_3)_2Cl_2]$	diamminedichloroplatinum(II)
$[Pt(NO_2)_4]^{2-}$	tetranitroplatinate(II) ion
$[Ni(CO)_4]$	tetracarbonylnickel(0)
	(commonly called "nickel carbonyl")

In naming a coordination compound, the name of the cation is given first as usual, followed by the name of the anion.

$K^+[Pt(NH_3)Cl_5]^-$	potassium amminepentachloroplatinate(IV)
$[Co(NH_3)_4SO_4]^+NO_3^-$	tetraamminesulfatocobalt(III) nitrate

Table 32.2
Common Ligands The donor atom in each ligand is shown in color. The NO_2^- ion can bond as a ligand through either the N atom (nitro) or the O atom (nitrito). The SCN⁻ group can bond as a ligand through either S or N, depending chiefly on the metal in the complex. In fact, the SCN⁻ or CN⁻ groups can attach themselves to two metal ions simultaneously.

Ligand	Name	Ligand	Name
F⁻	fluoro	O^{2-}	oxo
Cl⁻	chloro	CO_3^{2-}†	carbonato
Br⁻	bromo	$C_2O_4^{2-}$†	oxalato
I⁻	iodo	OSO_3^{2-}	sulfato (SO_4^{2-})
CN⁻	cyano	OSO_2^{2-}	sulfito (SO_3^{2-})
NCS⁻	isothiocyanato	NH_3	ammine
SCN⁻	thiocyanato	H_2O	aqua
ONO⁻	nitrito	CO	carbonyl
ONO⁻	nitro	NO	nitrosyl
OH⁻	hydroxo	PR_3	trialkyl- or triarylphosphine

† Carbonate and oxalate ions usually bond to the central metal atom through two oxygen atoms (see Section 32.3).

EXAMPLE 32.2
Nomenclature of Complexes

Write the names for the following two complexes: (a) $[Cd(CN)_4]^{2-}$ (b) $[Co(NH_3)_4(CO_3)]Cl$

(a) As a ligand, CN^- is named cyano (Table 32.2). With a total ligand charge of $4 \times (-1) = -4$ and a charge on the complex ion of -2, the cadmium ion must have a $+2$ charge. Naming the ligand first and changing "cadmium" to "cadmate" because the ion has a negative charge gives the compound name as tetracyano-cadmate(II) ion.

(b) In this coordination compound, the complex ion is the cation ($+1$ charge) and should be named first. The two types of ligands are CO_3^{2-}, carbonato, and NH_3, ammine. The total ligand charge is $1 \times (-2) = -2$ (for the single CO_3^{2-} ion), so the cobalt ion must have a $+3$ charge. The complete name is tetraamminecarbonatocobalt(III) chloride.

Exercise Name the following: (a) $K_4[Fe(CN)_6]$, and (b) $[Co(NH_3)_2(NO_2)_4]^-$. *Answer* (a) potassium hexacyanoferrate(II), (b) diamminetetranitrocobaltate(III) ion, or diamminetetranitritocobaltate(III) ion

EXAMPLE 32.3
Nomenclature of Complexes

Write the formulas for
(a) sodium tetrachlorodicyanochromate(III),
(b) pentaammineaquacobalt(III) chloride.

(a) In this coordination compound the "ate" ending shows that the complex ion is the anion. With six ligands, each with a charge of -1 (four Cl^- and two CN^-), the total ligand charge is -6. With chromate(III), Cr^{3+}, as the central ion, the complex ion must have a charge of -3. The formula is written as $Na_3[CrCl_4(CN)_2]$.

(b) Here, the complex ion is the cation. The ligands are H_2O and NH_3. The cobalt is present as the $+3$ ion and, as both ligands are neutral, this is the charge of the complex ion. The formula is, therefore, $[Co(H_2O)(NH_3)_5]Cl_3$.

Exercise Write formulas for the following: (a) hexaamminechromium(III) chloride, (b) pentaamminechlorochromium(III) chloride, (c) tetraaquanickel(II) ion, and (d) diiodocuprate(I) ion. *Answer* (a) $[Cr(NH_3)_6]Cl_3$, (b) $[Cr(NH_3)_5Cl]Cl_2$, (c) $[Ni(H_2O)_4]^{2+}$, (d) $[CuI_2]^-$

32.3 CHELATION

In many cases, two or more atoms with unshared pairs of electrons are present in the same ion or molecule, and if their spatial properties are favorable (that is, if they are not too close together or too far apart), they may coordinate to the same metal atom or ion to form a ring. The carbonate (CO_3^{2-}) and oxalate ($C_2O_4^{2-}$) ions usually behave in this way

carbonato complex   *oxalato complex*

but the carbonate ion does not form a very stable complex, for the four-membered ring is highly strained. Five- and six-membered rings are much less strained and are

Table 32.3
Some Common Chelating Agents The electron pairs available for donation are shown in color.

Formula	Abbreviation	Formula	Abbreviation
Form five-membered rings		**Form six-membered rings**	
$NH_2CH_2CH_2NH_2$	en	$NH_2CH_2CH_2CH_2NH_2$	tm
ethylenediamine *(bidentate)*		*trimethylenediamine* *(bidentate)*	
$(NH_2CH_2CO)^-$ with O above	gly	(acetylacetonate structure)	acac
glycinate ion *(bidentate)*		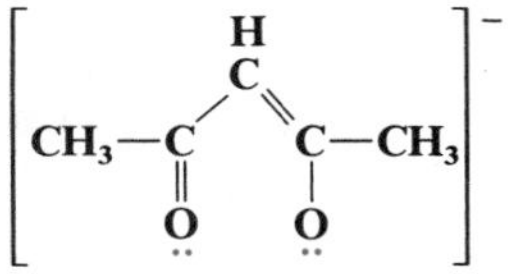 *acetylacetonate ion* *(bidentate)*	
$\begin{bmatrix} :O-C=O \\ :O-C=O \end{bmatrix}^{2-}$	ox		
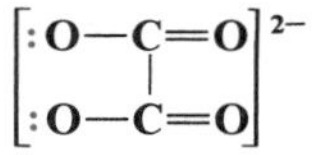 *oxalate ion* *(bidentate)*			
$NH_2CH_2CH_2NHCH_2CH_2NH_2$	dien		
diethylenetriamine *(tridentate)*			

very common. Most of the ligands that form such rings are organic molecules or anions. A few examples are listed in Table 32.3.

The phenomenon of ring formation by a ligand in a complex is called **chelation** and the ring formed is called a **chelate ring** (pronounced "key-late," from the Greek *kela* meaning "crab's claw"). A ligand which contains two donor atoms by which it can form a chelate ring is referred to as **bidentate.** The carbonato and oxalato ligands pictured above are bidentate.

If a molecule or ion contains more than two potential donor atoms (a polydentate ligand; Table 32.4), it may attach itself to the metal atom or ion through all of them and thus form several "fused" rings. (By "fused" rings, we mean rings that have one or more bonds in common.) For example, each diethylenetriamine molecule is **tridentate**—it has three donor atoms and forms two fused rings in the following complex:

Bidentate ligand: 2 donor atoms, forms chelate ring
Tridentate ligand: 3 donor atoms, forms 2 fused rings

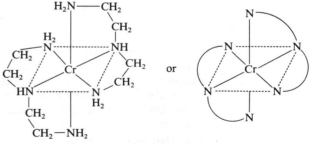

bis(diethylenetriamine)chromium(III) ion
$[Cr(dien)_2]^{3+}$, dien is tridentate

Table 32.4
Polydentate Ligands

Number of Donor Atoms	Name
2	**bidentate**
3	**tridentate**
4	**quadridentate**
5	**quinquedentate**
6	**sexidentate**

Note the use of the abbreviation for the chelating agent in the formula and also the use of "bis" as a prefix in the name where "di" would be confusing.

Chelation greatly increases the stability of a complex. This is of tremendous value in altering the properties of metal ions by complexation. Chelating agents, also known as sequestering agents, have a great many practical applications, some of which are discussed in Section 32.8. One of the most powerful chelating ligands known is the anion of ethylenediaminetetraacetic acid (edta) (Figure 32.1a). This ion is able to attach itself to a single metal ion through six donor atoms—both nitrogen atoms and one oxygen atom of each —CH_2COO^- (acetate) group. Five chelate rings

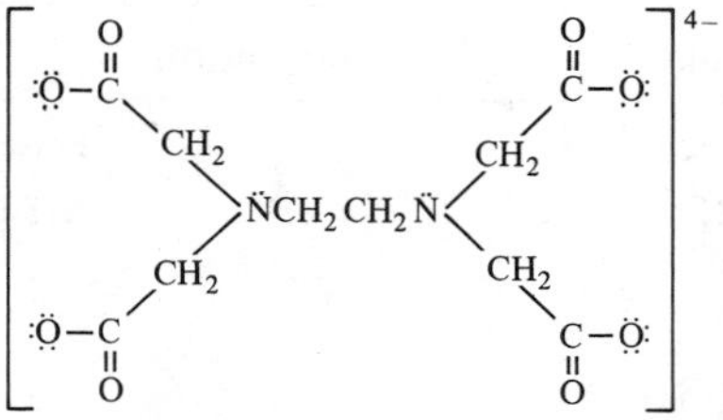

(a) Ethylenediamminetetraacetic acid (edta) anion

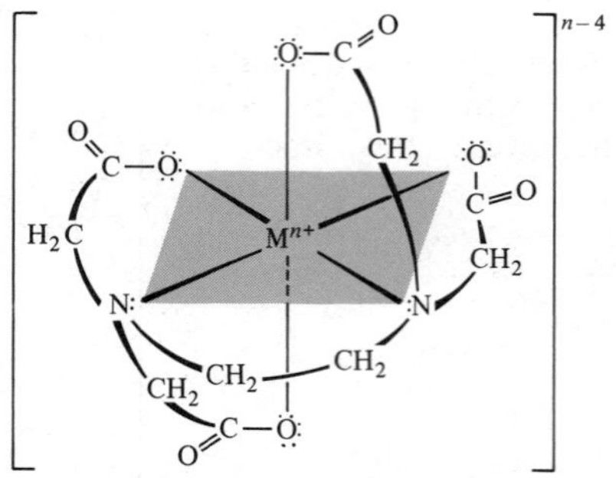

(b) edta-metal complex with five chelate rings

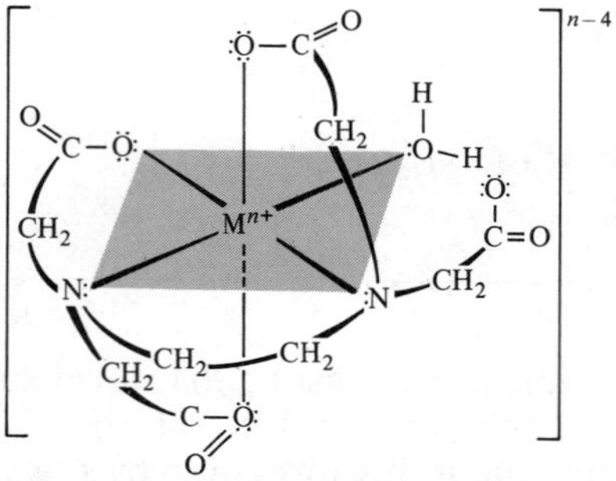

(c) edta-metal complex with four chelate rings

Figure 32.1
Ethylenediaminetetraacetic Acid and Complex Formation The edta can form five chelate rings (b), but one of the rings opens up (c) if the structure is strained.

are formed, with one central metal ion common to all of them (Figure 32.1b). The six atoms coordinated to the metal ion are located at the corners of an octahedron (see Figure 32.2). There is some strain in this structure, and this strain may overcome the stabilizing effect of the five rings. In such cases, one —CH_2COO— "arm" remains unattached, and a molecule of water or some other ligand takes its place (Figure 32.1c). If this ligand is water or another volatile neutral compound, it can be driven off by heating, with the formation of the fifth chelate ring. In aqueous solution this process may be reversed.

32.4 MOLECULAR GEOMETRY AND ISOMERISM

The metal atoms or ions and the ligands that make up a complex have definite spatial relationships with each other. As with the geometry of covalent molecules, the geometry of complexes is generally such as to allow the ligands to maintain the maximum possible distance from each other. The resulting shapes of complexes are like those of comparable covalent compounds (see Table 11.1). Complexes containing two unchelated coordinated groups, such as $[ClAgCl]^-$, are linear, and those containing four coordinated groups are either square planar, as is $[Pt(NH_3)_4]^{2+}$, or tetrahedral, as is $[Be(H_2O)_4]^{2+}$ (Figure 32.2). Two geometries occur with about equal frequency for five-coordinate complexes: square pyramidal (for example, $[CuCl_5]^{3-}$) or trigonal bipyramidal (for example, $[Ni(CN)_5]^{3-}$). Most six-coordinate complexes are octahedral, but a few are triangular prismatic.

The fixed positions of the ligands in a complex give rise to the possibility of both geometrical and optical isomerism. Geometrical, or *cis–trans,* isomers (Section 11.7b) are found when the same groups may assume different positions with respect to a rigid bond or a ring. Square-planar complexes such as $[Pt(NH_3)_2Cl_2]$ can form geometrical isomers in which the two like atoms are on adjacent *(cis)* or opposite *(trans)* corners of the square plane (Figure 32.3).

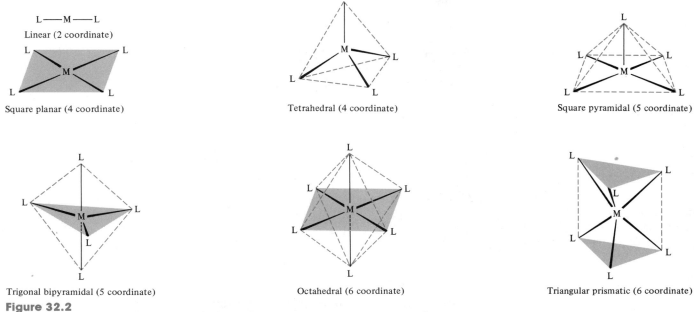

Figure 32.2
Geometry of Complexes The square planar, tetrahedral, and octahedral geometries are the most common.

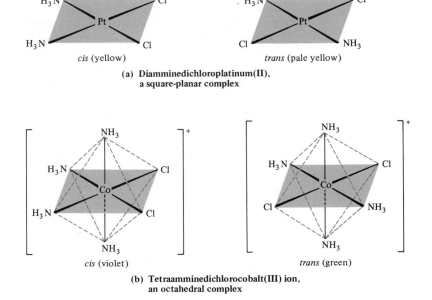

(a) Diamminedichloroplatinum(II), a square-planar complex

(b) Tetraamminedichlorocobalt(III) ion, an octahedral complex

Figure 32.3
Geometrical, *Cis-Trans,* Isomerism in Square Planar and Octahedral Complexes

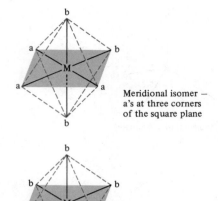

Meridional isomer —
a's at three corners
of the square plane

Facial isomer —
a's at corners of
triangular face

Figure 32.4
Geometrical Isomerism in an
Octahedral Complex of the General
Formula Ma₃b₃ A complex of this
type is $[Co(NH_3)_3(NO_2)_3]$.

The possible types of isomers of an octahedral complex depend upon how many ligands of different types are present. Octahedral complexes of the general formula Ma_2b_4, where a and b are different unidentate ligands, can have *cis* and *trans* isomers (Figure 32.3). With three of each type of ligand, $[Ma_3b_3]$, a different type of geometrical isomerism is possible, one in which the arrangements are designated as meridional *(mer)* and facial *(fac)* (Figure 32.4).

We have encountered optical isomerism, or chirality, as a property of asymmetrically substituted carbon atoms (Section 27.8). Asymmetrical isomers are not superimposable upon their mirror images. Complexes can also be optically active due to asymmetry and many of them are.

Optical activity is common in complexes that contain chelate rings. Tetrahedral four-coordinate complexes with two unsymmetrical rings are asymmetric and optically active. For example, the ligand benzoylacetonate coordinates through the two oxygen atoms to give a ring that is unsymmetrical because the two ends of the molecule are different. When two such molecules form a four-coordinate complex, as shown in Figure 32.5, the complex has two optically active isomers.

In six-coordinate complexes, if there are two chelate rings, the isomer in which the two nonchelated groups are in *cis* positions will have optical isomers. The *trans*

Figure 32.5
Optical Isomers of a Four-
Coordinate Complex Containing
Two Unsymmetrical Rings

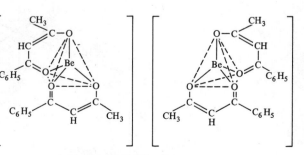

Benzoylacetonate ion

Bis(benzoylacetonate)beryllium(II)

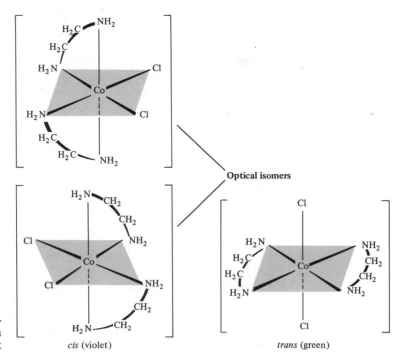

Figure 32.6
Isomers of Dichlorobis(ethylene-diammine)cobalt(III) ion, a Dichelate Octahedral Complex

cis (violet)   *trans* (green)

geometrical isomer of the same compound will not be optically active—it is superimposable on its mirror image (Figure 32.6).

If there are three chelate rings, the complex must be asymmetric, and *all* six-coordinate complexes with three chelate rings will have two optically active isomers (Figure 32.7).

It is also possible to achieve asymmetry without the presence of chelate rings. For example, an octahedral complex of the type $Ma_2b_2c_2$ is asymmetric if each donor group is adjacent to one like it (an "all *cis*" arrangement).

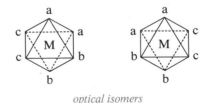

optical isomers

However, the synthesis of such compounds is difficult, and only a few are known.

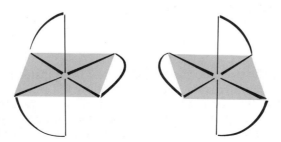

Figure 32.7
Optically Active Isomers of a Trichelate Octahedral Complex

As you might expect, with the many types of ligands that can be present in the same coordination compound, the possibility exists for structural isomerism—the occurrence of isomers in which the same groups are joined in different ways. There is linkage isomerism in which the same group can coordinate in more than one way (see NCS^- and SCN^-, or ONO^- and $NO_2{}^-$, in Table 32.2). There is also ionization isomerism, in which ligands and ions can change places, for example,

$$[Cr(NH_3)_5SO_4]Cl \qquad [Cr(NH_3)_5Cl]SO_4$$

EXAMPLE 32.4
Isomerism

How many isomers of what types would be possible for each of the following complexes?
(a) triamminetriaquacobalt(III) ion
(b) tris(ethylenediamine)cobalt(III) ion
(c) tetraamminediaquacobalt(III) ion
(d) dichlorobis(ethylenediamine)platinum(IV) chloride

(a) This complex contains three H_2O ligands and three NH_3 ligands. It is octahedral of the type Ma_3b_3 and has two geometrical isomers (facial and meridional) [see Figure 32.4].
(b) The ethylenediamine ligand is bidentate, so this is an octahedral complex with three chelate rings. It has two optically active isomers [see Figure 32.7].
(c) Here there are two H_2O ligands and four NH_3 ligands, to give an octahedral complex of the type Ma_2b_4. There are two possible *cis-trans*, geometrical isomers [see Figure 32.3].
(d) The two bidentate ethylenediamine ligands make this a dichelate, octahedral complex. There are two optical isomers—the *cis* isomers—and one *trans* isomer [see Figure 32.6].

Exercise   Describe the isomerism in (a) $K[Co(NO_2)_4(H_2O)_2]$, (b) $[NiBrCl(CN)_2]^{2-}$, and (c) $[Cr(C_2O_4)_3]^{3-}$. *Answer* (a) *cis* and *trans* isomers of the octahedral complex, (b) *cis* and *trans* isomers of the square-planar complex, (c) two optical isomers of the octahedral complex

EXAMPLE 32.5
Isomerism

Draw the structural formula for a second isomer of each of the following:

(a) The two chlorine ligands can be *trans* instead of *cis*. (The formulas of this and the other isomers are given below.)
(b) In the isomer shown, the two NH_3 ligands are *trans* and the two Cl^- ligands are *cis*. Two other isomers are possible: (a) NH_3 ligands *cis* and Cl^- ligands *trans*, or (b) both NH_3's and Cl's *cis* [this is a pair of optically active isomers].
(c) This is an example of the structural, or linkage, isomerism possible when a

ligand can coordinate in different ways. The nitrito group (ONO)⁻ could be a nitro group (NO₂)⁻.

(d) This complex illustrates ionization isomerism in which ligands and ions in a coordination compound can change places.

(a)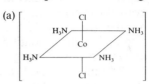

(b)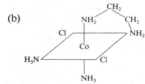

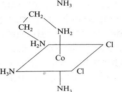 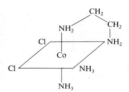

(c) 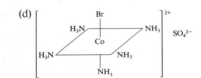 (d)

Exercise Draw the structural formulas for the isomers of $[Co(NH_3)Br(en)_2]^{2+}$.
Answer

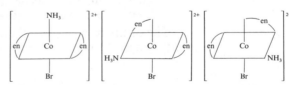

32.5 STABILITY AND LABILITY

<u>All metal ions have the ability to form complex ions.</u> Those with small radius and high charge, especially those that also have vacant d orbitals—the transition metal ions—do so most readily, but even the sodium ion, with its comparatively large radius and its small charge, forms complexes. Nearly all sodium complexes, however, are immediately destroyed by water, probably because of the formation of the more stable $[Na(H_2O)_x]^+$. The complexes of the beryllium ion, Be^{2+}, and the aluminum ion, Al^{3+}, are more stable toward dissociation in water than are those of the sodium ion. Ions of the heavier representative elements yield still more stable complexes. For example, the ions $[Zn(CN)_4]^{2-}$, $[Cd(NH_3)_4]^{2+}$, and $[SnS_3]^{2-}$ remain intact in aqueous solution, and their salts can be crystallized from these solutions.

In discussing chemical reactions we noted that when we refer to a substance as "stable" we are talking about thermodynamic stability. The dissociation constant of a complex is a measure of its thermodynamic stability (recall that $\Delta G° = -2.303RT$ log K). The smaller the value of K_d, the smaller the tendency for a complex to dissociate and the greater its thermodynamic stability.

The overall dissociation constants of some complexes are shown in Table 32.5. The data given in Table 32.5 illustrate several interesting facts about the stability of complexes:

1. Metal ions vary widely in the stability of the complex ions which they form, even those with the same ligand and those with the same coordination number (in Table 32.5, 2, 3, and 5; 7 and 8).

2. The higher the oxidation state of the metal, the more stable are the complexes it forms with a given ligand. This is illustrated by 16 and 17, 25 and 26, 27 and 28. The ligand–metal bond strength is greater for the higher metal oxidation states.

3. The stability of halide complexes often decreases in the order $I^- > Br^- > Cl^-$ (compare 7, 10, and 12).

4. The cyanide ion is like the halide ions in many respects, but far exceeds them in the stability of its complexes (compare 7, 10, and 12 with 14).

5. Chelate ring formation greatly increases the stability of complexes. Monoamines are rather poor coordinating agents (33), but diamines, if they can form five-membered rings, give extremely stable complexes (24). Much of the extra stabilization of complexes by chelation is attributable to the entropy factor (Section 22.5). Compare the K_d value for $[Cd(NH_3)_4]^{2+}$ (2), which has four unidentate ligands, with that of $[Cd(en)_2]^{2+}$ (24), which has two bidentate ligands. In the equilibrium

$$[Cd(NH_3)_4]^{2+} + 2en(aq) \rightleftharpoons [Cd(en)_2]^{2+} + 4NH_3(aq)$$

the formation of the chelate complex containing ethylenediamine is favored by entropy because the number of particles in the system increases. (There are three species in solution on the left in the equation above, and five on the right.)

6. The formation of fused chelate rings gives complexes that are more stable than those containing rings that are not fused (compare 29 and 31; 30 and 32). The complexing agents in these cases are amino acids that form five-membered chelate rings, but with glycine, no fused rings are formed; edta forms five fused rings if all of its possible donor atoms coordinate.

The distinction between thermodynamic stability and kinetic stability is nicely illustrated by the behavior of certain complexes. For example, the rates of exchange

---

Higher oxidation state of metal → more stable complexes

Chelate rings increase stability; fused rings are more stable than separate rings

---

Table 32.5
Overall Dissociation Constants of Some Common Complexes The names and structures of en, ox, and gly are given in Table 32.3. For edta, see Figure 32.1. A more extensive table of K_d is given in Appendix V4.

1. $[Ag(NH_3)_2]^+$	6.2×10^{-8}		19. $[Zn(OH)_4]^{2-}$	5×10^{-21}
2. $[Cd(NH_3)_4]^{2+}$	1×10^{-7}		20. $[CaP_2O_7]^{2-}$	1×10^{-5}
3. $[Cu(NH_3)_4]^{2+}$	1×10^{-13}		21. $[MgP_2O_7]^{2-}$	2×10^{-6}
4. $[Ni(NH_3)_6]^{2+}$	1×10^{-9}		22. $[CuP_2O_7]^{2-}$	2.0×10^{-7}
5. $[Zn(NH_3)_4]^{2+}$	3.46×10^{-10}		23. $[Ag(en)]^+$	1×10^{-5}
6. $[AgCl_2]^-$	9×10^{-6}		24. $[Cd(en)_2]^{2+}$	2.60×10^{-11}
7. $[CdCl_4]^{2-}$	9.3×10^{-3}		25. $[Co(en)_3]^{2+}$	1.52×10^{-14}
8. $[PdCl_4]^{2-}$	6×10^{-14}		26. $[Co(en)_3]^{3+}$	2.04×10^{-49}
9. $[AgBr_2]^-$	7.8×10^{-8}		27. $[Fe(ox)_3]^{4-}$	6×10^{-6}
10. $[CdBr_4]^{2-}$	2×10^{-4}		28. $[Fe(ox)_3]^{3-}$	3×10^{-21}
11. $[PdBr_4]^{2-}$	8.0×10^{-14}		29. $[Cu(gly)_2]$	5.6×10^{-16}
12. $[CdI_4]^{2-}$	8×10^{-7}		30. $[Zn(gly)_2]$	1.1×10^{-10}
13. $[Ag(CN)_2]^-$	1×10^{-22}		31. $[Cu(edta)]^{2-}$	1.38×10^{-19}*
14. $[Cd(CN)_4]^{2-}$	8.2×10^{-18}		32. $[Zn(edta)]^{2-}$	2.63×10^{-17}
15. $[Au(CN)_2]^-$	5×10^{-78}		33. $[Cd(CH_3NH_2)_4]^{2+}$	2.82×10^{-7}
16. $[Fe(CN)_6]^{4-}$	1.3×10^{-37}			
17. $[Fe(CN)_6]^{3-}$	1.3×10^{-44}			
18. $[Cu(OH)_4]^{2-}$	7.6×10^{-17}			

* Edta is the anion of ethylenediaminetetraacetic acid (Figure 32.1).

of ligands in some cyano complexes have been studied by using cyano ligands labeled with radioactive carbon. The presence of the radioactive CN^- group in the complex or in solution can be detected. The relative kinetic stabilities of substances are described by the terms "labile" and "inert." A **labile complex** undergoes rapid exchange of its ligands with, say, a reaction half-life of a minute or less.

$$[Ni(CN)_4]^{2-} + 4C^*N^- \rightleftharpoons [Ni(C^*N)_4]^{2-} + 4CN^-$$
$$t_{\frac{1}{2}} = \sim 30 \text{ s}$$

As is true of this tetracyanonickelate(II) complex, a labile complex can be thermodynamically stable and dissociated to only a very small extent (the K_d value for $[Ni(CN)_4]^{2-}$ is about 1×10^{-30}), and yet the ligands of such a complex may be continuously undergoing exchange at a very rapid rate.

By contrast, an **inert complex** has a slow rate of ligand exchange, for example

$$[Cr(CN)_6]^{3-} + 6C^*N^- \rightleftharpoons [Cr(C^*N)_6]^{3-} + 6CN^-$$
$$t_{\frac{1}{2}} = \sim 24 \text{ days}$$

The cations that most commonly form inert complexes are Cr^{3+}, Co^{3+}, Pt^{2+}, and Pt^{4+}.

An inert complex which is thermodynamically unstable in acidic solution is $[Co(NH_3)_6]^{3+}$. Its thermodynamic instability is demonstrated by its spontaneous transformation to the more stable hexahydrated species cobalt(II) complex:

$$4[Co(NH_3)_6]^{3+} + 20H^+ + 26H_2O(l) \longrightarrow 4[Co(H_2O)_6]^{2+} + 24NH_4^+ + O_2(g)$$

Its inertness is demonstrated by the fact that at room temperature this reaction takes several days.

32.6 EFFECT OF COMPLEX FORMATION ON PROPERTIES

When a metal ion becomes part of a complex, most of its properties are changed. For example, when an excess of aqueous ammonia is added to a solution of a copper(II) salt, the $[Cu(NH_3)_4]^{2+}$ ion is formed, and the solution becomes dark blue. The salts of this new ion have quite different solubilities from the corresponding salts of the "simple" copper(II) ion, and they crystallize in different forms. Changes of this sort are seen whenever a complex is formed.

Another example of a change in properties with complexation is shown by cobalt(III) hydroxide, $Co(OH)_3$, and tris(ethylenediamine)cobalt(III) hydroxide, $[Co(en)_3](OH)_3$. The former is polymeric, insoluble, and very weakly basic (Section 16.11); the latter is easily soluble and is as strong a base as sodium hydroxide. Again, metal ions like chromium(III), iron(III), and cobalt(III), when coordinated with the acetylacetonate ion $(CH_3COCHCOCH_3)^-$, give complexes which are volatile and can be distilled at moderate temperatures. In all such cases, the complex should be considered to be a distinctly different substance from the simple hydrated metal ion.

The reaction of tetraamminecopper(II) with cyanide ion is instructive, for it shows one complexing agent (ammonia) being displaced by a stronger one (cyanide ion). At the same time, the metal ion is reduced by the excess cyanide ion from Cu(II) to Cu(I).

$$2[Cu(NH_3)_4]^{2+} + 6CN^- \longrightarrow 2[Cu(CN)_2]^- + (CN)_2(aq) + 8NH_3(aq)$$

Such changes in oxidation state upon complex formation are not unusual. The reduction potential of a metal ion is always influenced by the nature of the complex in which it is held, though not always to the great extent that is shown by Cu^{2+},

$$Cu^{2+} + e^- \longrightarrow Cu^+ \qquad E° = 0.158 \text{ V}$$
$$Cu^{2+} + 2CN^- + e^- \longrightarrow [Cu(CN)_2]^- \qquad E° = 1.12 \text{ V}$$

Color and the presence of unpaired electrons are important characteristics of many transition metal ions and their complexes. Many such complexes are also colored (Sections 32.9–32.11). The cause of the color is the absorption by the complex of light in the visible range, due to transitions in energy level by the electrons.

It must be kept in mind that a complex ion in aqueous solution is in equilibrium with the simple hydrated metal cation. In most cases a solution of the complex ion contains a concentration of the metal ion that is small but sufficient for the reactions typical of that ion to take place. For example, a solution of $[Cu(NH_3)_4]^{2+}$ ($K_d = 1 \times 10^{-13}$) shows many of the chemical properties of the Cu^{2+} ion, including the precipitation of copper(II) sulfide when hydrogen sulfide is added

$$[Cu(NH_3)_4]^{2+} + H_2S(g) \longrightarrow CuS(s) + 2NH_4^+ + 2NH_3(aq)$$

32.7 METAL–OLEFIN COMPLEXES, METALLOCENES, AND METAL CLUSTERS

There are three groups of compounds which have many of the properties of complexes and which are considered to be complexes, although they do not exactly fit the definition of coordination compounds given earlier in this chapter. These are the metallocenes, the metal cluster compounds, and the compounds of olefins with heavy metals like platinum.

Typical of the metal–olefin complexes are $[PtCl_2(uns)]_2$ and $K[PtCl_3(uns)]$, where "uns" represents a molecule of an olefin—a hydrocarbon compound that contains a double bond (Section 27.6). In the formation of these compounds, the electrons of the π bond are shared by the metal atoms as well as the two carbon atoms of the double bond, for example, with ethylene,

$[PtCl_3(C_2H_4)]^-$

The olefin complexes are easy to prepare; $[PtCl_2(uns)]_2$, for example, is made by the direct addition of the olefin to platinum(II) chloride. They are quite stable compounds, but they are slowly destroyed by water and more rapidly by strong oxidizing agents.

Complex formation weakens the carbon–carbon double bond to the extent that it allows the easy addition of hydrogen or carbon monoxide. This makes $PtCl_2$ and $[PtCl_4]^{2-}$ valuable as catalysts for hydrogenation of olefins and similar reactions (Section 18.14).

Another group of compounds of metals and unsaturated hydrocarbons consists of the metallocenes, the best known of which contain the cyclic organic group $C_5H_5^-$. The compound cyclopentadiene, C_5H_6 (Figure 32.8a), readily loses a proton when treated with sodium to give the ionic compound $C_5H_5^-Na^+$, which contains the cyclopentadienyl group, $C_5H_5^-$ (abbreviated cp). This compound reacts with salts of many metals to give derivatives such as $[Fe(C_5H_5)_2]$, ferrocene; $[Co(C_5H_5)_2]$, cobaltocene; and $[Ru(C_5H_5)_2]$, ruthenocene. The bonding in these compounds, however, is covalent rather than ionic, as in the sodium compound. These metallocenes are insoluble in water but are soluble in nonpolar solvents, and they are volatile. In some metallocenes, the metal can be oxidized to give cationic complexes, for example, $[Fe(C_5H_5)_2]^+$. The organic rings can undergo a variety of substitution reactions, so a large number of different types of compounds can be formed.

In most metallocenes the metal atom lies between the two organic rings to form a sandwich (Figure 32.8b). The bonding of the metal atoms to the rings in such compounds has been the subject of much speculation. The cyclopentadienyl ring is a

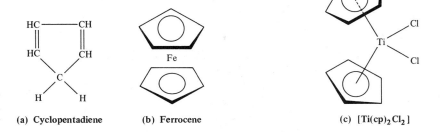

Figure 32.8
Metallocenes Derived from
Cyclopentadiene   (a) Cyclopentadiene   (b) Ferrocene   (c) $[Ti(cp)_2Cl_2]$

resonating structure; therefore, it is planar and all of the carbon atoms in it are equivalent. This is indicated by drawing a circle within the ring, as in Figure 32.8b and c. There is a concentration of electron density on each side of this ring which overlaps with the electron orbitals of the metal, and thus forms a chemical bond. The metal is not bonded to any specific carbon atom, but is bonded equally to all of them.

Large metal atoms can accommodate three or four cyclopentadiene rings, for example, $[U(C_5H_5)_4]$. Other compounds contain inorganic groups in addition to the cyclopentadiene rings, as is the case with $[Ti(C_5H_5)_2Cl_2]$ (Figure 32.8c). Finally, we should mention the cyclopentadiene carbonyls, which are numerous and which have been studied extensively, for example, $[Mn(C_5H_5)(CO)_3]$ and $[V(C_5H_5)(CO)_4]$.

In addition to the familiar compounds in which metal atoms are bonded to nonmetal atoms and the metallic materials in which metal atoms are united by metallic bonding, there is a group of chemical compounds containing metal–metal bonds. One example, which has been known for many years, is mercury(I) chloride, $:\ddot{C}l:Hg:Hg:\ddot{C}l:$, in which the two atoms of mercury share a pair of electrons in a covalent bond.

More recently, it has been discovered that there are many compounds in which metal atoms are bonded to each other. In some cases, as in Hg_2Cl_2 and $Mn_2(CO)_{10}$, the metal atoms are connected solely by covalent bonds (Figure 32.9a). In others, there are also neutral or negatively charged nonmetals binding the metal atoms together. One of the simplest of these is the dimer of chromium(II) acetate hydrate, $Cr_2(CH_3COO)_4 \cdot 2H_2O$ (Figure 32.9b). The two oxygen atoms of each acetate group

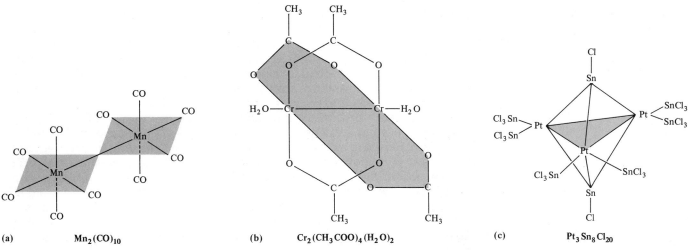

(a) $Mn_2(CO)_{10}$ (b) $Cr_2(CH_3COO)_4(H_2O)_2$ (c) $Pt_3Sn_8Cl_{20}$

Figure 32.9
Some Simple Metal Cluster Compounds

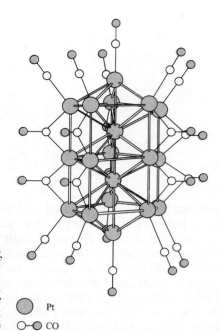

Figure 32.10
A Large Metal Cluster Anion,
$[Pt_{19}(CO)_{22}]^{4-}$ The dimensions of
this cluster are 80 by 110 nm.
(Source: Reprinted with permission
from *Chemical and Engineering
News,* Feb. 8, 1982, p. 13. Copyright
1982 American Chemical Society.)

Pt

CO

bind to separate chromium atoms, so that the four acetate groups form a paddle
wheel configuration. The existence of the metal–metal bond has been proven by
spectroscopy and x-ray crystal studies. In the corresponding molybdenum(II) acetate, there is evidence that the two molybdenum atoms share eight electrons—that
is, that there is a quadruple bond between them.

**Metal cluster compounds:
contain metal–metal bonds**

When two or more metal atoms are bonded to each other, the compound is
spoken of as containing a <u>metal cluster</u>. In some metal clusters different kinds of
metal atoms are joined together. An example is $Pt_3Sn_8Cl_{20}$, in which each platinum
atom is bonded to the other two, as well as to four tin atoms (Figure 32.9c). Some
clusters that are very large have been studied; their structures are quite beautiful
(Figure 32.10). Cluster compounds have received a great deal of attention in recent
years because of their usefulness as catalysts.

32.8 COMPLEXES IN
PRACTICAL APPLICATIONS
AND IN NATURE

Inorganic complexes, as we have seen, show a wide range of properties. Some of
them are extremely stable, while others are unstable; many have colors that are quite
different from the colors of their constituents; some are readily soluble in water,
whereas others are insoluble in that medium but dissolve easily in nonpolar solvents
such as benzene; some are volatile, whereas others are not. By proper "tailoring" of a
complex molecule or ion, almost any combination of properties can be built into it.
Because of this wide range of properties, complexes are used in many ways. They are
also essential to many processes in our natural environment, such as soil weathering.

Many uses of complexing agents depend upon their ability to selectively dissolve
or tie up metal ions or to remove them from solution. The calcium, magnesium, and
iron ions can be removed from hard water by complexing agents. In analytical
chemistry, an ion that would interfere with an analysis is held in solution as a
complex while other ions are detected or removed as precipitates. There are "com-
plexometric" titrations in which a complexing agent, frequently edta, is titrated into
a solution of a metal and the end point detected by the color change of another
complexing agent. We have already mentioned the use of complexes in hydrometallurgy (Section 28.4b).

Some metals and semimetals are essential to living things, while others are poisonous, and still others (e.g., Cu, Se, As) are essential in small amounts but toxic in larger amounts. Both essential metals and poisons can be dissolved and transported as complexes.

Humic acids are organic compounds formed in the soil by the decay of organic matter. They bind metal ions needed by plants, transport them through the soil, and make them available to the plant roots. Chlorosis is a condition caused by the lack of iron and results in yellowing of the leaves of orange trees and other acid-loving plants. Sprinkling an iron salt on the soil around an orange tree will not provide the needed iron. In the moist soil the iron is coverted to $Fe(OH)_3$ or Fe_2O_3, both of which are so insoluble that the roots cannot absorb them. Commercial fertilizers for acid-loving plants contain "chelated iron" which stays in solution in moisture in the soil and can be absorbed.

Several of the transition metals are essential to human life. In the body they are complexed with proteins in various metalloenzymes that catalyze crucial body functions. The heme portion of hemoglobin incorporates Fe^{2+}, and vitamin B_{12} binds Co^{2+}. Both heme, which functions in the transport of oxygen in the blood, and chlorophyll a, which is vital to the photochemical transfer of energy in plants, are members of the same class of compounds—the porphyrins (Figure 32.11). Health food stores all have large sections devoted to "chelated minerals"—iron, magnesium, copper, zinc, and other metal ions combined with complexing agents to render them soluble.

Many chelating, or sequestering, agents, including edta, remove unwanted metals from the body by forming stable, soluble complexes which can be eliminated with normal waste products. The chelating, or sequestering, agent British Anti-Lewisite (BAL), for example, was developed during wartime as an antidote to the arsenic-containing poisonous gas called Lewisite ($ClCH{=}CHAsCl_2$). BAL, which has the formula

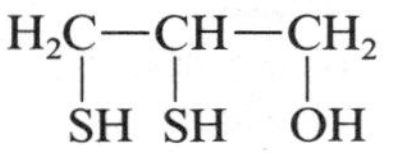

$$H_2C{-}CH{-}CH_2$$
$$\;\;|\;\;\;\;\;|\;\;\;\;\;|$$
$$SH\;\;SH\;\;\;OH$$

coordinates through the sulfur atoms. BAL is now used to treat poisoning by many elements, including arsenic, mercury, gold, bismuth, antimony, thallium, tellurium, and chromium.

Cadmium has been identified as a possible cause of hypertension (high blood pressure). We are born with virtually no cadmium in our bodies. It comes into our diet as a contaminant of the zinc used in various ways in our society. For example, we

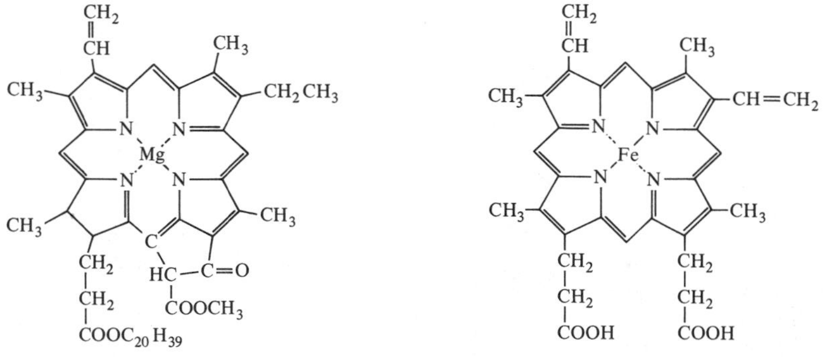

Figure 32.11
Structures of Chlorophyll a and Heme These compounds are both members of a class called porphyrins.

chlorophyll a

heme

inhale it in the dust from the wear and tear on tires (which contain zinc oxide) and ingest it with foods cooked in zinc-coated steel vessels. (Interestingly, in some undeveloped areas of the world where zinc-coated steel pots and pans are unknown, hypertension is very rare.) Sequestering agents for cadmium have been utilized as anti-hypertension drugs.

BONDING IN COMPLEXES

Bonding in complexes, as in other compounds, is rarely strictly ionic or strictly covalent. The valence bond approach to bonding in complexes emphasizes covalent bonding, the crystal field theory emphasizes ionic bonding, and the molecular orbital theory for complexes, which we discuss briefly, brings about a compromise between the two. Keep in mind that in the following sections, as in Sections 11.4–11.7 on valence bond theory and in Chapter 24 on molecular orbital theory, we are describing in words concepts based primarily on mathematical models.

32.9 VALENCE BOND THEORY

In valence bond theory, the metal–ligand bonds are looked upon as coordinate covalent bonds. Electron pairs from the donor atom are shared by entering vacant spaces in the outermost energy levels of the central metal atom or ion. Bonding is the overlap of atomic orbitals, and the atomic orbitals of the metal that are filled by the ligand electrons are viewed as hybridized and of equal energy. The number of hybridized orbitals is equal to the number of ligands in the complex.

The Be atom and Be^{2+} have the ground-state configurations shown in Figure 32.12a and b. In the $[Be(H_2O)_4]^{2+}$ ion, the $2s$ and $2p$ orbitals are hybridized (Figure 32.12c). The four pairs of ligand electrons have filled four equal sp^3 hybrid orbitals, an interpretation of bonding which is consistent with the observed tetrahedral geometry of such complexes.

The cobalt(III) ion contains six $3d$ electrons (Figure 32.13a). Since there are only five d orbitals to accommodate them, two electrons must be paired. The four unpaired electrons make the ion highly paramagnetic. This property is maintained in the cobalt(III) complex $[CoF_6]^{3-}$; therefore, it must be concluded that the six pairs of electrons furnished by the fluoride ligands do not interact with the unpaired electrons of cobalt. Instead, they utilize outer orbitals—the $4s$, the three $4p$, and two of the $4d$ orbitals, forming an sp^3d^2 (or "outer orbital") hybrid (Figure 32.13b).

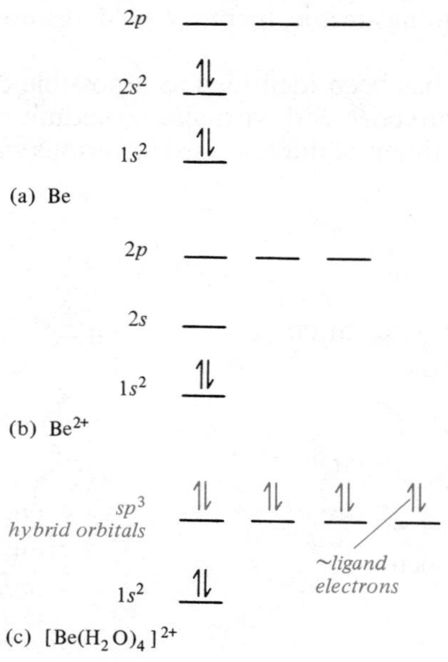

Figure 32.12
Bonding in the Beryllium Atom, the Be²⁺ Ion, and the Complex Ion [Be(H₂O)₄]²⁺ According to the Valence Bond Model

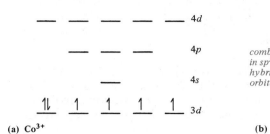

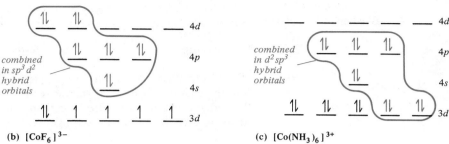

(a) Co^{3+} (b) $[CoF_6]^{3-}$ (c) $[Co(NH_3)_6]^{3+}$

Figure 32.13
Valence Bond Picture of Configuration in Cobalt(III) Complexes Ligand electrons are shown in color.

The $[Co(NH_3)_6]^{3+}$ complex ion, however, is diamagnetic, which indicates that it contains no unpaired electrons. The ammonia complex is also much more stable than the fluoride complex. It is believed that the energy liberated by coordination of ammonia with cobalt(III) is sufficient to cause the unpaired $3d$ electrons to form pairs. This empties two of the $3d$ orbitals and allows pairs of electrons from two of the ammonia molecules to utilize $3d$ orbitals. The pairs from the other four ammonia molecules then utilize the $4s$ and the three $4p$ orbitals, giving a d^2sp^3 (or "inner orbital") hybrid (Figure 32.13c).

The six equivalent orbitals available in d^2sp^3 or sp^3d^2 hybridized complexes are consistent with their observed octahedral geometry. Table 32.6 gives further examples of such complexes, as well as some in which ligand electrons use only s and p orbitals. (Bonding in the $[Co(NH_3)_6]^{3+}$ and $[CoF_6]^{3-}$ complexes is discussed from the crystal field and molecular orbital viewpoints in Sections 32.10 and 32.12.)

A somewhat different arrangement of electrons is possible in ions such as chromium(III) (Table 32.6). The simple ion contains three $3d$ electrons, so there are two vacant $3d$ orbitals. In the formation of hexacoordinate chromium(III) complexes, two pairs of electrons from the ligands can utilize these orbitals, the other four going into the $4s$ and the three $4p$ orbitals. Thus, the $3d$ orbitals are "filled," although three of them contain only one unpaired electron each. The presence of three unpaired electrons in the chromium complex is shown by the paramagnetism of this complex.

Table 32.6
Valence Bond Description of Electrons and Bonding in Some Transition Metal Complexes

Ion	Complex	Number of Electrons in Each Energy Level*						Type of Hybrid	Geometry†
		$3s$	$3p$	$3d$	$4s$	$4p$	$4d$		
Cr^{3+}	$[Cr(NH_3)_6]^{3+}$	2	6	3 +4	2	6		d^2sp^3‡	octahedral
Fe^{2+}	$[Fe(CN)_6]^{4-}$	2	6	6 +4	2	6		d^2sp^3	octahedral
Fe^{3+}	$[Fe(CN)_6]^{3-}$	2	6	5 +4	2	6		d^2sp^3‡	octahedral
Fe^{3+}	$[FeF_6]^{3-}$	2	6	5	2	6	4	sp^3d^2‡	octahedral
Co^{3+}	$[Co(NH_3)_6]^{3+}$	2	6	6 +4	2	6		d^2sp^3	octahedral
Co^{3+}	$[CoF_6]^{3-}$	2	6	6	2	6	4	sp^3d^2	octahedral
Ni^{2+}	$[Ni(CN)_4]^{2-}$	2	6	8 +2	2	4		dsp^2	square planar
Cu^+	$[Cu(NH_3)_2]^+$	2	6	10	2	2		sp	linear
Cu^+	$[Cu(CN)_4]^{3-}$	2	6	10	2	6		sp^3	tetrahedral
Cu^{2+}	$[Cu(NH_3)_4]^{2+}$	2	6	8 +2	2	4 + 1		dsp^2§	square planar

* Electrons supplied by the ligand are shown in color.

† Most complexes containing six coordinated groups are octahedral, whether the bonding is sp^3d^2 or d^2sp^3. In four-coordinate complexes, dsp^2 bonding is characteristic of the square-planar configuration, and sp^3 bonding, of the tetrahedral configuration.

‡ Since the metal ions in these complexes have an odd number of electrons, the complexes must have an odd number of electrons. On that account, they have unpaired electrons and are paramagnetic.

§ One electron in the $4p$ level of $[Cu(NH_3)_4]^{2+}$ has been promoted from the $3d$ level.

EXAMPLE 32.6
Bonding in Complexes

The cyanide ion is a strong ligand which will cause pairing of unpaired electrons in the d sublevel of the metal ion. Assuming d^2sp^3 hybridization for the Mn^{3+} ion in $[Mn(CN)_6]^{3-}$, determine whether $[Mn(CN)_6]^{3-}$ will be paramagnetic or diamagnetic.

The electron configurations are $[Ar]4s^23d^5$ for Mn and $[Ar]3d^4$ for Mn^{3+}. In order for the ligands to fill two of the d orbitals on the Mn^{3+} (as required for d^2sp^3 hybridization), one unpaired electron must be paired, leaving two unpaired electrons to give the following arrangement, in which color indicates ligand electrons:

$$\underline{\quad}\ \underline{\quad}\ \underline{\quad}\ \underline{\quad}\ \underline{\quad}\quad 4d$$
$$\underline{\uparrow\downarrow}\ \underline{\uparrow\downarrow}\ \underline{\uparrow\downarrow}\quad 4p$$
$$\underline{\uparrow\downarrow}\quad 4s$$
$$\underline{\uparrow\downarrow}\ \underline{\uparrow}\ \underline{\uparrow}\ \underline{\uparrow\downarrow}\ \underline{\uparrow\downarrow}\quad 3d$$

The hexacyanomanganate(III) ion should be paramagnetic. [It is.]

Exercise Briefly describe the bonding in $[Mn(H_2O)_6]^{3+}$ using the valence bond theory. The water molecule is not a strong ligand and no pairing of unpaired electrons in the d subshell of the metal ion will occur. *Answer* The electron configurations for Mn and Mn^{3+} are given above. Since no pairing of electrons occurs, the ligands will use the $4d$ subshell for the sp^3d^2 hybridization. The ion will be paramagnetic.

32.10 CRYSTAL FIELD THEORY

Crystal field theory views the interaction between metal ions and ligands in complexes in terms of electrostatic attraction and repulsion. The properties of the complex are explained by a rearrangement of the electrons of the metal ion. The bonding is considered to be completely ionic and interaction between the ligand electrons and the metal ion is *not* considered. "Crystal field theory" is so named because it derives from a theory developed for the energy relationships of ions in crystals. (A modification of crystal field theory that is corrected for small contributions from covalent bonding between the metal atom and the ligands is called ligand field theory. For our purposes, the differences between the two theories are not significant.)

We describe here how the crystal field theory explains the formation of octahedral complexes. Application of the theory to complexes of other coordination numbers and geometry would be similar.

We begin with an isolated Ti^{3+} ion, which has one $3d$ electron in addition to those in its filled shells. The d electron can reside in any of the five d orbitals (Figure 32.14), for they are of equal energy. As six ligands bearing electron pairs approach the metal ion, it becomes more difficult for an electron to occupy the d orbitals, because there is a repulsion between the electrons of the metal and the approaching ligand electrons. In other words, the energy level of the d orbitals is raised.

If the approaching ligand electrons had a perfectly symmetrical effect on the metal ion d orbitals, all of the d orbitals would be raised in energy equally. However, the ligands approach along the x, y, and z coordinates as shown in Figure 32.15, producing an octahedral field. Comparison with the arrangement of the d orbitals in Figure 32.14 shows that the two lobes of the d_{z^2} orbital and the four lobes of the $d_{x^2-y^2}$ orbital point directly toward the corners of the octahedron, where the negative charge of the approaching ligands is concentrated. These orbitals are therefore raised in energy relative to their positions in a symmetrical field. (Remember that orbitals represent regions of negative charge; because like charges repel each other, an increase in potential energy occurs when they are brought together.) The other three

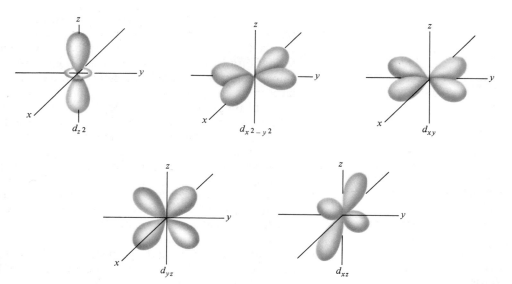

Figure 32.14
The Five *d* Orbitals

orbitals are further from the negative charge of the donor atom and are at a lower energy than they would be in a spherical field. The three orbitals of lower energy are called t_{2g} orbitals (pronounced "t-two-g") and the two of higher energy are called e_g orbitals (pronounced "e-g"). (These names are derived from spectroscopic terms.) The changes in energy levels can be pictured as follows:

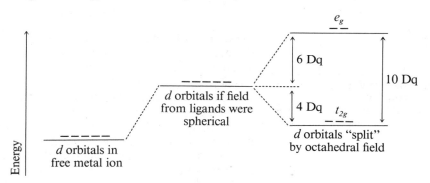

The single *d* electron in the Ti^{3+} ion will avoid the areas of higher energy and higher electronic repulsion at the corners of the octahedron and enter one of the t_{2g} orbitals. This increases the stability of the Ti^{3+} complex ion by lowering its energy.

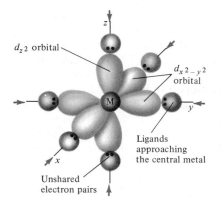

Figure 32.15
Six Ligands about to Form an Octahedral Complex

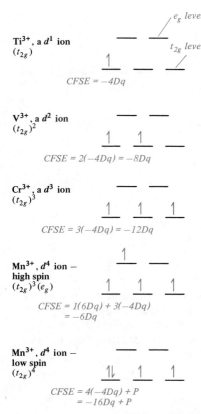

Figure 32.16
Crystal Field Picture of Configurations in d^1 through d^4 Ions in Octahedral Complexes P is a factor added because of energy used in pairing electrons.

The energy difference between the t_{2g} and e_g orbitals is called the *octahedral crystal field splitting* and is represented by the symbol 10 Dq (or sometimes by Δ). Crystal field splitting is a measure of the "crystal field strength" of the ligand. In the formation of these two energy levels, quantum theory requires that no energy be gained or lost. The decrease in energy of the set of orbitals that lies at the lower energy level must be balanced by a corresponding increase in the other set. Therefore, in terms of the total energy, 10 Dq, the energy of each of the two e_g orbitals is 6 Dq higher, and that of each of the three t_{2g} orbitals is 4 Dq lower than if the separation had not taken place [i.e., $2(+6\text{ Dq}) = +12$ Dq and $3(-4\text{ Dq}) = -12$ Dq].

The value of 10 Dq is measured spectroscopically. (It is inversely proportional to the wavelength of light absorbed when an electron is excited from the t_{2g} level to the e_g level; 10 Dq $= hc/\lambda$.) The amount of stabilization provided by the splitting of the d orbitals into two levels for a given ion—the **crystal field stabilization energy** (abbreviated CFSE)—can be calculated in terms of 10 Dq. It is the algebraic sum of -4 Dq per electron in a t_{2g} level and $+6$ Dq for each electron in an e_g level on the central ion of a complex.

The arrangement of the electrons and the CFSE for metal ions with from one to four d electrons, d^1 to d^4 ions, in octahedral complexes are summarized in Figure 32.16. The single electron in a t_{2g} level in Ti^{3+} gives a CFSE of -4 Dq.

In metal ions with four d electrons there are two possible arrangements of the electrons. Three of the electrons, according to the usual rules, occupy the lower energy t_{2g} orbitals and are unpaired. The fourth electron can either go into an e_g orbital or pair up with an electron in a t_{2g} orbital. If the fourth electron goes in at the higher energy level,

$$\text{CFSE} = 1(6\text{ Dq}) + 3(-4\text{ Dq}) = -6\text{ Dq}$$

In other words, in the $(t_{2g})^3 (e_g)$ configuration there is a stabilization energy from the three electrons in low-energy orbitals (-12 Dq), but it is decreased because the fourth electron occupies a higher energy orbital ($+6$ Dq), giving an overall CFSE of -6 Dq. The $[Mn(H_2O)_6]^{3+}$ ion is a typical example of an ion of this type. Since the four electrons occupy separate orbitals, their spins are not paired. A complex ion in which d electrons remain unpaired is called a **high-spin complex.**

In $[Mn(CN)_6]^{3-}$ and many other octahedral d^4 complexes, the fourth electron pairs up with one of the electrons in a t_{2g} orbital. A complex in which all d electrons are paired is called a **low-spin complex.** It might be expected that having *all* of the electrons in the lower energy orbitals would give added stability. However, a good deal of energy (represented by P; see Figure 32.16) is consumed in pairing the spins of two electrons, so some stability is lost.

The possibility of forming *either* high-spin or low-spin complexes exists for d^4 through d^7 ions. Whether a complex will be high spin or low spin depends upon the nature of the ligand. If the ligand is a strongly coordinating agent like CN^-—a **strong-field ligand**—its binding will provide enough energy to force a pairing of electrons and form the spin-paired system. A less strongly coordinating ligand such as Cl^-—a **weak-field ligand**—will form the high-spin system. It is easy to distinguish between the two cases, for the high-spin complexes are more highly paramagnetic than the low-spin complexes. Also, there is a marked difference in the position of the spectroscopic absorption bands.

To examine the crystal field approach for one more case, consider the d^6 cobalt complexes with ammonia molecules and with fluoride ion that were described from the valence bond viewpoint in the preceding section. In each case, at least two of the six d electrons must be paired, for there are only five orbitals. If only two electrons are paired, the complex has a high spin, $(t_{2g})^4(e_g)^2$ (where the superscripts indicate the number of electrons in each level). The $[CoF_6]^{3-}$ ion is a high-spin complex (Figure 32.17). It shows the presence of the two unpaired electrons by its paramagnetism and

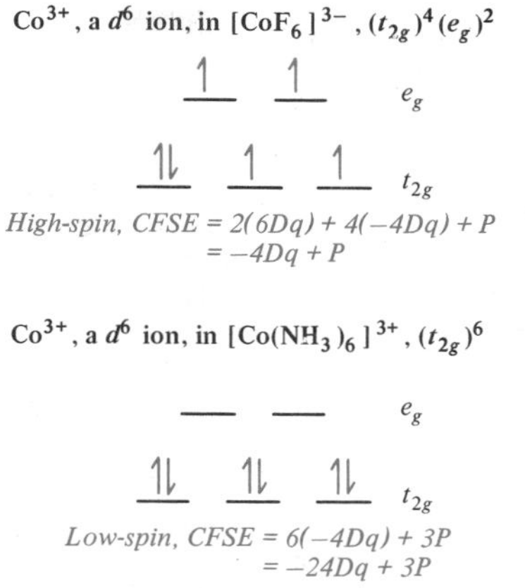

Co^{3+}, a d^6 ion, in $[CoF_6]^{3-}$, $(t_{2g})^4(e_g)^2$

High-spin, CFSE = 2(6Dq) + 4(−4Dq) + P
$\qquad\qquad$ = −4Dq + P

Co^{3+}, a d^6 ion, in $[Co(NH_3)_6]^{3+}$, $(t_{2g})^6$

Low-spin, CFSE = 6(−4Dq) + 3P
$\qquad\qquad$ = −24Dq + 3P

Figure 32.17
Crystal Field Picture of Configurations in d^6 High-Spin and Low-Spin Co^{3+} Octahedral Complexes

is not particularly stable, for its CFSE is low.

$$CFSE = 2(6\ Dq) + 4(-4\ Dq) + P = -4\ Dq + P$$

(where P is the energy consumed in pairing two electrons).

Most of the well-known Co^{3+} complexes are of the low-spin variety, with all of the electrons paired and occupying t_{2g} orbitals, $(t_{2g})^6$. The two e_g orbitals are empty. These low-spin Co^{3+} complexes are diamagnetic; the crystal field stabilization energy is high, so they are quite stable.

$$CFSE = 6(-4\ Dq) + 3P = -24\ Dq + 3P$$

Strong-field ligand →
low-spin complex
(paired d electrons)
Weak-field ligand → high-spin complex (unpaired d electrons)

The compound $[Co(NH_3)_6]Cl_3$, for example, is so stable that it does not lose ammonia even at 200 °C and can be recrystallized from hot concentrated hydrochloric acid without decomposition. In the valence bond nomenclature it is a d^2sp^3 complex. The two d orbitals are, of course, of the e_g type.

A d^7 ion can have either a low-spin configuration, $(t_{2g})^6(e_g)^1$, or a high-spin configuration, $(t_{2g})^5(e_g)^2$. From d^8 to d^{10} only one configuration is possible for each type of ion: for d^8, $(t_{2g})^6(e_g)^2$, with two unpaired electrons; for d^9, $(t_{2g})^6(e_g)^3$, with one unpaired electron; and d^{10}, $(t_{2g})^6(e_g)^4$, with no unpaired electrons.

32.11 COLOR, STABILITY, AND THE SPECTROCHEMICAL SERIES

One of the triumphs of the crystal field theory is its ability to correlate the stability of complexes with their colors. To illustrate how this is possible, we can consider a series of complexes of cobalt(III) in which there are six electrons in the $3d$ sublevel. In the simple, uncoordinated ion, all of these electrons have equal energy, but in the six-coordinate complexes, they are split between two levels. The difference in energy, 10 Dq, between the two levels depends upon the strength with which the ligands are bonded to the metal. In a complex containing "strong" ligands — that is, those that form strong bonds with the metal — the value of 10 Dq will be large, but if the ligands are "weak," 10 Dq will be small. Under the influence of external energy, such as light energy, an electron may be promoted from a lower level (t_{2g}) to a higher one (e_g). The smaller 10 Dq, the less the energy required. The absorbed energy, of course, is very quickly dissipated as heat as the electron falls back to the t_{2g} level. The energy of light depends upon the wavelength — the shorter the wavelength, the greater the energy. Visible light is a mixture of light of many wavelengths, ranging from blue (about 400 nm) to red (about 700 nm). The color which we see in a solution or a solid is due to the light which is *not* absorbed, but which is transmitted or reflected. A material

Table 32.7
Absorbed and Transmitted Colors

	Absorbed Wavelength (nm)	Absorbed Color	Transmitted Color
	410–490	violet/blue-green	yellow/red
	490–530	blue-green/green	red/violet
	530–580	green/yellow	violet/blue
	580–680	yellow/red	blue/blue-green

Table 32.8
Color and Bond Strength in Cobalt Complexes of the Type $[Co(NH_3)_5X]^{n+}$

Compound	Color		Wavelength of Light Absorbed (nm)
$[Co(NH_3)_5(NO_2)]Cl_2$	Yellow		455.9
$[Co(NH_3)_5(NH_3)]Cl_3$	Yellow		471.7
$[Co(NH_3)_5(H_2O)]Cl_3$	Rose-red	*Increasing strength of Co—X bond*	487.0
$[Co(NH_3)_5(NCS)]Cl_2$	Red		498.3
$[Co(NH_3)_5(OH)]Cl_2$	Carmine		501.7
$[Co(NH_3)_5(Cl)]Cl_2$	Reddish purple		521.8
$[Co(NH_3)_5(Br)]Br_2$	Reddish purple		540.5

which absorbs blue light (short wavelength), for example, appears to us to be orange (long wavelength) (Table 32.7).

The complex compounds of the transition metals are generally colored, which we believe indicates that electrons from the t_{2g} level are raised to the e_g level when visible light falls upon them. [Other changes in the quantum states of electrons are also induced, and light of different wavelengths is absorbed, but we are interested here only in the wavelengths that affect the $3d$ electrons.] Table 32.8 lists several complexes of the type $[Co(NH_3)_5X]^{n+}$, arranged in order of decreasing strength of the Co—X bond. The order of decreasing strength of the Co—X bond in this series, measured in a variety of ways, is the same as the order of decreasing energy (10 Dq) or increasing wavelength of the light absorbed.

$$Br^- < Cl^- < OH^- < NCS^- < H_2O < NH_3 < NO_2^-$$

Such a series of ligands arranged according to bond strength is called a "spectrochemical series." A tabulation including other ligands is given in Table 32.9. The $[Co(CN)_6]^{3-}$ ion, which contains six very strong ligands, is a pale yellow color. In the visible range only a small amount of radiation in the short-wavelength region is energetic enough to promote an electron in this ion from the t_{2g} level to the e_g level.

Among the types of reactions that complexes undergo, one of the most important is replacement of one ligand by another, and the stability series can be related to such reactions. For labile complexes, these reactions take place easily if the complex which is formed is more stable than the original one. Consider, for example, the reactions

$$[Cu(H_2O)_4]^{2+} + 4\ NH_3(aq) \longrightarrow [Cu(NH_3)_4]^{2+} + 4\ H_2O(l)$$

$$[Ni(NH_3)_4]^{2+} + 2\ NH_2CH_2CH_2NH_2(aq) \longrightarrow Ni\left(\begin{matrix}-NH_2CH_2\\-NH_2CH_2\end{matrix}\right)_2^{2+}(aq) + 4\ NH_3(aq)$$

$$[Zn(NH_3)_4]^{2+} + 4CN^- \longrightarrow [Zn(CN)_4]^{2-} + 4\ NH_3(aq)$$

In each of these reactions a weaker ligand is replaced by a stronger one (see Table 32.9).

Table 32.9
Spectrochemical Series Strongly binding ligands such as CN^- and NO_2^- are referred to as strong-field ligands. Weakly binding ligands such as Br^- and I^- are referred to as weak-field ligands.

CN^-
NO_2^-
ethylenediamine
pyridine
NH_3
H_2O
NCS^-
$C_2O_4^{2-}$
CH_3COO^-
OH^-
urea
F^-
Cl^-
Br^-
I^-

Increasing strength of binding as a ligand

If two complexes are of comparable stability, an equilibrium will be established which is governed by the relative concentrations of the reagents and the relative stabilities of the complexes. Examples are

$$[Ag(NH_3)_2]^+(aq) + 2\,Br^-(aq) \rightleftharpoons [AgBr_2]^-(aq) + 2\,NH_3(aq)$$
$$[Cd(NH_3)_4]^{2+}(aq) + 4\,CH_3NH_2(aq) \rightleftharpoons [Cd(CH_3NH_2)_4]^{2+}(aq) + 4\,NH_3(aq)$$

Inert complexes exchange ligands only slowly, and whether displacement takes place depends to a large extent upon the relative stabilities of the complexes in question. The hexaamminecobalt(III) ion, $[Co(NH_3)_6]^{3+}$, is not destroyed by hydrochloric acid, but it reacts with cyanide ion, a very strong ligand.

$$[Co(NH_3)_6]^{3+} + 6CN^- \longrightarrow [Co(CN)_6]^{3-} + 6\,NH_3(aq)$$

32.12 MOLECULAR ORBITAL THEORY

The molecular orbital theory uses a somewhat different explanation of high-spin and low-spin complexes. In the formation of an octahedral complex, molecular orbitals are formed by combination of the atomic orbitals of the metal with the orbitals that contain the available electron pairs of the ligands. When six ligands approach a d-transition metal atom or ion, the $4s$ and $4p$ orbitals of the metal are available for overlap with the ligand orbitals. Two of the five d orbitals are oriented in space so that they point toward the approaching ligands (see Figure 32.15), and these two are also available for bonding. The other three d orbitals cannot overlap ligand orbitals.

What happens is pictured this way: the $4s$, the three $4p$, and the two available d orbitals (a total of six orbitals) combine with the orbitals that hold the bonding electron pairs in each of the six ligands to give six bonding and six antibonding molecular orbitals. The remaining three d orbitals from the metal are nonbonding molecular orbitals—they are not properly oriented in space, and electrons residing in these orbitals make no contribution to bonding, nor is there any change in their energy levels.

According to this picture, in the $[Co(NH_3)_6]^{3+}$ ion, all of the outer shell electrons are paired and are in bonding orbitals, giving a stable diamagnetic complex. In the $[CoF_6]^{3-}$ complex ion, however, two of the nonbonding electrons have been displaced into the two lowest level antibonding orbitals. Thus, this ion is paramagnetic and is less stable than the amine complex.

SUMMARY

32.1 SOME DEFINITIONS **32.2** NOMENCLATURE OF COMPLEXES In a complex ion, a central metal cation is joined by coordinate covalent bonds to one or more molecules or anions (the ligands), which are the electron pair donors. A complex can be charged, or it can be neutral (if both the metal and the ligands are uncharged, or if the charge on the metal ion is balanced by opposite charges on the ligands). A compound containing a metal atom and its ligands is called a coordination compound. The number of nonmetal atoms bonded to a metal atom or ion in a complex is the coordination number of the metal. (The rules for naming complexes are described in Section 32.2.)

32.3 CHELATION Sometimes two or more atoms with unshared electron pairs, present in the same molecule, may coordinate to a single metal atom or ion, forming a chelate ring. Chelation greatly increases the stability of the complex. A bidentate ligand contains two donor atoms. A tridentate ligand contains three donor atoms and attaches itself to the metal at three points, forming two fused chelate rings. Edta, a powerful chelating agent, can attach itself to a single metal ion through six donor atoms.

32.4 MOLECULAR GEOMETRY AND ISOMERISM   The geometry of complexes is such as to allow for maximum separation between ligands. The fixed positions of the ligands in a complex create possibilities for both geometrical and optical isomerism. Optical activity is common in complexes that contain chelate rings. Structural isomerism can also exist; also the same group may coordinate in more than one way (linkage isomerism), or ligands and ions may change places (ionization isomerism).

32.5 STABILITY AND LABILITY   All metal ions have the ability to form complex ions, but these differ widely in their stability. The higher the oxidation state of the metal, the more stable are the complexes it forms with a given ligand. The CN^- ion tends to form highly stable complexes. Chelation increases the stability of a complex, and complexes with fused rings are more stable than complexes with separate rings. A labile complex undergoes rapid exchange of its ligands, while an inert complex has a slow rate of ligand exchange. (These terms refer to kinetic rather than thermodynamic stability.)

32.6 EFFECT OF COMPLEX FORMATION ON PROPERTIES   When a metal ion becomes part of a complex, most of its properties are changed. (A complex ion in solution, however, is in equilibrium with the simple hydrated metal cation, and so the solution may also exhibit the reactions characteristic of that ion.) Complex formation may be accompanied by changes in the oxidation state of the metal. Complexes of transition metal ions tend to be colored and some have unpaired electrons.

32.7 METAL–OLEFIN COMPLEXES, METALLOCENES, AND METAL CLUSTERS   Compounds of olefins with heavy metals, metallocenes, and metal cluster compounds have many of the properties of complexes. In metal–olefin complexes, electrons of the π bond in a carbon–carbon double bond are shared by a metal atom. Metallocenes are compounds in which a metal atom lies between two organic rings. Compounds in which two or more metal atoms are bonded to one another are said to contain a metal cluster.

32.8 COMPLEXES IN PRACTICAL APPLICATIONS AND IN NATURE   Complexing agents can be used in many ways; for example, they can be used to selectively dissolve metal ions or remove them from solution. Sequestering agents tie up toxic elements, allowing them to be eliminated from the human body, while organic complexing agents transport nutrients that are essential to plants. Many biologically important molecules, such as hemoglobin and chlorophyll, are complexes.

32.9 VALENCE BOND THEORY   **32.10** CRYSTAL FIELD THEORY   **32.11** COLOR, STABILITY, AND THE SPECTROCHEMICAL SERIES   **32.12** MOLECULAR ORBITAL THEORY   In valence bond theory, metal–ligand bonds are viewed as coordinate covalent bonds; electron pairs from the donor atom are shared by entering vacant spaces in the outermost energy levels of the metal atom or ion. Bonding occurs through the overlap of atomic orbitals, and the orbitals of the metal that are filled by the ligand electrons are viewed as hybridized and of equal energy, their number equal to the number of ligands. In crystal field theory, bonding is considered to be ionic. The approach of ligands with their electron pairs causes a splitting in the energy level of the metal atom or ion orbitals; the energy of some orbitals is raised and that of others is lowered. Electrons enter the orbitals with lower energy, making the complex more stable by an amount known as the crystal field stabilization energy, or CFSE. A strong-field ligand will create a low-spin complex, in which electrons are paired in the lower-energy orbitals. A weak-field ligand will create a high-spin complex, in which some electrons are unpaired in higher-energy orbitals. The crystal field theory makes it possible to relate the stability of complexes to their colors. The more strongly the ligands are bonded to the metal, the shorter the wavelength of light absorbed by the complex. (The color that we see is due to the wavelengths *not* absorbed.) According to molecular orbital theory, molecular orbitals are formed by combination of the atomic orbitals of the metal with the orbitals that contain the available electron pairs of the ligands.

SIGNIFICANT TERMS

complex
coordination compound
coordination number (complex)
chelation
chelate ring
bidentate
tridentate
labile complex
inert complex
crystal field stabilization energy
high-spin complex
low-spin complex
strong-field ligand
weak-field ligand

Some Coordination Compounds in Biochemistry

SOME COORDINATION COMPOUNDS IN BIOCHEMISTRY, by John C. Bailar, Jr.

Biochemists have long known that living bodies contain small amounts of metallic elements and have sought to learn the structures and functions of the compounds that contain these metals. In very recent years, this has become an exciting part of inorganic chemistry as well. . . . Chelating agents are widely prevalent in nature and are more powerful than is generally believed. Certain strains of soybeans growing in alkaline soil generate and secrete into the soil chelating agents that solubilize the iron needed by the plant. Similarly, mosses and lichens growing on solid rock extract the metals necessary for their growth through chelating agents which they generate. Microbiologists have often observed that bacteria growing in stainless-steel culture tanks etch the steel in order to get the iron they need for growth. . . . Many soils are deficient in cobalt, copper, zinc, and molybdenum, and the plants that grow in them are likewise deficient. This may not be important in the growth of the plant, but it may become important if the plants are used for human or animal food. For example, sheep raisers in Australia have known for many years that the sheep became ill if they grazed in certain areas. This illness, called sheep-sick, was finally traced to a deficiency of cobalt in the soil, and hence in the grass that grew there. The difficulty was quickly rectified by sprinkling the soil with solutions of cobalt salts, but this had to be done periodically and was inefficient in the use of cobalt. The problem is now avoided by forcing each sheep to swallow a pellet of cobalt metal and a small screw. These objects, being heavy, remain in the rumen indefinitely and give the animal all the cobalt it needs. The screw rubs against the pellet of cobalt and thus prevents it from becoming covered with an insoluble coat. When the sheep dies or is slaughtered, the cobalt pellet is recovered and given to another sheep — it may even become a family heirloom.

John C. Bailar, Jr., "Some Coordination Compounds in Biochemistry," *American Scientist* **59, 586** (1971).

QUESTIONS

Structure, Nomenclature, and Properties of Complexes

32.1 What do we call the constituents of a complex? What type of chemical bonding occurs between these constituents?

32.2 Define the term "coordination number" for the central atom or ion in a complex. What values of the coordination number for metals are most common?

32.3 Identify the ligands and give the coordination number and the oxidation number for the central atom or ion in each of the following: (a) $[Co(NH_3)_2(NO_2)_4]^-$, (b) $[Cr(NH_3)_5Cl]Cl_2$, (c) $K_4[Fe(CN)_6]$, and (d) $[Pd(NH_3)_4]^{2+}$.

32.4 Repeat Question 32.3 for (a) $Na[Au(CN)_2]$, (b) $[Ag(NH_3)_2]^+$, (c) $[Pt(NH_3)_2Cl_4]$, and (d) $[Co(en)_3]^{3+}$.

32.5 Briefly describe the rules for naming complexes. What does the suffix "o" signify? What does the suffix "ate" signify?

32.6 Name the following substances: (a) $K_3[Mn(CN)_6]$, (b) $[Pd(NH_3)_4](OH)_2$, (c) $[Ag(CN)_2]^-$, (d) $[Ag(NH_3)_2]^+$, and (e) $K_2[Fe(C_2O_4)_2] \cdot 2H_2O$.

32.7 Name the following substances: (a) $Na[Au(CN)_2]$, (b) $[Ni(NH_3)_4(H_2O)_2](NO_3)_2$, (c) $[CoCl_6]^{3-}$, (d) $[Co(H_2O)_6]^{3+}$, and (e) $Na_2[Pt(CN)_4] \cdot 3H_2O$.

32.8 Write formulas for the following: (a) diamminedichlorozinc(II), (b) tin(IV) hexacyanoferrate(II), (c) tetracyanoplatinate(II) ion, (d) potassium hexacyanochromate(III), and (e) tetraammineplatinum(II) ion.

32.9 Write formulas for the following: (a) diamminetetrachloroplatinum(IV), (b) hexaamminenickel(II) iodide, (c) magnesium tetracyanoplatinate(II) heptahydrate, (d) lead(II) tetrafluoroborate(III), and (e) iron(III) hexacyanoferrate(II).

32.10 What is the term given to the phenomenon of ring formation by a ligand in a complex? What numbers of atoms are found in stable rings?

32.11 Write a structural formula showing the ring(s) formed by a bidentate ligand such as the glycinate ion with a metal ion such as Fe^{3+}. How many members are in the ring?

32.12 Repeat Question 32.11 for a tridentate ligand such as diethylenetriamine.

32.13 Draw three-dimensional sketches showing the general geometries of complexes having coordination numbers of (a) two, (b) four (both forms), (c) five (both forms), and (d) six (both forms).

32.14 Choose which of the following structures can form geometrical isomers: (a) tetrahedral Mab_3, (b) tetrahedral Ma_2b_2, (c) square planar Mab_3, and (d) square planar Ma_2b_2. Name any geometrical isomers that can exist. Is it possible for any of these isomers to show optical activity?

32.15 How many geometrical isomers can be formed by the structures (a) octahedral Ma_2b_4 and (b) octahedral Ma_3b_3? Name any geometrical isomers that can exist. Is it possible for any of these isomers to show optical activity?

32.16 Write the structural formulas for (a) two isomers of $[Pt(NH_3)_2Cl_2]$, (b) four isomers (including linkage isomers) of $[Co(NH_3)_3(NO_2)_3]$, and (c) two isomers (including ionization isomers) of $[Pt(NH_3)_3Br]Cl$.

32.17 Determine the number and type of isomers that would be possible for each of the following complexes: (a) tetraamminediaquacobalt(III) ion, (b) triamminetriaquacobalt(III) ion, (c) tris(ethylenediamine) cobalt(III) ion, (d) dichlorobis(ethylenediamine)platinum(IV) chloride, and (e) diamminedibromodichlorochromate(III) ion.

32.18 For each pair of complexes, indicate whether the complexes are identical or are isomers:

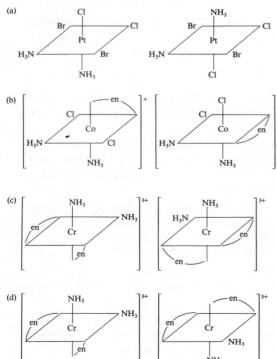

32.19 Werner studied the electrical conductance of aqueous solutions containing a series of platinum(IV) complexes having the general formula $Pt(NH_3)_xCl_4$, where x is an integer that varied from 2 to 6. His results can be summarized as

Formula of complex	Number of ions produced upon complete dissociation
$Pt(NH_3)_6Cl_4$	5
$Pt(NH_3)_5Cl_4$	4
$Pt(NH_3)_4Cl_4$	3
$Pt(NH_3)_3Cl_4$	2
$Pt(NH_3)_2Cl_4$	0

Assuming that Pt(IV) forms octahedral complexes, (a) write the formulas for the five compounds based on the dissociation results, (b) draw three-dimensional sketches of the complexes, (c) draw sketches of any isomers that are possible, and (d) name each compound.

32.20 What properties of the central metal ion increase the thermodynamic stability of a complex? What is the trend of stability of complexes with chelation?

32.21 Why is the dissociation constant smaller for (a) $[Co(en)_3]^{3+}$ than for $[Co(en)_3]^{2+}$, (b) $[Cu(gly)_2]$ than for $[Zn(gly)_2]$, and (c) $[Cd(en)_2]^{2+}$ than for $[Cd(NH_3)_4]^{2+}$?

32.22 Does the term "labile" imply that a complex is thermodynamically unstable? Does the term "inert" imply that a complex is thermodynamically stable? Briefly explain your answers.

32.23 Zinc will react with either hydrochloric or nitric acid. Copper will not react with hydrochloric acid, but reacts with nitric acid. Platinum will not react with either acid, but reacts with a mixture of the two. Explain.

32.24 A copper penny will not react with hydrochloric acid, but will react with hydroiodic acid to give $H_2(g)$. Is this behavior explained by the fact that $HI(aq)$ is a stronger acid than $HCl(aq)$? Explain your answer.

32.25 Briefly describe the bonding in the metal–olefin and metallocene complexes. How does the formation of these bonds change the properties of the ligands?

32.26 The ion $[PtCl_3(CH_2{=}CH_2)]^-$ is similar in many ways to $[PtCl_4]^{2-}$. What sort of bonding can exist in the former?

32.27 What is a metal cluster? What types of bonding are present in this type of complex?

32.28 People are born with almost no Cd^{2+} in their bodies, but this chemical is accumulated throughout their lives by those living in the United States and other "advanced" countries. Certain complexing agents, taken orally, can react with the Cd^{2+} so that it can be eliminated from the body through the urinary system. (In fact, the body can slowly excrete Cd^{2+} in the urine, but not as rapidly as it is absorbed.) What are some properties that might be important for an oral complexing agent?

Bonding in Complexes

32.29 Name the three theories that we use to explain the bonding in complexes. Briefly describe each of the theories.

32.30 Using the valence bond theory, describe the bonding in a Co^{3+} octahedral complex with ligands that can (a) occupy only the outer orbitals on the Co^{3+} and (b) occupy inner orbitals on the Co^{3+}. What types of hybridization of the atomic orbitals on Co^{3+} are proposed for each?

32.31 Using the valence bond theory, describe the bonding in a square planar Cu^{2+} complex in which the ligands can occupy inner orbitals on the Cu^{2+}. What type of hybridization of the Cu^{2+} atomic orbitals is envisioned?

32.32 How many unpaired electrons would you predict there to be in each of the following: (a) $[Fe(CN)_6]^{3-}$, (b) $[Fe(H_2O)_6]^{3+}$, (c) $[Mn(H_2O)_6]^{2+}$, and (d) $[Co(NH_3)_6]^{3+}$?

32.33 Consider the compound having the formula $[Co(NH_3)_5(H_2O)]^{3+}[Co(NO_2)_6]^{3-}$. In terms of valence bond theory, describe the bonding in each ion. Would you expect this substance to be paramagnetic or diamagnetic?

32.34 Draw a sketch of the crystal field splitting for octahedral complexes and label each of the energy levels. How many t_{2g} electrons and how many e_g electrons are there in (a) $[Mn(H_2O)_6]^{2+}$, (b) $[CoF_6]^{3-}$, and (c) $[Ti(H_2O)_6]^{3+}$?

32.35 Determine the electronic distribution in (a) $[Co(CN)_6]^{3-}$, a low-spin complex ion, and (b) $[CoF_6]^{3-}$, a high-spin complex ion. Express the crystal field stabilization energy for each complex.

32.36 Determine the crystal field stabilization energy for (a) $[Mn(H_2O)_6]^{3+}$, a high-spin complex, and (b) $[Mn(CN)_6]^{3-}$, a low-spin complex.

32.37 What determines the color of a complex? How can we use color to compile a list of ligands in order of metal–ligand bond strength?

32.38 What reactions will take place if samples of the labile complex $[Ni(H_2O)_4]^{2+}$ are mixed with solutions of (a) CN^-, (b) NH_3, (c) pyridine?

32.39 What reactions might take place if an aqueous solution of $[Co(NH_3)_5Cl]Cl_2$ and $NaNO_2$ is allowed to stand for several hours? Would you expect a reaction to occur between $Na_3[Co(CN)_6]$ and $NaNO_2$ in aqueous solution?

32.40* Which atomic orbitals are used to form the molecular orbitals for an octahedral complex? How many molecular orbitals are formed?

Answers to Selected Questions

32.4 (a) CN^-, 2, $+1$; (b) NH_3, 2, $+1$; (c) NH_3 and Cl^-, 6, $+4$; (d) ethylenediamine, 6, $+3$

32.7 (a) sodium dicyanoaurate(I), (b) tetraamminediaquanickel(II) nitrate, (c) hexachlorocobaltate(III) ion, (d) hexaaquacobalt(III) ion, (e) sodium tetracyanoplatinate(II) trihydrate

32.9 (a) $[Pt(NH_3)_2Cl_4]$, (b) $[Ni(NH_3)_6]I_2$, (c) $Mg[Pt(CN)_4] \cdot 7H_2O$, (d) $Pb[BF_4]_2$, (e) $Fe_4[Fe(CN)_6]_3$

32.15 (a) 2, *cis* and *trans*, no; (b) 2, meridional and facial, no

32.17 (a) 2 — *cis* and *trans* isomers; (b) 2 — meridional and facial isomers; (c) 2 — optical isomers; (d) 3 — *cis* (two optical isomers) and *trans* isomers; (e) 6 — all groups *trans*, Br's *trans* with others *cis*, Cl's *trans* with others *cis*, NH_3's *trans* with others *cis*, all groups *cis* (two optical isomers)

32.21 (a) The higher oxidation state of Co increases stability, (b) the smaller ionic size of Cu^{2+} increases stability, (c) ring formation increases stability.

32.24 No, the difference is that the very stable complex $[CuI_2]^-$ forms with HI.

32.26 An electron pair from the carbon-carbon double bond is shared with Pt.

32.31 Electron configuration is $[Ar]\,3d^{10}\,4s^1$ for Cu and $[Ar]\,3d^9$ for Cu^{2+}; one electron is promoted to the $4p$ subshell; the eight ligand electrons are envisioned as occupying, in pairs, the remaining $3d$ orbital, the $4s$ orbital, and two of the four $4p$ orbitals, which form four equivalent bonds by dsp^2 hybridization. The $4p$ energy level holds one unpaired electron.

32.33 d^2sp^3 for both ions, diamagnetic

32.36 (a) -6 Dq, (b) -16 Dq $+$ P

32.39 $[Co(NH_3)_5Cl]Cl_2 + NO_2^- \rightarrow [Co(NH_3)_5NO_2]Cl_2 + Cl^-$, $[Co(NH_3)_5NO_2]Cl_2$ will react further with NO_2^- to form $[Co(NO_2)_6]^{3-}$; no, CN^- is a stronger ligand than NO_2^-

PROBLEMS

Review of Principles

32.1 A compound synthesized in an inorganic preparation experiment was analyzed and found to contain 17.0 mass % Fe, 21.9 mass % C, 25.5 mass % N, and 35.6 mass % K. Find the empirical formula of the compound. The osmotic pressure exerted by a 0.0010 M solution at 25 °C of this compound was 0.095 atm. How many ions are present in this compound? Write the formula of the compound as a coordination compound. Name this substance.

32.2 The yellow complex $K_3[Rh(C_2O_4)_3]$ can be prepared from the wine-red complex $K_3[RhCl_6]$ by boiling a concentrated aqueous solution of $K_3[RhCl_6]$ and $K_2C_2O_4$ for two hours and then evaporating the solution until the product crystallizes.

$$K_3[RhCl_6](aq) + 3K_2C_2O_4(aq) \xrightarrow{\Delta}$$
$$K_3[Rh(C_2O_4)_3](s) + 6KCl(aq)$$

What is the theoretical yield of the oxalato complex if 1.00 g of the chloro complex is heated with 5.75 g of $K_2C_2O_4$? In an experiment, the actual yield was 0.83 g. What is the percent yield?   *Answer* 1.12 g, 74%

32.3 Consider the formation of the triiodoargentate(I) ion.

$$Ag^+ + 3I^- \longrightarrow [AgI_3]^{2-}$$

Would you expect an increase or decrease in the entropy of the system as the complex is formed? The standard state absolute entropy at 25 °C is 72.68 J/K mol for Ag^+, 111.3 J/K mol for I^-, and 253.1 J/K mol for $[AgI_3]^{2-}$. Calculate $\Delta S°$ for the reaction and confirm your prediction.

32.4 Molecular iodine reacts with I^- to form a complex ion.

$$I_2(aq) + I^- \rightleftharpoons [I_3]^-$$

Calculate the equilibrium constant for this reaction given the following data at 25 °C:

$$I_2(aq) + 2e^- \longrightarrow 2I^- \qquad E° = 0.535 \text{ V}$$
$$[I_3]^- + 2e^- \longrightarrow 3I^- \qquad E° = 0.5338 \text{ V}$$

32.5 Given the following standard reduction potential data:

$Co^{3+} + e^- \rightleftharpoons Co^{2+}$ $\hspace{2cm} E° = 1.808 \text{ V}$
$Co(OH)_3(s) + e^- \rightleftharpoons Co(OH)_2(s) + OH^-(aq)$
$\hspace{5cm} E° = 0.17 \text{ V}$
$[Co(NH_3)_6]^{3+} + e^- \rightleftharpoons [Co(NH_3)_6]^{2+}$
$\hspace{5cm} E° = 0.108 \text{ V}$
$[Co(CN)_6]^{3-} + e^- \rightleftharpoons [Co(CN)_5]^{3-} + CN^-$
$\hspace{5cm} E° = -0.83 \text{ V}$
$O_2(g) + 4H^+(10^{-7} \text{ M}) + 4e^- \rightleftharpoons 2H_2O(l)$
$\hspace{5cm} E° = 0.815 \text{ V}$
$2H_2O(l) + 2e^- \rightleftharpoons H_2(g) + 2OH^- \qquad E° = -0.828 \text{ V}$

Which cobalt(III) species among those listed would oxidize

water? Which cobalt(II) species among those listed would be oxidized by water?   *Answer* Co^{3+}; $[Co(CN)_5]^{3-}$

32.6 The overall dissociation constant for $[Fe(C_2O_4)_3]^{3-}$ is 3×10^{-21}. What would be the maximum concentration of Fe^{3+} in a solution containing 0.010 M $K_3[Fe(C_2O_4)]$ which also contains 1.5 M $C_2O_4^{2-}$?

32.7 Write the rate equation for the reaction

$$[Co(NH_3)_5F]^{2+} + H_2O(l) \longrightarrow [Co(NH_3)_5(H_2O)]^{3+} + F^-$$

in terms of concentrations of reactants. Experimentally it is found that doubling the concentration of $[Co(NH_3)_5F]^{2+}$ doubles the reaction rate. What is the order of reaction with respect to the complex?   *Answer* Rate $= k[Co(NH_3)_5F^{2+}]^m[H_2O]^n$, $m = 1$

32.8* At 25 °C, $\Delta H° = -46.4$ kJ, $\Delta G° = -42.84$ kJ, and $\Delta S° = -11.7$ J/K for the reaction

$$[Cu(H_2O)_4]^{2+} + 2NH_3(aq) \longrightarrow$$
$$[Cu(NH_3)_2(H_2O)_2]^{2+} + 2H_2O(l)$$

and $\Delta H° = -25.1$ kJ, $\Delta G° = -49.0$ kJ, and $\Delta S° = 79$ J/K for the reaction

$$[Cu(H_2O)_4]^{2+} + gly^- \longrightarrow [Cu(gly)(H_2O)_2]^+ + 2H_2O(l)$$

In each case, two Cu–water bonds are broken, but in the first reaction two Cu–NH_3 bonds are formed and in the second reaction a Cu–NH_2 and Cu–O bond are formed. Based on the $\Delta H°$ values, (a) which set of bonds is stronger? In each case, two water molecules are replaced—in the first reaction by two ligands and in the second reaction by one ligand. (b) Why does the entropy increase in the second reaction? Based on values of $\Delta G°$, (c) which complex ion is more stable?

CHAPTER 33

Organic Chemistry, Polymers, and Biochemistry

A few words are in order about the Thoughts on Chemistry at the end of this chapter. It is a bit different from those with other chapters, which are quotations that embody the thoughts of individuals of the past and the present. The "thoughts" in this case will be those of the reader.

The Thoughts on Chemistry with this chapter is a list of important topics in chemistry today. The Chemical Abstracts service of the American Chemical Society reviews publications that report on chemistry—about two million articles are looked at each year. In order to help individuals working in chemistry keep in touch with what is happening, collections of abstracts (short versions) of articles on different topics are assembled. Each topic on the list reproduced at the end of this chapter represents an area of chemistry in which enough people are interested to support issuing a collection of abstracts every two weeks.

Over 100 topics are covered. Read over the list. You may not know exact definitions of all of the terms, but that is not important. By now you have studied enough chemistry to grasp the significance of most of them. We cannot think of a better way to explore how diverse chemistry is and in how many ways it touches our lives than by reading through this list.

SOME INTRODUCTORY CONCEPTS

33.1 FUNCTIONAL GROUPS

If one of the hydrogen atoms in each of the compounds in the series of straight-chain hydrocarbons is replaced by an OH group, the following series of compounds is produced:

$$CH_3OH$$
$$CH_3CH_2OH$$
$$CH_3CH_2CH_2OH$$
$$CH_3CH_2CH_2CH_2OH$$
etc.

These compounds can all be represented by the general expression ROH, where R is an alkyl group (Section 27.5).

The chemistry of these compounds is dominated by the OH group. All compounds of the formula ROH exhibit similar chemical behavior, no matter how long the continuous chain of carbon atoms may be. Saturated hydrocarbons, you will recall, are relatively unreactive, so we should not expect the hydrocarbon part to overshadow the characteristic reactivity of the OH group. The compounds of the family represented by the formula ROH are collectively called alcohols, and the OH group is referred to as a functional group. A **functional group** is a chemically reactive atom or group of atoms that imparts characteristic properties to the family of organic compounds containing that group.

Table 33.1 lists the most common functional groups. In speaking or writing about an organic compound that includes an OH group, for example, we might refer to the compound as having a hydroxyl group or as being an alcohol or a phenol.

Table 33.1
Some Common Functional Groups

Compound Structure* (Functional Group in Color)	Functional Group Name	Compound Name
R—X	halo	Alkyl halide
R—OH	hydroxyl	Alcohol
Ar—OH	hydroxyl	Phenol
ROR	alkoxy	Ether
RNH$_2$, R$_2$NH, R$_3$N	amino	Amine†

R—C=O
   |
   H
	aldehyde or formyl	Aldehyde

R$_2$C=O	carbonyl, or keto, or oxo	Ketone

R—C=O
   |
   OH
	carboxyl	Carboxylic acid

R—C=O
   |
   NH$_2$
	amido	Amide

R—C=O
   |
   X
	carbonyl halide	Acyl halide

R—C—O—C—R
  | |
  O   O
	anhydride	Acid anhydride

R—C=O
   |
   OR
	ester	Ester

R—NO$_2$	nitro	Nitroalkane
R—SO$_3$H	sulfonic acid	Sulfonic acid
R—CN	cyano	Nitrile

* Ar is the abbreviation used for an aromatic group, such as the phenyl group (C_6H_5). X represents any halogen atom.

† RNH$_2$, a primary amine; R$_2$NH, a secondary amine; R$_3$N, a tertiary amine (Section 33.7).

Large and even not so large molecules can contain many functional groups of the same or different types. Such molecules are said to be polyfunctional.

In organic chemistry the power of a functional group should never be underestimated. Urea, the first synthetic organic chemical, a component of urine and a common fertilizer, differs by only one functional group, C=O versus C=S, from thiourea, a compound suspected of being a cancer-causing agent.

The arrangement of functional groups can also make a vast difference. The placement of the —NO$_2$ or —NH$_2$ groups significantly changes the taste of the following three compounds.

EXAMPLE 33.1
Organic Functional Groups

Many organic molecules contain several functional groups. In the following compounds, identify all of the functional groups.

(a) [structure with OH, NO₂, and C—CH₂CH₂OH groups]

(b) $H_2NCH_2CNHCH_2COCH_3$ (with two C=O groups)

The first of these compounds has four functional groups, the second has three.

(a) *hydroxyl group*, *nitro group*, *keto group*, *hydroxyl group*

(b) *amino group (primary)*, *amide group*, *ester group*

Exercise Identify the functional groups in the following molecules:

(a) $H-C$—[benzene ring]—$C-O-CCH_2CH_2CBr$ (with four C=O groups)

(b) HO—[benzene ring with H_3CO]—$CHCH_2NHCH_3$ (with OH group)

Answer (a) An aldehyde group, an anhydride group, and a carbonyl bromide group, (b) two hydroxyl groups, an alkoxy group, and a secondary amino group

---

33.2 CHEMICAL REACTIONS OF ORGANIC COMPOUNDS

It is beyond the scope of this chapter to discuss to any great extent the many possible types of chemical reactions of organic compounds and their functional groups. We can mention only a few of the common organic reactions. However, before we proceed in the following sections to discuss the properties and structures of some simple types of organic compounds, we want to provide an example of how organic reactions are pictured and explained. We can do this by discussing one general type of organic reaction: the substitution of a halogen atom in an alkyl halide (a compound with the general formula RX, where R is an alkyl group and X is a halogen; Section 33.3) by another atom or group, OH⁻ in our example. The overall reaction we have chosen is

$$NaOH(aq) + CH_3Br(l) \longrightarrow CH_3OH(aq) + NaBr(aq) \qquad (33.1)$$

methyl bromide   *methanol*

Most organic reactions involve making or breaking covalent bonds. The site of reaction in an organic compound is likely to be a multiple covalent bond in a functional group or a polar single covalent bond. Often an atom in an organic compound is somewhat deficient in electrons and therefore possesses a partial positive charge. Such an atom can become a site for reaction with an atom or group of atoms that possesses an available pair of electrons, such as a negative ion. In other words, electron-rich or electron-poor atoms or groups are potential reaction sites. A reactant that has a partial or complete positive charge and will bond with an atom that has an available electron pair is referred to as an **electrophile** ("electron-loving"). Similarly, a reactant that has a partial or complete negative charge that enables it to bond with an electron-deficient atom is referred to as a **nucleophile** ("nucleus-loving").

Referring back to Equation (33.1), the carbon–bromine bond in methyl bromide is polar because the bromine atom is more electronegative than the carbon atom. This makes the carbon atom somewhat electron deficient, and therefore an electrophilic reaction site.

$$\overset{\delta+}{\underset{}{\equiv}}C \overset{\delta-}{-} Br$$

The hydroxide ion from sodium hydroxide, with its negative charge, $:OH^-$, is a nucleophilic species.

In the reaction between hydroxide ion and methyl bromide, the nucleophilic OH^- approaches the electrophilic carbon atom in the C—Br bond. As the oxygen–carbon bond forms, the carbon–bromine bond breaks. The reaction can be represented as follows:

$$HO:^- + CH_3 - Br \longrightarrow HOCH_3 + :Br^-$$

where the arrows indicate the directions in which electron pairs move. In this reaction the breaking of the C—Br bond and the formation of the C—O bond occur simultaneously. This and other similar reactions have been shown to exhibit second-order kinetics, the rate being dependent upon the concentration of both hydroxide ion and methyl bromide. Many, but not all, alkyl chlorides, bromides, and iodides react with a variety of nucleophiles in this manner. This type of reaction is described as a "bimolecular nucleophilic substitution reaction."

In the equations for organic reactions, the formulas of simple reactants are often written over the arrows. The results are equations that are not stoichiometrically balanced, but show only the changes in the organic molecule or molecules of concern. The equation for the nucleophilic substitution reaction of hydroxide ion with methyl bromide, written in this way, would be

$$CH_3Br \xrightarrow{NaOH,\ H_2O} CH_3OH$$

FUNCTIONAL GROUPS WITH COVALENT SINGLE BONDS

33.3 HALOGEN DERIVATIVES OF HYDROCARBONS

Alkyl halides, RX
Aryl halides, ArX

Fluorine, chlorine, bromine, and iodine can all be found in organic molecules. The halides of hydrocarbons may be **alkyl halides,** RX, where R is a saturated hydrocarbon group; or **aryl halides,** ArX, where Ar is an aromatic group. They may also contain unsaturated R groups. Some common halogen derivatives of hydrocarbons are listed in Table 33.2 to illustrate their nomenclature (compare with the saturated hydrocarbons, Table 27.7) and the effect of molecular structure on boiling point.

Halogen atoms are more electronegative than the carbon atom, making the C—X bond polar and the carbon atom subject to attack by a nucleophilic reactant, as discussed in the preceding section. The reactions of alkyl halides with hydroxide bases (Equation 33.1), the cyanide ion, and ammonia are all of this type.

Table 33.2
Halogen Derivatives of Hydrocarbons The common name is given first; the systematic name is given in parentheses. The general molecular structure of these hydrocarbon halides is R—X.

	Boiling Point (°C)		Boiling Point (°C)

CH_3Br
methyl bromide
(bromomethane)
	5	CH_3CHCH_2
		    | |
		   Br Br
		propylene dibromide
		(1,2-dibromopropane)
			141

CH_3I *methyl iodide* *(iodomethane)*	42	$CH_2{=}CHCl$ *vinyl chloride* *(chloroethene)*	14
CH_3CH_2Br *ethyl bromide* *(bromoethane)*	38	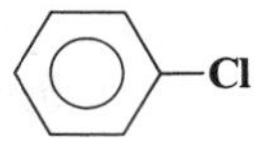 ◌—Cl *chlorobenzene*	132
$CH_3CH_2CH_2Br$ *(propyl bromide* *(1-bromopropane)*	71		

$$CH_3Br + NaCN \xrightarrow{H_2O} CH_3CN + NaBr$$

$$CH_3Br + 2NH_3 \xrightarrow{H_2O} CH_3NH_2 + NH_4Br$$

Halogen atoms bonded to aromatic rings are inert to such reactions.

Alkyl halides can also be induced to lose HX (where X is Cl, Br, or I) and form alkenes, for example,

$$CH_3CHBr + NaOH \xrightarrow[\Delta]{alcohol} CH_3CH{=}CH_2 + NaBr + H_2O$$
$$\quad\ \ |$$
$$\quad\ CH_3$$

isopropyl bromide   *propylene*

Many insecticides are highly chlorinated compounds. There can be no question as to the value of these compounds in agriculture in preventing insects from destroying crops. However, some of the compounds listed in Table 33.3 have come under criticism for (1) their long persistence in the environment and/or (2) their toxicity to both man and animals (see An Aside: Chlorinated Organic Compounds in the Environment).

Table 33.3
Chlorine-Containing Insecticides

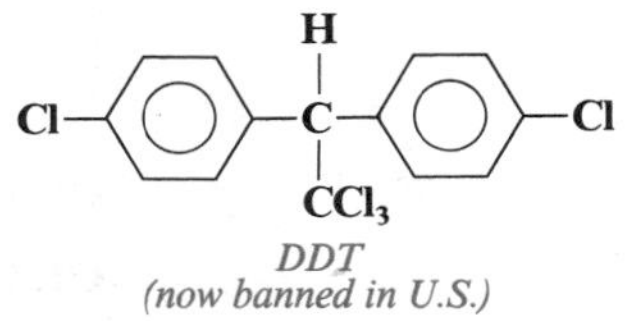

DDT
(now banned in U.S.)

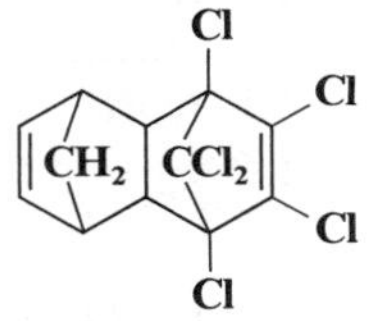

aldrin
(carcinogenic; now banned in U.S.)

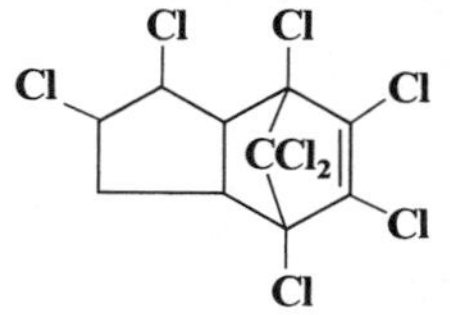

chlordane
(use in U.S. restricted)

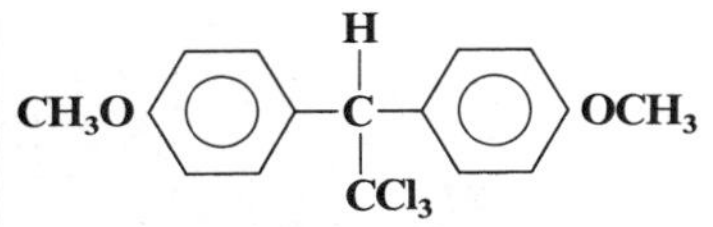

methoxychlor
(less persistent in environment than DDT)

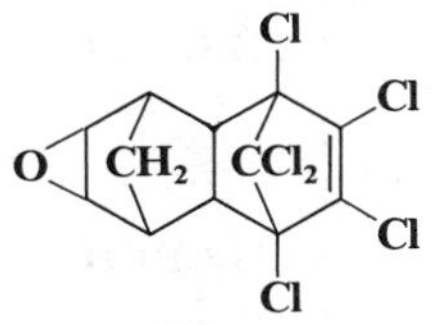

dieldrin
(carcinogenic; now banned in U.S.)

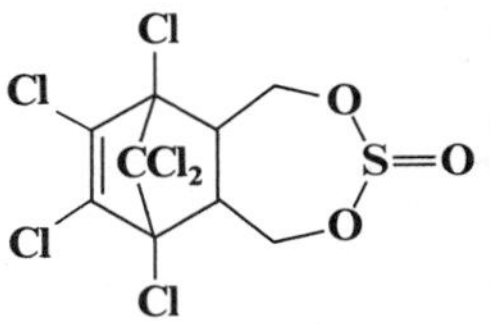

endosulfan
(widely used)

EXAMPLE 33.2
Organic Compounds:
Intermolecular Forces

The molecular structures of two different difluorobenzenes are

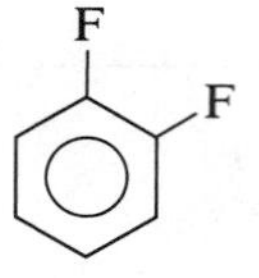

1,2-difluorobenzene   1,4-difluorobenzene

Which of these compounds would you predict to have the higher boiling point?

The boiling points will depend on the relative strengths of the intermolecular forces. Both molecules have the same mass and approximate structure, so we can eliminate any major difference in London forces. The structure of 1,2-difluorobenzene is such that it is a polar molecule, whereas 1,4-difluorobenzene is symmetrical and therefore nonpolar. Because of the additional dipole–dipole interactions in 1,2-difluorobenzene, we would predict it to have the higher boiling point. [This prediction agrees with observation—the boiling points are 91.2 °C for 1,2-difluorobenzene and 89 °C for 1,4-difluorobenzene.]

33.4 ALCOHOLS

In organic compounds, the OH group is usually covalently bonded and is called the **hydroxyl group.** The ending *ol* indicates the presence of a functional —OH in an organic molecule. **Alcohols** have the general formula ROH. (When R is aromatic, the compound is a phenol; next section.)

Alcohols, ROH

In the common system of nomenclature, the R group is named and the word *alcohol* follows, as in methyl alcohol (CH_3OH) and cyclohexyl alcohol ($C_6H_{11}OH$). Ethyl alcohol (C_2H_5OH) is the common beverage alcohol. In the IUPAC system of nomenclature, the name is derived from the longest hydrocarbon chain that includes the OH group by dropping the final *e* and adding *ol*, as in methanol, ethanol, and cyclohexanol. When necessary, a number is used to show the position of the OH group. Numbering starts at the end of the chain nearest to the OH group. Table 33.4 provides a few examples.

Alcohols are classified as primary, secondary, or tertiary, depending on whether the carbon atom to which the hydroxyl group is attached is primary, secondary, or

Table 33.4
Alcohols The general molecular formula for an alcohol is ROH.

	Boiling Point (°C)		Boiling Point (°C)
CH₃OH *methyl alcohol (methanol)*	65	**HOCH₂CH₂OH** *ethylene glycol (1,2-ethanediol)*	197
CH₃CH₂OH *ethyl alcohol (ethanol)*	78	**CH₂CHCH₂** | | | **OH OHOH** *glycerol (glycerin) (1,2,3-propanetriol)*	290 (dec)
CH₃CH₂CH₂OH *propyl alcohol (1-propanol)*	97	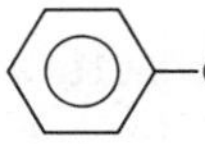	
CH₃CHCH₃ | **OH** *isopropyl alcohol (2-propanol)*	82	⬡—**CH₂CH₂OH** *β-phenylethyl alcohol (2-phenylethanol)*	219

tertiary. Like water, the alcohols exhibit hydrogen bonding, which causes their boiling points to be relatively high. The lower molecular mass alcohols are miscible with water because of hydrogen bonding between the alcohol and water molecules.

Like water, alcohols can also react as either acids or bases. As acids, they are even weaker than water, but in the presence of relatively strong bases, alcohols can give up protons. For example, reaction of alcohols with active metals such as sodium gives a class of compounds known as *alkoxides,* RO^-M^+. The reaction of ethyl alcohol with sodium can be used to dispose of waste sodium by converting it to sodium ethoxide, an alkaline ionic compound comparable to sodium hydroxide, and then allowing the alkoxide to react with water.

$$2CH_3CH_2OH + 2Na \longrightarrow 2CH_3CH_2ONa + H_2(g)$$
ethyl alcohol   *sodium ethoxide*

$$CH_3CH_2ONa + H_2O \longrightarrow CH_3CH_2OH + NaOH$$

In the presence of concentrated acids, alcohols act as bases in overall reactions such as

$$CH_3OH + HBr \longrightarrow CH_3Br + H_2O$$

Methanol, once known as wood alcohol because of its formation during wood distillation, is now made synthetically from carbon monoxide and hydrogen in quantities exceeding those of most other synthetic organic chemicals.

$$CO(g) + 2H_2(g) \xrightarrow[\text{catalyst}]{\text{heat, pressure}} CH_3OH(g)$$

Most of this methanol is converted to formaldehyde, much of it for use in phenol–formaldehyde polymers (Section 33.16b). Methanol is toxic and causes blindness or death when taken internally.

Ethanol, in addition to being a component of many beverages, is a valuable solvent and a frequently used reagent in organic synthesis. Ethylene glycol (see Table 33.4) is used as a permanent antifreeze and coolant in automobiles because of its relatively low volatility. Isopropyl alcohol is rubbing alcohol, and large quantities are converted into acetone (Section 33.8). Glycerol has a strong attraction for water, and because of this property it is used in lotions and other applications where moisture retention is desired. Glycerol is also used in the manufacture of paints, varnishes, explosives, and a variety of other products.

Fermentation of various grains, fruits, and other natural products that contain starch or sugars produces ethyl alcohol. Enzymes, which are the catalysts in biochemical systems, first convert starch to sugars, and the sugars are then coverted to ethyl alcohol and carbon dioxide by other enzymes.

At one time all ethyl alcohol was produced commercially by fermentation. It is now more economical to make ethyl alcohol by the reaction of water with ethylene, which is readily available from petroleum refineries.

$$CH_2{=}CH_2 + H_2O \xrightarrow[\text{pressure}]{\text{heat, catalysts,}} CH_3CH_2OH$$

Fermentation, however, is still the preferred method of obtaining ethyl alcohol for beverages, many of which retain flavors characteristic of the material that was fermented (Table 33.5). After fermentation, a solution contains up to 14% ethyl alcohol. Except for wines and beer, this solution is distilled, producing a distillate with increased alcohol content. Up to 95% ethyl alcohol by weight, which is the composition of a constant-boiling mixture of alcohol and water, can be obtained by distillation. The usual 80-proof beverage is a 40% solution (by volume) of ethyl alcohol.

Absolute ethyl alcohol, 100% or 200 proof, is made by removing the remaining water from 95% ethyl alcohol by distillation with benzene or by chemical means. (An

Table 33.5
Alcoholic Beverages

Beverage	Starting Material
Whiskey	Grains (rye, corn, wheat, oats, barley)
Rum	Molasses
Brandy	Grapes and other fruits
Gin	Grains (distilled and flavored with juniper berry)
Vodka	Potatoes and corn
Wines	Grapes
Sake	Rice
Mead	Honey
Beer	Barley, hops, and other grains
Tequila	Cactus

azeotropic mixture of benzene, alcohol, and water distills at 65 °C and removes the last few percent of water.) Ethyl alcohol for beverages is subject to a federal tax. In order to render industrial ethyl alcohol unfit for drinking, various toxic or objectionable materials (e.g., methanol) that are difficult to remove from ethyl alcohol are added. This *denatured alcohol* is tax free, hence much cheaper for industrial users.

As illustrated by the following example, an organic functional group will undergo many of the same reactions even though it is located in different kinds of molecules.

EXAMPLE 33.3
Reactions of Alcohols

Write the equations for the reactions of the following alcohols with sodium.

OH
|
(a) CH₃CHCH₂CH₃   (b) ⬠—OH   (c) CH₃—C—OH (with CH₃ above and CH₃ below)

2-butanol   *cyclopentanol*   *tert-butyl alcohol*

All alcohols can be expected to react with sodium in the manner shown at the beginning of this section for ethanol, although not necessarily at the same rate. The reactions would be as follows:

$$\text{(a) } 2\text{CH}_3\overset{\text{OH}}{\text{CHCH}_2}\text{CH}_3 + 2\text{Na} \longrightarrow 2\text{CH}_3\overset{\text{O}^-\text{Na}^+}{\text{CHCH}_2}\text{CH}_3 + \text{H}_2(g)$$

$$\text{(b) } 2\ ⬠\text{OH} + 2\text{Na} \longrightarrow 2\ ⬠\text{O}^-\text{Na}^+ + \text{H}_2(g)$$

$$\text{(c) } 2\text{CH}_3-\overset{\text{CH}_3}{\underset{\text{CH}_3}{\text{C}}}-\text{OH} + 2\text{Na} \longrightarrow 2\text{CH}_3-\overset{\text{CH}_3}{\underset{\text{CH}_3}{\text{C}}}-\text{O}^-\text{Na}^+ + \text{H}_2(g)$$

AN ASIDE

Chlorinated Organic Compounds in the Environment

Chlorinated hydrocarbons and pesticides in the environment present a problem. There is no doubt of this. Large amounts of such compounds have been released into the environment as a consequence of their widespread use in numerous valuable applications. Beginning in the 1940s with DDT (see Table 33.3), chlorinated pesticides have been spread and sprayed around the world. In addition, many industrially important compounds, such as vinyl chloride (CH_2=CHCl, a polymer raw material; Section 33.13) and trichloroethylene (ClCH=CCl₂, used in degreasing metal parts), have escaped into the environment by accident or along with waste materials. Also, the suspicion has arisen that chlorinated compounds can be produced by the reaction between chlorine used in water purification and organic pollutants present in the water.

As the number of chlorine atoms in a hydrocarbon is increased, the compounds become less flammable, more dense and viscous, less soluble in water and more soluble in organic solvents, and generally more stable to chemical attack. Compounds in which chlorine is bonded to a vinyl group or an aromatic ring are especially stable due to participation of lone-pair electrons from the chlorine in bonding, as represented by resonance structures such as

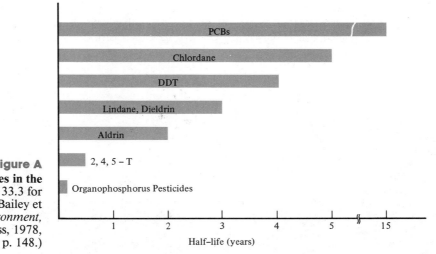

Because highly chlorinated compounds are not readily oxidized by air, hydrolyzed by water, degraded by sunlight, or broken down by bacterial action, those that get into the environment persist, accumulate, and can be distributed widely. DDT has been found in the polar ice and most of us have detectable amounts of DDT and PCBs (see below) in our bodies. The half-lives of some chloro-organic compounds in the environment are shown in Figure A.

In recent years, one substance after another has come to public attention as a toxic or harmful pollutant. The PCBs, in particular, have been in the news in the 1980s. The chlorination of biphenyl

produces a mixture of *polychlorinated biphenyls* (the PCBs) containing primarily the compounds in which three to five hydrogen atoms are replaced by chlorine atoms. The PCBs are *extremely* stable — they survive municipal incineration and can be destroyed only by burning at 1000–1600 °C or by oxidation by ozone and ultraviolet radiation.

Many of the uses of the PCBs have been based on their great thermal stability and their ability to conduct heat but not electricity. They are present in most electrical transformers. PCBs were first detected in the environment by a scientist searching for DDT and other pesticides in wildlife. Gas chromatography revealed, in addition to DDT, other chlorinated hydrocarbons which were shown from studies of the molecular masses to be PCBs. In 1968 one thousand people in Japan became ill from eating rice oil contaminated by PCBs leaking from a heat exchanger. Subsequently, the use and manufacture of PCBs were banned in many countries, includ-

Figure A
Half-lives of Some Pesticides in the Environment See Table 33.3 for structures. (Source: R. A. Bailey et al., *Chemistry of the Environment,* New York: Academic Press, 1978, p. 148.)

ing the United States. But for many years to come care must be exercised in the disposal of electrical equipment containing PCBs.

A wide range of toxic effects have been attributed to various chlorinated compounds, ranging from the possible carcinogenic effects of vinyl chloride and the now-banned insecticides aldrin and dieldrin (see Table 33.3) to the severe skin disease and other long-term effects caused by the PCBs. Many questions have been raised about the toxicity in humans of the compound known in the popular press as "dioxin." (All compounds derived from the six-membered ring $C_4H_4O_2$ are dioxins.) "Dioxin" is a contaminant produced in the manufacture of a number of chlorine-containing compounds, including the defoliant 2,4,5-T, which has been widely used.

2,4,5-T

"dioxin"
(2,3,7,8-tetrachlorodibenzo-p-dioxin)

2,4,5,-T was present in defoliants used during the Vietnam War, including the one known as Agent Orange. "Dioxin" has been the object of public concern because it has been found in animal tests to be extremely toxic in very low doses and because many individuals have been exposed to it through military service or by living near chemical manufacturing sites.

While exposure to large, obviously harmful concentrations of toxic compounds must always be avoided, the long-term effects of continued exposure to low levels of pollutants are of equally serious concern. Attention was first focused on such problems when DDT was identified as the cause of the decrease in the population of eagles, hawks, pelicans, and other large birds. DDT and other persistent compounds are concentrated by passage along a food chain (Figure B). Apparently DDT acts by increasing the formation of certain enzymes that catalyze the breakdown in birds of the steroid hormone estradiol. Low concentrations of estradiol mean later mating, causing the young to be born when food supplies are inadequate. Also, estradiol controls the storage of calcium in the bones, making less calcium available for the formation of eggshells.

The use of the chlorinated compounds that can persist in the environment has now been either banned or severely restricted in the United States. Chlorinated pesticides have been replaced by other types of compounds in many applications, for example, by organophosphorus compounds, which, although they are not

Figure B
Food Chain Concentration of DDT An example of how DDT concentration is increased by each species along a food chain. For example, in one study the following DDT concentrations were found: lake sediments, 0.0085 ppm; invertebrates, 0.40 ppm; fish feeding on invertebrates, 5 ppm; gulls feeding on fish, 3200 ppm.

without problems, are degraded more rapidly in the environment. The regulation of pesticides is, however, somewhat controversial. The health benefits of synthetic pesticides are great. The introduction of a DDT spraying program aimed at mosquitoes reduced the annual incidence of malaria in just one country from three million cases to about seven thousand cases. Also, the benefits to agriculture are not only desirable, but will become more and more necessary as world population grows. In agriculture, one answer lies in an approach called "integrated pest management": Conditions are controlled to favor natural predators and, rather than routine application of pesticides, pest populations are monitored so that spraying need only be done when the potential for crop damage is greatest.

33.5 PHENOLS

Phenols, ArOH

The attachment of a hydroxyl group to an aromatic ring gives a class of organic compounds known as **phenols**, ArOH. The simplest compound in the group is phenol itself, C_6H_5OH (Table 33.6). The structural similarity of phenols to alcohols is apparent, and like alcohols, the lower molecular mass phenols are water soluble. However, the aromatic ring modifies the chemical behavior of the hydroxyl group. Phenols are weak acids. Most of them have pK_a values of about 10, which makes them much stronger acids than alcohols. The acidity of phenols arises in part because the aromatic ring delocalizes the negative charge on the anion; for example,

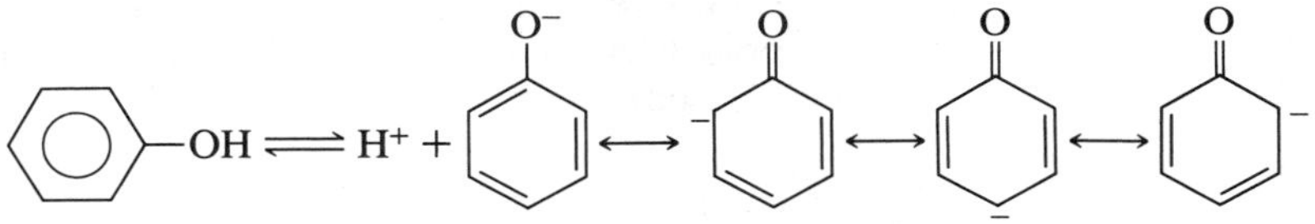

phenol

resonance structures of the phenoxide ion

Furthermore, the hydroxyl group causes the aromatic ring to be much more reactive toward substitution and oxidation. The Br, NO_2, and SO_3H groups are

Table 33.6
Phenols The general molecular formula of a phenol is ArOH.

	Melting Point (°C)		Melting Point (°C)
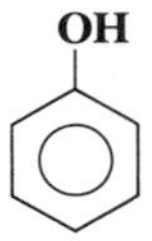 *phenol*	42	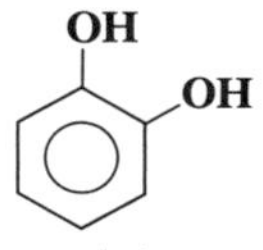 *catechol*	104
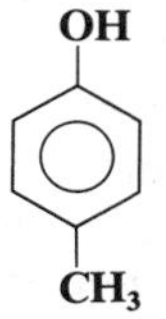 *p-cresol*	36	 *hydroquinone*	169
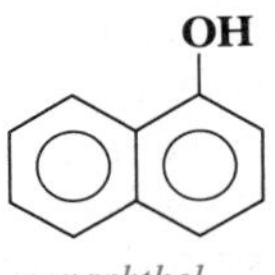 *α-naphthol (1-naphthol)*	94		

Table 33.7
Some More Complex Phenols Urushiol is a mixture of phenols that vary only in the amount of unsaturation in the side chain.

picric acid   *hexylresorcinol*   *urushiol*

readily substituted on ring carbon atoms in phenols under conditions that do not cause any reaction to occur with benzene.

Phenol itself is poisonous and also causes blisters on the skin. The biggest use for phenol is in the manufacture of phenol–formaldehyde polymers (Section 33.16b). Another important use of phenols is in bactericidal products. "Carbolic acid" is a name given to phenol and its aqueous solutions. Joseph Lister, applying Pasteur's theories about bacteria and infection in the late 1800s, did surgery under a spray of carbolic acid. Some of the more common antiseptic phenols are hexylresorcinol (Table 33.7) and the cresols (methylphenols) (Table 33.6). Phenols are also used in the manufacture of dyes, drugs, photographic developers, adhesives, and a large variety of other products. Picric acid (Table 33.7) is a strong acid and a high explosive. Many phenols occur naturally, for example, the active component in poison ivy (urushiol, Table 33.7) and several essential oils (oil of cloves, oil of aniseed).

33.6 ETHERS

Ethers, ROR′

An **ether,** which can be viewed as derived from water by replacing both hydrogen atoms with hydrocarbon groups, has the general formula ROR. If the two hydrocarbon groups are alike, the ether is a *simple* or *symmetrical* ether; if they are different, the ether is a *mixed* or *unsymmetrical* ether.

diethyl ether   *ethyl isopropyl ether*
a simple ether   *a mixed ether*

The common system of nomenclature names the groups attached to the oxygen atom followed by the word *ether,* as just shown. Sometimes the *di* is omitted when the groups are identical. Diethyl ether is then simply named ethyl ether. RO— is an *alkoxy group,* and in the IUPAC system of nomenclature, the ether is named as an alkoxy derivative of the longest chain hydrocarbon to which the alkoxy group is attached. The position of attachment is given by a number, starting at the end of the chain nearest the alkoxy group. Thus, ethyl isopropyl ether is 2-ethoxypropane. Table 33.8 gives several examples. Note that cyclic ethers are also known.

Ether molecules cannot form hydrogen bonds with one another. As a consequence, the boiling points of ethers are near those of hydrocarbons having the same molecular mass. The effect of hydrogen bonding is clearly illustrated by a comparison of the boiling points of ethylene glycol ($HOCH_2CH_2OH$, b.p. 197 °C) and 1,2-dimethoxyethane ($CH_3OCH_2CH_2OCH_3$, b.p. 85 °C).

Diethyl ether, a volatile flammable compound, is an anesthetic. The ethers are rather unreactive and are often used as solvents in carrying out reactions of organic compounds. However, ethers do have an unfortunate tendency to form peroxides (compounds containing —O—O—bonds) when exposed to the oxygen in air. These peroxides are susceptible to explosive decomposition. For this reason special

Table 33.8
Ethers The general molecular formula for an ether is ROR.

	Boiling Point (°C)		Boiling Point (°C)
CH_3OCH_3 *dimethyl ether* *(methoxymethane)*	−24	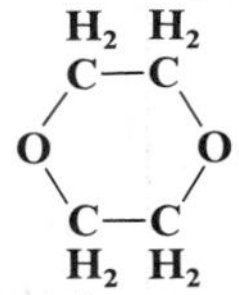 dioxane *(1,4-dioxin)*	101
$CH_3CH_2OCH_2CH_3$ *diethyl ether* *(ethoxyethane)*	35		
$CH_3OCH_2CH_2OCH_3$ *ethylene glycol dimethyl* *ether ("glyme")* *(1,2-dimethoxyethane)*	85	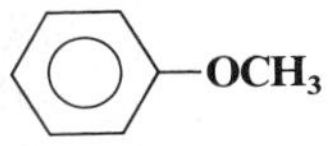 anisole *(methoxybenzene)*	154
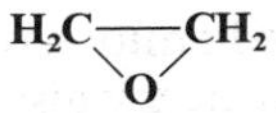 H_2C——CH_2 O *ethylene oxide* *(oxirane)*	11		

precautions must always be used when working with ethers, especially ethers from containers that have been opened and allowed to stand in the air.

33.7 AMINES

1° amine, RNH_2
2° amine, R_2NH
3° amine, R_3N

Amines can be thought of as formed by the replacement of the hydrogen atoms of an ammonia molecule by hydrocarbon groups. **Amines** are classified (Table 33.9) as primary (RNH_2), secondary (R_2NH), or tertiary (R_3N), according to the number of hydrogen atoms of the ammonia molecule that have been replaced by carbon atoms. Addition of a fourth hydrocarbon group yields a quaternary ammonium ion. The common system of nomenclature for amines is illustrated in Table 33.9. Such names as aniline, pyridine, and morpholine (Table 33.10) are nonsystematic names.

Aromatic amines are those with the nitrogen atom of the amine group attached to an aromatic ring, as in aniline. Such amines are usually prepared by the nitration of an aromatic compound and subsequent reduction of the nitro group, NO_2, with, for example, tin and concentrated hydrochloric acid.

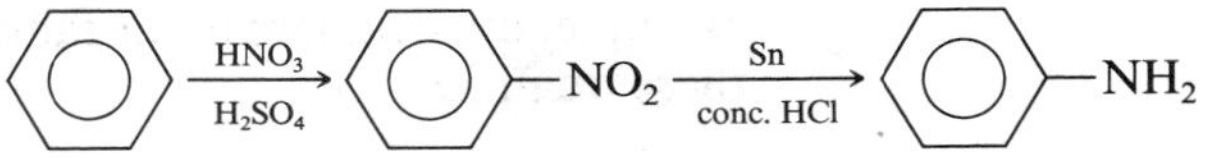

$$\text{benzene} \xrightarrow[H_2SO_4]{HNO_3} \text{nitrobenzene} (-NO_2) \xrightarrow[\text{conc. HCl}]{Sn} \text{aniline} (-NH_2)$$

benzene   *nitrobenzene*   *aniline*

Table 33.9
Classification of Amines

Primary amine, RNH_2
  CH_3NH_2
  methylamine
  b.p. −6 °C
Secondary amine, R_2NH
  $(CH_3)_2NH$
  dimethylamine
  b.p. 7 °C
Tertiary amine, R_3N
  $(CH_3)_3N$
  trimethylamine
  b.p. 3 °C
Quaternary ammonium salt, $R_4N^+X^-$
  $(CH_3)_4N^+I^-$
  tetramethylammonium iodide
  m.p. 230 °C (dec)

The amines are the most common organic bases. Simple amines such as the ethylamines

$CH_3CH_2NH_2$	$(CH_3CH_2)_2NH$	$(CH_3CH_2)_3N$
ethylamine	*diethylamine*	*triethylamine*
pK_b 3.33	pK_b 3.02	pK_b 3.28

are somewhat stronger bases than ammonia (NH_3, pK_b 4.7). The aromatic amines are weaker bases because resonance withdraws electron density from the nitrogen atom and stabilizes the amino group.

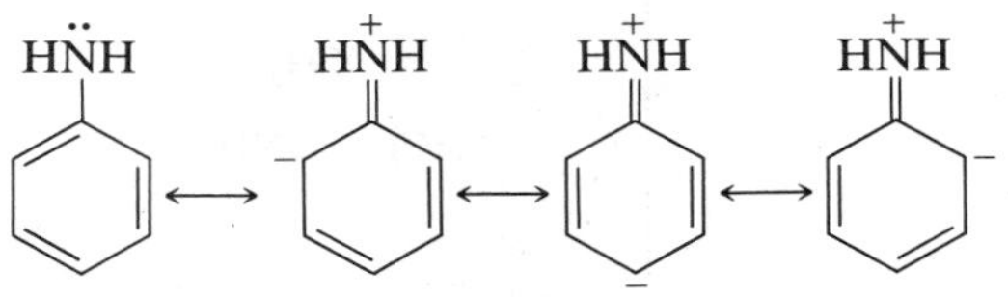

aniline, pK_b 9.38

Table 33.10
Aromatic and Cyclic Amines

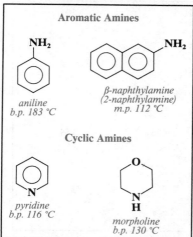

Aromatic Amines

aniline
b.p. 183 °C

β-naphthylamine
(2-naphthylamine)
m.p. 112 °C

Cyclic Amines

pyridine
b.p. 116 °C

morpholine
b.p. 130 °C

The salts of amines are odorless, water-soluble solids from which the free amines can be obtained by reaction with bases, for example,

$$CH_3NH_2 \xrightarrow{HCl} CH_3NH_3{}^+Cl^- \xrightarrow{NaOH} CH_3NH_2$$

methylamine   *methylammonium chloride*

By contrast with the amine salts, most free amines have fairly strong, unpleasant odors. Like the alcohols, amines of lower molecular mass (up to those with five carbon atoms) are water soluble.

Physiologically active amines (Table 33.11) found in plants are known as *alkaloids*. Nicotine is present in tobacco and is used as an insecticide. Morphine, a sedative and analgesic (pain killer), is a major component of opium. Codeine, another popular analgesic, is the methyl ether (at the phenolic hydroxyl group) of morphine. Heroin is also a derivative of morphine. Coniine, a relatively simple alkaloid, is the toxic substance in the hemlock that poisoned Socrates. The stimulating drugs amphetamine and methedrine are also amines. Note the structural similarity of these stimulants to epinephrine, also known as adrenalin, a naturally occurring stimulant that is released by the adrenal glands under conditions of fear or stress.

Aromatic primary amines react with a chilled acidic solution of a nitrite to form water-soluble and fairly unstable *diazonium salts*, $ArN_2{}^+X^-$. Much of the early incentive to study organic compounds arose from the desire to make synthetic dyes. An important class of dyes, the azo dyes, is formed by the coupling of diazonium salts with phenols or aromatic amines.

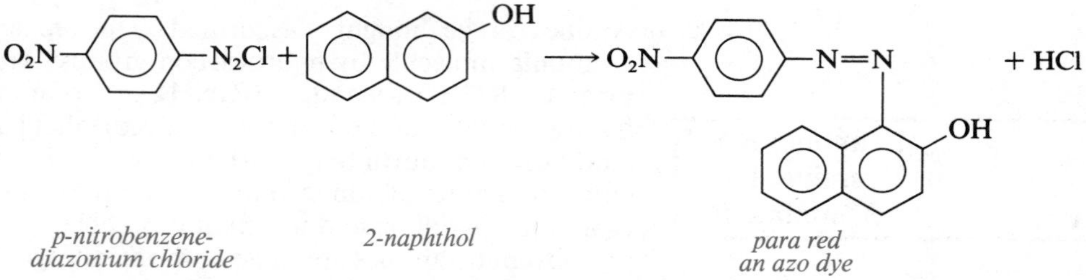

$$O_2N-\!\!\!\bigcirc\!\!\!-N_2Cl + \bigcirc\!\!\bigcirc\!\!OH \longrightarrow O_2N-\!\!\!\bigcirc\!\!\!-N\!=\!N-\!\!\bigcirc\!\!\bigcirc\!\!OH + HCl$$

p-nitrobenzene-diazonium chloride   *2-naphthol*   *para red an azo dye*

The *azo group,* $-N\!=\!N-$, is a *chromophoric group*, that is, a color-producing group. Any organic molecule that possesses a chromophoric group is colored. However, not all colored compounds are good dyes. A satisfactory fabric dye, for example, must adhere to the fabric and be stable to light, heat, and soap. Para red has these qualities.

Table 33.11
Some Physiologically Active Amines

nicotine   *morphine*   *coniine*

amphetamine (benzedrine)   *methedrine*   *epinephrine (adrenaline)*

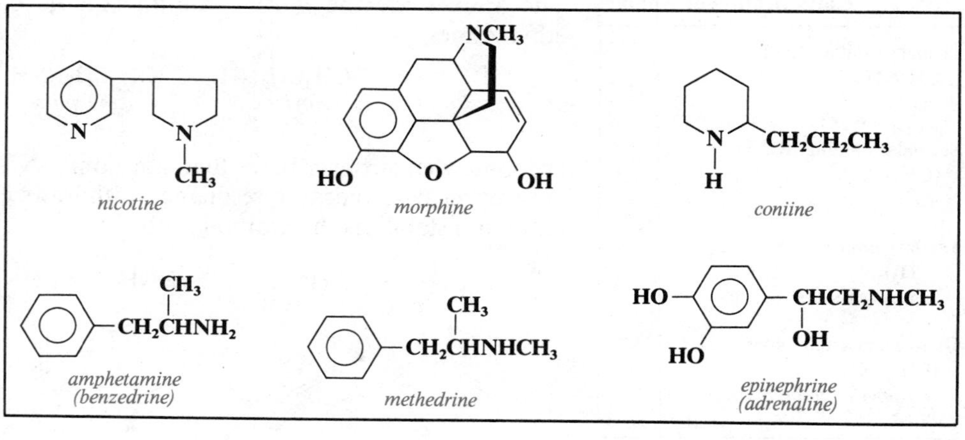

EXAMPLE 33.4
Alkaline Properties of Amines

What are the equilibrium concentrations of the various species present in a 0.100 M solution of aniline? $K_b = 4.2 \times 10^{-10}$ for

$$C_6H_5NH_2(aq) + H_2O(l) \rightleftharpoons C_6H_5NH_3^+ + OH^-$$

To solve this problem, we set up our usual equilibrium table with $x = [C_6H_5NH_3^+]$,

$$C_6H_5NH_2 + H_2O \rightleftharpoons C_6H_5NH_3^+ + OH^-$$

	$C_6H_5NH_2$	$C_6H_5NH_3^+$	OH^-
Initial	0.100	0	0
Change	$-x$	$+x$	$+x$
Equilibrium	$0.100 - x$	x	x

and substitute the equilibrium concentrations into the expression for K_b.

$$K_b = \frac{[C_6H_5NH_3^+][OH^-]}{[C_6H_5NH_2]} = \frac{(x)(x)}{(0.100 - x)} = 4.2 \times 10^{-10}$$

Assuming $(0.100 - x) \simeq 0.100$, we get $x = 6.5 \times 10^{-6}$ mol/L. Recognizing that the approximation is valid, the concentrations at equilibrium are

$$[C_6H_5NH_3^+] = [OH^-] = x = 6.5 \times 10^{-6} \text{ mol/L}$$
$$[C_6H_5NH_2] = 0.100 - x = 0.100 \text{ mol/L}$$

FUNCTIONAL GROUPS WITH COVALENT DOUBLE BONDS

33.8 ALDEHYDES AND KETONES

The **carbonyl group** consists of a carbon atom and an oxygen atom joined by a covalent double bond.

$$\diagdown_{\diagup}C{=}O$$

a carbonyl group

Like the covalent double bond between two carbon atoms, the covalent double bond in a carbonyl group is a combination of a σ bond and a π bond. The carbonyl group and its two attached groups lie in the same plane and include an sp^2-type carbon atom with bond angles near 120°. The carbon atom is slightly positive and the more electronegative oxygen atom is slightly negative.

Aldehydes, RCHO
Ketones, RCOR′

The carbonyl group is present in aldehydes and ketones, and in the rest of the functional groups discussed in this chapter.

An **aldehyde**, RCHO, is a compound in which a hydrogen atom and a hydrocarbon group are bonded to a carbonyl group (Table 33.12). The aldehyde group can be

Table 33.12
Aldehydes The general molecular formula for an aldehyde, often written as RCHO, is

$$R{-}C\diagup^{O}_{\diagdown H}$$

	Boiling Point (°C)		Boiling Point (°C)
HCHO *formaldehyde (methanal)*	−21	**CH₂=CHCHO** *acrolein (propenal)*	52
CH₃CHO *acetaldehyde (ethanal)*	21	—CHO *benzaldehyde*	179
CH₃(CH₂)₄CHO *caproaldehyde (hexanal)**	128		

* Note that the aldehyde group must be at the end of a chain, so it is unnecessary to write 1-hexanal.

Table 33.13

Ketones The general molecular formula for a ketone, often written as R_2CO or $RCOR'$ (in which R and R' may be the same or different) is

	Boiling Point (°C)
CH_3COCH_3 *dimethyl ketone (acetone)* *(2-propanone)*	56
$CH_3COCOCH_3$ *biacetyl* (dimethylglyoxal)* *(2,3-butanedione)*	88
$CH_3CH_2COCH_2CH_3$ *diethyl ketone* *(3-pentanone)*	102
$CH_3COCH_2CH_2CH_3$ *methyl n-propyl ketone* *(2-pentanone)*	102
$-COCH_3$ *methyl phenyl ketone* *(acetophenone)*	200

* This is one of the few colored (yellowish green) organic liquids. Practically all *pure* organic liquids are colorless; many pure organic solids are colored, however.

Table 33.14

Some More Complex Ketones

camphor

phenacyl chloride

methadone

found only at the *end* of a molecule. The general formula for an aldehyde may be written

(RCOH would look like an alcohol.)

In the simplest possible aldehyde, R is a hydrogen atom also (formaldehyde; see Table 33.12). The common names of the aldehydes are derived from the names of the carboxylic acids (next section) containing the same carbon skeleton by replacing the final *ic* by *aldehyde*. Thus, formaldehyde, HCHO, is the aldehyde corresponding to formic acid, HCOOH. The IUPAC system of nomenclature for aldehydes requires only the replacement of the final *e* of the name of the longest chain hydrocarbon including the aldehyde group by *al*. Substitutions or branches along this main chain are designated by numbers (the carbonyl carbon atom is numbered 1) and named by prefixes.

Formaldehyde is used mainly in the manufacture of phenol–formaldehyde and urea–formaldehyde polymers (Section 33.16b). It also finds some use as a disinfectant and a preservative, often as *formalin*, a 37% aqueous solution of formaldehyde. Several aldehydes have been isolated from fruits, to which they contribute characteristic odor and taste. Citral, a terpene aldehyde, is found in the oil from citrus fruits and in oil of lemon grass. It has a strong lemonlike odor. Vanillin is responsible for the flavor of the vanilla bean.

citral
 (3,7-dimethyl-2,6-octadienal)

vanillin

A **ketone**, R_2CO or $RCOR'$, contains two hydrocarbon groups attached to the carbon atom of the carbonyl group (Table 33.13). The general formula for a ketone may be written

In the common system of nomenclature, the two hydrocarbon groups are named, followed by the word *ketone,* as in methyl ethyl ketone, $CH_3COCH_2CH_3$. Dimethyl ketone is almost always referred to by its trivial name, *acetone*. In the IUPAC system of nomenclature, a ketone is designated by the suffix *one*, which replaces the final *e* of the name of the longest chain hydrocarbon containing the carbonyl group. A number is normally used to show the position of the carbonyl group, starting at the end of the chain nearest the carbonyl group. Thus, methyl ethyl ketone is 2-butanone in the IUPAC system. Substitutions and branches on the main chain are treated as is explained for hydrocarbons (Section 27.5).

Ketones are used extensively as solvents, especially in lacquers and other coatings. They frequently serve as starting materials for organic synthesis. Phenacyl chloride (Table 33.14), a potent lachrymator (tear inducer), is used in tear gas (Mace and CN). Camphor, from the camphor tree, is a ketone that has some use in medicine and plastics. Methadone is an addictive analgesic and is used in controlled programs to combat heroin addiction.

Alcohols are often the starting materials for the preparation of aldehydes and, especially, ketones. Sodium dichromate easily oxidizes a primary alcohol to an aldehyde and a secondary alcohol to a ketone.

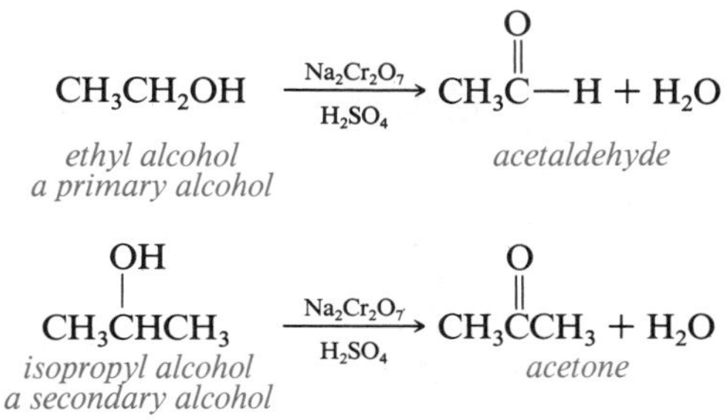

$$CH_3CH_2OH \xrightarrow[H_2SO_4]{Na_2Cr_2O_7} CH_3\overset{\displaystyle O}{\overset{\|}{C}}-H + H_2O$$

ethyl alcohol
a primary alcohol   *acetaldehyde*

$$CH_3\overset{\displaystyle OH}{\overset{|}{C}}HCH_3 \xrightarrow[H_2SO_4]{Na_2Cr_2O_7} CH_3\overset{\displaystyle O}{\overset{\|}{C}}CH_3 + H_2O$$

isopropyl alcohol   *acetone*
a secondary alcohol

A ketone is resistant to further oxidation under these conditions, but an aldehyde is readily oxidized to the corresponding carboxylic acid (Table 33.1); for example,

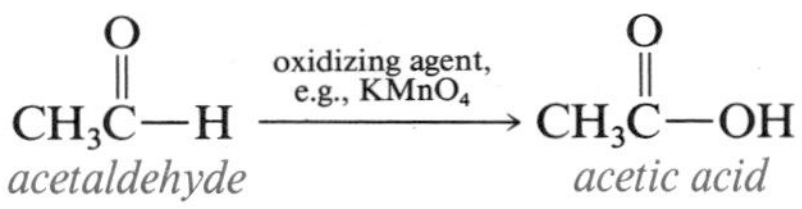

$$CH_3\overset{\displaystyle O}{\overset{\|}{C}}-H \xrightarrow[\text{e.g., KMnO}_4]{\text{oxidizing agent,}} CH_3\overset{\displaystyle O}{\overset{\|}{C}}-OH$$

acetaldehyde   *acetic acid*

Even atmospheric oxygen will convert many aldehydes to the corresponding acids. A very mild oxidizing agent, [Ag(NH$_3$)$_2$]OH, called Tollens' reagent, provides a diagnostic test for aldehydes.

$$RCHO + 2[Ag(NH_3)_2]OH \longrightarrow 2Ag(s) + RCOONH_4 + H_2O + 3NH_3$$

When this reaction is carried out in a clean test tube, the elemental silver that forms deposits as a silver mirror on the walls of the test tube. A process for the silvering of mirrors utilizes this reaction. [Solutions from this test must never be allowed to stand because of the possibility of the formation of silver azide, AgN$_3$, a *highly explosive* substance.]

33.9 CARBOXYLIC ACIDS

A **carboxylic acid,** RCOOH, has a functional group that is a combination of a carbonyl group and a hydroxyl group.

Carboxylic acids, RCOOH

$$R-C\overset{\displaystyle O}{\underset{\displaystyle OH}{\diagup}} \quad \text{or} \quad R\overset{\displaystyle O}{\overset{\|}{C}}OH \quad \text{or} \quad RCOOH$$

The more familiar carboxylic acids have common names that are associated with the sources from which they were first isolated. In the IUPAC system of nomenclature, the ending *oic* replaces the final *e* of the hydrocarbon name that is formed from the longest continuous chain of carbon atoms including the carboxyl group. The word *acid* follows this derived name. When this chain of carbon atoms is numbered, the carboxylic carbon atom is numbered 1. Table 33.15 shows the structures and names of some of the more common carboxylic acids.

Simple, unsubstituted monocarboxylic acids have pK_a values in the range 4–5; they are weaker as acids than sulfonic acids (RSO$_3$H) but stronger than phenols

Table 33.15
Carboxylic Acids The general molecular formula for a carboxylic acid, often written RCOOH, and in which R can be a hydrogen atom, is

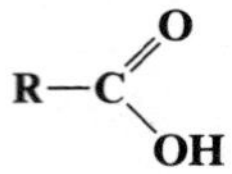

	Boiling Point (°C)		Boiling Point (°C)
HCOOH *formic acid (methanoic acid)*	101	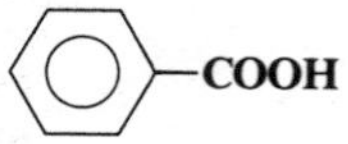 benzoic acid	121 m.p.
CH₃COOH *acetic acid (ethanoic acid)*	118	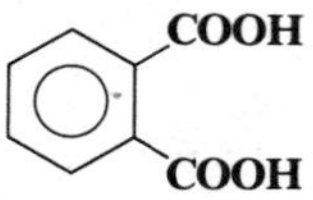 phthalic acid	230 m.p.
CH₃CH₂COOH *propionic acid (propanoic acid)*	140	terephthalic acid	>300 m.p. sublimes
CH₂=CHCOOH *acrylic acid (propenoic acid)*	140		
n-CH₃CH₂CH₂COOH *butyric acid (butanoic acid)*	163		

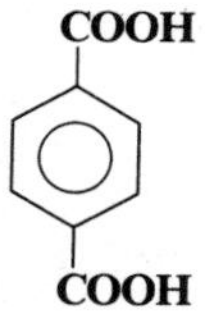

(Section 33.5). The ionization of a carboxylic acid, as shown, produces the **carboxylate ion**, $RCOO^-$.

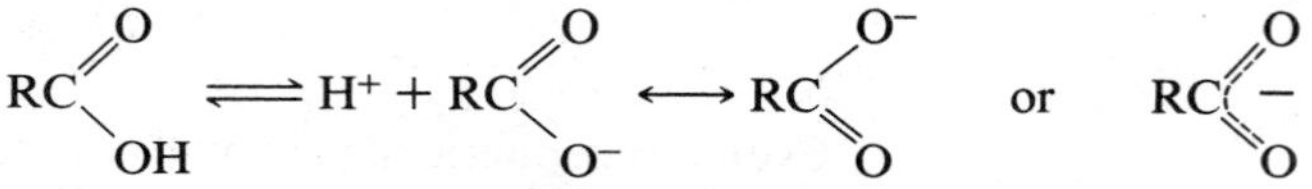

a carboxylate ion, resonance structures

This ion is stabilized by the delocalization of the negative charge over the two oxygen atoms.

All of the carboxylic acids form salts when they are treated with bases (e.g., hydroxides, carbonates, or hydrogen carbonates).

$$CH_3COOH + NaOH \longrightarrow CH_3COO^-Na^+ + H_2O$$

acetic acid (ethanoic acid) — *sodium acetate (sodium ethanoate)*

The name of the salt is obtained from the name of the cation, followed by the name of the carboxylic acid with the final *ic* replaced by *ate*.

Acetic acid is produced in large quantities (up to three billion pounds per year) for use in making plastics and solvents. Phthalic acid is also widely used in the production of varnishes, paints, and plastics.

Many carboxylic acids occur in nature, either free or combined in some form. The combination of hydroxyl groups and carboxylic acid groups in the same molecule to give hydroxy acids is very common in nature. Lactic acid (Table 33.16) is found in sour milk (racemic form) and in the muscles of man and animals (dextrorotatory isomer). Tartaric acid (dextrorotatory isomer) occurs in many fruits. Citric acid occurs in both plants and animals; lemon juice contains 5–8% citric acid.

Currently there is considerable interest in some physiologically active carboxylic acids called prostaglandins (Table 33.16). These substances are found in many body tissues and fluids, but they seem to occur in greatest amounts in human and sheep seminal plasma. Because of their broad physiological activity, high hopes are held for their use in medicine, particularly with respect to induced abortion, prevention of conception, and the regulation of menstruation and fertility.

Table 33.16
Some More Complex Carboxylic Acids The * denotes asymmetric carbon atoms.

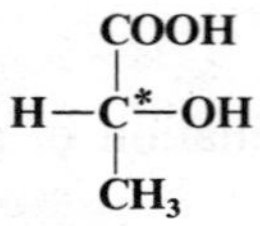

lactic acid

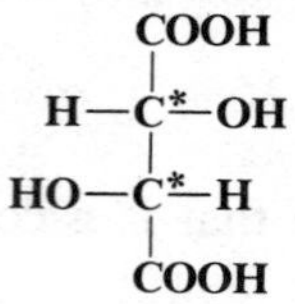

tartaric acid

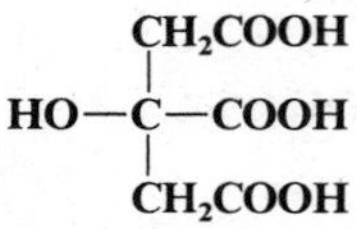

citric acid

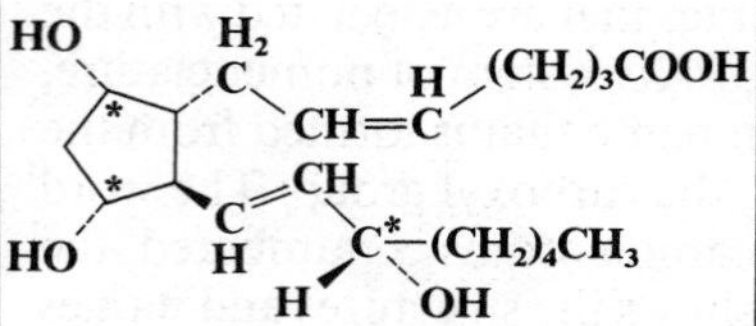

prostaglandin F₁ₐ (one of several prostaglandins)

33.10 ESTERS

A compound in which the acidic hydrogen atom of a carboxylic acid molecule is replaced by a hydrocarbon group is an **ester**, RCOOR′. The general formula for an ester can be written

---

Esters, RCOOR′

$$
R-C\!\!\underset{O-R'}{\overset{O}{\diagup}} \quad \text{or} \quad R\overset{O}{\overset{\|}{C}}OR' \quad \text{or} \quad RCOOR'
$$

In the two-word name for an ester, the first word is the name of the R′ group in RCOOR′. This word could be methyl (CH_3), ethyl (C_2H_5), phenyl (C_6H_5), or the like. The second word of the name is the name of the carboxylic acid with the final *ic* replaced by *ate,* identical with the name of the carboxylate anion. Table 33.17 illustrates the common and IUPAC system names.

A carboxylic acid and an alcohol form an ester in an *esterification reaction* when they are heated together in the presence of an acid catalyst.

$$
CH_3\overset{O}{\overset{\|}{C}}-OH + HOCH_2CH_3 \underset{}{\overset{H_2SO_4}{\rightleftharpoons}} CH_3\overset{O}{\overset{\|}{C}}-OCH_2CH_3 + H_2O
$$

acetic acid *ethyl alcohol* *ethyl acetate*

Table 33.17
Esters of Carboxylic Acids The general molecular formula for a carboxylic acid ester, often written as RCOOR′ or RCO_2R', and in which R and R′ may be alike or different, is

$$
R-C\!\!\diagdown^{O}_{OR'}
$$

	Boiling Point (°C)
HCOOCH₃	32
methyl formate (methyl methanoate)	
CH₃COOCH₃	57
methyl acetate (methyl ethanoate)	
CH₃COOCH₂CH₃	77
ethyl acetate (ethyl ethanoate)	
CH₂=CHCOOCH₃	85
methyl acrylate (methyl propenoate)	
⬡—COOCH₃	198
methyl benzoate	
⬡(COOC₂H₅)(COOC₂H₅)	298
diethyl phthalate	

The formation of an ester in such an equilibrium reaction is enhanced by the application of Le Chatelier's principle. An excess of either the carboxylic acid or the alcohol, or removal of water as it is formed, or both techniques together, are used to increase the yield of the ester.

The hydrolysis of an ester is the reversal of the reaction leading to its formation.

$$
CH_3\overset{O}{\overset{\|}{C}}-OCH_2CH_3 + H_2O \overset{H^+}{\rightleftharpoons} CH_3COOH + CH_3CH_2OH
$$

ethyl acetate *acetic acid* *ethyl alcohol*

Hot aqueous sodium hydroxide will also hydrolyze esters; the reaction is referred to as *saponification,* a term that is associated with the process for making soap (Section 15.20).

$$
CH_3COOCH_2CH_3 + NaOH \overset{H_2O}{\longrightarrow} CH_3COONa + CH_3CH_2OH
$$

ethyl acetate *sodium acetate* *ethyl alcohol*

Note that this reaction is not reversible; the salt of a carboxylic acid does not react with an alcohol.

Low molecular mass esters, for example, ethyl acetate and butyl acetate, are used extensively as solvents. Most esters of carboxylic acids have quite pleasant odors, even when derived from rather foul-smelling acids. Many fruits and flowers owe their flavor and fragrance to the esters present. For example, methyl salicylate is responsible for the flavor of wintergreen, and the ethyl ester of butyric acid (see Table 33.15) has the flavor of pineapple.

Aspirin, which is both a fever reducer and pain killer, is an ester formed between acetic acid and salicylic acid. When the aspirin reaches the alkaline environment of the intestines, the salicylic acid is liberated and absorbed by the body tissues. Salol (phenyl salicylate) is used to coat a pill when it is desired that the pill pass through the stomach unchanged and release its contents in the intestines. (Such a coating is called an enteric coating.) The salol coating is inert to the acidic conditions in the stomach, but it is hydrolyzed and dissolves in the alkaline intestines.

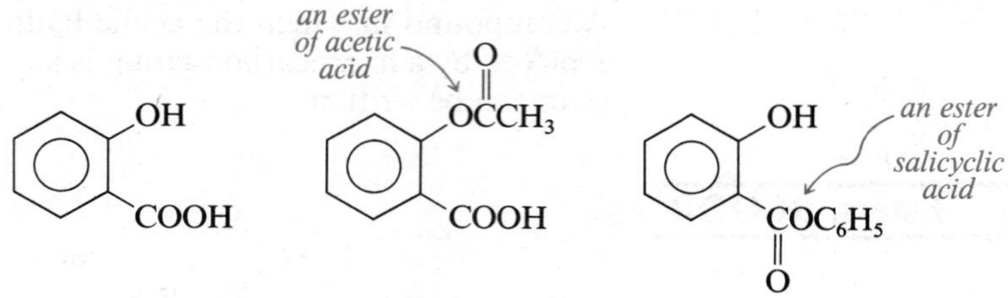

an ester
of acetic
acid

OH

OCCH₃
O

OH

an ester
of
salicylic
acid

COOH

COOH

COC₆H₅
O

salicylic
acid

aspirin
(acetylsalicylic acid)

salol
(phenyl salicylate)

33.11 ACYL HALIDES AND
CARBOXYLIC ACID
ANHYDRIDES

The replacement of the hydroxyl group of a carboxylic acid by a halogen atom gives
an **acyl halide**, RCOX, also called an acid halide (Table 33.18). An **acyl group**

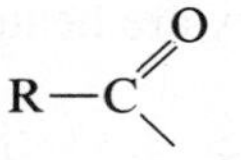

$$R-C\overset{\displaystyle O}{\underset{\displaystyle}{\big\|}}$$

an acyl group

is named by dropping the final *ic* from the name of the corresponding carboxylic
acid, and adding *yl*. The complete name of the acyl halide is then the name of the acyl
group, followed by the anionic name for the halogen atom.

The acyl halides are highly reactive compounds which do not occur in nature.
Those of lower molecular mass react rapidly with water, including moisture in the
air, undergoing hydrolysis to give the corresponding carboxylic acid, for example,

$$CH_3\overset{O}{\overset{\|}{C}}Cl \; + H_2O \longrightarrow CH_3\overset{O}{\overset{\|}{C}}OH + HCl$$

acetyl chloride   *acetic acid*

An **acid anhydride**, (RCO)₂O—the anhydride of a carboxylic acid—results
from the loss of water between two carboxyl groups.

$$R\overset{O}{\overset{\|}{C}}OH + HO\overset{O}{\overset{\|}{C}}R \longrightarrow R\overset{O}{\overset{\|}{C}}-O-\overset{O}{\overset{\|}{C}}R + H_2O$$

The anhydrides are given the name of the corresponding acid, followed by the
word *anhydride*. Mixed anhydrides, from two different carboxylic acids, and cyclic anhydrides, are named similarly, for instance, acetic butyric anhydride,
(CH₃CO)O(COC₃H₇) (Table 33.18).

Table 33.18
**Acyl Halides and Carboxylic Acid
Anhydrides**

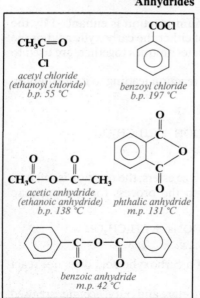

CH₃C=O
|
Cl

*acetyl chloride
(ethanoyl chloride)
b.p. 55 °C*

COCl

*benzoyl chloride
b.p. 197 °C*

CH₃C—O—C—CH₃
‖   ‖
O   O

*acetic anhydride
(ethanoic anhydride)
b.p. 138 °C*

*phthalic anhydride
m.p. 131 °C*

C—O—C
‖   ‖
O   O

*benzoic anhydride
m.p. 42 °C*

33.12 AMIDES

If an amino group or a substituted amino group is joined to an acyl group—that is, if
it replaces the OH group in a carboxylic acid—the resulting compound is an **amide**,
RCONH₂, or RCONHR′, or RCONR′R″:

Amides, RCONH₂

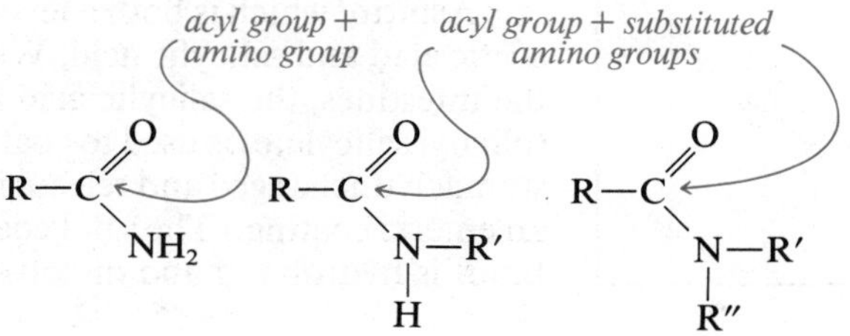

acyl group +
amino group

acyl group + substituted
amino groups

$$R-C\overset{\displaystyle O}{\big\|}$$
NH₂

$$R-C\overset{\displaystyle O}{\big\|}$$
N—R′
|
H

$$R-C\overset{\displaystyle O}{\big\|}$$
N—R′
|
R″

an amide

N-substituted amides

Table 33.19
Amides The general molecular formula for an amide, often written $RCONH_2$, is

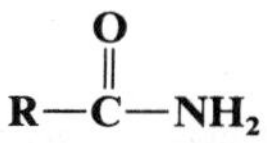

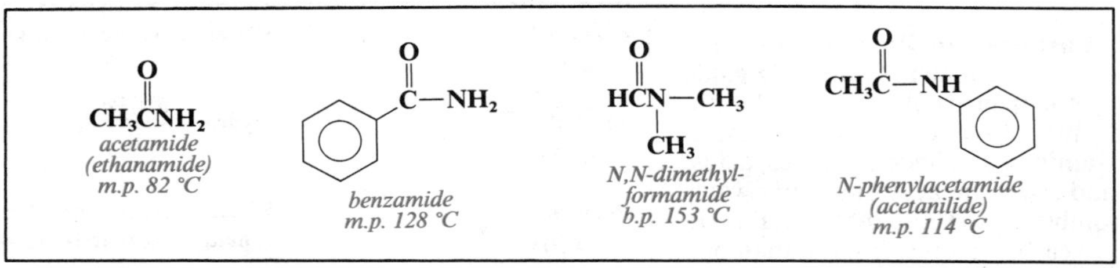

$$R-\overset{O}{\overset{\|}{C}}-NH_2$$

$$CH_3\overset{O}{\overset{\|}{C}}NH_2$$
acetamide
(ethanamide)
m.p. 82 °C

benzamide
m.p. 128 °C

$$H\overset{O}{\overset{\|}{C}}N-CH_3$$
$$\underset{CH_3}{}$$
N,N-dimethyl-
formamide
b.p. 153 °C

$$CH_3\overset{O}{\overset{\|}{C}}-NH$$
N-phenylacetamide
(acetanilide)
m.p. 114 °C

The common name for an amide is derived by replacing the *yl* of the acyl name by *amide*. Thus, acetamide is the name for CH_3CONH_2. Since the acyl group is named by replacing the *ic* of the carboxylic acid name by *yl*, one can equally well derive the amide name from the corresponding acid name by dropping the *ic* (or *oic* of the IUPAC name) and adding *amide*. If one or both of the hydrogen atoms on the amide nitrogen atom are replaced by hydrocarbon groups, the structure is named as an *N*-substituted amide (Table 33.19).

Amide molecules form intermolecular hydrogen bonds with themselves, or with other appropriate molecules such as water. Practically all of the amides are solids. *N,N*-Dimethylformamide (DMF), one of the few liquid amides, is an excellent solvent. Urea, H_2NCONH_2, is the diamide of carbonic acid.

p-Aminobenzenesulfonamide (sulfanilamide) (Table 33.20) and some of its *N*-substituted derivatives are known as the *sulfa drugs,* an important group of drugs that combat the growth of bacteria. The *penicillins,* which are also amides (see Table 33.20), were the first of the antibiotics to be discovered; they have to a great extent displaced sulfa drugs in the treatment of infectious diseases. Many penicillins are known; they differ only in the R group of the structure shown. *Aureomycin* is a representative of a group of tetracycline antibiotics, which are also amides.

Like acyl halides, amides react with water to give carboxylic acids

$$\overset{O}{\overset{\|}{R C} N H_2} + H_2O \xrightarrow{H^+ \text{ or } OH^-} \overset{O}{\overset{\|}{R C} O H} + NH_3$$

$$\overset{O}{\overset{\|}{R C} N H R'} + H_2O \xrightarrow{H^+ \text{ or } OH^-} \overset{O}{\overset{\|}{R C} O H} + R'NH_2$$

Amide hydrolysis is catalyzed by acids or bases and generally requires more vigorous reaction conditions than hydrolysis of acyl halides or acid anhydrides. The amide linkage is present in many molecules important in biochemistry (Section 33.21), and hydrolysis of this linkage plays a significant role in metabolism.

Some characteristic properties of the classes of organic compounds discussed in this chapter are summarized in Table 33.21.

Table 33.20
Some More Complex Amides

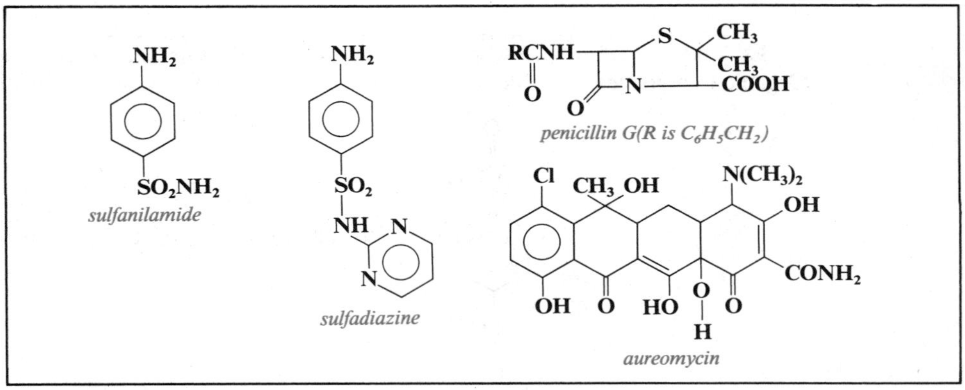

sulfanilamide

sulfadiazine

penicillin G (R is $C_6H_5CH_2$)

aureomycin

Table 33.21

Characteristic Properties of Some Common Types of Organic Compounds As a rule of thumb, monofunctional alcohols, ethers, amines, aldehydes, ketones, acids, and esters are at least slightly water soluble up to those that contain five carbon atoms. If more than one functional group is present, more carbon atoms can be carried into solution.

Alkyl halides RX	Water-insoluble, polar C—X bond subject to nucleophilic attack
Alcohols ROH	Hydrogen-bonded, very weak acid or base behavior
Phenols ArOH	Weak acids, lower molecular mass phenols are water soluble, aromatic ring reactive to substitution and oxidation
Ethers ROR	No hydrogen bonding, low boiling points, good solvents for organic compounds, relatively unreactive
Amines RNH_2, R_2NH, R_3N	Weak bases, foul odors, soluble in aqueous acids (salt formation)
Aldehydes and ketones $\overset{O}{\overset{\|}{RCH}}$ $\overset{O}{\overset{\|}{RCR'}}$	Polar C=O bond subject to nucleophilic attack, ketones good solvents for organic compounds
Carboxylic acids $\overset{O}{\overset{\|}{RCOH}}$	Weak acids, often biting odors, form salts with bases
Esters $\overset{O}{\overset{\|}{RCOR'}}$	Product of carboxylic acid + alcohol, pleasant odors, good solvents for organic compounds
Acyl halides $\overset{O}{\overset{\|}{RCX}}$	Reactive, not found in nature, lower molecular mass acyl halides hydrolyze in moist air
Acid anhydrides $\overset{O\ \ O}{\overset{\|\ \ \|}{RCOCR'}}$	Reactive, not found in nature
Amides $\overset{O}{\overset{\|}{RCNHR'}}$ $\overset{O}{\overset{\|}{RCNH_2}}$,	Hydrogen bonded, generally solids, hydrolyze under more vigorous conditions than acyl halides

EXAMPLE 33.5
Organic Compounds

Classify the following compounds according to the types of compounds listed in Table 33.21. Identify the functional groups and the R portions in each molecule.

(a) [benzene ring with COH (=O) top and COH (=O) bottom]   (b) $CH_3\overset{CH_3}{\underset{CH_3}{C}}OH$ (c) $CH_2{=}CHCOCH_2CH_2CH_2CH_3$ (with =O)   (d) [benzene ring with $\overset{O}{\overset{\|}{CCH_3}}$]

The R portions of each molecule are shown in color.

(a) 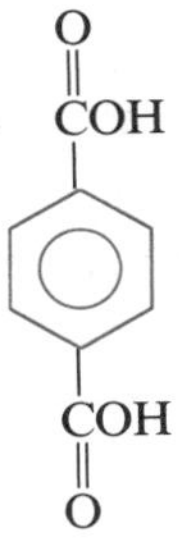 a dicarboxylic acid

(b) $CH_3-\underset{\underset{CH_3}{|}}{\overset{\overset{CH_3}{|}}{C}}OH$ *an alcohol*

(c) $CH_2=CH\overset{\overset{O}{\|}}{C}OCH_2CH_2CH_2CH_3$ *an ester*

(d) 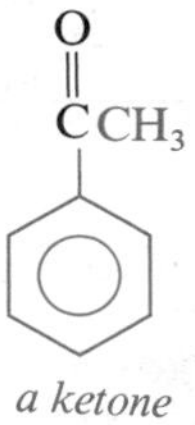 a ketone

Exercise Classify the following compounds and identify the functional groups and the R portions in each molecule.

(a) CH_2Cl_2

(b) 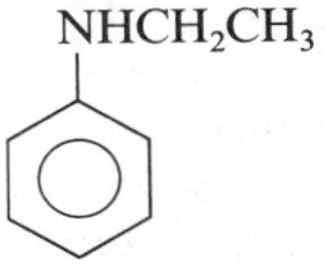 $NHCH_2CH_3$ (on benzene ring)

(c) $CH_3CH_2\overset{\overset{O}{\|}}{C}NH_2$

Answer (a) An alkyl chloride, R is CH_2, (b) an amine (secondary), R is C_6H_5 and CH_2CH_3, (c) an amide, R is CH_3CH_2

TOOLS OF CHEMISTRY

Infrared and Ultraviolet Spectroscopy

Absorption spectra arise when energy from incoming radiation is absorbed, causing atoms, molecules, ions, or electrons to move into higher energy states. Among the valuable tools of the organic chemist are infrared (IR) and ultraviolet (UV) absorption spectroscopy.

The infrared region of the electromagnetic spectrum extends from $2.5\,\mu m$ to $15\,\mu m$ ($1\,\mu m = 1 \times 10^{-4}$ cm = 1000 nm). Infrared spectra reflect increases in the energy of motion of atoms in a molecule relative to each other. The atoms in a molecule are never motionless. The bonds may, for example, bend or stretch (Figure A) or undergo other motions known as wagging, rocking, deformation, and so on. When the motion involves a change in dipole moment, and when the frequency of incoming radiation matches the frequency of the motion, absorption occurs and a "peak" appears in the infrared spectrum. Figure B shows the spectra of ethylene glycol and ethylenediamine with the origins of many of the peaks identified (str = stretching; def = deformation; wag = wagging). Customarily in infrared spectra the percent of the radiation *transmitted* (% transmittance) is

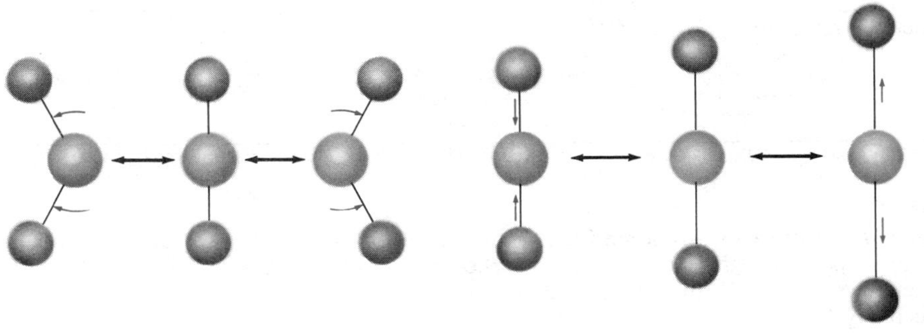

Figure A   (a)   (b)

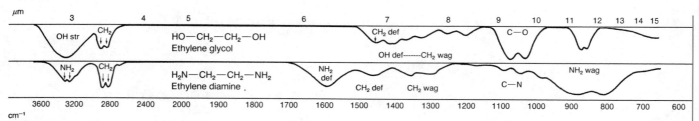

Figure B

Infrared Spectra of Ethylene Glycol (1,2-Ethanediol) and Ethylenediamine (1,2-Diaminoethane

plotted versus the wavelength (in μm, for example) or wave numbers (in cm⁻¹), so the absorption peaks actually appear as valleys.

The more complicated a molecule is, the more possibilities there are for relative motions of the atoms. Therefore, infrared spectra can be quite complex, and the larger the molecule the larger the number of peaks that appear in the spectrum. In spectra with many peaks, identification of the origin of all the peaks is difficult.

Infrared spectra are most useful in two ways. One depends upon the fact that the same functional groups cause absorption at the same wavelength (or very nearly so) in the spectra of all the molecules in which they occur. From the study of the spectra of thousands of compounds, "correlation charts" have been assembled. These charts show the locations of peaks that result from the presence of specific groups of atoms. A small portion of a correlation chart is shown in Figure C. This segment includes the location of the peaks of functional groups that contain a carbon–nitrogen single bond.

In the determination of the structure of an unknown compound, the infrared spectrum is used to indicate which functional groups are present by comparison of the spectrum with such charts. This is often not as simple and straightforward as it sounds, but with experience, much useful information about structure can be gleaned from infrared spectra. For example, an experienced observer would quickly know from the two spectra in Figure B that one compound contained OH groups and the other, NH₂ groups.

Infrared spectra, like mass spectra, are also used as fingerprints. It has been said that the infrared spectrum of a compound may be its most characteristic physical property. By comparison of the spectrum of a compound, say a reaction product that has not been identified, with the spectra of known compounds that might be products, identification can often be made. For example, if a compound was known to be either ethylenediamine or ethylene glycol, comparing its spectrum with the two known spectra in Figure B would quickly show which compound had been produced.

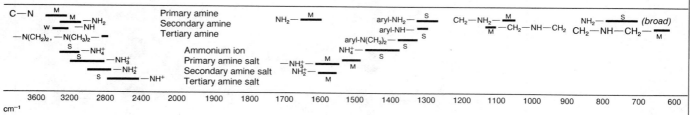

Figure C

Portion of an Infrared Correlation Chart This segment shows the location of peaks for groups that contain carbon-nitrogen single bonds. The letters S, M, and W indicate strong, medium, and weak bands, respectively.

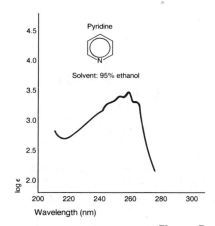

Figure D
Ultraviolet Spectrum of
Pyridine Source: R.M. Silverstein et
al., *Spectrometric Identification of*
Organic Compounds, New York:
Wiley, 1974.

The near-ultraviolet region of the electromagnetic spectrum extends from 200 to 400 nm. (Far-ultraviolet spectra, at shorter wavelengths, are difficult to measure experimentally and are of less practical value.) Ultraviolet radiation is of higher energy than infrared radiation. At such energy, absorption occurs by transitions of outer π or nonbonding electrons into higher energy levels, usually into unoccupied antibonding, σ^* or π^* orbitals.

A simple saturated hydrocarbon does not absorb in the near-ultraviolet region. The presence of carbon–carbon multiple bonds or of functional groups containing multiple bonds — that is, the presence of π electrons and π orbitals — is required for UV absorption. Ultraviolet spectra are much simpler than infrared spectra. They show a single peak or a few peaks for each isolated functional group or carbon–carbon multiple bond present in the molecule. Ultraviolet spectra are described in terms of λ_{max}, the wavelength of maximum absorption. Usually measured in solution, ultraviolet spectra are presented as plots of absorption versus wavelength or, as in the pyridine spectrum shown in Figure D, as the logarithm of the molar absorptivity, log ϵ, versus wavelength. Molar absorptivity, ϵ, is a function of the amount of radiation transmitted, the concentration of the substance in solution, and the length of the path of the light through the sample. Ultraviolet absorption peaks are shifted to longer wavelengths when a molecule contains conjugated systems, for example, $-CH=CH-CH=CH-$ or $-CH=CH-CH=O$.

Ultraviolet spectra can be used for structure analysis and compound identification in the same way that infrared spectra are used. However, their application in these ways is limited because there are fewer peaks in ultraviolet spectra and the peaks are broader. Spectra in the near-ultraviolet region are more often used in quantitative analysis, as are spectra in the visible region. The spectra are measured in solution and the intensity of the absorption varies with the concentration of the absorbing species. The relationship between the ultraviolet absorption and concentration is first determined experimentally. Then an unknown concentration can be found by comparison with the data for known concentrations. Titrations can be followed by spectral changes, and frequently, the concentration of a substance in a complex mixture can be measured by its characteristic absorption.

POLYMERS

33.13 WHAT IS A POLYMER?

Plastics, synthetic fibers, rubber, cellulose, proteins — these materials are all polymers. Polymers result when large numbers of smaller molecules, called **monomers,** chemically bond to each other. The individual large polymer molecules are known as **macromolecules.** In their simplest form, polymer molecules are long chains composed of one type of repeating structural unit. If a single paper clip were a monomer, then a chain of paper clips would constitute such a polymer, or macromolecule. Linear polyethylene is a polymer of this type. The monomer is ethylene, $CH_2=CH_2$, and the structure of a segment of the polymer chain is as shown:

the repeating unit from the monomer

$$-CH_2CH_2CH_2CH_2CH_2CH_2CH_2CH_2CH_2CH_2CH_2-$$

or $\quad +CH_2CH_2+_n \quad$ *n = a large number*

polyethylene

Table 33.22
Some Vinyl Polymers Examples of
the uses are given for each polymer.

Monomer	Polymer
Polypropylene	
$CH_2{=}CHCH_3$	$+CH_2CH+_n$ $\quad\quad\quad CH_3$
Carpeting, rope, molded automobile and appliance parts	
Polyvinyl chloride	
$CH_2{=}CHCl$	$+CH_2CH+_n$ $\quad\quad\quad Cl$
Phonograph records, exterior siding, pipe, floor tile	
Polystyrene	
$CH_2{=}CH$—⬡	$\left(CH_2CH\right)_n$ ⬡
Foam (Styrofoam), appliances, toys, furniture	

**Thermoplastic polymer:
softens when heated
hardens when cooled**

We encounter polyethylene almost every day in such items as flexible bottles, trash can liners, and the wrappings on food and meat in the supermarket.

The vinyl group, $CH_2{=}CH{-}$, is present in monomers which are structurally related to ethylene and form a large and widely used family of polymers known as vinyl polymers. In each of the vinyl polymers (Table 33.22) the repeating unit is CH_2CHX, where X varies according to the monomer that has been polymerized.

The materials from which many common articles such as toys, buckets, food containers, or garden hoses are made are often called "plastics." Strictly speaking, "plastic," or more precisely, a **thermoplastic polymer,** softens when it is heated and resolidifies when it is cooled. Such a material can be heated, then molded (as in making a toy) or extruded (forced through an opening to form a continuous shape, as in making a garden hose), and finally cooled to produce the desired article. But, although "plastics" are made from polymers, not all polymers are necessarily plastics, for many polymers do *not* soften when heated.

The size of the individual macromolecules in a polymeric substance is quite variable. Polymers are characterized by the *average molecular mass* of the chains. For the majority of synthetic polymers in common use as plastics or fibers, the average molecular masses are between 1×10^4 and 1×10^6 u. The number of repeating units in such polymers, known as the *degree of polymerization,* varies roughly from 100 to 5000.

Many naturally occurring polymers have been recognized for centuries, but an understanding of their true nature and properties has been acquired only in the last 50 years. The first synthetic polymer in commercial use was Bakelite, a phenol–formaldehyde polymer (see Figure 33.6) introduced in 1909. The use of synthetic polymers accelerated rapidly in the 1940s. Synthetic polymers are now produced in huge volume—on the order of 50 billion pounds per year in the United States alone.

Polymers have found a multitude of practical applications because of the great variation possible in their physical and mechanical properties. Some polymers are resistant to water, while others are water soluble. Some can be drawn into fibers and spread into very thin films. Some polymers are very hard and strong, while others are flexible and will return to their original shapes after being stretched or bent.

The chemistry of polymer formation and the physical properties of macromolecules are subject to the same influences as are the chemical and physical properties of smaller molecules. The differences between polymeric and nonpolymeric substances are due to variations in molecular structure, spatial arrangement, and the strength of intermolecular forces that result from the large size of polymer molecules. For example, flexible macromolecules are likely to be tangled and twisted together, and therefore cannot flow past each other as smaller molecules do. Large groups attached to the linear chain of a macromolecule can further inhibit the achievement of an orderly arrangement and the flow of the molecules past each other. Also, although the magnitude of intermolecular forces between individual small molecules is not great, the cumulative effect of such forces over the length of adjacent polymer chains can produce a very strong attraction between the chains.

The mechanical properties of polymers reflect the resistance of the chains to movement past one another. Therefore, strong intermolecular forces or molecular structures that inhibit molecular motion tend to strengthen and stiffen a polymer, and also to raise its melting point. When only weak dipole–dipole forces act between macromolecules, as in polyethylene, very long chains are needed to develop useful properties. At shorter chain lengths, strong intermolecular forces between chains, such as the hydrogen bonding between the polar amide groups in nylon, are required to provide mechanical strength (Figure 33.1; see Table 33.23). It is interesting to note that some polymers will deform if bent slowly enough for the molecules to move to new positions, but will break if bent so sharply that high local stresses occur. This

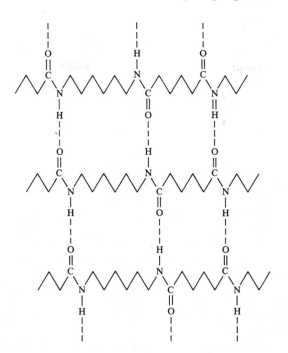

Figure 33.1
**Hydrogen Bonds between Amide
Groups on Adjacent Chains of
Nylon 66** (see Table 33.23)

behavior constitutes one of the principal differences between polymers and other
materials.

Because of the special techniques needed to form polymers and to study their
properties, polymer chemistry has developed into a distinct and separate branch of
chemistry. More than half of the chemists and chemical engineers in the United
States are employed in fields related in one way or another to polymer chemistry.

33.14 POLYMER STRUCTURE

A long chain of repeating units bonded together as in polyethylene forms a *linear
polymer* (Figure 33.2). In the natural course of polymerization or as the result of
intentional control of the reaction, other, often shorter, polymer chains of the same
or different composition can be attached to the main polymer chain, producing a
branched polymer. Both linear and branched polymers are generally thermoplastic.

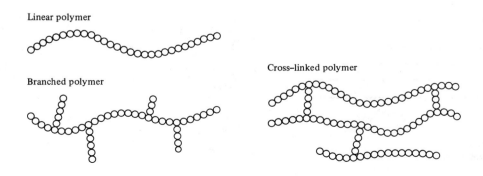

Figure 33.2
Polymer Structures Each circle
represents a single repeating unit.

Figure 33.3
Types of Copolymers Each circle represents a single repeating unit; the black and colored circles represent units from two different monomers.

Random copolymer

Block copolymer

Alternating copolymer

Graft copolymer

Thermoset polymers:
highly cross-linked
permanently rigid
do not melt when heated

Homopolymer: single
monomer
Copolymer: 2 or more
different monomers

If the "branches" on one polymer chain are bonded to other polymer chains, the result is a *cross-linked polymer*—a polymer in which long chains are interconnected by covalently bonded shorter chains.

The degree of branching or cross-linking has a significant effect on the properties of polymers. For example, linear polyethylene is much higher in density than polyethylene containing a significant number of branches. Highly cross-linked polymers, like network covalent substances, are rigid. They do not melt when heated, but instead, if heated to a high enough temperature, undergo chemical decomposition. Such substances are **thermoset polymers**—cross-linked polymers that are permanently rigid. To form articles with the desired shapes from thermosetting polymers, the cross-linking reaction must be allowed to take place during fabrication of the article.

A **homopolymer** is formed by the polymerization of a single type of monomer. The vinyl polymers illustrated in Table 33.22 are all homopolymers. By contrast, a **copolymer** is formed by the polymerization together (the "copolymerization") of two or more different monomers. Two monomers can combine in either regular fashion (although this is rare) or a random fashion. Figure 33.3 illustrates some of the ways in which two monomers can combine. Careful control of the polymerization reaction makes it possible to create polymers with exactly the desired properties by combination of different monomers in various ratios and geometric arrangements. Consequently, most of the synthetic polymers currently in practical use are copolymers.

As we know, crystallinity results from the packing together of molecules or ions in a regular arrangement. On the other hand, random arrangements of molecules produce amorphous substances, which have quite different properties from crystalline ones. Most polymers are either amorphous or semicrystalline. Because of the length of polymer chains, a fully ordered arrangement is not common.

In an amorphous polymer, the macromolecules are coiled and twisted together, not unlike a group of very long earthworms twisted together in a can. Crystallinity in polymers is possible when the chains can line up close together in parallel fashion (Figure 33.4). For this to happen, the individual polymer molecules must be of reasonably regular structure and without bulky substituents or branches that would get in the way. When the polymer chains pack together, they form *crystallites*—

Orientation of chains
in a crystalline polymer

Orientation of chains
in an amorphous polymer

Crystallite

Orientation of chains
in a semicrystalline polymer

Figure 33.4
Amorphous and Crystalline
Polymers

regions within the polymer that have crystalline properties such as sharp melting points. Only a portion of a given chain is likely to become part of a crystallite. A given chain may wander from one crystallite to another, with intermediate regions being amorphous.

33.15 THERMAL PROPERTIES OF POLYMERS

At low temperatures an amorphous polymer is a glass — only small groups, such as CH_3 side chains, can move at all. Glasses are rigid and brittle — they shatter if struck (like a mass of frozen worms).

As the temperature increases, it is possible for increasingly larger portions of the molecules to move. At what is called the **glass transition temperature**, T_g, there is a dramatic increase in the flexibility of a polymer as enough free volume becomes available to allow the cooperative motion of large segments of the polymer chains. Mechanical, electrical, and other properties also change at T_g.

Above their glass transition temperatures, polymers are flexible and rubbery. As the temperature increases beyond T_g, independent motion of the polymer chains becomes increasingly easier. At appropriate temperatures above T_g thermoplastic polymers can be molded and otherwise transformed into desired shapes. The increase in mobility with increasing temperature applies only to the amorphous regions of a semicrystalline polymer. Complete disentanglement of the molecules cannot occur until the melting point (T_m) of the crystalline region is reached. Below T_m the crystallites act like cross-links, inhibiting the mobility of the chains.

Rigid plastics: used below T_g
Flexible plastics: used above T_g

Rigid plastics have glass transition temperatures above the temperatures at which they are used. For example, polystyrene, a hard clear plastic used in housewares, plastic lenses, and Styrofoam, has a T_g of 100 °C, well above room temperature. On the other hand, polymers used in applications that require flexibility must have a T_g well below the temperature at which they will be used. Polyisobutylene, one of the butyl rubbers, has a T_g of -70 °C and is a tacky substance at room temperature. It is used in chewing gum and caulking compounds, as an adhesive, and as an oil additive, a use which provides a nice demonstration of the utilization of specific polymer properties. At ordinary temperatures lubricating oil is not a good solvent for polyisobutylene and the polymer molecules are coiled up. At higher temperatures, the oil becomes less viscous, an undesirable property. However it also becomes a better solvent for the polymer molecules. The molecules uncoil and counteract the decrease in viscosity of the oil, because the long chains tend to become entangled and thus resist movement past each other.

33.16 POLYMERIZATION REACTIONS

In order to participate in polymer formation, a molecule must be able to react at both ends so that the polymer chain can grow. Olefins polymerize by addition to both ends of the double bonds and conversion of the double bonds to single bonds. Difunctional molecules polymerize by reaction at each of their two functional groups. And cyclic compounds polymerize by reactions in which the ring is opened and addition takes place at both ends of the opened ring.

The two principal types of polymerization reactions are chain reaction polymerization (also referred to as addition polymerization) and step reaction polymerization (also referred to as condensation polymerization). The addition and condensation reactions involved in polymerization are no different from those we have encountered earlier in this chapter; however, they must be able to repeat thousands of times when the reactants are sufficiently pure.

a. Chain reaction polymerization **Chain reaction polymerization** is a rapid polymerization characterized by three reaction steps — initiation, propagation, and termination. The polymerization begins when a molecule of an *initiator* (I) is

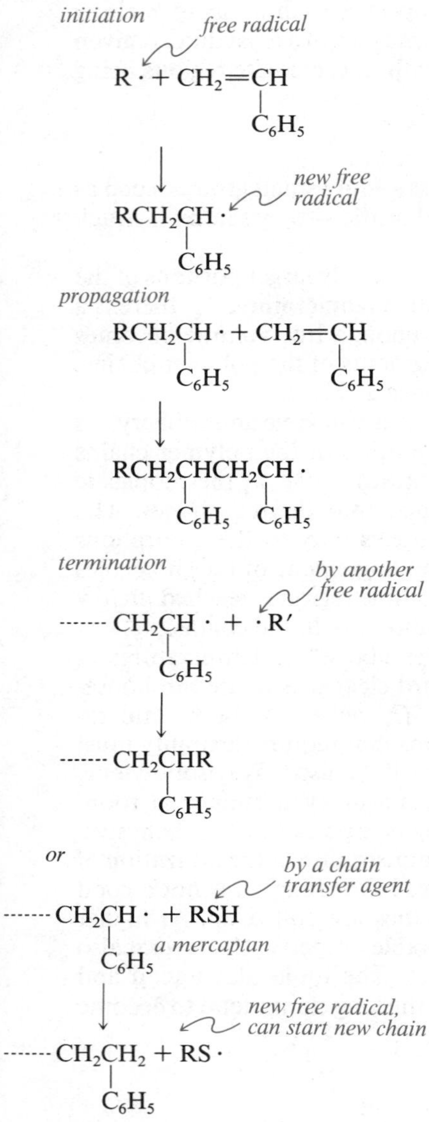

initiation

free radical

$$R \cdot + CH_2 = CH$$
$$\qquad\qquad | $$
$$\qquad\qquad C_6H_5$$

↓ *new free radical*

$$RCH_2CH \cdot$$
$$\quad\ \ |$$
$$\quad\ \ C_6H_5$$

propagation

$$RCH_2CH \cdot + CH_2 = CH$$
$$\quad\ \ | \qquad\qquad\quad |$$
$$\quad\ \ C_6H_5 \qquad\qquad C_6H_5$$

↓

$$RCH_2CHCH_2CH \cdot$$
$$\quad\ \ | \qquad\quad |$$
$$\quad\ \ C_6H_5 \ \ C_6H_5$$

termination

by another free radical

$$\text{------}\ CH_2CH \cdot + \cdot R'$$
$$\qquad\quad |$$
$$\qquad\quad C_6H_5$$

↓

$$\text{------}\ CH_2CHR$$
$$\qquad\quad |$$
$$\qquad\quad C_6H_5$$

or

by a chain transfer agent

$$\text{------}\ CH_2CH \cdot + RSH$$
$$\qquad\quad | \qquad\qquad \text{a mercaptan}$$
$$\qquad\quad C_6H_5$$

↓ *new free radical, can start new chain*

$$\text{------}\ CH_2CH_2 + RS \cdot$$
$$\qquad\quad |$$
$$\qquad\quad C_6H_5$$

Figure 33.5
Chain Reaction Polymerization of Styrene

converted to an active species (I*) that reacts with a monomer molecule (M) to give an active intermediate:

initiation

$$I \longrightarrow I*$$
$$I* + M \longrightarrow IM*$$

Propagation is the very rapid (10^{-1} to 10^{-6} s) growth of the polymer chain by the successive addition of monomer molecules.

propagation

$$IM* + M \longrightarrow IMM* + M \longrightarrow IMMM* \ldots I(M)_nM*$$

Propagation continues until the active end of the chain encounters a species (T) which reacts to give a molecule that is no longer active.

termination

$$I(M)_nM* + T \longrightarrow I(M)_nMT$$

Many important vinyl polymers are formed by chain reaction polymerization in which the active species that initiates the reaction is a free radical and the chain grows by successive addition of monomer to a free radical at the end of the chain (Figure 33.5). Other types of initiators lead to chain reaction polymerizations in which the reactive end of the chain is a cation, an anion, or a coordination complex.

b. Step reaction polymerization **Step reaction polymerization** proceeds by the reaction of difunctional monomers with each other. No initiator is necessary and each "step" is the same type of chemical reaction. Usually a small molecule, such as water or methanol, is eliminated in the combination of the two functional groups and the reaction takes place at both ends of the growing chain. For example, polyesters are formed by step reaction polymerization. Earlier we described the reaction between an alcohol and an acid to give an ester (Section 33.10). Polyesters result from the reaction between difunctional acids and difunctional alcohols as follows (where rectangles represent the molecules to which the functional groups are attached):

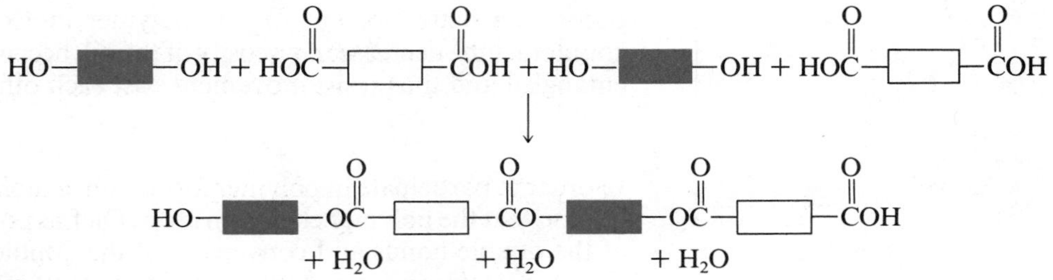

$$HO\text{---}\blacksquare\text{---}OH + HO\overset{O}{\overset{\|}{C}}\text{---}\square\text{---}\overset{O}{\overset{\|}{C}}OH + HO\text{---}\blacksquare\text{---}OH + HO\overset{O}{\overset{\|}{C}}\text{---}\square\text{---}\overset{O}{\overset{\|}{C}}OH$$

↓

$$HO\text{---}\blacksquare\text{---}O\overset{O}{\overset{\|}{C}}\text{---}\square\text{---}\overset{O}{\overset{\|}{C}}O\text{---}\blacksquare\text{---}O\overset{O}{\overset{\|}{C}}\text{---}\square\text{---}\overset{O}{\overset{\|}{C}}OH$$
$$\quad + H_2O \qquad\quad + H_2O \qquad\quad + H_2O$$

Some additional examples of polymers formed in this way are given in Table 33.23.

Bakelite, one of the older synthetic polymers, is a phenol–formaldehyde polymer formed by step reaction polymerization. Because both ortho positions and the para position in phenol are reactive sites, the polymerization reaction between phenol and formaldehyde can extend in three directions to form a network covalent type of polymer (Figure 33.6). Normally, the polymerization is stopped when the polymer is still soluble and fusible (able to melt without decomposition). A filler (usually wood flour) is added which will reinforce the final polymer, and then the cross-linked and infusible polymer is produced by the application of heat and pressure. This material is present as the bonding agent in such products as plywood and wood fiber boards (particle board).

Table 33.23
Some Copolymers Formed by Step Reaction Polymerization

Nylon 66, a polyamide

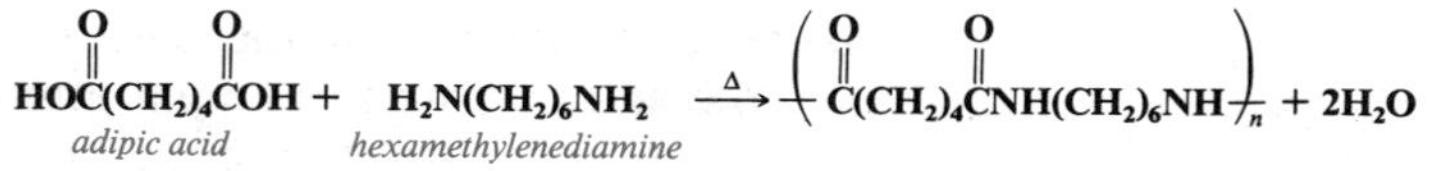

$$HOC(CH_2)_4COH + H_2N(CH_2)_6NH_2 \xrightarrow{\Delta} \left(C(CH_2)_4CNH(CH_2)_6NH \right)_n + 2H_2O$$

adipic acid   *hexamethylenediamine*

Used in fibers.

Poly(ethylene terephthalate), a polyester

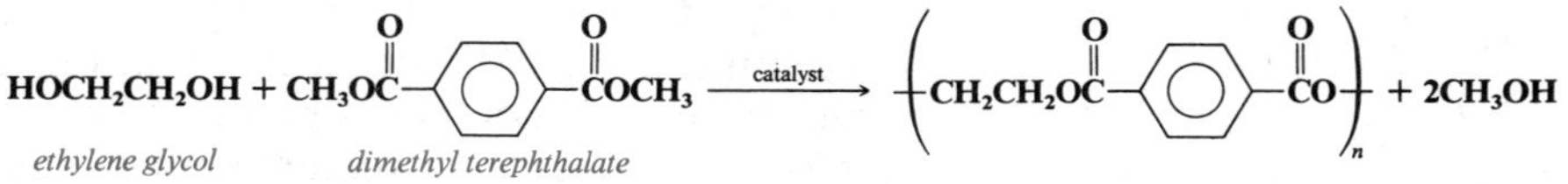

$$HOCH_2CH_2OH + CH_3OC\text{—}\bigcirc\text{—}COCH_3 \xrightarrow{catalyst} \left(CH_2CH_2OC\text{—}\bigcirc\text{—}CO \right)_n + 2CH_3OH$$

ethylene glycol   *dimethyl terephthalate*

Used in films (Mylar) and Fibers (Dacron)

A polycarbonate

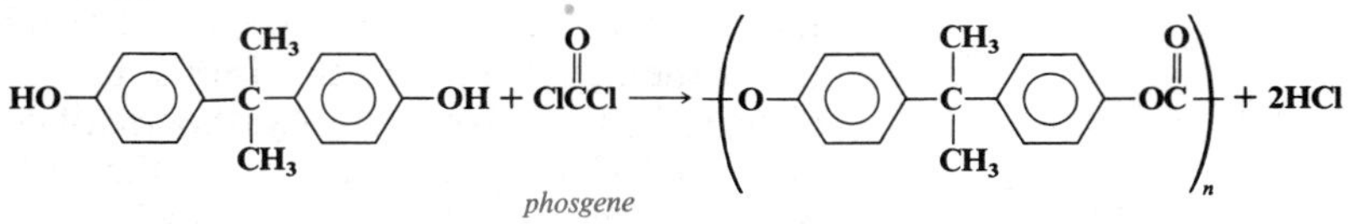

$$HO\text{—}\bigcirc\text{—}\overset{CH_3}{\underset{CH_3}{C}}\text{—}\bigcirc\text{—}OH + ClCCl \longrightarrow \left(O\text{—}\bigcirc\text{—}\overset{CH_3}{\underset{CH_3}{C}}\text{—}\bigcirc\text{—}OC \right)_n + 2HCl$$

phosgene

A very tough, transparent plastic (Lexan) used in, e.g., shatter-resistant windows

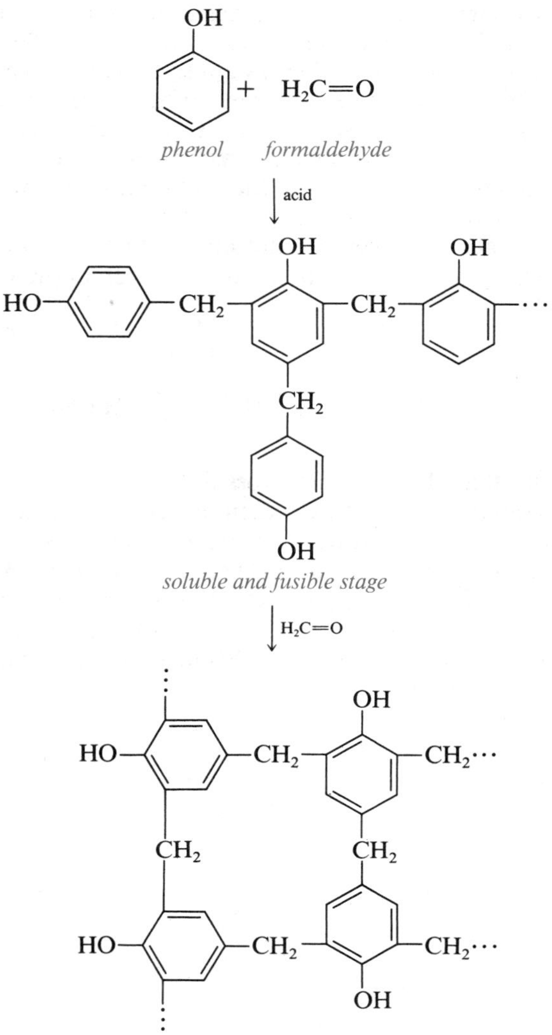

phenol   *formaldehyde*

acid

soluble and fusible stage

$H_2C=O$

Figure 33.6
Bakelite, a Phenol-Formaldehyde, Network Covalent, Cross-Linked Polymer These are generalized structures.

33.17 NATURAL POLYMERS

The unique properties of living things are in many ways the result of the properties of polymers. As is discussed further in the following sections, many of the molecules of biochemistry are macromolecules. Two natural polymers—cellulose and rubber—were the first polymers to be put into commercial use. Each had to be structurally modified to achieve useful properties.

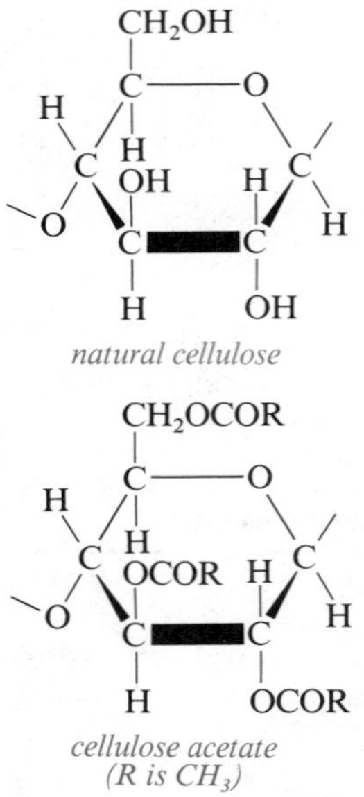

a. Cellulose The repeating unit in natural cellulose (Figure 33.7) is a ring structure with numerous hydroxyl groups which provide strong hydrogen bonding between the chains. Microcrystalline regions also help to hold the chains together. Natural cellulose is not thermoplastic. Before the hydrogen bonds are broken and the microcrystals melted—a requirement for plastic flow—the molecule undergoes thermal decomposition. By converting some of the hydroxyl groups to functional groups that do not form hydrogen bonds, it is possible to alter the properties of the natural polymer. The nitrate ester of cellulose was prepared and used commercially in lacquers and films in the 1800s, before the nature of polymers was understood. (Due to its high flammability, the use of cellulose nitrate in such applications is now obsolete.) Cellulose acetate and other cellulose esters are still used in fibers. (Garments made of such fibers are labeled "acetate.")

b. Natural rubber Polymers that have elasticity, like rubber, are referred to as **elastomers.** Such polymers are utilized above their glass transition temperatures. The polymer chains in an elastomer must be flexible and they must be joined by a moderate number of cross-links. In the unextended state, the molecules of an elastomer are tangled together. When a force is applied, the polymer chains move into an extended and more ordered arrangement (Figure 33.8). The cross-links are necessary to prevent the chains from slipping past each other when force is applied. When the force is released the chains return to their less ordered state, largely because of the concomitant increase in entropy.

Natural rubber is an unsaturated polymer in which the chain enters and leaves each covalent double bond in a *cis* orientation. (The *trans* isomer is not rubbery.)

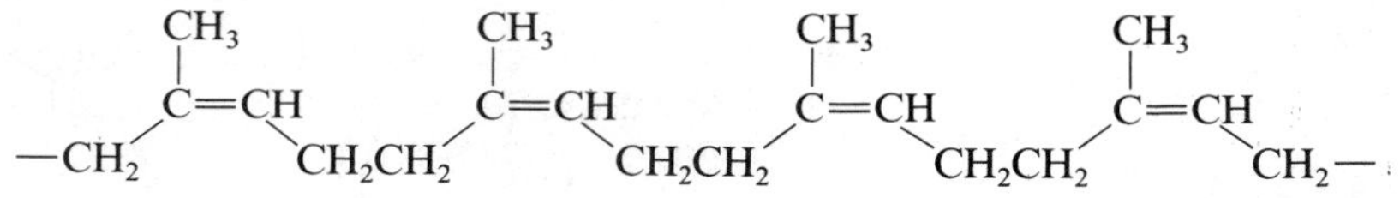

$$\begin{array}{c} CH_3 \\ | \\ C=CH \end{array} \qquad \begin{array}{c} CH_3 \\ | \\ C=CH \end{array} \qquad \begin{array}{c} CH_3 \\ | \\ C=CH \end{array} \qquad \begin{array}{c} CH_3 \\ | \\ C=CH \end{array}$$
$$-CH_2 \qquad CH_2CH_2 \qquad CH_2CH_2 \qquad CH_2CH_2 \qquad CH_2-$$

natural rubber

Note that there are no cross-links between the polymer chains. Natural rubber becomes soft and sticky when heated and tends to become permanently deformed when stretched. However, when natural rubber is heated with sulfur and a catalyst, sulfur cross-links are formed between the chains. This process is called *vulcanization;* it was discovered accidentally by Charles Goodyear in 1839. Introduction of a moderate number of sulfur cross-links converts natural rubber into a useful elastomer. A larger number of cross-links converts it into hard rubber, or ebonite, which is not an elastomer.

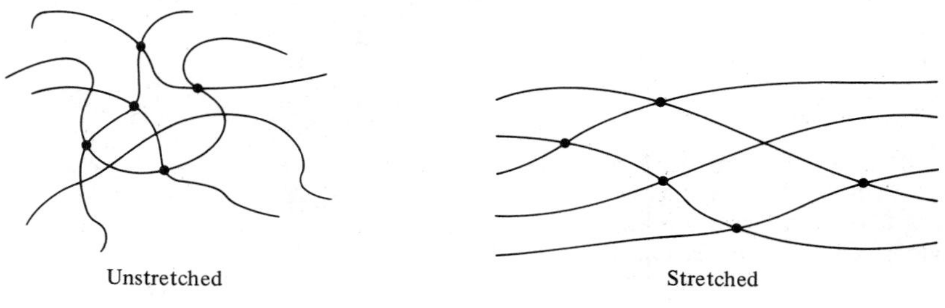

Figure 33.7
Natural Cellulose and Cellulose Acetate, a Thermoplastic Derivative

CH₂OH

natural cellulose

CH₂OCOR

cellulose acetate
(R is CH₃)

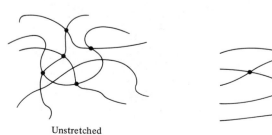

Figure 33.8
Vulcanized Rubber The black circles represent the sulfur cross-links.

Unstretched   Stretched

BIOCHEMISTRY

It is difficult to provide even the briefest introduction to a subject as broad and complex as biochemistry in the small space available to us here. Yet to omit this subject entirely would be a great pity. For one thing, everyone should know at least a little about the marvelous molecular machinery that not only keeps us alive, but enables us to solve quadratic equations, play the tuba, and read books such as this one. Moreover, biochemistry has become one of the most dynamic and exciting fields of modern science—one that attracts more and more students of chemistry, and that has had an enormous impact on the lives of all of us. So, for those of you who will not have the opportunity to study this subject at another time, as well as for those of you who will pursue the subject further, we give here a short introduction to the molecules of living things and how they function.

33.18 BIOLOGICAL MOLECULES: AN INTRODUCTION

Most biologically important substances are organic compounds, built up from skeletons of carbon atoms. Many of them are very large molecules, and most of these are polymers. In some cases these polymers consist of thousands of identical repeating units. Frequently, however, they are composed of several different monomers, which share only an overall structural similarity that allows them to be linked one to another. Moreover, the sequence in which the various monomers occur is not random but highly specific, and crucially important to the properties and function of such molecules.

In biological molecules we find a remarkably intimate relationship between structure and function. A seemingly small and insignificant change, involving only a few atoms in a giant molecule, can literally spell the difference between life and death for an organism. A single hemoglobin molecule, for example, contains some 8000 atoms; its molecular mass is nearly 65,000. The only difference between normal hemoglobin and the form of hemoglobin that causes sickle-cell disease—a painful and often fatal condition—is the following substitution at two places in the molecule:

**Hydrophilic: charged or polar
Hydrophobic: nonpolar**

$$-CH\diagup{}^{CH_3}_{CH_3} \qquad \text{replaced by} \qquad -CH_2CH_2COOH$$

A crucial concept for any understanding of how biomolecules interact and function is the distinction between hydrophilic and hydrophobic. **Hydrophilic** means, literally, "water-loving"; it refers to substances that are soluble in water and similar polar solvents. To be hydrophilic, a large organic molecule must generally have a great many charged groups or groups containing polar bonds. **Hydrophobic** means, literally, "water-fearing," and refers to substances that are insoluble in water but dissolve readily in nonpolar solvents such as benzene. Hydrophobic substances are generally composed chiefly of hydrocarbon chains, aromatic rings, and other nonpolar groups. Hydrophilic substances interact with other hydrophilic substances, and hydrophobic substances have an affinity for other hydrophobic substances, but molecules of the two classes do not readily interact with one another. In living systems, chemical reactions take place largely in aqueous solution, that is, in a hydrophilic environment. By contrast, most of the "architecture" of the living cell, including the membrane that surrounds it, is made of hydrophobic molecules. And as we shall see, some of the most important biomolecules are able to perform their special functions because they are "amphibious"—part hydrophilic and part hydrophobic.

The four major classes of organic compounds in living cells are proteins, carbohydrates, lipids, and nucleic acids. Table 33.24 shows the amounts of these substances that, together with water, inorganic ions, and smaller molecules, are

Table 33.24

Composition of cells. Amino acids are the monomers of which proteins are composed, and nucleotides are the monomers of which nucleic acids are composed.

Component	Bacterium *E. coli* (%)	Rat liver (%)
Water	70	69
Protein	15	21
Amino acids	0.4	—
Nucleic acids	7	1.2
Nucleotides	0.4	—
Carbohydrates	3	3.8
Lipids	2	6
Other small molecules	0.2	—
Inorganic ions	1	0.4

present in the cells of a microorganism and an animal. The ratios vary from species to species and among different types of cells. But the carbohydrates, lipids, proteins, and nucleic acids perform similar functions in all plants and animals.

33.19 CARBOHYDRATES

Carbohydrates are either simple sugars, called *monosaccharides; disaccharides,* composed of two simple sugars; or *polysaccharides,* which are polymers containing many sugar monomers. Monosaccharides are either polyhydroxy aldehydes (*aldoses*) or polyhydroxy ketones (*ketoses*) (Table 33.25).

Since most monosaccharides contain several asymmetrically substituted carbon atoms, monosaccharides and their derivatives form optically active isomers. In glyceraldehyde, for example (see Table 33.25), the middle carbon is attached to four different groups and the molecule therefore has two mirror-image enantiomers. A six-carbon aldose ($C_6H_{12}O_6$) has four such asymmetric carbon atoms and consequently forms 16 enantiomers. One of these, D-glucose (see Table 33.25), is the most biologically important simple sugar. Nearly all natural monosaccharides have the D configuration. (For historical reasons, D and L in the nomenclature of many biomolecules refer to absolute configurations, not to the direction of rotation of polarized light.)

Sugars with five carbon atoms (*pentoses*) or six carbon atoms (*hexoses*) are more stable as cyclic structures than in the open-chain structures depicted in Table 33.25. The ring is created by a reaction between the carbonyl oxygen of the sugar molecule and one of its hydroxyl groups. As Figure 33.9 shows, for D-glucose this reaction can give rise to two different ring structures, known as α-D-glucose and β-D-glucose, depending on the configuration at carbon atom 1. (When the ring forms, carbon atom 1 also becomes an asymmetric carbon, and the α and β forms are optical isomers of one another at that carbon atom.)

Monosaccharides combine with each other by the loss of water between two OH groups to form a *glycosidic linkage*. For example, sucrose, or common table sugar, is a disaccharide of glucose and fructose (Figure 33.10). Other common disaccharides include lactose, found in the milk of mammals (glucose linked to galactose), and maltose, or malt sugar (two linked glucose molecules).

Such reactions, in which monomers are joined by elimination of a water molecule, are known as *condensation reactions*. They are very important in the chemistry of living things, for many biopolymers are formed through condensation reactions. The reverse reaction, in which a bond between two monomers is broken by addition of the elements of water, is known as *hydrolysis*. The digestion of food

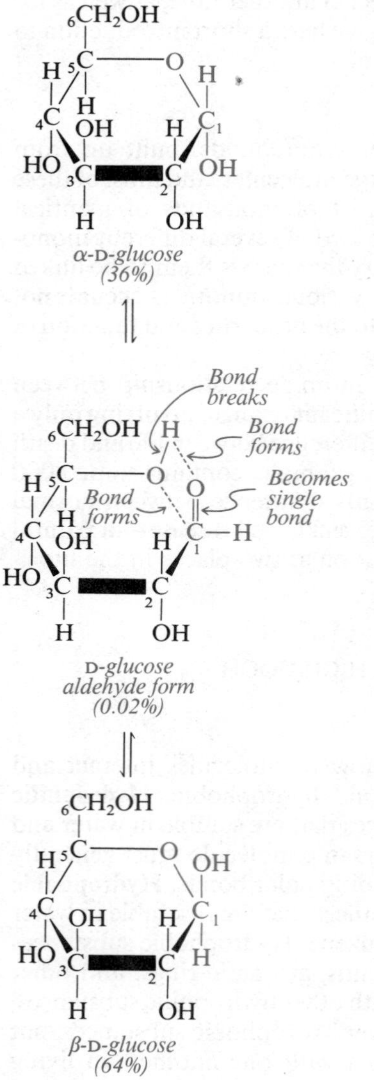

Figure 33.9
Formation of the Glucose Ring Structure In solution the aldehyde form of glucose is unstable. The aldehyde group reacts with one of the hydroxyl groups to give a ring structure, which can exist in two different configurations, the β configuration being slightly more stable.

Table 33.25
Some Monosaccharides The ketoses found in living things are almost always 2-ketoses—the second carbon atom in the chain is the carbonyl group carbon atom.

Aldoses (aldehydes)				Ketoses (ketones)	
		CHO	CHO		CH₂OH
CHO	CHO	HCOH	HCOH	CH₂OH	C=O
HCOH	HCOH	HOCH	HOCH	C=O	HOCH
CH₂OH	HCOH	HCOH	HOCH	HCOH	HCOH
D-*glyceraldehyde*	HCOH	HCOH	HCOH	HCOH	HCOH
	CH₂OH	CH₂OH	CH₂OH	CH₂OH	CH₂OH
	D-*ribose*	D-*glucose*	D-*galactose*	D-*ribulose*	D-*fructose*

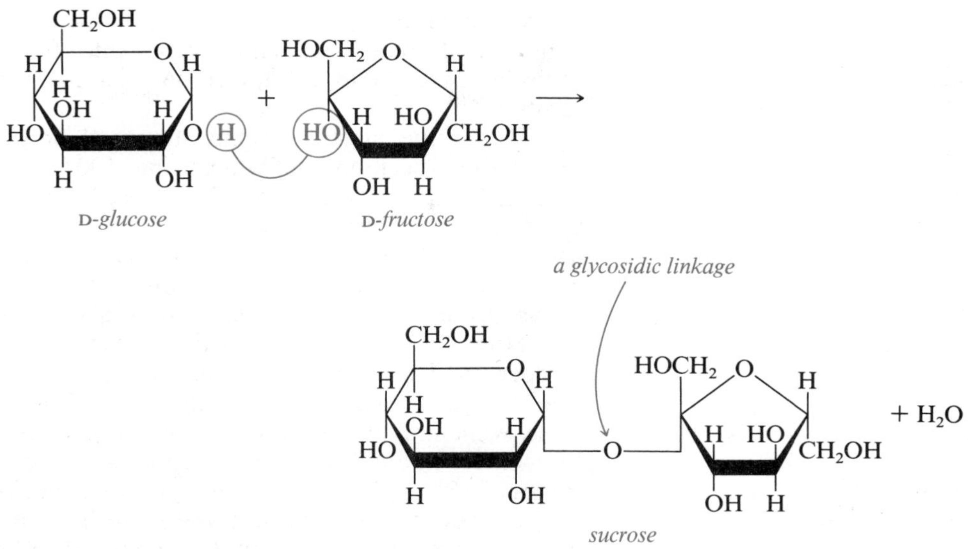

Figure 33.10
Formation of Sucrose (Table Sugar),
a Disaccharide

containing polymeric biomolecules such as starch or protein, always involves a series of hydrolysis reactions that break the starch or protein down into its component monomers.

Polysaccharides have two principal functions: energy storage and structural support. As we will see in Section 33.23, organisms use simple sugars, particularly glucose, as their main energy source, but they do not store such sugars in large quantities. For one thing, glucose is too reactive. For another, keeping huge numbers of glucose molecules inside a cell would create tremendous osmotic pressure (Section 15.16); water would flow into the cell, causing it to swell and burst. It is much more convenient to stockpile several thousand glucose units in the form of a single macromolecule. Plants store glucose molecules in the form of starch. The two chief forms of starch are amylose, a long, unbranched polymer of α-D-glucose monomers (Table 33.26), and amylopectin, an even larger molecule in which thousands of

Table 33.26
The Repeating Structural Units of
Some Polysaccharides.

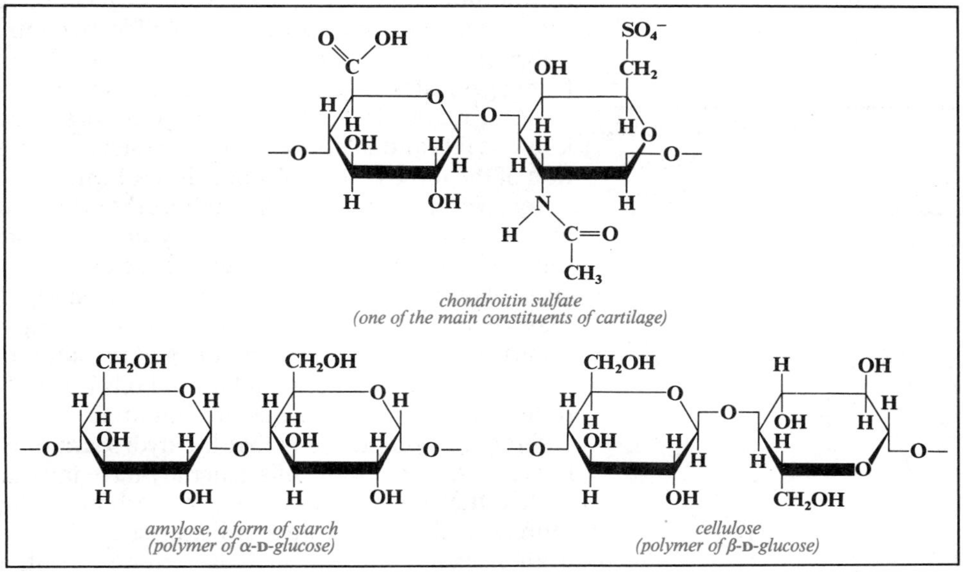

chondroitin sulfate
(one of the main constituents of cartilage)

amylose, a form of starch
(polymer of α-D-glucose)

cellulose
(polymer of β-D-glucose)

glucose monomers are arranged in a branching pattern. In animals, an excess of glucose in the bloodstream is converted into glycogen, which is stored in the liver and muscles. Like amylopectin, glycogen is a highly branched polymer of α-D-glucose units.

By far the most abundant structural polysaccharide, and one of the most interesting, is cellulose, of which some 100 billion tons are produced each year by plants. (Cotton, for example, is 99% cellulose, and the woody parts of trees are generally more than 50% cellulose.) Like amylose, cellulose is a polymer of glucose (see Table 33.26). In chemical composition the two substances are identical. Yet amylose is quite soluble in water, while cellulose is completely insoluble. (In fact, the transport of water through plant stems takes place in cellulose-lined tubes.)

How can two substances that are chemically identical have such different properties? The answer lies in their structures — specifically, in a small difference in the linkage of their glucose monomers. Cellulose is actually a polymer of β-D-glucose, while amylose is a polymer of α-D-glucose. The α orientation of the glucose monomers in amylose causes the polysaccharide chain to coil up into a helix (the shape of a Slinky toy). In this configuration, hydroxyl groups are positioned in such a way as to be available both to stabilize the helix by hydrogen bonding and to interact with water molecules. For cellulose, on the other hand, the most stable configuration is reached when the long molecules lie stretched out side by side, with hydrogen bonds between hydroxyl groups on *adjacent* chains. Cellulose fibers consist of many polysaccharide chains cross-linked in this way to form bundles that are exceptionally strong. Since the cross-linking leaves fewer hydroxyl groups exposed on the exterior of the fibers to interact with water, cellulose is insoluble in water.

Several of the structural polysaccharides used by animals are built from sugar monomers that have been chemicaly modified by the addition of other groups. (Such variations on a chemical theme are very common in the biological world.) One example is chondroitin sulfate (see Table 33.26), which is present in cartilage.

33.20 LIPIDS

Lipids: diverse, nonpolymeric, hydrophobic

"Lipid" is something of a catchall category for biochemical molecules; there are many different kinds of lipids that differ widely in structure. All **lipids** have one thing in common, however: They are all nonpolar compounds that contain large hydrocarbon segments and so are hydrophobic. In contrast to carbohydrates, lipids are not polymeric. Nevertheless, some lipid molecules are quite large, and lipids tend to form aggregates held together by hydrophobic interactions.

One major class of lipids is the glycerides, which include the compounds that we know as fats and oils. Glycerides are esters (Section 33.10) formed by the condensation of the three-carbon alcohol glycerol with one or more fatty acids (Figure 33.11). Fatty acids are long, straight-chain carboxylic acids that we encountered previously in soaps (Section 15.20). Since glycerol has three OH groups, it can form ester linkages with one, two, or three fatty acids, forming a monoglyceride, a diglyceride, or a triglyceride, respectively. In any one glyceride molecule, the fatty acid chains may be identical, or they may be different (a *mixed glyceride*). Most naturally occurring fats and oils are mixtures of several mixed glycerides.

The distinction between fats and oils is based on melting point: fats are solid at room temperature, and oils are liquid at room temperature. The reason for this difference in properties is that the hydrocarbon chains of the fatty acids in fats are largely *saturated,* while oils generally have fatty acid chains that are *unsaturated* — that is, they contain some carbon–carbon double bonds. Glycerides from animal sources, such as butter and lard, are usually high in saturated fatty acids, while those from vegetable sources, such as corn oil or safflower oil, are richer in unsaturated

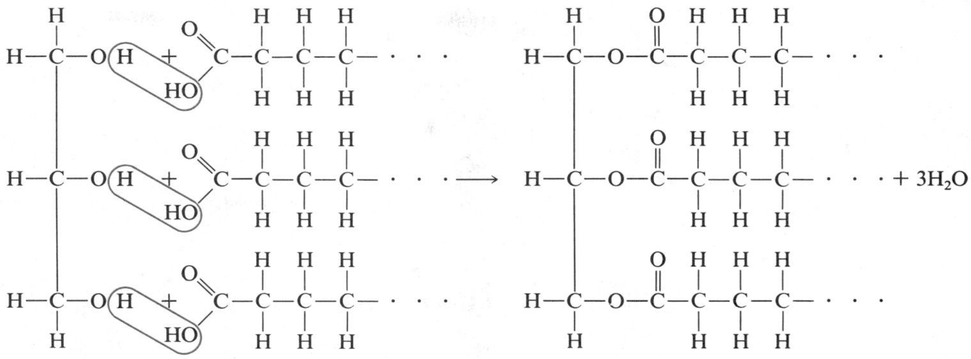

Figure 33.11
Formation of a Triglyceride Glycerol is esterified with three molecules of fatty acid. The fatty acid chains found in naturally occurring triglycerides all have an even number of carbon atoms because they are synthesized in two-carbon segments. The most common chains are 16 or 18 carbon atoms in length. When double bonds are present, the configuration of the chain with respect to the double bond is always *cis*.

glycerol   fatty acids (12–24 carbons)   a triglyceride (fat or oil) $+ 3H_2O$

fatty acids. Solid shortening for cooking and baking used to be made by hydrogenating vegetable oils — adding hydrogen across all the carbon–carbon double bonds to produce glycerides with completely saturated fatty acid chains. Today, however, there is evidence that a diet high in saturated fats contributes to "hardening" of the arteries — the buildup of fatty deposits in the walls of blood vessels, which may lead to high blood pressure, heart attacks, and strokes. Thus there has been a trend toward the use of *polyunsaturated* oils (those containing more than one double bond) in food products.

The chief function of fats in animals is energy storage. Unlike plants, animals are mobile and so must carry their energy stockpile around with them. It is therefore critically important to achieve the highest possible energy-to-weight ratio. Oxidation of a fat yields more energy than oxidation of the same weight of carbohydrate, which already contains many C—O and H—O bonds. Moreover, sugars and the storage polysaccharides (starch and glycogen) are hydrophilic, and in organisms are always hydrated. They thus impose an additional weight penalty on the organism, which must carry around extra water molecules. Fats, being hydrophobic, avoid this problem.

Phospholipids: hydrophilic heads, hydrophobic tails

Phospholipids — molecules of enormous biological importance — represent a variation on the triglyceride structure. In a phospholipid, two of the hydroxyl groups of glycerol are esterified with fatty acids, just as in a fat or oil. The third OH group, however, forms an ester link with phosphoric acid (H_3PO_4) or a derivative of phosphoric acid — usually one containing an amine group (Figure 33.12a). The two fatty acid chains make up a long, nonpolar "tail." The phosphate, however, carries a negative charge, while the amine group is usually in its cationic form ($-NH_3^+$ or $-NR_3^+$). Thus the molecule also has a compact, strongly dipolar "head." The overall structure of such a phospholipid is in fact very similar to that of a soap or detergent molecule (Section 15.20). Phospholipids, with their chemical "split personalities," are key constituents of biological membranes such as that which surrounds every living cell. These membranes are thought to consist principally of a double layer of phospholipid molecules (Figure 33.12b). The hydrophilic heads of the phospholipids can interact with substances in the aqueous interior of the cell and in the aqueous environment outside. These two aqueous regions, however, are separated by the hydrophobic tails of the phospholipids, which make up the interior of the membrane structure, and do not easily allow the passage of ions or most polar substances.

Waxes are also esters, but their structures are less complex than those of the glycerides and phospholipids. A molecule of wax is formed by a condensation

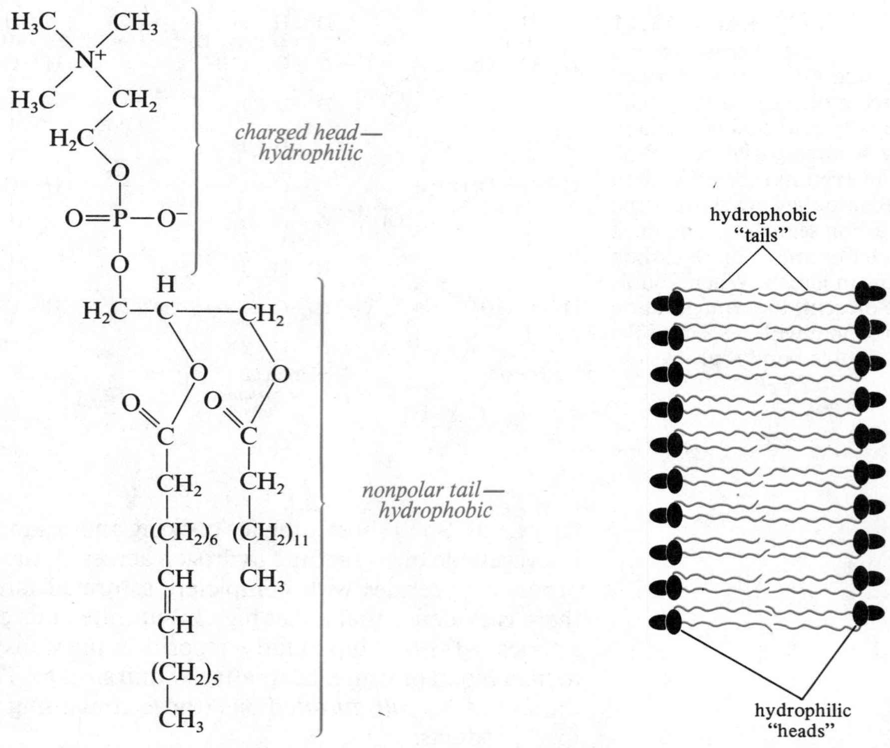

$$H_3C \quad CH_3$$

Figure 33.12
Phospholipids and the Structure of a Biological Membrane The basis of membrane structure is a phospholipid *bilayer*. The hydrophobic tails of the phospholipid molecules form the interior of the membrane, while the hydrophilic heads face outward toward the aqueous environment on either side of the membrane. The hydrophobic character of the membrane prevents the passage of most hydrophilic species such as ions or large polar molecules.

charged head — hydrophilic

nonpolar tail — hydrophobic

(a) Structure of a typical phospholipid

hydrophobic "tails"

hydrophilic "heads"

(b) Phospholipid bilayer

reaction between a long-chain monohydroxy alcohol and a long-chain fatty acid.

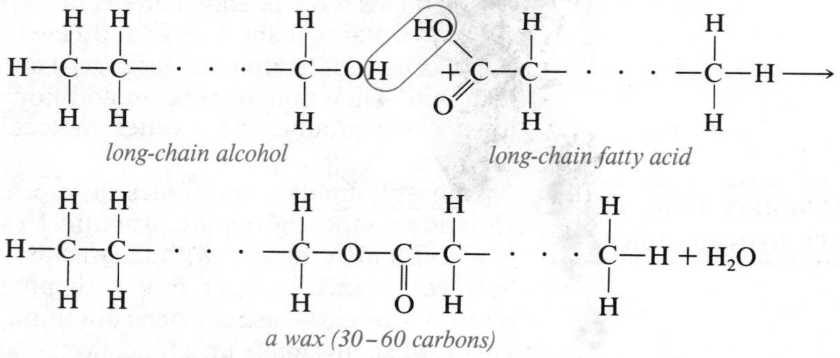

long-chain alcohol   *long-chain fatty acid*

$+ H_2O$

a wax (30–60 carbons)

The highly hydrophobic character of the hydrocarbon chain makes waxes useful as waterproofing materials for the skins, fur, or feathers of animals. A wax coating on the leaves and fruits of many plants helps slow the loss of water by evaporation in hot, dry conditions.

Structurally, steroids are very different from the lipids we have described so far, all of which consist in large part of hydrocarbon chains. Steroids are nevertheless classified as lipids because of their hydrophobic character. All steroids have structures based on four fused rings (Table 33.27). Very small variations in the bonding of atoms in the rings and in the groups attached to them give rise to compounds that are remarkably diverse in their biological function. Many steroids are hormones — chemical messengers that regulate various physiological processes. But notice in Table 33.27 how similar in structure are the male hormone testosterone and the adrenal hormone cortisone — compounds with drastically different biological activities. Another steroid, now rather notorious, is cholesterol, which, like the saturated glycerides, has been implicated in heart and circulatory disease.

Table 33.27
Some Steroids Testosterone and cortisone are both hormones. Despite their similarity in structure, they have totally different biological effects. Cholesterol, like the saturated triglycerides, has been implicated in heart and circulatory disease.

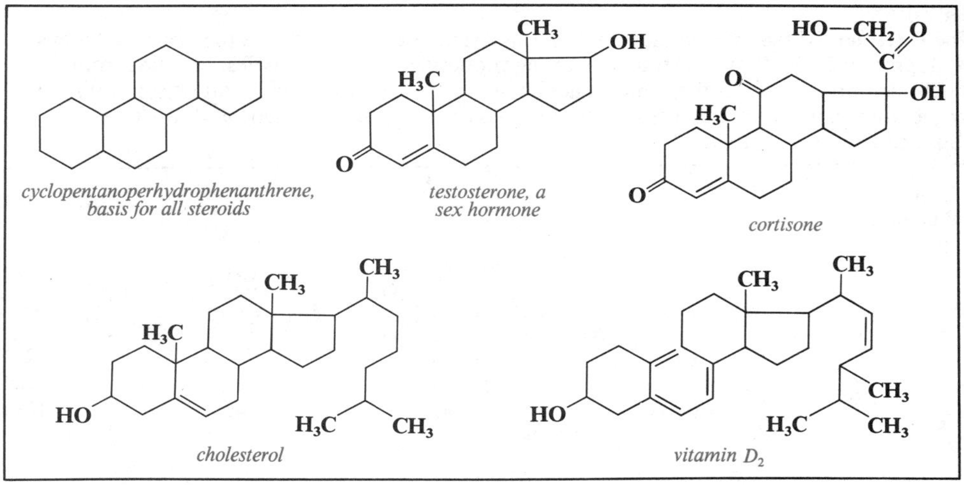

cyclopentanoperhydrophenanthrene, basis for all steroids

testosterone, a sex hormone

cortisone

cholesterol

vitamin D_2

33.21 PROTEINS

Proteins are in a very real sense the master molecules of living things. Virtually nothing happens in living organisms without their participation. The human body probably contains at least 10,000 different kinds of protein, and the number could well be higher. Some of the diverse functions of proteins are listed in Table 33.28.

a. Amino acids All **proteins** are polymers of α-amino acids. As the name implies, an **amino acid** contains both an amine group and a carboxylic acid group. (The designation α simply means that the amine group is attached to the carbon next to the carboxylic acid.) You can most easily think of an amino acid as consisting of a central carbon atom—the α *carbon*—to which are attached four different groups: the amine group (NH_2), the carboxylic acid group (COOH), a hydrogen atom, and a fourth variable group, commonly represented by R:

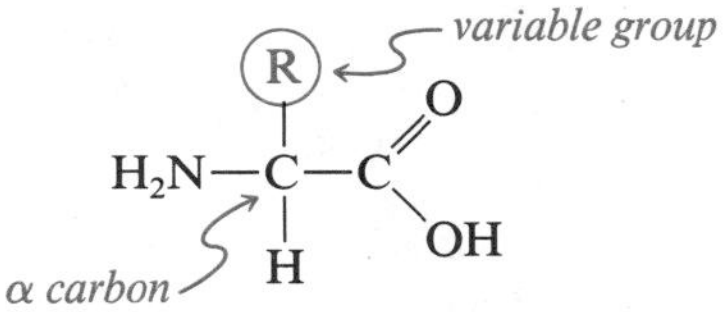

Table 33.28
Some Functions of Proteins

Enzymes	Catalyze biochemical reactions
Structural proteins	Virus coat proteins, cell wall proteins, insect silks, vertebrate protective tissues (skin, hair, feathers, scales, nails, hooves, horns, beaks, etc.), vertebrate connective tissues (bone, cartilage, tendons, ligaments, etc.)
Contractile proteins	Present in muscle fibers, cilia, flagella
Membrane proteins	Present in all cellular and intracellular membranes
Transport proteins	Bind and transport other molecules in bloodstream (e.g., hemoglobin)
Storage proteins	Release amino acids when needed, e.g., casein (milk protein), ovalbumin (egg white)
Protective proteins	Antibodies, blood-clotting agents
Hormones	Regulate growth and metabolism

The "R" group of the 20 common amino acids are shown in color in Table 33.29. (Note that the "R" group in amino acids is not always an alkyl group.)

Since the COOH group easily loses a proton and the NH_2 group easily gains one, an amino acid in solution can exist in several different ionic forms, the equilibrium concentrations varying with the pH:

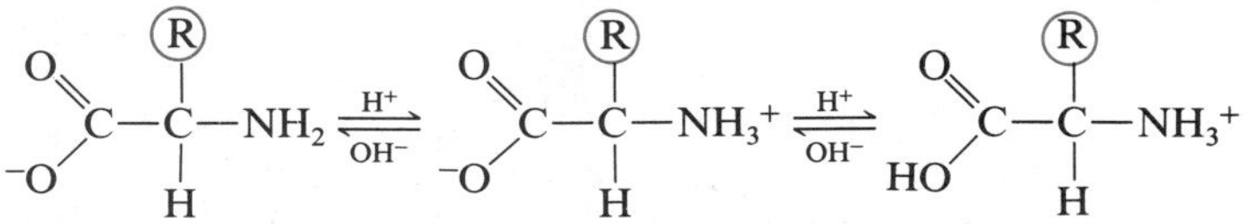

In near-neutral solutions (as well as in the crystalline state) the double-ion form is the one generally found.

It is evident from the above description that the α carbon must be a chiral, or asymmetric, carbon atom. This means that amino acids have optically active isomers, which, like sugars, are designated as either D or L forms. (The only exception is the amino acid glycine, in which the R group is another hydrogen atom.) All amino acids found in proteins are α-L-amino acids.

Table 33.29

The R Groups of the 20 Common Amino Acids These amino acids are the building blocks of all proteins. The R groups impart varying properties to the molecules. Proteins from different sources differ in their amino acid content. Some amino acids can be synthesized by the human body; others, the *essential amino acids,* cannot be made and must be obtained from the diet.

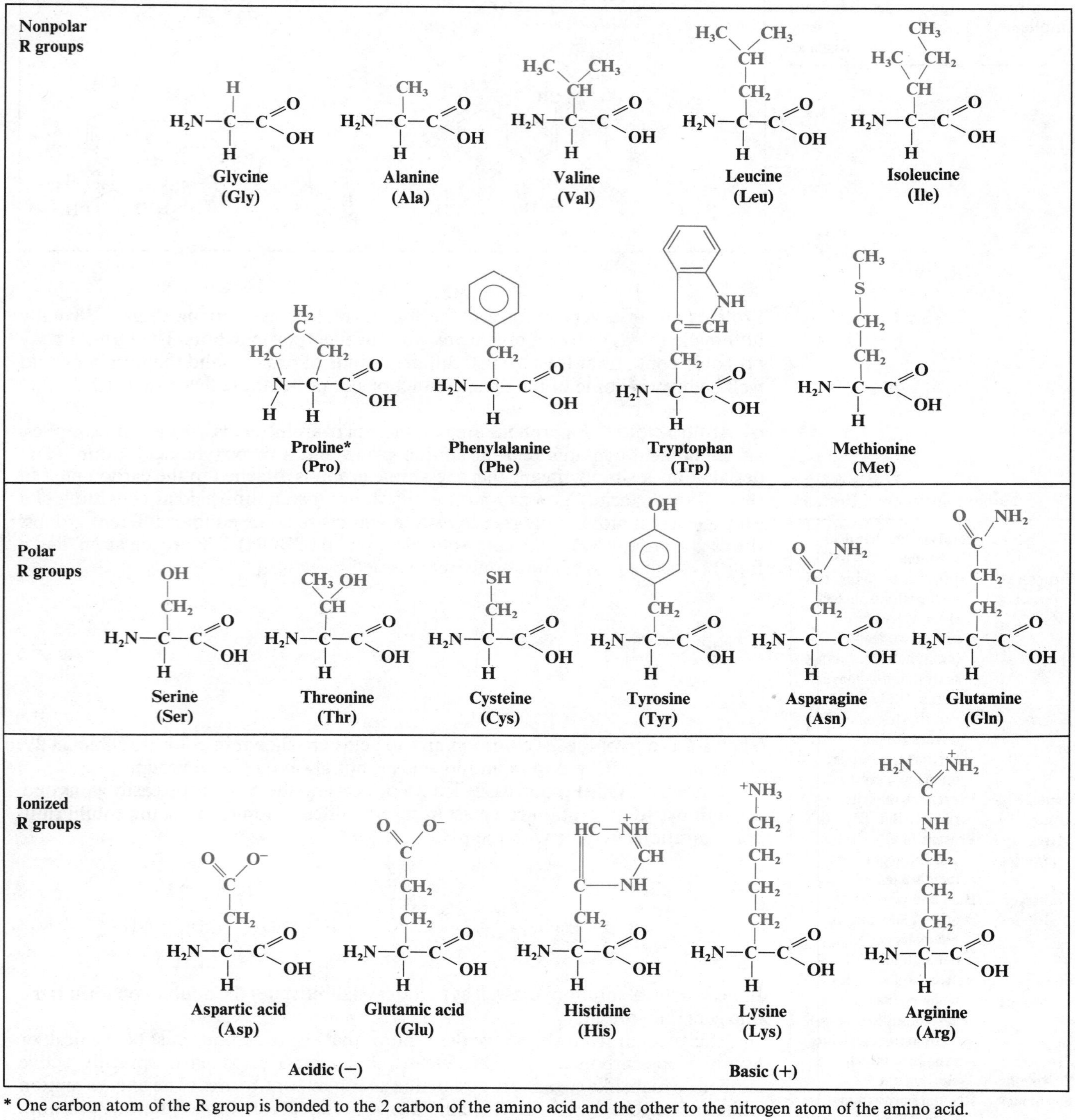

Nonpolar R groups

Glycine (Gly)

Alanine (Ala)

Valine (Val)

Leucine (Leu)

Isoleucine (Ile)

Proline* (Pro)

Phenylalanine (Phe)

Tryptophan (Trp)

Methionine (Met)

Polar R groups

Serine (Ser)

Threonine (Thr)

Cysteine (Cys)

Tyrosine (Tyr)

Asparagine (Asn)

Glutamine (Gln)

Ionized R groups

Aspartic acid (Asp)

Glutamic acid (Glu)

Histidine (His)

Lysine (Lys)

Arginine (Arg)

Acidic (−)

Basic (+)

* One carbon atom of the R group is bonded to the 2 carbon of the amino acid and the other to the nitrogen atom of the amino acid.

Figure 33.13

Formation of a Polypeptide Amino acids are linked by peptide bonds, formed by condensation reactions between the NH_2 group of one amino acid and the COOH group of the next.

Twenty different amino acids, each with a different "R" group, are commonly found in the proteins of living things. Since the rest of the molecule is the same in all amino acids, it is the R group that gives each amino acid its special properties— properties which it contributes to any protein molecule of which it becomes a part. As illustrated in Table 33.29, some R groups are hydrophobic and others are hydrophilic, either because they contain polar bonds, or because they are acidic or basic and under physiological conditions exist in ionized form.

Proteins consist of long, unbranched polymer chains made up of amino acid monomers. The link between adjacent monomers is formed by a condensation reaction between the amine group of one amino acid and the carboxylic acid group of another. As Figure 33.13 shows, a water molecule is removed, leaving the two amino acids joined by a **peptide bond.** A single chain of amino acids linked by peptide bonds is called a **polypeptide.** Some polypeptides contain as many as several thousand amino acid molecules. Every protein molecule consists of one or more polypeptide chains.

b. Protein structure The sequence of amino acids in the polypeptide chain constitutes the primary (1°) structure of a protein. To describe the structure of a functioning protein in an organism, however, it is necessary also to specify the three-dimensional shape that the polypeptide chain assumes (Figure 33.14). Functioning proteins can be divided on the basis of their structure into two broad classes: fibrous proteins and globular proteins.

In fibrous proteins, the polypeptide chains are relatively extended, and arranged so that they intertwine with or lie parallel to neighboring chains, like the strands of a rope or threads in a piece of fabric. Cross-links of various kinds hold the chains together, creating great strength. (Some fibrous proteins are as strong, for their size, as steel cable.) Most fibrous proteins have many hydrophobic R groups exposed on their surfaces, making them insoluble in water.

In globular proteins, by contrast, the polypeptide chain is wound and folded into a compact but irregular shape, like a tangled ball of yarn. Most globular proteins function in the aqueous interiors of cells or in the bloodstream, and so must be soluble. Consequently, they generally fold up so as to expose many hydrophilic R groups on the surface of the molecule.

Fibrous proteins are characterized by their secondary (2°) structures—the regular coiling or zigzagging of the polypeptide chains. Secondary structure is created by hydrogen bonding between N—H and C=O groups of amino acids near each other in the polypeptide backbone. Such bonding may occur between amino acids in neighboring chains or between amino acids in different regions of the same chain. One very common 2° structure found in many of the proteins of living things is the α

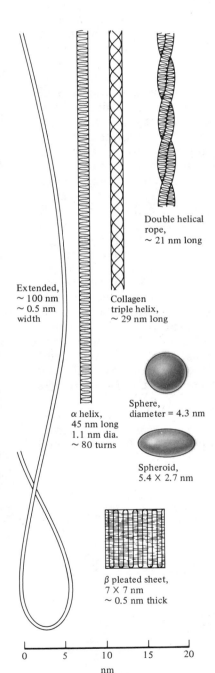

Double helical
rope,
~ 21 nm long

Extended,
~ 100 nm
~ 0.5 nm
width

Collagen
triple helix,
~ 29 nm long

α helix,
45 nm long
1.1 nm dia.
~ 80 turns

Sphere,
diameter = 4.3 nm

Spheroid,
5.4 × 2.7 nm

β pleated sheet,
7 × 7 nm
~ 0.5 nm thick

0   5   10   15   20
nm

Figure 33.14
Some Shapes a Protein Molecule of 300 Amino Acids Might Assume (From D. E. Metzler, *Biochemistry: The Chemical Reactions of Living Cells,* Academic Press, New York, 1977, p. 76.)

helix, in which the helical coiling of the polypeptide chain is maintained by intra-chain hydrogen bonds. Among the many α-helical proteins are the keratins, which are major structural components of animal skin, fur, wool, nails, hooves, and horns.

Although covalent bonds are not usually involved in the cross-linking of poly-peptide chains, there is one important exception to this rule: the disulfide bridge. You can see in Table 33.29 that the amino acid cysteine contains an R group with a terminal —SH. When two cysteine molecules are in proximity, they can react to form the double amino acid known as cystine (Figure 33.15), creating a covalent cross-link—a *disulfide bridge*. The smallest keratin fibers, for example, consist of three α helices coiled about each other and cross-linked by disulfide bridges. When these cross-links are few in number, as in the keratins of hair, the helical fibers are easily stretched and highly flexible. A larger number of cross-links makes for a tougher, less flexible form of keratin such as is found in the horns of animals. (To give hair a "permanent wave," the cross-links are chemically broken by treatment with a reducing agent and the hair is coiled on rollers to give it the desired degree of curl. New cross-links are then formed by treating the hair with an oxidizing solution, locking the fibers into their new shapes.)

The proteins that take part in the dynamic chemistry of living things—the enzymes, carriers, hormones, and so on—are nearly all globular proteins, and every globular protein is unique. The three-dimensional folding of the polypeptide chain in a globular protein constitutes the <u>tertiary (3°) structure</u> of the protein. In contrast to 2° structure, which involves hydrogen bonding of the N—H and C=O groups of the peptide links, 3° structure is created by interactions among the various R groups attached to the α carbons. These interactions include hydrogen bonds, the weaker intermolecular forces described in Sections 11.10 and 11.11, hydrophobic interactions, and the mutual attraction between oppositely charged groups. The interacting groups that determine 3° structure, unlike those that determine 2° structure, may be far from each other along the polypeptide backbone. The only covalent links involved are disulfide bridges, but because covalent bonds are stronger than the other kinds of interactions listed above, these bridges are very important factors in fixing the 3° structure of many proteins.

Many globular protein molecules—especially the larger ones—consist of several polypeptide chains. The way in which the chains are arranged and joined to one another constitutes the <u>quaternary (4°) structure</u> of the protein. Like 3° structure,

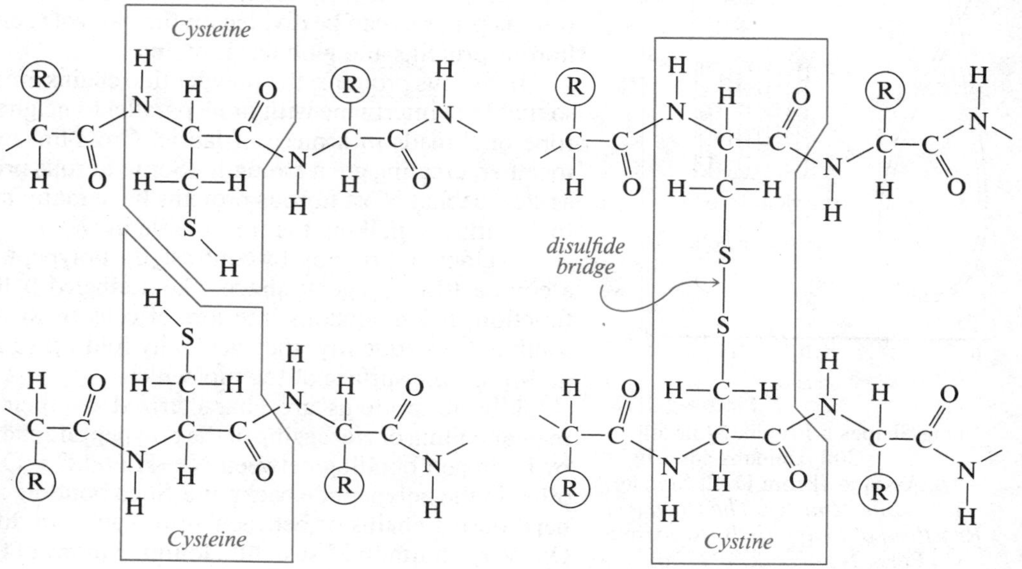

Figure 33.15
Formation of a Disulfide Bridge Disulfide bridges create covalent links between polypeptide chains, or between different regions of single chains. They play important parts in determining 2°, 3°, and 4° protein structure.

quaternary structure is usually created by weak interactions, but here too disulfide bridges may be involved.

The 3° and 4° structures of a globular protein can easily be disrupted by heat, extremes of pH, strongly oxidizing or reducing conditions, and the like. Under such conditions, the protein undergoes **denaturation** — it exhibits substantial changes in its physical properties, and its biological activity, which depends to a great extent on the maintenance of a precise spatial configuration, is usually lost. The most familiar example of denaturation is the change that takes place in albumin — the principal component of egg white — when you cook an egg. In this particular case the change is irreversible, but interestingly, this is not always the case. Often when the disruptive conditions are removed, a denatured polypeptide will spontaneously fold up and resume its original 3° and 4° structures. This suggests two things: that the original configuration is the most stable (i.e., lowest energy) state for that particular polypeptide, and that the polypeptide chain can "find" this configuration solely on the basis of its 1° structure. Indeed, it is now thought that the instructions for the manufacture of proteins in living cells specify *only* the 1° structure of each protein — the sequence of amino acids in the polypeptide chain (Section 33.22).

c. Enzymes Globular proteins play many roles in the chemistry of living things. By far the most important of the globular proteins are the **enzymes,** or biological catalysts. Without the assistance of enzymes, there would *be* no chemistry of living things.

It is important to keep in mind that even the simplest cell must perform hundreds of different chemical reactions *merely to stay alive.* To appreciate what this means, suppose for a moment that you are a chemical engineer, and that you are presented with the following assignment. You must devise a way of carrying out several hundred different reactions, simultaneously. Many of them are thermodynamically unfavorable and ordinarily would not take place at all to any significant extent. Most of the others, though spontaneous, are too slow to be useful. Nevertheless, you must get *all* of them to occur at very high rates and with very high yields. You cannot use powerful oxidizing or reducing agents, or strong acids or bases, nor can you vary the temperature or pressure very much; all the reactions must be carried out at atmospheric pressure, near room temperature, and within a relatively narrow range of pH. Moreover, the number of different vessels that you can use is quite limited, so many of the reactions must take place not only at the same time but in the same solution. Despite this, they must proceed without any of the side reactions that are usually so difficult to avoid in even the simplest chemical system.

No one would blame you if, faced with such a task, you quickly switched to another field to avoid a nervous breakdown. Yet cells can do all of the things we have just described — and continuously *adjust* the rate of most of the individual reactions into the bargain! This remarkable performance is made possible by enzymes.

Typically, enzymes are large molecules, with molecular masses ranging into the millions; often they consist of several polypeptide chains. Somewhere in its elaborately folded structure, each enzyme molecule possesses a region known as the *active site.* The active site may take the form of a groove along the surface of the molecule, or a deeper crevice or channel into the interior; its shape and location are unique in each enzyme. Physically, the **substrate** — the molecule or molecules with which an enzyme interacts — fits into the active site like a hand in a glove (Figure 33.16). Even more important than the physical fit, however, is the chemical fit. Various parts of the substrate molecule interact with the groups that line the active site. The bonds between enzyme and substrate are of the same sort that hold the folded protein chain in its three-dimensional shape: hydrogen bonds, hydrophobic interactions, electrostatic attraction between charged groups, even (in some cases) temporary covalent bonds. When a metal atom or ion is incorporated into the structure of the enzyme (as is often the case), it frequently participates in the binding of the substrate.

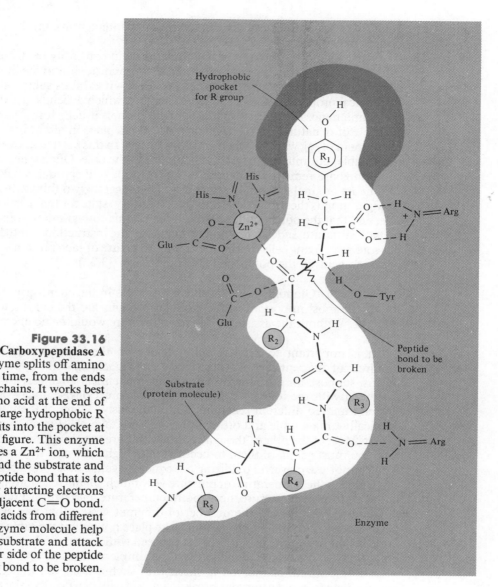

Figure 33.16

The Active Site of Carboxypeptidase A
This enzyme splits off amino acids, one at a time, from the ends of polypeptide chains. It works best when the amino acid at the end of the chain has a large hydrophobic R group, which fits into the pocket at the top of the figure. This enzyme incorporates a Zn^{2+} ion, which helps to bind the substrate and weakens the peptide bond that is to be broken by attracting electrons from the adjacent C=O bond. Other amino acids from different parts of the enzyme molecule help to position the substrate and attack atoms on either side of the peptide bond to be broken.

Interestingly the amino acids that make up the active site rarely lie near each other in the polypeptide chain. Indeed, they may be in different polypeptide chains. It is the folding of the protein molecule that brings these amino acids together to form the active site. This is why precise 3° and 4° structure is so essential to the biological activity of an enzyme molecule.

This precision of fit, chemical as well as physical, between the substrate molecule and the active site helps to account for the remarkable specificity of many enzymes —their extreme selectivity as to which molecules they will bind and which reactions they will catalyze. Most enzymes will not bind molecules that are almost identical to their substrates in form but possess slightly different functional groups, nor will they bind molecules that are similar to their substrates in chemical composition but are somewhat different in their three-dimensional structure.

Several factors are probably involved in catalysis by enzymes. One simple consideration is that by binding two substrate molecules (as many enzymes do), the enzyme serves as molecular "matchmaker." That is, it brings the reactants together, and ensures that the particular groups involved in the reaction are so oriented that the encounter will be effective (Section 18.2). Since the concentrations of reactants in living cells is often quite low, this is an important factor. Even more important, however, is the role of enzymes in weakening some of the bonds in the substrate or substrates so as to make the reaction easier. For one thing, an enzyme often undergoes a slight change in configuration upon binding the substrate. Such a change may physically strain the substrate molecule. Furthermore, binding of the substrate to the enzyme may withdraw electron density from the bond or bonds that are to be broken. An enzyme may also take a direct (though temporary) part in the reaction mechanism itself. For example, the enzyme may serve as an interim donor of an ion or group to one of the reactants (e.g., an H^+ ion in many common reactions), subsequently recovering its "loan" from another reactant. The efficiency of most enzymes is quite remarkable. Many enzyme molecules can handle thousands of substrate molecules per second, increasing the reaction rate by a factor of a million or more.

33.22 NUCLEIC ACIDS

Nucleic acids are the molecules of which genes are made. Their function is the preservation of the genetic information — the complete set of "blueprints" for all the actual and potential characteristics received by each organism from its parent or parents and passed on from generation to generation. Nucleic acids also make up most of the molecular machinery by which these genetic blueprints are "read" and the information they contain is translated into actual traits such as red hair, perfect pitch, or color-blindness.

Nucleic acids are polymers, the repeating units of which are complex structures called *nucleotides*. (Free nucleotides also play other important biochemical roles, especially in the transfer and utilization of energy, Section 33.23.) Each **nucleotide** has three parts: (1) a five-carbon sugar — either *ribose* or *deoxyribose,* (2) one of five different nitrogen-containing organic bases (Table 33.30), (3) a phosphate group ($-PO_4^{2-}$). The base replaces the OH group normally attached to the 1-carbon of the sugar ring, while the phosphate is bonded by an ester linkage to the 5-carbon (Figure 33.17).

A nucleic acid consists of several thousand nucleotides joined together by ester linkages between the 3-carbon of the sugar of one nucleotide and the phosphate group of another. The backbone of the molecule is thus a chain of alternating sugars

Nucleic acids: polymers of nucleotides

Nucleotides: sugar + base + phosphate

Table 33.30

The bases of DNA and RNA The double-ring structures are known as purines, the single-ring structures as pyrimidines.

Adenine

Guanine

Cytosine

Thymine (DNA only)

Uracil (RNA only)

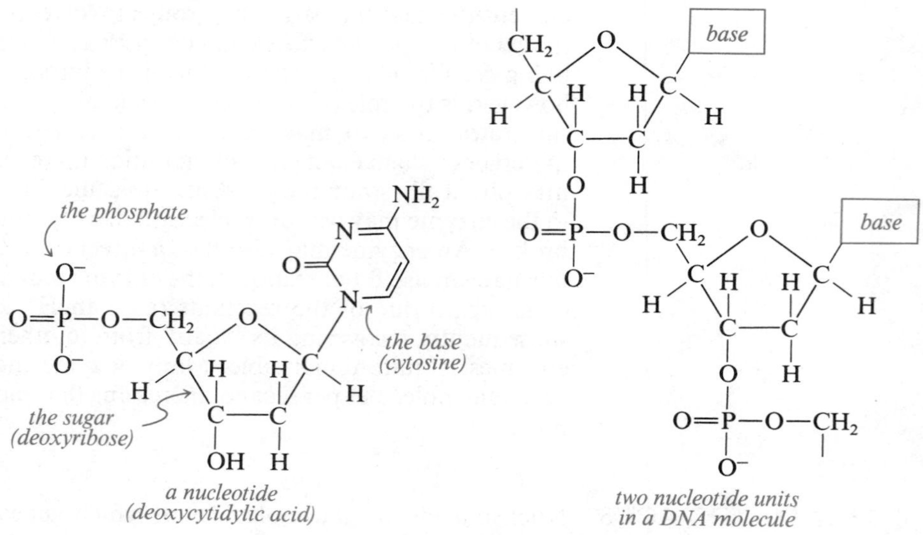

Figure 33.17
Components of a Nucleic Acid (a) A nucleotide, consisting of a sugar (ribose or deoxyribose), a phosphate group, and a nitrogen-containing base. (b) A portion of a DNA molecule, which consists of nucleotides linked by ester bonds between the sugar of one and the phosphate of the next.

and phosphate groups. Since each phosphate forms ester links to the preceding and the following sugar, successive sugars are said to be joined by *phosphodiester bonds*.

There are two major types of nucleic acid: **deoxyribonucleic acid, or DNA,** which carries the genetic information, and **ribonucleic acid, or RNA,** which is involved in putting this information to work in the cell. They differ in three ways:

DNA:
deoxyribose sugar
A, T, G, C bases
double-stranded
RNA:
ribose sugar
A, U, G, C bases
single-stranded

1. The sugar in RNA is ribose, while the sugar in DNA is 2-deoxyribose, in which the OH group on the 2-carbon atom in ribose has been replaced by a hydrogen atom.
2. Four different bases (see Table 33.30) are found in DNA: *cytosine* (abbreviated C), *thymine* (T), *adenine* (A), and *guanine* (G). In RNA, thymine does not occur; its place is taken by *uracil* (U).
3. DNA is nearly always double stranded (as described below), while RNA is usually single stranded.

You may be wondering exactly how a molecule such as DNA — indeed, any one molecule, no matter how complex — can determine specific traits of an organism. The answer is that traits are actually determined by what proteins each cell makes, and when and in what quantities it makes them . Proteins make up much of the structure of each living cell; more importantly, all enzymes are proteins, and enzymes control virtually every aspect of cell chemistry, including what *other* substances the cell can make. Nucleic acids, in turn, contain the coded information specifying the makeup of every one of the cell's thousands of different proteins. This information — the genetic information — is incorporated in *the sequence of bases of the cell's DNA*. (Strictly speaking, one should say "sequence of nucleotides"; however, since the nucleotides differ only in the bases attached to them, the phrase "base sequence" is commonly used in discussions of DNA and RNA.)

We have already mentioned that the 1° structure of a polypeptide seems sufficient to determine the 2°, 3°, and/or 4° structure that the protein molecule will ultimately assume. Thus the sequence of DNA bases must contain information that can be translated into a sequence of amino acids in each polypeptide chain. Since there are 20 different amino acids and only four DNA bases, it is obvious that a one-to-one correspondence between bases and amino acids is not possible. Instead, each amino acid is represented by a sequence of three consecutive bases, called a *codon*. There are 64 possible codons ($4 \times 4 \times 4$) — clearly more than enough to

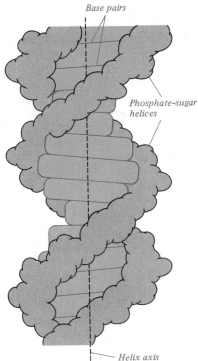

Base pairs

Phosphate-sugar helices

Helix axis

Figure 33.18
The DNA Double Helix The sugar-phosphate chains wind around the outside of the molecule, while the bases are stacked nearly perpendicular to the helix axis in the center.

specify the 20 different amino acids. In fact, most amino acids can be "spelled" by any of several different codons; in addition, some codons serve as "punctuation," indicating the start and the termination of polypeptide chains.

The key to the ability of DNA to preserve genetic information and to pass it on from generation to generation is its double-stranded structure, first deduced by James Watson and Francis Crick in 1953. This was the discovery that inaugurated the field of molecular biology, which has led to today's headlines about cloning and genetic engineering. The DNA molecule has often been likened to a "spiral staircase"—an apt comparison, though strictly speaking the shape should be described as helical rather than spiral. Each strand is coiled into a helix and the two strands wind about a common axis, forming the now-famous "double helix" structure (Figure 33.18). The sides of the staircase are the sugar–phosphate backbones, which lie on the outside of the molecule. (The presence of the phosphate groups on the outside is in fact what makes the nucleic acids acidic.) The bases lie between the two backbones, in the center of the structure—they form the "steps" of the staircase. The bases, which are flat, lie almost perpendicular to the axis of the double helix. Each base is joined to a base opposite it on the other strand by hydrogen bonds. Although individually these bonds are weak, their number gives the DNA molecule great stability. The sizes of the bases, and the location of the groups that can participate in hydrogen bonding, are such that adenine can pair only with thymine. Similarly, wherever guanine is present in one strand, it must be hydrogen bonded to a cytosine in the opposite strand (Figure 33.19). What this means is that the base sequences of the two strands are not independent. Rather, the two strands are *complementary*—once the sequence of one strand is given, that on the other strand is completely determined. The two strands carry the same information in the sense that a photographic print and the negative from which it was made carry the same information—either one could be used to reconstruct the other.

As Watson and Crick saw, this double-stranded structure provides a mechanism whereby the genetic information can be duplicated—something that must happen every time a cell divides. With the help of a number of highly specialized enzymes, the two strands are uncoiled from one another, and a new, complementary "partner" strand is synthesized for each. The bases for the new strands are assembled

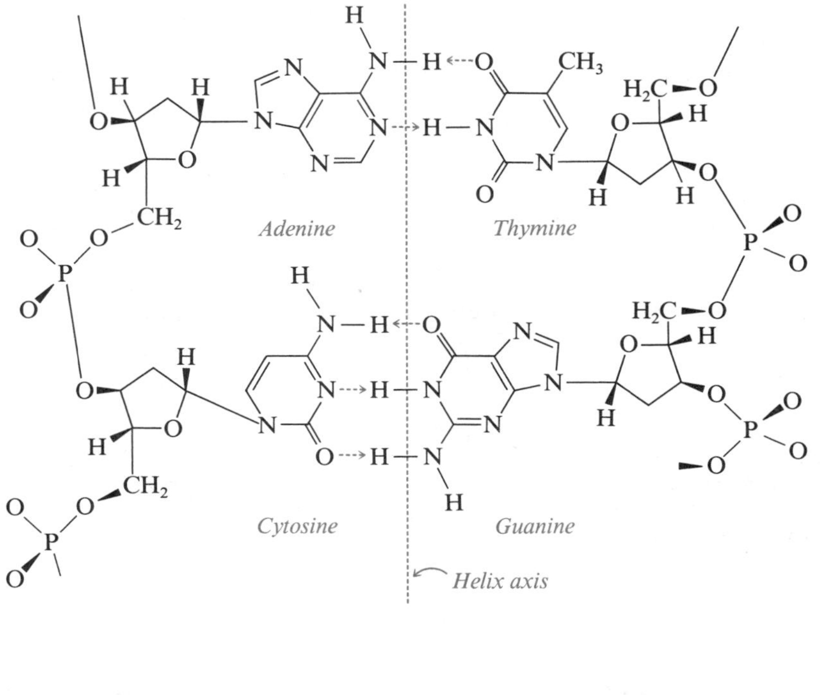

Figure 33.19
Base Pairing in DNA Because of the size of the bases and the location of their hydrogen-bonding groups, A can pair only with T, and C only with G. The hydrogen bonds are individually weak, but they are so numerous that collectively they impart great stability to the molecule—an essential characteristic if the genetic information is to be preserved unaltered from generation to generation.

Adenine   *Thymine*

Cytosine   *Guanine*

Helix axis

in the proper sequence in accordance with the base-pairing rules described above. Wherever thymine appears in an old strand, adenine is inserted opposite it in the new complementary strand, and so on. The eventual result is two new DNA molecules, each consisting of one new and one old strand (Figure 33.20). This process is called *replication*.

The synthesis of a polypeptide in accordance with the information contained in DNA is an intricate series of events, which we can sketch only in the most general way. First, in the process known as *transcription*, a single-stranded RNA molecule —a "transcript"—is made from a DNA gene—again, in accordance with the base-pairing rules. (In the RNA molecule, U takes the place of T, pairing with A.) This RNA molecule, known as messenger RNA (mRNA), becomes attached to

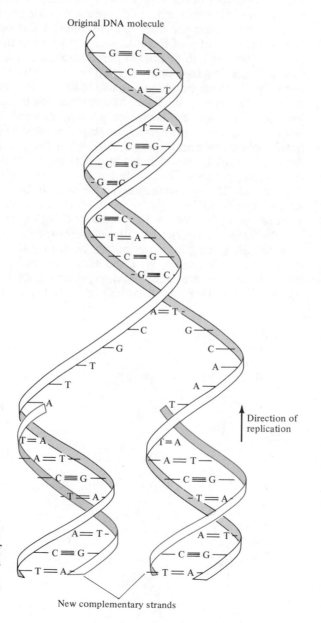

Original DNA molecule

Direction of replication

New complementary strands

Figure 33.20
Replication of DNA Each strand of the original DNA molecule acquires a new complementary strand, synthesized in accordance with the base-pairing rules.

Figure 33.21
Molecular Model of tRNA A tRNA molcule is linear and is folded into an L shape. At one end of the L is the point at which amino acids become attached. At the other end of the L is a sequence of bases that reads the codon. On each arm of the L is a segment in which base pairing forms a double helix. (Photo courtesy of Academic Press/Molecular Design, Inc., Orlando, Florida.)

structures called ribosomes, which are the cell's "protein factories." The key role in protein synthesis is played by another kind of RNA molecule, transfer RNA (tRNA), which serves as the link between the codons of the nucleic acid "message" and the amino acids that they stand for. There are many different species of tRNA molecules (Figure 33.21). Each has at one end a sequence of three bases — the anticodon — that can pair by hydrogen bonding with a complementary RNA codon. At the other end it binds a specific amino acid — the one called for by that particular codon. The mRNA transcript moves along the ribosome like a tape moving across the playback heads of a casette deck. As the tRNA molecules "read" successive mRNA codons, their amino acids are bound into the growing polypeptide chain by enzymes that are part of or attached to the ribosome, and the "empty" tRNA molecules are detached and released to bind new amino acids (Figure 33.22). When a "stop" codon is reached, the polypeptide chain (which in all likelihood has already begun to fold up into its final configuration) is detached from the ribosome. (Meanwhile, a whole succession of ribosomes may be bound to the same mRNA molecule, so that many copies of the same polypeptide may simultaneously be in various stages of completion.) The process of protein synthesis in accordance with a nucleic acid blueprint is called *translation*.

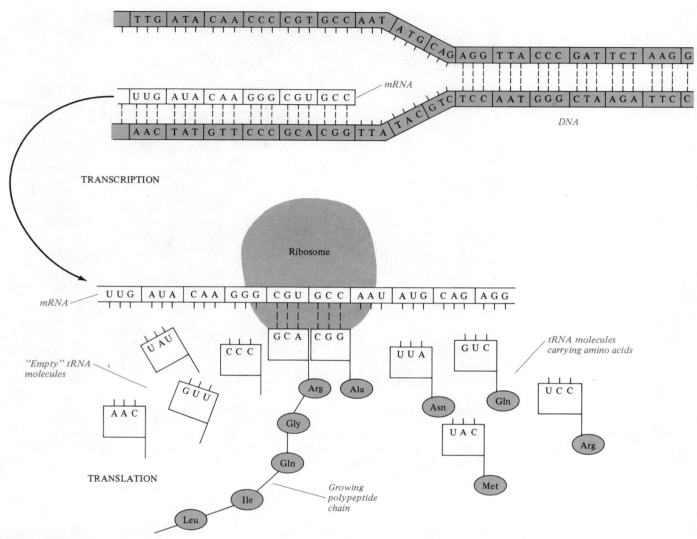

Figure 33.22

Transcription and Translation In transcription, a molecule of mRNA with a base sequence complementary to that of a DNA gene is synthesized. In translation, the mRNA transcript becomes attached to a ribosome—a protein factory incorporating many important enzymes. Each mRNA codon is "read" by a molecule of tRNA that has the complementary anticodon and so carries the amino acid specified by that codon. The amino acids are incorporated into the polypeptide chain in a complex sequence of enzyme-mediated steps.

33.23 ATP, ENERGY, AND METABOLISM

The chemical processes of a living organism, collectively called **metabolism,** can be divided into two parts. Organisms are constantly breaking down large molecules (such as those in foodstuffs) into smaller, simpler ones—a process known as **catabolism.** Catabolic reactions are usually accompanied by the release of free energy. At the same time, organisms are continuously synthesizing a great variety of large molecules from simpler molecules—a process known as **anabolism.** Most of

Catabolism: breakdown (releases energy)
Anabolism: synthesis (requires energy)
Metabolism: anabolism + catabolism

the macromolecules discussed above, for example, are assembled by organisms from the component monomers. Anabolic reactions generally cannot take place without an *input* of free energy. For simplicity, we shall refer to energy-requiring reactions as "uphill" and energy-yielding reactions as "downhill."

The overall strategy that is forced upon any organism by the laws of thermodynamics is obvious: it must somehow use the energy released by its downhill reactions to drive its uphill reactions. The question is, how? A complete answer (which would include much of what is known of biochemistry) would have to take into account a host of variations in different organisms, different types of cells, and different metabolic pathways. The basic pattern, however, is remarkably constant in all known organisms:

Whenever energy is available from the breakdown of a large molecule, it is immediately invested in making an energy-rich phosphate compound. Most commonly, it is used to add a third phosphate group to adenosine diphosphate (ADP) to make adenosine triphosphate (ATP).

Whenever a cell needs to do work—for example, to drive an uphill reaction—it obtains the necessary energy by splitting off a phosphate group from an energy-rich phosphate compound—most commonly, by removing one phosphate group from ATP to form ADP.

ATP: ribose + adenine + 3 phosphate groups

Adenosine diphosphate (ADP) is simply a nucleotide (Section 33.22) consisting of the sugar ribose, the base adenine, and two phosphate groups; **adenosine triphosphate (ATP)** has the same structure, but with a third phosphate group (Figure 33.23). For a number of reasons, chiefly having to do with its greater concentration of negative charge and fewer available resonance forms, ATP has a considerably higher energy content than ADP plus a free phosphate group. Stated another way, we can say that ATP has a high *free energy of hydrolysis:*

$$ATP + H_2O \longrightarrow ADP + P_i + H^+ \qquad \Delta G^\circ = -34.5 \text{ kJ (at pH 7)} \qquad (33.2)$$

ATP $\rightleftharpoons$ ADP + P$_i$ + energy

(The symbol P_i is used to stand for "inorganic phosphate," HPO_4^{2-}.) Splitting off a phosphate group from ATP is therefore a way of releasing free energy, while adding a third phosphate group to ADP requires energy. The third phosphate group in ATP, together with the second, which also has a relatively high free energy of hydrolysis, is often termed a "high-energy phosphate group", and the bonds joining these groups

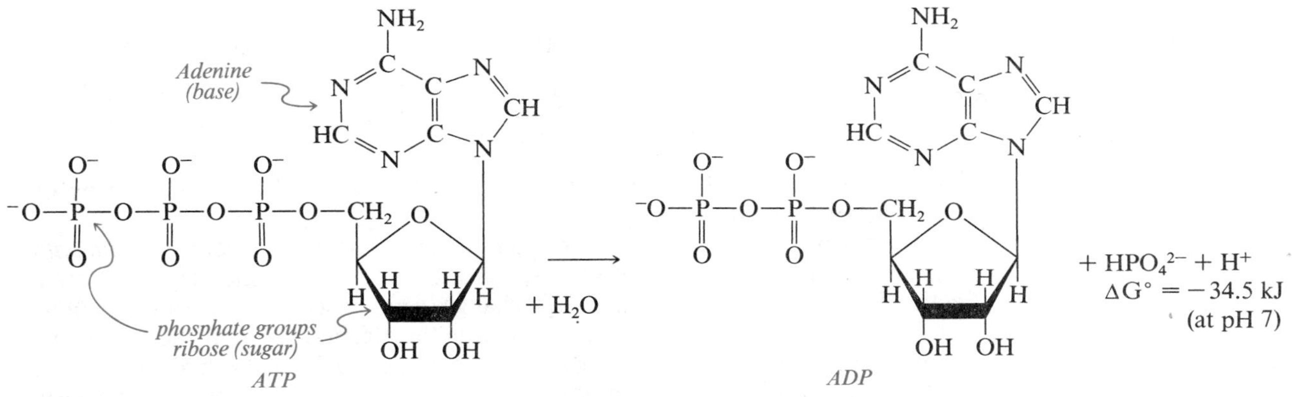

Figure 33.23
Hydrolysis of ATP When ATP loses its third phosphate group, forming ADP, a large amount of energy is released. This reaction is used to power much of the work done by living things, including the synthesis of large biomolecules.

to the rest of the molecule are referred to as "high-energy phosphate bonds." In fact, however, there is nothing unique about either the groups or the bonds; this is merely the biochemist's way of indicating the large free energy changes involved in the removal of these two phosphate groups by hydrolysis.

ATP is often called the "energy currency of the living cell." For the cell, using ATP as the medium of energy exchange has many of the same advantages that we derive from using money as a medium of exchange in everyday life. It would certainly not be convenient if, whenever you wanted to eat dinner at a restaurant, you had to work first for an hour in your office, or had to wash dishes for the chef to pay for your meal. It is much easier to pay cash from last week's salary, or write a check on your bank account.

Similarly, when a cell needs to carry out an uphill reaction, it can draw on its reserves of ATP—a stockpile of energy derived from quite unrelated reactions that may have taken place at various times in different parts of the cell. For example, most cells derive energy from the process known as respiration—the oxidation of energy-rich molecules (typically glucose) to CO_2 and H_2O:

$$C_6H_{12}O_6 + 6O_2 \longrightarrow 6CO_2 + 6H_2O \qquad \Delta G^\circ = -2872 \text{ kJ}$$

In cells, this overall reaction is carried out in a complex series of carefully controlled steps. The energy released in several of the most steeply downhill steps is used to make ATP from ADP and phosphate. The net yield is some 38 moles of ATP per mole of glucose oxidized. These ATP molecules can then be "spent" at any time and in any way that the needs of the cell dictate.

How does a cell use ATP to "pay" for uphill reactions? Here again, enzymes are the key. An enzyme can *couple* two different reactions, catalyzing both simultaneously so that they become in effect steps of a single overall reaction. In living cells, enzymes often combine an uphill reaction with the hydrolysis of ATP. The net energy change of the combined reaction is the algebraic sum of the energy changes of the two steps. Thus if the hydrolysis of ATP provides more energy than the uphill reaction requires, the overall reaction will be thermodynamically favorable, and will run downhill.

In a typical mechanism, an enzyme catalyzes the transfer of a phosphate group from ATP to a reactant molecule. This "activates" the reactant by increasing its energy. (You can think of the energy of ATP as being temporarily invested in the phosphorylated reactant.) Then, in the subsequent course of the reaction, the phosphate group is split off, and the energy released in this step drives the desired reaction. Schematically, if X is the reactant and Y is the product, we can write the reaction as

$$\text{ATP} + \text{X} \longrightarrow \text{ADP} + \text{X} - \textcircled{P} \quad \textit{activated reactant}$$

$$\frac{\text{X} - \textcircled{P} \longrightarrow \text{Y} + \textcircled{P}}{\text{ATP} + \text{X} \longrightarrow \text{ADP} + \textcircled{P} + \text{Y}}$$

The net result is clearly equivalent to the reaction $\text{X} \to \text{Y}$ accompanied by the hydrolysis of ATP and ADP.

Alternatively, enzymes can link reactions in sequences, called *metabolic pathways*, in which the products of one step are the reactants in the next. We saw in Section 22.7 that the overall free energy change of any reaction is independent of the number of steps. As in the previous case, it is the algebraic sum of the free energy changes of all the steps. Thus a downhill reaction (such as the hydrolysis of an energy-rich phosphorylated compound) *anywhere* in such a pathway can "push" subsequent reactions or "pull" preceding reactions, as long as it releases more free energy than they consume.

We can easily understand this in terms of Le Chatelier's principle (Section 17.2).

The equilibrium of the reaction B $\rightleftharpoons$ C may ordinarily favor B. Nevertheless, if a subsequent reaction continuously removes C, so that its concentration remains low, the reaction will be "pulled" to the right. Similarly, if a preceding reaction keeps producing B, the equilibrium will be constantly displaced by the appearance of more B, and the reaction will be "pushed" to the right.

You may at this point be wondering about the ultimate source of the energy-rich molecules that organisms use to drive their anabolic reactions and do the other work of staying alive. Cells can synthesize such molecules, of course—most cells can actually *make* glucose from simpler precursors—but only at the expense of breaking down other energy-rich substances. Such a cycle is the chemical equivalent of a perpetual motion machine. The second law of thermodynamics assures us that it is impossible to break even in this way. In fact, animals get their energy-rich molecules from eating plants (or eating other animals that have eaten plants). Plants *are* able to make energy-rich substances at a net profit, not because they can circumvent the laws of thermodynamics (for nothing can), but because they have a free, external energy source—the sun. In the process of photosynthesis, solar energy is captured in chemical form as the plant uses sunlight to drive an uphill reaction: the synthesis of sugar from CO_2 and H_2O. So virtually all the life energy on earth ultimately comes from the sun (Figure 33.24).

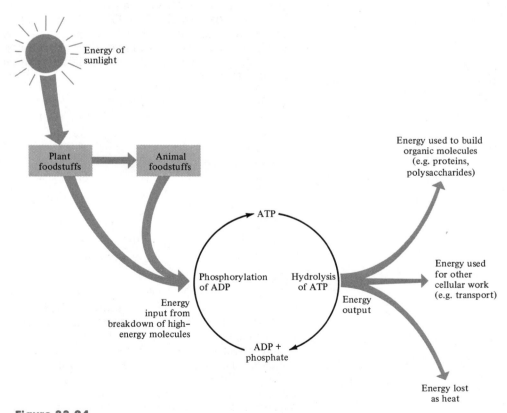

Figure 33.24
The Flow of Energy through the Living World Through photosynthesis, plants capture the energy of sunlight to make energy-rich molecules (carbohydrates) from CO_2 and H_2O. Organisms break down these molecules and use the energy released to make ATP. Hydrolysis of ATP then supplies the energy needed to drive "uphill" reactions and for other vital functions.

SUMMARY

SOME INTRODUCTORY CONCEPTS (Sections **33.1, 33.2**) A functional group is a chemically reactive atom or group of atoms that imparts characteristic properties to the family of organic compounds containing it. The site of reaction in an organic molecule is often a functional group, a multiple covalent bond, or a polar single bond. An electron-poor atom or group that will bond with an atom that has an available electron pair is called an electrophile. An electron-rich atom or group that will bond with an electron-deficient atom is called a nucleophile.

FUNCTIONAL GROUPS WITH COVALENT SINGLE BONDS (Sections **33.3–33.7**) Alkyl and aryl halides (RX, ArX), alcohols (ROH), phenols (ArOH), ethers (ROR, where the R's may be the same or different), and amines (primary, RNH_2, and secondary, R_2NH, or tertiary, R_3N, in which the R's may be the same or different) contain the following functional groups in which there are only single bonds: —X, —OH, —OR, and —NH_2, —NHR, —NR_2. Alcohols are classified as primary, secondary, or tertiary depending on whether the carbon atom to which the OH group is attached is primary, secondary, or tertiary. Alcohols exhibit hydrogen bonding and those with low molecular masses are miscible with water. Phenols are weak acids. Ethers tend to be unreactive, and low molecular mass ethers are often used as solvents. The amines are organic bases.

FUNCTIONAL GROUPS WITH COVALENT DOUBLE BONDS (Sections **33.8– 33.12**) Aldehydes and ketones (in which the R's may be the same or different) have carbonyl-containing functional groups. A secondary alcohol can be oxidized to a ketone. A primary alcohol can be oxidized to an aldehyde, and further oxidation yields a carboxylic acid (RCOOH) which contains the carboxyl group (—COOH). Carboxylic acids are generally weak acids and form salts when treated with bases. Esters, acyl halides, acid anhydrides, and amides are common types of organic compounds which have carbonyl-containing functional groups that are derived from carboxyl groups.

$$\underset{ketone}{\overset{\displaystyle O}{\overset{\displaystyle \|}{RCR}}} \qquad \underset{\substack{carboxylic\\acid}}{\overset{\displaystyle O}{\overset{\displaystyle \|}{RC-OH}}} \qquad \underset{\substack{acyl\\halide}}{\overset{\displaystyle O}{\overset{\displaystyle \|}{RCX}}}$$

$$\underset{aldehyde}{\overset{\displaystyle O}{\overset{\displaystyle \|}{RCH}}} \qquad \underset{amide}{\overset{\displaystyle O}{\overset{\displaystyle \|}{RC-NH_2}}} \qquad \underset{\substack{N\text{-}substituted\\amide}}{\overset{\displaystyle O}{\overset{\displaystyle \|}{RCNHR}}}$$

$$\underset{acid\ anhydride}{\overset{\displaystyle O \qquad\ O}{\overset{\displaystyle \|\qquad\ \|}{RC-O-C-R}}} \qquad \underset{ester}{\overset{\displaystyle O}{\overset{\displaystyle \|}{RCOR}}}$$

TOOLS OF CHEMISTRY: INFRARED AND ULTRAVIOLET SPECTROSCOPY Infrared spectra are produced when radiation in the infrared region of the spectrum (2.5 μm to 15 μm) is absorbed by the atoms in a molecule, increasing their energy of motion with respect to each other. The absorption peaks occur at characteristic wavelengths which reflect the stretching, bending, deformation, or other distortions of various bonds in the molecule. An IR spectrum can often be used as a "fingerprint" to identify an unknown compound, or at least to determine what functional groups it contains. Absorption in the near-ultraviolet region of the spectrum (200–400 nm) requires the presence of π electrons, that is, of multiple bonds. UV spectra, although simpler than IR spectra, can be used for structural analysis and compound identification, and also in quantitative analysis for determining the concentration of substances in solution.

SIGNIFICANT TERMS

functional group
nucleophile
electrophile
alkyl halide
aryl halide

hydroxyl group
alcohol
phenol
ether
amines
carbonyl group
aldehyde
ketone
carboxylic acid
carboxylate ion
ester
acyl halide
acyl group
acid anhydride
amide
monomers
macromolecules
thermoplastic polymer
thermoset polymer
homopolymer
copolymer
glass transition temperature
chain reaction polymerization
step reaction polymerization
elastomers
hydrophilic
hydrophobic
carbohydrate
lipid
protein
amino acid
peptide bond
polypeptide
denaturation
enzyme
substrate
nucleic acid
nucleotide
deoxyribonucleic acid (DNA)
ribonucleic acid (RNA)
metabolism
catabolism
anabolism
adenosine diphosphate (ADP)
adenosine triphosphate (ATP)

POLYMERS (Sections 33.13–33.17) Polymers, or macromolecules, are produced when large numbers of smaller molecules (monomers) are bonded together. A thermoplastic polymer (or "plastic") softens when heated and resolidifies when cooled. The majority of common synthetic polymers have molecular masses between 1×10^4 and 1×10^6 u and contain several hundred to several thousand monomers. The physical properties of a polymer are determined by such factors as the flexibility of the macromolecules, the sizes of the groups attached to the polymer chains, and the magnitude of intermolecular forces. Polymers may be linear or branched; if the branches of one polymer chain are covalently bonded to other chains, the polymer is said to be cross-linked. Thermoset polymers are cross-linked polymers that are permanently rigid; they do not melt when heated. A homopolymer is formed by polymerization of a single type of monomer, a copolymer by the polymerization of two or more different monomers. Most polymers are either amorphous or semicrystalline. At low temperatures an amorphous polymer is rigid and brittle. At the glass transition temperature, T_g, the flexibility of the polymer increases markedly. Rigid plastics are used at temperatures below T_g, flexible plastics at temperatures above T_g. To participate in polymerization, a molecule must be able to react at both ends. The principal types of polymerization reactions are chain reaction polymerization and step reaction polymerization.

BIOCHEMISTRY (Sections 33.18–33.23) Most biomolecules are organic polymers. The structure and function of biological molecules are intimately related. Cellular membranes and other structural elements are composed chiefly of hydrophobic substances. Most of the substances that take part in the chemical reactions of organisms are hydrophilic. *Carbohydrates* are simple sugars (monosaccharides), combinations of two sugars (disaccharides), or polymers of many sugars (polysaccharides). Simple sugars are polyhydroxy aldehydes or ketones. Glucose, like many monosaccharides, exists chiefly in a ring configuration in solution. Polysaccharides are used by organisms as storage forms for sugars (starch, glycogen) or to provide structural support (cellulose). *Lipids* are all nonpolymeric, hydrophobic substances. Among the lipids are the glycerides (fats and oils), esters of fatty acids, and the alcohol glycerol. Phospholipids play important roles in cellular membranes because they have polar, hydrophilic heads and nonpolar, hydrophobic tails. *Proteins* consist of one or more long, unbranched polymer chains of amino acids linked by peptide bonds (polypeptides). Fibrous proteins are generally hydrophobic, structural materials in which the polypeptide chains are relatively extended and cross-linked. Globular proteins are more compact, elaborately folded molecules, usually with hydrophilic exteriors that allow them to function in aqueous solution. Often they contain more than one polypeptide chain. Enzymes, the catalysts of living systems, are large protein molecules. Enzyme molecules possess a groove called the active site, where substrate molecules can be bound. An enzyme brings substrate molecules together in proper orientation for reaction, weakens bonds in the substrate(s), and may take a temporary part in the reaction mechanism.

Nucleic acids are polymers of nucleotides, each of which consists of a five-carbon sugar (ribose or deoxyribose), a nitrogen-containing base, and a phosphate group. DNA carries the genetic "blueprints" that specify what proteins an organism can make, while RNA is involved in "reading" the blueprints and guiding the synthesis of the proteins.

The breakdown of large molecules, which generally yields energy, is called catabolism; the synthesis of large molecules from simpler components, which generally requires energy, is called anabolism. Together these two processes make up the organism's metabolism. Organisms use the energy released by catabolic reactions to make ATP from ADP and phosphate. Enzymes couple the reverse of this reaction — the hydrolysis of ATP — to anabolic reactions so that the energy provided by the former can drive the latter.

THOUGHTS ON CHEMISTRY

Topics of Interest in Chemistry Today

CHEMICAL ABSTRACTS SELECTS

Adhesives
Amino Acids, Peptides & Proteins
Analytical Electrochemistry
Animal Longevity & Aging
Anti-Inflammatory Agents & Arthritis
Antioxidants
Antitumor Agents
Atherosclerosis & Heart Disease
Atomic Spectroscopy
Batteries & Fuel Cells
Biogenic Amines & the Nervous System
Biological Information Transfer
Blood Coagulation
Carbon & Heteroatom NMR
Carcinogens, Mutagens, & Teratogens
Catalysis (Applied & Physical Aspects)
Catalysis (Organic Reactions)
Chemical Hazards, Health, & Safety
Chemical Instrumentation
Chemical Processing Apparatus
Coal Science & Process Chemistry
Coatings, Inks & Related Products
Colloids (Applied Aspects)
Colloids (Macromolecular Aspects)
Colloids (Physicochemical Aspects)
Computers in Chemistry
Corrosion
Cosmetic Chemicals
Cosmochemistry
Crystal Growth
Detergents, Soaps & Surfactants
Distillation Technology
Drug & Cosmetic Toxicity
Electrochemical Reactions
Electrodeposition
Electron & Auger Spectroscopy
Electron Spin Resonance (Chemical Aspects)
Electrophoresis
Emulsion Polymerization
Energy Reviews & Books
Environmental Pollution
Epoxy Resins
Fats & Oils
Flammability
Flavors & Fragrances
Fluidized Solids Technology
Food Toxicity
Forensic Chemistry
Fuel & Lubricant Additives
Fungicides
Gas Chromatography
Gaseous Waste Treatment
Gel Permeation Chromatography
Heat-Resistant & Ablative Polymers
Herbicides
High Performance Liquid Chromatography
Infrared Spectroscopy (Organic Aspects)
Infrared Spectroscopy (Physicochemical Aspects)
Inorganic Analytical Chemistry
Inorganic & Organometallic Reaction Mechanisms
Inorganic Chemicals & Reactions
Inorganic Fluorine Chemistry
Insecticides
Ion-Containing Polymers
Ion Exchange
β-Lactam Antibiotics
Laser Applications
Lasers & Masers
Liquid Crystals
Liquid Waste Treatment
Macrocyclic Antibiotics
Mass Spectrometry
Metallo Enzymes & Metallo Coenzymes
New Books in Chemistry
Novel Sulfur Heterocycles
Nuclear Reactor Fuels
Optical & Photosensitive Materials
Optimization of Organic Reactions
Organic Analytical Chemistry
Organic Reaction Mechanisms
Organic Stereochemistry
Organoboron Chemistry & Boranes
Organofluorine Chemistry
Organophosphorus Chemistry
Organosilicon Chemistry

Organotin Chemistry
Organo-Transition
    Metal Complexes
Paper & Thin-Layer
    Chromatography
Photobiochemistry
Photochemistry
Plastic Films
Plastics Fabrication &
    Uses
Plastics Manufacture
    & Processing
Pollution Monitoring
Polymer Morphology
Porphyrins
Prostaglandins
Proton Magnetic
    Resonance
Psychobiochemistry

Radiation Chemistry
Radiation Damage
    (Material
    Aspects)
Raman Spectroscopy
Recovery & Recycling
    of Wastes
Silver Chemistry
Solar Energy
Solid & Radioactive
    Waste Treatment
Solvent Effects
Solvent Extraction
Steroids (Biochemical
    Aspects)
Steroids (Chemical
    Aspects)
Subatomic Particles
Surface Analysis

Surface Chemistry
    (Physicochemical
    Aspects)
Synfuels
Synthetic High
    Polymers
Synthetic Macrocyclic
    Compounds
Thermal Analysis
Thermochemistry
Trace Element
    Analysis
Ultrafiltration
Ultraviolet & Visible
    Spectroscopy
X-Ray Analysis &
    Spectroscopy
Zeolites

CA Selects (Columbus, Ohio: Chemical Abstracts Service (a division of the American Chemical Society)).

QUESTIONS

Functional Groups with Covalent Single Bonds

33.1 Write the general formula of an alkyl halide. How does this differ from the formula of an aryl halide? What type of reaction will alkyl halides undergo that aryl halides will not?

33.2 Write the structural formula for each compound: (a) 2-chloropentane, (b) 4-bromo-1-butene, (c) 1,2-dichloro-2-fluoro-propane, and (d) 1,4-dichlorobenzene.

33.3 Name the following halides:

(a)

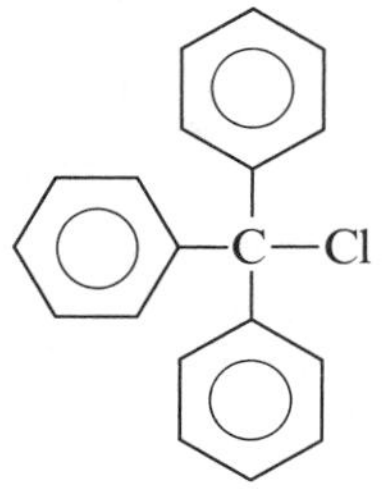

(b) $CH_3-\overset{\overset{\displaystyle CH_3}{|}}{CH}-CH_2Cl$

(c) $CHCl_3$

(d) $Cl-\overset{\overset{\displaystyle Cl}{|}}{C}=\overset{\overset{\displaystyle H}{|}}{C}-Cl$

33.4 Ethanol, like water, can act as a weak acid or a weak base. Write chemical equations showing CH_3CH_2OH acting (a) as a base with HCl and (b) as an acid with Na(*s*). (c) Name the compounds formed.

33.5 Write the general formula for (a) a primary alcohol, (b) a secondary alcohol, and (c) a tertiary alcohol.

33.6 Write the structural formula for each of the following compounds: (a) 1-butanol, (b) cyclohexanol, (c) 1,4-pentanediol, and (d) 3-hexyn-1-ol.

33.7 Name the following compounds:

(a) $CH_3\overset{\underset{\displaystyle CH_3}{|}}{CH}-CH_2OH$

(b) $HC{\equiv}C-CH_2OH$

(c) $CH_3-\overset{\underset{\displaystyle OH}{|}}{CH}-\overset{\underset{\displaystyle OH}{|}}{CH_2}$

(d) $CH_3-\overset{\overset{\displaystyle CH_3}{|}}{\underset{\underset{\displaystyle CH_3}{|}}{C}}-OH$

33.8* The molecular structure shown has the indicated IUPAC name with question marks where there should be numbers.

$$CH_3CHCH{=}CHCHC{\equiv}CCH_2OH$$
$$\overset{|}{Br}\qquad\overset{|}{CH_3}$$

?-bromo-?-methyl-?-octen-?-yn-?-ol

Write the name by putting the correct numbers where question marks now appear.

33.9 Which of the following compounds are phenols?

(a) 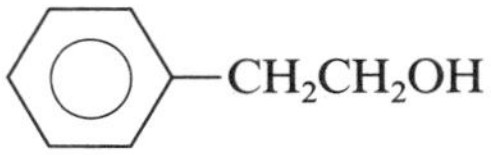 $-CH_2CH_2OH$

(b) 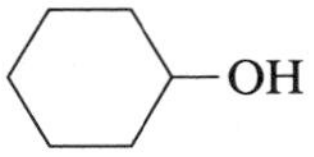 $-OH$

(c)

(d)

(e)

33.10 Write the structural formula for each of the following: (a) *p*-bromophenol, (b) 4-nitro-1-naphthol, and (c) *m*-nitrophenol.

33.11 What determines whether an ether is "symmetrical" or "unsymmetrical"?

33.12 Briefly describe the bonding around the oxygen atom in dimethyl ether. What intermolecular forces are found in this ether?

33.13 Write the structural formula for each of the following: (a) methoxymethane, (b) 1-ethoxypropane, (c) 1,3-dimethoxybutane, (d) ethoxybenzene, and (e) methoxycyclobutane.

33.14 Write the general formula for a compound that is (a) a primary amine, (b) a secondary amine, and (c) a tertiary amine. Is $(CH_3)_3CNH_2$ a tertiary amine? Give a reason for your answer.

33.15 Name the following amines:

(a)

(b) O_2N——NH_2

(c) —NH_2 (d) $CH_3CH_2CH_2CH_2$—$\overset{\displaystyle |}{\underset{\displaystyle CH_2CH_2CH_2CH_3}{N}}$—$CH_2CH_2CH_2CH_3$

33.16 Draw the structural formula for each of the following compounds: (a) *p*-bromotoluene, (b) cyclohexanol, (c) 2-methoxy-3-methylbutane, (d) diethylamine, (e) *o*-chlorophenol, and (f) 1,4-butanediol.

33.17 Name each of the following compounds:

(a) $CH_3CH_2CH_2CH_2OH$

(b)

(c) CH_3—$\overset{\displaystyle |}{\underset{\displaystyle NH_2}{CH}}$—$CH_3$

(d) CH_3—$\overset{\displaystyle |}{\underset{\displaystyle Cl}{C}}$=$CH_2$

(e) Br——Br

(f) $(CH_3CH_2)_3N$

(g) —O—

(h)

Functional Groups with Covalent Double Bonds

33.18 What is the basic arrangement of atoms that is common to both aldehydes and ketones? What is the difference between an aldehyde and a ketone?

33.19 What functional group is produced by the oxidation of a primary alcohol? Will this functional group undergo subsequent oxidation? If so, what new functional group will be produced? What functional group is produced by the oxidation of a secondary alcohol? Will this functional group readily undergo further oxidation?

33.20 Name the following compounds:

(a) $CH_3CH_2CH_2CH_2\overset{\displaystyle O}{\overset{\displaystyle \|}{C}}H$

(b) H—$\overset{\displaystyle Br}{\underset{\displaystyle Br}{\overset{\displaystyle |}{\underset{\displaystyle |}{C}}}}$—$CH_2$—$\overset{\displaystyle O}{\overset{\displaystyle \|}{C}}H$

(c) =O

(d) —$\overset{\displaystyle O}{\overset{\displaystyle \|}{C}}$—$CH_2$—$CH_3$

33.21 Write the structural formula for each of the following: (a) 2-methylbutanal, (b) propynal, (c) *o*-methoxybenzaldehyde, (d) 2-butanone, (e) bromopropanone, and (f) 3-hexanone.

33.22 Write the chemical equation for the reaction of benzoic acid with sodium hydroxide. Name the salt that is produced.

33.23 Write the structural formula for each of the following: (a) 2-methylpropanoic acid, (b) 3-bromobutanoic acid, (c) *p*-nitrobenzoic acid, (d) potassium benzoate, and (e) 2-aminopropanoic acid.

33.24 Name the functional groups that participate in an esterification reaction. What is the term given to the reverse of an esterification reaction?

33.25 Name the following esters:

(a) $CH_3\overset{\displaystyle O}{\overset{\displaystyle \|}{C}}$—$OCH_2CH_2CH_3$

(b) $CH_3\overset{\displaystyle O}{\overset{\displaystyle \|}{C}}OCH_3$

(c) —$\overset{\displaystyle O}{\overset{\displaystyle \|}{C}}$—$O$—

(d) $CH_3CH_2CH_2\overset{\displaystyle O}{\overset{\displaystyle \|}{C}}OCH_2CH_2CH_2CH_3$

(e) $CH_3C\equiv C\overset{\displaystyle O}{\overset{\displaystyle \|}{C}}$—$OCH_2CH_3$

33.26 What is the general formula for an acyl alide? What functional group is formed by the reaction of an acyl chloride and water?

33.27 What are the products of the reactions between an alcohol and (a) an acyl chloride and (b) an acid anhydride?

33.28 Write the structural formula for each of the following: (a) propanoic anhydride, (b) propanoyl chloride, (c) 2-propynoyl chloride, (d) 2-methylbutanoic anhydride, and (e) 3,5-dinitrobenzoyl chloride.

33.29 What is the structural difference between an amide and an amine? Contrast the chemical reactivity of these functional groups in their reactions with water.

33.30 Write the structural formula for each of the following: (a) N-methylformamide, (b) N-phenylethanamide, (c) N,N-dimethylacetamide, (d) p-phenylbenzamide, and (e) 3-butenamide.

33.31 Complete the following equations

(a) $CH_3CH_2\overset{\displaystyle O}{\overset{\|}{C}}-Cl + CH_3OH \longrightarrow$

(b) $CH_3CH_2\overset{\displaystyle O}{\overset{\|}{C}}O\overset{\displaystyle O}{\overset{\|}{C}}CH_2CH_3 + CH_3\overset{\displaystyle OH}{\overset{|}{C}}HCH_3 \longrightarrow$

(c) $\langle\bigcirc\rangle-\overset{\displaystyle O}{\overset{\|}{C}}-OH + CH_3OH \xrightarrow[\Delta]{H_2SO_4}$

(d) $CH_3CH_2\overset{\displaystyle O}{\overset{\|}{C}}H \xrightarrow[H^+]{MnO_4^-}$

33.32 Identify the major products of each reaction:

(a) [structure with OH and C—OH groups on benzene ring] $+ CH_3\overset{\displaystyle O}{\overset{\|}{C}}O\overset{\displaystyle O}{\overset{\|}{C}}CH_3 \longrightarrow$

(b) $\langle\bigcirc\rangle CH_2CH_2OH + $ [phthalic anhydride structure] $\longrightarrow$

(c) $CH_3CH_2\overset{\displaystyle O}{\overset{\|}{C}}OCH_3 \xrightarrow[\Delta]{\underset{conc\ HCl}{H_2O}}$

(d) [benzene ring with $O\overset{\displaystyle O}{\overset{\|}{C}}CH_3$ and C—OH groups] $\xrightarrow[\Delta]{NaOH(aq)}$

Polymers

33.33 What is necessary if a molecule is to be capable of polymerization? Name three types of molecules that can polymerize.

33.34 Describe the differences between thermosetting and thermoplastic polymers.

33.35 Using A and B for two different types of monomers, write structures which show how they might combine to form copolymers.

33.36 What changes could be made in the structures of polymer molecules that would increase the rigidity of the polymer and raise its melting point?

33.37 What is the glass transition temperature? What is its significance in determining the applications for which a polymer can be used?

33.38 Which of the following polymers might be chosen for use in (a) polishing wax, (b) molded automobile door handles? (i) Polystyrene, $T_g = 373$ K; (ii) poly(dimethyl siloxane), $T_g = 150$ K.

33.39 Which of the following polymers might be chosen for use in (a) rope, (b) skylights? (i) Polypropylene, $T_g = 253$ K; (ii) poly(methyl methacrylate), $T_g = 378$ K.

33.40 Using letters or symbols, schematically illustrate a chain reaction polymerization and the formation of a polyester by a step reaction polymerization.

Biochemistry

33.41 Name the four major classes of organic compounds found in living cells, and list some of the principal functions associated with each.

33.42 Give some examples of hydrophilic and hydrophobic biomolecules. Why is this distinction so important in the chemistry of living things?

33.43 What do we call the basic structural units of carbohydrates, and what is their chemical makeup? What terms are used to describe the carbohydrates formed by combinations of these units?

33.44 How do starch and cellulose differ in their properties? How can we account for these differences in terms of molecular structure?

33.45 List the principal types of lipids. What do they have in common? How do they differ from the other large biological molecules?

33.46 Give two reasons why fats are more efficient substances for energy storage than carbohydrates.

33.47 Describe the chemical structure of a phospholipid molecule. How is this structure related to the role of phospholipids in biological membranes?

33.48 Describe the structure of an amino acid. What kind of isomerism do most amino acids exhibit? Why?

33.49 How are the amino acids in a polypeptide joined together? What are the links called?

33.50 What is denaturation of a protein? What are some factors that can cause denaturation? Is this process reversible?

33.51 What is the active site of an enzyme? How does a substrate molecule bind to the active site?

33.52 Explain the mechanisms involved in the catalytic function of enzymes.

33.53 What are the basic structural units of nucleic acids? Describe the composition of these units. How are they linked together in a nucleic acid?

33.54 Briefly describe the structure of the DNA molecule. Explain the role of hydrogen bonding in the structure of DNA.

33.55* At one point, Watson and Crick were considering a possible structure for DNA in which the bases were on the outside of the molecule and the phosphate groups interacted with each other in the center. What chemical and functional objections to this model can you see?

33.56 How is genetic information encoded by nucleic acid molecules? Describe briefly how this information is duplicated.

33.57 What is ATP? Describe briefly the role of ATP in the utilization of energy by living cells.

33.58 Distinguish clearly among (a) hydrophilic and hydrophobic molecules, (b) aldoses and ketoses, (c) monosaccharides, disaccharides, and polysaccharides, (d) starch and cellulose, (e) condensation and hydrolysis, (f) fats and oils, (g) triglycerides and phospholipids, (h) fibrous proteins and globular proteins, (i) 1°, 2°, 3°, and 4° protein structure, (j) DNA and RNA, (k) replication, transcription, and translation, (l) anabolism and catabolism, (m) ADP and ATP.

Additional Questions

33.59 The structures of many of the classes of compounds discussed in this chapter can be "derived" from that of the water molecule, H_a-O-H_b, by replacing one or both of the hydrogens by various organic groups. Name the class of compound formed when (a) H_a is replaced by an alkyl group, (b) H_b is replaced by an aromatic group, (c) H_a and H_b are replaced by alkyl groups, (d) H_a is replaced by the $R-\overset{O}{\overset{\|}{C}}-$ group, (e) H_a is replaced by the $R-\overset{O}{\overset{\|}{C}}-O-$ group and H_b is replaced by an alkyl group, and (f) H_a and H_b are replaced by $R-\overset{O}{\overset{\|}{C}}-$ groups.

33.60 Identify and name the functional groups in the following:

(a) $HO-\overset{O}{\overset{\|}{C}}-$⟨benzene⟩$-\overset{O}{\overset{\|}{C}}-OH$

(b) $CH_2=CH-\overset{O}{\overset{\|}{C}}-O-CH_2CH_2CH_2CH_3$

(c) ⟨structure with OH, NO₂⟩

$O=C-CH_2CH_2OH$

33.61 Identify and name the functional groups in the following molecules:

(a) ⟨benzene⟩$-\overset{H}{\overset{|}{N}}-CH_2CH_3$

(b) $CH_3CH_2-\overset{O}{\overset{\|}{C}}-O-\overset{O}{\overset{\|}{C}}-CH_2CH_3$

(c) $HO-$⟨benzene with OCH_3⟩$-\overset{OH}{\overset{|}{C}}HCH_2-\overset{H}{\overset{|}{N}}-CH_3$

33.62 Identify the class of organic compound (ester, ether, ketone, etc.) to which each of the following belongs:

(a) ⟨benzene⟩$-CH_2OH$

(b) $\overset{O}{\underset{\|}{H_2C-\overset{\|}{C}}}\diagdown\!\!\overset{}{O}$ $H_2C-\overset{O}{\overset{\|}{C}}\diagup$

(c) ⟨benzene⟩$-O-$⟨benzene⟩

(d) $CH_3\overset{O}{\overset{\|}{C}}OC(CH_3)_3$

(e) ⟨benzene⟩⟨benzene⟩$-OH$

(f) $CH_3\overset{O}{\overset{\|}{C}}CH_2-$⟨benzene⟩

(g) ⟨cyclohexane⟩$-\overset{O}{\overset{\|}{C}}OH$

(h) ⟨benzene⟩$-CH_2-\overset{O}{\overset{\|}{C}}H$

(i) ⟨cyclohexane⟩$-\overset{O}{\overset{\|}{C}}NH_2$

(j) ⟨benzene⟩$-\overset{}{C}H-CH_2$ (with O bridge)

(k) ⟨benzene⟩$-CH_2CH_2\overset{O}{\overset{\|}{C}}Cl$

33.63 Xylocaine, a local anesthetic, has the following molecular structure:

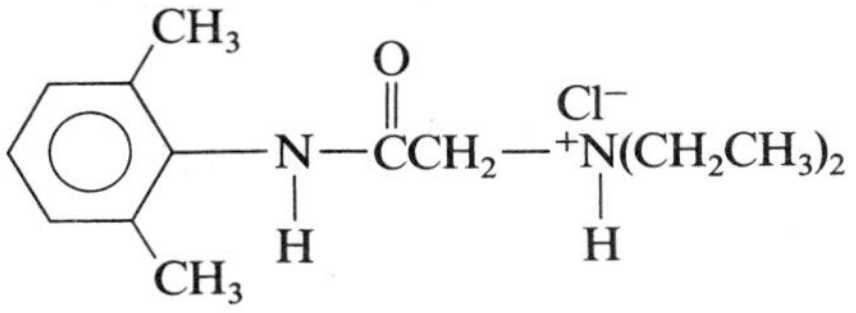

CH₃
$$\text{[structure with benzene ring, CH}_3\text{ groups, } -N-\overset{O}{\overset{\|}{C}}CH_2-\overset{Cl^-}{^+N}(CH_2CH_3)_2 \text{]}$$
H   H
CH₃

What functional groups are present in this compound?

33.64 Name each of the following compounds:

(a) CH₃CHCH₂OH
         |
         CH₃

(b) 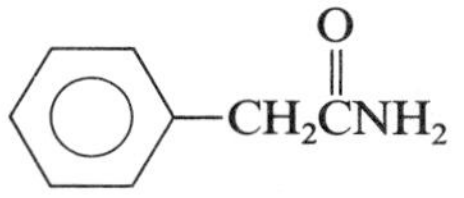 [benzene ring]–CH₂$\overset{O}{\overset{\|}{C}}$NH₂

(c) CH₃CH₂CH₂CH₂NH₂

(d) CH₃CH₂CH₂CH₂$\overset{O}{\overset{\|}{C}}$H

(e) 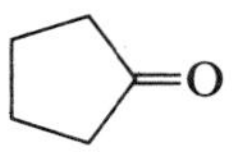 [cyclopentane ring]=O

(f) CH₃CH₂CHCH₃
              |
              OCH₃

(g) H₃C O
     | ‖
    CH₃C—COH
     |
    CH₃

(h) CH₃CH₂$\overset{O}{\overset{\|}{C}}$—Br

33.65 Give a molecular structure of a structural isomer of each of the following:

(a) CH₃CH₂OH

(b) ClCH₂$\overset{O}{\overset{\|}{C}}$H

(c) CH₃CH₂C=O
              |
              H

(d) CH₃CH₂CH₂$\overset{O}{\overset{\|}{C}}$—OH

(e) CH₃CH=CH$\overset{O}{\overset{\|}{C}}$—OH

(f) CH₃$\overset{O}{\overset{\|}{C}}$CH₂OH

(g) 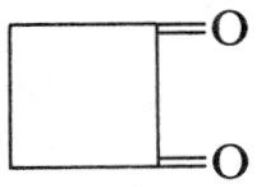 [cyclobutane ring with two =O]

(h) CH₃—$\overset{O}{\overset{\|}{C}}$—$\overset{O}{\overset{\|}{C}}$CH₃

33.66 Choose the compound that is the stronger acid in each set:

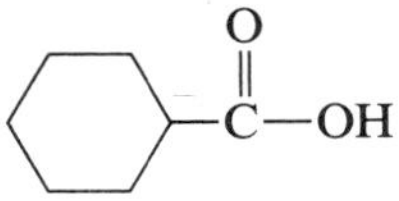

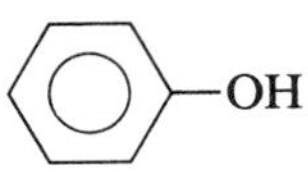

(a) CH₃CH₂CH₂OH   or   CH₃–[benzene ring]–OH

(b) CH₃CH₂OH   or   [cyclohexane ring]–$\overset{O}{\overset{\|}{C}}$–OH

(c) [benzene ring]–OH   or   [benzene ring]–$\overset{O}{\overset{\|}{C}}$–OH

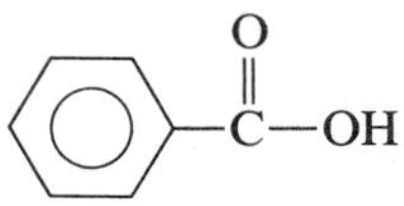

(d) 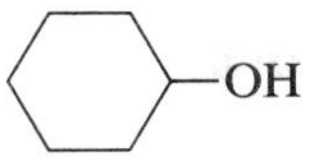 [cyclohexane ring]–OH   or   [benzene ring]–OH

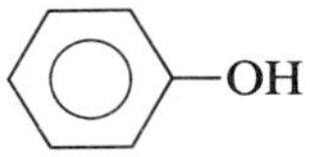

33.67* Alcohols can be used as starting reagents for producing many other types of compounds: (a) alkoxides, (b) ethers, (c) aldehydes and ketones, (d) acids, (e) esters, and (f) alkyl halides. Write a chemical equation illustrating the preparation of each of these types of compounds from an alcohol.

33.68 A student was given three bottles labeled A, B, and C. One of these contained acetic acid, one contained acetaldehyde, and one contained ethyl alcohol. (a) Write a structural formula for each of these compounds and (b) name them using the IUPAC nomenclature.

The student observed that substance A reacted with substance B to form an ester under certain conditions and that substance B formed an acidic solution when dissolved in water. (c) Identify which compound is in each bottle and (d) write balanced chemical equations for the reactions involving the formation of the ester and the ionization of the acid.

To confirm the identification, the student treated the compounds with a strong oxidizing agent and found that compound A required roughly twice as much oxidizing agent as compound C. (e) Write chemical equations for the reactions of compounds A and C with an acidic solution of MnO_4^-.

Answers to Selected Questions

33.3 (a) triphenylchloromethane, (b) 1-chloro-2-methylpropane, (c) trichloromethane, (d) trichloroethene

33.6

(a) CH₃CH₂CH₂CH₂OH

(b) 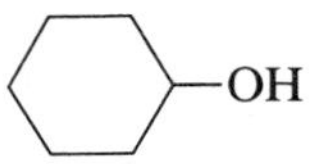 [cyclohexane ring]–OH

(c) CH₃CHCH₂CH₂CH₂
        | |
        OH   OH

(d) CH₃CH₂C≡CCH₂CH₂OH

33.12 sp^3 hybridization with two σ bonds and two lone pairs of electrons; London forces, dipole–dipole interactions

33.15 (a) diethylamine, (b) *p*-nitroaniline (or *p*-aminonitrobenzene), (c) cyclopentylamine, (d) tri-*n*-butylamine

33.17 (a) 1-butanol, (b) cyclopentanol, (c) 2-propylamine (isopropylamine or 2-aminopropane), (d) 2-chloropropene, (e) 1,4-dibromobenzene, (f) triethylamine, (g) diphenyl ether, and (h) 2,4,6-tribromoaminobenzene (or 2, 4,6-tribromoaniline)

33.21

(a) CH₃—CH₂—CH—$\overset{O}{\overset{\|}{C}}$—H
                       |
                       CH₃

(b) HC≡C—$\overset{O}{\overset{\|}{C}}$—H

(c) 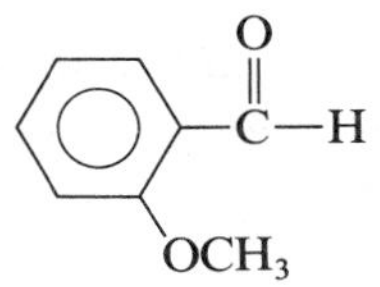 [benzene ring]–$\overset{O}{\overset{\|}{C}}$–H
         |
         OCH₃

(d) CH₃CH₂$\overset{O}{\overset{\|}{C}}$CH₃

(e) $CH_3\overset{\overset{\displaystyle O}{\|}}{C}-\overset{\overset{\displaystyle H}{|}}{\underset{\underset{\displaystyle H}{|}}{C}}-Br$

(f) $CH_3CH_2\overset{\overset{\displaystyle O}{\|}}{C}CH_2CH_2CH_3$

33.25 (a) propyl ethanoate (or propyl acetate), (b) methyl acetate, (c) phenyl benzoate, (d) butyl butanoate, (e) ethyl 2-butynoate

33.27 (a) an ester + HCl, (b) an ester + a carboxylic acid

33.32

(a)

(b)

(c)

$CH_3CH_2\overset{\overset{\displaystyle O}{\|}}{C}-OH + CH_3Cl$

(d)

$+ CH_3\overset{\overset{\displaystyle O}{\|}}{C}O^-Na^+$

33.36 Increase the crystallinity, or introduce chain linking, bulky substituents or branches on the chains, or groups that have strong intermolecular forces.

33.38 (a) ii; (b) i.

33.42 Hydrophilic: monosaccharides and disaccharides, some polysaccharides (starch), most globular proteins, nucleic acids; hydrophobic: some polysaccharides (cellulose), lipids, fibrous proteins; molecules interact with others of like nature — membranes and structural materials tend to be hydrophobic, molecules that take part in cellular metabolism tend to be hydrophilic.

33.46 Fats, which are mostly hydrocarbon, are more highly reduced than carbohydrates; fats are hydrophobic, and so do not attract water molecules, which add weight to carbohydrates.

33.48 Amino acids exhibit optical isomerism because they consist of an α carbon atom to which four different groups are attached: NH_2, COOH, H, and an R group (except glycine, in which R = H).

33.52 Enzymes bring substrate molecules together in correct orientation for reaction; weaken bonds in substrate by withdrawing electron density and/or stretching bonds that are to be broken; serve as intermediates in reaction mechanism.

33.53 Nucleotides consist of a pentose sugar (ribose or deoxyribose) with a nitrogenous base replacing the OH attached to carbon 1 and a phosphate group joined by an ester link to carbon 5; they are polymerized to form a nucleic acid by ester links between the phosphate of one nucleotide and carbon 3 of the sugar in the following nucleotide.

33.55 If bases were outside, there would be no need for base pairing by hydrogen bonding, and two strands of DNA would not have to be complementary; if phosphates were inside, DNA would not be acidic.

33.59 (a) alcohol, (b) phenol, (c) ether, (d) carboxylic acid, (e) ester, (f) carboxylic acid anhydride

33.61 (a) amino group; (b) anhydride group; (c) two hydroxyl, alkoxy, and amino groups

33.62 (a) alcohol, (b) anhydride, (c) ether, (d) ester, (e) phenol, (f) ketone, (g) carboxylic acid, (h) aldehyde, (i) amide, (j) cyclic ether, (k) acyl chloride

33.64 (a) 2-methyl-1-propanol, (b) phenylacetamide, (c) *n*-butylamine, (d) pentanal, (e) cyclopentanone, (f) 2-methoxybutane, (g) 2,2-dimethylpropanoic acid, (h) propionyl bromide

33.66

(a) CH_3-⬡$-OH$

(b) ⬡$-\overset{\overset{\displaystyle O}{\|}}{C}OH$

(c) ⬡$-\overset{\overset{\displaystyle O}{\|}}{C}OH$

(d) ⬡$-OH$

33.68

(a) $H_3C-\overset{\overset{\displaystyle O}{\|}}{C}-OH,$ $H_3C-\overset{\overset{\displaystyle O}{\|}}{C}H,$ $H_3C-\overset{\overset{\displaystyle H}{|}}{\underset{\underset{\displaystyle H}{|}}{C}}-OH;$

(b) ethanoic acid, ethanal, ethanol; (c) A is ethanol, B is acetic acid, C is acetaldehyde; (d) $CH_3CH_2OH + CH_3COOH \rightarrow CH_3COOCH_2CH_3 + H_2O$, $CH_3COOH + H_2O \rightarrow CH_3COO^- + H_3O^+$; (e) $5CH_3CH_2OH + 4MnO_4^- + 12H^+ \rightarrow 5CH_3COOH + 4Mn^{2+} + 11H_2O$, $5CH_3CHO + 6H^+ + 2MnO_4^- \rightarrow 2Mn^{2+} + 3H_2O + 5CH_3COOH$

PROBLEMS

Review of Principles

33.1 A laboratory procedure called for oxidizing 2-propanol to acetone using an acidic solution of $K_2Cr_2O_7$. However, an insufficient amount of $K_2Cr_2O_7$ was on hand, so the laboratory instructor decided to use an acidic solution of $KMnO_4$ instead. What mass of $KMnO_4$ was required to carry out the same amount of oxidation as 1.00 g of $K_2Cr_2O_7$?

33.2 A piece of glass 12 inches by 18 inches is to be silvered using the following reaction:

$$CH_3\overset{\overset{\displaystyle O}{\|}}{C}H(aq) + 2[Ag(NH_3)_2]OH(aq) \longrightarrow$$

$$2Ag(s) + CH_3\overset{\overset{\displaystyle O}{\|}}{C}ONH_4(aq) + 3NH_3(aq) + H_2O(l)$$

If the thickness of the silver is to be 0.0003 inch, what mass of acetaldehyde is needed for the reaction? The density of Ag is 10.5 g/cm³. *Answer 2 g*

33.3 The heat of combustion at 25 °C is −1367 kJ/mol for ethanol and −875 kJ/mol for acetic acid. Use Hess's law to predict the enthalpy change for the reaction

$$CH_3CH_2OH(l) + O_2(g) \longrightarrow CH_3\overset{\overset{O}{\|}}{C}OH(l) + H_2O(l)$$

Answer $\Delta H° = -492$ kJ

33.4 The standard state free energies of formation at 25 °C are −166.4 kJ/mol for methanol, −112.7 kJ/mol for dimethyl ether, and −237.2 kJ/mol for water. Calculate $\Delta G°$ for the following reaction

$$2CH_3OH(l) \longrightarrow CH_3OCH_3(g) + H_2O(l)$$

The enthalpy change for the reaction is 7.43 kJ. Calculate $\Delta S°$ for the reaction.

33.5 In aqueous solution, acetic acid exists mainly in the molecular form ($K_a = 1.745 \times 10^{-5}$). (a) Calculate the freezing point depression for a 0.10 molal aqueous solution of acetic acid neglecting any ionization of the acid. $K_f = 1.86$ °C kg/mol for water.

In nonpolar solvents such as benzene, acetic acid exists mainly as dimers

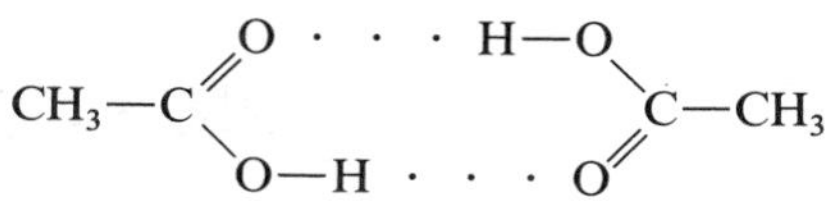

as a result of hydrogen bonding. (b) Calculate the freezing point depression for a 0.10 molal solution of acetic acid in benzene. $K_f = 4.90$ °C kg/mol for benzene.

33.6 Calculate the concentrations of the various species present in a 0.0123 M solution of diethylamine, $(C_2H_5)_2NH$. What is the pH of the solution? $K_b = 9.5 \times 10^{-4}$ for $(C_2H_5)_2NH$. *Answer* $[(C_2H_5)_2NH] = 0.0093$ mol/L, $[(C_2H_5)_2NH_2^+] = [OH^-] = 0.0030$ mol/L, pH = 11.48

33.7 Which solution would be the more acidic: a 0.10 M solution of aniline hydrochloride, $C_6H_5NH_3Cl$ ($K_b = 4.2 \times 10^{-10}$ for aniline, $C_6H_5NH_2$), or a 0.10 M solution of methylamine hydrochloride, CH_3NH_3Cl ($K_b = 3.9 \times 10^{-4}$ for methylamine, CH_3NH_2)?

33.8 What is the pH of a 0.10 M solution of sodium benzoate? $K_a = 6.6 \times 10^{-5}$ for benzoic acid, C_6H_5COOH. Would this solution be more or less acidic than a 0.10 M solution of sodium acetate? $K_a = 1.754 \times 10^{-5}$ for acetic acid, CH_3COOH. *Answer* pH = 8.59, more acidic than sodium acetate (pH = 8.88)

CHAPTER 34

Inorganic Qualitative Analysis: Chemical Principles Reviewed

The basis of qualitative analysis is chemical equilibrium. One guiding principle in making equilibrium reactions work for us appears over and over again — Le Chatelier's principle: If a system in equilibrium is subjected to a stress, a change that will offset the stress will occur in the system.

The man responsible for this principle, Henry Louis Le Chatelier, was born in Paris in 1850. He grew up in a home where the leading chemists of the day frequently came and went, visiting his father, who was Inspector General of Mines and who also had interests in the steel industry. His mother was a disciplinarian and enforced a strict schedule in her home.

Throughout his career, Le Chatelier maintained an equal interest in the practical developments of technology and their intrinsic scientific meaning. Much of his work grew from trying to solve industrial problems. His doctoral thesis was on the setting of cement, a process that includes complex and varied chemical reactions. This work has been called a classic of inorganic chemistry.

Le Chatelier went on to study the combustion of gases that causes mine explosions. From what he learned about acetylene gas came the development of the oxyacetylene torch used in welding. Further studies of reactions at high temperatures in the blast furnace led to his interest in equilibrium reactions. The outcome of that work, in 1884, was the famous principle now bearing Le Chatelier's name.

IONS IN AQUEOUS SOLUTION

34.1 AN OVERVIEW OF INORGANIC QUALITATIVE ANALYSIS

The goal of inorganic qualitative analysis is identification of the cations and anions present in a substance of unknown composition. Since solid substances are put into solution for most parts of the qualitative analysis scheme, qualitative analysis is based largely on the characteristic reactions of ions in aqueous solution.

The equilibrium properties of ions — strengths as Brønsted-Lowry acids and bases, oxidizing and reducing ability, solubilities of salts, and tendencies to form complex ions — provide an alternative to the periodic table in organizing the properties of ions in aqueous solution. This organization is the basis for inorganic qualitative analysis. The reactions of inorganic qualitative analysis provide excellent examples of how the principles of equilibria can be put to work to obtain desired results from chemical reactions.

Today we have an impressive array of instruments available for identifying the components of just about any type of mixture. However, "qual," as it is called, still remains of practical use in many circumstances. If the reagents are available, solution reactions often give the answer more quickly than do instrumental methods.

In addition, qualitative analysis maintains an important position in the study of general and inorganic chemistry. The laboratory work provides practice in observing chemical reactions and interpreting what you see in terms of theory. You will have to exercise judgment and make decisions when what you see does not correspond to what you expected, when you make a mistake, or when the experimental evidence is contradictory. The practical experience with equilibria and the behavior of ions in solution is a valuable addition to what is learned from the periodic table.

Qualitative analysis *can* be carried out in a cookbook fashion, merely by carefully following the directions given in the book. Although that approach may often lead to the correct answer, it is dull and time-consuming. However, if you take advantage of every clue, use your imagination to draw conclusions, and view qualitative analysis as a challenge, you will save much time and have more fun than someone who blindly follows directions. You will also learn more.

As the foundation for your laboratory work, we present in this chapter a review of the chemical principles upon which inorganic qualitative analysis is based. The examples in this chapter are all drawn from the chemistry of the ions chosen for inclusion in our qualitative analysis scheme. The scheme itself and the chemistry of the specific ions and groups of ions are discussed in detail in the next chapter. [The stepwise directions for the laboratory work are given in the separate laboratory manual.]

a. Some terms defined At this point, let's briefly go over some of the language of qualitative analysis. The **unknown,** the material to be analyzed, is a solution or solid of unknown composition. In a laboratory course in general chemistry, you probably will receive the unknown from the instructor. A **reagent** is any chemical used to bring about a desired chemical reaction. In cation analysis, the **group reagent** reacts simultaneously with all of the cations in a particular group. When we say an excess (*xs*) of a reagent is used, we mean that more than the stoichiometric amount of the reagent is made available.

A *precipitate* is any solid formed by a chemical reaction in solution. At many points in qualitative analysis we deal with the separation of solids and liquids. Precipitates are often driven to the bottom of a glass tube by centrifugation. The **supernatant solution,** which lies above the precipitate after centrifugation, can be removed by **decanting** it, which means carefully pouring the liquid off to separate it from the precipitate. This decanted solution is sometimes called the **centrifugate.** Precipitates can also be collected on a filter. The liquid that passes through the filter is called the **filtrate.**

What is left after part of a solid has dissolved or after a solution has been evaporated to dryness is often called the **residue.** And, in addition to separating solids from liquids, we frequently have to dissolve solids, a process called *dissolution.*

b. Anions and cations for analysis The eleven anions included in our analysis scheme are listed in Table 34.1. Anion analysis does not require separation of the ions. First, preliminary tests that indicate which anions or groups of anions may be present and which may be absent are carried out. Distinctive reactions for each individual anion then allow verification of the presence or absence of specific anions. These distinctive reactions are not done on separated anions or groups, but on the solution (or in some cases the solid) containing all of the anions.

Cation analysis is highly organized. Cations are first separated into groups by precipitating the ions in one group while leaving the ions of other groups in solution. The ions in each group are further separated by carefully chosen reactions under carefully controlled conditions. Finally, each ion is positively identified by a reaction that is characteristic of that ion.

Our cation analysis scheme deals with the 22 commonly encountered cations listed in Table 34.2. These cations are divided into five groups based on their reactions with the Cl^-, S^{2-}, OH^-, and CO_3^{2-} ions: The group reagents for Groups II to IV precipitate all of the members of each of the preceding groups as well as the members of their own groups. Therefore, systematic analysis of samples that may

Table 34.1
Anions for Analysis

Sulfide	S^{2-}
Sulfite	SO_3^{2-}
Carbonate	CO_3^{2-}
Nitrite	NO_2^-
Iodide	I^-
Bromide	Br^-
Chloride	Cl^-
Phosphate	PO_4^{3-}
Chromate	CrO_4^{2-}
Nitrate	NO_3^-
Sulfate	SO_4^{2-}

Table 34.2
Cations for Analysis

Ion	Symbol	Color in Solution
Aluminum	Al^{3+}	Colorless
Ammonium	NH_4^+	Colorless
Antimony(III)	Sb^{3+} or SbO^+	Colorless
Barium	Ba^{2+}	Colorless
Calcium	Ca^{2+}	Colorless
Chromium(III)	Cr^{3+}	Green or violet
Cobalt(II)	Co^{2+}	Pink or red
Copper(II)	Cu^{2+}	Blue
Iron(III)	Fe^{3+}	Yellow
Iron(II)	Fe^{2+}	Pale green
Lead(II)	Pb^{2+}	Colorless
Magnesium	Mg^{2+}	Colorless
Manganese(II)	Mn^{2+}	Pale pink
Mercury(II)	Hg^{2+}	Colorless
Mercury(I)	Hg_2^{2+}	Colorless
Nickel(II)	Ni^{2+}	Green
Potassium	K^+	Colorless
Silver	Ag^+	Colorless
Sodium	Na^+	Colorless
Tin(IV)	Sn^{4+}	Colorless
Tin(II)	Sn^{2+}	Colorless
Zinc(II)	Zn^{2+}	Colorless

contain cations from all of the groups must proceed by removal of each group in numerical order. [A flow chart summarizing the group separations is given in Figure 35.1.]

Cation Group I. *Cations precipitated as chlorides from cold dilute acidic solution.*

$$Pb^{2+}, Hg_2^{2+}, Ag^+$$

Cation Group II. *Cations not precipitated as chlorides from cold dilute acidic solution, but precipitated as sulfides from such a solution.*

$$Cu^{2+}, Pb^{2+}, Hg^{2+}, Sn^{4+}, Sn^{2+}, Sb^{3+} \text{ or } SbO^+$$

Cation Group III. *Cations not precipitated as chlorides or sulfides from dilute acidic solutions, but precipitated as hydroxides or sulfides from alkaline solutions containing ammonia and ammonium ion.*

$$Al^{3+}, Cr^{3+}, Co^{2+}, Fe^{3+} \text{ or } Fe^{2+}, Mn^{2+}, Ni^{2+}, Zn^{2+}$$

Cation Group IV. *Cations not precipitated as chlorides or sulfides from dilute acidic solutions or as hydroxides or sulfides from alkaline solutions containing ammonia and ammonium ion but precipitated as carbonates from alkaline solutions containing ammonia and ammonium ion.*

$$Ba^{2+}, Ca^{2+}$$

Cation Group V. *Cations not precipitated under any of the conditions described above.*

$$NH_4^+, Mg^{2+}, K^+, Na^+$$

The cation groups, the group reagents, and the color of the initial precipitate of each cation are summarized in Table 34.3. In reviewing the chemical principles applied in qualitative analysis, cations from this list are used in examples, and the place in the scheme where the various principles are applied is indicated.

Table 34.3
The Cation Groups

Cation Group	Group Reagent	Group Behavior	
		Ion	Product with Group Reagent
I	Cold dilute HCl	Ag^+	$AgCl(s)$, white
		Pb^{2+}	$PbCl_2(s)$, white
		Hg_2^{2+}	$Hg_2Cl_2(s)$, white
II	$CH_3C(S)NH_2$* in *ca.* 0.3 M HCl	Hg^{2+}	$HgS(s)$, black
		Pb^{2+}	$PbS(s)$, deep brown
		Cu^{2+}	$CuS(s)$, black
		SbO^+ or Sb^{3+}	$Sb_2S_3(s)$, orange
		$Sn^{4+}(Sn^{2+})$	$SnS_2(s)$, yellow (SnS, brown)
III	$CH_3C(S)NH_2$* + $NH_3(aq)$ + NH_4^+	Mn^{2+}	$MnS(s)$, pink
		$Fe^{2+}(Fe^{3+})$	$FeS(s)(Fe_2S_3(s))$, black
		Co^{2+}	$CoS(s)$, black
		Ni^{2+}	$NiS(s)$, black
		Zn^{2+}	$ZnS(s)$, white
		Al^{3+}	$Al(OH)_3(s)$, white
		Cr^{3+}	$Cr(OH)_3(s)$, gray-green
IV	$(NH_4)_2CO_3 + NH_3(aq)$ + NH_4^+	Ba^{2+}	$BaCO_3(s)$, white
		Ca^{2+}	$CaCO_3(s)$, white
V	None	Mg^{2+}	
		NH_4^+	
		K^+	
		Na^+	

* Thioacetamide, $CH_3C(S)NH_2$, is a source of H_2S and S^{2-} in solution.

34.2 NET IONIC EQUATIONS

Most of the reactions that are important in inorganic qualitative analysis involve ions. Therefore, it is best to describe these reactions by means of net ionic equations rather than molecular equations (Section 6.4). A net ionic equation includes only those ions and molecules that are necessary to describe completely the observed chemical reaction. The following conventions are used:

1. All soluble strong and moderately strong electrolytes are written as ions.
2. All soluble very weak electrolytes (e.g., H_2O, CH_3COOH) are written as molecules.
3. All solids and gases (e.g., PbS, CO_2) are written as molecules, even though the solids may be ionic (e.g., $BaSO_4$, $CaCO_3$).

In addition, we have chosen to omit (*aq*) for ions in solution in most cases. You can assume that all ions are in aqueous solution. Remember that *an ionic equation is not correctly balanced unless both atoms and ionic charges balance.*

Some typical reactions from cation qualitative analysis and their corresponding net ionic equations illustrate these points:

1. Mercury(II) sulfide precipitates when an acidic mercury(II) salt solution is saturated with hydrogen sulfide.

$$Hg^{2+} + H_2S(aq) \xrightarrow{H^+} HgS(s) + 2H^+$$
colorless   black

2. Manganese(IV) oxide is oxidized to permanganate ion by sodium bismuthate(V) in nitric acid solution.

$$2MnO_2(s) + 3NaBiO_3(s) + 10H^+ \rightleftharpoons 2MnO_4^- + 3Bi^{3+} + 5H_2O(l) + 3Na^+$$
black   violet
                                               or
                                               purple

3. A zinc salt solution when treated with excess sodium hydroxide solution gives an initial precipitate that redissolves.

$$Zn^{2+} + 2OH^- \rightleftharpoons Zn(OH)_2(s)$$
colorless   white

$$Zn(OH)_2(s) + 2OH^- \rightleftharpoons [Zn(OH)_4]^{2-}$$
colorless

4. Copper(II) sulfide dissolves in hot dilute nitric acid.

$$3CuS(s) + 8H^+ + 2NO_3^- \rightleftharpoons 3Cu^{2+} + 2NO(g) + 4H_2O(l) + 3S(s)$$
black   blue
or
brown

EXAMPLE 34.1
Net Ionic Equations

The separation and confirmation of Ag^+ involve (a) the precipitation of AgCl by adding HCl, (b) the formation of $[Ag(NH_3)_2]^+$ from the AgCl precipitate by adding NH_3, and (c) the reprecipitation of AgCl from the complex by adding HNO_3, which also forms NH_4NO_3. Write the net ionic equations for these reactions.

First we write the balanced equations for these reactions, using the complete formulas for the reactants and the products:

$$Ag^+ + HCl(aq) \longrightarrow AgCl(s) + H^+$$
$$AgCl(s) + 2NH_3(aq) \longrightarrow [Ag(NH_3)_2]^+Cl^-(aq)$$
$$[Ag(NH_3)_2]^+Cl^-(aq) + 2HNO_3(aq) \longrightarrow AgCl(s) + 2NH_4NO_3(aq)$$

The formulas of HCl, $[Ag(NH_3)_2]^+Cl^-$, HNO_3, and NH_4NO_3 should be written in ionic form in a net ionic equation because these compounds are strong electrolytes. However, the formulas of AgCl and NH_3 should not be written in the ionic form because AgCl is a solid and aqueous NH_3 is a weak electrolyte. Rewriting the equations and canceling ions common to each side of the equations,

$$Ag^+ + \cancel{H^+} + Cl^- \longrightarrow AgCl(s) + \cancel{H^+}$$
$$AgCl(s) + 2NH_3(aq) \longrightarrow [Ag(NH_3)_2]^+ + Cl^-$$
$$[Ag(NH_3)_2]^+ + Cl^- + 2H^+ + \cancel{2NO_3^-} \longrightarrow AgCl(s) + 2NH_4^+ + \cancel{2NO_3^-}$$

gives the net ionic equations

(a) $\qquad\qquad Ag^+ + Cl^- \longrightarrow AgCl(s)$
(b) $\qquad AgCl(s) + 2NH_3(aq) \longrightarrow [Ag(NH_3)_2]^+ + Cl^-$
(c) $[Ag(NH_3)_2]^+ + Cl^- + 2H^+ \longrightarrow AgCl(s) + 2NH_4^+$

Note that each equation is balanced with respect to number and type of each atom and with respect to ionic charges.

34.3 CHEMICAL EQUILIBRIUM
— THE BASIS FOR
QUALITATIVE ANALYSIS

The equilibrium constant expression is our major aid in understanding and controlling what happens in the reactions of ions in aqueous solution. For the general reaction

$$aA + bB + \cdots \rightleftharpoons cC + dD + \cdots$$

the concentrations of the reactants and products are related to the equilibrium constant K by the expression

$$K = \frac{[C]^c[D]^d \cdots}{[A]^a[B]^b \cdots}$$

In previous chapters we have studied the adaptations of this expression to water (K_w; Section 20.8), acids and bases (K_a, K_b; Sections 20.10–20.13; 21.2–21.9), solids in saturated solutions (K_{sp}; Sections 21.10–21.13), and complex ion equilibria (K_d; Section 21.14). All chemical reactions occur so that equilibria are achieved. Whatever the concentrations of reactants and products at equilibrium, they are related to each other so that their substitution into the equilibrium constant expression gives a value equal to K. The equilibrium constant expression can be used to find unknown concentrations from known concentrations at equilibrium. And nonequilibrium concentrations can be used to calculate the reaction quotient (Section 19.7) or the ion product (Section 21.12), thus allowing the prediction of whether a reaction will take place.

EXAMPLE 34.2
Equilibrium Concentrations

What is the concentration of acetate ion in equilibrium with a solution in which $[H^+] = 0.01$ mol/L and $[CH_3COOH] = 0.5$ mol/L? $K_a = 1.754 \times 10^{-5}$.

The reaction and the equilibrium expression are

$$CH_3COOH(aq) + H_2O(l) \rightleftharpoons CH_3COO^- + H_3O^+$$

$$K_a = \frac{[H^+][CH_3COO^-]}{[CH_3COOH]} = 1.754 \times 10^{-5}$$

Solving for $[CH_3COO^-]$ and substituting values of the concentrations gives

$$[CH_3COO^-] = K_a \frac{[CH_3COOH]}{[H^+]} = \frac{(1.754 \times 10^{-5})(0.5)}{(0.01)} = 9 \times 10^{-4} \text{ mol/L}$$

The acetate ion concentration is 9×10^{-4} mol/L.

EXAMPLE 34.3
Reaction Quotient

Will a precipitate of $PbCl_2$ form if $[Pb^{2+}] = 0.01$ mol/L and $[Cl^-] = 6$ mol/L? K_{sp} for $PbCl_2$ is 2×10^{-5} (at 25 °C).

The ion product for precipitation reactions takes the same form as the equilibrium constant expression. For

$$PbCl_2(s) \rightleftharpoons Pb^{2+} + 2Cl^-$$

the ion product is

$$Q_i = [Pb^{2+}][Cl^-]^2$$

Substituting the values of the concentrations gives

$$Q_i = (0.01)(6)^2 = 0.4$$

Because $Q_i > K_{sp}$, precipitation will occur.

Cation analysis is based on the controlled displacement of a series of equilibria in aqueous solution. The ions in the solution of the unknown are definitely not independent of each other, and Le Chatelier's principle is a powerful tool in controlling chemical reactions in such solutions. As soon as the concentration of one ion is changed, other concentrations must change.

The addition of more of a product ion causes the formation of more reactant as well as a decrease in the concentration of any other products.

$$A + B \underset{\longleftarrow C}{\rightleftharpoons} C + D$$

For example, at a point in cation analysis at which it is desirable for Sb^{3+} to stay in solution, the precipitation of SbOCl is inhibited by the presence of an excess of hydrogen ion.

$$Sb^{3+} + Cl^- + H_2O(l) \xrightleftharpoons[\quad\quad\quad\quad\quad H^+]{} SbOCl(s) + 2H^+$$

The addition of more of a reactant increases the concentration of the products of a reaction. This technique is used to ensure the complete removal of Ba^{2+} from solution as $BaSO_4$.

$$Ba^{2+} + SO_4^{2-} \xrightleftharpoons[]{\quad SO_4^{2-} \longrightarrow} BaSO_4(s)$$

A single ion may participate simultaneously in several equilibria. In fact, this is quite common. For example, carbonate ion (CO_3^{2-}) in a solution containing barium ion, lead ion, and hydrogen ion may participate in the precipitation of barium carbonate,

$$Ba^{2+} + CO_3^{2-} \rightleftharpoons BaCO_3(s) \tag{34.1}$$

the precipitation of lead carbonate,

$$Pb^{2+} + CO_3^{2-} \rightleftharpoons PbCO_3(s) \tag{34.2}$$

the formation of the conjugate acid of CO_3^{2-},

$$CO_3^{2-} + H^+ \rightleftharpoons HCO_3^- \tag{34.3}$$

or, with sufficient acid, in decomposition.

$$CO_3^{2-} + 2H^+ \rightleftharpoons CO_2(g) + H_2O(l) \tag{34.4}$$

At equilibrium in this solution, the concentration of carbonate ions remaining in solution will govern all of the equilibria in which carbonate ions participate. In other words, the same value of $[CO_3^{2-}]$ would be used to calculate how much Pb^{2+} is in solution (Equation 34.2), how much HCO_3^- has been formed (Equation 34.3), and so on.

Throughout cation analysis it is necessary to control competing equilibria so that the desired behavior of the ions can be achieved. This is accomplished by adding other ions that lead to (1) formation of precipitates, (2) altered solubilities, (3) formation of complexes, (4) changes in acid or base concentration, or sometimes (5) changes in oxidation numbers. The ultimate goal in most cases is the complete removal (or as nearly complete as possible) of all of one cation or of several cations from solution, while leaving behind other cations yet to be detected.

Competing equilibria are governed by a very important general principle: <u>An ion (X^+ or X^-) will form the precipitate, complex ion, or other species that is in equilibrium with the smallest concentration of that ion (X^+ or X^-) in solution.</u> This principle allows us to predict which of two or more products will form in a particular solution in which there are competing equilibria. For example, the K_{sp} value for two precipitates both containing, say, Hg^{2+} ion can be used to find out which precipitate will, at equilibrium, leave the smaller concentration of Hg^{2+} in solution. We do this by starting with comparable initial concentrations of the ions.

Table 34.4 gives sequences of precipitates and complex ions that have been determined in this way, using K_{sp} and K_d values. The table is based on initial ion concentrations normally encountered in qualitative analysis—0.1 M to 0.001 M for the unknown ions. Within each sequence the substance on the left leaves the largest concentration of the metal cation in solution at equilibrium and the substance on the right leaves the smallest.

What happens if a reagent containing Hg^{2+} is added to a solution that contains

Table 34.4
Equilibrium Concentrations of Cations

Cation	Concentration of Cation in Solution at Equilibrium
Pb^{2+}	$PbCl_2(s) > PbBr_2(s) > PbI_2(s) > PbSO_4(s) > Pb(OH)_2(s) > PbCO_3(s) > PbCrO_4(s) > PbS(s)$
Ag^+	$Ag_2SO_4(s) > Ag_2CO_3(s) > Ag_2CrO_4(s) > Ag_2O(s) > AgCl(s) > AgNCS(s) > AgBr(s) > [Ag(NH_3)_2]^+ > AgCN(s) > AgI(s) > [Ag(CN)_2]^- > Ag_2S(s)$
Hg_2^{2+}	$Hg_2SO_4(s) > Hg_2Cl_2(s) > Hg_2(NCS)_2(s) > Hg_2Br_2(s) > Hg_2I_2(s)$
Hg^{2+}	$HgBr_2(s) > Hg(NCS)_2(s) > HgO(s) > HgI_2(s) > [HgI_4]^{2-} > HgS(s)$
Cu^{2+}	$CuCO_3(s) > Cu(OH)_2(s) > [Cu(NH_3)_4]^{2+} > CuS(s)$
Sn^{2+}	$SnI_2(s) > Sn_3(PO_4)_2(s) > Sn(OH)_2(s) > [Sn(OH)_4]^{2-} > SnS(s)$
Sn^{4+}	$SnI_4(s) > SnO_2(s) > [Sn(OH)_6]^{2-} > SnS_2(s) > [SnS_3]^{2-}$
Mn^{2+}	$Mn(OH)_2(s) > MnCO_3(s) > MnNH_4PO_4(s) > MnS(s)$
Fe^{2+}	$Fe(OH)_2(s) > FeCO_3(s) > [Fe(CN)_6]^{4-} > KFe[Fe(CN)_6](s) > FeS(s)$
Fe^{3+}	$FePO_4(s) > Fe(OH)_3(s) > [Fe(CN)_6]^{3-} > KFe[Fe(CN)_6](s) > Fe_2S_3(s)$
Co^{2+}	$[Co(NCS)_4]^{2-} > Co(OH)_2(s) > CoCO_3(s) > [Co(NH_3)_6]^{2+} > CoS(s,\alpha)* > CoS(s,\beta)*$
Ni^{2+}	$NiCO_3(s) > Ni(OH)_2(s) > [Ni(NH_3)_6]^{2+} > NiS(s,\alpha)* > NiS(s,\beta)*$
Zn^{2+}	$ZnCO_3(s) > Zn(OH)_2(s) > [Zn(OH)_4]^{2-} > [Zn(NH_3)_4]^{2+} > ZnS(s)$
Al^{3+}	$AlPO_4(s) > Al(OH)_3(s) > [Al(OH)_4]^-$
Cr^{3+}	$CrPO_4(s) > Cr(OH)_3(s) > [Cr(OH)_4]^- > [Cr(NH_3)_5(OH)]^{2+}$

* The more soluble α form which precipitates initially changes on standing to the much less soluble β form.

both Br^- and I^-? From their relative positions in Table 34.4, we can predict that mercury(II) iodide, HgI_2, would precipitate rather than mercury(II) bromide, $HgBr_2$. A moment's thought will show why this is reasonable. Suppose that $HgBr_2$ formed instead. The concentration of Hg^{2+} in equilibrium with this solid,

$$HgBr_2(s) \rightleftharpoons Hg^{2+} + 2Br^-$$

will be greater than that required for precipitation of HgI_2. (Recall that precipitation begins when the product of the concentrations of the ions just exceeds the K_{sp} value.) Therefore, HgI_2 will begin to precipitate. As the Hg^{2+} concentration decreases, the $HgBr_2$ will dissolve to replenish the equilibrium concentration of Hg^{2+} ions. Essentially, the reaction will be

$$HgBr_2(s) + 2I^- \rightleftharpoons HgI_2(s) + 2Br^-$$

Therefore, HgI_2, and *not* $HgBr_2$, will be the precipitate formed. (If an *excess* of Hg^{2+} is added, some $HgBr_2$ will also form.)

EXAMPLE 34.4
Simultaneous Equilibria

Calculate the concentration of Zn^{2+} in equilibrium with a saturated solution of $Zn(OH)_2$ in which $[OH^-] = 0.1$ mol/L. $K_{sp} = 1.2 \times 10^{-17}$ for $Zn(OH)_2$. Find the concentration of Zn^{2+} in equilibrium with a solution containing $[OH^-] = 0.1$ mol/L and $[Zn(OH)_4]^{2-} = 0.1$ mol/L. $K_d = 5 \times 10^{-21}$ for $[Zn(OH)_4]^{2-}$. In which solution is $[Zn^{2+}]$ smaller? In a 0.1 M OH^- solution, would Zn^{2+} be more likely to form $Zn(OH)_2(s)$ or $[Zn(OH)_4]^{2-}$?

The concentration of zinc(II) ion in equilibrium with $Zn(OH)_2(s)$ is

$$Zn(OH)_2(s) \rightleftharpoons Zn^{2+} + 2OH^- \qquad K_{sp} = [Zn^{2+}][OH^-]^2 = 1.2 \times 10^{-17}$$

$$[Zn^{2+}] = \frac{K_{sp}}{[OH^-]^2} = \frac{1.2 \times 10^{-17}}{(0.1)^2} = 1 \times 10^{-15} \text{ mol/L}$$

and the concentration of zinc(II) in equilibrium with $[Zn(OH)_4]^{2-}$ is

$$[Zn(OH)_4]^{2-} \rightleftharpoons Zn^{2+} + 4OH^- \qquad K_d = \frac{[Zn^{2+}][OH^-]^4}{[Zn(OH)_4^{2-}]} = 5 \times 10^{-21}$$

$$[Zn^{2+}] = \frac{K_d[Zn(OH)_4^{2-}]}{[OH^-]^4} = \frac{(5 \times 10^{-21})(0.1)}{(0.1)^4} = 5 \times 10^{-18} \text{ mol/L}$$

Because the concentration of Zn^{2+} in solution at equilibrium is less with the hydroxo complex than with the hydroxide precipitate, the formation of $[Zn(OH)_4]^{2-}$ is preferred.

The equilibrium principle that we are discussing is illustrated in the progress of Zn^{2+} ion through the first few steps of the Cation Group III analysis. The colorless Zn^{2+} ion is present in the unknown solution. The group reagent solution contains $NH_3(aq)$, NH_4^+, and OH^- ions. Upon the first addition of the reagent, zinc hydroxide precipitates:

$$Zn^{2+} + 2OH^- \rightleftharpoons Zn(OH)_2(s)$$
white solid

However, further addition of the reagent dissolves the hydroxide to give the zinc(II)–ammonia complex, which is in equilibrium with a smaller concentration of Zn^{2+} (see Table 34.4).

$$Zn(OH)_2(s) + 4NH_3(aq) \rightleftharpoons [Zn(NH_3)_4]^{2+} + 2OH^-$$
colorless ion

Hydrogen sulfide, the next reagent in the sequence, leads to the reappearance of Zn^{2+} in the form of a white precipitate, that of zinc sulfide, one of the least soluble sulfides of the Group III cations.

$$[Zn(NH_3)_4]^{2+} + S^{2-} \rightleftharpoons ZnS(s) + 4NH_3(aq)$$
white

Such sequences of reactions in which cation concentration is gradually decreased are frequently used in qualitative analysis. From our knowledge of the principles of equilibrium and the equilibrium constant values, the decrease in concentration can be shown mathematically, as demonstrated in Example 34.5.

EXAMPLE 34.5
Successive Equilibria

Consider the following sequences of reactions performed on a 0.01 M solution of Ni^{2+}:

$$Ni^{2+} \xrightarrow{\text{NaOH}} Ni(OH)_2(s) \xrightarrow{\text{H}_2\text{S}} NiS(s)$$
green   pale green   black

Assuming that stoichiometric amounts of NaOH and H_2S were added, show that the concentration of Ni^{2+} in solution at equilibrium decreases in each reaction. $K_{sp} = 3 \times 10^{-16}$ for $Ni(OH)_2$; $K_{sp} = 3 \times 10^{-19}$ for NiS.

The first reaction, the formation of nickel(II) hydroxide, involves the equilibrium

$$Ni(OH)_2(s) \rightleftharpoons Ni^{2+} + 2OH^- \qquad K_{sp} = [Ni^{2+}][OH^-]^2 = 3 \times 10^{-16}$$

Letting $x = [Ni^{2+}]$ and recognizing that at equilibrium $[OH^-] = 2[Ni^{2+}] = 2x$ gives

$$(x)(2x)^2 = 3 \times 10^{-16}$$
$$x = [Ni^{2+}] = 4 \times 10^{-6} \text{ mol/L}$$

The concentration of Ni^{2+} has decreased from 0.01 M to 4×10^{-6} M.

The second reaction, the conversion of $Ni(OH)_2$ to NiS, involves the equilibrium

$$NiS(s) \rightleftharpoons Ni^{2+} + S^{2-} \qquad K_{sp} = [Ni^{2+}][S^{2-}] = 3 \times 10^{-19}$$

Letting $x = [Ni^{2+}]$ and recognizing that at equilibrium $[S^{2-}] = [Ni^{2+}] = x$, we write

$$(x)(x) = 3 \times 10^{-19}$$
$$x = [Ni^{2+}] = 5 \times 10^{-10} \text{ mol/L}$$

The concentration of Ni^{2+} has decreased from 4×10^{-6} M to 5×10^{-10} M.

The concentrations of ions in solution may be decreased by formation of precipitates and complex ions, as we have seen. They may also be decreased by formation of weakly ionized conjugate acids and bases, or by conversion to oxidation or reduction products. The remainder of this chapter is devoted to a review of such chemical equilibria, with special emphasis on applications in the cation analysis scheme.

ACID–BASE EQUILIBRIA

34.4 STRENGTHS OF ACIDS AND BASES

The Brønsted-Lowry definitions of acids and bases are most useful when we deal with aqueous solutions (Section 20.1). Remember that the water molecule can serve both as a proton acceptor, that is, as a *base,*

water as a base
$$HCl(aq) + H_2O(l) \rightleftharpoons H_3O^+ + Cl^-$$
$$NH_4^+ + H_2O(l) \rightleftharpoons H_3O^+ + NH_3(aq)$$
$$[Cu(H_2O)_4]^{2+} + H_2O(l) \rightleftharpoons H_3O^+ + [Cu(H_2O)_3(OH)]^+$$

and as a proton donor, that is, as an *acid,*

water as an acid
$$CO_3^{2-} + H_2O(l) \rightleftharpoons HCO_3^- + OH^-$$
$$NH_3(g) + H_2O(l) \rightleftharpoons NH_4^+ + OH^-$$

The water molecule is itself only slightly ionized. The ionization of water (Section 20.8),

$$H_2O(l) \rightleftharpoons H^+ + OH^-$$

leads to the ion product constant (at 25 °C) of

$$K_w = [H^+][OH^-] = 1.00 \times 10^{-14} \qquad (34.5)$$

These relationships make it clear that (1) in any aqueous solution both hydrogen and hydroxide ions are present, (2) the concentrations of the hydrogen and hydroxide ions are completely interdependent, and (3) in pure water (at 25 °C)

$$[H^+] = [OH^-] = 1 \times 10^{-7} \text{ mol/L}$$

To review briefly, we use K_w to establish a relative scale of acidity. By definition (Section 20.9)

$$pH = -\log [H^+] \qquad (34.6)$$
$$pOH = -\log [OH^-] \qquad (34.7)$$
$$pK_w = -\log K_w \qquad (34.8)$$
$$ = pH + pOH = 14.000 \text{ (at 25 °C)} \qquad (34.9)$$

Pure water is said to be neutral at $pH = pOH = 7$. Acidic solutions have $[H^+] > [OH^-]$ and alkaline solutions have $[OH^-] > [H^+]$ (see Table 20.5).

The strong acids (e.g., HCl, HBr, HI, HNO_3, $HClO_4$) are assumed to be completely ionized in 0.1 M, or less concentrated, solution. Thus, in a 0.1 M solution of any of these five acids, $[H^+] = 0.1$ mol/L. The weak acids (e.g., HSO_4^-,

H_3PO_4, HNO_2, HF, CH_3COOH, H_2CO_3, H_2S, NH_4^+, HS^-) are only partially ionized in terms of equilibria such as

$$HA(aq) + H_2O(l) \rightleftharpoons H_3O^+ + A^- \tag{34.10}$$

For weak acids, the equilibrium constant, or acid dissociation constant (Table 20.7), is

$$K_a = \frac{[H^+][A^-]}{[HA]} \tag{34.11}$$

Therefore, the hydrogen ion concentration for, say, a 0.1 M solution of a weak acid is less than 0.1 M. The relative strengths of weak acids are shown by their hydrogen ion concentrations in solutions of the same molarity.

The hydroxide ion is the strongest base that can exist in aqueous solution. Soluble ionic hydroxides (e.g., those of the alkali metals, Ba^{2+}, Sr^{2+}, and Ca^{2+}) give the hydroxide ion directly by dissolution and are essentially 100% dissociated; for example, $[OH^-] = 0.1$ mol/L in 0.1 M NaOH or KOH, and $[OH^-] = 0.02$ mol/L in 0.01 M $Ba(OH)_2$.

The anions of very weak acids, such as H_2CO_3, H_2S, and HCN, are relatively strong bases. They give alkaline aqueous solutions in their reactions with water as follows:

$$CO_3^{2-} + H_2O(l) \rightleftharpoons HCO_3^- + OH^-$$
$$S^{2-} + H_2O(l) \rightleftharpoons HS^- + OH^-$$
$$CN^- + H_2O(l) \rightleftharpoons HCN(aq) + OH^-$$

Such acid–base equilibria are sometimes referred to as hydrolysis equilibria (Section 21.1). Most other anions, ammonia, and many amines are somewhat weaker bases. For aqueous solutions of weak bases, the general equilibria are

$$B(aq) + H_2O(l) \rightleftharpoons BH^+ + OH^- \tag{34.12}$$

for example,

$$\underset{\text{methylamine}}{CH_3NH_2(aq)} + H_2O(l) \rightleftharpoons CH_3NH_3^+ + OH^-$$

or

$$B^{n-}(aq) + H_2O(l) \rightleftharpoons BH^{(n-1)-} + OH^- \tag{34.13}$$

for example,

$$F^-(aq) + H_2O(l) \rightleftharpoons HF + OH^-$$

(For K_a and K_b values, see Appendixes V.1 and V.2.)

EXAMPLE 34.6
Strengths of Acids

Compare the values of $[H^+]$ for 0.10 M solutions of HCl and of HCN. $K_a = 6.2 \times 10^{-10}$ for HCN.

Because HCl is a strong acid and is virtually completely ionized, $[H^+] = [HCl] = 0.10$ mol/L. For HCN, a weak acid, letting $x = [H^+]$, we find $[H^+]$ by our usual method for solving equilibrium problems. (To review this method, see Section 19.12.)

	$HCN(aq) \rightleftharpoons$	H^+ +	CN^-
Initial	0.10	0	0
Change	$-x$	$+x$	$+x$
Equilibrium	$0.10 - x$	x	x

$$K_a = \frac{[H^+][CN^-]}{[HCN]} = \frac{(x)(x)}{(0.10 - x)}$$

Assuming that $(0.10 - x) \approx 0.10$ (because K_a is significantly smaller than the known concentrations) gives

$$\frac{x^2}{0.1} = 6.2 \times 10^{-10}$$

$$x = \sqrt{(6.2 \times 10^{-10})(0.10)} = 7.9 \times 10^{-6} \text{ mol/L}$$

The assumption is valid (x is significantly smaller than 0.10) and therefore $[H^+] = 7.9 \times 10^{-6}$ mol/L. Thus the equilibrium concentration of H^+ in 0.10 M HCl is about 1.3×10^4 times greater than that found in 0.10 M HCN.

EXAMPLE 34.7
Simultaneous Equilibria

The separation of Fe^{3+} from Co^{2+} and Ni^{2+} is done by adding excess $NH_3(aq)$ so that Fe^{3+} precipitates as $Fe(OH)_3$, while Co^{2+} and Ni^{2+} are complexed as $[Co(NH_3)_6]^{2+}$ and $[Ni(NH_3)_6]^{2+}$. Assume a solution is 0.01 M in each of these ions and that sufficient concentrated ammonia solution has been added to make this solution 6 M in NH_3. Calculate the OH^- concentration in this solution.

Because K_{sp} for $Fe(OH)_3(s)$ is 3×10^{-39}, we can assume the reaction

$$Fe^{3+} + 3NH_3(aq) + 3H_2O(l) \longrightarrow Fe(OH)_3(s) + 3NH_4^+$$

to be essentially complete. From the stoichiometry we can assume that if the initial concentration of Fe^{3+} was 0.01 M, the concentration of NH_4^+ is 0.03 M.

The OH^- concentration is controlled by the equilibrium involving the aqueous ammonia, because OH^- does not enter into the formation of the cobalt and nickel complexes.

$$NH_3(aq) + H_2O(l) \rightleftharpoons NH_4^+ + OH^- \qquad K_b = \frac{[NH_4^+][OH^-]}{[NH_3]} = 1.6 \times 10^{-5}$$

Letting $x = [OH^-]$

	$NH_3(aq) + H_2O(l) \rightleftharpoons$	NH_4^+	$+ OH^-$
Initial	—	0.03	—
Change	—	$+x$	$+x$
Equilibrium	6	$0.03 + x$	x

$$K_b = \frac{[NH_4^+][OH^-]}{[NH_3]} = \frac{(0.03 + x)(x)}{6} \approx \frac{0.03x}{6} = 1.6 \times 10^{-5}$$

$$x = 3 \times 10^{-3} \text{ mol/L}$$

The concentration of OH^- is 3×10^{-3} mol/L.

In cation analysis, acids and bases are most often used in situations that involve several simultaneous equilibria. For example, acids and bases are essential in the buffered solutions used to control pH and thereby to control precipitation; these topics are discussed in Sections 34.6 and 34.10. Acids, in particular, are important in the displacement of equilibria for the purpose of the dissolution of solids; this topic is discussed in Section 34.11.

34.5 EFFECT OF AN ADDED COMMON ION

The addition of an ion common to a weak acid or a weak base such as ammonia in aqueous solution increases the equilibrium concentration of the undissociated acid or base. This change in concentration, called the common ion effect (Section 21.4), occurs by displacement of the dissociation equilibrium of the acid or the base, for example,

$$\underset{\longleftarrow A^-}{HA + H_2O \rightleftharpoons H_3O^+ + A^-}$$

As you can see, this is the principle of Le Chatelier at work again. As $[A^-]$ increases, $[H^+]$ decreases and $[HA]$ increases.

Ionization constant expressions for weak acids or weak bases can be used to find the changes in concentration that occur in the presence of a common ion, as illustrated in Example 34.8. The common ion effect is applied in buffer solutions, which are discussed in the next section. The effect is, of course, also applicable to the dissolution of slightly soluble salts and to any other equilibrium reaction.

EXAMPLE 34.8
Common Ion Effect

Find the effect on $[OH^-]$ and $[NH_3]$ of making a 0.010 M aqueous solution of ammonia also 0.050 M in ammonium chloride.

$$NH_3(aq) + H_2O(l) \rightleftharpoons NH_4^+ + OH^- \qquad K_b = 1.6 \times 10^{-5}$$

For the solution containing only aqueous ammonia, letting $x = [OH^-]$ gives

$$NH_3(aq) + H_2O(l) \rightleftharpoons NH_4^+ + OH^-$$

Initial	0.010	0	0
Change	$-x$	$+x$	$+x$
Equilibrium	$0.010 - x$	x	x

$$K_b = \frac{[NH_4^+][OH^-]}{[NH_3]} = \frac{(x)(x)}{(0.010 - x)} = 1.6 \times 10^{-5} \text{ mol/L}$$

We will assume that $(0.010 - x) \approx 0.01$. Therefore,

$$\frac{x^2}{0.010} = 1.6 \times 10^{-5} \qquad x = 4.0 \times 10^{-4} \text{ mol/L}$$

For the solution containing ammonia and additional NH_4^+, letting $x = [OH^-]$ gives

$$NH_3(aq) + H_2O(l) \rightleftharpoons NH_4^+ + OH^-$$

Initial	0.010	0.050	0
Change	$-x$	$+x$	$+x$
Equilibrium	$0.010 - x$	$0.050 + x$	x

$$K_b = \frac{(0.050 + x)(x)}{(0.010 - x)} = 1.6 \times 10^{-5}$$

Again assuming that $(0.010 - x) \approx 0.010$ and that $(0.050 + x) \approx 0.050$, we find

$$\frac{0.050x}{0.010} = 1.6 \times 10^{-5} \qquad x = 3.2 \times 10^{-6} \text{ mol/L}$$

The $[OH^-]$ has been decreased more than a hundredfold (from 4.0×10^{-4} to 3.2×10^{-6} mol/L) by the addition of the NH_4^+ ion, which is common to the NH_3 solution. Since in each case $[NH_3] = 0.010 - x$, the ammonia concentration is increased in the NH_4^+-containing solution.

34.6 BUFFER SOLUTIONS   When a salt containing the conjugate base of a weak acid is added to a solution of that acid, a buffer solution (Section 21.5) is produced. Similarly, the addition of a salt containing the conjugate acid of a weak base such as ammonia to a solution of that base yields a buffer solution. You can see that buffer solutions are made by adding a common ion. Buffer solutions serve the very important purpose of controlling the $[H^+]$ or the $[OH^-]$. The addition of small amounts of a strong acid or a strong base to a buffer solution causes only minor changes in the pH.

Acetic acid/sodium acetate is a frequently used buffer system. When a strong acid is added to this buffer, it reacts with the basic acetate ion:

$$H^+ + CH_3COO^- \rightleftharpoons CH_3COOH(aq)$$

When the strongly basic OH^- ion is added to the same solution, it reacts with the hydrogen ion to give water:

$$H^+ + OH^- \rightleftharpoons H_2O(l)$$

In each case the equilibrium between H^+ and CH_3COO^- is quickly restored, and the pH of the original solution comes back to nearly its original value.

By an appropriate choice of the ion/acid or ion/base buffer pair, pH can be maintained in any desired range. Buffers are most effective in the pH = pK_a (or pK_b) ± 1 range.

Buffer solutions play an essential role in cation analysis. It is only by controlling the pH with buffers that we are able, for example, to precipitate some sulfides while leaving others in solution. The applications of the common ion effect and buffer solutions to separations in cation analysis are usually of this kind—preventing the precipitation of one cation by a given anion while allowing another cation to precipitate. These applications also involve equilibria and are discussed in Section 34.10.

EXAMPLE 34.9
Buffer Solutions

We wish to make a buffer solution using HF and NaF. (a) What will be the most effective pH range of this buffer? (b) Knowing that buffers best resist change when the ratio of the acid concentration to the conjugate base concentration (or the base to the conjugate acid concentration) is between 1/10 and 10/1, what range of concentration can the NaF solution have if we wish to make the buffer solution by mixing equal volumes of the NaF solution and 0.200 M HF solution? (c) What will be the pH of the buffer solution made with equal volumes of 0.200 M HF and 0.200 M NaF? For HF, $K_a = 6.5 \times 10^{-4}$.

(a) From the relationship

$$pH = pK_a \pm 1$$

we find that the most effective pH range of the HF/F⁻ buffer is

$$pH = -\log(6.5 \times 10^{-4}) \pm 1 = 3.19 \pm 1$$

(b) The buffer solution should have an [HF]/[F⁻] ratio of between 10/1 and 1/10, or

$$\frac{0.200}{[F^-]} = \frac{10}{1} \qquad\qquad \frac{0.200}{[F^-]} = \frac{1}{10}$$

$$[F^-] = 0.0200 \text{ mol/L} \qquad [F^-] = 2.00 \text{ mol/L}$$

an NaF concentration between 0.0200 M and 2.00 M.

(c) For a 0.200 M HF/0.200 M NaF buffer the $[H^+]$ is found in the usual way, letting $x = [H^+]$. Note that we have doubled the volume and therefore divided the molarity in half.

	HF	$\rightleftharpoons$	H$^+$	+	F$^-$
Initial	0.100		0		0.100
Change	$-x$		$+x$		$+x$
Equilibrium	$0.100 - x$		x		$0.100 + x$

$$K_a = \frac{[H^+][F^-]}{[HF]} = \frac{(x)(0.100 + x)}{(0.100 - x)} \approx \frac{0.100x}{0.100} = 6.5 \times 10^{-4}$$

$$x = 6.5 \times 10^{-4} = [H^+]$$

$$pH = -\log(6.5 \times 10^{-4}) = 3.19$$

The pH is 3.19. [Whenever the ratio of the concentrations of the buffer pair is 1/1, the pH is equal to the pK_a.]

34.7 AMPHOTERISM

Any molecule or ion that can behave as either an acid or a base is said to be amphoteric. In the Brønsted-Lowry treatment of acids and bases, an amphoteric substance can either donate or accept one or more protons. The water molecule is thus a typical amphoteric molecule. Most commonly we encounter amphoterism in the oxides and hydroxides of representative metals and d-transition metals (Section 16.11). Using aluminum oxide and hydroxide as examples, the following equations, which give the metal ions in acid solution and the hydroxo complex ions in alkaline solution, illustrate the amphoteric behavior of such compounds:

as bases

$$Al_2O_3(s) + 6H^+ \longrightarrow 2Al^{3+} + 3H_2O(l) \tag{34.14}$$

$$Al(OH)_3(s) + 3H^+ \longrightarrow Al^{3+} + 3H_2O(l) \tag{34.15}$$

as acids

$$Al_2O_3(s) + 2OH^- + 3H_2O(l) \longrightarrow 2[Al(OH)_4]^- \tag{34.16}$$

$$Al(OH)_3(s) + OH^- \longrightarrow [Al(OH)_4]^- \tag{34.17}$$

Do not be confused if in various places you see the oxide, the hydroxide, or the hydrate written in equations representing the same reaction, such as

$$2Al^{3+} + 6OH^- \rightleftharpoons Al_2O_3(s) + 3H_2O$$

$$Al^{3+} + 3OH^- \rightleftharpoons Al(OH)_3(s)$$

$$2Al^{3+} + 6OH^- \rightleftharpoons Al_2O_3 \cdot 3H_2O$$

The hydroxide $Al(OH)_3(s)$ and the oxide $Al_2O_3(s)$ are chemically interchangeable, because the hydroxide is a hydrate of the oxide.

A similar relationship exists between the hydroxo complex ions such as $[Al(OH)_4]^-$ and the oxoanions such as AlO_2^-. Here again, the complex and the oxoanion are equivalent—dehydration of the complex yields the oxoanion. In writing an equation the two are interchangeable.

The amphoteric hydroxides that are part of the cation analysis scheme are listed in Table 34.5.

Table 34.5
Amphoteric Hydroxides The hydroxides can also be written as oxides. The hydroxo complexes can also be written as oxoanions.

Compound	Reaction with H$^+$ Produces	Reaction with OH$^-$ Produces
$Sb(OH)_3$	Sb^{3+} or SbO^+	$[Sb(OH)_4]^-$
$Sn(OH)_2$	Sn^{2+}	$[Sn(OH)_4]^{2-}$
$Pb(OH)_2$	Pb^{2+}	$[Pb(OH)_4]^{2-}$
$Sn(OH)_4$	Sn^{4+}	$[Sn(OH)_6]^{2-}$
$Al(OH)_3$	Al^{3+}	$[Al(OH)_4]^-$
$Cr(OH)_3$	Cr^{3+}	$[Cr(OH)_4]^-$
$Zn(OH)_2$	Zn^{2+}	$[Zn(OH)_4]^{2-}$

The acidic properties of amphoteric metal oxides and hydroxides can be utilized in separating them from nonamphoteric oxides and hydroxides. For example, in cation analysis Al^{3+} is separated from Fe^{3+} in this way. As aqueous sodium or potassium hydroxide solution is added slowly to a solution containing these ions, precipitation occurs first.

$$Al^{3+} + 3OH^- \rightleftharpoons Al(OH)_3(s) \qquad Fe^{3+} + 3OH^- \rightleftharpoons Fe(OH)_3(s)$$
colorless   white   yellow   red-brown

Then, as more hydroxide ion is added, aluminum(III) hydroxide dissolves,

$$Al(OH)_3(s) + OH^- \xrightleftharpoons{\text{excess OH}^-} [Al(OH)_4]^-$$
colorless

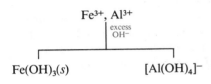

but the less acidic iron(III) hydroxide does not. This separation can be formulated in a single step as shown in the margin.

Amphoterism is not restricted to metal oxides and hydroxides. Sulfur, the element just below oxygen in the periodic table, also forms amphoteric compounds. The acid–base reactions of the amphoteric metal sulfides are illustrated by the following reactions of tin(IV) sulfide:

as a base

$$SnS_2(s) + 4H^+ \rightleftharpoons Sn^{4+} + 2H_2S(aq) \qquad \textbf{(34.18)}$$
yellow   colorless

as an acid

$$SnS_2(s) + 2HS^- \rightleftharpoons [SnS_3]^{2-} + H_2S(aq) \qquad \textbf{(34.19)}$$
sulfostannate(IV)
ion
(yellow)

The term "sulfoamphoteric" can be used for such compounds.

Certain metal cyanides are also amphoteric, for example,

as a base

$$Fe(CN)_2 + 2H^+ \rightleftharpoons Fe^{2+} + 2HCN(aq) \qquad \textbf{(34.20)}$$
white

as an acid

$$Fe(CN)_2 + 4CN^- \rightleftharpoons [Fe(CN)_6]^{4-} \qquad \textbf{(34.21)}$$
pale yellow

The equations involving sulfide and cyanide reactions as bases are consistent with Brønsted–Lowry acid-base definitions. The reactions as acids are more readily interpreted by Lewis definitions, for $Fe(CN)_2$ accepts electron pairs from the CN^- ions and SnS_2 accepts an electron pair from S^{2-}, making them Lewis acids.

EXAMPLE 34.10
Amphoterism

Write equations showing the sulfoamphoteric behavior of Sb_2S_3 to form Sb^{3+} and $[SbS_2]^-$.

The base reaction is

$$Sb_2S_3(s) + 6H^+ \rightleftharpoons 2Sb^{3+} + 3H_2S(aq)$$

and the acid reaction is

$$Sb_2S_3(s) + 2HS^- \rightleftharpoons 2[SbS_2]^- + H_2S(aq)$$

REDOX EQUILIBRIA

In a redox reaction, an oxidizing agent is reduced and a reducing agent is oxidized. Oxidation is shown by an increase in oxidation number and reduction by a decrease in oxidation number. The total increase and decrease in oxidation numbers in a redox reaction are equal to each other. A redox reaction can be represented as the sum of two electron-transfer reactions in which oxidation is represented by electron loss and reduction by electron gain. For example, the equation for the reaction of hydrogen sulfide with dilute nitric acid,

$$\overset{-2}{3H_2S}(aq) + \overset{+5}{2NO_3^-} + 2H^+ \longrightarrow \overset{+2}{2NO}(g) + 4H_2O(l) + \overset{0}{3S}(s) \qquad (34.22)$$

is the summation of equations for two half-reactions:

reduction   *oxidation*

$$NO_3^- + 4H^+ + 3e^- \longrightarrow NO + 2H_2O \qquad H_2S \longrightarrow 2H^+ + S + 2e^-$$

In balancing redox equations, electron gain and loss (Sections 23.1, 23.2) or oxidation number increase and decrease (Section 17.8) are equalized.

Quantitatively, the strengths of oxidizing and reducing agents under standard state conditions are measured by standard reduction potentials (Sections 23.8, 23.9). Recall that these potentials are always recorded for reduction reactions. Therefore, the relevant standard reduction potentials for the $H_2S - HNO_3$ reaction are

for the reduction of NO_3^- to NO
$$NO_3^- + 4H^+ + 3e^- \longrightarrow NO(g) + 2H_2O(l) \qquad E^\circ = 0.96 \text{ V} \qquad (34.23)$$

for the reduction of S(s) to H_2S
$$S(s) + 2H^+ + 2e^- \longrightarrow H_2S(aq) \qquad E^\circ = 0.142 \text{ V} \qquad (34.24)$$

A larger and more positive E° value indicates a stronger oxidizing agent, that is, the reactant in the couple is more easily reduced. The E° values show that in the $H_2S - HNO_3$ system, NO_3^- ion will be reduced, while H_2S will be oxidized to sulfur.

EXAMPLE 34.11
Redox Equilibria

Would adding Pb^{2+} to an aqueous solution of H_2S cause the H_2S to be oxidized to S? $E^\circ = -0.126$ V for the half-reaction

$$Pb^{2+} + 2e^- \longrightarrow Pb(s)$$

Combining the half-reactions involving Pb^{2+} and the sulfur (Equation 34.24) gives

$$Pb^{2+} + 2e^- \longrightarrow Pb(s) \qquad\qquad E^\circ = -0.126 \text{ V}$$
$$\underline{H_2S(aq) \longrightarrow S(s) + 2H^+ + 2e^- \qquad E^\circ = -0.142 \text{ V}}$$
$$Pb^{2+} + H_2S \longrightarrow Pb(s) + S(s) + 2H^+ \qquad E^\circ = -0.268 \text{ V}$$

Because E° is negative, this reaction would not be spontaneous under standard state conditions. [PbS(s) would form.]

The reduction potential values reveal which are likely to be the more stable oxidation states of ions in solution. An ion that is resistant to both oxidation and reduction will be found more commonly than an ion that is easily oxidized and/or reduced. For example, manganese(II) is more stable in aqueous solution than manganese(III), for manganese(II) is quite resistant to reduction,

$$Mn^{2+} + 2e^- \longrightarrow Mn(s) \qquad E^\circ = -1.185 \text{ V}$$

and also quite resistant to oxidation,

$$Mn^{3+} + e^- \longrightarrow Mn^{2+} \qquad E^\circ = +1.51 \text{ V}$$

(Remember that oxidation is the reverse of this reaction as it is written and that for the reverse reaction, $E^\circ = -1.51$ V.)

Using thermodynamics and our knowledge that at equilibrium $\Delta G = 0$ and $\Delta E = 0$, we have shown (Section 23.12, 23.13) that the equilibrium constant and the standard reduction potential are related by the following equation, derived from the Nernst equation:

$$\log K = \frac{n}{0.0592} E^\circ \qquad \text{(34.25)}$$

number of electrons transferred

This relationship can be used to calculate equilibrium constants from the potential data. For example, suppose that we wish to find the equilibrium constant for the reduction of nitric acid by hydrogen sulfide. First, we must find the overall E°. Note that the E° values are not multiplied by any factors because the standard state voltage does not depend on the actual quantities of the substances involved.

$2 \times [NO_3^- + 4H^+ + 3e^- \longrightarrow NO + 2H_2O]$	$E^\circ = 0.96$ V
$3 \times [H_2S \longrightarrow S + 2H^+ + 2e^-]$	$E^\circ = -0.142$ V
$\overline{3H_2S + 2NO_3^- + 2H^+ \longrightarrow 2NO + 4H_2O + 3S}$	$E^\circ = 0.82$ V

The positive E° value shows that the reaction will be spontaneous in the direction written.

From Equation (34.25)

$$\log K = \left(\frac{6}{0.0592}\right)(0.82) = 83$$

$$K = \frac{[NO]^2}{[H_2S]^3[NO_3^-]^2[H^+]^2} = 1 \times 10^{83} \qquad \text{(34.26)}$$

The very large value of K shows that equilibrium is established when the reaction is almost completely displaced toward nitrogen(II) oxide and sulfur. The next example makes use of this K value.

EXAMPLE 34.12
Redox Equilibria

Show that HNO_3 will dissolve $CuS(s)$, but that $HgS(s)$ will not dissolve.

The overall equations for the dissolution are

$$3HgS(s) + 2NO_3^- + 8H^+ \rightleftharpoons 3Hg^{2+} + 3S(s) + 2NO(g) + 4H_2O(l) \qquad \text{(a)}$$
$$3CuS(s) + 2NO_3^- + 8H^+ \rightleftharpoons 3Cu^{2+} + 3S(s) + 2NO(g) + 4H_2O(l) \qquad \text{(b)}$$

and the respective overall equilibrium constants are

$$K_{(a)} = \frac{[Hg^{2+}]^3[NO]^2}{[NO_3^-]^2[H^+]^8} \qquad K_{(b)} = \frac{[Cu^{2+}]^3[NO]^2}{[NO_3^-]^2[H^+]^8}$$

Each of the overall reactions can be considered to occur by the series of reactions described below. The overall equilibrium constants are the products of the respective equilibrium constants (see Section 19.6).

The first reactions in the series are those involving the solubility products of the sulfide precipitates.

$$HgS(s) \rightleftharpoons Hg^{2+} + S^{2-} \qquad K_{(c)} = K_{sp} = [Hg^{2+}][S^{2-}] = 4 \times 10^{-53} \qquad \text{(c)}$$
$$CuS(s) \rightleftharpoons Cu^{2+} + S^{2-} \qquad K_{(d)} = K_{sp} = [Cu^{2+}][S^{2-}] = 6 \times 10^{-36} \qquad \text{(d)}$$

The second reaction in the series is the dissociation of H_2S.

$$H_2S(aq) \rightleftharpoons 2H^+ + S^{2-} \qquad K_{(e)} = K_a = \frac{[H^+]^2[S^{2-}]}{[H_2S]} = 3 \times 10^{-20} \qquad \text{(e)}$$

The third reaction in the series is the oxidation of H_2S by NO_3^- for which K was found in Equation (34.26).

$$3H_2S(aq) + 2NO_3^- + 2H^+ \rightleftharpoons 2NO(g) + 4H_2O(l) + 3S(s) \qquad K_{(f)} = 1 \times 10^{83} \qquad \text{(f)}$$

The overall Equation (a) can be obtained by combining Equation (c) multiplied by 3 with Equation (e) inverted and multiplied by 3 and Equation (f).

$$3HgS(s) \rightleftharpoons 3Hg^{2+} + 3S^{2-} \qquad\qquad K = K_{(c)}^3$$
$$6H^+ + 3S^{2-} \rightleftharpoons 3H_2S(aq) \qquad\qquad K = 1/K_{(e)}^3$$
$$\underline{3H_2S(aq) + 2NO_3^-\; 2H^+ \rightleftharpoons 2NO(g) + 4H_2O(l) + 3S(s) \qquad K = K_{(f)}}$$
$$3HgS(s) + 2NO_3^- + 8H^+ \rightleftharpoons 3Hg^{2+} + 3S(s) + 2NO(g) + 4H_2O(l)$$
$$K_{(a)} = K_{(c)}^3 K_{(f)}/K_{(e)}^3$$

Thus,

$$K_{(a)} = \frac{K_{(c)}^3 K_{(f)}}{K_{(e)}^3} = \frac{(4 \times 10^{-53})^3 (1 \times 10^{83})}{(3 \times 10^{-20})^3} = 2 \times 10^{-16}$$

This low value of $K_{(a)}$ implies that greater concentrations of the reactants than of the products will be present at equilibrium, and for all practical purposes the reaction will not occur. For the overall Equation (b), we find

$$K_{(b)} = \frac{K_{(d)}^3 K_{(f)}}{K_{(e)}^3} = \frac{(6 \times 10^{-36})^3 (1 \times 10^{83})}{(3 \times 10^{-20})^3} = 8 \times 10^{35}$$

and because $K_{(b)}$ is very large we can expect that HNO_3 will dissolve $CuS(s)$.

In separating and identifying cations, advantage is taken of selective oxidation and reduction. For example, in Cation Group II, 2 M nitric acid oxidizes lead(II) and copper(II) sulfides, but not mercury(II) sulfide. This difference in oxidizability arises because of differences in solubility among these compounds. The lead(II) and copper(II) compounds are soluble enough to provide high enough concentrations of sulfide ion in solution to allow for its oxidation. The mercury(II) sulfide is so slightly soluble that oxidation in this manner is not possible. Analysis of Cation Group III provides another example of selective oxidation — $[Cr(OH)_4]^-$ is oxidized (to CrO_4^{2-}) by hydrogen peroxide, but $[Al(OH)_4]^-$ is not oxidized.

COMPLEXATION EQUILIBRIA

In aqueous solution, each complex ion is in equilibrium with its components, for example,

$$[Ag(NH_3)_2]^+ \rightleftharpoons Ag^+ + 2NH_3(aq)$$
$$[Cr(OH)_4]^- \rightleftharpoons Cr^{3+} + 4OH^-$$
$$[Fe(CN)_6]^{4-} \rightleftharpoons Fe^{2+} + 6CN^-$$

Each such reaction is described by an equilibrium constant which we call a dissociation constant (K_d) because the equilibria are written as dissociation processes. (Dissociation constant values are given in Appendix V.4.)

The smaller the numerical magnitude of K_d, the smaller is the equilibrium concentration of the metal ion in question. In addition, a smaller K_d indicates that the complex is more stable and forms more readily. Recall that the tabulated overall K_d values can only be used in calculations for reactions in the presence of excess ligand (Section 21.14). Both separations and identifications of cations may be effected via complexation.

EXAMPLE 34.13
Complexation Equilibria

As aqueous NH_3 is added to the mixture of Fe^{3+}, Co^{2+}, and Ni^{2+} described in Example 34.7, $Co(OH)_2$ and $Ni(OH)_2$ also form; but because the cation concentrations in equilibrium with the ammonia complexes are less than those in equilibrium with the hydroxide precipitates, these cations eventually form the ammonia complexes. Calculate the $[Co^{2+}]$ in equilibrium with $Co(OH)_2(s)$ and 0.01 M $[Co(NH_3)_6]^{2+}$ in 6 M NH_3 (which is an excess). For $Co(OH)_2$, $K_{sp} = 2 \times 10^{-16}$; for $[Co(NH_3)_6^{2+}]$, $K_d = 9 \times 10^{-6}$.

For the hydroxide precipitate that forms first

$$Co(OH)_2(s) \rightleftharpoons Co^{2+} + 2OH^- \qquad K_{sp} = [Co^{2+}][OH^-]^2 = 2 \times 10^{-16}$$

In Example 34.7 we found that $[OH^-] = 3 \times 10^{-3}$ mol/L in this solution. Therefore,

$$[Co^{2+}] = \frac{K_{sp}}{[OH^-]^2} = \frac{2 \times 10^{-16}}{(3 \times 10^{-3})^2} = 2 \times 10^{-11} \text{ mol/L}$$

For the dissociation of the ammonia complex

$$[Co(NH_3)_6]^{2+} \rightleftharpoons Co^{2+} + 6NH_3(aq) \qquad K_d = \frac{[Co^{2+}][NH_3]^6}{[Co(NH_3)_6{}^{2+}]} = 9 \times 10^{-6}$$

which upon substituting $[NH_3] = 6$ mol/L and $[Co(NH_3)_6{}^{2+}] = 0.01$ mol/L and solving for $[Co^{2+}]$ gives

$$[Co^{2+}] = \frac{K_d[Co(NH_3)_6{}^{2+}]}{[NH_3]^6} = \frac{(9 \times 10^{-6})(0.01)}{(6)^6} = 2 \times 10^{-12} \text{ mol/L}$$

The concentration of Co^{2+} in equilibrium with the complex is about one-tenth that of Co^{2+} in equilibrium with $Co(OH)_2$.

A separation can be achieved if one cation forms a complex under a particular set of conditions while another cation forms a precipitate. For example, cobalt(II), nickel(II), and zinc(II) ions form soluble ammine complexes, whereas under the same conditions, iron(II or III), aluminum, and chromium(III) ions are precipitated as hydroxides. Also, tin(II or IV), lead(II), zinc, and aluminum ions form soluble hydroxo complexes with excess hydroxide ion, whereas iron(II or III), nickel(II), and cobalt(II) ions form insoluble hydroxides.

Certain complex species are highly and distinctively colored and are thus useful for identifying the cations they contain. For example, in Cation Group III, each of the d-transition metals iron, cobalt, and nickel is positively identified by the characteristic colors of complexes. The Fe^{3+} ion is identified by the formation of both Prussian blue, $KFe[Fe(CN)_6]$ — the salt formed by Fe^{3+}, K^+, and the hexacyanoferrate(II) complex ion — and by the thiocyanatoferrate(III) ion, $[Fe(NCS)]^{2+}$, which gives a blood red solution. Cobalt is also identified by the color of a thiocyanato complex, $[Co(H_2O)_2(NCS)_4]^{2-}$, which is blue, or by a nitrito complex, $[Co(NO_2)_6]^{3-}$, which is yellow. The presence of Ni^{2+} is confirmed by the formation of the highly distinctive, bright red precipitate of the complex between nickel and dimethylglyoxime (DMG; see Figure 31.12). The colors of some characteristic complex ions and compounds are listed in Table 34.6.

Table 34.6
Colors of Some Complex Ions and Their Compounds

Species*	Color	Species*	Color
$[Cu(H_2O)_4]^{2+}$	Pale blue	$[Co(H_2O)_2(NCS)_4]^{2-}$	Blue to blue-green
$[Cu(NH_3)_4]^{2+}$	Dark blue	$[Co(NH_3)_6]^{3+}$	Yellow-brown
$[Cu(py)_2(NCS)_2]$	Light green	$[Co(NO_2)_6]^{3-}$	Yellow
$[Fe(H_2O)_6]^{2+}$	Pale green	$[Ni(H_2O)_6]^{2+}$	Green
$[Fe(H_2O)_6]^{3+}$	Yellow	$[Ni(NH_3)_6]^{2+}$	Deep blue
$[Fe(CN)_6]^{4-}$	Yellow	$[Ni(DMG)_2]$	Bright red
$[Fe(CN)_6]^{3-}$	Red	$[Mn(H_2O)_6]^{2+}$	Pale pink
$KFe[Fe(CN)_6]$	Dark blue	$[Cr(OH)_4]^-$	Green
$[Co(H_2O)_6]^{2+}$	Pink	$[Cr(NH_3)_6]^{3+}$	Yellow
$[Co(NH_3)_6]^{2+}$	Tan	$[Cr(NH_3)_5(OH)]^{2+}$	Violet

* Idealized formulas based on common coordination numbers; py = pyridine; DMG = dimethylglyoxime.

When the ions of a slightly soluble salt such as silver(I) chloride are brought together in aqueous solution in sufficient concentration, a precipitate forms:

$$Ag^+ + Cl^- \rightleftharpoons AgCl(s)$$

Once equilibrium is established and as long as the temperature remains unchanged, the mass of the precipitate does not change. But evidence for the movement of ions from the solution to the solid and back again can be seen in the gradual change from tiny crystals to larger ones.

The equilibrium between a slightly soluble solid and its ions in solution is represented by the solubility product constant, K_{sp}, which we have already used several times in this chapter. For silver(I) chloride

$$AgCl \rightleftharpoons Ag^+ + Cl^- \qquad K_{sp} = [Ag^+][Cl^-] = 1.8 \times 10^{-10}$$

As for all equilibrium constants, the concentration of the solid does not appear in the equilibrium expression. (An extensive list of K_{sp} values is given in Appendix V.3.)

Three kinds of information particularly useful for cation analysis can be found from K_{sp} values: (1) the concentrations of ions necessary for precipitation; (2) the means of controlling a precipitation by a second reaction; and (3) the conditions under which a solid will dissolve.

34.9 CONCENTRATIONS OF
IONS NECESSARY FOR
PRECIPITATION

For a given cation to be precipitated by a particular anion, the ion product of their molar concentrations, which takes the same form as the equilibrium constant expression, must exceed the solubility product constant. When solutions of the reacting cation and anion are mixed, precipitation begins when the product of the concentrations of the ions just exceeds the appropriate K_{sp} value. Precipitation continues as more ions are added but stops when the final ion product again equals the K_{sp} value.

To illustrate this, let's consider the addition, with adequate stirring, of 0.1 M aqueous ammonia solution to 25 mL of 0.10 M aluminum nitrate solution. The ultimate equilibrium that will be established is

$$Al(OH)_3(s) \rightleftharpoons Al^{3+} + 3OH^- \qquad K_{sp} = [Al^{3+}][OH^-]^3 = 3.5 \times 10^{-34}$$

A permanent precipitate of $Al(OH)_3$, that is, one that does not go back into solution, will result only when the product of the ion concentrations just exceeds the K_{sp} value. The $[OH^-]$ at which this occurs for the aluminum hydroxide solution is found as follows:

$$K_{sp} = [Al^{3+}][OH^-]^3$$
$$3.5 \times 10^{-34} = (0.10)[OH^-]^3$$
$$[OH^-]^3 = \frac{3.5 \times 10^{-34}}{(0.10)}$$
$$[OH^-] = 1.5 \times 10^{-11} \text{ mol/L}$$

As aqueous ammonia is added beyond this point the $[OH^-]$ increases and the $[Al^{3+}]$ is reduced accordingly until it is ultimately lowered to a small value. However, at all times the conditions of equilibrium defined by the K_{sp} expression must be satisfied.

EXAMPLE 34.14
Reaction Quotient

Is the OH^- concentration in a 6 M $NH_3(aq)$ solution great enough to produce precipitation of $Fe(OH)_3$ if the original solution is 0.01 M in Fe^{3+}? $K_{sp} = 3 \times 10^{-39}$ for $Fe(OH)_3$.

In Example 34.7 we calculated $[OH^-] = 3 \times 10^{-3}$ mol/L for the 6 M aqueous ammonia solution. For the equilibrium

$$Fe(OH)_3(s) \rightleftharpoons Fe^{3+} + 3OH^- \qquad K_{sp} = [Fe^{3+}][OH^-]^3 = 3 \times 10^{-39}$$

the ion product under these conditions is

$$Q_i = [Fe^{3+}][OH^-]^3 = (0.01)(3 \times 10^{-3})^3 = 3 \times 10^{-10}$$

Because the ion product exceeds the value of K_{sp}, precipitation of $Fe(OH)_3$ will occur.

34.10 CONTROLLED PRECIPITATION

A particularly valuable use of precipitation reactions is in *controlled precipitation.* The precipitation of cations can be controlled by controlling the concentrations of anions. Suppose two cations that form compounds of different solubilities with the same anion are present in a solution. Controlling the concentration of the anion permits the precipitation of one cation while leaving the other in solution. The separation of the cations is achieved because the K_{sp} of one of the possible compounds is never exceeded. Although a controlled precipitation can sometimes be carried out by merely limiting the quantity of the added precipitating reagent, this procedure is not generally useful. Localized high concentrations result where the reagent enters the solution, and subsequent equilibrations are slow and not necessarily complete.

A much more effective approach is to utilize a second chemical reaction to limit the concentration of the anion in solution. The second reaction maintains the concentration of the anion at the predetermined level that allows the precipitation of the less soluble compound while preventing that of the more soluble compound. In qualitative analysis cations are frequently separated by the controlled precipitations of hydroxides, carbonates, and sulfides. In the following sections we examine how these precipitations can be controlled by adding appropriate amounts of additional ions.

a. Hydroxide precipitations Aqueous ammonia is the reagent of choice for the precipitation of hydroxides. The hydroxide ion is provided by the acid–base reaction between ammonia and water.

$$NH_3(aq) + H_2O(l) \rightleftharpoons NH_4^+ + OH^- \qquad K_b = \frac{[NH_4^+][OH^-]}{[NH_3]} = 1.6 \times 10^{-5}$$

The concentration of the OH^- ion, and thereby the precipitation of hydroxides, is controlled by adding NH_4^+ to the solution. The added compound must be a salt between NH_4^+ and an anion that does not react with water and therefore does not affect the pH of the solution.

When we add NH_4^+ in this way we are adding an ion common to the reaction of NH_3 as a base with water and we are creating an NH_3/NH_4^+ buffer pair in the solution. This buffer pair maintains the $[OH^-]$ required for precipitation of the desired compounds while preventing the precipitation of other hydroxides. The "second reaction" being used to control the precipitation is the reaction between the added NH_4^+ and OH^- in the aqueous ammonia solution. We can calculate, for example, the concentration of ammonium ion necessary to prevent the precipitation of magnesium hydroxide when a 0.0010 M solution of Mg^{2+} is made 0.1 M in NH_3. The solubility product equilibrium is

$$Mg(OH)_2(s) \rightleftharpoons Mg^{2+} + 2OH^- \qquad K_{sp} = [Mg^{2+}][OH^-]^2 = 7.1 \times 10^{-12}$$

The concentration of OH^- at equilibrium, which must be exceeded for precipitation to occur, is then

$$[OH^-] = \sqrt{\frac{7.1 \times 10^{-12}}{[Mg^{2+}]}} = \sqrt{\frac{7.1 \times 10^{-12}}{1.0 \times 10^{-3}}} = 8.4 \times 10^{-5} \text{ mol/L}$$

From the K_b for ammonia, the $[NH_4^+]$ needed to limit $[OH^-]$ to this value is then

$$[NH_4^+] = (1.6 \times 10^{-5}) \times \frac{[NH_3]}{[OH^-]} = (1.6 \times 10^{-5}) \times \frac{1 \times 10^{-1}}{8.4 \times 10^{-5}}$$
$$= 0.02 \text{ mol/L}$$

The precipitation of magnesium(II) hydroxide is prevented by first adding to the 0.0010 M Mg^{2+} solution sufficient ammonium salt to give $[NH_4^+] = 0.02$ mol/L or more, and then making the solution 0.1 M in ammonia.

Similar calculations for a number of metal hydroxides give the data summarized in Table 34.7. Precipitation of the more soluble metal hydroxides can be prevented by ammonium ion concentrations readily attainable in the laboratory, but not precipitation of the less soluble ones. This technique is used to prevent the precipitation of $Mg(OH)_2$ in Cation Group III while allowing $Al(OH)_3$ and $Cr(OH)_3$ to precipitate.

b. Carbonate precipitations   The precipitation of carbonates can be controlled by controlling the carbonate ion concentration with ammonium ion by use of the equilibrium

$$NH_4^+ + CO_3^{2-} \rightleftharpoons NH_3(aq) + HCO_3^- \qquad K = \frac{[NH_3][HCO_3^-]}{[NH_4^+][CO_3^{2-}]} = 11.7$$

We can use the precipitation of magnesium carbonate as an example:

$$MgCO_3(s) \rightleftharpoons Mg^{2+} + CO_3^{2-} \qquad K_{sp} = [Mg^{2+}][CO_3^{2-}] = 1 \times 10^{-5}$$

For a 0.001 M magnesium salt solution, precipitation of the carbonate should occur if

$$[CO_3^{2-}] > \frac{K_{sp}}{[Mg^{2+}]} = \frac{1 \times 10^{-5}}{1 \times 10^{-3}} = 1 \times 10^{-2} \text{ mol/L}$$

From K for the ammonium ion–carbonate ion reaction used to control $[CO_3^{2-}]$, the quantity of ammonium ion required to reduce $[CO_3^{2-}]$ to this value for a solution with $[NH_3] = 0.1$ mol/L and $[HCO_3^-] = 0.1$ mol/L is

$$[NH_4^+] > \frac{[NH_3][HCO_3^-]}{[CO_3^{2-}]K} = \frac{(1 \times 10^{-1})(1 \times 10^{-1})}{(1 \times 10^{-2})(11.7)} = 0.09 \text{ mol/L}$$

Under these conditions, addition of sufficient ammonium salt to give $[NH_4^+] > 0.09$

Table 34.7
Effect of Ammonium Ion upon Precipitation of Hydroxides

Hydroxide	K_{sp}	$[OH^-]$ for Precipitation of $M(OH)_n$ ($[M^{n+}] = 0.001$ M) (mol/L)	$[NH_4^+]$ to Prevent Precipitation ($[NH_3] = 0.10$ M) (mol/L)
$Mg(OH)_2$	7.1×10^{-12}	8×10^{-5}	$>2 \times 10^{-2}$
$Mn(OH)_2$	2×10^{-13}	1×10^{-5}	$>1 \times 10^{-1}$
$Pb(OH)_2$	1.2×10^{-15}	1.1×10^{-6}	>1.5
$Fe(OH)_2$	8×10^{-16}	9×10^{-7}	>2
$Ni(OH)_2$	3×10^{-16}	5×10^{-7}	>3
$Co(OH)_2$	2×10^{-16}	4×10^{-7}	>4
$Zn(OH)_2$	1.2×10^{-17}	1.1×10^{-7}	>15
$Cu(OH)_2$	1.3×10^{-20}	3.6×10^{-9}	$>4.4 \times 10^2$
$Sn(OH)_2$	6×10^{-27}	2×10^{-12}	$>7 \times 10^5$
$Cr(OH)_3$	6×10^{-31}	8×10^{-10}	$>2 \times 10^3$
$Al(OH)_3$	3.5×10^{-34}	7.0×10^{-11}	$>2.3 \times 10^4$
$Fe(OH)_3$	3×10^{-39}	1×10^{-12}	$>1 \times 10^6$

Table 34.8
Effect of Ammonium Ion upon Precipitation of Carbonates

Carbonate	K_{sp}	$[CO_3^{2-}]$ for Precipitation of MCO_3 ($[M^{2+}] = 0.001$ M) (mol/L)	$[NH_4^+]$ to Prevent Precipitation of MCO_3 ($[NH_3] = [HCO_3^-] = 0.1$ M) (mol/L)
$MgCO_3$	1×10^{-5}	1×10^{-2}	$> 9 \times 10^{-2}$
$CaCO_3$	3.8×10^{-9}	3.8×10^{-6}	$>2.2 \times 10^2$
$BaCO_3$	2.0×10^{-9}	2.0×10^{-6}	$>4.3 \times 10^2$
$SrCO_3$	5.2×10^{-10}	5.2×10^{-7}	$>1.6 \times 10^3$
$PbCO_3$	7.4×10^{-14}	7.4×10^{-11}	$>1.2 \times 10^7$

mol/L will prevent precipitation of magnesium carbonate from a solution 0.001 M in Mg^{2+}.

Similar calculations give the additional data summarized in Table 34.8.

An ammonium ion-controlled carbonate precipitation is used in Cation Group IV to prevent the precipitation of $MgCO_3$ while allowing $CaCO_3$ and $BaCO_3$ to precipitate.

c. Sulfide precipitations Hydrogen sulfide in aqueous solution dissociates in two steps:

$$H_2S(aq) \rightleftharpoons HS^- + H^+ \qquad K_{a_1} = 1.0 \times 10^{-7}$$
$$HS^-(aq) \rightleftharpoons S^{2-} + H^+ \qquad K_{a_2} = 3 \times 10^{-13}$$

At atmospheric pressure an aqueous solution saturated with gaseous hydrogen sulfide has an H_2S concentration of 0.1 mol/L. In Section 21.7b we derived the following relationship of $[H^+]$ to $[S^{2-}]$ for such a solution:

$$K_{H_2S} = [H^+]^2[S^{2-}] = 3 \times 10^{-21} \qquad (34.27)$$

It is apparent from this equation that the sulfide ion concentration is strictly controlled by the hydrogen ion concentration. The smaller the $[H^+]$, the greater is the $[S^{2-}]$ and vice versa.

Table 34.9 summarizes the concentrations of hydrogen ion that must be exceeded to prevent precipitation of various sulfides from solutions 0.0010 M in metal ions (the average concentration in solutions used for cation analysis). Almost half of the cations in our analysis scheme are first precipitated as sulfides. The Group II sulfides, those of Hg^{2+}, Cu^{2+}, Pb^{2+}, Sb^{3+}, Sn^{2+}, and Sn^{4+}, are precipitated from an

Table 34.9
Effect of Hydrogen Ion upon Precipitation of Sulfides

Sulfide	K_{sp}	$[S^{2-}]$ for Precipitation of M_xS_y ($[M^{m+}] = 0.001$ M) (mol/L)	$[H^+]$ to Prevent Precipitation of M_xS_y (mol/L)
MnS	2.3×10^{-13}	2.3×10^{-10}	$>4 \times 10^{-6}$
FeS	4.2×10^{-17}	4.2×10^{-14}	$>3 \times 10^{-4}$
NiS(α)	3×10^{-19}	3×10^{-16}	$>3 \times 10^{-3}$
CoS(α)	4×10^{-21}	4×10^{-18}	$>3 \times 10^{-2}$
ZnS	2×10^{-24}	2×10^{-21}	>1
SnS	3×10^{-27}	3×10^{-24}	$>3 \times 10^1$
PbS	1×10^{-28}	1×10^{-25}	$>2 \times 10^2$
CuS	6×10^{-36}	6×10^{-33}	$>7 \times 10^5$
Ag_2S	7.1×10^{-50}	7.1×10^{-44}	$>2 \times 10^{11}$
HgS	4×10^{-53}	4×10^{-50}	$>3 \times 10^{14}$

acidic solution that does not provide a large enough $[S^{2-}]$ for the precipitation of the other cations present. The sulfides of the Group III cations, those of Mn^{2+}, Fe^{2+} or Fe^{3+}, Ni^{2+}, Zn^{2+}, and Co^{2+}, are precipitated from an alkaline solution of hydrogen sulfide, which has a higher $[S^{2-}]$ (see Figure 21.3).

EXAMPLE 34.15
Controlled Precipitation

What concentration of $[H^+]$ will keep Mn^{2+} (initially 0.1 M) in solution at a concentration of 0.1 M while Pb^{2+} (initially 0.1 M) precipitates as PbS?

Both precipitation reactions can be represented by the following general expressions:

$$MS(s) \rightleftharpoons M^{2+} + S^{2-} \qquad K_{sp} = [M^{2+}][S^{2-}]$$

As described above, for the H_2S–S^{2-} equilibrium in a solution saturated with H_2S at atmospheric pressure

$$K_{H_2S} = [H^+]^2[S^{2-}] = 3 \times 10^{-21}$$

which upon solving for $[S^{2-}]$ and substituting into the expression for K_{sp} gives

$$K_{sp} = [M^{2+}]\frac{K_{H_2S}}{[H^+]^2}$$

Solving for $[H^+]$ gives

$$[H^+] = \sqrt{\frac{K_{H_2S}[M^{2+}]}{K_{sp}}}$$

For MnS, $K_{sp} = 2.3 \times 10^{-13}$; therefore,

$$[H^+] = \sqrt{\frac{(3 \times 10^{-21})(0.1)}{2.3 \times 10^{-13}}} = 4 \times 10^{-5} \text{ mol/L}$$

For PbS, $K_{sp} = 1 \times 10^{-28}$, giving $[H^+] = 2 \times 10^3$ mol/L by a similar calculation. We can see that by keeping $[H^+]$ at a reasonable value between 2×10^3 mol/L and 4×10^{-5} mol/L—for example, 1 mol/L—the MnS will not precipitate and the Pb^{2+} will precipitate as PbS.

Hydrogen sulfide is a highly toxic substance. Exposure to 600 ppm of hydrogen sulfide in the air for 30 minutes can be fatal. The OSHA (Occupational Safety and Health Administration) standard for peak concentrations in the air is 20 ppm. Hydrogen sulfide should always be treated with respect; brief exposure to it deadens the sense of smell, making it possible to breathe large amounts of H_2S without realizing that it is still in the air.

The organic compound thioacetamide is used in many qualitative analysis procedures as the precipitating reagent for the sulfides. Heating an acidic thioacetamide solution yields directly an aqueous solution of hydrogen sulfide.

$$\underset{thioacetamide}{\overset{\overset{\displaystyle S}{\|}}{CH_3CNH_2}} + H^+ + 2H_2O \rightleftharpoons \underset{acetic\ acid}{\overset{\overset{\displaystyle O}{\|}}{CH_3COH}} + NH_4^+ + H_2S(aq) \qquad \textbf{(34.28)}$$

The hydrogen sulfide thus generated goes on to dissociate as discussed above. In alkaline solution, thioacetamide reacts to yield sulfide ion directly.

$$\overset{\overset{\displaystyle S}{\|}}{CH_3CNH_2} + 3OH^- \rightleftharpoons \overset{\overset{\displaystyle O}{\|}}{CH_3CO^-} + NH_3(aq) + H_2O(l) + S^{2-} \qquad \textbf{(34.29)}$$

The conditions for controlled precipitation of the sulfides are affected very little by the different sources of sulfide ion.

34.11 DISSOLUTION OF SOLIDS
A moment's thought about the general equilibrium

$$M_xA_y(s) \rightleftharpoons xM^{m+} + yA^{n-}$$

will reveal that the solid M_xA_y can be dissolved if the concentration of either the cation or the anion, or both, can be decreased sufficiently. Once again Le Chatelier's principle applies. As the product concentrations decrease, the equilibrium is shifted away from the solid. The concentration of the cation can be decreased by complexation or by oxidation or reduction. The concentration of the anion can be decreased by formation of a weak acid, by complexation, or by oxidation or reduction. While the principle is the same whether it is the cation concentration or the anion concentration that is decreased, it is generally more practical to decrease the concentration of the anion.

Dissolution of a solid by conversion of the anion to a weak acid depends upon a favorable relationship between K_{sp} and K_a and is best achieved when the anion is strongly basic, that is, when K_a is small. Dissolution of oxides, hydroxides, carbonates, and sulfites by the addition of strong acids is particularly effective for this reason.

EXAMPLE 34.16
Dissolution of Solids

To what pH must a solution containing a precipitate of $Cr(OH)_3$ be adjusted so that all of the precipitate dissolves, forming a solution such that $[Cr^{3+}] = 0.1$ mol/L?

The dissolution process is represented by the equilibrium

$$Cr(OH)_3(s) \rightleftharpoons Cr^{3+} + 3OH^- \qquad K_{sp} = [Cr^{3+}][OH^-]^3 = 6 \times 10^{-31}$$

Solving for $[OH^-]$ and substituting $[Cr^{3+}] = 0.1$ mol/L gives

$$[OH^-] = \sqrt[3]{\frac{K_{sp}}{[Cr^{3+}]}} = \sqrt[3]{\frac{6 \times 10^{-31}}{0.1}} = 2 \times 10^{-10} \text{ mol/L}$$

The corresponding $[H^+]$ is

$$[H^+] = \frac{K_w}{[OH^-]} = \frac{1.00 \times 10^{-14}}{2 \times 10^{-10}} = 5 \times 10^{-5} \text{ mol/L}$$

which gives

$$pH = -\log [H^+] = -\log(5 \times 10^{-5}) = 4.3$$

The precipitate of $Cr(OH)_3$ will be dissolved by adding H^+ until the pH $\leqslant 4.3$.

If either an anion or a cation can be oxidized or reduced and the resulting product does not itself give a product of low solubility with any other ion that is present, then dissolution will occur. An example of dissolution by a redox equilibrium in cation analysis is the oxidation of sulfur in the dissolution of CuS:

$$3CuS(s) + 8H^+ + 2NO_3^- \rightleftharpoons 3Cu^{2+} + 2NO(g) + 4H_2O(l) + 3S(s)$$

Dissolution by complexation is usually restricted to decreasing the equilibrium concentration of the cation and is dependent upon a favorable relationship between K_{sp} and K_d, the dissociation constant for the complex ion. Cations derived from the d-transition metals are most commonly involved. At various points in cation analysis, dissolution by complexation is carried out as follows:

$$AgCl(s) + 2NH_3(aq) \rightleftharpoons [Ag(NH_3)_2]^+ + Cl^-$$
$$Al(OH)_3(s) + OH^- \rightleftharpoons [Al(OH)_4]^-$$
$$SnS_2(s) + S^{2-} \rightleftharpoons [SnS_3]^{2-}$$

EXAMPLE 34.17
Dissolution of Solids

Compare the solubilities of silver chloride and silver iodide in 1.0 M NH_3. For AgCl, $K_{sp} = 1.8 \times 10^{-10}$; for AgI, $K_{sp} = 8.3 \times 10^{-17}$; for $[Ag(NH_3)_2]^+$, $K_d = 6.2 \times 10^{-8}$.

To solve this problem, we must express the solubilities of AgCl and AgI in terms of the known K_{sp} and K_d values. The dissolution of these silver halides in aqueous ammonia, which occurs by complex formation, is

$$AgX(s) + 2NH_3(aq) \rightleftharpoons \underset{x}{[Ag(NH_3)_2]^+} + \underset{x}{X^-} \qquad K = \frac{[Ag(NH_3)_2^+][X^-]}{[NH_3]^2}$$

where x is the molar solubility of AgX. We can show that, for this reaction, K is equal to the solubility product constant for the silver halide divided by the dissociation constant of the complex:

$$AgX(s) \rightleftharpoons Ag^+ + X^- \qquad K_{sp} = [Ag^+][X^-]$$

$$[Ag(NH_3)_2]^+ \rightleftharpoons Ag^+ + 2NH_3(aq) \qquad K_d = \frac{[Ag^+][NH_3]^2}{[Ag(NH_3)_2^+]}$$

We have

$$K_{sp} \times \frac{1}{K_d} = [Ag^+][X^-] \times \frac{[Ag(NH_3)_2^+]}{[Ag^+][NH_3]^2} = \frac{[Ag(NH_3)_2^+][X^-]}{[NH_3]^2} = K$$

We can see that $x = [Ag(NH_3)_2]^+ = [X^-]$ and $[NH_3] = 1.0 - 2x \approx 1.0$ mol/L. Thus

$$\frac{K_{sp}}{K_d} = \frac{(x)(x)}{(1.0)^2}$$

$$x^2 = (1.0)^2 \frac{K_{sp}}{K_d}$$

$$x_{AgCl} = \sqrt{(1.0)^2 \frac{(1.8 \times 10^{-10})}{(6.2 \times 10^{-8})}} = 5.4 \times 10^{-2} \text{ mol/L}$$

$$x_{AgI} = \sqrt{(1.0)^2 \frac{(8.3 \times 10^{-17})}{(6.2 \times 10^{-8})}} = 3.6 \times 10^{-5} \text{ mol/L}$$

Solid AgCl is 1500 times more soluble in NH_3 than is AgI.

EXAMPLE 34.18
Chemical Reactions in Qualitative Analysis

The following reactions are included in the qualitative analysis of Cation Group II. For each reaction state which of the chemical principles reviewed in this chapter is utilized.

(a) $Sn^{2+} + H_2O_2(aq) + 2H^+ \rightleftharpoons Sn^{4+} + 2H_2O(l)$

(b) $Sn^{4+} + 2H_2S(aq) \overset{H^+}{\rightleftharpoons} SnS_2(s) + 4H^+$

(c) $SnS_2(s) + 4H^+ + 6Cl^- \rightleftharpoons [SnCl_6]^{2-} + 2H_2S(aq)$

(d) $PbSO_4(s) + 4OH^- \rightleftharpoons [Pb(OH)_4]^{2-} + SO_4^{2-}$

(e) $[Pb(OH)_4]^{2-} + 4H^+ \rightleftharpoons Pb^{2+} + 4H_2O(l)$

(a) Tin is oxidized from the $+2$ to the $+4$ state, so this is an application of oxidation–reduction equilibrium.

(b) Here the Sn^{4+} ion and hydrogen sulfide are combined in sufficient concentration that the ion product exceeds the K_{sp} for tin(IV) sulfide, which precipitates. Note that the presence of hydrogen ion over the arrow shows that this is an example of controlled precipitation, in which the sulfide ion concentration is controlled by controlling the pH.

(c) The tin(IV) sulfide precipitate is dissolved in this reaction by the formation of a complex ion, making use of a complexation equilibrium.

(d) This reaction is also the dissolution of a precipitate by the formation of a complex ion. We can assume that lead(II) hydroxide is formed first but dissolves in excess base because it is an amphoteric hydroxide.

(e) Here the hydroxo complex is transformed to the uncomplexed Pb^{2+} ion in an acid–base reaction.

EXAMPLE 34.19
Chemical Reactions in Qualitative Analysis

Discuss each of the five reactions, (a)–(e), given in Example 34.18 in terms of the categories of chemical reactions included in Tables 17.2 and 17.7 and the flowchart in 17.10.

(a) This reaction involves ions in aqueous solution together with an oxidizing agent (hydrogen peroxide in acidic solution); it is a "more complex" redox reaction of ions.

(b) Writing net ionic equations obscures the reaction pattern, but a moment's thought shows that this is a partner-exchange reaction driven by the formation of a solid.

(c) This is a nonredox reaction involving ions and a solid. It can be thought of as a partner-exchange reaction driven by the formation of both the complex ion, which is only slightly dissociated, and a weak acid.

(d) Like reaction (c), this reaction can be categorized as a nonredox partner-exchange reaction.

(e) A nonredox reaction between ions, this partner exchange is an acid–base reaction driven by the formation of water.

SUMMARY

34.1 AN OVERVIEW OF INORGANIC QUALITATIVE ANALYSIS Inorganic qualitative analysis is organized around the equilibrium properties of ions in aqueous solution: strengths as Brønsted-Lowry acids and bases, oxidizing and reducing ability, solubilities of salts, and tendencies to form complex ions. Some of the terms used in qualitative analysis are defined in Section 34.1a. Anion analysis (Table 34.1) does not require separation of the ions. Preliminary tests indicate which anions or groups of anions may be present; the presence or absence of specific ions is then determined by distinctive reactions. Cations (Table 34.2) are first separated into groups by selective precipitation. The ions in each group are further separated, and ultimately each ion is positively identified by a characteristic reaction. The five cation groups of the analysis scheme used in this book are given in Table 34.3. [Figure 35.1 is a flow chart summarizing the group separations.]

34.2 NET IONIC EQUATIONS Most reactions that are important in qualitative analysis are best described by means of net ionic equations (Section 6.4), which include only those ions and molecules needed to describe completely the observed chemical reactions.

34.3 CHEMICAL EQUILIBRIUM — THE BASIS FOR QUALITATIVE ANALYSIS Whatever the concentrations of reactants and products at equilibrium, they are related in such a way that their substitution into the equilibrium constant expression (Sections 19.2, 19.3) gives a value equal to K, the equilibrium constant characteristic of the reaction. Cation analysis is based on the controlled displacement of a series of equilibria in aqueous solution, in accordance with Le Chatelier's principle. A single ion may participate simultaneously in several equilibria. In cation analysis, it is necessary to control competing equilibria in order to remove all of one or several cations from solution, leaving behind other cations that may be present. Competing equilibria are governed by the principle that an ion will form the precipitate, complex ion, or other species that is in equilibrium with the smallest concentration of that ion in solution (Table 34.4).

34.4 STRENGTHS OF ACIDS AND BASES   Water can serve as both a Brønsted-Lowry acid (a proton donor; Section 20.1) and a Brønsted-Lowry base (a proton acceptor). At 25 °C, water is only slightly ionized, in pure water, $[H^+] = [OH^-] = 1 \times 10^{-7}$ mol/L. The pH scale is defined by Equations (34.6)–(34.9) (see also Section 20.9 and Table 20.5). Pure water is considered neutral at pH 7; a higher pH represents an alkaline solution, a lower pH represents an acidic solution. Strong acids are assumed to be completely ionized in solutions of 0.1 M or less; weak acids are only partially ionized. The hydroxide ion is the strongest base that can exist in aqueous solution; soluble ionic hydroxides give the OH^- ion directly and are completely dissociated. The anions of very weak acids are relatively strong bases; most other anions, ammonia, and many amines are weaker bases.

34.5 EFFECT OF AN ADDED COMMON ION   **34.6** BUFFER SOLUTIONS   The addition of an ion common to a weak acid or a weak base in aqueous solution increases the equilibrium concentration of the undissociated acid or base (the common ion effect). A buffer solution, one that resists changes in pH, is produced when the salt of the conjugate base is added to a weak acid in solution and also when a salt of the conjugate acid is added to a weak base in solution. By the choice of an appropriate buffer pair, the pH of a solution can be maintained in any desired range, which is essential for the selective precipitations involved in qualitative analysis.

34.7 AMPHOTERISM   A molecule or an ion that can behave as either an acid or a base is said to be amphoteric (Section 16.11). Amphoterism is often encountered in the oxides and hydroxides of representative and d-transition metals (Table 34.5). The acidic properties of amphoteric metal oxides and hydroxides can be used to separate them from other compounds.

REDOX EQUILIBRIA   In a redox reaction, an oxidizing agent is reduced (shown by a decrease in oxidation number) and a reducing agent is oxidized (shown by an increase in oxidation number). The strengths of oxidizing and reducing agents are measured by standard reduction potentials (Sections 23.8, 23.9). A larger and more positive value of $E°$ indicates a stronger oxidizing agent. An ion that is resistant to both oxidation and reduction is likely to be stable in solution. The standard reduction potential and the equilibrium constant are related by the equation $\log K = nE°/0.0592$, where n is the number of electrons transferred. Selective oxidation and reduction are utilized in the analysis of cations.

COMPLEXATION EQUILIBRIA   In aqueous solution, each complex ion is in equilibrium with its components. The smaller the value of K_d, the smaller the equilibrium concentration of the metal ion, the more stable the complex, and the more readily it forms. The separation of cations can be achieved if one cation forms a complex under a particular set of conditions while another cation forms a precipitate. Certain complex ions are distinctively colored (Table 34.6).

34.8 THE SOLUBILITY PRODUCT CONSTANT   **34.9** CONCENTRATIONS OF IONS NECESSARY FOR PRECIPITATION   **34.10** CONTROLLED PRECIPITATION   **34.11** DISSOLUTION OF SOLIDS   The equilibrium between a slightly soluble solid and its ions in solution is represented by the solubility product constant, K_{sp}. For a given cation to be precipitated by a particular anion, their ion product, which takes the same form as the equilibrium constant expression, must exceed K_{sp}. Controlling anion concentration permits the precipitation of one cation while other cations remain in solution. A second chemi-

SIGNIFICANT TERMS

unknown
reagent
group reagent
supernatant solution
decanting
centrifugate
filtrate
residue

cal reaction is often used to maintain the concentration of the anion at the desired level for selective precipitation. Ammonium ion is used to control $[OH^-]$ in precipitating cations as hydroxides (Table 34.7) and to control $[CO_3^{2-}]$ in precipitating cations as carbonates (Table 34.8). Precipitation of sulfides from solutions of H_2S is controlled by the concentration of H^+ (Table 34.9). A salt can be dissolved if the concentration of the cation or anion can be decreased sufficiently. The concentration of the cation can be decreased by complexation, oxidation, or reduction; the concentration of the anion can be decreased in the same ways or by formation of a weak acid.

THOUGHTS ON CHEMISTRY

The Requisites of a Good Hypothesis

THE REQUISITES OF A GOOD HYPOTHESIS, by Robert Boyle

The Requisites of a Good Hypothesis are:

1. That it be Intelligible.
2. That it neither Assume nor suppose anything Impossible, Unintelligible, absurd, or demonstrably False.
3. That it be Consistent with it self.
4. That it be fit and sufficient to Explicate the Phaenomena, especially the chief.
5. That it be, at least consistent, with the rest of the Phaenomena it particularly relate to; and do not contradict any other known Phaenomena of Nature, or manifest Physical Truth.

The Qualityes & Conditions of an Excellent Hypothesis are

1. That it be not Precarious, but have sufficient Grounds in the Nature of the Thing itself, or at least be well recommended by some Auxiliary Proofs.
2. That it be the simplest of all the Good ones we are able to frame, at least containing nothing that is superfluous or Impertinent.
3. That it be the only Hypothesis that can Explicate the Phaenomena; or at least, that dos explicate them so well.
4. That it enable a skilful Naturalist to foretell future Phaenomena by their Congruity or Incongruity to it; and especially the events of such Experiments as are aptly devis'd to examine it, as Things that ought or ought not, to be consequent to it.

Robert Boyle, "The Requisites of a Good Hypothesis," *Royal Society Boyle Papers* **88**. (Quoted from p. 134, in *Robert Boyle on Natural Philosophy*, by Marie Boas Hall, Indiana University Press, 1965.)

QUESTIONS

Ions in Aqueous Solution

34.1 State the goal of inorganic qualitative analysis. Name the types of ionic equilibria that are used regularly in qualitative analysis.

34.2 List the cations and anions that are considered in the identification schemes presented in this book. Which metal appears in both the cation and anion schemes? What are the three elements that appear in the cation analysis with two oxidation states?

34.3 What are the two general steps in the analysis of anions? What are the three general steps in the analysis of cations?

34.4 Write the net ionic equations describing (a) S^{2-} reacting with $SnS_2(s)$ to produce $[SnS_3]^{2-}$; (b) HCl reacting with $SnS_2(s)$ to produce $[SnCl_6]^{2-}$; (c) Pb^{2+} reacting with H_2SO_4 to give $PbSO_4(s)$; (d) Fe^{2+} reacting with $NH_3(aq)$ to give $Fe(OH)_2(s)$; (e)

$NiS(s)$ reacting with HNO_3 to produce Ni^{2+}, $NO(g)$, and $S(s)$; and (f) Co^{2+} reacting with NaOH to give $Co(OH)_2(s)$.

34.5 Write the net ionic equations describing (a) Cu^{2+} reacting with $NH_3(aq)$ to produce the copper–ammonia complex which, in turn, (b) is converted to Cu^{2+} by acetic acid, followed by (c) the Cu^{2+} reacting with $K_4[Fe(CN)_6]$ to form $Cu_2[Fe(CN)_6](s)$.

34.6 Classify each of the reactions in Question 34.4 according to the reaction types listed in Tables 17.2 and 17.7.

34.7 Classify each of the reactions in Question 34.5 according to the reaction types listed in Tables 17.2 and 17.7.

34.8 Write the expression for the equilibrium constant for each of the following reactions:

(a) $Hg_2^{2+} + 2Cl^- \rightleftharpoons Hg_2Cl_2(s)$

(b) $Hg_2Cl_2(s) + 2NH_3(aq) \rightleftharpoons$
$$Hg(l) + Hg(NH_2)Cl(s) + NH_4^+ + Cl^-$$

(c) $AgCl(s) + 2NH_3(aq) \rightleftharpoons [Ag(NH_3)_2]^+ + Cl^-$

(d) $[Ag(NH_3)_2]^+ + Cl^- + 2H^+ \rightleftharpoons AgCl(s) + 2NH_4^+$

(e) $3HgS(s) + 8H^+ + 12Cl^- + 2NO_3^- \rightleftharpoons$
$\qquad 3[HgCl_4]^{2-} + 2NO(g) + 4H_2O(l) + 3S(s)$

(f) $[HgCl_4]^{2-} + Sn^{2+} + 2Cl^- \rightleftharpoons Hg(l) + [SnCl_6]^{2-}$

(g) $[Pb(OH)_4]^{2-} + 4H^+ \rightleftharpoons Pb^{2+} + 4H_2O(l)$

34.9 What is the general principle that governs competing equilibria?

34.10 A "chemical magician" performed the following series of "tricks" on a solution of $AgNO_3$: formed a black precipitate by adding a base, dissolved the precipitate by adding $S_2O_3^{2-}$ (to give $[Ag(S_2O_3)_2]^{3-}$), formed a cream-colored precipitate by adding Br^-, dissolved the precipitate by adding concentrated $NH_3(aq)$, and formed a yellow precipitate by adding I^-. Explain the theory behind this series of reactions and write equations describing each step.

Acid–Base Equilibria

34.11 Write the chemical equation for (a) the ionization of water, (b) the reaction with water of an anion such as F^- which will react to form an alkaline solution, and (c) the reaction with water of a cation such as NH_4^+ which will react to form an acidic solution.

34.12 What is the common ion effect? What effect would adding the common anion to a solution of a weak acid have on the pH of the solution? What effect would adding the common ion to a solution of NH_3 have on the pH of the solution? What are these special cases of the common ion effect called?

34.13 What is the effect of adding each of the following substances to a saturated solution of calcium oxalate, CaC_2O_4: (a) $Na_2C_2O_4$, (b) $H_2C_2O_4$, (c) $NaCl$, (d) $CaCl_2$, (e) additional CaC_2O_4, and (f) HCl? $K_{sp} = 6 \times 10^{-4}$ for CaC_2O_4 and $K_{a1} = 5.60 \times 10^{-2}$ and $K_{a2} = 6.2 \times 10^{-5}$ for $H_2C_2O_4$.

34.14 Nitrous acid, which is used in the analysis of Mn^{2+}, is unstable and must be freshly prepared by mixing $NaNO_2$ and HNO_3. Does the presence of Na^+ or NO_3^- affect the equilibrium

$$HNO_2(aq) \rightleftharpoons H^+ + NO_2^-$$

34.15 Write chemical equations illustrating the amphoteric behavior of (a) HS^- and (b) $Al(OH)_3$.

Redox and Complexation Equilibria

34.16 What is the quantitative measure of the oxidizing strength of an oxidizing agent (or the reducing strength of a reducing agent)? Briefly explain how nonstandard state conditions for a given reaction might influence this measure.

34.17 During the separation and identification of cations, selective oxidation and reduction is sometimes used. What does this statement mean? Give an example.

34.18 Briefly discuss how the formation of complexes can be used to separate and identify cations.

Solubility Equilibria

34.19 What is the relationship between the ion product and the solubility product (a) at equilibrium, (b) in order for precipitation not to occur, and (c) in order for precipitation to occur?

34.20 What common ion systems are used to control the precipitation of (a) hydroxides, (b) carbonates, and (c) sulfides?

34.21 Write the structural formula for thioacetamide. Write the chemical equations for the formation of H_2S in acidic solution and for the formation of S^{2-} in alkaline solution by heating thioacetamide.

34.22 Explain why $Al(OH)_3$ is formed when $(NH_4)_2S$ is added to a solution containing Al^{3+}.

34.23 Name some of the ways in which many insoluble oxides, hydroxides, carbonates, sulfides, and sulfates can be dissolved.

Answers to Selected Questions

34.5 (a) $Cu^{2+} + 4NH_3(aq) \rightarrow [Cu(NH_3)_4]^{2+}$, (b) $[Cu(NH_3)_4]^{2+} + 4CH_3COOH(aq) \rightarrow Cu^{2+} + 4NH_4^+ + 4CH_3COO^-$, (c) $2Cu^{2+} + [Fe(CN)_6]^{4-} \rightarrow Cu_2[Fe(CN)_6](s)$

34.7 (a) nonredox, displacement; (b) nonredox, not easily classified; (c) nonredox, partner exchange between aqueous ions

34.13 (a) Additional $[C_2O_4^{2-}]$ shifts equilibrium to reactants $(CaC_2O_4(s))$ side, (b) additional $[C_2O_4^{2-}]$ shifts equilibrium to reactants side, (c) no effect, (d) additional $[Ca^{2+}]$ shifts equilibrium to reactants side, (e) no effect on equilibrium—only more solid CaC_2O_4 present, (f) H^+ reacts with $C_2O_4^{2-}$, reduced $[C_2O_4^{2-}]$ shifts equilibrium to products side.

PROBLEMS

Review of Principles

34.1 What is the concentration of NO_2^- remaining in a solution that has been acidified with excess 6 M HCl? Assume that the original concentration of NO_2^- was 0.1 mol/L and that $[H^+]$ at equilibrium is 1 mol/L. $K_a = 7.2 \times 10^{-4}$ for HNO_2.

34.2* What is the concentration of HCO_3^- in equilibrium with $[H_2CO_3] = 0.01$ mol/L and $[H^+] = 0.01$ mol/L? What is the concentration of CO_3^{2-} in this system? $K_{a1} = 4.5 \times 10^{-7}$ and $K_{a2} = 4.8 \times 10^{-11}$ for H_2CO_3. *Answer* $[HCO_3^-] = 5 \times 10^{-7}$ mol/L, $[CO_3^{2-}] = 2 \times 10^{-15}$ mol/L

34.3 What is the pH of a buffer solution prepared by adding 10.0 mL of 0.100 M NH_4NO_3 to 15.0 mL of 0.100 M NH_3? $K_b = 1.6 \times 10^{-5}$ for NH_3.

34.4 What mole ratio of $Na(CH_3COO)$ to CH_3COOH would be needed to produce a buffer solution of pH 5.00? What would be the ratio for pH 5.50? $K_a = 1.754 \times 10^{-5}$ for acetic acid. *Answer* 1.8, 5.5

34.5 Assuming $Pb(OH)_2(s)$ to act as an acid, find $[H^+]$
$$Pb(OH)_2(s) \rightleftharpoons 2H^+ + PbO_2^{2-}$$
$$K_a = [H^+]^2[PbO_2^{2-}] = 4.6 \times 10^{-16}$$

and assuming $Pb(OH)_2(s)$ to act as a base, find $[OH^-]$

$$Pb(OH)_2(s) \rightleftharpoons Pb^{2+} + 2OH^-$$

$$K_b = K_{sp} = [Pb^{2+}][OH^-]^2 = 1.2 \times 10^{-15}$$

What is the pH of a solution in equilibrium with solid lead hydroxide?

34.6 Approximately how many drops (20 drops = 1 mL) of 1 M $NH_3(aq)$ are needed to neutralize 5 mL of a 0.1 M HCl solution? *Answer* 10 drops

34.7 Would adding Fe^{3+} to an acidic aqueous solution of H_2S cause the H_2S to be oxidized to S? $E° = 0.771$ V for $Fe^{3+} + e^- \xrightarrow{H^+} Fe^{2+}$ and 0.142 V for $S(s) + 2H^+ + 2e^- \rightarrow H_2S(aq)$.

34.8 An unknown was found to contain I^- and Fe. Using the following half-reactions and potentials:

$$I_2 + 2e^- \longrightarrow 2I^- \qquad E° = 0.536 \text{ V}$$
$$Fe^{3+} + e^- \longrightarrow Fe^{2+} \qquad E° = 0.771 \text{ V}$$

predict the formula of the compound. *Answer* FeI_2

34.9 Certain combinations of anions are incompatible. As an example, write the equation and describe what will happen in an acidic solution of SO_3^{2-} and S^{2-} using the following half-reactions and standard reduction potentials:

$$S(s) + 2H^+ + 2e^- \longrightarrow H_2S(aq) \qquad E° = 0.142 \text{ V}$$
$$H_2SO_3(aq) + 4H^+ + 4e^- \longrightarrow S(s) + 3H_2O(l) \qquad E° = 0.450 \text{ V}$$

34.10 Using values of $E°$, show that the oxidation of $Sn(s)$ by H^+ occurs only after any excess Al has reacted.

$$Sn^{2+} + 2e^- \longrightarrow Sn(s) \qquad E° = -0.136 \text{ V}$$
$$2H^+ + 2e^- \longrightarrow H_2(g) \qquad E° = 0.000 \text{ V}$$
$$Al^{3+} + 3e^- \longrightarrow Al(s) \qquad E° = -1.662 \text{ V}$$

Answer $E° = 1.662$ V for $2Al + 6H^+ \rightarrow 2Al^{3+} + 3H_2$, $E° = 0.136$ V for $Sn + 2H^+ \rightarrow Sn^{2+} + H_2$, and $E° = 1.526$ V for $2Al + 3Sn^{2+} \rightarrow 2Al^{3+} + 3Sn$; thus oxidation of Al by H^+ occurs first and tin oxidation by H^+ is less favorable; any Sn^{2+} formed will be reduced by Al.

34.11 Use the following half-reactions and standard reduction potentials to show that chlorine water will oxidize I^- to I_2, I_2 to IO_3^- and Br^- to Br_2:

$$Cl_2(aq) + 2e^- \longrightarrow 2Cl^- \qquad E° = 1.360 \text{ V}$$
$$Br_2(aq) + 2e^- \longrightarrow 2Br^- \qquad E° = 1.087 \text{ V}$$
$$I_2(aq) + 2e^- \longrightarrow 2I^- \qquad E° = 0.536 \text{ V}$$
$$2IO_3^- + 12H^+ + 10e^- \longrightarrow I_2(aq) + 6H_2O(l)$$
$$E° = 1.195 \text{ V}$$

[Note that reaction conditions during anion analysis testing are adjusted so that the oxidation of I_2 will occur before the oxidation of Br^-.]

34.12* What mass of solid $K_2S_2O_8$ is needed to react with the I^- and Br^- in a 2 mL sample in which $[I^-] = 1 \times 10^{-2}$ mol/L and $[Br^-] = 3 \times 10^{-2}$ mol/L? *Answer* 0.01 g $K_2S_2O_8$

34.13 At high concentrations of Cl^-, Ag^+ forms the complex $[AgCl_4]^{3-}$. Calculate the concentration of Ag^+ in equilibrium with $[Cl^-] = 6$ mol/L. Assume the complex is at a concentration of 0.01 mol/L. $K_d = 5 \times 10^{-6}$ for $[AgCl_4]^{3-}$.

34.14 Calculate the equilibrium constant for the reaction

$$HgS(s) + 2H^+ + 4Cl^- \rightleftharpoons [HgCl_4]^{2-} + H_2S(aq)$$

using the following equations and respective equilibrium constants:

$$HgS(s) \rightleftharpoons Hg^{2+} + S^{2-}$$
$$K_{sp} = [Hg^{2+}][S^{2-}] = 4 \times 10^{-53}$$
$$H_2S(aq) \rightleftharpoons 2H^+ + S^{2-}$$
$$K_a = [H^+]^2[S^{2-}]/[H_2S] = 3 \times 10^{-20}$$
$$[HgCl_4]^{2-} \rightleftharpoons Hg^{2+} + 4Cl^-$$
$$K_d = [Hg^{2+}][Cl^-]^4/[HgCl_4^{2-}] = 2 \times 10^{-16}$$

Will HgS dissolve in HCl? *Answer* 7×10^{-18}, no

34.15 Calculate the solubility in grams per liter of AgCl in water. $K_{sp} = 1.8 \times 10^{-10}$ for AgCl.

34.16 Compare the concentrations of Pb^{2+} and Hg^{2+} in a solution containing $[S^{2-}] = 0.01$ mol/L. $K_{sp} = 1 \times 10^{-28}$ for PbS and 4×10^{-53} for HgS. *Answer* $[Pb^{2+}]/[Hg^{2+}] = 3 \times 10^{24}$

34.17 Will a precipitate of Ag_2SO_4 form if $[Ag^+] = 0.01$ mol/L and $[SO_4^{2-}] = 0.1$ mol/L? $K_{sp} = 1.5 \times 10^{-5}$ for Ag_2SO_4.

34.18 A solution is 0.1 M in Ba^{2+} and 0.1 M in Ag^+. As CrO_4^{2-} is added, which cation will begin to precipitate first? $K_{sp} = 2.5 \times 10^{-12}$ for Ag_2CrO_4 and 1.2×10^{-10} for $BaCrO_4$. Repeat this problem for a solution that is 0.01 M in Ba^{2+} and 0.01 M in Ag^+. *Answer* Ag^+, Ba^{2+}

34.19 A solution is 0.01 M in CrO_4^{2-} and 0.01 M in Cl^-. Describe what will happen as a solution of Ag^+ is added dropwise. $K_{sp} = 1.8 \times 10^{-10}$ for AgCl and 2.5×10^{-12} for Ag_2CrO_4.

34.20 A solution is 0.01 M in Ag^+, 0.01 M in Pb^{2+}, and 0.01 M in Hg_2^{2+}. As HCl is added dropwise, which cation precipitates first and at what Cl^- concentration? $K_{sp} = 2 \times 10^{-5}$ for $PbCl_2$, 1.8×10^{-10} for AgCl, and 1.3×10^{-18} for Hg_2Cl_2. *Answer* Hg_2Cl_2 will precipitate first at $[Cl^-] = 1 \times 10^{-8}$ mol/L.

34.21 In many qualitative analysis schemes, Pb^{2+} appears twice because sufficient Pb^{2+} remains in solution after precipitation of the cations that form insoluble chlorides to be precipitated as the sulfide during subsequent tests. If an unknown solution contained 0.01 M Pb^{2+}, what would be the concentration of Pb^{2+} in solution after precipitation by 6 M HCl? Assume $[Cl^-] = 4$ mol/L at equilibrium. $K_{sp} = 2 \times 10^{-5}$ for $PbCl_2$. If $[S^{2-}] = 0.01$ M during the second precipitation, would PbS form? $K_{sp} = 1 \times 10^{-28}$ for PbS.

34.22 To what pH must a solution containing a precipitate of $Ni(OH)_2$ be adjusted so that 0.1 mol of the precipitate dissolves in 1 L? $K_{sp} = 3 \times 10^{-16}$ for $Ni(OH)_2$. *Answer* 6.7

34.23* The solubility of CO_2 in water is about 0.034 mol/L. Calculate $[CO_3^{2-}]$ and predict whether an appreciable amount of $PbCO_3$ will form in a 0.1 M Pb^{2+} solution. $K_{a1} = 4.5 \times 10^{-7}$ and $K_{a2} = 4.8 \times 10^{-11}$ for H_2CO_3 and $K_{sp} = 7.4 \times 10^{-14}$ for $PbCO_3$.

34.24* The anions of water-insoluble salts are brought into solution by boiling the solid with Na_2CO_3 solution, for example,

$$BaSO_4(s) + CO_3^{2-} \rightleftharpoons BaCO_3(s) + SO_4^{2-}$$

The SO_4^{2-} and CO_3^{2-} compete for Ba^{2+} as indicated by

$$K_{sp} = [Ba^{2+}][SO_4^{2-}] = 1.7 \times 10^{-10}$$
$$K_{sp} = [Ba^{2+}][CO_3^{2-}] = 2.0 \times 10^{-9}$$

Find the ratio of $[SO_4^{2-}]$ to $[CO_3^{2-}]$ at the point where the SO_4^{2-} is completely in solution by eliminating $[Ba^{2+}]$ from the above equations. What is the maximum concentration of SO_4^{2-} that can be present in a saturated solution of Na_2CO_3 where $[CO_3^{2-}] = 1.5$ mol/L? *Answer* 0.085, 0.13 mol/L

34.25* Repeat the calculations of Problem 34.24 for dissolving CuS with Na_2CO_3. $K_{sp} = 2.3 \times 10^{-10}$ for $CuCO_3$ and 6×10^{-36} for the reaction of CuS. If the limit of concentration for detection of the sulfide ions is 10^{-3} mol/L, will S^{2-} be detected using this technique?

34.26 What mass of thioacetamide is needed to quantitatively precipitate all of the Pb^{2+} and Sn^{4+} in a 5 mL sample originally containing these ions each at a concentration of 0.1 mol/L? *Answer* 0.2 g $CH_3C(S)NH_2$

34.27 How would you prepare 15 mL of a solution that is 0.10 M in Ag^+, 0.10 M in Pb^{2+}, and 0.10 M in Hg_2^{2+} from separate 0.50 M stock solutions of each ion?

34.28 What range of pH values could be used to separate 0.010 mol of Mn^{2+} from 0.010 mol of Zn^{2+} by selective precipitation of ZnS in 1 L of a saturated solution of H_2S? $K_{sp} = 2.3 \times 10^{-13}$ for MnS, $K_{sp} = 2 \times 10^{-24}$ for Zns, and $[H^+]^2[S^{2-}] = 3 \times 10^{-21}$ for a saturated solution of H_2S. *Answer* $-0.6 \leqslant pH \leqslant 5.0$

34.29* Is the concentration of $C_2O_4^{2-}$ in a 0.1 M $H_2C_2O_4$ solution large enough to produce a precipitate of CaC_2O_4 if the original solution was 0.01 M in Ca^{2+}? $K_{sp} = 1 \times 10^{-9}$ for CaC_2O_4 and $K_{a1} = 5.60 \times 10^{-2}$ and $K_{a2} = 6.2 \times 10^{-5}$ for $H_2C_2O_4$.

34.30 Calculate $[Ni^{2+}]$ in equilibrium with a saturated solution of $Ni[OH]_2$ such that $[NH_3] = 6$ mol/L. Likewise, find $[Ni^{2+}]$ in equilibrium with a solution in which $[Ni(NH_3)_6^{2+}] = 0.1$ mol/L

and $[NH_3] = 6$ mol/L. In which form, $Ni(OH)_2$ or $[Ni(NH_3)_6]^{2+}$, would the majority of the nickel be found in a solution of 6 M NH_3? $K_b = 1.6 \times 10^{-5}$ for $NH_3(aq)$, $K_{sp} = 3 \times 10^{-16}$ for $Ni(OH)_2$, and $K_d = 1 \times 10^{-9}$ for $[Ni(NH_3)_6]^{2+}$. *Answer* 3×10^{-12} mol/L, 2×10^{-15} mol/L, $[Ni(NH_3)_6]^{2+}$

34.31 Calculate the solubility of AgBr in 1.0 M NH_3. $K_{sp} = 4.9 \times 10^{-13}$ for AgBr and $K_d = 6.2 \times 10^{-8}$ for $[Ag(NH_3)_2]^+$.

34.32 To what final concentration of $NH_3(aq)$ must a solution be adjusted to just dissolve (a) 1 g of AgCl in 1 L of solution, (b) 1 g of AgBr in 1 L of solution, and (c) 1 g of AgI in 1 L of solution? Which of these silver halides can be separated from the others using 6 M $NH_3(aq)$? $K_{sp} = 1.8 \times 10^{-10}$ for AgCl, 4.9×10^{-13} for AgBr, and 8.3×10^{-17} for AgI, and $K_d = 6.2 \times 10^{-8}$ for $[Ag(NH_3)_2]^+$. *Answer* (a) 0.1 mol/L, (b) 2 mol/L, (c) 100 mol/L; AgI

34.33 Confirm that $[NH_4^+]$ must be larger than 0.1 mol/L to prevent precipitation of $Mn(OH)_2$ in a solution in which $[NH_3] = 0.1$ mol/L and $[Mn^{2+}] = 0.0010$ mol/L. $K_{sp} = 2 \times 10^{-13}$ for $Mn(OH)_2$ and $K_b = 1.6 \times 10^{-5}$ for $NH_3(aq)$.

34.34 A solution contains 0.1 M Zn^{2+} and 0.1 M Ni^{2+}. What concentration of H^+ is needed to keep Ni^{2+} in solution while Zn^{2+} precipitates as ZnS? $K_{sp} = 3 \times 10^{-19}$ for NiS, $K_{sp} = 2 \times 10^{-24}$ for ZnS, and $[H^+]^2[S^{2-}] = 3 \times 10^{-21}$ for a saturated solution of H_2S. *Answer* 0.03 mol/L $\leqslant [H^+] \leqslant 10$ mol/L

34.35 Show that concentrated HNO_3 (12 M) will dissolve PbS(s) to form a dilute solution. $K_{sp} = 1 \times 10^{-28}$ for PbS, $[H^+]^2[S^{2-}]/[H_2S] = 3 \times 10^{-20}$ for H_2S, and $K = 1 \times 10^{83}$ for the reaction

$$3H_2S(aq) + 2NO_3^- + 2H^+ \rightleftharpoons 2NO(g) + 4H_2O(l) + 3S(s)$$

CHAPTER 35

Inorganic Qualitative Analysis: Anions, Cations, and the Scheme

In 1840 Karl Remegius Fresenius, a 22-year-old German, went to Bonn to study chemistry. His early apprenticeship as a pharmacist had aroused an intense interest in chemical analysis — the determination of the composition of substances both qualitatively and quantitatively.

While in Bonn, Fresenius studied the chemical literature on analysis, which was extensive but filled with unrelated procedures. Just for practice, or so he thought, he wrote an Introduction to Qualitative Analysis in which he presented a systematic method for identifying qualitatively the anions and the cations present in a solid or a solution.

On the insistence of his professor, Fresenius published his work. The qualitative analysis scheme that he had devised turned out to be very successful in practice and it filled a great need. By the time Fresenius died in 1897 his book had seen 17 editions in German and numerous editions in other languages, including 8 in English. Most of the qualitative analysis schemes in use today are based substantially on Fresenius' work.

With the publication of his later textbook on quantitative analysis and his founding and editing of a journal for analytical chemistry, Fresenius earned the unofficial title of Father of Analytical Chemistry.

35.1 INTRODUCTION: FLOW CHARTS

Analysis for anions and for cations, the two parts of inorganic qualitative analysis, are carried out separately. Either part may be attacked first, but there is an advantage to analyzing for the anions first. Anion analysis is simpler, since there are fewer commonly encountered anions than cations. You will find that in anion analysis, the value of careful observation and the need to intelligently interpret what you see are particularly important.

In studying an unknown, a visual examination should come first. If the unknown is a solution, what color is it? Color is important, because some inorganic ions reveal their identities through color alone. You must be careful in drawing a conclusion too quickly, however, for the color of mixtures is sometimes deceptive. For example, a solution containing pink Co^{2+} and green Ni^{2+} may be almost colorless.

If the unknown is a solid, the color is also important, but it does not necessarily indicate the colors of the individual ions. Thus, Pb^{2+} and I^- are both colorless, but they combine to give the bright yellow PbI_2. It is a good idea to examine a solid unknown carefully, perhaps even under a magnifying glass. If the solid is a mixture, you may be able to see individual particles of the different substances. All such clues are helpful.

Flow charts are used to represent the steps in qualitative analysis, particularly for the analysis of cations, which is more systematic than the analysis of anions. A flow chart is a schematic outline that begins with the ions in question, indicates the reagents and the conditions for each step, and gives the formulas for the chemical products that result.

In considering qualitative analysis and in carrying out the procedures in the laboratory, keeping track of the steps in the analysis is essential. We recommend that you refer to the flow charts frequently.

Flow charts can be written in various ways. In this book we adopt the style illustrated below, in which precipitates or undissolved solids are carried to the left and ions in solution are carried to the right.

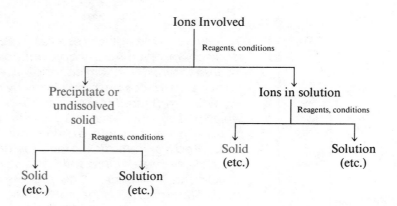

ANION ANALYSIS

Anion analysis begins with several preliminary tests that indicate the presence or absence of individual anions or groups of anions that have similar properties. With this information at hand, the analysis proceeds to specific tests that confirm the presence of individual anions. Physical separation of the anions is generally not necessary, because many of the specific tests allow detection of one anion in the presence of the others. However, when interference by one anion in detecting another is a possibility, the interfering ion must be removed before testing for the other.

Some of the preliminary tests and some of the specific tests can be carried out on solids. Eventually, however, the unknown must be put into solution. Table 17.1 gives some general rules about the solubilities of ionic compounds. You should be familiar with these rules because they can be helpful in deciding on the presence or absence of certain ions. Solubility or insolubility of a solid unknown in water will not eliminate any ions, but it will rule out certain combinations of anions and cations. For example, if a water-soluble unknown is found to contain carbonate ion (CO_3^{2-}), the only common inorganic cations that can be present are Na^+, K^+, and NH_4^+, because the carbonates of all the others are insoluble in water.

If the unknown is insoluble in water, it must be treated with a chemical reagent to convert it to soluble substances. Some anions are not stable in acidic solution, while other anions react with each other in the presence of acid. Consequently, anion analysis is usually performed on alkaline solutions. To prepare an insoluble solid for anion analysis, the solid is boiled with a saturated sodium carbonate solution. This treatment converts the anions to soluble sodium salts and leaves the cations as insoluble carbonates or their hydrolysis products. For example,

$$MA(s) + CO_3^{2-} \rightleftharpoons MCO_3(s) + A^{2-}$$
$$MA(s) + CO_3^{2-} + H_2O(l) \rightleftharpoons M(OH)_2(s) + CO_2(g) + A^{2-}$$

The sodium carbonate treatment is also desirable for mixtures which contain certain heavy metal cations that interfere with some of the anion tests.

Our qualitative analysis scheme includes 11 of the most common anions: sulfide (S^{2-}), sulfite (SO_3^{2-}), carbonate (CO_3^{2-}), nitrite (NO_2^-), iodide (I^-), bromide (Br^-), chloride (Cl^-), phosphate (PO_4^{3-}), chromate (CrO_4^{2-}), nitrate (NO_3^-), and sulfate (SO_4^{2-}).

35.2 PROPERTIES OF THE ANIONS

Qualitative analysis relies heavily on differences in equilibria to separate and identify ions that are similar in other ways. Acid–base equilibria, heterogeneous equilibria, redox equilibria, and complex ion equilibria are all ingeniously employed in the qualitative analysis scheme. An extensive review of these equilibria with emphasis on how they are used in cation analysis was given in Chapter 34. Here we briefly go over some of the pertinent properties of the anions included in our anion analysis scheme.

a. Acid–base behavior Water-soluble salts that contain strongly basic anions in combination with weakly acidic cations give alkaline solutions. Of the anions under consideration, three—S^{2-}, PO_4^{3-}, and CO_3^{2-}—are strong Brønsted-Lowry bases. Salts of these anions with cations such as Na^+ react with water as follows to give quite alkaline solutions. For example,

$$S^{2-} + H_2O(l) \rightleftharpoons HS^- + OH^- \tag{35.1}$$

Four of our anions—SO_3^{2-}, CrO_4^{2-}, NO_2^-, and SO_4^{2-}—are relatively weaker bases, as shown by the K_b's listed in Table 35.1. Their salts with weakly acidic cations give less alkaline solutions than do S^{2-}, CO_3^{2-}, and PO_4^{3-} salts. The remaining anions in our scheme are very weak bases. Essentially these anions do not react with water at all, and thus have no effect on the pH of the solution.

Three of the anions yield thermally unstable protonic acids that decompose to evolve gases when their solutions are acidified with a dilute, strong, nonoxidizing acid such as HCl or $HClO_4$. In some cases warming these acidified solutions is necessary to ensure evolution of the gas.

$$SO_3^{2-} + 2H^+ \longrightarrow H_2SO_3 \xrightarrow{\Delta} SO_2(g) + H_2O(l) \tag{35.2}$$

sulfurous
acid   _colorless_

$$CO_3^{2-} + 2H^+ \longrightarrow H_2CO_3 \xrightarrow{\Delta} CO_2(g) + H_2O(l) \tag{35.3}$$

carbonic
acid   _colorless_

$$2NO_2^- + 2H^+ \longrightarrow 2HNO_2 \xrightarrow{\Delta} NO(g) + NO_2(g) + H_2O(l) \tag{35.4}$$

nitrous   _colorless_   _brown_
acid

The sulfide ion also yields a gaseous product under the same acidic conditions:

$$S^{2-} + 2H^+ \longrightarrow H_2S(g) \tag{35.5}$$

colorless

The CrO_4^{2-} ion, the only colored anion in our list, is yellow in alkaline solution, but changes to the orange $Cr_2O_7^{2-}$ in acidic solution.

$$CrO_4^{2-} \underset{OH^-}{\overset{H^+}{\rightleftharpoons}} HCrO_4^- \underset{OH^-}{\overset{H^+}{\rightleftharpoons}} Cr_2O_7^{2-} + H_2O(l) \tag{35.6}$$

chromate ion   _dichromate ion_
(yellow)   _(orange)_

b. Redox properties The group of anions under consideration includes oxidizing agents, reducing agents, and two ions whose redox behavior depends upon the conditions.

The NO_3^- and CrO_4^{2-} ions are quite strong oxidizing agents in acidic solution (in which CrO_4^{2-} is converted to $Cr_2O_7^{2-}$; see Table 17.8). The I^-, S^{2-}, and SO_3^{2-} ions are reducing agents in acidic solution (in which S^{2-} is present as H_2S and SO_3^{2-} is present as H_2SO_3):

$$
\begin{aligned}
I_2(s) + 2e^- &\rightleftharpoons 2I^- & E° &= 0.536 \text{ V} \\
S(s) + 2H^+ + 2e^- &\rightleftharpoons H_2S(aq) & E° &= 0.142 \text{ V} \\
SO_4^{2-} + 4H^+ + 2e^- &\rightleftharpoons H_2SO_3(aq) + H_2O(l) & E° &= 0.172 \text{ V}
\end{aligned}
$$

Table 35.1
K_b Values of the Anions

S^{2-}	3×10^{-2}
PO_4^{3-}	1×10^{-2}
CO_3^{2-}	2.1×10^{-4}
SO_3^{2-}	2.0×10^{-7}
CrO_4^{2-}	3.1×10^{-8}
NO_2^-	1.4×10^{-11}
SO_4^{2-}	1.0×10^{-12}
NO_3^-	5×10^{-17}
Br^-	1×10^{-23}
Cl^-	3×10^{-23}
I^-	3×10^{-24}

The redox properties of the SO_4^{2-} ion vary with conditions. In dilute solution this ion shows virtually no oxidizing ability. However, in highly acidic concentrated solutions, the SO_4^{2-} ion, largely present as HSO_4^-, is a moderately strong oxidizing agent. (The oxidizing ability of concentrated sulfuric acid is made use of in one of the preliminary tests in anion analysis; Section 35.3.)

The nitrite ion, NO_2^-, can be either a strong oxidizing agent or a weak reducing agent in acidic solution. Only such strong oxidizing agents as permanganate ion (MnO_4^-) or chlorine (Cl_2) (see Table 17.8) are capable of oxidizing nitrite ion in acidic solution.

c. Solubility equilibria Precipitation reactions provide valuable information in the analysis for anions. In our scheme such reactions of several of the anions with barium ion, Ba^{2+}, are used in specific tests. Also the precipitation of anions with silver ion, Ag^+, is part of one of the preliminary tests.

Sulfite, carbonate, chromate, phosphate, and sulfate ions give barium salts that are only slightly soluble in water, as shown by their small K_{sp} values (Table 35.2). Of these salts, only barium sulfate, $BaSO_4$, can be precipitated from solutions that have been made acidic with dilute strong acid. In such solutions the other anions form weak conjugate acids, with ionization constants as shown in Table 35.2. Precipitation of an ionic compound from solution begins when the ion product exceeds the K_{sp} value. In the presence of the only slightly ionized conjugate acids, the concentrations of the anions are not sufficiently high for precipitation to occur. For example, the ionization of HPO_4^{2-} does not provide enough PO_4^{3-} ion for the following precipitation to occur:

$$3Ba^{2+} + 2PO_4^{3-} \rightleftharpoons Ba_3(PO_4)_2(s) \qquad K_{sp} = 3.2 \times 10^{-23}$$

As a further obstacle to precipitation, the carbonate and sulfite ions decompose to give CO_2 and SO_2 in solutions that have sufficiently high H^+ ion concentrations.

In neutral solutions all of the anions except NO_3^- give precipitates with silver ion. Two anions, NO_2^- and SO_4^{2-}, form precipitates with relatively large values for K_{sp}.

$$AgNO_2(s) \rightleftharpoons Ag^+ + NO_2^- \qquad K_{sp} = 6.0 \times 10^{-4}$$
$$Ag_2SO_4(s) \rightleftharpoons 2Ag^+ + SO_4^{2-} \qquad K_{sp} = 1.5 \times 10^{-5}$$

Ion concentrations must be quite high before the ion products can exceed these large K_{sp} values, so that silver sulfate and silver nitrite will precipitate.

One of the silver salts, Ag_2SO_3, changes from white to black when heated, as the SO_3^{2-} ion reduces the silver ion to elemental silver. Several silver salts are colored: Ag_2CO_3, pale yellow; $AgNO_2$, pale yellow; Ag_2S, black; $AgBr$, cream; AgI, pale yellow; Ag_2CrO_4, brown-red; Ag_3PO_4, yellow.

All the silver salts except Ag_2S, AgI, $AgBr$, and $AgCl$ dissolve in strongly acidic solution (dilute $HClO_4$ is used in the analysis). The anions of these acid-soluble silver salts are either destroyed ($NO_2^- \rightarrow NO + NO_2$; $CO_3^{2-} \rightarrow CO_2$; $SO_3^{2-} \rightarrow SO_2$) or tied up in the form of their weak conjugate acids. Whichever occurs, not enough anions remain in solution to allow the ion product to exceed the K_{sp} so that silver salts will precipitate.

We might expect that Ag_2S would dissolve in acidic solution, since the conjugate acids of the sulfide ion, HS^- and H_2S, are exceedingly weak acids. However, Ag_2S is so slightly soluble ($K_{sp} = 7.1 \times 10^{-50}$) that even these weakly acidic species supply enough S^{2-} ion to prevent the dissolution process. Silver sulfide can be dissolved only if S^{2-} is oxidized and thus effectively removed.

$$3Ag_2S(s) + 8H^+ + 2NO_3^- \longrightarrow 3S(s) + 2NO(g) + 6Ag^+ + 4H_2O(l) \qquad \textbf{(35.7)}$$

Of the silver halides, one, $AgCl$, is soluble in aqueous ammonia as a result of the reaction

Table 35.2
K Values Significant in SO_3^{2-}, CO_3^{2-}, CrO_4^{2-}, PO_4^{3-}, and SO_4^{2-} Analysis

Salt	K_{sp}
$BaSO_3$	1.0×10^{-8}
$BaCO_3$	2.0×10^{-9}
$BaSO_4$	1.7×10^{-10}
$BaCrO_4$	8.5×10^{-11}
$Ba_3(PO_4)_2$	3.2×10^{-23}

Conjugate Acid	K_a
HSO_3^-	5.0×10^{-8}
HCO_3^-	4.8×10^{-11}
$HCrO_4^-$	3.2×10^{-7}
HPO_4^{2-}	1×10^{-12}

$$AgCl(s) + 2NH_3(aq) \rightleftharpoons [Ag(NH_3)_2]^+ + Cl^- \tag{35.8}$$

The complex ion, $[Ag(NH_3)_2]^+$, is only slightly dissociated into Ag^+ and NH_3 (K_d, 6.2×10^{-8}), and the equilibrium concentration of silver ion is reduced to the point at which $[Ag^+][Cl^-] < K_{sp}$. The bromide and the iodide are much less soluble than the chloride (K_{sp} values: AgCl, 1.8×10^{-10}; AgBr, 4.9×10^{-13}; AgI, 8.3×10^{-17}), and complexation with dilute aqueous ammonia (6 M) does not remove sufficient Ag^+ for dissolution to occur. (AgBr will dissolve in a concentrated ammonia solution.)

35.3 THE PRELIMINARY TESTS FOR ANIONS

Separate preliminary tests detect the presence of anions with oxidizing or reducing properties, and of anions that fall into four different groups based on their reactions with *dilute* perchloric acid ($HClO_4$) and silver ion (Ag^+). Additional preliminary information is obtained from the action of concentrated sulfuric acid on the sample of unknown composition. In most cases, a positive result for a test consists of clearly observable phenomena such as a color change, the evolution of a gas, or the appearance of a precipitate. A flow chart for the preliminary tests for anions is given in Figure 35.1.

Table 35.3
Oxidizing and Reducing Anions

Oxidizing Anions
NO_2^-
CrO_4^{2-}
NO_3^-
Reducing Anions
S^{2-}
SO_3^{2-}
I^-
NO_2^-

Detection of the presence of oxidizing anions The development of a brown to black color when a few drops of an unknown solution are added to a solution of manganese(II) chloride ($MnCl_2$) in concentrated hydrochloric acid indicates the presence of oxidizing anions. Possibilities from our list of anions are NO_2^-, CrO_4^{2-}, and NO_3^- (Table 35.3). The manganese(II) is oxidized to the +3 state and the color change is due to the formation of complex ions such as $[MnCl_5]^{2-}$.

If the solution tested contains an oxidizing anion, reducing anions are probably absent, especially if the initial unknown solution is acidic. Oxidizing agents and reducing agents can coexist in neutral or alkaline solutions, but not in strongly acidic solutions.

Detection of the presence of reducing anions The appearance of a dark blue suspension or precipitate when the unknown solution is added to a solution containing $FeCl_3$, $K_3[Fe(CN)_6]$, and dilute HCl indicates the presence of reducing anions, which might be S^{2-}, SO_3^{2-}, I^-, or NO_2^-. The blue product is Prussian blue, $KFe[Fe(CN)_6]$, a material containing both iron(II) and iron(III). The reaction with iodide ion, for example, is

$$2K^+ + 2Fe^{3+} + 2[Fe(CN)_6]^{3-} + 2I^- \longrightarrow 2KFe[Fe(CN)_6](s) + I_2(aq) \tag{35.9}$$
Prussian blue

Detection of anion groups The characteristic acid–base and solubility equilibria reactions of the anions allow classification of the ions into groups based on their behaviors with perchloric acid and silver ion. The reactions observed and the

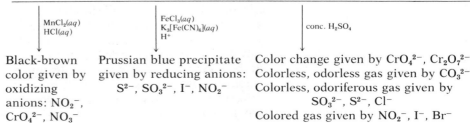

Figure 35.1
Flow Chart of Preliminary Tests for Anions

Group I

Anions decomposed in strongly
acidic solution (dilute $HClO_4$) with
the evolution, when the solution is
warmed, of gases having characteristic properties.

$S^{2-} \longrightarrow H_2S(g)$ *(colorless;*
odor of decayed eggs)
$SO_3^{2-} \longrightarrow SO_2(g)$ *(colorless;*
odor of burning sulfur)
$CO_3^{2-} \longrightarrow CO_2(g)$ *(colorless;*
odorless)
$NO_2^- \longrightarrow NO(g) + NO_2(g)$
(brown; sharp odor)

Group II

Anions stable in dilute $HClO_4$ and
precipitated from acid solution as
silver salts.

$[S^{2-} \longrightarrow Ag_2S$ *(black)*]
$I^- \longrightarrow AgI$ *(pale yellow)*
$Br^- \longrightarrow AgBr$ *(cream)*
$Cl^- \longrightarrow AgCl$ *(white)*

Group III

Anions stable in dilute $HClO_4$, but
precipitated as silver salts only
when the solution is neutralized.

$[CO_3^{2-} \longrightarrow Ag_2CO_3$ *(pale yellow)*]
$[NO_2^- \longrightarrow AgNO_2$ *(pale yellow;*
NO_2^- concentration
must be relatively
high)]
$PO_4^{3-} \longrightarrow Ag_3PO_4$ *(yellow)*
$CrO_4^{2-} \longrightarrow Ag_2CrO_4$ *(brownish*
red)
$SO_4^{2-} \longrightarrow Ag_2SO_4$ *(white; SO_4^{2-}*
concentration must be
relatively high)

Group IV

Anions stable in dilute $HClO_4$, but
give soluble silver salts in both
acidic and neutral media.

NO_3^-
SO_4^{2-}

ions in each group are listed in Table 35.4, and a flow chart is given in Figure 35.2.

The classification of anions into groups is designed only to give preliminary information about the presence or absence of individual ions. It is *not* designed as a scheme of separation. The group tests should be done in the following order:

1. Add 6 M perchloric acid to the sample, warm, and note any gases that are released.
2. Cool the acidic solution from step 1, add silver nitrate solution, and note the color of any precipitate that forms.
3. Remove any precipitate formed in step 2, make the solution just alkaline with 6 M ammonia, add more silver nitrate if necessary, and note the color of any precipitate that forms.

This sequence is necessary so that ions from one group do not interfere with ions from another group. For example, carbonate ion will precipitate in Group III as silver carbonate if the first test carried out is the addition of silver nitrate to a neutral solution of the sample. Anions that might interfere in this way are shown in brackets in Table 35.4.

Behavior toward concentrated sulfuric acid The use of concentrated sulfuric acid (18 M) in anion analysis depends partly upon its ability to function as a strong oxidizing agent and partly upon its acid behavior. Table 35.5 shows the observations that might be made for the addition of H_2SO_4 to an unknown, and their corresponding interpretations. The test with concentrated sulfuric acid must be performed on a solid—either a solid unknown or the solid remaining after an unknown solution is evaporated to dryness.

If the unknown is a mixture of salts, the results of this test may not be easy to interpret, because the gases that form may mask each other. Also, insoluble salts (e.g., the silver halides) and combinations of metal and nonmetal that have consider-able covalent character (e.g., CdI_2, $HgCl_2$) may react only slightly with the acid.

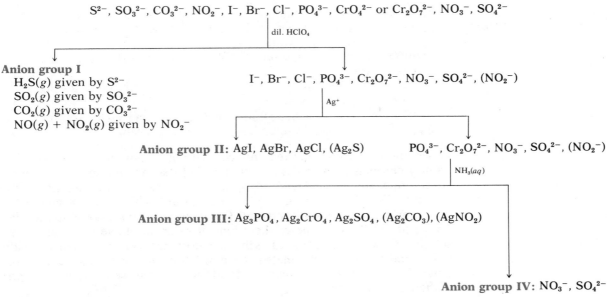

Figure 35.2
Flow Chart for Classifying the Anions into Groups The precipitates shown in parentheses will not appear if dilute $HClO_4$ has been added to the solution first. If the NO_2^- concentration is relatively high, NO_2^- will appear in Group III as well as in Group I.

Table 35.5
Behavior of Anions with Concentrated Sulfuric Acid*

Observation	Interpretation	
	Cold	Hot
No apparent change	PO_4^{3-}, NO_3^-, SO_4^{2-}	PO_4^{3-}, SO_4^{2-}
Color change	CrO_4^{2-} (yellow) $\longrightarrow$ $Cr_2O_7^{2-}$ (orange) $Cr_2O_7^{2-}$ $\longrightarrow$ CrO_3 (red)†	Same
Colorless, odorless gas evolved	CO_3^{2-} $\longrightarrow$ CO_2	Same
Colorless, odoriferous gas evolved	S^{2-} $\longrightarrow$ H_2S SO_3^{2-} $\longrightarrow$ SO_2 Cl^- $\longrightarrow$ HCl	Same
Colored gas evolved	NO_2^- $\longrightarrow$ NO_2 (brown) I^- $\longrightarrow$ I_2 (violet) Br^- $\longrightarrow$ Br_2 (red-brown)	Same Also, NO_3^- $\longrightarrow$ NO_2 (if the vapors are heated)

* Adapted from T. Moeller and R. O'Connor, *Ions in Aqueous Systems* (New York: McGraw-Hill Book Company, 1972), p. 215.

† The red CrO_3 is seldom formed.

EXAMPLE 35.1
Anion Analysis

What conclusion regarding the nature of the anion or anions present in a water-soluble substance may be drawn from each of the following observations?

(a) The substance is a white solid.

(b) Treatment of the solid with cold concentrated sulfuric acid gives no apparent change.

(c) Addition of dilute perchloric acid and silver nitrate to a solution of the substance gives no precipitate.

(d) When a few drops of a solution of the solid are added to a solution of $MnCl_2$ in concentrated hydrochloric acid, no color change occurs.

Observation (a) shows that the only colored ion among those being considered, namely chromate, CrO_4^{2-}, is absent. The fact that no change occurs when cold concentrated sulfuric acid is added (b) eliminates those ions that give gases with that reagent: CO_3^{2-}, S^{2-}, SO_3^{2-}, Cl^-, NO_2^-, I^-, and Br^-. This leaves the anions PO_4^{3-}, NO_3^-, or SO_4^{2-} as possibly present. Observation (c) does not eliminate PO_4^{3-}, NO_3^-, or SO_4^{2-}, for none of these ions gives an insoluble silver salt in acidic solution. Observation (d) indicates that the substance does not contain an oxidizing anion, and so NO_3^- is eliminated. We now know that the substance may contain either PO_4^{3-} or SO_4^{2-}. We cannot decide which of these two anions is present without specific tests.

35.4 THE SPECIFIC TESTS FOR ANIONS

Specific tests are described here for each of the 11 anions on our list. The preliminary tests may eliminate some anions from consideration. The specific tests for those anions suspected of being present are then performed.

S^{2-}

Sulfide ion   The test for sulfide ion is made directly on solid samples provided they are water soluble. If the sample is in solution, the solution is evaporated to dryness before testing. The addition of dilute hydrochloric acid results in the evolution of hydrogen sulfide if the sample contains S^{2-} (Equation 35.5). The H_2S is detected by its reaction with lead acetate, $Pb(CH_3COO)_2$. This test is usually carried out by exposing a piece of damp paper impregnated with lead acetate to the evolving gas.

$$Pb^2 + H_2S(g) \longrightarrow \underset{\substack{\textit{black or} \\ \textit{silvery}}}{PbS(s)} + 2H^+ \tag{35.10}$$

SO_3^{2-}

Sulfite ion   Acidification of the test solution, or a solid sample, with dilute sulfuric acid gives sulfur dioxide if sulfite ion is present (Equation 35.2). Passage of the sulfur dioxide gas into a solution containing dilute nitric acid (HNO_3), barium chloride ($BaCl_2$), and a small amount of potassium permanganate ($KMnO_4$) gives a white precipitate of barium sulfate ($BaSO_4$). The permanganate, a strong oxidizing agent, converts the $+4$ sulfur in SO_2 to the $+6$ state in SO_4^{2-}. The purple $KMnO_4$ is reduced to Mn^{2+}, which is pale pink or practically colorless in dilution solution. The sulfate formed is then converted to $BaSO_4$.

$$5SO_2(g) + 2MnO_4^- + 2H_2O(l) \longrightarrow 5SO_4^{2-} + 2Mn^{2+} + 4H^+ \tag{35.11}$$
$$\underset{\textit{purple}}{} \qquad\qquad\qquad\qquad \underset{\substack{\textit{pale} \\ \textit{pink}}}{\phantom{2Mn^{2+}}}$$

$$SO_4^{2-} + Ba^{2+} \longrightarrow \underset{\textit{white}}{BaSO_4(s)} \tag{35.12}$$

CO_3^{2-}

Carbonate ion   If the sample to be tested is in solution, the solution is heated until it evaporates *just* to dryness. (Many metal carbonates decompose on strong heating.) The residue, or the original solid unknown, is then treated with a small amount of zinc, dilute hydrogen peroxide (H_2O_2), and dilute sulfuric acid. The resulting mixture is warmed and any gas evolved is passed into a solution of barium hydroxide ($Ba(OH)_2$). The formation of a white precipitate of barium carbonate ($BaCO_3$) shows that the sample contains CO_3^{2-}.

$$CO_3^{2-} + 2H^+ \longrightarrow CO_2(g) + H_2O(l) \qquad \textbf{(35.13)}$$

$$CO_2(g) + Ba^{2+} + 2OH^- \longrightarrow BaCO_3(s) + H_2O(l) \qquad \textbf{(35.14)}$$
white

It is obvious that a solution prepared by sodium carbonate treatment of a sample cannot be used in this test to determine the presence of carbonate in the original unknown.

The hydrogen peroxide is added to oxidize any SO_3^{2-} that may be present to SO_4^{2-}, which is unaffected by the sulfuric acid.

$$SO_3^{2-} + H_2O_2(aq) \longrightarrow SO_4^{2-} + H_2O(l) \qquad \textbf{(35.15)}$$

Without the H_2O_2 addition, the SO_2 liberated upon acidification of SO_3^{2-} would also give a white precipitate, $BaSO_3$, with $Ba(OH)_2$. The zinc reacts with H_2SO_4 to generate hydrogen, and this gas helps sweep the CO_2 into the $Ba(OH)_2$ solution.

NO_2^{2-} **Nitrite ion** The test for nitrite ion makes use of this ion's ability to function as an oxidizing agent. The test solution is made very slightly acidic by addition of either dilute sulfuric acid or acetic acid. A few drops of freshly prepared iron(II) sulfate ($FeSO_4$) solution are then added. Part of the iron(II) is oxidized to iron(III) and the NO_2^- is reduced to NO. A reaction between this NO and some of the excess iron(II) in the solution yields a complex ion, $[Fe(NO)]^{2+}$, recognizable by its brown color.

$$NO_2^- + Fe^{2+} + 2H^+ \longrightarrow Fe^{3+} + NO(aq) + H_2O(l) \qquad \textbf{(35.16)}$$
oxidant reductant

$$Fe^{2+} + NO(aq) \longrightarrow [Fe(NO)]^{2+} \qquad \textbf{(35.17)}$$
brown

The NO_3^- ion behaves similarly, but only at high hydrogen ion concentrations.

I^-, Br^-, Cl^- **Iodide, bromide, and chloride ions** If two or more of these anions are present, the identificaton of each requires considerable care. The methods used for the detection of each in the presence of the others are based on the relative redox properties of the halogens. The sequence of reactions is made possible because iodide ion is more easily oxidized than bromide ion, and both are more easily oxidized than chloride ion.

The solution to be tested is first made slightly acidic with dilute hydrochloric acid; then a small amount of carbon tetrachloride (CCl_4) is added. This is followed by the addition, with shaking, of a few drops of chlorine water or sodium hypochlorite (NaOCl) solution. The appearance of a violet color in the CCl_4 (bottom) layer is proof of the presence of iodide ion.

$$2I^- + Cl_2(aq) \longrightarrow I_2(in\ CCl_4) + 2Cl^- \qquad \textbf{(35.18)}$$
violet

To test this solution for bromide ion, the iodine must first be oxidized to a colorless species (IO_3^-) by further addition of chlorine water.

$$I_2(in\ CCl_4) + 5Cl_2(aq) + 6H_2O(l) \longrightarrow 2IO_3^- + 10Cl^- + 12H^+ \qquad \textbf{(35.19)}$$

With still further addition of chlorine water, a yellow to brown color is formed in the CCl_4 solution if the original test solution contained bromide ion.

$$2Br^- + Cl_2(aq) \longrightarrow Br_2(in\ CCl_4) + 2Cl^- \qquad \textbf{(35.20)}$$
yellow to brown

To test for chloride ion in the presence of bromide and/or iodide ions, the bromide and iodide ions must be removed. This is done by preferential oxidation of these ions in acidic (H_2SO_4) medium at elevated temperature. Peroxodisulfate ion ($S_2O_8^{2-}$) oxidizes iodide and bromide to the free elements, but is not a strong enough oxidizing agent to produce chlorine from chloride ion.

$$\underset{(X = Br, I)}{2X^-} + S_2O_8^{2-} \xrightarrow{\ H_2SO_4\ } X_2 + 2SO_4^{2-} \qquad (35.21)$$

The free halogens are extracted into CCl_4. Silver nitrate is added to the acidified (HNO_3) water layer and AgCl is precipitated. Dissolution of the precipitate in aqueous ammonia unequivocally shows the presence of chloride ion (Equation 35.8).

Of course, if I^- and Br^- have been found to be absent, the test for Cl^- ion is greatly simplified. All that is necessary is to see whether a white precipitate forms when silver nitrate solution is added to a nitric acid solution of the sample and whether this precipitate dissolves when aqueous ammonia is added.

PO_4^{3-}   **Phosphate ion**   The presence of phosphate ion, PO_4^{3-}, is indicated if a bright yellow precipitate of ammonium molybdophosphate, $(NH_4)_3P(Mo_3O_{10})_4$, forms upon treatment of the test solution with ammonium molybdate–nitric acid reagent.

$$PO_4^{3-} + 12MoO_4^{2-} + 3NH_4^+ + 24H^+ \longrightarrow \underset{bright\ yellow}{(NH_4)_3P(Mo_3O_{10})_4(s)} + 12H_2O(l) \quad (35.22)$$

Any reducing agents present would interfere with this test by forming blue precipitates or colors with the reagent. Consequently, before the test is carried out, reducing agents are converted to other species by oxidation with hot concentrated sulfuric acid.

CrO_4^{2-}   **Chromate ion**   The presence of chromate ion, CrO_4^{2-}, is indicated by the yellow color of an alkaline sample solution. Addition of acid (e.g., dilute H_2SO_4) converts the CrO_4^{2-} to orange dichromate ion, $Cr_2O_7^{2-}$. The presence of CrO_4^{2-} ion is confirmed if a yellow precipitate of barium chromate ($BaCrO_4$) forms when the test solution is made slightly acidic with acetic acid and then treated with barium acetate, $Ba(CH_3COO)_2$, in solution.

$$CrO_4^{2-} + Ba^{2+} \longrightarrow \underset{yellow}{BaCrO_4(s)} \qquad (35.23)$$

NO_3^-   **Nitrate ion**   The ions NO_2^-, I^-, Br^-, and CrO_4^{2-} interfere with the detection of nitrate ion. If none of these ions is present, a dilute $FeSO_4$ solution is added to the acidified (with dilute H_2SO_4) test solution. Then *concentrated* H_2SO_4 is carefully introduced under the cooled solution so that it forms a separate layer. If after a few minutes a *brown ring* appears at the interface of the layers, nitrate ion is shown to be present.

$$NO_3^- + 3Fe^{2+} + 4H^+ \longrightarrow NO(aq) + 3Fe^{3+} + 2H_2O(l) \qquad (35.24)$$

$$Fe^{2+} + NO(aq) \longrightarrow \underset{brown}{[Fe(NO)]^{2+}} \qquad (35.25)$$

The brown ring forms at the interface between the solution and the sulfuric acid because the H^+ ion concentration there is highest.

Nitrite ion gives the same brown color, but does so throughout the entire solution because it does not require such a high H^+ ion concentration. The nitrite can be destroyed prior to testing for nitrate by reaction with solid sulfamic acid, H_2NSO_3H, in a test solution made slightly acidic with dilute H_2SO_4. Sulfamic acid is a strong acid in water. Undoubtedly there is initial proton transfer from it to NO_2^- ion, followed by oxidation of $H_2NSO_3^-$ to N_2.

$$H_2NSO_3H(aq) + NO_2^- \longrightarrow H_2NSO_3^- + HNO_2(aq) \qquad (35.26)$$

$$H_2NSO_3^- + HNO_2(aq) \xrightarrow{\text{heat}} N_2(g) + H^+ + H_2O(l) + SO_4^{2-} \qquad (35.27)$$

Iodide and bromide ions are oxidized by concentrated H_2SO_4 to the free halogens and these elements give brownish colors at the interface of the layers. The halide ions can be precipitated as silver salts by the addition of silver acetate, $Ag(CH_3COO)$, to a test solution acidified with acetic acid.

If CrO_4^{2-} is present in the solution it is reduced by the Fe^{2+} to dark green Cr^{3+}, thus obscuring the color of the brown ring. Chromate ion can be removed as insoluble $BaCrO_4$ by treatment of a weakly acidic (acetic acid) test solution with barium acetate.

SO_4^{2-} **Sulfate ion** Addition of $BaCl_2$ to a test solution made acidic with dilute HCl gives a $BaSO_4$ precipitate if SO_4^{2-} ion is present (Equation 35.12).

EXAMPLE 35.2
Anion Analysis

A colorless solid dissolves readily in water to give a solution that is neutral to litmus. Addition of cold concentrated sulfuric acid to the solution results in the liberation of a brownish gas. When dilute perchloric acid is added to a solution of the original solid and the mixture is warmed, a brown gas with a sharp odor is evolved. Addition of a few drops of a solution of the solid to a solution containing iron(III) chloride, potassium hexacyanoferrate(III), $K_3[Fe(CN)_6]$, and dilute hydrochloric acid gives a dark blue suspension. Treatment of the original solid with dilute sulfuric acid and passage of the gas evolved into a solution of barium chloride and potassium permanganate produces a white precipitate. Addition of barium chloride to an acidified (HCl) solution of the solid yields a white precipitate. Treatment of a solution of the solid with dilute nitric acid and silver nitrate gives a white precipitate that is completely soluble in aqueous ammonia.

What anion or anions are definitely present in the original solid? Justify your answer.

The absence of a yellow or orange color in the solid proves the absence of CrO_4^{2-} or $Cr_2O_7^{2-}$. The fact that an aqueous solution of the solid is neutral to litmus eliminates the strong Brønsted-Lowry bases: S^{2-}, CO_3^{2-}, and PO_4^{3-}. The brown gas liberated by the action of cold concentrated sulfuric acid is either NO_2 or Br_2, or both, indicating the presence of NO_2^- or Br^-, or both, and eliminating I^-, which gives I_2 as a violet vapor. However, those anions which form colorless gases when treated with concentrated sulfuric acid, SO_3^{2-} and Cl^-, have not been eliminated. (The CO_3^{2-} and S^{2-} ions also give colorless gases with sulfuric acid, but they have already been shown to be absent.) The evolution of a brown gas from the dilute perchloric acid shows the presence of NO_2^- ion, but does not eliminate SO_3^{2-}, which also falls in Group I in the anion group classification scheme.

The blue suspension (Prussian blue) formed in the next step shows the presence of a reducing agent and thus continues the possibility that SO_3^{2-} may be in the solid. (Remember S^{2-} and I^- have been eliminated.) The fact that a white precipitate ($BaSO_4$) is produced in the next step, which is

$$\text{unknown solution} + \text{dilute sulfuric acid} \longrightarrow \text{gas}$$
$$\text{gas} + KMnO_4(\text{oxidizing agent}) \longrightarrow SO_4^{2-}$$
$$SO_4^{2-} + Ba^{2+} \longrightarrow BaSO_4(s)$$

proves that SO_3^{2-} is present in the original solid. Sulfate ion, SO_4^{2-}, is also present, as evidenced by the formation of the white precipitate ($BaSO_4$) when a solution of the unknown is treated with an acidic solution of barium chloride. Finally, the white precipitate formed in the last test is silver chloride, $AgCl$; the complete solubility of the precipitate in dilute aqueous ammonia shows that Br^- ion is absent. These tests have shown that the anions in the solid are NO_2^-, SO_3^{2-}, SO_4^{2-}, and Cl^-. No conclusion can be drawn from these tests regarding the presence or absence of NO_3^- ion. The other six anions have all been shown to be absent.

CATION ANALYSIS

The steps in cation analysis fall into the following general sequence:

1. *Separation of the cations into a series of groups.* The cations of each successive group are precipitated as compounds with anions supplied by the group reagents. The precipitate containing the cations of one group is separated (usually by centrifugation followed by decantation). Then the group reagent for the next group is added to the remaining solution.

2. *Separation of the cations in each group from each other.* A series of reactions is carried out that eventually leads to the separation of each cation in a group from all of the others in that group. The reactions are carefully chosen to take advantage of similarities and differences in chemical properties.

3. *Identification of individual cations.* The presence of a cation is confirmed by one or more reactions characteristic of that cation.

Figure 35.3 is the flow chart for the separation of the groups from each other. Individual flow charts for the groups are given with the discussion of the ions in each group. In these group flow charts, each step is identified by a procedure number. Paragraphs in the text give further information about the chemistry and practical aspects of these steps. (The specific step-by-step directions for the laboratory work are given in the separate laboratory manual.)

CATION GROUP I (Hg_2^{2+}, Pb^{2+}, Ag^+)

Cation Group I brings together three metal ions that form chlorides that are insoluble in acidic solution. The group reagent is hydrochloric acid, and this group is sometimes known as the hydrochloric acid group, the chloride group, or the silver group. The chlorides of all the other cations in our cation analysis scheme are soluble in acidic solution.

The use of a moderate excess of hydrochloric acid to precipitate the group serves two purposes: (1) the excess chloride ion encourages the precipitation of the chlorides

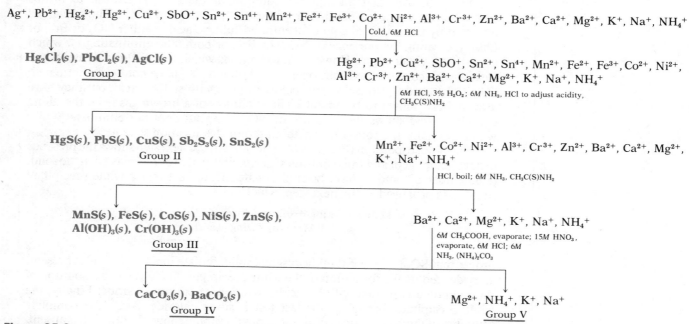

Figure 35.3

Flow Chart for Separation of Cations into Groups Details of the group separation procedures are discussed in the sections on the individual group analyses.

(by Le Chatelier's principle) and (2) the hydrogen ion prevents the interfering precipitation of the bismuth and the antimony oxochlorides, which would form if these ions were present.

$$Bi^{3+} + Cl^- + H_2O \rightleftharpoons BiOCl(s) + 2H^+ \qquad (35.28)$$

$$Sb^{3+} + Cl^- + H_2O \rightleftharpoons SbOCl(s) + 2H^+ \qquad (35.29)$$

Too large an excess of the acid, however, dissolves the silver and lead chlorides by complex formation. Mercury(I) chloride does not dissolve because the chloro complexes of mercury(I) are very unstable.

Lead chloride ($PbCl_2$) is by several thousandfold the most soluble of the three chlorides in this group. The use of a cool solution and the presence of excess chloride ion help to precipitate the maximum possible amount of $PbCl_2$ at this stage. However, lead chloride is soluble enough that it is impossible to avoid carrying some lead(II) over into the centrifugate and into Cation Group II. Therefore, provision is also made for the detection and removal of lead in the next analytical group.

35.5 MERCURY(I) ION $Hg_2{}^{2+}$

The colorless $Hg_2{}^{2+}$ ion is unique among the cations in our qualitative scheme because it contains a covalent metal–metal bond. The $Hg_2{}^{2+}$ ion is found in a number of solid compounds. In aqueous solutions, its existence is limited to the pH region below about 3 to 4. At higher pH values, a disproportionation reaction with water or hydroxide ion takes place:

$$Hg_2{}^{2+} + 2OH^- \rightleftharpoons Hg(l) + HgO(s) + H_2O(l) \qquad (35.30)$$

This reaction provides an example of the displacement of an equilibrium as the concentration of one ion is decreased by a competing reaction. The general equilibrium reaction is

$$Hg(l) + Hg^{2+} \rightleftharpoons Hg_2{}^{2+} \qquad (35.31)$$

$$K = \frac{[Hg_2{}^{2+}]}{[Hg^{2+}]} = 166 \qquad (35.32)$$

At equilibrium, the concentration of $Hg_2{}^{2+}$ is only 166 times that of Hg^{2+}. As $[Hg^{2+}]$ is decreased by the formation of the slightly soluble HgO, $[Hg_2{}^{2+}]$ is also decreased by further disproportionation. Disproportionation rather than mercury(I) compound formation occurs in several other reactions in which the concentration of Hg^{2+} in solution is decreased by the formation of slightly soluble compounds or of stable complexes:

$$Hg_2{}^{2+} + CO_3{}^{2-} \rightleftharpoons Hg(l) + HgO(s) + CO_2(g) \qquad (35.33)$$

$$Hg_2{}^{2+} + H_2S(aq) \rightleftharpoons Hg(l) + HgS(s) + 2H^+ \qquad (35.34)$$

$$Hg_2{}^{2+} + 4CN^- \rightleftharpoons Hg(l) + [Hg(CN)_4]^{2-} \qquad (35.35)$$

$$Hg_2Cl_2(s) + 2NH_3(aq) \rightleftharpoons Hg(l) + HgNH_2Cl(s) + NH_4{}^+ + Cl^- \qquad (35.36)$$

The elemental mercury formed in these reactions is so finely divided that it is black.

Of the common mercury(I) compounds, only the nitrate and perchlorate are soluble in water. Aqueous solutions of these compounds can be stabilized against disproportionation by adding elemental mercury, which converts any Hg^{2+} formed back to $Hg_2{}^{2+}$. Standard electrode potential data

$$2Hg^{2+} + 2e^- \longrightarrow Hg_2{}^{2+} \qquad E° = 0.920 \text{ V}$$

$$Hg^{2+} + 2e^- \longrightarrow Hg \qquad E° = 0.854 \text{ V}$$

$$Hg_2{}^{2+} + 2e^- \longrightarrow 2Hg \qquad E° = 0.788 \text{ V}$$

indicate that reduction of $Hg_2{}^{2+}$ to elemental mercury occurs more easily than oxidation of $Hg_2{}^{2+}$ to Hg^{2+}. The standard potentials of the Hg(II)–Hg(I) and

Hg(II) – Hg(0) couples are so close to that of the Hg(I) – Hg(0) couple that oxidation of mercury invariably gives mercury(II) unless an excess of the metal is present.

Reactions Important in the Separation and Identification of Hg_2^{2+}

Group precipitation

$$Hg_2^{2+} + 2Cl^- \rightleftharpoons Hg_2Cl_2(s) \qquad (35.37)$$
$$\text{\textit{white}}$$

Confirmatory test

$$Hg_2Cl_2(s) + 2NH_3(aq) \rightleftharpoons Hg(l) + Hg(NH_2)Cl(s) + NH_4^+ + Cl^- \qquad (35.38)$$
$$\qquad\qquad\qquad\quad \text{\textit{black}} \qquad \text{\textit{white}}$$

35.6 LEAD(II) ION
Pb^{2+}

Both lead(II) and lead(IV) compounds are known in the solid state. However, only lead(II) compounds are found in aqueous solution, for the lead(IV) compounds are very strong oxidizing agents and are easily reduced. These relationships are indicated by the standard potential data

$$PbSO_4 + 2e^- \longrightarrow Pb + SO_4^{2-} \qquad E^\circ = -0.359 \text{ V}$$
$$Pb^{2+} + 2e^- \longrightarrow Pb \qquad E^\circ = -0.126 \text{ V}$$
$$PbO_2 + 4H^+ + 2e^- \longrightarrow Pb^{2+} + 2H_2O \qquad E^\circ = +1.455 \text{ V}$$
$$PbO_2 + 4H^+ + SO_4^{2-} + 2e^- \longrightarrow PbSO_4 + 2H_2O \qquad E^\circ = +1.685 \text{ V}$$

The $+2$ oxidation state results even when elemental lead is treated with a relatively strong oxidizing agent such as dilute nitric acid.

$$3Pb(s) + 8H^+ + 2NO_3^- \longrightarrow 3Pb^{2+} + 2NO(g) + 4H_2O(l) \qquad (35.39)$$

Of the common lead(II) compounds, only the nitrate, acetate, and perchlorate are soluble in water. Lead(II) acetate is a weak electrolyte in solution because of the formation of acetato complexes such as $[Pb(CH_3COO)_4]^{2-}$. Lead(II) sulfate, an insoluble compound, dissolves in the presence of an excess of acetate ion by formation of such acetate complexes. Similarly, lead(II) hydroxide dissolves in strongly alkaline solutions by formation of the hydroxo complex ion, $[Pb(OH)_4]^{2-}$. In the presence of an excess of chloride ions, lead(II) chloride also forms a complex ion.

$$PbCl_2(s) + 2Cl^-(xs) \rightleftharpoons [PbCl_4]^{2-} \qquad (35.40)$$

Reactions Important in the Separation and Identification of Pb^{2+} in Cation Group I

Group precipitation

$$Pb^{2+} + 2Cl^- \xrightarrow{\text{cold}} PbCl_2(s) \qquad (35.41)$$
$$\text{\textit{white}}$$

Confirmatory tests

$$Pb^{2+} + SO_4^{2-} \rightleftharpoons PbSO_4(s) \qquad (35.42)$$
$$\text{\textit{white}}$$

$$Pb^{2+} + CrO_4^{2-} \rightleftharpoons PbCrO_4(s) \qquad (35.43)$$
$$\text{\textit{yellow}}$$

35.7 SILVER(I) ION
Ag⁺

Silver(II) and silver(III) compounds exist, but they are such strong oxidizing agents that they are difficult to prepare and are readily reduced. Even the silver(I) ion is readily reduced in acidic solution,

$$Ag^+ + e^- \longrightarrow Ag \qquad E° = 0.799 \text{ V}$$

In solution, the Ag^+ ion is colorless, but many solid silver(I) compounds that form with colorless anions are colored (e.g., AgBr, cream; AgI,. Ag_3PO_4, yellow; Ag_2S, Ag_2O, black; Ag_3AsO_4, reddish brown). The color of simple metal compounds deepens as the bonding becomes less ionic and more covalent. Apparently this is due to changes in the distribution of electron density in the anions.

The only common easily water-soluble silver(I) compounds are the nitrate, fluoride, and perchlorate; the nitrite, acetate, and sulfate are moderately soluble. Silver(I) nitrate solution is the usual source of Ag^+ in the laboratory. As a d-transition metal ion, silver(I) forms a number of complex ions, of which the most commonly encountered are $[Ag(NH_3)_2]^+$ and $[Ag(CN)_2]^-$.

Reactions Important in the Separation and Identification of Ag⁺

Group precipitation

$$Ag^+ + Cl^- \rightleftharpoons AgCl(s) \qquad \qquad \textbf{(35.44)}$$
white

Dissolution by complex ion formation

$$AgCl(s) + 2NH_3(aq) \rightleftharpoons [Ag(NH_3)_2]^+ + Cl^- \qquad \textbf{(35.45)}$$

Confirmatory test

$$[Ag(NH_3)_2]^+ + Cl^- + 2H^+ \rightleftharpoons AgCl(s) + 2NH_4^+ \qquad \textbf{(35.46)}$$

35.8 CATION GROUP I
ANALYSIS

The flow chart for Cation Group I is given in Figure 35.4. The procedures identified in the flow chart are discussed in the following paragraphs.

Procedure 1 Solubility product constants (Appendix V.3) indicate that lead(II) chloride is much more soluble than the chlorides of mercury(I) or silver(I). Because the solubility in water of $PbCl_2$ increases from about 0.036 mol/L at 20 °C to about 0.12 mol/L at 100 °C, cold solutions are used in this procedure to maximize precipitation of the lead(II) ion. Addition of excess hydrochloric acid initially reduces the solubility of each chloride by the common ion effect, but a large excess then increases the solubilities of AgCl and $PbCl_2$ as a consequence of the formation of chloro complex ions. In any event, a sufficiently large concentration of Pb^{2+} ion remains in solution to form PbS(s) in Cation Group II.

Procedure 2 Boiling the precipitate with water increases the rate of dissolution of lead(II) chloride and maximizes its removal. Mere washing with hot water is seldom completely effective.

Procedure 3 If crystals of lead(II) chloride separate as the solution cools, it is necessary to reheat until they dissolve so that enough Pb^{2+} is in solution to give a clear test. The tests are done on the hot solution. Lead(II) chromate is both a more distinctive precipitate and less soluble than lead(II) sulfate. Chromate precipitation is thus the better confirmatory test for the lead(II) ion.

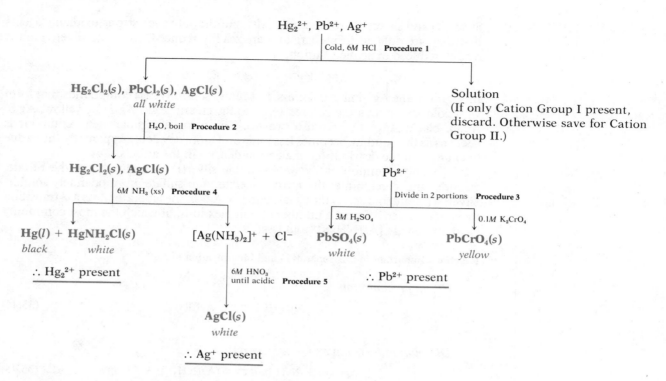

Hg_2^{2+}, Pb^{2+}, Ag^+

Cold, $6M$ HCl **Procedure 1**

$Hg_2Cl_2(s)$, $PbCl_2(s)$, $AgCl(s)$
all white

Solution
(If only Cation Group I present,
discard. Otherwise save for Cation
Group II.)

H_2O, boil **Procedure 2**

$Hg_2Cl_2(s)$, $AgCl(s)$

Pb^{2+}

$6M$ NH_3 (xs) **Procedure 4**

Divide in 2 portions **Procedure 3**

$3M$ H_2SO_4

$0.1M$ K_2CrO_4

$Hg(l)$ + $HgNH_2Cl(s)$
black   *white*

$[Ag(NH_3)_2]^+$ + Cl^-

$PbSO_4(s)$
white

$PbCrO_4(s)$
yellow

∴ Hg_2^{2+} present

$6M$ HNO_3
until acidic **Procedure 5**

∴ Pb^{2+} present

$AgCl(s)$
white

∴ Ag^+ present

Figure 35.4
Flow Chart for Analysis of Cation Group I The notation "xs" means "excess"; the symbol ∴ reads "therefore."

Procedure 4 Any lead(II) chloride not dissolved in Procedure 2 is converted by aqueous ammonia to a finely divided white basic salt [possibly Pb(OH)Cl] which gives a turbid suspension. Since this material dissolves in nitric acid, it causes no interference with the confirmatory test for the Ag^+ ion.

Formation of a gray to black residue is the confirmatory test for the Hg_2^{2+} ion. The easily complexed Ag^+ ion remains in solution. Therefore, aqueous ammonia serves to confirm both the presence and the absence of the Hg_2^{2+} ion and to separate silver(I) from mercury(I). Note that this solution should not be allowed to stand (see Procedure 5).

Procedure 5 Ammoniacal silver(I) solutions may deposit explosive residues. (Azides, containing N_3^-, may be formed. These can explode even when the solution is being poured.) Therefore, this procedure should be carried out without delay. Slow addition of nitric acid initially causes localized destruction of the complex ion and precipitation of white silver chloride, which then redissolves upon agitation because of the presence of excess ammonia. Consequently, nitric acid must be added until the solution is definitely acidic before the presence or absence of the Ag^+ ion can be confirmed.

EXAMPLE 35.3
Cation Group I

One of each of the following pairs of substances is known to be in a sample. What single reagent will show which species is present in each case?
(a) $PbCl_2$ and Hg_2Cl_2; (b) AgCl and $PbCl_2$; (c) $[Ag(NH_3)_2]Cl$ and $Pb(NO_3)_2$.

(a) Both compounds are water insoluble. Treatment of the sample with aqueous ammonia will give a black to gray material if Hg_2Cl_2 is present and no apparent change if the substance is $PbCl_2$.

$$Hg_2Cl_2(s) + 2NH_3(aq) \rightleftharpoons Hg(l) + HgNH_2Cl(s) + NH_4^+ + Cl^-$$
black   *white*

(b) AgCl will dissolve in aqueous ammonia; $PbCl_2$ will not. (Also, $PbCl_2$ will dissolve in hot water, but AgCl will not.)

$$AgCl(s) + 2NH_3(aq) \longrightarrow [Ag(NH_3)_2]^+ + Cl^-$$

(c) Both $[Ag(NH_3)_2]Cl$ and $Pb(NO_3)_2$ are water soluble. However, acidification of an aqueous solution of the sample with dilute HNO_3 will precipitate white AgCl if $[Ag(NH_3)_2]Cl$ is present. No effect is observed if HNO_3 is added to a solution of $Pb(NO_3)_2$.

$$[Ag(NH_3)_2]^+ + Cl^- + 2H^+ \longrightarrow AgCl(s) + 2NH_4^+$$

EXAMPLE 35.4
Cation Group I

A solution contains both Hg_2^{2+} and Pb^{2+} ions. A student suggested that these ions can be separated by adding a large excess of sodium hydroxide to the solution and thoroughly shaking the mixture. Was the student correct? Justify your answer.

The student was correct. The addition of a small amount of sodium hydroxide will cause both ions to precipitate.

$$Hg_2^{2+} + 2OH^- \longrightarrow Hg(l) + HgO(s) + H_2O$$
$$Pb^{2+} + 2OH^- \longrightarrow Pb(OH)_2(s)$$

The $Pb(OH)_2$ is amphoteric and will dissolve with complex formation when an excess of the base is added.

$$Pb(OH)_2(s) + 2OH^- \longrightarrow [Pb(OH)_4]^{2-}$$

CATION GROUP II
(Hg^{2+}, Pb^{2+}, Cu^{2+}, Sn^{2+} or Sn^{4+}, Sb^{3+} or SbO^+)

The sulfides of the cations in this group are precipitated by hydrogen sulfide in the presence of dilute (0.25 to 0.3 M) acid. This group is also sometimes called the copper–tin group or the acidic hydrogen sulfide group. Although we have not included them in our analysis scheme, cadmium, arsenic, and bismuth (all very toxic) would, if present, be part of this group.

The sulfides in this group are those with the smallest K_{sp} values (Appendix V.3). Therefore, they precipitate in the presence of a sulfide ion concentration that is kept low enough to avoid precipitation of the more soluble sulfides. Tin(IV) sulfide is the most soluble sulfide in this group. The sulfide ion concentration must exceed that required for precipitation of SnS_2, while remaining low enough to avoid the precipitation of ZnS, the least soluble sulfide in Cation Group III. As we have seen (Section 34.10c), the sulfide ion concentration is controlled by controlling $[H^+]$.

This large group is further separated by differences in the solubilities of the sulfides. The amphoteric sulfides of antimony and tin dissolve in alkaline solution in the presence of sulfide ion and ammonia, but the sulfides of mercury, lead, and copper remain undissolved in alkaline solution in the presence of ammonia. Lead and copper sulfides dissolve when the concentration of sulfide ion is decreased by its oxidation to elemental sulfur by nitric acid, while mercury sulfide is too slightly soluble to be affected by this procedure.

35.9 MERCURY(II) ION
Hg^{2+}

In most mercury(II) compounds the bonding is more nearly covalent than ionic. Mercury(II) ion probably exists in only a few compounds, such as the perchlorate or nitrate, or in the aqueous solutions of these two compounds. In aqueous solution, mercury(II) either reacts extensively with water or is strongly complexed. For example, in the presence of Cl^-, a series of complexes is formed: $[HgCl]^+$, $[HgCl_2]$, $[HgCl_3]^-$, $[HgCl_4]^{2-}$. Although the mercury(II) ion is colorless, solid compounds with colorless anions are often intensely colored as a consequence of covalency (e.g., HgO, red or yellow; HgS, red or black; HgI_2, red).

In aqueous solutions containing complex ions, the equilibrium concentration of Hg^{2+} *decreases* in the order

$$[HgCl_4]^{2-} > [Hg(NCS)_4]^{2-} > [HgBr_4]^{2-} > [HgI_4]^{2-} > [Hg(CN)_4]^{2-} > [HgS_2]^{2-}$$

The halo complex ions are sufficiently stable that even mercury(II) oxide can be dissolved in alkali metal chloride, bromide, or iodide solutions.

$$HgO(s) + 4X^- + H_2O(l) \longrightarrow [HgX_4]^{2-} + 2OH^- \tag{35.47}$$

Mercury(II) sulfide is the least soluble sulfide ($K_{sp} = 4 \times 10^{-53}$). It is not soluble in either dilute nitric acid or hydrochloric acid, but dissolves in hot aqua regia with the formation of a chloro complex.

Reactions Important in the Separation and Identification of Hg^{2+}

Group precipitation

$$Hg^{2+} + H_2S(aq) \xrightleftharpoons{H^+} HgS(s) + 2H^+ \tag{35.48}$$
$$\text{black}$$

Dissolution by oxidation of S^{2-} and complex ion formation

$$3HgS(s) + 8H^+ + 12Cl^- + 2NO_3^- \longrightarrow 3[HgCl_4]^{2-} + 2NO(g) + 4H_2O(l) + 3S(s) \tag{35.49}$$

Confirmatory tests

$$[HgCl_4]^{2-} + Sn^{2+}(xs) + 2Cl^- \longrightarrow Hg(l) + [SnCl_6]^{2-} \tag{35.50}$$
$$\text{black}$$
$$[HgCl_4]^{2-} + Cu(s) \longrightarrow Hg(l) + Cu^{2+} + 4Cl^- \tag{35.51}$$
$$\text{silvery}$$
$$\text{coating on Cu}$$

35.10 LEAD(II) ION Pb^{2+}

The chemistry of lead(II) ion presented in the discussion of Cation Group I need only be supplemented by equations for additional reactions that take place in the analysis of Cation Group II.

Reactions Important in the Separation and Identification of Pb^{2+} in Cation Group II

Group precipitation

$$Pb^{2+} + H_2S(aq) \xrightleftharpoons{H^+} PbS(s) + 2H^+ \tag{35.52}$$

Dissolution by oxidation of S^{2-}

$$3PbS(s) + 8H^+ + 2NO_3^- \longrightarrow 3Pb^{2+} + 2NO(g) + 4H_2O(l) + 3S(s) \tag{35.53}$$

Precipitation to separate from Cu^{2+}

$$Pb^{2+} + SO_4^{2-} \rightleftharpoons PbSO_4(s) \tag{35.54}$$
$$\text{white}$$

Dissolution as complex ion

$$PbSO_4(s) + 4OH^- \rightleftharpoons [Pb(OH)_4]^{2-} + SO_4^{2-} \tag{35.55}$$
$$\text{colorless}$$

Confirmatory test

$$[Pb(OH)_4]^{2-} + 4H^+ \rightleftharpoons Pb^{2+} + 4H_2O(l) \tag{35.56}$$
$$Pb^{2+} + CrO_4^{2-} \rightleftharpoons PbCrO_4(s) \tag{35.57}$$
$$\text{yellow}$$

35.11 COPPER(II) ION
Cu^{2+}

Copper(I), copper(II), and copper(III) are all known in solid compounds. However, copper(III) compounds are relatively rare, and copper(III) is so strongly oxidizing that it is reduced by water. Copper(II) is the only common species in aqueous solution. Copper(I) and copper(II) are related in terms of standard potentials by the following equilibria:

$$Cu_2O + H_2O + 2e^- \longrightarrow 2Cu + 2OH^- \qquad E° = -0.358 \text{ V}$$
$$2Cu(OH)_2 + 2e^- \longrightarrow Cu_2O + 2OH^- + H_2O \qquad E° = -0.080 \text{ V}$$
$$Cu^{2+} + e^- \longrightarrow Cu^+ \qquad E° = +0.153 \text{ V}$$
$$Cu^{2+} + 2e^- \longrightarrow Cu \qquad E° = +0.337 \text{ V}$$
$$Cu^+ + e^- \longrightarrow Cu \qquad E° = +0.521 \text{ V}$$

In acidic solution, Cu^+ and Cu^{2+} are related by a redox disproportionation equilibrium like that of mercury:

$$2Cu^+ \rightleftharpoons Cu(s) + Cu^{2+} \qquad K = \frac{[Cu^{2+}]}{[Cu^+]^2} = 1.4 \times 10^6 \qquad \textbf{(35.58)}$$

At equilibrium, the concentration of Cu^{2+} is always $(1.4 \times 10^6)[Cu^+]^2$, and Cu^+ can exist in solution only if its concentration is extremely small (e.g., in equilibrium with complex ion $[Cu(CN)_3]^{2-}$, the $K_d = 1 \times 10^{-35}$).

Water-soluble copper(II) compounds include the acetate, bromide, chloride, chromate, nitrate, perchlorate, and sulfate. Most other anions either form insoluble compounds with Cu^{2+} or reduce Cu^{2+} to Cu^+ or Cu^0. The equilibrium concentration of Cu^{2+} decreases in copper complex solutions as follows:

$$[Cu(H_2O)_4]^{2+} > [CuCl_4]^{2-} > [Cu(NH_3)_4]^{2+}$$
pale blue   *yellow*   *deep blue*

The volatile compounds of some elements give characteristic colors when the compound or its solution is exposed to a flame. This is usually done by dipping a clean platinum wire into the compound or its solution and holding the wire in the oxidizing part of a Bunsen burner flame (the pale flame). (Note that if the wire is held in the reducing flame, a brittle carbide is formed and the wire is ruined.) Copper(II) nitrate gives a bright blue flame color and copper(II) chloride, a green flame color.

Reactions Important in the Separation and Detection of Cu^{2+}

Group precipitation

$$Cu^{2+} + H_2S(aq) \rightleftharpoons CuS(s) + 2H^+ \qquad \textbf{(35.59)}$$
black

Dissolution by oxidation of S^{2-}

$$3CuS(s) + 8H^+ + 2NO_3^- \longrightarrow 3Cu^{2+} + 2NO(g) + 4H_2O(l) + 3S(s) \qquad \textbf{(35.60)}$$

Confirmatory tests

$$Cu^{2+} + 4NH_3(aq) \rightleftharpoons [Cu(NH_3)_4]^{2+} \qquad \textbf{(35.61)}$$
dark blue-purple

$$[Cu(NH_3)_4]^{2+} + 4H^+ \rightleftharpoons Cu^{2+} + 4NH_4^+ \qquad \textbf{(35.62)}$$

$$2Cu^{2+} + [Fe(CN)_6]^{4-} \rightleftharpoons Cu_2[Fe(CN)_6](s) \qquad \textbf{(35.63)}$$
reddish

$$Cu^{2+} + 2NCS^- + 2C_5H_5N(aq) \rightleftharpoons [Cu(NCS)_2(NC_5H_5)_2](s) \qquad \textbf{(35.64)}$$
pyridine   *green*

35.12 TIN(II) AND TIN(IV) IONS
Sn^{2+}, Sn^{4+}

Both tin(II) and tin(IV) are common, and both are encountered in aqueous solutions. These two oxidation states are related to each other and to elemental tin in terms of standard potentials as follows:

for acidic solutions

$$Sn^{2+} + 2e^- \longrightarrow Sn \qquad\qquad E^\circ = -0.136 \text{ V}$$
$$Sn^{4+} + 2e^- \longrightarrow Sn^{2+} \qquad\qquad E^\circ = +0.15 \text{ V}$$

for alkaline solutions

$$[Sn(OH)_4]^{2-} + 2e^- \longrightarrow Sn + 4OH^- \qquad E^\circ = -0.909 \text{ V}$$
$$[Sn(OH)_6]^{2-} + 2e^- \longrightarrow [Sn(OH)_4]^{2-} + 2OH^- \qquad E^\circ = -0.96 \text{ V}$$

Thus, tin(II) is a moderately strong reducing agent in alkaline solution, and tin(IV) is a weak oxidizing agent in acidic solution. Aqueous acidic tin(II) solutions are protected from atmospheric oxidation by adding elemental tin. Tin in both oxidation states reacts extensively with water. Both Sn^{2+} and Sn^{4+} oxides and hydroxides are amphoteric.

Tin(IV) compounds exhibit a greater degree of covalent bonding than the corresponding tin(II) compounds. Covalency in the solid compounds of tin is responsible for color (e.g., SnS, brown; SnS_2, yellow; SnI_4, red).

Reactions Important in the Separation and Identification of Sn^{2+} and Sn^{4+}

Group precipitation

$$Sn^{2+} + H_2O_2(aq) + 2H^+ \rightleftharpoons Sn^{4+} + 2H_2O(l) \tag{35.65}$$
$$Sn^{4+} + 2H_2S(aq) \xrightarrow{H^+} SnS_2(s) + 4H^+ \tag{35.66}$$
$$\text{yellow}$$

Dissolution by sulfoamphoterism

$$SnS_2(s) + S^{2-} \rightleftharpoons [SnS_3]^{2-} \tag{35.67}$$
$$\text{yellow}$$

Reprecipitation as sulfide

$$[SnS_3]^{2-} + 2H^+ (dil.) \rightleftharpoons SnS_2(s) + H_2S(g) \tag{35.68}$$

Dissolution as complex ion

$$SnS_2(s) + 4H^+ + 6Cl^- \rightleftharpoons [SnCl_6]^{2-} + 2H_2S(g) \tag{35.69}$$

Confirmatory test

$$3[SnCl_6]^{2-} + 4Al(s) \xrightarrow{HCl} 3Sn(s) + 4Al^{3+} + 18Cl^- \tag{35.70}$$
$$Sn(s) + 2H^+ \longrightarrow Sn^{2+} + H_2(g) \tag{35.71}$$
$$Sn^{2+} + 2Hg^{2+}(xs) + 2Cl^- \longrightarrow Hg_2Cl_2(s) + Sn^{4+} \tag{35.72}$$
$$\text{white}$$

35.13 ANTIMONY(III) ION
Sb^{3+}, SbO^+

Both antimony(III) and antimony(V) are known; however, antimony(V) is too strongly oxidizing to be stable in aqueous solution unless complexed (e.g., as $[Sb(OH)_6]^-$ or $[SbS_4]^{3-}$). Although we commonly describe antimony(III) in acidic solutions as Sb^{3+}, reaction with water to give oxoantimony(III), SbO^+, is pronounced

$$Sb^{3+} + H_2O(l) \rightleftharpoons SbO^+ + 2H^+ \tag{35.73}$$

and upon dilution such solutions precipitate oxoantimony(III) compounds, also known as antimonyl compounds. For example,

$$Sb^{3+} + Cl^- + H_2O(l) \rightleftharpoons \underset{\text{white}}{SbOCl(s)} + 2H^+ \qquad (35.74)$$

The oxide and anhydrous halides of antimony(V) are known, but salts with oxoanions are not known.

Reactions Important in the Separation and Identification of Sb^{3+}

Group precipitation

$$2Sb^{3+} + 3H_2S(aq) \rightleftharpoons \underset{\text{orange}}{Sb_2S_3(s)} + 6H^+ \qquad (35.75)$$

Dissolution by sulfoamphoterism

$$Sb_2S_3(s) + S^{2-} \rightleftharpoons 2[SbS_2]^- \qquad (35.76)$$

Reprecipitation as sulfide

$$2[SbS_2]^- + 2H^+(dil.) \rightleftharpoons Sb_2S_3(s) + H_2S(g) \qquad (35.77)$$

Dissolution as complex ion

$$Sb_2S_3(s) + 6H^+ + 8Cl^- \rightleftharpoons 2[SbCl_4]^- + 3H_2S(aq) \qquad (35.78)$$

Confirmatory test

$$2[SbCl_4]^- + 2S^{2-} + H_2O(l) \rightleftharpoons \underset{\text{orange}}{Sb_2OS_2} + 2H^+ + 8Cl^- \qquad (35.79)$$

35.14 CATION GROUP II ANALYSIS

The flow chart for Cation Group II is given in Figure 35.5. The procedures identified in the flow chart are discussed in the following paragraphs.

Procedure 1 Boiling with hydrogen peroxide oxidizes tin(II) to tin(IV), which forms a much less soluble sulfide than does tin(II). Only small quantities of tin(II) could coexist with mercury(II) without reaction to give Hg_2^{2+} or $Hg(l)$ and tin(IV). Adjustment of the H^+ concentration gives the approximately 0.3 mol/L concentration required to precipitate Group II sulfides without precipitating those of Fe^{2+}, Mn^{2+}, Co^{2+}, Ni^{2+}, or Zn^{2+}. For an unknown sample, the color of the precipitate can indicate the cations that are present or absent. If Group II cations are present, the precipitate will be yellow to brown or black. A light-colored precipitate is sulfur from the oxidation of sulfide ion.

Procedure 2 The separation is based on the acidic properties of Sb_2S_3 and SnS_2, which are amphoteric, as opposed to the very slightly acidic properties of HgS, PbS, and CuS, which are only slightly amphoteric. In the reaction between $SnS_2(s)$ and S^{2-}, for example, $SnS_2(s)$ is a Lewis acid and S^{2-} is a Lewis base. Polysulfide ion, S_x^{2-}, forms by oxidation of sulfide ion under alkaline conditions.

Procedure 3 Both PbS and CuS dissolve as the S^{2-} ions in solution are oxidized to $S(s)$. However, the solubility of HgS is so much less than the solubilities of PbS and CuS that there is not enough sulfide ion from HgS present to be oxidized by the warm (not boiling) approximately 2 M HNO_3 solution that remains at the end of the PbS and CuS dissolution.

Procedure 4 The solubility of HgS is increased by both the more concentrated acids and the removal of mercury(II) ions as the stable complex $[HgCl_4]^{2-}$.

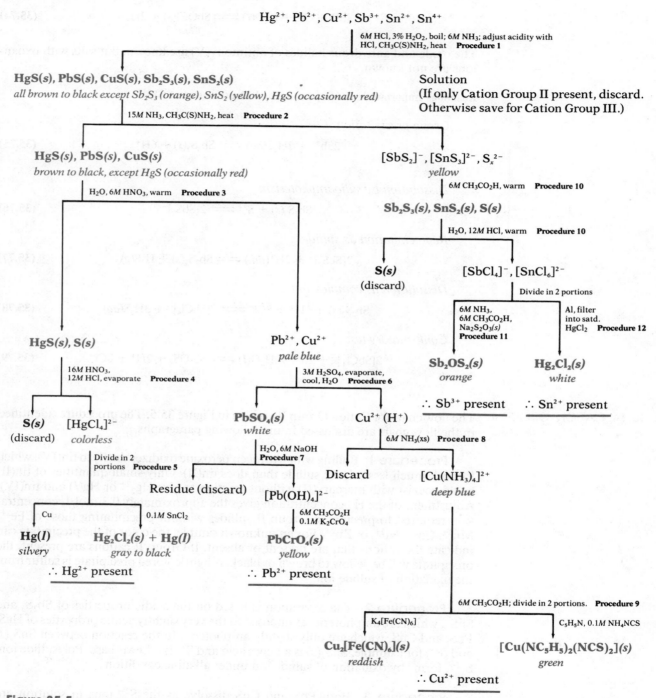

Figure 35.5
Flow Chart for Analysis of Cation Group II The initial solution of ions from separation of Cation Group I is acidic.

Procedure 5 Either test or both tests may be used to confirm the presence of mercury(II). In the reduction with copper, a silvery coating on the surface of the copper indicates the presence of mercury. Reduction by tin(II) is progressive, that is,

$$[HgCl_4]^{2-} \xrightarrow[\text{stoichiometric}]{\text{Sn}^{2+}} \underset{white}{Hg_2Cl_2(s)} \xrightarrow[\text{excess}]{\text{Sn}^{2+}} \underset{black}{Hg(l)} \tag{35.80}$$

Thus confirmation is positive if a white, a gray, or a black insoluble material results.

Procedure 6 Evaporation with H_2SO_4 removes nitric acid, in which $PbSO_4$ is soluble. Complete removal of nitric acid is assured if evaporation is continued until a dense white cloud of SO_3 is produced, showing that nitric acid and water have evaporated, the temperature has risen, and sulfuric acid is decomposing.

$$H_2SO_4(l) \xrightarrow{\Delta} SO_3(g) + H_2O(g) \tag{35.81}$$

(Note that SO_3 and HNO_3 vapors are highly corrosive, and this evaporation must be done under the hood.) Pouring the residue into water displaces the equilibrium:

$$Pb^{2+} + HSO_4^- + H_2O(l) \rightleftharpoons \underset{white}{PbSO_4(s)} + H_3O^+ \tag{35.82}$$

Procedure 7 The amphoteric nature of lead(II) is responsible for its ready solubility in a high concentration of hydroxide ion. The reaction of $[Pb(OH)_4]^{2-}$ with acetic acid yields Pb^{2+} in solution. Lead(II) chromate cannot be precipitated from strongly alkaline solution because the $[Pb^{2+}]$ in equilibrium with the hydroxo complex is lower than the $[Pb^{2+}]$ that would be in equilibrium with the chromate.

Procedure 8 This procedure serves a double purpose: (1) Small quantities of lead(II) ion or mercury(II) ion that remain are removed as hydroxides and discarded and (2) the presence of copper(II) ion is indicated by the color of the $[Cu(NH_3)_4]^{2+}$ complex ion. If a deep blue color results, it is unnecessary to carry out Procedure 9. However, small quantities of copper(II) ion cannot be positively detected in this way.

Procedure 9 Neither of the two confirmatory tests given is effective unless the $[Cu(NH_3)_4]^{2+}$ ion is first converted by acid to the Cu^{2+} ion. Either or both tests can then be used. The complex $[Cu(NC_5H_5)_2(NCS)_2]$ can be extracted into chloroform $(CHCl_3)$ to give a green solution.

Procedure 10 Acetic acid is strong enough to destroy the $[SbS_2]^-$ and $[SnS_3]^{2-}$ ions, but too weak to dissolve the resulting sulfides. Polysulfide ion reacts to give H_2S and elemental sulfur.

$$S_x^{2-} + 2H^+ \longrightarrow H_2S(aq) + (x - 1)S(s) \tag{35.83}$$

Hydrochloric acid redissolves the sulfides of antimony and tin but does not dissolve precipitated sulfur. Heating removes liberated hydrogen sulfide and prevents reprecipitation of the sulfides.

Procedure 11 The thiosulfate ion serves as a source of sulfide ion.

$$S_2O_3^{2-} + H_2O(l) \xrightarrow{H^+} SO_4^{2-} + H_2S(aq) \tag{35.84}$$

If solid $Na_2S_2O_3$ is added to the solution in a small test tube, two layers develop, with orange $Sb_2OS_2(s)$ forming at the interface where the ions come into contact. Tin(IV) does not interfere. A white to yellow precipitate of sulfur always forms, but is hidden if antimony(III) is present.

Procedure 12 Elemental aluminum reduces tin(IV) to elemental tin, which is then oxidized by hydrogen ion to tin(II). The oxidation of Sn(s) by hydrogen ion occurs *only after all of the aluminum has dissolved,* because the Al(s) is oxidized first, taking preference over Sn(s) oxidation. The tin(II) ion reacts as noted in Procedure 5, except that mercury(II) is always in excess and only white $Hg_2Cl_2(s)$ forms. Antimony(III) is reduced by aluminum to elemental antimony, but the latter is not oxidized by hydrogen ion.

EXAMPLE 35.5
Cation Group II

A colorless solution containing ions of Cation Group II in dilute HCl was treated with 3% H_2O_2 and the solution was then boiled. After adjustment of the acidity to about 0.3 M, thioacetamide was added and the solution heated. A black precipitate formed. Addition of concentrated aqueous ammonia and thioacetamide, followed by heating, left a precipitate that was still black (A) and a yellow solution (B). Precipitate A dissolved in warm dilute HNO_3, leaving behind a small amount of a whitish yellow material that proved to be sulfur. The resulting solution gave a white precipitate with dilute H_2SO_4. When solution B was made acidic with dilute acetic acid, a yellow precipitate formed. This precipitate was treated with concentrated HCl to give a solution (C), and the small residue of sulfur was discarded. Addition of powdered aluminum to solution C and filtration into a saturated $HgCl_2$ solution gave a white precipitate. Identify the ions present in the original solution.

The fact that the original solution was colorless shows that Cu^{2+} ion was absent. The solubility of the black precipitate A in warm dilute HNO_3 eliminated Hg^{2+}. The formation of the white precipitate with dilute H_2SO_4 showed Pb^{2+} to be present. The yellow precipitate produced when solution B was treated with acetic acid was probably SnS_2. If Sb^{3+} had been present, the precipitate would have had an orange (Sb_2S_3) color. The white precipitate (Hg_2Cl_2) produced when solution C was reduced by aluminum and added to $HgCl_2$ solution confirmed the presence of tin.

$$Sn^{2+} + 2Hg^{2+} + 2Cl^- \longrightarrow Hg_2Cl_2(s) + Sn^{4+}$$

The ions present were Pb^{2+} and Sn^{2+} or Sn^{4+} (or both of the latter two ions).

EXAMPLE 35.6
Cation Group II

Name a chemical reagent which will
(a) dissolve SnS_2, not but PbS;
(b) oxidize Sn^{2+} to Sn^{4+}, but not Sb^{3+} to Sb^{5+};
(c) distinguish between Hg_2^{2+} and Hg^{2+} ions;
(d) precipitate Pb^{2+}, but not Cu^{2+}.

(a) Sulfide ion, S^{2-}, will convert SnS_2 to the $[SnS_3]^{2-}$ complex, but will not react with PbS.
(b) In an acidic solution, 3% H_2O_2 will oxidize Sn^{2+} to Sn^{4+}, but not Sb^{3+} to Sb^{5+}. The Sb^{5+} ion is a strong oxidizing agent in aqueous solution and is readily reduced to Sb^{3+}.
(c) The Hg_2^{2+} ion is a member of Cation Group I and is precipitated as Hg_2Cl_2 by Cl^- ion. The Hg^{2+} ion forms water-soluble $HgCl_2$ with Cl^-.
(d) Dilute sulfuric acid will precipitate Pb^{2+} as white $PbSO_4$ but will leave Cu^{2+} in solution. Aqueous ammonia in excess also precipitates Pb^{2+}, but forms a complex ion with Cu^{2+}.

$$Pb^{2+} + 2NH_3(aq) + 2H_2O(l) \longrightarrow Pb(OH)_2(s) + 2NH_4^+$$
$$\textit{white}$$
$$Cu^{2+} + 4NH_3(aq) \longrightarrow [Cu(NH_3)_4]^{2+}$$
$$\textit{deep blue}$$

CATION GROUP III (Zn²⁺, Mn²⁺, Fe²⁺ or Fe³⁺, Co²⁺, Ni²⁺, Al³⁺, Cr³⁺)

The ions of Cation Group III are all precipitated by an ammonia/ammonium chloride-buffered hydrogen sulfide solution. This group has been called the basic hydrogen sulfide group, or the aluminum–iron group. The sulfides that did not precipitate in Group II appear here. These sulfides have larger K_{sp} values than the Group II cation sulfides and therefore require for precipitation the higher concentration of S^{2-} available in an alkaline hydrogen sulfide solution (pH about 9). None of the cations that remain form slightly soluble sulfides.

Two of the ions in this group, aluminum(III) and chromium(III), form very slightly soluble hydroxides. The concentration of hydroxide ion available in the group reagent ammonia solution is more than enough to almost completely precipitate these hydroxides. Why do the hydroxides form and not the sulfides? This is another case where the species is formed that is in equilibrium with the smallest cation concentration in solution (Section 34.3). The only remaining cation in our scheme that forms a precipitable hydroxide is magnesium. However, its hydroxide is much more soluble than those of aluminum and chromium, and for precipitation would require a larger concentration of hydroxide ion than is available in the presence of NH_4^+ ion.

With the exception of aluminum, which is a representative metal, and zinc, which has a filled d subshell, the elements in this group are transition metals and their atoms have incompletely filled d subshells. This leads to a variety of oxidation states. Some of the commonly encountered ions and compounds of elements of Cation Group III are listed in Table 35.6.

Table 35.6
Common Ions, Oxides, and Hydroxides of the Cation Group III Elements*

	Oxidation state				
	+2	+3	+4	+6	+7
Al		Al^{3+} Al_2O_3 $Al(OH)_3$ $[Al(OH)_4]^-$			
Cr		Cr^{3+} Cr_2O_3 $[Cr(OH)_4]^-$		CrO_4^{2-} $Cr_2O_7^{2-}$ CrO_3	
Mn	Mn^{2+} $Mn(OH)_2$	$MnO(OH)$	MnO_2	MnO_4^{2-}	MnO_4^-
Fe	Fe^{2+} $Fe(OH)_2$ $[Fe(CN)_6]^{4-}$	Fe^{3+} $Fe(OH)_3$ Fe_2O_3 $[Fe(CN)_6]^{3-}$			
Co	Co^{2+} $Co(OH)_2$ $[Co(NH_3)_6]^{2+}$	$Co(OH)_3$ $[Co(NH_3)_6]^{3+}$ $[Co(NO_2)_6]^{3-}$ $[Co(CN)_6]^{3-}$			
Ni	Ni^{2+} $Ni(OH)_2$ $[Ni(NH_3)_6]^{2+}$	$NiO(OH)$ Ni_2O_3	NiO_2		
Zn	Zn^{2+} $Zn(OH)_2$ $[Zn(NH_3)_4]^{2+}$ $[Zn(OH)_4]^{2-}$				

* Adapted from E. J. King, *Ionic Reactions and Separations* (New York: Harcourt Brace Jovanovich, 1973), p. 165, Table 9.2.

Table 35.7
Colors of Ions of Cation Group III Elements*

$[Al(H_2O)_6]^{3+}$	Colorless	$[Fe(H_2O)_6]^{3+}$	Pale violet
$[Cr(H_2O)_6]^{3+}$	Blue-violet	$[FeOH(H_2O)_5]^{2+}$	Amber
$[CrCl(H_2O)_5]^{2+}$	Green	$[FeCl(H_2O)_5]^{2+}$	Yellow
CrO_4^{2-}	Yellow	$[FeSCN]^{2+}$	Red (blood)
$Cr_2O_7^{2-}$	Orange	$[Mn(H_2O)_6]^{2+}$	Very pale pink
$[Co(H_2O)_6]^{2+}$	Rose red	MnO_4^{2-}	Deep green
$[Co(NH_3)_6]^{2+}$	Tan	MnO_4^{-}	Purple
$[Co(NCS)_4]^{2-}$	Blue-green	$[Ni(H_2O)_6]^{2+}$	Pale green
$[Co(DMG)_3]^{-\dagger}$	Brown	$[Ni(NH_3)_6]^{2+}$	Dark blue
$[Co(NH_3)_5(H_2O)]^{3+}$	Red	$[Zn(H_2O)_4]^{2+}$	Colorless
$[Fe(H_2O)_6]^{2+}$	Pale green	$[Zn(NH_3)_4]^{2+}$	Colorless

* *Source:* T. R. Hogness, W. C. Johnson, and A. R. Armstrong, *Qualitative Analysis and Chemical Equilibrium* (New York: Holt, Rinehart and Winston, 1966, 5th ed.), p. 418, Table 19.2.

† DMG = dimethylglyoxime.

The presence of unpaired electrons leads to a delightful array of colors for ions of the elements in this group (Table 35.7). Most of these elements have a great tendency to form complex ions. Careful observation of the color of the unknown solution and of colors produced along the way can provide useful clues in the analysis of this group. But remember, as we pointed out earlier (Section 35.1), colors can be misleading.

35.15 ZINC(II) ION Zn^{2+}

Zinc has the $+2$ oxidation state in all of its compounds. Elemental zinc is a moderately strong reducing agent. The bonding in zinc compounds is substantially covalent when the compounds are anhydrous, but saltlike if they are hydrated. Zinc hydroxide precipitates from a slightly alkaline solution, but dissolves as the [OH⁻] increases due to the formation of hydroxo complexes. The hydroxide also dissolves in aqueous ammonia by formation of the complex ion, $[Zn(NH_3)_4]^{2+}$. Zinc hydroxide is amphoteric, and in acidic solution yields the Zn^{2+} ion.

The Zn^{2+} ion forms complexes with numerous ligands, but the resulting species have much larger dissociation constants than the corresponding mercury(II) complexes. Association with halide ions is very weak. The species $[Zn(NH_3)_4]^{2+}$ ($K_d = 3.4 \times 10^{-10}$) and $[Zn(CN)_4]^{2-}$ ($K_d = 2.4 \times 10^{-20}$) are more stable than the halide complexes.

Water-soluble zinc salts include the acetate, bromide, chloride, iodide, nitrate, sulfate, and thiocyanate. Common water-insoluble compounds are the carbonate, hydroxide, double potassium hexacyanoferrate(II) ($K_2Zn_3[Fe(CN)_6]_2$) and sulfide (Table 34.3).

Reactions Important in the Separation and Identification of Zn^{2+}

Group precipitation

$$Zn^{2+} + 4NH_3(aq) \underset{}{\overset{\text{excess NH}_3}{\rightleftharpoons}} \underset{colorless}{[Zn(NH_3)_4]^{2+}} \tag{35.85}$$

$$[Zn(NH_3)_4]^{2+} + S^{2-} \rightleftharpoons \underset{white}{ZnS(s)} + 4NH_3(aq) \tag{35.86}$$

Dissolution in acid

$$ZnS(s) + 2H^+ \rightleftharpoons Zn^{2+} + H_2S(aq) \tag{35.87}$$

Complex formation

$$Zn^{2+} + 4OH^- \xrightleftharpoons{\text{excess OH}^-} [Zn(OH)_4]^{2-} \tag{35.88}$$

Confirmatory test

Repetition of the group precipitation reactions to give ZnS(s)

35.16 ALUMINUM(III) ION
Al³⁺

At ordinary temperatures and in aqueous solution, aluminum is stable only in aluminum(III) species. Anhydrous aluminum(III) compounds are generally covalently bonded, but when dissolved in water, they yield the colorless, hydrated aluminum ion. Because of its large charge and comparatively small size, this ion reacts extensively with water. However, only in the presence of such strongly basic anions as CO_3^{2-}, CN^-, or S^{2-} does hydrolysis result in the precipitation of the hydroxide. Aluminum hydroxide is amphoteric and dissolves in alkaline solutions above a pH of about 10 with the formation of $[Al(OH)_4]^-$. When first precipitated, aluminum hydroxide is a gelatinous substance that is hydrated. Upon standing in an open container, it gradually loses its water of hydration. The oxide, Al_2O_3, is obtained by heating the hydroxide.

Only a few complexes of aluminum are important in qualitative analysis, such as $[Al(OH)_4]^-$, $[AlF_6]^{3-}$, and $[Al(H_2O)_6]^{3+}$. Aluminon, the ammonium salt of aurintricarboxylic acid, gives an insoluble red complex with the Al^{3+} ion. This red complex is one of a type of colored complexes called "lakes." The term originated in the dye industry as the name for the colored substance formed by adding a metal hydroxide to an animal or vegetable dye. A lake is a colored precipitate, usually produced by making a solution of a dye and a metal ion alkaline. The ratio of dye to metal ion in the lake is variable. The aluminon lake with Al^{3+} can be represented as shown in the margin with two bonds to aluminum associated with each dye molecule. Ammine complex species of aluminum are unknown, and aqueous ammonia precipitates the hydroxide. The aluminum(III) ion is so weak an oxidizing agent that it gives no significant redox reactions in aqueous solutions.

Water-soluble aluminum(III) compounds include the acetate, bromide, chloride, iodide, nitrate, perchlorate, sulfate, and thiocyanate. Water-insoluble compounds include the hydroxide and phosphate.

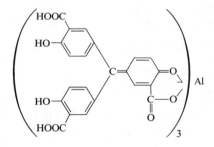

Reactions Important in the Separation and Identification of Al³⁺

Group precipitation

$$Al^{3+} + 3OH^- \rightleftharpoons Al(OH)_3(s) \tag{35.89}$$
$$\text{\textit{white}}$$

Dissolution in acid

$$Al(OH)_3(s) + 3H^+ \rightleftharpoons Al^{3+} + 3H_2O(l) \tag{35.90}$$

Complex ion formation and dissociation

$$Al^{3+} + 4OH^-(xs) \rightleftharpoons [Al(OH)_4]^- \tag{35.91}$$
$$\text{alkaline}$$
$$[Al(OH)_4]^- + 4H^+(xs) \xrightleftharpoons{\text{soln.}} Al^{3+} + 4H_2O(l) \tag{35.92}$$

Confirmatory test

$$Al^{3+} + \text{aluminon} \longrightarrow \text{red precipitate}$$

35.17 CHROMIUM(III) ION
Cr³⁺

Both chromium(II) and chromium(III) can exist as cations. However, standard potential data

$$Cr^{3+} + e^- \longrightarrow Cr^{2+} \qquad\qquad E° = -0.41 \text{ V}$$
$$Cr(OH)_3(s) + e^- \longrightarrow Cr(OH)_2(s) + OH^- \qquad E° = -1.1 \text{ V}$$

indicate clearly that chromium(II) is readily oxidized. Exposure of an aqueous solution of chromium(II) to air is sufficient to oxidize the chromium(II) ion.

Anhydrous chromium(III) compounds are molecular, but the hydrated compounds are saltlike, and aqueous solutions contain hydrated cations. The ion $[Cr(H_2O)_6]^{3+}$ is violet, but in the presence of chloride ion, the green complex ions $[Cr(H_2O)_5Cl]^{2+}$ and $[Cr(H_2O)_4Cl_2]^+$ form. Chromium(III) probably forms more stable complex species than any other common cation except cobalt(III). Many of these complexes are distinctively colored and have very small dissociation constants. Common examples are $[Cr(NH_3)_6]^{3+}$, yellow; $[Cr(NH_3)_5Cl]^{2+}$, red; $[Cr(NH_3)_5(OH)]^{2+}$, pink; and $[Cr(NH_3)_2(SCN)_4]^-$, red.

Water-soluble chromium(III) salts include the acetate, bromide, chloride, iodide, nitrate, perchlorate, and sulfate. Difficultly soluble compounds include the hydroxide and the phosphate. The hydroxide is amphoteric and is readily soluble in strongly alkaline solutions and in acidic solutions. Its solubility is small enough ($K_{sp} = 6 \times 10^{-31}$) that strongly basic anions such as S^{2-} and CO_3^{2-} yield sufficient hydroxide ion concentration by reaction with water to cause precipitation.

$$2Cr^{3+} + 3S^{2-} + 6H_2O(l) \longrightarrow 2Cr(OH)_3(s) + 3H_2S(aq) \qquad \textbf{(35.93)}$$
$$2Cr^{3+} + 3CO_3^{2-} + 3H_2O(l) \longrightarrow 2Cr(OH)_3(s) + 3CO_2(g) \qquad \textbf{(35.94)}$$

Oxidation to chromium(VI) is much easier to carry out in alkaline media than in acidic media, as indicated by standard potential data.

$$Cr_2O_7^{2-} + 14H^+ + 6e^- \longrightarrow 2Cr^{3+} + 7H_2O \qquad E° = +1.33 \text{ V}$$
$$CrO_4^{2-} + 4H_2O + 3e^- \longrightarrow Cr(OH)_3 + 5OH^- \qquad E° = -0.13 \text{ V}$$

The dichromate ($Cr_2O_7^{2-}$) and chromate (CrO_4^{2-}) ions exist in solution in a pH-dependent equilibrium, with dichromate ion more stable in acidic solutions and chromate ions more stable in alkaline solutions (see Figure 31.7).

Reactions Important in the Separation and Identification of Cr³⁺

Group precipitation

$$Cr^{3+} + 3OH^- \rightleftharpoons Cr(OH)_3(s) \qquad \textbf{(35.95)}$$
$$\text{\small gray-green}$$

Dissolution in acid

$$Cr(OH)_3(s) + 3H^+ \longrightarrow Cr^{3+} + 3H_2O(l) \qquad \textbf{(35.96)}$$

Complex ion formation and oxidation

$$Cr^{3+} + 4OH^-(xs) \rightleftharpoons [Cr(OH)_4]^- \qquad \textbf{(35.97)}$$
$$\text{\small dark green}$$

$$2[Cr(OH)_4]^- + 2OH^- + 3H_2O_2(aq) \overset{OH^-}{\rightleftharpoons} 2CrO_4^{2-} + 8H_2O(l) \qquad \textbf{(35.98)}$$
$$\text{\small yellow}$$

$$2CrO_4^{2-} + 2H^+ \rightleftharpoons Cr_2O_7^{2-} + H_2O(l) \qquad \textbf{(35.99)}$$
$$\text{\small orange}$$

Confirmatory tests

$$Ba^{2+} + CrO_4^{2-} \rightleftharpoons BaCrO_4(s) \qquad \textbf{(35.100)}$$
$$\text{\small yellow}$$

$$2BaCrO_4(s) + 2H^+ \rightleftharpoons 2Ba^{2+} + Cr_2O_7^{2-} + H_2O(l) \qquad \textbf{(35.101)}$$
$$Cr_2O_7^{2-} + 4H_2O_2(aq) + 2H^+ \rightleftharpoons 2CrO_5(amyl\ alcohol) + 5H_2O(l) \qquad \textbf{(35.102)}$$
$$\text{\small blue}$$

35.18 MANGANESE(II) ION
Mn^{2+}

Manganese(II) and manganese(III) both exist as cations. From the standard potential data, however, it is clear that manganese(II) is resistant to both oxidation and reduction and is therefore the stable species in aqueous solution.

$$Mn^{2+} + 2e^- \longrightarrow Mn \qquad\qquad E° = -1.185 \text{ V}$$
$$Mn(OH)_2(s) + 2e^- \longrightarrow Mn + 2OH^- \qquad E° = -1.55 \text{ V}$$
$$Mn^{3+} + e^- \longrightarrow Mn^{2+} \qquad\qquad E° = +1.51 \text{ V}$$
$$MnO_2(s) + 4H^+ + 2e^- \longrightarrow Mn^{2+} + 2H_2O \qquad E° = +1.23 \text{ V}$$
$$MnO_4^- + 8H^+ + 5e^- \longrightarrow Mn^{2+} + 4H_2O \qquad E° = +1.51 \text{ V}$$

Manganese(II) ion does not react extensively with water. Its hydroxide is among the more soluble and more basic of the precipitable hydroxides, and in these respects it closely resembles magnesium hydroxide. Manganese(II) ion is pale pink in hydrated salts and in aqueous solution, but the color is so delicate as to be undetectable in dilute solutions. The ion forms few stable complexes. Water-soluble compounds include the acetate, bromide, chloride, iodide, nitrate, sulfate, and thiocyanate. The hydroxide, carbonate, and sulfide are insoluble in water, but the sulfide is soluble in acidic solutions. Manganese(II) compounds resemble magnesium compounds very closely. Like magnesium hydroxide, manganese(II) hydroxide fails to precipitate in the presence of moderate concentrations of ammonium ion.

Oxidation is effected only by powerful oxidants. Conversion to purple MnO$_4^-$ ion by oxidants like sodium bismuthate(V) or lead(IV) oxide is an excellent confirmatory reaction. Oxidation to black, insoluble MnO$_2$ by chlorate ion in nitric acid solution is specific to Mn^{2+} ion and is an excellent means of separating manganese from other species in this cation group. The manganese(II) ion does not produce a flame color.

Reactions Important in the Separation and Identification of Mn^{2+}

Group precipitation

$$Mn^{2+} + NH_3(aq) + NH_4^+ \longrightarrow \text{no observed reaction} \qquad \textbf{(35.103)}$$
$$Mn^{2+} + S^{2-} \rightleftharpoons \underset{pink}{MnS(s)} \qquad \textbf{(35.104)}$$

Dissolution in acid

$$MnS(s) + 2H^+ \longrightarrow Mn^{2+} + H_2S(g)$$

Oxidation and reduction of Mn (Procedures 3 and 4)

$$\underset{pale\ pink}{Mn(OH)_2(s)} + H_2O_2(aq) \longrightarrow \underset{black}{MnO_2(s)} + 2H_2O \qquad \textbf{(35.105)}$$
$$MnO_2(s) + H_2O_2(aq) + 2H^+ \longrightarrow Mn^{2+} + 2H_2O(l) + O_2(g) \qquad \textbf{(35.106)}$$

Oxidation and reduction of Mn (Procedures 5 and 6)

$$3Mn^{2+} + 3H_2O(l) + ClO_3^- \xrightarrow[\Delta]{HNO_3} 3\underset{black}{MnO_2(s)} + 6H^+ + Cl^- \qquad \textbf{(35.107)}$$
$$MnO_2(s) + HNO_2(aq) + H^+ \xrightarrow{\Delta} Mn^{2+} + H_2O(l) + NO_3^- \qquad \textbf{(35.108)}$$

Confirmatory test

$$2Mn^{2+} + 14H^+ + 5NaBiO_3(s) \xrightarrow{HNO_3} 2\underset{\substack{purple\ to\\violet}}{MnO_4^-} + 5Bi^{3+} + 7H_2O(l) + 5Na^+ \qquad \textbf{(35.109)}$$

Both Fe^{2+} and Fe^{3+} cations are encountered in aqueous solution, where they are hydrated, and in a variety of compounds. Pertinent standard potential data are

$$Fe^{2+} + 2e^- \longrightarrow Fe \qquad E° = -0.440 \text{ V}$$
$$Fe(OH)_2 + 2e^- \longrightarrow Fe + 2OH^- \qquad E° = -0.877 \text{ V}$$
$$Fe^{3+} + e^- \longrightarrow Fe^{2+} \qquad E° = +0.771 \text{ V}$$
$$Fe(OH)_3 + e^- \longrightarrow Fe(OH)_2 + OH^- \qquad E° = -0.56 \text{ V}$$

Oxidation of elemental iron to iron(II) and of iron(II) to iron(III) are both easier to carry out under alkaline conditions than under acidic conditions. Elemental iron reacts with H^+ ion to form Fe^{2+} ion, but conversion of Fe^{2+} to Fe^{3+} ion under acidic conditions requires a much stronger oxidizing agent. Because of the reduction of iron(III) by elemental iron,

$$Fe(s) + 2Fe^{3+} \rightleftharpoons 3Fe^{2+} \qquad K = 7.3 \times 10^{39} \qquad (35.110)$$

addition of elemental iron to an iron(II) salt solution prevents the oxidation of the solution by reducing any Fe^{3+} that is formed.

Iron(II) compounds closely resemble those of manganese(II), cobalt(II), and nickel(II). Iron(III) compounds most closely resemble those of aluminum(III) and chromium(III). In aqueous solution, the hydrated iron(II) ion is green, but the color is apparent only in concentrated solution. The hydrated iron(III) ion probably has a faint violet color, but in solution sufficient colloidal iron(III) oxide is formed to impart a yellow or even reddish color. Neither hydroxide dissolves in excess OH^- ion, but the iron(III) compound is more acidic than the iron(II) compound. Both cations form a variety of complexes. Characteristic ones are the anions $[Fe(CN)_6]^{4-}$, hexacyanoferrate(II), which is yellow; $[Fe(CN)_6]^{3-}$, hexacyanoferrate(III), which is red; and $[Fe(NCS)]^{2+}$, which is red. Ammine complexes do not form in aqueous solution.

Water-soluble iron(II) and iron(III) compounds include the acetates, chlorides, bromides, nitrates, perchlorates, and sulfates. Water-insoluble iron(II) and iron(III) compounds include the hydroxides, phosphates, and sulfides. Iron(II) carbonate is insoluble, but, as with the Al^{3+} and Cr^{3+} ions, reaction of CO_3^{2-} ion with Fe^{3+} ion yields the hydroxide as a consequence of hydrolysis. Under acidic conditions, reaction with hydrogen sulfide or thioacetamide reduces iron(III) to iron(II) but does not precipitate iron(II) sulfide. Under alkaline conditions, however, both FeS and Fe_2S_3 are precipitated.

Either the Fe^{2+} or the Fe^{3+} ion or both ions can be present in a sample received for analysis. Any Fe^{2+} is ultimately oxidized in the Cation Group III analysis to Fe^{3+}, which is separated and identified.

Reactions Important in the Separation and Identification of Fe²⁺ and Fe³⁺

Group precipitation

$$Fe^{2+} + 2OH^-(xs) \rightleftharpoons Fe(OH)_2(s) \qquad (35.111)$$
$$\textit{green} \rightarrow \textit{black} \rightarrow \textit{reddish brown}$$
$$\textit{on exposure to air}$$

$$Fe^{3+} + 3OH^-(xs) \rightleftharpoons Fe(OH)_3(s) \qquad (35.112)$$
$$\textit{reddish brown}$$

$$Fe(OH)_2(s) + S^{2-} \xrightarrow{\text{OH}^-} FeS(s) + 2OH^- \qquad (35.113)$$
$$\textit{black}$$

$$2Fe(OH)_3(s) + 3S^{2-} \xrightarrow{\text{OH}^-} Fe_2S_3(s) + 6OH^- \qquad (35.114)$$
$$\textit{black}$$

Dissolution in acid

$$FeS(s) + 2H^+ \longrightarrow Fe^{2+} + H_2S(g) \tag{35.115}$$

$$Fe_2S_3(s) + 4H^+ \longrightarrow 2Fe^{2+} + 2H_2S(g) + S(s) \tag{35.116}$$

Oxidation

$$3Fe^{2+} + NO_3^- + 4H^+ \longrightarrow 3Fe^{3+} + NO(g) + 2H_2O(l) \tag{35.117}$$

Confirmatory tests

$$Fe^{3+} + K^+ + [Fe(CN)_6]^{4-} \rightleftharpoons KFe[Fe(CN)_6](s) \tag{35.118}$$
dark blue

$$Fe^{3+} + NCS^- \rightleftharpoons [Fe(NCS)]^{2+} \tag{35.119}$$
blood red

35.20 COBALT(II) ION
Co^{2+}

Although both cobalt(II) and cobalt(III) are known in many compounds, only cobalt(II) is stable as the simple hydrated ion in aqueous solution. In the presence of many complexing ligands, however, cobalt(II) is readily oxidized to cobalt(III), and the cobalt(III) complexes are among the most stable and most numerous of all known complexes. These relationships are indicated by standard potential data such as

$$
\begin{array}{ll}
Co^{3+} + e^- \longrightarrow Co^{2+} & E^\circ = +1.808 \text{ V} \\
Co(OH)_3(s) + e^- \longrightarrow Co(OH)_2(s) + OH^- & E^\circ = +0.17 \text{ V} \\
[Co(NH_3)_6]^{3+} + e^- \longrightarrow [Co(NH_3)_6]^{2+} & E^\circ = +0.11 \text{ V} \\
[Co(CN)_6]^{3-} + e^- \longrightarrow [Co(CN)_6]^{4-} & E^\circ = -0.83 \text{ V}
\end{array}
$$

Thus, we are concerned primarily with reactions of the Co^{2+} ion, but oxidation in the presence of OH^- ion or complexing groups is readily effected, even by atmospheric oxygen.

In many of its reactions, the rose-colored Co^{2+} ion so closely resembles the pale green Fe^{2+} and bright green Ni^{2+} ions that separations are not easy to carry out. Water-soluble cobalt(II) compounds include the acetate, bromide, chloride, iodide, nitrate, sulfate, and thiocyanate. Water-insoluble compounds include the hydroxide, carbonate, and sulfide. Two forms of the sulfide exist—initial precipitation gives black α-CoS, which is readily soluble in 6 M HCl, but on standing this form converts spontaneously to black β-CoS, which is only very slightly soluble in 6 M HCl. Cobalt(II) ion forms numerous complex ions, for example, $[Co(NH_3)_6]^{2+}$, tan; $[CoCl_4]^{2-}$, blue; and $[Co(CN)_6]^{4-}$, brown. In aqueous solution, these species are generally unstable with respect to either conversion to the hydrated species, for example,

$$[CoCl_4]^{2-} + 6H_2O(l) \rightleftharpoons [Co(H_2O)_6]^{2+} + 4Cl^- \tag{35.120}$$
blue   rose

or oxidation, for example,

$$4[Co(NH_3)_6]^{2+} + 2H_2O(l) + O_2(g) \rightleftharpoons 4[Co(NH_3)_6]^{3+} + 4OH^- \tag{35.121}$$
tan   yellow

Cobalt(II) ion is not extensively hydrolyzed, and its hydroxide is not amphoteric.

Reactions Important in the Separation and Identification of Co²⁺

Group precipitation

$$Co^{2+} + 2OH^-(xs) \rightleftharpoons Co(OH)_2(s) \qquad (35.122)$$
rose   *blue → pink*

$$Co(OH)_2(s) + 6NH_3(aq) \rightleftharpoons [Co(NH_3)_6]^{2+} + 2OH^- \qquad (35.123)$$
tan

$$[Co(NH_3)_6]^{2+} + S^{2-} \rightleftharpoons CoS(s) + 6NH_3(aq) \qquad (35.124)$$

Dissolution by oxidation of S^{2-}

$$3CoS(s) + 8H^+ + 2NO_3^- \longrightarrow 3Co^{2+} + 2NO(g) + 4H_2O(l) + 3S(s) \qquad (35.125)$$

Oxidation

$$4Co(OH)_2(s) + 2H_2O_2(aq) \xrightarrow[\text{neutral soln.}]{\text{alkaline or}} 4Co(OH)_3(s) \qquad (35.126)$$
blue or pink   *black*

Reduction

$$2Co(OH)_3 + 4H^+ + H_2O_2(aq) \xrightarrow[\text{soln.}]{\text{acidic}} 2Co^{2+} + 6H_2O(l) + O_2(g) \qquad (35.127)$$

Confirmatory tests

$$Co^{2+} + 4NCS^- \rightleftharpoons [Co(NCS)_4]^{2-} \text{ (amyl alcohol)} \qquad (35.128)$$
blue to blue-green

$$Co^{2+} + 7KNO_2(s) + 2H^+ \longrightarrow K_3[Co(NO_2)_6](s) + NO(g) + 4K^+ + H_2O(l) \qquad (35.129)$$
bright yellow

35.21 NICKEL(II) ION
Ni²⁺

Only the $+2$ oxidation state of nickel is known in solution. One example of a higher oxidation state is found in the black solid formulated variously as Ni_2O_3, $NiO \cdot NiO_2$, or NiO_2,

$$NiO_2 + H_2O + 2e^- \longrightarrow Ni(OH)_2 + 2OH^- \qquad E° = +0.490 \text{ V}$$

However, in solution in acids NiO_2 gives the Ni^{2+} ion. Except in resistance to oxidation and in color, nickel(II) compounds resemble those of cobalt(II), and most of what was said about cobalt in the preceding section also applies to nickel. A precipitate of nickel(II) sulfide, unlike cobalt(II) sulfide, is readily converted into a brown colloidal sol by sulfide ion in alkaline solutions. A sol of this type is flocculated by adding an ammonium salt and then heating. Nickel(II) complexes closely resemble those of cobalt(II), but do not undergo atmospheric oxidation. A complex characteristic of the nickel(II) ion is the bright red dimethylglyoxime (HDMG) derivative, with two DMG⁻ ions for each Ni²⁺ (see Figure 31.12). Precipitation of this compound from a buffered acetate solution can detect 5×10^{-5} mol Ni²⁺ /L without interference from other common cations.

Reactions Important in the Separation and Identification of Ni²⁺

Group precipitation

$$Ni^{2+} + 2OH^-(xs) \rightleftharpoons Ni(OH)_2(s) \tag{35.130}$$
green   green

$$Ni(OH)_2(s) + 6NH_3(aq) \rightleftharpoons [Ni(NH_3)_6]^{2+} + 2OH^- \tag{35.131}$$
deep blue

$$[Ni(NH_3)_6]^{2+} + S^{2-} \rightleftharpoons NiS(s) + 6NH_3(aq) \tag{35.132}$$
black

Dissolution by oxidation of S²⁻

$$3NiS(s) + 8H^+ + 2NO_3^- \longrightarrow 3Ni^{2+} + 2NO(g) + 4H_2O(l) + 3S(s) \tag{35.133}$$

Dissolution in acid

$$Ni(OH)_2(s) + 2H^+ \longrightarrow Ni^{2+} + 2H_2O(l) \tag{35.134}$$

Confirmatory test

$$Ni^{2+} + 2HDMG(aq) + 2CH_3COO^- \rightleftharpoons Ni(DMG)_2(aq) + 2CH_3COOH(aq) \tag{35.135}$$

35.22 CATION GROUP III ANALYSIS

The flow chart for Cation Group III is given in Figure 35.6 (the initial solution of ions from the separation of Cation Group II is acidic). The procedures identified in this flow chart are discussed in the following paragraphs.

Procedure 1 The centrifugate from Group II is first boiled to remove sulfide ion as hydrogen sulfide so that the rather distinctive reactions with aqueous ammonia can be observed before being obscured by the formation of sulfide precipitates. These reactions are

$$Fe^{2+} \xrightarrow{NH_3} Fe(OH)_2(s) \xrightarrow{NH_3(xs)} \text{no change} \tag{35.136}$$
dark green $\xrightarrow{O_2}$ red brown

$$Co^{2+} \xrightarrow{NH_3} Co(OH)_2(s) \xrightarrow{NH_3(xs)} [Co(NH_3)_6]^{2+} \tag{35.137}$$
blue → pink $\xrightarrow[\text{slowly}]{O_2}$ brown   tan

$$Ni^{2+} \xrightarrow{NH_3} Ni(OH)_2(s) \xrightarrow{NH_3(xs)} [Ni(NH_3)_6]^{2+} \tag{35.138}$$
      pale green   deep blue

$$Zn^{2+} \xrightarrow{NH_3} Zn(OH)_2(s) \xrightarrow{NH_3(xs)} [Zn(NH_3)_4]^{2+} \tag{35.139}$$
      white   colorless

$$Al^{3+} \xrightarrow{NH_3} Al(OH)_3(s) \xrightarrow{NH_3(xs)} \text{no change} \tag{35.140}$$
      white

$$Cr^{3+} \xrightarrow{NH_3} Cr(OH)_3(s) \xrightarrow{NH_3(xs)} \text{no change} \tag{35.141}$$
      gray-green

$Mn(OH)_2$ does not precipitate because the $[OH^-]$ is controlled by the NH_4^+ ion present (see Table 34.7). The precipitation of magnesium hydroxide in this group is also prevented by the presence of ammonium ion (see Table 34.7).

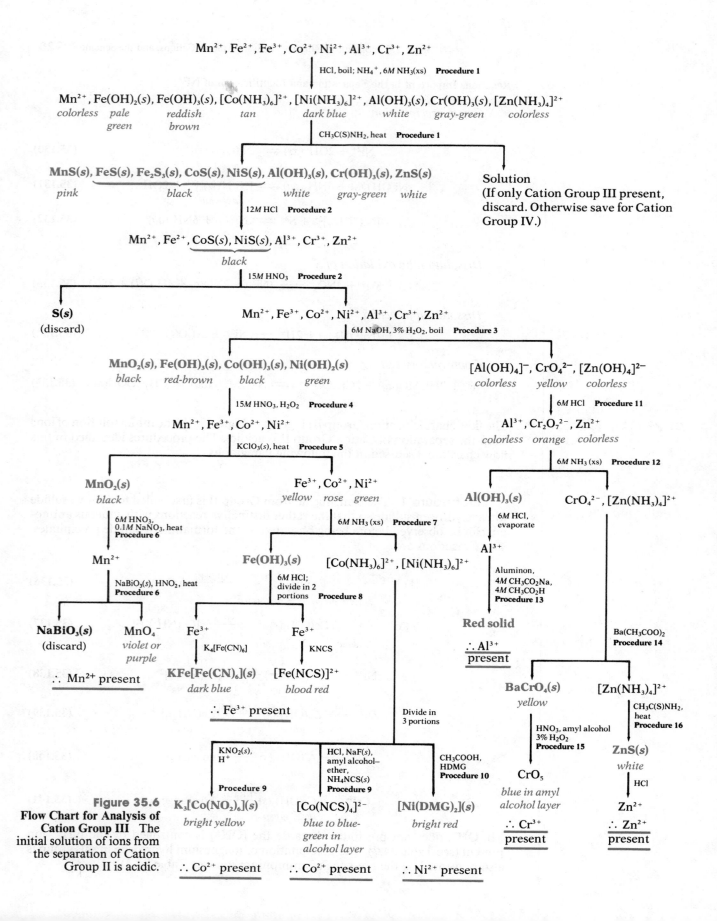

Figure 35.6
Flow Chart for Analysis of Cation Group III The initial solution of ions from the separation of Cation Group II is acidic.

Procedure 2 The β forms of CoS and NiS are insoluble in 12 M hydrochloric acid, but dissolve when nitric acid is added because of the oxidation of sulfide to elemental sulfur. A black residue remaining after addition of hydrochloric acid suggests the presence of Co^{2+} or Ni^{2+} ion or both (unless not all of the FeS or Fe_2S_3 has dissolved).

Procedure 3 This separation is based on the amphoteric properties of aluminum, chromium, and zinc hydroxides as compared to the nonamphoteric properties of the other hydroxides. Slow addition of the sodium hydroxide solution precipitates all of the hydroxides first and then causes dissolution of the amphoteric ones. Careful observations at this point may give useful information when an unknown sample is being analyzed. The appreciable solubility of $Mn(OH)_2$ and the tendency of $[Cr(OH)_4]^-$ ion to yield $Cr(OH)_3(s)$ decrease the effectiveness of a separation involving only sodium hydroxide. Oxidation with hydrogen peroxide yields insoluble, black $MnO_2(s)$ and the stable, distinctively colored CrO_4^{2-} ion. Simultaneously, distinctive red-brown $Fe(OH)_3(s)$ and black $Co(OH)_3(s)$ are produced by oxidation.

Procedure 4 Neither $MnO_2(s)$ nor $Co(OH)_3(s)$ is appreciably soluble in nitric acid. Reduction of each with hydrogen peroxide enhances solubility.

Procedure 5 Oxidation of Mn^{2+} to $MnO_2(s)$ by ClO_3^- ion in acidic solution is a unique reaction and provides adequate proof of the presence of manganese in a sample.

Procedure 6 Manganese(IV) oxide again dissolves in acidic solution only as a consequence of reduction — this time by nitrous acid. Oxidation to intensely colored MnO_4^- ion is also a unique reaction of manganese.

Procedure 7 The separation utilizes the equilibrium

$$NH_3(aq) + H_2O(l) \rightleftharpoons NH_4^+ + OH^- \tag{35.142}$$

The Fe^{3+} ions react with the OH^- ions, and the Co^{2+} and Ni^{2+} ions react with the NH_3 molecules. When the ammonia solution is first added, the hydroxides all precipitate. Excess ammonia takes cobalt(II) and nickel(II) back into solution as complexes.

Procedure 8 Reactions of Fe^{3+} ions with $[Fe(CN)_6]^{4-}$ and NCS^- ions are specific and extremely sensitive. The Fe^{2+} ion gives a bluish white precipitate with the $[Fe(CN)_6]^{4-}$ ion and gives no apparent reaction with the NCS^- ion.

Procedure 9 The Ni^{2+} ion does not interfere with the formation of blue to blue-green $[Co(NCS)_4]^{2-}$, nor with the yellow precipitate of $K_3[Co(NO_2)_6]$. Fluoride ion removes any Fe^{3+} ion as the $[FeF_6]^{3-}$ complex, and thus cuts out interference by the red $[Fe(NCS)]^{2+}$ ion.

Procedure 10 Dimethylglyoxime gives only a brown color with the Co^{2+} ion, so that the Ni^{2+} ion can be detected in the presence of the Co^{2+} ion.

Procedure 11 The addition of HCl neutralizes the hydroxo complexes of Al^{3+} and Zn^{2+}, and converts CrO_4^{2-} to $Cr_2O_7^{2-}$.

Procedure 12 The same principle noted for Procedure 7 applies here — the Al^{3+} ions react with the OH^- ions and the Zn^{2+} ions react with the NH_3 molecules. Making the solution alkaline forms the CrO_4^{2-} ion from $Cr_2O_7^{2-}$.

$$\underset{\text{orange}}{Cr_2O_7^{2-}} + 2OH^- \rightleftharpoons 2\underset{\text{yellow}}{CrO_4^{2-}} + H_2O(l) \tag{35.143}$$

Procedure 13 The formation of the red lake is described in Section 35.16.

Procedure 14 Barium chromate is not as intensely colored as lead(II) chromate (Cation Groups I and II). A yellow acid-soluble precipitate at this point can only be $BaCrO_4$.

Procedure 15 Formation of the blue peroxochromate is inhibited by excess acid, excess peroxide, or heat. Assignment of the formula CrO_5 to this compound is not certain. Even a fleeting blue color confirms the presence of chromium in a sample.

Procedure 16 Zinc sulfide is the only common insoluble white sulfide. It dissolves readily in hydrochloric acid. A faint white cloudiness that is unchanged upon the addition of acid is colloidal sulfur formed by oxidation of sulfide ion by chromate ion.

EXAMPLE 35.7
Cation Group III

A solution was known to contain the following Group III cations: Mn^{2+}, Fe^{3+}, and Al^{3+}. Show by a flow chart how you would separate these ions.

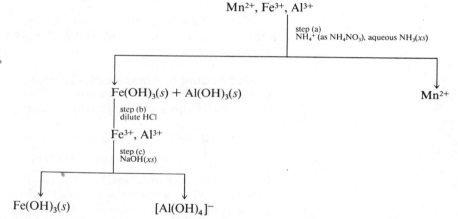

(a) Manganese(II) hydroxide is insoluble, but in the presence of an excess of NH_4^+, insufficient OH^- ion is supplied to precipitate the hydroxide.
(b) The precipitated iron(III) and aluminum hydroxides are redissolved in acidic solution.
(c) Separation of Fe^{3+} and Al^{3+} is effected by taking advantage of the amphoteric nature of $Al(OH)_3$.

EXAMPLE 35.8
Separation of Ions

Show the chemical reagent or reagents that will separate each of the following pairs of ions:

(a) Pb^{2+} and Zn^{2+}; (b) Hg^{2+} and Fe^{2+}; (c) Mn^{2+} and Co^{2+}; (d) Al^{3+} and $Cr_2O_7^{2-}$.

(a) An excess of aqueous ammonia will precipitate Pb^{2+} as $Pb(OH)_2$ and leave Zn^{2+} in solution as the $[Zn(NH_3)_4]^{2+}$ complex.
(b) In a solution 0.3 M in HCl, Hg^{2+} can be precipitated as HgS, while Fe^{2+} remains in solution. (Hg^{2+} is a member of Cation Group II, and Fe^{2+} is a member of Group III.)
(c) In concentrated nitric acid solution, Mn^{2+} is oxidized to black, insoluble MnO_2 by $KClO_3$, and Co^{2+} is unaffected.
(d) Aqueous ammonia will precipitate $Al(OH)_3$ and convert the $Cr_2O_7^{2-}$ (dichromate) ion to CrO_4^{2-} (chromate) ion (Equation 35.143).

**CATION GROUP IV
(Ca²⁺, Ba²⁺)**

35.23 CALCIUM(II) AND
BARIUM(II) IONS
Ca²⁺, Ba²⁺

Calcium and barium are members of the same periodic family. They have very similar chemical properties and, as a result, are difficult to separate. Because there are only two ions in this cation group, and because as individuals they have few distinctive characteristics, we have combined the discussion of the group and the properties of the individual ions.

The chlorides, sulfides, and hydroxides of barium and calcium are so soluble that these ions are in no danger of being separated with the earlier groups. These ions are precipitated as carbonates with an ammonium chloride/ammonia-buffered ammonium carbonate solution. Sometimes this group of cations is known as the ammonium carbonate group or the alkaline earth group.

Strontium, which we have chosen not to include in our analysis scheme, would also, if present, precipitate as a carbonate in this group. Magnesium is the only ion remaining in our scheme that might interfere here. However, precipitation of $MgCO_3$ is suppressed by the presence of ammonium ion (see Table 34.8).

Only the $+2$ oxidation states of calcium and barium are known. Almost without exception, calcium and barium compounds are ionic. Both cations are colorless and give white or colorless salts unless the anion is colored. Water-soluble salts include the acetates, bromides, chlorides, iodides, perchlorates, and nitrates. Slightly soluble compounds include the carbonates, fluorides, oxalates, and sulfates. The equilibrium concentrations of calcium and barium ions in saturated aqueous solutions *decrease* in the following series:

$$CaCrO_4 > Ca(OH)_2(s) > CaSO_4(s) > CaF_2(s) > CaCO_3(s) > CaC_2O_4(s)$$
$$Ba(OH)_2(s) > BaF_2(s) > BaC_2O_4(s)\ BaCO_3(s) > BaSO_4(s) > BaCrO_4(s)$$

An analytically useful difference in solubility lies between the two chromates — barium chromate can be precipitated while calcium ion is left in solution. Almost no complex species of calcium and barium are known.

These ions give distinctively different flame colors. The Ca^{2+} flame is brick red, and the Ba^{2+} flame is yellow-green.

Reactions Important in the Separation and Identification of Ba²⁺ and Ca²⁺

Group precipitation (M = Ba²⁺, Ca²⁺)

$$M^{2+} + CO_3^{2-} \rightleftharpoons MCO_3(s) \tag{35.144}$$

Dissolution by acid (M = Ba²⁺, Ca²⁺)

$$MCO_3(s) + 2H^+ \rightleftharpoons M^{2+} + CO_2(g) + H_2O(l) \tag{35.145}$$

Confirmatory tests

$$Ba^{2+} + CrO_4^{2-} \rightleftharpoons BaCrO_4(s) \tag{35.146}$$
$$Ca^{2+} + C_2O_4^{2-} \rightleftharpoons CaC_2O_4(s) \tag{35.147}$$

35.24 CATION GROUP IV
ANALYSIS

The flow chart for Cation Group IV is given in Figure 35.7. The procedures that are identified on the flow chart are discussed in the following paragraphs.

Procedure 1 This procedure is designed to remove ammonium ion primarily by the following oxidation–reduction:

$$NH_4^+ + NO_3^- \xrightarrow{\Delta} N_2O(g) + 2H_2O(g) \tag{35.148}$$

It may be omitted if ammonium salts are known to be absent. If the solution used is a centrifugate from Cation Group III and is brown due to colloidal NiS, prior neutralization with acetic acid and evaporation to flocculate and remove this material may be necessary.

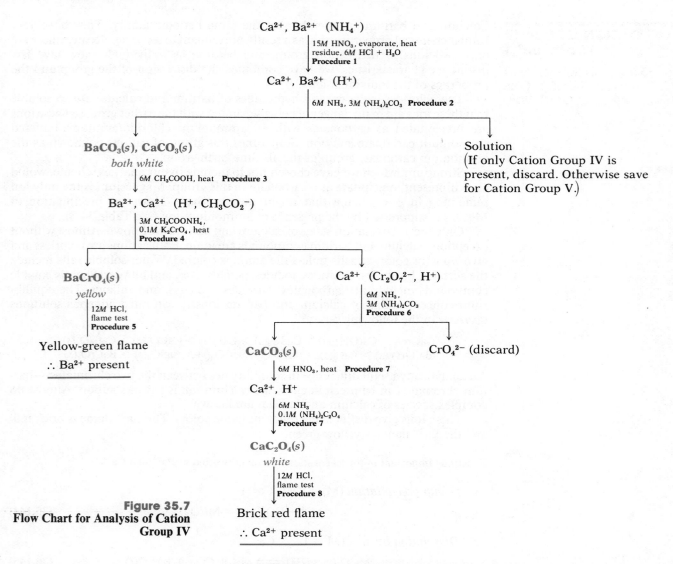

Figure 35.7
Flow Chart for Analysis of Cation Group IV

Procedure 2 The concentration of the NH_4^+ ion is adjusted to prevent precipitation of magnesium carbonate but allow precipitation of the less soluble carbonates of calcium and barium.

Procedure 3 Acetic acid, rather than a strong acid, is used to permit buffering to an optimum pH in the next step.

Procedure 4 Because of the solubility of $BaCrO_4$ at low pH, an acetic acid/acetate ion buffer is used to ensure complete precipitation of the Ba^{2+} ion.

Procedure 5 Although the formation of a yellow precipitate in the preceding step is usually adequate proof of the presence of the Ba^{2+} ion, a flame test is more sensitive and provides confirmation. Flame tests are usually made on chlorides because of their greater volatilities. The only other cation in the series studied here that gives a green flame color is the Cu^{2+} ion. That flame is bright green to blue.

Procedure 6 This step is necessary only to separate Ca^{2+} from the yellow CrO_4^{2-} ion that was introduced in Procedure 4.

Procedure 7 Calcium oxalate, CaC_2O_4, is best precipitated from neutral or slightly alkaline solution.

Procedure 8 Although the formation of a precipitate in the previous step proves the presence of the Ca^{2+} ion, the flame test gives added evidence. This flame color is not particularly distinctive and should be compared with that obtained with pure calcium chloride.

EXAMPLE 35.9
Cation Group IV

The Mg^{2+}, Ca^{2+}, and Ba^{2+} ions exhibit similar behavior in the solubilities of their salts; for example, all three form insoluble carbonates. Explain why Ca^{2+} and Ba^{2+} ions can be separated from Mg^{2+} by means of an appropriate $NH_4Cl-(NH_4)_2CO_3-NH_3$ aqueous mixture.

The compounds $CaCO_3$ and $BaCO_3$ (K_{sp}, 4.7×10^{-9} and 1.6×10^{-9}, respectively) are much less soluble than $MgCO_3$ (K_{sp}, 4.0×10^{-5}). The CO_3^{2-} concentration in solution is controlled with NH_4^+ ion:

$$NH_4^+ + CO_3^{2-} \rightleftharpoons NH_3 + HCO_3^-$$

The additional NH_4^+ ion from the NH_4Cl reduces the CO_3^{2-} ion concentration (common ion effect) to the point where the ion product $[Mg^{2+}][CO_3^{2-}]$ does not exceed the solubility product and Mg^{2+} remains in solution. On the other hand, the CO_3^{2-} concentration remains sufficiently high that the K_{sp} values of $CaCO_3$ and $BaCO_3$ are exceeded by the corresponding ion products.

CATION GROUP V (Mg^{2+}, Na^+, K^+, NH_4^+)

The collection of these somewhat different ions into a single qualitative analysis group is based solely on the sizable solubilities of many of their compounds. Not surprisingly, this is sometimes referred to as the soluble group. Because of the high degree of solubility of most compounds of these cations with simple anions, no single group reagent is available. Ammonium ion is identified in the original unknown sample by production of gaseous ammonia. For the other ions, we resort to unusual reagents for the formation of individually distinctive precipitates. Additional confirmation of the presence of sodium and potassium can be made by their colors in flame tests.

35.25 MAGNESIUM(II) ION Mg^{2+}

Magnesium is a member of Representative Group II, suggesting that the properties of the colorless Mg^{2+} ion closely resemble those of the Ca^{2+} and Ba^{2+} ions. The smaller Mg^{2+} ion is more acidic and more readily complexed than the Ca^{2+} and Ba^{2+} ions. Magnesium sulfate and chromate are very soluble in water, but the hydroxide is slightly soluble except in the presence of the ammonium ion (Section 30.10). The same is true of the carbonate. The double ammonium phosphate, $MgNH_4PO_4 \cdot 6H_2O$, has limited solubility in water. In saturated aqueous solutions, the equilibrium concentration of Mg^{2+} *decreases* in the order

$$MgC_2O_4(s) > MgCO_3(s) > MgF_2(s) > MgHPO_4(s) > Mg(OH)_2(s) > MgNH_4PO_4 \cdot 6H_2O(s)$$

A distinctive reaction of the Mg^{2+} ion is the formation of an intensely blue lake of $Mg(OH)_2$ with *p*-nitrobenzeneazoresorcinol (see margin), known as Magneson I or as S and O reagent (for Suitzu and Okuma, who studied it).

35.26 SODIUM AND POTASSIUM IONS Na^+, K^+

The Na^+ and K^+ cations are derived from closely related Representative Group I metals and have very similar properties. Both are large, colorless ions that cannot be reduced chemically to the free metals in aqueous solution. They are very weak acids and thus do not react appreciably with water. They do not form complexes in

Formula	Solubility (mol/L)	Formula	Solubility (mol/L)
$KClO_4$	0.15	$(NH_4)_2[PtCl_6]$	ca. 0.005
$K[BF_4]$	0.036	$(NH_4)_2Na[Co(NO_2)_6]$	0.001
KIO_4	0.03	$NH_4[B(C_6H_5)_4]$	Very small
$K_2[PtCl_6]$	0.016		
$K_2[SiF_6]$	0.006	Na_2SiF_6	0.03
$K_2Na[Co(NO_2)_6]$	ca. 0.001	$NaZn(UO_2)_3 \cdot$	0.02
$K[B(C_6H_5)_4]$	ca. 10^{-6}	$(CH_3COO)_9 \cdot 9H_2O$	
NH_4ClO_4	2.0	$Na[Sb(OH)_6]$	0.002

aqueous systems. With few exceptions, their compounds dissolve extensively in water. A few compounds have reduced solubilities, as noted in Table 35.8, but precipitation reactions are not particularly sensitive. However, selective precipitations of the two cations can be used for identification. Flame tests (bulky yellow for Na^+, fleeting violet for K^+) are much more sensitive, but contamination by Na^+ ion is so common that its identification in this manner presents problems. The sodium flame color masks that of potassium. The potassium color can best be seen under this circumstance by viewing through a didymium or cobalt glass filter, which absorbs yellow light.

35.27 AMMONIUM ION
NH_4^+

The NH_4^+ ion has roughly the same radius as the K^+ ion (0.143 nm compared to 0.133 nm for K^+) and thus forms many compounds of comparable crystal structures and solubilities (see Table 35.8). For this reason, removal of the NH_4^+ before the K^+ ion can be identified by precipitation is essential. Similarities to the Na^+ ion are much less striking.

All solid ammonium compounds undergo thermal decomposition. If the anion present is nonoxidizing, ammonia is a product, for example,

$$NH_4Cl(s) \xrightarrow{\Delta} NH_3(g) + HCl(g) \tag{35.149}$$

$$(NH_4)_2CO_3(s) \xrightarrow{\Delta} 2NH_3(g) + H_2O(g) + CO_2(g) \tag{35.150}$$

If the anion present is oxidizing, an oxidation product of the NH_4^+ ion results, for example,

$$NH_4NO_3(s) \xrightarrow{\Delta} N_2O(g) + 2H_2O(g) \tag{35.151}$$

$$3(NH_4)_2SO_4(s) \xrightarrow{\Delta} N_2(g) + 4NH_3(g) + 3SO_2(g) + 6H_2O(g) \tag{35.152}$$

$$(NH_4)_2Cr_2O_7(s) \xrightarrow{\Delta} N_2(g) + 4H_2O(g) + Cr_2O_3(s) \tag{35.153}$$

A distinctive reaction of the NH_4^+ ion is that with OH^- ion, which liberates ammonia, particularly when heated.

$$NH_4^+ + OH^- \xrightarrow{\Delta} H_2O(l \text{ or } g) + NH_3(g)$$

Liberated ammonia is identified by odor (with CARE, for ammonia in high concentrations is toxic), by the change in moist red litmus to blue, or by its reaction with an alkaline solution containing the $[HgI_4]^{2-}$ ion (Nessler's reagent).

$$4NH_3 + 2[HgI_4]^{2-} \underset{}{\overset{OH^-}{\rightleftharpoons}} \underset{\substack{\text{yellow to orange} \\ \text{to brown}}}{Hg_2NI(s)} + 7I^- + 3NH_4^+ \tag{35.154}$$

Reactions of Importance in the Separation and Detection of Mg^{2+}, Na^+, K^+, and NH_4^+

Confirmatory tests

$$NH_4^+ + OH^- \xrightarrow{\Delta} NH_3(g) + H_2O(g) \tag{35.155}$$

$$Mg^{2+} + NH_4^+ + PO_4^{3-} + 6H_2O(l) \rightleftharpoons MgNH_4PO_4 \cdot 6H_2O(s) \qquad \textbf{(35.156)}$$

magnesium ammonium phosphate hexahydrate

$$MgNH_4PO_4 \cdot 6H_2O(s) + 2H^+ \rightleftharpoons Mg^{2+} + NH_4^+ + H_2PO_4^- + 6H_2O(l) \quad \textbf{(35.157)}$$

$$Mg^{2+} + \text{Magneson I} \longrightarrow \text{blue lake} \qquad \textbf{(35.158)}$$

$$K^+ + [B(C_6H_5)_4]^- \longrightarrow K[B(C_6H_5)_4](s) \qquad \textbf{(35.159)}$$

potassium tetraphenylborate

$$Na^+ + Zn^{2+} + 3UO_2^{2+} + 9CH_3COO^- + 6H_2O(l) \rightleftharpoons$$
$$NaZn(UO_2)_3(CH_3COO)_9 \cdot 6H_2O(s) \qquad \textbf{(35.160)}$$

sodium zinc uranyl acetate hexahydrate

35.28 CATION GROUP V ANALYSIS   The flow chart for the separation and identification of the cations of this group is given in Figure 35.8. The following procedures are identified in the flow chart.

Procedure 1   Only a sample to which neither aqueous ammonia nor an ammonium salt has been added can be used for this procedure. It is recommended that a portion of the original sample be used directly for this test. Boiling must be avoided because the alkaline solution can spatter on the litmus paper and thus give misleading results. Proper procedure requires that the moist red litmus contact only the vapors released from the warm solution or suspension.

Procedure 2   This procedure is designed only to remove any remaining traces of cations from Groups I to IV which would precipitate in the next step. It may be omitted for samples containing only Group V cations.

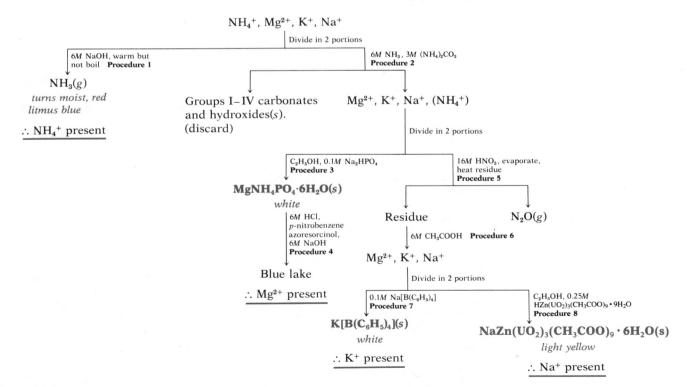

Figure 35.8
Flow Chart for Analysis of Cation Group V

Procedure 3   White crystalline $MgNH_4PO_4 \cdot 6H_2O$ is less soluble in ethanolic solutions than in aqueous systems. Supersaturation sometimes occurs and can be relieved by scratching the inner walls of the reaction vessel with a glass rod.

Procedure 4   A blue solid, a lake, identifies the Mg^{2+} ion. The reagent itself may give a bluish solution when sodium hydroxide is added.

Procedure 5   Complete removal of any NH_4^+ ion present is necessary because, like the K^+ ion, it forms an insoluble tetraphenylborate.

Procedure 6   A weak acid is used to avoid subsequent problems with precipitations. Flame tests for the K^+ and Na^+ ions can be run on the residue before dissolution in acetic acid.

Procedure 7   No other common ion except the NH_4^+ will form a precipitate at this point. A flame test for the K^+ ion can be made for confirmation.

Procedure 8   This reaction is specific for the Na^+ ion. Adding ethanol improves its sensitivity. Again a flame test can be made.

THOUGHTS ON CHEMISTRY

The Epigrams of Karl Remigius Fresenius

THE EPIGRAMS OF REMIGIUS FRESENIUS

(Karl Remigius Fresenius loved to take walks. He built a long covered gallery beside his house and walked there when the weather was bad. Thinking as he walked, he occasionally stopped to write an epigram—a distillation of his philosophy of life—on the wall. Some of these epigrams are given here in both the original German and in a free translation.)

Forsche gründlich,
Rede wahr,
Schreibe bündig,
Lehre klar.

Research thoroughly,
speak truthfully,
write concisely,
teach clearly.

Nach goldner Frucht vom Baum
    des Lebens
Greift der Müssiggang vergebens.

The golden fruit from the tree of
    life
will not be reached by laziness.

Musst Du Dich in der Jugend
    müh'n,
So wolle nicht darüber klagen,
Nur Bäumme, die im Lenze blühn,
Können im Herbste Früchte tragen.

Do not complain if you have to
struggle in your youth;
only trees that bloom in spring
will bear fruit in fall.

Wünschest Du ein froh Geschick,
Nütze auch den Augenblick.

To lead a happy life
take advantage of each moment.

Glauben was man hofft,
Führt ze Täuschung oft.

To believe what one expects
often leads to disappointment.

Legst Du Abends Dich zur Ruh',
Mazh' das Sorgenkästchen zu.
Drückst Du noch so fest darauf,
Morgens springt von selbst es auf.

When you go to bed at night,
close your little box of sorrow,
but even if you lock it tight,
'twill open up again tomorrow.

The German quoted from Ralph E. Oesper, "The Epigrams of Remigius Fresenius," *J. Chem. Educ.* **14**, 313 (1937). English translation by Winfried J. Fremuth.

QUESTIONS

Anion Analysis

35.1 How can an anion analysis be performed on an unknown that is insoluble in water? Write chemical equations for the dissolution process.

35.2 Identify which of the anions in the schemes are (a) strong Brønsted-Lowry bases, (b) weak Brønsted-Lowry bases, (c) strong oxidizing agents, and (d) reducing agents.

35.3 Briefly describe the preliminary tests used to obtain information about an anion unknown. Identify which anions fall into the various groups based on their reactions in these tests.

35.4 The presence of the oxidizing anions (NO_3^-, NO_2^-, and CrO_4^{2-}) can be detected using aqueous KI instead of $MnCl_2$. Write the equations representing reactions of these ions with I^- in aqueous acidic solution.

35.5 A mixture is known to contain one or more of the halide ions (I^-, Br^-, and Cl^-). Describe how you could test for each of these ions and write equations for the various reactions used.

35.6 A student wishes to determine whether a solution known to contain Br^- also contains I^-. A friend tells the student that this can be done simply by acidifying the solution with dilute sulfuric acid, adding $NaNO_2$ and CCl_4, and shaking the mixture. From what you can find out in the text about the redox chemistry of I^-, Br^-, and NO_2^-, do you think the friend's suggestion is a reasonable one? Defend your answer. $E° = 1.00$ V for HNO_2/NO.

35.7 Why will anion unknowns which give strong positive tests for NO_2^- often give faint tests for NO_3^-, and those containing S^{2-} or SO_3^{2-} give faint tests for SO_4^{2-}?

35.8 In each pair of ions, the second interferes with the detection of the first: (a) NO_3^- and NO_2^- and (b) X^- (Cl^-, Br^-, or I^-) and S^{2-}. In each case, give the reason for the interference and tell how the offending ion may be removed. Include pertinent equations.

35.9 A white substance is a mixture of salts containing either Na^+ or K^+ as the cation. Among the anions possibly present are CO_3^{2-}, PO_4^{3-}, NO_3^-, S^{2-}, and SO_3^{2-}. Describe how you would determine which of these anions are actually present in the salt mixture and write equations for the reactions that confirm the presence of the ions.

35.10 Identify the anion(s) present in an unknown from the following observations made on a Na_2CO_3 solution: (a) A dark color did not form when the solution was acidified and tested with $MnCl_2$. (b) A dark blue precipitate formed when the solution was acidified and tested with a mixture of $FeCl_3$ and $K_3Fe(CN)_6$. (c) Bubbles of an odorless gas were observed when $HClO_4$ was added to the original solid sample. (d) A light-colored precipitate was produced when $AgNO_3$ was added to an acidic solution. (e) After separation of the silver precipitate in Step (d), negative results were obtained for the anions in Groups III and IV. (f) A dark odoriferous gas, in addition to the gas described in Step (c), was generated by the addition of H_2SO_4 to the original solid sample. (g) The sample gave a white precipi-

tate when tested with Zn, H_2O_2, H_2SO_4, and $Ba(OH)_2$. (h) The solution was acidified and a violet color was observed in a CCl_4 layer after the addition of chlorine water. (i) The solution was acidified and a red-brown color was observed in the CCl_4 layer after the addition of a considerable amount of chlorine water. (j) The tests for Cl^- were negative.

35.11 Identify the anion(s) present in an unknown from the following observations made on a colorless, water-soluble sample: (a) A dark color was formed when the solution was acidified and tested with $MnCl_2$. (b) A blue precipitate did not form when the solution was acidified and tested with a mixture of $FeCl_3$ and $K_3Fe(CN)_6$. (c) No noticeable gases were generated upon addition of $HClO_4$ to the original solid sample. (d) A white precipitate formed when the acidic solution was treated with $AgNO_3$. (e) After separation of the silver precipitate, a second silver precipitate formed after the solution was made slightly alkaline with aqueous NH_3. (f) A colorless odoriferous gas was generated upon addition of H_2SO_4 to the original solid sample. (g) Addition of chlorine water to an acidified solution of the sample did not produce a violet or red-brown color in a CCl_4 layer. (h) The white precipitate produced in Step (d) dissolved upon addition of NH_3. (i) A precipitate did not form when the unknown was tested with ammonium molybdate. (j) A brown ring test was positive. (k) A white precipitate formed upon addition of $BaCl_2$ to the acidic solution.

35.12 Tell what conclusions can be drawn from the result of parts (a) through (f) regarding anions not present, anions possibly present, and anions definitely present in the original solid. (a) A white solid was partially soluble in water and the resulting solution was neutral to litmus paper. The original solid gave no gaseous product when treated with dilute $HClO_4$. A small amount of the solid was boiled with saturated Na_2CO_3 solution and the resulting mixture was filtered. Portions of the filtrate were treated with various reagents with the following results: (b) Addition to a dilute solution of $MnCl_2$ in concentrated HCl gave no color change. (c) Addition to an aqueous mixture of $FeCl_3$, $K_3[Fe(CN)_6]$, and HCl resulted in the formation of a deep blue precipitate. (d) Acidification with dilute $HClO_4$, followed by warming of the solution and the addition of $AgNO_3$, yielded a pale yellow precipitate. (e) Acidification with dilute HCl, addition of CCl_4, and dropwise addition of Cl_2 water accompanied by vigorous shaking produced a violet color in the CCl_4 (lower) layer. (f) Acidification with a slight excess of dilute HCl followed by addition of dilute $BaCl_2$ solution gave a white precipitate.

Cation Group I (Hg_2^{2+}, Pb^{2+}, Ag^+)

35.13 Why must a large excess of Cl^- be avoided during the precipitation of the cations in Group I? Write equations illustrating (a) the precipitation and (b) what happens if the Cl^- concentration is too high.

35.14 If the concentration of Ag^+ in equilibrium with $AgCl(s)$ is larger than the concentration of Ag^+ in equilibrium with $[Ag(NH_3)_2]^+$, why does AgCl reprecipitate upon the addition of HNO_3 to a solution containing the ammine complex?

35.15 An unknown solution contained only Pb^{2+}, Ag^+, or Hg_2^{2+}. A student decided to use only one confirmatory test to identify the ion present — namely the addition of K_2CrO_4 to the unknown solution. Look up the colors of the chromate precipitates of Pb^{2+}, Ag^+, and Hg_2^{2+} and comment on this procedure. A second student decided to use an excess of NaOH. Explain the expected observations.

Cation Group II (Hg^{2+}, Pb^{2+}, Cu^{2+}, Sn^{2+} or Sn^{4+}, Sb^{3+} or SbO^+)

35.16 Why does Pb^{2+} appear in both Cation Groups I and II? Is this the same reason that mercury appears in both of these groups? Explain.

35.17 If a light-colored sulfide precipitate is obtained for Cation Group II, what cations are probably not present in the sample?

35.18 Write equations illustrating the amphoteric behavior of $Sn(OH)_2$ with HCl and NaOH.

35.19 Why will CuS dissolve in HNO_3, but not in HCl?

35.20 A student felt that her separation of Hg^{2+} from Pb^{2+} and Cu^{2+} by treatment of the sulfides with warm HNO_3 might have been in error and wanted to run a one-step test on the filtrate as a check. She added excess $NH_3(aq)$ and found that a white precipitate and blue solution formed. Were Pb^{2+} and Cu^{2+} in the filtrate?

35.21 An unknown was found to contain either Sn^{2+} or Sn^{4+}. A student decided to precipitate the sulfide using $Na_2S(aq)$ and determine the oxidation state by the color of the sulfide. How would this test have distinguished between the two ions?

35.22 Which cations in Group II would you report for an unknown that was analyzed as follows? (a) Part of the sulfide precipitate dissolved in ammoniacal thioacetamide, leaving a dark precipitate A and a supernatant B. (An ammoniacal solution is one that contains NH_3.) (b) The supernatant B was treated with acetic acid and concentrated HCl and then divided into two portions. (c) One portion gave an orange precipitate with NH_3, acetic acid, and $Na_2S_2O_3$. The other portion did not form a precipitate with Al and $HgCl_2$. (d) Precipitate A was dissolved in HNO_3, to give solution C. (e) Solution C did not form a precipitate upon addition of H_2SO_4. (f) Solution C formed a deep blue complex with NH_3. After acidification with acetic acid, the solution was divided into two portions. A red precipitate formed in one portion when treated with $K_4[Fe(CN)_6]$ and a green precipitate formed in the other portion when treated with C_5H_5N and NH_4NCS.

Cation Group III (Zn^{2+}, Mn^{2+}, Fe^{2+} or Fe^{3+}, Co^{2+}, Ni^{2+}, Al^{3+}, Cr^{3+})

35.23 Using the flow chart for Cation Group III, identify those steps in which oxidation–reduction reactions occur and write the overall net ionic equation for each case.

35.24 Which reagent(s), NaOH, $NH_3(aq)$, or $(NH_4)_2S$, would you use to distinguish between (a) Co^{2+} and Ni^{2+}, (b) Zn^{2+} and Fe^{2+}, (c) Fe^{2+} and Ni^{2+}, and (d) Mn^{2+} and Fe^{3+}?

35.25 Why does aluminum hydroxide readily dissolve in concentrated NaOH? Why is it insoluble in concentrated $NH_3(aq)$?

35.26 A Group III unknown formed a dark precipitate A upon the addition of NaOH and H_2O_2. The colorless supernatant B was treated with HCl and then NH_3, with no effect. When the supernatant B was heated with thioacetamide, no precipitate formed. Precipitate A dissolved in HNO_3 and H_2O_2 to form a colored solution C. No precipitate formed when $KClO_3$ was added to C and the mixture heated. Solution C was treated with NH_3, without apparent effect. What ions are possibly present? What additional tests would you like to perform on this sample?

Cation Groups IV and V (Ca^{2+}, Ba^{2+} and Mg^{2+}, Na^+, K^+, NH_4^+)

35.27 Which reagent can be used to distinguish Ca^{2+} from Ba^{2+}: Na_2CO_3, K_2CrO_4, $NH_3(aq)$, NaOH, or $(NH_4)_2C_2O_4$?

35.28 Why must any NH_4^+ in an unknown be removed before performing the confirmation test for K^+? How is this done? Why should the test for NH_4^+ be performed on the original sample?

35.29 What reagent is specific only for Na^+ among the Group V cations?

35.30 A student decided to determine the presence of NH_4^+ in an acidic solution by adding Cu^{2+} and observing whether or not the dark blue copper–ammonia complex formed. The results were negative. Did this experiment prove the absence of the ammonium ion? Explain.

Additional Questions

35.31 Write chemical formulas for the following substances: (a) mercury(I) chloride, (b) diamminesilver(I) ion, (c) antimony(III) sulfide, (d) tetrachlorohydrargyrate(II) ion (or tetrachloromercurate(II) ion), (e) manganese(IV) oxide, (f) chromate ion, (g) sodium nitrite, (h) potassium hexacyanoferrate(II), (i) ammonium carbonate, (j) thioacetamide, (k) hydrosulfuric acid.

35.32 Write names for the following substances: (a) $PbCl_2$, (b) SnS_2, (c) $[SnS_3]^{2-}$, (d) $[Cu(NH_3)_4]^{2+}$, (e) $PbCrO_4$, (f) NH_4NCS, (g) $Cr_2O_7^{2-}$, (h) $[Zn(OH)_4]^{2-}$, (i) $KFe[Fe(CN)_6]$, (j) $NaBiO_3$, (k) $(NH_4)_2C_2O_4$, (l) $MgNH_4PO_4 \cdot 6H_2O$.

35.33 Which anions cannot be present in a water-soluble sample known to contain Cu^{2+} and Zn^{2+}? (Hint: Look up the solubilities of the various compounds containing the anions considered in the scheme.)

35.34 A student analyzed a solid sample and reported that it contained Hg_2^{2+} and S^{2-}. Are these results reasonable? Explain.

35.35 Write the net ionic equations describing (a) Al^{3+} reacting with excess NaOH to give $[Al(OH)_4]^-$; (b) Ni^{2+} reacting with NH_3 to produce the nickel–ammonia complex, which, in turn, is converted to Ni^{2+} by acetic acid, and then the Ni^{2+} reacting with HDMG to form the bright red precipitate; (c) ZnS(s) reacting with HCl; (d) Ca^{2+} reacting with $(NH_4)_2CO_3$ to give $CaCO_3(s)$; (e) K^+ reacting with $Na[B(C_6H_5)_4]$ to give a white precipitate; (f) $Hg_2Cl_2(s)$ reacting with excess $NH_3(aq)$; (g) $Sb_2S_3(s)$ reacting with S^{2-} to give $[SbS_2]^-$, which in turn, reacts with acetic acid to give $Sb_2S_3(s)$.

35.36 Why do certain metallic ions give flame tests, whereas others do not?

35.37 What is meant by a "lake"? Cite two cases in which lakes are used in the confirmatory tests for the scheme presented in this book.

35.38 You are given a sample of a solder which could contain one or more of the elements Pb, Sn, Cu, and Ag. Devise a flow chart to determine which metals are present. The first step will be the dissolving of the metal in aqua regia.

35.39 A sample of German silver was dissolved in acid and subjected to analysis. The following results were obtained: (a) No precipitate was formed in the presence of Cl^-. (b) A dark precipitate A was formed with acidic thioacetamide, leaving supernatant B. (c) A dark precipitate C was formed from B in ammoniacal thioacetamide. (d) Subsequent treatment of the supernatant from Step (c) indicated no other ions present. (e) Treatment of A with ammoniacal thioacetamide produced no change. (f) Precipitate A dissolved in HNO_3 to form solution D. (g) Treatment of D with H_2SO_4 had no effect, but addition of NH_3 produced a bluish solution E. (h) Solution E was separated into two portions. Treatment of one portion with H^+ and $K_4[Fe(CN)_6]$ gave a reddish solid and treatment of the other portion with C_5H_5N and NH_4NCS gave a green precipitate. (i) Treatment of C with HCl caused part of the precipitate to dissolve and the remainder dissolved in HNO_3, forming solution F. (j) Addition of NaOH and H_2O_2 to F gave a green precipitate G and a colorless solution H. (k) Precipitate G dissolved in HNO_3 and H_2O_2. The resulting solution did not form a precipitate with $KClO_3$ nor with NH_3. Division of the solution into three portions and treatment of one portion with HDMG gave a red solid. No color was formed in the other portions upon addition of HCl, NaF, amyl alcohol, ether, and NH_4NCS or upon the addition of NaOH, CH_3COOH and KNO_2. (l) Solution H was acidified and NH_3 was added without effect. A white precipitate was formed upon heating the solution with thioacetamide. The precipitate dissolved when HCl was added. Identify the metals that make up this alloy.

35.40 Identify the metals found in Wood's metal (which is used in automatic sprinkler systems, electric fuses, and safety valves for steam boilers) from the following information: (a) A sample of the metal was dissolved in acid to produce solution A. (b) A white precipitate B was formed upon addition of HCl to A, leaving supernatant C. (c) A dark precipitate D was formed upon treatment of C with HCl and a source of S^{2-}, leaving solution E. (d) Treatment of E with the NH_4Cl–NH_3 buffer and a source of S^{2-} gave no precipitate. (e) No precipitate formed upon the addition of $(NH_4)_2CO_3$ to the buffered solution prepared in Step (d). (f) Flame tests and other evidence indicated that ions from Group V were absent. (g) Precipitate B dissolved in hot water. Half of the resulting solution gave a yellow precipitate upon addition of K_2CrO_4 and the other half gave a white precipitate upon addition of H_2SO_4. (h) Precipitate D was treated with additional S^{2-}, and a new precipitate F was formed in contact with a solution, G. (i) Addition of HCl to G gave a precipitate. The precipitate dissolved in excess HCl. (j) The

solution of G found in Step (i) only gave a gray precipitate after reduction with aluminum and addition of $HgCl_2$. (k) Precipitate F dissolved in HNO_3. A white precipitate H was separated from the solution I upon addition of H_2SO_4. (l) Further analysis of the precipitate H showed it to be soluble in NaOH. A yellow precipitate formed upon acidification of the solution with acetic acid and addition of K_2CrO_4. (m) A white precipitate J formed upon addition of NH_3 to solution I, indicating the presence of Bi^{3+}. (n) A colorless solution K remained after removal of J. (o) A yellow precipitate formed upon addition of CN^- and S^{2-} to solution K, indicating the presence of Cd^{2+}.

35.41* In an extended scheme of cation analysis, additional ions could be separated in the groups considered in the scheme presented in this book. Look up solubility data for the compounds such as chlorides and sulfides of the following elements and predict into which cation group each would belong: As, Au, Be, Cs, Li, Mo, Pt, Rb, Se, Sr, Te, Ti, Tl, U, V, Zr, and the lanthanides.

Answers to Selected Questions

35.4 $6I^- + 2NO_3^- + 8H^+ \rightarrow 3I_2 + 2NO + 4H_2O$, $2I^- + 2HNO_2 + 2H^+ \rightarrow I_2 + 2NO + 2H_2O$, $18I^- + Cr_2O_7^{2-} + 14H^+ \rightarrow 3I_2 + 2[CrI_6]^{3-} + 7H_2O$

35.6 $E° = -0.09$ V (nonspontaneous at standard state conditions) for $2Br^- + 2HNO_2 + 2H^+ \rightarrow Br_2 + 2NO + 2H_2O$, $E° = 0.46$ V (spontaneous at standard state conditions) for $2I^- + 2HNO_2 + 2H^+ \rightarrow I_2 + 2NO + 2H_2O$

35.10 Br^-, I^-, CO_3^{2-}

35.15 $PbCrO_4$ is yellow, Ag_2CrO_4 is red-brown, Hg_2CrO_4 is red, procedure should work; $[Pb(OH)_4]^{2-}$ is colorless, Ag_2O is brown, Hg_2O is black, procedure should work.

35.21 SnS is brown, SnS_2 is yellow.

35.22 Sb^{3+}, Cu^{2+}

35.24 (a) NaOH gives pink $Co(OH)_2$ and green $Ni(OH)_2$ or NH_3 gives tan $[Co(NH_3)_6]^{2+}$ and blue $[Ni(NH_3)_6]^{2+}$, (b) NaOH gives colorless $[Zn(OH)_4]^{2-}$ and green $Fe(OH)_2$ or NH_3 gives colorless $[Zn(NH_3)_4]^{2+}$ and green $Fe(OH)_2$ or S^{2-} gives white ZnS and black FeS, (c) NH_3 gives green $Fe(OH)_2$ and blue $[Ni(NH_3)_6]^{2+}$, (d) NaOH gives pink $Mn(OH)_2$ and red-brown $Fe(OH)_3$ or NH_3 gives red-brown $Fe(OH)_3$ and no reaction with Mn^{2+} or S^{2-} gives pink MnS and black Fe_2S_3.

35.26 Co^{2+} and Ni^{2+}; split solution C into three portions —treat one with HCl, NaF(s), amyl alcohol–ether, $NH_4NCS(s)$ to test for Co^{2+}, treat one with NaOH, CH_3COOH, $KNO_2(s)$ to test for Co^{2+}, and treat one with CH_3COOH and HDMG to test for Ni^{2+}

35.33 S^{2-}, CO_3^{2-}, PO_4^{3-}

35.39 Cu, Zn, Ni

35.41 Cation Group I: Tl; Cation Group II: As, Au, Mo, Pt, Se, Te; Cation Group III: Be, Ti, U, V, Zr, lanthanides; Cation Group IV: Sr; Cation Group V: Cs, Li, Rb

LOGARITHMS AND GRAPHS

I.A LOGARITHMS

Logarithms and antilogarithms are used in chemistry when working with pH and with many equations in kinetics, nuclear chemistry, thermodynamics, and electrochemistry. It is important that you know how to work with logarithms and antilogarithms even though your electronic calculator may make finding the values of these mathematical functions quite easy.

There are several commonly used "bases" such as 2, 10, 12, and e ($e = 2.718281828459$) for expressing logarithms. Logarithms to the base 10, called "common logarithms" and abbreviated "log," are used throughout this book. Sometimes the mathematics by which an equation is derived gives the equation in the form of a logarithm to the base e. Such a logarithm is called a "natural logarithm" and abbreviated "ln." In equations we can replace "ln x" by "(2.303)log x" because

$$\ln x = (2.302585092994)\log x$$

The *common logarithm* of a number is the power to which 10 must be raised to get that number

$$a = 10^b$$

the logarithm of a
number

For example, we can easily see that the logarithm of 10 is 1 because $10 = 10^1$, and the logarithm of 100 is 2 because $100 = 10^2$. Similarly, the logarithm of 50.00 is 1.6690 because $50.00 = 10^{1.6990}$.

The usual way to express the logarithm of a number is to write

$$\log a = b$$

read as "the logarithm of a equals b"

Thus,

$$\log 10 = 1 \quad \log 100 = 2 \quad \log 50.00 = 1.6990$$

Logarithms can be used to multiply and divide numbers, to raise a number to some power, and to find the nth root of a number. Because logarithms are exponents, the rules for exponents are followed in performing these operations. In each case, the desired calculation is restated in logarithmic form as follows:

desired calculation	logarithmic form
$(a)(b)$	$\log(a)(b) = \log a + \log b$
a/b	$\log(a/b) = \log a - \log b$
a^n	$\log(a^n) = n \log a$
$\sqrt[n]{a}$	$\log(\sqrt[n]{a}) = (\log a)/n$

The logarithms of the numbers are found, the calculation is performed using the logarithms, and the value of the answer is found by taking the antilogarithm of the result of the calculation.

The logarithm of any number contains two parts called the "characteristic" and the "mantissa." The *characteristic*, the number to the left of the decimal point in the logarithm, is based upon the location of the decimal point in the original number. The *mantissa*, the number to the right of the decimal point in the logarithm, is based upon the exact value of the digits in the original number. For example,

$$\log 50.00 = 1.6990 \quad \log 500. = 2.699$$

characteristic   mantissa   characteristic   mantissa

The mantissa should be given to the same number of significant digits as the original number, as shown above. In using a calculator to find a logarithm, keep this rule in mind:

$$\log 959 = 2.982 \quad (\text{not } 2.981818607)$$

When the logarithm of a number appears in an equation and is to be treated like any other factor in the calculation, the usual rules of significant figures apply, once the logarithm has been supplied with the correct number of digits. For example,

$$\log z = \frac{(96.5)(0.8401)}{(8.314)} = 9.75$$
$$z = 5.6 \times 10^9$$

and also,

$$x = (0.8401) - \frac{(8.314)(2.303)}{(96.5)} \log(7.6 \times 10^3)$$
$$= (0.8401) - \frac{(8.314)(2.303)(3.88)}{(96.5)}$$
$$= (0.8401) - (0.770) = 0.070$$

In the absence of a calculator, logarithms are found by using a log table as described below. The logarithms of numbers with up to four significant digits are found from a four-place common logarithm table like Table I.1. Note that logarithms of negative numbers are undefined because there is no power to which 10 can be raised that will generate a negative number.

1. *Finding the logarithm of a number between 1 and 10* The logarithm of 1 is zero ($10^0 = 1$), and the logarithm of 10 is one ($10^1 = 10$). The logarithm of a number between 1 and 10 is between zero and one. In other words, the characteristic is 0 and the logarithm is the same as the mantissa. A table of four-place common logarithms (see Table I.1) is used to find the mantissa as follows:

(a) Move downward in the column labeled "number" until you reach the row containing the first two digits of the original number.

(b) Move across the row until you reach the column containing the third digit of the original number. Write down the four-digit number that appears in the table in that column.

TABLE I.1 **Four-Place Common Logarithms**

Number	0	1	2	3	4	5	6	7	8	9	1	2	3	4	5	6	7	8	9
											Proportional Parts								
10	0000	0043	0086	0128	0170	0212	0253	0294	0334	0374	4	8	12	17	21	25	29	33	37
11	0414	0453	0492	0531	0569	0607	0645	0682	0719	0755	4	8	11	15	19	23	26	30	34
12	0792	0828	0864	0899	0934	0969	1004	1038	1072	1106	3	7	10	14	17	21	24	28	31
13	1139	1173	1206	1239	1271	1303	1335	1367	1399	1430	3	6	10	13	16	19	23	26	29
14	1461	1492	1523	1553	1584	1614	1644	1673	1703	1732	3	6	9	12	15	18	21	24	27
15	1761	1790	1818	1847	1875	1903	1931	1959	1987	2014	3	6	8	11	14	17	20	22	25
16	2041	2068	2095	2122	2148	2175	2201	2227	2253	2279	3	5	8	11	13	16	18	21	24
17	2304	2330	2355	2380	2405	2430	2455	2480	2504	2529	2	5	7	10	12	15	17	20	22
18	2553	2577	2601	2625	2648	2672	2695	2718	2742	2765	2	5	7	9	12	14	16	19	21
19	2788	2810	2833	2856	2878	2900	2923	2945	2967	2989	2	4	7	9	11	13	16	18	20
20	3010	3032	3054	3075	3096	3118	3139	3160	3181	3201	2	4	6	8	11	13	15	17	19
21	3222	3243	3263	3284	3304	3324	3345	3365	3385	3404	2	4	6	8	10	12	14	16	18
22	3424	3444	3464	3483	3502	3522	3541	3560	3579	3598	2	4	6	8	10	12	14	15	17
23	3617	3636	3655	3674	3692	3711	3729	3747	3766	3784	2	4	6	7	9	11	13	15	17
24	3802	3820	3838	3856	3874	3892	3909	3927	3945	3962	2	4	5	7	9	11	12	14	16
25	3979	3997	4014	4031	4048	4065	4082	4099	4116	4133	2	3	5	7	9	10	12	14	15
26	4150	4166	4183	4200	4216	4232	4249	4265	4281	4298	2	3	5	7	8	10	11	13	15
27	4314	4330	4346	4362	4378	4393	4409	4425	4440	4456	2	3	5	6	8	9	11	13	14
28	4472	4487	4502	4518	4533	4548	4564	4579	4594	4609	2	3	5	6	8	9	11	12	14
29	4624	4639	4654	4669	4683	4698	4713	4728	4742	4757	1	3	4	6	7	9	10	12	13
30	4771	4786	4800	4814	4829	4843	4857	4871	4886	4900	1	3	4	6	7	9	10	11	13
31	4914	4928	4942	4955	4969	4983	4997	5011	5024	5038	1	3	4	6	7	8	10	11	12
32	5051	5065	5079	5092	5105	5119	5132	5145	5159	5172	1	3	4	5	7	8	9	11	12
33	5185	5198	5211	5224	5237	5250	5263	5276	5289	5302	1	3	4	5	6	8	9	10	12
34	5315	5328	5340	5353	5366	5378	5391	5403	5416	5428	1	3	4	5	6	8	9	10	11
35	5441	5453	5465	5478	5490	5502	5514	5527	5539	5551	1	2	4	5	6	7	9	10	11
36	5563	5575	5587	5599	5611	5623	5635	5647	5658	5670	1	2	4	5	6	7	8	10	11
37	5682	5694	5705	5717	5729	5740	5752	5763	5775	5786	1	2	3	5	6	7	8	9	10
38	5798	5809	5821	5832	5843	5855	5866	5877	5888	5899	1	2	3	5	6	7	8	9	10
39	5911	5922	5933	5944	5955	5966	5977	5988	5999	6010	1	2	3	4	5	7	8	9	10
40	6021	6031	6042	6053	6064	6075	6085	6096	6107	6117	1	2	3	4	5	6	8	9	10
41	6128	6138	6149	6160	6170	6180	6191	6201	6212	6222	1	2	3	4	5	6	7	8	9
42	6232	6243	6253	6263	6274	6284	6294	6304	6314	6325	1	2	3	4	5	6	7	8	9
43	6335	6345	6355	6365	6375	6385	6395	6405	6415	6425	1	2	3	4	5	6	7	8	9
44	6435	6444	6454	6464	6474	6484	6493	6503	6513	6522	1	2	3	4	5	6	7	8	9
45	6532	6542	6551	6561	6571	6580	6590	6599	6609	6618	1	2	3	4	5	6	7	8	9
46	6628	6637	6646	6656	6665	6675	6684	6693	6702	6712	1	2	3	4	5	6	7	7	8
47	6721	6730	6739	6749	6758	6767	6776	6785	6794	6803	1	2	3	4	5	5	6	7	8
48	6812	6821	6830	6839	6848	6857	6866	6875	6884	6893	1	2	3	4	4	5	6	7	8
49	6902	6911	6920	6928	6937	6946	6955	6964	6972	6981	1	2	3	4	4	5	6	7	8
50	6990	6998	7007	7016	7024	7033	7042	7050	7059	7067	1	2	3	3	4	5	6	7	8
51	7076	7084	7093	7101	7110	7118	7126	7135	7143	7152	1	2	3	3	4	5	6	7	8
52	7160	7168	7177	7185	7193	7202	7210	7218	7226	7235	1	2	2	3	4	5	6	7	7
53	7243	7251	7259	7267	7275	7284	7292	7300	7308	7316	1	2	2	3	4	5	6	6	7
54	7324	7332	7340	7348	7356	7364	7372	7380	7388	7396	1	2	2	3	4	5	6	6	7
55	7404	7412	7419	7427	7435	7443	7451	7459	7466	7474	1	2	2	3	4	5	5	6	7
56	7482	7490	7497	7505	7513	7520	7528	7536	7543	7551	1	2	2	3	4	5	5	6	7
57	7559	7566	7574	7582	7589	7597	7604	7612	7619	7627	1	2	2	3	4	5	5	6	7
58	7634	7642	7649	7657	7664	7672	7679	7686	7694	7701	1	1	2	3	4	4	5	6	7
59	7709	7716	7723	7731	7738	7745	7752	7760	7767	7774	1	1	2	3	4	4	5	6	7
60	7782	7789	7796	7803	7810	7818	7825	7832	7839	7846	1	1	2	3	4	4	5	6	6
61	7853	7860	7868	7875	7882	7889	7896	7903	7910	7917	1	1	2	3	4	4	5	6	6
62	7924	7931	7938	7945	7952	7959	7966	7973	7980	7987	1	1	2	3	3	4	5	6	6

Table I.1   **A-3**

TABLE I.1   **Four-Place Common Logarithms (continued)**

Number	0	1	2	3	4	5	6	7	8	9	Proportional Parts 1	2	3	4	5	6	7	8	9
63	7993	8000	8007	8014	8021	8028	8035	8041	8048	8055	1	1	2	3	3	4	5	5	6
64	8062	8069	8075	8082	8089	8096	8102	8109	8116	8122	1	1	2	3	3	4	5	5	6
65	8129	8136	8142	8149	8156	8162	8169	8176	8182	8189	1	1	2	3	3	4	5	5	6
66	8195	8202	8209	8215	8222	8228	8235	8241	8248	8254	1	1	2	3	3	4	5	5	6
67	8261	8267	8274	8280	8287	8293	8299	8306	8312	8319	1	1	2	3	3	4	5	5	6
68	8325	8331	8338	8344	8351	8357	8363	8370	8376	8382	1	1	2	3	3	4	4	5	6
69	8388	8395	8401	8407	8414	8420	8426	8432	8439	8445	1	1	2	2	3	4	4	5	6
70	8451	8457	8463	8470	8476	8482	8488	8494	8500	8506	1	1	2	2	3	4	4	5	5
71	8513	8519	8525	8531	8537	8543	8549	8555	8561	8567	1	1	2	2	3	4	4	5	5
72	8573	8579	8585	8591	8597	8603	8609	8615	8621	8627	1	1	2	2	3	4	4	5	5
73	8633	8639	8645	8651	8657	8663	8669	8675	8681	8686	1	1	2	2	3	4	4	5	5
74	8692	8698	8704	8710	8716	8722	8727	8733	8739	8745	1	1	2	2	3	4	4	5	5
75	8751	8756	8762	8768	8774	8779	8785	8791	8797	8802	1	1	2	2	3	3	4	5	5
76	8808	8814	8820	8825	8831	8837	8842	8848	8854	8859	1	1	2	2	3	3	4	5	5
77	8865	8871	8876	8882	8887	8893	8899	8904	8910	8915	1	1	2	2	3	3	4	4	5
78	8921	8927	8932	8938	8943	8949	8954	8960	8965	8971	1	1	2	2	3	3	4	4	5
79	8976	8982	8987	8993	8998	9004	9009	9015	9020	9025	1	1	2	2	3	3	4	4	5
80	9031	9036	9042	9047	9053	9058	9063	9069	9074	9079	1	1	2	2	3	3	4	4	5
81	9085	9090	9096	9101	9106	9112	9117	9122	9128	9133	1	1	2	2	3	3	4	4	5
82	9138	9143	9149	9154	9159	9165	9170	9175	9180	9186.	1	1	2	2	3	3	4	4	5
83	9191	9196	9201	9206	9212	9217	9222	9227	9232	9238	1	1	2	2	3	3	4	4	5
84	9243	9248	9253	9258	9263	9269	9274	9279	9284	9289	1	1	2	2	3	3	4	4	5
85	9294	9299	9304	9309	9315	9320	9325	9330	9335	9340	1	1	2	2	3	3	4	4	5
86	9345	9350	9355	9360	9365	9370	9375	9380	9385	9390	1	1	2	2	3	3	4	4	5
87	9395	9400	9405	9410	9415	9420	9425	9430	9435	9440	0	1	1	2	2	3	3	4	4
88	9445	9450	9455	9460	9465	9469	9474	9479	9484	9489	0	1	1	2	2	3	3	4	4
89	9494	9499	9504	9509	9513	9518	9523	9528	9533	9538	0	1	1	2	2	3	3	4	4
90	9542	9547	9552	9557	9562	9566	9571	9576	9581	9586	0	1	1	2	2	3	3	4	4
91	9590	9595	9600	9605	9609	9614	9619	9624	9628	9633	0	1	1	2	2	3	3	4	4
92	9638	9643	9647	9652	9657	9661	9666	9671	9675	9680	0	1	1	2	2	3	3	4	4
93	9685	9689	9694	9699	9703	9708	9713	9717	9722	9727	0	1	1	2	2	3	3	4	4
94	9731	9736	9741	9745	9750	9754	9759	9763	9768	9773	0	1	1	2	2	3	3	4	4
95	9777	9782	9786	9791	9795	9800	9805	9809	9814	9818	0	1	1	2	2	3	3	4	4
96	9823	9827	9832	9836	9841	9845	9850	9854	9859	9863	0	1	1	2	2	3	3	4	4
97	9868	9872	9877	9881	9886	9890	9894	9899	9903	9908	0	1	1	2	2	3	3	4	4
98	9912	9917	9921	9926	9930	9934	9939	9943	9948	9952	0	1	1	2	2	3	3	4	4
99	9956	9961	9965	9969	9974	9978	9983	9987	9991	9996	0	1	1	2	2	3	3	3	4

(c) Move further across the same row into the proportional parts section of the table until you reach the column containing the fourth digit of the original number. Add this number to the four-digit number you found in the table in the second step.

(d) Place a decimal point before the final four-digit number calculated in the third step.

If the original number contains fewer than four significant digits, the procedure is terminated at the appropriate place and the mantissa is given to the correct number of significant figures (rounded off, if necessary).

The following examples illustrate this technique:

To find log 4.683:
(a) move down the number column to 46
(b) move across the row to 8 and write down 6702
(c) move further across the row to 3 in the proportional parts section and add 3 to get 6705
(d) log 4.683 = 0.6705

To find log 7.2:
(a) move down the number column to 72 and write down 8573
(b) round off to give log 7.2 = 0.86

[To find the mantissa of a number which has more than four significant digits, "five-place log tables" or calculators must be used.]

2. *Finding the logarithm of a number greater than 10*   As we saw above, log 10 = 1. The logarithm of a number greater than 10 is greater than 1 and has a characteristic of 1 or more. To see this, we can rewrite the number in standard scientific notation and convert this logarithm of a product into the sum of the logarithms according to the rule for multiplying with logarithms.

$$\log (a \times 10^n) = \log a + \log 10^n = (\log a) + n$$

The desired logarithm consists of a mantissa determined by log a and a characteristic equal to n. The following examples illustrate the technique

$$\begin{aligned}\log (107) &= \log (1.07 \times 10^2)\\ &= \log (1.07) + \log (10^2)\\ &= 0.029 + 2 = 2.029\end{aligned}$$

$$\begin{aligned}\log (6.022 \times 10^{23}) &= \log (6.022) + \log (10^{23})\\ &= 0.7797 + 23 = 23.7797\end{aligned}$$

[In the above addition steps, n is an exact number.]

3. *Finding the logarithm of a number between 0 and 1*   The logarithm is negative for a number less than 1, but greater than 0. To see this, we can rewrite the number in standard scientific notation and use logarithms as was done above.

$$\log (a \times 10^{-n}) = \log a + \log 10^{-n} = (\log a) - n$$

Because n is always greater than log a, the desired logarithm is always a negative number. The following examples illustrate the technique:

$$\begin{aligned}\log (0.362) &= \log (3.62 \times 10^{-1})\\ &= \log (3.62) + \log (10^{-1})\\ &= 0.559 + (-1)\\ &= 0.559 - 1 = -0.441\end{aligned}$$

$$\begin{aligned}\log (4.7 \times 10^{-16}) &= \log (4.7) + \log (10^{-16})\\ &= 0.67 + (-16)\\ &= 0.67 - 16 = -15.33\end{aligned}$$

Some of you may have learned other ways to represent logarithms for numbers less than 1, such as 1.559 and 16.67 or 9.559 − 10 and 4.67 − 10. These notations are very difficult to use in the types of calculations performed in chemistry.

The *antilogarithm* (or inverse logarithm) is the value of the number to which the logarithm corresponds. For example, if log a = 2, the antilogarithm of log a is 100 (i.e., log 100 = 2). The value of the antilogarithm is found by essentially reversing the above procedures for finding logarithms:

1. *Finding the antilogarithm for log a between 0 and 1*   The antilogarithm is a number between 1 and 10 if the logarithm is greater than 0, but less than 1. The following examples illustrate the use of a logarithm table in finding the antilogarithm:

$$\log x = 0.6952$$

$$x = \text{antilog} (0.6952)$$

(a) look for 6952 in the table and write down 49 as the first two digits, because 6952 would be in this row if it appeared in the table

(b) 6952 is between 6946 and 6955, so, taking the number at the top of the column, write down 5 as the third digit
(c) the difference 6952 − 6949 = 6 appears in the proportional parts section, giving the fourth digit as 7
(d) $x = 4.957$

$$\log y = 0.438$$

$$y = \text{antilog} (0.438)$$

(a) look for 4380 in the table and write down 27 as the first two digits
(b) 4380 is between 4378 and 4393, so write down 4 as the third digit
(c) the difference 4380 − 4378 = 2 appears in the proportional parts section, giving the fourth digit as 1
(d) rounding off 2.741 gives $y = 2.74$

2. *Finding the antilogarithm for log a greater than 1*   The antilogarithm of 1 is 10 and the antilogarithm of a logarithm greater than 1 is greater than 10. For example,

$$\begin{aligned}\log x &= 6.9372\\ x &= \text{antilog} (6.9372)\\ &= \text{antilog} (0.9372 + 6)\\ &= [\text{antilog} (0.9372)][\text{antilog} (6)]\\ &= 8.654 \times 10^6\end{aligned}$$

$$\begin{aligned}\log y &= 173.26\\ y &= \text{antilog} (173.26)\\ &= \text{antilog} (0.26 + 173)\\ &= [\text{antilog} (0.26)][\text{antilog} (173)]\\ &= 1.8 \times 10^{173}\end{aligned}$$

3. *Finding the antilogarithm if log a is negative*   The antilogarithm is a number less than 1, but greater than 0 if the logarithm is negative. To find the antilogarithm of a negative logarithm, it is first necessary to restate the logarithm with a positive mantissa so that the logarithm table can be used. This is like knowing the punchline to a joke but having no idea how the story goes. The procedure is to first subtract the mantissa of the logarithm in question from 1, for example,

$$\log x = -1.36 \quad 1 - 0.36 = 0.64$$

and then combine it with the negative number equal to the characteristic plus 1, which in this case is 2.

$$0.64 - 2 (= -1.36)$$

The problem now is simply to find the antilogarithm of 0.64 − 2 as follows:

$$\begin{aligned}\log x &= -1.36\\ x &= \text{antilog} (-1.36)\\ &= \text{antilog} (0.64 - 2)\\ &= \text{antilog} [0.64 + (-2)]\\ &= [\text{antilog} (0.64)][\text{antilog} (-2)]\\ &= 4.4 \times 10^{-2}\end{aligned}$$

The step in which the negative logarithm is restated with a positive mantissa can be summarized by the equation

$$-X.Y = (1 - 0.Y) - (X + 1)$$

For example, in the above example we find that $(-1.36) = [(1 = 0.36) - (1 + 1)] = (0.64 - 2)$. Following is another example:

$$\log y = -17.963$$
$$y = \text{antilog}\,(-17.963)$$
$$= \text{antilog}\,(0.037 - 18)$$
$$= \text{antilog}\,[0.037 + (-18)]$$
$$= [\text{antilog}\,(0.037)][\text{antilog}\,(-18)]$$
$$= 1.09 \times 10^{-18}$$

In Section 2.3 we discussed the rules of significant figures for calculations involving addition (or subtraction) and multiplication (or division). For example, we know that each answer to the following problems should contain three significant digits:

$$z = (16.3)(7.942) \quad y = (6.32 \times 10^{-36})^3$$

Solving these problems using logarithms should not change this conclusion. By applying our usual rules to *only the mantissas*, we obtain the correct answers

$$\log z = (\log 16.3) + (\log 7.942)$$
$$\qquad\quad 12\ 3 \qquad\quad 1.234$$
$$= (1.212) + (0.8999)$$
$$\quad 123 \qquad 1234$$
$$= 2.112 \qquad \text{addition rule}$$
$$\quad 123 \leftarrow \text{applied only}$$
$$\qquad\qquad\qquad \text{to mantissa}$$
$$z = 129$$
$$\quad 123$$

$$\log y = (3)(\log 6.32 \times 10^{-36})$$
$$= (3)(-35.199)$$
$$\qquad\qquad 123 \qquad \text{multiplication}$$
$$= -105.597 \nwarrow \begin{array}{l}\text{rule applied}\\ \text{to mantissa}\end{array}$$
$$\qquad\qquad 123$$
$$y = 2.53 \times 10^{-106}$$
$$\quad 1\ 23$$

Problems

1. Find the logarithm of (a) 7.42, (b) 5.288, (c) 0.276, (d) 4.99×10^{-132}, (e) 5×10^{26}, and (f) 6.022×10^{317}. *Answer* (a) 0.870, (b) 0.7233, (c) -0.559, (d) -131.302, (e) 26.7, (f) 317.7797

2. Find the antilogarithm of (a) 0.2635, (b) 0.9988, (c) -5.2955, (d) -104.7, (e) 5.3153, and (f) 421.2. *Answer* (a) 1.834, (b) 9.972, (c) 5.064×10^{-6}, (d) 2×10^{-105}, (e) 2.067×10^5, (f) 2×10^{421}

3. Perform the following calculations using logarithms: (a) $(7.290)(18.26)$, (b) $(9.435)/(0.8888)$, (c) $(9.35)^{3.5}$, (d) $\sqrt[3]{6.293}$. *Answer* (a) 133.3, (b) 10.62, (c) 2.50×10^3, (d) 1.796

I.B GRAPHS

Many chemical experiments are designed to determine the relationship between two measurable quantities known as variables. For example, we could gather data to describe the pressure of an ideal gas as a function of the absolute temperature, the potential of an electrochemical cell as a function of pH, or the concentration of a reactant as a function of time. If the variable y can be expressed as a function of the variable x [written mathematically as $y = f(x)$], then y is known as the dependent variable and x is known as the independent variable.

One of the best ways to quickly communicate the general behavior of the relationship between two variables is with a graph. The dependent variable is plotted along the vertical axis, the *ordinate*, and the independent variable is plotted along the horizontal axis, the *abscissa*, (see Figure I.1) [We say that "y is plotted against x" or that the figure is "a plot of y versus x."]

Here are a few tips for making good graphs:

1. Choose a good quality graph paper. For most graphs, paper that has 10 divisions per centimeter works nicely. Although cross-ruled notebook paper is suitable for rough plots, it should not be used for final laboratory reports or for solutions to problems. [Occasionally "semi-log" or "log-log" paper is used to construct graphs involving logarithms of variables. The logarithm scales on these styles of graph paper eliminate having to determine the logarithms of numbers before making the plot. However, when analyzing the data (for example, to determine the slope of a straight line), the actual numerical values of the logarithms must be used.]

2. The axes should be clearly marked and labeled using units. The numeric divisions along the axes should be linear (evenly spaced) and clearly indicated. Choose ranges for the numeric divisions for the variables so that the set of data will occupy most of the area of the graph rather than being concentrated into one small area. It is not necessary to have an origin (0) on the graph. Leave suitable blank margins along the edges of the graph paper.

3. All data points should be accurately plotted and clearly marked on the graph. Draw a circle or some other geometric figure around each data point so that it is highly visible. [The size of the geometric figures is sometimes used to represent the precision of the measurement.] If more than one set of data appears on the graph, indicate each set by a characteristic geometric symbol or color.

4. Use mechanical drawing devices ("irregular" or drawing curves and straight edges) to draw the "best curves" through the data. Usually a "smooth curve" should be drawn through the data instead of connecting individual data points (see Figure I.1). Depending on the data, the "best curve" may not actually pass through the data points, but rather it will lie so that the points make equal positive and negative deviations from the curve.

5. A short, but complete description of the graph should appear.

Once the "best curve" is drawn through the data, the graph can be used to determine the value of one of the variables for a given value of the other variable. For example, in Figure I.1 we can see that the value of y that corresponds to x_3 will be y_3.

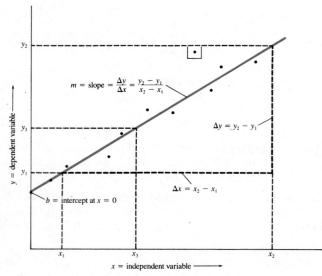

Figure I.1   Plot of y vs. x; $y = mx + b$

A graph can readily reveal the presence of inaccurate data points. For example, the data point indicated by the square in Figure I.1 lies too far from the curve compared to the other data and should not be included in the analysis of the set of data. [There are statistical tests available to indicate whether or not a data point should be included, but we will not concern ourselves with them.]

Often the variables that are plotted in a graph are related by the linear function $y = mx + b$ where the value of m is the slope of the straight line and b is the intercept of the straight line with the y axis at $x = 0$. [The slope and intercept are often related to physical quantities. For example, in the study of kinetics, the slope could be an activation energy or a rate constant.] The graphical method for determining the slope and intercept of the line is shown in Figure I.1. To improve the accuracy in calculating the slope, the points (x_1, y_1) and (x_2, y_2) should be chosen from the "best" straight line through the data rather than being chosen from among the actual data points. To improve the precision in calculating the slope, these points should be chosen near the extremes of the values of the variables. The slope should be reported with any units that Δy and Δx have.

Many electronic calculators have a linear least-squares regression program which determines the equation for the straight line through a set of data points. This program eliminates any guessing about where the "best" straight line in a graph should be drawn and automatically gives the values of the slope and intercept. Obviously, any inaccurate data should not be included in the regression analysis.

UNITS AND CONSTANTS

TABLE II.1   **Fundamental Constants.** The numbers in parentheses represent the standard deviation in the last significant figures cited. Values based on *J. Phys. Chem. Ref. Data*, **2**, 663–734 (1973).

Symbol	Quantity	Value	Common Rounded-Off Value
a_0	Bohr radius	$5.2917706(44) \times 10^{-11}$ m	5.29×10^{-11} m
c	Velocity of light	$2.99792458(12) \times 10^{8}$ m/s	3.00×10^{8} m/s
e	Electronic charge	$1.6021892(46) \times 10^{-19}$ C	1.602×10^{-19} C
F	Faraday's constant	$9.648456(27) \times 10^{4}$ C/mol	9.65×10^{4} C/mol
g	Gravitational acceleration	9.80665 m/s^2	9.81 m/s^2
h	Planck's constant	$6.626176(36) \times 10^{-34}$ J s	6.626×10^{-34} J s
k	Boltzmann's constant	$1.380662(44) \times 10^{-23}$ J/K	1.381×10^{-23} J/K
L	Avogadro's number	$6.022045(31) \times 10^{23}$ /mol	6.022×10^{23} /mol
m_e	Electron rest mass	$9.109534(47) \times 10^{-31}$ kg	9.11×10^{-31} kg
m_n	Neutron rest mass	$1.6749543(86) \times 10^{-27}$ kg	1.675×10^{-27} kg
m_p	Proton rest mass	$1.6726485(86) \times 10^{-27}$ kg	1.673×10^{-27} kg
R	Gas constant	$8.31441(26)$ J/K mol	8.314 J/K mol
		$8.20568(26) \times 10^{-2}$ L atm/K mol	0.0821 L atm/K mol
		$8.20568(26) \times 10^{-5}$ m^3 atm/K mol	8.21×10^{-5} m^3 atm/K mol
R	Rydberg's constant	$1.097373177(83) \times 10^{7}$ /m	1.097×10^{7} /m
		$2.179907(12) \times 10^{-18}$ J	2.18×10^{-18} J
$\bar{V}$	Ideal gas molar volume	$22.41383(70)$ L/mol	22.4 L/mol
		$2.241383(70) \times 10^{-2}$ m^3/mol	0.0224 m^3/mol

TABLE II.2   **Commonly Used Prefixes**

Decimal Location	Prefix	Prefix Symbol
$1,000,000,000,000 = 10^{12}$	tera	T
$1,000,000,000 = 10^{9}$	giga	G
$1,000,000 = 10^{6}$	mega	M
$1,000 = 10^{3}$	kilo	k
$100 = 10^{2}$	hecto	h
$10 = 10^{1}$	deka	da
$0.1 = 10^{-1}$	deci	d
$0.01 = 10^{-2}$	centi	c
$0.001 = 10^{-3}$	milli	m
$0.000\,001 = 10^{-6}$	micro	μ
$0.000\,000\,001 = 10^{-9}$	nano	n
$0.000\,000\,000\,001 = 10^{-12}$	pico	p
$0.000\,000\,000\,000\,001 = 10^{-15}$	femto	f
$0.000\,000\,000\,000\,000\,001 = 10^{-18}$	atto	a

<u>TABLE II.3</u>   **Base Units of the International System of Units** The SI units are shown in boldface. Selected conversion factors for non-SI units are given. The numbers in parentheses represent the standard deviation in the last significant figures cited. Factors marked with an asterisk are exact. Values based on *J. Phys. Chem. Ref. Data,* **2,** 663–734 (1973).

Physical Quantity, Unit	Abbreviation	Selected Conversion Factors (Common Rounded-Off Conversion Factor)	Physical Quantity, Unit	Abbreviation	Selected Conversion Factors (Common Rounded-Off Conversion Factor)
Length			*Time*		
Meter	**m**		**Second**	**s**	
Ångstrom	Å	$1\ \text{Å} = 1 \times 10^{-10}\ \text{m}^*$	*Electrical current*		
Inch	inch	$1\ \text{inch} = 2.54 \times 10^{-2}\ \text{m}^*$	**Ampere**	**A**	
Mass			*Temperature*		
Kilogram	**kg**		**Kelvin**	**K**	
Atomic mass unit	u	$1\ \text{u} = 1.6605655(86) \times 10^{-27}\ \text{kg}$ $(1.6606 \times 10^{-27}\ \text{kg})$	Degree Celsius	°C	$T(\text{K}) = T(°\text{C}) + 273.15^*$
Metric ton		$1\ \text{metric ton} = 1 \times 10^3\ \text{kg}^*$	Degree Fahrenheit	°F	$T(°\text{C}) = [T(°\text{F}) + (40\ F\ \text{degrees})]$ $\times \left(\dfrac{5\ C\ \text{degrees}}{9\ F\ \text{degrees}}\right) - (40\ C\ \text{degrees})^*$
Pound (avoir.)	lb	$1\ \text{lb} = 4.5359237 \times 10^{-1}\ \text{kg}^*$ $(0.454\ \text{kg})$	*Amount of substance mole*		
Ounce (avoir.)	oz	$1\ \text{oz} = 2.8349523125 \times 10^{-2}\ \text{kg}^*$ $(0.0283\ \text{kg})$	**Mole**	**mol**	
Ounce (troy or apoth.)	oz	$1\ \text{oz} = 3.11034768 \times 10^{-2}\ \text{kg}^*$ $(0.0311\ \text{kg})$	*Luminous intensity* **Candela**	**cd**	

Table II.4   A-9

TABLE II.4   **Derived Units of the International System of Units.** The SI units are shown in boldface. Selected conversion factors for non-SI units are given. The numbers in parentheses represent the standard deviation in the last significant figures cited. Factors marked with an asterisk are exact. Values based on *J. Phys. Chem. Ref. Data,* **2,** 663–734 (1973).

Physical Quantity Unit	Abbreviation	Selected Conversion Factors (Common Rounded-Off Conversion Factor)
Area		
Square meter	**m^2**	
Density		
Kilogram per cubic meter	**kg/m^3**	
Grams per milliliter	$g/mL = g/cm^3$	$1\ g/cm^3 = 1 \times 10^3\ kg/m^3*$
Dipole moment		
Coulomb meter	**C m**	
Debye	D	$1\ D = 3.335641(14) \times 10^{-30}\ C\ m$
		$(3.34 \times 10^{-30}\ C\ m)$
Electrical resistance		
Ohm	$\Omega = V/A = kg\ m^2/A^2 s^3$	
Electricity, quantity		
Coulomb	$C = A\ s$	
Electrostatic unit	$esu = cm^{3/2}\ g^{1/2}/s$	$1\ C = 3.335641(14) \times 10^{-10}\ esu$
		$(3.34 \times 10^{-10}\ esu)$
Electromotive force		
Volt	$V = kg\ m^2/A\ s^3$	
Energy		
Joule	$J = kg\ m^2/s$	
Erg	$erg = g\ cm^2/s^2$	$1\ erg = 1 \times 10^{-7}\ J*$
Calorie	cal	$1\ cal = 4.184\ J*$
Electron volt	eV	$1 eV = 1.6021892\ (46) \times 10^{-19}\ J$
		$(1.602 \times 10^{-19}\ J)$
Liter atmosphere	L atm	$1\ L\ atm = 1.01325 \times 10^2\ J*$
Wave number	cm^{-1}	$1\ cm^{-1} = 1.986477(10) \times 10^{-23}\ J$
		$(1.986 \times 10^{-23}\ J)$
Atomic mass unit	u	$1\ u = 1.492442(6) \times 10^{-10}\ J$
		$(1.492 \times 10^{-10}\ J)$
Entropy		
Joule per Kelvin	**J/K**	
Entropy unit, Gibb	cal/K	$1\ cal/K = 4.184\ J/K*$

Physical Quantity Unit	Abbreviation	Selected Conversion Factors (Common Rounded-Off Conversion Factor)
Force		
Newton	$N = kg\ m/s^2$	
Dyne	$dyne = g\ cm/s^2$	$1\ dyne = 1 \times 10^{-5}\ N*$
Pound force	lbf	$1\ lbf = 4.4482216152605\ N*$
		$(4.45\ N)$
Frequency		
Hertz	$Hz = s^{-1} = /s$	
Cycles per second	cps	$1\ cps = 1\ Hz*$
Pressure		
Pascal	$Pa = N/m^2$	
	$= kg\ m^2/s$	
Atmosphere	atm	$1\ atm = 1.01325 \times 10^5\ Pa*$
Bar	bar	$1\ bar = 1 \times 10^5\ Pa*$
Pounds per square inch	$psi = lb/in^2$	$1\ psi = 6.894757293167 \times 10^3\ Pa$
		$(6.89 \times 10^3\ Pa)$
Torr, millimeter of mercury	Torr = mm Hg	$1\ Torr\ 1.33322368421 \times 10^2\ Pa$
		$(133.3\ Pa)$
		$1\ atm = 760\ Torr*$
Radiation, activity		
Becquerel	$Bq = disintegration/s$	
Rutherford	Rd	$1\ Rd = 1 \times 10^6\ Bq*$
Curie	Ci	$1\ Ci = 3.7 \times 10^{10}\ Bq*$
Radiation, dosimetry		
Coulomb per kilogram	**C/kg**	
Roentgen	R	$1\ R = 2.57976 \times 10^{-4}\ C/kg*$
		$(2.58 \times 10^{-4}\ C/kg)$
Radiation, energy absorbed		
Gray	$Gy = J/kg$	
Rad	rad	$1\ rad = 1 \times 10^{-2}\ Gy*$
Volume		
Cubic meter	**m^3**	
Liter	L	$1\ L = 1 \times 10^{-3}\ m^3*$
Quart (US liq.)	qt	$1\ qt = 9.4635295 \times 10^{-4}\ m^3$
		$(9.46 \times 10^{-4}\ m^3)$
Milliliter	mL	$1\ mL = 1\ cm^3*$
Cubic centimeter	$cm^3 = cc$	$1\ cm^3 = 1 \times 10^{-6}\ m^3*$

Properties of Atoms

TABLE III.1 **Ionization Energy and Electron Affinity at 0 K.** (Data mainly from T. Moeller, *Inorganic Chemistry*, New York: Wiley 1982, pp. 76–79 and 81–84.)

Element Z Symbol	Ionization Energy (kJ/mol)	Electron Affinity (kJ/mol)	Element Z Symbol	Ionization Energy (kJ/mol)	Electron Affinity (kJ/mol)
1 H	1312.0	−72.7	41 Nb	664	
2 He	2372.3	21	42 Mo	684.9	−96
			43 Tc	702	
3 Li	520.2	−59.8	44 Ru	711	
4 Be	899.4	240	45 Rh	720.	
5 B	800.6	−83	46 Pd	805	
6 C	1086.4	−122.5	47 Ag	731.0	−125.7
7 N	1402.3	0.0	48 Cd	867.7	
8 O	1313.9	−141.4	49 In	558.3	−34
9 F	1681.0	−322.2	50 Sn	708.6	−121
10 Ne	2080.6	29	51 Sb	833.7	−101
			52 Te	869.2	−183
11 Na	495.6	−52.9	53 I	1008.4	−295.3
12 Mg	737.7	230	54 Xe	1170.4	41
13 Al	577.6	−50	55 Cs	375.7	−45.5
14 Si	786.4	−120.	56 Ba	502.9	52
15 P	1011.7	−74	57 La	538.1	
16 S	999.6	−200.4	58 Ce	528	
17 Cl	1251.1	−348.7	59 Pr	523	
18 Ar	1520.5	35	60 Nd	530.	
			61 Pm	535	
19 K	418.8	−48.3	62 Sm	543	
20 Ca	589.8	156	63 Eu	547	
21 Sc	631		64 Gd	564	
22 Ti	658	−37.7	65 Tb	564	
23 V	650.	−90.4	66 Dy	572	
24 Cr	652.8	−64	67 Ho	581	
25 Mn	717.4		68 Er	589	
26 Fe	759.3	−56.2	69 Tm	596	
27 Co	758	−90.3	70 Yb	603.4	
28 Ni	736.7	−123.1	71 Lu	523.5	
29 Cu	745.4	−123.1	72 Hf	680	
30 Zn	906.4		73 Ta	761	−80
31 Ga	578.8	−36	74 W	770.	−50
32 Ge	762.1	−116	75 Re	760.	−14
33 As	947	−77	76 Os	840	
34 Se	940.9	−195	77 Ir	880	
35 Br	1139.9	−324.5	78 Pt	870	−205.3
36 Kr	1350.7	39	79 Au	890.1	−222.75
			80 Hg	1007.0	
37 Rb	403.0	−46.88	81 Tl	589.3	−50
38 Sr	549.5	168	82 Pb	715.5	−101
39 Y	616		83 Bi	703.3	−101
40 Zr	660.		84 Po	818	−170

Table III.2   **A-11**

Element Z Symbol	Ionization Energy (kJ/mol)	Electron Affinity (kJ/mol)	Element Z Symbol	Ionization Energy (kJ/mol)	Electron Affinity (kJ/mol)
85 At		− 270			
86 Rn	1037.0	41			
87 Fr		− 44.0			
88 Ra	509.3				
89 Ac	670				
90 Th					
91 Pa					
92 U					
93 Np					
94 Pu	560				
95 Am	580				

TABLE III.2   **Atomic and Ionic Radii of the Elements, in nm.** (Data mainly from T. Moeller, *Inorganic Chemistry,* New York: Wiley, 1982, pp. 70–72 and 141–147.)

Element Z Symbol	Anion Radius − 4	Anion Radius − 3	Anion Radius − 2	Anion Radius − 1	Atomic Radius	Cation Radius + 1	Cation Radius + 2	Cation Radius + 3
1 H				0.208	0.037			
2 He					0.05			
3 Li					0.152	0.068		
4 Be					0.111		0.035	
5 B					0.080			
6 C	0.260				0.077			
7 N		0.171			0.074			
8 O			0.140		0.074			
9 F				0.136	0.071			
10 Ne					0.065			
11 Na					0.186	0.097		
12 Mg					0.160		0.066	
13 Al					0.143			0.051
14 Si					0.118			
15 P		0.212			0.110			
16 S			0.184		0.103			
17 Cl				0.181	0.099			
18 Ar					0.095			
19 K					0.227	0.133		
20 Ca					0.197		0.099	
21 Sc					0.161			0.081
22 Ti					0.145		0.080	0.076
23 V					0.131		0.088	0.074
24 Cr					0.125		0.083	0.063
25 Mn					0.137		0.080	0.066
26 Fe					0.124		0.074	0.064
27 Co					0.125		0.072	0.063
28 Ni					0.125		0.069	

Element Z Symbol	Anion Radius −4	−3	−2	−1	Atomic Radius	Cation Radius +1	+2	+3
29 Cu					0.128	0.096	0.072	
30 Zn					0.133		0.074	
31 Ga					0.122			0.062
32 Ge					0.123			
33 As		0.222			0.125			
34 Se			0.191		0.116			
35 Br				0.196	0.114			
36 Kr					0.110			
37 Rb					0.248	0.147		
38 Sr					0.215		0.112	
39 Y					0.178			0.092
40 Zr					0.159			
41 Nb					0.143			0.070
42 Mo					0.136			0.067
43 Tc					0.135			
44 Ru					0.133			0.68
45 Rh					0.135			0.068
46 Pd					0.138		0.080	
47 Ag					0.145	0.126	0.089	
48 Cd					0.149		0.097	
49 In					0.163			0.081
50 Sn					0.141		0.093	
51 Sb		0.245			0.145			0.076
52 Te			0.218		0.143			
53 I				0.220	0.133			
54 Xe					0.130			
55 Cs					0.265	0.167		
56 Ba					0.217		0.134	
57 La					0.187			0.114
58 Ce					0.183			0.107
59 Pr					0.182			0.106
60 Nd					0.181			0.104
61 Pm					~0.181			0.106
62 Sm					0.180		0.110	0.100
63 Eu					0.199		0.109	0.098
64 Gd					0.179			0.097
65 Tb					0.176			0.093
66 Dy					0.175			0.092
67 Ho					0.174			0.091
68 Er					0.173			0.089
69 Tm					~0.173		0.094	0.087
70 Yb					0.194		0.093	0.086
71 Lu					0.172			0.085
72 Hf					0.156			
73 Ta					0.143			0.67
74 W					0.137			
75 Re					0.137			
76 Os					0.137			
77 Ir					0.136			0.73
78 Pt					0.139		0.080	
79 Au					0.144	0.137		0.085
80 Hg					0.150		0.110	
81 Tl					0.170	0.147		0.095
82 Pb					0.175		0.120	
83 Bi					0.155			0.096
84 Po					0.118		0.230	
85 At								

Table III.2   **A-13**

| Element | | Anion Radius | | | Atomic | | Cation Radius | |
Z Symbol	−4	−3	−2	−1	Radius	+1	+2	+3
86 Rn					0.145			
87 Fr						0.180		
88 Ra							0.143	
89 Ac					0.188			0.118
90 Th					0.180			0.108
91 Pa					0.161			0.113
92 U					0.139			0.101
93 Np								0.110
94 Pu					0.151			0.108
95 Am					~0.131			0.107
96 Cm								0.095
97 Bk								0.094
98 Cf								0.095
99 Es								

Thermodynamic Data

TABLE IV.1 ΔH_f°, ΔG_f°, S°, and C_p° for Selected Substances at 25 °C. Most of the data are from *NBS Technical Note 270–3* (1968), *270–4* (1969), *250–5* (1971), and *270–7* (1973) and from *NBS Circular 500* (1952).

Substance	ΔH_f° (kJ/mol)	ΔG_f° (kJ/mol)	S° (J/K mol)	C_p° (J/K mol)
Aluminum				
$Al(s)$	0.0	0.0	28.33	24.35
$Al_2O_3(\alpha\text{-solid})$	−1675.7	−1582.4	50.92	79.04
$AlF_3(s)$	−1504.1	−1425.1	66.44	75.10
$AlCl_3(s)$	−704.2	−628.9	110.67	91.83
$Al_2Cl_6(g)$	−1290.8	−1220.5	490	
$Al_2(SO_4)_3(s)$	−3440.84	−3100.13	239.3	259.41
Antimony				
$Sb(\text{solid III})$	0.0	0.0	45.69	25.23
$Sb(g)$	262.3	222.2	180.16	20.79
$Sb_4O_6(\text{solid II})$	−1440.6	−1268.2	220.9	
$Sb_4O_6(\text{solid I})$	−1417.1	−1253.1	246.0	202.76
$Sb_2O_5(s)$	−971.9	−829.3	125.1	
$SbCl_5(l)$	−440.2	−350.2	301	
$SbCl_3(s)$	−382.17	−323.72	184.1	107.9
$SbOCl(s)$	−374.0			
Argon				
$Ar(g)$	0.0	0.0	154.7335	20.7857
Arsenic				
$As(\alpha\text{-solid})$	0.0	0.0	35.1	24.64
$As(g)$	302.5	261.1	174.10	20.786
$As_4(g)$	143.9	92.5	314	
$H_3As(g)$	66.44	68.91	222.67	38.07
$As_2O_5(s)$	−883.03	−782.4	105.4	116.52
$As_4O_6(\text{monoclinic})$	−1309.6	−1154.03	234	
$H_3AsO_3(aq)$	−742.2			
$H_3AsO_4(aq)$	−902.5			
$AsCl_3(l)$	−305.0	−259.4	216.3	
Barium				
$Ba(s)$	0.0	0.0	67	26.36
$Ba(g)$	175.56	144.77	170.285	20.7861
$BaO(s)$	−558.1	−528.4	70.3	47.45
$Ba(OH)_2(s)$	−946.4			
$Ba(OH)_2(aq)$	−998.22	−875.3	−8	
$BaCl_2(s)$	−860.06	−810.9	126	75.3
$BaCO_3(s)$	−1218.8	−1138.9	112.1	85.35
$Ba(NO_3)_2(s)$	−991.86	−795.0	213.8	151.0
$BaSO_4(s)$	−1465.2	−1353.1	132.2	101.75
$BaCrO_4(s)$	−1428.0			
Beryllium				
$Be(s)$	0.0	0.0	9.54	17.82
$BeCl_2(s)$	−511.7			

Table IV.1   **A-15**

Substance	ΔH_f° (kJ/mol)	ΔG_f° (kJ/mol)	S° (J/K mol)	C_p° (J/K mol)
Bismuth				
Bi(s)	0.0	0.0	56.74	25.52
$Bi_2O_3(s)$	−573.88	−493.7	151.5	113.51
$BiCl_3(s)$	−379.1	−315.1	177.0	105
BiOCl(s)	−366.9	−322.2	120.5	
Boron				
B(β-solid)	0.0	0.0	5.86	11.09
B(g)	562.7	518.8	153.34	20.799
$B_2H_6(g)$	35.6	86.6	232.00	56.90
$B_2O_3(s)$	−1272.77	−1193.70	53.97	62.93
$H_3BO_3(s)$	−1094.33	−969.01	88.83	81.38
$[B(OH)_4]^-(aq)$	−1344.03	−1153.32	102.5	
BN(s)	−254.4	−228.4	14.81	19.71
$BF_3(g)$	−1137.00	−1120.35	254.01	50.46
$BCl_3(l)$	−427.2	−387.4	206.3	106.7
$NaBH_4(s)$	−183.34	−119.54	104.68	86.6
Bromine				
Br(g)	111.884	82.429	174.912	20.786
$Br_2(l)$	0.0	0.0	152.231	75.689
HBr(g)	−36.40	−53.43	198.585	29.142
HBr(aq)	−121.55	−103.97	82.4	−141.8
$BrO_3^-(aq)$	−83.7	1.7	163.2	
HBrO(aq)	−113.0	−82.4	142.3	
BrF(g)	−93.85	−109.16	228.86	32.97
BrCl(g)	14.64	−0.96	239.99	34.98
Cadmium				
Cd(γ-solid)	0.0	0.0	51.76	25.98
Cd(g)	112.01	77.45	167.636	20.786
CdO(s)	−258.2	−228.4	54.8	43.43
CdS(s)	−161.9	−156.5	64.9	
Calcium				
Ca(s)	0.0	0.0	41.63	26.28
Ca(g)	192.63	158.91	154.779	20.786
CaO(s)	−635.5	−604.2	39.7	42.80
$Ca(OH)_2(s)$	−986.6	−896.76	76.1	84.5
$CaC_2(s)$	−62.8	−67.8	70.3	62.34
$CaCO_3$(calcite)	−1206.87	−1128.76	92.9	81.88
$CaCO_3$(aragonite)	−1207.04	−1127.72	88.7	81.25
$Ca(NO_3)_2(s)$	−937.22	−741.99	193.3	149.33
$CaSO_4(s)$	−1432.69	−1320.30	106.7	99.6
$CaCl_2(s)$	−795.0	−750.2	113.8	72.63
$CaCl_2 \cdot 6H_2O(s)$	−2607.26			
$Ca(NO_3)_2(s)$	−937.22	−741.99	193.3	149.33
$Ca_3(PO_4)_2(s)$	−4137.6	−3899.5	236.0	227.82
Carbon				
C(graphite)	0.0	0.0	5.740	8.527
C(diamond)	1.8966	2.8995	2.377	6.1149
$CH_4(g)$	−74.81	−50.75	186.155	35.309
$C_2H_2(g)$	226.73	209.20	200.83	43.93
$C_2H_4(g)$	52.26	68.12	219.45	43.56
$C_2H_6(g)$	−84.68	−32.89	229.49	52.63
CO(g)	−110.525	−137.152	197.564	29.117
$CO_2(g)$	−393.509	−394.359	213.64	37.11

Substance	ΔH_f° (kJ/mol)	ΔG_f° (kJ/mol)	S° (J/K mol)	C_p° (J/K mol)
HCN(g)	108.87	124.7	201.67	35.86
$CS_2(l)$	89.70	65.27	151.34	75.7
$CF_4(g)$	−925	−879	261.50	61.1
$CCl_4(l)$	−135.44	−65.56	216.40	131.75
$CH_3Cl(g)$	−80.83	−57.40	234.47	40.75
$CH_2Cl_2(l)$	−121.46	−67.32	177.8	100.0
$CHCl_3(l)$	−134.47	−73.72	201.7	113.8
$CH_3COOH(l)$	−484.5	−389.9	159.8	124.3
$CH_3COOH(aq)$	−485.76	−396.56	178.7	
$CH_3OH(l)$	−238.66	−166.36	126.8	81.6
$CH_3CH_2OH(l)$	−277.70	−174.89	160.7	112.30
cis-CHClCHCl(l)	−27.6	22.05	198.41	113
trans-CHClCHCl(L)	−23.14	27.28	195.85	113
$CH_3NH_2(l)$	−47.3	35.6	150.21	
Chlorine				
Cl(g)	121.679	105.696	165.088	21.841
$Cl_2(g)$	0.0	0.0	222.957	33.907
HCl(g)	−92.307	−95.299	186.799	29.12
HCl(aq)	−167.159	−131.260	56.5	−136.4
$HClO_4(aq)$	−129.33	−8.62	182.0	
HClO(aq)	−120.9	−79.9	142	
ClF(g)	−54.48	−55.94	217.78	32.05
$ClF_3(g)$	−163.2	−123.0	281.50	63.85
Chromium				
Cr(s)	0.0	0.0	23.77	23.35
$CrO_3(s)$	−589.5			
$Cr(OH)_3(s)$	−1064.0			
$[Cr(H_2O)_6]^{3+}$	−1999.1			
Cobalt				
Co(hexagonal)	0.0	0.0	30.04	24.81
CoO(s)	−237.94	−214.22	52.97	55.23
$Co_3O_4(s)$	−891	−774	102.5	123.4
$CoCl_2(s)$	−312.5	−269.9	109.16	78.49
Copper				
Cu(s)	0.0	0.0	33.150	24.435
CuO(s)	−157.3	−129.7	42.64	42.30
$Cu_2O(s)$	−168.6	−146.0	93.14	63.64
CuS(s)	−53.1	−53.6	66.5	47.82
$Cu_2S(s)$	−79.5	−86.2	120.9	76.32
$CuCl_2(s)$	−220.1	−175.7	108.07	71.88
CuCl(s)	−137.2	−119.87	86.2	48.5
$CuSO_4(s)$	−771.36	−661.9	109	100.0
$CuSO_4 \cdot 5H_2O(s)$	−2279.65	−1880.055	300.4	280.
$Cu(NO_3)_2(s)$	−302.9			
Fluorine				
F(g)	78.99	61.92	158.645	22.744
$F_2(g)$	0.0	0.0	202.67	31.30
HF(g)	−271.1	−273.2	173.669	29.133
HF(aq)	−320.08	−296.85	88.7	
Helium				
He(g)	0.0	0.0	126.0405	20.7857
Hydrogen				
H(g)	217.965	203.263	114.604	20.7857
$H_2(g)$	0.0	0.0	130.574	28.824

Table IV.1   **A-17**

Substance	ΔH_f° (kJ/mol)	ΔG_f° (kJ/mol)	S° (J/K mol)	C_p° (J/K mol)
Iodine				
$I(g)$	106.838	70.283	180.682	20.786
$I_2(s)$	0.0	0.0	116.135	54.438
$[I_3]^-(aq)$	−51.5	−51.5	239.3	
$HI(g)$	26.48	1.72	206.485	29.158
$HIO(aq)$	−138.1	−99.2	95.4	
$IO_3^-(aq)$	−221.3	−128.0	118.4	
$IF_5(l)$	−864.8			
$ICl_3(s)$	−89.5	−22.34	167.4	
$IBr(s)$	−10.5			
Iron				
$Fe(\alpha\text{-solid})$	0.0	0.0	27.28	25.10
$FeO(s)$	−272.0			48.12
$Fe_2O_3(s)$	−824.2	−742.2	87.40	103.85
$Fe_3O_4(s)$	−1118.4	−1015.5	146.4	143.43
$Fe(OH)_2(s)$	−569.0	−486.6	88	
$Fe(OH)_3(s)$	−823.0	−696.6	106.7	
$FeCl_2(s)$	−341.79	−302.34	117.95	76.65
$FeCl_3(s)$	−399.49	−334.05	142.3	96.65
$FeSO_4(s)$	−928.4	−820.9	107.5	100.58
$FeSO_4 \cdot 7H_2O(s)$	−3014.57	−2510.27	409.2	394.47
$Fe_2(SO_4)_3(s)$	−2581.5			
$K_3[Fe(CN)_6](s)$	−173.2			
$K_4[Fe(CN)_6](s)$	−523.4			
Lead				
$Pb(s)$	0.0	0.0	64.81	26.44
$PbO(yellow)$	−217.32	−187.90	68.70	45.77
$PbO(red)$	−218.99	−188.95	66.5	45.81
$PbO_2(s)$	−277.4	−217.36	68.6	64.64
$Pb_3O_4(s)$	−718.4	−601.2	211.3	146.9
$PbS(s)$	−100.4	−98.7	91.2	49.50
$PbCl_2(s)$	−359.41	−314.13	136.0	
$Pb(NO_3)_2(s)$	−451.97			
$PbSO_4(s)$	−919.94	−813.20	148.57	103.207
Lithium				
$Li(s)$	0.0	0.0	28.03	23.64
$Li(g)$	155.10	122.13	138.633	20.7861
$LiH(s)$	−90.42	−69.96	24.7	34.7
$LiOH(s)$	−487.23	−443.9	50	
$LiF(s)$	−612.1	−584.1	35.86	42.01
$LiCl(s)$	−408.78			51.0
$LiAlH_4(s)$	−101.3			76.1
Magnesium				
$Mg(s)$	0.0	0.0	32.51	23.89
$MgO(s)$	−601.83	−569.57	26.8	37.40
$Mg(OH)_2(s)$	−924.66	−833.75	63.14	77.03
$Mg_3N_2(s)$	−461.24			104.56
$MgCl_2(s)$	−641.83	−592.33	89.5	71.30
$MgBr_2(s)$	−517.6			
$MgI_2(s)$	−359.8			
$MgCO_3(s)$	−1113	−1029	65.7	75.52
$Mg(NO_3)_2(s)$	−789.60	−588.40	164.01	142.00
$Mg_3(PO_4)_2(s)$	−4022.9			
$MgSO_4(s)$	−1278.2	−1173.6	91.6	96.27
Manganese				
$Mn(\alpha\text{-solid})$	0.0	0.0	32.01	26.32

Substance	$\Delta H_f°$ (kJ/mol)	$\Delta G_f°$ (kJ/mol)	$S°$ (J/K mol)	$C_p°$ (J/K mol)
$MnO(s)$	−385.22	−362.92	59.71	45.44
$MnO_2(s)$	−520.03	−465.18	53.05	54.14
$Mn_2O_3(s)$	−959.0	−881.2	110.5	107.65
$Mn_3O_4(s)$	−1387.8	−1283.2	155.6	139.66
$MnO_4^-(aq)$	−541.4	−447.3	191.2	
$MnO_4^{2-}(aq)$	−653	−500.8	59	
Mercury				
$Hg(l)$	0.0	0.0	76.02	27.983
$Hg^{2+}(aq)$	171.1	164.43	−32.2	
$Hg_2^{2+}(aq)$	172.4	153.55	84.5	
$HgO(red)$	−90.84	−58.555	70.29	44.06
$HgO(yellow)$	−90.46	−58.425	71.1	
$HgCl_2(s)$	−224.3	−178.7	146.0	
$Hg_2Cl_2(s)$	−265.22	−210.777	192.5	
$HgS(red)$	−58.2	−50.6	82.4	48.41
$HgS(black)$	−53.6	−47.7	88.3	
Neon				
$Ne(g)$	0.0	0.0	146.2187	20.7857
Nickel				
$Ni(s)$	0.0	0.0	29.87	26.07
$NiO(s)$	−239.74	−211.71	37.99	44.31
$NiS(s)$	−82.0	−79.5	52.97	47.11
$NiCl_2(s)$	−305.332	−259.065	97.66	71.67
$[Ni(NH_3)_6]^{2+}(aq)$	−630.1	−256.1	394.6	
Nitrogen				
$N_2(g)$	0.0	0.0	191.50	29.125
$NH_3(g)$	−46.11	−16.49	192.34	35.06
$NH_3(aq)$	−80.29	−26.57	111.294	
$NH_4^+(aq)$	−132.51	−79.37	113.4	79.9
$N_2H_4(l)$	50.63	149.24	121.21	98.87
$NO(g)$	90.25	86.57	210.652	29.844
$NO_2(g)$	33.18	51.30	239.95	37.20
$N_2O(g)$	82.05	104.18	219.74	38.45
$N_2O_3(g)$	83.72	139.41	312.17	65.61
$N_2O_4(g)$	9.16	97.82	304.18	77.28
$N_2O_5(s)$	−43.1	113.8	178.2	143.1
$N_2O_5(g)$	11.3	115.1	355.6	84.5
$HNO_3(l)$	−174.10	−80.79	155.60	109.87
$HNO_3(aq)$	−207.36	−111.34	146.4	−86.6
$NH_4NO_3(s)$	−365.56	−184.01	151.08	139.3
$NH_4NO_2(s)$	−256.5			
$NH_4Cl(s)$	−314.43	−202.97	94.6	84.1
$NH_4Cl(aq)$	−299.66	−210.62	169.9	−56.5
$(NH_4)_2SO_4(s)$	−1180.85	−901.90	220.08	187.49
$NOCl(g)$	51.71	66.07	261.58	44.69
$NOBr(g)$	82.17	82.42	273.55	45.48
$NH_4(CH_3COO)(s)$	−616.14			
Oxygen				
$O(g)$	249.170	231.785	160.946	21.912
$O_2(g)$	0.0	0.0	205.029	29.355
$O_3(g)$	142.7	163.2	238.82	39.20
$OH^-(aq)$	−229.994	−157.293	−10.75	−148.5
$H_2O(l)$	−285.830	−237.178	69.92	75.291

Table IV.1   A-19

Substance	ΔH_f° (kJ/mol)	ΔG_f° (kJ/mol)	S° (J/K mol)	C_p° (J/K mol)
$H_2O(g)$	−241.818	−228.589	188.715	33.577
$H_2O_2(l)$	−187.78	−120.42	109.6	89.1
Phosphorus				
$P(g)$	314.64	278.28	167.268	20.786
$P(white)$	0.0	0.0	41.09	23.840
$P(red)$	−17.6	−12.1	22.80	21.21
$P(black)$	−39.3			
$P_4(g)$	58.91	24.48	279.87	67.15
$PH_3(g)$	5.4	13.4	210.12	37.11
$P_4O_6(s)$	−1640.1			
$P_4O_{10}(s)$	−2984.0	−2697.8	228.86	211.71
$HPO_3(s)$	−948.5			
$H_3PO_2(s)$	−604.6			
$H_3PO_3(s)$	−964.4			
$H_3PO_4(s)$	−1279.1	−1119.22	110.50	106.06
$H_3PO_4(l)$	−1266.9			
$H_3PO_4(aq)$	−1288.34	−1142.65	158.2	
$H_4P_2O_7(s)$	−2241.0			
$PF_5(g)$	−1595.8			
$PF_3(g)$	−918.8	−897.5	273.13	58.70
$PCl_5(g)$	−374.9	−305.0	364.47	112.80
$PCl_5(s)$	−443.5			
$PCl_3(l)$	−319.7	−272.4	217.2	
$PCl_3(g)$	−287.0	−267.8	311.67	71.84
Potassium				
$K(s)$	0.0	0.0	63.6	29.16
$K(g)$	90.00	61.17	160.230	20.786
$KOH(s)$	−425.85			
$KOH(aq)$	−481.16	−439.575	9.20	
$KCl(s)$	−435.868	−408.325	82.68	51.51
$KBr(s)$	−392.17	−379.20	96.44	53.85
$KI(s)$	−327.65	−322.29	104.35	55.06
$K_2CO_3(s)$	−1146.12			
$KNO_3(s)$	−492.71	−393.13	132.93	96.27
$K_2SO_4(s)$	−1433.69	−1316.37	175.7	130.1
$K_2SO_4(aq)$	−1409.92			
$KMnO_4(s)$	−813.4	−713.8	171.71	119.2
$K_2Cr_2O_7(s)$	−2033.01			
Selenium				
$Se(black)$	0.0	0.0	42.442	25.363
$Se(red)$	6.7			
$Se(g)$	227.07	187.07	176.61	20.828
$H_2Se(g)$	29.7	15.9	218.91	34.73
$SeO_2(s)$	−225.35			
$SeO_3(s)$	−166.9			
$H_2SeO_4(s)$	−530.1			
$SeF_6(g)$	−1117	−1017	313.76	110.5
$SeCL_4(s)$	−183.3			
Silicon				
$Si(s)$	0.0	0.0	18.83	20.00
$Si(g)$	455.6	411.3	167.86	22.251
$SiH_4(g)$	34.3	56.9	204.51	42.84
$SiO_2(\alpha\text{-quartz})$	−910.94	−856.67	41.84	44.43
$H_2SiO_4(s)$	−1481.1	−1333.0	193	

Substance	$\Delta H_f°$ (kJ/mol)	$\Delta G_f°$ (kJ/mol)	$S°$ (J/K mol)	$C_p°$ (J/K mol)
$H_2SiO_3(s)$	−1188.7	−1092.4	134	
$SiF_4(g)$	−1614.94	−1572.68	282.38	73.64
$SiCl_4(l)$	−687.0	−619.90	239.7	145.31
$SiBr_4(l)$	−457.3	−443.9	277.8	
SiC(cubic)	−65.3	−62.8	16.61	26.86
Silver				
$Ag(s)$	0.0	0.0	42.55	25.351
$Ag_2O(s)$	−31.05	−11.21	121.3	65.86
Ag_2S(orthorhombic)	−32.6	−40.67	140.01	76.53
$AgCl(s)$	−127.068	−109.805	96.2	50.80
$[AgCl_2]^-(aq)$	−245.2	−215.5	231.4	
$AgI(s)$	−61.84	−66.19	115.5	56.82
$AgNO_3(s)$	−124.39	−33.47	140.92	93.05
$[Ag(MH_3)_2]^+(aq)$	−111.29	−17.24	245.2	
Sodium				
$Na(s)$	0.0	0.0	51.0	28.41
$Na(g)$	108.70	78.12	153.616	20.7861
$NaOH(s)$	−426.73			80.3
$NaOH(aq)$	−469.595	−419.170	49.8	
$Na_2S(s)$	−373.2			
$NaCl(s)$	−411.003	−384.028	72.4	49.71
$NaCl(aq)$	−407.112	−393.041	115.5	
$Na_2CO_3(s)$	−1130.9	−1047.7	136.0	110.50
$NaHCO_3(s)$	−947.7	−964.8	102.1	87.61
$Na_2SO_4(s)$	−1384.49	−1266.83	149.49	127.61
$Na_2S_2O_3(s)$	−1117.1			146.0
$NaClO_4(s)$	−385.68			100.8
$NaCH_3COO(s)$	−710.4			
Strontium				
$Sr(s)$	0.0	0.0	54.4	25.1
$SrO(s)$	−590.4	−559.8	54.4	45.02
$SrCO_3(s)$	−1218.4	−1137.6	97.1	81.42
$SrCl_2(s)$	−828.4	−781.2	117	79.1
Sulfur				
S(rhombic)	0.0	0.0	31.80	22.64
S(monoclinic)	0.33			
$S(g)$	278.805	238.283	167.711	23.673
$S_8(g)$	102.30	49.66	430.87	156.44
$H_2S(g)$	−20.63	−33.56	205.69	34.23
$SO_2(g)$	−296.830	−300.194	248.11	39.87
$SO_3(s)$	−454.51	−368.99	52.3	
$SO_3(g)$	−395.72	−371.08	256.65	50.67
$H_2SO_4(l)$	−813.989	−690.101	156.904	138.91
$H_2SO_4(aq)$	−909.27	−744.63	20.1	−293
$SCl_2(l)$	−50.21			
$S_2Cl_2(l)$	−59.41			
Tellurium				
$Te(s)$	0.0	0.0	49.71	25.73
$H_2Te(g)$	99.6			
$TeO_2(s)$	−322.6	−270.3	79.5	
Tin				
Sn(white)	0.0	0.0	51.55	26.99
Sn(gray)	−2.09	0.13	44.14	25.77
$SnO(s)$	−285.8	−256.9	56.5	44.31
$SnO_2(s)$	−580.7	−520.5	52.3	52.59

Table IV.2   **A-21**

Substance	ΔH_f° (kJ/mol)	ΔG_f° (kJ/mol)	S° (J/K mol)	C_p° (J/K mol)
$SnCl_4(l)$	−511.3	−440.2	258.6	165.3
$SnCl_2(s)$	−325.1			
$SnCl_2 \cdot 2H_2O(s)$	−921.3			
Uranium				
U	0.0	0.0	50.33	27.49
$UO_2(s)$	−1130	−1075	77.8	
$UO_3(s)$	−1264	−1184	98.62	
$UF_6(g)$	−2113	−2029	379.74	
Xenon				
$Xe(g)$	0.0	0.0	169.5394	20.7857
$XeF_4(s)$	−261.5			
Zinc				
$Zn(s)$	0.0	0.0	41.63	25.40
$ZnO(s)$	−348.28	−318.32	43.64	40.25
$Zn(OH)_2(s)$	−644	−552	81.6	
ZnS(wurtzite)	−192.63			
ZnS(sphalerite)	−205.98	−201.29	57.7	46.0
$ZnCl_2(s)$	−415.05	−369.430	111.46	71.34
$ZnSO_4(s)$	−982.822	−874.5	119.66	

TABLE IV.2   **Vapor pressure of water below 100°C**

Temperature (°C)	Vapor Pressure (Torr)	Temperature (°C)	Vapor Pressure (Torr)	Temperature (°C)	Vapor Pressure (Torr)
0.0	4.579	35.0	42.175	70.0	233.7
1.0	4.926	36.0	44.563	71.0	243.9
2.0	5.294	37.0	47.067	72.0	254.6
3.0	5.685	38.0	49.692	73.0	265.7
4.0	6.101	39.0	52.442	74.0	272.2
5.0	6.543	40.0	55.324	75.0	289.1
6.0	7.013	41.0	58.34	76.0	301.4
7.0	7.513	42.0	61.50	77.0	314.1
8.0	8.045	43.0	64.80	78.0	327.3
9.0	8.609	44.0	68.26	79.0	341.0
10.0	9.202	45.0	71.88	80.0	355.1
11.0	9.844	46.0	75.65	81.0	369.7
12.0	10.518	47.0	79.60	82.0	384.9
13.0	11.231	48.0	83.71	83.0	400.6
14.0	11.987	49.0	88.02	84.0	416.8
15.0	12.788	50.0	92.51	85.0	433.6
16.0	13.634	51.0	97.20	86.0	450.9
17.0	14.530	52.0	102.09	87.0	468.7
18.0	15.477	53.0	107.20	88.0	487.1
19.0	16.477	54.0	112.51	89.0	506.1

Temperature (°C)	Vapor Pressure (Torr)	Temperature (°C)	Vapor Pressure (Torr)	Temperature (°C)	Vapor Pressure (Torr)
20.0	17.535	55.0	118.04	90.0	525.76
21.0	18.650	56.0	123.80	91.0	546.05
22.0	19.827	57.0	129.82	92.0	566.99
23.0	21.068	58.0	136.08	93.0	588.60
24.0	22.377	59.0	142.60	94.0	610.90
25.0	23.756	60.0	149.38	95.0	633.90
26.0	25.209	61.0	156.43	96.0	657.62
27.0	26.739	62.0	163.77	97.0	682.07
28.0	28.349	63.0	171.38	98.0	707.27
29.0	30.043	64.0	179.31	99.0	733.24
30.0	31.824	65.0	187.54	100.0	760.00
31.0	33.695	66.0	196.09		
32.0	35.663	67.0	204.96		
33.0	37.729	68.0	214.17		
34.0	39.898	69.0	223.73		

Equilibrium Constants

TABLE V.1 K_a, **Ionization Constants of Acids at 25 °C** The acids are arranged in alphabetical order of the nonmetal atom. (Data mainly from *Stability Constants of Metal-Ion Complexes*, Special Publications **17** (1964) and **25** (1971), The Chemical Society, London.)

Name	Formula	K_a	Name	Formula	K_a
Inorganic and organic acids			*Oxygen*		
Arsenic			Hydrogen peroxide	H_2O_2	2.2×10^{-12}
Arsenic	H_3AsO_4	6.5×10^{-3}	*Phosphorus*		
	$H_2AsO_4^-$	1.1×10^{-7}	Phosphoric	H_3PO_4	7.5×10^{-3}
	$HAsO_4^{2-}$	3×10^{-12}		$H_2PO_4^-$	6.6×10^{-8}
				HPO_4^{2-}	1×10^{-12}
Boron			Phosphorous	H_3PO_3	3×10^{-2}
Boric	H_3BO_3	6.0×10^{-10}		$H_2PO_3^-$	1.6×10^{-7}
Bromine			Hypophosphorous	H_3PO_2	1.23×10^{-2}
Hydrobromic	HBr	large	Pyrophosphoric	$H_4P_2O_7$	1.2×10^{-1}
Hypobromous	$HBrO$	2.2×10^{-9}		$H_3P_2O_7^-$	7.9×10^{-2}
Carbon				$H_2P_2O_7^{2-}$	2.0×10^{-7}
Acetic	CH_3COOH	1.754×10^{-5}		$HP_2O_7^{3-}$	4.8×10^{-10}
Benzoic	C_6H_5COOH	6.6×10^{-5}	*Silicon*		
Carbonic	H_2CO_3	4.5×10^{-7}	Metasilicic	H_2SiO_3	3.2×10^{-10}
	HCO_3^-	4.8×10^{-11}		$HSiO_3^-$	1.5×10^{-12}
Chloroacetic	$CH_2ClCOOH$	1.40×10^{-3}	*Sulfur*		
Cyanic	$HNCO$	3.3×10^{-4}	Hydrosulfuric	H_2S	1.0×10^{-7}
Dichloroacetic	$CHCl_2COOH$	3.32×10^{-2}		HS^-	3×10^{-13}
Formic	$HCOOH$	1.772×10^{-4}	Sulfuric	H_2SO_4	large
Hydrocyanic	HCN	6.2×10^{-10}		HSO_4^-	1.0×10^{-2}
Oxalic	$H_2C_2O_4$	5.60×10^{-2}	Sulfurous	H_2SO_3	1.43×10^{-2}
	$HC_2O_4^-$	6.2×10^{-5}		HSO_3^-	5.0×10^{-8}
Propionic	CH_3CH_2COOH	1.3×10^{-5}	Thiosulfuric	$H_2S_2O_3$	2.0×10^{-2}
Thiocyanic	$HNCS$	large		$HS_2O_3^-$	3.2×10^{-3}
Trichloroacetic	CCl_3COOH	2×10^{-1}	**Amphoteric hydroxides**		
Chlorine			Aluminum hydroxide	$Al(OH)_3$	4×10^{-13}
Hydrochloric	HCl	large	Antimony(III) hydroxide	$SbO(OH)$	1×10^{-11}
Perchloric	$HClO_4$	large	Chromium(III) hydroxide	$Cr(OH)_3$	9×10^{-17}
Chloric	$HClO_3$	large	Copper(II) hydroxide	$Cu(OH)_2$	1×10^{-19}
Chlorous	$HClO_2$	1.1×10^{-2}		$HCuO_2$	7.0×10^{-14}
Hypochlorous	$HClO$	2.90×10^{-8}	Lead(II) hydroxide	$Pb(OH)_2$	4.6×10^{-16}
Chromium			Tin(IV) hydroxide	$Sn(OH)_4$	10^{-32}
Chromic	H_2CrO_4	1.8×10^{-1}	Tin(II) hydroxide	$Sn(OH)_2$	3.8×10^{-15}
	$HCrO_4^-$	3.2×10^{-7}	Zinc hydroxide	$Zn(OH)_2$	1.0×10^{-29}
Fluorine			**Metal cations**		
Hydrofluoric	HF	6.5×10^{-4}	Aluminum ion	Al^{3+}	1.4×10^{-5}
Iodine			Ammonium ion	NH_4^+	6.3×10^{-10}
Hydroiodic	HI	large	Bismuth(III) ion	Bi^{3+}	1×10^{-2}
Periodic	HIO_4	5.6×10^{-9}	Chromium(III) ion	Cr^{3+}	1×10^{-4}
Iodic	HIO_3	1.6×10^{-1}	Copper(II) ion	Cu^{2+}	1×10^{-8}
Hypoiodous	HIO	2.3×10^{-11}	Iron(III) ion	Fe^{3+}	4.0×10^{-3}
Manganese			Iron (II) ion	Fe^{2+}	1.2×10^{-6}
Permanganic	$HMnO_4$	large	Magnesium ion	Mg^{2+}	2×10^{-12}
Nitrogen			Mercury(II) ion	Hg^{2+}	2×10^{-3}
Nitric	HNO_3	large	Zinc ion	Zn^{2+}	2.5×10^{-10}
Nitrous	HNO_2	7.2×10^{-4}			

TABLE V.2 K_b, **Ionization Constants of Bases at 25 °C**   For sparingly soluble bases, see Table V.3. The ions are arranged in alphabetical order. (Data mainly from *Stability Constants of Metal-Ion Complexes*, Special Publications **17** (1964) and **25** (1971), The Chemical Society, London.)

Name	Formula	K_b	Name	Formula	K_b
Inorganic and organic bases			Cyanide ion	CN^-	1.6×10^{-5}
Ammonia	NH_3	1.6×10^{-5}	Fluoride ion	F^-	1.5×10^{-11}
Aniline	$C_6H_5NH_2$	4.2×10^{-10}	Formate ion	$HCOO^-$	5.643×10^{-11}
Diethylamine	$(C_2H_5)_2NH$	9.5×10^{-4}	Nitrite ion	NO_2^-	1.4×10^{-11}
Dimethylamine	$(CH_3)_2NH$	5.9×10^{-4}	Oxalate ion	$C_2O_4^{2-}$	1.6×10^{-10}
Ethylamine	$C_2H_5NH_2$	4.7×10^{-4}		$HC_2O_4^-$	1.79×10^{-13}
Methylamine	CH_3NH_2	3.9×10^{-4}	Phosphate ion	PO_4^{3-}	1×10^{-2}
Triethylamine	$(C_2H_5)_3N$	5.2×10^{-4}		HPO_4^{2-}	1.5×10^{-7}
Trimethylamine	$(CH_3)_3N$	6.3×10^{-5}		$H_2PO_4^-$	1.3×10^{-12}
			Phosphite ion	HPO_3^{2-}	6.3×10^{-8}
Anions				$H_2PO_3^-$	3×10^{-13}
Acetate ion	CH_3COO^-	5.701×10^{-10}	Metasilicate ion	SiO_3^{2-}	6.7×10^{-3}
Arsenate ion	AsO_4^{3-}	3.3×10^{-3}		$HSiO_3^-$	3.1×10^{-5}
	$HAsO_4^{2-}$	9.1×10^{-8}	Sulfate ion	SO_4^{2-}	1.0×10^{-12}
	$H_2AsO_4^-$	1.5×10^{-12}	Sulfite ion	SO_3^{2-}	2.0×10^{-7}
Borate ion	$H_2BO_3^-$	1.6×10^{-5}		HSO_3^-	6.99×10^{-13}
	$B_4O_7^{2-}$	10^{-3}	Sulfide ion	S^{2-}	3×10^{-2}
Carbonate ion	CO_3^{2-}	2.1×10^{-4}		HS^-	1.0×10^{-7}
	HCO_3^-	2.2×10^{-8}	Thiocyanate ion	NCS^-	1.4×10^{-11}
Chromate ion	CrO_4^{2-}	3.1×10^{-8}	Thiosulfate ion	$S_2O_3^{2-}$	3.1×10^{-12}

TABLE V.3 K_{sp}, **Solubility Products of Sparingly Soluble Salts and Bases at 25 °C**   The substances within each group are arranged in order of decreasing K_{sp}.

Salt	K_{sp}	Salt	K_{sp}	Salt	K_{sp}
Acetates		*Chlorides*		*Hydroxides*	
$Ag(CH_3COO)$	4.4×10^{-3}	$PbCl_2$	2×10^{-5}	$Ba(OH)_2$	1.3×10^{-2}
$Hg_2(CH_3COO)_2$	4×10^{-10}	$CuCl$	1.2×10^{-6}	$Sr(OH)_2$	6.4×10^{-3}
Arsenates		$AgCl$	1.8×10^{-10}	$Ca(OH)_2$	4.0×10^{-5}
Ag_3AsO_4	1×10^{-22}	Hg_2Cl_2	1.3×10^{-18}	Ag_2O	2×10^{-8}
Bromides		*Chromates*		$Mg(OH)_2$	7.1×10^{-12}
$PbBr_2$	3.9×10^{-5}	$CaCrO_4$	6×10^{-4}	$BiO(OH)$	1×10^{-12}
$CuBr$	5.2×10^{-9}	$SrCrO_4$	2.2×10^{-5}	$Be(OH)_2$	4×10^{-13}
$AgBr$	4.9×10^{-13}	Hg_2CrO_4	2.0×10^{-9}	$Mn(OH)_2$	2×10^{-13}
Hg_2Br_2	5.8×10^{-23}	$BaCrO_4$	1.2×10^{-10}	$Cd(OH)_2$	8.1×10^{-15}
Carbonates		Ag_2CrO_4	2.5×10^{-12}	$Pb(OH)_2$	1.2×10^{-15}
$MgCO_3$	1×10^{-5}	$PbCrO_4$	2.8×10^{-13}	$Fe(OH)_2$	8×10^{-16}
$NiCO_3$	1.3×10^{-7}	*Cyanides*		$Ni(OH)_2$	3×10^{-16}
$CaCO_3$	3.84×10^{-9}	$AgCN$	2.3×10^{-16}	$Co(OH)_2$	2×10^{-16}
$BaCO_3$	2.0×10^{-9}	*Ferrocyanides*		$Zn(OH)_2$	1.2×10^{-17}
$SrCO_3$	5.2×10^{-10}	$KFe[Fe(CN)_6]$	3×10^{-41}	$SbO(OH)$	1×10^{-17}
$MnCO_3$	5.0×10^{-10}	$Ag_4[Fe(CN)_6]$	2×10^{-41}	$Cu(OH)_2$	1.3×10^{-20}
$CuCO_3$	2.3×10^{-10}	$K_2Zn_3[Fe(CN)_6]_2$	1×10^{-95}	$Hg(OH)_2$	4×10^{-26}
$CoCO_3$	1.0×10^{-10}	*Fluorides*		$Sn(OH)_2$	6×10^{-27}
$FeCO_3$	2.1×10^{-11}	BaF_2	1.0×10^{-6}	$Cr(OH)_3$	6×10^{-31}
$ZnCO_3$	1.7×10^{-11}	MgF_2	6.8×10^{-9}	$Al(OH)_3$	3.5×10^{-34}
Ag_2CO_3	8.1×10^{-12}	SrF_2	2.5×10^{-9}	$Fe(OH)_3$	3×10^{-39}
$CdCO_3$	1.0×10^{-12}	CaF_2	2.7×10^{-11}	$Sn(OH)_4$	10^{-57}
$PbCO_3$	7.4×10^{-14}	ThF_4	4×10^{-28}		

Table V.4 **A-25**

Salt	K_{sp}	Salt	K_{sp}	Salt	K_{sp}
Iodides		CdC_2O_4	2×10^{-8}	*Sulfates*	
PbI_2	7.1×10^{-9}	ZnC_2O_4	2×10^{-9}	$CaSO_4$	2.5×10^{-5}
CuI	1.1×10^{-12}	CaC_2O_4	1×10^{-9}	Ag_2SO_4	1.5×10^{-5}
AgI	8.3×10^{-17}	$Ag_2C_2O_4$	3.5×10^{-11}	Hg_2SO_4	6.8×10^{-7}
HgI_2	3×10^{-26}	PbC_2O_4	4.8×10^{-12}	$SrSO_4$	3.5×10^{-7}
Hg_2I_2	4.5×10^{-29}	$Hg_2C_2O_4$	2×10^{-13}	$PbSO_4$	2.2×10^{-8}
Nitrates		MnC_2O_4	1×10^{-15}	$BaSO_4$	1.7×10^{-10}
$BiO(NO_3)$	2.8×10^{-3}	$La_2(C_2O_4)_3$	2×10^{-28}	*Sulfides*	
Nitrites		*Phosphates*		MnS	2.3×10^{-13}
$Ag(NO_2)$	6.0×10^{-4}	Li_3PO_4	3×10^{-13}	FeS	4.2×10^{-17}
Oxalates		$Mg(NH_4)PO_4$	3×10^{-13}	NiS	3×10^{-19}
MgC_2O_4	8×10^{-5}	Ag_3PO_4	1.4×10^{-16}	CoS	4×10^{-21}
$CoCrO_4$	4×10^{-6}	$AlPO_4$	5.8×10^{-9}	ZnS	2×10^{-24}
FeC_2O_4	2×10^{-7}	$Mn_3(PO_4)_2$	1×10^{-22}	SnS	3×10^{-27}
NiC_2O_4	1×10^{-7}	$Ba_3(PO_4)_2$	3×10^{-23}	CdS	2×10^{-28}
SrC_2O_4	5×10^{-8}	$BiPO_4$	1.3×10^{-23}	PbS	1×10^{-28}
CuC_2O_4	3×10^{-8}	$Ca_3(PO_4)_2$	10^{-26}	CuS	6×10^{-36}
BaC_2O_4	2×10^{-8}	$Sr_3(PO_4)_2$	4×10^{-28}	Cu_2S	3×10^{-48}
		$Mg_3(PO_4)_2$	10^{-32}	Ag_2S	7.1×10^{-50}
		$Pb_3(PO_4)_2$	7.9×10^{-43}	HgS	4×10^{-53}
				Fe_2S_3	1×10^{-88}

TABLE V.4

K_d, **Dissociation Constants for Complexes at 25 °C** The complexes for a given metal ion are arranged in order of decreasing K_d. The following abbreviations are used to represent ligands: (en) is the ethylenediamine molecule, $H_2NCH_2CH_2NH_2$; (nta) is the nitrilotriacetate ion, $N(CH_2COO)_2^{3-}$; (gly) is the glycine ion, $H_2NCH_2COO^-$; and (edta) is the ethylenediaminetetraacetate ion, $(OOCCH_2)_2NCH_2CH_2N(CH_2COO)_2^{4-}$.

Complex	K_d	Complex	K_d	Complex	K_d
Aluminum		*Copper*		*Mercury*	
$[AlF_6]^{3-}$	3×10^{-20}	$[Cu(SCN)_2]$	1.8×10^{-4}	$[HgCl_4]^{2-}$	2×10^{-16}
Calcium		$[CuCl_2]^-$	1.15×10^{15}	$[Hg(SCN)_4]^{2-}$	2.0×10^{-22}
$[Ca(P_2O_7)]^{2-}$	1×10^{-5}	$[Cu(P_2O_7)]^{2-}$	2.0×10^{-7}	*Nickel*	
$[Ca(nta)_2]^{4-}$	2.44×10^{-12}	$[Cu(C_2O_4)_2]^{2-}$	6×10^{-11}	$[Ni(NH_3)_6]^{2+}$	1×10^{-9}
Cadmium		$[Cu(NH_3)_4]^{2+}$	1×10^{-13}	*Palladium*	
$[CdCl_4]^{2-}$	9.3×10^{-3}	$[Cu(gly)_2]$	5.6×10^{-16}	$[PbBr_4]^{2-}$	8.0×10^{-14}
$[Cd(SCN)_4]^{2-}$	1×10^{-3}	$[Cu(OH)_4]^{2-}$	7.6×10^{-17}	$[PdCl_4]^{2-}$	6×10^{-14}
$[CdBr_4]^{2-}$	2×10^{-4}	$[Cu(eta)]^{2-}$	1.38×10^{-19}	*Silver*	
$[Cd(NH_3)_6]^{2+}$	1×10^{-5}	*Gold*		$[Ag(OH)_3]^{2-}$	1.7×10^{-5}
$[CdI_4]^{2-}$	8×10^{-7}	$[Au(CN)_2]^-$	5×10^{-39}	$[Ag(en)]^+$	1×10^{-5}
$[Cd(CH_3NH_2)_4]^{2+}$	2.82×10^{-7}	*Iron*		$[AgCl_2]^-$	9×10^{-6}
$[Cd(NH_3)_4]^{2+}$	1×10^{-7}	$[Fe(C_2O_4)_3]^{4-}$	6×10^{-6}	$[AgCl_4]^{3-}$	5×10^{-6}
$[Cd(en)_4]^{2+}$	2.60×10^{-11}	$[Fe(SCN)_3]$	5×10^{-7}	$[AgBr_2]^-$	7.8×10^{-8}
$[Cd(CN)_4]^{2-}$	8.2×10^{-18}	$[Fe(C_2O_4)_2]^{2-}$	2×10^{-8}	$[Ag(NH_3)_2]^+$	6.2×10^{-8}
Cobalt		$[Fe(C_2O_4)_3]^{3-}$	3×10^{-21}	$[Ag(SCN)_4]^{3-}$	2.1×10^{-10}
$[Co(NH_3)_6]^{2+}$	9×10^{-6}	$[Fe(CN)_6]^{4-}$	1.3×10^{-37}	$[Au(CN)_2]^-$	1×10^{-22}
$[Co(C_2O_4)_3]^{4-}$	2.2×10^{-7}	$[Fe(CN)_6]^{3-}$	1.3×10^{-44}	*Zinc*	
$[Co(en)_3]^{2+}$	1.52×10^{-14}	*Lead*		$[Zn(NH_3)_4]^{2+}$	3.46×10^{-10}
$[Co(en)_3]^{3+}$	2.04×10^{-49}	$[Pb(SCN)_2]$	3×10^{-3}	$[Zn(gly)_2]$	1.1×10^{-10}
		Magnesium		$[Zn(edta)]^{2-}$	2.63×10^{-17}
		$[Mg(P_2O_7)]^{2-}$	2×10^{-6}	$[Zn(CN)_4]^{2-}$	2.4×10^{-20}
		$[Mg(nta)_2]^{4-}$	6.3×10^{-11}	$[Zn(OH)_4]^{2-}$	5×10^{-21}

Standard Reduction Potentials at 25 °

TABLE VI.1 **Acidic Media** (Data adapted from T. Moeller, *Inorganic Chemistry*, New York: Wiley, 1982, p 789–803.)

Reduction Half Reaction	E°, V	Reduction Half Reaction	E°, V
$Li^+ + e^- \rightarrow Li(s)$	−3.045	$PbCl_2(s) + 2e^- \rightarrow Pb(s) + 2Cl^-$	−0.268
$Rb^+ + e^- \rightarrow Rb(s)$	−2.925	$V^{3+} + e^- \rightarrow V^{2+}$	−0.256
$K^+ + e^- \rightarrow K(s)$	−2.925	$Ni^{2+} + 2e^- \rightarrow Ni(s)$	−0.250
$Cs^+ + e^- \rightarrow Cs(s)$	−2.923	$AgI(s) + e^- \rightarrow Ag(s) + I^-$	−0.1518
$Ra^{2+} + 2e^- \rightarrow Ra(s)$	−2.916	$Sn^{2+} + 2e^- \rightarrow Sn(s)$	−0.136
$Ba^{2+} + 2e^- \rightarrow Ba(s)$	−2.906	$Pb^{2+} + 2e^- \rightarrow Pb(s)$	−0.126
$Sr^{2+} + 2e^- \rightarrow Sr(s)$	−2.888	$P(s) + 3H^+ + 3e^- \rightarrow PH_3(g)$	−0.063
$Ca^{2+} + 2e^- \rightarrow Ca(s)$	−2.866	$Fe^{3+} + 3e^- \rightarrow Fe(s)$	−0.036
$Na^+ + e^- \rightarrow Na(s)$	−2.714	$2H^+ + 2e^- \rightarrow H_2(g)$	0.000
$La^{3+} + 3e^- \rightarrow La(s)$	−2.522	$AgBr(s) + e^- \rightarrow Ag(s) + Br^-$	+0.0713
$Ce^{3+} + 3e^- \rightarrow Ce(s)$	−2.483	$Si(s) + 4H^+ + 4e^- \rightarrow SiH_4(g)$	+0.102
$Mg^{2+} + 2e^- \rightarrow Mg(s)$	−2.363	$Hg_2Br_2(s) + 2e^- \rightarrow 2Hg(l) + 2Br^-$	+0.1397
$H_2(g) + 2e^- \rightarrow 2H^-$	−2.25	$S(s) + 2H^+ + 2e^- \rightarrow H_2S(aq)$	+0.142
$Sc^{3+} + 3e^- \rightarrow Sc(s)$	−2.077	$Sn^{4+} + 2e^- \rightarrow Sn^{2+}$	+0.15
$[AlF_6]^{3-} + 3e^- \rightarrow Al(s) + 6F^-$	−2.069	$Sb_2O_3(s) + 6H^+ + 6e^- \rightarrow 2Sb(s) + 3H_2O(l)$	+0.152
$Be^{2+} + 2e^- \rightarrow Be(s)$	−1.847	$Cu^{2+} + e^- \rightarrow Cu^+$	+0.153
$V^{3+} + 3e^- \rightarrow V(s)$	−1.798	$SO_4^{2-} + 4H^+ + 2e^- \rightarrow H_2SO_3(aq) + H_2O(l)$	+0.172
$Hf^{4+} + 4e^- \rightarrow Hf(s)$	−1.700	$AgCl(s) + e^- \rightarrow Ag(s) + Cl^-$	+0.2222
$Al^{3+} + 3e^- \rightarrow Al(s)$	−1.662	$[Hg_2Br_4]^{2-} + 2e^- \rightarrow Hg(l) + 4Br^-$	+0.223
$Ti^{2+} + 2e^- \rightarrow Ti(s)$	−1.628	$Hg_2Cl_2(s) + 2e^- \rightarrow 2Hg(l) + 2Cl^-$	+0.2676
$Zr^{4+} + 4e^- \rightarrow Zr(s)$	−1.529	$Cu^{2+} + 2e^- \rightarrow Cu(s)$	+0.337
$V^{4+} + 4e^- \rightarrow V(s)$	−1.50	$SO_4^{2-} + 8H^+ + 6e^- \rightarrow S(s) + 4H_2O(l)$	+0.3572
$[SiF_6]^{2-} + 4e^- \rightarrow Si(s) + 6F^-$	−1.24	$VO^{2+} + 2H^+ + e^- \rightarrow V^{3+} + H_2O(l)$	+0.359
$[TiF_6]^{2-} + 4e^- \rightarrow Ti(s) + 6F^-$	−1.191	$[Fe(CN)_6]^{3-} + e^- \rightarrow [Fe(CN)_6]^{4-}$	+0.36
$Mn^{2+} + 2e^- \rightarrow Mn(s)$	−1.185	$H_2SO_3(aq) + 4H^+ + 4e^- \rightarrow S(s) + 3H_2O(l)$	+0.450
$V^{2+} + 2e^- \rightarrow V(s)$	−1.175	$Cu^+ + e^- \rightarrow Cu(s)$	+0.521
$Cr^{2+} + 2e^- \rightarrow Cr(s)$	−0.913	$I_2(s) + 2e^- \rightarrow 2I^-$	+0.5355
$H_3BO_3(s) + 3H^+ + 3e^- \rightarrow B(s) + 3H_2O(l)$	−0.869	$MnO_4^- + e^- \rightarrow MnO_4^{2-}$	+0.564
$SiO_2(s) + 4H^+ + 4e^- \rightarrow Si(s) + 2H_2O(l)$	−0.857	$Hg_2SO_4(s) + 2e^- \rightarrow 2Hg(l) + SO_4^{2-}$	+0.6151
$Zn^{2+} + 2e^- \rightarrow Zn(s)$	−0.7628	$Cu^{2+} + Br^- + e^- \rightarrow CuBr(s)$	+0.640
$Cr^{3+} + 3e^- \rightarrow Cr(s)$	−0.744	$Po^{2+} + 2e^- \rightarrow Po(s)$	+0.65
$Te(s) + 2H^+ + 2e^- \rightarrow H_2Te(aq)$	−0.739	$[PtCl_6]^{2-} + 2e^- \rightarrow [PtCl_4]^{2-} + 2Cl^-$	+0.68
$U^{4+} + e^- \rightarrow U^{3+}$	−0.607	$O_2(g) + 2H^+ + 2e^- \rightarrow H_2O_2(aq)$	+0.6824
$As(s) + 3H^+ + 3e^- \rightarrow AsH_3(g)$	−0.607	$[PtCl_4]^{2-} + 2e^- \rightarrow Pt(s) + 4Cl^-$	+0.73
$Ga^{3+} + 3e^- \rightarrow Ga(s)$	−0.529	$Fe^{3+} + e^- \rightarrow Fe^{2+}$	+0.771
$Fe^{2+} + 2e^- \rightarrow Fe(s)$	−0.4402	$Hg_2^{2+} + 2e^- \rightarrow 2Hg(l)$	+0.788
$Cr^{3+} + e^- \rightarrow Cr^{2+}$	−0.408	$Ag^+ + e^- \rightarrow Ag(s)$	+0.7991
$Cd^{2+} + 2e^- \rightarrow Cd(s)$	−0.4029	$Rh^{3+} + 3e^- \rightarrow Rh(s)$	+0.80
$Se(s) + 2H^+ + 2e^- \rightarrow H_2Se(aq)$	−0.399	$2NO_3^- + 4H^+ + 2e^- \rightarrow N_2O_4(g) + 2H_2O(l)$	+0.803
$Ti^{3+} + e^- \rightarrow Ti^{2+}$	−0.369	$Cu^{2+} + I^- + e^- \rightarrow CuI(s)$	+0.86
$PbI_2(s) + 2e^- \rightarrow Pb(s) + 2I^-$	−0.365	$2Hg^{2+} + 2e^- \rightarrow Hg_2^{2+}$	+0.920
$PbSO_4(s) + 2e^- \rightarrow Pb(s) + SO_4^{2-}$	−0.3588	$NO_3^- + 3H^+ + 2e^- \rightarrow HNO_2(aq) + H_2O(l)$	+0.94
$In^{3+} + 3e^- \rightarrow In(s)$	−0.343	$NO_3^- + 4H^+ + 3e^- \rightarrow NO(g) + 2H_2O(l)$	+0.96
$Tl^+ + e^- \rightarrow Tl(s)$	−0.3363	$Pd^{2+} + 2e^- \rightarrow Pd(s)$	+0.987
$PbBr_2(s) + 2e^- \rightarrow Pb(s) + 2Br^-$	−0.284	$[AuCl_4]^- + 3e^- \rightarrow Au(s) + 4Cl^-$	+1.00
$Co^{2+} + 2e^- \rightarrow Co(s)$	−0.277	$Br_2(l) + 2e^- \rightarrow 2Br^-$	+1.0652

Table VI.2 **A-27**

Reduction Half Reaction	E°, V	Reduction Half Reaction	E°, V
$Br_2(aq) + 2e^- \rightarrow 2Br^-$	+1.087	$MnO_4^- + 8H^+ + 5e^- \rightarrow Mn^{2+} + 4H_2O(l)$	+1.51
$SeO_4^{2-} + 4H^+ + 2e^- \rightarrow H_2SeO_3(aq) + H_2O(l)$	+1.15	$2BrO_3^- + 12H^+ + 10e^- \rightarrow Br_2(l) + 6H_2O(l)$	+1.52
$ClO_4^- + 2H^+ + 2e^- \rightarrow ClO_3^- + H_2O(l)$	+1.19	$Ce^{4+} + e^- \rightarrow Ce^{3+}$	+1.61
$2IO_3^- + 12H^+ + 10e^- \rightarrow I_2(s) + 6H_2O(l)$	+1.195	$2HClO(aq) + 2H^+ + 2e^- \rightarrow Cl_2(g) + 2H_2O(l)$	+1.63
$Pt^{2+} + 2e^- \rightarrow Pt(s)$	~1.2	$HClO_2(aq) + 2H^+ + 2e^- \rightarrow HClO(aq) + H_2O(l)$	+1.645
$ClO_3^- + 3H^+ + 2e^- \rightarrow HClO_2(aq) + H_2O(l)$	+1.21	$Au^+ + e^- \rightarrow Au(s)$	+1.691
$O_2(g) + 4H^+ + 4e^- \rightarrow 2H_2O(l)$	+1.229	$H_2O_2(aq) + 2H^+ + 2e^- \rightarrow 2H_2O(l)$	+1.776
$MnO_2(s) + 4H^+ + 2e^- \rightarrow Mn^{2+} + 2H_2O(l)$	+1.23	$Co^{3+} + e^- \rightarrow Co^{2+}$	+1.808
$2HNO_2(aq) + 4H^+ + 4e^- \rightarrow N_2O(g) + 3H_2O(l)$	+1.29	$Ag^{2+} + e^- \rightarrow Ag^+$	+1.980
$Cr_2O_7^{2-} + 14H^+ + 6e^- \rightarrow 2Cr^{3+} + 7H_2O(l)$	+1.33	$S_2O_8^{2-} + 2e^- \rightarrow 2SO_4^{2-}$	+2.01
$Cl_2(g) + 2e^- \rightarrow 2Cl^-$	+1.3595	$O_3(g) + 2H^+ + 2e^- \rightarrow O_2(g) + H_2O(l)$	+2.07
$PbO_2(s) + 4H^+ + 2e^- \rightarrow Pb^{2+} + 4H_2O(l)$	+1.455	$F_2(g) + 2e^- \rightarrow 2F^-$	+2.87
$Au^{3+} + 3e^- \rightarrow Au(s)$	+1.498	$F_2(g) + 2H^+ + 2e^- \rightarrow 2HF(aq)$	+3.06

TABLE VI.2   **Alkaline Media** (Data adapted from T. Moeller, *Inorganic Chemistry,* New York: Wiley, 1982, pp. 789–803.)

Reduction Half Reaction	E°, V	Reduction Half Reaction	E°, V
$Ca(OH)_2(s) + 2e^- \rightarrow Ca(s) + 2OH^-$	−3.02	$SbO_2^- + 2H_2O(l) + 3e^- \rightarrow Sb(s) + 4OH^-$	−0.66
$Sr(OH)_2(s) + 2e^- \rightarrow Sr(s) + 2OH^-$	−2.88	$PbO(s) + H_2O(l) + 2e^- \rightarrow Pb(s) + 2OH^-$	−0.580
$Ce(OH)_3(s) + 3e^- \rightarrow Ce(s) + 3OH^-$	−2.87	$TeO_3^{2-} + 3H_2O(l) + 4e^- \rightarrow Te(s) + 6OH^-$	−0.57
$Mg(OH)_2(s) + 2e^- \rightarrow Mg(s) + 2OH^-$	−2.690	$Fe(OH)_3(s) + e^- \rightarrow Fe(OH)_2(s) + OH^-$	−0.56
$BeO(s) + H_2O(l) + 2e^- \rightarrow Be(s) + 2OH^-$	−2.613	$S(s) + 2e^- \rightarrow S^{2-}$	−0.447
$Al(OH)_3(s) + 3e^- \rightarrow Al(s) + 3OH^-$	−2.30	$Cu_2O(s) + H_2O(l) + 2e^- \rightarrow 2Cu(s) + 2OH^-$	−0.358
$U(OH)_4(s) + e^- \rightarrow U(OH)_3(s) + OH^-$	−2.20	$TlOH(s) + e^- \rightarrow Tl(s) + OH^-$	−0.343
$U(OH)_3(s) + 3e^- \rightarrow U(s) + 3OH^-$	−2.17	$CrO_4^{2-} + 4H_2O(l) + 3e^- \rightarrow Cr(OH)_3(s) + 5OH^-$	−0.13
$H_2PO_2^- + e^- \rightarrow P(s) + 2OH^-$	−2.05	$2Cu(OH)_2(s) + 2e^- \rightarrow Cu_2O(s) + H_2O(l) + 2OH^-$	−0.080
$SiO_3^{2-} + 3H_2O(l) + 4e^- \rightarrow Si(s) + 6OH^-$	−1.697	$Tl(OH)_3(s) + 2e^- \rightarrow TlOH(s) + 2OH^-$	−0.05
$Mn(OH)_2(s) + 2e^- \rightarrow Mn(s) + 2OH^-$	−1.55	$MnO_2(s) + 2H_2O(l) + 2e^- \rightarrow Mn(OH)_2(s) + 2OH^-$	−0.05
$Cr(OH)_3(s) + 3e^- \rightarrow Cr(s) + 3OH^-$	−1.34	$NO_3^- + H_2O(l) + 2e^- \rightarrow NO_2^- + 2OH^-$	+0.01
$Zn(OH)_2(s) + 2e^- \rightarrow Zn(s) + 2OH^-$	−1.245	$SeO_4^{2-} + H_2O(l) + 2e^- \rightarrow SeO_3^{2-} + 2OH^-$	+0.05
$Te(s) + 2e^- \rightarrow Te^{2-}$	−1.143	$HgO(s) + H_2O(l) + 2e^- \rightarrow Hg(l) + 2OH^-$	+0.098
$PO_4^{3-} + 2H_2O(l) + 2e^- \rightarrow HPO_3^{2-} + 3OH^-$	−1.12	$PbO_2(s) + H_2O(l) + 2e^- \rightarrow PbO(s) + 2OH^-$	+0.247
$WO_4^{2-} + 4H_2O(l) + 6e^- \rightarrow W(s) + 8OH^-$	−1.05	$IO_3^- + 3H_2O(l) + 6e^- \rightarrow I^- + 6OH^-$	+0.26
$MoO_4^{2-} + 4H_2O(l) + 6e^- \rightarrow Mo(s) + 8OH^-$	−1.05	$ClO_3^- + H_2O(l) + 2e^- \rightarrow ClO_2^- + 2OH^-$	+0.33
$In(OH)_3(s) + 3e^- \rightarrow In(s) + 3OH^-$	−1.00	$Ag_2O(s) + H_2O(l) + 2e^- \rightarrow 2Ag(s) + 2OH^-$	+0.345
$PbS(s) + 2e^- \rightarrow Pb(s) + S^{2-}$	−0.93	$ClO_4^- + H_2O(l) + 2e^- \rightarrow ClO_3^- + 2OH^-$	+0.36
$SO_4^{2-} + H_2O(l) + 2e^- \rightarrow SO_3^{2-} + 2OH^-$	−0.93	$O_2(g) + 2H_2O(l) + 4e^- \rightarrow 4OH^-$	+0.401
$Se(s) + 2e^- \rightarrow Se^{2-}$	−0.92	$IO^- + H_2O(l) + 2e^- \rightarrow I^- + 2OH^-$	+0.485
$P(s) + 3H_2O(l) + 3e^- \rightarrow PH_3(g) + 3OH^-$	−0.89	$NiO_2(s) + 2H_2O(l) + 2e^- \rightarrow Ni(OH)_2(s) + 2OH^-$	+0.490
$Fe(OH)_2(s) + 2e^- \rightarrow Fe(s) + 2OH^-$	−0.877	$MnO_4^- + 2H_2O(l) + 3e^- \rightarrow MnO_2(s) + 4OH^-$	+0.588
$2H_2O(l) + 2e^- \rightarrow H_2(g) + 2OH^-$	−0.8281	$BrO_3^- + 3H_2O(l) + 6e^- \rightarrow Br^- + 6OH^-$	+0.61
$Cd(OH)_2(s) + 2e^- \rightarrow Cd(s) + 2OH^-$	−0.809	$BrO^- + H_2O(l) + 2e^- \rightarrow Br^- + 2OH^-$	+0.761
$Co(OH)_2(s) + 2e^- \rightarrow Co(s) + 2OH^-$	−0.73	$ClO^- + H_2O(l) + 2e^- \rightarrow Cl^- + 2OH^-$	+0.89
$Ni(OH)_2(s) + 2e^- \rightarrow Ni(s) + 2OH^-$	−0.72	$O_3(g) + H_2O(l) + 2e^- \rightarrow O_2(g) + 2OH^-$	+1.24

TABLE V.3   **Elemental Listing of Standard Reduction Potentials at 25 °C**   (Data adapted from T. Moeller, *Inorganic Chemistry*, New York: Wiley, 1982, pp. 789–803.)

Reduction Half Reaction	E°, V	Reduction Half Reaction	E°, V
Aluminum		*Copper*	
$Al(OH)_3(s) + 3e^- \rightarrow Al(s) + 3OH^-$	-2.30	$Cu_2O(s) + H_2O(l) + 2e^- \rightarrow 2Cu(s) + 2OH^-$	-0.358
$[AlF_6]^{3-} + 3e^- \rightarrow Al(s) + 6F^-$	-2.069	$2Cu(OH)_2(s) + 2e^- \rightarrow Cu_2O(s) + H_2O(l) + 2OH^-$	-0.080
$Al^{3+} + 3e^- \rightarrow Al(s)$	-1.662	$Cu^{2+} + e^- \rightarrow Cu^+$	$+0.153$
Antimony		$Cu^{2+} + 2e^- \rightarrow Cu(s)$	$+0.337$
$SbO_2^- + 2H_2O(l) + 3e^- \rightarrow Sb(s) + 4OH^-$	-0.66	$Cu^+ + e^- \rightarrow Cu(s)$	$+0.521$
$Sb_2O_3(s) + 6H^+ + 6e^- \rightarrow 2Sb(s) + 3H_2O(l)$	$+0.152$	$Cu^{2+} + Br^- + e^- \rightarrow CuBr(s)$	$+0.640$
Arsenic		$Cu^{2+} + I^- + e^- \rightarrow CuI(s)$	$+0.86$
$As(s) + 3H^+ + 3e^- \rightarrow AsH_3(g)$	-0.607	*Fluorine*	
Barium		$F_2(g) + 2e^- \rightarrow 2F^-$	$+2.87$
$Ba^{2+} + 2e^- \rightarrow Ba(s)$	-2.906	$F_2(g) + 2H^+ + 2e^- \rightarrow 2HF(aq)$	$+3.06$
Beryllium		*Gallium*	
$BeO(s) + H_2O(l) + 2e^- \rightarrow Be(s) + 2OH^-$	-2.613	$Ga^{3+} + 3e^- \rightarrow Ga(s)$	-0.529
$Be^{2+} + 2e^- \rightarrow Be(s)$	-1.847	*Gold*	
Boron		$[AuCl_4]^- + 3e^- \rightarrow Au(s) + 4Cl^-$	$+1.00$
$H_3BO_3(s) + 3H^+ + 3e^- \rightarrow B(s) + 3H_2O(l)$	-0.869	$Au^{3+} + 3e^- \rightarrow Au(s)$	$+1.498$
Bromine		$Au^+ + e^- \rightarrow Au(s)$	$+1.691$
$BrO_3^- + 3H_2O(l) + 6e^- \rightarrow Br^- + 6OH^-$	$+0.61$	*Hafnium*	
$BrO^- + H_2O(l) + 2e^- \rightarrow Br^- + 2OH^-$	$+0.761$	$Hf^{4+} + 4e^- \rightarrow Hf(s)$	-1.700
$Br_2(l) + 2e^- \rightarrow 2Br^-$	$+1.0652$	*Hydrogen*	
$Br_2(aq) + 2e^- \rightarrow 2Br^-$	$+1.087$	$H_2(g) + 2e^- \rightarrow 2H^-$	-2.25
$2BrO_3^- + 12H^+ + 10e^- \rightarrow Br_2(l) + 6H_2O(l)$	$+1.52$	$2H^+ + 2e^- \rightarrow H_2(g)$	0.000
Cadmium		*Indium*	
$Cd(OH)_2(s) + 2e^- \rightarrow Cd(s) + 2O\lambda$	-0.809	$In(OH)_3(s) + 3e^- \rightarrow In(s) + 3OH^-$	-1.00
$Cd^{2+} + 2e^- \rightarrow Cd(s)$	-0.4029	$In^{3+} + 3e^- \rightarrow In(s)$	-0.343
Calcium		*Iodine*	
$Ca(OH)_2(s) + 2e^- \rightarrow Ca(s) + 2OH^-$	-3.02	$IO_3^- + 3H_2O(l) + 6e^- \rightarrow I^- + 6OH^-$	$+0.26$
$Ca^{2+} + 2e^- \rightarrow Ca(s)$	-2.866	$IO^- + H_2O(l) + 2e^- \rightarrow I^- + 2OH^-$	$+0.485$
Cerium		$I_2(s) + 2e^- \rightarrow 2I^-$	$+0.5355$
$Ce(OH)_3(s) + 3e^- \rightarrow Ce(s) + 3OH^-$	-2.87	$2IO_3^- + 12H^+ + 10e^- \rightarrow I_2(s) + 6H_2O(l)$	$+1.195$
$Ce^{3+} + 3e^- \rightarrow Ce(s)$	-2.483	*Iron*	
$Ce^{4+} + e^- \rightarrow Ce^{3+}$	$+1.61$	$Fe(OH)_2(s) + 2e^- \rightarrow Fe(s) + 2OH^-$	-0.877
Cesium		$Fe(OH)_3(s) + e^- \rightarrow Fe(OH)_2(s) + OH^-$	-0.56
$Cs^+ + e^- \rightarrow Cs(s)$	-2.923	$Fe^{2+} + 2e^- \rightarrow Fe(s)$	-0.4402
Chlorine		$Fe^{3+} + 3e^- \rightarrow Fe(s)$	-0.036
$ClO_3^- + H_2O(l) + 2e^- \rightarrow ClO_2^- + 2OH^-$	$+0.33$	$[Fe(CN)_6]^{3-} + e^- \rightarrow [Fe(CN)_6]^{4-}$	$+0.36$
$ClO_4^- + H_2O(l) + 2e^- \rightarrow ClO_3^- + 2OH^-$	$+0.36$	$Fe^{3+} + e^- \rightarrow Fe^{2+}$	$+0.771$
$ClO^- + H_2O(l) + 2e^- \rightarrow Cl^- + 2OH^-$	$+0.89$	*Lanthanum*	
$ClO_4^- + 2H^+ + 2e^- \rightarrow ClO_3^- + H_2O(l)$	$+1.19$	$La^{3+} + 3e^- \rightarrow La(s)$	-2.522
$ClO_3^- + 3H^+ + 2e^- \rightarrow HClO_2(aq) + H_2O(l)$	$+1.21$	*Lead*	
$Cl_2(g) + 2e^- \rightarrow 2Cl^-$	$+1.3595$	$PbS(s) + 2e^- \rightarrow Pb(s) + S^{2-}$	-0.93
$2HClO(aq) + 2H^+ + 2e^- \rightarrow Cl_2(g) + 2H_2O(l)$	$+1.63$	$PbO(s) + H_2O(l) + 2e^- \rightarrow Pb(s) + 2OH^-$	-0.580
$HClO_2(aq) + 2H^+ + 2e^- \rightarrow HClO(aq) + H_2O(l)$	$+1.645$	$PbI_2(s) + 2e^- \rightarrow Pb(s) + 2I^-$	-0.365
Chromium		$PbSO_4(s) + 2e^- \rightarrow Pb(s) + SO_4^{2-}$	-0.3588
$Cr(OH)_3(s) + 3e^- \rightarrow Cr(s) + 3OH^-$	-1.34	$PbBr_2(s) + 2e^- \rightarrow Pb(s) + 2Br^-$	-0.284
$Cr^{2+} + 2e^- \rightarrow Cr(s)$	-0.913	$PbCl_2(s) + 2e^- \rightarrow Pb(s) + 2Cl^-$	-0.268
$Cr^{3+} + 3e^- \rightarrow Cr(s)$	-0.744	$Pb^{2+} + 2e^- \rightarrow Pb(s)$	-0.126
$Cr^{3+} + e^- \rightarrow Cr^{2+}$	-0.408	$PbO_2(s) + H_2O(l) + 2e^- \rightarrow PbO(s) + 2OH^-$	$+0.247$
$CrO_4^{2-} + 4H_2O(l) + 3e^- \rightarrow Cr(OH)_3(s) + 5OH^-$	-0.13	$PbO_2(s) + 4H^+ + 2e^- \rightarrow Pb^{2+} + 2H_2O(l)$	$+1.455$
$Cr_2O_7^{2-} + 14H^+ + 6e^- \rightarrow 2Cr^{3+} + 7H_2O(l)$	$+1.33$	*Lithium*	
Cobalt		$Li^+ + e^- \rightarrow Li(s)$	-3.045
$Co(OH)_2(s) + 2e^- \rightarrow Co(s) + 2OH^-$	-0.73	*Magnesium*	
$Co^{2+} + 2e^- \rightarrow Co(s)$	-0.277	$Mg(OH)_2(s) + 2e^- \rightarrow Mg(s) + 2OH^-$	-2.690
$Co^{3+} + e^- \rightarrow Co^{2+}$	$+1.808$	$Mg^{2+} + 2e^- \rightarrow Mg(s)$	-2.363

Table VI.3 **A-29**

Reduction Half Reaction	E°, V	Reduction Half Reaction	E°, V
Manganese		*Scandium*	
$Mn(OH)_2(s) + 2e^- \rightarrow Mn(s) + 2OH^-$	-1.55	$Sc^{3+} + 3e^- \rightarrow Sc(s)$	-2.077
$Mn^{2+} + 2e^- \rightarrow Mn(s)$	-1.185	*Selenium*	
$MnO_2(s) + 2H_2O(l) + 2e^- \rightarrow Mn(OH)_2(s) + 2OH^-$	-0.05	$Se(s) + 2e^- \rightarrow Se^{2-}$	-0.92
$MnO_4^- + e^- \rightarrow MnO_4^{2-}$	$+0.564$	$Se(s) + 2H^+ + 2e^- \rightarrow H_2Se(aq)$	-0.399
$MnO_4^- + 2H_2O(l) + 3e^- \rightarrow MnO_2(s) + 4OH^-$	$+0.588$	$SeO_4^{2-} + H_2O(l) + 2e^- \rightarrow SeO_3^{2-} + 2OH^-$	$+0.05$
$MnO_2(s) + 4H^+ + 2e^- \rightarrow Mn^{2+} + 2H_2O(l)$	$+1.23$	$SeO_4^{2-} + 4H^+ + 2e^- \rightarrow H_2SeO_3(aq) + H_2O(l)$	$+1.15$
$MnO_4^- + 8H^+ + 5e^- \rightarrow Mn^{2+} + 4H_2O(l)$	$+1.51$	*Silicon*	
Mercury		$SiO_3^{2-} + 3H_2O(l) + 4e^- \rightarrow Si(s) + 6OH^-$	-1.697
$HgO(s) + H_2O(l) + 2e^- \rightarrow Hg(l) + 2OH^-$	$+0.098$	$[SiF_6]^{2-} + 4e^- \rightarrow Si(s) + 6F^-$	-1.24
$Hg_2Br_2(s) + 2e^- \rightarrow 2Hg(l) + 2Br^-$	$+0.1397$	$SiO_2(s) + 4H^+ + 4e^- \rightarrow Si(s) + 2H_2O(l)$	-0.857
$[Hg_2Br_4]^{2-} + 2e^- \rightarrow Hg(l) + 4Br^-$	$+0.223$	$Si(s) + 4H^+ + 4e^- \rightarrow SiH_4(g)$	$+0.102$
$Hg_2Cl_2(s) + 2e^- \rightarrow 2Hg(l) + 2Cl^-$	$+0.2676$	*Silver*	
$Hg_2SO_4(s) + 2e^- \rightarrow 2Hg(l) + SO_4^{2-}$	$+0.6151$	$AgI(s) + e^- \rightarrow Ag(s) + I^-$	-0.1518
$Hg^{2+} + 2e^- \rightarrow 2Hg(l)$	$+0.788$	$AgBr(s) + e^- \rightarrow Ag(s) + Br^-$	$+0.0713$
$2Hg^{2+} + 2e^- \rightarrow Hg_2^{2+}$	$+0.920$	$AgCl(s) + e^- \rightarrow Ag(s) + Cl^-$	$+0.2222$
Molybdenum		$Ag_2O(s) + H_2O(l) + 2e^- \rightarrow 2Ag(s) + 2OH^-$	$+0.345$
$MoO_4^{2-} + 4H_2O(l) + 6e^- \rightarrow Mo(s) + 8OH^-$	-1.05	$Ag^+ + e^- \rightarrow Ag(s)$	$+0.7991$
Nickel		$Ag^{2+} + e^- \rightarrow Ag^+$	$+1.980$
$Ni(OH)_2(s) + 2e^- \rightarrow Ni(s) + 2OH^-$	-0.72	*Sodium*	
$Ni^{2+} + 2e^- \rightarrow Ni(s)$	-0.250	$Na^+ + e^- \rightarrow Na(s)$	-2.714
$NiO_2(s) + 2H_2O(l) + 2e^- \rightarrow Ni(OH)_2(s) + 2OH^-$	$+0.490$	*Strontium*	
Nitrogen		$Sr^{2+} + 2e^- \rightarrow Sr(s)$	-2.888
$NO_3^- + H_2O(l) + 2e^- \rightarrow NO_2^- + 2OH^-$	$+0.01$	$Sr(OH)_2(s) + 2e^- \rightarrow Sr(s) + 2OH^-$	-2.88
$2NO_3^- + 4H^+ + 2e^- \rightarrow N_2O_4(g) + 2H_2O(l)$	$+0.803$	*Sulfur*	
$NO_3^- + 3H^+ + 2e^- \rightarrow HNO_2(aq) + H_2O(l)$	$+0.94$	$SO_4^{2-} + H_2O(l) + 2e^- \rightarrow SO_3^{2-} + 2OH^-$	-0.93
$NO_3^- + 4H^+ + 3e^- \rightarrow NO(g) + 2H_2O(l)$	$+0.96$	$S(s) + 2e^- \rightarrow S^{2-}$	-0.447
$2HNO_2(aq) + 4H^+ + 4e^- \rightarrow N_2O(g) + 3H_2O(l)$	$+1.29$	$S(s) + 2H^+ + 2e^- \rightarrow H_2S(aq)$	$+0.142$
Oxygen		$SO_4^{2-} + 4H^+ + 2e^- \rightarrow H_2SO_3(aq) + H_2O(l)$	$+0.172$
$2H_2O(l) + 2e^- \rightarrow H_2(g) + 2OH^-$	-0.8281	$SO_4^{2-} + 8H^+ + 6e^- \rightarrow S(s) + 4H_2O(l)$	$+0.3572$
$O_2(g) + 2H_2O(l) + 4e^- \rightarrow 4OH^-$	$+0.401$	$H_2SO_3(aq) + 4H^+ + 4e^- \rightarrow S(s) + 3H_2O(l)$	$+0.450$
$O_2(g) + 2H^+ + 2e^- \rightarrow H_2O_2(aq)$	$+0.6824$	$S_2O_8^{2-} + 2e^- \rightarrow 2SO_4^{2-}$	$+2.01$
$O_2(g) + 4H^+ + 4e^- \rightarrow 2H_2O(l)$	$+1.229$	*Tellurium*	
$O_3(g) + H_2O(l) + 2e^- \rightarrow O_2(g) + 2OH^-$	$+1.24$	$Te(s) + 2e^- \rightarrow Te^{2-}$	-1.143
$H_2O_2(aq) + 2H^+ + 2e^- \rightarrow 2H_2O(l)$	$+1.776$	$Te(s) + 2H^+ + 2e^- \rightarrow H_2Te(aq)$	-0.739
$O_3(g) + 2H^+ + 2e^- \rightarrow O_2(g) + H_2O(l)$	$+2.07$	$TeO_3^{2-} + 3H_2O(l) + 4e^- \rightarrow Te(s) + 6OH^-$	-0.57
Palladium		*Thallium*	
$Pd^{2+} + 2e^- \rightarrow Pd(s)$	$+0.987$	$TlOH(s) + e^- \rightarrow Tl(s) + OH^-$	-0.343
Phosphorus		$Tl^+ + e^- \rightarrow Tl(s)$	-0.3363
$H_2PO_2^- + e^- \rightarrow P(s) + 2OH^-$	-2.05	$Tl(OH)_3(s) + 2e^- \rightarrow TlOH(s) + 2OH^-$	-0.05
$PO_4^{3-} + 2H_2O(l) + 2e^- \rightarrow HPO_3^{2-} + 3OH^-$	-1.12	*Tin*	
$P(s) + 3H_2O(l) + 3e^- \rightarrow PH_3(g) + 3OH^-$	-0.89	$Sn^{2+} + 2e^- \rightarrow Sn(s)$	-0.136
$P(s) + 3H^+ + 3e^- \rightarrow PH_3(g)$	-0.063	$Sn^{4+} + 2e^- \rightarrow Sn^{2+}$	$+0.15$
Platinum		*Titanium*	
$[PtCl_6]^{2-} + 2e^- \rightarrow [PtCl_4]^{2-} + 2Cl^-$	$+0.68$	$Ti^{2+} + 2e^- \rightarrow Ti(s)$	-1.628
$[PtCl_4]^{2-} + 2e^- \rightarrow Pt(s) + 4Cl^-$	$+0.73$	$[TiF_6]^{2-} + 4e^- \rightarrow Ti(s) + 6F^-$	-1.191
$Pt^{2+} + 2e^- \rightarrow Pt(s)$	~ 1.2	$Ti^{3+} + e^- \rightarrow Ti^{2+}$	-0.369
Polonium		*Tungsten*	
$Po^{2+} + 2e^- \rightarrow Po(s)$	$+0.65$	$WO_4^{2-} + 4H_2O(l) + 6e^- \rightarrow W(s) + 8OH^-$	-1.05
Potassium		*Uranium*	
$K^+ + e^- \rightarrow K(s)$	-2.925	$U(OH)_4(s) + e^- \rightarrow U(OH)_3(s) + OH^-$	-2.20
Radium		$U(OH)_3(s) + 3e^- \rightarrow U(s) + 3OH^-$	-2.17
$Ra^{2+} + 2e^- \rightarrow Ra(s)$	-2.916	$U^{4+} + e^- \rightarrow U^{3+}$	-0.607
Rhodium		*Vanadium*	
$Rh^{3+} + 3e^- \rightarrow Rh(s)$	$+0.80$	$V^{3+} + 3e^- \rightarrow V(s)$	-1.798
Rubidium		$V^{4+} + 4e^- \rightarrow V(s)$	-1.50
$Rb^+ + e^- \rightarrow Rb(s)$	-2.925	$V^{2+} + 2e^- \rightarrow V(s)$	-1.175

Reduction Half Reaction	$E°$, V
$V^{3+} + e^- \rightarrow V^{2+}$	-0.256
$VO^{2+} + 2H^+ + e^- \rightarrow V^{3+} + H_2O(l)$	$+0.359$
Zinc	
$Zn(OH)_2(s) + 2e^- \rightarrow Zn(s) + 2OH^-$	-1.245
$Zn^{2+} + 2e^- \rightarrow Zn(s)$	-0.7628
Zirconium	
$Zr^{4+} + 4e^- \rightarrow Zr(s)$	-1.529

INDEX

Boldface entries denote definitions of significant terms listed at ends of chapters.

Table of atomic masses and electron configurations listed by atomic number

Scaled to the relative atomic mass $^{12}C = 12$ exactly. A number in parentheses is the atomic mass number of the isotope of longest known half-life.

Atomic number	Element	Symbol	Atomic mass	Electron configuration
1	Hydrogen	H	1.0079	$1s^1$
2	Helium	He	4.00260	$1s^2$
3	Lithium	Li	6.941	$1s^2\ 2s^1$
4	Beryllium	Be	9.01218	$1s^2\ 2s^2$
5	Boron	B	10.81	$1s^2\ 2s^2\ 2p^1$
6	Carbon	C	12.011	$1s^2\ 2s^2\ 2p^2$
7	Nitrogen	N	14.0067	$1s^2\ 2s^2\ 2p^3$
8	Oxygen	O	15.9994	$1s^2\ 2s^2\ 2p^4$
9	Fluorine	F	18.998403	$1s^2\ 2s^2\ 2p^5$
10	Neon	Ne	20.179	$1s^2\ 2s^2\ 2p^6$
11	Sodium	Na	22.98977	$1s^2\ 2s^2\ 2p^6\ 3s^1$
12	Magnesium	Mg	24.305	$1s^2\ 2s^2\ 2p^6\ 3s^2$
13	Aluminum	Al	26.98154	$1s^2\ 2s^2\ 2p^6\ 3s^2\ 3p^1$
14	Silicon	Si	28.0855	$1s^2\ 2s^2\ 2p^6\ 3s^2\ 3p^2$
15	Phosphorus	P	30.97376	$1s^2\ 2s^2\ 2p^6\ 3s^2\ 3p^3$
16	Sulfur	S	32.06	$1s^2\ 2s^2\ 2p^6\ 3s^2\ 3p^4$
17	Chlorine	Cl	35.453	$1s^2\ 2s^2\ 2p^6\ 3s^2\ 3p^5$
18	Argon	Ar	39.948	$1s^2\ 2s^2\ 2p^6\ 3s^2\ 3p^6$
19	Potassium	K	39.0983	$1s^2\ 2s^2\ 2p^6\ 3s^2\ 3p^6\ 4s^1$
20	Calcium	Ca	40.08	$1s^2\ 2s^2\ 2p^6\ 3s^2\ 3p^6\ 4s^2$
21	Scandium	Sc	44.9559	$1s^2\ 2s^2\ 2p^6\ 3s^2\ 3p^6\ 3d^1\ 4s^2$
22	Titanium	Ti	47.88	$1s^2\ 2s^2\ 2p^6\ 3s^2\ 3p^6\ 3d^2\ 4s^2$
23	Vanadium	V	50.9415	$1s^2\ 2s^2\ 2p^6\ 3s^2\ 3p^6\ 3d^3\ 4s^2$
24	Chromium	Cr	51.996	$1s^2\ 2s^2\ 2p^6\ 3s^2\ 3p^6\ 3d^5\ 4s^1$
25	Manganese	Mn	54.9380	$1s^2\ 2s^2\ 2p^6\ 3s^2\ 3p^6\ 3d^5\ 4s^2$
26	Iron	Fe	55.847	$1s^2\ 2s^2\ 2p^6\ 3s^2\ 3p^6\ 3d^6\ 4s^2$
27	Cobalt	Co	58.9332	$1s^2\ 2s^2\ 2p^6\ 3s^2\ 3p^6\ 3d^7\ 4s^2$
28	Nickel	Ni	58.69	$1s^2\ 2s^2\ 2p^6\ 3s^2\ 3p^6\ 3d^8\ 4s^2$
29	Copper	Cu	63.546	$1s^2\ 2s^2\ 2p^6\ 3s^2\ 3p^6\ 3d^{10}\ 4s^1$
30	Zinc	Zn	65.38	$1s^2\ 2s^2\ 2p^6\ 3s^2\ 3p^6\ 3d^{10}\ 4s^2$
31	Gallium	Ga	69.72	$1s^2\ 2s^2\ 2p^6\ 3s^2\ 3p^6\ 3d^{10}\ 4s^2\ 4p^1$
32	Germanium	Ge	72.59	$1s^2\ 2s^2\ 2p^6\ 3s^2\ 3p^6\ 3d^{10}\ 4s^2\ 4p^2$
33	Arsenic	As	74.9216	$1s^2\ 2s^2\ 2p^6\ 3s^2\ 3p^6\ 3d^{10}\ 4s^2\ 4p^3$
34	Selenium	Se	78.96	$1s^2\ 2s^2\ 2p^6\ 3s^2\ 3p^6\ 3d^{10}\ 4s^2\ 4p^4$
35	Bromine	Br	79.904	$1s^2\ 2s^2\ 2p^6\ 3s^2\ 3p^6\ 3d^{10}\ 4s^2\ 4p^5$
36	Krypton	Kr	83.80	$1s^2\ 2s^2\ 2p^6\ 3s^2\ 3p^6\ 3d^{10}\ 4s^2\ 4p^6$
37	Rubidium	Rb	85.4678	[Krypton core] $5s^1$
38	Strontium	Sr	87.62	[Krypton core] $5s^2$
39	Yttrium	Y	88.9059	[Krypton core] $4d^1\ 5s^2$
40	Zirconium	Zr	91.22	[Krypton core] $4d^2\ 5s^2$
41	Niobium	Nb	92.9064	[Krypton core] $4d^4\ 5s^1$
42	Molybdenum	Mo	95.94	[Krypton core] $4d^5\ 5s^1$
43	Technetium	Tc	(98)	[Krypton core] $4d^5\ 5s^2$
44	Ruthenium	Ru	101.07	[Krypton core] $4d^7\ 5s^1$
45	Rhodium	Rh	102.9055	[Krypton core] $4d^8\ 5s^1$
46	Palladium	Pd	106.42	[Krypton core] $4d^{10}$
47	Silver	Ag	107.868	[Krypton core] $4d^{10}\ 5s^1$
48	Cadmium	Cd	112.41	[Krypton core] $4d^{10}\ 5s^2$
49	Indium	In	114.82	[Krypton core] $4d^{10}\ 5s^2\ 5p^1$
50	Tin	Sn	118.69	[Krypton core] $4d^{10}\ 5s^2\ 5p^2$
51	Antimony	Sb	121.75	[Krypton core] $4d^{10}\ 5s^2\ 5p^3$
52	Tellurium	Te	127.60	[Krypton core] $4d^{10}\ 5s^2\ 5p^4$
53	Iodine	I	126.9045	[Krypton core] $4d^{10}\ 5s^2\ 5p^5$
54	Xenon	Xe	131.29	[Krypton core] $5s^2\ 5p^6$